The Law of the European Union

The Law of the European Union

FIFTH EDITION

Formerly titled

Kapteyn & VerLoren van Themaat
The Law of the European Union and the European Communities

Edited by

Pieter Jan Kuijper

Fabian Amtenbrink

Deirdre Curtin

Bruno De Witte

Alison McDonnell

and

Stefaan Van den Bogaert

Wolters Kluwer

Published by:
Kluwer Law International B.V.
PO Box 316
2400 AH Alphen aan den Rijn
The Netherlands
Email: international-sales@wolterskluwer.com
Website: lrus.wolterskluwer.com

Sold and distributed in North, Central and South America by:
Wolters Kluwer Legal & Regulatory U.S.
7201 McKinney Circle
Frederick, MD 21704
United States of America
Email: customer.service@wolterskluwer.com

Sold and distributed in all other countries by:
Air Business Subscriptions
Rockwood House
Haywards Heath
West Sussex
RH16 3DH
United Kingdom
Email: international-customerservice@wolterskluwer.com

Printed on acid-free paper.

ISBN 978-90-411-5411-8

e-Book: ISBN 978-90-411-5412-5
web-PDF: ISBN 978-90-411-8958-5

Printed in the United Kingdom.

THE AUTHORS AND EDITORS

Maarten Aalbers

Europa Institute, Law Faculty, University of Leiden

Fabian Amtenbrink

Erasmus School of Law, Erasmus University Rotterdam

Ilektra Antonaki

Europa Institute, Law Faculty, University of Leiden

Jürgen Bast

Law Faculty, Justus-Liebig University of Giessen

Monica Claes

Law Faculty, Maastricht University

K.J. Cseres

Amsterdam Centre for European Law and Governance, University of Amsterdam

D.M. Curtin

Law Department, European University Institute, Law Faculty, University of Amsterdam

Armin Cuyvers

Europa Institute, Law Faculty, University of Leiden

Bruno De Witte

Law Faculty, Maastricht University; Law Department/Robert Schuman Centre of the European University Institute (EUI)

Sacha Garben

College of Europe, Bruges

Willem Geelhoed

Faculty of Law, University of Groningen

Morag Goodwin
Law Faculty, University of Tilburg

Matthias Haentjens
Hazelhoff Centre for Financial Law of Leiden University

Leigh Hancher
University of Tilburg and EUI, Florence

Jan Inghelram
Legal Adviser for Administrative Cases, Court of Justice of the EU

Suzanne Kingston
School of Law, University College Dublin

Xandra Kramer
Erasmus University Rotterdam and Utrecht University

P.J. Kuijper
Law Faculty, University of Amsterdam

Alison McDonnell
Europa Institute, Law Faculty, University of Leiden

Joana Mendes
Law Faculty, University of Luxembourg

Pablo Mendes de Leon
Law Faculty, University of Leiden

K.J.M. Mortelmans†
Formerly: Council of State, The Netherlands

Tom Ottervanger
Europa Institute, Law Faculty, University of Leiden

Jannemieke Ouwerkerk
Law Faculty, University of Leiden

Ana Ramalho
Department of International and European Law, Maastricht University

Jorrit J. Rijpma

Europa Institute, Law Faculty, University of Leiden

Felix Ronkes Agerbeek

Legal Service of the European Commission

Sarah Schoenmaekers

Law Faculty, Maastricht University

Annette Schrauwen

Law Faculty, University of Amsterdam

Ben Smulders

European Commission

Christof R.A. Swaak

Practice Group Competition & Regulation at Stibbe, Amsterdam & Brussels

Jouke Tegelaar

Hazelhoff Centre for Financial Law of Leiden University

C.W.A. Timmermans

Formerly: European Court of Justice

Christa Tobler

Europa Institutes of the Universities of Leiden and Basel

Thomas Vandamme

Amsterdam Centre for European Law and Governance, Law Faculty, University of Amsterdam

Pieter Van Cleynenbreugel

Law Faculty, University of Liège

Stefaan Van den Bogaert

Europa Institute, Law Faculty, University of Leiden

Anne Pieter van der Mei

Maastricht Centre for European Law (MCEL), Maastricht University

Pieter Van Nuffel

Legal Service, European Commission

R.H. van Ooik

Law Faculty, University of Amsterdam

Thomas van Rijn

Formerly: Legal Service, European Commission

Marc van der Woude

General Court of the European Union and Erasmus School of Law of the Erasmus University in Rotterdam

M.A. Verbrugh

Erasmus School of Law at the Erasmus University Rotterdam, the Netherlands

Dorine Verheij

Hazelhoff Centre for Financial Law of Leiden University

Ellen Vos

Law Faculty, Maastricht University

Dennis Weber

Amsterdam Centre for Tax Law (ACTL) of the University of Amsterdam

Maria Weimer

Law Faculty, University of Amsterdam

Kassandra Wetz

Law Faculty, Justus-Liebig University of Giessen

SUMMARY OF CONTENTS

The Authors and Editors v

List of Abbreviations xli

Foreword xlix

Chapter 1
THE GENESIS AND HISTORICAL DEVELOPMENT OF THE EUROPEAN COMMUNITIES AND THE EUROPEAN UNION 1
C.W.A. Timmermans

Chapter 2
STRUCTURE AND EVOLUTION OF UNION LAW 43
Bruno De Witte

Chapter 3
SYSTEM OF COMPETENCES 69
Jürgen Bast and Kassandra Wetz

Chapter 4
FUNDAMENTAL RIGHTS 95
Monica Claes

Chapter 5
THE POLITICAL INSTITUTIONS 129
D.M. Curtin, P.J. Kuijper and R.H. van Ooik

Chapter 6
SOURCES OF EUROPEAN UNION LAW 193
Bruno De Witte and Ben Smulders

Chapter 7
LAW-MAKING 235
Pieter Van Nuffel and Felix Ronkes Agerbeek

Chapter 8
THE EU ADMINISTRATION 267
Joana Mendes

Chapter 9
BUDGET AND FINANCES 313
Jan Inghelram

Chapter 10
THE COURT OF JUSTICE OF THE EUROPEAN UNION SUPRANATIONAL ADJUDICATOR AND ACCOUNTABILITY FORUM 357
Deirdre Curtin and Maria Weimer

Chapter 11
APPLICATION AND ENFORCEMENT OF EU LAW IN THE MEMBER STATES 413
Alison McDonnell

Chapter 12
THE FUNCTIONING OF THE INTERNAL MARKET: THE FREEDOMS 469
K.J.M. Mortelmans

Chapter 13
FREE MOVEMENT OF GOODS 485
Stefaan Van den Bogaert and Pieter Van Cleynenbreugel

Chapter 14
FREE MOVEMENT OF SERVICES, ESTABLISHMENT AND CAPITAL 539
Stefaan Van den Bogaert, Armin Cuyvers and Ilektra Antonaki

Chapter 15
FREE MOVEMENT OF WORKERS AND COORDINATION OF SOCIAL SECURITY 587
Anne Pieter van der Mei

Chapter 16
CITIZENSHIP OF THE UNION 611
Annette Schrauwen

Chapter 17
EUROPEAN MIGRATION AND ASYLUM LAW 639
Jorrit J. Rijpma

Chapter 18
JUDICIAL COOPERATION IN CIVIL MATTERS 673
Xandra Kramer

Chapter 19
EU CRIMINAL LAW 691
Jannemieke Ouwerkerk and Willem Geelhoed

Chapter 20
COMPETITION LAW AND POLICY 715
Christof R.A. Swaak and Marc van der Woude

Chapter 21
STATE AID LAW 779
Tom Ottervanger and Maarten Aalbers

Chapter 22
PUBLIC PROCUREMENT 805
Sarah Schoenmaekers

Chapter 23
TAXATION 829
Dennis Weber

Chapter 24
INTELLECTUAL PROPERTY 849
Ana Ramalho

Chapter 25
COMPANY LAW 867
M.A. Verbrugh

Chapter 26
ECONOMIC AND MONETARY UNION 883
Fabian Amtenbrink

Chapter 27
FINANCIAL MARKET REGULATION AND SUPERVISION 951
Matthias Haentjens, Jouke Tegelaar and Dorine Verheij

Chapter 28
EU SOCIAL LAW AND POLICY 995
Sacha Garben

Chapter 29
EQUAL TREATMENT AND NON-DISCRIMINATION 1017
Christa Tobler

Chapter 30
AGRICULTURE AND FISHERIES 1047
Thomas van Rijn

Chapter 31
TRANSPORT POLICY 1067
Pablo Mendes de Leon

Chapter 32
EUROPEAN ENERGY LAW – FROM MARKET TO UNION? 1089
Leigh Hancher

Chapter 33
THE REGIONAL DIMENSION OF EU LAW: COHESION POLICY AND GEOGRAPHICAL DIFFERENTIATION 1107
Thomas Vandamme

Chapter 34
EU HEALTH LAW AND POLICY 1129
Anne Pieter van der Mei and Ellen Vos

Chapter 35
CONSUMER PROTECTION IN THE EU 1145
K.J. Cseres

Chapter 36
ENVIRONMENTAL POLICY 1165
Suzanne Kingston

Chapter 37
RESEARCH AND TECHNOLOGY 1185
Morag Goodwin

Chapter 38
SUPPORTING POLICIES 1199
Sacha Garben

Chapter 39
AN INTRODUCTION TO UNION EXTERNAL ACTION, ITS SCOPE, ITS INSTITUTIONS AND ITS INSTRUMENTS 1231
Pieter Jan Kuijper

Chapter 40
THE COMMON FOREIGN AND SECURITY POLICY AND THE COMMON SECURITY AND DEFENCE POLICY 1263
Pieter Jan Kuijper

Chapter 41
UNION EXTERNAL ACTION UNDER THE TFEU 1291
Pieter Jan Kuijper

Table of Selected Cases (Numerical Order) 1349

Subject Index 1369

TABLE OF CONTENTS

The Authors and Editors v

List of Abbreviations xli

Foreword xlix

Chapter 1
THE GENESIS AND HISTORICAL DEVELOPMENT OF THE EUROPEAN COMMUNITIES AND THE EUROPEAN UNION 1
C.W.A. Timmermans

1. The Schuman plan and its background 1
   1.1 The power vacuum in Europe and the aim of European integration 2
   1.2 The problem of Franco-German relations and the commitment of the German Federal Republic to Western Europe 3
   1.3 Economic considerations 4
2. The ECSC Treaty of 18 April 1951 5
3. The failure of plans for a European Defence Community (EDC) and a European Political Community (EPC) 7
   3.1 Background and content of these plans 7
   3.2 Failure of these plans and "relance européenne" 8
4. The Spaak Report and the conclusion of the treaties establishing the European Economic Community (EEC) and the European Atomic Energy Community (Euratom) 10
   4.1 The contents of the Spaak Report 10
   4.2 The conclusion of the EEC and Euratom Treaties 12
5. The Communities, the United Kingdom, and enlargement to include other democratic European countries 12
6. European Political Cooperation (EPC); The European Council and the Single European Act 18
   6.1 EPC and the European Council 18
   6.2 The Single European Act (1986) 21
7. The Treaties of Maastricht (1992), Amsterdam (1997) and Nice (2001) 23
   7.1 The Treaty of Maastricht (1992) 23
   7.2 The Treaty of Amsterdam (1997) 27
   7.3 The Treaty of Nice 29
8. The Treaty establishing a Constitution for Europe and the Treaty of Lisbon 31
   8.1 The Treaty establishing a Constitution for Europe 31

8.2 The Treaty of Lisbon 33
8.3 Post Lisbon 35
Further reading 38

Chapter 2
STRUCTURE AND EVOLUTION OF UNION LAW 43
Bruno De Witte
1. Introduction: A special legal system 43
2. Evolution of the Treaty architecture 45
2.1 Treaty architecture prior to Maastricht 45
2.2 Creation of the pillar structure by the Maastricht Treaty 46
2.3 Evolution of the pillar structure from Maastricht to Lisbon 48
3. The evolution of differentiation and variable geometry 51
3.1 Pre-Maastricht closer cooperation 51
3.2 The birth of variable geometry in the Maastricht Treaty 52
3.3 The creation and evolution of enhanced cooperation 53
3.4 The multiplication of structured opt-out regimes and the revival of inter se agreements 56
3.5 The permanence of many-faced differentiation 57
4. Mechanisms of constitutional change: Treaty revisions, accession treaties, withdrawal agreements 59
4.1 Treaty revisions 59
4.2 Accession to the European Union 64
4.3 Withdrawal from the European Union 66
Further reading 67

Chapter 3
SYSTEM OF COMPETENCES 69
Jürgen Bast and Kassandra Wetz
1. Introduction 69
2. The evolution of the legal discourse on the EU's competence 70
2.1 1970s until the Maastricht Treaty 70
2.2 Mid-1990s until the Convention of 2002/2003 71
2.3 Post-Constitutional Treaty until present 72
3. The principle of conferral 73
3.1 Functions of the principle of conferral 73
3.2 Scope of the principle of conferral 76
3.3 Judicial control over compliance with the principle of conferral 78
4. The typology of competences 79
4.1 Exclusive competence 79
4.2 Shared competence with pre-emptive force (concurrent competences) 80
4.3 Shared competence without pre-emptive force (parallel competences) 81
5. Requirements for lawful exercise of competences 82
5.1 Principle of subsidiarity 82
5.2 Principle of proportionality 84
5.3 Principle of sincere cooperation 84
6. The role of national parliaments and constitutional courts 85
6.1 National parliaments 86
6.2 National constitutional courts 88
7. The (limited) role of the individual 90

8. Three layers of imbalance in the system of competences 91
Further reading 92

Chapter 4
FUNDAMENTAL RIGHTS 95
Monica Claes
1. Introduction 95
2. EU fundamental rights law as part of human rights law 97
3. The genesis of EU fundamental rights law 98
4. Sources of EU fundamental rights 102
4.1 The Charter of Fundamental Rights 103
4.1.1 Origins 103
4.1.2 The scope of application of the Charter 104
4.1.3 Limitations 110
4.1.4 Rights and principles 111
4.2 The ECHR 112
4.2.1 The ECHR as a source of EU fundamental rights 112
4.2.2 Accession of the EU to the ECHR 113
4.2.3 The position of EU law under the ECHR 117
4.3 General principles of EU law 118
5. The enforcement of EU fundamental rights 119
6. The coexistence of EU, ECHR and national fundamental rights law 120
6.1 Coexisting human rights: The EU perspective 121
6.2 The coexistence of national constitutional rights, the ECHR and EU fundamental rights: The national perspective 125
Further reading 127

Chapter 5
THE POLITICAL INSTITUTIONS 129
D.M. Curtin, P.J. Kuijper and R.H. van Ooik
1. Introduction 129
2. The European Council 130
2.1 Internal organization 130
2.1.1 Establishment 130
2.1.2 Composition 131
2.1.3 Voting arrangements 132
2.1.4 Auxiliary bodies 132
2.2 Political powers and functions 133
2.2.1 Agenda setting 133
2.2.2 Legislation 133
2.2.3 Non-legislation: administration/governance 134
3. The Council (of Ministers) of the European Union 135
3.1 Internal organization 135
3.1.1 Establishment 135
3.1.2 Composition 136
3.1.3 Voting arrangements 136
3.1.4 Auxiliary bodies 138
3.2 Political powers and functions 141
3.2.1 Agenda setting 141
3.2.2 Legislation 141

3.2.3 Non-legislation: administration/governance 142
4. The European Commission 143
4.1 The College of Commissioners 143
4.1.1 Composition, appointment and censure 143
4.1.2 Characteristics of the Commission 144
4.2 The Commission and its services 149
4.2.1 The organization of the Commission's services 149
4.2.2 The Commission services as part of the EU civil service 151
4.3 The Commission's tasks and functions 154
4.3.1 Participation in the legislative process 154
4.3.2 Administration 156
4.3.3 Supervision 157
5. The European Parliament 159
5.1 Composition and election 159
5.1.1 The members of the European Parliament (MEPs) and their statute 159
5.1.2 Elections 161
5.1.3 European political groups and parties 163
5.2 Internal organization 165
5.2.1 Internal organs of the parliament 165
5.2.2 The General Secretariat of the parliament 167
5.2.3 The plenary meeting 168
5.3 Powers and functions 169
5.3.1 Parliament's role in the legislative process 169
5.3.2 Other powers and functions of the European Parliament 171
5.4 The relation with national parliaments 173
6. The relations between the four political institutions 174
6.1 Formal relations of appointment, representation, and responsibility 174
6.2 Political inter-institutional relations 175
6.2.1 In the budgetary process 175
6.2.2 In legislative matters and questions of responsibility 176
6.3 Final reflections 183
7 Advisory bodies 184
7.1 Common provisions 184
7.2 Economic and Social Committee 185
7.3 Committee of the Regions 186
8. Common rules 186
8.1 Privileges and immunities 186
8.2 Seat of the Institutions 188
8.3 Linguistic régime 189
Further reading 191

Chapter 6
SOURCES OF EUROPEAN UNION LAW 193
Bruno De Witte and Ben Smulders

1. Introduction: The hierarchy of sources 193
2. Primary Law: The Treaties, the Charter and General Principles of Law 194
2.1 The Treaties and their Protocols 194
2.2 The Charter of Fundamental Rights 195
2.3 General Principles of Union Law 196
3. Secondary Law: Legal instruments 198

3.1 EU legal instruments: A general view 198
3.1.1 Article 288: An incomplete list of instruments 199
3.1.2 The reform of the legal instruments by the Lisbon Treaty 200
3.1.3 The general regime for the adoption and publication of EU legal acts 203
3.2 Regulations 206
3.3 Directives 208
3.4 Decisions 211
3.5 Interinstitutional agreements and Acts of the European Council 214
3.5.1 Interinstitutional agreements 214
3.5.2 Acts of the European Council 215
3.6 Legal instruments of the former Second and Third Pillars 216
3.7 Non-binding instruments 218
4. Agreements concluded between Member States inter se 221
4.1 Introduction 221
4.2 Typology and examples of agreements between Member States 223
4.2.1 Agreements concluded by EU Member States prior to EU membership 223
4.2.2 Agreements concluded by Member State governments meeting within the Council 224
4.2.3 Agreements concluded by EU Member States having a nexus with primary EU law 225
4.2.4 Agreements concluded by EU Member Status having a nexus with international agreements concluded by the EU 227
4.2.5 Agreements concluded by EU Member States having a nexus with secondary EU law 227
4.2.6 Agreements concluded by EU Member States using EU institutions 230
4.2.7 Agreements concluded by EU Member States following an empowerment by the EU 232
4.3 Concluding remarks 232
Further reading 234

Chapter 7
LAW-MAKING 235
Pieter Van Nuffel and Felix Ronkes Agerbeek
1. Introduction 235
2. Legal basis 236
3. Legislative and non-legislative acts 237
4. Decision-making process 239
4.1 General framework 239
4.2 Initiative 242
4.3 Consultation 248
4.4 Adoption of the Act 251
4.4.1 Decision making power in the hands of two institutions 251
4.4.2 Decision making by a single institution 256
4.4.3 Approval by Member States 259
5. Democratic legitimacy 260
5.1 A different kind of democracy 260
5.2 Scale 261
5.3 Pluralism 262
5.4 Sense of political community 264
5.5 Conclusion 264

Further reading 265

Chapter 8
THE EU ADMINISTRATION 267
Joana Mendes

1. Introduction 267
2. Executive federalism and the EU administration 268
2.1 The "executive federalism" model 268
2.2 Facing a complex reality 270
2.3 The constitutional framework of the EU administration 271
3. Comitology committees 273
3.1 Origins, rationale and tensions 273
3.2 The Lisbon Treaty: Comitology and implementing acts 275
3.2.1 Organic traits 276
3.2.2 Functions and functioning 276
3.2.3 Formal powers: The comitology procedures 277
3.2.4 Appeal Committee 278
3.2.5 Transparency 279
3.3 Scope of comitology: The dividing line between implementing and delegated acts 279
3.4 Committees and delegated acts 282
4. Agencies 283
4.1 Rationales and types 283
4.2 Organization 285
4.3 Powers 287
4.4 Legal bases 291
4.5 Legal limits to the agencies' powers 292
4.6 Accountability 294
4.7 The international dimension 294
5. Networks 295
5.1 Legally mandated 296
5.2 Informal networks 297
6. The Member States' administration: Framed autonomy 298
6.1 Institutional and procedural autonomy 299
6.2 Direct administrative effect 300
6.3 Transnational effects of national administrative acts 301
7. Commission and Council (administrative functions) 301
8. Integrated or composite administration: Legal issues 305
8.1 Composite procedures, procedural rights and judicial review 306
8.2 Transparency, accountability and efficiency 308
8.3 Procedures between fragmentation and codification 309
9. Conclusions 311
Further reading 311

Chapter 9
BUDGET AND FINANCES 313
Jan Inghelram

1. Historical development 313
1.1 The situation under the founding treaties 313
1.2 The first budgetary treaty of 21 April 1970 and the first own resources decision 314

1.3 The Second Budgetary Treaty of 22 July 1975 315
1.4 The Delors I Package of 1988 315
1.5 The Treaty of Maastricht 317
1.6 The Treaty of Amsterdam 318
1.7 The Treaty of Nice 318
1.8 The Treaty of Lisbon 319
2. Legal framework 319
3. Budgetary principles 321
3.1 Principles of unity and budgetary accuracy 321
3.2 Principle of annuality 322
3.3 Principle of equilibrium 323
3.4 Principle of unit of account 323
3.5 Principle of universality 324
3.6 Principle of specification 324
3.7 Principle of sound financial management 324
3.8 Principle of transparency 325
4. Own resources 325
4.1 The own resources decision 325
4.2 The juste retour discussion 328
4.3 The collection of own resources 329
5. The Multi-Annual Financial Framework 331
5.1 Procedure 331
5.2 Contents 332
6. The budgetary procedure 333
7. The implementation of the budget 335
7.1 Responsibility and methods of implementation 335
7.2 Financial actors and internal auditor 336
7.3 The need for a basic act 337
8. The European Court of Auditors 338
9. The discharge procedure 341
10. The protection of the financial interests of the EU 342
10.1 Origins 342
10.2 The PFI Convention of 1995 and the PFI Directive of 2017 343
10.3 The PFI Regulation of 1995 345
11. The European Anti-Fraud Office (OLAF) 347
11.1 Creation and legal framework 347
11.2 Structure and organization 348
11.3 Competences 349
11.4 Conduct of investigations 351
11.5 Procedural guarantees 353
11.6 Supervision 354
11.7 Judicial control 354
12. Final remarks 355
Further reading 356

Chapter 10
THE COURT OF JUSTICE OF THE EUROPEAN UNION SUPRANATIONAL ADJUDICATOR AND ACCOUNTABILITY FORUM 357
Deirdre Curtin and Maria Weimer
1. Introduction: Institutional structure and functions 357

2. Direct judicial protection before the CJEU 361
2.1 Infringement proceedings 361
2.1.1 The administrative stage 362
2.1.2 The judicial stage 364
2.1.3 Financial sanctions 367
2.1.4 Infringement procedures: Fit for the future? 368
2.2 The action for annulment 369
2.2.1 Time limits 370
2.2.2 Reviewable acts 370
2.2.3 Grounds for annulment 371
2.2.4 Standing 373
2.3 The action for failure to act 383
2.4 The plea of illegality, Article 277 TFEU 385
2.5 The action for damages 386
3. Cooperation with national courts through the preliminary reference procedure 388
3.1 Types of preliminary references 391
3.2 The separate functions of the Court of Justice and national courts 392
3.3 National courts and tribunals: power and obligation to refer 395
3.3.1 Courts and tribunals in the sense of Article 267 TFEU 395
3.3.2 Obligation to refer 396
3.4 Effects of a preliminary ruling 398
3.5 Interim measures 400
4. Reforming EU Judicial Adjudication and Architecture 401
4.1 Inter-institutional accountability? 401
4.2 Reform of the Judicial Selection Committee 402
4.3 Docket reform? 403
4.3.1 Introduction 403
4.3.2 Reform due to increase in workload of the CJEU 403
4.3.3 Reform due to increase in workload of the General Court 405
4.4 Openness in judging 407
4.4.1 Access to documents 407
4.4.2 Case publicity 408
4.4.3 The oral hearing 409
4.4.4 Judging the CJEU secrecy 409
5. Conclusion 411
Further reading 411

Chapter 11
APPLICATION AND ENFORCEMENT OF EU LAW IN THE MEMBER STATES 413
Alison McDonnell
1. Application and enforcement in a composite legal order 413
1.1 The composite EU legal order 413
1.2 Effective application and enforcement 416
1.3 Role of founding values 416
2. Primacy of EU Law: Relation of EU law to national constitutional law 417
2.1 Primacy announced 417
2.2 Unconditional primacy and the duty of national courts to set aside conflicting national law 418
2.3 Beyond conflicts of substantive rules of EU and national law 419

2.4 Reactions of national constitutional courts to the ECJ's doctrine of primacy of EU law 421
3. The effect of Union law in the national legal systems: Direct effect 427
3.1 General 427
3.2 Direct effect of primary Union law 428
3.2.1 Treaty provisions 428
3.2.2 EU Charter of Fundamental Rights: General principles 429
3.3 Reliance before national courts on secondary EU law 430
3.3.1 Conditions for direct effect 430
3.3.2 Decisions addressed to Member States: Directly applicable Regulations 432
3.3.3 Directives 432
3.3.4 International agreements binding on the Union 435
3.4 Indirect effect: Duty of consistent interpretation 435
3.5 Horizontal direct effect: General principles 437
4. Judicial protection in national courts 442
4.1 National courts are EU courts 442
4.2 Enforcement of EU law or of EU law-based rights as a duty of Member States 443
4.3 Principle of effective judicial protection: Charter Article 47 444
4.4 National procedural autonomy, principles equivalence and effectiveness 446
4.5 Res judicata 450
5. Sanctions in domestic law for EU law infringements 452
5.1 Responsibility of Member States 452
5.2 Choice of sanctions 453
5.3 Penal sanctions 456
5.4 Enforcement by means of civil remedies 457
6. Liability of Member States for damage suffered by individuals as a result of infringements of Union law which can be attributed to a Member State including judicial shortcomings 458
6.1 The fall-back remedy: Damages 458
6.2 Francovich liability: An EU law right to damages from Member States 459
6.3 Judicial errors 465
6.4 Limits of a remedy in damages 467
7. Concluding remarks 467
Further reading 468

Chapter 12
THE FUNCTIONING OF THE INTERNAL MARKET: THE FREEDOMS 469
K.J.M. Mortelmans
1. Introduction 469
1.1 The internal market and the fundamental freedoms 469
1.2 Fundamental freedoms and fundamental rights 470
1.3 Types of barriers to free movement 471
1.4 Crucial role of the Court of Justice of the EU and the national courts 471
2. The realization of the internal market: prohibitions and justifications 473
2.1 The four freedoms: prohibitions 473
2.1.1 Vertical direct effect as a weapon 474
2.1.2 Horizontal direct effect as a weapon 474
2.2 Justifications 474
2.3 The convergence of the freedoms and exceptions 475
2.4 External aspects of the internal market 476

3. The realization of the internal market: Positive integration and mutual recognition 477
3.1 Harmonization and uniform legislation 477
3.2 The mutual recognition principle 479
4. Growing pains affecting the internal market 480
4.1 Purely internal situation 481
4.2 Re-importation and strategic migration 482
4.3 Reverse discrimination 482
4.4 Abuse of law 483

Chapter 13
FREE MOVEMENT OF GOODS 485
Stefaan Van den Bogaert and Pieter Van Cleynenbreugel

1. Preliminary observations 485
1.1 The concept of a customs union 485
1.2 The term "goods" 486
1.3 Goods coming from third countries 487
1.4 Cross-border movement of goods 487
1.5 Direct effect 489
1.5.1 Measures adopted by states and EU institutions 489
1.5.2 Horizontal direct effect? 491
2. Financial restrictions: tariff barriers 492
2.1 Customs duties 493
2.2 Charges having an equivalent effect 493
2.3 Permissible charges 494
2.3.1 Duty for inspection required by EU law 494
2.3.2 Payment for a service rendered 495
2.4 Recovery of unlawful charges 496
3. Financial restrictions: internal taxation 496
3.1 Article 110(1) TFEU 497
3.1.1 Similar products 497
3.1.2 Discrimination 499
3.1.3 Justification 500
3.2 Article 110(2) TFEU 501
3.3 Remedies 503
4. Boundaries between Articles 30 and 110 TFEU 503
5. Non-tariff barriers: quantitative restrictions 505
6. Non-tariff barriers: measures having the equivalent effect of quantitative restrictions 506
6.1 Defining MEEQR in Dassonville 507
6.2 Clarifying MEEQR in Cassis de Dijon 509
6.2.1 Mutual recognition of national product rules 509
6.2.2 The post-Cassis case law of the Court 510
6.3 Containing the tide in Keck & Mithouard 514
6.3.1 Keck: "selling arrangements" 515
6.3.2 Judicial qualifications of "selling arrangements" 516
6.3.3 Exclusionary rules after Keck: "Rules of use", market access and remoteness 519
6.4 Import versus export restrictions 522
7. Boundaries between non-tariff and tariff restrictions 523
8. Overview of restrictions 524
9. Justifications 525

9.1 Absence of EU harmonization legislation 525
9.2 Two sets of justifications 526
9.2.1 Article 36 TFEU derogations 526
9.2.2 "Mandatory requirements in the general interest" 529
9.2.3 Towards a singular justifications regime? 530
9.3 Principle of proportionality 531
9.3.1 Test of suitability 532
9.3.2 Test of necessity 532
9.4 Balancing fundamental freedoms and fundamental human rights 533
10. Burden of proof 534
11. Free movement of goods and state-backed commercial monopolies 534
12. Conclusion 536
Further reading 537

Chapter 14
FREE MOVEMENT OF SERVICES, ESTABLISHMENT AND CAPITAL **539**
Stefaan Van den Bogaert, Armin Cuyvers and Ilektra Antonaki
1. Introduction 539
2. Free movement of services and the freedom of establishment 540
2.1 Treaty basis 540
2.2 The concept of establishment 541
2.3 The concept of a service 541
2.3.1 An economic activity 541
2.3.2 Distinguishing services from establishment 544
2.3.3 Distinguishing between services and goods 545
2.4 Beneficiaries and scope 545
2.4.1 Nationality and establishment in the EU 546
2.4.2 The cross-border element 546
2.4.3 The inclusion of service recipients 547
2.4.4 Horizontal direct effect of Articles 49 and 56 TFEU 548
2.5 Restrictions on freedom of establishment and the freedom to provide services 549
2.5.1 Discriminatory restrictions 549
2.5.2 Beyond discrimination: The Säger approach 551
2.5.3 Limits to the concept of restrictions 552
2.5.4 Some specific examples of restrictions 553
2.6 Justification of restrictions 556
2.6.1 Pursuing a legitimate aim 557
2.6.2 The proportionality assessment 562
2.6.3 Compliance with fundamental rights 566
2.7 The Services Directive 567
2.7.1 Scope 568
2.7.2 Administrative simplification and cooperation 568
2.7.3 Authorizations, prohibited and suspect restrictions to establishment 569
2.7.4 Restrictions on services 570
3. Free movement of capital 570
3.1 Historical overview 571
3.2 Scope and effect of the current Treaty provisions 572
3.2.1 Direct effect 572
3.2.2 Territorial scope 572
3.2.3 Material scope 574

3.3 Relationship with the other freedoms 575
3.3.1 Capital versus Services 575
3.3.2 Capital versus Establishment 576
3.4 Restrictions 577
3.4.1 Discriminatory measures 577
3.4.2 Non-discriminatory measures 578
3.5 Justifications 580
3.5.1 Treaty derogations 581
3.5.2 Judicial derogations 583
3.5.3 Proportionality 584
3.5.4 Legal certainty 585
Further reading 586

Chapter 15
FREE MOVEMENT OF WORKERS AND COORDINATION OF SOCIAL SECURITY 587
Anne Pieter van der Mei
1. Introduction 587
2. Aim and historical development 588
3. The right to work in other Member States 592
3.1 The right to work 592
3.2 The public service exception 593
4. The status of worker 594
5. Social advantages 595
6. Prohibition of direct discrimination, indirect discrimination, discrimination on grounds of migration and non-discriminatory obstacles to free movement 597
7. Enforcement 599
8. Coordination of social security 599
8.1 Introduction 599
8.2 Scope 601
8.2.1 Personal scope 601
8.2.2 Substantive scope 602
8.3 Rules determining the applicable legislation 603
8.4 Principles of coordination 605
8.5 Coordination rules for specific types of social security benefits 606
8.5.1 Health care and health insurance 606
8.5.2 Unemployment benefits 608
Further reading 610

Chapter 16
CITIZENSHIP OF THE UNION 611
Annette Schrauwen
1. The concept of "citizenship of the Union" 611
1.1 European citizenship before the Treaty of Maastricht 612
1.2 Citizenship in the Treaty of Maastricht 613
1.2.1 Why a notion of citizenship? 613
1.2.2 Definition of citizenship of the Union 614
1.2.3 Reception of the concept 614
1.3.3 Citizenship of the Union in the Lisbon Treaty 615
2. Acquisition and loss of Union citizenship 616

3. Union citizenship as a legal status 617
3.1 Directive 2004/38: Personal scope and beneficiaries 617
3.2 Relationship between the Directive and the Treaty provisions 619
4. Free movement rights 619
4.1 Rights of exit and entry 620
5. Residence rights 622
5.1 Residence rights under the Treaty provisions 622
5.2 Residence rights under Directive 2004/38 623
5.2.1 Residence up to three months 624
5.2.2 Residence longer than three months and up to five years 624
5.2.3 Right of permanent residence 626
6. Limiting the right of residence and expulsion 628
7. The right to equal treatment 630
7.1 The right to equal treatment under the Treaty provisions 630
7.2 The Right to equal treatment under the Directive 631
8. The position of family members under the Directive 633
9. Political rights 634
9.1 Electoral rights 634
9.2 The citizens' initiative 635
10. The right to diplomatic protection and the right to address the institutions 636
11. Citizenship reports and the possibility of extending citizenship rights 636
12. Concluding remarks 637
Further reading 638

Chapter 17
EUROPEAN MIGRATION AND ASYLUM LAW 639
Jorrit J. Rijpma
1. Introduction 639
2. The rationale behind a European migration and asylum policy 640
2.1 Free movement and spill-over 641
2.2 Security 641
2.3 Economics 642
2.4 Solidarity, mutual recognition and trust 643
2.5 International human rights obligations and Union values 645
3. Union competences in asylum and migration 646
3.1 Treaty framework 646
3.2 Variable geometry 647
3.3 The EU's policy agenda on migration and asylum 649
4. EU migration and asylum law: Substantive rules 651
4.1 Borders and Visa 651
4.1.1 Borders 651
4.1.2 Visa 653
4.1.3 Entry-exit system and ETIAS 654
4.2 Irregular migration 655
4.2.1 Preventing access to territory 655
4.2.2 Preventing human smuggling and trafficking 655
4.2.3 Return 656
4.3 Asylum policy 658
4.3.1 Dublin Regulation 659
4.3.2 Temporary Protection Directive and relocation decisions 660

4.3.3 Qualification Directive 661
4.3.4 Procedures Directive 663
4.3.5 Reception Directive 664
4.3.6 A third phase for the Common European Asylum System 665
4.4 Legal migration 666
4.4.1 Family reunification 667
4.4.2 Long Term Residents Directive 668
4.4.3 Blue Card Directive 670
5. Concluding remarks 671
Further reading 672

Chapter 18
JUDICIAL COOPERATION IN CIVIL MATTERS 673
Xandra Kramer

1. Introduction and institutional development 673
2. Policy background and pillars of judicial cooperation 675
3. Institutional framework: Scope and limits of Article 81 TFEU 677
3.1 Civil matters and judicial cooperation 677
3.2 Cross-border dichotomy 678
3.3 Decline of the internal market requirement 680
3.4 Special position of family law 681
4. Key areas of civil justice and the legislative framework 682
4.1 Key areas and the existing legislative framework 682
4.1.1 Private international law instruments 682
4.1.2 Instruments on specific procedural issues and European procedures 685
4.1.3 General measures to support the area of civil justice cooperation 686
4.2 Legislative approach: In search of coherence 686
4.3 Contribution of ECJ case law 687
5. Current debates and prospects 688
Further reading 690

Chapter 19
EU CRIMINAL LAW 691
Jannemieke Ouwerkerk and Willem Geelhoed

1. The evolution of criminal law into an area of EU competence 691
1.1 Integration within the Schengen framework and the ne bis in idem principle 692
1.2 From Maastricht to Amsterdam: Criminal law on an intergovernmental basis 693
1.3 Criminal law competences under the Lisbon Treaty 693
1.4 Jurisdiction of the ECJ over criminal law matters 695
1.5 Opt-out arrangements for the UK, Ireland, and Denmark 695
2. Substantive criminal law of the EU 695
2.1 Influence of the EU on the general part of criminal law 695
2.2 Euro crimes 696
2.3 Regulatory criminal law 700
3. EU norms of criminal procedure 702
3.1 Minimum standards of procedural rights for suspects and accused persons 702
3.2 Minimum standards of procedural rights for victims of crime 704
4. Judicial cooperation on the basis of mutual recognition 705
4.1 Mutual recognition as a cornerstone principle 705
4.2 European arrest warrant 706

4.3 Cross-border gathering and use of evidence 706
4.4 Cross-border supervision of non-custodial pre-trial measures 706
4.5 Transfer of execution of sanctions 707
4.6 Taking account of foreign convictions 708
4.7 The protection of fundamental rights in cross-border cooperation 708
5. European agencies and bodies for criminal justice cooperation 710
5.1 Europol 710
5.2 Eurojust 711
5.3 The European Judicial Network 712
5.4 OLAF 712
5.5 The future European Public Prosecutor's Office 712
Further reading 713

Chapter 20
COMPETITION LAW AND POLICY 715
Christof R.A. Swaak and Marc van der Woude
1. General part: A system of undistorted competition 715
1.1 The place of competition rules in the Treaty 715
1.2 The actors involved 716
1.3 The sources of law 718
1.4 The objectives and effectiveness of the competition rules 719
1.5 Market definition 721
2. Anti-competitive collusion 722
2.1 The structure of Article 101 TFEU 722
2.2 The concept of undertaking 726
2.3 The concept of collusion 730
2.4 The concept of effect on trade 732
2.5 Within the internal market 734
2.6 Restriction of competition 735
2.7 Horizontal agreements 737
2.7.1 Introduction 737
2.7.2 Various common types of horizontal cooperation 739
2.8 Cartels 741
2.9 Vertical agreements 743
2.10 Licensing agreements 746
3. Abuses of dominant position 747
3.1 The structure of Article 102 TFEU 747
3.2 The concept of dominance 748
3.3 Proof of dominance 751
3.4 The concept of abuse 753
3.5 Exclusionary practices 756
3.6 Exploitative abuses 763
4. Enforcement of antitrust rules 765
4.1 The system set up by Regulation 1/2003 765
4.2 Enforcement by the Commission 766
4.3 Enforcement by NCAs and the ECN 768
4.4 Enforcement by national courts 769
4.5 Judicial review 771
5. Concentration control 772
5.1 Setting up the system 772

5.2 Concentrations with a Community dimension 774
5.3 The notification system 775
5.4 The substantive test 776
Further reading 778

Chapter 21
STATE AID LAW 779
Tom Ottervanger and Maarten Aalbers
1. Introduction 779
2. Developments in EU state aid law 2005–2017 781
3. Article 107(1) TFEU 782
3.1 Advantage 782
3.1.1 The concept of an advantage 782
3.1.2 The market economy investor test 783
3.1.3 The Altmark test 784
3.2 State resources 784
3.2.1 Transfer of state resources 784
3.2.2 Imputability to the state 786
3.3 The selectivity criterion 786
3.4 Effect on interstate trade 789
3.5 Distortion of competition 789
4. Exemptions 790
4.1 Automatic exemptions: Article 107(2) TFEU 790
4.2 Exemptions granted by the Commission: Article 107(3) and Article 106(2) TFEU 790
4.2.1 General exemption regime under Article 107(3) TFEU 790
4.2.2 Categories of exemptions under Article 107(3) TFEU 791
4.2.3 Exemption under Article 106(2) TFEU for services of general economic interest 793
4.2.4 Special derogation 794
5. Article 108 TFEU enforcement 794
5.1 Introduction 794
5.2 Ex-post supervision for existing aid 795
5.3 Ex-ante supervision of new aid 796
5.3.1 Administrative procedure 796
5.3.2 Preliminary examination 797
5.3.3 Formal investigation procedure 797
6. Unlawful aid 798
6.1 Definition 798
6.2 Recovery 799
6.3 Procedure 800
7. Judicial protection 800
7.1 National courts 800
7.2 The General Court and the Court of Justice 801
8. State Aid Modernization Programme: New enforcement priorities 803
Further reading 804

Chapter 22
PUBLIC PROCUREMENT 805
Sarah Schoenmaekers
1. Introduction 805
2. History and international context of the EU public procurement regime 805
3. Objectives of the EU public procurement regime 808
4. Principles and treaty provisions underlying the EU public procurement regime 809
4.1 The principle of non-discrimination 809
4.2 The equal treatment principle 810
4.3 The principle of transparency 811
4.4 Treaty provisions 811
5. Public sector procurement: The new General Directive 2014/24/EU 812
5.1 Introduction and rationale of the Directive 812
5.2 Scope of application 812
5.2.1 Procurement of public contracts and design contests 812
5.2.2 Contracting authority 813
5.2.3 Thresholds 815
5.2.4 Exceptions 815
5.3 Selection 817
5.3.1 Grounds for exclusion 817
5.3.2 Selection criteria 818
5.3.4 Reduction of the number of candidates 819
5.4 Award criteria 819
5.5 Procedures 820
5.5.1 Open procedure 820
5.5.2 Restricted procedure 820
5.5.3 Competitive procedure with negotiation 821
5.5.4 Competitive dialogue 821
5.5.5 Innovation partnership 822
5.5.6 Negotiated procedure without prior publication 822
5.6 Procurement tools 822
5.6.1 Framework agreements 822
5.6.2 Dynamic purchasing systems 823
5.6.3 Electronic auctions 823
5.6.4 Electronic catalogues 824
5.6.5 Centralized procurement and joint procurement 824
5.7 Contract performance 824
6. Utilities procurement 825
7. Concessions 825
8. Remedies 826
9. Future outlook and conclusion 827
Further reading 827

Chapter 23
TAXATION 829
Dennis Weber
1. Introduction 829
2. EU treaty freedoms in taxation cases 829
2.1 Introduction 829
2.2 Tax restrictions in the case law of the court 830

2.2.1 (Indirect) discrimination on grounds of nationality 830
2.2.2 Allowances related to personal and family circumstances 830
2.2.3 Horizontal discrimination 832
2.2.4 Restriction of free movement 833
2.3 Tax disparities in the case law of the Court 835
2.4 Per country versus overall approach – always somewhere approach – neutralisation of restrictions 837
2.5 Balanced allocation of the power to tax, prevention of tax avoidance, effectiveness of fiscal supervision: Justifications for restrictions 838
2.5.1 Balanced allocation of the power to tax 838
2.5.2 Prevention of tax avoidance 838
2.5.3 Effectiveness of fiscal supervision 839
3. State aid rules and harmful tax competition 840
3.1 Harmful tax competition 840
3.2 State Aid 841
4. Harmonization in taxation 842
4.1 Decision-making in tax matters 842
4.2 Harmonization in direct taxation 843
4.2.1 Corporate taxation 843
4.3 Indirect taxation 845
4.3.1 Union Customs Code 845
4.3.2 Value Added Tax (VAT) 845
4.3.3 Excises and energy taxation 846
4.4 Administrative cooperation and recovery of tax claims 846
5. Conclusion 847
Further reading 847

Chapter 24
INTELLECTUAL PROPERTY 849
Ana Ramalho
1. Introduction 849
2. Intellectual property in the context of the EU Treaties 850
2.1 Negative integration: National IP rights and Treaty provisions 851
2.2 Positive integration: The legal basis to regulate intellectual property in the EU 852
3. The development of an intellectual property acquis 854
3.1 Trademarks 855
3.2 Patents and rights similar to patents 858
3.3 Copyright and related rights 861
4. Conclusion 865
Further reading 866

Chapter 25
COMPANY LAW 867
M.A. Verbrugh
1. Introduction 867
2. Freedom of establishment and case law 867
2.1 Introduction 867
2.2 Articles 49 and 54 TFEU 867
2.3 Incorporation doctrine and real seat doctrine 869
2.4 Case law 870

2.4.1 Introduction 870
2.4.2 Cross border transfer of the real seat 870
2.4.3 Cross border merger and cross border conversion 871
2.4.4 Recognition of foreign companies using a branch 872
2.4.5 Conclusion 873
3. Harmonization of company law 873
3.1 Introduction 873
3.2 Company Law Directives 874
3.3 Conclusion 877
4. Supranational companies 877
4.1 Introduction 877
4.2 SE, SCE and EEIG 878
4.3 SPE, SUP and FE 879
5. Modernization of company law 880
Further reading 881

Chapter 26
ECONOMIC AND MONETARY UNION 883
Fabian Amtenbrink
1. A brief history of Economic and Monetary Union 883
1.1 The original EEC Treaty 883
1.2 Werner Report: The first plan to form a European Economic and Monetary Union 884
1.3 The European Monetary System: An interlude 886
1.4 From the Single European Act to the Treaty on European Union and the single European currency 887
2. EMU as structured by the Treaty on European Union and the Treaty on the Functioning of the European Union 891
3. The *ad hoc* and structural European regulatory response to the European sovereign debt crisis 892
4. Legal status of non-euro area Member States and the legal and economic conditions for joining the single currency (convergence criteria) 895
4.1 Member States outside the euro area 895
4.2 Legal and economic criteria for joining the single currency (convergence criteria) 898
5. Economic policy inside and outside the euro area 902
5.1 Objectives and principles of economic policy coordination in the EU 902
5.2 The rules on deficit financing according to market principles 906
5.3 Economic policy coordination inside and outside the euro area 910
5.3.1 The European Semester 911
5.3.2 Multilateral surveillance of deficits, debts and macroeconomic (im)balances 912
5.3.3 Excessive deficit and excessive macroeconomic imbalances procedures 914
5.3.4 Scope of judicial review in the multilateral surveillance, excessive deficit and macroeconomic imbalances procedure 921
5.4 Powers to deal with extraordinary economic circumstances inside and outside the euro area 923
6. Monetary policy in the euro area 928
6.1 Legal nature, organizational structure and constitutional position of the ESCB and the ECB 929
6.1.1 Legal nature 929

6.1.2 Organizational structure 931
6.1.3 ECB independence and accountability 934
6.2 Objectives and scope of monetary policy 942
6.3 Tasks of the ESCB and of the ECB 945
6.4 The ECB's legal instruments 949
Further reading 950

Chapter 27
FINANCIAL MARKET REGULATION AND SUPERVISION 951
Matthias Haentjens, Jouke Tegelaar and Dorine Verheij

1. Introduction 951
2. Institutional structure and its development 951
2.1 Lamfalussy Report: 2001 951
2.2 De Larosière Report: 2009 954
2.3 Banking Union, single supervision and crisis management: 2014–present 955
2.3.1 Banking Union 955
2.3.2 Single supervision 955
2.3.3 Crisis management 956
2.4 Future developments 957
3. Regulation 958
3.1 Introduction 958
3.2 Banks 959
3.3 Securities and markets 963
3.4 Insurers and pension funds 972
4. Supervision and enforcement 974
4.1 Introduction 974
4.2 European Supervisory Authorities 975
4.2.1 Supervisory powers 977
4.2.2 Joint Committee of the ESAs 982
4.3 Banking Union 982
4.3.1 Single Supervisory Mechanism: ECB 982
4.3.2 Single Resolution Mechanism: SRB 986
5. Legal protection 988
5.1 Introduction 988
5.2 ESAs 989
5.3 ECB and SRB 990
Further reading 993

Chapter 28
EU SOCIAL LAW AND POLICY 995
Sacha Garben

1. Social policy in the Treaties 995
2. Rationale of EU action 997
3. The EU social *acquis* at a glance 998
3.1 Overview of main legislative and policy measures 998
3.1.1 Posting of workers 998
3.1.2 Working time 1001
3.1.3 Non-standard forms of employment 1002
3.1.4 Structural changes in the company 1004
3.1.5 Information and consultation of workers 1007

3.1.6 OSH 1008
3.1.7 Social OMC 1009
3.1.8 The European Pillar of Social Rights 1010
3.2 Cross-cutting considerations 1012
3.2.1 A uniform application of the labour law directives? 1012
3.2.2 The role of the EU Charter 1013
3.2.3 A social deficit? 1015
4. Final considerations 1015
Further reading 1016

Chapter 29
EQUAL TREATMENT AND NON-DISCRIMINATION 1017
Christa Tobler
1. Introduction 1017
2. The larger context of international law 1019
3. The layered system of Union non-discrimination law 1020
4. Field of application 1021
4.1 Personal scope 1022
4.2 Material scope 1022
4.2.1 The oldest field: Pay 1022
4.2.2 Other issues related to employment and occupation 1023
4.2.3 Employment-related social security 1024
4.2.4 Other matters, in particular goods and services 1024
5. Equal treatment and non-discrimination 1025
5.1 Equality and discrimination under EU law: An Aristotelian understanding 1025
5.2 Discrimination grounds 1026
5.3 Multi-dimensional discrimination 1028
5.4 Forms of discrimination 1029
5.4.1 Direct discrimination 1029
5.4.2 Indirect discrimination 1031
5.4.3 Harassment 1032
5.4.4 Instruction to discriminate 1033
6. Duty to treat differently 1033
7. Grounds allowing for differential treatment (justification) 1034
7.1 Open system: Objective justification 1034
7.2 Half-closed system for age discrimination: Objective justification under Article 6(1) of Directive 2000/78 1035
7.3 Closed system of statutory grounds 1036
7.3.1 Genuine occupational requirements 1037
7.3.2 Positive action 1038
7.3.3 Protection of women as regards pregnancy and maternity 1039
7.3.4 Occupational social security under Article 6(2) of Directive 2000/78 and under Article 9(1)(g) of Directive 2006/54 1040
7.3.5 Article 2(5) of Directive 2000/78 1040
7.4 An overarching issue: Proportionality 1041
8. Enforcement 1042
8.1 Enforcement under specific secondary law 1042
8.2 General elements of enforcement of non-discrimination law 1043
9. Conclusion 1044
Further reading 1045

Chapter 30
AGRICULTURE AND FISHERIES 1047
Thomas van Rijn

1. The nature of the agricultural problems 1047
2. The place of the common agricultural and common fisheries policies in the TFEU 1049
 2.1 Agriculture and fisheries 1049
 2.2 Internal market and common policy 1049
3. Objectives 1051
4. Scope 1052
5. Instruments and their development 1053
 5.1 Common market organization 1054
 5.2 Structural measures 1055
 5.3 Approximation of laws 1056
 5.4 Competition rules 1057
6. Pillars of the actual agricultural law 1057
 6.1 Direct income support 1058
 6.2 Regulation of the market 1059
 6.3 Rural development support 1059
 6.4 Promotion of product quality 1059
 6.5 Measures combating animal and plant diseases and promoting animal welfare 1060
7. Pillars of the actual fisheries law 1060
 7.1 Conservation 1061
 7.2 Fleet restructuring 1062
 7.3 International relations 1062
 7.4 Market regulation 1063
8. Decision making 1063
9. Implementation, application, control 1064
10. Financing 1064
11. Outlook 1065
Further reading 1066

Chapter 31
TRANSPORT POLICY 1067
Pablo Mendes de Leon

1. Particularities of transport services 1067
2. The development of a common transport policy 1067
3. The relationship between the general principles of the TFEU and the special provisions of the transport title 1068
4. Principal provisions of the title on transport 1068
 4.1 Establishment of a common transport policy 1068
 4.2 Articulation of the characteristics of transport 1069
 4.3 Equal treatment of transporters 1069
 4.4 Measures on State aid 1069
 4.5 Establishment of charges, rates and conditions 1070
 4.6 Specific procedures for sea and air transport 1070
5. Particular subjects pertaining to transport 1070
 5.1 Public services and services of general economic interest 1070
 5.2 Competition 1071
 5.3 State aid 1071
 5.4 External Relations 1072

6. Measures applying to the transport modes 1072
6.1 Road transport 1072
6.1.1 Economic regulation 1072
6.1.2 Safety and security 1073
6.1.3 Protection of the environment 1073
6.1.4 Social policies 1074
6.1.5 External relations 1074
6.2 Rail transport 1074
6.2.1 Economic regulation, including social policies and consumer protection 1074
6.2.2 Safety and security 1075
6.2.3 External relations 1075
6.3 Inland waterway transport 1075
6.3.1 Economic regulation, including social policies and consumer protection 1075
6.3.2 Safety and security 1076
6.3.3 Protection of the environment 1076
6.3.4 External relations 1076
6.4 Maritime transport 1076
6.4.1 Economic regulation, including consumer protection 1076
6.4.2 Safety and security 1078
6.4.3 Protection of the environment 1079
6.4.4 Infrastructure 1079
6.4.5 Social policies 1080
6.4.6 External relations 1080
6.5 Air transport 1081
6.5.1 Economic regulation, including social policies 1081
6.5.2 Safety and security 1083
6.5.3 Protection of the environment 1083
6.5.4 Infrastructure 1084
6.5.6 Consumer protection 1085
6.5.7 External relations 1085
7. Combined Transport and Trans-European Networks 1086
Further reading 1087

Chapter 32
EUROPEAN ENERGY LAW – FROM MARKET TO UNION? 1089
Leigh Hancher
1. Introduction 1089
2. The constitutional framework 1090
2.1 The Treaty of Lisbon 1091
2.2 Nuclear energy: The Euratom Treaty 1093
2.2.1 Nuclear safety 1093
2.2.2 The Supply Agency 1094
2.3 Energy, SGEI and the Lisbon Treaty 1094
2.4 The inter-relationship between Article 194 and climate change policy 1095
2.4.1 Article 192 TFEU: Renewables, emissions and efficiency 1095
2.5 Energy networks 1096
2.6 Article 194 TFEU: What difference does it make? 1097
3. The third energy package legislation – building the internal market 1097
3.1 The third energy package 1097
3.1.1 The unbundling regime 1098

3.1.2 National regulatory authorities 1099
3.2 The New Agency – the ACER 1100
3.3 ACER, network codes and comitology 1101
3.4 REMIT 1101
3.5 The gas security of supply regulation 1102
3.6 Conclusion 1102
4. External energy policy 1102
4.1 Introduction 1102
4.2 Shared competence 1103
4.2.1 Strategic Partnerships 1103
4.2.2 The Energy Community Treaty 1104
4.3 Foreign direct investment 1104
5. The future of EU energy law and policy 1104
6. Conclusion 1105
Further reading 1106

Chapter 33
THE REGIONAL DIMENSION OF EU LAW: COHESION POLICY AND GEOGRAPHICAL DIFFERENTIATION 1107
Thomas Vandamme

1. Introduction: "A Europe of the Regions"? 1107
2. Economic, social and territorial cohesion 1109
3. Funding economic, social and territorial cohesion 1110
3.1 Structural Funds and Cohesion Fund: General and operational principles 1112
3.1.1 The additionality principle 1114
3.1.2 The complementarity principle 1114
3.1.3 The programming principle 1114
3.1.4 The principle of partnership 1115
3.2 The Structural Funds and Cohesion Fund 1116
3.2.1 The European Regional and Development Fund 1116
3.2.2 The European Social Fund 1116
3.2.3 The Cohesion Fund 1117
3.3 Other financial instruments 1118
3.3.1 The European Agricultural Fund for Rural Development 1118
3.3.2 The European Maritime and Fisheries Fund 1118
3.4 The European Investment Bank 1119
4. Geographical differentiation: "Overseas Europe" 1120
4.1 Introduction 1120
4.2 The passerelle clause to change a territory's status 1122
4.3 The Outermost Regions 1123
4.4 The Overseas Countries and Territories 1124
Further reading 1128

Chapter 34
EU HEALTH LAW AND POLICY 1129
Anne Pieter van der Mei and Ellen Vos

1. Introduction 1129
2. EU health law and policy: A brief history 1130
3. Health and the internal market 1133
3.1 Pharmaceuticals 1134

3.2 Foodstuffs 1136
3.3 Tobacco 1138
3.4 Healthcare providers 1139
3.5 Patients 1140
4. Health policy *stricto sensu* 1142
5. EU health law and policy: Future 1143
Further reading 1144

Chapter 35
CONSUMER PROTECTION IN THE EU **1145**
K.J. Cseres
1. Introduction 1145
2. The development of consumer law in the EU 1146
2.1 First phase: No legal basis – consumer law as soft law 1146
2.2 Second phase: Establishing a legal basis 1147
2.3 Third phase: Re-orientation of the internal market 1150
2.3.1 Full harmonization: A new regulatory approach 1152
3. EU regulatory model of consumer protection 1154
3.1 Regulatory approach: Information paradigm 1155
3.2 The normative concept of the consumer in EU law 1156
3.2.1 The average consumer 1157
3.2.2 The vulnerable consumer 1158
4. Enforcement of consumer law 1159
Further reading 1163

Chapter 36
ENVIRONMENTAL POLICY **1165**
Suzanne Kingston
1. History and development 1165
2. Aims 1169
3. Competence and external action 1170
4. Principles 1171
4.1 The precautionary principle 1172
4.2 The preventive principle 1173
4.3 The rectification at source principle 1173
4.4 The polluter pays principle 1174
4.5 The integration principle 1175
5. Legal bases and environmental guarantee provisions 1176
5.1 General legal bases 1176
5.2 Environmental guarantee provisions and minimum harmonization 1177
5.3 Governance and enforcement 1178
6. Overview of selected sectoral environmental policies 1181
6.1 Climate and energy 1181
6.2 Industrial pollution control 1181
6.3 Control of chemical substances 1182
6.4 Environmental impact assessment and Strategic environmental impact assessment 1182
6.5 Biodiversity and nature conservation 1183
Further reading 1184

Chapter 37
RESEARCH AND TECHNOLOGY 1185
Morag Goodwin
1. Introduction 1185
2. Legal framework 1186
3. Decision-making procedure 1188
4. European Research Area 1189
4.1 The Framework Programmes and Horizon 2020 1191
4.2 Competitiveness and Innovation Programme 1194
4.3 European Institute of Innovation and Training 1194
4.4 Joint Programming, JTIs and ETPs 1195
4.5 European Research Council 1196
5. European Space Policy 1196
Further reading 1198

Chapter 38
SUPPORTING POLICIES 1199
Sacha Garben
1. Introduction 1199
1.1 Complementary competences 1199
1.2 The place of supporting policies in the Treaties 1199
1.3 Between authorization and restraint 1201
2. European integration in supporting policy areas 1202
2.1 Limited competence but extensive integration? 1202
2.2 Negative integration 1203
2.3 Positive integration 1205
3. The protection and improvement of human health 1208
3.1 The place of health in the Treaties 1208
3.2 Specific areas of EU health law and policy 1209
3.2.1 Free movement of patients 1210
3.2.2 Tobacco regulation 1210
3.2.3 Protection of workers' health and safety: The Working Time Directive 1211
3.2.4 Fiscal sustainability of national health care systems 1212
4. Education, vocational training, youth and sport 1213
4.1 Education and vocational training 1213
4.1.1 ERASMUS 1213
4.1.2 Professional diploma recognition 1214
4.1.3 Academic diploma recognition 1215
4.1.4 Student residence 1216
4.1.5 Education of migrant children 1217
4.1.6 Cost-effectiveness of education systems 1217
4.2 Youth 1218
4.3 Sport 1219
5. Culture 1221
6. Industry 1223
7. Tourism 1224
8. Civil protection 1225
9. Administrative cooperation 1227
10. Concluding Remarks 1228
Further reading 1229

Chapter 39
AN INTRODUCTION TO UNION EXTERNAL ACTION, ITS SCOPE, ITS INSTITUTIONS AND ITS INSTRUMENTS **1231**
Pieter Jan Kuijper
1. The background to the Treaty provisions 1231
2. Union external powers: Their structure and foundations in the EU treaties 1234
3. The instruments of external action 1236
4. External relations powers in the system of exclusive, shared and supplementary powers of the TFEU 1238
5. The Union's institutions and decision-making in the field of external action 1242
6. Mixed agreements and mixed membership of international organizations 1248
   6.1 Mixed agreements 1248
   6.2 Mixed membership in international organizations 1252
7. Loyalty and sincere cooperation in external relations 1254
8. The place of international law in the law of the EU 1255
   8.1 International law as law of the Union 1255
   8.2 Harmonious interpretation and direct effect 1258
   8.3 Agreements of the Member States 1260
9. Conclusion. Great expectations inspired and frustrated by the two Treaties 1261
Further reading 1262

Chapter 40
THE COMMON FOREIGN AND SECURITY POLICY AND THE COMMON SECURITY AND DEFENCE POLICY **1263**
Pieter Jan Kuijper
1. Background and introduction 1263
2. Bodies, Institutions and Agencies 1264
3. CFSP and CSDP policies and actions 1270
   3.1 Introductory remarks 1270
   3.2 CFSP: The common policy with respect to the International Criminal Court (ICC) 1272
   3.3 CSDP military common policy: The EU's non-proliferation policies 1275
   3.4 CFSP/CSDP Civilian Action: EU-Lex Kosovo 1279
   3.5 Military CSDP mission: Atalanta 1283
4. Conclusion 1288
Further reading 1289

Chapter 41
UNION EXTERNAL ACTION UNDER THE TFEU **1291**
Pieter Jan Kuijper
1. Introduction 1291
2. The common commercial policy 1292
   2.1 The commercial policy competence of the Community 1292
      2.1.1 The concept of commercial policy and its scope. Article 207 TFEU 1292
      2.1.2 The exclusivity of Community competence in the field of commercial policy 1296
   2.2 Principles and development of the common commercial policy 1298
   2.3 Commercial policy arrangements 1301
      2.3.1 Autonomous commercial policy: Regulation of imports and exports 1301
      2.3.2 Autonomous commercial policy: Safeguard measures 1304

2.3.3 Anti-dumping duties and countervailing duties 1307
2.3.4 The exercise of the EU's rights and implementation of its duties under International Trade Agreements 1311
2.3.5 EU policy on foreign direct investment: Two preconditions 1314
2.4 Conclusion 1318
3. Development and other cooperation policies 1319
3.1 Development cooperation and other cooperation policies 1319
3.1.1 Objectives and scope of development cooperation and other cooperation policies. A brief overview 1319
3.1.2 Autonomous measures: Financing instruments 1322
3.1.3 Contractual measures: International Agreements 1325
3.2 Conclusion 1325
4. The System of European Union Agreements 1326
4.1 The system viewed geographically 1326
4.2 Agreements based on Article 217 TFEU 1327
4.2.1 Article 217 TFEU 1327
4.2.2 The EEA Agreement 1328
4.2.3 The Association Agreements with the Eastern European and Southern Caucasus countries 1330
4.2.4 Association with a view to accession 1331
4.2.5 Development association 1333
4.3 Other cooperation agreements 1335
4.3.1 Partnership agreements with Russia and Central Asia 1335
4.3.2 Diverse trade and cooperation agreements 1336
4.4 Conclusion 1339
5. Restrictive measures 1339
5.1 Introduction and overview of restrictive measures (sanctions) 1339
5.2 Legal basis and adoption of sanctions regimes 1341
5.3 Judicial review of restrictive measures: The Kadi cases and beyond 1343
5.4 Restrictive measures: Some conclusions 1346
6. Overall conclusion 1346
Further reading 1347

Table of Selected Cases (Numerical Order) 1349

Subject Index 1369

LIST OF ABBREVIATIONS

AAC	Average Avoidable Cost
AB	Appellate Body (WTO)
ACER	Agency for the Cooperation between Energy Regulators
ACP	Africa, Caribbean and Pacific group of countries.
ADR	Alternative Dispute Resolution
AER	Application and Enforcement Regulation
AFSJ	Area of Freedom, Security and Justice
AG	Advocate General
AIFMs	Alternative Investment Fund Managers
ALDE	Alliance of Liberals and Democrats for Europe
ATC	Agreement on Textiles and Clothing (WTO)
AVC	Average Variable Cost
BEREC	Body for European Regulators for Electronic Communications
BGPL	Bodies Governed by Public Law
BIT	Bilateral Investment Treaty
BoS	Board of Supervisors
BRICs	Brazil, Russia, India, China
BRRD	Bank Resolution and Recovery Directive
CAP	Common Agricultural Policy
CCP	Common Commercial Policy
CDDH	Steering Committee for Human Rights (Council of Europe)
CDU-CSU	Christian Democratic Union – Christian Social Union (German political party)
CEAS	Common European Asylum System
CEDAW	Convention on the Elimination of Discrimination against Women
CEDEFOP	European Centre for the Development of Vocational Training
CEE	Charges having Equivalent Effect
CEF	Connecting Europe Facility
CEPOL	European Union Agency for Law Enforcement Training
CETA	Comprehensive Economic and Trade Agreement (with Canada)
CF	Cohesion Fund
CFI	Court of First Instance (Former Lower Court of the CJEU, see also GC)
CFP	Common Fisheries Policy

CFREU	Charter of Fundamental Rights of the EU
CFSP	Common Foreign and Security Policy
CISA	Convention on the Implementation of the Schengen Agreement
CITES	Convention on International Trade in Endangered Species
CJ	(European) Court of Justice (Upper Court of the CJEU)
CJEU	Court of Justice of the European Union
CMO	Common Market Organization
CoC	Committee of Contributors
CoR	Committee of the Regions
Coreper	Committee of Permanent Representatives
COSAC	Conference of the Committees of the national parliaments of the EU Member States specializing in EU matters.
CPC	Community Patent Convention
CPVO	Community Plant Variety Office
CRA	Credit Rating Agencies
CRD	Capital Requirements Directive
CRP	Council Rules of Procedure
CRPD	Convention on the Rights of Persons with Disabilities
CSDP	Common Security and Defence Policy
CSDR	Central Securities Depositary Regulation
DAC	Development Assistance Committee (OECD)
DCFTA	Deep and Comprehensive Free Trade Agreement
DG	Directorate General or Director General
DGS	Deposit Guarantee Scheme
DSU	Understanding on Rules and Procedures governing the Settlement of Disputes (WTO)
EAA	European Asylum Agency
EAEC	European Atomic Energy Community (Euratom)
EAFRD	European Agricultural Fund for Rural development
EAGF	European Agriculture Guarantee Fund
EASA	European Aviation Safety Agency
EASO	European Asylum Support Office
EBA	European Banking Authority
EC	European Community
ECA	European Court of Auditors
ECAA	European Common Aviation Area
ECB	European Central Bank
ECDC	European Centre for Disease Control
ECHA	European Chemicals Agency
ECHR	European Convention of Human Rights
ECJ	European Court of Justice (also referring to CJEU as a whole; see also CJ)
ECN	European Competition Network
ECOFIN	Council of Ministers for Economic and Financial Matters
ECOSOC	Economic and Social Committee (see also ESC)
ECR	European Conservatives and Reformists

ECSB	European System of Central Banks
ECSC	European Coal and Steel Community
ECtHR	European Court of Human Rights
ECU	European Currency Unit
EDA	European Defence Agency
EDC	European Defence Community
EDF	European Development Fund
EDP	Excessive Deficit Procedure
EEA	European Economic Area
EEA	European Environment Agency
EEAS	European External Action Service (EU diplomatic service)
EEC	European Economic Community
EFDD	Europe of Freedom and Direct Democracy
EFRD	European Fund for Regional Development
EFSA	European Food Safety Agency
EFSF	European Financial Stability Facility
EFSM	European Financial Stability Mechanism
EFTA	European Free Trade Agreement
EIA	Environmental Impact Assessment
EIB	European Investment Bank
EIDHR	European Instrument for Democracy and Human Rights
EIOPA	European Insurance and Occupational Pensions Authority
EIP	Excessive Imbalance Procedure
EJN	European Juridical Network
EMA	European Medicine Agency
EMCDDA	European Monitoring Centre for Drugs and Drug Addiction
EMCF	European Monetary Cooperation Fund
EMI	European Monetary Institute
EMIR	European Market Infrastructure Regulation
EMMF	European Maritime and Fisheries Fund
EMS	European Monetary System
EMU	European Monetary Union
EMU	Economic and Monetary Union
ENISA	European Agency for Network and Information Security
ENP	European Neighbourhood Policy
ENPI	European Neighbourhood Policy Instrument
EP	European Parliament
EPA	Economic Partnership Agreement
EPC	European Political Cooperation
EPC	European Patent Convention
EPC	European Political Community
EPO	European Patent Office
EPPO	European Public Prosecutor's Office
EPU	European Political Union
ERA	European Research Area

ERAC	European Research Area Committee
ERC	European Research Council
(E)RDF	(European) Regional Development Fund
ERM	Exchange Rate Mechanism
ERTA	European Road Transport Agreement (see Case 22/70)
ESA	European Space Agency
ESA	European Supervisory Authority/ies
ESC	European Social Charter
ESC	Economic and Social Committee (see also ECOSOC)
ESF	European Social Fund
ESI	European Structural and Investment (Funds)
ESM	European Stability Mechanism
ESMA	European Securities and Market Authority
ESRB	European Systemic Risk Board
ETIAS	European Travel Information and Authorization System
ETP	European Technology Programme
ETS	Emissions Trading System
EU	European Union
EUIPO	European Union Intellectual Property Office (see OHIM)
EUMC	EU Military Committee
EUNAVFOR	European Union-led Naval Force (Somalia)
EU-OSHA	European Occupational Safety and Health Agency
EURES	European Network for Employment Services
EUROFOUND	European Foundation for the Improvement of Living and Working Conditions
EUSR	EU Special Representative
FAO	Food and Agriculture Organization
FCC	Federal Constitutional Court (Germany, see also GCC)
FDI	Foreign Direct Investment
FE	Fundatio Europea (European Foundation)
FET	Fair and Equitable Treatment
FP	Framework Programme
FPI	Foreign Policy Instruments (Service for)
FR	Financial Regulation
FRA	Fundamental Rights Agency
FRO	Fundamental Rights Officer
FTA	Free-Trade Agreement
GAC	General Affairs Council
GATS	General Agreement on Trade in Services
GATT	General Agreement on Tariffs and Trade
GBER	General Block Exemption Regulation
GC	General Court (Lower Court of the CJEU, see also CFI)
GCC	German Constitutional Court (see also FCC)
GDP	Gross Domestic Product
GDR	German Democratic Republic (formerly East Germany)

GHG	Greenhouse gas
GNI	Gross National Income
GNP	Gross National Product
GPA	Government Procurement Agreement (WTO)
GSA	European GNSs Agency (linked to Galileo)
GSP	Generalized Scheme of Preferences
GUE/NGL	European United Left/Nordic Green Left
HCCH	Hague Conference on Private International Law
HHI	Herfindahl-Hirschman Index
HICP	Harmonized Index of Consumer Prices
HR/VP	High Representative/Vice President (for external action) (see also VP/HR)
IAEA	International Atomic Energy Agency
IATA	International Air Transport Association
ICAO	International Civil Aviation Organization
ICC	International Criminal Court
ICCPR	International Covenant of Civil and Political Rights
ICERD	International Convention on the Elimination of all Forms of Racial Discrimination
ICESCR	International Covenant of Economic, Social and Cultural Rights
ICSD	Investment Compensation Scheme Directive
ICTY	International Criminal Tribunal for the former Yugoslavia
IGC	Inter-Governmental Conference
ILO	International Labour Organization
IMF	International Monetary Fund
IMO	International Maritime Organization
IORP	Institution for Occupational Retirement Provisions
IP	Intellectual Property
IPA	Pre-Accession Instrument
IPR	Intellectual property Right
ISDS	Investor to State Dispute Settlement
ITLOS	International Tribunal on the Law of the Sea
JHA	Justice and Home Affairs
JTI	Joint Technology Initiative
KFOR	Kosovo Force (NATO)
MAD	Market Abuse Directive
MAR	Market Abuse regulation
MEEQR	Measures having Equivalent Effect to Quantitative Restrictions
MEIP	Market Economy Investor Principle
MEP	Member of the European Parliament
MFF	Multi-annual Financial Framework
MiFID	Market in Financial Instruments Directive
MiFIR	Market in Financial Instruments Regulation
MMFs	Money Market Funds
NATO	North-Atlantic Treaty Organization

NCA	National Competent Authorities
NCA	National Competition Authority
NCB	National Central Bank
NGO	Non-Governmental Organization
NPT	Treaty on the Non-Proliferation of Nuclear Weapons
NRA	National Regulatory Authority
OCTs	Overseas Countries and Territories
ODA	Official Development Assistance
ODR	Online Dispute Resolution
OECD	Organization for Economic Cooperation and Development
OEEC	Organization for European Economic Cooperation
OHIM	Office for the Harmonization in the Internal Market (see also EUIPO)
OLAF	Office européen de lutte antifraud/ European Anti-Fraud Office
OMC	Open Method of Coordination
OMRs	Outermost Regions
OMT	Outright Monetary Transactions
OPCW	Organization for the Prohibition of Chemical Weapons
OSCE	Organization for Security and Cooperation in Europe
PCI	Project of Common Interest
PFI	Protection of the Financial Interests (of the EU)
PPE/EPP	Parti Populare Européen/European People's Party (Christian Democrats)
PPI	Protocol on Privileges and Immunities
PRD	Patient's Rights Directive
PRIIP(s)	Packaged Retail and Insurance-based Investment Product(s)
PSC	Political and Security Committee
PSO	Public Service Obligation
QMV	Qualified Majority Voting
R(E)IO	Regional (Economic) Integration Organization
REACH	Registration, Evaluation, Authorization and Restriction of Chemicals
RQMV	Reversed Qualified Majority Voting
S&D	Socialists and Democrats
SAA	Stabilization and Association Agreement
SAAP	State Aid Action Plan
SAC	Special Area of Conservation
SAM	State Aid Modernization
SBC	Schengen Borders Code
SCCI	Single Complex and Continuous Infringement
SCE	Societas Cooperativa Europea (European Cooperative Society)
SCIFA	Strategic Committee on Immigration, Frontiers and Asylum
SDS	Sustainable Development Strategy
SE	Societas Europea (European Company)
SEA	Single European Act
SES	Single European Sky
SGEI	Service(s) of General Economic Interest
SIS	Schengen Information System

SME	Small and Medium-sized Enterprises
SOFA	Status of Forces Agreement
SOLVIT	Internal Market Problem Solving Network
SOMA	Status of Mission Agreement
SPA	Special Protection Area
SPC	Supplementary Protection Certificate
SPE	Societas Privata Europea (European Private Company)
SPS	Agreement on the Application of Sanitary and Phytosanitary Measures (WTO)
SRB	Single Resolution Board
SRM	Single Resolution Mechanism
SSM	Single Supervisory Mechanism
SUP	Societa Unius Personae (Single Member Limited Liability Company)
TBR	Trade Barrier Regulation
TBT	Agreement on Technical Barriers to Trade (WTO)
TCN	Third Country National
TEC	Treaty of the European Community
TEU	Treaty on European Union
TFEU	Treaty on the Functioning of the European Union
TPD	Tobacco Products Directive
TRIPs	Agreement on Trade-related Intellectual Property Rights
TSCG	Treaty on Stability, Coordination and Governance
TSO	Transmission System Operator
TTIP	Transatlantic Trade and Investment Pact (with the US)
UCC	Union Customs Code
UCITS	Undertaking for Collective Investment in Transferable Securities
UCLAF	Unité de coordination de la lutte antifraude/Unit for the coordination of the fight against fraud
UE	Union Européenne (see also EU)
UK	United Kingdom
UN	United Nations
UNCLOS	UN Convention on the Law of the Sea
UNCTAD	United Nations Conference for Trade and Development
UNHCR	United Nations High Commissioner for Refugees
UNMIK	UN Mission in Kosovo
UNRWA	UN Relief and Works Agency (for Palestine)
UNSC	UN Security Council
US	United States
VAT	Value Added Tax
VIS	Visa Information System
VP/HR	Vice President/High Representative (for external action) (see also HR/VP)
WCO	World Customs Organization
WEU	Western European Union
WMD	Weapons of Mass Destruction
WTO	World Trade Organization

FOREWORD

This manual of European Law can hardly any longer legitimately be called the fifth English edition of what once started as Kapteyn & VerLoren van Themaat *Introduction to the Law of the European Communities* back in the 1970s, and continued until the fourth edition published in 2008. Its content and authors have simply changed too much. However, it still stands in that lineage. It still pays attention to the historical development of European Union law; it still attempts to place positive Union law against its political, economic and social background. It has no longer been written exclusively by Dutch authors – the diversity of nationalities among the authors has grown exponentially with this book – but all authors are or have been connected to Dutch universities and they have all attempted to go beyond only sources in the English language as the basis for their contributions. With the large number of authors, it has become very difficult, if not impossible, to have full coherence in approach throughout the book, but the editors have done their very best to ensure such coherence at least within distinct sectors of Union law (institutional law, internal market, economic and monetary union etc.).

Of the editors of the fourth edition of Kapteyn/VerLoren van Themaat, sadly Kamiel Mortelmans is no longer with us. He passed away in the spring of 2017, after a long illness, during much of which he continued his work as a Counselor of State of the Netherlands. His short introductory chapter to the internal market section of the book is his last publication. We dedicate this book to his memory. Fortunately, Professor and Judge Kapteyn is still with us. He has watched our efforts to continue in the spirit of the initial authors of the *Introduction* from a distance, but with keen interest. It is a great pleasure to the editors that he will be able to read the result of the collaboration between so many people. We also want to pay homage to one of the long-serving editors of various editions of Kapteyn/VerLoren van Themaat, Christiaan Timmermans, also a former judge of the European Court of Justice, who, once again, was ready to update his introductory chapter to this work.

Work on this book was started in earnest in late 2013, when the various consequences of the Lisbon Treaty were becoming more and more visible in EU legislative and regulatory acts and in the case law of the Union Courts. During the last years of writing and revising the contributions (2016–2017) the so-called Brexit raised its head and indeed began its course. The editors then decided that, since the way in which Brexit would finally be consummated remained largely unclear, any attempt to take it into account at that stage would result in pure speculation, which likely would be overtaken by events at the moment of publication. Moreover, there was no doubt in the minds of the editors that the British, who would soon be from the outside looking in, would be best served by a solid manual of European Union law, describing and analysing that law as it stood at the moment of cutting themselves off from the Union to which especially their best lawyers had so much contributed. In a way this book also hopes to be a homage to the contribution that our British brother and sister lawyers have made to European Union law in many different capacities.

The editors have made an effort to limit the length of footnotes somewhat, where that was possible, and to make the lists of suggested further reading as informative, but at the same time as brief as possible. Now that it has been normal practice for such a long time already to find and consult the case law of the Union Courts without any difficulty by case number on the website of the Court of Justice, the time has come to do away with complicated tables of cases. There is just an index of the most important cases, listed by number.

The editors are grateful to all authors for their patience and support, supplying us with drafts, re-drafts and updates of their contributions over many years. We want to single out in particular those who were ready, at an advanced stage of the project to fill in for, or assist, others and to produce high quality drafts under great time pressure: Jannemieke Ouwerkerk, Pim Geelhoed, Felix Ronkes Agerbeek, Kassandra Wetz. We also want to extend our gratitude to Miluska Kooij, who served as secretary to the editors in the early stages of the project. The editors are particularly grateful to Sherin Seyda, who took over as secretary to the editors, when the project went into a higher gear and saw it through to the end; her work was invaluable. Special thanks to Maureen Posthuma Mantje and Andrew Faughnan, who provided language editing assistance for selected chapters. We are also grateful to Wendy Rodger for her help at proof stage. Financial support for this project in its different phases was extended by the Stichting Europa Instituut, Amsterdam, the Professor H.F. Van Panhuys Fonds, Amsterdam, and the Europa Instituut, Leiden. Finally, as always, the staff of Kluwer Law International, with all its professionalism, could be counted on to bring the book to market in expeditious fashion. The state of the law is broadly that of end of summer/autumn 2017. Individual authors have done their best to put in brief references to later developments.

The editors,
Pieter Jan Kuijper
Fabian Amtenbrink
Deirdre Curtin
Bruno De Witte
Alison McDonnell
Stefaan Van den Bogaert

CHAPTER 1
THE GENESIS AND HISTORICAL DEVELOPMENT OF THE EUROPEAN COMMUNITIES AND THE EUROPEAN UNION

*C.W.A. Timmermans**

1. The Schuman plan and its background

On 9 May 1950 a press conference took place at the Quay d'Orsay to make public a proposal by the French Government which was to have far-reaching importance for European integration. The French Foreign Minister, Robert Schuman, read a sensational declaration. It contained the proposal to place the whole of Franco-German coal and steel output under a common High Authority, in an organization open to the participation of other countries of Europe.

This proposal was sensational in two respects. In the first place it meant a turn of the tide in French policy with regard to Western Germany, a policy which had so far been directed at a continued tutelage by the Western Allies of the defeated enemy. A proposal for a Franco-German partnership in a limited but vital economic field, as the nucleus of a broader European co-operation, broke through this post-war policy. The form which was to be given to this cooperation was equally revolutionary: the grouping of coal and steel production under the direction of a common High Authority (composed of independent persons), capable of taking decisions binding on France, Germany, and any other participating countries, and which could be implemented in their territory. This proposal introduced a new element into the pattern according to which the promotion of common interests by states was traditionally organized in international society.

The typical feature of this latter pattern had been an *intergovernmental* organization, commonly based on three principles. In the first place, decisions of the organization are taken by organs composed of government representatives. Second, participating states are not legally bound by these decisions against their will; even if the basic treaty provides for binding decisions, unanimity will be required to arrive at them; decisions having no binding effect by virtue of the treaty itself will only obtain this effect in relation to states accepting them. Third, the implementation of decisions is reserved to the participating states themselves. There are, of course, exceptions to each of these three principles. But it is the abandonment of these principles as a starting point for the association of states in an international organization which justifies the *supranational*[1] label which was later to be given to the form of organization which was developed on the basis of the Schuman Declaration.

---

* Former Judge European Court of Justice.

1. This term occurred in the original version of the ECSC Treaty (Art. 9), but disappeared during a later revision.

1.1 *The power vacuum in Europe and the aim of European integration*

What was the background to this Declaration, which broke both with a main feature of post-war French foreign policy and with traditional views concerning the organization of cooperation between states?

In the spring of 1950 the world presented a grim picture, especially seen from Western Europe. The eastern part of Europe had been brought firmly within the Russian sphere of influence. The *coup d'état* of 20 February 1948 in (then) Czechoslovakia and the Berlin blockade from 24 June 1948 to 12 May 1949 had enhanced the fear of Russian expansionism. The explosion of the first Russian A-bomb in August 1949, three to four years earlier than the West had anticipated, and the strengthening of the monolithic communist block which was expected to result from the final victory of the party of Mao Zedong in China in the autumn of 1949, tended to foster even further the widely prevalent opinion in the West that the chances of a third world war had increased considerably.

The risk that Europe itself might once more be at the centre of a future conflict was recognized by many people. Indeed, armed forces of the two super-powers confronted each other there. The fuel for a conflict lay piled high: the artificial division of Germany and the militarily weak position of the garrisons of the Western Allies in West Berlin. The countries of Western Europe were busily engaged in restoring their economies with American financial aid under the Marshall Plan (1947). Politically, however, they were still at a stage of relative insignificance, while militarily they were making a first modest attempt to put up a coordinated defence of their territory against an attack from the East. Being helpless against superior Russian military power and without hope of ever being able to establish any adequate defence against it, they depended on the military and financial aid of the United States under the North Atlantic Treaty, concluded on 4 April 1949. The impulse for this Treaty came on the one hand from the Brussels Treaty of 17 March 1948, on the part of the United Kingdom, France and the Benelux countries, and on the other hand from the so-called Vandenberg Resolution. This Resolution had been adopted on 11 June 1948 by the U.S. Senate and recommended an association of the United States with "such regional and other collective arrangements as are based on continuous and effective self-help and mutual aid".

The international political situation which had developed after the war gave all the more impetus to a political trend which, by taking up pre-war plans and ideas, aimed at a firmly organized political and economic partnership of European nations. Europe on the basis of this partnership should muster enough strength to play its part in international politics once again, instead of being at its mercy. The vacuum which had arisen in Europe had to be filled with a new political structure which would diminish the Russian threat and reduce the dependence on the United States. Winston Churchill was the first to give full publicity to the idea of European integration after the war. On 19 September 1946, in an address at Zurich University, he submitted that it was necessary to build "a kind of United States of Europe" for which he saw a partnership between France and Germany as the first step.

The year 1948 formed a climax for the numerous political groups which advocated a united Europe. On 7 May 1948 they jointly convened the Congress of Europe in the Hague. A great many prominent parliamentarians, scholars and statesmen not in office at the time took part. In a series of resolutions they made an appeal for the formation of a political and economic union, the calling of a European Assembly whose members were to be appointed by the national parliaments, the framing of a Charter of Human Rights, and the creation of a Court of Justice to supervise the observance of the Charter.

At the instigation of the Belgian and French Governments, these proposals were studied in the Council of the Brussels Treaty to ascertain to what extent they could be carried into effect.

These discussions resulted in the Statute of the Council of Europe, signed on 5 May 1949, in which, in addition to the countries of the Brussels Treaty, Sweden, Norway, Denmark, Ireland, and Italy took part. The Statute was the result of a laboriously reached compromise, the British participants in particular having doggedly held out for an organization along purely intergovernmental lines. The British concession concerned the establishment of a Consultative Assembly in addition to the classic Committee of Ministers. This Assembly was composed of representatives of the Member States, who were to be designated in a way to be determined by each government. Although it was not expressly stated in the Statute, the intention of the framers was to pave the way for an organ in which the national parliaments might be represented, a novelty in the set-up of an international organization. It was not until 1951 that the logical consequence was drawn from this intention and the Statute was amended in the sense that henceforth each parliament, at least as a general rule, was to appoint the number of delegates in the Assembly assigned to the respective country.

For the rest, the Council of Europe turned out to be a disappointment for the champions of firm European partnership. The Consultative Assembly was only able to make recommendations to the Committee of Ministers, which in turn could do little more than frame recommendations to the Member States, in practically all important cases on the basis of unanimity. Nevertheless, the Consultative Assembly, which consisted of a select group of parliamentarians, played a particularly important political role during the first few years. It was indeed from the midst of this body that the initiative came for the framing of a treaty which was eventually signed in Rome on 4 November 1950 as the European Convention for the Protection of Human Rights and Fundamental Freedoms and which entered into force on 3 September 1953. In the Assembly, the first great debates in public concerning the form and substance of future European cooperation also took place. There the different groups which had already manifested themselves at the Hague Congress became clearly apparent: the unionists, the federalists and the functionalists. The unionists desired a further development of intergovernmental cooperation between European countries. The federalists held that a European federation should be the ultimate aim. The boldest among them, the constitutionalists, wished to proceed to convene a *Constituante Européenne* which would draft and proclaim a constitution for a United States of Europe. The more prudent of the federalists, the functionalists, advocated a merger of sovereign national rights on concrete points, for instance heavy industry.

1.2 *The problem of Franco-German relations and the commitment of the German Federal Republic to Western Europe*

It was this last approach which the French Government followed up when making public its plan for the establishment of a High Authority for coal and steel. Although men like Schuman and Monnet (the intellectual father of the plan) no doubt nursed conceptions of the future political structure of Europe, it was not only such conceptions which incited the French to action. The central problem was that of Franco-German relations.

The aim of French European policy was to obtain effective guarantees against a revival of a German menace to French security. Such guarantees had been sought by successive French Governments in a permanent restriction of the scope of development of German economic and political power after the collapse of the Third Reich in 1945. Especially after the final breach between the four Great Powers about the course of action to be taken with regard to Germany, this restrictive French policy appeared less and less feasible in an atmosphere of growing tension between East and West. The United States, in particular, followed by the United Kingdom, was bent on an early reconstruction of economic and political life in the Western zones of occupation of Germany. In Anglo-American circles a thriving Germany closely allied to the West was increasingly regarded as an essential condition for the recovery of Europe and as an indispensable bulwark against the dreaded Russian expansionism. With many reservations therefore, French diplomats had to acquiesce in a series of preliminary measures which led to the establishment in May 1949 of the German Federal Republic. Within, as yet, fairly narrow limits, the Occupation Statute introduced in May of that year made the Germans in the Western zones masters in their own house again.

Early in 1950, French policy reached an impasse. The negative attitude towards German economic and political recovery taxed relations with the new German state – which to an increasing degree was becoming a European political and economic reality to be reckoned with. The position of the Saar, a politically autonomous area, but economically associated with France, bade fair to become a bone of contention. The German Federal Republic, in view of the inequality involved, took a very reserved attitude towards the Ruhr Statute, which was agreed by the end of 1948 particularly at the instigation of France and which ensured allied supervision over the coal and steel industry in this district by means of an international authority. The United States and the United Kingdom showed themselves less and less willing to give an effective shape to this supervision. Finally, the French Government realized that, with the aggravation of antagonism between East and West, it would hardly be possible in the long run to resist American insistence on permitting the German Federal Republic to play its potential role in the economic, political and even military sphere among the nations of Europe to the full.

The Schuman Plan constituted a brilliant attempt to break through this impasse. The policy aim remained the same: effective guarantees against a revival of a German menace to French security. But the means for achieving this aim were changed drastically. Instead of the former negative policy, directed at a continued allied tutelage of Germany, efforts were directed towards a far-reaching partnership on a basis of parity of the two countries within a European setting. It was precisely the coal and steel sector, the traditional basis of every form of power politics, which seemed an excellent starting-point for such an association. The unilateral supervision over the German coal and steel industry, embodied in the Ruhr Statute, which had not proved viable, would make way for a coal and steel regime on a broader basis, which would subject this industry in France, Germany, and other European countries which wished to participate, to supervision on an equal footing by a common High Authority. This arrangement would also place the Saar problem in a different perspective.

Thus the Schuman Plan was a political answer to a series of political problems of the first order: the existence of a power vacuum in Europe, viewed by many people as one of the sources of the cold war; the more effective shaping of European integration, which was widely deemed necessary; the settlement of Franco-German relations; and finally the cementing of the German Federal Republic, which was once again developing into a European power, into Western Europe on a basis of equality, but with maximum guarantees against independent German power politics, with all the dangers to Europe and world peace this could involve, also in view of the division of the former German territory into a Western and an Eastern sector.

1.3 *Economic considerations*

Considerations of a more economic character were not absent, but they played a rather subsidiary part compared to the political considerations mentioned above, some of which were acute. Thanks to Marshall Aid, but also as a result of the activities of the Organization for European Economic Co-operation (the OEEC, which later became the OECD), the economic prospects for the European countries at the beginning of 1950 were not unfavourable. At the instigation of the United States and in spite of initial objections, particularly on the part of the United Kingdom, the OEEC had been established on 16 April 1948 in connection with Marshall Aid as a "continuous organization", meaning that after termination of this aid it would still have the task of shaping economic cooperation between the participating countries of Europe. A Dutch suggestion that the OEEC be entrusted with the task of setting up a customs union on the model of the Benelux Treaty of 1944, and a French attempt to equip the organization with strong institutions had come to nothing, despite U.S. support. These ideas had been strongly opposed in particular by the United Kingdom, but with regard to the French proposal also by Benelux, which feared excessive influence by the larger European countries.

Within the limits thus set on it, this intergovernmental organization of the traditional type had nevertheless taken the first important steps on the road towards the liberalization of trade and payments and towards a better mutual adjustment of national economic policies. However, aspirations for a far-reaching economic partnership based on abolition of tariff frontiers between the participating states, hopes widely cherished at least on the continent, could not be satisfied by the OEEC. Not only was there great difference of opinion among Member States about the nature of and the methods appropriate to a European economic partnership, but the institutional structure of the OEEC did not seem adapted to bear the load of the development and pursuance of a common policy in an economic union. Indeed, in the view of many people, this union would be the indispensable complement of the abolition of trade barriers between the countries of Europe.

Both in institutional respects and with regard to methods of European economic integration, the Schuman Plan suggested new roads. A free movement of coal and steel products might be a first step on the road towards a series of sector markets which might finally lead to full economic integration. The production and sale of coal and steel seemed a good starting point also because this sector demonstrated the striking inappropriateness of national frontiers, which cut up artificially the area where the greatest concentration of coal and iron ore in Western Europe was to be found.

2. The ECSC Treaty of 18 April 1951

The French initiative, which was particularly sympathetically received by the United States, met with a favourable reception in several European capitals, especially Bonn. On 20 June 1950 there was a conference in Paris of the six countries (the German Federal Republic, France, Italy and the three Benelux countries) which had subscribed to the principles of the Schuman Plan. An attempt to persuade the United Kingdom to join as well had failed. The fear of being impeded in the development of its own welfare state and in the maintenance of the bonds with the Commonwealth, as well as an insufficient realization of the importance of the French proposal and the vistas it opened, caused the British Government to cling to its standpoint that only a cooperation based on coordination of national policies within the framework of an intergovernmental organization like the OEEC was acceptable.

After nine months of negotiations, the Treaty establishing the European Coal and Steel Community (ECSC) was signed in Paris on 18 April 1951. On 25 July 1952 it entered into force. According to its Article 97, it was concluded for 50 years. The basis of the common market for coal and steel thus called into being was formed by the prohibition within this market, of:

(i) duties on importation or exportation or charges having equivalent effect, and quantitative restrictions;
(ii) measures and practices discriminating between producers, purchasers or consumers or interfering with the purchaser's free choice of supplier;
(iii) subsidies or aids granted by states, or special charges;

(iv) restrictive practices tending towards the sharing or exploiting of markets.[2]

In accordance with the Schuman Plan, the High Authority occupied a central place in the institutional structure of the Community. It was composed of independent persons jointly designated by the governments, had its own financial resources from a levy on coal and steel production, and was provided with powers for binding the Member States and companies coming under the Treaty regime. Thus it became a governmental authority operating in this new market, instead of or alongside the six national governments.

This breakthrough from the classic pattern of international organization, which in itself was quite revolutionary, was, however, attended by many safeguards. In the first place the powers of the High Authority were bound up strictly with the provisions of the Treaty.[3] In these provisions, the policy to be pursued in the coal and steel sector was laid down fairly precisely. As the French delegation reported after the negotiations: *"la loi ici, c'est le Traité"*. A Court of Justice was charged, in particular, with ensuring the observance of the law in the implementation of the Treaty.[4]

In the second place, the High Authority was obliged to consult governments and other interested parties frequently and cooperate closely with them. This was to be done either directly,[5] or in concert with the Special Council of Ministers,[6] or the Consultative Committee[7] as the case might be. The Council, which was created as a result of a Dutch initiative, was entrusted with the coordination between on the one hand the policy of the High Authority and on the other hand that of the governments responsible for the general economic policy of their countries,[8] a problem which indeed had to be provided for in a system of partial integration such as that of the ECSC system. Only in exceptional cases did the Council of Ministers itself have the power to intervene in the coal and steel market (e.g. under certain conditions in crisis situations[9]). Its task consisted chiefly in giving its opinion – unanimously or by a qualified majority vote – to the High Authority on the decisions to be taken by the latter.[10] On a number of important issues the High Authority was obliged to obtain the prior consent of the Council to its decision by means of an assent. The Council then acted as co-regulator.

Finally, the Treaty provided for a Common Assembly[11] originally composed of members of the national parliaments nominated by them, to which the High Authority was politically responsible for the implementation of the Treaty. This Assembly was given the right to dismiss the members of the High Authority collectively by the adoption of a motion of censure.[12]

The desire of the Contracting Parties not to give the High Authority too great a freedom of manoeuvre (and to this end obliging it to consult the governments and to respect democratic principles and the rule of law) only partly accounts for the heavy institutional structure of the Coal and Steel Community. Indeed, considering the strong commitment to the detailed provisions of the Treaty, the High Authority was given only modest scope for the development of a freely determined policy. The extensive institutional provisions were thus primarily justified by

2. Art. 4 ECSC.
3. Art. 14 ECSC. See, generally, P. Reuter, *La Communauté Européenne du Charbon et de l'Acier* (LGDJ, 1953).
4. Arts. 7 and 31 et seq. ECSC.
5. Art. 46 ECSC.
6. Arts. 26–30 ECSC.
7. Arts. 18 and 19 ECSC.
8. Art. 26 ECSC.
9. Arts. 58 and 59 ECSC.
10. Art. 28 ECSC laid down special voting requirements relating to decisions and assents.
11. Arts. 20–25 ECSC.
12. Art. 24 ECSC.

the political perspective, stated in the preamble of the Treaty, which was strongly influenced by the Schuman Declaration: namely the resolve "to lay the foundations for institutions which will give direction to a destiny henceforward shared".

Article 97 ECSC provided that the Treaty was concluded for a fixed period of fifty years. Since the Treaty was never prolonged, it lapsed definitively in 2002.[13] Coal and steel products are now in principle subject to the provisions of the EU Treaties.[14]

3. The failure of plans for a European Defence Community (EDC) and a European Political Community (EPC)

The Schuman Declaration of 9 May 1950 ushered in an era of ambitious attempts to give shape to European integration in a variety of other fields following the same model. Two of these attempts reached the stage of elaborated texts: the Treaty establishing a European Defence Community (EDC) and the draft Statute for a European Political Community (EPC).

3.1 *Background and content of these plans*

The Treaty establishing the EDC originated in the Pleven Plan, which derived its name from the proposals of the then French Minister of Defence in October 1950. Shortly after the Schuman Declaration, the Korean conflict had broken out, a conflict which made a deep impression within Europe. To many people in the West it seemed that convincing evidence had thus been produced of the aggressive designs of Moscow-led international communism. What had happened in Korea, might be repeated in Europe. The future appeared gloomier than ever.

In August 1950 Winston Churchill (then in Opposition) launched, in the Consultative Assembly of the Council of Europe, the idea of a European army under a European Minister of Defence, although he left the British role in the dark. In September the North Atlantic Treaty Council met in New York. The U.S. Secretary of State announced that his country was going to station more armed forces in Western Europe. His Government, however, regarded German rearmament as urgent and essential for the defence of that part of the world. The German forces would have to form part of an integrated Atlantic force which would be set up, under a common supreme command, and which was to receive political and strategic guidelines from NATO.

France vigorously opposed this proposal for German rearmament. In October, Pleven submitted counter-proposals; these attempted to safeguard the objectives of French policy with regard to Germany by the methods of the Schuman Plan, and at the same time to make possible the German rearmament stubbornly urged by the U.S. Government. A European army, composed of the smallest possible national units, would be placed under the control of a European ministry of defence, embedded in an institutional structure similar to that of the ECSC. As such, this European army would form part of the integrated Atlantic force which the North Atlantic Council had decided in September to proceed to form.

After a period of great confusion, the French proposal was ultimately adopted in principle, partly under the influence of the recently appointed Atlantic commander-in-chief, the U.S. General Eisenhower, whose support had been enlisted for the idea. Laborious negotiations between the ECSC countries (with the United Kingdom again holding aloof) finally resulted on 27 May 1952 in the signing of the EDC Treaty, in which an institutional structure somewhat resembling that of the ECSC was provided for.

---

13. Cf. the Protocol on the financial consequences of the expiry of the ECSC Treaty annexed to the Treaty of Nice.

14. The Treaty on European Union and the Treaty on the Functioning of the European Union, both of 2009 (*infra* section 8).

This new Treaty met with opposition from many quarters on widely different grounds, partly of a political, partly of a more pragmatic nature. One of the major political objections, which was also raised in the circles of those wishing to promote European integration, was the fact that a European army was being created without any provision for the framing of a European defence policy and military strategy or a European foreign policy bound up therewith. Another objection concerned the weak democratic character of the EDC.

In order to meet these objections, the six foreign ministers resolved on 10 September 1952 (anticipating ratification) already to implement Article 38 of the EDC Treaty. This Article had been included in the Treaty at the instigation of Italy and provided for proposals from the Parliamentary Assembly of the EDC concerning institutional reform, *inter alia*, to ensure a stronger democratic character of this Community. These proposals were to be seen in the perspective of a later federal or confederal structure, founded on the principle of division of powers and containing, in particular, a system of bicameral representation. The Common Assembly of the ECSC was supplemented by co-opted persons so as to give it a composition similar to that of the Parliamentary Assembly provided for in the EDC Treaty. The resulting "*ad hoc* Assembly" was requested by the Ministers to draft a Statute for a European Political Community: a request which went even further than the mandate contained in Article 38 of the EDC Treaty.

The invitation of the Ministers also spoke of the connection between on the one hand the establishment of such a Community and on the other hand the laying of common foundations for economic development and a fusion of essential interests of the Member States. This passage responded to a suggestion from the Dutch Foreign Minister, Beyen, who wanted to give the Latin tendency to set up institutional structures a firm starting-point in economic reality. His ideas about this were embodied in two Dutch memoranda, of December 1952 and February 1953, in which the outlines of a European common market were sketched. This so-called Beyen Plan, which broke with the then still prevalent idea of a progressive integration of the European economy sector by sector, was later to form the basis of a successful Benelux initiative which in 1957 led to the conclusion of the EEC Treaty.[15]

The so-called "*ad hoc* Assembly" under the chairmanship of Paul Henri Spaak, the Belgian statesman, accomplished its task energetically. In March 1953 the Statute for a European Political Community, drafted by the Assembly and adopted by a very large majority, was handed to the six Ministers. This Community would be endowed with an institutional structure resembling that of the ECSC and the EDC, although a more important role than in either of these Communities was allotted to the supranational policy-making institution and to the parliamentary element. The institutions of the EPC were to take over, on the basis of the respective treaties, the powers of those of the existing ECSC and the future EDC. Procedures were provided to ensure the realization of a coordinated foreign policy of the participating countries, which might in course of time become a common policy, the introduction of a Community tax to defray Community expenses, and the establishment of a common market.

A solitary opponent, the French Gaullist Michel Debré, had vainly championed a different conception in the "*ad hoc* Assembly": that of a Political Union on purely intergovernmental lines, with a Conference of Heads of Government as the top organ.

3.2 *Failure of these plans and "relance européenne"*

The draft Statue for an EPC was not to get beyond the phase of being an object of study. The chances of ratification of the EDC Treaty by France were gradually dwindling. On 30 August 1954 the French National Assembly finally resolved to adjourn the debate on the acceptance of

15. See, generally, R. Griffiths (Ed.), *The Netherlands and the Integration of Europe 1945–1957* (NEHA, 1990).

the EDC Treaty *sine die* – and with that, the draft statute for an EPC also disappeared. Various factors led to this French attitude. A coalition of communists and Gaullists (whose numbers had greatly increased) had hotly opposed the EDC. The former resolutely rejected German rearmament. The latter turned against the abandonment of the instrument, *par excellence*, of national sovereignty: the French army. Moreover, in French circles there was a widespread fear of a confrontation with growing German power within an EDC without the United Kingdom.

The international situation, too, had changed. A political thaw in East-West relations appeared to set in after Stalin's death and the Korean Armistice in 1953. Besides, after the fall of Dien-Bien-Phu in August 1954, the French Government of Pierre Mendès-France had some interest in giving the Soviet Government, which was waging a vehement campaign against acceptance of the EDC, as little cause for irritation as possible, because it badly needed its support in an honourable liquidation of the French empire in Indo-China. To this should be added the French resentment of U.S. pressure to accept the EDC Treaty. The U.S.A. had far overshot the mark when, in December 1953, the U.S. Secretary of State, Foster Dulles, had threatened an "agonizing reappraisal of basic U.S. policy" if the EDC should fail to be established owing to French refusal.

The efforts towards European integration had been dealt a severe blow by the decision of the French Parliament. However, thanks to an initiative of the British Foreign Secretary, Anthony Eden, the essential matter which had formed the primary concern could be settled: the admission of the German Federal Republic as a partner on terms of equality in the Atlantic alliance. The so-called Paris Agreement of 23 October 1954, which had been reached at his instigation, provided, *inter alia*, for the creation of a Western European Union (WEU), equipped with a Parliamentary Assembly and an Agency for arms control, on the basis of a modification of the Brussels Treaty of 1948, to which Italy and the German Federal Republic now also became parties. In this looser European association, the German Federal Republic, with due observance of certain restrictions, was allowed to proceed to rearmament and to make its contribution to the integrated Atlantic armed forces.[16] The occupation regime of Western Germany, now to be admitted to NATO, was terminated, although the three Western occupying powers reserved to themselves their rights with regard to Berlin and to Germany as a whole. An agreement between France and the German Federal Republic finally provided for a settlement of outstanding disputes between the two countries. With reference to the matter of the future position of the Saar, the prospect of a plebiscite was offered, which in 1955 was to turn out in favour of confederation with the German Federal Republic.

The dismay amongst the champions of European integration about the rejection of the EDC treaty did not, however, last long. A "*relance européenne*" was started. A Benelux memorandum of 20 May 1955 resumed the thread of the Beyen Plan: economic integration should precede political integration. The memorandum proposed the convening of a conference for the purpose of working out texts for a treaty which would give shape to far-reaching collaboration in the fields of transport infrastructure, coordination of energy policies, development of the peaceful use of atomic energy, and creation of a common market. In the two last-mentioned fields an important task was intended for a common Authority.

The reaction of the other ECSC countries was not unfavourable, although the French Government displayed an aversion to supranational institutions. The German Government also showed some reserve in this field, possibly because it was apprehensive of the *dirigiste* tendency which it felt was already embodied in the ECSC in the powers of the High Authority. The main

16. In 2010, the mutual defence clause of the WEU Treaty having been integrated in the EU Treaty (Art. 42(7)) by the Treaty of Lisbon, the WEU Member States decided to dissolve that organization.

interest shown on the French side was for cooperation in the field of atomic energy. On 1–2 June 1955 the six foreign ministers of the ECSC countries met in Messina to discuss the Benelux memorandum. It was broadly approved, although in the resolution of the Ministers the institutional provisions relating to cooperation in the field of atomic energy and the establishment of a common market were mentioned only in vague terms. It was decided to convene one or more conferences for working out treaties, and also to entrust the preliminaries for these conferences to a committee of government representatives. This was to be assisted by experts and to be presided over by a political personality who was to coordinate the activities. Paul-Henri Spaak was found willing to undertake the latter task. The United Kingdom, being a member of the WEU and a power allied with the ECSC in a somewhat superficial association (meant to keep a door open) was invited to take part in the activities. This invitation was accepted, although the United Kingdom Government did not subscribe to the Messina Resolution. British participation in the work of the Intergovernmental Committee was to be only short-lived. Already in November 1955 it came to an end. The plans which had matured in the Committee could not be reconciled with the British preference for intergovernmental cooperation, preferably in the OEEC, and for a free-trade area rather than a customs union.

4. The Spaak Report and the conclusion of the treaties establishing the European Economic Community (EEC) and the European Atomic Energy Community (Euratom)

4.1 *The contents of the Spaak Report*

On the basis of the Messina Resolution the Intergovernmental Committee, led with great political imagination and dynamism by Paul Henri Spaak, had set to work on 9 July 1955. In April 1956 the Spaak report was completed in its final form.[17] In the Schuman Plan, the matter of the institutions had taken priority. However, the Spaak Plan – particularly in the light of the widespread reticence about setting up supranational structures after the *débâcle* of the EDC – only dealt with this question following analysis of the substantive problems to be solved in relation to the establishment of a common market and the promotion of the peaceful use of atomic energy. The measures required for the establishment of a common market and the underlying philosophy are traced in broad outline. "The purpose of a common market must be the creation of a large area with a common economic policy, so that a powerful unit of production is formed and continuous expansion is made possible, as well as an increased stability, an accelerated increase of the standard of living, and the development of harmonious relations between the Member States thus united."[18] For this, a fusion of the separate national markets was absolutely essential. The division of labour on a larger scale could put an end to the waste of economic resources. A greater certainty that the requisite sources of supply are permanently accessible makes it possible to abandon productive activities which pay no attention to costs.

This grand design is worked out further in the report around three topics. The *fusion of markets* involves the establishment of a customs union, the abolition of quantitative restrictions, free movement of services and a common agricultural policy. This fusion of markets should be accompanied by a *policy for a common market*. Indeed, in the present economic situation an expansion of markets and of competition *per se* would not yet be sufficient to ensure the more rational division of economic activities and the most favourable degree of expansion. A

17. *Rapport des Chefs de Délégations aux Ministres des Affaires Etrangères* (Secretariat of the Intergovernmental Conference, Brussels, 21 Apr. 1956).
18. Ibid., at 13 (unofficial translation).

common competitive regime would be needed and also provisions for harmonization of laws and the development of a common transport policy. Another essential point was the coordination of national economic policies, so as to avoid difficulties with the balance of payments, if possible, and also common action for eliminating these difficulties, should they arise. *To ensure the development in this common market of European economic resources and their full use*, financial aid for investments and retraining of workers would be necessary in order to promote the transformation of enterprises, the development of economically backward regions, and professional mobility. Freedom of movement should also be given to the production factors – labour and capital.

The report further contended that the realization of this ambitious programme could only take place during a transitional period divided into stages. A multitude of tasks embracing supervision, coordination, legislation, and administration would have to be carried out, which could not possibly all be regulated in detail in the text of the treaty. Moreover, it was felt essential to ensure that flexible methods could be used in implementing the programme, because economic conditions are apt to change rapidly. A good deal therefore would have to be left to institutions, the powers of which would be clearly defined in the treaty, and to procedures, the diversity of which would match that of the problems which might arise. With regard to the institutional structure and the division of powers the report subsequently developed four principles:

(i) pending a closer unity of monetary, budgetary, and social policies of the participating countries it would be necessary to make a distinction between:
  a. matters of general policy, which would remain the reserved domains of the governments, and
  b. problems relating to the functioning of the common market;

(ii) the creation of an organ furnished with authority and Community responsibility would be inevitable, since:
  a. the interest of producers and their legal certainty would demand a direct procedure (*i.e. not via* the governments) for the application and supervision of the rules concerning competition;
  b. the supervision of the fulfilment by the states of their obligations and the control of clauses which permit them to be temporarily relieved of these obligations under certain conditions (safeguard clauses) could hardly be subjected to voting by governments;

(iii) the general policy measures falling within the competence of the governments have so decisive an effect on the functioning of the common market that agreement between the governments should be facilitated and the coordination of these measures more effectively ensured through the use of proposals from a common institution. Certain decisions are even so indispensable for the functioning and development of the common market that, at the suggestion of this institution, acting objectively in the general interest, the rule of unanimity of the governments might be put aside, either in a strictly specified number of cases or after a given period had elapsed;

(iv) it would be necessary to provide for appeal to a judicial body and for organization of parliamentary supervision.

On the basis of these principles the report reached the conclusion that four different institutions were needed: a Council of Ministers, a European Commission, a Court of Justice, and a Parliamentary Assembly. The functions of the two last institutions could be performed by the Court and the Common Assembly of the ECSC. A similar conclusion was drawn in the report with regard to an organization for the peaceful development of atomic energy.

By giving priority to the practical problems involved in the objectives to be reached over the problem of the institutional structure, the Spaak Report succeeded – and this is not the least of its numerous great merits – in demonstrating in a tactical but convincing way the advantages of an institutional structure coordinated with that of the ECSC. A Commission composed of independent persons and serving the Community interest was to be the pivot around which the institutional structure would revolve. It would be able to ensure an efficient discharge of functions of supervision and administration. It would have the task of stimulating and initiating common policies and common rules, and of stimulating the coordination of national policies and national laws. Thanks to the guarantee of impartiality implied in its composition and the formulation of its task, it would even be possible to break through the rule of unanimity in the collective determination of policy measures by the governments.

4.2 *The conclusion of the EEC and Euratom Treaties*

On 29 May 1956 the six foreign ministers met in Venice. At this conference they adopted the Spaak Report as basis for negotiations to frame the requisite treaties. An intergovernmental conference, again under the leadership of Paul-Henri Spaak, was convened for this purpose on 26 June 1956. The negotiations naturally did not proceed without difficulties. Formidable problems had to be solved. Fitting the weak French economy into a common market caused great concern. On the French side all sorts of guarantees were demanded on this point. Moreover, the French Government wished its partners to share in the commercial and financial liabilities of France with regard to the overseas territories and countries associated with that country, particularly those in Africa. Nevertheless, on 25 March 1957 the Treaty establishing the European Economic Community and the Treaty establishing a European Atomic Energy Community were signed in Rome; unlike the ECSC Treaty, they were concluded for an indefinite period.[19] A smooth ratification procedure followed. The long-standing fear that the French Parliament might ultimately refuse to accept the establishment of a common market was found to be unjustified. This fear had even helped to cause questions relating to the peaceful use of atomic energy (which after the Suez crisis of 1956 in the view of many people was of even greater importance than the common market) to be settled in a separate treaty. The partners wished to prevent the fate of cooperation in this field being dependent upon that of a common market.

The successful course of the negotiations and of ratification – the treaties entered into force on 1 January 1958 – was due primarily to the indefatigable efforts of the Action Committee for the United States of Europe, a very effective European pressure group set up by Jean Monnet. Monnet, who in 1952 had been appointed the first President of the High Authority, had tendered his resignation from this office after the failure of the EDC Treaty in the French Parliament so that he might devote his full energy to the "*relance européenne*". In the Action Committee he had managed to unite a large number of influential politicians and trade union leaders from the six countries, who had declared their willingness to make a joint effort to gain the support of their groupings for the federalist basic idea and for the specific resolutions of the Committee.

5. The Communities, the United Kingdom, and enlargement to include other democratic European countries

As was to be expected, there was a reaction on the part of the other OEEC countries to the establishment of the EEC and Euratom. On a British initiative, an enquiry was started in the OEEC in the course of 1957 into the possibilities of bringing about an association in the form

---

19. Arts. 312 EC and 208 Euratom. So far no state has ceased to be a member.

of a free-trade area between the OEEC countries, in which the Six would participate as one economic unit. Great differences of opinion turned out to exist on various issues about which the Six – who were apprehensive of the possibility that the integration process they had started might be watered down – were very much concerned. The problems which worried them included: the necessary degree of harmonization of economic and social policies, the settlement of the problem of the agricultural sector, the consequences of the lack of a common external tariff and a common external trade policy, and the institutional form for such an association. The negotiations (which started in the autumn of 1957, after the termination of the ratification procedure of the EEC Treaty) took place in the Intergovernmental Committee set up by the OEEC Council, under the leadership of the British Minister, Reginald Maudling. They came to an abrupt end in November 1958. The French Minister of Information, Jacques Soustelle, on behalf of the government of General de Gaulle, who had meanwhile come into power, informed the press (without any previous consultation with the five partners) that it was not possible to create a free-trade area without a common external tariff and without harmonization in the economic and social spheres. Thus, the door was closed to the other OEEC countries. Seven among them, *viz.* the United Kingdom, Denmark, Norway, Sweden, Austria, Switzerland and Portugal, decided in July 1959 to go their own way: on 4 January 1960, in Stockholm, the Treaty establishing a European Free Trade Association (EFTA) was concluded. Greece and Turkey associated themselves with the Community in agreements of 9 July 1961 and 12 September 1963 respectively, both based on then Article 238 EEC (now renumbered Art. 217 TFEU).

However, after a few years a radical change took place in the British attitude towards the Communities. On 31 July 1961 Prime Minister Harold Macmillan informed the House of Commons that in the opinion of his government "it would be right for the United Kingdom to make a formal application, under Article 237 of the EEC Treaty for negotiations with a view to joining the Community if satisfactory arrangements could be made to meet the special needs of the United Kingdom, the Commonwealth, and EFTA".[20] A solution of these problems, including, for the United Kingdom, those of British agriculture, would have to be found in conformity with the broad principles and purposes which inspired the concept of European unity and which were embodied in the Rome Treaty. The United Kingdom Government subsequently submitted a request to the Council of Ministers of the EEC to open negotiations with a view to a possible accession. Denmark, Norway, and Ireland followed the British example. The other EFTA countries (Austria, Sweden, Switzerland, and Portugal) on the other hand made a request for negotiations with a view to the establishment of an association or some other economic arrangement.

The negotiations with the United Kingdom started in the autumn of 1961. After 16 months of laborious and often detailed negotiations, which did result in preliminary agreement on many points, the French Government dramatically put an end to the negotiations. At his press conference of 14 January 1963, General de Gaulle plainly showed that he considered British membership of the Community premature and saw no purpose in continuing the negotiations. He alleged that the United Kingdom had not appeared ready to accept a genuine common external tariff, to renounce Commonwealth preferences, to abandon the claim that her agriculture must be privileged, and to cut her ties with the EFTA countries. If the United Kingdom (and with her, inevitably the other EFTA applicant countries) were to join the Community, its character would change and its cohesion be lost. In the long run, General de Gaulle feared the Community would be swallowed up in a colossal Atlantic community, dependent on and controlled by the United States. In the General's view, the Nassau Agreements of December 1962, according to

20. H.C Deb. Vol. 645, Col. 930.

which American aid to the development of the British Skybolt Missile was stopped and the British were to receive the American Polaris Missile as a substitute, had confirmed and reinforced the dependence of the United Kingdom on the United States. With the United Kingdom, the American horse would be dragged into the European Troy. Two weeks after this press conference, on 29 January 1963, it was stated in Brussels that the existing differences of opinion with France made further negotiations impossible.

Rather more than four years after this failure, the Wilson Government considered the time ripe for the United Kingdom to apply once again. On 2 May 1967, Harold Wilson declared in the House of Commons that his Government had decided to make an application for membership of the EEC and parallel applications for membership of the ECSC and Euratom. He reported the readiness of his Government "to accept the Treaty of Rome, subject to the necessary adjustments consequent upon the accession of a new member and provided that we receive satisfaction on the points about which we see difficulty."[21] These points concerned in particular the operation of the Community Common Agricultural Policy: its potential effects on the cost of living, and on the structure and well-being of British agriculture; the budgetary and balance-of-payments implications of its system of financing; and certain Commonwealth problems, in particular those of New Zealand and of the sugar-producing countries, whose needs were safeguarded by the Commonwealth Sugar Agreement. Other points about which questions arose were capital movements and regional policies. However, as Wilson stated, the Government believed "that there is nothing either in the Treaty of Rome or in the practical working of the Community which need make these problems insoluble".[22]

The reactions of the countries of the Community to the British request for accession, followed by those of Ireland, Denmark, and Norway,[23] were again divided. From a communiqué of 19 December 1967, issued by the Council of the European Communities, it finally became evident that although no Member State had raised any fundamental objection to the enlargement of the Community, nevertheless France, unlike the European Commission and her five partners, was unwilling to start negotiations with the four countries which had sought membership. The French Government considered it desirable that the recovery of the British economy should be completed before the request of the United Kingdom could be considered. The requests for accession presented by the four countries remained on the Council's agenda.

The resignation of General de Gaulle and the coming into office of a new French President, a confirmation of the United Kingdom's pledge to Europe by the new Heath Government and the definitive arrangement by the Community of the financing of the Common Agricultural Policy after the expiry of the transitional period finally helped to create the conditions for the re-opening of negotiations on the enlargement of the Communities. The communiqué of the meeting of the Heads of State or Government of the Six at The Hague, on 1–2 December 1969,[24] in which a conception of the future development of the Communities is set out, mentions as one of the elements of agreement the opening of negotiations with the applicant States insofar as they accept the Treaties and their political aims, the decisions taken since the entry into force of the Treaties and the choices made in the sphere of further development. After preliminary discussions within the circle of the Six, negotiations started in the summer of 1970. In the early

---

21. H.C Deb. Vol. 746, Col. 311.
22. Ibid., Col. 313.
23. Sweden, too, intimated a desire to seek a form of participation in the Community which could be reconciled with its policy of neutrality.
24. Bull. EC. 1-1970, 11 at 16 (point 13 of the communiqué). See, generally, H. von der Groeben, *The European Community: The Formative Years* (European Perspectives, 1985).

summer of 1971 they resulted in general agreement between the Six and the United Kingdom. On 22 January 1972 the Final Act embodying the instruments of accession was signed by the six Member States, the United Kingdom, Ireland, Denmark and Norway. After the necessary ratification procedures had been completed, the United Kingdom, Ireland and Denmark acceded to the Communities on 1 January 1973.[25] Norway did not accede, the referendum on accession having gone against membership of the Communities. In the course of 1972 and 1973 free trade agreements principally relating to industrial products, were concluded with the remaining EFTA countries, Austria, Portugal, Sweden, Switzerland, Finland, Norway and Iceland.[26]

The enlargement of the Communities did not stop with the Community of Nine. Greece applied to accede in 1975 and became the tenth Member State on 1 January 1981.[27] In 1977 Spain and Portugal sought membership of the Communities and after long and difficult negotiations acceded on 1 January 1986.[28] Turkey made formal application for membership on 14 April 1987,[29] as did Morocco on 8 July 1987.[30]

The not inconsiderable problems relating to readiness and ability to take decisions apparent in a Community of nine increased substantially in a Community of twelve. Enlargement poses particular difficulties for the maintenance and expansion of a common market and Community policy, as the divergence in the level of development and economic structure within the Community is significantly increased.[31] In these circumstances it is understandable that attempts were resumed in the 1980s (having already been undertaken in the previous decade as part of efforts towards a European Union) to reform the Community in order to prevent a watering-down of the integration process and give it, if possible, a new impetus. These efforts resulted in the Single European Act of 1986.[32]

The new dynamism in the integration process in the late 1980s, with the completion of the internal market (the so-called "1992 effect"), made the Community more attractive to those

---

25. For the United Kingdom see the European Communities Act 1972 (as amended). After various renegotiations conducted by the Labour Government a referendum was held in the United Kingdom which indicated considerable majority support for Community membership (see R. Irving, "United Kingdom Referendum", 1 EL Rev. (1975–76)).
26. For Austria see O.J. 1972, L 300/2; Portugal O.J. 1972, L 301/65 (this lapsed on Portuguese accession on 1 Jan. 1986); Sweden O.J. 1972, L 300/98; Switzerland O.J. 1972, L 300/189; Finland O.J. 1973, L 328/2; Norway O.J. 1973, L 171/2 and Iceland O.J. 1972, L 301/2. These Agreements (and particularly the Protocols thereto) were amended from time to time; the agreements with Austria, Finland, Iceland, Norway and Sweden lapsed on the entry into force of the EEA Agreement on 1 Jan. 1994.
27. O.J. 1979, L 291.
28. O.J. 1985, L 302.
29. Bull. EC 4-1987, points 1.3.1 and 1.3.2. See *infra*.
30. Bull. EC 7/8-1987, point 2.2.35. This was put to one side on the ground that Morocco was not a European country (*Europa-Archiv* 1987, Z 207).
31. See Bull EC Supp. 1-3/78 as revised in COM(83)116 final. The Committee of Three Wise Men set up as a result of the European Council's discussions in Dec. 1978 in anticipation of a future enlargement to twelve Member States reported in Oct. 1979 on the adaptations to the mechanisms and procedures of the Institutions which would be necessary (Report on European Institutions presented by the Committee of Three to the European Council). See, generally, P. VerLoren van Themaat, "Enkele kanttekeningen bij de rapporten van de drie 'Wijzen' en van de Commissie-Spierenburg", (1980) SEW, 144. As to two-speed integration see, *inter alia*, *Gedifferentieerde Integratie in de Europese Gemeenschappen* (14th session of the Asser Instituut Colloquium Europees Recht (1984), The Hague, 1985); C.-D. Ehlermann "How flexible is Community law? An unusual approach to the concept of two speeds", 82 *Michigan Law Review* (1984), 1274; E. Grabitz and B. Langeheine, "Legal problems related to a proposed 'Two Tier System' of integration within the European Community", (1981) CML Rev., 33.
32. See section 6.2, *infra*.

states outside it. Another contributory factor was the collapse of the Soviet hegemony in Central and Eastern Europe, first through the end of the tutelage imposed on the satellite states of Czechoslovakia, Hungary, Poland, Bulgaria and Romania, and later through the implosion of the Soviet Union itself. In the resulting turbulence, political unrest and economic insecurity, the European Community stood out as a beacon of economic prosperity and political stability.

The first territorial expansion eastward resulted from German unification on 3 October 1990. This took place without the need for a Treaty amendment, as the new German *Länder* became part of the Federal Republic of Germany, which was already a Member State.[33] Immediately prior to unification, economic and monetary union was achieved between the old German Democratic Republic and the Federal Republic, which meant that the Community Treaties could be applied immediately in the new *Länder*.[34] The old German Democratic Republic achieved the necessary transformation of its legal system and legislation extremely quickly.

In response to the desire of the EFTA countries to strengthen their economic ties with the Community, the then President of the Commission, Jacques Delors, launched the concept of what eventually became the European Economic Area[35] on 17 January 1989. This would involve the expansion of the Community's internal market and the relevant Community legislation to embrace the EFTA countries. The negotiations which followed were difficult, as the highest possible degree of homogeneity of legislation and its adaptation in the future by the Community and the EFTA countries had to be reconciled with maintaining the independence of the Community system of decision-making and judicial protection.[36] On 2 May 1992 the EEA Agreement was signed in Oporto.[37] As a result of a referendum, Switzerland did not ratify the Agreement, which was then adapted by means of a Protocol.[38] The EEA Agreement thus entered into force on 1 January 1994, a year behind the original schedule. The EEA Agreement obliged the participating EFTA countries, to receive into their legal systems a large body of Community law and, although they would be consulted, they did not attain any power of co-decision on future amendments of that body of law by the Community. It is thus understandable that the majority of the participating EFTA countries regarded the EEA as a step on the way to actual membership of the Communities.

Accession negotiations were opened with Austria, Finland, Norway and Sweden on 1 February 1993[39] and, given the preparatory work in the EEA Agreement and the high degree of afflu-

33. See C. Tomuschat, "A united Germany within the European Community", (1990) CML Rev., 415; C.W.A. Timmermans, "German unification and Community law", (1990) CML Rev., 437, and W. Sinninghe Damsté and W. Wedekind, "De eenwording van Duitsland en de EG, een tussenstand", (1991) SEW, 455.
34. As to the package of transitional measures agreed in certain fields (e.g. trade, agriculture, transport and the environment) see O.J. 1990, L 353.
35. In an address to the European Parliament, Bull. EC Supp. 1/89. For discussion of the development of the EFTA-EC relationship, see S. Norberg et al., *EEA Law* (Fritzes, 1993), 35–69. See Ch. 41, "Union external relations under the TFEU", section 4.2.2, of this book.
36. See Opinion 1/91 *EEA I*, and Opinion 1/92 *EEA II*. See also the contributions by R. Barents and W. van Gerven in J. Stuyck and A. Looijestijn-Clearie (Eds.) *The European Economic Area EC-EFTA* (Kluwer, 1994), 57 and 33, respectively.
37. For the text of the EEA Agreement, see O.J. 1994, L 1/3. See S. Norberg et al., op. cit. *supra* note 35; T. Blanchet et al., *The Agreement on the European Economic Area (EEA)* (OUP, 1994); J. Stuyck and A. Looijestijn-Clearie (Eds.), op. cit. *supra* note 36; S. Norberg, "The agreement on a European Economic Area", (1992) CML Rev., 1171, and J. Steenbergen, "Het EER-Verdrag, een beknopte samenvatting", (1993) SEW, 140.
38. Concluded on 17 Mar. 1993, Bull. EC 3-1993, point 1.3.2. The Protocol contained special provisions permitting Liechtenstein to accede, and this took place on 1 May 1995, Bull. EC 3-1995, point 1.4.49, and 4-995, point 1.4.59.
39. Bull. EC 1/2-1993, point 1.3.1.

ence of the candidate countries, came to a very speedy resolution, so that the Treaty of Accession could be signed on 24 June 1994.[40] For a second time, however, the Norwegian people decided in a referendum against accession. On 1 January 1995, Austria, Finland and Sweden acceded to the European Union,[41] leaving only Norway, Liechtenstein and Iceland as partners in the EEA. The Treaty and Act of Accession and the Protocols attached thereto were set out on the same basis as earlier accessions, namely acceptance by the new Member States of the so-called *acquis communautaire*,[42] but with technical adaptation of existing legislation on institutional as well as substantive aspects. Exceptions to the *acquis* were for a limited period only.

Unlike with previous accessions, no general transitional period was necessary, as the legal arrangements relating to the internal market were already in place in the context of the EEA Agreement. The customs union and the Common Agricultural Policy applied in principle as from the date of accession. As far as institutional adaptations were concerned, the United Kingdom and Spain refused to agree to a mechanical adjustment of the provisions concerning qualified majority voting in the Council[43] and the resulting change in the number of votes required for a blocking minority. This problem was resolved in a somewhat unorthodox manner in the Ioannina Declaration.[44]

The dismantling of the Soviet empire cleared the way for new relations with the former satellite states in Central and East Europe. Sooner or later, most of them declared their desire for full membership of the European Union. As a first stage, the so-called Europe Agreements created the framework for close association with these countries.[45] In June 1993, the European Council of Copenhagen agreed in principle to accession of these countries, but set a number of general prior conditions; these conditions were, first, of a political nature, amounting to respect for the principles of democracy and the rule of law (as confirmed later in Art. 49(1) TEU) and, secondly, the general economic condition of a well-functioning market economy. Applications for membership were subsequently received from Poland and Hungary in 1994; from Romania, Slovakia, Estonia, Latvia, Lithuania and Bulgaria in 1995; from the Czech Republic and Slovenia in 1996. Cyprus and Malta had already applied for membership in 1990. During the European Council in Luxembourg in December 1997, it was decided to deal with all these applications in one total process, and to develop a so-called pre-accession strategy for each individual candidate state, within the framework of which considerable financial and technical assistance is given, in particular for the development of the rule of law and good governance and the strengthening of the infrastructure which this requires.[46] In spring 1998, the formal accession negotiations started

---

40. See O.J. 1994, C 241/9. See also D. Booß and J. Forman, "Enlargement: Legal and procedural aspects", 95 CML Rev. (1995); and M. Jorna, "The accession negotiations with Austria, Sweden, Finland and Norway: A guided tour", 20 EL Rev. (1995), 131.
41. As will be explained further in section 7.1 *infra*, in 1991 the Treaty of Maastricht created the European Union, which included and is "founded on" the European Communities, so that from then on accession was to that body.
42. I.e. the total legislative achievement of the Community, including the relevant interpretations relating to this given by the Court of Justice. See C. Curti Gialdino, "Some reflections on the *acquis communautaire*", (1995) CML Rev., 1089–1121.
43. Art. 205 EC.
44. Bull. EU 3-1994, point 1.3.28, O.J. 1994, C 105/1, as adapted to take account of Norway not acceding, O.J. 1995, C 1/1. See further, Ch. 5, "The political institutions", section 3.1.3 and Ch. 9, "Budget and finances", section 1.4, of this book.
45. Described further in Ch. 41, "Union external relations under the TFEU", of this book.
46. See Reg. 622/98 on assistance to the applicant States in the framework of the pre-accession strategy, and in particular on the establishment of Accession Partnerships, O.J. 1998, L 85, and Regs. 1266 to 1268/99 on coordinating aid to the applicant countries in the framework of the pre-accession strategy, O.J. 1999, L 161.

with Cyprus, Estonia, Hungary, Poland, Slovenia and the Czech Republic; in February 2000 with Malta and the other East European countries (Bulgaria, Latvia, Lithuania, Romania and Slovakia). The European Council in Helsinki (December 1999) accepted the application for membership made earlier by Turkey, and decided to treat it in the same way as that of the other countries.[47]

The Member States agreed at an early stage that the scale of the forthcoming enlargement necessitates a reform of the institutional structure of the European Union; it was more difficult to win agreement on the substance of the reform. This was one of the most important points on the agenda for the Intergovernmental Conference convened in 1996, in conformity with Article N(2) of the Treaty on European Union (in the Maastricht version), which led to the Treaty of Amsterdam.[48] However, the parties at the negotiations did not manage to reach agreement on the required institutional changes. In 2000, a new Intergovernmental conference was convened in order to resolve the so-called "leftovers" of Amsterdam. In December of that year, these negotiations were concluded somewhat laboriously in Nice. The national ratification procedures concerning the Treaty of Nice were only completed in October 2002, after a second Irish referendum (a first referendum in Ireland rejected the Treaty). With this, the path was cleared for the new accessions. The accession negotiations were successfully completed during the European Council of Copenhagen in December of the same year for Cyprus and Malta, the three Baltic States (Estonia, Lithuania and Latvia), Hungary, Poland, the Czech Republic, Slovakia and Slovenia. These countries acceded on 1 May 2004. Negotiations with Bulgaria and Romania were completed at the end of that same year. Both countries acceded on 1 January 2007.

With the accession of these twelve new Member States – bringing the membership of the EU to a total of twenty-seven states – the accession process has not come to an end. Formal negotiations with Turkey were opened in October 2005, but are generally expected to be lengthy; their outcome is uncertain, also because of the still unresolved problem of Cyprus. The EU and its Member States have also agreed that the Western Balkans have their future in the EU.[49] Croatia became the 28th EU Member State on 1 July 2013. Accession negotiations are ongoing with Montenegro and Serbia. Remain as further potential candidates for accession in the Western Balkans: the Former Yugoslavian Republic of Macedonia, Bosnia and Herzegovina, Albania and Kosovo. Finally, accession negotiations with Iceland, which were opened in 2010, have been put on hold by Iceland after a change of government.

6. European Political Cooperation (EPC); The European Council and the Single European Act

6.1 *EPC and the European Council*

A solitary opponent, the French Gaullist Michel Debré had in vain at the beginning of 1953 championed a different idea in the "*Ad Hoc* Assembly" than the proposal for a supranational Political Community which it accepted.[50] He argued in favour of a Political Union on purely intergovernmental lines, with a Conference of Heads of Government as the top organ. Debré's

---

47. In the meantime, a pre-accession strategy for Turkey has been established, Reg. 390/2001, O.J. 2001, L 58.
48. See 7.2 *infra*.
49. See Declaration and Thessaloniki agenda for the Western Balkans of 21 June 2003. Bull. EU 6-2003, point 1.6.70.
50. See *supra* at the end of section 3.1.

proposal, which was viewed sceptically by his fellow-members of the Assembly, was revived in essence in 1960–1962 in General de Gaulle's proposals for the formation of a Political Union.[51]

In de Gaulle's view it was the states which were the only foundations on which Europe could be built: only the states had the necessary legitimacy to exercise authority over the peoples of Europe. Political decisions could only be taken with the agreement of those in power in those states, i.e. national governments – although according to de Gaulle's concepts of political leadership this principally meant the Heads of State or Government of all participating countries. Specialized organisms, such as the three Communities, could do useful work relating to common problems but would clearly be subordinate to unanimous political decision-making by governments. The final version of the French proposals envisaged a Political Union with the aim of approximating, coordinating and unifying policies of the Member States in the spheres of foreign policy, the economy, culture and defence, under the general leadership of a Council of Heads of State or government.

De Gaulle's plans were discussed at two Summits, one in Paris on 10–11 January 1961 and the other in Bonn on 18 July 1961; the discussion continued thereafter in the so-called Fouchet Commission, although in April 1962 this had to suspend its work without agreement having been reached. There were a number of stumbling-blocks: the intergovernmental framework, the fear of encroaching on the competence of the existing Communities, the still uncertain relations with the United Kingdom, and the possible weakening of relations with the United States within NATO as a result of the proposed defence cooperation. The inflexible attitude of the Netherlands, supported by Belgium, contributed substantially to the failure of the negotiations. These countries argued, in essence, that the principle of the supranational character of a political union could only be discussed if the United Kingdom participated from the outset (the negotiations on the first attempt by the United Kingdom to accede to the Communities had begun in Autumn 1961). France was resolutely opposed to this.

Often the word "political" in relation to de Gaulle's proposed union is thought to indicate that it concerned only external relations. This is not, however, the case; the French plans also envisaged this union laying down the powers of the governments acting by mutual agreement to take all important (i.e. political) decisions in the economic sphere. The Communities, acting under the supranational formula, would merely execute these decisions. Thus, it was always inherent in the French view that there was no place in the Communities for qualified majority decisions on important matters, nor was there any room for an independent political role for the Commission.[52]

The rigour of the French position became apparent during the constitutional crisis provoked by France in 1965 as a result of certain proposals for financing agriculture which the Commission had submitted to the Council and which were supported by the other members of the Council but were unacceptable to the French. The main reason for this crisis, however, was the possibility for the Council to decide on matters of agricultural policy with qualified majority as from 1 January 1966. The crisis took the form of a boycott by France of Council meetings (the so-called "empty chair policy") and only came to an end with the Luxembourg Accord of January 1966. This recorded French dissent from the views of the other Member States on majority

51. See *Le dossier de l'Union Politique* (Political Committee of the European Parliament, 1964) and H. Nijenhuis, "De Nederlands tactiek in de onderhandelingen over een Europese politieke unie (1960–1962): Nee tegen De Gaulle!", (1986) *Internationale Spectator*, 41.

52. See P.J.G. Kapteyn, "De politieke verschraling van de Europese Gemeenschappen; de EEG: Een politiek verschijnsel?", (1966) *Internationale Spectator*, 51.

voting and was thus in reality an agreement to disagree. As a result of this Accord, the Council thenceforth avoided voting.[53]

After the failure of French plans for a Political Union and the French veto of the United Kingdom's application in January 1963, the three-monthly consultations on external policy which the foreign ministers had held since the end of 1959 were discontinued. To the great annoyance of the French Government the *other* five Member States of the Communities wanted to discuss external policy only within the framework of the WEU Council (i.e. with the United Kingdom being involved).

Only after de Gaulle's resignation, when the French position on United Kingdom accession changed, were the conditions fulfilled for a closer cooperation between the Member States in foreign policy. At the Summit at The Hague on 1–2 December 1969, at which it was decided to open negotiations with the four countries which had applied to accede to the Communities, the foreign ministers were requested to study the best method of making progress in the field of "political integration". This task resulted in a report of a committee of Directors-General for political affairs in the six foreign ministries under the chairmanship of Davignon (from Belgium). Six-monthly meetings of the foreign ministers to discuss matters of foreign policy were proposed, to be preceded by meetings of a Political Committee of directors-general. The governments approved this report at the Luxembourg Summit on 27 October 1970 (hence it is often called the Luxembourg report); it laid the basis for European Political Cooperation (EPC). This was further expanded through the report approved at the Copenhagen Summit on 23 July 1973.[54] The report accepted by the foreign ministers in London on 13 October 1981 envisaged still further improvements in the EPC procedure.[55]

The foreign ministers of the Member States met at least four times a year. The preparation of and follow-up to the ministerial meetings was in the hands of the above-mentioned Political Committee. Discussions in EPC covered all important questions of foreign policy of concern to the Member States as a whole. The coordination of the positions of the Member States concerning the political and economic aspects of security fell within the field of EPC.[56] The European Parliament was associated with EPC, albeit often subject to restrictions because of the confidential nature of the discussions.

Cooperation in EPC was purely intergovernmental in nature. Nevertheless, coordination between Community and EPC affairs was inevitable. Economic measures affecting the Community internally, the Community's commercial policy and the way in which relations with developing countries concerning development aid were and are handled, affect the foreign policies of the Member States and are, in turn, influenced by them. Thus the Copenhagen report of 1973, with an eye to this point, envisaged the Commission being invited to give its views on subjects which could have an influence on Community activities. In practice the Commission was represented at all ministerial EPC meetings and all meetings of the Political Committee.[57]

---

53. This Accord and its consequences are discussed further in Ch. 9, "Budget and finances", section 1.4, of this book.
54. See *Seventh General Report on the activities of the European Communities* (Brussels, Luxembourg, 1973), 502 et seq.
55. See Bull. EC supp. 3/81, at 14 et seq.
56. Solemn Declaration on European Union agreed at the Stuttgart Summit in 1983 section 1.4.2. (Bull. EC 6-1983, 1.6.1). The reports and the Solemn Declaration were confirmed and supplemented by Title III of the Single European Act, later repealed and replaced by provisions of the Treaty of Maastricht. See, generally, S. Nuttall, *European Political Co-operation* (OUP, 1992) and G. Edwards. "European political cooperation", 12 YEL (1992); and A. Pijpers et al. (Eds.), *European Political Co-operation in the 1980s* (Nijhoff, 1988).
57. B. Bot, "Waarheen met de Europese politieke samenwerking?", (1977) *International Spectator*, 788.

The connection between the activities of the Communities and the work on political cooperation was expressly recognized at the Paris Summit of 9–10 December 1974. This also prompted setting up the European Council. It was decided that the Heads of State and Government would meet at least three times a year, accompanied by their foreign ministers, as the Council of the Communities and, at the same time, in the context of political cooperation. The foreign ministers, in order to ensure consistency in Community activities and continuity of work, were instructed to act as initiators and coordinators, meeting in the Council; at the same time they may hold political cooperation meetings. It was expressly provided that these arrangements did not affect the rules and procedures laid down in the Treaties or the provisions on political cooperation in the Luxembourg and Copenhagen reports. The Commission was to exercise its powers at all these meetings and play the part assigned to it in the various texts concerned.[58]

The setting up of the European Council institutionalized the Summit conferences which had taken place since December 1969, after de Gaulle's resignation, from time to time and with varying degrees of success.[59] At the same time, these meetings, in so far as they related to questions falling within the competence of the Communities, were at least informally incorporated into the institutional scheme of the Communities.

The formation of the European Council with, on the one hand, EPC organized on an intergovernmental basis and, on the other hand, the Council's practice since the Luxembourg Accord of not applying the qualified majority voting principle, at least in important matters, amounted to a recognition of the accuracy of some of de Gaulle's views. The thought of extending political cooperation into a more wide-ranging union was taken up again in the 1970s. At the Paris Summit in October 1972, the Heads of State and Government "assigned themselves the key objective of converting, before the end of this decade and in absolute conformity with the signed Treaties, all the relationships between Member States into a European Union."[60] At the Paris Summit in December 1974 the then Belgian Prime Minister, Tindemans, was asked to prepare a report on the basis of reports from the Community Institutions and his discussions with governments and circles representative of public opinion in the Community. This report on European Union, presented in December 1975,[61] was neither accepted nor rejected by the European Council. It was simply agreed that the foreign ministers and the Commission would produce an annual report to the European Council about results achieved and the feasible advances in the short term which could be made in various fields of the Union.[62]

6.2 *The Single European Act (1986)*

Conversion of all the relations between the Member States into a European Union was impossible in the 1970s. Only in 1981 was the thread taken up again. The German Foreign Minister Genscher and his Italian colleague Colombo put forward a draft "European Act" which envisaged an improvement of the institutional provisions and an intensification and expansion of cooperation, also in the field of foreign policy, on the way to a European Union. Although this was not the original intention, their initiative resulted not in an amendment of the Treaties but

---

58. See Bull. EC 12-1974, at 7 (point 3, 4th para, of the communiqué from the Dec. 1974 Paris Summit).
59. The Hague (Dec. 1969), Paris (Oct. 1972), Copenhagen (Dec. 1973) and Paris (Dec. 1974). See, generally, J. Werts, *The European Council* (Elsevier Science Publishers, 1992) and H.-J. Glaesner, "The European Council" in D. Curtin and T, Heukels (Eds.), *Institutional Dynamics of European Integration, Essays in honour of Schermers* (Nijhoff, 1994), 101.
60. Bull. EC 10-1972, at 23. (point 16 of the communiqué).
61. Bull. EC Supp. 1/76. As to the reports from the Commission, the Parliament, the Court of Justice and the Economic and Social Committee, see Bull. EC Supps. 5/75 and 9/75.
62. Bull. EC 11-1976 point 2501 (at 93).

in the Solemn Declaration on European Union adopted by the European Council at Stuttgart on 19 June 1983, which largely got bogged down in intentions about the policy to be pursued and the procedures to be applied.[63]

In the meantime there was a movement in circles in the European Parliament,[64] led by the Italian member Spinelli, which sought to achieve a fundamental reform of European cooperation. This led to the drawing up of a Draft Treaty establishing the European Union which was adopted by the European Parliament on 14 February 1984 by a large majority.[65]

The Draft Treaty attracted a great deal of attention, not only in academic circles[66] but also in political circles in the Community. It was difficult for the governments not to react in some way. At the meeting in Fontainebleau on 25–26 June 1984, the European Council decided to set up an *ad hoc* Committee, composed of personal representatives of the Heads of State and Government on the lines of the Spaak Committee. This *ad hoc* Committee, under the chairmanship of Dooge, Chairman of the Irish Senate, was requested to make suggestions for improving European cooperation: in the Community field, in the field of political cooperation and in any other field. In March 1985 the Committee produced its report, albeit not a unanimous one in all parts.[67] Partly as a result of this report the European Council, at its meeting in June 1985 in Milan, and despite objections from Denmark, Greece and the United Kingdom, decided to convene a conference within the meaning of Article 236 EEC to draw up the text of a treaty on common foreign and security policy and on amendments to the EEC Treaty. This conference commenced work in September 1985 and the candidate Member States (Spain and Portugal) were invited to participate.

The conference had various materials before it: the report of the Dooge Committee; the report of the *ad hoc* Committee on a People's Europe (the Adonnino Committee which had also been established as a result of the Fontainebleau Summit);[68] the decisions of the Milan European Council on the realization of a single internal market by 1992,[69] and a draft revision of the treaties prepared by Luxembourg, then president-in-office of the Council. The result of the Committee's work, out of all the proposals before it, was the Single European Act which was signed on 17 February 1986 by nine Member States and on 28 February 1986 by Denmark, Italy and Greece. Both Denmark and Ireland needed to hold a referendum before ratification.[70]

The Single European Act (SEA), which came into force on 1 July 1987[71] made on the one hand a number of amendments to the existing Community Treaties. On the other hand, it con-

63. Bull. EC 6-1983, point 1.6.1.
64. The Assembly became formally known as the Parliament in 1987.
65. O.J. 1984, C 77/33; Bull. EC 2-1984, point 1.1.2.
66. E.g. R. Bieber et al. (Eds.), *An Ever Closer Union* (European Perspectives, 1985); F. Capotorti et al., *The European Union Treaty* (OUP, 1986) (also published in French as *Le Traité d'Union Européenne* (Université de Bruxelles, 1985) and in German as *Der Vertrag zur Grundung der Europäischen Union* (Nomos, 1986); J. Schwarze et al. (Eds.), *Eine Verfassung für Europa* (Nomos, 1984); I. Pernice, "Verfassungsentwurf für eine Europäische Union", (1984) EuR, 126; and J. Weiler and Modrall, "Institutional reform: Consensus or majority?", (1985) EL Rev., 316; J.P. Jacqué, "The Draft Treaty establishing the European Union", (1985) CML Rev., 19–42.
67. See Bull. EC 3-1985, point 3.5.1.
68. Bull. EC supp. 7/85.
69. See the Commission's White Paper *Completing the Internal Market,* COM(85)310 final, presented to the Milan European Council, June 28–29, 1985 (Bull. EC 6-1985, point 1.2.5).
70. Bull. EC Supp. 2/86. The Court of Justice has produced a collection of documents relating to the ratification process of the SEA.
71. See e.g. J. De Ruyt, *L'Acte Unique Européen,* 2nd ed. (Université de Bruxelles, 1989); A. Arnull, "Current survey, I. European Communities, 2. Institutional and jurisdictional questions. The Single European Act",

tained a number of independent provisions relating to the European Council[72] and one, very detailed Article (Art. 30 SEA) which by and large confirmed the existing practice on EPC.[73] A new development was that a secretariat was set up in Brussels to assist the Presidency of EPC in preparing and implementing EPC's activities and in administrative matters. Of the amendments made to the Community Treaties, the inclusion of the internal market concept in Article 8a EEC, and the envisaged completion of the internal market by 31 December 1992 were of particular significance. To enable this completion, a new legal basis for harmonization measures was introduced in Article 100a EEC, permitting decision-making by qualified majority. New policy areas, in which the Community was already active on the basis of Article 235 EEC (now Art. 352 TFEU), were given a specific Treaty basis, such as environmental protection and research and technological development. The cohesion policy, designed to strengthen economic and social cohesion between the Member States of the Community, was itself strengthened. On the institutional side, the introduction of the cooperation procedure which gave the European Parliament more say in Community decision-making was particularly noteworthy, as was the attachment to the Court of Justice of a Court of First Instance, designed to deal with staff cases and to give first instance judgments on cases regularly involving complex assessment of factual issues, such as competition cases.

7. The Treaties of Maastricht (1992), Amsterdam (1997) and Nice (2001)

7.1 *The Treaty of Maastricht (1992)*

After the entry into force of the Single European Act on 1 July 1987, and inspired by the progress of the market integration process, the drive towards an economic and monetary union (EMU), which had started in the early 1970s but had quickly appeared unattainable because of global monetary developments, was resumed. A completed internal market cannot continue to function without the keystone of an EMU. In a system of fixed but adaptable exchange rates, to

(1986) EL Rev., 358; R. Bieber et al. "Implications of the Single Act for the European Parliament", (1986) CML Rev., 767; A. Campbell, "The single European Act and the implications", (1986) ICLQ, 932; D. Edward, "The impact of the Single Act on the institutions", (1987) CML Rev., 19; C.D. Ehlermann, "The internal market following the Single European Act", (1987) CML Rev., 361; N. Forewood and M. Clough, "The Single European Act and free movement – Legal implications of the provisions for the completion of the internal market", (1986) EL Rev., 383; D. Freestone and S. Davidson, "Community competence and part III of the Single European Act", (1986) CML Rev., 793; H.-J. Glaesner, "Die Einheitliche Europäische Akte", (1986) EuR 119, id., "The Single European Act", (1986) YBEL, 283; C. Gulmann, "The Single European Act – Some remarks from a Danish perspective", (1987) CML Rev., 31; H.G. Krenzler, "Die Einheitliche Europäische Akte als Schritt auf dem Wege zu einer gemeinsamen europäischen Außenpolitik", (1986) EuR, 384; P. Pescatore, "Die 'Einheitliche Europäische Akte': Eine ernste Gefahr für den gemeinsamen Markt", (1986) EuR, 153 and "Some critical remarks on the 'Single European Act'", (1987) CML Rev., 9; A. Toth, "The legal status of the declarations annexed to the Single European Act", (1986) CML Rev., 803; P. VerLoren van Themaat, "De Europese Akte", (1986) SEW, 464, and J. De Zwaan, "The Single European Act: Conclusion of a unique document", (1986) CML Rev., 747. See also the 12th. Report of the House of Lords Select Committee on the European Communities, Session 1985–86 (HL 149). As to the SEA and environmental policy, see L. Krämer, "The Single European Act and environmental protection: Reflections on several provisions in Community law", 24 CML Rev. (1987), 659 and D. Vandermeersch, "The Single European Act and the environmental policy of the European Economic Community", (1987) EL Rev., 407. As to the views of the Dutch government, see F. Kellermann, "Current Survey. II Member States of the European Communities. Netherlands; The views of the Netherlands Government on the Single European Act", (1987) EL Rev., 221.

72. Art. 2 SEA. See F. Capotorti in F. Capotorti et al. (Eds), *Du droit international au droit de l'intégration* (Nomos, 1987) 79 and T. Oppermann in ibid., 537.

73. See *supra* section 6.1. See J. Frowein in F. Capotorti et al., ibid., 247 and T. Oppermann, ibid.

say nothing of a system of fluctuating exchange rates, so much uncertainty remains as to the results of cross-border investments, that the economic advantages of market integration cannot be optimally utilized. Moreover, an internal market without an EMU is never a safe haven, as the risk of unilateral intervention by a Member State disturbing the market remains. These economic realities caused the Hanover European Council in June 1988 to entrust to a committee of specialists, chaired by the President of the Commission, Jacques Delors, the task of studying and proposing concrete stages towards EMU.[74] The Delors Committee Report was presented in April 1989;[75] in December 1989, the Strasbourg European Council[76] decided that the first phase of EMU could begin on 1 July 1990 with the full liberalization of capital movements. At the same time it was decided to convene an intergovernmental conference before the end of 1990, for the purpose of drawing up a treaty basis with a view to the final stages of EMU.

At the same time the collapse of Soviet hegemony began. The breathtaking progress of German unification and the revolutions in the neighbouring Central and East European countries created a climate of hope, but also of considerable political and economic unrest and uncertainty. The German Chancellor, Kohl, strove to anchor a united Germany firmly in a strengthened European Community, strengthened into political unity in order to support the far-reaching restructuring in the former Eastern Bloc countries and to support an effective peace and security policy in Europe. Kohl linked German cooperation on EMU (which meant that Germany would have to surrender its much-prized monetary autonomy, just like the other participants) to a real strengthening of the Community in political terms. After initial hesitation, Mitterrand, then French President, supported this idea. In a joint initiative, they presented to a special European Council in Dublin in April 1990 a proposal for the development of a common foreign and security policy.[77] In June 1990, during the regular Dublin European Council, it was agreed to convene a conference on political union to open in December 1990, alongside the intergovernmental conference on EMU.[78] The work of the two conferences was to run in parallel and to be concluded rapidly and at the same time.[79] The Dublin European Council thus confirmed the Franco-German linkage of these subjects.

Both conferences opened on 15 December 1990, following on from the Rome European Council.[80] For the conference on EMU much preparatory work had already been undertaken, including a draft treaty drawn up by the Commission.[81] With barely six months prior to its opening, the conference on political union was much less well prepared; there was merely a list of subjects which had been drawn up on the basis of contributions by the Commission[82] and some Member States.[83] On that basis, the Rome European Council requested the conference to pay particular attention to a number of issues: strengthening democratic legitimacy as well as the

74. Bull. EC 6-1988, point 3.4.1.
75. Bull. EC 4-1989, points 1.1.1–1.1.9.
76. Bull. EC 12-1989, point 1.1.11.
77. Bull. EC 4-1990, point I.12 (alongside their paper on political union, a paper from the Belgian Government on the subject was also considered).
78. Bull. EC 6-1990, points I.11 and Annex I (political union); I.10 (EMU).
79. This point was specifically confirmed at the Rome European Council in Dec. 1990, Bull. EC 12-1990, point I.10.
80. Bull. EC 12-1990, points 1.1.7 and 1.1.8. As to the problems of coherence between the two conferences, see the contributions by J.-V. Louis and G. Maganza in J. Monar et al. (Eds.), *The Maastricht Treaty on European Union* (European Interuniversity Press, 1993) 163 and 173 respectively.
81. Bull. EC Supp. 2/91, 13–38, as to the draft treaty, see 39–62.
82. See Bull. EC Supp. 2/91, 85–179. The Commission's Opinion of 21 Oct. 1990 is set out in *ibid.*, 75–82.
83. See, generally, J. Cloos et al., *Le Traité de Maastricht: genèse, analyse, commentaire* (Bruylant, 1993) 59–83 (particularly at 75 et seq.).

functioning of the Institutions; a common foreign and security policy; European citizenship (an idea of the Spanish Prime Minister Gonzales); extension of Community action and also further and deeper cooperation, in the context of the Union, in the area of justice and home affairs (for instance, immigration policy; organized crime; the fight against drugs, and cooperation in criminal matters), at the request of Chancellor Kohl.[84]

The negotiations proceeded pretty speedily – but at the expense of the ambitions of devotees of a Union concept, who had hoped that competence in more areas would be transferred to the Union level, and that the Community method would operate (rather than the intergovernmental method) at that level too. The United Kingdom in particular maintained its strident opposition to such a development, reflecting a certain continuity in its distrust of supranational institutions. Thus the common foreign and security policy and cooperation in justice and home affairs remained outside the Community framework, almost wholly along intergovernmental lines. An attempt by the Dutch – at the time holding the Presidency – to bring the political union and the three Communities into a unitary structure, as had been intended with EMU all along, backfired dramatically. On 30 September 1991 (Black Monday), apart from Belgium, the other Member States were not even prepared to accept the Dutch text as a basis for discussion. During the European Council at Maastricht on 9–10 December 1991 the negotiations were concluded, after certain concessions to a number of Member States, in particular to the United Kingdom in relation to social policy and EMU, and to the poorer Member States, which, led by Spain, forced a larger transfer of resources in their direction through a new cohesion fund.[85] The final text of the Treaty of Maastricht – also called the Treaty on European Union – was agreed and signed at Maastricht on 7 February 1992.[86]

The structure chosen for the Union was tripartite. The most important part, consisting of the three Communities, was strictly separated from the other two, common foreign and security policy (CFSP) and cooperation in the field of justice and home affairs (JHA), which operate in a much more intergovernmental framework. This tripartite structure – the three parts commonly being referred to as the respective "pillars" supporting the Union as a whole – was to be regarded as an interim phase in the development of the Union. Article N(2) TEU provided for a new intergovernmental conference to be convened in 1996, *inter alia* to review this structure. The Union established by the TEU was not itself granted legal personality. It did not replace the European Communities, but brought them, as a separately organized and still autonomous part, together with the two other parts into a relationship which in legal terms was rather weakly set up. However, new Member States accede to the Union, and only thereby to the Communities. This differs from the approach of the Single European Act, which still foresaw accessions to the various Communities. The relationship between the three parts was demonstrated by the single institutional framework, the purpose of which was to ensure the consistency and continuity of the activities carried out in order to attain the Union's objectives, while respecting and building upon the *acquis communautaire*.[87] The most important body in political terms was the European Council, for which the TEU lays down the tasks. The CFSP was determined by the Council, within the principles and general guidelines laid down by the European Council.[88] The Com-

84. Bull. EC 12-1990, points I.4-I.9.
85. Bull. EC 12-1991, points I.1 and I.3.
86. See J. Cloos et al., op. cit. *supra* note 83; see further the literature cited at the end of Ch. 2, "Structure and evolution of Union law", of this book.
87. Art. C(1) TEU, Maastricht version.
88. Art. J.8 (1) and (2) TEU, Maastricht version. See also Art. J.3 (1) TEU, Maastricht version.

mission had a right of initiative, but not an exclusive one,[89] and the European Parliament was to be consulted by the Presidency on the main aspects and basic choices of CFSP.[90] The Court of Justice was carefully excluded from the picture.[91] As a whole, CFSP was somewhat more "Communitarized" than was EPC, although even the institutional model of CFSP was – and is – still essentially intergovernmental, not least because decision-making is based on unanimity.

The TEU altered the name of the European Economic Community (EEC) to make it simply the European Community (EC), reflecting the long-standing reality that the Community's tasks are not solely economic in nature. The new provisions of the EC Treaty relating to EMU were set out in detail, so that this part of the Treaty in fact is a second *traité-loi,* like the ECSC Treaty, rather than a *traité-cadre,* like its other provisions. The separate preparation of the EMU and political union texts, which were integrated only in the final stages of the negotiations, was detrimental to the clarity of the final version of the Treaty. In addition to the inclusion of the principle of subsidiarity and the creation of Union citizenship, the major features of the TEU on the institutional side are the strengthening of the powers of the European Parliament – through the introduction of the co-decision procedure, the right to set up temporary Committees of Inquiry, the creation of a European Ombudsman, the formalization of the right of petition to the Parliament, the extension of the assent procedure to certain categories of international agreements, and participation in the appointment of members of the Commission – and finally the inclusion of certain new areas of activity.

The ratification of the TEU[92] met with unexpectedly severe problems in certain Member States. The negative result of the first Danish referendum was followed by fierce discussions in most Member States about the nature of the Community. In these discussions it became very apparent how weakly legitimized in the Member States Community action is, and just how much misunderstanding exists about the Community's structure and functioning. A second referendum in Denmark produced a positive result, after the Edinburgh European Council in December 1992 had given the Danish Government support through a felicitous interpretation of certain parts of the TEU.[93] In France and the United Kingdom the ratification process proved extremely contentious, but was also ultimately successful.[94] After the German Federal Constitutional Court had ruled that German ratification would not be incompatible with the

---

89. Art. J.8 (3) provides that any Member State or the Commission may refer questions or make proposals to the Council within the ambit of CFSP. The Commission must be fully associated with work in the field of CFSP, Art. J.9 TEU, Maastricht version.
90. Art. J.7 TEU, Maastricht version. The Presidency must ensure that the views of the European Parliament must be taken into consideration; the Parliament must be kept regularly informed by the Presidency and the Commission of the development of CFSP, may ask questions of the Council or make recommendations to it, and holds an annual debate on progress in implementing CFSP, ibid.
91. See Art. M TEU, Maastricht version. In JHA the only involvement of the Court is if Conventions adopted by the Member States confer jurisdiction upon it, Art. K.3(2)(c), 3rd para, TEU, Maastricht version.
92. See F. Laursen and S. Vanhoonacker (Eds.), *The Ratification of the Maastricht Treaty: Issues, Debates and Future Implications* (Nijhoff, 1994).
93. Bull. EC 12-1992, 1.3. See, further, D. Howarth, "The compromise on Denmark and the Treaty on European Union: A legal and political analysis", (1994) CML Rev., 765; D. Curtin and R. van Ooik, "De bijzondere positie van Denemarken in de Europese Unie – Een juridisch Fata Morgana?", (1993) SEW, 675 and, as to the Edinburgh European Council in general, P. VerLoren van Themaat, "De Europese Raad van Edinburgh als goudmijn voor juristen", (1993) SEW, 423. On 6 Apr. 1998 the Danish Supreme Court dismissed an action claiming that the implementation of the EC Treaty as amended by the TEU was incompatible with Art. 20 of the Danish constitution, *Carlsen et al. v. Rasmussen,* see English translation in A. Oppenheimer (Ed.) *The Relationship Between European Community Law and National Law: The Cases* (CUP, 2003),175.
94. As to England and Wales, see *R. v. Secretary of State for Foreign and Commonwealth Affairs, ex parte Rees Mogg* (1993) 3 CMLR, 101 and as to Scotland, see *Monckton v. Lord Advocate,* (1994) *The Times* 12 May; see also

Constitution,[95] the Treaty on European Union finally came into force, nearly a year later than envisaged, on 1 November 1993.[96]

7.2 *The Treaty of Amsterdam (1997)*[97]

A new intergovernmental conference was already foreseen in the Treaty of Maastricht, in order to reconsider a number of (mainly) institutional problems that had not been resolved at Maastricht (structure of the Union, co-decision procedure, CFSP).[98] Subsequently, two important main themes were added to the agenda of this conference. First, how the Union could be brought closer to its citizens – the necessity of which had emerged so clearly in the ratification process for the Treaty of Maastricht, which had been highly problematic in a number of Member States. A second new point on the agenda was the need for reform in order to prepare the Union for the expected large number of new accessions.

The Conference started in March 1996, with at its disposal preparatory material[99] in the form of separate reports drawn up by the Parliament, the Council and the Commission, about the experiences in the application of the Treaty of Maastricht, as well as the end report of the so-called Reflection Group, presided over by Carlos Westendorp, and composed of personal representatives of the ministers of foreign affairs and the President of the European Commission, as well as two representatives of the European Parliament.

The Westendorp report comprised an inventory of the negotiation positions. The conference was concluded, as planned, in June 1997 in Amsterdam. The working method was still mainly that of classic, international diplomatic consultation, although this time with more transparency than during earlier conferences and moreover, as an interesting novelty, a certain amount of say being given to representatives of the European Parliament. Perhaps here a cautious development can be signalled which might eventually lead to a certain constitutionalization of the treaty amendment procedure, in the sense that the democratic legitimacy for these

---

European Communities (Amendment) Act 1993, and E. Szyszczak, 18 EL Rev. (1993), 248. As to France, see the discussion by N. Cohen, 18 EL Rev. (1993), 233.

95. *Brunner* (1994) 1 CMLR, 57. See e.g. J. Frowein, "Das Maastricht-Urteil und die Grenzen der Verfassungsgerichtsbarkeit", (1994) ZaÖRV, 1; M. Herdegen, "Maastricht and the German Constitutional Court: Constitutional restraints for an 'ever closer union'", (1994) CML Rev., 235; H. Ipsen, "Zehn Glossen zum Maastricht-Urteil", (1994) EuR, 1; B. Meyring "Intergovernmentalism and supranationality: Two stereotypes for a complex reality", (1997) EL Rev., 221; C. Tomuschat, "Die Europäische Union unter Aufsicht des Bundesverfassungsgerichts", (1993) EuGRZ, 489; J. Wieland, "Germany in the European Union – The Maastricht Decision of the Bundesverfassungsgericht", (1995) EJIL, 259; J. Weiler, "Der Staat 'über alles': Demos, Telos und die Maastricht-Entscheidung des Bundesverfassungsgerichts" (Harvard Jean Monnet Paper, 1995); J. Weiler, "Does Europe need a constitution? Reflections on Demos, Telos and the German Maastricht Decision", (1995) ELJ, 219; and M. Zuleeg, "The European Constitution under constitutional constraints: The German Scenario", (1997) EL Rev., 19.
96. The Court of Justice has produced a series of documents on the ratification of the Treaty of Maastricht.
97. See D. O'Keeffe and P. Twomey (Eds.), *Legal Issues of the Amsterdam Treaty* (Hart, 1999); Editorial: "The Treaty of Amsterdam: Neither a bang nor a whimper", (1997) CML Rev., 767–772, G. Berthu and D. Souchet, *Le Traité d'Amsterdam contre la démocratie. Texte intégral comparé et commenté* (François-Xavier de Guibert, 1998); R. Barents, *Het Verdrag van Amsterdam in Werking* (Kluwer, 1999); Theme issue in (1997) *SEW*, 343 et seq. with contributions by R. Barents, J. Donner, H. Posthumus Meyjes and C. Timmermans.
98. Cf. Art. N(3) TEU, Maastricht version.
99. See, with further references, J. Winter et al. (Eds), *Reforming the Treaty on European Union* (TMC Asser Instituut, 1996).

amendments would also be set at the level of the Union itself (cf. also the required assent of the European Parliament for accession of a new Member State, Art. 49 TEU).[100]

It is hard to give an overall judgement on the results of the Treaty of Amsterdam. As far as the necessary reforms with a view to enlargement are concerned, the negotiations were a failure (composition of the Commission, weighting of votes in the Council, drastic reduction of the number of cases where the Treaties provide for voting by unanimity). The solution to these problems (the so-called "leftovers" of Amsterdam) had to be postponed for a new conference, convened in 2000. The negotiators did manage to include in the Treaty a general solution to the issue of a multi-speed Europe, that is a procedure allowing a limited number of Member States (but at least a majority of them) to use the existing institutional framework and the existing procedures to cooperate more closely in the framework of the EC and the Third pillar (i.e. police and judicial cooperation in criminal matters) of the Union.[101] The structure of the Union was not really changed by the Treaty of Amsterdam; attempts to weld the Union and the three Communities into a single organization failed. The Union itself – the organizational construct which embraces the Communities together with the Common Foreign and Security Policy (CFSP) and police and judicial cooperation in criminal matters[102] – was structured in more detail, even though it was not explicitly accorded legal personality.[103] For instance, the CFSP was now called a policy of the Union and no longer – as in the Treaty of Maastricht – a matter for the Union together with the Member States. The concept of the Union began to acquire a constitutional significance with the explicit requirement for the Union to respect the principles of democracy and the rule of law in Article 6 TEU. The Union moreover was entrusted with the task of supervising respect for these principles, including fundamental rights, in the Member States by means of the sanction mechanism of Article 7 TEU, which enables the Union to act in situations of serious and persistent breach of these principles.

As for the development of the *acquis communautaire*, which according to Article 2, 5th indent, TEU,[104] is an objective of the Union, Amsterdam saw some positive achievements. The most significant of these was the transfer to the EC (in a new Title IV) of migration policy and judicial cooperation in civil cases, as well as international private law, which the Treaty of Maastricht had allocated to the Third Pillar. This "Communitarization" was not perfect, however, as the decision-making procedures in this area were made more intergovernmental than the normal Community methods (requiring unanimity in the Council, and granting a joint right of initiative to the Member States) and the competence of the Court of Justice to deliver preliminary rulings was limited.[105] Denmark, Ireland and the United Kingdom decided in principle not to participate in this new area of EC policy (a so-called "opt-out" was agreed), but with a proviso that they could later "opt in" under certain conditions (this possibility was more restricted for Denmark). In the context of these arrangements, the Schengen regime[106] was also incorporated

100. Cf. in this context also the procedure followed for the establishment of the Charter of Fundamental Rights for the European Union, for which the drafting was put in the hands of a "convention" composed of representatives of the national parliaments and the European Parliament, the governments of the Member States and the European Commission. A similar body was later set up in order to prepare a draft treaty for the Intergovernmental Conference convened in 2004 (see *infra* section 7.3 and 8).
101. See Ch. 2, "Structure and evolution of Union law", section 3.3, of this book.
102. This was the new wording used in the title of the Third Pillar, which had previously referred to Justice and Home Affairs.
103. See Ch. 2, "Structure and evolution of Union law", section 1, of this book.
104. This objective was already contained in the Treaty of Maastricht, as Art. B, 5th indent.
105. See Arts. 67 and 68 EC.
106. The so-called Schengen arrangements (mainly concerning abolishing internal borders and increased cooperation on external controls) were originally between a number of Member States. See Ch. 12, The

into the Union framework, and the various legislative provisions allocated between Title IV EC and the Third Pillar according to the respective division of competence. The Third Pillar was given a dose of the Community method insofar as the role of the European Parliament and the Commission was strengthened, and the Court of Justice was also granted a limited jurisdiction. This was, however, not the case for the CFSP, where the intergovernmental decision-making model was maintained and even strengthened, to the extent that executive tasks were entrusted to the secretariat of the Council, under the direction of a secretary general, who received a new responsibility as High Representative for CFSP. The Court was still not granted any jurisdiction in this area. Finally, in institutional terms it should also be noted that the role of the European Parliament was strengthened within the system of the Community. The Parliament became a full-fledged co-legislator in the framework of the co-decision procedure, and the scope of application of that procedure was considerable extended; in other areas, the Parliament's influence was strengthened – for instance the nomination of the intended President of the Commission.

To bring the Union closer to its citizens, the principle of open government was included in the Treaty and was made subject to further regulation.[107] In this context, mention may also be made of the new coordination mechanisms concerning employment policy and the fine-tuning of the EC Treaty provisions concerning public health (Art. 152) and consumer protection (Art. 153). A far-reaching consequence for lawyers was also the re-numbering of provisions of the EU and EC treaties, in the framework of a simplification of these texts, whereby in the EC Treaty in particular a number of obsolete or superfluous provisions were removed.

7.3 *The Treaty of Nice*[108]

The Intergovernmental Conference (IGC) which had the particular task of elaborating the necessary institutional reforms to prepare the Union for the accession of ten or more new Member States, began in spring 2000 and came to an extremely laborious conclusion in December of that same year, in Nice. The results achieved for the three Amsterdam leftovers provoked mixed reactions, but at least the door was opened to a historic enlargement of the Union extending into Central and East Europe. The agreement reached on the weighing of votes in the Council met the French demand that the weight of French and German votes should remain equal. There is an additional possibility, however, of an extra condition being set for a qualified majority,[109] which is that this represents at least 62 % of the total population of the Union, so that account can be taken of the considerable difference between these two Member States in demographic terms. The threshold for reaching a qualified majority is raised slightly. The compromise reached

---

functioning of the internal market", of this book.

107. Art. 1 TEU and 255 EC, Arts. 28 and 41 TEU.

108. V. Constantinesco, Y. Gautier and D. Simon (Eds.) *Le traité de Nice, premières analyses* (PUS, 2001); M. Andenas and J. Usher, *The Treaty of Nice and Beyond, Enlargement and Constitutional Reform* (Hart, 2003), R. Barents, "Some observations on the Treaty of Nice", 8 MJ, 121–132, R. Barents, "Het Verdrag van Nice: Een eerste indruk", NJB 2001, 113, M. Borchmann, "Der Vertrag von Nizza", 12 EuZW, 170–173, J. M. Favret, "Le traité de Nice du 26 février 2001: Vers un affaiblissement irréversible de la capacité d'action de l'Union européenne?", 37 RTDE, 271–304, J. Shaw, "The Treaty of Nice: Legal and constitutional implications", 7 EPL, 195–215, W. Wessels, "Nice results: The millennium IGC in the EU's evolution", 39 JCMS, 197–220, T. Wiedmann, "Der Vertrag von Nizza – Genesis einer Reform", 36 EuR, 185–215, J. Wouters, "Institutional and constitutional challenges for the European Union: some reflections in the light of the Treaty of Nice", 26 EL Rev., 342–356, J.W. de Zwaan, "Het Verdrag van Nice, Een bescheiden stap in het proces van Europese integratie", (2001) SEW, 42.

109. The formulation of Art. 3 of the Protocol on the enlargement of the European Union indicates that application of this condition must be explicitly requested by a member of the Council. In the absence of such a request, a decision may be taken by qualified majority without the population criterion being met.

in regard to the composition of the Commission is not very satisfactory, insofar as the rule that there is one Commissioner per Member State is maintained until the Commission reaches the size of twenty-seven members. If and when that situation is reached, there will be new negotiations about the ultimate size and a system of rotation. Such a large number of members involves risks for the effective operation of the Commission, and an attempt was made to compensate these risks by strengthening considerably the powers of the President of the Commission. The Commission will from now on be appointed by the Council by qualified majority, and no longer by a common decision of the governments of the Member States; the appointment will still require the approval of the European Parliament. From an institutional point of view – consider the autonomy of the Commission and the institutional balance – the appointment by the Council is unsatisfactory, but it illustrates the Member States' view of the Commission's position. As for the third Amsterdam leftover, reduction in the number of matters requiring decision-making by unanimity, the achievement at Nice was minimal. Leaving aside the common commercial policy – which from now on, barring a few exceptions, also includes trade in services and trade aspects of intellectual property law – the Member States did not manage to break through the unanimity requirement for important matters such as direct and indirect taxes, social security, and asylum and immigration legislation.

Of the other subjects dealt with in the Treaty of Nice, mention must certainly be made of the reform of the Union's judicial apparatus.[110] The Treaty lays the basis for fundamental reorganization, including the possible establishment of new judicial panels for specific areas of law (e.g. staff cases), so that the overload on the Court of Justice and Court of First Instance can be tackled (Arts. 220 and 225a EC).[111] On the whole, these developments concern the creation of legal bases, and require further decision-making by unanimity. Another achievement concerns the multi-speed regime introduced by the Treaty of Amsterdam ("enhanced cooperation"). Such a possibility is now also – to a limited extent – introduced for the CFSP. In addition, the application of this regime is made easier, as the possibility of a veto by a single Member State is removed.

Concurrently with the IGC, negotiations were taking place in another forum on a Charter of fundamental rights for the European Union. This group, called the Convention, composed of representatives of the national governments, the national parliaments, the European parliament, the European Commission and others, succeeded in drafting, in a relatively short space of time, a text which was favourably received in many circles. The Charter of Fundamental Rights was not actually included in or attached to the Treaty of Nice. The idea of according binding legal effects to the Charter was abandoned following opposition by the United Kingdom, but also the Netherlands.[112] In the end, the Charter was "solemnly proclaimed" by the European Parliament, the Council and the Commission.[113]

---

110. A. Johnston, "Judicial reform and the Treaty of Nice", (2001) CML Rev., 499–523; P.J.G. Kapteyn, "De rechterlijke organisatie van de Europese Unie en de Intergouvernementele Conferentie 2000", (2001) NJB, 1.
111. As a first judicial panel The European Union Civil Service Tribunal was established by Council Decision of 2 Nov. 2004 (O.J. 2004, L 333/7).
112. Cf. the extremely critical advisory report by the Netherlands *Raad van State* of 4 Oct. 2000, Kamerstukken Tweede Kamer (Parliamentary papers Lower House) 2000–2001, No. 21501-20 A.
113. The text of the Charter was published in O.J. 2000, C 364/3.

8. The Treaty establishing a Constitution for Europe and the Treaty of Lisbon

8.1 The Treaty establishing a Constitution for Europe

Even if the Member States, in agreeing on the Treaty of Nice, considered the institutional reforms brought about by that Treaty sufficient to prepare the Union for enlargement, they adopted at the same time a Declaration on the future of the Union announcing a new round of negotiations for treaty amendments of a more constitutional nature.[114] This declaration demonstrates that the Union is in an ongoing process of reform.[115] An impetus for reform also came from the discussions triggered in 2000 by Joshka Fischer, the then German Minister for foreign affairs, on the ultimate shape of the Union, and the ensuing debate on a European Constitution.[116] It should moreover be noted that the German Länder had made their approval of the Treaty of Nice in the German Bundesrat conditional on the convening of a new intergovernmental conference to reach a more clear-cut division of competences between the Union and its Member States. This IGC was indeed announced at Nice for 2004.

An essential step towards the preparation of that conference was made by the Laeken Declaration on the Future of the European Union adopted by the European Council on 15 December 2001.[117] This declaration starts by sketching the contours of the agenda for the conference by listing a large number of questions grouped under four headings: a better division and definition of competence in the EU; simplification of the Union's instruments; more democracy, transparency and efficiency in the EU, including the question of the role of national parliaments; towards a constitution for European citizens. This fourth theme raises questions such as the simplification of the patchwork of existing treaties, the structure of the Union (the three pillars), the possible inclusion of the Charter of Fundamental Rights, to end up with the ultimate question, cautiously phrased, whether the simplification and reorganization of the treaties might not lead eventually to the adoption of a constitutional text for the Union.

The Laeken Declaration set out the process to be followed for the preparation of the IGC. In that respect, the Laeken Declaration breaks new ground, is really innovative and confirms the seriousness of the commitment of the Heads of States and Government to bringing the Union closer to its citizens. The preparation of the IGC was entrusted to a convention composed of 15 representatives of the Heads of State and Government of the Member States, 30 Members of national parliaments, 16 Members of the European Parliament and 2 Commission representatives; the accession candidate countries were also to be fully involved in the Convention's proceedings. The former President of France, Valéry Giscard d'Estaing was appointed as chairman of the Convention. The Convention's discussions and all its official documents should be public. The Convention did indeed work in full openness, its documents and discussion reports systematically being made available on the internet. Moreover, a Forum was set up to organize the debate with organizations representing civil society. This procedure, which in fact builds on the

114. Declaration No. 23 on the future of the Union.

115. B. De Witte, "Simplification and reorganization of the European treaties", (2002) CML Rev., 1255–1287.

116. Cf. E. U. Petersmann, "Proposals for a new constitution for the European Union: Building-blocks for a constitutional theory and constitutional law of the EU", (1995) CML Rev., 1123–1175; I. Pernice, "Multilevel constitutionalism and the Treaty of Amsterdam: European constitution-making revisited", (1999) CML Rev., 703–750; K. Lenaerts and M. Desomer, "New models of constitution-making in Europe: The quest for legitimacy", (2002) CML Rev., 1217–1253; A. Von Bogdandy and J. Bast, "The European Union's vertical order of competences: The current law and proposals for its reform", (2002) CML Rev., 227–268, and already much earlier G.F. Mancini, "The making of a Constitution for Europe", (1989) CML Rev., 595–614. See also S. Prechal, "Een constitutionele 'post-Nice' agenda?", (2001) NJB, 384.

117. Bull. EU, 12-2001, I-27.

experience made with the convention for the elaboration of the EU Charter on fundamental rights, breaks with the traditional preparatory process of treaty amendments by secret negotiations at diplomatic level, and constitutionalizes the treaty-making process at Union level, by making it transparent and giving the process in itself a democratic legitimacy. Indeed, more than two thirds of the members of the convention were members of parliament.

The mandate given to the Convention was an open one: the final document to be produced could comprise different options, indicating the degree of support which they received, or recommendations if consensus was achieved. However, the authors of the Laeken Declaration made it quite clear that the final document would only provide the starting point for the IGC, the ultimate decisions being taken by that conference.

The Convention, which had its inaugural session in March 2002, was asked to complete its work within one year. President Giscard d'Estaing was able to submit on 18 July 2003 to the President of the European Council in Rome the final document of the Convention consisting not of a list of options but the text of a draft Treaty establishing a Constitution for Europe which the Convention had been able to adopt by consensus.[118] That draft was welcomed by the European Council as a good starting point for the IGC which began its work in October 2003. Agreement on a draft treaty establishing a Constitution for Europe was reached on 18 June 2004. The Treaty was signed in Rome on 29 October of that same year.[119] In reality, the draft treaty as adopted by the Convention was much more than a starting point for the IGC; the latter, apart from an important technical and legal revision, mainly limited its work to the most delicate institutional issues such as the system of qualified majority voting in the Council and the composition of the European Commission.[120]

The Constitution consists of four parts. Part I lays down the basic foundations, values, general objectives of the Union, its competences and institutional structure. Together with Part II, which contains the Charter of Fundamental Rights of the Union, the rules of Part I are of a more constitutional nature whereas Part III (The Policies and Functioning of the Union) mainly consolidates the existing provisions of the EU and EC Treaty – with sometimes important modifications. Part IV, finally, contains general and final provisions. Added to the Constitution are 36 Protocols and 2 Annexes which form an integral part thereof.

The Constitution does not constitute a completely new text. The impression given by its grand title: "A Constitution for Europe" might be somewhat misleading. The Constitution is a step, in some regards an important step, in the continuous evolution of the European Communities and the European Union, Although without any doubt it brings important innovations and improvements, particularly at the institutional level[121] – most of which have been taken over by the Treaty of Lisbon (see below 8.2) – it nevertheless fully fits into that evolution and can certainly not be qualified as a revolutionary new departure. Indeed, the Constitution codifies and consolidates to a very large extent existing treaty texts, taking into account the principles developed in the case law of the Court of Justice like the basic principle of primacy of Union law over national law. That the Constitution does not dramatically change the basic characteristics

---

118. The text of this draft treaty is published in O.J. 2003, C 169/1.
119. The text of the Treaty is published in O.J. 2004, C 310/1.
120. See more particularly on the work of the IGC, J.P. Jacqué, "De la Convention à la Conférence intergouvernementale, le projet de la Convention à l'épreuve des réalités politiques", (2005) RTDE, 227.
121. See for an analysis of the Constitution J.C. Piris, *The Constitution for Europe: A Legal Analysis*, (CUP, 2006); R. Barents, *Een Grondwet voor Europa, Achtergronden en commentaar* (Kluwer, 2005); K. Lenaerts and P. van Nuffel, "La Constitution pour l'Europe et l'Union comme entité politique et ordre juridique", (2005) CDE, 1–2; G. Amato, H. Bribosia and B. De Witte (Eds.), *Genèse et destinee de la Constitution européenne/Genesis and destiny of the European Constitution* (Bruylant, 2007).

of the EU is well illustrated by the emphasis put on the preservation of the Member States as basically sovereign states, and the need to preserve that quality as one of the constitutional principles of the EU (Art. I-5, para 1).

At the beginning of 2007, the Constitutional Treaty had been ratified by 18 of the 27 Member States. However, in 2005 the Treaty had been rejected by referendum in France and The Netherlands. The negative results of these referenda to some extent repeat the experiences of the ratification process of the Maastricht Treaty. The European Union continues to suffer from a fundamental problem of legitimacy within its Member States. The Union, its operation and its policies are met with much mistrust within some Member States. Lack of knowledge and understanding of the Union's objectives and functioning can easily be exploited to sow distrust and use the Union as a scapegoat for more general societal problems, such as caused for instance by globalization and the resulting difficulties of adaptation of national economies. What obviously also played a role both in France and The Netherlands were feelings of anxiety and uncertainty about enlargement. Another striking feature of the debate in both Member States is that objections against the Constitution did not just address its innovative parts, but also principles and rules regarding the common market which had been introduced already by the EEC Treaty of 1957. Presenting the new Treaty as a constitutional text might also have sent a wrong signal by possibly suggesting that the Constitution would entail a quantum leap and initiate a completely new phase in the process of integration. Paradoxically, Member States had chosen the constitutional language with the expectation of, by doing so, bringing the Union closer to its citizens.

8.2 *The Treaty of Lisbon*

After a pause for reflection imposed by the European Council, the German presidency during the first half of 2007 prepared initiatives to sort out the crisis caused by the negative referenda on the European Constitution. The European Council of June 2007 decided to convoke a new IGC which was instructed to elaborate, within a few months, and in any event before the end of 2007, a new draft Treaty, on the basis of a detailed mandate adopted by the European Council. The mandate makes clear that this new Treaty instead of replacing the existing treaties by one single text will apply the traditional method of amending the existing treaties which will thus continue to exist. All constitutional language, including the references to the symbols of the Union (the flag, the anthem etc., contained in Art. I-8 of the Constitution) will have to be dropped. However, in substance the major institutional innovations of the Constitution, will be maintained. That explains the ambitious timetable set for this new IGC and justifies at the same time the decision not to convoke a new convention. Nevertheless, a representative of the European Commission and three Members of the European Parliament participated in this IGC.

After the IGC had concluded its work on 19 October 2007, the new Treaty was signed at Lisbon on 13 December of that same year and baptized accordingly. Again the ratification process appeared laborious. Ireland needed a second referendum for its ratification. After the German *Bundesverfassungsgericht* had given the green light,[122] and the last ratification by Czechia had arrived in November 2009, the Lisbon Treaty could enter into force on 1 December of that same year.

The Treaty of Lisbon amends the Treaty on European Union and the EC Treaty, moreover by way of a Protocol annexed to it also the Euratom Treaty. Under the Lisbon Treaty, the European Union and the European Community are merged into one single organization, the European Union, which replaces and succeeds the European Community. The EC Treaty is renamed

122. Decision of 30 June 2009, BVERFG, 2 BvE 2/08.

Treaty on the Functioning of the European Union (TFEU). This Treaty and the TFEU have the same legal value (Arts. 1 TEU and TFEU).

As to the structure of both treaties and their interrelationship, it might be tempting to regard the TEU, in laying down the objectives, principles and values of the Union as well as the main features of its institutional structure, as the basic text, somewhat comparable with Part I of the Constitution. Such a comparison would, however, only partly be correct and at all events too simplistic. In fact, insofar as the innovative provisions of Part I and Part III of the Constitution have been maintained – which has largely been the case – the authors of the Treaty of Lisbon have dispersed them over both the TEU and the TFEU. In doing so, they respected fairly closely the present structure of both the EU and the EC Treaties. For instance, the detailed provisions on the common foreign and security policy have all been kept in the TEU, whereas the fundamental provisions on the delimitation of competences and the various categories of competence appear in the TFEU (Arts. 2 to 6). Likewise, some of the general provisions from Part I of the Constitution, such as those on the principle of non-discrimination on grounds of nationality, transparency, protection of personal data and the churches, are also placed in the Treaty on the Functioning of the European Union (Arts. 10 to 13 TFEU).

Like the Constitution, the Treaty of Lisbon abandons the complex and, indeed, in the long run almost unworkable distinction between the European Community and the European Union as separate but interlinked organizations and abolishes the architecture of the three pillars. This is one of its most important innovations. The European Community and the European Union are being merged into one single, unitary structure, the European Union, with one single legal personality. However, the Euratom Treaty and with that the European Community for atomic energy will continue to exist. The former third pillar, on police and judicial cooperation in criminal matters, is almost completely made subject to the Community method, both as to the decision-making procedure and the system of judicial protection; the Common Foreign and Security Policy, however, remains governed by more intergovernmental procedures with a minimal role for the Court of Justice.

Democracy and guarantees for the respect of the rule of law within the Union's legal order are reinforced. The position of the European Parliament in the Union's decision-making is further strengthened as the co-decision procedure becomes the ordinary legislative procedure; the number of areas to which this procedure applies is substantially increased, for instance, to include not just the former third pillar subjects, but also common agricultural and commercial policies. The Charter of Fundamental Rights, albeit not a part of the Treaties themselves, but having the same legal value, becomes binding (Art. 6 TEU).[123] Moreover, the TEU provides that the Union shall accede to the European Convention for the Protection of Human Rights and Fundamental Freedoms (Art. 6(2) TEU).

An important institutional modification is furthermore the introduction of the office of President of the European Council in order, *inter alia,* to improve the representation of the EU on the international level. The president, who cannot be at the same time a head of state or government, is appointed for a term of two and a half years, renewable once (Art. 15 TEU). As an institutionally fairly drastic measure to ensure coherence of the external action of the EU in the various fields of EU external competence (e.g. trade policy, development cooperation, CFSP), the function of the High Representative of the EU on foreign and security policy is merged with that of Vice-president of the European Commission responsible for external relations. The High Representative will at the same time be the permanent chairman of the Foreign Affairs Council

---

123. The Charter was solemnly (re)proclaimed at a plenary session of the European Parliament by the Presidents of the Parliament, the Council and the Commission on 12 Dec. 2007 (O.J. 2007, C 303).

and Vice-president of the European Commission (so-called "double hatting") (Art. 18 TEU). For the problem of qualified majority voting in the Council, one of the most contentious problems to be solved, the system of weighed voting which was basically maintained by the Treaty of Nice is replaced by a system of double majority: to obtain a qualified majority at least 55 % of the Member States, comprising at least sixteen of them and representing at least 65 % of the population of the Union must be in favour. Higher percentages apply when the Council does not act on a proposal from the Commission (Art. 238(2) TFEU). However, this new voting system will only enter into force as from 2014 with a further derogation period until 2017 during which Member States may require recourse to the voting rules of the Treaty of Nice (Art. 16(4) and (5) TEU and Arts. 3 and 4 of the Protocol on transitional provisions).

As to the composition of the European Commission, the system of one Member per Member State will continue until 2014. The Commission to be appointed that year will be composed of a number of Members corresponding to two thirds of the number of Member States unless the European Council decides to alter this number. The Members will be chosen from among the nationals of the Member States on the basis of a system of rotation treating all Member States equally (Art. 17(5) TEU). However, referring to a commitment taken after the first, negative, referendum in Ireland on the Lisbon Treaty, the European Council decided in 2013 to provisionally maintain the system of one member of the Commission per Member State as from 2014.[124]

Another important innovation is the role granted to national parliaments, not only by allowing them to be directly informed about legislative proposals of the European Commission, but also by giving them a specific responsibility for controlling respect of the principle of subsidiarity, providing as a measure of last resort also the possibility of an appeal before the Court of Justice.[125] These mechanisms are important because they could improve the legitimacy of EU action as seen at the national level by fostering national parliaments to become more actively involved in the discussion of EU actions and policies.

8.3 *Post Lisbon*

The evolution of the Union after the entering into force of the Lisbon Treaty has been greatly marked by the financial crisis starting in 2007 as a banking crisis but quickly developing into a fiscal, a sovereign debt and economic crisis. The crisis particularly affected the members of the Eurozone. When some of these members in fact lost access to the financial markets to finance their sovereign debts, even the survival of the euro as a common currency was put into question. Action was taken, often, inevitably, after politically difficult and last minute decision-making, on three fronts more particularly: assisting Member States in financial difficulties, strengthening the discipline of the Stability and Growth Pact by enhancing surveillance and coordination mechanisms for national budgetary and economic policies and reforming banking and financial markets legislation, improving supervision and laying down the foundations for a Banking Union. Indeed, during the period 2011–2014 far reaching, sometimes highly complex legislation has been adopted for these purposes.[126]

On the institutional level it is interesting to note that for some of the new instruments Member States preferred to have recourse to traditional international treaties instead of applying the

124. Decision of 22 May 2013 concerning the number of members of the European Commission, O.J. 2013, L 165/98.
125. See Protocol 1 on the role of national parliaments in the EU and Protocol 2 on the application of the principles of subsidiarity and proportionality, annexed to the treaties.
126. See Ch. 27, "Financial market regulation and supervision", of this book.

Union method, but at the same time entrusting important competences to the Union institutions, the Commission and the Court of Justice particularly, for the implementation of these treaties: the Treaty on the European Stability mechanism,[127] the Treaty on Stability, Coordination and Governance (also called the Fiscal Compact), both of 2013, and the Agreement on a Single Resolution Fund of 2014.[128] This use of the intergovernmental method is the more remarkable because many of the rules concerned could, quite probably, have been enacted by Union legislation.

For the time being, these new measures and mechanisms have brought the euro into calmer waters, also due to the interventions of the European Central Bank.[129] One may note in this context that Latvia became the 18th member of the Eurozone on 1 January 2014, whereas Lithuania has joined as from 1 January 2015.

In the longer term, the substance of the intergovernmental instruments just mentioned should be integrated into the Union legal system, as already envisaged by some of them, and if legally necessary, by amending the existing treaties. This would at the same time allow ensuring for the European Parliament a role in the decision-making on these issues commensurate with the position it now has acquired in the legislative process of the EU. Further amendments of the Treaties might also be considered to strengthen the economic part of the EMU, more particularly within the context of the Eurozone. The debate on this issue is well prepared.[130] Indeed, the coordination method, which the Treaties have at present foreseen with regard to national economic policies, and this mainly by soft law instruments, has become an anachronism. New initiatives recently announced by President Macron of France, possibly to be presented in tandem with Germany, will give a new impetus to the debate on strengthening the governance of the Eurozone.

A second event that has profoundly shaken up the Union and will mobilize considerable administrative and political resources in the coming years to avoid potential economic, social and political damage is of course Brexit. Indeed, as Shakespeare was justly quoted, "true is it, that we have seen better days".[131] By the 23 June 2016 referendum a narrow majority of the people of the United Kingdom (51,9% of a turnout of 72%) supported the UK leaving the EU after a campaign appealing more to emotion than to reason. It may be said that about forty years of largely negative and often incorrect press coverage of the EU and its policies had well prepared the ground for this outcome.[132] The concessions David Cameron had obtained, after laborious negotiations, for a "new settlement" for the UK in the EU appeared of no avail.[133] The UK has triggered the

127. Member States considered it necessary first to amend Art. 136 TFEU adding a third paragraph explicitly allowing setting up such a stability mechanism. This treaty amendment was validated by the Court in case C-370/12, *Pringle*.
128. It is highly regrettable that both treaties and the agreement, which are of such importance for the economic and financial governance of the EU, and the functioning of the Eurozone in particular, have not been published on EUR-Lex. These texts can be found (with some effort) on the website of the European Council, available at <www.european-council.europa.eu/media>.
129. See C-62/14, *Gauweiler and Others*.
130. See the Van Rompuy Report of 2012, "Towards a genuine Economic and Monetary Union", the Commission's Blueprint, also of 2012, "A Blueprint for a deep and genuine Economic and Monetary Union – Launching a European debate" (COM(2012)777), the Five Presidents Report of 2015, "Completing Europe's Economic and Monetary Union", Report by J.-C. Juncker in close cooperation with D. Tusk, J. Dijsselbloem, M. Draghi and M. Schulz.
131. Editorial Comments, (2016) CML Rev., 875.
132. See the excellent analysis in the Editorial Comments, *supra* note 131.
133. Decision of the Heads of State or Government, meeting within the European Council, concerning a new settlement for the United Kingdom within the European Union.

withdrawal procedure of Article 50 TEU by notifying to the European Council in March 2017 its intention to withdraw from the EU and the Euratom treaty. The UK Government originally intended to decide withdrawal without involving Parliament by using the royal prerogative of the executive to decide on issues of external relations. This position was attacked in the courts. For an outsider the outcome of this litigation is not so astonishing considering the high ranking status of the principle of the Sovereignty of Parliament in the UK constitutional order. Indeed, the Supreme Court largely confirmed the decision of the Divisional Court according to which the decision to withdraw required the consent of Parliament.[134] The notification of the withdrawal decision has started the two years time limit provided for by Article 50. During this period a withdrawal agreement should be negotiated setting out the arrangements for withdrawal. Withdrawal will be a fact as from the date of the entry into force of the agreement or in the absence of such agreement at the end of the two years period. However, that period may be extended by a unanimous decision of the European Council and in agreement with the UK. Article 50 does not impose a limit to such extension.

The withdrawal agreement will have to establish the terms of withdrawal, a highly complex exercise after over forty years of ever closer economic and financial relationships and involvement of the UK in EU policies and EU legislation in fields as diverse as the internal market (free movement of persons), agriculture, environment, (nuclear) energy, (air-) transport, labour law, judicial cooperation, immigration, trade policy. The Council, acting by a qualified majority, after obtaining the consent of the European parliament, will decide the withdrawal agreement on behalf of the Union. The agreement, at least in principle, will not have to be mixed, that is require to be approved by the Member States individually. According to Article 50, par. 2, the arrangements for withdrawal will have to be negotiated "taking account of the framework of its (the UK's) future relationship with the Union." Thus, the details of that relationship will not have to be decided by the withdrawal agreement, if at all possible in view of the complexities involved. Quite probably, if negotiations succeed, the agreement will also provide for a transitional regime to avoid a cliff-edge at the date of Brexit. The most obvious and negotiation time saving solution would be for the UK continuing to apply during that interim period parts of the acquis with conditions attached such as accepting future evolution of that acquis and the relevant jurisdiction of the EU Court of Justice, paying an annual contribution into the EU budget etc.[135] An important question, which Article 50 leaves unanswered, is of whether and under which conditions the UK could still change its mind preferring to remain a member of the EU and withdraw its notification under Article 50. Legal opinions on that question differ. One may say that this question is in the end more a political than a legal one.[136]

With regard to that future relationship many models are being discussed.[137] They range from the European Economic Area (EEA)-, Swiss-, CETA- (EU-Canada Agreement), a bespoke Free Trade Agreement "plus" model to a fall-back on the WTO regime. Whatever the outcome, one thing seems to be certain. Brexit will indeed mean Brexit. Continuing access to the Customs

---

134. *R (Miller) v. Secretary of State for exiting the EU et al*, (2017) UKSC 5.
135. Cf. European Council Negotiation Guidelines of 29 Apr. 2017, para 3 and Council Negotiation Directives of 22 May 2017, para 19.
136. See on this question and others regarding the interpretation of Art. 50 TEU, also with further references, P. Eeckhout and E. Frantziou, "Brexit and Article 50 TEU: A constitutionalist reading", (2017) CML Rev.
137. See more particularly J.-C. Piris, "Which options would be available to the United Kingdom in case of a withdrawal from the EU?", (2015) CSF-SSUP Working Paper; M.T. Cremades and P. Novak, "Brexit and the European Union: General institutional and legal considerations", (2017) *Study for the EP Committee on Constitutional Affairs.*

Union and the internal market with the UK at the same time "taking back control" of legislation, court jurisdiction and the budget is not a possible model.

Brexit and growing voices of citizens' dissatisfaction with the Union in other Member States have prompted the remaining 27 Member States to reopen the debate about the future of the Union.[138] We mentioned already the ongoing discussion on the strengthening of the Eurozone. At the same time the internal cohesion of the Union is seriously challenged by conflicts about how to handle the refugee crisis, even about the implementation of measures already decided.[139] Further challenges are caused by constitutional developments in Hungary and Poland affecting basic democratic values (e.g. independence of the media) and the rule of law (independence of the judiciary in Poland). May it again be confirmed that it is in periods of crisis that the Union succeeds in deciding the necessary reforms.

Further reading

History of European integration

Beach, D., *The Dynamics of European Integration: Why and When EU Institutions Matter* (Palgrave Macmillan, 2005).

Berglund, S. and J. Ekman et al., *The Making of the European Union: Foundations, Institutions and Future Trends* (Edward Elgar, 2006).

Bitsch, M.-T., *Histoire de la construction européenne de 1945 à nos jours* (Complexe, 2004).

Blair, A., *The European Union Since 1945*, 1st ed. (Pearson Longman, 2005

Booker, C. and R. North, *The Great Deception: Can the European Union survive?*, 2nd ed. (Continuum, 2005).

Brugmans, J., *L'idée européenne, 1920–1970*, 3rd ed. (De Tempel, 1970).

Chryssochoou, D.N., *Theory and reform in the European Union*, 2nd ed. (Manchester University Press, 2003).

Courty, G. and G. Devin, *La construction européenne* (La Découverte, 2005).

Devuyst, Y., *The European Union at the Crossroads: An Introduction to the EU's Institutional Evolution*, 2nd ed. (Peter Lang, 2003).

Dinan, D., *Europe Recast: A History of European Union* (Palgrave Macmillan, 2004).

Dinan, D., *Ever Closer Union: An Introduction to European Integration*, 3rd ed. (Palgrave MacMillan, 2005).

Dinan, D., *Origins and Evolution of the European Union* (OUP, 2006).

Duff, A., *Reforming the European Union* (Federal Trust, 1997).

Gerbet, P., *La construction de l'Europe*, 3rd ed. (Imprimerie Nationale Éditions, 1999).

Van Gerven, W., *The European Union: A polity of States and Peoples* (Hart, 2005).

Gillingham, J.R., *European Integration, 1950–2003: Superstate or New Market Economy?* (CUP, 2003).

Griffiths, R.T. (Ed.), *The Netherlands and the Integration of Europe 1945–1957* (NEHA, 1990).

Groeben, H. von der, *Aufbaujahre der Europäischen Gemeinschaft: Das Ringen um den Gemeinsamen Markt und die Politische Union (1958–1966)* (Nomos, 1982).

Haas, E.B., *The Uniting of Europe: Political, Social and Economic Forces 1950–1957*, 2nd ed. (Stanford University Press, 1968).

---

138. See the Bratislava Declaration of 27 Member States (16 Sept. 2016) and the Rome Declaration of the leaders of 27 Member States and of the European Council, the European Parliament and the European Commission (25 Mar. 2017). See also the European Commission White Paper on the future of Europe and the way forward (1 Mar. 2017) followed up by President Juncker's State of the Union Address to the European Parliament of 13 Sept. 2017.

139. Cf. Joined Cases C-643/15 and C-647/15, *Slovak Republic and Hungary v. Council.*

Kaiser, W. and P. Starie, *Transnational European Union: Towards a Common Political Space* (Routledge, 2005).
Koolhaas, R. and T. Deutinger et al., *History of Europe and the European Unio* (Archis Foundation, 2005).
Mayne, R., *The Community of Europe* (Victor Gollancz, 1962).
Meerssche, P. van de, *Europese integratie en desintegratie 1945-heden* (Standaard Uitgeverij, 1978).
Meerssche, P. van de, *Van Jalta tot Malta: Politieke geschiedenis van Europa*, 1st ed. (Het Spectrum, 1990).
Meunier, S. and K.R. MacNamara, *Making History: European Integration and Institutional Change at Fifty* (OUP, 2007).
Middlemas, K., *Orchestrating Europe. The Informal Politics of European Union 1973- 1995* (Fontana Press, 1995).
Milward, A.S., *Politics and Economics in the History of the European Union* (Routledge, 2005).
Milward, A.S., *The Reconstruction of Western Europe, 1945–51* (Methuen, 1984).
Milward, A.S. et al., *The Frontier of National Sovereignty* (Routledge, 1993)
Monnet, J., *Mémoires* (Fayard, 1976).
Moravcsik, A. and U. Harvard et al., *Europe without illusions: The Paul-Henri Spaak Lectures, 1994–1999* (University Press of America, 2005).
Pinder, J., *The Building of the European Union*, 3rd ed. (OUP, 1998).
Quermonne, J.-L., *Le système politique de l'Union européenne: Des Communautés économiques à l'Union politique*, 4th ed. (Montchrestien, 2001).
Reuter, P., *La Communauté Européenne du Charbon et de l'Acier* (Librairie Générale de Droit et de Jurisprudence, 1953).
Rogowski, R. and C. Turner, *The shape of the new Europe* (CUP, 2006).
Rücker, K. and L. Warlouzet, *Quelle(s) Europe(s)?: Nouvelles approches en histoire de l'intégration européenne = Which Europe(s)?: New approaches in European integration history* (P. Lang, 2007).
Ruyt, J. de, *L'Acte unique européen*, 2nd ed. (Université Bruxelles, 1989).
Snyder, F. G., *Constitutional dimensions of European economic integration* (Kluwer Law International, 1996).
Spierenburg, D. and R. Poidevin, *Histoire de la Haute Autorité de la Communauté Européenne du charbon et de l'acier: une expérience supranationale* (Bruylant, 1993).
Tsoukalis, L., *What kind of Europe?* (OUP, 2005).
Urwin, D., *The Community of Europe. A History of European Integration since 1945*, 2nd ed. (Longman, 1997).
Vanthoor, W.F.V., *A Chronological History of the European Union 1946–2001*, 2nd ed. (Edward Elgar, 2002).
Vembulu, R.P., *Understanding European Integration: History, Culture, and Politics of Identity* (Aakar Books, 2003).
Wilkens, A. (Ed.), *Le Plan Schuman dans l'Histoire; Intérêts nationaux et projet européen* (Bruylant, 2004).
Wood, D.M. and B.A. Yesilada, *The emerging European Union*, 4th ed., (Pearson/Longman, 2007).
Zorgbibe, C., *Histoire de l'Union Européenne* (Fondation Robert Schuman, 2005).
de Zwaan, J.W. and A.E. Kellermann, *The European Union: An Ongoing Process of Integration: Liber Amicorum Alfred E. Kellermann* (T.M.C. Asser Press, 2004).

Economic integration

Diebold Jr., W., *The Schuman Plan: A Study in Economic Cooperation, 1950–1959* (Praeger, 1959)
Dyson, K.H.F. and K. Featherstone, *The Road to Maastricht: Negotiating Economic and Monetary Union* (OUP, 1999).

McDonald, F. and S. Dearden, *European Economic Integration*, 4th ed. (Financial Times Prentice Hall, 2004).

Nello, S.S., *The European Union: Economics, Policies and History* (MacGraw-Hill, 2005).

Pelkmans, J., *European Integration: Methods and Economic Analysis*, 3rd ed. (Prentice Hall/Financial Times, 2006).

Zervoyianni, A. and G. Argiros et al., *European integration* (Palgrave Macmillan, 2006).

Treaty of Maastricht

Cloos, J. et al., *Le traité de Maastricht: Genèse, analyse, commentaires* (Bruylant, 1993).

Constantinesco, V. et al. (Eds.), *Traité sur l'Union Européenne* (Economica, 1995).

Corbett, R.G., *The Treaty of Maastricht: From Conception to Ratification: A Comprehensive Reference Guide* (Longman, 1993)

Dehousse, R. (Ed.), *Europa After Maastricht. An Ever Closer Union?* (Beck, 1994).

Devroe, W. and J. Wouters, *De Europese Unie: Het Verdrag van Maastricht en zijn uitvoering: analyse en perspectieven* (Peeters, 1996).

Duff, A. and J. Pinder, *Maastricht and Beyond: Building the European Union* (Routledge, 1994).

Hrbek, R. (Ed.), *Der Vertrag von Maastricht in der wissenschaftlichen Kontroversen: Beitr. für das Jahreskolloquium des Arbeitskreises Europäische Integration e.V., 12./14. November 1992 in Bonn* (Nomos, 1993).

Ingelaere, F., *Grondlijnen van de Europese Politieke, Economische en Monetaire Unie: een verkenning van het Europese Unieverdrag* (Story-Scientia, 1992).

Lane, R., "New Community competences under the Maastricht Treaty, 30 CML Rev. (1993), 939

Maillet, P. (Ed.), *Trois défis de Maastricht: convergence, cohésion, subsidiarite* (L'Harmattan, 1993).

Monar, J., W. Ungerer and W. Wessels (Eds.), *The Maastricht Treaty on European Union. Legal Complexity and Political Dynamic* (European University Press, 1994).

O'Keeffe, D., P.M. Twomey (Eds.), *Legal Issues of the Maastricht Treaty* (Chancery, 1994).

Schwarze, J. (Ed.), *Vom Binnenmarkt zur Europäischen Union: Beiträge zur aktuellen Entwicklung des Gemeinschaftsrechts* (Nomos, 1993).

Treaty of Amsterdam

Barents, R., *Verdrag van Amsterdam in werking* (Kluwer, 1999).

Heukels, T. and N.M. Blokker et al., (Eds.), *The European Union after Amsterdam: A Legal Analysis* (Kluwer, 1998).

Monar, J. and W. Wessels, *The European Union after the Treaty of Amsterdam* (Continuum, 2001).

O'Keeffe, D. and P.M. Twomey (Eds.), *Legal issues of the Amsterdam treaty* (Hart, 1999).

Winter, J.A., *Reforming the Treaty on European Union: The Legal Debate* (Kluwer Law International, 1996).

Treaty of Nice

Andenas, M.T. and J.A. Usher, *The Treaty of Nice and Beyond: Enlargement and Constitutional Reform* (Hart, 2003).

Bond, M. and K. Feus, *The Treaty of Nice explained* (Federal Trust for Education and Research, 2001).

Bradley, K.St.C., "Institutional design in the Treaty of Nice", 38 CML Rev. (2001), 1095–1123.

Constantinesco, V., Y. Gautier and D. Simon (Eds.) *Le traité de Nice, premières analyses* (Presses Universitaires de Starsbourg, 2001).

Melissas, D.K. and I. Pernice, *Perspectives of the Nice Treaty and the Intergovernmental Conference in 2004* (Nomos, 2002).

The EU Charter on fundamental rights

Arnull, A., "From Charter to Constitution and beyond: Fundamental rights in the new European Union", (2003) *Public Law*, 774–793.

Eriksen, E.O., J.E. Fossum et al., *The Chartering of Europe: The European Charter of Fundamental Rights and Its Constitutional Implications* (Nomos, 2003).

Feus, K., *An EU Charter of Fundamental Rights: Text and Commentaries* (Federal Trust, 2000).

Hervey, T.K. and J. Kenner (Eds.), *Economic and Social Rights under the EU Charter of Fundamental Rights: A Legal Perspective* (Hart, 2003).

Knook, A., The Court, the Charter and the vertical division of powers in the European Union, 42 CML Rev. (2005), 367–398.

Peers, S. and A. Ward, *The European Union Charter of Fundamental Rights* (Hart, 2004).

Quinn, G. and L. Flynn, *EU Charter on Fundamental Rights* (OUP, 2001).

Schönlau, J., *Drafting the EU Charter: Rights, Legitimacy and Process* (Palgrave Macmillan, 2005).

Treaty Establishing a Constitution for Europe

Albi, A. and J. Ziller, *The European Constitution and National Constitutions: Ratification and Beyond* (Kluwer Law International, 2007).

Amato, G. and H. Bribosia et al., *Genesis and destiny of the European Constitution: Commentary on the Treaty Establishing a Constitution for Europe in the Light of the Travaux Préparatoires and Future Prospects = Genèse et destinée de la Constitution européenne: commentaire du Traité établissant une Constitution pour l'Europe à la lumière des travaux préparatoires et perspectives d'avenir* (Bruylant, 2007).

Barnier, M. and G. Dimitrakopoulos et al., *A New Constitutional Settlement for the European People* (Bruylant, 2004).

Blankart, C.B. and D.C. Mueller, *A Constitution for the European Union* (MIT Press, 2004).

Bogdandy, A.v. and J. Bast, *Principles of European Constitutional Law* (Hart, 2006).

Brand, M., *Affirming and refining European constitutionalism: Towards the Establishment of the First Constitution for the European Union* (European University Institute, 2004).

Church, C.H. and D. Phinnemore, *Understanding the European Constitution: an introduction to the EU Constitutional Treaty* (Routledge, 2006).

Constantinesco, V. and Y. Gautier et al., *Le Traité établissant une Constitution pour L'Europe: analyses & commentaires* (Presses universitaires de Strasbourg, 2005).

Cowgill, A. and A. Cowgill, *The European Constitution in Perspective: Analysis and Review of 'The Treaty Establishing a Constitution For Europe'* (British Management Data Foundation, 2004).

Curtin, D.M. and A.E. Kellermann et al., *The EU Constitution: The Best Way Forward?* (T.M.C. Asser Press, 2005).

Curtin, D.M. and W. Devroe, *Mind the Gap: The Evolving EU Executive and the Constitution* (Europa Law Publishing, 2004).

De Búrca, G. and W. Devroe, *The EU Constitution: In Search of Europe's International Identity* (Leuven Centre for a Common Law of Europe etc., 2005)

De Schutter, O. and P. Nihoul et al., *Une constitution pour l'Europe: réflexions sur les transformations du droit de l'Union européenne* (Larcier, 2004).

De Witte, B., *Ten reflections on the Constitutional Treaty for Europe* (European University Institute, 2003).

Dehousse, R., *Une constitution pour l'Europe?* (Presses de Sciences Po, 2002).

Devuyst, Y., *The European Union Transformed: Community Method and Institutional Evolution from the Schuman Plan to the Constitution for Europe* (Peter Lang, 2005).

Dony, M. and E. Bribosia, *Commentaire de la Constitution de l'Únion européenne* (Editions de l'Université Libre de Bruxelles, 2005).

Eriksen, E.O. and J.E. Fossum et al., *Developing a Constitution for Europe* (Routledge, 2004).
Fischer, K.H., *Der Europäische Verfassungsvertrag: Texte und Kommentar* (Stämpfli, 2005).
FitzGerald, G. and A. O'Rourke, Europe Re-united: A Constitutional Treaty: An Analysis (Institute of European Affairs, 2004).
Häberle, P., *Europäische Verfassungslehre* (Nomos, 2005).
Inglis, K. and A. Ott, *The Constitution for Europe and an Enlarging Union: Unity in Diversity?* (Europa Law Publishing, 2005).
Jacobs, A., *The European Constitution: How it Was Created, What it Will Change* (Wolf Legal Publishers), 2005.
MacCormick, N., *Who's Afraid of a European Constitution?* (Imprint Academic, 2005).
Milton, G. and J. Keller-Noëllet et al., *The European Constitution: Its Origins, Negotiation and Meaning* (John Harper Publishing, 2005).
Norman, P., *The Accidental Constitution: The Making of Europe's Constitutional Treaty* (EuroComment, 2005).
Pernice, I. and J. Zemánek, A Constitution for Europe: The IGC, the Ratification Process and Beyond (Nomos, 2005).
Piris, J.-C., *The Constitution for Europe: A Legal Analysis* (CUP, 2006).
Schwarze, J., *The Birth of a European Constitutional Order: The Interaction of National and European Constitutional Law* (Nomos, 2001).
Timmermans, C.W.A., "The constitutionalisation of the European Union", (2002) *Yearbook of European Law*, at 1–11.
Verhoeven, A., *The European Union in Search of a Democratic and Constitutional Theory* (Kluwer Law International, 2002).
Weiler, J.H.H., *The Constitution of Europe: "Do the New Clothes Have an Emperor?" and other essays on European integration* (CUP, 1999).
Ziller, J. and M. Marquis, *The European Constitution* (Kluwer Law International, 2005).

Brexit

Cremades, M.T. and P. Novak, "Brexit and the European Union: General institutional and legal considerations", (2017) *Study for the EP Committee on Constitutional Affairs.*
Eeckhout, P. and E. Frantziou, "Brexit and Article 50 TEU: A constitutionalist reading", (2017) CML Rev.
Piris, J.-C., "Which options would be available to the United Kingdom in case of a withdrawal from the EU?", (2015) *CSF-SSUP Working Paper.*

CHAPTER 2
STRUCTURE AND EVOLUTION OF UNION LAW

*Bruno De Witte**

1. Introduction: A special legal system

The European Communities, and later the European Union, came into being as creatures of international law, as they were established by means of international treaties concluded by states. Today still, the Treaty on European Union (TEU) and the Treaty on the Functioning of the European Union (TFEU) form the basic documents of the EU legal order. One could logically conclude from this that the European Union is still, in terms of its legal nature, an international organization, albeit a very distinctive and advanced one. There are, however, also good reasons for thinking that the European Union is now so different from any other international organization in the world that it has become "something else", more like the central unit of a European federal state. This discussion on the proper legal nature of the European Union, and of EU law, has been going on for decades, and it is indeed a curious characteristic of EU law that its precise place within the legal universe is not firmly established. This chapter will not engage with that discussion, as not many practical consequences flow from the abstract question of whether the European Union legal order belongs to the world of international law or not. Suffice it to say that there are two credible options for explaining the legal nature of the European Union. The first option consists in saying that, in view of its basis in a set of international treaties, the European Union is still an international organization and EU law is part of international law. This option must necessarily come with the recognition that the European Union is an international organization unlike any other that has existed before, in view of the width and depth of the limitations that are put on the sovereignty of its Member States. But this option allows for other experiments of international cooperation to adopt some or all of the distinctive features of EU law in order to create similarly advanced organizations elsewhere in the world. This option is based, in other words, on a belief in the flexibility and dynamic potential of international law.[1] The second option consists in arguing that, because of its particular legal features, the "European legal order has [...] cut the umbilical cord with the international legal order".[2] There is no entity that resembles the EU elsewhere in the world, and there is no realistic prospect for it to be

---

* Law Faculty, Maastricht University; Law Department/Robert Schuman Centre of the European University Institute (EUI).

1. For a fuller articulation of this view, see B. de Witte, "The European Union as an international legal experiment" in G. de Búrca and J.H.H. Weiler (Eds.), *The Worlds of European Constitutionalism* (CUP, 2012), 19–56; see also T.C. Hartley, "International law and the law of the European Union – A reassessment", 72 *British Yearbook of International Law* (2001) 1–35, and J. Klabbers, "Straddling the fence: The EU and international law" in A. Arnull and D. Chalmers (Eds.), *The Oxford Handbook of European Union Law* (OUP, 2015), 52–71.
2. R. Schütze, *European Constitutional Law* (CUP, 2012), at 66.

created any time soon. As it is not a credible option to argue that the European Union has become a federal state, the authors defending this view argue that the European Union finds itself on a middle ground. It is more than an international regime and not (yet) a federal state, but it possesses features stemming from both sides.[3]

The controversy on the legal nature of the European Union does not stand in the way of a widespread tendency, in the legal literature, to use constitutional terminology to describe and understand EU law. It is often claimed, also occasionally by the European Court of Justice, that EU law forms a "constitutional" legal order. Only a minority of scholars object against this usage, on the ground that Constitutions are the basic legal instruments of sovereign states, and that constitutional terminology should therefore be reserved for states and not extended to non-state entities such as the European Union.[4] Around the turn of the century, the use of constitutional terminology to describe central features of the EU legal order had become commonplace in legal writing.[5] This approach was transferred from legal scholarship to practical politics in 2002–2003, when the Convention on the Future of the Union set out to draft a new treaty text that would be called Treaty establishing a Constitution for Europe. Most EU legal scholars applauded this project to formalize the EU's informal constitutional arrangements, but it failed. During the so-called period of reflection that followed the negative referenda in France and the Netherlands and the demise of the Constitutional Treaty, the Member State governments came to the conclusion that part of the Treaty's failure to take force was due to its overambitious constitutional design. In order to save most of the content of the reforms, they stated in June 2007 that "the constitutional concept, which consisted in repealing all existing Treaties and replacing them by a single text called "Constitution" was to be abandoned".[6] They also scrapped from the text of the Lisbon Treaty, which was subsequently agreed, some of the terminology used in the Constitutional Treaty that seemed too redolent of national constitutional texts, such as "law" (instead of regulation or directive) or "minister of foreign affairs" (instead of High Representative of the European Union) and "primacy of European Union law".

The constitutional perspective on EU law continues, however, to make sense even after the demise of the Constitutional Treaty, and we find several textbooks of EU law that flaunt constitutional terms in their titles.[7] By using constitutional language, these authors seek to emphasize that the European Treaties perform many of the same functions as a national constitution: they establish public authority, and allocate powers between different political institutions; they establish a division of competences between the EU and the Member States, in a way which is reminiscent of similar delimitations of competences in federal constitutions; they set out the basic values of the EU legal order, and the fundamental rights of persons; they organize a system of judicial review for the enforcement of EU law obligations and for the review of the validity

---

3. Among the authors who have recently exposed this view, we can mention R. Schütze, op. cit. *supra* note 2, and M. Avbelj, "Theory of European Union", 36 ELR (2011), 818–836.
4. See for example D. Grimm, "Does Europe need a constitution?", 1 ELJ (1995), 282–302.
5. Among the many writings from that period in which the terms constitution and constitutional were used in relation to EU law, see J.H.H. Weiler, *The Constitution of Europe* (CUP, 1999); K. Lenaerts, P. Van Nuffel and R. Bray, *Constitutional Law of the European Union* (Sweet and Maxwell, 1999); J.C. Piris, "L'Union européenne a-t-elle une Constitution? Lui en faut-il une?", 35 *Revue trimestrielle de droit européen* (1999), 599–635; P. Craig, "Constitutions, constitutionalism, and the European Union", 7 ELJ (2001) 125–150; A. Peters, *Elemente einer Theorie der Verfassung Europas* (Duncker & Humblot, 2001).
6. Those were the words used in the European Council's mandate for the intergovernmental conference that was to elaborate the Lisbon Treaty (Annex 1 of the European Council Conclusions of 21/22 June 2007, 1).
7. A. Rosas and L. Armati, *EU Constitutional Law – An Introduction*, 2nd ed. (OUP, 2012); R. Schütze, op. cit. *supra* note 2; A. von Bogdandy and J. Bast (Eds.), *Principles of European Constitutional Law*, 2nd ed. (OUP, 2011); K. Tuori, *European Constitutionalism* (CUP, 2015).

of EU action. In other words: the usage of constitutional terminology seeks to underline the close similarity (or analogy) between some of the legal issues that arise under EU law and those that arise in the constitutional law of states (especially federal states). These similarities will be explored in the following chapters of this book. This chapter will rather discuss some very idiosyncratic overall features of the EU legal order, which one will hardly find in the universe of constitutional law. Those are: the curious Treaty architecture, with the basic norms of the EU legal order being spread over various treaty instruments (section 2), and the prominent role of differentiation and variable geometry, implying that not all Member States participate in all EU policies (section 3). Both these features are deeply embedded in the history of the European integration process, and we will therefore adopt an evolutionary approach in discussing them. Finally, section 4 will describe the three main ways in which the EU's legal foundations change, namely through treaty revisions, accessions and withdrawals. These are mechanisms of "constitutional change" that strongly denote the international law character of the European Union. They illustrate very well the special nature of the EU legal order, situated in an intermediate position between international and constitutional law, and containing features of both.

2. Evolution of the Treaty architecture

In Article 1 of the Treaty on European Union, it is stated that "the Union shall be founded on the present Treaty and on the Treaty on the Functioning of the European Union" and that those two Treaties "shall have the same legal value". This fragmentation of the Union's basic legal norms over two different instruments is a curious feature of the EU legal order. It has also been a constant feature of the history of the European Communities and the European Union, although the precise form of that fragmentation has changed over time through a historical evolution of the so-called "Treaty architecture". The latter is a term of art among European Union scholars and politicians. It refers to the way in which the Treaties and annexed Protocols and other documents (the Charter of Rights) on which the European Union is founded are arranged in relation to each other, and also to the internal structure of those Treaties. It refers, one could say with some exaggeration, to the way the Treaties look before one examines their actual content. This may seem a rather technical-legal matter, but it has in fact been a matter of core constitutional politics in the history of European integration. The adoption, at Maastricht, of a Treaty on the European Union alongside the existing European Community Treaty was an example of such politics-inspired Treaty architecture. Similarly, the Lisbon Treaty was also an attempt to use Treaty architecture in order to make a statement of constitutional politics: in this case, the dismemberment of the Constitutional Treaty into two separate treaties (the TEU and the TFEU), which the Lisbon Treaty effected, was a way for the governments of the Member States to tell their public opinion that the "constitutional moment" was over. The main episodes of this historical evolution will be traced in the following pages.

2.1 *Treaty architecture prior to Maastricht*

From its early days, the integration process of the "small Europe" (as it was then known in contrast with the larger Council of Europe) was marked by the coexistence of several international organizations. In 1957, the Treaty of Rome established the European Economic Community (EEC) and the European Atomic Energy Community (EAEC) alongside each other and alongside the existing Coal and Steel Community (ECSC), instead of forming a single consolidated organization based on a single treaty. The multiplicity of treaties was, at first, accompanied by a duplication of certain institutions: the Commission (EEC) operated alongside the High

Authority (ECSC), and there were two separate Councils.[8] This was quickly remedied by the *Traité de fusion* of 1965.[9] This "Merger Treaty" created a set of common institutions for the Communities but did not merge those Communities themselves.

As time went by, the ECSC and EAEC were increasingly perceived as rather marginal "annexes" of the EEC. The centrality of the latter organization, and the relatively small differences between the rules governing the three organizations, encouraged the use of the term Community legal order in the singular.[10] When the Court of Justice used the term "new legal order" in its seminal judgments *Van Gend en Loos*[11] and *Costa v. ENEL*[12] of the early 1960s, that term referred, strictly speaking, to the EEC's legal order, but in the course of time it came to refer to the *ensemble* of Community law across the three organizations. Beyond the variety of sources of Community law and the variety of law-making modes, there was a deep sense of the unity of the Community legal order, and of the existence of common principles underlying it. One finds a synthetic rendering of this vision in a paragraph of the Court's Opinion 1/91 (dealing with the proposed European Economic Area Agreement), which was given at the time of the Maastricht summit, and in which the Court referred to the existence of several "Community Treaties" but one single "Community legal order", of which the EEC Treaty was declared to form the "constitutional charter".[13]

This sense of unity of the legal order was deeply challenged by the Treaty of Maastricht. That Treaty added to the European Community a new organization called the European Union (EU), whose relationship with the EC was not clearly defined, and which gave legal cover to the creation of two forms of inter-state cooperation – common foreign and security policy (CFSP); and justice and home affairs (JHA) – that did not possess some of the key legal characteristics undergirding the Community legal order, such as: Commission initiative for legislation; full judicial review; primacy and direct effect in the domestic legal orders. The EC/EU dichotomy introduced by the Maastricht Treaty was gradually eroded, leading eventually to the merger of the two organizations through the Lisbon Treaty; we will trace, in the next two sections, this evolutionary process of emergence and demise of the so-called pillar structure.

2.2 *Creation of the pillar structure by the Maastricht Treaty*

The Maastricht Treaty created, alongside the existing three European Communities, a new entity called the European Union. This more complex Treaty architecture became known almost immediately as the "pillar structure" although that term was not used in the official documents at the time.[14] This hybrid structure, with two intergovernmental pillars joining the existing supranational pillar (itself consisting of three different organizations, EEC, ECSC and EAEC)

8. On the contrary, a single Parliament and a single Court of Justice were set up right from the beginning, through the Convention on certain institutions common to the European Communities, which entered into force at the same time as the EEC and EAEC Treaties.
9. See F. Laursen, "The 1965 Merger Treaty: The first reform of the founding European Community Treaties" in F. Laursen (Ed.), *Designing the European Union – From Paris to Lisbon* (Palgrave Macmillan, 2012), 77–97.
10. One factor in this evolution was the existence, from the start, of a single legal service covering the three Communities; it consciously promoted the vision of an integrated and coherent legal order. See A. Vauchez, *L'Union par le droit – L'invention d'un programme institutionnel pour l'Europe* (Presses de Sciences Po, 2012), at 52–62.
11. Case 26/62, *NV. Algemene Transport- en Expeditie Onderneming van Gend & Loos v. Nederlandse administratie der belastingen.*
12. Case 6/64, *Flaminio Costa v. ENEL.*
13. Opinion 1/91 on the creation of the European Economic Area.
14. The term "pillars" was acknowledged by the European Council some years later; see Conclusions of the Dublin European Council, 13 and 14 Dec. 1996.

under the new roof of the EU, had been originally proposed by the French representative in the intergovernmental conference (IGC) on European Political Union; it was then developed by the Council Secretariat and formally presented in the first Draft Treaty submitted by the Luxembourg presidency on 12 April 1991.[15] The proposed structure built on existing developments in European integration. In particular, what was henceforth called Common Foreign and Security Policy had been known in previous years as European Political Cooperation in foreign affairs (EPC).[16] As for cooperation in justice and home affairs (JHA), this had also started long before the Maastricht Treaty, although in a wholly informal intergovernmental framework made up of ad-hoc working groups of national civil servants, the most prominent of which was the Trevi Group.[17] So, both for CFSP and JHA, the Draft Treaty of the Luxembourg Presidency was a step forward, in that it sought to connect two mechanisms of intergovernmental cooperation more closely to the core cooperation framework formed by the European Community.

The Dutch government, which took over the presidency of the IGC in the second half of 1991, presented a new Draft Treaty text in September 1991 which was much more ambitious. It proposed to include the new policy fields of CFSP and JHA fully *within* the existing institutional framework of the European Community. The Dutch Draft was quickly rejected by most of the other governments, the main reason being their fear that the existing "Community method", as practiced in the framework of the EC, could not sufficiently accommodate the intergovernmental mode of decision-making that they preferred to use in the two new fields of cooperation. In the end, the Member States agreed to confirm the hybrid institutional structure adopted in the Luxembourg Draft which included the new policy domains within the framework of a newly created European Union, thus keeping them *outside* the existing European Community framework, although both organizations were linked to each other by a set of common provisions included in the EU Treaty.

Even though the reasons for the creation of the pillar structure at Maastricht were rather contingent, the "separate paths" approach taken at that time had long-term implications for the structural evolution of European law. At first, legal writers struggled to make sense of the new post-Maastricht Treaty architecture. In fact, many Community lawyers reacted defensively by taking the view that the European Community remained, after Maastricht, an autonomous organization with its own institutions, and that those institutions were simply "borrowed" for the purpose of complementary action in foreign and home affairs. The European Union was seen as a kind of "flag of convenience" framework for inter-state cooperation that "currently has no legal personality, has no powers of its own and does not have its own institutions, but uses the traditional institutions of the European Community to achieve its aims".[18] Other observers, however, emphasized the unitary elements of the Maastricht Treaty which linked the pillars rather tightly together. In particular, the important common provisions and final provisions of the Treaty on European Union did not just deal with CFSP or JHA, but covered both the intergovernmental pillars *and* the European Community. For example, after Maastricht, the revision of both Treaties and the accession of new States to both organizations (the EC and EU) was determined

---

15. D. Beach, *The Dynamics of European Integration* (Palgrave Macmillan, 2005), at 109.
16. On the institutional practice of the early years of EPC, see S. Nuttall, "Interaction between European political cooperation and the European Community", 7 *Yearbook of European Law* (1987), 211.
17. On the pre-Maastricht origins of cooperation in the field of Justice and Home affairs, see E. Denza, *The Intergovernmental Pillars of the European Union* (OUP, 2002), Ch. 3; and J. Monar, "Justice and home affairs: The Treaty of Maastricht as a decisive intergovernmental gate opener", 34 *European Integration* (2012), 717, 718–721.
18. T. Heukels and J. de Zwaan, "The configuration of the European Union: Community dimensions of institutional interaction" in D. Curtin and T. Heukels (Eds.), *The Institutional Dynamics of European Integration – Essays in Honour of Henry G Schermers* (Nijhoff, 1994), 227.

by provisions included in the final part of the EU Treaty, and the EC Treaty did no longer have its own rules on those matters. Therefore, the better legal view – which slowly won ground in the following years – was to conceive of the European Union as an overarching but layered organization *within* which the European Community, the European Atomic Energy Community and (until its demise) the European Coal and Steel Community operated as autonomous sub-organizations with their own legal personality, including the capacity to conclude international agreements with third countries.[19]

2.3 *Evolution of the pillar structure from Maastricht to Lisbon*

The evolution after Maastricht, both in political practice and in scholarly understanding, was marked by two complementary trends. First, there was a gradual acknowledgement that the European Union, far from being a transitional construction, was a stable legal reality that was not going to disintegrate easily. Secondly, there was a growing understanding that the European Union was not radically different from the European Community, and that both organizations had many principles and practices in common.

This evolution had implications for the way in which a future merger of the Treaties was viewed. At first, the main goal of those advocating a merger was to bring the intergovernmental pillars back in "from the cold", into the safe haven of the European Community, whereas the idea of a merger was resisted by the intergovernmental camp fearing that the distinctive institutional characteristics of the second and third pillar would thereby be lost. Later on, towards the end of the 1990s, the prospect of a merger of the Treaties became gradually less controversial: on the one hand, the *communautaristes* bore little hope that the intergovernmental features of the second and third pillars could be wiped out entirely; and on the other hand, the intergovernmental-minded could not deny that all three pillars were part of a single institutional framework and subject to a set of common legal principles, and they had become increasingly aware of the practical complications caused by the separation in two Treaties.

However, the first post-Maastricht Treaty revision conference, which resulted in the Treaty of Amsterdam, came too early for the idea of a consolidation of the Treaties to have garnered sufficient support, but that Treaty nevertheless showed the robustness and power of attraction of the first pillar. The Member States had come to recognize (some more willingly than others) that they had been overly imaginative in the autumn of 1991 in breaking with the European Community mould and in developing unprecedented procedures and entirely new legal instruments. The procedures of the second and third pillars had proved to be cumbersome and inefficient, and the new legal instruments, particularly those chosen for the third pillar, had proved to be blunt and legally ambiguous.[20] A more acute understanding of the long-term national interests of the Member States led them, in Amsterdam, to inject into the two intergovernmental pillars an extra dose of *méthode communautaire*, and also to transfer half of the third pillar (the part dealing with immigration and asylum policy) from the third to the first pillar.

The Nice Treaty, which was agreed in December 2000, lacked ambition and the question of Treaty architecture was not even broached during the negotiations, although a Declaration on

---

19. For a summary of that developing discussion on the degree of unity of the EU legal order, see C. Herrmann, "Much ado about Pluto? The unity of the European Union legal order revisited" in M. Cremona and B. de Witte (Eds.), *EU Foreign Relations Law: Constitutional Fundamentals* (OUP, 2008), 20–51; and D. Curtin and I. Dekker, "The European Union from Maastricht to Lisbon: Institutional and legal unity from the shadows" in P. Craig and G. de Búrca (Eds.), *The Evolution of EU Law*, 2nd ed. (OUP, 2011), 155–185.
20. For a discussion of the institutional weaknesses of the second and third pillar regimes after Maastricht, see E. Denza, op. cit. *supra* note 17, Ch. 4 and 6.

the Future of the Union was adopted by the Nice summit in December 2000 which included the question of "simplification of the Treaties" (as it was called) among the four reform themes on which the governments would start a "wider and deeper debate" after the entry into force of the Nice Treaty. One year later, the European Council, at its meeting of Laeken, convened the Convention on the Future of the Union which started its constitution-drafting work soon afterwards, in February 2002. A consensus on merging the EC Treaty and EU Treaty into one common text was reached fairly early in the Convention's life. The impulsion came from the working group on Legal Personality which was steered by its chair Giuliano Amato towards the conclusion that a full-scale merger of the two separate organizations (the EC and the EU) was needed, which would imply a consequent merger of the two Treaties by which those organizations were established. The decisive moment for the adoption of this revolutionary approach to Treaty architecture occurred when the Praesidium of the Convention, in October 2002, presented its "Draft European Constitution".[21] From that moment onwards, the basic choice for a merger and reorganization was no longer called into question and survived until the signing, in October 2004, of the Constitutional Treaty. That Treaty also incorporated, in its Part II, the Charter of Fundamental Rights which had been adopted in 2000 but had remained a legally non-identified object since then.

A merger of the European Community and the European Union inevitably involved a choice about the name of the unified organization. The hallowed name "Community" may have sounded more appealing to many people, but it was very quickly decided that the new organization would instead be called the European Union. The Member State governments and the European institutions themselves had by now adopted the habit of speaking about the European Union in generic terms, even when they referred to policies or measures that were adopted in the framework of the Community. The merger was formally laid down in two provisions of the Constitutional Treaty. Article IV-437, one of its final provisions, was entitled "Repeal of earlier Treaties" and stated that "This Treaty establishing a Constitution for Europe shall repeal the Treaty establishing the European Community and the Treaty on European Union". In order to fill the void created by this repeal, Article I-1 stated that "this Constitution establishes the European Union", which was to succeed to the previously existing European Community and European Union.

The merger of the EC and EU Treaties was a very welcome reform, and one that did not provoke any opposition from the side of individual governments during the IGC that adopted the Constitutional Treaty. Nor was it controversial during the French and Dutch referendum campaigns. However, when the European Council of June 2007 decided formally to bury the Constitutional Treaty, it also decided to undo the merger and instead to use the two existing Treaties as the recipients within which most of the substantive reforms contained in the Constitutional Treaty would be re-inserted, whereas the Charter of Fundamental Rights was expelled from the Treaties. At the same time, however, the European Council confirmed the fusion of the European Community and the European Union into one single organization, because that move had seemed so obviously right to everyone. This, in turn, meant that the EC Treaty could stay alive only by shedding its name, since the "Community" that gave it its name was disappearing, and it was decided that the revised EC Treaty would instead be – awkwardly – called the Treaty on the Functioning of the European Union.

---

21. CONV. 369/02 of 28 Oct. 2002. On the background of the Praesidium's proposal for unification of the treaties, see H. Bribosia, "De la simplification des traités au traité constitutionnel" in G. Amato, H. Bribosia and B. de Witte (Eds.), *Genesis and Destiny of the European Constitution* (Bruylant, 2007), 187–222, 195–202.

So, with the entry into force of the Lisbon Treaty, in December 2009, the organizational dichotomy created at Maastricht was terminated. The Lisbon Treaty left in existence two separate treaties (the EU Treaty and the Treaty on the Functioning of the EU), but only one single organization, the European Union.[22] The "two-treaties-for-one-organization" idea was rendered as follows in the new Article 1(3) TEU:

> "The Union shall be founded on the present Treaty and on the Treaty on the Functioning of the European Union (hereinafter referred to as 'the Treaties'). Those two Treaties shall have the same legal value. The Union shall replace and succeed the European Community."

One may note that the two Treaties are knitted more closely together than before Lisbon. This results from the frequent use, throughout both instruments, of the term "the Treaties" to refer to both of them in an indistinct manner, and also from the adoption of a single set of overall objectives (in Arts. 2 and 3 TEU) that irradiate both Treaty texts.[23]

There is, in fact, no logical explanation for the decision to keep two separate Treaties, the only explanation being of a tactical-political nature: in order to make it appear to the public of a number of key countries that the Constitutional Treaty was effectively dead and buried, it seemed advisable to "artificially" keep in place the pre-existing Treaties, even though one of the amendments to the "existing" EC Treaty was to modify its name and thereby to end the long and successful life of the European Community. The European Union, on the other hand, continued its strange trajectory: the term has started its life as the embodiment of the political dream of European federalists; it then became an unidentified legal object at Maastricht; it was later gradually conceived of as the overarching organization of the European integration process; and it now absorbed and replaced the European Community.

As for the former intergovernmental pillars, they were incorporated into the common regime of competences, legal instruments, decision-making, judicial review and legal effect. Probably the most visible change in daily legal practice is the fact that the separate range of legal instruments, which the EU Treaty had provided for CFSP and for criminal justice, has now disappeared. The general typology of legal instruments contained in Article 288 TFEU now applies to the whole of EU law.[24] Still, CFSP has remained a very distinct institutional field that is, as Article 24(1) TEU quaintly states, "subject to specific rules and procedures".[25] Criminal law and criminal procedure, on the other hand, have become barely distinguishable from other policy areas in institutional terms, although the pre-Lisbon instruments of "third pillar law" (such as the Framework Decisions) continue to exist as long as they are not revised or deleted.

Finally, a continued sense of legal fragmentation – despite the new organizational unity – results from the many Protocols added to the Treaties, which sometimes contain very crucial institutional provisions,[26] and also from the decision to "expel" the Charter of Rights from the

22. In fact, and to be entirely accurate, the European Atomic Energy Community (EAEC) continues to exist even after the Lisbon Treaty so that we still have two organizations existing alongside each other. This dichotomy is hardly noticeable, though, given the negligible legal and political importance of the EAEC.
23. See, on this point, M. Cremona, "The two (or three) treaty solution: The new treaty structure of the EU" in A. Biondi, P. Eeckhout and S. Ripley (Eds.), *EU Law after Lisbon* (OUP, 2012), 40–61, at 45–46.
24. See Ch. 6, "Sources of EU law", of this book.
25. See the discussion by M. Cremona op. cit. *supra* note 23, at 49–54.
26. Consider, for example, Protocol no. 2 on subsidiarity and proportionality.

Treaty text and to make it into a *sui generis* legal instrument which is not part of the Treaties but is given the same legal force as the Treaties by virtue of Article 6 TEU.[27]

3. The evolution of differentiation and variable geometry

In the course of time, the EU legal order has gradually moved away from the ideal of unity and now accommodates various forms of "variable geometry" whereby some Member States are allowed not to participate in the making of EU law norms, and are consequently not bound either to apply such norms. Strong functional and normative reasons explain this evolution and make it very likely that this complex regime of territorial differentiation is there to stay and (probably) to expand further. The *functional* reason is that variable geometry has proved essential for allowing European integration to proceed. Widening, deepening and uniformity could not go together. The choice for widening-with-deepening made repeatedly in the past thirty years of the EU's existence, led to sacrificing the aspiration to the creation of a uniform legal order. But differentiation is also *normatively* attractive since it allows for the diverse preferences of national governments and national public opinions to be accommodated. Some countries can decide to move ahead with the European integration process without being stopped by the more reluctant countries, but also without forcing the latter to participate in new cooperation ventures.

A wide variety of forms of differentiation currently exists, and some policy areas are more clearly marked by their use than others. A simple distinction can be made between mechanisms of differentiation laid down in the Treaty text (and therefore having a formal constitutional status) and the forms of differentiation that were developed beyond the text of the Treaties, through the practice of the EU institutions and the Member States. The current coexistence of these different forms can best be understood by tracing their evolution, which we will do in the following pages.

3.1 *Pre-Maastricht closer cooperation*

The idea that some countries could form the vanguard of the European integration process, clearing the path for others to follow, is as old as that process itself. The Schuman Plan of 9 May 1950 was specifically addressed only to France and Germany, but other European states were invited to join the proposed Coal and Steel Community which was designed to be, in Robert Schuman's words, the first basis of a European federation. The Treaty establishing the Coal and Steel Community, signed in 1951 by six states, contained an open-ended invitation to all European states to join the Six. The EEC Treaty, signed in Rome in 1957, was similarly designed to set in place a nucleus of economic integration that could be joined by others. This, of course, is also what has effectively happened through the gradual extension of membership of the European Communities first, and the European Union later, from six to 28 Member States.

As membership of the European Union grew, the "vanguard" idea became gradually posed in a very different way: it no longer referred to the vanguard role of the members of the "Community club" in relation to the rest of Europe, but rather to the special role that could possibly be played by a smaller group of countries *among the Member States* of the EU. In view of the fact that many important policy decisions (including, especially, revisions of the founding Treaties) continued to be subject to the unanimous agreement of all Member State governments, there was a growing sense that countries unwilling to accept a further deepening of European integration were taking the others hostage. The United Kingdom became the archetypical laggard,

---

27. On the position of the Charter of Rights in the current system of sources of EU law, see Ch. 6, "Sources of EU law", section 2.2., of this book.

particularly under the long series of Conservative governments starting in 1979, but soon also other countries appeared to be consistently less keen than others to extend EC powers, or to make EC decision-making more supranational.

The traditional legal instrument allowing to deal with this problem was the conclusion of international treaties "on the side" between a limited number of EU Member States. This may be called "old-fashioned flexibility",[28] as this mechanism was based on the simple fact that the EU Member States continue to be sovereign states having the capacity to conclude international treaties with third countries but also with each other; a capacity which was not affected, in principle, by the creation of the European Communities and the European Union. Even during the negotiation of the EEC Treaty, and in the period immediately afterwards, several such *inter se* agreements[29] were concluded, also on matters related to those covered by the EEC Treaty; a prominent example was the Treaty establishing the Benelux Economic Union which was concluded on 3 February 1958, that is, only one month after the entry into force of the EEC Treaty. In anticipation of this, Article 233 EC stated – and Article 350 TFEU still states today – that the Treaties do not preclude "the existence or completion of regional unions between Belgium and Luxembourg, or between Belgium, Luxembourg and the Netherlands […]".

Benelux cooperation was not the only form of international cooperation between small groups of states. For many years, the hegemonic position of the EC was not well established, and the history of relationships between European countries was also one of special partnerships between small groups of countries. There are numerous examples of international agreements concluded between EU Member States ever since the 1950s, in areas such as tax law, environmental protection, defence, culture and education. One such *inter se* agreement could truly be seen as a "pioneer group initiative" from a European integration perspective, namely the Schengen cooperation regime, composed of a first Agreement signed in 1985, an implementing Convention adopted in 1990, and numerous specific decisions adopted by the Schengen Executive Committee after that. Schengen cooperation was started at a time when a general consensus on abolishing the controls on persons at the intra-Community borders could not be reached. The same reasons which justified the rule of Article 233 EEC Treaty, whereby the Benelux countries could adopt more advanced measures of integration, could be applied to Schengen. Yet, already from the start, there was a concern that Schengen could develop from a transitional laboratory into a stable institutional regime functioning *alongside* the European Union in a durable fashion, which seemed unattractive due to its important deficits in terms of transparency and judicial protection and due also to its proximity, content-wise, with the core idea of the internal market. The time had come for a new reflection on how to institutionalize closer cooperation within the main Treaty framework rather than outside it.

3.2 *The birth of variable geometry in the Maastricht Treaty*

The urge to neutralize the obstructive power of single countries (that is, their power to prevent the others from deepening their cooperation) became very acute during the twin intergovernmental conferences (the EMU and EPU conferences) that eventually led to the Treaty of Maastricht. Until the very end, the United Kingdom, in particular, opposed essential elements

28. B. de Witte, "Old-fashioned flexibility: International agreements between Member States of the European Union" in G. de Búrca and J. Scott (Eds.), *Constitutional Change in the EU – From Uniformity to Flexibility?* (OUP, 2000), 31–58.
29. The term "*inter se* agreements" stands for agreements concluded between less than all the member states of the EC/EU. The term is traditionally used in international law for agreements concluded between some, but not all, parties to an earlier agreement.

of the package that the other countries came to support, namely the creation of the Economic and Monetary Union and the rather less spectacular plan to transfer new competences in social policy. In both cases, a compromise was brokered at the very final stage of the negotiations, and was indeed crucial for reaching the final agreement on the text of the Treaty. In the case of EMU, an opt-out was agreed for the UK but also for Denmark; this opt-out was presented as temporary, although no time path was laid down for those countries to join the EMU. As regards social policy, the legal construction was seemingly the opposite, as the Maastricht Treaty comprised a Protocol by which all the Member States enabled 11 of them (that is, all members except the United Kingdom) to opt in to a separate Social Policy Agreement laying down new competences in the field of social policy. Both stratagems had one major element in common: they allowed for the creation of new norms of secondary EC law that would be adopted by the Council in a *reduced* composition but with the participation of the other institutions acting in their *normal* composition, and resulting in EC law that had all the qualities of "normal" EC law,[30] except that it did not apply in the dissenting Member States. The Maastricht Treaty thus set the legal model for the way in which closer cooperation is still practiced today: there is structural differentiation between Member States both at the time of law-making and at the time of its application.

3.3 *The creation and evolution of enhanced cooperation*

The institutional asymmetries created by the Maastricht Treaty in the fields of Economic and Monetary Union and social policy were presented at the time as, possibly temporary, exceptions and were not vindicated as a new structural way of addressing the problem of "unity in diversity" in European integration. Not long after the entry into force of the Maastricht reforms, however, the debate on the constitutional codification of a general regime of "flexibility" began rather abruptly with a series of speeches and papers presented by leading politicians in the summer of 1994. Right from the start, this debate was linked to the future enlargement of the EU, flexibility being seen in some quarters as a means of sidelining unknown and possibly unpredictable newcomers. However, the debate was also linked, more immediately and pressingly, to the fear of irreconcilable differences of views between the existing Member States. In his William and Mary Lecture given in Leiden in September 1994, John Major, the then British Prime Minister, welcomed the enlargement of the EU to the east and stated that the continuing growth in size and diversity of the Union should lead to greater *à la carte* flexibility, whereby overlapping groups of countries would be allowed to cooperate in specific fields of common interest *outside* the main EU institutional framework.[31] Other countries, particularly France and Germany, started canvassing, around the same time, the alternative idea of enabling a *stable core group* of countries to cooperate across a broad range of policy fields, either within or outside the

30. The characteristic of being "normal EC law" was far from obvious with regard to the measures adopted under the Social Policy Agreement. This was apparently an agreement of public international law, under which the EC institutions were "borrowed" to adopt binding measures, but the legal nature of this legislative output was not clearly defined in the Agreement. See discussion of this question, immediately after the adoption of the Maastricht Treaty, by D. Curtin, "The constitutional structure of the Union: A Europe of bits and pieces", 30 CML Rev. (1993), 17–69, at 52–61; and P. Watson, "Social policy after Maastricht", 30 CML Rev. (1993), 481–513, at 491–494. In the following years, the Court of Justice implicitly assumed (without any discussion) that this legislative output was perfectly "normal" EU law, with its normal characteristics (such as primacy and direct effect), and subject to the normal judicial review procedures. The only difference was that it did not apply to, and in, the United Kingdom.
31. J. Major, "Europe, a future that works" (William and Mary Lecture, Leiden Town Hall), *Agence Europe*, No 6312, 10 Sept. 1994.

institutional framework of the European Union. In particular the so-called Lamers-Schäuble paper presented by the CDU-CSU fraction of the *Bundestag*, while never put forward as official German government policy, became a key document in this political debate.[32] The paper promoted the idea of a core Europe (*Kerneuropa*) of pioneer countries; it seemed to envisage a group composed of the original six Member States (minus Italy, possibly), which caused immediate opposition in the other Member States.

As a result of those debates in 1994, most governments saw both options (*à la carte* cooperation outside the EU framework, and a structured core group either inside or outside) as threats to the cohesion of the European Union, and to the principle of uniform rights and duties of states which had characterized the European integration process so far. The consensus emerging from the 1996 Intergovernmental Conference, after long and extenuating negotiations, was that some general mechanism of institutional flexibility could be put in place, but it would be encapsulated within the existing EU framework and made subject to rather strict conditions.[33] Agreement was eventually reached, in the Treaty of Amsterdam, on a very cautious general mechanism allowing a group of willing states to undertake closer cooperation among themselves while using the institutional mechanisms of the European Union, but, crucially, only if the others would allow them to do so.[34] So, this was neither *à la carte* cooperation, nor the creation of a fixed vanguard group. Indeed, according to one observer, "much of the debate about flexibility during the IGC focused on a set of regulatory conditions which were designed to prevent the creation of a *directoire* or an *avant garde* group which would forge ahead towards deeper integration, leaving behind those which were either not willing or not able".[35]

In fact, the conditions for closer cooperation imposed by the Amsterdam Treaty were so rigid that, only one year after the Treaty's entry into force, and before the new regime had even been tested in practice, the Member State governments started a process of reviewing and, ultimately, redrafting the relevant rules during the next intergovernmental conference that took place in 2000. General agreement was eventually reached, in the final stages of the Nice Treaty negotiations, on facilitating recourse to closer cooperation.[36] The new Treaty texts allowed for what was now named "enhanced cooperation" to be launched by a qualified majority vote in the Council, except in common foreign and security policy. The substantive conditions for closer cooperation were also somewhat relaxed compared to the Amsterdam regime.

The potential political energy needed to exploit the enhanced cooperation mechanism was diverted, immediately after the signature of the Treaty of Nice, into the new constitutional reform process launched by the Convention on the Future of the Union. Within that context of across-the-board constitutional reform, flexibility did not emerge as a central issue. The few changes proposed in the Draft Treaty, which were then carried forward to the final text of the Constitutional Treaty and, much later, to the Lisbon Treaty, once again aimed at facilitating enhanced cooperation compared to the post-Nice situation. Enhanced cooperation initiatives can now be started on request of at least nine Member States and the authorization is given by

---

32. CDU/CSU Group in the *Bundestag, Reflections on European Policy*, 1 Sept. 1994.
33. For a political analysis of the negotiation of the Amsterdam flexibility regime, see A. Stubb, *Negotiating Flexibility in the European Union. Amsterdam, Nice and Beyond* (Palgrave Macmillan, 2002), Ch. 4.
34. For a legal analysis of the Amsterdam rules, see, among others, H. Kortenberg, "Closer cooperation in the Treaty of Amsterdam", 35 CML Rev. (1998), 833–854; and G. Gaja, "How flexible is flexibility under the Amsterdam Treaty?", 35 CML Rev. (1998), 855–870.
35. A. Stubb, op. cit. *supra* note 33, 49.
36. For a comment on the new rules introduced by the Treaty of Nice see J. Shaw, "Enhancing cooperation after nice: Will the Treaty do the trick?" in M. Andenas and J.A. Usher (Eds.), *The Treaty of Nice and Beyond. Enlargement and Constitutional Reform* (OUP, 2003), 207.

a qualified majority vote of the Council; they can cover all areas of non-exclusive EU competence.[37] The most striking element was, possibly, the emphasis on closer cooperation in the field of CFSP and particularly defence. Whereas the latter policy field was previously off-limits for closer cooperation initiatives, it was now turned into a privileged area for experimentation with a range of flexibility regimes, denoting perhaps a greater acceptance of the European Union as a policy-making venue for military matters.[38] The post-Lisbon developments have, however, not concretized this possibility, since no major pioneer groups in defence matters have been created as yet.

Another specific regime of enhanced cooperation created by the Lisbon Treaty, which was less prominently discussed in its preparatory phase but proved to be more important in practice, concerns the field of economic governance, where it was grafted upon the existing variable geometry between Eurozone and non-eurozone countries. The legal basis allowing for the adoption of euro-area specific legislation on economic governance (Art. 136(1) TFEU) was used for important parts of the "six-pack" and "two-pack" economic governance reforms; and more recently, unprecedented forms of variable geometry were experimented for banking supervision, where the new ECB-centred mechanism, while legally mandatory only for euro-area states, is opened up for "closer cooperation" with non-euro states who wish to join.[39]

What also happened, in the years since the Lisbon Treaty, is that the *general* enhanced cooperation regime was finally used, for the first time since its creation by the Treaty of Amsterdam. A first and rather uncontroversial application occurred for conflicts of law on divorce.[40] A second, much more controversial application related to the new EU patent system, where two countries (Italy and Spain) challenged the recourse to enhanced cooperation before the Court of Justice.[41] In its judgment, the Court confirmed that the function of enhanced cooperation is indeed to advance European cooperation even where (or rather, *especially* where) the unanimity requirement makes "normal" decision-making too difficult. Since then, a third piece of enhanced cooperation law was adopted, namely the twin Regulations on judicial cooperation in matters of matrimonial property and registered partnership property.[42] A fourth Council authorization for enhanced cooperation was given for the creation of a financial transaction tax, but the directive itself was not yet adopted.[43]

---

37. Art. 20 TEU. The conditions and procedures are spelled out in considerable detail in Arts. 326 to 334 TFEU.
38. See, for an analysis of the Lisbon changes in this policy area, M. Cremona, "Enhanced cooperation and the common foreign and security and defence policy", *EUI Working Papers* LAW 2009/21.
39. See G. Lo Schiavo, "From national banking supervision to a centralized model of prudential supervision in Europe", 21 MJ (2014), 110–140, at 135–137.
40. Council Reg. 1259/2010 of 20 Dec. 2010 implementing enhanced cooperation in the area of the law applicable to divorce and legal separation, O.J. 2010, L 343/10. The authorization had been given by Council Decision 2010/405 of 12 July 2010, O.J. 2010, L 189/12. See S. Peers, "Divorce European style: The first authorization of enhanced cooperation", 6 EuConst (2010), 339–358.
41. Joined Cases C-274/11 and C-295/11, *Spain and Italy v. Council*. The Council had authorized enhanced cooperation in this area by a Decision adopted (despite negative votes of Italy and Spain) on 10 Mar. 2011, O.J. 2011, L 76/53, on which see S. Peers, "The constitutional implications of the EU patent", 7 EuConst (2011), 229–266.
42. Council Reg. 2016/1103, O.J. 2016, L 183/1, and Council Reg. 2016/1104, O.J. 2016, L 183/30.
43. Council Decision 2013/52, O.J. 2013, L22/11.

3.4 *The multiplication of structured opt-out regimes and the revival of inter se agreements*

At the same time as creating the closer cooperation mechanism, the Amsterdam Treaty had also "repatriated" the Schengen regime within the legal order of the European Union,[44] but the price that had to be paid for this move – given the lack of unanimous support among all Member States – was a new opt-out Treaty regime for the United Kingdom and Ireland, and another one for Denmark.[45] A system of differentiation between EU Member States that had existed *outside* the EU legal framework was thus brought *inside* that framework, but without modifying the degree and content of the differentiation and creating, indeed, a number of frictions in the institutional functioning of the EU's immigration and border control policies.[46] This vast new opt-out area established by the Amsterdam Treaty joined the Maastricht-based opt-out regime for EMU, and it "replaced", so to speak, the social policy opt-out which was terminated at Amsterdam in view of the fact that the Labour government, that had recently come to power in the UK, had agreed to accept the additional social policy competence which the other 11 Member States had already agreed at Maastricht.

A few years later, the Convention on the Future of the Union was convened by the European Council. Despite its general ambition to simplify and consolidate the existing constitutional law of the European Union, the Convention did not seriously attempt to absorb the existing opt-out mechanisms, which were kept practically intact in the Constitutional Treaty first, and in the Lisbon Treaty later. In the end, the Lisbon Treaty even *added* a major new opt-out regime in the field of police cooperation and criminal justice where, in return for the introduction of the "Community method" in that policy area, the United Kingdom obtained an opt-out from future developments and even a right to unilaterally pull out from *existing* third pillar instruments by which the UK was bound.[47]

The fact that the Amsterdam Treaty had terminated the separate legal life of the Schengen Agreement and Convention, by transforming their content into EU law, and that it had also established a system of enhanced cooperation within the EU institutional framework, seemed

---

44. That regime was laid down in the Protocol integrating the Schengen *acquis* into the framework of the European Union, annexed by the Treaty of Amsterdam to the EC and EU Treaties. That Protocol was later modified by the Treaty of Lisbon and has now become Protocol No 19 annexed to the Treaties. The many tricky legal issues raised by this integration of the "Schengen *acquis*" into EU law proper were discussed by S. Peers, "*Caveat Emptor?* Integrating the Schengen *Acquis* into the European Union legal order", 2 CYLS (2000), 87–123, and by P.J. Kuijper, "Some legal problems associated with the communitarization of policy on visas, asylum and immigration under the Amsterdam Treaty and the incorporation of the Schengen acquis", 37 CML Rev. (2000), 345–366.
45. As Monar put it, in the title of his analysis of the new mechanism, the Amsterdam Treaty had achieved "reform at the price of fragmentation" (J. Monar, "Justice and home affairs in the Treaty of Amsterdam: Reform at the price of fragmentation", 23 EL Rev. (1998), 320–335).
46. The special position of those countries was laid down partly in special Protocols applying to them (known today, after the Lisbon Treaty, as Protocols No 21 and 22 annexed to the Treaties) and partly in special provisions within the Schengen Protocol (No 19). On the ultra-complex legal position of the opt-out countries in relation to the Schengen *acquis,* see J. Schutte, "UK v. EU: A continuous test match", 34 *Fordham International Law Journal* (2011), 1346–1376. For an example of the institutional frictions caused by the Schengen opt-out, see the judgment of the Court of Justice in Case C-482/08, *United Kingdom v. Council,* as to whether a contested measure came within the development of the Schengen *acquis* (in which the UK does not take part) or within the field of police cooperation (in which the UK fully participated at the time).
47. The latter right applied to *all* existing third pillar instruments taken together, hence the commonly used expression of a *block opt-out.* The United Kingdom exercised that right in 2014 although it "opted back in" (with the agreement of the EU institutions and the other Member States) into a selected number of instruments which the British governments considered useful, such as the European Arrest Warrant. See Commission Decision of 1 Dec. 2014, O.J. 2014, L 345/6.

to have relegated *inter se* agreements to the footnotes of the European integration story. It has even been argued that, where the conditions for use of enhanced cooperation are met (namely, a group of nine states, and a proposal coming within the scope of EU competences), and if authorization can be obtained for it, then the conclusion of an *inter se* agreement should not be held permissible. Yet, recent practice shows that the EU Member States consider that they have retained the capacity and the right to conclude international treaties among themselves, even when the subject matter of their agreement is closely connected to European Union matters. The conclusion of the "Fiscal Compact" between 25 Member States, and of the Treaty establishing the European Stability Mechanism between the 17 Euro-states, are recent and spectacular examples of the use of international law as a mechanism of differentiated integration.[48]

3.5 *The permanence of many-faced differentiation*

The existence of a controlled system for differentiation and variable geometry has now become a stable characteristic of EU law. As rightly noted by Rosas and Armati, it is "one of the defining features of the EU, setting it apart from established nation states. It is crucial to a description of what the Union legal order is".[49] It affects many different policies of the EU,[50] and each of the particular forms of the flexibility design seems likely to last, and to flourish. First, there is no reason to think that the major *opt-out area* of Economic and Monetary Union will disappear any time soon. In addition, now that *enhanced cooperation* has been experimented a few times, one can expect it to become a regularly used instrument in the EU's law-making toolbox, in particular in order to circumvent single country veto positions in policy matters where the unanimity rule continues to apply. Thirdly, recourse to *international agreements* between groups of Member States outside the EU legal framework has been confirmed to be a valid option, although the difficult conditions under which the ESM Treaty and Fiscal Compact came about and were ratified will not necessarily encourage the governments to make frequent use of this differentiation instrument. Finally, we might see a continued and increasing use of the omnipresent *micro-flexibility* that has been part of Community law for decades, namely the recourse to minimum harmonization, to soft law and to tailor-made derogations.[51]

The unity of the EU legal order is not formally affected by the many forms of flexibility that have spread profusely since Maastricht. There are rather firm criteria to determine whether a legal norm belongs to the EU legal order or not. Thus, measures of enhanced cooperation are part of EU law, although they are binding only upon, and within, the Member States that participated in their adoption. Similarly, legal measures from which some countries opt out are also part of the EU legal order, despite their limited geographical scope. Also, what is still sometimes

48. On the political and legal circumstances explaining this recourse to extra-EU international agreements, see B. de Witte, "Using international law in the Euro crisis – Causes and consequences", (2013) ARENA Working Paper No 4. For a detailed discussion of inter se agreements as somewhat atypical sources of EU law, see Ch. 6 "Sources of EU Law", section 4, of this book.
49. A. Rosas and L. Armati, *EU Constitutional Law: An Introduction* (OUP, 2010), 98. Similarly, for the author of a recent Italian textbook of EU law, variable geometry has become one of the three fundamental characteristics of the EU legal order: J. Ziller, *Diritto delle politiche e delle istituzioni dell'Unione europea* (Il Mulino, 2013), 283 et seq.
50. The range of policy areas affected by forms of differentiation is documented in a recent collection of essays: B. de Witte, A. Ott and E. Vos (Eds.), *Between Flexibility and Disintegration – The Trajectory of Differentiation in EU Law* (Edward Elgar Publishing, 2017).
51. For discussion of this kind of differentiation in secondary EU law, see e.g. G. de Búrca, "Differentiation within the "core"? The case of the internal market" in G. de Búrca and J. Scott, op. cit. *supra* note 28, 133–171; E. Vos and M. Weimer, "Differentiated integration or uniform regime? National derogations from EU internal market measures" in B. de Witte, A. Ott and E. Vos, op. cit. *supra* note 50, 304–335.

called "Schengen law" has become regular EU law after the incorporation of the Schengen regime in Amsterdam. On the contrary, international agreements concluded by a limited set of Member States (such as the ESM treaty and the Fiscal Compact) are not part of the EU legal order, and the Court of Justice cannot review the decisions adopted by organs set up under such an agreement.

Thus, if the formal criteria for deciding what belongs to the EU legal order still function well, the content of that EU legal order presents a very unusual shape. Its degree of fragmentation, in terms of participation of states in decision-making, and of applicability of legal norms across the EU territory, is rather unique and sets the European Union firmly apart from the federal constitutional systems to which it resembles in other respects. The Court's old ideal of EU legal rules being "fully applicable at the same time and with identical effects over the whole territory of the Community"[52] has become unattainable. This, in itself, may not be such a great loss; but the easy and almost insouciant recourse to flexibility also comes with lack of transparency, complicated accountability mechanisms, and neglect of intra-state solidarity, and those are serious challenges for the constitutional integrity of the European Union.[53]

The history of differentiation, flexibility and variable geometry in the European Union is closely linked with the presence of an 'awkward member" of the EU, namely the United Kingdom.[54] Indeed, it is largely because of the positions adopted, in the course of time, by successive UK governments that the EU legal order gradually moved away from the ideal of unity and started to accommodate various forms of non-participation of some States in the making of EU law norms. Given this history, one might expect that the announced withdrawal of the UK will diminish the attraction of variable geometry as a model for the future development of the EU. But this will not necessarily be the case, for two contrasting reasons. On one view, the distrust of the EU expressed by a majority of British voters reflects similar feelings in other parts of the European Union, and this implies that Union should evolve towards a less centralized and more flexible organization so as to reassure the growing mass of Eurosceptic citizens across Europe. On another view, the defection of the UK may act as an incentive for other countries to advance the integration project more vigorously, but given that it is unlikely that all 27 states would join that project and agree to a major revision of the EU treaties to strengthen the EU institutions, a division between a core Europe and the rest becomes an attractive option for the future. In this respect, we have seen a recent revival of the multi-speed and/or concentric circles models. In particular, it is suggested that euro area countries could form a core group, advancing into new areas of cooperation, whilst the remaining countries would stay behind in a less-integrated rest group. This model had been canvassed already at the time the UK was still part of the Union, and with a view essentially to circumvent the obstructive power of that country,[55] but it was revived after the Brexit referendum since some other non-euro area countries, such as Hungary and

52. Case 48/71, *Commission v. Italy*, para 8.
53. For a general constitutional perspective on the recent differentiation practice, see D. Thym, "Competing models for understanding differentiated integration" in B. de Witte, A. Ott and E. Vos, op. cit. *supra* note 50, 28–75.
54. S. George, *An Awkward Partner: Britain in the European Community*, 3rd ed. (OUP, 1998).
55. See, for a carefully developed model of this kind, J.C. Piris, "It is time for the Euro area to develop further closer cooperation among its members", *Jean Monnet Working Papers* 05/11, and also, J.C. Piris, *The Future of Europe: Towards a Two-Speed EU?* (CUP, 2012).

Poland, have in turn become "awkward partners"[56] which the other states may want to "neutralize" by means of a Euro-area based closer cooperation.[57]

4. Mechanisms of constitutional change: Treaty revisions, accession treaties, withdrawal agreements

Like any legal system, the EU legal system has mechanisms of change, allowing for the evolution of the law. In this section, we will examine the legal mechanisms allowing for changes of the EU's constitutional law, and in particular the *founding Treaties*. As will be explained in a later chapter,[58] EU primary law consists not only of the Treaties and the Charter of Rights (that is, written primary law) but also of the general principles of Union law (unwritten primary law). The latter source of law has been recognized by the Court of Justice through its case law; the discovery of new general principles, or modifications in the meaning of some existing principles, are decided by the Court of Justice through its case law.

Changes in the founding Treaties take essentially two forms, which have politically been termed as "deepening" and "widening": the adoption of *revisions of the Treaties* (which have historically been tools for the deepening of the integration process), and the adoption of *accession agreements* (which have been the tools for the expansion of membership of the EC and EU from 6 to 28 Member States). Since the Treaty of Lisbon, there is now also a third legal instrument for the modification of primary EU law, namely the *withdrawal agreement* leading to the reduction of EU membership; the first application of this new mechanism is likely to happen soon with the United Kingdom's Brexit. We will examine the legal characteristics of each of these three forms of constitutional change in turn.[59]

4.1 *Treaty revisions*

The European Communities were founded, back in the 1950s, by means of international treaties concluded between their Member States. Since then, the deepening of the European integration process took place essentially by means of new treaties between the Member States "revising" (or "amending", which has the same meaning) the existing treaties. The main revision treaties were the Single European Act, the Treaty of Maastricht, the Treaty of Amsterdam, the Treaty of Nice and most recently the Treaty of Lisbon. Revision treaties have led to major changes in the institutional set-up and policy scope of the European Communities and the European Union.

The procedure for revision of the Treaties is laid down in Article 48 TEU. It is an example of the common practice of international law whereby multilateral treaties contain rules on how to amend them later on. The international legal regime of treaty amendment is one of utmost flexibility; the Contracting Parties are free to arrange for the later amendment of "their" treaty in the way they wish.[60] Indeed, a large and increasing number of multilateral treaties contain such a special amendment procedure, which is generally aimed at facilitating adaptation to changing circumstances, often by allowing for the amendment of a treaty without the agreement of all

56. See A. Szczerbiak, *Poland within the European Union: The New Awkward Partner?* (Routledge, 2012).
57. See for example the proposal to create a new parliamentary assembly for the Eurozone: S. Hennette, T. Piketty, G. Sacriste and A. Vauchez, *Pour un traité de démocratisation de l'Europe* (Seuil, 2017).
58. See Ch. 6, "Sources of EU law", of this book.
59. For the description of the actual processes of revision and accession in the course of the EU's history, see Ch. 1, "Genesis and historical development of the European Communities and the EU", of this book.
60. See A. Aust, *Modern Treaty Law and Practice*, 3rd ed. (CUP, 2013), at 233–234: "It is wrong to think that the Vienna Convention is a rigid structure which places obstacles in the way of treaty modification: rather, it allows states to include in treaties such amendment provisions (good or bad) as they wish or, indeed, nothing at all".

the states.[61] Article 48 EU Treaty is an example of a specific amendment clause but, contrary to most others, it does *not* provide more flexibility than the default rule, contained in Article 39 of the Vienna Convention on the Law of Treaties whereby treaties can be modified at any time by agreement between their parties. Article 48 does require the agreement of *all* the parties (in this case, the Member States of the EU) for the valid adoption of the amendments and, *in addition*, it requires some involvement of the EU institutions in the preparatory phase and, in almost every case, the separate approval of the amendments by each state according to its own constitutional requirements.

The European Union's "rule of change" is thus particularly rigid, not because this rigidity is prescribed by general rules of international law, but because its Member States have committed themselves to such a rigid mechanism. The original rule that the European Community treaties could only be revised with the agreement of all the Member States, which made perfect sense when the EC counted only six states, was left untouched on each later occasion, despite the fact that membership grew from 6 to 28, which has rendered the unanimity requirement an ever more cumbersome obstacle in the way of treaty change.[62]

As to the *content* of the treaty amendments, the Member States have traditionally acted, to use a famous German expression, as the *Herren der Verträge* ("Masters of the Treaties"), bound by nothing else than the limits posed by their respective constitutions; they acted as "independent and sovereign states having freely decided [...] to exercise in common some of their competences".[63] The fact that the Member State governments acted as "masters" of the treaty text did not mean that they could also control what happened under the new treaty once it had entered into force. The dynamic evolution of EU law in between treaty revisions partly escaped their control, and they could correct unwanted evolutions only on the occasion of a further treaty revision and on the unlikely condition that they found a consensus to overrule, say, a particular interpretation of the treaty text adopted by the Court of Justice.

The close control exercised by the Member State governments on the revision process has been diluted somewhat in the course of time. Compared to the previous revision clauses, the new rules enacted by the Lisbon Treaty for future revisions of the European Treaties innovate in two limited respects: they prescribe the use of the "Convention method" for future revisions, and they provide for two so-called simplified revision procedures, in addition to the ordinary revision procedure.[64]

The most significant change, compared to the previous text of Article 48, is the formal integration of the Convention method as a normal feature of future revisions. Those future Conventions shall be "composed of representatives of the national Parliaments, of the Heads of State or Government of the Member States, of the European Parliament and of the Commission", that is, the same components as the 2002/3 Convention that prepared the ill-fated Constitutional Treaty. It is clearly confirmed that the Convention will not affect the formal power of treaty

61. For a survey of the wide variety of those special amendment procedures, see J. Brunnée, "Treaty amendments" in D.B. Hollis (Ed.), *The Oxford Guide to Treaties* (OUP, 2012), 347–366.
62. For an analysis of how, in particular, the requirement that each treaty revision should be separately ratified by each State has placed obstacles in the way of Treaty change on many occasions, see C. Closa, *The Politics of Ratification of EU Treaties* (Routledge, 2013).
63. This phrase was used by the member state governments in the introductory part of the Decision on Denmark, adopted at the Edinburgh summit of 12 Dec. 1992, but it referred back to their earlier adoption of the Treaty of Maastricht.
64. On the current, post-Lisbon, EU treaty amendment regime, see also S. Peers, "The future of EU Treaty amendments", 31 *Yearbook of European Law* (2012), 17–111; B. de Witte, "Treaty revision procedures after Lisbon" in A. Biondi, P. Eeckhout and S. Ripley (Eds.), *EU Law after Lisbon* (OUP, 2012), 107–127.

negotiation and conclusion that will be entrusted, as before, to an intergovernmental conference. The Convention's role is modestly defined as that of adopting "by consensus a recommendation to a conference of representatives of the governments of the Member States". However, the Convention's role had been described in equally modest terms by the Laeken Declaration of 2001, and this did not prevent the 2002/3 Convention from adopting a complete draft text of the treaty rather than a mere "recommendation". The new Article 48 thus creates a new ad-hoc organ of the European Union, the Convention, to be convened for a single purpose, namely the revision of the Constitution. A degree of direct parliamentary involvement in treaty reforms is thereby entrenched for the future.

However, it will be possible for the European Council to propose that revisions should be decided directly by an IGC without a prior Convention, if the nature of the revision does not justify the setting-up of a cumbersome Convention. The European Council can decide such a change of track towards the "old" (pre-Lisbon) Article 48 procedure by a simple majority but subject to the consent of the European Parliament, which seems an effective means of ensuring that the European Council will not abuse this possibility of acting without a Convention. The very first Treaty revision after the entry into force of the Treaty of Lisbon made use of this "abbreviated ordinary procedure": a Protocol was adopted and signed by the member states allowing for 18 extra members of the European Parliament to be elected or appointed, in addition to those who were elected in June 2009 according to the Nice Treaty rules on the composition of the Parliament.[65] As the Lisbon Treaty had not yet entered into force in June 2009, the new rules on the EP's composition contained in it could not yet be applied, and the Protocol was meant to remedy that problem.

The second innovation of the Lisbon treaty regarding future revisions is the creation of a distinction between one *ordinary* Treaty revision procedure and several *simplified* procedures. Paragraphs 2 to 5 of Article 48 TEU, as amended by the Lisbon Treaty, are entitled *Ordinary revision procedure.* The word "ordinary" indicates that the procedure described there is applicable to any amendment of the Treaties and their Protocols, unless the amendment comes within the scope of one of the simplified revision procedures described in paragraphs 6 and 7 or provided for in specific articles of the Treaties.

Simpler ways to amend particular bits of primary EU law had existed before. For example, the Statute of the Court of Justice, which was annexed to the EC Treaty in the form of a Protocol (and therefore with full Treaty status) could be amended, already long before Lisbon, by means of a unanimous Council decision[66] – with the exception of the most sensitive part, Title I of the Statute, which could only be modified through the ordinary revision procedure of Article 48 TEU. Such mini-revision clauses continue to exist under the Treaty of Lisbon. In the case of the Statute of the Court of Justice, Article 281 TFEU now states that amendments will be decided (again, with the exception of some parts of the Statute) by means of the co-decision procedure. This creates a unique situation in which the European Parliament will become the co-author of Treaty amendments.

The novelty brought by the Lisbon Treaty is that we now have two *standard* simplified procedures, applicable to a wider range of cases, and whose legal regime is now incorporated within

65. Protocol amending the Protocol on Transitional Provisions annexed to the Treaty on European Union, to the Treaty on the Functioning of the European Union and to the Treaty establishing the European Atomic Energy Community, signed on 23 June 2010, O.J. 2010, C 263/1. The mini-IGC that adopted this amendment was convened by a European Council decision of 17 June 2010 (O.J. 2010, L 160/5) which refers, in its recital 4, to the European Parliament's consent on the choice of not convening a Convention.

66. See, for example, the Council Decision of 20 Dec. 2007 amending the Protocol on the Statute of the Court of Justice, O.J. 2008, L 24.

Article 48 TEU, rather than being mentioned in the particular corner of the Treaty to which a simplified mechanism applies. Of those two procedures, only the one described in *paragraph* 7 introduces a genuine measure of flexibility in treaty amendment. It is commonly called the *passerelle* (which can be translated as "footbridge" or, perhaps more appropriately, as "gateway") because it allows the EU institutions to shift from one decision-making system to another within a given policy area. In all the areas and cases where the Treaties continue to provide that the Council must act by unanimity, a European Council decision (itself taken by unanimity and with the consent of the European Parliament) will be enough to remove the unanimity lock in a particular case or area, and allow the Council to act henceforth by qualified majority. Similarly, the European Council will be able to introduce the "ordinary legislative procedure" (that is: co-decision) in all the areas and cases in which the Treaties still provide for a different (normally, more intergovernmental) procedure. In other words, a further deepening of integration by making EU decision-making less intergovernmental is, to some extent, possible without the need for setting up an IGC and, above all, without the need for constitutional ratification of these changes by all the Member States separately. The scope of application of this simplified procedure is limited by Article 353 TFEU (to which, confusingly, Article 48 fails to cross-refer): decisions about the EU's own resources and about its multiannual financial framework, decisions based on the "flexibility" clause of Article 352 TFEU (ex-Article 308 TEC) and sanctions against states violating fundamental rights or the EU's other fundamental values, cannot be made subject to the co-decision procedure and/or qualified majority voting by means of the *passerelle.* In addition, one must note the existence, scattered throughout the Treaties, of the so-called *passerelles spéciales* which apply to specific policy areas instead of the general clause of Article 48(7).[67] When all is said and done, the scope of application of the general *passerelle* is actually quite limited.

Moreover, each national parliament will be able to stop any such simplified amendment based on Article 48(7) by expressing its opposition within a six-month period following the European Council decision (that decision will, obviously, not enter into force during this period). The two-phased approach to treaty revision is thus not entirely abandoned.[68] The difference with the ordinary revision mechanism is that national parliaments, instead of being required to give their positive approval to proposed amendments, will have the option of expressing their disagreement by vetoing a proposed amendment. Despite the preservation of a single-parliament veto power, this reform is significant because it puts the responsibility for formally approving an amendment on the shoulders of the Member State representatives in the European Council (and the members of the EP). The Treaties will, in this case, no longer be amended by another international agreement but by a unilateral decision of an organ of the European Union. This phenomenon, which is quite common in the law of international organizations, had remained exceptional in the EU legal order thus far.

The other simplified revision procedure, which is laid down in Article 48, *paragraph 6,* has a broader scope. It applies to amendments of "Part Three of the Treaty on the Functioning of

67. Those Treaty provisions are, again, not cross-referred to by Art. 48. See Art. 81(3) TFEU (measures concerning family law), Art. 153(2) (certain fields of employment and social security law), Art. 192(2) TFEU (certain environmental policy matters), Art. 312(2) TFEU (multiannual financial framework). The broadest of the *passerelles spéciales* is included in Art. 31(3) TEU and refers to the whole common foreign and security policy. See S. Peers, op. cit. *supra* note 64, at 48–59; and R. Böttner, "The Treaty amendment procedures and the relationship between Art. 31(3) TEU and the general bridging clause of Art. 48(7)", 12 EuConst (2016), 499–519.

68. The national parliaments do not possess a similar veto power under the *passerelles spéciales* mentioned in the previous footnote (except for the one about family law), so that those *passerelles* are actually easier to use.

the European Union relating to the internal policies and action of the Union", all together some 171 treaty articles – subject to one major exception: if the proposed amendment of an internal policy provision leads to an increase in the European Union's competences, then the ordinary revision procedure will have to be used instead. So, for example, if the member states wanted to modify the current Article 153(5) TFEU, and remove the sentence which currently excludes the use of the EU's social policy competences with regard to the right of association and the right to strike, they could not do so according to the simplified procedure, because that amendment would involve an expansion of EU competences. The scope of this simplified procedure, unlike the one in paragraph 7, seems rather fuzzy and may give rise to controversies, as was shown when this procedure was used for the first time, namely in 2011, for the addition of a new paragraph 3 to Article 136 TFEU so as to allow the creation of the European Stability Mechanism.[69] In the *Pringle* case, the applicants challenged the use of the simplified procedure in this case, arguing that the amendment led to an expansion of EU competences. The Court of Justice rejected that argument mainly for the reason that the new paragraph authorized the euro-area *Member States* (and not the EU itself) to create a stability mechanism.[70] Yet, interestingly, the Court of Justice found the challenge admissible, thereby recognizing that it has jurisdiction to control whether the EU institutions respect the dividing line between the ordinary and the simplified revision procedures.[71]

Upon a closer examination of the procedure prescribed by paragraph 6, it soon appears that it is not simple at all. As in the paragraph 7 procedure, discussed above, there is no need for a Convention or an IGC; the amendment is rather "adopted" directly by the European Council acting by unanimity of its members. But – and here is the crucial difference with paragraph 7 – that decision will be subject to "approval" by each member state under its own constitutional requirements. One may expect these constitutional requirements to involve, in most if not all member states, a consultation of the national parliament and probably also a positive vote of approval by the parliament. If one also considers the fact that adopting a unanimous European Council decision is not necessarily a simpler feat than reaching an agreement at an IGC (the actors being essentially the same ...),[72] one may well wonder whether the paragraph 6 procedure is really any simpler than the ordinary revision procedure without a Convention.[73] Moreover, unlike the latter, it does not require the consent of the European Parliament, thus making it also a distinctly less democratic revision procedure.

The innovations brought to the revision procedures by the Lisbon Treaty do not affect the fundamental legal and political rule of the game, namely that all Member States must give their unanimous consent to future amendments of the Treaties. The EU's rules of change thereby continue to be much more rigid than those applying to national constitutions, but also more rigid than those applying to the founding instruments of other, less integrated, international

---

69. European Council Decision of 25 Mar. 2011 amending Art. 136 of the Treaty on the Functioning of the European Union with regard to a stability mechanism for Member States whose currency is the euro, O.J. 2011, L 91/1. For the legal reasons explaining the perceived need for this Treaty amendment, see B. de Witte, "The European Treaty amendment for the creation of a financial stability mechanism", (2011) *SIEPS European Policy Analysis*.
70. Case C-370/12, *Pringle*.
71. Case C-370/12, *Pringle*, paras. 30–37.
72. The fact that an Intergovernmental Conference can act as rapidly as the European Council if there are no serious divergences between the EU countries is illustrated by the first post-Lisbon Treaty amendment, mentioned above, which took only six days between the convening of the IGC and the signature of the amendment (see *supra* note 65).
73. Indeed, the "simplified" amendment of Art. 136 TFEU, although adopted in Mar. 2011, entered into force only in May 2013, because of the slow national ratifications, in particular by the Czech Republic.

organizations.[74] They are a powerful confirmation of the fact that European Union law is anchored in international law and that the Union's legal fate remains in the hands of the states that have created it, or joined it later on.

4.2 *Accession to the European Union*

The enlargement of the European Communities and the European Union, throughout the decades of their existence, has taken the form of a series of accession treaties between the existing Member States and the candidates for accession. Those treaties have organized the way in which the new Member States could join the existing organization. Seven accession treaties were concluded so far.[75] They were invariably based on the simple principle that the newcomers must accept the existing legal order (the so-called *acquis*) with only little room for institutional accommodation and derogations.

The conditions and procedure for accession are laid down in Article 49 TEU. As regards the *conditions*, the first thing of note in the text of Article 49 is that applications for accession will only be examined if made by a European state (this condition did not stand in the way of the opening of accession negotiations with Turkey, since part of the territory of that country is situated in Europe). Another, more substantial, condition is that the applicant State must respect and promote the values referred to in Article 2 TEU (such as democracy, the rule of law and the protection of fundamental rights). This condition was first added to the text of Article 49 by the Amsterdam Treaty and was modified to its current version by the Lisbon Treaty. It reflects the existing practice adopted by the EU institutions which had been based on the so-called "Copenhagen criteria" (after the city where the European Council first formulated this set of enlargement conditions, in the year 1993). These criteria introduced a form of political conditionality that extends beyond the question of whether the applicant States is able to adapt to the existing rules of EU law. Political conditionality was applied to the enlargement operations that have taken place since then[76] and continues to be, today, an important hurdle for the possible accession of Turkey and of countries from the Western Balkans.

As regards the *procedure* to be followed for accession, Article 49 states that applications for accession must be addressed to the Council, which, after obtaining the opinion of the Commission and the assent of the European Parliament, "shall act unanimously". Following this, "the conditions of admission and the adjustments to the Treaties" form the subject of an agreement (i.e. an international treaty) concluded between the existing Member States and the State(s) applying for accession. This agreement has to be ratified by all the State Parties in accordance with their respective constitutional requirements.

The text of Article 49 thus gives the impression of a clear distinction between the early part of the process (ending with the Council's unanimous decision to open negotiations) and the later part (when negotiations are conducted by the Member States). Yet, that impression is misleading. In reality, the EU institutions and the Member States act in combination at both stages of the process.

---

74. For this comparison, see W. Lehmann, *Federal States and International Organizations: A Short Comparison of their Amending Rules with the European Union*, European Parliament studies, Dec. 2011, available at <www.europarl.europa.eu/studies>.
75. See Ch. 1, "Genesis and historical development of the European Communities and the EU", of this book, for the historical detail of the successive enlargements of the EU.
76. See K. Smith, "The evolution and application of EU membership conditionality" in M. Cremona (Ed.), *The Enlargement of the European Union* (OUP, 2003), 105–139.

At the first stage, the actual decision to accept a request for accession and open the negotiations is, in fact, taken by the European Council (not the Council) once every Member State has expressed its willingness to go ahead, and without awaiting (despite what the text of Art. 49 says) a formal opinion of Commission or Parliament.[77] However, that decision of the European Council is preceded by much previous activity, including monitoring reports by the Commission on the legal, economic and political situation in the applicant State, and the passage through intermediate stages such as that of "potential candidates", that is, States of whom the European Council declares that they are on their way to EU membership but not quite ready to engage in actual negotiations.[78]

Also the second stage of the process, namely the negotiations properly speaking, offers a mixed picture of Member State and EU activity. Whereas the Member States must sign the eventual final deal, the negotiation process itself is entrusted to the EU institutions. The Council decides on common positions of the Union on all matters that arise in the negotiations, and the Commission is invited to make the necessary proposals for those positions. Moreover, the Commission is sometimes entrusted with the discussion of a solution to specific problems with the applicant states and then reports back to the Council. As for the European Parliament, its consent power which Art. 49 seems to situate at the start of the process is now exercised at the final stage, namely when an agreement has been reached but before its signature. The existence of this veto right at the end of the road allows the EP to weigh in on the negotiation process. All in all, the accession mechanism includes both strong (inter-) state and EU components at every stage.[79]

The conditions of admission usually cover in particular the transitional measures that have to be taken in order that the gradual integration of the new Member State in the Union in the economic and legal fields may proceed as smoothly as possible. The "Eastern" accessions of 2004 and 2007 were particularly rich in safeguard clauses and transitional arrangements of various kinds, including with respect to the free movement of persons.[80] Accession treaties also, inevitably, make some limited adjustments to the Treaties and to the institutional functioning of the EU, for example with respect to the composition of the institutions, voting rules and budgetary contributions, and the EU's personnel and language regime.

When a State joins the European Union, EU law applies in principle to its entire territory and if the territory of the State is later modified, that modification automatically extends the territorial scope of application of EU law. Thus, on 3 October 1990, the day of German unification, the European Treaties became applicable to the new *Länder* from the former GDR.[81] Similarly, if part of a Member State were to secede, that part would no longer be within the

77. C. Hillion, "EU enlargement" in P. Craig and G. de Búrca (Eds.), *The Evolution of EU Law*, 2nd ed. (OUP, 2011), 187–216, 205–206.
78. C. Hillion op. cit. *supra* note 77, 207.
79. C. Hillion, "Accession and withdrawal in the law of the European Union" in A. Arnull and D. Chalmers (Eds.), *The Oxford Handbook of European Union Law* (OUP, 2015), 126–152, at 134.
80. For a general legal analysis of the Treaties of accession leading to the 2004 and 2007 enlargements, see respectively C. Hillion, "The European Union is dead. Long live the European Union [...] A commentary on the Treaty of accession 2003", 29 EL Rev. (2004), 583–612, and A. Lazowski, "And then they were twenty-seven [...] A legal appraisal of the sixth accession treaty", 44 CML Rev. (2007), 401–430. On the question of the derogations to free movement, see A. Ott, "Differentiation through accession law: Free movement rights in an enlarged European Union" in B. de Witte, A. Ott and E. Vos, op. cit. *supra* note 50, 146–178.
81. C. Tomuschat, "A united Germany within the European Community", 27 CML Rev. (1990), 415–436; C.W.A. Timmermans, "German unification and community law", 27 CML Rev. (1990), 437–449. As to the package of transitional measures agreed in certain fields, see O.J. 1990, L 353.

European Union.[82] As an exception to the general rule, Article 355 TFEU contains a series of specific provisions dealing with particular territories.[83]

4.3 *Withdrawal from the European Union*

The Lisbon Treaty innovated by inserting into the Treaties a procedure whereby Member States can withdraw from the EU. Before Lisbon, the text of the Treaties made no reference to withdrawal, and it was a somewhat controversial, though mainly theoretical, issue whether withdrawal was allowed, taking account of the general international law rules on the termination of treaties but also of the special nature of the European integration project.[84] That uncertainty was removed by the Lisbon Treaty, which provided for a procedure for withdrawal. When the United Kingdom started the withdrawal process, in the wake of the Brexit referendum of June 2016, it was clear to all parties involved that the procedure of Article 50 TEU would be followed.

The main element of the procedure is that, upon the notification of a wish to withdraw, the exiting State and the European Union start negotiations for a withdrawal agreement to settle the legal and financial conditions for the termination of that country's membership. On the EU side, that agreement is concluded by the Council acting by qualified majority, which means that single EU States do not have a veto right concerning the terms of withdrawal. Importantly, the absence of such an agreement is not an impediment to withdrawal. Indeed, Article 50(3) TEU provides that "the Treaties shall cease to apply" either after the entry into force of the withdrawal agreement or, in the absence of an agreement, two years after the date of notification. This "guillotine clause" may serve to protect the right of the withdrawing State to effectively exit even against the resistance of the rest of the EU, but it may also put the withdrawing State under severe pressure to accept the terms of withdrawal preferred by the EU, as exiting without an agreement may cause great difficulties. Some elements of the process are not clearly spelled out by the text of Article 50, though. For example, it is not specified whether the exiting State may decide to withdraw its notification at a later stage of the negotiations and decide to remain within the EU after all. Also, Article 50(2) mentions that, when agreeing the terms of withdrawal, the parties shall be "taking account of the framework for [its] future relationship with the Union". This rather vague clause seems to imply that the agreement(s) governing that future relationship are separate legal instruments, but it is left open whether these should enter into force at the same time as the withdrawal agreement or only at a later stage, once the country has effectively left the Union. In the latter case, it would seem necessary for the withdrawal agreement to provide for a transitional period, during which parts of EU law continue to apply to the exiting State, so as not to interrupt brutally all existing relations between that State and the rest of the EU. It is also not spelled out whether these agreement(s) on future relations shall be concluded by the European Union, or by its (remaining) Member States, or by both. This is a matter that, presumably, shall be decided in accordance with the applicable rules on the EU's *external* relations (as, by this stage, the existing State will have left the Union). These and other elements of legal uncertainty have come to the fore in the content of the ongoing Brexit negotiations.[85]

---

82. On this question, which has recently been discussed with respect to a possible secession of Scotland from the UK and of Catalonia from Spain, see C. Closa, "Secession from a Member State and EU membership: The view from the Union", 12 EuConst (2016), 240–264.
83. On this, see Ch. 33, "Cohesion policy and geographic differentiation", of this book.
84. See, on that discussion, C. Hillion op. cit. *supra* note 79, 146–148.
85. In addition to the abundant Brexit commentary in the blogosphere, the legal and political issues of the UK's withdrawal are discussed by K. Armstrong, *Brexit Time – Leaving the EU – Why, How and When?* (CUP, 2017). See also A. Cuyvers, "Artikel 50 VEU en Brexit: de juridische contouren voor een politiek drama", (2016) *Nederlands tijdschrift voor Europees recht*, 221–229.

Further reading

Cremona, M., "The two (or three) treaty solution: The new treaty structure of the EU" in A. Biondi, P. Eeckhout and S. Ripley (Eds.), *EU Law after Lisbon* (OUP, 2012), 40–61.

Curtin, D. and I. Dekker, "The European Union from Maastricht to Lisbon: Institutional and legal unity from the shadows" in P. Craig and G. de Búrca (Eds.), *The Evolution of EU Law*, 2nd ed. (OUP, 2011), 155–185.

Hillion, C., "EU enlargement" in P. Craig and G. de Búrca (Eds.), *The Evolution of EU Law,* 2nd ed. (OUP, 2011), 187–216.

Hillion, C., "Accession and withdrawal in the law of the European Union" in A. Arnull and D. Chalmers (Eds.), *The Oxford Handbook of European Union Law* (OUP, 2015), 126–152.

Lazowski, A., "Withdrawal from the European Union and alternatives to membership", 37 EL Rev. (2012), 523–540.

Peers, S., "The future of EU Treaty amendments", 31 *Yearbook of European Law* (2012), 17–111.

De Witte, B., "Treaty revision procedures after Lisbon" in A. Biondi, P. Eeckhout and S. Ripley (Eds.), *EU Law after Lisbon* (OUP, 2012), 107–127.

De Witte, B., A. Ott and E. Vos (Eds.), *Between Flexibility and Disintegration – The Trajectory of Differentiation in EU Law* (Edward Elgar Publishing, 2017).

Further reading

[illegible]

[illegible]

[illegible]

[illegible]

[illegible]

CHAPTER 3
SYSTEM OF COMPETENCES

*Jürgen Bast and Kassandra Wetz**

1. Introduction

The discourse on the competences of the European Union is, in its essence, about the role of the Member States in the European constitutional settlement. At first sight, this seems only natural, as the relationship between EU and Member State powers follows the inexorable logic of communicating vessels. This view may be a little too simplistic, though. The assumed mutual exclusivity of competences is conceptually weak, since the mere existence of a Union competence neither does away with a Member State competence nor necessarily blocks its exercise.

Yet there is some truth to the imagery of communicating vessels. A competence vests its holder with the legal capacity to act. It determines the scope of the *potential* exercise of power, a "space of possibilities". In EU law, this space is usually described in broad and general language, open-ended in terms of policy. Joseph Weiler's narrative of the Transformation of Europe[1] largely holds true for the European Union of today. His core observation was that, from a Member State's perspective, the shift in the 1980s from an intergovernmental, consensus-bound mode of decision-making to a supranational, majoritarian mode has turned the EU's scope of powers into a source of incalculable risk. The shift implies a loss of political control over the production of the law ("voice") that, once adopted, unleashes overwhelming, supranational legal force, leaving little room for selective non-compliance ("exit").

This uneasy combination of decisional and legal supranationalism explains why the rules governing the EU system of competences are highly significant for the Members States. After the loss of an exclusive "voice" in the EU's decision-making procedures and the legal possibility of "exit" by way of non-compliance when implementing EU law, these rules are a rare guarantee that the law-making by EU institutions will not lead to a complete loss of Member States' autonomy. In contrast to the EU, in most international organizations States have ensured for themselves sufficient options of "voice", "exit", or both. This is why hardly any meaningful legal discourse on the competence of international organizations exists, and why States are so lenient in accepting informal changes to the scope and contents of their mandates.[2] In the EU, competence has been an issue since the transformation of Europe materialized by the Single European Act, and it came into full swing after the Treaty of Maastricht. It has remained on the agenda ever since.

---

* Law Faculty, Justus-Liebig University of Giessen. The chapter partly builds on works co-authored by Armin von Bogdandy. The authors would like to thank Jasmin Schnitzer for her support concerning literature research.

1. J.H.H. Weiler, "The Transformation of Europe", 100 Yale Law Journal (1991), 2403.
2. Cf. J. Klabbers, "The transformation of international organizations law", 26 EJIL (2015), 9.

The following chapter will discuss the relevant rules of the system of competences in more detail. It starts with an overview of the various phases legal scholarship on competences has gone through (section 2). The ensuing sections are doctrinal, providing a legal analysis of the post-Lisbon system of competences and the respective roles of national parliaments, courts, and individuals in that system (section 3 to 7). The final part provides a brief normative evaluation of the imbalances in the current system (section 8).

A preliminary remark on the terminology seems appropriate. The terms "competences" and "powers" are used interchangeably in this chapter. As far as the EU is concerned, this refers to the legal capacity of Union institutions to adopt legal acts within the framework of the EU Treaties. It does not include everything deriving from EU law that affects what happens in the Member States, such as directly applicable Treaty provisions (like in the UK Review of 2012).[3] Unless indicated otherwise, competence here means legislative competence in the substantive sense of enacting abstract and general rules (not necessarily in the formal sense of Art. 289 TFEU), and as far as external competences are concerned, treaty-making powers. This chapter leaves aside the powers of administrative bodies to implement the relevant rules, as well as judicial powers.[4] A crucial element determining the powers of the EU courts is the concept of "scope (of application) of EU law", which is different from the "scope of EU competences" discussed here, though not totally unrelated.[5]

2. The evolution of the legal discourse on the EU's competence

Three periods can be distinguished in the scholarly writings on issues of competence, demarcated by the Maastricht Treaty of 1992 and the draft Constitutional Treaty of 2003.

2.1 *1970s until the Maastricht Treaty*

In the early 1970s, the notion of "Community law" as a distinct, supranational legal order gained ground in legal scholarship. Pioneering studies by *Jean-Victor Luis* (1969),[6] *Manfred Zuleeg* (1969),[7] *Pierre Pescatore* (1972),[8] *Hans-Peter Ipsen* (1972)[9] and *R.H. Lauwaars* (1973)[10] highlighted the autonomy of the Community legal order and supported the functional need of its claim to primacy. The emergence of a multinational legislature fascinated those authors. Remarkably little research was devoted to the limits of powers of the early Communities. Exceptional studies, such as the ones by *Manfred Zuleeg* (1971)[11] and *Vlad Constantinesco* (1974),[12] tended to present the Communities' competence vis-à-vis its Member States as a well-defined system that pertains to a limited range of matters.

---

3. Foreign & Commonwealth Office of the United Kingdom (Ed.), Review of the Balance of Competences between the United Kingdom and the European Union (2012), <www.gov.uk/government/uploads/system/uploads/attachment_data/file/35431/eu-balance-of-competences-review.pdf>.
4. See Ch. 8, "The EU administration" and Ch. 10, "The Court of Justice of the EU", of this book.
5. See S. Prechal, H. de Vries and S. van Eijken, "The principle of attributed powers and the 'scope of EU law'" in L.F.M. Besselink, F. Pennings and S. Prechal (Eds.), *The Eclipse of the Legality Principle in the European Union* (Wolters Kluwer, 2011), 213.
6. J.-V. Louis, *Les règlements de la Communauté économique européenne* (Bruxelles Presses Universitaires, 1969).
7. M. Zuleeg, *Das Recht der Europäischen Gemeinschaften im innerstaatlichen Bereich* (Carl Heymanns, 1969).
8. P. Pescatore, *Le droit de l'intégration* (Bruylant, 1972, repr. 2005).
9. H.P. Ipsen, *Europäisches Gemeinschaftsrecht* (Mohr Siebeck, 1972).
10. R.H. Lauwaars, *Lawfulness and Legal Force of Community Decisions* (Sijthoff, 1973).
11. M. Zuleeg, "Die Kompetenzen der Europäischen Gemeinschaften gegenüber den Mitgliedstaaten", 20 *Jahrbuch des öffentlichen Rechts n.F.* (1971), 1.
12. V. Constantinesco, *Compétences et pouvoirs dans les Communautés européenne* (Libr. Générale de Droit et de Jurisprudence, 1974).

The collection on "Thirty Years of Community Law", edited by the Commission (1983) with a view to consolidating the established knowledge on the new body of law, still did not include a chapter on competence.[13] Behind the scenes, however, the building blocks of a more critical view gradually emerged in the course of the 1970s and 1980s. One of the main issues of concern was the Court's jurisprudence on implied powers to conclude external agreements, following the ERTA judgment of 1971.[14] The central question in this case was whether the EC had the competence to conclude an international agreement in the area of transport policy. The Court held that although the Treaties did not explicitly confer the competence to conclude international agreements in this area on the EC, the competence followed implicitly from the exercise of the internal competence. Another issue at the time was the insistence on the exclusive nature of the Common Commercial Policy and Common Fisheries Policy, even in the face of the Community institutions' apparent difficulty in living up to these mandates.[15] Moreover, the expansive activity of the Community in matters such as private law, education, and cultural policy triggered critical comments from proponents of the respective field. In that period, the claim of transgressions of the limits of Community competence, well-known as it is today, emerged as an argument.[16] Particular attention was paid to the expansive use of Article 235 EEC Treaty (now Art. 352 TFEU) after the Paris summit of 1972.[17] According to this provision, if action by the EC is necessary to attain the objectives set out in the EEC Treaty but the Treaty has not provided sufficient competences, the Council may adopt the appropriate measures. The prevailing view at the time was that such a provision was justified to fill in the gaps not thought of when the Treaty was drafted, and to foster European integration.[18] The implied dynamics of the system of competences was not yet seen as a major issue.[19]

2.2 *Mid-1990s until the Convention of 2002/2003*

The heyday of scholarly debate on the system of competences started in the mid-1990s and lasted for almost a decade. Its catalyst was the Maastricht Treaty, which by inserting Article 3b EEC Treaty (now Art. 5 TEU) codified the principle of conferral and introduced the principle of subsidiarity. With regard to the latter, virtually no prior debate in academic circles had taken place,[20] and very little with regard to the former.[21] The Article and the ensuing discussion re-

---

13. Commission of the European Communities (Ed.), *Thirty years of Community law* (EC Commission, 1983). Note that even in the previous edition of this volume, the system of competences did not form a separate chapter. It figured among the "The basic principles" in Ch. III.
14. Case 22/70, *Commission v. Council (ERTA)*.
15. For a summary, see R. Schütze, "Parallel external powers in the European Community: From 'cubist' perspectives towards 'naturalist' constitutional principles?", 23 YBEL (2004), 225.
16. Cf. J.H. Kaiser, "Grenzen der EG-Zuständigkeiten", (1980) Europarecht, 97.
17. See Communiqué of the Paris Summit of the Heads of States or Government, 19–21 Oct. 1972, Bulletin EC 10-1972, 15, 23; also available at <aei.pitt.edu/1919/02/paris_1972_communique.pdf>.
18. See e.g., the special issue of the journal Europarecht (1976), with contributions *inter alia* by U. Everling, C. Tomuschat, and R.H. Lauwaars; see further D.-W. Dorn, "Art. 235 EWGV: Prinzipien der Auslegung" (Engel, 1986); for a critical voice, see P. Lachmann, "Some Danish Reflections on the Use of Art. 235 of the Rome Treaty", 18 CML Rev. (1981), 447.
19. For an account of the expansive development in that periods, see J.H.H. Weiler, op. cit. *supra* note 1, at 2442–2453.
20. See L.A. Geelhoed, "Het subsidiariteitsbeginsel: een communautair principe?" (1991) S.E.W., 422.
21. For early studies, see J.-L. Dewost, "Décisions des institutions en vue du développement des compétences et des instruments juridiques" in R. Bieber and G. Ress (Eds.), *Die Dynamik des Gemeinschaftsrechts* (Nomos, 1987), 321; H.-P. Kraußer, *Das Prinzip begrenzter Ermächtigung im Gemeinschaftsrecht als Strukturprinzip des EWG-Vertrages* (Duncker & Humblot, 1991).

flected the political unease in certain quarters over the loss of autonomy that was set in motion by the Single European Act and accelerated by the Maastricht Treaty.[22] For the first time, the role of the Member States in the constitutional settlement of European integration required attention. A seminal work that gave a kick-start to the post-Maastricht discussion was the study by *Alan Dashwood* (1996).[23]

It is fair to say that the post-Maastricht debate was dominated by German authors. The hostile language in the Federal Constitutional Court's Maastricht decision (internationally known as the *Brunner* case) had polarized the scholarly community.[24] In its judgment, which concerned the compliance of the Maastricht Treaty with the German Basic law, the Federal Constitutional Court asserted its power to review whether acts adopted by EU institutions remained within the limits of EU competence (whether they were not so-called *ultra vires* acts). This doctrine undermined the exclusive competence of the Court of Justice to review the compliance of EU legal acts with Treaty provisions. In hindsight, it is remarkable to see that both critics and defenders of the EU/EC system of competences by and large relied on a federal paradigm. The former claimed that a proper federal order of competences, as "ideally" represented in the German Basic Law, was lacking. They called for a competence catalogue and enforceable restraints on the EC/EU's "functional" competences.[25] The latter argued that precisely such a system had emerged in the jurisprudence of the Court of Justice, the transparency of which would benefit from codification or restatement.[26]

Intense debate unfolded – also on the subsidiarity principle, its origins and legal elements and the ensuing deference of the Court in enforcing it, representative of which are the monographic studies by *Christian Calliess* (1999)[27] and *Antonio Estella* (2002).[28]

2.3 *Post-Constitutional Treaty until present*

Much of our discipline's current insight into the EU system of competences dates back to the period described above. It has left visible traces in the draft Constitutional Treaty, which the European Convention adopted in 2003 responding to the call of the IGC Declaration of 2001 to provide for "a more precise delimitation of powers between the European Union and the Member States".[29]

22. See D.Z. Cass, "The word that saves Maastricht? The principle of subsidiarity and the divisions of powers within the European Community", 29 CML Rev. (1992), 1107.
23. A. Dashwood, "The limits of European Community powers", 21 EL Rev. (1996), 113; for corresponding contributions from other jurisdictions, see H.D. Jarass, "Die Kompetenzverteilung zwischen der Europäischen Gemeinschaft und den Mitgliedstaaten", 121 *Archiv des öffentlichen Rechts* (1996), 173; J. Martín y Pérez de Nanclares, *El sistema de competencias de la Comunidad Europea* (McGraw-Hill, 1997).
24. *Entscheidungen des Bundesverfassungsgerichts* Vol. 89, 155 (Maastricht).
25. E. Steindorff, *Grenzen der EG-Kompetenzen* (Verlag Recht und Wirtschaft, 1990); P. Kirchhof, "Gewaltenbalance zwischen staatlichen und europäischen Organen", (1998) *Juristenzeitung*, 965; U. Di Fabio, "Some remarks on the allocation of competences between the European Union and its Member States", 39 CML Rev. (2002), 1289.
26. I. Pernice, "Kompetenzabgrenzung im Europäischen Verfassungsverbund", (2000) *Juristenzeitung*, 866; F.C. Mayer, "Die drei Dimensionen der europäischen Kompetenzdebatte", 61 *Zeitschrift für ausländisches öffentliches Recht und Völkerrecht* (2001), 577; A. von Bogdandy and J. Bast, "The European Union's vertical order of competences", 39 CML Rev. (2002), 227.
27. C. Calliess, *Subsidiaritäts- und Solidaritätsprinzip in der Europäischen Union*, 2nd ed. (Nomos, 1999).
28. A. Estella, *The EU Principle of Subsidiarity and its Critique* (OUP, 2002).
29. Declaration (No. 23) on the future of Europe, O.J. 2001, C 80, 85. Cf. G. de Búrca and B. de Witte, "The delimitation of powers between the EU and its Member States" in A. Arnull and D. Wincott (Eds.), *Accountability and Legitimacy in the European Union after Nice* (OUP, 2002), 201; V. Michel, "2004: Le défi de la répartition des compétences", (2003) CDE, 17.

The Convention's draft, notably its typology of competences, marks the second watershed in the scholarly debate, and for a while, it attracted almost exclusive attention.[30] In studies that look at the broader picture, insights gained from comparative federalism are prominent,[31] most notably in the works of Robert Schütze. In a series of articles on particular types of competence, and in his ensuing monograph (2009),[32] Schütze has demonstrated that in the EU system exclusive legislative competence is the exception rather than the rule, hence the notion of "cooperative federalism".

A second major theme is provided by the mechanisms of competence control. The new role of national parliaments in monitoring competence compliance has triggered rich debate on the "early warning system" and the role of national parliaments in the EU's constitutional setting at large. Suffice it to mention the studies of Steven Weatherill on the "competence creep" deeply embodied in Brussel's institutional culture.[33]

In recent years, a further topic has emerged that approaches the Union's competence from a different angle: from below, as it were. It concerns the justification of a "self-defence" of national constitutional courts against competence encroachments by the Union and its reluctant Court. The ultra vires doctrine of the German Federal Constitutional Court is particularly visible in this regard, e.g. in the OMT case concerning the powers of the ECB.[34]

3. The principle of conferral

The principle of conferral is the main principle guiding the EU system of competences. It is laid down in the second paragraph of Article 5 TEU. The legal contents of this principle are best explained by distinguishing its various functions (1.). On that basis, the scope of the principle can be determined (2.), as well as the framework for judicial control of compliance with the principle (3.).

3.1 *Functions of the principle of conferral*

The principle of conferral serves four main functions: a constitutive, a constraining, a stabilizing, and a structuring function.

(i) The constitutive function of the principle implies that the Union is entrusted with its own independent competences. The keyword phrase that most closely approximates this function is "attribution of competences".

In the European Union, as in many federal States, the authorities of the upper ("Union") level of the composite polity do not have original powers. The original, autonomous powers

30. See e.g. S. Weatherill, "Competence" in B. de Witte (Ed.), *Ten Reflections on the Constitutional Treaty for Europe* (EUI, 2003) 45; P. Craig, "Competence: Clarity, containment and consideration", 29 EL Rev. (2004), 323; M. Nettesheim, "Die Kompetenzordnung im Vertrag über eine Verfassung für Europa", (2003) *Europarecht*, 511; F.C. Mayer, "Competences – Reloaded?", 3 *International Journal of Constitutional Law* (2005), 493; R. Mastroianni, "Le competenze dell'Unione" in G. Morbidelli and F. Donati (Eds.), *Una costituzione per l'Unione europea* (Torino, 2006) 131.

31. See e.g., T. von Danwitz, "Vertikale Kompetenzkontrolle in föderalen Systemen", 131 *Archiv des öffentlichen Rechts* (2006), 510; S. Oeter, "Federalism and democracy" in A. von Bogdandy and J. Bast (Eds.), *Principles of European Constitutional Law*, 2nd ed. (Hart Publishing, 2010), 55.

32. See, *inter alia*, R. Schütze, "Supremacy without pre-emption?", 43 CML Rev. (2006), 1023; R. Schütze, "Cooperative federalism constitutionalised: The emergence of complementary competences in the EC legal order", 31 EL Rev. (2006), 167; R. Schütze, *From Dual to Cooperative Federalism* (OUP, 2009).

33. S. Weatherill, "Competence creep and competence control", 23 YBEL (2004), 1; S. Weatherill, "Better competence monitoring", 30 EL Rev. (2005), 23.

34. See e.g., the special issue of the German Law Journal (Vol. 15 No. 2, (2014)) on the OMT Decision of the German Federal Constitutional Court; cf. the ECJ's response: Case C-62/14, *Gauweiler*.

rest with the component states that have – historically or at least conceptually, as the case may be – joined or "pooled" their sovereign forces. Legally and conceptually, it is important to distinguish between the genesis of a competence and its validity. As regards the genesis, a Union competence is dependent on the act of conferral by the collective of the Member States, by way of making or amending the founding treaties of the EU. In the language of the Court of Justice, the relevant provisions in the EU Treaties that establish a Union competence are called "a legal basis". Once a competence is conferred, however, its validity is independent of the will of the Member States, individually or collectively. The Union exercises conferred competences on its own behalf as a distinct legal personality both under international and domestic law. Theoretical conceptions such as the "pooling of sovereignty" or "shared exercise" of Member State competences tend to misconceive this point.[35] Likewise, the concept of "delegation" used in the principle-agent model of political science is legally speaking not precise, as it implies that the agent (delegatee) exercises powers of the principal(s).

The constitutive function of the principle of conferral is also helpful for understanding the fate of Member State's competence after the act of conferral. The wording of Article 5(2) TEU could be understood to mean that Member States lose the relevant competence when it is conferred on the Union, like a commodity that cannot be in two places at the same time. This is actually not the case. Conferring a competence means creating it, rather than transferring it in a literal sense. Consequentially, a Member State competence remains in force but, depending on the type of Union competence involved, the State may be pre-empted from exercising it.[36]

The constitutive function is reserved for Union competences. The EU Treaties entrust plenty of tasks to the Member States, but they do not attribute Member State competences, for the latter are original (see Art. 4(1) and 5(2)(2) TEU). The system of competences established in the Treaties is not "bipolar" in nature.[37] Accordingly, provisions such as Article 136(3) TFEU, which states that Member States whose currency is the euro may establish a stability mechanism, cannot be construed as creating a competence of the Member States that did not exist previously. In terms of competences, they are of a declaratory nature. They clarify the scope of already existing competences in view of the relevant Union competences.[38] Likewise, provisions such as Article 165(1) TFEU do not establish competences attributed to the Member States. Such clauses are best perceived as negative elements that limit a competence conferred on the Union; they operate in conjunction with the relevant legal basis.[39] Hence, they are not applicable cross-sectorally to limit the powers of the Union when acting on a different legal basis. The same holds true for prohibitions on harmonization laid down in legal bases such as Articles 167(5) or 168(5) TFEU relating to culture and public health, respectively.[40]

(ii) The principle of conferral also serves a constraining function; it limits the powers of the Union. The keyword phrase is "delimitation of competences". The EU institutions have to rely on a specific legal basis and respect the boundaries laid down therein. They are the only source from which the legitimacy of the EU to exercise public authority can flow. Any increase in Union competence has to follow the amendment procedures provided for in the Treaties,

35. Cf. Art. 88-1 of the French Constitution of 1958: "l'Union européenne constituée d'États qui ont choisi librement d'exercer en commun certaines de leurs compétences".
36. For details, see *infra* section 4.
37. A. von Bogdandy and J. Bast, "The federal order of competences" in A. von Bogdandy and J. Bast (Eds.), *Principles of European Constitutional Law*, 2nd ed. (Hart Publishing, 2010), 275, at 286.
38. Case C-370/12, *Pringle*, paras. 72 and 184.
39. See e.g., Case C-76/05, *Schwarz*, para 70; Case C-73/08, *Bressol*, para 28.
40. Case C-376/98, *Germany v. Parliament and Council (Tobacco Advertising)*, paras. 78 and 88; Case C-434/02, *André*, para 32; Case C-210/03, *Swedish Match*, para 76.

usually involving both the Member States (which have the final say) and the EU institutions. The Union does not possess *Kompetenz-Kompetenz,* i.e., the power to define the scope of its own powers, according to a theoretical conception of German constitutional jurisprudence.[41]

The principle of conferral does not imply a presumption in favour of a competence being attributed to the Member States, nor should a competence attributed to the Union necessarily be construed narrowly. Such rules of interpretation are not part of EU law.[42]

(iii) A third function of the principle of conferral may be called the stabilizing function. Its main purpose is securing the federal balance of powers. The keyword phrase is "distribution of competences". The contents of the order of competences is subject to change only by way of the regular Treaty amendment procedures. Failing activation of such an amendment procedure, political actors from the Member States and at the Union level are bound to act within the framework of the competences as it stands at a given point in time. Informal amendments or unilateral modifications are strictly precluded.[43] The system of competences creates relatively stable political spaces in which democratic political processes can unfold.

This is not to say that any changes to the system of competences brought about by means of new interpretation are unlawful; the meaning of the law, including the law of competences, changes over time. A certain degree of flexibility is inevitably needed to fill in unforeseen gaps or to react to changed circumstances.[44] But such constitutional change by way of interpretation does not alter the wording of the constitutional treaties and is only possible within the established doctrinal and institutional framework.

(iv) The principle of conferral structures the law of the Union both vertically and horizontally. The keyword phrase is "order according to competences". In vertical terms, the EU system of competences builds on the premise of a hierarchy of law between the Treaties and the general principles of EU law ("primary law"), one the one hand, and acts adopted by the EU institutions ("secondary law"), on the other.[45] This relationship is functionally equivalent to the supremacy of national constitutions in the Member States. In horizontal terms, all acts of secondary law are derived from a legal basis that lays down specific procedural and substantive requirements for its enactment. Most legal bases are related to specific policies, providing the Union with the necessary powers to fulfil the objectives stated in the relevant section of the Treaties. In some instances, the objectives are a defining element of the competence (e.g., Art. 192 TFEU). These sectoral objectives and standards remain significant for construing the provisions of an act and its relationship with other acts in the relevant field, even after its adoption.[46]

Accordingly, the choice of legal basis is of "constitutional significance".[47] The legal basis determines the competent institution, the procedure to be followed, and the substantive standards the act has to meet. It establishes the type of competence (exclusive or shared; legislative or non-legislative) and the instruments at the disposal of the acting institutions (regulations, directives,

41. S. Oeter, op. cit. *supra* note 31, at 68.
42. S. Kadelbach, "Art. 5 TEU" in H. von der Groben, J. Schwarze and A. Hatje (Eds.), *Europäisches Unionsrecht* (Nomos, 2015), paras. 17–18.
43. See e.g., Case 43/75, *Defrenne,* para 56/58; Case 59/75, *Manghera,* para 21; Case 68/86, *United Kingdom v. Council,* para 24; Case C-27/04, *Commission v. Council,* para 81.
44. M. Nettesheim, "Kompetenzen" in A. von Bogdandy and J. Bast (Eds.), *Europäisches Verfassungsrecht,* 2nd ed. (Springer, 2009), 389, at 400–401.
45. See Art. 263(2) TFEU; see Opinion 2/15, *FTA EU-Singapore,* para 235; Case C-25/02, *Rinke,* paras. 25–26; Case 26/78, *Viola,* para 9/14.
46. See e.g., Case C-17/16, *El Dakkak,* para 37.
47. See Op. 2/00, *Cartagena Protocol on Biosafety,* para 5; Case C-370/07, *Commission v. Council (CITES),* paras. 47–49; Case T-529/09, *in 't Veld v. Council,* para 47.

decisions, or all of them). Hence, the legal basis defines the mode and degree of how the Union impacts on the legal order of the Member States. In some instances, even the territorial scope of the application is altered by the choice of legal basis. Given this constitutional significance, it is only natural that the Court of Justice denies any discretion on the part of the EU institutions to choose between competing legal bases and has developed a huge body of case law to guide the legally correct choice.[48]

3.2 *Scope of the principle of conferral*

According to a broad (and preferable) interpretation, the principle of conferral applies to *all* actions by the Union. This view is supported by the unqualified language of Article 5(2) TEU. After the former "pillars" of the Union were merged by the Treaty of Lisbon, the scope of the principle has undoubtedly come to comprise the Common Foreign and Security Policy (see Art. 2(4) TFEU). While it still enjoys special status to some degree, that policy is a part of the EU legal order and subject to its constitutional principles unless indicated otherwise.[49]

(i) However, legal scholarship has deliberated on possible exceptions to this principle. The first issue concerns Article 352 TFEU and its predecessors. The so-called "flexibility clause" raises doubts as to whether it is effectively governed by the principle of conferral. It entrusts a very broad competence to the Union. When relying on Article 352 TFEU, the Union institutions are empowered to act even though they do not have a specific competence at their disposition. Still, this provision is not placed outside the system of competences. Article 352 TFEU neither gives the Union *Kompetenz-Kompetenz* nor is it the equivalent of a simplified amendment procedure.[50] Essentially defined by reference to objectives rather than bound to any particular subject matter, the scope of this competence is broad, but not without limits. This is demonstrated by the fact that the Court of Justice has at least once decided that a planned measure would transgress these limits. In its first Opinion in 1994 on the accession to the European Convention of Human Rights, the Court held that the general framework created by the Treaties would be fundamentally altered and, hence, Article 352 TFEU could not be used as the legal basis for the accession.[51]

It would be a misunderstanding of the principle of conferral to surmise that it required a Union competence to be defined in narrow terms or that the content of the prospective measures be foreseeable. Nevertheless, it may be contentious whether Article 352 TFEU disposes of sufficiently clear limits. The constraining and stabilizing functions of the principle of conferral are less marked here. To a certain extent, the broad scope of the competence and the vagueness of its substantive requirements are offset by the high procedural requirements set out in Article 352(1) and (2) TFEU. Anyway, while Article 352 TFEU has been highly instrumental to expand

48. See R.H. van Ooik, *De keuze der rechtsgrondslag voor besluiten van de Europese Unie* (Kluwer, 1999); C. Schwartz, *Die Wahl der Rechtsgrundlage im Recht der Europäischen Union* (Nomos, 2013).

49. C. Hillion, "A powerless Court? The European Court of Justice and the Common Foreign and Security Policy" in M. Cremona and A. Thies (Eds.), *The European Court of Justice and External Relations Law* (Hart Publishing, 2014), 69. On the delimitation of competences in relation to justice and home affairs, see A. Engel, "Delimiting competences in the EU: CFSP versus AFSJ legal bases", 21 *European Public Law* (2015), 47.

50. For a different view, see German Federal Constitutional Court, *Entscheidungen des Bundesverfassungsgerichts* Vol. 123, 267, at 393–395 (Lissabon).

51. Op. 2/94, *ECHR I*, paras. 27–35; see also Case C-376/98, *Germany v. Parliament and Council (Tobacco Advertising)*, para 83.

the Community's scope of activity in the 1970s and 1980s, its significance today arguably has diminished in view of the wide range of specific competences provided for in the Treaties.[52]

(ii) So-called implied powers are a second matter of concern. Union competences can be either expressly provided for or they can be non-written, i.e. implied. This category has been developed by the Court: first, in relation to the Coal and Steel Community,[53] and later, applied mainly with regard to external agreements of the Communities.[54] There are various ways to argue in favour of an implied power. One is to maintain that an expressly provided competence cannot be exercised effectively without being extended to areas not covered by the wording of the relevant legal basis.[55] Another argument refers to the nature of a matter that can only be regulated at the level of the Union, e.g. the internal organization of Union institutions (in French called *pouvoir d'organisation interne*).[56]

Neither do implied powers constitute an exception to the principle of conferral.[57] Implied powers can only be derived with reference to express provisions of the Treaties and are subject to the procedural rules and substantive limits set out therein. The acceptance of implied powers as part of the EU system of competences amounts to a rule of interpretation rather than a licence to invent new competences: implied powers are conferred, albeit tacitly.

For these reasons, mere objectives of the Union, be they sectoral policy objectives or the general objectives established in Article 3 TEU, do not necessarily imply the existence of a corresponding competence (see Art. 3(6) TEU). While it is common in international organizations to derive competences from objectives ("mandates"), such a doctrine would not comply with the EU's brand of the principle of conferral, although it had originally been accepted to some degree by the Court.[58] In light of the advanced state of constitutional development of the Union, implied powers based on objectives can no longer be justified.[59] This is confirmed rather than denied by Article 352 TFEU, since otherwise the provision would be redundant.

(iii) Some scholars have argued that only acts that bear binding force are subject to the principle of conferral.[60] They consider it superfluous to subject non-binding acts such as recommendations or resolutions to the discipline of the system of competences. The concept of "act" in the sense of Article 5 TEU would then only refer to acts entailing legal effect vis-à-vis third parties.

This view tends to underestimate the significance of non-binding acts as effective instruments of governance. Recent studies of the public authority exercised by international organizations, which oftentimes takes the form of soft law and information measures, confirm the

---

52. T. Konstadinides, "Drawing the line between circumvention and gap-filling: An exploration of the conceptual limits of the Treaty's flexibility clause", 31 YBEL (2012), 227, at 258–259.
53. Case 8/55, *Fédération Charbonnière*, 299–300.
54. Case 22/70, *Commission v. Council (ERTA)*, paras. 15 et seq.; Op. 1/76, *Laying-up fund for inland waterway vessels*, paras. 3 et seq.; cf. T. Konstadinides, "EU foreign policy under the doctrine of implied powers", 39 EL Rev. (2014), 511.
55. Case 440/05, *Commission v. Council (Ship-Source Pollution)*, para 66; Case C-295/90, *Council v. Parliament (Student Right of Residence Case)*, para 18.
56. See Case C-58/94, *Netherlands v. Council*, para 37.
57. Op. 2/94, *ECHR I*, paras. 23–27.
58. Joined Cases 281, 283 to 285 & 287/85, *Germany v. Commission*, paras. 28–30.
59. J. Larik, "From specialty to a constitutional sense of purpose: On the changing role of the objectives of the European Union", 63 ICLQ (2014), 935.
60. B. Biervert, *Der Mißbrauch von Handlungsformen im Gemeinschaftsrecht* (Nomos, 1999), 90; H. Kraußer, *Das Prinzip begrenzter Ermächtigung im Gemeinschaftsrecht als Strukturprinzip des EWG-Vertrags* (Duncker & Humblot, 1991), 88–89.

opposite view.[61] Also, in the EU, non-binding measures make up a significant proportion of the acts published in the Official Journal (roughly 10 % of all acts), let alone the multitude of non-published acts.[62] The EU Treaties take non-binding measures rather seriously. They appear in the list of standard instruments of the Union (Art. 288 TFEU). The Treaties mention specific powers to adopt recommendations or deliver opinions in various provisions (e.g., in Art. 121 TFEU on the coordination of economic policies). Other specific competences authorize the Commission to take non-binding initiatives to promote coordination (e.g., in Art. 181(2) TFEU concerning research and technological development, an example of the famous "method of open coordination").[63]

Hence, it would jeopardize the functions of the principle of conferral, in particular the constraining and stabilizing functions, to recognize non-binding acts as a general exception to the principle. Any act attributed to a public authority that aims at influencing the behaviour of private actors or public authorities requires legitimacy, whether or not it comes with the threat of a sanction. Admittedly, implied powers concerning non-binding measures are easier to justify than powers concerning legally binding measures, e.g., the power of the European Parliament to adopt resolutions regarding all matters that are of concern to the Union.[64]

3.3 *Judicial control over compliance with the principle of conferral*

The principle of conferral is subject to judicial review (see Art. 263(2) TFEU).[65] There is but one exception: with regard to the Common Foreign and Security Policy according to Article 275 TFEU. The lack of competence can be invoked in any proceedings before the ECJ in which the lawfulness of a Union act can be assessed. Whoever has legal standing in the respective action or procedure can raise such a plea, or the Court can judge it ex officio. To enable the Court to exercise the function of a competence court, the institutions have to state the legal basis as part of the requirement to state reasons referred to in Article 296(2) TFEU.[66]

With an eye to possible reform, some scholars have suggested establishing a special court outside the Union scheme with special jurisdiction over competence issues.[67] This proposal responds to the alleged tendency of the Court to rule pro-Union and to support a broad understanding of Union competence. It also responds to the abovementioned concerns raised by national courts. Since the ECJ and national constitutional or supreme courts tend to have diverging views on how to interpret Treaty provisions on EU competences, a new "hybrid" judicial body which is not clearly assigned to either the EU or national jurisdictions could prove to

---

61. M. Goldmann, *Internationale öffentliche Gewalt* (Springer, 2015); B. Kingsbury and L. Casini, "Global administrative law dimensions of international organizations law", 6 *International Organizations Law Review* (2009), 319; A. von Bogdandy, Ph. Dann and M. Goldmann, "Developing the publicness of public international law: Towards a legal framework for global governance activities", 9 GLJ (2008), 1375.
62. A. von Bogdandy, F. Arndt and J. Bast, "Legal instruments in European Union Law and their reform: A systematic approach on an empirical basis", 23 YBEL (2004), 91, at 112.
63. On OMC, see G. de Búrca, "The constitutional challenge of new governance in the European Union", 28 EL Rev. (2003), 814–839.
64. Case 230/81, *Luxembourg v. Parliament*, para 39.
65. On the constitutional function of the ECJ to resolve competence conflicts, see M. Claes and M. de Visser, "The Court of Justice as a federal constitutional court" in E. Cloots, G. de Baere and S. Sottiaux (Eds.), *Federalism in the European Union* (Hart Publishing, 2012), 83, at 98–99.
66. Case C-363/14, *Parliament v. Council (Europol)*, para 41; Case C-130/10, *Parliament v. Council (Al-Qaeda Sanctions)*, para 42.
67. J.H.H. Weiler, "The European Union belongs to its citizens: Three immodest proposals", 22 EL Rev. (1997), 150, at 155–156; cf. G. Davies, "Subsidiarity: The wrong idea, in the wrong place, at the wrong time", 43 CML Rev. (2006) 63, at 63–65.

be a more impartial judge in this controversial matter. It is up for debate whether the Court has meanwhile developed a more balanced approach to competence issues.[68] However that may be, the Member States have mainly codified ECJ case law in subsequent Treaty revisions, instead of attempting to overrule or side-line the Court.[69] It would anyway be hard to disentangle the jurisdiction of a new, separate court exercising a competence review from the other grounds of review exercised by the ECJ.

4. The typology of competences

The competences of the Union can be categorized in various ways. The Treaty of Lisbon opted for a typology for distinguishing Union competences according to how they affect the capacity of Member States to take action in a field covered by a Union competence. This typology is based on case law of the ECJ. Its codification in Articles 2 to 6 TFEU responded to demands for more transparency and clarity in the system of competences, notably with regard to the list of exclusive competences.[70]

The Treaty distinguishes exclusive competences from shared competences, the latter encompassing further sub-categories. It is important to note that Articles 2 to 6 TFEU do not provide a competence catalogue in the sense that Union institutions can directly rely on it to act. The legal bases of the respective measures are to be found in other sections of the Treaties (see Art. 2(6) TFEU).

4.1 *Exclusive competence*

Exclusive competences entail a prohibition for Member States to act in the entire area (see Art. 2(1) TFEU). The mere existence of the competence causes this effect, irrespective of whether the Union actually exercises the competence. Uniformity of law is considered crucial here, in all cases and from the outset. This uniformity can only be achieved by action taken at the Union level, assuming that the regulatory machinery of the Union is able to satisfy the need for regulation. It is telling that most policies listed in Article 3(1) TFEU have only been introduced after a transitional period, in order to avoid a legal gap.[71] Apart from implementing measures referred to in Article 291(1) TFEU, Member States are only exceptionally permitted to act if and when the Union has authorized such action. The list of fields of exclusive competence provided in Article 3(1) TFEU is meant to be exhaustive.[72] Nevertheless, implied powers can be exclusive as well, e.g. the internal organization of the Union institutions. The innovative potential of Article 3(1) TFEU as compared to previous case law is up for debate, in particular regarding

---

68. See Case C-376/98, *Germany v. Parliament and Council (Tobacco Advertising)*; but see also, e.g. Case C-210/03, *Swedish Match*; Case C-380/03, *Germany v. Parliament and Council (Tobacco Advertising II)*; Joined Cases C-154/04 & 155/04, *Alliance for Natural Health*; Case C-58/08, *Vodafone*. Cf. M. de Visser, *Constitutional Review in Europe* (Hart Publishing, 2015), 198–199; R. Schütze, "Limits to the Union's 'internal market' competence(s): Constitutional comparisons" in L. Azoulai (Ed.), *The Question of Competence in the European Union* (OUP, 2014), 215, 224–231.
69. R. Zbíral, "Restoring tasks from the European Union to Member States: A bumpy road to an unclear destination?", 52 CML Rev. (2015), 61.
70. Laeken Declaration of Dec. 15, 2001 on the Future of the European Union. For an early evaluation of the Lisbon typology, see R. Schütze, "Lisbon and the federal order of competences: A prospective analysis", 33 EL Rev. (2008), 709, at 721 et seq.
71. This was not always successful, see e.g., Case 804/79, *Commission v. United Kingdom*; cf. M. Pechstein, *Die Mitgliedstaaten der EG als "Sachwalter des gemeinsamen Interesses"* (Nomos, 1987), 77–79.
72. See Art. 4(1) TFEU.

competition law (lit. b). This competence was previously seen as non-exclusive.[73] Accordingly, national regulatory powers are recognized in Regulation 1/2003 (pre-dating the Lisbon Treaty but still in force). Under the new regime, this recognition constitutes an authorization in the sense of Article 2(1) TFEU.[74] Pursuant to this provision, Member States may legislate in an area covered by Union exclusive competence if Union legislation explicitly empowers them to do so.

With regard to external competences, Article 3(2) TFEU codifies three strands of case law. The Union has exclusive competence for the conclusion of an international agreement when its conclusion is provided for in a legislative act, is necessary to enable the Union to exercise its internal competence or in so far as its conclusion may affect common rules or alter their scope. The provision gives rise to several problems. Article 3(2) TFEU could be read as *establishing* competences although according to the system of the Treaties it should only *classify* them as exclusive. Moreover, it is difficult to draw a distinction between Article 3(2) TFEU and the actual competence provision of Article 216(1) TFEU, which is worded slightly differently.[75] According to the latter provision, the Union may conclude an international agreement where the Treaties so provide, where the conclusion of an agreement is necessary to achieve, within the framework of the Union's policies, one of the objectives referred to in the Treaties, where the conclusion is provided for in a legally binding Union act or is likely to affect common rules or alter their scope. According to the Court, not all external competences recognized in Article 216 TFEU are exclusive.[76] Yet another problem is the deviation from the language of settled case law; it is not entirely clear whether this intentionally constitutes a deviation in meaning.[77] The main conceptual weakness of Article 3(2) TFEU is that it confuses external competences that are exclusive independent of their actual use ("necessary to enable the Union to exercise its internal competence"), with situations where an external competence has become exclusive as a result of Union legislative activity (the first and third alternatives mentioned in Article 3(2) TFEU). The latter situation may be called "subsequent exclusivity" and is actually a feature of a shared competence with pre-emptive force (see next section).[78]

4.2 *Shared competence with pre-emptive force (concurrent competences)*

According to the residual clause in Article 4(1) TFEU, a competence is to be classified as a shared competence unless stated otherwise. A shared competence is described in Article 2(2) TFEU as being exercised by both the Union and the Member States. Just to be clear, this does not mean that competences affiliated with this type could be attributed to either the Union or to the Member States. The Treaties only confer competences on the Union, as the system of competences is not bipolar (see above). Article 4(2) TFEU comprises a list of areas assigned to the category of shared competences, but it is clear from Article 4(1) TFEU that this list is not exhaustive.

---

73. Relying on Case 14/68, *Walt Wilhelm*, para 3, as an authority.
74. M. Dougan, "The Convention's draft Constitutional Treaty: Bringing Europe closer to its lawyers?", 28 EL Rev. (2003) 763, at 770.
75. For a detailed analysis, see I. Govaere, "'Setting the international scene': EU external competence and procedures post-Lisbon revisited in the light of ECJ Opinion 1/13", 52 CML Rev. (2015), 1277.
76. See Opinion 2/15, *FTA EU-Singapore*, para 242.
77. Concerning an apparently broader approach to the second situation and an apparently narrower approach to the established ERTA doctrine in the third situation. The Court held that Art. 3(2) TFEU should be interpreted in line with previous case law, see C-114/12, *Commission v. Council*, paras. 66–67; Opinion 2/15, *FTA EU-Singapore*, paras. 171 and 231.
78. R. Schütze, *From Dual to Cooperative Federalism* (OUP, 2009), 305–307.

The effect of shared competences is that they empower the Union to act but do not automatically prevent the Member States from acting in the same field. More specifically, the Member States are not pre-empted as long as and to the extent that the Union has not exercised its competence (Art. 2(2) TFEU). Once it does, Member States are pre-empted from legislating or concluding international agreements pertaining to the same matter. However, according to the Protocol (No. 25) on the Exercise of Shared Competences, this does not preclude the Member States from acting in the policy field as a whole, but only within the scope regulated by the respective Union measure. Still, it is possible for the Union to block the Member States by mere inaction if a particular aspect was intentionally omitted from the relevant act. Strictly speaking, this is not inaction, as it is only possible if the Union has acted to some degree.[79] Concerning the time limit, it is not entirely clear whether pre-emption of Member States ceases by the inaction of the Union over time, or whether it is necessary for the Union to revoke its measure expressly. In light of the principle of legal certainty, it would seem necessary that the Union formally repeals the legislative act in order to cease pre-emption, even though attaining the necessary quorum could prove politically difficult. Declaration (No. 18) in Relation to the Delimitation of Competences attached to the Treaties confirms this.

As regards external competences, it is not quite clear how far the non-exclusive treaty-making powers of the Union extend. The terms of Article 3(2) TFEU are framed so broadly that it seemingly leaves no room for external powers *not* being exclusive.[80] In some instances, however, the Treaty drafter left no doubt that the mere existence of an external Union competence does not prevent the Member States from exercising their treaty-making powers (e.g., Art. 191(4) TFEU on environmental policy). Arguably, an external Union competence is of a non-exclusive nature whenever the internal Union competence is confined to minimum harmonization (e.g. in the field of social policy, cf. Article 153(4) TFEU), as international commitments of the Member States to higher standards would not interfere with the Union exercising its internal or external competences.[81]

4.3 *Shared competence without pre-emptive force (parallel competences)*

In the language borrowed from other federal jurisdictions, the above category of shared competence that potentially entails Member States' pre-emption could be termed "concurrent competences". It is actually a subcategory of the larger category which the Treaties equally refer to as shared competence. On closer inspection, some shared competences of the Union are not vested with pre-emptive force in accordance with the second clause of Article 2(2) TFEU. They could be called "parallel competences", to distinguish them from concurrent competences.[82]

The Treaties do not expect a conflict between the two levels of government to arise in the relevant fields. Accordingly, exercise of that competence shall not result in Member States being prevented from exercising theirs. If in a concrete situation a case of conflict were nevertheless to arise, the Union measure would prevail according to the principle of primacy, which applies as a general rule of conflict. Some of the parallel competences are mentioned in Article 4(3) and (4) TFEU (research, technological development, space, development cooperation and humanitarian aid); the parallel nature of the respective external competences is also made

---

79. See Case 60/86, *Commission v. United Kingdom (Dim-dip)*, paras. 9–12.
80. But see Opinion 1/13, *Convention on the civil aspects of child abduction*, paras. 69–74; Opinion 1/03, *Lugano Convention*, para 115; cf. T. Konstadinides, op. cit., supra note 54.
81. Cf. Opinion 2/91, *ILO Convention*, paras. 18 and 21.
82. On this distinction, see C.W.A. Timmermans, "ECJ doctrines on competences" in L. Azoulai (Ed.), *The Question of Competence in the European Union* (OUP, 2014), 159.

explicit (see e.g., Article 209(2) TFEU regarding development cooperation policy). Likewise, the legislative powers to set minimum harmonization can be categorized as parallel, e.g. those set out in criminal matters (Articles 82 and 83 TFEU).

Further types of parallel competence are foreseen in the catalogues of Articles 5 and 6 TFEU. Article 5 mentions certain coordinating competences (with regard to economic and employment policies), and Article 6 TFEU refers to supplementing, supporting, and further coordinating competences (with regard to health, culture, education, industry etc.). They all would comply with the definition of a shared competence in the first clause of Article 2(2) TFEU, but the lack of pre-emptive force is even more marked here compared to the competences discussed in the previous paragraph. Union competence to support, coordinate or supplement the actions of the Member States does not "supersede" their competence in these areas, and does not entail harmonization of their laws and regulations, as Article 2(5) TFEU explains. For want of a generic term provided by the Treaty, these competences may be called "non-regulatory competences". The listing in Articles 5 and 6 TFEU is not exhaustive, either, as legal bases of this type can be found in many other fields.

5. Requirements for lawful exercise of competences

The exercise of competences conferred on the Union must be treated separately from the question of the existence of a competence. Requirements for that matter are laid out in the specific legal basis. However, some requirements for the lawful exercise of competences apply cross-sectorally to all competences in addition to the specific requirements, in particular EU fundamental rights and the general principles of EU law. This section will focus on the principles mentioned in Article 5 TEU: the principles of subsidiarity and proportionality. It will also briefly assess the meaning of the principle of sincere cooperation with regard to the exercise of competences.

5.1 *Principle of subsidiarity*

The principle of subsidiarity is enshrined in Article 5(3) TEU. It applies only within the ambit of shared competences and serves as a safeguard for ensuring their balanced exercise. Its introduction signifies the defeat of the view that a Union competence should be exercised to the fullest extent possible. The principle is an expression of the paradigm of cooperative federalism, according to which it is normal that the respective spheres of competence overlap, not just during a transitional period.

This principle comprises two conditions which need to be complied with cumulatively: one negative – the objectives of the proposed action cannot be sufficiently achieved by the Member States; and one positive – the proposed action can be better achieved at Union level. The negative condition refers to a regulatory deficit at the Member State level, and a negative expectation regarding their ability to remedy the situation. The positive condition requires demonstrating the added value of action at the Union level, in light of the scale or effects of the proposed action. Assessing each and every provision of an act with regard to its compliance with the principle is not required.[83] Concerning the regulatory deficit, it is not necessary that it be deemed present in every Member State; the condition is fulfilled if even only a few Member States are currently facing the problem.[84]

---

83. See Case C-508/13, *Estonia v. Parliament and Council*, paras. 51 and 60.
84. See Case C-508/13; *Estonia v. Parliament and Council*, para 53; Joined Cases C-358/13& C-181/14, *D. and G.*, para 119.

All Union institutions are obliged to respect this principle (with the exception of the ECJ; its jurisdiction is always exclusive in nature[85]). Further specifications are laid down in the Protocol on Subsidiarity regarding proposed legislative acts in the meaning of Article 289 TFEU.[86] These include procedural requirements such as those that oblige the Commission to undertake a consultation prior to proposing legislation (Art. 2) and to notify the national parliaments of any draft legislative act (Art. 4). The Protocol also requires a statement explaining the presumed compliance with the principle (Art. 5).

Ever since the principle of subsidiarity was introduced, it has attracted scholarly attention, raising expectations regarding its potential as a means to oppose "competence creep" by Union institutions.[87] It has also attracted a lot of criticism, either for being drafted inadequately or for being applied inadequately by the Union legislature and the Court. Critique concerning its design considers its wording unclear, and disapproves of its reference to the achievement of objectives instead of the objectives themselves.[88] With regard to its application, it has been argued that the Union legislature barely engages with the subsidiarity conditions in any detail. Instead, the institutions only superficially claim compliance with the principle while referring to objectives such as harmonization that can logically only be achieved at the Union level.[89] The Court has been criticized for not reviewing subsidiarity conditions thoroughly enough.[90]

The present authors do not share the disappointment with the latter point. True, the subsidiarity principle is a legal principle and, hence, compliance is subject to judicial review. Nevertheless, questions of whether the capacity of the Member States is not "sufficient" to achieve a political goal and whether the Union is "better" equipped to do so, are essentially political and hardly amenable to judicial review. The principle of subsidiarity is best perceived as procedural, leaving it to the political institutions at the Union and Member State levels to engage with it in substance.[91] The Court as controlling authority rightly acknowledges the political significance of the principle by applying a low level of scrutiny, which respects the political institutions' discretion.[92] The procedural nature of the principle has been reinforced by the modifications of the Treaty of Lisbon. These focus on the procedures instead of the content of the principle, i.e. the "political safeguards of federalism", to employ a term common in U.S. constitutionalism.[93] The Treaty introduced a new, dialogical mechanism involving the national parliaments, which will be discussed below (see section 6).

---

85. See Joined Cases 31/62 & 33/62, *Wöhrmann et al. v. Commission*, 1042; Case 281/84, *Zuckerfabrik Bedburg v. Council and Commission*, para 12; Case C-377/09, *Hanssens-Ensch*, para 17; cf. R.W. Wegener, "Der Numerus Clausus der Klagearten", (2008) *Europäische Grundrechte-Zeitschrift*, 354.
86. Protocol (No. 2) on the Application of the Principles of Subsidiarity and Proportionality.
87. P. Craig, "Subsidiarity: A political and legal analysis", 50 JCMS (2012), 72, at 72–73.
88. P. Kiiver, *The Early Warning System for the Principle of Subsidiarity* (Routledge, 2012), 75; G. Davies, op. cit. *supra* note 67, at 74–75.
89. S. Weatherill, "The limits of legislative harmonization: Ten years after Tobacco advertising", 12 GLJ (2011) 827, at 844–855.
90. S. Weatherill, "Competence and legitimacy" in C. Barnard and O. Odudu (Eds.), *The Outer Limits of European Union Law* (OUP, 2009), 21–22. Craig counters the alleged significance of the role of the Court by arguing, *inter alia*, that during the 20 years of the establishment of the principle, only about ten substantiated claims have been brought before the Court: P. Craig, op. cit. *supra* note 87.
91. I. Cooper, "Is the subsidiarity early warning mechanism a legal or political procedure? Three questions and a typology", *EUI Working Papers RSCAS 2016/18*, 10–11.
92. See Case C-547/14, *Philip Morris*, paras. 214–227; Case C-477/14, *Pillbox 38 (UK) Ltd.*, paras. 148–151.
93. X. Groussot and S. Bogojevic, "Subsidiarity as a procedural safeguard of federalism" in L. Azoulai (Ed.), *The Question of Competence in the European Union* (OUP, 2014), 234; on the U.S. jurisprudence, see F.C. Mayer, *Kompetenzüberschreitung und Letztentscheidung* (Beck, 2000), 275 et seq.

5.2 *Principle of proportionality*

The principle of proportionality is enshrined in Article 5(4) TEU. It is a codification of the general principle of proportionality developed by the Court.[94] The codification is only partial; it is clear from the context that Article 5(4) TEU is not aimed at ensuring the liberty of the individual against public authority.[95] Rather, it serves to safeguard the balance of the system of competences and thereby the autonomy of the Member States. Although Article 5 TEU clearly states that the principle is independent of the principle of subsidiarity, it is not easy to draw a distinction between them as the two principles overlap. In contrast with the principle of subsidiarity, the principle of proportionality is applicable to all Union actions and not confined to areas of shared competence.

According to the principle, the means used by the Union have to be appropriate for attaining the legitimate objectives pursued and must not extend beyond what is necessary to achieve those objectives. The term "objectives" here is not a reference to the objectives in Article 3 TEU. Rather, it relates to the specific objectives pursued by the measure; the wording is slightly misleading.[96] The principle of proportionality applies to the form and substance of the measure. As regards form, i.e. the legal instruments at the disposal of the institutions, there is no simple hierarchy of types of acts in the sense that directives are always less intrusive than regulations. Prior to the Treaty of Lisbon, the former Subsidiarity Protocol[97] stated that directives were preferable to regulations (para 6). It makes sense that this was repealed in the new Protocol. Proportionality essentially relates to the density of the regulation, which by no means depends on the type of act chosen for the measure.[98]

Compliance with the principle is subject to judicial review, albeit restrained in order to allow political institutions broad discretion in cases entailing political, social and economic choices and complex assessments. This means that a measure is only unlawful if it is manifestly inappropriate or excessive in relation to the objective pursued.[99]

5.3 *Principle of sincere cooperation*

The principle of sincere cooperation is laid down in Article 4(3) TEU and is directed at both the Union and the Member States. With regard to the order of competences, it obliges the Union to remain cognizant of the implications of the measures it takes on the powers of the Member States, and to respect those powers.[100] By this principle, the Union shall also support and assist Member State authorities when they exercise implementing powers,[101] including Member State

94. Case 122/78, *Buitoni*, para 16/18; Case 15/83, *Denkavit Nederland*, para 25; Case C-58/08, *Vodafone*, para 51; Joined Cases C-293/12 & C-594/12, *Digital Rights Ireland*, para 46.
95. For reviews of the jurisprudence, see V. Trstenjak and E. Beysen, "Das Prinzip der Verhältnismäßigkeit in der Unionsrechtsordnung", (2012) *Europarecht*, 265; T. von Danwitz, "Thoughts on proportionality and coherence in the jurisprudence of the Court of Justice" in P. Cardonnel, A. Rosas and N. Wahl (Eds.), *Constitutionalising the EU Judicial System* (Hart Publishing, 2012), 367; J. Saurer, "Der kompetenzrechtliche Verhältnismäßigkeitsgrundsatz", (2014) *Juristenzeitung*, 281–286.
96. K. Lenaerts and P. van Nuffel, *European Union Law*, 3rd ed. (Sweet & Maxwell, 2011), para 7-040.
97. Protocol (No. 30) on the application of subsidiarity and proportionality (1997).
98. J. Bast, "Legal instruments and judicial protection" in A. von Bogdandy and J. Bast (Eds.), *Principles of European Constitutional Law*, 2nd ed. (Hart Publishing, 2010), 345, at 357–358 and 385.
99. Case 265/87, *Schräder*, para 22; Case C-58/08, *Vodafone*, para 52; Case C-176/09, *Luxembourg v. Parliament and Council*, para 62; Case C-508/13, *Estonia v. Parliament and Council*, para 29.
100. Case 230/81, *Luxembourg v. Parliament and Council*, para 38; Joined Cases 358/85 & 51/86, *France v. Parliament (Brussels Meetings)*, paras. 34–35.
101. Case 94/87, *Alcan I*, para 9; Case C-404/00, *Commission v. Spain*, para 46; Case C-505/09 P, *Commission v. Estonia*, para 86.

courts.[102] Broadly speaking, the principle of sincere cooperation aims at ensuring the effectiveness of Union acts and the functioning of the Union as well as the exercise of Member State powers.

The principle of sincere cooperation thus may establish additional obligations for the Union, with which it must comply when exercising its competences. Nevertheless, the principle does not alter the scope of Union competences. Notably, failure to comply with the auxiliary obligations that follow from the principle does not necessarily make an action unlawful.[103]

6. The role of national parliaments and constitutional courts

The previous parts have focused on EU institutions. Yet, as the system serves to limit the scope of Union competences and, more broadly, to stabilize the federal balance of power, the role of national institutions is of interest.

National institutions play a vital role in the exercise of Union competences. The national governments are responsible for forming the intergovernmental institutions of the EU, most notably the Council. The national administrations are involved in a myriad of comitology committees and Council working parties. Above all, they bear the main responsibility for implementing EU law, forming the basic layer of European composite administration besides the Commission and EU agencies. The national courts are institutionally independent of the EU judiciary, but the two are interlinked via the preliminary ruling procedure of Article 267 TFEU. As the Court puts it, national courts are "ordinary courts within the European Union legal order" as they adjudicate disputes regarding the implementation of Union law where the Court does not have direct competence and, as they case may be, make preliminary references to the Court.[104]

The involvement of national legislative institutions in the exercise of EU competences is less obvious. They do play a role in transposing and complementing EU legislation, but this is only a functional role, one hardly appealing to members of representative bodies that are accountable to voters.[105] As opposed to other branches, national legislatures lack a strong link to their European counterpart which to some degree would compensate their loss of autonomous decision-making powers following the increase in Union competences and their extensive use. Hence, national parliaments were considered the "losers of Europeanization".[106] The Treaty of Lisbon has attempted to remedy both setbacks, the "missing link" and the "extensive use", with a single stroke. It formalized a political dialogue on draft EU legislation by attributing a role to national parliaments in safeguarding the subsidiarity principle. This section will evaluate the new role as "subsidiarity watchdog" below.

There is yet another type of institution that struggles with its decline of autonomy and lack of participatory compensation: the national constitutional courts (or the national supreme courts exercising constitutional functions, as the case may be). These courts are oftentimes proud institutions that have good reason to mourn the loss of their right to have the last word on matters relating to their own constitutions.

---

102. Order of 13 July 1990 in Case C-2/88, *Zwartveld*, paras. 17–18; C-275/00, *First and Franex*, para 49.
103. Case C-149/96, *Portugal v. Council*, para 67.
104. Op. 1/09, *Patent Court*, para 80.
105. S. Kadelbach, *Allgemeines Verwaltungsrecht unter europäischem Einfluß* (Mohr Siebeck, 1999), 299–301. On the role of national parliaments, see L. Besselink, "EU constitutionalism and national parliaments: Insiders or outsiders?" in D. Jancic (Ed.), *National Parliaments after the Lisbon Treaty and the Euro Crisis* (OUP, 2017), 25–35.
106. J. O'Brennan and T. Raunio, "Introduction" in J. O'Brennan and T. Raunio, *National Parliaments within the Enlarged European Union* (Routledge, 2007), 2–8; A. Cygan, *Accountability, Parliamentarism and Transparency in the EU* (EE, 2013), 35–39.

6.1 *National parliaments*

Articles 6 and 7 of the Subsidiarity Protocol prescribe a procedure often referred to as the "early-warning system".[107] Its scope is limited to legislative acts in the formal sense of Article 289 TFEU. The procedure starts with the notification of a draft legislative act to the national parliaments. They are in turn entitled to deliver a reasoned opinion within eight weeks if they believe that the proposal does not comply with the principle of subsidiarity. If the sum of critical opinions represents one third of all possible "votes" by the national parliaments or their chambers ("yellow card"), the legislative institutions of the Union are obliged to reconsider the draft. Since the Commission enjoys a near-monopoly of initiative in legislative matters, the duty to give reasons explaining a decision to maintain, amend or withdraw the proposal will usually fall to the Commission. If a simple majority of "votes" is reached and the proposal is deliberated under the ordinary legislative procedure ("orange card"), the Commission – if it chooses to move on with the draft – has to justify, by giving a reasoned opinion, why it considers its proposal to be in compliance with the principle. In this case, the European Parliament as well as the Council can reject the proposal outright, as prescribed by Article 7 of the Protocol (which deviates from the regular decision-making procedure laid down in Art. 294 TFEU).

In the first few years after introduction, there was a steady rise in the number of reasoned opinions sent by parliaments. The numbers then strongly declined starting in 2014, but have risen again recently.[108] The decline thus does not necessarily imply that national parliaments are less engaged with the issue. A sharp decrease in new initiatives by the Commission may also serve as a partial explanation.[109] The "yellow card" threshold has been reached three times.[110] In the case of the Monti II Regulation, the result was a withdrawal of the proposal (which, according to the Commission, was not for reasons of non-compliance with the principle of subsidiarity but because it would not have the necessary support from the Council and the European Parliament).[111]

When assessing the impact of the mechanism, it should be noted that many of the opinions issued by national parliaments include a variety of objections unrelated to subsidiarity. In the view of the present authors, this is more indicative of the procedure's success than of failure. At

---

107. On this procedure, see e.g., D. Jancic, "The game of cards: National parliaments in the EU and the future of the early warning mechanism", 52 CML Rev. (2015), 939; A. Cygan, *Accountability, Parlamentarism and Transparency in the EU* (EE 2013), 156; P. Kiiver, op. cit. *supra* note 88; T. Raunio, "National legislatures in the EU Constitutional Treaty" in J. O'Brennan and T. Raunio, *National Parliaments within the Enlarged European Union* (Routledge, 2007), 85.
108. The number of opinions amounts to 34 in 2010, 64 in 2011, 70 in 2012, 88 in 2013, 21 in 2014, 8 in 2015 and 65 in 2016; see annual reports from the Commission on subsidiarity and proportionality 2010 to 2016, COM(2011)344, COM(2012)373, COM(2013)566, COM(2014)506, COM(2015)315, COM(2016)469, COM(2017)600.
109. See annual reports from the Commission on subsidiarity and proportionality 2014 and 2015, COM(2015)315 and COM(2016)469, and annual report from the Commission on relations between the European Commission and national parliaments 2015, COM(2016)471.
110. In 2012 with regard to the proposed Regulation on the exercise of the right to take collective action within the context of freedom of establishment and freedom to provide services (Monti II), COM(2012)130, in 2013 concerning the proposed Regulation on the establishment of the European's Public Prosecutor's Office, COM(2013)534, and in 2016 with regard to the proposed Directive amending the Posting of Workers Directive, COM(2016)128.
111. Annual report from the Commission on subsidiarity and proportionality 2012, COM(2013)566; see F. Fabbrini and K. Granat, "Yellow card, but no foul: The role of the national parliaments under the Subsidiarity Protocol for an EU Regulation on the right to strike", 50 CML Rev. (2013), 115, arguing its consistency with the principle of subsidiarity.

face value, the subsidiarity mechanism involves monitoring compliance with the subsidiarity principle as a legal principle, i.e. a mechanism of ex ante monitoring the legality of EU legislation. However, the test itself largely requires political assessment. In view of their composition and procedures, parliaments are ill-equipped to provide legal assessment. They are politically accountable institutions that engage with political questions and deliberate on them in an open-ended, public procedure.[112]

Therefore, the subsidiarity mechanism is best perceived as institutionalizing a formalized political dialogue between national parliaments and Union institutions.[113] The terms of the subsidiarity principle are broad enough to couch almost any argument on the merits of proposed legislation in the language of subsidiarity. If we view the mechanism as an instrument for enhancing political dialogue with the legislative institutions of Europe, use of the mechanism can be rated as a moderate success.[114] It complements other, more informal instruments intended to enhance the dialogue between national parliaments and Union institutions, such as the Barroso initiative of 2006.[115] Irrespective of failures to meet the "yellow" and "orange card" thresholds, there is obviously steady engagement by the national parliaments with legislative drafts of the Union, although some parliaments are very active and others not at all.[116] A high number of critical opinions from the national parliaments may indeed provide the Commission with an "early warning" of a potential lack of political support in the EU institutions. Otherwise, one misses the point when the national parliaments are collectively construed to be a consultative chamber of the Union legislature, a 'Conseil d'État' for Europe.[117] The subsidiarity mechanism should rather be seen as giving the national parliaments, acting individually, a formal voice in the political process that results in EU legislation.

While such proceduralization and politicization of the subsidiarity principle may be welcomed, the Lisbon Treaty also made a half-hearted attempt at strengthening its justiciability, again involving national parliaments. Article 8 of the Subsidiarity Protocol states that Member States may bring an action before the ECJ on behalf of their national parliaments claiming an infringement of the principle of subsidiarity. This action relates to legislative acts already adopted. Article 8 does not actually introduce a new procedure since it refers to the action for annulment according to Article 263 TFEU. This Article determines the admissibility of the action, save for the grounds of review which are limited to an "infringement of the principle of subsidiarity" (which would anyway be covered by the catchall clause of "infringement of the Treaties" laid down in Article 263(2) TFEU). Notably, Article 8 of the Protocol does not grant national

112. Cf. J. von Achenbach, "The European Parliament as a forum of national interest?", 55 JCMS (2017), 193–202.
113. For a similar view, see M. Nettesheim, "Subsidiarität durch politische Verhandlungen: Art. 5 Abs. 3 EUV als Verständigungsauftrag" in D. König and D. Uwer (Eds.), *Grenzen europäischer Normgebung* (Bucerius Law School Press, 2015), 35, at 36 and 50–51, and I. Cooper, "Is the subsidiarity early warning mechanism a legal or political procedure? Three questions and a typology", *EUI Working Papers RSCAS 2016/18*, 5–11.
114. D. Fromage, *Les parlements dans l'Union Européenne après le Traité de Lisbonne* (L'Harmattan, 2015), 300, 408, 415. For a more critical perception, see D. Jancic, op. cit. *supra* note 107, 939, and D. Jancic, "EU Law's grand scheme on national parliaments: The third yellow card on posted workers and the way forward" in D. Jancic (Ed.), *National Parliaments after the Lisbon Treaty and the Euro Crisis* (OUP, 2017), 306–309.
115. COM(2006)211; see D. Jancic, "The Barroso initiative: Window dressing or democracy boost?", 8 *Utrecht Law Review* (2012), 78.
116. See annual reports from the Commission on subsidiarity and proportionality 2010 to 2016, COM(2011)344, COM(2012)373, COM(2013)566, COM(2014)506, COM(2015)315, COM(2016)469, COM(2017)600; for a study of the very active Swedish parliament, see A.J. Cornell, "The Swedish *Riksdag* as scrutiniser of the principle of subsidiarity", 12 EuConst (2016), 294.
117. This view is taken by P. Kiiver, "The early warning system for the principle of subsidiarity: The national parliament as a Conseil d'Etat for Europe", 36 EL Rev. (2011), 98; P. Kiiver, op. cit. *supra* note 88, 126–133.

parliaments standing before the Court, as the action has to be "notified" by the respective Member State. It is a matter of national law to lay down the conditions for triggering the action and to implement the representation of national parliaments in the proceedings. To institute proceedings, it is not required first to deliver an opinion in the early warning procedure; these are two distinct mechanisms.[118] Until now, no such action has been brought before the Court.

6.2 *National constitutional courts*

Some national constitutional courts claim for themselves a role in safeguarding the limits of EU competences, as well. It has to be stressed, though, that the ECJ has jurisdiction over all aspects relating to the conformity with and interpretation of Union law (see Art. 19 TEU). The ECJ has consistently held that its jurisdiction to declare invalid provisions of EU law is exclusive.[119] By implication, the ECJ claims for itself to be the only court that is competent to adjudicate the EU system of competences.

National apex courts (constitutional or supreme) find this difficult to digest. After all, the ECJ is a Union institution exercising competences conferred on it by the Member States. A considerable number of apex courts has expressed reservations to protect elements of their constitutional order that they deem essential, thus establishing national (constitutional) law standards to review the exercise of Union competence.[120] The conferral of competence on the Union was never meant to enable it to interfere with these essential elements, they argue. It is highly questionable whether this reasoning is compatible with the primacy of EU law, as that principle relates to all parts of national law, including constitutional law.[121]

The frontrunner in this type of constitutional reasoning is the Federal Constitutional Court of Germany (FCC), although recently a more illiberal brand of "constitutional identity" has emerged in the jurisprudence of Central European courts.[122] Besides protecting the "constitutional identity" of the German constitution against any interference by EU institutions, the FCC has developed a concept of "ultra vires review". This deserves brief explanation here as it involves a direct challenge to the ECJ. The FCC has declared itself competent to review any question of Union competence, irrespective of their impact on essential elements of the German constitution. This is conceptualized as reviewing whether the use of competences by Union institutions, including the European Court, transgresses the limits set in the national act giving assent to the conclusion of, or an amendment to, the EU Treaties.[123] The FCC acknowledges that the ECJ must first have had the chance to remedy the transgression of powers, i.e. a violation of the principle of conferral, in a preliminary ruling. However, the FCC does not consider itself bound by this ruling if, in the FCC's perception, the relevant legal act or judgment "manifestly" transgresses the limits set in the EU Treaties and it is "structurally significant" for

118. P. Kiiver, op. cit. *supra* note 88, 43.
119. Case 314/85, *Foto-Frost*, paras. 14–19; Case C-119/05, *Lucchini*, para 53.
120. For an overview, see F.C. Mayer, "Multilevel constitutional jurisdiction" in A. von Bogdandy and J. Bast (Eds.), *Principles of European Constitutional Law*, 2nd ed. (Hart Publishing, 2010), 399; on details, see A. von Bogdandy, P. Cruz Villalón and P. Huber (Eds.), *Handbuch Ius Publicum Europaeum* Vol. II (C.F. Müller, 2007).
121. For an attempt at justifying a restrained version of such "identity review" in light of Art. 4(2) TEU, see A. von Bogdandy and S. Schill, "Overcoming absolute primacy: Respect for national identity under the Lisbon Treaty", 48 CML Rev. (2011), 1417.
122. K. Kovács, "The rise of an ethnocultural constitutional identity in the jurisprudence of the East Central European Courts", 18 GLJ (2017), 1703.
123. *Entscheidungen des Bundesverfassungsgerichts* Vol. 134, 366, at 382 et seq. (OMT); Vol. 126, 286, at 304–305 (Honeywell); Vol. 123, 267, at 353–354 (Lissabon); Vol. 89, 155, at 188 (Maastricht).

the vertical balance of powers. This approach clearly interferes with the power of the European Court to have the final say in interpreting the Treaties.[124]

Inspired by the doctrine of the FCC, the Czech Constitutional Court has even held a decision of the ECJ to be ultra vires.[125] The decision of the European Court in Case C-399/09 (Landtóva), a preliminary reference by the Czech Supreme Administrative Court, concerned retirement pensions for working periods before the dissolution of Czechoslovakia. According to the ECJ, there was discrimination based on nationality in that only Czech nationals residing in Czech territory were entitled to a supplement, which violated EU law.[126] The Czech Constitutional Court argued that the EU regulation was not even applicable as the case did not involve cross-border employment but was rather a specific consequence of the dissolution of Czechoslovakia.[127]

Another approach to monitoring the observance of the limits of EU competence has been applied by the Danish Supreme Court. In a recent case, after having submitted a preliminary reference to the ECJ,[128] the Danish Court found that the Danish law was so clear that any interpretation in accordance with the relevant Employment Directive would be *contra legem* and thus not possible. As a consequence, Danish law was not to be disapplied but, to the contrary, according to the Danish Court, it takes precedence.[129] The Court relied on the argument that the scope of EU competences and thus the scope of the direct applicability of Union acts is limited by the Danish Act of Accession. This Act does not, according to the Danish Court, include competence for the direct applicability of the general principle of prohibition of discrimination on grounds of age not explicitly provided for in the Treaties, which the Danish law in the present case was in conflict with.[130]

Finally, the most recent threat to the exclusivity of the EU Court of Justice's competence is a preliminary reference by the Italian Constitutional Court in *M.A.S. (Taricco II)*. In its judgment, the ECJ made some concessions to the referring court.[131] The Italian Constitutional Court challenged the ECJ's view on the extent to which national courts must ensure the effectiveness of sanctions for VAT fraud under the broad and open-ended competence conferred in Article 325 TFEU to combat fraud. It held that the obligation stemming from Article 325 TFEU to disregard the statutory limitation periods for VAT fraud prosecution may encroach upon the Italian constitutional identity, namely the constitutional principle of legality of criminal sanctions as well as the separation of powers.[132] Leaving aside the constitutional dimension, especially the alleged violation of the Italian constitutional identity, the ECJ agreed with the Italian Constitutional Court that national courts do not necessarily have to ensure the effectiveness of Article 325

---

124. J. Bast, "Don't act beyond your powers: The perils and pitfalls of the German Constitutional Court's ultra vires review", 15 GLJ (2014), 167.
125. Judgment of 31 Jan. 2012, Pl. ÚS 5/12, *Slovak Pensions XVII*, Part VII.
126. Case 399/09, *Landtóva*, paras. 31–54.
127. For assessment of the rather hostile positioning against the European Court, see case notes by J. Komárek, *"Czech Constitutional Court: Playing with Matches"*, 8 EuConst (2012), 323–337, and R. Zbíral, *"A legal revolution or negligible episode? Court of Justice decision proclaimed ultra vires"*, 49 CML Rev. (2012), 1475–1491.
128. See Case C-441/14, *Dansk Industri*.
129. Judgment of 6 Dec. 2016, Case 15/2014, *DI, acting on behalf of Ajos A/S*.
130. See M. R. Madsen, H. P. Olsen and U. Sadl, "Competing supremacies and clashing institutional rationalities: The Danish Supreme Court's decision in the *Ajos* case and the national limits of judicial cooperation", 23 ELJ (2017), 140.
131. Case C-42/17, *M.A.S. (Taricco II)*.
132. See D. Sarmiento, "An instruction manual to stop a judicial rebellion (before it is too late, of course)", *Despite our Differences*, 1.2.2017, available at <despiteourdifferencesblog.wordpress.com/2017/02/01/an-instruction-manual-to-stop-a-judicial-rebellion-before-it-is-too-late-of-course/>.

TFEU if this would incur a violation of the principle of legality – quite a remarkable statement in light of the particular importance the ECJ usually attaches to the principle of effectiveness (*effet utile*).[133] Although the ECJ relied on EU law and the ECHR, rather than national constitutional law, to argue for the significance of the principle of legality, it stated that national courts can apply the principle even if this leads to a situation which is not compatible with Union law, thus allowing them to give preference to national law. It would be the task (and duty) of the national legislature to remedy the situation.[134]

7. The (limited) role of the individual

Having considered the functions of Union and Member State institutions in the system of competences, this section discusses the individual. What role, if any, do private parties play in the EU system of competences, either as beneficiaries or, in a more active capacity, as citizens?

Assuming such a role is indeed anything but self-evident. The system of competences primarily serves to regulate relations between public authorities. To some degree, the Court has recognized that maintaining the institutional balance, i.e. the horizontal order of competences, serves the purpose of protecting the interests of individuals. It did so particularly (but not exclusively) with regard to the prerogatives of the European Parliament, which the Court reads as a means of involving the citizens in the political process of the Union.[135] The present authors were not able to detect a comparable line of reasoning with regard to the vertical order of competences. On the contrary, in the context of actions for damages (Art. 340(2) TFEU) the Court held that the division of competences between the Union and the Member States does not intend to confer rights on individuals.[136] Accordingly, transgressions of the limits of powers cannot as such incur the liability of either the Union or the Member States.

Some authors have argued, however, that the principle of conferral serves to protect the interests of the individual because any lawful interference with individual rights by a Union institution requires a proper legal basis.[137] While the starting point of this argument adequately reflects the principle of legality in the EU legal order, the conclusion tends to assume an overly narrow scope of the principle of conferral, which is actually not limited to acts that interfere with individual rights.

Another approach links the system of competences to the concept that decisions should be "taken as closely as possible to the citizen" (see Arts. 1(2) and 10(3) TEU). The principle of subsidiarity is particularly charged with that idea (see, *inter alia*, the Preamble of the Subsidiarity Protocol).[138] Again, the aim of ensuring proximity to the citizens only partially captures the nature of the EU system of competences. As explained above, the principle of subsidiarity is only

133. Case C-42/17, *M.A.S. (Taricco II)*.
134. Case C-42/17, *M.A.S. (Taricco II)*, para 61.
135. Case 9/56, *Meroni*, 152; Case 138/79, *Roquette Frères (Isoglucose)*, para 33; Case C-300/89, *Commission v. Council (Titanium Dioxide)*, para 20.
136. See Case C-221/10 P, *Artegodan*, para 82.
137. H. Kraußer, *Das Prinzip begrenzter Ermächtigung im Gemeinschaftsrecht als Strukturprinzip des EWG-Vertrags* (Duncker & Humblot, 1991), 27 and 77; for a similar analogy to the domain reserved for parliamentary legislation (Gesetzesvorbehalt), see J. Schwarze, *Europäisches Verwaltungsrecht* (Nomos, 1988), 219 and 238 et seq. See also FCC's procedural doctrine entailing that any German citizen has standing to challenge an ultra vires act because a significant transgression of EU competences encroaches upon the powers of the German parliament and, as a consequence, upon the constitutionally protected political rights of citizens who elect this parliament, see *Entscheidungen des Bundesverfassungsgerichts* Vol. 134, 366, at 380–381(OMT).
138. G. de Búrca, "Reappraising subsidiarity's significance after Amsterdam", *Harvard Jean Monnet Working Paper 7/99*, 13; N.W. Barber, "Subsidiarity in the Draft Constitution", 11 EPL (2005), 197.

concerned with the use of EU competences. The question of allocating competences is settled in the Treaties, which do not imply a preference for action at the national level.

General principles, recognized as a non-written source of EU law, might also be relevant for the protection of the individual in the context of competences. For instance, the transparency of the distribution of competences and the predictability of their use could be seen as an expression of the principle of legal certainty. This principle requires, according to the Court, that legal rules be clear and precise, and aims to ensure that situations and legal relationships governed by EU law remain foreseeable.[139] However, the principle of legal certainty has as yet only been used with regard to action of Union institutions and implementing action of Member State authorities, but not with regard to the construction of Treaty provisions. The rationale for the principle is that the persons concerned must know, without ambiguity, what their rights and obligations are and be able to take steps accordingly.[140] Such rights and obligations of private parties may arise from EU legislation but not from a legal basis as such. Hence, the predictability of the use of competence is not governed by the principle of legal certainty, according to the jurisprudence of the Court.

A similar line of argumentation would be applicable with regard to the protection of legitimate expectations, yet another general principle of EU law. Claims that legitimate expectations have not been protected can only be invoked in the case a Union institution has acted in a way to establish those expectations.[141] In this way, prior action of a Union institution can indeed cause a limit to the further exercise of a competence. However, the principle of the protection of legitimate expectations does not have the effect of modifying the distribution of competences laid down in the Treaties. Because of the principle of primacy, there can be no legitimate expectations in the lawfulness of national legal acts that in fact do not comply with EU law.[142]

Eventually, individuals may come to play a role in the system of competences not only as passive beneficiaries but also as Union citizens and nationals of a Member State, in whose names public authority is exercised at either level of governance. From this point of view, the principle of conferral connects with the principle of democracy, in particular the function of the former to stabilize the federal balance of power and to create distinct political spaces. The system of competences covers protecting the interest of citizens in tracing the responsibility of public authorities and holding them to account. The contents of the order of competences, i.e. the actual distribution of powers, is conceptually neutral in view of the principle of democracy. From the perspective of the citizens it does not matter which level of public authority is competent since both levels have to meet standards of democracy, according to Article 2 TEU.[143]

8. Three layers of imbalance in the system of competences

The remainder of this chapter will briefly evaluate potential weaknesses in the EU system of competences. The section will be limited to identifying three layers of imbalance in the current system. A full account would go beyond the scope of this chapter.

The first and by far the oldest layer of imbalance, and a matter for concern, is the claim that the system of competences is too flexible and open-ended, so much so that it lacks an effective

139. Case C-63/93, *Duff*, para 20.
140. Case 169/80, *Gondrand Frères and Garancini*, para 17.
141. Case C-606/10, *ANAFE*, para 78.
142. Case C-606/10, *ANAFE*, paras. 79–81.
143. For a different view, see the German Federal Constitutional Court, *Entscheidungen des Bundesverfassungsgerichts* Vol. 123, 267, at 370–381 (Lissabon), arguing that the EU builds on an inferior version of the principle of democracy.

means of and measures for control. References to this claim have come up repeatedly in this chapter. Appropriate remedies are less evident as long as high expectations of performance are directed at the Union. Calls for a simple "repatriation" of powers have repeatedly turned out to be unsustainable in the face of the largely overlapping spheres of competence, which are in many respects less problematic than a precise delimitation of jealously guarded, mutually exclusive competences.

The second layer of imbalance is less concerned with the architecture than the substance of EU competences. Critics from that school of thought claim that the EU actually has too few competences that really matter. They hold that a social asymmetry between positive and negative integration exists, implying that the deregulatory effects of market freedoms and competition policy are not adequately balanced by Union competences sufficient to re-regulate the markets, pursue macro-economic policies and create the infrastructure of a pan-European welfare state.[144] Industrial relations are a case in point, and a core issue of concern. Article 153(5) TFEU may prevent the Union legislature from regulating these matters but it does not shield arrangements made at the national level from the interference of market freedoms.[145] Obviously, this ambiguity could be resolved going in either direction.

The third layer of imbalance is seen in a concept of Union competence that is too narrow to constrain European governance by alternative means. In reaction to the economic and financial crises since 2008, the EU and its Member States have developed (or rediscovered) instruments for exercising public authority that tend to evade the discipline of the EU system of competences. The list of instruments includes: "recommendations" on economic policies in the Eurozone which, if disregarded, entail financial sanctions;[146] the use of "conditionalities" attached to loans granted to a Member State, the contents of which are well in excess of Union competences;[147] and the conclusion of international agreements between Member States which set up bodies whose task is to exercise economic governance at the European level.[148] The "voluntary" character of compliance or the lack of attribution to the Union may render such measures lawful. And yet, they obviously constitute a challenge to the EU system of competences, whose boundaries they push.

Further reading

Azoulai, L. (Ed.), *The Question of Competence in the European Union* (OUP, 2014).

von Bogdandy, A. and J. Bast, "The federal order of competences" in A. von Bogdandy and J. Bast (Eds.), *Principles of European Constitutional Law*, 2nd ed. (Hart, 2010), 275.

Craig, P. "Subsidiarity: A political and legal analysis", 50 JCMS (2012), 72.

Dashwood, A., "The limits of European Community powers", 21 EL Rev. (1996), 113.

144. F. Scharpf, *Governing in Europe: Effective and Democratic?* (OUP, 1999), 50–83; A. Somek, *Engineering Equality: An Essay on European Anti-Discrimination Law* (OUP, 2011), 21–52; F. Rödl, "The Labour Constitution" in A. von Bogdandy and J. Bast (Eds.), *Principles of European Constitutional Law*, 2nd ed. (Hart Publishing, 2010), 623, at 633–639.
145. Case 438/05, *Viking*; Case 341/05, *Laval*; cf. C. Joerges and F. Rödl, "Informal politics, formalised law and the 'social deficit' of European integration", 15 ELJ (2009), 1.
146. For an evaluation from the perspective of competences, see J. Bast and F. Rödl, "Jenseits der Koordinierung? Zu den Grenzen der EU-Verträge für eine Europäische Wirtschaftsregierung", (2012) *Europäische Grundrechte-Zeitschrift*, 269–278.
147. M. Ioannidis, "Europe's new transformations: How the EU economic constitution changed during the eurozone crisis", 53 CML Rev. (2016), 1237–1316.
148. M. Dawson, "Opening Pandora's Box? The crisis and the EU institutions" in M. Dawson, H. Enderlein and C. Joerges (Eds.), *Beyond the Crisis: The Governance of Europe's Economic, Political and Legal Transformation* (OUP, 2015), 85; K. Tuori, *European Constitutionalism* (CUP, 2015), 202.

Kiiver, P., *The Early Warning System for the Principle of Subsidiarity* (Routledge, 2012).
Konstadinides, T., "EU foreign policy under the doctrine of implied powers", 39 EL Rev. (2014), 511.
Nettesheim, M., "Kompetenzen" in A. von Bogdandy and J. Bast (Eds.), *Europäisches Verfassungsrecht*, 2nd ed. (Springer, 2009), 389.
Schütze, R., "Lisbon and the federal order of competences: A prospective analysis", 33 EL Rev. (2008), 709.
Schütze, R., *From Dual to Cooperative Federalism* (OUP, 2009).
Trstenjak V. and E. Beysen, "Das Prinzip der Verhältnismäßigkeit in der Unionsrechtsordnung", (2012) Europarecht, 265.
Weiler, J.H.H., "The transformation of Europe", 100 *Yale Law Journal* (1991), 2403.

CHAPTER 4
FUNDAMENTAL RIGHTS

*Monica Claes**

1. Introduction

The European Union is a relative newcomer in the area of fundamental rights protection, but the Union has now become an important player in the field, and it can no longer be denied that the EU is a human rights organization of some sorts. The protection and promotion of fundamental rights have climbed relatively high on the Union's agenda and policy issues are increasingly debated through the lens of fundamental rights. Increasingly, the EU is expected to not only *respect*, but also *protect* and *fulfil* human rights. While the EU still lacks a general human rights competence, fundamental rights must inform and shape every action of the EU.

The protection of human rights now features prominently among the foundational values of the European Union: in the preamble of the Treaties, in the body of the Treaties, in the Charter – the EU's own Bill of Rights – and increasingly fundamental rights appear also in secondary legislation and policy documents. The growing awareness of the importance of fundamental rights translates into institutional arrangements, aimed at mainstreaming fundamental rights into all EU policies and actions. The upsurge of fundamental rights discourses is also reflected in the case law of the European courts and the references made by national courts.

According to Article 2 TEU, the EU is *based on* the values of human dignity, freedom, democracy, equality, the rule of law and *respect for* human rights, including the rights of persons belonging to minorities, values it *aims to promote*, not only in the EU but also in its relations with the wider world, as is stated in Article 3 TEU. Since the Treaty of Lisbon, the Union now has its own binding bill of rights, the EU Charter of Fundamental Rights, that has the same legal value as the TEU and the TFEU. Article 6(2) TEU contains a legal obligation to join the ECHR.[1] The EU now has a Fundamental Rights Agency, based in Vienna. The Commission has a Commissioner with a fundamental rights portfolio, and Justice and fundamental rights is one of ten priorities of the Juncker Commission (2014–2019). The EU works to mainstream fundamental rights in all its policies, and is developing human rights policies and adopting legislation aimed specifically at shaping fundamental rights in various fields (mainly concerning the right to equal treatment and the freedom from discrimination, the right to privacy and the rights of the defence in criminal law).[2] Increasingly, national courts turn to the CJEU for guidance on human rights issues, while NGOs and human rights groups have discovered EU law as a new forum for

---

* Law Faculty, Maastricht University.

1. As will be explained further below, since Opinion 2/13 of the ECJ, it has become less likely that the EU will actually join, despite the Treaty obligation to do so.
2. For a discussion of the mechanisms through which EU fundamental rights are protected and enforced beyond the judicial arena, see M. Dawson, *The Governance of EU Fundamental Rights* (CUP, 2017).

advocacy and strategic litigation. As a consequence, the CJEU is increasingly asked to decide human rights issues and review societal choices in the light of fundamental rights. Thus, while the EU still has no general competence in the area of fundamental rights, the Court of Justice has decided cases concerning virtually all fundamental rights, including the freedom from torture and inhuman and degrading treatment (especially in the context of asylum),[3] the freedom of religion (headscarves in the workplace),[4] the right to privacy,[5] and the right to a fair trial. In some areas, the European Union even takes the lead in shaping fundamental rights and developing human rights policies, and the CJEU is sometimes more protective than the ECtHR.[6]

The TEU furthermore places human rights at the heart of the European Union's *external relations*. As Article 21 TEU spells out, the Union's "action on the international scene shall be guided by the principles which have inspired its own creation, development and enlargement, and which it seeks to advance in the wider world: democracy, the rule of law, the universality and indivisibility of human rights and fundamental freedoms [...]".

Finally, the EU institutions are increasingly called upon to enforce fundamental rights *against the Member States*. In some instances, the EU acts merely to enforce specific EU law obligations which touch upon fundamental rights. Thus, the Commission opened infringement proceedings against Hungary in 2017, claiming that its law on foreign funding of non-governmental organizations infringed the TFEU provisions on the free movement of capital but also several provisions of the Charter of Fundamental Rights, such as the freedom of association.[7] But the EU is increasingly also called upon to intervene when the human rights situation in its Member States seems to be deteriorating more generally, even beyond the scope of EU law.[8] And while Member States in general are hesitant to grant the EU competences to monitor compliance with fundamental rights generally, and have for this reason settled with a rather weak Fundamental Rights Agency, there are increasing calls for EU monitoring of fundamental rights situation in the Member States.[9] So, despite the lack of a general human rights competence, one can clearly see an extension of the EU's concerns with human rights issues.

---

3. See e.g. Joined Cases C-411/10 and C 493/10, *N.S. v. Secretary of State for the Home Department M.E. et al. v. Refugee applications Commissioner et al.*; C-63/15, *Ghezelbash v. Staatssecretaris van Veiligheid en Justitie*; in relation to the EAW, see Joined Cases C-404/15 and C-659/15 PPU, *Aranyosi and Căldăraru*.
4. Case C-157/15, *Samira Achbita and Centrum voor gelijkheid van kansen en voor racismebestrijding v. G4S Secure Solutions NV*; Case C-188/15, *Asma Bougnaoui and Association de défense des droits de l'homme (ADDH) v. Micropole SA*. Note however, that the ECJ approached these cases more as an equal treatment than as a freedom of religion issue.
5. Joined Cases C-293/12 and C-594/12, *Digital Rights Ireland Ltd v. Minister for Communications, Marine and Natural Resources and Others and Kärntner Landesregierung and Others*; Case C-131/12, *Google Spain SL and Google Inc. v. Agencia Española de Protección de Datos (AEPD) and Mario Costeja González*.
6. For a comparison between the respective performance of the ECHR and the EU in the fields of migration and refugee law, see C. Costello, *The Human Rights of Migrants and Refugees in European Law* (OUP, 2016).
7. European Commission Press Release IP/17/1982 of 13 July 2017.
8. Cases in point are the calls for EU intervention on the basis of Art. 7 TEU in Hungary and Poland. The main concern here is rule of law, but fundamental rights issues, mainly the freedom of the press, minority rights and the rights of asylum seekers also play a role. See e.g. European Parliament resolution of 17 May 2017 on the situation in Hungary (2017/2656(RSP)).
9. See e.g. the EU's concerns with media pluralism, leading to the establishment of a High Level Group on Media Freedom and Pluralism (2011–2013) and the continuing preoccupation of the EU with media freedom and pluralism in the context of the digital market, see <ec.europa.eu/digital-single-market/en/policies/media-freedom-and-pluralism>.

Nevertheless, it is obvious that the EU still is a newcomer, and is, so to speak, still learning to be a human rights organization, and so is its Court.[10] The Union institutions and the Member States have not yet fully accepted the new reality, and are at times hesitant to recognize the EU as a human rights actor. Furthermore, the EU does not step into uncharted waters: the area of fundamental rights protection is rather crowded, and the EU competes with both national and international systems of fundamental rights protection.

This chapter is structured as follows. The next section situates EU fundamental rights law in the broader context of human rights law. The third section looks into the genesis and development of EU fundamental rights law from the foundation of the European Communities until today. Indeed, in order to understand the current complex system of fundamental rights protection in the EU, it is important to examine its genesis. The fourth section analyses the sources of EU fundamental rights law, and discusses the Charter, the ECHR, general principles of EU law and secondary EU law in turn. Section five examines how EU fundamental rights can be enforced, while section six investigated the complex relationships between EU, ECHR and national fundamental rights law.

2. EU fundamental rights law as part of human rights law

Fundamental or human rights are generally perceived as rights that any individual enjoys by virtue of her humanity against the exercise of public authority.[11] All public authorities are precluded from violating these fundamental rights (these are known as negative obligations). But there is more: fundamental rights should also inform and shape all actions of public authorities, and may oblige them to act, i.e. to do something in order to ensure that individuals can enjoy their rights (positive obligations).[12] A few fundamental rights are considered absolute in the sense that no interferences with those rights are admitted. Most fundamental rights can be limited and interferences can be justified, if certain conditions are complied with. Interferences must usually be provided for by law, they must aim to protect a legitimate interest, and be proportionate. It should be emphasized that fundamental rights are not just about the rights and claims of individuals. They often concern fundamental, sensitive and sometimes divisive societal issues, and ultimately turn on how societies are shaped and how polities are organized: Can an employer prohibit the wearing of a headscarf? Do workers have a right to strike? Can intelligence services, the police or commercial actors collect, use and sell personal data? Do prisoners have the right to vote? Is there a right to social welfare? Can asylum seekers or illegal migrants claim such rights? And who should decide such questions?

---

10. For critical appraisals, see e.g. N. Ferreira and D. Kostakopoulou (Eds.), *The Human Face of the European Union: Are EU Law and Policy Humane Enough?* (CUP, 2016); A. Williams, "Human rights and the EU" in D. Chalmers and A. Arnull (Eds.), *The Oxford Handbook of EU Law* (OUP, 2015), 249–270; G. de Búrca, "After the EU Charter of Fundamental Rights: The Court of Justice as a human rights adjudicator?", 20 MJ (2013), 168–184; A. von Bogdandy, "The European Union as a human rights organization? Human rights and the core of the European Union", 37 CML Rev. (2000), 1307–1338.
11. See e.g. the preamble and Art. 1 of the Universal Declaration of Human Rights. In this chapter, I use the terms "human rights" and "fundamental rights" interchangeably. I use the concept as a legal term of art, leaving aside more philosophical and political conceptions of human rights.
12. In international human rights law, this is referred to as the "duty to respect, protect and fulfil human rights": The obligation to respect means that States must refrain from interfering with or curtailing the enjoyment of human rights; the obligation to protect requires States to protect individuals against human rights abuses; the obligation to *fulfil* means that States must take positive action to facilitate the enjoyment of basic human rights.

Human rights law is, first of all, national law. The constitutional documents of all EU Member States contain fundamental rights bills of some kind, often in the first chapter of the constitution, sometimes in a separate document.[13] Fundamental rights are thus entrenched, and are beyond the reach of everyday politics: they cannot be diminished or abolished by the majority of the day, and they bind all public authorities. They are, in other words, higher up in the hierarchy of laws than legislative acts. While the EU Member States converge on the content and substance of rights, there is still quite some diversity in the manner in which they can be enforced. Some Member States provide for special judicial procedures aimed specifically at protecting fundamental rights, while in other Member States fundamental rights protection is a joint responsibility of all courts.[14]

But fundamental rights are no longer the business of states alone. Especially since 1945, international human rights law has expanded immensely. All EU Member States are parties to a wide range of human rights treaties, both at the international level (e.g. the International Covenant on Civil and Political Rights (ICCPR), the International Covenant on Economic, Social and Cultural Rights (ICESCR), the International Convention on the Elimination of All Forms of Racial Discrimination (ICERD), or the Convention on the Elimination of All Forms of Discrimination against Women (CEDAW)), and regionally, treaties adopted in the context of the Council of Europe, such as the European Convention for the Protection of Human Rights and Fundamental Freedoms (ECHR) and the European Social Charter (ESC). Given the variety of approaches to the domestic effect of international treaty law and the diversity in justice systems, the precise impact of international treaty law in their national law may vary from one Member State to the next. But it is safe to say today that international human rights law is firmly embedded in national law.

It is in this already rather crowded field that EU fundamental rights law is developing, adding its own logic to the multi-sourced field of human rights law.

3. The genesis of EU fundamental rights law[15]

The current prominence of fundamental rights in the EU Treaties and EU law stands in stark contrast to the original treaties, none of which contained a bill of rights, or a reference to fundamental rights.[16] The protection or promotion of human rights was not mentioned as one of the organization's aims. The Treaties did contain certain rights commonly understood as human rights (mainly the prohibition of discrimination on grounds of nationality and the right to equal treatment between men and women and),[17] but these were not presented in the form of a catalogue. The protection of human rights became the specialty of that other European organization, the Council of Europe, in the context of which the European Convention of Human

---

13. On fundamental rights protection in constitutional law, see e.g. S. Gardbaum, "The structure and scope of constitutional rights" in T. Ginsburg and R. Dixon (Eds.), *Comparative Constitutional Law* (Edward Elgar, 2011), 387–405.
14. Thus, in Germany and Spain a constitutional complaint (*Verfassungsbeschwerde* and *amparo* respectively) can be brought before the Constitutional Court against a decision of any public authority on grounds that fundamental rights have been infringed. See M. de Visser, *Constitutional Review in Europe – A Comparative Analysis* (Hart Publishing, 2014).
15. On the history of EU fundamental rights law see G. de Búrca, "The evolution of EU human rights law" in P. Craig and G. de Búrca, *The Evolution of EU Law*, 2nd ed. (OUP, 2011), 465–497; see also P. Alston (Ed.), *The EU and Human Rights* (OUP, 1999).
16. The Statute of the Council of Europe, in contrast, stated "the safeguard and development of human rights and fundamental freedoms" as one of the Council's aims.
17. Arts. 7 and 119 of the EEC Treaty respectively.

Rights (ECHR) had been concluded, and which all the founding Member States of the EC had signed.[18] This is not to say that human rights were never on the agenda during the negotiation processes that led to the creation of the European Communities. Quite to the contrary, as Gráinne de Búrca has convincingly demonstrated, the plan for a European Political Community contained quite a robust system of human rights protection.[19] Yet, with the failure of the European Defence Community, the plans for the EPC were shelved, and the choice was made for an incremental approach to European integration, beginning with the integration of the economies of its Member States and the creation of an internal market. International human rights protection in Europe became the main task of the Council of Europe and its ECtHR.

The European Communities were however soon forced to acknowledge the importance of developing their own system of human rights protection, as the absence of a bill of rights and the lack of a system of judicial protection of such rights proved to be problematic. In several early ECSC and EEC cases, the Court of Justice had taken the view that it could not review the compatibility of ECSC and EEC measures with *national* constitutional rights: the validity of acts of the Community institutions could only be reviewed in the light of Community law.[20] When the Court of Justice, soon after, developed the principles of direct effect and primacy, claiming that Community law is part of the law of the land of the Member States and takes precedence over all conflicting measures of national law, including also national fundamental rights, this led to a situation that could be detrimental for fundamental rights. National constitutional rights could not be invoked, while the EC Treaties did not contain a human rights bill, leaving individuals without protection of their fundamental rights in the face of Community law.

The European Court of Justice assumed a guiding role in the process that led to the creation of a European system of fundamental rights protection from the early 1970s onwards. It developed a famous line of cases positing that fundamental rights were included in the general principles of Community law.[21] Accordingly, while *national* constitutional rights could not be invoked to oppose the application of EC law because of the primacy of EC law, fundamental rights would still be protected as part of the general principles *of EC law*. In other words, it would not be necessary to invoke national constitutional rights, as EC law would offer similar protection at the European level. At the same time, the Court managed to protect the autonomy of the EU system, by not submitting it to the purview of national courts with reference to national constitutional rights. Such a system would have threatened the unity of EU law, given disparities in the national systems of fundamental rights protection.

Yet, these decisions did not immediately manage to convince the Italian and German constitutional courts. In a 1973 decision *Frontini*, the Italian *Corte costituzionale* held that in the exceptional case where secondary Community law were to infringe fundamental principles of the constitutional order or the fundamental rights of the individuals, the constitutional court would step in. Similarly, the German *Bundesverfassungsgericht* held in the 1974 landmark case *Solange I*, that despite the decisions of the ECJ, as long as ("*so lange*") fundamental rights were not granted adequate protection compared to the standards set by the German Basic law, the court would

---

18. Note that not all Member States had *ratified* the ECHR: France only ratified by 1978.
19. G. de Búrca, "The road not taken: The European Union as a global human rights actor", 105 AJIL (2011), 649–693.
20. Case 1/58, *Stork v. High Authority*; Cases 36–38/59, *Ruhrkohlen-Verkaufsgesellschaft and others v. High Authority*; Cases 36, 37, 38 and 40/59, *Geitling v. High Authority*; Case 40/64, *Sgarlata and others v. Commission*.
21. Case 29/69, *Erich Stauder v. City of Ulm – Sozialamt*; Case 11/70, *Internationale Handelsgesellschaft mbH v. Vorratstelle für Getreide und Futtermittel Frankfurt am Main*; Case 4/73, *Nold*; Case 44/79, *Hauer v. Land Rheinland Pfalz*.

not accept the unconditional precedence of Community law. In exceptional cases of conflict, it would offer protection of constitutional fundamental rights as against the application of Community law in Germany. This reluctance of the constitutional court to fully accept the absolute and unconditional primacy of EU law and to relinquish jurisdiction in favour of the European Union persists until this day, even if it has been toned down in a later decision nicknamed *Solange II*, where the *Bundesverfassungsgericht* held that it would not exercise its jurisdiction as long as the general level of fundamental rights protection offered in the EU remained adequate (even if not fully identical to the standard of protection offered in Germany). Many other constitutional courts have since adopted a similar stance, and have announced that if the EU should fail to offer adequate protection of fundamental rights, they would step in to guarantee them, even if this meant setting aside EU law (and thus not respecting the principle of primacy as set out by the Court of Justice).[22] So far, however, national courts have not actually insisted on their national standards, and have – sometimes reluctantly – accepted the standards set by the CJEU, even when they considered the standard of protection offered by EU law lower than their national standard.[23]

When defining European fundamental rights as general principles of EU law, the Court claimed to draw on the "common constitutional traditions of the Member States as a source of inspiration". Recourse to common constitutional traditions has the advantage of anchoring European principles in *national* traditions, thus ensuring the ideological continuity that is essential for their acceptance and legitimacy.[24] The EU general principles are thus tied in with the past of the Member States, and acknowledge the national roots of the EU and of European fundamental rights. In addition, they prevent the image of "European imperialism" and accusations of excessive judicial creativity or activism on the part of the CJEU. The Court could claim that it did not "invent" these principles, but merely drew from and built on the common heritage of the national constitutional traditions. Yet, the Court did not *actually* conduct thorough comparative analysis of the constitutional traditions of the Member States, not even in the early cases with only six or nine systems to compare. In fact, the early cases usually concerned individuals or undertakings invoking economic rights, such as the right to property or the freedom the conduct a business.[25] Especially the latter right was *not* clearly embedded in the common constitutional traditions of the Member States, but was protected mainly in Germany, as an

22. For comparative analyses of the current situation, see A. Albi and S. Bardutzky (Ed.), *National Constitutions in European and Global Governance: Democracy, Rights, the Rule of Law* (Asser Press, 2018). See most recently the Italian constitutional court in Order no 24/2017, where the *Corte Costituzionale* made a reference to the ECJ, indicating that the ECJ's interpretation of EU law in Case C-105/14, *Taricco* could infringe the Italian constitutional requirement to respect inalienable human rights, with particular reference to the principle of legality in criminal matters. See also decision of Nov. 2016 of the Hungarian constitutional court on relocation of asylum seekers, Decision 22/2016. (XII. 5.) AB on the Interpretation of Art. E) (2) of the Fundamental Law.
23. See e.g. the national responses to Case 399/11, *Melloni*, commented in A. Torres Pérez, "Melloni in three Acts: From dialogue to monologue", 10 *European Constitutional Law Review* (2014), 308–331; and to Case C-303/05, *Advocaten voor de Wereld,*, commented in E. Cloots, "Germs of pluralist judicial adjudication: Advocaten voor de wereld and other references from the Belgian Constitutional Court", 47 CML Rev. (2010), 645–672.
24. T. Tridimas, "Primacy, fundamental rights and the search for legitimacy" in M.P. Maduro and L. Azoulai (Eds.), *The Past and Future of EU Law. The Classics of EU Law Revisited on the 50th Anniversary of the Rome Treaty* (Hart Publishing, 2010), 98–105, at 98.
25. Also dubbed as the "right to economic initiative", "right of private initiative", freedom of enterprise", "freedom of trade", "freedom to pursue an occupation", and a "professional activity", see A. Usai, "The freedom to conduct a business in the EU, its limitations and its role in the European legal order: A new engine for deeper and stronger economic, social, and political integration", 14 GLJ (2013), 1869–1888.

expression of ordo-liberalism.[26] It is well known that, a few exceptions left aside, the Court still does not conduct a thorough analysis of the constitutional traditions of the Member States.[27]

From 1989 onwards, the Court consistently recognized the particular significance of the ECHR,[28] and referred more often to the ECHR than to any other international treaty, when establishing general principles. The underlying logic is evident: the ECHR can be seen as a reflection of common standards, to which moreover all Member States are bound.

The first fundamental rights cases typically dealt with challenges of the validity of decisions and acts *of the European institutions*, often in the light of the right to property and the right freely to pursue trade and professional activities. This is indeed what had been most problematic from the Member States' perspective: that European law could not be reviewed in the light of fundamental rights, and still claimed primacy over national law, including constitutional rights. In a second move, the Court of Justice expanded the reach of general principles to cover also *Member State action*, and extended its purview to acts of the Member States done "within the scope of EC law". When the Member States act as agents of the Communities, their actions have to comply with the same general principles of European law, including fundamental rights.

European fundamental rights protection also found its way onto the political agenda. The commitment to fundamental rights was considered as an important element of the European identity in the political discourse fairly early on.[29] The European Parliament,[30] the Council and the Commission[31] confirmed their commitment to fundamental rights and pledged to respect them in the exercise of their competences.[32] In addition, in 1978, the European Council made explicit what had been implicit before, i.e. that membership of the European Communities was conditional on respect of fundamental rights.[33] This position would later be developed into the Copenhagen criteria for the accession of new Member States, at the occasion of the European Council of Copenhagen in 1993.

Fundamental rights entered the preamble of the Treaties with the Single European Act, and the body of the Treaties with the Treaty of Maastricht. Article F of that Treaty stated that "The Union shall respect fundamental rights, as guaranteed by the European Convention for the Protection of Human Rights and Fundamental Freedoms signed in Rome on 4 November 1950 and as they result from the constitutional traditions common to the Member States, as

---

26. M. Everson and R. Correia Gonçalves, "Art. 16 – Freedom to conduct a business" in S. Peers, T. Hervey, J. Kenner and A. Ward (Eds.), *The EU Charter of Fundamental Rights. A Commentary* (Hart, 2014), 437–463.
27. At least it does not give evidence of such analysis. Advocate Generals do sometimes conduct a comparative analysis, which the Court may implicitly follow. See e.g. Joined Cases C-387/02, C-391/02 and C-403/02, *Berlusconi and Others*; Case C-550/07 P, *Akzo Nobel Chemicals and Akcros Chemicals v. Commission*. On the ECJ and the comparative method in the field of fundamental rights, see e.g. C. McCrudden, "Using comparative reasoning in human rights adjudication: The Court of Justice of the European Union and the European Court of Human Rights compared", 15 CYELS (2013), 383–415.
28. Cases 46/87 and 227/88, *Hoechst*, para 13.
29. Declaration on European Identity (Copenhagen 1973).
30. The 1984 draft European Union Treaty elaborated by the EP stated that: "The Union shall protect the dignity of the individual and grant every person coming within its jurisdiction the fundamental rights and freedoms derived in particular from the common principles of the Constitutions of the Member States and from the ECHR". A 1989 EP resolution, Report on the Declaration of fundamental rights and freedoms (doc. A2-0003/89) of 20 Mar. 1989, general rapporteur Karel De Gucht, containing the first ever EC bill of rights was unsuccessfully submitted to the IGC preparing the Maastricht Treaty.
31. The Commission termed the protection of fundamental rights "an essential element of the Community legal order", Commission report of 4 Feb. 1976 on the protection of fundamental rights in the European Community – Supplement 5/76 -Bull. EC.
32. Joint Declaration on fundamental rights, O.J. 1977, C 103.
33. European Council of Copenhagen, Declaration on Democracy (1978) 3 Bulletin of the EC 6.

general principles of Community law", while at the same time excluding this provision from the purview of the Court. The latter exclusion was corrected by the Treaty of Amsterdam.

In the course of time, it was felt that more was needed in order to ensure fundamental rights in the EU, for several reasons: to convince the Member States that the EU was "safe" and would not disrespect fundamental rights; to make it clear to candidate states that the EU values fundamental rights and a fundamental rights culture; to make the EU more legitimate to its citizens, as well as to repair the imbalance between the internal and the external human rights discourse of the EU. Two options were considered and discussed for many years: accession of the EU to the ECHR and a home-grown bill of rights. The first option was rejected by the Court of Justice when it held in Opinion 2/94 that the Treaties did not provide a legal basis for accession.[34] In 1999, the European Council set up a Convention which drafted a bill of rights for the EU: the EU Charter of Fundamental Rights. When the Treaty of Nice was signed, the European institutions (but not the Member States) solemnly proclaimed the Charter of Fundamental Rights. At that stage, the Charter was not a legally binding document. It became binding when the Lisbon Treaty entered into force on 1 December 2009. Since then, the *Charter* has acquired a central place in the EU's system of fundamental rights protection. At the same time, the Lisbon Treaty provided the legal basis for accession to the *ECHR* that the CJEU has asked for in Opinion 2/94. Finally, the Treaty confirms that fundamental rights, as they derive from the common constitutional traditions of the Member States and the ECHR, are *general principles of EU law*. It is to these three various sources of EU fundamental rights that we shall now turn.

4. Sources of EU fundamental rights

Article 6 TEU attests to the multi-sourced nature of EU fundamental rights law. It sets out three main strands of EU fundamental rights protection under EU law. Paragraph 1 states that the Union shall respect the *Charter of Fundamental Rights*, which has the same legal value as the Treaties; paragraph 2 holds an obligation for the EU to *accede to the ECHR*, while the third paragraph confirms that fundamental rights, as guaranteed by the ECHR and as they result from the common constitutional traditions of the Member States, constitute *general principles of EU law*. This latter source of EU fundamental rights is "multi-layered" in itself, since these general principles are drawn from the ECHR and the common constitutional traditions of the Member States. Interestingly, Article 6 TEU is silent on the relationship between Charter and general principles, and seems to assume that Charter and general principles (and thus indirectly also the ECHR and the common constitutional traditions) will normally coincide, or at least, that they will not conflict. The reality proves to be much more complex. But before looking into the relations between the various sources of EU fundamental rights law, we will look at each of them in turn.

In addition to the sources of EU fundamental rights listed in Article 6 TEU, one should not forget that EU secondary law may also shape fundamental rights. To be sure, the EU does not have general fundamental rights competence, and Article 6 TEU and the Charter explicitly confirm that the Charter does not extend the powers and competences of the EU. But, as is confirmed by Article 3 TEU and Article 51(1) of the Charter, the EU is under an *obligation to promote* the application of the rights and principles included in the Charter in accordance with the powers and competences conferred to it.[35] Accordingly, it must exercise its competences with a view to promoting the Charter rights. Moreover, several legal bases in the Treaties, especially in the

---

34. Opinion 2/94, *Accession ECHR*.
35. Art. 51(1) Charter states that "They shall therefore respect the rights, observe the principles and *promote the application thereof* in accordance with *their respective powers* and *respecting the limits* of the powers of the Union as *conferred* on it in the Treaties" (my italics).

Area of Freedom, Security and Justice, give the EU competences to develop policies which aim at protecting fundamental rights. This has resulted for instance in directives on child abuse and trafficking in human beings,[36] data protection,[37] equality law,[38] and procedural rights of suspects and accused persons in criminal proceedings.[39] These examples show that, while not having a general fundamental rights competence, the EU does have competences to actively develop bits and pieces of a fundamental rights policy. While the Charter and EU general principles do not grant the EU *additional* powers, they do attribute the duty to contribute to the realization of fundamental rights in the exercise of its existing competences.

4.1 *The Charter of Fundamental Rights*

4.1.1 *Origins*

Despite the gradual expansion of general principles of EU law in the jurisprudence of the Court of Justice, the ideas of accession to the ECHR and of a homegrown bill of rights never really disappeared from the agenda. In 1999 the European Council set up a body, called Convention, composed of representatives of the Heads of State and Government and of the President of the Commission as well as of members of the European Parliament and national parliaments, and tasked it with the mandate to draft a fundamental rights charter.

The drafters decided to bracket the issue of the legal force of the Charter, and immediately started debating the substantive rights to be contained in the Charter. The Convention adopted its draft on 7 October 2000. The Member States, not keen on being bound by yet another supranational bill of rights, shied away from the document. The EU institutions did however embrace it, and solemnly proclaimed it at the occasion of the signing of the Nice Treaty. The Charter thus existed in legal limbo for a while: while the institutions proclaimed to be committed to it, it was not legally binding, because the Member States did not want it to be. This is most likely also

---

36. Directive 2011/92/EU of 13 Dec. 2011 on combating the sexual abuse and sexual exploitation of children and child pornography, O.J. 2011, L 335/1; Directive 2011/36/EU of 5 Apr. 2011 on preventing and combating trafficking in human beings and protecting its victims, O.J. 2011, L 101/1 (both based on Art. 82(2) and Art. 83(1) TEU).
37. Reg. (EU) 2016/679 of the European Parliament and of the Council of 27 Apr. 2016 on the protection of natural persons with regard to the processing of personal data and on the free movement of such data, and repealing Directive 95/46/EC (General Data Protection Reg.), O.J. 2016, L 119/1; Directive (EU) 2016/680 of the European Parliament and of the Council of 27 Apr. 2016 on the protection of natural persons with regard to the processing of personal data by competent authorities for the purposes of the prevention, investigation, detection or prosecution of criminal offences or the execution of criminal penalties, and on the free movement of such data, and repealing Council Framework Decision 2008/977/JHA, O.J. 2016, L 119/89.
38. See e.g. Directive 2010/41/EU of the European Parliament and of the Council of 7 July 2010 on the application of the principle of equal treatment between men and women engaged in an activity in a self-employed capacity and repealing Council Directive 86/613/EEC, O.J. 2010, L 180/1; Directive 2006/54/EC of the European Parliament and of the Council of 5 July 2006 on the implementation of the principle of equal opportunities and equal treatment of men and women in matters of employment and occupation (recast), O.J. 2006, L 204/23.
39. See e.g. Directive 2013/48/EU of the European Parliament and of the Council of 22 Oct. 2013 on the right of access to a lawyer in criminal proceedings and in European arrest warrant proceedings, and on the right to have a third party informed upon deprivation of liberty and to communicate with third persons and with consular authorities while deprived of liberty, O.J. 2013, L 294/1; Directive 2012/13/EU of the European Parliament and of the Council of 22 May 2012 on the right to information in criminal proceedings, O.J. 2012, L 142/1.

the reason why the Court of Justice – contrary to its Advocates General and the Court of First Instance – did not make reference to the Charter until 2006.[40]

The Charter featured prominently as part II of the Treaty establishing a Constitution for Europe. It was one of the elements that gave the Treaty constitutional appearance and accordingly, it was deleted when the Treaty was de-constitutionalized and transformed into the Treaty of Lisbon. The Charter is, thus, not part of the body of the EU Treaties. Instead, Article 6 TEU states that "the Union recognizes the rights, freedoms and principles set out in the Charter of Fundamental Rights of the European Union of 7 December 2000, as adapted at Strasbourg, on 12 December 2007, which shall have the same legal value as the Treaties". The Charter therefore has the same legal value as it would have had if it were part of the Treaties: it is primary EU law.

4.1.2 *The scope of application of the Charter*

The Charter is primarily addressed to the EU, and its institutions, bodies, offices and agencies should respect and promote the rights and principles it contains. EU secondary law must hence be in conformity with the Charter to be valid, and it must be interpreted and applied in accordance with the Charter. But the Charter also binds the Member States, be it "only when they are implementing EU law".

The Charter and the EU institutions & bodies

Under Article 51(1) of the Charter, its provisions are addressed to "the *institutions, bodies, offices and agencies of the Union* with due regard for the principle of subsidiarity and to the *Member States* only when they are implementing Union law". The first part of the sentence thus makes the Charter binding on all authorities set up by the Treaties or under secondary law and requires all those authorities to respect and promote the rights of the Charter.[41] It therefore binds the European Council, Council, Commission, Parliament, CJEU, European Central Bank, and Court of Auditors, all EU bodies, offices and agencies, and their legislative and decision-making work must always respect the Charter. The Charter has acquired an increasingly prominent place in the policy cycle of the EU. The Council,[42] the Commission,[43] the European Parliament[44] have

40. Case C-540/03, *Parliament v. Council (Family Reunification Directive)*.
41. See the Explanations to the Art. 51 of the Charter, O.J. 2007, C 303/02. According to Art. 6 TEU and Art. 52(7) of the Charter, these Explanations, drafted by the Legal Service of the Council must be given due regard by the courts of the Union and of the Member States in the interpretation of the Charter.
42. Council of the European Union, Guidelines on methodological steps to be taken to check fundamental rights compatibility at the Council's preparatory bodies, Council Doc. No. 10140/11; revised guidelines in Council of the EU doc. 16957/14 (16 Dec. 2014), reissued as doc. 5377/15.
43. Commission of the European Union, Strategy for the effective implementation of the Charter of Fundamental Rights by the European Union, COM(2010)573/4; Commission Staff Working Paper, Operational Guidance on taking account of Fundamental Rights in Commission Impact Assessments, SEC(2011)567 final. For an appraisal see I. Butler, "Ensuring compliance with the Charter of Fundamental Rights in legislative drafting: The practice of the European Commission", 37 EL Rev. (2012), 397–418.
44. European Parliament resolution of 8 June 2011 on guaranteeing independent impact assessments, 2010/2016(INI), 8 June 2011. The European Parliament's Rules of Procedure provide for a mechanism further strengthening its ability to ensure full respect for Charter rights: the Committee on Civil Liberties, Justice and Home Affairs (LIBE) of the European Parliament may be requested by the committee responsible for the subject matter, a political group or at least 40 Members, "if they are of the opinion that a proposal for a legislative act or parts of it do not comply with rights enshrined in the Charter" to provide its opinion on the matter, which "shall be annexed to the report of the committee responsible for the subject-matter". The procedure was put in effect only once. LIBE is normally involved in legislative files that touch upon fundamental rights issues dealt with by other committees through the production of "normal" opinions.

made adjustments to their procedures in order to enhance verification of compliance with the Charter during the drafting and negotiation of legislation and policy. In early 2016, the institutions concluded an Inter-institutional Agreement on Better Law-Making, which provides for fundamental rights impact assessments, to be applied to legislative and non-legislative initiatives, delegated acts and implementing measures expected to have significant economic, environmental and social impacts.[45] Such *ex ante* reviews are important to develop "a fundamental rights culture", and to mainstream fundamental rights into the entire legislative and policy process.

However, in these instances, the Charter is used mainly in a manner that is *reactive* (following legislative proposals and policy initiatives and preventing violations), rather than *proactive* (examining how fundamental rights could inform the legislative agenda and policy-making). Critics have pointed to the danger that these exercises may be reduced to formalistic "ticking the boxes", and may limit themselves to merely predicting what the courts will say and preventing judicial review of the relevant measures.[46] In addition, while fundamental rights have begun to influence the legislative process, progress has been much slower in other contexts.[47]

In addition to the EU institutions, *bodies, offices and agencies* are under the same duty to respect, observe and promote the Charter. There is a wide variation in the manner in which agencies, bodies and offices give effect to this duty. Fundamental rights were initially absent from their operation and were not on their radar, but gradually, agencies seem to become aware of their fundamental rights obligations. A case in point is the European Border and Coast Guard Agency (previously Frontex). At the outset, and despite the fact that it operates in an area that is prone to fundamental rights violations, Frontex was very much set up as a border guard agency, while fundamental rights concerns were not brought to the fore. The Agency is now developing a human rights culture.[48] As required by the 2011 Regulation,[49] Frontex adopted a Fundamental Rights Strategy, a code of conduct, a Fundamental Rights Officer (FRO) who monitors possible violations of fundamental rights and a Consultative Forum on Fundamental Rights made up of representatives of the FRA, the UNHCR, and several other governmental and non-governmental human rights organizations, which serves as an independent body advising the Agency in all fundamental rights matters. As required by the new 2016 Regulation,[50] the Agency, now rebranded European Border and Coast Guard Agency, has in addition set up a complaints mechanism, to monitor and ensure the respect for fundamental rights in all the activities of the Agency. Despite the continuing focus on border control and migration management, the Agency is increasingly and actively employing the language of human rights in its training courses for border guards and in its organizational structure. Whether the language of fundamental rights

---

45. Interinstitutional Agreement between the European Parliament, the Council of the European Union and the European Commission on Better Law-Making, O.J. 2016, L 123.
46. For an extensive discussion see M. Dawson, *The Governance of EU Fundamental Rights* (CUP, 2017), Ch. 3.
47. O. de Schutter, "The implementation of the Charter of Fundamental Rights in the EU institutional framework", Study for the AFCO Committee of the EP, 2016, PE 571.397.
48. See the analysis in K. Franko Aas and H. Gundhus, "Policing humanitarian borderlands: Frontex, human rights and the precariousness of life", 55 *British Journal of Criminology* (2015), 1–18; R. Mungianu, *Frontex and Non-Refoulement: The International Responsibility of the EU* (CUP, 2016), Ch. 9. See also O. de Schutter, "The implementation of the Charter of Fundamental Rights in the EU institutional framework", Study for the AFCO Committee of the EP, 2016, PE 571.397, 42–46; M. Dawson, *The Governance of EU Fundamental Rights* (CUP, 2016), 111–114.
49. Reg. 1168/2011/EU establishing a European Agency for the Management of Operational Cooperation at the External Borders of the Member States of the European Union, O.J. 2011, L 304/1.
50. Reg. 2016/1624 of 14 Sept. 2016, O.J. 2016, L 251/1.

and the accompanying organizational structure are sufficient to improve the compliance with the Charter remains to be seen.

The Charter binds the EU institutions, bodies, offices and agencies even when they are acting *outside the scope of the Treaties*. Thus, the Court of Justice has pointed out that the Charter applies to the Commission and the European Central Bank also when acting in the context of the ESM Treaty, despite the fact that those actions are not governed by the TEU.[51]

A final question concerns the territorial scope of application of the Charter: does it also apply when the EU acts *outside the territory of the Member States*? Fundamental rights protection is clearly among the guiding principles and objectives of the EU's actions on the international scene.[52] Under Articles 3(5), Article 21(1) first paragraph, 2)(b), and (3) and Article 23 TEU and Article 205 TFEU, the EU shall seek to advance the principles of democracy, the rule of law, the universality and indivisibility of human rights and fundamental freedoms, respect for human dignity, the principles of equality and solidarity, and respect for the principles of the United Nations Charter and international law.[53] The obligation to promote and support fundamental rights thus equally applies in the external relations of the European Union, both in trade and investment policies and in the area of Common Foreign and Security Policy.[54] In order to put this obligation into effect and promote human rights globally, the EU has developed a range of legal and policy instruments. The Strategic Framework and the Action Plan on Human Rights and Democracy constitute the backbone, and together with the Guidelines on key human rights issues they form the human rights and democracy agenda of the EU. The EU includes human rights, as well as democracy and the rule of law, into its agreements with external partners. So-called human rights clauses in such agreements provide that the respect for human rights, democracy and the rule of law constitutes the basis for the agreement and represents an "essential element" of the agreement on which the reciprocal obligations of the parties are premised, so that human rights violations of a certain scale by one of them can amount to a material breach of the agreement and justify suspension or other counter-measures. This mechanism is known as human rights conditionality. However, many commentators have shown that the good intentions of the EU do not often deliver the intended outcomes, and that too often they remain exactly that: good intentions.[55]

The EU is not a party to many international human rights treaties: it is not a party to the UN human rights treaties, nor to the ECHR or the European Social Charter.[56] However, this does not exclude the EU from *unilaterally* considering itself bound by these instruments through internal

51. Joined Cases C-8/15 P to C-10/15 P, *Ledra Advertising et al v. European Commission and European Central Bank*, para 67.
52. For more on the role of human rights in the EU's external relations, see Ch. 41, "Union external relations under the TFEU", of this book.
53. Action Plan on Human Rights and Democracy (2015–2019) "Keeping human rights at the heart of the EU agenda".
54. Case C-366/10, *Air Transport Association of America and Others*, para 101, and Case C-263/14, *Parliament v. Council*, para 47.
55. See e.g. N. Ferreira and D. Kostakopoulou, *The Human Face of the European Union: Are EU Law and Policy Humane Enough?* (CUP, 2016); S. Poli (Ed.), *The European Neighbourhood Policy – Values and Principles* (Routledge, 2016); P. Leino, "Journey towards all that is good and beautiful. Fundamental rights and 'common values' as guiding principles of EU foreign relations law" in M. Cremona and B. de Witte (Eds.), *EU Foreign Relations Law: Constitutional Fundamentals* (Hart Publishing, 2008). K.E. Smith, *European Union Foreign Policy in a Changing World* (Wiley, 2013); L. Bartels, *Human Rights Conditionality in the EU's International Agreements* (OUP, 2005).
56. The EU is however a party to the UN Convention on the Rights of Persons with Disabilities (CRPD).

measures.[57] Indeed, the Court of Justice has confirmed that the EU must respect international law in the exercise of its powers, including also international human rights law. In practice, this implies that the question of the conformity of the agreement at issue with international law must be taken into account in the prior examination of all the relevant facts to be conducted by the institutions *before* concluding an international agreement.[58] In addition, the EU institutions must examine the human rights situation in the other party to the agreement and the impact which the conclusion of the agreement could have in this regard.[59] It is clear, thus, that the EU is *as a matter of EU law* bound to respect and promote human rights in the conduct of foreign relations.

So then, is the EU bound *by the EU Charter* when acting on the international plane? This raises the question of extraterritorial application of the Charter. There seems to be no reason why the EU institutions would not be so bound, since Article 51(1) of the Charter does not limit its scope of application to the territory of the Member States. On the other hand, Article 52 TEU and Article 355 TFEU do limit the application of the *Treaties* to the territories of the Member States (with the exceptions explicitly provided for in the Treaties), and the Charter coincides, in principle, with the scope of the Treaties. The General Court addressed the question in the case of the *Front Polisario,* concerning the validity of the Council Decision concluding a trade liberalization agreement between the EU and the Kingdom of Morocco. The General Court held – without much argumentation – that the Council must examine whether an agreement does not entail infringements of fundamental rights under the Charter. On appeal before the Court of Justice, Advocate General Wathelet confirmed the obligation imposed on the EU to respect and promote fundamental rights in the conduct of foreign relations and the conclusion of international agreements, both as a matter of EU law and as a matter of international law.[60] He also referred to the decision of the European Ombudsman who, in her decision on the trade agreement with Vietnam, found the Commission's failure to provide valid reasons for not conducting a prior human rights impact assessment a case of maladministration.[61] But the Advocate General rejected the view of the General Court and denied what he called the extraterritorial effect *of the Charter,* on the ground that neither the EU nor the Member States exercise control over the Western Sahara and EU law is not applicable in the Western Sahara. The CJEU overruled the decision of the General Court on other grounds, dismissing the action of Front Polisario as inadmissible, but it remained silent on the general question of the application of the Charter outside the territory of the Member States.

The Charter and the EU Member States

The more difficult question, however, is to define the scope of application of the Charter to the *Member States.* In its pre-Lisbon case law on general principles of EU law, the Court of Justice had gradually extended the application of general principles, first to acts of the Member States "implementing EU law", then to the Member States derogating from EU law, and finally, using very broad terminology, to the states when "acting within the scope of EU law".[62] The

---

57. For an argument in favour of considering the EU bound by international human rights law, see *The European Union and International Human Rights Law* (OHCRH Regional Office for Europe, available at <www.ohcrh.org>).
58. See Case 286/90, *Poulsen and Diva Navigation,* para 9; Case C-162/96, *Racke,* para 45; Cases C-402/05 P and C-415/05 P, *Kadi and Al Barakaat International Foundation v. Council and Commission,* para 291.
59. Case T-512/12, *Front Polisario v. Council.*
60. Opinion of A.G. Wathelet in Case C-104/16 P, *Front Polisario v. Council.*
61. European Ombudsman, Decision of 26 Feb. 2016 in Case 1409/2014/MHZ.
62. For a thorough analysis see M. Dougan, "Judicial review of member state action under the general principles and the Charter: defining the scope of EU law", 52 CML Rev. (2015), 1201–2015.

first situation – the Member State implementing EU law – is fairly straightforward and the rationale is obvious: when giving effect to a regulation or a decision, and when implementing a directive, the Member State is in fact acting as an agent of the EU, and accordingly, it is as much bound by EU fundamental rights as the institutions themselves.[63] The Member States thus share the responsibility with the EU institutions to guarantee compliance with fundamental rights. This has led the Court of Justice on several occasions to confirm the validity of EU measures that were rather vague on the fundamental rights implications, on the ground that it was for the Member States to ensure that fundamental rights were protected.[64] A wide discretionary power for the Member States does not allow them to escape the application of EU fundamental rights.

The second category, of the Member States derogating from EU law, is much more controversial. The Court's reasoning is as follows: when EU law allows a Member State to derogate from its obligations under the Treaties, such derogation should not go unfettered. The EU could not allow a Member State to violate fundamental rights when, in the absence of the derogation, EU fundamental rights would apply to protect those same rights. The Member State is therefore acting "within the field of EU law", and hence, so the Court held, EU fundamental rights restrict the discretion of the Member State.[65]

The application of the EU fundamental rights to Member State action is often seen with suspicion, since the Member States each have their own systems of fundamental rights protection and are moreover parties to the ECHR and other human rights treaties. When the protection offered under EU law deviates from the choices the Member States make under their own human rights law, EU fundamental rights law is seen as displacing national constitutional guarantees. An overly broad interpretation of the application of EU fundamental rights, to national acts that have limited connection with EU law, would imply that the EU could be seen as interfering with the autonomy of the Member States to make choices on sensitive issues. A link with EU law is accordingly always required, but in some cases that link has been very weak. A case in point is *Carpenter*, which has been considered a form of competence creep through fundamental rights, interfering with the sovereignty and internal affairs of the Member State beyond the competences transferred in the Treaties.[66]

63. Case 5/88, *Wachauf*; Case C-292/97, *Karlsson and others*; Joined Cases C-20/00 and C-64/00, *Booker Aquaculture Ltd et al. v. Scottish Ministers*; Case C-540/03, *Parliament v. Council (Family Reunification Directive)*; Case 101/01, *Lindqvist*.
64. Case C-540/03, *Parliament v. Council (Family Reunification Directive)*; Case 101/01, *Lindqvist*.
65. See e.g. Case C-260/89, *ERT*; Case C-368/95, *Familiapress*; Case C-112/00, *Schmidberger*; Joined Cases C-482&493/01, *Orfanopoulos*; Case C-244/06, *Dynamic Medien*, EU:C:2008:85; Case C-145/09, *Tsakouridis*; Joined Cases C-422, 425 & 426/09, *Vandorou*; Case C-390/12, *Pfleger*; Case C-98/14, *Berlington Hungary*.
66. Case C-60/00, *Carpenter*; the effects of the ruling in Carpenter have been curtailed in Case C-457/12, *S and G*. Mr. Carpenter was a British citizen living in the UK and married to a third country national. Mrs. Carpenter's residence permit was not renewed and she was therefore supposed to go back to her home country and reapply for a residence permit from there. The UK government argued that the case concerning the residence permit of a third country national married to its own non-moving citizen was purely internal and should be decided on the basis of national law. But the applicants claimed that since Mr. Carpenter provided services also in other EU countries, the expulsion of his wife would force him to follow her, would thus interfere with his free movement rights and hence came within the scope of EU law. Even if the UK rules would be considered a justified interference with free movement rights on public policy grounds (i.e. to deter irregular migration), the application of these rules to the Carpenters should respect the right to family life as a general principle of Union law and should be proportionate. The ECJ held that since Mr. Carpenter provided services in other Member States (and thus exercised his free movement rights), the case came indeed within the scope of EU law, and EU fundamental rights applied. In this case, the decision

Since Lisbon, the new fundamental rights provisions of the TEU and the Charter clearly demonstrate the will of the Member States to prevent EU fundamental rights to be used to extend the reach of EU law. Article 6 TEU states that the provisions of the Charter "shall not extend in any way the competences of the Union as defined in the Treaties". The duty to pay "due regard to the powers and competences of the Union" and to the principle of subsidiarity is repeated in the preamble to the Charter, and in Article 51(2) of the Charter, which states that "The Charter does not extend the field of application of Union law beyond the powers of the Union or establish any new power or task for the Union, or modify powers and tasks as defined in the Treaties". To remove all possible doubts, Declaration 1 annexed to the Charter repeats that "The Charter does not extend the field of application of Union law beyond the powers of the Union or establish any new power or task for the Union, or modify powers and tasks as defined by the Treaties".

Article 51(1) of the Charter clearly intends to preclude the judicial expansion of the Charter to fields that are not covered by EU law. The wording of Article 51(1) ("only when implementing EU law") raised doubts as to whether the Member States intended to detract from the generous approach of the CJEU and limit the scope of EU rights. The Explanations, which have to be taken into account when interpreting the Charter, suggest that the provision confirms the existing case law of the Court of Justice. In *Åkerberg Fransson*, a case concerned with VAT fraud, the Court clarified the meaning of Article 51(1) of the Charter, specifying that the scope of the Charter fully overlaps with the scope of EU law: whenever a situation is covered by EU law, the Charter applies. This means that the Charter is applicable in all situations governed by EU law and must be complied with where national legislation falls within the scope of EU law, for instance where national legislation is such as to obstruct one or more of the fundamental freedoms guaranteed by the Treaty and the Member State concerned relies on overriding reasons in the public interest in order to justify such an obstacle.[67]

The scope of the Charter thus coincides with the scope of EU law. Since the fundamental rights guaranteed by the Charter must therefore be complied with where national legislation falls within the scope of European Union law, situations cannot exist which are covered by European Union law without those fundamental rights being applicable. But when a legal situation does not come within the scope of European Union law, the Court does not have jurisdiction to rule on it and any provisions of the Charter relied upon cannot, of themselves, form the basis for such jurisdiction. The Court has rejected the applicability of the Charter when no sufficient link with EU law was established in cases such as *Siragusa*, *Hernandez*, and *Torralbo Marcos*.[68]

This position seems reasonable.[69] Nevertheless, the *Åkerberg Fransson* decision received quite a bit of criticism, and many considered the link with EU law too tenuous in the case at

---

to deport Mrs. Carpenter did not strike a fair balance between the right to respect for the family life of Mr. Carpenter and the maintenance of public order and public safety. The weak link with EU law – namely, the fact that Mr. Carpenter provided services in other countries – was sufficient for the Court to apply EU fundamental rights and review the expulsion as a matter of EU law, rather than leaving it to the national courts to be decided under national law.

67. So the Court in Case 201/15, *AGET*, paras. 62–64.

68. Case C-206/13, *Siragusa*; Case C-198/13, *Hernández and others*; Case C-265/13, *Torralbo Marcos*. In *Siragusa*, the ECJ stated that "In order to determine whether national legislation involves the implementation of EU law for the purposes of Art. 51 of the Charter, some of the points to be determined are whether that legislation is intended to implement a provision of EU law; the nature of that legislation and whether it pursues objectives other than those covered by EU law, even if it is capable of indirectly affecting EU law; and also whether there are specific rules of EU law on the matter or capable of affecting it" (at para 25).

69. See e.g. M. Dougan "Judicial review of member state action under the general principles and the Charter: Defining the scope of Union law", (2015) CML Rev., 1201–1245.

hand. The Court saw a sufficient link in the fact that VAT is partially harmonized and that the Member States have an obligation under EU law to ensure the collection of VAT and prevent evasion. In addition, Article 325 TFEU obliges the Member States to counter illegal activities affecting the financial interests of the European Union through effective deterrent measures, and to counter fraud affecting the financial interests of the European Union. The decision seems to be in line with pre-Lisbon case law, which established that Member States are bound by EU fundamental rights when they are acting to enforce Union law.[70] The German Federal Constitutional Court, for one, which has always instigated the CJEU to protect fundamental rights in the first place, saw the decision as proof of a "federalizing effect" of the Charter, and warned the CJEU not to go beyond the limits of its competences.[71]

The Charter is part of EU primary law and hence, it is part of the law of the land of the Member States. Under EU law, individuals can rely on the Charter before national courts, but only in cases coming within the scope of EU law. The decision as to whether the Charter applies remains a very tricky one, and national bodies and courts struggle with the issue, as is also repeatedly confirmed by the Fundamental Rights Agency and the Commission in their Annual Reports on the application of the Charter. National legislative and administrative bodies do not yet systematically include the Charter in their human rights impact assessments. National courts sometimes apply the Charter to cases not coming within the scope of EU law, while there are also (many) instances where the Charter is not applied while it should have been.[72] Courts often do not explain why the Charter does or does not apply in a case before them, also when making reference to the CJEU. There is a clear lack of knowledge and awareness of the Charter in the Member States. In order to assist national actors and potential litigants, the FRA and the Commission are developing tools to provide information on the Charter and its scope.[73]

4.1.3 *Limitations*

Article 52(1) of the Charter accepts that limitations may be imposed on the exercise of rights enshrined by the Charter as long as the limitations are provided for by law, respect the essence of those rights and freedoms and, in accordance with the principle of proportionality, are necessary and genuinely meet objectives of general interest recognized by the European Union or the need to protect the rights and freedoms of others. This limitation clause thus combines the system of a "core" or "essence of the right", with a system based on a proportionality test.[74]

---

70. E.g. Case 77/81, *Zuckerfabrik Franken*; Case 222/84, *Johnston*; Case 222/86, *Heylens*; Case C-326/88, *Hansen*; Case C-349/07, *Sopropé*.
71. *Bundesverfassungsgericht*, Judgment of 24 Apr. 2013 – 1 BvR 1215/07 – (Counter-Terrorism Database).
72. See e.g. the 2016 Fundamental Rights Report of the Fundamental Rights Agency, Ch. 1, "EU Charter of Fundamental Rights and its use by the Member States".
73. See e.g. Charterpedia, an online tool providing easy-to-access information on the Charter, <fra.europa.eu/en/charterpedia>; EU Charter app, a fundamental rights one-stop-shop for mobile devices, both designed by FRA. See also Charterclick, <www.charterclick.eu/>, funded by the European Commission.
74. For instance in Case C-362/14, *Maximillian Schrems v. Data Protection Commissioner*, the ECJ invalidated the Commission Safe Harbour Decision because it violated the essence both of the right to privacy and the protection of personal data as it arises from Arts. 7 and 8 of the Charter as well as the essence of the right to an effective judicial remedy under Art. 47 Charter, see T. Ojanen, "Making the essence of fundamental rights real: The Court of Justice of the European Union clarifies the structure of fundamental rights under the Charter: ECJ 6 Oct. 2015, Case C-362/14, *Maximillian Schrems v. Data Protection Commissioner*", 12 EuConst (2016), 318–329.

4.1.4 Rights and principles

The EU Charter is famous for being the most modern and inclusive bill of rights, containing not only classic civil and political rights, but also economic and social, and even collective rights. The distinction is well-known in international human rights law, and roughly coincides with the distinction between negative and positive obligations. The inclusion of social rights was initially considered a victory for those who favoured a progressive Charter, which could contribute to making the EU more social, against those (Member States) who feared the costly social rights that are meant to be only aspirational. Yet, the old distinction did re-enter the Charter text via the backdoor, through the distinction between "rights" and "principles". Article 52(5) stipulates that principles "may be implemented by legislative and executive acts taken by institutions, bodies, offices and agencies of the Union, and by acts of Member States when they are implementing Union law, in the exercise of their respective powers. They shall be judicially cognizable only in the interpretation of such acts and in the ruling on their legality."[75] So, while rights are enforceable and justiciable, principles require further action by the European and national authorities and are not justiciable. They become significant for the courts only when implementing acts are interpreted or reviewed. Yet, the Charter is imprecise as to which of its provisions should be viewed as "rights" and which other as "principles". The Explanations are of little help and merely state, by way of illustration, that Articles 25 (rights of the elderly), 26 (integration of persons with disabilities) and 37 (environmental protection) contain principles, and that in some cases, an article of the Charter may contain both elements of a right and of a principle, as is the case for Articles 23 (equality between men and women), 33 (family and professional life) and 34 (social security and social assistance). These examples show that the wording is not decisive: "rights" can contain principles and vice-versa. The absence of a clear distinction in the Charter is primarily the result of the inability of the drafters to arrive at a consensus on the matter.[76] It was decided to leave it to the Court of Justice to flesh out the distinction between rights and principles and the impact of the distinction on a case-by-case basis.

Yet, so far, the Court has not been particularly helpful in settling the distinction between rights and principles and clarifying the impact of the distinction.[77] In cases like *Dominguez* and *Heimann*[78] on the right to annual leave, *Kamberaj* on the right to housing assistance and *AMS* on workers' rights to information and consultation within the undertaking, the Court used concepts as "right", "principle" and "general principle" interchangeably, and did not elaborate on the impact of principles.[79] In *Glatzel*, a case concerning discrimination on grounds of disability, the Court expressed itself for the first time on Article 51(1) and Article 52(5) of the Charter.[80] The case turned on the principle of equal treatment (Art. 20 of the Charter), more specifically, the principle of non-discrimination on the grounds of disability (Art. 21(1)) and the principle of integrating persons with disabilities (Art. 26). The Court confirmed that Article 26 contains a

75. On the distinction between rights and principles, see J. Krommendijk, "Principled silence or mere silence on principles? The role of the EU Charter's principles in the case law of the Court of Justice", 11 EuConst (2015), 321–356.
76. Ibid., at 331.
77. M. de Mol, "Dominguez: A deafening silence", 8 EuConst (2012) 280–303.
78. Joined Cases C-229/11 and C-230/11, *Heimann*. See also L. Pech, "Between judicial minimalism and avoidance: The Court of Justice's sidestepping of fundamental constitutional issues in *Römer* and *Dominguez*", 49 CML Rev. (2012), 1841–1880.
79. For critical discussion of these cases, see D. Gudmundsdottir, "A renewed emphasis on the Charter's distinction between rights and principles: Is a doctrine of judicial restraint more appropriate?", 52 CML Rev. (2015), 685–720.
80. ECJ, Case C-356/12, *Wolfgang Glatzel v. Freistaat Bayern.*

principle, referring in passing to the Explanations, and stated that it "cannot itself confer on individuals a subjective right which they may invoke as such". Yet, the Court did not provide much guidance as to what principles do allow the Court to do. It seemed to adopt a narrow interpretation of Article 52(5) by limiting judicial review to measures implementing Article 26 and did not pay attention to the role of principles as standard for legal review or tools of interpretation.

4.2 *The ECHR*

4.2.1 *The ECHR as a source of EU fundamental rights*

The EU is not (yet) a party to the ECHR, and is thus not bound to comply with the ECHR *under international law*. Applications directed against the EU are not admissible before the Strasbourg court. Nevertheless, the ECHR and the case law of the ECtHR are of fundamental importance for the EU, and do serve as a source of EU fundamental rights, *as a matter of EU law*. First, Article 6(3) TEU mentions the ECHR as a source of EU fundamental rights, namely as constituting general principles of EU law. This is a confirmation of the standing case law of the CJEU, which has used the ECHR as a source of inspiration and as an indication of common constitutional traditions of the Member States for a long time. The sentence can also be read in a stronger way, as indicating that the EU considers itself bound *unilaterally*, as a matter of EU law, despite the fact that the EU as such is not a party to the ECHR, in a similar way as the EU considers itself bound, unilaterally, to the 1951 Refugee Convention by means of Article 78 TFEU. The CJEU, however, has not favoured this interpretation. It has consistently held that the ECHR is *as such* not a source of EU fundamental rights: as long as the European Union has not acceded to it, it is not a legal instrument which has been formally incorporated into European Union law.[81] Since it is not as such part of EU law, EU law also does not govern the relations between the ECHR and the legal systems of the Member States, nor does it determine the conclusions to be drawn by a national court in the event of conflict between the rights guaranteed by the ECHR and a rule of national law. In other words, the ECHR does not assume the characteristics of EU law, including direct effect and primacy.[82] As we shall see, this defensive interpretation of Article 6 (3) TEU by the Court has limited practical consequences, as there are other ways in which the ECHR shapes EU fundamental rights.

Indeed, the Convention that drew up the Charter was tasked to draw on the ECHR, among other sources. More importantly, Article 52(3) of the Charter states that "in so far as this Charter contains rights which correspond to rights guaranteed by the ECHR, the meaning and scope of those rights shall be the same as those laid down by the said Convention. This provision shall not prevent Union law providing more extensive protection".[83] The provision thus essentially contains an obligation to follow the ECHR, and since the latter is interpreted by the ECtHR, it contains an obligation to follow the case law of the ECtHR. The Court of Justice does indeed refer to the case law of the ECtHR, but it does not do so consistently, and it often does so in a summary fashion.[84]

---

81. Case C-571/10, *Kamberaj*; Case C-617/10, *Åklagaren v. Hans Åkerberg Fransson*, at para 44.
82. This is not to say that ECHR law cannot have direct effect and primacy in the domestic legal orders of the Member States. It only means that *EU law* does not give them these characteristics, and it is a matter of ECHR and national law. As a consequence, the domestic effect of ECHR law may differ from one Member State to the next.
83. The Explanations of the Charter contain a list of Charter articles whose meaning and scope are the same as the corresponding articles of the ECHR, as well as a list of articles where the meaning is the same as the corresponding articles of the ECHR, but where the scope is wider.
84. See *infra*, section 6.1.

So, while the Court may insist that the ECHR is not binding on the EU,[85] it is still under a Treaty obligation to comply with the Convention itself and with the case law of the ECtHR.

4.2.2 *Accession of the EU to the ECHR*

Background

The idea of accession to the ECHR dates back to the 1970s, when the European Communities, in search of a European identity, pointed to the importance of human rights protection. In 1979 the Commission issued a memorandum on accession of the EC to the ECHR. The Commission perceived a growing demand to counterbalance increased EU competences with formal subjection to clear and well-defined fundamental rights, and given the disagreement among Member States on a proper catalogue of fundamental rights, the Commission proposed that the EC would accede to the ECHR.[86] In 1994, the Council asked the Court of Justice to deliver an opinion on whether the Community had competence to accede to the ECHR. The Court denied such competence holding that the EC Treaty did not contain provisions conferring a general power on the Community to enact rules or conclude international agreements on human rights, and that Article 235 EC (the "flexibility" clause, now Art. 352 TFEU) could not be used given the constitutional significance of accession both for the EC and its Member States.

That basis was finally provided by the Lisbon Treaty in Article 6(2) TEU, which holds that "The Union shall accede to the European Convention for the Protection of Human Rights and Fundamental Freedoms. Such accession shall not affect the Union' s competences as defined in the Treaties". In addition, Protocol 8 was added to the Treaties,[87] stating that the accession agreement should ensure that accession "shall not affect the competences of the Union or the powers of its institutions", and also shall not affect "the situation of Member States in relation to the European Convention, in particular in relation to the Protocols thereto, measures taken by Member States derogating from the European Convention in accordance with Article 15 thereof and reservations made by Member States in accordance with Article 57 thereof". It further stated that accession should not affect Article 344 TFEU, which grants the Court of Justice an exclusive jurisdiction for disputes between EU Member States relating to EU law. In addition, the Final Act of the Lisbon Treaty included a Declaration to Article 6(2) TEU according to which accession "should be arranged in such a way as to preserve the specific features of Union law".

On May 26, 2010, the Committee of Ministers of the Council of Europe gave an ad hoc mandate to its Steering Committee for Human Rights (CDDH) to develop, in co-operation with the European Commission, the necessary legal instruments for accession. The CDDH entrusted that task to an informal working group CDDH-UE, composed of 14 experts from the Council of Europe states (7 from EU Member States and 7 from non-EU states). On the side of the EU, the Council gave the Commission a mandate to conduct the negotiations on behalf of the Union.

---

85. Thus, when a national court asks about the compatibility of EU law with the ECHR, the ECJ will insist that it solely reviews the compatibility with the Charter, but then adds that under Art. 52(3) Charter it must ensure the consistency between the Charter and the ECHR when corresponding rights are at stake, "without thereby adversely affecting the autonomy of Union law and [...] that of the Court of Justice of the European Union", Case C-601/15 PPU, *J.N. v. Staatssecretaris van Veiligheid en Justitie*, at para 47.
86. Accession of the Communities to the European Convention on Human Rights Commission Memorandum, Supplement 2/79 of Bulletin of the EC. In 1990, the Commission made a formal proposal to the Council to start accession negotiations (Commission Communication, SEC(90)1087 final).
87. Protocol (No 8) relating to Art. 6(2) of the Treaty on European Union on the accession of the Union to the European Convention on the Protection of Human Rights and Fundamental Freedoms.

Official talks on the EU's accession to the ECHR commenced in July 2010.[88] The Accession Agreement was finalized in June 2013.[89]

The Draft Accession Agreement

The key features of the Agreement were the co-respondent and prior involvement mechanisms, both suggested by the CJEU at an early stage of the negotiations, and genuine novelties in the ECHR system. The co-respondent mechanism sought to ensure that proceedings by non-Member States and individual applications are correctly addressed to Member States and/or the Union as appropriate, and thus to address the concern mentioned in point (b) of Article 1 of Protocol 8. Where a complaint would be directed against one or more EU Member States challenging the compatibility of a provision of (secondary) EU law with the ECHR, the Union would become a co-respondent with the defendant State(s). Conversely, where a complaint would be brought against the EU, but actually challenged the compatibility of a provision of the EU Treaties with the ECHR, all Member States would become co-respondents with the defendant EU. Becoming co-respondent was voluntary, either at the invitation of the ECtHR or at the EU's or the Member States' own request. In case of a request by the EU or its Member States, the ECtHR would decide whether it was "plausible" that the conditions triggering the co-respondent mechanism were met.[90]

The prior involvement mechanism aimed to avoid situations where the ECtHR would be asked to review actions of the EU or the Member States acting as agents on their compatibility with the ECHR, in cases where the CJEU has not been involved. It introduced the possibility of prior involvement of the CJEU in proceedings before the ECtHR where the EU has joined as a co-respondent, allowing the CJEU to examine whether, as a matter of EU law, human rights have been breached. If the CJEU did not find a human rights violation, the ECtHR would then proceed with its own assessment of the case, in the light of the CJEU's views but without being bound by it. The prior involvement procedure thus would function as a kind of replacement for the preliminary reference that did not take place.[91]

The Agreement further provided that proceedings before the CJEU should not be understood as "means of dispute settlement" in the meaning of Article 55 of the ECHR so as to avoid the perceived difficulty of the double exclusivity of both courts under Article 55 ECHR and Article 344 TFEU. In addition, it contained adaptations to the rules of the ECHR to accommodate the special position of the EU as a non-state.

---

88. On the negotiation process and the Draft Accession Agreement, see J. Callewaert, *The Accession of the European Union to the European Convention on Human Rights* (Council of Europe, 2014); P. Gragl, "A giant leap for European Human Rights? The final agreement on the European Union's accession to the European Convention on Human Rights", 51 CML Rev. (2014), 13–58; V. Kosta, N. Skoutaris and V. Tzevelekos (Eds.), *The EU Accession to the ECHR* (Hart Publishing, 2014); T. Lock, "End of an epic? The draft agreement on the EU's accession to the ECHR", 31 YEL (2012), 162–197.
89. Draft Agreement on the Accession of the EU to the ECHR and Draft Explanatory Report, see <www.coe.int/t/dghl/standardsetting/hrpolicy/accession/Meeting_reports/47_1(2013)008rev2_EN.pdf>.
90. Accession Agreement, Art. 3(5).
91. On the procedure see R. Baratta, "Accession of the EU to the ECHR: The rationale for the ECJ's prior involvement mechanism", 50 CML Rev. (2013), 1305; C. Timmermans, "Some personal comments on the accession of the EU to the ECHR" in V. Kosta, N. Skoutaris and V. Tzevelekos (Eds.), *The EU Accession to the ECHR* (Hart Publishing, 2014), 333–339; Critical of the procedure is e.g. A. Torres Perez, "Too many voices? The prior involvement of the ECJ", 4 *European Journal of Human Rights* (2013).

Opinion 2/13

The adoption of the Agreement required unanimity in the Council and the consent of the European Parliament, in accordance with Article 218(6)(a) and (8) TFEU, and would then require ratification by all the EU Member States in accordance with their national constitutional requirements (Art. 218(8) TFEU), as well as the approval of all the other State Parties to the Convention (Art. 50 ECHR). Yet, before the ratification process began, the CJEU was asked to give its Opinion on the compatibility of the Accession Agreement with EU law pursuant to Article 218(11) TFEU. On 18 December 2014, much to the surprise and dismay of many, the CJEU declared the Accession Agreement to be incompatible with EU primary law. It did so on a number of grounds, which it grouped under five headings.[92] First, the CJEU held the Agreement liable to adversely affect the specific characteristics of EU law and its autonomy, for three main reasons: a) the Agreement failed to coordinate Article 53 ECHR – which gives contracting parties the power to set higher standards of protection than those guaranteed by the ECHR – with Article 53 of the EU Charter, which the CJEU in *Melloni* has interpreted as meaning that the Member States could apply higher standards of fundamental rights protection than the EU Charter except where, by doing so, they would fail to respect the primacy, unity and effectiveness of EU law; b) the Agreement failed to allow for the application of the principle of mutual trust, according to which EU Member States are obliged to trust each other's systems of fundamental rights protection, except in exceptional circumstances; indeed, the ECHR, as interpreted by the Strasbourg court, requires its contracting parties to check each other's compliance with human rights, which may force EU Member States to disregard the mutual trust principle in their relations; and c) the Accession Agreement lacked a provision ensuring the compatibility of Protocol No.16 to the ECHR, according to which the highest courts of the Member States may request advisory opinions from the ECtHR, with the CJEU's preliminary ruling procedure.

Second, the Court found a breach of Article 344 TFEU, since the Accession Agreement did not explicitly exclude from the ECtHR's jurisdiction inter-State disputes relating to the application of Convention rights which come within the scope of EU law. Upon accession, the ECHR would become part of EU law and hence, any dispute between the Member States, or between the Member States and the EU, concerning compliance with the ECHR "where EU law is at issue" would fall within the exclusive jurisdiction of the Court of Justice. By not excluding these cases from the jurisdiction of the ECtHR, the draft Agreement violated Article 344 TFEU.

Third, the arrangements concerning the co-respondent mechanism did not ensure that the specific characteristics of the EU and EU law were preserved. An assessment by the ECtHR of the conditions triggering the co-respondent mechanism necessarily presupposed an assessment of EU law governing the division of powers between the EU and its Member States and would thus be liable to interfere with the division of powers between the EU and its Member States. Moreover, the Agreement lacked a provision precluding a Member State from being held responsible jointly with the EU for the violation of a provision of the ECHR in respect of which that Member State may have made reservations at the time it ratified the ECHR. And finally, by allowing the ECtHR to adopt decisions on the apportionment of responsibility between the EU and its Member States, even if based solely on the reasons given by the respondent and the

92. For a discussion of Opinion 2/13 see among many others B. De Witte and Š. Imamović, "Opinion 2/13 on accession to the ECHR: Defending the EU legal order against a foreign human rights court", 40 EL Rev. (2015), 683–705; S. Peers, "The EU's accession to the ECHR: The dream becomes a nightmare", 16 GLJ (2015), 213–222; P. Eeckhout, "Opinion 2/13 on EU accession to the ECHR and judicial dialogue – Autonomy or autarky?", 38 *Fordham Int'l L.J.* (2015), 955.

co-respondent jointly, the Agreement could adversely affect the division of powers between the EU and its Member States.

Fourth, the Court held that the procedure for prior involvement failed to preserve the specific characteristics of the EU and EU law. Allowing the ECtHR to decide whether the CJEU had already given a ruling on a particular question would mean conferring on it jurisdiction to interpret the case law of the Court of Justice. The Court stated that the prior involvement procedure should be set up in such a way as to ensure that, in any case pending before the ECtHR, the EU was fully and systematically informed, so that the competent EU institution would be able to assess whether the Court of Justice has already given a ruling on the question at issue in that case and, if it has not, to arrange for the prior involvement procedure to be initiated. The Court further held that the Agreement limited the scope of the prior involvement procedure to questions of validity of EU secondary law. By excluding questions of interpretation of EU secondary law before the CJEU, the Agreement adversely affected the competences of the EU and the powers of the Court.

Finally, the Court noted that certain acts adopted in the context of the CFSP fell outside the ambit of judicial review by the Court of Justice. Upon accession under the Agreement, the ECtHR would be empowered to rule on their compatibility with the ECHR. Referring to Opinion 1/09 the Court stated that such jurisdiction could not be conferred exclusively on an international court outside the institutional and judicial framework of the EU. Accordingly, the Accession Agreement failed to consider the specific characteristics of EU law with regard to the judicial review of acts, actions and omissions on the part of the EU in CFSP matters.

The Court thus concluded that the Accession Agreement was not compatible with Article 6(2) TEU or with Protocol No 8. The Opinion was met with disbelief and outright horror. Despite the Court of Justice's record of defying international treaties that grant judicial powers to international courts competing with its own, very few had expected the Court to actually block accession. Indeed, the Agreement had been carefully prepared by the negotiators, with the Court involved in the process, and all the Member States as well as the other institutions supported accession under this Agreement. The Advocate General, while critical of some elements in the Agreement, had taken the view that the EU could join on the basis of this Accession Agreement provided that a number of additional safeguards were added to it.

After Opinion 2/13

In the case of a negative Opinion of the Court, an EU agreement may not enter into force, under Article 218(11) TFEU, unless it is amended or the EU Treaties are revised. To be sure, some of the objections of the Court do not require Treaty amendment or a revision of the Accession Agreement, but other objections might require either or both these operations to take place.

Revision of the EU Treaties is not a very attractive option in the current political climate and with the debacle of the Constitutional Treaty and given protracted negotiation and ratification process of the Lisbon Treaty not so long ago.[93] For the time being, the prospects for accession are rather grim. Despite the consistent commitment to accession on the part of the European Commission, no real progress has been made, and given Brexit, the tense relationship between the EU, Russia and Turkey, and the lack of political will on both sides to proceed with the negotiations, it seems unlikely that accession will happen any time soon.

93. Revision of the Treaties could for instance aim to effectively eliminate the objections of the ECJ, e.g. by amending Protocol No 8; or alternatively, it could aim to accommodate the wishes of the Court, e.g. by expanding the ECJ's jurisdiction in the field of CFSP.

4.2.3 The position of EU law under the ECHR

As has been explained before, while the EU is not a party to the ECHR, all its Member States are. This raises the question whether they remain bound by the ECHR when acting in the scope of EU law, and whether they can be held to account before the Strasbourg Court for acts done in the fulfilment of their obligations under EU law. From the perspective of the Member States, such an approach may put them in an extremely difficult position. They would be caught between conflicting treaty obligations, when complying with EU law obligations would cause them to breach ECHR rights. The position of the Strasbourg Court on this question has been clarified over the years.

In the *Matthews* case,[94] the ECtHR held the UK responsible for a violation of the right to vote under Article 3 of Protocol 1 to the ECHR, of Denise Matthews, a UK citizen residing in Gibraltar. She was denied the right to vote in the European elections since the UK did not organize elections in the territory of Gibraltar. However, the UK Government claimed that it did so, because of Council Decision 76/787 and the 1976 Act concerning elections to the European Parliament, in which it was agreed among the Member States that the UK would not include Gibraltar. The question thus arose whether the UK could be held liable for an act done in compliance with EU law. The Court noted that acts of the European Community as such could not be challenged before it as the European Community was not a Contracting Party. However, notwithstanding the transfer of competences to the European Community, Contracting States remained responsible for ensuring that ECHR rights were guaranteed. The UK had freely entered into these obligations. Indeed, the relevant acts are acts of international law, and part of *primary law*. The UK thus remained fully responsible under the ECHR.

The situation was different in the later case of *Bosphorus v. Ireland*.[95] In that case, the Irish Government implemented a Council Regulation (which in turn implemented a UN Security Council Regulation). Would the ECtHR still maintain that the Member States of the EU continued to be bound by the ECHR, even when they were bound by *secondary EU law*? In such a case, the infringement of the ECHR seems attributable to the EU, rather than the Member State that merely implements the EU regulation. The Strasbourg Court introduced the "presumption of equivalent protection". It highlighted the fact that States are bound to respect fundamental rights in all cases coming within their jurisdiction. Since the alleged infringement (the impounding of an aircraft in violation of the right to property) was committed by the Irish authorities, it could be attributed to the defendant State. However, the Court then examined whether Ireland could justify the infringement by stating that it was merely complying with an EU obligation under an EU regulation. The ECtHR emphasized the importance of international cooperation, and recalled that the EU itself was not a party to the ECHR. On the other hand, a State remained responsible under the Convention for all acts and omissions of its organs regardless of whether the act or omission in question was a consequence of domestic law or of the necessity to comply with international legal obligations. The Court then stated that State action in compliance with an international obligation (in this case the implementation of an EU Regulation) was justified, as long as the relevant international organization (the EU) could be considered to offer equivalent protection, as regards both the substantive guarantees and the mechanisms controlling their observation. And the Court concluded that if such *equivalent protection* is considered to be provided by the organization, the presumption will be that a State has not departed from the requirements of the Convention when it does no more than implement legal obligations

94. ECtHR, *Matthews v. United Kingdom*, Application no. 24833/94, 18 Feb. 1999.

95. ECtHR, *Bosphorus Hava Yollari Turizm ve Ticaret Anonim şirketi v. Ireland*, Application no. 45036/98, 30 June 2005.

flowing from its membership of the organization. However, the presumption can be rebutted if, in the circumstances of a particular case, it is considered that the protection of Convention rights was *manifestly deficient*. In such cases, the interest of international cooperation would be outweighed by the Convention's role as a "constitutional instrument of European public order" in the field of human rights.[96]

The *Bosphorus* doctrine was refined in later case law, and a full picture has now emerged. Thus, when Member States have no discretion and merely implement an EU law obligation, the *Bosphorus* doctrine applies and the Member State will be excused for infringing the ECHR, unless the applicant can demonstrate before the Strasbourg Court that the system of fundamental rights protection in the EU is no longer equivalent to the protection offered by the ECHR system. This has not happened so far.

However, in cases where EU law does allow the Member States a measure of discretion, and they can comply with their EU law obligations without thereby infringing their obligations under the ECHR, they will not be excused. This was the case in *MSS v. Belgium and Greece*. Since the Dublin Regulation contained a so-called sovereignty clause, allowing the Member States not to return an asylum seeker to the country where they had first entered the Union, they could not be considered to be under an EU law obligation that could excuse them from complying with their obligations under the ECHR. The *Bosphorus* presumption accordingly did not apply, and Belgium was found to be in breach of the ECHR for returning an asylum seeker to Greece, while it could and should have known that there were systemic deficiencies in the Greek asylum system.[97]

In *Michaud*, the Strasbourg Court clarified that the presumption would also not apply, when the national courts have failed to make a reference for a preliminary ruling to the CJEU. In such a case, the EU system for the protection of fundamental rights has not functioned properly, and cannot be considered to be equivalent to the system of protection offered by the ECHR.[98]

The Bosphorus doctrine will have come as a relief to the EU and its CJEU, as the ECtHR will not, except in highly exceptional circumstances, review the compatibility of EU law with the ECHR in cases brought against EU Member States. It will also have been welcomed by the Member States, who will not easily find themselves caught between EU obligations and the ECHR. When implementing EU law obligations, they can act on the presumption that the EU offers equivalent protection. Only when they retain discretion under EU law, they must ascertain that ECHR obligations are complied with. For the individual, however, the *Bosphorus* presumption implies that a "mere" infringement of her ECHR rights does not suffice to hold the Member State liable before the ECHR, when that infringement takes place in the fulfilment of EU law obligations. In such a case, the applicant will have to demonstrate that the protection offered by the EU was manifestly deficient. Accordingly, the ECtHR seems to apply double standards to the benefit of EU Member States. This is remarkable, especially since the EU presents itself as a human rights champion in the international arena.

4.3 *General principles of EU law*

General principles of EU law were the first sources of EU fundamental rights law. In the absence of a human rights bill in the Treaties, and without a formal link between the EU and the ECHR, the Court of Justice discovered fundamental rights as general principles of EU law, deriving from the common constitutional traditions of the Member States and (later) international

96. Ibid., at para 156.
97. ECtHR, *M.S.S. v. Belgium and Greece*, Application no. 30696/09, 21 Jan. 2011.
98. ECtHR, *Michaud v. France*, Application no. 12323/11, 6 Dec. 2012.

treaties to which the Member States are parties. The rationale of the reasoning is obvious. In order to satisfy the concerns of the national courts which had expressed concerns about the lack of protection of fundamental values under EU law, and had indicated that they would offer such protection unilaterally on the basis of their own national Constitution, the Court promised to offer equivalent protection on the basis of EU law.[99]

EU fundamental rights as general principles were first developed in the case law of the Court of Justice, but later confirmed in the Treaties. In the Lisbon Treaty, the reference to fundamental rights as general principles of EU law is maintained, despite the fact that the Charter has now become binding and that there is now a duty to join the ECHR.[100] The confirmation of general principles may well have had an impact on the extensive interpretation of the Charter: it would be awkward if the Charter did not coincide with the general principles of EU law.

Since 2009, the Charter has become the prime point of reference for the CJEU and for the other institutions in defining fundamental rights. While general principles continue to exist as sources of fundamental rights in the Treaties, their added value is rather limited. Their continued presence in Article 6 TEU is mostly to make it clear that the introduction of the Charter does not intend to detract from the existing role of fundamental rights in EU law. Since the Charter has acquired binding status, general principles of EU law have become much less prominent in the case law of the Court. Moreover, when the Court does refer to common constitutional traditions of the Member States, it does so in an imprecise manner. The Court does not supply proof of the existence of a common tradition by referring to national provisions, practices or jurisprudence. This stands in contrast to the practice of the ECtHR which tends to make a *tour d'horizon* when it is examining whether consensus or common ground exists among the contracting parties. The ECtHR analyses whether consensus exists between the contracting parties when deciding whether it will interpret the Convention dynamically and set a common standard for all contracting parties, or rather, leave the States a margin of appreciation to make their own value judgments.[101]

5. The enforcement of EU fundamental rights

The Treaty and the Charter do not introduce a special procedure for the enforcement of EU fundamental rights. There is thus no European "human rights complaint procedure", as is the case for instance before the ECtHR, or before certain domestic constitutional courts. Instead, the normal enforcement procedures apply.

When it comes to alleged infringements of EU fundamental rights *by the EU institutions*, standing may be problematic. Indeed, the standing requirements under Article 263 TFEU are strict, and may preclude private individuals from challenging EU acts directly before the European Courts. Private applicants may be more successful when challenging acts of the EU institutions indirectly through national courts. Thus, Digital Rights Ireland successfully challenged the data retention directive before the Irish High Court, claiming that it violated the right to privacy and the right to data protection under Articles 7 and 8 of the Charter.[102]

---

99. See the discussion *supra*.
100. Art. 6(3) of the TEU reads: "Fundamental rights, as guaranteed by the European Convention for the Protection of Human Rights and Fundamental Freedoms and as they result from the constitutional traditions common to the Member States, shall constitute general principles of the Union's law".
101. K. Dzehtsiarou, *European Consensus and the Legitimacy of the European Court of Human Rights* (CUP, 2015).
102. ECJ, Joined Cases C-293/12 and C-594/12, *Digital Rights Ireland Ltd v. Minister for Communications et al* and *Kärtner Landesregierung, Michael Seitlinger et al.*

When it comes to *Member State acts* within the scope of EU law, the Commission may bring infringement actions *against Member States* who have allegedly failed to comply with their Charter obligations. This is possible only when the Charter applies, and the Commission will usually link the complaint to the infringement of another obligation under EU law.

Private enforcement before national courts is equally possible. Private actors can claim before a national court that the State must take account of EU fundamental rights when implementing EU law, as was the case for instance in *A, B and C*. In that case concerning three asylum seekers who claimed to be prosecuted on the ground of homosexuality, the Court held that the directive had to be read in the light of the Charter, and that the assessment of whether the asylum seekers were indeed homosexual, had to be done in accordance with the Charter.[103] The Charter thus provides an additional mechanism in the toolbox of human rights actors.

Finally, when it comes to more systematic infringements of human rights, Article 7 TEU introduces a novel mechanism, which has not been put to use today. Indeed, on a reasoned proposal by one third of the Member States, by the European Parliament or by the European Commission, the Council, acting by a majority of four fifths of its members after obtaining the consent of the European Parliament, may determine that there is a clear risk of a serious breach by a Member State of the values referred to in Article 2, including also the values of respect for human dignity, freedom, democracy, equality, the rule of law and respect for human rights, including the rights of persons belonging to minorities, all of which have a human rights component. The procedure has two steps, and may finally, after a process of negotiation, end in a unanimous decision to suspend voting rights in the Council. As said, the procedure has not yet been put to the test with regard to fundamental rights, although the European Commission launched in 2016 a pre-Article 7 dialogue with Poland relating to rule of law questions.

6. The coexistence of EU, ECHR and national fundamental rights law

EU fundamental rights are multi-sourced: laid down in the Charter, drawn from and informed by the ECHR, international treaties and common constitutional traditions and shaped in EU legislation; but they are not the only fundamental rights individuals enjoy. These EU fundamental rights often overlap with national constitutional rights and with rights deriving from international human rights treaties, most conspicuously the ECHR, which is itself deeply embedded in domestic legal systems. As we have seen, EU fundamental rights apply only in cases coming within the scope of EU law. They are addressed to the EU and to the Member States when acting in the scope of EU law. But both the EU and the Member States are also bound by other human rights systems. The *EU* is bound by international human rights law: ius cogens, international customary law relating to human rights,[104] and international human rights treaties to which the EU is a party.[105] Moreover, the EU Treaties may make other human rights treaties binding on the EU institutions by referring to them. Thus, Article 78 TFEU provides that the "common policy on asylum, subsidiary protection and temporary protection [...] must be in accordance with the Geneva Convention", and the most recent pieces of legislation in the field of asylum law similarly make reference to the Convention.

For the *Member States*, the situation is even more complex. They are bound by their own constitutional mechanisms, by the ECHR and other human rights treaties to which they are

---

103. ECJ, Joined Cases C-148 to 150/13, *A, B and C v. Staatssecretaris van Veiligheid en Justitie.*
104. ECJ, Case C-308/06, *Intertanko*, para 51.
105. Namely, the UNCRPD, the United Nations Convention on the Rights of Persons with Disabilities, which the EU ratified along with all the Member States.

parties, which apply to all their actions whether within or outside the scope of EU law, and they are also bound by EU fundamental rights but only when acting within the scope of EU law.

In many cases, therefore, human rights systems overlap, and a case can be governed simultaneously by several norms. At the same time, these systems have different legal status and the judicial bodies that have responsibility to ensure respect for these human rights (the ECtHR, national (constitutional) courts and the CJEU) have very different institutional positions. So, how do these human rights bills deriving from different sources relate to one another? The question is not a purely academic one. Each of these bills is ultimately interpreted by a different court, which has a different role in its own institutional setting, and may favour different interpretations, make different value choices, and balance rights differently. These differences do not only follow from different choices and preferences, but also from their different situational logic. The ECtHR is an international court with a very broad geographical reach, extreme diversity among its contracting parties, a low compliance pull, and a subsidiary role, protecting only the common minimum standards. At the same time, it is "only" a human rights court, with an exclusive focus on fundamental rights protection. The CJEU on the other hand, is not only a human rights court ensuring respect for EU fundamental rights, but also the EU's supreme court, ensuring respect for EU law more broadly and fostering the uniform interpretation of EU law. Upholding fundamental rights is only part of the CJEU's mission. At the same time, the CJEU has the advantage that the Member States of the EU are less diverse than those of the Council of Europe. EU law also has a stronger enforcement system and compliance pull, EU law is part of the law of the land of the Member States, and the national courts are deeply involved in the enforcement of EU law. In addition, the EU has an institutional machinery which allows it to further flesh out and develop fundamental rights in secondary legislation, which in turn can inform the interpretation of the Charter by the CJEU.

Now, divergences may occur between the national human rights mechanisms, the ECHR and the EU. Given the differences just set out, this should not in principle be problematic. Ideally, fundamental rights are protected within each of the spheres within which public authorities act, with Strasbourg guaranteeing a common minimum standard, and the EU developing a more robust human rights system, going beyond the Strasbourg minimum, where appropriate. But the reality is not as straightforward. The plurality of human rights sources and the overlapping of systems may lead to divergences and tensions, both between Strasbourg and Luxembourg, and between each of the European Courts and national (constitutional) courts. What is more, there are no shared rules about the way in which the systems relate to one another. Each of them – national, EU and ECHR – contain rules to deal with conflicts and divergences. They usually aim to achieve coherence, avoid divergences and increase the level of protection. We will look, below, at how this interaction is construed from the points of view of EU law and national constitutional law.

6.1 *Coexisting human rights: The EU perspective*

A number of principles of EU law and provisions of the Charter explicitly deal with the issue. First, it should be remembered that the Charter was drawn up by reference to the ECHR and the common constitutional traditions of the Member States which moreover, remain *indirect* sources of EU fundamental rights in their own right (Article 6 TEU). In 1999, the European Council explicitly mandated the Convention to incorporate the rights protected in the ECHR and in the common constitutional traditions of the Member States, and to take account of the ESC and the Community Charter of the Fundamental Social Rights of Workers (Article 136

TEC), insofar as they do not merely establish objectives for action by the Union.[106] So, when drawing up the Charter, the Convention clearly drew on the ECHR and the common constitutional traditions of the Member States.

These sources of Charter rights retain relevance now that the Charter has acquired full legal force. According to Article 52(3) of the Charter, the meaning and scope of Charter rights that correspond to rights guaranteed by the ECHR shall be the same as those laid down by the said Convention, but Union law may offer higher protection. Accordingly, since the ECHR is interpreted and fleshed out by the ECtHR, the Charter in a sense instructs the CJEU to draw on the case law of the ECtHR when interpreting the Charter.[107] The CJEU's practice in this respect is, however, not very consistent. The Court does not systematically refer to the case law of the ECtHR, but it often does do so, especially in landmark cases.[108] These references are always very short, and do not engage with the case law of the Strasbourg Court. They are usually presented as an afterthought and serve to demonstrate to the CJEU's audience that it follows the case law, and that the CJEU sees no discrepancies between its position, and the case law of the Strasbourg Court. The absence of citation of the Strasbourg case law should not be taken to demonstrate that the CJEU as a matter of principle disapproves of or detracts from that case law. Yet, there is a danger that the perception exists of inconsistencies between the CJEU case law and the ECtHR. In addition, the practice of the CJEU not to truly engage with the Strasbourg case law, and at most make reference to it almost as an afterthought, also precludes constructive dialogue. In many cases, where the interpretation of the CJEU initially seems to detract from the Strasbourg case law, the CJEU later on seems to re-align itself to that case law. This has been the case for instance in the context of returns under the Dublin Regulations, to countries in where fundamental rights of asylum seekers where threatened. When the ECtHR decided that a country would violate the ECHR when returning an asylum seeker in such circumstances in *M.S.S. v. Belgium and Greece*, the CJEU followed suit in its judgment in *N.S.*[109] In that case, however, the CJEU restricted the rule to cases of systemic infringements. When the ECtHR in *Tarakhel v. Switzerland* held that the rule would also apply in individual cases concerning vulnerable groups, the CJEU followed suit in *CK v. Slovenia*.[110] In these cases, it is striking that the ECtHR takes the lead, while under the ideal picture described above, one would expect the CJEU to be ready to offer more protection than the pan-European minimum requires.

Essentially, Article 52(3) Charter operates as a rule of conflict: in case of divergence in the approach of both Courts on a specific right such a conflict must be solved in one way only: EU law should align with ECHR law.

Likewise, in so far as this Charter recognizes fundamental rights as they result from the constitutional traditions common to the Member States, those rights shall be interpreted in harmony with those traditions (Art. 52 (4) Charter).[111] To be sure, only *common* constitutional traditions of the Member States inform general principles of EU law and the interpretation of the

106. Conclusions of the European Council meeting in Cologne 3 and 4 June 1999.
107. See e.g. Case C-578/16 PPU *CK, HF and AS v. Slovenia*; Case C-400/10 PPU, *J. McB. v. L.E.*
108. See e.g. Case C-105/14, *Criminal proceedings against Ivo Taricco and Others*; Case C-578/16 PPU, *CK, HF and AS v. Slovenia*; Case C-617/10, *Åklagaren v. Hans Åkerberg Fransson*; Joined Cases C-411/10 and C-493/10 *NS v. Secretary of State for the Home Department and M. E. and Others v. Refugee Applications Commissioner and Minister for Justice, Equality and Law Reform.*
109. Joined Cases C-411/10 and C-493/10, *N.S. v. Secretary of State for the Home Department and M. E. and Others v. Refugee Applications Commissioner and Minister for Justice, Equality and Law Reform.*
110. Case C-578/16 PPU, *CK, HF and AS v. Slovenia.*
111. Note that there is no mention of the possibility for the EU to offer higher protection. There is no reason, however, why the EU should not be so able.

Charter. This is not so for the traditions of individual Member States. It should be remembered that the principle of primacy of EU law also governs the relationship between EU fundamental rights law and national law of individual Member States (including also rules of constitutional rank). As a consequence, national constitutional rights cannot be invoked against EU law.[112]

While Article 52 is aimed to achieve coherence between the Charter on the one hand and the ECHR and common constitutional traditions of the Member States as sources of general principles on the other, Article 53 is meant to ensure that the Charter is not used to lower existing levels of protection. Article 53 is a so-called non-regression clause, and was adopted mainly in order to make it clear beyond doubt that the Charter does not intend to decrease existing levels of protection offered either by the ECHR or by national constitutions. With regard to the ECHR, the provision does not seem to cause any problems. Indeed, Article 53 of the *ECHR* allows contracting parties to offer more protection in their national laws, and the Convention should not be used as a pretext to decrease existing levels of protection. Article 53 of the *Charter* proclaims that the Charter should not as be interpreted as restricting or adversely affecting human rights and fundamental freedoms as recognized by the ECHR (or other international treaties to which all Member States are parties). Article 53 of the ECHR thus allows more protection under the Charter (but does not oblige it), while Article 53 of the Charter prohibits a decrease of the protection offered by the ECHR. The two provisions seem to be perfectly compatible.[113]

Article 53 of the Charter has given rise to much more controversy in the relation between EU law and Charter rights on the one hand and *national constitutional protection* on the other. The aim of the provision is to ensure that the Charter should not be used as a pretext for national authorities, *within their own scope of application*, to decrease the level of protection offered when the Charter was adopted. When viewed in this way, the provision has a rather limited effect, and does not change the usual relationship between EU law (including the Charter) and national law (including constitutional rights). The normal rule in case of conflict between EU law and national law is straightforward: under the principle of primacy, EU law trumps national law, and national law has to be set aside when it conflicts with EU law. This general rule of primacy also applies in cases of alleged conflict between EU law and national constitutional rights. Such cases usually arise in the context of individuals seeking to invoke their constitutional rights against the application of EU law. In those cases, the Court has consistently held ever since *Internationale Handelsgesellschaft*, that constitutional rights cannot be invoked against EU law.

Article 53 of the Charter has sometimes been interpreted as introducing an exception to this simple rule of primacy, and as allowing for unilaterally setting aside EU law where it lowers national constitutional protection. This is not, however, the way in which the Court has interpreted Article 53. In the *Melloni* case referred by the Spanish *Tribunal constitucional*, the Court of Justice had to answer the question whether, based on Article 53, a national court could refuse to apply the framework decision on the European Arrest Warrant where its application would breach national constitutional rights. The Court of Justice rejected the view that Article 53 of the Charter can be read as a general authorization to a Member State to apply the higher national constitutional standard of protection, and to give it priority over the application of provisions of EU law, because this would undermine the principle of the primacy of EU.[114] The Court's answer

---

112. This is a simple application of the principle of primacy as proclaimed in Case 11/70, *Internationale Handelsgesellschaft*. There is still uncertainty as to whether an exception could be made when the national fundamental right at stake is part of national identity or the core of the Constitution. Many constitutional courts maintain that that is indeed the case.
113. Nevertheless the Court of Justice sees a problem in the coexistence of both Arts. 53 and requires them to be coordinated, Opinion 2/13 on Accession to the ECHR, see *supra*.
114. ECJ, Case C-399/11, *Melloni v. Ministerio Fiscal*.

is somewhat circular: Article 53 Charter does not contain an exception to primacy, because of the primacy of EU law.[115] But in the Court's view, Article 53 of the Charter confirms that national fundamental rights continue to apply when Member States implement EU law, subject to two conditions: the application of the national constitution may not lower the level of protection offered by the Charter as interpreted by the Court and secondly, it may not compromise the primacy, unity and effectiveness of EU law. Two situations can thus be distinguished. Where EU law leaves a margin of discretion to the Member States, they remain free to apply their constitutions in addition to the Charter, and they can offer more protection, within the space left by EU law. This is evident and does not require the permission of Article 53 of the Charter: where EU law leaves the Member States a choice between two options, one of which would be unconstitutional and the other constitutional, it is evident that EU law does not preclude a choice for the constitutional option. Take for example the decision of the German *Bundesverfassungsgericht* where it annulled the German law transposing the data retention directive, because the legislature had not used the discretion left in the directive to choose an implementation that was in conformity with the Basic Law.[116] This is perfectly in line with EU law, as was also stated in *Åkerberg Fransson*, handed on the same day as *Melloni*, where the Court held that national fundamental rights may serve as a standard of review to be used by national courts when "the action of the Member States is not entirely determined by EU law", subject to the conditions mentioned above.[117] It could even be argued that Article 53 Charter imposes an obligation under EU law to maintain the "higher" national level of protection in such cases.

Where, on the other hand, EU law does not leave any discretion to the Member States, and the national constitution offers a higher level of protection, the latter cannot be invoked against EU law. The level of protection is then defined exclusively by EU law, more specifically, by the Charter and EU general principles, and where relevant by EU secondary law. In these cases, the Charter has the effect of harmonizing fundamental rights in the scope of EU law, and Member States are not allowed under EU law to deviate from the common standard. They can, however, have recourse to other techniques and mechanisms offered by EU law to derogate from EU obligations. The famous Omega case illustrates this nicely. In that case, the CJEU permitted derogation from the free movement rules, since the protection of fundamental rights was considered a legitimate interest capable of justifying a restriction of the obligations imposed by EU law. The harmonizing effect of EU fundamental rights is thus not absolute, and is subject to exceptions, in so far as allowed under EU law.

This harmonizing effect of the Charter imposes a great responsibility on the Court of Justice, in view of the promise contained in *Internationale Handelsgesellschaft* that EU law would, instead of the national courts protecting national constitutional rights, ensure such protection on the basis of general principles of EU law. If the Court offers to replace the constitutional

115. For arguments as to why Art. 53 Charter should not be read as restricting the primacy of EU law, see B. De Witte, "Art. 53" in S. Peers, T. Hervey, J. Kenner and A. Ward (Eds.), *The EU Charter of Fundamental Rights – A Commentary* (Hart, 2014), 1523–1538.
116. *Bundesverfassungsgericht*, decision of 2 Mar. 2010 (*data retention*), see A. Kaiser, "German Federal Constitutional Court – German data retention provisions unconstitutional in their present form: Decision of 2 Mar. 2010", 6 EUConst (2010), 503–517. See also the decision of the *Czech* constitutional court, decision of 22 Mar. 2011, Pl. ÚS 24/10 (*data retention*) with references to the German, Romanian, Bulgarian and Cypriot constitutional courts which had similarly annulled the implementing legislation, and, strikingly, a reference to Joined Cases C-92/09 and C-93/09, *Schecke and Eifert*, where the Court emphasized the necessity to provide, in a manner as stringent as possible, the guarantees and instruments for protecting the fundamental rights of individual when handling their personal data generated in course of electronic communications.
117. ECJ, Case C-617/10, *Åklagaren v. Hans Åkerberg Fransson.*

courts, it must take its role of guardian of fundamental rights seriously. And it is here that the decision in *Melloni* is most disappointing. The Court rejected the application of the Spanish standard on the ground that the framework decision reflected "the consensus reached by all the Member States regarding the scope to be given under EU law to the procedural rights enjoyed by persons convicted in absentia who are the subject of a European arrest warrant." This, however, is not the point: it is the mission of the Court to review whether that consensus reached by the Member States[118] in a legislative document complies with the EU fundamental rights as laid down in the Charter, protected under general principles and as informed by the ECHR. To state that the Member States (i.e. the governments convening in the Council) have consented to the legislation is hardly convincing. The real question was whether they were allowed to do so under the Charter. Furthermore, the Court should have reiterated that when executing an EAW, the Member States are implementing EU law and hence, are bound to respect fundamental rights (Articles 6 TEU and 51(2) Charter). More specifically with respect to the position of the Spanish constitutional court, it is disappointing that the Court does not show awareness of the problem the referring court is confronted with and does not engage with its arguments.

6.2 *The coexistence of national constitutional rights, the ECHR and EU fundamental rights: The national perspective*

The *ECHR* has been made effective in one way or other in most of its Contracting Parties and in all member States of the European Union.[119] There are many different ways of giving effect to the ECHR. In some countries, the ECHR (like other international treaties) is as such part of the law of the land, and has been awarded a higher rank in the legal order, allowing national courts to use it as a standard for review, such as in Belgium, France and the Netherlands. In the Netherlands, the ECHR (and other international human rights treaties) operates as virtually the only standard for review, at least in relation to Acts of Parliament, as the Constitution does not have the same bite as international treaties. In France and Belgium, ordinary courts and constitutional courts compete for legal authority over fundamental rights cases. In France, the *contrôle de constitutionnalité* (*Conseil constitutionnel*) and *contrôle de conventionnalité* (ordinary courts) are separated. In Belgium, both the Constitutional Court and the ordinary courts apply and enforce the ECHR. In most of these countries, the courts seek to interpret the Constitution in light of the ECHR.

In other countries, the courts are under a constitutional obligation to interpret national law and/or the national constitution in line with the ECHR. Sometimes, this is prescribed in the Constitution, as is the case in Article 10 of the Spanish Constitution. In Austria, for instance, human rights protection, both of constitutional rights and of the ECHR, used to be the business

---

118. Or rather: the EU legislature, in which the Member States governments play a crucial role. It is important to stress here that the Member States are represented in the Council *by their governments*. The Spanish government voted in favour of a framework decision that infringed the constitutional rights as expounded by its constitutional court. See on this point L. Besselink, "The parameters of constitutional conflict after *Melloni*", (2014) EL Rev., 531–552.

119. Appendix to Recommendation Rec(2004)6 of the Committee of Ministers to Member States on the improvement of domestic remedies (12 May 2004), at 3–4: Convention has "become an integral part of the domestic legal orders of all states parties". On the impact of the ECHR in the domestic legal orders of EU Member States see the comparative essays in J. Gerards and J. Fleuren (Eds.), *Implementation of the European Convention on Human Rights and of the Judgments of the ECtHR in National Case Law. A Comparative Analysis* (Intersentia, 2014); H. Keller and A. Stone Sweet, *A Europe of Rights. The Impact of the ECHR on National Legal Systems* (OUP, 2008); and G. Martinico and O. Pollicino (Eds.), *The National Judicial Treatment of the ECHR and EU Laws. A Comparative Constitutional Perspective* (Europa Law Publishing, 2010).

of the *Verfassungsgerichtshof*. The ECHR has, indeed, been granted constitutional rank in Austria. Ordinary courts can and must interpret national laws in so far as possible in line with the ECHR, but when such conform interpretation is impossible, courts of first instance are obliged to apply the law even if it seems to infringe the ECHR. Courts of appeal must refer such cases to the *Verfassungsgerichtshof* as the sole court competent to strike down the law on grounds of its unconstitutionality.[120]

In other countries, the ECHR has been incorporated by intervention of the legislature, given a special status in the legal order, and put in the hands of the courts, such as in the UK and in Sweden. In Sweden, the UK and in the Netherlands, the courts tend to follow the case law of the Strasbourg Court meticulously. Since there is no traditional of strong courts and review of legislation, they tend to restrictively interpret their role as ECHR courts, applying the ECHR minimum as a maximum.

All this is different for the *Charter*, which is part of primary EU law and thus takes on its characteristics, including direct effect and primacy. In contrast to the ECHR, EU law does dictate the effect and rank of the Charter in the domestic legal orders of the Member States. Most national courts do apply the Charter, but they struggle with defining its scope. National courts may also find themselves caught between conflicting obligations, when there is a discrepancy between EU law and the Charter as interpreted by the CJEU on the one hand, and the ECHR as interpreted by the ECtHR on the other. When they do find themselves in such a situation, the only court they can turn to is the CJEU, as there is no preliminary reference procedure before the ECtHR. Several courts have made references to the CJEU indicating that they had doubts about the compatibility of EU law with the ECHR. The Court of Justice generally rephrases these kinds of references, and stresses the autonomy of EU law and EU fundamental rights law (while admitting that the Charter must be interpreted in accordance with the ECHR as interpreted by the ECtHR). In a sense, this approach is to be commended in the light of the subsidiary character of the ECHR, which assumes that ECHR rights are protected in the domestic systems of the Contracting Parties, and by extension, by the EU. The ECHR and the ECtHR only step in when the domestic systems have failed to respect the rights protected in the ECHR, and only provide minimum protection. Converging on the ECtHR level of protection implies aligning with the ECHR minimum. Yet, at the same time, and since EU fundamental rights law is by nature multi-sourced, the CJEU should pay due regard to the case law of the ECtHR, and engage with it, since this is for many national courts their first point of reference when it comes to fundamental rights protection.

A case in point is *J.N.*, where the Dutch Council of State raised a question concerning the validity, in the light of Article 6 of the Charter and point (e) of the first subparagraph of Article 8(3) of Directive 2013/33, pointing out that, according to the Explanations relating to the Charter, the rights provided for in Article 6 thereof correspond to those guaranteed by Article 5 of the ECHR and have, by virtue of Article 52(3) of the Charter, the same meaning and scope as those laid down by the ECHR. The referring court pointed out that Article 5(1)(f) ECHR as interpreted by the ECtHR suggested that the Directive must be invalid, since it allows for the detention of an asylum seeker only if such detention was imposed with a view to removal. The CJEU went out of its way to emphasize the autonomy of EU law and the CJEU, and stated that it would solely review the conformity of the directive with the Charter, and not with the ECHR which as such does not form part of EU law. It did concede that the Charter had to be

120. See P. Cede, "Report on Austria and Germany" in G. Martinico and O. Pollicino (Eds.), *The National Judicial Treatment of the ECHR and EU Laws. A Comparative Constitutional Perspective* (Europa Law Publishing, 2010), at 63.

interpreted in conformity with the ECHR, but it then quickly added that EU measures must be interpreted, as far as possible, in such a way as not to affect their validity and in conformity with primary law as a whole and, in particular, with the provisions of the Charter.[121] Such conform interpretation is widely used by many courts, including constitutional courts, in order to save legislation from annulment, while at the same time upholding the constitution. However, it can be argued that the technique is less convincing in multi-layered systems such as the EU, where fundamental rights systems coexist, and legislative and regulatory power is shared between actors belonging to different systems. The CJEU thus aims to maintain the validity of the Directive, but shifts the responsibility for compliance with the Charter (and hence with the ECHR) to the EU legislature and the national implementation.

While the CJEU's approach on the relationship between the EU and the ECHR may be technically correct, its insistence on the autonomy is unnecessary to say the least, and is not helpful for national courts, especially in those systems where these courts are in their own national system expected to apply the ECHR directly. By overemphasizing the autonomy of the Charter and then offering its own interpretation of the ECHR and the case law of the ECtHR, the CJEU may alienate the national courts.

Further reading

De Búrca, G., "After the EU Charter of Fundamental Rights: The Court of Justice as a human rights adjudicator?", 20 MJ (2013), 168–184.

Dawson, M., *The Governance of EU Fundamental Rights* (CUP, 2017).

Dougan, M., "Judicial review of member state action under the general principles and the Charter: Defining the scope of Union law", (2105) CML Rev., 1201–1245.

Kuijer, M., "Fundamental rights protection in the legal order of the European Union" in A. Lazowski and S. Blockmans (Eds.), *Research Handbook on EU Institutional Law* (Edward Elgar, 2016), 220–259.

de Mol, M., *De directe werking van de grondrechten van de Europse Unie* (Wolf Legal Publishers, 2014).

Peers, S., T. Hervey, J. Kenner and A. Ward (Eds.), *The EU Charter of Fundamental Rights. A Commentary* (Hart, 2014).

Spaventa, E., "Fundamental rights in the European Union" in C. Barnard and S. Peers (Eds.), *European Union Law*, 2nd ed. (OUP, 2017), 227–261.

de Vries, S., U. Bernitz and S. Weatherill (Eds.), The EU Charter of Fundamental Rights as a Binding Instrument – Five Years Old and Growing (Hart Publishing, 2015).

121. ECJ, Case C-601/15 PPU, *J.N. v. Staatssecretaris van Veiligheid en Justitie.*

CHAPTER 5
THE POLITICAL INSTITUTIONS

*D.M. Curtin, P.J. Kuijper and R.H. van Ooik**

1. Introduction

After its establishment by the Maastricht Treaty in 1993, the European Union as such had only one organ of its own: the European Council (former Art. 4 TEU). For the rest, the Union "made use of" or "borrowed" the five Institutions of the former European Communities: the European Parliament, the Council, the Commission, the Court of Justice and the Court of Auditors. Together with the European Council they formed a "single institutional framework" which should ensure the consistency and continuity of all of the Union's activities, while respecting and building upon the *acquis communautaire* (former Art. 3 TEU). Today, after the Treaty of Lisbon has entered into force, things are less complicated: the European Council as the only organ of the previous EU and the five Institutions of the European Communities are now all Institutions of the (revised) *Union*. The European Central Bank was added to the list of official institutions so that currently the Union has seven institutions (Art. 13 TEU).

Of these seven EU institutions only the "political" ones will be examined in some depth in this chapter, i.e. those institutions that are involved in the setting of the agenda for, and the making and the implementation of, the Union's most important policy decisions. These political institutions are the European Council, the Council, the Commission and the European Parliament. The other main institutions – Court of Justice, Court of Auditors and European Central Bank – are dealt with in other chapters of this book. Independent bodies, closely linked to, or inside the broad ambit of, other institutions, such as the Ombudsperson, OLAF, and the Independent Data Supervisor, will be mentioned in passing in this chapter or elsewhere in this book. At the end of the chapter some space is reserved for two Advisory Bodies, the Economic and Social Council and the Committee of the Regions, which are directly linked to the legislative process of the Union, because their advice on many subjects is a formal legal requirement, when legislation is being considered. The chapter concludes with a brief discussion of three subjects that are directly relevant to all institutions of the Union: privileges and immunities, the seat of the institutions and their linguistic regime.

In view of its importance and overarching status the *European Council* is examined first (section 2, below). The institutional structure is of decisive importance for the balance of powers within the Union, and the two most important actors involved in the legislative process are still the *Council* and the *Commission*, even after the various Treaty changes. The latter institution has also been given important non-legislative tasks (sections 3 and 4, below). At the outset, the

---

* D.M. Curtin: Law Department, European University Institute, Law Faculty, University of Amsterdam. P.J. Kuijper: Law Faculty, University of Amsterdam. R.H. van Ooik: Law Faculty, University of Amsterdam.

European Parliament played only a modest role on the European stage, but since 1979 the Parliament has been directly elected and its role in the Union has gradually grown in importance, in particular when it comes to the adoption of EU legislation (section 5).

The discussion of each of these four institutions focuses on (1) its internal organization, including its composition and applicable voting rules (2) its tasks and powers, and (3) its relations to other institutions. Thus, each institution is discussed separately (or "vertically") but from the perspective of these three important "horizontal" themes.

2. The European Council

2.1 *Internal organization*

The European Council, just like the Council of the European Union (Section 3 below), is a body composed of the Heads of State or Government – together with the Presidents of the Commission and of the European Council itself. They do not act in their personal capacity, but rather as representatives of their respective national interests. The Treaties make this profusely clear by stating that "Member States are represented in the European Council by their Heads of State or Government and in the Council by their governments..."[1] The background, composition, decision-making procedures, and auxiliary bodies of the European Council are examined in detail below.

2.1.1 *Establishment*

The European Council was established, on 9–10 December 1974. According to the communiqué issued at the conclusion of that Summit, the Heads of State or Government announced that henceforth they would meet three times a year, accompanied by their Foreign Ministers, as a formation of the Council of the European Communities, for the work on political cooperation.[2] Although the European Council was established outside the Community framework, it acquired an explicit Treaty basis in 1987, in the Single European Act (SEA). Article 2 SEA provided that the European Council brought together the Heads of State or Government of the Member States and the President of the Commission; it was assisted by the Foreign Ministers and by a Member of the Commission, and met at least twice a year. Article D TEU (Maastricht) and later Article 4(2) TEU (Nice) maintained this provision more or less word-for-word, adding that the chairmanship of the European Council was to be held by the Head of State or Government which held the Presidency of the Council, for a period of six months.[3] With the entry into force of the Treaty of Lisbon, the European Council became one of the seven institutions of the Union and acquired a permanent president. The provisions governing it under the current legal order are Article 15 TEU, Articles 235–236 TFEU and the Rules of Procedure of the European Council.[4]

1. Art. 10(2) TEU, second subpara.
2. European Commission, "8th General Report on the activities of the European Communities 1974", Bull-EC 12-1974, Annex, 347, 7. See, generally, J. Werts, *The European Council,* (John Harper, 2008); W. Wessels, *The European Council,* (Palgrave-MacMillan, 2015), and the extensive literature cited therein, and H.J. Glaesner, "The European Council" in D. Curtin and T. Heukels (Eds.) *Institutional Dynamics of European Integration* (Festschrift for Schermers, Vol. II, 1994), 101.
3. See further U. Puetter, *The European Council and the Council: New Intergovernmentalism and Institutional Change* (OUP, 2014), section 3.3.
4. European Council Decision 2009/882 of 1 Dec. 2009 adopting its Rules of Procedure, O.J. 2009, L 315/51.

2.1.2 *Composition*

Presently, the European Council is composed of thirty members: its President, the Heads of State or Government of the 28 Member States, and the President of the Commission. The High Representative of the Union for Foreign Affairs and Security Policy also takes part in its work,[5] but is not an official member. "When the agenda so requires", the members of the European Council may each be assisted by a minister, and the Commission President may be assisted by a member of the Commission.[6] Prior to Lisbon, the Ministers of Foreign Affairs and a Commission member had a right to assist these respective members of the European Council (ex Art. 4 TEU). Hence, since Lisbon the foreign ministers no longer automatically take part in the European Council meetings.[7] The Treaties provide that the European Council shall meet twice every six months, but that the President shall convene special meetings when the situation so requires.[8] In practice, since early 2000s and especially since 2008 (start of the financial crisis), the meetings of the European Council have been much more frequent, reaching up to ten times per year in 2011 and 2012.[9]

President of the European Council

As stated above, under the Lisbon Treaty, the European Council has a permanent President who is elected by the European Council by qualified majority for a term of two and a half years, which may be renewed once.[10] The President is officially a technical chairman: his task is to chair and stimulate the work of the European Council and to ensure the preparation and continuity of its work. He also represents the Union, "at his level", on issues concerning the common foreign and security policy and "without prejudice to the powers of the High Representative of the Union for Foreign Affairs and Security Policy".[11] Whether *in reality* the President has more far-reaching (political) influence, is very much dependent on the personality and professional skills of the individual in office. The President does not hold a national office.[12] The first President of the European Council was Herman van Rompuy, a former Prime Minister of Belgium. He was elected on 1 December 2009; his term was renewed in 2012; and it ended in November 2014. His term of office was dominated by the euro crisis and he regarded himself, and was, a confidence builder.[13] His successor sought international visibility and had quite a lot to do with the EU's eastern border – a task facilitated by Donald Tusk's previous role as Prime Minister of Poland.

---

5. Art. 15(2) TEU.
6. Art. 15(3) TEU.
7. See also *infra* section 3.3.
8. Art. 15(3) TEU.
9. U. Puetter, "The European Council – The new centre of EU politics", Swedish Institute for European Policy Studies, 16 EPA (2013), 7.
10. Art. 15(5) TEU.
11. Art. 15(6) TEU.
12. Ibid.
13. P. de Schoutheete, "The European Council after van Rompuy", Jacques Delors Institute, Notre Europe (2015), 2. Available at <www.institutdelors.eu/media/europeancouncil-deschoutheete-jdi-april15.pdf?pdf=ok>.

2.1.3 *Voting arrangements*

Decisions in the European Council are taken by consensus "except where the Treaties provide otherwise".[14] Thus, in certain cases, it acts by simple majority[15] or by qualified majority.[16] The rules governing voting in the Council apply to the European Council when it acts by qualified majority.[17] When votes are cast, any member of the European Council may also act on behalf of *one* other member; the European Council President and the President of the Commission do not take part in the vote; and abstentions by members do not prevent the adoption of acts by unanimity.[18] Since the High Representative is formally not a member of the European Council, he or she does not participate in the vote. The European Council Rules of Procedure also provide for a written vote procedure for decisions on urgent matters.[19] The procedure may be used when all members of the European Council having the right to vote agree to that procedure.

2.1.4 *Auxiliary bodies*

Some commentators describe the European Council as a "power station not connected to the grid"[20] as it depends on the Council and the Commission to implement its decisions. Indeed, unlike the pre-Lisbon President of the European Council, the new permanent President cannot rely on national administrative resources to carry out his will.[21] Instead, the European Council depends on the General Affairs Council (GAC) and the General Secretariat of the Council for support. Article 15(6)(b) TEU states that the President of the European Council must ensure the preparation and continuity of the work of the European Council "on the basis of the work of the General Affairs Council" while Article 16(6) TEU provides that the GAC "shall prepare and ensure the follow-up to meetings of the European Council, in liaison with the President of the European Council and the Commission".

The European Council is also to be assisted by the General Secretariat of the Council under Article 235(4) TFEU. Further details on the nature of this assistance are supplied in the Rules of Procedure of the European Council. Thus, the Secretary-General of the Council attends the European Council meetings and takes all the necessary measures for the organization of proceedings.[22] This key role of the Council Secretariat, which functions as interface and communication channel between the European Council presidency and the largely more transient six-month Council presidency, has increased the role and significance of this already increasingly powerful (but somewhat hidden) actor.[23] The European Council has moved in early 2017 to the new Europa building, which it shares with the Council (of Ministers). There both institutions will

---

14. Art. 15(4) TEU.
15. E.g. for procedural matters and for the adoption of its Rules of Procedure – Art. 235(3) TFEU.
16. E.g. deciding on the Council configurations and the presidency of those configurations – Art. 236 TFEU.
17. Art. 235(1) TFEU, second subparagraph. See also *infra* section 3.1.3.
18. Art. 235(1) TFEU. There is not a maximum of abstentions that will invalidate a decision, as is the case in Art. 31(1), second subpara TEU in connection with the so-called constructive abstention in the CFSP. On the other hand there is the quorum that has to be present, when voting takes place, namely two-thirds of the Members, without weighting their votes. See Art. 6(3) Rules of Procedure of the European Council, op. cit. *supra* note 4.
19. Art. 7 Rules of Procedure of the European Councils, op. cit. *supra* note 4.
20. Cited in P. Bocquillon and M. Dobbels, "An elephant on the 13th floor of the Berlaymont? European Council and Commission relations in legislative agenda setting", 21 JEPP (2014), 20–38, 24.
21. Ibid.
22. Art. 13 Rules of Procedure of the European Council, op. cit. *supra* note 4.
23. D. Curtin, *Executive Power of the European Union: Law Practices and the Living Constitution* (OUP, 2009), 77.

continue to be serviced by the Council Secretariat and to present themselves to the outside world effectively as one entity.[24]

2.2 *Political powers and functions*

When it comes to the powers and the functions of the European Council, it is noteworthy that there is a significant discrepancy between the powers listed in the Treaty and the powers that this institution exercises in practice.[25] What is certain is that "[t]he European Council is central to the EU's decision-making process" and "no important developments internally or externally occur without having been considered by the European Council".[26] The role of the European Council in agenda setting, legislation, administration, and the Union budget are discussed below.

2.2.1 *Agenda setting*

Article 15(1) TEU clearly sets out the agenda-setting powers of the European Council by stating that it "shall provide the Union with the necessary impetus for its development and shall define the general political directions and priorities thereof". The term "priorities", which was introduced by the Lisbon Treaty,[27] underlines the agenda-setting role of the European Council. Another Lisbon innovation, the permanent presidency of the European Council, is also said to further enhance its powers in this area.[28] Aside from the general mandate in Article 15(1) TEU, there are also policy-specific provisions, which highlight the agenda-setting powers of the European Council. In two areas of Union policy, the European Council is specifically tasked with identifying "the strategic interests and objectives of the Union' in the Union's external action[29] and with defining "the strategic guidelines for legislative and operational planning within the area of freedom, security and justice".[30]

2.2.2 *Legislation*

The Lisbon Treaty precludes legislation by the European Council as is evident from the text of Article 15(1) TEU, which provides that the European Council "shall not exercise legislative functions". However, there is a difference between formal and informal legislative agenda setting, and some commentators argue that while the Commission is in charge of formally proposing and drafting legislation,[31] the European Council does play a key part in informal legislative agenda setting.[32] Moreover, the European Council has an important role in resolving differences between Member States in key areas such as multi-annual budget legislation, and it sometimes sets deadlines for the adoption of (and adopts guidelines on the content of) legislation such as the post-crisis measures in the area of the Economic and Monetary Union.[33]

The instances when the European Council intervenes in legislative decision-making, also in the TFEU domain, usually entail a "deadlock in the Council or a slowdown in important

---

24. One street address, one website and one e-mail address for the two institutions.
25. U. Puetter, op. cit. *supra* note 3, 78–79.
26. P. Craig and G. de Búrca, *EU Law: Text, Cases and Materials*, 5th ed. (OUP, 2011), 49.
27. P. Craig, *The Lisbon Treaty, Revised Edition: Law, Politics, and Treaty Reform*, (OUP, 2013), 85.
28. Ibid., 105.
29. Art. 22(1) TEU.
30. Art. 68 TFEU.
31. See *infra* section 4.2.1.
32. P. Bocquillon and M. Dobbels, op. cit. *supra* note 20, 21–23.
33. S. Peers, "The EU's political institutions" in C. Bernard and S. Peers (Eds.), *European Union Law* (OUP, 2014), 67.

legislative processes", and in these cases the European Council assumes the role of a "steering committee" and "final arbiter" at times coordinating the legislative work of the Council also horizontally.[34] A good recent example is the finalization (late December 2016) of the Commission proposals on the modernization of the so-called trade-defence legislation, before it was sent to the European Parliament. Part of these proposals had been in the Council's drawers for three years.[35]

2.2.3 *Non-legislation: administration/governance*

Under the Treaty of Lisbon, the European Council exercises a wide range of non-legislative functions. First, it decides on certain *constitutional* matters: it plays a key part in the Treaty revision process under Article 48 TEU and serves an important function in enlargement as it specifies the conditions of eligibility for EU membership under Article 49 TEU and withdrawal of a Member State from the Union under Article 50 TEU. Second, it decides on a number of key *institutional* matters such as the composition of the EP and the Commission, the appointment and dismissal of the High Representative, the configurations and the presidency of the Council, and the selection of the President and the Board of the ECB.[36]

In addition, a recent study suggests that in the post-Maastricht era, the European Council has gained increasing *prominence in new areas of EU activity*, which are governed through policy coordination by the top leaders of the EU Member States rather than through the classic "Community" method. According to the study, currently the three main areas where the European Council plays a crucial role are economic governance; foreign, security and defence policy; and social and employment policies.[37] Unsurprisingly, these were the fields in which the Maastricht Treaty defined the policy-making role of the European Council in more specific terms than its general mandate of providing impetus for the development of the EU.[38] With regard to the Common Foreign and Security Policy, the Treaties provide that the European Council (along with the Council) shall define and implement the Union's policy in this field.[39] It also "shall identify the Union's strategic interests, determine the objectives of and define general guidelines for the common foreign and security policy, including for matters with defence implications".[40]

Non-legislative decision-making by the European Council often takes the form of decisions. Article 12 of the European Council Rules of Procedure provides:

> 1. Decisions adopted by the European Council shall be signed by its President and by the Secretary-General of the Council. Where they do not specify to whom they are addressed, they shall be published in the Official Journal of the European Union. Where they specify to whom they are addressed, they shall be notified to those to whom they are addressed by the Secretary-General of the Council.

---

34. U. Puetter, op. cit. *supra* note 3, 77.
35. Council Proposal of 10 Apr. 2013 for a Regulation of the European Parliament and of the Council amending Council Reg. 1225/2009 on protection against dumped imports from countries not members of the European Community, 2013/0103(COD) and Council Reg. 597/2009 of 9 Dec. 2016 on protection against subsidized imports from countries not members of the European Community, 2013/0103(COD). See on the deadlock in the Council: E. Zalan, "EU countries agree to reinforce trade defence", (2016) *EUobserver.* Available at <euobserver.com/economic/136260>.
36. Respectively Arts. 14(2) TEU, 17 TEU, 18(1) TEU, 236(a) and (b) TFEU, and 283(2) TFEU.
37. U. Puetter, op. cit. *supra* note 9. See also Puetter, op. cit. *supra* note 3.
38. U. Puetter, op. cit. *supra* note 3, 80.
39. Art. 24(1) TEU. See further on the CFSP Ch. 40, "Common foreign and security policy and common security and defence policy", of this book.
40. Art. 26(1) TEU.

2. The provisions concerning the form of acts set out in Annex VI to the Rules of Procedure of the Council shall apply mutatis mutandis to decisions of the European Council.

One noteworthy aspect of these provisions is that they highlight the role of the Secretary-General of the Council in non-legislative decision-making by the European Council.

3. The Council (of Ministers) of the European Union

3.1 *Internal organization*

The Council is the Institution of the Union in which the Member States are represented as such and by means of which they participate in the political and legal activities of the Union. The members of the Council do not sit in a personal capacity, but as representatives of their Member State (Art. 16(3) TEU). Each of them acts on the instructions, and by a mandate, of his or her government.

In this the Council differs from the Commission, whose members are independent.[41] In the Council, therefore, the Union's interest, which the Council as an institution is as much required to protect as the Commission, will be viewed through the lens of national interests. According to the subject matter and the political climate in the EU, the lens will be more or less tinted. A pure protection of national interests which encroaches upon essential interests of the Union, however, conflicts with the responsibility which the Member States making up the Council bear for the protection of the interests of the Union.[42]

In practice the Member State governments nowadays have extensive contacts with their national parliament's relevant committees in preparation for Council meetings. The United Kingdom was the first Member State to practice systematic "parliamentary scrutiny"; other Member States followed over the years. It has become a normal practice in the Council and its preparatory bodies, such as Coreper, to place a parliamentary scrutiny reservation on a particular decision and to lift it at a later date, once the relevant parliamentary committee has finished its consideration or lifted its objection. In some instances this can lead to considerable delays in the decision-making.

The background, composition, decision-making procedures, and auxiliary bodies of the Council are discussed below.

3.1.1 *Establishment*

The Council of the European Union gave itself this name soon after the 1992 Treaty on European Union (i.e. Maastricht Treaty) had entered into force.[43] Prior to that, it was known as the Council of Ministers (of the European Communities). By giving itself this new name, the Council wanted to emphasize that it had acquired important powers (of decision making) in the so-called second and third pillars of the European Union, as established by the Maastricht Treaty. Its official name according to the Treaties was, and is, however simply "the Council".

The Council of the EU should not be confused with the *European Council* which is an entirely different institution of the Union (see Section 2 above), nor should this Council be confused with the *Council of Europe*, which is an entirely different international organization (with now 47

41. Art. 17(3) TEU and Art. 245 TFEU. See further *infra* section 4.1.2.
42. See Joined Cases 2 & 3/60, *Niederrheinische Bergwerks-AG et al. v. High Authority* on this responsibility.
43. Council Decision 93/591 of 8 Nov. 1993 concerning the name to be given to the Council following the entry into force of the Treaty on European Union, O.J. 1993, L 281/18.

members). Under the current legal regime, the Council is governed by Article 16 TEU, Articles 237–243 TFEU and its Rules of Procedure.[44]

3.1.2 *Composition*

Article 16(2) TEU provides that the Council is composed of "a representative of each Member State at ministerial level, who may commit the government of the Member State in question and cast its vote". This provision, formulated as such since the Maastricht Treaty, makes it possible for members of *regional* governments to be the representatives of the Member States, provided that the minister in question is competent to commit the Member State as a whole.[45] The provision also makes clear that only persons holding a political office, rather than civil servants, may be members of the Council.[46] The composition of the Council is not static: it meets in various configurations, which, under the current legal regime, are determined by the European Council in accordance with Article 236 TFEU.[47] The Treaty mentions two of these configurations – the General Affairs Council and the Foreign Affairs Council.[48] Both of these are composed of the foreign ministers of the EU Member States. Presently, there are eight other configurations: Agriculture and Fisheries; Justice and Home Affairs; Economic and Financial Affairs; Employment; Social Policy, Health and Consumer Affairs; Competitiveness; Education, Youth, Culture and Sport; Transport, Telecoms and Energy; and Environment.[49] The current practice is that the General Affairs, Agriculture and Fisheries, Foreign Affairs Council and Economic and Financial Affairs Councils meet every month, while the other configurations meet every two or three months.[50]

The members of the Council hold the Presidency of the Council on the basis of equal rotation, the conditions of which are determined by a European Council decision.[51] This rule does not apply to the Presidency of the Foreign Affairs Council, which is held by the High Representative.[52]

3.1.3 *Voting arrangements*

The Council votes according to three different voting procedures: qualified majority, unanimity and simple majority. Article 16(3) TEU provides that the Council must act by qualified majority unless the Treaties provide otherwise. Thus, since the entry into force of the Treaty of Lisbon,

---

44. Council Decision 2009/937 of 1 Dec. 2009 adopting the Council's Rules of Procedure, O.J. 2009, L 325/35 (CRP).
45. R.H. Lauwaars, "De institutionele bepalingen in het EU-Verdrag", (1992) SEW, 678–679; see also J.W. de Zwaan, *The Permanent Representatives Committee – its role in European Union decision-making* (T.M.C. Asser, 1995).
46. A. Dashwood et al., *European Union Law*, 6th ed. (Hart Publishing, 2011), 46.
47. Art. 16(6) TEU. See also *supra* section 2.2.3.
48. Art. 16(6) TEU, second and third subparas.
49. Decision of the Council (General Affairs) 2009/878 of 1 Dec. 2009 establishing the list of Council configurations in addition to those referred to in the second and third subparagraphs of Art. 16(6) of the Treaty on European Union, O.J. 2009, L315/46, amended by European Council Decision 2010/594 of 16 Sept. 2010 amending the list of Council configurations, O.J. 2010, L 263/12.
50. S. Peers, op. cit. *supra* note 33, 55.
51. Art. 16(9) TEU and Art. 236(b) TFEU. European Council Decision 2009/881 of 1 Dec. 2009 on the exercise of the Presidency of the Council, O.J. 2009, L 315/50; further details in Council Decision 2009/908 of 1 Dec. 2009 laying down measures for the implementation of the European Council Decision on the exercise of the Presidency of the Council, and on the chairmanship of preparatory bodies of the Council, O.J. 2009, L 322/28.
52. Art. 18(3) TEU.

qualified majority has become the default voting procedure in the Council. Before Lisbon, voting by a simple majority was the default procedure, defined as voting by a majority of the votes of the Council's component members – and so *not* of the Council members actually present and voting (see ex Art. 205 EC). After Lisbon, this definition of "simple" has not changed (see Art. 238(1) TFEU).

Hence, when the Treaties explicitly mention this voting modality, the Council can act by a *simple* majority, which is the case with some minor, mainly procedural, issues.[53] The same goes for *unanimous* voting: it only applies when the Treaty basis in question explicitly mentions it. This is the case for some sensitive areas such as common foreign, security and defence policy, taxation, parts of employment law and environmental law and – last but not least – deciding under the legal basis for "unforeseen cases" of Article 352 TFEU.

The minimum quorum required for proceeding to a vote is more than half of the Members who are entitled to vote, i.e. those members who are represented at ministerial level.[54] It is also worth mentioning that any member of the Council may vote on behalf of one other member,[55] and abstentions do not prevent the adoption of acts that require unanimity.[56]

Qualified majority

With regard to the rules on *qualified majority* voting, under the Treaty of Lisbon these rules have been modified[57] so that qualified majority is defined as "at least 55% of the members of the Council, comprising at least fifteen of them and representing Member States comprising at least 65% of the population of the Union". Moreover, a blocking minority must include at least four Member States.[58] The rules are slightly different in the (rare) cases when the Council is not acting based on a proposal from the Commission or from the High Representative;[59] when not all members of the Council are participating in voting (for example in the case of "enhanced cooperation");[60] or when both of the aforementioned conditions are present.[61]

It must be noted however that these changes to the definition of qualified majority have become applicable only gradually, passing through two transitional regimes between 1 December 2009 and 31 October 2014[62] and between 1 November 2009 and 31 March 2017.[63] During this second period, both the pre- and post-Lisbon rules were concurrently applicable,[64] and the Lisbon regime entered into force completely only on 1 April 2017.

It is often said that Council chairs in reality continue to look for consensus. In practice, however, looking for consensus has become much easier, now that the asterisk rule has been introduced into the Rules of Procedure.[65] The placing of this asterisk next to a point on the agenda

53. E.g. Arts. 4, 6, 13, 150, 160, 240, 241, 245, 247 and 337 TFEU.
54. Art. 11(4) CRP, cited *supra* note 44.
55. Art. 239 TFEU.
56. Art. 238(4) TFEU. There is the exception in case of constructive abstention, Art. 31(1) 2nd subpara TEU.
57. Art. 16(3)–(5) TEU, Art. 238(2)–(3) TFEU and Protocol (No 36) on Transitional Provisions annexed to the Lisbon Treaty govern the new qualified majority voting regime.
58. Art. 16(4) TEU.
59. Art. 238(2) TFEU.
60. Art. 238(3)(a) TFEU.
61. Art. 238(3)(b) TFEU.
62. See Art. 3(3) of Protocol (No 36) on Transitional Provisions, annexed to the Lisbon Treaty. During this period the pre-Lisbon qualified majority voting, with its weighting of votes, depending of the seize of the population, was still in place even after the entry into force of the Lisbon Treaty.
63. Ibid., Art. 3(2).
64. S. Peers, op. cit. *supra* note 33, 59.
65. Art. 3(2) CRP, cited *supra* note 44.

indicates that voting is possible on that point. The placing itself is a notarial task, performed by the Council Secretariat, and indicates that "all the procedural requirements provided by the Treaties have been complied with". This removes the onus of putting an item up for voting from the Presidency alone and makes pressure from the Commission on the Presidency to this effect unnecessary. As soon as the asterisk appears, all Member States and the Commission can ask for a vote, which the Presidency must proceed with. This has made voting easier and the readiness to compromise of a minority, which is not sure that it will have the votes to block, greater, as soon as the asterisk appears with an item on the agenda. This greater readiness to compromise often leads to consensus in the end.

Ioannina compromise

It should be mentioned here that in the so-called *Ioannina Compromise*, further rules were set in relation to the acceptance of qualified majority voting in the Council.[66] The current, revised version of the Compromise is contained in Council Decision 2009/857.[67] It states that if a certain minority of Member States indicate their opposition to the Council adopting an act by a qualified majority, the Council shall "discuss the issue". Next, the Council shall, in the course of these discussions, "do all in its power to reach a satisfactory solution" to address concerns raised by the minority. To this end, the President of the Council shall undertake any initiative necessary to facilitate a wider basis of agreement in the Council. The members of the Council shall lend him or her their assistance.[68] But that is it. Accordingly, as some authors have correctly pointed out, "a small number of Member States can delay the adoption of legislation by qualified majority, the Council being required to undertake further discussion in an attempt to address their concerns".[69] However, in the end that small number cannot prevent the majority from adopting the Council act and hence they can still be outvoted.

Despite this rather limited importance, the Ioannina Compromise Decision enjoys a great degree of "constitutional protection" as Protocol No. 9 annexed to the Lisbon Treaty effectively aims to prevent it from being amended or repealed: a preliminary deliberation on the European Council on the proposal to amend or repeal is required.[70]

3.1.4 *Auxiliary bodies*

The Council is assisted by three types of auxiliary bodies: the Committee of Permanent Representatives (commonly referred to as Coreper); working groups and committees; and its General Secretariat.

Coreper

Coreper is composed of the ambassadors of the EU Member States. The task of this committee is to prepare the work of the Council and to carry out any other duties assigned to it by the

---

66. The Ioannina compromise takes its name from an informal meeting of foreign ministers in the Greek city of Ioannina on 27 Mar. 1994. The text of the Compromise was published in *Agence Europe*, Document No. 1879 of 14 Apr. 1994. The Council Decision, which was part of the compromise, was also published in O.J. 1994, C 105/1; it was amended by a Decision at Brussels on 1 Jan. 1995, O.J. 1995, C 1/1.
67. Council Decision 2009/857 of 13 Dec. 2007 relating to the implementation of Art. 9C(4) of the Treaty on European Union and Art. 205(2) of the Treaty on the Functioning of the European Union between 1 Nov. 2014 and 31 Mar. 2017 on the one hand, and as from 1 Apr. 2017 on the other, O.J. 2009, L 314/73.
68. Ibid.
69. E. Berry, M. J. Homewood and B. Bogusz, *Complete EU Law: Text, Cases, and Materials* (OUP, 2013), 33.
70. A. Dashwood et al., op. cit. *supra* note 46, 50.

Council.[71] Coreper adopts procedural decisions in cases provided for in the Council's Rules of Procedure.[72] Moreover, according to Article 19(2) of the Rules of Procedure, "[a]ll items on the agenda for a Council meeting shall be examined in advance by Coreper unless the latter decides otherwise. Coreper shall endeavour to reach agreement at its level to be submitted to the Council for adoption". If agreement is reached indeed, the issue will appear on the agenda of the Council as a so-called "A" item.

Coreper is divided in two: Coreper I is made up of deputy heads of the Permanent Representations and deals with technical and legal questions; Coreper II consists of the Permanent Representatives themselves and deals with political, financial and institutional questions.[73] Matters relating to the CFSP and CDSP are followed and prepared in the Political and Security Committee (PSC), consisting of junior ambassadors of the member States, which functions *de facto* almost as a Coreper for this sector, although formally it has to report to the Foreign Affairs Council through Coreper II.[74] The two Corepers and PSC together form a permanent two-way transmission belt for the exchange of information between the national administrations and the institutions of the Union. Within the Member States, the individual members of Coreper participate in the shaping, among different departments of government, of the national positions, which they will have to defend in Coreper. At the same time they have to convince their governments of certain "realities" inherent in the negotiations in Coreper. J. Linthorst Homan, the first occupant of the Dutch seat in Coreper II, characterized his function as a Janus-like ambassadorship: envoy of the Netherlands to the EEC and envoy of the EEC to the Dutch government.[75]

Coreper does not, however, have independent powers of decision, except for the procedural decisions mentioned above.[76] This is slightly different for the PSC, which during so-called crisis management operations may take the necessary decisions on the political control and strategic direction of such operations.[77] Together the two Corepers and the PSC, as the bodies preparing the decision-making of the Council, *de facto* play an important and influential role.

Working groups and committees

The role of working groups and committees is evident from Article 19(3) of the Rules of Procedure which provides that "[c]ommittees or working parties may be set up by, or with the approval of, Coreper with a view to carrying out certain preparatory work or studies defined in advance". In practice, these working groups agree on the texts of many measures to be formally adopted by the Council. The more politically sensitive issues are referred to Coreper, and if the latter is unable to reach an agreement, the measure is referred to the ministers as a "B" item.[78]

However, empirical research has shown some time ago that a very large proportion of decisions pass through the upper ministerial and sectoral levels as "A" items on the agenda.[79] An "A" items implies that the issue has been settled at a lower level, and it will usually be passed as a matter of course at the higher level with no further discussion required. Ministers, when meeting in

71. Art. 240(1) TFEU.
72. Art. 240(1) TFEU. The list of procedural decisions is provided in Art. 19(7) CRP, cited *supra* note 44.
73. J.W. De Zwaan, op. cit. *supra* note 45, 140–144.
74. See Art. 38 TEU, which contains a "no prejudice" clause with respect to Art. 240 TFEU.
75. J. Linthorst Homan, *Wat zyt gy voor een vent. Levensherinneringen* (Koninklijke van Gorcum B.V., 1974).
76. See Case C-25/94, *Commission v. Council*, where the Court ruled that Coreper cannot take decisions under Art. 145 EC (now Art. 202 TFEU). However, the Council's vote confirming Coreper's decision can have legal effects and can thus be subjected to an act of annulment and reviewed by the Court, para 21 et seq.
77. See Art. 38 TEU *in fine*.
78. S. Peers, op. cit. *supra* note 33, 63.
79. M.P.C.M. van Schendelen, "The Council decides: Does the Council decide?", 33 JCMS (1996), 531–548.

the Council, will therefore concentrate on the "B" items of the agenda, indicating the – much smaller – number of items on which officials or permanent representatives have not been able to reach agreement in their preparatory meetings. This means that the decisions (taken by the lower echelons in the hierarchy) are approved as such without any substantive negotiation or even discussion in the *political* forum of the Council of the EU. In effect, it follows that a large proportion of Council decisions are being taken by either the lower-level civil servants sitting in working parties or the higher-level national civil servants sitting in committees, regardless of the actual impact of these "Council" decisions on the lives of ordinary European citizens and businesses. The high number of legal acts passed in the so-called "A" item procedure thus shows the importance of Coreper as well as the whole committee system behind it for the ability of the Council to actually take decisions.[80]

General Secretariat

The Council is also assisted by a General Secretariat,[81] under the leadership of the Secretary-General appointed by the Council by qualified majority.[82] The General Secretariat is "closely and continually involved in organising, coordinating and ensuring the coherence of the Council's work and implementation of its 18-month programme. Under the responsibility and guidance of the Presidency, it [assists] the latter in seeking solutions".[83] It is worth mentioning that following the Treaty of Amsterdam and until the entry into force of the Lisbon Treaty (and thus the creation of a permanent post of a High Representative), the Secretary-General formally was also the High Representative for the Common Foreign and Security Policy.[84]

At a general level, it should be noted that the Council machinery (and the Commission machinery for that matter) is geared to produce a decision at the lowest possible level, in the different working groups and committees, after which the rest of the procedure follows a paper trail before being officially sealed at the political level in the Council, without further debate. Exceptionally there are so-called *"faux points B"* for those cases in which a decision is basically reached, but requires one or more Member State to make a statement.[85]

---

80. See further J. Lempp and J. Altenschmidt, "The prevention of deadlock through informal processes of "supranationalization": The Case of COREPER", 30 EI (2008), 511–26; D. Curtin, op. cit. *supra* note 23.
81. For a more detailed discussion on the General Secretariat, see D. Curtin, op. cit. *supra* note 23, 84; T. Christiansen and S. Vanhoonacker, "At a critical juncture? Change and continuity in the institutional development of the Council secretariat", 31 WEP (2008), 751–770.
82. Art. 240(2) TFEU; Art. 23(1) CRP, cited *supra* note 44. Before the Treaty of Nice he was appointed by unanimity.
83. Art. 23(3) CRP, cited *supra* note 44.
84. See D. Edward and R. Lane, *Edward and Lane on European Union Law* (Edward Elgar, 2013), para 3.38. The Treaty of Amsterdam, however, also created the new post of Deputy Secretary-General of the Council, who was to take care of the running of the General Secretariat so as to allow the Secretary-General to devote himself largely to the duties of HR. This prepared the way for the complete split between these functions in the Treaty of Lisbon. The first occupant of this job, Pierre de Boissieu, was in the mold of earlier Secretaries-General, a highly experienced diplomat, whereas Javier Solana, as SG/HR, had a much more political profile, see M. Westlake and D. Galloway, *The European Council,* (John Harper, 2006), 343 et seq.
85. See F. Lavadoux and M-V Grasset, "Strategic planning tools for European negotiators to defend their national interests in the Council of the European Union", (2013) EIPA, 71.

3.2 Political powers and functions

3.2.1 Agenda setting

The Council's agenda-setting role is inextricably linked to its presidency, as the president controls the Council's agenda and vote.[86] More specifically, in accordance with Article 2(6) of its Rules of Procedure, the Council's 18-month programme is prepared by the group of three Member States holding the Council Presidency for that period. It is also noteworthy that the programme is prepared in cooperation with the Commission, the President of the European Council, and the High Representative.[87] As each Member State sets out its programme and priorities for its six-month presidency, this is "an opportunity for the Member State concerned to make its mark on the direction of the EU, EU policy, and legislation".[88]

3.2.2 Legislation

The Council used to be the principal legislator of the Union. However, with successive Treaty amendments, the European Parliament has gained increasing legislative powers. Currently, Article 16(1) TEU explicitly provides that the Council shall exercise legislative functions jointly with the EP, and the ordinary legislative procedure, which entails joint decision-making by the Council and the EP, has become the default legislative procedure in the EU.[89] In the specific cases provided for by the Treaties, the Council legislates through a special legislative procedure, which predominantly stands for Council decision-making on its own, but usually with consultation or the consent of the EP.[90]

All these Council acts are directly based on the Treaties (often the TFEU) and they all constitute "legislation" in Lisbon terminology, whether they were adopted under the ordinary legislative procedure or under a special legislative procedure. This can be inferred from Article 289(3) TFEU which states that "legal acts adopted by legislative procedure shall constitute legislative acts". The ordinary legislative procedure is provided in the Treaty provisions on, for example, transport, agriculture and the internal market.[91] Legislative acts (of general application) of the Council alone can be found in the area of competition,[92] State aid,[93] the Area of Freedom, Security and Justice,[94] et cetera.

The provisional agenda of the Council meetings is divided into two parts: a part entitled "Legislative deliberations" which deals with deliberations on legislative acts and a part entitled "Non-legislative activities" which deals with non-legislative activities. Article 16(8) TEU mandates that the Council meet in public "when it deliberates and votes on a draft legislative act". In reality, this part of the deliberative meetings are telecasted to a large room elsewhere in the Council building, which is open to the press and to the public. Furthermore the Council meetings are broadcasted using video streaming, remaining available for at least a month.[95] However, the usefulness of such "open legislative meetings" is not great. Many legislative items are "A"

86. Ibid.
87. Art. 2(6) CRP, cited *supra* note 44. P. Craig, op. cit. *supra* note 27, 104.
88. E. Berry, M.J. Homewood and B. Bogusz, op. cit. *supra* note 69, 34.
89. Art. 289 TFEU.
90. A. Turk, "Lawmaking after Lisbon" in A. Biondi, P. Eeckhout and S. Ripley (Eds.), *EU Law after Lisbon* (OUP, 2012), 69.
91. Arts. 91, 43(2) and 114 TFEU, respectively.
92. Art. 103(1) TFEU.
93. Art. 109 TFEU.
94. For example, Arts. 70 and 74 TFEU.
95. Arts. 7(3) CRP, cited *supra* note 45.

items and often the discussion on legislative "B" items are perfunctory, when not yet "ripe" for decision, or shift to informal meetings in smaller groups or "confessionals" with the Presidency, outside the Council Chamber, when a qualified majority is not immediately there.[96] There is nothing surprising about this; the Council has become too large to continue to function as a small club, where everything is discussed in the plenary, and has become subject to the decision-making dynamics that is well-known in national parliaments and in the European Parliament itself.[97]

Next to the legislative deliberations, the Council has opened up the initial discussions concerning non-legislative matters, insofar as these will result in legally binding rules for the Member States. The Presidency is charged with deciding which non-legislative matters should be discussed in public and for which length of time, but Coreper or the Council may modify that decision by a simple majority.[98] Moreover, the Council is bound to have public deliberations on its own and the Commission's long-term agenda of activities and legislation. Furthermore the Council or Coreper may decide by qualified majority to open other deliberations to the public on important issues affecting the interests of the European Union and its citizens. The means for opening up the meetings are the same as in the case of legislative deliberations.[99]

3.2.3 *Non-legislation: administration/governance*

Article 16(1) TEU provides that the Council "shall carry out policy-making and coordinating functions as laid down in the Treaties". As to the Council's coordinating powers, under Article 5 TFEU, it coordinates the economic,[100] employment[101] and social policies of the Member States.[102] As regards the Council's policy-making functions, Article 291(2) TFEU is relevant: it states that the Council also exercises – at "tertiary" level – implementing powers "in duly justified cases".

Some authors argue that certain binding acts of the Council following the special legislative procedure do not constitute legislation.[103] However, as was pointed out above, Article 289(3) TFEU seems to exclude this possibility since it states that all acts adopted by a legislative procedure (ordinary *and* special) are automatically legislative acts. This would have been relevant for the standing requirements for private parties seeking an action for annulment before the Court under Article 263(4) TFEU, as the standing requirements for "regulatory acts" are more relaxed than for legislative acts.[104]

96. J-P. Jacqué, *Droit Institutionnel de l'Union européenne*, 8th ed. (Dalloz, 2015), 352 -355.
97. Ibid., 354.
98. Art. 8(1) CRP, cited *supra* note 44.
99. Art. 8(2),(3) and (4) CRP, op. cit. *supra* note 44.
100. In this regard, Art. 121(1) TFEU provides: "Member States shall regard their economic policies as a matter of common concern and shall coordinate them within the Council [...]".
101. Art. 146(2) TFEU provides: "Member States, having regard to national practices related to the responsibilities of management and labour, shall regard promoting employment as a matter of common concern and shall coordinate their action in this respect within the Council [...]".
102. S. Peers, op. cit. *supra* note 33, 56.
103. See, E. Best, "Legislative procedures after Lisbon: Fewer, simpler, clearer?", 15 MJ (2008), 85–96, 93–95.
104. See Ch. 10, "The Court of Justice of the EU", section 2.2.4.

4. The European Commission

4.1 The College of Commissioners

4.1.1 Composition, appointment and censure

As opposed to the Council and the European Council, discussed above, the European Commission is not there to defend national interests of Member States but the "general interest of the EU' instead. It was already established in the original Treaty of Rome (1958) and in fact even earlier, in 1952, in the European Coal and Steal Community (ECSC) Treaty – though under the name of "High Authority". It was precisely the establishment of this independent institution, with its power to adopt binding decisions for the coal and steel industry, which did not have to be ratified, that made the ECSC call itself a "supranational" organization.

The European Commission – which in Article 13 TEU is referred to, simply, as "the Commission" – now consists of twenty-eight members who have to be nationals of a Member State, one from each Member State. In the past two nationals of each of the five large countries were appointed, and one national of each of the smaller countries.[105] However, the Nice Treaty abolished the second commissioner from the larger Member States, by stating that when the Union would reach 25 Member States, the number of commissioners was to be reduced to the number of Member States.[106] This number of commissioners was later increased to 27 as a result of the accession of Bulgaria and Rumania on 1 January 2007 and then to 28 as a result of the accession of Croatia on 1 July 2013.[107]

The Commission has a President and a number of Vice-Presidents, the latter being appointed by the President,[108] except for the Vice-President/High Representative, who is appointed by the European Council in agreement with the President of the Commission. The European Council can discontinue the HR/VP according to the same procedure (Art. 18 TEU). The Commission adopts its own Rules of Procedure so as to ensure that both it and its departments operate in accordance with the provisions of the relevant Treaty.[109]

Since the entry into force of the Lisbon Treaty, the members of the Commission are appointed in accordance with the following procedure (Art. 17(7) TEU). First of all, the European Council nominates a person for appointment as the new president of the Commission; it must take into account the outcome of the elections to the European Parliament and after having held the appropriate consultations. Next, this nomination must be approved by the European Parliament. Then the Council, in agreement with the nominated president, draws up a list of the other candidates for membership of the Commission. Finally, the composition of the Commission as a whole is submitted for the approval of the European Parliament; only following this approval the new Commission may be appointed by the Council.[110] The appointment is for five years and may be renewed.

---

105. Former Art. 213(1) EC as it read until the entry of the Protocol on Enlargement on 1 February 2003, annexed to the Treaty of Nice, O.J. 2001, 080/49.
106. As a result of Art. 4(1) Protocol on Enlargement, attached to the Nice Treaty, – now non-existent.
107. See below for the Lisbon provision stating that the number of commissioners would be reduced to two thirds (Art. 17 TFEU) and the EU's response to the Irish "no" to Lisbon.
108. Art. 17(6)(c) TEU. The Vice-President(s) deputize for the President, chairing the weekly meeting of the Commission in his absence.
109. Art. 249(1) TFEU. See European Commission Rules of Procedure, O.J. 2000, L 308/26, last amended by Commission Decision 2011/737 of 9 Nov. 2011, O.J. 2011, L 296/58.
110. This right of Parliament to approve the Commission recalls the French system of investiture, i.e. a vote of confidence in the new government.

In practice the European Parliament requests *individual* candidates to submit to hearings concerning their political ideas, their work program for the years to come and also their knowledge of EU affairs. In case of unsatisfactory answers, the EP may threaten to refuse to approve the entire Commission team – after which the candidate's country will probably come up with a less controversial figure. For example, in October 2004 the Parliament refused to agree with the appointment of the proposed Italian commissioner Buttiglioni because of his views on non-discrimination (Art. 19 TFEU); the nominated President, Mr Barroso, thereupon had to withdraw his proposal for the new Commission. Only after Mr Buttiglioni had been replaced by another Italian (Mr Frattini), did Barroso succeed in obtaining Parliament's approval.

All decisions of the Council in the appointment process shall be adopted by qualified majority. This is important since in this way it is made impossible for one Member State to prevent the appointment or reappointment of a President or Member of the Commission it does not like.[111]

While in the end the Council appoints the members of the Commission, it cannot remove them during their five-year term of office. The *Court of Justice* alone, on the application of the Council or the Commission, may compulsorily retire an individual member of the Commission from office if he or she no longer fulfils the conditions required for the performance of his duties or if he has been guilty of serious misconduct (Art. 247 TFEU).[112]

In addition, the European Parliament can compel the Commission to resign as a body by adopting a motion of censure on its activities (Art. 234 TFEU).[113] If such a motion of censure on the activities of the Commission is put before the European Parliament, it shall observe a "cooling off" period of at least three days after the motion has been tabled before deciding by open vote. If the motion of censure is supported by at least a two-thirds majority of the votes cast, representing a majority of the component members of Parliament, the members of the Commission *shall* resign as a body, while the High Representative shall resign only from duties that she carries out as a member of the Commission. All these Commission members shall remain in office and continue to deal with current business until they are replaced by a new team. The term of office of the members of the Commission appointed to replace them shall expire on the date on which the term of office of the members of the censured Commission would have expired.

4.1.2 *Characteristics of the Commission*

Independence

Strictly speaking, the attention given to the division of the seats of the Commission according to nationality ought to be unnecessary, for these nationals are not representatives of the Member States. On the contrary, they have the right and the duty to perform their tasks with complete independence in the general interest of the Union, and Member States shall ensure their independence and are forbidden to seek to influence them in the performance of their tasks.[114] They are to refrain from any action incompatible with the nature of their duties. Also the other EU institutions, bodies, offices and entities are prohibited from influencing the Commissioners. The only exception relates to the High Representative, who is also one of the vice-presidents of

---

111. For instance, one may recall the problems surrounding the appointment of the president of the Commission in 1995, after the United Kingdom used its veto to block the appointment of Mr. Dehaene, the Belgium Prime Minister. Instead, Mr. Santer, the Prime Minister of Luxembourg, was nominated.
112. The power of the President to force a member of the Commission to resign, is discussed below, see 132 below and accompanying text.
113. See also R. Corbett et al. *The European Parliament*, 4th ed. (John Harper, 2000).
114. Arts. 17(3) TEU and 245 TFEU.

the Commission; she may receive instructions from the Council in the area of the CFSP (Art. 18(2) TEU).

During their term of office, Commissioners may not engage in any other occupation, and even after they have ceased to hold office they are required, just as ordinary Commission officials, "to behave with integrity and discretion as regards the acceptance [...] of certain appointments or benefits".[115] Privileges and immunities ensure undisturbed performance of their duties.[116] The Commissioners are, however, subject to a special Code of Conduct[117] that was first developed by the Prodi Commission in the aftermath of the 1999 abdication of the *Santer* Commission in connection with widespread integrity problems *inter alia* due to certain actions by Commissioners Bangemann and Cresson.[118] The Prodi Commission at that time (2000) undertook a broad administrative overhaul of the Commission with a view to bringing it up-to-date with modern approaches to public sector management.[119]

The principle of collegiality when taking decisions

All decisions of the Commission are taken by the college of Commissioners and are attributable to the Commission as a whole;[120] they are taken by simple majority (Art. 250 TFEU).[121] The Commission as a whole is responsible to the European Parliament (Art. 17(6) TEU) and the President has to safeguard collegiality (Art. 17(8) TEU). The Commissioners are thus forced into strong solidarity; this reinforces their independence and protects them at the same time. Any attempt at untoward influence by a Member State on "its" Commissioner is counteracted by the influence, always, of other Commissioners during deliberations in the College. At the same time, any attempt to single out a specific Commissioner as politically responsible for a specific decision will fail because all decisions are taken collectively.[122] This does not mean that the Commission cannot empower individual Members to take certain categories of decisions

---

115. This provision (now Art. 245 TFEU) was relevant when the member of the *Santer* Commission, Bangemann, who was responsible for telecommunications, announced in June 1999 that he would accept a position with the Spanish telecom firm Telefónica. The Council asked the Court of Justice in that case to deprive Bangemann of his pension rights (Case C-290/99, *Council v. Bangemann*, see Council Decision of 9 July 1999 on the referral of the case of Mr. Bangemann to the Court of Justice, O.J. 1999, L 192/55). Bangemann requested the annulment of this Council Decision in the Court of First Instance (Case T-208/99, *Bangemann v. Council*). Both cases were withdrawn in the framework of a compromise reached between the two parties, after Bangemann finally did not take the job (Council Decision of 17 Dec. 1999 on the settlement of the Bangemann case, O.J. 2000, L 16/73). Another relevant case is that of Edith Cresson, also a member of the *Santer* Commission, which abdicated after her misbehaviour came to light thanks to the whistleblower Paul Van Buitenen, see Case C-432/04, *Commission v. Cresson*. The Court condemned her for favouritism, but did not impose the sanction of deprivation of pension rights. The case of former President Barrroso, who accepted a job at *Goldman Sachs International* twenty months after his Commission ended, was put in the hands of the Commission's Ad hoc Ethical Committee. In its report, the Committee remonstrated Mr. Barroso for his ill-considered judgment, but could not find legal reasons to decide that he had violated his duty of integrity and discretion, since the so-called cooling-off period of 18 months had elapsed. See <ec.europa.eu/transparency/ethics-for-commissioners/index_en.htm> (last visited 10 February 2017).
116. Protocol (No. 7) on Privileges and Immunities of the European Union, annexed to the consolidated version of the Treaty of Lisbon, O.J. 2012, C 326/1, Arts. 19 and 11–14.
117. European Commission, "Code of Conduct for Commissioners", C(2011)2904 final, is the present version.
118. See 116.
119. See D. Curtin, op. cit. *supra* note 23, 113 et seq. and literature mentioned there.
120. The importance of the principle of collegiality is demonstrated by the fact that Art. 1 Rules of Procedure of the Commission, cited *supra* note 109, is devoted to repeating it.
121. The quorum of the Commission for taking valid decisions is a majority of the Members.
122. J.-P. Jacqué, op. cit. *supra* note 96, 390–391, with a reference to Case C-137/92 P, *Commission v. BASF*, for the Court's principled view of collegiality at paras. 63 and 64.

in their field of competence,[123] as long as such empowerments (*habilitations* in French) are of a purely administrative nature and explicitly granted by the college. As the Court puts it, this is necessary "in order to prevent the rule requiring collective deliberation from having a paralysing effect on the full Commission".[124]

In addition, the Commission may delegate the adoption of management or administrative measures to Directors-General or Heads of Department acting on its behalf, again under the conditions imposed by the college.[125] Both empowerments and delegations can be sub-delegated, in particular for individual decisions awarding grants and contracts.[126]

Much more important decisions, proposed by one or more Commissioners, may be taken by written procedure, provided that the relevant departments of the Commission, among which always the Legal Service, have approved it beforehand. Here the collegial deliberation is replaced by collegial written approval by all Commissioners.[127]

Attempts to reduce the number of Commissioners

For obvious reasons, the Member States are anxious that the Commission is composed in such a way that a certain insight into and sympathy for the various national ways of thinking, the – sometimes divergent – national aspirations and the very real problems which beset various parts of the Union are guaranteed to a reasonable extent.

A reduction in the number of commissioners appears, however, desirable both from the point of view of internal cohesion and to ensure a more even distribution of portfolios. Such reduction was envisaged by the Treaty of Nice after the enlargement to 27 Member States. The number of commissioners would "be less than the number of Member States"; the members of the Commission would be chosen according to a system of rotation to be adopted by the Council acting unanimously.[128] Current Article 17(5) TEU, as amended by the Lisbon Treaty, provides that the number of commissioners shall, as of 1 November 2014, correspond to *two thirds* of the number of Member States. The members of the Commission will be chosen on the basis of a system of equal rotation between the Member States, whereby the following principles must be respected: Member States must be treated on a strictly equal footing, and the composition of the Commission will at all times sufficiently reflect the demographical and geographical differences between the Member States.

However, a concession was made to Ireland in order for it to ratify the Lisbon Treaty after the holding of a second referendum,[129] consisting in the use by the European Council of the last part of Article 17(5) TEU, namely its competence "to alter this number" (of two thirds), by a unanimous decision. Hence, quite peculiarly, this "safeguard clause" was already activated *before*

123. Art. 13 Rules of Procedure of the Commission, cited *supra* note 109.
124. This is the case, for instance, with a number of procedural decisions in the process of taking individual competition decisions, see Case 5/85, *Akzo v. Commission,* para 31 et seq. These are standing empowerments. Individual empowerments can also be granted by the Commission, for instance in order to finalise the text of a document already fully discussed during a Commission meeting.
125. Art. 14 Rules of Procedure of the Commission, cited *supra* note 109. Such delegations are granted primarily in the framework of procurement procedures, the selection of development projects etc.
126. Ibid., Art.15.
127. Ibid., Art. 12. If a Commissioner or his cabinet objects, and the problem is not solved, an oral deliberation and a vote may become necessary.
128. Former Art. 4(2) Protocol on Enlargement to the Treaty of Nice, cited *supra* note 50.
129. See S. Quinlan, "The Lisbon Treaty Referendum 2008", 24 Irish Pol. Stud. (2009), 107–121, 111; M. De Bruyn, "The Irish referendums on the Lisbon Treaty: Did the recession save Lisbon?", 20 JCER (2012), 91–101, 94; D. Curtin, "Ierland en het Verdrag van Lissabon: Van 'nee' naar 'ja'?" in R.H. van Ooik & R.A. Wessel (Eds.), *De Europese Unie na het Verdrag van Lissabon* (Europa in beeld 6, 2009), 85.

the entry into force of the Lisbon Treaty. As a consequence, that the number of commissioners in the Juncker Commission (2014–2019) has remained one per Member State, thus guaranteeing Ireland "its" Commissioner.[130] The possibility of reintroducing a reduction of the number of Commissioners, however, remains open.

The Commission's President

As a result of the Treaty of Nice, the position of the *President* of the Commission was strengthened. Former Article 217 EC stated that the President had the power of political guidance and that he decided on the internal organization and on the distribution of portfolios among the members of the Commission. Currently, Article 17(6) TEU provides that the President shall: (a) lay down guidelines within which the Commission is to work; (b) decide on the internal organization of the Commission, ensuring that it acts consistently, efficiently and as a collegiate body; (c) appoint Vice-Presidents, other than the High Representative of the Union for Foreign Affairs and Security Policy, from among the members of the Commission. Furthermore, a member of the Commission shall resign if the President so requests.[131] The High Representative of the Union for Foreign Affairs and Security Policy shall resign, in accordance with the procedure of Article 18(1), if the President so requests. That is to say that the President will have to seek approval by two-thirds majority of the European Council.

Under Barroso the Commission indeed has become more presidential, with stronger control by the President of the activities of the individual Commissioners, who are supposed to follow the line of the Commission's legislative programme and have less freedom to develop initiatives in their own corner. In particular, the Secretariat-General of the Commission has been transformed from an administrative machinery shepherding documents and proposals through the weekly Commission meetings and following their progress through the Council and the Parliament into a kind of Cabinet Office in British style, maintaining control and exercising discipline over the Commissioners and their cabinets and services in implementing the Commission programme and executing the President's orders.[132]

Juncker was elected to head the Commission as one of the so-called *Spitzenkandidaten* on the basis of the result of the elections for the European Parliament. He vowed to make the Commission more politically responsive, presumably to the EP. At the same time, the Council to reckon looms large as co-legislator and with Member States often more oriented towards defending their national interest than a primarily politically inspired viewpoint.[133] His way of organizing the Commission is unique, partly inspired by finding a remedy for the too large number of members and partly by seeking to avoid that discussions between 28 Commissioners

---

130. Council Decision of 2 Oct. 2012 concerning the number of members of the European Commission, EUCO 176/12. Available at <register.consilium.europa.eu/doc/srv?l=EN&f=ST%20176%202012%20INIT> (last visited May 2017).
131. See also Art. 3(6) Rules of Procedure of the Commission, cited *supra* note 109. The use of this power was contested in the case of ex-Commissioner Dalli, who as Health Commissioner had had unofficial and confidential meetings with representatives of the tobacco industry without his services being informed of them. President Barroso put Mr Dalli before the choice of being dismissed under Art. 17(6) TEU or to resign voluntarily. Mr Dalli took the latter option, but later asserted that his resignation was in reality a dismissal. Both the General Court and, on appeal, the Court of Justice disagreed and did not see the brandishing of the power of Art. 17(6) as an actual exercise of it, see Case T-562/12, *Dalli v. Commission,* paras. 126–159 and Case C-395/15 P, *Dalli v. Commission,* paras. 74–84.
132. See D. Curtin, op. cit. *supra* note 23.
133. See J. Peterson, "Juncker's political European Commission and an EU in crisis", 55 JCMS (2016), 349–367.

would become a prefiguration of the Council discussions by giving prominent coordinating positions to members from smaller countries. This will be further explained below.

Involvement in national affairs

While it is the duty of the Commission to serve the general interest of the Union as a whole, this does not mean that it has to neglect *national* interests in performing its duties. It will, however, have to consider all matters from the viewpoint of the EU's general interest. Thus, in making its contribution to the policy-making in the Council, where national interests are very much to the fore and frequently clash with each other, it will have to try to find, for these antitheses, solutions which do justice to the Union interest.

It should be noted, though, that just as the Council, which is the natural representative of the various national interests, has nevertheless to protect the essential interests of the Union (see section 3.1. above), the Commission for its part also has to take account of the vital interests of individual Member States. The Commission, therefore, should never help to outvote a Member State if the latter's vital interests might – in the opinion of the Commission – be prejudiced. The Commission bears this responsibility in particular because in most cases under the TFEU and Euratom Treaty qualified majority decisions of the Council can only be reached with its cooperation.[134]

The fact that members of the Commission are obliged to perform their duties in complete independence, in the general interest of the Union, forbids their being prejudiced in favour of or against particular national standpoints or interests, but they may remain politically active and be members of national or European political parties, but their loyalty to the Commission and its positions should prevail over party loyalty.[135] This includes conducting personal discussions with parliamentarians or members of government of their own or other countries, if they wish to do so.[136] However, Commissioners should abstain from public statements or interventions on behalf any political party or trade union of which they are members, except when they are standing for election.[137] Under certain circumstances, e.g. if the free democratic system in a Member State is at issue, there could even be an obligation on members of the Commission, and indeed of the Commission as an institution, to comment.[138]

It is a typical obligation for an *official* to refrain from interference in political questions in the performance of his duties. The Commission, however is not a body of officials which is

---

134. See also Ch. 7, "Law-making", section 2.5, of this book.
135. See Code of Conduct for Commissioners, cited *supra* note 117, point 1.1.
136. See European Parliament, "Written Question No. 10/71 of Mr. Vredeling to the Commission of the European Communities", O.J. 1971, C 61/1. See also Art. 245 TFEU.
137. See Code of Conduct for Commissioners, op. cit. *supra* note 117, point 1.1. For election campaigns they may take "unpaid electoral leave", during which they will be temporarily replaced by a colleague Commissioner.
138. According to the German Secretary of State, Moersch, answering a question by a German Parliamentarian, 21 *Agenor* (1971), 10. In connection with the participation of the FPÖ in the Austrian government, the Commission declared that it shared the concerns of the other Member States, but for its own part strove for a workable relationship with Austria. It based itself in this on its role as guardian of the European Treaties, 3 Europa van Morgen (2000), 25. More recently, see the Communication from the Commission on a procedure for better enforcing the Rule of Law in the EU member States, which procedure lies in between the Art. 258 TFEU infringement procedure and the Art. 7 TEU fundamental values sanction mechanism: European Commission, "A new EU Framework to strengthen the Rule of Law", COM(2014)158 final. The Commission is presently applying this procedure for the first time in the case of Poland; it has issued recommendations to Poland on 27 July and 21 Dec. 2016 based on this procedure, see Commission Press Releases, "Rule of Law: Commission issues recommendation to Poland", IP/16/2643 and "Rule of Law: Commission discusses latest developments and issues complementary Recommendation to Poland", IP/16/4476.

hierarchically subordinate to the Council. It is not subject to instructions from the Council, but is a body bearing its own political responsibility. This is made clear by the provision that it must resign *en bloc* if a political body, the European Parliament, censures its policy (Art. 17(8) TEU and Article 234 TFEU, see also the section below). Moreover it is entrusted, particularly under the TFEU, with a task which has not only an administrative, but also a political content, as appears from the role conferred on it in the formulation of Union *policies*.

It is incorrect, therefore, to equate the Commission with the secretariat of a traditional international organization, in the service of the body representing the member States of the organization. The Commission is one of the EU Institutions; it is a body with its own political responsibility, its own political task. If there is a sort of international secretariat in the Union, it is the civil service structure of the various Institutions and other bodies.[139]

4.2 *The Commission and its services*

4.2.1 *The organization of the Commission's services*

How the Commission is organized internally as a political organ will have repercussions on how it deals with its services and the other institutions of the EU. As briefly mentioned already, President Juncker created six Vice-Presidents, next to the High Representative for Foreign Affairs, Mrs. Mogherini. They were all tasked with co-ordinating a certain field of activity (or "project team"), just as the Treaty had already given this task to the High Representative in the field of Foreign Affairs. One Vice-President, Frans Timmermans (NL), was given the title First Vice-President and charged with inter-institutional relations, with the rule of law and the Charter of Fundamental Rights, and with continuing and reinforcing the *Better Regulation* programme that had been initiated by the Barroso Commission.[140] The other Vice-Presidents are in charge of "project teams"[141] that reflect the political priorities of the Juncker Commission: Digital Single Market, Energy Union, Euro and Social Dialogue and Jobs, Growth and Competitiveness.[142] All these Vice-presidents, except one, Mr. Oettinger (Germany) came from small countries, whereas the Commissioners from important Member-States were given heavy portfolios, like Monetary Union (Moscovici), Financial Markets (Hill), etc. The intention was to turn the Commission, which is much too large at 28 and with not enough work to go around, nevertheless into a well-integrated whole that would pursue a number of broad priority objectives. Ideally this cohesiveness at the political level should be reflected at the administrative level. The jury is still out on this reform of the political level of the Commission.

The most important instruments that the Commission has at its disposal to ensure its political cohesion in pursuing certain objectives and its services' adherence to these objectives are

---

139. E.g. the Council's General Secretariat (see Art. 240(2) TFEU and *supra* section 3.1.4).

140. *Better Regulation* under Barroso (see Communication from the Commission, "Better Regulation for Growth and Jobs in the European Union", COM(2005)97 final,) became *Better Lawmaking* under Juncker and it has culminated for the moment in "Inter-Institutional Agreement on Better Lawmaking" between the European Parliament, the Council and the Commission, O.J. 2016, L 123/1. Note that the European Council is not a party and not bound by it, presumably because it may not exercise legislative functions.

141. Art. 3(4) of the Rules of Procedure, cited *supra* note 109, allows the President to set up such groups of Commissioners.

142. Budget and Human Resources was the one portfolio comprising two Directorates-General that remained what they always were, although it was declared a "project group" including all Commissioners.

respectively the Commissioners' cabinets[143] and the General Secretariat of the Commission. Its head, the Secretary-General, is the head of the Commission civil service.[144]

Each member of the Commission has a personal staff – his or her *cabinet* – which assists him or her, not least by enabling the commissioner to keep abreast of matters falling within his colleagues' portfolios and thus to participate in the collegiate responsibility for the Commission's policies.[145] The *chefs de cabinet* meet weekly to prepare the Commission's meetings. There are meetings of the *chefs de cabinet* at a lower level to prepare specific points on the agenda of the Commission; these meetings include representatives of the service(s) that is (are) responsible for the proposed Commission decision. Members of the General Secretariat are always present at these meetings of the *chefs* at different levels and prepare the report. Their service is responsible for the administrative functioning of the Commission and for guiding the Commission's legislative proposals through the Council and the Parliament, but – as stated earlier – it has become more and more like a UK cabinet office, keeping track of the proper execution of Commission's programme by the other services of the Commission. Two other horizontal services are also represented at the meetings of the chefs de cabinet in different compositions and at the weekly Commission meeting, the Legal Service[146] and the Spokesman's Service.

All these preparatory meetings serve to set the agenda for the weekly Commission meeting, first by separating the agenda (as in the Council) into the items which do not need to be discussed by the Commissioners ("A" items) and those which do ("B" items). And, second, after verifying if the latter are indeed ripe for a decision, preparing the discussion on these "B" items. Very often a consensus is reached, but if not, the Commission acts by a "simple" majority of its Members (Art. 250 TFEU). As the quorum of the Commission is equal to this number, currently at least 15 votes in favour, out of a total number of 28 votes, are needed for the Commission to adopt valid decisions.[147] Thus the Commissioners' cabinets and the General Secretariat, under the watchful eyes of Legal Service and the Spokesman's Group, together function as the transmission belt between the Commission as a political college and the different Directorates General (DGs) of the Commission.

There are at present 19 policy DGs, for example Competition, Climate Action, Health and Food Safety, Economic and Financial Affairs, Mobility and Transport, Maritime and Fisheries etc. Next to the horizontal services already mentioned above, there are eight other such DGs, mainly concerned with the internal servicing of the Commission, such as DGs Budget, Interpretation, Translation, Informatics etc. Finally, there are four DGs occupied with external relations: Trade, Development Cooperation, Neighbourhood and Enlargement, and Humanitarian Aid and Civil Protection. The size of DGs varies between a few hundred and over 2300 for

143. The Commissioners' cabinets and their relations with their DGs are laid down in Art. 19 Rules of Procedure.
144. The powers of the Secretary-General are described in some detail in Art. 20 Rules of Procedure. The present occupant of the post is Alexander Italianer, a Dutchman. His predecessor was Catherine Day (Ireland), who held the post for 10 years and left a strong imprint on the organization.
145. There are rules on the number of members a Cabinet may have and on their nationality: at least three nationalities must be represented and either the chef of cabinet or his deputy shall not have the same nationality as the Commissioner, Communication from the President to the Commission, "The Working Methods of the European Commission 2014–2019", C(2014)9002. In the past cabinets were almost completely single nationality units.
146. The Legal Service combines the vetting of the legality of the Commission's acts that will have legal consequences in the light of the Treaties, the Charter of Fundamental Rights and, if necessary, international law (Art. 23(4) Rules of Procedure) with defending the Commission's and the Union's interests before the EUCJ, national and international courts and tribunals. In these preparatory meetings it serves primarily in the first capacity.
147. Art. 7 and 8(2) Rules of Procedure, op. cit. *supra* note 110. After Brexit, 14 out of 27 votes will be enough.

Translation (due to the 24 official languages). The DGs and Services are headed by Directors-General, who work together with one or more Deputy-Directors-General and also often have one or more special assistants. Below this level DGs are divided in Directions, headed by a Director, and these Directions are each divided into units, each under a Head of Unit, sometimes assisted by a Deputy.[148] There is thus a clear three-layered hierarchical structure in each DG.[149] At the level of the Director-General and his/her team there is constant contact with the cabinet of the responsible Commissioner and with the Commissioner him/herself.

Every time the Commission changes, and in particular when there is a change of President, there is an opportunity to overhaul the Commission's structure, not only where the portfolios of the Commissioners are concerned, but also to create new DGs (e.g. the DG Climate Action in the Juncker Commission) or to redistribute the tasks differently between the DGs (which normally entails a redistribution of Directions or Units). Ideally there should be a close correspondence between Commissioners' portfolios and DG's so that a Commissioner is responsible for one, two, or three full DGs. It is this "requirement" which often leads to shifting Directions from one DG to another, as from a management perspective it is better to avoid two Commissioners sharing a DG.

4.2.2 *The Commission services as part of the EU civil service*

Next to the Commission, each of the Institutions, independent and other Union bodies has its own staff of officials. Some 58,000 staff members (including those employed at research centres) are employed on a permanent or temporary basis by the Union.[150] The majority (about 32,500) are employed in the Commission's services.[151] Irrespective of the Institution for which they work, all officials and other servants form part of a single Union administration in the sense that they are subject to the same set of legal rules, namely the Staff Regulations and Conditions of Employment of other Servants of the EU.[152]

Under the Staff Regulations, an "official of the Union" means "any person who has been appointed, as provided for in these Staff Regulations, to an established post on the staff of one of the Institutions of the Union by an instrument issued by the Appointing Authority of that institution".[153] The legal status of officials is governed entirely by public law (i.e. by the Treaties and the Staff Regulations and rules made thereunder) and is not a contractual relationship.

---

148. This structure is laid down in ibid., Art. 21.
149. Except in the Legal Service, which has a flatter structure with only directions that service one or more DG's, as well as the Commission as a college.
150. This number is based on an estimate of 56,000 made by Maros Sefcovic, the then Commission Vice-President for Interinstitutional Relations and Administration in a speech "A European Civil Service fit for the 21st Century" held on 10 May 2012, and the growth in employment, including temporary staff, of the Commission and of the other institutions and agencies, which could be verified on their websites. Available at </europa.eu/rapid/press-release_SPEECH-12-349_en.htm?locale=en> (last visited May 2017).
151. See the entities mentioned in: European Commission, "HR Key Figures Staff Members", (2017). Available at <ec.europa.eu/civil_service/docs/hr_key_figures_en.pdf>(visited Mar. 2017).
152. Art. 1a, Reg. 31 laying down the Staff Regulations of Officials of the European Communities and Conditions of Employment of other servants of the European Communities, last amended by European Parliament and Council Regulation 423/2014, O.J. 2014, L 129/12.
153. This also applies to persons appointed by Community bodies ("agencies") to whom the Staff Regulations apply under the Community acts establishing them. A number of bodies, including the European External Action Service, Economic and Social Committee and the Committee of the Regions, the offices of the European Ombudsman and of the European Data Supervisor are to be treated as institutions for the purposes of the Staff Regulations (Cf. Art. 1b Staff Reg., cited *supra* note 152).

Other members of staff (referred to as "Contract Staff") are employed on a contractual basis. Most of the latter are employed as local agents performing manual labour or auxiliary services.

The European Ombudsman has arrived at five public service principles that, with slight adaptations, are valid for any public administration. They are: (1) Commitment to the European Union and its citizens; (2) Integrity; (3) Objectivity; (4) Respect for others; and (5) Transparency.[154] Actually principle (1) can simply be reduced to the principle of loyalty, but it is that notion that often causes the most problems for international civil servants themselves and for outsiders.

It is the duty of every EU official, just as of any national official, to be loyal to the authority, which has appointed him, and to the public interest of the Union and its citizens, for the benefit of which he is working.[155] For an international official this duty takes on a special dimension because it means that he must also show himself independent of the government of the state whose nationality he possesses, and that he must not be guided by considerations of national interest. It has, therefore, been laid down that the Union official, in discharging his functions and in determining his conduct, should keep in mind solely the interests of the European Union, without seeking or accepting instructions from any government or from any authority, organization or person outside his Institution.[156]

As a rule, two criteria that are not always easy to combine are applied in recruiting officials of international organizations; they have to satisfy the most exacting demands as to ability, efficiency, and integrity, and at the same time the filling of these posts should be spread as widely and as fairly as possible over all the Member States. In several organizations the latter requirement is in practice a euphemistic expression covering a system of strict national quotas for the division of the posts at every level. These two criteria are also applied in the recruitment of Community officials.[157] Each Institution attempts to maintain a broad and reasonable balance of nationalities across the range of posts.[158] Unlike in most international organizations, the quota system is of subsidiary importance, although it is no secret that the Member States take an active interest in senior appointments. However, the career principle is laid down in Articles 29–31 of the Staff Regulations; and these also provide in Article 7(1) that an official is to be appointed solely in the interests of the service and irrespective of his nationality, and in Article 27 that no single post may be reserved for nationals of a particular Member State.[159]

The *privileges and immunities* of the officials and other servants are laid down in the Protocol on the Privileges and Immunities of the European Union.[160] The Council determines the

---

154. See European Ombudsman, "Public Service Principles for the EU civil service", (2012), which contains further explanations. Available at <www.ombudsman.europa.eu/en/resources/publicserviceprinciples.faces> (visited Mar. 2017).
155. See Case C-274/99 P, *Connolly v. Commission*, and the Order and judgment in Case T-203/95 R and Case T-203/95, *Connolly v. Commission*. See also European Parliament Debates No. 475, 192 (Commission's answer to a question by Bonde concerning Connolly, *The Rotten Heart of Europe* (London, 1995)). It also results from these cases that the duty of "discretion and integrity" continues after leaving the EU civil service or during a leave of absence for personal reasons.
156. Art. 11 Staff Reg., cited *supra* note 152.
157. Ibid., Art. 27.
158. For statistics relating to the distribution of nationalities and gender according to age, category and grade in the Commission civil service, see European Commission, "Staff figures", (2016). Available at <ec.europa.eu/civil_service/about/figures/index_en.htm> (last visited May 2017).
159. These provisions have been regularly relied on in proceedings brought before the Court of Justice and the CFI, see e.g. Case 85/82, *Bernhard Schloh v. Council* (reservation of a particular post for a particular nationality).
160. Protocol on Privileges and Immunities, cited *supra* note 116, also see *infra* section 8.1.

categories of servants to which these privileges and immunities are granted.[161] According to Article 17 of the Protocol, this is in the interest of the Union, not their own personal interest and the relevant institution shall be *required* to waive immunity, if maintaining it is not in the interest of the institution. It was also with reference to this provision that the Court decided, in the first Order in the *Zwartveld* case, that the privileges and immunities have a purely "functional character, inasmuch as they are intended to avoid any interference with the functioning and independence of the [Union]" – and the same applies for the officials of the Union.[162]

The most important immunity for EU civil servants is the immunity from suit and legal process,[163] and the most important privilege is exemption from national taxes.[164]

The immunity from suit and legal process relates to acts performed by the officials in their official capacity. The phrase "in their official capacity" should, according to the Court, be interpreted restrictively. This immunity, therefore, covers only acts which, by their nature, represent a participation of the person entitled to the immunity in the performance of the tasks of the institution to which he belongs.[165]

EU officials and other servants are exempt from national taxes on salaries, wages and emoluments paid by the Union but are, however, liable to a tax levied by the EU itself, which goes into the general budget.[166] The combination of exemption from national taxation but subjection to a Union tax prevents the effective remuneration of EU officials and other servants "firstly and chiefly, [...] from differing according to their nationality or fiscal domicile as a result of the assessment of different national taxes, and secondly [...] from being inordinately taxed as a result of double taxation".[167]

Union officials and other servants are subject to disciplinary rules[168] and can also be held financially liable for any losses suffered by the Union through gross negligence on their part in the exercise of their function or in connection with it.[169] The Court of Justice has unlimited jurisdiction over disputes, which arise in this respect – which means in first instance the General Court. Indeed, pursuant to Article 91 of the Staff Regulations, any dispute concerning the legality of a decision affecting any person to whom the Staff Regulations apply[170] can be brought before the General Court, without prejudice to the right of appeal to the Court of Justice.

---

161. Ibid., Art. 15.
162. Case 2/88 Imm., *J.J. Zwartveld et al.* para 19.
163. Protocol on Privileges and Immunities, op. cit. *supra* note 116, Art. 12(a).
164. Ibid., Art. 12, 2nd para.
165. Case 5/68, *Sayag et al. v. Leduc et al.* In case of criminal acts by the Institution in question, this immunity may be lifted; see Art. 17, 2nd para Protocol on Privileges and Immunities, and the Commission Decision of 1 Mar. 1995, 6431 *Agence Europe* (1995), 8.
166. The tax is levied on the basis of Protocol on Privileges and Immunities, op. cit. *supra* note 117, Art. 12, 1st para, by Council Reg. 260/68 laying down the conditions and procedure for applying the tax for the benefit of the European Communities, O.J. 1968, 56/8, last amended by Council Reg. 1750/2002 of 30 Sept. 2002, O.J. 2002, L 264/15. See Case 3/83, *Abrias et al.* v. *Commission.*
167. Case 32/67, *Van Leeuwen v. City of Rotterdam*, at para 3. See further on national taxation and Community officials also Case 23/68, *Johannes Gerhardus Klomp v. Inspectie der Belastingen*; Case 85/85, *Commission v. Belgium* and Case 260/86, *Commission v. Belgium*. These principles also imply that exempted EU remunerations or pensions cannot be taken into account for the calculation of the income tax of a partner or of a wealth tax, see resp. Case 6-60, *Humblet v. Belgian State* and Case C-558/10, *Bourgès-Manoury v. Direction des services fiscaux d'Eur-et-Loir.* On European Schools and national taxation see Case 44/84, *Hurd v. Jones*. If a national tax is entirely separate from the EU remuneration, it can be levied without problem: Case C-293/91 *Kristoffersen v. Skatteministeriet.*
168. Arts. 86–80 Staff Reg., cited *supra* note 152.
169. Ibid., Art. 22.
170. Which includes an unsuccessful candidate: Case 130/75, *Prais v. Council.*

4.3 The Commission's tasks and functions

According to Article 17(1) TEU, the Commission shall promote the general interest of the Union and take appropriate initiatives to that end. It shall ensure the application of the Treaties, and of measures adopted by the institutions pursuant to them. It shall oversee the application of Union law under the control of the Court of Justice of the European Union. It shall execute the budget and manage programmes. It shall exercise coordinating, executive and management functions, as laid down in the Treaties. With the exception of the common foreign and security policy, and other cases provided for in the Treaties, it shall ensure the Union's external representation. Finally, it shall initiate the Union's annual and multiannual programming with a view to achieving interinstitutional agreements. From all these Commission tasks and functions, we will make a selection and discuss the most important ones more extensively: its role in proposing legislation, its non-legislative tasks, its supervisory role. As the Commission's role in the budgetary procedure and in external representation are discussed in some detail in the relevant chapters,[171] the discussion below will be concentrated primarily on the other tasks and functions mentioned in Article 17(1) TEU.

4.3.1 Participation in the legislative process

The Commission's participation in the legislative activities of the Union is particularly evident in the role it takes in the adoption of EU legislation, since Lisbon officially referred to as "legislative" acts and which are directly based on the Treaties. In practically all cases in which decision-making power is conferred on the Council, or on the Council and the European Parliament together, it/they can act only on the basis of a proposal from the Commission. The Commission thus has the *right of initiative*. This right is, moreover, exclusive – no Commission proposal, no act by the Council.[172] The right of initiative is given even greater significance by the fact that normally the Council may amend such a Commission proposal only by unanimous vote,[173] and the fact that as long as the Council has not taken a decision the Commission may alter its proposal.[174] Moreover it has been accepted by the Court of Justice that the Commission may withdraw a proposal even quite late in the interaction between the Council and the European Parliament, if one of the co-legislators, or both together, have perverted (*"dénaturé"*) the Commission's original proposal from its original function and objective to such an extent that the Commission's proposal lost its *raison d'etre*.[175] In this way the Court put a limit – be it a broad one

171. See Ch. 19, "Budget and finances", and Ch. 39, 40, 41 on the European Union's external action, of this book.
172. There are exceptions to this exclusivity, Art. 129(4) TFEU e.g. permits the Council to adopt certain provisions relating to the European Central Bank on the basis of a proposal from the Commission *or* a recommendation from the ECB. See also Art. 129(3) TFEU. The European Parliament only has a quasi-right of initiative, see section 5.2.1, *infra*.
173. Art. 293(1) TFEU, which however also mentions a few exceptions relating to the ordinary legislative procedure and to some provisions on adopting the budget. The exception in Art. 294(10), for example, concerns decisions of the Council adopting a joint text agreed in the Conciliation Committee with the European Parliament, which can be taken by qualified majority without the Commission having altered its proposal to reflect that joint text. See Case C-344/04, *The Queen ex parte International Air Transport Association (IATA), European Low Fares Airline Association (ELFAA) v. Department for Transport*.
174. Art. 293(2) TFEU.
175. Case C-409/13, *Council v. Commission*, paras. 82–95. See P.J. Kuijper, "Commission's right of withdrawal of proposals: Curtailment of the Commission's Right or Acceptance by the Court of the Commission's long-standing position?", (2015) Acelg, available at <acelg.blogactiv.eu/2015/06/01/>. In this case the Council and Parliament were seeking a compromise, while combining the first and second readings of the proposal and thus formally the Council had not yet acted under Art. 293(2) TFEU, when the Commission withdrew its proposal. The withdrawal was caused by the likelihood that the Council and the Parliament would agree

– to the amending power of the Council and the Parliament as co-legislators, thus protecting the essence of the Commission's right of proposal.[176]

The Commission's participation in the shaping of measures taken by the Council and the European Parliament, however, does not always take the form of a proposal. In some cases the Commission is only empowered to adopt non-binding *recommendations* or *opinions*. Article 17(1) TEU therefore speaks, broadly, of "appropriate initiatives", a term which includes (Commission) proposals, recommendations and opinions. As opposed to proposals, the Council may amend these "atypical" forms of Commission's initiatives not only by unanimity but also by qualified majority, at least if the Treaty legal basis in question states that the Council is to decide by that majority. Such opinions are provided for in, for instance, some articles on EMU.[177] Recommendations forming the basis for action by the Council can be found in some provisions on, for example, (other aspects of) EMU and also in provisions on the Union's external actions.[178] It is not yet clear if such preparatory acts of the Commission are also protected against *"dénaturation"*, but it is not to be excluded.

The Commission may be influenced in its power to make proposals or recommendations by other institutions.[179] First of all, the European Council can use its general power to determine the direction and priorities of the Union (Art. 15 TEU) to ask the Commission to make certain proposals. Secondly the *European Parliament* and the *Council* have a more limited right to ask for proposal from the Commission. Parliament may, acting by a majority of its component Members, request the Commission to submit any appropriate proposal on matters on which it considers that a Union act is required for the purpose of implementing the Treaties (Art. 225 TFEU). The Council acting by simple majority may request the Commission to undertake any studies the Council considers desirable for the attainment of the common objectives and to submit to it any appropriate proposals (Art. 241 TFEU). In both instances, if the Commission does not submit a proposal, it shall inform the European Parliament of the reasons. Thirdly, in the field of the EMU not only the Council, but also a Member State may request the Commission to make a recommendation or a proposal, as appropriate, for the economic and monetary matters indicated. The Commission must examine such request, and since time is of the essence in these matters, submit its conclusions without delay (Art. 135 TFEU).[180] It is evident that such

---

that each case of Macro-Financial Assistance (Balance of Payments support) would have to be decided by normal legislative procedure, while the core of the Commission proposal was that such decisions would be taken by implementing decisions of the Commission, given the time pressure normally involved in such cases, while collaborating with other States and organizations, such as the IMF.

176. The three institutions later agreed in their 2016 Inter-institutional Agreement on Better Lawmaking, point 9, cited *supra* note 140, how such withdrawals should be made henceforth.

177. E.g. Arts. 126(5) TFEU (excessive deficits) and 144(3) TFEU (protective measures in balance of payments crises).

178. E.g. Arts. 121(2) and (4) TFEU (broad guidelines of economic policies of the Member States and the Union); 126(13) TFEU (excessive deficits); 219 TFEU (exchange-rate system); 138 TFEU (common positions on matters of particular interest for economic and monetary union); 207(3) TFEU (negotiation of international agreements in the field of the common commercial policy) and 218(3) TFEU (negotiations leading to international agreements).

179. For a study in the Commission's power of initiative, see: P. Ponzano, C. Hermann and D. Corona, "The power of initiative of the European Commission: A progressive erosion?", 89 *Notre Europe, Studies and Research* (2012).

180. As to the meaning of "proposals" in this context, see Ch. 7, "Law-making", section 4.2, of this book. See also Case C-27/04, *Commission v. Council*, where the Court held that, when the Council has adopted recommendations under (now) Art. 126(7) TFEU (excessive deficit procedure), it cannot subsequently modify them without a fresh recommendation from the Commission since the latter has a right of initiative in the excessive deficit procedure.

conclusions may consist of a refusal to make a proposal or recommendation. Hence, in all three cases, the Commission remains free not to make any proposal or recommendation and thus the right to make proposals and recommendation remains entirely its own.

On the other hand, it is true to say that the Commission nowadays abridges its own "unfettered" right of proposal by launching white papers, green papers or action plans before coming up with its final proposal. In this way, it tests the waters for its proposal beforehand with the co-legislators and the Member States, as well as with stakeholders. This last aspect is important, because it will give the Commission additional information for its impact assessment that must accompany any substantive Commission proposal that is expected to have significant economic, environmental or social impacts.[181] In addition, the Commission is obliged to accompany all its legislative proposals with an assessment of subsidiarity and proportionality.

Another element that hems in the Commission's freedom of making proposals without fundamentally affecting it, is the long-term legislative planning. Every five years, when a new Commission and Parliament are elected, together with the Council, they agree on a five-year legislative programme that the Commission converts into Annual Work Programmes. This annual programme is coordinated every year with the Council and the Parliament, resulting in a "joint declaration" signed by the presidents of the three institutions.

In conclusion, it is fair to say that the Commission's "exclusive" right to make proposals remains largely unscathed because the Court has upheld the Commission's right to modify and withdraw its proposals, when they risk to be robbed of their essence by the co-legislators, while this right has been put into a corset of planning and programming that is not unusual in the modern administrative state.

4.3.2 *Administration*

In the new Lisbon terminology of Articles 289–291 TFEU, the Commission enjoys extensive and very important tasks relating to non-legislative acts. These acts can be divided in delegated acts and implementing acts. It is the Commission and the Commission only that may enact such *delegated* acts: "A legislative act may delegate to the Commission the power to adopt non-legislative acts of general application to supplement or amend certain non-essential elements of the legislative act" (Art. 290(1) TFEU). With respect to *implementing* acts the Commission does not enjoy such exclusivity, since in principle the Member States are charged with implementing Union law (Art. 291(1) TFEU). However, "where uniform conditions for implementing legally binding Union acts are needed, those acts shall confer implementing powers on the *Commission*". Only, in duly justified specific cases and in the cases provided for in Articles 24 and 26 TEU) the Council itself or the co-legislators can confer such powers on the Council (Art. 291(2)).[182]

If Treaty based acts that do not have general application are also considered to be non-legislative acts (see section 2.2.3 above), it can be said that the Commission, next to the Council, equally enjoys the right to adopt such non-legislative acts. These "administrative" activities of the Commission, which are directly based on the TFEU, fall mainly in the fields of the customs union, competition policy and safeguard clauses. These are in fact the main areas in which the TFEU exhibits the characteristics of a treaty-law or management treaty.[183]

---

181. Interinstitutional Agreement on Better Lawmaking, cited *supra* note 140, point 13.
182. See further on this Arts. 289–291 system, Ch. 8, "The EU administration", of this book.
183. Note also the Commission's original administrative function in adopting conservatory measures in the event of delays in the annual decision-making process in the Council concerning agricultural prices. This is based on former Arts. 10 and 211 EC (replaced, in substance by Arts. 4(3) TEU and 17(1) TEU).

The Treaty of Lisbon has clarified that the Commission disposes of clearly defined powers to take non-legislative acts, either by virtue of non-essential legislative powers delegated to it on an ad hoc basis by the co-legislators, or as standard implementing measures, in most other areas of Union law beyond competition and State aids. The relative clarity of the situation[184] should not lead to the conclusion that these powers are unimportant as to the number or the weight of the non-legislative acts taken by the Commission. Delegated legislation and implementing measures are adopted by the Commission in such areas as trade and environmental law, where – as in competition and State aids – the economic importance of such measures can be huge. And the numbers of implementing acts in areas such as the agricultural and the common commercial policy are considerable.

4.3.3 *Supervision*

In accordance with Article 17(1) TEU (cited above), the Commission ensures "the application of the Treaties" and the "measures adopted by the institutions pursuant to them".

This supervision extends in the first place to ensuring the observance by the *Member States* of their obligations under the Treaties. If the Commission considers that a Member State has failed to fulfil its obligations, it may institute infringement proceedings, which may lead to a condemnation by the Court of Justice, which may ultimately impose fines and penalty payments.[185] Such supervision is also exercised indirectly through the Commission's systematic interventions in preliminary questions cases, especially when a possible conflict between Union law and national law is underlying the question posed by the national court.[186] Another way in which the Commission uses the Court in its role as guardian of the treaties is by starting from time to time annulment proceedings against acts of the other major institutions (mostly the Council) or defending itself against such proceedings[187] or, exceptionally, by initiating actions for failure to act.[188] In the area of external relations a similar function is fulfilled by asking the Court for an Opinion under Article 218(11). Such requests may serve the purpose of obtaining clarification about both the horizontal and the vertical division of powers, when concluding international agreements of the EU.[189]

The Commission also watches over the distortions of competition caused by Member States in the internal by market through public undertakings (Art. 106 TFEU) and by granting state aids to private undertakings (Arts. 107–109 TFEU). Broadly speaking, in both cases the Commission can address the necessary decisions to the Member States and, if necessary go directly before the Court.[190]

Moreover, Member States are subject to new disciplines on democratic values under Article 7 TEU and, in respect of their (excessive) deficits and their drawing on the stability mechanism, in the framework of the EMU. In both the Commission plays a certain role of surveillance and

---

184. Except that the EUCJ has left the distinction between delegation of legislation and implementing powers largely to the political judgment of the Council and the Parliament.
185. Arts. 258 and 260 TFEU. See on the infringement proceeding, Ch. 10, "The Court of Justice of the EU", section 2.1, of this book.
186. The most dramatic examples are those where an individual breaches national criminal law provisions in order to have them struck down by the EUCJ in the light of Union law, e.g. see Case 8/74, *Procureur de Roi v. Benoît and Gustave Dassonville.*
187. Case C-3/95, *Commission v. Council (Ecowas)* and Case C- 409/13, *Council v. Commission*, see *supra* note 175.
188. A classic case is: Case 13/83 *European Parliament and Commission v. Council.*
189. Most recent example: Opinion 2/15, *FTA Singapore,* see Ch. 41, "Union external relations under the TFEU", section 2.3.5, of this book.
190. See Ch. 20, "Competition law and policy", of this book.

control. As was already briefly mentioned, the Commission has created a special procedure for exercising its role in the Article 7 procedure.[191] In the framework of EMU the Commission was bestowed with new surveillance functions in the excessive deficit procedure (Two-Pack and Six-Pack) and, outside the Union framework, in the ESM treaty.[192]

The supervisory function of the Commission also extends to ensuring the observance by *private parties* of their EU obligations. This appears, e.g., from its powers in relation to violations of the principle of non-discrimination in transport matters[193] or of breach of the rules of competition by "undertakings" (companies).[194] In the Council regulations in these fields, control by the Commission has taken the form of a series of specific powers, particularly those by which it can oblige an undertaking to put an end to an infringement[195] and those by which it can impose fines (considered to be administrative) and/or periodic penalty payments for breaches of the competition rules.[196]

Necessary information for performing the supervisory function

In order to exercise its supervisory function the Commission must possess the necessary *information.*[197] For this purpose, in addition to the data which it obtains through complaints by Member States or private parties, or through questions asked by members of the European Parliament, the Commission may at all times request the Member States to provide it with the requisite information. The Member States are obliged by virtue of Article 4(3) TEU to comply with such requests.[198] Many legislative acts of the Council (and Parliament), particularly harmonization directives, impose a duty on Member States to provide information permitting the Commission to judge whether or not they are fulfilling their obligations. An obligation to provide information to the Commission and a right of investigation by it may also arise in relation to private companies[199] or procedures may be set up which give the Commission the requisite data[200] in some other way. Article 337 TFEU[201] contains a general provision according to which the Commission (within the limits and under the conditions laid down by the Council in accordance with the provisions of the Treaty) may collect any information and carry out any necessary checks. This provision has not so far led to a general regulation of the Commission's powers in this field, and initially only formed the basis for decisions of the Council relating to a series of statistical enquiries to be carried out by the Commission.[202]

---

191. See Ch. 11, "Application and enforcement of EU law in the Member States", of this book.
192. It is obvious that these new surveillance functions do not have the same "hardness" as the supervisory functions mentioned earlier and they do not lead to a clear decision by the Union courts. See O. Clerc, "La Commission dans l'UEM: une redynamisation fondée sur un magistère d'influence" in J. Auvret – Finck, *La Commission européenne en voie de redynamization* (Pedone, 2017), 103–119.
193. Arts. 95(3) and (4) TFEU.
194. Arts. 101 and 103(2)(a) TFEU.
195. E.g. Council Reg. 1/2003 of 16 Dec. 2002 on the implementation of the rules on competition laid down in Arts. 81 and 82 of the Treaty, O.J. 2003, L 001, Art. 7.
196. Ibid., Arts. 23 and 24. See further Ch. 20, "Substantive law of the EU", of this book.
197. See, generally, G. Ibanez, *The Administrative Supervision and Enforcement of EC Law: Powers, Procedures and Limits* (Hart, 1999).
198. See also Art. 192 Euratom.
199. E.g. Reg. 11, Arts. 11 and 13 of Reg. 1/2003, cited *supra* note 195, see also Arts. 17 and 20.
200. E.g. under the old competition rules, notification of agreements in accordance with Reg. 17, Arts. 4 and 5.
201. Cf. Art. 187 Euratom, and also the extensive powers of the Commission concerning inspections for safeguard controls under Title II, Ch. VII Euratom.
202. Art. 337 TFEU does not prevent the Commission from imposing a duty on the Member States to provide information on the basis of specific provisions: Joined Cases 188-190/80, *France et al. v. Commission;* Case

Finally, it should be mentioned that with regard to information, which is by nature confidential, an obligation of secrecy has been imposed on the members of the Commission as well as on members of the other institutions, members of committees, and officials and other servants of the Community.[203] The obligation of secrecy is not absolute as far as the Commission is concerned. Thus, in cases before it the Commission must weigh the interest of secrecy against interests such as the proper course of investigation proceedings, the rights of the defence and the duty to state reasons for Commission decisions.[204] In addition, in accordance with Article 16 TFEU, since 1 January 1999, personal data processed by the institutions and bodies set up by, or on the basis of, the EC Treaty are covered by Community acts on the protection of individuals with regard to the processing and movement of such data.[205]

5. The European Parliament

5.1 *Composition and election*

Before entering into the details of the composition, election, internal organization and powers of the European Parliament, it should be pointed out that, though the Parliament has maintained its principal function, i.e. providing the policies and legislation of what is now called the European Union with democratic legitimacy, there is no Institution that has seen its composition change and its powers grow so radically as the European Parliament. From a smallish purely consultative assembly composed of people who were the delegates of the Parliaments of the Member States, it has become a truly parliamentary machinery of 751 members, elected by direct universal suffrage, which is a full-co-legislator with the Council of Ministers in virtually all domains of the vastly expanded powers of the EU.

5.1.1 *The members of the European Parliament (MEPs) and their statute*

The European Parliament, as it is now called in Article 13 TEU (but which was originally called "the Assembly"),[206] consists of "representatives of the Union's citizens".[207] As representatives of these citizens, the members of the European Parliament are not bound by instructions of their governments, or of the national parliaments.[208] As representatives of the citizens they exercise their duties without instructions or obligation to consult. By the use of the words "representatives

C-426/93, *Germany v. Commission.*

203. Art. 339 TFEU and, extensively, Arts. 24–27 and 194 Euratom.

204. See Case 53/85, *AKZO Chemie BV et al. v. Commission* and Joined Cases 296 & 318/82, *Netherlands and Leeuwarder Papierwarenfabriek BV v. Commission*. See, though, Case 145/83, *Adams v. Commission*: Art. 339 enshrines a general principle. See also Commission Notice on the internal rules of procedure for processing requests for access to the file in cases pursuant to Arts. 85 and 86 of the EC Treaty, O.J. 1997, C 23/3 and D. Curtin, "Top secret Europe" (inaugural speech), (University of Amsterdam, 2011).

205. H. Hijmans, "The European data protection supervisor: The institutions of the EC controlled by an independent authority", 43 CML Rev. (2006), 1313–1342. See also Reg. 45/2001 of 18 Dec. 2000 on the protection of individuals with regard to the processing of personal data by the Community institutions and bodies and on the free movement of such data, O.J. 2001, L 8/1, and, already from an earlier date, Directive 95/46 of 24 Oct. 1995 on the protection of individuals with regard to the processing of personal data and on the free movement of such data, O.J. 1995, L 281/31.

206. In fact it re-christened itself long before its name was formally changed; see European Parliament Resolution on renaming of the Parliament, O.J. 1958, 1/6 and European Parliament Resolution on the renaming of the Parliament, O.J. 1962, 31/1045. Art. 3(1) Single European Act (SEA) brought the name "European Parliament" into the Treaties where it changed or supplemented them.

207. Arts. 14(2) TEU.

208. See already the Council Act concerning the election of the representatives of the Assembly by direct universal suffrage, O.J. 1976, L 278/05, as amended by Council Decision 2002/772 of 25 June 2002 amending the

of the Union's citizens" the modern concept of representation, as laid down in the constitutional law of Member States, has also been incorporated in the Treaties.

The Lisbon Treaty (Art. 14(2) TEU) has fixed the European Parliament at a maximum of 750 members and its chairperson, in which function the Italian Antonio Tajani succeeded the German Martin Schulz at the beginning of 2017. The European citizens will be represented by a digressively proportional system of repartition over the Member States, varying between at least 6 MEPs for the smallest member States (Luxemburg, Cyprus and Malta) and at most 96 seats for the largest Member State (Germany). This repartition is not stable because of shifts in the population numbers of Member States in relation to each other. Germany's population is shrinking relatively the most and hence the difference in the number of seats between Germany (96) and France (74) and Italy (73) will have to be reduced over time.[209] Moreover, the number of citizens represented by a Maltese MEP is about ten times as small as the number of people represented by a German MEP. This has led the German Constitutional Court to put the legitimacy of the European Parliament in doubt.[210]

The Statute of the European Parliament is laid down in a decision of the Parliament itself, adopted in conformity with Article 223(2) TFEU.[211] It is in part a consolidation and development of existing provisions from the Treaties and the Rules of Procedure and a large number of provisions on a uniform salary, pension and benefits scheme for MEPs. The latter provisions constituted an important step forward from the old system of highly unequal remuneration of MEPs based on their national parliamentary salaries.[212] They are complemented by a Code of Conduct for MEPs, which enjoins them to make an extensive declaration of their financial interests and which their possibility to accept gifts above a certain value.[213]

Being an MEP is incompatible with a large number of other high political and judicial functions in EU institutions or in their administration, as is being minister in a government of a Member State. Since 2004 it is also incompatible with a national parliamentary mandate[214] and, moreover, should probably be incompatible too with membership of regional parliaments of the Member States, insofar as these have substantive legislative functions.[215] Such incompatibilities flow quite naturally from the function that Parliament fulfils in the balance between the institutions and from the Union outlook that an MEP must have in contradistinction to members of national governments. The Member States may declare, at national level, other positions to be incompatible with membership of the European Parliament.[216]

Act concerning the election of the representatives of the European Parliament by direct universal suffrage, annexed to Council Decision 76/787, O.J. 2002, L 283/1.

209. European Parliament, Report on a proposal for a modification of the Act concerning the election of the Members of the European Parliament by direct universal suffrage of 20 Sept. 1976, (2009/2134(INI)), 40.
210. See 2 BvE 2/08, *Lissabon Urteil*, para 285.
211. European Parliament Decision 2005/684 of 28 Sept. 2005 adopting the Statute for the Members of the European Parliament, O.J. 2005, L 262/1. This statute entered into force with the election of the 2009–2014 Parliament.
212. Ibid., Arts. 9–19. It also contains important provisions on the reimbursement of expenses incurred in the exercise of their mandate and for their personal assistance, subject to further regulation by Parliament. Such reimbursements can now be better controlled, while in the past they often served as a supplement to inadequate compensation based on national standards.
213. This Code of Conduct is attached as Annex 1 to the European Parliament Rules of Procedure, (2015). Available at www.europarl.europa.eu/sides/getDoc.do?pubRef=-//EP//NONSGML+RULES-EP+20150909+0+DOC+PDF+V0//EN&language=EN (last visited May 2017).
214. Art. 7(1) and (2) of the Direct Elections Act, cited *supra* note 208.
215. A proposal to this effect is being considered.
216. Ibid., Arts. 6(2) and 7(2).

MEPs are protected in the discharge of their parliamentary functions, and in any activity which cannot be separated from the exercise of those functions by parliamentary immunity, as laid down in the Protocol on the Privileges and Immunities of the European Communities (PPI).[217] Requests for lifting this immunity,[218] filed mostly by the judicial authorities of the Member States, are a fairly regular occurrence. Such requests are handled by the Committee on Legal Affairs of the Parliament and granted in about a quarter of the cases.[219] The Committee has laid down some principles and a procedure for treating such requests, in which it emphasizes that parliamentary immunity is a guarantee of the independence of the Parliament as a whole and of its Members and is not a Member's personal privilege.[220] In the end the Parliament decides by simple majority, on proposal of the Committee, whether or not to lift the immunity of an MEP. Such decisions may end up before the ECJ, for instance because they emerge in national courts in defamation procedures, raising questions of whether and when national courts should ask preliminary questions and, once such questions have been asked, whether the decision to lift immunity was valid.[221]

5.1.2 *Elections*

Up until 1979, members of the European Parliament were appointed by and from the national parliaments in accordance with the procedure laid down by each Member State, the number of delegates per country being specified in the Treaty. This method of appointing members was envisaged as being only temporary, as was clear from the old Article 138(3) EEC (now, modified, Art. 14(1)–(3) TEU and Art. 223 TFEU) which required the Parliament to draw up proposals for elections by direct universal suffrage in accordance with a uniform procedure in all Member States. It also provided that the Council, acting unanimously, was to lay down the appropriate provisions which it would "recommend to Member States for adoption in accordance with their respective constitutional requirements".

On the basis of these provisions, the Council decided on 20 September 1976 to recommend to the Member States provisions in the form of an Act concerning the election of the representatives of the Assembly by direct universal suffrage.[222] The Act was accepted by all the Member States in accordance with their respective constitutional requirements and thus is part of EU primary law.

---

217. Arts. 7–9, PPI op. cit. fn. 116.

218. See also Direct Elections Act, cited *supra* note 208, Art. 4(2). See also Rules 5–9 of the Rules of Procedure, cited *supra* note 213. The Court interprets the period of immunity mentioned in Art. 9 in the Protocol on Privileges and Immunities of the European Communities in a wide sense: it is valid "during the sessions" (and while travelling to and from the place of meeting of the Parliament). See Case 149/85, *Wybot v. Faure et al.* As to jurisdiction in relation to actions for non-contractual liability for acts committed on the European Parliament's premises, see Case C-201/89, *Le Pen et al. v. Puhl et al.*

219. Based on numbers given in O. Costa and F. Saint Martin, *Le Parlement européen,* 2nd ed. (La documentation française, 2011), 30.

220. European Parliament, Committee on Legal Affairs, Notice to Members (0011/2016), *Principles for Immunity Cases,* para 1.

221. See resp. Joined Cases C-200-201/2007, *Alfonso Luigi Marra v. Eduardo De Gregorio and Antonio Clemente* and Case C-163/10, *Aldo Patriciello.* In the latter case the Court came to a different conclusion than the Parliament, ruling that a statement from an MEP made outside the Parliament and resulting in a prosecution for uttering false accusations in his country of origin did not fall under Art. 8 of the PPP, unless there was a direct and obvious connection with the exercise of his parliamentary duties – which was in all likelihood not the case, but left to the determination of the national court.

222. See *supra* note 209.

The Act on direct elections originally did not prescribe a uniform electoral procedure for all the Member States. Hence elections for the EP were governed in each Member State by its *national* provisions.[223] The preference for a particular electoral system, whether of proportional representation (with either a list system or a single transferable vote) or majoritarian ("first past the post" in each electoral district) and equipped with a minimum threshold for parties or not, is deeply ingrained in national traditions and political power relationships. Under the old Treaty provisions, the task of finding a consensus on a *uniform* procedure fell upon the Parliament and the Council, with the former having the right of initiative.[224] Several attempts at fashioning such a uniform procedure failed.[225] Hence the Treaty of Amsterdam added the possibility of creating an election procedure "in accordance with principles common to all Member States".[226] Making use of this new possibility, the Parliament drew up a number of such principles in July 1998.[227] In the end the Act concerning elections was modified so as to include principles from different electoral systems of the Member States. Proportional representation became the leading principle, but with a considerable possibility of choice for the Member States. They could choose between a list system or a single transferable vote system; they could introduce a threshold, but not higher than 5 per cent of the votes cast; they could even institute constituencies, but without generally affecting the proportional nature of the voting system.[228]

The elections must be held on dates fixed by the Member States but within a particular period beginning on a Thursday morning and ending on the following Sunday. Results shall be made public only after the end of polling in the last Member State.[229]

Members of the European Parliament are elected for five years.[230] Their credentials are verified by the Parliament; the Parliament decides whether the members elected, taking note of the results declared officially by the Member States, may be admitted according to the provisions of the Act concerning Elections.[231] Evaluation of whether members elected satisfy the conditions laid down in national legislation takes place under national provisions, again, pending the entry into force of a uniform electoral procedure or one based on common principles. Until that moment the filling of seats falling vacant during the Parliament's term of office occurs according to national procedures.[232]

The Act concerning Elections contains no provisions relating to active and passive voting rights; the modalities remain matters for the Member States, subject now to the obligations resulting from Directive 93/109, on voting rights for EU citizens not residing in their own State;[233]

---

223. Ibid., Art. 7(2): i.e. national provisions established or declared applicable for the elections.
224. Ibid.
225. See e.g, the Reports Patijn (1975), Seitlinger (1982) and De Gucht (1991 and 1993) mentioned in Costa and Saint Martin, cited *supra* note 219, 12.
226. Art 190(4) in its Amsterdam version, presently Art. 223(1), first sentence TFEU.
227. European Parliament Resolution on a draft electoral procedure incorporating common principles for the election of Members of the European Parliament, O.J. 1998, C 292/66. Following this up, the Council amended the Act on direct elections, on 25 June/23 Sept. 2002 in the sense that as of 2004, elections would be on the basis of proportional representation; see Direct Elections Act, cited *supra* note 208.
228. Arts. 1–3 Direct Elections Act, cited *supra* note 208.
229. Ibid. Art. 10.
230. Art. 10(3) TEU.
231. Art. 12 Direct Elections Act, op. cit. *supra* note 209.
232. Ibid. Art. 13. As to some of the difficulties in this regard, see K. Bradley and A. Feeney, "Legal developments in the European parliament", 13 YEL (1993), 383–425, 412–413 and K. Bradley and A. Feeney, "Legal developments in the European parliament", 14 YEL (1994), 401–438, 428–429.
233. Council Directive 93/109 of 6 Dec. 1993 laying down detailed arrangements for the exercise of the right to vote and stand as a candidate in elections to the European Parliament for citizens of the Union residing in

this Directive implements the right conferred by Article 22 TFEU for every citizen of the Union – i.e. according to Article 20 TFEU, every person holding the nationality of a Member State – residing in a Member State of which he is not a national, to vote and to stand as a candidate in elections to the European Parliament in that Member State under the same conditions as nationals of that State.[234]

5.1.3 *European political groups and parties*

Article 10(4) TEU states that "political parties at European level contribute to forming European political awareness and to expressing the will of citizens of the Union". This sentiment is repeated in Charter Article 12 on freedom of assembly and association.[235] Moreover, Article 8 of the Statute for MEPs confirms that Members may form themselves into political groups and that the Rules of Procedure will contain the conditions for the exercise of this right. This last provision is merely the recognition of an ancient reality: the formation of European political groups already took place in the old Assembly of the European Coal and Steel Community (ECSC).[236] These groups rather than the national parties put their stamp on the work of the Parliament from the very beginning. This is evident in the parliamentary debates as well as in the composition of the various parliamentary bodies. These parliamentary groups over the years have spawned political parties at European level, whose existence has now been recognized in Articles 10 TFEU and 12 of the Charter.

The conditions for official recognition of groups are political affinity between the members of the Group, the "European" character of the Group, expressed in at least 25 members having been elected in at least 7 Member States.[237] The creation of a group comprising independent members of the Parliament – a mixed group ("groupe mixte") – consisting of a number of non-attached members, was found by the Committee on Constitutional Affairs and then by the Parliament itself to be in conflict with Article 32(1) Rules of Procedure, since the members of this group maintained their political independence and thus showed a lack of political affinity. This interpretation of Article 32(1) by the Parliament was upheld by the Court of First Instance, after an initial suspension by its President.[238] In the meantime the Parliament has issued an interpretation of the relevant rule of procedure that there is a presumption of political affinity among members forming a political group, which can only be refuted if the members of the group themselves deny that there is such political affinity.[239] Therefore, as long as the rule "don't ask, don't tell" is followed by a non-affiliated group and the Parliament, it can obtain financial assistance.

---

a Member State of which they are not nationals, O.J. 1993, L 329/34. See Ch. II, section 6.2, *supra*. See the Resolutions of the European Parliament, on voting rights for citizens of the Union in the European elections, O.J. 1994, C 44/159 and, on obstacles to, and discrimination against, EU citizens participating in the European elections, O.J. 1994, C 128/316.

234. See also Ch. 16 "Citizenship of the Union", of this book.

235. Art. 12(2) of the Charter on Fundamental Rights: "Political parties at Union level contribute to expressing the political will of the citizens of the Union".

236. See P.J.G. Kapteyn, *L'Assemblée commune de la Communauté européenne du charbon et de l'acier: un essai de parlementarisme européen* (Aspects Européens. Série C. Études politiques 9, 1962), 64–103. The ECSC Treaty expired on 23 July 2002.

237. Rule 31, Rules of Procedure, cited *supra* note 213. According to Rule 32(1), Members may form themselves into groups according to their political affinities. These groups must include persons elected "in a quarter of the Member States".

238. Joined Cases T-222, 327 & 329/99, *Martinez and De Gaulle v. European Parliament.*

239. See the declaration attached to Rule 32(1), Rules of Procedure, cited *supra* note 213.

In the present Parliament (2014–2019) there are eight Parliamentary groups: two big ones, the Christian-Democrats (PPE, 219 seats) and the Social-Democrats (S&D, 191 seats); two intermediate size groups, the European Conservatives and Reformists (ECR, 71 seats)[240] and the Liberals (ALDE, 68 seats); and four smaller groups, the Unitary Left/Nordic Greens (GUE/NGI, Communists and ultra-left, 52 seats), the Greens (Greens/EFA, 50 seats), the European Freedom and Direct Democracy Party (EFDD, the hard "Leave" party, 48 seats), and finally a non-affiliated group of 52 MEPs. These groups, in spite of their multi-national, multi-lingual and multi-cultural character generally show great cohesiveness during votes and basically determine the political life in the European Parliament. As in any Parliament, the bigger the group, the bigger the influence and this is supported by the rules for dividing up the leadership jobs in Parliament, such as Committee chairmanships etc., and the rules on the allocation of money from the budget of the Parliament for political and administrative assistance. There is therefore an incentive to form big political groups in the European Parliament, since this means more jobs and more money.[241] This may put the cohesiveness of such groups to the test.

As to European political parties, the Treaty of Nice introduced a new provision (Art. 191(2) TEC) providing for regulation of such political parties, and in particular their funding. Parliament and Council succeeded in passing such a regulation, primarily dealing with funding, just in time for the elections of 2004.[242] Ten years later Parliament and Council passed a much more comprehensive piece of legislation replacing this regulation.[243] It lays down a statute for European political parties and European political foundations, which often exist to support these parties.[244] In order to be officially registered as a European political party an applicant organization (usually an alliance of parties that already exist in the Member States) must fulfil certain existential and governance requirements, most prominently among which is the observance, in its programme and in its activities, of the foundational values of the EU, as laid down in Article 2 TEU.[245] The Register shall be kept by the Authority for European Political Parties, which shall examine any application for registration and decide on the inscription of the European political party in question in the register.[246] It shall also verify the continued compliance of the registered parties with the conditions of registration. If a possible breach of the foundational values of the Union is involved, the Authority shall be advised by a Committee of six independent eminent persons (to which the Council, the Commission and the Parliament each appoint two such persons).[247] The Court of Justice shall review the legality decisions of the Authority and shall also have the power to award damages and to enjoin the authority to act, if it was under an obligation to do so.[248]

An important legal benefit of the registration is that European political parties shall have European legal personality as from the date of publication of their registration and thus can

240. The future of this moderate eurosceptic group, which consists *inter alia* of a large contingent of British Tories will be uncertain after Brexit.
241. Money is allocated to political groups not only on the basis of size, but also on the basis of linguistic diversity.
242. Reg. 2004/2003 of 4 Nov. 2003 on the regulations governing political parties at European level and the rules regarding their funding, O.J. 2003, L 297/1.
243. Reg. 1141/2014 of 22 Oct. 2014 on the statute and funding of European political parties and European political foundations, O.J. 2014, L 317/1.
244. In the following everything that is said about European political parties can be taken to apply to European political foundations as well.
245. Arts. 3,4, and 5 of Reg. 1141/2014, cited *supra* note 243.
246. Ibid., Arts. 7–9.
247. Ibid., Art. 11. In its opinions the Committee shall give full consideration to the fundamental right of freedom of association and to the need to ensure pluralism of political parties in Europe.
248. Ibid., Art. 6(11).

easily operate throughout the Member States of the Union.[249] The funding of European political parties is based on a budget that will be distributed for 15% equally among all parties and for 85% in proportion to their share of elected members of the European Parliament. Any support to the parties is limited to 85% of the reimbursable expenditure indicated in the budget of the European political party concerned.[250] The latter 85% rule has the function of ensuring that the parties are at least partially capable of providing for themselves from other sources and thus represent a non-negligible number of European citizens. The provisions on control of the expenses of the subsidized parties and possible sanctions have been considerably extended compared to the predecessor regulation.[251]

5.2 *Internal organization*

By way of introduction, it is important to point out that the European Parliament is fairly autonomous as far as its own organization is concerned. It can decide on its Rules of Procedure by a majority of its Members without approval by the Council, while the Court of Justice requires such approval for the adoption of its Rules of Procedure.[252] Like most other major institutions, it can propose its own functioning budget and expect that the Commission and the Council will not substantially interfere with it. The only important point that strongly influences its functioning, namely its seat and the place of its General Secretariat, is totally outside its power. Protocol 6 to the TFEU, laying down Strasbourg as its seat, Luxemburg as the location of its General Secretariat and Brussels as the place, where the EP's committees meet is part of primary law. France and Luxemburg have resisted any attempt to change this.

5.2.1 *Internal organs of the parliament*

The *President* has as primary duty the overall direction of the activities of the EP and presiding over its proceedings. He "shall enjoy all the powers necessary... to ensure that [the proceedings] are properly conducted". This strong and broad language is necessary to keep a Parliament of 750 MEPs on the rails and moving forward. He is also the representative of the Parliament on ceremonial occasions and in international relations and responsible for security and the inviolability of its premises (Rule 22). A task that has given the President additional visibility and authority is his appearance before the European Council at the beginning of each meeting in order to put forward the position of Parliament on the issues to be discussed (Art. 235(2) TFEU).

The President may be replaced by 14 Vice-Presidents, to whom he can delegate, not only the task of presiding parliamentary proceedings, but also (parts of) his other duties. There are also five so-called Quaestors, who are responsible for administrative and financial matters directly concerning MEPs and who can also be entrusted with other tasks (Rule 28). Together the President and the 14 Vice-Presidents form the Bureau, with the Quaestors in an advisory capacity. The Bureau has a multitude of tasks (Rule 25), which are primarily of a financial and administrative nature, such as making the implementing rules of the Statute for European political parties and the application of the Statute for Members. It is the Bureau that decides on the applications from European political parties for funding, on the distribution of appropriations between the different political parties and, if necessary, on the recovery of amounts wrongly paid (Rule 209). The Bureau decides by simple majority; if necessary the President has the casting vote. The Bureau appoints the Secretary-General of the Parliament and works closely

---

249. Ibid., Arts. 12–16.
250. Ibid., Arts. 17–19. See Art. 17(4) for the 85% limit on the subsidy as a whole.
251. Ibid., Art. 23 et seq.
252. Contrast Art. 232 TFEU with Art. 253 TFEU.

with him. All the above-mentioned officers of the European Parliament are elected by simple majority of the votes cast; their mandate is for the duration of two and a half years, i.e. half a parliamentary mandate.

Next to the Bureau there is the Conference of Presidents, consisting of the President and the leaders of the different political groups represented in the Parliament (Rule 26). The responsibilities of the Conference of the Presidents are linked primarily to the political functioning of the Parliament: the organization of the Parliament's work, relations with other institutions and bodies of the Union and parliaments of the Member States, relations with non-member countries and other international organizations, the composition of committees etc. The Conference of the Presidents normally decides by consensus (Rule 27).

The Standing Committees form the lynch pin on which most parliamentary activities turn and within a Committee the most important persons, next to the chair, are the rapporteurs on the relevant subjects having been allocated to that Committee. There are committees corresponding to the different fields of action of the Union, e.g. for international trade, for foreign affairs, for the environment, public health and food safety, for the budgets, for industry, research and energy, for the EMU, for the internal market and consumer protection for legal affairs etc. Altogether there are twenty standing committees.[253]

Proposals from the Commission or other issues on the agenda of a session of Parliament are allocated to the relevant committee, which takes the lead on the proposal in question. Under the guidance of a rapporteur the committee will prepare a report and a resolution, after having received so-called opinions from other interested committees.[254] It is on the basis of the rapporteur's work that first the Committee fixes the report and the proposed amendments, if it concerns a legislative proposal, and that, later, the plenary decides the definitive position of the Parliament. If at a later stage the Council and the Parliament need to reconcile their positions on a proposal of the Commission, the rapporteur and the chair of the competent committee will be part of the delegation of the Parliament to the conciliation committee or the trilogue with the other two institutions.

Next to the standing committees there are special committees, which are instituted for a period of no more than a year; they have a specific mandate. Recent examples are the two successive Special Committees on Tax rulings (TAXE 1 and 2).[255] If the EP is of the view that its special powers of inquiry[256] need to be used with a view to shedding light on alleged contraventions against, or maladministration in, the implementation of Union law, a Committee of Inquiry may be created at the request of a quarter of the component members of the EP (Art. 226 TFEU). Recent examples are, first, the Commissions of Inquiry on Emission Measurement

253. These Committees and their areas of responsibility are described in Annex V to the Rules of Procedure, op. cit. *supra* note 214. Nineteen cover specific fields of EU competence. Committee XX is the Committee on Petitions, responsible for petitions, citizens' initiatives and relations with the European Ombudsman.
254. Rapporteurs can receive help from so-called shadow rapporteurs designated by each political group in order to arrive at a compromise in the committee on a Commission proposal, which will be reflected in the report. See Rule 205a. Political groups also designate members as coordinators in each Committee (Rule 205) who help the Chair of the Committee with decisions on procedures or on the appointment of rapporteurs etc. See Costa and Saint Martin, op. cit. *supra* note 219, 77–82.
255. See <europarl.europa.eu/committees/en/taxe/home.html>. The work of these committees was related to the reports in the press, commonly called Lux-leaks.
256. European Parliament, Council, Commission Decision 95/167 of 19 Apr. 1995 on the detailed provisions governing the exercise of the European Parliament's right of inquiry, O.J. 1995 L 113/2.

in the Automotive Sector[257] and, second, the Commission on Money Laundering, Tax Avoidance and Tax Evasion.[258]

The European Parliament also elects so-called delegations, which have the task to maintain relations with the parliaments of third States with which the EU has special relations or to participate in the work of mixed inter-parliamentary commissions, created in the framework of pre-accession association agreements or of association agreements concluded with the so-called neighbourhood States. In the case of the ACP/EU Cooperation Agreement of Cotonou there is even a full-fledged Inter-parliamentary Assembly of which a delegation from the EP forms part together with parliamentary delegations of all the ACP countries.[259]

5.2.2 *The General Secretariat of the parliament*

As was already mentioned above the Bureau appoints the Secretary-General of the Parliament. From the very beginning of the ECSC it was the wish of the European Parliament to have its own General Secretariat. As a matter of fact, the General Secretariat has grown to considerable size (about 6700 persons). This is easy to explain. The EP is confronted with draft legislation that is usually more technical than that national parliaments deal with. Hence MEPs need more expert support and this is provided by the Secretariat. For reasons of democracy every MEP must be able to express him- or herself in his (her) mother tongue and, if at all possible, also have the possibility to listen to other MEPs also in his/her mother tongue. The same is true for written documents and any draft legislation before Parliament. The possibility to use *de facto* working languages, as are used in the Commission or in the working groups of the Council, simply does not exist for the EP. Hence the translation and interpretation services are relatively larger than in other institutions. Finally the dispersion of the meetings over Strasbourg and Brussels and the location of the General-Secretariat in Luxemburg create the need for more personnel compared to other EU institutions, which are largely stationary.[260]

The General Secretariat is divided into 12 Directorates-General and a Legal Service. Four and a half of those Directorates-General are devoted to the direct support of the work of the President and the MEPs: the DG's for the Presidency, for the Internal, respectively the External EU Policies, the Parliamentary Research Service and half of the Legal Service. All the other DG's are related to the functioning of the General Secretariat (Personnel, budget, Security, IT,) and the indirect support of the MEPs (Translation, Interpretation, Infrastructure and Logistics).[261]

The Secretary-General is the head of this civil service of the Parliament. As already mentioned above, he is appointed by the Bureau and works closely with it. He and his Secretariat are there to see to it that the Parliament as a political institution that exists primarily through its meetings, works smoothly during those meetings, notably the monthly plenary meetings. During the plenary he also fulfils a personal role as an important adviser to the President and as the person, who is responsible for the formal details, such as the adoption of Union acts or of the positions of the Parliament on proposals, and the proper way of certifying and signing them. In a way he is the master of the European Parliament, but at the same time the Parliament, through

257. See <.http://www.europarl.europa.eu/committees/en/emis/home.html>. The Committee issued its final report on 28 February 2017, which was discussed in plenary during the Apr. 2017 session.
258. See <http://www.europarl.europa.eu/committees/en/PANA/home.html>. This committee deals with the consequences of the so-called Panama papers.
259. On these international agreements, see Ch. 41, "Union external relations under the TFEU", of this book.
260. In the same vein O. Costa and F. Saint Martin, op. cit. *supra* note 218, 74–76.
261. See <www.europarl.europa.eu/the-secretary-general/en/organisation.html> (last visited Mar. 2017).

the Bureau, is the master of the Secretary-General, who is responsible before the Bureau for the way he runs his administration.

5.2.3 *The plenary meeting*

As the role of the Parliament in the legislative and budgetary procedures and its other powers will be explained briefly in section 5.3 below, this paragraph concentrates rather on the constraints under which the Parliament has had to develop its method of work in its plenary composition. The EP has 750 Members and meets in plenary formation only for a week (actually four working days) every month, except that in May and in November there are two meetings (one of which is a two-day meeting) and in August there is no meeting. During three and a half days the plenary is in session, usually from 9 am to midnight, with an hour reserved at noon for voting only. The normal plenary meetings show a very limited attendance, as usually only the rapporteur, the shadow rapporteurs and the chair of the competent committees are present. During the voting hour the Assembly room is nearly full, which shows that the actual attendance at the monthly plenary sessions is very high, but that most of those present are in other meetings, of political groups, of standing committees and delegations, which are going on in parallel with the plenary.[262]

It has been calculated that with so many MEPs and about 30 hours of meeting time per parliamentary week, each MEP in theory could not have more than about 30 minutes of speaking time a year.[263] Hence speaking time in the Plenary is strictly rationed and mostly parcelled out in portions of 5 and 2 minutes. The agenda of a session of a week is carefully planned and the discussion of each agenda item is strictly scripted, indicating the names of the intervenors in the debate and their allotted speaking time. The President is normally very strict in enforcing respect for the planning and breaking into the agenda by a MEP not on the list of speakers is "inconceivable". The Rules of Procedure[264] are extremely detailed and their most recent amendments of January 2017 nicely reflect the preoccupations of the Parliament with rationalizing its procedures to the utmost, while at the same time trying to find openings for new ways to discuss hot topics and to minimize the risk of reputational damage.[265] Therefore, a brief overview of these amendments follows.

An example of rationalization is the uniformization of the thresholds requiring a certain number of MEPs and political groups for valid procedural requests. They are now limited to three such thresholds: a "low" one, consisting of 5% of total MEPs (i.e. 38 MEPs) or a political group; a "medium threshold" corresponding to 10% of total MEPs comprising MEPs from one or more political groups; and a "high" one corresponding to one or more political groups or Members, who together constitute 20% of total MEPs. There is also the limitation of requests for roll call votes by the same political group to 100 per week, of the number of oral explanations of vote by any Member to three per week, and of motions for resolution to one per Member per month. Written declarations by Members will cease to exist. Written questions are limited

262. A slightly less than 90 % attendance rate can be calculated from figures collected by *Votewatch Europe* for the 2014–2019 Parliament until 16 February 2016. Available at <www.votewatch.eu/en/term8-political-group-participation.html> (last visited May 2017).

263. O. Costa and F. Saint Martin, op. cit. *supra* note 218, 88.

264. European Parliament Rules of Procedure, Provisional Edition, (Jan. 2017). The Rules of Procedure count 231 articles and seven annexes. See: <www.europarl.europa.eu/sides/getDoc.do?pubRef=-//EP//NONSGML+RULES-EP+20170116+0+DOC+PDF+V0//EN&language=EN> (last visited May 2017).

265. General Revision of the Rules of Procedure, A brief overview of the main changes, available at <www.europarl.europa.eu/sed/doc/ext/manual/L004678-BROC-A5-MEP-New%20Rules%202017_web_EN.pdf>.

to twenty over a rolling period of three months, but these questions may be supported by other MEPS than the author. On the other hand the amendments introduce a new instrument the so-called minor and major interpellations, which are actually a series of interdependent questions about a specific issue, accompanied in the case of major interpellations by a short explanatory memorandum. The first one seems to be very close to a question for written answer, but the major interpellation may lead to a debate in Plenary. This new instrument of interpellation can be seen as a "compensation" for the limitation of the number of questions for written answer, while encouraging MEPs to come up with more coherent questioning about bigger problems. The amendments are rounded out with new provisions tightening up Annex I containing the Code of Conduct on the financial interests and conflicts of interests of MEPs.

That a Parliament does most of its actual legislative work in its standing committees is not unusual, but the extreme regimentation of its plenary proceedings, and the lack of room for interventions in plenary debates by Members from outside the circle of the committee, i.e. rapporteur and shadow rapporteurs, that dealt with the legislation in question is exceptional and linked to the very large size of the Plenary and the multilingualism of the institution.[266]

5.3 *Powers and functions*

According to Article 14(1) TEU, the European Parliament shall, jointly with the Council, exercise legislative and budgetary functions; it shall exercise functions of political control and consultation as laid down in the Treaties; and Parliament shall elect the President of the Commission.

5.3.1 *Parliament's role in the legislative process*

The way in which the European Parliament is involved in the legislative process has developed remarkably since the coming into force of the EEC and Euratom Treaties in 1958. The decision-making process is discussed fully in another chapter,[267] but a brief explanation of the Parliament's role is appropriate here.

Apart from special cases, the Treaties envisages four general ways in which the European Parliament participates in the Council's decision-making, which are most conveniently discussed chronologically.

(1) The original, and least far-reaching involvement is the *consultation* procedure, whereby the Council consults the Parliament to ascertain its views on a Commission proposal. Such consultation was not generally required: the obligation to consult existed only where specifically laid down in the legal basis used by the Commission in its proposal, i.e. the Treaty provision conferring competence on the Council to act in relation to the matter concerned. In practice, however, the Council often sought the advisory opinion of the Parliament even where this was not required by the Treaties. Moreover, the Parliament itself sometimes addresses opinions to the Council on its own initiative.[268] When consultation of the Parliament is required but has not in fact taken place, the relevant measure may be annulled by Court of Justice on the ground of

266. It is important to realize that maintaining the unrestricted possibility to speak 23 languages makes hundreds of language combinations possible, some of which can be realized only through one or two intermediate interpreters. This is an important consideration in keeping strictly to the planning of a debate and also an element which eliminates much spontaneity and vivacity from the debate in plenary.

267. See Ch. 7, "Law-making", of this book.

268. E.g. European Parliament Resolution of 11 May 1979 on measures to promote the development of fish farming, O.J. 1979, C 140/117, accompanied by a draft proposal for a Council regulation, O.J. 1979, C 140/120, in which it invited the Commission to submit to the Council. Parliament now has the express right to request the Commission to submit appropriate proposals, see the end of this section, *infra*.

infringement of an essential procedural requirement.[269] The consultation procedure, and thus the advisory role of the Parliament, is now only relevant in a very limited number of policy areas; very often the consultation procedure has been replaced by a right of co-decision of Parliament (now called the ordinary legislative procedure, see below) or by a right of assent for the EP.

(2) With the coming into force of the SEA on 1 July 1987, a second procedure was established, the *cooperation* procedure. This procedure was designed to permit the Parliament a second reading of a proposed act. This permitted the Parliament to reject the common position of the Council, after which the Council could only act by unanimity during the second reading. Moreover, where amendments put forward by the Parliament[270] were taken on board by the Commission in its re-examined proposal, the Council can only deviate from them by unanimity.[271] The Treaty of Amsterdam replaced the cooperation procedure in nearly all cases by the co-decision procedure; and subsequently it was abolished with the entry into force of the Lisbon Treaty.

(3) The Treaty of Maastricht introduced a third procedure: the so-called *co-decision* procedure, renamed the "*ordinary legislative procedure*" by the Lisbon Treaty without fundamentally changing its substance. The term is used in the various substantive Treaty provisions (legal bases) but the exact content of the procedure is laid down in Article 294 TFEU. The two characteristic elements in this procedure are the convocation of a Conciliation Committee and the Parliament's right of co-decision. The Conciliation Committee is convened when the Council declines to adopt all or some of the amendments proposed by Parliament at the end of the first phase of the procedure – which more or less corresponds to the cooperation procedure described above (Art. 294(3–6) TFEU). The Parliament's right of co-decision concerns a joint draft text drawn up by the Conciliation Committee.[272] This text must be approved by both the Council and the Parliament; if one of the two does not approve it, then the draft text is deemed not to be adopted (Art. 294(13) TFEU). Nor is an act adopted if the Conciliation Committee fails to reach agreement on a joint text (Art. 294(12) TFEU).

The ordinary legislative procedure now applies to almost all areas of EU policy; if this is (still) not the case the term "special legislative procedure is used (Art. 289 TFEU). Acts adopted under the ordinary procedure are signed by the Presidents of the Council *and* the Parliament;[273] they are referred to as "legal acts" or "legislative acts".[274]

(4) Finally, there are a number of cases in which the Council needs the "assent" of the European Parliament before it could formally adopt the act. The Lisbon Treaty refers to it as the "*consent*" of Parliament. This procedure was introduced by the Single European Act (SEA), and initially only concerned the accession of new Member States[275] and the conclusion of associa-

269. Case 138/79, *SA Roquette Frères v. Council* and Case 139/79, *Maizena GmbH v. Council*. See F. G. Jacobs, "Isoglucose resurgent: Two powers of the European Parliament upheld by the Court", 18 CML Rev. (1981), 219–226, and K. Lenaerts, "Zaken 138/79 en 139/79, resp. Roquette Frères S.A. en Maizena GmbH, aan wier zijde het Europees Parlement tegen Raad van de Europese Gemeenschappen, aan wiens zijde Commissie van de Europese Gemeenschappen; Vorderingen to nietigverklaring van 's Raads Verordening nr 1293/79. ("Isoglucose – Produktiequota" zaken)", 6 SEW (1981), 397–410. See also e.g. Case 817/79, *Buyl et al. v. Commission* in relation to examination to see if this essential requirement had been met.

270. Parliament uses the term "amendments", but old Art. 252(c) makes it clear that these are proposed amendments.

271. Old Art. 252 EC.

272. See Case C-344/04, *IATA and ELFAA*, on the broad powers of the conciliation committee in drawing up a text.

273. Art. 297(1) TFEU.

274. Art. 296 TFEU. See also Art. 230(1) EC.

275. See now Art. 49 TEU.

tion agreements.[276] Since Lisbon, apart from these two cases, the consent procedure applies to the conclusion of nearly all other international agreements, including trade agreements and the European Convention of Human Rights (Art. 218(6) and 207(3) TFEU);[277] to the imposition of sanctions on a Member State for violating EU values (Art. 7 TEU), and to decisions taken under Article 352 TFEU (the so-called flexibility clause). Under this procedure, the Parliament must explicitly give its consent to the Council acts mentioned in the relevant provisions, but it is the Council alone – not Council and EP – that decides. It can be discussed whether, from the viewpoint of the EP, the ordinary legislative procedure or the consent procedure is "the best".[278]

5.3.2 *Other powers and functions of the European Parliament*

General power of deliberation

Like most parliaments in the world, the EP has the function of deliberating about important political and social questions that preoccupy the citizens and their representatives and also about issues that will come before them in the form of draft legislation or an international agreement to be approved. The favoured instrument of parliaments at large, and also of the EP, in such situations is the motion or the resolution.

Long before the EP had been given the formal power, now enshrined in Article 225 TFEU, to invite the Commission to come forward with a proposal on a given matter, the Parliament regularly exerted pressure on the Commission to do so by adopting resolutions.[279] Similarly the Parliament has long tried to influence the progress of important international negotiations conducted by the Commission (and therewith the attitude of the Council that was supervising how the Commission executed its directives for the negotiations in question) by adopting resolutions relative to these negotiations, even before its powers of consent were as broad as they are now.[280] Resolutions were similarly used in domains where the Commission lacked legislative powers in the past, such as agriculture and fisheries (two important policies run largely by the Commission within the framework of Council only regulations), and presently in such areas as the CFSP and CSDP.[281]

Budgetary powers

Article 16(1) TEU states that the European Parliament, jointly with the Council, shall exercise budgetary functions. Articles 312–316 TFEU give further details on the nature of these functions. Thus, under Article 312(2) TFEU, the Council adopts a regulation laying down the multiannual

---

276. See now, as amended, Art. 217 read with 218(6)(a) TFEU.

277. There have been examples where the Parliament has denied its consent to certain international agreements. The best-known recent examples are the Swift agreement with the US and the multilateral Anti-Counterfeiting Trade Agreement (ACTA).

278. Cf. R. H. Lauwaars and R. H. Van Ooik, "De problematiek van de dubbele rechtsgrondslagen in het Europese recht", 7/8 SEW (2010) 294–306.

279. So-called "own initiative reports". E.g. European Parliament, D-G for Research, "Options for a definitive VAT system", (*Economic affairs series E – 5*, 1995). Available at: <www.europarl.europa.eu/RegData/etudes/etudes/join/1995/165529/DG-4-ECON_ET(1995)165529_EN.pdf>. See further the European Parliament study, "European Commission follow-up to European Parliament requests. A Rolling Check-List", (*EPRS*, 2017). Available at <file:///C:/Users/11110104/Downloads/QA0117037ENN_002.pdf>.

280. European Parliament Resolution of 24 Mar. 1994 on the results of the Uruguay Round of the GATT Multilateral Trade Negotiations, O.J. 1994, C 114/5, and European Parliament Resolution of 8 July 2015 containing the European Parliament's recommendations to the European Commission on the negotiations for the Transatlantic Trade and Investment Partnership (TTIP), (2014/2228(INI)).

281. E.g. European Parliament Resolution of 22 Nov. 2016 on the European Defence Union, (2016/2052(INI)).

financial framework, according to a special legislative procedure. This special procedure obliges the Council to decide by unanimity (or by qualified majority, if the European Council unanimously so authorizes), after consent of the EP given by a majority of its component Members.[282] Similarly the Union's annual budget is adopted by the EP and the Council jointly, on proposal of the Commission, acting in accordance with a special legislative procedure. This procedure is in outline close to the normal legislative procedure, with two readings of the budget proposal in Council and Parliament, the (early) establishment of a conciliation committee and an obligation of the EP to decide in many instances by a majority of its component Members to either adopt or reject (amendments to) the budget.[283]

Powers of supervision and control

Obviously, the instruments and powers of control and supervision that are at the disposal of the Parliament serve primarily to control the Commission in all its activities, since the Commission is politically responsible to the Parliament. Some of these instruments are also used in the Parliament's relations with the Council, but then rest primarily on what has become a "constitutional custom". An example is the instrument of parliamentary questions (and, presumably, the new closely related instrument of interpellations), which have been equally directed at the Commission and the Council, even in the absence of any political responsibility of the latter to the Parliament. There is the one restriction that questions to the Council may not deal with an ongoing ordinary legislative procedure or with the Council's budgetary functions,[284] since such questions should find a solution in the framework of the normal legislative and budgetary processes between the two institutions.

Another instrument that serves to help the EP to exercise oversight over the Commission, the Council, the Court of Auditors, the Ombudsperson, other institutions and agencies, is the reporting that these institutions are supposed to do. Annually the Parliament is nowadays inundated with a large number of such reports. The Commission alone, next to its Annual Report, produces quite a few specialized reports, *inter alia* on the application of Union law, on EU competition policy etc. This requires from the Parliament a careful parsing of these reports and deciding on their priority for discussion.

Furthermore the Parliament disposes of a Committee on Petitions[285] for looking into all kinds of complaints that are brought by petitioners and searching for information concerning these complaints. A similar role is played by the Special Committees that the EP institutes from time to time in order to look into specific problems relating to the functioning of the Union and its institutions or of the Member States, such as the recent scandals concerning emissions standards for diesel engines for cars and relating to tax rulings by Member State authorities and excessive techniques of tax avoidance, or even tax evasion.[286]

The above techniques of supervision and control are based on obtaining information or being given information and then using it to good effect. The big guns come out, when the actual instruments of political responsibility of the Commission are being resorted to. The first of those, coming up on a yearly basis, is the need for the Commission to obtain parliamentary discharge of its execution of the budget (Art. 319 TFEU). Both the Council and the Parliament

---

282. Art. 312(2) TFEU,
283. Art. 314 TFEU. See for a more extensive discussion of the EU budget, Ch. 9, "Budget and finances", of this book.
284. Annex II, point 2, relative to Arts. 130 -131A of the Rules of Procedure, op. cit. *supra* note 4.
285. See *supra* note 252.
286. See *supra* note 254 and accompanying text.

examine the accounts presented by the Commission and commented on the report of the Court of Auditors. In the end the EP gives a discharge or not. Even when the EP gives a discharge, that is often accompanied by points of criticism and desired improvements, to which the Commission must react. Refusal of a discharge in principle has no fatal effects for the Commission, but the Parliament has often argued that it should lead the Commission to resign. However, there is no indication in the Treaty to that effect, although a Commission will be seriously weakened, if it is obvious that the reasons why discharge is being refused are extremely serious. This was the case for the refusal of a discharge for the 1998 budget, which was related to certain payments made by Commissioner Cresson and thus contributed to the demise of the Santer Commission in the spring of 1999.

The ultimate sanction in the arsenal of the EP is the motion of censure of the Commission (Art. 234 TFEU). The Parliament can only vote on such a motion after three days of reflection and the required majority is two-thirds, comprising more than half of the statutory number of MEPs. So far all motions of censure have either been withdrawn before the vote or have not reached the required majority.[287] That the required majority for the motion of censure in the case of Mme. Cresson was only just missed was another contributing factor to the end of the Santer Commission.

5.4 *The relation with national parliaments*

It has rightly been pointed out that representatives of national parliaments, through the Convention format, in which they occupied more than half of the Convention's seats, have had considerable influence on the Constitution for Europe, and thus also on the Treaty of Lisbon. They have certainly had a hand in promoting the expansion of the powers of the European Parliament. However, their ideas about giving a greater influence to national parliaments, for instance by mixing members of national parliaments with the European Parliament or by creating a second chamber of the European Parliament consisting of members of national parliaments, have not had any resonance, as they were firmly resisted by the governments of the Member States.[288]

In the end, Protocol 1 of the Treaty of Lisbon, on the role of national parliaments, does not really go beyond earlier such Protocols attached to the Maastricht and Amsterdam Treaties. It lays down obligations on the part of the Union institutions, primarily the Commission, to provide national parliaments with all the important policy papers, the annual legislative programme and all draft legislative acts at the same time as such documents the European institutions send such documents to each other. The same goes for the Council agendas and the minutes of the Council meetings.[289] For draft legislative acts there should be a period of scrutiny for the national parliaments before the European institutions can take action on them. This will permit national parliaments to give a reasoned opinion on whether the proposed legislative act has respected the subsidiarity principle (further developed in Protocol 2).[290]

Many models have been suggested and tried for a kind of combined cooperative institution between the EP and the national parliaments. Protocol 1 merely suggests that the EP and national parliaments shall together make another attempt of agreeing on such an inter-parliamentary institution. Nothing has come of this. What does function is the Conference of Parliamentary Committees for Union Affairs (COSAC), which may submit any contribution to the three

287. See O. Costa and F. Saint Martin, op. cit. *supra* note 218, 148 et seq.

288. Ibid., 206 et seq.

289. Arts. 1,2 and 5 of Protocol (No 1) on the role of national parliaments, annexed to the consolidated version of the Treaty of Lisbon, O.J. 2016, C 202/1.

290. Ibid., Arts. 3 and 4.

institutions involved in producing EU legislation. It may also organize inter-parliamentary conferences to discuss specific topics of Union policies and promote the exchange of information on best practices between national Parliaments and the EP.[291]

Protocol 2 on the application of the principles of subsidiarity and proportionality lays down a much more thorough procedure for the vetting of subsidiarity by the national parliaments than Article 3 of Protocol 1. This includes the so-called "yellow card" and "orange card" procedures, which leads to a formal exchange of positions between national parliaments and the Commission. This is discussed in greater detail in the chapter on law-making.[292]

6. The relations between the four political institutions

In this section, we will venture to give an impression of the relations between the four political institutions, as we have described and analysed them above. These relations can be divided into relations of appointment, representation and responsibility, and political relations, as they have been fixed in the Treaties. The political relations as laid down in the Treaties can be distinguished in the legislative process and the budgetary process. Finally, these inter-institutional relations will be analysed in the light of their actual application in practice and be placed in the context of the notion of the "balance between the institutions", as developed by the Court of Justice, and the classical idea of the separation of powers.

6.1 Formal relations of appointment, representation, and responsibility

As already described above the European Council and the European Parliament together take care of the selection and appointment of the President of the Commission. The European Council takes the result of the elections for the European Parliament into account and consults widely, presumably with the Member States and the political groups within the Parliament, and then puts forward a candidate by qualified majority. The EP elects this candidate with the required majority or not. In the latter case the process is repeated.

Once the Commission President is elected, the European Council consults with him and, with his agreement appoints, the High Representative for Foreign Affairs and Security Policy, who is also Vice-President of the Commission. The European Council may end her term of office in the same way.

The Commission President is *ipso facto* a member of the European Council and the VP/HR takes part in its foreign affairs activities. Thus, the European Council, which also elects its own President, exercises a certain control over its own composition, insofar as its members are not legitimized as Heads of State or government of a Member State. The President of the European Parliament is present in the European Council, normally only at the beginning,

The Council of Ministers will fashion a common agreement with the President elect on the list of commissioners to propose to the EP and subsequently request the Parliament's consent with the whole Commission, including its President and the HR/VP. After this *investiture* the Commission, as proposed, shall be appointed by the European Council.

The Commission is formally politically responsible, as a whole, to the European Parliament, which can adopt a motion of censure, after which the Commission has to step down (except for the VP/HR, who only resigns in respect of her activities within the TFEU context). As has been mentioned above, motions of censure have at best had indirect success, most notably in the case of the Santer Commission.

291. Ibid., Arts. 9 and 10.
292. See Ch. 7, "Law-making", of this book.

As far as the choice of the President of the Commission is concerned, the Parliament and the European Political Parties clearly have had success limiting the freedom of the European Council by relentlessly propagating the idea of the *Spitzenkandidaten* during the 2014 election campaign for the European Parliament, making the selection of J.C. Juncker almost inevitable.

On a formal level, however, it remains remarkable how strongly the Commission is sandwiched between the European Council and Council of Ministers on the one side and the European Parliament on the other. There is no such political control of the institutions that are composed of the representatives of the Member States (except possible political control by their national parliaments); there is only a little bit of countervailing influence through the membership of the President of the Commission of the European Council. Only judicial control from outside this political quartet can correct acts with legal consequences from the side of the European Council and the Council of Ministers, and then only for their acts within the ambit of the TFEU.

In the section below it will be seen to what extent the picture is changed by looking at the political processes between these four institutions.

6.2 *Political inter-institutional relations*

6.2.1 *In the budgetary process*[293]

Even though the text of the Treaties does not grant any explicit powers to the European Council in setting the Union's budget, the reality is that the negotiations on the final, most controversial details of the multiannual financial framework take place in the European Council.[294] In fact, one of the key reasons for the institutional evolution of the European Council was its important role in conflict resolution (since the early 1980s) in matters of "who contributes how much, and who gets what financial benefits".[295] Thus, the Union's multiannual budget "cannot be concluded without the direct involvement of the European Council"[296] as it has a "de facto role as a forum for resolving deadlock during the final phase of budget negotiations".[297]

Article 16(1) TEU affirms that the Council and the European Parliament jointly shall exercise budgetary functions. Articles 312 ff. TFEU go into greater detail on these functions. Thus, under Article 312(2) and under the shadow of the European Council's decisions, the Council, on proposal of the Commission,[298] must adopt a regulation laying down the multiannual financial framework, according to a special legislative procedure with the consent of the EP.[299] As Article 312(1) TFEU now makes the multi-annual financial framework binding for the annual budgets, the EP has lost some budgetary autonomy in respect of the annual budget. Before the Lisbon Treaty, when Inter-institutional Agreements were the instrument by which the multi-annual budgetary framework was adopted, the Parliament was party to these agreements and thus directly influenced their contents and the subsequent annual budgets. Now it can only withhold its consent.[300]

---

293. For more details, see Ch. 9, "Budget and finances", of this book.
294. S. Peers, op. cit. *supra* note 33, at 61 and 68.
295. P. Craig and G. De Búrca, op. cit. *supra* note 26, 49.
296. U. Puetter, op. cit. *supra* note 3, 76.
297. Ibid., 90.
298. Presumably the Commission's proposal rests on Art. 17(2) TFEU, as it is not mentioned in Art. 312(2) TFEU.
299. The last such instrument is Council Reg. 1311/2013, laying down the multi-annual framework for the years 2014–2020, O.J. 2013, L 347/884. Art. 312(2), second subparagraph mentions the possibility of using QMV.
300. See below Ch. 9, "Budget and finances", of this book.

Similarly, the Union's *annual* budget is also adopted by the EP and the Council acting jointly, on proposal of the Commission, in accordance with a special legislative procedure. This procedure is in outline close to the ordinary legislative procedure, with two readings of the budget proposal in Council and Parliament, the (early) establishment of a conciliation committee and an obligation of the EP to decide in many instances by a majority of its component Members to either adopt or reject (amendments to) the budget.[301] Ultimately the EP has the power with a reinforced majority to adopt its amendments against the will of the Council.[302] However, Parliament remains subject to the discipline of the multi-annual financial framework and, moreover, Article 324 prescribes that the whole budgetary procedure should be governed by regular meetings between the presidents of the three concerned institutions called at the initiative of the Commission in order to foster consultation and reconciliation between the positions of the Commission, Council and Parliament.

6.2.2 *In legislative matters and questions of responsibility*

Preliminary remark

It is clear from the preceding paragraphs that all major political institutions have been affected in their functioning by the increase in their membership over the years since 2003. The Lisbon Treaty was supposed to provide a response to that challenge. However, the institutions in which all Member States are represented and the Commission have evolved necessarily from an atmosphere and style of leadership that could still be called "clubby" to a functioning that is closer to the so-called parliamentary diplomacy that characterizes large regional and worldwide organizations.[303] In particular the European Parliament has become so huge that it can only function through a very regimented style of leadership and meetings that are scripted to the last detail with very limited speaking time in the plenary, leaving very little room for spontaneous interventions during debates. These are consequences of size that the Lisbon Treaty could perhaps edulcorate, but never undo.

After this preliminary remark we will turn to a further analysis of the relations between the four political institutions from the perspective of each of these institutions relying on the description of each institution and its role in the legislative process given in sections 2 through 5, and drawing upon the summaries of the political responsibility relations between those institutions and of the budgetary process set out immediately above.

From the perspective of the European Council

It is important to realize, first of all, that the European Council, having become an institution of the Union, is henceforth subject to the duty of sincere cooperation just like the other institutions. The significance of this change has not yet fully sunk in whether with the European Council itself or the other institutions concerned, notably in those cases where the European Council has gone particularly far in setting out what ought to be the outcome of the legislative procedures, in which it has been called upon to arbitrate. There is a potential tension here between the European Council being used as a chamber of political appeal for the Council and the prohibition of exercising legislative functions by the European Council.[304]

---

301. Art. 314 TFEU.
302. Art. 314(7)(d) TFEU. See on this possibility in greater detail Ch. 9, "Budget and finances", of this book.
303. On parliamentary diplomacy, see J. Kaufmann, *Conference Diplomacy,* 2nd ed. (Nijhoff, 1988), and more recently S. Stavridis and D. Jancic, *Parliamentary Diplomacy in European and Global Governance* (Brill, 2017).
304. Art. 15(1), TEU, second sentence.

As stated earlier, the European Council is supported by what originally was the Council's General Secretariat.[305] And we have seen that the European Council and the Council have created a common identity towards the outside world. Since both the European Council President and the Council Presidency rely on the same body for support and assistance, this is a major factor in ensuring cooperation and coordination between the two presidents, one more permanent in nature and the other rotating periodically (with the exception of the presidency of the Foreign Affairs Council).[306]

Nothing terribly explicit is said in the Treaty of Lisbon regarding the issue of relationship between the presidencies of the European Council and the Council of Ministers other than in the context of the tasking of the GAC, when the European Council presidency would seem to have a leading role.[307] Unlike some proposals made in the context of the European Convention, there is no overlap with the work of the Council itself—the only explicit interface is with the GAC and in one direction: it must prepare and implement European Council work. Given, however, the fact that one presidency is permanent (and supported by the same Council Secretariat) and the other changes every six months (even if embedded in teams of three), it is relatively clear that the latter will *de facto* be in a subordinate position. This is also made apparent in a number of explicit provisions, such as that it is the European Council that adopts the decision establishing further formations in which the Council may meet and the Presidency of those Council formations (other than the General Affairs and the Foreign Affairs Councils).[308] Moreover, the rather Janus-faced figure of the new High Representative of the Union for Foreign Affairs and Security Policy does not only chair the Foreign Affairs Council but at the same time is also one of the vice presidents of the Commission.[309]

Particularly noteworthy is the fact that under the Lisbon Treaty, the foreign ministers no longer take part in the European Council meetings as a matter of course. However, Article 15(3) TEU provides that European Council members "may decide" to be assisted by a minister. In addition, the permanent presidency of the European Council means that all meetings of the European Council are held in Brussels rather than in individual Member States, when they are holding the Council Presidency. Both of these post-Lisbon changes have reduced the ability of the Council to exercise leadership when it comes to major political decisions of the EU.[310] As Christiansen observes, "[t]he outcome might be a kind of division of labour", with the European Council President concentrating on the "high politics" issues whereas the rotating Presidency takes care of routine business [the legislative work of the Union] and as such is focused on "low politics".[311]

Various arrangements aim to contribute to harmonious relations between the Commission and the European Council in the post-Lisbon legal order. As stated above, the President of the Commission is a member of the European Council, albeit without a right to vote. It must also be recalled that the High Representative, who is one of the Vice-Presidents of the Commission,

---

305. Art. 13 Rules of Procedure of the European Council, cited *supra* note 4.
306. D. Curtin, op. cit. *supra* note 23, 77–78.
307. The Member of the European Council, whose country holds the Presidency of the Council reports back to the European Council on the work of the Council, Art. 4(1) Rules of Procedure of the European Council, cited *supra* note 4.
308. Art. 236 TFEU.
309. See further D. Curtin, op. cit. *supra* note 23, 85 et seq.
310. T. Christiansen, "The European Union after the Lisbon Treaty: An elusive "institutional balance"?" in A. Biondi et al., op. cit. *supra* note 90, 238.
311. Ibid. 239. This distinction between "high politics" and "low politics" applies in particular in the field of external action.

also takes part in the work of the European Council. Moreover, according to the Rules of Procedure of the European Council, the President of the European Council "shall establish *close cooperation and coordination* with the Presidency of the Council and the President of the Commission, particularly by means of regular meetings" (emphasis added).[312] With regard to agenda setting, while the European Council is given the power to define the priorities of the Union, the Commission retains the power to initiate the multi-annual agenda of the EU.[313]

However, it is well known that the establishment of the post of the permanent President of the European Council was strongly opposed by the Commission and perceived as a threat to its powers.[314] The Commission was until then the only one of the four political institutions to have a permanent President that could speak for the Union both externally and internally without much challenge from the other institutions. Now this monopoly by default has fallen away. Again, the division between "high politics" and "low politics" applies: The President of the European Council maintaining the contacts with third States at the level of heads of State and government and the Commission representing the Union in the TFEU domain.

The relation between the European Council and the European Parliament is one at arm's length, which is to be expected in a situation where the Parliament has no formal controlling power over the European Council and the latter has only a limited duty to report to the Parliament. Its President generally represents the European Council before the EP; he is charged with reporting to the EP after each meeting of the European Council.[315] Moreover, the member of the European Council representing the Member State holding the Presidency of the Council shall present to the European Parliament the priorities of its Presidency and the results achieved during the six-month period.[316] According to Article 235(2) TFEU, the President of the EP may be invited to be heard by the European Council. However, this is a long-standing practice as the EP President has addressed the plenary session of the European Council since 1988.[317]

From the perspective of the Council

It has been demonstrated above, how the Council of Ministers, now simply called the Council, is working hand in glove with the European Council, following its guidelines and reporting back, through the European Council member holding the rotating Presidency of the Council. Moreover, it has become embedded more and more, like the other two institutions that are involved in the legislative and budget cycles, in a relationship of mutual dependency, planning and coordination. The budget cycle has its own seven-yearly and yearly cycles, which require constant coordination meetings between the protagonists, which have been formalized in Article 324 TFEU. The legislative work of the Union is also increasingly planned in annual legislative programmes (Commission), rolling three-Presidency cycles of 18 months (Council) and parliamentary year cycles (EP) that have to mesh with each other. Collaboration on synchronizing these cycles is more and more laid down in informal agreements and formal inter-institutional agreements.[318] Thus, both the Commission and the European Council have a say in the long-

312. Art. 2(3) Rules of Procedure of the European Council, cited *supra* note 4.
313. P. Craig, op. cit. *supra* note 27, 107.
314. Ibid., 84.
315. Art. 15(6)(d) TEU and Art. 5 Rules of Procedure of the European Council, cited *supra* note 4.
316. Ibid., Art. 5.
317. P. Craig and G. De Búrca, op. cit. *supra* note 26, 49.
318. E.g. European Parliament and Council Decision 2013/108 of 21 Nov. 2012 on mobilization of the European Union Solidarity Fund, O.J. 2013, L 56/15; Interinstitutional Agreement of 17 May 2006 on budgetary discipline and sound financial management; Commission proposal of 18 Mar. 2013 for a European Parliament and Council Decision amending the Interinstitutional Agreement of 17 May 2006 on budgetary discipline

term agenda of the Council. On the other hand, as we have already seen, the Council, and also the European Parliament, can strongly influence the Commission's so-called exclusive legislative initiative under Articles 241 and 225 TFEU. In in respect of both co-legislators the Commission must give reasons why it does not want to follow their requests.[319] In practice it may thus be very difficult for the Commission to resist such requests.

As to the Council's relationship with the EP, it is clear that under the Lisbon Treaty in particular, the EP's powers have been greatly expanded, placing it on more of an equal footing with the Council, while the Commission's role in the legislative procedure has declined with every reform of the Treaties since Maastricht. Most of the times the ordinary legislative procedure applies, after Lisbon also in the important area of agriculture and fisheries (Art. 43(2) TFEU). In addition, in the field of external action, the consent of the EP is required for nearly all international agreements outside the domain of the CFSP, as the exception for trade agreements has fallen away. As a result, the Council can no longer legislate alone or dictate its terms to the Commission and instead has to cooperate with the EP in exercising its legislative, budgetary and foreign affairs powers. This changed power relation between the Council and the Parliament, has also had its influence on the position of the Commission to the extent that it has become more difficult for the Council, under the watchful eye of the Parliament, to bury certain Commission proposals forever in its desk drawers, if the interest of Parliament in these proposals is broad and strong enough.[320]

The only area of Union power, where the Council, under the guidelines of the European Council, has retained its near unfettered powers after Lisbon, is the Common Foreign and Security Policy (CFSP) and the Common Security and Defence Policy (CSDP). Because the operational aspects of this policy were hardly paid out of the Union budget, but mostly by the Member States, the Council remained largely unrestrained in this domain by any counter-power. Only the Parliament retained its right of at least being informed of the CFSP and the CSDP and exercising a minimum of scrutiny over it.[321] Moreover, the Court had and has the power to watch over the frontier between the CFSP/CSDP and the Union policies and did so effectively already before Lisbon.[322] On the other hand in this field the Council Secretariat lost its Commission-like tasks of conception combined with execution because of the creation of the European External Action Service under the High Representative for Foreign Affairs *cum* Vice-President of the Commission, which was placed between Council and Commission.

From the perspective of the European Parliament

There can be little doubt that the European Parliament has gained most in power relative to the other political institutions, except perhaps the European Council, both in the long run and after the latest amendments of the Union treaties. The "democratic deficit" of the EU, the increasing

---

and sound financial management as regards the multiannual financial framework, to take account of the expenditure requirements resulting from the accession of Croatia to the European Union, COM(2013)157 final; Inter-institution Declaration on Democracy, Transparency and Subsidiarity, Bull-EC 10-1993.

319. The Council's discretion in doing so is much larger than that of the Parliament, which must show that a Union act is required for the purpose of implementing the treaties.

320. See, for instance, the Commission proposals in respect of foreign direct investment, which could very well have fallen into oblivion but for the avid interest of Parliament in them. See Ch. 41, "External relations", section 2, of this book. On the other hand, if the Council is near-unanimously of the view that a Commission proposal should not go further, the EP has no final sanction against the Council, if the latter truly wants to bury that proposal.

321. Case C-658/11, *Parliament v. Council.*

322. Case C-91/05, *Commission v. Council (Ecowas).*

democratization of the Member States' governments, in particular in the field of foreign affairs, have stimulated the granting of more and more powers to the EP in the course of successive treaty reforms. The Lisbon Treaty has been, as far as one can see, the crown on this work, except for the exclusion of CFSP and CSDP from the Parliament's participation in decision-making. The legislative and the budgetary procedure, as well as the approval of international agreements, begin approaching the model of some federal states, with an upper chamber, consisting of delegations of the Member States, and a lower house representing the population of the federation as a whole.[323] Both chambers must come to an agreement, if necessary through protracted negotiations in so-called conciliation committees.

When looking at the Parliament from the Council's vantage point, it was indeed clear that both branches of the Union's legislative power now stand on an equal footing with each other and that they are condemned to close collaboration, if the Union is to have a workable budget and good legislation. From the EP's side the perspective cannot be much different, except that the Parliament is probably conscious that formally it has the last word in budgetary matters, which can tilt the balance of power ever so slightly its way.

As far as the relation between the EP and the European Council is concerned, it was shown that, in spite of a certain amount of mutual participation by the Presidents from both sides on the occasion of the meetings of the European Council, the two institutions keep each other at arm's length. The European Council has no strong relation to the European Parliament, since it cannot participate in legislative functions, but on the other side the EP tries to subject the European Council to its general power of political scrutiny, although it does not dispose of any political sanction that has a basis in the EU Treaties.

Insofar as the power of political approval and censure of the Parliament over the Commission is concerned, the Parliament has been busy, from as soon as it obtained these powers, to chip away at their collective character. *De facto* the EP has now acquired a right of individual approval over the nomination of Commissioners, simply by threatening the Commission President elect with using the collective sanction otherwise. It remains to be seen whether the Parliament can obtain a right of individual censure over Commissioners in a similar way, by once again threatening to use the nuclear option of collective censure unless the President uses his power of requesting a Member of the Commission to resign (Art. 17(6) *in fine* TFEU).[324]

In the same vein the European Parliament has attempted to reinforce the link of political accountability between itself and the Commission and to turn the latter into more of a European Union government by introducing the idea of the "*Spitzenkandidaten*" (party leaders) in the campaign for the EP elections and thus forcing the European Council to give some real content to the words "taking into account the elections to the European Parliament"[325] when selecting the Commission President and in the subsequent "formation" of the full Commission. This experiment has had a mixed reception in the literature,[326] but it has emboldened the Commission in several respects.

---

323. As the reader is well aware from the preceding paragraphs on the individual institutions, this is only a rough approximation of the reality.
324. Such attempts by the EP to bend the rules of the Treaties with a view to making the control of the Parliament over the Commission more proportional to the seriousness of the "political sins" committed by one or more Commissioners raise delicate questions about the formation of constitutional custom, as it has happened also in national constitutional systems, that might be regarded by the Court as unconstitutional in the light of the explicit wording of Art. 17(7) and (8) TEU.
325. Art. 17(7) TEU.
326. M. Goldoni, "Politicising EU lawmaking? The Spitzenkandidaten experiment as a cautionary tale", 22 ELJ (2016), 279–295.

The fact that the EP has the final word in the budgetary procedure seems to give it a slight edge within the triangle of Commission-Council-Parliament that deals with these matters. The Commission which in the past was involved in the legislative procedure until the last moment in a constant dialogue with the Council, now has become mostly an honest broker and is under constant risk of being marginalized, especially during the second reading of its proposal. This is even more so, when Council and Parliament proceed to the second reading almost immediately without formally closing the first reading, as has become a frequent occurrence lately. Hence it is of great importance that the Commission's right of withdrawing its proposal has been recognized also in such situations by the ECJ.[327] This practice of proceeding almost immediately to the second reading of a legislative proposal as between Parliament and Council has been severely criticized for reasons related to transparency and proper procedure.[328]

When the Parliament has availed itself of its right to have the last word, it has done so forcefully, *inter alia* by turning down a number of important treaties for reasons related to fundamental rights and self-determination.[329]

From the perspective of the Commission

Inevitably a lot has already been said about the Commission from the perspective of the other political institutions. It has often been painted in the literature as the great loser of the successive treaty reforms, notably of the Lisbon Treaty.[330] It is undeniable that the Commission has indeed lost power in relation to the other two institutions implicated in the legislative and budgetary cycles, principally to the European Parliament, which has become a real co-legislator, a role that before Maastricht was played in large part by the Commission through its interaction with the Council. And also to the European Council in respect to agenda-setting.

Views differ as to how the Lisbon changes affected the power balance between these two institutions in practice. Some commentators argue that the rise in the powers of the European Council (through the more frequent meetings, the permanent presidency, and the more limited composition which excludes foreign ministers)[331] does not impinge on the powers of the Commission as the European Council has merely used the policy-making space created by *new* areas of EU activity.[332]

327. See Case C-409/13, *Commission v. Council (Right of Withdrawal)*.
328. See D. Curtin, op. cit. *supra* note 23; A. Berthier, "Transparency in EU Lawmaking", (2016) *ERA Forum*.
329. The cases in question were: Swift and the relevant agreement with the US concerning the equivalence of data protection rules in the US and the EU; the Fisheries Agreement with Morocco because of Morocco's implied extension of that agreement to the Economic Zone in the Atlantic off the coast of Western Sahara; and the Anti-Counterfeiting Trade Agreement (ACTA). See further: G. Rosén, "The impact of norms on political decision-making: how to account for the European Parliament's empowerment in EU external trade policy", JEPP (2016). Available at <www.tandfonline.com/doi/full/10.1080/13501763.2016.1227357> (last visited May 2017).
330. See O. Höing and W. Wessels, "The European Commission's position in the post-Lisbon institutional balance. Secretariat or partner to the European Council?" in M. Chang et al. (Eds.), *The European Commission in the Post-Lisbon Era of Crises: Between Political Leadership and Policy Management* (Peter Lang, 2013). T. Christiansen, op. cit. *supra* note 309.
331. U. Puetter, op. cit. *supra* note 9, 8–9.
332. Ibid., U. Puetter states that "[e]specially in the areas of economic governance and foreign policy, the Commission has become an actor besides rather than above the member state executives that commands some of the relevant resources for policy development and implementation".

Others claim that the enhanced powers of the European Council have led to diminished powers for the Commission, especially in the area of legislative agenda-setting.[333] While yet others hold that the power relationship between the European Council and the Commission in the area of legislative agenda setting can be characterized as one of "competitive cooperation" where elements of both the hierarchical principal-agent model and the more cooperative joint agenda-setting model are present.[334] While opinions on this issue vary, the potential for tensions between the two institutions is quite tangible in a Union characterized by shared executive power.[335]

Nevertheless, the Commission's (exclusive) power as an initiator of legislation and of the budget remains indispensable. This has been clearly demonstrated by the real-life experiment during the period (1992–1998), when the then new domain of Justice and Home Affairs was run entirely as an intergovernmental affair, where the proposals for legislation had to be made by the Member States, mostly the one holding the six-month presidency of the Council, and had to be adopted by unanimity. The proposals that were put forward by the Member States were often hobby horses of their governments, drafted too much in their national traditions and taking little account of the traditions and needs of other Members of the Union. The negotiations, which had to be achieved by unanimity, usually led to a tasteless lowest common denominator.[336] After having had the experience of this system for several years, Member States decided by the Treaty of Amsterdam, to apply the "Community method" to Justice and Home Affairs, including the Commission monopoly of proposal.[337]

Seen in this perspective, it is extremely important that the Commission, with the help of the ECJ, has been able to safeguard the right of withdrawal of its proposals, when the co-legislators are about to amend it so completely that it is "perverted", i.e. that its original objective can impossibly be reached any longer.[338] This is the only weapon that the Commission still has to maintain the original intention of its proposals, when the two co-legislators proceed on their own without heeding the Commission's advice. The possible withdrawal is thus a vital protection of a true right of proposal.

Furthermore, the Commission's position as author of delegated legislation and as implementer of basic regulations, has been better regulated in the Lisbon Treaty (Arts. 191 and 192 TFEU) and considerably reinforced its position in relation to the co-legislators. Although the literature has tended to argue, especially in respect of implementing powers, that some habits of the old "comitology" die hard and that thus the "revolution" is not what it has been made out to be,[339] there is little doubt that the leeway for the Council to reserve implementing powers to itself has been diminished and that as a consequence the Commission in such fields as agriculture, fisheries and trade has become much more solidly entrenched as the implementer of important policies of the Union.

---

333. M. Dawson and F. de Witte, "Constitutional balance in the EU after the Euro-crisis", 76 MLR (2013), 817–844, 830.
334. P. Bocquillon and M. Dobbels, op. cit. *supra* note 20, 34.
335. For a detailed discussion on shared executive power in the EU, see P. Craig, op. cit. *supra* note 27, 101–120.
336. P.J. Kuijper, "Some legal problems associated with the communitarization of policy on visas, asylum and immigration under the Amsterdam Treaty and incorporation of the Schengen acquis", 37 CML Rev. (2000), 345–366, 345; S. Peers, "Mission accomplished? EU Justice and Home Affairs law after the Treaty of Lisbon", 48 CML Rev. (2011), 661–693, 661.
337. In reality there were still quite some deviations from the full Community method in the Amsterdam Treaty, but these have been successively removed by subsequent treaty modifications until only very few remained.
338. Case C-409/13, *Council v. Commission (Right of Withdrawal).*
339. See M. Chamon, "Institutional balance and Community method in the implementation of EU legislation following the Lisbon Treaty", 53 CML Rev. (2016), 1501 -1544.

6.3 *Final reflections*

After the above description and analysis, it is pretty clear that of the four political institutions there are three that seem permanently and inevitably linked to each other in constant collaborative combat in the framework of the budgetary and legislative procedures. The European Council stands a bit apart from the other three, which are subject to its power of setting priorities and giving guidance. Moreover, it is not subject to any formal mechanism of political control from the other three, of which the Council of Ministers is simply completely subservient to it. The Parliament is the only countervailing power that tries to get a grip on the European Council through the latter's obligation to appear from time to time before it, and to report on its actions and intentions. Supported by a Court ruling, the Parliament also tries to bring its general power of scrutiny to bear on the European Council, also in the field of the CFSP.

Indeed, the European Council is not *legibus solutus*, as it is hemmed in by the prohibition on its participating in legislative activity and by the duty of sincere cooperation. These legal restrictions on the European Council's powers may become relevant, if it tries to prescribe solutions for certain problem in such detail as to *de facto* prescribing legislative texts that the Council of Ministers and, implicitly, also the Parliament should adopt. There are reports in the literature that warrant the conclusion, not merely that this might happen, but that it has actually happened already.[340] In such cases guidance is transformed into actual, forbidden, participation in the legislative process. The Court of Justice would be the final arbiter in such a case, which would most likely be brought by the Parliament. There is a delicate balance to be achieved between powers of guidance and powers of legislation.

The European Council, after its full integration into the Union legal system after Lisbon, is no doubt a mighty, if not the mightiest, player in the quartet of the Union's political institutions. However, this further constitutionalization of the European Council also brings some restraints on its powers, as we have seen.

As between the other three political institutions, constantly engaged in their political work in the framework of the legislative and budgetary procedures, a formal political sanction is operative only between two of them, namely between the European Parliament and the Commission. As was already signalled earlier, it is, once again, the organ that is composed of Member State representatives, the Council, which escapes legally formalized political control. On the other hand, as we have shown, the EP subjects the Council to its general scrutiny (questions, interpellations, reports by special committees) broadly in the same way as the Commission, in spite of the absence of any possible political sanction.

In the end, it remains a bit of an anomaly that the EU organs with national representation are subject to judicial control, but not to political control except by the general scrutiny powers of the European Parliament. Even if composed of national representatives, these organs remain organs of the Union, not organs of the Member States. If they can be subject to a judicial sanction at the behest of Parliament, why can they not be exposed to political control by the same Parliament?

The Council has lost a lot of its autonomy with the European Council directly above it and both being served by the same administrative machinery. Moreover, it must now, after Lisbon, share its legislative, budgetary and treaty-making powers, which it still exercised virtually alone in quite some domains, with the co-equal European Parliament. The Council also lost an important part of its executive power in the field of the AFSJ to the Commission and some Agencies,

340. 'Editorial Comments: The EU Quest for Unity', 54 CML Rev., 681–694, 685.

and in the CFSP to the EEAS – which now plays a Commission-like role in that domain, albeit without a monopoly of proposal.

The Commission has shed quite some feathers as *the* agenda setter of the EU, whereas the European Council has now taken quite a bit of this role in practice. The Commission's remaining "freedom" not to follow the guidance of the European Council and not make certain proposals is largely illusory in reality. Recently the Commission has attempted to take back some of the initiative in the post-Brexit discussion about the future of Europe, but it is characteristic that it has done so in the form of an options paper without giving clear guidance. The Commission has gained in regulatory and executive power in the AFSJ and in trade, but lost such powers in CFSP. It has gained in general, with delegated legislation and implementing powers. This is due to the introduction of Articles 291 and 292 in the Lisbon Treaty, combined with considerable effort to have these procedures introduced in many existing basic regulations.

There is little doubt that over the years the EP has gained substantially in powers by the simple force of the argument that more direct democratic legitimation of Union legislation was necessary. It has profited from this sentiment as the application of what is now called the co-legislative procedure and the cases in which assent/consent of the EP was required were extended with every modification of the European Treaties ever since Maastricht. Moreover, its rights as co-legislator have been well protected by the procedures for delegated legislative power and implementing powers as laid down in the Lisbon Treaty.

In the light of the above synthesis, it is evident that the two principal political organs of yore, the Commission and the Council have, relatively speaking, declined in power and influence in comparison with the European Council, now fully integrated into the Union system, and the steadily rising European Parliament. This is now the new "balance between the institutions" created by the Lisbon Treaty and, as usual, upheld by the EUCJ.[341] As it is quite likely that the Treaty of Lisbon will not be modified for quite some time because of the basic impossibility to have any modification ratified by all Member States simultaneously, the crucial question will be how the necessary adjustments and adaptations to the balance between the political institutions will be possible in the decades to come. In national constitutional systems constitutional custom has been formed without modifying the written text of constitutions or basic laws. Can the EUCJ forget its standard approach to such claims, namely that "mere practice cannot change the Treaty"?[342] Can it be convinced that certain practice is not "mere" practice? Can Member States use post-Treaty interpretative declarations under the classic international law of treaties in order to *de facto* modify the balance between the institutions?[343]

7 Advisory bodies

7.1 *Common provisions*

The treaty of Lisbon created a separate chapter for what it called "the Union's Advisory Bodies", which serves to distinguish them from the institutions. These are the Economic and Social Committee (ESC), which has existed from the beginning of the EEC, and the Committee of the Regions (CoR), which was introduced by the Treaty of Maastricht. The ESC was based on

341. It would seem that "the balance between the institutions does not exist", see B. De Witte, "The institutional balance in the European Union: Is there a need for a new horizontal division of powers?" in R. Herzog and S. Hobe (Eds.), *Die Europäische Union auf dem Weg zum verfassten Staatenverbund: Perspektiven der europäischen Verfassungsordnung* (C.H. Beck, 2004).

342. E.g. Opinion 1/94.

343. In the institutional core of the TFEU it will not be possible to use the technique of intergovernmental agreements next to the TFEU, as with respect to EMU.

a model that existed in many founding Members of the EEC; it reflected a reality of the socio-economic relations in the Member States at the time. The Committee of the Regions was created at the request of the federal or strongly decentralized Member States, and Member States that were starting a process of decentralization or devolution.[344] These two Committees have a number of identical Treaty provisions in common. They have the same maximum number of Members (350), who must be independent, receive no instructions from anyone, and shall exercise their functions only in the Union's interest. The Council, acting unanimously, on a proposal from the Commission, will fix the actual composition of both Committees; this concerns the distribution of the seats among the Member States.[345] The members of both Committees will have a mandate of five years, which is renewable. The chair and the officers of the Committees serve for two and a half years after having been elected by the members. The Committees adopt each their rules of procedure and they are served by the same Secretariat.[346] Both Committees shall be consulted by one of the three legislative institutions, when that is prescribed in the TFEU and whenever the Commission, Council or Parliament so request.

7.2 *Economic and Social Committee*

The composition of the ESC has been adapted over the years from a straightforward representation of employers and employed to include new groups. Article 300(2) speaks of "other parties representative of civil society, notably in socio-economic, civic, professional and cultural areas". In reality the ESC nowadays consists of an employers group (117 members from various employers organizations from all Member States), a workers group (116 members from organized labour organizations) and a third group (consisting of 111 members of different civic groups, including consumers' organizations, volunteer organizations etc.). The Council appoints these members in accordance with the proposals made by each Member State; it consults the Commission on these appointments, which in turn may obtain the views of the European bodies of employers, workers and representatives of civil society.

The ESC has to be consulted, according to the TFEU, by the co-legislators (Council and European Parliament together), when they are about to legislate in the different areas of the internal market,[347] in relation to harmonization measures[348] and in the framework of the transport and agricultural policies.[349] Moreover, the ESC's advice is obligatory with respect to measures relating to the flanking policies of the internal market, such as Employment, Social Policy, Public Health, Consumer Protection, Industry, Structural Funds, Research and the Environment.[350] The legislative institutions may subject the advice to a deadline and continue the legislative procedure if that deadline is not kept.[351] It is striking that advice about legislative proposals in the field of competition and State aids has never been added. It is likely that advice by the ESC could have been very useful indeed on these policies.

---

344. Even traditionally strongly centralized Member States, like France and the UK have gone through such a process over the last three decades. It bears pointing out that the European Movement has included from the beginning a strong regionalist stream that emphasized federalism from the bottom up and trans-frontier regionalism. See P. Wagstaff, *Regionalism in the European Union* (Exeter, 1999).
345. See Arts. 300(4), 301 and 305 TFEU. See also Art. 7 of Protocol (No 36) to the Treaty of Lisbon (Transitional provisions).
346. Arts. 302, 303, 306 and 307 TFEU.
347. Art. 46 TFEU (free movement of persons), Art. 50(1) TFEU (establishment), Art. 59(1) TFEU (services).
348. Art. 113 TFEU, (harmonization of indirect taxes) and Art. 114 and 115 TFEU (general harmonization).
349. Art. 43(2), (common organizations of the markets) and Art. 91(2) (common transport policy).
350. Respectively Arts 148(2), 153(2), 168(4), 169(3), 172,173(3), 177, 182(4) and 192(1) and (2) TFEU.
351. Art. 304 TFEU. This rule is also applicable to the CoR, see Art. 307 TFEU.

The three institutions involved in the ordinary legislative procedure may each ask the ESC, if they see fit, for advice on other matters. Finally, the ESC has acquired a right to give *sua sponte* advice to these three institutions, in cases in which it considers this appropriate.[352]

There is no denying that in most Member States the social dialogue has often been neglected in decision-making and that organs which embody the social dialogue have lost influence. Inevitably this has had repercussions on the weight that has been given to the advice of the ESC. It is uncertain if the "modernization" of Group 3 of the ESC has been able to improve this situation.

7.3 *Committee of the Regions*

The CoR was brought into the Treaty at Maastricht and has to be consulted on many subjects on which the ESC is obligatorily consulted as well: in the fields of employment and social policy, public healthy, trans-European networks, structural funds and the environment.[353] As can be seen, these subjects have a regional dimension or concern areas where powers have been devolved by Member States to the regions, such as the environment. The CoR may also issue advice on other subjects on which the ESC has been consulted, if it believes that these subjects have a specific regional interest. Moreover, the CoR, like the ESC, may issue and opinion on its own initiative.

The CoR consists of representatives of the regions and local bodies; they must hold a local or regional electoral mandate or be politically accountable to an elected assembly. The way in which the members are appointed is identical to that of the members of the ESC, but the Treaty also provides for alternate members. For obvious reasons there is an incompatibility with the membership of the European Parliament.[354]

It is common knowledge that the number of regional, provincial and local representative offices from all Member States in Brussels is considerable and that the Commission and other institutions are intensely lobbied by these offices, if their interests may be affected by actions of the institutions. There is reason to pose the question whether the CoR has much of a value-added, if so many regional and local authorities prefer to deal with the EU institutions on their own.

8. Common rules

8.1 *Privileges and immunities*

The uniform rules on the privileges and immunities of the EU, necessary for the performance of its tasks in the territories of the Member States are laid down in Protocol (No. 7) on the Privileges and Immunities (PPI) of the European Union to the Lisbon Treaty (Art. 343 TFEU).[355] It deals with the privileges and immunities of the Union (and Euratom, see Art. 191 of the EAEC Treaty), of the members of its institutions, its officials and other servants, the representatives of the Member States taking part in the work of the institutions, and of the missions accredited to the Union. The provisions of the Protocol also apply in relation to the Union's supplementary policies and forms of cooperation to the extent that the Union institutions are entrusted with a decision-making role; to the European Investment Bank (Art. 28 Protocol No. 5 on the EIB) and the European Central Bank (Art. 39 Protocol No 4 on the ECSB and the ECB).[356] The members

352. Art. 302(2) TFEU. This provision was added at Maastricht, when also many of the new provisions on flanking policies containing an obligation to seek advice from the ESC were introduced into the Treaty.
353. See *supra* note 349.
354. Art. 305 TFEU.
355. This Protocol was originally attached to the Merger Treaty and entered into force on 1 Jan. 1967. It has only been subject to technical modifications since then.
356. See also Arts. 21 and 22 PPI.

of the Court of Auditors are placed on the same footing as members of the Court of Justice (Art. 247(9) EC), as is the President of the European Council.[357]

Articles 1 and 2 of the PPI lay down rules concerning the inviolability of the premises, the buildings, and the archives of the Communities. They further provide that their property and assets may not be the subject of any administrative or legislative measure of constraint without the authorization of the Court of Justice. The Court's authorization is required in order to prevent an untimely or inappropriate encroachment on the independent functioning of the Community in favour of private interests.[358] Articles 3 and 4 PPI contain rules on the exemption of the Communities from direct and indirect taxes or sales taxes and from customs duties or import or export prohibitions and restrictions. Articles 5 and 6 PPI relates to freedom of communication and to travel documents (*laissez-passer*) for the members of the institutions and officials and other servants. Articles 7 through 9 relate to the specific phenomenon of parliamentary immunity of members of the European Parliament. This kind of immunity is not to be compared to state or diplomatic immunity; it guarantees a higher level of freedom of speech and of action for members of parliament in the exercise of their function than usual in society.[359]

The privileges and immunities of officials and other servants of the EU are laid down in Articles 11 through 13. This includes the non-application of Member States' rules on entry, residence and importation of personal effects, when they move to another Member State or take up residence there in connection with their work for the Union. Freedom from direct taxes in that country is guaranteed to officials and servants of the Union, but other taxes, such as wealth tax and death duties remain due in the country whence they came.[360] It is up to the co-legislators to determine in accordance with the ordinary legislative procedure which categories of officials or other servant will come under the protection of Articles 11–13 (Art. 15 PPI). The order of the Court in *Zwartveld et al.*[361] illustrates that the protection afforded by the Protocol is not absolute but functional in nature, and does not extend further than is necessary to avoid any interference with the functioning and independence of the Union (Art. 17(1) PPI).[362]

The immunity from the jurisdiction of its Member States, which is normally granted to other international organizations, is lacking. In principle, the Union can also be summoned to appear before national courts in the Member States without their consent, at least in so far as the Court of Justice has not been declared competent in the matter by or in pursuance of the Treaties (see Arts. 274 TFEU, 155 Euratom). In view of the extensive competence of the Court this will only very rarely occur. The Court of Justice has jurisdiction in disputes concerning the Community's non-contractual liability (Arts. 268 TFEU, 151 Euratom).[363] Articles 270 TFEU and 152 Euratom declare that the Court also has jurisdiction in any dispute between the Communities and their

357. See also Arts. 19 and 20 PPI.
358. Case 4/62, *Application for authorization to enforce a garnishee order against the High Authority.*
359. See also *supra* section 5.1.1 *in fine.*
360. The Court has taken the position that Arts. 12 and 13 (formerly 13 and 14) PPI "establish a division of fiscal powers between the EU and the Member State in which the official (...) had his domicile for tax purposes before entering the service of the EU [...]", Case C-270/10, *Lotta Gistø,* para 14.
361. Case C-2/88, *Zwartveld.*
362. Further see *supra* section 4.2.2.
363. Such actions are fairly rare; since 2000, there have been some 8 of which 2 were appealed (Case C-460/09 P, *Inalca & Cremonini v. Commission* and C-282/05, *Holcim*) and 2 were concerned with non-contractual responsibility for lawful conduct (both rejected: T-69/00, *FIAMM et al v. Council and Commission* and T-138/03, *E.R. et al. v. Commission*). Two others concerned the costly aftermath of the so-called Mulder litigation, on the unlawful refusal of milk quota to certain Netherlands producers.

servants.[364] It is important to recall here that the European Civil Service Tribunal was split off from the General Court in 2004[365] and was reintegrated into that Court again in September 2016.[366] Moreover, in many contracts of a public law or private law nature, or in general conditions applicable thereto, an arbitration clause confers jurisdiction on the Court to hear disputes relating to such contracts (see Arts. 272 TFEU, 153 Euratom).[367]

8.2 *Seat of the Institutions*

The Treaties contain identical provisions concerning the seat of the Community Institutions: it "shall be determined by common accord of the governments of the Member States". (Cf. Arts. 341 TFEU, 189 Euratom). After repeated decisions on provisional working places, a definitive decision was adopted in 1992 at Edinburgh by common agreement of the governments of the Member States.[368] This decision, updated with the ECB and Europol, was attached as a Protocol to the Treaty of Amsterdam and is now Protocol (No 6) to the Lisbon Treaty.[369] What initially was intended to be an intergovernmental decision of the Member States based on the Treaty has now been included in part in the primary law of the Union.[370]

Protocol 6 confirms the existing situation at the time of the Edinburgh decision, except for the two new additions. Parliament has its seat in Strasbourg, where the 12 periods of monthly plenary sessions, including the budget session must be held. Periods of additional plenary sessions are held in Brussels, where the Parliament's Committees also meet. The Parliament's General Secretariat and its departments remain in Luxembourg. The Council has its seat in Brussels, but its meetings are held in Luxembourg during the months of April, June and October. The Commission also has its seat in Brussels, but certain departments are established in Luxembourg. The Economic and Social Committee (ECOSOC) and the Committee of the Regions (which shares an organizational structure with ECOSOC) also have their seat in Brussels. The Court of Justice, the Court of Auditors, and the European Investment Bank all have their seat

---

364. To illustrate both the diversity of EU institutions and services that can be involved and the diversity of the subject matter of the cases, the following recent cases are highlighted: Case C-417/14 RX-II, *Livio Missir Mamachi de Lusignano v. Commission* relative to damages in connection with the tragic murder of an EU diplomat and his wife *en poste* and illustrating the complicated relation between Court of Justice, General Court and Civil Service Tribunal; Joined Cases T-504 and 505/16, *Jean-Pierre Bodson et al. v. EIB* concerning the annulment of salary decisions contrary to earlier commitments; Case T-569/16, *OU v. Commission*, seeking the repayment of sums withheld subsequent to a disciplinary procedure; Case T-585/16, *Carina Skareby v. EAAS* relative to the refusal of permission to publish an article.
365. Council Decision 2004/752/EC, establishing the European Civil Service Tribunal, O.J. 2004, L 333/7.
366. Reg. (EU, Euratom) 2016/1192 on the transfer to the General Court of jurisdiction at first instance in disputes between the European Union and its servants, OJ. 2016, L 200/137.
367. Since the entry into force of the Lisbon Treaty, there have been 9 cases under Art. 272 TFEU handled by the General Court, of which 2 have been appealed to the Court of Justice: Case C-78/14 P, *Commission v. ANKO* and Case C-564/13, P *Planet v. Commission.*
368. O.J. 1992, C 341/1. The decision was adopted on the occasion of the Edinburgh European Council in December 1992, Bull. EC 12-92, points I.14 and I.32.
369. Protocol (No 6) on the Location of the Seats of the Institutions and of Certain Bodies, Offices, Agencies and Departments of the European Union.
370. It interesting to note that the ECB and Europol were already assigned their seat together with 7 other agencies. Offices and bodies in a decision based on Art. 341 TFEU (then 216 EEC): Dec. 93/C 323/01, Decision by Common Agreement between the Representatives of the Governments of the Member States meeting at Head of State and Government Level, on the Location of the Seats of Certain Bodies and Departments of the European Communities and of Europol, O.J. 1993, C 323/1.

in Luxembourg. The European Central Bank has its seat in Frankfurt and Europol is domiciled in The Hague.[371]

The European Council is the only main institution that is not mentioned in the Protocol. Originally the European Council met in the capitals of the rotating half-yearly Presidency of the Council. Once it became clear that the European Council was to become a full-fledged institution under the Lisbon Treaty, a separation from the Presidency imposed itself. Since the European Council was to be serviced by the Council Secretariat, Brussels has become its *de facto* seat, where special accommodation has been created for it, next to the existing Council building.

The three other main institutions, which are those intensely involved in the legislative process, thus remain spread throughout Luxembourg, Brussels and Strasbourg. This situation – most unsatisfactory in terms of efficiency and rational financial policy – may be explained on the basis of considerations of national prestige, but also financial and economic interests, which prevent a rational decision regarding the seat of the institutions.[372] A rational decision will be all the more difficult because Protocol 6 has anchored the seats of only certain institutions and one agency in primary law. The seat of other EU agencies and bodies is still governed by intergovernmental decisions based on Article 341 TFEU.

8.3 *Linguistic régime*

Finally, a few observations are appropriate about the Union's linguistic régime. The texts of the EU, FEU and Euratom Treaties are equally authentic in twenty four languages.[373] The first regulation of the EEC in 1958 laid down the language regime on the basis of what is now Article 342 TFEU; it determined that all these languages would be official and working languages.[374] Irish (Gaelic), however, has a special status.[375] The *Official Journal* appears in these languages, Irish excepted. Each institution has the power to lay down in its rules of procedure which of the languages are to be used in specific cases, that is to say to limit the number of internal working languages. Most major institutions accordingly have limited their working languages to English, French and German. The European Central Bank is effectively mono-lingual: English. The major institutions have not formally done so in their Rules of Procedure, as suggested in Regulation 1.[376] Only the Court has done so, because on the one hand it needs an official language of procedure, which may be different in in every single case and, on the other hand, it also needs one

---

371. Europol is presently the only non-institution that is listed in the Protocol. Ten years after the decision mentioned in the preceding fn., Dec. 2004/97 was adopted by common agreement between the Representatives of the Member States meeting at the Head of State or Government Level, which assigned seats to 9 agencies and bodies that had been established in the years 2000–2003, including Eurojust, EASA and the Chemicals Agency, O.J. 2004, L 29/15.

372. Any attempt by the Parliament to change this situation unilaterally has had to be rebuffed by the Court on the instigation of France or Luxemburg, insofar as transfer of personnel to Brussels could not be justified as necessary for the support of the meetings that the Protocol had accepted as legitimate Brussels meetings. See Joined Cases C-237 and 238/11, *France & Luxemburg v. European Parliament,* with a reference in para 20 to three earlier cases.

373. Arts. 55 TEU, 358 TFEU and 225 Euratom. Art. 55 TEU contains the full list of languages.

374. See Reg. 1. of 1958 (O.J. 17/1958 at 385) as amended.

375. Reg. 920/2005, O.J. 2005, L 156/3. After its recognition as an official language more than 30 years after Ireland's accession, the application of Irish (Gaelic) was "suspended" in renewable terms of five years. The present suspension runs out in early 2021. It proves extremely difficult to recruit sufficient translators and interpreters for Gaelic. Moreover, the use of Maltese is *de facto* very restricted.

376. Art. 6 Reg. 1/1958.

single language of deliberation between the judges so that they can discuss cases without help of interpreters, as otherwise the secrecy of the deliberation would be breached.[377]

The costs of translation work (and simultaneous interpretation)[378] are extremely high, and delays in decision-making inevitably arise because of translation problems. The use of languages in the system of the European Union has major political and cultural implications, but given the enormous costs, the question whether it is now time to apply more widely the practice of using one or more working languages becomes ever more pressing. The major institutions, however, must have the courage to decide formally on such restrictions.[379] If they do so, it remains crucial that, in so far as Community acts have legal effect, they be available to Community citizens in their own language.[380] Similarly, it is important to safeguard the use of a person's own language in the European Parliament and, in so far as litigants are concerned, before the Court.

The use of languages in the Court is laid down in the Rules of Procedure (Arts. 29, 30 and 31).[381] The *official languages* of the Court are the 24 languages referred to above. Which of these is to be the language of the proceedings depends upon the plaintiff's choice, with the reservation that if the defendant is a Member State or a natural or legal person from a Member State, the language is the official language of that Member State. If there is more than one official language in this Member State, as in the case of Belgium, the plaintiff may choose whichever suits him. Upon joint request of the parties the Court may authorize the use of another official language. In special cases the Court may further authorize the total or partial use of another official language as the language of the case. If a national court makes a request for a preliminary ruling (Arts. 234 EC, 150 Euratom), the language of the proceedings shall be that of this court. Member States may use their own official language if intervening in a preliminary procedure. The publications of the Court of Justice appear in the official languages, Irish excepted. However, in principle only the text of the Court's decision in the language of the proceedings has force of law.

Equally authentic texts in 24 languages may cause the Court serious problems, when it is called upon to interpret and apply Union law. It will always have to be presumed that the texts have the same meaning in all the authentic languages. If upon comparison there is found to be a difference in meaning which cannot be eliminated by application of the usual methods of interpretation, the meaning to be adopted will have to be one which reconciles the texts with each other as much as possible, sometimes with the help of the preponderance of meaning among the 24 versions.[382]

---

377. Art. 7 Reg. 1/1958. The language of deliberation of the Court has always remained French.
378. The complications of simultaneous interpretation in 23 languages (not counting Gaelic) are staggering. There are over 500 dyadic language relations with this number of languages and hence many of them have to be covered through one or more intermediate languages. Planning the presence of interpreters at a Council of Ministers, where one must be able to serve each minister in his own language, thus becomes a major puzzle.
379. That they have not dared do so in clearly reasoned fashion has handicapped them in cases concerning the limitation of the use of languages in e.g. recruitment competitions. See Case C-556/10 P, *Italian Republic v. Commission,* para 86 and Joined Cases T-124/13 and T-191/13 *Italy and Spain v. Commission,* paras. 113 et seq. and 146. This stands in contrast to the cases against OHIM where such reasoned official limitation of the use of languages was available, see *infra* note 380.
380. Case C-361/01 P, *Kik v. OHIM,* and annotation thereof by N. Shuihbne, "*Kik v. Office* for Harmonization in the internal market", (2004) CML Rev., 1093–1111.
381. See Art. 64 Statute for the Court of Justice in the version established by the Treaty of Nice. The Rules of Procedure for the Court of First Instance contain similar rules in Arts. 35–37.
382. Cf. Art. 33, Vienna Convention on the Law of Treaties, United Nations, *Treaty Series,* Vol. 1155, at 331. See Case 29/69, *Erich Stauder v. City of Ulm-Sozialamt;* Case 30/77, *Régina v. Pierre Bouchereau* at para 14: "The different language versions of a Community text must be given a uniform interpretation and hence in the

Further reading

Auvret-Finck, J., *La Commission européenne en voie de redynamization* (Pedone, 2017).
Bocquillon, P., and M. Dobbel, "An elephant on the 13th Floor of the Berlaymont? European Council and Commission relations in legislative agenda setting", 21 JEPP (2014), 20–38.
Christiansen, T., and S. Vanhoonacker, "At a critical juncture? Change and continuity in the institutional development of the Council Secretariat", 31 WEP (2008), 751–770.
Corbett, R., F. Jacobs and D. Neville, *The European Parliament*, 9th ed. (John Harper, 2016).
Costa, O. and F. Saint Martin, *Le parlement européen*, 2nd ed. (La documentation française, 2011).
Craig, P., *The Lisbon Treaty, Revised Edition: Law, Politics, and Treaty Reform* (OUP, 2013).
Curtin, D., *Executive Power of the European Union: Law Practices and the Living Constitution* (OUP, 2009).
Feugier, J.-L. and M.-H. Pradines, *La function publique européenne en perspective* (La documentation française, 2015).
Höing, O., and W. Wessels, "The European Commission's position in the post-Lisbon institutional balance. Secretariat or partner to the European Council?" in M Chang et al. (Eds.), *The European Commission in the Post-Lisbon Era of Crises: Between Political Leadership and Policy Management* (Peter Lang, 2013).
Jacqué, J-P., *Droit institutionnel de l'Union européenne,* 8th ed. (Dalloz, 2015).
Nugent, N. and M. Rhinard, *The European Commission,* 2nd ed. (Palgrave 2015)
Peers, S., "The EU's political institutions" in C. Bernard and S. Peers (Eds.), *European Union Law* (OUP, 2014).
Peterson, J., "Juncker's political European Commission and an EU in crisis", 55 JCMS (2016), 349–367.
Ponzano, P., C. Hermann and D. Corona, "The power of initiative of the European Commission: A progressive erosion?", 89 *Notre Europe, Studies and Research* (2012).
Puetter, U., *The European Council and the Council: New Intergovernmentalism and Institutional Change* (OUP, 2014).
Puetter, U., "The European Council – The new centre of EU politics", Swedish Institute for European Policy Studies, 16 EPA (2013).
Rittberger, B., *Building Europe's Parliament, Democratic Representation beyond the Nation-State* (OUP 2007).
Van Schendelen, M.P.C.M., "The Council decides: Does the Council decide?", 33 JCMS (1996), 531–548.
Stavridis, D. and D. Jancic, *Parliamentary Diplomacy in European and Global Governance* (Brill, 2017).
Turk, A., "Lawmaking after Lisbon" in A. Biondi, P. Eeckhout and S. Ripley (Eds.), *EU Law after Lisbon* (OUP, 2012).
Werts, J., *The European Council* (John Harper, 2008).
Westlake, M. and D. Galloway, *The Council of the European Union*, 3rd ed. (John Harper, 2006).
De Zwaan, J.W., *The Permanent Representatives Committee – its Role in European Union Decision-making* (Elsevier, 1995).

---

case of divergence between the versions the provision in question must be interpreted by reference to the purpose and general scheme of the rules of which it forms a part". In circumstances in which one or more of the texts involved may have to be interpreted in a manner at variance with the natural and usual meaning of the words it is preferable, in the interests of legal certainty, to explore the possibilities of solving the points at issue without giving preference to any one of the texts involved, Case 80/76, *North Kerry Milk Products Ltd. v. Minister for Agriculture and Fisheries.*

CHAPTER 6
SOURCES OF EUROPEAN UNION LAW

*Bruno De Witte and Ben Smulders**

1. Introduction: The hierarchy of sources

The European Union legal order is, like national legal orders, a structured system of norms. The question whether a particular normative statement is part of European Union law is determined by the EU legal order's rule of recognition. Normative statements belong to EU law if they are recognized as one of the *sources of EU law.* The list of recognized sources of EU law is to be found partly in the Treaties and partly outside, namely in the institutional and judicial practice of the EU institutions. EU law is not made exclusively by the EU institutions. In fact, the highest source of the EU legal order, namely the basic Treaties, stems from the Member States. Also, the general principles of Union law, an important unwritten source of EU law, is not "made" by any EU institution, but is "discovered" by the Court of Justice within the broader international and comparative legal environment in which EU law is situated; and finally, the international agreements of the EU, another important source of EU law, are not made by the EU institutions on their own but by those institutions together with third states or other international organizations.

This system of sources is marked by a clear *hierarchy* between what is commonly called primary law and secondary law. *Primary law* is the law that is "given" to the EU institutions, by setting the framework for their activity: this category is constituted first of all by the basic Treaties of the European Union (the TEU, the TFEU, the Treaties of Accession and also, but playing only a marginally role, the Euratom Treaty); additional sources of primary law, operating alongside the Treaties and having the same rank in the hierarchy of norms, are the EU Charter of Fundamental Rights and the (unwritten) general principles of Union law. *Secondary law* is the law "made" by the EU institutions on the basis of the powers given to them by the Treaties, and within the limits set by the sources of primary law. It takes the form, essentially, of regulations, directives and decisions. The priority of primary law over secondary law is not merely theoretical. It can be judicially enforced before the Court of Justice by means of an action for annulment, an action for damages or a preliminary reference on validity. Because of the existence of this judicial enforcement, the EU institutions are constantly aware of the need for their acts to be in accordance with primary law norms, so that the hierarchy of the sources of law becomes a routine reality of the EU's institutional practice

This basic hierarchy is rendered more complex by the existence of a source of EU law that occupies an intermediate position between primary and secondary law, namely the international

---

* Bruno De Witte [Law Faculty, Maastricht University; Law Department/Robert Schuman Centre of the European University Institute (EUI)] is the principal author of sections 1 to 3, and Ben Smulders [European Commission] is the principal author of section 4.

agreements concluded by the European Union. According to Article 216 paragraph 2 TFEU, those agreements "are binding upon the institutions of the Union"; this means that they occupy a higher rank in the hierarchy of sources than the acts of secondary law adopted by the EU institutions. At the same time, those agreements can only be concluded under the conditions set by the Treaties, and they must comply with the substantive provisions of the Treaties, and with the Charter and the general principles of Union law. In other words, international agreements rank lower than primary law in the hierarchy of sources.

Within secondary law, there is no hierarchical relation between regulations, directives and decisions. These are different but equivalent legal instruments, and the choice among them in a given case is determined either by the Treaty text or by the nature of the matter to be dealt with, as will be explained below in sub-section 3.1. Yet, among the instruments of secondary law, a hierarchy exists when one of them is adopted to implement another, pre-existing, one. This hierarchical ordering within secondary law corresponds to the relationship, in national legal orders, between legislative acts and the administrative acts adopted for their implementation; the latter must comply with the former, and that same hierarchy exists also in the EU legal order between what are sometimes called "basic acts" and the acts adopted for their implementation.

The hierarchy of sources leads to two important rules in legal practice. The first one is that norms of secondary law must be interpreted in conformity with primary law, that is to say, that they must as far as possible be interpreted and applied in a way which does not affect their validity and is compatible with primary law.[1] The second rule is that, where there is a conflict that cannot be "interpreted away", the norm of primary law will prevail, and the conflicting norm of secondary law will be declared invalid (in the context of a preliminary reference on validity) or null and void (in the context of a direct action for annulment).

2. Primary Law: The Treaties, the Charter and General Principles of Law

2.1 *The Treaties and their Protocols*

The basic Treaties (the TEU and the TFEU) are the equivalent of a written constitution for the European Union: these legal documents establish the organization as a whole (the European Union), create the institutions of the EU, attribute powers to those institutions, and define how those powers should be exercised; they also organize a system of judicial protection. Given those functional characteristics, it is not uncommon for the combination of the TEU and the TFEU to be referred to as the "constitutional charter" of the European Union. Even though this analogy with a national constitution is, in many respects, appropriate and illuminating, one should also note some crucial differences. *First* of all, the two Treaties taken together count 413 articles, some of which are very long, and this makes them a legal ensemble that is much longer and much more detailed than a normal national constitution; one consequence of this is that the activity of the EU institutions is probably more often constrained or affected by the existence of Treaty rules than the activity of national institutions is determined or affected by their constitution. *Secondly,* whereas the protection of fundamental rights is usually a prominent part of a written national constitution, the Treaties refer to fundamental rights only sporadically, and the EU's "bill of rights" rather takes the form of a separate document, the Charter of Fundamental Rights; that Charter was kept deliberately outside the Treaties by the Lisbon revision treaty, although it was given the same rank as the Treaties in the hierarchy of norms. A *third* characteristic refers to the nature of the Treaties as international treaties; unlike a national constitution,

---

1. This rule of interpretation is a true mantra in the Court's case law; see e.g. Case C-149/10, *Chatzi*, para 43; Case C-12/11, *McDonagh*, para 44.

they did not come into being through an act of the sovereign people, but were agreed by means of a series of international treaties spread in time, each of which was concluded and ratified by the EU's Member States. This implies that, even though the Treaties may be the principal source of primary EU law, this position at the top of the hierarchy of EU law does not mean that they necessarily prevail over any other source of law. In particular, many constitutional courts of the EU Member States take the view that the EU Treaties are, indeed, "just" international treaties (even though weightier than most others), and that EU law therefore cannot claim to prevail over the core principles of their own national constitution.

According to Article 51 TEU, and following the established practice of international treaty law, "the *Protocols* and Annexes to the Treaties shall form an integral part thereof". The Treaty of Rome (1957) was already accompanied by a number of protocols, and other protocols were added at each later treaty revision, so that we now have a large number of, often lengthy, protocols attached to the Treaties. The Lisbon Treaty put some order in the jumble of accumulated protocols by numbering them: 37 Protocols altogether are listed in the Final Act of the Treaty of Lisbon. It is not always obvious why certain matters are dealt with in a separate protocol rather than directly in the Treaty text. For example, Protocol no. 2 on the application of the principles of subsidiarity and proportionality consists of nine Articles, which could easily have been fitted in the text of the TFEU, for example following the initial articles of that Treaty dealing with the categories of EU competence. If one adds all these Protocols to the corpus of primary EU law, as one should in view of Article 51 TEU, then the first distinctive characteristic noted above, namely that the Treaties are much longer and much more detailed than an average national constitution, becomes even more obvious.

2.2 *The Charter of Fundamental Rights*

The emergence, content and present role of the Charter of Rights is discussed in a separate chapter of this volume.[2] The most important contribution of the Treaty of Lisbon to the system of sources of EU law was probably the fact that it gave to the Charter of Rights the rank of primary law. Whereas the text of the Charter itself was hardly changed compared to its original version adopted in 2000, its legal value was profoundly modified. From 2000 until December 2009, the Charter had a twilight existence in legal terms, as a formally non-binding document, which nevertheless displayed some legal effects. The Court of Justice often referred to it, but as a source of interpretation for other norms, rather than as a separate source of law itself. Article 6, paragraph 1 TEU, as amended by the Treaty of Lisbon, modified the legal position with a stroke by stating that "[t]he Union recognises the rights, freedoms and principles set out in the Charter of Fundamental Rights of the European Union of 7 December 2000, as adapted at Strasbourg, on 12 December 2007, which shall have the same legal value as the Treaties". Since 1 December 2009 (the date of entry into force of the Lisbon Treaty), the Charter displays the same legal force as the Treaties themselves. In particular, it can act as a source for the judicial review of the legality of EU measures; also, like all other binding norms of EU law (whether of primary or of secondary law) it has primacy over national law. Yet, the Charter remains a *separate* source of primary EU law. Whereas the Constitutional Treaty had included the Charter as one of its constitutive parts, that solution was rejected by the drafters of the Lisbon Treaty, in their effort to make it seem that the Lisbon Treaty was "just" an ordinary revision treaty without the constitutional ambitions of its unfortunate predecessor. So, the Charter remained a separate document. It was re-enacted in Strasbourg on the very same day as the revision Treaty was agreed in Lisbon, and by a separate set of authors: not by the Member State representatives but by the presidents of

---

2. See Ch. 4, "Fundamental rights", of this book.

the three political institutions of the EU, the Commission, Council and Parliament, who had already adopted the first, almost identical, version of the Charter in 2000. Those presidents, obviously, do not have the power to make primary EU law; the force of primary law was given to the Charter by the separate decision of the Member States to grant it the same legal value as the Treaty. They did so by virtue of the little phrase in Article 6, paragraph 1 TEU, quoted above. The formal non-treaty nature of the Charter does not have many practical consequences, except perhaps for the fact that it is unclear how the Charter could be amended in the future. The Treaty revision procedures apply to the Treaties, and not to the Charter; yet, the rank of primary law is accorded to the version of the Charter *as adapted on 12 December 2007*, so that later modifications of the Charter would become part of primary EU law only if the text of Article 6 TEU were amended accordingly.

2.3 *General Principles of Union Law*

The most characteristic feature of general principles of Union law is that they are *unwritten* norms of EU law that have primary law rank. The fact that they are unwritten means that they were not enacted by the authors of written primary law (the Member States), but by the Court of Justice that decided, early on in its existence, that the Treaty norms needed to be supplemented, mainly in the interest of the legal protection of individuals, by a set of unwritten norms which it called "general principles of Community law". Still today, the text of the Treaties only refers in passing to this judge-made source of EU law, namely in Article 6, paragraph 3, where it is said that "[f]undamental rights, as guaranteed by the European Convention [...] and as they result from the constitutional traditions common to the Member States, shall constitute general principles of the Union's law". That reference was included in the Treaties, in a slightly different formulation, at the time of the Maastricht Treaty revision. Another textual reference has been there ever since the original version of the EEC Treaty, and is now to be found in Article 340 TFEU where it is stated that the non-contractual liability of the Union shall be governed by "the general principles common to the laws of the Member States". A more general, and very much implicit, reference can be read in Article 19 TEU where it is stated: "It (= the Court) shall ensure that in the interpretation and application of the Treaties *the law* is observed". This provision has been read as meaning that the Court's task involves more than simply the application of the Treaty provisions, but allows it to supplement the Treaties with additional unwritten norms drawn from the common legal experience of the Member States.[3]

In the course of the years, the Court has discovered a large set of such general principles, the most common among which were, and still are, the principles of proportionality, of equality, of legal certainty, of legitimate expectations, and of effective judicial protection (the latter also referred to as the "rights of the defence"). A major development happened in 1969, when the Court of Justice decided, in the *Stauder* case, that fundamental rights, as recognized by the constitutions of the Member States and by the ECHR, were part of the general principles of Community law and would henceforth be protected by the Court against their breach by the Community institutions (and, as later became clear, also against violations by the Member States when acting within the scope of EC law).[4]

The typical function of all these general principles is to protect individuals (and companies) against unlawful action by the EU or national institutions. In relation to EU and Member State administrative action, the principles of proportionality, equality and legitimate expectations are very frequently invoked; as for the principle of effective judicial protection, it is often invoked

---

3. Cf. T. Koopmans, "The birth of European law at the crossroads of legal traditions", 39 AJCL (1991), at 495–6.
4. Case 29/69, *Stauder v. Stadt Ulm*.

in competition cases, as well as in the context of financial sanctions imposed as part of the EU's foreign policy. In the course of time, though, the Court of Justice, also discovered what may be called "institutional principles", i.e. unwritten norms of primary law that govern the relations between EU institutions, or between EU institutions and the Member States. The most prominent among those are the principle of institutional balance and the principle of sincere cooperation, also called the principle of loyalty.[5] The principle of institutional balance is often mentioned in the Court's case law, but its practical significance is rather limited, as it is mostly used by the Court as shorthand for the division of powers among the EU institutions laid down in the Treaties. Primacy, direct effect and state liability are also commonly referred to as "principles", but they are not general principles of EU law in the sense discussed here. Indeed, they are not separate sources of EU law, but rather qualities attached to norms of EU law. Primacy, direct effect and state liability are always, and necessarily, invoked in conjunction with another norm of EU law and have no independent existence.

The role of general principles as separate sources of EU law has shrunk somewhat over the years due to the fact that many of them were gradually spelled out as written norms of primary law. This is most clearly the case of the general principles protecting fundamental rights. Now that fundamental rights are contained in a written document of primary law, the Charter of Fundamental Rights, there seems no justification any more for treating them as unwritten principles of the EU legal order. When nowadays the CJEU mentions, say, the freedom of expression, it refers to Article 11 of the Charter and no longer to an unwritten general principle of freedom of expression. And yet, the role of general principles is not entirely played out, even in this domain. Indeed, Article 6 TEU continues to refer to general principles as a source of fundamental rights protection, alongside the Charter, and this has prompted the view that certain rights could receive protection as unwritten principles in situations that are not covered by the Charter. A good example of this is the right to good administration which, according to Article 41 (1) Charter implies that "[e]very person has the right to have his or her affairs handled impartially, fairly and within a reasonable time by the institutions, bodies, offices and agencies of the Union". This particular right of the Charter, unlike most others, is therefore not applicable to *Member State* action, but it has been argued that a similar unwritten right to good administration should bind the Member States when acting within the scope of EU law, and it should do so as a general principle of Union law.[6]

Apart from the fundamental rights, other unwritten principles have at some point been included in written primary law. This is the case with the principle of sincere cooperation, which for a long time operated as an unwritten norm, but is now written down in Article 4 TEU, and for the principle of proportionality, one of the oldest general principles, which was included in primary law by the Treaty of Maastricht and is now included in Article 5 TEU and in the Protocol no. 2 on subsidiarity and proportionality. Yet, in the case of proportionality, the Court of Justice continues to refer to it as a general principle rather than as a Treaty norm. Something similar happened with the principle to effective judicial protection, to which the European Courts continue to refer as a general principle, simply adding that it has "been reaffirmed" by Article 47 of the Charter.[7]

In addition, certain legal norms that originated in the text of the Treaties (and were therefore written norms from the start) are nevertheless labelled "principle". This is the case, for example,

---

5. See M. Klamert, *The Principle of Loyalty in EU Law* (OUP, 2014).
6. See H. Hofmann and B. Mihaescu, "The relation between the Charter's fundamental rights and the unwritten general principles of EU law: Good administration as the test case", 9 EuConst (2013), 73–101.
7. One among many examples is Case T-720/14, *Rotenberg*, para 144.

for the principle of conferral and the principle of subsidiarity, both of which are laid down in Article 5 TEU (with subsidiarity being spelled out further in a separate Protocol). Here, the word "principle" does not refer to a separate source of law, but to a written Treaty norm with a broad scope and special importance for the EU legal order. More generally, one should distinguish between the use of the term "general principle" as a source of unwritten law, and the use of the word "principle" as the label or denomination of particular written norms of either primary or secondary law. To complicate matters, sometimes elements of a principle take a written form, but the overarching principle continues to apply in situations not covered by the written norms. This is the case with the *general principle of equality*. Many aspects of the principle of equality or non-discrimination are nowadays covered by written norms of primary and secondary law; indeed, right from the time of the Treaty of Rome, the principle of non-discrimination on grounds of nationality and the right to equal pay for men and women were laid down in the EEC Treaty. Yet, even today, there are many situations that are not covered by any of the written norms of EU law and in which the Court applies the general principle of equality (or the interchangeably used term "principle of non-discrimination"). This is particularly the case where the ground of unequal treatment is not one of the "suspect grounds" covered by written norms of EU law. The CJEU has consistently adopted a broad definition of equality, according to which that principle "requires that comparable situations must not be treated differently and different situations must not be treated in the same way unless such treatment is objectively justified";[8] this definition basically allows for the contestation of any measure of EU law for either making or failing to make distinctions, and it should therefore not come as a surprise that the principle of equality is, together with the principle of proportionality, the most frequently invoked general principle in judicial challenges of the legality of EU measures.

3. Secondary Law: Legal instruments

3.1 *EU legal instruments: A general view*

In addition to the founding Treaties, the Charter and the general principles of Union law that, together, constitute the primary law of the European Union, there is a body of secondary law, made up of the legal acts adopted by the institutions of the European Union. These acts can be adopted by several institutions acting together (the most prominent example being legislative acts adopted by the European Parliament and the Council acting jointly under the ordinary legislative procedure), or, more commonly, by single institutions. These acts take different legal forms and those legal forms are commonly known as *legal instruments,* which is also the term we will employ in this chapter even though the Treaty text does not use it. In addition to these legal instruments, the EU institutions also adopt, together with third countries or other international organizations, a large number of *international treaties, conventions and agreements*. These are also considered to be part of secondary law, since the conclusion of such external agreements depends on an authorization given, expressly or impliedly, by the Treaties; but, as was mentioned in section 1, they occupy a higher rank in the hierarchy of sources of EU law than secondary law adopted unilaterally by the EU institutions. Also, these agreements are not *just* sources of EU law but also sources of public international law, and therefore subject to the legal regimes of both EU law and international law; their legal status and regime will not be discussed in this chapter,

---

8. This formula is repeated in many rulings of the Court. See e.g. Case C-176/09, *Luxembourg v. European Parliament and Council*, para 31; Case C-596/14, *Ana de Diego Porras*, para 35.

but in connection with the external relations of the Union, in Chapter 39.[9] In the last section of this Chapter, attention will be paid to the agreements concluded between the Member States of the EU; these are not, formally speaking, acts of the European Union institutions, but they are often closely related to the functioning of the EU and can be seen as a "satellite" source of EU law.

3.1.1 *Article 288: An incomplete list of instruments*

The TFEU contains a provision (Art. 288) setting out the principal categories of legal acts of the Union, and specifying their nature and their legal effects. Other articles in the same Treaty chapter contain rules relating to the formulation, publication, entry into force and enforcement of these acts, which we will discuss in subsection 3.1.3.

Article 288 TFEU, first paragraph, lists the legal instruments of the EU:

> "To exercise the Union's competences, the institutions shall adopt regulations, directives, decisions, recommendations and opinions".

The other paragraphs of Article 288 give a general indication of the nature of each of the instruments, from which it becomes clear, first of all, that only regulations, directives and decisions have binding legal force, while recommendations and opinions are not legally binding. This shows that the category of "legal acts", in EU law at least, comprises both binding law and soft law.[10] The following pages will principally deal with the three types of binding instruments, whereas recommendations and opinions (and other kinds of non-binding acts not mentioned in Art. 288) are discussed separately in sub-section 3.7.

According to the first paragraph of Article 288, these acts are to be adopted by "the institutions". That term is under-inclusive, inasmuch as EU agencies (that do not belong to the list of "institutions" of Art. 13 TEU) also adopt some of the legal instruments of Article 288; they usually adopt decisions.[11] The general reference to "institutions" should not be taken to mean that the EU institutions (or agencies) may freely choose to adopt any of these instruments in any of the policy domains in which they act. Whether they may adopt a legal act, and in what form they can do so, will depend on the description of the powers granted to them in specific Treaty provisions, according to the principle of conferral (or, in the case of agencies, in the regulation by which they are established). Sometimes, the specific empowering provision in the Treaty (the "legal basis") mentions one legal instrument by name, thus eliminating the possibility of choice; and in the policy domain of CFSP, there is a general rule imposing the use of one single binding instrument, namely the decision.[12] When the legal basis article does not prescribe the use of a specific instrument, then the choice of legal instrument is determined on a case-by-case basis, depending on the nature of the measure to be taken.[13] For example, Article 16 TFEU states that the EU can "lay down rules" on data protection, and this generic indication allowed the

---

9. Furthermore, treaties concluded by the Union may provide for the establishment of bodies that may be empowered to take decisions for the implementation of those treaties (e.g. Decisions of the Joint Committee of the EEA, and decisions of the association councils established in the association agreements concluded by the EU with third countries). These decisions are often binding and are published in the "Official Journal" and have been recognized by the Court of Justice as formal sources of EU law; they are also dealt with in Ch. 39, "An introduction to Union external action", of this book.
10. Indeed, the Treaty section to which Art. 288 belongs is entitled "The legal acts of the Union".
11. The fact that agencies may adopt binding legal acts is not written with so many words in the Treaties, but was found by the Court of Justice to follow implicitly from the language of Articles 263 and 277 TFEU referring to the judicial review of "acts" of Union bodies, offices and agencies. See Case C-270/12, *United Kingdom v. Parliament and Council*, para 65.
12. Art. 25 TEU.
13. This rule was laid down in Art. 296 TFEU by the Lisbon Treaty reform.

EU to adopt on that basis, on the same day of 27 April 2016, both a Regulation on general data protection[14] (replacing an earlier directive of 1995) and a Directive on the processing of personal data for crime fighting purposes,[15] a distinction reflecting the more sovereignty-sensitive nature of criminal policy.

There is a certain specialization, in practice, among the institutions in terms of the instruments they adopt. The nature of the Commission's powers implies that the Commission generally adopts acts of an executive nature, and it uses mainly regulations (for generally applicable measures) or decisions (for measures addressed to States or individuals) for that purpose, although there are also examples of implementing directives adopted by the Commission.[16] The Council and the Parliament are more obviously endowed with a legislative role, and therefore typically act by means of directives and regulations; however, the Council also often acts as an executive institution and, in that capacity, it frequently adopts decisions. When the ordinary legislative procedure applies, the act will be co-authored by Council and Parliament and this co-authorship implies that challenges of the legality of such acts will have to be directed against both institutions. As for the European Council, it only occasionally adopts binding acts and does not have legislative powers, which explains that those binding acts invariably take the form of decisions (see subsection 3.5, below).

Special arrangements regarding legal instruments are contained in Article 132 TFEU, where the categories of acts of the European Central Bank (ECB) are listed: regulations, decisions, recommendations and opinions (so, directives are not included in the list). The Statute of the ECB also gives it the power to issue guidelines and instructions addressed to central banks. Both of these are, somewhat counterintuitively, binding legal instruments.[17]

It should furthermore be noted that, quite apart from these specific arrangements in monetary policy, the text of Article 288 TFEU gives only an incomplete picture of the legal instruments which are used in practice in the EU. The text of Article 288 still corresponds by and large to the original text of the Treaty establishing the EEC, but during the intervening sixty years of institutional practice other instruments have been invented and used which are not mentioned in Article 288. They are mostly of the soft law variety and are often described, in the Brussels jargon, as "atypical acts";[18] but some of them may have a binding legal character, in particular the interinstitutional agreements that will be discussed in subsection 3.5 below.

3.1.2 *The reform of the legal instruments by the Lisbon Treaty*

When the Laeken Declaration launched, in December 2001, the process of Treaty reform that would lead to the enactment of the Constitutional Treaty, the question of whether and how to "simplify" the existing system of legal instruments was firmly put on the reform agenda. A

14. Reg. 2016/679 on the protection of natural persons with regard to the processing of personal data and on the free movement of such data, O.J. 2016, L 119/1.
15. Directive 2016/680 on the protection of natural persons with regard to the processing of personal data by competent authorities for the purposes of the prevention, investigation, detection or prosecution of criminal offences or the execution of criminal penalties, and on the free movement of such data, O.J. 2016, L 119/89.
16. Furthermore, the Treaty exceptionally empowers the Commission to adopt autonomous directives, i.e. directives that do not implement a legislative act adopted by the Parliament and/or Council. See for example Art. 106(3) TFEU.
17. Protocol 4 on the Statute of the European System of Central Banks and of the European Central Bank, Art. 12 and Art. 14.3. Regarding legal instruments in the field of monetary policy, see Ch. 26, "Economic and Monetary Union", of this book.
18. For a comprehensive discussion (but prior to the Lisbon Treaty), see S. Lefèvre, *Les actes communautaires atypiques* (Bruylant, 2006).

working group of the Convention for the future of the Union was set up for this purpose, and in its final report of November 2002, that working group proposed a number of fundamental changes, in particular the abolition of the separate range of legal instruments for the Third Pillar (following logically from the proposed abolition of that pillar), a change in the denomination of the most important instruments (so that in future a legislative regulation would instead be a "law of the EU" and a directive would be called a "framework law of the EU"), and the introduction of a clear hierarchy between legislative and administrative (or implementing) acts.[19] These various reforms found their way into the final text of the Constitutional Treaty, but later modifications in the Lisbon Treaty meant that the new denominations "law" and "framework law" were not introduced after all, and that instead the familiar instruments "regulation" and "directive" were retained. However, other changes in the system of legal instruments were carried over into the Lisbon Treaty.[20]

a. *Disappearance of second and third pillar instruments* – The most obvious change made by the Lisbon Treaty was the disappearance of the special set of legal instruments for what used to be known as the Third Pillar. Framework decisions and conventions are, since the entry into force of the Lisbon Treaty, no longer available as instruments for the European Union's policy in the field of police and criminal justice cooperation. In this field, the "mainstream" legal instruments are now used. The field of Common Foreign and Security Policy remained distinctive after Lisbon, in that regulations and directives are not available in this area of EU policy; the central legal instrument in this field has become the *decision,* which, under the Lisbon Treaty, has replaced the variety of binding instruments previously in use for CFSP, namely the joint actions, common positions and decisions. This was a major terminological simplification, although it should be kept in mind that these CFSP decisions are still being used for a variety of different purposes[21] corresponding to the purposes for which different CFSP instruments had been used in pre-Lisbon times. In subsection 3.6, below, we will describe in greater detail this change in the field of the former third pillar, as well as the "afterlife" that many of the single pre-Lisbon instruments still have today, eight years after the Lisbon reforms.

b. *New distinction between legislative, delegated and implementing acts* – The Lisbon Treaty also accomplished an important reform of the regime of "mainstream" legal instruments. As was mentioned above, the Constitutional Treaty had accomplished a radical terminological novelty by introducing the new instruments of "laws" and "framework laws" to replace regulations and directives having a legislative nature. This innovation was undone by the Lisbon Treaty, so that regulations and directives continue to be the main legislative instruments of the European Union. However, the related ambition of introducing a clearer hierarchy within the system of EU acts was not abandoned. The amorphous system operating pre-Lisbon, in which the distinction between legislative and executive acts was not made visible by the use of different denominations for the acts (thus, a regulation could be used both for very important legislative measures

---

19. The European Convention, Final report of Working Group IX on Simplification, 29 Nov. 2002, CONV 42/02.

20. For commentaries on the reforms proposed in the Constitutional Treaty, see K. Lenaerts and M. Desomer, "Towards a hierarchy of legal acts in the European Union? Simplification of legal instruments and procedures", 11 ELJ (2005), 744–765; S. Prechal, "Adieu à la Directive?", 1 EuConst (2005), 481–494; P. Stancanelli, "Le système décisionnel de l'Union" in G. Amato, H. Bribosia, B. de Witte (Eds.), *Genèse et destinée de la Constitution européenne* (Bruylant, 2007), 485–543.

21. See Art. 25 (b) TEU.

taken in co-decision and for very lowly implementing measures taken by the Commission), was replaced by a more detailed typology of acts in which that distinction is more clearly expressed.

The upper tier is formed by what the Treaty text calls "legislative acts". This term does not indicate a formal instrument, but the normative nature of some regulations, directives or decisions. This particular legislative nature will be determined by the use of a particular procedure, as is stated by the curiously worded Article 289(3) TFEU: "Legal acts adopted by legislative procedure shall constitute legislative acts". There is not one single legislative procedure, though. Whereas the co-decision procedure became the ordinary legislative procedure, there are still many cases in which special legislative procedures are prescribed, mainly for allowing the Council to act as sole author of legislation. The identification of legislative acts is not a purely formal matter. Practical legal consequences flow from this identification: for example, the rule that the Council shall meet in public is limited to its deliberations on legislative acts;[22] the new role of national parliaments in monitoring respect for the principle of subsidiarity relates to draft legislative acts only;[23] and the broadening of the individual right to challenge EU acts before the European Court refers to "regulatory acts", a term which according to the Court of Justice excludes legislative acts.[24]

An intermediate level of law-making, between the legislative and purely executive, was introduced, namely the adoption of delegated acts. Such acts are adopted by the Commission in order to "supplement or amend certain non-essential elements of the legislative acts" (Art. 290(1) TFEU). In contrast with implementing acts, these delegated acts may thus actually modify a legislative act, albeit only on non-essential points, provided that there is a specific delegation within the relevant legislative act, and subject to control by the institutions that have adopted that act, that is, normally speaking, by Council and Parliament. In pre-Lisbon practice, the Commission was already frequently given the power to amend or supplement legislative acts, but that practice was covered by its general implementation powers and had no explicit Treaty basis. The creation of a formal distinction between delegated acts and "pure" implementing acts was introduced in order to enhance the transparency and accountability of EU decision-making, although the incipient post-Lisbon practice shows that it also creates additional complexity and is a source of inter-institutional disputes.[25]

So, as a result, we now have nine different binding legal instruments of "mainstream" EU law: "ordinary" regulations, directives and decisions (that is, acts whose denomination is not further specified); delegated regulations, directives, and decisions; and implementing regulations, directives and decisions. The nature of the act is to be visible from its title. Indeed, it is specified by the TFEU that the adjective "delegated" shall be inserted in the title of delegated acts and that the word "implementing" shall be inserted in the title of implementing acts.[26] This will certainly add to the transparency of EU law, compared to the present situation. There are two important limits, though, to this new transparency.

First, one should not assume that regulations, directives or decisions without an adjective in their title are always legislative acts. Indeed, as was mentioned above, the qualification as a legislative act results exclusively from the fact that the act's legal basis prescribes its adoption by means of either the ordinary or a special legislative procedure. There are, however, a number of

---

22. Art. 16 (8) TEU.
23. Protocol on the application of the principles of subsidiarity and proportionality.
24. Case C-583/11 P, *Inuit Tapiriit Kanatami and others v. European Parliament and Council.*
25. See, for further discussion, Ch. 8, "The EU administration", of this book.
26. See respectively Art. 290(3) and Art. 291(4) TFEU.

legal bases in the Treaties that allow for the adoption of what could be called *autonomous non-legislative acts,* that is, acts that do not count as legislative acts because their adoption procedure does not say so, but also do not count as delegated or implemented acts, because the power to adopt those acts comes directly from the Treaties and not from some earlier legislative act. Examples of such autonomous non-legislative acts are the Council Decision of 2015 on the relocation of asylum seekers[27] and the Council Regulation of 2015 on the application of state aid rules to certain categories of horizontal state aid.[28] The latter, in particular, would deserve to be called a legislative act in the ordinary meaning of that term, but it is not a legislative act under EU law, for the simple reason that its legal basis does not refer to the use of a legislative procedure for its adoption. These autonomous non-legislative acts may very well require further measures by either the Member States or by the Commission, but in the latter case the Commission measures will not be identified as either delegated or implementing.

The *second* limit to transparency is the fact that the instruments dating from before 1 December 2009 (the date of entry into force of the Lisbon Treaty) do not carry those specifications, so that their legislative, delegated or implementing nature is not immediately visible from their title; in addition, many of the current (post-Lisbon) legal acts that implement or supplement basic acts dating from before Lisbon also do not carry those specifications. The reason for this is that pre-Lisbon legislative acts could not specify whether follow-up acts by the Commission should be of the delegated or implementing variety, since that dichotomy did not exist at the time. Therefore, in case of doubt, post-Lisbon acts based on that pre-Lisbon legislation may still be called "regulation" or "decision" without specification, even when they have an implementing nature.

c. *Merger of the two types of decisions* – Finally, the Lisbon Treaty accomplished another reform in the regime of legal instruments that passed largely unnoticed because it lacks visibility in the English and the French language. As will be explained further in subsection 3.4, the pre-Lisbon regime was marked by the existence of two different instruments which, in English (and French), were both called "Decision" but which had different names in some other official languages; for example, in German they were respectively called *Entscheidung* and *Beschluss,* and in Dutch they were called *beschikking* and *besluit.* The former of the two was mentioned in the Treaty, whereas the latter had been developed through institutional practice. The Lisbon Treaty removed that distinction. Henceforth, there is one single instrument called Decision (in German: *Beschluss* and in Dutch *besluit),* which combines the different functions of the two previously existing instruments. This has improved terminological clarity, but at the cost of clouding the distinctive nature of that instrument, as we shall see in subsection 3.4.

3.1.3 *The general regime for the adoption and publication of EU legal acts*

The TFEU chapter entitled "Legal acts of the Union, adoption procedures and other provisions" (Arts. 288 to 299) contains rules that define some of the formalities of the adoption and publication process for the various types of instruments.

---

27. Council Decision 2015/1601 establishing provisional measures in the area of international protection for the benefit of Italy and of Greece, O.J. 2015, L 248/80. Its legal basis is Art. 78 (3) TFEU, which has a decision-making procedure that does not mention the word "legislative".
28. Council Reg. 2015/1588 on the application of Articles 187 and 188 of the Treaty on the Functioning of the European Union to certain categories of horizontal State aid, O.J. 2015, L 248/1. Its legal basis is Art. 109 TFEU, which does not foresee a legislative procedure.

a. *Duty to state reasons* – Probably the most important rule, from a legal perspective, is that all regulations, directives and decisions must *state the reasons* on which they are based and refer to any proposals or opinions which were required to be obtained in accordance with the Treaties (Art. 296 TFEU, second sentence). The requirement to refer to proposals or opinions makes it possible to check whether the decision-making procedure required by the Treaties was followed for the adoption of the act. The duty to state the reasons for the adoption of the act serves to put interested parties in a position to know why the measure was adopted and to allow the Court to exercise its review function.[29] If no reasons or inadequate reasons are given, this is an infringement of an essential procedural requirement – and therefore a ground for annulment of the contested act under Art. 263 TFEU).

One remarkable characteristic of this norm is that it applies to *all* acts, including legislative acts, whereas it is rather uncommon, in comparative constitutional law, for the legislator to be subject to a duty to state reasons. In order to compensate for this all-embracing character of the duty, the case law of the European Courts – which is very copious and detailed as regards the requirement to give reasons – has made clear that the extent of the duty to provide a statement of reasons depends on the nature of the measure in question.[30]

The statement of reasons of a *regulation or directive or a general decision* need not be as detailed as that of an individual act. It may be confined to a statement about the overall situation that led to the adoption of the regulation or directive, and about the general weighing of interests by the Union legislator. It is not required to provide a detailed listing of the sometimes numerous and complicated facts which led to its adoption, together with a more or less complete assessment of these facts and a specific explanation of all the provisions of the act,[31] but the legislator does have a specific duty, at least when it acts within a field of shared competence, to explain why the act complies with the principle of subsidiarity;[32] in this case, however, the standard of review is not the duty to state reasons but directly the principle of subsidiarity.

In the case of individual *decisions*, it is necessary to mention all the various elements which are relevant in law or as facts. However, the required degree of precision of the statement of reasons for a decision will be weighed against practical realities and the time and technical facilities available for making the decision.[33] The actual circumstances under which measures have to be adopted may sometimes be relevant in that they may lead to a reduction of the pretty rigorous demands that the Court usually makes of the reasoning of decisions. In particular, if the Member State or undertaking concerned has been closely involved in the process leading to the adoption of the decision (as is the case in competition and state aid cases), the reasoning may be less detailed.[34] A decision following a well-established line of decisions may be less fully reasoned and may simply refer to the standing administrative practice of the Commission.[35] Nevertheless, the breach of the duty to state reasons remains one of the favourite arguments of applicants claiming the illegality of an EU act, especially in competition cases, and that argument is not infrequently successful.

---

29. E.g. Case 250/84, *Eridania*; Case C-84/94, *United Kingdom v. Council (Working time directive)*.
30. E.g. Joined Cases 142 & 156/84, *British-American Tobacco et al. v. Commission*; Case C-76/01 P, *Eurocoton and others v. Council*.
31. Case 5/67, *W. Beus GmbH and Co. v. Hauptzollamt München*. See also Case 167/88, *APGB v. ONIC*.
32. Case C-377/98, *Netherlands v. Parliament and Council*.
33. E.g. Case C-350/88, *Delacre. v. Commission* (citing earlier case law).
34. E.g. Case 13/72, *The Netherlands v. Commission*; Case 9/83, *Eisen und Metall Aktiengesellschaft v. Commission*.
35. Case 73/74, *Groupement des fabricants de papiers peints de Belgique et al. v. Commission*; Joined Cases 142 & 156/84, *British-American Tobacco*.

The extent of the duty to state reasons also depends on the subject matter to which the measure relates, but there is no justification for the total absence of a statement of reasons of decisions that have a negative impact on individuals, firms or states, as the case may be. This simple rule was applied in the high profile cases relating to the freezing of funds of suspected supporters of terrorist groups. The General Court annulled several Council decisions listing such suspects because of the absence, in the preamble of the decision, of any statement of the actual reasons why *they* were listed.[36]

b. *Publication* – As regards the publication of EU legal instruments, the Treaty provides for a differentiated regime. All *legislative* acts must be published in the *Official Journal of the European Union* (Art. 297 TFEU). Other (that is, non-legislative) regulations and directives must also be published if they are addressed to all Member States, as is most commonly the case. The same goes for decisions that do not specify to whom they are addressed (Art. 297 (2) TFEU). All these acts enter into force on the date specified by them or, failing this, on the twentieth day following their publication (Art. 297 (1) TFEU). Limits have been set on the freedom of the institutions to fix the date of entry into force. Entry into force on the date of publication, and *a fortiori* on an earlier date, is permitted only if there are adequate reasons for this.[37] The Court has emphasized on several occasions that whereas "in general the principle of legal certainty precludes a Community measure from taking effect from a point in time before its publication, it may exceptionally be otherwise where the purpose to be achieved so demands and where the legitimate expectations of those concerned are duly respected".[38]

Directives that are addressed only to specific Member States, and decisions addressed either to specific States or to individuals need not be published. They must instead be notified to their addressees and take effect upon such notification (Art. 297 (2) last sentence TFEU). Notification takes place on communication of the measure to the addressee on the condition that the latter is in a position to take cognizance of it.[39] In view of the importance which some of those directives and decisions may have for parties other than their addressees, the EU institutions may decide to publish them in the *Official Journal* even when this is not obligatory. The Commission is also obliged to publish its decisions in competition cases, on the basis of secondary law.[40] Article 132(2) TFEU specifies that the ECB *may* decide to publish its decisions, recommendations and opinions. As regulations are not listed in that provision, the general rules of Article 297 TFEU apply to ECB regulations.

All instruments of EU law, whether contained in the *Official Journal* or not, have their own identification number. This is not a matter dealt with by the Treaties, but which has developed through practice, with frequent changes in the ways the various instruments were numbered, The current method of numbering applies to all acts adopted after 1 January 2015, whereas previously adopted acts are numbered according to older, partly different, methods.[41]

36. Case T-228/02, *Organisation des Modjahedines du peuple d'Iran v. Council*; Case T-47/03, *Sison v. Council*.
37. Case 17/67, *Firma Max Neumann*.
38. Case 98/78, *Racke*, para 20; see also Case 110/81, *Roquette Frères v. Council*.
39. Case 6/72, *Europemballage Corporation and Continental Can Company Inc. v. Commission*.
40. See Reg. 1/2003 on the implementation of the rules on competition laid down in Articles 81 and 82 of the Treaty, O.J. 2003, L 1/1, Art. 30.
41. The new method of numbering is explained on the eur-lex website, available at <eur-lex.europa.eu/content/tools/elaw/OA0614022END.pdf>.

3.2 *Regulations*

When they were first mentioned in the text of the EEC Treaty, regulations were seen as a remarkable legal innovation. Indeed, it was until then very rare for an international organization (as the European Communities were) to have the power to adopt binding acts, and even rarer to adopt *generally* binding acts which were to be directly applicable within the legal system of the Member States. Although the use of the word "laws" was avoided in favour of the more innocuous sounding word "regulations", what was in fact created was an instrument for the exercise of true legislative and executive powers by the European Community institutions.

Regulations are very frequently used in the EU legal system, both as legislative and administrative instruments. The three characteristic elements of a regulation that are mentioned in Article 288 are: (a) their general application; (b) their entirely binding character; and (c) their direct applicability in each Member State.[42] These three characteristics supposedly distinguish regulations from the other two binding instruments listed in Article 288, although, as we shall see, the dividing line between regulations and decisions, in particular, is not clearly traced.

The general application of a regulation refers to the impersonal, non-individualized character of the situations to which it applies, as well as the legal effects it entails for the legal subjects to whom it is addressed. As the ECJ put it in an early case, a measure has general application provided that "it is applicable [...] to objectively determined situations and involves legal consequences for categories of persons viewed in a general and abstract manner".[43]

A regulation not only has general application, but it is also binding in its entirety; it thus differs from a directive, which is only binding as to the result to be achieved. Moreover, a regulation is directly applicable in all Member States.[44] This means that, once a regulation has entered into force, it forms part of the national legal system of each Member State, in the same way as its domestic legislation, but that it retains its character of being EU law, which means *inter alia* that the regulation has primacy over conflicting national law. A consequence from the direct applicability of regulations is that the Member States may not adopt measures applying the regulation which modify its scope or add provisions to it, unless this is provided for in the regulation itself.[45] Likewise, the Member States are not permitted to transform the contents of a regulation into national legislative provisions, since by doing so they would create uncertainty about the legal nature of the applicable provisions and the time of their entry into force.[46]

In practice, however, the text of a regulation frequently provides that implementing measures must be taken either by a Union institution (usually the Commission) or the Member States, or both.[47] Implementation by the Commission frequently takes place by means of decisions, but

---

42. Art. 288, para 2 TFEU.
43. Case 6/68, *Zuckerfabrik Watenstedt GmbH v. Council.* Cf. earlier, with a somewhat different formulation, Joined Cases 16 & 17/62, *Confédération nationale.*
44. This does not mean that a regulation cannot contain rules concerning the situation in only one of the Member States or even in a part of its territory. This is implicit in the judgment in Case 30/67, *Industria Molitoria Imolese SpA et al. v. Commission.* Despite the limited territorial field of application such a regulation has Union-wide validity.
45. Case 40/69, *Hauptzollamt Hamburg-Oberelbe v. Firma Paul G. Bollmann.*
46. See e.g. Case Case 94/77, *Fratelli Zerbone Snc v. Amministrazione delle Finanze dello Stato,* para 26.
47. An example of a regulation requiring (quite complex) implementing measures by the Member States is Council Reg. 1/2003 on the implementation of the rules on competition laid down in Arts. 81 and 82 of the Treaty, O.J. 2003, L 1/1. An example of a regulation requiring implementation both by the Commission and by the Member States is Reg. 1760/2000 establishing a system for the identification and registration of bovine animals and regarding the labelling of beef and beef products, O.J. 2000, L 204/1.

often also by means of (further) regulations;[48] in the latter case, the implementing regulation must obviously be in conformity with the basic regulation. When implementation is entrusted to the Member States, the forms and procedures of national law apply. In particular, national law should determine whether for the implementation of a regulation an act of the national legislature (i.e. a statute) is needed, or some other legal instrument can be used. In general, the Member States are empowered, as well as being obliged under their duty of sincere cooperation, to lay down the necessary administrative and procedural rules to ensure compliance with the EU regulations and to prescribe sanctions for non-compliance. In fact, the duties of the Member States when they have to implement regulations are very similar to the duties imposed on them when they implement directives, which are discussed in the next sub-section. The fact that many regulations require further implementing measures, either by the Member States or by the EU institutions themselves, means that private individuals are not always able automatically to rely on provisions of regulations before national courts. In other words: the direct applicability of regulations does not necessarily mean that all provisions of regulations have direct effect.[49]

This being said, the regulation is not primarily used as an instrument for the harmonization of national laws, but rather for other purposes. Broadly speaking, two main usages may be distinguished: (i) for the creation of European-level institutional regimes; (ii) for the direct regulation of certain sectors of economic or non-economic activity in the member states. Examples of the first category include: the creation of European Union agencies;[50] the enactment of European funding programmes in diverse fields such as regional development, education, migration or development policy; the establishment of complex mechanisms of fiscal policy governance,[51] and the creation of the single supervisory mechanism for banks.[52] Examples of the second category include the market regulation in the field of agriculture and fisheries, the central legal elements of the EU's competition policy, the system for the registration and authorization of chemicals,[53] and the system for the allocation of responsibility among Member State to deal with asylum requests (the "Dublin regulation"); in all those cases, even though Member States may have to adopt implementing measures, the main lines of the relevant legal regime are laid down in the EU regulation rather than in national law. This feature continues to distinguish regulations from directives, where the EU-origin of the measure is embedded in a legal regime that is mainly one of national law.

---

48. For example: Commission Implementing Reg. 793/2013 establishing measures in respect of the Faeroe Islands to ensure the conservation of the Atlanto-Scandian herring stock, O.J. 2013, L 223/1, which implements the legislative Reg. 1026/2012.
49. See, for a case in which the Court of Justice declared that a provision of a regulation lacked direct effect: Case C-403/98, *Azienda Agricola Monte Arcosu Srl v. Regione Autonoma della Sardegna*. For the question of the direct effect of the various EU instruments, see Ch. 11, "Application and enforcement in the Member States", of this book.
50. For example, Reg. 1093/2010 establishing a European Banking Authority, O.J. 2010, L 331/12; Reg. 2016/1624 on the European Border and Coast Guard, O.J. 2016, L 251/1.
51. For example, Reg. 1176/2011 on the prevention and correction of macroeconomic imbalances, O.J. 2011, L 306/25 (one of several regulations comprising the "Six-Pack" and "Two-Pack" reforms of economic governance).
52. Reg. 1024/2013 conferring specific tasks on the European Central Bank relating to prudential supervision, O.J. 2013, L 287/63.
53. Reg. 1907/2006 concerning the registration, evaluation, authorization and restriction of chemicals (REACH) and establishing a European Chemicals Agency, O.J. 2006, L 396/1 (maybe the longest regulation ever, as it occupies 850 pages of the EU's Official Journal).

3.3 *Directives*

A directive has binding force in relation to the result to be achieved for each Member State to which it is addressed but it leaves the Member States free to choose the form and methods for implementing it.[54] Along with regulations, directives are the most important instruments of EU legislation. The term "directive", and corresponding terms in the various other European languages, may not suggest intrinsically that directives have binding force, but they clearly do in the European system. However, the binding force of directives is of a special kind, differing from that of regulations. This legal instrument, for which there is no clear parallel in national or international law, has raised many questions about its legal nature and the obligations it imposes on the Member States. These questions have been repeatedly brought to the attention of the Court of Justice, and have been extensively treated in legal writing.[55] One obvious question was the meaning of the indication, in the text of the Treaty, that the binding force of directives is limited to the result to be achieved. The distinction between "result" and "form and method" is not very clear, so that the question arose whether a directive can go into details and whether it could go as far as introducing uniform rules in Member State law.

In EU institutional practice, the directive has developed into an important instrument for the harmonization of national legislation, whenever such harmonization appears necessary for the proper functioning of the European internal market. In such cases EU intervention is limited; not in the sense that the consequences of intervention may not be very considerable, but in the sense of a limitation of the purpose of the intervention: the European Union legislator may oblige the national legislature to amend national law only to the extent necessary for the functioning of the internal market. This limitation is expressed in the concrete Treaty provisions that serve as legal basis for harmonization directives, such as Article 113 TFEU ("to the extent that such harmonization is necessary") or Article 114 TFEU ("for the achievement of the objectives set out in Art. 26", which is to say the establishment of the internal market). Limitations are also expressed, although in a different way, in relation to directives in other areas than the internal market, such as environmental protection, consumer protection, social policy or migration: here the directive must make a concrete contribution to the achievement of the policy objectives which the TFEU (or TEU) formulates for each policy sector separately. Thus, the "result to be achieved", imposed by the directive, may be defined as a legal or factual situation which promotes the Union interest which the directive is aimed to ensure. This may be, for instance, the free movement of food or cars in the common market, or a high level of consumer protection, or an effective protection against discrimination.

Yet, as long as the directive remains within the limits of the policy domain and the policy objectives defined by its legal basis, there is nothing (as the Court of Justice recognized early on[56]) to preclude it from containing extremely detailed substantive provisions, and thus in fact requiring the introduction of uniform rules in the law of all the Member States. The degree of uniformity imposed by a directive will depend on the nature of the problem being regulated, and on the circumstances and the political conditions for its adoption at the EU level. Sometimes, the desired result can only be achieved by far-reaching rules that limit the autonomy of

---

54. Art. 288, para 3.
55. S. Prechal, *Directives in EC Law*, 2nd ed. (Oxford European Community Law Library, 2005), Ch. 2–5; also C.W.A. Timmermans, "Community Directives revisited", 17 YEL (1997), 1.
56. See Case 38/77, *Enka BV v. Inspecteur der Invoerrechten en Accijnzen Arnhem*, in which the Court concluded that harmonization in the customs field could necessitate ensuring the absolute identity of provisions governing the treatment of goods imported into the Community whatever the Member State across whose frontier they are imported.

the Member States to a large extent, while in other cases the text of the directive leaves more freedom of manoeuvre to the Member States. What also happens regularly is that first a so-called "framework directive"[57] is adopted, which is then later filled in by means of specific directives, so that in the end the national authorities have little left to regulate.

There is one situation, however, where directives cannot impose truly uniform rules, namely where the legal basis in the Treaties only allows for *minimum harmonization*, that is, where Member States, by virtue of the Treaty, preserve the competence to adopt additional rules. For example, directives in the field of social policy "shall not prevent any Member State from maintaining or introducing more stringent protective measures compatible with the Treaties".[58]

Each directive sets a date by which it must be transposed by the Member States, and this formal characteristic continues to distinguish directives from regulations and decisions. The period of time thus given to the Member States to take the necessary measures for ensuring compliance with the directive varies from case to case, depending on the complexity of the content and the urgency of the matter; it is often one year or less, but the term may occasionally amount to up to three years, as was the case with the General Services Directive.[59] The Commission is to be informed of the Member State's implementation, and of the text of the provisions of national law that were enacted to implement the directive. In addition, the Member States are required to include a reference to the directive when they adopt or publish the transposition measures, so as not to "hide" the EU-origin of these measures. If a Member State fails to implement a directive within the term prescribed, and to inform the Commission accordingly, the latter may bring an action for failure to fulfil treaty obligations against that Member State under Article 258 TFEU. Also, the Court of Justice has held that the Member States are not entirely free to act in the period preceding the deadline for transposition: they are not allowed to take measures, within that period, that are "liable seriously to compromise the result prescribed" by the directive.[60] This duty was, rather controversially, extended by the CJEU to national courts who must, during that intermediate period, "refrain as far as possible from interpreting domestic law in a manner which might seriously compromise, after the period for transposition has expired, attainment of the objective pursued" by the directive.[61]

The Member State's choice of form and method is, in the end, mainly a choice of the kind of legal instruments that will be adopted to transpose the content of the directive into national law, and of the competent authorities that will be in charge of the transposition and further implementation of the directive. The Member State has the freedom to delegate powers to its domestic authorities as it considers fit and in doing so to determine the extent to which implementation will take place by means of legislation or by administrative measures (the same is true, of course, for EU regulations that require implementation by the Member States). This choice takes place on the basis of the relevant rules of constitutional law, which will differ from one Member State to another, so that in one Member State a directive may have to be implemented by parliament by means of a statute, while in another Member State the same directive can be implemented by the government (i.e. the administration) autonomously. The free choice

57. The term "framework directive" is a label attached to certain directives, but it does not constitute a separate category of legal instruments.
58. Art. 153, para 4 TFEU. Similar clauses exist for the domains of consumer protection (Art. 169, para 4 TFEU) and of environmental policy (Art. 193 TFEU).
59. Directive 2006/123 of the European Parliament and of the Council of 12 Dec. 2006 on services in the internal market, O.J. 2006, L 376/36 (Art. 44: transposition deadline fixed at 28 Dec. 2009).
60. Case C-129/96, *Inter-Environnement Wallonie*, para 45; Case C-422/05, *Commission v. Belgium*, para 62; Case C-439/16 PPU, *Emil Milev*, para 31.
61. Case C-212/04, *Adeneler*, para 123.

of form and methods also includes the freedom for the legislature to choose whether to implement a directive by enacting a specific new piece of legislation, or by amending existing legislation in the area of the directive.[62]

The Member States are also free to determine the role played by regional or local authorities in implementing directives; in Member States with a federal or quasi-federal structure (such as Belgium, Germany and Spain), that role may be very extensive, whereas in Member States which are more centralized (such as Netherlands and France) this role may be more limited. Often though (for instance in the field of environmental protection), even in centralized states the local authorities will have a role to play in a second phase: the general lines for the implementation of the directive are set at national level (in a statute, or government order), and the application and enforcement will be left to regional or local authorities. The bottom line is that, whereas each Member State has the freedom to allocate powers to implement directives (or regulations) within its domestic legal system as it considers fit, that internal allocation of powers will not release the State from the obligation to ensure that the provisions of the directive concerned are properly implemented in national law,[63] or, to put this in other terms, the Member States "enjoy institutional autonomy" in this context, but "that autonomy may be exercised only in accordance with the objectives and obligations laid down in [the] directive".[64]

A firm line of case law makes it clear that each Member State is obliged to implement directives in a manner which satisfies the requirement of legal certainty and thus to transpose the provisions of the directive into national provisions having binding force,[65] which must also be enforceable *vis-à-vis* private parties where appropriate.[66] Transposition need not necessarily require enactment in precisely the same words in an express legal provision; thus, existing legal rules may be sufficient, as long as the full application of the directive is ensured in a sufficiently clear and precise manner.[67] Mere circulars, official instructions or administrative practices, which by their nature can always be changed as and when the authorities please and which are not sufficiently public, are not enough to constitute proper fulfilment of the obligation to implement directives.[68] In particular, if a directive creates rights which may be relied on by individuals, high demands are made for the transposition into the national legal order, so that beneficiaries may be aware of their rights and can exercise them before their national courts if necessary.[69] In the specific case of social policy directives, implementation may be left by the Member States to management and labour acting by means of collective agreements; this possibility may even be explicitly mentioned in the text of a directive,[70] but it will not discharge the Member States

62. For example, directives dealing with questions of private law are sometimes, and in some countries, transposed by means of amendments to a general Civil Code, and at other times, and in other countries, they are transposed by specific new statutes.
63. Joined Cases 227 to 230/85, *Commission v. Belgium*.
64. Case C-424/15, *Xabier Ormaetxea Garai*, para 30.
65. Case 239/85, *Commission v. Belgium*; Case C-340/96, *Commission v. United Kingdom of Great Britain and Northern Ireland*.
66. An example of a directive that obliges the national government to ensure that its provisions are enforceable, both in relation to the authorities and in relation to private parties, is Council Directive 2000/78, establishing a general framework for equal treatment in employment and occupation, O.J. 2000, L 303/16, Art. 16.
67. Case C-360/87, *Commission v. Italy*; Case C-131/88, *Commission v. Germany*; and Case C-190/90, *Commission v. The Netherlands*.
68. This is very often repeated in the Court's case law; see, for example: Case 102/79, *Commission v. Belgium*; Case C-296/01, *Commission v. France*; Case C-132/04, *Commission v. Spain*.
69. E.g. Case C-361/88, *Commission v. Germany*.
70. E.g. Art. 18 of Directive 2000/78 establishing a general framework for equal treatment in employment and occupation, O.J. 2000, L 303/16.

from their obligation to ensure that all workers are afforded in full the protection required by the directive, so that the state guarantee forms a residual guarantee of effective protection where this is not ensured by other means.[71] The same rules apply in areas of EU law other than employment law with regard to implementation by means of covenants and self-regulation by private organizations.[72]

Increasingly, EU directives give concrete guidance as to the institutional arrangements that Member States must adopt when implementing a directive. In those cases, the substantive harmonization is accompanied by procedural or administrative harmonization.[73] Occasionally even, the EU adopts directives aiming exclusively at the harmonization of national procedural or administrative rules, as for example with the directive on the enforcement of intellectual property rights, the directive on the budgetary frameworks of the Member States, the directive on antitrust damages actions, and the directive on the exercise of the right to free movement of workers.[74] In such cases, and given the procedural nature of the directive itself, the choice of form and method can be very limited indeed.

The direct effect of provisions of directives and their application in general by national courts is discussed in detail in Chapter 11. Here it should merely be noted that the possibility for private parties to rely, in certain cases, on a provision of a directive before a national court, does not discharge a Member State from the obligation to adopt appropriate implementing measures within the period prescribed in the directive.[75]

Finally, it may be noted that, although directives are primarily directed at the Member States, this does not exclude the possibility for a directive to entrust the Commission with the adoption of implementing measures that will contribute to the smooth implementation of the directive by the Member States. For example, the Directive of 1995 on data protection required the Commission to decide which third states offered sufficient guarantees for the protection of data so as to allow the export of those data.[76]

3.4 *Decisions*

According to Article 288 TFEU, fourth sentence, "[A] decision shall be binding in its entirety. A decision which specifies those to whom it is addressed shall be binding only on them". Unlike with regulations and directives, the Treaty text does not really attempt to define the legal

71. Case 143/83, *Commission v. Denmark*; Case 235/84, *Commission v. Italy*; Case C-430/98, *Commission v. Luxembourg*.
72. Case C-340/96, *Commission v. United Kingdom*.
73. For discussion of this phenomenon, see M. Eliantonio and E. Muir, "Concluding thoughts: Legitimacy, rationale and extent of the incidental proceduralization of EU Law", *Review of European Administrative Law* (2015), 177–204 (and other contributions, dealing with specific directives, in that same journal issue).
74. Directive 2004/48 on the enforcement of intellectual property rights, O.J. 2004, L 157/45; Directive 2011/85 on requirements for budgetary frameworks of the Member States, O.J. 2011, L 306/41; Directive 2014/104 on certain rules governing actions for damages under national law for the infringement of the competition law provisions of the Member States and of the European Union, O.J. 2014, L 349/1; Directive 2014/54 on measures facilitating the exercise of rights conferred on workers in the context of freedom of movement for workers, O.J. 2014, L 128/8.
75. Case 102/79, *Commission v. Belgium*, and Case C-197/96, *Commission v. France*.
76. Directive 95/46 on the protection of individuals with regard to the processing of personal data and the free movement of such data, O.J. 1995, L 281/31, Art. 25. One well-known EU-level implementing measure of that directive was Commission Decision 2000/520 on the adequacy of the protection provided by the safe harbour privacy principles and related frequently asked questions issued by the US Department of Commerce, O.J. 2000, L 215/7 (annulled by the ECJ in Case C-362/14, *Schrems*, and replaced by Commission Implementing Decision 2016/1250, O.J. 2016, L 207/1).

characteristics of decisions, which reflects the fact that they are a rest category which is used for a wide variety of purposes, e.g. for prohibiting a cartel or state aid measure; for funding a project from the EU budget; for making appointments in the EU institutions; for the conclusion of the EU's external agreements; for rule-making on institutional matters; and for any kind of binding act of Common Foreign and Security Policy.

As was mentioned above (in sub-section 3.1.2), this instrument of EU law is the continuation of what were, prior to the entry into force of the Lisbon Treaty, two different legal instruments both called "Decision" in English, although they were different in nature and had different names in other official languages. The first of those was mentioned in Article 249 EC (the predecessor of Art. 288 TFEU), namely the Decision as an individual act addressed either to private persons or to Member States; the other one was not mentioned in the Treaty text but was developed through the practice of the institutions and was sometimes called "Decision *sui generis*" so as to distinguish it from the other category.

Decisions in the sense of Article 249 EC (the first category) were the means by which the Community adopted individual administrative acts. Given the fact that the Commission is the principal executive organ of the EU, most of these individual decisions emanated from the Commission, but there were also decisions adopted by other institutions and bodies, such as the Council or one of the agencies. Decisions were binding in all respects on their addressees.[77] The other category of decisions (which effectively formed a fourth type of binding legal act in pre-Lisbon Community law) played an important and often underestimated role.[78] Decisions *sui generis* were used for the enactment of detailed institutional arrangements in the internal operation of the European Union, such as for laying down rules of procedure for the institutions, or setting up new committees or new administrative bodies.[79] The adoption of the budget also took the form of a decision *sui generis*, as well as the acts through which the Council approved international agreements.[80] *Sui generis* decisions were furthermore used for the adoption of multi-annual funding programmes to be implemented by the EU together with the Member States, such as the Socrates programme for mobility of students and teachers.[81]

Today, after the Lisbon Treaty, these two instruments have been merged into a single one. This is reflected by the text of Article 288 which no longer presupposes (as its predecessor Art. 249 EC did) that it has specific addressees, but now assumes (as can be seen from its text quoted

---

77. According to former Art. 249 EC, para 4.
78. Among academic writers who drew attention to this legal instrument, see A. von Bogdandy, J. Bast, F. Arndt, "Legal instruments in European Union law and their reform: A systematic approach on an empirical basis", (2004) YEL, 91, at 103–106, and, in greater detail, J. Bast, *Grundbegriffe der Handlungsformen der EU, entwickelt am Beschluss als praxisgenerierter Handlungsform des Unions- und Gemeinschaftsrechts* (Springer, 2006), at 146–435.
79. For example: Council Decision of 28 June 1999 laying down the procedures for the exercise of implementing powers conferred on the Commission, O.J. 1999, L 184/23 (the "Comitology" decision that applied until its recent post-Lisbon reform); Commission Decision of 11 Nov. 2003 on establishing the European Regulators Group for Electricity and Gas, O.J. 2003, L 296/34; Commission Decision of 14 Jan. 2005 setting up the Education, Audiovisual and Culture Executive Agency, O.J. 2005, L 24/35. An example of an institutional act adopted by various institutions and bodies was the Decision of the European Parliament, the Council, the Commission, the Court of Justice, the Court of Auditors, the Economic and Social Committee and the Committee of the Regions of 20 July 2000 on the organization and operation of the Office for Official Publications of the European Communities, O.J. 2000, L 183/12.
80. See, alongside numerous other examples, the Council Decision of 7 Nov. 2000 concerning the conclusion, on behalf of the Community, of the Convention for the Protection of the Rhine, O.J. 2000, L 289/30 (the text of the convention itself is published in the Official Journal as an attachment to the decision).
81. Decision 253/2000/EC of the European Parliament and of the Council of 24 Jan. 2000 establishing the second phase of the Community action programme in the field of education "Socrates", O.J. 2000, L 28/1.

above) that some decisions can have individual addressees and others not. In both cases, decisions are binding. Decisions that do not have individual addressees are generally binding and directly applicable in the national legal orders; whether they can also have direct effect, i.e. whether their provisions can be invoked by individuals before national courts, depends entirely on the formulation of these provisions.

As a result, the decision-new style has become a ubiquitous legal instrument, which is used in many different contexts and basically whenever a directive or regulation is either not appropriate or not permitted by the Treaty text. The core function of the decision is still to contain individual acts, addressed to individualized persons or companies or to single Member States. Its traditional area of application is competition law, where the Commission addresses antitrust and merger decisions to companies, and state aid decisions to the Member States. Some decisions authorize parties to do things, for instance Commission decisions authorizing a planned merger under the Merger Regulation, or authorizing a Member State to implement a programme of state aid. Other decisions may impose obligations, for example where a Member State is required to abolish or modify a particular state aid measure because it infringes the prohibition contained in Article 107 TFEU, or where undertakings are required to put an end to an infringement of the competition rules. More generally, beyond the field of competition law, the decision is the instrument by which the EU institutions apply EU legislation to specific situations, today often in the form of Implementing Decisions. Given the nature of the horizontal division of powers, many such decisions are adopted by the Commission, but also by agencies (when they are equipped with regulatory powers) and also rather frequently by the Council, an institution which plays an executive role instead of, or alongside, the Commission in some policy domains.[82]

Decisions may also, on occasion – just like regulations and directives – require national implementing measures. Indeed, decisions addressed to Member States may contain an authorization, a prohibition, or a refusal to grant an authorization, and this then leads to the adoption, abolition, or non-adoption of national rules. Sometimes, decisions require States to set in place a complete regulatory scheme at the national level, for example with the so-called Cooperation and Verification Mechanisms imposed on Romania and Bulgaria after their accession (and based on their Treaty of Accession),[83] or with the Council decision on relocation of asylum seekers, which requires all Member States (except those having an opt-out in this policy area) to organize the transfer of asylum seekers from Greece and Italy into their own territory.[84] In such cases, the reasons to use a decision rather than a regulation are rather elusive.

General decisions, which are not addressed to either individuals or Member States, continue to fulfil the various functions of the pre-Lisbon *sui generis* decisions. They are thus used for measures relating to the EU's internal institutional framework,[85] and it should therefore not come as a surprise that every EU institution occasionally adopts them. Even the Court of

82. For instance in the field of economic governance, e.g. Council Implementing Decision 2013/463 on approving the macroeconomic adjustment programme for Cyprus, O.J. 2013, L 250/40.
83. Commission Decisions of 13 Dec. 2006, published in the O.J. 2006, L 354/56 (Romania) and O.J. 2006, L 354/58 (Bulgaria).
84. Council Decision 2015/1601 establishing provisional measures in the area of international protection for the benefit of Italy and of Greece, O.J. 2015, L 248/80.
85. For example: Commission Decision 2015/1937 establishing an independent advisory European Fiscal Board, O.J. 2015, L 282/37.

Justice, which certainly cannot adopt regulations or directives, does adopt decisions to regulate its own activities.[86]

Finally, it should be noted that decisions are, as was mentioned above in subsection 3.1.2, the only available binding instrument in the field of Common Foreign and Security Policy (apart, of course, from the adoption of external agreements with third parties). Decisions in this policy domain are distinguished from the others by the adjunction of the letters "CFSP" to the title.[87] The fact that regulations and directives are not available in the CFSP domain serves to emphasize that the Union does not exercise legislative powers in this policy domain.

3.5 *Interinstitutional agreements and Acts of the European Council*

3.5.1 *Interinstitutional agreements*

Interinstitutional agreements (IIAs) play an important role in regulating the relations between the EU institutions in the legislative and budgetary field. As the name indicates, these are agreements concluded between two or more of the EU institutions. They are intended to "oil the wheels" of the inter-institutional processes by adding more detailed rules of behaviour to the often very laconic Treaty language. Among the main illustrations are the Agreements of 29 October 1993 and 6 May 1999 on budgetary discipline and the improvement of the budgetary procedure,[88] later replaced by the IIA on budgetary discipline and sound financial management of 2006, and later again by a similarly called IIA of 2013;[89] the Interinstitutional Declaration of 25 October 1993 on democracy, transparency and subsidiarity and the Interinstitutional Agreement (annexed thereto) on procedures for implementing the principle of subsidiarity,[90] and the Interinstitutional Agreement on better law-making of 2003, now replaced by an identically named agreement of 13 April 2016.[91] These agreements were in the past usually published in the C series of the *Official Journal*, and do not create legal obligations for third parties. Between the institutions themselves, it was not clear whether the agreements had binding legal force,[92] but they certainly were considered by their signatories as authoritative guidance for their action. The existence of this instrument was finally recognized in the text of the Treaties by the Lisbon reform. Article 295 TFEU, which is part of the chapter on Legal Acts, states that "[t]he European Parliament, the Council and the Commission shall consult each other and by common agreement make arrangements for their cooperation. To that end, they may, in compliance with the

86. For example: European Court of Justice Decision of 11 Dec. 2012 concerning public access to documents held by the Court of Justice of the European Union in the exercise of its administrative functions, O.J. 2013, C 38/2.
87. For example: Council Decision 2014/145/CFSP concerning restrictive measures in respect of actions undermining or threatening the territorial integrity, sovereignty and independence of Ukraine, O.J. 2014, L 78/16.
88. O.J. 1993 C 331/1 and O.J. 1999, C 172/1. The 1999 Agreement replaced that of 1993.
89. O.J. 2006, C 139/1, and O.J. 2013, C 73/1, respectively. For discussion of the evolution of the institutional budget rules see Ch. 9, "Budget and finances", of this book.
90. Bull. EU 10-1993 point 2.2.1 (approved by the European Parliament O.J. 1993, C 329/132).
91. O.J. 2003, C 321/1, and O.J. 2016, L 123/1.
92. This was a controversial point. On the practice of interinstitutional agreements, and their legal qualification prior to the Lisbon Treaty reform, see J. Monar, "Interinstitutional agreements: The phenomenon and its new dynamics after Maastricht", 31 CML Rev. (1994), 693–719; F. Snyder, "Interinstitutional agreements: Forms and constitutional limitations" in G. Winter (Ed.), *Sources and Categories of European Law* (Nomos, 1996), 453–466; F. von Alemann, *Die Handlungsform der interinstitutionellen Vereinbarung* (Springer, 2006); B. Driessen, *Interinstitutional Conventions in EU Law* (Cameron May, 2007); and the special issue of the 13th volume of the European Law Journal (2007), no. 1.

Treaties, conclude interinstitutional agreements which may be of a binding nature". Whereas the Treaty text seems to imply that IIAs can be either binding or not, the practice rather shows that the institutions choose the label "Agreement" only when they aim at concluding binding arrangements, and use other denominations when they seek a softer kind of understanding.[93] The Treaty text also could be read as implying that IIAs must necessarily be concluded between all three institutions, but again the practice points to the existence of *bilateral* IIAs as well. A famous example of a bilateral IIA is the Framework Agreement between the Commission and the Parliament concluded in 2010[94] which lays down far-reaching cooperation mechanisms between the two institutions, and which was objected against by the Council for affecting the institutional balance between the *three* institutions.[95] More recently, the ECB has concluded a bilateral IIA with the European Parliament on procedures for ensuring the democratic accountability of the ECB's new tasks in banking supervision,[96] whereas the ECB concluded a Memorandum of Understanding with the Council on their cooperation in the same field. In the latter case, the choice of the name of this instrument seems to indicate that the two institutions did not wish to conclude a binding agreement.

3.5.2 *Acts of the European Council*

The results of the deliberations of the European Council take the form of "Conclusions" which are published on that institution's website but not in the *Official Journal of the European Union*. Indeed, the European Council conclusions are policy documents, and not formal acts, and they do not have binding legal force. Nevertheless, in addition to a number of inconsequential but politically desirable statements, the conclusions may contain important policy guidelines, which are subsequently translated into binding legal instruments by the other institutions according to the rules and procedures laid down in the Treaties. European Council conclusions may also occasionally contain soft law measures in separate annexes.

In addition to these conclusions, which are adopted at each European Council meeting, the institution also occasionally adopts formal acts, which are almost always called Decision. This occurred already prior to the Lisbon Treaty, as the Treaty of Amsterdam had bestowed concrete tasks on the European Council, which were fulfilled by means of formal acts:[97] in particular, the adoption of common strategies in the field of foreign policy, and the (non-binding) conclusions on economic policy[98] and employment.[99] Since the Treaty of Lisbon, there are many more Treaty provisions providing for the adoption of formal decisions by the European Council. First of all, the European Council acts by means of decisions to make a number of high-level appointments, such as those of its own President, of the High Representative of the Union for Foreign Affairs and Security Policy,[100] and of the President and board members of the European Central

93. A good illustration of this practice is the fact that the Interinstitutional Agreement on Better Law-Making of 2016 (*supra* note 91), contains in an Annex the Common Understanding between the Parliament, the Council and the Commission on Delegated Acts. The choice of the names ("Agreement" v. "Understanding") seems to express a deliberate distinction between a binding and a non-binding instrument.
94. O.J. 2010, L 304/47.
95. See Council Statement on the Framework Agreement on relations between the European Parliament and the Commission, O.J. 2010, C 287/1.
96. O.J. 2013, L 320/2.
97. See A. Dashwood, "Decision-making at the summit", 3 CYELS (2000–2001), 79–105.
98. Former Art. 99, para 2 EC.
99. Former Art. 128, para 1 EC.
100. On 1 Dec. 2009, the very first day after the entry into force of the Treaty of Lisbon, the European Council already adopted three decisions: the Decision electing the President of the European Council (O.J. 2009,

Bank; it also decides, together with the European Parliament, on the president and members of the Commission. Other cases in which formal decisions by the European Council are required relate to various aspects of membership of the Union,[101] to the composition of the European Parliament,[102] and to common foreign and security policy.

Since the Treaty of Lisbon, the Treaties themselves can be revised, in some instances, according to simplified revision procedures which are characterized by the fact that the Treaty amendment is not made by means of another treaty between the Member States, but by means of a unanimous European Council decision (which then has to be approved by each State separately). This has happened already once, with the European Council decision of 25 March 2011 amending Article 136 TFEU.[103] From the perspective of the system of sources of EU law, this is an important innovation since it implies that an act of a EU institution (the European Council) can become part of primary EU law.

3.6 *Legal instruments of the former Second and Third Pillars*

When new forms of cooperation between the Member States were set up outside the existing framework of the European Community by the Treaty of Maastricht, in the fields of common foreign and security policy (commonly known then as the "Second Pillar") and of justice and home affairs (known as the "Third Pillar"), the Member States decided to adopt a whole new terminology for the legal instruments which were to be used in these new policy areas. In this intergovernmental policy domain, regulations and directives were not to be used, but instead instruments that carried different names, and whose legal nature was different. The former (pre-Lisbon) Article 12 TEU listed the means by which the *Common Foreign and Security Policy* (Second Pillar) should be given form.[104] The main binding instruments were the joint actions and the common positions. *Joint actions* did "address specific situations where operational action by the Union is deemed to be required" (former Art. 14(1) TEU). This refers to a concrete "foreign" action of the EU,[105] or measures of a financial nature,[106] although in practice the joint action instrument was also used to set up specialized EU bodies, such as the European Defence Agency,[107] which can be called an "operational action" only with some stretch of the imagination. *Common positions* on the other hand were not operational; former Article 15 TEU stated – rather vaguely – that in these common positions, the "approach of the Union to a particular matter of a geographical or thematic nature" was defined. This "approach" could later lead to specific operational measures: for instance, sanctions were usually adopted by means of com-

---

L 315/48), the Decision appointing the High Representative (O.J. 2009, L 315/49) and the Decision on the exercise of the Presidency of the Council (O.J. 2009, L 315/50).

101. See Articles 7 and 50 TEU, and Art. 355 para 6 TFEU.
102. Art. 14 para 2 TEU.
103. European Council Decision 2011/199 amending Art. 136 of the TFEU with regard to a stability mechanism for Member States whose currency is the Euro, O.J. 2011, L 91/1. The Decision entered into force in May 2013, after approval by all the Member States.
104. See e.g. R. Wessel, *The European Union's Foreign and Security Policy – A Legal Institutional Perspective* (Kluwer Law International, 1999), Ch. 5, for a thorough study of the legal nature of the acts under the Second Pillar, with examples from practice; see also P. Koutrakos, *EU International Relations Law*, 1st ed., (Hart, 2005), 393–404.
105. E.g. Council Joint Action of 29 July 1999 concerning the installation of the structures of the United Nations Mission in Kosovo (UNMIK), O.J. 1999, L 201/1.
106. Council Joint Action of 16 Nov. 2000 on the holding of a meeting of Heads of State or of Government in Zagreb (Zagreb Summit), O.J. 2000, L 290/54.
107. Council Joint Action of 12 July 2004 on the establishment of the European Defence Agency, O.J. 2004, L 245/17. That instrument is now replaced by Council Decision (CFSP) 2015/1835, O.J. 2015, L 266/55.

mon positions,[108] which were then actually implemented by an act of the European Community (insofar as economic sanctions were concerned) or by national measures (whether or not preceded by an EU implementing act).

As for the legal instruments of the Third Pillar, they were described in former Article 34(2) TEU.[109] *Common positions* were comparable with the instrument with the same name in the Second Pillar: they defined "the approach of the Union to a particular matter". The two other legal instruments, the *decisions* and *framework decisions* were closer to the instruments of Community law. *Framework decisions* were clearly similar to EC directives; they had the purpose "of approximation of the laws and regulations of the Member States" in the area of criminal procedure and even substantive criminal law.[110] Framework decisions were "binding upon the Member States as to the result to be achieved but shall leave to the national authorities the choice of form and methods". After this definition, it was explicitly stated, however, that they did not have direct effect. In this way, the Member States sought to exclude the possibility that the Court of Justice might have transposed its case law on the direct effect of directives to the framework decision instrument. However, this exclusion of direct effect did not alter the fact that framework decisions, like directives, imposed a duty on Member States to take all measures that were necessary for the correct and complete implementation at the national level. Furthermore, the Court of Justice held, in *Pupino*,[111] that the national courts have a duty to interpret their national law in conformity with framework decisions, as far as they can, which may come close in practice to framework decisions having direct effect within the national legal order.

The entry into force of the Lisbon Treaty, which caused the merger of the EC and the EU and consequently also of the three "pillars", led to the disappearance of the separate range of instruments for the domain of criminal justice and police cooperation. Yet, the existing instruments of third pillar law were kept into being and will continue to exist for as long as they are not amended or replaced by one of the new post-Lisbon instruments. This rule on the "afterlife" of third pillar instruments is laid down in Article 9 of Protocol no. 36 on transitional provisions, which provides that the legal effects of such acts "shall be preserved until those acts are repealed, annulled or amended in implementation of the Treaties". Some of those acts have indeed been transformed into mainstream EU law since the entry into force of the Lisbon Treaty,[112] but others still exist today, including some of the most important ones such as the Framework Decision on the European arrest warrant.[113] Not only can they continue to display their legal effects

---

108. E.g. Council Common Position 98/240 of 19 Mar. 1998 on restrictive measures against the Federal Republic of Yugoslavia, O.J. 1998, L 95/1; Council Common Position 2001/931 on the application of specific measures to combat terrorism, O.J. 2001, L 344/90 (still in force today, but many times amended and updated since by means of Council Decisions).
109. See S. Peers, *EU Justice and Home Affairs Law*, 2nd ed. (Oxford European Union Law Library, 2006), 31–37.
110. E.g. Council Framework Decision of 29 May 2000 on increasing protection by criminal penalties and other sanctions against counterfeiting in connection with the introduction of the euro, O.J. 2000, L 140/1; Council Framework Decision of 13 June 2002 on combating terrorism, O.J. 2002, L 164/3; Council Framework Decision of 13 June 2002 on the European arrest warrant and the surrender procedures between Member States, O.J. 2002, L 190/1.
111. Case C-105/03, *Pupino*, para 43; see also more recently Case C-554/14, *Ognyanov*, para 58.
112. For example: Directive 2012/29 establishing minimum standards on the rights, support and protection of victims of crime, and replacing Council Framework Decision 2001/220/JHA, O.J. 2012, L 315/57.
113. See *supra* note 110. The Directory of European Union Legislation (made available on the Eur-Lex website) lists the third pillar instruments that remain in force.

at the EU and national level, but they can still serve as the legal basis for new implementing measures.[114]

3.7 *Non-binding instruments*

In addition to the adoption of binding acts, all the EU institutions also adopt non-binding acts. Some EU bodies can *only* adopt non-binding acts, in the absence of the attribution of the power to adopt binding acts; for example, the Euro Group, composed of the ministers of finance of the Euro area states, is a politically powerful body but it cannot adopt binding legal acts.[115]

As was already mentioned in section 2.1, above, Article 288 TFEU mentions two types of *non-binding instruments*, namely recommendations and opinions, but in practice there are far more such instruments. We will start by discussing the two *named* instruments, after which we will mention some of the main *un-named* ones.

Opinions are usually preparatory acts forming one step in the procedure leading to the adoption of a definitive act. The most well-known are the opinions on proposals for EU legislation given by the Economic and Social Committee, and the Committee of the Regions, and above all the opinions given by the European Parliament – the last mentioned being given in the form of a particular legal instrument which the Parliament itself calls a "resolution". In addition to opinions, there are other kinds of preparatory acts which are not mentioned in Article 288 TFEU, but are mentioned elsewhere in the Treaties: proposals by the Commission for regulations or directives, and "positions at first reading" adopted by the Council in the course of the ordinary legislative procedure.[116] All these acts exist only in function of the definitive acts for which they form a preparatory step; they do not have an independent existence, and as such cannot be challenged before the Courts.[117] Alongside their main role as preparatory acts, opinions are sometimes used in different contexts and occasionally even display rather anomalous binding legal effects: for example, in the context of the procedure by which Member States must inform the Commission about new technical standards that may create obstacles to the free movement of goods, the Commission is empowered to send an opinion to a Member State forcing it to postpone the application of the new standard.[118]

Recommendations are mostly, unlike opinions, independent and definitive acts.[119] Although they do not have binding force for the institution or Member States to which they are addressed, nevertheless in certain circumstances they may be an aid to the interpretation of EU and national provisions.[120] Recommendations, when addressed to the Member States, act as a kind of surrogate directive: they often lay down very detailed standards and encourage the Member

114. The latter consequence is not spelled out in Protocol no. 36 but was logically drawn by the ECJ in its judgment of 16 Apr. 2015, *Parliament v. Council*, C-540/13, para 47.
115. The Euro Group is set up under a Protocol to the Treaties, but that protocol states, rather confusingly, that it "shall meet informally". Euro Group meetings often adopt written documents, which are mostly called "statements"; these are in no way binding, since the Euro Group has not been given any powers of decision-making in the Protocol.
116. See Art. 294, para 5 TFEU.
117. It is possible, though, to challenge the final act on the ground that a preparatory step was not taken, or was taken incorrectly. In this case there may be an "infringement of an essential procedural requirement" in the sense of Art. 263 TFEU.
118. Directive 98/34 laying down a procedure for the provision of information in the field of technical standards and regulations, O.J. 1998, L 204/37, Art. 9(2).
119. An example of recommendations that are *not* definitive acts are those addressed by the Commission to the Council with a view of opening the negotiation of an external agreement (as provided by Art. 218 TFEU, para 3).
120. Case C-322/88, *Salvatore Grimaldi v. Fonds des maladies professionnelles*, para 18.

States to comply with them, but any "implementing" national legislation is adopted on a voluntary basis.[121] In several places of the Treaty, the EU institutions are specifically allowed, or even required, to adopt recommendations and sometimes rather elaborate decision-making rules are provided for that purpose. This is the case, for example, of the recommendations of the Council setting out the broad guidelines of economic policy[122] of the Member States, or concerning their employment policy.[123] These recommendations characterize a method of governance that has become known as the *open method of coordination.*[124] An indication of their quasi-binding nature is the fact that they are published in the L series of the *Official Journal*. Apart from the many cases in which specific Treaty provisions allow for, or require, the adoption of recommendations, Article 292 TFEU also seems to grant to both the Council and the Commission a general power to adopt recommendations, independently from a particular basis in one of the policy chapters of the TFEU. The institutional practice confirms this, as we can observe that both institutions adopt recommendations for which the only legal basis, mentioned in their preamble, is Article 292.[125]

In addition to the opinions and recommendations, there are – as was said – many other types of *soft law*[126] to be found in the legal practice of the Community.

It is not unknown for *declarations* to be included in the minutes of meetings of the Council, relating to acts which have been adopted. Insofar as they contain declarations or reservations on the part of one or more members of the Council, they have no significance in the eyes of the Court of Justice.[127] If such declarations emanate from the Council itself, the Court declines to use them for the purpose of interpreting a provision of Community secondary legislation where no reference is made in the wording of the provision involved to the content of the declaration.[128]

Resolutions are the typical form taken by acts of the European Parliament, both for its contribution to the legislative process (i.e. for expressing opinions, proposing amendments, expressing rejections), and for political declarations outside the legislative process.[129] The Council also makes use of resolutions from time to time, for instance in order to lay down the principles of Union action in a certain area, when it does not have the competence to set binding rules, or when it does not (yet) have sufficient political support for binding measures.[130] Resolutions thereby help to shape the Council's policy in a given area. The Court of Justice has stated that resolutions can sometimes have binding legal force if they are intended to have legal effects and,

---

121. See, for example, Recommendation of the European Parliament and of the Council of 20 Dec. 2006 on the protection of minors and human dignity and on the right of reply in relation to the competitiveness of the European audiovisual and online information services industry, O.J. 2006, L 378/72.
122. Art. 121, para 2 TFEU.
123. Art. 148, para 4 TFEU.
124. See European Council, Lisbon, 23 and 24 Mar. 2000, Conclusions of the Presidency, para 37, Bull EU 2000-3.
125. For example, Commission Recommendation 2015/914 on a European resettlement scheme, O.J. 2015, L 148/32. This recommendation deals with the resettlement of asylum seekers, but its legal basis is Art. 292 rather than, as one would expect, one of the articles in the Treaty chapter on immigration and asylum.
126. The term soft law is not official, and will not be found in the Official Journal. It is a commonly used term in the literature for indicating a variety of non-binding acts that do have some kind of legal effect. See F. Snyder, "Soft law and institutional practice in the European Community" in S. Martin (Ed.), *The Construction of Europe. Essays in Honour of Emile Noël* (Kluwer Academic Publishers, 1994), 197; L. Senden, *Soft Law in European Community Law* (Hart, 2004).
127. See Case 38/69, *Commission v. Italy*.
128. Case C-292/89, *The Queen v. Immigration Appeal Tribunal, ex parte Antonissen*.
129. An example of the latter kind is the Resolution of the European Parliament of 22 Nov. 2012 on the elections to the European Parliament in 2014, 2012/2829 (RSP).
130. See A. von Bogdandy et al., op. cit. *supra* note 78, at 115–117.

moreover, if the power to attach such legal effects is conferred by or through the Treaties.[131] Usually it will be clear simply from the name "resolution" that the first of these two conditions is not fulfilled. In long-standing case law, the Court of Justice regards these resolutions as expressions of the Council's political will and nothing more: the failure to comply with such a resolution cannot in itself give rise to an infringement of Union law;[132] and private parties cannot rely on such a resolution,[133] nor can it be invoked against them.[134] Resolutions can, though, be an aid to the interpretation of legal acts of the institutions connected to them.[135]

Yet another category consists of the *notices, communications and guidelines* of the Commission, in which this institution sets out the framework for dealing with individual cases, for example in the field of competition and state aid, or describes the kind of Member State measures or behaviour which it considers to be compatible with EU law in a given area (such as the internal market freedoms).[136] Although these instruments do not have any intrinsic binding force with regard to private parties, and they cannot deviate from the Treaty or secondary law,[137] they can – in combination with the principle of legitimate expectations – impose a self-limitation on the Commission with regard to its individual decisional practice in the area covered by the guideline or notice;[138] and these communications and guidelines themselves can also be challenged for conflict with fundamental rights or general principles.[139]

However, most communications published by the Commission do not seek to control the behaviour of firms or Member States, but rather set out the policy ideas of the Commission, or describe a set of inter-related proposals for legislation.[140] This is part of a broader category composed of a wide range of variously named documents published by the various EU institutions (strategies, agendas, high level reports, green and white papers, work programmes, etc.) that all share the characteristic of being policy documents rather than normative instruments seeking to guide behaviour. Although such documents are sometimes included, in the literature, under the heading of soft law, this would be a misnomer, as these documents do not display any legal characteristics, whether hard or soft. They often announce or foreshadow legal develop-

---

131. E.g. the Court of Justice recognized the binding force of Annex VI of the Hague Resolution of 3 Nov. 1976 on the introduction of a fisheries zone: Case 141/78, *France v. United Kingdom*, and Case 32/79, *Commission v. United Kingdom*. Resolutions of the European Parliament may also have such legal effects, in particular when based on its power to regulate its own internal affairs, see Joined Cases C-213/88 & 39/89, *Luxembourg v. European Parliament*.
132. Joined Cases 90 & 91/63, *Commission v. Luxembourg and Belgium*.
133. Case 9/73, *Carl Schlüter v. Hauptzollamt Lörrach*.
134. Case 59/75, *Manghera*.
135. Case 43/72, *Merkur Außenhandel-GmbH & Co. v. Commission*.
136. Examples of the former include: Commission Notice on Guidelines on the applicability of Art. 81 of the EC Treaty to horizontal cooperation agreements, O.J. 2001, C 3/2; Community framework for State aid in the form of public service compensation, O.J. 2005, C 297/4. An example of the latter type is Commission Communication on the implementation of the services directive, COM(2012)261 of 8 June 2012.
137. Case C-169/95, *Spain v. Commission*.
138. See e.g. Joined Cases C-189/02 P, C-202/02 P, C-205/02 P to C-208/02 P, and C-213/02 P *Dansk Rørindustri and others v. Commission*, in relation to the Commission's fining policy in competition cases. On the important and quasi-binding role of soft law instruments in competition policy, see O. Stefan, *Soft Law in Court. Competition Law, State Aid and the Court of Justice of the European Union* (Kluwer Law International, 2013).
139. As for example in Case C-526/14, *Tadej Kotnik and others*.
140. Such policy communications are very numerous; see for example Communication from the Commission, "A blueprint for a deep and genuine economic and monetary union", COM(2012)777; Communication from the Commission, "Strategy for the effective implementation of the Charter of Fundamental Rights by the European Union", COM(2010)573; Communication from the Commission, "Towards a reform of the Common European Asylum System and enhancing legal avenues to Europe", COM(2016)197.

ments, but are not sources of law themselves. It is true, though, that this distinction is sometimes blurred by the fact that certain policy documents are contained in formal, even binding, acts; for example, the Multiannual Framework 2013–2017 for the Fundamental Rights Agency is laid down in a Council Decision, the reason being presumably that the Agency is thus legally constrained in not exceeding the scope of activity laid down in the document.[141]

Finally, it may be noted that the EU institutions use a separate range of soft law instruments in their relations with third countries or international organizations, corresponding to the established practice of public international law. Typical examples thereof are the "memorandum of understanding[142] and the "memorandum of cooperation.[143]

In the context of its judicial review of the legality of EU acts, the European Courts have tended to take a non-formalist view of the distinction between binding and non-binding instruments. Whereas the Courts could have taken the line that non-binding instruments can never impose any legal obligations on Member States or individuals, they have rather taken the view that instruments with a non-binding label could nevertheless aim at imposing legal obligations, in which case the Courts would examine their legality in the context of a direct action or a preliminary reference.[144] This attitude by the Courts seems inspired by the wish to offer extensive judicial protection against EU measures but it has the disadvantage of blurring the distinction between binding and non-binding acts.

4. Agreements concluded between Member States inter se

4.1 *Introduction*

Another, often overlooked, legal instrument of the process of European integration consists of the *treaties and conventions concluded by the Member States between themselves,* which may be of great importance for the realization of the objectives of the EU, and are concluded precisely with this in mind.

The EC and EU Treaties, prior to the Lisbon reform, explicitly provided for the conclusion of conventions between the Member States in a number of named areas: under Article 293 EC, for the abolition of double taxation within the Community, the mutual recognition of companies or firms, the retention of legal personality in the event of transfer of a company's seat from one country to another, and the possibility of mergers between companies or firms governed by the laws of different countries, and the simplification of formalities governing the reciprocal recognition and enforcement of judgments of courts or tribunals and of arbitration awards. Only three treaties have come into being on this basis: the Convention of 27 February 1968 on the Mutual Recognition of Companies and Firms,[145] the Convention of 27 September 1968 on Jurisdiction and the Enforcement of Judgments in Civil and Commercial Matters (usually called the Brussels Convention)[146] and the Convention of 23 July 1990 on the Elimination of Double

141. Council Decision 252/2013, O.J. 2013, L 79/1.
142. E.g. the Memorandum of Understanding between the Council of Europe and the European Union, Strasbourg, 13 May 2007.
143. E.g. the Memorandum of Cooperation between the European Union and the International Civil Aviation Organisation providing a framework for enhanced cooperation, O.J. 2011, L 232/2.
144. See for example Case C-410/09, *Polska Telefonia Cyfrowa,* paras. 30–35: the Court examines in detail the content of Commission Guidelines in the field of electronic communications before concluding that they do not lay down binding obligations, instead of stating that Guidelines can *never* constitute binding norms.
145. Bull EC Suppl. 2/1969. This treaty has never entered into force.
146. O.J. 1972, L 299/32. Now replaced by Reg. 44/2001, O.J. 2001, L 12/1, except with regard to Denmark (the Reg. does not apply to Denmark due to its opt-out from the Area of Freedom, Security and Justice, so the

Taxation in connection with the adjustment of profits of associated enterprises.[147] In addition, the pre-Lisbon EU Treaty provided for the possibility of conventions being concluded between the Member States, in all areas covered by the Third Pillar. In the years following the entry into force of the Treaty of Maastricht (when this possibility was introduced), a large number of such conventions were concluded, but only one of these actually entered into force, which was the Europol Convention.[148]

Today, after the Lisbon Treaty, these explicit references in the Treaty text have disappeared. But this does not mean that inter se agreements no longer exist, quite to the contrary. In fact, quite apart from the "authorizations" that used to figure in the text of the Treaties, the Member States had always preserved the power to conclude such agreements "on the side". The classic approach towards the power of Member States to conclude agreements between themselves is reflected in the ECJ judgment in joined Cases C-181/91 and C-248/91[149] and can be summarized as follows:[150] in matters coming within their competence, Member States may exercise their powers individually or collectively and in doing so they may therefore conclude agreements amongst themselves. If such agreements do not have a basis in the Treaties, they do not form part of EU law and cannot be interpreted by the Court of Justice. If, however, such agreements do fall within the competences of the EU and appear to be in contradiction with EU law, the general principle of supremacy applies. In such cases of incompatibility, at least three different consequences are conceivable:[151]

- The agreement is clearly incompatible with EU law with the consequence that the former remains valid but cannot be applied to justify a breach of the latter.[152]
- The agreement is replaced by EU law. In these cases, the Court of Justice suggests that the agreement has been abrogated by the Member States when adhering to the EU.[153]
- The agreement, though conferring rights to nationals of the contracting parties only, is, by virtue of EU law principle of non-discrimination, extended to nationals of the other Member States.[154]

By concluding agreements among themselves, Member States run the risk of circumventing the EU's legislative and other procedures or at least interfering with them in a way that could amount to a breach of their duty of loyal cooperation under Article 4(3) TEU. This is likely to happen in cases of exclusive EU competence but may also occur in cases of shared competence where the principle of pre-emption prevails.[155] The reality of today, however, is not that clear cut.

Convention remains in force in relation to that country).

147. O.J. 1990, L 225/10.
148. Convention on the establishment of a European Police Office, O.J. 1995, C 316/1 (entered into force 1 Oct. 1998). Now replaced by Reg. 2016/794, O.J. 2016, L 135/53.
149. Joined Cases C-181 and C-248/91, *European Parliament v. Council.*
150. K. Lenaerts and P. Van Nuffel, *European Union Law* (Sweet & Maxwell, 2011), paras. 22–110.
151. Compare P.J. Kuijper et al. (Eds.), *The Law of EU External Relations: Cases, Materials and Commentary on the EU as International Legal Actor* (OUP, 2013), 1059–1068.
152. See e.g. Case 10/61, *Commission v. Italy*; Case 286/86, *Ministère Public v. Deserbais*; Case C-473/93, *Commission v. Luxemburg*; Joined Cases C-241/91 P and C-242/91 P, *RTE and ITP v. Commission*; Case C-28/04 *Tod's Spa et Tod's SARL v. Heyrau SA*; Case C-533/08 *TNT Express v. Axa.*
153. See e.g. Case C-475/93, *Thevenon and Stadt Speyer Sozialamt v. Landesversicherungsanstalt Rheinland-Pfalz.*
154. See e.g. Case C-235/87, *Matteucci v. Communauté française of Belgium.* See for the special case of double taxation agreements authorized under former Art. 293 EC: Case C-374/04, *Test Claimants v. Commissioners of the Inland Revenue.*
155. See e.g. C. Timmermans, "ECJ Doctrines on Competences" in L. Azoulai (Ed.), *The Question of Competence in the European Union* (OUP, 2014), 155–167. Compare also A. Rosas, "The Status in EU Law of International Agreements concluded by EU Member States", (2011) *Fordham International Law Journal*, 1317–1320.

Indeed, many agreements between Member States are not explicitly acknowledged by, based on, or empowered by – and thus not clearly regulated by – the EU Treaties. In such cases, they nevertheless often have a *nexus* with the EU legal order and give therefore rise to complex issues at the interface between EU law, international law and national constitutional law which do not allow a simple EU law compatibility check. This is due to the fact that in practice they concern a wide range of arrangements, taking different forms, some dating back to before accession of the Member States concerned to the EU, some concluded very recently, often having a very different impact on EU primary and secondary law, sometimes without any involvement of EU institutions and sometimes attributing to them an important role in the implementation of the agreements. The doctrine has made several attempts to categorize them but given the increased recourse to such instruments over the last years, in particular in an attempt to meet the unprecedented challenges posed by the banking crisis and the sovereign debt crisis, these typologies entail the risk of being quickly outdated.[156] Member States are, in principle, not allowed to amend the Union treaties through agreements *inter se* that do not respect the rather cumbersome and lengthy provisions set out in those Treaties concerning amendments thereto, but in the current, rather exceptional circumstances the temptation to do so nevertheless exists.[157] The growing complexity of this phenomenon calls for integrating in due course the substance of these instruments into the EU legal system, if need be following amendment of the Treaties. In doing so, Member States would considerably improve legal certainty and enhance the enforceability of the rules laid down in the instruments in question. At the same time, they would avoid maintaining inconsistencies with substantive EU law and duplication of EU institutions and procedures and more generally problems of pre-emption of EU action. As long as such integration has not taken place in the formal sense, the agreements cannot be considered norms of primary Union law or provisions of secondary Union law *stricto sensu*, but that has not prevented some authors from holding that they give shape to the Union legal order in a broader sense.[158]

4.2 *Typology and examples of agreements between Member States*

Without trying to be in any way exhaustive, one can discern the following, partially overlapping categorization of the most important types of agreements concluded by Member States *inter se*. They are illustrative of the wide variety of this phenomenon.

4.2.1 *Agreements concluded by EU Member States prior to EU membership*

The Treaties regulate explicitly some agreements concluded prior to accession. For instance, reference is made in Article 350 TFEU to the possibility of regional unions between Belgium and Luxembourg and between Belgium, the Netherlands and Luxembourg. Another example is the Common Travel Area between Ireland and the United Kingdom (cf. Protocol 20 on the application of Article 26 TFEU). Failing such explicit provisions of primary law, these agreements must be brought in line with the Treaties. Article 351 TFEU, allowing for a derogation from the principle of primacy of both secondary and primary EU law in relation to agreements concluded prior to EU membership in so far as such agreements have established an obligation

156. See e.g. B. de Witte, "Internationale verdragen tussen lidstaten van de Europese Unie", (2001) *Mededelingen van de Nederlandse Vereniging voor Internationaal Recht*, 79–131; B. de Witte, "Chameleonic Member States: Differentiation by means of partial and parallel international agreements" in B. de Witte, D. Hanf and E. Vos (Eds.), *The Many Faces of Differentiation in EU* (Intersentia, 2001), 231–267.

157. See e.g. A. Rosas, op. cit. *supra* note 155, at 1319.

158. K. Lenaerts and P. Van Nuffel, op. cit. *supra* note 150, paras. 22–110 *in fine*.

that the EU Member States in question cannot honour a norm of EU law fully, is no avail in the case of agreements concluded between Member States *inter se.* Indeed, according to established case law,[159] agreements concluded between Member States *inter se* prior to accession fall outside the scope of Article 351 TFEU, since the latter only cover agreements concluded between one or more EU Member States, on the one hand, and, one or more third countries on the other. Illustrative in this respect is the Commission's decision to initiate infringement procedures against the Netherlands, Austria, Slovakia, Romania and Sweden requesting them to terminate intra-EU bilateral investment treaties between them.[160] Many of these agreements were agreed in the nineties, before the EU enlargements of 2004, 2007 and 2013. According to the Commission, these agreements constitute violations of the general principles of primacy, unity, effectiveness and non-discrimination on grounds of nationality as well as the freedom of establishment and the free movement of capital.

4.2.2 *Agreements concluded by Member State governments meeting within the Council*

From the very beginning of the Communities, Member States have felt a need to conclude agreements between themselves which had no clear legal basis in the Treaties. Decisions to that effect have often been taken in the context of formal meetings of the Council or the European Council by "representatives of the Governments of the Member States within the Council" or "the Heads of State or Government within the European Council" respectively. *Ratione materiae* these decisions, which have taken the form of "acts", "declarations", "resolutions" or "statements", relate in practice not only to subjects clearly falling outside the ambit of the Treaties, where nevertheless some form of cooperation or coordination between EU Member States is deemed opportune or even necessary, but also to subjects giving rise to disputes between these Member States as to the existence and/or scope of EU competence and where recourse to such type of decision-making has been considered an easy way out. A third category constitutes so-called hybrid acts, where the subject matter falls partly within the remit of the Member States and partly within that of the EU. In these cases, the denomination "Decision of the Council and the Ministers meeting within the Council" has been used. In particular in the area of external representation, some such acts have been challenged successfully by the Commission before the Court of Justice.[161]

The traditional view is that the agreements concluded by Member States' representatives meeting within the Council have no legal effect other than under public international law in so far as the content and the purpose of these acts would justify such conclusion.[162] Whether they have in addition effect under national law is to be decided by each Member State individually in accordance with the constitutional requirements of that Member State.[163] Not being part of EU law, such decisions cannot be enforced as such within the EU legal order but according to

159. See e.g. Case C-478/07, *Budvar v. Ammersin.* See also P. Manzini, "The priority of pre-existing treaties of EC member states within the framework of international law", 12 EJIL (2001), 781–792; C. Franklin, "Flexibility v. legal certainty: Art. 307 EC and other issues in the aftermath of the Open Skies Cases", 10 EFA Rev. (2005), 79–115.
160. Press release of the European Commission of 18 June 2015.
161. In Case C-28/12, *Commission v. Council,* the Court annulled a hybrid act for the provisional application of the Open Skies Agreement with the US.
162. H. Schermers and D. Waelbroeck, *Judicial Protection in the European Union,* 6th ed. (Kluwer Law International, 2001), paras. 670–671.
163. K. Lenaerts and P. Van Nuffel, op. cit. *supra* note 150, paras. 20–111 *in fine.*

some authors may serve to the Court of Justice as a source of interpretation when "confirming" obligations of Member States under EU law.[164]

4.2.3 *Agreements concluded by EU Member States having a nexus with primary EU law*

Member States' agreements in the sense of the previous paragraph have been used *inter alia* to settle issues of major political importance related to the ratification of changes to primary EU law.[165] For instance, in December 2008, the European Council agreed to give certain legal guarantees on the concerns of the Irish people relating to the interface between the Lisbon Treaty and the right to life, family and education, taxation, security and defence. It did so in return for a commitment from the Irish government to seek ratification of the Lisbon Treaty. The European Council agreed – at its meeting of June 2009 – on arrangements which were annexed to the Presidency conclusions, one of which was a Decision of the Heads of State or Government, meeting within the European Council, on the concerns of the Irish people on the Lisbon Treaty. In many respects, the solution resembled the arrangements agreed at the Edinburgh European Council of December 1992 in order to solve certain problems raised by Denmark about the Maastricht Treaty ("the Edinburgh Decision").[166] In both cases, the Presidency conclusions of the European Council meeting had, as an annex, a "Decision", which was drafted in legal form. In this respect, it is noteworthy that in the June 2009 conclusions, reference was made to the fact that the Heads of State or Government had declared that in the Irish case the "Decision was legally binding". In both cases, the "final provisions" said that the Decision would take effect on the date of entry into force of the Treaty – a typical final clause used in international treaty-making. Moreover, the United Kingdom and Denmark registered the Decision in the Danish case as an international treaty to the UN Secretary-General, according to Article 102 of the UN Charter[167] – a procedure which is reserved to international treaties. Some commentators concluded that the "Decision" in the Danish case constituted therefore an international treaty in simplified form.[168] Another view is that the primary purpose of the exercise was only to clarify the existing treaty text, without reopening it. Hence, the intention might have been primarily to reassure Denmark that it could rely on a legally binding interpretation of the Maastricht Treaty. In that view, the Decision constituted an "agreement relating to the treaty which was made between all the parties in connexion with the conclusion of the treaty".[169] Whatever view may prevail, the December 1992 conclusions clearly stated that the aim was to conclude the process of ratification in accordance with the respective constitutional requirements of Member States "without

164. Ibid., referring to Case 43/75, *Defrenne*. However, looking more closely at that case, it is difficult to draw from it such a general conclusion. A Member States' resolution was held contrary to the Treaty text and the Court clearly stated that neither this resolution nor a Council Directive of 1975 was capable of changing the date of effectiveness of the principle of equal pay as per 1 Jan. 1962 and hence it would not seem to attribute to the resolution a confirming effect of EU obligations at all.

165. See Editorial Comments, "An ever mighty European Council – Some recent institutional developments", 46 CML Rev. (2009), 1385–1387.

166. O.J. 1992, C 348.

167. See 1765 UN Treaty Series 98 (30685) UK Treaty Series (1994) 2.

168. See Art. 11 of the Vienna Convention on the Law of the Treaties. See for a commentary B. de Witte, "The Process of ratification of the constitutional treaty and the crisis options: A legal perspective", 16 *EUI Working Paper Law* (2004), 13; W. Hummer and W. Obwexer, "Ireland's "Nein zu Nizza"- Konsequenzen aus dem negativen irischen Referendum von 7. Juni 2001", (2011) *Integration*, 237–249.

169. See Art. 31(2)(a) of the Vienna Convention. See in defence of this view A. Aust, *Modern Treaty Law and Practice* (CUP, 2007, at 24 (fn. 52). See also Case C-192/99, *Kaur*, attaching a certain weight to the 1972 unilateral UK declaration on its nationals in interpreting the scope of Community citizenship.

re-opening the present text" of the Maastricht Treaty,[170] while the June 2009 conclusions stated in relation to the Irish case that the arrangements were "fully compatible with the Treaty".[171] Nevertheless, in the Danish case the provisions of the Decision were eventually integrated into the Amsterdam Treaty. In the Irish case, the Heads of State or Government declared that at the conclusion of the next Accession treaty, the provisions of the Decision would be set out "in a Protocol to be attached, in accordance with their respective constitutional requirements, to the TEU and the TFEU".

As regards the issue of the legally binding effect, reference should be made also to the Court's judgment in its 2010 *Rottmann* case, where it stated that the Edinburgh Decision was intended to clarify a specific issue (i.e. the concept of a national of a Member State) and that it "[had] *to be taken into consideration as being* [an instrument] *for the interpretation of the* [Treaties]".[172] Arguably, this draws on Article 31(3)(a) of the Vienna Convention under which a subsequent agreement between the parties on the interpretation of a previous treaty is part of the context to be taken into account for interpreting that treaty.

A more recent example is the "New Settlement for the United Kingdom within the European Union"[173] concluded in a vain attempt to help the UK government in February 2016 to win the *Brexit* referendum. It was very much inspired by the Danish and Irish cases in that it took again the form of a Decision of the Heads of State of Government, meeting within the European Council, and was presented as an instrument of international law, by which the 28 Member States agreed on a joint interpretation of certain provisions of the EU Treaties (e.g. the references therein to the notion of "an ever closer Union", the notion of "national security" in the sense of Article 4(2) TUE, the relationship between social benefits and the free movement of citizens and workers in the sense of Article 22 TFEU and Article 45 TFEU respectively) and on principles and arrangements in certain policy areas governed by primary law (e.g. economic governance and competitiveness). In case of national parliaments were to issue a "yellow card" in the sense of Article 7(1) of Protocol no 2 on the application of the principles of subsidiarity and proportionality, it was agreed that, in the absence of substantive modifications, the Council would discontinue the consideration of the draft legislative action in question. In addition, the Decision "took note" of the Commission's commitment to submit proposals for amending existing EU secondary legislation with a rather detailed content.

Adopting an act as the Decision in question, through an agreement concluded in a simplified form, is considered by the Heads of State and Government a prerogative recognized by international law, and notably by Article 31 of the 1969 Vienna Convention on the Law of Treaties, to the signatories of international treaties. This could explain why the first paragraph of the Preamble of the Decision spelled out that the Heads of States or Government represented Governments that "are signatories of the Treaties on which the Union is founded".

Under Article 11 of the Vienna Convention, the consent of a State to be bound by an agreement may be expressed by any means agreed by the parties. In the present case, the final provision of the Decision in paragraph 2 of Section E does not require any formality for the parties to express their consent to be bound. It does not require any formality such as signing or notification of having accomplished a formal ratification or another procedure in accordance with

---

170. Edinburgh Conclusions on Denmark, para 1.
171. Para 4.
172. See Case C-135/08, *Rottmann v. Freistaat Bayern*, para 40.
173. See the European Council conclusions of 18–19 Feb. 2016, to which is attached the Decision of the Heads of State of Government, meeting within the European Council concerning a new settlement for the United Kingdom within the European Union (O.J. 2016, C 69 I/1).

constitutional requirements. The only condition provided for the Decision to take effect is that the UK informs the Council that it has decided to remain a member of the European Union, a condition of which we now know it will not be met.

4.2.4 *Agreements concluded by EU Member Status having a nexus with international agreements concluded by the EU*

Following the negative outcome of a consultative referendum on 6 April 2016 on the bill approving the ratification by the Netherlands of the mixed Association Agreement between the EU and the EAEC and their Member States, of the one part, and Ukraine, of the other part, the Heads of State or Government of the 28 Member States, the Prime Minister of the Netherlands managed to convinced his colleagues to conclude an agreement *inter se* in order to facilitate such ratification after all. The agreement, concluded on 15 December 2016,[174] took again the form of a Decision of the Heads of State or Government, meeting within the European Council. It covered areas, falling both under EU and Member States' competence, such as security, mobility of citizens, financial support, corruption and human rights and it was agreed that it would become only legally binding on the signatories once the Netherlands would have ratified the Association Agreement with Ukraine.

With regard to its legal nature and effects, the view taken was that the Decision should, in this case as well as in previous instances, be regarded as an instrument of public international law, by which the EU Member States agreed on how they understood and would apply, within their competences, certain provisions of an act by which they were otherwise all bound. It followed the line of previous comparable Decisions aimed at clarifying certain issues and interpreting certain provisions of the EU Treaties, although in this case these clarifications pertained for the first time to a mixed international agreement and the (formal) agreement of the third country in question was not sought. It remains to be seen how this can be reconciled with the Court's finding in the so-called hybrid acts case where it ruled:" The contracting parties to a mixed agreement concluded with third countries are, first, the European Union and, second, the Member States. When such an agreement is negotiated and concluded, each of those parties must act within the framework of the competences which it has while respecting the competences of any other contracting party".[175] That said, in its conclusions, the European Council stated that this way of addressing the Dutch concerns was "in full conformity with the Association agreement and the EU treaties".[176]

4.2.5 *Agreements concluded by EU Member States having a nexus with secondary EU law*

Probably more problematic for the integrity and autonomy of the EU legal order are a series of recent agreements concluded between Member States which interfere with instruments of EU secondary law to an extent that makes it hard to claim that the latter instruments can exist and *a fortiori* can be applied autonomously, that is to say independently from the Member States' agreements related thereto. A more indirect interference occurs where Member States agree among themselves on an interpretation of EU secondary law.[177]

---

174. The Decision is annexed to the European Council conclusions of 15 Dec. 2016.
175. Case C-28/12, *Commission v. Council*, para 47.
176. Para 23 of the European Council conclusions of 15 Dec. 2016.
177. See e.g. the "Specifications on the implementation of the Stability and Growth Pact and guidelines on the format and content of stability and convergence programs", of 3 Sept. 2012, agreed in the context of the Euro group and available at <ec.europa.eu/economy_finance/economic_governance/sgp/pdf/coc/code_of_conduct_en.pdf>.

Internal Market: the case of Uniform Patent Protection

On essentially formal grounds the Court of Justice declined to examine this issue in a case brought by Spain against the European Parliament and the Council in connection with the creation of unitary patent protection through Regulation (EU) No 1257/2012 and the more or less concomitant conclusion by some Member States of an agreement on a Unified Patent Court ("the UPC Agreement")[178] playing a key role in the proper functioning of the protection scheme set up by the Regulation.[179] In this case, Spain argued *inter alia* that safeguarding the autonomy of the EU required that "the essential character of the EU and of its institutions should not be altered by any international treaty" but that this was the consequence of the UPC Agreement.[180] Spain took the view that, in acceding to that agreement, Member States were exercising a competence which was now an exclusive competence of the EU, in breach of the principles of sincere cooperation and autonomy of EU law. However, in its judgment, as a preliminary point, the Court found that in an action brought under Article 263 TFEU, it had no jurisdiction to rule on the lawfulness of an international agreement concluded by Member States, nor did it have jurisdiction in such an action to rule on the lawfulness of a measure adopted by a national authority. Moreover, it recalled its case law, according to which the direct application of a regulation means that its entry into force and its application in favour of or against those subject to it were independent of any measure of reception into national law "unless the regulation in question leaves it to the Member States themselves to adopt the necessary [...] measures to ensure the application of the provisions of that regulation".[181] Arguably, had Spain launched an infringement procedure on the basis of Article 259 TFEU against the Member States on the ground that by concluding the UPC Agreement they had breached *inter alia* the principle of autonomy of the EU legal order, the Court would not have been able to declare Spain's action inadmissible and would have had to address the substantive merit of its claim. From the perspective of EU law autonomy interesting to note is also the fact that eventually the EU legislature, following an explicit European Council "suggestion" to that effect[182] but contrary to the Commission's original proposal, decided not to include in the EU regulation provisions defining the substantive scope of the unitary protection and accepted that these were integrated in the parallel Member States' agreement instead. Eventually, the Commission decided not to stand in the way of this agreement between Council and Parliament and intervened partially in support of these two institutions in the case brought by Spain.

Banking crisis: the case of the Single Resolution Mechanism

In the context of reforms following the 2008 banking crisis, the Euro Area Member States concluded an agreement *inter se* interfering with EU secondary law, in particular the Council and

178. For decades, attempts had been made to create a system of unified patent protection within the Union all of which had failed. See in particular the Court's (negative) Opinion 1/09.
179. See Case C-146/13, *Spain v. European Parliament and Council*, and Reg. (EU) 1257/2012 of the European Parliament and the Council of 17 Dec. 2012 implementing enhanced cooperation in the area of the creation of unitary patent protection (O.J. 2012, L 361). The Member States' Agreement on a Unified Patent Court was signed in Brussels on 19 Feb. 2013 (O.J. 2013, C 175).
180. Case C-146/13, paras. 89–93.
181. Case C-146/13, paras. 100–107.
182. See para 3 of the European Council conclusions of 28/29 June 2012, illustrating the relativity of Art. 15 TEU, according to which this institution "shall not exercise legislative functions". The text of § 33 is rather confusing since it could also be interpreted as reflecting instead an agreement between the Heads of State and Government of the Member States participating in the enhanced cooperation concerning uniform patent protection.

Parliament regulation creating a Single Resolution Mechanism and a Single Resolution Fund.[183] The adoption of that regulation was preceded, on 18 December 2013, by a Decision of the representatives of the Euro Area Member States meeting within the Council on the organization of the negotiations and conclusion of an intergovernmental agreement concerning the Single Resolution Fund to be established by that EU regulation. That Decision, taken in the middle of an ordinary legislative procedure, involving therefore both Council and European Parliament on an equal footing, made it clear that the scope of the Commission proposal for that regulation, based on Article 114 TFEU, could not be accepted by a majority in the Council in that it covered not only the setting up and certain modalities of use of a resolution fund but also the transfer and mutualization of contributions raised at national level necessary in order to finance that fund. In particular Germany contested Article 114 TFEU as the legal basis to regulate the latter, was willing to accept Article 352 TFEU for that purpose but managed eventually, through the Decision, to convince the other Euro Area Member States to deal with the contributions in a parallel Member States' agreement. The ensuing agreement[184] was signed on 21 May 2014, i.e. before the adoption of the EU regulation, the scope *ratione materiae* of which was substantially more limited than the Commission's original proposal. The final texts of both instruments contain many cross references and it is obvious that neither of them can operate autonomously but one depends fully on the existence and application of the other, raising thus comparable questions of autonomy of the EU legal order as the UPC Agreement. Another interesting feature of the SRM are two "Declarations of intent by the contracting parties and observers of the Intergovernmental Conference that are members of the Council of the EU to be deposited with the Agreement". Declaration no 1 "freezes" certain aspects of EU legislation, irrespective as to whether in the future the Commission proposes to amend or repeal and the European Parliament, as co-legislator, agrees with such a proposal. Declaration no 2 states that the signatories of the Member States' Agreement, i.e. the Euro Area Member States, will strive to complete ratification of this instrument so as to permit the SRM to be fully operational by 1 January 2016. This again illustrates operational dependence of EU legal instruments on the will of a limited number of EU Member States to effectively ratify the agreement concluded *inter se*. In a statement for the Council minutes, the Commission regretted the wording of Article 88 of the EU regulation which made the application of Union law dependent on conditions laid down in an international treaty, maintaining the view that Article 114 TFEU was the correct legal base for establishing all aspects of the Single Resolution Mechanism and the Single Resolution Fund.

Sovereign debt crisis: The case of the European Stability Mechanism

Another example of Member States concluding an agreement amongst themselves with the intent to limit the use of a legal base foreseen in the Treaties can be found in the annex to the European Council conclusions of 16–17 December 2010. In the context of the sovereign debt crisis, it was agreed at the level of Heads of State or Government of the EU Member States meeting within the European Council that, through a treaty, a permanent mechanism would be established by the Euro Area Member States in order to safeguard the financial stability of the Euro Area a whole. This led to the creation of the European Stability Mechanism ("ESM") having legal personality under public international law. In their statement annexed to the European Council conclusions the Heads of State or Government declared that following the creation

183. Reg. 806/2014 of 15 July 2014, O.J. 2014, L 225.

184. Agreement on the transfer and mutualization of contributions in the Single Resolution Fund ("SRF agreement"), Council document 8457/14. See e.g. its Art. 15, illustrating how much this agreement is intertwined with the application of the SRM regulation.

of the ESM outside the EU Treaty framework, Article 122(2) TFEU should no longer be used for safeguarding the stability of the euro area. It is interesting to note that the President of the Commission refused to adhere to the statement, which explains why it could not be integrated into the conclusions of the European Council, of which he is a formal member. That such intergovernmental intent to "freeze" secondary EU law has limited effect was confirmed five years later when, despite this statement, the Council decided on a proposal of the Commission on the basis of Article 122(2) TFEU to provide assistance to Greece in the form of a bridge loan so as to enable it to reimburse certain debts to the IMF and the ECB granted in the context of the financial stability of the Euro Area.[185]

Migration: The case of the relocation scheme

The latest example where Member States meeting in the Council decided to move key elements from a Commission proposal to an agreement *inter se* is in the politically very sensitive area of migration management. Following the massive loss of life in the Mediterranean during the Spring of 2015, the Commission proposed *inter alia* a Council regulation on the basis of Article 87(3) TFEU in order to set up an emergency response mechanism to assist Italy and Greece, which would take the form of a scheme allowing 40,000 persons in need for international protection to be relocated from these two Member States to other EU Member States.[186] The proposal included a distribution key for that purpose based on the size of the population, the total GDP and the unemployment rate of Member States. Following difficult discussions in the June 2015 European Council, the Justice and Home Affairs Council of 20 July 2015 agreed on a General Approach regarding the Commission proposal pending the Opinion of the European Parliament. In parallel, Representatives of the Governments of (all) the Member States meeting within the Council adopted a resolution on 32,256 persons to be relocated and the distribution of that figure between them, the intention being that the EU instrument would build on that Resolution and would therefore contain multiple references to it, both in its recitals and operative part, raising complex questions about the actual binding force or not of these key elements of the relocation scheme.[187] The EU instrument was eventually adopted, by unanimity, two months later.[188] Interestingly, a week later, as migration flows had continued over the Summer, the Council adopted, this time by qualified majority, another Decision on the basis of Article 78(3) TFEU establishing an additional relocation scheme for the benefit of Italy and Greece, the distribution key of which, however, was not made the subject of a separate intergovernmental resolution but remained an integral part of this second EU instrument.[189]

4.2.6 *Agreements concluded by EU Member States using EU institutions*

The issue of Member States using EU Institutions outside the EU legal framework has given rise to much controversy in the academic world following the conclusion of two Member States'

185. See e.g. S. Blockmans and R. Wessel (Eds.), *The EU Legal Order under the Influence of International Organisations. Between Autonomy and Dependence* (TMC Asser Press, 2013), 297–312.
186. COM(2015)286 final of 27 May 2015.
187. Press release of the Council 11097/15 of 20 July 2015.
188. Council Decision (EU) 2015/1523 of 14 Sept. 2015, O.J. 2015, L 239/146.
189. Council Decision (EU) 2015/1601 of 22 Sept. 2015, O.J. 2015, L 248/80. This Decision was challenged by Hungary and Slovakia before the Court (pending Cases C-643/15 and C-647/15) on the ground that it should have been a legislative and not a non-legislative act. They also claimed that the Decision should have been taken by unanimity in light of the European Council Statement of 23 Apr. 2015, which they interpreted as including the guideline that no quota would be imposed by EU law on a Member State against its will.

agreements in 2013: the ESM Treaty and the Fiscal Compact.[190] The phenomenon is not new, however. Already in the *Bangladesh* and *Lomé* cases of the early nineties, in which the European Parliament opposed the Council and the Commission in relation to a decision by all Member States, meeting within the Council, to grant aid to third countries and to confer power upon the Commission to manage that aid, the Court of Justice had to deal with it.[191] More recently in the *Pringle* case, the Court has had the opportunity to refine its doctrine in this respect but seized it only in a rather limited way.[192]

In light of this case law, it is submitted that, save special Treaty provisions conferring specifically powers to the Court itself such as Article 273 TFEU,[193] starting point of any analysis of this issue is the principle of conferral of powers (cf. Art. 13(2) TFEU). This implies that in so far as the Court's case law has allowed EU institutions to be mandated to carry out certain tasks outside the EU legal framework, such a possibility must be interpreted in a restrictive way. From this follows at least three consequences:

Such a mandate must be compatible with the tasks and powers conferred by the EU treaty to that institution and should in no way alter their nature ("essential character"). In relation to these activities, the Union should not have exclusive competence.

The tasks are to be carried out in the name the Member States which have been authorized to entrust such a task to an EU institution. They should not entail any power to make decisions of their own. From the case law it follows that this implies that only certain types of action are amenable to being fulfilled on the basis of a "Bangladesh" mandate. In principle it should be a mandate to carry out management and coordination tasks, notably in connection with financial management as recognized explicitly by the Court in *Bangladesh* and *Lomé* though not repeated in *Pringle*. In other words, the EU institution can only act as an agent of these Member States. However, in its judgment in *Ledra*[194] the Court explicitly acknowledged that in specific circumstances an EU institution may engage in some form of wrongdoing in the exercise of its mandate, triggering the EU's non-contractual responsibility in the sense of Article 340 TFEU and not only engage the liability of the mandating Member States.

The administrative tasks which can be the subject of a "*Bangladesh*" mandate to an EU institution are to be distinguished from the exercise of any of the powers which the EU treaty confers on such an institution. An example of the latter is the case of the Fiscal Compact, in the context

---

190. See e.g. S. Peers, "Towards a new form of EU law?: The use of EU institutions outside the EU legal framework", 9 EuConst (2013) 37–72; P. Craig, "Pringle and use of EU institutions outside the EU legal framework: Foundations, procedure and substance", 9 EuConst (2013), 263–284. In relation to the scope *ratione materiae* of both treaties, it has been claimed that EU competence existed (see Ch. 1, "Genesis and historical development of the European Communities and the EU", section 8.1, of this book). With respect to the ESM Treaty, the Court held in Case C-370/12 *Pringle,* that the activities of the ESM fell within the EU's competence regarding coordination of the Member States' economic policies but complied with the measures adopted by the EU in that area (see paras. 68 and 69 of the judgment).

191. Case C-181/91 and C-181/91, *European Parliament v. Council and Commission* ("*Bangladesh*"), and Case C-316/91, *European Parliament v. Council* ("*Lomé*").

192. See cited *supra* note 188.

193. In a series of agreements between Member States, which since 2010 have been concluded in the context of the banking and sovereign debt crisis, this Treaty provision has enabled the contracting parties in question to grant the Court of Justice the power to settle disputes between them in connection with the interpretation and application of these instruments given the fact that the latter have, as required by Art. 273 TFEU, a *nexus* with the EU Treaties. In the case of the Fiscal Compact this provision has been interpreted widely so as to allow granting the Court a power analogous to its powers in infringement cases under Articles 258–260 TFEU (cf. Art. 8 Fiscal Compact). See for a commentary e.g. L. Azoulai et al., "Another legal monster? An EUI debate on the fiscal compact treaty", 9 *EUI Working Papers Law* (2012).

194. Judgment of 20 Sept. 2016 in Joined Cases C-8/15 P to C-10/15 P, *Ledra Advertsing et alii v. Commission.*

of which the Commission's role to be engaged in monitoring and surveillance of the budgetary in the Member States is based on Articles 121, 126 and 136 TFEU and therefore did not require a "*Bangladesh*" mandate. Conversely, in the context of the ESM Treaty, the Commission role cannot be linked to one of the powers conferred to it by the EU Treaties. Instead, it is limited, in essence to negotiating, concluding and monitoring compliance with a Memorandum of Understanding concerning the conditionality which the Euro Area Member State receiving financial assistance must accept as a *quid pro quo* for this assistance.[195]

4.2.7 *Agreements concluded by EU Member States following an empowerment by the EU*

According to Article 2 (2) TFEU in areas of competence the EU shares with Member States, the EU and Member States may legislate and adopt legally binding acts but the Member States shall exercise that competence *to the extent* the Union has not exercised its competence. Conversely, the Member States shall again exercise their competence *to the extent* that the Union has decided to cease exercising its competence. Nothing in the text of this treaty provision suggests that in such a situation of "retro-cession" Member States could not, in principle, decide to exercise jointly their regained competence through an agreement *inter se.* According to Article 2 TFEU, in cases of exclusive EU competence, only the EU is authorized to legislate and adopt legally binding acts, the Member States being able to do so themselves only if also empowered by the Union or for the implementation of Union acts. At least in one case of EU exclusive competence, i.e. the conservation of maritime biological resources under the common fishery policy (cf. Art. 3(1)(d) TFEU), the EU legislature adopted Regulation (EU) No 1380/2013, giving some scope for agreements between Member States.[196] According to its recital 39 read in conjunction with Article 18, Member States sharing a direct management interest are authorized to adopt joint recommendations for achieving the objectives of certain Union conservation measures. Pending such recommendations, allowing for this form of regional cooperation between groups of Member States on conservation measures, the Commission will refrain from adopting delegated or implementing acts in connection with these measures.

Although the current Treaties no longer refer to conventions between Member States as a policy instrument, the existing ones (e.g. the Europol Convention), empowered under the former Third Pillar, keep their legal force, including any interpretative jurisdiction conferred on the Court.

Finally, there seems nothing in the text of Article 291 TFEU preventing Member States from fulfilling, through a joint agreement, their respective obligation under that Article, according to which they "shall adopt all measures of national law necessary to implement legally binding Union acts", providing of course, such agreements produce legal effects under their respective national law and there is no contradiction with the implementing measures the Commission has been empowered to take under Article 291(2) TFEU.

4.3 *Concluding remarks*

The recent developments described above seem to suggest that the harmonious times, during which agreements between Member States could be considered as a temporary phenomenon in essence aimed at promoting closer cooperation between them with a view to subsequent conversion into EU instruments,[197] are over and that the phenomenon has a more structural

195. See Art. 1 ESM Treaty.
196. O.J. 2013, L 354.
197. See A. Rosas, *supra* note 155, at 1318–1319, pointing at the examples of the *Schengen* Agreement on the gradual abolition of internal border controls of 1985 (cf. Protocol on the Schengen *Acquis* Integrated into

nature. The *vires* provided by the EU Treaties are so wide that the possibilities to act within the EU legal framework are virtually unlimited and for those Member States that wish to constitute an *avant garde* in terms of deeper cooperation and integration, the same Treaties provide for a sophisticated but nevertheless generous framework for enhanced cooperation.[198] Still, Member States show an increasing willingness to choose for a, at least partially, different route than the one offered by the EU. The motives to do so vary and range from political sensitivities at national level, issues of constitutional pluralism, disputes about EU legal basis, concerns about the relative easiness with which EU instruments can be amended or repealed now that QMV has become the voting rule by default, to reluctance to allow the more "supranational" EU institutions, such as the Court, the Commission and the European Parliament, to play fully the role conferred to them by the Treaties. In such circumstances, the EU legal framework with its elaborated system of judicial, political and financial checks and balances and despite the possibilities it offers in terms of secondary legislation amendments and its various forms of delegation seems to be felt by some as a straitjacket not allowing for the necessary flexibility in dealing with the complex problems of modern society. Also to note is that where the EU Treaties and secondary legislation prescribe openness to other Member States joining in cases of e.g. enhanced cooperation, the euro and the banking union, the fact is that a Member State would have to sign up to an intergovernmental agreement which – unless that intergovernmental agreement provides for an automaticity for others to join – would imply that every "in" has a *de facto* veto right on a new Member State. If such an intergovernmental agreement interferes with the operation of an EU instrument, the exercise or not of the veto right by an "in" might affect the legal position of an "out" under that EU instrument. Attempts have even been made to conceptualize at the highest political level the phenomenon, the best known example being the promotion of the idea of the *Union method* as an alternative (or even succession) to the *Community method*, which, upon closer examination, does not convince that much as it based on the rather simple, pragmatic premise: "better something than nothing", *viz.* sticking to the Community method may in certain circumstances for whatever reason, legitimate or not, lead to no action at all at European level, whereas recourse to *intergovernmentalism* at least does to some extent.[199] More difficult to explain in light of that *rationale* though are some of the hybrid actions described earlier leading to situations where EU law and intergovernmental agreements are so intertwined that there is a risk of creating a relationship of subordination affecting the autonomy of the EU legal order at its heart. Or to put it more prosaically: "the EU legal and institutional system is a self-standing composite whole, not a menu from which the Member States can pick and choose according to their *gusto*".[200] At the same time, one cannot ignore the fact that the Court of Justice itself, by being flexible about agreements concluded between Member

---

the Framework of the European Union, O.J. 2010, C 83/290) and the *Prüm* Convention of 2005 relating to increased cross-border cooperation as regards combatting terrorism, cross-border crime, and illegal migration.

198. See the rather flexible interpretation given by the Court to the conditions for enhanced cooperation in Joined Cases C-274/11 and C-295/11, *Spain and Italy v. Council*, relating to uniform patent protection, and Case C-209/13, *UK v. Council*, relating to financial transaction tax.

199. See e.g. Chancellor Merkel's speech delivered at the opening ceremony of the 61st academic year of the College of Europe in Bruges on 2 Nov. 2010, 5–8.

200. See C. Timmermans, *supra* note 155, at 165; see in the same sense M. Dawson and F. de Witte, "Constitutional balance in the EU after the Euro-crisis", 76 *Modern Law Review* (2013), 817–844; E. Chiti and M. Teixeira, "The constitutional implications of the European responses to the financial and public debt crisis", 50 CML Rev. (2013), 683–708.

States *inter se*, in particularly those that "use" EU institutions, has relativized somewhat its own pretentions with respect to the constitutional character of the EU edifice.[201]

Further reading

Bast, J., *Grundbegriffe der Handlungsformen der EU* (Springer, 2006).
Bast, J., "New categories of acts after the Lisbon reform: Dynamics of parliamentarization in EU Law", (2012) CML Rev., 885–928.
Curtin, D. and T. Manucharyan, "Legal acts and hierarchy of norms in EU law" in A. Arnull and D. Chalmers (Eds.), *The Oxford Handbook of European Union Law* (OUP, 2015), 103–125.
De Witte, B., "Legal instruments and law-making in the Lisbon Treaty" in S. Griller and J. Ziller (Eds.), *The Lisbon Treaty: EU Constitutionalism without a Constitutional Treaty?* (Springer, 2008), 79.
Lenaerts, K. and P. Van Nuffel, *European Union Law*, 3rd ed. (Sweet & Maxwell, 2011), Ch. 22 and 23.
Prechal, S., *Directives in EC Law*, 2nd ed. (OUP, 2005).
Tridimas, T., *The General Principles of EU Law*, 3rd ed. (OUP, 2016).

201. See, however, its (negative) Opinion 2/13 on the draft agreement concerning accession of the EU to the ECHR, delivered a few months before its judgment on uniform patent protection, going very much in the opposite direction as regards the need to protect the constitutional character of the EU legal framework and its ensuing autonomy.

CHAPTER 7
LAW-MAKING

*Pieter Van Nuffel and Felix Ronkes Agerbeek**

1. Introduction

In addition to the founding treaties which constitute the "primary" law of the European Union, there is an impressive[1] body of "secondary" law, made up of the legal instruments adopted by the institutions of the European Union. Indeed, law-making has become the most important activity of the European Union. In the first decades of European integration, the implementation and application of the basic principles of the treaties – in particular the "four freedoms" and the competition rules – attracted most attention. However, now that the single market is in place, not in the least due to the Court's case-law on primacy and direct effect, the most striking characteristic of the Union is its continuing process of law-making. As its financial resources remain very limited in the current phase of European integration, the Union aims at attaining its objectives by adopting laws, to facilitate the functioning of the internal market and to shape the common policies that complement it, as well as the new policies that transformed the Union into a political union.

This Chapter focuses on the "legislative" activity of the Union, as opposed to its "executive" activities, which are discussed in the next Chapter. That said, the contrast between the Union's legislative and executive activities should not be exaggerated. The institutional structure of the Union does not correspond to the classic *trias politica.* It is impossible, therefore, to make a strict distinction between the powers and acts of the Legislature and those of the Executive. The Treaties have, rather, created a continuum. Moreover, many of the principles discussed in this Chapter apply regardless of whether the activity in question is legislative or non-legislative. In particular, all activities of the Union are governed by the *principle of conferral*, according to which the Union shall act only within the limits of the competences conferred upon it in the Treaties (Art. 5 TEU). Furthermore, each institution shall act within the limits of the powers conferred on it in the Treaties, and in conformity with the procedures, conditions and objectives set out in them (Art. 13 TEU). By virtue of these fundamental principles, the *legal basis* is the linchpin of any decision-making process of the Union. It determines which procedure must be followed and what type of instrument can be used; in addition, the legal basis shapes the content of the envisaged act.

---

* Pieter Van Nuffel is the principal author of sections 1 to 4, and Felix Ronkes Agerbeek the principal author of section 5. They are respectively Principal Legal Adviser and Member of the Legal Service of the European Commission. Any views expressed are personal and cannot be attributed to the Commission.

1. At the moment of the accession of Croatia to the EU, the "*acquis*" counted some 144,000 pages (COM(2012)161 – Comprehensive Monitoring Report on Croatia 2012, at 17).

This Chapter accordingly starts by summarizing the rules for determining the legal basis (section 2). It then explains the formal distinction, introduced by the Treaty of Lisbon, between "legislative acts" and other acts (section 3). The longer section 4 sets out the procedures for Union law-making and describes the roles of, in particular, the European Parliament, the Council and the Commission in the law-making process. However, law-making is not just a matter of rules and procedures: the last section concludes the Chapter with remarks on law-making and democratic legitimacy in the European Union.

A number of topics that arguably fall under the rubric of "law-making" will be dealt with in other chapters:

- The *form* that Union law can take, namely the various *instruments* (Regulations, Directives and Decisions).[2]
- *Delegated and implementing acts.* The measures are essentially "executive acts" that implement a legislative act.[3]
- *International agreements.* Although international agreements concluded by the Union with third countries or international organizations do form part of the Union secondary law – and are steadily growing in importance, as the Union is very active in international law-making – these legal instruments[4] will not be discussed at length here.[5]
- *Decisions adopted by the representatives of the governments of the Member States* or *agreements concluded between the Member States.*[6] The present Chapter will only deal with secondary Union law in the strict sense, namely the acts of the EU institutions.

2. Legal basis

The competences of the Union are governed by the principle of conferral (Art. 5(1) TEU). Therefore, any act of the Union needs a legal basis, i.e. a treaty provision[7] that will empower the Union to act. The choice of legal basis is essential in the law-making process. It has, in the words of the Court, "constitutional significance".[8]

Indeed, the legal basis determines the *existence* of a competence and the *nature* of that competence,[9] the *legislative* or *non-legislative* form of the envisaged act;[10] the *procedure* to be followed to adopt that act, i.e. the respective role of the institutions in the adoption of the

2. See Ch. 6, "Sources of EU law", of this book.
3. This will be discussed in Ch. 8, "The EU administration", of this book.
4. Bilateral and multilateral international agreements, treaties, conventions, exchange of letters or international legal transactions by whatever other name they may be referred to, concluded by the Union or by the Union and its Member States (so-called "mixed agreements"), as well as the decisions of bodies set up an international agreement which have the power to adopt acts having legal effects for the Union (Art. 218(9) TFEU), such as decisions of Association Councils established in the Association agreements.
5. Instead they will be discussed Ch. 39, 40 and 41, on the Union's external actions, of this book.
6. These are dealt with in Ch. 6, "Sources of EU law", of this book.
7. Or the relevant provision of an act adopted on the basis of the treaties, allowing for the adoption of delegated acts or of implementing acts by the Commission (or, as the case may be, by the Council), or for the adoption of an act by a Union Agency. A Union act based on the treaty cannot provide for a "secondary legal basis" whereby the legislature would provide that a matter can be decided in accordance with another (lighter) procedure than the procedure provided for by the treaties (Case C-133/06, *EP v. Council*, paras. 54–60).
8. Case C-370/07, *EP v. Council*, para 47; Opinion 1/08, para 110; Opinion 2/00, para 5.
9. See Ch. 3, "System of competences", of this book.
10. See *infra* subsection 3.

act;[11] and lastly the type of *instrument* which can or has to be used, and therefore the legal effect of the act.[12]

It is therefore not surprising that most litigation between institutions concerns the choice of legal basis. The Court of Justice has in a long series of judgments and opinions [13] clearly laid down the rules for determining the legal basis of an act:

(i) The choice of the legal basis must rest on objective factors amenable to judicial review, which include the aim and content of that measure.[14]

(ii) If examination of the measure reveals that it pursues a twofold purpose or that it has a twofold component and if one of these is identifiable as the main or predominant purpose or component, whereas the other is merely incidental, the measure must be founded on a single legal basis, namely, that required by the main or predominant purpose or component.[15]

(iii) By way of exception, if it is established that the measure pursues several objectives which are inseparably linked without one being secondary and indirect in relation to the other, the measure must be founded on the various corresponding legal bases.[16]

(iv) No dual legal basis is possible, however, where the procedures required by each legal basis are incompatible with each other.[17] In such a case, the legislature will have to adopt two separate acts, each adopted on its own legal basis, in accordance with the procedure it provides for.

The legal basis or bases of an act must be expressly indicated in the act.[18] Normally the legal basis is referred to in the citations at the beginning of the preamble, following the words "Having regard to".

3. Legislative and non-legislative acts

Although the original treaties did not refer to "Community legislation" or a "Community legislature", the Court has used these expressions from the early days[19] without, however, giving them any precise definition. Despite this lack of clarity it is possible to infer from practice that these

---

11. See *infra* subsection 4.
12. See Ch. 6, "Sources of EU law", of this book.
13. See, most recently, Case C-377/12, *Commission v. Council*, para 34; Case C-658/11, *EP v. Council*, para 43; Case C-490/10, *EP v. Council*, paras. 44–47; Case C-130/10, *EP v. Council*, paras. 42–45; Case C-411/06, *Commission v. EP and Council*, paras. 45–47; Case C-155/07, *EP v. Council*, paras. 34–37; Opinion 2/00, paras. 22–23.
14. For example: Case C-43/12, *Commission v. Council*; Case C-656/11, *UK v. Council*; Case C-490/10, *EP v. Council*. In addition, where the Treaty contains a more specific provision that is capable of constituting the legal basis for the measure in question, the measure must be founded on that provision (Case C-490/10, *EP v. Council*, para 44; Case C-155/07, *EP v. Council*, para 34).
15. For example: Case C-377/12, *Commission v. Council*; Case C-137/12, *Commission v. Council*.
16. For example: Case C-166/07, *EP v. Council*; Case C-411/06, *Commission v. EP and Council*; Case C-155/07, *EP v. Council*, para 34; Case C-94/03, *Commission v. Council*.
17. Case C-300/89, *Commission v. Council* ("*Titanium dioxide*"), paras. 17–21. The ordinary legislative procedure is compatible with a procedure which provides for simple consultation of the European Parliament (Case C-155/07, *EP v. Council*), unless the other procedure would involve unanimous decision making in the Council (Case C-130/10, *EP v. Council*, paras. 46–48; see however Case C-166/07, *EP v. Council*, para 69). The Court has not yet decided whether a legislative procedure is compatible with a non-legislative procedure.
18. Case C-370/07, *Commission v. Council*, para 39.
19. In Case 20-59, *Italy v. High Authority*, the Court referred to the "legislative" power ("*compétence légiférante*") of the High Authority; in Case 41-69, *ACF Chemiefarma*, to the "Community legislature" (para 20); in Case 52-69, *Geigy*, to "Community legislation" (para 11). Later, the Court has considered that regulations have

expressions were used to refer to acts formulated in general terms and adopted directly on the basis of a provision in the treaties. Such acts can be differentiated from acts adopted on the basis of a provision in an act adopted by the institutions. According to settled case-law, the adoption of rules essential to the subject-matter envisaged is reserved to the legislature. Such rules must be laid down in the "basic legislation"; the power to adopt them cannot be delegated.[20]

Apart from this simple distinction between, on the one hand, acts adopted on the basis of primary law and, on the other, acts adopted on the basis of secondary law, there has also been a tendency in European politics to use the word "legislation" in a substantive sense, as in the national context. The first few references to the concept of "legislation" in the treaties, notably the Treaty of Amsterdam[21] must be understood in that sense. This approach was also very much present in the work on constitutional reform that took place at the beginning of this century.[22] As a consequence and on the basis of the work undertaken by the European Convention,[23] the *Treaty establishing a Constitution for Europe* proceeded to a new classification and denomination of Union legal acts.[24] This system was partially introduced by the Treaty of Lisbon. In particular, it created the category of "legislative acts" and introduced a clear distinction between *legislative* and *non-legislative acts*.

It should be stressed from the outset, however, that the distinction, introduced by the Treaty of Lisbon, between legislative acts and other acts is a strictly formal one. An act does not qualify as a legislative act due to its supposed legislative content. Nor does it qualify as such on account of having been adopted by the European Parliament and the Council, the institutions that exercise "legislative functions" (Art. 14(1) and 16(1) TFEU). Instead, the determining factor is the decision-making procedure that has been followed. Put quite simply, any act adopted in accordance with the *ordinary legislative procedure* or a *special legislative procedure* is a legislative act (Art. 289(3) TFEU). Any other act, regardless of its content, is a non-legislative act.

This does not mean that the distinction is purely arbitrary. On the contrary, the Convention examined every legal basis in the treaties to determine whether acts adopted on the basis of the provision concerned would be legislative in nature. However, the result was not perfect. In particular, the legislative procedure was not introduced, at all, into the Euratom Treaty, despite the evident legislative powers of the Euratom Community, notably the power to adopt health and safety standards. Furthermore, it can be argued that some provisions of the TFEU, in particular in the area of competition policy,[25] allow for the adoption of measures that would, in a national context, probably be considered of a legislative nature. Be that as it may, under

---

a "legislative nature" as they are of general application (Case C-298/89, *Gibraltar*, para 17; Case T-306/01, *Yusuf*, para 185).

20. Case C-355/10, *EP v. Council* (para 64 and case law cited there).
21. Art. 207(3) EC referred to cases in which the Council was "acting in its legislative capacity"; and also the Protocol on the role of the national parliaments in the EU provided for certain obligations with respect to "legislative proposals"). However, the definition of that concept was left to the Council who made a (not very successful) attempt in its then applicable Rules of Procedure.
22. See for instance the *Laeken Declaration on the Future of the European Union* (15 Dec. 2001).
23. See notably the Final Report of Working Group IX on Simplification (CONV 424/02).
24. In particular, Arts. I-33 to I-35 of the draft Constitution provided for "Legislative acts" ("European laws" and "European framework laws") and "Non-legislative acts" (all other acts, in particular the "European regulations" and "European Decisions"). See more in detail P. Stancanelli, "Le système décisionnel de l'Union" in G. Amato, H. Bribosia and B. De Witte (Eds.), *Genesis and destiny of the European Constitution* (Bruylant, 2007), 485–543.
25. Acts based on Art. 103 and 109 TFEU. Other examples might be acts based on Art. 31, 155 and 188 TFEU (concerning the common customs tariff, implementation of agreements between management and labour, joint undertakings). Further, the restrictive definition of the special legislative procedure (Art. 289(2)

the system introduced by the Treaty of Lisbon, such measures are considered non-legislative acts. Only where the legal basis requires that the applicable procedure for the adoption of an envisaged act is the ordinary legislative procedure or a special legislative procedure (Art. 289(3) TFEU), the act will be considered a legislative act.[26]

The fact that an act qualifies as a legislative act has a number of consequences and effects:

- Legislative acts are adopted on a proposal from the Commission (Art. 17(2) TEU).[27]
- Not only the European Parliament, but also the Council must meet in public when it deliberates and votes on a legislative act (Art. 16(8) TEU and Art. 15(2) TFEU). In the course of the legislative procedure, these institutions must refrain from adopting other acts in that area (Art. 296 TFEU).
- Draft legislative acts must be submitted to the subsidiarity control of national parliaments and cannot be adopted within the first eight weeks after their transmission to national parliaments (Art. 12(a) TEU, Protocols No 1 and 2).
- For the review of legality by the Court of Justice on grounds of infringement of the principle of subsidiarity, the Committee of Regions has *locus standi* for the legislative acts on which it was consulted (Art. 8 Protocol No 2).
- With respect to directives adopted under a legislative procedure, the Commission can, in case of failure to notify transposition measures, request the Court already in the first infringement procedure to impose the payment of a lump sum or a penalty (Art. 260(3) TFEU).
- The power to conclude an international agreement provided for in a legislative act creates exclusive competence in that area (Art. 3(2) TFEU).
- The adoption of legislative acts in the Common Foreign Security Policy (CFSP) is excluded (Art. 24(1), second paragraph, and Art. 31(1) TEU).
- Only a legislative act can provide for the possibility to adopt delegated acts (Art. 290 TFEU).

Despite all of these special features, there is no hierarchy between legislative and non-legislative acts. And a legislative act can, like non-legislative acts, take the form of a Regulation, a Directive or a Decision, depending on what its legal basis provides for.[28]

4. Decision-making process

4.1 *General framework*

The Union has the reputation of operating very complex decision-making procedures. This reputation is only partially justified. It is true that a decision [29] is only seldom the feat of a single

---

TFEU) makes it impossible that any act of the European Central Bank, or of the Commission, would receive the label "legislative act".

26. Joined Cases C-643/15 and C-647/15 *Slovakia and Hungary v. Council*, paras. 58–63. Arts. 203, 349 and 352 TFEU leave the Council the choice whether to adopt the envisaged measures as a legislative or as a non-legislative act.
27. Except in the very few cases in which the treaties provide otherwise (cf. Arts. 223(1), 226, 228(4) and 308 TFEU), as well in case of an initiative of a quarter of the Member States in the areas of judicial cooperation in criminal matters and of police cooperation (cf. Art. 76(b) TFEU).
28. The legislative instruments will indicate in the preamble of the act, in the last sentence before the recitals, that the European Parliament and/or the Council are/is acting "in accordance with the ordinary legislative procedure" or "in accordance with a special legislative procedure".
29. In this subsection, the word "decision" is used in its generic meaning (what has been decided); for a discussion of the instruments which take the form of a "Decision", see Ch. 6, "Sources of EU law", of this book.

institution, due essentially to the supranational nature of the Union. Most decisions consequently require the involvement of at least two institutions, and in many instances, they require the involvement, in one way or another, of a whole range of institutional actors. The impression of complexity is created by the fact that the roles of these actors, i.e. their respective power to influence the end-result, are not always the same, but may be quite different depending on the procedure provided for by the legal basis of the envisaged measure. The upshot is that decision-making in the Union is a theme with many variations. Nevertheless, the basic structures of the decision-making procedures are fundamentally simple and easy to understand.

This subsection will not offer an exhaustive enumeration of all possible variants; instead, it will focus on the possible roles in which the institutions may appear in the procedure at the stages of *initiative*, *consultation* and *adoption*.

The original decision-making scheme, as laid down in 1957 in the EEC Treaty and the Euratom treaty was straightforward:[30] save for the few cases where the treaties conferred decision-making powers directly on the Commission (in particular in the area of competition law), Community law was essentially adopted by the Council, acting by unanimity or in some cases by a qualified majority, on a proposal from the Commission, and, in many areas, after consulting the European Parliament. Today, however, the *ordinary legislative procedure*, first introduced as the "co-decision procedure" for a limited number of areas by the Treaty of Maastricht, is applicable in most policy areas. In accordance with this procedure, legislative acts are adopted, on a proposal from the Commission, by the European Parliament and the Council acting jointly, with the Council voting by qualified majority.

The normal decision-making procedure for acts, which are today legislative acts, has thus drastically evolved in the fifty years between the Treaties of Rome and the Treaty of Lisbon, through successive treaty changes. The rise of the European Parliament from a mere consultative organ to a real co-legislature, as well as the generalization of qualified majority voting in the Council are the most striking developments. Formally, the involvement of the Commission has not changed over the years, however the changes in institutional balance between the European Parliament and the Council have to an extent altered the role of the Commission in the decision-making process: what was formerly a dialogue between the Commission and the Council, has in present-day law-making become a multiparty endeavour in which the Commission must navigate the cross-currents of politics in the Council and the Parliament.

In the areas where the ordinary legislative procedure is not applicable, the respective treaty legal bases provide for either a *special legislative procedure* or a *non-legislative procedure.* A special legislative procedure entails that one or more elements of the ordinary legislative procedure are modified (for example, the Council deciding with unanimity). A non-legislative procedure usually corresponds to the original scheme (Council decision on a proposal of the Commission, after consulting the European Parliament), be it that successive treaty changes have also here extended qualified majority voting in Council; but the denomination non-legislative procedure covers also all other cases, such as the decision making by the European Central Bank (ECB).

Further, Union law comprises a large number of measures deriving from acts adopted on the basis of the treaties, in particular the *delegated acts* adopted by the Commission (Art. 290 TFEU), the *implementing acts* adopted by the Commission or, in specific cases, by the Council (Art. 291 TFEU), decisions adopted by the Council to implement acts in the area of the

30. But different from the European Coal and Steel Community, which laid decision-making essentially in the hands of the High Authority (the Commission), be it for essential decisions after an *avis conforme* of the Council.

CFSP (Art. 31(2) TEU), as well as measures adopted by bodies established by Union legislation (agencies).[31]

The complex division of powers between the institutions, which has emerged as a result of the historical evolution, is an important element of the institutional balance created by the treaties.[32] The fact that most decision-making procedures require the involvement of two or more institutional actors, and depend on their cooperation, increases, however, the potential for conflicts between institutions. Indeed, on a regular basis, the Court of Justice is requested to resolve differences of views between the institutions on what may seem merely procedural matters, but which in reality concern the division of powers between the institutions. That said, the risk of such conflicts is mitigated by the principle that the institutions must practice *mutual sincere cooperation* (Art. 13(2) TEU). Obviously, that principle cannot be relied upon to change the powers as conferred by the treaties to the institutions,[33] but each institution should exercise its powers in such a way that it allows the other institutions to fully exercise theirs.[34] This may entail, depending on the case at hand, early information on its position,[35] mutual consultation,[36] or avoidance of unjustified delays.[37]

Furthermore, the absence of details in the treaties regarding how the different decision-making procedures should actually be run has led the institutions to lay down in inter-institutional agreements (whether labelled as such or otherwise) a number of practical arrangements and working methods, aimed at facilitating the application of the procedures, in particular the Joint Declaration of 13 June 2007 on practical arrangements for the co-decision procedure,[38] [39] and at enhancing the quality of the content and of the texts of Union legislation.[40] Since the Treaty of

---

31. These measures will be essentially discussed in Ch. 8, "The EU administration", of this book; however, many of the elements treated in the following are equally relevant for all or some of these "third layer" Union measures.
32. That being said, law-making is almost always decided by the normal procedures, i.e. if not the ordinary legislative procedure (applicable to most cases), by the Council acting by qualified majority or unanimity on a proposal by the Commission after consulting the European Parliament. It is rather with respect to institutional decisions that the drafters of the treaties have tried to establish in each case an appropriate balance of powers between the institutions, which sometimes results in rather complex procedures, as for example in Art. 223(2) TFEU, where the European Parliament may decide, on its own initiative, the statute of the members of Parliament, but after having obtained an opinion of the Commission and consent by the Council; the Council adopts this consent with a qualified majority, or with unanimity with respect to rules and conditions relating to taxation.
33. Case C-48/14, *EP v. Council*, paras. 58–60; Case C-77/11, *Council v. EP*, para 67; Case C-73/14, *Council v. Commission*, para 84.
34. Or, in other words, each institution must ensure that the institutional balance is respected (observance of the institutional balance means that each of the institutions must exercise its powers with due regard for the powers of the other institutions: Case C-133/06, *EP v. Council*, para 57; Case C-409/13, *Council v. Commission*, para 64).
35. Case C-409/13, *Council v. Commission*, paras. 97–105.
36. Case C-73/14, *Council v. Commission*, paras. 86–88.
37. Case C-65/93, *EP v. Council*, paras. 26–27.
38. O.J. 2007, C 145/5. The Declaration was adopted before the entry into force of the treaty of Lisbon, but is still applied, now with respect to the ordinary legislative procedure.
39. See also the Framework Agreement of 20 Oct. 2010 on relations between the European Parliament and the European Commission (O.J. 2010, L 304/47), the Interinstitutional Agreement of 20 Dec. 1994 on accelerated working method for official codification of legislative texts (O.J. 1996, C 102/2), the Interinstitutional Agreement of 28 Nov. 2001 on a more structured use of the recasting technique for legal acts (O.J. 2002, C 77/1).
40. See in particular the Interinstitutional Agreement of 13 Apr. 2016 on Better Law-Making (O.J. 2016, L 123/1), which replaced the 2003 Interinstitutional Agreement (O.J. 2003, C 321/1). See further the Interinstitutional

Lisbon, Article 295 TFEU explicitly provides that the European Parliament, the Council and the Commission shall consult each other and by common agreement make arrangements for their cooperation, the three institutions may decide that such inter-institutional agreements may be of a binding nature.

This subsection concentrates on the inter-institutional aspects of decision-making, and will not enter into the detailed internal rules and procedures for adopting a decision or position, unless relevant for the balance between institutions. Suffice it to recall that the Commission takes its decisions by a simple majority of its members (Art. 249(1) TFEU), the European Parliament by a majority of the votes cast, unless the treaty provides for a majority of its component members (the "absolute" majority of 376 members, Art. 231 TFEU) and the Council by a qualify majority, unless the treaty provides otherwise (Art. 16(3) TEU).[41]

4.2 *Initiative*

All decision-making procedures start with the tabling of a draft measure. It is an important step in law-making as (i) it gives concrete and precise form to a political idea, which may be until then general or vague, and (ii) the draft legal act determines the scope of the discussions during the decision making process. One of the essential, and at that time truly original, features of the founding treaties was to entrust this task quasi exclusively to an independent institution created to act solely in the general interest of the Union: the European Commission. This is doubtless a key aspect of the "Community method", and one of the reasons why the Union is so much more successful in decision-making than classic international organizations.

Almost all legal bases in the original treaties required that measures be adopted following a proposal from the Commission. Although this "monopoly of legislative initiative" has been questioned regularly, in particular in favour of a right of initiative for members of the European Parliament,[42] it has been maintained in successive institutional reforms, and even reinforced by the Treaty of Lisbon. Indeed, henceforth, the Commission's exclusive right of initiative is, with respect to the legislative acts, expressed in Article 17(2) TEU as a general principle.[43] Moreover, with respect to non-legislative acts, almost all treaty provisions provide that measures are adopted on a proposal from the Commission, with the noteworthy exceptions of the role of the ECB in the area of monetary policy and of High Representative in the CFSP (the exceptions to the principle that Union measures are adopted on a proposal from the Commission are treated below, at the end of this sub-section).

This right of initiative means that it is for the Commission to decide whether or not to submit a proposal for an act,[44] and if so at what time, and to determine the subject-matter, objective

---

Agreement of 22 Dec. 1998 on common guidelines for the quality of drafting Community legislation (O.J. 1999, C 73/1) and the Joint Practical Guide for persons involved in the drafting of EU legislation, drawn up by the Legal Services of the three institutions pursuant to that agreement.

41. For a more detailed discussion of these notions, and in particular the evolution of the Council's "qualified majority", see Ch. 5, "The political institutions", of this book.
42. J.C. Piris, "After Maastricht, are the Community Institutions more efficacious, more democratic and more transparent?", EL Rev. 1994, 449–487 at 466.
43. The general principle applies "except where the Treaties otherwise provide", but this exception refers only to a handful of cases (Arts. 75, 223(1) and (2), 226, 228(4) and 308 TFEU, as well as Art. 40.1 of Protocol No 4). As a consequence, the treaty provisions which allow the adoption of legislative acts do not mention anymore that they are to be adopted on a proposal from the Commission, since this follows from Art. 17(2) TEU.
44. Except in cases where an abstention to present the necessary proposals would amount to a failure to act in the sense of Art. 265 TFEU; this requires, however, that there is a binding time-line and that subject-matter

and content of that proposal.[45] This may seem quite exorbitant, but the Commission does not act in a political vacuum.[46]

It was a deliberate choice of the drafters of the original treaties to grant the right of initiative to the Commission alone; at the same time, these treaties, in particular the EEC treaty, contained for most of the (limited number of) policies programmatic provisions with clear and precise objectives to be achieved within a fixed time-limit,[47] or envisaged the establishment of a programme which would guide the concrete implementation of the policy.[48] Over the years, it has become well-established practice that, before the Commission tables major concrete proposals, the further development of Union policy concerned is discussed between the institutions, which gives rise to the adoption of programmatic Council conclusions and European Parliament resolutions. These documents are not binding upon the Commission, but considered by the latter as important guidance for its action. Besides, such policy documents are, in turn, usually a response to Commission communications on the issue, which may take the form of Green or White Papers.

The Commission has indeed traditionally been considered as the "engine" of the European construction. This is a role that it certainly still plays, be it with varying degrees of success,[49] despite the growing importance of the European Council. Since the Treaty of Maastricht, the latter is formally entrusted with providing the Union "with the necessary impetus" for its development, and defining the Union's general political directions and priorities (Art. 15(1) TEU).[50] The question whether these political guidelines, usually embodied in the conclusions of its meetings, are legally binding when they invite the Commission to make a proposal, can be left unanswered.[51] In practice, the European Council conclusions constitute for the Com-

---

and the nature of the act to be adopted may be determined with a sufficient degree of precision (Case 13/83, *EP v. Council*, paras. 53 and 68).
The question whether the legislature, when empowering the Commission, pursuant to Arts. 290 and 291 TFEU, to adopt delegated or implementing acts (sometimes within specific time-limits), can actually create an obligation for the Commission in the sense of Art. 265 TFEU to act, has until now not been raised before the Court of Justice.

45. Case C-409/13, *Council v. Commission*, para 70. Joined Cases C-643/15 and C-647/15, *Slovakia and Hungary v. Council*, para 146. In the particular case of Art. 155(2) TFEU where the Commission can propose to the Council to decide the implementation of an agreement concluded at Union level between management and labour, the content of the measure is obviously integrally determined by the agreement concerned.
46. J.P. Jacqué, "La Commission européenne après Lisbonne, déclin ou changement de paradigm?" in F. Berrod et al., *Europe(s), droit(s) européen(s): Une passion d'universitaire* (Bruylant 2015), 241; P. Ponzano, C. Hermanin and D. Corona, "The Power of Initiative", available at <www.institutdelors.eu/media/commission_power_of_initiative_ne_feb2012_01.pdf?pdf=ok>.
47. In particular, the EEC Treaty provided for a transitional period of twelve years, in which the common market was to be achieved in three stages (Art. 8 EEC); the custom duties and quantitative restrictions were to be reduced in accordance with a strict timetable (Arts. 14 and 33 EEC).
48. See the general programmes on the right of establishment and the freedom to provide services (Arts. 54 and 63 EEC); the broad lines of the common agricultural policy were established at a conference of Member States (the 1958 conference at Stresa), pursuant to Art. 43(1) EEC.
49. S. Bailer, "An agent dependent on the EU Member States? The determinants of the European Commission's legislative success in the European Union", (2014) Journal Eur. Int., 37–53.
50. In the Area of Freedom, Security and Justice, Art. 68 TFEU requires the European Council more specifically to define the strategic guidelines for legislative and operational planning; the European Council has done so by adopting the successive "Tampere" (1999), "The Hague" (2005) and "Stockholm" (2010) programmes (O.J. 2010, C 115/8), and recently in the European Council Conclusions of 27 June 2014.
51. Since the treaty of Lisbon, the argument (defended in the previous of this book) that the tasks of the European Council were laid down in the treaty on European Union, which was without prejudice to the EC treaty (then Art. 47 TEU), cannot be relied upon anymore. On the other hand, the treaty now expresses very

mission the inescapable political framework for its action, including the exercise of its right of initiative.[52] The President of the Commission, however, is a member of the European Council, which adopts its conclusions by consensus; and, again, these conclusions are often a response to a communication or report by the Commission. This is because the Commission not only has the task of presenting draft measures, but more generally, it has to "take appropriate initiatives" (Art. 17(1) TEU).

In particular, the Treaty of Lisbon entrusted the Commission with the task of initiating the Union's multiannual programming; until now, this has not yet been achieved.[53] But the Commission adopts at the end of each year its annual work programme, which announces all major proposals it will present next year. This annual work programme is subject of a dialogue with the European Parliament and the Council respectively, both before and after its adoption.[54] Moreover, in respect of the way it exercises its right of initiative, the Commission is politically responsible to the European Parliament (Art. 17(8) TEU); and the Parliament elects the Commission's President who sets the Political Guidelines for his or her Commission, and gives a vote of consent to the College before its appointment by the European Council (Art. 17(7) TFEU). To sum up, the "monopoly of initiative" of the Commission must be seen in the overall European political context.

Despite these political constraints, the Commission remains totally independent in legal terms to decide whether to present a proposal, and if so when and with what content. It has only to respect the treaty provisions. The Commission is regularly "invited" by the European Council, the European Parliament or the Council to present a proposal for legislation, but it can refuse to do so.[55]

The Treaty of Lisbon has introduced the "citizen's initiative": one million European citizens, from at least seven Member States, may invite the Commission to submit any appropriate proposal on matters where these citizens consider that a legal act of the Union is required for the purpose of implementing the Treaties (Art. 11(4) TFEU).[56] However, once again, the Commission is not obliged to present a proposal.[57]

---

clearly the principle that the European Council shall not exercise legislative functions (Art. 15(1) TEU). See also Joined Cases C-643/15 and C-647/15 *Slovakia and Hungary v. Council*, para 145.

52. See further: P. Bocquillon and M. Dobbels, "An elephant on the 13th floor of the Berlaymont? European Council and Commission relations in legislative agenda setting", (21) *Journal of European Public Policy* (2014), 20–38.
53. Point 5 of the Interinstitutional Agreement of 13 Apr. 2016 on Better Law-Making (O.J. 2016, L 123/1) constitutes a first step in that direction: it provides that upon appointment of a new Commission, the three institutions shall sign joint conclusions on principal policy objectives and priorities for the new term, with an indicative timing and a mid-tem review.
54. Point 6 of the Interinstitutional Agreement mentioned in previous footnote. See also point 35 and Annex 4 to the Framework Agreement of 20 Oct. 2010 on relations between the European Parliament and the European Commission (O.J. 2010, L 304/47).
55. Arts. 225 and 241 TFEU confer upon the European Parliament and the Council the right to request the Commission to submit an appropriate proposal, but they cannot actually oblige the Commission: it must either comply or explain. A formal request under these provisions is however seldom, and the Commission has in recent years not taken any negative decision in this respect.
56. A. Karatzia, "The European citizen's initiative and the EU Institutional balance: On realism and the possibilities of affecting EU law-making", 54 CML Rev. (2017), 177–208.
57. Rules and conditions for the citizens' initiative are laid down in Reg. 211/2010 (O.J. 2011, L 65/1). Until the end of 2016, there have been three successful initiatives, but in all cases, the Commission has limited itself to explain why it would not present a legislative proposal on the issue; quite a few initiatives fail or are withdrawn by their organizers (available at <ec.europa.eu/citizens-initiative/public/welcome>). Besides, the Commission refuses to register an initiative when it manifestly falls entirely outside the Commission's

The Commission must consult widely before proposing legislative acts (Art. 2 of Protocol No. 2 on the application of the principles of subsidiarity and proportionality). Any draft legislative act must be accompanied by an assessment of its financial impact and a detailed statement demonstrating its compatibility with the principles of subsidiarity and proportionality (Art. 4 of Protocol No. 2). Therefore, before tabling any major initiative, the Commission as a rule will have sounded out the attitude of the Member States and the political groups in the European Parliament, and its services will have had, at a more technical level, necessary contacts with Member States' experts. Over the years, the Commission has developed a number of additional supporting practices to prepare the draft proposals, in order to ensure their quality. Known collectively as "Better Regulation",[58] these supplementary practices go well beyond ordinary political preparation. First, the preparatory work usually starts long before the actual proposal is presented. As a rule, the Commission carries out impact assessments of its initiatives that are expected to have significant economic, environmental or social impacts. An "inception impact assessment" or "roadmap" is beforehand made public in order to inform stakeholders and to allow them to provide feedback. The quality of the final assessments is controlled by an independent Regulatory Scrutiny Board,[59] and often an open, or a targeted, stakeholder consultation is also organized.

All proposals for acts adopted on the basis of the treaty are accompanied by an explanatory memorandum, a financial statement, in case the act might have an impact on the budget, as well as, if it has been established, the impact assessment and the opinion of the Regulatory Scrutiny Board. These documents are not part of the proposal proper. They serve as information, but are not adopted or approved by the legislature. Having said that, the explanatory memorandum in particular, may remain useful after the adoption of the proposal by the legislature as it can help to clarify the intended meaning or purpose of a particular provision of the act.

Much of the preparatory actions are also applied, *mutatis mutandis*, to drafts for delegated acts, and even in some instances to the drafts of implementing acts, drawn up by the Commission services for adoption by the College. In the area of the supervision of financial institutions, however, the preparation and drafting of technical standards for these institutions, in the form of draft delegated acts or draft implementing acts, has been entrusted by the regulations establishing the European Supervisory Authorities (ESAs) to those authorities.[60] Such regulations provide for specific procedures governing the handling by the Commission of the draft acts, thereby limiting to some extent the freedom the Commission has generally in elaborating draft delegated and implementing acts.

The presentation of a proposal for a legislative or non-legislative act to be adopted on the basis of the treaty forms not only the formal starting-point of the decision-making procedure, but furthermore determines the scope for future discussions and the final adoption of the measure. Obviously, the legislature is not obliged to adopt an act in the exact wording proposed by the Commission (it is rather exceptional that a proposal is not somewhere amended); but

---

powers to submit a proposal for a legal act (such refusals are regularly challenged, not always unsuccessfully: Case T-754/14, *Effler*); the Commission needs to motivate carefully any refusal to register (Case T-646/13, *Bürgerinitiative Minority Safepack*). See also J. Organ, "Decommissioning direct democracy? ", (2014) EuConst, 422–443.

58. See the Commission staff working document *Better Reg. Guidelines* (SWD(2015)111) and points 12–24 of the Interinstitutional Agreement of 13 Apr. 2016 on Better Law-Making (O.J. 2016, L 123/1); M. Dawson, "Better regulation and the future of EU regulatory law and politics", 53 CML Rev. (2016), 1209–1236.

59. Commission Decision C(2015)3263.

60. See Arts. 10 to 15 of respectively Reg. 1093/2010 (on the European Banking Authority), Reg. 1094/2010 (on the European Insurance and Occupational Pensions Authority) and Reg. 1095/2010 (on the European Securities and Markets Authorities), O.J. 2010, L 331/12, 48 and 84.

the legislature cannot depart from the subject matter or alter the objective of the proposal.[61] Moreover, the Council, acting alone or in co-decision with the European Parliament, can only adopt a measure which amends the Commission's proposal, be it an amendment to its substantive provisions, its recitals (the motivation) or its legal basis, by acting unanimously (Art. 293(1) TFEU). This rule suffers only limited exceptions. Most importantly, it does not apply in the ordinary legislative procedure when a measure is adopted in third reading – which is, in practice, very uncommon; nor does it apply in the context of budgetary matters, specifically, the multi-annual framework and the budget.[62]

The rule from Article 293(1) TFEU by no means guarantees that the outcome of the decision-making in the Council accords with what the Commission considers to be the general interest of the Union (and in areas for which the Council must in any event decide by unanimity the rule has no practical effect). But it none the less constitutes a very important element in the institutional balance between the Council and the Commission.

As the treaty expressly provides (Art. 293(2) TFEU), the Commission may alter its proposal at any time during the procedure leading to the adoption of the act. Taking into account the course the debates take in the European Parliament and in the Council, the Commission very often does so, in order to make the adoption of the measure possible. Indeed, when the Council (or the European Parliament and the Council) envisage adopting a text that differs from the original proposal, the Commission can, by modifying its proposal in that sense, allow the Council to act by qualified majority.[63] The Commission is, therefore, in the course of the discussions within the European Parliament and the Council not a passive participant. Its role is not limited to submitting a proposal and subsequently promoting contact and seeking to reconcile the positions of the European Parliament and the Council. As the final act has to be adopted "on a proposal" from the Commission, the latter will not only actively defend its initiative, but also remain attentive throughout the procedure whether it needs to modify its proposal, and if so in what direction and to what extent.[64]

The Commission not only has the power to alter its proposal, but also, if need be, to withdraw it: according to the Court of Justice, "[the] power of the Commission to withdraw a proposal is inseparable from the right of initiative with which that institution is vested".[65] The Commission's power of withdrawal is not, however, unfettered. The Commission must state the reasons for the withdrawal and must respect the principle of sincere cooperation.[66]

61. Case 355/87, *Commission v. Council*, para 44; Case C-408/95, *Eurotunnel*, para 39.
62. Further, as the text of Art. 293(1) TFEU is taken literally ("on a "proposal" from the Commission"), this rule does not apply in the rare cases where the treaty provides that the Council acts on a "recommendation" from the Commission (see in particular the decision to authorize the opening of international negotiations, Art. 207(3) and 218(3) TFEU, and further in some instances in economic policy, Art. 121, 126 and 144 TFEU, employment policy, Art. 148 TFEU, and monetary agreements, Art. 219 TFEU).
63. The Commission can formally modify its proposal by presenting a full-fledged modified proposal. It can also modify it more informally by accepting, at the end of the negotiations, the Council's "presidency compromise", or the agreement reached in a "trilogue" between the European Parliament and the Council. Joined Cases C-643/15 and C-647/15 *Slovakia and Hungary v. Council*, paras. 179–185.
64. To that effect, the Commission has organized internally the "GRI" procedure ("*groupe des relations interinstitutionnelles*") which follows evolution of the different ongoing legislative and non-legislative procedures and prepares the decisions of the College concerning ongoing legislative procedures. The GRI is in particular responsible for preparing the positions to be adopted by the Commission within the framework of the ordinary legislative procedure, vis-à-vis both Parliament and the Council.
65. Case C-409/13, *Council v. Commission*, para 96.
66. The Commission undertook to provide the European Parliament a detailed explanation before withdrawing a proposal (Framework Agreement of 20 Oct. 2010 on relations between the European Parliament and

Not all Union measures originate in a Commission initiative. Three policy areas require particular attention. First, in the CFSP, the right of initiative belongs to the High Representative for Foreign Affairs and Security Policy, as well as to any Member State (Art. 30(1) TEU).[67] International agreements in this area are negotiated and concluded at the initiative of the High Representative (Art. 218(3) and (5) TFEU). Second, in the areas of judicial cooperation in criminal matters and of police cooperation, measures may be adopted on a proposal from the Commission or on the initiative of a quarter of the Member States (Art. 76 TFEU).[68] Third, the monetary union presents several specific features. In view of the independence of the European Central Bank (ECB), the latter adopts its measures on the Union's monetary policy on its own initiative (Art. 282(4) TFEU and Protocol No 4). Where the decision-making power in that area has been given to the European Parliament and the Council, not only the Commission but also the ECB may take the initiative in some instances (Art. 129(3) and (4) TFEU, Art. 40 and 41 of Protocol No 4).

In a limited number of cases, where a measure is of direct concern to a particular institution, that institution has the right of initiative. Examples are the European Parliament's right of initiative in relation to measures concerning its composition, its election, the statute of its members, the rules concerning Committees of Inquiry and the Ombudsman, and the Court of Justice's right of initiative to request the Council to increase the number of Advocates-General.[69] In some cases both the Commission and the institution concerned have a right of initiative which either of them may exercise. Examples are the right of initiative of the Commission or the Court of Justice to initiate a modification of the Statute of the Court or the establishment of a specialized court and the right of initiative of the Commission or the European Investment Bank to request the Council to amend the Statute of that Bank.[70] Finally, in a case whereby the treaties only indicate which institution is to take a certain decision, it is for that institution to act on its own initiative.[71]

the European Commission (O.J. 2010, L 304/47).

67. Before the Treaty of Lisbon, the Commission had, formally, a right of initiative – shared with the Member States – in the area of CFSP (then Art. 22 TEU), which it never used. In reality, initiatives were tabled by the Member State holding the Council's presidency, assisted by the High Representative who was also the Secretary-General of the Council (then Art. 18(3) TEU). The "loss" of this right of initiative for the Commission is largely compensated by the fact that the High Representative is, since the Treaty of Lisbon, a member of the Commission; and the treaty foresees now that the High Representative may submit proposals to the Council "with the Commission's support". The treaties provide also in two instances for "joint proposals" from the High Representative and the Commission: Art. 215 TFEU on restrictive measures against third countries or persons, groups and non-state entities and Art. 222(3) TFEU on the "solidarity clause"; the possibility to present joint proposals is recognized more generally in Art. 22(2) TEU.
68. Art. 76 TFEU is a remainder of the right to initiate legislation which the Member States had in the former "Third Pillar" (Art. K3 TEU under the Maastricht Treaty; Art. 34(2) TEU under the Amsterdam Treaty), abrogated by the Treaty of Lisbon, and an echo of the right of initiative the Member States shared with the Commission during a transitional phase of five years (between 1999 and 2004) in the areas of immigration, visas, asylum and cooperation in civil law, when these areas had been transferred into Community competence by the Treaty of Amsterdam (then Art. 67(1) EC).
69. For the EP: see Art. 14(2) TEU, Arts. 223(1) and (2), 226 and 228(4) TFEU; for the Court: Art. 252 TFEU.
70. See Arts. 281, 257 and 308 TFEU.
71. For example the Council determines, on its own initiative, the languages of the institutions (Art. 342 TFEU) and the salaries of the members of the institutions (Art. 243 TFEU). The institutions decide their own rules of procedure (Art. 232, 235, 240, 249 and 285 TFEU and Art. 12.3 of Protocol No 4) – but the Court of Auditors requires further the approval of the Council.

4.3 *Consultation*

In numerous cases, the treaties provide that before a measure can be adopted, one or more institutions or bodies need to be consulted.[72] The purpose of these consultations is to ensure that the voice of specific interests is formally heard in the law-making process. A clear distinction has to be made between, on the one hand, general consultation provisions or the possibility for Union bodies to deliver opinions on request or on their own initiative[73] and, on the other, the obligatory consultations provided for in the legal basis of the proposed measure.[74] This subsection only deals with the latter.[75] Such consultations must be referred to in the act (Art. 296, 2nd para TFEU); they constitute an essential procedural requirement within the meaning of Article 263 TFEU.

After the Commission (or the institution entrusted with the initiative) has presented its proposal, it is the responsibility of the legislature – the institution(s) called upon to adopt the proposed act, usually the European Parliament and the Council, or the Council – to request the opinion of any other institution, committee or body for which the legal basis of the act provides its consultation. The essential character of a consultation is that the legislature is to have due regard to the opinion(s) issued, but is not bound by it.

Originally, this consultation phase was an important part of the decision-making process. It was essentially the only way in which the European Parliament participated in law-making. The original treaties provided in most – but not all – policy areas for an obligatory consultation of the European Parliament before the Council could adopt the envisaged measure on a proposal of the Commission. Although the opinion of the European Parliament was not binding, it was an important step in the procedure, as the Commission had the practice to indicate, before the vote in the plenary, which of the Parliament's amendments (if adopted) it would take over in a formally amended proposal. As a consequence, the Council was in many instances called upon to decide on a proposal modified after the Parliament's opinion.[76]

With the growing importance of the European Parliament, in particular through the introduction of the cooperation procedure by the Single European Act, the co-decision procedure by the Treaty of Maastricht and the further extension of the co-decision procedure in the successive treaty changes to most policy areas, the number of cases in which the European Parliament is only consulted have drastically diminished. That does not mean, however, that mere consultation of the European Parliament has become an exceptional procedure: the European Parliament is consulted in all special legislative procedures where the decision is left to the Council; it is consulted before the adoption of some non-legislative acts where the measures

72. Usually indicated in the legal basis of the act by the expression "after consulting [...]"; in some instances the equivalent expression "after seeking an opinion from [...]" is used.
73. See the consultation of the European Parliament on the main aspects of the CFSP (Art. 36 TEU), the opinions on request or on their own initiative of the Court of Auditors, Economic and Social Committee and the Committee of the Regions (Art. 287(4), 304 and 307 TFEU), or the right to deliver opinions on request or on their own initiative, in their respective fields of competence, foreseen for the Political and Security Committee, the Economic and Financial Committee, the Employment Committee and the Social Protection Committee (Art. 38 TEU, Art. 134(2), 150 and 160 TFEU).
74. Or, in the case of the ECB, the general provision of Art. 127(4) TFEU, concerning any measure in its field of competence.
75. The consultation of representatives of Member States on draft Commission delegated acts, and on draft Commission implementing acts ("comitology") is discussed in Ch. 8, "The EU administration", of this book.
76. This course of events was expressly referred to in the original version of Art. 293(2) TFEU, as it provided that "as long as the Council has not acted, the Commission may alter its original proposal, in particular where the [European Parliament] has been consulted on that proposal" (then Art. 149 EEC).

are, in substance, of a legislative nature;[77] in some cases it must be consulted before the adoption of a decision to conclude an international agreement (though for most international agreements the treaty requires that the European Parliament must give its consent).[78]

The institutional framework of the Union further comprises two advisory bodies, the Economic and Social Committee and the Committee of Regions, who must be consulted in many instances. The Economic and Social Committee, set up by the original EEC and Euratom treaties, consists (now) of representatives of the employers, of the employed and of civil society,[79] and must be consulted on measures related to the establishment of the internal market and most flanking policies. The Committee of the Regions, created by the Treaty of Maastricht, consists of representatives of regional and local bodies of the Member States,[80] and must be consulted on measures in a series of flanking policies. Despite their relative prominent place in the treaties, these two committees have in practice little influence on the decision-making process. The preparatory bodies of the Parliament and the Council usually start their work as soon as the Commission presents its proposal, and do not await the opinions of these Committees. Furthermore, on major initiatives, the Commission will already have taken into consideration the views of stakeholders (see remarks on "Better Regulation" in the previous subsection). Besides, and perhaps even more importantly, the interests represented in these Committees are nowadays often more successfully promoted by the direct efforts of stakeholders to influence the decision-making process (i.e. by lobbying the members of the European Parliament and the Member States). This all undermines the potential interest for, and the weight of, formal opinions of these Committees.

Not only the European Parliament and the advisory bodies, but any institution can be required under the applicable treaty legal basis to give its opinion on an envisaged measure. Article 336 TFEU even requires that the legislature consults all other institutions before modifying the Staff Regulations of the EU Officials and the conditions of employment of the other servants. Particular attention must be given to the position of the ECB; not only is its opinion provided explicitly in a number of treaty provisions,[81] but Article 127(4) TFEU provides that it shall be consulted on any proposed Union act in its field of competence.

With respect to the consultation of the European Parliament, the Court has ruled that due consultation in the cases provided for by the Treaty constitutes an essential formal requirement, the breach of which renders the concerned measure void.[82] Further, the Court has strengthened this right by deciding that the requirement to consult the European Parliament means that it must be consulted *again* whenever the text to be finally adopted, taken as a whole, differs in essence from the text on which the Parliament has already been consulted (except in cases in which the amendments substantially correspond to the wishes of the Parliament itself).[83] This

77. See for example Art. 103 and 109 TFEU (competition law), Art. 128(2), 129(4) and 140(2) TFEU (monetary policy), Art. 153(2)3d subparagraph (some measures in social policy), Art. 188 TFEU (joint undertakings) or Art. 322(2) TFEU (rules on making own resources available).
78. Art. 218(6) TFEU.
79. See Ch. 5, "The political institutions", section 7.2, of this book.
80. See Ch. 5, "The political institutions", section 7.3, of this book.
81. For example, outside the monetary policy *stricto sensu*, for measures reducing the free movement of capital with third countries, modifying Protocol No 13 on the excessive deficit procedure or conferring to the ECB of prudential supervision over financial institutions, establishing common positions and a unified representation in IFIs (Art. 66, 126(14), 127(6) TFEU) and institutional treaty changes in the monetary area (Art. 48(3) and (6) TEU).
82. Case 138/79, *Roquette*, para 33; Case C-392/95, *EP v. Council*, para 14; Case C-408/95, *Eurotunnel*, para 45.
83. Case C-388/92 *EP v. Council*, para 10; Case C-280/93, *Germany v.* Council, para 38; Case C-392/95, *EP v. Council*, para 15; Case C-408/95, *Eurotunnel*, para 46; Joined Cases C-643/15 and C-647/15 *Slovakia and*

will be the case, in particular, when the Council modifies the legal basis of the envisaged measure, even if the decision-making procedure would not be affected by the change of legal basis. Finally, it follows from the Court's case-law that where the institution or body requested to give an opinion refuses to do so, or simply does not take any position, the legislature can adopt the measure without the necessary opinion, as such a refusal constitutes a breach of the obligation of sincere cooperation,[84] provided that the legislature has exhausted all possibilities of obtaining the opinion, for example by using the internal rules of the institution concerned to request an emergency procedure, or an extraordinary session.[85] Article 218(6)(b) TFEU gives the Council the possibility to set an express time-limit for the opinion of the European Parliament on an international agreement in the (rare) cases where the latter is only requested to give an opinion.

It is submitted here that the principle, according to which the disregard of an obligatory consultation constitutes an essential procedural requirement in the sense of Article 263 TFEU, applies not only in respect to the European Parliament, but also with regard to the Economic and Social Committee and the Committee of Regions or any other institution or body which needs to be consulted. Although the Court laid much emphasis in its reasoning on the fact that consultation of the European Parliament reflects the fundamental democratic principle that the people should take part in law-making through the intermediary of a representative assembly, the explicit reference to an obligatory consultation of another institution or body in the legal basis, seems to make it unavoidably an essential procedural requirement, regardless of the nature of the body concerned.

An omission to consult properly could certainly be raised in a preliminary reference to question the validity of a Union measure;[86] moreover the ECB, the Court of Auditors and the Committee of the Regions (but not the Economic and Social Committee) can enforce their right to be consulted where the treaties provide so, because they have the right to bring a case before the Court of Justice to review the legality of an act for the purpose of protecting their prerogatives.[87] The question arises whether they could also demand re-consultation in case the legislature envisages to adopt a text which differs in essence from the text on which they have given their opinion. In practice, the Council has never proceeded to a re-consultation, except with regard to the European Parliament.

Finally, the Treaty of Lisbon has established a particular form of consultation of the national parliaments.[88] All draft legislative acts are to be forwarded to the national parliaments. Thereby commences an eight-week period during which any national parliament may issue a reasoned opinion stating why it considers that the proposal does not comply with the principle of subsidiarity; although sometimes national parliaments make objections on other grounds, in particular by reference to the principle of proportionality, the procedure covers only compliance of legislative proposals with the principle of subsidiarity. If a third [89] of the national parliaments issues a reasoned opinion (the so-called "yellow card"),[90] the Commission (or the institution that has presented the initiative) must review its proposal, and decide whether to maintain, amend or withdraw it, stating the reasons for the response. If half of the national parliaments (the so-called

---

Hungary v. Council, paras. 160–169.

84. Case C-65/93, *EP v. Council*, paras. 27–28.
85. Case 138/79, *Roquette*, para 36, Case C-65/93, *EP v. Council*, para 22.
86. Cases cited in previous footnote, and Joined Cases C-13 to 16/92, *Driessen*, para 23.
87. Art. 263, subpara 3 TFEU; Art. 8 of Protocol No 2 on the application of the principles of subsidiarity and proportionality.
88. Art. 12 TEU; Protocol No 2 on the application of the principles of subsidiarity and proportionality.
89. A quarter of the national parliaments in judicial cooperation in criminal matters and police cooperation.
90. Each national parliament has two votes; in case of a bicameral system, each chamber shall have one.

"orange card") issues a reasoned opinion, the proposal must not only be reviewed by the Commission (or the institution that has presented the initiative), but if the Commission maintains its proposal, the legislature must consider whether it is compatible with the principle of subsidiarity (Art. 7(3) Protocol No 2).[91] [92]

4.4 *Adoption of the Act*

The third possible role in which an institution may be called upon to participate in the decision-making process is that of author of the act, or co-participant in the decision to adopt the act concerned. One can make a distinction between the straightforward situation where the decision-making power lies with one institution, and the politically more complex procedures whereby two institutions need to agree in order for the act to be adopted, namely the ordinary legislative procedure and the consent procedure. The exceptional case where an act adopted by a Union institution must be approved by the Member States before it can enter into force will be discussed at the end of this subsection.

4.4.1 *Decision making power in the hands of two institutions*

The ordinary legislative procedure

The *ordinary legislative procedure*,[93] whereby acts are adopted jointly by the European Parliament and the Council (Art. 289(1) TFEU), is described in detail in Article 294 TFEU.[94] It is a more elaborate version of the co-decision procedure,[95] which was introduced by the Treaty

---

91. Until now, the threshold for an orange card was never reached; the yellow card has been drawn only three times: with respect to the proposal for a Reg. on the exercise of the right to take collective action within the context of the freedom of establishment and the freedom to provide services (COM(2012)130); to the proposal for a Reg. on the establishment of the European Public Prosecutor's Office (COM(2013)534); and to the proposal for a Directive amending the Directive on the posting of workers (COM(2016)128). In all three cases, the Commission considered, after thorough analysis, that there was no incompatibility with the principle of subsidiarity (cf. COM(2013)851, COM(2016)505); it nevertheless decided to withdraw the first proposal because it clearly lacked political support (see F. Fabbrini and K. Granat, "'Yellow card, but no foul': The role of the national parliaments under the subsidiarity protocol and the Commission proposal for an EU Reg. on the right to strike", 50 CML Rev. 2013, 115–144).
92. It had been envisaged, as part of the "New Settlement for the United Kingdom within the European Union", to provide for i.a. a "red card" mechanism under which in case reasoned opinions were issued by 55% of national parliaments, the Member States would discontinue the consideration of the proposal unless it would have been amended to accommodate the concerns expressed. See Section C.3 of the Decision of the Heads of State or Government of 19 Feb. 2016 concerning a new settlement for the UK within the EU (O.J. 2016, C 69i). This decision, however, did not enter into force, so that the legal nature of this addition and its relation with the procedure laid down in Protocol No 2 can remain unclarified.
93. A. Rasmussen, "Twenty years of co-decision since Maastricht", (2012) Journal Eur. Int., 735–751, and literature cited.
94. See also Rules 49–78 of the Rules of Procedure of the European Parliament, the Joint Declaration of Practical arrangements for the co-decision procedure (O.J. 2007, C 145/5), as well as the "Guide to the ordinary legislative procedure" edited by the General Secretariat of the Council (Nov. 2011, available at <www.consilium.europa.eu/en/documents-publications/publications/2011/guide-ordinary-legislative-procedure>). The indication in a legal basis that measures are adopted by "the European Parliament and the Council, acting in accordance with the ordinary legislative procedure" is a reference to the procedure of Art. 294 TFEU.
95. The ordinary legislative procedure in Art. 294 TFEU corresponds in substance to the last version (Treaty of Amsterdam) of the so-called *co-decision procedure* described in Art. 251 EC. The original version of the procedure, laid down by the Treaty of Maastricht (then Art. 189b EC), was slightly different (and more

of Maastricht for, essentially, the legal bases for establishing the internal market.[96] By means of successive treaty changes (Amsterdam, Nice, and Lisbon[97]), the co-decision procedure has been generalized. As it is now applicable to most policy areas (it is referred to in more than 80 provisions), it is indeed justified to call it the "ordinary" legislative procedure.

The European Parliament and the Council participate on an equal footing in the ordinary legislative procedure. Acts adopted under this procedure are, as indicated in their title, acts "of the European Parliament and of the Council" and are signed by the presidents of the two institutions (Art. 297(1) TFEU). It means that actions for annulment against such acts must be addressed to the two Institutions.[98] The ordinary legislative procedure, with up to three readings, may seem complicated, but corresponds to the legislative procedures in a classic bi-cameral parliamentarian system: the Commission's proposal is discussed and amended successively by the European Parliament and the Council until they agree on a common text; if, in the third reading, no agreement can be found, the proposal is deemed not to have been adopted.

The *first reading* (paras. 3 to 6 of Art. 294 TFEU) starts when the Commission proposes a legislative act to both the Parliament and the Council.[99] After having received, where applicable, the opinions of bodies which needed to be consulted, the European Parliament, acting by majority of votes cast, adopts its "position" at first reading in the form of a legislative resolution, which may contain amendments to the proposal. Then follows the first reading in the Council: if the Council approves the Parliament's position, the act is adopted.[100] In all other cases, the Council must adopt its position at first reading and communicate it to the Parliament. The Council informs the European Parliament of "the reasons which led it to adopt its position at first reading"; the Commission informs the Parliament of its position.

The first reading (unlike the second and the third) does not have a deadline. This has created the possibility to develop a practice, whereby through informal consultation the positions of the three institutions are already approximated, where possible, during the first reading, with the

---

complicated) in its original version (for the procedure as it applied between 1993 and 1999, see the 3rd edition of this book, at 430–439).

96. The co-decision procedure was preceded by the so-called "cooperation procedure", introduced by the Single European Act (then Art. 149 EEC) for these single market legal bases. The cooperation procedure provided for the examination of the Commission's proposal in two readings with as most striking feature the rule that, in case the European Parliament rejected the Council's common position, the Council could only adopt the act with unanimity (even if the Commission would have agreed to the final draft, so that, with respect to the Commission's position, no unanimity requirement existed).
The treaty of Maastricht extended the use of the cooperation procedure (Art. 189C EC, renumbered to Art. 252 EC) to a number of other policy areas, but made at the same time the co-decision procedure applicable to the internal market legal bases. The treaties of Amsterdam and Nice further reduced the use of the cooperation procedure for the benefit of the co-decision procedure. The treaty of Lisbon has eliminated the cooperation procedure which was until then only applicable in a handful cases in the EMU.
97. The treaty of Lisbon has essentially introduced the changes proposed by the European Convention, on the basis of Working Group IX on Simplification (doc CONV 424/02), which found their way into the Treaty establishing a Constitution for Europe.
98. Art. 21 and 23 of the Protocol on the Statute of the Court of Justice have been modified by the Treaty of Nice to take that situation into account. The European Parliament and the Council, while both being defendant, will bring each their own defence.
99. Para 15 of Art. 294 TFEU provides for the necessary (small) adaptations to the procedure in the exceptional cases that the ordinary legislative procedure is initiated by a group of Member States, the ECB or the Court of Justice (cf. *supra*, subsection 4.1).
100. The Council decides, in principle, by qualified majority. However, in case the Parliament's position comprises an amendment to the Commission's proposal, the Council must decide by unanimity (Art. 293(1) TFEU), unless the Commission would have modified its proposal accordingly (see *supra* subsection 4.1).

aim to conclude the legislative procedure already in that reading. Once the examination of the proposal within the preparatory bodies of the European Parliament and the Council has reached a certain degree of maturity, representatives of these two institutions meet, together with representatives of the Commission, for direct, face-to-face negotiations. These informal tripartite meetings are called "trilogues".[101] As the formal position of the Parliament must be totally identical to that of the Council in order for the act to be adopted in first reading, the negotiations in the trilogue meetings take place before any formal first reading positions are adopted, on the basis of provisional views. The representatives of the Parliament (in particular the chairperson of the relevant parliamentary committee and the *rapporteur* for the file) will discuss the proposal on the basis of the report adopted by the committee, or in some cases on the basis of amendments adopted by the plenary (but not as attachment to a formal legislative resolution). The Council, represented by its (rotating) presidency, will negotiate on the basis of an informal "common approach" on the matter adopted by Coreper. Any agreement reached in a trilogue only becomes law when it is formally approved by the European Parliament and by the Council in accordance with Article 294 TFEU.

This informal trilogue procedure has been very successful. Indeed most legislative acts are adopted at first reading, despite the fact that the original views are in some cases very distant from each other. The institutions know that, in the ordinary legislative procedure, they will have to agree sooner or later; and it is easier to reach agreements without the time constraints of second and third readings. This trilogue practice is certainly laudable in terms of efficiency; however, it also has a downside. The fact that the negotiations are conducted on the basis of informal mandates, which, moreover, with regard to the European Parliament, do not necessarily reflect the position of the institution as a whole, but only of the relevant committee, may be considered to affect the democratic quality of the legislative debate. Trilogues also render the legislative process less transparent, as an agreement is reached before the European Parliament and the Council have stated publicly their formal positions on the Commission's proposal. Moreover, trilogues take place behind closed doors, which is difficult to reconcile with the principle that the Council and the European Parliament "shall meet in public" when deliberating and voting on a draft legislative act (Art. 16(8) TEU and Art. 15(2) TFEU).[102]

In about a dozen cases per year,[103] the ordinary legislative procedure is continued in a *second reading*. At the beginning of the second reading, the ball is in the court of the European Parliament. It must act within a time-limit of three months (which may be extended by a maximum of one month). There are three possibilities:

---

101. The term "trilogue" ("three-speak") is a pseudo-etymological wordplay on "dialogue" ("through speaking"). Trilogues are not limited to first reading, but may be held at all stages of the procedure (see points 7–9, 14 and 23–25 of the Joint Declaration of Practical arrangements for the co-decision procedure, O.J. 2007, C145/5). These trilogues are in fact an informal version of the Conciliation Committee provided for in Art. 294(10) TFEU for the conciliation phase of the procedure, after the second reading. See also C. Bultena, "Negotiations in the ordinary legislative procedure : The perspective of the European Parliament" in F. Goudappel and E. Hirsch Ballin (Eds.), *Democracy and Rule of Law in the European Union* (Asser Press, 2016), 93–108.

102. See the Decision of the European Ombudsman of 12 July 2016 setting out proposals following her strategic inquiry OI/8/2015/JAS concerning the transparency of Trilogues (available at <www.ombudsman.europa.eu/>). See also Case T-540/15, *De Capitani*, concerning the European Parliament's refusal to provide access to certain documents pertaining to a trilogue. For the question whether the general public can have access to legal advice provided in the context of a trilogue, see Case T-755/14, *Herbert Smith Freehills*.

103. Available at <www.europarl.europa.eu/code/about/statistics_en.htm>.

- First, the European Parliament may approve (by a majority of votes cast) the Council's position at first reading or may fail to take a decision within the time-limit. In those cases, the act shall be deemed adopted in the wording that corresponds to the position of the Council, that is to say, the legislative act is definitively adopted without the Council considering it anew.
- Second, the European Parliament may, by a majority of its component members, reject the Council's position. In that case, the act shall be deemed not to have been adopted; the legislative procedure is terminated.
- Third, the European Parliament may adopt, in this case by a majority of its component members, amendments to the Council's position at first reading. In that case, the procedure continues and the Commission is requested to deliver an opinion on those amendments.

The fact that, unless it simply decides to approve the Council's position at first reading, the European Parliament is faced in the second reading with a higher threshold for its decisions is another reason for the Parliament to favour an agreement at first reading (the majority of its component members is a significantly higher threshold than a majority of votes cast). It may, however, in some cases harden the Council's attitude in the trilogues at first reading, as the Council knows that the situation for the Parliament at second reading may be more difficult.

Where the Parliament proposes amendments to the Council's position at first reading, the Council must, in its turn, act within a time-limit of three months (which may be extended by a maximum of one month). If the Council approves all of the European Parliament's amendments by qualified majority – or by unanimity with respect to those amendments on which the Commission delivered a negative opinion – the act in question shall be deemed adopted. If, however, the Council fails to approve all of the amendments proposed by the Parliament, a Conciliation Committee is convened.

The *Conciliation Committee* is composed of the twenty-eight members of the Council and an equal number of members representing the European Parliament. The task of this Committee is to reach an agreement on a joint text, by a qualified majority of the Council's representatives and a simple majority of the representatives of the European Parliament. The Commission takes part in the proceedings of the Conciliation Committee and takes "all necessary initiatives with a view of reconciling the positions" (Art. 294(11) TFEU). However, the Commission can at that stage no longer force the Council to act by unanimity if both branches of the legislature want to depart from the Commission's proposal (Art. 293(1) TFEU). The Conciliation Committee has six weeks to reach a joint text (this time-limit may be extended by a maximum of two weeks). If the Conciliation Committee fails to approve a joint text within the time-limit, the proposed act is deemed not adopted and the legislative procedure is terminated. This happened until now in two cases, for a proposal to modify the Working Time Directive and a proposal on Novel Foods.[104]

If, by contrast, the Conciliation Committee approves a joint text, the *third reading* commences. The European Parliament, acting by a majority of the votes cast, and the Council acting by a qualified majority, each have six weeks to adopt the act in accordance with the joint text (this time-limit too may be extended by a maximum of two weeks). This approval should normally be a formality, but the treaty is precise, and states that if they fail to do so, the proposed act shall be deemed not to have been adopted.[105]

---

104. Respectively COM(2004)607 and COM(2007)872.
105. Proposals that failed (in the Parliament) in the third reading are the Takeover Bids Directive (2001) and the Port Services Directive (in 2003).

Failure to reach sooner or later an agreement remains the exception though. For instance, in almost all cases during the 2009–2014 Parliamentary term, an agreement between the Council and the Parliament was reached in first reading (85%), second reading (13%) or in conciliation and third reading (2%).[106]

A last remark on the ordinary legislative procedure: in the areas of coordination of social security of migrant workers (Art. 48 TFEU) and judicial cooperation in criminal matters (Art. 82 and 83 TFEU), the Treaty of Lisbon has introduced a so-called "emergency brake": a Member State has the right to suspend the ordinary legislative procedure where it considers that the draft act would affect, respectively, "important aspects of its social security system" or "fundamental aspects of its criminal justice system". A Member State may request that the matter be referred to the European Council, for "discussion" (the European Council has no legislative functions, Art. 15(1) TEU). Within four months, the European Council can, by consensus, refer back the proposal, and the ordinary legislative procedure can continue. If, however, the European Council fails to reach consensus, the proposed act is not adopted. In other words, although the treaty does not provide for unanimity in the Council, in the cases concerned the emergency brake gives *de facto* the power to any Member State to veto the envisaged measure.[107] The emergency brake has until now never been triggered (but its mere existence may possibly affect the dynamics of the decision-making process).

The consent procedure

The other procedure where two[108] institutions participate in the actual decision is the *consent procedure*,[109] whereby the act is adopted by one institution, but after having obtained the consent of the other on the actual text of the act to be adopted. The institution with the right to consent, usually the European Parliament, cannot amend the proposed text: it can only consent to that text or reject it. The classic example is when the European Parliament gives its consent for the conclusion, on behalf of the Union, of an international agreement (Art. 218(6)(a) TFEU).[110]

Yet, although the consent procedure means in principle a simple yes or no, in practice (outside the case of international agreements)[111] the text, on which the Council will formally request

106. Available at <www.europarl.europa.eu/code/information/activity_reports/activity_report_2009_2014_en.pdf>.

107. In the case of Art. 82 and 83 TFEU, the treaty provides, though, that in case of disagreement, an authorization to establish an enhanced cooperation shall be deemed to be granted, in case at least nine Member States formulate such a request (a similar provision has been introduced for the establishment of the European Public Prosecutor (Art. 86(1) TFEU) and for operational cooperation between police authorities (Art. 87(3) TFEU).

108. Or three, in the particular case of Art. 226 TFEU, where the European Parliament adopts the detailed provisions governing the exercise of its right of inquiry, after obtaining the consent of both the Council and the Commission.

109. The word "consent" (in French *approbation*) has been introduced by the Treaty of Lisbon, to replace the previous "assent" (in French *avis conforme*). This change of expression evokes the idea that the role of the other institution (usually the European Parliament) in this decision-making procedure is not of an advisory nature (be it a binding one), but a real participation (cf. Art. 289(2) TFEU). This change has, however, no legal consequences (besides, in German, the expression *Zustimmung* has remained unchanged).

110. Similarly to the situation of a national parliament, called upon to approve, in order to allow their ratification, international agreements which are already negotiated and signed by the government, the European Parliament can only consent to, or reject, the conclusion of the international agreement.

111. That being said, the European Parliament is kept fully informed on international negotiations (Art. 214(10) TFEU), and disposes of political means to influence those negotiations, which are backed precisely by the threat that it may reject the international agreement if it does not correspond to its expectations. See Ch. 39, 40 and 41, on the Union's external relations, of this book.

the European Parliament's consent, is often pre-negotiated. On the basis of the proposal or the initiative, the institutions will try to reach agreement in informal trilogue meetings. In those meetings, however, the European Parliament will be less powerful compared to the situation under the ordinary legislative procedure, in particular where the treaties provide that the Council must act with unanimity.

For internal law-making, the consent procedure is only used in three cases (the Council must act with unanimity in each case): for measures under Article 352 TFEU, the legal basis for measures to attain the Union's objectives when the treaties do not provide for the necessary powers; for measures to combat discrimination (Art. 19(1) TFEU); and for the establishment of the European Public Prosecutor's Office (Art. 86(1) TFEU).[112] The consent procedure is also required for various measures of an institutional nature (for instance for the appointment of the Commission, for authorizing enhanced cooperation between Member States in one of the areas covered by the Treaties, or for the determination that there is a clear risk that a Member State seriously breaches the values on which the Union is founded) and for certain amendments to the treaties, with a great variety of procedural requirements.[113] And it is the normal procedure for concluding international agreements (Art. 218(6)(a) TFEU).

The Treaty of Lisbon has provided for a variant on the consent procedure for the adoption by the Commission of *delegated acts* (Art. 290 TFEU). However, in that case, the Commission actually adopts the act, but postpones its publication in the Official Journal, and hence its entry into force. The Commission then submits that act to the European Parliament and the Council for a period set in the act on the basis of which the delegated act is adopted (usually two months). If the European Parliament (by a majority of its component members) or the Council (by a qualified majority) express an objection within that period, the delegated act will not enter into force. If no objection is raised within that period, the Commission can publish the delegated act, which can than enter into force. The delegated acts will further be discussed in the next Chapter 8, on the Executive.

4.4.2 *Decision making by a single institution*

The other decision-making procedures are straightforward as they require *only one institution to decide to adopt the act*. That institution is free to decide on the content and precise text of the act. However, as indicated above (subsections 4.1 and 4.2), that institution will have to respect the rights of the institution which has taken the initiative (usually the Commission) – in particular

---

112. These three legal bases provide for a decision by the Council by unanimity, in accordance with a special legislative procedure (thus: on a proposal of the Commission, Art. 17(2) TEU), after obtaining consent of the European Parliament (adopted a majority of the votes cast). The Council may also choose to adopt a measure under Art. 352 TFEU as a non-legislative act.

113. In particular, consent of the European Parliament is required for the adoption by the European Council (acting as the case may be by unanimity, qualified majority or simple majority) of decisions under Art. 7(2), 14(2), 17(7), 48(3) and 48(7) TEU and Art. 86(4) TFEU. Further, consent of the European Parliament is necessary for decisions adopted by the Council, acting unanimously, under Art. 49 TEU, Art. 25, 82(2), 83(1), 312(2) TFEU, for a decision of the Council acting by a majority of four fifths under Art. 7(1) TEU, and for decisions of the Council acting by a qualified majority adopted under Art. 50(2) TEU and Art. 311, 4th subpara, and 329(1) TFEU. In all these cases, the European Parliament can adopt its consent by a majority of the votes cast; however, for the consent under Art. 48(7) and 49 TEU, Art. 223(1), and 312(2) TFEU, it needs to reach a majority of the component members. Consent of the Council is necessary for measures adopted by the European Parliament under Art. 223(2), 226 and 228 TFEU ; the Council acts by qualified majority, save in the case of the last sentence of Art. 223(2) TFEU. Consent of the Commission is necessary for a decision of the Council under Art. 27(3) TEU and for a decision of the European Parliament under Art. 226 TFEU.

the fact that the decision-making institution cannot depart from the subject matter or alter the objective of the proposal – and the rights of the institutions and bodies whose consultation is obligatory – in particular, at least with respect to the European Parliament, that the final text taken as a whole should not differ in essence from the text on which the consultation took place.

As indicated at the beginning of this subsection, the original decision-making scheme, as laid down in original Treaties of Rome conferred decision-making powers essentially on the Council, acting on a proposal of the Commission and after consulting the European Parliament.[114] The scope of the original scheme has been, over the successive treaty changes, largely reduced, to the benefit of the ordinary legislative procedure. Yet, outside the areas where the ordinary legislative procedure is applicable, the original scheme is still the most frequent. But it is certainly not the only one: the Commission has maintained the few decision-making powers it had under the original treaties; and with the development of the Union, other institutions, in particular the European Council and the ECB, have also received the power to adopt certain acts.[115]

In many instances, the treaties provide that the *Council* adopts measures in accordance with a special legislative procedure. Such measures are "legislative acts", with all the legal consequences and effects thereof (see Subsection 3 above); other measures which the Council may adopt are non-legislative acts. Politically speaking, however, the important question is not whether an act of the Council is "legislative" or "non-legislative", but whether the Council must adopt the act by qualified majority or by unanimity.[116] Unanimity is obviously more difficult to attain, as it requires all members of the Council to agree or at least abstain. But, perhaps even more importantly, the unanimity requirement fundamentally changes the dynamic of the decision-making process. Voting by qualified majority requires each Member State to be mindful of the collective interest of other Member States; it incentivizes Member States to engage actively with each other and to consider the common good. Voting by unanimity, by contrast, provides each Member State with the ability to block common action regardless of the consequences for the other Member States; it incentivizes each Member State to concentrate only on its individual interest as defined by the vagaries of its domestic politics.[117]

---

114. The decision-making in the Euratom treaty has never been changed: all measures are adopted by the Council (acting with a qualified majority or unanimously, on a proposal from the Commission) or by the Commission. The European Parliament has remained with a purely consultative role, on a limited number of matters, essentially with regard to the establishment of health and safety basic standards (Art. 31 EAEC), the conclusion of international agreements (Art. 206 EAEC) and Art. 203 EAEC (the equivalent of Art. 352 TFEU); see also Art. 96 and 98 EAEC.

115. This evolution was reflected in the text of (now) Art. 288 TFEU, which enumerates the instruments of the Union: the original version (Art. 189 EEC) referred only to the Council and the Commission as authors of the instruments; the treaty of Maastricht added "the European Parliament acting jointly with the Council". The current text indicates simply "the institutions".

116. It should be recalled that, as indicated *supra* in subsection 4.1, when the Council acts on a proposal of the Commission, it may amend that proposal only by acting unanimously (Art. 293 (1) TFEU). As a consequence, this institutional weapon for the Commission to defend its original proposal, or at least what it considers to be the general interest of the Union, will only be an effective one where the treaty legal basis provides for qualified majority.

117. For a more in-depth discussion of the notion qualified majority (and its evolution) and unanimity, as well as the difference between qualified majority on a proposal of the Commission or not, "constructive abstention" in CFSP, Council Decision 2009/857 (O.J. 2009, L 314/73), etc. see Ch. 5, "The political institutions", of this book.

Therefore, the importance of the extension of qualified majority voting since the Single European Act[118] over the successive treaty changes, by the extension of the scope of the ordinary legislative procedure, but also outside that procedure, cannot be overestimated.

After the Treaty of Lisbon, unanimity for law-making is required for:

- decisions under the Common Foreign and Security Policy (Art. 31 TEU)
- the harmonization of national tax provisions (Art. 113, 115 and 192(2)(a) and 194(3) TFEU)
- some measures related to social protection, social security or the protection of workers (Art. 21(3) and 153 (2))
- arrangements regarding the right of Union citizens (who reside in a Member State of which they are not a national) to vote and to stand as a candidate at municipal elections and at elections to the European Parliament (Articles 22(1) and (2) TFEU)
- measures which "constitute a step backwards" in Union law as regards the liberalization of the free movement of capital to or from third countries (64(3) TFEU)
- provisions concerning passports, identity cards, residence permits or any other such document that are necessary to facilitate the right of Union citizens to move and reside freely within the territory of the Member States (Art. 77(3) TFEU)
- measures concerning family law with cross-border implications (Art. 81(3) TFEU)
- measures concerning operational cooperation between law enforcement authorities in relation to the prevention, detection and investigation of criminal offences (Art. 87(3) TFEU)
- measures laying down the conditions and limitations for police operations in the territory of another Member State (89 TFEU)
- language arrangements for the European intellectual property rights (Art 118(2) TFEU)
- the conferral of specific tasks upon the ECB concerning policies relating to the prudential supervision of credit institutions and other financial institutions (Art 127(6) TFEU)
- actions to achieve the Union's policy on the environment insofar as they constitute provisions primarily of a fiscal nature, measures affecting town and country planning, water resources or land use, or measures significantly affecting a Member State's choice between different energy sources and the general structure of its energy supply (Art. 192(2) TFEU).

For each of these acts, except for decisions under the CFSP,[119] the treaty requires adoption by the Council in accordance with a special legislative procedure. Together with the three cases to which the consent procedure applies, they constitute the full range of legislative acts for which the Council must vote by unanimity. In addition, unanimity remains the rule for a variety of Council decisions, essentially in institutional matters.[120]

118. The original treaties provided already for qualified majority voting from 1966 in a number of policies (in particular agricultural policy), but due to the *compromis de Luxembourg* (see Ch. 1, "Genesis and historical development of the European Communities and the EU", of this book), qualified majority voting was not applied in practice until the mid-80s. Moreover, the essential legal basis for the completion of the internal market, Art. 100 EC (approximation of national legislations that directly affect the "common market"), provided for unanimity.

119. The adoption of legislative acts in the Common Foreign Security Policy (CFSP) is excluded (Art. 24(1), second para, and Art. 31(1) TEU).

120. For example: the determination of the Multiannual Financial framework (Art. 312(2) TFEU), the composition of the advisory Committees (Art. 301 and 305 TFEU) (Art. 252 TFEU), the rules governing the

The *European Central Bank* (ECB) has, since its establishment in 1998, decision-making powers in the area of monetary policy of the Union (Art. 132 and 181(4) TFEU, Protocol No 4). A particular aspect of the ECB's decision-making is that, differently from almost all other decision-making procedures provided for in the treaties, it takes its decisions on its own initiative, without any implication of another institution.[121]

The *Commission* plays an essential role in law-making through its proposals[122] and through the delegated and implementing acts it adopts in accordance with Articles 290 and 291 TFEU.[123] The original treaties have entrusted the Commission also with some decision-making powers, directly on the basis of the Treaty. Most of these powers serve to execute its task to ensure the application of Union law,[124] in particular in the area of competition law and state aid. But there are cases in which the treaty has entrusted upon the Commission the right to lay down general rules, such as the directives on the application of competition rules by public undertakings.[125]

Finally,[126] since it has been created as a separate institution by the Treaty of Lisbon, the *European Council* also possesses some formal decision-making powers, but, as Article 15(1) TEU expressly states, it does not have legislative functions. Consequently, the (formal) powers of the European Council are limited to institutional matters and treaty changes, as well as strategic decisions and general guidelines in the CFSP (Art. 26(1) TEU).

4.4.3 *Approval by Member States*

It is the essence of the supranational nature of the European Union that the measures to realize its objectives are not taken in a diplomatic conference of its members,[127] but by the Union's institutions. Nevertheless, in a very small number of cases, which amount, directly or in essence, to a modification of the treaties, a decision of the European Council or of the Council enters only into force upon *approval by the Member States* "in accordance with their respective

---

languages of the institutions (Art. 342 TFEU). Unanimity remains also applicable for the conclusion of certain international agreements (Art. 218(8) and 219(1) TFEU) in particular association agreements, as well for the decision on the association of the Overseas Countries and Territories (Art. 203 TFEU).

121. See further Ch. 27, "Financial market regulation and supervision", of this book.
122. See *supra* subsection 4.1.
123. See on the Executive, Ch. 8, "The EU administration", of this book.
124. Also dealt with in Ch. 8, "The EU administration", of this book.
125. See also Art. 105(3) and 108(4) TFEU on block exemptions. Art. 45(3)d TFEU grants moreover the Commission the power to adopt regulations to lay down the conditions under which migrant workers are entitled to remain on the territory of a Member State after having been employed in that state. However, the Commission has renounced to exercise that power: although it had adopted such rules in the past (Reg. 1251/70), it has repealed them (Reg. 635/2006), since the legislature had, by Directive 2004/38, adopted a general legislation on the right of residence for EU citizens, which granted the beneficiaries of the right to stay a more privileged status.
126. The *Court of Justice* has the power to adopt its Rules of Procedure, but needs the approval of the Council (Art. 253 TFEU). The same applies for the General Court (and the specialized courts) acting in agreement with the Court of Justice (Art. 254 and 257 TFEU).
127. Yet, the treaties provide for two instances in which decisions necessary for the operation of the Union are taken "by common accord of the governments of the Member States": the appointment of Judges and Advocates-General (Art. 19(2) TEU and Art. 253 and 254 TFEU) and the determination of the seat of the institutions (Art. 341 TFEU). The original treaties foresaw the same procedure for the appointment of the Commission and of the members of the ECB Executive Board, but these appointments are made since the Lisbon treaty by the European Council. For agreements concluded *inter se* by the EU Member States, see Ch. 6, "Sources of EU law", of this book.

constitutional requirements". This means in practice that the decision concerned needs to be approved by all national parliaments.

Such an approval is required for some simplified treaty revisions (Art. 48(6) TEU and Art. 40.2 of Protocol No 4)[128] and decisions which in substance constitute such an amendment (Art. 42(2) TEU: establishment of a common defence; Art. 25 TFEU: new rights for EU citizens; Art. 262 TFEU: extension of the jurisdiction of the Court to disputes on European intellectual property rights). The approval of Member States is further required for the accession of the EU to the ECHR (Art. 218(8) TFEU), the rules concerning the direct election of the European Parliament (Art. 223(1) TFEU) and the decision on the Own Resources of the Union (Art. 311 3d subpara TFEU).

In particular the latter case makes clear that this exceptional supplementary procedural requirement has not as purpose to ensure that all Member States agree with the measure – in any event for all these decisions unanimity is required in the European Council or the Council – but to ensure that the *national parliaments'* rights are preserved, whatever their governments may decide.[129] These cases are basically a limitation to the transfer of competences to the EU institutions.

5. Democratic legitimacy

5.1 A different kind of democracy

In the previous subsection the various procedures have been discussed that govern law-making in the European Union. These rules, admittedly sometimes complicated, have been laid down, and through successive treaty changes modified and supplemented with additional guarantees not just to make law-making possible for a Union composed of a large number of sovereign states, but to ensure that these laws are considered legitimate by the European citizens.

Ensuring the democratic legitimacy of its laws is a perennial concern of any democratic society. People tend to obey the law if they believe that it is legitimate and that the authorities making and enforcing it have the right to dictate behaviour. To achieve "a normative commitment through legitimacy", the perception of fairness of the methods used to make decisions is crucial.[130] It is not enough, therefore, to argue that the results of the legislative process promote the common good. Democratic legitimacy depends on a variety of additional factors, including participation and voice as well as accountability, transparency and efficiency.[131]

Meeting the various – and sometimes conflicting – demands of democratic legitimacy is challenging in any society, and even more so in a polity as comprehensive and multifaceted as the European Union.[132] The question of how to strengthen the Union's democratic qualities has been a preoccupation from the outset of European integration,[133] has prompted several adjust-

128. Not all simplified treaty changes require approval by the Member States: see Art. 355(6) and Art. 252 TFEU.
129. A similar logic underpins the (questionable) practice of the Council to insist on the conclusion of "mixed agreements" even where the Union has competence to conclude the agreement on its own (See further Ch. 39, 40 and 41, on Union external relation, of this book).
130. T. R. Tyler, *Why People Obey the Law* (Princeton University Press, 2006).
131. F. Scharpf, *Governing in Europe* (OUP, 1999) and V. Schmidt, "Democracy and legitimacy in the European Union" in E. Jones et al. (Eds.), *The Oxford Handbook of the European Union* (OUP, 2012), 661–675.
132. E. Stein, "International integration and democracy: No love at first sight", 95 AJCL (2001), 489–543.
133. See, for instance, M. Gaudet, "The Challenge of the changing institutions", speech of 23 Apr. 1965, available at the Archive of European Integration: <aei.pitt.edu/id/eprint/13532>.

ments to the Treaties,[134] and has lost none of its relevance today.[135] What adds to the complexity is that democratic theory and democratic sensibilities have developed almost exclusively in the context of nation states.[136] The European Union, however, is a legal and political system of its own kind that affects but also to a very large extent relies on national-level democracy and legitimacy.[137] The Union's unique, compound system of governance[138] is difficult to capture accurately using traditional notions about democracy and legitimacy.[139] This is one of the reasons why scholars remain divided over the question of whether the Union suffers from a "democratic deficit".[140] But apart from causing "problems of translation",[141] the specific characteristics of the European Union pose important real-world challenges. These challenges relate to: the scale of the polity, its pluralist nature, and its relatively abstract sense of political community. A brief look at these three characteristics of the Union, which are interrelated, reveals both strengths and weaknesses as regards the Union's ability to enable its citizens "to control all those, their national governments included, who combine to exercise the powers of the EU".[142]

5.2 *Scale*

The European Union's size provides a potential for political inclusion that no single Member State's democracy can match. But it also poses a challenge in terms of ensuring democratic legitimacy. The larger a polity is, the more complicated it becomes in practice to, in one way or another, involve in the decision-making process all those touched by its laws.[143] That there is no simple solution to this problem is reflected in the circumstance that many people feel alienated from EU politics despite the variety of ways in which citizens have the right "to participate in the democratic life of the Union" (Art. 10(3) TEU).

The Treaty on European Union provides that "[t]he functioning of the Union shall be founded on representative democracy" and that "[c]itizens are directly represented at Union level in the European Parliament" (Art. 10(1) and (2) TEU). Every EU citizen accordingly has the right to vote and to stand as candidates in elections to the European Parliament.[144] Citizens are also represented in the EU law-making process via their governments and national parliaments.[145] Beyond participation through formally entitled representatives, or through bodies such as the Economic and Social Committee or the Committee of Regions, there are many

---

134. See Ch. 1, "Genesis and historical development of the European Communities and the EU", of this book.
135. As demonstrated, for instance, by the adoption of a new Interinstitutional Agreement on Better Law-Making (O.J. 2016 L 123/1).
136. J. Weiler, "European democracy and its critics: Polity and system" in J. Weiler, *The Constitution of Europe: 'Do the New Clothes Have an Emperor?' And other Essays on European Integration* (CUP, 1999), 264–285, at 279.
137. J. Coultrap, "From parliamentarism to pluralism: Models of democracy and the European Union's democratic deficit", 11 *Journal of Theoretical Politics* (1999), 107–135.
138. V. Schmidt, *Democracy in Europe* (OUP, 2006); S. Fabbrini, *Compound Democracies* (OUP, 2007).
139. Former Commission President Jacques Delors quipped that the Union is an "unidentified political object" (speech of 9 Sept. 1985). See also, C. Lord (Ed.), *A different kind of democracy?* (Open Society Foundations 2015).
140. Compare, for instance, Y. Meny, "De la democratie en Europe: Old concepts and new challenges", 41 JCMS (2002), 1–13, with A. Moravcsik, "In defence of the 'democratic deficit': Reassessing legitimacy in the European Union", 40 JCMS (2002), 603–624.
141. J. Weiler, op. cit. *supra* note 136, at 264.
142. C. Lord, *A Democratic Audit of the European Union* (Palgrave, 2004).
143. R. Dahl, *On Democracy* (Yale University Press, 1998).
144. Arts. 20(2)(b) and 22(2) TFEU, as well as Art. 39(1) Charter of Fundamental Rights.
145. Art. 12 TEU and Protocol No 1 on the role of National Parliaments in the European Union. See also sections 4.3 and 4.4.3 *supra*.

other means of getting involved in EU law-making.[146] They include the possibility to launch a citizen's initiative[147] or to provide information and comments to the Commission – in practice often via the intermediary of interest groups such as consumer organizations or industry associations – in the context of structured dialogues or open consultations on envisaged or existing legislation.[148] The Union has 24 official languages, in which all laws and other documents of general application are drafted, each language version being equally authentic.[149] Citizens have the right to write to a Union institution in any of these official languages and may expect an answer in the same language.[150]

While all these opportunities for participation carry the promise of enhancing democratic legitimacy, they add to the costs and complexity of the law-making process, and they might nurture a sense that it is almost impossible to exercise influence in the European maelstrom of political representatives, interest groups and other intermediaries, unless one happens to be a well-resourced and well-connected transnational actor.[151] The upshot is that, in a very large polity, enhancing participation and closeness to the citizen while assuring the transparency, efficiency and efficacy of the overall machinery of law-making is not an easy task.[152]

5.3 *Pluralism*

The European Union is a "plural society" in which each Member State constitutes a separate subsociety with its own language(s), political parties, interest groups and media. If the European Union were to function simply according to majority rule and government-versus-opposition politics, some of these subsocieties might find themselves continuously in the minority, being denied access to power; they would feel excluded and discriminated against and would have little or no reason to remain committed to the Union. This implies that the European Union requires a system of governance "that emphasizes consensus instead of opposition, that includes rather than excludes, and that tries to maximize the size of the ruling majority instead of being satisfied with a bare majority".[153]

---

146. See section 4.2 and 4.3 *supra*. Art. 11 TEU, which was introduced by the Lisbon Treaty (based on Art. I-47 of the Treaty establishing a Constitution for Europe), provides that "the institutions shall, by appropriate means, give citizens and representative associations the opportunity to make known and publicly exchange their views in all areas of Union action" and that the institutions "shall maintain an open, transparent and regular dialogue with representative associations in civil society".
147. See section 4.2 *supra*.
148. See section 4.2 *supra* on the Commission's obligation to consult widely before proposing legislative acts and on the Commission's practices under the rubric of "Better Regulation" (which include a "feedback mechanism" and the REFIT Platform for improving existing EU legislation). See also D. Obradovic and J. Alonso Vizcaino, "Good governance requirements concerning the participation of interest groups in EU consultations", (43) CML Rev. (2006), 1049–1085.
149. Reg. 1 of 15 Apr. 1958, determining the languages to be used by the [then] European Economic Community (O.J. 1958, 385). Reg. 1 was last amended by Reg. 517/2013 (O.J. 2013, L 158/1); see also Case C-161/06, *Skoma-Lux*, paras. 38–40 and 59. For Irish, a temporary derogation applies: only regulations adopted jointly by the European Parliament and the Council need to be adopted also in Irish (Reg. 920/2005, O.J. 2005, L 156/3; Reg. 1257/2010 (O.J. 2010, L 343/5).
150. Art. 24 TFEU; Art. 41(4) Charter of Fundamental Rights; Art. 2 of Reg. 1.
151. The technical nature of much EU legislation and the complexity of the law-making process may indeed work in favour of organized interests which, in turn, raises the risk of "minoritarian bias", that is to say, "an inordinate power of the few at the expense of the many": M. Poiares Maduro, *We, the Court* (Hart Publishing, 1998), 117–121.
152. K. Lenaerts and P. Van Nuffel, *European Union Law* (Sweet & Maxwell, 2011), 735–736.
153. A. Lijphart, *Patterns of Democracy* (Yale University Press, 2012), Ch. 3.

The emphasis on "consensus democracy" is visible in the Union's institutional structure and in its law-making process. Each institution has members from each Member State (and, in practice, from the left, centre and right of the political spectrum in Europe). The idea that Member States are the primary political units is embodied in the Council, where each Member State is equally represented through its government. But even the European Parliament, the most "majoritarian" institution at Union level, combines the principles of proportional representation and of national representation.[154] The concern for inclusion of Member State voices is reflected in the EU law-making process in the central role played by the Council, in features such as the "emergency brake" procedure,[155] in the method for calculating a qualified majority,[156] but also in the Council's general practice to strive for consensus.[157] The Council and the European Parliament could be said to confer "dual democratic legitimacy" on EU legislation: a wide consensus among Member States (whose representatives in the Council are accountable to their national parliaments) and, in addition, the support from a political majority at Union level (consisting of directly elected representatives in the European Parliament).[158] In the ordinary legislative procedure, which applies to most law-making in the Union, the Commission must, for each legislative proposal, gather support from at least a qualified majority in the Council and a majority in the European Parliament. The overall result is that EU law-making requires consensus among a large number of interlocutors and across a wide range of the political spectrum.

The consensual, pluralist nature of its decision-making processes is one of the Union's greatest assets, but it has various side effects. Having a relatively high number of interlocutors with strong bargaining positions can make it more difficult to find compromises. It may result in public policies that are costly, as they try to satisfy all interests involved, and difficult to reverse or amend.[159] It may also inhibit transparency during the decision-making process, at least if the hypothesis is accepted that a degree of confidentiality is sometimes desirable to enable participants in that process to strike a compromise.

The need to achieve consensus among a high number of interlocutors raises the likelihood, moreover, that important issues either are "delegated" to the EU-judiciary or remain within the discretion of national authorities. Neither outcome is objectionable in and of itself, though each has its complications. Leaving matters to the EU-judiciary may be inevitable as a way out of intractable political problems, but it puts a strain on the legitimacy and credibility of the courts.[160] Leaving matters to the national authorities is, as the Treaties recognize,[161] desirable for those matters that are better dealt with at national or local level, but for those that are better dealt with at Union level it is an unsatisfactory end result.

Finally, the notion of "dual democratic legitimacy" raises at least as many questions as it answers. The European Parliament's ability to strengthen the Union's democratic legitimacy depends on whether and to what extent that assembly accurately reflects European public opinion and is able to connect with the people it represents. The Council's ability to strengthen the

154. See Ch. 5, "The political institutions", section 5, of this book.
155. See section 4.2.1, *supra*.
156. See Ch. 5, "The political institutions", section 2, of this book.
157. See Ch. 5, "The political institutions", section 2, of this book.
158. K. Lenaerts and P. Van Nuffel, op. cit. *supra* note 152, 743.
159. F. Scharpf, "The joint decision trap: Lessons from German federalism and European integration", 66 *Public Administration* (1988), 239.
160. M. Poiares Maduro, "In search of a meaning and not in search of the Meaning: Judicial review and the constitution in times of pluralism", (2013) *Wisconsin Law Review*, 541–563, at 549.
161. Art. 5(3) TFEU, Art. 10(3) TFEU, and Protocol No 2 on the application of the principles of subsidiarity and proportionality.

Union's democratic legitimacy depends on the quality of the democratic structures in the Member States and, in particular, on how well those structures enable the citizens of each Member State to control their government's actions within the Council.[162] It also depends on the willingness and the ability of those governments to defend and justify the compromises they have reached in Brussels to their respective national constituencies.[163] And while ensuring the inclusion of all Member State voices is crucial to maintain the cohesion and stability of the Union's fragmented political community, it also preserves those very fragments by cementing the power of Member States' governments.[164] In sum, the strong emphasis in the EU law-making process on inclusiveness and pluralism constitutes an important democratic quality of the Union, but it also signals the vulnerabilities of the Union's system of governance.

5.4 *Sense of political community*

The European Union does not have the same sense of political community that characterizes most nation states. It essentially lacks a common language, common media, shared political parties and a common political debate. Nor does it have "a drive towards, or an acceptance of, an overarching organic-cultural national identity displacing those of the Member States".[165] This should not lead to the conclusion, however, that the Union cannot be truly democratic.[166] The fact that public discourse in the EU is fragmented along national and linguistic lines certainly poses a challenge. The lack of a Union-wide "public sphere" may make it more difficult, for instance, for European citizens to recognize their shared interests across national boundaries.[167] It also makes it more difficult to overcome parochialism and to examine one's national laws, beliefs and practices from an outside point of view.[168] But those problems should not be confused with the mistaken – and potentially dangerous – idea that a strong sense of political community and a cultural identity shared by all the members of that community is a precondition for democratic legitimacy. In fact, the weak sense of a Union-wide political community and cultural identity is an essential aspect of democratic legitimacy in the European Union, rather than an obstacle to it.[169] Insofar as the Treaties are not merely an agreement among the Member States, but a social contract among the nationals of those states, the Union stands for a notion of citizenship that invites individuals to see themselves as simultaneously belonging to national and transnational communities, and for a notion of democracy that does not require uniformity or cultural homogeneity, but that is grounded in a basic sense of solidarity which paves the way for conciliation, mutual accommodation and compromise.

5.5 *Conclusion*

Ensuring the democratic legitimacy of EU legislation is an important but difficult endeavour. Despite the challenges the EU faces in this regard, it is wrong to say that the Union is undemocratic

162. J. Weiler, op. cit. *supra* note 136, at 264–285, 282.
163. F. Scharpf, "Legitimacy in the multilevel European polity", 1 *European Political Science Review* (2009), 173–204.
164. Ibid.
165. J. Weiler, op. cit. *supra* note 136, at 324–357, at 346.
166. As the German Constitutional Court essentially held in its decision of 12 Oct. 1993, BVerfGE 89, 155, *Brunner v. European Union Treaty*, CMLR (1994) 57.
167. J. Habermas, "Democracy in Europe: Why the development into a transnational democracy is necessary and how it is possible", 21 ELJ (2015), 546–557.
168. On the importance of overcoming parochialism: A. Sen, *The Idea of Justice* (Allen Lane, 2009), 130.
169. F. Cheneval and F. Schimmelfennig, "The case for democracy in the European Union", 51 JCML (2013), 334–350.

or that it is inevitably less democratic than national systems. Democracy comes in many shapes and forms and is never perfect.[170] In some respects, the EU is democratic in ways that national political systems are not. Transnational issues – such as migration, pollution, financial crises or cross-border crime – are not just difficult for a national system to handle; such systems cannot provide truly democratic decisions in these areas. In that sense, the European Union offers a potential for democratic legitimacy that a national democracy cannot emulate. Moreover, the EU law-making process, geared as it is towards maintaining the cohesion and stability of a highly fragmented political community, puts a strong emphasis on inclusiveness and pluralism; unlike some national systems, the Union does not concentrate executive or legislative power in bare-majority institutions, but requires that each legislative proposal satisfies many diverse interests and has support across a wide range of the political spectrum. Finally, unlike many traditional political communities, the Union exemplifies an idea of democracy that does not seek its roots in a myth of a unique identity shared by all its citizens, but that is founded on "common values" in a diverse society (Art. 2 TEU). It expressly recognizes the plurality of peoples' affiliations and embraces "the universe of plural and diverse classifications that characterize the world in which we actually live".[171] The upshot is that one should be neither complacent nor alarmist about the democratic legitimacy of the European Union. The project of perfecting the Union can never be completed, but it can be carried on so long as a basic sense of solidarity prevails.

Further reading

Best, E., *Understanding EU Decision-Making* (EIPA/Springer, 2016).

Lijphart, A., *Patterns of Democracy*, 2nd ed. (Yale University Press, 2012).

Lord, C., *A Different Kind of Democracy? Debates about Democracy in the European Union*, (Open Society Foundations, 2015).

Türk, A.H., "Lawmaking after Lisbon" in A. Biondi & P. Eeckhout, *EU Law After Lisbon* (OUP, 2012).

Weiler, J.H.H., *The Constitution of Europe: "Do the New Clothes Have an Emperor?" And Other Essays on European Integration* (CUP, 1999).

170. R. Dahl, *Democracy and its Critics* (Yale University Press, 1989).

171. A. Sen, *Identity and Violence: The Illusion of Destiny* (Allen Lane, 2006), 17.

CHAPTER 8
THE EU ADMINISTRATION

*Joana Mendes**

1. Introduction

It has been the conventional view that the EU administration includes, at least, the national administrations of the Member States and the Commission to the limited extent that the Treaty gave it administrative functions (namely, in the areas of competition, state aids and staff management). The proliferation of comitology committees, EU agencies, and formal and informal networks of national and EU bodies, as well as the diversification of the functions of the Council, has fundamentally blurred this picture. Nevertheless, the predominant view remained that, as in the original institutional model of the European Community, the functions that public administrations perform in a state setting essentially remained with the Member States. Only in the past decade has there been a more systematic effort to make sense of the complex web of entities that proliferated in the "EU administrative space" and of the ensuing legal problems.[1] Nevertheless, "EU administration" as such has to a great extent remained outside of the main textbooks on the EU, largely in the shadow of its political institutions – a tendency that only recently started to change.[2]

---

* Law Faculty, University of Luxembourg.

1. The pioneer work of E. Schmidt-Assmann, "Verwaltungskooperation und Verwaltungskooperationsrecht in der Europäischen Gemeinschaft", (1996) *Europarecht*, 270–301, and E. Chiti and C. Franchini, *L'integrazione amministrativa europea* (Mullino, 2003), was followed and taken further by others. The first monographs on EU administrative law (J. Schwarze, *Europäisches Verwaltungsrecht*, (Nomos, 1988), M. Chiti, *Diritto amministrativo europeo*, (Giuffrè, 1999); P. Craig, *EU Administrative Law*, 2nd ed. (OUP, 2012)) and collective works (J.B. Auby and J. Dutheil de la Rochère (Eds.), *Traité de Droit Administratif Européen*, (Bruylant, 2014); M. Chiti and G. Greco (Eds.), *Trattato di Diritto Amministrativo Europeo* (Giuffrè, 2007); H. Hofmann, G. Rowe and A. Türk, *Administrative Law and Policy of the European Union* (OUP, 2011)) gave further visibility to the administrative functions of the EU. See also D. Curtin, *Executive Power of the European Union: Law, Practices and the Living Constitution* (OUP, 2009) and J. Dutheil de la Rochère (Ed.), *L'éxecution du droit de l'Union, entre mécanismes communautaires et droits nationaux* (Bruylant, 2009). The term "European Administrative Space" seems to have its origin in the SIGMA group of OECD (see OECD, "Preparing Public Administrations for the European Administrative Space", (1998) SIGMA Papers, available at <dx.doi.org/10.1787/5kml6143zd8p-en>), the aim of which was to prepare the public administrations of the acceding countries to European integration.
2. P. Craig and G. de Búrca, *The Evolution of EU Law*, 2nd ed. (OUP, 2014); D. Chalmers, G. Davies and G. Monti, *European Union Law: Text and Materials*, 3rd ed. (CUP, 2014) (but see at 78–80 and 144–150); C. Blumann, *Droit institutionnel de l'Union européenne*, 5th ed. (LexisNexis, 2013); J. Jacqué, *Droit institutionnel de l'Union européenne*, 7th ed. (Dalloz, 2012). The exceptions are in: R. Schütze, *European Union Law* (CUP, 2015), Ch. 9; A. Arnull and D. Chalmers (Eds.), *Oxford Handbook of European Union Law* (OUP, 2015), with a chapter on Comitology by A. Türk, at 327–349; and C. Barnard and S. Peers, *European Union Law* (OUP,

After briefly explaining how a distinct administration slowly emerged in the shadow of the Treaty of Rome and identifying its foundational traits (section 1), this chapter maps and characterizes the core administrative structures and entities that compose the EU administration, as well as the main legal issues they raise (sections 2 to 4). It situates the role of national administrations within the EU administration (section 5) and it points out the administrative functions of the Commission and the Council (section 6). Finally, it explains the legal problems that arise from the tension between two basic foundational features of the EU composite administration: separation and collaboration (section 7).

2. Executive federalism and the EU administration

2.1 *The "executive federalism" model*

The existence of an EU executive power, distinct from the EU's norm production function, and of an EU administration was largely a foreign element to the original institutional structure of the European Communities. Following the same basic institutional set-up as the European Coal and Steel Community, the institutions of the EEC were a Council, a Commission, an Assembly and a Court. Although their functions and relative weight were different in the ECSC and in the EEC, like in the ECSC each institution had to operate according to the procedures defined in the Treaty (and those created on the basis of the Treaty), within the competences and legal acts therein specified. European integration, which then essentially meant the creation of an internal market, was anchored in this unique institutional system. In this context, only by virtue of a misplaced analogy with the constitutional organization of powers within the state, most would argue, could one speak of an executive and of an administration subject to its political orientations.[3]

The Community was mainly a "norm production machine".[4] The Council had a vaguely defined "power of decision", in addition to the specification that it coordinated the general economic policies of the Member States (Art. 145 EECT). The Commission had the power to monitor compliance with those norms and to initiate the Community's decision-making procedures (Art. 155 EECT); it also exercised the implementing competences the Council would confer on it (Art. 155 EECT). Since the outset, it directly regulated competition in the internal market, it monitored anti-dumping practices during an initial transitional period, and controlled the existing regimes and award of state aids (Arts. 89, 91 and 93 EECT); it managed its own staff, as did the other institutions (Art. 246(3) EECT); it implemented the budget (Art. 205 EECT); it managed the European Social Fund (Art. 124 EECT). Only to this extent could one say that the

---

2014), with a chapter on "General principles of EU law and EU administrative law" by H. Hofmann, at 196–225.

3. See P. Pescatore, "L'exécutif communautaire: Justification du quadripartisme institué par les traités de Paris et de Rome", 14 *Cahiers de droit européen* (1978), at 387–406. See, however, K. Lenaerts, "Some reflections on the separation of powers in the European Community", 28 CML Rev., at 11–35, at 14. "Executive" and "administrative" are terms often used interchangeably referring to the same reality albeit from different perspectives (cf., e.g., D. Curtin, op. cit. *supra* note 1 and H. Hofmann and A. Türk, *Legal Challenges in EU Administrative Law towards an Integrated Administration* (Edward Elgar, 2009)). They may co-exist within the same institution, as is the case with the Commission and the Council (on the terms, see *infra*, section 7).
4. The argument has been made many times, most notably by G. Majone, *Regulating Europe* (Routledge, 1996). Azoulai eloquently refers to a "machine à édicter des norms generals, centralisées et uniformisantes" (L. Azoulai, "Pour un droit de l'éxecution de l'Union Européenne", at 1–23, in J. Dutheil de la Rochère (Ed.), *L'éxecution du Droit de l'Union, entre Mécanismes Communautaires et Droits Nationaux* (Bruylant, 2009), at 2).

Commission had executive powers, including administrative powers, i.e. to implement norms, to ensure compliance and to manage programmes.

Even if it was possible to identify in the powers attributed to the Council and to the Commission those that could more closely resemble executive powers,[5] the duty of Member States to "take all appropriate measures, whether general or particular, to ensure fulfilment of the obligations arising out of [the] Treaty or resulting from action taken by the institutions" (Art. 5 EECT) reflected a fundamental political choice. The Member States retained the competence to implement the policies and norms defined by the EU institutions.[6] Such competence included the transposition of directives, such as those adopted "for the approximation of such provisions laid down by law, regulation or administrative action in Member States as directly affect the establishment or functioning of the common market" (Art. 100 EECT),[7] and the adoption of the measures necessary to ensure the application of regulations. The deployment of the Member States' administrative structures and powers (as well as their judiciary, via the preliminary reference procedure) at the service of enforcing the law of the Community was subject to a duty of loyal cooperation also with the EU institutions. Member States had the duty to "facilitate the achievement of the Community's tasks" and to "abstain from any measure which could jeopardize the attainment of the objectives of [the] Treaty" (Art. 5 EECT).

The model was thus one of "executive federalism".[8] The division of powers between the Member States and the Community was not only grounded on the attribution of competences. This principle was coupled with a vertical division between "the legislative power" that belonged to the Community and "the executive power" that remained with the Member States – one that conveyed the idea that "execution begins where legislation stops".[9] In this model, the Member States were the primary "executive branch" of the Community.[10] This meant that their procedures and their administrations (in addition to their courts) were at the service of Community law. In principle, Member States retained their procedural and institutional autonomy in implementing the norms produced by the Community. Such autonomy was, however, subject to restrictions (in particular, via the principles of equivalence and effectiveness).[11]

There were, as mentioned above, a few exceptions to the model of executive federalism. The powers which the Treaty attributed to the Commission in the area of competition enabled the Commission to put an end to possible infringements of competition law by addressing

---

5. P. Pescatore, op. cit. *supra* note 3.
6. This choice corresponded both to the model of European integration conceived by Jean Monnet and to the interests of the Member States that created the EEC – see C. Franchini, "Les notions d'administration indirecte et de coadministration", at 335–355, in J.B. Auby and J. Dutheil de la Rochère, op. cit., *supra* note 1, at 337.
7. E. Chiti and C. Franchini consider this article to be the cornerstone of the administrative system of the EEC, op. cit. *supra* note 1, at 11–12.
8. J. Frowein, "Integration and the federal Experience in Germany and Switzerland", at 573–600 in M. Cappelletti, M. Seccombe and J. Weiler, (Eds.), *Integration Through Law* (De Gruyter, 1986), at 586–587; P. Dann, "European Parliament and executive federalism: Approaching a parliament in a semi-parliamentary democracy", 9 ELJ (2003), 549–574; B. Dubey, "Administration indirecte et fédéralisme d'exécution en Europe", 39 *Cahiers de Droit Européen* (2003), 87–134; J. Jacqué, "Introduction: Pouvoir législatif et pouvoir exécutif de l'Union Européenne" in J.B. Auby and J. Dutheil de la. Rochère, op. cit. *supra* note 1, at 43–67; R. Schütze, "From Rome to Lisbon: "Executive Federalism in the (New) European Union", 47 CML Rev. (2010), 1385–1427.
9. K. Lenaerts, "Regulating the regulatory process: "Delegation of powers" in the European Community", 18 ELR (1993), 23–49, at 28.
10. Idem.
11. See further, *infra*, sub-section 6.1.

individual decisions to the undertakings operating in the internal market. The Commission could also instruct a Member State to end or modify a state aid scheme, subject to a prior hearing of interested parties. But these exceptions – as important as they were for the creation and functioning of the internal market – only confirmed the rule: the administration of the law of the Community remained in the hands of the Member States. They had the primary competence in this regard. In the silence of the Treaty, the EEC was largely deprived of the competences that would allow it to carry out the implementation of its norms, expect in specific cases.

2.2 *Facing a complex reality*

This basic grid remains valid in the EU 60 years later, despite the deep institutional changes, the deepening of the internal market regulation, and the expansion of EU competences that have transformed the EEC into the current EU.[12] However, since the outset the reality of EU administration has been more complex and intricate than what the model of executive federalism lets envisage. In particular, this model conveys a vertical separation between implementation by Member States and the limited administrative competences of the EU, which reflects a partial and imperfect view of the EU administration.

First, the functional distinction between norm production and surveillance of compliance therewith, on the one hand, and norm implementation, on the other hand, did not prevent the Commission from acquiring from the very beginning implementing tasks also in the areas where these seemed to have been left to the Member States, in particular in the management of the common policies.[13] Emile Noël, then the secretary general of the Commission, noted in a speech of 1967 that the progressive implementation of common policies had reduced the degree of decentralization originally built into the Community system.[14] He noted in particular the effects of the adoption of the first regulations on the common agriculture policy. Far from being only the initiator and overseer of a policy essentially developed by the Member States (Arts. 40(1) and 43(1) EECT), the Commission became directly involved in the management of agricultural policy.[15] As Nöel had predicted, the widening of competences of the Community progressively multiplied the administrative tasks of the institutions, in particular those of the Commission. This expansion had organizational consequences: it led not only to administrative differentiation within the Commission, but also to the proliferation of committees that assisted it in carrying out its functions.[16] The EU administration was extending beyond the internal bureaucratic structures of the Commission that supported its limited powers of direct administration.

12. On the validity of the distinction between direct and indirect administration, despite the composite nature of the EU administration, see J. Ziller, "Les concepts d'administration directe, d'administration indirecte et de co-administration et les fondements du droit administratif européen" in J.B. Auby and J. Dutheil de la Rochère, op. cit. *supra* note 1, at 327–334 and 332–334. For a contrary view, see, e.g., C. Franchini, op. cit. *supra* note 6, 340.
13. E. Chiti and C. Franchini, op. cit. *supra* note 1, 22–23.
14. E. Noël and H. Etienne, "Quelques considérations sur la déconcentration et la délégation du pouvoir de décision dans la Communauté Economique Européenne", point 8 in Historical Archives of the European Union (Emile Noël Fonds, 1967), "Discours d'Emile Noël", available at <archives.eui.eu/en/fonds/111338?item=EN.03-01-808>.
15. E.g. Art. 2 of Reg. (EEC) 2115/71 of the Council of 28 Sept. 1971 laying down the conditions for applying protective measures in the market in milk and milk products (O.J. 1971, L 222, 5–7).
16. E. Chiti and C. Franchini, op. cit. *supra* note 1.

Secondly, the fact that "more rules were needed to ensure uniform application"[17] led to the differentiation of the norm production function of the Community. In addition to the measures directly based on the Treaty – at the time enacted mostly by the Council – there was "derived law intended to ensure their implementation" which implied a distinction between legislative acts and executive acts of the institutions.[18] Despite the difficulties in fitting EU powers in a frame of separation of powers, the distinction between these two layers of EU acts provoked a discussion on whether the Council or the Commission was the holder of "executive power".[19] The distinction between the "legislative" and the "executive" was no longer only a matter of vertical separation, as the term "executive federalism" largely conveys, but also of horizontal separation between the powers if the Commission and those of the Council.

Thirdly, administrative structures and procedures that involve in various degrees and forms national administrations and EU institutions have multiplied, giving effect to the duty of loyal cooperation between the Member States and the EU institutions to ensure the fulfilment of EU law obligations, and in the shadow of direct effect and supremacy of EU law. Collaboration (if not integration) between the administrations of the Member States and the EU institutions is therefore an essential element of the EU administration.[20] As will be seen in more detail below, collaboration has had important organic and legal consequences.[21]

2.3 *The constitutional framework of the EU administration*

The Lisbon Treaty confirmed and made more visible the main lines along which an EU administration has developed overtime. The vertical separation between norm production and implementation is, for the first time, acknowledged in the Treaty. Article 291(1) TFEU – according to which "Member States shall adopt all measures of national law necessary to implement legally binding Union acts" – thus confirms the main tenet of the model of executive federalism: when it comes to implementation, the primary competence belongs to the Member States, the Union having only the competences specifically defined in the Treaty or intervening when uniform conditions of implementation are required.[22]

The Treaty also acknowledges a differentiation between a legislative power and an executive power at the Union level, even if the distinction can only be made on the basis of organic and procedural criteria (Arts. 289, 290 and 291(2), (3) and (4) TFEU). The Commission has the power to adopt delegated acts – i.e. "non-legislative acts of general application to supplement or amend certain non-essential elements of the legislative act" (Art. 290(1) TFEU) – and

---

17. E. Noël and H. Etienne, op. cit. *supra* note 14, point 8.
18. Judgment in Case 25/70, *Köster*, para 6. On the scope of implementing powers, see Judgment in Case 23/75, *Rey Soda*, where the Court referred to "an appreciably wide power of implementation" at para 13 and at para 14 to "an extensive power"; see also Judgment in Case 16/88, *Commission v. Council*, para 11.
19. For an account of the distinction before the entry into force of the Lisbon Treaty, see E. Schmidt-Assmann, "Introduction: European composite administration and the role of European administrative law" in O. Jansen and B. Schoendorf-Haubold (Eds.), *The European Composite Administration* (Intersentia, 2011), at 11–13 (reprinted text). For an overview of the horizontal distribution of executive powers, see J. Jacqué, op. cit. *supra* note 8, 43–67, in particular 45–47 and 49–50.
20. E. Schmidt-Assmann, op. cit. *supra* note 19, at 1, H. Hofmann and A. Türk, op. cit. *supra* note 3, E. Chiti and C. Franchini, op. cit. *supra* note 1, and J. Ziller, op. cit. *supra* note 12.
21. See *supra*, sub-sections 2.1, 2.2, 2.3 and *infra*, section 3.
22. According to J. Ziller, "Exécution centralisée et execution partagée" in J. Dutheil de la Rochère (Ed.), *L'exécution du droit de l'Union, entre mécanismes communautaires et droits nationaux* (Bruylant, 2009), at 113, the added value of Art. 291(1) TFEU, in relation to the general clause of Art. 4(3), 2nd paragraph TEU (duty of Member States to ensure the fulfilment of their obligations under the Treaty) is precisely the fact that it clarifies this division of competences.

implementing acts, "where uniform conditions for implementing legally binding Union acts are needed" (Art. 291(2) TFEU). The Council may adopt implementing acts "in duly justified specific cases" and under the Common Foreign and Security Policy.[23]

Administrative collaboration was given its own legal basis (Art. 197 TFEU). This provision concretizes the general principle of sincere cooperation (Art. 4(1) TEU) for administrative matters.[24] Importantly, it stresses that effective implementation of Union law by the Member States "is essential for the proper functioning of the Union" and "shall be regarded as a matter of common interest" (paragraph 1). The Union can therefore "support the efforts of Member States to improve their administrative capacity to implement Union law", including the exchange of information and of civil servants and training facilities.

Thus, vertical separation of executive competences, collaboration between the Member States and the Union, horizontal differentiation between legislative and executive powers are the main lines, now enshrined in the Treaty, that define the institutional framework of the EU administration, both in an organic and functional sense. But the Lisbon Treaty did more than giving visibility to the EU administration. It also determined its attributes – open, efficient and independent (Art. 298 TFEU);[25] made the fundamental right of good administration binding (Art. 41 of the Charter); explicitly subjected the EU institutions, bodies, offices and agencies to the principles of equal treatment of citizens (Art. 9 TEU), transparency and democratic participation (Arts. 11 TEU and 15 TFEU), and protection of personal data (Art. 16 TFEU); and formalized the possibility to challenge before the EU courts the acts and omissions of its bodies, offices or agencies or to request a preliminary ruling on their validity and interpretation (Arts. 263, 265, 267(b) TFEU). If the EU administration had been hitherto "ungraspable", "unthought-of", "hidden",[26] these developments delineated a normative framework to the functioning of the EU administration that justifies a different approach to some of the legal problems it raises. The current debate on a possible EU law on the administrative procedure is but a manifestation thereof.[27]

Yet, which are the organic entities that are part of this administration, which is also made of the public administrations of twenty-eight states? And which functions do those entities and national public administrations perform? The following sections will discuss the organic and functional profiles of the main bodies, entities and structures that form part of the EU administration. The analysis of comitology committees, agencies and networks will illustrate the complex links of collaboration that are one characteristic trait of the EU administration. The chapter will also discuss the role of the Member States' administrations, of the Commission and of the Council. These two institutions will be discussed in less detail, since they are analysed in other chapters of the book. This chapter only intends to tease out, in general terms, their core administrative functions.

---

23. See, e.g., J. Jacqué, op. cit. *supra* note 8, at 48, on continuity and change in this matter. See, further, *infra*, sub-section 2.6.
24. J. Ziller, "L'autorité administrative dans l'Union Européenne" in L. Azoulai et L. Burgorgue-Larsen (Eds.), *L'autorité de l'Union européenne* (Bruylant, 2006), 119–153, at 148.
25. On the various interpretations of this provision as a possible legal basis for an EU law on the administrative procedure, see P. Craig, "A General Law on Administrative Procedure, Legislative Competence and Judicial Competence", 19 EPL (2013), 503–524. See also, E. Nieto Garrido, "Possible developments of Art. 298 TFEU: Towards an open, efficient and independent European administration", 18 EPL (2012), 373–397.
26. See L. Azoulai, op. cit. *supra* note 4, 1–2 and D. Ritleng, "L'identification de la function executive dans l'Union Européenne" in J. Dutheil de la Rochère, op. cit. *supra* 22, at 35.
27. See *infra*, sub-section 3.3.

3. Comitology committees

3.1 *Origins, rationale and tensions*

Comitology committees – composed of representatives of Member States' administrations and chaired by a member of the Commission – are one of the oldest forms of administrative collaboration between the EU institutions and national administrations. Since the 1960s, they have intervened in the making of secondary acts adopted mainly by the Commission to implement legal acts adopted by the institutions (initially, primarily the Council) on the basis of the Treaty. Although this practice initiated in the field of agriculture policy, it rapidly expanded to other fields.[28] The reasons to introduce a differentiation between primary and secondary – implementing – legal acts are very similar to those that in general justify the delegation of powers. As an early commentator pointed out, "with ever-increasing business, the Council ha[d] to be relieved of some of its burden, and decision-making powers [needed to] be delegated to the Commission".[29] The Court ratified this practice, recognizing that "the Commission alone is able continually to follow with attention trends on the agricultural markets and to act with urgency as the situation requires".[30]

Comitology committees both brought to the Community procedures the expertise that the Commission lacked and enabled the administrations of Member States to influence the decisions that the Commission would adopt. The intervention of national administrations in Community procedures was also a way of ensuring the effectiveness of the measures adopted, since national administrations needed to implement them on the ground. In this respect, they were not fundamentally different from other committees that normally supported the work of the Commission. Writing as Executive Secretary of the Commission, Emile Noël indicated in 1963:

> "[...] when the Commission has to determine the practical conditions of application of a previously defined policy or [to make] essentially technical decisions, it resorts, in a systematic way, to the collaboration of national experts designated by each of the concerned national administrations. [...] [They] may usefully guide the services of the Commission in their search for solutions that are technically sound and generally acceptable by the six governments. [...] They also enable a dialogue at the administrative level between European and national civil servants".[31]

Comitology committees were born out of this practice. Their distinctive feature, however, were the powers of control that the Council retained over the powers it delegated to the Commission, without which systematic delegation would have been politically unfeasible.[32] In essence, comitology committees were the response to political problems that the conferral of powers of the Council to the Commission could pose in an institutional system carefully crafted to balance the "intergovernmental institution" and the "supranational institution" that were at the time the

28. A series of Council regulations on several agriculture markets adopted on the 4th of Apr. of 1962 established the first management committees. On the origins of the comitology system, see C.F. Bergström, *Comitology: Delegation of Powers in the European Union and the Committee System* (OUP, 2005), 43–57. Regulatory committees – which gave different powers to the opinion of the committee – appeared first in the common commercial policy (see C.F. Bergström, at 78–85).
29. C. Bertram, "Decision-Making in the E.E.C.: The Management Committee Procedure", 5 CML Rev. (1968), 246–264, at 246.
30. Judgment in Case 23/75, *Rey Soda*, para 11.
31. E. Noël, "Comment fonctionnent les institutions de la Communauté Économique Européenne", 6 *Revue du Marché Commun* (1963), 14–21, at 20.
32. C. Bertram, op. cit. *supra* note 29, 262.

motor of European integration.[33] The opinion of the committees on the Commission's drafts could trigger the intervention of the Council, in different terms depending on the procedure followed in each case.[34] A negative opinion of the committee could block the adoption of the act by the Commission. The tasks the Council delegated to the Commission remained within the Council's reach. Collaboration – including the provision of expertise and the mutual accommodation of the positions of national administrations – and control were hence the main rationales for the creation of comitology committees. They explain the organic and functional features that these committees retain still today.[35]

As widespread as comitology was, it was far from being consensual. It soon became clear that comitology procedures had the potential to fundamentally alter the distribution of powers between the institutions that the Treaty had established. The history is intricate and long. It will be briefly explained here, to the extent that it is an important element to understand the current regime of comitology. Despite the powers of control of the Council, comitology effectively transformed the role of the Commission as it had initially been envisaged in the Treaty. Since the Commission drafts discussed in the committees would rarely be referred to the Council, the Commission was, in fact, "no longer a merely proposal-making body" but also a "decision-making body".[36] The Council reacted by setting up other procedures that would strengthen its position.[37] The position of the Parliament was particularly weak. Under the Treaty, the Parliament often needed to be consulted in the adoption of primary acts, but it was fully excluded from comitology procedures.[38] This summary sets the scene of the institutional struggles involving the Council, the Commission and the Parliament over the adoption of implementing measures, which were fought both on the political and on the legal front. While the Court settled the legality of comitology procedures,[39] the institutional concerns they raised were not appeased. The Commission predominantly considered that, according to the Treaty, the possibility of delegation was an injunction addressed at the Council more than a mere option for the Council.[40]

The Single European Act further specified the relative position of the Council and of the Commission in this matter, but still ambiguously.[41] The first comitology decision adopted on a new Treaty basis re-arranged and reduced the wide variety of committees that had proliferated

---

33. E. Noël, op. cit. *supra* note 31, at 15.
34. For a more detailed account of these procedures, see P. Craig, op. cit. *supra* note 1, at 110–139 and H. Hofmann, G. Rowe and A. Türk, op. cit. *supra* note 1, at 223–255.
35. See *infra,* sub-section 3.2.2.
36. C. Bertram, op. cit. *supra* note 29, at 251 and 262 and C.F. Bergström, op. cit. *supra* note 28.
37. C. Bertram, op. cit. *supra* note 29, at 263–264.
38. C.F. Bergström, op. cit. *supra* note 28, at 54–57.
39. Famously in the Judgment in Case 25/70, *Köster,* the Court validated the legality of the management procedure. See also Judgment in Case 23/75, *Rey Soda,* para 12, emphasis added. On the possible consequences vis-à-vis private parties, see Judgment in Case 5/77, *Tedeschi v. Denkavit,* para 51–57.
40. See e.g. E. Noël, *Quelques considérations sur la déconcentration et la délégation du pouvoir de décision dans la CEE* (European University Institute, 1967), available at <archives.eui.eu/en/fonds/111338?item=EN.03-01-808>, point 9. The Court's pronouncement in the Judgment in Case 25/70, *Köster,* stressing that the Council's power to delegate was optional contradicted this position (see *supra* note 18).
41. It added a provision to Art. 145 EECT that seemingly enshrined the Council's duty to confer powers of implementation to the Commission, but this interpretation was also contested (see C.F. Bergström, op. cit. *supra* note 28, at 183, n. 252). The English version (the Council "shall [...] confer") indicated perhaps more strongly than the French version that delegation was a duty of the Council. On the significance of the change, see K. Bradley, "Comitology and the law: Through a glass, darkly", 29 CML Rev. (1992), 693–721, at 713.

in the meanwhile by defining a typology of procedures.[42] The Treaty change and the decision had a fundamental political importance: they were meant to avoid lengthy discussions during the legislative process on the specific design of comitology procedures, and thus facilitate delegation, at a time in which the legislative production of the Council was particularly intensive, in view of the goal to complete the internal market by January 1993.[43] However, they did not placate the divergent institutional concerns.[44]

The quest of the Parliament for more powers in comitology procedures became an important trigger of change in the regime of comitology in the following years. Having progressively acquired more powers in the adoption of primary acts, the Parliament sought to strengthen its position as well in the adoption of implementing measures. Its quest ultimately led to the creation in 2006, of a new procedure – the regulatory procedure with scrutiny – that gave the Parliament the possibility to veto, on specified grounds, draft implementing measures of general scope that amended non-essential elements of acts adopted under the co-decision procedure.[45]

The 2006 amendment was the last important episode in the comitology saga before the entering into force of the Lisbon Treaty. It was not only the result of the fight of the Parliament for increased powers in the adoption of implementing acts that would parallel its legislative role, but also the outcome of the reforms that the failed Constitutional Treaty would have introduced.[46] It made the transition to the regime of non-legislative acts that the Lisbon Treaty enshrined, notably, by introducing the embryo of the distinction between two instances of implementation (as it singled out a procedure for the amendment of legislative acts).[47]

3.2 *The Lisbon Treaty: Comitology and implementing acts*

The Lisbon Treaty introduced significant changes in the system of secondary acts. It created a distinction between delegated acts – acts of general application that supplement or amend non-essential elements of the legislative act (Art. 290(1)) TFEU – and implementing acts – measures that implement legal acts of the Union (Art. 291(1)) TFEU. In addition, the Treaty made explicit that the Member States had the primary competence of implementation and the Union a subsidiary competence triggered by the need to "ensure uniform conditions of implementation" (Art. 291(1) and (2) TFEU). While not being a novelty, the explicit attribution of the primary competence of implementation to the Member States brought to the forefront the vertical separation of powers between the Union and the Member States. Both aspects affected the comitology regime in three fundamental ways.

First, the distinction between delegated and implementing acts withdrew from the scope of comitology the acts that supplement or amend legislative acts, thereby reducing the scope

---

42. Council Decision 87/373/EEC, of 13 July 1987, laying down the procedures for the exercise of implementing powers conferred on the Commission (O.J. 1987, L 197/33). However, only the second Comitology Decision, adopted in 1999, would establish non-binding criteria for the choice of the type of procedure (see Judgment in C-378/00, *Commission v. Parliament and Council*, para 50 and 62).
43. J. Jacqué, op. cit. *supra* note 1, 459–460.
44. C.F. Bergström, op. cit. *supra* note 28, at 209–212.
45. Art. 2(2) of the amended Decision.
46. On the 2006 decision, see K. Caunes, "Et la fonction exécutive européenne créa l'administration à son image: Retour vers le futur de la comitologie", 43 *Revue trimestrielle de droit européen* (2007), 297–346. For more detail of the context of the 2006 reform, see J. Blom-Hansen, "Interests, instruments and institutional preferences in the EU comitology system: The 2006 comitology reform", 17 EJL (2011), 344–365.
47. On the links between the regulatory procedure with scrutiny and delegated acts, see M. Keading and A. Hardacre, "The European Parliament and the future of comitology after Lisbon", 19 ELJ (2013), 382–403, at 384–388 and 399–402.

of implementation scricto sensu.[48] Yet, this effect largely hinges on the demarcation between "supplement" and "implement", which, being far from clear, opened the new front of institutional struggles.[49] Second, the primary competence of Member States to implement legal acts of the Union changed the locus of control in the comitology regime: control of the Commission's exercise of implementing powers would no longer belong to the Council but to the Member States (Art. 291(3)) TFEU).[50] A third significant change was that the rules and principles that govern the mechanisms of control – the comitology procedures – were now to be established by the Council and the Parliament via the ordinary legislative procedure (no longer by the Council alone). For the first time, the Parliament shared with the Council the power to define the legal regime of comitology committees (Art. 291(3)) TFEU). Yet, empirical research of the negotiations that led to Regulation 182/2011 shows that the Parliament's input in this process was not decisive for the solutions finally adopted.[51]

3.2.1 *Organic traits*

Comitology committees retained in the new regime the same organic features they had before. They are composed of representatives of Member States' administrations and are chaired by a member of the Commission. They are adjunct bodies that assist the Commission while being legally detached from it.[52] Formally, they are also not part of the Member States' administrations. They are thus intermediate bodies, an aspect that in the past has raised the issue of whether access to committee documents held by the Commission was subject to the rules on access to documents.[53] The matter is now settled: it is the duty of the Commission to decide on requests on access to documents, except if the request is addressed to a Member State.[54]

The specific composition of the committees is decided by the Member States. They define who will be part of their delegation.[55] However, the chair has also a formal say in defining the final composition insofar as it may object to the presence of experts that are not part of the delegation proposed by the Member States and it may invite representatives of acceding countries and of other third parties (e.g. representatives of US agencies) as well as other experts.[56]

3.2.2 *Functions and functioning*

As mentioned above, comitology committees enable the Member States' administrations to participate in, and control, the Commission's exercise of implementing powers. The account of the institutional struggles that preceded the current regime emphasizes the aspect of control (as

48. See D. Ritleng, *La Délégation du Pouvoir Législatif de l'Union Européenne* (Dalloz, 2010), 559–576.
49. See *infra,* sub-section 3.3.
50. See, *infra,* however, the observations on the role of the Appeal Committee.
51. See T. Christiansen and M. Dobbels, "Comitology and delegated acts after Lisbon: How the European Parliament lost the implementation game", 16 *European Integration Online Paper* (2012), available at <eioator.at/eiop/pdf/2012-013.pdf>, according to whom the Parliament failed to "[translate] treaty gains into legislative success", at 13. For a different analysis of the negotiation process, see G.J. Brandsma and J. Blom-Hansen, "Negotiating the post-Lisbon comitology system: Institutional battles over delegated decision-making", 50 JCMS (2012), 939–957.
52. See (Art. 3(2) Reg. 182/2011 and Arts. 5(3), 9 and 12 of for Standard Rules of Procedure Committees (O.J. 2011, C 206, at 11–13).
53. Judgment in Case T-188/97, *Rothmans v. Commission,* para 56 to 60. The Court's solution to place comitology committees under the responsibility of the Commission was only determined by the need to avoid an excessive restriction to the right on access to documents (para 61).
54. Art. 13 of the Standard Rules of Procedure.
55. Art. 5 (1) and (2) of the Standard Rules of Procedure.
56. Arts. 5 (2) and 7 of the Standard Rules of Procedure.

does the Treaty in Art. 291(3) TFEU). However, this focus hides another important functional trait of comitology committees: collaboration. As pointed out by Bergström, comitology committees have functioned – and arguably function – as "working [groups] [where] colleagues of different nationalities, representing different administrative traditions, meet in the spirit of mutual respect to agree on common solutions to their problems".[57] They have institutionalized the links of collaboration between the Member States' administrations and the Commission.[58]

The formal rules that define the internal decision-making procedures of comitology committees confirm the centrality of collaboration. The purpose of their deliberations is to "find solutions which command the widest possible support within the committee" (Art. 3(4) of Reg. 182/2011). Consensus may prevail over formal voting (Art. 4(4) of the Standard Rules of Procedure)[59] and written procedure applies only in "duly justified cases" (Art. 3(5) of Reg. 182/2011). In addition, the chair has the duty to explain its decision – within the committee – in the light of the "suggestions and amendments" made, in particular those that "have been largely supported within the committee" (Art. 3(4) of Reg. 182/2011). Beyond formal rules, the actual functioning of procedures has been studied from different perspectives and subject to various interpretations and normative constructions.[60] This rich doctrinal debate indicates at least the difficulty in reducing the complexity of comitology into single explanatory models.

Irrespective of the variety of ways in which committees may effectively function, they act within the formal framework set by Regulation 182/2011. Their role and powers need also to be understood in the light of the procedures defined therein. The different types of comitology procedures define, now as before, the extent to which the Commission is formally constrained by the opinion of the committee or the lack thereof.

3.2.3 *Formal powers: The comitology procedures*

The 2011 Comitology Regulation defines two basic procedures: the advisory and the examination procedure (Art. 2). Under the advisory procedure, the Commission is obliged to "take the utmost account of the conclusions drawn from the discussions within the committee and the opinion delivered" (Art. 4(2)). Under the examination procedure, a negative opinion of the committee prevents the Commission from adopting the draft implementing act; the absence of an opinion of the committee may prevent it from doing so (Art. 5(3) and (4)). However, a more careful reading of the Regulation reveals additional procedures, which are presented as derogations from the general rules.[61] In addition, the regulatory procedure with scrutiny, which the 2006 revision of the comitology decision had introduced, still governs the adoption of implementing acts in one type of situations: when legislative acts in force refer to the provisions of

57. C.F. Bergström, op. cit. *supra* note 28.
58. C. Blumann, op. cit *supra* note 1, at 31; E. Chiti and C. Franchini, op. cit. *supra* note 1, at 61–62. See also R. Dehousse, A. Fernández Pasarín and J. Plaza, "How consensual is comitology?", 21 *Journal of European Public Policy* (2014), 842–859, showing that consensus does not mean lack of contestation in committee deliberations. On the constitutional difficulties this raises, see A. Türk, "Comitology" in A. Arnull and D. Chalmers (Eds.), *Oxford Handbook of European Union Law* (OUP, 2015), at 338–341.
59. For the formal voting rules see Arts. 4(1) and 5(1) of the Reg. (EU) 182/2011 of the European Parliament and of the Council of 16 Febr. 2011 laying down the rules and general principles concerning mechanisms for control by Member States of the Commission's exercise of implementing powers, (O.J. 2011, L 55/13).
60. C. Joerges and J. Neyer famously argued, in a study of comitology in the food sector, that committees were the setting for deliberative political processes, C. Joerges, and J. Neyer, "From intergovernmental bargaining to deliberative political processes: The constitutionalization of comitology", 3 ELJ (1997), 273–99. For an account of the literature on the functioning of comitology committee, see R. Dehousse, op. cit. *supra* note 58, at 842–843.
61. See Arts. 5(5) (and 8(5)), 7 and 8.

the previous Comitology Decision enshrining the regulatory procedure with scrutiny.[62] These variants and specifications thus show that the apparent simplification of the binary division between advisory and examination procedures is misleading.

The advisory procedure applies "as a general rule" to implementing acts not specified in the Regulation (Art. 2(3)). At first sight, the examination procedure thus appears to be the exception, since it applies "in particular" in the situations indicated in Article 2(2). However, not only does this provision not establish an exhaustive list, but also it specifies that the examination procedure applies to a broad range of implementing acts: those of general scope (al. a)), and those adopted in specific policy areas ("programmes with substantial implications", agriculture, fisheries, environment, security, safety, public health, common commercial policy and taxation – al. b)). Article 2(2) specifies the general clause according to which the criteria to choose between the advisory and the examination procedure are the nature and the impact of implementing acts (Art. 2(1)). The openness of Article 2(2) and the ambiguity of Article 2(3) – which indicates that "in duly justified cases" the advisory procedure may also apply in the situations mentioned in Article 2(2) – indicate that the choice of procedures is left, to a large extent, to legislative negotiations.[63]

3.2.4 *Appeal Committee*

One of the novelties of the 2011 Comitology Regulation was the introduction of an appeal committee. Given that Article 291 TFEU explicitly placed the exercise of implementing powers under the control of Member States, controversial cases could no longer be referred to the Council as in the past. An appeal committee, meeting "at the appropriate level" (recital 7), intervenes when the Commission decides to submit it a draft implementing act that was blocked in the first instance committee.[64] Referral to the appeal committee may also occur when the lack of an opinion from the committee may prevent the Commission from adopting the draft implementing act, in the terms of Article 5(4).[65] The persistence of "no opinion" outcomes after the intervention of the Appeal Committee in politically sensitive cases led the Commission to propose "targeted" modifications to the 2011 Comitology Regulation, not yet adopted at the time of the writing, to clarify the "ownership" of politically sensitive implementing acts.[66]

The appeal committee is currently composed of high-level Member States representatives. It is up to the Member States to indicate the level of representation that they consider appropriate, in accordance with legally specified criteria.[67] The Commission chairs this committee and decides its concrete composition taking into account the Member States' suggestions.[68] In line with the consensual approach mentioned above, when deciding, the committee should "find solutions which command the widest possible support" of its members (Art. 6(2)). Voting results are not disclosed.[69] One main question discussed with regard to the appeal committee

62. Art. 12. On the transition, see Art. 13. For the problems it raised, see P. Craig, op. cit. *supra* note 1, 675–677.
63. See, in more detail, P. Craig, "Delegated acts, implementing acts and the new comitology regulation", (2011) ELR, at 671–687.
64. Art. 5(3).
65. Art. 7 indicates another instance in which the appeal committee intervenes.
66. See Proposal for a Regulation of the European Parliament and of the Council amending Reg. (EU) 182/2011, COM(2017) 85 final, Strasbourg, 14.2.2017.
67. Art. 1 (5) of the Rules of procedure for the appeal committee (Reg. (EU) 182/2011) (O.J. 2011, C 183/13). See, further, Commission's Proposal, cit., *supra* note 66, at 8.
68. Art. 3(7) of the Comitology Regulation and Art. 1 (5) of the Rules of procedure, cited *supra* note 67.
69. Arts. 9(2) and 12(2) of the Standard Rules of Procedure. See, further, Commission's Proposal, cit., *supra* note 66, at 7 and 8.

is the extent to which this may be "the Council in disguise", as there appears to be little difference in practice between the appeal committee and the role the Council played in comitology procedure pre-Lisbon.[70] The Commission's proposed reform may mitigate further the formal distinction, as it intends to introduce the possibility to refer matters to the Council in case of a 'no opinion' result in the Appeal Committee.[71]

3.2.5 *Transparency*

The lack of information on the deliberations of committees – and, for a long time, the absence of information on the committees themselves – has been in the past an issue of concern, in particular because it hindered the possibility of parliamentary oversight. The Parliament put the transparency of comitology committees on the agenda.[72] In fact, the steady consolidation of its powers of scrutiny over the adoption of implementing measures began with the right to be informed about the activities of comitology committees.[73]

A major step in improving the transparency of comitology committees was the creation of the Comitology Register of the Commission in 2003. The register has been gradually consolidated.[74] The Comitology Regulation specifies the information that it needs to contain: *inter alia*, the agendas of committee meetings; the implementing acts, both the drafts and the final measures; the minutes and attendance lists of meetings; the voting results (Art. 10(1)). In addition to the register, the Commission needs to publish an annual report on the work of the committees, and transmit information on the working of the committees to the Council and to the Parliament.[75] It is noteworthy that the standard rules of procedure of comitology committees, which govern the conditions on access to documents, in accordance with Regulation 1049/2001, include confidentiality clauses. Thus, the committees' discussions are confidential, as are the documents submitted to members of the committees, experts and representatives of third parties unless the Commission itself discloses them, or, in an apparently paradoxical fashion, if access is granted after a request on access to documents.[76] These documents will therefore not be placed in the register, but a request on access to documents will trigger an assessment of whether the document should or not be disclosed under Regulation 1049/2001.

3.3 *Scope of comitology: The dividing line between implementing and delegated acts*

Comitology procedures apply only to the adoption of implementing acts. These exclude acts of general application that amend or supplement a legislative act, which, since the Lisbon Treaty, are adopted as delegated acts.[77] Implementing acts can be acts of general application or indi-

70. T. Christiansen and M. Dobbels, "Delegated powers and inter-institutional relations in the EU after Lisbon: A normative assessment", 36 *West European Politics* (2013), 1159–1177, at 1168. See also P. Craig, op. cit. *supra* note 63, at 686.
71. See, further, Commission's Proposal, cit., *supra* note 66, at 8 and 9.
72. C.F. Bergström, op. cit. *supra* note 28, at 274–278.
73. Art. 7(3) to (5) of Council Decision 1999/468/EC (see also recitals 10 and 11).
74. Available at <ec.europa.eu/transparency/regcomitology/index.cfm?CLX=en>. Cf. G.J. Brandsma, D. Curtin and A. Meijer, "How transparent are EU "comitology" committees in practice?", 14 ELJ (2008), 819–838, highlighting the shortcomings of the register on the basis of an empirical study based on data up to 2005; and R. Dehousse, op. cit. *supra* note 58, 847–848, using the register as a dataset for their research, assuming, therefore the reliability of this source.
75. The reports are available at <ec.europa.eu/transparency/regcomitology/index.cfm?do=Report.Report>.
76. Art. 13 of the Standard Rules of Procedure for Committees (O.J. 2001, L 206/11).
77. With the exception of the acts still subject to the regulatory procedure with scrutiny.

vidual measures.[78] The parent act on which they are based does not need to be a legislative act, since the Treaty refers to the implementation of "legally binding Union acts".[79]

However, beyond these two aspects, the delimitation between the scope of application of implementing acts and of delegated acts is far from settled. The core dispute involving the distinction is the meaning to be attributed to implementing and to supplementing an act. This has been one of the main debates on the scheme of Articles 290 and 291 TFEU, which dates back to the Treaty establishing a Constitution for Europe.[80] There is both a horizontal and a vertical dimension to the problem. On the one hand, the European Parliament and the Council have different powers of control over delegated acts and over implementing acts.[81] On the other, the adoption of measures necessary for the implementation of EU law is primarily the competence of the Member States; the Commission (or, in some cases, the Council) exercises this competence "where uniform conditions for implementing legally binding Union acts are needed".[82]

The Court addressed the distinction between delegated and implementing acts in the *Biocides* judgment, but, in essence, left the matter in the hands of the legislative institutions.[83] In fact, the Court provided a very thin criterion (if it is a criterion at all) for the distinction: by delegated acts, the Commission adopts "rules *coming within the regulatory framework* as defined by the basic legislative act"; implementing acts "*provide further detail* in relation to the content of a legislative act".[84] In addition, the Court considered that the choice between conferring a delegated or an implementing power on the Commission falls within the discretion of the legislator. While doing so, the Court did not include the requirement – to which it had referred in a previous case – that such choice would need to abide to objective criteria amenable to judicial review.[85] As a result of discretion, "judicial review is limited to manifest errors of assessment".[86]

---

78. Delegated acts, on the contrary, can only be acts of general application, by force of the Treaty (Art. 290(1), first paragraph TFEU).
79. Art. 291(2) TFEU. On the contrary, the parent act of delegated acts is always a legislative act (Art. 290(1) TFEU).
80. See, e.g., K. Lenaerts and M. Desomer, "Towards a hierarchy of legal Acts in the European Union? Simplification of legal instruments and procedures", 11 ELJ (2005), 744–765; D. Ritleng, "Les Actes de l'Union" in V. Constantinesco et al. (Eds.), *Le traité établissant une constitution pour l'Europe: analyses & commentaries* (Presses Universitaires de Strasbourg, 2005), at 203–220; P. Ponzano, "'Executive' and 'delegated' acts: The situation after the Lisbon Treaty" in S. Griller and J. Ziller (Eds.), *The Lisbon Treaty: EU Constitutionalism without a Constitutional Treaty?* (Springer, 2008), 135–141; H. Hofmann, "Legislation, delegation and implementation under the Lisbon Treaty: Typology meets reality", 15 ELJ (2009), 482–505; P. Craig, *The Lisbon Treaty. Law, Politics, and Treaty Reform* (OUP, 2010), 48–57, 260–282; J. Jacqué, op. cit. *supra* note 8; R. Schütze, "'Delegated' legislation in the (new) European Union: A constitutional analysis", 74 *Modern Law Review* (2011), 674–689; J. Bast, "New categories of Acts after the Lisbon reform: Dynamics of parliamentarization in EU law", 49 CML Rev. (2011), 345–397, at 388–394.
81. Cf. Art. 290(2) TFEU and Arts. 10(3)(4) and 11 of Reg. (EU) 182/2011, cited *supra* note 66.
82. Art. 291 TFEU.
83. Judgment in C-427/12, *Biocides*. See also Judgment in Case C-88/14, *Commission v. European Parliament and Council* (Visa requirements), paras. 28 to 32 (on what constitutes an amendment of a legislative act) and Judgment in Case C-286/14, *European Parliament v. Commission*, paras. 30, 40 to 46, 52 to 58 and 62 (on the distinction between supplementing and amending an act and its consequences).
84. Judgment in C-427/12, *Biocides*, paras. 38 and 39.
85. Confront the Judgment in C-427/12, *Biocides*, para 40 with the Judgment in C-355/10, *Schengen Borders*, para 67. AG Villalón both stressed the need of judicial review over this question and emphasized its limits (Opinion in C-355/10, *Schengen Borders*, paras. 70 to 72). He concluded that the legislator has "full discretion" to choose between delegated and implementing acts (Opinion in *Schengen Borders*, para 77).
86. For a critical assessment, see D. Ritleng "The dividing line between delegated and implementing acts: The Court of Justice sidesteps the difficulty in *Commission v. Parliament and Council (Biocides)*", 52 CML Rev. (2015), 243–257).

The scope of discretion given to the legislator, combined with limited judicial review and the lack of an effective criterion of distinction, may call into question the very significance of the distinction between delegated and implementing acts.[87]

Therefore, while it remains the case that comitology committees apply only to implementing acts, in practice it may be hard to determine *a priori* which acts "supplement" or "amend" a legal act, and, to this extent, which acts may fall within the scope of comitology. At present, in these cases, whether the Commission will be given delegated or implementing powers is essentially a matter for negotiation between the Commission, the Parliament and the Council in each instance. In this process, each institution may sacrifice its position on what type of act should apply in exchange for accommodation by the other institutions on substantive points of the legislative act.[88]

One final point regards the nature of implementing powers. The institutions often present them as purely technical. They can be of such nature. For example, implementing acts frequently define templates that national administrations should use to provide information to the Commission.[89] But implementing acts can also deal with significantly more complex issues. It is via implementing acts that the Commission declares and terminates the recognition of "a situation of public health emergency in relation to [...] epidemics of human influenza considered to have pandemic potential" and to a "serious cross-border threat to health [that] endangers public health at the Union level", in accordance with Articles 12(1) and 14 of the EU Decision on serious cross-border threats to health.[90]

---

87. D. Ritleng, op. cit. *supra* note 83, at 254–256; M Chamon, 'Institutional balance and Community method in the implementation of EU legislation following the Lisbon Treaty' (2016) 53 *Common Market Law Review* 1524. Note the laconic statement of the Court in C-427/12, *Biocides* regarding whether the parent act required uniform conditions for implementation – Judgment in *Biocides,* para 53 and confront with Judgment in Case C-146/13, *Spain v. European Parliament and Council,* paras. 76 to 82 (on whether implementation should be remain with the Member States or be a task of the Commission). On the relevance of this requirement, see the different opinions of R. Schütze, "'Delegated' Legislation in the (new) European Union: A Constitutional Analysis", 74 *The Modern Law Review* (2011), 661–693, at 690–691 and of J. Bast, "New categories of Acts after the Lisbon reform: Dynamics of parliamentarization in EU law", 49 CML Rev. (2012), 885–928, at 919–924.
88. See the initial observations of T. Christiansen and M. Dobbels, "Non-legislative rule making after the Lisbon Treaty: Implementing the new system of comitology and delegated Acts", 19 ELJ (2013), 42–53. See also Secretary General of the Commission, Note for the Attention of Directors General and Heads of Service on Delegated and Implementing acts – further guidance, SEC(2012)537, 2–3, where the Commission mentions negotiations regarding delegated and implementing acts as a practice to be avoided, because it impacts on its institutional prerogatives. On the different institutional preferences of the institutions in the new system, see G.J. Brandsma and J. Blom-Hansen, "Controlling delegated powers in the post-Lisbon European Union", 23 *Journal of European Public Policy* (2016), 531–549.
89. Commission Implementing Decision of 25 July 2014 implementing Decision 1082/2013/EU of the European Parliament and of the Council with regard to the template for providing the information on preparedness and response planning in relation to serious cross-border threats to health (O.J. 2014, L 223/25).
90. Decision 1082/2013/EU of the European Parliament and of the Council of 22 Oct. 2013 on serious cross-border threats to health (O.J. 2013, L 293/1) According to Art. 13 of the decision, as a result of the recognition of a threat, the Commission "may exceptionally and temporarily accept a variation to the terms of a marketing authorization for a human influenza vaccine, where certain non-clinical or clinical data are missing" (Art. 21 of Reg. (EC) 1234/2008) and market authorizations may be issued to medicinal products to be used in emergency situations (point 2 of Art. 2 of Reg. (EC) 507/2006).

3.4 Committees and delegated acts

As mentioned, delegated acts are formally outside the scope of comitology procedures. In addition, the Commission is not bound to consult any other type of committees in the adoption of delegated acts (with the exception of specific legislative provisions stating otherwise). Yet, consultation with experts coming from national authorities is crucial in the preparation of delegated acts – if for no other reason than to provide the Commission with an important, if not indispensable, source of information – and was never discarded by the Commission.[91]

Since the beginning, the Commission's position on this matter was clear: in making use of its powers under Article 290 TFEU, it could form new expert groups or use existing ones.[92] This means that comitology committees may also be involved in the adoption of delegated acts. However, the main difference is that such consultation occurs outside the framework of comitology procedures (i.e. outside the framework of Reg. 182/2011).

The consultation of experts has been a bone of contention between the Commission, the Council and the Parliament. The Commission has systematically insisted that the opinion of these experts does not bind it in any way.[93] Any legal obligation in this respect, even in the form of an advisory procedure, would amount to re-introducing the comitology system, where it cannot exist by force of the Treaty. This position means that it is the Commission's discretion to "decide whether or not to summon and consult them and what functions to give them"[94] The Council has complained about insufficiencies in the way the Commission consults experts.[95] The European Parliament has struggled with being properly involved in the preparatory phase of delegated acts.[96] The Common Understanding on Delegated Acts attached to the Inter-institutional Agreement on Better Lawmaking provides a basis to avoid contention on matters of procedure.[97] Nevertheless, five decades after the first institutional clashes on the use of comitology committees, history seems to repeat itself.

---

91. The Commission expressly stated that it "intends systematically to consult experts from the national authorities of all the Member States". Apart from the fact that implementation of delegated acts is a task of national authorities, consultations are important to "establish an effective partnership at the technical level with experts in the national authorities" (Commission Communication, "Implementation of Art. 290 of the Treaty on the Functioning of the European Union", COM(2009)673 final, 6–7). Cf. the observations above in section 3.2.1 on the rationales of comitology committees.
92. Idem, at 7.
93. According to the Commission, "these experts will have a consultative rather than an institutional role in the decision-making procedure. At the end of the consultations, the Commission will inform the experts of the conclusions it believes should be drawn from the discussions, its preliminary reactions and how it intends to proceed" (Commission Communication, 2009, 7). See also Letter from Mr Maroš Šefčovič, Vice-President of the European Commission of 12 Mar. 2014, attached to Council Doc. 7792/14, JUR163-DELACT 71-INST 156, Brussels, 17 Mar. 2014.
94. The citation is from C. Bertram, op. cit. *supra* note 29, at 254. T. Christiansen and M. Dobbels, "Inter-institutional tensions in the EU's system of delegated powers after Lisbon" in C.F. Bergström and D. Ritleng (Eds.), *Rulemaking by the European Commission: The New System for Delegation of Powers* (OUP, 2016), making the parallelism between the early days of comitology and the current state of delegated acts.
95. The Council's initiative of 2014 to revise the Common Understanding on Delegated Acts.
96. European Parliament Resolution of 25 Febr. 2014 on follow-up on the delegation of legislative powers and control by Member States of the Commission's exercise of implementing powers (2012/2323(INI), points 12 and 13.
97. Interinstitutional Agreement between the European Parliament, the Council of the European Union and the European Commission on Better Law-Making (O.J. 2016, L 123/1).

4. Agencies

4.1 *Rationales and types*

The possibility of creating specialized agencies with their own legal personality appears to have been considered for the first time during the negotiations of the first regulations on the common agriculture policy, in December 1961. It was, however, rejected: instead of entrusting the daily management of market organizations to ad hoc bodies with "*pouvoirs propres*", the Council would rather make use of the possibilities of delegation that Article 155 EEC provided.[98] The issue was considered again in the mid-1960s, during the negotiations of the Merger Treaty, as a means to tackle the workload that the Commission and the Council had acquired in the management of the common policies. The creation of agencies was equally rejected then.[99] The first would appear in 1975, with limited and non-politically salient functions.[100] Many were created during the 1990s and their number continued to rise steadily during the 2000s and beyond. Half a century after the creation of bodies of this type was first considered and rejected, more than forty agencies act in significant policy fields – control of external borders, chemicals, pharmaceuticals, environment, fundamental rights, police cooperation, intellectual property, energy, electronic communications, financial services, among others – with a wide variety of powers.[101] What made this "model" so successful?[102]

European agencies have been predominantly perceived as the result of a compromise between the need to increase the administrative capacity of the Union in specialized fields and the need to avoid excessive centralization that would be politically and practically undesirable or unfeasible.[103] Agencies were often created by legislative acts setting up new regulatory regimes, thereby receiving tasks that were previously performed by Member States.[104] But there are more reasons behind the creation of agencies. They provide scientific and technical expertise while being at arms' length from political influence; they enhance the credibility of policy to the extent that they perform their functions outside the direct political influence.[105] They are also

---

98. E. Noël and H. Etienne, op. cit. *supra* note 14, at 2.
99. E. Noël and H. Etienne, op. cit. *supra* note 14, at 2.
100. The European Centre for the Development of Vocational Training (CEDEFOP) and the European Foundation for the Improvement of Living and Working Conditions (EUROFOUND). CEDEFOP assists the Commission in the development of vocational training policy and contributes to its implementation; EUROFOUND knowledge production. Art. 2 of Reg. (EEC) 1365/75 of the Council of 26 May 1975 on the creation of a European Foundation for the improvement of living and working conditions, as amended (O.J. 1975, L 139, at 1).
101. A list is available at <europa.eu/about-eu/agencies/index_en.htm>. The proliferation, "mushrooming" of agencies in the EU, or "agencification process" in the EU has been conventionally analysed in "waves": see, e.g., X.A. Yataganas, "Delegation of regulatory authority in the European Union. The relevance of the American model of independent agencies", (2001) *Jean Monnet Working Paper*; H. Hofmann, op. cit. *supra* note 3, 286–292.
102. On whether European agencies can considered a single model, see E. Chiti, "An important part of the EU's institutional machinery: Features, problems and perspectives of European agencies", 46 CML Rev. (2009), 1395–1442, at 1427–1433.
103. E.g. R. Dehousse, "Regulation by networks in the European Community: The role of European agencies", 4 *Journal of European Public Policy* (1997), 246–261, at 251–254.
104. The European Food and Safety Authority is one example among many. See, E. Chiti, "Decentralization and integration into the Community administrations: A new perspective on European agencies", 10 ELJ (2004), 402–438, at 432–433.
105. See further G. Majone, "The credibility crisis of Community regulation", 38 JCMS (2000), 273–302, and G. Majone, "Europe's 'democratic deficit': The question of standards", 4 ELJ (1998), 5–28 (referring, more broadly, to the rationales of delegation of policy-making powers, including to agencies).

useful institutionalized forms of collaboration between the Member States' administrations and contribute to ensuring compliance with EU law.[106]

They are, today, undoubtedly "an important part of the EU's institutional machinery".[107] In reality, the term "European agencies" encompasses different types of bodies. As recently pointed out by the European Ombudsman "there are no simple answers to the questions 'what is an EU agency?' and 'what do EU agencies do?'".[108] There are various ways of classifying them. Officially, they are currently divided into two main categories: decentralized and executive agencies.[109] The term "decentralized" refers to agencies that have legal personality, are created by EU legislation and are given instrumental powers in support of the EU institutions, in particular the Commission and the Council, or final decision-making powers in given instances.[110] They remain autonomous from the institutions. They have their own governing bodies and powers to manage their budget (which consists, generally, of a financial contribution from the general EU budget).[111] Hence, they have administrative and financial autonomy vis-à-vis the Commission or the Council services.[112] Yet, both the Commission and the Member States – represented in the agencies' governing boards – retain significant influence over their action, thereby challenging the assumption that they would be independent bodies.[113] Another trait that may challenge the assumed independence of agencies is the "stable and institutionalized dialogue" that some maintain with the private sector.[114]

---

106. See, in more detail, R. Dehousse, op. cit. *supra* note 103; G. Majone, "Delegation of regulatory powers in a mixed polity", 8 ELJ (2002), 319–339; E. Chiti, op. cit. *supra* note 104, 423–431; M. Thatcher, "The creation of European regulatory agencies and its limits: A comparative analysis of European delegation", 18 *Journal of European Public Policy* (2011), 790–809 (adding the perspective of sociological theories and defending an historical-rationalist explanation to the creation of agencies); M. Busuioc, *European Agencies: Law and Practices of Accountability* (OUP, 2013), at 24–37.
107. E. Chiti, op. cit. *supra* note 102.
108. Report on visits to Agencies, Dec. 2014, at 1, available at <www.ombudsman.europa.eu/activities/visitreport.faces/en/59248/html.bookmark#_ftn2>.
109. Available at <europa.eu/about-eu/agencies/index_en.htm>. The Commission had classified them as "regulatory agencies" (e.g. Commission of the European Communities (2002), Communication from the Commission. The operating framework for the European Regulatory Agencies, COM(2002)718 final; Commission of the European Communities (2008), Communication from the Commission to the European Parliament and the Council. European agencies – The way forward, COM(2008)135 final. On the difficulties of this terminology, see P. Craig, op. cit. *supra* note 25, 148–149.
110. Not all these features differentiate the "decentralized agencies" from the executive agencies. Thus, for instance, executive agencies also have legal personality by force of their regulation (Art. 4(2) of Reg. 58/2003, of 19 Dec. 2002 laying down the statute for executive agencies to be entrusted with certain tasks in the management of Community programmes (O.J. 2003, L 11/1).
111. On the internal structure of agencies, see sub-section 3.2.2 *infra*.
112. Some agencies can generate their own funds, but these are only a part of their budget (see M. Busuioc and M. Groenleer, "The theory and practice of EU agency autonomy and accountability: Early day expectations, today's realities and future perspectives" in M. Everson, C. Monda and E. Vos (Eds.), *European Agencies in between Institutions and Member States* (Kluwer, 2014), 175–200, at 186).
113. On means of influence by the Commission, see E. Chiti, op. cit. *supra* note 102, at 1399–1400. Critically on the claimed "independence" of agencies, see M. Busuioc and M. Groenleer, op. cit. *supra* note 112, at 180–181, and 185–191. See also M. Thatcher, op. cit. *supra* note 106, at 791, pointing out that depending on their institutional configuration, agencies may be "closer to being networks incorporating the Commission and national policy-makers" rather than free standing bodies with clear formal autonomy". The degree of agencies' independence varies, also in view of the relation of some of the agencies with national regulatory authorities – see E. Chiti, op. cit. *supra* note 102, at 1429–1430 (on ACER), and M. Busuioc, op. cit. *supra* note 106, at 17.
114. E. Chiti, op. cit. *supra* note 102, at 1401–1402.

"Executive agencies", unlike the "decentralized agencies", are not independent bodies and are set up on a temporary basis.[115] They perform their tasks under the "control and responsibility" of the Commission, who establishes them for a limited period of time (subject to extensions and renewals) to manage Union programmes, in accordance with the common statute defined in Regulation 58/2003.[116] The Commission also reviews the legality of the acts of these agencies, on its own initiative or by application of a person "directly or individually concerned" or by a Member State.[117] The following sections will explain the organic traits and powers of the so-called decentralized agencies, as well as some selected legal problems (namely, the legal bases for the creation of agencies, the legal limits to their powers, accountability and the external dimension of agencies' action).

4.2 *Organization*

European agencies are created in an *ad hoc* manner. They are associated to specific legal regimes, being instrumental to policy development or implementation in the EU. As a result, they do not have a uniform organic structure, which is each time defined in the founding regulation. Nevertheless, it is possible to identify some common traits in this respect.[118] The governing bodies of the European agencies typically consist of a Management Board and a Director.[119] The Management Board takes the core management decisions (including budget powers) and defines the strategic priorities of the agency; the Director is the legal representative of the agency.

The Management Board typically includes representatives of the Member States, appointed either by the Member States or by the Council, and a varied number of Commission representatives that may or may not have voting rights. Some Management Boards count also with representatives of the European Parliament, of interested persons, and of non-EU countries.[120] This mixed composition confirms the "in between" nature of agencies: while Member States are represented in the EU agencies, these are EU bodies created by a Union legislative act to fulfil EU functions.[121] The large number of Management Boards' members has raised concerns regarding the effective fulfilment of their tasks. One problem is whether they are capable of counterbalancing the powers of the Director.[122] Among other administrative tasks, the Manage-

---

115. But notice that the Joint Statement of the European Parliament, the Council of the EU and the Commission on decentralized agencies mentions the possibility of closing down or merging decentralized agencies (at points 4 and 5, available at <europa.eu/agencies/documents/joint_statement_and_common_approach_2012_en.pdf>).
116. Arts. 1, 2, 3, and 6(3) of Reg. 58/2003, cited *supra* note 107. Art. 6 specifies some of the tasks of the agencies and excludes from their realm "tasks requiring discretionary powers in translating political choices into action" (Art. 6(1)). On executive agencies, see further P. Craig, op. cit. *supra* note 25, at 148–153.
117. Art. 22 of Reg. 58/2003, cited *supra* note 107.
118. The following refers only to those agencies that in the new official terminology are termed "decentralized agencies". The executive agencies have different organic structure (Art. 7 of Council Reg. (EC) 58/2003, cited *supra* note 107).
119. "Management Board" and "Director" are not uniform designations – see Analytical Fiche n. 5, note 1, available at <europa.eu/agencies/documents/fiche_5_sent_to_ep_cons_2010-12-15_en.pdf>.
120. See, in more detail, Analytical Fiche no. 5, 1–3 and Annex, cited *supra* 119. Also, see further M. Busuioc, op. cit. *supra* note 106, at 35–36.
121. See E. Chiti, op. cit. *supra* note 102, at 1398, who considers this model "functional to the exigency of political compromise between the Member States and the Commission" but also "excessively baroque" (at 1400), See, further, E. Vos, "European agencies and the composite EU executive" in M. Everson, C. Monda and E. Vos (Eds.), *European Agencies in between Institutions and Member States* (Kluwer, 2014), at 26–30.
122. Analytical Fiche n. 5, at 5, questioning, in particular, whether one representative per Member State is always needed. The Common Approach attached to the Joint Statement of the Parliament, the Council and the Commission indicates how sensitive this issue is: Management Boards are to keep on representative from

ment Board appoints and dismisses the agency's Director and has disciplinary powers in his or her regard. In addition, it has budgetary tasks (it adopts the budget, as well as the financial rules applicable to the agency, and issues an opinion on the agency's accounts). Importantly, it adopts the agency's multiannual work programme, it may define its strategic aims and priorities and establish the agency's internal bodies (scientific committees and working parties, an executive board that assists the Management Board and possibly the Director, advisory boards). The Director's tasks are the daily administration of the agency. Among other powers, he or she prepares and implements the decisions of the Management Board, manages the staff and the budget and binds legally the agency.[123]

Some agencies have scientific committees.[124] They may directly adopt the scientific opinions of the agency (as in the case of EFSA) or assist the governing bodies on scientific issues related to the work of the agency. As a rule, their members may be appointed directly by the management board, but they can also be appointed by the Member States.[125] The agencies that have final decision-making powers (e.g. OHIM, CPVO, EASA, ECHA, ACER, SRB) include a Board of Appeal in their organic structure, which, as the name indicates, decide on appeals against the agencies' decisions.[126] The Board can usually replace the initial decision, and its decision is subject to appeal to the General Court.[127]

Finally, some of the agencies created since 2009 – namely, the Agency for the Cooperation of Energy Regulators (ACER), the Body of European Regulators for Electronic Communications (BEREC) and the financial agencies – confirm that "decentralized agencies" is far from being a homogeneous group. The main decision-making body of the financial agencies is a board

---

each Member State in the future (see point 10 of the Joint Statement on a Common Approach, cited *supra* note 115.

123. For example, the Director of EASA can decide on appeals (Art. 47 of the Reg. (EC) 216/2008 of the European Parliament and of the Council of 20 Febr. 2008 on common rules in the field of civil aviation and establishing a European Aviation Safety Agency (O.J. 2008, L 79/1) a decision which is then subject to the board of appeals.
124. E.g. EEA, EFSA, EMCDDA, FRA, GSA, ECHA, EMA.
125. This seems to be the case only for the EMA (see Art. 61(2) of Reg. (EC) 726/2004 of the European Parliament and of the Council of 31 Mar. 2004 laying down Community procedures for the authorization and supervision of medicinal products for human and veterinary use and establishing a European Medicines Agency, (O.J. 2004, L 136/1). For cases where members are appointed by the management board, see, e.g., Art. 28(5) of Reg. (EC) 178/2002 of the European Parliament and of the Council of 28 Jan. 2002 laying down the general principles, requirements and procedures of food law and establishing the European Food Safety Authority (O.J. 2002, L 31/1); and Art. 14(1) of Council Reg. (EC) 168/2007 of 15 Febr. 2007 establishing a European Union Agency for Fundamental Rights, (O.J. 2007, L 53/1).
126. Arts. 58 to 65 of Council Reg. (EC) 207/2009 of 26 Febr. 2009 on the Community trade mark (O.J. 2009, L 78/1), Arts. 45 to 48 of Council Reg. (EC) 2100/94 of 27 July 1994 on Community plant variety rights (O.J. 1994, L 227/1), Arts. 40 to 51 of Reg. (EC) 216/2008, cited *supra* note 123, Arts. 89 to 94 of Reg. (EC) 1907/2006 of the European Parliament and of the Council of 18 Dec. 2006 concerning the Registration, Evaluation, Authorization and Restriction of Chemicals (REACH) and establishing a European Chemicals Agency (O.J. 2006, L 396/1), and Arts. 18 to 20 of Reg. (EC) 713/2009 of the European Parliament and of the Council of 13 July 2009 establishing an Agency for the Cooperation of Energy Regulators after Reg. (EC) 713/2009; Art. 85 of Reg. (EU) 806/2014 of the European Parliament and of the Council of 15 July 2014 establishing uniform rules and a uniform procedure for the resolution of credit institutions and certain investment firms in the framework of a Single Resolution Mechanism and a Single Resolution Fund and amending Reg. (EU) 1093/2010 (O.J. 2014, L 225/1).
127. E.g. Judgment of the General Court (Eighth Chamber) of 11 Dec. 2014 in Case T-102/13, *Heli-Flight GmbH & Co. KG v. European Aviation Safety Agency (AESA)*.

of supervisors where national regulatory authorities are represented.[128] Thus, for example, the boards of supervisors "give guidance to the work of the [agencies]" and adopt the opinions, recommendations, decisions, and advice that the agencies are empowered to adopt.[129] ACER and BEREC have a similar organic structure, but only insofar as a board of regulators equally features next to a management board and a director. The internal allocation of powers and controls are different in each case.[130] The inclusion of such a board in the agencies' governing structure is a reflection of the regulatory specificities of the financial, energy and communications sectors and of the networks of regulators that were in place before the creation of these agencies.[131] The different schemes of appointing the members of the boards of regulators (or supervisors) and of the other governing bodies, as well as the different accountability links between the governing bodies of the agencies – and between them and the EU institutions – imply a varying degree of distance vis-à-vis the influence of national interests. The founding regulations of the financial agencies, as those of ACER and BEREC, emphasize their "independence" and that of the members of the respective governing bodies.[132] At the same time, however, the existence of a governing body like a board of regulators may question the independence of these agencies vis-à-vis national interests.[133]

4.3 *Powers*

Except in some individual decision-making procedures, European agencies have powers that formally support the adoption of decisions and legal acts of the EU institutions and national authorities, or the development of EU policies.[134] The immediate legal reason to attribute them instrumental powers lies in the *Meroni* judgment, which placed limits on delegation of powers to bodies different from the EU institutions (see below). But instrumental powers also fit the "in

---

128. Art. 43 of Reg. (EU) 1095/2010 of the European Parliament and of the Council of 24 Nov. 2010 establishing a European Supervisory Authority (O.J. 2010, L 331/84), Art. 43 of Reg. (EU) 1094/2010 of the European Parliament and of the Council of 24 Nov. 2010 establishing a European Supervisory Authority (European Insurance and Occupational Pensions Authority) (O.J. 2010, L 331/48) and Art. 43 of Reg. (EU) 1093/2010 of the European Parliament and of the Council of 24 Nov. 2010 establishing a European Supervisory Authority (European Banking Authority) (O.J. 2010, L 331/12). On the Single Resolution Board, see Art. 43(1) of Reg. (EU) 806/2014, cited *supra* note 126.
129. Art. 43(1) and (2) of Reg. (EU) 1095/2010, cited *supra* note 128, Art. 43(1) and (2) of Reg. (EU) 1094/2010, cited *supra* note 128, and Art. 43(1) and (2) of Reg. (EU) 1093/2010, cited *supra* note 128.
130. Regarding ACER, see Arts. 13, 15 and 17 of Reg. (EC) 713/2009, cited *supra* note 126 (Board of Regulators, Administrative Board and Director, respectively); concerning BEREC, see Arts. 5, 7 and 9 of Reg. (EC) 1211/2009 of the European Parliament and of the Council of 25 November 2009 establishing the Body of European Regulators for Electronic Communications (BEREC), after Reg. (EC) 1211/2009 (Board of Regulators, Management Committee and Administrative Manager, respectively). On ACER and its possible impact on the regulatory structure of energy, see D. Haverbeke, B. Naesens and W. Vandorpe, "European energy markets and the new agency for cooperation of energy regulators", 28 *Journal of Energy & Natural Resources Law* (2010), 403–430, at 414.
131. See M. Thatcher, op. cit. *supra* note 106, at 804–805. On ACER, see further D. Haverbeke, op. cit. *supra* note 130.
132. Art. 42 of Reg. (EU) 1095/2010, cited *supra* note 125, Art. 42 of Reg. (EU) 1094/2010, cited *supra* note 128, Art. 42 of Reg. (EU) 1093/2010, cited *supra* note 128, as amended, and Art. 47(1) of Reg. (EU) 806/2014 cited *supra* note 129. On BEREC, see Art. 4 of Reg. (EC) 1211/2009, cited *supra* note 130. See, however, the more nuanced provision on the independence of the ACER board of regulators at Art. 14(5) Reg. (EC) 713/2009, cited *supra* note 126 (but see also Art. 12(7)).
133. See, on financial agencies, N. Moloney, "The European securities and markets authority and institutional design for the EU financial market: Part 1 – rule-making", 12 *European Business Organization Law Review* (2011), 41–86, at 63, according to whom "ESMA's independence becomes more illusory on closer inspection".
134. For examples, see *infra*.

between" nature of European agencies: they ensure common administrative action, while not encroaching upon the competences of the Commission and of the Member States.[135]

Yet, instrumental powers can be determinative of the content of the final decisions in various degrees. In some cases, the line between the instrumental powers of the agencies and the final Union acts that they ground may be quite thin.[136] This may be mainly due to practical reasons (e.g. they collect the information on the basis of which the final decision is adopted; they have the expertise that the Commission does not have). In some cases, legal requirements reinforce practical reasons (e.g. when the EU legislation imposes on the Commission the duty to justify draft decisions that are not in accordance with the scientific opinion of the agency).[137]

Thus, a general characterization of the agencies' powers as instrumental – even if duly nuanced by an explicit reference to the cases in which agencies have final decision-making powers – hides a wide variety of powers, which tend to escape easy classifications. In reality, the powers of agencies depend very much on the needs of each regulated sector.[138] A typology is, nonetheless, useful as an analytical framework.[139] The following will distinguish, according to the core tasks they perform, between information-providing agencies, advisory agencies, agencies that have adjudicatory powers, and operational agencies.[140]

Some agencies are mainly tasked with gathering, analysing and providing information that both the EU institutions and the Member States can use when defining or implementing policy, or, generally, in the performance of other tasks. Their work may include the dissemination of information to the public,[141] and the management of information networks.[142] These are the primary tasks of the Fundamental Rights Agency, the European Environment Agency, and the European Monitoring Centre for Drugs and Drug Addiction, among others.[143] Other agencies,

---

135. E. Chiti, op. cit. *supra* note 102, at 1405.
136. E. Chiti, op. cit., *supra* note 102, at 1405, See also Judgment of 26 Nov. 2002 in Joined Cases T-74/00, T-76/00, T-83/00, T-84/00, T-85/00, T-132/00, T-137/00 and T-141/00, *Artegodan GmbH and Others v. Commission*, para 198–199.
137. E.g. Art. 7(3) of Reg. 1331/2008, concerning the opinion of EFSA. On the powers of the financial agencies, see below text accompanying footnotes 146 to 148. In other cases, legislative provisions aside, the agencies' opinion may become *de facto* the final decision. On the importance of the instrumental powers of the agencies, see E. Chiti, op. cit. *supra* note 102, at 1405.
138. H. Hofmann and A. Morini, "Constitutional aspects of the pluralization of the EU executive through "agencification" ", 37 ELR (2012), 419–443, at 430.
139. For a classification of agencies according to their powers, see P. Craig, op. cit. *supra* note 25, at 148–149, and references.
140. Outside of this account are agencies that support the internal functioning of the institutions (such as the Centre of Translation).
141. E.g. ENISA, Arts. 1(1) and 3(a)(b)(c)(d) of Reg. (EC) 526/2013 of the European Parliament and of the Council of 21 May 2013 concerning the European Union Agency for Network (O.J. 2013, L 165/41) and Information Security; EU-OSHA, Art. 3(1) of Council Reg. (EC) 2062/94 of 18 July 1994 establishing a European Agency for Safety and Health at Work, as amended (O.J. 2003, L 245/38).
142. E.g. EFSA (Arts. 23(g) and 36 of Reg. (EC) 178/2002, cited *supra* note 125; EU-OSHA (Arts. 3(1)(f) and 4 of Reg. 2062/94, cited note *supra* 141).
143. See, respectively Arts. 4(1) and 6(1)(a)) of Council Reg. (EC) 168/2007, cited *supra* note 125; Arts. 1(2) and 2) of Reg. (EC) 401/2009, cited *supra* note 125; and Arts. 1(2), 2(a)(b)(c) and 5 of Reg. (EC) 1920/2006 of the European Parliament and of the Council of 12 Dec. 2006 on the European Monitoring Centre for Drugs and Drug Addiction (O.J. 2006, L 376/1). See, further, E. Chiti, "European agencies' rulemaking: Powers, procedures and assessment", 19 ELJ (2013), at 98–99; O. de Schutter, "The EU fundamental rights agency: Genesis and potential" in K. Boyle (Ed.), *New Institutions for Human Rights Protection* (OUP, 2009), at 93–136.

which have primarily other types of functions, also have an important role in providing information or in managing information systems.[144]

Others' core task is the provision of technical and scientific assistance to the Commission. This is the case of EMSA, EFSA, ERA, EMA, and BEREC, among others. They mainly intervene in decision-making procedures with an advisory function – they issue formally non-binding opinions that constitute preparatory acts of Commission's decisions.[145] They also regulate their respective sectors via informal regulatory instruments (such as best practices).[146] One of the tasks of the financial agencies is to provide guidelines and recommendations to national authorities and financial institutions to ensure consistent and effective supervisory practices.[147] Specific to this case is that the addressees of such guidance "shall make every effort to comply with those guidelines and recommendations and need to provide reasons for non-compliance".[148] This provision stresses the thin line between having merely instrumental powers and having de facto final decision-making powers. The financial agencies make draft regulatory and implementing standards, which are adopted by the Commission, respectively, as delegated and implementing acts.[149] Yet, if the Commission intends not to endorse one such draft or introduce amendments, it needs to justify its position; furthermore, it cannot introduce amendments without first asking the agency to adopt them.[150] As many scholars have observed, these powers very much stretch the limits of "technical and scientific assistance", and, in particular, the legal limits usually placed on the powers of agencies.[151]

Some agencies have mainly or also the power to adopt individual decisions that are legally binding on third parties. Thus, OHIM decides on Union trademarks and registered designs, the CPVO decides applications for plant variety rights. ECHA verifies whether the applications made by manufacturers and importers for the registration of chemical products are complete and rejects them in case of lacking documents.[152] EASA issues air-worthiness specifications

---

144. E.g. Frontex "develop[s] and operate[s] information systems that enable swift and reliable exchanges of information regarding emerging risks at the external borders" (Art. 2(1)(h) of Council Reg. (EC) 2007/2004 of 26 Oct. 2004 establishing a European Agency for the Management of Operational Cooperation at the External Borders of the Member States of the European Union (O.J. 2004, L 349).
145. See, e.g., Art. 10(3) of Commission Reg. (EU) 1299/2014 of 18 Nov. 2014 on the technical specifications for interoperability relating to the "infrastructure" subsystem of the rail system in the European Union (O.J. 2014, L 356/1) in the case of the ERA; Art. 7a(3) of Directive 2002/21/EC of the European Parliament and of the Council of 7 Mar. 2002 on a common regulatory for electronic communications networks and services as amended by Directive 20097140/EC of 25 Nov. 2009 (O.J. 2002, L 108/33).
146. E.g. ECHA provides "technical and scientific guidance and tools where appropriate for the operation of [the Chemicals Reg.] in particular to assist the development of chemical safety reports [...] by industry and especially by SMEs" (Art. 77(2)(g) of Reg. (EC) 1907/2006, cited *supra* note 126; Art. 2(a) of Reg. (EC) 1211/2009, cited *supra* note 130; and Arts. 8(1)(e) and 16 of Reg. (EU) 1095/2010, cited *supra* note 128.
147. Art. 16(1) of Reg. (EU) 1095/2010, cited *supra* note 128, Art. 16(1) of Reg. (EU) 1094/2010, cited *supra* note 128, and Art. 16(1) Reg. 1093/2010, cited *supra* note 128.
148. Art. 16(3) of Reg. (EU) 1095/2010, cited *supra* note 128, Art. 16(3) of Reg. (EU) 1094/2010, cited *supra* note 128, and Art. 16(3) Reg. 1093/2010, cited *supra* note 128.
149. Arts. 8 and 1(2) of Reg. (EU) 1095/2010, cited *supra* note 128, Arts. 8 and 1(2) of Reg. (EU) 1094/2010, cited *supra* note 128, and Arts. 8 and 1(2) Reg. 1093/2010, cited *supra* note 128, as amended.
150. Arts. 10(1) and 15(1) of Reg. (EU) 1095/2010, cit. *supra* note 128, Arts. 10(1) and 15(1) of Reg. (EU) 1094/2010, cited *supra* note 128, and Arts. 10(1) and 15(1) Reg. 1093/2010, cited *supra* note 128.
151. See, e.g., M. Busuioc, "Rule-Making by the European Financial Supervisory Authorities: Walking a tight rope", 19 ELJ (2013), 111–125, at 114. On the legal limits of the powers of agencies, see sub-section 3.2.5.
152. Arts. 25 to 45 of Council Reg. (EC) 207/2009, cited *supra* note 128; Arts. 49 to 63 of Council Reg. (EC) 2100/94, cited *supra* note 126; Art. 20 of Reg. (EC) 1907/2006, cited *supra* note 126, respectively.

that determine, *inter alia*, whether aircrafts can fly.[153] In emergency situations, ESMA can adopt decisions directed at market operators, including the power to prohibit or condition "financial activities that threaten the orderly functioning and integrity of financial markets or the stability of the whole or part of the financial system in the Union";[154] it can also address individual decisions to national authorities.[155] The Single Resolution Board, created in the framework of the European Banking Union, draws up resolution plans and adopts related decisions applicable to some of the banks that fall under its jurisdiction.[156] ACER may decide on the terms and conditions for access to cross-border energy infrastructure, albeit with the involvement of national regulators.[157]

Distinct from the former are the agencies in charge of operational activities. FRONTEX, EASO and the former third pillar agencies – EUROJUST, EUROPOL and CEPOL – are the most paradigmatic examples. FRONTEX coordinates Member States' actions in the management of external borders, assists them when "increased technical and operational assistance" is required at the external borders, but also carries out joint operations and pilot projects in cooperation with the Member States, deploying for this effect guards from the European Border Guard Teams constituted by the Agency.[158] FRONTEX may have significant powers regarding third country nationals that are illegally present in a Member State, since, while not deciding on the merits of return decisions, it may "ensure the coordination or the organisation of joint return operations".[159] EASO conducts several activities aimed at supporting the EU and the Member States in the field of asylum. Among other tasks, it supports the Member States in the relocation of asylum seekers within the EU and those Member States that find themselves particularly under pressure due to the arrival of a large number of third-country nationals (e.g. via the deployment of support teams).[160] EUROJUST was created to support and strengthen coordination and cooperation between national authorities investigating and prosecuting serious crimes affecting more than one Member States or requiring a common prosecution.[161] Thus, among other powers, it may (i) ask the competent authorities of Member States concerned to consider undertaking an investigation or prosecution of specific acts or setting up a joint investigation team; (ii) ensure that authorities of the Member States inform each other of the investigations or prosecutions which have repercussion at the EU level or may affect Member States; (iii) assist the EUROPOL.[162] EUROPOL's mission is to support and strengthen action of the police authorities of the Member States and other law enforcement services and their mutual cooperation in the prevention and combat of serious crimes affecting more than one Member States, terrorism or crimes that would affect the interests of the EU policy.[163] For this purpose, it may (i) collect, store, process, analyse and exchange information and intelligence; (ii) ask the

---

153. Art. 5(4) of Reg. (EC) 216/2008, cited *supra* note 123.
154. Art. 9(5) of Reg. (EU) 1095/2010, cited *supra* note 128, Art. 9(5) of Reg. (EU) 1094/2010, cited *supra* note 128, and Art. 9(5) Reg. 1093/2010, cited *supra* note 128.
155. Art. 18(3) of Reg. (EU) 1095/2010, cited *supra* note 128, Art. 18(3) of Reg. (EU) 1094/2010, cited *supra* note 128, and Art. 18(3) Reg. 1093/2010, cited *supra* note 128.
156. Art. 7(2) of Reg. (EU) 806/2014 cited *supra* note 126.
157. Art. 8 of Reg. (EC) 713/2009, cited *supra* note 126.
158. See, in more detail, Arts. 2(1) and 3 to 3c of Council Reg. (EC) 2007/2004, cited *supra* note 144.
159. Art. 9 of Council Reg. (EC) 2007/2004, cited *supra* note 144.
160. Arts. 5, 8 of Reg. (EU) 439/2010 of the European Parliament and of the Council of 19 May 2010 establishing a European Asylum Support Office (O.J. 2010, L 132/11).
161. Art. 85 of the TFEU.
162. Arts. 6 and 7 of Council Reg. of 28 Febr. 2002 setting up Eurojust with a view of reinforcing the fight against serious crime, as amended (O.J. 2002, L 63/1).
163. Art. 88 of the TFEU.

authorities of Member States to initiate, conduct or coordinate investigations and suggest setting up join investigations teams; and (iii) provide intelligence and analytical support to Member States.[164] Finally, CEPOL was created to function as a network for the cooperation of national training institutions of senior police officers in the Member States. Among other powers, it (i) provides training sessions based on common standards; (ii) disseminates best practices and research findings; and (iii) develops electronic networks.[165]

4.4 *Legal bases*

Until the Lisbon Treaty, European agencies were not even mentioned in the Treaties. Whether or not the EU had competence to create bodies of this kind was an issue that cast a gloom over their legal legitimacy, even if the issue was somewhat mitigated by the instrumental nature of the agencies' powers. The case brought by the UK in 2012 against the powers of the ESMA on short-selling activities confirms that, despite the fact that agencies are ubiquitous in EU law, their legal basis still remains an issue. In fact, the Treaties acknowledge the existence of agencies – an acknowledgment that has important legal consequences, among which the fact that the agencies' acts can now formally be subject to judicial review[166] – but it does not provide an explicit legal foundation for their creation.[167]

The founding regulations of many agencies, in particular those adopted until the end of the 1990s, were based on what is now Article 352 TFEU.[168] This was no longer always the case for agencies created in the 2000s (e.g. European Aviation Safety Agency, the European Food Safety Authority, the European Chemicals Agency), partially due to the pressure of the Parliament, which had only a consultative role under Article 308 ECT.[169]

One legal basis that has been commonly used is Article 114 TFEU.[170] This choice has led to court disputes triggered by the UK in two cases. In the *ENISA* case, the UK contested that the creation of agencies could be considered a harmonization measure within the meaning of Article 114 TFEU.[171] The Court, however, followed the path it had opened in a previous judgment (*Smoke Flavourings*), where it had held that the EU legislator has a margin of discretion in choosing the most appropriate technique to achieve harmonization. The Court specified that, under Article 114 TFEU,

---

164. Art. 5 of Council Decision of 6 Apr. 2009 establishing the European Police Office (Europol) (O.J. 2009, L 121/37).
165. Arts. 1, 4 and 7 of Council Decision 2005/681/JHA of 20 Sept. 2005 establishing the European Police College (CEPOL) (O.J. 2005, L 256/63).
166. Art. 263, 265, 267 TFEU. See also Art. 9 TEU, Arts. 15(1), 16(2) and 228 TFEU.
167. With the exception of the European Defence Agency (Arts. 42 and 45 TEU), EUROJUST (Art. 85 TFEU) and EUROPOL (Art. 88 TFEU).
168. In 2008, the Commission reported "Out of the 23 agencies under the EC Treaty, 12 of them have their legal basis under Art. 308 EC, the other ones being created under a sectoral Treaty basis, 8 agencies' basic acts being adopted under co-decision" (Communication from the Commission to the European Parliament and the Council – European agencies – The way forward, COM/2008/0135 final, note 7).
169. But FRA, for instance, was created on the basis of Art. 308 EC. On the consequences of this change to the powers of the Parliament in the agencies' structures, see M. Busuioc and M. Groenleer, op. cit. *supra* note 112, at 18. On the role of the Parliament, see F. Jacobs, "EU Agencies and the European Parliament" in M. Everson, C. Monda and E. Vos (Eds.), *European Agencies in between Institutions and Member States* (Kluwer, 2014), 201–228, and also, D. Curtin, op. cit. *supra* note 1, 150–155.
170. E.g. ACER, BEREC, EBA, ECHA, EFSA, EIOPA, EMA, ENISA, ESMA and SRB were created on the basis of this Treaty article.
171. The case concerned only ENISA but the UK's plea was formulated more broadly: see Judgment in C-217/04, *United Kingdom v. Parliament and Council*, para 11.

> "The legislature may deem it necessary to provide for the establishment of a Community body responsible for contributing to the implementation of a process of harmonisation in situations where, in order to facilitate the uniform implementation and application of acts based on that provision, the adoption of non-binding supporting and framework measures seems appropriate".[172]

It added that "the tasks conferred on such a body must be closely linked to the subject-matter" of the harmonization measure.[173] A similar plea in the *ESMA* case, more recently, met the same fate. Here the UK contested that ESMA could lawfully have the power to adopt decisions addressed at natural or legal persons under Article 114 TFEU. The Court disagreed. It followed from the previous cases that a Union body, office or agency established under that Treaty article, may have "powers for the implementation of the harmonisation sought [...], in particular where the measures to be adopted are dependent on specific professional and technical expertise and the ability of such a body to respond swiftly and appropriately".[174]

4.5 *Legal limits to the agencies' powers*

Since European agencies started "mushrooming" in the EU institutional landscape, the judgment in *Meroni* has been invoked as an impediment to give them more than instrumental powers. *Meroni* was pronounced in 1958 and concerned the legality of a delegation of powers from the High Authority of the European Coal and Steal Community to private bodies. In this judgment, the Court had held that, despite the lack of a specific provision allowing for a delegation of powers, delegation was permissible if it was necessary for the performance of the tasks of the High Authority specified in the Treaty. However, only "clearly defined executive powers" subject to "to strict review in the light of objective criteria determined by the delegating authority", could be delegated to bodies not foreseen in the Treaty. The delegation of "wide discretionary powers", which made possible "the execution of actual economic policy", would result in a "transfer of responsibility" from the delegator to the delegate, and would thus render ineffective the guarantees stemming from the balance of powers that characterized the institutional structure of the Community.[175]

Is this reasoning applicable under a different Treaty to agencies created by the EU legislator, the powers of which have been defined in a founding regulation and were not delegated in the *Meroni* sense?[176] If one gives a positive answer to this question, do the powers of the existing agencies comply with the strictures of *Meroni*? These two questions have been at the core of a decade-long debate.[177] Yet, it is hard to deny that, at least, the agencies that have final

---

172. Judgment in C-217/04, *United Kingdom v. Parliament and Council*, para 44.
173. Judgment in C-217/04, *United Kingdom v. Parliament and Council*, para 45.
174. Judgment in C-270/12, *United Kingdom v. Parliament and Council*, para 105; see also 107. The Court also considered that the purpose of the power attributed to the ESMA was indeed to "improve the conditions for the establishment and functioning of the internal market in the financial field" in accordance with Art. 114 TFEU, as interpreted in the ENISA case (see paras. 113 to 116). For a different view, see Opinion of A.G. Jääskinen in C-270/12, *United Kingdom v. Parliament and Council*, para 51–54.
175. Judgment in Case 9/56, *Meroni*.
176. See, e.g. R. Dehousse, op. cit. *supra* note 103; E. Chiti, op. cit. *supra* note 102; M. Chamon, "EU agencies: Does the Meroni Doctrine make sense?", 17 MJ (2010), 281–305.
177. More extensive accounts of the debate can be found in S. Griller and A. Orator "Everything under control? The 'way forward' for European agencies in the footsteps of the Meroni doctrine", 31 ELR (2010), 3–35; M. Chamon, op. cit. *supra* note 176; T. Zwart, "La poursuite du Père Meroni ou pourquoi les agences pourraient jouer un rôle plus en vue dans l'Union Europèenne" in J. Dutheil de la Rochère (Ed.), *L'exécution du droit de l'union, entre mécanismes communautaires et droits nationaux* (Bruylant, 2009), 159–73.

decision-making powers have discretionary powers, even if limited to adjudicating an individual case.[178]

Equally relevant to the discussion on the legal limits of agencies' powers is *Romano*. In this judgment, the Court had been asked to assist a national court on how to interpret a decision of an administrative commission that had been created by the Council and, *inter alia,* dealt with administrative questions and questions of interpretation arising from the regulations on the social security of migrant workers. The decision at issue defined one of the conditions for the attribution of social benefits to migrant workers listed in the regulation. While the request for a preliminary ruling did not contend with the validity of the decision, the Court held that "a body such as the administrative commission may not be empowered by the Council to adopt *acts having the force of law*", by which it seemed to refer to acts of general application.[179]

The debate on the legal limits of agencies' powers has had a practical reflection, notwithstanding the doubts regarding the applicability of the two judgments to EU agencies. The limits of *Meroni* and *Romano* are a plausible explanation for the procedural scheme that currently grounds the making of delegated and implementing rules in the financial sector.[180] The influence of *Meroni* is also visible in the regulation governing the executive agencies, which specifies that these agencies may not perform "tasks requiring discretionary powers in translating political choices into action".[181]

The relevance of *Meroni* and *Romano* was more recently at stake in the *ESMA* case on short-selling activities.[182] While pointing out the difference between the bodies underlying *Meroni* and "a European Union entity, created by the EU legislator", the Court went on to review the powers of ESMA in the light of *Meroni,* thus considering that this judgment applies in this instance and, indirectly, to current agencies.[183] The ruling thus seems to contradict those that, pointing out the differences, doubted that the *Meroni* doctrine could be relevant to EU agencies. It now seems clear that, formally at least, delegation of powers to EU agencies must be restricted to "clearly defined executive powers". However, a closer reading of the judgment leaves room to more nuanced conclusions. The legality of the ESMA's powers at issue hinges more on the definition of conditions and criteria that delimit its discretion in accordance with the ESMA's founding regulation – which make those powers "amenable to judicial review" – than on a distinction between "clearly defined executive powers" and "wide discretionary powers", which is

178. See Judgment of 19 Nov. 2008, Case T-187/06, *Schräder v. CPVO*, paras. 59–67; and commentary in M. Chamon, op. cit. *supra* note 176, at 294–295.
179. Judgment in Case 98/80, *Giuseppe Romano v. Institut national d'assurance maladie-invalidité,* para 20. The interpretation of the ruling is contested. The original "atti di carattere normativo", translated into French as "actes revêtant un caractère normative", indicates that it referred to acts of general application. The Court invoked Art. 155 EECT (on delegation of powers by the Council to the Commission) and the judicial system of the Treaty, which only envisaged judicial review of acts of the institutions (see also Opinion of AG Werner in Case 98/80, *Giuseppe Romano v. Institut national d'assurance maladie-invalidité,* 1263–1266).
180. L. Dragomir, *European Prudential Banking Reg. and Supervision: The Legal Dimension* (Routledge, 2010); M. Busuioc, op. cit. *supra* note 151.
181. Art. 6(1) of Council Reg. (EC) 58/2003, cited *supra* note 110.
182. On both aspects there has been abundant commentary. See, *inter alia*; M. Chamon, "The empowerment of agencies under the Meroni doctrine and Art. 114 TFEU: Comment on *United Kingdom v. Parliament* and Council (Short-selling) and the proposed Single Resolution Mechanism", 39 ELR (2014), 380–403; M. Scholten and M. van Rijsbergen, "The ESMA-short selling Case: Erecting a new delegation doctrine in the EU upon the Meroni-Romano remnants", 41 *Legal Issues of Economic Integration* (2014), 389–405; C.F. Bergström, "Shaping the new system for delegation of powers to EU agencies: *United Kingdom v. European parliament and Council (Short Selling),* 51 CML Rev. (2015), 219–242.
183. Judgment in C-217/04, *UK v. Parliament and Council,* paras. 43 and 44 to 53.

arguably questionable.[184] The ruling, in fact, entrusts the EU legislator a wide margin of discretion in defining a given regulatory regime, in the light of which the powers of the agencies will ultimately be assessed.[185] When assessing the validity of ESMA's powers in view of *Romano*, the Court acknowledged that ESMA had powers to adopt measures of general application. But one difference between the decision at stake in that judgment and the decisions that the ESMA is entitled to adopt under the current regulation was enough to enable the Court to conclude that the ESMA's powers did not breach "the principle established in *Romano*": unlike the decisions of the administrative commission at stake in *Romano*, the decisions of ESMA are subject to judicial review.[186] Thus, the *Romano* prohibition would hold in a scenario in which the acts of entities established under EU law would not be subject to judicial review.

4.6 *Accountability*

One main concern regarding European agencies has been their accountability. Since they were institutionally separate from the EU institutions and from the Member States, how to ensure that agencies would give account of their actions, to whom, and via which mechanisms?

Empirical research has shown that this concern has resulted in both "overloads" and deficits.[187] Most European agencies have been given a variety of account-giving obligations both to the EU institutions (often in the from of reports and hearings to and before the European Parliament and/or the Council), and within the structure of the agency (to the management board). However, partially overlapping obligations do not seem to have been tailored to the different degrees of autonomy and to the variety of powers that the agencies have been entrusted with.[188]

4.7 *The international dimension*

EU agencies often liaise with international bodies that are active in their respective fields of action, as well as with the agencies of other countries. The establishment of cooperation links with other specialized entities is often grounded on an explicit legal provision,[189] which, nonetheless, may not capture the way the external action of EU agencies may evolve. It ranges from memoranda of understanding that the agencies establish directly with their international counterparts to informal contacts. While far from being a new phenomenon, the "thickening" web of global regulatory collaboration has possibly intensified this aspect of the activity of EU agencies.

International regulatory cooperation between agencies may constitute a necessary condition for the effective performance of their tasks (think, for example, of climate change, pandemics, food regulation) but it is far from being unproblematic. Agencies' embeddedness in transnational networks may strengthen their autonomy vis-à-vis the EU institutions, which also raises the issue of the legal limits to which such interactions should be subject (beyond the formal mandates they are given).[190] At the same time, they enable international regulatory

184. Judgment in C-217/04, *UK v. Parliament and Council*, paras. 45, 49 and 53. The Court seems to assume that technical assessments are incapable of grounding discretion, which is a problematic postulation.
185. See C.F. Bergström, op. cit. *supra* note 182, at 241.
186. Judgment in C-217/04, *UK v. Parliament and Council*, para 64 and 65.
187. M. Busuioc and M. Groenleer, op. cit. *supra* note 112, at 264–269.
188. M. Busuioc and M. Groenleer, op. cit. *supra* note 112, at 195, indicating that "differences in agency powers have mostly not resulted in variations in the design of accountability obligations".
189. See, for examples, E. Chiti, op. cit. *supra* note 102, 1413–1414.
190. E. Chiti, op. cit. *supra* note 102, 1416. M. Groenleer, "Linking up levels of governance: Agencies of the European Union and their interaction with international institutions" in O. Costa and K.-E. Joergensen (Eds.), *The Influence of International Institutions on the European Union. When Multilateralism Hits Brussels* (Palgrave Macmillan, 2012), 135–154. Pointing out some issues of concern, see Joint Statement of the European

bodies or agencies from third countries to partially influence the outcome of EU policy-making processes, thus potentially affecting the conduct of the EU institutions and, indirectly, of the Member States.[191]

5. Networks

Networks are not a fully separate phenomenon from agencies. As seen above, some agencies are formally institutionalized networks of national regulators, and started their life as networks;[192] others have as one of their main tasks to constitute and manage networks.[193] But the term "networks" is broader than this link to agencies. Networks are often created informally or outside hierarchical structures to allow coordination between actors situated at different levels of government, at different stages of policy-making. In some cases, they are open to the participation of private parties.[194] Yet, they constitute a central aspect of the EU administration: they both reflect one of its structural characteristics pointed out above – collaboration – and are one of the dynamic forces behind administrative integration.[195]

"Networks" is a loose concept that encompasses various realities: networks of national independent authorities (regulators); of departments of national administrations created in the framework of mutual assistance, or of departments of national administrations integrated in the same decision-making procedure; of experts in a given field (including national officials, but often encompassing private persons outside a public capacity); partnerships between local, regional, national and European authorities, or involving only regional or local authorities; networks of governmental departments that support the Open Method of Coordination. Their functions include information generation and management, both to inform policy-making (e.g. European Information Observation Network) and ensure coordinated implementation (e.g. European Competition Network) as well as regulatory convergence (via, e.g. adopting best practices, peer review).[196] The problems they may pose in terms of legal framing of their often "soft" powers and accountability are hence quite varied. Their function, organization and regime

---

Parliament, the Council of the EU and the Commission on decentralized agencies, cited *supra* note 112, point 25. On specific examples, see D. Curtin, op. cit. *supra* note 1, 158–160 (Europol), and A. Ott, E. Vos and F. Coman-Kund, "European agencies on the global scene: EU and international law perspectives" in M. Everson, C. Monda and E. Vos (Eds.), *European Agencies in between Institutions and Member States* (Kluwer, 2014), 87–122, at 101–113.

191. M. Groenleer and S. Gabbi, "Regulatory agencies of the European Union as international actors legal framework, development over time and strategic motives in the case of the European Food Safety Authority", 13 *European Journal of Risk Reg.* (2013), 479–492, at 480, who also indicate that international collaboration between agencies may also "advance the [EU's] political and strategic goals in the international arena in a more efficient and effective way" and may be "instrumental to the support and credibility of EU policies" (at 483). On the procedural effects of the reception of decisions of international bodies in EU law, see J. Mendes, "EU law and global regulatory regimes: Hollowing out procedural standards?", 10 *International Journal of Constitutional Law* (2012), 988–1022.

192. See, on this point, M. Thatcher, op. cit. *supra* note 106, at 798, noting that networks of national regulators both hindered and made possible the development of new agencies (804–805). On the similarities between agencies and networks, see W. Weib, "Agencies versus networks: From the divide to convergence in the administrative governance in the EU", 61 *Administrative Law Review* (2009), 45–70.

193. E.g. EIONET (Arts. 1 and 2 of Reg. (EC) 401/2009, cited *supra* note 131).

194. For a broader perspective on networks in EU governance, see T. Börzel, "European governance: Negotiation and competition in the shadow of hierarchy", 48 JCMS (2010), 191–219, arguing that networks are often dominated by governmental actors.

195. In general, see H. Hoffman and A. Türk (Eds.), *EU Administrative Governance* (Edward Elgar, 2006), Ch. 3 and conclusions.

196. H. Hofmann, G. Rowe and H. Türk, op. cit. *supra* note 1, at 307–312.

vary across policy areas. In these circumstances, it is not easy to provide a systematic overview of networks. This section maps the phenomenon by distinguishing those networks that were created by force of an EU legal act from networks that emerged outside a formal legal framework, while illustrating within these two categories the functions that networks may perform in the implementation of EU law. The examples below exclude networks of which European and national authorities may be part together with non-EU states.[197]

5.1 *Legally mandated*

Networks are often information-gathering structures, which support in various degrees decision-making and enforcement. Thus, for instance, within the European Information Network on Drugs and Drug Addiction (Reitox), Member States and the Commission collect and analyse relevant information on drugs and drug addiction, on policies and solutions adopted, on new psychoactive substances or combinations thereof that entail risks to public health.[198] The information generated by this network has both public health and criminal law relevance. It may eventually lead to control measures and criminal penalties adopted by the Member States, upon decision of the Council adopted in a procedure that involves the Europol, the European Monitoring Centre on Drugs and Drug Addiction, and national competent authorities.[199] Information exchange networks are often supported by databases set up and managed by the Commission and Member States.[200]

Another example of an information network is the epidemiological surveillance network established by the EU decision on serious cross-border threats to health.[201] It comprises the Commission, national competent authorities and an EU agency (the European Centre for Disease Control), which also operates and coordinates the network. Via the network they share information on epidemiological surveillance of communicable diseases and related health issues, on the progression of epidemic situations, unusual epidemics and new communicable diseases. The network is only one element of broader coordination duties between the Commission and the Member States, and among the Member States, to tackle serious cross border-threats to health, including in emergency situations.

The European network of employment services (EURES), established and operated by the Commission and the Member States explicitly combines information exchange with the

197. E.g. the Information Network on Capacity Building set up by the Intergovernmental Forum on Chemical Safety, in which the EU and Member States participate by force of Art. 20 of Reg. (EC) 304/2003 of the European Parliament and of the Council of 28 Jan. 2003 concerning the export and import of dangerous chemicals (O.J. 2003, L 63/1).
198. Art. 5(2) of Reg. (EC) 1920/2006, cited *supra* note 140, see e.g. Proposal for a Council Decision on submitting 4-methylmethcathinone (mephedrone) to control measures, COM(2010)583 final.
199. Arts. 8 and 9 of Council Decision 2005/387/JHA of 10 May 2005 on the information exchange, risk-assessment and control of new psychoactive substances (O.J. 2005, L 127/32) (following a risk assessment report – see Art. 6 of the same decision). Another example of a predominantly information-gathering network is the European Crime Prevention Network (Council Decision 2009/902/JHA of 30 Nov. 2009 setting up a European Crime Prevention Network, O.J. 2009, L 321/44).
200. For examples, see D.-U. Galetta, H. Hoffman and J.-P. Schneider, "Information exchange in the European Administrative Union: An introduction", 20 *European Public Law* (2014), 65–70, at 67. See also the Anti-Counterfeit and Anti-Piracy Information System, set up in the context of Reg. (EU) 608/2013 of the European Parliament and of the Council of 12 June 2013 concerning customs enforcement of intellectual property rights (O.J. 2013, L 181/15) in relation to Council Resolution of 25 Sept. 2008 on a comprehensive European anti-counterfeiting and anti-piracy plan (point 16).
201. Art. 6 of Decision 1082/2013/EU, cited *supra* note 89.

provision of services.[202] The main function of this network is to promote mobility of workers by exchanging and processing vacancies and applications for employment, which includes "the development of measures to encourage and facilitate the mobility of workers".[203] For this purpose, the network provides, via a tripartite institutional structure, services such as recruitment, job matching and placement.[204] The network even has its own Management Board, which the Commission needs to consult, *inter alia*, when developing "strategies, operational objectives and work programmes" for the network.[205]

Information is explicitly instrumental to enforcement of EU law in the case of the European Competition Network, one of the most conspicuous examples of networks including the Commission and national regulatory authorities.[206]

5.2 *Informal networks*

Informal networks may emerge as a result of EU sectorial legislation, often at the initiative of the Member States as a means to facilitate their implementation and compliance with EU law. A case in point is the Common Strategy of Implementation created to implement the Water Framework Directive. The Common Strategy is a collaborative network that includes public and private experts and enables Member States to exchange information necessary for the implementation of the Directive, test the different approaches and develop good practices. It aims at reducing disparities in the techniques involved in the application of the Directive, which could impact on its uniform application. With this purpose, working groups composed of Member States experts prepare guidance documents, possibly with the participation of NGOs and stakeholders under the orientation of a coordination group composed of the Commission and of Member States. Such guidance documents both "clarify the meaning and implications of the open-ended framework norms and to facilitate comparative evaluation of Member States' performance in the implementation of this"[207] The Common Strategy of Implementation was developed very much at the margin of the norms of the directive.

In other cases, the creation of informal networks may be the result of administrative collaboration mandated by EU law. For example, the Platform of European Market Surveillance Authorities for Cosmetics facilitates cooperation, including the exchange of information and

---

202. Arts. 1 and 2 of the Commission Implementing Decision 2012/733/EU of 26 Nov. 2012 implementing Reg. (EU) 492/2011 of the European Parliament and of the Council as regards the clearance of vacancies and applications for employment and the re-establishment of EURES (O.J. 2012, L 328/21).
203. Art. 2(d) of the Commission Implementing Decision 2012/733/EU, cited *supra* note 202.
204. Art. 7 (see also Arts. 4, 5 and 6) of the Commission Implementing Decision 2012/733/EU, cited *supra* note 202.
205. Art. 8(7) of the Commission Implementing Decision 2012/733/EU, cited *supra* note 202. The powers mentioned in the text, among others, were challenged in Court by the Parliament, on the grounds that the Commission had exceeded its implementing powers by adopting this decision (Judgment in C-65/13, *Parliament v. Commission*). The Court dismissed the action of annulment.
206. Commission notice on the cooperation within the network of competition authorities (O.J. 2004, C 101/43). See, e.g., I. Maher, "Regulation and modes of governance in EC Competition Law: What's new in enforcement?", 31 *Fordham International Law Journal* (2008), 1713–1740, at 1719, 1731–1732; Y. Svetiev, "Networked competition governance in the EU: Delegation, decentralization, or experimentalist architecture" in C. Sabel and J. Zeitlin (Eds.), *Experimentalist Governance in the European Union: Towards a New Architecture* (OUP, 2010), 79–120, at 95–114; more descriptively, L. Lianos and A. Andreangeli, "The European Union" in E.M. Fox and M.J. Trebilcock (Eds.), *The Design of Competition Law Institutions: Global Norms, Local Choices* (OUP, 2013), 385–443, at 429–432.
207. J. Scott, "In legal limbo: Post-legislative guidance as a challenge for European administrative law", 48 CML Rev. (2011), 329–355, at 338–339, 342 and 347.

expertise as well as the development and implementation of joint projects, between (mainly) national authorities responsible for the surveillance of the cosmetics market.[208] The network thus seems to concretize the duties of administrative collaboration that bind national administrations by force of the EU Regulation on cosmetic products, in view of its "proper application and due enforcement", and of the Commission to foster that collaboration. Nevertheless, there is no explicit reference in that regulation or in another EU legal act to the creation of a network.[209]

A prominent example of informal networks is SOLVIT, the Internal Market Problem Solving Network. The Commission describes SOLVIT as "a network of centres set up by Member States within their own national administrations, as a fast and informal means of resolving problems individuals and businesses encounter when exercising their rights in the internal market".[210] SOLVIT constitutes an alternative mechanism to tackle alleged infringements of internal market law by public authorities, when they are not being handled judicially.[211] Its role is thus to contribute to better enforcement of EU law. The cases are handled informally by the centre of the home country (defined, *inter alia*, on the basis of nationality or residence of the person concerned) and by the lead centre, i.e. of the Member State where the alleged breach arose. Although SOLVIT is mainly a horizontal mechanism, the Commission plays a central role, *inter alia*, by managing and monitoring the database, providing case-handling assistance and, potentially, intervening if it considers that the solution proposed does not comply with EU law.[212]

6. The Member States' administration: Framed autonomy

The sections above have characterized the "in between" structures – comitology committees, agencies and networks – that currently populate what some have called a "European administrative space".[213] They have emerged largely at the margin of the Treaties, showing how political expediency may stretch the limits of what would prima facie be legally permissible and consolidate practices than may eventually be legally acknowledged in the future. The half-hearted way

208. Available at <ec.europa.eu/growth/sectors/cosmetics/market-surveillance/index_en.htm>. The platform is registered as in the Commission register of expert groups, available at <ec.europa.eu/transparency/regexpert/index.cfm?do=groupDetail.groupDetail&groupID=1465>.

209. Art. 29(1) and (2) of Reg. (EC) 1223/2009 of the European Parliament and of the Council of 30 Nov. 2009 on cosmetic products (O.J. 2009, L 342/59).

210. Recital 3 of Commission Recommendation 2013/461/EU of 17 Sept. 2013 on the principles governing SOLVIT Text with EEA relevance (O.J. 2013, L 249/10). It was created by Commission Recommendation of 7 Dec. 2001 on principles for using SOLVIT, (O.J. 2011, L 331/79).

211. Point II of Commission Recommendation 2013/461/EU, cited *supra* note 210.

212. Recital 4 and Point VI of Commission Recommendation 2013/461/EU, cited *supra* note 210. For an analysis of the advantages and problems that SOLVIT poses, see M. Lottini, "La rete SOLVIT: uno strumento di risoluzione delle controversie transfrontaliere", (2006) *Rivista italiana di diritto pubblico comunitario*, 1089–1106, D-U. Galletta, "Informal information processing in dispute resolution networks: Informality versus the protection of individual's rights?", 20 *European Public Law* (2014), at 73–77.

213. The term "European administrative space" has been used, among others, by J. Olsen as "convergence on a common European model" (J. Olsen, "Towards a European administrative space?", 10 *Journal of European Public Policy* (2003)), by H. Hofmann as a "space in which European, national and sub-national administrations and interested parties act together in agenda setting, rule-making and implementation" (H. Hofmann, "Mapping the European administrative space", 31 *West European Politics* (2008), 662–676), and by J. Trondal and G. Peters as "an emergent common administrative order in Europe through the development of new institutional constellations and configurations" (J. Trondal and B. G. Peters, "The rise of European administrative space: Lessons learned", 20 *Journal of European Public Policy* (2013), 295–307).

in which the Lisbon Treaty has recognized the existence of agencies illustrates this dynamic of administrative integration.

Yet, notwithstanding the importance of the various more or less institutionalized ways in which national administrations are entangled under EU law, vertical separation of norm production and norm implementation – and, as a result, decentralization of the latter – remains, formally, the core organizational principle. According to the Treaty, implementation of EU law is indubitably a competence of the Member States.[214] But in an integrated legal system, the implementing competences of national administrations are framed and constrained by EU law, as will be explained next.

6.1 *Institutional and procedural autonomy*

In implementing EU law, Member States retain institutional and procedural autonomy. Even if they are bound by a duty of loyal cooperation, it is for the Member States to "determine which institutions within [their] national system" will have the competence to adopt the substantive measures needed to comply with their obligations under the Treaty.[215] How "specific national bodies" exercise those competences is "solely a matter for the constitutional system of each state".[216] This principle applies to the implementation of EU law via legislative means (notably, the transposition of directives),[217] via judicial procedures, as well as to administrative implementation.

Nevertheless, the extent of Member States' institutional and procedural autonomy may be considerably limited. First, the principle applies "insofar as [EU law], including its general principles, does not include common rules [regarding implementation]".[218] Secondly, institutional and procedural autonomy are subject to requirements of effectiveness and equivalence.[219] On the first point, it would likely be difficult to find instances where EU legislative acts do not spell out in some detail the duties of Member States when giving effect to EU law. The extent to which they do will expand or reduce national administrative autonomy. One example among many is the Water Framework Directive, which determines that Member States need to adopt river basin management plans (the main legal instrument though which the goals of the Directive are to be attained), specifies in considerable detail the information that they ought to include as well as important procedural rules for their adoption (concerning access to information and

---

214. Arts. 291(1) and 197(1) TFEU (insofar as it refers to "effective implementation by Member States").
215. Judgment in Joined Cases 51, 54/71, *International Fruit Company NV and others v. Produktschap voor groenten en fruit*, para 3.
216. Idem., para 4. Grounding such principle on the need to preserve the sovereignty of Member States, see R. Mehdi, "Le principe d'autonomie institutionelle et procédurale et le droit administratif" in J.B. Auby and J. Dutheil de la Rochère, op. cit. *supra* note 1, 887–936, at 888.
217. But see, R. Mehdi, op. cit. *supra* note 216, 904–910, on the impact of EU integration on the relative position of the French parliament and the executive, and 910–914, on the pressure that the duties of implementation of EU law (and in particular, the transposition of directives) place on national structures.
218. Judgment in Joined Cases 205 to 215/82, *Deutsche Milchkontor GmbH and others v. Germany*, paras. 17 and 20.
219. Judgment in Case 39/70, *Norddeutsches Vieh- und Fleischkontor GmbH v. Hauptzollamt Hamburg-St. Annen*, (procedure regarding the application of special import terms for frozen meats for processing) and Judgment in Case 94/71, *Schlüter & Maack v. Haupzollamt Hamburg-Jonas*, paras. 10 and 11 (procedure regarding export refunds on products subject to the same price system, in the realm of the common organization of the market in sugar). Judgment in Joined Cases 205 to 215/82, *Deutsche Milchkontor GmbH and others v. Germany*, paras. 17 and 21–24.

participation).[220] Frequently, in addition, sectorial legislation contains provisions that directly or indirectly affect the organic structures of Member States.[221]

The requirements of effectiveness and equivalence constitute a second important limit to national procedural autonomy. They determine that national rules deployed for the implementation of EU law must not be "less favourable than those governing similar domestic situations (principle of equivalence) or render impossible in practice or excessively difficult the exercise of rights conferred by [EU] law (principle of effectiveness)".[222] Thus, Member States must apply national procedures and substantive law in a way that is not discriminatory when compared to national situations. In addition, the application of national law must not affect the effectiveness of EU law. Both requirements have been initially formulated and abundantly applied to judicial procedures, but they equally govern the use of administrative procedures.[223] Depending on how the EU Courts apply both requirements, administrative procedural autonomy may, in fact, become quite restricted, even where the absence of specific EU rules would seem to suggest that national procedural rules would remain unaffected.[224]

6.2 *Direct administrative effect*

As results from the above, both national law and EU law apply in instances where national administrations implement EU law. That EU law frames the competences of national administrations is also an effect of the direct applicability of EU law.[225] But there are further consequences of such direct applicability, in particular in cases in which national administrations may be faced with national laws that contradict EU law. What happens when EU law and national law collide? In the case of *Costanzo*, the Court considered that also administrative authorities are bound to apply provisions of a directive that, being unconditional and sufficiently precise, have direct effect and, as a result, set aside conflicting national provisions.[226] Specifically, "when the conditions under which the Court has held that individuals may rely on the provisions of a directive before the national courts are met, *all organs of the administration, including decentralized authorities such as municipalities*, are obliged to apply those provisions".[227] If it is not possible to interpret the national norm in a way that makes it consistent with EU law, both national administrative bodies and courts need to apply EU law and protect the rights that it confers on individuals,

---

220. Arts. 13 and 14(1) of Directive 2000/60/EC of the European Parliament and of the Council of 23 Oct. 2000 establishing a framework for Community action in the field of water policy (O.J. 2000, L 327/1).
221. E.g. the creation of single contact points imposed by Directive 2006/123/EC of the European Parliament and of the Council of 12 Dec. 2006 on services in the internal market (O.J. 2006, L 376/36).
222. E.g. Judgment in Case C-1/06, *Bonn Fleisch Ex- und Import GmbH v. Hauptzollamt Hamburg-Jonas*, para 41.
223. Judgment in Joined Cases C-608/10, C-10/11 and C-23/11, *Südzucker and Others v. Hauptzollamt Hamburg-Jonas*, para 62; Judgment in Case C-201/02, *Wells*, para 67. For a critical assessment of the requirements of equivalence and effectiveness in the case law of the Court regarding judicial procedural autonomy, see M. Bobek, "Why there is no principle of "procedural autonomy" of the Member States" in B. de Witte and H. Micklitz (Eds.), *The European Court of Justice and the Autonomy of the Member States* (Intersentia, 2010). See also D.U. Galetta, *L'autonomia Procedurale Degli Stati Membri dell'Unione Europea: "Paradise Lost"*? (Giapichelli, 2009).
224. For an account of the constraints that national competition authorities face in the implementation of competition law in view of the "effective and uniform" application of EU competition law, see S.B. Volcker, "Ignorantia legis non excusat and the demise of national procedural autonomy in the application of the EU competition rules: Schenker", 51 CML Rev. (2014), 1497–1519, at 1515–1519.
225. J. Ziller, op. cit. *supra* note 12, at 328 and 333.
226. Judgment in Case 103/88, *Fratelli Costanzo SpA c. Comune di Milano*, para 30.
227. Judgment in Case 103/88, *Fratelli Costanzo SpA c. Comune di Milano*, para 31. See also Judgment in C-297/03, *Sozialhilfeverband Rohrbach*, para 27; Judgment in Case C-6/05, *Medipac-Kazantzidis AE v. Venizeleio-Pananeio (PE.S.Y. KRITIS)*, para 43.

"disapplying, if necessary, any contrary provision of national law".[228] In this way, EU law also intrudes into the administrative organization of Member States, imposing obligations directly on its organs and decentralized authorities.

6.3 *Transnational effects of national administrative acts*

In an integrated market, the legal acts of Member States – including those of their administrations – are bound to produce legal effects beyond their borders. In EU law this is very much the case as a result of the principle of mutual recognition, according to which every product that is legally produced and traded within a Member State must also be freely marketed in the other Member States, except if considerations of public interest would justify otherwise.[229] It is thus by force of EU law – and irrespective of the will of the States involved – that administrative acts have cross-border effects.[230]

The obligation to recognize the legal effects of acts adopted by the administrative bodies of other Member States may result directly from EU legislation, which often gives competence to one of the Member States to adopt acts that automatically produce effects throughout the territory of the EU. Thus, the decision of a Member State to attribute a Schengen visa allows the person concerned to circulate in the whole Schengen area.[231] Frequently, EU legislation defines a procedure for the adoption of national administrative acts that involves the other Member States and the Commission. For instance, the determination of whether a given product is a novel food may involve consultation among the different Member States and the Commission.[232] EU legislation may also allow the Commission to extend the legal effects of a national administrative act,[233] or national administrations to conduct inspections in the territory of other Member States.

7. Commission and Council (administrative functions)

As part of the EU executive, both the Commission and the Council exercise functions of an administrative nature, i.e., in a broad sense, those that entail policy-making and discretion in the definition and implementation of strategies by various means in view of the pursuance of predefined public interests, as well as the setting up of the organic structures and the mobilization of resources ancillary to these functions.[234] This notion does not apply to the whole European Union, contrary to what its quick reading in light of the principle of attributed competences

---

228. Judgment in Case 103/88, *Fratelli Costanzo SpA v. Comune di Milano*, para 33. See also Case C-208/05, *ITC*, para 68 and 69; Judgment in C-429/09, *Günter Fuß v. Stadt Halle*, para 40; Judgment in C-239/09, *Seydal and Vereinigte Agrarbetriebe GmbH & Co.*, para 52. See, further, M. Verhoeven, *The Costanzo Obligation. The Obligations of National Administrative Authorities in the Case of Incompatibility between National Law and European Law* (Intersentia, 2011).
229. Case 8/74, *Dassonville*, and Case 120/78, *Rewe Central AG v. Bundesmonopolverwaltung für Branntwein.*
230. See M. Gautier, "Acte administratif transnational et droit de l'Union Europeén" in J.B. Auby and J. Dutheil de la Rochère, op. cit. *supra* note 1, 1303–1315, at 1308–1310.
231. Arts. 5 and 23 of Reg. (EC) 810/2009 of the European Parliament and of the Council of 13 July 2009 establishing a Community Code on Visa (O.J. 2009, L 243/1). The decision may be subject to prior consultation of the authorities of other Member States (Art. 22).
232. Art. 4 of Reg. (EU) 2015/2283 of the European Parliament and of the Council of 25 Nov. 2015 on novel foods (O.J. 2015, L 327/1).
233. Art. 12 of Reg. (EC) 258/97, cited *supra* note 229, does not explicitly envisage this possibility, but it appears to fall within the scope of the powers of the Commission under the regulation (available at <ec.europa.eu/food/food/biotechnology/novelfood/index_en.htm>).
234. On the broader institutional role of the Commission and the Council, see Ch. 5, "The political institutions", of this book.

could convey.[235] While the EU is confined to the competences attributed by the Treaty, those competences are carried out in an institutionally, procedurally and functionally differentiated way, as defined in various Treaty provisions.[236] The distinction between executive and administrative functions is often drawn along the political/administrative divide, even when the complementarity between the two is acknowledged.[237] The distinction may have explanatory value, but the many grey zones and circular influences between what may be considered "directing" and what would fall under "implementing" often question its analytical purchase.[238]

As mentioned above, since the outset of the European integration process, the Commission has exercised functions that, with hindsight, one could consider to be of administrative nature.[239] These are better captured in the current Treaty description of the Commission's role. In addition to ensuring "the application of the Treaties, and of the measures adopted by the institutions pursuant to that end", Article 17(1) TEU specifies that the Commission executes the budget, manages programmes, exercises coordinating, executive and management functions, and ensures the Union external representation (unless otherwise provided in the Treaties and with the exception of the common foreign and security policy). As was seen above, the Commission carries out some of these functions, namely, the exercise of coordinating, executive and management functions, with the involvement of EU agencies, comitology committees and networks.

The various functions of the Commission are distributed per policy area and are attributed, accordingly, to different Directorates-General (DGs). Policy fragmentation also means that the DGs have different functions. In fact, the different competences of the EU per policy area result in different powers attributed to the Commission by sector EU legislation. As a result, considering their predominant functions, it is possible to distinguish DGs that are mainly concerned with regulation and enforcement of EU law including vis-à-vis private persons – this is the case of competition, agriculture, fisheries, internal market, health and consumer protection, economic and financial affairs, taxation and customs union – from those DGs that are mainly tasked with preparing legislative initiatives or conducting infringement procedures against Member States.[240] Yet, core issues that the Commission needs to address cut across the policy areas attributed to each DG, requiring internal coordination between services.[241] Thus, for example, the implementation of the European Semester involves all the DGs.

The Commission's complex internal bureaucratic structure is, nevertheless, too thin to support the manifold functions and areas of action of the Commission. The Commission is

235. For an elaboration of the EU as administrative, see P. Lindseth, *Power and Legitimacy: Reconciling Europe and the Nation-State* (OUP, 2011).
236. Namely in Title III of the Treaty on European Union, but also in Arts. 289 to 291 TFEU.
237. D. Curtin, op. cit. *supra* note 1, at 38–40.
238. The discussion is relevant for legal purposes (see Arts. 15(3) TFEU and 298(1) TFEU).
239. Historically, the unique functions of the Commission that made it "the motor of integration" are its formally exclusive power of legislative initiation and the power to bring infringement procedures as "guardian of the Treaties" – see R. Dehousse, "The "Community Method" at Sixty" in R. Dehousse (Ed.), *The "Community Method" Obstinate or Obsolete?* (Palgrave Macmillan, 2011).
240. The observation is made by H. Kassim et al., *The European Commission of the Twenty-First Century*, (OUP, 2013), at 24, who place in the second group the DGs dealing with employment, environment, justice and home affairs, transport, and energy.
241. H. Kassim, op. cit. *supra* note 240, at 82. Internal coordination is crucial to ensure compliance with the principle of collegiality (idem, 183–187, 205), even if the complex internal organization of the Commission and the sheer breadth of its tasks has required expedited procedures of decision-making, other than only collective deliberation in the College of Commissioners (Rules of Procedure of the Commission, C(2000) 3614, O.J. 2000, L 308/26).

therefore dependent on the knowledge of experts and national officials, but also of private actors, associations, NGOs, who are external to its organization. The heavy reliance on external expertise – outside comitology committees and agencies – transforms the DGs into "strategic nodes in political-administrative networks" involving various natural and legal persons.[242] It also raises important issues of transparency and impartiality of the working of the Commission.

By contrast to the Commission, the way the Treaty of Lisbon generally describes the role of the Council would seem to indicate that this institution would not have functions that could be considered "administrative".[243] The fact that the Council has no longer the primary competence for implementing EU legal acts would reinforce this first impression. In fact, under the Lisbon Treaty, only in duly justified cases and in the area of common security and foreign policy will the Council have the competence to adopt implementing acts.[244] However, one can only start perceiving the variety of functions that the Council exercises by examining the provisions of the Treaty that attribute specific competences to the Council, and, more deeply, by discerning what may effectively be involved in the deployment of those functions.[245] As will become clear from the examples given below, the competence to adopt implementing acts does not exhaust the range of administrative functions that the Council may perform. These functions may not presuppose a basic legislative act that requires implementation.

Thus, the Council defines the conditions under which certain funds will operate and may also be involved in the management of funds falling within the realm of its external action;[246] decides on the allocation of fishing opportunities;[247] defines and suspends the Common Customs Tariff duties that apply to the import of goods into the EU (varying according to product and provenience);[248] determines the psychoactive substances that are subjected to control measures across the Union;[249] adopts restrictive measures against natural or legal persons and groups or non-State entities;[250] decides and oversees whether Member States have excessive deficits in

242. D. Spence, *The European Commission* (Harper, 2006), at 129.

243. Art. 16 TEU provides "The Council shall, jointly with the European Parliament, exercise legislative and budgetary functions. It shall carry out policy-making and coordinating functions as laid down in the Treaties".

244. Art. 291(2) TFEU (the power of the Council under former Art. 202 ECT was considerably different – see J. Jacqué, op. cit. *supra* note 8, at 106–107).

245. On the first point, see J. Jacqué, op. cit. *supra* note 8, at 105–106 (referring to Art. 202 ECT).

246. Arts. 14(3) third paragraph, 15(b)–(d)–(e) and 18 of Council Reg. (EU) 2015/322 of 2 Mar. 2015 on the implementation of the 11th European Development Fund (O.J. 2015, L 58/1). It should be noticed that Commission has the main implementing tasks under this regulation.

247. Art. 43(3) TFEU. See, e.g., Council Reg. (EU) 2015/104 of 19 Jan. 2015 fixing for 2015 the fishing opportunities for certain fish stocks and groups of fish stocks, applicable in Union waters and, for Union vessels, in certain non-Union waters, amending Reg. (EU) 43/2014 and repealing Reg. (EU) 779/2014 (O.J. 2015, L 22/1).

248. Art. 31 TFEU. See, e.g., Council Reg. (EU) 1387/2013 of 17 Dec. 2013 suspending the autonomous Common Customs Tariff duties on certain agricultural and industrial products and repealing Reg. (EU) 1344/2011 (O.J. 2013, L 354/201).

249. Council Implementing Decision 2014/688/EU of 25 Sept. 2014 on subjecting 4-iodo-2,5-dimethoxy-N-(2-methoxybenzyl)phenethylamine (25I-NBOMe), 3,4-dichloro-N-[[1 (dimethylamino) cyclohexyl]methyl]benzamide (AH-7921), 3,4-methylenedioxypyrovalerone (MDPV) and 2-(3-methoxyphenyl)-2-(ethylamino)cyclohexanone (methoxetamine) to control measures (O.J. 2014, L 287/22).

250. Art. 215 TFEU. See, e.g., Council Reg. (EU) 833/2014 of 31 July 2014 concerning restrictive measures in view of Russia's actions destabilizing the situation in Ukraine (O.J. 2014, L 229, at 1).

breach of the budgetary limits defined under the Stability and Growth Pact;[251] decides who are independent external auditors entitled to audit the accounts of the European Central Bank and of the national central banks of the Eurosystem;[252] adopts specific measures defining the conditions of application of the Treaties to the outermost regions of the EU;[253] decides and adopts implementing measures with regard to the system of own resources of the Union;[254] decides on the rate of contribution to the pension scheme of EU officials.[255] Importantly, the Council also defines the position to be adopted on behalf of the EU in administrative bodies set up by an international agreement of which the EU is a party. Prima facie, these decisions would seem to fall purely in the realm of the EU international relations. Yet, they ultimately lead to the adoption of decisions by those bodies that will produce legal effects in the EU legal order similar to administrative decisions of the Commission.[256] They define, for example, the chemicals that should be banned or severely restricted for health or environmental reasons.[257]

In addition, while the Council only has implementing powers in exceptional cases, these are far from being trivial powers. Via its implementing powers the Council establishes and amends the list of person and entities suspected of terrorist association whose funds, financial assets and economic resources will be frozen;[258] makes some of the provisions of the Schengen acquis operational with regard to the United Kingdom;[259] authorizes derogations of certain EU law

---

251. Art. 126(6) TFEU. See, e.g., Council Decision 2014/404/EU of 20 June 2014 abrogating Decision 2010/282/EU on the existence of an excessive deficit in Austria (O.J. 2014, L 190, at 66).
252. Council Decision 1999/70/EC of 25 Jan. 1999, concerning the external auditors of the national central banks (O.J. 1999, L 22/69), last amended in 2014.
253. Art. 349 TFEU. Some of these measures may be adopted under the special legislative procedure defined in this Treaty article. Even where that is the case, one may argue that some of these measures have an administrative character, where, e.g., they define specific conditions applicable to a closed category of products [see Council Decision 376/2014/EU of 12 June 2014 authorizing Portugal to apply a reduced rate of excise duty in the autonomous region of Madeira on locally produced and consumed rum and liqueurs and in the autonomous region of the Azores on locally produced and consumed liqueurs and eaux-de-vie (O.J. 2014, L 182).
254. Council Reg. (EU, Euratom), 608/2014 of 26 May 2014 laying down implementing measures for the system of own resources of the European Union (O.J. 2014, L 168/29).
255. Council Reg. (EU) 1201/2014 of 7 Nov. 2014 adjusting, with effect from 1 July 2011, 1 July 2012 and 1 July 2013, the rate of contribution to the pension scheme of officials and other servants of the European Union (O.J. 2014, L 325, at 1).
256. On the impact of decisions of international bodies in EU administrative procedure, see J. Mendes, "EU law and global regulatory regimes: Hollowing out procedural standards?", (2012) *International Journal of Constitutional Law*, 988–1022.
257. See, e.g., Council Decision (EU) 2015/423 of 6 Mar. 2015 establishing the position to be adopted on behalf of the European Union within the seventh meeting of the Conference of the Parties to the Rotterdam Convention as regards the amendments of Annex III to the Rotterdam Convention on the Prior Informed Consent Procedure for certain hazardous chemicals and pesticides in international trade (O.J. 2015, L 68/48). Council Decision 2014/832/EU, of 7 Nov. 2014, establishing the position to be adopted on behalf of the European Union in the Administrative Committee of the United Nations Economic Commission for Europe on the draft new Regulation on hydrogen and fuel cell vehicles (O.J. 2014, L 341/15).
258. E.g., Council Implementing Regulation (EU) 2015/513 of 26 Mar. 2015 implementing Art. 2(3) of Regulation (EC) 2580/2001 on specific restrictive measures directed against certain persons and entities with a view to combating terrorism and repealing Implementing Reg. (EU) 790/2014 (O.J. 2015, L 82/1).
259. Council Implementing Decision (EU) 2015/215 of 10 Febr. 2015 on the putting into effect of the provisions of the Schengen acquis on data protection and on the provisional putting into effect of parts of the provisions of the Schengen acquis on the Schengen Information System for the United Kingdom of Great Britain and Northern Ireland (O.J. 2015, L 36/8).

provisions to specific Member States.[260] It was also via this means that the Council approved the macroeconomic adjustment programme for Cyprus and Greece.[261]

Another aspect worth highlighting is that the Council's function of policy coordination has not only led to the attribution of important powers to the Council under the economic governance structure put in place to respond to the Eurocrisis, but also to the creation of new administrative structures that support the work of the Council. Committees such as the Eurogroup Working Group and the Economic and Financial Committee – composed of senior representatives of the administrations of the Member States and of the Commission – ensure the coordination between Member States' administrations and between them and the Commission. They have a core role in supporting both policy initiation and implementation.

8. Integrated or composite administration: Legal issues

In a model of executive federalism, the administrative implementation of EU law is a task of national administrations (indirect administration). When giving effect to EU law, their powers are framed by EU law and are subject to the jurisdiction of national courts and of the Court of Justice, via infringement procedures and preliminary rulings, as well as to the control of national ombudsmen. In the specific cases determined by the Treaty, the EU institutions (as a rule, the Commission) have direct powers of implementation subject to the jurisdiction of the Court of Justice and the control of the EU Ombudsman (direct administration).[262]

The validity of this distinction has been extensively discussed in the legal literature.[263] Wherever one may stand in the discussion, it is important to retain two aspects. First, as pointed out above, the distinction remains a structural legal feature of the EU administration; it also has both budgetary and jurisdictional implications.[264] Second, in reality one is hard pressed to find instances of decision-making that do not involve both national administrative entities and EU institutions or bodies in various combinations and with various powers.[265] To express this reality, different authors have used different terms. Composite administration and integrated administration are the terms that seem to have become more widespread in English written literature.[266] Composite administration stresses a "network" structure that combines elements of cooperation and hierarchy, where the generation and management of

260. E.g. Council Implementing Decision 2014/796/EU, of 7 Nov. 2014, authorizing the Republic of Latvia to apply a measure derogating from Art. 287 of Directive 2006/112/EC on the common system of value added tax (O.J. 2014, L 330/46); Council Implementing Decision 2014/695/EU of 29 Sept. 2014 authorizing Italy to apply, in determined geographical areas, reduced rates of taxation on gas oil and LPG used for heating purposes in accordance with Art. 19 of Directive 2003/96/EC (O.J. 2014, L 291/16).

261. Council Implementing Decision 2013/463/EU, of 13 Sept. 2013, on approving the macroeconomic adjustment programme for Cyprus (O.J. 2013, L 250/40); Council Implementing Decision (EU) 2015/1411, of 19 Aug. 2015, approving the macroeconomic adjustment programme of Greece (O.J. 2015, L 219/12).

262. See, *inter alia*, J. Ziller, op. cit. *supra* note 12.

263. In addition to the reference in the footnote above, see works cited *supra* notes 6 and 20.

264. J. Ziller, op. cit. *supra* note 12.

265. For examples, see, *inter alia*, the contributions in O. Jansen and B. Schoendorf-Haubold (Eds.), *The European Composite Administration* (Intersentia, 2011). See also S. Cassese, "European administrative proceedings", 68 *Law and Contemporary Problems* (2004), 21–36.

266. Other terms may be co-administration, decentred integration, decentralized administration, network governance (more common in political science literature), "European administrative space" (used in public administration studies). On composite administration in international law, see A. von Bogdandy and P. Dann, "International composite administration: Conceptualizing multi-level and network aspects in the exercise of international public authority" in A. von Bogdandy et al. (Eds.), *The Exercise of Public Authority by International Institutions. Advancing International Institutional Law* (Springer, (2010), 883–912.

information, decision-making and control of implementation depend on both national and EU bodies.[267] Integrated administration emphasizes that the EU administration is anchored in "multilevel cooperative governance structures" that involve institutionally independent bodies and, not being limited to implementation, cover also agenda-setting and policy-making.[268]

8.1 *Composite procedures, procedural rights and judicial review*

Instances of decision-making that involve national administrative entities and EU institutions and bodies result in composite decision-making procedures. They encompass one or more intertwined sub-procedures and intermediary acts of both national and EU administrative bodies, which are instrumental in the adoption of the final decision.[269] Their concrete design – that is, the allocation of powers between various national and EU administrative bodies, vertically, horizontally in each level and diagonally, often in polycentric schemes – depends on each legal regime. The scheme will be tailored according to the structural specificities of the policy area (including those specified in the legal bases) and to the regulatory needs of each sector. For this reason, composite procedures tend to escape taxonomies.[270] They are both a cause and an effect of the evolutionary nature of the EU administration.[271]

Composite procedures are one expression of the tension between separation and integration that characterize the EU administration.[272] Formally, the authors of final legal acts are indicated in sectoral legal regimes, which thus make it possible to allocate formal legal responsibility for the acts adopted, either at the national or at the EU level. Yet, depending on the legal rules and practice, instrumental and intermediate procedural acts adopted during the procedure by entities situated at different levels of governance may, in fact, determine the content of the final decision, in a way that may hinder both effective procedural and judicial protection of those affected.[273] There may be a mismatch between, on the one hand, the formal attribution of decision-making to national or EU institutions and bodies, each following their own rules of administrative procedure and controlled by different jurisdictions (even if linked via preliminary reference procedures); and, on the other hand, the reality of administrative cooperation and intertwined decision-making, where it might be difficult to identify the material author (or authors) of the final act.

---

267. E. Schmidt-Assmann, op. cit. *supra* note 19, at 6–8, and 22. See also G. della Cananea, "La questione della comitologia", (1990) *Rivista trimestrale di diritto pubblico,* at 691 and 700, mentioning "amministrazioni composte".
268. H. Hofmann and A. Türk, "Conclusions – Europe's Integrated Administration" in H. Hofmann and A Türk (Eds.), *EU Administrative Governance* (Edward Elgar, 2006), 573–596, at 580–584.
269. See G. della Cananea, "The European Union's mixed administrative proceedings", 68 *Law and Contemporary Problems* (2004), 197–217; H. Hofmann, "Composite decision making procedures in EU administrative law" in H. Hofmann and A. Türk, op. cit. *supra* note 3, 168–176, who considers that cooperation in generating and managing information is the substance of these procedures.
270. See, however, G. della Cananea, op. cit. note *supra* 269, at 199–205, who suggests a grid of top-down procedures (in which the final act is adopted by national administrations), bottom-up procedures (leading to a final act of an EU institution or body), and hybrid procedures (that combine the first two types).
271. H. Hofmann and A. Türk characterize the EU's integrated administration as heterarchical, evolutionary and fragmented, op. cit. *supra* note 267, at 583–584. On the evolutionary character of the EU administration, see also C. Franchini, op. cit. *supra* note 6, at 3338.
272. On separation and cooperation as essential elements of EU law implementation, E. Schmidt-Assmann, op. cit. *supra* note 19, at 1.
273. For a distinction of different types of intermediary or instrumental acts, see Judgment in Case 60/81, *IBM v. Commission*, para 9.

The separation of jurisdictions in composite decision-making procedures poses challenges both to procedural protection and to judicial review, possibly leading to gaps.[274] Thus, composite procedures may hinder the possibility to exercise the right to be heard before the deciding bodies that effectively determine the content of the decision.[275] Nevertheless, the case law of the EU Courts shows a concern for effective compliance with the right to be heard, beyond the way in which the EU legislation formally splits the procedure between the national and the EU institutions.[276] If by force of EU law, a natural or legal person only establishes a direct relation with national administrative authorities, this does not mean that the right to be heard should not also be respected in the stage of the procedure that takes place before the Commission, where the content of the Commission's decision so requires.[277] Thus, for example, in a case involving the payment of agricultural levies, the Court has held that the right to be heard ought to be guaranteed both at the national and EU stages of the procedure; in this instance the Commission's discretion in adopting a decision required that also the Commission would comply with the right to be heard.[278]

The challenges that composite procedures entail to effective judicial review seem to be more intractable.[279] *Borelli* illustrates the problems that may arise in cases where the Commission has limited or no discretion and decides on the basis of a national decision.[280] The case concerns the granting of funding that was decided by the Commission, but depended on a favourable decision of the Member States' authorities on whether the requests for funding is justified. The Commission had no discretion on the matter, thus a negative decision of the Member State authorities led to a Commission decision refusing the granting of aid. Borelli challenged the Commission's decision before the Court of Justice alleging the unlawfulness of the decision of the Region of Liguria under EU law. Under Italian law this decision was not reviewable, because it was a preparatory measure. The Court upheld the Commission's decision, because it lacked jurisdiction to review the legality of a national measure even if it formed part of a Community decision-making procedure and the national measure was binding on the Commission.[281] Given the way the decision-making procedure was split "any irregularity that [could] affect the opinion [could not] affect the validity of the decision by which the Commission refused the aid applied for".[282] The conundrum was to be solved by national courts: even if the domestic rules of jurisdiction did not provide for review of the legality of the national measure, the national court

274. For a compelling argument on the essential (possibly, foundational) character of collaboration in the EU administration, and speaking of "common administrative systems", see S. Cassese, op. cit. *supra* note 265, at 22.
275. J. Mendes, *Participation in EU Rule-Making: A Rights-Based Approach* (OUP, 2011), at 159–160.
276. Judgment of 9 Nov. 1995, in Case T-346/94, *France-Aviation v. Commission*, para 36 (holding that the Commission had "a duty to arrange for the applicant to be heard by the French authorities"); Judgment of 19 Febr. 1998 in Case T-42/96, *Eyckeler & Malt AG v. Commission*, para 84 to 88; Judgment of 6 Dec. 1994 in Case T-450/93, *Lisrestal—Organizac¸a˜o Gesta˜o de Restaurantes Colectivos Ldª and others v. Commission*, para 48, and Judgment in Case C-32/95 P, *Commission v. Lisrestal*, paras. 28 and 33. For an analysis of these cases, see, *inter alia*, J. Mendes, op. cit. *supra* note 275, at 177–183.
277. See, to this effect, Case T-42/96, *Eykeler & Malt*, paras. 84–88; Judgment in Case T-50/96, *Primex Produkte Import-Export GmbH & Co and others v. Commission*, paras. 67–71.
278. Judgment in Case T-290/97, *Mehibas Dordtselaan BV v. Commission*, para 45 and 46.
279. See L. Azoulai, op. cit. *supra* note 4, at 15.
280. Judgment in Case C-97/91, *Oleificio Borelli SpA v. Commission*.
281. Case C-97/91, *Oleificio Borelli SpA v. Commission*, paras. 9 and 10.
282. Case C-97/91, *Oleificio Borelli SpA v. Commission*, paras.11 and 12.

should review this intermediary act as if it were a final act.[283] This rule seems to apply only in instances where the EU institutions have a "limited or non-existent discretion" in the adoption of a measure that depends on a prior national act.[284]

The judgment was heavily criticized on the grounds that, in effect, it left the applicant without judicial protection, given the lack of remedies in Italian law for preparatory acts.[285] In addition, the Court compelled Member States to change their system of remedies, while itself excluding preparatory measures from the concept of reviewable act.[286] *Borelli* illustrates the problems that may arise from the tension between integration and separation in EU composite procedures: the EU and the Member States authorities implement EU law jointly, but judicial protection relies on a jurisdictional division between national and EU courts that preliminary reference procedures do not bridge. The problem is not limited to actions of annulment. Also in liability actions, the division means that Member States, EU institutions and bodies are responsible for the damages that they may have separately caused before different jurisdictions.[287]

8.2 *Transparency, accountability and efficiency*

The proliferation of centres of decision in the EU administrative space characterized by structural and functional interdependencies poses challenges not only to judicial control of administrative action, but to other forms of accountability, to transparency and efficiency. The intertwinement between the EU institutions, national and EU bodies composed of national and EU public officials and private parties (in various combinations) indicates that the transparency, accountability and efficiency of the various arrangements cannot rely only on the rules governing each of these bodies, and, possibly, also not on the rules governing each decision-making process.

Few rules are applicable across sectors, and the sectoral rules may rapidly gain new contours. The identification of who decides on what may not be clear-cut, even after an expert reading of the schemes defined in EU legislation. Lack of transparency, in this broad sense, may hinder effective accountability mechanisms. It may lead to gaps, but also to misplaced and partially overlapping modes of accountability. Whichever modes of accountability are put in place to render accountable the various entities and bodies who collaborate in the implementation of EU law, they need to be suitable to the specific structural characteristics of the EU administration.[288] In

283. Case C-97/91, *Oleificio Borelli SpA v. Commission*, paras. 13–15. See also Judgment in Case C-269/99, *Carl Kühne and others v. Jütro Konservenfabrik*, C-269/99, paras. 52–53, and 58, and Judgment in Case C-343/07, *Bavaria NV and Bavaria Italia v. Bayerischer Brauerbund*, para 57.
284. Judgment in Case C-269/99, *Carl Kühne and others v. Jütro Konservenfabrik*, para 57; see also Judgment in Case C-343/07, *Bavaria NV and Bavaria Italia v. Bayerischer Brauerbund*, paras. 65–67, 70.
285. L.F. Maseo Seco, "I procedimenti composti comunitari: riflessioni intorno alla problematica della impossibilità di difendersi ed eventuali alternative" in G. della Cananea and M. Gnes (Eds.), *I procedimenti amministrativi dell'Unione Europea. Un'indagine. Atti del convegno di Studio, Urbino, 14 Marzo 2003* (Giappichelli, 2004), 11–32, at 12 and 29.
286. H. Hofmann, op. cit. *supra* note 80, at 154. For an overview of the discussion and a different view on Case C-97/91, *Borelli*, see F. Brito Bastos, "The *Borelli* Doctrine Revisited: Three Issues of Coherence in a Landmark Ruling for EU Administrative Justice", 8 *Review of European Administrative Law* (2015), 269–298.
287. See further, C. Broyelle, "L'imputation de la responsabilité dans les situtaions d'exécution nationale du droit de l'Union" in J.B. Auby and J. Dutheil de la Rochère, op. cit. *supra* note 1, 1035–1044.
288. On this point, regarding the possibilities of parliamentary control of the EU integrated administration (in their analysis not limited to implementation). See H. Hofmann and A. Türk, op. cit. *supra* note 268, at 588.

this respect, the creation of accountability networks, which exist in an embryonic form, may be a propitious way forward.[289]

Efficiency of administrative action is also an issue.[290] The EU legislator – who is largely responsibly for the way decision-making procedures are structured – acknowledges its concern regarding the possible overlaps. Such concern may lead to a meta-level of coordination, implying additional time and resources. Thus, for example, there are various systems of notifications and alerts put in place to ensure the protection of public health. It is also the role of the Commission to ensure that these systems are linked to each other "so that the competent authorities of the Member States can avoid as much as possible notifying the same alert through different systems at Union level."[291]

8.3 *Procedures between fragmentation and codification*

As much as EU law has evolved according to the needs of EU integration, also the rules that govern its decision-making procedures have been tailored to the specific characteristics of each policy area. As mentioned, the combinations in which Member States, the Commission, the Council, EU agencies and a wide range of committees of officials, experts and private entities contribute to decision-making in the EU outside legislative procedures differ from each policy sector to the next. Common rules applicable horizontally apply to selected aspects of decision-making: access to documents (Reg. 1049/2001), comitology (Reg. 182/2011), and the rules of procedure of each institution. The Code of Good Administrative Behaviour of the EU Ombudsman has a broader scope: it applies to instances of maladministration. The risks and merits of this fragmentation are valued differently. Some scholars stress the disadvantages of excessive "juridification", which would provide a rights-based claim to already powerful corporations giving them direct access to court, and distort the administrative process by possibly fashioning them along the model of trial-type judicial procedures.[292] Others stress the advantages of shaping the administrative procedure not only according to judicially set principles but also in view of the specificity of the administrative process; of covering possible gaps in the procedural protection of individuals; of clarifying the content of the law and granting better easier access to the law; and the ability of general rules of procedure to concretize the constitutional rules that define the relationship between the EU institutions, bodies, offices and agencies, on the one hand, and the citizens, on the other.[293]

These two main approaches have been feeding the debate on a possible codification of the EU administrative procedure. It was intense in the mid-1990s, triggered by the first references

289. See C. Harlow and R. Rawlings, "Promoting accountability in multilevel governance: A network approach", 13 ELJ (2007), 542–562. In a similar fashion, though not using the term, H. Hofmann and A. Türk, op. cit. *supra* note 268, at 590.
290. See C. Franchini, op. cit. *supra* note 6, at 350.
291. Recital 16 of Decision 1082/2013/EU, cited *supra* note 89.
292. See, e.g., C. Harlow, "Codification of EC administrative procedures? Fitting the foot to the shoe or the shoe to the foot?", 2 ELJ (1996), 3–25; and C. Harlow and R. Rawlings, *Process and Procedure in the EU Administration*, (Hart, 2014), 331–335.
293. See, ReNEUAL Model Rules on EU Administrative Procedure, 2014, "Introduction to the ReNEUAL Model Rules – Book I: General Provisions" (available at <www.reneual.eu/publications/ReNEUAL%20Model%20Rules%202014/Book%20I%20%20general%20provision_2014-09-03%20individualized_final.pdf>); J. Ziller, "Is a law of administrative procedure for the Union institutions necessary? Introductory remarks and prospects", (2011) *EP Briefing Note PE 432.771*; O. Mir, "Arguments in favour of a general codification of the procedure applicable to EU administration", (2011) *EP Briefing Note PE 432.776*. On the argument of constitutional value of procedural rules regarding rulemaking, see D. Curtin, H. Hoffman and J. Mendes, "Constitutionalising EU executive rule-making procedures: A research agenda", 19 ELJ (2013), 1–21.

in the 1992 Treaty on European Union to citizenship, rule of law and the efficient and democratic functioning of the institutions.[294] The European Ombudsman – whose office was also established then – was particularly proactive in this regard.[295] The discussion then abated for a while, but the Lisbon Treaty provisions on the principles that ought to bind the functioning of the EU institutions, bodies, offices, and in particular Article 298 TFEU, revived the debate. On this ground, the Parliament asked the Commission to submit a proposal on an EU Law on the Administrative Procedure.[296] However, the Parliament's resolution was minimalist: it amounted to a restatement of the judicially established general principles of EU law (resembling the non-binding Code on Good Administrative Behaviour) and was restricted to single case decision-making. Arguably, such a limited future law on the administrative procedures of the European would have been too narrow. The initial work of the Parliament was resumed after the 2014 European elections and brought a significant innovation: this time the Parliament drafted the regulation that, in its view, the Commission should propose to the EU legislator.[297] As the explanatory memorandum of the Parliament's draft regulation indicates, the Parliament's proposal is more ambitious than its previous resolution. It translates principles and rights into rules that govern the administrative procedure in its various stages, from its initiation to its conclusion, including provisions on the rectification and withdrawal of acts. Its scope remains limited to "administrative activities", understood in a narrow sense, and thus excluding the adoption of delegated and implementing acts as well as non-legislative acts adopted directly on the basis of the Treaty.[298] Despite the fact that a large share of administrative activities remain outside this proposal,[299] the Parliament is, nevertheless, treading new ground, both in terms of the content of its proposal, and also, significantly, by going as far as drafting the regulation. It remains to be seen whether a sceptical Commission will adopt a legislative proposal on this matter.[300]

---

294. C. Harlow, op. cit. *supra* note 292.

295. Resolution A5-0245/2001, on the European Ombudsman's Special Report to the European Parliament on a Code of Good Administrative Behaviour (C5-0438/2000 – 2000/2212(COS), 6 September 2001 – See J. Mendes, "Good administration in the EU law and the European Code of Good Administrative Behaviour", (2009) *EUI Working Papers*.

296. European Parliament resolution of 15 Jan. 2013 with recommendations to the Commission on a Law of Administrative Procedure of the European Union (2012/2024(INI)). The Commission's reaction can be read here: "Follow up to the European Parliament resolution with recommendations to the Commission on a Law of Administrative Procedure of the European Union, adopted by the Commission on 24 Apr. 2013", available at <www.europarl.europa.eu/oeil/popups/ficheprocedure.do?lang=en&reference=2012/2024%28INL%29#tab-0>.

297. Proposal for a Regulation of the European Parliament and of the Council on the Administrative Procedure of the European Union's institutions, bodies, offices and agencies, discussed at the Hearing of the Committee on Legal Affairs (28 Jan. 2016,), available at <www.europarl.europa.eu/committees/en/juri/events.html;jsessionid=D97214D54ADC0B228E1A402456118936.node2?id=20160128CHE00181>; see also D.-U. Galetta et al., "The context and legal elements of a proposal for a regulation on the administrative procedure of the European Union's institutions, bodies, offices and agencies", *Study for the Juri Committee*, available on the same link.

298. See Arts. 2 and 26 of the Proposal cited.

299. Cf. ReNEUAL Model Rules on EU Administrative Procedure, Books II (rulemaking), IV (contracts), V (mutual assistance), VI (administrative information management), but also the much more detailed Book III on single case decision-making. For a critical assessment of the 2013 Resolution of the European Parliament, see J. Mendes, "The making of delegated and implementing acts" in C.F. Bergström and D. Ritleng (Eds.), *Rule-making by the European Commission: The New System* (OUP, 2015).

300. See the answer by Vice-President Timmermans to a written question by the Parliament at <www.europarl.europa.eu/sides/getAllAnswers.do?reference=E-2016-001249&language=EN>.

9. Conclusions

The Lisbon Treaty has acknowledged the existence of an EU administration. It referred for the first time to the bodies, offices and agencies that, in supporting the work of the EU institutions, often adopt acts capable of having external legal effects. In doing so, it only timidly lifted the veil of the under-world of collaborative structures that make the daily implementation of EU law possible. Comitology committees, agencies, networks are the most established structures of institutionalized collaboration, and also they (agencies and networks) are in flux, in a political system where expediency is a creative source of new forms of administrative action that often test the limits of what is legally admissible.

At the same time, the Treaty also appeared to solidify the vertical separation between norm-production – a centralized task of the institutions – and implementation – decentralized in the Member States – that, formally, had been a structural feature of the EU since the outset. However, given the ability of EU norms to affect national laws, integration via the production of common rules has significantly limited the autonomy of Member States in carrying out the implementation of EU law. Separation exists by force of the Treaty, and is embodied in a jurisdictional division between national and European courts, national and European ombudsmen. But this legal feature is at odds with the effective intertwinement between national administrations and EU institutions via composite procedures, and with the involvement in decision-making of various "in between" bodies composed of both national and EU officials (whose legal acts, to the extent that those bodies may formally enact them, are nonetheless EU acts, subject to the EU law). The complex links that have created a composite or integrated administration also challenge transparency, accountability and efficiency.

The constitutional principles of the Treaty that now explicitly apply also to the EU administration – equal treatment of citizens (Art. 9 TEU), transparency and democratic participation (Arts. 11 TEU and 15 TFEU), protection of personal data (Art. 16 TFEU) – have inspired a move one step further, namely to consider the possibility of a law on the EU administrative procedure – that could concretize EU constitutional principles and norms that should shape EU administrative action.

Further reading

Auby, J.-B., and J.D. de la Rochère (Eds.), *Traité de Droit Administratif Européen*, 2nd ed. (Bruylant, 2014).

Chiti, M. (Ed.), *Diritto amministrativo europeo* (Giuffrè Editore, 2013).

Craig, P., *EU Administrative Law*, 2nd ed. (OUP, 2012).

Harlow, C. and R. Rawlings, *Process and Procedure in the EU Administration* (Hart, 2014).

Hofmann, H., G. Rowe and A. Türk, *Administrative Law and Policy of the European Union* (OUP, 2011).

Conclusions

[illegible]

[illegible]

[illegible]

Further reading

[illegible]

CHAPTER 9
BUDGET AND FINANCES

*Jan Inghelram**

EU budget and finances do not often attract lawyers' attention. Legislation and case-law are indeed limited in this area, compared to other areas of EU activity. It is, however, an area of major political importance, which is confirmed, for instance, by the long and often difficult discussions, among the Member States themselves as well as between the EU institutions, preceding the adoption of each multi-annual financial framework, by which limits to EU revenue and expenditure are defined for a period of several years to come. It is also an area which has contributed in an important way to the EU institutional landscape as it exists now. The current powers of the European Parliament indeed cannot be understood without taking into account the development and exercise of its budgetary powers. Moreover, rules in relation to budget and finances do not only affect the internal functioning of the EU, but are capable of affecting individuals, in particular in the area of the protection of the financial interests of the EU and combating fraud.

At the Treaty level, budget and finances are essentially governed by the financial provisions of the TFEU (Arts. 310–325). These provisions cover budgetary matters, except for Article 325 TFEU which specifically deals with the protection of the financial interests of the EU and combating fraud. The different legal issues raised by those provisions will be dealt with hereinafter, whereby attention will be given to their political and institutional implications, taking also into account their historical development. Furthermore, a substantial part of this contribution deals with the protection of the financial interests of the EU, and OLAF in particular. Finally, the European Court of Auditors (Arts. 285–287 TFEU) will also be covered by this chapter because of its importance in the budgetary area.

1. Historical development

1.1 *The situation under the founding treaties*

Whereas international organizations are usually financed by contributions from their members, the authors of the ECSC Treaty provided for a revolutionary system of funding. The ECSC received own resources in the form of levies imposed on the production of coal and steel. Those levies could, in principle, not exceed 1% of the average value of the products on which they were assessed.[1] Their collection was done directly by the High Authority (later the Commission).

---

* Dr. iur., LL.M, Director, Legal Adviser on Administrative Matters of the Court of Justice of the EU. The views expressed in this contribution are strictly personal.

1. Arts. 49 and 50(2) ECSC.

The EEC and Euratom were not granted the same power to impose levies. A system of financial contributions from the Member States was provided for,[2] but the prospect of a system of own resources was immediately held out.[3] As of 1962, agricultural levies were gradually introduced, although not yet in the form of own resources of the EEC.[4]

In the beginning, there were also several separate budgets. The ECSC budget was divided into two budgets, one for operational expenditure and the other for administrative expenditure. There was a similar division for Euratom with an operating budget and a research and investment budget. The EEC had one single budget from the start. With the entry into force of the Merger Treaty of 1965, one general budget was introduced, which included the administrative expenditure and the related revenue of the ECSC, the revenue and expenditure of the EEC, and the revenue and expenditure of Euratom as previously entered in its operating budget.[5]

This general budget was adopted by the Council. Before this adoption, each institution drew up estimates of its expenditure, which the Commission consolidated in a preliminary draft budget, on the basis of which the Council established the draft budget. The European Parliament had the right to propose modifications to the draft budget, but the final decision-making power was in the hands of the Council. The latter was also the sole authority competent to give discharge in respect of the implementation of the budget.

1.2 *The first budgetary treaty of 21 April 1970 and the first own resources decision*

Negotiations held in Luxembourg in April 1970 resulted in the First Budgetary Treaty of 21 April 1970[6] and Council Decision 70/243 of 21 April 1970 on the replacement of financial contributions from Member States by the Communities' own resources.[7] Both instruments introduced important changes to the financial system of the European Communities.

Council Decision 70/243, also called the first own resources decision, introduced as of 1971 the already announced system of own resources for the general budget. Initially, those own resources comprised customs duties, agricultural levies, and a percentage of the value-added tax (VAT) levied by the Member States. This percentage was limited to a 1% ceiling calculated on a uniform basis, and was gradually applied as progress was made in harmonizing the VAT basis. After a transitional period during which the Member States paid contributions in a decreasing way to balance the general budget of the European Communities, the 1980 budget was the first one to be entirely financed by own resources.[8]

The First Budgetary Treaty granted to the European Parliament its first decision-making powers in the budgetary procedure. It conferred on the President of the European Parliament the power to declare that the budget was finally adopted and it provided that the discharge in respect of the implementation of the budget would be given by a joint decision of the European

---

2. Arts. 200 EEC and 172 Euratom.
3. Arts. 201 EEC and 173 Euratom.
4. Reg. 25 of 20 Apr. 1962 on the financing of the common agricultural policy, O.J. 1962, 30/991, and Reg. 130/66/EEC of the Council of 26 July 1966 on the financing of the common agricultural policy, O.J. 1966, 165/2965.
5. Art. 20(1) of the Merger Treaty, O.J. 1967, 152/2. The First Budgetary Treaty of 21 Apr. 1970 added to this general budget the revenue and expenditure of the research and investment budget of Euratom. The operational budget of the ECSC remained outside the general budget until the ECSC Treaty expired in 2002.
6. O.J. 1971, L 2/1. See on the exact date of that Treaty, H. Matthijs, "De begroting van de Europese Unie", (2010) SEW, 51–60, 51, note 4.
7. O.J. 1970, L 94/19.
8. B. Kerremans and H. Matthijs, *De begroting en de openbare financiën van de Europese Unie*, 2nd ed. (Intersentia, 2004), at 19.

Parliament and the Council. This Treaty also introduced the distinction between compulsory and non-compulsory expenditure,[9] which would continue to exist until the entry into force of the Treaty of Lisbon.

1.3 *The Second Budgetary Treaty of 22 July 1975*

The Second Budgetary Treaty of 22 July 1975[10] further increased the powers of the European Parliament in the budgetary procedure. The decision-making power on budgetary matters was henceforth shared between the European Parliament and the Council, which became the two arms of the budgetary authority, and the former obtained, within limits, the last word over non-compulsory expenditure. The European Parliament also obtained the power to grant discharge in respect of the implementation of the budget. Furthermore, the Second Budgetary Treaty established the European Court of Auditors.

1.4 *The Delors I Package of 1988*

In the 1980s, the Community budget was faced with two major problems.

First, shortly after the full implementation of the first own resources decision in 1980, the budgetary ceiling already began to loom uncomfortably close. On the one hand, there was a decline of revenue both from customs duties, as a result of tariff reductions within the GATT, and from agricultural levies, as a result of the increasing Community self-sufficiency for most agricultural products. Furthermore, revenue from VAT stagnated because of the declining share of consumer expenditure in the Gross National Product (GNP) of the Member States. On the other hand, expenditure of the Community continued to grow, particularly in the agricultural sector. In addition, in 1981 and 1986, three relatively less prosperous Member States acceded to the Community (Greece, Spain and Portugal), making greater calls on the structural funds, while contributing proportionally less. In 1984, the financial possibilities resulting from the first own resources decision were exhausted. The VAT ceiling was raised to 1.4 % by the second own resources decision in May 1985,[11] but this reform did not solve the budgetary problems. Already in 1987, expenditure threatened to exceed revenues, again primarily because of the agricultural expenditure, the proportion of which rose to more than 70% of the Community budget.

Secondly, serious tension developed between the European Parliament and the Council for several reasons. The European Parliament sought to compensate its limitations in the sphere of policy-making and legislation by inserting a number of new budget headings and entering appropriations which could be used to commence new actions. This raised the question whether a prior basic act is necessary to implement expenditure.[12] Other sources of tension were the difference in views on the distinction between compulsory and non-compulsory expenditure, the latter being interpreted in a broad way by the European Parliament and in a narrow way by the Council; the maximum rate of increase for non-compulsory expenditure,[13] which was an important restriction on the European Parliament's freedom of action; and the expansion of compulsory expenditure, particularly in the sphere of agricultural expenditure, which was to the detriment of non-compulsory expenditure.

---

9. Compulsory expenditure was expenditure necessarily resulting from the Treaty or from acts adopted in accordance therewith, whereas non-compulsory expenditure was all other expenditure.
10. O.J. 1977, L 359/1.
11. Council Dec. 85/257/EEC, Euratom of 7 May 1985, O.J. 1985, L 128/15.
12. See also *infra*, section 7.3.
13. Art. 203(9) EEC, later Art. 272(9) EC; abolished by the Treaty of Lisbon.

Consequently, the budgetary procedure between 1980 and 1987 was characterized by recurring friction between the European Parliament and the Council, which repeatedly culminated in litigation before the ECJ.[14] Although the Commission attempted to mediate in those conflicts within the limits of its role in the budgetary process, its efforts had little success. Even the Joint Declaration of the European Parliament, the Council, and the Commission of 30 June 1982,[15] which dealt with the distinction between compulsory and non-compulsory expenditure and by which those institutions recognized that a legal basis was required for the utilization of appropriations, did not lead to a more harmonious collaboration.

Against this background, the Commission presented in February 1987 a package of comprehensive proposals for the reform of the Community's public finances, known as the Delors I package.[16] These proposals resulted in two important innovations.[17]

First, a new "fourth own resource" was introduced by the 1988 own resources decision.[18] Intended to keep the Community budget in balance, this new resource, based on the Member States' GNP,[19] was calculated by applying to a base, made up of the sum of the Member States' GNP, a rate to be determined during the budgetary procedure in the light of the total of all other revenue. Initially a rather modest EU own resource (10.6% in 1988), it has meanwhile become the most important source of EU revenue (71% in 2018).

Secondly, the budgetary process was to take place within a financial framework of a period of five to seven years, which would determine the financial ceilings for the most important categories of expenditure during that period. Decided upon by the European Council, this financial framework would become part of an interinstitutional agreement (IIA) between the European Parliament, the Council and the Commission and be accompanied by an own resources decision laying down the contributions of the Member States. In practice, financial frameworks have been adopted through this procedure for the periods 1988–1992,[20] 1993–1999,[21] 2000–2006,[22] and 2007–2013.[23]

---

14. See Case 34/86, *Council v. European Parliament*; Case 377/87, *European Parliament v. Council*, and Case 383/87, *Commission v. Council*.
15. Joint declaration by the European Parliament, the Council and the Commission on various measures to improve the budgetary procedure, O.J. 1982, C 194/1.
16. These were set out in two communications: *The Single European Act: A new frontier for Europe* (COM(87)100), and *Report on the financing of the Community Budget* (COM(87)101). The broad lines of the proposed reform were adopted by the Brussels European Council of Febr. 1988 and were then given concrete shape in various proposals culminating in a package of measures agreed in June 1988. See further European Commission, *European Union Public Finance*, 5th ed. (Publications Office, 2014), at 33–43, and L. Kolte, "The Community budget: New principles for finance, expenditure planning and budget discipline", 25 CML Rev. (1988), 487–501.
17. Other changes brought forward by the Delors I package were a reform of the structural funds and the adoption of secondary legislation on budgetary discipline (most recently Council Reg. (EC) 2040/2000 of 26 Sept. 2000 on budgetary discipline, O.J. 2000, L 244/27, meanwhile repealed).
18. Art. 2(1)(d) of Council Dec. 88/376/EEC, Euratom of 24 June 1988, O.J. 1988, L 185/24.
19. Gross National Income (GNI) since the 2007 own resources decision, Council Dec. 2007/436/EC, Euratom of 7 June 2007, O.J. 2007, L 163/17.
20. IIA of 29 June 1988, O.J. 1988, L 185/33, and Council Dec. 88/376/EEC, Euratom of 24 June 1988 on the system of the Communities' own resources, O.J. 1988, L 185/24. See P. Zangl, "The interinstitutional agreement on budgetary discipline and improvement of the budgetary procedure", 26 CML Rev. (1989), 675–685.
21. IIA of 29 Oct. 1993, O.J. 1993, C 331/1, and Council Dec. 94/728/EC, Euratom of 31 Oct. 1994 on the system of the European Communities' own resources, O.J. 1994, L 293/9. This IIA was preceded by the so-called Delors II package, see COM(92)2000 & 2001.
22. IIA of 6 May 1999, O.J. 1999, C 172/1, and Council Dec. 2000/597/EEC, Euratom of 29 Sept. 2000 on the system of the European Communities' own resources, O.J. 2000, L 253/42.
23. IIA of 17 May 2006, O.J. 2006, C 139/1, and Council Dec. 2007/436/EC, Euratom of 7 June 2007 on the system of the European Communities' own resources, O.J. 2007, L 163/17. See A. Montagnon, "L'accord sur

Apart from laying down the financial framework, the IIAs also contained agreements on issues such as the distinction between compulsory and non-compulsory expenditure,[24] and the need for a prior basic act to implement expenditure.[25] Furthermore, procedural arrangements were made to ensure close cooperation during the budgetary procedure. In this respect, the IIA of 17 May 2006[26] provided for a conciliation procedure in which the European Parliament, the Council and the Commission participated and the purpose of which was to continue discussions on the general trend of expenditure and to secure agreement between the former two institutions on different issues in relation to the adoption of the budget.

Notwithstanding uncertainties as to their legal effects,[27] the IIAs have been a powerful instrument of regulation of the budgetary procedure between 1988 and 2014, when the first multiannual framework adopted under the new provisions of the Treaty of Lisbon entered into force.

1.5 *The Treaty of Maastricht*

The most important amendments made by the Treaty of Maastricht in relation to EU finances concerned the control of financial management. The European Court of Auditors was raised to the status of a Community Institution.[28] Accordingly, the provisions relating to its composition and powers were moved from Title II of Part Five (financial provisions) to Title I of that Part (provisions governing the Institutions).[29] Furthermore, the Court of Auditors was given the new task of drawing up a "statement of assurance" on the reliability of the accounts and the regularity and the legality of the underlying transactions.[30] Those changes, the origin of which were British proposals,[31] were intended to place more emphasis than hitherto on the legality, regularity and soundness in accounting terms of the Community's financial management, and thus to sharpen the responsibilities of the European Parliament as well as of the Court of Auditors. The greater emphasis on sound financial management and control was also reflected by a change of the rules relating to the implementation of the budget by the Commission,[32] as well as by a new provision on the discharge procedure.[33]

Further changes involved including a provision on charging expenditure occasioned for the Community Institutions by the provisions in the TEU relating to CFSP and JHA to the

---

le cadre financier 2007–2013", (2006) RMC, 441–444.

24. In this respect, the Joint Declaration of 30 June 1982, O.J. 1982, C 194/1, was replaced by the IIA of 6 May 1999 (see paras. 7 and 30–31 as well as Annex IV). See also the IIA of 17 May 2006, paras. 34–35 and Annex III.
25. See the IIA of 13 Oct. 1998 on the legal basis and implementation of the budget, O.J. 1998, C 344/1, replaced by the IIA of 6 May 1999. Since 2003, the subject matter is governed by the Financial Regulation. See further *infra*, section 7.3.
26. Part II and Annex II.
27. The ECJ indirectly addressed the question of the legal nature of IIAs in Case 204/86, *Greece v. Council*, paras. 16–17. See also J. Monar, "Interinstitutional agreements: The phenomenon and its new dynamics after Maastricht", 31 CML Rev. (1994), 693–719, and H.-J. Timmann, "La procédure budgétaire pour l'exercice 1989 et la première application de l'accord interinstitutionnel", (1989) RMC, 235–242.
28. Art. 7 EC. See further D. O'Keeffe, "The court of auditors" in D. Curtin and T. Heukels (Ed.), *Institutional Dynamics of European Integration, Essays in Honour of Henry G. Schermers* (Nijhoff, 1994), at 177–194.
29. To become Arts. 188a, 188b and 188c EC.
30. See further *infra*, section 8.
31. J. Cloos, G. Reinesch, D. Vignes and J. Weyland, *Le Traité de Maastricht, Génèse Analyse, Commentaires*, 2nd ed. (Bruylant, 1994), at 439.
32. The words "having regard to the principles of sound financial management" were added to Art. 205 EC.
33. The newly drafted Art. 206 EC set out the discharge procedure, which was previously summarily stated in Art. 206b EEC.

Community budget;[34] repealing the old Article 200 EEC (on the financial contributions from the Member States) and redrafting Article 201 EC to reflect the existence of the Community's own resources; as well as adding a new Article 201a EC on budgetary discipline in the wake of the Delors I package and a new Article 209a EC on the protection of the Community's financial interests.

The Treaty provisions on the budgetary procedure remained, however, unchanged. Furthermore, attempts by various delegations to the Intergovernmental Conference to include the own resources system in the Treaties themselves, to strengthen the role of the European Parliament in the determination of the Community's own resources, to abolish the distinction between compulsory and non-compulsory expenditure, and to introduce a Community tax were unsuccessful.

1.6 The Treaty of Amsterdam

The Treaty of Amsterdam continued in the same direction as set out by the Treaty of Maastricht. The Treaty provisions on the budgetary procedure remained unchanged, but further changes were brought to the provisions on the control of financial management and the Community action against fraud.

In this context, a provision was added to Article 248(1) EC[35] requiring the "statement of assurance" of the European Court of Auditors to be published in the Official Journal and Article 248(3) EC was amended to strengthen this institution's powers of access to information. Furthermore, Article 274 EC[36] was modified to introduce an obligation on the Member States to cooperate with the Commission in order to ensure that the Community appropriations were used in accordance with the principles of sound financial management. Finally, Article 280 EC[37] on the protection of the Community's financial interests introduced new obligations on the Member States and the Commission and became a legal basis for the adoption of measures in that area.

1.7 The Treaty of Nice

The Treaty of Nice, which primarily aimed at reforming the institutional provisions in view of the upcoming enlargement, introduced only very limited changes to the financial Treaty provisions. In relation to the European Court of Auditors, Article 247 EC laid down new rules on the composition and appointment of its members and Article 248(4) EC introduced the possibility for that institution to create chambers to adopt certain categories of reports or opinions under the conditions laid down by its rules of procedure, which, in the same way as for the EU Courts, would have to be approved by the Council.[38] Furthermore, Article 279 EC was amended to allow the Financial Regulation to be adopted by a qualified majority.

A major change would have occurred if the Intergovernmental Conference had accepted the Commission's proposal to add to the financial Treaty provisions an Article 280a EC, by which a European Public Prosecutor would have been established.[39] This was, however, not the case.

---

34. Art. 199, second para, EC. Administrative expenditure occasioned by the implementation of those provisions was automatically charged to the Community budget. Under the Maastricht Treaty, operating expenditure could be charged to the budget (Arts. J.11(2) and K.8(2) TEU) and, under the Amsterdam Treaty, operating expenditure was charged to the budget, save exception (Arts. 28(3) and 41(3) TEU).
35. Previously Art. 188c EC.
36. Previously Art. 205 EC.
37. Previously Art. 209a EC.
38. The rules of procedure of the Court of Auditors have been published in O.J. 2010, L 103/1.
39. COM(2000)608.

1.8 *The Treaty of Lisbon*

The Treaty of Lisbon has introduced the most important changes to the financial Treaty provisions since the Second Budgetary Treaty of 22 July 1975.[40] However, as to their substance, those changes have, to a large extent, codified at the level of the Treaty budgetary practice as it had developed since the Delors I package of 1988.

The financial framework has thus become the "multiannual financial framework" provided for by Article 312 TFEU. Moreover, even if this framework is no longer laid down in an interinstitutional agreement but in a regulation, the subtle balance of powers which existed since 1988 has been maintained by the Treaty of Lisbon. Indeed, whereas the European Parliament could and can exercise a certain influence over the content of the (multi-annual) financial framework,[41] the Member States have always had and still have a predominant role in the decision-making process.[42]

In the same way, Article 314 TFEU has placed the European Parliament and the Council on an equal footing in the annual budgetary procedure, while, at the same time, putting an end to the legendary distinction between compulsory and non-compulsory expenditure. However, in practice, those institutions had already been cooperating closely within the context of the arrangements made by the interinstitutional agreements. The conciliation procedure under the Interinstitutional Agreement of 17 May 2006[43] has thus, in fact, become the Conciliation Committee under Article 314 TFEU. Another example of codification is Article 310(3) TFEU, which has written into the Treaty the requirement of a prior basic act to implement expenditure.

In the sensitive area of EU revenue, the Treaty of Lisbon has not brought about any changes, except for the possibility to adopt implementing measures for the own resources decision.[44] Finally, an important change introduced by the Treaty of Lisbon is the possibility for the Council to establish a European Public Prosecutor's Office, primarily intended to combat crimes affecting the financial interests of the EU. However, contrary to what the Commission had proposed during the negotiations of the Treaty of Nice, the new provision in this respect (Art. 86 TFEU) does not form part of the financial Treaty provisions, but of the provisions on judicial cooperation in criminal matters.

2. Legal framework

At the level of primary EU law, budgetary matters are essentially governed by Title II, "Financial Provisions", of Part Six, "Institutional and Financial Provisions", of the FEU Treaty.[45] After an

---

40. See further C. Viessant, "Le budget de l'Union européenne après l'entrée en vigueur du traité de Lisbonne", (2010) RMC, 524–532; U. Bux, "Das EU-Haushaltsverfahren nach Lissabon", 45 EuR (2010), 711–718; M.-L. Houbé, "La procédure budgétaire à l'épreuve du Traité de Lisbonne", (2012) RMC, 370–374.
41. Before the Treaty of Lisbon, the European Parliament exercised this influence by being a party to the IIA in which the financial framework was laid down. Since the Treaty of Lisbon, it has to consent to the regulation laying down the multiannual financial framework (Art. 312(2) TFEU).
42. Before the Treaty of Lisbon, the financial framework has always been decided upon by the Heads of State or Government of the Member States before it was laid down in an interinstitutional agreement. Since the Treaty of Lisbon, the multi-annual framework is decided upon by the European Council before being laid down in a regulation adopted by the Council acting unanimously (Art. 312(2) TFEU). See also further *infra*, section 5.1.
43. See *supra*, section 1.4.
44. Art. 311, last para, TFEU.
45. Few provisions of the EU Treaty refer to the EU budget. The most important one is Art. 41 TEU on CFSP expenditure (see further *infra*, section 3.1). Furthermore, Arts. 14(1), 16(1) and 17(1) TEU merely announce the respective competences of the European Parliament, the Council and the Commission in budgetary matters.

introductory provision (Art. 310 TFEU), this title includes six chapters which respectively deal with own resources (Art. 311 TFEU), the multiannual financial framework (Art. 312 TFEU), the EU budget (Arts. 313 to 316 TFEU), the implementation of the budget and discharge (Arts. 317 to 319 TFEU), common provisions (Arts. 320 to 324 TFEU) and combating fraud (Art. 325 TFEU).

Secondary legislation mainly exists in three areas. First, in relation to EU revenue, Article 311 TFEU provides for the adoption of the own resources decision and of implementing measures thereof, whereas Article 322(2) TFEU allows for the adoption of rules on collecting EU revenue.[46]

Secondly, Article 322(1) TFEU is the legal basis for the adoption of the Financial Regulation, which is the most important secondary law with regard to the establishment and the implementation of the EU budget. The current version of the Financial Regulation (hereinafter "FR") is laid down in Regulation (EU, Euratom) No 966/2012 of the European Parliament and of the Council of 25 October 2012,[47] with implementing measures provided for by Commission Delegated Regulation (EU) No 1268/2012 of 29 October 2012.[48] Both regulations define rules which are relevant not only for the EU institutions in the exercise of their budgetary powers, but also for private persons, in particular those on procurement and grants.[49] Furthermore, substantive legislation in certain policy areas may also contain detailed provisions related to the implementation of the budget, which are specific to that area.[50] More fundamentally, this raises the question as to where the scope of Article 322(1) TFEU as a legal basis stops in budget-related matters and that of substantive Treaty provisions begins.

Thirdly, Article 325(4) TFEU[51] has given rise to the adoption of secondary legislation in the field of the protection of the EU's financial interests, in particular the OLAF Regulation.[52]

Finally, a specific category of rules governing EU budgetary matters are the budgetary principles. They find expression in several Treaty provisions and are systematically set out in the Financial Regulation.[53]

---

46. See further *infra*, section 4.
47. Reg. (EU, Euratom) 966/2012 of the European Parliament and of the Council of 25 Oct. 2012 on the financial rules applicable to the general budget of the Union and repealing Council Reg. (EC, Euratom) 1605/2002, O.J. 2012, L 298/1, last amended by Reg. (EU, Euratom) 2015/1929 of the European Parliament and of the Council of 28 Oct. 2015, O.J. 2015, L 286/1. See also U. Bux, "Das Haushaltsrecht und die neue Haushaltsordnung der EU", 54 *Zeitschrift für Europarecht, internationales Privatrecht und Rechtsvergleichung* (2013), 54–62.
48. Commission Delegated Reg. (EU) 1268/2012 of 29 Oct. 2012 on the rules of application of Reg. (EU, Euratom) 966/2012 of the European Parliament and of the Council on the financial rules applicable to the general budget of the Union, O.J. 2012, L 362/1, last amended by Commission Delegated Reg. (EU) 2015/2462 of 30 Oct. 2015, O.J. 2015, L 342/7.
49. Titles V (Arts. 101–120) and VI (Arts. 121–137) of the FR.
50. See, e.g., in relation to structural funds, Reg. (EU) 1303/2013 of the European Parliament and of the Council of 17 Dec. 2013 laying down common provisions on the European Regional Development Fund, the European Social Fund, the Cohesion Fund, the European Agricultural Fund for Rural Development and the European Maritime and Fisheries Fund and laying down general provisions on the European Regional Development Fund, the European Social Fund, the Cohesion Fund and the European Maritime and Fisheries Fund and repealing Council Reg. (EC) 1083/2006, O.J. 2013, L 347/320, last amended by Reg. (EU) 2017/2305 of the European Parliament and of the Council of 12 Dec. 2017, O.J. 2017, L 335/1.
51. Including its predecessor, Art. 280(4) EC. Before the existence of a specific legal basis in the Treaty, Art. 235 EC was used as a legal basis, e.g., for the adoption of the PFI Reg.
52. See further *infra*, section 11.
53. Title II (Arts. 6–35) of the FR.

3. Budgetary principles

3.1 Principles of unity and budgetary accuracy

Article 310(1), first paragraph, TFEU states that all items of revenue and expenditure of the Union shall be shown in the budget, and thus gives expression to the budgetary principles of unity and accuracy, further defined by Articles 7 and 8 of the Financial Regulation. As a result, no EU revenue shall be collected and no EU expenditure effected unless booked to a line in the budget.[54] Together with the principle of annuality, the principle of unity is a fundamental principle in budgetary matters.[55]

There are, however, some exceptions to the budgetary principles of unity and accuracy. First, whereas administrative CFSP expenditure is automatically charged to the EU budget, operating CFSP expenditure is not charged to the EU budget if it arises from operations having military or defence implications or if the Council, acting unanimously, so decides. In that case, such expenditure, although deriving from EU legal instruments, is charged to the Member States.[56]

Secondly, the borrowing-and-lending operations, by which the EU contracts borrowings on the capital markets or with financial institutions to on-lend either to Member States[57] or to third countries,[58] are not included in the EU budget. In 1978, the Commission, at the instigation of the European Parliament, proposed that these operations be shown in full in the budget, but this proposal was rejected by the Council.[59] Until today, the borrowing-and-lending operations are not included in the budget but information thereon appears in an annex, with a description of their effect on the budget.[60]

Furthermore, there are some exceptions to the budgetary principles of unity and accuracy which are not really exceptions, since revenue and expenditure involved do not derive from EU legal instruments but from international agreements concluded by the Member States. Therefore, technically, they are not revenue and expenditure of the EU.[61] This is the case, in particular, for aid granted to the ACP[62] countries within the context of the European Development Funds. This aid is not financed out of the EU's own resources, but out of contributions made by the Member States according to a special allocation system, set out in an international agreement

54. Art. 8(1) FR.
55. Case C-284/90, *Council v. European Parliament*, para 26.
56. Art. 41(2) TEU.
57. See Council Reg. (EC) 332/2002 of 18 Febr. 2002 establishing a facility providing medium-term financial assistance for Member States' balances of payments, O.J. 2002, L 53/1, last amended by Council Reg. (EC) 431/2009 of 18 May 2009, O.J. 2009, L 128/1, as well as Council Reg. (EU) 407/2010 of 11 May 2010 establishing a European financial stabilization mechanism, O.J. 2010, L 118/1, last amended by Council Reg. (EU) 2015/1360 of 4 Aug. 2015, O.J. 2015, L 210/1. Under the former, the Commission is empowered to raise funds on behalf of the EU and on-lend to Member States which have not yet adopted the euro. Under the latter, the EU can borrow up to 60 billion euro to on-lend to any Member State.
58. See, in this context, Council Reg. (EC, Euratom) 480/2009 of 25 May 2009 establishing a Guarantee Fund for external actions, O.J. 2009, L 145/10.
59. It was one of the reasons why the European Parliament rejected the draft budget for 1979, see European Commission, cited *supra* note 16, at 286–287.
60. Art. 35(1) FR. However, the budget records the guarantees for such operations, see Art. 7(2) FR. See further M. Vitsentzatos, "Loans and guarantees in the European Union budget", 15 ERA Forum (2014), 131–144.
61. See Joined Cases C-181 & 248/91, *European Parliament v. Council and Commission*, para 30 (which concerned an aid granted to Bangladesh within the framework of a collective action of the Member States financed directly by them).
62. African, Caribbean and Pacific.

concluded by them and reflecting their historical and political ties with the ACP countries.[63] Attempts by the European Parliament and the Commission to include this aid in the EU budget have up to now been unsuccessful.[64]

Finally, even if they are part of the EU, separate legal entities have their own budget, which is not part of the EU budget. This is, for instance, the case for the ECB, the EIB, and the satellite agencies, notwithstanding the fact that the latter may receive important funding from the EU budget.[65] As for the ESM, which is formally a separate international organization,[66] it logically has a separate budget.

3.2 *Principle of annuality*

According to the principle of annuality,[67] budget operations must relate to a specific financial year, which coincides with a calendar year. Its aim is to enable, at regular intervals, a full supervision of EU activities which have financial consequences. To reconcile the rule of annuality with the need to engage in multiannual operations, a system of differentiated appropriations exists, which consist of commitment appropriations and payment appropriations.[68] Commitment appropriations cover, in a particular financial year, the total cost of the legal obligations entered into in respect of operations to be carried out over a period of more than one financial year. Payment appropriations cover expenditure, up to the amount entered in the budget, resulting from the commitments entered into during the financial year and/or previous financial years.

In the interests of good management, it is not always possible to have these appropriations match calendar years exactly. For practical reasons, Article 316 TFEU, therefore, allows appropriations, other than those relating to staff expenditure, to be carried over to the next financial year.[69] By contrast, sums recovered in one financial year can no longer be used in the context of a previous financial year which has already been closed.[70]

Article 315 TFEU provides for a system of provisional twelfths in case no budget has been adopted at the beginning of a financial year. This means that no more than the equivalent of one-twelfth of the preceding financial year's budget appropriations may be spent in respect of any chapter of the budget in any one month.[71] In the period up to 1988, the Community was frequently forced to resort to this emergency solution.

---

63. Internal Agreement between the Representatives of the Governments of the Member States of the European Union, meeting within the Council, on the financing of European Union aid under the multiannual financial framework for the period 2014 to 2020, in accordance with the ACP-EU Partnership Agreement, and on the allocation of financial assistance for the Overseas Countries and Territories to which Part Four of the Treaty on the Functioning of the European Union applies, O.J. 2013, L 210/1, last amended by Council Dec. (EU) 2015/334 of 2 Mar. 2015, O.J. 2015, L 58/75.
64. European Commission, cited *supra* note 16, at 299–300.
65. See also A. Boissenin, "Le démembrement budgétaire par les agences européennes", (2014) *Revue française de finances publiques*, 15–22.
66. Set up by an intergovernmental treaty signed on 2 Febr. 2012 by the euro area Member States.
67. See Arts. 310(1) and 313(1) TFEU as well as Arts. 9–16 FR.
68. Art. 10 FR.
69. See also Art. 13 FR.
70. Case T-186/98, *Inpesca v. Commission*, para 68.
71. Art. 16 FR. See further J. Pipkorn, "Legal implications of the absence of the Community budget at the beginning of a financial year", 18 CML Rev. (1981), 141–167.

3.3 *Principle of equilibrium*

According to the principle of equilibrium, revenue and expenditure shown in the EU budget must be in balance.[72] With reference to that principle, Article 17(2) FR states that the EU may not raise loans, which means that it cannot borrow for budgetary purposes. This should be distinguished from the borrow-and-lending activities of the EU, in the framework of which it borrows not to cover EU expenditure but to on-lend to Member States or third countries.[73] Furthermore, there is one limited exception, recently provided for by Article 203(8) FR, which allows for the acquisition by the EU of a building to be financed through a loan.[74]

In the course of implementing the budget, it may turn out that actual expenditure is lower or higher than predicted, thus giving rise to a surplus or a deficit at the end of the financial year.[75] A surplus or a deficit is entered, by way of an amending budget, in the budget of the following year, either as revenue (in the case of a surplus) or as a payment appropriation (in the case of a deficit).[76] In case of a surplus, the entire surplus has to be carried over to the next financial year, and not only a part of it corresponding to the own resources based on the Member States' GNI.[77] In practice, a surplus occurs more frequently than a deficit. The surplus carried over from one financial year to the next leads to a decrease of the revenue originally entered in the budget of the next financial year and thus, in fact, diminishes the financial burden on the Member States.

3.4 *Principle of unit of account*

From the very beginning, there has been a need for a common, and constant, monetary reference value for drawing up the Community budget and for its implementation. When the ECSC first existed, and in the initial years of the EEC, use was made of the US dollar, which provided a sufficiently stable reference value until the end of the 1960s. After the collapse of the Bretton Woods system, which resulted in fluctuating exchange rates, it was finally decided, in 1981, to express the Community budget in the currency unit of the European Monetary System, called the ECU. This solution was satisfactory to the extent that the ECU was used as a unit of account, but it revealed shortcomings in relation to payments, since the ECU was not universally accepted as a means of payment.[78] The introduction of the euro has solved this problem. Article 320 TFEU explicitly provides that the multiannual framework and the annual budget shall be drawn up in euro.[79]

---

72. Art. 310(1), last para, TFEU. See also Arts. 17–18 FR.
73. See *supra*, section 3.1.
74. The fact that, before, the EU could not borrow to finance investments obliged EU institutions to use complex methods of financing property acquisitions which were not always cost efficient and transparent, see Special Report 2/2007 of the Court of Auditors concerning the Institutions' expenditure on buildings, O.J. 2007, C 148/1, para 57.
75. For the calculation and budgeting of the balance of a given financial year, see Art. 1 of Council Reg. (EU, Euratom) 608/2014 of 26 May 2014 laying down implementing measures for the system of own resources of the EU, O.J. 2014, L 168/29.
76. Art. 18 FR.
77. Case C-284/90, *Council v. Parliament*, paras. 17–19.
78. See further X. Yataganas, in Commentaire J. Mégret, *Le droit de la CE et de l'union européenne, Les finances de l'Union européenne* (Université de Bruxelles, 1999), at 360–365.
79. See also Art. 19 FR.

3.5 Principle of universality

According to the principle of universality, total revenue shall cover total payment appropriations.[80] The setting aside of certain revenue for certain expenditure is therefore not allowed. This principle also implies that all income and expenditure must be entered separately, and may not be adjusted against each other.[81] The FR defines some exceptions to the principle of universality.[82]

The principle of universality does not prevent that reciprocal claims between the EU and a third party give rise to a set-off.[83] This set-off is not subject to a prior obligation to ascertain that the use of the EU funds concerned for the purposes prescribed and the completion of the activities which justified the granting of the EU funds concerned will remain assured in spite of the proposed set-off.[84]

3.6 Principle of specification

The principle of specification requires that appropriations are earmarked for specific purposes by title and chapter.[85] It allows the budgetary authority to express its policy and political priorities in the budget, and to check whether those priorities are followed up in the subsequent stages of the budget cycle. As a result of this principle, the budget is structured according to a certain nomenclature (titles, chapters, articles, items).

In order to guarantee sufficient flexibility in the implementation of the budget, Article 317, third paragraph, TFEU allows for appropriations to be transferred, within certain limits laid down in the FR.[86] The remarks included in the budget cannot limit the possibility to carry out transfers of appropriations under the conditions laid down in the FR.[87]

3.7 Principle of sound financial management

Whereas, for a long time, legality was the predominant criterion for determining whether expenditure was appropriate, sound financial management has constantly gained in importance. As a concept, it was first introduced at the level of the Treaty by the Second Budgetary Treaty of 22 July 1975, as one of the audit criteria for the European Court of Auditors.[88] With the Treaty of Maastricht, it became a principle guiding the implementation of the budget.[89] The Treaty of Lisbon has further stressed its importance by including an additional reference to the principle of sound financial management in the introductory article of the financial Treaty provisions.[90]

The principle of sound financial management is, in fact, composed of three separate principles, namely of economy, efficiency and effectiveness (the three "E's"). The principle of economy, which concerns the input, requires that the resources used by the institution in the pursuit of its activities are made available in due time, in appropriate quantity and quality and at the best price. The principle of effectiveness, which relates to the output, is concerned with attaining

80. Art. 20 FR.
81. Ibid.
82. Arts. 21–23 FR.
83. Art. 80(1) FR.
84. Case C-87/01 P, *Commission v. CEMR*, para 29.
85. See Art. 316, second para, TFEU and Art. 24 FR.
86. Arts. 25–29 FR.
87. Case 204/86, *Greece v. Council*, paras. 25–26.
88. Together with legality and regularity, see Art. 206a(2), first para, EEC, now Art. 287(2), first para, TFEU.
89. Art. 205 EC, now Art. 317 TFEU.
90. Art. 310(5) TFEU.

the specific objectives set and achieving the intended results. The principle of efficiency is concerned with the best relationship between input and output.[91]

One of the requirements, in practice, of the principle of sound financial management is that any legislative proposal which may have an impact on the budget must be accompanied by a financial statement and an *ex ante* evaluation.[92] The importance of the principle of sound financial management also finds expression in the reports of the European Court of Auditors.[93]

However important the principle of sound financial management has become over the decades, it mainly concerns the authorities in charge of the implementation of the EU budget and thus, above all, the European Commission. It is of less practical importance for beneficiaries of EU funds. Sound financial management is indeed not a criterion for entitlement to EU funds. This entitlement is subject to the legal conditions for obtaining the EU funds being met. It cannot result from the mere fact that the funding would achieve the objective of the financing set by the EU.[94]

3.8 *Principle of transparency*

The principle of transparency implies that the budget, the accounts and the reports on budgetary and financial management are published in the Official Journal of the European Union.[95] Furthermore, in accordance with this principle, it is provided for that information is published on borrowing-and-lending operations contracted by the EU as well as on recipients of EU funds, with due observance of the requirements of confidentiality and security, in particular the protection of personal data.[96]

4. **Own resources**

4.1 *The own resources decision*

Since the first own resources decision of 1970,[97] the EU is financed by "own resources". This implies that those resources are attributed to the EU at source and cannot therefore be entered in the budget of a Member State. It does not necessarily mean that the EU is entitled to collect those resources or that it may decide to raise taxes.[98]

Since 1988, the adoption of a new multi-annual financial framework (MFF) has been accompanied by the adoption of a new own resources decision.[99] The adoption of the 2014–2020 MFF has given rise to the adoption of Council Decision 2014/335/EU, Euratom of 26 May 2014 on the system of own resources of the EU (hereinafter "the 2014 own resources decision").[100]

---

91. Art. 30(2) FR.
92. Art. 31 FR.
93. See, e.g., Special Reports 25/2015 on "EU support for rural infrastructure: potential to achieve significantly greater value for money", available at <www.eca.europa.eu/Lists/ECADocuments/SR15_25/SR_RURAL_EN.pdf> (last accessed on 20 Mar. 2018), and 6/2014 on "Cohesion policy funds support to renewable energy generation – has it achieved good results?" available at <www.eca.europa.eu/Lists/ECADocuments/SR14_06/SR14_06_EN.pdf> (last accessed on 20 Mar. 2018).
94. See, to that effect, Case C-240/03 P, *Comunità montana della Valnerina v. Commission*, para 145.
95. Art. 34 FR.
96. Art. 35 FR.
97. See *supra*, section 1.2.
98. C.-D. Ehlermann, "The financing of the Community: The distinction between financial contributions and own resources", 19 CML Rev. (1982), 571–589, 588.
99. See also *supra*, section 1.4.
100. O.J. 2014, L 168/105.

A special legislative procedure provided for by Article 311, second paragraph, TFEU governs the adoption of the own resources decision. This decision is adopted unanimously by the Council, after consultation of the European Parliament, and it does not enter into force until it is approved by the Member States in accordance with their respective constitutional requirements. It remains, however, secondary EU legislation.[101] The unanimity rule, combined with the implication of the national parliaments in the decision-making process and the absence of a real decision-making power for the European Parliament, reflects the intention of the Member States to keep the subject-matter of EU financing firmly under control. The Treaty of Lisbon has provided for the possibility to attenuate the Member States' influence somewhat by allowing the Council to adopt implementing measures for the EU own resources system.[102] When adopting those measures, the Council acts by a qualified majority, it has to obtain the consent of the European Parliament and there is no approval by the Member States in accordance with their respective constitutional requirements. The first regulation to be adopted under that provision is Council Regulation (EU, Euratom) No 608/2014 of 26 May 2014 laying down implementing measures for the system of own resources of the EU.[103] However, the most important provisions, including those defining the EU own resources, continue to form part of the own resources decision itself.

Currently, the following sources of revenue are EU own resources: (1) customs duties and sugar levies, (2) a standard percentage levied on the harmonized value-added tax (VAT) base of each Member State (hereinafter the "VAT own resource"), and (3) a standard percentage levied on the gross national income (GNI) of each Member State (hereinafter the "GNI-based own resource").[104] Other sources of revenue (some 1% of the budget) are taxes on EU staff salaries, contributions from non-EU countries towards certain EU programs, and fines imposed on companies in breach of competition law or other rules.

Customs duties and sugar levies, also called the "traditional own resources", are own resources since 1970. They essentially result from the existence of a unified customs area. Over the decades, the traditional own resources have decreased in importance, mainly because of the reduction of customs duties negotiated within the context of the World Trade Organization. Whereas they still accounted for almost 30% of EU revenue in 1988, they represent 15.8% in 2018. A certain percentage of those duties may be deducted as collection costs by the Member States, before the revenue is passed on to the EU.[105]

In the same way as the traditional own resources, the VAT own resource is an own resource since 1970. Its importance has also decreased,[106] due to changes in the way it is calculated. Whereas the maximum contribution (as a percentage) from the VAT own resource was fixed at 1.4 % in 1985,[107] it is fixed at 0.30% since the 2007 own resources decision.[108] Furthermore, since 1988, the VAT base to be used for the calculation may not exceed a certain percentage (initially

101. G. Wilms, "Die Reform des EU-Haushaltes im Lichte der Finanziellen Vorausschau 2007–2013 und des Vertrages von Lissabon – neue Perspektiven für die Europäische Union?", 42 EuR (2007), 707–743, 710. The requirement of an approval by the Member States in accordance with their respective constitutional requirements is also provided for by Arts. 25, 218(8) and 223(1) TFEU.
102. Art. 311, last para, TFEU.
103. O.J. 2014, L 168/29.
104. Art. 2 of the 2014 own resources decision.
105. 10%, later 25%, and now 20%, see Art. 2(3) of the 2014 own resources decision.
106. From 57.2% of EU revenue in 1988 to 11.9% in 2018.
107. Art. 3(2) of Council Dec. 85/257/EEC, Euratom of 7 May 1985 on the Communities' system of own resources, O.J. 1985, L 128/15.
108. Art. 2(4) of Council Dec. 2007/436/EC, Euratom of 7 June 2007 on the system of the European Communities' own resources, O.J. 2007, L 163/17.

55% and since the 2000 own resources decision[109] 50%) of the Member States' GNP/GNI. This capping of the VAT percentage and the VAT base tends to work in favour of less prosperous Member States, because in those States the proportion of the VAT base in relation to GNI is relatively high.

Notwithstanding the complex way of calculating the VAT own resource, there is a direct link between, on the one hand, the collection of VAT revenue in compliance with the applicable EU law[110] and, on the other, the availability to the EU budget of the corresponding VAT own resources, since any lacuna in the collection of the first potentially causes a reduction in the second.[111] This is of particular relevance for the EU's competence in relation to VAT fraud.[112]

The GNI-based own resource was first introduced by the 1988 own resources decision.[113] It is intended to keep the EU budget in balance and has meanwhile become the most important source of EU revenue (71% in 2018). Because of its link with the GNI of the Member States,[114] the GNI-based own resource matches each Member State's ability to pay, but it stimulates the *juste retour* discussion.

The own resources decision also sets an overall ceiling of EU revenue. The total amount of own resources to cover annual appropriations for payments may not exceed 1.23% of the sum of all the Member States' GNIs, whereas the total amount of appropriations for commitments may not exceed 1.29%.[115] This ceiling, which is not the same as the overall ceiling of EU expenditure, set by the MFF,[116] corresponds to the upper limit of what the Member States can be called upon to contribute to the EU. It explains why it would have been difficult, if not impossible, to create the ESM (and its predecessor – the temporary EFSF) through an EU legal instrument. In the case of the ESM, the total subscribed capital of 704.8 billion euro and the maximum lending capacity of 500 billion euro largely exceed the own resources ceiling (for payment appropriations), which, for 2018, amounts to 196 billion euro.[117] Integrating the ESM in the EU would, therefore, require a modification of the own resources system, which proves to be one of the most difficult undertakings in EU politics.[118]

---

109. Art. 2(1)(c) of Council Dec. 2000/597/EC, Euratom of 29 Sept. 2000 on the system of the European Communities' own resources, O.J. 2000, L 253/42.
110. Council Dir. 2006/112/EC of 28 Nov. 2006 on the common system of VAT, O.J. 2006, L 347/1, last amended by Council Dir. (EU) 2017/2455 of 5 Dec. 2017, O.J. 2017, L 348/7.
111. Case C-539/09, *Commission v. Germany*, para 72.
112. See also *infra*, section 10.2.
113. Council Dec. 88/376/EEC, Euratom of 24 June 1988 on the system of the Communities' own resources, O.J. 1988, L 185/24. At that time, it was still referred to as the "fourth own resource", since the traditional own resources comprised the agricultural levies (and sugar levies), on the one hand, and the customs duties, on the other. See also *supra*, section 1.4.
114. The GNI is calculated by the Commission in accordance with Reg. (EU) 549/2013 of the European Parliament and of the Council of 21 May 2013 on the European system of national and regional accounts in the EU, O.J. 2013, L 174/1, last amended by Commission Delegated Reg. (EU) 2015/1342 of 22 Apr. 2015, O.J. 2015, L 207/35.
115. Art. 3 of the 2014 own resources decision.
116. See *infra*, section 5.2.
117. The situation is different for EU assistance under the EFSM, in the context of which the EU can borrow up to 60 billion euro to on-lend to the Member States (see also *supra*, section 3.1). Moreover, it is expressly provided for in Art. 2(2) of Council Reg. (EU) 407/2010 of 11 May 2010 establishing a European financial stabilization mechanism, O.J. 2010, L 118/1, last amended by Council Reg. (EU) 2015/1360 of 4 Aug. 2015, O.J. 2015, L 210/1, that the outstanding amount of loans or credit lines to be granted to Member States under the EFSM is limited to the margin available under the own resources ceiling for payment appropriations.
118. See further *infra*, section 4.2.

Finally, the own resources decision is a measure of budgetary law whose purpose is to define own resources allocated to the EU budget. As such, it cannot create taxes or duties. They can only be established by the EU legislature in the exercise of powers based on the provisions of the FEU Treaty, e.g. in relation to the common agricultural policy.[119] This expresses the fundamental idea that budgetary measures do not by themselves allow for revenue to be collected or expenditure to be made, but that, as a general rule, a "basic act", adopted on the basis of Treaty provisions in policy areas, is needed in this respect.[120]

4.2 *The juste retour discussion*

The introduction of a system of own resources in 1970 created a problem of apportionment between the Member States. Member States which imported a relatively large quantity of agricultural products from outside the Community and themselves had a relatively small agricultural sector ended up contributing more to the Community and received comparatively little benefit from the Community's agricultural spending in return. The financial burden created by the own resources system was also proportionately heavier for the Member States with a relative high VAT base in relation to GNP, which were primarily the less prosperous Member States.

As early as 1974, such a structural imbalance in the United Kingdom's financial relationship with the Community became a major political issue. Attempts were made to define some form of correction mechanism. Two mechanisms were agreed upon in 1976[121] and in 1980,[122] but the conditions for their application were never met. The third attempt led to the current correction mechanism. It was originally embodied in Article 3 of the second own resources decision in 1985,[123] and has been repeated in the own resources decisions since. Currently, three key elements are involved:

- first, two thirds of the difference between the United Kingdom's percentage share in VAT own resources and its percentage share in allocated EU expenditure, multiplied by total allocated expenditure, is refunded to the United Kingdom by way of a reduction of its share in the GNI-based own resource;[124]
- secondly, the reduction in the United Kingdom's contribution is made up by all the other Member States in accordance with their respective percentage share in the GNI-based own resource;[125]
- thirdly, an exception applies to Germany, the Netherlands, Austria and Sweden whose financing share of the UK rebate is restricted to one fourth of their normal share.[126] Those four Member States as well as Denmark also benefit from a reduced rate of call of the VAT own resources[127] and/or certain gross reductions of their share in the GNI-based own resource, to be financed by all Member States.[128]

---

119. Case C-335/12, *Commission v. Portugal*, para 66.
120. See further, in relation to expenditure, *infra*, section 7.3.
121. Council Reg. (EEC) 1172/76 of 17 May 1976 setting up a financial mechanism, O.J. 1976, L 131/7.
122. Council Reg. (EEC) 2743/80 of 27 Oct. 1980 amending Reg. (EEC) 1172/76 setting up a financial mechanism, O.J. 1980, L 284/1, and Council Reg. (EEC) 2744/80 of 27 Oct. 1980 establishing supplementary measures in favour of the United Kingdom, O.J. 1980, L 284/4.
123. Council Dec. 85/257/EEC, Euratom of 7 May 1985 on the Communities' system of own resources, O.J. 1985, L 128/15.
124. For further details, see Art. 4 of the 2014 own resources decision.
125. Art. 5(1)(a) of the 2014 own resources decision.
126. Art. 5(1)(b) of the 2014 own resources decision.
127. 0.15% instead of 0.30%.
128. Art. 2(4)–(5) of the 2014 own resources decision.

The combination of those rebates for certain Member States with the important share of GNI-based own resources in EU revenue stimulates the *juste retour* discussion, whereby Member States calculate the difference between what they pay to the EU budget by way of own resources and what they receive from it as expenditure. Such a mathematical approach has certain flaws since it fails to recognize the economic impact of EU own resources as well as many indirect advantages of the process of European integration. For instance, the contribution to traditional own resources tends to be higher for a Member State which has a main EU entry point on its territory,[129] but the actual financial burden of the resources collected by that Member State is not necessarily borne there since the goods are often destined for other Member States. In the same way, companies in the "net contributor" Member States benefit from the demand triggered in other Member States by EU expenditure, in particular structural funds expenditure.[130]

It is, however, true that, in its current form, the own resources system resembles a system of national contributions negotiated on a country by country basis.[131] Notwithstanding the significant changes proposed by the Commission in 2011,[132] the Council, by adopting the 2014 own resources decision, kept unchanged the existing own resources system. However, during the negotiations on the 2014–2020 MFF, the European Parliament obtained the setting up of a high level group in charge of examining the reform of the own resources system.[133] In its final report, published on 17 January 2017, the high level group recommends a comprehensive and viable reform of the system of own resources based on a combination of new resources stemming from production, consumption and environmental policies. It also points out that withdrawal of the United Kingdom from the EU will entail the discontinuation of the UK correction mechanism and the related "rebates on rebate". More generally, the high level group proposes that any correction mechanism on the revenue side be abolished.[134]

4.3 *The collection of own resources*

Separate rules govern the collection of EU own resources. In this respect, Article 322(2) TFEU provides that the Council, acting on a proposal from the Commission and after consulting the European Parliament and the European Court of Auditors, determines the methods and procedure whereby the EU own resources are made available to the Commission. Currently, the

129. For instance, a seaport. This effect is therefore also called the "Rotterdam effect".
130. This is the so-called "knock-on effect", see further J. Le Cacheux, "The poisonous budget rebate debate", (2005) *Notre Europe, Studies & Research*, at 13 et seq., available at <www.notre-europe.eu/media/etud41-en.pdf?pdf=ok> (last accessed on 20 Mar. 2018).
131. See also Opinion 2/2006 of the European Court of Auditors on a proposal for a Council Decision on the system of the European Communities' own resources, O.J. 2006, C 203/50, para 16. See for further analysis of the current own resources system and the possibilities for change, P. Cattoir, "Tax-based EU own resources: An assessment" in European Commission, Taxation Papers, Working Paper 1/2004 (Publications Office, 2004); S.R.F. Plasschaert, "Towards an own tax resource for the European Union?: Why? How? And when?", 44 *European Taxation* (2004), 470–479; J. Inghelram, "Welke toekomst voor de financiering van de EU?", (2007) SEW, 191–200; S. Hiernaux-Fritsch and A. F. W. Moonen, "Financiering van de begroting van de Europese Unie", (2010) SEW, 192–197; A.R. Leen, "De Europese identiteit en de financiering van de EU", (2011) SEW, 447–454; V. Constantinesco, "Le financement de l'Union européenne: contributions nationales ou impôt européen?", (2012) *Revue française d'administration publique*, 1079–1084; V. Dussart, "L'impossible création d'un impôt européen?", (2012) *Revue française d'administration publique*, 1085–1091.
132. COM(2011)510 and COM(2011)739.
133. European Parliament resolution of 3 July 2013 on the political agreement on the MFF 2014–2020 (2012/2799(RSP)), para 13.
134. See final report, at 12–13, available at <ec.europa.eu/budget/mff/hlgor/library/reports-communication/hlgor-report_20170104.pdf> (last accessed on 20 Mar. 2018). See also COM(2017)358.

collection of own resources is governed by Council Regulation (EU, Euratom) No 609/2014 of 26 May 2014 on the methods and procedure for making available the traditional, VAT and GNI-based own resources and on the measures to meet cash requirements.[135]

In relation to traditional own resources, the obligation of Member States to establish the EU's entitlement to own resources arises as soon as the conditions provided for by the customs regulations have been met.[136] The established amounts must be entered in the accounts at the latest on the first working day after the nineteenth day of the second month following the month during which the entitlement was established. In case of problems of recovery, the amounts are shown in separate accounts.[137] The traditional own resources are made available by the Member States to the Commission by crediting the amounts involved to an account opened in the name of the Commission with their treasury or national central bank.[138] The Member States deduct 20% in order to cover the collection costs of traditional own resources borne by them. They are released of their obligation to make traditional own resources available to the Commission only if the established amounts prove irrecoverable for reasons of *force majeure*, for other reasons not attributable to them or to avoid prejudicing a criminal investigation affecting the EU's financial interests.[139]

For VAT and GNI-based own resources, Member States inform the Commission of the calculations made under the relevant legislation.[140] One-twelfth of the total amount of such resources appearing in the EU budget must be entered in the accounts on the first working day of each month. The balances of VAT and GNI-based resources are adjusted each year.[141] Those resources are made available in the same way as traditional own resources.[142]

Any delay in making available own resources gives rise to payment of interest by the Member State concerned.[143] That interest may be claimed regardless of the reason for which the own resources are paid too late onto the Commission's account.[144] In particular, the following

135. O.J. 2014, L 168/39, last amended by Council Reg. (EU, Euratom) 2016/804 of 17 May 2016, O.J. 2016, L 132/85. See also COM(2015)447.
136. Art. 2(1) of Council Reg. 609/2014 and Case C-392/02 *Commission v. Denmark*, para 58. For sugar levies, the relevant date is that of the notification provided for in the EU regulations governing the sugar sector, see Art. 2(2).
137. Art. 6(3) of Council Reg. 609/2014.
138. Arts. 9–10 of Council Reg. 609/2014.
139. Art. 13(2) of Council Reg. 609/2014 and Case C-19/05 *Commission v. Denmark*, para 32. This condition is not fulfilled if the amounts corresponding to the entitlements prove irrecoverable because of Binding Tariff Information documents issued by the customs authorities themselves, see Case C-60/13, *Commission v. United Kingdom*, paras. 55–56.
140. Arts. 10a–10b of Council Reg. 609/2014. For VAT own resources, Council Reg. (EEC, Euratom) 1553/89 of 29 May 1989 on the definitive uniform arrangements for the collection of own resources accruing from VAT, O.J. 1989, L 155/9, last amended by Council Reg. (EC) 807/2003 of 14 Apr. 2003, O.J. 2003, L 122/36, and for GNI-based own resources, Council Reg. (EC, Euratom) 1287/2003 of 15 July 2003 on the harmonization of gross national income at market prices, O.J. 2003, L 181/1.
141. Art. 6(3) of Council Reg. 609/2014. In 2014, these adjustments resulted in very high amounts to be paid by some Member States, among which the United Kingdom. A solution was found by allowing the payment of the adjustment to be postponed, in certain exceptional circumstances, from Dec. 1st to Sept. 1st of the following year, see Council Reg. (EU, Euratom) 1377/2014 of 18 Dec. 2014 amending Reg. (EC, Euratom) 1150/2000 implementing Decision 2007/436/EC, Euratom on the system of the European Communities' own resource, O.J. 2014, L 367/14.
142. Without prior deduction of collection costs.
143. Art. 12 of Council Reg. 609/2014.
144. Case C-442/08, *Commission v. Germany*, para 93.

circumstances cannot justify a late payment: the fact that the delay was not intentional,[145] that the EU budget was not adversely affected,[146] or that the delay was due to an error or to fraud committed by the customs authorities of a Member State.[147]

The strict interpretation by the case-law of the rules on the collection of own resources is clearly motivated by the fact that, due to the principle of equilibrium,[148] any shortfalls in revenues of own resources has to be offset either by another own resource or by an adjustment of expenditure, which can put to the test the delicate agreement arrived at by the European Council with regard to the MFF and the corresponding own resources decision.[149]

5. The Multi-Annual Financial Framework

5.1 *Procedure*

The multi-annual financial framework (hereinafter "MFF") sets annual ceilings for EU expenditure, divided over the main policy areas, over a period of at least five years. This budgetary instrument has been introduced by the Delors I package of 1988[150] and it is provided for at the level of the Treaty since the entry into force of the Treaty of Lisbon. Whereas the MFF previously formed part of an interinstitutional agreement between the European Parliament, the Council and the Commission, it is now laid down in a Council regulation, adopted according to the procedure provided for in Article 312 TFEU. The first one to be adopted under that provision is Council Regulation (EU, Euratom) No 1311/2013 of 2 December 2013 laying down the MFF for the years 2014–2020.[151]

The special legislative procedure for adopting the MFF is laid down in Article 312(2) TFEU. The Council acts unanimously after obtaining the consent of the European Parliament, which is given by a majority of its component members. Furthermore, the European Council may, unanimously, authorize the Council to act by a qualified majority.

In practice, the procedure has turned out to be essentially the same as before the entry into force of the Treaty of Lisbon. The political decision on the MFF is taken by the European Council.[152] After that decision, notwithstanding the fact that the European Parliament's power is formally limited to giving (or refusing to give) its consent, a negotiation phase starts between the European Parliament and the Council. Regarding the 2014–2020 MFF, even if these negotiations have not fundamentally changed the political decision taken by the European Council and, in particular, the ceilings of EU expenditure set by it, the European Parliament obtained certain flexibility within those ceilings and a mid-term review/revision of the MFF.[153] Furthermore, an

145. Case 93/85, *Commission v. United Kingdom*, para 37.
146. Case C-348/97, *Commission v. Germany*, para 62.
147. Case C-392/02, *Commission v. Denmark*, para 63, and Case C-334/08, *Commission v. Italy*, paras. 45–49.
148. See *supra*, section 3.3.
149. See Case C-392/02, *Commission v. Denmark*, para 54, and the Opinion of the A.G. in that case, para 7.
150. See *supra*, section 1.4.
151. O.J. 2013, L 347/884, last amended by Council Reg. (EU, Euratom) 2017/1123 of 20 June 2017, O.J. 2017, L 163/1.
152. For the 2014–2020 multi-annual framework, this decision was adopted by the European Council on 8 Febr. 2013.
153. The political agreement was reached on 27 June 2013, see the European Parliament resolution of 3 July 2013 on the political agreement on the MFF 2014–2020 (2012/2799(RSP)). On 14 Sept. 2016, the Commission made several proposals for a mid-term review/revision of the MFF, see COM(2016)603.

interinstitutional agreement is still concluded, as before, between the European Parliament, the Council and the Commission, although this agreement no longer lays down the MFF itself.[154]

Apart from these procedural similarities, there is, nevertheless, an important difference as to the legal consequences of the MFF, compared to the pre-Lisbon situation. During the latter period, the MFF, being part of an interinstitutional agreement, could not affect the European Parliament's powers in budgetary matters,[155] whereas the MFF is now binding on that institution when it exercises its powers in relation to the establishment of the budget.[156]

The way in which the MFF is adopted and its legal consequences, together with the exclusive power of the Council to decide on own resources, show the predominant influence which the Member States still have in relation to the financing of the EU and its expenditure. This situation, which confirms the important role of finances in EU politics, has not really changed with the Treaty of Lisbon.

5.2 *Contents*

The most important part of Council Regulation No 1311/2013 is its Annex I, which contains the actual MFF. For each year between 2014 and 2020, the MFF states, per heading and subheading, the maximum amounts for which financial commitments may be undertaken (total commitment appropriations) as well as the maximum amounts of payments which can be made (total payment appropriations). Six separate headings of expenditure are identified:

(1) "Smart and inclusive growth", with subheadings 1a "Competitiveness for growth and jobs" (an important part of which is expenditure for research and development; also the Erasmus programme falls under this subheading; between 15.6 billion euro (in 2014) and 21.1 billion euro (in 2020) per year) and 1b "Economic, social and territorial cohesion" (i.e. structural funds and cohesion fund expenditure) (between 34.1 billion euro (in 2014) and 47.9 billion euro (in 2020) per year);

(2) "Sustainable growth: natural resources", which refers in essence to agricultural expenditure (between 47 billion euro (in 2014) and 50.6 billion euro (in 2020) per year);

(3) "Security and citizenship" (among others expenditure for the Asylum, Migration and Integration Fund and for the Internal Security Fund; between 1.6 billion euro (in 2014) and 2.5 billion euro (in 2020) per year);

(4) "Global Europe", which refers to expenditure for external action (between 7.9 billion euro (in 2014) and 8.8 billion euro (in 2020) per year);

(5) "Administration", mainly administrative expenditure of the EU institutions (between 8.2 billion euro (in 2014) and 9.4 billion euro (in 2020) per year);

(6) "Compensations", which refers to certain expenditure related to the accession of Croatia (0.03 billion euro in 2014 and none afterwards).

The overall ceiling for commitment appropriations during the period 2014–2020 has been fixed at 960 billion euro, which equals 1% of gross national income (GNI) and at 908.4 billion euro for payment appropriations (0.95% of GNI). The MFF is adjusted annually (by the Commission), on the basis of a fixed deflator of 2% a year.[157] In nominal terms, the ceilings are higher than those

---

154. Interinstitutional Agreement of 2 Dec. 2013 between the European Parliament, the Council and the Commission on budgetary discipline, on cooperation in budgetary matters and on sound financial management, O.J. 2013, C 373/1. The legal basis for this IIA is Art. 295 TFEU, which allows those three institutions to conclude IIAs in general.

155. See, to that effect, Case 204/86, *Greece v. Council*, para 17.

156. Art. 312(1), last para, TFEU.

157. Art. 6(2) of Council Reg. 1311/2013.

of the 2007–2014 MFF.[158] However, expressed in 2011 prices, the 2014–2020 ceilings are lower than the 2007–2014 ceilings. This reflects the economic austerity considerations underlying the adoption of the 2014–2020 MFF. A practical consequence is that EU expenditure, after a period of constant increase, decreased in 2014 in order to achieve in 2018 the same level as in 2013.[159]

Furthermore, in terms of percentage of GNI, the ceilings in the MFF per budgetary year[160] are lower than the own resources ceilings,[161] which implies that, in fact, the EU spends less than the income to which it can be entitled. However, the MFF ceilings may be exceeded under certain strict conditions, for example to mobilize guarantees given under the EU budget within the context of borrowing-and-lending operations implying Member States,[162] whereas the own resources ceilings may not.[163] In the same way, the MFF can be revised in the event of unforeseen circumstances, but while respecting the own resources ceilings.[164]

The Interinstitutional Agreement of 2 December 2013 between the European Parliament, the Council and the Commission[165] contains complementary provisions related to the MFF and provisions on special instruments not included in the MFF (Part I), provisions on interinstitutional cooperation during the budgetary procedure (Part II) and provisions related to the sound financial management of EU funds (Part III). It does not differ that much from the previous IIAs, apart from the fact that it does not include the MFF itself.[166]

Finally, the MFF not only affects the relationship between the Member States and the EU but also the relationship between the Member States themselves because of the ceilings per main area of EU expenditure. The allocation of EU expenditure between the Member States indeed greatly varies from one policy area to the other. For instance, Poland is a major beneficiary of the structural funds, whereas France receives important EU funding for its agricultural sector.

6. The budgetary procedure

The budgetary procedure is the annual procedure by which the EU budget is established. It is governed by Article 314 TFEU, which establishes a special legislative procedure for the adoption of the EU budget. The Treaty of Lisbon has introduced important changes to the budgetary procedure, at least if one compares Article 314 TFEU to the previously applicable Treaty texts.[167] It has put an end to the distinction between compulsory and non-compulsory expenditure, which had been an important source of conflict between the European Parliament and the Council,[168] it has reduced the number of readings of the draft budget in those two institutions from two to one and the Commission received a right of initiative to propose the draft budget,

158. Interinstitutional Agreement between the European Parliament, the Council and the Commission of 17 May 2006 on budgetary discipline and sound financial management, O.J. 2006, C 139/1, Annex I.
159. Expenditure in 2013 was 144.5 billion euro, whereas, in 2014, it was 135.5 billion euro, in 2015 141.3 billion euro, in 2016 136.6 billion euro, and in 2017 134.5 billion euro.
160. Between 1.03% in 2014 and 0.98% in 2020 for commitment appropriations (average of 1% for 2014–2020) and between 0.98% in 2014 and 0.91% in 2020 for payment appropriations (average of 0.95% for 2014–2020).
161. 1.29% for commitment appropriations and 1.23% for payment appropriations, see *supra*, section 4.1.
162. To which the European financial stabilization mechanism belongs, see *supra*, section 3.1.
163. Recital 6 of the preamble to Council Reg. 1311/2013 and Arts. 3(3) and 4(1).
164. Art. 17(1) of Council Reg. 1311/2013.
165. O.J. 2013, C 373/1.
166. The 2013 IIA is also different in some other ways, taking into account the entry into force of the Treaty of Lisbon. For instance, it includes no longer any reference to the distinction between compulsory and non-compulsory expenditure, see *supra*, section 1.8.
167. The changes are less important if one takes into account budgetary practice, see *supra*, section 1.8.
168. See *supra*, section 1.4.

identical to its right of initiative in legislative matters.[169] The European Parliament no longer has the last word it traditionally had over non-compulsory expenditure, which, in fact, was its most important budgetary power in the pre-Lisbon period,[170] but it has obtained joint power with the Council over all expenditure in the budget and can, in very exceptional circumstances, impose a budget against the will of the Council.[171] However, limits to its powers in the budgetary procedure follow from the requirement, laid down in Article 312(1) TFEU, that the annual budget must comply with the multiannual financial framework.[172]

The budgetary procedure has three stages. The first stage is that of the preparation of the draft budget. Before July 1 of the year n–1, all the institutions draw up estimates of their expenditure for the year n, which are consolidated by the Commission in a draft budget. According to Article 314(2) TFEU, the draft budget is submitted to the European Parliament and the Council not later than 1 September of the year n–1, but, in practice, it is sent earlier to allow as much time as possible for the second stage of the budgetary procedure.

During the second stage, the actual decision-making process takes place. Before 1 October of the year n-1, the Council adopts its position on the draft budget. In doing so, it acts by a qualified majority.[173] Once the European Parliament has received the Council's position, it has forty-two days to determine its own position. If it approves the Council's position or if it has not taken a decision, the budget is (deemed to have been) adopted. If, however, the European Parliament adopts amendments by a majority of its component members, the amended draft budget is submitted to the Conciliation Committee, unless the Council informs the European Parliament, within ten days, that it has approved Parliament's amendments.

The Conciliation Committee is composed of the members of the Council or their representatives and an equal number of members representing the European Parliament. It has the task of reaching agreement on a joint text on the basis of the positions of the European Parliament and the Council. Decisions are taken by a qualified majority of the members of the Council or their representatives and by a majority of the representatives of the European Parliament. The Commission takes part in the Conciliation Committee's proceedings with the explicit purpose of reconciling the positions of the European Parliament and the Council.

The Conciliation Committee has twenty-one days to agree on a joint text. If there is no agreement, the Commission must submit a new draft budget. If, however, an agreement on a joint text is found, the European Parliament and the Council have a period of fourteen days to approve that text. In this respect, Article 314(7) TFEU mentions four possible outcomes. First, if both institutions approve the joint text or fail to take a decision, or if one of them approves the joint text and the other fails to take a decision, the budget is deemed to be adopted in accordance with the joint text. Secondly, if the European Parliament, acting by a majority of its component members, and the Council, acting by a qualified majority, both reject the joint text, or if one of them rejects the joint text and the other fails to take a decision, the Commission must submit a new draft budget. Thirdly, if the European Parliament rejects the joint text while the Council approves it, the Commission must also submit a new draft budget. Fourthly, if the European Parliament approves the joint text whilst the Council rejects it, the former may,

169. Previously, the Council established the draft budget, see *supra*, section 1.1.

170. Non-compulsory expenditure was an important category of expenditure. Whereas it represented 8% of the budget in 1970, it increased to more than 60% in the 2010 budget, when the distinction was last made. Moreover, contrary to compulsory expenditure, which were the consequence of legal obligations and allowed for little flexibility, policy priorities could be set with non-compulsory expenditure.

171. Art. 314(7)(d) TFEU, see further *infra*.

172. See *supra*, section 5.1.

173. Art. 16(3) TEU.

within fourteen days and acting by a majority of its component members and three-fifths of the votes cast, decide to confirm all or some of its previously adopted amendments. If that is not the case, the position agreed in the Conciliation Committee in relation to that amendment prevails.

The third and last stage is that of the formal adoption of the budget. When the second stage has been completed, the President of the European Parliament declares that the budget has been definitively adopted. Once this declaration is made, the budget ranks among the acts which are capable of producing legal effects vis-à-vis third parties.[174] The Treaty of Lisbon has not brought along any changes to this power of the President of the European Parliament.[175]

The functioning of the budgetary procedure is essentially based on a dialogue and cooperation between the European Parliament, the Council and the Commission.[176] This is also stressed by Article 324 TFEU, introduced by the Treaty of Lisbon, according to which regular meetings between the Presidents of the European Parliament, the Council and the Commission are convened, on the initiative of the Commission. These Presidents shall take all the necessary steps to promote consultation and the reconciliation of the positions of their institutions in budgetary matters.[177] Moreover, even if, since the Treaty of Lisbon, the European Parliament has the power to ultimately impose its amendments and thus to decide on the content of the budget, dialogue and cooperation remain of primary importance. Indeed, the procedural hurdle for exercising that power is high, while the agreement reached within the Conciliation Committee functions as a fall-back position.[178] It is, therefore, likely that, in practice, that agreement will determine the content of the relevant budget headings.

7. The implementation of the budget

7.1 *Responsibility and methods of implementation*

Article 317 TFEU provides that the Commission implements the budget in cooperation with the Member States but on its own responsibility. The final responsibility for implementing the budget is, therefore, carried by the Commission.[179]

In accordance with the Financial Regulation,[180] the power to implement the budget is conferred by the Commission to the EU institutions insofar as their section of the budget is concerned.[181] Furthermore, the Commission can implement its own section of the budget in three different ways. First, it can directly implement the budget, by its departments, including its staff

---

174. Case 34/86, *Council v. European Parliament*, para 6. However, a natural or legal person is not directly concerned by the adoption of the budget and, therefore, cannot introduce an action for the annulment of that adoption, see Case 297/83, *Parti écologiste "Les Verts" v. Council*, para 7. In the same way, remarks in the budget can neither confer individual rights nor give rise to any legitimate expectation, see Joined Cases 87/77, 130/77, 22/83, 9/84 and 10/84, *Vittorio Salerno and others v. Commission*, para 59.

175. After the entry into force of the Treaty of Lisbon, the Council took the view that the President of the Council and the President of the Parliament were both required to sign the act establishing the EU's annual budget, since those two institutions had become co-authors of that act. This view was, however, rejected in Case C-77/11, *Council v. European Parliament*, para 50. See further F. Le Bot, "La procedure budgétaire, une procedure legislative très spéciale", 20 *Revue des affaires européennes* (2013), 563–569.

176. See also Case 204/86, *Greece v. Council*, para 16.

177. Interinstitutional cooperation during the budgetary procedure is also an important subject-matter in the legal instruments on the multi-annual financial framework, see Art. 23 of Council Reg. 1311/2013, O.J. 2013, L 347/884 and Part II of the Interinstitutional Agreement of 2 Dec. 2013, O.J. 2013, C 373/1.

178. Art. 314(7)(d) TFEU.

179. See also Art. 58(2) FR.

180. See also *supra*, section 2.

181. Arts. 317, second para, TFEU and 55 FR. The EU budget has ten sections: Section 1 Parliament; Section 2 Council; Section 3 Commission; Section 4 Court of Justice; Section 5 Court of Auditors; Section 6

in the EU delegations in third countries, or through executive agencies. This is called "direct management".[182] If the Commission delegates powers to executive agencies, Council Regulation (EC) No 58/2003 of 19 December 2002 laying down the statute for executive agencies to be entrusted with certain tasks in the management of Community programmes[183] applies.[184]

Secondly, the budget can be implemented under "shared management" with the Member States.[185] This is the most common way of implementing the budget. Member States authorities indeed collect all own resources for the EU and manage some 80% of EU expenditure.

Thirdly, the budget can be implemented indirectly (also called "indirect management") by entrusting budget implementation tasks to, amongst others, third countries, international organizations, the EIB and the EIF, and public as well as certain private law bodies.[186]

The detailed rules on the ways in which the budget can be implemented as well as, in particular, on delegation of powers in that context[187] were first introduced by the Financial Regulation of 2002.[188] They were a response to problems of delegation of powers[189] which became an important subject-matter in the discharge procedure relating to the financial year 1996, which culminated in the collective resignation of the Commission in 1999.

7.2 *Financial actors and internal auditor*

A crucial role in the process of implementing the budget is played by the financial actors, namely the authorizing officer, the accounting officer and, to a lesser extent, the imprest administrator. An important principle is that of the separation of functions between the authorizing officer and the accounting officer.[190] The authorizing officer, which is the EU institution itself and whose powers are delegated or subdelegated to staff,[191] is responsible for implementing revenue and expenditure in accordance with the principles of sound financial management and for ensuring that the requirements of legality and regularity are complied with.[192] The accounting officer, appointed by each institution, is responsible for adequate accounting and management of the financial means.[193] Finally, the imprest administrator is competent for the collection of revenue other than own resources and for the payment of small sums.[194] The financial actors are subject to specific liability rules.[195]

Economic and Social Committee; Section 7 Committee of the Regions; Section 8 European Ombudsman; Section 9 European Data Protection Supervisor; and Section 10 European External Action Service.

182. Art. 58(1)(a) FR.
183. O.J. 2003, L 11/1.
184. Art. 62 FR.
185. Arts. 58(1)(b) and 59 FR.
186. Arts. 58(1)(c) and 60 FR.
187. See also Art. 63 FR.
188. Council Reg. (EC, Euratom) 1605/2002 of 25 June 2002 on the Financial Regulation applicable to the general budget of the European Communities, O.J. 2002, L 248/1.
189. See, e.g., Special Report 1/96 of the European Court of Auditors on the MED programmes, O.J. 1996, C 240/1, para 52.
190. Art. 64 FR.
191. Art. 65 FR. The powers of authorizing officer can be delegated or subdelegated only to staff, see Art. 65(4) FR. This implies that those powers cannot be delegated to persons outside the EU institutions or to members of an EU institution.
192. Art. 66 FR.
193. Art. 68 FR.
194. Art. 70 FR.
195. Arts. 71–75 FR.

Until the entry into force of the Financial Regulation of 2002, the financial controller was also a financial actor. He exercised an *ex ante* control function through the explicit advance authorization (visa) which had to be obtained from him for each individual budget commitment, payment order or recovery order. The financial controller has been replaced, with a change of competences, by the internal auditor.

The internal auditor advises the EU institution by which he or she is appointed[196] on dealing with risks by issuing independent opinions on the quality of management and control systems as well as recommendations for improving the conditions of implementation of operations and promoting sound financial management.[197] Each year, the EU institution concerned must forward to the discharge authority (the European Parliament and the Council) a report on the internal audit of financial management.[198] The internal auditor enjoys a position of functional independence within the EU institution to which he or she belongs. If his or her independence is at stake, the internal auditor can bring an action before the ECJ.[199]

7.3 *The need for a basic act*

In the past, important interinstitutional discussions took place on the question whether the budget was a sufficient legal basis for expenditure.[200] The European Parliament and the Commission proposed an affirmative answer to that question, which would maximize their budgetary powers, whereas the Council took the view that implementation of the budget in relation to expenditure also required a "basic act", which is an act adopted pursuant to a legal basis provided for by the Treaty.

The case-law gave the answer to that question. In *Commission v. Council*,[201] the ECJ already held that "under the scheme of the Treaty the conditions under which legislative and budgetary powers are exercised are not the same." Some months later, in *Commission v. Council*,[202] the ECJ noted that the Commission's power to implement the budget is not such as to modify the Treaty division of powers whereby general or individual measures may be adopted within certain areas. Consequently, even though an individual measure might almost inevitably entail the commitment of expenditure, that measure and the commitment have to be distinguished, particularly since the power to adopt the administrative decision and the power to commit the expenditure might be entrusted, within the internal organization of each institution, to different officials. Finally, in *United Kingdom v. Commission*,[203] the ECJ ruled that implementation of Community expenditure relating to any significant Community action presupposes not only the entry of the relevant appropriation in the budget of the Community, which is a matter for the budgetary authority, but in addition the prior adoption of a basic act authorizing that expenditure, which is a matter for the legislative authority. Implementation of budgetary appropriations for Community action which does not fall within that category – namely non-significant Community action – does not require prior adoption of such a basic act.

Following this judgment, the European Parliament, the Council and the Commission reached agreement on what was to be understood under non-significant Community actions for which expenditure can be authorized without prior adoption of a basic act, e.g., pilot schemes of

196. Art. 98(1) FR.
197. Art. 99(1) FR.
198. Art. 99(5) FR.
199. Art. 100 FR.
200. See also *supra*, section 1.4.
201. Case 242/87, *Commission v. Council*, para 18.
202. Case 16/88, *Commission v. Council*, paras. 16–17.
203. Case C-106/96, *United Kingdom v. Commission*, para 26.

an experimental nature, preparatory actions and one-off actions.[204] Currently, the exceptions to the need for a basic act are defined by the Financial Regulation.[205]

The Treaty of Lisbon has consolidated the solution which already followed from the above-mentioned case-law. Article 310(3) TFEU now expressly mentions that the implementation of expenditure in the budget requires the prior adoption of a legally binding Union act providing a legal basis for its action and for the implementation of the corresponding expenditure. Exceptions can still be provided for in secondary legislation.

The result of this solution is that particular care is required in the exercise of the budgetary and legislative powers, as the one set of powers has implications for the other. Since there is no basis in the Treaties for the legislative powers to take precedence over the budgetary powers, or *vice versa*, the institutions concerned must exercise their powers in such a way as to respect each other's sphere of competence. In practice, this implies that the European Parliament cannot, acting as budgetary authority, define normative provisions of EU policy, whereas the Council cannot, in the exercise of its legislative powers, adopt normative provisions outside the limits set by the budgetary authority. In this respect, Article 310(4) TFEU also imposes on the EU in general a duty not to adopt any act which is likely to have appreciable implications for the budget without providing an assurance that the expenditure arising from such an act is capable of being financed within the limit of the EU's own resources and in compliance with the multiannual financial framework.

8. The European Court of Auditors

The European Court of Auditors,[206] the "external auditor" of the EU, was created by the Second Budgetary Treaty of 22 July 1975[207] and was constituted in 1977. With the Treaty of Maastricht, it became an EU institution.

The Court of Auditors consists of one national of each Member State. Its members are appointed for a renewable term of six years by a qualified majority vote of the Council after consultation of the European Parliament. They elect one of their number as president for a three-year term. The president may be re-elected. In the general interest of the Union, the members of the Court of Auditors are to be completely independent in the performance of their duties, in the same way as the members of the Commission and the Court of Justice. They can only be compulsorily retired by a ruling of the Court of Justice. The same privileges and immunities as for the judges of the Court of Justice apply to them.[208]

Article 287 TFEU defines the Court of Auditors' mission and powers.[209] According to Article 287(1) TFEU, it examines the accounts of all revenue and expenditure of the EU[210] as well as

204. See the Interinstitutional Agreement of 13 Oct. 1998 on the legal basis and implementation of the budget, O.J. 1998, C 344/1, replaced by the IIA of 6 May 1999, O.J. 1999, C 172/1.
205. Art. 54 FR.
206. See further C. Kok, "The Court of Auditors of the European Communities: 'The other Court in Luxembourg'", 26 CML Rev. (1989), 345–367; M.B. Engwirda and A.F.W. Moonen, "De Europese Rekenkamer: Positie, bevoegdheden en toekomstperspectief", (2000) SEW, 246–257; M. Freytag, *Der Europäische Rechnungshof* (Nomos, 2005); and J. Inghelram, "The European Court of Auditors: Current legal issues", 37 CML Rev. (2000), 129–146.
207. See *supra*, section 1.3.
208. See further Arts. 285–286 TFEU.
209. See also further Arts. 158–163 FR.
210. The audit powers of the Court of Auditors are not limited to revenue and expenditure mentioned in the EU budget but cover also, for example, the European Development Funds, see the First Declaration to the Second Budgetary Treaty of 22 July 1975.

the accounts of all revenue and expenditure of bodies set up by the EU in so far as the relevant constituent instrument does not preclude such examination. These bodies are the so-called satellite agencies. In relation to the ECB, the Court of Auditors' audit task is shared with an independent external auditor recommended by the Governing Council and approved by the Council.[211]

According to Article 287(2) TFEU, the Court of Auditors examines the legality and regularity of all revenue[212] and expenditure and examines whether the financial management has been sound. In doing so, it reports in particular on any cases of irregularity. This reporting obligation was added by the Treaty of Amsterdam in the wake of the adoption of the PFI-Convention and the PFI-Regulation,[213] thereby stressing the Court of Auditors' role in the area of the protection of the financial interests of the EU.[214]

The Treaty of Maastricht assigned to the Court of Auditors the task of drawing up a "statement of assurance" on the reliability of the accounts and the regularity and the legality of the underlying transactions.[215] Whereas such a statement on the reliability of the accounts is a typical audit exercise, a statement on the reliability of the regularity and the legality of the underlying transactions is more delicate, because of the enormous amount of transactions involved and the question of which transactions exactly "underlie" a specific item of EU revenue or expenditure. Even a statistically relevant sample of transactions already results in an important number of transactions to be examined. In the absence of any further details in the Treaty or in secondary legislation, it belongs to the Court of Auditors to further define this task. Moreover, since the Treaty of Nice, Article 287(2), first paragraph, TFEU mentions that the statement of assurance may be supplemented by specific assessments for each major area of Union activity. This seems to allow for some form of general statement of assurance every year, supplemented by more detailed assessments covering each year different areas of EU activity.

According to Article 287(3) TFEU, the audit is based on records and, if necessary, performed on the spot in the other institutions, on the premises of any body which manages revenue or expenditure on behalf of the EU and in the Member States, including on the premises of any natural or legal person in receipt of payments from the budget.[216] The audit is carried

211. Art. 27 of Protocol (4) on the Statute of the European System of Central Banks and of the European Central Bank. The Court of Auditors examines "the operational efficiency of the management" of the ECB. The wording of this provision as well as the fact that the ECB's resources and their use are of evident financial interest to the EU and its objectives (see Case C-11/00, *Commission v. ECB*, para 93) suggest that this includes more than merely auditing the efficiency of the ECB's administration. This interpretation seems further confirmed by Art. 20(7) of Council Reg. (EU) 1024/2013 of 15 Oct. 2013 conferring specific tasks on the European Central Bank concerning policies relating to the prudential supervision of credit institutions, O.J. 2013, L 287/63, according to which the Court of Auditors takes into account the supervisory tasks conferred on the ECB by that regulation when auditing the latter.

212. This includes the competence to audit administrative cooperation between the Member States in the VAT area, see Case C-539/09, *Commission v. Germany*, para 81.

213. See further *infra*, sections 10.2 and 10.3.

214. See also Case T-277/97, *Ismeri Europa v. Court of Auditors*, para 123, according to which it was the Court of Auditors' obligation to denounce a serious irregularity it had discovered without having to conclude whether this irregularity was the result of a simple lack of precaution or of a fraudulent intention.

215. See further I. Harden, F. White and K. Donnelly, "The Court of Auditors and financial control and accountability in the European Community", 1 EPL (1995), 599–632; B. Friedmann, "Défis de la certification DAS au contrôle des finances publiques communautaires", (1996) *Revue française de finances publiques*, 7–14; and J. Belle, "Institutions nationales de contrôle et Cour des comptes européenne: déclaration d'assurance annuelle et certification", (2006) *Revue française de finances publiques*, 147–160. The Treaty of Amsterdam added the obligation to publish the statement of assurance.

216. Art. 287(3), first para, TFEU.

out in liaison with national audit bodies (or, if these do not have the necessary powers, with the competent national departments). The expression "in liaison with" was deliberately chosen to bring about a minimum of obligations between the national audit bodies and the Court of Auditors.[217] In practice, it means that the Court of Auditors notifies the national audit body of an audit in the Member State. The latter informs the former whether it intends to take part in the audit. The fact that it can but is not obliged to take part in the audit confirms the autonomous nature of the Court's audit rights in the Member States.[218] The Court of Auditors also has a right to obtain, at its request, any document or information necessary to carry out its task[219] and a right of access to information held by the EIB in respect of the EIB's activity in managing EU expenditure and revenue.[220]

According to Article 287(4) TFEU, the Court of Auditors draws up an annual report after the close of each financial year, which it forwards to the other EU institutions. This report is published in the Official Journal, together with the reactions of the institutions.[221] Furthermore, the Court of Auditors also publishes special reports, which examine certain areas of EU policy. These reports too are usually published. The Court of Auditors may, under certain circumstances, identify third parties in its reports but has to enable them to make observations on those points in such reports which refer to them by name, before those reports are definitively drawn up.[222] Annual reports, special reports and opinions are adopted by a majority of the members of the Court of Auditors. Internal chambers may however be established in order to adopt certain categories of reports or opinions under the conditions laid down by the Court of Auditors' rules of procedure. In practice, all reports and opinions except for the annual report are adopted by such chambers, unless the latter refer their adoption to the Court.[223]

Apart from the above-mentioned internal and external audits at the EU level, EU revenue and expenditure are also subject to audits carried out at the national level, because of the important role of the Member States' authorities in managing EU revenue and expenditure.[224] In order for these audits to be as efficient as possible, "single audit" principles have been developed by

217. C.-D. Ehlermann, *Der Europäische Rechnungshof* (Nomos, 1976), at 35.
218. Ibid.
219. Art. 287(3), second para, TFEU, and Art. 161 FR.
220. Art. 287(3), third para, TFEU. This right is governed by a tripartite agreement between the Court, the EIB and the Commission. However, it is stipulated that, in the absence of such an agreement, the Court shall nevertheless have access to information necessary for the audit of Community expenditure and revenue managed by the EIB. See further D. Skiadas, "European Court of Auditors and European Investment Bank: an uneasy relationship", 5 EPL (1999), 215–225.
221. Art. 287(4) TFEU read with Art. 162(4) FR.
222. Case C-315/99 P, *Ismeri Europa v. Court of Auditors*, para 29. See further J.-F. Bernicot and J.-M. Champomier, "L'auditeur et le juge: Cour de justice des Communautés européennes, 10 juillet 2001: Ismeri Europa Srl c/ Cour des comptes des Communautés européennes (Affaire C-315/99 P)", (2002) *Revue française de finances publiques*, 185–195; O. Mader, *Verteidigungsrechte im Europäischen Gemeinschaftsverwaltungsverfahren* (Nomos, 2006); J. Inghelram, "L'arrêt Ismeri: quelles conséquences pour la Cour des comptes européenne? ", 37 CDE (2001), 707–728.
223. Art. 11 of the rules of procedure, O.J. 2010, L 103/1.
224. See, e.g., Art. 127 of Reg. (EU) 1303/2013 of the European Parliament and of the Council of 17 Dec. 2013 laying down common provisions on the European Regional Development Fund, the European Social Fund, the Cohesion Fund, the European Agricultural Fund for Rural Development and the European Maritime and Fisheries Fund and laying down general provisions on the European Regional Development Fund, the European Social Fund, the Cohesion Fund and the European Maritime and Fisheries Fund and repealing Council Reg. (EC) 1083/2006, O.J. 2013, L 347/320, last amended by Reg. (EU) 2017/2305 of the European Parliament and of the Council of 12 Dec. 2017, O.J. 2017, L 335/1.

the European Court of Auditors,[225] allowing one (internal) audit authority to rely on the work of another. They have meanwhile been put into practice in the structural funds area.[226]

9. The discharge procedure

Discharge, governed by Article 319 TFEU, is the final approval of how the budget for a specific year has been implemented. The power to give discharge lies with the European Parliament, acting on a recommendation by the Council. Although the Treaty mentions that discharge is given to the Commission, separate discharge decisions are taken in relation to the implementation by each EU institution of their own section of the budget. This is a consequence of the powers conferred on them by the Commission in this respect.[227]

The European Parliament and the Council examine the accounts, the financial statement, and the evaluation report referred to in Article 318 TFEU, as well as the annual report by the Court of Auditors together with the replies of the institutions, the statement of assurance, and the special reports by the Court of Auditors. The European Parliament can ask the Commission to give evidence or information on the execution of expenditure or the operation of financial control systems. The Commission must take appropriate steps to act on the observations made by the European Parliament and the Council in the context of the discharge procedure, and must report on the measures taken.

The power of the European Parliament to give discharge to the Commission also implies that it can refuse to give discharge. Although the political effect may be similar, the refusal to give discharge is not the same as a motion of censure against the Commission, which is subject to different procedural requirements.[228] Up to now, the European Parliament has not given discharge on two occasions.[229] In order to put pressure, it can also postpone its decision to grant a discharge until its requests are met. This is a more often used instrument by the European Parliament.

The scrutiny of the implementation of the budget is the conclusion of the budget cycle. For a long time, this scrutiny was simply a formal accounting exercise. However, it has gradually gained importance and has resulted in a series of measures to improve financial accountability and control. The creation of OLAF and the introduction by the Financial Regulation of 2002 of clear rules on delegation of powers in the process of implementing the budget are a consequence of the discharge procedure in relation to the financial year 1996.[230]

---

225. Opinion 2/2004 on the "single audit" model (and a proposal for a Community internal control framework), O.J. 2004, C 107/1.
226. See further Special Report 16/2013 of the Court of Auditors on "Taking stock of 'single audit' and the Commission's reliance on the work of national audit authorities in Cohesion", available at <www.eca.europa.eu/Lists/ECADocuments/SR13_16/SR13_16_EN.pdf> (last accessed on 20 Mar. 2018). See also Special Report 7/2017 on "The certification bodies' new role on CAP expenditure: a positive step towards a single audit model but with significant weaknesses to be addressed", available at <www.eca.europa.eu/Lists/ECADocuments/SR17_7/SR_CERTIFICATION_BODIES_EN.pdf> (last accessed on 20 Mar. 2018).
227. Art. 55 FR. See further on this issue, M. Rossi, "Zur Entlastungsbefugnis des Europäischen Parlaments", 48 EuR (2013), 170–193.
228. Arts. 17(8) TEU and 234 TFEU.
229. In Nov. 1984 and Dec. 1998. The latter episode led to the collective resignation of the Commission in Mar. 1999. See further "Editorial Comments, The report of the Committee of Independent Experts: an ill wind [...]", 36 CML Rev. (1999), 269–272, and P. Craig, "The fall and renewal of the Commission: Accountability, contract and administrative organisation", 6 ELJ (2000), 98–116.
230. See also *supra*, section 7.1 and *infra*, section 11.1.

10. The protection of the financial interests of the EU

10.1 Origins

EU money is to a large extent paid to beneficiaries under a system of shared management and on the basis of a large variety of – usually complex – rules and conditions. Such a system of indirect financing increases the risk of irregularities and fraud to the detriment of the EU budget.[231] Moreover, irregular and fraudulent actions to the detriment of the EU budget are frequently cross-border. Cooperation between the administrative and judicial bodies of the Member States is, therefore, particularly important.

Already in 1976, the Commission launched a proposal, which included a modification of the existing Treaties, to allow for the adoption of common rules on the protection under criminal law of the financial interests of the European Communities and the prosecution of infringements of the provisions of those Treaties, as well as on the liability and protection under criminal law of officials and other servants of the European Communities.[232] Although this ambitious proposal was never adopted, it has had, to a certain extent, a precursory role, since it highlighted the need for an appropriate degree of judicial cooperation in criminal matters, in order for the protection of the EU's financial interests to be fully effective. This same idea now finds expression in Article 86 TFEU, which was introduced by the Treaty of Lisbon and which allows for the establishment of a European Public Prosecutor's Office.

The protection of the EU's financial interests became gradually more important with the adoption of several sectoral rules[233] since the 1970s, in particular in the areas of agriculture and structural funds, which are important areas of EU expenditure. Furthermore, the reform of the Community finances in the 1980s[234] was accompanied by an increased focus on the protection of its financial interests. This resulted, amongst others, in the creation in 1988 of UCLAF,[235] a unit within the Commission coordinating anti-fraud activities.

The incentive for the development of general rules on the protection of the EU's financial interests was given by the landmark ruling in *Commission v. Greece*,[236] in which the ECJ held that, when EU legislation does not specifically provide any penalty for an infringement of EU law, Member States have to ensure that these infringements are penalized under the same conditions as infringements of national law and they have to ensure that, in any event, the penalties are effective, proportionate and dissuasive.

Shortly after, the Treaty of Maastricht introduced Article 209a EC, which included the first explicit reference in the Treaty to the protection of the EU's financial interests and imposed on the Member States, in line with the ruling in *Commission v. Greece*, a duty to take the same

---

231. See further the Commission's annual reports on the protection of the EU's financial interests, e.g., for 2015, COM(2016)472.
232. Draft for a Treaty (1) amending the Treaties establishing the European Communities so as to permit the adoption of common rules on the protection under criminal law of the financial interests of the Communities and the prosecution of infringements of the provisions of those Treaties, and (2) amending the Treaty establishing a Single Council and a Single Commission of the European Communities so as to permit the adoption of common rules on the liability and protection under criminal law of officials and other servants of the European Communities, O.J. 1976, C 222/2.
233. They are specific to certain policy areas, as opposed to general rules with regard to the protection of the EU's financial interests, which are applicable to all policy areas.
234. See *supra*, section 1.4.
235. Abbreviation of *Unité de coordination de la lutte anti-fraude*.
236. Case 68/88, *Commission v. Greece*.

measures to counter fraud affecting the EU's financial interests as they take to counter fraud affecting their own financial interests.

The Treaty of Amsterdam further developed the Treaty provision on the protection of the EU's financial interests, which became Article 280 EC. The obligation on the Member States to assimilate measures to counter fraud affecting the EU's financial interests to those which they take to counter fraud affecting their own financial interests was supplemented by an obligation on the EU and the Member States to counter fraud and any other illegal activities affecting the EU's financial interests through measures which act as a deterrent and be such as to afford effective protection in the Member States. Most importantly, however, Article 280(4) EC became a specific legal basis for the adoption of legislative measures in the area of the protection of the EU's financial interests. The first measure to be adopted on the basis of that provision was the OLAF Regulation.

The Treaty of Nice did not bring any changes to Article 280 EC. The Commission had proposed to make it the legal basis for the creation of a European Public Prosecutor, but this proposal was not accepted.[237] The Treaty of Lisbon deleted the last sentence of Article 280(4) EC, according to which the measures adopted under that provision "shall not concern the application of national criminal law or the national administration of justice". This sentence became obsolete with the changes brought by the Treaty of Lisbon in the area of judicial cooperation in criminal matters.

10.2 *The PFI Convention of 1995 and the PFI Directive of 2017*

In parallel with the above developments, the criminal law aspects of the protection of the financial interests were dealt with under the former third pillar of the EU. One of the first conventions to be drawn up under that pillar was the PFI[238] Convention of 26 July 1995.[239] Article 1 contains a definition of the concept of fraud affecting the EU's financial interests. The Member States undertake the obligation to take the necessary and appropriate measures to ensure that the conduct covered by the definition, as well as participation in, instigation of, or attempt at such conduct, all constitute criminal offences in their national penal law systems. They are obliged to set effective, proportionate and dissuasive criminal penalties for such conduct, with a distinction being made between serious and minor fraud.[240] The Convention also contains provisions on criminal liability of heads of businesses, jurisdiction of the Member States, extradition and prosecution, cooperation in relation to cross-border fraud, and the principle of *ne bis in idem*.[241]

Three supplementary protocols have been annexed to the PFI Convention in the subsequent years. The Protocol of 27 September 1996[242] contains a definition of both passive corrup-

---

237. See *supra*, section 1.7.
238. The abbreviation "PIF", acronym of the French term "*protection des intérêts financiers*", is often also used.
239. Convention drawn up on the basis of Art. K.3 of the Treaty on European Union, on the protection of the European Communities' financial interests, O.J. 1995, C 316/49, with Explanatory Report, O.J. 1997, C 191/1. See further, e.g., F. C. M. A. Michiels, "Nieuwe instrumenten ter bescherming van de financiële belangen van de Europese Gemeenschappen", (1996) SEW, 362–371.
240. Art. 2 of the PFI Convention.
241. Arts. 3–7 of the PFI Convention.
242. O.J. 1996, C 313/2. See also Explanatory Report, O.J. 1998, C 11/5. See also, with a more general scope than the protection of the Communities' financial interests, the Convention on the fight against corruption involving officials of the European Communities or officials of Member States of the European Union, drawn up by the Council in 1997, O.J. 1997, C 195/1. For a more general view on the subject-matter, see the EU Anti-Corruption Report, COM(2014)38, and the European Court of Auditors' view on that report, available at <www.eca.europa.eu/Lists/ECADocuments/PL14_LETTER/PL14_LETTER_EN.PDF> (last accessed on 20 Mar. 2018).

tion of officials (both EU and national), and active corruption (bribery), as a result of which the financial interests of the EU are or may be damaged, as well as the obligation on Member States to make these forms of corruption subject to penal sanctions. The Second Protocol of 19 June 1997[243] obliges the Member States to establish money laundering as a criminal offence, and to take necessary measures to ensure that legal persons can be held liable as well as ensuring that the confiscation or removal of the instruments and proceeds of these offences is possible. Finally, the Protocol of 29 November 1996[244] governs the interpretation of the PFI Convention and the protocols annexed thereto.[245] This jurisdictional protocol provides for voluntary acceptance by the Member States, by means of a declaration, of the jurisdiction of the ECJ to give preliminary rulings. The Member States can choose whether only courts of last instance may make preliminary references to the Court of Justice, or all their courts.

The ratification of the PFI Convention and the protocols took several years.[246] Partly for that reason, the Commission made a proposal for a PFI Directive in 2001.[247] This proposal was based on Article 280(4) EC and included elements from the PFI Convention and its protocols.[248] After the entry into force of the Treaty of Lisbon, which left the PFI Convention and its protocols unaffected,[249] the Commission submitted a new proposal for a PFI Directive.[250] After several years of negotiation, the PFI Directive was adopted in July 2017.[251]

The PFI Directive defines, for the first time, the notion of "financial interests of the EU". They are all revenues and expenditures covered by, acquired through, or due to the EU budget or the budgets of institutions, bodies, offices and agencies established under the Treaties or budgets managed and monitored by them.[252] This definition is clearly inspired by the rulings in *Commission v. ECB*,[253] and *Commission v. EIB*.[254] In response to the argument of the ECB and the EIB that the OLAF Regulation did not apply to them on the grounds that the notion of "financial interests of the EU" only referred to the EU budget, the ECJ held that that notion is not restricted exclusively to the EU budget in the strict sense, but also covers the resources and expenditure of all bodies, offices or agencies which owe their existence to the Treaty.[255] This being said, the PFI Directive appears more restrictive than the ECJ's ruling, which refers to all resources and expenditure of those bodies and not only, as the PFI Directive does, to resources and expenditure included in their budgets.[256]

243. O.J. 1997, C 221/12. See also Explanatory Report, O.J. 1999, C 91/8.
244. O.J. 1997, C 151/1.
245. The jurisdictional protocol also applies to the Second Protocol, drawn up at a later date, see Art. 13(3) of the Second protocol.
246. The Convention and the protocols entered into force on 17 Oct. 2002, with the exception of the second protocol, which entered into force on 19 May 2009.
247. COM(2001)115.
248. See further, e.g., D. E. Comijs, "Communautair strafrecht?", 7 NTER (2001), 267–271.
249. See Art. 9 of Protocol (36) on Transitional Provisions.
250. Proposal for a Directive of the European Parliament and the Council on the fight against fraud to the Union's financial interests by means of criminal law, COM(2012)363/2.
251. Dir. (EU) 2017/1371 of the European Parliament and of the Council of 5 July 2017 on the fight against fraud to the Union's financial interests by means of criminal law, O.J. 2017, L 198/29. The PFI Directive replaces the PFI Convention with effect from 6 July 2019, see Art. 16..
252. Art. 2(1)(a) of the PFI Directive.
253. Case C-11/00, *Commission v. ECB*.
254. Case C-15/00, *Commission v. EIB*.
255. See respectively paras. 91 and 122.
256. See on this difference, Opinion 8/2012 of the European Court of Auditors on the Commission's proposal, O.J. 2012, C 383/1, para 7.

The Commission's proposal intended to solve the question, which arose in the context of the PFI Convention, whether fraud affecting the EU's financial interests includes VAT fraud.[257] With reference to *Commission v. Germany*,[258] the Commission considered that this is actually the case, because of the direct link between the collection of VAT revenue in compliance with EU law and the availability to the EU budget of the corresponding resources.[259] Meanwhile, the case-law has interpreted the PFI Convention as being also applicable to VAT fraud.[260] As a compromise, the PFI Directive applies to cross-border VAT fraud with damages over 10 million euro.[261]

10.3 *The PFI Regulation of 1995*

In the same year as the PFI Convention, the Council adopted the PFI Regulation.[262] Whereas the former provides for criminal law PFI measures, which, at that time, could only be adopted under the third pillar of the EU, the latter provides for administrative PFI measures, for which a legal basis existed under the first pillar of the EU.[263]

By adopting the PFI Regulation, the Council laid down a series of general principles and required that, as a general rule, all sectoral regulations comply with those principles.[264] The PFI Regulation contains the first general definition of the concept "irregularity". It is defined as "any infringement of a provision of [EU] law resulting from an act or omission by an economic operator, which has, or would have, the effect of prejudicing the general budget of the [EU] or budgets managed by them, either by reducing or losing revenue accruing from own resources collected directly on behalf of the [EU], or by an unjustified item of expenditure".[265] This definition also covers the concept of "fraud" as defined by the PFI Convention.[266] Even irregularities having no specific financial impact may be seriously prejudicial to the financial interests of the EU and thus constitute an "irregularity" in the sense of the PFI Regulation. This is, for instance, true for non-compliance with public procurement rules[267] or for depriving the EU of potential revenue.[268]

The PFI Regulation makes a distinction between "administrative measures" and "administrative penalties". Any irregularity should in principle lead to the withdrawal of the wrongly obtained advantage either by the obligation to pay or repay the amounts due or wrongly received, or by the total or partial loss of the security lodged. Those "administrative measures" are not regarded as penalties.[269] Intentional irregularities or those caused by negligence may lead to "administrative penalties", listed in Article 5(1) of the PFI Regulation, such as the payment

---

257. See also Special Report 8/2007 of the European Court of Auditors concerning administrative cooperation in the field of VAT, O.J. 2008, C 20/1, para 91.
258. Case C-539/09, *Commission v. Germany*.
259. See Recital 4 in the preamble to the proposal.
260. Case C-105/14, *Taricco and Others*, para 41.
261. Art. 2(2) of the PFI Directive.
262. Council Reg. (EC, Euratom) 2988/95 of 18 Dec. 1995 on the protection of the European Communities financial interests, O.J. 1995, L 312/1.
263. The legal basis of the PFI Reg. was Art. 235 EC. Art. 280(4) EC (now Art. 325(4) TFEU) did not yet exist.
264. Case C-420/06, *Jager*, para 61.
265. Art. 1(2) of the PFI Reg. This definition also constitutes a reference for defining the European Court of Auditors' task, introduced by the Treaty of Amsterdam, to report in particular on any cases of irregularity (Art. 287(2), first para, TFEU), see also *supra*, section 8.
266. See Recital 6 in the preamble to the PFI Reg.
267. Case C-465/10, *Chambre de commerce et d'industrie de l'Indre*, para 46.
268. Case C-669/11, *Société ED et F Man Alcohols*, para 37.
269. Art. 4 of the PFI Reg.

of an administrative fine or the exclusion from a subsidy scheme. The administrative measures and penalties may be applied to the economic operators who have committed the irregularity and to those who are under a duty to take responsibility for the irregularity or to ensure that it is not committed.[270]

The PFI Regulation also lays down rules on the limitation period for proceedings,[271] which equally apply to administrative measures and penalties.[272] The limitation period for proceedings is four years from the time when the irregularity was committed.[273] In the case of continuous or repeated irregularities, the limitation period runs from the day on which the irregularity ceases. This is the case when the irregularity is committed by an operator who derives economic advantages from a body of similar transactions which infringe the same provision of EU law.[274] Sectoral rules may make provision for a shorter period which may not be less than three years, whereas Member States retain the possibility of applying a period which is longer than four years. However, this longer period must be proportionate in light of the objective of protecting the EU's financial interests.[275]

The penalty, provided for by EU law, consisting in excluding an operator from a subsidy scheme because of a false declaration, is not criminal in nature. Therefore, combining that penalty with a criminal penalty is not forbidden by the *ne bis in idem* principle.[276] If a penalty is provided for by national law, it is up to the national court to determine whether this penalty is criminal in nature and thus to assess whether it can be combined with a criminal penalty. However, even if this combination is not allowed, the remaining penalties must remain effective, proportionate and dissuasive.[277]

The PFI Regulation contains some general rules on checks and inspections,[278] which are further developed in sectoral rules as well as in Council Reg. (Euratom, EC) No 2185/96 of 11 November 1996 concerning on-the-spot checks and inspections carried out by the Commission in order to protect the European Communities' financial interests against fraud and other irregularities.[279] This regulation grants the Commission far-reaching powers to carry out checks and inspections for the detection of serious or transnational irregularities, in special cases where such checks are necessary in order to improve the effectiveness of the protection of financial interests and so to ensure an equivalent level of protection within the EU, or at the request of a Member State.[280] The Commission inspections are carried out under the Commission's authority and responsibility by its officials and other servants.[281] These inspectors have access, under

270. Art. 7 of the PFI Reg.
271. Art. 3 of the PFI Reg.
272. Case C-278/02, *Handlbauer*, para 34.
273. See further Case C-59/14, *Firma Ernst Kollmer Fleischimport und –export*, paras. 29 and 33.
274. Case C-279/05, *Vonk Dairy Products*, para 44. See also Case C-52/14, *Pfeifer & Langen*, paras. 56 and 69.
275. Joined Cases C-201/10 and C-202/10, *Ze Fu Fleischhandel and Vion Trading*, para 51.
276. Case C-489/10, *Bonda*, para 45. The judgment contains a detailed analysis of the case-law of the European Court of Human Rights in this respect (paras. 36–44). See for an earlier opposite view, J. Pradel, G. Corstens and G. Vermeulen, *Droit Penal Européen*, 3rd ed. (Dalloz, 2009), at 725.
277. Case C-617/10, *Åkerberg Fransson*, paras. 36–37.
278. Art. 9 of the PFI Reg.
279. O.J. 1996, L 292/2. See further L. Kuhl and H. Spitzer, "Die Verordnung (Euratom, EG) Nr. 2185/96 des Rates über die Kontrollbefugnisse der Kommission im Bereich der Betrugsbekämpfung", 9 EuZW (1998), 37–44, and S. Ulrich, "Kontrollen des Europäischen Amtes für Betrugsbekämpfung (OLAF) bei Wirtschaftsbeteiligten: Befugnisse, Verfahrensrechte und Rechtsschutzmöglichkeiten bei Kontrollen vor Ort nach der VO (Euratom, EG) Nr. 2185/96", (2000) *Europäisches Wirtschafts- & Steuerrecht*, 137–147.
280. Art. 2 of Council Reg. 2185/96.
281. Art. 6 of Council Reg. 2185/96. In practice, they are carried out by OLAF, see further *infra*, section 11.3.

the same conditions as national administrative inspectors and in compliance with national legislation, to all the information and documentation on the operations concerned which are required for the proper conduct of the on-the-spot checks and inspections.[282] The officials of the Member State concerned "may participate in the on-the-spot checks and inspections",[283] which implies that they are not obliged to do so. This confirms the autonomous nature of the Commission's on-the-spot checks and inspections in the Member States.

11. The European Anti-Fraud Office (OLAF)

11.1 Creation and legal framework

OLAF[284] is the most visible expression of the measures taken until now in the area of the protection of the EU's financial interests.[285] It was preceded by UCLAF, a unit responsible for coordinating anti-fraud activities, which the Commission created within its own structure in 1988.[286] However, in the context of the discharge procedure of the financial year 1996, which ultimately led to the collective resignation of the Commission in 1999, the European Parliament called for the creation of an independent anti-fraud office. In December 1998, the Commission submitted a proposal to create an independent anti-fraud agency,[287] which, after several changes negotiated within a high-level group of representatives of the European Parliament, the Council and the Commission, led to the creation of OLAF and the definition of its competences.

---

282. Art. 7 of Council Reg. 2185/96.
283. Art. 4 of Council Reg. 2185/96.
284. Abbreviation of *Office européen de lutte antifraude.*
285. See further on OLAF, e.g., F. H. Brüner and H. Spitzer, "OLAF-Reform II – Kosmetischer Eingriff oder Großer Wurf?", 43 EuR (2008), 859–872; V. Covolo, "The legal framework of OLAF investigations. What lessons for the European penal area?", 2 *New Journal of European Criminal Law* (2011), 201–219; V. Covolo, *L'émergence d'un droit pénal en réseau. Analyse critique du système européen de lutte antifraude* (Nomos, 2015); S. Gleß, "Das Europäische Amt für Betrugsbekämpfung (OLAF)", 10 EuZW (1999), 618–621; X. Groussot and Z. Popov, "What's wrong with OLAF? Accountability, due process and criminal justice in European anti-fraud policy", 47 CML Rev. (2010), 605–643; J. Inghelram, *Legal and Institutional Aspects of the European Anti-Fraud Office (OLAF) – An Analysis with a Look Forward to a European Public Prosecutor's Office* (Europa Law Publishing, 2011); J. Inghelram, "Judicial review of investigative acts of the European Anti-Fraud Office (OLAF): A Search for a Balance", 49 CML Rev. (2012), 601–628; J. Inghelram, "Fundamental Rights, the European Anti-Fraud Office (OLAF) an a European Public Prosecutor's Office (EPPO): Some selected issues", (2012) *Kritische Vierteljahresschrift für Gesetzgebung und Rechtsprechung,* 67–81; J. Inghelram, "Het Europees Bureau voor Fraudebestrijding (OLAF): Actuele juridische uitdagingen", (2015) SEW, 233–244; J. Inghelram, "Procedural guarantees in OLAF investigations: Reflections on the impact of the Charter of Fundamental Rights of the EU" in V. Bazzocchi (Ed.), *EPPO and OLAF: The Judicial Review and Procedural Guarantees,* (Fondazione Basso – OLAF, 2015), at 109–117; G. Kratsas, "A case for OLAF: The place and role of the Anti-fraud Office in the European Union Context", 18 EPL (2012), 65–97; M. Niestedt and H. Boeckmann, "Verteidigungsrechte bei internen Untersuchungen des OLAF: Das Urteil Franchet und Byk des Gerichts erster Instanz und die Reform der Verordnung (EG) Nr. 1073/1999", 20 EuZW (2009), 70–74; B. Sarrot Reynaud de Cresseneuil, "Le rôle de l'OLAF dans la lutte contre la fraude à la TVA intracommunautaire", (2007) *Revue de droit fiscal,* 3, 45–48; C. Stefanou, S. White and H. Xanthaki, *OLAF at the Crossroads – Action against EU fraud* (Hart, 2011); R. Trașcă, "La place de l'Office européen de lutte antifraude dans la répression de la fraude au budget communautaire", 44 CDE (2008), 7–82; J. A. E. Vervaele, "Towards an independent European agency to fight fraud and corruption in the EU?", (1999) *European Journal of Crime, Criminal Law and Criminal Justice,* 331–346; and J. Wakefield, "Good governance and the European Anti-Fraud Office", 12 EPL (2006), 549–575.
286. See *supra,* section 10.1.
287. COM(98)717.

OLAF has been created by a decision adopted by the Commission on 28 April 1999 (hereinafter the "OLAF-Decision").[288] The most important instruments governing its competences were, however, two regulations adopted on 25 May 1999,[289] which have meanwhile been replaced by one single regulation adopted on 11 September 2013 (hereinafter the "OLAF Regulation").[290]

Furthermore, on 25 May 1999, the European Parliament, the Council and the Commission signed an Interinstitutional Agreement concerning internal investigations by OLAF (hereinafter: the "1999 IIA").[291] This Agreement contains in its annex a model decision, to be adopted by an EU institution, body, office or agency, concerning the terms and conditions for internal investigations by OLAF in relation to the prevention of fraud, corruption and any illegal activity detrimental to the EU's interests.

Finally, OLAF's investigations are also governed by guidelines adopted by the Director-General of OLAF pursuant to Article 17(8) of the OLAF Regulation. These guidelines are published on OLAF's internet site.[292]

11.2 *Structure and organization*

Whereas the Commission initially proposed that OLAF be an independent agency, OLAF is structurally still a part of the Commission. However, insofar as the investigation function is concerned, OLAF has far-reaching independence.[293] This is expressed, amongst others, by the fact that the Director-General of OLAF cannot seek nor take instructions from any government or any institution, body, office or agency in the performance of his duties with regard to the opening and carrying-out of external and internal investigations or to the drafting of reports following such investigations and that he can bring an action against the Commission before the ECJ if his independence is at stake.[294] This far-reaching independence is limited to investigations and does not apply when OLAF exercises other competences.[295] In the latter case, OLAF is to be compared to a Directorate-General of the Commission. In order to guarantee its independence, OLAF also has budgetary and administrative autonomy in practice.[296]

---

288. Commission Dec. 1999/352/EC, ECSC, Euratom of 28 Apr. 1999 establishing the European Anti-Fraud Office (OLAF), O.J. 1999, L 136/20, last amended by Commission Dec. (EU) 2015/2418 of 18 Dec. 2015, O.J. 2015, L 333/148.
289. Reg. (EC) 1073/1999 of the European Parliament and of the Council of 25 May 1999 concerning investigations conducted by the European Anti-Fraud Office (OLAF), O.J. 1999, L 136/1, and Council Reg. (Euratom) 1074/1999 of 25 May 1999 concerning investigations conducted by the European Anti-Fraud Office (OLAF), O.J. 1999, L 136/8. Both had the same contents, but the former, adopted on the basis of Art. 280(4) EC (now Art. 325(4) TFEU), applied in EC matters and the latter in Euratom matters.
290. Reg. (EU, Euratom) 883/2013 of the European Parliament and of the Council of 11 Sept. 2013 concerning investigations conducted by the European Anti-Fraud Office (OLAF) and repealing Reg. (EC) 1073/1999 of the European Parliament and of the Council and Council Reg. (Euratom) 1074/1999, O.J. 2013, L 248/1, last amended by Reg. (EU) 2016/2030 of the European Parliament and of the Council of 26 Oct. 2016, O.J. 2016, L 317/1.
291. O.J. 1999, L 136/15. This IIA is still in force.
292. <ec.europa.eu/anti-fraud/sites/antifraud/files/docs/body/gip_18092013_en.pdf> (last accessed on 20 Mar. 2018).
293. Art. 3 of the OLAF Decision.
294. Art. 17(3) of the OLAF Reg.
295. See *infra*, section 11.3.
296. The Director-General of OLAF acts as the appointing authority for the staff members of OLAF (Art. 6(1) of the OLAF Decision). Moreover, the budget appropriations for OLAF are entered under a specific budget line (Arts. 6(2) of the OLAF Decision8 and 18 of the OLAF Reg.) and the Director-General of OLAF acts as authorizing officer for the implementation of that budget line (Art. 6(3) of the OLAF Decision). In order

OLAF is headed by a Director-General, appointed by the Commission after consultation with the European Parliament and the Council. His term of office is seven years and not renewable.[297] He may delegate in writing certain of his functions to one or more members of the staff of OLAF.[298] Currently, OLAF has four Directorates, two of which deal with investigations, one with investigation support and one with policy. OLAF has some 420 members of staff.

11.3 *Competences*

OLAF's most important competences are its investigation competences. They are the rationale of its existence. A distinction must be made between "external investigations" (in the Member States and in third countries) and "internal investigations" (within EU institutions, bodies, offices and agencies).

When carrying out external investigations, OLAF exercises the investigation powers which the relevant legislation confers upon the Commission.[299] With regard to investigations carried out in the Member States, these are the powers defined in Council Reg. (EC) No 2185/96,[300] in Article 9(1) of the PFI Regulation, as well as in the relevant sectoral rules.[301] In relation to investigations carried out in third countries, the investigation powers are those defined by the cooperation and mutual assistance agreements and any other legal instrument in force.

Internal investigations are governed, in part, by Article 4 of the OLAF Regulation, which requires each EU institution, body, office and agency to adopt a decision containing additional rules on the conduct of such investigations.[302] A model decision is annexed to the 1999 IIA, which has been taken over by or which has inspired many of the decisions adopted by the EU institutions, bodies, offices and agencies pursuant to Article 4 of the OLAF Regulation.[303]

---

to safeguard the independence of the OLAF Supervisory Committee, special rules apply to the appointment of staff of its secretariat, see Art. 15(8) of the OLAF Reg.

297. Art. 17(1)–(2) of the OLAF Reg.
298. Art. 17(6) of the OLAF Reg.
299. Art. 3 of the OLAF Reg.
300. See *supra*, section 10.3.
301. These are primarily the following: for EU own resources, Art. 3 of Council Reg. (EU, Euratom) 608/2014 of 26 May 2014 laying down implementing measures for the system of own resources of the EU, O.J. 2014, L 168/29; for mutual administrative assistance, Council Reg. (EC) 515/97 of 13 Mar. 1997 on mutual assistance between the administrative authorities of the Member States and cooperation between the latter and the Commission to ensure the correct application of the law on customs and agricultural matters, O.J. 1997, L 82/1, last amended by Reg. (EU) 2015/1525 of the European Parliament and of the Council of 9 Sept. 2015, O.J. 2015, L 243/1; for the common agricultural policy, Art. 47 of Reg. (EU) 1306/2013 of the European Parliament and of the Council of 17 Dec. 2013 on the financing, management and monitoring of the common agricultural policy and repealing Council Reg. (EEC) 352/78, (EC) 165/94, (EC) 2799/98, (EC) 814/2000, (EC) 1290/2005 and (EC) 485/2008, O.J. 2013, L 347/549, last amended by Reg. (EU) 2017/2393 of the European Parliament and of the Council of 13 Dec. 2017, O.J. 2017, L 350/15; for the structural funds, Art. 75 of Reg. (EU) 1303/2013 of the European Parliament and of the Council of 17 Dec. 2013 laying down common provisions on the European Regional Development Fund, the European Social Fund, the Cohesion Fund, the European Agricultural Fund for Rural Development and the European Maritime and Fisheries Fund and laying down general provisions on the European Regional Development Fund, the European Social Fund, the Cohesion Fund and the European Maritime and Fisheries Fund and repealing Council Reg. (EC) 1083/2006, O.J. 2013, L 347/320, last amended by Reg. (EU) 2017/2305 of the European Parliament and of the Council of 12 Dec. 2017, O.J. 2017, L 335/1; and for direct expenditure, the Financial Reg.
302. Art. 4(1) and (7) of the OLAF Reg. See further on this requirement, Case C-11/00, *Commission v. ECB*, and Case C-15/00, *Commission v. EIB*.
303. For the Council, see Dec. 1999/394/EC, Euratom of 25 May 1999 concerning the terms and conditions for internal investigations in relation to the prevention of fraud, corruption and any illegal activity detrimental to the Communities' interests, O.J. 1999, L 149/36. For the Commission, see Dec. 1999/396/EC, ECSC,

Internal investigations can be conducted for the purpose either to combat fraud, corruption and any other illegal activity affecting the EU's financial interests, or to investigate serious matters relating to the discharge of professional duties by members or staff of EU institutions, bodies, offices and agencies.[304] They can therefore fall either within or outside the scope of the protection of the EU's financial interests. This distinction is important since the OLAF Regulation only applies to internal investigations which fall within that scope. This derives from the fact that the legal basis of this regulation is Article 280(4) EC (now Art. 325(4) TFEU), which only allows for the adoption of "measures in the fields of the prevention of and fight against fraud affecting the [EU's] financial interests".[305]

Therefore, the only legal basis for internal investigations which fall outside that same scope would be the acceptance by the EU institution concerned, on the basis of its administrative autonomy,[306] of OLAF – which, from an institutional point of view, remains a Commission service – carrying out such investigations on its premises. The institutions which have taken over the model decision annexed to the 1999 IIA have thereby also made this acceptance. On the contrary, some other institutions or bodies have adopted a decision on OLAF internal investigations which is limited to the protection of the EU's financial interests.[307] In their case, OLAF would not be competent to carry out internal investigations on their premises which fall outside the scope of the protection of the EU's financial interests, unless they decided otherwise on an *ad hoc* basis.

When carrying out internal investigations, OLAF has the right of immediate and unannounced access to any information held by the EU institutions, bodies, offices and agencies, as well as to their premises, and it is empowered to inspect their accounts. OLAF may also make a copy of and obtain extracts from any document or the contents of any data medium held by the EU institutions, bodies, offices and agencies and, if necessary, assume custody of such documents or data to ensure there is no danger of their disappearance.[308] This includes the right to seize an EU official's computer or to copy the contents of the computer's storage devices.

Euratom of 2 June 1999 concerning the terms and conditions for internal investigations in relation to the prevention of fraud, corruption and any illegal activity detrimental to the Communities' interests, O.J. 1999, L 149/57. For the European Parliament, see Rule 12 of the Rules of Procedure which refers to the Dec. of the European Parliament of 18 Nov. 1999 on the amendments to the Rules of Procedure following the Interinstitutional Agreement of 25 May 1999 on the internal investigations conducted by the European Anti-Fraud Office (OLAF), O.J. 2000, C 189/209. Not all Members of the European Parliament agreed with that decision. Their action for annulment against that decision was, however, unsuccessful, see Case T-17/00, *Rothley and Others v. Parliament*, and Case C-167/02 P, *Rothley and Others v. Parliament*.

304. Arts. 2(1) of the OLAF Decision and 1(4) of the OLAF Reg.
305. This is not changed by the wording of Art. 1(4) of the OLAF Reg., which seems to refer to internal investigations falling outside the scope of the protection of the EU's financial interests. Indeed, three words ("to that end") added to the second sentence of that provision confirm that the OLAF Reg. is a legal basis only for OLAF investigations falling within that scope, in conformity with Art. 325(4) TFEU.
306. See Recital 4 to the preamble of the 1999 IIA and Case T-530/12 P, *Moises Bermejo Garde v. Economic and Social Committee*, para 105. It does not seem that Art. 86(2) of the EU Staff Reg., according to which OLAF may launch administrative investigations in disciplinary matters, can replace the decision adopted by each EU institution, body, office and agency in this respect. In contrast with this decision (and with the OLAF Reg.), this provision does not include any rule on the conduct of investigations or on procedural guarantees.
307. This seems to be the case, e.g., for the European Court of Auditors (see <www.eca.europa.eu/Lists/ECADocuments/DEC98_2004/DEC98_2004_EN.PDF>, and <www.eca.europa.eu/Lists/ECADocuments/DEC99_2004/DEC99_2004_EN.PDF> (last accessed on 20 Mar. 2018)), the ECB (see O.J. 2016, L 79/34), and the EIB (see <www.eib.org/attachments/general/pv_cg_olaf_en.pdf> (last accessed on 20 Mar. 2018)).
308. Art. 4(2)(a) of the OLAF Reg.

Moreover, OLAF may request oral information, including through interviews, and written information from officials, other servants, members of institutions or bodies, heads of offices or agencies, or staff members.[309]

Some restrictions to these broad access rights may follow from the decisions adopted by the EU institutions, bodies, offices and agencies. For instance, the ECJ has excluded from the scope of internal investigations documents and information held or created in the course of legal proceedings by reference to its tasks, its independence and the secrecy of its deliberations as set out in the Treaties and the Statute of the Court.[310]

OLAF's investigative competences are supplemented by a duty to inform OLAF which applies to the EU institutions, bodies, offices and agencies, as well as, insofar as national law allows, to the competent authorities of the Member States.[311] Furthermore, in the context of internal investigations, EU personnel have a duty to cooperate with OLAF and a duty to supply information. The latter is, in essence, an obligation of whistle-blowing. Both duties are provided for by the decisions adopted by each EU institution, body, office and agency,[312] as well as by Article 22(a) of the EU Staff Regulations. In return, the persons concerned are protected against inequitable or discriminatory treatment as a result of having communicated information to OLAF.[313] The duty to cooperate with OLAF and the duty to supply information find their limit in the fundamental right not to incriminate oneself.

Apart from carrying out investigations, OLAF also has other tasks, the most important of which is the assistance and coordination task. This task consists of providing the Member States with assistance from the Commission in organizing close and regular cooperation between their competent authorities in order to coordinate their activities for the purpose of protecting the EU's financial interests.[314] In doing so, OLAF exercises for the Commission the coordinating task in the area of the protection of the EU's financial interests, which the latter has under Article 325(3) TFEU. Furthermore, OLAF exercises some other tasks, such as developing a strategy for fighting fraud; preparing the Commission's legislative and regulatory anti-fraud initiatives; developing the necessary means to tackle fraud; collecting and analysing information; and providing technical assistance, especially in the field of training, to the other EU institutions and bodies and to the national authorities concerned with the protection of the EU's financial interests.[315] The distinction between investigative and other tasks is important since OLAF's far-reaching independence vis-à-vis the Commission and the other EU institutions only applies insofar as it exercises investigative competences.[316]

11.4 *Conduct of investigations*

The Director-General may open an investigation when there is a sufficient suspicion that there has been fraud, corruption or any other illegal activity affecting the EU's financial interests. However, such a suspicion does not in itself oblige the Director-General to open an investigation. Investigation policy priorities, proportionality and the fact that internal investigations may be better conducted by the EU institution, body, office or agency concerned also play a role

309. Art. 4(2)(b) of the OLAF Reg.
310. A.G. Jacobs, at para 167, in Case C-11/00, *Commission v. ECB*.
311. Art. 8 of the OLAF Reg.
312. See Art. 4(7) of the OLAF Reg.
313. On the EU courts' vigilance to protect whistle-blowers, see e.g. Case F-2/09, *Menghi v. ENISA*, para 138.
314. Arts. 2(2) of the OLAF Decision and 1(2) of the OLAF Reg.
315. See Arts. 2(3)–(5) of the OLAF Decision and 1(2) of the OLAF Reg.
316. See also *supra*, section 11.2.

when deciding whether or not to open an investigation.[317] Investigations are opened by a decision of the Director-General of OLAF, acting on his own initiative or following a request from a Member State or from an EU institution, body, office or agency.[318]

The Director-General of OLAF directs the conduct of investigations[319] and provides OLAF's employees with the necessary written authority for each intervention.[320] In order to enable the staff of OLAF to fulfil their tasks effectively, the competent authorities of the Member States, in conformity with national rules, and the EU institutions, bodies, offices and agencies provide for the necessary assistance.[321] In the case of the Member States, this obligation boils down to a duty to take appropriate measures to enforce, if necessary, OLAF's powers of investigation. Precautionary measures, in particular measures for the safeguarding of evidence, are taken by the competent authorities of the Member States in conformity with their national law or by the EU institution, body, office or agency concerned, in close cooperation with OLAF.[322]

Investigations have to be conducted continuously over a period proportionate to the circumstances and complexity of the case.[323] There is no precise and imperative deadline for OLAF investigations to be completed.[324] However, where an investigation has been in progress for more than twelve months, the Director-General of OLAF must inform the Supervisory Committee of the reasons for which OLAF has not yet been able to conclude the investigation and the expected timeframe for completion.[325] Moreover, the need to act within a reasonable period of time in conducting administrative proceedings, which is set forth in Article 41(1) of the Charter of Fundamental Rights of the EU, as an element of the right to good administration, also applies to OLAF investigations.[326]

On completion of an investigation, OLAF draws up a report under the authority of its Director-General specifying, amongst others, the facts established and their preliminary classification in law as well as the conclusions of the investigation. The report is accompanied by recommendations of the Director-General on the action that should be taken.[327] This report is sent by OLAF, together with any useful related documents, to the competent authorities of the Member States concerned or to the EU institution, body, office or agency concerned.[328]

If the procedural requirements laid down by the national laws of the Member State concerned have been respected, OLAF's reports constitute admissible evidence in administrative or judicial proceedings of the Member State in which their use proves necessary in the same way and under the same conditions as administrative reports drawn up by national administrative inspectors. They are subject to the same rules of evaluation as those applicable to administrative reports drawn up by national administrative inspectors and have the same evidentiary value as such reports.[329] This evidentiary value awarded to OLAF reports exists independently of what

317. Art. 5(1) of the OLAF Reg.
318. Art. 5(2) of the OLAF Reg. See further Art. 5(3)–(6) on the decision whether or not to open an investigation and its consequences.
319. Art. 7(1) of the OLAF Reg.
320. Art. 7(2) of the OLAF Reg.
321. Art. 7(3) of the OLAF Reg.
322. Arts. 7(6)–(7) of the OLAF Reg.
323. Art. 7(5) of the OLAF Reg.
324. Case T-48/05, *Franchet and Byk v. Commission*, para 272.
325. Art. 7(8) of the OLAF Reg.
326. Case T-48/05, *Franchet and Byk v. Commission*, paras. 273 and 274.
327. Art. 11(1) of the OLAF Reg.
328. Art. 11(3)–(4) of the OLAF Reg.
329. Art. 11(2) of the OLAF Reg.

national law provides in this respect. As a regulation, the OLAF Regulation is binding in its entirety and directly applicable in all Member States.[330]

This obligation on the Member States to give OLAF reports the same status as national administrative reports does not, however, include any obligation to initiate judicial or disciplinary proceedings. The national judicial authorities indeed remain free, in the context of their own powers, to assess the content and significance of the information obtained from OLAF and, thus, the action to be taken if necessary.[331] In the same way, an OLAF report does not include an obligation for the EU institution, body, office or agency concerned to take disciplinary measures.[332]

11.5 *Procedural guarantees*

Especially in relation to internal investigations, OLAF has far-reaching powers of investigation, which are likely to affect the lives and careers of persons under investigation. Furthermore, although qualified as being administrative,[333] OLAF investigations often merely precede those of national prosecuting authorities, which use the OLAF findings in national criminal law proceedings. In such a context, the importance of procedural guarantees is undeniable.

Whereas no procedural guarantees were provided for in the 1999 version of the OLAF Regulation,[334] they are now mentioned in Article 9 of the OLAF Regulation. This provision refers to several fundamental rights such as the right to an impartial treatment, the principle of the presumption of innocence, the right to avoid self-incrimination, the right to be assisted by a person of his or her choice, the right to be informed and the right to be heard.[335] It also sets out the conditions under which several of those rights can be exercised in the context of OLAF investigations. The right of access to the file is, however, not mentioned.[336]

Moreover, procedural guarantees directly flow from several provisions of the Charter of Fundamental Rights of the EU.[337] In relation to those provisions, Article 9 of the OLAF Regulation has the role of a "law" under Article 52(1) of the Charter, which is necessary for limitations to the exercise of certain fundamental rights to be valid.[338] Such limitations can be found in Article 9(3) of the OLAF Regulation, in relation to the right to be informed, and in Article 9(4),

330. See Art. 288, second para, TFEU.

331. Case T-193/04, *Tillack v. Commission*, para 70. See further on this case the annotation by J. Wakefield, 45 CML Rev. (2008), 199–221.

332. Case T-503/04, *Pessoa e Costa v. Commission*, para 97.

333. Art. 2(4) of the OLAF Reg.

334. Procedural guarantees were intended to form part of the decision taken by each EU institution, body, office or agency.

335. See also, on the latter right, Art. 12(2), third para, of the OLAF Reg. As a rule, the right to be informed and the right to be heard do not apply at the stage of the preliminary investigation carried out by the EU institution, body, office or agency before the file is sent to OLAF, see Case C-220/13 P, *Nikolaou v. Court of Auditors*, paras. 94–96.

336. See on the right of access to the file in the context of OLAF investigations, e.g., Case T-48/05, *Franchet and Byk v. Commission*, para 255, and Case T-447/11, *Catinis v. Commission*, para 63. For a critical view, see S. Braum, "Justizförmigkeit und europäische Betrugsermittlung – Bemerkungen zum Fall Eurostat (EuG T-48/05, Urteil vom 8. 7. 2008)", (2009) *Juristenzeitung*, 298–304, 303.

337. E.g., Arts. 41 on the right to good administration (which includes the right to be heard and the right of access to the file), and 48 on the presumption of innocence and right of defence. Before the entry into force of the Charter, the case-law had already derived some procedural guarantees in the context of OLAF investigations from the general principles of EU law, see, e.g., on the right to impartial treatment, Case T-309/03, *Camós Grau v. Commission*, para 102, and on the principle of the presumption of innocence, Case T-48/05, *Franchet and Byk v. Commission*, paras. 209 et seq.

338. See, e.g., Case C-129/14 PPU, *Spasic*, paras. 56–57.

in relation to the right to be heard. From a legal point of view, Article 9 of the OLAF Regulation is, therefore, as important for OLAF as it is for persons under investigation.

11.6 *Supervision*

At the time of OLAF's creation, the absolute priority was its independence from the Commission and the other EU institutions in the exercise of its investigative task. This is reflected in the way in which control is exercised over OLAF.

Although OLAF is a Commission service, the latter cannot exercise control over the former, except, as a last resort, through a (special) disciplinary procedure against the Director-General of OLAF.[339] Control is essentially exercised by the Supervisory Committee,[340] which is composed of five independent persons who possess the qualifications required for the appointment in their respective countries to senior posts relating to OLAF's areas of activity. They are appointed by common accord of the European Parliament, the Council and the Commission for a period of five years. Their term of office is not renewable. The Committee addresses opinions and, where appropriate, recommendations to the Director-General concerning the investigative activities of OLAF and it adopts reports which it sends to the EU institutions. Although the Supervisory Committee has an important role to play in supervising how OLAF investigators respect fundamental rights and procedural guarantees, the supervision exercised by it remains essentially an *ex post* control since it cannot intervene in on-going investigations.

A sufficient and immediate remedy to redress potential violations of rights and procedural guarantees of persons under investigation is, therefore, currently not provided for by the OLAF legal framework.[341] The Commission has proposed the creation of a Controller of procedural guarantees who would have the two-fold task of reviewing complaints lodged by persons under investigation about violation of their procedural guarantees and of authorizing OLAF to conduct certain investigative measures in respect of members of EU institutions.[342] However, apart from this authorizing competence, only applicable to members of EU institutions, the powers of the Controller of procedural guarantees would be limited to issuing non-binding recommendations to the Director-General of OLAF. Actually redressing potential violations would, therefore, not be part of its competences.[343]

11.7 *Judicial control*

Until now, judicial control over OLAF's investigative activities has been exercised by the EU courts through action for damages cases.[344] On the contrary, considering that they do not bring

339. Art. 17(9) of the OLAF Reg.
340. See Art. 15 of the OLAF Reg. and COM(2016)113.
341. Opinion 6/2011 of the European Court of Auditors on the amended proposal for a Reg. of the European Parliament and of the Council amending Reg. (EC) 1073/1999 concerning investigations conducted by the European Anti-Fraud Office (OLAF) and repealing Reg. (Euratom) 1074/1999, O.J. 2011, C 254/1, paras. 15 and 37–40, and Opinion 2/2013 of the OLAF Supervisory Committee on establishing an internal OLAF procedure for complaints, para 4 (<europa.eu/supervisory-committee-olaf/sites/default/files/documents/publications/opinions/2-2013_opinion_complaints_procedure_en.pdf> (last accessed on 20 Mar. 2018)).
342. COM(2014)340.
343. See further Opinion 6/2014 of the European Court of Auditors concerning a proposal for a Reg. of the European Parliament and of the Council amending Reg. (EU, Euratom) 883/2013 as regards the establishment of a Controller of procedural guarantees, O.J. 2014, C 419/1.
344. Arts. 268 and 340, second para, TFEU. See, e.g., Case T-309/03, *Camós Grau v. Commission*, and Case T-48/05, *Franchet and Byk v. Commission*.

about a distinct change in the applicant's legal position, the case-law has thus far considered an action for annulment[345] to be inadmissible against OLAF investigative acts such as a decision to open an investigation[346] and the acts performed in the course of an investigation,[347] a final report drawn up by OLAF and a decision to close an investigation,[348] a decision of OLAF not to annul investigative acts which have been accomplished by one of its investigators who was allegedly in a situation of conflict of interest,[349] a refusal by OLAF to inform a person of certain investigative acts concerning the latter and to allow the latter to defend himself in the context of the investigation,[350] and OLAF's forwarding to an EU institution of the report concluding an internal investigation[351] or to national prosecuting authorities of information on internal investigations.[352]

Due to this inadmissibility, the legality of an OLAF investigative act can only be contested before the court reviewing the decision subsequently taken on the basis of that act (provided such a decision is taken).[353] Furthermore, this inadmissibility deprives, in practice, the applicant of the possibility to ask for interim measures[354] in the context of such an action, and, thus, of an effective remedy in urgent matters. It is not sure whether such a situation would, in each and every circumstance, be compatible with the fundamental right to an effective remedy, enshrined in Article 47 of the Charter of Fundamental Rights of the EU.[355] In any case, the admissibility of an action for the annulment of an OLAF investigative act always has to be examined on a case by case basis.[356]

12. Final remarks

The area of EU budget and finances has undergone important changes over the decades. With regard to budgetary matters, the institutional balance has undoubtedly shifted in favour of the European Parliament, but decisions which are crucial for EU finances (and, therefore, for its functioning) are, in fact, still taken by the Member States. This is particularly true for the

345. Art. 263 TFEU (or, in the case of EU staff, Art. 270 TFEU).
346. Case T-690/13, *In vivo v. Commission*, para 24.
347. Case T-215/02, *Gómez-Reino v. Commission*, para 50.
348. Case T-29/03, *Comunidad Autónoma de Andalucía v. Commission*, para 40, Case T-4/05, *Strack v. Commission*, para 51, and Case C-237/06 P, *Strack v. Commission*, para 63.
349. Case T-96/03, *Camós Grau v. Commission*, para 38.
350. Case T-215/02, *Gómez-Reino v. Commission*, paras. 55–56.
351. Ibid., para 50.
352. Case T-193/04, *Tillack v. Commission*, para 82, and Case T-261/09 P, *Commission v. Violetti and Others*, para 73.
353. If that court is a national court and has doubts about the validity of the OLAF investigative act, it has to ask for a preliminary ruling by the ECJ on the validity of that act, see, to that effect, Case 314/85, *Foto-Frost*, para 20.
354. Art. 279 TFEU. See, e.g., Case T-193/04 R, *Tillack v. Commission*, paras. 46–47.
355. See, in this respect, the judgment of the European Court of Human Rights of 21 Dec. 2010 in the case *Société Canal Plus and Others v. France* (no. 29408/08), in which it found that Art. 6 ECHR was violated in a situation where the applicants could only contest search and seizure measures if an appeal was lodged against the decision on the merits (taken by a competition authority). According to the Court, this made the possibility of obtaining judicial review of these measures uncertain, since both the adoption of a decision on the merits and the introduction of an appeal against that decision were first required. Moreover, several years passed between the search and seizure measures and the decision on the merits. The Court stressed that Art. 6 ECHR requires appropriate redress, which necessarily implies the certainty, in practice, that effective judicial review can be obtained and, moreover, within a reasonable period of time (see para 40).
356. See, to that effect, Case C-314/11 P, *Commission v. Planet*, para 44.

decision on the multi-annual financial framework as well as for the (politically related) decision on EU own resources.

The current situation in relation to budgetary matters is not expected to change in the near future. Today's budgetary practice dates back to the 1980s and has, in fact, merely been consolidated at Treaty level by the Treaty of Lisbon. It is, however, practice which is essentially based on cooperation between the EU institutions and has thus constantly proven to be able to solve conflicts between them.

An area in which discussion is nevertheless ongoing is that of EU own resources. Although modifying the EU own resources system has turned out to be one of the most difficult exercises in EU politics, there is a more or less general consensus that the current system is inappropriate, since it depends too much on contributions due by each Member State, the level of which is subject to endless discussions. Moreover, the withdrawal of the United Kingdom from the EU will inevitably lead to changes to the current EU own resources system, since the UK correction mechanism is an essential part of that system.

Finally, further developments can most likely be expected in the area of the protection of the financial interests of the EU. The European Public Prosecutor's Office will have a major impact on the protection of the financial interests of the EU and on OLAF, notwithstanding the fact that the creation and functioning of the EPPO falls outside the scope of the financial Treaty provisions.

Further reading

Becker, S.,M.W. Bauer and A. De Feo (Eds.), *The New Politics of the European Union Budget,* (Nomos, 2017).

Bux, U., "Das EU-Haushaltsverfahren nach Lissabon", 45 EuR (2010), 711–718.

Covolo, V., *L'émergence d'un droit pénal en réseau. Analyse critique du système européen de lutte antifraude* (Nomos, 2015).

European Commission, *European Union Public Finance*, 5th ed. (Publications Office, 2014), available at <ec.europa.eu/budget/library/biblio/publications/2014/EU_pub_fin_en.pdf>.

Hiernaux-Fritsch, S. and A.F.W. Moonen, "Financiering van de begroting van de Europese Unie", (2010) SEW, 192–197.

Houbé, M.-L., "La procédure budgétaire à l'épreuve du Traité de Lisbonne", (2012) RMC, 370–374.

Inghelram, J., *Legal and Institutional Aspects of the European Anti-Fraud Office (OLAF) – An Analysis with a Look Forward to a European Public Prosecutor's Office* (Europa Law Publishing, 2011).

Inghelram, J., "Het Europees Bureau voor Fraudebestrijding (OLAF): Actuele juridische uitdagingen", (2015) SEW, 233–244.

Leen, A.R., "De Europese identiteit en de financiering van de EU", (2011) SEW, 447–454.

Matthijs, H., "De begroting van de Europese Unie", (2010) SEW, 51–60.

Stefanou, C., S. White and H. Xanthaki, *OLAF at the Crossroads – Action against EU Fraud* (Hart, 2011).

CHAPTER 10
THE COURT OF JUSTICE OF THE EUROPEAN UNION SUPRANATIONAL ADJUDICATOR AND ACCOUNTABILITY FORUM

*Deirdre Curtin and Maria Weimer**

1. Introduction: Institutional structure and functions

In the system of the treaties, the Court of Justice of the EU (hereafter: CJEU) acts as the independent and ultimate arbiter of the law (both Treaties and secondary legislation and any other rules), and enjoys a formal separation of its overarching judicial power from the other institutions or actors and from the national courts who enforce and apply Union Law. There has been a great deal of discussion as to the precise nature of that judicial power.[1] Part of that debate has been on its propensity, in a variety of ways, to "judicial activism" in fulfilling these varied and discretionary tasks.[2] According to Article 19(1) TEU, the CJEU includes the Court of Justice (hereafter: CJ), the General Court (hereafter: GC) and specialized courts. In accordance with Article 19(2) TEU, the CJ consists of 28 judges, one from each Member State, and is supported by 8 Advocates General.[3] The number of Advocates General can be increased by the Council, acting unanimously, upon request of the CJ. Currently, the CJ is supported by 11 Advocates General. Under Article 19(2) TEU, the GC consists of at least one judge from each Member State, and under Article 254(1) TFEU the precise number is determined by the Statute of the CJEU. At present, the GC is undergoing a process of doubling the number of its judges. Since 1 September 2016, it consists of 44 judges. The target number of two judges from each Member State will be reached in 2019.[4] The only specialized court to have been established, the Civil Service Tribunal (hereafter: CST), ceased to exist on 31 August 2016. The enlarged General Court took over its jurisdiction over staff cases.

The institutional structure, jurisdiction, remedies and procedures before the CJEU are determined by Articles 251–281 TFEU, the Statute of the CJEU and the rules of procedure of the CJ and GC. The Statute is attached to the Treaties as Protocol No 3. However, it can be amended

---

* D. Curtin: Law Department, European University Institute; Law Faculty, University of Amsterdam. M. Weimer: Law Faculty, University of Amsterdam.

1. K. Lenaerts, "Some reflections on the separation of powers in the European Union", 28 CML Rev. (1991), at 11–35, 32 and M. Adams et al. (Eds.), *Judging Europe's Judges: The Legitimacy of the Case Law of the European Court of Justice* (Hart Publishing, 2013).
2. See recently two book length discussions on judicial activism and the legitimacy of the CJEU and its case law: M. Dawson, B. De Witte and E. Muir (Eds.), *Judicial Activism at the European Court of Justice* (Edward Elgar, 2013) and M. Adams op. cit. *supra* note 1.
3. Art. 252 TFEU.
4. See section 4. See Art. 48 of the Statute of the CJEU.

following the ordinary legislative procedure, upon request of the CJ and after consultation of the Commission, or on a proposal from the Commission and after consultation of the CJ.[5]

The main task of the CJEU, as determined by Article 19(1) TEU, is to "ensure that in the interpretation and application of the Treaties the law is observed". This provision also contains the very core of what has developed over time to become the Union legal order. It expresses the fact that – unlike the usual situation in inter-state legal transactions – the interpretation and application of the relevant agreement is not just a matter for the contracting parties individually and, in cases where an international organization is created, the policy organs of that organization. The lawfulness of actions of the contracting parties on the basis of the Treaties is subject to the supervision of the CJEU.

To allow the CJEU to fulfil its main task, the Treaty authors have conferred upon it jurisdiction over multiple types of disputes arising under EU law. This jurisdiction is shared between the CJ and the GC.[6] The Court of Justice fulfils the function of a "constitutional" and "supreme" court of the EU. It hears infringement cases, decides on preliminary references from national courts and adopts opinions on the compatibility with the Treaties of envisaged international agreements. It also rules on actions for annulment or failure to act brought by a Member State against the European Parliament, Council or both, or brought by one EU institution against another. Moreover, it rules on appeals against decisions of the GC. It is also a fundamental rights court inasmuch as it interprets and applies the EU Charter of Fundamental Rights.[7] The GC rules on the actions for annulment and failure to act brought against EU institutions and bodies by natural and legal persons. It deals (in the first instance) primarily with the cases concerning competition, state aid, anti-dumping, intellectual property, public procurement, access to documents as well as international anti-terrorist sanctions transposed to the EU legal order.

The reference to observance of the law in Article 19(1) TEU shows that the CJEU's task involves more than simply the application of the Treaty provisions.[8] Interpretation and application of national laws by national courts takes place within the framework of an established legal order and legal tradition, in which these laws are embedded. The national courts may invoke the legal principles and concepts embedded in their legal orders when interpreting and applying the provisions of national legislation in any dispute brought before them. Such support, taken for granted in the national system, is not at the disposal of the CJEU for interpreting and applying Treaty provisions. Yet it is essential, since the countless questions which arise in the context of the Court's work cannot be answered, or cannot be answered fully in legal terms, on the basis merely of the Treaty. The CJEU is therefore faced with the task of deriving from the Treaty texts a legal order which can provide a framework within which the law contained in the treaties can be interpreted and applied, and on the basis of which the decisions and judgments concerning that law can be accepted and regarded as law by the Member States and their organs (including their judiciaries), the other institutions and the individual holders of Union legal rights and obligations.[9]

The CJEU performs this task mainly by giving form to unwritten Union law. In its case law there are regular references to general principles of law, such as good faith, legal certainty, due diligence, the principle of equality, legitimate expectations, abuse of rights and the principle of

5. Art. 281 TFEU.
6. Art. 256 TFEU and Art. 51 of the Statute of the CJEU.
7. A. Peripoli, "Is the ECJ finally putting the Charter to work?", 128 LQR (2012), 212–216.
8. Cf. T. Koopmans, "The birth of European Law at the crossroads of legal traditions", 39 AJCL (1991), 493–507, 495–496.
9. See R. Barents, *Remedies and Procedures before the EU Courts* (Wolters Kluwer, 2016), 113–115. See also e.g. Joined Cases C-46/93 and C-48/93, *Brasserie du Pêcheur*, para 27.

proportionality.[10] In the words of Kapteyn, a former Judge at the ECJ: "the Court's finding of law [...] is largely an exercise in comparative law. This use of the comparative technique is not governed by an *a priori* intent to find the highest common denominator; rather is it governed by an intent to trace elements from which it is possible to build Community legal principles and rules which will offer an appropriate, fair and viable solution for the questions with which the Court is confronted. Comparative law in this sense also forms the source of inspiration for the determination of the autonomous meaning of many legal terms occurring in written Community law [...] as a rule it will naturally take place *in camera* during the deliberations between judges who, each of them educated and initiated in their own national legal system and way of thinking, together have to give effect to written and unwritten Community law".[11] According to Lenaerts and Gutman, the Court uses the comparative method instrumentally: its overarching aim is "to find, through the examination of the laws of the Member States [...], the solution which "best suits" the objectives of the Union and which is "acceptable" for the national legal orders responsible for implementing Union law".[12]

Union law is still today law in the making. It is law which often has to be developed by Union legislation and continually adapted to changing circumstances and views. The Union legislature means, in principle, the Council and Parliament together, or the Council in specific circumstances acting alone. In all too many cases the legislature fails to fulfil its functions as a result of failure to take decisions, sometimes through a failure to achieve unanimity. In these circumstances the Court is sometimes obliged with the aid of the systematic teleological method of interpretation to deduce solutions from primary Union law for concrete problems which should have been dealt with by the Union legislature.[13] Such judicial creativity is open to objection on the ground of the lack of legal certainty,[14] and also the possible absence of consensus in broad societal terms for the Court's decisions.

This function of the Court as filling gaps in legislative provisions remains relevant today even in a context where the decision-making capacity of the legislative institutions whose role is to decide on policy has increased. The Court's role in the process of integration since the mid-1980s has sometimes led to sharp criticism retrospectively and indeed this criticism continues today. Critics found that the Court had sought inspiration in "guidelines which are essentially political in nature and hence, not judicially applicable", and had thus been guilty of the kind of "judicial activism which may be an usurpation of power".[15] This kind of criticism neglects the fact that the

---

10. See A. Arnull, *The General principles of EEC Law and the Individual* (LUP, 1990); H.G. Schermers and D. Waelbroeck, *Judicial Protection in the European Communities,* 6th ed. (Kluwer, 2001), paras. 53–238 and literature cited therein; J. Usher, *General Principles of EC Law* (Longman, 1998) and T. Tridimas, *The General Principles of EC Law* 3rd ed. (OUP, 2017).
11. P.J.G. Kapteyn and P. VerLoren van Themaat, *Introduction to the Law of the European Communities. From Maastricht to Amsterdam* (Kluwer Law International, 1998), 277.
12. K. Lenaerts, and K. Gutman, "The comparative law method and the Court of Justice of the European Union. Interlocking legal orders revisited" in D. Fairgrieve and M. Adenas (Eds.), *Courts and Comparative Law* (OUP, 2015), 152. A.G. Kokott calls this approach "evaluative comparison". See her Opinion in Case C-550/07 P, *Akzo Nobel Chemicals*, para 94.
13. See e.g. Case 804/79, *Commission v. United Kingdom.*
14. Perhaps with a view to this point, in its judgments in Case 22/70, *Commission v. Council (ERTA)* and Case 6/72, *Continental Can et al. v. Commission*, in which it developed a "new" rule, the Court concluded that on the facts the "new" rule was inapplicable.
15. H. Rasmussen, *On Law and Policy in the European Court of Justice: A Comparative Study in Judicial Policymaking* (Brill, 1986), 62. One of the most serious attacks on the way in which the Court fulfils its function came from the Warden of All Souls College, Oxford, (then) Sir Patrick Neill: *The European Court of Justice: A Case Study in Judicial Activism, London* (European Policy Forum, 1995). See also, very critically, T.C. Hartley,

Court has a duty – like the other institutions – to ensure that the tasks entrusted to the Union are carried out; but also, in the words of Lord Howe, it neglects the fact that "the Court had no pre-existing legal system to work with. The treaty provisions it was called upon to interpret were often general in scope and silent on detail. The option of operating in a 'non-activist' manner, merely interpreting the meaning of words, was simply not open to the Court of Justice".[16]

The CJEU is by design very independent in interpreting what the law means.[17] Admittedly, judges are appointed for the relatively short term of office of 6 years and can be reappointed,[18] which could theoretically encourage them to seek support of their governments. And yet, in their extra-judicial writings the judges illustrate strong levels of psychological independence but also of considerable freedom from inter-institutional constraints. The independence of individual CJEU judges from external pressures seems to be sufficiently secured by the principle of collegial adjudication combined with the lack of possibility to submit dissenting opinions by individual judges. Consequently, Member States – when deciding on a reappointment – cannot associate a candidate with a specific judicial decision. Also, in general, there is little real checking from the outside as to the exercise of this judicial function nor indeed on the whole is there the means to do so. When the CJ decides upon inter-institutional conflicts or about the division of powers for example, it receives input and information in the context of the court procedures and there may be a dialogue of sorts with a limited number of representatives of other institutions at the oral hearing, but this does not affect its "independence" in reaching a judgment.

In the context of a general chapter, only limited space can be given to the discussion of the conditions under which and the way in which the Court exercises its multifarious jurisdiction. The present discussion deals only with those proceedings which concern the core of the Court's jurisdiction. It thus takes as a starting point the basic division between direct actions (section 2) and preliminary references (section 3). Direct actions and preliminary rulings are naturally imbued with a different philosophy in terms of the role played by the CJEU. In direct actions the CJEU adjudicates in concrete cases on disputes between parties (including between institutions) whereas in preliminary ruling proceedings the Court rules only on a specific point of EU law, leaving the final resolution of the case to the national court. However, it may be the case that at times the actual role of the national court is rather limited, the CJ having effectively determined the outcome of the case before it. There are clear links between direct actions and indirect actions through the national courts. In effect, the judicial system of the EU must be viewed holistically and in an integrated manner.

Constitutional Problems of the European Union (OUP, 1999), Ch. 2 and 3, more specifically note 71 and note 72.

16. G. Howe, "Euro-Justice: Yes or No?", 21 EL Rev. (1996) 187–198. See also M. Capelletti, "Is the European Court of Justice "running wild"?, (1987) EL Rev., 311–322; J.H.H. Weiler, "The Court of Justice on trial", 24 CML Rev. (1987), 555; T.C. Hartley, "The European Court, judicial objectivity and the constitution of the European Union", 112 *Law Quarterly Review* (1996), 95–109; A. Arnull, "The European Court and judicial objectivity and the constitution of the European Union", 112 *Law Quarterly Review* (1996), 411–423. Having examined the scholarly discussion on judicial activism at the CJEU, two authors concluded that "at present [...] a broad consensus seems to exist in legal doctrine that the ECJ has been faithfully interpreting the rules, legitimately filled some gaps, and has never engaged in excessive activism"; see H. de Waele and A. van der Vleuten, "Judicial activism in the European Court of Justice — the Case of LGBT Rights", 19 *Michigan State Journal of International Law* (2013), 639–666.
17. K. Lenaerts, "The Court's outer and inner selves: Exploring the external and internal legitimacy of the European Court of Justice" in M. Adams, op. cit. *supra* note 1.
18. Their counterparts in the US Supreme Court are appointed for life and in the European Court of Human Rights for a single, non-renewable term of office of 9 years (from 2010).

An integrated perspective leads back to the functioning of the CJEU as an institution and the challenges it faces in exercising the tasks conferred upon it. One thing is clear from the analysis of both direct and indirect actions and that is that the CJEU is, as an institution, overburdened and under pressure, almost chronically so. The consequences of such overburdening are indeed not minor and include delayed justice, and inadequate and even bad reasoning which cannot but ultimately affect the legitimacy of the case law as a whole. With time the problems seem to get more pressing, not less, especially since the extension of the jurisdiction of the Court in the Treaty of Lisbon. While the Court in recent case law still restricts the access of private applicants in annulment proceedings, this results in more pressure on the preliminary ruling procedure to provide for individual protection against invalid EU acts. In section 4 we discuss the institutional aspects of the EU judicial architecture including docket reform, and issues of accountability and transparency.

2. Direct judicial protection before the CJEU

This section deals with the direct actions before the Court. First, those procedures which require the Court to judge whether the acts and omissions of the Member States (section 2.1) and the institutions (sections 2.2, 2.3, 2.4) are in conformity with EU law will be explained. Special attention will be devoted to the right of action of private parties against EU acts. Furthermore, the possibilities for individuals to bring actions for damages before the Court on the ground of the Union's non-contractual liability will be discussed (section 2.5).

2.1 *Infringement proceedings*

Infringement proceedings (Arts. 258–260 TFEU) may lead to a pronouncement of the Court on the question whether a Member State has failed to fulfil one of its obligations under the Treaty. As such, their main function[19] is to ensure compliance with EU law,[20] and thereby to uphold the rule of law in the EU. According to the Court, infringement proceedings are essential in "enabling the Community interests enshrined in the Treaty to prevail over the inertia and resistance of Member States".[21] In these proceedings a very important function has been assigned to the Commission as the "guardian of the Treaty" (Art. 17(1) TEU).[22] Although the Member States themselves may also take the initiative for such a procedure (Art. 259 TFEU),[23] in practice they have tended to leave this initiative almost entirely to the Commission.[24] The centralized enforcement of EU law against the Member States via Articles 258–260 TFEU complements the de-centralized enforcement via the assertion of individual rights before national courts. While preliminary references pursuant to Article 267 TFEU enable individuals to obtain indirect

19. There are other functions, such as public policy enforcement and a forum for interaction and political negotiation, see D. Chalmers, G. Davies, G. Monti, *European Union Law: Text and Materials,* 3rd ed. (CUP, 2014), 340–351.
20. See Joined Cases C-20 & 28/01, *Commission v. Germany.*
21. Case C-25/59, *Netherlands v. High Authority.*
22. See Case C-333/99, *Commission v. France,* para 23, Case C-394/02, *Commission v. Greece,* paras. 14–15, Case C-33/04, *Commission v. Luxembourg,* para 65.
23. Before such a procedure can get to Court, the complaining Member State must bring the matter before the Commission which has to deliver a reasoned opinion after each of the States involved has had the opportunity to submit observations.
24. E.g. Case 141/78, *France v. United Kingdom*; Case C-388/95, *Belgium v. Spain*; Case C-145/04, *Spain v. United Kingdom*; Case C-364/10, *Hungary v. Slovakia*. For a discussion of why there has been a very limited use of Art. 259 TFEU see C. Harlow and R. Rawling, "Accountability and law enforcement: The centralized EU infringement procedure", (2006) EL Rev., 447–475, 452.

control of the compliance of national laws with EU law,[25] infringement proceedings are the only mechanism in which the Court can directly review national laws and Member State conduct more generally for their compatibility with EU law.[26]

The infringement procedure before the CJ constitutes only the last step thereof, and a measure of last resort. According to Smith, "The real interest in Article 258 TFEU is not what happens in the Court (not much does) but rather all the points in the process before a judgment is handed down".[27] Of crucial importance for the resolution of infringement cases is the administrative pre-litigation stage,[28] in which the Commission and the Member States communicate, and often settle infringements outside of the Courtroom. Furthermore, since the Maastricht Treaty, the infringement procedure has been complemented with the so-called sanctions procedure (Art. 260(2–3) TFEU), which has developed dynamically over time in the interaction between the Commission and the Court.

2.1.1 *The administrative stage*

The administrative stage of the infringement procedure has three aims: to give the Member State the chance to end the (possible) infringement, to exercise its rights of defence, and to delimit the substance of the dispute with a view to possible proceedings before the Court.[29] The Commission has full discretion to decide on when to open or close the infringement procedure.[30] The decision to open the procedure can be based either on the Commission's own initiative or be triggered by an individual complaint.[31] If the Commission, in the light of the information it has received and gathered,[32] is of the view that a Member State has failed to fulfil the obligations imposed on it by the Treaties or the measures for their implementation, it must give this state a

25. It is the national courts who ultimately judge the compatibility of national law with EU law based on the interpretation provided by the Court.
26. See L. Prete and B. Smulder, "The coming of age of infringement proceedings", 47 CML Rev. (2010), 9–61, 9–10. See further below at section 2.2.
27. M. Smith, "The evolution of infringement and sanction procedures: of pilots, diversions, collisions and circling" in A. Arnull and D. Chalmers (Eds.), *The Oxford Handbook of European Union Law* (OUP, 2015), 354.
28. In certain areas, such as state aid control (Art. 108(2) TFEU), harmonization (Art. 114(9) TFEU) and security exceptions (Art. 348 TFEU), the Commission may bring the matter directly to the Court of Justice without going through the normal Art. 258 or 259 TFEU procedure (the right is also available to any interested Member State under 108(2) TFEU and to any Member State under Arts. 114(9) TFEU and 348 TFEU; see also Arts. 38 and 92 Euratom).
29. Case C-362/01, *Commission v. Ireland* and Case C-456/03, *Commission v. Italy*, recently also Case C-274/07, *Commission v. Lithuania*, para 20.
30. Case 48/65, *Lütticke v. Commission*; Case C-205/98, *Commission v. Austria.*
31. In 2014, 777 EU Pilot investigations were launched, while 3715 new individual complaints were registered, see: European Commission, "Monitoring the application of Union law, 2014 Annual Report", available at <www.ec.europa.eu/atwork/applying-eu-law/docs/annual_report_32/com_2015_329_en.pdf>.
32. See *infra* section 4.4.3. on the oral hearing. Nowadays, most information is gathered via the "EU Pilot", a system introduced in 2008 to better handle the Commission's workload. It is aimed at resolving compliance problems without having to resort to infringement procedures and thus precedes the formal opening of the pre-litigation stage. The member states have to reply to the Pilot within 10 weeks, thus making the information exchange between the Commission and the member states more efficient and manageable, see also M. Smith, op. cit. *supra* note 27, 359–366. In 2014, 1336 EU pilot files were processed. After the response by the member states, the Commission was able to close around 75% of the files, see Commission's 2014 Annual Report, cited *supra* note 31. For an account on alternative problem-solving mechanisms, EU Pilot and SOLVIT for dealing with complaints and Internal Market Scoreboard (IMS) as a peer-pressure inducing mechanism through the publication of half-yearly reports on implementing and infringement procedures, see C. Koops, *Contemplating Compliance, European compliance mechanisms in international perspective* (ACIL/ACELG, 2014), Ch. 4.

prior opportunity to submit its observations. This is done in a letter of formal notice (*lettre de mise en demeure*) designed to set out the points at issue and to put the state in a position in which it can prepare its defence, or fulfil the obligation imposed on it by EU law.[33] The letter of formal notice defines the subject matter of the dispute, which may not subsequently be extended, without breaching the defence rights of the Member State concerned.

If the Member State refuses to put an end to the infringement and the Commission adheres to its original view, the Commission then decides on its final position. This is done by means of a (non-binding) reasoned opinion, which further delineates the subject-matter of the procedure. The Commission sets out its views, giving the reasons for them,[34] which must be sufficiently precise to enable the Court to ascertain whether a violation of EU law has taken place. According to the Court, the Commission is obliged "to specify precisely [...] the grounds of complaint which it already raised more generally in the letter of formal notice and alleges against the Member State concerned, after taking cognizance of any observations submitted by it".[35] This is an essential requirement to delimit the subject-matter of the dispute, and to ensure that the Member State in question can either end the alleged infringement or defend itself before the Court. The reasoned opinion invites the Member State to take the appropriate measures[36] within a period, which the Commission determines,[37] to remedy its default. By formally stating the infringement of the Treaty with which the Member State concerned is charged, the Commission's reasoned opinion[38] concludes the administrative pre-litigation procedure.[39]

If the Member State does not comply with the reasoned opinion within the given period,[40] the Commission may bring the matter before the Court. The Commission enjoys discretionary power in this.[41] It is also for the Commission to decide at which moment it wishes to bring proceedings before the Court.[42] The Commission does not have to show the existence of a legal interest "since, in the general interest of the Community, its function is to ensure that the provisions of the Treaty are applied by the Member States and to note the existence of any failure to

33. Case C-473/93, *Commission v. Luxembourg*. An opinion of the Commission relating to draft measures does not constitute a formal notice under Art. 226 TFEU; moreover, draft measures may not be the object of infringement proceedings: see Order in Case C-341/97, *Commission v. Netherlands*.
34. I.e. the reasoned opinion must contain "a coherent statement of the reasons which led the Commission to believe that the state in question has failed to fulfil an obligation under the Treaty", Case 7/61, *Commission v. Italy*. See also Case C-365/10, *Commission v. Slovenia*; Case C-34/11, *Commission v. Portugal*.
35. Case C-350/02, *Commission v. Netherlands,* para 21.
36. The Commission is not obliged to indicate what specific action should be taken, cf. Case C-247/89, *Commission v. Portugal*.
37. The Commission will usually give two months (see e.g. Case C-376/00, *Commission v. Italy*), although a period of one month or even less is not unknown in urgent cases. See Case 293/85, *Commission v. Belgium*.
38. The decision to issue a reasoned opinion cannot be described as a measure of administration or management and may not be delegated; see Case C-191/95, *Commission v. Germany*. The same applies to the decision to commence proceedings before the Court under Art. 258; see Case C-191/95, *Commission v. Germany*.
39. Case 74/82, *Commission v. Ireland*.
40. The Commission tends to give Member States a period of two months unless a departure from this practice is justified, see Case C-196/07, *Commission v. Spain,* paras. 29 et seq.
41. The Court usually does not question the way in which it was exercised, see Case 416/85, *Commission v. United Kingdom*. See also Case 200/88, *Commission v. Greece*; Case C-431/92, *Commission v. Germany*; Case C-236/99, *Commission v. Belgium* and, more recently, Case C-255/05, *Commission v. Italy*, para 38.
42. Case 7/71, *Commission v. France*. The time between the infringement taking place or commencing and being brought to the Court can vary enormously: the Court has noted that the excessive duration of the pre-litigation procedure may make it more difficult for the Member State concerned to rebut the Commission's arguments, and may thus infringe the rights of the defence, see Case C-490/04, *Commission v. Germany*. See further, H.G. Schermers and D. Waelbroeck, op. cit. *supra* note 10, paras. 1285–1288.

fulfil the obligations deriving therefrom, with a view to bringing it to an end".[43] The Commission must always ensure that the complaints in both its reasoned opinion and its application to the Court are based on the same grounds, arguments and submissions, and are formulated with coherence and precision.[44]

2.1.2 *The judicial stage*

The objective of infringement proceedings is to obtain a formal pronouncement by the Court that a Member State has failed to fulfil its obligations flowing from EU law. It aims to demonstrate *objectively* the failure to fulfil these obligations, and it is therefore irrelevant whether the failure to fulfil obligations is the result of intention or negligence on the part of the Member State responsible, or of technical difficulties encountered by it.[45] It is also irrelevant whether the subjects harmed by the alleged infringement have already acted before national courts,[46] or whether the infringement resulted in any particular harm at all. The objective nature of the infringement procedure means that "where a Member State fails to fulfil its obligation, [...] the infringement exists regardless of the frequency or the scale of the circumstances complained of".[47]

It is relatively seldom that infringement cases will lead to an action before the CJ. The procedure is clearly intended to avoid rather than obtain a condemnation of the defaulting state. The number of actual judgments of the Court on infringement proceedings is considerably smaller than the number of cases in which the Commission deals with matters relating to the failure of Member States to fulfil obligations under the Treaty. The judgments of the Court form the tip of an iceberg: in most cases an amicable settlement is reached before the matter goes to the Court.[48] Melanie Smith critically assesses however the overall lack of transparency and accountability. There is a lack of judicial scrutiny as the Commission possesses such wide discretion in steering the procedure.[49]

Within infringement proceedings, the Court must judge the behaviour of the Member State as a whole and, in so doing, must take into account all relevant facts, such as the question of whether in the given circumstances the State has been given sufficient time to take the appropriate measures for remedying its failure.[50]

The obligations referred to in Article 258 TFEU may flow, with the general exceptions under Articles 275 and 276 TFEU, from primary or secondary EU law, from international law which

---

43. Case 167/73, *Commission v. France*.
44. E.g. Case C-98/04, *Commission v. United Kingdom*. For infringements consisting in violations of EU Directives, see Cases C-66/06, *Commission v. Ireland*, paras. 58–59, and C-59/04, *Commission v. France*, para 12, 31 et seq.
45. Case C-71/97, *Commission v. Spain*. Pending the proceedings before the Court, the Commission may apply to the Court under Art. 279 TFEU, asking it to order the Member State in question to withdraw or suspend certain measures pending delivery of the judgment in the main proceedings, see Case C-195/90 R, *Commission v. Germany*.
46. Cases C-275/08, *Commission v. Germany*, paras. 36 and 37; and C-87/02, *Commission v. Italy*, para 39.
47. C-226/01, *Commission v. Denmark*.
48. In 2014, 893 new infringement procedures were launched by sending a letter of formal notice, as well as 256 reasoned opinions to member states, see 2014 Annual Report, cited *supra* note 31.
49. See further, M. Smith, *Centralised Enforcement, Legitimacy and Good Governance in the EU* (Routledge, 2009), Ch. 1. The rights of third parties are limited in infringement proceedings, e.g. to obtain access to infringement files, see e.g. Case T-309/97, *Bavarian Lager Company v. Commission*.
50. Whether or not the periods allowed the Member State by both the formal notice and the reasoned opinion are reasonable depends on the circumstances in the actual case. See Case 293/85, *Commission v. Belgium*.

is binding on the Union,[51] but also from general principles of unwritten Union law which must be respected when a Member State acts within the scope of application of EU law.[52] A failure to fulfil such an obligation may consist of a positive action or an omission on the part of a Member State.

It is settled case law that a Member State is responsible for a failure under Article 258 TFEU irrespective of the question of which national agency actually breached EU law, even if this agency is independent under national constitutional law.[53] Hence, decisions of national courts may give rise to a breach of a Member State's obligations,[54] although the use of the infringement procedure will tend to be appropriate only where there is a widely-held judicial construction which has not been disowned by a supreme court, but rather confirmed by it and which constitutes a breach of EU law that can only be brought to an end through legislation.[55]

Moreover, the Court also held that an administrative practice can be the subject-matter of an action for failure to fulfil obligations if it is, to some degree, of a consistent and general nature.[56] Such a failure may be deduced from a series of infringements that have persisted over a protracted period. Also, as the Court has held,[57] nothing prevents the Commission from seeking, in parallel to a finding of a series of such infringements, a declaration that these were due to a general and persistent practice.[58] Insofar as the Commission's action also seeks such a more general finding, the Court seems willing to adapt the procedural conditions under which it might be justifiable.[59]

The Court is prepared to guarantee effective use of the Commission's power to initiate infringement proceedings. Thus, a Member State may not rely on the alleged failure by one or more other Member States in order to justify its own failure to fulfil its obligations under EU law.[60] The Court has also rejected any attempt by a Member State to justify its failure to implement provisions of EU law on the ground that the provisions have direct effect.[61] Furthermore, a Member State may not rely on national provisions or practices to justify its failure to fulfil its obligations or to comply with time-limits laid down in EU acts.[62] The Member States are obliged to take the necessary steps to fulfil their EU obligations by the due date, even in circumstances

---

51. Case C-13/00, *Commission v. Ireland*, regarding the Bern Convention.
52. Cf. Case C-260/89, *Elliniki Radiophonia Tileorassi AE v. Dimotiki Etairia Pliroforissis and Sotirios Kouvelas.*
53. E.g. action by local authorities can be attacked by infringement proceedings against the State concerned, e.g. Case 301/84, *Commission v. United Kingdom.*
54. Case C-154/08, *Commission v. Spain*, with comment by M. Lopez Escudero in 48 CML Rev. (2011), 227–242. See also M. Taborowski, "Infringement proceedings and non-compliant national courts", 49 CML Rev. (2012), 1881–1914.
55. See Case C-129/00, *Commission v. Italy*. Infringement of EU law by judicial bodies may also be the subject of cases involving Member State liability, cf. Case C-224/01, *Köbler v. Republik Österreich* and Case C-173/03, *Traghetti del Mediterraneo.*
56. See Case C-387/99, *Commission v. Germany* and the case law cited in para 42 of that judgment; Case C-287/93, *Commission v. Belgium*; Case C-489/06 *Commission v. Greece.*
57. See Case C-494/01, *Commission v. Ireland (Irish Waste).*
58. See also Case C-265/95, *Commission v. France (Spanish Strawberries)*; Case C-189/07, *Commission v. Spain*; Case C-150/07, *Commission v. Portugal (Medicinal Herbs Products)*; Case C-88/07, *Commission v. Spain.*
59. See P. Wennerås, "A new dawn for Commission enforcement under Art. 226 and 228 EC: General and Persistent (GAP) infringements, lump sums and penalty payments", 43 CML Rev. (2006), 31–62, 33–50. It should be noted, however, that in order to demonstrate structural non-compliance, the Commission must do more than refer to a few individual cases only, see Case C-248/05, *Commission v. Ireland.*
60. E.g. Case 52/75, *Commission v. Italy*; Case 90-91/63, *Commission v. Belgium and Luxemburg*, paras. 1–2; Case 78/76, *Firma Steinike und Weinlig v. Germany*, and Case C-38/89, *Ministère public v. Guy Blanguernon.*
61. Case 168/85, *Commission v. Italy.*
62. Already in Case 30/72, *Commission v. Italy.*

of political crisis.[63] Only an appeal to absolute impossibility to fulfil its obligations properly will be accepted by the Court as defence.[64] One may question whether this extremely strict position should not be qualified somewhat if it cannot reasonably be expected of a Member State that it fulfils its obligations within the required term, as a result of circumstances which are not due to action or failure to act of that Member State.[65] This discussion became particularly prominent in the course of the ongoing economic and financial crisis. Several countries such as Ireland and Greece alleged that the Commission should consider the current status of their economy when assessing the amount of penalty payments.[66]

If the action brought by the Commission is not dismissed by the Court, the latter will rule in its judgment that the Member State has failed to fulfil its obligations. In that case, the State is obliged to take the necessary measures to comply with the judgment (Art. 260(1) TFEU). The process of compliance must, in the interest of the immediate and uniform application of EU law, be initiated immediately and must be completed as soon as possible.[67] For the competent national authorities (a term which includes national courts as well as administrative authorities) this entails a prohibition against applying a national rule recognized as incompatible with the Treaty and, if the circumstances so require, an obligation on them to take all appropriate measures to facilitate the full application of EU law.[68] A judgment can, moreover, form the basis for liability incurred by a Member State as a result of its default, as regards other Member States, the Union or private parties.[69]

In practice, the implementation of the CJ's judgments has never been challenged by a categorical and definitive refusal to comply by the Member State concerned – although very occasionally it may have looked like it.[70] However, the number of instances in which the procedure for failure to take measures to comply with a judgment of the CJ has had to be initiated is substantial, particularly as a result of the late implementation of directives by the Member States.[71] It has been repeatedly necessary for the Court to hand down a second judgment in which the failure to comply with Article 260(1) TFEU is established.[72] The cause of the failure

63. Case 79/72, *Commission v. Italy*; Case 52/75, *Commission v. Italy*, Case 10/76, *Commission v. Italy* and Case 123/76, *Commission v. Italy*.
64. See e.g. Case 52/84, *Commission v. Belgium*; Case C-121/07, *Commission v. France*, para 72.
65. See in more detail L. Prete and B. Smulders, op. cit. *supra* note 26, 43–45 and P. Wennerås, op. cit. *supra* note 59, 54–61.
66. See Case C-407/09, *Commission v. Greece*, para 26; Case C-374/11 *Commission v. Ireland*, para 31; Case C-279/11, *Commission v. Ireland*, para 42. In these cases, the Court held that the current economic status of the Member States should be taken into account, e.g. recent developments of GDP and inflation. Yet, it also stated that this was already included in the Commission's 2010 communication (SEC(2010)923/3) regarding the data used to calculate lump sum and penalty payments.
67. See e.g. Case 169/87, *Commission v. France*; Case C-387/97, *Commission v. Greece*.
68. E.g. Case 48/71, *Commission v. Italy*; Joined Cases 314-316/81 & 83/82, *Procureur de la République et al. v. Waterkeyn et al.*; Case C-101/91, *Commission v. Italy*.
69. See e.g. Case 263/88, *Commission v. France*; Case 39/72, *Commission v. Italy*. See also Case C-243/89, *Commission v. Denmark*. See Ch. 11, "Application and enforcement in the Member States", section 7, of this book.
70. Cf. the notorious case when France, in the late 1970s, refused the import of mutton from the UK, Case 232/78, *Commission v. France* and Joined Cases 24 & 97/80 R, *Commission v. France*. Case C-1/00, *Commission v. France* (refusal to end the ban on British beef).
71. The details can be found in annual Commission's reports and factsheets on monitoring the application of EU law, available at the Commission's website. E.g. on 31 Dec. 2006 the Art. 228 EC procedure had been launched in 94 cases (Table 2.3). See also T.C. Hartley, op. cit. *supra* note 15, Ch. 6.
72. Spectacular examples include Joined Cases 227-230/85, *Commission v. Belgium*; Case 169/87, *Commission v. France*.

by the Member States to fulfil its obligations is often to be found in the need for long drawn-out and difficult legislative procedures.[73]

2.1.3 *Financial sanctions*

A remarkable achievement[74] of the Treaty of Maastricht was that it introduced a provision (now Art. 260(2) TFEU) for the imposition by the CJ of a lump sum or penalty payment on the defaulting Member State, if the latter is indeed found not to have taken the necessary measures to comply with an earlier judgment. The objective of the sanctions procedure is complementary to the overall objective of the infringement procedure, namely to induce a defaulting Member State to comply with a judgment establishing a failure to fulfil obligations, thereby ensuring that EU law is applied.[75]

The Lisbon Treaty simplified the infringement procedure in two ways. Firstly, in the procedure under Article 260(2) TFEU enforcing compliance with a previous finding of an infringement by the CJ, a reasoned opinion by the Commission is no longer required. The Commission merely has to give the Member State the opportunity to submit its observations. Secondly, in the case of alleged failure of the Member State to notify measures transposing a directive the Commission can now request the imposition of a financial penalty already in its initial application to the CJ (Art. 260(3) TFEU).

In the first proceeding in which the Commission proposed that a penalty payment should be imposed,[76] the Court considered that "[i]n the absence of provisions in the Treaty, the Commission may adopt guidelines for determining how the lump sums or penalty payments which it intends to propose to the Court are calculated, so as, in particular, to ensure equal treatment between the Member States"[77] and the foreseeability and proportionality of sanctions.[78] The Commission has indeed developed a set of guidelines.[79] In determining the amount of the lump sum or periodic penalty payment, the Commission takes into account three criteria: the seriousness of the infringement, the duration and the need to ensure the deterrent effect of the penalty, to end the infringement in question and prevent further infringements.[80] However, the Commission's guidelines and submissions do not bind the CJ.

---

73. For an empirical study of national responses to EU infringement proceedings, see T. Börzel, T. Hofmann, and D. Panke, "Caving in or sitting out: Longitudinal patterns of non-compliance in the European Union", 19 JEPP (2012), 454, 467.
74. See for a more detailed discussion M. Smith, "Inter–institutional dialogue and the establishment of enforcement norms: A decade of financial penalties under Art. 228 EC (now 260 TFEU)", 16 EPL (2010), 547–570, who describes both procedures under Art. 258 and 260 as "sister provisions".
75. Cases C-304/02, *Commission v. France (Fisheries Control)*, para 80; C-121/07, *Commission v. France* para 57.
76. Case C-387/97, *Commission v. Greece*. See, Case C-584/14, *Commission v. Greece*. See also, an infringement procedure against Germany for the recycling of electronic waste (O.J. 2012, L 197/38). Proceedings in the latter were discontinued because Germany complied with the Directive: Case C-545/15 (order of 10.3.2016), *Commission v. Germany*.
77. Ibid., para 84.
78. See Case C-387/97, *Commission v. Greece*, para 87.
79. See European Commission, "Application of Art. 228 of the EC Treaty, replacing two earlier communications of 1996 and 1997" SEC(2005)1658. See after Lisbon, "Application of Art. 260 of the Treaty on the Functioning of the European Union" SEC(2010)923/3, Updating of data used to calculate lump sum and penalty payments to be proposed by the Commission to the Court of Justice in infringement procedures. Since 2010, the Commission published an annual update of the data.
80. See Communication from the Commission: Updating of data used to calculate lump sum and penalty payments to be proposed by the Commission to the Court of Justice in infringement proceedings, C(2016) 5091 final. See also M. Smith, op. cit. *supra* note 27, 369; N. Kilbey, "Financial penalties under Art. 228(2) EC: Excessive complexity?", 44 CML Rev. (2007), 743–758 and S. Peers, "Sanctions for infringements of

2.1.4 *Infringement procedures: Fit for the future?*

The relative lack of legal evolution in the infringement procedures begs the question of whether the latter continue to provide for both an adequate and legitimate instrument of law enforcement in the EU as it stands today. As has been shown above, the legal framework for infringement proceedings has barely evolved beyond its original conception in the Treaty of Rome as an elite-circle quasi-diplomatic procedure reigned almost entirely by the Commission. And yet, today the infringement procedure operates in an entirely different constitutional and political framework. There is growing concern over the accountability of the EU's exercise of its powers.[81] At the latest with the Lisbon Treaty the principles of openness, transparency, and access to documents have become inherently linked to the Union's commitment to democratic principles.[82] Even before Lisbon, the Commission has been promoting principles of good governance and good administration.[83] Against the background of these constitutional evolutions both the secretive nature and almost unlimited discretionary power of the Commission in steering the outcome of an infringement procedure[84] stand out as issues of concern.

The practical relevance of the administrative stage is illustrated by the fact that many infringement cases are being settled through negotiations between the Commission and the Member State concerned during that stage.[85] This could, on the one hand, be read as a sign of success of the infringement procedure. On the other hand, it contributes to a lack of accountability and sound administration on the part of the Commission.

The Commission has wide discretion in deciding on when to open, close or refer the infringement case to the Court. Moreover, this discretion remains largely outside of the purview of judicial scrutiny.[86] Both the Commission's discretion and the Court's deference to it are being justified by the need to secure the "essential power"[87] of the Commission to make use of the infringement procedure, thereby acting in its capacity as the "guardian of the Treaty".[88] However, the strongly increased infringement workload especially after the 2004 enlargement has required the Commission not only to reorganize the way in which it handles infringements,[89]

EU Law after the Treaty of Lisbon", 18 EPL (2012), 31–62, 33. It should also be noted that the Court accepted that a lump sum and a penalty payment may be ordered in the same case. See Case C-304/02, *Commission v. France*.

81. Especially executive powers, see D. Curtin, *Executive Power in the European Union* (OUP, 2009). See also C. Harlow, *Accountability in the European Union,* (OUP, 2002).
82. See Arts. 1(2), 10 and 11 TEU and Art. 15(3) TFEU; see also Case C-280/11 P, *Council v. Access Info Europe*, for access to documents in legislative procedures as an expression of democratic principles. D. Curtin, H. Hofmann, and J. Mendes, "Constitutionalising EU executive rule-making procedures: A research agenda", 19 ELJ (2013), 1–21; A. Alemanno and O. Stefan, "Openness at the Court of Justice of the European Union: Toppling a taboo", 51 CML Rev. (2014), 97–139.
83. See European Commission, "European Governance – A White Paper" COM(2001)428; Art. 41 Charter of Fundamental Rights of the European Union (CFR).
84. See L. Prete and B. Smulders, op. cit. *supra* note 26 and also D. Chalmers and G. Davies, G. Monti, op. cit. *supra* note 19, 343–348 on the public policy use of the infringement procedure by the Commission.
85. See Report from the Commission: "Monitoring the application of European Union law 2016 Annual Report", available at <www.eur-lex.europa.eu/legal-content/EN/TXT/PDF/?uri=COM%3A2017%3A370%3AFIN&from=EN> at 21. In 2016, 72% (630) of infringement cases were closed during the administrative "pilot" stage because the Commission considered the answers by member states concerned "satisfactory".
86. See the Case 48/65, *Lütticke v. Commission*; Case C-205/98, *Commission v. Austria.*
87. See Joined Cases 2 & 3/62, *Commission v. Luxembourg and Belgium.*
88. See Joined Cases C-20 & 28/01, *Commission v. Germany,* para 30.
89. By introducing the EU Pilot, a special database for handling the communication between the Commission and Member States was established, see European Commission, "A Europe of results – Applying Community law" COM(2007)502; see for a discussion M. Smith, op. cit. *supra* note 27, 359.

but also to intensify priority setting. In other words, the concern is that when deciding which infringements to pursue or not to pursue the Commission might be guided by either political or economic considerations, which might potentially conflict with the principle of rule of law and citizens' rights.[90]

The confidentiality of all documents relating to an active infringement procedure[91] further aggravates this problem, as citizens in general, and complainants in particular, are not able to understand the reasoning which has led the Commission to either drop or settle a particular infringement case. The lack of transparency has been strongly criticized in an inquiry made by the European Ombudsman. Some Member States provide access to their infringement files. While recognizing the approach to non-disclosure in current EU case law, the Ombudsman criticizes the fact that the Commission generally presumes non-disclosure without providing convincing reasons on a case-by-case basis for how disclosure would compromise the infringement process.[92]

Finally, a related concern is the lack of third parties' rights in the pre-litigation phase. Complainants cannot challenge the Commission's decision not to commence a proceeding by means of an annulment procedure (Art. 263(4) TFEU).[93] Also here, inquiries of the European Ombudsman have drawn critical attention to the lack of due process in the way the Commission deals with complainants, in particular with regard to lack of information and reason giving vis-à-vis the complainant.[94] The pressure from the Ombudsman has had some effect, with the Commission ultimately adopting certain procedural entitlements for complainants. These include a commitment to a timely handling of cases, information about each procedural step, and in the case of closure of an infringement case, the opportunity to comment on the Commission decision.[95] However, these are only minimal guarantees based on the Commission's voluntary commitments. It is doubtful whether they allow the complainant to provide for an effective input into the infringement proceeding, and even less so to hold the Commission to account for its decisions.[96]

2.2 *The action for annulment*

The action for annulment is, in practice, a central judicial remedy provided for in the Treaties.[97] It aims to obtain a decision from the Court that an act adopted by an EU institution breaches EU law. Article 263 TFEU lays down the legal requirements for the filing of an action for annulment. There are four pivotal questions that will be examined by the GC or the CJ following Article 263.

---

90. See M. Smith, *Centralised Enforcement, Legitimacy, and Good Governance in the EU* (Routledge 2009), 136–137.
91. On access to infringement documents see Case T-105/95, *WWF UK v. Commission*; Case C-514/07, *API and Sweden v. Commission*. On access to documents from past infringements, see Case T-59/09, *Germany v. Commission*.
92. European Ombudsman, "Draft recommendations of the European Ombudsman in his inquiry into complaint 2207/2010/PB against the European Commission", Decision of 26 Sept. 2013, paras. 47–71.
93. Case 247/87, *Star Fruit v. Commission*, paras. 11–14.
94. See European Ombudsman, "Own-initiative inquiry into the Commission's administrative procedures for dealing with complainants under Art. (258)" in Annual Report 1997, 270; European Ombudsman, "Decision of the European Ombudsman on Complaint 995/98/OV against the European Commission", 30 Jan. 2001.
95. See European Commission, "On relations with the complainant in respect of infringements of community law" COM(2002)141; European Commission, "Updating the handling of relations with the complainants in respect of the application of Union Law", COM(2012)154, at 4–7.
96. D. Chalmers, G. Davies, G. Monti, op. cit. *supra* note 19, 370.
97. See Arts. 263 TFEU and 19(3) TEU. See also previously Arts. 230 EC and 146 Euratom.

The first question concerns the compliance with the time limits for bringing an action.[98] The second is whether the act of the Union for which annulment is sought constitutes a reviewable act.[99] Third, the Court will examine whether the party bringing the action may ask for judicial review, and therefore has standing. Paragraphs 2–4 of Article 263 TFEU distinguish between three classes of applicants in this regard, namely between "privileged", "semi-privileged" and "non-privileged" applicants. Lastly, the Court will examine the existence of possible grounds for the annulment of the act.[100] In the following we will explore these four key issues of an action for annulment, in a slightly different order, reversing the last two.

2.2.1 *Time limits*

According to Article 263(6) TFEU an action for annulment can be brought within a period of two months, dating, as the case may be, either from the publication of the act concerned[101] or from its notification to the applicant or, failing that, from the day on which the applicant had knowledge of that act.[102] This requirement is of great practical importance given that annulment actions brought outside the time limit are inadmissible. The deadline for lodging an action preserves legal certainty. However, after the deadline, the legality of the contested EU measure can still be reviewed in the preliminary reference procedure.[103]

2.2.2 *Reviewable acts*

The essential requirement as to the nature of reviewable acts under Article 263 TFEU is that they should be *legally binding*. Article 263(1) TFEU explicitly mentions legislative acts in the sense of Article 289(3) TFEU. However, also other acts of EU institutions including the Council, the Commission (e.g. in the sense of Arts. 290 and 291 TFEU), the European Central Bank, the European Parliament, and post-Lisbon also the European Council as well as of other EU bodies, offices and agencies are reviewable insofar as they are intended to produce *legal effects vis-à-vis third parties*. The Lisbon Treaty, therefore, has extended the jurisdiction of the Court with regard to reviewable acts.[104] Annulment actions may also be directed against "sui generis" acts of the institutions.[105] In the determination of legal effects of an act the Court adopts a non-formalist approach directed at examining the wording, context and substance of an act as well as the intention of its author.[106]

---

98. Art. 263(6) TFEU.
99. Art. 263(1) TFEU.
100. Art. 263(2) TFEU.
101. Cf. Art. 297 TFEU.
102. As to the details, see Art. 49–52 of the Rules of Procedure of the Court of Justice of 25 Sept. 2012 (O.J. 2012, L 265) as amended on 18 June 2013 (O.J. 2013, L 173/65) and on 19 July 2016 (O.J. 2016, L 217/69, hereafter: The CJ's Rules of Procedure); Art. 58–61 of the Rules of Procedure of the General Court of 4 Mar. 2015 (O.J. 2015, L 105/1) as amended on 13 July 2016 (O.J. 2016, L 217/71, hereafter: GC's Rules of Procedure). See also Practice directions relating to direct actions and appeals" O.J. 2004, L 361/15. For a strict application of the time-limits see, e.g. Case C-406/01, *Germany v. Parliament and Council*, in which a German action was found inadmissible because it was lodged one day too late.
103. R. Schütze, *An Introduction to European Law* (CUP, 2012), 263. See however the last paragraph in the section 3.1.
104. For an overview see M. Dougan, "The Treaty of Lisbon 2007: Winning minds, not hearts", 45 CML Rev. (2008), 617–703.
105. E.g. Case C-316/91, *Parliament v. Council*; for an annulment of an atypical act of the ECB see Case T-496/11, *United Kingdom v. ECB*.
106. See Case T-496/11, *United Kingdom v. ECB*, at para 31 with further case-law references.

Regulations, directives and decisions, the three types of binding legal acts mentioned in Article 288 TFEU, are unproblematic examples of reviewable acts in an annulment procedure. In contrast, mere recommendations and opinions, confirmatory measures and implementing measures in relation to decisions already taken are not reviewable, nor, in principle, internal instructions,[107] or communications and acts of an internal character. As the Court noted in its judgment in *Reynolds* "it is settled case law that only measures the legal effects of which are binding on, and capable of affecting the interests of, the applicant by bringing about a distinct change in his legal position are acts or decisions which may be the subject to an action for annulment".[108] As long as the act is capable of affecting the applicant by bringing about a distinct change in her legal position, it can constitute a reviewable act under Article 263 TFEU.[109]

The Court opted for the wide interpretation of the concept of reviewable act. In the *ERTA* case the Court accepted that annulment proceedings may be brought against "all measures adopted by the institutions, whatever their nature and form, which are intended to have legal effects".[110] Furthermore, in *Les Verts*[111] and *Chernobyl*[112] the Court has recognized the capacity of the European Parliament to sue and to be sued despite the fact that at that time the Treaty text did not refer to that institution. According to Arnull, both rulings "remain of the utmost importance as examples of the extent to which the Court has been prepared to stretch the Treaty".[113] The need to adopt a wide interpretation of the requirements of the annulment procedure in those cases was justified by the need to maintain the rule of law. On several occasions, the Court stated that it would be inconsistent with the objectives of the Treaty, in particular with Article 19 TEU, to interpret the conditions under which an action for annulment is admissible restrictively.[114]

2.2.3 *Grounds for annulment*

Article 263(2) TFEU lays down four grounds for the annulment of an EU act. The first ground is lack of competence. The EU institutions must respect the principle of conferral,[115] which means that they can only act within the limits of the competences conferred upon them by the Member States and laid down in the Treaties. Therefore, an EU act for which there is no legal basis under the Treaty can be annulled by the Court on the ground of lack of competence. The issue of the gradual expansion of regulatory powers at EU level as well as so-called "competence creep" has

107. Case C-131/03 P, *R. J. Reynolds Tobacco Holdings Inc. and Others,* para 55.
108. Ibid., para 54. For these purposes the Court will look to see whether such acts, although adopted e.g. in the form of internal instructions to EU officials or codes of conduct for the Member States, aim to impose obligations which do not already flow from EU law, see e.g. Case C-180/96, *United Kingdom v. Commission,* and Case C-443/97, *Spain v. Commission.* On Council conclusions that are intended to have legal effects, see Case C-27/04, *Commission v. Council (stability pact).*
109. Ibid. For a recent example of this approach see Case C-362/08 P, *Internationaler Hilfsfonds v. Commission,* para 52. See also the discussion in A. Albors-Llorens, *Private Parties in European Community Law* (OUP, 1996), 266.
110. Case C-22/7022/70, *Commission v. Council (ERTA),* para 42.
111. Case 294/83, *Parti écologiste "Les Verts" v. Parliament* Case C-294/83, *Les Verts.*
112. Case C-70/88, *Parliament v. Council.*
113. A. Arnull (1995), "Private applicants and the action for annulment under Article 173 of the EC Treaty", 32 CML Rev. (1995), 7–49 at 19.
114. E.g. Case 25/62, *Plaumann v. Commission,* para 107 and Case 22/70, *Commission v. Council (ERTA),* paras. 40 and 41.
115. Art. 5(1) and (2) TEU and 13(2) TEU.

been a matter of growing concern not only among legal scholars[116] and practitioners but also among the wider public.[117] Despite the fact that lack of competence is often argued before the Court, only once has the Court annulled an EU legislative act on that ground.[118] With regard to non-legislative measures, the lack of competence has been successfully invoked in the case of an excessive delegation of power to an EU agency or institution[119] or where an implementing EU act has gone beyond the limits of mere implementation of a legislative act.[120]

The second ground is infringement of an essential procedural requirement. The EU institutions when adopting acts must follow the applicable procedural rules laid down in the Treaties. This requirement is closely linked to the principle of conferral insofar as the relevant procedure for the adoption of an EU act is specified in the legal basis laid down in the Treaty, and conferring the power to adopt that act.[121] Non-compliance with the relevant procedural rules in the adoption of an act can lead to its annulment.[122]

The third ground for review is the infringement of "any rule of law relating to the application of the Treaty". This ground has the widest scope and is in practice the most important one. It includes infringements of the Treaties as the primary sources of EU law, as well as provisions of secondary legislation, provided it is hierarchically superior to the contested act.[123] This ground also includes provisions of international agreements by which the Union itself is bound.[124] Moreover, rules of law relating to the application of the Treaty also encompass general principles of law[125] as well as, since the entry into force of the Lisbon Treaty, the rights provided in the EU Charter of Fundamental Rights.[126] It should also be noted that the Lisbon Treaty emphasized the role of the Court in reviewing EU legislative acts on the ground of breach of the principle of subsidiarity. Article 8 of Protocol No 2 on subsidiarity confers on the Court the jurisdiction for such subsidiarity actions brought by the Member States, or notified by them in accordance with their legal order on behalf of their national Parliament, or a chamber thereof. This provision is part of the new system of monitoring and enforcement of the subsidiarity principle in the EU legal order.[127]

---

116. E.g. S. Weatherill, "Competence creep and competence control", 23 YEL (2004), 1–55. For a defence of the broad approach to competences taken by the Court, see B. de Witte, "A competence to protect. The pursuit of non-market aims through internal market legislation" in P. Syrpis (Ed.), *The Judiciary, the Legislature, and the EU Internal Market* (CUP, 2012).
117. E.g. the UK's initiative on Review of the Balances of Competences between the United Kingdom and the European Union, presented to the Parliament in July 2012.
118. See Case C-376/98, *Germany v. Parliament and Council (Tobacco Advertising)*. See also Case T-496/11, *United Kingdom v. ECB*.
119. Case 9/56, *Meroni & Co., Industrie Metallurgiche, SpA v. High Authority* (*Meroni I*), paras. 150–152. For a recent example where no excessive delegation of powers to an EU agency has been found, see Case C-270/12, *United Kingdom v. Parliament and Council ("Short Selling")* of 22 Jan. 2014, not yet reported.
120. Case 22/88, *Industrie- en Handelsonderneming Vreughenhil BV v. Minister van Landbouw en Visserij*, paras. 16–26; See recently Case C-355/10, *European Parliament v. Council*.
121. Case T-240/10, *Hungary v. Commission*, Case C-132/12 P, *Stichting Woonpunt and Others v. Commission*.
122. See for examples: Case 138/79, *Roquette Frères v. Council*; Case C-405/07 P, *Netherlands v. Commission*: Case C-269/90, *Technische Universität München v. Hauptzollamt München-Mitte*: Case C-291/89, *Interhotel v. Commission*; Case T-240/10, *Hungary v. Commission*.
123. E.g. Joined Cases 113-118/77, *NTN Toyo Bearing Co Ltd and Others v. Council*.
124. E.g. Joined Cases 21-24/72, *International Fruit Company*, Cf. *supra* section 1.2.
125. E.g. Case C-309/89, *Codorníu v. Council*.
126. In Case C-583/11 P, *Inuit Tapiriit Kanatami and Others v. Parliament and Council*, Art. 47 CFR was invoked as a ground for annulment.
127. Art. 5(3) TEU and Protocol No. 2 on the application of the principles of subsidiarity and proportionality. See in more detail M. Dougan, op. cit. *supra* note 104, 657.

The fourth ground, misuse of powers (*détournement de pouvoir*), refers to a concept known in the law of each of the Member States, although its content varies rather widely between the different legal systems. From the case law of the Court it appears that in its interpretation of the concept, the Court has taken the various national systems of law as sources of inspiration, but pursued its own course, finding that "a measure is only vitiated by misuse of powers if it appears, on the basis of objective, relevant and consistent evidence to have been taken with the exclusive or main purpose of achieving an end other than that stated or evading a procedure specifically prescribed by the Treaty for dealing with the circumstances of the case".[128]

If the action for annulment is justified on one of the above-mentioned grounds the Court will declare the act concerned wholly or partly void.[129] The act is then void as of the moment it originated and with respect to everyone (*ex tunc* and *erga omnes* effects).[130] When annulling an act the Court is entitled to state which of the effects of the annulled act shall be definitive.[131] This means that in the interest of legal certainty the Court can decide to maintain in force the effects of an act until it is replaced, including implementing acts which have been adopted on the basis of the annulled act.[132] The Court has applied its power to maintain the legal effects of an annulled act in respect of acts of the EU institutions by analogy in the context of preliminary references from national courts.

2.2.4 *Standing*

Initially, only the Member States,[133] the Council and the Commission had a general right to bring an action for annulment. The Treaty of Maastricht extended this right also to the European Parliament and to the European Central Bank for the purpose of protecting their prerogatives. The Treaty of Amsterdam did the same for the Court of Auditors,[134] and the Treaty of Lisbon for the Committee of Regions.[135] The Treaty of Nice had in the meantime granted the European Parliament a general right to bring an action for annulment. Post-Lisbon, the Member States, the European Parliament, the Council and the Commission are so-called "privileged" applicants since they are deemed to act in the general interest (Art. 263(2) TFEU). The European Central Bank, the Court of Auditors and the Committee of the Regions are "semi-privileged" applicants as they may solely bring review proceedings "for the purpose of protecting their prerogatives" (Art. 263(4) TFEU). The right of action has also been granted to a limited extent to private parties, (Art. 263(4) TFEU). The right of individuals to file an action for annulment before the Court is a subject of particular constitutional importance. The role of the Court in interpreting the Treaty requirements for non-privileged applicants has for

---

128. Case C-110/97, *Netherlands v. Council*, para 137 and the cases cited.
129. Art. 264(1) TFEU.
130. However, the Court will sometimes consider requests for limiting the ex tunc effect of its ruling, see Case C-178/05, *Commission v. Greece* and Case C-475/07, *Commission v. Poland*. See also C. Waldhoff "Recent developments relating to the retroactive effect of decisions of the ECJ", 46 CML Rev. (2009), 173–190, 173.
131. Art. 264(2) TFEU.
132. Case 59/81, *Commission v. Council*. See also Case 81/72, *Commission v. Council*.
133. The Lisbon Treaty opens the possibility that Member States, in accordance with their legal order, notify *on behalf of their national Parliament or a chamber of it* actions for annulment on grounds of infringement of the principle of subsidiarity by a legislative act, see Art. 8 of the Draft Protocol No. 2 on the application of the principles of subsidiarity and proportionality. According to the same Article the Committee of the Regions may bring such actions against legislative acts for the adoption of which the Treaty on the Functioning of the EU provides that it be consulted.
134. Cf. Art. 173 EC. This codifies, in respect of the European Parliament, the case law of the Court of Justice, see Case 70/88, *European Parliament v. Council (Chernobyl)*.
135. See Art. 263(3) TFEU.

many years been a bone of contention among scholars and practitioners, and it continues to be so under the Lisbon Treaty. In the following section we therefore discuss the standing of non-privileged applicants in more detail.

Standing of non-privileged applicants (private parties)

The Lisbon Treaty introduced important changes regarding the right of private parties to challenge potentially unlawful EU acts directly before the Court. Article 263(4) TFEU[136] distinguishes three situations when natural or legal persons have standing to bring an action for annulment. Firstly, private parties who are *addressees* of the act in question automatically have standing, and can bring an action before the Court within the time limit set out in Article 263(6) TFEU. Secondly, parties seeking the annulment of an act, which is not addressed to them, but to other parties, have to show that they *are directly and individually concerned* by it (general test). The third category, which represents the main change introduced by the Lisbon Treaty, are private parties, who are *non-addressees* and seek to challenge a so-called *regulatory act.* These applicants have to show that they are *directly concerned* by the act, and that the latter *does not entail implementing measures* (Lisbon test).[137]

The general (Plaumann) standing test: Direct and individual concern

According to Article 263(4) TFEU any natural or legal person[138] may file an action of annulment "against an act […], which is of *direct and individual concern* to them" (emphasis added). In the Court's case law the requirement of "direct and individual concern"[139] indicates that it is not enough that a private party is affected in their interests by an act addressed to someone else. For an action to be admissible a more qualified test needs to be fulfilled.

Direct concern. Of the two requirements of "direct and individual concern", the former has been relatively unproblematic. The non-addressee is directly concerned when its legal position is affected directly, or *ipso facto,* by the act in question without there being other intermediary steps necessary to create the effect on the applicant. In *Les Verts* the Court found that the European Parliament's decision directly concerned the applicants because it constituted "a complete set of rules which are sufficient in themselves and which require no implementing provisions since the calculation of the share of the appropriations to be granted to each of the political groupings concerned is automatic and leaves no room for any discretion".[140] Therefore, the necessity for the addressees of a contested act, typically the Member States, to adopt implementing measures

136. Art. 263(4) TFEU states: "Any natural or legal person may, under the conditions laid down in the first and second paragraphs, institute proceedings against *an act addressed* to that person or which is of *direct and individual concern* to them, and against a *regulatory act* which is of *direct concern* to them and *does not entail implementing measures*" (emphasis added).

137. For a more detailed discussion, see K. Lenaerts, I. Maselis, K. Gutman, *EU Procedural Law* (OUP, 2014), 309–364 and R. Barents, op. cit. *supra* note 9, 213–291. See also previous works: A. Albors-Llorens, op. cit. *supra* note 109; A. Arnull, "Private applicants and the action for annulment since *Codorniu*", 38 CML Rev. (2001), 7–52; A. Ward, *Judicial Review and the Rights of Private Parties in EU Law* (OUP, 2007).

138. The Court defined a legal person as someone who "has acquired legal personality in accordance with the law governing its constitution […] or if it has been treated as an independent legal entity by the Community institutions […]", Case T-161/94, *Sinochem Heilongjiang v. Council,* para 31.

139. It also applies to associations which base their standing on the circumstance that the persons they represent are directly and individually concerned, see e.g. Case C-321/95 P, *Greenpeace and Others v. Commission.*

140. Case 294/83, *Parti écologiste "Les Verts" v. Parliament,* para 31.

generally excludes direct concern.[141] If, however, the national authorities have no discretion as to how to implement the act, these measures may be equated to Union acts, which accordingly may affect private parties directly.[142]

Individual concern. The Court's interpretation of the second element of the general test, namely "individual concern," has been much more controversial. The Court's case law in this regard has been criticized on two main grounds: its inconsistency on the one hand, and its restrictiveness on the other. Both criticisms have raised further concerns over the respect for fundamental legal principles, namely the principle of legal certainty and the principle of effective judicial protection in the EU legal order. However, it should be noted that the system of legal protection provided for in the Treaties consists of two pillars, the CJEU and the national courts. Thus, there are various options for individuals to obtain review of the legality of a Union act.[143]

Since the Court's ruling in *Plaumann* in 1964[144] it has held that "[i]n order for a measure to be of individual concern to the persons to whom it applies, it must affect their legal position because of a factual situation which differentiates them from all other persons and distinguishes them individually in the same way as a person to whom it is addressed".[145] This interpretation remains authoritative also under the new Article 263(4) TFEU given that for non-addressees it maintains the formulation of an act "which is of direct and individual concern".[146] It is therefore important to provide a brief overview of the development of the case law since *Plaumann*.

The Court developed the *Plaumann* test on the basis of the original wording of ex Article 173(2) EC (as laid down in the Rome Treaty), and which in its formulation remained unchanged until the Lisbon treaty. Article 173(2) EC stated:

> "Any natural or legal person may [...] institute proceedings against a decision addressed to that person or against a *decision* which, *although in the form of a regulation or a decision addressed to another person,* is of *direct and individual concern* to the former" (emphasis added).

The requirement of "individual concern" was therefore strongly linked to the legal form of the contested act, namely a decision. Over time, the Court has adopted a wide interpretation of the word "decision" as encompassing acts of general application, such as true regulations and directives.[147] In other words the Court looked at the substance and not the form of the contested

---

141. See Case 96/71, *R. & V. Haegeman v. Commission*, paras. 5–8 and 9–13; Case 92/78, *SpA Simmenthal v. Commission*, paras. 27–30.
142. E.g. Case C-417/04 P, *Regione Siciliana v. Commission*, para 28; Joined Cases 113-118/77, *NTN Yoyo Bearing Company v. Council*, para 11.
143. See Case C-583/11 P, *Inuit Tapiriit Kanatami and Others v. Parliament and Council*, Opinion of A.G. Kokott, paras. 116–117. This can be done indirectly, in the course of an action for annulment through Art. 277 TFEU when the Union act is implemented by the EU authorities or through a preliminary question when the Member State is implementing the EU act. See further section (2) Evaluation.
144. Case 25/62, *Plaumann v. Commission*. The case concerned the requirements for the admissibility of an action brought by a German importer of clementines against a Commission decision addressed to Germany. The Commission decision concerned the application of customs duties in relation to clementines, and therefore affected the economic interests of Plaumann. However, as a non-addressee the company had to show that the Commission decision addressed to Germany was also of individual and direct concern to it.
145. Case 25/62, *Plaumann v. Commission*.
146. With the exception of "regulatory acts" see "The Lisbon test" below.
147. Case C-309/89, *Codorniu*, T-135/96, *UEAPME*. A. Arnull, "Judicial review in the European Union" in A. Arnull and D. Chalmers (Eds.), *Oxford Handbook of European Union law* (OUP, 2015), 377–402. For a detailed review of the Court's previous practice in this respect see Opinion in Case C-358/89, *Extramet* (A.G. Jacobs), pages 2515–2519.

measure. Provided that applicants could establish direct and individual concern, they were allowed to challenge the validity of any measure adopted by a Union institution, whatever form it took, as long as it was intended to have legal effects.[148] This was originally a significant departure from the text of the Treaty. However, the drafters of the Lisbon Treaty decided to codify this line of case law, replacing the word "decision" in Article 263(4) TFEU with the word "act".

The early case law was characterized by a strict application of the *Plaumann* test; as a consequence, the barrier of individual concern could only be overcome by private applicants in a few cases.[149] This was due to the high degree of individualization of the applicant required by the Court ever since *Plaumann*. To be individualized by the contested measure in the same way as an addressee, the applicant had to be the member of a "closed class" of persons, the membership of which was fixed at the time of adoption of the contested act, and could therefore be established *ex ante*.[150] A negative impact of the contested act on the applicant's economic position on its own was not considered sufficient, even in cases of grave adverse impact.[151]

In the late 1970s, however, the Court while maintaining the *Plaumann* formula, gradually began to provide for several exceptions thereto, confined to specific categories of cases. Most literature mentions the first case where the Court departed from the *Plaumann* formula, the *Les Verts v. European Parliament* case. In this case, a new political party challenged the practice for reimbursement of expenditure by the European Parliament, which was alleged to discriminate against new parties. *Locus standi* was granted, as the party would otherwise not have any possibility to challenge the legal act.[152]

In a series of cases, the Court found applicants to be individually concerned by measures that particularly adversely affected applicants' positions as market participants. In *Extramet*,[153] the Court found that an importer of a product is individually concerned by a Council regulation imposing anti-dumping duties on that product, because this seriously affected his economic activity. The case was still confined to the field of anti-dumping, and was later distinguished by the Court due to its underlying "exceptional circumstances".[154] The later *Codorníu* case, however, seemed at first to indicate a more fundamental change in approach. *Codorníu* involved a Spanish manufacturer of sparkling wine named "*crémant*" who challenged a Council regulation restricting the use of this term to certain sparkling wines produced in France and Luxembourg. The specificity of the applicant's position in this case was that Codorníu had held a trademark including the term "*crémant*" since 1924. Without giving a lengthy explanation about how this fitted into the usual "closed category" test, the Court found the applicant to be individually concerned given that the regulation effectively prevented him from using his trademark.[155]

---

148. See A. Arnull, op. cit. *supra* note 137, 23.
149. Case 112/77, *Aug. Töpfer & Co. GmbH v. Commission*; Case 88/76, *Société pour l'exportation des sucres SA v. Commission*.
150. Even if the number and identity of the importers affected by the consequences of such a decision could be determined, this still does not constitute a factual situation which is, as compared with all other persons, particularly relevant to them, if this results from purely fortuitous circumstances. Case 38/64, *Getreide-Import Gesellschaft v. Commission*. Even if a party is the only importer affected by a Commission decision addressed to a Member State, that party will not be found individually concerned (unless he or she forms part of a closed class, as is explained in the text); see, in this very restrictive sense, e.g. Case 231/82, *Spijker Kwasten BV v. Commission*.
151. Case T-173/98, *Union de Pequeños Agricultores v. Council*, para 50.
152. Case 294/83, *Parti écologiste "Les Verts" v. Parliament*.
153. Case C-358/09, *Extramet Industrie SA v. Council*, para 17.
154. T-598/97, *British Shoe Corporation v. Council*, paras. 48–50.
155. Case C-309/89, *Codorníu SA v. Council*, at para 21. In later case law this interpretation was explained as meaning that the applicant has had a "specific right" obtained before the entry into force of the challenged

The CJ's ruling in *UPA*, however, disappointed hopes of a more liberal approach.[156] In that case a Spanish trade association representing small agricultural producers challenged a Council regulation that discontinued agricultural aid for small producers. The measure not only adversely affected small producers in economic terms, but was also a so-called self-executing regulation, i.e. a regulation that did not require implementing measures at national level. The alternative path of challenging the Council regulation indirectly through the preliminary ruling procedure was thus unavailable to the applicants. At the same time, given that they belonged to an open category of people, the applicants would not be considered "individually concerned" under the *Plaumann* test. Advocate General Jacobs therefore argued that to deny standing to private parties in such cases would effectively lead to a denial of justice.[157] This in turn would violate the principle of effective judicial protection,[158] as well as running counter to the claim, often repeated in the Court's case law on the annulment procedure, that the Treaty provides for a *complete* system of judicial protection.

The Advocate's General's suggestion was followed in an unprecedented way by the GC in the somewhat similar *Jégo-Quéré*[159] case, decided a couple of months after the Opinion in *UPA* but prior to the CJ's decision. In the much-expected ruling in *UPA*, however, the CJ declined to follow the lead of its Advocate General and reverse *Plaumann*. The CJ's main argument was based on the architecture of the EU system of judicial protection as laid down in the Treaties, which it said prevented the CJ from adopting a legal interpretation of ex Article 230(4) EC, 4th limb, 4th limb (now Art. 263(4) TFEU) that was *contra legem*,[160] and thus a *de facto* Treaty amendment. These pronouncements showed a non-activist Court, exercising judicial self-restraint and raising arguments based on the separation of powers between the EU's treaty-making and judicial authority. Unsurprisingly, the sudden self-restraint was met with sharp criticism in the literature, which criticized the CJ not only for disregarding the principle of effective judicial protection, but also for being inconsistent.[161]

How did the Treaty makers respond to these stipulations when drafting the Treaty of Lisbon? Firstly, the newly introduced subparagraph of Article 19(1) TEU incorporates into the Treaty text the CJ's admonition, by obliging the Member States to provide remedies sufficient to ensure effective legal protection under EU law. Secondly, Article 263(4) TFEU reforms the system of individual judicial protection by abolishing the requirement of individual concern for so-called "regulatory acts", while keeping it for all other acts (see below). However, given that no definition of this term is provided in the Treaty, this has produced new interpretative problems. In the words of Schütze "The dividing line between the second and third category is thus poised to become *the* post-Lisbon interpretative battlefield within Article 263(4) TFEU".[162]

---

act, see Case C-87/95 P, *Cassa Nazionale di Previdenza ed Assistenza a favore degli avvocati e dei Procuratori v. Council*, at para 36 and Case T-99/94 at para 20.

156. Case C-50/00 P, *Unión de Pequeños Agricultores (UPA) v. Council.*
157. Case C-292/00 P, *Davidoff & Cie SA and Zino Davidoff SA v. Gofkid Ltd*, Opinion of A.G. Jacobs, paras. 38–44.
158. Now enshrined in Art. 47 CFR.
159. Case T-177/01, *Jégo-Quéré & Cie SA v. Commission*, paras. 49–51.
160. Case C-50/00 P, *Unión de Pequeños Agricultores (UPA) v. Council*, paras. 44–45.
161. P. Craig, "Standing, rights, and the structure of legal argument", 9 EPI (2003), 493–508; C. Kombos, "A paradox in the making: Detecting something positive in *UPA* under the *Ten Kate* effect",15 ELJ (2009), 506–535.
162. R. Schütze, op. cit. *supra* note 104, 198.

The Lisbon test: What are "regulatory acts"?

It did not take long for the Court to get the opportunity to define the notion of "regulatory acts" under Article 263(4) TFEU, and thereby also clarify whether it would accept a more relaxed standing test for private applicants wishing to challenge general legislative measures. In the *Inuit Tapiriit Kanatami* case, concerning an action to annul the so-called *Seals* Regulation, the CJ had to decide whether "regulatory acts" in the sense of Article 263(4) also cover legislative acts, with the consequence that the requirement of "individual concern" would no longer be applicable. The Court held that the concept of "regulatory acts" provided for in Article 263(4) TFEU does not encompass legislative acts. Relying on textual interpretation, the CJ explained that "regulatory acts" "cannot [...] refer to all acts of general application but relates to a more restricted category of such acts. To adopt an interpretation to the contrary would amount to nullifying the distinction made between the term "acts" and "regulatory acts" by the second and third limbs of the fourth paragraph of Article 263 TFEU".[163]

Consequently, given that the contested *Seals* Regulation is a legislative act, it fell under the second limb of Article 263(4) TFEU. The applicants, therefore, had to pass the test of "direct and individual" concern. The Court rejected the applicants' call to abandon the *Plaumann* test, with the argument that the wording of the second limb was not altered by the Treaty of Lisbon. Heavily relying on the *travaux préparatoires,* the Court concluded that "there is nothing to suggest that the authors of the Treaty of Lisbon had any intention of altering the scope of the conditions of admissibility already laid down in Article 230(4) EC,"[164] and one should add, as interpreted by the Court in its case law since *Plaumann.*

Finally, the Court did not feel compelled to change its approach by the constitutional enshrinement of the right to an effective remedy in Article 47 of the Charter. In this regard, the Court repeated the well-known pronouncements from previous case law regarding the complete system of legal remedies and procedures laid down in the Treaties[165] especially referring to the new Article 19(1) TEU, which now reaffirms the Member States' responsibility for providing sufficient judicial remedies for individuals to challenge EU acts via the preliminary procedure. Article 47 of the Charter, according to the Court, "is not intended to change the system of judicial review laid down by the Treaties, and particularly the rules relating to the admissibility of direct actions brought before the Courts of the European Union".[166]

Thus, in *Inuit Tapiriit Kanatami* the Court rejected the idea that Article 263(4) third limb TFEU read together with Article 47 of the Charter should be interpreted so as to create a remedy for individuals to directly challenge the constitutionality of EU legislative acts,[167] which would be a sort of individual constitutional complaint such as that existing in some, but not all legal orders of the Member States.[168]

---

163. Case C-583/11 P, *Inuit Tapiriit Kanatami and Others v. Parliament and Council*, para 58.
164. Ibid., para 70.
165. Ibid., paras. 92–96.
166. Ibid., para 97.
167. Ibid., see in particular paras. 105–106.
168. For criticism of this approach see F.-V. Guiot, "L'affaire *Inuit*: Une illustration des interactions entre recours individuel et équilibre institutionnel dans l'interprétation de l'article 263 du TFUE", (2014) RTDE, 389–408. For the defence, drawing the parallel with analogous national systems for the constitutional review of legislation functioning in accordance with the "preliminary reference" model, see A. Popov, "La complémentarité entre les recours en annulation formés par des particuliers et les renvois préjudicielles en appréciation de validité avant comme après l'entrée en vigueur du traité de Lisbonne et l'accès au prétoire de l'Union européenne", 48 CDE, (2012), 167–194.

The Lisbon test: Standing requirements

This brings us to the newly defined conditions for the admissibility of "regulatory acts" as laid down in the third limb of Article 263(4) TFEU, namely the requirement that those acts must be of *direct concern* to the applicant and must *not entail implementing measures*. Also here the Court has had the opportunity to clarify those conditions in a series of post-Lisbon cases.

As explained above, in *Inuit Tapiriit Kanatami* the Court defined "regulatory acts" as "acts of general application apart from legislative acts".[169] Moreover, in its ruling in *Telefónica*, the CJ defined the meaning of the two other conditions of the third limb of Article 263(4) TFEU.

Because of the potential overlap between both requirements some scholars suggested that the "requirement that an act not "entail implementing measures" may have been inserted simply to clarify the meaning of "direct concern" rather than posing an additional hurdle to the standing of private applicants.[170] However, the Court adopted a different interpretation in *Telefonica*.[171] The case concerned a Commission decision addressed to Spain, which declared an aid scheme to be incompatible with the common market, and required Spain to recover the aid. The applicant, a large Spanish telephone operator, was a recipient under this scheme, and now risked having to pay back the aid received. The declaration in the Commission's decision that the aid scheme was unlawful therefore directly affected the applicant's legal position, and no discretion was left to Spain in this regard. However, the Court nonetheless dismissed the action as inadmissible, because the Commission decision still entailed implementing measures. The Court went on to restate that implementing measures can be challenged either directly or indirectly. Where the responsibility for implementation lies at EU level a direct action via Article 263 TFEU coupled with a plea of illegality of the basic act at issue on the basis of Article 277 TFEU is available. Where implementation is a matter for the Member States, the route via the preliminary ruling pursuant to Article 267 TFEU is open to the applicant.[172] As a result, the condition of no implementing measures adds a further hurdle to the condition of direct concern.[173] To sum up, the Lisbon reform of Article 263(4) TFEU only minimally broadened the access of private applicants to EU courts. As Barents concludes: "the mountain laboured and brought forth a mouse".[174]

Evaluation

It is clear from the above post-Lisbon cases that in interpreting the newly defined standing requirements for regulatory acts under the Lisbon test the Court remains firmly rooted in its understanding of the EU system of individual judicial protection as expressed in its case law before Lisbon, most notably *UPA*: namely, as "a complete system of legal remedies and procedures designed to ensure judicial review of the legality of acts of the institutions" either directly via Article 263 or indirectly via Article 267 TFEU.

169. Case T-18/10, *Inuit Tapiriit Kanatami and Others v. Parliament and Council*, para 56.

170. See S. Peers and M. Costa, "Court of Justice of the European Union (General Chamber), Judicial review of EU Acts after the Treaty of Lisbon; Order of 6 Sept. 2011, for a counterview see C. Werkmeister, S. Pötters and J. Traut, "Regulatory acts within Art. 263(4) TFEU – A dissonant extension of *locus standi* for private applicants", 13 CYELS (2010–2011), 311 and W. Cremer, "Art. 263 AEUW" in C. Calliess and M. Ruffert (Eds.), *EUV/AEUV Kommentar*, 4th ed. (C.H. Beck, 2011), 2324.

171. Case C-295/12 P, *Telefònica SA and Telefònica de Espana SAU v. Commission.*

172. Ibid., para 29.

173. See also C-456/13 P, *T&L Sugars*. For propositions of alternative interpretations see Opinion of A.G. Cruz Villalón in C-456/13 P, *T&L Sugars*, 16–48; and Opinion of A.G. Wathelet in C-132/12 P, *Stichting*, 69–76.

174. R. Barents, op. cit. *supra* note 9, 284.

In this understanding, the preliminary reference procedure is seen as a central instrument for judicial review of EU acts. In the Court's interpretation, the Lisbon reform of the annulment procedure, in Article 263(4), third limb, was supposed to liberalize the access to the Court by individual applicants only with regard to so-called "self-executing" non-legislative regulations. In contrast, non-legislative directives or other measures requiring implementation fall outside the scope of the Lisbon test (Art. 263(4) third limb). For those measures, applicants must either satisfy the *Plaumann* test of "direct and individual concern" (Art. 263(4), second limb), or challenge them indirectly by bringing actions against the respective implementing measures before the national courts. Moreover, legislative measures generally remain outside the purview of private applicants under Article 263(4), unless in those exceptional cases where they are able to demonstrate "direct and individual concern".

It is therefore not surprising that critical commentators have referred to the new Lisbon test as a "partial gap-plugging mechanism"[175] or a "minimalist solution"[176] to the problem of effective judicial protection under EU law. Taking Article 19 TEU as a confirmation of its approach, the Court remains unimpressed by the concerns regarding the deficiencies of individual judicial protection through preliminary references, as expressed most prominently by Advocate General Jacobs in *UPA*. At the same time, it accepts the difficulties of individuals to challenge EU legislative measures even in those situations, such as previously in *UPA*, where there are no implementing measures that can be challenged either before the EU or the national courts. It follows, therefore, that the main concern with regard to the Court's case law on the standing of private applicants under Article 263 TFEU, namely the problem of access to the Court, and therefore the risk of a denial of justice, remains valid also since the Lisbon Treaty.

How can such an approach to individual judicial protection be explained, especially given that it comes from the EU's highest and most powerful court, which in the past invoked the principle of judicial protection in order to considerably widen its own jurisdiction under Article 263 against the Treaty text?[177]

An important argument often invoked in favour of excluding EU legislative measures from a direct challenge under Article 263(4) refers to the higher democratic legitimation of such measures. In the *Inuit Tapiriit Kanatami* case, Advocate General Kokott summarized this argument as follows: "The absence of easier direct legal remedies available to individuals against legislative acts can be explained principally by the *particularly high democratic legitimation of parliamentary legislation*. Accordingly, the distinction between legislative and non-legislative acts in respect of legal protection cannot be dismissed as merely formalistic; rather, it is attributable to a qualitative difference. In many national legal systems individuals have no direct legal remedies, or only limited remedies, against parliamentary laws".[178] (emphasis added)

While this argument holds true for national constitutional systems, it does not withstand further scrutiny in the specific context of the EU's legal and political system. As observed by other commentators, EU legislative measures do not enjoy the same degree of democratic legitimacy as national legislation.[179] The persisting problem in this respect is, in particular, the lack of transparency and democratic accountability in law-making procedures, due to the practice of

175. A. Albors-Llorens, op. cit. *supra* note 109; A. Albors-Llorens, "Remedies against the EU Institutions after Lisbon: An era of opportunity?", 71 CLJ (2012), 507–536.
176. M. Dougan, op. cit. *supra* note 104, 677.
177. E.g. in Case 294/83, *Parti écologiste "Les Verts" v. Parliament* and Case 70/88, *European Parliament v. Council (Chernobyl)*.
178. Case C-583/11 P, *Inuit Tapiriit Kanatami and Others v. Parliament and Council*, Opinion of A.G. Kokott, para 38.
179. See e.g. S. Peers and M. Costa, op. cit. *supra* note 170, 95; M. Dougan, op. cit. *supra* note 104, 678.

settling most pressing political controversies in closed meetings with the representatives of the Parliament, the Council and the Commission (trilogues) instead of a transparent parliamentary assembly. Moreover, there are many special legislative procedures laid down in the Treaty,[180] which do not require the participation of the European Parliament further aggravating the problem of democratic legitimation. The argument of Advocate General Kokott could therefore easily become a double-edged sword. As noted by Dougan, "If anything, one might argue that the rule of law – through the medium of effective judicial review, directly at the behest of the citizen, in respect of all Union measures, legislative as well as non-legislative – plays an even more important role in legitimizing the existence and exercise of Union power than it does within the ordinary national legal systems".[181]

Through the argument about the democratic legitimacy of EU legislative measures, however, shines another much more pragmatic and functionalist rationale in granting those measures a special treatment under Article 263(4) TFEU. As noted by Arnull, the Court's interpretation of the Treaty has since early on been concerned with strengthening the EU and its institutions.[182] This tendency is present until this day, and has led to criticism about the Court engaging in judicial activism.[183] Given the cumbersome, lengthy, and politically complex process of negotiating new EU legislation, it is therefore not far fetched to assume that the Court is particularly reluctant to extend the possibilities of private applicants to directly challenge EU legislation, just as it has often been reluctant to strike down EU legislation,[184] or has second-guessed legislative choices in order to uphold a legislative measure.[185] This more pragmatic concern with the functioning of the EU legislature seems highly problematic in the context of today's Union, in which the question as to the limits and ways of EU legal integration has become an equally salient concern. It could therefore be argued that by shielding EU legislation from direct individual challenge, the Court fails to adjust its case law to the expansion of EU legislative powers over time. On the other hand, the argument can also be made that a direct individual challenge would undermine the existing institutional balance.

Either way, it can also be argued that effective judicial protection against EU legislative measures does not require that an individual should be entitled to challenge those measures directly before the EU courts.[186] After all, EU courts and national courts share the responsibility for the application and development of EU law. The EU judicial system does not only depend on the CJEU, but also on national courts, which are not only more numerous, but also have greater resources in providing access to court for private litigants. Therefore, the Court's insistence on the national courts as an important second pillar of the EU system of individual judicial review is likely to be influenced by its conception of the preliminary reference procedure as fundamental for the development of the Union legal order. The judicial dialogue through Article

---

180. See e.g. Arts. 21(3), 64(3), 77(3) TFEU.
181. M. Dougan, op. cit. *supra* note 104, 678.
182. A. Arnull, op. cit. *supra* note 137, 44.
183. See M. Dawson et al., op. cit. *supra* note 2.
184. For example on the ground of lack of legal basis. A striking recent counter-example is the ruling on the Data Retention Directive, Joined Cases C-293 & 594/12, *Digital Rights Ireland and Seitlinger and Others.*
185. See Joined Cases C-402 & 432/07, *Christopher Sturgeon, Gabriel Sturgeon and Alana Sturgeon v. Condor Flugdienst GmbH and Stefan Böck and Cornelia Lepuschitz v. Air France SA*; see also J.H.H. Weiler, "Epilogue: Judging the judges – Apology and critique" in M. Adams, H. de Waele, J. Meeusen and G. Straetmans (Eds.), *Judging Europe's Judges* (Hart, 2013). P. Craig, "Legality, standing and substantive review in Community law", 14 OJLS (1994), 507–537; See also the conclusions of H. Schepel, E. Blankenburg, "Mobilizing the European Court of Justice" in J.H.H. Weiler and G. de Búrca (Eds.), *The European Court of Justice* (OUP, 2002), 9–42.
186. Case C-583/11 P, *Inuit Tapiriit Kanatami and Others v. Parliament and Council,* para 105.

267 between the Court and national courts has empowered lower national courts, in particular, by granting them the authority to interpret and apply EU law, and to refer questions to the CJ irrespective of domestic procedures or hierarchies.[187] This enabled national courts to deviate from established domestic jurisprudence, and to use EU law to achieve new legal outcomes. At the same time, it created new opportunities for the Court to expand its jurisdiction. In the words of Alter, "lower courts were the motors of EC legal integration into the national order, and legal expansion through their referrals to the ECJ".[188] Similarly, Chalmers, Davies and Monti observe that the preliminary reference procedure "sets out numerous decentralized laboratories for the testing and exploration of EU law, in the form of national courts and tribunals, which are, by and large, accessible to private parties. [...] It is, thus through the preliminary reference procedure that the Court of Justice has been able to open up and widen the horizons of EU law through the establishment of new doctrines and principles; systematize EU law through bringing disparate cases under unifying schema and categories; and revisit case law in the light of experience in national arenas".[189]

Against this background, the Court's understanding of the EU judicial system as expressed in *UPA,* and again emphasized in *Inuit Tapiriit Kanatami,* appears consequential. From the Court's perspective, the possible deficiencies of indirect legal protection of individuals via the preliminary reference procedure are outweighed by the fundamental importance of the latter in the Union legal order. Adopting a more liberal approach on the standing of individual applicants under Article 263(4) would reduce the importance of preliminary references on the validity of EU acts, channelling more cases directly to the Court.

This links up to the more practical argument sometimes invoked by the proponents of a more restrictive approach to the standing of private applicants, namely that a liberal approach would open the gates to a flood of litigation at EU level. This argument is often dismissed with the reference to the overriding constitutional value of effective judicial protection, which should not be subordinated to practical concerns. However, the Court's post-Lisbon case law on standing of individual applicants should arguably be seen in the broader context of the changes contained in the Lisbon treaty regarding the widened jurisdiction of the Court, for example with regard to reviewable Union acts or in the Area of Freedom, Security and Justice.[190] In the words of Jacobs "The various extensions of the jurisdiction of the Courts under the Lisbon Treaty are to be welcomed in a Union based on the rule of law. [...] But it cannot be denied that they also present challenges of a novel kind for the Courts; and they may even require, sooner or later, some re-shaping of the Union's judicial system".[191]

A final remark seems important in order to understand the Court's post-Lisbon approach. Apart from the disagreement as to what an effective EU judicial protection of individuals entails, the Court also disagrees on what could be called the empirical assessment of the risks and gaps of protection arising from its narrow interpretation of Article 263(4). In other words, the Court seems to assume that a situation in which implementing acts of a legislative EU act are lacking, and thereby a situation of a denial of justice is practically very unlikely in the present state of the Union. The Opinion of Advocate General Kokott in *Inuit Tapiriit Kanatami* is insightful in this regard. On the one hand, she agreed with the applicants that in view of the EU fundamental

---

187. See e.g. Case C-416/10, *Krizan v. Slovenska,* para 69.
188. K. Alter, "The European Court's political power", 19 WEP (1996), 466–467.
189. D. Chalmers, G. Davies, G. Monti, op. cit. *supra* note 19, 174 et seq.
190. See in more detail F. Jacobs, "The Lisbon Treaty and the Court of Justice" in A. Biondi, P. Eeckhout and S. Ripley (Eds.), *EU Law After Lisbon* (OUP, 2012).
191. Ibid., 212–213.

right to an effective remedy, an individual cannot be forced to act unlawfully and possibly run the risk of a penalty, merely in order to provoke an implementing act that could be challenged before the national courts.[192] On the other hand, she found that "such a situation is not to be feared in the system of the European Treaties with regard to EU legislative acts".[193] According to the Advocate General, an individual is always free to write to the competent authority either at EU or at national level, and to request confirmation that the requirement or ban laid down in a self-executing legislative EU act is not applicable to him. In case of a negative decision of a national authority, national courts would be obliged to review this decision, and possibly to refer the question of validity of the underlying EU act to the CJ for a preliminary ruling. In view of Article 19(1) TEU, the conditions for admissibility of actions before national courts, including possible preventive actions for declarations or injunctions, may not be excessively restrictive.[194] It is true that today most EU legislative measures, due to their often broad and open-ended nature, require implementation either at EU or national level. In *Inuit Tapiriit Kanatami*, the challenged regulation was implemented by a Commission Regulation, against which the applicants filed a parallel legal challenge before the Court.[195] Therefore, the practical extent of the problem of denial of justice with regard to potentially invalid EU legislative acts is not entirely clear.

2.3 *The action for failure to act*

As well as the action for annulment, the Treaties in Article 265 TFEU also provide for an action against failure to act where such failure is contrary to EU law. Articles 263 and 265 TFEU are seen as expressions of one and the same legal recourse.[196] While the former provides for the possibility of control in respect of positive actions of EU institutions, the latter allows a remedy for situations where the institutions have evaded their obligations by failing to act. The action for failure to act is meant to induce action by the institution (Art. 266 TFEU) that failed to act, and can be directed at all EU institutions, bodies, offices and agencies with the exception of the Court of Auditors and the CJEU. Article 265(2) contains an important pre-litigation requirement: the institution in question must first be formally called upon to act. This should be done within a reasonable period of it having become clear that the institution is not going to act.[197] If the institution has not defined its position within two months, an action may be brought before the Court within a further period of two months.

Like the action for annulment, the action for failure to act distinguishes between privileged and non-privileged applicants. The first category encompasses EU institutions and Member States, and is therefore wider than the notion of privileged applicants under Article 263(2) TFEU. With regard to the nature of "inactions" that can be challenged by privileged applicants, the wording of Article 265(1) TFEU suggests that an act that an EU institution failed to adopt, does not have to be a legally binding one. This reading is confirmed by the Court, which found that actions for failure to act can also be brought in relation to "preparatory acts".[198]

In contrast, regarding the standing of non-privileged private parties, the wording of Article 265(3) TFEU indicates that the failure to act must concern an act intended to have legal

192. C-432/05, *Unibet*.
193. Case C-583/11 P, *Inuit Tapiriit Kanatami and Others v. Parliament and Council*, Opinion of A.G. Kokott, para 119.
194. Ibid., paras. 118–123.
195. Case T-526/10, *Inuit Tapiriit Kanatami and Others v. Commission (Inuit Tapiriit II)*.
196. Case 15/70, *Amedeo Chevalley v. Commission*; Case C-68/95, *T. Port GmbH & Co. KG v. Bundesanstalt für Landwirtschaft und Ernährung*, para 59.
197. Cf. Case 59/70, *Netherlands v. Commission*.
198. Case 377/87, *Parliament v. Council*.

effects (literally, an act other than a recommendation or opinion).[199] Furthermore, the Treaty text speaks of acts that an institution, body, office or agency of the Union "has failed to address" to the private applicant. At first sight this indicates a narrower framing of standing of private applicants as compared to Article 263(4) TFEU. However, according to case law of the Court the standing requirements for the annulment procedure and the failure to act procedure should be interpreted in parallel.[200] This means that Article 265(3) TFEU should be read as allowing private parties to have standing when they are: potential addressees of an act; when they are directly concerned by a regulatory act; or directly and individually concerned by a non-regulatory act which should have been adopted.

A further "unwritten" condition for an action for failure to act for both privileged and non-privileged applicants is that the institution was under an *obligation to act*. Therefore, applicants cannot successfully challenge a EU institution for its failure to act where the latter has "the right, but not the duty" to act.[201] This means, for example, that an action is inadmissible where it is aimed at obtaining from the Court a ruling that the Commission has failed to fulfil its Treaty obligations by not commencing infringement proceedings against a Member State under Article 258 TFEU. The Commission is not under an *obligation* to start such proceedings nor, where the Commission's reasoned opinion is not complied with, is it *obliged* to bring proceedings before the Court against the Member State in question.[202] The Commission's discretion with regard to the decision on whether or not to commence an infringement procedure excludes an obligation to act.

Another situation in which there is no obligation to act is where there is no legal obligation to adopt *specific* measures, but only a *general* obligation, e.g. to develop a Union policy. In *Parliament v. Council (Common Transport Policy)*, the Court rejected the Parliament's right to bring an action for failure to act against the Council on the ground that the latter had failed to lay down a framework for the common transport policy. According to the Court, the failure to act has to be "sufficiently defined", which would be the case where the act to be adopted could be "identified individually".[203]

If the act that was the object of the action for failure to act is in fact adopted between the action being brought and the judgment being given, the action becomes devoid of purpose. After all: the remedy in Article 265 TFEU is based on the premise that a declaration can be obtained from the Court that the failure to act is contrary to the Treaty, insofar as it has not been repaired by the institution(s) concerned. The institution(s) concerned must then, under Article 266 TFEU, take the necessary measures to comply with the judgment, without prejudice to any actions in respect of non-contractual liability which may result from the judgment.[204] Such a declaration by the Court has no further point if the result has, in fact, already been achieved.[205]

---

199. Case 15/70, *Amadeo Chevalley v. Commission* and Case 6/70, *Gillberto Borromeo Arese et al. v. Commission.*
200. Ibid., Case C-107/91, *Empresa Nacional de Urânio SA v. Commission* (in relation to Art. 148 Euratom); Case C-68/95, *T. Port GmbH & Co. KG v. Bundesanstalt für Landwirtschaft und Ernährung*; Case T-395/04, *Air One v. Commission* and Case C-167/04, *Asklepios Klinken v. Commission.*
201. Cf. Case 247/87, *Star Fruit Company SA v. Commission*. As for infringement procedures against Member States under Art. 86(3) EC, see Case C-141/02 P, *Commission v. T-Mobile Austria GmbH*. Private parties may complain to the Commission about infringements of Community law, see the Report from the Commission (op. cit. *supra* note 85), at 4.
202. See *supra* section 2.1.4; Case 247/87, *Star Fruit Company SA v. Commission*, para 11.
203. Case 377/87, *Parliament v. Council*, para 37.
204. Under Art. 288(2) read with Art. 235 EC (Arts. 188(2) and 151 Euratom).
205. See Case 377/87, *Parliament v. Council*; Case 383/87, *Commission v. Council* and Case C-25/91, *Pesqueras Echebastar SA v. Commission* (an incorrect declaration of inadmissibility); see also Joined Cases C-15 &

Finally, one point should be made about the judgment of the Court. In its judgment, the Court may decide that the failure to act constitutes an infringement of the Treaty. The institution is then obliged to take the necessary measures to comply with the judgment (Art. 266 TFEU),[206] which is to say to take a decision or at the very least to define its position. Regarding the time limit for such compliance, the Court requires that the institution "has a reasonable period for that purpose".[207] As to the possibility of bringing an action for damages in the event of an unlawful failure to act, see section 2.5. below.

2.4 *The plea of illegality, Article 277 TFEU*

As explained above, a private party will rarely have the right to lodge a direct action for annulment of an EU legislative act. Moreover, parties might often experience difficulties to challenge regulatory acts (e.g. delegated and implementing acts) on the ground that the parent measure is illegal, for example, due to the expiry of time limits under Article 263(6) TFEU. The plea of illegality laid down in Article 277 TFEU allows parties in proceedings initiated against acts of general application adopted by an institution, body, or agency of the Union, to plead the illegality of its parent measure. This procedure, therefore, is not an independent one, but is attached to another proceeding before the Court, in which the time limits and standing requirements have been observed.[208]

Parties can invoke the plea of illegality on the same grounds as those applying to an action for annulment and notwithstanding the expiry of the time limit for appeal laid down in Article 263(6) TFEU.[209] The act whose legality is called into question must be applicable, directly or indirectly, to the issue with which the application is concerned.[210] A recent example is the *Inuit Tapiriit* litigation, where the applicants, besides challenging the legislative parent regulation via Article 263(4) (see above), also lodged an action against a Commission implementing regulation and simultaneously raised the plea of illegality against the parent regulation.[211]

If the plea is admitted, the Court will not apply the provisions of the parent act in that specific case, thus leading to the annulment of the implementing act based on those provisions.[212] The parent act itself, however, is not annulled,[213] although the institution that issued it will, naturally, draw the appropriate conclusions and take measures to replace the illegal act.

As "any party" may invoke the plea of illegality, the text of Article 277 TFEU does not exclude Member States and institutions from the right to invoke the possible illegality of a general act under that Article.[214] Although the Court seems to have sought the ratio of Article 277 TFEU particularly in the limited right of direct appeal for private parties, there is no indication that it

---

108/91, *Josef Buckl & Söhne OHG and others v. Commission* and Joined Cases T-194/97 and 83/98, *Branco v. Commission*.

206. Arts. 233 EC and 149 Euratom (1st para in each case).
207. Ibid., Case 377/87, *Parliament v. Council*, para 69.
208. Joined Cases 31 & 33/62, *Wöhrmann v. Commission*.
209. Arts. 241 EC and 156 Euratom. This plea of illegality is often called "the exception of illegality" (after the French).
210. Case 32/65, *Italy v. Council and Commission*.
211. Case T-526/10, *Inuit Tapiriit Kanatami and Others v. Commission (Inuit Tapiriit II)*.
212. See Case C-9/56, *Meroni & Co., Industrie Metallurgiche, SpA v. High Authority* (*Meroni I*).
213. See Joined Cases 31 & 33/62, *Milchwerke Heinz Wöhrmann & Sohn KG et al. v. Commission* and Joined Cases 15-33/73, *Roswitha Schots, née Kortner et al. v. Council et al.*
214. The majority view in the literature is that they may. See M. Waelbroeck, D. Waelbroeck and G. Vandersanden, "La Cour de Justice" in J.V. Louis et al. (Eds.), *Commentaire Mégret, Le Droit de la CEE*, 2nd ed. (Éditions de l'Université de la Bruxelles, 1993), 132–133 and the literature mentioned therein. Support for this view can be found in Case 32/65, *Italy v. Council and Commission*, and Case C-135/93, *Spain v. Commission*.

should be interpreted otherwise. Unlike private parties, Member States and institutions do have the right to challenge legislative acts, but that is not a decisive argument to deny them access to the plea of illegality. Irregularities in an act may appear after the time limit for challenging it has passed when measures of implementation are adopted, as was confirmed by the Court.[215]

2.5 *The action for damages*

Articles 268 and 340(2) TFEU lay down the conditions for an action for damages. This action allows any party that has suffered damage or loss caused by illegal action of a Union institution or its civil servants to seek compensation before the Court (so-called non-contractual liability). It is recognized that the action for damages constitutions an independent action, the success of which does not depend on the prior success of another action.

In *Lütticke*, the Court laid down certain conditions, based on Article 340(2) TFEU and the general principles to which it refers, which must be satisfied in order for the Union (then, Community) to be liable.[216] These conditions relate to:

(1) the illegality[217] of the conduct of which the Union institution is accused,
(2) the existence of actual damage,
(3) a causal link between the damage claimed and the conduct alleged against the institution.

Conduct does not just cover purely substantive acts, but also legal acts (including the failure to adopt or execute legal acts). The act (or omission) must however be an official act, that is, it must be attributable to the Union. Proceedings against the Union in matters arising from non-contractual liability are barred after a period of five years from the event giving rise thereto,[218] namely the occurrence of the damage.[219] Unlike under Article 264 TFEU, the applicants for an action for damages do not have to fulfil any standing conditions. Any party that has suffered damage through an illegal Union (in)action may bring proceedings under Article 340(2) TFEU, although in practice actions are usually brought by private applicants.[220] The coming into force of the Treaty of Lisbon altered the Court's jurisdiction regarding actions for damages in certain policy fields. Acts in areas formerly falling under the Third Pillar (formerly "Police and Judicial Cooperation in Criminal Matters") are now open to actions for damages. The Court may not, however, review acts in the field of CFSP, except for compliance with Article 40 TEU (non-affectation) and review of the legality of restrictive measures, Article 263(4) TFEU.

In *Bergaderm*[221] the Court established that for liability of the Union three conditions must be fulfilled: 1) the rule of law infringed must be intended to confer rights on individuals 2) the breach of the rule must be sufficiently serious and 3) there must be a direct causal link between

215. Case C-11/00, *Commission v. European Central Bank*. See also A. Barav, "The exception of illegality in Community Law: A critical analysis", 11 CML Rev. (1974), 366–386, 371.
216. Case 4/69, *Alfons Lütticke GmbH v. Commission*.
217. Case C-257/90, *Italsolar v. Commission*. Infringement of unwritten law can also lead to liability of the Community, see Case 74/74, *CNTA v. Commission*, on infringement of the principle of legitimate expectations.
218. Art. 46 Statute of the Court of Justice.
219. Cf. Case C-9/56, *Meroni & Co., Industrie Metallurgiche, SpA v. High Authority* (*Meroni I*) and Case C-10/56, *Meroni & Co., Industrie Metallurgiche, società in accomandita semplice v. High Authority (Meroni II)*.
220. Compare an action for damages declared admissible in Case C-8/15 P to C-10/15 P, *Ledra Advertising et al. v. Commission and ECB* and action for annulment declared inadmissible in Case C-105/15 to C-109/15 P, *Mallis v. Commission and ECB*.
221. Case C-352/98 P, *Bergaderm et al. v. Commission*. See also Case C-472/00 P, *Commission v. Fresh Marine* and Case C-282/05 P, *Holcin v. Commission*.

the infringement of the rule and the damage suffered by the applicant.[222] Development in the area of liability of *Member States* for infringements of Union law,[223] had consequences for the case law on liability of the *Union* for such infringements. In its judgment in *Brasserie du Pêcheur and Factortame III*,[224] the Court stated the principle that "the conditions under which the State may incur liability for damage caused to individuals by a breach of Community law cannot, in the absence of particular justification, differ from those governing the liability of the Community in like circumstances".

The jurisdiction to find the Union non-contractually liable is now vested in the General Court by virtue of Article 256 TFEU. As in cases of liability of Member States on the basis of EU law, the degree of discretion enjoyed by the institution is not determined by whether the act is general or individual – a condition which always led to problems in the past. The decisive test is therefore not the individual nature of the act in question, but the discretion available to the institution when it was adopted.[225] A general requirement is now that the breach of the rule should be sufficiently serious – that is, a manifest and serious infringement by the institution of the limits of its powers. If the institution only enjoys a very limited margin of discretion – or none at all – the breach of EU law itself is already a sufficiently serious infringement.

The application of the new test (*Bergaderm*) was an improvement (compared with the previous case law) as it embodied a less opaque, and less restrictive approach. It entailed the application of the factors laid down in the case law on state liability for determining the existence of a sufficiently serious breach.[226] Potentially these factors are more generous than the factors the Court had looked to in the past (in relation to the Union's non contractual liability).[227]

As mentioned above, the existence of actual damage is necessary, as well as a causal link between the damage and the illegal conduct. The point of departure is complete compensation for damage suffered: not merely actual losses suffered, but also – in the absence of particular circumstances warranting a different assessment – loss of earnings.[228] The damage does not already have to have occurred: compensation for imminent damage is possible if this is foreseeable with sufficient certainty.[229] The damage may also be immaterial.[230] The requirement of causality means that the damage must be a direct consequence of the illegal conduct.[231] If the damage is partially caused by the conduct of the person suffering the damage, then responsibility may be shared.[232]

---

222. For one of the first cases in which the CFI applied the new set of conditions, see Case T-18/99, *Cordis v. Commission.*
223. See Ch. 11, "Application and enforcement in the Member States", section 7, of this book.
224. Joined Cases C-46 & 48/93, *Brasserie du Pêcheur SA v. Bundesrepublik Deutschland* and *The Queen v. Secretary of State for Transport, ex parte: Factortame Ltd and Others.*
225. See C. Hilson, "The role of discretion in EC law on non-contractual liability", 42 CML Rev. (2005), 677–695, who observes, however, that the case law on state liability now appears to be moving away from the previous emphasis on discretion.
226. See Joined Cases C-46 & 48/93, *Brasserie du Pêcheur SA v. Bundesrepublik Deutschland* and *The Queen v. Secretary of State for Transport, ex parte: Factortame Ltd and Others*, paras. 56–57. See T. Tridimas, "Liability for breach of Community law: Growing up and mellowing down?", 38 CML Rev. (2001), 301–332, at 321–331.
227. See on this subject C. Hilson, op. cit. *supra* note 225.
228. Joined Cases C-104/89 & C-37/90, *Mulder v. Council and the Commission (Mulder II).*
229. Joined Cases 56-60/74, *Kampffmeyer v. Commission and Council.*
230. Joined Cases 7/56 & 3-7/57, *Algera et al. v. Common Assembly* and e.g. Case C-259/96 P, *Council v. De Nil en Impens.*
231. See for examples of an insufficient causal link Joined Cases 64 & 113/76, 167& 239/78, 27-28 & 45/79, *P. Dumortier Frères SA et al. v. Council*; Case T-7/96, *Perillo v. Commission* and Case T-149/96, *Coldiretti et al. v. Council and Commission.*
232. Case 308/87, *Alfredo Grifoni v. European Atomic Energy Community.*

The CJEU's jurisdiction to hear and determine an action for damages differs according to the contractual or non-contractual nature of the liability involved. To determine jurisdiction under Article 268 TFEU, the Union judicature must assess whether the applicant's claim for compensation is contractual or non-contractual in nature.[233] Specifically the Union courts must examine, through an analysis of the various matters in the file, such as, for example the legal rule allegedly infringed, the nature of the damage claimed, the conduct complained of and the legal relations between the parties in question, whether there exists between them a genuine contractual context, linked to the subject-matter of the dispute, the in-depth examination of which proves to be indispensable for the resolution of the said action".

Since the judgment in *Bergaderm*, the CJEU has expressly (or sometimes indirectly) recognized the following general principles of Union law as being rules of law conferring rights on individuals: the principle of non-discrimination, the principle of proportionality, the principle of protection of legitimate expectations, the principle of good faith and rule against abuse of rights, and the prohibition of unjust enrichment.[234] Notably, as far as the principle of sound administration is concerned, it does not in itself confer rights on individuals, except where it constitutes the expression of specific rights for the purposes of Article 41 of the Charter of Fundamental Rights.[235]

3. Cooperation with national courts through the preliminary reference procedure

Under Article 267 TFEU, the Court of Justice has jurisdiction to give preliminary rulings relating in particular to the interpretation of the Treaty and the validity and interpretation of acts of the institutions, bodies, offices and agencies of the Union. The preliminary reference procedure constitutes an important mechanism for judicial cooperation and dialogue between the CJ and national courts.[236] In the words of the Court, Article 267 TFEU establishes "a special field of judicial cooperation which requires the national court and the Court of Justice, both keeping within their respective jurisdiction, and with the aim of ensuring that Community law is applied in a unified manner, to make direct and complementary contributions to the working out of a decision".[237] This definition reveals an understanding of the CJ as not being placed hierarchically as the highest court above the national courts, but as cooperating with them, each exercising its own jurisdiction.[238] Moreover, it is widely acknowledged, and also strongly emphasized by the Court,[239] that the main function of Article 267 is to ensure *uniform application* of EU law in all

233. See Case C-214/08 P, *Guidard v. Commission*, paras. 35–44, Case T-424/08, *Nexus Europe (Ireland) v. Commission*, paras. 58–60.
234. See K. Lenaerts et al., op. cit. *supra* note 137, 519 and cases cited there.
235. Ibid.
236. According to R. Schütze it is the "cornerstone of the Union's judicial cooperative federalism", R. Schütze, op. cit. *supra* note 104, 289–290.
237. Case 16/65, *Firma C. Schwarze v. Einfuhr- und Vorratsstelle für Getreide und Futtermittel*, at 886 of the English edition.
238. For a critical view see T. De la Mare and C. Donnelly, "Preliminary rulings and EU legal integration: Evolution and stasis" in P. Graig and G. de Búrca, *Evolution of EU law* (OUP, 2011), 377 who state with reference to J. Komarek, "Federal elements in the Community judicial system: Building coherence in the Community legal order", 42 CML Rev. (2005), that over the years "the role of preliminary references shifted from the cooperational to the coordinational; yet this is only minimally reflected by the express wording of the case law which still seeks to identify "national courts as partners, not inferiors", and is not reflected at all in the Treaty language".
239. See e.g. Case 166/73, *Rheinmühlen-Düsseldorf v. Einfuhr- und Vorratsstelle für Getreide und Futtermittel*, para 2; recently in Case C-495/03, *Intermodal Transports v. Staatssecretaris van Financiën*; Case C-458/06,

Member States, both as regards the interpretation of this law by the national courts and in relation to the validity or invalidity of Union acts.[240]

In addition to that, as noted in the previous section, the CJ sees the preliminary reference procedure as a fundamentally important mechanism for the *development* of EU law. Article 267 fosters the inclusion of Union law in the national legal orders, having direct effect and priority over national law. National courts, especially lower national courts, are crucial in this respect. The Court's interpretation of Article 267 reveals the idea that in order to protect the autonomous nature of the EU legal order, national courts must be able to interpret and apply EU law in an unimpeded manner. Thus, in the famous *Costa v. ENEL* judgment, the Court found that "Article 267 is to be applied regardless of any domestic law, whenever questions relating to the interpretation of the Treaty arise".[241] Subsequently, the Court used these points to declare that a lower court is entitled to refer to the CJ a point of law covered by a ruling of a higher court, even though the lower court may in national law be bound by the ruling of the higher court; the mere existence of such a rule in national law cannot deprive the lower court of its right to make a reference.[242] The fact that a national court or tribunal, at any level of the national judicial hierarchy, and at any stage of its judicial procedure, is entitled to refer a preliminary question to the CJ, has made the preliminary reference procedure a powerful driver of legal integration.[243]

Last but not least, Article 267 also fulfils an important function in legal protection.[244] As we have seen in the previous section, the Court considers the preliminary reference procedure to be the central instrument for indirect judicial protection of individuals challenging the validity of EU acts,[245] and therefore for the effective judicial protection of individual rights. This becomes particularly important for challenges to the validity of EU *legislative* acts, given that the latter can only be challenged by private applicants via the direct annulment procedure (Art. 263(4) TFEU) in the exceptional cases of "direct and individual concern" (see above section 2).

However, both judicial actors[246] and academics[247] have questioned the aptness of the preliminary reference procedure as an instrument of effective judicial protection of individuals.

Skatteverket. v. Gourmet Classic Ltd.

240. For a critical view discussing the drawbacks of the Court's focus on uniformity see T. De la Mare and C. Donnelly, op. cit. *supra* note 228, 391–393; D. Chalmers, "The dynamics of judicial authority", Jean Monnet Working Paper 5/04.
241. Case 6/64, *Costa v. ENEL.*
242. See Case 146/73, *Rheinmühlen-Düsseldorf v. Einfuhr- und Vorratsstelle für Getreide und Futtermittel (III)*; see more recently See e.g. Case C-416/10, *Krizan v. Slovenska*; Joined Cases C-188 & 189/10, *Aziz Melki and Sélim Abdeli*; Case C-210/06, *Cartesio Oktató és Szolgáltató bt.* where the court found that national courts are entitled to continue with their reference even if their decision has been overturned on appeal by a higher domestic court.
243. See also discussion above at Section 2.2.4. (2).
244. On shortcomings in this regard, however, Case C-50/00 P, *Unión de Pequeños Agricultores (UPA) v. Council*, Opinion A.G. Jacobs. See also on the costs of referral T. De la Mare and C. Donnelly, op. cit. *supra* note 228, 375.
245. As recently confirmed in Case C-583/11 P, *Inuit Tapiriit Kanatami and Others v. Parliament and Council.*
246. See Case T-177/01, *Jégo-Quéré & Cie SA v. Commission*; Case C-50/00 P, *Unión de Pequeños Agricultores v. Council*, Opinion of A.G. Jacobs. The ECtHR has also dealt with the question whether there is an unreasonable delay in EU proceedings of preliminary reference in breach of Art. 6(1) of the ECHR, finally answering in the negative. See ECtHR, *Pafitis v. Greece*, para 95.
247. A. Albors-Llorens, op. cit. *supra* note 109, 177; A. Albors-Llorens, "The standing of private parties to challenge Community measures: Has the European Court missed the boat?", 62 CLJ (2003), 72–92; E. Berry and S. Boyes, "Access to justice in the community courts: A limited right", 24 CJQ (2005), 224–225. See the comprehensive discussion on the matter between a supporter and opponents of the preliminary ruling procedure as a means for effective judicial protection of private parties: P. Nihoul, "La recevabilité des

Most notably, in his opinion to the *UPA* case, Advocate General Jacobs listed a number of reasons,[248] such as that national courts are not competent to declare EU law invalid; that the decision to refer is not in the hands of the applicant, but depends on a discretionary decision by the national court (with the exception of courts of last instance); that there is a risk of a denial of justice where no national implementing measures are available for challenge at the national level as well as where the applicant would be forced to breach the law in order to provoke a challengeable implementing act, such as in the case of so-called "self-executing" EU measures banning a product or activity.

Given the rejection of these arguments by the Court in the *UPA* ruling as well as the recent confirmation of the *UPA* approach[249] in the post-Lisbon case law of the Court, most notably in *Inuit Tapiriit Kanatami*,[250] a change of course with regard to the Court's interpretation of the system of EU judicial protection including the right to an effective remedy seems unlikely just now. In the Court's present interpretation of the post-Lisbon constitutional settlement, private applicants get direct access to the Court via the annulment procedure only in exceptional cases of "self-executing" non-legislative regulations.[251] For all other measures, the preliminary reference procedure remains crucial. At the same time, however, the Court has addressed some of the criticism regarding the shortcomings of individual legal protection under this procedure by increasing the pressure on the national legal systems to ensure a "complete system of legal remedies and procedures designed to ensure judicial review of the legality of acts of the institutions".[252] This, in turn, raises the question what kind of measures exactly are required, following the Court's understanding of an effective system of judicial protection, on the part of the Member States as well as the national courts? In particular, to what extent do the Court's pronouncements in UPA, and recently in *Inuit Tapiriit Kanatami*, require reform of national procedural rules? Referring to previous case law, the Court stated that "it is for the domestic legal system of each Member State to designate, with due observance of [...] the principles of effectiveness and equivalence, the courts and tribunals with jurisdiction, and to lay down the detailed procedural rules governing actions brought to safeguard rights which individuals derive from European Union law".[253]

In fact, this is a reference to a line of previous case law on national remedies for enforcement of EU law, in which the Court has already required extensive changes in national rules of procedure in order to ensure the effectiveness of EU law.[254] It may therefore be assumed that an interpretation of Article 19(1) TEU in the light of Article 47 of the Charter of Fundamental Rights would require proactive changes in national rules of procedure, and/or their interpretation by national courts, in order to provide for access of individuals to judicial review (by e.g.

---

recours en annulation introduits par un particulier à l'encontre d'un acte communautaire de portée Générale", (1994) RTDE, 171; D. Waelbroeck, A.-M. Verheyden, "Les conditions de recevabilité des recours en annulation des particuliers contre les actes normatifs communautaires", 31 CDE (1995), 399–441. See also a recent piece: R. Mastroianni, A. Pezza, "Striking the right balance: Limits on the right to bring an action under Art. 263(4) of the Treaty on the Functioning of the European Union", 30 *The American University International Law Journal* (2015), 770–780.

248. See A.G. Jacobs, op. cit. *supra* note 245, paras. 41–43.
249. See in more detail above section 2.2.4.
250. Case C-583/11 P, *Inuit Tapiriit Kanatami and Others v. Parliament and Council.*
251. See above section 2.2.4.
252. Case C-50/00 P, *Unión de Pequeños Agricultores v. Council;* Case C-583/11 P, *Inuit Tapiriit Kanatami and Others v. Parliament and Council,* para 100.
253. Case C-583/11 P, *Inuit Tapiriit Kanatami and Others v. Parliament and Council,* para 102.
254. See Case C-432/05, *Unibet (London) Ltd and Unibet (International) Ltd v. Justitiekanslern,* paras. 40–44; and the case note of A. Arnull, 44 CML Rev. (2007) 1763–1780.

broadening national standing requirements) in cases where such access would otherwise be problematic. This goes in particular to situations in which national implementing measures are not available, and possibly even where national law would normally not provide for a judicial remedy.[255]

3.1 *Types of preliminary references*

Article 267 TFEU provides for two types of preliminary references. Firstly, the Court has jurisdiction to give preliminary rulings relating to the *interpretation* of EU law including both Treaty provisions and acts of the institutions, bodies, offices and agencies of the Union. Under this type of reference, the Court has adopted a broad understanding of the concept of "acts of the institutions". They include regulations, directives and decisions irrespective of whether they have direct effect.[256] They also cover treaties concluded by the EU with third countries or international organizations[257] or which are binding on the Union in other ways,[258] as in the case of mixed agreements to which the EU and the Member States are parties – even covering, in these mixed agreements, obligations of the Member States thereunder.[259] The Court can also interpret acts that do not produce legal effects, such as recommendations.[260] Moreover, questions of interpretation can relate to the clarification of unwritten legal principles inherent in EU law.[261] Even if a provision of EU law, as a result of being referred to in a national law[262] or in an agreement concluded between the parties,[263] is in substance used to determine the rules applicable in a situation not governed by EU law (being a purely domestic matter within the Member State involved), the Court will regard itself as competent to respond to questions relating to provisions of EU law posed by a national court or tribunal.

Secondly, the CJ can also make a preliminary ruling on the *validity* of EU acts. Here, it can pronounce itself only on the validity of acts of the institutions, bodies, offices and agencies of the

---

255. See in more detail on reform proposals following the Court's approach S. Peers and M. Costa, op. cit. *supra* note 170, 97–103.
256. See Case C-491/01, *The Queen v. Secretary of State for Health ex parte British American Tobacco (Investments) Ltd and Imperial Tobacco Ltd (Tobacco advertising II)*.
257. Implementing rules adopted by a Joint Committee on the basis of such agreements also form part of Community law and can be interpreted by the Court under Art. 234 EC, see e.g. Case C-237/91, *Kazim Kus v. Landeshauptstadt Wiesbaden* and Case C-188/91, *Deutsche Shell AG v. Hauptzollamt Hamburg-Harburg*.
258. See, *inter alia*, Joined Cases 21-24/72, *International Fruit Company* and, further, Joined Cases 267-269/81, *Amministrazione delle Finanze dello Stato v. Società Petrolifera Italiana SpA (SPI) et al.*
259. Case C-18/90, *Office national de l'emploi (Onem) v. Kziber*. The Court has no jurisdiction under Art. 267 TFEU to rule on the interpretation of provisions of international law binding Member States outside the framework of Community law, Case 130/73, *Magdalena Vandeweghe et al. v. Berufsgenossenschaft für die Chemische Industrie*, para 2. The Court does accept jurisdiction if such provisions may be applicable in situations which come within the scope of both national law and Union law (Case C-53/96, *Hermès International v. FHT Marketing Choice BV*, annotated by A. von Bogdandy, 36 CML Rev. (1999), 663–672, 635 and Joined Cases C-300 & 392/98, *Dior et al. v. Tuk Consultancy BV et al.*
260. See Case 322/88, *Grimaldi v. Fonds des maladies professionnelles*; See also Case T-109/06, *Vodafone Espana and Vodafone Group v. Commission*.
261. E.g. Case 11/70, *Internationale Handelsgesellschaft* (respect for human rights) and Case 84/78, *Ditta Angelo Tomandini Snc v. Amministrazione delle Finanze dello Stato* (protection of legitimate expectations).
262. Joined Cases 297/88 & C-197/89, *Dzodzi v. Belgian State*, annotated by M. Bravo-Ferrer-Delgrado and N. La Casta Muñoa in 29 CML Rev. (1992), 152–159, and Case C-231/89, *Gmurzynska-Bscher v. Oberfinanzdirektion Köln*. For a limit to this case law, see Case C-346/93, *Kleinwort Benson v. City of Glasgow District Council*, annotated by G. Betlem, 33 CML Rev. (1996), 137–147.
263. See Case C-88/91, *Federazione Italiana dei Consorzi Agrari (Federconsorzi) v. Azienda di stato per gli Interventi nel mercato Agricolo (AIMA)*.

Union, and only on those acts that are legally binding. The Court's jurisdiction is not limited as to the grounds upon which the validity of the measures at issue in the Article 267 proceedings may be contested;[264] thus it has jurisdiction to examine all grounds capable of invalidating those measures, including examining their compatibility with rules of international law.[265]

Given that lower national courts have, in principle, no obligation under Article 267 to refer preliminary questions to the CJ (but see below), for many years it was wondered whether they could thus declare a Union measure invalid independently of a judgment of the CJ. This question was decided in the seminal *Foto-Frost v. Hauptzollamt Lübeck-Ost*[266] ruling. Following that ruling, national courts do not have jurisdiction to declare EU measures invalid. Divergences between national courts in different Member States as to the validity of EU acts would be liable to jeopardize the unity of the EU legal order and detract from the fundamental requirement of legal certainty. Moreover, the necessary coherence of the complete system of legal remedies established by the Treaties would be undermined. While national courts are entitled to *confirm* the validity of EU acts without referring to the CJ, the latter is the only body empowered, under Article 267, to declare an EU act invalid. From this it follows that where national courts have doubts about the legality of a Union act they are always obliged to refer a question on validity to the CJ. The exclusive power of the CJ to declare EU measures invalid also follows logically from the Court's exclusive jurisdiction to declare EU acts void under Article 263 TFEU.[267]

Finally, the possibility for a party to challenge the validity of earlier acts on which a contested decision is based by means of national proceedings exists only "if that party was not entitled under Article 263 to bring a direct action challenging those acts by which it was thus affected without having been in a position to ask that they be declared void".[268] If it is perfectly clear that the parties would have had standing to challenge the act directly, but failed to do so, then they may not later on rely on the illegality of the EU decision before the national court.[269] Under the same reasoning, on grounds of legal certainty, a Member State may not rely before a national court on the illegality of a EU decision addressed to it if it did not lodge an action for annulment against that decision within the time limits set by Article 263(5).[270]

3.2 *The separate functions of the Court of Justice and national courts*

According to a consistent line of case law, Article 267 TFEU is based "on a clear separation of functions between national courts or tribunals and the Court of Justice".[271] The jurisdiction of the Court based on Article 267 is confined to a decision on the interpretation of Union law and on the validity of Union acts; it does not enable the Court to investigate the facts.[272] In particular, the Court does not pronounce on the application of EU law to the facts of the case referred in the proceedings before the national court.[273] It does not, for example, have jurisdiction under Article 267 to pronounce on the question whether particular laws or administrative acts of a

264. Joined Cases 21-24/72, *International Fruit Company.*
265. See Case C-162/96, *Racke v. Hauptzollamt Mainz,* annotated by J. Klabbers, 36 CML Rev. (1999), 179–189.
266. Case 314/85, *Foto-Frost v. Hauptzollamt Lübeck-Ost.*
267. Ibid., paras. 14–17.
268. Case C-239/99, *Nachi Europe GmbH v. Hauptzollamt Krefeld,* para 36.
269. Case C-370/12, *Thomas Pringle v. Governement of Ireland.* See further D. Wyatt, "The relationship between actions for annulment and references on validity after TWD Deggendorf" in J. Lombay and A. Biondi (Eds.), *Remedies for Breach of EC Law* (Wiley, 1996).
270. Case C-241/01, *National Farmers' Union v. Secrétariat général du gouvernement.*
271. See e.g. Case C-30/93, *AC-ATEL Electronics Vertriebs GmbH.*
272. Case 6/64, *Costa v. ENEL.*
273. See, *inter alia,* Joined Cases 28-30/62, *Da Costa en Schaake.*

Member State are compatible with EU law.[274] However, the Court's task is to provide the referring national court with all the elements for the interpretation of EU law which may enable the national court to judge the issue of compatibility of the national laws or acts with EU law.[275] In order to do so it may reformulate the questions asked.[276]

The strict separation between interpretation on the one hand and application of EU law *in concreto* on the other tends to give rise to considerable difficulties in practice.[277] The process of thought leading to a judicial decision cannot be readily separated into two independent parts: the interpretation of general rules on the one hand, and the subsequent application of the rules thus interpreted to the facts on the other. The interpretation given by a court is also determined by the facts. A study of the various judgments given by the Court pursuant to Article 267 makes it obvious that the Court was inspired by the facts of the case in its interpretation of EU law and has given an interpretation for a concrete case, which bordered on judging the validity of national legislation.[278] In some cases, the Court deliberately adopted a broader understanding of its own role. While stating that it was for the national court to decide the factual question whether objective justification for discrimination existed, the Court added in one case that it could "provide guidance based on the documents in the file and on the written and oral observations which have been submitted to it, in order to enable the national court to give judgment".[279]

The Court has repeatedly emphasized that national courts must explain on what grounds they consider an answer to their questions to be necessary for the judgment in the main proceedings, if those grounds are not unequivocally evident from the file on the case. Moreover, in order to give an interpretation of EU law which will be of use to the national court, it is essential that the national court defines the factual and legal context in which the interpretation is requested, or at the very least explains the assumptions of fact on which the preliminary questions are based. The absence of this information may lead to the reference being found inadmissible. There is another procedural reason why it is important that the referring court includes this information in its reference: the Court, by means of its Registrar, informs the governments of the Member States and other interested parties of the order making the reference, and that order provides the basis on which they may submit observations in accordance with Article 23 of the Statute of the Court.[280]

Where a national court makes its request in very concrete terms,[281] following the spirit of cooperation embodied in the preliminary reference procedure the CJ usually exercises a minimum of formality. From the request of the national court, even if it is loosely phrased,[282] it selects those questions of interpretation or validity with respect to which it has jurisdiction. Even if questions of interpretation asked by a national court are in reality questions of the validity

274. See, *inter alia*, Case 6/64, *Costa v. ENEL* and Case 20/64, *Albatros v. Société des pétroles et des combustibles liquides (Sopéco)*.
275. See Case 112/75, *Directeur régional de la sécurité sociale de Nancy v. Hirardin et al.*
276. See for an early example Case 1/71, *SA Cadillon v. Firma Höss, Maschinenbau KG.*
277. See the findings of H.-W. Micklitz, *The Politics of Judicial Cooperation in the EU. Sunday Trading, Equal Treatment and Good Faith* (CUP, 2005).
278. See Case C-294/97, *Eurowings Luftverkehrs AG v. Finanzamt Dortmund-Unna*; Case C-147/04, *De Groot en Slot Allium BV and Bejo Zaden BV v. Ministre de l'Économie, des Finances et de l'Industrie and Ministre de l'Agriculture, de l'Alimentation, de la Pêche et des Affaires Rurales.*
279. Case C-77/02, *Erika Steiiiicke v. Bundesanstalt für Arbeit.*
280. Cf. Joined Cases C-320-322/90, *Telemarsicabruzzo et al. v. Circostel et al.* An overview of the case law may be found in the order in Case C-116/00, *Criminal proceedings against Claude Laguillaumie.*
281. E.g. in Case 13/61, *Kledingverkoopbedrijf de Geus en Uitdenbogerd v. Robert Bosch GmbH and Maatschappij tot voortzetting van de zaken der Firma Willem van Rijn.*
282. See e.g. Case 251/83, *Haug-Adrion v. Frankfurter Versicherungs-AG.*

of Union acts, "it is appropriate for the Court to inform the national court at once of its view without compelling the national court to comply with purely formal requirements which would uselessly prolong the procedure under Article 267 and would be contrary to its very nature".[283]

The jurisdiction of the CJ is subject solely to the existence of a request within the meaning of Article 267, without it being required to examine whether the decision of the national court has become *res judicata* under the provisions of the latter's domestic law.[284] Article 267 does not prevent an order making a reference from being subject to the normal appeal procedure of national law;[285] the preliminary ruling procedure will continue, however, "as long as the request of the national court has neither been withdrawn nor become devoid of object".[286] The distribution of functions between the CJ and the national court means that it is not for the former to determine whether the decision to make the reference was in accordance with the rules of national law on court organization and procedure.[287] The national court enjoys wide discretion when deciding whether a preliminary reference is necessary to enable it to give judgment in the action. In the words of the Court "questions on the interpretation of Union law referred by a national court in the factual and legislative context which that court is responsible for defining and the accuracy of which is not a matter for the Court to determine, enjoy a presumption of relevance".[288]

There are, however, exceptional cases, in which the Court has defined limits on the discretion of the national courts to refer.[289] In *Foglia v. Novello II*,[290] the Court pointed out that it could not remain indifferent to the assessments made by national courts in the exceptional cases in which those assessments may affect the proper working of the Article 267 procedure. It refused to accept the reference on the grounds that there was no genuine dispute between the parties before the national court. Rather, the parties filed the action before the national court with the exclusive aim to trigger a reference, and to obtain a ruling from the Court, which would show the incompatibility with EU law of a national provision of another country (France) than of the Member State (Italy) where the case was brought. The CJ argued that in Article 267 proceedings it does not consider that its function is to deliver advisory opinions on general or hypothetical questions, or to answer questions in the framework of procedural constructions set up with the aim of obtaining a decision on certain issues of EU law;[291] rather its duty is to assist in the administration of justice.[292] Thus it does not have jurisdiction to reply to questions which are manifestly unconnected to a real dispute, and which therefore do not correspond to an objective

283. Case 16/65, *Firma C. Schwarze v. Einfuhr- und Vorratsstelle für Getreide und Futtermittel.*
284. Case 13/61, *Kledingverkoopbedrijf de Geus en Uitdenbogerd v. Robert Bosch GmbH and Maatschappij tot voortzetting van de zaken der Firma Willem van Rijn.*
285. Case 146/73, *Rheinmühlen III*; *contra* Opinion of A.G. Warner, in Case 166/73, *Rheinmühlen II.*
286. See Case 106/77, *Amministrazione delle Finanze dello Stato v. Simmenthal SpA*, the Court refers to this as "its unvarying practice".
287. Joined Cases C-332, 333 & 335/92, *Eurico Italia Srl et al. v. Ente Nazionale Risi*; Case C-62/14, *Peter Gauweiler et al. v. Deutscher Bundestag*, para 15.
288. Joined Cases C-94 & 202/04, *Federico Cipolla and Others*, para 25. See also: Case C-104/10, *Kelly*, paras. 61, 63–66; C-312/12, *Adjini*, para 18; C-416/10, *Krizan*, paras. 67–68.
289. For an overview of the case law on the Court's criteria, see Case C-112/00, *Schmidberger v. Republic of Austria*, paras. 30–33.
290. Case 244/80, *Foglia v. Novello II.*
291. See e.g. Case 93/78, *Mattheus v. Doego Fruchtimport und Tiefkühlkost eG*; Case C-83/91, *Meilicke v. ADV/ORGA AG*; Joined Cases C-430 & 431/99, *Inspecteur van de Belastingdienst Douane, Rotterdam district v. Sea-Land Service Inc. et al.*
292. E.g. (citing earlier judgments) Case C-415/93, *Union Royale Belge des Sociétés de Football Association ASBL et al. v. Bosman et al.*

requirement inherent in the resolution of a dispute.[293] Further exceptional circumstances, in which the Court has limited the discretion of national courts to refer have been found when referred questions were manifestly irrelevant,[294] incomprehensible or unintelligible,[295] or where references lacked an adequate factual or legal basis.[296]

3.3 *National courts and tribunals: power and obligation to refer*

Which courts or tribunals are entitled or obliged to ask the CJ for a preliminary ruling, and under what conditions are they obliged to refer the matter? These questions relate to the interpretation of Article 267; they are, therefore, questions which may or must themselves be the subject of a request for a preliminary ruling when a national court or tribunal is confronted with them.

3.3.1 *Courts and tribunals in the sense of Article 267 TFEU*

First of all, what is to be understood by the term "any court or tribunal of a Member State" under Article 267? It clearly covers those bodies, which according to the commonly used terminology in each of these Member States belong to the judiciary in the wide sense; it thus includes administrative courts.[297] Administrative bodies which decide on administrative appeals against decisions of bodies to which they are organizationally linked will not be considered "courts or tribunals" for the purposes of Article 267 references, even if in the national system they are regarded as exercising an appellate function, as they are not acting as third parties in relation to the authority which adopted the decision under appeal.[298]

Moreover, it is clear from the case law that it is not necessary to wait until the substantive trial of the action; a court or tribunal seized of an interlocutory point may make a reference.[299] The nature of the case before a court does not restrict the right to refer; thus Article 267 can be used in the framework of voluntary jurisdiction and in non-contentious proceedings, providing these are intended to lead to a decision of a judicial nature.[300]

---

293. Case 244/80, *Foglia v. Novello II*; Case 286/88, *Falciola Angelo SpA v. Commune di Pavia*, and Case C-281/98, *Roman Angonese v. Cassa di Risparmio di Bolzano SpaA.*

294. See Case C-343/90, *Lourenço Dias v. Director da Alfandega do porto* and Joined Cases C-430 & 431/99, *Sea-Land Service;* Case C-11/07, *Hans Eckelkamp and Others v. Belgische Staat.*

295. Case C-318/00, *Bacardi-Martini SAS and Cellier des Dauphins v. Newcastle United Football Company Ltd;* Case C-116/00, *Criminal proceedings against Claude Laguillaumie.*

296. Case C-250/06, *United Pan-Europe Communications Belgium.*

297. It embraces even courts in associated countries and territories to which only part of the Treaties apply. Cf. Joined Cases C-100 & 101/89, *Kaefer and Procacci v. French State,* Case C-260/90, *Leplat v. Territory of French Polynesia (French Polynesia)* and Case C-163/90, *Administration des douanes et droits indirects v. Legros and Others (La Réunion).* See A. Arnull, "The evolution of the Court's jurisdiction under Art. 177 EEC", 18 EL Rev. (1993), 129–137, 132. As to the Isle of Man, see Case C-355/89, *Department of Health and Social Security v. Barr et al.* (and in particular the Opinion of A.G. Jacobs). For a recent case see: Case C-175/11, *D. and A.*, paras. 83, 88, 95–97, 105.

298. Case C-24/92, *Corbiau v. Administration des Contributions du Grand-Duché de Luxembourg.* See also: Case C-517/09, *RTL Belgium*, paras. 36, 39–42, 44–46; Case C-465/11, *Forposta*, paras. 17–18; Case C-555/13, *Merck*, paras. 19, 23–25; Case C-396/14, *MT Højgaard et Züblin*, paras. 23–26, 31–32. In contrast, see: Case C-385/09, *Nidera Handelscompagnie*, paras. 35–36, 40; C-118/09, *Koller*, paras. 22–23.

299. Case 107/76, *Hoffmann-La Roche v. Centrafarm Vertriebsgesellschaft Pharmazeutischer Erzeugnisse mbH.*

300. See Case C-111/94, *Job Centre Coop. ARL.* See further, e.g. Case C-53/03, *Synetairismos Farmakopoion Aitolias & Akarnanias (Syfait) and Others. v. GlaxoSmithKline plc. and. GlaxoSmithKline AEVE.* See however: Case C-497/08, *Amiraike Berlin*, paras. 17–21.

Classification problems arise particularly for professional disciplinary bodies, which act at the borderline between private and public law.[301] In order to determine whether a body making a reference is a court or tribunal for the purposes of Article 267, the Court takes account of a number of factors, such as whether the body is established by law, whether it is permanent, whether its jurisdiction is compulsory, whether its procedure is *inter partes*, whether it applies rules of law and whether it is independent.[302] Case law of the Court demonstrates that this test is applied globally, and the Court does not apply strict criteria to the various factors individually.[303]

However, arbitrators to whom parties have agreed to submit their dispute for resolution are not a court or tribunal in the sense of Article 267 EC.[304] In general, there will be an insufficiently close link between such an arbitration and the general system of judicial protection of the Member State to qualify such an arbitrator as a court or tribunal under that Article.[305] This case law is of particular interest in countries where a not insignificant proportion of the administration of justice is conducted by arbitration; such arbitration may involve the application of EU law, particularly in the competition field. The effect of refusing Article 267 references from arbitrators is that the Court's ability to ensure the uniform application and maintenance of EU law for, *inter alia*, the benefit of the judicial protection of those affected by EU law is restricted.[306]

3.3.2 *Obligation to refer*

The next question concerns the obligation of national courts to refer a question to the CJ. Such obligation exists, according to Article 267(3) TFEU for all courts or tribunals of a Member State "against whose decisions there is no judicial remedy under national law". This obligation extends not only to highest courts in the hierarchy of the national judicial system, such as the German Federal Constitutional Court, but also to lower courts which act as courts of last instance *in the particular case*. This can be the case, for instance, when in a concrete case no further remedy exists because a claim is below a certain sum,[307] or with regard to appellate courts. However, the Court has established that where the decision of an appellate court can be challenged before a supreme court, the appellate court is not under an obligation to refer according to Article 267(3) TFEU.[308]

Are national courts of last resort always obliged to refer as soon as a question of EU law has been raised before them? Firstly it should be noted that a combined reading of both paragraphs two and three of Article 267 shows that an obligation to refer only exists if the national court considers that a decision on the point of EU law is necessary to enable it to give judgment. In other words, Article 267 only establishes an obligation to refer *relevant* questions to the CJ.[309]

---

301. See e.g. Case 138/80, *Jules Borker (Paris Bar Council)*; Case 246/80, *Broekmeulen v. Huisarts Registratie Commissie*. See also Case C-58/13 and C-59/13, *Torresi*, 17–19.
302. Case C-53/03, *Synetairismos Farmakopoion Aitolias & Akarnanias (Syfait) and Others. v. GlaxoSmithKline plc. and. GlaxoSmithKline AEVE*, referring to earlier case law.
303. For a recent controversial case see Case C-394/11, *Valeri Hariev Belov v. CHEZ Elektro Balgaria AD and Others*.
304. Case 102/81, *Nordsee v. Reederei Mond*.
305. Case 246/80, *Broekmeulen v. Huisarts Registratie Commissie* and Case 102/81, *Nordsee v. Reederei Mond*. See W. Alexander and E. Grabandt, "National courts entitled to ask preliminary rulings under Art. 177 of the EEC Treaty: The case law of the Court of Justice", 19 CML Rev. (1982), 413–420.
306. Case C-126/97, *Eco Swiss China Time Ltd. v. Bennetton International NV*, annotated by A. Komninos, 37 CML Rev. (2000), 459–478.
307. In Case 6/64 *Costa v. ENEL*.
308. Case C-99/00, *Kenny Roland Lyckeskog*. See however: Case C-416/10, *Križan*, para 72; Case C-119/15, *Biuro Podróży Partner*, para 54.
309. See Case 283/81, *Srl CILFIT et al. v. Ministry of Health*, paras. 9 and 10.

The mere fact that a question of EU law is raised, however irrelevant or absurd, cannot oblige the court of highest instance in the case to refer to the CJ. This also implies that a national court cannot be (or, as the case may be, is not) obliged to refer to the CJ if it is able to settle the dispute exclusively on grounds of national law.[310]

Secondly, in its case law the Court has also developed certain exceptions to this duty to refer relevant questions. The first exception refers to a situation of a so-called "*acte éclairé*". A national court of last resort is not obliged to refer if the question referred is substantially identical to a question that has already been answered in a preliminary ruling.[311] According to the Court, the "authority of an interpretation under Article 267 already given by the Court may deprive this obligation of its purpose and thus empty it of its substance". The Court took this further in *CILFIT*,[312] noting that the same effect (i.e. that the obligation to refer becomes devoid of purpose) "may be produced where previous decisions of the Court have already dealt with the point of law in question, irrespective of the nature of the proceedings which led to those decisions, even though the questions at issue are not strictly identical".[313] Thus it is clear that the previous decisions do not need to have been given in Article 267 rulings. The Court went on to stress, though, "that in all such circumstances national courts and tribunals, including those referred to in the third paragraph of Article 267, remain entirely at liberty to bring a matter before the Court of Justice if they consider it appropriate to do so".[314] The Court always retains the possibility of reconsidering its case law.[315]

In *CILFIT* the Court also added a second, more controversial exception to the obligation to refer, based on the so-called "*acte clair*" doctrine. This follows French legal practice known as the "*théorie de l'acte clair*". This theory holds that the obligation to refer does not apply if the highest court concerned is of the opinion that there can be no reasonable doubt about the answers to the questions raised. Put in the words of the Court in *CILFIT*, "the correct application of Union law may be so obvious as to leave no scope for any reasonable doubt as to the manner in which the question raised is to be resolved".[316] But the Court has warned that it is not enough that the highest court concerned thinks that the answer is evident. Before it comes to a conclusion that there is no reasonable doubt on the point, "the national court or tribunal must be convinced that the matter is equally obvious to the courts of the other Member States and to the Court of

---

310. See in the Netherlands KIM-Sieverding, Hoge Raad, NJ 1961, 245. Cf. Case 283/81, *Srl CILFIT et al. v. Ministry of Health*, para 10.
311. Joined Cases 28-30/62, *Da Costa en Schaake*, at 31 of the English edition.
312. It is important to note that the *CILFIT* ruling only concerns questions of interpretation, and not questions relating to the validity of EU acts. See Case C-461/03, *Gaston Schul Douane-expediteur.*
313. Case 283/81, *Srl CILFIT et al. v. Ministry of Health*, para 14. See also: Case C-72/14 and C-197/14, *X*, paras. 59–63.
314. Ibid. at para 15. If a reference arrives on a point already decided, the Court's registry will draw the attention of the referring court to the earlier judgment and ask it if it wishes to maintain the reference. That the national court may then nevertheless still fail correctly to deduce the solution under EU law to the case in hand is evident from Case C-224/01, *Köbler v. Republik ÖsterreiCH.*
315. E.g. redefinition of scope of free movement of goods provisions following Joined Cases C-267 & 268/91, *Keck and Mithouard*; but see already generally, A. Arnull, "Owing up to fallibility: Precedent and the Court of Justice", 30 CML Rev. (1993), 247–266.
316. Case 283/81, *Srl CILFIT et al. v. Ministry of Health*, para 16 et seq. See H. Rasmussen, "The European Court's acte clair strategy in C.I.L.F.I.T. Or: Acte clair, of course! But what does it mean?", 9 EL Rev. (1984), 242–259; G. Bebr, "The rambling ghost of "Cohn-Bendit": Acte clair and the Court of Justice", 20 CML Rev. (1983), 439–472; and D. Wyatt, "Art. 177(3)-the Court cautiously endorses the *acte clair* doctrine", 8 EL Rev. (1983). Cf. Art. 6(4) of the Treaty concerning the establishment and the Statute of a Benelux Court 13 *European Yearbook* (1965), 259–266, which, however, prohibits reference to this court in such a case. For a recent case see: Case C-160/14, *Ferreira de Silva e Brito*, paras. 37–45.

Justice". The national court or tribunal must assess this "on the basis of the characteristic features of Union law and the particular difficulties to which its interpretation gives rise".[317] In order to prevent abuse of this exception by national courts of last resort, the Court stipulated highly strict requirements, which the former have to fulfil before finding that a reference is not necessary, namely

- they must compare all the different language versions of the provision of EU law that is being interpreted;
- even when the different language versions completely agree, they must consider the special EU law terminology; and the different use and meaning of legal concepts in EU law and in the law of the various Member States;[318]
- they must place every provision of EU law in its context and interpret it in the light of the provisions of EU law as a whole, of the objectives of EU law and its state of evolution at the date on which the provision involved is to be applied.

It follows that the freedom *not* to refer a question to the CJ will have to be used with great circumspection by highest national courts. The danger of the "*acte clair*" exception is that even apparently clear texts, or seemingly technical terms can have different meanings for lawyers coming from 28 different countries, and legal cultures. It has also been observed that national courts have sometimes used the "*acte clair*" doctrine to avoid making a reference, even where the *CILFIT* criteria are not fully complied with.[319] At the same time, recognizing the cooperative relationship between the CJ and national courts, there is arguably also a need for some flexibility for the latter. It would not be conducive to proper cooperation between the CJ and the highest judicial bodies in the Member States, if the latter are subject so strongly to the control of the Court that they are automatically obliged to refer, even if there cannot be the slightest doubt on the interpretation of the text of EU law.[320]

3.4 *Effects of a preliminary ruling*

The preliminary ruling of the CJ "is binding on the national court hearing the case in which the decision is given".[321] This does not mean that the court may not make a new preliminary reference to the CJ in the same dispute. Such a new preliminary reference may be justified if the national court encounters problems in interpreting or applying the judgment on the first reference, or if the national court puts a new question of law to the CJ, or if it submits new facts to the latter, which could lead to the CJ giving a different answer to a question on which it had already pronounced.[322] For national courts other than those hearing the case in which the decision is given, the judgment in the preliminary ruling has "authority of interpretation".[323] The Court has expressly held in *Firma C. Schwarze v. Einfuhr- und Vorratsstelle für Getreide und Futtermittel*[324] that although in Article 267 TFEU proceedings it can decide on the validity of a measure (i.e. it

---

317. Case 283/81, *Srl CILFIT et al. v. Ministry of Health*, paras. 16–17.
318. See e.g. Case 36/75, *Rutili v. Ministre de l'intérieur.*
319. See T. De la Mare and C. Donnelly, op. cit. *supra* note 228, with further references; see also M. Bobek, "Learning to talk preliminary rulings, the courts of the new member states and the Court of Justice", 45 CML Rev. (2008), 1611–1643, 1631.
320. See also Case C-338/95, *Wiener S.I. GmbH v. Hauptzollamt Emmerich*, Opinion of A.G. Jacobs, para 64.
321. Case C-446/98, *Fazenda Pública v. Câmara Municipal do Porto.*
322. Cases C-356/98, *Arben Kaba v. Secretary of State for the Home Department* and C-466/00, *Arben Kaba v. Secretary of State for the Home Department.*
323. Cf. Joined Cases 28-30/62, *Da Costa en Schaake NV et al. v. Nederlandse Belastingadministratie.*
324. Case 16/65, *Firma G. Schwarze v. Einfuhr- und Vorratsstelle für Getreide und Futtermittel.*

can declare a measure invalid), it has no jurisdiction in such proceedings to declare a measure void. While a preliminary ruling in which the Court declares a measure of an institution invalid is addressed only to the referring court, it is a sufficient legal basis for any other court to regard the measure as invalid. Indeed, this results from the particularly imperative requirements of legal certainty in addition to those of the uniform application of EU law.[325] Therefore, national courts should follow the interpretation given, but retain the power to make a reference to the CJ, if they have grounds to doubt this interpretation.

Is a Member State obliged on the basis of Article 4(3) TEU (the duty of loyal cooperation) to amend a rule of which it has become apparent in a preliminary ruling that it is not in conformity with EU law, and to amend it according to the preliminary ruling? In general, such a question will not arise, since the national court will set aside the national rule on the basis of the preliminary ruling, and the Member State will draw the appropriate consequences from this and amend the rule. The declaration that an act is invalid is definitive and binding on the national court to which it is made. While no written obligation of the Member State exists to adapt legislative measures, existing case law confirmed that national courts are no longer allowed to apply that act and all national authorities have to draw the necessary conclusions from the decision.[326] In some cases, the Court explicitly stated what consequences should follow its ruling in the national legal order.[327]

The preliminary reference judgment is declaratory, and has effect *ex tunc*, even if it concerns an interpretation. The interpretation given clarifies and defines the meaning of the rule of EU law which should have been applied and understood since its coming into force. Thus the national court ought to apply the rule as so interpreted even to legal relationships that commenced before the preliminary ruling was handed down.[328] A recent example of an *ex tunc* declaration of invalidity is Joined Cases 293/12 and 594/12 *Digital Rights Ireland,* in which the Court in a preliminary ruling procedure declared invalid *ab initio* an EU Directive (the Data Retention Directive) for breach of the fundamental rights to the protection of private life and to the protection of personal data laid down in the EU Charter of Fundamental Rights. The *ex tunc* declaration of invalidity of the whole Directive in this case has created practical difficulties for those Member States that already imposed it into national law, raising questions regarding the status of those national implementing measures under EU law. On the one hand, there is no uniform standard and it has to be decided under national law whether the invalidity of the Directive has any effect on the imposed measure.[329] At the same time, it is also not clear whether an invalid directive has an effect on prior infringements. In particular, after the invalidity of the EU Data Retention directive, it remains to be seen whether Member States might challenge their prior infringement rulings. The Commission reimbursed Sweden its 3 million Euro fine for non-transposition in 2013.[330]

---

325. Case 66/80, *International Chemical Corporation v. Amministrazione delle Finanze dello Stato*; see also Case 112/83, *Société des produits de maïs SA v. Administration des Douanes et droits indirects.*
326. Case 23/75, *Rey Soda v. Cassa Conguaglio Zucchero*, para 50–51 ; K. Lenaerts et al., op. cit. *supra* note 137, 471–473.
327. See Case C-333/07, *Sociètè Regie Networks v. Direction de contrôle fiscal Rhône-Alpes Bourgogne*, paras. 119–121, 124, 126.
328. Even administrative bodies may in some cases be bound to apply the rule as interpreted by the Court to legal relationships which arose or were formed before the Court gave its ruling, see Case C-453/00, *Kühne & Heitz NV v. Produktschap voor Pluimvee en Eieren.*
329. Case 23/75, *Rey Soda v. Cassa Conguaglio Zucchero*, paras. 50–51, Case 199/86, *Raiffeisen Hauptgenossenschaft eG v. Bundesanstalt für landwirtschaftliche Marktordnung (BALM)*, para 29.
330. Case C-270/11, *Commission v. Kingdom of Sweden.*

It is only in very exceptional cases[331] that the CJEU restricts the retroactive effect of its judgment for interested parties. This will tend to only happen where it is felt that full retroactive effect would seriously disturb legal relations entered into in the past in good faith.[332]

Sometimes there is little point in declaring an act invalid because the unlawfulness does not lie so much in what the text contains as in what it omits. In such cases, the Court contents itself with a declaration that the relevant provision is incompatible with EU law and that the competent EU institution is obliged to adopt the necessary measures to correct the incompatibility.[333] In this sense, the Court implicitly recognizes that a declaration of invalidity in the context of Article 267 TFEU proceedings brings into operation the duty laid down in Article 266 TFEU to take the necessary measures to comply with the judgment; this analogous application of the terms of Article 266 (which applies on the annulment of an act or condemnation of a failure to act) is justified, as the Court has expressly indicated,[334] by the necessary consistency between the preliminary ruling procedure and the procedure of an action for annulment as two mechanisms for reviewing the legality of acts of the EU institutions.

3.5 *Interim measures*

The Court's exclusive competence to declare a Union act invalid does not prevent a national court,[335] in interlocutory proceedings, from suspending the enforcement of a national measure based on a Union act, such as a regulation,[336] or from granting other interim measures,[337] if it has serious doubts about the validity of the Union act involved. However, the interim measures in question may only last until the Court has delivered its ruling on the validity of the Union act concerned. If the question has not yet been referred to the CJ, the national court granting interim relief must make a reference itself, setting out why it believes the regulation concerned to be invalid. Moreover, the uniform application of EU law requires that identical conditions apply in all Member States with regard to the granting of suspensory relief (even though the making and examination of the application for such relief is a matter for national law). The Court has found that the conditions applying to the grant of interim relief by the Court itself in actions for annulment should also apply to the grant of interim relief by national courts. This means that the criterion of urgency has to be satisfied: it must be necessary for the suspensory measures to be adopted and take effect before the decision on the substance of the case, in order to avoid serious and irreparable damage to the party seeking such measures. Furthermore, the national court must take full account of the Union interest,[338] so that EU regulations should not be set aside too easily. Finally, in reaching its decision the national court must respect the case law of

---

331. E.g. in the Case 43/75, *Defrenne v. SABENA*.
332. Case 43/75, *Defrenne*. See also Case C-242/09, *Albron Catering*, 36–40 and Case C-464/11, *Forposta*, 44–45. For an early critical analysis of this case law, see M. Waelbroeck, "May the Court of Justice limit the retrospective operation of its judgments?", 1 YEL (1981), 115–123. For a more recent case, see e.g. Case C-372/98, *The Queen v. Ministry of Agriculture, Fisheries and Food*.
333. E.g. Joined Cases 124/76 & 20/77, *SA Moulins et Huileries de Pont-à-Mousson v. Office National Interprofessionnel des Céréales*.
334. Case 112/83, *Société des produits de maïs SA v. Administration des douanes et droits indirects*.
335. Case C-453/03, *ABNA and Others v. Secretary of State for Health and Food Standards Agency*.
336. Joined Cases 143/88 & C-92/89, *Zuckerfabrik Süderdithmarschen AG et al. v. Hauptzollamt Itzehoe et al.*
337. Case C-465/93, *Atlanta Fruchthandelsgesellschaft and Others (I) v. Bundesamt für Ernährung und Forstwirtschaft*.
338. It is up to the national court to decide, in accordance with its own rules of procedure, which is the most appropriate way of obtaining all relevant information on the Union act in question. It is not *obliged* to give the institution which adopted the act an opportunity to express its views, see Case C-334/95, *Krüger v. Hauptzollamt Hamburg-Jonas*, paras. 45–46.

the CJ and GC as to the validity of the Union act, as well as any interim orders in which similar interim relief has been granted at the EU level.

Finally, with regard to interim measures in the case of preliminary references on interpretation, the national court may grant interim relief on the basis of applicable national rules while a preliminary reference is pending before the CJ. In contrast to interim relief in preliminary references on validity, there are thus no binding requirements of EU law for granting interim relief for references on interpretation. However, national rules must be both effective and non-discriminatory.[339]

4. Reforming EU Judicial Adjudication and Architecture

4.1 *Inter-institutional accountability?*

The CJEU when exercising its judicial function is not itself subject to inter-institutional accountability processes. There is no contestatory inter-institutional engagement that is not dominated by the Court throughout the procedure. In the institutional rule-making context, however, the Court is more dependent on processes of articulation, explanation and clarification to some of the other institutions, in particular those with legislative and budgetary power. The Court needs some of the other institutions (the Council and the Parliament in particular) in order, for example, to amend its Statute.[340] This is done on the basis of a draft by the CJEU itself, which is agreed among its several courts[341] and is only subsequently sent to the Member States in Council for discussion and debate. The extent to which this can be considered a contestatory inter-institutional dialogue is open to question. Up until now the practice has been to largely accept the technical input by the Court.[342] As for the Rules of Procedure of the Court of Justice, these are established by the Court and "approved" by the Council.[343] This may also require some dialogue and negotiation in practice.

The CJEU is even more dependent on other actors such as the Council and the Parliament when it comes to its budget, and also with regard to more general efforts to deal with its backlog, involving a change in the CJEU architecture and rules of procedures. This all means that the CJEU as an institution is more than ever required to engage in extra-judicial processes of consultation, negotiation and even approval with the Council and the Parliament in particular. The (Vice-) President of the Court now spends considerable time talking on behalf of the CJEU with these institutions in order to put the rules it wants in place.[344] The Parliament in particular would like to see more intensive accountability processes evolve, for example in the direction of more openness during court procedures (at least of the observations and hearings) and selection hearings of judges before the European Parliament itself. The selection committee put in place by the Lisbon Treaty[345] does provide some supranational check on Member State appointments and could be considered a nascent part of a wider system of checks and balances on the

339. See Case C-213/89, *The Queen v. Secretary of State for Transport (Factortame I)*.
340. Art. 281 TFEU.
341. The Commission can also propose an amendment to the CJEU Statute.
342. For the criticism of this solution referring to the need of keeping the judicial and law-making competences separate see: A. Alemanno and L. Pech, "Thinking justice outside the docket: A critical assessment of the reform of the EU's court system", 54 CML Rev. (2017), 129–175, 146–148.
343. Art. 253 TFEU.
344. See *infra* section 4.3.
345. Art. 255 TFEU.

CJEU itself or, quite the opposite, judicial self-governance at the EU level.[346] This will now be examined more closely.

4.2 *Reform of the Judicial Selection Committee*

The novelty of the Lisbon Treaty with regard to judicial appointments to the CJ and GC is that these are now made after consultation with the 255 Panel, which provides an opinion on candidates' suitability to perform their duties.[347] The Panel is composed of seven persons chosen from among former members of the CJ and GC, members of national supreme courts, and lawyers of recognized competence, one of whom is proposed by the European Parliament. The Council must adopt a decision establishing the Panel's operating rules and a decision appointing its members.[348] The Panel acts on the initiative of the CJ's President.[349] Even though judges are selected after consultation with the Panel, Member States do not propose a list of candidates, but just one candidate, so there is not much substantive selection choice.[350] The Panel assesses candidates individually ranks them or recommends the best ones. It has been proposed that a list of at least three names should be required for each vacant judgeship position.[351] Currently, the selection panel is shrouded in secrecy both in terms of their input and output.[352] One way of remedying this transparency deficit would be to require (or develop the practice of) circulating the opinions of the panel prior to the actual appointment of judges[353] as well as publicizing their output and process after the appointment is made. A further problem is that the criteria for the assessment of candidates, some rather intuitive and obvious, others more specific – expertise in EU law, professional experience of at least 20 years for the CJ and 12–15 years for GC, adequate language skills, ability to work in an international environment – are not established in a legally binding act but developed by the Panel itself. There have been 6 negative opinions of the 64 new candidates over 2014, 2015 and 2016.[354] So far, a person who received a negative opinion from the Panel has never been appointed. Therefore, according to Kuijper, "the dynamic of 'nomination equals appointment' has been broken", and the Panel has been effective in contributing

346. A. Alemanno, L. Pech, op. cit. *supra* note 342, 130; T. Dumbrovský, B. Petkova, M. Van Der Sluis, "Judicial appointments: The Art. 255 TFEU advisory panel and selection procedures in the Member States", 51 CML Rev. (2014), 455–482, 481–482. On the problems stemming from combining within the CJEU both judicial and administrative functions see M. van der Woude, "Towards a European Council of the judiciary: Some reflections on the administration of the EU Courts" in F.A.N.J. Goudappel, E.M.H. Hirsch Ballin, *Democracy and Rule of Law in the European Union. Essays in Honour of Jaap W. de Zwaan* (Springer, 2016), 63–79.
347. Art. 255 TFEU.
348. See Council Decision of 25 Feb. 2010 relating to the operating rules of the panel provided for in Art. 255 of the Treaty on the Functioning of the European Union (O.J. 2010, L 50) and Council Decision of 11 Feb. 2014 appointing the members of the panel provided for in Art. 255 of the Treaty on the Functioning of the European Union (O.J. 2014, L 41).
349. See also P. Craig, "Courts, continuity, and change" in P. Craig, *The Lisbon Treaty, Revised Edition: Law, Politics, and Treaty Reform* (OUP, 2013).
350. H. Rasmussen, "Present and future European judicial problems after enlargement and the post-2005 ideological revolt", 44 CML Rev. (2007), 1661–1687, 1677.
351. Ibid., 1677.
352. A. Alemanno, "How transparent is transparent enough? Balancing access to information against privacy in European judicial selection" in M. Bobek, *Selecting Europe's Judges* (OUP, 2014).
353. Ibid.
354. "Fourth Activity Report of the Panel Provided for by Art. 255 of the Treaty on the Functioning of the European Union" (2017). Available at <curia.europa.eu/jcms/upload/docs/application/pdf/2017-03/rapport_activite___c255_-_en.pdf>.

to higher quality judges at the CJEU.[355] Another positive contribution of the Panel is that its establishment prompted some Member States to introduce selection procedures at the national level.[356] Still, the Member States do not use the potential of the Panel to the fullest: it can only eliminate bad candidates, but not select or even recommend the best ones.

The functioning of the Article 255 Panel has arguably led to an increase in the powers of the judiciary at the expense of the executive. The working methods of the Panel are not transparent; and all of its members are chosen "at the will of" the CJ's President.[357] With these deficits in mind, a more diverse membership of the Panel would be welcome. Further involvement of the Parliament in a tangible way at some stage of the appointment procedure would be a step forward, also in legitimacy terms.[358] Given the impact of the CJ's President on the composition of 255 Panel, the CJ's dominant influence on the CJEU's Statute and the rules of procedure, there is some talk about the emerging and yet unexplored "self-government of the EU judicial system".[359]

4.3 *Docket reform?*

4.3.1 *Introduction*

The need to reform the EU Judicial architecture received little attention in the European Convention discussions on Treaty reform. The discussions on it lasted only one month.[360] Yet the debate on the need to reform the EU judicial system is an older one, and the topic was more substantively considered in the debate preceding the Nice Treaty, which resulted in two reports.[361] These earlier official reports distilled three fundamental requirements that should be taken into account when thinking about the future of the judicial system: the need to secure the unity of EU law by means of a supreme court; the need to ensure that the judicial system is transparent, comprehensible, and accessible to the public; and the need to dispense justice without unacceptable delay.[362] Craig adds two further considerations to this list: the division of judicial power between the CJ and GC should be as coherent and symmetrical as possible; and the system should be structured to ensure that the most important points of law are decided by the CJ, and that it is, as far as possible, not troubled by less important cases. These criteria can provide the foundation for a rational system of Union judicial architecture. In Craig's view: "A significant step in this direction would be for the GC's jurisdiction to reflect its nomenclature and become a real general court of first instance for all direct actions, with limited rights of appeal to the ECJ".[363]

4.3.2 *Reform due to increase in workload of the CJEU*

According to Craig, the Court's increased caseload is due to four factors: enlargement, extended EU competence with each treaty revision, the success of the harmonization initiatives, and the

355. P.J. Kuijper, "The Court of Justice of the European Union", not yet published, 9.
356. For a detailed overview see T. Dumbrovský et al., op. cit. *supra* note 346.
357. Ibid., 481–482.
358. Ibid.
359. A. Alemanno and L. Pech, op. cit. *supra* note 342, 130 et seq.
360. P. Craig, op. cit. *supra* note 349, 134–136.
361. "The future of the judicial system of the European Union (Proposals and Reflections)" (1999), available at <www.alanuzelac.from.hr/Pdf/eu-postdip/Buducnost%20suda%20Europskih%20zajednica%20-%20ave.pdf>; "Report by the Working Party on the Future of the European Communities' Court System" (2000). Available at <ec.europa.eu/dgs/legal_service/pdf/due_en.pdf>.
362. See The Future of the Judicial System of the European Union (op. cit. *supra* note 361), 17. See also Report by the Working Party on the Future of the European Communities (op. cit. *supra* note 361), 10.
363. P. Craig, op. cit. *supra* note 349, 137.

growing awareness of EU law by lawyers.[364] De la Mare and Donnelly[365] state that in recent years "docket reform has been at the core of commentary and thinking about the CJEU. [...] Delays are not, however, the only challenge created by an overburdened docket. Two further consequences must be considered, namely the impact of the current situation on the continued effective functioning of the preliminary ruling procedure, and how the CJEU's concern for uniformity and effectiveness of EU law, which, as has been noted, underpins its approach to preliminary rulings, reflects on the nature of EU law more generally".

Sharpston highlighted the fact that nowadays the focus is (often) on speed of case-processing, as this is what is demanded of the Court. "[I]n a difficult case, speed may come at the expense of quality". This poses a major risk, especially in AFSJ, as this was "an uncharted and sensitive territory" with not much case law for the Court to draw on. Sharpston has suggested that the Court takes account of the differences between relatively straightforward infringement cases and complex cases, when it comes to pressuring for speed. She argues that speed of turnaround and conciseness are not ends in themselves, but that the quality of the ruling is. "The target must always be the properly *reasoned judgment* [...] An incoherent judgment, swiftly produced, that gives rise to a series of further references, damages the Court's authority and squanders Member State goodwill is a very bad bargain".[366]

The discussion of different kinds of procedural solutions in recent literature has largely concentrated on the role of the GC in direct actions and it is (often) proposed to extend the jurisdiction of GC over all direct actions under Article 263 and 265 TFEU regardless of who the applicant is.[367] This still leaves open the issue of preliminary rulings. Possible reform of the preliminary ruling procedure raises important issues concerning the nature of the relationship between the national courts and the Union courts. It also has implications for the relationship between the CJ and GC.[368] The Nice Treaty for the first time gave the GC the power to hear preliminary rulings in specific areas laid down by the Statute.[369] Craig, along with many other scholars,[370] suggests giving GC power to hear preliminary references. Weiler also suggests that the CJ should give up its "fetishistic attachment to the preliminary reference procedure".[371] Jacobs favours instituting a variant of the "green light" system for preliminary references: a national court states its provisional answer to the question(s) it refers to the CJ, and the CJ, following an abbreviated procedure, can give the national court the green light to decide the case on its own.[372]

---

364. P. Craig, "The jurisdiction of the Community Courts reconsidered" in G. de Búrca and J.H.H. Weiler, *The European Court of Justice* (OUP, 2001), 554–586, 561 et seq.
365. G. de Búrca and P. Craig, op. cit. *supra* note 238, 387.
366. E. Sharpston, "Transparency and clear legal language in the European Union: Ambiguous legislative texts, laconic pronouncements and the credibility of the judicial system", 12 CYELS (2010), 409–423, 421.
367. P. Craig, op. cit. *supra* note 349, 139.
368. Ibid., 140.
369. Ibid., 141. See Art. 256(3) TFEU.
370. De Búrca and P. Craig, op. cit. *supra* note 365; A. Alemanno and L. Pech, op. cit. *supra* note 343, 174–175. For the opposite view, although expressed in 2005, see: J. Komárek, "Federal elements in the EU Community judicial system: Building coherence in the Community legal order", 42 CML Rev. (2005), 9–34, 33.
371. J.H.H. Weiler, op. cit. *supra* note 186, at 252. See however H. Rasmussen, op. cit. *supra* note 350, 1679–1680, who argues that with the increased number of judges (since 2004), arguments in favour of a shared preliminary ruling jurisdiction (between the CJ and GC) are weakened as the CJ no longer has the manpower problem it had before the 2004 enlargement.
372. F. Jacobs, "The Court of Justice in the twenty-first century: Challenges ahead for the judicial system?" in A. Rosas, E. Levits, and Y. Bot, *The Court of Justice and the Construction of Europe: Analyses and Perspectives on Sixty Years of Case-law* (Asser Press, 2013), 49–59.

The creation of a unified patent court could also be a solution in reducing the workload of the CJ.[373]

4.3.3 *Reform due to increase in workload of the General Court*

The Court of Justice submitted draft amendments to the EU legislature on 28 March 2011 regarding the CJEU's Statute. In response to the GC's inability to deal with the volume of cases lodged every year, the CJ expressed a clear preference for an increase in judges rather than the establishment of specialized courts.[374] The Court therefore proposed to increase the number of judges from 27 to 39, an increase of 12.[375] The Commission welcomed the proposal and adopted its opinion on 30 September 2011.[376] However, it was not until April 2014 that the Parliament adopted a position on the report.[377] At this point, the CJ's President, Vassilios Skouris highlighted that the "situation is even more serious than [...] when the legislative initiative of the CJ was put forward".[378] Skouris highlighted recent cases brought before the CJ regarding the GC's breach of the duty to adjudicate within a reasonable time and estimated 20 million euros in claims for damages in this regard.[379] Skouris declared that the Court did not consider the establishment of specialized courts to constitute a viable alternative.[380] Specialized courts are generally considered to be less flexible and suffer from structural weaknesses in their method of appointment in judges.[381]

The proposal indicated a three-stage process to increase the number of judges to 56 at the end of the process by September 2019.[382] The Council officially backed the proposal on 23 June 2015,[383] whereas the European Parliament was critical.[384] The Parliament criticized the Council's "deep contempt for European taxpayers' money" and argued that "it makes no sense for the EU to increase spending so frivolously" and that this "would be poorly received by the European

373. See also D. Chalmers, G. Davies, G. Monti, *European Union Law*, 2nd ed. (CUP, 2010), 178–183.
374. Court of Justice, "Draft Amendments to the Statute of the Court of Junstice of the European Union and to Annex I Thereto" available at <www.data.consilium.europa.eu/doc/document/ST-8787-2011-INIT/en/pdf> (last visited 10 Jan. 2016).
375. Ibid 5.
376. European Commission, "Opinion of 30 Sept. 2011 on the requests for the amendment of the Statute of the Court of Justice of the European Union, presented by the Court" COM(2011)596 final.
377. F. Dehousse, "Reform of the EU court system (II): Abandoning the management approach by doubling the general court", (Egmont Royal Institute for International Relations, 2016) 18. Available at <tepsa.eu/wp-content/uploads/2016/03/paper.pdf>.
378. S. Vassilios, "Response of the Court of Justice to the presidency's invitation to present new proposals on the procedures for increasing the number of judges at the general court of the European Union", 3. Available at <d ata.consilium.europa.eu/doc/document/ST-14448-2014-REV-1/en/pdf>.
379. Ibid.
380. Ibid., 6.
381. Ibid., 5–6.
382. Council of the European Union, "Position of the Council at first reading in view of the adoption of a Regulation amending Protocol No 3 on the Statute of the Court of Justice of the European Union" (2011/0901B(COD)), preamble (8).
383. Council of the European Union, "European Court of Justice: Council Backs Reform of General Court" (EU Press statement, 2015). Available at <consilium.europa.eu/en/press/press-releases/2015/06/23-gac-court-justice-reform/> (last visited 11 Jan. 2017).
384. European Parliament, "Draft Recommendation for Second Reading of 10 Sept. 2015 with a view to the adoption of a regulation of the European Parliament and of the Council amending Protocol No 3 on the Statute of the Court of Justice of the European Union" (2011/0901B(COD). Available at <europarl.europa.eu/sides/getDoc.do?pubRef=-%2f%2fEP%2f%2fNONSGML%2bCOMPARL%2bPE-567.628%2b01%2bDOC%2bPDF%2bV0%2f%2fEN>.

public".[385] The Parliament furthermore questioned the Court's argument of urgency and interpretation of judicial statistics.[386]

The Reform Regulation received further criticism from some of the GC's sitting judges.[387] They considered the reform to be "yesterday's solution for yesterday's problem"[388] and asked that "in the interest of the institution and the public interest generally" a more efficient and less costly long-term solutions should be found.[389] They countered the official position of the CJ regarding the enormous backlog in cases and argued that approximately 80% of the backlog from 2010 had been liquidated; progress which was achieved without additional judges.[390] The judges furthermore questioned the extent to which this solution would help productivity, given that the number of judges would double while their staff would be reduced.[391] The proposal was also criticized by academics and professionals. Alemanno and Pech highlighted the productivity argument and noted that the doubling of the GC's judges was simply an "unnecessary distraction from less visible and arguably more decisive issues such as case management and productivity per personnel unit".[392] Arguably, the alternative proposed by the Parliament in 2015 – consisting of the appointment of additional *référendaires* – would enhance the GC's adjudication capacity at a much lower cost. Such an alternative solution would also be easily reversible.[393] Alemanno and Pech further criticized the top-down and authoritarian approach taken by Skouris, particularly given the "lack of any proper prospective impact assessment" on the proposal.[394] Steve Peers was also critical of the approach taken by Skouris,[395] particularly for blaming Members of the European Parliament for listening to the "rebel judges" (the aforementioned dissenting GC judges[396]) and threatening to retaliate against them. Peers did however recommend that the EP agree to the proposal with the introduction of a sunset clause. The sunset clause would be the appointment of additional judges for a single term, followed by an evaluation of whether this measure is as effective as it has been claimed to be.[397] Moreover, Weiler, among others, observes

385. Ibid.
386. Ibid., 16.
387. G. Berardis at al., "Doubling the general court's judges: Why progressive, reversible and more economical solutions are far better" (2015). Available at <g8fip1kplyr33r3krz5b97d1.wpengine.netdna-cdn.com/wp-content/uploads/2015/04/EP-Strasbourg-Summary-and-costs.pdf>.
388. Ibid., 2.
389. Ibid., 1.
390. Ibid., 3.
391. Ibid., 3–4.
392. A. Alemanno and P. Laurent, "Reform of the EU's court system: Why a more accountable – not a larger – court is the way forward", (*Verfassungsblog*, 2015). Available at: <verfassungsblog.de/reform-of-the-eus-court-system-why-a-more-accountable-not-a-larger-court-is-the-way-forward/>.
393. A. Alemanno, L. Pech, op. cit. *supra* note 342, 174, referring to the Recommendation for Second Reading on the Council position (09375/1/2015 – C8-0166/2015 – 2011/0901B(COD)), Committee on Legal Affairs (Rapporteur: António Marinho e Pinto), A8-0296/2015, 14 Oct. 2015.
394. Ibid. See also for a detailed examination of the reform's legislative history and shortcomings: A. Alemanno, L. Pech, op. cit. *supra* note 342.
395. S. Peers, "Don't mention the extra judges! When the CJEU reform turns into farce" (European Law Analysis, 2015). Available at <eulawanalysis.blogspot.nl/2015/07/dont-mention-extra-judges-when-cjeu.html> (last visited 12 Jan. 2017).
396. G. Berardis, op. cit. *supra* note 387.
397. S. Peers, op. cit. *supra* note 397. For a detailed overview of the academic and media criticism surrounding the reform see F. Dehousse, B. Marsicola, "The reform of the EU Courts (II). Abandoning the management approach by doubling the general court", 83 *Egmont Paper* (2016).

that what is really troubling is the docket of the CJ, constantly growing because of preliminary references.[398]

The Reform Regulation was eventually passed by the European Parliament on 28 October 2015 and was approved by the Council on 3 December 2015. Regulation 2015/2422 officially amended the CJEU's Statute and introduced the revised Article 48,[399] which stipulates that GC shall consist of: a) 40 judges as from 25 December 2015; b) 47 judges as per 1 September 2015; and c) two judges per Member State as from 1 September 2019.

Daniel Sarmiento also weighs in on the consequences of the reform and how to "learn to cope with it".[400] He wonders if the huge overall number of judges and staff that are to join GC may lead to a certain amount of friction. In the proposal for the additional judges, some argued that the CJEU should rather set up specialized courts. Sarmiento considers that, while the current approach is centred on the appointment of new judges, a 56-judge General Court may result in the emergence of specialist chambers, which focus on preliminary references. Sarmiento also worries that the CJ will be unable to process the amount of appeals brought by unhappy parties against GC decisions. The higher number of appeals cases may result in a tendency of the CJ to make use of Article 181 of its Rules of Procedure, which allows it to strike out an appeal if that appeal is manifestly inadmissible or unfounded.[401] Also Alemanno and Pech, in their detailed study of both the merits and course of the reform, criticized "the underlying diagnosis and the cure administered". On procedural grounds, Alemanno and Pech reproached the CJ for a rudimentary assessment of the problems faced by the CJEU, non-involvement of any external stakeholders and independent experts, and lobbying by EU judges with political decision-makers. With regard to the merits, they criticize the reform as being disproportionate and inadequate in light of governance challenges facing the EU judicial system as a whole. They claimed that a more efficient and flexible (reversible) solution would be to enhance the CJEU's staff instead of doubling the number of GC's judges.[402] It may indeed be considered problematic that the CJ – a judicial body – is given a power to make legislative proposals of amendments to the CJEU's Statute and its own and the GC's rules of procedure. The need is to ensure the transparency and objectivity of such legislative initiatives. As Alemanno and Pech have rightly observed, the CJ should precede such initiatives with external impact assessments and entrust the representation of the EU judicial branch in political law-making procedures to independent experts who do not hold judicial office.

4.4 *Openness in judging*

4.4.1 *Access to documents*

Article 15(1) TFEU expressly extended the application of the principle of openness to the work of the CJEU, yet the fourth subparagraph of paragraph 3 indicates that the courts are subject to this principle "only when exercising their administrative tasks". Indeed, the CJEU is the only EU institution today that does not have formal rules on access to documents in line with the provisions of the Access regulation. The provisions of the Access regulation do not grant access

398. J.H.H. Weiler, "Editorial: A Faustian deal", 14 *International Journal of Constitutional Law* (2016), 323.
399. European Parliament and Council, "Regulation 2015/2422 amending Protocol No. 3 on the Statute of the Court of Justice of the European Union", O.J. (2015, L 341/14.
400. D. Sarmiento, "The reform of the general court: Unleashing the forces of change", (EU Law Analysis, 2015). Available at: <eulawanalysis.blogspot.nl/2015/12/the-reform-of-general-court-unleashing.html> (last visited 12 Jan. 2017).
401. Ibid.
402. A. Alemanno, L. Pech, op. cit. *supra* note 342.

to court documents as such (only to Council, Commission and European Parliament documents) and contain an exception (Art. 4(2) second indent), where disclosure would undermine "court proceedings", unless there is "an overriding interest in disclosure". This is in line with general thinking that openness of the judicial activity of the European courts would interfere (too much) with the secrecy of the judges' own deliberations on how to resolve specific cases while they are ongoing, which is regarded as sacrosanct. The limited "judicial transparency" in the CJEU is exacerbated by the fact that there are no dissenting opinions and by the terse and often highly selective nature of the Courts' own reasoning; this is in spite of the fact that the opinions of the Advocate Generals to the CJEU might be considered to foster a more open dialogue.[403] Yet Article 15 TFEU must also be interpreted in the light of more general fundamental norms regarding the judiciary, such as the right to a fair trial and the requirement of independence.

4.4.2 *Case publicity*

Traditionally, following registration of a case, a notice is published in the Official Journal containing the date of registration of an application initiating proceedings, the names and addresses of the parties, the subject matter of the proceedings, the form of order sought by the applicant, and a summary of the pleas in law and of the main supporting arguments.[404] This publication represents the only information made available to the general public about pending cases, with much more information being made available to the parties (the full file). Information is also restricted in the context of preliminary rulings when the judgment of the national court referring questions to the CJEU is not disclosed in public at the supranational level (there are different practices at the national level) even though it is made available to the governments of the Member States (both in the original form and with a translation). More recently it seems to be the practice to only make a (non-public) translated *summary* of the referring court's order available to all the Member State governments (because of the length of the referring court's decisions).[405] However, the French translation of a full referring order is always available to the Member States.

When it comes more specifically to the observations made by the various parties to the procedures, such as national governments and public Union institutions (as well as the litigants themselves), the practice was for a long time to prepare an extensive "Report for the Hearing", the court's summary of the various arguments submitted and under consideration by the CJ, which was moreover *published* alongside the CJ's judgment in the European Court Reports. It has however been many years since this (traditionally public) report prepared by the *juge rapporteur* was published, and it had become in recent years a very "thin" document with only a very brief summary of the main arguments. Nonetheless, those who physically attended court hearings in Luxembourg were privy to the kinds of arguments made and the questions asked by the judges and could collect a physical copy of the *Report for the Hearing*. The *Report for the Hearing* has in any event become a collector's item. Since 1 November 2012, the CJ's new Rules of Procedure have entered into force.[406] The CJ, unlike GC, no longer produces these (quasi-public) documents, thin or otherwise.[407] Rather, the various arguments submitted by a string

403. See e.g. the rather idealized view in this regard of M. Lasser, *Judicial Deliberations: A Comparative Analysis of Judicial Transparency and Legitimacy* (OUP, 2004).

404. Art. 21(4) of the CJ's Rules of Procedure; Art. 79 of the GC's Rules of Procedure.

405. Art. 98 of the CJ's Rules of Procedure (in effect from 1/11/2012).

406. See the CJ's Rules of Procedure, op. cit. *supra* note 102.

407. The CJ's Judge A. Rosas, writing extra-judicially, stated that this document was not "indispensible", yet it constituted too big a burden for the CJ's translation services. See A. Rosas, "L'organisation des audiences

of public actors such as EU institutions or Member State governments will remain hidden to a large extent even after a case has been closed by the CJ (unless they grant public access on request which the Member States rarely do; the EU institutions have a much better track record on this, once the case is closed, see further below). Yet, such observations constitute salient input from public actors and governments on core issues.

4.4.3 *The oral hearing*

Public access to the oral hearing is a matter of principle;[408] it presumes however literally physical presence in Luxembourg. The website of the Court publishes a judicial calendar with information on the dates of public hearings. Special provision is made for hearings *in camera*. According to Article 84 of the (new) CJ's Rules of Procedure, minutes of the hearing are drawn up by the Registrar and constitute official record and these can be "inspected" by the parties to the proceedings; third parties can inspect these minutes and obtain copies. The minutes are very short and no substitute for a transcript of the hearing itself. Article 85 of the new Rules provides that a party to the proceedings or "an interested person *who has participated in the proceedings*" can listen to the recording made in the language used by the speaker at the hearing. The Courts however prepare a transcript of the hearing which is available internally within the Court (also in translations made on the day). These are not made available to the public nor is there any "live" recording (via web cam) or otherwise of the hearings themselves. The extent to which either the Advocate General or the Court itself will in individual cases publicly summarize the arguments of the parties and all the intervening institutions and governments is variable and flexible and at best often very brief. In judgments that may be particularly terse in terms of the reasoning given by the Courts, it may be relevant for the interested (and affected) public to know who was putting what arguments when and how that led to the decision in question. As the 37-page report for the hearing in the *Kadi II* case[409] illustrates, it does open a window on the issues at stake and the arguments being made by public actors in a timely fashion. As the case may be, public actors may be subject to accountability processes both nationally (for national governments) and supranationally (for EU executive actors). That is why public access is important and relates to the overall democracy arguments the Court itself makes with regard to other institutions. It does not affect the Court itself in its rightfully secret internal judicial *deliberations* on the actual resolution of individual cases nor indeed on its initial internal *preliminary report* on the initial assessment of the reporting judge.[410]

4.4.4 *Judging the CJEU secrecy*

The principled question is why a constitutional court that is "interpreting" the law including very loose human rights and due process requirements should not be more open and modern and less inward-looking to its own internal interests and constraints, in line with best practice elsewhere in Europe including by the Strasbourg court?[411] The gap in terms of openness between the CJEU on the one hand and the European Court of Human Rights, where one can consult online on the site of the court itself, the video of pleadings in more important cases, is

---

de plaidoires devant la Cour de Justice" in A. Tizzano et al., *La Cour de justice de l'Union européenne sous la présidence de Vassilios Skouris (2003–2015). Liber amicorum Vassilios Skouris* (Bruylant, 2015), 539.

408. Art. 47 CFR.

409. Case C-584/10 P, *Commission v. Kadi*, hearing of 16 Oct. 2012.

410. Art. 59 of the CJ's Rules of Procedure.

411. Joined Cases C-514, 528 & 532/07 P, *Kingdom of Sweden v. API, European Commission*, Opinion of A.G. Maduro.

widening. It can therefore come as no surprise that there has been a call by the European Bars and other actors for the CJ to make available at least a recording ("audio file") of hearings.[412] Moreover the ECtHR gives public access to all documents deposited with its Registrar in both pending and closed cases.

The situation in the CJEU is very different from that of the ECtHR, with significantly less public access both during and even after the judicial proceedings are over. The observations by the institutions and by the Member states are in principle not formally classified in security terms but are "controlled" by the Court itself during the proceedings and, after the case has closed, by the originator of the document – by the national governments who apply their own national law and by the Union institutions in question, who apply the Union rules. This can be considered even more surprising in the context of preliminary rulings, where only points of law are at issue before the supranational courts.

There is however a certain irony that at the same time that the Court is interpreting and determining the often quite extensive scope of the provisions of the Access Regulation with regard to other institutions, it seems to be becoming ever more restrictive as a matter of practice and procedure in relation to public access to its own documents during the course of its own procedures. Of course, it can be argued that this is comparing apples and oranges: courts are quite different to legislatures and executives, both of whom act on behalf of the citizen in a democratic chain of delegation, whereas courts relate to "legal subjects" and strictly circumscribed legal procedures and competences. But this argument is too one-sided. Courts, and especially the CJEU, operate within the overall democratic and constitutional context. As stated recently by Advocate General Bobek, the general principle of openness enshrined in Article 15 TFEU and anchored also in the Charter of Fundamental Rights (Art. 11 – freedom to receive information including public documents), applies to all institutions of the EU, without exceptions, the CJEU included.[413] Bobek, however, instead of focusing on the list of provisions on the basis of which the CJ is obliged to guarantee openness proposes to approach the issue differently: "what might a court at the beginning of the 21st century *want* to do by itself, in order to reasonably engage with its wider audience?"[414] The Court's "interpretation" of the law (Treaty provision or otherwise) may and often is an act of norm creation or refinement. Why should the public not know on the basis of what arguments (input into the process) it has come to its decision (even if it can go beyond these arguments in its judgment)? And even more importantly in the democratic context, why should citizens not know what arguments public actors are putting before the Courts both on points of law (preliminary references) and in order to resolve specific cases (which often have more far-reaching effects beyond one limited factual constellation)? Should public institutions and national governments be able to rely on their own interest in keeping such pleadings (written and oral) secret? We opine that they should not. Last but not least, it should be emphasized that the openness of judicial bodies, in particular the highest judicial bodies whose decisions are final and irreversible, as is the case of the CJ, allows them to be held accountable to the general public as well as the legal scholarship, the latter being particularly called to scrutinize the decisions of highest judicial bodies. In lack of the access to the case-file even after the case is closed, lawyers cannot

412. See CCBE comments on the draft rules of procedure of the General Court, 4, available at <www.ccbe.eu/fileadmin/speciality_distribution/public/documents/PD_LUX/PDL_Position_papers/EN_PDL_20140716_CCBE-Comments-on-the-Draft-Rules-of-Procedure-of-the-General-Court.pdf (accessed on 21/09/2017).

413. Art. 42 of the Charter does not apply to the Court when it exercises its judicial powers. See Case C-213/15 P, *Commission v. Patrick Breyer*, Opinion of A.G. Bobek, paras. 81–82.

414. Ibid., para 91.

fully assess the quality of judicial reasoning: check whether all arguments have been properly addressed, the background of the case properly considered, etc. Neither can citizens monitor and further understand the exercise of judicial power (input legitimacy).[415] Arguably, the public access to the case file would exert a positive pressure on judges, increasing their care for the highest possible quality of judicial decisions and their motives (output legitimacy). In sum, the lack of the CJEU's openness weakens its legitimacy by missing the chance for increasing its democratic accountability and the care of judges for the highest possible quality of their decisions.[416]

5. Conclusion

The CJEU adjudicates on matters of structural importance to the nature of the European Union and the manner in which it is evolving as a polity. It acts as an important forum of accountability in the EU. This happens particularly, but not only, in constitutional type litigation either referred from national (constitutional) courts or in cases directly involving the EU institutions. The role of the courts is to produce a fine-grained analysis of the facts in a particular case and to do so serially, without having to look at the bigger picture across these cases or their inter-relationship also in terms of the evolving European integration process as a whole. It is clear however that courts and the CJEU in particular do more than simply interpret a given set of rules; they fill gaps, explain ambiguities and decide who wins and who loses,[417] not only with regard to individual litigants but also much more structurally and politically in an institutional sense. The courts clearly exercise both political *and* legal discretion.

Further reading

Alemanno, A., "How transparent is transparent enough? Balancing access to information against privacy in European judicial selection" in M. Bobek, *Selecting Europe's Judges* (OUP, 2014).

Arnull, A., "Judicial review in the European Union" in A. Arnull and D. Chalmers (Eds.), *Oxford Handbook of European Union Law* (OUP, 2015).

Bobek, M., "Learning to talk preliminary rulings, the courts of the new member states and the Court of Justice", 45 CML Rev. (2008), 1611–1643.

Craig, P., "Courts, continuity, and change" in P. Craig *The Lisbon Treaty, Revised Edition: Law, Politics, and Treaty Reform* (OUP, 2013).

Dumbrovský, T., B. Petkova and M. van der Sluis, "Judicial appointments: The Article 255 TFEU advisory panel and selection procedures in the Member States", 51 CMLR (2014), 455–482.

Jacobs, F., "The Court of Justice in the twenty-first century: Challenges ahead for the judicial system?" in A. Rosas, E. Levits, and Y. Bot, *The Court of Justice and the Construction of Europe: Analyses and Perspectives on Sixty Years of Case-law* (Asser Press, 2013), 49–59.

Koopmans, T., "The birth of European Law at the crossroads of legal traditions", 39 AJCL (1991), 493–507.

Lenaerts, K., Maselis I., and Gutman, K., *EU Procedural Law* (OUP, 2014).

Peers, S., "Sanctions for infringements of EU Law after the Treaty of Lisbon", 18 EPL (2012) 31–62.

Peripoli, A., "Is the ECJ finally putting the Charter to work?", 128 LQR (2012), 212–216.

Smith, M., *Centralised Enforcement, Legitimacy, and Good Governance in the EU,* (Routledge, 2009).

415. Ibid., para 98.

416. Ibid., para 96.

417. J. Heliskoski and P. Leino, "Darkness at the break of noon: The case law on Regulation 1049/2001 on access to documents", 43 CML Rev. (2006), 735–781, 781.

Tridimas, T., "Liability for breach of Community law: Growing up and mellowing down?", 38 CML Rev. (2001), 301–332.

Weiler, J.H.H., "Epilogue: Judging the judges – Apology and critique" in M. Adams et al. (Eds.) *Judging Europe's Judges: The Legitimacy of the Case Law of the European Court of Justice* (Hart Publishing, 2013), 235–253.

CHAPTER 11
APPLICATION AND ENFORCEMENT OF EU LAW IN THE MEMBER STATES

*Alison McDonnell**

The law of the European Union forms "its own legal system which, on the entry into force of the treaty, became an integral part of the legal systems of the Member States".[1] How does this integration of EU law in the national legal systems take place? What provisions are made for the application of EU law? What mechanisms ensure the effective application in practice of EU legal norms in the Member States? The present chapter concerns these questions.

In this introductory section, the overall composite structure of the Union's legal order is briefly recalled, and the Member States' general responsibility to ensure that EU law is effectively applied; the extra task of ensuring that application is effective in practice is covered here by the term enforcement. The relevance of the founding values of the EU legal order in this context is mentioned. Thereafter, section 2 of this chapter deals with the primacy of EU law within the national legal systems, and the dialogue with national highest or constitutional courts. The next section covers the effect of EU law in general, and direct effect in particular (section 3). The following sections deal with access to remedies and proceedings in the national legal systems in order to guarantee the effectiveness of EU law and effective judicial protection (section 4), the sanctions to be established in the national legal systems for infringements of EU law (section 5), and the liability of Member States for damage to individuals resulting from infringements of EU law for which the Member State is responsible, including its judicial branch (section 6).

1. Application and enforcement in a composite legal order

1.1 *The composite EU legal order*

Although application of EU law is a responsibility entrusted to the European Commission by Article 17(1) TEU, the way EU law actually works in practice is through the Member States. According to Article 4(3) TEU, first sentence, "Pursuant to the principle of sincere cooperation, the Union and the Member States shall, in full mutual respect, assist each other in carrying out tasks which flow from the Treaties". This duty is then further specified with regard to the Member States, as being to take any appropriate measure, general or particular, to ensure fulfilment of the obligations arising out of the Treaties or resulting from the acts of the institutions

---

* Europa Institute, Law Faculty, University of Leiden. This chapter makes extensive use of the text by Jos Kapteyn in previous editions of this work. Particular thanks to Darinka Piqani for her updating of section 2. And to Leonard Besselink, for his comments.

1. Case 6/64, *Costa v. E.N.E.L.* See Ch. 2, "Structure and evolution of Union law", of this book. See also B. de Witte, "Direct effect, primacy and the nature of the legal order" in P. Craig and G. de Búrca (Eds.), *The Evolution of EU Law*, 2nd ed. (OUP, 2011).

of the Union. This is all part of the expression of the principle of loyal or sincere cooperation.[2] The Member States are obliged to ensure, in their respective territories, the application of and respect for European Union law.[3] Moreover, "as is evident from Article 19(1) TEU, the guardians of [the EU] legal order and the judicial system of the European Union are the Court of Justice and the courts and tribunals of the Member States".[4] The EU legal order thus works through and depends on the Member States. Only in the field of fraud and the Union's financial interests, is responsibility formally and specifically shared between Member States and Union.[5]

Seen the other way round, the policy, administration and legislation in the Member States are extensively influenced by decisions taken in the context of the EU. Particularly since the development of the doctrines of direct effect and primacy, as well as the extension of Union competences, the national legal orders are permeated with EU law.[6] Where competences are retained by the Member States, these must be exercised with regard to the duties imposed by EU law. The success of supranational rules was based on a combination of these factors, together with the system of preliminary references, and backed up by *Francovich* damages and the possibility of infringement proceedings brought by the Commission.

All authorities of Member States are covered by the obligation to ensure effective application of EU law: the government and the judiciary, but also parliaments and the administration, including decentralized authorities.[7]

In relation to national administrations, the efforts to reform and clarify the executive and implementing arrangements for EU law with the Treaty of Lisbon led to a new provision, Article 291(1) TFEU, which states: "Member States shall adopt all measures of national law necessary to implement legally binding Union acts".[8] However, the duty – or the power – to apply and implement EU law is shared between the Union and the Member States.[9] Under Article 197(1) TFEU, "effective implementation of Union law by the Member States, which is essential for the proper functioning of the Union, shall be regarded as a matter of common interest".[10] The Union may, under this article, support the Member States in order to "improve their administrative capacity

2. This principle is an even stronger version of the international law principle of *pacta sunt servanda*. See further M. Klamert, *The Principle of Loyalty in EU Law* (OUP, 2014).
3. Opinion 1/09, *Patent Court*, para 68, citing Case C-298/96, *Oelmühle and Schmidt Söhne*, para 23 and Case C-432/05, *Unibet* para 38.
4. Opinion 1/09, *Patent Court*, para 66.
5. Art. 310 TFEU states: "The Union and the Member States, in accordance with Article 325, shall counter fraud and any other illegal activities affecting the financial interests of the Union". The protection of the financial interests of the Union against fraud is discussed in Ch. 9, "Budget and finances", of this book.
6. L. Besselink, *A Composite European Constitution* (Europa Law Publishing, 2007).
7. Cf e.g. Case C-518/11, *UPC Nederland BV v. Gemeente Hilversum*, para 59, with reference to the duty of a local authority, to ensure fulfilment of EU obligations and refrain from measures which could jeopardize the attainment of EU objectives, citing Case 85/85, *Commission v. Belgium*, para 22; Case C-344/01, *Germany v. Commission*, para 79; and Case C-61/11 PPU, *El Dridi*, para 56. This chapter does not examine the particular arrangements regarding criminal law; for these, see Ch. 19, "EU criminal law", of this book.
8. Case C-146/13, *Spain v. European Parliament and Council* paras. 76–77. This is the only place in the TFEU which obliges the Member States, in so many words, actually to adopt measures. Art. 291 further provides the basis for implementation measures to be adopted by the Commission or Council, as exceptions to the general rule of implementation by the Member States.
9. R. Schutze, *From Dual To Cooperative Federalism: The Changing Structure Of European Law* (OUP, 2009).
10. Art. 197 is the sole article in Title XXIV, on Administrative cooperation, TFEU. It is one of 4 "supporting" competences which were given a specific legal basis by the Treaty of Lisbon; the others are tourism, civil protection and sport, see Arts. 195, 196 and 165 TFEU. It could possibly be used as a basis for a regulation on EU administrative law and procedure. See also "The General Principles of EU Administrative Procedural Law", report to JURI committee of European Parliament, 2015.

to implement Union law", including facilitating exchange of information. It should use regulations for this, but harmonization is excluded. Moreover, this article is "without prejudice to the obligations of the Member States to implement Union law or to the prerogatives and duties of the Commission", and also without prejudice to "other provisions of the Treaties providing for administrative cooperation among the Member States and between them and the Union". The exclusion of harmonization under Article 197(1) TFEU is limited in practice, since in specific areas – such as the internal market (Art. 115 TFEU), or customs (Art. 33 TFEU) – there are explicit legal bases for approximation of laws, regulations or administrative provisions of the Member States. Article 197(1) TFEU has not been used much so far.[11]

Under the principle of loyal cooperation, the EU institutions must also provide assistance to the Member States, in relation to their enforcement duties in the field of EU law.[12] The interplay between national and EU institutions in the joint application of EU law crops up in many areas, for instance competition law (where leniency rules and rules on access to documents need to be coordinated)[13] and protection of the Union's financial interests (where the activities of OLAF must be coordinated with national criminal authorities),[14] but not forgetting registration of protected designations of origins, customs law, and many more.

The place of national parliaments within the EU legal order was formalized in Protocol 1 attached to the Lisbon Treaty, by which they were given powers in relation to the scrutiny of EU legislative proposals.[15] Parliaments can issue reasoned opinions if they consider that proposals breach the principle of subsidiarity, obliging the Commission to reconsider its proposal.[16] Arguably, parliaments cannot be bound in the same way as governments by the principle of sincere cooperation, as this would interfere with their role in the democratic process.[17] States remain liable for actions (or failures to act) of their legislatures. As to the role of parliaments in implementing EU law, Member States enjoy a great deal of flexibility in transposing directives into national law, including by reference to pre-existing legislation, or to judicial interpretation, or by various combinations of old and new legislative and judicial measures, as long as they achieve the result prescribed.[18] Legislation may be struck down for incompatibility with EU law, but – in accordance with the principle of separation of powers – courts should normally not direct the legislature as to what to do in order to fulfil obligations.[19]

---

11. See Commission Proposal for a Regulation of the European Parliament and of the Council Establishing for the Period 2014 to 2020 the Rights and Citizenship Programme, COM(2011)758 final; Commission Proposal for a Regulation of the European Parliament and of the Council on the establishment of the Structural Reform Support Programme for the period 2017 to 2020, COM(2015)701 final, based on Art. 175(3) TFEU and Art. 197(2) TFEU.
12. The leading case is Case C-2/88 Imm., *J. J. Zwartveld and Others*.
13. See further Ch. 20, "Substantive law of the EU", of this book.
14. Case T-193/04, *Tillack v. Commission*.
15. The Protocol on the Role of National Parliaments attached to the Amsterdam Treaty only went as far as allowing them to "express their views". National parliaments also exert some influence through various interparliamentary fora, such as the Conference of European Community Affairs Committees (COSAC).
16. See Ch. 7, "Lawmaking", of this book; F. Fabbrini and K. Granat, "'Yellow card, but no foul': The role of the national parliaments under the subsidiarity protocol and the commission proposal for an EU regulation on the right to strike", 50 CML Rev. (2013), 115–144.
17. Cf. G. Van der Loo and R. Wessel, "The non-ratification of mixed agreements: Legal consequences and solutions", 54 CML Rev. 735–770, on whether national parliaments are under a duty to ratify external agreements of the EU.
18. Cf., e.g. Case C-81/05, *Cordero Alonso*; Case C-617/10, *Fransson*. See further, e.g. S. Prechal, *Directives in EC Law*, 2nd ed. (OUP, 2005), Ch. 5.
19. Though some courts may make attempts: L.F.M. Besselink, annotation of "*Stichting Waterpakt, Stichting Natuur en Milieu, Vereniging Consumentenbond and three others v. State of the Netherlands*", 41 CML Rev. (2004),

1.2 Effective application and enforcement

Generally speaking, in the early years of the Community, the focus was on drawing up common rules. The development of the principles of direct effect and primacy by the Court of Justice allowed such rules to achieve their full effect within the Member States. Gradually more emphasis was laid on how to make application of this new body of law really effective, and strengthen enforcement mechanisms; these were centrally guided, if not centralized themselves.[20] Still more recently, the aims of better implementation and application of existing rules have been highlighted, particularly since the Juncker Commission entered office.[21] The Commission provides guidance in many areas (in the form of soft law, communications or recommendations), for instance on the collaborative economy, or on a deeper and fairer single market. The enforcement aspects of common rules can also be regulated in separate acts: see examples of directives with regard to posted workers, intellectual property rights, public procurement.[22] In addition to judicial remedies, the Union has encouraged and established alternative forms of enforcement and dispute settlement.[23]

1.3 Role of founding values

The Treaty of Amsterdam included arrangements in order to review developments within the Member States in relation to the essential values underlying the Union, such as the rule of law and democracy. This trend was strengthened with the Treaty of Lisbon, so that now a kind of enforcement mechanism is also established. Under Article 7 TEU, the Council may determine that there is a clear risk of a serious breach by a Member State of the values referred to in Article 2 TEU, which are the founding values of the Union, i.e. "respect for human dignity, freedom, democracy, equality, the rule of law and respect for human rights, including the rights of persons belonging to minorities". To do so, the Council acts by a majority of four fifths of its members after obtaining the consent of the European Parliament. (Art. 7(1) TEU).[24] Proposals may come from the Parliament, the Commission or one third of the Member States. Article 7(2) TEU lays down the possibility actually to establish a serious and persistent breach of those values (and not merely the risk of such a breach); in that case, it is the European Council which must decide, by unanimity. Certain rights of the Member State which breaches these values may be

---

1429–1455.

20. H. Micklitz and A. Wechsler, *The Transformation of Enforcement—European Economic Law in Global Perspective* (Hart, 2017).
21. Communication from the Commission: EU law: Better results through better application (O.J. 2017, C 18/02).
22. Directive 2004/48/EC on the enforcement of intellectual property rights (civil remedies); Directive 2014/67/EU on the enforcement of Directive 96/71/EC concerning the posting of workers; Remedies Directive for the utilities sector (Directive 92/13/EEC); Remedies Directive for the public sector (Directive 89/665/EEC) (the latter two as amended by Directive 2007/66/EC, O.J. 2007, L 335/31).
23. E.g. the SOLVIT system, intended to prompt national public authorities to overcome obstacles without claimants needing to litigate, and involving national Coordination Centres to help ascertain the rights at stake, and then work with the authorities to solve problems, see C(2013)5869 final Commission recommendation of 17 Sept. 2013 on the principles governing SOLVIT, addressed to the Member States.
24. The first paragraph of the present Art. 7 was inserted by the Nice Treaty, i.e. concerning a determination that there is "a clear risk of a serious breach" by a Member State of the values referred to in Art. 2. It was introduced in order to monitor Member States, with the aim to prevent the actual occurrence of a "serious and persistent breach". See L. Besselink, "The bite, the bark and howl: Article 7 TEU and the rule of law initiatives" in A. Jakab and D. Kochenov (Eds.), *The Enforcement of EU Law and Values: Ensuring Member States' Compliance* (OUP, 2017).

suspended (Art. 7(3) TEU).[25] It was widely held that the main point of Article 7 was the impossibility to use it – which led the then President of the Commission, Barroso, in 2012, to call it "the nuclear option".

The Article 7 procedure is an example of centralized enforcement, but the assumption that the founding values are respected in all Member States is essential to the operation of the decentralized system of enforcement on which the EU legal order is based. The values in Article 2 TEU crucially include the rule of law and democracy. If these are seriously threatened, the system cannot function, neither within individual states nor between states, under the principle of mutual trust. Unlike Article 258 TFEU, concerning failure to fulfil Treaty obligations, the Article 7 procedure does not need any further link with EU law to bring a national situation within the scope of the provision. The very fact that the conditions to trigger Article 7 TEU are so hard to fulfil may also indicate the fundamental nature of these issues.

The Commission took steps to demonstrate the possibility of strengthening the mechanism, launching a Rule of Law Initiative in a communication of March 2014, setting out "A new EU Framework to strengthen the Rule of Law".[26] It adopts a three-step mechanism for addressing "systemic threats" to rule of law in Member States, which should precede recourse to Article 7; the key element is "dialogue". The Union, and this is most visible in the Commission, struggles with the developments in Hungary and Poland, where, at the time of writing, reactionary political developments threaten fundamental values of the EU.[27] These developments tend to undermine the working of the internal market, the harmonized response to the refugee crisis, etc., through government policy which other national bodies are too weak to compensate.[28] In Poland the Constitutional Court and independence of the judiciary are particularly under threat. The Union depends on functioning national legal systems which share the most basic values, enabling mutual trust, for its very existence.[29]

2. Primacy of EU Law: Relation of EU law to national constitutional law

2.1 *Primacy announced*

The nearest the principle of primacy has got to a Treaty basis is its reaffirmation in Declaration No. 17 concerning primacy, attached to the Lisbon Treaty, by which the Intergovernmental Conference recalled that the Treaties and the law adopted on the basis of the Treaties have primacy over the law of Member States, under the conditions laid down by the settled case law of the Court of Justice.

25. The voting arrangements for the purposes of this Article are laid down in Art. 354 TFEU.
26. COM(2014)158 final.
27. Commission recommendation regarding the Rule of Law in Poland (27 July 2016). It expired 27 Oct. 2016. In December 2016, the Commission issued further recommendations. In December 2017, the Commission proposed that the Council adopt a decision under Art. 7(1) with regard to the rule of law in Poland, see IP/17/5367.
28. Cf. M. Varju and M. Papp, "The crisis, national economic particularism and EU law: What can we learn from the Hungarian case?", 53 CML Rev. (2016), 1647.
29. "As a supranational polity, the EU relies on the binding force of legal rules being implemented by the Member States. [...] the euro crisis and then the refugee crisis exposed difficulties in the design and enforcement of European rules which transcend simple phenomena of disrespect [...]", D. Thym, "The 'refugee crisis' as a challenge of legal design and institutional legitimacy", 53 CML Rev., 1545. K. Lenaerts, "La vie après l'avis: Exploring the principle of mutual (yet not blind) trust", 54 CML Rev. (2017), 805.

The principle of primacy[30] in the EU dates from the 1964 ECJ judgment in *Costa v. ENEL*,[31] which laid down both that European law has precedence over national laws, and that the resolution of possible conflicts between EU law and the law of the Member States is itself a matter of EU law. Together with the recognition less than a year earlier, in *Van Gend en Loos*,[32] of direct effect for provisions of EU law, the foundations of the "new legal order" were laid. In *Costa v. ENEL*, the ECJ established the "special" character of EU law (Community law at the time) and the autonomous nature of this "new" legal order, invoking several arguments, such as that "the EEC Treaty has created its own legal system", that "[...] the Member States have limited their sovereign rights, [...] and have thus created a body of law which binds both their nationals and themselves". The Court emphasized the contrast between EU law and ordinary international treaties whose *internal* mode of application remains at the discretion of states.[33]

In *Costa v. ENEL* the ECJ also coined the principle of autonomy of the EU legal order, which is closely linked to primacy. Autonomy, as an inherent characteristic of the "new" legal order, distinguishes EU law from national sources of law, and therefore serves to render it immune to judicial review under national law.

2.2 *Unconditional primacy and the duty of national courts to set aside conflicting national law*

The unconditional nature of the principle of primacy of EU law over national law is already present in *Costa v. ENEL*, where the Court ruled that EU law could not be "overridden by domestic legal provisions, however framed, without being deprived of its character as [EU law]".[34] This was later confirmed in *Internationale Handelsgesellschaft*, where the ECJ stated that the validity of EU law measures cannot be challenged on grounds of fundamental rights as formulated by the national constitution *or* constitutional principles,[35] and in *Simmenthal II*.[36]

Simmenthal II showed that the principles of direct effect and primacy of EU law are indissolubly linked. The Court was clear about the logical consequences of the priority of directly effective EU law over national law: "Those provisions and measures [EU law] not only by their entry into force render automatically inapplicable any conflicting provisions of current national law but – in so far as they are an integral part of, and take precedence in, the legal order applicable in the territory of each of the Member States – also preclude the valid adoption of new

30. Also called "principle of precedence", or "supremacy" – though arguably supremacy implies more than a practical tool for settling conflicts of law. See generally, on the history, K. Alter, *Establishing the Supremacy of European Law, the Making of an International Rule of Law* (OUP, 2001). See also B. de Witte, "Direct effect, supremacy, and the nature of the legal order" in P. Craig and G. de Búrca (Eds.), *The Evolution of EU Law*, 2nd ed. (OUP, 2011).
31. Case 6/64, *Costa v. E.N.E.L.*
32. Case 26/62, *Van Gend en Loos.*
33. M. Claes, *The National Constitutional Mandate in the European Constitution* (Hart Publishing, 2006), at 97: "No rule in international law [...] imposes supremacy of the international norm before national courts". According to De Witte, internal primacy, due to supremacy of international law, already existed in international law, but was neglected: B. de Witte, "Retour à Costa: la primauté du droit communautaire à la lumière du droit international", (1984) RTDE, 428.
34. Case 6/64, *Costa v. E.N.E.L*, at 594. The phrase "however framed" was used as an English translation (made much later, in 1973, when the UK joined the EC) for the French phrase "quel qu'il soit". A better translation would have been "of whatever kind".
35. Case C-11/70, *Internationale Handelsgesellschaft v. Einfuhr- und Vorratsstelle Getreide und Futtermittel*, para 3.
36. Case 106/77, *Amministrazione delle finanze dello Stato v. Simmenthal* (*Simmenthal II*). (Strictly speaking, this is the third *Simmenthal* judgment, but the first (Case 35/76, *Simmenthal SpA v. Ministero delle Finanze italiano*) was not as memorable as the later two).

national legislative measures to the extent to which they would be incompatible with Community provisions".[37] Precedence of EU law thus applies to all national acts, whether they were adopted before or after the EU act in question: despite the different wording in the judgment in *Simmenthal II* between existent ("render inapplicable") and new measures ("preclude the valid adoption"), the intended effect is the same: the national court must set aside any provision of national law which may conflict with it, whether prior or subsequent to the EU rule.[38] Conflicting national law is not repealed, but its binding force is suspended.

This case law has been further refined: not only national courts but all organs of the state, including administrative authorities,[39] have the duty to *disapply*[40] not only general abstract rules but also specific individual administrative decisions which contravene EU law.[41]

Although this case law means that national courts may not review EU law measures in the light of national constitutional provisions or principles, the Court was willing to examine whether any analogous guarantee inherent in EU law itself was disregarded. The Court aimed to show that EU law affords guarantees comparable to those found in national constitutional law, and that it has the task hereby of ensuring that such guarantees (notably respect for fundamental rights) are protected in the EU legal order, also through preliminary references. Since there was no Treaty basis to protect fundamental rights at the time, the ECJ introduced the concept of "general principles of Community law", including "respect for fundamental rights", and ruled that "the protection of such rights, whilst inspired by the constitutional traditions common to the member states, must be ensured within the framework of the structure and objectives of the Community".[42] This was an effort to reconcile an absolute version of primacy with national concerns on the erosion of constitutional standards. More space has been given to these national concerns since then: the Treaties contain references to national constitutions and national (constitutional) identity.[43]

2.3 *Beyond conflicts of substantive rules of EU and national law*[44]

The consequences were far-reaching: national courts were required to give immediate effect to EU law in a case before them, on their own initiative without having to wait for a decision from the parliament or a constitutional court repealing or declaring unconstitutional those conflicting national provisions, which in some Member States is a fundamental rule of constitutional law.[45] This also meant that any national procedural rule or legislative, administrative or judicial practice that could hinder this immediate effect of EU law before national courts would be incompatible with EU law and its principles. The same is true if that procedural rule is of

37. Case 106/77, *Simmenthal II*, para 17.
38. Case 106/77, *Simmenthal II* at para 21.
39. Cf. Case 103/88, *Fratelli Costanzo*. See M. Verhoeven, *The Costanzo Obligation* (Intersentia, 2011).
40. Joined Cases C-10-22/97, *IN.CO.GE.'90*, para 21.
41. Case C-224/97, *Erich Ciola and Land Vorarlberg*, Case C-118/00, *Gervais Larsy and Inasti*, and Case C-198/01, *CIF v. Autorità Garante della Concorrenza e del Mercato*.
42. Case C-11/70, *Internationale Handelsgesellschaft*, para 4. This method is still applied: see Case C-42/17, *M.A.S.*
43. See e.g. Art. 4(2) TEU (national identity), Art. 6(3) TEU (fundamental rights as general principles of Union law). Both provisions were introduced with the Treaty of Maastricht, later amended. Other provisions in the Treaty, its Protocols and Declarations refer to national "constitutional requirements" in a more procedural sense.
44. Part of the analysis in this section will appear in D. Piqani, "Constitutional/Supreme Courts and their relationship to EU Courts" in R. Wolfrum, F. Lachenmann and R. Grote, *Max Planck Encyclopedia of Comparative Constitutional Law*, (OUP online) forthcoming.
45. *Simmenthal II*, para 24.

constitutional character or if the judicial practice is established by constitutional courts. In *Filipiak* certain tax law provisions were declared unconstitutional by the Polish Constitutional Tribunal (PCT). However, based on Article 190(3) of the Polish Constitution, the PCT decided to defer the effects of its judgment. A Polish administrative court had concerns about the compatibility of these national provisions (declared unconstitutional, but whose effect was kept intact) with Article 49 TFEU (freedom of establishment). The architecture of national legal systems – with constitutional courts at the apex of the national judicial system – and the binding nature of their decisions would in principle mean that lower courts must follow the decision by the Constitutional Tribunal. However, this deferral decision by the PCT prevented national courts giving immediate effect to EU law. The ECJ ruled that national courts must set aside conflicting national law "irrespective of the judgment of the national constitutional court which has deferred the date on which those provisions, held to be unconstitutional, are to lose their binding force".[46] The implications of this line of case law are twofold: first, it reinstates the "unconditional and absolute"[47] version of primacy of EU law according to the ECJ; second, it undermines the authority of constitutional courts whose (deferral) decisions may not be followed by lower courts for the sake of effectiveness of EU law.[48]

Similarly, national procedural rules of hierarchy within the judiciary must not prevent lower courts from referring a question for a preliminary ruling to the Court of Justice if they consider this necessary. Lower courts should be free to reach out to the Court of Justice on issues of interpretation or validity of EU law notwithstanding the fact that a superior court may have ruled on the issue and despite the obligation of these same courts, under national procedural law, to follow the law as established in those rulings of superior courts.[49] More recently, in a bold statement in *Križan*, the ECJ ruled that "[...]the national court, having exercised the discretion conferred on it by Art. 267 TFEU, is bound, for the purposes of the decision to be given in the main proceedings, by the interpretation of the provisions at issue given by the Court of Justice and must, if necessary, disregard the rulings of the higher court if it considers, in the light of that interpretation, that they are not consistent with European Union law".[50]

Primacy is also relevant in situations in which a national provision is allegedly in conflict, simultaneously, with a provision of EU law and with a provision of the Constitution. Several dilemmas for national courts emerge: should they first ask a question concerning constitutionality (assuming there is an appropriate national court and procedure)? Does a decision on the

46. Case C-314/08, *Filipiak*, para 85. For a similar case and outcome see Case C-409/06, *Winner Wetten*, and annotation by T. Beukers, (2011) CML Rev., 1985.
47. M. Claes, op. cit. *supra* note 33, at 387.
48. Note, however, the line of case law in which the ECJ has considered whether the obligation to enforce Union law can be temporarily suspended as to its effects within the national legal order when retroactive annulment of a national measure could give rise to a gap in environmental protection, thus failing to achieve the effectiveness of EU environmental law as laid down in other provisions, i.e. when another EU objective is at stake. See K. Sowery, "Does environmental protection provide a (special) basis for suspending the normal consequences of a breach of Union law?", annotation of Case C-379/15, *Association France Nature Environnement v. Premier ministre and Ministre de l'Écologie, du Développement durable et de l'Énergie*, (2017) CML Rev., at 1157. In Case C-25/14, *UNIS*, the Court held that the interest in preventing legal uncertainty may justify putting the stability of contractual arrangements already in the course of performance in the area of public procurement above the observance of EU law.
49. See Case 166/73, *Rheinmülen*, para 4. See more recently Case C-210/06, *Cartesio* and Case C-173/09, *Elchinov* (and commentary by A.-P. van der Mei on Case C-512/08, *Commission v. France*, and Case C-173/09, *Elchinov*, (2011). CML Rev., 1297.
50. Case C-416/10, *Križan*, para 69. See also M. de Visser, *Constitutional Review in Europe: A Comparative Analysis* (Hart Publishing, 2014), at 424–427.

constitutionality of the national provision by the constitutional court preclude a further referral to the ECJ? Already in *Mecanarte*, the ECJ ruled that the existence and mandatory nature of a domestic interlocutory procedure should not become an obstacle for the national court to refer questions to the ECJ.[51] In wanting to deal with simultaneous claims of unconstitutionality and incompatibility with EU law, some national jurisdictions provide for *priority of the constitutional question*.[52] The ECJ has ruled on such a system and concluded that the priority given to the constitutional question is not incompatible with EU law as long as national courts and tribunals remain free to refer to the ECJ any question they considered relevant at whatever stage of the proceedings; that national courts are free to adopt any interim measure for the protection of rights conferred under EU law; and lastly, that national courts remain free to disapply, at the end of the interlocutory procedure, the provision of national law considered contrary to EU law.[53] This was confirmed by the Court in *A v. B and others*[54] and *Kernkraftwerke Lippe-Ems*,[55] in which the Court emphasized that primacy entailed that national courts should be free to refer a question for a preliminary ruling to the ECJ at any stage of the proceedings "[…] even at the end of an interlocutory procedure for the review of constitutionality".[56]

2.4 *Reactions of national constitutional courts to the ECJ's doctrine of primacy of EU law*

The ECJ's narrative on the unconditional primacy of EU law met with resistance[57] in many highest national courts.[58] One fundamental tension concerns the *locus* of primacy of EU law: according to the ECJ, primacy is "an essential feature of the EU legal order"[59] and a characteristic "arising from the very nature of EU law".[60] For some highest national courts, such as the German Constitutional Court, however, the source for primacy of EU law is the national constitution itself, more specifically constitutional provisions that allow for limitations of sovereignty or transfer of sovereign powers to the EU.[61] The Italian *Corte Costituzionale* took the view that it alone – and no other Italian court – was competent to decide whether a national provision was incompatible with EU law, as it had sole jurisdiction in constitutional questions; the conflict

51. Case C-348/89, *Mecanarte*, paras. 46–47.
52. See e.g. in France Art. 23-2 of Order 58-1067 of 7 November 1958 on the organic law governing the Constitutional Council as amended by Organic Law No. 2009-1523 of 10 December 2009 on the Application of Article 61-1 of the Constitution or Art. 26(4) of the Belgian Special Majority Act.
53. Joined Cases C-188 & 189/10, *Melki and Abdeli*, para 57.
54. Case C-112/13, *A v. B and Others*. See M. de Visser, "Juggling centralized constitutional review and EU primacy in the domestic enforcement of the Charter: *A.v. B*", (2015) CML Rev., 1309; D. Paris, "Constitutional courts as guardians of EU fundamental rights?", 11 EuConst (2015), 389.
55. Case C-5/14, *Kernkraftwerke Lippe-Ems GmbH v. Hauptzollamt Osnabrück*. See R. García and E. Ferreiro Serre, "Hardening the preliminary reference procedure in a Union in crisis: *Kernkraftwerke Lippe-Ems*", (2016) CML Rev., 819.
56. Case C-112/13, *A v. B and Others*, para 39.
57. See e.g. M. Kumm, "The jurisprudence of constitutional conflict: Constitutional supremacy in Europe before and after the Constitutional Treaty", (2005) ELJ, 262.
58. Both constitutional courts and highest courts entrusted with the review of constitutionality of laws. On the impact of *Simmenthal II* specifically on the position of constitutional courts see M. Bobek, "The impact of the European mandate of ordinary courts on the position of constitutional courts" in M. Claes et al., *Constitutional Conversations in Europe. Actors, Topics and Procedures* (Intersentia, 2012), 287. The analysis here looks mainly at the German and Italian courts, with limited references to other Member States.
59. See Case C-399/11, *Melloni*, para 59.
60. See Opinion 2/13, *Accession ECHR*, para 166.
61. *Lisbon Treaty* Decision 2BvE 2/08 etc., 30 June 2009 at para 231: "In a functional sense, the source of Community authority, and of the European constitution that constitutes it, are the peoples of Europe with their democratic constitutions in their states".

between national law and EU law was "translated" into an infringement of constitutional law.[62] This line was also followed by the French *Conseil d'État*.[63] Article 55 of the French Constitution expressly gave priority to norms of written international law, but the *Conseil d'État* felt it lacked jurisdiction to consider the issue, on the ground that it would then have to consider the compatibility of the decree with the Constitution. The *Conseil d'État* later revised its standpoint and accepted the primacy of the law of international agreements, including EU law, even above subsequent national law.[64] In the UK, the European Communities Act 1972 was the vehicle for the entry of EU law into the national legal system, but it has always been debated whether the priority of EU law occurs by virtue of EU law, or by virtue of the 1972 Act.[65]

The ECJ's view, as already clear from *Simmenthal II*, is that a conflict between a provision of EU law and a subsequent national law may not be solved by "an authority with a discretion of its own, other than the court called upon to apply Community law, even if such an impediment to the full effectiveness of Community law were only temporary".[66]

As a rule, national courts will try to avoid an outright choice of one rule over another by interpreting them in such a way that they do not conflict: they will not readily assume that the national legislature has acted contrary to the state's international obligations. In this context, it may be less relevant whether the courts concerned do or do not consider themselves obliged to give priority to the rule of EU law as a matter of national constitutional law or EU law. The national court is in any case bound to interpret national rules as far as possible in conformity with EU law, in order to avoid conflicts with provisions of EU law lacking direct effect.[67] It is, though, crucial that national courts refer the interpretation of the rule of EU law to the ECJ under Article 267 TFEU. The Court of Justice can ensure that the EU rule will not be interpreted too narrowly so as to prevent conflict with the rule of national law: if the national court wishes to avoid a conflict, it must do so by interpreting the national rule narrowly. Consequently, in *Costa v. ENEL*, the ECJ was obliged to argue forcefully, on the basis of an exhaustive explanation of the primacy of EU law, that "Article [267] is to be applied regardless of any domestic law whenever questions relating to the interpretation of the Treaty arise".[68]

A second and important implication deriving from the understanding of the source of primacy of EU law is in the context of a conflict between EU law and a norm of constitutional rank. If the constitution is the basis for primacy, precedence of EU law provisions may only be accepted if it does not conflict with fundamental constitutional principles, implying that EU

---

62. I.e. was infringement of EU law a breach of Art. 11 of the Italian Constitution which permits restrictions of sovereignty in favour of international organizations; *Simmenthal*. Other highest courts in the EU have refrained from translating the issue of incompatibility between EU law and national law into a constitutional issue: e.g. French Constitutional Council (Decision 2010-605 DC, 12 May 2010); German Constitutional Court (*Alfons Lütticke*, Case No. 2 BvR225/69, 1971); Hungarian Constitutional Court (Judgment 1053/E/2005 AB, 16 June 2006); Estonian Supreme Court (Judgment Case 3-4-1-1-05, 19 April 2005).
63. Conseil d'État N° 62814, *Syndicat général des fabricants de semoules de France*, 1 March 1968.
64. In the judgment of 20 Oct. 1989, *Nicolo*, Rec. Lebon at 190, for Treaty law in general. For EU law in particular, see the judgments of 24 Sept. 1990, *Boisdet*, and of 28 Feb. 1992, *Philip Morris*. Primacy was however based on Art. 55 of the French Constitution, which granted precedence to international law, and not on the very nature of the treaties. This position of the *Conseil* was confirmed in *Société Arcelor Atlantique et Lorraine et autres*, No. 287110, 8 Feb. 2007. The *Cour de Cassation* took a different view: *Cafés Jacques Vabre*, 24 May 1975.
65. Some conceptual clarity came from the Supreme Court's judgment in *Miller, R (on the application of Miller and another) v. Secretary of State for Exiting the European Union* [2017] UKSC 5.
66. Case 106/77, *Simmenthal II*, at para 23. The Corte Costituzionale later accepted the ECJ's approach: Judgment No. 170 of 8 June 1984, *Granital*.
67. See *infra* section 3.
68. Case 6/64, *Costa v. E.N.E.L.*

law may be challenged or reviewed in the light of the Constitution; however, this was excluded in *Simmenthal II* and *Internationale Handelsgesellschaft*[69] and more recently in *Melloni.*[70] In *Melloni* the ECJ reiterated its previous case law, concluding that Member States are free to apply national constitutional standards on the condition that "the level of protection provided for by the Charter, as interpreted by the Court, and the *primacy*, unity and effectiveness of EU law are not thereby compromised".[71]

Problems on this point arose initially in Germany and Italy. The ECJ's theory of the restriction of national sovereignty *vis-à-vis* the EU legal order was gradually accepted: but in both countries, the constitutional courts continually held that their constitutions place limits on the transfer of sovereignty.[72] The essential elements of the constitutional order, particularly fundamental rights, may not be affected by any such transfer.[73] In 1973, the Italian *Corte Costituzionale* introduced its *controlimiti* doctrine: it regarded the conflict between European and national law as a theoretical problem, but reserved the right to intervene if the EEC, contrary to its expectations, were to be given an unacceptable power to violate the fundamental principles of the Italian constitutional order or inalienable human rights.[74] However, at the same time the *Corte Costituzionale* declined to control the constitutionality of each individual Community regulation.[75] In Germany, the *Bundesverfassungsgericht* regarded itself as having jurisdiction to review regulations against the fundamental rights laid down in the German Constitution *as long as* (hence the popular name "*Solange* judgment") the process of integration had not developed far enough for Community law to contain a codified catalogue of fundamental rights, decided by a democratically legitimate and elected parliament and offering the same guarantees as those afforded by the German Constitution.[76] Later, in 1986, the German Court believed this protection had been achieved,[77] and said that "as long as" this guarantee is present (hence: *Solange II*) it would not hear cases seeking to challenge the constitutionality of secondary EU law in the light of fundamental rights guaranteed by the German Basic Law.

For many years, the solution adopted in *Solange II* remained intact: applications for review were not admissible as long as EU protection of fundamental rights was not demonstrated to

---

69. Case 11/70, *Internationale Handelsgesellschaft*, see *supra*.
70. Case C-399/11, *Melloni*.
71. *Melloni*, para 60 (emphasis added). See further, e.g. L. Besselink "The parameters of constitutional conflict after *Melloni*", 39 EL Rev., 531.
72. Support for this is in Art. 24(1) *Grundgesetz*, which permits the transfer of sovereignty to a supranational organization, and Art. 11 of the Italian Constitution which allows for the limitation of sovereignty to the benefit of international organizations having the aim of assuring peace and justice between nations. With a view to the ratification of the Treaty of Maastricht, the entirely revised version of Art. 23 of the *Grundgesetz* now contains a number of conditions for and limitations on the transfer of sovereign powers to the European Union. M. Herdegen, "Maastricht and the German Constitutional Court: Constitutional Restraints for an 'an ever closer Union'", (1994) CML Rev., 235, at 236 with references in note 6.
73. *International Handelsgesellschaft* BVerfGE 37, 271 (*Solange I*); see H. Ipsen, "BVerfG versus EuGH re 'Grundrechte' Zum Beschluss des Zweiten Senats des BVerfS vom 29.05.1974", (1975) EuR, 1.
74. Decision No. 183/73, 18 Dec. 1973 (*Frontini*), para 9. *Controlimiti* were confirmed later in *Granital* (Decision No. 170/84, 8 June 1984) and *Fragd* (Decision 232/89, 21 April 1989). In *Fragd*, the Constitutional Court repeated explicitly that it reserved to itself the right to review EU law against the fundamental principles of the Italian constitutional order and inalienable human rights. See G. Gaja, "New developments in a continuing story: The relationship between EEC law and Italian law", (1990) CML Rev., 83–95.
75. Ibid., para 9.
76. Order of 29 May 1974, *International Handelsgesellschaft* (*Solange I*), BVerfGE 37.
77. Decision of 22 Oct. 1986, *Wünsche Handelsgesellschaft* (*Solange II*), BVerfGE 73; (1987) EuR 51 (with note by Ipsen).

be below the national level.[78] The judgment of the *Bundesverfassungsgericht* in *Atlanta* confirmed this.[79] However, it seems that the *Bundesverfassungsgericht* has now "offered a route to bypass the admissibility hurdle"[80] by applying a constitutional identity review in cases in which human dignity as a fundamental right is at stake. In a case concerning surrender procedures under the European Arrest Warrant, the German Constitutional Court declared the constitutional complaint brought by Mr. R as *admissible* on grounds of alleged violation of human dignity as part of its constitutional identity review. According to the *Bundesverfassungsgericht:* "If a violation of the guarantee of human dignity is asserted, the Federal Constitutional Court reviews such a serious violation of a fundamental right in the context of the identity review [...] – notwithstanding its past jurisprudence declaring inadmissible both constitutional complaints and referrals in specific judicial review proceedings that assert a violation of fundamental rights under the Basic Law by secondary Community law or Union law respectively [...]".[81]

The German *identity review,* initially introduced in the *Lisbon* decision, protects the core of constitutional identity of the German *Grundgesetz,* reflected in its Articles 23(1) and 79(3). Whereas it is for the Court of Justice to interpret the challenged EU act, it is for the *Bundesverfassungsgericht* "to determine the inviolable core content of the constitutional identity, and to review whether the act (in the interpretation determined by the Court of Justice) interferes with this core".[82] The Italian Constitutional Court has also invoked the notion of constitutional identity in a preliminary reference[83] asking the ECJ to clarify a previous judgment in Case C-105/14, *Taricco*. *Taricco* concerned national rules on limitation periods for criminal offences and the EU objective of combatting fraud contained in Article 325(1) TFEU. In 2015, the ECJ ruled that national provisions on limitation periods whereby perpetrators escape punishment in a significant number of cases of serious fraud, may have an adverse effect "[...] on the fulfilment of the Member States' obligations under Article 325(1) and (2) TFEU".[84] National courts should then set aside, if need be, those provisions in order to give full effect to EU law.[85] According to the Italian Constitutional Court, the ECJ judgment in *Taricco* could conflict with the principle of legality enshrined in Article 25 of the Italian Constitution.[86] Another problematic element was the discretion given in *Taricco* to national courts on setting aside national limitation periods.[87] The Italian Constitutional Court did not immediately apply its *controlimiti* doctrine, but asked the

---

78. In its *Maastricht* decision (1993, BVerfGE 89), the *Bundesverfassungsgericht* remarked that it exercises its jurisdiction over the applicability of secondary Community law in Germany in a "Kooperationsverhältnis" (relationship of cooperation) with the European Court of Justice. Since the latter guarantees the protection of fundamental rights in concrete cases throughout the whole territory of the Community, the Bundesverfassungsgericht can "limit itself to providing a general guarantee of the unalterable standards of fundamental rights" (our translation) (Part B.2(b)).
79. Decision of 7 June 2000, 2 BvL 1/97, also known as the *Banana Market* Case; annotated by F. Hoffmeister, (2001) CML Rev., 791, Cf. Case C-466/93, *Atlanta Fruchthandelsgesellschaft et al. v. Bundesamt für Ernährung und Forstwirtschaft* (*Atlanta II*).
80. J. Nowag, "EU law, constitutional identity, and human dignity: A toxic mix? Bundesverfassungsgericht: Mr R", 53 CML Rev. (2016), at 1449.
81. *Bundesverfassungsgericht,* Identity Review Order, 2 BvR 2735/14, 15 Dec. 2015, para 34.
82. Order of 14 Jan. 2014, 2BvR2728/13 (*Gauweiler*), para 27.
83. Italian Constitutional Court, Ordinanza n. 24, 26 Jan. 2017 (*Taricco*). Case C-42/17, *M.A.S. and M.B.*
84. *Taricco,* para 58. For a comment see M. Timmerman, "Balancing effective criminal sanctions with effective fundamental rights protection in cases of VAT fraud: *Taricco*", 53 CML Rev. (2016), 779.
85. For a comment see P. Faraguna, "The Italian Constitutional Court in re Taricco: Gauweiler in the Roman campagna", available at <verfassungsblog.de/the-italian-constitutional-court-in-re-taricco-gauweiler-in-the-roman-campagna/>.
86. Italian Constitutional Court, Ordinanza n. 24, 26 Jan. 2017 (Taricco), para 4.
87. Ibid., para 7.

ECJ for clarification, or even a revisitation[88] of *Taricco* in order to avoid constitutional conflict, using nuanced language and highlighting interpretations that would avoid a conflict between legality as part of Italian constitutional identity and the *Taricco* judgment.[89] The ECJ "clarified" in *M.A.S.* that in such situations, the national court does not need to disapply national provisions on limitation if this would conflict with the principle that offences and penalties must be defined by law.[90] It argued on the basis that the relevant limitation rules had not been completely harmonized at EU level, and that the principle that offences and penalties must be defined by law is also found in the Charter, the common constitutional traditions of the Member States, and the ECHR. The ECJ could thus avoid engaging with the question of Italian national constitutional identity.[91]

The ECJ would have difficulty in the adjudication and enforcement of the national identity clause in Article 4(2) TEU, if every Member State was in charge of invoking and applying its own national identity as a limit to primacy of EU law. From that point of view, the willingness to engage in dialogue through the preliminary reference proceedings is essential, as well as awareness of difference in scope. The *Bundesverfassungsgericht* takes care to distinguish between the concept of national identity in Article 4(2) and the concept of constitutional identity within the meaning of Article 79(3) of the Basic Law; protection of the latter is a task for the German Constitutional Court alone, and it cannot be balanced against any other legal interest.[92]

The *Bundesverfassungsgericht* regards it as one of its tasks to ensure that the EU Institutions, including the Court, do not exceed the sovereign powers transferred by the German law ratifying the Treaties. In *Kloppenburg*[93] it examined whether, in according vertical direct effect to certain provisions of directives, the ECJ had remained within the bounds of what it regarded as acceptable judicial creativity. The explicit statement, in its *Maastricht* judgment, that legal acts of EU institutions which, in its opinion, were no longer covered by transfer of competences would not be binding on German territory was perhaps no surprise.[94] The *Bundesverfassungsgericht* seeks to guard the limits of EU competence.[95] This approach of *ultra vires* review was

88. F. Fabbrini and O.Pollicino, "Constitutional identity in Italy: European integration as the fulfilment of the Constitution", EUI Working Paper LAW 2017/06, at 12.
89. See e.g. para 7 of the Ordinanza. The Constitutional Court also seems to indicate that *Taricco* should be clarified as a requirement of legal certainty forming part of the common constitutional traditions of the Member States.
90. Case C-42/17, *M.A.S.*, para 61. A.G. Bot, in his Opinion, had advocated a strict application of primacy, which could only have led to a collision.
91. Case C-42/17, *M.A.S.*, para 44 (lack of harmonization), paras. 51–55, and 63.
92. As done in the interpretation of national identity by the ECJ, Order 2BvR2728/13, para 29. "[...] as an interest which may be balanced against others, the respect of national identity [under Art. 4(2) TEU] does not meet the requirements of the protection of the core content of the Basic Law [...] which may not be balanced against other legal interests. The protection of the latter is a task of the Federal Constitutional Court alone".
93. Decision of 8 April 1987, BVerfGE 75.
94. *Maastricht* judgment, see esp. part C.I.3. For the text, see M. Herdegen, op. cit. *supra* note 73, at 251–262. For a critical analysis, see T. Koopmans, "Rechter, D-mark en democratie: Het Bundesverfassungsgericht en de Europese Unie", (1994) NJB, at 245–251.
95. Cf. C. Tomuschat, "Die Europäische Union unter der Aufsicht des Bundesverfassungsgerichts", (1993) Eur. Gr.Z., 489–496. Cf. M. Kumm, "Who is the final arbiter of constitutionality in Europe?", (1990) CML Rev., 351. The Danish Højesteret (Supreme court) took a similar position in its judgment of 6 April 1998, *Carlsen v. Rasmussen*, see K. Høegh, "The Danish judgment", (1999) EL Rev., 80. According to the Danish Supreme Court, Danish courts could only declare *ultra vires* EU acts inapplicable in Denmark in extraordinary situations and if established "with required certainty" (*Carlsen v. Rasmussen*, para 9.6); confirmed in the DKSK's *Lisbon* Decision, Case 199/2012 of 20 Feb. 2013, part 3.

further elaborated in its *Lisbon* and *Honeywell* decisions.[96] The German court pledges to act as the final arbiter: its jurisdiction will be *exceptional* – "if obvious transgressions take place" – and *subsidiary* to legal protection at EU level –"if legal protection cannot be obtained at the Union level".[97] In *Honeywell*, the *ultra vires* threshold was set high: the breach of competences has to be obvious and the challenged EU act lead to a "structurally significant shift to the detriment of Member State competences".[98] Despite the controversy surrounding the judgment in Case C-144/04, *Mangold* – which was at the heart of the constitutional complaint in *Honeywell* – the *Bundesverfassungsgericht* concluded that it was not *ultra vires.*[99] A similar outcome was reached in the context of *Gauweiler,*[100] which was the first reference for a preliminary ruling to come from the *Bundesverfassungsgericht.*[101] Despite the critical tone in the order for a reference – which gave the impression that the German court viewed the Outright Monetary Transactions (OMT) programme as a manifest transgression of Union competences – the German Court indicated that subject to a particular interpretation the OMT was not *ultra vires.*[102] So far, the threat by the *Bundesverfassungsgericht* to rule an act of an EU institution *ultra vires* has never materialized.

The view of the *Bundesverfassungsgericht* or any other national constitutional court that the direct effect and supremacy of EU law can only be recognized within the boundaries of the powers conferred on the Union is in itself correct. However, the core issue is who is the final arbiter, in other words who decides on whether these boundaries have been respected? As a question of interpretation of EU law, this is for the ECJ to determine. However, from the perspective of some constitutional courts, it is a matter for constitutional law, as it is the national constitution that validates the transfer of powers to the EU. The willingness of highest national courts to engage in structured dialogue with the ECJ can be useful,[103] as it can provide an opportunity to

---

96. *Lisbon*, Case 2BvE 2/08, 5/08, 2BvR 1010/08, 1022/08, 1259/08, 182/09, 30 June 2009; see D. Thym, "In the name of sovereign statehood: A critical introduction to the *Lisbon* judgment of the German Constitutional Court", 46 CML Rev 2009, 1795. *Honeywell* 2 BvR 2661/06 German Constitutional Court, 6 July 2010; cf. M. Payandeh, "Constitutional review of EU law after *Honeywell*: Contextualizing the relationship between the German Constitutional Court and the EU Court of Justice", 48 CML Rev. (2011), 9.
97. *Lisbon* Decision, para 238.
98. *Honeywell* Decision, para 64.
99. In support, see M. Mahlmann, "The politics of constitutional identity and its legal frame: The ultra vires decision of the German federal constitutional court", (2010) GLJ, 1407. The *Bundesverfassungsgericht* found that giving legal effects to directives before the transposition period expired, and determining that prohibition of discrimination on grounds of age constitutes a general principle of EU law, are not manifest transgressions of competences, see *Honeywell* paras. 75–77 and 78–79.
100. *Bundesverfassungsgericht,* Order of 14 Jan. 2014, 2BvR2728/13 (reference for a preliminary ruling); Case C-62/14, *Gauweiler* (ECJ preliminary ruling); *Bundesverfassungsgericht* 2 BvR 2728/13, etc., 21 June 2016 (final decision). On Case C-62/14 see V. Borger, "Outright monetary transactions and the stability mandate of the ECB: *Gauweiler*", 53 CML Rev, 2016, 139; on the *Bundesverfassungsgericht* decision, see A. Pliakos and G. Anagnostaras, "Saving face? The German Federal Constitutional Court decides *Gauweiler*", (2017) GLJ, 213; also Special Issue: "The European Court of Justice, the European Central Bank and the supremacy of EU law", 23 MJ (2016).
101. The *Bundesverfassungsgericht* already admitted the possibility of a preliminary reference in its *Lisbon* and *Honeywell* decisions.
102. *Bundesverfassungsgericht* 2 BvR 2728/13.
103. The Belgian Constitutional Court has the highest number of references to the ECJ. Some constitutional courts (the Czech, Croatian, Latvian, Hungarian, Maltese, Portuguese and Romanian) have not yet used this "channel" for dialogue, although they have not excluded the possibility. The Italian Constitutional Court sent its first reference for a preliminary ruling in 2008, see Decision No. 102, 15 April 2008 and Order No. 103, 15 April 2008; see O. Pollicino, "From partial to full dialogue with Luxembourg: The last cooperative step of the Italian Constitutional Court", 10 EuConst (2014), 143. The French Constitutional Council made its first reference in a case concerning the EAW, see Decision No. 2013-314P QPC, 4 April 2013, see

accommodate constitutional concerns;[104] such exchanges are not totally without risks, however, if the national court disagrees strongly with the ECJ's finding.[105]

3. The effect of Union law in the national legal systems: Direct effect

3.1 General

The doctrine of direct effect may be explained historically as the means of improving the enforcement and application of EU law, by involving the national courts, and therefore laying the basis for the effective application of this law in all Member States. Given the variety of rules and traditions in the Member States concerning the direct application of provisions of international agreements by national courts, the Court of Justice developed a doctrine for EU law which could be applied by the courts in all Member States in the same way, despite these divergences.

In *Van Gend en Loos*[106] the Court of Justice observed that the preliminary reference procedure, laid down in the Treaty, "confirms that the states have acknowledged that [Union] law has an authority which can be invoked by their nationals before [their] courts and tribunals".

Under international law, a state traditionally is free to decide for itself in what way it will comply with treaty obligations within its national legal order. Under a monist approach, international obligations are directly incorporated in a domestic legal order, and can be invoked in a national court if they fulfil appropriate conditions (in the language of public international law: if they are self-executing).[107] Under the dualist approach,[108] written rules of international law can be applied within the domestic legal order only after their transformation into national rules. The regulation of the internal effect of rules of international law is thus left to national constitutional law. The Court of Justice took quite a different position. Although this is not explicitly stated in any of the Treaties, the Court found that Treaty provisions[109] and some secondary EU law provisions[110] enter the internal national legal order without the aid of any particular national measure, to the extent that their character makes this appropriate.

F.-X. Millet, "How much lenience for how much cooperation? On the first preliminary reference of the French Constitutional Council to the Court of Justice", 51 CML Rev. (2014), 195. E.g. also Polish Constitutional Tribunal in Case K 61/13, 7 July 2015; Slovenian Constitutional Court Case U-I-295/13, 6 Nov. 2014. See further CJEU *Annual report 2016*, at 109–111.

104. E.g. in Case C-62/14, *Gauweiler* and Case C-42/17, *M.A.S.*

105. The Danish Supreme Court decided that it was unable to comply with the preliminary ruling of the ECJ in Case C-441/14, *Ajos;* Case 15/2014, decision 6 Dec. 2016 of the DKSC: it concluded that the Danish Accession Act does not confer powers on the EU to allow unwritten general principles to overrule a provision in Danish legislation in a dispute between two private parties, and it would act *ultra vires* if it set aside Danish legislation in this situation. The Czech Constitutional Court, which embraced the *ultra vires* review of the *Bundesverfassungsgericht,* once ruled that the ECJ (in Case C-399/09, *Landtová)* exceeded its competences: Czech Constitutional Court, Slovak Pensions Pl. ÚS 5/12, 31 Jan. 2012.

106. Case 26/62, *NV Algemene Transport- en Expeditie Onderneming Van Gend en Loos v. Administratie der Belastingen.*

107. See *infra.*

108. Still prevalent e.g. in Germany, Italy and the United Kingdom.

109. E.g. Case 26/62, *Van Gend & Loos* and Case 28/67, *Firma Molkerei-Zentrale Westfalen/Lippe GmbH v. Hauptzollamt Paderborn.* See Ch. 13, "Free movement of goods", and Ch. 14, "Free movement of services, establishment and capital", of this book.

110. E.g. Case 9/70, *Franz Grad v. Finanzamt Traunstein,* Case 33/70, *SpA SACE v. Finance Minister of the Italian Republic* and Case 41/74, *Yvonne Van Duyn v. Home Office.*

Regulations, which by their nature and function in the system of Union sources of law are directly applicable,[111] and other provisions of EU law which leave the EU institutions and the Member States no discretionary freedom in their application or implementation, must be applied by the national courts even without the intervention of a legal measure transposing EU law (as a whole or in respect of particular provisions) into domestic law.

The terms "direct applicability" and "direct effect" are sometimes confused, but usually the term "direct applicability of EU law" deals with the question whether or not EU law has to be *transformed* into domestic law; the term "direct effect" tends to be used to describe a situation in which a private individual can invoke or rely on a provision of EU law in national judicial proceedings.[112] Note, however, that it is not only courts which are obliged to apply directly effective provisions: the obligation applies to all government bodies, including the administration, and also decentralized entities, such as municipalities.[113] A further remark is appropriate here: the question whether a provision of EU law applies in the national legal system as such does not correspond exactly to the question whether such provisions can be relied on before the national courts. Whether a provision of EU law can be relied on before the national courts also depends on whether the provision lends itself to such reliance.

3.2 *Direct effect of primary Union law*

3.2.1 *Treaty provisions*

In the 1960s, there were two points of view as to when treaty provisions can be directly applied by the national courts.[114] The predominant view was inspired by an Opinion of the Permanent Court of International Justice from 1928, which stated that "according to a well-established principle of international law an international agreement cannot, as such, create direct rights and obligations for private individuals. But undoubtedly the very object of an international agreement, according to the intention of the contracting parties, may be the adoption by the parties of some definite rules creating individual rights and obligations and enforceable by the national courts".[115] Thus: treaty provisions can have direct effect if they create *rights and obligations for individuals.* The national court must ascertain the intention of the contracting parties in this respect. The second view is associated with the concept of "self-executing", a concept stemming from American practice.[116] In this view, national courts apply treaty provisions which can have effect on their own, that is to say can be applied by the courts without the intervention beforehand of legislative or administrative

111. See Ch. 7, "Lawmaking", of this book. See Art. 266 TFEU and e.g. Case 43/71, *Politi s.a.s. v. Ministry for Finance of the Italian Republic.*
112. Certainly in earlier years, the terms "direct applicability" and "direct effect" were sometimes used interchangeably also in English translations made ex post. E.g. Case 43/71, *Politi,* Case 50/76, *Amsterdam Bulb v. Produktschap voor siergewassen* and Case 31/78, *Francesco Bussone v. Ministère italien de l'agriculture* where the ECJ uses both direct applicability and direct effect (for regulations). See generally, J.A. Winter, "Direct applicability and direct effect: Two distinct and different concepts in Community Law", (1972) CML Rev., 425–438; A. Hinarejos, "On the legal effects of framework decisions and decisions: Directly applicable, directly effective, self-executing, supreme?", (2008) ELJ, 620.
113. Cf. Case 103/88, *Fratelli Costanzo v. Comune di Milano.* See M. Verhoeven, *The Costanzo Obligation: The Obligations of National Administrative Authorities in the Case of Incompatibility Between National Law and European Law* (Intersentia, 2011). See also B. de Witte, op. cit. *supra* note 1.
114. See the – old but still relevant – monograph by M. Waelbroeck, *Traités internationaux et juridictions internes dans les pays du Marché commun,* CIDC (1969), para 151–156, with further references.
115. Permanent Court of International Justice, Jurisdiction of the Courts of Danzig, Advisory Opinion 1928, Series B, No. 15, at 17–18.
116. J. J. Paust, "Self-executing treaties", (1988) AJIL, at 760–783.

bodies. That will depend on the formulation of the provision in question. This view can lead to a much broader application of treaty provisions than the first view, and the emphasis shifts from the (subjective) issue of the intention of the contracting parties, to the (objective) issue whether the treaty provision lends itself by its very nature to application by a national court.

In *Van Gend en Loos,* the referring court asked whether Article 12 EEC[117] "has direct application within the territory of a Member State, in other words, whether nationals of such a state can, on the basis of the Article in question, lay claim to individual *rights which the courts must protect*".[118] The Court of Justice answered that the provision "produces direct effects and creates individual rights which national courts must protect". The Court stated that the fundamental principles and objectives of the Treaty demonstrate that "the Community constitutes a new legal order of international law, for the benefit of which the States have limited their sovereign rights, albeit within limited fields, and the subjects of which comprise not only the Member States but also their nationals". Whether international treaty provisions have direct effect depends on their spirit, their general scheme and their wording. The Court concluded that EU law intends to confer rights on individuals, from the very spirit of the Treaty.[119] The Court also ruled that the Treaty provision at issue was one of the essential provisions on which the Community was based. Finally, the wording of the provision also favoured direct effect, as it was a Treaty article imposing negative obligations on the Member States – certain action was prohibited, so the obligation was very clear.[120]

The explicit finding in *Van Gend en Loos* that the question whether a provision has direct effect is a question of *interpretation* of that provision, is of essential importance for the uniform interpretation and application of Union law within the legal systems of the Member States. It implies that it is not the national courts but the Court of Justice which has the final say on the question, in the framework of the preliminary reference procedure of Article 267 TFEU.[121]

3.2.2 *EU Charter of Fundamental Rights: General principles*

Since the Treaty of Lisbon entered into force, the Charter of Fundamental Rights of the European Union has "the same legal value as the Treaties" (Art. 6 TEU).[122] The question of effect within the national order becomes one of scope, and the prior question of the applicability of some other provision of EU law: Charter rights can only be triggered if there is a right granted by EU law to be invoked before a national court. The ECJ provided some clarity in *Åkerberg Fransson,* where it stated that "situations cannot exist which are covered in that way by European Union

---

117. Art. 12 EEC prohibited increasing customs duties between Member States. In its present form (Art. 30 TFEU) the provision prohibits all customs duties between Member States.
118. Case 26/62, *Van Gend en Loos* (emphasis added).
119. The "very object" of the EU Treaties is "the adoption [...] of some definite rules creating individual rights and obligations and enforceable by national courts".
120. Case 28/67, *Firma Molkerei-Zentrale Westfalen-Lippe* expanded this to cover "rights [...] by reason of obligations which the Treaty imposes in a clearly defined way upon individuals as well as upon the Member States and upon the institutions of the [Union]". Certain principles, such as the principle that offences and penalties must be defined by law, may also limit the effect of Treaty provisions in the national order, cf. Case C-42/17, *M.A.S.*
121. Intervening States argued that direct effect of the relevant provision was not a question of interpretation but of application; this was firmly rejected by the ECJ. Historical research has also brought to light that the extensive pleadings of the Commission Legal Service were highly influential: this was a considered attempt to revolutionize and strengthen the legal order of the EEC in its early years, cf. M. Rasmussen, "Revolutionizing European law: A history of the *Van Gend en Loos* judgment", 12 *International Journal of Constitutional Law* (2014), at 136–163.
122. See further Ch. 4, "Fundamental rights", of this book. The Charter was first solemnly proclaimed in 2000.

law without those fundamental rights being applicable. The applicability of European Union law entails applicability of the fundamental rights guaranteed by the Charter".[123] In principle, therefore, everything within the scope of EU law is subject to protection of fundamental rights under the Charter.[124] However, the Charter itself contains "rights, freedoms and principles" of various kinds. The effect of the Charter provisions depends further on the content of the right or principle in question.

It was already laid down in case law that national courts must review the application of national provisions within the scope of EU law, having regard to all the rules of EU law, including general principles of EU law;[125] prior to the granting of binding force to the Charter, this was also how fundamental rights were protected as a matter of EU law. In certain cases, as explained in section 3.5 below, a general principle of EU law has been combined with a provision of secondary law in order to safeguard an individual right in a case before a national court, where the norm of secondary law on its own could not have such effect.

3.3 *Reliance before national courts on secondary EU law*

3.3.1 *Conditions for direct effect*

The case law on the conditions for direct effect first developed in preliminary references asking whether private parties could rely in national courts on various Treaty provisions against the national authorities.[126] Later, the Court had to look at the effect of provisions of acts of the Union, including regulations, directives and decisions, as well as international agreements binding the EU. It was also asked to what extent provisions of EU law may be relied upon by private parties against other private parties (so-called horizontal direct effect). The special aspects of the case law on these issues are examined below. This section first deals with some general aspects of the doctrine of direct effect as developed in the Court's case law.

A consistent line of case law shows that for a provision to have direct effect it must be unconditional and sufficiently precise. It is unconditional where it is not subject, in its implementation or effects, to the taking of any measure either by the EU institutions or by the Member States, and it is sufficiently precise to be relied on by an individual and applied by the court where the obligation which it imposes is set out in unequivocal terms.[127]

An EU law rule must be available for the court, meaning a sufficiently clear and unconditional norm which is not dependent on a discretionary implementing measure. That rule is necessary for the court in two ways. First, as an alternative to be applied instead of a national rule with which it is in conflict (or where a national rule is lacking). Second, as a standard against which a national measure can be reviewed, when the court is asked to declare a particular national measure to be in conflict with that rule, in order to have it annulled or set it aside.

This does not mean that provisions which depend on discretionary measures by the Member States can never be relied on before the national courts. The national courts can review the legality of acts on the basis of such provisions to the extent that they set sufficiently clear limits

123. Case C-617/10, *Åkerberg Fransson*, para 21.
124. On the scope of application of the Charter: M. Dougan, "Judicial review of Member State action under the general principles and the Charter: Defining the 'scope of Union law'", (2015) CML Rev., 1201–1246. See also Case C-682/15, *Berlioz*, on the rights protected.
125. Case C-260/89, *Elliniki Radiophonia Tiléorassi (ERT) v. Dimotiki Etairia Pliroforissis*, para 44.
126. Exceptionally, Case 13/61, *De Geus en Uitdenbogerd v. Bosch*, concerned the effects in litigation between private parties of the provisions on anti-competitive agreements, now Art. 101 TFEU.
127. In that sense, see e.g. Case 44/84, *Hurd v. Jones;* also Case C-236/92, *Comitato di Coordinamento per la Difesa della Cava and others v. Regione Lombardia*. Cf. already A.G. Mayras Opinion in Case 41/74, *Van Duyn*.

to the margin of discretion allowed to Member States where these limits may have been exceeded.[128] This can even be in relation to implementing measures by the EU itself, also before national courts under certain conditions.[129] They can use a superior rule of EU law in order to review the EU implementing act against the limits which that provision imposes on the margin of discretion.[130] This is no different where the implementation of an obligation lying on the Member States depends on discretionary measures taken by them. If the court is free under national law to review measures implementing national laws against those national laws, this possibility of review may not be withheld in the case of EU laws.[131] Direct effect can thus be defined broadly as "the obligation of a court or another authority to apply the relevant provision of [EU] law, either as a norm which governs the case or as a standard for legal review".[132]

The way provisions of EU law are given direct effect varies, also depending on the procedural rules and the context of substantive legal rules involved in the concrete dispute. Consequently, the requirements for direct effect of a particular provision will also vary. Ultimately, the question will always be whether the provision relied on is sufficiently "operational" in the context of an actual dispute so as to be applied by the court, without the court exceeding the limits of its judicial function.[133]

The ECJ case law essentially followed the view inspired by the concept of "self-executing" provisions, elaborating that in its own way.[134] The other view (that direct effect resulted from the creation of rights and obligations for individuals) gradually faded.[135]

Some commentators argue that there is no reason to set special conditions for the application of EU rules by the national courts: why should EU rules be treated differently from national rules? The situation is the same in both cases.[136] The ECJ, however, attaches importance to the instrument containing the relevant provisions. As mentioned above, the ECJ has found the EU Treaties appropriate for direct effect ever since *Van Gend en Loos*. However, for directives there are specific limitations (see further below). For international agreements binding the Union, the question of spirit and general scheme is also still relevant.[137]

---

128. Also sometimes referred to as the objective review of legality. See further section 3.3.2. *infra*, especially on Case C-72/95, *Kraaijeveld et al. v. Gedeputeerde Staten van Zuid-Holland.*
129. Providing the plaintiffs cannot appeal against such acts directly (under Art. 263 TFEU), cf. Case C-188/92, *TWD Textilwerke Deggendorf GmbH v. Bundesrepublik Deutschland.* The national court may not annul the EU implementing act itself, but must make a preliminary reference to the ECJ.
130. Cf. Case 77/72, *Capolongo v. Azienda Agricola Maya,* para 6.
131. This is especially likely when implementing directives. Cf. Case 51/76, *Verbond Nederlandse ondernemingen v. Inspecteur der invoerrechten en accijnzen* (VNO). See section 3.3.2 *infra.*
132. S. Prechal, op. cit. *supra* note 18, at 241.
133. In this sense, cf. already P. Pescatore, "The doctrine of direct effect: An infant disease of Community Law", (1983) EL Rev., at 176–177; and Opinion of A.G. Van Gerven in Case C-128/92, *Banks v. British Coal,* para 27, referring to the Court's flexible interpretation of the conditions for direct effect. See recently Case C-413/15, *Elaine Farrell v. Minister for the Environment, and Motor Insurers' Bureau of Ireland (MIBI).*
134. See e.g. already Case 8/81, *Becker v. Finanzamt Münster-Innenstadt,* in which the Court distinguishes between the possibility to rely on unconditional and sufficiently precise provisions and the specific case if the provisions define rights of individuals against the state (para 25). In Joined Cases C-100/89 and C-101/89, *Kaefer & Procacci,* the ECJ recalled that "an unconditional provision is one which leaves no discretion to the Member States", though the substantive obligation may depend on a condition being satisfied (paras. 26, 27).
135. Rather, there remains a (procedural) right to rely on a directly effective provision before a national court (see section 4 *infra*). See the judgments in the Case C-63/99, *Glosczuk,* para 38; Case C-257/99, *Barkoci and Malik,* and Case C-268/99, *Jany.*
136. S. Prechal, "Does direct effect still matter?", 37 CML Rev. (2000), at 1059.
137. Case 181/73, *Haegemann v. Belgian State* (*Haegeman II*). See Ch. 41, "Union external relations under the TFEU", of this book.

3.3.2 *Decisions addressed to Member States: Directly applicable Regulations*

Provisions of decisions addressed to Member States can be relied upon directly before national courts.[138] This is based on the binding effect attributed to Union decisions by Article 288 TFEU, which provides that: "A decision shall be binding in its entirety…" That provision also lays down the binding nature and direct applicability of regulations. As the Court has often said, "the direct application of a [Union] regulation means that its entry into force and its application in favour of or against those subject to it are independent of any measure of reception into national law";[139] thus regulations can create individual rights which national courts must protect, also *vis-à-vis* other private parties.[140] When a national court is called to apply a provision of a regulation in a particular case, it will assess whether and to what extent, the provision can be applied without the court exceeding its judicial function, just as when it applies national law. Sometimes regulations provide for implementing or further measures to be taken by the Union or by the Member States; these may involve some discretion for the body adopting them.[141] In certain cases, this discretion may mean that the provision of the regulation cannot be applied.[142] If a regulation does not prescribe national implementing measures, national law which does require such implementing measures may not be applied: this would prevent "the uniform application of regulations throughout the [Union]".[143]

3.3.3 *Directives*

The Court of Justice decided early on – and very controversially – that, just as decisions addressed to Member States should have direct effect due to their binding nature, this must also apply to directives.[144]

---

138. Cf. Case 9/70 *Grad v. Finanzamt Traunstein;* Case 20/70, *Transports Lesage & cie. v. Hauptzollamt Freiburg;* Case C-156/91, *Hansa Fleisch;* a provision of a decision addressed to a Member State may be relied on as against that Member State where the provision imposes an obligation which is unconditional and sufficiently clear and precise. If the provision must be implemented within a specified period, it may be relied on by individuals against a Member State only after that period has expired. Such decisions may not have horizontal effect (see below) cf. Case C-80/06, *Carp*. Decisions of EU institutions addressed to individuals determine the application of a provision of Union law in individual cases; we do not use the term direct effect for such decisions.
139. Cf. Case 50/76, *Amsterdam Bulb,* para 4; Case 43/71, *Politi v. Ministero delle finanze*; Case 34/73, *Fratelli Variola v. Amministrazione delle finanze dello Stato.* In the English translation of early case law the term "direct effect" is sometimes used.
140. Provided the individuals are aware of the precise extent of the obligations imposed on them by the regulation; Case C-108/01, *Consorzio del Prosciutto di Parma & Salumificio S. Rita v. Asda Stores & Hygrade Foods.*
141. Cf. Case 230/78, *Eridania-Zuccherifici nazionali et al. v. Minstero dell' Agricoltura e Foreste et al.*: in such a case, the manner in which this competence is exercised is regulated by national public law; the national courts decide whether the measures taken are in conformity with the content of the regulation.
142. Cf. Case C-403/98, *Azienda Agricola Monte Arcosu Srl v. Regione Autonoma della Sardegna,* where the Member State had to define a particular kind of farmer. In other cases, it may be necessary explicitly to indicate which bodies are entrusted with national implementation. In Case C-528/15, *Al Chodor,* the ECJ ruled that a provision of the Dublin Regulation could not be applied directly, since it requires Member States to establish objective criteria (for determining the Member State responsible). The need for detailed implementing rules does not always preclude direct effect, especially in case of prohibitions, cf. Case 87/82, *Rogers v. Arthenay.*
143. Case 93/71, *Leonesio*. The Court stated that national budgetary rules may not frustrate the direct application of a provision of EU law, nor the exercise of pecuniary rights of individuals.
144. Case 41/74, *Van Duyn.* See "Direct Effect of Directives" (Ch. 9) in S. Prechal, op. cit. *supra* note 18. Generally: S. Prechal, "Direct effect, indirect effect, supremacy and the evolving constitution of the European

The doctrine on direct effect of provisions of directives can be summarized as follows. The basic principle is that in cases where a directive is correctly implemented "its effects extend to individuals through the medium of the implementing measures adopted by the Member State concerned".[145] However, when a Member State fails to implement a directive in national law within the time period allowed, or when the directive is not correctly implemented, then private individuals may rely on the provisions of that directive before the national courts as against the Member States concerned in all cases when the content of these provisions is unconditional and sufficiently precise. This is called *vertical direct effect*. Member State cannot rely on the provisions of the directive itself against an individual: so-called *inverse vertical direct effect* is excluded.[146]

With regard to the direct effect of a provision of a directive, the Court ruled that a provision of EU law is unconditional when the obligation it imposes is not subject, in its implementation or effects, to the taking of any measure either by the EU Institutions or the Member States; and, according to the Court, the provision is sufficiently precise to be relied on by an individual and applied by the court where the obligation which it imposes is set out in unequivocal terms.[147] Private parties can rely on provisions of directives which meet these conditions both in relation to the state as governing authority, and the state in its capacity as employer "against any national provision which is incompatible with the directive or in so far as the provisions define rights which individuals are able to assert against the state".[148]

The state also embraces organizations or institutions which come under its authority or supervision, or which enjoy special powers. Such organizations and institutions include, for instance, the tax authorities,[149] regional authorities,[150] an independent police authority,[151] and regional bodies with responsibility for public health.[152] They also include – regardless of the legal form – bodies which are responsible for providing a public service under the control of the state and have for that purpose special powers beyond those resulting from the normal rules applicable in relations between individuals (also called "exorbitant powers"), such as a nationalized company (in the leading case this was the British Gas Corporation).[153] This occurs wherever a state has delegated the performance of a task in the public interest: the conditions that the organization concerned must be subject to the authority or control of the state, and that they must possess special powers beyond those which result from the normal rules applicable to relations between individuals are not conjunctive.[154]

Direct effect of provisions of directives is based on several arguments: first, it would be incompatible with the binding effect which Article 288 TFEU ascribes to directives to exclude as a matter of principle the possibility of the obligation imposed on the Member State being

Union" in C. Barnard (Ed.), *The Fundamentals of EU Law Revisited: Assessing the Impact of the Constitutional Debate?* (OUP, 2007), at 35, 37–38.

145. Case 8/81, *Becker v. Finanzamt Münster-Innenstadt*, para 19; see also Case 222/84, *Johnston v. Chief Constable of the Royal Ulster Constabulary*, at para 51, in which the Court spoke of effects that "reach" individuals.
146. Case 80/86, *Kolpinghuis Nijmegen*: "a national authority may not rely, as against an individual, upon a provision of a directive whose necessary implementation in national law has not yet taken place". Other limits are discussed *infra*.
147. For this "didactic" summary of the case law, see Case C-236/92, *Comitato di coordinamento per la difesa della Cava*.
148. Case 8/81, *Becker*, at para 25.
149. Case 8/81, *Becker*.
150. Case 103/88, *Fratelli Costanzo*.
151. Case 222/84, *Johnston*.
152. Case 152/84, *Marshall v. Southampton and South-West Hampshire Area Health Authority (Marshall I)*.
153. Case C-188/89, *Foster v. British Gas*. See also the Opinion in this case. Cf. Case C-279/12, *Fish Legal*.
154. Case C-413/15, *Elaine Farrell v. Minister for the Environment, and Motor Insurers' Bureau of Ireland (MIBI)*.

relied upon by persons concerned. Second, in particular in cases where directives impose on Member States a duty to adopt a certain course of action, their effectiveness ("*effet utile*") would be impeded if persons were prevented from relying on them before a court, and national courts were prevented from taking them into consideration. Article 288 TFEU speaks of direct applicability in relation to regulations, but this does not mean that other categories of acts never have similar effects.[155] The binding nature of a directive exists in relation to "each Member State to which it is addressed".[156] Third, a Member State which has not adopted the implementing measures required by the directive within the prescribed period may not plead in its defence its own failure to perform the obligations which the directive entails as against persons who have acted in accordance with the provisions of a directive.[157]

Direct effect of provisions of directives was far from obvious. By definition, directives require legislative intervention by Member States, so the Court has understandably only wished to make exceptions to this where an individual relies on a directive against the Member State which has failed to implement that directive on time, or correctly, into its domestic law, "vertical" effect. Even with this limitation, the Court's case law initially met with opposition in some national courts, for instance in Germany[158] and France.[159]

As to the provision in question being sufficiently precise, even provisions of directives which entail discretionary measures by national authorities may be relied on in the national courts to the extent that they set sufficiently precise *limits* to the discretion enjoyed by Member States regarding implementation, and it is alleged that these limits have been exceeded.[160] If such discretion has been exceeded, individuals may use those provisions to have the national rules or measures set aside, since national authorities have the duty to take all the general or particular measures necessary to ensure that the result sought by the directive is achieved.[161] The Court ruled on this in the 1970s,[162] and confirmed it in *Kraaijeveld*,[163] nearly twenty years later. In such cases, not only does EU law permit a review in the light of provisions of a directive, but even

155. Case 41/74, *Van Duyn*; Case 8/81, *Becker* and Case 152/84, *Marshall I*.
156. Case 152/84, *Marshall I*.
157. Case 148/78, *Criminal proceedings against Tullio Ratti*. This is a form of "estoppel" argument, *nemo turpitudinem suam allegans auditur* i.e. states should not profit from their failure to implement a directive.
158. The German Bundesfinanzhof's resistance to direct effect of provisions of the Sixth VAT Directive was finally overcome through the intervention of the *Bundesverfassungsgericht*: *Bundesfinanzhof* 25 April 1985, (1981) *Europarecht*, 442 and *Bundesverfassungsgericht*, 8 April 1987, BVerfGE 75; Case 70/83, *Kloppenburg v. Finanzamt Leer*.
159. A directive could not be relied on to oppose individual administrative decisions (*Cohn-Bendit*, Conseil d'Etat 22 Dec. 1978). For later developments, see J. Gerkrath, "Direct effect in Germany and France: A constitutional comparison" in J.M. Prinssen and A. Schrauwen (Eds.), *Direct Effect: Rethinking a Classic of EC Legal Doctrine* (Europa Law Publishing, 2002).
160. See already C.W.A. Timmermans, "Directives: Their effect within the national legal systems", (1979) CML Rev., 533, 544 et seq. Not only implementing legislation, but any measure taken by national authorities, see Case C-127/02, *Landelijke Vereniging tot Behoud van de Waddenzee*.
161. Case 435/97, *WWF and Others v. Autonome Provinz Bozen and Others*. As to the limits to the direct effect of directives in "triangular" and horizontal relations, see *infra*, section 3.5.
162. Case 51/76, *VNO*, para 24; Case 38/77, *Enka v. Inspecteur der invoerrechten en accijnzen* and Case 21/78, *Delkvist v. Anklagemyndigheden*.
163. Case C-72/95, *Kraaijeveld et al. v. Gedeputeerde Staten van Zuid-Holland*. Case C-287/98, *State of the Grand Duchy of Luxembourg v. Linster* concerned review on the basis of a directive which had not been fully implemented on time.

obliges the court to carry out a review under Union law *ex officio* if it is under a similar obligation under national law concerning binding rules of national law.[164]

As mentioned, inverse vertical direct effect is excluded: while Treaty provisions and regulations may impose obligations directly on individuals *vis-à-vis* public authorities,[165] unimplemented or incorrectly implemented directives cannot of themselves do so, since a directive imposes obligations only on "each Member State to which it is addressed".[166] In the specific context of criminal proceedings, a directive "cannot, of itself and independently of a national law adopted by a Member State for its implementation, have the effect of determining or aggravating the liability in criminal law of persons who act in contravention of the provisions of that directive".[167]

3.3.4 *International agreements binding on the Union*

International agreements concluded by the Union, and by the Union together with the Member States form an integral part of the Union legal order.[168] Hence, all the problems of direct effect set out above are also encountered in this field too, as well as the consequences when direct effect is not possible. The details and case law in relation to these agreements are dealt with elsewhere in this book.[169]

3.4 *Indirect effect: Duty of consistent interpretation*

"The most obvious example of the applicability of a rule of Union law's not being synonymous with its having direct effect can be seen in the obligation to interpret national law in conformity with Union law".[170]

In the interpretation of national law, the national court is obliged to take the greatest possible account of EU law; this is particularly relevant to provisions of directives which do not fulfil the conditions for being directly effective.[171] *Von Colson and Kamann v. Land Nordrhein-Westfalen*[172] shows that the obligation on Member States to achieve a particular result envisaged by a directive, as well as the obligation to take all general or particular measures to ensure fulfilment of that obligation (Art. 4(3) TEU) is binding on all the authorities of Member States including,

---

164. Case C-72/95, *Kraaijeveld*. The judgment (at para 57) refers in that context to Joined Cases C-430 & 431/93, *Van Schijndel and Van Veen v. Stichting Pensioenfonds voor Fysiotherapeuten*. There is some lack of clarity on the question of the criteria for deciding whether a rule of EU law involves binding law in the sense of "mandatory law" (French: règles contraignantes); see S. Prechal, "Community law in national courts: The lessons from *Van Schijndel*", 35 CML Rev. (1998), 681, at 689–700.
165. E.g. in the field of competition or agriculture.
166. Case 152/84, *Marshall I*; Case C-106/89, *Marleasing* and Case C-168/95, *Arcaro*.
167. Case 14/86, *Pretore di Salò*, para 20; see also Case 80/86, *Kolpinghuis Nijmegen*; Joined Cases C-387, 391 & 403/02, *Berlusconi and Others*, paras. 73–74. Case C-105/14, *Taricco and others*.
168. Constant case law since Case 181/73, *Haegeman II*. See Ch. 39, 40 and 41, on Union external action and relations, of this book.
169. See Ch. 39, "An introduction to Union external action" and Ch. 41, "Union external relations under the TFEU", of this book.
170. Opinion of A.G. Cruz Villalón in Case C-306/12, *Spedition Welter*.
171. The duty exists not only in relation to directives, but to any provision of EU law. See, in relation to the EC Treaty, Case C- 165/91, *Van Munster v. Rijksdienst voor Pensioenen*. See, in relation to external agreements Joined Cases 300 & 392/98, *Parfum Christian Dior*, requiring national judges to apply national rules as far as possible in the light of the wording and purpose of Article 50 of TRIPs despite the fact that under EU law the provision lacked direct effect (para 47). See further Ch. 41, "Union external relations under the TFEU", of this book. All national authorities are bound to follow such interpretation.
172. Case 14/83, *Von Colson and Kamann v. Land Nordrhein-Westfalen*. See also Case C-355/96, *Silhouette International Schmied v. Hartlauer Handelsgesellschaft*.

for matters within their jurisdiction, the courts. Also following that reasoning, the Court ruled in *Marleasing*[173] that it follows that in applying national law, national courts are required to interpret national law[174] – applying interpretative methods recognized by that law – as far as possible in the light of the wording and purpose of a directive in order to achieve the result required by Article 288(3) TFEU.[175] This obligation holds regardless of whether the national provisions are of earlier or later date than the directive. It exists once the period for transposition of the directive has expired.[176] It is usually referred to as the duty of consistent interpretation, but sometimes other terms are used (e.g. compliant interpretation, conform interpretation, etc.).

The duty of consistent interpretation is inherent in the system of the Treaty, "since it permits the national court, for the matters within its jurisdiction, to ensure the full effectiveness of [Union] law when it determines the dispute before it".[177] The national court may first examine whether it can interpret the national provisions in a manner which is consistent with the relevant provision of the directive concerned, before looking at whether the latter provision can be relied upon as such against the national provisions.[178] This is particularly important when direct effect of a directive is prevented in disputes between private parties (see following section). Certain other EU acts are precluded from having direct effect: in *Pupino,* the Court extended the duty of consistent interpretation which existed in EC law in relation to directives, to framework decisions taken under (former Third Pillar) EU law, which are precluded from having direct effect.[179]

The duty to interpret national law in conformity with EU law is not absolute, but has inherent limits. The Court has ruled that the duty to interpret and apply national legislation in conformity with EU law is subject to general principles of law, such as legal certainty and non-retroactivity, certainly when these provide individual protection. It is possible for interpretation in conformity with a directive to have a negative influence on the legal position of individuals, even though provisions of directives cannot of themselves impose obligations on individuals.[180] The principles of legal certainty and non-retroactivity preclude the obligation of consistent interpretation from leading to the criminal liability of individuals being determined or aggravated,

173. Case C-106/89, *Marleasing v. Comercial Internacional de Alimentación.* For an example of an obligation to interpret in conformity with the Treaty, see Case C-165/91, *Van Munster.*
174. Not only the domestic provisions enacted in order to implement the directive in question, but national law as a whole, see Joined Cases C-397-403/01, *Bernhard Pfeiffer,* para 115.
175. The duty of consistent interpretation implies that a national court is bound to use all possible methods of interpretation in order to achieve the result sought by the directive (Joined Cases C-397-403/01, *Pfeiffer,* para 116).
176. Case C-212/04, *Konstantinos Adeneler And Others v. ELOG.* A Member State does not have to adopt measures implementing a directive before the period for its transposition has expired, but a directive does produce legal effects for the Member State – and all national authorities – on publication or from the date of its notification (ibid., para 119). During the transposition period, Member States may not take any measures liable seriously to compromise the attainment of the result prescribed by it (Case C-129/96, *Inter-Environnement Wallonie,* para 45). This a parallel to the international law obligation in Art. 18 of the Vienna Convention on the Law of Treaties, 1969.
177. Joined Cases C-397-403/01, *Pfeiffer,* para 114.
178. It is for the national court to interpret and apply domestic law in accordance with Union law and, to the extent this is not possible, to disapply provision of domestic law contrary Union law, Case C-208/05, *ITC Innovative Technology Center GmbH v. Bundesagentur für Arbeit,* para 70.
179. Case C-105/03, *Maria Pupino*; see S. Peers, "Salvation outside the church: Judicial protection in the third pillar after the *Pupino* and *Segi* judgments", (2007) CML Rev., 883–929. Cf. Art. 10 of Declaration 50 to the Lisbon Treaty on amending or replacing pre-Lisbon legislation where appropriate. Not all such acts have been replaced, cf. Case C-579/15, *Popławski,* on Framework Decision 2002/584.
180. The Court recalled this in Case C-106/89, *Marleasing,* referring to Case 152/84, *Marshall I.* See also Case C-168/95, *Criminal proceedings against Arcaro.*

on the basis of a framework decision alone,[181] or on that of an unimplemented directive.[182] The duty is limited by certain fundamental rights such as the right to a fair trial.[183] Finally, the national court is under the obligation to interpret national law "as far as possible"[184] in conformity with the directive. The principle that national law must be interpreted in a manner consistent with European Union law requires national courts to do whatever lies within their jurisdiction, taking the whole body of domestic law into consideration.[185] Whether an interpretation in conformity with the directive is possible, depends on the flexibility of the provision of national law to be interpreted. An obligation to interpret national law *contra legem* is excluded.[186]

If a national court "considers that it is impossible for it to interpret the national provision at issue in a manner that is consistent with EU law, the national court must disapply that provision", since it is under an obligation to provide, within the limits of its jurisdiction, the legal protection which individuals derive from EU law and to ensure the full effectiveness of that law, which may include disapplying any provision of national legislation contrary to that principle.[187] In *Ajos*, the ECJ ruled that a national court cannot rely on the principle of the protection of legitimate expectations in order to continue to apply a rule of national law that conflicts with the general principle prohibiting discrimination on grounds of age.[188] The requirement to interpret national law in conformity with EU law also entails the obligation for national courts to change their established case law, where necessary, if it is based on an interpretation of national law that is incompatible with the objectives of a directive.[189]

3.5 *Horizontal direct effect: General principles*

How far may private parties rely on provisions of Union law not just against national authorities but also against other private parties (so-called horizontal situations)?[190] A distinction must be made in this context between Treaty provisions and provisions of directives, and the special

---

181. Case C-554/14, *Ognyanov*, paras. 62 to 64 and the case law cited.
182. Cf. Case 80/86, *Criminal proceedings against Kolpinghuis Nijmegen*, referring to Case 14/86, *Pretore di Salò v. Persons unknown*, at para 20. See also Case C-60/02, *Criminal proceedings against X*, where this protection was also extended to cover regulations requiring some degree of national implementing measures. Cf. Case C-168/95, *Arcaro* and Case C-384/02, *Grongaard and Bang*.
183. See Case C-105/03, *Maria Pupino*, paras. 58–60.
184. See Joined Cases C-397-403/01, *Pfeiffer*, para 113 and case law cited.
185. C-282/10, *Dominguez*, para 27, and Case C-42/11, *Lopes Da Silva Jorge*, para 56. In Case C-306/12, *Spedition Welter* the Court seemed to tilt the balance in favour of the effectiveness of EU law; C. Franklin, "Limits to the limits on the principle of consistent interpretation? Commentary on the Court's decision in *Spedition Welter*", 40 EL Rev. (2015); M. Brenncke, "Hybrid methodology for the EU principle of consistent interpretation", (2017) *Statute Law Rev.*, argues that EU obligations change the legal methodology that national courts have to employ.
186. Case C-294/16 PPU, *JZ*; Case C-282/10, *Dominguez*, para 25; and C-176/12, *Association de médiation sociale*, para 39. See Case C-212/04, *Adeneler*, para 110 and, by analogy, Case C-105/03, *Pupino*, paras. 44 and 46. Case C-441/14, *Ajos*, para 32; this case led to problems in Denmark, also as to the question which court, national or ECJ, decides whether a particular interpretation would be contra legem; see next footnote.
187. Case C-555/07, *Kücükdeveci*, para 51, Case C-441/14, *Ajos*, para 37. The referring court in *Ajos* (Danish Supreme Court) concluded that the Danish Accession Act does not confer powers to the EU to allow the unwritten general principle prohibiting discrimination on the grounds of age to *overrule* a provision in Danish legislation in a dispute between two private parties; the court would act *ultra vires* if it set aside Danish legislation in this situation. (Case No. 15/2014 *Dansk Industri (DI) acting for Ajos A/S v. The estate left by A*).
188. Case C-441/14, *Ajos*, para 38.
189. Case C-456/98, *Centrosteel*, para 17.
190. See generally M. Dougan, "When worlds collide! Competing visions of the relationship between direct effect and supremacy", 44 CML Rev. (2007), 931–963.

situation of the EU Charter of Fundamental Rights. The implication that the Court did not *exclude* reliance on Treaty provisions in horizontal situation was already apparent from the Court's case law on the free movement of goods under Articles 34 et seq. TFEU in conjunction with the Article 4(3) TEU. This case law involved actions in national courts between private parties about the limits which the provisions placed on the exercise of exclusive rights under national legislation on protection of industrial and commercial property.[191]

The Court has expressly held that the prohibition of discrimination on grounds of nationality under Articles 18, 45, 49 and 56 TFEU has horizontal direct effect. It covers collective agreements or rules in the employment field and in the field of the supply of services, e.g. *Walrave*, or *Laval.*[192] Such cases involve situations where a group or organization can exercise a certain power over private individuals, and is able to impose conditions as a result of which the exercise of the fundamental freedoms may be hindered;[193] this also extends to trade unions.[194] Following *Angonese,*[195] in principle a private party can also rely on these non-discrimination provisions against another private party which is not a collective body (in this case a bank), in a situation concerning access to employment. Possibly employment relations may be seen as a special case.[196] In *Defrenne II* the principle of equal pay for men and women for equal work in Article 157 TFEU was declared applicable not only to the action of public authorities but also "to all agreements which are intended to regulate paid labour collectively, as well as to contracts between individuals",[197] despite the fact that the provision explicitly addresses Member States, and also that it deals with a principle rather than a clear prohibition.

Such horizontal application also raises another issue: in the case of application of Treaty provisions against a Member State, the state has certain possibilities of justification of its action, based on Treaty derogations or other public interests. Private bodies, even trade unions, do not have access to these exemptions.

If such Treaty provisions can apply horizontally, the next question was whether this also held for provisions of *directives,* which specifically impose obligations on the Member States. In *Marshall I,* the Court firmly rejected this: "it must be emphasized that [...] the binding nature of a directive, which constitutes the basis for the possibility of relying on the directive before a national court, exists only in relation to 'each Member State to which it is addressed'. It follows that a directive may not of itself impose obligations on an individual and that a provision of a directive may not be relied upon as such against such a person".[198] Despite much

191. Cf. e.g. Case 78/70, *Deutsche Grammophon v. Metro SB.*
192. Case 36/74, *Walrave and Koch v. Association Union Cycliste Internationale et al.* and Case C-415/93, *Union royale belge des sociétés de football association et al. v. Bosman et al.* See moreover Joined Cases C-51/96 & C-191/97, *Deliège v. Ligue francophone de judo et disciplines associées,* and Case C-176/96, *Lehtonen and et al. v. Fédération royale belge des sociétés de basketball.* See further Ch. 13, "Free movement of goods" and Ch. 14, "Free movement of services, establishment and capital", of this book.
193. Cf. Case C-411/98, *Ferlini v. Centre Hospitalier de Luxembourg.*
194. Case C-438/05, *Viking* and Case C-341/05, *Laval.*
195. Case C-281/98, *Angonese v. Cassa di Risparmio di Bolzano,* concerning Art. 45 TFEU.
196. Case 43/75, *Defrenne II.* Case C-144/04, *Mangold.*
197. Case 43/75, *Defrenne II,* para 39. This caused a stir: see W. van Gerven, "La contribution de l'arrêt Defrenne au développement du droit communautaire", (1977) CDE, 131 et seq.
198. Case 152/84, *Marshall v. Southampton and South West Hampshire Area Health Authority (Marshall I),* para 48. See further Case C-192/94, *El Corte Inglés,* Case C-97/96, *Daihatsu-Händler* and Case C-456/98, *Centrosteel.*

criticism, the Court has maintained this stance.[199] Objections against this position have been extensively set out in the literature and in Opinions of a number of advocates general.[200]

Recognition of horizontal direct effect for provisions of directives which are not correctly implemented or not implemented on time would without doubt benefit the effectiveness of EU law, and strengthen the judicial protection of individuals. However, it should not be forgotten that direct effect is itself an exception – and a controversial one – to the rule that directives have effects as a result of their implementation by national authorities. This also explains why the type of direct effect recognized in *Defrenne II* for Treaty provisions imposing obligations on the Member States cannot be transferred to directives imposing such obligations: Treaty provisions are not subject to a "higher" rule opposing such effect. Stretching the exception in the case of directives would confer a new power on the EU "to enact obligations for individuals with immediate effect, whereas it has competence to do so only where it is empowered to adopt regulations".[201]

Given the extremely broad interpretation of the concept "state body", so as to include undertakings which have been made responsible for the provision of public services, horizontal direct effect of directives may result: provisions may be relied on by private parties against other private parties. There are difficulties in determining whether an undertaking is to be included in this category,[202] and it leads to tricky distinctions between undertakings that must be assimilated to branches of the state, and others.[203]

In *Portgás*, a chamber of the Court allowed the *state* to rely on the direct effect of an unimplemented provision of a directive against a private entity holding a public service concession. Portgás provided a public service, with the grant of special powers, and therefore fell within the category of undertaking against which the provisions of Directive 93/38 (public procurement) may be relied on by *an individual*. The Court stated that "the authorities of the Member States must be in a position to ensure that [...] bodies comply with the provisions of Directive 93/38",[204] if necessary before national courts. This finding has not been confirmed. The formulation of the conditions for direct effect have always been in relation to the possibilities for *individuals* to rely on unimplemented provisions before courts, since they lack other means of enforcing their protection. For state authorities, this is not the same: they can enact rules, issue decisions etc.

Permitting a private party to rely on a provision of a directive in a proceeding against the State may have effects for the legal position of third parties.[205] Since "a directive may not of itself impose obligations on an individual",[206] the question is where, in such triangular relations, the division lies between a permitted effect on the legal position of third parties, and

---

199. Case C-91/92, *Faccini Dori v. Recreb*, at paras. 22–24. Joined Cases C-397-403/01, *Pfeiffer*, para 108. Case C-441/14, *DI, acting on behalf of Ajos*,
200. See A.G. Lenz Opinion in Case C-91/92, *Faccini Dori*.
201. Case C-91/92, *Faccini Dori*, at para 24.
202. The formula used by the Court in Case C-188/89, *Foster v. British Gas* only gives an indication, but does not contain criteria to be used elsewhere. See also in this context Joined Cases C-253-258/96, *Kampelman*.
203. Cf. on this problem, D. Curtin, "Directives: The effectiveness of judicial protection of individual rights", (1990) CML Rev., 709–737.
204. Case C-425/12, *Portgás*, para 34.
205. Possibly disadvantageous: see the not entirely successful attempt by the Court to deny this in Case 8/81, *Becker*, at para 44. See also Case 103/88, *Fratelli Costanzo* and Case C-201/94, *The Queen v. The Medicines Control Agency, ex parte Smith & Nephew Pharmaceuticals* as good examples of such "horizontal" effects. Certain horizontal effects also result from consistent interpretation of national law (section 3.4 *supra*).
206. Case C-192/94, *El Corte Inglés v. Blázquez Rivero*, at para 15 (our emphasis), confirming the constant case law.

the forbidden imposition of obligations on such parties, i.e. acceptable or unacceptable horizontal effects.[207] *CIA Security* and *Unilever* reveal that a directive can be relied on in proceedings between private parties in certain circumstances.[208] CIA Security concerned Directive 83/189/EEC, which requires notification of national technical standards and regulations. The ECJ found that a national court should not apply a national technical regulation which has not been notified in accordance with Directive 83/189, even in a dispute between private parties; it thus acquired "indirect" horizontal effect. The Directive makes the entry into force of national technical regulations which should have been notified dependent on the agreement or lack of objection of the Commission; the Court ruled that the non-applicability of national regulations adopted contrary to the Directive may be relied on in civil proceedings between private parties concerning contractual rights and obligations.[209] In *Delena Wells*, the Court specified that an individual "may not rely on a directive against a Member State where it is a matter of a State obligation directly linked to the performance of another obligation falling, pursuant to that directive, on a third party"; however, "mere adverse repercussions on the rights of third parties" do not justify preventing an individual from invoking the provisions of a directive against the Member State concerned.[210] Academic efforts to order the Court's case law on this point systematically tend to get wrecked each time by new judgments which do not wholly fit the system designed.[211]

In relation to triangular situations, mention should also be made of the so-called "New Approach Directives", referring to harmonized standards established by private bodies. Whereas in *Fra Bo*[212] it seemed that, in such cases, there was an indirect effect in horizontal situations, the Court in *Elliott* seems to have returned to a more orthodox approach, as far as horizontal effects are concerned[213] – it guaranteed the required judicial protection of individuals by deciding that it can itself review the standard involved.

The Court has made special efforts in the field of non-discrimination, following the adoption of Directive 2000/78.[214] It has aimed to achieve the result of the (unimplemented) directive in horizontal situations, while still not actually applying the directive. In these cases it identified an underlying general principle, which the directive in question embodies, and applied

207. Cf. C.W.A. Timmermans, "Community Directives revisited", (1997) YEL, 1–28, at 17.
208. Case C-194/94, *CIA Security International v. Signalson and Securitel* and Case C-443/98, *Unilever Italia v. Central Food.*
209. In Case C-226/97, *Johannes Martinus Lemmens,* however, Mr Lemmens challenged his conviction for drunken driving on the ground that the breathalyser had not been notified under the Directive; he was unsuccessful. The Court stated in Case C- 443/98, *Unilever Italia* that "Directive 83/189 does not in any way define the substantive scope of the legal rule on the basis of which the national court must decide the case before it. It creates neither rights nor obligations for individuals".
210. Case C-201/02, *Delena Wells.* paras. 56–58.
211. See for an overview, the critical annotation by M. Dougan of Case C-443/98, *Unilever Italia,* 38 CML Rev. (2001), 1503- 1517; for a new attempt to find a theoretically convincing explanation, see M. Dougan, op. cit. *supra* note 190.
212. In Case C-171/11, *Fra.bo SpA v. Deutsche Vereinigung des Gas- und Wasserfaches eV (DVGW) – Technisch Wissenschaftlicher Verein,* it seemed that the market freedoms might apply to certification bodies that monitor compliance with technical standards, cf. R. van Gestel and H. Micklitz, "European integration through standardization: How judicial review is breaking down the club house of private standardization bodies", 50 CML Rev. (2013), 145–182.
213. Case C-613/14, *James Elliott Construction Limited.* Cf. Annotation by A. Volpato, 54 CML Rev. (2017), 591–603. Cf. also Opinion of A.G. Trstenjak in Case C-80/06, *Carp v. Ecorad,* para 34; Opinion of A.G. Mazák in Case C-254/05, *Commission v. Belgium.*
214. Council Directive 2000/78/EC of 27 Nov. 2000 establishing a general framework for equal treatment in employment and occupation, O.J. 2000, L 303/16.

the general principle rather than the directive – even though the direct application of general principles is in some jurisdictions also contentious.[215] As is well known, since Case C-260/89, *ERT,* general principles of unwritten EU law must be respected by Member States within the scope of application of EU law. National courts must appraise the application of national provisions within the scope of EU law also against general principles of EU law. In this case law, the ECJ found that the limitation in respect of the application of provisions of unimplemented directives when horizontal situations are concerned, does not operate when general principles are concerned. Thus, in *Mangold,* concerning non-discrimination in respect of age, the Court found that Directive 2000/78 aims only "to lay down a general framework for combating discrimination on the grounds of religion or belief, disability, age or sexual orientation", but that the source of the actual principle underlying the prohibition of those forms of discrimination was found in various international instruments and in the constitutional traditions common to the Member States.[216] As it later summarized: "Directive 2000/78 does not itself lay down the general principle prohibiting discrimination on grounds of age but simply gives concrete expression to that principle".[217] The situation in *Mangold* involved two separate difficulties preventing the directive from being effective: the period prescribed for transposition had not yet expired, and the conflict was between two private parties. Since the general principle was used, both these hurdles were overcome, and the national provision at odds with the directive had to be disapplied; the Court ruled: "It is the responsibility of the national court to guarantee the full effectiveness of the general principle of non-discrimination in respect of age, setting aside any provision of national law which may conflict with Community law, even where the period prescribed for transposition of that directive has not yet expired".[218]

The Court's decision that horizontal direct effect may result from a general principle of EU law is remarkable – even though this meant setting aside *incompatible national law,* rather than applying a principle directly. General principles are a means to "fill gaps", but are usually considered a means to protect private individuals *vis-à-vis* public authorities. Moreover, their unwritten and abstract nature may conflict with legal certainty; they raise similar problems if applied to impose obligations on individuals to those attaching to directives. Moreover, the general principles of EU law are also derived from various international instruments, while horizontal direct effect in such a context is not usual.

One argument supporting horizontal direct effect of directives is that national courts are bound to apply directives in their capacity as branches of the state; arguably, they are bound by provisions of a directive when resolving a dispute between private parties. Nevertheless, in *AKT,* concerning Directive 2008/104/EC on temporary agency work, the Court made an explicit distinction between the obligation imposed on national competent authorities under that directive and any obligation on the courts to disapply national rules which are not justified.[219] This reasoning may seem to contradict the Court's usual view that the obligation on Member States to take all measures necessary to achieve the result prescribed by a directive also extends to their judiciary.[220]

---

215. E.g. in Denmark: DKSC Case No. 15/2014 *Dansk Industri (DI) acting for Ajos A/S vs. The estate left by A.*
216. Case C-144/04, *Mangold,*
217. Case C-441/14, *Ajos* para 23.
218. Case C-144/04, *Mangold,* operative part. This was confirmed in Case C-555/07, *Kücükdeveci,* Case C-176/12, *Association de médiation sociale,* and Case C-441/14, *Ajos.*
219. Case C-533/13, *AKT.* See generally A. Davies, "The legal nature of the duty to review prohibitions or restrictions on the use of temporary agency work: *AKT*", 53 CML Rev. (2016), 493.
220. E.g. Case C-72/95, *Kraaijeveld et al.* and Case C-106/89, *Marleasing.* An alternative solution in Case C-533/13, *AKT* would have been to find the relevant provision not sufficiently precise to be applied directly.

One question which is not resolved is whether the Charter of Fundamental Rights can be applied in horizontal situations. In *AMS*, the Court did not rule this out in general terms, but examined specifically the provision at issue in that case, finding that it needed "more specific expression in European Union or national law".[221]

4. Judicial protection in national courts

4.1 National courts are EU courts

In the Union's decentralized structure, the application and enforcement of EU law takes place principally in the day-to-day legal activities within the Member States. The national courts thus occupy a central position in this process. There is a distinction between the competence of the EU to establish rights and remedies, and the role of national procedural law in providing for them. It is the task of national courts to decide whether national rules and administrative acts are compatible with EU law, whether individuals have acted in accordance with the obligations incumbent on them under EU law, and to give effect to the consequences of such decisions under national law or, in some cases, under EU law itself.[222] Where necessary, they are guided in this by the Court of Justice through a preliminary ruling under Article 267 TFEU. The national courts may also be faced with the question whether acts of the Union institutions are compatible with the EU law on which they are based, including the protection of fundamental rights (though they may not answer this question themselves).[223] It is their responsibility in particular to provide the legal protection which individuals derive from the rules of EU law and to ensure that those rules are fully effective. The national courts can thus be seen as the ordinary courts of the Union, and "are closely involved in the correct application and uniform interpretation of European Union law and also in the protection of individual rights conferred by that legal order".[224] This role is so important that the ECJ precluded the establishment of a separate court which would deal with litigation on patents, because this would "deprive [national] courts of their task, as 'ordinary' courts within the European Union legal order, to implement European Union law and, thereby, of the power provided for in Article 267 TFEU, or, as the case may be, the obligation, to refer questions for a preliminary ruling in the field concerned".[225] National courts must be able to deal with the full range of EU law, in order to ensure the full application of EU law in all Member States and to ensure judicial protection of an individual's rights under that law; the tasks attributed to the national courts and to the Court of Justice respectively are indispensable to the preservation of the very nature of the law established by the Treaties.[226] The EU must have a "complete system of legal remedies", so that any measure adopted by the Union's institutions can be reviewed, either directly in an action before the ECJ or through a preliminary reference coming from a case before the domestic courts.[227]

221. The Charter article and a directive could not be combined to require that national law breaching the directive had to be set aside, because the Charter article by itself did not confer a right which individuals could rely on as such, so it could not be different in conjunction with the directive. Case C-176/12, *AMS*, para 49.
222. E.g. the nullity of certain contracts under competition rules in Art. 101(2) TFEU (nullity), or liability of Member States for damage resulting from infringements of EU law attributable to them, discussed *infra* (section 6).
223. Joined Cases C-397-403/01, *Pfeiffer*, para 111. National courts may decide that they do not doubt the compatibility of such acts.
224. Opinion 1/09, *Patent Court*, para 84.
225. Ibid. para 80. See also Case C-284/16, *Achmea*, paras. 31-37.
226. Ibid. para 85.
227. Case 294/83, *Les Verts v. Parliament*, para 23. See on the preliminary reference system and the Court's rules on standing, Ch. 10, "The Court of Justice of the EU", of this book. Special problems may also arise in

As explained above, national courts are obliged to interpret national law as far as possible in conformity with EU law, to apply directly effective provisions of EU law, and, in the case of conflict between the latter and national provisions, to set aside national law.[228] However, the degree to which the national court can apply EU law also depends on the possibilities offered by its national legal order. In the Union, "when provisions of the Treaty or of regulations confer power or impose obligations upon the states for the purposes of the implementation of [Union] law, the question of how the exercise of such powers and the fulfilment of such obligations may be entrusted by Member States to specific national bodies is solely a matter for the constitutional system of each state"; this is known as the *principle of national procedural autonomy*.[229]

National law is the conduit for EU law to work in the Member States. Whether Union law can actually be enforced depends on what legal remedies are afforded by the national legal system, and under what conditions these remedies may be used. Various questions arise. Can someone who believes that another party has acted in breach of EU law seek damages for loss suffered, or an injunction restraining the conduct concerned, or repayment of sums paid but not due, or the quashing or suspension of the relevant decision of an authority? Which appeal or limitation periods apply? And before which court must they appeal – the civil courts or some kind of administrative court?

4.2 *Enforcement of EU law or of EU law-based rights as a duty of Member States*

Member States have a duty to cooperate in achieving the full effect of EU law – a duty which is also put in terms of effectiveness, or *effet utile*.[230] They also have a duty to ensure the effective protection of rights derived from EU law. Furthermore, although Member States are responsible for the procedural rules within their legal order, one of the limits on their freedom in doing this is that they should not make it impossible for EU rights to be exercised – and this is also referred to as the principle of effectiveness. These various concepts of effectiveness overlap to a great extent, but are not precisely the same.[231] In some cases, the need for effectiveness of a policy may lead to a less favourable situation for some individuals: examples are in the recovery of State aid, or competition leniency programmes.[232]

In many leading cases, the emphasis is on the protection of rights based on EU law; the national courts have a special role within the EU legal order for the protection of such rights. A new sentence introduced by the Treaty of Lisbon, in Article 19(1) TEU, states that Member States shall provide remedies sufficient to ensure effective legal protection in the fields covered by Union law. This provision codifies the Court's case law on decentralized judicial protection, in particular its finding in *UPA* that "it is for the Member States to establish a system of legal remedies and procedures which ensure respect for the right to effective judicial protection".[233] The

---

providing judicial protection in relation to administrative acts adopted in so-called composite procedures, involving national and EU authorities, see F. Brito Bastos, "Derivative illegality in European composite administrative procedures", (2018) CML Rev., 101-134, and Case C-97/91, *Borelli*.

228. Sections 2 and 3 of this Chapter.
229. Joined Cases 51 & 54/71, *International Fruit Company et al. v. Produktschap voor Groenten en fruit* (*International Fruit Company II*), at para 4. See further *infra* section 4.4.
230. Case 14/68 *Walt Wilhelm* "practical effectiveness"; Case 106/77, *Simmenthal*. Also called "full effect".
231. S. Prechal and R. Widdershoven, "Redefining the relationship between 'Rewe-effectiveness' and effective judicial protection", 4 *Review of European Administrative Law* (2011), 31–50; J. Krommendijk, "Is there light on the horizon? The distinction between "*Rewe* effectiveness" and the principle of effective judicial protection in Article 47 of the Charter after *Orizzonte*", 52 CML Rev. (2016), 1395–1418.
232. Case C-119/05, *Lucchini*; C-428/14, *DHL Express (Italy) v. Autorita' Garante della Concorrenza e del Mercato*.
233. Case C-50/00, *UPA*, para 41.

new sentence is intended to help solve the problems of access to judicial review for individuals who lack standing before the Court of Justice to contest Union measures directly, but have no means to challenge national implementing measures either, so as to obtain indirect access to the ECJ through a preliminary reference.[234] According to the Court, regardless of the national judicial arrangements, the Member States must ensure the protection of rights of individuals based on EU law: "the Member States [have] none the less responsibility for ensuring that those rights are effectively protected in each case".[235]

Article 19(1)(2) TEU is not generally intended to require new remedies to be created; this may be necessary, though, where it is not otherwise possible to guarantee rights conferred on individuals under EU law or if the only way to have access to a court is by infringing the law.[236] Member States should not prevent national courts from performing their task as EU courts, which means there is also a duty for the legislature. According to Opinion 1/09, Article 19(1)(2) TEU requires Member States to integrate national courts as EU courts in national systems with a view to complying with their mandate under EU law pursuant to Article 4(3) TEU.[237] This obligation on the Member States has also meant in the past that direct review of a discriminatory rule of national procedural law against Article 18 TFEU had to be possible.[238]

One area where the extent of judicial protection as a matter of EU law – whether afforded by the ECJ or in cooperation with the national courts – is far from clear is that of measures taken in the context of the sovereign debt crisis and the eurocrisis. Measures such as Memoranda of Understanding (MoU) were not EU law, even though EU institutions were involved. In all cases, the ECJ has ruled that national measures were not implementing EU law; remedies must be sought in national law (or under the ECHR).[239] It should also be noted that the jurisdiction of the CJEU is limited in the field of CFSP,[240] leaving a special role for national courts.

4.3 *Principle of effective judicial protection: Charter Article 47*

As the Court summarized in *Unibet*: "the principle of effective judicial protection is a general principle of [Union] law stemming from the constitutional traditions common to the Member

234. Case C-50/00 *UPA*; Case C-263/02 P. *Jégo-Quéré*, especially Opinion of A.G. Jacobs. At the same time, other changes were introduced, to relax slightly the standing requirements for individuals in relation to so-called "regulatory acts", under Art. 263(4) TFEU; see Ch. 10, "The Court of Justice of the EU", of this book.
235. Case C-93/12, *ET Agrokonsulting-04-Velko Stoyanov*, para 35; citing Case C-224/01, *Köbler*; Case C-268/06, *Impact*; Case C-12/08, *Mono Car Styling*; and Joined Cases C-317-320/08, *Alassini and Others*. See also A.G. Wathelet Opinion in Case C-682/15, *Berlioz*, para 67: "[...] it is on the Member States that the second paragraph of Article 19 TEU imposes the obligation to provide 'remedies sufficient to ensure effective legal protection in the fields covered by Union law'".
236. Case C-583/11 P, *Inuit*, para 105; Case C-432/05, *Unibet*, para 40.
237. Opinion 1/09, *Patent Court*, paras. 68–70; see C. Lacchi, "Multilevel judicial protection in the EU and preliminary references", 53 CML Rev., 679–707.
238. This related to *cautio judicatum solvi* in Case C-43/95, *Data Delecta Aktiebolag and Ronny Forsberg v. MSL Dynamics*; see also Case C-323/95, *Hayes v. Kronenberger* and Case C-122/96, *Saldanha and MTS Securities Corporation v. Hiross*, involving claims based on national law brought by nationals of other Member States.
239. Joined Cases C-8/15 P, to C-10/15 P, *Ledra and Mallis*. National measures implementing MoU do not implement EU law, as the MoU are not EU law. Cf. also *Pringle*, C-370/12. Nevertheless, the Charter should apply to *all* acts of the institutions. See also Case C-128/12, *Sindicato dos Bancários do Norte and others* – in these Portuguese cases, in which questions regarding the Charter were referred, the ECJ declared that it lacked jurisdiction, since the national legislation providing for salary reductions for public sector workers was not a measure implementing EU law.
240. Art. 24 TEU. See, however, Case C-72/15, *Rosneft*, para 74, where the ECJ found that it had jurisdiction in preliminary rulings. See Ch. 40, "Common foreign and security policy and security and defence policy", of this book.

States", and enshrined in Articles 6 and 13 ECHR "and which has also been reaffirmed by Article 47 of the Charter of fundamental rights of the European Union".[241] Since the Treaty of Lisbon, the Charter is binding, with the same force as the treaties. Article 47 guarantees the right to an effective remedy and to a fair trial.

Under the principle of cooperation laid down in Article 4(3) TEU, Member States have to ensure judicial protection of an individual's rights under EU law.[242] Not only must an appeal be possible against a decision of a national authority denying a person the exercise of those rights, but the judicial control must also be effective.[243] EU law does not require a Member State to establish a procedure which involves a more extensive review than that carried out by the Court of Justice in similar cases.[244]

Alongside the principle of effective judicial protection, it is now Article 47 of the Charter which is the major source, sometimes in the form of a double reference to the "fundamental right to effective judicial protection, as enshrined in Article 47 of the Charter".[245] The Charter applies to all EU institutions and bodies, and to the Member States only when they are implementing Union law (see Charter Art. 51(1)).[246] National courts have made many preliminary references regarding this provision, but the ECJ has often declared that it lacks jurisdiction.[247] Moreover, in various judgments, the Court of Justice has restricted its consideration of the remedies required to those set out in secondary EU law, rather than applying Article 47 of the Charter, even if the referring court asks questions about that provision.[248] Article 47 is also used to interpret the rules laid down in secondary law, so that rights granted therein can be effectively enforced,[249] and has been used to push national courts towards providing remedies in the environmental field in accordance with Aarhus Convention obligations.[250]

Berlioz confirmed that Article 47 of the Charter has a wider scope *ratione materiae* than Article 6 ECHR, as it applies where "[the] rights and freedoms guaranteed by the law of the Union are violated" (whether or not they are set out in the Charter.[251] In that case, the link to EU law

---

241. Case C-432/05, *Unibet (London) Ltd, Unibet (International) Ltd v. Justitiekanslern,* para 37, citing Case 222/84, *Johnston*; Case 222/86, *Heylens and Others*; Case C-424/99, *Commission v. Austria*; Case C-50/00 P, *Unión de Pequeños Agricultores*; and Case C-467/01, *Eribrand.* See also Ch. 10, "The Court of Justice of the EU" and Ch. 4, "Fundamental rights", of this book.
242. Case C-432/05, *Unibet,* para 38.
243. See Cases 222/84, *Johnston* ("an effective judicial remedy"), 222/86, *Unectef v. Heylens*, C-13/94, *P v. S and Cornwall County Council* and C-185/97, *Coote v. Granada Hospitality*. In this sense also Case 36/75, *Rutili v. Ministre de l'intérieur*.
244. Case C-120/97, *Upjohn v. The Licensing Authority et al.*, at para 36; where national authorities have a wide measure of discretion in implementing EU law, any national procedure for judicial review of relevant decisions of national authorities must enable the court or tribunal seized of an application for annulment of such decisions effectively to apply the relevant principles and rules of EU law when reviewing their legality.
245. Case C-362/14, *Maximillian Schrems,* para 95.
246. See Ch. 4, "Fundamental rights", of this book on the scope of application of the Charter, and M. Dougan, op. cit. *supra* note 124.
247. E.g. Joined Cases C-532/15 and C-538/15, *Eurosaneamientos SL*.
248. See e.g. on Dublin Regulation: Case C-63/15, *Mehrdad Ghezelbash v. Staatssecretaris van Veiligheid en Justitie* and Case C-155/15, *George Karim v. Migrationsverket*. A.G. Sharpston in *Ghezelbash* considered that the right to an effective remedy has a very broad scope in the EU legal order, and that it must apply in all proceedings likely to culminate in a measure adversely affecting a person, paras. 82–83.
249. Case C-239/14, *Abdoulaye Amadou Tall v. Centre public d'action sociale de Huy*; Case C-396/13, *Sähköalojen ammattiliitto ry v. Elektrobudowa Spółka Akcyjna,* on the possibility to bring claims for minimum wages with regard to posted workers.
250. C-243/15, *Lesoochranarske zoskupenie VLK II*.
251. Case C-682/15, *Berlioz Investment Fund,* see esp. paras. 53–59.

was the implementation of Directive 2011/16, on cooperation between tax authorities. The ECJ had ruled earlier that that directive does not confer rights on individuals;[252] however, if a party is sanctioned for not providing information requested on the basis of the directive – because it is disputed whether the request fulfils conditions laid down in the directive – there must be a right to judicial protection. That "right" is the protection against arbitrary or disproportionate intervention by public authorities.

Despite the fact that neither the obligation in Article 19 TEU nor the Charter are intended to create new remedies, it has been argued that the principle of effective judicial protection could work as a standard entailing positive (procedural) obligations, giving rise to new remedies and national powers.[253] In this sense, it is "more encompassing", and could entail obligations to provide reasons for a decision, legal aid or interim relief.[254] It has also been argued that the principle of effective judicial protection includes a party's right to a preliminary reference.[255]

4.4 *National procedural autonomy, principles equivalence and effectiveness*

Pursuant to the principle of sincere cooperation, in Article 4(3) TEU, the national courts must protect EU rights. It is, however, for the national legal system of each Member State to fix the procedures.[256]

In the leading case, *Rewe*, the ECJ ruled "in the absence of [Union] rules on this subject, it is for the domestic legal system of each Member State to designate the courts having jurisdiction and to determine the procedural conditions governing actions at law intended to ensure the protection of the rights which citizens have from the direct effect of [Union] law, it being understood that such conditions *cannot be less favourable than those relating to similar actions of a domestic* nature". It went on to say "the position would be different only if the conditions and time-limits made it *impossible in practice* to exercise the rights which the national courts *are obliged to protect*".[257]

Thus *three* elements apply. The *first* is the *duty to afford judicial protection,* deduced from Article 4(3) TEU, which obliges the Member States and their organs, including national courts, to ensure compliance with the obligations resulting from EU law, also reflected at individual level by the fundamental right to an effective remedy laid down in Article 47 Charter. The *second* element concerns the *procedural autonomy* of the Member States' legal systems. The concept of procedure covers all substantive and organizational rules and principles applicable to actions brought, and the determination of the courts having jurisdiction. This applies to the extent there are no provisions of EU law dealing with the point or harmonizing national provisions.[258] The *third* element is composed of the *two conditions* laid down in the case law, from *Rewe* onwards:

---

252. Case C-276/12, *Sabou.*
253. J. Krommendijk, op. cit. *supra* note 231.
254. S. Prechal and R. Widdershoven, op. cit. *supra* note 231, at 40. Case C-562/13, *Abdida,* para 50, gives an example of interim relief where enforcement of a return decision "may expose the third country national concerned to a serious risk of grave and irreversible deterioration in his state of health".
255. C. Lacchi, op. cit. *supra* note 237. There could also be a right to a preliminary reference under national law.
256. Case 33/76, *Rewe v. Landwirtschaftskammer für das Saarland,* Case 45/76, *Comet v. Produktschap voor Siergewassen;* Case 265/78, *Ferwerda v. Produktschap voor Vee en Vlees,* at para 10, Case C-343/96, *Dilexport Srl v. Amministrazione delle Finanze dello Stato.* See, critically, A. Biondi, "The European Court of Justice and certain national procedural limitations: Not such a tough relationship, (1999) CML Rev., at 1271–1287. C. Kakouris, "Do the Member States possess judicial procedural 'autonomy'?", 34 CML Rev. (1997), 1389–1412.
257. Case 33/76, *Rewe v. Landwirtschaftskammer für das Saarland,* para 5 (emphasis added).
258. Many procedural details are contained in secondary EU law, especially regarding state aid, public procurement, agricultural subsidies, and – more recently – migration and asylum, see elsewhere in this book.

conditions for claims brought under EU law may not be less favourable than claims brought purely under national law (*principle of equivalence*), and the exercise of the rights must not be made "virtually impossible" or excessively difficult (*principle of effectiveness*).[259]

In *Peterbroeck* and *Van Schijndel*[260] the Court developed guidelines on how to resolve conflicts between the principles of effectiveness and equivalence on the one hand and the procedural autonomy of the Member States on the other. A balance must be sought between the interests served by the national rule that makes the application of EU law impossible or excessively difficult, and the interest of effective protection of rights which individuals derive from the direct application of EU law. The basic principles of the domestic judicial system, such as protection of the rights of the defence, the principle of legal certainty and the proper conduct of procedure, must be taken into consideration by the national court, which must have reference to the role of the provision in question in the procedure, its progress and its special features, viewed as a whole, before the various national instances.

The principle of *equivalence* is an application of the principle of non-discrimination on grounds of nationality (Art. 18 TFEU)[261] in the specific field of procedural rules guaranteeing the EU law rights of individuals in the domestic legal systems of the Member States. It requires that provisions should be applied to claims based on EU law which are no less favourable than for "similar" claims based on national law.[262] The question what claims under national law are "similar" to claims based on EU law can be problematic. The national courts are the only courts directly acquainted with the national procedural rules, and the Court of Justice can assist them in this with information on the interpretation of EU law. For instance, it is important that the national courts examine both the subject and the main characteristics of the national claims which are alleged to be "similar".[263] The Court has found that actions alleging breaches of EU may be "similar [...] in the light of their purpose and their essential characteristics" to actions alleging breach of the national constitution.[264]

Review of national procedural rules in the light of the principle of *effectiveness* has led to case law in many areas. Rules of evidence which had as a consequence that it was practically impossible or excessively difficult to have taxes, duties or dues which were levied in infringement of EU law reimbursed were found contrary to EU law – even if the rules themselves were applied

---

259. For the consequences of these principles for national law, see e.g. Case 68/79, *Just v. Danish Ministry for Fiscal Affairs*; Case 170/84, *Bilka v. Weber von Hartz*; Case 222/84, *Johnston*, and Case 109/88, *Handels- og Kontorfunktionærernes Forbund i Danmark v. Dansk Arbejdsgiverforening, acting on behalf of Danfoss* (law on evidence), and Case 130/79, *Express Dairy Foods v. Intervention Board for Agricultural Produce* and Case 54/81, *Fromme v. BALM* (calculation of interest).

260. Case C-312/93, *Peterbroeck, Van Campenhout & Cie v. Belgian State*, and Joined Cases C-430 & 431/93, *Van Schijndel and Van Veen*. See generally M. Hoskins, "Tilting the balance: Supremacy and national procedural rules", (1996) EL Rev., 365–377.

261. A direct review of the discriminatory rule of national procedural law (*cautio judicatum solvi*) against Art. 18 TFEU was needed in Case C-43/95, *Data Delecta Aktiebolag and Ronny Forsberg v. MSL Dynamics*; Case C-323/95, *Hayes v. Kronenberger* and Case C-122/96, *Saldanha and MTS Securities Corporation v. Hiross*. These cases involved EU law claims brought by nationals of other Member States.

262. Case C-93/12, *ET Agrokonsulting-04-Velko Stoyanov*, para 38; Case C-3/16, *Aquino*, para 50, citing, Case C-429/12, *Pohl*, para 26, and C-429/15, *Danqua*, para 30. It does not mean, of course, that a Member State is obliged to apply the most favourable national rule to EU law claims (Case C-231/96, *Edilizia Industriale Siderurgica v. Ministero delle Finanze*).

263. See on this problem in particular Case C-326/96, *Levez v. Jennings* and Case C-78/98, *Preston et al. v. Fletcher et al.*, and the Opinion of the A.G. in these cases. See also M. Bobek, "Why there is no principle of 'procedural autonomy' of the Member States" in B. de Witte and H.-W. Micklitz (Eds.), *The European Court of Justice and the Autonomy of the Member States* (Intersentia, 2011).

264. See Case C-118/08, *Transportes Urbanos v. Administración del Estado*; also Case C-69/14, *Târşia*, para 34.

without distinction.[265] The burden of proof must be reversed when this is necessary to prevent employees who suffer from factual discrimination from being deprived of any effective means of enforcing the principle of equal pay.[266] The national court may be obliged to ignore national rules which prevent it from granting interim relief in a case where the ECJ has yet to judge on the existence of rights claimed under EU law, alleged to be breached by national provisions.[267] A certificate or declaration by a national authority may not be treated as conclusive evidence excluding the exercise of any power of review by the courts.[268] National legislation determining an individual's standing and legal interest in bringing proceedings may not undermine the right to effective judicial protection.[269] An individual must be able to bring a separate action on the basis of Directive 93/13 on unfair terms in consumer contracts, regardless of a pending collective action.[270]

There is extensive case law on the admissibility of time-limits for bringing claims based on EU law in relation to effectiveness. The ECJ upholds the principle of legal certainty, and "it is compatible with [EU] law to lay down reasonable time-limits for bringing proceedings in the interests of legal certainty".[271] *Emmott* was a rare exception to the predominance of legal certainty;[272] here the ECJ ruled that a period laid down by national law within which proceedings must be initiated can only start to run as of the moment at which a directive is correctly implemented. Later case law showed that this exception is very limited: even when a Member State has not properly implemented a directive (in time), EU law does not prevent a restriction on the retroactive effect of claims to unpaid benefits or the application of a limitation period on claims to reimbursement of duties levied contrary to the directive.[273]

National courts may be obliged to apply directly effective provisions of EU law of their own motion (*ex officio*).[274] This could oblige them to abandon their passive role, and rely on facts and circumstances other than those invoked by the parties.[275] National courts must, of their

265. Case 199/82, *San Giorgio;* Joined Cases 331, 376 & 378/85, *Les Fils de Jules Bianco and J. Girard Fils v. Directeur Général des douanes et droits indirects*. These cases concerned assumptions and rules of evidence.
266. Case 109/88, *Danfoss*; Case C-127/92, *Enderby v. Frenchay Health Authority et al.* and Case C-400/93, *Specialarbejderforbundet i Danmark v. Dansk Industri.*
267. Case C-213/89, *R. v. Secretary of State for Transport, ex parte Factortame*: at the time, the common law ruled that an interim injunction did not lie against the Crown to suspend the effect of an Act of Parliament.
268. Case 222/84, *Johnston*. For the strict limits under the principle of effectiveness for the application of hardship clauses under national fiscal law in relation to agricultural levies, see Case C-290/91, *Peter v. Hauptzollamt Regensburg.*
269. Case C-432/05, *Unibet*, para 42 and the case law cited. See also Case C-174/02, *Streekgewest Westelijk Noord-Brabant v. Staatssecretaris van Financiën.*
270. Joined Cases C-381/14 & C-385/14, *Jorge Sales Sinués and Youssouf Drame Ba v. Caixabank et al.*
271. Case C-343/96, *Dilexport*, at para 26, with reference to earlier case law. The fact that reasonable time-limits may prevent an appeal being brought is also not considered sufficient to turn a lower court into a court adjudicating at last instance in the sense of Art. 267(3) TFEU, cf. Case C-3/16, *Aquino*, para 44.
272. Case C-208/90, *Emmott v. Minister for Social Welfare and Attorney General.*
273. The Court later distinguished *Emmot*, due to its particular circumstances, where the time-bar had the result of depriving the applicant of any opportunity whatever to rely on her right, Case C-188/95, *Fantask and others v. Industriministeriet*, para 51. Cf. also Case C-338/91, *Steenhorst-Neerings v. Bestuur van de Bedrijfsvereniging voor Detailhandel, Ambachten en Huisvrouwen*; Case C-410/92, *Johnson v. Chief Adjudication Officer* (*Johnson II*). In Case C-231/96, *Edilizia Industriale Siderurgica*, para 48, the Court explicitly distinguished the case from *Emmott.*
274. Case 166/73, *Rheinmühlen Düsseldorf v. Einfuhr- und Vorratsstelle für Getreide und Futtermittel* (*Rheinmühlen II*); Joined Cases C-87-89/90, *Verholen et al. v. Sociale Verzekeringsbank Amsterdam.* Joined Cases C-430 & 431/93, *Van Schijndel*, Case C-312/93, *Peterbroeck, Van Campenhout & Cie v. Belgian State.*
275. Joined Cases C-430 & 431/93, *Van Schijndel*, para 22.

own motion,[276] raise points of law based on binding EU law rules not just if rules of national law *oblige* them to raise of their own motion points of law based on binding domestic rules, but also if these national rules *enable* them to do so.[277] A rule of national law preventing the procedure laid down in Article 267 TFEU from being followed must be set aside.[278] In *Eco-Swiss*, the ECJ ruled that if domestic rules of procedure require a national court to grant an application for annulment of an arbitration award where such an application is founded on failure to observe national rules of public policy, it must also grant such an application where it is founded on failure to comply with the prohibition laid down in Article 101 TFEU; presumably such rules are thus public policy.[279]

In the area of consumer protection, the need to ensure that consumers are given the effective protection which Council Directive 93/13/EEC on unfair terms in consumer contracts seeks to achieve, was a reason to require courts to apply EU rules *ex officio*.[280] In *Asturcom*, a Spanish case, the Court gave strong "guidance" to the national court, to steer it towards finding that certain provisions of Directive 93/13 had the same rank as domestic provisions of public policy;[281] the national court would therefore be obliged to apply these of its own motion, and also to give due effect, in accordance with national law, to the consequences of its finding. These cases can be seen in terms of the principle of equivalence, but with some centralizing tendencies.

The national courts have a substantial degree of flexibility in determining whether national measures are compatible with the principles of equivalence and effectiveness.[282] At the same time, it is constant case law that, to the extent that courts enjoy discretion, they must use that discretion in favour of EU law.[283] The procedural autonomy of the Member States is far from absolute.[284] The principles of equivalence and effectiveness require the national courts, informed by the case law of the Court of Justice, particularly in the context of Article 267 TFEU, to apply the rules and principles of national law in such a way as to ensure the full application of EU law. Of course, the national court must not step beyond its judicial function; it cannot simply create new national rules; the extent to which the national legislature awards its courts discretion is thus also relevant.[285] What courts can and must do is apply EU law, as interpreted by the ECJ, if necessary setting aside any obstacles arising from national law. Even in relation to the recovery of taxes levied by a Member State in breach of EU law, the Member States are also free to designate the courts and tribunals having jurisdiction and to lay down the detailed procedural rules governing actions at law for safeguarding the rights which taxpayers derive from EU law.[286]

---

276. See also Case C-72/95, *Kraaijeveld*, Case C-435/97, *World Wildlife Fund et al.*, and Case C-287/98, *Linster*.
277. Joined Cases C-430 & 431/93, *Van Schijndel*, para 15.
278. Cf. Case 166/73, *Rheinmühlen II*.
279. Case C-126/97, *Eco Swiss China Time Ltd v. Benetton International NV*. See Case C-518/11, *UPC Nederland BV v. Gemeente Hilversum*, where the referring court asked about this though the ECJ did not give an answer.
280. Joined Cases C-240-244/98, *Océano Grupo Editorial and Salvat Editores*, and Cases C-473/00, *Cofidis* and C-168/05, *Mostaza Claro*.
281. Case C-40/08, *Asturcom Telecomunicaciones*, paras. 51, 52: Art. 6 of Directive 93/13 must be regarded as a provision of equal standing to national rules of public policy; the Directive is essential for certain tasks entrusted to the EU.
282. Cf. Case C-93/12, *ET Agrokonsulting-04-Velko Stoyanov*, para 38, also citing Case C-326/96 *Levez* and Case C-63/08 *Pontin*; Joined Cases C-222-225/05, *J. van der Weerd and others v. Minister van Landbouw, Natuur en Voedselkwaliteit*, paras. 39 and 40.
283. Case C-453/00, *Kühne & Heitz*.
284. M. Bobek, op. cit. *supra* note 263.
285. A. Wallerman, "Towards an EU law doctrine on the exercise of discretion in national courts? The Member States' self- imposed limits on national procedural autonomy", 53 CML Rev. (2016), 339–360.
286. Case C-69/14, *Dragoş Constantin Târşia v. Statul român*, para 23.

However, it is ultimately the Member States – not just their judiciary – which have "responsibility for ensuring that those rights are effectively protected in each case".[287]

Overall, there can remain differences in judicial protection between different Member States.[288] The ECJ case law sets limits and guidelines for the procedural autonomy of the Member States where EU provisions harmonizing procedure are lacking,[289] but uniformity does not result. National procedural law will never be completely harmonized, but the current situation suffers from its case-driven nature, and leads to many preliminary references to the ECJ. The differences in judicial protection within the EU threaten the uniformity of judicial *protection*, but also the uniform *enforcement* of EU law. To overcome this to some extent, EU secondary law increasingly includes provisions on procedural issues.[290]

Ideally, the principle of effective judicial protection and Article 47 of the Charter should remedy the lack of uniformity to some extent, without being too intrusive. In the current situation it is far from being predictable when the ECJ will solve a case using Article 47 of the Charter or the principles of effective judicial protection, or procedural autonomy as limited by the principles of equivalence and effectiveness, or a combination. In *Orizzonte Salute*, the ECJ examined the Italian scheme at issue in the context of procedural autonomy and the limitations thereto read in the light of Article 47 of the Charter. The Advocate General primarily approached the matter from the point of view of the fundamental right to an effective remedy under Article 47 of the Charter.[291] In *ET Agrokonsulting-04-Velko Stoyanov*, the ECJ used the principles of equivalence and effectiveness *as well as* Article 47 of the Charter – although the detailed analysis is based on principles of equivalence and effectiveness.[292]

4.5 *Res judicata*

The rules implementing the principle of *res judicata* are a matter for the national legal order, in accordance with the principle of the procedural autonomy of the Member States.[293] Within the EU legal order, an EU act can only be invalidated, and a provision of EU law only authoritatively interpreted, by the Court of Justice. The effects of such judgments are however binding throughout the EU and are also *ex tunc* – it is therefore highly likely that certain situations may have been judged in national courts (or by national administrative authorities) under erroneous assumptions. When can these be revisited?

In principle the national legal order decides what is covered, whether it is the same matter, same persons, and time limits for acquiring *res judicata* etc.[294] The Court has itself dealt with ob-

---

287. Case C-93/12, *ET Agrokonsulting-04-Velko Stoyanov*, para 35.
288. See K. Lenaerts, I. Maselis, K. Gutman, *EU Procedural Law*, 2nd ed. (OUP, 2015); W. Van Gerven, "Of rights, remedies and procedures", (2000) CML Rev., 501–536.
289. This absence was characterized as "regrettable": Case 130/79, *Express Dairy Foods*, at para 12. Since the Treaty of Maastricht, there have been considerable developments in harmonization of civil procedural law, currently on the basis of the Treaty provisions on judicial cooperation in civil matters, see Ch. 18, "Judicial cooperation in civil matters", of this book.
290. In many areas directives have been issued to this end, e.g. Directive 2004/35/EC on environmental liability with regard to the prevention and remedying of environmental damage, O.J. 2004, L 143/56-75; Directive 92/13/EEC coordinating the laws, regulations and administrative provisions relating to the application of Community rules on the procurement procedures of entities operating in the water, energy, transport and telecommunications sectors, O.J. 1992, L 76/14-20 (as amended by Directive 2007/66/EC).
291. Case C-61/14, *Orizzonte Salute*, cf. J. Krommendijk, op. cit. *supra*, note 231.
292. Case C-93/12, *ET Agrokonsulting-04-Velko Stoyanov*, esp. para 61. Case C-73/16, *Puškár*.
293. See judgment in *Fallimento Olimpiclub*, C-2/08, paras. 22 and 24.
294. For an overview of national rules governing the scope of *res judicata*, A. Kornezov, "Res judicata of national judgments incompatible with EU law: Time for a major rethink?", 51 CML Rev. (2014), 809–842.

jective limits of the authority of *res judicata* on a number of occasions. In *Köbler*, the Court said an action for damages (against the state) following an incorrect judgment by a highest court did not have the same purpose as an appeal against such a judgment, so did not fall under *res judicata*.[295] In *Lucchini* the national courts had manifestly exceeded their substantive jurisdiction in the case at hand, so that the principle of primacy of EU law precluded *res judicata* being accorded to those judgments.[296] In *Fallimento Olimpiclub*, the ECJ implicitly chose a narrow conception of *res judicata* covering only the operative part of a judgment, so that findings of fact or of law on a fundamental issue which formed the underpinning of the operative part were not immune from reassessment in another proceeding.[297]

Generally, the principles of equivalence and effectiveness also apply in this field. With regard to equivalence, the situation is fairly straightforward: where national law imposes an obligation on a court or administrative body to reopen a case in order to remedy an infringement of domestic law, the principle of equivalence requires it to do the same in order to remedy an EU law infringement. In *Kühne & Heitz*.[298] the Court applied this reasoning to an administrative decision, albeit under strict conditions, and stressing the fact that Dutch law empowers administrative authorities to reopen proceedings. The ECJ reasoned in terms of the principle of loyal cooperation. A later ruling confirmed that the decision in *Kühne & Heitz* must be seen as to be confined to the exceptional facts of that case. As far as national administrative bodies are concerned,[299] in accordance with the principle of legal certainty, the EU principle of effectiveness does not impose, apart from such exceptional circumstances, an obligation to reopen an administrative decision which has become final upon expiry of the reasonable time-limits for legal remedies or by exhaustion of those remedies.[300]

In contrast to some other procedural principles, *res judicata* is also seen as a general principle of EU law, and closely linked to the need, firmly recognized in the EU legal order, for legal certainty. This may explain why, in relation to the principle of effectiveness, there is a more deferential approach to national bodies. In *Kapferer*[301] the ECJ said that a national court is not required to disapply domestic rules of procedure conferring finality on a decision, even if to do so would enable it to remedy an infringement of EU law by the decision at issue. In *Târşia*,[302] such weight was accorded to *res judicata* that the Court permitted a situation whereby it was impossible to recover a tax levied in conflict with EU law, after a subsequent judgment clearly revealed the illegality of the national tax,[303] because the final decision (even involving the public authority) had been given in the course of civil proceedings, and under national law there was no possibility to revise civil judgments, though such a possibility existed as regards final decisions incompatible

295. See *Köbler*, C-224/01, and section 6 of this chapter.
296. Case C-119/05, *Ministero dell'Industria, del Commercio e dell'Artigianato v. Lucchini.*
297. Case C-2/08, *Fallimento Olimpiclub.*
298. Case C-453/00, *Kühne & Heitz NV and Productschap voor Pluimvee en Eieren.*
299. See in general F. Becker, "Application of Community law by Member States' public authorities: Between autonomy and effectiveness", (2007) CML Rev., 1035–1056.
300. Joined Cases C-392 & 422/04, *i-21 Germany GmbH en Arcor AG & Co. KG v. Bundesrepublik Deutschland*, para 51. See annotation by M. Taborowski, (2007) CML Rev., 1463.
301. Case C-234/04, *Rosmarie Kapferer v. Schlank & Schick GmbH.* "the principle of cooperation [...] EC does not require a national court to disapply its internal rules of procedure in order to review and set aside a final judicial decision if that decision should be contrary to [Union] law".
302. Case C-69/14, *Târşia.*
303. The illegality of the tax was established in Case C-402/09, *Tatu*, in 2011 – 3 years later than the final decision in Mr Târşia's original case. The question of reasonable time-limits was mentioned in the Opinion in relation to *res judicata:* A.G. Jääskinen in Case C-69/14, *Târşia*, para 20.

with EU law made in the course of administrative proceedings.[304] The Court recalled in *Târşia* that EU law does not require a judicial body automatically to go back on a judgment having the authority of *res judicata* in order to take into account the interpretation of a relevant provision of EU law adopted by the Court after delivery of that judgment.[305]

Nevertheless, the question of effectiveness does play a role in certain situations. For instance, the question of whether time limits are reasonable has been addressed: such time limits may not be liable to render practically impossible or excessively difficult the exercise of rights conferred by EU law.[306]

In *Fallimento Olimpiclub*, a national rule was precluded "to the extent that it would prevent the national court seized of that dispute from taking into consideration the rules of Community law concerning abusive practice in the field of value added tax", which is an argument of effectiveness.[307] Notably, in the context of consumer protection the principle of effectiveness can override *res judicata*. This happened in particular in a series of cases involving mortgage cases in Spain. Because the protection to consumers afforded by the Directive on Unfair Terms in Consumer Contracts, Directive 93/13, should be given by national courts *ex officio*, the ECJ refused to grant the authority of *res judicata* to cases in which the national courts had not fulfilled their obligations in this way.[308]

5. Sanctions in domestic law for EU law infringements

5.1 Responsibility of Member States

From the earliest case law, it has been clear that in order to fulfil their Treaty obligations, Member States must ensure that implementation of EU law is *actually effective*. This involves real enforcement of the application of EU law, and includes setting sanctions or penalties under national law, of a civil, administrative, penal or disciplinary nature, for infringement of rules of EU law. Appropriate proceedings must be made available.[309] Infringements of directly applicable EU law provisions are covered, as well as infringements of domestic provisions implementing EU law obligations. Sanctions include all measures which remove a benefit from or impose a disadvantage on a person for failure to abide by certain rules. Civil law may also provide effective means for enforcing compliance. The special remedy of liability in damages of the Member States themselves for infringements of EU law is dealt with separately (see section 6).

The primary responsibility for the enforcement of all these provisions lies with the Member States. It is constant case law that "where EU legislation does not specifically provide any

304. Case C-217/16, *Commission v. Zagoriou*, confirmed that the choice of competent court is a matter of national law.

305. Citing *Impresa Pizzarotti*, C-213/13, para 60. The ECJ declined to use the principle of equivalence, because the two courses of action (civil and administrative) were both domestic, so it was not a case of prejudicing an action based on EU law.

306. Case C-2/06 *Kempter*, paras. 58 and 59.

307. Case C-2/08, *Fallimento Olimpiclub*, paras. 30–31: here, the argumentation in one case would determine all subsequent cases on the same matter. The ECJ limited the scope of the authority of *res judicata*. In Case C-505/14, *Klausner Holz Niedersachsen*, the national court had to be able to draw all the consequences of establishing a breach of State aid rules, in spite of another judicial decision which had become definitive, if that decision had not examined the issue of state aid.

308. Most recently, Case C-49/14, *Finanmadrid*, para 48, the rules of *res judicata* must comply with the principles of equivalence and effectiveness, citing Case C-40/08, *Asturcom Telecomunicaciones*, para 38. The original leading case in relation to Spanish mortgages, Case C-415/11, *Aziz v. Caixa d'Estalvis de Catalunya*, concerns limited jurisdiction of the national court rather than *res judicata*.

309. See section 4 of this chapter.

penalty for an infringement or refers for that purpose to national legislation, [Article 4(3) TEU] requires the Member States to take all the measures necessary to guarantee the application and effectiveness of EU law".[310] These are national sanctions, within the sphere of national procedural autonomy. The principles of equivalence and effectiveness apply: the Member States "must ensure that infringements of EU law are penalized under conditions, both procedural and substantive, which are analogous to those applicable to infringements of national law of a similar nature and importance and which, in any event, make the penalty effective, proportionate and dissuasive".[311] That last phrase confirms that the obligation of effectiveness is predominant. Nevertheless, "proportionate" may also protect an infringer from fines which the Court considers too high.[312] The obligation under Article 4(3) TEU includes proceedings for the collection or recovery of duties or levies which have been fraudulently evaded or for damages.[313] Finally, the national authorities should proceed, with respect to infringements of EU law, with the same diligence as that which they bring to bear in implementing corresponding national laws.[314] The obligations described by the Court apply to all bodies in the Member States in whom authoritative power is vested.

5.2 *Choice of sanctions*

Member States may, in principle, choose which sanctions to use, but always ensuring a real and effective protection of legal rights, and with a deterrent effect *vis-à-vis* the infringer. This was clarified in early case law on the Directive on equal treatment of men and women in relation to access to employment.[315] Compensation as a sanction must at least be adequate in relation to the damage sustained, and may not be purely nominal; a national rule setting a ceiling *a priori* is unlawful.[316] Where a Member State employs civil law sanctions, EU law may affect the applicable rules for finding liability: infringement of the prohibition of discrimination is in itself sufficient as a basis for engaging the full liability of the person who committed the discrimination, and no regard may be had to the grounds of exemption envisaged by national law.[317] In the field of air passengers' rights, the Court has ruled that if a system of civil liability has been established, a public authority is not required to use further administrative law measures in individual cases: the national authority is responsible by means of general monitoring activities, without a duty

310. E.g. Case C-382/09, *Stils Met SIA v. Valsts ieņēmumu dienests*, para 44, citing Case C-36/94, *Siesse*, para 20, and Case C-91/02, *Hannl-Hofstetter*, para 17 (on customs infringements); also Case C-382/92, *Commission v. UK*, para 55, on directives.
311. Case C-443/13, *Ute Reindl v. Bezirkshauptmannschaft Innsbruck*, at para 38, citing Case C-315/05, *Lidl Italia*, para 58, and Joined Cases C-387/02, C-391/02 and C-403/02, *Berlusconi and Others*, para 65. In this sense already Case 50/76, *Amsterdam Bulb*, Case 14/83, *Von Colson*; Case 68/88, *Commission v. Greece (Greek Maize)* (on regulations), Case C-7/90, *Vandevenne and Others (also on regulations)*.
312. E.g. Case C-255/14, *Robert Michal Chmielewski*, where a Hungarian rule (implementing Regulation 1889/2005 on controls of cash) which imposed an administrative fine of 60% of the amount of undeclared cash, even with no hint of fraudulent or unlawful activities, but solely a breach of the obligation to declare, was forbidden.
313. Case C-352/92, *Milchwerke Köln and Wuppertal v. Hauptzollamt Köln-Rheinau*, para 23, referring to the Opinion of A.G. Van Gerven.
314. Case 68/88, *Commission v. Greece (Greek Maize)*.
315. Directive 76/207/EEC, O.J. 1976, L 39/40, now replaced by Equal Treatment Directive 2006/54/EC.
316. Case 14/83, *Von Colson*. Case C-271/91, *Marshall II*. See e.g. also Case C-180/95, *Draehmpaehl v. Urania Immobilienservice*.
317. Case C-177/88, *Dekker v. Stichting VJV-Centrum*. The question of direct horizontal effect was not raised by the Hoge Raad (Dutch Supreme Court) in this case. See also Case C-180/95, *Draehmpaehl*. In Case C-338/91, *Steenhorst Neerings*, the Court accepted the need to preserve the financial equilibrium of the social security system as justification for limiting retroactive claims.

to act on individual complaints by taking enforcement action against a third party, where the damages can already be claimed before the civil courts.[318]

The EU rule to be sanctioned may leave the choice of sanctions entirely open[319] or contain further indications about, for instance, which persons should be subject to sanctions for which infringements,[320] the result to be achieved with the sanctions,[321] or the procedures to be made available.[322] A rule of Union law may provide for specific sanctions and oblige the Member States to apply these in case of infringements – these are then EU sanctions.[323] The establishment of EU sanctions obviously serves uniform enforcement of Union law better than leaving this to the Member States. Implementation of sanctions which vary between Member States as regards their nature and severity[324] for infringements of the same EU rules may disturb the proper functioning of the internal market, and is difficult to reconcile with the idea that citizens of the Union should receive equal treatment before the (same) law.[325]

Including specific sanctions in a directive could be seen as contrary to the character of the directive as a legal instrument, since, under Article 288 TFEU, the choice of form and methods for achieving the result prescribed by the directive is left to the national authorities. The obligation to impose specific sanctions was initially encountered in regulations, and where the Union had a particular financial interest in the strict enforcement of the rules, such as in agriculture[326] or VAT.[327] The sanctions prescribed by the Union may aim to ensure that the EU rules concerning the levying of amounts or the receipt of premiums and subsidies are complied with. In the course of time, the EU has developed an arsenal of *administrative sanctions,* including: fines, non-payment of EU subsidies and premiums, recovery of subsidies and premiums, ex post recovery of EU duties and levies, possible with a surcharge, loss of deposits, temporary exclusion from the advantages of a premium or subsidy scheme.

According to Case C-240/90, *Germany v. Commission*, the Union can set sanctions for traders who have committed fraud, even if the trader then suffers a loss that is greater than the mere

318. Joined Cases C-145/15 and C-146/15, *Ruijssenaars, Jansen, Dees-Erf* v. *Staatssecretaris van Infrastructuur en Milieu.*
319. E.g. a standard clause in a regulation: "Member States shall take appropriate legal or administrative measures in case of non-compliance with the provisions of this Regulation" or in a directive: "The Member States shall determine the penalties applicable to breaches of the national provisions adopted pursuant to this Directive".
320. E.g. Art. 16 Reg. 11/60 concerning the abolition of discrimination in transport rates and conditions, O.J. 1960, 52/1121.
321. See e.g. Commission Communication reinforcing sanctioning regimes in the financial services sector, COM(2010)716. Reg. (EU) 909/2014 on improving securities settlement in the European Union and on central securities depositories and amending Directives 98/26/EC and 2014/65/EU and Reg. (EU) 236/2012, Recital 62. O.J. 2014, L 257/1.
322. See Art.11 of Directive 2005/29/EC concerning unfair business-to-consumer commercial practices in the internal market, O.J. 2005, L 149/22. On problems in Member States where public procurement comes under contract law and not administrative law, see Case C-81/98, *Alcatel Austria et al. v. Bundesministerium für Wissenschaft und Verkehr.*
323. Of course, these are not sanctions (restrictive measures) imposed as a foreign policy instrument on countries or individuals, on which see Ch. 41, "Union external relations under the TFEU", of this book.
324. See Case C-273/90, *Meico-Fell v. Hauptzollamt Darmstadt*, at para 12.
325. For the specific problems in relation to different fining policies under the competition rules, see N. Dunne, "Convergence in competition fining practices in the EU", 53 CML Rev., 453–492.
326. See Case C-240/90, *Germany v. Commission.*
327. The Member States have retained powers in relation to sanctions for infringements of VAT rules, subject to the principle of proportionality, see Case 299/86, *Criminal proceedings against Drexl*, and Case C-276/91, *Commission v. France.*

repayment of the wrongly received amounts. The ECJ rejected the argument that sanctions by which the trader is excluded from the right to a benefit are penal sanctions: the Court considered such sanctions to be a specific administrative instrument. This qualification has been upheld by the Court in *Bonda*,[328] in the context of national proceedings against Mr Bonda for fraud in his declaration of the agricultural area eligible for an agricultural subsidy.[329] Mr Bonda could not rely on the principle of *ne bis in idem* in order to avoid his prosecution for fraud, as the EU penalties were administrative in nature.

Notwithstanding the Court's rulings, these are *punitive* sanctions aiming at the imposition of an extra disadvantage and deterrence. In principle, in that case the guarantees of Article 6 ECHR concerning "criminal charges" could be applicable, in addition to the possible application of the *ne bis in idem* rule.[330] Yet, the ECJ seems to deny that these sanctions are punishments in the sense of that provision, stressing the administrative nature of the sanctions, and maintaining that they are not penal sanctions because they merely guarantee that an undertaking voluntarily assumed will be carried out,[331] or because the right to EU aid must be subject to the condition that the beneficiary offers all guarantees of probity and trustworthiness.[332] This is due to the fear that too heavy an emphasis on the penal character of the sanctions could lead to such material and procedural requirements in relation to the imposition of the sanctions, that it would be impossible to apply them effectively. A tension arises between the need for effectiveness in implementing policies, on the one hand, and the requirements of the modern liberal state based on the rule of law, on the other.

The principle of effectiveness of Union law may lead to a restriction of the application of national rules and principles intended to protect the interests of individuals. If effective enforcement requires national coercive measures, a Member State may not plead an objection raised under national law.[333] The national courts must also respect this requirement. In *Taricco*, in the area of VAT fraud, the Court found that a national rule in relation to limitation periods was liable to have an adverse effect on fulfilment of Member States' obligations under Article 325(1) and (2) TFEU if it prevented the imposition of effective and dissuasive penalties in a significant number of cases of serious fraud affecting the financial interests of the European Union.[334] The Court later acknowledged that this obligation could be limited by the principle of legality.[335]

The imposition and application of sanctions to infringements of Union law, whether or not transposed into national law, may be reviewed on the basis of general legal principles, such as the requirements of legality, proportionality and non-discrimination.[336] The principle of pro-

328. Case C-489/10, *Criminal proceedings against Łukasz Marcin Bonda*.
329. Art. 138(1) of Commission Reg. (EC) 1973/2004 of 29 Oct. 2004 laying down detailed rules for the application of Council Reg. (EC) 1782/2003 as regards the support schemes provided for in Titles IV and IVa of that Regulation and the use of land set aside for the production of raw materials (O.J. 2004, L 345/1).
330. Cf. ECtHR App. 8544/79, *Oztürk* and App. 12547/86 *Bendenoun*, and the leading case Application Nos. 5100/71 etc., *Engel*. The ECtHR has elaborated on the consequences associated with sanctions in competition law in ECtHR, *A. Menarini Diagnostics srl v. Italy*, Appl. 43509/08.
331. Cf. Case 117/83, *Könecke v. Balm*, at para 14.
332. Case C-240/90, *Germany v. Commission*, at para 26.
333. Case C-217/88, *Commission v. Germany*, concerning decisions imposing on winegrowers an obligation to distil certain qualities of table wine, in implementation of EU rules.
334. Case C-105/14, *Taricco*.
335. Case 42/17, *M.A.S.*
336. E.g. Case 117/83, *Könecke* (criminal or other sanctions may only be imposed if there is a clear and unambiguous legal basis for doing so) and Case 240/78, *Atalanta Amsterdam v. Produktschap voor Vee en Vlees* (the sanctions should be proportionate to the degree of failure to implement the contractual obligations or to the seriousness of the breach of those obligations). See also Case C-29/95, *Pastoors and Trans-Cap v.*

portionality is thus a two-edged sword – the requirement that the sanction is proportional to the gravity of the infringement serves the interest not just of the enforcement of EU law – the sanction must be sufficiently severe to be effective and deterrent – but also of judicial protection of persons accused of infringements – the sanction may not be more severe than is necessary.[337]

5.3 *Penal sanctions*

With the Treaty of Lisbon, in Article 83 TFEU, the Union gained competences in the field of criminal law. The article distinguishes between interests related to the fight against cross-border offences, on the one hand, and "inherently European interests" or "direct federal interests", reflected in the two different paragraphs. Article 83(1) permits the Union legislature to establish minimum rules on the definition of criminal offences and sanctions in a listed number of areas of particularly serious crime with a cross-border dimension.[338]

Article 83(2) TFEU creates a competence for the Union to establish minimum rules, in directives, for the definition of criminal offences and sanctions, if the approximation of criminal laws and regulations of the Member States is essential to ensure the effective implementation of a Union policy in an area which has been subject to harmonization measures. This provision clarifies, to some extent, a situation under which the ECJ had found the EU to enjoy certain implicit competences with regard to requiring the use of criminal law. In *Commission v. Council (environmental crimes)*, the ECJ accepted arguments of the Commission that it would be possible to adopt a directive under what was then Article 175(1) EC in order to ensure effective deterrence against infringements of Community environmental measures.[339] This was despite criminal law and criminal procedural law being the competence of the Member States.[340] The Court later clarified, in *Ship Source pollution*, another environmental case, that "the determination of the type and level of the criminal penalties to be applied does not fall within the Community's sphere of competence".[341] It remained unclear whether this implicit competence to require use of penal sanctions was general, or only in relation to the environment. In any case, the Community competence was limited to the use of penal sanctions as such, a minimum level, and the elements of the crime. The new legal basis, Article 83(2) TFEU, may now be considered the "lex specialis in the field of harmonizing criminal sanctions for the enforcement of substantive Union policies", and the derived competence based on case law, on the ground of effectiveness, is "dormant".[342] In *Taricco*, the Court stated that "criminal penalties may nevertheless be essential" for Italy to fulfil its duty to ensure effective and dissuasive penalties for VAT fraud,

---

Belgische Staat, for review against the prohibition of indirect discrimination and against the principle of proportionality; Case C-177/95, *Ebony Maritime* (a system of strict criminal liability for sanctioning infringements of a regulation is not per se incompatible with EU law).

337. As was evident in Case C-255/14, *Chmielewski*. See further Ch. 19, "EU criminal law", section 2.3, of this book.
338. See further Ch. 19, "EU criminal law", section 2.3, of this book.
339. Case C-176/03, *Commission v. Council (environmental crimes);* The ECJ annulled a decision to act based on an intergovernmental competence, because former Art. 47 TEU protected Community competences from such encroachment.
340. Union law could – and can – set limits to the exercise of this competence: Case 203/80, *Criminal proceedings against Casati* and Case C-226/97, *Lemmens*. Recently, also in the field of irregular migration, Case C-290/14, *Skerdjan Celaj;* Case C-329/11, *Achughbabian*. Case C-430/11, *Sagor*. See already H.G. Sevenster, "Criminal law and EC law", (1992) CML Rev., at 29–70.
341. Case C-440/05, *Commission v. Council*, para 70.
342. M. Dougan, "From velvet glove to the iron fist: Criminal sanctions for the enforcement of EU law" in M. Cremona (Ed.), *Compliance and the Enforcement of EU Law* (OUP, 2012), at 111.

even though the relevant Directive did not call explicitly for criminal sanctions; this may imply that the residual basis has not disappeared.[343]

5.4 *Enforcement by means of civil remedies*

Member States can use private enforcement as a way of ensuring the full implementation of EU law, by allowing civil remedies such as actions for damages, injunctive relief, contractual remedies and interim relief. This may even be required by EU law, in order to ensure its full effect.[344]

In some areas, even where strong EU-based rights are at stake, the civil remedies may be predominant: in consumer protection, for instance, the essential instruments of EU consumer law[345] do not require *public* enforcement of consumer law; in some Member States (e.g. Germany) no consumer protection authorities exist. In these Member States, consumer protection rules such as the provisions transforming the EU directives into national law are exclusively subject to private enforcement (possibly with standing for consumer protection organizations).

The civil remedies, in particular the nature and severity of contractual sanctions, are determined by national law (subject to the principles of equivalence and effectiveness.[346]

In recent years, a growing body of secondary EU law enabling and promoting this form of enforcement has been enacted.[347] This development covers most of EU law – notably in the field of competition law,[348] consumer protection,[349] intellectual property[350] and public procurement.[351] Most of the substantive rules promote the internal market, and the legal basis used is Article 114 TFEU. The EU rules have introduced some harmonization (e.g. regarding legal standing, disclosure of evidence, interim measures, injunctive relief, actions for damages, and

343. The matter is however complicated by the Court in the next paragraph citing the PIF Convention on fraud against the Union's resources which does explicitly call for criminal penalties. See Case C-105/14, *Criminal proceedings against Ivo Taricco and Others*, paras. 39–40.

344. Case C-253/00, *Antonio Muñoz v. Frumar*.

345. E.g. Directive 93/13 on unfair terms in consumer contracts, O.J. 1993, L 95/29, and Directive 2005/29 on unfair business- to-consumer commercial practices, O.J. 2005, L 149/22.

346. Cf. Case C-159/00, *Sapod Audic v. Eco-Emballages SA*, "the severity of the sanction under the applicable national law, such as nullity or unenforceability of the contract between [the parties] is a question governed by national law, in particular as regards the rules and principles of contract law [...]", para 52. See also Case C-219/15, *Schmitt*.

347. See generally F. Wilman, *Private Enforcement of EU Law Before National Courts: The EU Legislative Framework* (Edward Elgar, 2015).

348. Directive 2014/104/EU on certain rules governing actions for damages under national law for infringements of the competition law provisions of the Member States and of the European Union, O.J. 2014, L 349/1.

349. Directive 85/374/EEC on the approximation of the laws, regulations and administrative provisions of the Member States concerning liability for defective products, O.J. 1985, L 210/29; Directive 2009/22, (Consumer Injunctions Directive), originally adopted in 1998 and codified in 2009, also sets out rules on legal standing and provides for certain specific remedies, most notably injunctions, O.J. 2009, L 110/30.

350. Directive 2004/48/EC on the enforcement of intellectual property rights, O.J. 2004, L 195/45: Art. 3(1), Member States must ensure that their civil procedures on the infringement of intellectual property rights are not "unnecessarily complicated or costly, or entail unreasonable time-limits or unwarranted delays". The Directive harmonizes rules on standing, evidence, interlocutory measures, seizure and injunctions, damages and costs and judicial publication. See also Case C-453/99, *Courage v. Crehan* and Joined Cases C-295-298/04, *Vincenzo Manfredi v. Lloyd Adriatico Assicurazioni.*

351. Directive 89/665/EEC on the coordination of the laws, regulations and administrative provisions relating to the application of review procedures to the award of public supply and public works contracts, O.J. 1989, L 395/33.

legal costs[352]). With regard to environmental protection, the Environmental Liability Directive (2004/35) aimed to establish a framework based on the "polluter-pays" principle.[353]

The use of private enforcement has a dual advantage: it adds to the limited availability of centralized resources to ensure implementation (basically the Commission, but in some cases also national bodies have a duty to enforce parts of EU law[354]); and it provides a means to protect the individual rights involved. The development in the case law granting horizontal effect to the fundamental freedoms laid down in Treaty provisions (see above) opens up the way to damage claims on that basis. Although the remedy of private damages should be seen mainly as that of providing compensation, there can also be severe deterrent effects. For instance, in the *Laval* and *Viking* cases, where trade unions were found to be bound by Treaty freedoms, damages claims followed. This is subject to criticism, as industrial action is a fundamental right, and yet the prospect of (unlimited) damages undoubtedly has a "chilling effect".[355] Moreover, the cumulation of private remedies and public sanctioning may in itself lead to a disproportionate effect on infringers of EU law, whereas there is no satisfactory forum for discussing such cumulation.

6. Liability of Member States for damage suffered by individuals as a result of infringements of Union law which can be attributed to a Member State including judicial shortcomings

6.1 *The fall-back remedy: Damages*

It is an established principle of EU law that "a Member State is obliged to make good damage caused to individuals as a result of breaches of European Union law for which it is responsible".[356] If there is no possibility to rectify an irregular situation, the "safety-net" is the possibility to provide financial compensation, in the form of damages. In *Dominguez*, the ECJ found "if the national court is unable to achieve the objective laid down in Article 7 of Directive 2003/88, the party injured as a result of domestic law not being in conformity with European Union law can none the less rely on the judgment in *Francovich and Others* in order to obtain, if appropriate, compensation for the loss sustained".[357]

As shown below, the system of state liability in damages was developed as a consequence of the need to ensure the effectiveness of EU law, but specifically in relation to protection of individual rights derived from EU law. The ECJ emphasized, for instance in *A.G.M.-COS.MET*, that the aim in such situations "is not deterrence or punishment but compensation for the damage suffered by individuals as a result of breaches of [Union] law by Member States".[358] In a series of cases on the scope of the EU Charter of Fundamental Rights in relation to the extent to which

352. Directive 2004/48, cited *supra* note 350.
353. See Ch. 36, "Environmental policy", of this book.
354. National competition authorities, but also other regulatory bodies, e.g. on data protection, fundamental rights, financial services, etc. See, e.g., Ch. 5, "The political institutions", of this book.
355. E.g. the BALPA saga, in which a trade union withdrew its plans for strike action and from related legal proceedings regarding the setting up of a British Airlines subsidiary in another Member State, after British Airlines stated that it would seek unlimited damages, relying on *Viking*, quoted in S. Reynolds, "Explaining the constitutional drivers behind a perceived judicial preference for free movement over fundamental rights", 53 CML Rev. (2016), 643–677, citing K. Apps, "Damages against trade unions after *Viking* and *Laval*", 34 EL Rev. (2009), 141–154.
356. Opinion 1/09, *European and Community Patents Court*, para 86.
357. Case C-282/10, *Dominguez*, paras. 43, 44. Similarly, A.G. Wahl's Opinion in C-455/14 P, *H. v. Council*: a national court can award damages although it cannot annul an EU act (Case 314/85, *Foto-frost*).
358. Case C-470/03, *A.G.M.-COS.MET*, para 88. See also, e.g. Case C-118/08, *Transportes Urbanos*, para 36.

a directive applied to a particular situation,[359] the ECJ referred to the possibility to obtain, if appropriate, compensation for the loss sustained if a directive has apparently not been implemented correctly (so national law is not in conformity with EU law) but where the provisions of the directive may not be invoked and consistent interpretation is not possible.[360] The ECJ considers this to be a last option however: the possibility to claim compensation cannot alter the obligation of the national court to uphold the interpretation of national law that is consistent with a directive or, if such an interpretation is not possible, to disapply the national provision that is at odds with the relevant general principle.[361] It seems unlikely that breach of the Charter as such could give rise to a right to reparation, since in all cases where the Charter applies, some other provision of EU law must be involved.

Other circumstances may also make it impossible to redress a situation which is not in conformity with EU law, such as domestic procedural rules or the principle of *res judicata*. Here too, damages may be an ultimate remedy.[362]

Damages actions may exist in parallel with infringement proceedings brought by the Commission under Article 260, but they are separate.[363] Ensuring deterrence and punishment should be the duty of the Commission under TFEU.[364] The possibility of being held liable for (substantial) damages can obviously also have a deterrent effect.[365] Moreover, as the Court pointed out in *Van Gend & Loos*, there is added value in having a role for citizens in ensuring that EU law is (correctly) applied.[366] It is doubtful whether there is one "correct" answer as to whether Member State liability is only about protection of individual rights or also about enforcement.

6.2 *Francovich liability: An EU law right to damages from Member States*

The ECJ first enunciated the principle of Member State liability in damages for breaches of EU law in *Francovich.*[367] This became a remedy under EU law (then Community law), opening the possibility for uniform conditions.[368] It was extremely important that the Court anchored the principle of state liability for damage suffered by individuals through breach of EU law for which a Member State is responsible firmly in EU law itself, even though the Treaties do not

359. Case C-282/10, *Dominguez;* C-176/12, *AMS,* para 50.
360. As well as *Dominguez* and *AMS,* also e.g. Case C-316/13, *Fenoll,* Case C-291/13, *Papasavvas v. O Fileleftheros Dimosia Etairia.*
361. Case C-441/14, *Dansk Industri (DI), acting on behalf of Ajos A/S, v. Estate of Karsten Eigil Rasmussen,* para 42.
362. E.g. Case C-69/14, *Târşia.* A final judicial decision obliged Mr Târşia to pay a tax which was subsequently declared incompatible with EU law: his rights under EU law could not be corrected by a new judicial decision in his earlier case, so he should have the possibility of rendering the State liable in order to obtain recovery. See K. Sowery, "Equivalent treatment of Union rights under national procedural law: *Târşia*", 53 CML Rev. (2016), 1705.
363. Cf. Case C-445/06, *Danske Slagterier,* para 38.
364. See Ch. 10, "The Court of Justice of the EU", of this book.
365. The dual theme of individual compensation plus Member State deterrence/punishment has regularly been discussed in the literature, e.g. C. Harlow, "*Francovich* and the problem of the disobedient state", 2 ELJ (1996), 199; P. Craig, "Once more unto the breach: The Community, the State and damages liability", 113 LQR (1997); Similar debates also apply to private law liability in damages: e.g. P. Nebbia, "Damages actions for the infringement of EC Competition Law: Compensation or deterrence?", 22 EL Rev. (2008), 23.
366. Case 26/62, *Van Gend en Loos,* "The vigilance of individuals concerned to protect their rights amounts to an effective supervision in addition to the supervision entrusted by Articles [258 and 259] to the diligence of the Commission and of the Member States".
367. Joined Cases C-6/90 & C-9/90, *Francovich and Bonifaci v. Italy.* Italy failed to implement Directive 80/987 on the protection of employees in the event of the insolvency of the employer.
368. See Case 60/75, *Russo v. AIMA.*

mention this remedy explicitly.[369] Two bases were given for the principle of state liability. First, the Court found it was inherent in the system of the Treaties, because of the requirements of the full effectiveness of EU rules. Secondly, the Court noted that Member States are required, under Article 4(3) TEU, to take all appropriate measures, whether general or particular, to ensure the implementation of EU law.

The *conditions* under which liability gives rise to a remedy in damages depend on the nature of the breach of EU law at stake. *Francovich* concerned a failure by a Member State to implement a Directive; the Court ruled that where a Member State fails to fulfil its obligation under Article 249(3) EC to take all the measures necessary to achieve the result prescribed by a directive, a right to obtain reparation exists when three conditions are fulfilled: (I) the result prescribed by the directive should entail the grant of rights to individuals; (ii) it should be possible to identify the content of those rights on the basis of the provisions of the directive; and (iii) there should be a causal link between the breach of the state's obligation and the loss and damage suffered by the injured party. The Court confirmed that the reparation had to be made on the basis of national law on liability.

In a series of cases in 1996, the ECJ was able to clarify its earlier judgment and apply the principle of state liability to other forms of breach of EU law. The major judgment was *Brasserie du Pêcheur and Factortame*,[370] where the Court could pronounce on the principle and conditions in a broader context. The provisions at issue in *Brasserie du Pêcheur* were directly effective Treaty articles on free movement of goods and freedom of establishment: Article 34 TFEU and Article 49 TFEU. This judgment confirms that liability in damages does not only arise when the provisions infringed are not directly effective: it also applies when a directly applicable provision of EU law is breached. In this case, right to reparation is a necessary corollary of the direct effect recognized for the EU provisions whose breach has caused damage (and which is a minimum guarantee).[371] The Court also confirmed in *Brasserie du Pêcheur* that the obligation for Member States to make good damage suffered by individuals as a result of infringements of EU law attributable to them even applies to cases where it is the national legislature which is responsible for the infringement.[372] Since the uniform application of Union law is a fundamental requirement of the EU legal order, liability for decisions of constitutional authorities cannot be made dependent on domestic rules on the division of powers between national authorities. The ECJ introduced the phrase "attributable to the state", clarifying the broader nature of potential liability. Finally, in *Brasserie du Pêcheur* the Court made an important statement about the conditions establishing liability; it drew a parallel between the liability regime in relation to infringements attributable to Member States and the rules laid down in its case law on Article 340 TFEU concerning the non-contractual liability of the Union. The conditions for liability of Member States "cannot, in the absence of particular justification, differ from those governing the liability of the [Union] in like circumstances" (para 42). The harmonization of the two forms of liability may not be so obvious from the point of view of legal theory, but from that of legal policy, the Court's argument is convincing: the protection of the rights which individuals derive from Union law

369. See, *inter alia*, F. Schockweiler, "La responsabilité de l'autorité nationale en cas de violation de droit communautaire", 27 RTDE (1992), and J. Steiner, "From direct effects to *Francovich*", 18 EL Rev. (1993), 3.
370. Joined Cases C-46 & 48/93, *Brasserie du Pêcheur/Factortame III;* see also Case C-392/93, *The Queen v. H.M. Treasury, ex parte British Telecommunications;* Case C-5/94, *The Queen v. Ministry of Agriculture, Fisheries and Food, ex parte Hedley Lomas (Ireland)* and Joined Cases C-178, 179 & 188-190/94, *Dillenkofer et al. v. Deutschland,* annotated by P. Oliver, (1997) CML Rev. 635, On state liability for acts of the judiciary, see *infra* and Case C-224/01, *Köbler v. Österreich.*
371. Joined Cases C-46 & 48/93, *Brasserie du Pêcheur/Factortame III*, paras. 20 to 22.
372. Recently confirmed in relation to Art. 56 TFEU in Case C-98/14, *Berlington Hungary*, para 106.

cannot vary depending on whether a national authority or a Union authority is responsible for the damage.

With this harmonization in mind, the Court transposed – in a different wording – the essence of the so-called *Schöppenstedt* formula,[373] concerning the EU's non-contractual liability, to the field of liability of Member States. If the breach of EU law committed by a Member State is attributable to the national legislature acting in a sphere where it has a wide discretion in making normative choices, EU law grants a right to reparation under certain conditions.

After *Dillenkofer*,[374] it was clarified that this right to reparation arises where *three* conditions are met. The *first* condition is that the rule of EU law which was infringed was intended to confer rights on individuals. That will tend to be the case in general if the Member State acts contrary to a directly effective provision of EU law. A special case is that of incorrect implementation of directives, or failure to implement within the time-limit set. The rule of law infringed is then the EU law rule that obliges a Member State under Article 288(3) TFEU to take all the measures necessary to achieve the result prescribed by a directive. In that case, a right to damages arises if the result prescribed by the relevant provision involves the conferral of rights on individuals, and the content of the rights in question can be ascertained purely on the basis of the provisions of the directive.

The case law on the application of this first condition in the case of directives is not extensive[375] but is stable, and shows that the rights involved must be those of the individuals who claim damages. The provision of a directive at issue does not need to refer explicitly to a right of the beneficiaries to claim the result prescribed; it may also involve a certain discretion, provided it is possible to establish the minimum guarantees or rights. Note that the conditions are cumulative: the obligation to make good damage caused by the national authorities' disregard of the limits on their discretion only arises if the condition as to the intended conferral of rights whose content can be determined is met. If the national court, in the framework of a so-called objective review of legality, concludes that the competent national authority, in the exercise of its discretion in implementing a directive, has exceeded the limits of that discretion, it does not automatically mean that the Member State is liable under EU law to make reparation for damage – even if the act exceeding discretion amounts to a sufficiently serious breach of EU law and has caused damage to individuals. It must also be demonstrated that the result prescribed by the directive involves the conferral of rights on individuals and that the content of these rights can be established solely on the basis of the directive's provisions.[376] It is also apparent that the breached obligation is not necessarily the same as the substantive right conferred on the individual: as mentioned, this is most obvious in the case of failure to implement directives, where

---

373. See Ch. 10, "The Court of Justice of the EU", of this book. See generally A. Biondi and M. Farley, *The Right to Damages in European Law* (Kluwer Law International, 2009). In Case C-352/98 P, *Bergaderm*, a case concerning non-contractual liability of the Union, the ECJ recalled its reasoning in *Brasserie* that the protection of rights of individuals should not vary depending on whether a national authority or an EU authority is responsible. It thus confirmed that, absent a particular justification, the conditions for liability must be the same for the Union and Member States.

374. Joined Cases C-178, 179 & 188-190/94, *Dillenkofer*.

375. See Joined Cases C-6 & 9/90, *Francovich*; Case C-91/92, *Dori*; Joined Cases C-178, 179 & 188-190/94, *Dillenkofer*, and Case C-127/95, *Norbrook Laboratories v. Ministry of Agriculture, Fisheries and Food;* Case C-470/03, *A.G.M.-COS.MET;* Joined Cases C-501/12 to C-506/12, C-540/12 and C-541/12, *Specht*.

376. For a case in which the conferral of rights on individuals by a directive was denied, see Case C-222/02, *Paul and others v. Bundesrepublik Deutschland*. See M. Dougan "Addressing issues of protective scope within the *Francovich* right to reparation", (2016) EuConst, 124. This does not, of course, exclude an obligation to compensate damage on the basis of national law – which after all may set less restrictive conditions.

the directive lays down the relevant right – but the obligation on the Member State is that contained in Article 288 TFEU, to implement the directive.[377]

The first condition also means that this is essentially a public law remedy, and not intended to resolve conflicts *between* private parties,[378] even though damages are often referred to as providing the necessary protection in horizontal conflicts involving EU law which cannot be invoked directly.

The *second* condition is that the breach of EU law must be sufficiently serious. In cases involving the exercise of normative powers – for instance, implementing directives or setting rules where EU law leaves the national legislature a wide margin of discretion – that condition is fulfilled where the Member State manifestly and gravely exceeds the limits within which it should remain in the exercise of its powers.[379] When the Member State at the moment of the infringement was not faced with normative choices, and had only considerably reduced, or even no, discretion, then the mere infringement of EU law may qualify as sufficiently serious – as in the case of the failure to implement directives within the time limit set – but this is not necessarily so.[380] It should be borne in mind that the existence and the extent of the margin of discretion are determined by EU law and not national law.[381]

In determining whether a breach is sufficiently serious, the factors characterizing the situation include:[382]

- the clarity and precision of the rule infringed,
- the extent of the margin of discretion which the rule infringed allowed,[383]
- whether the infringement was committed intentionally, or damage caused intentionally,
- whether an error of law was excusable or inexcusable,[384]
- whether the behaviour of a Union institution may have contributed to the infringement,
- whether or not national measures or practices which are contrary to EU law are being maintained.

Regardless of other factors, a breach of EU law should be considered manifest and sufficiently serious if it continues despite a judgment establishing the infringement in question, or despite a preliminary ruling or constant case law of the Court in the area, from which it is apparent that the relevant action is an infringement. In relation to the relevant time period during which a Member State may be considered to be in error, the ECJ confirmed in *Specht*, that although the interpretation that the Court gives to a rule of EU law, in the context of a request for a preliminary ruling, clarifies and defines the meaning and implications of that rule as it ought to have been understood and applied from the time of its entry into force, the nature and extent of the obligations on Member States under the relevant provision may sometimes be considered to be

377. See extensively M. Dougan, op. cit. previous note.
378. See section 5.4 of this Chapter on other remedies to be established.
379. Confirmed by e.g. Case C-452/06, *Synthon*; Joined Cases C-501/12 etc., *Specht*.
380. Cf. Case C-127/95, *Norbrook Laboratories*. See also explicitly Case C-424/97, *Salomone Haim v. Kassenzahnärztliche Vereinigung Nordrhein*, at para 41.
381. Cf. case C-424/97, *Haim*, at para 40.
382. Case C-224/01, *Gerhard Köbler v. Republik Österreich*, paras. 53 to 56. Case C-173/03, *Traghetti del Mediterraneo*, para 43.
383. Joined Cases C-501/12 etc., *Specht*, para 102, citing C-278/05, *Robins and Others*, para 72.
384. Case C-392/93, *The Queen v. H.M. Treasury, ex parte British Telecommunications*. The Court ruled that the infringement was not sufficiently serious, as it was based on the interpretation in good faith of a provision of a directive which could be interpreted in different ways; see also Joined Cases C-283, 291 & 292/94, *Denkavit Internationaal et al. v. Bundesamt für Finanzen*.

clear and precise only after the date of the judgment.[385] Furthermore, the Court has emphasized that the preliminary ruling procedure should be seen in a different light from proceedings to establish state liability; thus, the fact that a national court found it necessary to seek a preliminary ruling on a question concerning the EU law at issue in the proceedings on the substance is not a decisive factor in determining whether there was an obvious infringement of that law on the part of the Member State.[386]

On the other hand, the reparation of damage cannot be made dependent on the prior establishment by the Court of an infringement of EU law attributable to a Member State, and national courts do not need to await the outcome of infringement proceedings.[387] Nor may it depend on a condition derived from the concept of fault (in French: "*notion de faute*") going further than the sufficiently serious breach of Union law.

These factors are partly objective, and partly subjective.[388] Objective, insofar as they concern the extent to which the rule of law infringed determines the content and scope of the obligation imposed on the Member State; subjective, insofar as they refer to factors, (incriminatory or mitigating), which could have influenced the behaviour of the Member State in its failure to fulfil its obligation.

It is not clear whether the Charter of Fundamental Rights may influence the conditions for liability: the Court has used wording in the context of the Charter that seems to offer a lower threshold than "serious breach", but it referred to *Francovich* as well.[389]

In relation to certain exceptional measures taken in order to respond to the financial and economic crises of 2006 and onwards, the Court has accepted the need to preserve the financial stability of the European Union as a broad justification for what may otherwise seem to be clear infringements of EU law.[390] It is therefore difficult to imagine such acts being treated as sufficiently serious breaches for an action for State liability.[391]

The *third* condition for Member State liability to be engaged is that there is a direct causal link between the breach of the state's obligation and the damage suffered. The Court tends to leave the assessment of the causal link to the referring court, without giving much further guidance.[392] It is for the national court to assess whether the loss and damage claimed flows sufficiently directly from the infringement.[393] The Court has also clarified that national requirements relating to a direct causal link must comply with effectiveness; thus, in situations where a tax has

385. Joined Cases C-501/12 etc., *Specht*, para 105.
386. Case C-244/13, *Ewaen Fred Ogieriakhi v. Minister for Justice and Equality* (para 55 and operative part).
387. Case C-445/06, *Danske Slagterier*, also stated that where the Commission has brought infringement proceedings, the limitation period laid down by national legislation for a damages claim does not need to be interrupted or suspended during those proceedings.
388. Cf. Joined Cases C-46 & 48/93, *Brasserie du Pêcheur/Factortame III*, at para 78, where in this context the Court speaks of certain objective and subjective elements which are relevant for deciding whether the infringement of EU law is sufficiently serious, and which may be linked with the notion of fault in the national legal system.
389. Case C-176/12, *AMS:* "Domestic law not being in conformity with European Union law", para 50.
390. Cf. Case C-41/15, *Gerard Dowling*.
391. In Cases C- 8-10/15 P, *Ledra*, para 67, the Court ruled that national acts in the context of the ESM Treaty do not implement EU law. The ECJ did find that a violation of Charter rights by a Memorandum of Understanding could in principle trigger non-contractual liability of the EU, on the basis of an omission of the Commission to "oversee the application of Union law" as required by Art. 17(1) TEU. Ibid.
392. For an exception, where the Court itself decided that there was no causal link, see Case C-319/96, *Brinkmann Tabakfabriken v. Skatteministeriet*. In principle, national courts review whether the conditions for state liability for infringement of EU law have been fulfilled, on the basis of the Court's guidelines, e.g. Case C-278/05, *Robins v. Secretary of State for Work and Pensions*.
393. Case C-446/04, *Test claimants in the FII Group Litigation*, para 218.

been passed on, a final consumer's claim against the State – on grounds that the tax infringed EU law – may only be barred provided it is not impossible or excessively difficult for the consumer to obtain reimbursement from the taxable person.[394]

When all these three conditions imposed by EU law are met, the Member State must make good the damage caused, in the framework of *national* law on liability. This has been constant case law ever since *Francovich*. The conditions imposed by the national legal rules concerning compensation for damage must, of course, not be less favourable than those applicable to similar national claims. Nor may they make it virtually impossible or excessively difficult to receive compensation for damage.[395] These are the usual conditions of the *Rewe* and *Comet* case law, discussed above. At all events, the compensation must be adequate in relation to the damage suffered, so that the rights of the persons suffering the damage are effectively guaranteed.[396]

A Member State cannot plead the distribution of powers and responsibilities between the bodies within its national legal order in order to escape liability.[397] In Member States, whether they are federal in structure or not, where decentralized (territorial) authorities with a certain degree of autonomy or other autonomous bodies under public law perform certain legislative or administrative tasks, problems may arise if the latter cause damage to individuals as a result of applying national law in conflict with Union law. The underlying idea must be the obligation of each Member State to ensure that damage is compensated, regardless of which body committed the relevant infringement and regardless of which body should, in principle, under the law of the Member State in question, be liable to make compensation. There is no objection under Union law to decentralized authorities making good the damage suffered by individuals, either alone or together with central authorities.[398] The fulfilment by the Member State of its EU law obligations, therefore, does not necessarily require the federal or central authorities themselves to compensate damage which individuals have suffered as a result of application by decentralized bodies of national measures enacted in conflict with EU law.[399] In *A.G.M.-COS.MET*, the Court found that statements made by an official could also be attributable to a Member State, and therefore engage liability.[400] These elements are all in line with the responsibility of states under public international law.

The system of non-contractual liability of a Member State for damage caused by a breach of EU law does not apply to internal situations, i.e. a situation which is confined in all respects within a single Member State. Although there may be situations where national legislation that is applicable without distinction to a state's own nationals and those of other Member States potentially breaches a fundamental freedom laid down in Article 49, 56 or 63 TFEU, this does not provide a sufficient nexus for a national to bring a claim in damages against his own State with regard to that legislation, where there is no link between the subject or circumstances of the

394. C-94/10, *Danfoss*, paras. 28, 37, 28.
395. See e.g. C-429/09 *Fuss*, where the ECJ did not allow certain national requirements which impaired effectiveness.
396. Joined Cases C-94 & 95/95, *Bonifaci et al. and Berto et al. v. INPS*. See also on the question of limitation periods, Case C- 445/06, *Danske Slagterier.*
397. Case C-302/97, *Klaus Konle v. Republik Österreich*, para 62.
398. In any case, it is open to question whether the magic formula in the *Rewe-Comet* case law (Case 33/76, *Rewe* and Case 45/76, *Comet*) can prevent the person who suffered the damage being sent from pillar to post in this situation. See B. Hessel, "European integration and the supervision of local and regional authorities: Experiences in the Netherlands with requirements of European Community law", (2006) *Utrecht Law Review*, 91–110.
399. See Case C-302/97, *Konle*, and Case C-424/97, *Haim*.
400. Case C-470/03, *A.G.M.-COS.MET*,

dispute in the main proceedings and those articles.[401] The reasoning on this in *Ullens de Schooten* is rather minimal, but states that those provisions "are intended to protect persons making actual use of the fundamental freedoms". This may sit somewhat uneasily with the constant case law regarding the obstacles to free movement in terms of potential effects. On the other hand, it is undeniable that damages are intended to redress an actual harm experienced. Insofar, a difference in the scope of EU law in these different areas may be warranted.

Finally, it should be noted that there have been some studies on the extent to which the award of damages on this basis actually takes place in national courts, finding mixed results.[402]

6.3 *Judicial errors*

A special case of breach of EU law by a Member State is that of error by the judiciary. In this context the ECJ added an extra condition in order to cross the "sufficiently serious" threshold.

A Member State incurs liability as a result of breaches of EU law, whatever the organ of the State whose act or omission was responsible for the breach.[403] It was not strange, therefore, that in *Köbler*[404] the Court decided that Member States may, in principle, be liable for damage caused to individuals by infringements of EU law consisting of decisions of a national court adjudicating at last instance.[405]

According to *Köbler,* state liability arising from action of national courts is governed by the same three conditions as any other state violation of EU law: the intention to confer rights on individuals, a sufficiently serious breach, and a causal link between the breach and the damage. As to the second condition, "regard must be had to the specific nature of the judicial function and to the legitimate requirements of legal certainty," so liability of a Member State "can be incurred only in the exceptional case where the court has manifestly infringed the applicable law".[406] Thus, a national court cannot be found to have committed a manifest error by not applying a provision of EU law *ex officio* even before a judgment of the ECJ declared that national courts have this particular duty.[407] On the other hand, EU law precludes a provision of national law which requires, as a precondition for an action in damages, the setting aside of the decision given by the court or tribunal which caused the loss or damage, when such setting aside is, in practice, impossible.[408]

---

401. C-268/15, *Ullens de Schooten v. Belgium,* para 57.

402. E.g. R. Condon and B. van Leeuwen, "Bottom up or rock bottom harmonization? Francovich state liability in national courts", EUI Working Papers, LAW 2015/03, find that the success rate in national courts is low, but this could mean it is a good deterrent. Zs. Varga, "National remedies in the case of violation of EU law by Member State courts", 54 CML Rev. (2017), 51, finds that the remedy of retrial may sometimes be more effective.

403. Case C-46/93, *Brasserie du Pêcheur,* paras. 31–32. Opinion 1/09, *Patent court,* para 86; Case C-154/08, *Commission* v. *Spain,* para 125.

404. Case C-224/01, *Köbler,* confirmed in Case C-173/03, *Traghetti del Mediterraneo v. Italy,* where the Court ruled that, although national law may define certain criteria, these may not be stricter than those set out in *Köbler*. See B. Beutler, "State liability for breaches of Community law by national courts: Is the requirement of a manifest infringement of the applicable law an insurmountable obstacle?", 46 CML Rev. (2009), 773–804.

405. A wrong judgment of a lower court can, in theory, be repaired in appeal: Member State liability is engaged only where the relevant decision is from a court adjudicating at last instance, confirmed in Case C-168/15, *Milena Tomášová v. Ministerstvo spravodlivosti SR, Pohotovosť.*

406. Case C-224/01, *Köbler,* para 53.

407. Case C-168/15, *Tomášová.* At the time of the national court's enforcement decision, the relevant ECJ judgment explaining the duty of the national court to act ex officio, had not yet been handed down.

408. Case C-160/14, *Ferreira da Silva e Brito and Others v. Portugal.*

Even though the application of the principle of state liability to judicial decisions has been accepted in one form or another by most Member States[409] the Court's judgment in *Köbler* caused quite a stir and was strongly criticized.[410] Even the extra hurdle resulting from the requirement for a serious breach to be "manifest" in this area was not enough. It was feared that the combination of the *Köbler* liability threat and the rigid *CILFIT* criteria[411] would induce courts of last instance to flood the Court with preliminary questions, anxious to avoid any risk of incurring liability. The national court hearing a claim for reparation must also consider the non-compliance by the court in question with its obligation to make a reference for a preliminary ruling under Article 267(3) TFEU. The case law gives no basis for finding that the failure to refer can *in itself* engage liability, however. It is the violation of substantive EU law by a judicial ruling which may cause damage to individuals. Disregard of the duty to refer is only one of the several factors, albeit an important one, for assessing the manifest nature of the infringement. Failure to make a preliminary reference cannot in and of itself entail damages, since the outcome of the reference is, by definition, unknown.[412] Moreover, since the ECJ refines its case law continually, it is hard to claim that the error of failing to refer by a national court is sufficiently manifest to incur actual *Köbler* liability. It is remarkable that the ECJ, for the first time, has actually ruled that in the particular circumstances of a case – characterized by the fact that there were conflicting decisions of lower courts regarding the interpretation of a relevant concept and the fact that the concept frequently gave rise to difficulties of interpretation in various Member States – the court of last instance had been obliged to make a reference to the Court.[413]

At the time of *Köbler*, commentators saw an action for damages against a judicial decision at highest instance as posing problems with regard to *res judicata*, finding that it calls into question the final decision.[414] The ECJ firmly rejects this argument: "recognition of the principle of State liability for a decision of a court adjudicating at last instance does not in itself have the consequence of calling in question that decision as *res judicata*. Proceedings seeking to render the State liable do not have the same purpose and do not necessarily involve the same parties as the proceedings resulting in the decision which has acquired the status of *res judicata*".[415]

A particular aspect of breach of EU law in relation to judicial errors is the case of excessive length of proceedings. In the context of non-contractual liability of the EU, the General Court has recently, for the first time, ordered the EU to pay damages to companies involved.[416] This may open a new avenue in certain Member States, if an EU right is at stake before national courts.

---

409. Cf. *Köbler*, para 48 and Opinion of A.G. Léger, paras. 77 to 82.
410. See e.g. P. Wattel, "*Köbler, Cilfit* and *Welhgrove:* We can't go on meeting like this", (2004), CML Rev. 177; with more sense of proportion, e.g. C.D. Classen's annotation of *Köbler* in (2004) CML Rev., at 813.
411. Case 283/81, *CILFIT v. Ministry of Health,* where the ECJ set out the conditions under which a national court needs to make a preliminary reference.
412. There may be other paths to condemn a state for a failure of its court to make a reference, cf. *Dhahbi v. Italy,* ECtHR, No. 17120/09 (but here the fault was in failing to provide reasons), or the right to one's "lawful judge", as e.g. under German constitutional law.
413. Case C-160/14, *Ferreira da Silva,* para 45.
414. P. Wattel, op. cit. *supra* note 410.
415. Case C-160/14, *Ferreira da Silva,* para 50.
416. Case T-577/14, *Gascogne Sack Deutschland and Gascogne.* This included a small amount for non-material harm. Under appeal: Case C-146/17 P, pending.

6.4 Limits of a remedy in damages

A drawback of reparation in damages is that it is based on economic loss. In certain situations this may be inappropriate or insufficient. For instance, in cases relating to asylum law, infringements of EU law may bring a loss of opportunity or well-being – for instance if family members are not allowed to join each other. The loss of an opportunity to have a judgment from the ECJ, because no preliminary reference was made, may involve feelings of frustration without material damage. The ECJ has recognized that there may be an interest in bringing proceedings in order simply to establish the illegality of a contested act; that cannot, as such, compensate for material harm or for interference with one's private life, but may nevertheless provide a means of rehabilitation or constitute a form of reparation for the non-material harm which an applicant has suffered.[417] In *Safa Nicu Sepahan*, the General Court awarded non-material damages against the EU, as a result of damage to the applicant's "personality rights" and in particular to its reputation.[418]

In certain areas, such as air passengers' rights, EU law requires national systems of remedies to be established; provided the Member State has put in place the required arrangements, there is virtually no possibility of claiming damages in individual cases under *Francovich*.[419]

7. Concluding remarks

The EU legal order, whereby law developed by supranational bodies is given effect through national legal systems, judicial and administrative, has developed a high degree of sophistication, attempting to balance the requirements of effectiveness of EU initiatives with the characteristics of individual, sovereign States. In general, it involves a high level of judicial protection for individuals, thanks both to legislation and cooperation between courts. In terms of legislation, harmonization of civil procedure has progressed, but most rules are still national, so that national procedural autonomy, while limited by the ECJ case law, still has a central role. Indeed, the ECJ plays a crucial role in relation to application of EU law within the Member States, and advances many centralizing tendencies. The vexed question, in relation to primacy, of whether the ECJ or the (highest) national courts are the "ultimate arbiter" has in practice not led to unsurmountable difficulties, and the judicial dialogue continues.

While direct effect of EU law in the Member States is generally accepted, and has been indispensable in the development of the EU legal order, there are issues which deserve reflection: in particular how to allow for the fact that certain private parties may be subject to obligations similar to those imposed on Member States, without enjoying similar possibilities for exemptions through justifications, despite the fact that they may defend more or less public interests (e.g. trade unions).

The national courts seem to take well to their role as EU courts, including the "judicial dialogue" – it was only in 2015 (in Case C-160/14, *Ferreira da Silva*) that the ECJ ruled for the first time that a national court had breached its duty to make a preliminary reference.

Currently, a salient question is whether the founding values of the EU, as expressed in Article 2 TEU, can also be "enforced".

---

417. C-239/12 P, *Abdulrahim v. Council and Commission.*

418. Case T-384/11, *Safa Nicu Sepahan Co., v. Council.* Confirmed on appeal: Case C-45/15 P, *Safa Nicu Sepahan v. Council.*

419. Case C-568/08, *Combinatie Spijker Infrabouw*, for public procurement; Joined Cases C-145/15 and C-146/15, *Ruijssenaars, Jansen, Dees-Erf v. Staatssecretaris van Infrastructuur en Milieu* for air passengers' rights.

Further reading

Alter, K.J., *Establishing the Supremacy of European Law: The Making of an International Rule of Law in Europe* (OUP, 2001).

Barav, A., *Judicial Enforcement and Implementation of European Union Law* (Larcier, 2017).

Claes, M., *The National Constitutional Mandate in the European Constitution* (Hart Publishing, 2006)

Claes, M., "The primacy of EU law in European and in national law" in A. Arnull and D. Chalmers (Eds.), *The Oxford Handbook of European Law* (OUP, 2015), 178–211.

Claes, M., "The validity and primacy of EU law and the 'cooperative relationship' between national constitutional courts and the European Court of Justice", 23 MJ (2016).

Cloots, E., *National Identity in EU Law* (OUP, 2015).

Corkin, N., *Europeanization of Judicial Review* (Routledge, 2015).

De Witte, B., J.A. Mayoral and U. Jaremba (Eds.), *National Courts and EU Law – New Issues, Theories and Methods* (Edward Elgar Publishing, 2016).

Gilliker, P., *Research Handbook on EU Tort Law* (Edward Elgar Publishing, 2017).

Gutman, K., "Liability for breach of EU law by the Union, Member States and individuals: Damages, enforcement and effective judicial protection" in A. Lazowski and S. Blockmans (Eds.), *Research Handbook on EU Institutional Law* (Edward Elgar Publishing, 2016).

Harlow, C., P. Leino and G. della Cananea, *Research Handbook on EU Administrative Law* (Edward Elgar Publishing, 2017).

Lenaerts, K., I. Maselis and K. Gutman (Ed. J. Nowak), *EU Procedural Law*, 2nd ed. (OUP, 2015).

Lenaerts, K. and T. Corthaut. "Of birds and hedges: The role of primacy in invoking norms of EU law", (2006) EL Rev., 287–315.

Micklitz, H.-W. and A. Wechsler *The Transformation of Enforcement* (Hart Publishing, 2016).

Poltorak, N., *European Union Rights in National Courts* (Kluwer Law International, 2014).

Prechal, S., *Directives in EC Law*, 2nd ed. (OUP, 2005).

Prinssen, J.M. and A.A.M. Schrauwen, *Direct Effect: Rethinking a Classic of EC Legal Doctrine* (Europa Law Publishing, 2002).

Schütze, R., *From Dual to Cooperative Federalism: The Changing Structure of European Law* (OUP, 2009).

Tridimas, T., *The General Principles of EU Law*, 2nd ed. (OUP, 2007).

Van Gerven, W., "Of rights, remedies and procedures", (2000) CML Rev., 501–536.

Wilman, F., *Private Enforcement of EU Law Before National Courts: The EU Legislative Framework* (Edward Elgar, 2015).

CHAPTER 12
THE FUNCTIONING OF THE INTERNAL MARKET: THE FREEDOMS

*K.J.M. Mortelmans†**

1. Introduction

1.1 The internal market and the fundamental freedoms

The functioning of the internal market is fundamentally important for the achievement of the objectives of the European Union,[1] as is apparent from the initial provisions of the Treaty on European Union. Article 3(3) TEU provides that the Union "shall establish an internal market".[2] Article 4(2) TFEU provides that the Union and the Member States have shared competence in the area of the internal market. The Protocol on the Internal Market and Competition, annexed to the TEU and to the TFEU, includes the consideration "that the internal market as set out in Article 3 of the Treaty on European Union includes a system ensuring that competition is not distorted".

In its Opinion on the accession of the EU to the European Convention for the Protection of Human Rights and Fundamental Freedoms, the Court of Justice of the European Union stressed that the pursuit of the EU's objectives, as set out in Article 3 TEU, is entrusted to a series of fundamental provisions, such as those providing for the free movement of goods, services, capital and persons, citizenship of the Union, the area of freedom, security and justice, and competition policy. According to the Court, "those provisions, which are part of the framework of a system that is specific to the EU, are structured in such a way as to contribute – each within its specific field and with its own particular characteristics – to the implementation of the process of integration that is the *raison d'être* of the EU itself".[3]

Article 3(3) TEU does not include a description of the internal market, but Article 26 TFEU describes the internal market as "an area without internal frontiers in which the free movement of goods, persons, services and capital is ensured in accordance with the provisions of this Treaty".

* Formerly: Council of State, The Netherlands.

1. See W. Molle, *The Economics of European Integration* (Dartmouth Publishing Company, 2006). C. Barnard, *The Substantive Law of the EU. The Four Freedoms*, 4th ed. (OUP, 2013), 8.
2. The terms internal market and common market were both used in the EC Treaty, with related but distinct meanings. The term "single market" was not used in the EC Treaty, but does occur in the literature. See K. Mortelmans, "The Common Market, the Internal Market and the Single Market: What's in a Market?", (1998) CML Rev., 101–136. In the Lisbon Treaty the term "common market" is replaced in the TFEU by the term "internal market", cf. Art. 2(2)(g) Lisbon Treaty.
3. Opinion 2/13, paras. 172 and 191.

The definition of the internal market is vague. It avoids taking any clear position on what sorts of obstacles to trade are attacked and who should attack them, judicial or legislative institutions.[4] The emphasis is on the case law of the Court of Justice. In countless judgments, the Court has interpreted and refined its interpretation of the central provisions. In handing down judgments, the Court is primarily concerned with solving legal disputes, and not with drafting a textbook.[5] Nevertheless, certain clear lines in the approach of the Court can be traced.[6]

The realization of the internal market does not only come about by means of case law; the Union legislature also has an important task – as is revealed by Article 26(3) TFEU. It is impossible, within the confines of this work, to mention all the directives and regulations which are directed at the functioning of the internal market, let alone discuss them individually. In other chapters of this book the most important internal market instruments will be discussed.

In the next paragraphs general themes of EU Free Movement Law will be analysed.[7]

1.2 *Fundamental freedoms and fundamental rights*

In German literature[8] and later, to some extent in English-language literature,[9] a distinction was made between fundamental rights and fundamental freedoms. In an increasing number of cases, the Court made a link between free movement and human rights, such as freedom of expression,[10] family life[11] or the right to strike.[12] Potential conflicts between fundamental freedoms and fundamental rights are to be resolved by determining the right balance between the protected guarantees and interests at issue.[13]

The case law on the EU Charter of Fundamental Rights in relation to the freedoms establishing the internal market gives the Court of Justice the opportunity to refine this relationship.[14] In the *Pfleger* case, the Court considered that, "where it is apparent that national legislation is such as to obstruct the exercise of one or more fundamental freedoms guaranteed by the Treaty, it may benefit from the exceptions provided for by EU law in order to justify that fact only in so far as that complies with the fundamental rights enforced by the Court. That obligation to comply with fundamental rights manifestly comes within the scope of EU law and, consequently, within

4. S. Weatherill, "The Court's case law on the internal market: A circumloquacious statement of the result, rather than a reason for arriving at it?" in M. Adams, H. de Waele, J. Meeusen and G. Straetmans (Eds.), *Judging Europe's Judges, The Legitimacy of the Case Law of the European Court of Justice* (Hart, 2013), 90.
5. R.H. Lauwaars and C.W.A. Timmermans, *Europees Gemeenschapsrecht in kort bestek*, 6th ed. (Noordhoff, 2003), 198.
6. The Opinions of the Court's Advocates General are very useful for gaining insight into the main lines of the case law. They set out the case law, and sometimes suggest (more or less radical) new lines of analysis, e.g. A.G. Van Gerven on selling arrangements in Case 145/88, *Torfaen Borough Council* or A.G. Sharpston on the internal situation in Case C-34/09, *Zambrano*. Sometimes the A.G.s criticize the Court's previous stance, see e.g. A.G. Jacobs in Case C-413/92, *Leclerc-Siplec*. See K. Mortelmans, "The Court under the Influence of its Advocates General: An analysis of the case law on the Functioning of the internal market", (2005) YEL, 127–172.
7. See in more detail N. Nic Shuibhne, *The Coherence of EU Free Movement Law. Constitutional Responsibility and the Court of Justice* (OUP, 2013).
8. Gemeinschaftsgrundrechte and Grundfreiheiten: see J. Gebauer, *Die Grundfreiheiten des EG-Vertrages als Gemeinschafsgrundrechte* (Duncker & Humblot, 2004).
9. P. Oliver and W.-H. Roth, "The internal market and the four freedoms", (2004) CML Rev., 407–441.
10. See, e.g. Case C-112/00, *Schmidberger*.
11. See, e.g. Case C-60/00, *Carpenter*.
12. Case C-348/05, *Viking line*.
13. V. Trstenjak and E. Beysen, "The growing overlap of fundamental freedoms and fundamental rights in the case law of the CJEU", (2013) EL Rev., 312.
14. K. Lenaerts, "Exploring the limits of the EU Charter of Fundamental Rights", (2012) EU Const., 392–393.

that of the Charter. The use by a Member State of exceptions provided for by EU law in order to justify an obstruction of a fundamental freedom guaranteed by the Treaty must, therefore, be regarded as "implementing Union law" within the meaning of Article 51(1) of the Charter".[15]

1.3 *Types of barriers to free movement*

The obstacles caused by actions of the Member States are of various types: those discussed in this chapter are tariff and non-tariff barriers and fiscal barriers. The obstacles examined here are dealt with in various places in the TFEU, but only the Title on the free movement of goods gives a complete picture. For the other freedoms, the system is not explicitly elaborated in the TFEU. Nevertheless, the Court partly filled the gap for the other freedoms.[16]

In general, there is a stricter system for tariff barriers (Arts. 28–32 TFEU) and non-tariff barriers (Arts. 34–37 TFEU) than there is for fiscal barriers (Arts. 110–113 TFEU): the first two types of barriers must be removed, save where an exception may be relied upon; but fiscal systems have to be applied in a non-discriminatory, non-protectionist manner.

The various approaches (tariff or non-tariff, import or export) work through into the case law of the Court of Justice. For example, if cattle are subject to veterinary checks and a fee is charged for the inspection, the inspection and the fee fall within the ambit of different provisions of the TFEU. Veterinary inspections in relation to export are considered under Article 35 TFEU; inspections on importation are assessed under Article 34 TFEU, and the fee in both cases is examined under Article 30 TFEU or possibly Article 110 TFEU. An inspection fee cannot be justified on the basis of an exception which justifies the inspection itself, although if both result from Union measures (as opposed to unilateral national measures) they will both be governed in the first instance by those Union measures.[17]

1.4 *Crucial role of the Court of Justice of the EU and the national courts*

The realization and functioning of the internal market are essentially based, in the first instance, on a number of pivotal "negative integration" Treaty provisions[18] and their interpretation by the Court of Justice.[19] The success of the internal market lies in that, from the very beginning, the Court of Justice brought national courts on board.[20] The majority of cases where the Court has given an interpretation of the free movement provisions are preliminary reference proceedings. Comparative research on judicial decisions from a number of Member States shows that the national courts in many cases, whether or not after a preliminary reference, apply the relevant Treaty provisions correctly.[21]

---

15. Case 390/12, *Pfleger*, para 36.
16. Art. 56 TFEU is silent on non-tariff barriers, but see Case C-18/93, *Corsica Ferries* and Case C-384/93, *Alpine Investment*. Art. 56 TFEU is also silent on fiscal measures, but see Case C-49/89, *Corsica Ferries.*
17. Case 46/76, *Bauhuis*.
18. Arts. 30, 34, 35, 45, 49, 56, 63 and 110 TFEU. "Negative integration" entails that when national law violates a Treaty provision, it cannot be applied and must be set aside.
19. The EFTA Court interprets the parallel provisions of the EEA Agreements. The CJEU sometimes refers to relevant case law of the EFTA Court; see Case C-192/01, *Commission v. Denmark*. See P. Christiansen, "The EFTA Court", (1997) EL Rev., 539. The General Court is only occasionally faced with such internal market provisions; see, e.g. Case T-69/89, *Radio Telefis Eireann v. Commission*; Case T-113/96, *Dubois v. Council and Commission*; Case T-266/97, *VTM v. Commission*; Case T-313/02, *Meca-Medina.*
20. K. Lenaerts, "The Court's outer and inner selves: Exploring the external and internal legitimacy of the European Court of Justice" in M. Adams, H. de Waele, J. Meeusen and G. Straetmans (Eds.), *Judging Europe's Judges, The Legitimacy of the Case Law of the European Court of Justice* (Hart, 2013), 40.
21. M.A. Jarvis, *Application of EC Law on the Free Movement of Goods by National Courts of the Member States* (OUP, 1998); W. Lichtenwalder, *Die Anwendung von Art. 30 EGV in der mitgliedstaatlichen Rechtsprechung*

The case law of the Court of Justice on the prohibitions and exceptions is constantly evolving. More and more market operators rely on Treaty prohibitions in judicial actions, so the Court must give an (indirect) answer in innumerable preliminary references to the question whether a certain national rule conflicts with a directly effective Treaty prohibition – even if at first sight the rule has nothing to do with e.g. obstacles to the free movement of goods or services.[22]

The Court's answers in these cases concerning the functioning of the internal market are not always unambiguous.[23] On the one hand, the Court works in a framework of convergence, using the technique of assimilation. In this way, the case law acquires some structure. A market operator can see how a line of approach in relation to one of the freedoms may be extrapolated to apply to other freedoms, such as the extensive effect of the Treaty prohibition. On the other hand, a large number of judgments by the Court do not fit in these structures.

This is illustrated by a few examples, which are worked out in detail below. The *Keck* case law has not (yet) been transposed to other freedoms.[24] Since *Keck,*[25] the Court also uses other techniques in order to exclude national rules from the scope of the prohibition. In the *Italian trailers* case[26] on goods, the Court favoured the market access approach, in line with its earlier case law on establishment in *Gebhard*.[27] In *Mickelsson*, the Court stressed the considerable influence of a national measure on the behaviour of consumers.[28]

Moreover, the condition that the rule-of-reason exceptions only hold for measures which apply indistinctly to national and non-national goods is no longer adhered to in a number of cases concerning, *inter alia,* environment and taxation. There are a number of reasons for this departure from a straight line of case law. First, as was already pointed out in the introduction to this chapter, the Court of Justice is primarily concerned with solving legal disputes, not writing a textbook. Secondly, the composition of the Court has changed over the years – and perhaps new judges (and Advocates General) have a new vision of the realization of the internal market. Thirdly, the Court clearly finds it difficult to rule on the obstacles it is currently confronted with on the basis of a Treaty framework which was – and even after Lisbon is – not designed for them, or at least not sufficiently. The best example is environmental protection. This exception is not listed in Article 36 TFEU, while over the years a great number of provisions on the environment have been included in the Treaty. In the absence of clear and direct footholds in the Treaty, the Court has to tie itself in knots in order to save directly discriminatory measures aimed at

---

(Lang, 1996). H. van Harten, "National judicial autonomy: the example of national European law precedents in the Dutch case law on the free movement of services and the freedom of establishment", (2009) *Review of European Administrative Law*, 135.

22. Cf. Joined Cases C-267 & 268/91, *Keck and Mithouard.*
23. P. Oliver, "Could the wording of the Court's judgments be improved?", (2001), EuZW, 257; T. Von Danwitz, "Der richterliche Dialog in der Gerichtspraxis des Vorabentscheidungsverfahrens: Herausforderungen für die Zukunft" in U. Becker, A. Hatje, M. Potacs and N. Wunderlich (Eds.), *Verfassung und Verwaltung in Europa – Festschrift für Jürgen Schwarze zum 70. Geburtstag* (Nomos, 2013), at 675–678; N. Nic Shuibhne, *supra* note 7.
24. See J. Snell, "The legitimacy of free movement case law: Process and substance" in M. Adams, H. de Waele, J. Meeusen and G. Straetmans (Eds.), *Judging Europe's Judges, The Legitimacy of the Case Law of the European Court of Justice* (Hart, 2013), 116.
25. Joined Cases C-267 & 268/91, *Keck and Mithouard.*
26. Case C-110/05, *Commission v. Italy.*
27. Case C-55/94, *Gebhard.* See also Barnard, *supra* note 1, 19; N. Nic Shuibhne, *supra* note 7, 211.
28. Case C-142/05, *Mickelsson.* See on this development S. Weatherill, *supra* note 4, 95 and J. Snell, *supra* note 24, 114.

environmental protection.[29] To a certain extent, this reasoning also applies for the "tax system" exception which was introduced in *Bachmann*, and for the exception "a social security system's financial balance" which was introduced in *Smits and Peerbooms*.[30] Advocates General, who are sometimes caught between case-by-case approaches on the one hand and theory on the other, at times urge the Court to clarify things.[31]

2. The realization of the internal market: prohibitions and justifications

2.1 *The four freedoms: prohibitions*

Article 26(2) TFEU mentions four freedoms (goods, persons, services, capital). The free movement of capital comprises also the free movement of payments, as appears from Article 63(2) TFEU.[32]

According to the Treaty, restrictions shall be prohibited (goods, services, establishment, capital and payments) or discriminations on nationality shall be abolished (workers). None of the Treaty articles gives information on the scope of the restriction. It appears from the case law of the Court that not only directly discriminatory measures (or distinctly applicable measures) are prohibited, but also indirectly discriminatory or (certain)[33] non-discriminatory measures (or indistinctly applicable measures).[34]

During the transitional period of the common market (1958–1969), the freedoms relating to goods, persons, services and payments were realized on the basis of the relevant provisions in the EEC Treaty and through directly effective prohibitions on the introduction of new restrictions on these freedoms, and the instruction to abolish existing restrictions ("negative integration").[35] The free movement of capital was phrased in different terms in the EEC Treaty (see old Art. 67 EEC) until the amendments made by the Treaty of Maastricht brought it into line with the other freedoms. The free movement of persons resulted from, on the one hand, the free movement of workers (employees) and on the other, the freedom to exercise a trade or profession.

The Treaty of Maastricht introduced into the EC Treaty the concept of citizenship of the Union. The rights of these citizens are now included in Articles 20–25 TFEU. This extension, effected by the Treaty of Maastricht and developed by the Court of Justice, means that it is no longer only economically active persons that come within the scope of the Treaty, but as a rule all citizens of the Union now have the right to reside freely in the territory of another Member State, and to travel within the Union. Sometimes, the Treaty provisions on citizenship are being referred to as "a fifth freedom", operating under the dynamics of free movement law.[36] Title V of Part 3 of the TFEU, introduced by the Treaty of Amsterdam, contains rules concerning the movement of persons from third countries (see Arts. 77–80 TFEU).

---

29. Case C-2/90, *Commission v. Belgium*; Case C-379/98, *PreussenElektra AG*.
30. Case C-204/90 *Bachmann*; Case C-157/99, *Geraets-Smits and Peerbooms*.
31. E.g. A.G. Jacobs in Case C-379/98, *PreussenElektra*.
32. Joined Cases C-286/82 and C-26/83, *Luigi Carbone*.
33. Joined Cases C-267/91 and C-268/91, *Keck and Mithouard*.
34. See N. Nic Shuibhne, *supra* note 7, 189.
35. The Treaty articles which concerned this process, e.g. Art. 7 EC, originally Art. 8 EEC, were repealed by the Treaty of Amsterdam.
36. K. Lenaerts, "EU citizenship and the European Court of Justice's '*stone-by-stone*' approach", (2015) *International Comparative Jurisprudence*, 1–10.

2.1.1 *Vertical direct effect as a weapon*

In the course of the 1960s and 1970s, the Court indicated that the provisions prohibiting obstacles to free movement have vertical direct effect – at least as of the end of the transitional period of the common market (1 Jan. 1970).[37] In the 2000s, the Court declared that Article 18(1) EC (now Art. 20(1) TFEU) has direct effect and that "Union citizenship is destined to be the fundamental status of nationals of the Member States, enabling those who find themselves in the same situation to enjoy the same treatment in law irrespective of their nationality, subject to such exceptions as are expressly provided for".[38]

2.1.2 *Horizontal direct effect as a weapon*

The question whether or not the Treaty prohibitions concerning free movement have horizontal direct effect has not been absolutely decided.[39] Cases such as *Walrave, Bosman, Deliege, Wouters* and *Laval*[40] clearly indicate that this is the case with respect to free movement of workers and services where private organizations such as football associations are concerned. In *Angonese*, the Court went one step further, declaring Article 45 TFEU to be applicable in a purely private conflict between an individual and a bank.[41] For the other freedoms, there is no explicit case law, and the opinions in academic literature are divided.[42]

In *Sapod Audic*, the Court came to the conclusion, without any further reasoning, that Article 28 EC (now Art. 34 TFEU) is not applicable to private agreements.[43] The *Spanish strawberries* case[44] brought a variant – one which is to be welcomed – from the point of view of free movement of goods. In this case, France was found to have infringed Article 10 EC (now Art. 4 (3) TEU) read with Article 28 EC (now Art. 34 TFEU), because it had not acted (sufficiently) against obstacles organized by market operators (angry farmers).[45]

2.2 *Justifications*

The Treaty provisions on the five freedoms are not absolute.[46] The available justifications can be conveniently grouped in several types.[47]

The first group comprises economic safeguard clauses. The amendments made by the Treaty of Maastricht revised this group in accordance with the current state of integration. These concern provisions dealing with economic policy (Art. 122 TFEU), and provisions on balance of payments difficulties (Arts. 143 and 144 TFEU), which are temporary in nature.

---

37. E.g. Case 2/74, *Reyners.*
38. Case C-184/99, *Grzelczyk* and Case C-413/99, *Baumbast.*
39. N. Nic Shuibhne, *supra* note 7, 100.
40. Case 36/74, *Walrave*; Case C-415/93, *Bosman*; Joined Cases C-51/96 & C-191/97, *Deliège*; Case C-309/99, *Wouters*; Case C-341/05, *Laval.*
41. Case C-281/98, *Angonese.*
42. C. Barnard, *supra* note 1, 77; see also S. Van den Bogaert, "Horizontality" in C. Barnard and J. Scott (Eds.), *The Legal Foundations of the Single market: Unpacking the Premises* (Hart, 2002), 123–152.
43. Case C-159/00, *Sapod Audic.* For more elaboration, see chapter 3.2. in this volume.
44. Case C-265/95, *Commission v. France (Spanish strawberries)*.
45. Idem.
46. C. Barnard, "Derogations, justifications and the four freedoms" in C. Barnard and O. Odudu (Eds.), *The Outer Limits of European Union Law* (OUP, 2009).
47. Another group, which concerned the transitional period of the common market, such as Arts. 26 and 226 EEC, has now been repealed. See Case C-212/96, *Chevassus-Marche v. Conseil régional de la Réunion.*

The second group comprises Articles 36, 45, 52, 62, 65, 72 and 345–347 TFEU.[48] Exceptions to free movements are from the point of view of the Member States national measures of general interest: no free movement for unsafe products or criminals. The exceptions contained in these provisions, most of which lose their effect where harmonization takes place, are non-economic in nature. As long as the focus was not on labour relations, the case law of the Court had no direct effect on national economic models. The rulings of the Court in *Viking* and *Laval*,[49] which regulate corporations and their governance, are much more sensitive and their impact is potentially more far reaching than those dealing with goods.[50]

As a counterbalance to the broad definition (including non-discriminatory measures) of the Treaty prohibition, the Court introduced in the *Cassis de Dijon* case also so-called "mandatory requirements" or "rule of reason" derogations.[51] These case-law-based justifications, such as consumer protection, are as a rule only applicable for indistinctly applicable national measures.[52]

In addition to these groups of general justifications, there are a number of specific exceptions relating to undertakings with special tasks[53] or certain specific sectors.[54]

In many cases the reasoning of the Court concentrates on the application of the principle of proportionality.[55] As part of the proportionality test, the Court stresses the importance of coherence or consistency.[56] Although the final judgment in principle rests on the national judge who has to apply the interpreted provision, the Court does not hesitate in some sensitive cases, such as coffee shops and soft drugs, to apply its interpretation to the case in question.[57]

The Charter of Fundamental Rights of the EU embeds the case law of the Court on the relationship between fundamental rights, national interests and the freedoms.[58]

2.3 *The convergence of the freedoms and exceptions*

Under the influence of the case law of the Court there has been a growing unity in the effect of the prohibitions[59] as well as of the justifications.[60] The judgment in *Futura*, concerning the freedom to provide services, gives a fine example.[61] In this judgment, references are made to the fundamental case law on establishment, workers, and goods in the context of both the prohibitions and the justifications. Not just the Court of Justice, but also the General Court uses

48. See Case C-186/01, *Dory*.
49. Case C-438/05, *Viking* and C-341/05, *Laval*.
50. J. Snell, *supra* note 24, 120.
51. Case C-120/78, *Cassis de Dijon*.
52. Exceptions are cases on environmental protection, see Case C-2/90 and on social security, see Case C-157/99, *Geraets-Smits*.
53. Arts. 37 and 106(2) TFEU.
54. Art. 42 TFEU in relation to agriculture, Art. 96 TFEU in relation to transport.
55. See recently Case C-573/12, *Alands*.
56. Joined Cases C-338/04, 359/04 and C-360/04, *Placanica*; Case C-169/07, *Hartlauer*.
57. Case C-137/09, *Josemans*.
58. Compare Case C-36/02, *Omega Spielhallen* with Case C-208/09, *Sayn-Wittgenstein*.
59. P. Oliver, "Goods and services: Two freedoms compared" in M Waelbroeck, M. Dony and A de Walsche, *Mélanges en hommage à Michel Waelbroeck* (Bruylant, 1999), 1365; J. Snell, *Goods and Services in EC Law. A Study of the Relationship between the Freedoms* (OUP, 2002); H.D. Jarass, "A unified approach to the fundamental freedoms" in M. Andenas and W.-H. Roth (Eds.), *Services and Free Movement in EU Law* (OUP, 2002), 141; M. Poiares Maduro, "Harmony and dissonance in free movement" in M. Andenas and W.-H. Roth (Eds.), *Services and Free Movement in EU Law* (OUP, 2002), 41.
60. K.J.M. Mortelmans, "Excepties bij non-tarifaire intracommunautaire belemmeringen: Assimilatie in het nieuwe EG-Verdrag?", (1997) SEW, 182; N. Nic Shuibhne, *supra* note 7, 185.
61. Case C-250/95, *Futura Participations*. See also Case C-503/99, *Commission v. Belgium (Golden Shares)*.

the technique of assimilation.[62] In some judgments, a convergence between the free movement rules and the competition rules can also be identified.[63]

However, important differences continue to exist, as will become apparent from an analysis of the different freedoms and, as mentioned earlier, depending on whether or not horizontal direct effect is recognized.[64] This is only logical, since there are in fact differences between the freedoms themselves. For instance, services – which are intangible unlike goods – cannot be stored, so there can be no time element between production and consumption. Persons have different characteristics from capital. These differences also affect the scope of the freedoms: while the free movement of capital also applies to capital from third countries,[65] the free movement provisions can in principle only be relied upon by nationals of EU Member States, and not by third-country nationals.

The starting point for the convergence of the prohibitions is the Court of Justice's case law on Article 34 TFEU. The judgment in *Cassis de Dijon* was a milestone in this respect.[66] In *Cassis*, the Court brought national measures (concerning product requirements) which did not distinguish between national and imported products within the scope of the prohibition. This broad definition of the prohibition under Article 34 TFEU was gradually taken over in relation to the interpretation of Article 56 TFEU and subsequently Articles 45 TFEU and 49 TFEU. The new text concerning free movement of capital (Art. 56 EC, now Art. 63 FTEU), introduced by the Treaty of Maastricht, has brought opportunities for a further convergence of the prohibitions.

The starting point for the convergence of the justifications, on the other hand, is to be found in the Treaty itself. Article 63(1)(b) TFEU includes a provision which is extremely similar to Articles 36, 45(3) and 52 TFEU. All these provisions concern public policy, public security and – with the exception of capital – public health.

Article 36 TFEU has also acted as a catalyst for the convergence of the rule of reason derogations. The "mandatory requirements" formulated in *Cassis de Dijon* for the free movement of goods have also been accepted, as "overriding requirements in the general interest", in relation to the freedom to provide services,[67] and they are gradually finding their way into other freedoms, such as the free movement of persons,[68] although this is certainly not an automatic development.[69]

2.4 *External aspects of the internal market*

In the analysis of the various obstacles to free movement, a distinction should be drawn between intra-Union movement and movement between a Member State and a third country.[70] The rules which apply in respect of the European Economic Area (EEA) are very similar to

62. Case T-266/97, *VTM*; the case law on services is used in relation to a situation concerning establishment.
63. Case C-309/99, *Wouters*. See on this, K.J.M. Mortelmans, "Towards convergence in the application of the rules on free movement and on competition", (2001) CML Rev., 613.
64. N. Nic Shuibhne, *supra* note 7, 32.
65. Case C-452/04, *Fidium*.
66. Case 120/78, *Cassis de Dijon*.
67. Compare Case C-120/78, *Cassis de Dijon* with Case C-353/89, *Commission v. the Netherlands (TV advertising)*.
68. See e.g. Case C-379/87, *Groener*; Case C-340/89, *Vlassopoulou*; and Case C-19/92, *Kraus*.
69. Case C-484/93, *Svensson and Gustavsson*. Here the Court did not accept the transposition of an argument about coherence of fiscal policy, taken from freedom to provide services, for freedom of capital movements.
70. Cf. Art. 206 TFEU. M. Cremona, "The external dimension of the single market: Building (on) the foundations" in C. Barnard and J. Scott (Eds.), *The Law of the Single European Market: Unpacking the Premises* (Hart, 2002), 351.

those applicable within the Union itself.[71] This is to some extent also true for Switzerland.[72] The Europe Agreements also contained, for some policy areas such as establishment,[73] rules which had the same content as the internal market and the EEA rules. After the accession of a number of East European countries in 2004 and 2007, similar international agreements remain relevant for countries such as Russia, with whom the Union has concluded a Partnership and Cooperation Agreement.[74] The freedom of movement between the Union and other third countries is subject to different sets of rules; these depend on *inter alia* international rules (e.g. GATT/ WTO).[75]

Now that the internal market has been (more or less) realized, and economic controls at the internal frontiers of the Member States within the European Union are no longer possible in theory, the external frontier, e.g. the common commercial policy and immigration policy, has become of crucial importance. It is thus of major significance to indicate which persons, goods, services and capital are permitted to enter the internal market and subject to what conditions. This dimension is examined in the chapter of this book on external relations.

3. The realization of the internal market: Positive integration and mutual recognition

3.1 *Harmonization and uniform legislation*

In a number of instances, the negative integration provisions aimed at achieving free movement go hand in hand with acts adopted by the institutions of the Union. The abolition of obstacles by one Member State will in many cases be insufficient to achieve an area without internal frontiers. Quality rules for goods (health requirements) and for persons (diplomas) will remain necessary in a number of instances. In many cases, these rules differ from one Member State to another – the requirement of an alcohol percentage in *Cassis de Dijon* of 15% in France and 20% in Germany is an example.[76] Such dissimilarities between the legislation of the Member States cause distortions which need to be removed.[77] The institutions of the Union are granted powers

71. See S. Norberg et al., *EEA Law: A Commentary on the EEA Agreement* (C.E. Fritzes AB, 1993); P. Oliver, assisted by M. Jarvis, *Free Movement of Goods in the European Community* (Sweet & Maxwell, 2003), 503. See also Case C-452/01, *Ospelt.*
72. See "EC-Switzerland Agreements on Free Movement" (2002), O.J. L 114/6; S. Breitenmoser, "Sectoral agreements between the EC and Switzerland: Contents and context", (2003) CML Rev., 1137–1186; C. Kaddous, C. Tobler and A. Zapedowska, "Chronik droit européen: Suisse–Union européenne/Europarecht: Schweiz–Europäische Union", 26 *Swiss Review of International and European Law* (2016), 526–560. See also Case C-452/04, *Fidium.*
73. See, e.g. Case C-268/99, *Jany.*
74. Decision 97/800 [1997] O.J. L 327/1. See Case C-265/03, *Simutenkov.*
75. For a systematic analysis and a comparison between EC and GATT law, see J. Tumlir, "GATT Regeln und Gemeinschaftsrecht. Ein Vergleich wirtschaftlicher und rechtlicher Funktionen" in M. Hilf, F.G. Jacobs, and E.U. Petersmann (Eds.), *GATT und die Europaïsche Gemeinschaft* (Nomos, 1986), 87. See also G. de Búrca, "Unpacking the concept of discrimination in EC and international trade law" in C. Barnard and J. Scott (Eds.), *The Law of the Single European Market: Unpacking the Premises* (Hart, 2002), 181; J. Scott, "Mandatory or imperative requirements in the EU and the WTO" in C. Barnard and J. Scott, *The Law of the Single European Market: Unpacking the Premises* (Hart, 2002), 269; J.W. van de Gronden, (Ed.), *The EU and WTO Law on Services* (Kluwer, 2009); P. Van den Bossche, *The Law and Policy of the World Trade Organization* (CUP, 2008).
76. Case 210/78, *Cassis de Dijon.*
77. On distortions see Art. 116 TFEU. As to the difference between distortion and discrimination; see also Case 14/68, *Walt Wilhelm*; Case C-379/92, *Peralta*; Case C-384/93, *Alpine Investments*; and Case C-376/98, *Germany v. Parliament and Council (Tobacco advertising I).*

to adopt harmonization measures or uniform measures. These rules (secondary law) must conform to the Treaty provisions on free movement (primary law), although in a number of cases the Court has granted the legislature of the Union a margin of discretion.[78] These rules contain, in a number of cases, exceptions which are substantively equivalent to those of the Treaty. Here too, these exceptions in secondary law must match the exceptions in primary law, as interpreted by the Court of Justice.[79]

Many proposals for Union measures failed to be adopted prior to the coming into force of the Single European Act (SEA) on 1 July 1987 because of the requirement of unanimity in Article 100 EEC. In the absence of Union measures, the Court of Justice reviewed national measures purely on the basis of the Treaty prohibitions.[80] To cope with this problem, the new Article 100A EEC (now Art. 114 TFEU) permitted harmonization measures for the completion of the internal market to be adopted by qualified majority. By the target date of the end of 1992, most of the 300 proposals presented by the Commission as part of its internal market programme[81] had been approved by the European Parliament and Council.[82] Some of these concern situations involving full or exhaustive harmonization. The Court, after having established this, then restricts itself to an interpretation of the relevant secondary legislation. Examples of this approach are particularly prevalent in the agricultural sector.[83] In such situations, there is no longer a possibility of relying on the Treaty exceptions in the TFEU, or only in very limited circumstances.[84] In many cases, though, harmonization is still partial or incomplete, so that primary law (the free movement principle and the recognized exceptions) may still be invoked in the non-harmonized areas.[85] That is the case for a large number of minimum harmonization directives in the environmental sector and concerning consumer protection. Here, the Court applies a double test. First, it looks at the content of the directive and – for national measures which go further – at the Treaty-based prohibition and the exceptions. In all cases involving the interpretation of a directive, the Court considers that the directive in question must be interpreted in the light of the Treaty provisions on free movement. In a number of judgments, the Court has considered the difference between exhaustive, full and minimum harmonization.[86] In a number of cases concerning directives, adopted by the legislature of the Union, on the sales and advertising of tobacco products, the Court has indicated the limits of the application of Article 114 TFEU. Article 114 TFEU does not confer on the legislature of the Union an exclusive competence to

78. Case 37/83, *Rewe-Zentral AG v. Direktor der Landwirtschaftskammer Rheinland*; Joined Cases C-427, 429 & 436/93, *Bristol-Myers Squibb, C. H. Boehringer Sohn, Boehringer Ingelheim KG and Boehringer Ingelheim A/S, and Bayer Aktiengesellschaft and Bayer Danmark A/S v.Paranova A/S*; See K.J.M. Mortelmans, "The relationship between the Treaty rules and Community measures for the establishment and functioning of the internal market: Towards a concordance rule" (2002) CML Rev., 1303–1346.
79. K. Lenaerts, *supra* note 20, 37.
80. Case 8/74, *Dassonville*; Case 2/74, *Reyners*.
81. Completing the Internal Market (COM(85)310 final), also called the White Paper.
82. See Commission Recommendation of 12 Jul. 2004 on the transposition into national law of directives affecting the internal market, O.J. 2005, L 98/47.
83. Case C-128/94, *Hans Hönig v. Stadt Stockach*; Case C-1/96, *The Queen v. Minister of Agriculture, Fisheries and Food.*
84. Cf. Art. 95 EC. See Case 5/77, *Tedeschi*. Constant case law, see Case C-222/91, *Philip Morris Belgium SA*.
85. Case C-573/12, *Alands Vindkraft*.
86. See, e.g. Case C-1/96, *The Queen v. Minister of Agriculture, Fisheries and Food, ex parte Compassion in World Farming*. See S. Weatherill, "Why harmonize?" in T. Tridimas and P. Nebbia (Eds.), *European Union Law for the Twenty-First Century: Rethinking the New Legal Order, Vol. 2, Internal Market and Free Movement. Community Policies* (OUP, 2004), 11; S. Weatherill, "Maximum versus minimum harmonization: Choosing between unity and diversity in the search for the soul of the internal market" in N. Nic Shuibhne and L.W. Gormley (Eds.), *From Single Market to Economic Union: Essays in Memory of John A. Usher* (OUP 2012), 175.

regulate the economic activities in the internal market. This provision is intended to improve the conditions for the establishment and functioning of the internal market. This provision may be used as a legal basis to prevent future obstacles, but the existence of those obstacles must be likely and the measure in question must actually aim to prevent those obstacles.[87] Recent case law of the Court is (almost) entirely marked by judicial green lights for legislative harmonization.[88] However, the application of the Charter of Fundamental Rights may lead to some limitations in this respect.[89]

3.2 *The mutual recognition principle*

The widespread failures in the years 1970–1986 of the attempts to adopt Community measures were partially compensated by the case law of the Court of Justice on the mutual recognition of national rules. The celebrated judgment in *Cassis de Dijon* is something of a landmark in this respect.[90] In this case, the Court introduced a number of mandatory requirements of general interest (so-called rule-of-reason exceptions) as a counterbalance to an overbroad definition of Article 34 TFEU. This judgment was also the basis for the rule of mutual recognition (or mutual acceptance).[91] This rule means that Member State A must admit goods or services coming from Member State B to its territory, if those goods or services have been lawfully produced and marketed in Member State B, according to the rules applicable in Member State B.[92] Member State A may hinder the free movement of such goods only on grounds of the exceptions provided in Article 36 TFEU or the judicially created overriding public interest requirements, for instance in relation to consumer protection. In this way, free movement may be achieved without the need for harmonization. The application of this home state (or state of origin) principle[93] leads to competition between legal systems.[94]

In the application of the mutual recognition principle, the rules on conflict of laws from international private law play an important role. In sensitive areas, such as health protection

---

87. Case C-376/98, *Germany v. Parliament and Council (Tobacco advertising I)*; Case C-491/01, *British American Tobacco*; Case C-434/02, *Andre v. Landrat des Kreises Herford*; Case C-210/03, *Swedish Match AB*; Joined Cases C-154 & 155/04, *The Queen, on application of Alliance for Natural Health (C-154/04) and Nutri-Link Ltd v. Secretary of State for Health, and the Queen, on application of National Association of Health Stores (C-155/04) and Health Food Manufacturers Ltd v. Secretary of State for Health and National Assembly for Wales.*
88. S. Weatherhill, *supra* note 4, 103 mentioning e,g. Case C-58/08, *Vodafone*.
89. Case C-293/12 and Case C-593/12, *Digital Rights*.
90. Case 120/78, *Cassis de Dijon*. A. Mattera, "L'article 30 du traité CEE, la jurisprudence 'Cassis de Dijon' et le principe de la reconnaissance mutuelle: Instruments au service d'une Communauté plus respectueuse des diversités nationales", (1992) RMC, 13–71. The mutual recognition principle was also formulated a month before the judgment in *Cassis* in Joined Cases 110 & 111/78, van Wesemael. This approach, best known from *Cassis de Dijon*, was in fact also used in Case 8/74, *Dassonville*.
91. V. Hatzopoulos, *Le principe communautaire d'équivalence et de reconnaissance mutuelle dans la libre prestation de services* (Bruylant, 1999); K. Armstrong, "Mutual recognition" in C. Barnard and J. Scott (Eds.), *The Law of the Single European Market: Unpacking the Premises* (Hart, 2002), 225.
92. For the concepts "lawfully produced and marketed", see B. O'Connor, "The free movement of foodstuffs in EC law" (1993) EFLR, 177. Cf. Case 59/82, *Schutzverband gegen Unwesen in der Wirtschaft v. Weinvertriebs*; Case C-296/00, *Carbone*.
93. See W.H. Roth, "Wettbewerb der Mitgliedstaaten oder Wettbewerb der Hersteller? Pladoyer fur eine Neubestimmung des Art 34", 159 *Zeitschrift für das gesamte Handelsrecht und Wirtschaftsrecht* (1995), 85 and 91.
94. See T. Koopmans, "Concurrentie tussen rechtsstelsels", (1992) SEW, 446; N. Reich, "Competition between legal orders: A new paradigm of EC law?", (1992) CML Rev., 861; R. Van den Bergh, "Towards an institutional legal framework for regulatory competition in Europe", (2000) *Kyklos*, 435; S. Weatherill, "Preemption, harmonization and the distribution of competence to regulate the internal market" in C. Barnard and J. Scott (Eds.), *The Law of the Single European Market: Unpacking the Premises* (OUP, 2002), 41.

and safety, the Union still tends to adopt harmonization measures dealing with essential requirements.[95] In these areas, there is a danger that too broad an interpretation of the mutual recognition principle would cause a reduction in national standards.[96] In its internal market programme, the Commission consciously presented the mutual recognition principle as a new strategy.[97] As part of the Commission's Package on Internal Market of Goods of 9 July 2008,[98] the so-called Mutual Recognition Regulation 764/2008 was adopted.

Depending on the subject-matter involved, the internal market is achieved through this rule of mutual recognition or through harmonized or uniform rules.[99] The Services Directive[100] illustrates the tension between mutual recognition rules and the Treaty rules on freedoms.[101]

4. Growing pains affecting the internal market

While 1992 was undoubtedly an important milestone in the history of the European Union (see Art. 14(1) EC), the internal market was not completed by 31 December 1992, neither in law nor in fact.[102] The Court of Justice ruled, in the area of free movement of persons, that in the absence of the required measures of harmonization, Article 14 EC does not have direct effect.[103] Partly as a result of this, the Court took on a much less prominent role in relation to the realization of the internal market, than it did in relation to the realization of the common market.[104] In the realization of the internal market, it is the Union legislature which takes a central role.

Article 26 TFEU contains the same definition of internal market as its predecessor Article 14 EC: an area without internal frontiers. What is, under current internal market law, the legal position of goods, persons, services or capital, that do not cross internal frontiers? Is there still a need for an inter-state element?

Recent developments complicate the answer to this question. Firstly, the growing case law of the Court of Justice in the slipstream of Directive 2004/38 on Citizens of the European Union and their family originating from a Third Country: the *Zambrano* route. Secondly, the entry into force of the Services Directive.

These growing pains will be examined in four themes: purely internal situation, re-importation and strategic migration, reverse discrimination and abuse of law.

---

95. Cf. the White Paper COM(85)310 final, para 39.
96. This view surfaced principally in the German literature. See E. Steindorff, Probleme des Art. 30 EWG-Vertrag (1984) *ZHR*, 338–355; J. Sedemund, "'Cassis de Dijon' und das neue Harmonisierungskonzept der Kommission" in J. Schwarze (Ed.), *Der Gemeinsame Markt Bestand und Zukunft in wirtschaftsrechtlicher Perspektive* (Nomos, 1987), 37. Cf. Case C-320/93, *Lucien Ortscheit*.
97. COM(85) 310 final, para 61. See on this R. Bieber, R. Dehousse, J. Pinder, and J.H.H. Weiler (Eds.), *1992: One European Market* (Nomos, 1988). See also A. Bernel, *Le principe d'équivalence ou de reconnaissance mutuelle en droit communautaire* (Schulthess Polygraphischer Verlag, 1996); D.C. Horng, "The principle of mutual recognition: The European Union's practise and development", (1999) *World Competition*, 135.
98. O.J. 2008, L 218.
99. In respect of *Cassis de Dijon*, Community legislation now governs the matter; see Reg. 1576/89, O.J. 1989, L 160/1, most recently amended by Reg. 3378/94, O.J. 1994, L 366/1.
100. 2006/123, O.J. 2006, L 376/36.
101. J. Snell, *supra* note 24, 113–114.
102. See T. Koopmans, "De paradox van 1992", (1989) RMT, 472; E. Steindorff, "Unvollkommener Binnenmarkt", (1994) ZHR, 149; S. Weatherill, "The Common Market: Mission accomplished?" in V. Heiskanen and K. Kulovesi (Eds.), *Function and Future of European Law* (Helsinki University Press, 1999), 33.
103. Case C-297/92, *Baglieri*; Case C-378/97, *Wijsenbeek*.
104. See Case 2/74, *Reyners*. In that judgment, the expiry of the transitional period for the common market was an essential element allowing the Court to recognize the direct effect of Art. 49 TFEU.

4.1 *Purely internal situation*

The prohibitions (on obstacles to free movement) and exceptions (to free movement) concern restrictions imposed on transborder economic activities: for instance, Cassis de Dijon from France that may not be marketed in Germany as Cassis de Dijon. If all the relevant aspects of an economic activity occur within one Member State (for instance, Dutch regulations concerning prices for bread baked and sold in the Netherlands by Dutch bakers) and there are no relevant provisions of secondary law, then according to the Court we are confronted with an "internal situation", and the prohibitions of Articles 45, 49, 56 TFEU cannot be relied upon.[105] In the discussion of the various Treaty provisions imposing prohibitions, the application of the internal situation doctrine to the various freedoms will be examined in detail. The main lines are as follows.

Cases such as *Pistre, Kos* and *Lancry*,[106] concerning tariffs, are no longer based on country borders, but declare the prohibitions to apply to regional or similar barriers. In a few cases concerning Article 30 TFEU, the Court ruled that regional rules come within the scope of application of this prohibition on tariffs.[107] The Court's judgment in *Carbonati Apuani* includes a general consideration which relates to non-tariff barriers, even though the case concerned tariff barriers.[108]

Since *Guimont*[109] (free movement of goods) and *Reisch*[110] (free movement of capital), the Court regularly gave an answer to the preliminary questions on free movement put to it, even though it was evident from the file that all the relevant aspects were situated within one Member State. The Court wanted to assist the national court, because it could not be excluded that the relevant national legislation might also be applicable to intra-Union (cross-border) situations.[111] In *Pistre*, the Court ruled that although the national rule in fact had no link with the import of goods, this could not exclude the applicability of Article 34 TFEU EC: there was an obstacle to trade because the French regulations could also apply to products from other Member States.[112] Likewise, in *Trijber and Harmsen*, concerning the scope of the Services Directive, the Court found that there was a cross-border element because the services concerned "may also be enjoyed by nationals of other Member States".[113]

In cases where the national measure is a copy of a Treaty provision, e.g. Article 101 TFEU, the Court of Justice has held that it has jurisdiction to give preliminary rulings on questions concerning EU law in situations in which the facts in the main proceedings fell outside the direct scope of that law, provided always that those provisions had been rendered applicable by the national law, which adopted, for solutions applied to purely internal situations, the same approach as that for solutions provided for under EU law. In such cases, according to settled case

105. See, e.g., Case 52/79, *Debauve*; Case C-41/90, *Höfner and Elser*; Case C-60/91, *Batista Morais*; Case C-112/91, *Werner v. Finanzamt Aachen-Innenstadt*; Case C-448/98, *Guimont*; Case C-186/12, *Impacto Azul Lida*. A variant is that another country is involved, but that it is a third country, e.g. Joined Cases C-64 & 65/96, *Uecker and Jacquet*.
106. Joined Cases C-321-324/94, *Pistre*; Joined Cases C-485 & 486/93, *Kos*; Joined Cases C-363 & 407–411/93, *Lancry*.
107. Joined Cases C-363 & 407–411/93, *Lancry*; Joined Cases C-485 & 486/93, *Kos*; Case C-212/96, *Chevassus*.
108. Case C-72/03, *Carbonati Apuani*. See also Case C-441/04, *A-Punkt Schmuckhandel* and Case C-293/02, *Jersey Produce Marketing Organisation v. States of Jersey et al.*
109. Case C-448/98, *Guimont*.
110. Joined Cases C-515, 519–524 & 526–540/99, *Reisch*.
111. See also Case C-212/06, *Belgian Social Security System*; Case C-367/12, *Sokoll-Seebacher*.
112. Joined Cases C-321-324/94, *Pistre*. See also Case C-448/98, *Guimont*.
113. Joined Cases C-340 & 341/14, *Trijber and Harmsen*, para 41.

law, it is clearly in the interests of the European Union that, in order to forestall future differences of interpretation, provisions or concepts taken from EU law should be interpreted uniformly, irrespective of the circumstances in which they are to apply.[114]

4.2 *Re-importation and strategic migration*

A person, product or service in Member State A may benefit from the rules on free movement if activities are performed in Member State B, or if the product was in circulation in Member State B. If a Belgian national exercises his or her right of free movement by, say, exercising his profession in France, and later wishes to exercise that profession in Belgium, he or she is a beneficiary of Union rights. This is not an internal situation and he or she may exercise his or her profession in Belgium under the same conditions as a Frenchman who wishes to exercise that profession in Belgium.[115] This case law has given rise to the application of re-importation or return constructions.[116] In many cases a product, person or service may return to its home Member State after a stay in another Member State.

The case law of the Court on third-country nationals and their children who could rely on their Union citizenship led to a special application of the internal situation. In *Zambrano*, the Court of Justice relied on Article 20 TFEU to prevent a Columbian national living in Belgium and a failed asylum seeker himself, and thus his family, from being deported from Belgium.[117] The Court considered that the refusal to grant Mr Zambrano a residence permit would lead to a situation where his children, citizens of the Union (who did not leave Belgium), would have to leave the territory of the Union in order to accompany their parents. It looked as if the Court was shedding the purely internal rule, but subsequent case law in *Dereci*[118] and *McCarthy*[119] attenuated the *Zambrano* approach.[120]

4.3 *Reverse discrimination*

In cases concerning internal situations, a person, service or product may well suffer from reverse discrimination. This means that a product, service or person from Member State A is discriminated against by that same Member State A compared with a product, service or person from Member State B, C etc. The Court has consistently found[121] that Union law is not applicable in cases where a Member State – in a field in which no common rules apply and there is no harmonization of legislation – treats national products or its own citizens less favourably than imported products or persons who make use of their rights of free movement.[122] In the *Belgian social security* case, the Court added that interpretation of provisions of Union law might possibly be of use to the national court, also having regard to situations classified as purely internal, in particular if the law of the Member State concerned were to require every national of that State

114. Case C-32/11, *Allianz Hungaria*; Case C-413/13, *FNV Kunsten*.
115. Case 115/78, *Knoors*.
116. Case C- 61/89, *Bouchacha*; Case C-370/90, *Singh*; Case C-291/05, *Eind*.
117. Case C-34/09, *Zambrano*.
118. Case C-256/11, *Dereci*.
119. Case C-434/09, *McCarthy*.
120. C. Barnard, *supra* note 1, 239.
121. See, e.g. Case 86/78, *SA des Grandes Distilleries Peureux*; Joined Cases 35 & 36/82, *Morson and Jhanjan*; Case 355/85, *Cognet*; Case 308/86, *Lambert*.
122. See further N. Nic Shuibhne, *supra* note 7, 85. This point is also at issue in the relations between the EU and global organizations; see W. Weiss, "Gibt es eine EU-Inländerdiskriminierung?: Zur Kollision von Gemeinschaftsrecht mit Welthandelsrecht und Assoziationsrecht", (1999) EuR, 499.

to be allowed to enjoy the same rights as those which a national of another Member State would derive from Union law in a situation considered to be comparable by that court.[123]

4.4 *Abuse of law*

Sometimes, the purpose of the operation described in the previous paragraph is to escape stricter national rules on matters such as minimum prices or establishment requirements by using Articles 34, 49 or 56 TFEU. The Court will not permit these provisions to be relied upon if it appears from objective circumstances that the goods or services were exported simply in order to be re-imported and thereby to escape a legal requirement with which they would otherwise have had to comply.[124] In that case, a Member State is entitled to take measures designed to prevent certain of its nationals from attempting, under cover of the rights created by the Treaty, to improperly circumvent their national legislation or to prevent individuals from improperly or fraudulently taking advantage of provisions of Union law.[125]

The *Centros* case, from which the preceding passage is taken, contains a reference to earlier case law, which illustrates the fact that this phenomenon has been manifest in a wide number of policy areas.[126] There is obvious tension between legitimately profiting from the competition between national legal orders, and the abuse of this. A number of judgments on the transfer of a company's seat reveal how restrictively the Court applies the concept of abuse of law, and what a commotion this entails.[127]

In recent years, the Court was regularly confronted with cases where citizens of the Union relied on Directive 2004/38 in order to obtain the right of residence. This Directive establishes a derived right of residence for third-country nationals who are family members of a Union citizen, within the meaning of Article 2(2) of that directive, only where that citizen has exercised his right of freedom of movement by becoming established in a Member State other than the Member State of which he is a national.[128] In two cases, the Court elaborated on the concept of "genuine residence" and added that the scope of Union law cannot be extended to cover abuses. Proof of such an abuse requires, first, a combination of objective circumstances in which, despite formal observance of the conditions laid down by the European Union rules, the purpose of those rules has not been achieved, and, secondly, a subjective element consisting in the intention to obtain an advantage from the European Union rules by artificially creating the conditions laid down for obtaining it.[129]

---

123. Case C-212/06, *Belgian Social Security*. See also Case C-250/03, *Mauri* and Case C-451/03, *Servizi Ausiliari Dottori Commercialisti.*
124. Case 229/83, *Leclerc. v. "Au blé vert"*; Case C-370/90, *Surinder Singh*, and Case C-23/93, *TV 10 SA v. Commissariaat voor de Media.*
125. Case C-212/97, *Centros*; Case C-208/00, *Uberseering.*
126. A. Kjellgren, "On the borders of abuse: The jurisprudence of the European Court of Justice on circumvention, fraud and abuses of Community law" in M. Andenas and W.-H. Roth (Eds.), *Services and Free Movement in EU Law* (OUP, 2002), 245.
127. Case C-212/97, *Centros*; Case C-208/00, *Uberseering*. See also Case C-109/01, *Akrich.*
128. Case C-127/08, *Metock*; Case C-256/11 *Dereci*; Joined Cases C-356/11 and C-357/11 *O. and Others*. See Art. 35 of Directive 2004/38: Member States may adopt the necessary measures to refuse, terminate or withdraw any right conferred by this Directive in the case of abuse of rights or fraud, such as marriages of convenience.
129. Case C-456/12, *O. and B.* and Case C-457/12, *S. and G.* See also Case C-110/99, *Emsland-Stärke*, Case C-303/08 *Bozkurt*, Case C-364/10, *Hungary v. Slovakia.*

CHAPTER 13
FREE MOVEMENT OF GOODS

*Stefaan Van den Bogaert and Pieter Van Cleynenbreugel**

1. Preliminary observations

One of the fundamental objectives of the EU is the establishment of an internal market,[1] which has been defined as "an area without internal frontiers in which the free movement of goods, persons, services and capital is ensured in accordance with the provisions of the Treaties".[2] In *Gaston Schul*, the Court of Justice of the EU (ECJ) famously held that the concept of a "common market", which it had defined in a consistent line of decisions and which was replaced by the concept of an "internal market" in the 1986 Single European Act, involved "the elimination of all obstacles to intra-Community trade in order to merge the national markets into a single market bringing about conditions as close as possible to those of a genuine internal market".[3] The free movement of goods, laid down in Title II (Arts. 28–37 TFEU) in Part Three on Union Policies and Internal Actions of the Treaty of the Functioning of the European Union is of quintessential importance to the fulfilment of this aim.

This chapter outlines and analyses the Treaty framework of this fundamental freedom as interpreted and applied by the ECJ in its extensive case law, resulting in the removal from the Member State legal orders of many a national measure found to restrict the free movement of goods (negative integration).[4] The other side of the coin, namely the adoption of EU secondary legislation harmonizing national legislation to ensure and promote free circulation of goods between EU Member States (positive integration), largely falls outside the scope of this chapter.[5]

1.1 The concept of a customs union

Article 28 TFEU indicates that the Union shall comprise a customs union covering all trade in goods. The customs union has both an external and an internal dimension. The *external* dimension relates to the adoption of a common customs tariff for goods coming from third countries

* S. Van den Bogaert: Europa Institute, Law Faculty, University of Leiden. P. Van Cleynenbreugel: Law Faculty, University of Liège.

1. Art. 3(3) TEU.
2. Art. 26(2) TFEU.
3. Case 15/81, *Schul*, para 33.
4. For detailed analyses of this dimension of EU free movement of goods law, see also a.o, C. Barnard, *The Substantive Law of the EU* (OUP, 2016); L.W. Gormley, *EU Law of Free Movement of Goods and Customs Union* (OUP, 2009); F. Peraldi-Leneuf, Y. Petit, B. Bertrand, L. Grard, C. Soulard and C. Blumann, *Introduction au marché intérieur. Libre circulation des marchandises* (Éditions de l'Université de Bruxelles, 2015); N. Nic Shuibhne, *The Coherence of EU Free Movement Law* (OUP, 2013), 304; S. Weatherill, *Cases & Materials on EU Law* (OUP, 2016).
5. This aspect is covered in Ch. 12, "The functioning of the internal market", of this book.

(Art. 31 TFEU) and the establishment of a common commercial policy in trade with third countries (Art. 207 TFEU).[6] The *internal* dimension focuses on the abolition, as between Member States, of obstacles to the free movement of goods. These obstacles can be of a financial nature, concerning pecuniary or fiscal measures, or have a non-financial character, dealing with measures imposing other types of obligations. On the one hand, the financial restrictions comprise firstly, border charges on imports and exports and the charges having an equivalent effect (Art. 30 TFEU), and secondly, discriminatory or protectionist measures of internal taxation (Art. 110 TFEU). Although internal tax measures are not formally addressed in the Title in the Treaty dedicated to the free movement of goods, in practice they are invariably seen as complementary to the prohibitions incorporated in that Title. On the other hand, the non-financial restrictions cover quantitative restrictions as well as measures having an equivalent effect to quantitative restrictions on imports and exports (Arts. 34–36 TFEU).

1.2 *The term "goods"*

The concept of "goods" has not been defined in the Treaty. In *Commission v. Italy*, the ECJ has explained the scope of the terms as follows: "By goods […], there must be understood products which can be valued in money and which are capable, as such, of forming the subject of commercial transactions".[7] This definition is not considered to be exhaustive, resulting in a very wide array of products being captured by the "goods" notion. From the Court's case law, it appears, in particular, that agricultural products such as strawberries have been qualified as goods,[8] just like animals;[9] gold;[10] waste, regardless of whether it has any intrinsic commercial value;[11] coins which are no longer legal tender;[12] human corpses and body parts;[13] or, perhaps surprisingly, electricity, even though it is not tangible.[14] Conversely, in *Jägerskiöld v. Gustafsson*, the Court held that even though the granting of fishing rights and the issuing of fishing permits could be valued in money and could be the subject of trade, "this was not sufficient to bring them within the scope of the provisions relating to the free movement of goods".[15] The granting of rights and the issuing of permits were not deemed tangible products; they were intangible benefits, even if they were laid down in a document.[16] The same goes for lottery tickets.[17] In a similar fashion, the

---

6. These matters shall be tackled in Ch. 41, "Union external relations under the TFEU", of this book.
7. Case 7/68, *Commission v. Italy*.
8. Case C-265/95, *Commission v. France*, paras. 17–18.
9. Case C-67/97, *Criminal proceedings against Bluhme*, para 19.
10. Case C-166/03, *Commission v. France*, paras. 2–3, dealing with French legislation obliging certain gold products to be named gold alloy, whereas those products were marketed as gold in their Member State of origin.
11. Case C-2/90, *Commission v. Belgium* (*Walloon Waste*), para 23. See for other illustrations also Case C-324/93, *The Queen/Secretary of State for the Home Department, ex parte Evans Medical and Macfarlan Smith*; Joined Cases C-418/97 and C-419/97, *ARCO Chemie Nederland Ltd*; Case C-221/06, *Stadtgemeinde Frohnleiten*; Case C-28/09, *Commission v. Austria*.
12. Case 7/78, *Regina v. Thompson, Johnson and Woodiwiss*, para 25. Coins and banknotes that are legal tender do not constitute goods, see also Case C-358/93, *Bordessa* para 12.
13. Case C-203/99, *Veedfald*; Case C-421/09, *Humanplasma*.
14. Case C-379/98, *PreussenElektra*.
15. Case C-97/98, *Jägerskiöld*, para 36. The Court nevertheless considered the provision of those fishing rights to constitute a service which is covered by Art. 56 TFEU if it has a cross-frontier character.
16. Rules concerning the tax deductibility of gifts in kind equally do not concern goods, which may however be the object of the gift, see Case C-318/07, *Persche*, para 29.
17. See Case C-275/92, *Schindler*, confirmed in Case C-124/97, *Läärä*, para 20.

Court held in *Vereniging van Vlaamse Reisbureaus* that the sale of travel should not be qualified as a good, but rather as a service provided by a travel agency.[18]

1.3 Goods coming from third countries

The Treaty provisions on the free movement of goods apply regardless of the nationality or the residence of the owner, the trader or the purchaser.[19] In this regard, they differ from the other fundamental freedoms. The Treaty provisions on goods apply in the first place to products originating in Member States. By virtue of Article 29(2) TFEU, these provisions also apply to products coming from third countries which are in free circulation in the Member States. The same principle also applies to Article 110 TFEU, even though the Treaty does not explicitly state this anywhere.[20]

Goods originating in a third country shall be considered to be in free circulation in a Member State if the import formalities have been complied with and any customs duties or charges having an equivalent effect which are payable have been levied in that Member State, and if they have not benefited from a total or partial drawback of such duties or charges.[21] In *Donckerwolke*, the Court held that goods originating in third countries and placed in free circulation "are definitively and wholly assimilated to products originating in Member States".[22]

In practice, this means that products coming from third countries must first pass the EU Common Customs Wall. Upon arrival in the EU, a customs duty is to be paid according to the Common Customs Tariff. Detailed rules are to be found in Regulation 952/2013 on the Union Customs Code.[23] The amount of the duty is fixed by the Council and is determined depending on the origin and the value of the good. Since the entry into force of the Common Customs Tariff in 1969, the customs union is regarded as an area of exclusive EU competence.[24] Duties recovered under the Common Customs Tariff are collected by the competent national authorities but belong to the Union's "own resources", accruing to the general budget of the EU.[25]

1.4 Cross-border movement of goods

Article 30 TFEU prevents Member States from levying customs duties and charges having an equivalent effect on goods *imported* from another Member State, on goods in transit within its territory[26] as well as on products *exported* to another Member State. Article 110 TFEU prohib-

---

18. Case 311/85, *Vereniging van Vlaamse Reisbureaus*, para 32.
19. Joined Cases 2/69 and 3/69, *Sociaal fonds voor de Diamantarbeiders*, paras. 24–26.
20. Case 193/85, *Cooperativa Co-Frutta*, para 25.
21. Art. 28(2) TFEU, which states that the provisions of Art. 30 and of Chapter 3 of this Title shall apply to products originating in Member States and to products coming from third countries which are in free circulation in Member States. On the notion of free circulation, see Art. 29 TFEU. For illustrations, see Case 288/83, *Commission v. Ireland*; Case 69/84, *Padovani*; Case 125/88, *Nijman*, para 11 and Case C-216/01, *Budvar*, para 95.
22. Case 41/76, *Donckerwolcke*, para 17.
23. Reg. 952/2013 of the European Parliament and of the Council of 9 Oct. 2013 laying down the Union Customs Code, O.J. 2013, L 269/1, which will apply from 1 May 2016 onwards. This Regulation will repeal the previous Reg. (EC) 450/2008 of the European Parliament and of the Council of 23 Apr. 2008 laying down the Community Customs Code, O.J. 2008, L 145/1.
24. Art. 3(1) (a) TFEU.
25. On the EU's own resources, see Council Decision 2007/436/EC of 7 June 2007 on the system of the European Communities' own resources, O.J. 2007, L 163/17. See also Ch. 9, "Budget and finances", of this book for more information on the EU's budget.
26. See for examples Case 266/81, *Società Italiana per l'Oleodotto Transalpino (SIOT)*, para 20; Case C-16/94, *Dubois*; Case C-23/99, *Commission v. France*; Case C-112/00, *Schmidberger*; Case C-320/03, *Commission v.*

its discriminatory or protectionist treatment negatively impacting on products imported from other Member States via national taxation. Likewise, Articles 34–36 TFEU prohibit quantitative restrictions or measures having an equivalent effect *between* Member States. A cross-border element is thus required to trigger the application of the relevant Treaty provisions. This entails that measures wholly internal to one Member State, restricting the importation or exportation of goods from one region of a Member State to another region of the same Member State are in principle not captured by those provisions.[27] EU law allows for situations of reverse discrimination to arise or remain in place.[28] In this specific context, reverse discrimination refers to a situation where goods imported from or exported to other Member States are treated more favourably than goods circulating only domestically.[29]

Whilst the Court formally never departed from the wholly internal situation doctrine, it nevertheless managed to interpret the Treaty provisions sufficiently widely and flexibly so as to avoid the application of the doctrine on a number of occasions. In *Lancry*, a case concerning dock dues imposed in the French overseas departments on imports, the Court unequivocally stipulated that a charge levied at a regional frontier in a Member State constitutes an obstacle to the free movement of goods which is "at least as serious" as a charge levied at the national frontier of the Member State.[30] The establishment of a regional customs frontier undermines the unity of the EU customs territory, regardless of whether the products subjected to the charger are domestic or imported from other Member States.[31] In a similar fashion, in *Carbonati Apuani*, a case in which the Court was asked to adjudicate on whether a local tax on all marble from Carrara that crosses the municipality's territorial boundaries infringes the Treaty free movement rules, the Court issued the sweeping statement that the "very principle of a customs union [...] requires the free movement of goods to be ensured within the union generally, not in trade between Member States alone, but more broadly throughout the territory of the customs union. If Articles 28 and 30 TFEU make express reference only to trade between Member States, that is because the framers of the Treaty took it for granted that there were no charges exhibiting the features of a customs duty in existence within the Member States".[32]

In *Pistre*, the Court has made it clear that Article 34 TFEU cannot be considered inapplicable simply because all the facts of the specific case before the national court are confined to a single Member State.[33] Also in such a situation, the application of the national measure may have an effect on the free movement of goods between Member States, "in particular when the measure in question facilitates the marketing of goods of domestic origin to the detriment of imported goods".[34] In such circumstances, the application of the national measure, even if it merely applies

Austria.

27. The same goes for goods produced in a Member State and subsequently re-imported, where the export and re-import had the sole purpose of circumventing stricter national rules, see Case 229/83, *Leclerc*.
28. For an early illustration, see Case 86/78, *SA des grandes distilleries Peureux*.
29. Joined Cases 314/81, 315/81, 316/81 and 83/82, *Waterkeyn*, para 11; Case 286/81, *Oosthoek*, para 9 and Case 355/85, *Cognet*, para 10. See for additional examples, Case 98/86, *Mathot* and Case 237/82, *Jongeneel Kaas*. On the concept of reverse discrimination, see P. Oliver, "Some further reflections on the scope of Articles 28–30 (ex 30–36 EC)", 36 CML Rev. (1999), 783 and A. Tryfonidou, *Reverse Discrimination in EC Law* (Kluwer, 2009), 31–40.
30. See Case C-363/93, *Lancry*, para 26; See also Case C-163/90, *Legros*, para 16.
31. Case C-363/93, *Lancry*, para 27; Case C-163/90, *Legros*, para 17.
32. Case C-72/03, *Carbonati Apuani*, para 22.
33. Joined Cases C-321/94 to C-324/94; Case C-321/94, *Pistre*; Case C-322/94, *Barthes*; Case C-323/94, *Milhau*; and Case C-324/94, *Oberti*, para 44.
34. Joined Cases C-321/94 to C-324/94; Case C-321/94, *Pistre*; Case C-322/94 *Barthes*; Case C-323/94 *Milhau*; and Case C-324/94, *Oberti*, para 45.

to domestic producers, can be said to create and maintain a difference of treatment between domestic and foreign goods, hindering, at least potentially, intra-Community trade.[35]

1.5 *Direct effect*

The Treaty free movement provisions explicitly target measures adopted by Member States impeding the free movement of goods. From the expiry of the transitional period establishing the common market,[36] the Court consistently held that the free movement provisions have direct effect. As a result, those provisions can be invoked by natural or legal persons as well as Member States in proceedings before national courts against restrictive measures adopted by a Member State as the principal addressee of the provisions.[37] The provisions can equally be invoked against private bodies exercising regulatory functions akin to the state.[38]

1.5.1 *Measures adopted by states and EU institutions*

All state measures amounting to a customs duty, a levy of equivalent effect, a quantitative restriction, a measure having equivalent effect or an internal tax can be prohibited. The ECJ consistently adhered to a wide view of what constitute state measures. Firstly, this set of rules includes all statutes, rules, practices[39] and in some cases even statements[40] emanating from public or

---

35. The mere potentiality of such effects has been considered sufficient for the Court to accept jurisdiction in a request for a preliminary ruling dealing with a purely internal situation, see Case C-448/98, *Guimont*, para 22. In that case, the rule at stake was nevertheless applicable to both domestic and imported products, though in practice it had so far only been applied to domestic goods. It cannot therefore be maintained that the Court would proceed in the same fashion if a national rule explicitly provided for a different treatment *to the detriment of* domestic goods.
36. Art. 8(1) EEC Treaty stated that "[t]he Common Market shall be progressively established in the course of a transitional period of twelve years. The transitional period shall be divided into three stages of four years each; the length of each stage may be modified in accordance with the provisions set out below. Art. 8(7) EEC Treaty determined that the expiry of the transitional period shall constitute the final date for the entry into force of all the rules laid down and for the completion of all the measures required for the establishment of the Common Market". In Case 2/74, *Reyners* and Case 33/74, *Van Binsbergen*, the Court made clear that the freedom of establishment and freedom to provide services provisions in the Treaty were to be considered as having direct effect following the expiry of the transitional period. In doing so, it also paved the way for other freedoms to be invoked before (national) judges.
37. Art. 30 TFEU (formerly Art. 12 EEC) was at stake in the landmark judgment of *van Gend & Loos*, which laid the foundations for the concept of direct effect. The direct effect of Art. 34 TFEU was established in Case 74/76, *Iannelli*; that of Art. 35 TFEU in Case 83/78, *Pigs Marketing Board* and that of Art. 110 (1) and (2) TFEU in Case 7/65, *Lütticke* and Case 27/67, *Fink-Frucht*, respectively. Prior to explicitly acknowledging so, the Court already accepted the direct applicability and direct effect of those provisions, e.g. in the *Dassonville* judgment itself.
38. Case C-171/11, *Fra.bo.*
39. See for examples of administrative practices *inter alia* Case 249/81, *Commission v. Ireland*, including a practice to promote the buying of domestic products into the definition; Joined Cases 266/87 and 267/87, *The Queen v. Royal Pharmaceutical Society of Great Britain* para 15; Case C-192/01, *Commission v. Denmark*, para 40; Case C-212/03, *Commission v. France*, para 17; Case C-88/07, *Commission v. Spain*, para 54.
40. Case C-470/03, *Lehtinen*, para 58. In para 66, it was held that "statements which, by reason of their form and circumstances, give the persons to whom they are addressed the impression that they are official positions taken by the State, not personal opinions of the official, are attributable to the State. The decisive factor for the statements of an official to be attributed to the State is whether the persons to whom those statements are addressed can reasonably suppose, in the given context, that they are positions taken by the official with the authority of his office".

regulatory authorities,[41] including rules prescribed by international agreements[42] or administrative practices that have no national law legal basis.[43] However, a mere intention to adopt restrictive measures is not sufficient; the rules or measures have to be "enacted by" the Member States authorities concerned. Secondly, the authorities enacting these measures can be legislative or administrative, public or private and situated at national, regional or local levels.[44]

In addition, the ECJ established two further categories of measures that can also be captured by the free movement provisions. Firstly, it recognized that not only state action, but also inaction by the state may trigger the application of the Treaty prohibitions.[45] This way, private actions could be brought under the Court's scrutiny. In these circumstances, Member States will be regarded by the Court as having failed to ensure compliance with the Treaty free movement provisions by not effectively acting against certain private actions hindering free movement. The classic example here is the *Spanish strawberries* case, in which the Commission commenced enforcement proceedings against France for not taking sufficient measures to avoid farmers from committing acts of violence directed against agricultural products originating in other Member States.[46] The Court acknowledged the difficulty for the competent authorities to deal with these types of cases, but nevertheless found that the French Government had "manifestly and persistently abstained from adopting appropriate and adequate measures to put an end to the acts of vandalism which jeopardize the free movement" of certain agricultural products on its territory and to prevent the recurrence of such acts.[47] France was held to have infringed Article 34 TFEU, read in conjunction with the principle of sincere cooperation.[48] In *Schmidberger*, the Court confirmed that a Member State should take all necessary measures against actions that prevent the effective transit of goods through its territory as a result of actions by individuals.[49] As a result, the fact that the competent authorities of a Member State "did not ban a demonstration which resulted in the complete closure of a major transit route such as the Brenner motorway for almost 30 hours on end is capable of restricting intra-Union trade in goods".[50] However, the Court in this case, paying due regard to the wide discretion to be accorded to national authorities matters like this, concluded that the Austrian authorities were reasonably entitled to consider that the legitimate objective of the demonstration could not be have been

41. This includes the judiciary, see Case 58/80, *Dansk Supermarked*, and Case 434/85, *Allan and Hanbury's Ltd.*
42. See for examples Case 144/81, *Keurkoop*; Case 286/86, *Deserbais*; Case C-3/91, *Confiserie du Tech SA*; Case C-324/93, *The Queen v. Secretary of State for Home Department, ex parte Evans Medical Ltd and Macfarlan Smith Ltd.*
43. See e.g. Case 21/84, *Commission v. France*, para 13.
44. Case 222/82, *Apple and Pear Development Council*; Case 21/88, *Du Pont de Nemours Italiana*; Joined Cases C-1/90 and C-176/90, *Aragonesa*; Case C-416/00, *Morellato*; Case C-255/03, *Commission v. Belgium*, not published in the ECR. For an overview and several hypotheses, see P. Oliver (Ed.), *Oliver on Free Movement of Goods in the European Union* (Hart, 2010), 56–60. Private bodies entrusted with regulatory functions equally fall within the scope of Arts. 34–35 TFEU measures, see for example Joined Cases 266/87 and 267/87, *The Queen v. Royal Pharmaceutical Society of Great Britain*, paras. 15–16 and Case C-16/94, *Dubois* para 20. See also Case C-292/92, *Hünermund*, where a national private body without sanctioning powers was nevertheless entrusted with authorization decisions.
45. See *inter alia* Case 249/81, *Commission v. Ireland*; Case C-325/00, *Commission v. Germany*; Case C-227/06, *Commission v. Belgium*, not published in the ECR. An example of intellectual property entitlements being considered measures attributed to a Member State is Case 144/81, *Keurkoop*.
46. Case C-265/95, *Commission v. France*, paras. 31–32.
47. Case C-265/95, *Commission v. France*, para 65.
48. Formerly laid down in Art. 10 EC, now replaced, in substance, by Art. 4(3) TEU.
49. Case C-112/00, *Schmidberger*, para 60.
50. Case C-112/00, *Schmidberger*, para 64.

achieved in the present case by measures less restrictive of intra-EU trade.[51] Recently, the Court in *Ålands Vindkraft* noted again that failure by a Member State to adopt adequate measures to prevent barriers to the free movement of goods created through the actions of traders but made possible by specific legislation of that state "is just as likely to obstruct intra-Community trade as is a positive act".[52] Swedish legislation providing for the award of tradable certificates to producers of green electricity solely in respect of green electricity produced in the territory of that state was regarded as capable of impeding imports of green electricity from other Member States.[53] Ultimately, the Court held that the Swedish system could be objectively justified.

Secondly, also quantitative restrictions or measures having an equivalent effect adopted by EU institutions could be subject to Articles 34–35 TFEU scrutiny. In *Denkavit*, the Court stated that export restrictions could equally emanate from EU institutions.[54] This has been confirmed in subsequent case law.[55] In all situations, the Court confirmed that the prohibition laid down in Articles 34–35 TFEU not only covers national measures, but also supranational measures adopted by the EU institutions. EU institutions nevertheless appear to be granted more leeway than Member States in restricting the free movement of goods. In most judgments, the Court indeed held that the supranational rules actually contributed to the free movement of goods, and therefore did not fall foul of the prohibitions in Articles 34–35 TFEU.[56]

1.5.2 *Horizontal direct effect?*

The Treaty provisions on free movement of goods are vertically directly effective. They can be invoked in national proceedings against the Member States or the EU institutions which adopted them or to which they can be attributed. This could happen even in an incidental way in disputes between private litigants, where the compatibility of a national measure with EU free movement provisions is called into question.[57] A Member State national may rely on those provisions against his or her own Member State.[58] In a similar fashion, a Member State may invoke the provisions against a fellow Member State on the basis of Articles 259–260 TFEU.[59]

What is less clear is whether the Treaty provisions are also horizontally directly effective, i.e. whether they capture also private measures, such as contractual arrangements between private parties limiting in themselves the importation or exportation of goods in the territory of a Member State. In *Dansk Supermarked*, the Court did hold that it is "impossible in any circumstances for agreements between individuals to derogate from the mandatory provisions of the Treaty

51. Case C-112/00, *Schmidberger*, para 93. For instance, the Court took into account that the obstacle to the free movement of goods resulting from that demonstration was "limited by comparison with both the geographic scale and the intrinsic seriousness of the disruption", para 85.
52. Case C-573/12, *Ålands Vindkraft*, para 74.
53. Case C-573/12, *Ålands Vindkraft*, para 75.
54. Case 15/83, *Denkavit*, para 15, by analogy with Joined Cases 80/77 and 81/77, *Les fils de Ramel*, which already maintained likewise for tariff restrictions.
55. Case C-51/93, *Meyhui*, para 11; Case C-284/95, *Safety Hi-Tech*, para 63; Case C-114/96, *Kieffer and Thill*, para 27; Case C-210/03, *Swedish Match*, para 59; Joined Cases C-154/04 and C-155/04, *Alliance for Natural Health*, para 47; Case C-59/11, *Kokopelli*, para 80.
56. For background, see K.J.M. Mortelmans, "The relationship between the treaty rules and community measures for the establishment and functioning of the internal market: Towards a concordance rule?", 39 CML Rev. (2002), 1303–1346.
57. An example can be found in Case 261/81, *Rau*.
58. One only has to think of the seminal judgments in *Dassonville* (Case 8/74), and *Groenveld* (Case 15/79) to find examples of the Court implicitly accepting this position.
59. Case C-388/95, *Belgium v. Spain*, offers an example in this regard.

on the free movement of goods".[60] However, this statement was never reiterated by the Court in later case law. To the contrary, on several occasions, the Court has explicitly rejected horizontal direct effect for Article 34 TFEU. In *Sapod Audic,* the Court stated that "a contractual provision cannot be regarded as a barrier to trade for the purposes of Article [34 TFEU] since it was not imposed by a Member State but agreed between individuals".[61] In this regard, the Court generally maintains a strict distinction between the addressees of the free movement rules on goods and the competition rules.[62] In *Vlaamse Reisbureaus,* the Court emphasized that "Articles [101 and 102 TFEU] concern the conduct of undertakings and not laws or regulations of the Member States", whereas Article [34 TFEU] "concern[s] only public measures and not the conduct of undertakings".[63] Private agreements between market operators or unilateral business decisions amounting to quantitative restrictions or measures having equivalent effect would in practice thus not be covered by Articles 34–36 TFEU, but rather fall under the Articles 101–102 TFEU prohibitions on anticompetitive behaviour instead.

In 2012 the Court reignited the debate on the horizontal direct effect of Articles 34–35 TFEU in its *Fra.Bo* judgment. The dispute concerned a decision from the German certification body "DVGW" (the Deutsche Vereinigung des Gas- und Wasserfaches) to withdraw or refuse to extend the certificate for copper fittings – intended in particular for piping for water or gas – produced and distributed by the Italian company Fra.bo. The ECJ held that Article 34 TFEU "applies to standardization and certification activities of a private-law body, where the national legislation considers the products certified by that body to be compliant with national law and that has the effect of restricting the marketing of products which are not certified by that body".[64]

In so arguing, the Court confirmed and at the same time extended to the domain of goods a line of case law relating to other fundamental freedoms that already acknowledged the direct effect of the Treaty provisions in relation to professional or private bodies exercising regulatory functions akin to the state.[65] As a result, traders can now under certain circumstances directly rely on Articles 34–35 TFEU before national courts vis-à-vis private (standardization) bodies. Beyond the specific situation of private associations endowed with (quasi-) regulatory powers, the Court has not accepted the invocation of Articles 34–35 TFEU directly against a private defendant in national proceedings.[66]

2. Financial restrictions: tariff barriers

Within the category of the financial restrictions to the free movement of goods, a distinction needs to be made between on the one hand the customs duties and the charges having an

---

60. Case C-58/80, *Dansk Supermarked,* para 17. This case concerned the scope of IP entitlements, which were held only to exist if and to the extent that the national judiciary was willing to acknowledge and protect them, see para 12.
61. Case C-159/00, *Sapod Audic,* para 74.
62. 177/82 and 178/82, *Van de Haar;* Case 65/86, *Bayer.*
63. Case 311/85, *Vereniging voor Vlaamse reisbureaus,* paras. 11 and 30.
64. Case C-171/11, *Fra.bo,* para 32.
65. See Case 36/74, *Walrave;* Case C-415/93, *Bosman,* para 83; Case C-438/05 *Viking;* Case C-341/05, *Laval.* See for an overview, S. Van den Bogaert, "Horizontality" in C. Barnard and J. Scott (Eds.), *The Legal Foundations of the Single Market: Unpacking the Premises* (Hart, 2002), 123–152 and H. Schepel, "Constitutionalising the market, marketising the constitution, and to tell the difference: On the horizontal application of the free movement provisions in EU law", 18 ELJ (2012), 177–200.
66. See also C. Krenn, "A missing piece in the horizontal effect 'jigsaw': Horizontal direct effect and the free movement of goods", 49 CML Rev. (2012), 177–216. See also, more generally, L.W. Gormley, "Private parties and the free movement of goods: Responsible, irresponsible, or a lack of principles?", 38 *Fordham International Law Journal* (2015), 993–1016.

equivalent effect (Art. 30 TFEU), and on the other hand the internal taxation measures (Art. 110 TFEU). The former will be addressed in this section, the latter in the next.

Article 30 TFEU unequivocally prohibits customs duties on imports and exports as well as charges having an equivalent effect between Member States. The prohibition applies equally to customs duties of a fiscal nature.

2.1 *Customs duties*

Customs duties are pecuniary or fiscal charges levied on goods at the time or by reason of the fact that they cross a border between Member States.[67] As the Court held in *Capolongo*, these charges have the negative effect of altering the cost price of the product in question.[68] Customs duties between Member States are therefore strictly prohibited. They are viewed as figuring among the most blatant barriers to the achievement of the internal market, the abolition of which is therefore essential. The Court has not often had to deal with customs duties in the strict sense, the landmark case of *Van Gend & Loos* being one of the notable exceptions.[69] Since border controls on goods in the EU have been lifted by the Single European Act, customs duties now belong to a distant past.

2.2 *Charges having an equivalent effect*

Aside from customs duties, Article 30 TFEU also prohibits charges having the equivalent effect of customs duties (CEEs). The motivation for this inclusion is straightforward: in the absence of a prohibition on CEEs, Member States would have been in a position relatively easily to circumvent the prohibition of customs duties by imposing fiscal barriers to trade that do not constitute a customs duty in the strict sense. The CEEs have thus been regarded as necessarily complementary to customs duties, allowing for a significant increase in the effectiveness of the Article 30 TFEU prohibition.[70]

Unsurprisingly, the Court has given a wide interpretation to this term. In *Commission v. Belgium,* the Court stated that any measure which leads to the same discriminatory or protective results as customs duties falls within the CEEs definition.[71] Building on this definition, it stated in *Commission v. Italy* that "any pecuniary charge, however small and whatever its designation and mode of application, which is imposed unilaterally on domestic or foreign goods by reason of the fact that they cross a frontier, and which is not a customs duty in the strict sense, constitutes a charge having equivalent effect within the meaning of [...] the Treaty".[72] The Court added that this is so, "even if the charge is not imposed for the benefit of the State, is not discriminatory or

67. It does not matter whether the charge is levied at the border or subsequently; the mere fact that it is levied as a consequence of having crossed the border suffices, see Case 78/76, *Steinike.*
68. Case 77/72, *Capolongo,* para 12.
69. Case 26/62, *Van Gend & Loos.*
70. Joined Cases 2/62 and 3/62, *Gingerbread,* at 432.
71. Joined Cases 2/62 and 3/62, *Gingerbread,* at 432.
72. Case 24/68, *Commission v. Italy,* para 9. The definition remained in use in among others Joined Cases 2/69 and 3/69, *Diamantarbeiders,* para 15–18; Case 29/72, *Marimex,* para 7; Case 90/79, *Commission v. France,* para 13; Case 158/82, *Commission v. Denmark,* para 18; Case C-163/90, *Legros,* para 13; Case C-266/91, *Celulose Beira,* para 10; Case C-426/92, *Milch-Kontor,* para 50; Case C-130/93, *Lamaire,* para 13; Joined Cases C-485/93 and C-486/93, *Simitzi,* para 15; Case C-90/94, *Haahr Petroleum,* para 20; Case C-347/95, *Fazenda Pública* para 18; Case C-213/96, *Outokumpu Oy.,* para 20; Case C-109/98, *CRT France International,* para 11; Case C-389/00, *Commission v. Germany,* para 22; Case C-387/01, *Weigel,* para 64; Case C-72/03, *Carbonati Apuani,* para 20; Joined Cases C-393/04 and C-41/05, *Air Liquide Industries Belgium,* para 51; Case C-173/05, *Commission v. Italy,* para 42 and Case C-254/13, *Orgacom,* paras. 22 and 24.

protective in effect and if the product on which the charge is imposed is not in competition with any domestic product".[73] In other words, it is the *effect* of the measure, the actual levying of the charge, and not the *purpose or the motivation behind it*, which determines the scope of application of Article 30 TFEU.[74] This was subsequently reiterated by the Court in *Diamantarbeiders*. It held that it "follows from the system as a whole and from the general and absolute nature of the prohibition [...] that customs duties are prohibited independently of any consideration of the purpose for which they were introduced and the destination of the revenue obtained therefrom".[75] The Court added that the Treaty rules apply regardless of whether the contested national measures adversely affect certain Member States and their nationals, or all EU citizens, or only the nationals of the Member State which was responsible for the measures in question.[76]

Just like with customs duties, the prohibition laid down in Article 30 TFEU has also with regard to CEEs been construed as a fundamental rule which does not permit any exceptions: charges are effectively prohibited *per se*.[77]

2.3 *Permissible charges*

Despite the clear and absolute wording of the prohibition of Article 30 TFEU, charges have nevertheless been deemed permissible in two particular situations: 1) when the payment is levied to cover the costs of a mandatory inspection required by EU law; and 2) when the payment constitutes a consideration for a service rendered. These are not exceptions to the prohibition of customs duties or CEEs. In those circumstances, the charges are rather not considered to be customs duties or charges having an equivalent effect at all.

2.3.1 *Duty for inspection required by EU law*

Firstly, where EU law *requires* inspections to be carried out on imported goods, the costs for such an inspection may be recovered and will escape the prohibition of Article 30 TFEU. National authorities are however not entitled to levy duties on traders for inspections merely *permitted* under EU law.[78]

In *Commission v. Germany*, the Court laid down the precise conditions that need to be fulfilled for a charge not to be classified as a CEE:[79]

(a) they do not exceed the actual costs of the inspections in connection with which they are charged;
(b) the inspections in question are obligatory and uniform for all the products concerned in the Union;
(c) they are prescribed by EU law in the general interest of the Union;
(d) they promote the free movement of goods, in particular by neutralizing obstacles which could arise from unilateral measures of inspection adopted in accordance with Article [36] of the Treaty".

73. Case 24/68, *Commission v. Italy*, para 9.
74. See also Case C-45/95, *Ayuntamiento de Ceuta*, para 28.
75. Joined Cases 2/69 and 3/69, *Diamantarbeiders*, paras. 11–14.
76. Joined Cases 2/69 and 3/69, *Diamantarbeiders*, paras. 24–26.
77. Case 24/68, *Commission v. Italy*, para 10. Art. 36 TFEU cannot be relied upon to justify them, see Case 46/76, *Bauhuis*, para 12.
78. Case 314/82, *Commission v. Belgium*. See also Case C-389/00, *Commission v. Germany*, para 35.
79. Case 18/87, *Commission v. Germany*, para 8.

2.3.2 *Payment for a service rendered*

Secondly, the Court has been open to the argument that, in principle, a charge can be justified because it merely constitutes a payment for a service the state rendered to the importer. In *Commission v. Belgium,* the Court held that a charge shall not be viewed as a CEE if it is "the consideration for a service actually rendered to the importer and is of an amount commensurate with that service".[80] Belgium had provided for the possibility of completing customs formalities at in-country customs posts rather than at the border itself. At these in-country customs posts, public warehouses provided temporary storage facilities for the imported goods while the import formalities were taken care of. The importer was also given the option to store his goods for an extended period. The Court ruled that only in this latter instance, a service is rendered directly to the importer and hence Belgium could impose a charge, not exceeding the costs incurred when providing the service.[81] Conversely, storage charges imposed when the imported goods were presented at the public warehouses solely for the completion of customs formalities were not acceptable.[82]

At the same time, this case also demonstrates that the Court closely scrutinizes the circumstances under which charges are imposed exclusively in exchange for such services.[83] In practice the Court has indeed been very reluctant to accept the "exchange argument". Mostly, it has proven unsuccessful. In *Ford España v. Spain,* the Court held that a levy cannot escape the qualification as a CEE, even if it is to be regarded as a remuneration for a service rendered to the importer, if its amount is not proportionate to the service or does not correspond to the costs incurred. Spain had levied a flat-rate duty, amounting to a percentage of the declared value of imported cars and other goods, for customs clearance services.[84] In *Commission v. Italy,* a small charge had been imposed on exports, arguably with the purpose of collecting statistical information to discern trade patterns.[85] The Italian government argued that the charge should be regarded as a *quid pro quo* for a service rendered, and thus not as a CEE. The Court rejected the argument, asserting that the statistical information was beneficial to the whole of the economy, but not to the individual importer or exporter.[86] It continued holding that even "if the competitive position of importers and exporters were to be particularly improved as a result, the statistics still constitute an advantage so general, and so difficult to assess, that the disputed charge cannot be regarded as the consideration for a specific benefit actually conferred".[87] Also in *Bresciani,* the Court was found unwilling to take financial charges imposed for compulsory veterinary and public health inspections carried out on imported animals outside the scope of Treaty scrutiny.[88] Firstly, it indicated that it is of no importance that a duty is proportionate to the quantity of the goods and not to their value: *any* charge imposed on a good because of the fact that it has crossed a border is prohibited.[89] Secondly, it also unequivocally stated that the costs of public health inspections imposed in the general interest should be borne by the general

---

80. Case 132/82, *Commisison v. Belgium,* para 8.
81. Case 132/82, *Commisison v. Belgium,* para 10.
82. Case 132/82, *Commisison v. Belgium,* para 14.
83. See also Case 266/81, *Società Italiana per l'Oleodotto Transalpino (SIOT) v. Ministero delle finanze, Ministero della marina mercantile, Circoscrizione doganale di Trieste and Ente autonomo del porto di Trieste,* para 23.
84. Case 170/88, *Ford España SA v. Estado español.* See also Case C-389/00, *Commission v. Germany,* para 45 and Joined Cases C-260/06 and C-261/06, *Daniel Escalier* and *Jean Bonarel,* para 49.
85. Case 24/68, *Commission v. Italy,* para 1.
86. Case 24/68, *Commission v. Italy,* para 15.
87. Case 24/68, *Commission v. Italy,* para 16.
88. Case 87/75, *Bresciani.*
89. Case 87/75, *Bresciani,* para 9.

public.[90] Thirdly, the argument that domestic products are subject to similar burdens is only valid if the charge falls within a system of internal taxation applying "systematically and in the same way" to domestic and imported products.[91]

2.4 *Recovery of unlawful charges*

Customs duties and CEEs that have been imposed by a Member State in breach of the prohibition of Article 30 TFEU must be eliminated. Moreover, traders who have paid such an unlawful duty are entitled to repayment.[92] Repayment is subject to the conditions of form and substance laid down in the applicable national legislation, but the Court has emphasized that these conditions may not be less favourable than those relating to similar claims regarding national charges and they may not render repayment virtually impossible or excessively difficult.[93]

There is however, an exception to this principle: repayment may not lead to the unjust enrichment of the traders.[94] In that regard, the Court has indicated that repayment may be disallowed when the unduly levied charges have been incorporated in the price of the goods and have thus been passed on to other persons. In *Comateb*, it was made clear that this exception may need to be qualified further: the trader himself may have actually suffered damages as a result of the very fact that he has passed on the unlawful charge, because the increase in the price of the product brought about by passing on the charge has led to a decrease in sales.[95] In such circumstances, a trader may justly claim that reimbursement would not lead to him being unjustly enriched. It is then for the national court to give an appropriate effect to this claim.[96] Furthermore, traders may not be prevented from filing a claim seeking to obtain reparation of losses caused by the Member State's unlawful levying of the charge in accordance with the appropriate procedures of national law and subject to the conditions laid down in the Court's *Brasserie du Pêcheur and Factortame* judgments.[97]

3. Financial restrictions: internal taxation

In principle, and to the extent that no harmonized secondary legislation has been adopted at EU level, Member States are entitled to set up their own system of internal taxation. Article 110 TFEU only prevents Member States from adopting internal taxes which discriminate against products that are in free circulation or afford protection to domestic products.[98] According to the ECJ, Article 110 TFEU supplements the provisions on the abolition of customs duties and charges having equivalent effect. Its aim is to ensure free movement of goods between the Member States in normal conditions of competition by eliminating all forms of protection which may result from the application of internal taxation that discriminates against products from other Member States.[99] Articles 28–30 TFEU would indeed have been of little use had it been open

90. Case 87/75, *Bresciani*, para 10.
91. Case 87/75, *Bresciani*, para 11.
92. Case 199/82, *San Giorgio*, para 12.
93. Case C-343/96, *Dilexport*.
94. Case 199/82, *San Giorgio*, para 13.
95. Joined Cases C-192/95 to C-218/95, *Comateb*, paras. 30–31.
96. Joined Cases C-192/95 to C-218/95, *Comateb*, para 32.
97. Joined Cases C-192/95 to C-218/95, *Comateb*, paras. 33–34.
98. Member States can subject imported products to a diferent taxation regime, as long as the charge to be paid is the same or lower than the one imposed on domestic products. As such, national fiscal sovereignty is safeguarded, see Case 127/75, para 3 and Case 15/81, *Schul*, para 21.
99. Case 168/78, *Commission v. France*; Case 169/78, *Commission v. Italy* and Case 171/78, *Commission v. Denmark*.

to Member States to favour domestic products over imported ones via differentiated taxation, once the latter had entered the national territory. Article 110 TFEU therefore demands complete neutrality of internal taxation between domestic and imported products.[100]

The Court has consistently adopted a wide interpretation of Article 110 TFEU "so as to cover all taxation procedures which, directly or indirectly, conflict with the principle of equality of treatment of domestic products and imported products".[101] The prohibition of Article 110 TFEU applies "whenever a fiscal levy is likely to discourage imports of goods originating in other Member States to the benefit of domestic production".[102] Furthermore, Article 110 TFEU only refers to "products from other Member States". The Court has made it clear in *Co-Frutta*, however, that the provision equally applies to goods originating in third countries which are in free circulation in the EU.[103] The provision also applies when it actually is the *export* which constitutes the chargeable event giving rise to a fiscal charge.[104] This is a perfectly logical decision, as the Treaty effectively prohibits customs duties and CEEs, as well as quantitative restrictions and measures having an equivalent effect to quantitative restrictions on *either* imports or exports.

Article 110 TFEU consists of two paragraphs, prohibiting respectively 1) discrimination between similar domestic and imported products; and 2) indirect protection of domestic products over competing imported products. Both prohibitions will be addressed in turn.

3.1 *Article 110(1) TFEU*

Article 110(1) TFEU provides that "[n]o Member State shall impose, directly or indirectly, on the products of other Member States any internal taxation of any kind in excess of that imposed directly or indirectly on similar domestic products".

Two cumulative conditions must be met to trigger the application of the Article 110(1) TFEU prohibition: firstly, there must be similarity between the domestic and the imported product; and secondly, there must be discrimination.

3.1.1 *Similar products*

In the early case of *Fink-Frucht*, the Court held that similarity between products exists "when the products in question are normally to be considered as coming within the same fiscal, customs or statistical classification".[105] Some years later, in *Rewe-Zentral*, the Court adhered to a less formalistic approach, stipulating that "a comparison must be made between the taxation imposed on products which, at the same stage of production or marketing, have similar characteristics and meet the same needs from the point of view of consumers".[106] In *Commission v. France*, the Court reiterated this stance, emphasizing the necessity to interpret the concept of "similar products" with sufficient flexibility and pointing out that the scope of Article 110(1) TFEU must be determined on the basis "not of the criterion of the strictly identical nature of the products but

---

100. Among others, Case 47/88, *Commission v. Denmark*, paras. 8 and 9; Case C-313/05, *Brzeziński*, para 27; Case C-387/01, *Weigel*, para 66; Case C-2/09, *Kalinchev*, para 37; Case C-402/09, *Tatu*, paras. 34–35.
101. Case 252/86, *Bergandi*, para 25 (tax on the use of gaming machines); Case C-221/06, *Stadtgemeinde Frohnleiten*, para 40 (waste taxation).
102. Case 252/86, *Bergandi*, para 25; Case 29/87, *Denkavit*, para 25 (health inspections); Case C-90/94, *Haahr Petroleum*, para 27 (port duties).
103. Case 193/85, *Cooperativa Co-Frutta*, para 28; see Case C-130/92, *OTO*, para 18 and Case C-90/94, *Haahr Petroleum*, para 26.
104. Case 142/77, *Larsen*, para 25.
105. Case 27/67, *Fink-Frucht*, at 232.
106. Case 45/75, *Rewe-Zentrale*, para 12.

on that of their similar and comparable use".[107] Most recent case law still confirms that products are similar if "their characteristics and the needs which they serve place them in a competitive relationship".[108]

In *Johnnie Walker*, the compatibility with Article 110 TFEU of a system of differential taxation applied under Danish tax legislation to Scotch whisky and fruit wine of the liqueur type was at stake.[109] To determine whether these two categories of beverages are similar, the Court looked at certain objective characteristics, such as their origin, the method of manufacture and their organoleptic properties, in particular taste and alcohol content, and considered whether these categories of beverages are capable of meeting the same consumer needs. The Court observed that the beverages exhibit manifestly different characteristics (amongst others different processes of manufacturing, different alcoholic strengths) and concluded that they could not be considered similar products.[110] In *Commission v. Italy*, an Italian tax on the consumption of fresh and dried bananas and on banana meal was under scrutiny. As the Italian banana production was completely negligible and therefore left out of account, the Court assessed the similarity between bananas and other table fruit typically produced in Italy, such as, in particular, apples, pears, peaches, plums, apricots, cherries, oranges and mandarins.[111] It thereby came to the conclusion that the two categories of fruits possessed different characteristics and could not be regarded as similar products as a result. The Court specifically mentioned the different organoleptic characteristics and water content of the two categories of product. It illustrated this by pointing at the higher water content of pears and other fruit typically grown in Italy which give them "thirst-quenching properties which bananas do not possess".[112] Conversely, in *Commission v. France*, in which a different rate of taxation for dark- and light-tobacco cigarettes was at stake, the Court did establish the similarity of the two products in question, holding that the difference between them was merely one of degree.[113]

In recent years, the Court was asked on a number of occasions to assess the similarity – for tax purposes – of domestic and imported used cars.[114] The Court maintained that the similarity between a domestic and imported used car in a specific case is to be derived from their characteristics and the needs they serve.[115] To the extent that those characteristics and needs allow to consider both cars as interchangeable,[116] they are similar for the purposes of Article 110(1) TFEU.[117] On the one hand, the Court in that respect lists the price, size, comfort, performance,

107. Case 168/78, *Commission v. France*, para 5.
108. Case C-437/12, *X*, para 23.
109. Case 243/84, *John Walker*.
110. Case 243/84, *John Walker*, paras. 12–14.
111. Case 184/85, *Commission v. Italy*, para 8.
112. Case 184/85, *Commission v. Italy*, para 10.
113. Case C-302/00, *Commission v. France*, para 25.
114. Case 47/88, *Commission v. Denmark*; Case C-345/93, *Nunes Tadeu*; Case C-375/95, *Commission v. Greece*; Case C-393/98, *Gomes Valente*; Case C-101/00, *Tulliasiamies and Antti Siilin*; Case C-387/01, *Weigel*; Joined Cases C-290/05 and C-333/05; Case C-290/05, *Ákos Nádasdi* and Case C-333/05, *Németh;* Case C-313/05, *Brzeziński*; Case C-74/06, *Commission v. Greece*; Case C-2/09, *Kalinchev*; Case C-402/09, *Tatu*; Case C-437/12, *X*; Case C-586/14, *Budişan*.
115. Case C-437/12, *X*, para 23.
116. Case C-101/00, *Tulliasiamies and Antti Siilin*, para 75–76; Case C-74/06, *Commission v. Greece*, para 37; Case C-437/12, *X*, para 23.
117. To counter any claims that cars were not similar, the Court additionally advised Member States to put in place rules to avoid such discriminatory effects from materializing. In the context of car registration taxes levied on imported used cars, this includes reliance on "detailed and statistically based scales relating to the age and actual annual average kilometrage of the vehicle", possibly supplemented by an "inspection of the

fuel consumption, durability, reliability, drive and equipment, age and mileage, general condition and brand as exemplary criteria.[118] On the other hand, the mere fact that two vehicles were put in service on the same date would not automatically classify them as similar, "as their wear and tear may differ".[119]

The abovementioned case law overview makes clear that the concept of similarity is interpreted widely by the Court. However, that does not preclude the concept from still being surrounded by a certain degree of uncertainty or lack of clarity. As Oliver and Martinez Navarro correctly point out, so far there has been no attempt to draw inspiration from the systematic and rigorous economic analysis carried out to define the concept of the relevant product market in the field of competition law for the purposes of Article 110 TFEU.[120] In any event, when the Court reaches the conclusion that domestic and imported products are not similar, it will still proceed to the examination of whether they are nevertheless in some kind of competition with each other under Article 110(2) TFEU.[121]

3.1.2 *Discrimination*

Article 110(1) does not prescribe any particular system of taxation. However, where the Court has established similarity between domestic and imported products, it will subsequently examine whether the system of taxation in a given Member State respects the requirement of neutrality. It is settled case law that a system of taxation is compatible with Article 110 TFEU "only if it is so arranged as to exclude any possibility of imported products being taxed more heavily than similar domestic products, so that it cannot in any event have discriminatory effect".[122] Article 110(1) TFEU catches direct as well as indirect discrimination.

Direct discrimination entails unequal treatment expressly on the basis of the origin of products. Instances of blatant discrimination do not occur often in practice. Examples nevertheless include situations where taxes are only levied on imported products;[123] where tax burdens are heavier on imported products than on domestic products;[124] where tax reliefs are available only to domestic products;[125] where procedures for tax collection are more favourable for domestic goods than for these coming from other Member States;[126] or where penalties for tax offences are more severe for imported products than for domestic ones.[127]

Indirect discrimination occurs when measures are neutral at face value, i.e. seem to apply equally to domestic and imported products, but in practice place a greater burden on the latter and thus affect them adversely.[128] The case of *Humblot* is illustrative in this respect: France imposed an annual car tax, the amount of which hinged upon the power rating (fiscal horsepower)

---

general condition of the vehicle and its content" in order to determine this value, see Case C-402/09, *Tatu*, para 44 and 47.

118. Case C-437/12, *X*, para 25.
119. Case C-437/12, *X*, para 24.
120. P. Oliver and M. Martínez Navarro, "Free Movement of Goods" in C. Barnard and S. Peers (Ed.), *European Union Law* (OUP, 2014), 348.
121. Confirmed in Case 168/78, *Commission v. France*, para 6. See also section 3.2.
122. Case C-90/94, *Haahr Petroleum*, para 34; Case C-375/95, *Commission v. Greece*, para 29. See also, more recently, Case C-198/14, *Visnapuu*, para 54.
123. Case 57/65, *Lütticke*.
124. Case C-90/94, *Haahr Petroleum*. See also Case 127/75, *Bobie Getränkevertrieb* and Case C-213/96, *Outokumpu Oy*.
125. Case 148/77, *H. Hansen jun.* and Case 21/79, *Commission v. Italy*.
126. Case 55/79, *Commission v. Ireland*.
127. Case 299/86, *Drexl*.
128. Case C-402/09, *Tatu*, para 37.

of the car. Below 16 cylinder volume (CV), the tax increased gradually up to a maximum of 1100 French francs. From 16 CV onwards, a flat-rate amount of 5000 francs was imposed. In practice, only imported cars were subject to the flat-rate tax, as no car manufactured in France had a power rating exceeding 16 CV. Humblot was charged 5000 francs when he imported a car with a 36 CV power rating. He claimed the tax breached Article 110 TFEU and sought a refund. The Court signalled that as such, France was at liberty to subject cars to a progressive road tax, but stressed that the system of taxation had to be free from discriminatory or protective effect. It proceeded holding that although "the system embodies no formal distinction based on the origin of products, it manifestly exhibits discriminatory or protective features contrary to Article [110 TFEU], since the power rating determining liability to the special tax has been fixed at a level such that only imported cars, in particular from other Member States, are subject to the special tax, whereas all cars of domestic manufacture are liable to the distinctly more advantageous differential tax".[129] It concluded that the "resultant additional taxation is liable to cancel out the advantages which certain cars imported from other Member States might have in consumers' eyes over comparable cars of domestic manufacture, particularly since the special tax continues to be payable for several years. In that respect, the special tax reduces the amount of competition to which cars of domestic manufacture are subject and hence is contrary to the principle of neutrality with which domestic taxation must comply".[130] France subsequently amended its legislation, but also the new legislation has already been subject to the Court's scrutiny on several occasions.[131] In *Tatu*, the Court likewise confirmed that the levying of a pollution tax upon first registration of a car in Romania resulted in "discouraging the placing in circulation in that Member State of second-hand vehicles purchased in other Member States without discouraging the purchase of second-hand vehicles of the same age and condition on the domestic market".[132] The latter cars were already registered previously and were not therefore subject to the pollution tax now levied upon registration of the car in Romania.

3.1.3 *Justification*

Article 110(1) TFEU is an absolutely worded Treaty prohibition. It provides no possibilities for justification of discriminatory internal taxation measures. The Court also made it clear that Article 36 TFEU cannot be helpful in this context.[133] In practice, even though the Court does not always distinguish between direct and indirect discrimination, it may nevertheless be necessary to determine which type of discriminatory action is precisely at stake in a particular case. This has to do with the fact that direct discrimination on grounds of nationality cannot be justified, whereas apparently neutral national tax rules that tend to favour domestic products may be upheld if there is some objective justification available. This would prevent Article 110(1) TFEU from being applied too harshly. It must be stated that so far, there is no explicit case law on this point, however. The Court has limited itself to stating that differentiated taxation may be acceptable if it is based on objective criteria. In *Chemial Farmaceutici v. DAF*, the Court explained that differentiation is compatible with Union law if it pursues economic policy objectives which are themselves in conformity with the requirements of EU law.[134] Admittedly, the Court

129. Case 112/84, *Humblot*, para 14.
130. Case 112/84, *Humblot*, para 15.
131. Case 433/85, *Feldain*; Case 76/87, *Seguela and Lachkar* Case C-265/99, *Commission v. France*.
132. Case C-402/09, *Tatu*, para 61.
133. Case 29/72, *Marimex*, para 4–5; Case 46/76, *Bauhuis*, para 12–14 and Case C-302/00, *Commission v. France*, para 33.
134. Case 140/79, *Chemial Farmaceutici v. DAF*, para 14.

also required that the contested rules must be devoid of any discrimination, whether direct or indirect;[135] but notwithstanding this, the judgment can be understood to support the argument that the Court is willing to accept objective justifications in situations of indirect discrimination.

3.2 *Article 110(2) TFEU*

If domestic and imported products are not considered similar, the next step is to examine whether the tax provisions are nevertheless caught under Article 110(2) TFEU. That provision maintains that "no Member State shall impose on the products of other Member States any internal taxation of such a nature as to afford indirect protection to other products". This prohibition is triggered when two cumulative conditions are satisfied: first, there must be a competitive relationship between the domestic and the foreign products; and secondly, the tax must be protective of the domestic product.[136] The threshold for meeting those conditions is lower than for those in Article 110(1) TFEU. In its early *Fink-Frucht* judgment, the Court established that domestic and foreign products do not have to be in direct competition. However, it proceeded holding that, in the interests of legal certainty, it is necessary for the economic relationship covered by Article 110(2) to be "not merely fortuitous, but lasting and characteristic".[137] In the recent case of *Commission v. Sweden*, the Court held that the purpose of Article 110(2) TFEU is "to prevent any form of indirect fiscal protectionism affecting imported products which, although not similar to domestic products, nevertheless compete with some of them, even if only partially, indirectly or potentially".[138]

The *Commission v. UK* case nicely illustrates how the Court adjudicates on Article 110(2) TFEU. The Commission started enforcement proceedings against a UK taxation scheme that differentiated between beer and wine. The tax on certain wines was almost five times higher than that on beer in terms of volume. The UK produces a lot of beer, whereas almost all wine is imported. In view of the difficulties encountered when establishing whether these products were actually in competition and whether the tax scheme was protective of beer, the Court initially declined to rule on the issue and invited the parties to re-examine the case.[139] Ultimately, it would render judgment only five years later.[140]

Firstly, when determining the possible competitive relationship between beer and wine, the Court tried to measure the degree of substitution, i.e. the cross-elasticity between the products concerned. It did also compare the manufacturing processes and the natural properties of those beverages.[141] Furthermore, the Court pointed out that attention should not only be paid to consumer habits in a Member State or in a given region, as it regarded these as essentially variable in time and space and therefore not immutable. Hence, "the tax policy of a Member State must not crystallize given consumer habits so as to consolidate an advantage acquired by national industries concerned to respond to them".[142] Product substitutability being considered the essential criterion, the Court established that the decisive competitive relationship between a popular

135. Case 140/79, *Chemial Farmaceutici v. DAF*, para 14.
136. See for examples Case 170/78, *Commission v. UK*, para 8 and 27 and Case 184/85, *Commission v. Italy*, paras. 11–15.
137. Case 27/67, *Fink-Frucht* at 232–233.
138. Case C-167/05, *Commission v. Sweden*, para 41; see also Case 356/85, *Commission v. Belgium*, para 7, and Joined Cases C-367/93 to C-377/93, *Roders*, para 38.
139. Case 170/78, *Commission v. UK*, para 24.
140. Case 170/87, *Commission v. UK*.
141. Case 170/87, *Commission v. UK*, para 8.
142. Case 170/87, *Commission v. UK*, para 8.

and widely consumed beverage such as beer and wine must be established by reference to the lightest and cheapest varieties of wine which are the most accessible to the public at large.[143]

Secondly, the Court had to ascertain whether the tax system afforded protection to domestically produced beer.[144] The Court looked at the tax burdens by reference to the volume, the alcoholic strength and the price of the products. It quickly became apparent that precisely those wines which, in view of their price, are most directly in competition with domestic beer production are subject to a considerably higher tax burden: 400% by reference to volume and 100 % by reference to alcoholic strength. It was clear, therefore, that the UK tax system has the effect of subjecting wine imported from other Member States to an additional tax burden so as to afford protection to domestic beer production. According to the Court, wine has been stamped "with the hallmarks of a luxury product" which can "scarcely constitute in the eyes of the consumer a genuine alternative to the typical domestically produced beverage".[145] As a consequence, the UK tax system was found in breach of Article 110(2) TFEU.

Differentiated taxation of competing products is only problematic whenever the national tax measure has the effect of protecting domestic goods to the detriment of competing imported products. Member States do retain significant autonomy to structure their tax system and to differentiate their tax rates according to their own preferences.[146] In *Johnnie Walker*, the Court confirmed that Member States may lay down tax arrangements which differentiate between certain products on the basis of objective criteria, such as the nature of the raw materials used or the production processes employed, as long as such differentiations pursue objectives of economic policy which are themselves compatible with the requirements of the Treaty and its secondary legislation.[147] In *Commission v. Sweden*, the Court seemingly adopted a more functional approach: having established a competitive relationship between wine and strong beer, the Court went on to determine whether the higher taxation of wine as compared with strong beer was such as to have the effect on the market of reducing potential consumption of imported products (wine) to the advantage of competing domestic products (beer).[148] The Court stated that a mere slight tax differentiation between strong domestic beers and competing imported wines does not automatically produce protective effects.[149] Since statistical evidence demonstrated no significant substitution of imported wine purchases with competing domestic beer purchases, it concluded that the Commission had not sufficiently made clear that the tax differentiation in the case at hand was in itself likely to influence consumer behaviour to the advantage of domestically produced strong beers.[150]

---

143. Case 170/87, *Commission v. UK*, para 12.
144. Case 170/87, *Commission v. UK*, paras. 13–27.
145. Case 170/87, *Commission v. UK*, para 27.
146. This includes the imposition of higher taxes on domestic products, see Case 86/78, *distilleries Peureux*, paras. 32–33.
147. Case 243/84, *John Walker*, para 22. See also already Case 46/80, *Vinal*, para 13; Case C-213/96, *Outokumpu Oy*, para 30.
148. Case C-167/05, *Commission v. Sweden*, para 52.
149. Case C-167/05, *Commission v. Sweden*, paras. 57–59.
150. The Court also pointed out that, for the purposes of applying Art. 110 (2) TFEU, it is impossible to require, in each case, that the protective effect of internal tax arrangements be shown statistically. It suffices that a given tax mechanism is likely, in view of its inherent characteristics, to bring about such an effect. In the case at hand, the Commission had failed to demonstrate this. (Case C-167/05, *Commission v. Sweden*, paras. 60–62).

3.3 Remedies

In the past, the Court has not always clearly distinguished between the first and the second paragraph of Article 110 TFEU when rendering judgments condemning national tax rules. Some early enforcement actions, better known as the "spirits cases", involving Member States tax rules allegedly contravening Article 110 TFEU, are illustrative in this respect.[151] In *Commission v. France*, the Commission challenged a French tax scheme differentiating between spirits based upon fruit or wine (such as cognac, calvados or armagnac) and spirits based on grain (such as whisky, gin and vodka).[152] France was a major producer of the former category of spirits, whereas the latter category was predominantly imported. This latter category was subject to higher tax rates. The Court first acknowledged that in this specific case, classifying certain beverages as "similar products" within the meaning of Article 110(1) TFEU may be difficult "in view of the nature of the factors implied by distinguishing criteria such as flavour and consumer habits".[153] Subsequently, it deemed it unnecessary for the purposes of solving the dispute to rule on the question of whether or not certain domestic and imported spirits are wholly or partially similar products "when it is impossible reasonably to contest" that they are at least in partial competition and that "it is impossible to deny the protective nature of the French tax system" in the meaning of Article 110(2) TFEU.[154]

This approach to take Article 110 TFEU "as a whole"[155] is however not unproblematic. It overlooks the different legal consequences attached to a finding of a violation of the first and the second paragraph of this Article. The former prohibits discrimination, the latter protectionism. In case of an infringement of Article 110(1) TFEU, the Member State must equalize the taxes on the similar domestic and imported products.[156] A breach of Article 110(2) TFEU means that the Member State must merely remove the protectionist effect of the tax, without necessarily having to equalize the tax on the domestic product and the competing imported product.

Be that as it may, in later case law, the Court has been more rigorous in the application of the first and the second paragraph of Article 110 TFEU.[157] As a result, both paragraphs are applied more or less independently from each other.

4. Boundaries between Articles 30 and 110 TFEU

The relationship between Article 30 and Article 110 TFEU is one of complementarity and mutual exclusivity.[158] Both Treaty provisions deal with the imposition of fiscal charges by the state. One the one hand, Article 30 TFEU prohibits duties and charges levied because goods cross a border. Contrary to similar domestic products, foreign products are subjected to the duty or the charge as a result of being imported in a given country. These duties and charges are in principle unlawful. On the other hand, Article 110 TFEU rules out measures of internal taxation, applying both to domestic and imported products, which are discriminatory or protectionist. The

---

151. Case 168/78, *Commission v. France*; Case 169/78, *Commission v. Italy*; Case 171/78, *Commission v. Denmark*. See for background, C. Tobler, *Indirect Discrimination. A Case Study into the Development of the Legal Concept of Indirect Discrimination under EC Law* (Intersentia, 2005), 125–129.
152. Case 168/78, *Commission v. France*, para 11.
153. Case 168/78, *Commission v. France*, para 12.
154. Case 168/78, *Commission v. France*, para 39.
155. Case 168/78, *Commission v. France*, para 13.
156. In Case C-586/14, *Budişan* para 43, the Court did not seem willing to accept, in the specific context of second-hand cars, an alternative remedy, in accordance with which a Member State temporarily exempts payment of a related tax in order to compensate for overtaxation of imported goods.
157. Case C-198/14, *Visnapuu*, para 58.
158. See for a recent confirmation, Case C-198/14, *Visnapuu*, para 50.

discriminatory or protective effect must be eliminated. The Court of Justice has confirmed that provisions relating to charges having equivalent effect and those relating to discriminatory or protective internal taxation cannot be applied together, with the result that, under the system established by the Treaty, one charge cannot belong to both categories at the same time.[159]

In most circumstances, it is relatively straightforward to determine whether a contested fiscal charge constitutes a duty or a charge in the meaning of Article 30 or conversely, amounts to a measure of internal taxation that needs to be addressed under Article 110 TFEU. Some situations however, are more difficult.

A first situation which may be problematic is when a charge imposed on imported products – which will, in principle, simply be qualified as an unlawful tax under Article 30 TFEU – is also imposed on domestic products. In *Denkavit*, the Court ruled that an annual levy imposed in the same manner on importers of feeding-stuffs containing additives and national manufacturers of such products needs to be assessed under Article 110 TFEU if "it relates to a general system of internal dues applied systematically and in accordance with the same criteria to domestic products and imported products alike".[160] In *Mikhailidis*, the Court stressed that a charge levied at the frontier when the export operation takes place, will come under Article 30 TFEU scrutiny, "unless the allegedly comparable charge levied on national products is applied at the same rate, at the same marketing stage and on the basis of an identical chargeable event".[161] In *Orgacom*, the Court confirmed that the use of different methods of calculation can additionally be taken into account when determining the different nature of charges.[162]

A second borderline case between Articles 30 and 110 TFEU concerns the situation that a Member States levies a fiscal charge on an imported product while it does not produce or manufacture this product or only in negligible quantities. Such a levy will not necessarily have to be regarded as a charge having an equivalent effect to a customs duty. In *Co-Frutta*, the Court made it clear that such a charge constitutes internal taxation within the meaning of Article 110 TFEU "if it relates to a general system of internal dues applied systematically to categories of products in accordance with objective criteria irrespective of the origin of the products".[163] This solution makes perfect sense. If any fiscal charge on imported products which are not produced locally were to have to be classified as an *ipso facto* unlawful charge under Article 30 TFEU, this would entail a far-reaching and unwarranted intervention in the internal taxation policy of that Member State. Furthermore, as has also been demonstrated in *Co-Frutta*, the classification of the charge as internal taxation does not automatically mean that it is lawful. It will subsequently have to be examined under Article 110 TFEU.

A third situation in which the classification of a fiscal charge under Article 30 or 110 TFEU may be disputed involves the so-called "para-fiscal" charges. These charges concern taxes the proceeds of which are selectively refunded or come to the benefit of a particular domestic industry. If this refund or benefit to the national producers completely offsets the tax levied, the tax will be regarded as a charge under Article 30 TFEU, because in fact it only affects imported products. If, conversely, the refund or benefit is only partial, then it will be assessed whether the

159. Among others, Joined Cases 2/62 and 3/62, *Commission v. Luxemburg and Belgium*, at 432; Case 10/65, *Deutschmann*; Case 57/65, *Lütticke*, at 210; Case 105/76, *Interzuccheri*, para 9; Case C-90/94 *Haahr Petroleum*, para 19; Case C-387/01 Case C-387/01, *Weigel*, para 63 and Joined Cases C-393/04 and C-41/05, Case C-393/04, *Air Liquide Industries Belgium* and Case C-41/05, *Province de Liège*, para 50; Case C-254/13, *Orgacom*, para 20.
160. See Case 132/78, *Denkavit*, para 7 and Case 29/87, *Dansk Denkavit*, para 33.
161. Joined Cases C-441/98 and C-442/98, *Michaïlidis* para 23.
162. Case C-254/13, *Orgacom*, para 32.
163. Case 193/85, *Cooperativa Co-Frutta*, para 14.

tax is not discriminatory under Article 110 TFEU.[164] The Court has further specified that the criterion of whether the burden is offset "presupposes a check, during a reference period, on the financial equivalence of the total amounts levied on national products processed or marketed on the domestic market in connection with the charge in question and the advantages afforded exclusively to those products".[165] According to the Court, it is then for the national court to ascertain that national products processed or marketed domestically do not in fact derive an exclusive benefit or a proportionally greater benefit than imported or exported products from the services of the body to which the charge in dispute accrues, which might offset entirely or partially the burden constituted by that charge.[166]

5. Non-tariff barriers: quantitative restrictions

In addition to tackling national fiscal and tariff barriers to the free movement of goods, EU law also addresses quantitative import and export restrictions, and measures having the equivalent effect of such quantitative restrictions. Article 34 TFEU states that quantitative restrictions on imports and all measures having equivalent effect shall be prohibited between Member States. Article 35 TFEU similarly maintains that quantitative restrictions on exports and all measures having equivalent effect shall be prohibited between Member States. Those restrictions and measures are prohibited, unless they can be justified in accordance with specific Treaty exceptions outlined in Article 36 TFEU or with judicially created "mandatory requirements in the public interest" and comply with the principle of proportionality.[167]

The concept of quantitative restrictions has not been defined in the Treaty. In *Geddo*, the Court described quantitative restrictions as "measures which amount to a total or partial restraint of, according to the circumstances, imports, exports or goods in transit".[168] Such legislative or administrative measures or administrative rules restrict the importation, exportation or transit of one or more goods according to *numbers* or their value. These restrictions can be total (in case of a ban) or partial (when quotas are imposed). It is clear that the concept applies equally to imports and exports.

The most obvious examples of quantitative restrictions are total bans on the importation of particular goods. The case of *Henn and Darby* is a clear example in this regard, as the United Kingdom prohibited the importation of any kind of pornographic material.[169] The Court in this judgment referred to an import ban as "the most extreme form of restriction".[170] Other examples include, in particular, a limit on the amount of goods imported,[171] limits on the amounts of products that can be exported,[172] the refusal to grant an export license for the transportation of livestock,[173] restrictions on the amount of alcoholic products that can be imported by a private

---

164. Case 77/72, *Capolongo*; Case 77/76, *Cucchi* Case C-94/74, *Industria Gomma Articoli vari*; Case 73/79, *Commission v. Italy*; Case C-72/92, *Scharbatke*; Cases C-78/90 to C-83/90, *Compagnie Commerciale de l'Oues*; Case C-234/99, *Nygårdi*; Case C-347/95, *Leite de Lisboa*; Case C-28/96, *Fricarnes*; Case C-517/04, *Koornstra*.
165. Case C-28/96, *Fricarnes*, para 27, Case C-234/99, *Nygård*, para 43.
166. Case C-347/95, *Leite de Lisboa*, para 26 and Case C-28/96, *Fricarnes*, para 29.
167. Those provisions have also been covered extensively in specialized treatises on the matter. See among others P. Oliver, op. cit. *supra* note 44, at 534, which entirely focuses on Arts. 34–37 TFEU. See also C. Barnard, *The Substantive Law of the EU. The Four Freedoms*, 4th ed. (OUP, 2013), 71–197.
168. Case 2/73, *Geddo*, para 7.
169. Case 34/79, *R. v. Henn and Darby*.
170. Case 34/79, *R. v. Henn and Darby*, para 12.
171. See for example Case 13/68, *Salgoil*; Case 231/78, *Commission v. UK*.
172. Case C-47/90, *Établissements Delhaize*; Case C-388/95, *Belgium v. Spain*.
173. Case C-5/94, *Hedley Lomas* and Case C-1/96, *Compassion in World Farming*.

distributor as opposed to a state commercial monopoly[174] and a total ban on landing fish in Ireland by vessels flying another Member State's flag.[175]

Quantitative restrictions feature only rarely in the case law of the Court. In many instances, the Court relies on the more open ended notion of measures having an equivalent effect to quantitative restrictions to bring under the scope of application of the free movement of goods measures that really are quantitative restrictions.[176] The case of *Romkes* is illustrative in this respect. The Court analysed whether measures directly reducing in the short term the quantities of fish that can be traded between the Member States, but which are designed in the long term to ensure an optimum yield from fishing and therefore to increase such trade, constituted measures having an equivalent effect to quantitative restrictions.[177] This case also clearly indicates that Member States can, under certain circumstances, temporarily restrict the import, export or transit of goods. The Treaty prohibitions will not apply in such a situation.[178]

It is regrettable that the Court essentially subsumes the concept of quantitative restrictions under the wider notion of measures having an equivalent effect to quantitative restrictions, thereby virtually leaving it devoid of practical purpose. The rationale behind this is also unclear. A plausible explanation might lie in the issue of justification. Quantitative restrictions generally differentiate between domestic and foreign products. From an orthodox point of view, they are prohibited, unless they can be justified with the Treaty exceptions of Article 36 TFEU. Measures having an equivalent effect to quantitative restrictions can also be justified with mandatory requirements in the general interest, at least if they are found not to be directly discriminatory. By categorizing a quantitative restriction as a measure having an equivalent effect, and explicitly leaving aside the issue of direct discrimination as part of its analysis, the Court *de facto* has broadened the avenues of justification for the measure at stake. This does not have to be problematic as such, but more orthodox, clear and elegant ways to achieve a similar result exist.

6. Non-tariff barriers: measures having the equivalent effect of quantitative restrictions

Judicial developments relating to Articles 34–35 TFEU have mostly centred on the concept of measures having the equivalent effect of quantitative restrictions (MEEQR). As this notion has not been defined in the Treaty itself, the Court developed an extensive and at times confusing body of judgments outlining, applying and circumscribing the concept. This section analyses the constituent MEEQR elements as found in the *Dassonville* judgment. *Dassonville* bore the

174. Case C-170/04, *Rosengren*.
175. Case C-535/03, *The Queen on the application of Unitymark Ltd and North Sea Fishermen's Organisation v. Department for Environment, Food and Rural Affairs*.
176. Case 40/82, *Commission v. UK*; Case 59/82, *Schutzverband gegen Unwesen in der Wirtschaft v. Weinvertriebs-GmbH*; Case 74/82, *Commission v. Ireland*; Case 172/82, *Syndicat National des Fabricants Raffineurs d'Huile de Graissage v. Inter-Huiles*; Case 261/85, *Commission v. UK*; Case C-131/93, *Commission v. Germany*; Case C-67/97, *Bluhme*; Case C-473/98, *Kemikalieninspektionen v. Toolex Alpha AB*; Case C-172/00, *Arzneimittel v. Eurim-Pharm Arzneimittel*; Case C-421/09, *Humanplasma*, para 30, where the Court maintained that a ban on the import of blood which had been donated in return for some monetary compensation in a different Member State amounted to an MEEQR rather than a proper quantitative restriction. Although the Court qualified the import ban as an MEEQR, the measure in effect amounted to a quantitative restriction in its own right in accordance with the definition set out in this section; Case C-142/09 See also Case C-142/09, *Lahousse and Lavinchy*, and Case C-161/09, *Stafidas*, where the Court did not properly classify the quantitative or equivalent nature of the restriction at hand.
177. Case 46/86, *Romkes*, para 24, where the Court held that the contested measure did not constitute an MEEQR; this has been confirmed in Case C-535/03, *Unitymark*, para 50.
178. Case C-535/03, *Unitymark*, para 51.

seeds of further evolutions, which fully emerged in the wake of the *Cassis de Dijon* judgment. That judgment established a regime of "mutual recognition" of goods produced in another Member State and introduced the "rule of reason" doctrine into free movement law. As a result, an unprecedentedly wide array of national measures was brought under the Court's free movement of goods scrutiny. The seemingly uncontrollable influx of free movement of goods claims to which *Dassonville* and *Cassis de Dijon* sparked a lot of academic commentary,[179] calling for a review of the Court's case law on the matter. Ultimately, the judgment in *Keck and Mithouard* would offer a solution by excluding certain non-discriminatory selling arrangements from the scope of Article 34 TFEU. The exclusion of such measures did however not solve everything and moreover created new delineation problems, as for instance the legal disputes in relation to so-called "rules of use" in *Commission v. Italy* and *Mickelsson & Roos* demonstrate.

6.1 *Defining MEEQR in Dassonville*

The Court's judgment in *Dassonville* is generally considered to have provided the definition of MEEQR still in operation today. The case addressed the difficulties encountered by Belgian parallel importers of Scotch whisky to obtain an authenticity certificate that the importers' distributors were not required to obtain on the basis of French legislation. The Court acknowledged that the Belgian rules did not explicitly differentiate between domestic and imported products, but had the effect of indirectly discriminating against products on the basis of their (imported) origin in another Member State.[180] In its judgment, the Court stated that the concept of MEEQR encompasses "all trading rules enacted by Member States which are capable of hindering, directly or indirectly, actually or potentially, intra-Community trade".[181] On the basis of that definition, the Court concluded that "the requirement by a Member State of a certificate of authenticity which is less easily obtainable by importers of an authentic product which has been put into free circulation in a regular manner in another Member State than by importers of the same product coming directly from the country of origin constitutes a measure having an effect equivalent to a quantitative restriction as prohibited by the Treaty".[182]

In order to be considered an MEEQR, Member States rules or practices have to meet three cumulative requirements: to consist of trading rules (1), to be enacted by Member States (2) and to be capable of hindering intra-Union trade in direct, indirect, actual or potential ways (3). All three requirements have been developed further throughout the Court's case law.

Firstly, the Court did not faithfully stick to the "*trading rules*" concept. Subsequent case law omitted the "trading" epithet and only referred to "rules"[183] or even to "measures".[184] In doing so, the Court made clear that national rules governing not only the trading as such, but also the production, format, size and labelling of products can be considered MEEQR.[185]

Secondly, MEEQR consist of rules *enacted by a Member State*. As previously mentioned in section 1.5 of this chapter, the Court has invariably taken a wide view on what constitute state

179. For overviews and references to more abundant literature, see C. Barnard, "Sunday trading: A drama in five acts", (1994) *Modern Law Review*, 449–460; J. Tillotson, "Sunday trading and free movement of goods in the EEC. Clarification at community level", (1993) *World Competition*, 139–143; R. Joliet, "The free circulation of goods: The Keck and Mithouard decision and the new directions in the case law", 1 CJEL (1995), 437–451; W. Wils, "The search for the rule in Art. 30 EEC: Much ado about nothing?", 18 EL Rev. (1993), 475–492.
180. Case 8/74, *Dassonville*, paras. 6–7.
181. Case 8/74, *Dassonville*, para 5.
182. Case 8/74, *Dassonville*, para 9.
183. Joined Cases 177/82 and 178/82, *van de Haar*, para 12, referring to rules or national provisions.
184. Case C-324/93, *Evans Medical and Macfarlan Smith*, para 21.
185. See references cited *infra* notes 203–228.

measures.[186] Furthermore, it has equally accepted that a failure to act by a Member State comprises the enactment of a potentially restrictive rule. Actions by private associations entrusted with a public mandate or by individuals whose behaviour can be attributed to the state and could thus equally have been "enacted by Member States".[187]

Thirdly, the "direct or indirect, actual or potential" hindrance requirement outlined in *Dassonville* did not readily clarify to what extent both distinctly and indistinctly applicable measures could qualify as an MEEQR. Originally, Commission Directive 70/50/EEC clearly distinguished between different types of measures having the equivalent effect of quantitative *import* restrictions.[188] According to Article 2(1) of the Directive, "measures, *other than those applicable equally to domestic or imported products*, which hinder imports which could otherwise take place, including measures which make importation more difficult or costly than the disposal of domestic production", were to be considered MEEQR. Article 3 subsequently also prohibited "measures governing the marketing of products which deal, in particular, with shape, size, weight, composition, presentation, identification or putting up and which are equally applicable to domestic and imported products, where the restrictive effect of such measures on the free movement of goods exceeds the effects intrinsic to trade rules", at least to the extent that those measures were disproportionate and the same effects could be reached by means of less restrictive measures. As a result, distinctly applicable measures were automatically considered to qualify as MEEQR, whereas only disproportionate indistinctly applicable measures would come within the scope of the Directive's prohibitions. The Court did not refer to this distinction in *Dassonville*, creating uncertainty as to whether the MEEQR concept not only applied to all distinctly applicable national measures, but also to the indistinctly applicable ones.

At the very least, the notion of "hindrance" reflects the *effects-focused* nature of the MEEQR notion.[189] Whilst a measure may have as its purpose to restrict intra-Union trade, the *Dassonville* judgment signals the Court's approach of also looking beyond the Member States' intentions and focus primarily on the effects produced by the rule or measure at hand. Although the Court sometimes takes the purpose of a measure into account, this will in principle not be decisive in determining the existence of an MEEQR.[190] At the same time, the *Dassonville* definition does not as such provide for a quantifiable *de minimis* threshold below which a measure is not considered to be an MEEQR worthy of EU law's attention.[191] The Court has overall been willing to apply Articles 34–35 TFEU to any rule or practice falling within the definition of an MEEQR, without quantifying the actual practical effects those rules or practices may have.[192]

---

186. See references cited *supra* notes 39–45.
187. See references cited *supra* notes 44–47.
188. Commission Directive 70/50/EEC of 22 Dec. 1969 based on the provisions of Art. 33 (7), on the abolition of measures which have an effect equivalent to quantitative restrictions on imports and are not covered by other provisions adopted in pursuance of the EEC Treaty, O.J. 1970, L 13/29. The Directive only applied during the transitional period, which formally ended on 31 Dec. 1969.
189. See C. Barnard, op. cit. *supra* note 167, at 79 for the same argument.
190. See for cases where the purpose of the measure or the Member State's intent played some role in the assessment, Cases 60/84 and 61/84, *Cinéthèque*, para 21; Joined Cases C-267/91 and C-268/91, *Keck and Mithouard,* para 14; Case C-379/92, *Peralta*, para 24; Case C-110/05, *Commission v. Italy*, para 37. In *Groenveld,* para 7, references are made to both the object and effect of measures. This could imply that the object or purpose of the measure at stake could at least provide an indication of the effects generated by that measure.
191. Joined Cases 177/82 and 178/82, *van de Haar*, para 14. For a critique as to that approach and advocating the introduction of a *de minimis test*, see the Opinion of A.G. Jacobs in Case C-412/93, *Leclerc-Siplec*, para 42–44.
192. The particular strand of case law relating to selling arrangements in the *Keck and Mithouard* judgment (Joined Cases C-267/91 and C-268/91), comprises an exception in that regard. In the wake of A.G. Jacobs' opinion in *Leclerc-Siplec* mentioned in the previous footnote, two other Advocates General have also

6.2 *Clarifying MEEQR in Cassis de Dijon*

The seminal *Cassis de Dijon* judgment further clarified the scope of the Court's MEEQR definition. The case concerned a prohibition by the German authorities to import and sell French "Cassis de Dijon" liquor in Germany. According to German law, "the marketing of fruit liqueurs, such as "Cassis de Dijon", was conditional upon a minimum alcohol content of 25%, whereas the alcohol content of the product in question, which was freely marketed as such in France, is between 15 and 20%".[193] The German rule did not make a distinction between imported and domestically produced liquors in that respect. The Court held that "disparities between the national laws relating to the marketing of the products" could indirectly present obstacles to the free movement qualifying as an MEEQR.[194] As a result, "the unilateral requirement imposed by the rules of a Member State of a minimum alcohol content for the purposes of the sale of alcoholic beverages constitutes an obstacle to trade which is incompatible with the provisions of the Treaty".[195]

A direct consequence of the Court's approach in *Cassis de Dijon* has been that measures which do not on their face distinguish between domestic and imported/exported products, but do however have the effect of making the market importation or exportation of goods more difficult, also fall within the MEEQR definition. Such indistinctly applicable measures can either indirectly discriminate against imported/exported goods or could merely make the potential acquisition, distribution, marketing and packaging of those goods in another Member State *more burdensome* than is the case for domestic products.[196] Both indirectly discriminatory and non-discriminatory rules that target or affect "foreign" products and thus make import/export more difficult, could have an equivalent effect of quantitative restrictions.[197]

6.2.1 *Mutual recognition of national product rules*

Cassis de Dijon clarified that national rules are problematic from the point of view of EU free movement law to the extent that they impose an additional or "dual" burden on imported goods.[198] If those goods have already been subject to inspections and regulated product rules in their Member State of origin, the Member State of importation should no longer impose unreasonable additional rules that in essence duplicate or replicate the already regulated processes in the Member State of origin. This means that if products have been inspected on their compliance with rules in the state of origin, the scope for additional inspections relating to the

---

sought to introduce a more general *de minimis*-like restriction test, see Opinion of A.G. Stix-Hackl in Case C-322/01, *Deutscher Apothekerverband*, para 78 and Opinion of A.G. Kokott in Case C-142/05, *Mickelsson And Roos*, para 66, advocating a quantifiable or otherwise more predictable market access test.

193. Case 120/78, *Rewe-Zentral AG v. Bundesmonopolverwaltung für Branntwein (Cassis de Dijon)*, para 3.

194. Case 120/78, *Cassis de Dijon*, para 8.

195. Case 120/78, *Cassis de Dijon*, para 14.

196. For a critique as to the lack of a discrimination test, see G. Marenco, "Pour une interprétation traditionnelle de la notion de mesure d'effet equivalent à une restriction quantitative", (1984) *Cahiers de Droit Européen*, 349.

197. See among others Joined Cases 177/82 and 178/82, *van de Haar*, para 13; Case C-184/96, *Commission v. France*, para 17; Joined Cases C-277/91, C-318/91 and C-319/91, *Ligur Carni* para 37–39; Case C-67/97, *Bluhme*, para 20.

198. See in that regard e.g. the requirement that margarine be packaged in cube-shaped (and not truncated cone shaped) packages, Case 261/81, *Rau*, paras. 13–14, holding that "a particular form of packaging also used for imported products is of such a nature as to render the marketing of those products more difficult or more expensive either by barring them from certain channels of distribution or owing to the additional costs brought about by the necessity to package the products in question in special packs which comply with the requirements in force on the market of their destination".

shape, size, weight and packaging of products in the Member State of importation ought to be limited.[199] The Court here directly developed the basic features of a system of "mutual recognition" of goods produced or previously imported in another Member State. According to the Court, "provided that they have been lawfully produced and marketed in one of the Member States, [...] the sale of such products may not be subject to a legal prohibition on the marketing of beverages with an alcohol content lower than the limit set by the national rules".[200] As a result, goods produced lawfully in one Member State should be recognized as complying with EU safety and technical standards. Any indistinctly applicable national product rule that would create an additional regulatory burden in that respect would be captured by Article 34 TFEU.[201]

It is not surprising that Member States have been obliged mutually to recognize the rules and practices governing the production and marketing of goods across different Member States. The Commission even built its programme for the further development of the internal market on this principle, entrusting the Member State in which the product entered the internal market with the determination, application and enforcement of its technical standards. Other Member States to which the good was subsequently transferred had to consider those rules to be sufficient and compatible with the standards set in their own legal order.[202]

6.2.2 *The post-Cassis case law of the Court*

On the basis of its *Cassis* reasoning, the Court has subsequently been confronted with an astonishingly wide variety of rules, measures and practices that fell under the classification of MEEQR. The most notable examples include rules regulating prices of (domestic and) imported products,[203] rules requiring import authorizations, licenses or certificates,[204] the obligation

---

199. Not doing so would amount to a *de iure* or *de facto* protection of national products over imported products, see Case 16/83, *Prantl*, para 21.
200. Case 120/78, *Cassis de Dijon*, para 14.
201. See for that argument e.g. Case C-239/90, *Boscher, Studer et Fromentin*, para 16. See also K.E. Sorensen, "Non-harmonized technical regulation and the free movement of goods", 23 EBLR (2012), 163–212.
202. See for that framework, Case 120/78, *Cassis de Dijon*, para 14 and the Commission Communication on the consequences of *Cassis de Dijon*, O.J. 1980, C 256/2.
203. In this instance, the Court accepted that measures imposing fixed prices generally affect all products; only in instances where national rules make a distinction between domestic and imported products will the measure be considered an MEEQR, or otherwise when it can be ascertained that imported products are disadvantaged by the pricing regime. See *inter alia*, Case 65/75, *Tasca*; Joined Cases 88/75, 89/75 and 90/75, *SADAM*; Case 13/77, *GB-Inno*; Case 82/77, *van Tiggele*; Joined Cases 177/82 and 178/82, *van de Haar*; Case 181/82, *Roussel Laboratoria*; Case 229/83, *Leclerc v. Au Blé Vert*; Joined Cases 80/85 and 159/85, *Nederlandse Bakkerij Stichting*; Case 56/87, *Commission v. Italy*; Case 249/88, *Commission v. Belgium*; Case C-531/07, *Fachverband der Buch- und Medienwirtschaft*; most recently, see Case C-333/14, *Scotch Whisky Association*, concerning a rule imposing a minimum price per unit on alcohol sold for retail purposes in Scotland, Case C-221/15, *Colruyt*, concering fixed prices for the sale of cigarettes and Case C-148/15, *Deutsche Parkinson Vereinigung* concerning the sales of prescription-only medicines by pharmacies.
204. On licenses, see *inter alia* Cases 51–57/71, *International Fruit Company*; Case C-212/03, *Commission v. France*; Case C-434/04, *Ahokainen and Leppik*; for the particular case of exports, see Case 237/82, *Jongeneel Kaas*; on authorizations, see among others Case C-344/90, *Commission v. France*; Case C-400/96, *Harpegnies*, para 30; Case C-387/99, *Commission v. Germany*; Case C-24/00, *Commission v. France*, para 23; Case C-150/00, *Commission v. Austria*; Case C-95/01, *Greenham Abel*; Case C-192/01, *Commission v. Denmark*; Case C-270/02, *Commission v. Italy*; Case C-219/07, *Nationale Raad van Dierenkwekers en Liefhebbers*, para 21; Case 524/07, *Commission v. Austria* (summary publication); Case C-333/08, *Commission v. France*; Case C-198/14, *Visnapuu*, see Case 8/74, *Dassonville*; Case 251/78, *Denkavit*; Case 272/80, *Frans-Nederlandse Maatschappij voor Biologische Producten*; Case 25/88, *Bouchara (Wurmser)*; Case C-205/89, *Commission v. Greece*; Case C-385/10, *Elenca Srl v. Ministero dell'Interno*; Case C-484/10, *Ascafor and Asidac*. For a measure having the equivalent effect of licenses, authorizations or certificates, see Case 59/82, *Schutzverband gegen Unwesen in*

to register prior to importation,[205] the obligation to have a more or less permanent or fixed establishment in the Member State of importation,[206] inspections upon importation without taking into account inspections or authorizations already carried out in the state of origin,[207] rules restricting the usage of languages on packaged products,[208] deposit requirements,[209] restrictions on the possession or use of particular goods or ingredients necessary for the production of those goods,[210] advertising bans,[211] rules specifically regulating the conditions of production of particular goods[212] and more generally governing different "product features" such as the shape, size, weight, composition,[213] presentation or identification (including designations of origin protected by national law)[214] of the products concerned,[215] or the imposition of sanctions or fines on

---

der Wirtschaft v. Weinvertriebs-GmbH; Case C-325/00, *Commission v. Germany*; Case C-166/03, *Commission v. France*, and Case C-481/12, *"Juvelta"* in relation to exports, see Case C-272/95, *Deutsches Milch-Kontor*.

205. Case C-55/99, *Commission v. France*; Case C-390/99, *Canal Satélite Digital*.
206. Joined Cases 87/85 and 88/85, *Gyselinx*; C-189/95, *Franzén*; Case C-254/98, *TK-Heimdienst* on the requirement to have an appointed representative in the Member State of importation, see Case 155/82, *Commission v. Belgium*.
207. See among many others, Case 104/75, *De Peijper*; Case 45/87, *Commission v. Ireland*; Case 21/88, *Du Pont de Nemours*; Case C-172/00, *Ferring Arzneimittel*; Case C-14/02, *ATRAL SA v. Belgium*; Case C-112/02, *Kohlpharma*; Case C-443/10, *Bonnarde*; Case C-150/11, *Commission v. Belgium*.
208. Case 27/80, *Fietje*; Case C-369/89, *Piageme*; Case C-51/93, *Meyhui*; Case C-85/94, *Piageme v. Peeters*; Case C-385/96, *Goerres*; Case C-33/97, *Colim v. Bigg's Continent Noord*; Case C-169/99, *Schwarzkopf*.
209. Case 95/81, *Commission v. Italy*; Case 192/84, *Commission v. Greece*.
210. Case C-323/93, *Crespelle*; Case C-293/94, *Brandsma*, para 6. In the same vein, the requirement of goods being stocked could also fall within the ambit of Art. 34 TFEU, see Case 13/78, *Freie Hansestadt Bremen*. On restrictions of use in particular, see Case C-110/05, *Commission v. Italy*; Case C-142/05, *Mickelsson And Roos*; Case C-433/05, *Sandström*; Case C-114/15, *Audace*.
211. Case 286/81, *Oosthoek's Uitgeversmaatschappij*; Case C-362/88, *GB-Inno*; Case C-126/91, *Yves Rocher*; Joined Cases C-1/90 and C-176/90, *Aragonesa*; Case C-292/92, *Hünermund*; Case C-320/93, *Ortscheit*; Case C-412/93, *Leclerc-Siplec*; Case C-470/93, *Mars*; Joined Cases C-34/95 to C-36/95, *KO v. De Agostini*; Case C-337/95, *Parfums Christian Dior*; Case C-368/95, *Vereinigte Familiapress*; Case C-6/98, *ARD v. PRO Sieben Media*; Case C-405/98, *Gourmet International*; Case C-71/02, *Karner*; Case C-239/02, *Douwe Egberts*.
212. Joined Cases C-158/04 and C-159/04, *Alfa Vita*. Similarly, rules inciting the purchase of domestically produced or distributed products falls within the ambit of Art. 34 TFEU, see Case 249/81, *Commission v. Ireland*; Case 222/82, *Apple and Pear Development Council*, and Case C-325/00, *Commission v. Germany*; and more recently, the purchase of green energy certificates, see Case C-573/12, *Ålands Vindkraft*. The same goes for rules restricting the distribution of goods that would otherwise not easily obtain access to the market, see Case C-108/09, *Ker-Optika*.
213. See for national recipe rules and ingredient requirements in particular, Case 120/78, *Cassis de Dijon*; Case 788/79, *Gilli and Andres*; Case 53/80, *Kaasfabriek Eyssen*; Case 130/80, *Kelderman*; Case 94/82, *De Kikvorsch Groothandel-Import-Export*; Case 174/82, *Sandoz*; Case 94/83, *Albert Heijn*; Case 97/83, *CMC Melkunie BV*; Case 216/84, *Commission v. France*; Case 304/84, *Muller and others*; Case 407/85, *3 Glocken GmbH and Kritzinger*; Case 76/86, *Commission v. Germany*; Case 52/88, *Commission v. Belgium*; Case 67/88, *Commission v. Italy*; Case C-169/89, *Gourmetterie Van den Burg*; Case C-269/89, *Bonfait BV*; Joined Cases C-13/91 and C-113/91, *Debus*; Case C-17/93, *Van der Veldt*; Case C-51/94, *Commission v. Germany*; Case C-358/95, *Morellato*; Case C-12/00, *Commission v. Spain*; Case C-14/00, *Commission v. Italy*; Case C-121/00, *Hahn*; Case C-416/00, *Morellato*; Case C-358/01, *Commission v. Spain*; Case C-41/02, *Commission v. The Netherlands*.
214. See among others Case 12/74, *Commission v. Germany*; Case 41/76, *Donckerwolcke*; Case 13/78, *Freie Hansestadt Bremen*; Case 113/80, *Commission v. Ireland*; Case 193/80, *Commission v. Italy*; Case 16/83, *Karl Prantl*; Case 207/83, *Commission v. UK*; Case 178/84, *Commission v. Germany*; Case 182/84, *Miro*; Case 286/86, *Deserbais*; Case 298/87, *Smanor*; Case 47/90, *Établissements Delhaize*; Case C-3/91, *Confiserie du Tech*; Case C-315/92, *Clinique Laboratoires SNC and Estée Lauder Cosmetics*; Case C-184/96, *Commission v. France*; Case C-448/98, *Guimont*; Case C-491/01, *British American Tobacco and Imperial Tobacco*; Case C-6/02, *Commission v. France*; Case C-478/07, *Budvar v. Ammersin*.
215. See for that overview of categories, Joined Cases C-267/91 and C-268/91, *Keck and Mithouard*, para 15.

imported goods[216] for failure to comply with national regulations.[217] The rules under scrutiny can either be substantive or procedural in nature: the Court has made it clear that evidentiary rules making it more difficult for an importer to prove the compatibility of imported products with domestic rules are equally captured by Article 34 TFEU.[218]

Summarizing, in the wake of *Cassis de Dijon* the Court has predominantly focused on rules concerning product requirements, i.e. rules governing the intrinsic and extrinsic characteristics of a specific product.[219] Product requirement rules essentially condition the ingredients, shape, size, weight, packaging or format of goods.[220] To the extent that those rules effectively prevent a product lawfully manufactured in a Member State from being marketed on the territory of another Member State, intra-Union trade in those particular goods is liable to be hindered. Essentially, such rules impose additional requirements on goods lawfully produced in another Member State and result in additional costs for traders. In doing so, they effectively impose a dual regulatory burden (home state burden and host state burden) on the products concerned. As a result, these measures should be classified as MEEQR.

While certain dual burden situations (e.g. demanding products to be repackaged or ingredients to be changed or unnecessary formalities to be fulfilled) are relatively straightforward, in other situations it is less clear-cut whether a dual burden has been imposed. The judgment in *Alfa Vita* exemplifies this. In this case, national legislation obliged sellers of "bake-off" products (products that have been prepared and pre-baked at a different venue, requiring them to be baked-off briefly prior to sales) to comply with all requirements imposed on traditional bakeries, including, in particular, the requirement of having a flour store, an area for kneading equipment and a solid-fuel store. According to the Court, such a rule does not take the specific nature of those products into account and entails additional costs, thereby making the marketing of those products more difficult.[221] As those national rules also targeted imported bake-off products, they qualified as an MEEQR. In this particular scenario, the Court presupposed that the additional costs that would have to be made for the sales and marketing of the imported bake-off products amounted to an additional burden imposed by the Member State of importation. The burden in this situation is however that shops – and not products – needed to be re-arranged or restructured in order to accommodate for the national rule. As such, it would seem that the Court interpreted the concept and scope of dual burden in a very flexible and open-ended way. It could even be argued that any measure imposing any kind of "additional costs" on importers compared to what domestic producers would have to bear would qualify under the "dual burden" test applied in the wake of *Cassis de Dijon*.[222] Any such rule would go against the framework of mutual recognition promoted by the Court in this regard.

---

216. Case 41/76, *Donckerwolcke*; Case 52/77, *Cayrol v. Rivoira*; Case 179/78, *Rivoira*; Case 65/79, *Chatain*; Case C-367/89, *Richardt*; Case C-276/91, *Commission v. France*; Case C-378/97, *Wijsenbeek*; Case C-224/00, *Commission v. Italy*.
217. The abovementioned categories and case law illustrations only represent the most salient examples of MEEQR identified by the Court. For a more elaborate overview and an assessment of different examples and attempts at categorization, see P. Oliver op. cit. *supra* note 44, 157–213.
218. See e.g. Joined Cases 89/74, 18/75 and 19/75, *Arnaud* and Joined Cases 10/75–14/75, *Lahaille*.
219. For an attempt at defining product requirement rules, see Opinion of A.G. Van Gerven in Joined Cases C-401/92 and C-402/92, *Tankstation 't Heukske*, para 16.
220. According to Art. 3 of Directive 70/50/EEC, product requirement rules relate to measures governing the marketing or distribution of products which deal, in particular, with shape, size, weight, composition, presentation, identification or putting up.
221. Joined Cases C-158/04 and C-159/04, *Alfa Vita*, para 19.
222. See for that expression, Joined Cases C-158/04 and C-159/04, *Alfa Vita*, para 19.

The extensive interpretation of the concept of MEEQR by the Court did leave much room for – at times perhaps even frivolous – litigation against undesirable national rules of economic regulation.[223] Rules that did not affect intra-Union trade but merely sought to regulate the exercise of commercial freedom within a particular territory – "market circumstances rules"[224] – were also considered as MEEQR and thus brought under the Court's scrutiny. Consequently, on each and every occasion the Court was called upon to adjudicate whether the contested national measure, having easily taken the MEEQR hurdle, could be justified and complied with the principle of proportionality. In *Cinéthèque,* for example, the Court held that French legislation banning the sale or hire for private use of recordings of cinematographic works before the expiry of a period between 6 and 18 months after the release of the film did come within the scope of application of Article 34 TFEU for "it may create barriers to intra-Union trade in video-cassettes". The Court came to this conclusion, despite acknowledging that the French system did "not have the purpose of regulating trade patterns" and its effect was "not to favour national production as against the production of other Member States, but to encourage cinematographic production as such".[225] Ultimately, the Court found that the French system could be justified.[226] In the illustrious "Sunday trading" cases, the Court followed the same conceptual approach: rules governing opening times of shops were held to fall within the scope of Article 34 TFEU, only to subsequently escape the prohibition of Article 34 TFEU provided the measures could be justified and were held to be proportionate.

This case law of the Court provoked a lot of academic debate on the precise boundaries of Article 34.[227] The wide interpretation of what constitute MEEQR resulted in a perceived increase of the workload of the Court.[228] Moreover, it entailed the risk that Member States would lose all powers to regulate commercial activities (e.g. imposing mandatory Sunday closures, restricting times and methods of sales, regulating promotions and advertising etc.) with the Court meddling with national provisions that did not as such have as their object or purpose the limitation of intra-Union trade, but mainly sought to establish a playing field within which commercial freedom could be exercised throughout a Member State. It could genuinely be questioned whether the Court was the best suited institution or even whether it was competent under EU law to do so.

At the same time, it must be acknowledged that the concept of MEEQR, how large it may have been interpreted by the Court, is not all-encompassing. Precisely seeking to limit the scope of the MEEQR definition, the Court maintained in a string of cases that Articles 34–35 TFEU do not apply in instances where a national measure's effect on trade is "too uncertain and indirect"

223. See Case 145/88, *Torfaen Borough Council*; Case C-306/88, *Rochdale Borough Council v. Stewart John Anders*; Case C-312/89, *Conforama,*; Case C-332/89, *Ministère Public v. Marchandise*; C-304/90, *Reading Borough Council v. Payless DIY Ltd* and C-169/91, *Stoke-on-Trent*. In later judgments, the Court stated that those rules qualified as selling arrangements falling outside the scope of Art. 34 TFEU in accordance with the *Keck and Mithouard* criteria, see among others Joined Cases C-69/93 and C-258/93 *Punto Casa*, para 15; Joined Cases C-418/93 to C-421/93, C-460/93 to C-462/93, C-464/93, C-9/94 to C-11/94, C-14/94, C-15/94, C-23/94, C-24/94 and C-332/94, *Semeraro Casa Uno and Others*, para 28 and Case C-483/12, *Pelckmans*, para 24.

224. See for that concept, K.J.M. Mortelmans, "Art. 30 of the EEC Treaty and legislation relating to market circumstances: Time to consider a new definition", 28 CML Rev. (1991), 116.

225. Cases 60/84 and 61/84, *Cinéthèque,* para 21.

226. Cases 60/84 and 61/84, *Cinéthèque,* para 23.

227. See among others E. White, "In search of the limits to Art. 30 of the EEC Treaty", 26 CML Rev. (1989), 235; A. Arnull, "What shall we do on Sunday?", 26 EL Rev. (1991), 112; J. Steiner, "Drawing the line: Uses and abuses of Art. 30 EEC", 29 CML Rev. (1992), 749.

228. See K.J.M. Mortelmans, op. cit. *supra* note 224.

to even consider the measure to be of equivalent effect to a quantitative restriction.[229] The most obvious example in this respect has been the Court's judgment in *Peralta*. In that case, the Court maintained that national legislation prohibiting vessels from discharging chemical substances in a Member State's territorial waters fell outside the scope of the free movement provisions, as the purpose of such regulation was "not to regulate trade in goods with other Member States and the restrictive effects which it might have on the free movement of goods are too uncertain and indirect for the obligation which it lays down to be regarded as being of a nature to hinder trade between Member States".[230] Additional cases applying the *Peralta* remoteness test have included rules on urban planning,[231] rules requiring the seizure of goods by tax collectors in case of fiscal debts,[232] legislative provisions limiting the sale of strong spirits for consumption on the premises to places open to the public without dealing with imports of spirits,[233] measures limiting summary debt payment procedures to inhabitants in a particular Member State[234] and measures prohibiting the production and distribution of bakery products during certain hours of the night.[235] The *Peralta* remoteness test did not however allow to clearly and precisely predict types of situations in which national rules will always escape Articles 34–35 TFEU scrutiny.[236] It rather enabled the Court to refrain, on a case-by-case basis, from applying the free movement of goods provisions to situations where the applicant makes a mere egregious statement as to free movement rights being infringed.[237]

6.3 *Containing the tide in Keck & Mithouard*

In the wake of the "Sunday trading" saga and cases such as *Cinéthèque* and *Peralta*, a more general and systematic assessment of measures as MEEQR – rather than continuing on the basis of a case-by-case approach – was increasingly suggested in legal doctrine, with the Court of Justice being invited to provide clarity on the boundaries of the concept of MEEQR.[238] The Opinion of Advocate General Tesauro in *Hünermund* can be seen as a culmination point in that regard. In unequivocal terms, the A.G. opined that "the purpose of Article [34 TFEU] is to ensure the free movement of goods in order to establish a single integrated market, eliminating therefore

229. Case 69/88, *Krantz*; Case C-339/89, *Sulzer*; Joined Cases C-277/91, C-318/91 and C-319/91, *Ligur Carni* Case C-379/92, *Peralta*; Case C-96/94, *Centro Servizi Spediporto*; Case C-134/94, *Esso Española*; Joined Cases C-140/94, C-141/94 and C-142/94, *DIP SpA v. Comune di Bassano del Grappa*; Case C-266/96, *Corsica Ferries France*; Case C-44/98, *BASF*. See for background on those cases, E. Spaventa, "The outer limits of the treaty free movement provisions: Some reflections on the significance of *Keck, Remoteness* and *Deliège*" in C. Barnard and O. Odudu (Eds.), *The Outer Limits of European Union Law* (Hart, 2008), 245–272.

230. Case C-379/92, *Peralta*, para 24.

231. Joined Cases C-140/94, C-141/94 and C-142/94, *DIP SpA v. Comune di Bassano del Grappa*.

232. Case 69/88, *Krantz*.

233. See in that regard already, without explicitly referring to the remoteness test, Case 75/81, *Blesgen*.

234. Case C-412/97, *ED v. Fenocchio*, para 11.

235. Case 155/80, *Oebel*, para 16, also confirmed in Case C-412/97, *ED v. Fenocchio*. *Oebel* in effect found its par later on in the general exclusion of non-discriminatory selling arrangements from the scope of Art. 34 TFEU in Joined Cases C-267/91 and C-268/91, *Keck and Mithouard*.

236. A.G. Jacobs referred to this test as a *de minimis* test in disguise, see Opinion of A.G. Jacobs in Case C-112/00, *Schmidberger*, para 65. See for the most developed critique, Opinion of A.G. Kokott in Case C-142/05, *Mickelsson And Roos*, para 46.

237. Clear examples in that regard can be found in Case C-93/92, *Baskiciogullari*, para 11, claiming that the restrictive effect resulted from the refusal of dealers to repair products that had been the subject of parallel importation rather than from a rule of national law. See also Case C-23/89, *Quietlynn* and Case C-350/89, *Sheptonhurst*, on the licensed sale of sex products. Similarly, the Court recently argued that shop opening hours fall within the same category, see Case C-483/12, *Pelckmans*, para 24.

238. See references cited *supra* note 227.

those national measures which in any way create an obstacle to or even mere difficulties for the movement of goods; its purpose is not to strike down the most widely differing measures in order, essentially, to ensure the greatest possible expansion of trade".[239] Inviting the Court to interpret Article 34 TFEU in this light, A.G. Tesauro proposed to leave room to the Member States to organize and regulate the organization of sales, promotional and marketing activities in accordance with a state's or region's socio-cultural characteristics.[240]

6.3.1 *Keck: "selling arrangements"*

In November 1993, the Court explicitly addressed the issue in its *Keck and Mithouard* judgment. The case concerned a French prohibition on selling at a loss. Keck and Mithouard argued that the prohibition on selling at a loss impeded the import of goods in France, as it made it more difficult for imported goods to gain access to and exposure on the market. As such, the rule would qualify as an MEEQR. The Court – well aware of the criticism voiced against too extensive an MEEQR interpretation – used this opportunity to develop new limits on the *scope of Article 34 TFEU*, thereby seeking to close the floodgates of litigation opened by *Cassis de Dijon*.

The Court commenced in very unusual fashion, indicating that "[i]n view of the increasing tendency of traders to invoke Article [34] of the Treaty as a means of challenging any rules whose effect is to limit their commercial freedom even where such rules are not aimed at products from other Member States", it considered it "necessary to re-examine and clarify its case-law on this matter".[241]

First, it simply reiterated its established case law since *Cassis de Dijon* that "in the absence of harmonization of legislation, obstacles to free movement of goods which are the consequence of applying, to goods coming from other Member States where they are lawfully manufactured and marketed, rules that lay down requirements to be met by such goods (such as those relating to designation, form, size, weight, composition, presentation, labeling, packaging) constitute measures of equivalent effect prohibited by Article [34] TFEU. This is so even if those rules apply without distinction to all products unless their application can be justified by a public-interest objective taking precedence over the free movement of goods".[242]

Subsequently, however, the Court explicitly departed from its previous case law, stating that "contrary to what has previously been decided, the application to products from other Member States of national provisions restricting or prohibiting certain selling arrangements is not such as to hinder directly or indirectly, actually or potentially, trade between Member States within the meaning of the *Dassonville* judgment, so long as those provisions apply to all relevant traders operating within the national territory and so long as they affect in the same manner, in law and in fact, the marketing of domestic products and of those from other Member States".[243] As a result, measures that can be qualified as "selling arrangements" do not fall under Article 34 TFEU. In the words of the Court, "the application of such rules to the sale of products from another Member State meeting the requirements laid down by that State is not by nature such as to prevent their access to the market or to impede access any more than it impedes the access of domestic products. Such rules therefore fall outside the scope of Article [34] of the Treaty".[244]

---

239. Opinion of Advocate General Tesauro in Case C-292/92, *Ruth Hünermund and others v. Landesapothekerkammer Baden-Württemberg*, para 28.
240. Opinion A.G. Tesauro in Case C-292/92, *Hünermund*, para 15.
241. Joined Cases C-267/91 and C-268/91, *Keck and Mithouard*, para 14.
242. Joined Cases C-267/91 and C-268/91, *Keck and Mithouard*, para 15.
243. Joined Cases C-267/91 and C-268/91, *Keck and Mithouard*, para 16.
244. Joined Cases C-267/91 and C-268/91, *Keck and Mithouard*, para 17.

As the Court in *Keck* did not provide a definition of selling arrangements, subsequent case law gradually clarified the rules that were to be captured by that notion. Selling arrangements now certainly include selling at a loss rules,[245] shop opening (and closing) hours,[246] legislation restricting channels of distribution and sales (e.g. only through established pharmacists or opticians),[247] rules requiring retailers to have premises in a particular territory,[248] rules regulating sales rounds,[249] rules prohibiting sales in private premises,[250] rules fixing retail prices of e.g. books,[251] rules on selling at low profit margins[252] and rules on marketing through advertising.[253] As the Court itself summarized it in *Karner*, rules relating to the place and time of sales as well as to the marketing of specific products are in principle considered to be selling arrangements.[254] In essence, any rule regulating the specific sales and promotion conditions of goods therefore is to be considered a selling arrangement subject to the Court's *Keck* check.[255]

6.3.2 *Judicial qualifications of "selling arrangements"*

In the early years post *Keck*, the Court further clarified the boundaries of the selling arrangement definition.[256] Firstly, in *Familiapress*, Court held that rules which concern the selling of a product but at the same time also affect the content of that product, fall within the scope of Article 34 TFEU. The case concerned a prohibition in Austrian law to offer consumers free gifts linked to the sale of products or the provision of services. A German distributor of magazines marketed and sold German magazines containing prize-winning crossword puzzles in Austria. The mere

245. Joined Cases C-267/91 and C-268/91, *Keck and Mithouard*, para 18.
246. Joined Cases C-401/92 and C-402/92, *Tankstation 't Heukske*; Joined Cases C-69/93 and C-258/93, *Punto Casa*; Joined Cases C-418/93 to C-421/93, C-460/93 to C-462/93, C-464/93, C-9/94 to C-11/94, C-14/94, C-15/94, C-23/94, C-24/94 and C-332/94, *Semeraro Casa Uno*.
247. Case C-391/92, *Commission v. Greece*; Case C-387/93, *Banchero*; Case C-162/97, *Nilsson, Hagelgren and Arrborn*; Case C-108/09, *Ker-Optika*.
248. Case C-254/98,. *TK-Heimdienst*.
249. Case C-20/03, *Burmanjer, Van Der Linden and De Jong*.
250. Case C-322/01, *DocMorris*.
251. Case C-93/94, *Commission v. the Netherlands*; Case C-531/07, *Fachverband der Buch- und Medienwirtschaft*.
252. Case C-63/94, *Groupement National des Négociants en Pommes de Terre de Belgique* for sales yielding low profit margins.
253. Case C-292/92, *Hünermund*; Case C-412/93, *Leclerc-Siplec*; Joined Cases C-34/95, C-35/95 and C-36/95, Case C-34/95, *Konsumentombudsmannen (KO) v. De Agostini*; Case C-34/95 and Case C-35/95 *TV-Shop i Sverige AB*; Case C-6/98, *Arbeitsgemeinschaft Deutscher Rundfunkanstalten (ARD)*; Case C-405/98, *Gourmet International Products* ; Case C-71/02, *Karner*. See also, Case C-315/92, *Clinique Laboratoires and Estée Lauder Cosmetics*; Case C-470/93, *Mars*; Case C-51/94, *Commission v. Germany*; Case C-368/95, *Vereinigte Familiapress*; Case C-143/03, *Commission v. Italy*; Case C-309/02, *Radlberger*; Case C-463/01, *Commission v. Germany*.
254. Case C-71/02, *Karner*, para 38.
255. See J. Stuyck, "Annotation of Case C-71/02, *Herbert Karner Industrie-Auktionen GmbH v. Troostwijk GmbH*, Judgment of the Fifth Chamber of 25 Mar. 2004", 41 CML Rev. (2004), 1696. See for another example, Case C-441/04, *A-Punkt Schuckhandel v. Schmidt*, para 9 and 26.
256. See for literature relating to *Keck* and its progeny, S. Weatherill, "Recent case law concerning the free movement of goods: Mapping the frontiers of market deregulation", 36 CML Rev. (1999), 51–85; N. Nic Shuibhne "The free movement of goods and Art. 28 EC: An evolving framework", 27 EL Rev. (2002), 408–425; F. Leidenmuhler, "The free movement of goods within an EC-wide market: Still a work in progress", 12 *Cardozo Journal of International & Comparative Law* (2004), 163–186; P. Oliver and S. Enchelmaier, "Free movement of goods: Recent developments in the case law", 44 CML Rev. (2007), 649–704; A. Dawes, "Importing and exporting poor reasoning: Worrying trends in relation to the case law on the free movement of goods", 8 GLJ (2007), 761–776; S. Enchelmaier, "The ECJ's recent case law on the free movement of goods: Movement in all sorts of directions", 26 *Yearbook of European Law* (2007), 115–156.

fact that the magazine offered the opportunity to win prizes by completing the crossword puzzle was sufficient for the Austrian government to prohibit the magazine's distribution on Austrian territory in accordance with national law. It subsequently argued that such prohibition did not go against Article 34 TFEU, as the "possibility of offering readers of a periodical the chance to take part in prize competitions [was] merely a method of promoting sales" falling within the boundaries of the *Keck* exception.[257] The Court disagreed with this position, holding that "even though the relevant national legislation is directed against a method of sales promotion, in this case it bears on the actual content of the products, in so far as the competitions in question form an integral part of the magazine in which they appear. As a result, the national legislation in question as applied to the facts of the case is not concerned with a selling arrangement within the meaning of the judgment in Keck and Mithouard".[258] To the extent that a producer or distributor of magazines would be obliged to alter the contents of the magazine and thus to re-produce its product tailored to the Austrian market, Austrian legislation imposed a regulatory burden on foreign-produced magazines that impeded access to the Austrian market for goods lawfully produced in another Member State. Such burden would fall within the MEEQR definition.[259]

Secondly, the Court also clarified that if national selling arrangements have a differential impact, in law or in fact, on domestic and foreign traders – and thus do not comply with the conditions by the Court imposed in paragraph 16 of *Keck* – they are caught under Article 34 TFEU. A number of cases concerning restrictions on advertising are illustrative in this respect. Whilst the Court confirmed that advertising restrictions essentially comprise rules relating to selling arrangements, it held in *De Agostini* that an outright ban on advertising, applying in one Member State, of a type of promotion for a product which is lawfully sold there might have a greater impact on products from other Member States.[260] This was the case especially in relation to products sold by De Agostini, an encyclopedic magazine which contains information about dinosaurs and a related model dinosaur aimed at children.[261] De Agostini claimed that television advertising was the only effective method of promotion which could enable it to reach children and their parents and thus to penetrate the market. An outright ban on television advertising aimed at children under 12 years could effectively negatively affect de Agostini's access to the Swedish market.[262] While in *De Agostini*, the Court ultimately left it to the national court to make the final assessment in this regard, in *Gourmet*, a case also concerning a Swedish law prohibiting advertising of alcohol on radio and tv, the Court explicitly stated that total bans on advertising constitute an obstacle to trade between Member States and are to be construed as MEEQR.[263]

The situation is thus as follows: when it can be established that the contested national measure amounts to a selling arrangement, the prohibition in Article 34 TFEU *prima facie* does not apply, as selling arrangements do not constitute MEEQR.[264] The mere classification of a rule as a *prima facie* selling arrangement is however not sufficient to escape the Article 34 prohibition. The Court imposed a two-step check to assess whether or not selling arrangements are ultimately to be considered as MEEQR anyway. In paragraph 16 of *Keck*, it held that selling arrangements do not fall within the scope of Article 34 TFEU if (1) they apply to all relevant traders operating

257. Case C-368/95, *Vereinigte Familiapress*, para 10.
258. Case C-368/95, *Vereinigte Familiapress*, para 11.
259. Case C-368/95, *Vereinigte Familiapress*, para 12.
260. Joined Cases C-34/95, C-35/95 and C-36/95, *Konsumentombudsmannen (KO) v. De Agostini*, para 42.
261. Joined Cases C-34/95, C-35/95 and C-36/95, *Konsumentombudsmannen (KO) v. De Agostini*, para 16.
262. Joined Cases C-34/95, C-35/95 and C-36/95, *Konsumentombudsmannen (KO) v. De Agostini*, para 43.
263. Case C-405/98, *Gourmet*, paras. 20–24. D. Kraft, "Advertising restrictions and the free movement of goods – The case law of the ECJ", 18 EBLR (2007), 517–523.
264. Joined Cases C-267/91 and C-268/91, *Keck and Mithouard*, para 18.

within the national territory and (2) if they affect in the same manner, in law and in fact, the marketing of domestic products and of those from other Member States.[265] The added value of the first condition has rightly been questioned.[266] It seemingly does not add anything to the second condition, which essentially means that rules which, at face value or in fact, distinguish between domestic and imported goods, are captured by Article 34 TFEU, as such distinctions are presumed to make trading in imported goods more difficult and thus to affect intra-Union trade in those goods. Basically, in paragraph 16 of *Keck*, the Court has brought the principle of non-discrimination back into its scrutiny of the boundaries of Article 34 TFEU. Rules relating to selling arrangements that indirectly affect the marketing of imported products more than the marketing of domestic products are thus covered under Article 34 TFEU.[267]

The Court further developed the second condition in more recent case law. In *Ker-Optika*, it was confronted with national legislation authorizing the sale of contact lenses only in shops which specialize in the sale of medical devices, and thus prohibiting the sale of contact lenses via the Internet.[268] The Court held that it was clear that the prohibition on selling contact lenses by mail order "deprives traders from other Member States of a particularly effective means of selling those products and thus significantly impedes access of those traders to the market of the Member State concerned".[269] National legislation banning internet sales (also from other countries) thus qualifies as an MEEQR.

In cases such as *De Agostini*, *Gourmet* or *Ker-Optika*, the contested measures involved total bans. In *Heimdienst*, Article 34 TFEU was held to encapsulate also measures merely impeding access to the market.[270] The case involved an Austrian rule obliging bakers, butchers and grocers organizing sales on rounds to have a permanent establishment in the same or an adjacent administrative district. The Court made it clear that in order for goods from other Member States to enjoy the same access to the market of the Member State of importation as domestic goods, they should not have to bear additional costs.[271] And that is precisely what the Austrian legislation did, imposing the requirement on economic operators in another Member State to have a permanent establishment in Austria.[272]

The factual circumstances of this case are similar to those in *Alfa Vita*, where additional costs were considered to impose an additional "regulatory" burden on importers.[273] The main difference between both cases is however that *Heimdienst* considered a prima facie legal selling arrangement (sales on rounds), whereas the rules in *Alfa Vita* governed the conditions for the production of (imported) goods and therefore fell within the "product requirements" rules scheme of *Cassis*. In both cases, the outcome was the same, i.e. both measures being MEEQR, as they imposed additional costs on importers (dual burden threshold).

In essence, the *Keck* discrimination check thus provides an additional safeguard against unwarranted exclusion of some selling arrangement rules from the Article 34 TFEU prohibition. Rules relating to selling arrangements are excluded from Article 34 TFEU unless they either discriminate between domestic and imported products or they impose additional burdens (in

---

265. Joined Cases C-267/91 and C-268/91, *Keck and Mithouard*, para 16.
266. See P. Oliver, op. cit. *supra* note 47, 117–118 and references included therein.
267. See for a similar assessment, Opinion of A.G. Van Gerven in Joined Cases C-401/92 and C-402/92, *Tankstation 't Heukske*, para 21.
268. Case C-108/09, *Ker-Optika*.
269. Case C-108/09, *Ker-Optika*, para 54.
270. Case C-254/98, *TK-Heimdienst*.
271. Case C-254/98, *TK-Heimdienst*, para 26.
272. Case C-254/98, *TK-Heimdienst*, paras. 29–30.
273. Joined Cases C-158/04 and C-159/04, *Alfa Vita*, para 19.

the sense of the *Cassis* line of cases) on imported goods. As such, the classification of rules as a selling arrangement creates a kind of presumption of non-application of Article 34 TFEU that can be rebutted on the basis of the relatively modest "dual burden" conditions reflected in the *Cassis* test.

6.3.3 *Exclusionary rules after Keck: "Rules of use", market access and remoteness*

The distinction between product requirement and selling arrangement rules has been termed rigid and artificial, and moreover difficult to maintain in practice, primarily since not all national rules can easily fit either the product requirement or the selling arrangement rule boxes. Despite the Court's attempt to distinguish selling arrangements from other product requirements, it has been unable to draw a clear distinction between rules that escape from Article 34 TFEU scrutiny and those that do not.[274] Particularly relevant in this regard is the remarkable recent case law relating to rules restricting the use of a particular good.[275]

This saga initiated with the opinion of A.G. Léger in *Commission v. Italy* (*"Towing Trailers"*), in which he qualified the prohibition in the Italian Highway Code on the towing of trailers by mopeds as an MEEQR. This was unsurprising, as restrictions on the use of goods had already been caught under Article 34 TFEU in previous case law.[276] In *Mickelsson and Roos*, a case concerning Swedish legislation prohibiting the use of personal watercraft other than on general navigable waterways, however, A.G. Kokott suggested the Court follow another approach. She proposed to extend the Court's *Keck* case-law on selling arrangements to arrangements for use and thus to exclude such arrangements from the scope of Article 34 TFEU.[277]

These two cases, on the use of trailers in Italy and on the use of jet skis in Sweden, clearly illustrate the limits of the formal distinction between product requirements and selling arrangements. In both instances, national rules essentially sought to restrict the use that could be made of particular goods. In the Italian case, the national highway code determined that trailers could not be towed by motorcycles, but only by at least four wheel automobiles.[278] As a result, trailers designed to be towed by motorcycles could not be used in Italy.[279] In the Swedish case, national legislation allowed for jet skis only to be used in general navigable waters or in other waters designated as fit for jet skis by local authorities.[280] Once again, national legislation sought to

---

274. See for that particular critique, S. Weatherill, "After *Keck*: Some thoughts on how to clarify the clarification", 33 CML Rev. (1996), 885–906. A recent illustration of those difficulties can be found in Case C-483/12, *Pelckmans Turnhout NV v. Walter Van Gastel Balen NV and Others*, para 24 jo. 15, where the Court did not directly categorize national rules concerning shop opening times as a selling arrangement, nor did it refer explicitly to the *Keck and Mithouard* judgment; See on that subject matter also T. Horsley, "Unearthing Buried Treasure: Art. 34 TFEU and the *Exclusionary Rules*". 37 EL Rev. (2012), 734–757. See also L. W. Gormley, "Inconsistencies and misconceptions in the free movement of goods", 40 EL Rev. (2015), 925–939; I. Lianos, "In memoriam *Keck*: The reformation of the EU law on the free movement of goods", 40 ELJ (2015), 225–248.
275. For more elaboration, see P. Oliver, "Of trailers and jetskis: Is the case law on Art. 34 TFEU hurtling in a new direction?", 33 *Fordham International Law Journal* (2009–2010), 1423–1471.
276. See, e.g. Case 119/78, *Grandes Distilleries Peureux*; Case C-473/98, *Toolex Alpha.*
277. Opinion of A.G. Kokott in Case C-142/05, *Mickelsson And Roos*, para 66. The A.G. opinion caused some commotion at the Court. The *Towing Trailers* case was referred to the Grand Chamber, and the oral phase of the proceedings was reopened. A.G. Bot delivered a second opinion, also qualifying the Italian rules as an MEEQR. Somewhat surprisingly, perhaps, *Mickelsson And Roos* itself was not referred to the Grand Chamber.
278. Case C-110/05, *Commission v. Italy*, para 7.
279. Case C-110/05, *Commission v. Italy*, para 8.
280. Case C-142/05, *Mickelsson And Roos*, para 2 and paras. 10–12.

constrain the use of goods, this time to avoid nuisance caused by those goods. In both cases, it was unclear whether those rules should be captured by the lenient product requirement restriction test outlined in *Cassis de Dijon* and its progeny or whether a *Keck*-like exemption from the Article 34 TFEU prohibition should be developed.

In its judgment, the Court began by generally outlining three types of MEEQR within the meaning of Article 34 TFEU: firstly, measures adopted by a Member State the object or effect of which is to treat products coming from other Member States less favourably; secondly, rules that lay down requirements to be met by goods lawfully produced and marketed in another Member State; and thirdly, [a]ny other measure which hinders access of products originating in other Member States to the market of a Member State.[281] The Court also contrasted between these measures and the national provisions restricting or prohibiting certain selling arrangements from *Keck*, which are not such as to hinder directly or indirectly, actually or potentially, trade between Member States and thus remain outside Article 34 TFEU scrutiny, provided the conditions in paragraph 16 of *Keck* have been satisfied.[282]

This typology of MEEQR is new. The Court, however, refrained from providing any further guidance or clarification, which would have been most helpful in this context. The first two categories of MEEQR appear relatively straightforward, even though partially overlapping; the third category is rather vague; arguably it purports to be a rest category of rules that do not relate to product requirements nor selling arrangements. As a result, for now it remains somewhat unclear whether this typology primarily constitutes a confirmation of existing case law or rather whether it heralds a departure from it. Future case law will have to tell.

In any event, applying the law to the facts, the Court observed that a prohibition on the use of a product in the territory of a Member State exerts a considerable influence on the behaviour of consumers.[283] Consumers are not interested in products they cannot use.[284] Consequently, it held that the Italian legislation, to the extent that its effect is to hinder access to the Italian market for trailers, constitutes an MEEQR within the meaning of Article 34 TFEU.[285] In so arguing, the Court rejected Advocate General Kokott's proposal to extend the scope of the selling arrangement exception to rules of use.

Similarly, in *Mickelsson and Roos*, the Court ruled that "where the national regulations for the designation of navigable waters and waterways have the effect of preventing users of personal

---

281. Case C-110/05, *Commission v. Italy*, para 37. See among others also T. Horsley, "Anyone for *Keck*? – Comment on Case C-110/05, *Commission v. Italy, Judgment of the Court (Grand Chamber)* of 10 Feb. 2009; Case C-142/05, *Åklagaren v. Percy Mickelsson and Joakim Roos, Judgment of the Court (Second Chamber)* of 4 June 2009; Case C-265/06, *Commission v. Portugal, Judgment of the Court (Third Chamber)* of 10 Apr. 2008", 46 CML Rev. (2009), 2001–2019; I. Lianos, "Shifting narratives in the European internal market: Efficient restrictions of trade and the nature of 'economic integration'", EBLR (2010), 724. See for background on the scope of Art. 34 TFEU in this respect, P. Oliver, op. cit. *supra* note 275; L. Gormley, "Free movement of goods and their use – What is the use of it?", 33 *Fordham International Law Journal* (2011), 1589–1628; E. Spaventa, "Leaving *Keck* behind? The free movement of goods after the rulings in *Commission v. Italy and Mickelsson and Roos*", 35 EL Rev. (2009), 914–932; C. Barnard, "Trailing a new approach to free movement of goods", 68 CLJ (2009), 288–290; A. Tryfonidou, "Was Keck a half-baked solution after all?", 34 *Legal Issues of Economic Integration* (2007), 167–182; P. Wenneras and B. Ketil, "Selling arrangements, keeping *Keck*", 35 EL Rev. (2010), 387–400.
282. Case C-110/05, *Commission v. Italy*, para 36.
283. Case C-110/05, *Commission v. Italy*, para 56.
284. Case C-110/05, *Commission v. Italy*, para 57.
285. Case C-110/05, *Commission v. Italy*, para 58. In Case C-265/06, *Commission v. Portugal*, para 36, revolving around a Portugese rule prohibiting car windows to be tainted, the Court reached the same conclusion, albeit without any reflection on the scope of the rule limiting the use of tainted windows in this regard.

watercraft from using them for the specific and inherent purposes for which they were intended or of greatly restricting their use, which is for the national court to ascertain, such regulations have the effect of hindering the access to the domestic market in question for those goods and therefore constitute, save where there is a justification pursuant to Article [36 TFEU] or there are overriding public interest requirements, measures having equivalent effect to quantitative restrictions on imports prohibited by Article [34 TFEU]".[286] Consequently, after *Towing trailers* and *Mickelsson & Roos,* it seems now clear that "residual" rules, such as, in particular, restrictions on use, – which cannot be captured by the notions of product requirement rules or selling arrangement rules – can also be qualified as MEEQR and thus come within the scope of Article 34 TFEU.[287] Furthermore, the following three types of restrictions on use can be identified as being caught under Article 34 TFEU: firstly, total prohibitions on use; secondly, rules preventing goods from being used for the specific and inherent purposes for which they were intended; and thirdly, rules which greatly restrict the use of goods. The latter two types of restrictions are rather imprecise and leave the national authorities ample room for appreciation.

Furthermore, in *Towing Trailers,* the Court also appears to have confirmed its adherence to a market access formula,[288] without however providing further guidance on this issue.[289] In legal doctrine, it has been submitted that judicial references to market access indicate that the Court is willing to engage in more empirical assessments of the extent to which access to a market is in effect impeded. That assessment is said to constitute the expression of a nascent *de minimis* test claiming that negligible impediments on market access should not fall within the MEEQR definition.[290] This submission certainly is not without merit. Former A.G. Jacobs advocated the introduction of a *de minimis* test in this context in his opinion in *Leclerc-Siplec.*[291] However, the submission that a market access test is taking shape and that a *de minimis* rule flows from it cannot be read in the Court's case law. The Court does indeed refer to access to the market as a precondition for falling under the residual category of rules to be considered as MEEQR, but so far, it has not explicitly considered the application of a *de minimis* test in that regard. Arguably, access to the market should rather be seen as referring to the open-ended "dual burden" or "additional costs" concepts identified in the context of the mutual recognition principle in *Cassis*. If a national measure imposes "additional costs" – an additional regulatory or economic burden – on imported goods and cannot be classified as a certain selling arrangement, EU law considers the measure to fall within the MEEQR definition. MEEQR are in principle prohibited, unless they can be justified in accordance with Article 36 TFEU and/or mandatory requirements or unless their effects are too uncertain or indirect to impede intra-Union trade.[292] The Court confirmed this approach in its 2016 *Deutsche Parkinson Vereinigung* judgment. That case concerned German

286. Case C-142/05, *Mickelsson And Roos,* para 28.
287. For a similar approach, see Case C-456/10, *ANETT*, para 35.
288. Case C-110/05, *Commission v. Italy,* paras. 34 and 36. See also Case C-456/10, *ANETT*, para 35 and M. Jesse, "What about Sunday trading…? The rise of market access as an independent criterion under Art. 34 TFEU", 3 EJRR (2012), 440. See also L. W. Gormley, "Silver threads among the gold … 50 years of the free movement of goods", 31 *Fordham International Law Journal* (2008), 1637–1691; L. Prete, "Of motorcycle trailers and personal watercrafts: The battle over *Keck*", 35 *Legal Issues of Economic Integration* (2008), 133–155; G. T. Davies, "The Court's jurisprudence on free movement of goods: Pragmatic presumptions, not philosophical principles", 2 *European Journal of Consumer Law* (2012), 25–38.
289. For differing opinions as to the value of market access as a self-standing test, compare S. Weatherill, op. cit. *supra* note 274 with J. Snell, "The notion of market access: A concept or a slogan", 47 CML Rev. (2010), 437–472.
290. J. Snell, op. cit. *supra* note 289, 448–449.
291. Opinion of A.G. Jacobs in Case C-412/93, *Leclerc-Siplec,* para 42.
292. See Opinion of A.G. Kokott in Case C-142/05, *Mickelsson And Roos,* para 46.

legislation prescribing fixed prices for prescription-only medicinal products. According to the Court, that legislation has "a greater impact on the sale of prescription-only medicinal products by pharmacies established in other Member States than on the sale of the same medicinal products by pharmacies established within the national territory".[293] As this legislation imposes additional costs on and impedes the market access of pharmacies established in another Member State,[294] it had to be considered an MEEQR.

6.4 *Import versus export restrictions*

The bulk of the Court's case law on quantitative restrictions and MEEQR has always focused on imports. Occasionally, however, the Court has also dealt with restrictions on exports. Parallels between the two strands of case law have gradually become clearly visible. Whilst the *Cassis de Dijon* approach of covering both distinctly and indistinctly applicable measures has consistently been applied to national measures liable to restrict imports, the case law on export restrictions relied on a seemingly more narrow definition of MEEQR. After having confirmed *Dassonville* in relation to exports at first,[295] the *Groenveld* judgment proclaimed that export-related measures could only qualify as MEEQR if they "have as their specific object or effect the restriction of patterns of exports and thereby [result in] the establishment of a difference between the domestic trade of a Member State and its export trade in such a way as to provide a particular advantage for national production or for the domestic market of the State in question at the expense of the production or of the trade of other Member States".[296] According to that definition, measures affecting exports to other Member States only fall within the scope of the Articles 34–35 TFEU prohibitions if they directly distinguish between goods destined for exportation and those meant to be traded domestically.[297] Measures that do not on their face distinguish between domestic and export situations would in that understanding never qualify as an MEEQR, despite any potentially restrictive effects on intra-Union trade that may be brought about by those rules. The Court consistently confirmed this more narrow export MEEQR definition in subsequent case law.[298]

More recently however, the Court seems to have abandoned its previous strict adherence to this narrow definition in relation to exports. In *Gysbrechts,* the Court had to consider the legality of a national rule prohibiting a supplier from requiring an advance or any payment before expiry of the period for withdrawal that had to be offered to certain categories of consumers.[299] It was submitted that such a national rule made exports of goods subject to the withdrawal period more difficult, as traders would be less willing to carry the risks of non-payment in rela-

293. Case C-148/15, *Deutsche Parkinson Vereinigung,* para 27.
294. Case C-148/15, *Deutsche Parkinson Vereinigung,* para 26.
295. Case 53/76, *Les Sieurs Bouhelier,* para 11, although the Court did not explicitly refer to *Dassonville* in this judgment and the rule at stake was discriminatory in scope, the judgment did not explicitly deviate from the *Dassonville* formula by proposing an alternative export MEEQR definition; Case 68/76, *Commission v. France,* para 16, where the imposition of an export formality is considered an obstacle to trade, without it being deemed discriminatory on nationality per se.
296. Case 15/79, *Groenveld* para 7.
297. Case 15/79, *Groenveld,* para 7, final sentence.
298. See among others Case C-9/89, *Spain v. Council,* para 21, and Case 339/89, *Alsthom Altantique;* see also Case 155/80, *Oebel;* Case C-80/92, *Commission v. Belgium,* para 24; Case C-47/90, *Établissements Delhaize frères;* Case C-388/95, *Belgium v. Spain;* Case C-203/96, *Dusseldorp* and Case C-209/98, *FFAD* v. *Københavns Kommune,* para 34; C-137/00, *Milk Marque* paras. 114–115; Case C-108/01, *Consorzio del Prosciutto di Parma;* Case C-469/00, *Bellon and Biraghi;* Case C-12/02, *Grilli* where the formula has essentially been replicated, albeit with slight modifications.
299. Case C-205/07, *Gysbrechts).*

tion to consumers residing in a different Member State.[300] In its judgment, the Court first of all confirmed the *Groenveld* definition.[301] It subsequently nevertheless added that the consequences of the national prohibition on advance payments are generally "more significant in cross-border sales made directly to consumers, in particular, in sales made by means of the internet, by reason, *inter alia*, of the obstacles to bringing any legal proceedings in another Member State against consumers who default, especially when the sales involve relatively small sums.[302] As the actual effects of the prohibition were more readily felt in relation to exports, the prohibition was to be considered a *prima facie* prohibited MEEQR.[303] In doing so, the Court seemed – albeit implicitly – to extend the obstacle- or burden-focused definition used in relation to imports to the realm of exports as well.

In its 2016 Grand Chamber *New Valmar* judgment, the Court confirmed this approach. The case concerned Belgian legislation imposing the use of the Dutch language in invoices drawn up by companies established in the Flemish region.[304] The Court ruled that the contested legislation constituted an MEEQR prohibited by Article 35 TFEU, for it produces restrictive effects on trade which are likely to deter the initiation or continuation of contractual relationships with an undertaking established in the Dutch-speaking region of Belgium.[305] The Court came to this conclusion on the ground that, even if such legislation – indistinctly applicable to all invoices issued by an undertaking in Flanders – can affect domestic trade within Belgium as well as cross-border trade, "the fact remains that it is more likely to affect the latter, [...], given that a purchaser established in a Member State other than the Kingdom of Belgium is less likely to be able to understand Dutch than a purchaser established in the latter Member State, where that language is one of the official languages".[306] In the interest of coherence in the application of an EU standard on MEEQR, the full equation between import and export MEEQR definitions should be applauded.[307]

By contrast, the exclusion from the scope of Article 34 TFEU of certain selling arrangements developed in *Keck* has only been applied in relation to rules restricting the sales and promotion of imported goods. This makes sense, as sales and promotion rules are not generally targeting goods destined for export in the state of production. States to which the goods are exported would rather adopt rules structuring the conditions under which those goods can be sold there. In that situation, the *Keck* conditions could apply to those rules, which are essentially rules governing the sales and marketing of imported products in the other Member State.

7. Boundaries between non-tariff and tariff restrictions

The Court of Justice consistently maintains a strict boundary between the tariff and non-tariff restriction categories. The prohibition on quantitative restrictions and MEEQR in Article 34 TFEU does not therefore extend to obstacles of trade covered by other specific provisions of

300. Case C-205/07, *Gysbrechts*, para 15.
301. Case C-205/07, *Gysbrechts*, para 40.
302. Case C-205/07, *Gysbrechts*, paras. 42 and 44.
303. Case C-205/07, *Gysbrechts*, para 43; for a focus on effects in this regard, see W. Henning-Roth, "Annotation of Case C-205/07, *Lodewijk Gysbrechts, Santurel Inter BVBA*, Judgment of the Court of Justice (Grand Chamber) of 16 Dec. 2008, not yet reported", 47 CML Rev. (2010), 515.
304. Case C-15/15, *New Valmar*, para 17.
305. Case C-15/15, *New Valmar*, para 42.
306. Case C-15/15, *New Valmar*, para 43.
307. For the development of that argument, see M. Szydlo, "Export restrictions within the framework of the free movement of goods. Reconsideration of an old paradigm", 47 CML Rev. (2010), 753–789.

the Treaty, including Articles 30 and 110 TFEU.[308] In *De Danske Bilimportører,* the Court held that a registration charge for new cars could not fall within the scope of application of Article 34 TFEU.[309] Even when such a charge could place an additional burden on the importation of cars from other Member States – all the more so in the absence of domestic car production –, its restrictive effects were to be assessed from the point of view of Article 110 TFEU, since the measure qualified as internal taxation.[310]

8. Overview of restrictions

The concepts of quantitative restrictions and of measures having an equivalent effect of import/export restrictions (MEEQR) have been defined broadly in the Court's case law. Starting from *Dassonville* and further developed in *Cassis de Dijon,* the MEEQR notion covers any national rule or measure that has the effect of impeding intra-Union trade in direct or indirect, actual or potential ways. Some national rules do however escape the MEEQR definition. More specifically, six categories of rules can be distinguished throughout the Court's body of case law.

Firstly, measures containing restrictions on quantities of imported or exported products can be classified as quantitative restrictions. In practice, the Court frequently treats such measures as MEEQR.

Secondly, measures that on their face discriminate between domestic and imported/exported products are to be considered MEEQR. The same goes for measures that are indistinctly applicable in law but in fact establish a distinction between domestic and imported/exported goods. Situations of direct and indirect discrimination on the basis of "nationality" of the product always qualify as MEEQR.

Thirdly, indistinctly applicable rules that do not indirectly discriminate between domestic and foreign products can also be qualified as MEEQR if and to the extent that those rules impose an additional regulatory or economic burden on goods lawfully produced and marketed in another Member State. To the extent that a trader importing those goods incurs extra costs (e.g. by having to repackage the product or by losing profits due to unavailability of traditional advertising channels), the Court deems access to the market for those products and intra-Union trade to be negatively affected. Throughout the Court's case law, this testing framework has been applied in relation to product requirement rules governing shape, size, weight and packaging of products.

Fourthly, in *Towing Trailers,* the Court extended this testing framework to a third, residual, category of MEEQR, comprising other measures, which do not relate to product characteristics and do not concern certain selling arrangements, but nevertheless hinder access of products originating in other Member States to the market of a Member State, such as the rules on the use of products as regulated by national law.

Fifthly, the Court exempts rules governing certain selling arrangements (i.e. rules determining the conditions of sales, the opportunities for promoting a product, sales channels etc.) from the MEEQR prohibition. Starting with *Keck and Mithouard,* the Court ruled that selling arrangements are only to be considered MEEQR if they do not apply equally to all traders and if they affect the marketing of imported goods more in law or in fact than is the case for domestic products.

---

308. See among others Joined Cases C-78/90 to C-83/90, *Compagnie Commerciale de l'Ouest,* para 20, and Case C-228/98 *Dounias,* para 39.
309. Case C-383/01, *De Danske Bilimportører,* para 34.
310. Case C-383/01, *De Danske Bilimportører,* para 35.

Finally, national measures that have too remote or indirect an effect on intra-Union trade are considered to fall outside the scope of Articles 34–35 TFEU. Whereas the Court so far refrained from developing a full-fledged *de minimis* test in this field of EU law, the remoteness test seeks to exclude some measures from the scope of EU free movement of goods law. The application of the test in practice nevertheless gives rise to legal uncertainty and the test has proven hardly practical in effectively limiting the scope of the MEEQR definition.

9. Justifications

Once it has been established that particular rules or practices amount to quantitative import or export restrictions or measures having the equivalent effect of such restriction, these rules or practices are in principle prohibited under EU law. Under certain circumstances, Member States can nevertheless justify *prima facie* prohibited measures if they serve a specific public interest purpose. Two different types of justifications can be distinguished: on the one hand, the Treaty-based exceptions laid down in Article 36 TFEU, and on the other hand, the judicially created derogations or "mandatory requirements in the general interest". It must be observed, however, that the grounds of justification can only be invoked in the absence of EU harmonization legislation. Moreover, in view of the fundamental nature of the Treaty right to free movement of goods, these defences are to be interpreted restrictively and remain confined to the protection of non-economic interests. They must also comply with the requirements of the principle of proportionality.

9.1 *Absence of EU harmonization legislation*

Articles 34 and 35 TFEU have a deregulatory effect. Essentially, they impose negative obligations on Member States (and on EU institutions). These obligations only relate to Member State measures that have not been the subject of harmonization at the EU level[311] or are not subject to a special regime provided for in the Treaties themselves.[312] In instances where EU secondary law exhaustively regulates the free movement of particular goods, the Court will refrain from applying Articles 34–35 TFEU. The same holds true for Article 36 TFEU: this provision can only be invoked if EU law did not harmonize or did not fully harmonize the conditions Member States can rely upon to limit the free circulation of particular goods.[313] The Court is called upon to determine, on a case-by-case basis, the extent to which a harmonizing measure exhaustively regulates the free movement of a particular product.[314] If national rules have to be assessed on the basis of harmonized EU law provisions, Member States cannot rely on Article 36 TFEU derogations or on mandatory requirements exceptions to justify a restrictive measure.[315]

311. Case C-309/02, *Radlberger*, para 14 and Case C-265/06, *Commission v. Portugal*, para 29. See *inter alia* Case 193/80, *Commission v. Italy*, para 17–18 on the relationship between Art. 34 TFEU and harmonized legislation. For more recent illustrations, see also C-573/12, *Ålands Vindkraft*, para 57–58; Case C-95/14, *UNIC*, para 33 and the Opinion of A.G. Bot in Case C-492/14, *Essent Belgium*, para 77; see also Case C-198/14, *Valev Visnapuu*, para 40.

312. Reference can in that regard be made to Arts. 346–351 and 355 TFEU, which provide for exception regimes in relation to particular areas, as well as to specific derogation mechanisms outlined in Art. 114 (4)–(5) TFEU.

313. Case 5/77, *Tedeschi*; Case 148/78, *Ratti*; see also Case C-473/98, *Toolex Alpha*.

314. Compare Case C-84/06,. *Antroposana* with Case C-319/05, *Commission v. Germany*. For an example as to where national rules were not covered by harmonization, see Case C-446/08, *Solgar Vitamin's France* and Case C-142/09, *Lahousse and Lavinchy*.

315. See *inter alia*, Case C-257/06, *Roby Profumi*, para 14 and also implicitly Case C-37/92, *Vanacker and Lesage*, para 9; Case C-324/99, *DaimlerChrysler*, para 32; Case C-322/01, *Deutscher Apothekerverband*, para 64; Case

EU secondary legislation instruments can nevertheless also directly allow reliance on Article 36 TFEU derogations or mandatory requirements exceptions to be invoked. In that case, these defences could still be relied upon, yet only by virtue of the explicit or implicit mandate given in a particular EU secondary legislation instrument.[316] If the harmonizing instrument grants room to the Member States to rely on specific national justifications not covered by harmonizing provisions, Article 36 TFEU will still govern and restrain the scope of those justifications. That is the case at least if and to the extent the instrument of secondary legislation expressly refers to concepts such as environmental protection, public order, public safety or health protection, which also appear in Article 36 TFEU.[317]

9.2 *Two sets of justifications*

9.2.1 *Article 36 TFEU derogations*

Firstly, Article 36 TFEU provides that the provisions of Articles 34 and 35 TFEU shall not preclude prohibitions or restrictions on imports, exports or goods in transit that can be justified on certain specific grounds of public interest. As a result, either quantitative restrictions as well as MEEQR can still escape the prohibition if they fall within one of the derogations offered by Article 36 TFEU. Moreover, the list of grounds of derogation in Article 36 TFEU is exhaustive. Objectives not explicitly mentioned therein cannot be invoked.[318] Grounds for derogation are:

- *Public morality*: this ground is often invoked in relation to indecent or presumably immoral products.[319] The Court acknowledges that different Member States may entertain different views on public morality within their respective territories, but held that this should not be used to prohibit or restrain the importation of contentious goods that are actually produced within these Member States themselves as well and thus lead to a harsher treatment of imported goods vis-à-vis domestic goods. The judgments in *Henn and Darby* and *Conegate* clearly exemplify this position.[320] In the former case, the Court accepted that the UK prohibition on the import of pornographic material could be justified under Article 36 TFEU, because "on a comprehensive view, there was no lawful trade in such goods in the UK".[321] Conversely, in the latter case, the UK could not prohibit the importation of life size inflatable rubber dolls, as these products were also produced within the United Kingdom itself.[322]

C-463/01, *Commission v. Germany*, para 36; Case C-484/10, *Ascafor and Asidac*, para 47 and Case C-216/11, *Commission v. France*, para 27. Measures adopted on the basis of Art. 114 TFEU in particular rely on a specific derogations regime outlined in Art. 114(4)–(5) TFEU. See in that regard, N. De Sadeleer, "Procedures for derogation from the principle of approximation under Art. 95 EC", 40 CML Rev. (2003), 889–915. To the extent that EU secondary legislation does not fully harmonize specific product requirements, Member States can continue to use the grounds outlined in Art. 36 TFEU, see Case C-249/07, *Commission v. the Netherlands*, para 41–43.

316. In e.g. related fields not covered by the harmonizing instrument, Case C-132/08, *Lidl Magyarország Kereskedelmi*, paras. 44–45 or in fields where the Commission did not yet adopt implementing measures, see Case C-446/08, *Solgar Vitamin's France*, para 48.
317. Case C-324/99, *DaimlerChrysler*, para 31; Case C-249/07, *Commission v. the Netherlands* offers another recent example in this respect.
318. Case 113/80, *Commisision v. Ireland*; Case 229/83, *Leclerc v. Au Ble Vert*.
319. Case 34/79, *R v. Henn and Darby*.
320. Case 121/85, *Conegate*.
321. Case 34/79, *Henn and Darby*, para 21.
322. Case 121/85, *Conegate*, para 16.

- *Public policy:* contrary to what this concept might suggest, this ground is interpreted in a very narrow fashion, only to include matters that are deemed so important that they touch upon a Member State's *ordre public.*[323] Examples of this exception include the need to protect the interests of the state in minting coinage[324] or the responsibility of a state to guarantee a sufficient exercise of fundamental rights such as the freedom of expression.[325]
- *Public security*: this derogation surfaced mainly in relation to limits imposed on producers or distributors of oil, natural gas or other energy resources to maintain minimum supplies as a matter of national law.[326] The Court is willing to accept such measures, as long as they do not impose unreasonable burdens on private traders.[327]
- *The protection of the life and health of humans, animals and plants:*[328] Member States have often tried to defend national measures on this ground. The Court investigates the issue closely. The *Sandoz* case illustrates the Court's approach in this respect. The case concerned the refusal from the Dutch authorities to allow the sale of muesli bars containing added vitamins on public health grounds. In other countries, such as Belgium and Germany, these muesli bars were readily available. The Court accepted that, in the absence of harmonization at EU level, Member States must be accorded a wide discretion to decide what degree of protection of the health and life of humans they intend to assure. They must however pay due regard to the requirements of the free movement of goods within the EU, in particular the principle of proportionality underlying the last sentence of Article 36 TFEU.[329] Hence it ruled that national rules could prohibit the marketing of foodstuffs lawfully marketed in another Member State to which vitamins have been added, "provided that the marketing is authorized when the addition of vitamins meets a real need, especially a technical or nutritional one".[330] Furthermore, it should be noted that consumer protection cannot be equated with human health per se, even though measures protective of human health can also be protective of consumers.[331] Similarly, the protection of animals' and plants' health covers specific protective

---

323. Case 113/80, *Commission v. Ireland*; Case 95/81, *Commission v. Italy*; Case 177/83, *Ringelhan & Rennett* ; Case 229/83, *Leclerc v. Au Blé Vert*; Case 231/83, *Cullet*; Case 288/83, *Commission v. Ireland*; Case C-265/95, *Commission v. France*.
324. Case 7/78, *Thompson, Johnson and Woodiwiss*.
325. Case C-112/00, *Schmidberger*.
326. Case 72/83, *Campus Oil*, is prominent in this regard. See also Case C-227/06, *Commission v. Belgium*, summary publication, where the Court held that public security only covers the most fundamental interests of a society.
327. See Case 231/83, *Cullet*; Case 174/84, *Sun Oil*; Case 50/85, *Schloh*; Case 406/85, *Gofette and Gilliard*; Case 25/88, *Bouchara (Wurmser)*; Case C-347/88, *Commission v. Greece*; Case C-367/89, *Richardt*; Case C-157/94, *Commission v. the Netherlands*; Case C-398/98, *Commission v. Greece*; Case C-186/01, *Dory*. See also Case C-67/97, *Bluhme* (protection of endangered species) and Joined Cases 141/81, 142/81 and 143/81, *Holdijk* (protecting animal welfare).
328. See Case 104/75, *De Peijper* for a clear example in this respect. See also Case 251/78, *Denkavit*; Case 174/82, *Sandoz*; Case C-293/94, *Brandsma*; Case C-432/03, *Commission v. Portugal*; Case C-121/00, *Hahn*; Case C-172/00, *Ferring Arzneimittel*; Case C-15/01, *Paranova Läkemedel*; Case C-112/02, *Kohlpharma*; Case C-239/02, *Douwe Egberts*; C-319/05, *Commission v. Germany*; C-421/09, *Humanplasma* and Case C-484/10, *Asociación para la Calidad de los Forjados (Ascafor)*, for other and more recent examples.
329. Case 174/82, *Sandoz BV*, para 16.
330. Case 174/82, *Sandoz BV*, para 20.
331. Case C-39/90, *Denkavit*.

situations and should not be read to encapsulate a general justification on the basis of environmental protection.[332]

- *The protection of national treasures possessing artistic, historic or archaeological value.*[333]
- *The protection of industrial and commercial property.*[334]

The Court has construed these defences to the free movement of goods narrowly so as to avoid intra-Union trade to be hampered more than necessary to achieve the public interest aims a Member State wants to promote.[335] In particular, the Court has been adamant to confirm that economic objectives or motives can never be used when invoking one of the Treaty exceptions.[336] It nevertheless accepts the invocation of the abovementioned derogations to also have consequences for economic objectives pursued by a Member State.[337]

Secondly, besides the fact that national measures can only be justified if they pursue a legitimate aim, Article 36 TFEU states that even justifiable restrictions or prohibitions may not constitute "a means of *arbitrary discrimination* or a disguised restriction on trade between Member States". This latter condition is confusing at first sight as distinctly applicable measures in and of themselves "discriminate" against imported or exported products and could nevertheless be justified on the basis of Article 36 TFEU. The references to "arbitrary discrimination" or "disguised restriction" in this provision should rather be understood as prohibiting that abuse is being made of the possibilities offered by Article 36 TFEU to uphold *prima facie* restrictive national measures.[338] A similar situation could arise where Member States invoke those derogations in an incoherent or inconsistent manner.[339] The Court scrutinizes whether the invoked ground of derogation actually corresponds to the real purpose of the national measure, or whether it is intended to favour domestic products over imported ones.[340] The abovementioned prohibition on the importation of pornographic materials also produced in the Member State concerned is a clear example of such a disguised restriction. The *Commission v. UK (Christmas poultry)* case is another example: measures that would impose unnecessary and burdensome public health inspections – without having regard to similar inspections already conducted at the Member State of origin – could thus be considered as a disguised restriction on trade, using the public health derogation as a sham to restrict imports of specific goods.[341] In more recent case law,

332. Case C-379/98, *PreussenElektra AG*.
333. See e.g. Case 7/68, *Commission v. Italy*; A. Biondi, "The merchant, the thief and the citizen: The circulation of works of art within the European Union", 34 CML Rev. (1997), 1173–1195.
334. See separate chapter in this volume by Ana Ramalho. This type of justification mostly takes place against the background of EU secondary legislation measures, see *inter alia* Joined Cases C-427/93, C-429/93 and C-436/93, *Boehringer*; see also recently Case C-478/07, *Budvar*.
335. Case 7/61, *Commission v. Italy*. See also for that reasoning also Case 72/83, *Campus Oil Limited*.
336. See also Case 72/83, *Campus Oil Limited;* Case C-254/98 *TK-Heimdienst* and Case C-109/04 *Kranemann*; Case C-456/10, *ANETT*, para 53.
337. See Case C-120/95, *Decker*.
338. See on that notion, S. Weatherill, "Fitting "abuse of rights" into EU law governing the free movement of goods and services" in R. De La Feria and S. Vogenauer (Eds.), *Prohibition of Abuse of Law: A New General Principle of EU Law?* (Hart, 2011), 49–62.
339. Case C-161/09, *Stafidas*, para 42–48. Similar case law on incoherence or inconsistency in the invocation of justifications has also been developed in relation to the freedom of establishment and the freedom to provide services, e.g. in Case C-500/06, *Corporación Dermoestética Media* (incoherent advertising standards for the advertisement of medical services) and Case C-169/07, *Hartlauer,* (incoherent reimbursement procedures for similar treatments under national social security law).
340. See for examples, Case 34/79, *Henn and Darby*; Joined Cases C-1/90 and C-176/90, *Aragonesa.*
341. Case 40/82, *Commission v. UK*, para 24.

the Court incorporates those more specific conditions within the proportionality test read into Article 36 TFEU.[342]

9.2.2 *"Mandatory requirements in the general interest"*

The development of an open-ended MEEQR definition resulted in an extensive set of national rules and practices potentially being captured by the Articles 34–35 prohibitions. The ensuing narrow interpretation of the Article 36 TFEU derogations and the closed list of public interest exceptions included therein posed a threat to Member States' regulatory autonomy and limited the scope of national measures that could be adopted without frustrating EU free movement of goods principles. Plainly aware of the strains this legal framework could put on national autonomy, the Court of Justice already in *Cassis de Dijon* recognized that indistinctly applicable MEEQR could escape the Article 34 TFEU prohibition in "so far as those provisions may be recognized as being necessary in order to satisfy mandatory requirements relating in particular to the effectiveness of fiscal supervision, the protection of public health, the fairness of commercial transactions and the defence of the consumer".[343] In so holding, the Court decided that measures *prima facie* qualifying as MEEQR can nevertheless be exempted from the Treaty prohibition if they contribute to "overriding reasons in the public interest".[344]

Contrary to the closed list of Treaty derogations in Article 36 TFEU, the list of mandatory requirements is not exhaustive. On a case-by-case basis, the Court has the opportunity to identify additional mandatory requirements and to allow Member States to claim that their rules are justified on the basis of those freshly asserted overriding reasons in the public interest. Currently acknowledged mandatory requirements are:

- The effectiveness of fiscal supervision, avoidance of tax evasion and combating fraud in general;[345]
- The protection of public health, (which is also captured by Art. 36 TFEU);[346]
- The fairness of commercial transactions and of fair commercial practices;[347]
- Consumer protection;[348]

342. For a recent illustration, see Case C-333/14, *Scotch Whisky Association*, para 51, which clearly establishes this position.
343. Case 120/78, *Cassis de Dijon*, para 8.
344. The Court now frequently refers to the notion of "overriding reasons in the public interest", see Joined Cases C-34/95 to C-36/95, *KO v. De Agostini*, para 54; Case C-368/95, *Vereinigte Familiapress*, para 18 and 24; for recent examples, see C-150/11, *Commission v. Belgium*, para 55 and case law references therein and C-573/12, *Ålands Vindkraft*, para 76.
345. Case 120/78, *Cassis de Dijon*; Case 823/79, *Carciati*; Case 134/83, *Abbink*; Case C-184/96, *Commission v. France*; Case C-443/10, *Bonnarde*.
346. Case 53/80, *Koninklijke Kaasfabriek Eyssen BV*; Case 178/84, *Commission v. Germany*.
347. Case 58/80, *Dansk Supermarked*; Case 6/81, *Beele Handelmaatschappij BV*; Case 220/81, *Robertson*; Case 286/81, *Oosthoek's Uitgeversmaatschappij*; Case 179/85, *Commission v. Germany*; Case 52/88, *Commission v. Belgium*; Case C-238/89, *Dahlhausen*; Case C-77/97, *Smithkline Beecham Markenartikel*; Case C-366/98, *Geffroy and Casino France SNC*; Case C-448/98, *Guimont*; Case C-166/03, *Commission v. France*.
348. Case 27/80, *Fietje*; Case 6/81, *Beele Handelmaatschappij BV*; Case 220/81, *Robertson*; Case 261/81, *Rau*; Case 286/81, *Oosthoek's Uitgeversmaatschappij*; Case 179/85, *Commission v. Germany*; Case 25/88, *Bouchara (Wurmser)*; Case 52/88, *Commission v. Belgium*; Case C-196/89, *Nespoli and Crippa*; Case C-51/93, *Schott Zwiesel Glaswerke AG*; Case C-313/94, *F.lli Graffione*; Case C-184/96, *Commission v. France*; Case C-210/96, *Gut Springenheide GmbH and Tusky*; Case C-77/97, *Smithkline Beecham Markenartikel G*; Case C-383/97, *van der Laan*; Case C-220/98, *Estée Lauder Cosmetics GmbH,*; Case C-366/98, *Geffroy and Casino France SNC*; Case C-448/98, *Guimont*; Case C-3/99, *Cidrerie Ruwet SA*; Case C-358/01, *Commission v. Spain*; Case C-166/03, *Commission v. France*; Case C-108/09, *Ker-Optika* ; Case C-161/09, *Stafidas*; Case C-481/12, *UAB "Juvelta"*.

- The protection of the environment and of biological resources;[349]
- Balancing national (social security) budgets;[350]
- Rules related to economic planning and advertising;[351]
- Rules aimed at improving employment conditions and the working environment;[352]
- Protection of regional or national culture, socio-cultural practices or languages;[353]
- Safety standards on the road or in navigable waters;[354]
- Product safety standards;[355]
- Maintenance of a plurality of opinions within media and press;[356]
- The rights of the child;[357]
- Freedom of expression.[358]

A successful invocation of overriding reasons in the public interest in principle requires that the national rules or practices concerned do not fall within the scope of harmonized EU legislation and are indistinctly applicable (even though they may indirectly discriminate against imported goods). In addition, the mandatory requirements relied upon should not disproportionately restrain the free movement of goods. In checking this, the Court essentially applies the same proportionality test to mandatory requirements as it does to Article 36 TFEU derogations, as will be explained below.[359] Consequently, it developed a judicially structured *rule of reason* framework in accordance with which national MEEQR can escape from the Treaty prohibition if they impose a reasonable public interest obstacle to freedom of movement.

9.2.3 *Towards a singular justifications regime?*

Whilst both the Article 36 TFEU derogations and the judicial "mandatory requirements" exceptions offer Member States the opportunity to justify obstacles to the free movement of goods on similar "public interest" grounds, the scope of application of both defences is substantially different. On the one hand, it is undisputed that the Article 36 TFEU derogations can be invoked in relation to both distinctly and indistinctly applicable measures.[360] On the other hand, however, in its 1982 *Commission v. Ireland* judgment, the Court explicitly stated that measures which apply

349. Joined Cases 3/76, 4/76 and 6/76, *Kramer*; Case 172/82, *Syndicat National des Fabricants Raffineurs d'Huile de Graissage*; Case 240/83, *Association de défense des brûleurs d'huiles usagées (ADBHU)*; Case 302/86, *Commission v. Denmark, Commission v. Belgium*; Case C-159/94, *Commission v. France*; Case C-341/95, *Bettati*; Case C-203/96, *Dusseldorp*; Case C-389/96, *Aher-Waggon*; Case C-67/97, *Bluhme*; Case C-314/98, *Snellers Auto's*; Case C-309/02, *Radlberger*; Case C-463/01, *Commission v. Germany*; C-433/05, *Sandström*; Case C-265/06, *Commission v. Portugal*; Case C-286/07, *Commission v. Luxembourg*; Case C-142/05, *Mickelsson and Roos*; Case C-443/10, *Bonnarde*.
350. Case C-120/95, *Decker*; Case C-158/96, *Kohll*.
351. Case C-412/93, *Leclerc-Siplec*; Case C-159/94, *Commission v. France*.
352. Case 155/80, *Oebel*; Case C-312/89, *SIDEF Conforama,*; Case C-332/89, *Ministère Public v. Marchandise*.
353. Case 229/83, *Leclerc v. Au Blé Vert*; Joined Cases 60/84 and 61/84, *Cinéthèque*; Joined Cases C-153/88 to C-157/88, *Fauque and Others*; Case C-369/89, *Piageme*; Case C-169/91, *Stoke-on-Trent*; Joined Cases C-418/93 to C-421/93, C-460/93 to C-462/93, C-464/93, C-9/94 to C-11/94, C-14/94, C-15/94, C-23/94, C-24/94 and C-332/94, *Semeraro Casa Uno*.
354. Case C-18/93, *Corsica Ferries Italia Srl*; Case C-55/93, *van Schaik*; Case C-314/98, *Snellers Auto's BV*.
355. Case 188/84, *Commission v. France*.
356. Case C-368/95, *Vereinigte Familiapress*.
357. Case C-244/06, *Avides Media AG*.
358. Case C-112/00, *Schmidberger*; Case C-71/02, *Karner*.
359. For an overview of those conditions and the similarities between them and Art. 36 TFEU analysis, see already the Opinion of A.G. Van Gerven in Joined Cases C-1/90 and C-176/90, *Aragonesa*, para 14.
360. See Art. 36 TFEU itself referring to the provisions of Art. 34 and 35, which naturally also includes indistinctly applicable MEEQR. See also Joined Cases C-34/95, C-35/95 and C-36/95, *De Agostini*, paras. 45–46.

only to imported products and are therefore discriminatory on their face cannot be justified by "mandatory requirements".[361] As a result, mandatory requirements could only be invoked to justify indistinctly applicable measures restricting imports. In *New Valmar*, the Court confirmed that mandatory requirements could equally be relied upon to justify indistinctly applicable export restrictions.[362] At the same time, the Court also acknowledged that measures that apply without distinction to domestic and imported products yet nevertheless indirectly discriminate against imported goods could be justified on the basis of mandatory requirements.[363] A similar acknowledgement has been made in relation to indirectly discriminatory export restrictions in *Gysbrechts*.[364]

Whilst the distinction between directly discriminatory and other measures remains good law for the purposes of determining the scope of justificatory requirements, it has not always been rigorously maintained in practice. On several occasions, the Court has allowed Member States to invoke a mandatory requirement in relation to a directly discriminatory measure. In those instances, the Court (deliberately?) generally chose to ignore the discriminatory scope of the measure and proceed as if the measure was merely indistinctly applicable or restrictive of free movement.[365] The judgment in *Ålands Vindkraft* exemplifies this approach. National legislation required Swedish energy suppliers to hold on to a certain number of tradable green electricity certificates. The legislation at stake only recognized certificates awarded in relation to green electricity produced in the territory of Sweden itself. Despite the plainly discriminatory nature of the measure, the Court qualified it as a mere "restriction" to free movement before subsequently analysing a possible justification on the basis of the mandatory requirements of environmental protection.[366] Conversely, in other recent cases such as *Aher-Waggon*,[367] *Commission v. Finland*[368] and *Commission v. Austria*[369] the Court did acknowledge the discriminatory nature of national measures, but this nevertheless did not prevent it from subsequently considering Member States' justifications on the basis of mandatory requirements such as environmental protection or road safety.

As a result, it can be submitted that with regard to directly discriminatory national measures, the Court appears willing to tear down the strict separation between Article 36 Treaty derogations and mandatory requirements exceptions. The law on the free movement of goods seems to be evolving towards a unitary justifications approach, in accordance with which any quantitative restriction or MEEQR could be justified by either Article 36 derogations or mandatory requirements.

9.3 *Principle of proportionality*

The Court requires public interest justifications to impose only reasonable – proportionate – restrictions on the free movement of goods. In *FEDESA*, it was held that "[b]y virtue of that principle [of proportionality], the lawfulness of the prohibition of an economic activity is

361. Case 113/80, *Commission v. Ireland*, para 11.
362. Case C-15/15, *New Valmar BVBA*, paras. 48–51.
363. Case 113/80, *Commission v. Ireland*, para 14; see equally Case 16/83, *Prantl*; Case 207/83, *Commission v. UK*; Case 274/87, *Commission v. Germany*; Case C-238/89, *Dahlhausen* evocating the same position.
364. Case C-205/07, *Gysbrechts*, para 47.
365. See Case C-2/90, *Commission v. Belgium ("Walloon Waste")*, para 32; Case C-120/95, *Decker*, para 39 and Case C-158/96, *Kohll*, para 41.
366. Case C-573/12, *Ålands Vindkraft*, paras. 76–77.
367. Case C-389/96, *Aher-Waggon*, para 19.
368. Case C-54/05, *Commission v. Finland*, para 40.
369. Case C-524/07, *Commission v. Austria* (summary publication), para 56–57.

subject to the condition that the prohibition measures are appropriate and necessary in order to achieve the objectives legitimately pursued by the legislation in question; when there is a choice between several appropriate measures, recourse must be had to the least onerous, and the disadvantage caused must not be disproportionate to the aims pursued".[370] The proportionality assessment conducted by either the Court or the national courts essentially comprises two stages: an assessment of the suitability or the appropriateness of the measure, followed by an inquiry into its necessity.

9.3.1 *Test of suitability*

In order for a national restrictive measure to be justifiable, that measure must firstly have a "reasonable connection" with the public interest to be protected.[371] To the extent that a national measure is not suitable or appropriate for the achievement of a particular public interest goal, the Court will not proceed to investigating the necessity of the measure at hand.[372] In practice, the first hurdle of the proportionality test is generally easily taken. The Court often even refrains from explicitly relying on the suitability standard, as the measures invoked happen to be generally and *prima facie* suitable to achieve the public interest aim. Also, in areas of moral sensitivity, where societies genuinely differ on the need and scope of protection, the Court tends to be rather deferential, refraining from substituting the Member State's assessment for its own.[373]

As mentioned above, Article 36 TFEU specifically states that measures which in effect arbitrarily discriminate against imported/exported products or which contain disguised restrictions on trade cannot be justified. Whilst the Court did not formally state so, it could be submitted that such measures – which in effect serve another purpose than the public interest objectives they seem to address on their face – would not be suitable justificatory measures, simply by virtue of their arbitrarily discriminatory or protectionist purpose or effect.[374]

9.3.2 *Test of necessity*

The second limb of the proportionality assessment seeks to determine whether the national rule or practice was not only suitable, but also indispensable to reach or maintain the public interest objective invoked by the Member State.[375] In this context, Member States have to be able to demonstrate that the restrictive measure adopted is actually the least restrictive measure that could have been adopted in the interest of protecting the public interest objective at hand, and that the restrictive or disadvantageous effects caused the measure yielded remain limited, and in any event reasonable in light of the aims pursued.[376] Whereas the Court acknowledged that Member States retain a margin of discretion in this regard,[377] and often left it to the national

---

370. Case 331/88, *FEDESA*, para 13.
371. See already Case 8/74, *Dassonville*, para 6 and Case 120/78, *Cassis de Dijon*, para 8 only refers to necessity.
372. For a recent example, see Case C-148/15, *Deutsche Parkinson Vereinigung*, in which a German rule providing for a system of fixed prices for the sale by pharmacies of prescription-only medicinal products for human use was not considered suitable to protect public health.
373. Case 121/85, *Conegate*, paras. 16–18 for an example.
374. Case 34/79, *Henn and Darby*, para 21.
375. See e.g. Case C-385/99, *Müller-Fauré*, para 68.
376. Case 104/75, *De Peijper*, para 18 and para 32; C-161/09, *Stafidas*, para 60. Sometimes, this limb of the test of necessity is considered a third stage of the proportionality test entertained by the Courts – the proportionality *sensu stricto* stage. We do however subsume this stage under the test of necessity.
377. Case C-394/97, *Heinonen*, para 43; Case C-434/04, *Ahokainen and Leppik*, para 32; Case C-141/07, *Commission v. Germany*, para 51.

courts to adjudicate, it has also not shied away from considering the availability of alternative – and potentially less restrictive or more appropriate – measures achieving the same goals.[378]

Specifically, national measures requiring additional authorizations or licenses, imposing bans on particular foreign products or ingredients or mandating double safety checks or registrations can serve a public interest purpose, but may also be inappropriate and unnecessary given that licenses, inspections and authorizations have already been conducted or granted within the Member State of origin. The *Canal Satélite Digital* judgment is a case in point in this regard. The Court claimed that authorization requirements prior to marketing in the Member State of importation can only be considered appropriate and necessary if four cumulative conditions had been fulfilled: an authorization scheme (1) has to be based on objective, non-discriminatory criteria which are known in advance, in such a way as to circumscribe the exercise of the national authorities' discretion, so that it is not used arbitrarily; (2) cannot duplicate controls which have already been carried out in the context of other procedures, either in the same state or in another Member State; (3) would have to be the best solution as any subsequent control would occur too late to be genuinely effective and to enable it to achieve the aim pursued and (4) cannot, on account of its duration and the disproportionate costs to which it gives rise, be such as to deter the operators concerned from pursuing their business plan.[379] Those conditions, set out by the Court in considerable detail, make clear that a mere replication of authorization procedures, which have already occurred in the Member State of origin, can never meet the necessity limb of the proportionality assessment. As a result, Member States are obliged to acknowledge prior authorizations and controls granted or undertaken in the Member State of origin. Restrictive measures will only be justifiable if they truly add control or authorization requirements to which the goods at hand have not been subjected before.

9.4 *Balancing fundamental freedoms and fundamental human rights*

More recently, attention has also been paid to the need to reconcile the requirements of the protection of fundamental rights in the EU with those arising from the fundamental freedoms enshrined in the Treaty. The Court engages in this exercise by relying on fundamental rights as a possible justification for a restriction of the fundamental freedoms. This approach was exemplified in *Schmidberger*, where the national court raised the question whether the principle of the free movement of goods guaranteed by the Treaty prevailed over the freedom of expression and freedom of assembly, guaranteed by Articles 10 and 11 of the ECHR. It held that "the interests involved must be weighed having regard to all the circumstances of the case in order to determine whether a fair balance was struck between those interests".[380] A balancing exercise is thus of prime importance in this context. The competent authorities enjoy a wide margin of discretion. Nevertheless, they must ensure that the restrictions imposed on intra-EU trade are proportionate to the legitimate objective of fundamental rights protection.[381] In this case, the Court was deferential to the Member State's autonomy in structuring the exercise of fundamental rights, considering that the national authorities had done everything in their power to minimise the impact on intra-Union trade whilst maximizing the orderly exercise of fundamental

378. E.g. in Case C-387/99, *Commission v. Germany*, para 81; Case C-297/05, *Commission v. the Netherlands*, para 79; Case C-110/05, *Commission v. Italy*, para 67.
379. Case C-390/99, *Canal Satélite Digital*, paras. 35–42.
380. Case C-112/00, *Schmidberger*, para 81.
381. Case C-112/00, *Schmidberger*, para 82.

rights such as the freedom of expression.[382] The balance struck in such a situation always remains highly case-dependent and is generally left open to national authorities and courts for final decision-making.[383]

10. Burden of proof

The Commission in Article 258 TFEU infringement proceedings or a private complainant in national proceedings can suffice with demonstrating that the measure at stake qualifies as a quantitative restriction or an MEEQR in accordance with Articles 34–35 TFEU as interpreted by the ECJ in its case law. It will then be upon the Member State concerned to prove that a public interest reason warrants a proportionate restriction on the free movement of goods. The Member State has to offer sufficient evidence allowing for its arguments on the appropriateness and necessity of the measure to be demonstrated. Hereupon, the burden of proof shifts again to the other party in the proceedings to refute those claims. The Court maintains that a mere general proposition that a national rule contributes to a public interest goal is insufficient. More detailed analysis as to why that measure has been chosen and whether alternative solutions have been considered need to be adduced by the Member State in that regard. However, the Court does not go as far as requiring that Member States establish that the restrictive measure adopted by them and falling within one of the justifications is the least restrictive alternative measure in that regard. According to the case law, "the burden of proof cannot be so extensive as to require the Member State to prove, positively, that no other conceivable measure could enable that objective to be attained under the same conditions".[384] As long as the Member State concerned can demonstrate convincingly that the measure adopted is a suitable, necessary and proportionate measure to be taken, it is not required to prove that no other measure could have attained the same public interest objective. In *Scotch Whisky Association*, the Court further added that the review of proportionality of a national measure is not to be confined to examining only information, evidence or other material available to the national legislature at the time when it adopted the measure. In assessing the proportionality of a national measure, attention also needs to be paid to, at least to the extent that national law permits this, evidence or other material available to the national court on the date on which it renders its judgment, even when, in the face of scientific uncertainty, the legislature did not have such information in its possession.[385]

11. Free movement of goods and state-backed commercial monopolies

The prohibitions in Articles 34–35 TFEU also directly affect the operations of state-owned or state-backed commercial monopolies entrusted (often for national tax purposes) with the procurement, marketing, sales, promotion or distribution of products such as alcoholic beverages,[386] tobacco products and postal stamp outlets[387] at wholesale or retail level.[388] Where-

382. Case C-112/00, *Schmidberger*, paras. 87–88. See Case C-71/02, *Karner*, paras. 48–53, where the Court analysed the scope of fundamental rights protection in relation to a measure which was deemed to be a selling arrangement thus falling outside the scope of Art. 34 TFEU.
383. For similar assessments in relation to other fundamental free movement rights, see Case C-341/05, *Laval*; Case C-438/05, *Viking*. Case C-36/02, *Omega*.
384. Among others Case C-110/05, *Commission v. Italy*, para 66; Case C-333/14, *Scotch Whisky Association*, para 55.
385. Case C-333/14, *Scotch Whisky Association*, para 65.
386. The Swedish monopoly has frequently been considered by the Court in that regard, see Case C-189/95, *Franzén*; Case C-170/04, *Rosengren*.
387. The Spanish system is a case in point, see e.g. Case C-456/10, *ANETT*.
388. Case 90/82, *Commission v. France*.

as the Treaty does not require such commercial monopolies to be abolished, their operations need to comply with Articles 34–35 TFEU and Article 37 TFEU. This latter provision especially requires Member States to adjust state monopolies of a commercial character so as to ensure that no discrimination regarding the conditions under which goods are procured and marketed exists between nationals of Member States. In practice, this means that the existence and operation of state-backed commercial monopolies could remain in place. At the same time however, Member States are no longer able to introduce new measures that would discriminate against imported or exported goods.[389] In addition, those monopolies could no longer maintain the exclusive right to import particular products from other Member States, as such exclusive right could discriminate against imported products, to the advantage of domestic products.[390] A similar reasoning has been developed in relation to exclusive export rights.[391]

To the extent that state monopolies remain in place, Article 37(1) TFEU requires them to guarantee that imported (or exported) goods can be distributed and marketed under the same conditions as local goods within the system set up by the monopoly. The Court interpreted this provision only to cover rules applicable to the exercise of exclusive rights conferred on the monopoly.[392] In *Franzén*, the Court clarified this position. Mr. Franzén sold wine without a licence. A Swedish state company, Systembolaget, had a monopoly on retail sales of alcoholic beverages. Franzén claimed that the monopoly hindered his own trading activities and impeded the importation of foreign alcoholic beverages and promoted the sales of local products. The Court stated that "the purpose of Article 37 of the Treaty is to reconcile the possibility for Member States to maintain certain monopolies of a commercial character as instruments for the pursuit of public interest aims with the requirements of the establishment and functioning of the common market. It aims at the elimination of obstacles to the free movement of goods, save, however, for restrictions on trade which are inherent in the existence of the monopolies in question".[393] In this case, the Court concluded that the existence of the monopoly did not make the importation of foreign alcoholic beverages more difficult, but that the licensing system itself constituted an obstacle in that it imposed additional costs on such beverages, such as intermediary costs, payment of charges and fees for the grant of a licence, and costs arising from the obligation to maintain storage capacity in Sweden.[394]

The Court has not yet clearly stated what kind of trade restrictions would be inherent to the existence of a state monopoly, and as such escape the Court's scrutiny. Those rules, which relate to the existence and the operation of a particular state-backed monopoly,[395] could determine whether foreign or imported products may be sold, the conditions under which they can be procured and marketed, or other limits or quotas imposed on those products that differentiate them from similar national products also subject to the commercial monopoly.[396] Such rules cannot discriminate against imported or exported products. A remaining question, however, is

389. Art. 37(1) TFEU. As such, that provision does not impede the imposition of an additional levy or temporary reductions of sales on both national and imported products, see e.g. Case 253/83, *Kupferberg*, para 21.
390. Case 59/75, *Manghera*, para 33 is the most clear example and has since been confirmed in *inter alia* Case C-347/88, *Commission v. Greece*, para 44.
391. Case C-159/94, *Commission v. France*, para 34.
392. Case 91/75, *Miritz*, para 5; Case 120/78, *Cassis de Dijon*, para 7; Case 91/78, *Hansen*, para 9 and 10; Case C-387/93, *Banchero*, para 29, Case C-189/95, *Franzén*, para 35 and Case C-170/04, *Rosengren*, para 17.
393. Case C-189/95, *Franzén*, para 39.
394. Case C-189/95, *Franzén*, para 71.
395. Case C-456/10, *ANETT*, para 24.
396. See for that assessment as well, J. Buenda Sierra, *Exclusive Rights and State Monopolies under EC Law: Art. 86 (former Art. 90) of the EC Treaty* (OUP, 1998), 119–122.

to what extent indistinctly applicable rules regulating the sales of both local and foreign products can be considered to be part of rules governing the exercise of a state monopoly.[397] In proclaiming in *Franzén* that trade in goods from other Member States may not be put at a disadvantage in law or in fact, the Court seems to hint that indistinctly applicable rules accompanying a state monopoly, yet having a greater impact on imported goods, could not qualify as rules governing the existence of a state monopoly exempted from Articles 34–35 TFEU.[398] As a result, it seems that indirectly discriminatory measures cannot benefit from the Article 37 TFEU exemption.[399]

Rules that do not directly govern the existence and operation of a state-backed commercial monopoly also do not fall within the scope of Article 37. Consequently, they are to be assessed on their compliance with Articles 34–35 TFEU.[400] In *Asociación Nacional de Expendedores de Tabaco y Timbre (ANETT)*, the Court stated that national rules preventing tobacco retailers from importing particular tobacco products on to the Spanish territory affected the free movement of goods within the European Union and did not as such govern the exercise of the exclusive right relating to the state-backed commercial monopoly in question.[401] It even argued that measures which do not target either the sales network of the monopoly in question or the marketing or advertising of the products distributed by the monopoly can be separated from the operations of the monopoly.[402] It does not matter whether the rules at hand affect private individuals or the licensees of a state-backed monopoly themselves; as long as the rules can be separated from the actual operations of a monopoly, Article 34 TFEU will apply. Absent further clarifications offered by the Court, it remains difficult to draw a clear dividing line between the operations of state-backed monopolies and national rules not directly governing such operations.

12. Conclusion

The Treaty provisions on the free movement of goods are and remain a cornerstone of the EU internal market and, by extension, of the entire European integration project. The role of the ECJ has been crucial in this respect. Through its extensive, at times far-reaching and controversial body of case law, the Court has contributed directly to the shaping of the EU internal market as we know it today.

Although the Court's body of case law on the free movement of goods continues to grow, its scope and limits are now relatively carved out. This relatively stable outlook notwithstanding, a number of as yet unsettled issues remain to be addressed, more than 40 years after the Court's virtually all-encompassing proclamation about measures having an equivalent effect to quantitative restrictions in *Dassonville*. To name but two, firstly, the dividing line between national rules or practices covered by the Articles 34–35 TFEU prohibitions and measures which are not to be qualified as quantitative restrictions or MEEQR remains contentious. The Court's recent struggles with rules on the use of goods clearly illustrate this problem. Secondly, it also remains unclear which type of justifications can be invoked to justify directly discriminatory national measures. In some cases, the Court has accepted mandatory requirements to uphold directly

397. In Case C-189/95, *Franzén*, para 39, the Court indeed also appeared also to acknowledge the existence of a set of restrictions inherent in the existence of state monopolies; the Court did not however develop a positive list of such inherent restrictions.
398. Case C-189/95, *Franzén*, para 40 and Case C-158/94, *Commission v. Italy*, para 32. This has been confirmed in Case C-438/02, *Hanner*, para 43.
399. C-438/02, *Hanner*, para 37.
400. Case C-189/95, *Franzén*, para 36 and Case C-170/04, *Rosengren*, para 18. See also Case C-198/14, *Valev Visnapuu*, para 91.
401. Case C-456/10, *ANETT*, para 26.
402. Case C-456/10, *ANETT*, para 29.

discriminatory national measures, but it has not yet explicitly acknowledged this. This results in uncertainty about the scope of application of the mandatory justifications and their possibly distinctive features in relation to Article 36 TFEU. Those issues occasionally still stir controversy and demonstrate that the demarcation of the scope and the full realization of the free movement of goods remains a work in progress.

Further reading

Barnard, C., *The Substantive Law of the EU: The Four Freedoms*, 5th ed. (OUP, 2016).

Jansson, M. and H. Kalimo, "*De minimis* meets "market access": Transformations in the substance – and the syntax – of EU free movement law?", 51 CML Rev. (2014), 523–558.

Oliver, P., "Of trailers and jet skis: Is the case law on Article 34 TFEU hurtling in a new direction?", 33 *Fordham International Law Journal* (2011), 1423–1471.

Oliver, P. and S. Enchelmaier, *Oliver on Free Movement of Goods in the Union*, 5th ed. (Hart, 2010).

Shuibhne, N. Nic, *The Coherence of EU Free Movement Law, Constitutional Responsibility and the Court of Justice* (OUP, 2014).

Weatherill, S., "After *Keck*: Some thoughts on how to clarify the clarification", 33 CML Rev. (1996), 887–908.

Weiler, J., "From *Dassonville* to *Keck* and beyond: An evolutionary reflection on the text and context of the free movement of goods" in P. Craig and G. de Búrca (Eds.), *The Evolution of EU Law* (OUP, 1999), Ch. 10.

CHAPTER 14
FREE MOVEMENT OF SERVICES, ESTABLISHMENT AND CAPITAL

*Stefaan Van den Bogaert, Armin Cuyvers and Ilektra Antonaki**

1. Introduction

In the early days of European integration, trade in goods formed the lion's share of European GDPs. Unsurprisingly, many of the seminal cases of the Court of Justice of the EU (ECJ) on freedom of movement concentrated on obstacles concerning the free circulation of goods. Initially, the other fundamental freedoms largely remained in the shadow of their "big brother". Often, developments first witnessed in the field of goods only occurred at a later stage in the other freedoms. Services were expressly conceived as a residual freedom, whereas the Treaty provisions relating to capital even lacked direct effect.[1]

Times have changed. Nowadays, services account for more than 73% of European GDPs.[2] The services sector has taken centre stage in national economies and EU internal market law alike. At the same time, market integration in services is lagging behind, and a true internal market for services has not been established.[3] The Monti report on the future of the internal market specifically points to services as one of the sectors where further progress can still be achieved.[4] In several ways, free movement of services is even more legally challenging than goods. Services are generally more pluriform and flexible than goods, and with the advent of modern technology such as the Internet, they have become increasingly mobile and transnational. Many services now literally cross borders at the speed of light, and, as Airbnb and Uber illustrate, this can have major disruptive effects at national level. Services are increasingly proving to be a complex target to tackle with the standard internal market law approach, largely developed by the ECJ with goods in mind. What should be done with online gambling, abortion or soft drugs, to mention but some of the more challenging areas where the free movement of services has been of concern to the ECJ. Moreover, "public" services such as healthcare and education have been taken to come under the scope of the Treaty's free movement rules, setting the scene for a clash

* Europa Institute, Law Faculty, University of Leiden.

1. See Arts. 60, 67 and 68 EEC Treaty. Also note that the ECJ no longer considers the freedom to provide services as residual; see Case C-452/04, *Fidium Finanz*, para 32.
2. ECB Statistics Pocket Book, Sept. 2014, at 7, available at <www.ecb.europa.eu/pub/pdf/stapobo/spb201409en.pdf>.
3. "Completing the Euro, A roadmap towards fiscal union in Europe", Report of the "Tommaso Padoa-Schioppa Group" (Notre Europe, 2012), para 41: only 20% of the services provided in the EU have a cross-border dimension.
4. M. Monti, "A new strategy for the single market, report to President of the European Commission Barroso", of 9 May 2010 (the Monti report), at 53 a.o.

between EU free movement rights and highly sensitive areas of national social organization and welfare. With the proposal for a directive on the liberalization of services in the internal market, an attempt was undertaken to come to a comprehensive coordinated approach in this area. Yet the much watered-down services directive which ultimately saw the light falls short of its original objectives, leaving many problems unresolved.

The freedoms of establishment and capital have equally acquired a whole new significance since their inception. In the field of establishment, companies are increasingly exploring the limits of this freedom to find the optimum regulatory environment, creating tensions with *inter alia* collective labour agreements and national tax systems in the process.[5] The free movement of capital has developed from the "ugly duckling" of the fundamental freedoms to an increasingly mature, important and wide-ranging freedom that creates a host of legal questions, not in the least in the context of taxation. It is the only freedom that applies to third countries, and whose scope extends beyond the boundaries of the EU.

This chapter firstly discusses the freedom to provide services and the freedom of establishment. Considering the similarities and the close connection between both freedoms, as well as their gradual convergence in the case law of the Court, both freedoms are discussed jointly.[6] The discussion will start from an analysis of the relevant Treaty provisions as developed by the ECJ, followed by an analysis of the Services Directive, which also applies to establishment.[7] Importantly, under the *Tedeschi* principle, relevant specific secondary EU legislation must be applied before primary EU law.[8] In practice, therefore, it must first be assessed whether the Services Directive, or any other secondary law, applies to a given situation before applying the Treaty provisions on services or establishment. Moreover, the Services Directive largely codifies the case law of the ECJ. Its generally poor drafting, however, tends to create confusion and legal uncertainty. For a coherent and accessible exposition of the freedom of services and establishment, it therefore remains useful to start with an overview of primary law, which then provides the necessary background to understand and apply the Services Directive. Subsequently, the chapter elaborates on the free movement of capital and its significant development over time.

2. Free movement of services and the freedom of establishment

2.1 *Treaty basis*

Chapter 2 of Title IV on Free movement of persons, services and capital in the Treaty on the Functioning of the EU deals with the right of establishment (Arts. 49–55 TFEU). The freedom to provide services is primarily dealt with in Chapter 3 (Arts. 56 to 62 TFEU).

5. The freedom of establishment of companies will be dealt with separately, in Ch. 25, "Company law", of this book.
6. Questions surrounding the freedom of companies to relocate or reincorporate themselves, for example, including the multitude of tax and corporate law issues this raises, have developed into a field of their own, and are discussed separately in Ch. 12, "The functioning of the internal market", of this book.
7. Specific secondary EU legislation adopted to supplement the general Treaty framework will largely be left out of consideration in this chapter, unless and to the extent explicitly mentioned. Certain instruments are dealt with separately in more specific chapters. The sectoral regulation of telecom or transport services is dealt with in Ch. 31, "Transport services" the new regulation of financial services is covered in Ch. 27, "Financial market supervision and regulation", of this book.
8. Case 5/77, *Tedeschi*, para 35.

2.2 The concept of establishment

The concept of "establishment" is closely connected with that of "services". The main similarity consists in the *self-employed* capacity in which EU nationals, who have established themselves in a host Member State or are providing services there, are working. This sets them apart from the category of workers (Art. 45 TFEU), who perform work in an *employed* capacity. In the contexts of services and establishment, the element of subordination is missing.

The concept of "establishment" has been defined by the ECJ as "the actual pursuit of an economic activity through a fixed establishment in another Member State for an indefinite period".[9] "Establishment" is a very broad concept, allowing an EU national "to participate, on a stable and continuous basis, in the economic life of a Member State other than his state of origin and to profit therefrom, so contributing to economic and social interpenetration within the Union in the sphere of activities as self-employed persons".[10] In *Klopp*, the ECJ held that the freedom of establishment "is not confined to the right to create a single establishment, but includes the freedom to set up and maintain more than one place of work within the EU".[11] Importantly, in *AGET Iraklis*, the Court added that the actual exercise of establishment entails not only, "the freedom to determine the nature and extent of the economic activity that will be carried out in the host Member State, in particular the size of the fixed establishments and the number of workers required for that purpose, but also, the freedom subsequently to scale down that activity or even the freedom to give up, should it so decide, its activity and establishment".[12]

The two defining elements of establishment are thus 1) the fixed establishment in the host Member State and 2) the stable and continuous basis on which the work is carried out. Herein lies precisely the crucial difference with the Treaty provisions on services, in particular the third paragraph of Article 57, which envisages the provider of services moving to another Member State to pursue his activity there on a temporary basis.[13]

2.3 The concept of a service

The concept of a service under EU law includes economic activities that are normally provided for remuneration, and that are not covered by any of the other freedoms. The qualification of an activity as a service depends on two issues: 1) the economic nature of the activity which is normally provided for remuneration and 2) its temporary nature.[14]

2.3.1 An economic activity

In line with its general approach of interpreting the scope of the fundamental freedoms expansively, the ECJ has given a broad definition to the concept of an economic activity.

Firstly, the specific nature of a certain activity, be it recreational or sporting, or the presence of an element of chance, does not remove it from the ambit of free movement.[15] What matters principally is that the activity is "genuine and effective and not such as to be regarded as purely marginal and ancillary".[16] In *Deliège*, the ECJ demonstrated its willingness to look beyond the formal classification by a sports federation of its members as amateur athletes and stipulated

---

9. Case C-221/89, *Factortame*, para 20.
10. Case C-55/94, *Gebhard*, para 25.
11. Case 107/83, *Klopp*, para 19.
12. Case C-201/15, *AGET Iraklis*, para 53.
13. *Gebhard*, para 26; Case C-70/95, *Sodemare*.
14. See for the delineation between goods and services section 2.3.3. *infra* and Case C-275/92, *Schindler*.
15. Case 279/80, *Webb*, para 10.
16. Case 53/81, *Levin*, para 17.

that "sporting activities, and in particular, a high-ranking athlete's participation in an international competition are capable of involving the provision of a number of separate, but closely related services within the scope of Article 56 TFEU".[17]

Secondly, the Court did not set the threshold for remuneration very high. Firstly, relatively low levels of compensation may suffice for the qualification of a given activity as a service. In *Jundt*, for example, the ECJ found that a compensation of DEM 1612 (about €500) was sufficient to qualify 16 hours of teaching as a service, even though this course was given in a quasi-honorary capacity.[18] Secondly, even quid-pro-quo transactions without any payment may constitute remuneration. In *Steymann*, the ECJ held that it was "impossible to rule out *a priori* the possibility" that work carried out by members of a religious community – which concerned, *inter alia*, plumbing work and general household duties – constitutes an economic activity within the meaning of the Treaty: "in so far as the work, which aims to ensure a measure of self-sufficiency for the Bhagwan Community, constitutes an essential part of participation in that community, the services which the latter provides to its members may be regarded as being an *indirect quid pro quo* for their work".[19] Thus, in spite of the absence of conventional payment in money, the Court qualified Steymann's activities as the provision of services, in view of the fact that Steymann's work played a relatively important role in the way of life in the community and that the community provided for his material needs, including pocket money, in return.[20]

Thirdly, the consideration does not necessarily have to be paid by those for whom the services are performed.[21] For example, the Court has held on several occasions that the fact that health care treatment received by an EU citizen in a hospital is paid for by an insurance company or the national health service does not prevent the qualification of that treatment as a service.[22]

Fourthly, in this context, the ECJ has been confronted with the complex question of what the legal situation is when the service is provided by the state itself. Early on, in *Humbel*, the Court ruled that courses taught under the national education system did not constitute services within the meaning of the Treaty. The Court reasoned as follows: firstly, in establishing such a system, the state "is not seeking to engage in gainful activity but is fulfilling its duties towards its own population in the social, cultural and educational fields. Secondly, the system in question is, as a general rule, funded from the public purse and not by pupils or their parents".[23] The Court added that the "nature of the activity is not affected by the fact that pupils or their parents must sometimes pay teaching or enrolment fees in order to make a certain contribution to the operating expenses of the system".[24] For these same reasons, the Court concluded in *Wirth* that courses given in an establishment of higher education which seek to make an economic profit and which are financed essentially out of private funds, particularly out of payments made by students or their parents, do constitute services within the meaning of Article 56 TFEU.[25] Education can

17. Joined Cases C-51/96 & C-191/97, *Deliège*, para 56.
18. Case C-281/06, *Jundt*.
19. Case 196/87, *Steymann*, paras. 11–12.
20. See also Case 263/86, *Humbel*, para 17; Case C-422/01, *Skandia and Ramstedt*, para 23; Case C-76/05, *Schwarz*, para 38.
21. Case 352/85, *Bond van Adverteerders*, para 16; Joined Cases C-51/96 & C-191/97, *Deliège*, para 56; Case C-157/99, *Smits and Peerbooms*, para 58.
22. Case C-157/99, *Smits and Peerbooms*, para 55, Case C-385/99, *Müller-Fauré*, para 103, and especially Case C-372/04, *Watts*. Note, however, that *Watts* did not concern the healthcare provided by the NHS in the UK. It only concerned the compensation sought from the NHS for health care provided in another state. It was this healthcare in the different state that was qualified as a service.
23. Case 263/86, *Humbel*, para 18.
24. Case 263/86, *Humbel*, para 19.
25. Case C-109/92, *Wirth*, para 17.

thus be a service, but the public-private divide is not always easy to draw. This has become readily apparent as well in the Court's case law regarding access to cross-border health care. In the seminal *Kohll* case, the Court explicitly held that the fact that the contested national rules concerned social security cannot exclude the application of Article 56 TFEU.[26] The treatment provided by an orthodontist established in another Member State than the patient, outside any hospital infrastructure, was subsequently regarded as a service provided for remuneration.[27] This principled decision of the Court to bring public health care under the scope of the fundamental freedoms where the treatment is provided for remuneration, which has been consistently reiterated in subsequent case law, potentially has an enormous impact on the organization of national social welfare systems.[28] To ensure that Member States retain the necessary leeway to organize their welfare systems, however, the Court also recognized the need to ensure stable financing of national social security systems and to maintain a balanced national health care system as overriding requirements in the general interest, capable of justifying restrictions to free movement.[29]

Fifthly, the ECJ has consistently held that the morally questionable or socially sensitive nature of an activity does not in itself prevent its qualification as a service. This expansive approach has led the ECJ into many a challenging field. In *Grogan*, the ECJ had to decide whether abortion qualified as a service.[30] The case concerned student activists handing out information on UK abortion clinics in Ireland. At that time, abortions were illegal in Ireland, as was leaving Ireland for the purpose of having an abortion abroad. This prohibition reflected a deep-seated moral conviction of a majority of Irish citizens, which had voted in a referendum to provide constitutional protection to the life of the unborn. Referring to this constitutionally embedded moral conviction, the Society for the Protection of Unborn Children in Ireland (SPUC) argued before the ECJ that, even though it was legal in other Member States, abortion could not qualify as a service because it was "grossly immoral".[31] The ECJ chose to pre-empt any discussion on morality by only looking at legality and remuneration: "Whatever the merits of those arguments on the moral plane, they *cannot influence* the answer to the national court's first question. It is not for the Court to substitute its assessment for that of the legislature in those Member States where the activities in question are practised legally".[32] As abortion was a "medical activity which is normally provided for remuneration" and was "lawfully practiced in several Member States", it qualified as a service under Article 56 TFEU.[33]

The Court adopted a similar approach with regard to games of chance. In *Schindler*, many Member States argued that games of chance should not constitute services, amongst other things because of their dubious morality.[34] The ECJ finely pointed out that these apparently immoral games of chance were not illegal, but in fact "commonplace" in various Member States.

---

26. Case 158/96, *Kohll*, para 21.
27. Case 158/96, *Kohll*, para 29. See also Case C-255/09, *Commission v. Portugal*.
28. J. van den Gronden et al. (Eds.), *Health Care and EU law* (Asser, 2011); S. de la Rosa, "The Directive on cross-border healthcare or the art of codifying complex case law", 49 CML Rev. (2012), 15; A. Andreangeli, "Healthcare services, the EU single market and beyond: Meeting local needs in an open economy – How much market or how little market?", 43 *Legal Issues of Economic Integration* (2016), 145.
29. For a flexible approach of the ECJ in this regard, see Case C-512/08, *Commission v. France*. See generally for the issue of justification, *infra* para 2.6.
30. Case C-159/90, *Grogan*. See for a detailed analysis of EU and ECHR law in such ethically and medically complex fields also N. Koffeman, *Morally Sensitive Issues and Cross-Border Movement in the EU* (2015, Intersentia).
31. *Grogan*, para 19.
32. *Grogan*, para 20, emphasis added.
33. *Grogan*, paras. 18 and 21.
34. Case C-275/92, *Schindler*.

In contrast to *Grogan*, where the ECJ abstained from a moral qualification, the ECJ did explicitly recognize that lotteries are morally "questionable". This conclusion, however, did not prevent the Court from qualifying lotteries as economic activities normally organized for remuneration, and hence as services.[35]

In *Jany*, the Court described prostitution as "an activity by which the provider satisfies a request by the beneficiary in return for consideration", consequently holding that it can also be regarded as a service provided for remuneration.[36] As to the possible immorality of the activity, the Court again observed that far from being prohibited in all Member States, prostitution is tolerated, and even regulated, by most states.

Conversely, in *Josemans*, the Court ruled that the Treaty provisions on services did not apply to a municipal regulation in the Netherlands restricting access to coffee shops to residents only. The Court stressed that narcotic drugs, by their very nature, are subject to a prohibition on importation and marketing in all Member States.[37] The fact that some Member States describe a narcotic drug as a "soft" drug, or that the sale of cannabis is tolerated in practice, despite being formally prohibited by law, did not call that finding into question.[38]

Concluding, in qualifying certain activities as services within the Treaty, the ECJ takes a very liberal approach. As long as an activity is legal in one or more Member States, and as long as it is normally provided for some form of remuneration, it constitutes a service. At the same time, as will be seen further below, the ECJ often "compensates" for this liberal approach by giving considerable leeway to Member States when it comes to *justifying* restrictive measures. The consequence is that free movement of services has a broad scope of application, including many sensitive areas, but that the precise application of this freedom may vary considerably depending on the service involved. This adds to the complexity of the free movement of services.

2.3.2 *Distinguishing services from establishment*

The crucial difference between services and establishment lies in the temporary nature of the provision of services, as opposed to the more permanent nature of establishment.[39] According to the Court in *Gebhard*, the temporary nature of the activities at issue has to be determined "in the light, not only of the duration of the provision of the service, but also of its regularity, periodicity or continuity".[40] Furthermore "the fact that the provision of services is temporary does not mean that the provider of services within the meaning of the Treaty may not equip himself with some form of infrastructure in the host Member State (including an office, chambers or consulting rooms) in so far as such infrastructure is necessary for the purposes of performing the services in question".[41]

In *Schnitzer*, the Court offered further guidance: "services" within the meaning of the Treaty may cover services varying widely in nature, including services which are provided over an extended period, even over several years, where, for example, the services in question are supplied in connection with the construction of a large building. Services within the meaning of the Treaty may likewise be constituted by services which a business established in a Member State

35. The Court has repeated this stance ever since in its still expanding body of case law relating to gambling, see e.g. Case C-42/07, *Liga Portuguesa* and Joined Cases C-316/07, C-358/07, C-359/07, C-360/07, C-409/07 & C-410/07, *Stoß*.
36. Case C-268/99, *Jany*, para 48.
37. Case C-137/09, *Josemans*, para 41.
38. Case C-137/09, *Josemans*, para 42.
39. Case C-55/94, *Gebhard*, para 26; Case C-70/95, *Sodemare*.
40. *Gebhard*, para 27.
41. *Gebhard*, para 27. Cf. also Case C-347/09, *Dickinger and Ömer*.

supplies with a greater or lesser degree of frequency or regularity, even over an extended period, to persons established in one or more other Member States, for example the giving of advice or information for remuneration. No provision of the Treaty affords a means of determining, in an abstract manner, the duration or frequency beyond which the supply of a service or of a certain type of service in another Member State can no longer be regarded as the provision of services within the meaning of the Treaty".[42]

No single or simple criterion exists, therefore, to distinguish between services and establishment. Services can include even very long term and regular activities.[43] A UK lawyer can, for example, provide regular legal advice to a French company for over a decade, even visiting France several weeks a year, yet still fall under the free movement of services.[44] For the rules on establishment to come into play, it seems indispensable that some infrastructure is established and that part of the economic activity, including the search for additional customers, is carried out from that infrastructure.

2.3.3 *Distinguishing between services and goods*

The provision of services may also involve goods, e.g. a lottery ticket. In such a scenario, it is not always straightforward which fundamental freedom is applicable. It is established case law that, where a national measure relates to both the free movement of goods and the freedom to provide services, the Court will in principle examine it "in the light of one only of those two fundamental freedoms if it is apparent that one of them is entirely secondary in relation to the other and may be considered together with it".[45] However, when those two aspects are intimately linked, one not capable of being regarded as entirely secondary in relation to the other, it is appropriate to examine both fundamental freedoms simultaneously. In particular, this may be the case in the field of telecommunications.[46]

2.4 *Beneficiaries and scope*

Once it is determined that a certain activity amounts to a service, the question arises who may rely on the right to freedom of movement granted under Articles 49 and 56 TFEU. On this question, the ECJ has generally also adopted an expansive approach, further widening the scope and impact of the fundamental freedoms. Five elements are of particular importance: 1) the requirements that the self-employed are EU nationals, 2) are established in the EU, 3) the requirement of a cross-border element, 4) the inclusion of service recipients, and 5) the issue of horizontal direct effect.

---

42. Case C-215/01, *Schnitzer*, paras. 30–31.
43. See also Case 63/86, *Commission v. Italy*, para 19, which already implied that a service provider might remain in the host Member State for an extended time.
44. Member States may, however, exceptionally treat an entity wholly or principally providing services to that state as established in their own territory where these entities are only established in another Member States to purposely evade professional rules. As the ECJ is very hesitant to accept abuse of free movement rights, the burden of proof in such cases lies with the Member State, which faces the uphill battle proving that this is really a case of abuse and not just use of free movement rights. See Case 33/74, *Van Binsbergen*, para 13, Case C-148/91, *Omroep Veronica*; Case C-23/93 *TV10*; Case C-367 and 369/96, *Arblade* para 32. For the entire discussion on the use or abuse of free movement rights when relocating legal entities, see the discussion of the *Centros* case law in Ch. 25, "Company law", of this book.
45. Case C-275/92, *Schindler*, para 22; Case C-71/02, *Karner*, para 46; Case C-36/02, *Omega*, para 26; Case C-452/04, *Fidium Finanz*, para 34; Case C-137/09, *Josemans*, paras. 49–50; Case C-108/09, *Ker-Optika*, para 43.
46. Case C-390/99, *Canal Satélite Digital*, paras. 29–33; Case C-403/08 *Football Association Premier League*, para 79.

2.4.1 *Nationality and establishment in the EU*

Article 49 TFEU can only be invoked by nationals of a Member State. Similarly, Article 56 TFEU only prohibits restrictions on the freedom to provide services "in respect of nationals of Member States who are established in a Member State other than that of the person for whom the services are intended". In other words, in order to benefit from the right to free movement of services, a service provider must (1) have the nationality of an EU Member State and (2) also be established in an EU Member State.[47] In the case of legal persons, which also fall under the scope of Article 56 TFEU,[48] both requirements are usually met simultaneously, as legal entities generally acquire the nationality of a Member State by setting up establishment in that Member State.

The double requirement of nationality and establishment, however, only applies to service *providers* and not to service *recipients*. Third-country nationals or entities who are established within the EU can rely on Article 56 TFEU when receiving a service from an EU provider.[49] For example, a Chinese lawyer living in Brussels cannot rely on Article 56 TFEU to provide legal services in Sweden. He or she can, however, rely on Article 56 TFEU to receive legal services from a Swedish law firm.

On the basis of Article 56, paragraph 2 TFEU, the freedom to provide services may be extended to "nationals of a third country who provide services and who are established within the Union". A Commission proposal to this end was, however, withdrawn, meaning that the scope of the freedom to provide services on this point is still determined by the case law of the ECJ.[50]

2.4.2 *The cross-border element*

In line with the general case law of the ECJ concerning free movement, Articles 49 and 56 TFEU only cover situations that involve some form of cross-border element, as EU law is not concerned with purely internal situations.[51]

With regard to establishment, the Court has clarified that Article 49 TFEU cannot be interpreted in such a way that Member State nationals are excluded from the benefit of EU law in their state of origin, "when they find themselves in a situation which may be assimilated to that of any other persons enjoying the rights and liberties guaranteed by the Treaty".[52] Whenever EU nationals have obtained a qualification in another Member State and subsequently return to their home state to practise, for example, the situation is no longer wholly internal and thus Article 49 TFEU can be relied upon in the home state. Conversely, when there is no "EU

47. Natural persons have alternative options to benefit from free movement law. They may enjoy derived rights as family members of an EU citizen who has made use of his free movement rights under Reg. 492/2011 and Directive 2004/38. Additionally, both legal and natural entities may benefit from rights conferred upon them in international agreements concluded between the EU and their country of origin, for example in association or partnership agreements, see Ch. 41, "Union external relations under the TFEU", of this book.
48. See the General Programme for the abolition of restrictions on the freedom to provide services, title I, O.J. 1962, at 32.
49. Case C-484/93, *Svensson and Gustavsson*. See on this P. Oliver, "Goods and services: Two freedoms compared" in *Mélanges en hommage à Michel Waelbroeck* (Bruylant, 1999), at 1371.
50. Case C-113/89, *Rush Portuguesa*; Case C-164/99, *Portugaia Construçoes*; Case C-43/93, *Van der Elst*; Case C-445/03, *Commission v. Luxembourg*; Case C-244/04, *Commission v. Germany*. See further Case C-341/05, *Laval* and Case C-438/05, *Viking*, as well as the further discussion *infra*. For the proposal see O.J. 1999, C 67/17, as withdrawn by the Communication from the Commission "Withdrawal of Commission Proposals which are no longer of Topical Interest" COM (2004)542 Final/2.
51. Case 52/79, *Debauve*, or Case C-108/98 *RI.SAN.* for examples where a cross-border element was absent.
52. Case 115/78, *Knoors*, para 24.

element" present in the situation, EU nationals cannot invoke Article 49 TFEU against their state of origin.[53]

In relation to services, the Court has distinguished four distinct scenario's with a cross-border element. The first scenario, and the only one expressly envisioned in Article 56 TFEU, involves a service provider who travels to another Member State to provide a service.[54] The second scenario is where the service recipient travels to another Member State to receive a service.[55] In the third scenario, the service provider and the service recipient both travel to another Member State. This scenario is almost customarily typified by organized bus travels where the bus driver, the tourists and the tour guide travel together around Europe and are confronted with all forms of holiday-wrecking restrictions.[56] The fourth and final scenario is where it is the service itself that crosses a border, even though the provider and the recipient do not.[57] With the advent of telecommunications and the Internet, this fourth scenario has become increasingly important. A German company banking in Estonia, a Belgian citizen participating in a French online lottery, or a Swedish football fan watching a match in the English Premier League online are just a few of the many examples that permeate our daily lives.

In practice, this requirement of a trans-frontier element does not often pose problems. The decision in *Trijber and Harmsen* exemplifies this.[58] Mr Trijber was refused a licence for organizing small canal tours of Amsterdam with his 34-person sloop. The referring Dutch court had stressed that his services were expected to be provided "mainly to residents of the Netherlands" and therefore seemingly presented a purely internal situation.[59] The ECJ, however, found that there was a cross-border element because the services of Trijber "may also be enjoyed by nationals of other Member States […]".[60] Even the likelihood of a small number of non-national customers may thus be enough to bring a service under the scope of Article 56 TFEU, even where it is provided by a service provider in its home state.[61] Evidently, this potentially significantly broadens the scope of the relevant Treaty provisions.[62]

2.4.3 *The inclusion of service recipients*

The typical scenario envisioned by Article 56 TFEU is that of a service provider wanting to provide a service in another Member State.[63] In its early case law, it seems the scenario of the service

53. Case C-118/09, *Koller*.
54. It is not required that the specific service recipient in the other MS has already been identified. Mere offers of services, without any already identified customers, also fall under the freedom. See Case C-384/93, *Alpine Investments*, para 19.
55. Case 15/78, *Koestler*.
56. Case C-154/89, *Commission v. France*; Case C-180/89, *Commission v. Italy*; Case C-198/89, *Commission v. Greece*; Case C-398/95, *Ypourgos Ergasias*.
57. Case C-384/93, *Alpine Investments*; Joined Cases C-403/08 & C-429/08, *Football Association Premier League (Murphy)*.
58. Joined Cases C-340/14 & C-341/14, *Trijber and Harmsen*. Although this judgment concerned the scope of the Services Directive, its findings also apply to services under Art. 56 TFEU.
59. Idem, para 28. The key question the Dutch court invited the ECJ to answer was whether the services directive would even apply in a purely internal situation. The ECJ refused the invitation by finding a cross-border element.
60. Idem, para 41. Equally, the prostitution services provided by Harmsen also had a cross-border element as his customers included non-residents.
61. Case C-265/12, *Citroën Belux*, para 33.
62. For an example where the ECJ did not discern a cross-border element, see Case C-245/09, *Omalet*.
63. Case 33/74, *Van Binsbergen*.

provider travelling abroad was the only one the ECJ was thinking of as well.[64] Subsequently, however, in *Luisi and Carbone*,[65] the Court famously established that service *recipients* may also rely on Article 56 TFEU: "[…] the freedom to provide services includes the freedom, for the recipients of services, to go to another Member State in order to receive a service there, without being obstructed by restrictions, even in relation to payments and that tourists, persons receiving medical treatment and persons travelling for the purpose of education or business are to be regarded as recipients of services".[66]

As a result, all individuals that travel to another Member State to receive some kind of service, be it healthcare, education or even general tourism, might in principle invoke the free movement of services to challenge any restrictions they encounter.[67] In addition, service providers that attend to these "incoming" service recipients in the host Member State may also rely on Article 56 TFEU. To trigger the application of Article 56 TFEU, it may suffice that only "a number of customers" are from other Member States, for instance because they are holidaying.[68]

2.4.4 *Horizontal direct effect of Articles 49 and 56 TFEU*

The final element affecting the scope of the fundamental freedoms is the issue of horizontal direct effect. To what extent can Articles 49 and 56 TFEU be relied upon against private entities?

In *Reyners*, the ECJ ruled that Article 49 TFEU has direct effect, notwithstanding the fact that the criteria for direct effect established in *Van Gend & Loos* were arguably not fulfilled. According to the ECJ, Article 49 TFEU imposes the attainment of a precise result, namely the prohibition of discrimination on grounds of nationality, by the end of the transitional period, the fulfilment of which was not made dependent on the implementation of a programme of progressive measures.[69] A couple of months later, in *Van Binsbergen*, the ECJ accorded *vertical* direct effect to Article 56 TFEU on the same grounds.[70] The *horizontal* direct effect of both freedoms, however, remains as yet uncertain.

In this respect, three different situations, or "extensions" to traditional vertical direct effect, must be distinguished. Firstly, the ECJ extended vertical direct effect by adopting a broad conception of "the state": any public body is bound by EU law, not just national governments.[71] Articles 49 and 56 TFEU may therefore be relied upon against any public body, including regional, local or municipal governments or independent public bodies. Secondly, the ECJ ruled that free movement rights can also be invoked against private (non-public) entities that wield some form of public or collective authority. Examples include bar associations, sports federations, trade unions or standard-setting bodies with authority to regulate their sector.[72] Residency requirements imposed by a bar association may, after all, restrict free movement just as much as a national law imposing the same requirement. The authority with which these entities are vested grants

---

64. Case 33/74, *Van Binsbergen*; Case 16/78, *Choquet*; Case 279/80, *Webb*; Case 76/81, *SA Transporoute et travaux*.
65. Joined Cases 286/82 & 26/83, *Luisi and Carbone*; Case 186/87, *Cowan*; Case C-159/90, *Grogan*; Case C-55/93, *Van Schaik*; Case C-274/96, *Bickel and Franz*; Case C-348/96, *Calfa*.
66. Joined Cases 286/82 & 26/83, *Luisi and Carbone*, para 16.
67. See also Case C-158/96, *Kohll*; Case C-372/04, *Watts* and especially Case 186/87, *Cowan*, where the specific services received by a British tourist did not even have to be specified.
68. Case C-98/14, *Berlington*, paras. 25–26.
69. Case 2/74, *Reyners*, paras. 24–27.
70. Case 33/74, *Van Binsbergen*, paras. 26–27.
71. Case 152/84, *Marshall*, para 49; Joined Cases C-1/90 & C-176/90, *Aragonesa*.
72. Case 71/76, *Thieffry*; Case C-309/99, *Wouters*, para 120; Case 36/74, *Walrave and Koch*; Joined Cases C-51/96 & C-191/97, *Deliège*; Case C-171/11, *Fra.bo*.

them a function *akin to that of the state*. These could therefore be described as "quasi-horizontal" situations.

In the third situation, the parties involved in the dispute are private and do not possess any public or collective regulatory authority. The application of the free movement provisions in such a "purely" horizontal situation is more controversial. On the one hand, one could ask why purely private entities should be bound by Articles 49 or 56 TFEU. These provisions are primarily aimed at Member States, whereas the competition sanction is aimed at private behaviour. On the other hand, following the effectiveness logic underlying much of EU law, one could equally ask why private entities should be allowed to frustrate free movement, and with it the effectiveness of the internal market, if they have the capacity to do so.

Until now, only Article 45 TFEU on the free movement for workers has unequivocally been held to be fully horizontally directly effective.[73] While certain parts of the reasoning concerning workers could unquestionably be transposed to the other freedoms, such as the risk that free movement is "neutralized by obstacles" created by private entities, so far the ECJ has not unambiguously extended the purely horizontal application of Article 45 TFEU to Articles 49 or 56 TFEU. In *Viking* (concerning establishment) and *Laval* (on services), the Court had to determine the application of these Treaty articles to collective action organized by trade unions.[74] The Court did hold that there is no indication in its case law that could validly support the view that Articles 49 and 56 TFEU apply "only to associations or to organizations exercising a regulatory task or having quasi-legislative powers".[75] This could be taken as an argument in favour of the application of Articles 49 and 56 to purely private behaviour as well. The precise impact of this ruling is however still unclear. The ECJ also pointed out that trade unions, "in exercising their autonomous power to negotiate with employers or professional organizations the conditions of employment and pay of workers, [...] participate in the drawing up of agreements seeking to regulate paid work collectively".[76] Further clarification on the purely horizontal effect of Articles 49 and 56 TFEU would therefore be desirable. Until then, the divergence between the fundamental freedoms on this issue continues.

2.5 *Restrictions on freedom of establishment and the freedom to provide services*

This section focuses on the meaning, the scope and the limitations of the concept of restriction in the fields of establishment and services.

2.5.1 *Discriminatory restrictions*

Initially, the wording of Articles 46 and 56–57 TFEU may have given rise to some doubts as to the specific role of the principle of non-discrimination within the context of establishment and services. However, the text of Article 61 TFEU[77] and the definitions of restrictions in the General Programmes for the abolition of restrictions on the freedom of establishment and the

73. Case C-281/98, *Angonese*. Interestingly, the contested measure amounted to indirect discrimination.
74. Case C-438/05, *Viking*; Case C-341/05 *Laval*.
75. Case C-438/05, *Viking*, para 65.
76. See also P. Craig and G. de Búrca, *EU Law. Text, Cases & Material*, 6th ed. (OUP, 2015) at 796–798.
77. Art. 61 TFEU provides that "As long as restrictions on freedom to provide services have not been abolished, each Member State shall apply such restrictions *without distinction on grounds of nationality or residence* to all persons providing services within the meaning of the first paragraph of Art. 56". Admittedly though, the ECJ seems to have never invoked this provision to interpret Art. 56. See also Warner A.G. in Case 52/79, *Debauve*, and the Court's subsequent rejection of his Opinion in para 16 of its judgment.

freedom to provide services[78] leave no doubt that the prohibition of discrimination on grounds of nationality in effect lies at the basis of the provisions concerning these fundamental freedoms. This conclusion is further strengthened by the early judgments of the ECJ on the matter.[79] The ECJ views the freedom of establishment and the freedom to provide services as a specific expression of the general principle of equal treatment or non-discrimination.[80]

The prohibitions of Articles 49 and 56 TFEU target both directly and indirectly discriminatory measures.[81] Directly discriminatory measures make a distinction explicitly based on nationality or the place of establishment. The concept of direct discrimination is therefore rather limited.[82] In *Sjöberg*, for instance, Sweden appeared to impose stricter penalties for promoting illegal gambling with foreign providers than for promoting illegal gambling with Swedish providers.[83]

Indirectly discriminatory measures formally apply irrespective of nationality or place of establishment but may *in fact* lead to differential – adverse – treatment of non-nationals because the requirements imposed are more easily satisfied by nationals.[84] Common examples include residency or language requirements. Such requirements do not refer to nationality directly, but are usually easier to meet for nationals or entities established in a host state.[85]

---

78. General Programme for the abolition of restrictions of freedom to provide services of 18 Dec. 1961, *Official Journal of 15 Jan. 1962, Special Editions, Second Series*, IX, at 32: Restrictions are defined as "any measure which, pursuant to any provision laid down by law, regulation or administrative action in a Member State, or as a result of the application of such a provision, or of administrative practices, prohibits or hinders the person providing services in his pursuit of an activity as a self-employed person *by treating him differently from nationals of the State concerned*". Furthermore, are also to be regarded as restrictions, "any requirements imposed, pursuant to any provision laid down by law, regulation or administrative action or in consequence of any administrative practice, where, although *applicable irrespective of nationality, their effect is exclusively or principally to hinder the provision of services by foreign nationals*" (Title III) (emphasis added).
79. Case 33/74, *Van Binsbergen*, para 25.
80. Case 39/75, *Coenen*.
81. Case C-288/89, Gouda, para 10: Art. 56 TFEU entails "*in the first place*, the abolition of any discrimination (…)." (emphasis added). Also see, on the fundamental importance of non-discrimination in EU law, Joined Cases 117/76 and 16/77, *Ruckdeschel*, para 7; Case 39/75 *Coenen*. For further examples relating to services see Case 168/85, *Commission v. Italy*; Case 63/86, *Commission v. Italy*; Case C-154/89, *Commission v. France*; Case C-180/89, *Commission v. Italy*; Case C-198/89, *Commission v. Greece*; Case C-260/89, *ERT*; Case C-353/89, *Commission v. Kingdom of the Netherlands*; Case C-58/90, *Commission v. Italy*; Case C-17/92, *Federación de Distribuidores Cinematográficos*; Case C-45/93, *Commission v. Spain*.
82. Unequal treatment of entities in equal situations may also form discrimination. See Case C-390/96, *Lease Plan Luxembourg*. Also, G. Davies, *Nationality Discrimination in the European Internal Market* (Kluwer, 2003), 22–31.
83. Case C-447/08 and C-448/08, *Sjöberg*, para 57.
84. Case C-73/08, *Bressol*, para 41, in the context of equal treatment of EU Citizens: "a provision of national law must be regarded as indirectly discriminatory if it is intrinsically liable to affect nationals of other Member States more than nationals of the host State and there is a consequent risk that it will place the former at a particular disadvantage". Also Case C-195/98, *Österreichischer Gewerkschaftsbund*, para 40; Case C-212/05, *Hartmann*, para 30.
85. In the context of services, Case 33/74, *Van Binsbergen*, imposing a residency requirement on lawyers in the Netherlands; Case 205/84, *Commission v. Germany*, requiring establishment and authorization in Germany for insurance companies; Case C-337/97, *Meeusen*, paras. 23 and 24, more generally on residency requirements.

2.5.2 *Beyond discrimination: The Säger approach*

In *van Binsbergen*, the ECJ already laid the foundations for a broader approach, going beyond discrimination.[86] In the wake of the *Dassonville* and *Cassis de Dijon* judgments concerning goods,[87] in *Säger* the ECJ for the first time held that Article 56 TFEU "requires not only the elimination of discrimination against a provider of services on the ground of his nationality, but also the abolition of any restriction, even if it applies without distinction to national providers of services and to those of other Member States, when it is liable to prohibit or otherwise impede the activities of a provider of services established in another Member State where he lawfully provides similar services".[88] On the same day, the Court based its judgment in *Collectieve Antennevoorziening Gouda* on exactly the same grounds, clearly signalling its determination to abandon its traditional discrimination-based analysis in favour of a broader approach to restrictions within the field of the free movement of services.[89] As a result, the key question is no longer whether a measures amounts to discrimination, but whether there is a chance that a measure will make it more difficult, in any way, shape or form, to provide or receive cross-border services. In *Alpine Investments*, for example, a Dutch ban on cold-calling was held to constitute a restriction to freedom of movement, despite the genuinely non-discriminatory nature of the prohibition.[90] In the field of establishment, the ECJ followed suit shortly afterwards. Cases such as *Kraus* or *Gebhard* established that national measures which are "liable to hinder or make less attractive the exercise of fundamental freedoms" amount to an infringement of Article 49 TFEU unless they can be justified, even though they are applicable without discrimination on grounds of nationality.[91]

The *Säger* conception of a restriction, comprising not only directly and indirectly discriminatory measures, but also genuinely non-discriminatory measures, casts a very wide net. It virtually encapsulates almost any national norm regulating establishment and the provision of cross-border services. The long tentacles of the concept of restriction are perfectly illustrated by the ECJ's approach to the so-called dual burden problem and the principle of home state control in the field of services. Usually service providers are regulated in their home state. When offering cross-border services, they are likely to have to comply with the regulations of the host states as well, which might very well differ. This dual (or multiple) regulatory burden would put cross-border service providers at a clear competitive disadvantage vis-à-vis national service providers, which only have to comply with their own national regulation. To prevent such a double burden, which would *de facto* undermine the internal market for services, the ECJ has held that Member States may in principle not impose "all the conditions required for establishment" on a service provider, even if they apply indiscriminately to all service providers. As a general rule, Member States should trust the regulations in the home state of the service provider and avoid regulatory duplication. The dual regulatory burden resulting from a host Member State nevertheless imposing its own regulation on an issue which is already subject to regulation in the home Member State, may therefore amount to a restriction. Even completely non-discriminatory measures that in themselves do not hinder free movement can consequently become restrictions if they duplicate regulations in the home state of the service provider. This also means that Member States are not just prohibited from imposing stricter norms on foreign providers, but that they

86. Case 33/74, *Van Binsbergen*, para 10.
87. Case 8/74, *Dassonville*; Case 120/78, *Rewe-Zentral AG v. Bundesmonopolverwaltung für Branntwein (Cassis de Dijon)*.
88. Case C-76/90, *Säger*, para 12.
89. Case C-288/89, *Stichting Collectieve Antennevoorziening Gouda.*
90. Case C-384/93, *Alpine Investments.*
91. Case C-19/92, *Kraus*, para 32; Case C-55/94, *Gebhard*, para 37.

may be obligated to apply fewer national norms to foreign providers than to national providers, so as to avoid a dual burden. In the context of establishment, the situation is somewhat different, as the self-employed establishes himself in the host Member State on a stable basis, and must thus in principle comply with the host state regulations, but also here, the firm approach of the ECJ conveys the message loud and clear that Member States should abstain from imposing unnecessary or disproportionate restrictions.[92]

The *Säger* approach also captures relatively "minor" restrictions. In his opinion on *Leclerc-Siplec*, AG Jacobs called for the introduction of a kind of *de minimis* test in free movement law, entailing that only measures substantially hindering access to the market would amount to a restriction of free movement. So far, the Court has not taken up this suggestion. In *Josemans*, for instance, the Netherlands Government argued that the marketing of non-alcoholic beverages and food in coffee shops – which represented between 2.5% and 7.1% of the turnover of coffee shops in Maastricht – is altogether secondary to the marketing of cannabis and therefore should not have any bearing on the outcome of the main proceedings.[93] The ECJ however, refused to accept this argument. While acknowledging that coffee shops are primarily dedicated to the sale and consumption of cannabis, it stressed that the marketing of non-alcoholic beverages and food constitutes "a not inconsiderable economic activity".[94] The municipal regulation preventing proprietors of coffee shops from providing catering services to persons residing in other Member States was therefore regarded as a restriction to Article 56 TFEU, albeit one that could be justified.

Interestingly, the ECJ, to some extent curiously and contrary to expectations, has also refrained from transposing its *Keck* ruling to the field of services, despite clearly having had the opportunity to do so. The clearest rejection of *Keck* for services can be seen in *De Agostini*, a case concerning a Swedish ban on misleading advertising and advertising aimed at children under 12.[95] Under this ban, Sweden prohibited a certain advertisement for a children's magazine on dinosaurs. The ban affected both the free movement of goods (the magazine), and the free movement of services (the broadcasting of the advertisement). The ECJ did apply *Keck* to the potential restriction on goods, but refrained from doing so with regard to the services involved. If all *Keck* criteria were met, the same ban would therefore not constitute a restriction for goods, but would form a restriction for services that would need to be justified. This rejection of *Keck* for services preserves the very broad scope of Article 56 TFEU.

2.5.3 *Limits to the concept of restrictions*

Its wide interpretation notwithstanding, on a number of occasions the ECJ has made it clear that the concept of restriction does have its limits.[96] In *Deliège*, a case concerning the non-selection of an athlete to take part in an international sporting event, the ECJ ruled that even though selection rules "inevitably have the effect of limiting the number of participants in a tournament, such a limitation is viewed as *inherent* in the conduct of an international high-level sports event", which necessarily involves certain selection criteria.[97] Therefore, such rules do not amount to a prohibited restriction. The Court added that, for the purposes of an international

---

92. Case 143/87, *Stanton v. INASTI*; Case C-107/94, *Asscher*; Case C-19/92, *Kraus*; Case C-64/08, *Engelmann*; Case C-384/08 *Attanasio Group*; Case C-438/08, *Commission v. Portugal*.
93. Case C-137/09, *Josemans*, para 45.
94. Idem, para 46.
95. Joined Cases C-34/95, C-35/95 and C-36/95, *De Agostini*.
96. For an exceptional example where the ECJ allowed a Member State to temporarily keep in place a restriction which had been found *unjustified* see Case C-409/06, *Winner Wetten*.
97. Joined Cases C-51/96 & C-191/97, *Deliège*, para 64.

sports tournament, the choice of one system for selecting participants over another is based "on a large number of considerations unconnected with the personal situation of any athlete, such as the nature, the organization and the financing of the sport concerned".[98] Even if one selection system proves more favourable to one category of athletes than another, "it cannot be inferred from that fact alone that the adoption of that system constitutes a restriction on the freedom to provide services".[99] In other words, if a rule, in view of the overall context and the objectives it pursues, is to be regarded as an inherent limitation, it does not qualify as a restriction and falls outside the scope of Article 56 TFEU. This line of reasoning bears a striking resemblance to the approach adopted by the Court in *Wouters* and *Meca-Medina* in the field of competition law.[100]

Moreover, the Court also established that certain effects ensuing from the application of a particular rule may simply be "too uncertain and indirect" for such a rule to be considered as a restriction to the freedom to provide services.[101] *Commission v. Spain*, for example, concerned the Spanish refusal to reimburse expenses incurred for medical treatment in a hospital in another Member State of persons insured under the Spanish national health scheme who had made use of their free movement rights and who had unexpectedly become ill, in so far as the level of cover applicable in the Member State where the treatment is administered is lower than that provided for under the Spanish legislation. The Court ruled that the possibility that the difference in level of cover would interfere with free movement in a case of unexpected illness abroad appeared "too uncertain and indirect" for the Spanish legislation to constitute a restriction to freedom of movement.[102] The Court rendered a similar judgment in *Grogan*, a case evolving around the prohibition in Ireland for student associations to distribute practical information about the lawful medical termination of pregnancy in clinics in another Member State. The ECJ established that the students' associations distributing the contested information did not work for the clinics and ruled on that basis that the link between the activity of the students' associations and the medical terminations of pregnancies in clinics in another Member State "is *too tenuous* for the prohibition on the distribution of information to be capable of being regarded as a restriction" within the meaning of Article 56 TFEU.[103]

2.5.4 *Some specific examples of restrictions*

Recognition of diplomas and professional qualifications

The issue of recognition of diplomas and professional qualifications has been the subject of both extensive case law from the ECJ and intense EU legislative action. Initially, in *Thieffry*, a Belgian national whose Belgian diploma had been officially recognized in France as equivalent to the French law degree, and who passed the special qualifying examination for the profession of *avocat* in France, was nevertheless refused admission to the Paris Bar on the ground that he did not possess the prescribed national diploma. The ECJ established that this refusal constituted a restriction incompatible with the freedom of establishment, even in the absence of specific secondary EU legislation.[104] In subsequent case law, the Court went so far as to impose positive

98. *Deliège*, para 65.
99. *Deliège*, para 66.
100. Case C-309/99, *Wouters*; Case C-519/04 P, *Meca-Medina*. See further Ch. 20, "Substantive law of the EU", of this book.
101. Case C-190/98, *Graf*; Case C-565/08, *Commission v. Italy*, where the Italian rules setting maximum tariffs for lawyers were held not to restrict market access.
102. Case C-211/08, *Commission v. Spain*, para 72.
103. Case C-159/90, *Grogan*, paras. 24–25.
104. Case 71/76, *Thieffry*.

obligations on responsible authorities concerning the recognition of foreign qualifications, in the absence of specific EU or national legislation. In *Vlassopoulou*, the ECJ established that national requirements concerning qualifications may have the effect of hindering nationals of the other Member States in the exercise of their right of establishment, even if they apply without discrimination, if they fail to take into account the knowledge and qualifications acquired in other Member States.[105] National authorities are therefore required to examine to what extent the knowledge and qualifications attested by a foreign diploma correspond to those required in the host state. If that comparative examination of diplomas results in a finding of equivalence, the foreign diploma must be recognized. In case of only partial equivalence, national authorities are entitled to require proof that the missing knowledge and qualifications have been acquired.[106] If completion of a period of preparation or training is required for entry into a profession in the host Member State, it must be determined whether professional experience acquired in the Member State of origin or in the host Member State may be regarded as satisfying that requirement in full or in part.[107]

After the ECJ had made the first step, the EU legislature undertook further action to promote and regulate freedom of movement in this respect. Initially, a vertical or sectoral approach was followed, separately harmonizing or coordinating the qualification requirements for specific professions. Directive 77/249 on lawyers' services and Directive 98/5 on the right of establishment for lawyers are paradigm examples.[108] In view of the slow and relatively limited progress made, this approach was abandoned in favour of a horizontal approach, characterized by mutual recognition. Directive 89/48 provided for a general system for the recognition of higher-education diplomas awarded on completion of professional education and training of at least three years' duration.[109] Permission to pursue a regulated profession in the host state was only given to EU nationals who were fully qualified to practise in the state where they obtained the qualifications.[110] This directive also contained provisions on the completion of an adaptation period or the taking of an adaptation test in the event of substantial differences between the home and host state's regulations. In 2005, the three mutual recognition directives and most of the sectoral directives (though not the two lawyers' directives) were replaced by Directive 2005/36 on the recognition of professional qualifications.[111] This Directive, which essentially consolidates the mutual recognition approach, and endeavours to create a general legal framework for recogni-

105. Case 340/89, *Vlassopoulou*, para 15; Case C-575/11, *Eleftherios-Themistokis Nasiopoulos*.
106. *Vlassopoulou*, para 23.
107. *Vlassopoulou*, para 21.
108. Directive 77/249/EEC to facilitate the effective exercise by lawyers of freedom to provide services O.J. 1977, L 78/17 and Directive 98/5/EC to facilitate practice of the profession of lawyer on a permanent basis in a Member State other than that in which the qualification was obtained O.J. 1998, L 77/36.
109. Council Directive 89/48/EEC on a general system for the recognition of higher-education diplomas awarded on completion of professional education and training of at least three years' duration O.J. 1989, L 19/16. See e.g. Case C-47/08, *Commission v. Belgium*; Case C-51/08, *Commission v. Luxembourg*; Case C-61/08, *Commission v. Greece*; Case C-118/09, *Koller*; Case C-359/09, *Ebert*; Joined Cases C-422/09, C-425/09 & C-426/09, *Vandorou*; Case C-424/09, *Toki*.
110. Case C-313/01, *Morgenbesser*.
111. Directive 2005/36/EC on the recognition of professional qualifications O.J. 2005, L 255/22. See e.g. Case C-52/08, *Commission v. Portugal*; Case C-53/08, *Commission v. Austria*; Case C-54/08 *Commission v. Germany*; Case C-492/1,2 *Conseil national de l'ordre des médecins*; Case C-477/13 *Eintragungsausschuss*. See further M. Van Riemsdijk, "Obstacles to the free movement of professionals: Mutual recognition of professional qualifications in the European Union", 15 *European Journal of Migration and Law* (2013), 47, T. Heremans, "Free movement of lawyers in the European Union", 47 CML Rev. (2010), 1867; M. Peeters "Free movement of medical doctors in the EU", 26 *Medicine and law* (2007), 231.

tion, forms the current frame of reference on this matter. In circumstances not covered under this Directive or the other EU legislation on recognition, one falls back on primary law and the principles established by the ECJ.

Interestingly, qualifications obtained by an EU national outside the EU are considered as evidence of formal qualifications if the holder has three years' professional experience in the Member State which has recognized the non-EU qualification.[112] Conversely, qualifications obtained by third-country nationals are not protected under the Directive.

Posting of workers

The right of service providers to enter and reside in the Member State where they provide a service extends to their staff involved in providing the service, including third-country nationals. In principle, Member States are not entitled to restrict the use of non-EU staff with requirements such as work permits, fees or other administrative obstacles.[113] The inclusion of posted workers under the scope of Article 56 TFEU raised important social welfare concerns amongst Member States. In response, the Court held in *Rush Portuguesa* that EU law "does not preclude Member States from extending their legislation, or collective labour agreements entered into by both sides of industry, to any person who is employed, even temporarily, within their territory, no matter in which country the employer is established; nor does [it] prohibit Member States from enforcing those rules by appropriate means".[114] Subsequently, the situation was – at least partially – regulated by the Posted Workers Directive.[115] Directive 96/71 imposes on Member States the obligation to guarantee workers posted to their territory minimum protection as regards certain terms and conditions of employment, including, in particular maximum work periods and minimum rest periods, minimum paid annual holidays or minimum rates of pay. In *Laval*, the list in Article 3 of the Directive of host Member States' labour standards that may be imposed on posted workers was held to be exhaustive. Moreover, these minimum standards may only be imposed via the methods indicated in the Directive, excluding for example the Swedish system of determining wages via negotiations between management and labour on a case-by-case basis. The Posted Workers Directive thus offers only limited protection. Any standard that does not fall under the seven limitative grounds, exceeds the minimum protection, or is not imposed via one of the methods prescribed by the Directive, is excluded from its scope, and a result may form a restriction that is in principle prohibited under Article 56 TFEU.[116] In March 2016, the European Commission proposed a targeted revision of the rules on posting of workers within the European Union to ensure they remain fit for purpose.[117] If adopted, the proposal would introduce changes in three main areas: remuneration of posted workers, including in situations of subcontracting; rules on temporary agency workers; and long-term posting.

---

112. Art. 3(3) of Directive 2005/36.
113. Case C-113/89, *Rush Portuguesa*.
114. Idem, para 18.
115. Directive 96/71/EC concerning the posting of workers in the framework of the provision of services O.J. 1997, L 18/1.
116. See e.g. Case C-549/13, *Bundesdruckerei*; Case C-522/12, *Isbir*; Case C-515/08, *Dos Santos Palhota*; Case C-346/06, *Rüffert*; Case C-319/06, *Commission v. Luxembourg*; Case C-490/04, *Commission v. Germany*. In 2016 the European Commission adopted a proposal for a new Directive on posted workers, yet this proposal has run into severe political difficulties, largely along an East-West divide. See the proposal amending Directive 96/71/EC concerning the posting of workers in the framework of the provision of services COM(2016)128.
117. (COM(2016)0128 final) – procedure file 2016/0070 (COD).

Transparency

The requirement of transparency when awarding public contracts forms an atypical restriction on Article 56 TFEU. For the most part, the award of public contracts is covered by the EU rules on public procurement.[118] In some cases, however, public contracts wholly or partially fall outside the procurement rules, for example because the total sum involved remains below the monetary threshold, or because the content or nature of the contract has been excluded from the scope of the procurement directives. To the extent that these public contracts might be of interest to providers in other Member States, they must, however, still comply with internal market rules and the general principles of EU law.[119] These include especially the principles of equal treatment and non-discrimination on grounds of nationality. From these principles, the ECJ has derived an obligation of transparency, which concretely requires "ensuring, for the benefit of any potential tenderer, a degree of advertising sufficient to enable the services market to be opened up to competition and the impartiality of the procedures to be reviewed".[120] Any failure to provide sufficient advertising, or to award the contract via an impartial procedure amenable to judicial review, violates the principle of transparency.[121] In the case of a contract for services, such a failure hence forms a restriction on the free movement of services.[122]

2.6 *Justification of restrictions*

In practice, because of the very broad interpretation given to the concept of restriction by the ECJ, the test of justification is often decisive for the outcome of a legal dispute. As with the other freedoms, a national measure which is regarded as a restriction on Article 49 or 56 TFEU can be justified if it serves a legitimate aim in a proportionate manner and does not violate fundamental rights. Two different types of legitimate aims can be distinguished: firstly, the Treaty-based derogations laid down in Articles 51 and 52 TFEU,[123] and secondly, the judicially created exceptions or "overriding requirements in the general interest". These exceptions can only be invoked in the absence of EU harmonization legislation and are to be interpreted narrowly, so that their scope cannot be determined unilaterally by each Member State without any control by the EU institutions.[124] As a rule, it is up to the Member State to substantiate that a restrictive national measure is justified.[125]

118. See Ch. 22, "Public procurement", of this book.
119. Case C-324/98, *Telaustria;* Case C-231/03, *Coname;* Case C-458/03, *Parking Brixen;* Case C-64/08, *Engelmann;* Case C-221/12, *Belgacom.* See also the Commission interpretative communication on the Community law applicable to contract awards not or not fully subject to the provisions of the Public Procurement Directives O.J. 2006, C 179/02.
120. Case C-458/03, *Telaustria,* para 62; Case C-324/98, *Parking Brixen,* para 49. For the requirement that the content and conditions of the contract are also sufficiently clear and predictable, see Joined Cases C-660/11 & C-8/12, *Biasci.* Rather flexible on this last point, Case C-470/11, *Garkalns.*
121. The obligation of transparency does not apply to in-house or quasi-in-house situations where the contracting authority *inter alia* exercises control similar to that which it exercises over its own departments over the entity acquiring a contract. See Case C-107/98, *Teckal;* Case C-573/07, *Sea Srl.* For the inclusion of a private minority shareholder in a semi-public company directly receiving a contract, see Case C-196/08, *Acoset.*
122. This restriction may still be justified: see Case C-113/13, *Azienda sanitaria locale,* where contracts were awarded directly to voluntary associations.
123. For Art. 51 TFEU in the context of services, see M. Hensler and M. Kilian, "Die Ausübung hoheitlicher Gewalt im Sinne des Art. 45 EG", (2005) EuR, 192.
124. For services, e.g. Case C-355/98, *Commission v. Belgium,* para 28; Case C-465/05, *Commission v. Italy* (security guards), para 49.
125. Case 352/85, *Bond van Adverteerders.*

Importantly, in most cases, it will be the national court that eventually rules on the compatibility of an alleged restriction with EU law. In the context of an Article 267 TFEU procedure, the ECJ only provides – more or less detailed – guidance on the interpretation of EU law.[126] Only in the context of an infringement procedure, does the ECJ formally determine the conformity of a national measure with EU law itself. This key role for national courts adds an important dynamic to the application of the free movement provisions in practice.

2.6.1 *Pursuing a legitimate aim*

Treaty-based derogations

In the context of establishment, Articles 51 and 52 TFEU establish that the Treaty provisions shall "not apply to activities within a Member State which are connected, even occasionally, with the exercise of official authority" and shall furthermore "not prejudice the applicability of provisions laid down by law, regulation or administrative action providing for special treatment for foreign nationals on grounds of public policy, public security or public health". Via Article 62 TFEU, the four justificatory aims exhaustively enumerated in Articles 51 and 52 TFEU also apply to services.[127] By now, the different aims of public policy,[128] public security,[129] public health,[130] and public authority[131] have all been adjudicated upon by the ECJ.

In *Reyners*, the Court stated that a whole profession could only be exempt from the fundamental freedom on the basis of Article 51 TFEU when the activities connected with the exercise of official authority are inseparable from the professional activity in question taken as a whole.[132] Concretely, the most typical activities of the profession of *avocat*, such as consultation and legal assistance and also representation and the defence of parties in court, were not considered as connected with the exercise of official authority, as "the exercise of these activities leaves the discretion of judicial authority and the free exercise of judicial power intact".[133] In a series of infringement proceedings against several Member States, the Court confirmed the narrow interpretation of the official authority exception, holding that the activities of notaries are not connected with the exercise of official authority within the meaning of Article 51.[134] Consequently, by imposing a nationality requirement for access to the profession of notary, the six Member States concerned had failed to fulfil their obligations under Article 49 TFEU. In *Hiebler*, the ECJ

126. See Ch. 8, "The EU administration", of this book, on the preliminary reference procedure. For an example of very detailed guidance by the ECJ that is intended to leave very little space for the national court's proportionality assessment, see e.g. Case C-49/98, *Finalarte*; Case C-341/05, *Laval*; Case C-539/11, *Ottica New Line*; Joined Cases C-338/04, C-359/04 & C-360/04, *Placanica*.

127. For Art. 51 TFEU in the context of services see M. Hensler and M. Kilian, op. cit. *supra* note 123.

128. Case 352/85, *Bond van Adverteerders*; Case C-260/89, *ERT*; Case C-348/96, *Calfa*; Case C-36/02, *Omega*; Case C-244/11, *Commission v. Greece*.

129. Case 427/85, *Commission v. Germany*; Case C-266/96, *Corsica Ferries III*; Joined Cases C-430 & 431/99, *Sea-Land Service*. See also Case C-205/99, *Analir*, where the exception was identified in the cabotage regulation.

130. Case C-158/96, *Kohll*; Case C-157/99, *Smits and Peerbooms*; Case C-451/99, *Cura Anlagen*; Case C-262/02, *Commission v. France*; Case C-429/02, *Bacardi*; Case C-89//09, *Commission v. France*; Case C-539/11, *Ottica New Line*.

131. Case C-3/88, *Commission v. Italy*; Case C-198/89, *Commission v. Greece*; Case C-593/13, *Rina Services and Others*.

132. Case 2/74, *Reyners*, paras. 46–47.

133. Case 2/74, *Reyners*, paras. 52–53.

134. Case C-47/08, *Commission v. Belgium*; Case C-50/08, *Commission v. France*; Case C-51/08, *Commission v. Luxembourg*; Case C-53/08, *Commission v. Austria*; Case C-54/08, *Commission v. Germany*; Case C-61/08, *Commission v. Greece*.

recently also established that the fire safety regulation tasks performed by chimney sweeps in the Land of Corinthia are not, as such, connected with the exercise of official authority.[135]

Sometimes, the application of these grounds may require an analysis of the ECHR as well.[136] In *Omega*, the Court held that local authorities could legitimately prohibit the commercial exploitation of games simulating acts of homicide on grounds of protecting public policy, by reason of the fact that "playing at killing people" is an affront to human dignity. Furthermore, Member States have also relied on Article 106(2) TFEU as a justification ground for restricting free movement of services, arguing that a restriction was necessary for the operation of a service of general economic interest.[137]

Judicially created exceptions

Besides the Treaty-based exceptions, the ECJ has recognized an additional category of legitimate aims, the so-called "overriding requirements in the general interest", which may be relied upon to justify restrictive national measures. These "rule of reason" exceptions form an open category: Member States are free to proffer any aim that in their view justifies limiting free movement.[138] Ultimately, it is up to the ECJ, as the final arbiter of EU law, to determine whether a certain objective can indeed form a legitimate aim. The ECJ is usually rather generous in accepting an aim as legitimate, reserving most scrutiny for the proportionality assessment. Importantly, however, the legitimate aim may not be purely economic in nature, i.e. it may not pursue an economic objective such as increasing revenue or protecting a certain economic sector.[139] In the context of services, moreover, the overriding objective that the Member State wants to safeguard may not "already be protected by the rules to which the person providing the services is subject in the Member State in which he is established".[140]

Over the years, the ECJ has considered a great variety of overriding objectives. In particular, the following have been considered and mostly accepted in principle as overriding requirements in the general interest:

– Avoiding the risk of crime.[141]
– Coherence of the fiscal system and effectiveness of fiscal supervision.[142]

---

135. Case C-293/14, *Hiebler*, para 39: this case is situated in the framework of the Services Directive.
136. Case C-36/02, *Omega*.
137. Case C-55/96, *Job Centre*; Case C-266/96, *Corsica Ferries III*; Joined Cases C-147 & 148/97, *Deutsche Post*; Case C-309/99, *Wouters*.
138. For the standard language in the context of services, see Case C-76/90, *Säger*, para 15. The Member State is not formally obliged to explicitly mention the legitimate aim in the act imposing the restriction, but an explicit discussion of the aim relied on may make it easier to justify the measure before the ECJ.
139. Joined Cases 62 & 63/81, *Seco*; Case 352/85, *Bond van Adverteerders*; Case C-353/89, *Commission v. Kingdom of the Netherlands*; Case C-17/92, *Federación de Distribuidores Cinematográficos*; Case C-398/95, *SETTG*; Case C-158/96, *Kohll*; Case C-224/97, *Ciola*; Case C-49/98, *Finalarte*; Case C-221/12, *Belgacom*; Case C-338/09, *Yellow Cab*; or Case C-347/09, *Dickinger*. The risk of seriously undermining the financial balance of the social security system may constitute a legitimate aim. See Case C-158/96, *Kohll*; Case C-157/99, *Smits and Peerbooms*; Case C-372/04, *Watts* or Case C-385/99, *Müller-Fauré*. Moreover, in Case C-448/08, *Sjöberg* the ECJ indirectly seems to allow an economic justification by accepting the objective of preventing private profit from a moral evil (gambling), which indirectly means that all profit from gambling should end up in the public coffers.
140. Case C-76/90, *Säger*, para 15; *Commission v. Italy (security guards)*, para 63; Case C-272/94, *Guiot*. In some contexts, such as gambling, however, the ECJ does not require the Member States to recognize home state controls, allowing them to impose their own rules instead. See very explicitly on this point *Ligua Portuguesa*.
141. Case C-124/97, *Läärä*; Joined Cases C-186/11 & C-209/11, *Stanleybet*; Case C-225/15, *Politanò*.
142. Case C-204/90, *Bachmann*; Case C-300/90, *Commission v. Belgium*; Case C-484/93, *Svensson and Gustavsson*; Case C-451/99, *Cura Anlagen*; Case C-422/01, *Försäkringsaktiebolaget Skandia (publ)*; Case C-334/02,

- Combating concealed employment.[143]
- Combating drug tourism and the accompanying public nuisance.[144]
- Consumer protection.[145]
- Cultural policy.[146]
- Employment conditions.[147]
- Ensuring the adequacy of regular maritime transport services to, from and between islands.[148]
- Ensuring that the provision of medicinal products to the public is reliable and of good quality.[149]
- Ensuring the trustworthiness of persons authorized to trade in military weapons and munitions (in relation to Article 346(1)(b) TFEU).[150]
- Ensuring security of supply as regards defence material.[151]
- Financial balance of the social security system.[152]
- Good reputation of the financial sector.[153]
- Guaranteeing the quality of skilled trade work and protecting those commissioning such work.[154]
- Guaranteeing the lawfulness and legal certainty of documents entered into by individuals.[155]
- Human Dignity[156]
- Linguistic protection.[157]

Commission v. France; C-303/07, *Aberdeen Property Fininvest Alpha Oy*; Case C-311/08, *Société de Gestion Industrielle SA (SGI)*; Case C-337/08, *X Holding*; Case C-35/11, *Test Claimants;* Case C-350/11, *Argenta;* Case C-375/12, *Bouanich*; Case C-591/13, *Commission v. Germany*; Case C-657/13, *Verder*; Case C-66/14, *Finanzamt Linz*; Case C-388/14, *Timac Agro Deutschland.*

143. Case C-255/04, *Commission v. France*, para 52.
144. Case C-137/09, *Josemans*, para 65.
145. Case 220/83, *Commission v. France*; Case 252/83, *Commission v. Denmark*; Case 205/84, *Commission v. Germany*; Case C-154/89, *Commission v. France*; Case C-180/89, *Commission v. Italy*; Case C-198/89, *Commission v. Greece*; Case C-353/89, *Commission v. Kingdom of the Netherlands*; Case C-76/90, *Säger*; Case C-275/92, *Schindler*; Case C-384/93, *Alpine Investments*; Case C-412/93, *TF-1*; Case C-222/95, *Parodi*; Case C-366/97, *Romanelli*; Case C-393/05, *Commission v. Austria*; Case C-404/05, *Commission v. Germany;* Case C-265/12, *Citroën Belux.*
146. Case C-154/89, *Commission v. France*; Case C-180/89, *Commission v. Italy*; Case C-198/89, *Commission v. Greece*; Case C-353/89, *Commission v. Kingdom of the Netherlands*; Case C-211/91, *Commission v. Belgium*; *Commission v. Infront* 2008 ECR I-1451; Case C-250/06, *UPAC v. Belgium*; Case C-195/06, *KommAustria v. ORF.*
147. Case C-272/94, *Guiot.*
148. Case C-205/99, *Analir*, para 27.
149. Case C-141/07, *Commission v. Germany*, para 47; Case C-531/06, *Commission v. Italy*, para 52; Joined Cases C-171/07 & C-172/07, *Apothekerkammer des Saarlandes*; Joined Cases C-570/07 & C-571/07, *Blanco Pérez*; Case C-84/11 *Susisalo and Others.*
150. Case C-474/12, *Schiebel Aircraft GmbH.*
151. Idem.
152. Case C-158/96, *Kohll*; Case C-368/98, *Vanbraekel*; Case C-157/99, *Smits and Peerbooms*; Case C-385/99, *Müller-Fauré*; Case C-372/04, *Watts*; Case C-169/07, *Hartlauer.*
153. Case C-384/93, *Alpine Investments*; Case C-42/02, *Lindman.*
154. Case C-58/98, *Corsten*, para 38.
155. Case C-50/08, *Commission v. France.*
156. Case C-36/02, *Omega.*
157. Case C-211/91, *Commission v. Belgium*, or more recently Case C-222/07, *UTECA*, para 27 (defending and promoting one or several official languages).

- Maintenance of order in society.[158]
- Medical and hospital service of high quality, open to all.[159]
- National, historical and artistic heritage.[160]
- Navigational safety.[161]
- Pluralism in a bilingual region.[162]
- Port safety.[163]
- Preserving the system of administration of justice.[164]
- Preventing abuse of free movement of services.[165]
- Preventing addiction[166]
- Preventing fraud.[167]
- Preventing social dumping.[168]
- Preventing the disclosure of strategic information.[169]
- Preventing unfair competition on the part of undertakings paying their workers at a rate less than the minimum rate of pay.[170]
- Professional rules protecting the recipient of services.[171]
- Proper administration of justice.[172]
- Protection against advertising.[173]
- Protection of the environment.[174]
- Protecting of litigants and the sound administration of justice.[175]
- Protection of workers and the employment market.[176]
- Protection of intellectual property rights.[177]

---

158. Case C-275/92, *Schindler*; Case C-67/98, *Zenatti*.
159. Case C-158/96, *Kohll*, para 50; Case C-157/99, *Smits and Peerbooms*, para 73; Case C-385/99, *Müller-Fauré*, para 73; Case C-496/01, *Commission v. France*; Case C-169/07, *Hartlauer*.
160. Case 180/89, *Commission v. Italy*.
161. Case C-18/93, *Corsica Ferries II*.
162. Case C-250/06, *United Pan-Europe Communications*.
163. Joined Cases C-128/10 & 129/10, *Navtiliaki Etairia Thasou AE*.
164. Case C-3/95, *Sandker*, para 38.
165. Case C-244/04, *Commission v. Germany*, para 38. See for the general ground of preventing abuse of EU law as such also Case C-147/03 *Commission v. Austria*, para 70.
166. Case C-243/01, *Gambelli*, Case C-42/07, *Liga Portuguesa*, Joined Cases C-316/07, C-358/07 to C-360/07, C-409/07 & C-410/07, *Stoß*.
167. Case C-275/92, *Schindler*; Case C-67/98, *Zenatti*.
168. Case C-244/04, *Commission v. Germany*, para 61.
169. Case C-474/12, *Schiebel Aircraft GmbH*.
170. Case C-60/03, *Wolff*, para 41. For the overriding objective of avoiding disturbances on the labour market, see also Case C-445/03, *Commission v. Luxembourg*, para 38.
171. Case 33/74, *Van Binsbergen*; Joined Cases 110 & 111/78, *Van Wesemael*; Case 279/80, *Webb*; Case C-76/90, *Säger*; Case C-106/91, *Ramrath*; Case C-19/92, *Kraus*; Case C-309/99, *Wouters*.
172. Case C-289/02, *AMOK*.
173. Case C-412/93, *TF-1*.
174. Case C-384/08, *Attanasio Group*; Case C-18/93, *Corsica Ferries II* and Case C-17/00, *De Coster*. A.G. Lenz in his Opinion in Case C-37/92, *Vanacker*, comes to the conclusion, on the basis of his analysis of the ECJ's judgment in Case 240/83, *ADBHU*, that this exception does indeed hold for services.
175. Joined Cases C-372/09 & C-73/09 *Peñarroja Fa*.
176. Case 279/80, *Webb*; Joined Cases 62 & 63/81, *Seco*; Case C-113/89, *Rush Portuguesa*; Case C-272/94, *Guiot*; Joined Cases C-369 & C-376/96, *Arblade*.
177. Case 62/79, *Coditel*; Case 395/87, *Tournier*; Joined Cases C-92 & 326/92, *Phil Collins*, and more recently also Case C-403/08, *Football Association Premier League* and Case C-351/12, *OSA*.

- The necessity of complying with the principle of legal certainty.[178]
- The right to take collective action for the protection of the workers of the host state against possible social dumping.[179]
- The quality of postgraduate education.[180]
- Rationalization of the service provided to users.[181]
- Road safety.[182]
- Social policy objectives.[183]
- Social policy reasons.[184]
- Social protection of workers.[185]
- Technical aspects of life assurance taxation.[186]

Justifying discriminatory restrictions under the rule of reason?

According to traditional doctrine, directly discriminatory measures can only be justified under Treaty-based exceptions, whereas indirectly and non-discriminatory measures can also be justified under "rule of reason" objectives.[187] In its 2009 *Commission v. Spain* ruling, the Court was very outspoken on the issue, holding that "although a certain number of overriding reasons in the public interest have indeed been recognized [...] the fact remains that those objectives cannot be relied upon to justify discriminatory restrictions".[188] However, as with goods, this doctrine has not always been adhered to that rigorously by the ECJ.[189] Where it prefers a more flexible approach, the ECJ usually does not confront the discriminatory nature of a measure directly, but rather sidesteps it by categorizing a national measure generally as a restriction to freedom of movement instead of specifically as a discrimination. A clear and unequivocal statement from the Court on this point would be beneficial for legal certainty.

Combining multiple legitimate aims

Often, the assessment of a restriction focuses on one legitimate aim. The ECJ, however, has accepted that measures can serve multiple legitimate aims simultaneously.[190] Where the different

178. Case C-347/06, *ASM Brescia SpA* 2008, para 64; Case C-98/14 *Berlington.*
179. Case C-341/05, *Laval.*
180. Case 523/12, *Dirextra Alta Formazione.*
181. Case C-384/08, *Attanasio.*
182. Case C-55/93, *Van Schaik*; Case C-451/99, *Cura Anlagen*; C-384/08, *Attanasio.*
183. Case C-355/00, *Freskot.*
184. Case C-275/92, *Schindler.*
185. Case C-255/04, *Commission v. France*, para 47.
186. Case C-118/96, *Safir.*
187. Case C-353/89, *Commission v. Kingdom of the Netherlands*; Case C-288/89, *Gouda*, para 11, Case C- 17/92, *FDC*, para 15; Case C-224/97, *Ciola*; Case C-451/99, *Cura Anlagen*; Case C-341/05, *Laval*, paras. 116–117, Case C-546/07, *Commission v. Germany*, para 47 (but also see paras. 43 and 51), as well as S. O'Leary and J.M. Fernández-Martín, "Judicially-created exceptions to the free provision of services" in M. Andenas, W.-H. Roth, *Services and Free Movement in EU Law* (OUP, 2002), 163.
188. Case C-153/08, *Commission v. Spain*, paras. 36–37.
189. This especially in the context of taxation, see eg. Case C-118/96, *Safir*. But also *Smits Peerebooms* and Case C-42/02, *Lindman* 2003.
190. A difference should be made here between 1) the different political aims that may underlie the adoption of a national measure, 2) the aim or aims that a Member State formally relies on to justify a measure before a court, and 3) the aim or aims that the relevant court actually identifies and uses for the proportionality test. It is for example possible that the ECJ only focuses on one of the multiple aims mentioned in the legislative history, or that it accepts a new aim not even mentioned at all. See Case C-203/08, *Betfair* or Joined Cases C-447/08 & C-448/08, *Sjöberg.*

objectives do not interfere, for example protecting the environment and protecting consumers, such a combination is normally unproblematic. Sometimes, however, the different aims may conflict, such as where a measure aims to both limit gambling opportunities and to create a sufficient and attractive legal supply of games of chance to pre-empt illegal gambling.[191] This then gives rise to complex questions on proportionality, and especially consistency.[192]

2.6.2 *The proportionality assessment*

To be justified, a restriction must comply with the principle of proportionality. As with the other freedoms, this means that the restriction must be both *suitable* and *necessary* to achieve the desired aim(s).[193] The formally one-size-fits-all test of proportionality involves a balancing act for the national court or the ECJ, which inevitably presupposes a degree of latitude. It has the advantage of being flexible, allowing the ECJ to vary its level of scrutiny according to the particular context. In complex, sensitive areas, the ECJ often grants more leeway to the Member States. But this flexibility comes at a price, as it creates a level of legal uncertainty.

Suitability and consistency

For a restriction to be suitable, it must firstly be "appropriate for ensuring attainment of the objective pursued".[194] In *IPTM*, for example, in which the refusal to admit EU citizens not resident in Portugal to the examination for the award of a recreational boating licence was at issue, the ECJ found that the residence condition, which bears no relation to training or to the ability to sail, "is not in itself appropriate for attaining the objective pursued, that is to ensure safety of navigation at sea".[195] In contrast, in *Commission v. France*, a prohibition on broadcasting advertising for alcoholic beverages during sporting events was found suitable to combat alcohol abuse and therefore protect public health.[196]

In *Gambelli*, the ECJ further developed the concept of suitability by including a consistency requirement. The case concerned the Italian regulation of games of chance, which formally served the legitimate aims of protecting consumers and preventing fraud and gambling addiction. The referring court, however, also "pointed out that the Italian State is pursuing a policy of substantially expanding betting and gaming at national level with a view to obtaining funds [...]".[197] The actual policy of the Italian Government, awarding e.g. a large number of new licences, therefore seemed partially at odds with the legitimate aims it claimed to pursue. Confronted with these facts, the ECJ held that the Italian restriction could only be considered suitable where it served "to limit betting activities in a *consistent and systematic* manner".[198] This requirement became known as the *consistency* or *hypocrisy* test: a restriction is not suitable where the aim it pursues is simultaneously contradicted or undermined by other actions of the Member State.[199] First developed in the context of gambling, this test has now been generalized. In

191. Case C-203/08, *Betfair*.
192. See the discussion in the gambling cases further *infra*.
193. Case C-49/98, *Finalarte*.
194. Case C-76/90, *Säger*, para 15, Case C-433/04, *Commission v. Belgium*, para 33; Case C-164/99, *Portugaia Construções*, para 19; Case C-279/00, *Commission v. Italy*, para 33; Case C-445/03, *Commission v. Luxembourg*, para 21; Case C-53/13, *Strojírny Prostějov. and ACO Industries Tábor*, para 44.
195. Case C-509/12, *IPTM*,; Case C-53/13, *Strojírny Prostějov. and ACO Industries Tábor*.
196. Case C-262/02, *Commission v. France (Loi Evin)*, para 30.
197. Case C-243/01, *Gambelli*, para 68; Case C-212/08, *Zeturf*, para 70.
198. Case C-243/01, *Gambelli*, para 67.
199. In a sense one can compare this logic to cases such as *Jany* and *Conegate* where the ECJ finds that a Member State cannot prohibit the import of products or services that may be legitimately produced or offered

Hartlauer, which concerned the Austrian requirement of prior authorization for the establishment of new outpatient dental clinics, the ECJ formulated it as follows: "national legislation is appropriate for ensuring attainment of the objective pursued only if it genuinely reflects a concern to attain it in a consistent and systematic manner".[200]

The ECJ can be seen to police consistency with differing degrees of rigour. In *Gambelli*, and in other gambling cases, for example, the ECJ left the consistency assessment to the national of courts, contenting itself with subtle or less subtle hints.[201] Conversely, in *Hartlauer*, the ECJ was rather strict on consistency: Austria did not require prior authorization for the setting up of group practices, which were considered sufficiently equivalent to outpatient dental clinics; therefore the Austrian measure did not consistently pursue its aim of preventing the risk of serious harm to the financial balance of the social security system, and the measure was not suitable.[202]

Where the ECJ allows Member States to pursue multiple yet contradictory aims with one measure, the test seemingly shifts from consistency to one of "balance" between the different contradictory aims.[203] In *Ladbrokes*, the Court first observed that the fact that the objective of protecting consumers from gambling addiction "is, in principle, difficult to reconcile" with a policy of expanding games of chance, does not render the Dutch policy in itself inconsistent. It then added that "a fair balance has to be drawn between demand for the controlled expansion of authorized games of chance with the aim of making the provision of such games attractive for the public and the need to reduce as far as possible consumer addiction to such games".

This discretion for the ECJ to choose the intensity of its consistency review generally appears justified: often national measures must serve multiple, competing objectives, which need to be reconciled. At the same time, the test applied may become so flexible as to lose most of its limiting effect.

Necessity

In addition to being suitable, a restriction "must not go beyond what is necessary in order to attain the objective pursued".[204] This necessity test essentially asks whether the legitimate aim cannot be achieved in a less restrictive manner, and therefore at a lower cost to free movement. Generally, it also encapsulates a possible third limb of proportionality, concerning the proportionality *sensu strictu*, meaning that the restrictive or disadvantageous effects of a measure must remain limited, and in any event reasonable in view of the aims pursued. The necessity test is a very factual and contextual one, requiring an assessment of possible alternatives for the

---

nationally. National production is not consistent with an import ban and actually contradicts the aim of the import ban, which is to make a product unavailable, Case C-268/99, *Jany* and Case 121/85, *Conegate*.

200. Case C-169/07, *Hartlauer*, para 55; Cases C-570/07 and C-571/07, *Blanco Pérez*, para 94; Case C-539/11, *Ottica*, para 47; Case C-367/12, *Sokoll-Seebacher*, para 39; Case C-293/14 *Hiebler*, para 65; Case C-500/06, *Corporación Dermoestética*, para 39.
201. In the case of Italy, moreover, these increasingly obvious indications of inconsistency were ignored by the Italian Supreme Court in judgment 111/04 of 26 Apr. 2004, *Gesualdo*, but even then the ECJ did not go so far as applying the consistency test itself in the context of gambling. Similarly, see Case C-262/02, *Commission v. France (Loi Evin)*, especially paras. 33–39.
202. Case C-169/07, *Hartlauer*, para 63. Here one can also detect a certain link or at least resemblance between consistency and equal treatment.
203. Cf. the language of the ECJ in Case C-258/08, *Ladbrokes*, paras. 30–32.
204. Case C-678/11, *Commission v. Spain*, para 42. See also Case C-523/12, *Dirextra Alta Formazione*, para 24; Case C-341/05, *Laval*, para 101; Case C-76/90 *Säger*, para 15; Joined Cases C-369/96 & C-376/96, *Arblade*, para 35; Case C-58/98 *Corsten*, para 39; Case C-390/99, *Canal Satélite Digital*, para 33.

contested restrictive measure.[205] In most cases, the necessity test forms the real stumbling block for justification. As with the other freedoms, where the ECJ has recognized that Member States retain a margin of discretion in this regard, and often leaves it to the national courts to adjudicate, it has also not refrained from considering available alternatives and applying the necessity test rather strictly in some cases either.[206]

A nice illustration of a strict application of necessity can be found in several of the cases concerning cross-border health care.[207] In *Kohll*, the ECJ held that Article 56 TFEU precludes national rules which make reimbursement of the cost of dental treatment provided by an orthodontist established in another Member State, in accordance with the rates of the state of insurance, subject to prior authorization by the insured person's social security institution. Luxembourg submitted that the requirement of prior authorization was necessary to safeguard public health, to control health expenditure, and to protect the financial balance of the social security scheme.[208] The ECJ was not convinced, however, about the necessity of the measure. As regards the need to protect public health, it pointed out that the professions of doctor and dentist had been harmonized and that Member States should trust the quality of doctors and dentists established in other Member States, which "must be afforded *all guarantees* equivalent to those accorded to doctors and dentists established on national territory, for the purposes of freedom to provide services".[209] As regards the necessity to control health expenditure and to protect the financial balance of the social security scheme, the Court merely pointed out that remuneration for expenses was requested at the Luxembourg rate, meaning there would be no increased costs. As regards the necessity to provide a balanced medical and hospital service accessible to all, the Court concluded that it had not been demonstrated that the measure was *indispensable* for the maintenance of an *essential* treatment facility or medical service on national territory.[210] In *Geraets-Smits*, the ECJ did accept, in view of the same objectives as in *Kohll*, that the requirement of prior authorization could be justified in the case of assumption of costs for hospital treatment in another Member State, subject however to the normality and the necessity of the treatment. It further specified that "normal treatment" means that authorization cannot be refused when the treatment concerned is sufficiently tried and tested by international medical science, and that authorization can only be refused on the ground of lack of medical necessity if the same or equally effective treatment can be obtained without undue delay at an establishment in the home Member State.[211]

Evidently, a strict check of proportionality in general or necessity in specific is not confined to the context of health care. In *dos Santos Palhota*, for example, concerning the posting of workers, the Court established that a prior declaration of secondment would be "just as effective

205. In the context of services, necessity also looks at possible supervision and control by other Member States. As the ECJ held in Case C-465/05, *Commission v. Italy (security guards)*, para 63: "Thus, a measure introduced by a Member State, which in effect duplicates supervision which has already been carried out in the Member State where the service provider is established, cannot be considered necessary to attain the objective pursued".
206. See also Case C-389/05, *Commission v. French Republic* (Artificial insemination centre for bovine animals). Note that these centers had already been the subject of earlier judgments, only then in relation to the free movement of goods. See Case 271/81, *Béarn* and Case C-323/93, *Crespelle*; Case C-465/05, *Commission v. Italy* (*Security Guards*).
207. In the context of cross-border health care, Directive 2011/24 on the application of patients' rights was adopted, *inter alia* codifying much of the precious ECJ case law: see O.J. 2011, L 88/45.
208. Case 158/96, *Kohll*, paras. 37–38.
209. Idem, para 48.
210. Idem, para 52, our italics.
211. Case C-444/05, *Stamatelaki*.

whilst being less restrictive" and thus a more proportionate means for attaining the goal of ensuring compliance with social welfare and wage legislation of the host Member State than a work licensing mechanism, prior checks or a confirmation of posting.[212]

One particular way for the ECJ to be strict on necessity is to set a high standard of proof. It is always up to the Member State that wants to justify a restriction to provide "all the evidence of such a kind as to enable the court to be satisfied that the measure does indeed comply with the requirements deriving from the principle of proportionality".[213] The ECJ can therefore ask the Member State to substantiate its claims about the actual risks addressed and the effectiveness of the restrictive measures imposed. In *Blanco and Fabretti,* the ECJ did not accept the general claims that casinos in other Member States were connected with criminal activities, and that most of the proceeds of organized crime were made outside Italy, but required actual proof to support these claims.[214] Just how much and what kind of "evidence" is required can differ. In *Pfleger,* the ECJ indicated that the mere fact that a "Member State is not able to produce studies serving as the basis for the adoption of the legislation at issue" does not automatically mean a measure cannot be justified.[215] In other circumstances, the ECJ may require objective, detailed evidence.[216]

Conversely, the ECJ can also be very flexible in applying proportionality. It has given Member States and national courts unprecedented leeway to justify restrictive measures when regulating games of chance.[217] Regulation of gambling is complex and contested as financial, social and moral compasses seemingly do not point in the same direction. In *Liga Portuguesa* the ECJ stated that "in the absence of Community harmonization in the field, it is for each Member State to determine in those areas, in accordance with its own scale of values, what is required in order to ensure that the interests in question are protected".[218] This *general* discretionary margin to regulate gambling is subsequently used to virtually dismantle the necessity test within the proportionality assessment.[219] For example, both the Commission and many providers of gambling services have argued that multi-licence systems with strict licence conditions and supervision can protect public order and consumers just as well as exclusive licences or state monopolies.[220] This is a classic necessity argument, entailing that the overriding aims relied on by the Member States may be achieved by less restrictive means. In the context of gambling, however, the ECJ almost invariably leaves the assessment of the necessity of a restriction to the discretion of the

212. Case C-515/08, *dos Santos Palhota,* paras. 51–53.
213. Case C-98/14, *Berlington,* para 65.
214. Case C-98/14, *Berlington,* paras. 41–42. Note that this case concerns the taxation on gambling profits, and therefore not the regulation of gambling itself, which seems to translate immediately into a stricter necessity test.
215. Case C-390/12, *Pfleger,* para 51.
216. Case C-390/12, *Bressol,* para 71 (our italics). Although this case concerned EU citizenship, the sections on the evidence required to justify a restriction are also relevant for services.
217. This leeway only concerns the regulation of gambling itself, not the *procedure* to award any licences for games of chance that are available. In this formal aspect the ECJ takes a much stricter approach, *inter alia* applying a very strict necessity test. See Joined Cases C-338/04, C-359/04 & C-360/04, *Placanica,* later confirmed in, e.g. Case C-347/09, *Dickinger and Ömer* and Cases C-72/10 and C-77/10, *Costa and Cifone.*
218. Case C-42/07, *Liga Portuguesa,* para 57. This formulation links to the earlier formulations in Case C-275/92, *Schindler* para 32 and *Placanica* para 47. This formulation is also used verbatim in, e.g., Joined Cases C-447/08 & C-448/08, *Sjöberg,* para 37;, Joined Cases C-186/11 & C-209/11, *Stanleybet,* para 24; Case C-156/13, *Digibet,* para 24, and Case C-98/14, *Berlington,* para 56, although there the "scale of values" is replaced with the even more far reaching "in principle, free". For a mix of both lines, see Joined Cases C-316/07, C-358/07, C-359/07, C-360/07, C-409/07 & C-410/07, *Stoß,* para 76.
219. See especially Case C-42/07, *Liga Portuguesa* para 57; or Case C-275/92, *Schindler,* para 61.
220. Case C-275/92, *Schindler,* para 55, Case C-124/97, *Läärä,* para 11.

Member States.[221] In *Liga Portuguesa*, for example, the ECJ held that it was up to the Member State to determine *what is required* to ensure protection of the interests in question.[222] In *Carmen Media*, it seemingly even went one step further, holding that the *choice of methods* for controlling gambling "falls within the margin of discretion which the national authorities enjoy".[223] As a consequence, providers are pre-empted from relying on examples from other Member States to show that similar levels of control and protection may be achieved via less restrictive alternatives, and therefore that gambling regulation in particular Member States may go beyond what is necessary.[224]

Strikingly, the ECJ also does not require Member States to take existing home state controls into account, rejecting the requirement of mutual recognition, even where providers are already under strict supervision in their home state that matches or exceeds supervision in the host state. The mere fact that an operator lawfully offers gambling opportunities via the Internet from a Member State where it is subject to regulation and control, "cannot be regarded as amounting to a sufficient assurance that national consumers will be protected against the risks of fraud and crime, in the light of the difficulties liable to be encountered in such a context by the authorities of the Member State of establishment in assessing the professional qualities and integrity of operators".[225]

Equally, the standard of proof imposed on Member States is often set at a remarkably low level, certainly in comparison to other free movement cases.[226] The ECJ, for example, is willing to accept claims that foreign gambling operators cannot effectively be supervised and controlled or that national measures actually achieve their stated objectives without requiring any substantial evidence, even where these statements are contested and challenged with evidence.[227]

Consequently, the example of gambling clearly evidences the flexibility with which the ECJ can adapt the formally speaking one-size-fits-all internal market test to different freedoms.[228] This flexibility may be necessary in light of the enormous diversity in services, but at the same time exacts a price in legal certainty.

2.6.3 *Compliance with fundamental rights*

Finally, a restriction can only be justified when it also complies with fundamental rights, which now includes all rights guaranteed under the Charter, the general principles of EU law, and the European Convention of Human Rights. Although the ECJ does not often refer to this requirement explicitly, it can be used as a separate requirement that must be met to justify a restriction. In *ERT*, for example, in the context of establishment, the ECJ held that "the national rules in question can fall under the exceptions provided for by the combined provisions of Articles 56

---

221. See Case C-275/92, *Schindler*, para 61; Case C-124/97, *Läärä* para 39; Case C-67/98, *Zenatti*, para 33; Case C-6/01, *Anomar* para 87 and Case C-243/01, *Gambelli*, para 63.
222. Case C-42/07, *Liga Portuguesa*, para 57.
223. Case C-46/08, *Carmen Media*, para 59. Similarly see C-448/08, *Sjöberg*, paras. 40 and 45 and C-410/07, *Stoß*, paras. 79–82, and 92.
224. Case C-42/07, *Liga Portuguesa*, para 68.
225. Case C-42/07, *Liga Portuguesa*, paras. 68–69. See also A. Dawes and K. Struckmann, "Rien ne va plus? Mutual recognition and the free movement of services in the gambling sector after the Santa Casa judgment", 35 El Rev. (2010), at 236, as well as the general case law of the ECJ on double burdens discussed above.
226. On the required level of evidence-based proof see S. Planzer, "ECJ on gambling addiction – Absence of an evidence-oriented approach", 1 *European Journal of Risk Regulation* (2010), at 289.
227. See for example Case C-410/07, *Stoß*, para 72, holding that it is not necessary to produce a study serving as the basis for the adoption of the legislation at issue.
228. In a different context, see for example Case C-262/02, *Commission v. France (Loi Evin)*, para 33 or Case C-222/07, *UTECA*, para 36, as well as the discussion in D. Chalmers et al., *EU Law* (CUP, 2006), 833–834.

and 66 only if they are compatible with the fundamental rights the observance of which is ensured by the Court".[229] This finding was later confirmed, also for services, in *Carpenter*, where it was held that the decision to deport Mrs Carpenter constituted an interference with the exercise by Mr Carpenter of his right to respect for his family life within the meaning of Article 8 ECHR.[230]

2.7 The Services Directive

In 2006, the Directive on services in the internal market was adopted.[231] Importantly, and contrary to what its name suggests, the Services Directive also contains rules on establishment. It is one of the most contested pieces of legislation in EU history, *inter alia* because it developed into a symbol of the perceived clash between a "market" Europe and a "social" Europe.[232] From an ambitious proposal intended to liberalize the services sector based on the country of origin principle, it was gradually watered down to a rather underwhelming instrument. The Directive that emerged does comprise important provisions concerning administrative simplification and cooperation, but also contains a lot of opt-outs from its scope and in terms of substance essentially largely codifies the case law of the ECJ.[233] The hard-fought political compromises contained in the Directive, moreover, have led to convoluted and sometimes unclear language. This creates legal uncertainties, especially where the Directive, intentionally or not, does seem to deviate from the case law of the ECJ. These different flaws further cement the status of the Services Directive as a missed opportunity to further complete the EU's internal market.[234] Be that as it may, under the *Tedeschi* principle, it does now form the default legal framework applicable to those services not excluded from its scope, and hence the first port of call when assessing a potential restriction on services or establishment.

This section briefly discusses four main elements of the Directive, being its scope, administrative simplification and cooperation, prohibited and suspect restrictions to establishment, and the test for restrictions to services under Article 16 of the Directive.[235]

---

229. Case C-260/89, *ERT*, para 43.
230. Case C-60/00, *Carpenter*, para 40. In the context of goods see Case C-368/95, *Familiapress*, para 24. Even though this last case only mentions that justifications "must also be interpreted in the light of the general principles of law and in particular of fundamental rights", it does refer back to the clearer language in *ERT*.
231. Directive 2006/123/EC on services in the internal market, O.J. 2006, L 376/37.
232. On the preceding debates, see Editorial Comments, (2006) CML Rev., 307–311.
233. On the evolution of the proposal, see J.-V. Louis and S. Rodrigues (Eds.) *Les services d'intérêt général et l'Union européenne* (Bruylant, 2006); O. de Schutter and S. Francq, "La proposition de directive relative aux services dans le Marché intérieur: reconnaissance mutuelle, harmonisation et conflicts de lois dans l'Europe élargie", (2005) CDE, 603–660., C. Barnard, "Unravelling the Services Directive", 45 CML Rev. (2008), 323; K. Nicolaïdis and S. Schmidt, "Mutual recognition on trial : The long road to services liberalization", 14 *Journal of European Public Policy* (2007), 717.
234. See very critically for example B. de Witte, "Setting the scene: How did services get to Bolkestein and why?" EUI Working Paper 20/2007.
235. So far the ECJ has applied the Services Directive in the following cases: Joined Cases C-340/14 & C-341/14, *Trijber and Harmsen*; Case C-293/14, *Hiebler*; Case C-179/14, *Commission v. Hungary*; Case C-593/13, *Rina Services*; Case C-57/12, *Femarbel*; Case C-119/09, *Société fiduciaire nationale d'expertise comptable*. The Services Directive was held not to be applicable in the following cases: Case C-342/14, *X-Steuerberatungsgesellschaft*; Case C-168/14, *Grupo Itevelesa and Others*; Case C-315/13, *De Clercq and Others*; Case C-351/12, *OSA*; Case C-162/12, *Airport Shuttle Express*; Case C-539/11, *Ottica New Line*; Case C-197/11, *Libert*; Joined Cases C-357/10 to C-359/10, *Duomo Gpa*; Case C-458/08, *Commission v. Portugal*; Case C-61/08, *Commission v. Greece*; Case C-53/08, *Commission v. Austria*; Case C-52/08, *Commission v. Portugal*; Case C-50/08, *Commission v. France*; and Case C-47/08, *Commission v. Belgium*.

2.7.1 *Scope*

In principle, the Directive applies to services supplied by providers established in a Member State.[236] The political controversy surrounding the Services Directive was partially solved by carving out many areas of the supposedly general scope of the Directive. Article 1 of the Directive already excludes multiple areas, including, in particular, services of general economic interest, measures to protect or promote cultural or linguistic diversity or media pluralism, Member States' rules of criminal law, labour law, or the right to negotiate, conclude and enforce collective agreements.

Article 2 excludes multiple categories of services as well, including non-economic services of general interest, financial services, electronic communications services, services in the field of transport, audiovisual services, gambling, social services, private security services, and services provided by notaries and bailiffs. Importantly, it also excludes services of temporary work agencies and healthcare services.[237] The Directive also does not apply to the field of taxation.

Concerning the Directive's relationship with other provisions of EU law, Article 3 confirms that in the event of a conflict between provisions of the Services Directive with a provision of another EU act governing specific aspects of access to or exercise of a service activity, the latter shall prevail. This is an application of the *lex specialis generalis derogat* adage. This includes Directive 96/71 on posted workers,[238] former social security Regulation 1408/71 on Directive 89/552 on television broadcasting,[239] and Directive 2005/36 on the recognition of professional qualifications.[240] Article 3 further stipulates that the Directive does not concern rules of private international law.

Summarizing, service activities come within the scope of the Services Directive, unless they fall under one of the many exceptions.

2.7.2 *Administrative simplification and cooperation*

One of the main contributions of the Services Directive concerns administrative simplification.[241] Member States must simplify procedures and formalities applicable to access to a service activity where necessary.[242] More concretely, Article 5(3) of the Directive obligates Member States to recognize certificates or any other documents attesting a certain requirement has been met by the service provider in another Member State. In principle, Member States may not require originals or certified copies or translations, which should make it easier for service providers to rely on their home state qualifications.

Member States are also obligated to create a so-called "point of single contact". They have to ensure that all relevant practical information is easily accessible to providers and recipients through these points of single contact. A service provider must be able to complete all formalities "needed for access to his service activities, in particular, all declarations, notifications or applications necessary for authorization from the competent authorities, including applications

---

236. Art. 2(1) Services Directive.
237. See for Art. 2(2)(d) of the Services Directive Joined Cases C-340/14 & C-341/14, *Trijber and Harmsen*, 40–42 and Case C-168/14, *Grupo Itevelesa and Others*. For 2(2)(f) see Case C-57/12, *Femarbel*and; and Case C-539/11, *Ottica New Line*. For 2(2)(i) see Case C-293/14, *Hiebler*, paras. 27–47. For 2(2)(j) see Case C-57/12, *Femarbel*and; and Case C-197/11, *Libert*.
238. O.J. 1997, L 18/1.
239. O.J. 1989, L 298/23.
240. O.J. 2005, L 255/22.
241. Ch. II of the Services Directive.
242. Art. 5(1) of the Services Directive. For further evaluation requirements also see Arts. 5, 9(2), 15(5), 25(3) and 39 of the Services Directive.

for inclusion in a register, a roll or a database, or for registration with a professional body or association".[243] All Member States have complied with this obligation by establishing online "e-government portals".[244]

Besides procedural simplification, the Directive also provides for administrative cooperation. Chapter VI establishes that Member States shall give each other mutual assistance and shall put in place measures for effective cooperation, with a view to ensuring the supervision of the provision of services. The assistance may take the form of information supply, supervision, involve an alert mechanism when service activities could cause serious damage to the health or safety of persons or to the environment, etc.[245]

2.7.3 *Authorizations, prohibited and suspect restrictions to establishment*

Chapter 3 of the Services Directive deals with the freedom of establishment. Articles 9–13 provide general criteria for authorization schemes, the granting of authorizations, the duration of authorizations, award procedures, and the selection of candidates, basically codifying the case law of the ECJ in this respect.

Article 14 of the Directive provides a list of requirements that are always prohibited.[246] The prohibited requirements include discriminatory requirements based directly or indirectly on nationality or, in the case of companies, the location of the registered office. The prohibition encompasses discriminatory requirements concerning the provider, his staff, persons holding the share capital or members of the provider's management or supervisory bodies. It also captures any requirement that the provider, his staff, persons holding the share capital or members of the provider's management or supervisory bodies be resident within the territory. In addition, further prohibited requirements include prohibitions on having an establishment in more than one Member State, restrictions on the freedom of a provider to choose between a principal or a secondary establishment, an obligation to provide or participate in a financial guarantee, or an obligation to have been pre-registered. This list of prohibited requirements is based on existing case law of the ECJ, but does provide more legal certainty to service providers.

Additionally, Article 15 provides a list of requirements that are "suspect". Member States are under the obligation to evaluate existing suspect requirements, and as of 28 December 2006 have to notify any new suspect requirements they wish to introduce to the Commission.[247] Suspect requirements include, *inter alia*, quantitative or territorial restrictions, in particular in the form of limits fixed according to population or of a minimum geographical distance between providers, an obligation on a provider to take a specific legal form, requirements which relate to the shareholding of a company or fixed minimum and/or maximum tariffs with which the provider must comply. Such suspect requirements are only allowed if they meet the requirements of Article 15(3), meaning that they may not discriminate directly or indirectly, and must proportionately serve an overriding reason relating to the public interest.[248]

243. Art. 6 of the Services Directive.
244. Available at <ec.europa.eu/internal_market/eu-go/index_en.htm>.
245. Arts. 28–36 of the Directive.
246. For applications of Art. 14, see Case C-179/14, *Commission v. Hungary*, paras. 42–48 and Case C-593/13, *Rina Services*, paras. 25–40.
247. Art. 15(6) and (7) of the Services Directive.
248. Art. 15(3) of the Services Directive, just like Art. 16, defines the concept of necessity as serving an overriding reason, just one example of unnecessary legal confusion. For an application of Art. 15, see Case C-293/14, *Hiebler*, paras. 48–79 and Case C-179/14, *Commission v. Hungary*.

2.7.4 *Restrictions on services*

Article 16 is the main provision concerning restrictions on services. It stipulates firstly that Member States shall in principle ensure free access to and free exercise of a service activity in their territory. Exceptions to this general obligation must comply with the requirements of non-discrimination, transparency and proportionality.[249] Subsequently, Article 16 also contains a list of prohibited restrictions, which include, *inter alia*, any obligation on the provider to have an establishment in the host Member State, or a ban on setting up a certain form or type of infrastructure.[250]

Seemingly, the test for justification under Article 16(1) follows the standard justification test for free movement as developed by the ECJ. There is however one important *caveat*: Article 16(1) only mentions four possible grounds for justification, being the three traditional grounds of public policy, public security and public health that already appear in in Article 52(1) TFEU, with the sole addition of environmental protection. Besides these justificatory grounds, Article 17 contains several additional – general – derogations from the freedom to provide services, stipulating that Article 16 does not apply to, e.g. services of general economic interest which are provided in another Member State, matters covered by Directive 96/71, acts requiring the involvement of a notary, or the registration of vehicles in another Member State.[251] Moreover, "by derogation from Article 16, and in exceptional circumstances only", Article 18 allows additional "case-by-case" derogations, but only relating to "the safety of services".

This limited set of grounds for justification raises the question whether Member States may still rely on the many other overriding requirements in the general interest recognized by the ECJ to justify restrictions to services falling under the scope of the Directive.[252] So far this question has not been answered by the ECJ. The issue did arise in *OSA*, but the ECJ did not have to rule on it as ultimately the copyright issues at stake were excluded from the scope of the Directive under Article 17.[253] Consequently, it currently remains an open question whether Member States can only rely on the justificatory grounds expressly enumerated in Article 16(1), or whether they can also invoke other grounds. On the one hand, the explicit addition of environmental protection could be taken to imply that the legislator intended to exclude other overriding objectives of public concern. On the other hand, the far-reaching consequences of such a reading, combined with the general poor level of drafting of the Services Directive argue for the conclusion that Member States may still rely on an open category of justificatory grounds as well. Excluding all other ground for justification would drastically reduce the regulatory space of Member States and undermine the unity in the legal framework for services. After all, the rule of reason was created by the ECJ precisely in response to a (too) imitative list of Treaty exceptions, and if the ECJ can complement the Treaty itself, it may be argued it could certainly complement a Directive as well.

3. Free movement of capital

Nowadays, the free movement of capital and the creation of a Capital Markets Union are regarded as factors of crucial importance for the achievement of financial stability and sustainable

249. For an application of Art. 16, see Case C-179/14, *Commission v. Hungary*, paras. 102–117.
250. Art. 16(2) of the Services Directive. See also Art. 19 for prohibited restrictions on recipients of services.
251. See on Art. 17(6), Case C-342/14, *X-Steuerberatungsgesellschaft* and on 17(11), Case C-351/12, *OSA*.
252. See *supra* section 2.6.1 for an overview of these objectives.
253. Case C-351/12, *OSA*.

growth in the European Union.[254] This was not always the case, however. In comparison with the other fundamental freedoms, the free movement of capital followed a slow development. Only with the Maastricht Treaty, capital developed into a fully-fledged freedom.

The present section analyses the current legal framework on capital and payments as enshrined in Chapter 4 of Title 4 of the TFEU (Arts. 63–66 TFEU) and interpreted by the ECJ.

3.1 *Historical overview*

Originally, Article 67 EEC was formulated differently from the other Treaty provisions on goods, persons and services, in the sense that it contained a qualified obligation: the abolition of capital restrictions between Member States was to be achieved only "to the extent necessary to ensure the proper functioning of the common market". Also Article 71 EEC merely required Member States to "endeavour to avoid" the introduction of new exchange restrictions on capital movements. As a result, the ECJ in *Casati* refused to recognize the direct effect of Article 67 EEC, holding that complete freedom of capital could "undermine the economic policy of the Member States or create an imbalance of payments, thereby impairing the proper functioning of the common market".[255] In this way, it refrained from applying the classic negative integration approach developed in the framework of the other freedoms.[256]

Initially, the abolition of capital restrictions was thus left to the Council, which adopted three directives on the basis of Article 69 EEC Treaty. The first two were adopted in 1960[257] and 1963.[258] They essentially divided capital movements into four annexed lists (A, B, C and D), which would follow a different degree of liberalization. The third directive, Directive 88/361,[259] was the most important one as it "brought about the full liberalization of capital movements".[260] Its first article required Member States to abolish restrictions on movements of capital taking place between persons resident in Member States. In *Bordessa*, the Court ruled that this prohibition of capital restrictions was directly effective and could thus be relied on before national courts by individuals.[261]

Ultimately, capital would mature into a fully-fledged freedom only with the entry into force of the Maastricht Treaty in 1993 and the establishment of the EMU. At the 1988 European Council in Hannover, a committee, under the chairmanship of European Commission president Delors, was entrusted with the task of preparing a report on the realization of the EMU. The Delors report would greatly influence the legal set-up for the EMU that found its way into the Treaty on the European Union.[262] The report considered a complete liberalization of capital movements an indispensable requirement for the creation of a monetary union.[263] To achieve this, Article

---

254. Commission Staff Working Document on the movement of capital and the freedom of payments, SWD(2015)58 final, Brussels, 5 March 2015.
255. Case 203/80, *Casati*, para 9.
256. J. Snell, "Free movement of capital: Evolution as a non-linear process" in P. Craig and G. De Búrca (Eds.), *The Evolution of EU Law* (OUP, 2011), 547–574.
257. "First Council Directive for the implementation of Art. 67 of the Treaty", O.J. 1960, 43, at 921–932.
258. "Second Council 63/21/EEC Directive of 18 Dec. 1962 adding to and amending the First Directive for the implementation of Art. 67 of the Treaty", O.J. 1963, 9, 62–74.
259. Council Directive 88/361/EEC of 24 June 1988 for the implementation of Art. 67 of the Treaty, O.J. 1988, L 178, at 5–18.
260. Joined Cases C-358/93 & C-416/93, *Bordessa*, para 17.
261. Ibid., paras. 33–35.
262. The EMU is dealt with in Ch. 26 of this book.
263. Committee for the Study of Economic and Monetary Union, "Report on economic and monetary union in the European Community" (1989), at 11.

73b of the Maastricht Treaty provided that all restrictions on capital movements and payments were to be prohibited.

3.2 *Scope and effect of the current Treaty provisions*

3.2.1 *Direct effect*

Article 63 TFEU unequivocally prohibits all restrictions on the movement of capital between Member States and between Member States and third countries. The waiting for the recognition of direct effect of Article 63 TFEU was not long and came in *Sanz de Lera*.[264] This has substantially accelerated the evolution of the case law in this area.[265]

Until now, the ECJ has refrained from expressly ruling on the issue of horizontal direct effect of Article 63 TFEU. This has been explained by the fact that a substantial part of the capital case law concerns taxation, "a quintessentially vertical subject matter".[266] In the golden shares case law, the Court has avoided the question by qualifying the contested special rights as "state measures".[267] Interestingly, in an *obiter dictum* in the *EDP* case, the Court seemed to rule out the horizontal applicability of Article 63 TFEU.[268] It has been argued that this should be interpreted as meaning that if the Member State merely makes use of the rights available to all shareholders, this might not be a restriction falling within the scope of Article 63 TFEU.[269]

3.2.2 *Territorial scope*

The most important distinguishing feature of the free movement of capital is the fact that it applies not only to Member States but also to third countries. The prohibition of Article 63 TFEU extends also to all restrictions on the movement of capital between Member States and third countries.[270] The Court has observed that the external dimension of the free movement of capital may pursue objectives other than that of establishing the internal market, such as, in particular, that of ensuring the credibility of the single currency on world financial markets and maintaining financial centres with a world-wide dimension within the Member States.[271] In subsequent case law, this has been interpreted so as to cover restrictions on capital movements involving the provision of financial services between Member States and third countries,[272] national measures which restrict payments of dividends deriving from investments to or from

264. Joined Cases C-163/94, C-165/94 & C-250/94, *Sanz de Lera*, para 41. Equally, Case C-101/05, *Skatteverket v. A*, para 21.
265. See J. Usher, "The evolution of the free movement of capital", 31 *Fordham International Law Journal* (2007), 1533–1570; S. Peers, "Free movement of capital: Learning lessons or slipping on spilt milk?" in C. Barnard and J. Scott (Eds.), *The Law of the Single European Market: Unpacking the Premises* (Hart, 2002), 333–350; J. Snell, op. cit. *supra* note 256. L. Flynn, "Free movement of capital" in C. Barnard and S. Peers (Eds.), *European Union Law* (OUP, 2014), 443–472.
266. C. Barnard, *The Substantive Law of the EU: The Four Freedoms* (OUP, 2016), at 526.
267. Case C-112/05, *Commission v. Germany*. For an academic discussion see in particular C. Gerner-Beuerle, "Shareholders between the market and the state. The VW law and other interventions in the market economy", 49 CML Rev. (2012), 97–144; D. Saam & P. Zumbansen, "The ECJ, Volkswagen and European corporate law: Reshaping the European varieties of capitalism", 8 GLJ (2007), 1027–1052.
268. Case C-543/08, *Commission v. Portugal*, para 62.
269. K. Engsig Sørensen, "Company law as a restriction to free movement – Examination of the notion of "restriction", using company law as the frame of reference", 11 ECL (2014), 178–188 at 186. See also the cited books S. Grundmann, *European Company Law – Organization, Finance and Capital Markets* (Intersentia, 2012); A. Dashwood et al., *Wyatt and Dashwood's European Union Law* (Hart, 2011).
270. See also Case C-439/97, *Sandoz*, para 18.
271. Case C-101/05, *Skatteverket v. A*, para 31.
272. Case C-560/13, *Wagner-Raith*, para 37.

third countries,[273] or national tax legislation under which the dividends paid by companies established in a Member State to an investment fund established in a non-Member State are not the subject of a tax exemption, while investment funds established in that Member State receive such an exemption.[274]

Article 63 TFEU conveys the impression that capital movements between Member States and between Member States and third countries are treated in the same way. That is however not completely the case. Other Treaty provisions impose a number of limits on capital movements to or from third countries, creating a less liberal framework for extra-EU capital flows.

Firstly, the "grandfather clause" contained in Article 64(1) TFEU allows Member States to maintain restrictions that existed on 31 December 1993 under national or Union law on capital movements to or from third countries involving direct investment – including in real estate – establishment, the provision of financial services or the admission of securities to capital markets.[275] According to the same article, in respect of restrictions existing under national law in Bulgaria, Estonia and Hungary, the relevant date is 31 December 1999, and in respect of restrictions existing under national law in Croatia, the relevant date is 31 December 2002.

Secondly, Articles 64(2) and (3) and Article 65(4) TFEU are legal bases for further legislative action at EU level. Article 64(2) merely requires the European Parliament and the Council to "endeavour to achieve" the objective of free movement of capital between Member States and third countries "to the greatest extent possible". Article 64(3) TFEU allows for the adoption of measures which constitute a step backwards in Union law as regards the liberalization of the movement of capital to or from third countries. Article 65(4) TFEU allows the Council to adopt a decision stating that restrictive national tax measures concerning one or more third countries are nevertheless to be considered compatible with the Treaties in so far as they are justified by one of the objectives of the Union and compatible with the proper functioning of the internal market.[276] This clause, conferring on the Council the competence to rule on the legality of national measures, something that is normally reserved for the Court, was inserted in the Lisbon Treaty. It is said to signal a distrust on the part of the Member States towards the ECJ when it comes to capital movements with third countries.[277]

Thirdly, in exceptional circumstances, Article 66 TFEU allows the adoption of safeguard measures where movements of capital to or from third countries cause, or threaten to cause, serious difficulties for the operation of the Economic and Monetary Union.[278] These safeguard measures must be strictly necessary and may last for a maximum of six months.

---

273. Case C-446/04, *Test Claimants in the FII Group Litigation*, para 183.
274. Case C-190/12, *Emerging Markets Series of DFA Investment Trust Company*, para 35.
275. Recently, the Court ruled that the opening of a securities account by a resident of a Member State with a banking institution outside the EU (*in casu* in Switzerland) comes within the concept of a movement of capital involving the provision of financial services, within the meaning of Art. 64(1) TFEU. Furthermore, it held that Art. 64(1) TFEU applied even where the capital restriction imposed by the national legislation could also be applied to situations which have nothing to do with direct investment, establishment, the provision of financial services or the admission of securities to capital markets. See Case C-317/15 *X v. Staatssecretaris van Financiën*, paras. 31 and 25.
276. It has been observed that Art. 65(4) TFEU bears a certain resemblance to Art. 108(2)(3) TFEU. See J. Snell, op. cit. *supra* note 256, at 553.
277. Ibid. See also C. Barnard op. cit. *supra* note 266, at 524–525.
278. The case law on Art. 66 TFEU (previously Art. 59 EC) relates to the failure of some Member States to adopt appropriate steps to eliminate incompatibilities between BITs concluded with third countries prior to accession to the EU and the Treaties (see, for instance, Case C-118/07 *Commission v. Finland*). However, it does not provide any examples as to what measures could be adopted under this provision. Legal scholarship has tried to identify various scenarios which could potentially trigger the application of Art. 66 TFEU.

Finally, Article 75 TFEU provides for the definition of a framework for administrative measures with regard to capital movements and payments, such as the freezing of assets, as part of the fight against terrorism. This provision was amended in the Lisbon Treaty and moved to Title V on the area of freedom, security and justice. Before Lisbon, Article 60 (2) EC empowered Member States to take unilateral measures against a third country with regard to capital movements and payments for serious political reasons and on grounds of urgency, provided that the Council had not acted and that they had informed the Commission and the other Member States. This provision was repealed by the Lisbon Treaty. However, Article 215 TFEU currently provides a legal basis for the interruption or reduction, in part or completely, of the Union's economic and financial relations with one or more third countries, where such restrictive measures are necessary to achieve the objectives of the Common Foreign and Security Policy.

3.2.3 *Material scope*

Contrary to the previous regime, in which there were two different provisions – Article 67 EEC on capital movements and Article 106 EEC on payments –, Article 63 TFEU covers both capital movements and payments. The difference between these two notions is that "capital movements" refer to financial operations essentially concerned with the investment of funds, rather than to remunerations for a service, whereas "payments" refer to the transfers of foreign exchange which constitute the consideration for an underlying transaction. This distinction was first made in *Luisi and Carbone*, concerning fines imposed on two Italian residents for purchasing various currencies for tourism and medical treatment abroad in excess of the maximum amount permitted by Italian law.[279] The Court clarified that the physical transfer of bank notes may therefore not be classified as a movement of capital where the transfer in question corresponds to an obligation to pay arising from a transaction involving the movement of goods or services.[280]

The Treaty provisions refrain from offering any indication as to what financial transactions fall within the scope of the free movement of capital. In the absence of any Treaty definition of capital movements, the ECJ uses the non-exhaustive nomenclature in Annex I of Directive 88/361 as having indicative value for the purposes of defining capital movements.[281] This list includes a wide variety of capital movements, such as direct investments,[282] investments in real estate,[283] operations in securities (e.g. resale of shares,[284] bonds,[285] receipt of dividends[286]), fi-

---

These include undesired interest rate developments, currency instability, heavy foreign exchange speculation, extreme imbalance of payments and overheated economic expansion. See U. Becker, *European Fundamental Rights and Freedoms* (Walter de Gruyter, 2007), at 359.

279. Joined Cases 286/82 & 26/83, *Luisi and Carbone*.
280. Ibid., paras. 21–22. The same approach was followed in Case 308/86, *Lambert*. See also Case C-412/97, *ED Srl v. Italo Fenocchio*.
281. Case C-222/97, *Trummer and Mayer*, para 21; Joined Cases C-105/12 to C-107/12, *Essent NV*, para 40.
282. Case C-282/04, *Commission v. Kingdom of the Netherlands*, para 19; Case C-367/98, *Commission v. Portugal*, para 38; Case C-174/04, *Commission v. Italy*, para 12; Case C-39/11, *VBV – Vorsorgekasse*, para 21; Case C-483/99, *Commission v. France*, para 37; Case C-503/99, *Commission v. Belgium*, para 38.
283. Case C-370/05, *Festersen*, para 23; Case C-452/01, *Ospelt*, para 7; Joined Cases C-515/99, C-519/99 to C-524/99 & C-526/99 to C-540/99, *Reisch and others*, para 29; Case C-386/04, *Centro di Musicologia Stauffer*, paras. 23–24.
284. Case C-265/04, *Bouanich v. Skatteverket*, para 29.
285. Case C-329/03, *Trapeza tis Ellados*, para 34.
286. Case C-35/98, *Verkooijen*, paras. 28–30. Although not expressly mentioned in the nomenclature annexed to Directive 88/361, the receipt of dividends necessarily presupposes participation in undertakings referred to in Heading I (2) of the nomenclature and therefore it is indissociable from a "capital movement" according

nancial loans and credits,[287] mortgages and other guarantees,[288] gifts and endowments[289] and inheritances.[290]

3.3 *Relationship with the other freedoms*

In practice, it is sometimes difficult to determine which fundamental freedom is applicable to a given situation. According to well-established case law, the *purpose* of the legislation at issue must be taken into consideration.[291] Where a national measure relates to several fundamental freedoms at the same time, the Court will in principle examine the measure in relation to only one of those freedoms if it appears, in the circumstances of the case, that the other freedoms are entirely secondary in relation to the first and may be considered together with it.[292] However, when the contested national measure is generally applicable with no principal purpose related to a particular freedom, the Court applies the relevant Treaty provisions simultaneously.[293]

3.3.1 *Capital versus Services*

In *Fidium Finanz*,[294] the Court had the opportunity to clarify the demarcation between services and capital. The case concerned the authorization requirement under German legislation for the operation of lending activities in Germany by the Swiss undertaking Fidium. The Court first examined whether the activity of granting credit on a commercial basis was a service or a capital movement. In that regard, it noted that the business of a credit institution consisting of granting credit constitutes a service within the meaning of Article 56 TFEU.[295] This conclusion was reinforced by reference to Directive 2000/12/EC relating to the taking up and pursuit of the business of credit institutions, which sought to regulate the activity of granting loans, *inter alia*, from the point of view of both the freedom of establishment and the freedom to provide financial services. At the same time, the Court acknowledged that loans and credits granted by non-residents to residents feature under Heading VIII of Annex I to Directive 88/361. Thus, the granting of credit on a commercial basis is an activity falling within the scope of both Article 56 and Article 63 TFEU.[296]

Nevertheless, the "predominant consideration" was freedom to provide services, as the rules impeding access to the German financial market for companies established in non-member

---

to the judgment in *Verkooijen*. In fact, in the case of dividends from a company established in another Member State and quoted on the stock exchange, this can even qualify as "acquisition by residents of foreign securities dealt in on a stock exchange" as referred to in Heading III. A (2) of Annex I to Directive 88/361.

287. Case C-452/04, *Fidium Finanz*, para 42; Case C-282/12, *Itelcar*, para 14; Case C-578/10, *van Putten and Others*, para 36; Case C-478/98, *Commission v. Belgium*.
288. Case C-222/97, *Trummer and Mayer*, paras. 24, 34; Case C-279/00, *Commission v. Italy*, para 37.
289. Case C-318/07, *Persche*, paras. 24, 25.
290. Case C-256/06, *Jäger*, para 25; Case C-513/03, *van Hilten-van der Heijden*, para 42; Case C-364/01, *Barbier*, para 58.
291. Case C-157/05, *Holböck*, para 22; Case C-196/04, *Cadbury Schweppes*, paras. 31–33; Case C-452/04, *Fidium Finanz*, paras. 34, 44–49; Case C-374/04, *Test Claimants in Class IV of the ACT Group Litigation*, paras. 37 and 38; Case C 446/04, *Test Claimants in the FII Group Litigation*, para 36; Case C-524/04, *Test Claimants in the Thin Cap Group Litigation*, paras. 26–34.
292. Case C-233/09, *Dijkman*, para 33; Case C-42/07, *Liga Portuguesa*, para 47; Case C-452/04, *Fidium Finanz*, para 34.
293. Joined Cases C-155/08 & C-157/08, *X and E.H.A. Passenheim-van Schoot*.
294. Case C-452/04, *Fidium Finanz*.
295. Ibid., para 39. See also the case law cited: Case C-484/93, *Svensson and Gustavsson*, para 11; Case C-222/95, *Société civile immobilière Parodi*, para 17.
296. Case C-452/04, *Fidium Finanz*, para 43.

countries affected primarily the freedom to provide services.[297] The effect of reducing cross-border financial traffic relating to credit services was merely an *unavoidable consequence* of the restriction on the freedom to provide services.[298] However, the Court concluded that the Treaty provisions of services could not be relied on by an undertaking established in a third country and there were no grounds for examining the compatibility of the national rules with the free movement of capital.[299] It has been suggested that the "predominant consideration" criterion was intentionally fashioned by the Court in order to limit the scope of the third-country dimension of Article 63 TFEU.[300]

3.3.2 *Capital versus Establishment*

The crucial criterion to distinguish between capital and establishment is the exercise of definite influence over the management of the company. Provisions of national law which apply to the possession, by nationals of a Member State, of holdings in the capital of a company established in another Member State allowing them to exert a definite influence on the company's decisions and to determine its activities, fall within the ambit of Article 49 TFEU.[301] Conversely, "direct investments", i.e. investments of any kind made by natural or legal persons which serve to establish or maintain lasting and direct links between the persons providing the capital and the company to which that capital is made available in order to carry out an economic activity, fall within the scope of Article 63 TFEU.[302] National legislation which is not limited to those shareholdings which enable the holder to have a definite influence on a company's decisions and to determine its activities, but which applies irrespective of the size of the holding which the shareholder has in a company, may come under both Articles 49 and 63 TFEU.[303]

The Court introduced a further distinction between "direct" and "portfolio" investments: on the one hand, "direct investments" are investments in the form of participation in an undertaking through the holding of shares, which confers the possibility of effectively participating in its management and control; on the other hand, "portfolio" investments are investments in the form of the acquisition of shares on the capital market solely with the intention of making a financial investment without any intention to influence the management and control of the undertaking.[304] Both direct and portfolio investments are referred to in Annex I of Directive 88/361 and thus fall within the scope of Article 63 TFEU, blurring somehow the distinction between shareholdings falling within the scope of establishment and those falling within the scope of capital.

It has been suggested that when the Court wants to limit the scope of its rulings to investors coming from Member States and exclude third country investors, it upholds the application of

297. Ibid., para 49.
298. Ibid.
299. Ibid., paras. 47, 51.
300. O'Brien, "Case C-452/04, Fidium Finanz AG v. Bundesanstalt für Finanzdienstleistungsaufsicht, judgment of the Court of Justice (Grand Chamber) of 3 Oct. 2006, 2006 ECR I-9521", 44 CML Rev. (2007), 1483–1499, at 1495.
301. Case C-244/11, *Commission v. Greece*, para 21; Case C-212/09, *Commission v. Portugal*, para 42; Case C-326/07, *Commission v. Italy*, para 34; Case C-543/08, *Commission v. Portugal*, para 41; Case C-251/98, *Baars*, para 22; Case C-436/00, *X and Y*, paras. 37, 66–68.
302. Case C-212/09, *Commission v. Portugal*, para 43; Case C-112/05, *Commission v. Germany*, para 18; Case C-326/07, *Commission v. Italy*, para 35; Case C-543/08, *Commission v. Portugal*, para 42; Case C-446/04, *Test Claimants in the FII Group Litigation*, paras. 36–38; Case C-157/05, *Holböck*, paras. 23–25.
303. Case C-81/09, *Idryma Typou*, para 49; Case C-326/07, *Commission v. Italy*, para 36.
304. Joined Cases C-105/12 to C-107/12, *Essent NV*, para 40; Case C-182/08, *Glaxo Wellcome*, para 40; Case C-81/09, *Idryma Typou*, para 49; Case C-201/15, *AGET Iraklis*, para 58.

the freedom of establishment, as the latter does not apply to third country investments.[305] Overall, however, the Court's case law appears to indicate a preference for capital over establishment, especially in the context of taxation.[306]

3.4 *Restrictions*

The long-standing debate on the distinction between non-discrimination and market access does not resonate – at least not to the same extent – in the field of capital.[307] The wording of Article 63 TFEU goes beyond the mere elimination of unequal treatment on grounds of nationality and prohibits all restrictions on the movement of capital between Member States and between Member States and third countries.[308]

3.4.1 *Discriminatory measures*

Although rare, cases of direct discrimination do exist in the capital case law. They are regarded as overt restrictions on capital movements. Thus, the Court has set aside a Portuguese provision precluding investors from other Member States from acquiring more than a given number of shares in certain Portuguese undertakings,[309] an Austrian provision exempting only Austrian nationals from having to obtain authorization before acquiring a plot of land,[310] or an Italian provision exempting only Italian nationals from the requirement of obtaining an authorization to buy a property in certain parts of the national territory.[311]

With respect to indirectly discriminatory measures, the Court has found that Danish legislation on agriculture imposing a residence requirement, which could be waived only with the authorization of the minister responsible for agriculture, restricted the free movement of capital.[312] Furthermore, Belgian rules which resulted in an inheritance consisting of immovable property situated in Belgium being subject to transfer duties that were higher than the inheritance duties payable if the person whose estate was being administered had been residing in that Member State at the time of death, were found to have the effect of restricting the movement of capital.[313] Similarly, the Court held that a Portuguese provision under which the amount of capital gains realized by residents when transferring immovable property was to be taken into account as to only 50% of its amount, whereas for non-residents the full amount of capital gains was subject to tax, constituted a capital restriction.[314]

---

305. See for example the outcome of Case C-244/11, *Commission v. Greece*, para 26, where the contested Greek legislation was intended primarily to control speculative hostile acquisitions by sovereign wealth funds established in non-member countries.
306. See indicatively the recent Case C-157/05, *Holböck*, paras. 22–24; Case C-47/12, *Kronos International*. See also W. Schön, "Free movement of capital and freedom of establishment", 17 EBOR (2016), 229–260.
307. L. Flynn, "Freedom to fund?: The effects of the internal market rules, with particular emphasis on free movement of capital" in U. Neergaard et al. (Eds.), *Social Services of General Interest in the EU* (Springer, 2013), at 188.
308. Case C-98/01, *Commission v. UK*.
309. Case C-367/98, *Commission v. Portugal*, para 40.
310. Case C-302/97, *Konle*, para 23.
311. Case C-423/98, *Albore*, para 16.
312. Case C-370/05, *Festersen*, para 25.
313. Case C-11/07, *Eckelkamp*, paras. 45–46.
314. Case C-443/06, *Hollmann*, paras. 36, 40.

3.4.2 *Non-discriminatory measures*

Direct investments

The Court has adopted a broad interpretation of the concept of capital restriction. This can be evidenced especially in the *golden shares* case law.[315] The Court has consistently ruled that the special rights retained by the state in privatized undertakings restrict capital movements, as they are liable to deter or discourage foreign investors form investing in the undertakings at issue. This rigorous application of the free movement of capital has far-reaching implications for national corporate governance systems. This is why Member States have tried to argue that, under certain conditions, golden shares should be placed beyond the reach of free movement rules through the application of a *Keck*-inspired approach. However, so far the Court has not accepted this argument, without however dismissing it in principle.[316]

Another important restriction on capital movements is the *authorization requirement* which is usually imposed by national legislation for certain types of investments. According to settled case law, a requirement of prior authorization is a disproportionate restriction on capital movements, as it causes the exercise of the free movement of capital to be subject to the discretion of the administrative authorities and can thus be such as to render that freedom illusory.[317] Instead of prior authorization, the national authorities can adopt less restrictive measures, such as a system of declaration.[318]

Also national legislation imposing qualification requirements, e.g. providing that members of companies and firms operating pharmacies can only be pharmacists, amounts to a restriction on the freedom of establishment and the free movement of capital, for it prevents investors from other Member States who are not pharmacists from acquiring stakes in companies and firms of that kind.[319]

Investments in real estate

With respect to investments in real estate, the Court has primarily qualified authorization and residence requirements as capital restrictions. Thus, it has ruled that a prior authorization procedure is likely to discourage non-residents from making investments in immovable property and therefore such an obligation constitutes a restriction under Article 63 TFEU.[320] Moreover, the Court has held that Article 63 TFEU precludes national legislation which lays down, as a

315. Case C-58/99, *Commission v. Italy*; Case C-367/98, *Commission v. Portugal*; Case C-483/99, *Commission v. France*; Case C-503/99, *Commission v. Belgium*; Case C-463/00, *Commission v. Spain*; Case C-98/01, *Commission v. UK*; Case C-174/04, *Commission v. Italy*; Joined Cases C-282/04 & C-283/04, *Commission v. Kingdom of the Netherlands*; Case C-112/05, *Commission v. Germany*; Joined Cases C-463/04 & C-464/04, *Federconsumatori*; Case C-274/06, *Commission v. Spain*; Case C-207/07, *Commission v. Spain*; Case C-326/07, *Commission v. Italy*; Case C-171/08, *Commission v. Portugal*; Case C-543/08, *Commission v. Portugal*; Case C-212/09, *Commission v. Portugal*; Case C-244/11, *Commission v. Greece*; Case C-95/12, *Commission v. Germany*.
316. Case C-463/00, *Commission v. Spain*; Case C-98/01, *Commission v. UK*; Case C-171/08, *Commission v. Portugal*; Case C-543/08, *Commission v. Portugal*; Case C-219/09, *Commission v. Portugal*.
317. Joined Cases C-358/93 and C-416/93, *Bordessa*, para 25; Joined Cases C-163/94, C-165/94 and C-250/94, *Sanz de Lera*, para 141; Case C-54/99, *Eglise de Scientologie de Paris*, para 14; Case C-302/97, *Konle*, para 39; Joined Cases C-515/99 et al., *Reisch*, para 32; Case C-567/07, *Sint Servatius*, para 22; Case C-197/11, *Libert*, paras. 46–47; Case C-39/11, *VBV – Vorsorgekasse*, paras. 22, 27.
318. Joined Cases C-358/93 & C-416/93, *Bordessa*, paras. 26–27.
319. Case C-531/06, *Commission v. Italy*, paras. 47–48.
320. Case C-302/97, *Konle*, para 39; Case C-567/07, *Sint Servatius*, para 39; Case C-197/11, *Libert*, paras. 46–47; Case C-452/01, *Ospelt*, para 34.

condition for acquiring an agricultural property, the requirement that the acquirer take up fixed residence on that property.[321]

Mortgages

With respect to mortgages, the Court has found that the prohibition on the creation of a mortgage in a foreign currency constitutes a restriction on capital movements, for it deprives the private parties concerned of a right which constitutes a component element of the free movement of capital and payments.[322] The effect of such a prohibition is to weaken the link between the debt to be secured, payable in the currency of another Member State, and the mortgage, whose value may, as a result of subsequent currency exchange fluctuations, come to be lower than that of the debt to be secured. This can only reduce the effectiveness of such a security, and thus its attractiveness.[323]

Financial loans and credits

The Court has also found that provisions, implying that a bank must be established in a Member State in order for recipients of loans residing in its territory to obtain an interest rate subsidy from the state out of public funds, are liable to dissuade those concerned from approaching banks established in another Member State and therefore constitute an obstacle to movements of such capital.[324] Furthermore, provisions which discriminate according to the place where the loan is contracted are likely to deter residents from contracting loans with persons established in other Member States and therefore constitute a restriction on the movement of capital.[325] Finally, national legislation which prohibits the acquisition by persons resident in a Member State of securities of a loan issued abroad constitutes a restriction of the free movement of capital.[326]

Taxation

The case law on taxation is very rich and covers different types of taxes and transactions. To mention but some examples, firstly, in relation to the sale of shares, the Court has ruled that national legislation under which the *profits from sales of shares* in foreign limited companies are taxable as soon as the shareholding amounted to 1%, whereas the profits from sales of shares in limited companies governed by national law were taxable only when that shareholding amounted to 10%, introduces a difference in treatment on the basis of the place of investment of the capital and has the effect of discouraging a shareholder from investing his capital in a company established in another state.[327]

Secondly, the Court has ruled that Article 63 TFEU precludes national legislation on *dividends taxation* which makes the granting of a tax advantage (e.g. tax exemption or reduced tax rate) subject to the condition that the dividends are paid by companies established within national territory.[328]

---

321. Case C-370/05, *Festersen*, paras. 25, 48; Case C-302/97, *Konle*, para 40; Joined Cases C-515/99 et al., *Reisch*, para 33; Case C-452/01, *Ospelt*, para 34.
322. Case C-222/97, *Trummer and Mayer*, paras. 26–28.
323. Ibid.
324. Case C-484/93, *Svensson and Gustavsson*, para 10.
325. Case C-439/97, *Sandoz*, para 31.
326. Case C-478/98, *Commission v. Belgium*, paras. 15, 19.
327. Case C-436/06, *Grønfeldt*, paras. 13–14; Case C-446/04, *Test Claimants in the FII Group Litigation*, para 166.
328. Case C-35/98, *Verkooijen*, paras. 34–36; Case C-194/06, *Orange European Smallcap Fund*, para 65; Case C-513/04, *Kerckhaert and Morres*, para 24; Case C-379/05, *Amurta*, paras. 15, 25–28; Case C-101/05, *Skatteverket v. A*, paras. 41–43; Case C-446/04, *Test Claimants in the FII Group Litigation*, para 74.

Thirdly, in *corporate taxation*, a taxpayer's right to deduct from his taxable profits the losses relating to the partial reduction in value of the shares held in the company, where the reduction in value of the shares results from the distribution of the profits, undeniably constitutes a tax advantage.[329] The Court has ruled that the granting of that advantage to a resident taxpayer only where he acquires shares in a resident company from a resident shareholder makes shares held by non-residents less attractive and is, therefore, likely to dissuade the resident taxpayer from acquiring them. In addition, such a difference in treatment is also likely to dissuade non-resident investors from acquiring shares in the resident company and therefore to represent an obstacle to that company's accumulation of capital from other Member States. Thus, it constitutes a restriction on the free movement of capital.[330] Moreover, national legislation under which a resident company cannot deduct from its taxable revenue reductions in profit resulting from the partial write-down of holdings in non-resident companies, whereas it can do so in relation to holdings in resident companies, has a restrictive effect on capital movements.[331]

Fourthly, in relation to *income from capital and movable property*, the Court found that the Belgian tax legislation, which established less favourable tax treatment of income from capital and movable property received by non-resident investment companies with no permanent establishment in Belgium in comparison with income earned by resident investment companies or non-resident companies with a permanent establishment in Belgium, constituted a capital restriction.[332] In the same vein, regarding immovable property, the Portuguese provision, laying down a basis of assessment of 50% applicable only to capital gains, realized by taxable persons residing in Portugal and not to those realized by non-resident taxable persons was found to be a restriction on the movement of capital.[333]

Finally, the Court has developed a rich case law on *inheritance taxation* which in essence prohibits national provisions whose effect is to reduce the value of the inheritance of a resident of a State other than the Member State in which the assets concerned are situated and which taxes the inheritance of those assets.[334] In particular, the Court found that EU law precludes national legislation according to which, in order to assess the property's value, the fact that the person holding legal title was under an unconditional obligation to transfer it to another person who has financial ownership of that property, may be taken into account if, at the time of his death, the former resided in that Member State, but may not be taken into account if he resided in another Member State.[335] Furthermore, the Court ruled that Belgian legislation making a distinction in relation to the limitation period for the valuation of registered shares for the purposes of inheritance tax according to the location of the issuing company's centre of effective management constituted a restriction on the free movement of capital.[336]

3.5 *Justifications*

As with the other fundamental freedoms, restrictions on the free movement of capital can be justified either by express Treaty derogations or by the judicial "overriding reasons in the public

329. Case C-182/08, *Glaxo Wellcome*, paras. 53–59.
330. Ibid., paras. 53–59.
331. Case C-377/07, *STEKO Industriemontage*, paras. 25–27.
332. Case C-387/11, *Commission v. Belgium*, paras. 38–40.
333. Case C-443/06, *Hollmann*, paras. 35–36, 39.
334. Case C-484/93, *Svensson and Gustavsson*, para 10; Case C-222/97, *Trummer and Mayer*, para 26; Case C-439/97, *Sandoz*, para 19; Case C-364/01, *Barbier*, para 62; Case C-513/03, *van Hilten-van der Heijden*, para 44; C-43/07, *Arens-Sikken*, para 37; Case C-11/07, *Eckelkamp*, para 44; Case C-256/06, *Jäger*, para 30.
335. Case C-364/01, *Barbier*, para 62.
336. Case C-132/10, *Halley*, paras. 23–25.

interest". According to orthodox doctrine, the first category is an exhaustive list of derogations applying to both distinctly (i.e. directly discriminatory) and indistinctly (i.e. both indirectly and non-discriminatory) applicable measures, whereas the second category is open-ended and applies only to indistinctly applicable measures. Moreover, the justification grounds must comply with the principles of legal certainty and proportionality.

3.5.1 *Treaty derogations*

Article 65 TFEU contains two express derogation: one specific (Art. 65(1)(a) TFEU) and one general (Art. 65(1)(b) TFEU).

Firstly, Article 65(1)(a) TFEU specifically allows Member States to apply national legislation which distinguishes between resident and non-residents taxpayers in relation to matters of direct taxation. Considering the relative lack of fiscal harmonization at EU level, Member States felt the need to introduce into the Maastricht Treaty (then Art. 73d (1) (a) of the Treaty) a derogation that allows for a certain degree of fiscal differentiation of taxpayers according to their place of residence (fiscal non-residents benefit from tax exemptions in most Member States) or the place where the capital is invested (usually, foreign investments will be discriminated against through less favourable tax treatment).[337] As explained in *Verkooijen*,[338] even before the entry into force of the Maastricht Treaty, national tax legislation differentiating between resident and non-resident taxpayers was justified on the condition that it applied to situations which were not objectively comparable, or it could be justified by overriding reasons in the general interest, in particular in relation to the cohesion of the tax system. This was essentially the codification of the *Schumacker* and *Bachmann* case law.[339]

This derogation has been strictly interpreted by the ECJ. In most circumstances, the situations of resident and non-resident taxpayers are found to be comparable, excluding the application of this derogation. In *Lenz*,[340] which concerned an Austrian legislation providing for half-rate taxation only in relation to revenue from capital of Austrian origin, the Court emphasized that Article 65(1)(a) TFEU does not render automatically any tax legislation making a distinction between taxpayers by reference to the place where they invest their capital compatible with the Treaty.[341] The derogation should be read in conjunction with the third paragraph of Article 65 TFEU, according to which the national legislation shall not constitute a means of arbitrary discrimination or a disguised restriction on the free movement of capital.[342] *In casu*, the Court found that in relation to a tax rule designed to attenuate the effects of double taxation of the profits distributed by the company in which the investment was made, shareholders, who were fully taxable in Austria and received revenue from capital from a company established in another Member State, were therefore in a situation comparable with that of shareholders who were likewise fully taxable in Austria but received revenue from capital from a company established in Austria.[343] Thus, the national legislation at issue could not be justified. Similarly, in *Grünewald*,[344] the Court found that the German Income Law which discriminated against non-residents in relation to the deductibility of annuities paid in the context of anticipated suc-

337. European Commission, *European Economy* (Directorate-General for Economic and Financial Affairs, 6/2003), 321.
338. Case C-35/98, *Verkooijen*, para 43.
339. Case C-279/93, *Schumacker*; Case C-204/90, *Bachmann*; Case C-300/90, *Commission v. Belgium*.
340. Case C-315/02, *Lenz*.
341. Ibid., para 26.
342. Ibid.
343. Ibid., para 32.
344. Case C-559/13, *Grünewald*.

cession infringed the free movement of capital. By reference to *Schröder*,[345] the Court explained that, in relation to direct taxes, the situations of residents and of non-residents are generally not comparable, firstly because non-residents in most cases only receive part of their total income in the Member State in question, and secondly because it is easier to assess their ability to pay tax at the place of their residence.[346] However, the situations are comparable where the non-resident receives no significant income in the state of his residence and obtains the greater part of his taxable income from an activity performed in the other Member State concerned.[347] Furthermore, with respect to expenses directly linked to an activity that has generated taxable income in a Member State, residents of that state and non-residents are in a comparable situation.[348] The Court found that in the case at hand the situations were comparable and thus the difference in treatment was not justified by Article 65(1)(a) TFEU.

Secondly, Article 65(1)(b) TFEU contains a general derogation from the free movement of capital, similar to the ones contained in Articles 36, 45(3) and 52 TFEU concerning the other freedoms. This general derogation recognizes three legitimate objectives that Member States can invoke in order to justify the imposition of a restriction on capital movements. First, they are allowed to adopt restrictive measures in order to prevent infringements of national law and regulations in particular in the field of taxation and prudential supervision of financial institutions. Secondly, the Treaty permits procedures for declarations of capital movements for purposes of administrative or statistical information. Those two derogations are also to be found in Article 4 of the Third Capital Directive. Finally, as with the other freedoms, reasons related to public policy or public security can provide a safety net for national regulatory measures.

The first ground of justification was successfully invoked in the *Sandoz* case,[349] which concerned the compatibility with EU law of an Austrian rule under which the tax authorities could levy a stamp duty of 0.8% on the value of loans contracted by resident borrowers with non-resident lenders. The Court ruled that the Austrian legislation deprived residents of a Member State of the possibility of benefiting from the absence of taxation, which may be associated with loans obtained outside the national territory.[350] Therefore, this measure was likely to deter such residents from obtaining loans from persons established in other Member States and as such constituted an obstacle to the free movement of capital.[351] Nevertheless, the duty was regarded as justified on the ground of Article 65(1)(b) TFEU. In particular, the Court accepted the arguments brought forward by the Austrian Government that first, due to the partial harmonization of tax law, the imposition of an indirect tax was within the competence of the Member States and second, the contested tax was justified by the need to observe the principle that residents should be treated equally for tax purposes.[352] The purpose of the legislation was to prevent taxable persons from evading the requirements of domestic tax legislation through the exercise of the freedom of movement of capital. The Court also found that the contested measure was not a means of arbitrary discrimination, as it applied to all borrowers resident in Austria without distinction on grounds of nationality or the place where the loan was contracted.[353] Thus, the measure was considered to be essential in order to prevent infringements of national tax law, as

345. Case C-450/09, *Schröder*, para 37.
346. Case C-559/13, *Grünewald*, para 25.
347. Ibid., para 27.
348. Ibid., para 29.
349. Case C-439/97, *Sandoz*.
350. Ibid., para 19.
351. Ibid., para 20.
352. Ibid., para 23.
353. Ibid., paras. 25–26.

provided for in Article 65(1)(b) TFEU. It has been suggested that this case should be treated with considerable caution, as the Court appears to be extremely generous in permitting essentially all equally applicable national tax rules.[354]

As evidenced by the words *in particular*, the list of grounds on which Member States are allowed to take restrictive measures in order to prevent infringements of national law and regulations is non-exhaustive. The reference to taxation and prudential supervision of financial institutions is a mere indication of the purpose which this derogation provision serves. This was underlined in *Bordessa*,[355] where the Court said that measures in other fields were also accepted, as long as they were designed to prevent "illegal activities of comparable seriousness, such as money laundering, drug trafficking or terrorism". In this way, the Court added new concrete elements to the non-exhaustive list of Article 65 (1) (b) TFEU.

There has been no case law in relation to the second ground of justification.[356] However, it is interesting to note that national tax authorities are entitled, within reasonable limits, to require taxpayers to declare money transfers abroad for administrative or statistical purposes.[357]

Public policy and public security are two traditional grounds of justification applicable to all four freedoms in a similar way. In relation to capital, the ECJ has explained in *Eglise de Scientologie* that although Member States are free to determine the requirements of public policy and public security in the light of their national needs, they must nonetheless be interpreted strictly, and their scope cannot be determined unilaterally by each Member State without any control of the Union institutions.[358] It also held that public policy and public security might be relied on only if there is a genuine and sufficiently serious threat to a fundamental interest of society, and insisted that those derogations must not be misapplied so as to serve purely economic ends and that any persons affected have access to legal redress.[359]

In the summer of 2015, Greek authorities introduced temporary restrictions on the free movement of capital (capital controls) in an attempt to avoid financial panic and massive capital outflows after the announcement of the notorious referendum on the deal with the creditors. In its immediate preliminary assessment, the Commission expressed the view that the contested measures were prima facie justified. The stability of the financial and banking system in Greece constituted a matter of overriding public interest and public policy that would appear to justify the imposition of temporary restrictions on capital flows. However, the Commission emphasized that the free movement of capital should be reinstated as soon as possible in the interests of the Greek economy, the Eurozone and the EU's single market as a whole.[360]

3.5.2 *Judicial derogations*

Apart from the express Treaty derogations, the ECJ has created a number of overriding requirements in the public interest that also serve to justify restrictions on capital movements. This list is open-ended and covers various legitimate objectives, such as resisting pressure on land or at

354. J. Snell, op. cit. *supra* note 256, at 557.
355. Joined Cases C-358/93 & C-416/93, *Bordessa*, para 21.
356. C. Barnard op. cit. *supra* note 266, at 610.
357. See European Commission website, in the FAQ section regarding free movement of capital.
358. Case C-54/99, *Eglise de Scientologie*, para 17. An example of a perhaps somewhat broader interpretation is the ECJ's acceptance that safeguarding supplies of petroleum products in the event of a crisis is a matter of public security capable of justifying restrictions on free movement: Case C-483/99, *Commission v. France*; Case 72/83, *Campus Oil*.
359. Case C-54/99, *Eglise de Scientologie*, para 17.
360. European Commission, Statement/15/5271, Brussels, 29 June 2015. See also European Commission, Statement IP/13/298, Brussels, 28 Mar. 2013 on the capital controls imposed by Cyprus.

maintaining, as a town and country planning measure, a permanent population in rural areas,[361] the protection of the environment[362] or the promotion of research and development.[363]

Requirements related to a national public housing policy and to the financing of that policy are also regarded as a public interest reason. This was explicitly stated in *Sint Servatius*,[364] which concerned a Dutch institution active in the public housing sector in the Netherlands (and thus able to contract loans on particularly favourable terms) that did not obtain the required authorization for a construction project in Belgium on the ground that the project would not be beneficial to the Netherlands housing market. The Court qualified the system of prior authorization as a restriction, before accepting that it could be justified on reasons related to the Netherlands' public housing policy.[365]

Interestingly, the list of overriding requirements may even include considerations of an economic nature. In principle, it is settled case law that grounds of a purely economic nature cannot constitute overriding reasons in the public interest justifying a restriction of a fundamental freedom.[366] National legislation may nevertheless constitute a justified restriction on the freedom of capital when it is dictated by reasons of an economic nature in the pursuit of an objective in the public interest.[367] More precisely, in the recent *Essent* case regarding the prohibition of the Dutch energy distribution system, the Court acknowledged that the reasons underlying the choice of the property ownership rules adopted by the national legislation within the scope of Article 345 TFEU constitute factors which may be taken into consideration as overriding reasons in the public interest capable of justifying restrictions on the free movement of capital.[368] Contrary to the golden shares case law, the Court accepted that Article 345 TFEU could justify a prohibition of privatization. Furthermore, it was also acknowledged that the objectives of combating cross-subsidization in the broad sense, including exchange of strategic information, in order to achieve transparency in the electricity and gas markets, and to prevent distortions of competition could be regarded as overriding reasons in the public interest.

3.5.3 *Proportionality*

Once the Court has established that a restriction on capital movements is capable of being justified, it proceeds to the final step, i.e. it examines whether the contested measure is proportionate to the objective pursued. As with the other freedoms, the principle of proportionality consists of two tests: (1) the *suitability* and (2) the *necessity* test. These two tests reveal the complicated and sometimes sensitive balancing act performed by the Court: the former requires that the measure is appropriate to achieve the objective pursued; the latter involves a balancing of competing interests and requires that there are no less restrictive measures to achieve the proposed goal.[369]

Systems of prior authorization are usually regarded to be disproportionate when they lack precision or when a system of declaration could have achieved the same objective.[370] An

361. Case C-370/05, *Festersen*, paras. 27–28; Case C-302/97, *Konle*, para 40.
362. Joined Cases C-515/99 et al., *Reisch*, para 34.
363. Case C-10/10, *Commission v. Austria*, para 37.
364. Case C-567/07, *Sint Servatius*.
365. Ibid., para 30.
366. Joined Cases C-105/12 to C-107/12, *Essent NV*, para 51; Case C-388/01, *Commission v. Italy* para 22; Case C-109/04, *Kranemann v. Land Nordrhein-Westfalen*, para 34.
367. Joined Cases C-105/12 to C-107/12, *Essent NV*, para 52.
368. Ibid., paras. 53 and 55.
369. T. Tridimas, *The General Principles of EU law* (OUP, 2006), at 139.
370. See also Joined Cases 286/82 & 26/83, *Luisi and Carbone*, para 34; and Joined Cases C-163/94, C-165/94 & C-250/94, *Sanz de Lera*, para 25; Case C-302/97, *Konle*, para 44.

example can be drawn from the *Bordessa* case,[371] which concerned two sets of criminal proceedings for exporting a certain amount of money from Spain without the requisite authorization from the Spanish authorities. The Court found that although the requirement of prior authorization could be justified on grounds of prudential supervision, the effectiveness of tax controls and the fight against illegal activities, such as tax evasion, money laundering, drug trafficking and terrorism, it was nevertheless disproportionate as it would cause the exercise of the free movement of capital to be subject to the discretion of the administrative authorities and thus be such as to render that freedom illusory.[372] Instead of prior authorization, the Spanish authorities could have adopted a less restrictive measure such as a system of declaration. Such a system did not entail suspension of the transaction in question but still allowed the national authorities to exercise effective supervision in order to prevent infringements of their laws and regulations.[373]

That is not to say, however, that a system of prior authorization can never be justified, "particularly where such authorization is in fact necessary for the protection of public policy or public security".[374] In *Commission v. France (golden shares)*, the ECJ stated that a system of prior authorization could be proportionate if it was based on objective, non-discriminatory and known in advance criteria and it provided legal remedies to the persons affected.[375] *In casu*, the authorization procedure was, however, again held to be disproportionate, as the discretionary power of the Minister to approve any shareholding exceeding certain limits was regarded as a serious interference with the free movement of capital that went beyond what was necessary to attain the objective of securing petroleum supplies in the event of a real threat.[376]

So far, from the infringement procedures involving golden shares, only in the *Belgian* case[377] was the proportionality hurdle successfully taken. The Belgian legislation at issue allowed the government to retain certain privileges in the management of the privatized undertakings in the gas and energy sector. The ECJ ruled that these privileges were justified by the objective of safeguarding of supplies of petroleum products in the event of a crisis, and more importantly, were also in conformity with the principle of proportionality. The rights of the Belgian Government to oppose any transfer, use as security, or change in the destination of certain strategic assets and to oppose certain management decisions were carefully circumscribed, based on objective criteria and subject to judicial review.

3.5.4 *Legal certainty*

Legal certainty is a fundamental principle of EU law which requires that rules should be clear and precise so that individuals may ascertain unequivocally what their rights and obligations are and may take steps accordingly. In the Court's case law, it sometimes appears as an additional factor to be taken into consideration when assessing the justification of a restrictive measure. In *Eglise de Scientologie*, the Court held that the French system of prior authorization for certain categories of direct foreign investments was not consistent with the principle of legal certainty and as such violated the free movement of capital.[378] Although the system was justifiable on public policy and public security grounds, the investors concerned were given no indication as to the specific circumstances in which prior authorization was required. Such lack of precision

---

371. Joined Cases C-358/93 & C-416/93, *Bordessa*.
372. Ibid., para 25.
373. Ibid., paras. 25–27.
374. Case C-54/99, *Eglise de Scientologie*, para 19; Case C-302/97, *Konle*, paras. 45–46.
375. Case C-483/99, *Commission v. France*, para 48.
376. Ibid., para 51.
377. Case C-503/99, *Commission v. Belgium*.
378. Case C-54/99, *Eglise de Scientologie*, para 21.

did not enable individuals to be apprised of the extent of their rights and obligations deriving from Article 63 TFEU and, therefore, it was contrary to the principle of legal certainty.[379]

Further reading

Barnard, C., *The Substantive Law of the EU*, 5th ed. (OUP, 2016).

Flynn, L., "Free movement of capital" in C. Barnard and S. Peers (Eds.), *European Union Law* (OUP, 2014), at 443–472.

Hatzopoulos, V., *Regulating Services in the European Union* (OUP, 2012).

Lianos I., and O. Odudu, *Regulating Trade in Services in the EU and the WTO: Trust, Distrust and Economic Integration* (CUP, 2012).

Schön, W., "Free movement of capital and freedom of establishment", 17 EBOR (2016), at 229–260.

Snell, J., "Free movement of capital: Evolution as a non-linear process" in P. Craig and G. De Búrca (Eds.), *The Evolution of EU Law* (OUP, 2011), at 547–574.

Usher, J., "The evolution of the free movement of capital", 31 *Fordham International Law Journal* (2007), at 1533–1570.

Van den Bogaert S., and A. Cuyvers, "Money for nothing: The case law of the EU Court of Justice on the regulation of gambling", 48 CML Rev. (2011), at 1175–1213.

Wiberg, M., *The EU Services Directive – Law or Simply Policy* (Springer, 2014).

379. Ibid., para 22. See also Case C-483/99, *Commission v. France*, para 50.

CHAPTER 15
FREE MOVEMENT OF WORKERS AND COORDINATION OF SOCIAL SECURITY

*Anne Pieter van der Mei**

1. Introduction

Article 45 TFEU stipulates that "[f]reedom of movement for workers shall be secured within the Union" (para 1) and that it "shall entail the abolition of any discrimination based on nationality between workers of the Member States as regards employment, remuneration and other conditions of work and employment" (para 2). The provision is supplemented by Article 48 TFEU, which confers upon the EU legislature the task and power to "adopt measures in the field of social security [...] necessary to provide freedom of movement for workers".

The text of Article 45 TFEU has remained largely unchanged ever since the provision was included (as Art. 48) in the original EEC Treaty. In terms of substance, however, free movement of workers has changed in the course of the last decades. Both the EU legislature and the Court of Justice have construed this freedom broadly and expanded its scope far beyond the wording of Article 45 TFEU. Today, the provision entitles nationals of the Member States to gain access not only to the labour markets but also to the social security and welfare systems of other Member States and it enables them, together with their families, to integrate in the host State's society. The progressive development of free movement of workers has even paved the way for the extension of free movement and equal treatment rights to all Member States' nationals and the creation of Union citizenship.[1] Free movement of workers now is part of the broader topic of EU law on free movement of persons and the legal status of workers is now also partially governed by legal instruments applicable to all Union citizens, notably including Directive 2004/38 on Union citizens' right to move and reside freely.[2]

This is not to say that separate discussion of free movement of workers has become redundant. First, formally, where Article 45 TFEU is applicable, the situation at hand is governed by this provision without there being a need to have recourse to the general rules applicable to

* Associate Professor, Maastricht Centre for European Law (MCEL), Maastricht University.

1. Art. 20 TFEU. See further E. Guild et al. (Eds.), *The Reconceptualization of European Union Citizenship* (Brill Nijhoff, 2014); M. Condinanzi et al. (Eds.), *Citizenship of the Union and Free Movement of Persons* (Nijhoff, 2008); S. O'Leary, *The Evolving Concept of Community Citizenship – From the Free Movement of Persons to Union Citizenship* (Kluwer Law International, 1996) and M. Everson, "The legacy of the market citizen" in J. Shaw and G. More (Eds.), *New Legal Dynamics of European Union* (OUP, 1995), 73–90.
2. Directive of the European Parliament and of the Council of 29 Apr. 2004 on the right of citizens of the Union and their family members to move and reside freely within the territory of the Member States amending Reg. (EEC) 1612/68 and repealing Directives 64/221/EEC, 68/360/EEC, 72/194/EEC, 73/148/EEC, 75/34/EEC, 75/35/EEC, 90/364/EEC, 90/365/EEC and 93/96/EEC, O.J. 2004, L 158, at 77.

Union citizens, such as Article 21 TFEU (freedom of movement) or Article 18 TFEU (non-discrimination).[3] Second, in terms of substance, Union citizens may derive from the rules on free movement of workers, rights they do not enjoy in their mere capacity as Union citizens. This chapter discusses the current rules on free movement of workers, and focuses on their added legal value in comparison with the general rules applicable to all Union citizens.[4]

2. Aim and historical development

For a proper understanding of how free movement of workers has evolved and what it precisely entails today, it is useful to first establish why EU law actually provides for this freedom. Remarkably, for this purpose not much can be learned from the EEC's foundational years. The Spaak-report, which served as the basis for the negotiations on the EEC Treaty,[5] spoke in macro-economic terms of a free mobility for the production factor labour.[6] However, the Member States that actually negotiated and ultimately concluded the EEC Treaty did not subscribe to free factor mobility. In fact, France, Germany and the Benelux countries firmly opposed it and rather insisted on retaining the power to regulate labour mobility in accordance with the needs of their national labour markets. Only Italy had a concrete interest in introducing free movement for workers, seeing it as a means to solve its unemployment problem.[7]

In the end, the six founding States did agree to include a provision on free movement of workers in the EEC Treaty, but they did not do so to realize free factor mobility. Two examples illustrate the point.

First, if the Member States had really wanted such mobility, Article 48 EEC should have provided for free movement rights for all workers established in the Member States regardless of their nationality. Article 48 EEC spoke of "workers of the Member States", but this did not reflect an intention to possibly include third country nationals in the free movement regime. Rather, a nationality clause was left out because Member States did not wish to include all nationals, and especially not those coming from the overseas territories, in the free movement regime.[8]

Second, a free mobility of the production factor labour would have required a right to move other Member States in order to look for work there. The Northern Member States opposed, however, as they feared a large inflow of job-hunting Italian nationals. These States stuck to the

3. Case C-100/01, *Oteiza Olazabal* and Case C-392/05, *Alevizos*.
4. See further the contribution of A. Schrauwen to this volume.
5. Art. 69 ECSC Treaty already called for a freedom of movement for miners and steel workers (para 1) as well as cooperation to ensure that "social security arrangements" would not inhibit labour mobility (para 4). Art. 69 served primarily a social goal: in the long term the creation of a common market was expected to increase employment, but, in the short term, the restructuring of production processes could cause problems of temporary unemployment, which freedom of movement could help to solve. S. Goedings, *Labor Migration in an Integrating Europe – National Migration Policies and Free Movement of Workers, 1950–1968* (Sdu, 2005), at 41. Within the ECSC, however, free movement of workers was never a key issue. Its creation was hampered by the same conflict of interests and positions taken by the various Member States as in the case of the EEC. Art. 69 ECSC was implemented but only for highly skilled workers. Its practical impact remained minimal. For example, in the period 1957–1963 only 451 of the approximately 1,400,000 workers in the coal and steel sectors actually exercised this freedom. See S. Goedings, op. cit., at 100.
6. Rapport des Chefs de Délégation aux Ministres des Affaires etrangères (1956), at 17–18. An unofficial English translation is available at <aei.pitt.edu/995/1/Spaak_report.pdf>.
7. On the role of Italy during the Treaty negotiations, and how it persuaded the other five States to have free movement of workers included in the EEC Treaty, see F. Romero, "Migration as an issue in European interdependence and integration: The case of Italy" in A. Milward et al. (Eds.), *The Frontier of National Sovereignty – History and Theory 1945–1992* (Routledge, 1993), at 33–58, and S. Goedings, op. cit. *supra* note 5.
8. S. Goedings, op. cit. *supra* note 5, at 128–135.

view that labour movement should be driven by the needs of national labour markets. As a result, Article 48(3) EEC merely mentioned a right to move to other States in order to "accept offers of employment actually made".

Article 48 EEC was the product of a political compromise between States which had no common view on why free movement of workers was actually needed and what it should precisely encompass. The six did commit themselves to free movement of workers but essentially postponed discussion on what it should precisely entail to the 1958–1970 transitional period during which it was to be realized.

During this period notable progress was made. Free movement of workers was created well before the 1970 deadline and given more substance than the wording of Article 48 EEC demanded. Thus, a right to look for work was recognized[9] and workers were granted a right to equal treatment as regards vocational training,[10] social advantages,[11] trade union rights[12] and public housing[13] as well as a right to be joined by their family members.[14]

Many factors may account for this progress, but the most important is that Article 48 EEC could be implemented during a time of almost full employment. In the course of the 1960s, economic growth had largely solved the Italian unemployment problem. Like the other Member States, Italy started to recruit workers from outside the Community. Labour mobility between Member States and third countries increased considerably, whilst labour mobility of European workers between the Member States virtually came to a standstill. As a result, Member States no longer had strong motives for obstructing or delaying the realization of free movement of workers, provided third country nationals and workers from overseas territories would not be included in the free movement regime.

This development in the labour markets paved the way for the European Commission, which through its right of initiative, could take the lead in the negotiations on free movement of workers. From the beginning the Commission had rejected the view that this freedom should be conceived in terms of free factor mobility. Possible problems of unemployment should not be solved by promoting labour mobility, but rather through other means such as the free movement of capital and a regional policy. Work should be brought to the unemployed, not *vice versa*.[15] In the Commission's view, another role was envisaged for the free movement of workers. It should be seen as a personal freedom, as a fundamental individual right for European citizens to choose the place where they wish to work.[16]

---

9. The Member States had informally recognized this right by including a declaration in the minutes of the Council meeting at which Reg. 1612/68 was adopted. The declaration read: "[N]ationals of a Member State [...] who move to another Member State in order to seek work there shall be allowed a minimum period of three months for the purpose; in the event of their not having found employment by the end of that period, their residence on the territory of this second State may be brought to an end". The fact that the right was not mentioned in the Regulation itself is probably explained by the fact that France, Germany and the Benelux countries were only willing to entitle job-seekers to assistance in the search of work (Art. 5 Reg. 1612/68) but were firmly opposed to giving them a right to social welfare rights. The last sentence of the above-mentioned declaration stated that "if the abovementioned persons should be taken charge of by national assistance (social welfare) in the second State during the aforesaid period they may be invited to leave the territory of this second State". S. Goedings, op. cit. supra note 5, at 259.
10. Art. 7(3) Reg. 1612/68.
11. Art. 7(2) Reg. 1612/68.
12. Art. 8 Reg. 1612/68.
13. Art. 9 Reg. 1612/68.
14. Arts. 10 and 12 Reg. 1612/68.
15. See Commission Recommendation and Opinion of 7 July 1965 (O.J. 1965, 2293).
16. A. Evans, "European citizenship", (1982) *Modern Law Review*, 497–515, at 498–500.

Free movement of workers was realized in 1968 when the Council adopted Regulation 1612/68[17] (now replaced by Reg. 492/2011).[18] In the preamble to Regulation 1612/68 freedom of movement was referred to as a fundamental right for workers which may be exercised in "freedom and dignity".[19] While free movement also serves "to satisfy the requirements of the economies of the Member States", it is above all a means to guarantee workers "the possibility of improving their living and working conditions and promoting their social advancement". Thus, freedom of movement for workers was primarily seen as an individual right that gives nationals of the Member States the opportunity "to pursue the activity of their choice"[20] in the Member State of their choice, and that they were wholly free to make use of or not. Free movement of workers was not so much viewed as a tool for achieving macro objectives of economic growth or social progress. Rather, it was construed as an "embryonic form of European citizenship".[21]

This view of free movement of workers as an individual right conferred on nationals of the Member States as European citizens has driven the development of free movement of workers since the late 1960s. Both the Court and the EU legislature have subscribed to the view. The Court strengthened the notion of "Market Citizenship"[22] embedded in Article (48 EEC, then 39 EC and now) 45 TFEU by giving broad interpretations of concepts like "discrimination", "worker" and "social advantages". The EU legislature picked up the notion of European citizenship and transformed "Market Citizenship" into a broader legal-political status, Union citizenship, which *inter alia* entitles all Member States' nationals, including the ones that are not economically active, to move and reside freely among the Member States.[23]

Until the end of the last century, this progressive development of free movement of workers appeared not to be particularly controversial. Of course, not all of the Court's rulings were welcomed by all and Member States did express concerns about benefit tourism and the financial implications of free movement for their welfare states. Most of the concerns and critique, however, concerned the judicial strengthening of the legal status of economically inactive Union citizens.[24] Free movement of workers did not rank high on the list of politically sensitive topics of EU law.

This can largely be explained by three factors. First, it was recognized that workers contribute to the host State's economy, often will make tax contributions there too and, hence, they were not so likely to become a genuine netto burden on the host State.

Second, while the Court has expanded the scope of workers' and their families' right to equal treatment so as to capture access to social security and welfare systems, it did not sacrifice Member States' legitimate interest in protecting and keeping up these systems. For example, the Court offered Member States protection against social tourism by allowing them to deny

17. Reg. (EEC) 1612/68 of the Council of 15 Oct. 1968 on freedom of movement for workers within the Community. O.J., English Special Edition 1968(II), at 475.
18. Reg. (EU) 492/2011 of the European Parliament and of the Council of 5 Apr. 2011 on freedom of movement for workers within the Union, O.J. 2011, L 141, at 1.
19. See fifth recital of the preamble to Reg. 1612/68.
20. See third recital to the preamble to Reg. 1612/68.
21. L. Levi-Sandri, "Free movement of workers in the European Community", 11 Bulletin EC (1968), at 5. The reference to European Citizenship was not wholly new. In 1961 the European Commission had already held that the right to work in other Member States granted by Art. 39 EC was to be regarded as "le premier aspect d'une citoyenneté européenne". Debs. EP no. 48, 135, 22 Nov. 1961.
22. The term "Marktbürgerschaft" was first introduced by Ipsen. See H. Ipsen, "Europäisches Gemeinschaftsrecht", (1964) *Neue Juristische Wochenschrift*, at 340 (note 2). See further M. Everson, op. cit. *supra* note 1.
23. Arts. 20 and 21 TFEU.
24. Case C-85/96, *Martínez Sala.*

worker status and rights linked to it to nationals of other Member States who only perform "marginal and ancillary activities".[25]

Third, and probably most importantly, European citizens did not make much use of their right to work elsewhere in the Union.[26] The differences between the level of social security benefits and wages in the original Member States appeared not huge enough to overcome workers' preference to live with family and friends in a place they know and speak the language of. Worker mobility remained low and this created a political setting in which EU law on free movement of workers could be realized and shaped without triggering too much opposition.

Since the turn of the millennium, however, the political climate has changed. While the EU rules on free movement of workers were extended without much opposition to the nationals and territories of the EEA States Iceland, Liechtenstein and Norway[27] as well as Switzerland,[28] the accession of many Eastern European States has made free movement of persons and workers a quite controversial topic. The nationals of these new Member States were expected, and indeed have appeared, to be more mobile than their fellow citizens from Western Europe, especially because of the difference between wage levels in the Eastern and Western Member States are smaller than among the latter. This triggered fears for benefit tourism[29] and an influx of "cheap" Eastern European workers that would take up jobs "meant" for national workers or might drive down wage levels. The "old" Member States thus insisted on transitional arrangements to be included in accession treaties allowing them to postpone the full application of free movement of Eastern European workers for a maximum of seven years.[30]

Even though there are no signs that the increase in mobility since enlargement has had a disturbing impact on wages, employment or social benefit systems,[31] political and public support for a further strengthening of the legal status of Union citizens, including workers, has declined. In fact, in some States there is outright opposition with calls being made for ceilings to be imposed on the number of migrant workers to be admitted per year[32] and EU free movement rules to be restricted. Whether it is for this reason or perhaps because free movement of workers has reached its outer limits of its potential development, the law governing it now seems to have entered a stage of fine-tuning, consolidating and, perhaps above all, safeguarding the *acquis communautaire* mainly developed in the last decades of the last century.[33]

---

25. Case 53/81, *Levin.* and Case 139/85, *Kempf.*
26. S. Koikkalainen, "Free movement in Europe: Past and present", (2011) *Migration Policy Institute,* available at <www.migrationpolicy.org/article/free-movement-europe-past-and-present>.
27. Arts. 28–35 Agreement on the European Economic Area, O.J. 1994, L 1.
28. Art. 8 Agreement between the European Community and its Member States, of the one part, and the Swiss Confederation, of the other, on the free movement of persons, O.J. 2002, L 114.
29. E.-M. Poptcheva, *Freedom of Movement and Residence of EU Citizens – Access to Social Benefits,* European Parliament Research Service, 2014, available at <www.europarl.europa.eu/RegData/bibliotheque/briefing/2014/140808/LDM_BRI(2014)140808_REV1_EN.pdf>.
30. D. Kraleva, "Free movement of workers in the EU – Legal aspects of the transitional arrangements", (2013) ZEI Discussion Paper 217, available at <http://aei.pitt.edu/43307/>.
31. On the contrary, the migration of Eastern European workers even seems to have had an positive impact on economic growth. Communication from the Commission to the European Parliament, the Council, the European Economic and Social Committee and the Committee of Regions, *The Impact of Free Movement of Workers in the Context of EU Enlargement.* COM(2008)765 and E.-M. Poptcheva, op. cit. *supra* note 29, at 20–27.
32. Editorial Comments, "The free movement of persons in the European Union: Salvaging the dream while explaining the nightmare", (2014) CML Rev., 729–740, at 730–731.
33. Compare M. Dougan, "Social security and the internal market – The contribution of union citizenship and the relevance of the Lisbon Treaty" in U. Becker and J. Schwarze (Eds.), *Gemeinwohlverantwortung im Binnenmarkt* (Mohr Siebeck, 2010), 97–135, at 134 and E. Spaventa, "The constitutional impact of union

3. The right to work in other Member States

3.1 *The right to work*

Today, free movement of workers may entail more than (could have been) anticipated six decades ago, but its hard core still consists of a right to work in other Member States. More specifically, Article 45 TFEU provides for a right to look for, to accept and to perform paid economic activities for and under the direction of a self-employed person[34] established in another Member State.[35]

Even though Article 45(3) TFEU still only mentions a right "to accept offers of employment actually made", it does now entitle Union citizens to move to and to look for work in other Member States. Jobseekers may stay in the host State for a reasonable period (of at least three months) and perhaps longer if, and for as long as, they can demonstrate to have "genuine chances of being engaged."[36] Jobseekers are entitled to the same assistance from employment offices as nationals of the host State,[37] free to exchange with potential employers applications and offers for employment and to conclude with them employment contracts.[38] They may even have a right to claim "benefits of a financial nature which are intended to facilitate access to the labour market of a Member State" to the exclusion of social assistance benefits.[39] National laws, rules or practices which directly or indirectly discriminate against or hinder nationals of other Member States from obtaining employment are prohibited.[40] Once Union citizens have entered into an employment relationship with an employer in another Member State, they are entitled to be treated equally in all matters related to employment, including remuneration, dismissal,[41] conditions of employment,[42] vocational training,[43] social advantages awarded to workers,[44]

---

citizenship" in N. Neergaard et al., *The Role of Court in Developing a European Social Model: Theoretical and Methodological Perspectives* (DJOF Publishing, 2010).

34. Art. 45 TFEU also entitles employers to hire workers. Case C-208/05, *ITC*; Case C-379/11, *Caves Krier Frères* and Case C-202/11, *Las*.
35. The essential feature of an employment relationship is "that for a certain period of time a person performs services for and under the direction of another person in return for which he receives remuneration". Case 66/85, *Lawrie-Blum*.
36. Case C-292/89, *Antonissen*, as now codified in Art. 6(1) *juncto* Art. 14(1) and (4) Dir. 2004/38.
37. Art. 5 Reg. 492/2011.
38. Art. 2 Reg. 492/2011. Case C-67/14, *Alimanovic*, at 44- 46, and Case C-299/14, García-Nieto, at 37.
39. Case C-67/14, *Alimanovic*, at 44- 46 and Case C-299/14, García-Nieto, at 37.
40. Art. 3 Reg. 492/2011. These include including rules or practices that prescribe specific recruitment procedures for foreign nationals, restrict the advertising of vacancies, impose additional registration duties on non-residents (Art. 3) or limit the number of foreign nationals by number of percentage (Art. 4). See Case 167/73, *Commission v. France*. (requiring a ratio of three French seamen to one non-French seaman). Conditions relating to linguistic knowledge required by reason of the nature of the post to be fulfilled may be permissible though. Art. 3(1), last sentence, Reg. 492/2011; Case C-379/87, *Groener* (upholding language requirement for teachers) and Case C-202/11, *Las* (disproportionality of rule requiring employment contracts to be drafted in a given language). The same holds true for requirements concerning possession of diploma's or other qualifications. See Directive 2005/36/EC of the European Parliament and of the Council of 7 Sept. 2005 on the recognition of professional qualifications, O.J. 2005, L 255, at 22.
41. Case 44/72, *Marsman*.
42. Case 15/69, *Ugliola* (disadvantages resulting from obligations to fulfil military service); Case 152/73, *Sotgiu* (separation allowances); Case 225/85, *Commission v. Italy* (duration and extension of labour contracts); Case 33/88, *Allué* (temporary employment contracts); Case C-90/96, *Petrie* (fulfilment of specific tasks) and Case C-35/97, *Commission v. France* (supplementary pension rights in cases of early retirement).
43. Art. 7(3) Reg. 492/2011.
44. Art. 7(2) Reg. 492/2011 and Case C-57/96, *Meints* (redundancy benefit for agricultural workers).

membership of trade unions and related rights,[45] and, should they become unemployed, re-instatement of re-employment.[46]

The right to work in other Member States is subject to a few conditions. First, the work must be performed for and under the direction of a self-employed person. This condition of subordination demarcates free movement of workers from the right to establish in other Member States as a self-employed person. Put simply, a worker has a boss, who gives instructions on what to do and how to work and pays him/her a salary. A self-employed person is his/her own boss and is paid by those who buy his/her products or receive his/her commercial services.

Second, the activities must be performed for an employer based in another Member State.[47] The required cross-border element is not only present when a national of Member State enters into an employment relationship with an employer in another Member State, but also when a Union citizen has (first) been employed,[48] self-employed,[49] living[50] or studying[51] in another Member State and subsequently returns to his/her home State to work.

Third, the activities performed must be remunerated. It is immaterial how much remuneration is paid,[52] how it is calculated,[53] from which funds it is paid[54] or whether it is offered in cash or in kind.[55] Yet, a remuneration must be paid; unpaid voluntary work is not covered.

Fourth, the activities performed must be economic in nature. Often, the mere fact that a remuneration is paid will suffice. The nature of the work or the specific context in which is performed is in principle of no relevance. Thus, sport activities,[56] prostitution[57] and work performed for religious communities[58] or international organizations[59] may come within the scope of Article 45 TFEU. Exceptions exist, however. For example, work performed in the context of sheltered employment programmes primarily serving social objectives[60] may fall outside the scope of free movement of workers just like certain posts within the public service do.

3.2 *The public service exception*

The right to work in other Member States does not "apply to employment in the public service" (Art. 45(4) TFEU). This exception reflects the classic notion that States may reserve posts in the public service for their own nationals so as to ensure that their sovereign powers are exercised by persons who may be assumed to have a specific bond of solidarity with or loyalty to the State.[61] Initially, Member States held the view that it was up to them to establish which posts or functions are covered by the exception. They essentially favoured an institutional approach,

---

45. Art. 8 Reg. 492/2011. Case C-213/90, *ASTI* (taking part in the management of bodies).
46. Art. 7(1) Reg. 492/2011.
47. The rules do not apply in wholly internal situations. Case C-332/90, *Steen.*
48. Case C-18/95, *Terhoeve.*
49. Case C-107/94, *Asscher.*
50. Case C-212/05, *Hartmann.*
51. Case C-224/98, *D'Hoop.*
52. Case C-456/02, *Trojani.*
53. Case 3/87, *Agegate.*
54. Case C-10/05, *Mattern and Cikotic* and Case C-109/04, *Kranemann.*
55. Case 196/87, *Steymann.*
56. Case 36/74, *Walrave and Koch* and Case C-415/93, *Bosman.*
57. Joined Cases 115 and 116/81, *Adoui and Cornaille.*
58. Case 196/87, *Steymann* and Case C-456/02, *Trojani.*
59. Case C-310/91, *Schmid* and Case C-411/98, *Ferlini.*
60. Case 344/87, *Bettray.*
61. N. Beenen, *Citizenship, Nationality and Access to the Public Service – The Impact of European Community Law* (Europa Law Publishing, 2011).

according to which the question of whether a Member State is entitled to reserve certain posts to its own nationals should be answered on the basis of national law and in accordance with the specific manner in which States have organized their public services. The Court, however, has rejected this view[62] and rather opted for a functional approach. Article 45(4) TFEU only applies to posts:

> "which involve direct of indirect participation in the exercise of powers conferred by public law and duties designed to safeguard the general interests of the State or of other public authorities. Such posts in fact presume on the part of those occupying them the existence of a special relationship of allegiance to the State and reciprocity of rights and duties which form the foundation of the bond of nationality".[63]

According to the Court, on a case-by-case basis, it must be established whether a given post is indeed exempted from free movement of workers and whether the "very strict conditions"[64] of Article 45(4) TFEU are met. From the case law one may conclude that the exemption may apply to posts in the police and other forces of order, the armed forces, the judiciary, tax authorities and the diplomatic service. However, posts in education,[65] healthcare,[66] utilities,[67] public transport,[68] post and telecommunications, and broadcasting generally are assumed to fall outside the scope of Article 45(4) TFEU. Article 45(4) cannot be relied upon for economic ends and certainly does not allow Member States in times of high unemployment to invoke it "as a convenient reservoir of posts".[69]

It is inherent in the functional approach chosen by the Court that it is of no relevance whether a given person is appointed as a civil servant or employed on the basis of a private employment contract.[70] Further, once a national of another Member State has been admitted to a certain post, s/he is entitled to be treated equally as regards all employment conditions.[71] However, if that person wishes to gain access to another post, the State in question may (again) rely on Article 45(4) TFEU.

4. The status of worker

The right to work in other Member States is granted to all Union citizens. Those who exercise this right, however, are not necessarily entitled to all the rights and benefits awarded by Article 45 TFEU, notably including the right to reside for more than three months[72] and equal treatment as regards social advantages.[73] The Court has established that Union citizens only acquire[74]

---

62. Case C-270/13, *Haralambidis*.
63. Case 149/79, *Commission v. Belgium*. Logically, Member States cannot rely on Art. 45(4) TFEU in order to exclude one of its own nationals. Case C-298/14, *Brouillard*.
64. Case C-473/93, *Commission v. Luxembourg*.
65. Case 66/85, *Lawrie-Blum*.
66. Case 307/84, *Commission v. France*.
67. Case C-290/94, *Commission v. Greece*.
68. Ibid.
69. Opinion of 15 Apr. 1986, A.G. Mancini, Case 307/84, *Commission v. France*, at 2.
70. Case 152/73, *Sotgiu*. In fact, activities performed for private employers may fall with the scope of Art. 45 TFEU when they for a not insignificant part involve the exercise of public authority. Case C-47/02, *Anker*.
71. After all, the mere fact that s/he has been admitted demonstrates that the grounds for possibly invoking the exception are not applicable in the case at hand. Case 152/73, *Sotgiu*.
72. Art. 7(1)(b) Dir. 2004/38.
73. Art. 7(2) Reg. 492/2011.
74. A Union citizen who has acquired worker status does not necessarily loose it, in case s/he becomes wholly or partially unemployed. Art. 7(3) Dir. 2004/38. In addition, the status of worker may be retained when

worker status when the activities performed are "effective and genuine" and not on such a small scale as to be regarded as purely "marginal and ancillary".[75] Part-time work may suffice, but the Court has never indicated how many hours must actually be worked for.[76]

5. Social advantages

Article 7(2) of Regulation 492/2011 provides that workers "shall enjoy the same [...] social advantages as nationals workers".[77] Whereas in the late 1960s the EEC legislature only had work related rights or benefits in mind, the Court has broadened the concept of "social advantages" so as to capture all rights or benefits which:

> "whether or not linked to a contract of employment, are generally granted to national workers primarily because of their objective status as workers or by virtue of the mere fact of their residence on the national territory and whose extension to workers who are nationals of other Member States therefore seems likely to facilitate the mobility of such workers within the Community".[78]

The Court has classified as "social advantages" *inter alia* social assistance[79] and numerous other social benefits,[80] study grants,[81] benefits to cover funeral expenses,[82] the right to live together in the host State with an unmarried partner[83] and the right to use one's own language in Court.[84] In essence, the case law on Article 7(2) implies that workers are to treated as equal members of the host State's socio-economic society who can participate in the labour market and have access to welfare state regimes under the same conditions as nationals of the host State.[85] However,

---

a women has to give up work because of the physical constraints of the late stages of pregnancy and the aftermath of childbirth. Case C-507/12, *Saint Prix.*

75. Case 53/81, *Levin.* In interpreting the concept of worker the Court has taken account of changing conditions on the labour market. Various categories, however, remain in a precarious situation, like persons learning on the job, apprentices, persons in an low-paid or unpaid internship. See C. O'Brien, "Social blind spots and monocular policy making: The ECJ's migrant worker model", 4 CML Rev. (2009), 1107–1141.
76. Ten hours a week may do, however, depending on and taking into account all other relevant factors. Case C-213/05, *Geven.* A low number of working hours or the short duration of employment (Case C-413/01, *Ninni-Orasche*) may be indications that the work is to be regarded as marginal and ancillary, but this presumption may be rebutted by other factors such as the number of days of paid leave, possible entitlement to payment of wages in the event of sickness, whether or not employment is covered by a collective labour agreement or the duration of the employment relationship. Case C-14/09, *Genc.*
77. In addition, to social advantages Art. 7(2) confers upon workers a right to equal treatment as regards "fiscal advantages". This provision is primarily meant to prevent that the right to equal treatment as regards remuneration (Art. 45(2) TFEU) would be rendered ineffective and be undermined by discriminatory national provisions on income tax. Case C-175/88, *Biehl.* For discussion of the quite technical and specialist case law of the Court see M. Schaper, *The Structure and Organisation of EU law in the Field of Direct Taxes* (IBFD, 2013), and K. Daxkobler, "*Die grundfreiheitliche Rechtsprechung des EuGH zum Recht der direkten Steuern und zum Sozial- und Sozialversicherungsrecht im Vergleich*" (Dissertation WU Wien, 2014).
78. Case 207/78, *Even.*
79. Case 249/83, *Hoeckx.*
80. These include e.g. childbirth loans, Case 65/81, *Reina,* minimum income benefits for old people, Case 261/83, *Castelli,* special old-age allowances, Case 157/84, *Frascogna,* unemployment benefits Case 94/84, *Deak* and family benefits, Case C-85/96, *Martínez Sala.*
81. Case 39/86, *Lair.*
82. Case C-237/94, *O'Flynn.*
83. Case 59/85, *Reed.*
84. Case 137/84, *Mutsch.*
85. In addition, the Court has held that workers cannot be denied social advantages because they, by participating in the labour market and paying taxes in the state of employment, create a link with the society of that

workers do not have to be regarded as equal and full-fledged members of the host State's "political community". Rights of a more "political" nature, such as the rights to vote and to stand as a candidate in elections as well as certain rights linked to the performance of military service[86] fall outside the scope of Article 7(2).

The broad meaning given to the concept of social advantages has raised issues concerning benefit tourism, especially in relation to social assistance, maintenance grants and other non-contributory benefits. The Court has recognized that some threshold had to be included in the free movement regime so as to avoid imposing on host State's excessive financial burden that could affect the financing of benefit tax-funded benefit schemes. It has not done so by permitting Member States to make entitlement to benefit conditional upon a minimum period of employment of residence in national territory. From the moment a worker takes up employment, s/he is entitled to claim social advantages on equal terms as nationals of the host State.[87] Rather, the Court has safeguarded the interests of the host State by reserving the right to equal treatment as regards social advantages to Union citizens who hold the status of worker, and who thus perform "effective and genuine activities".[88] Hence, Union citizens who merely perform "marginal and ancillary" activities or who are still looking for their first employment[89] are excluded from Article 7(2).

The case law on social advantages, which extends to their family members in as far as the benefits can be said to constitute an advantage for the worker him- or herself,[90] has been crucial for the development of free movement of workers. The practical significance of Article 7(2) of Regulation 492/2001, however, has decreased because Article 24(1) Directive 2004/38 confers upon all Union citizens residing in the territory of another Member State a right to equal treatment with nationals of the host State "within the scope of the Treaty". For workers, Article 7(2) still has added value in situations in which Directive 2004/38 does not apply or guarantee equal treatment. It involves the following situations.

First, Article 24(2) of Directive 2004/38 permits Member States to deny social assistance to Union citizens during the first three months of residence.[91] This limitation, however, does not affect workers' right to rely on Article 7(2) of Regulation 492/2011 to claim social assistance[92] from the moment they acquire their privileged status.[93]

Second, Union citizens who (wish to) reside in another Member State for a period of three months up to five years are, in case they do not hold the status of worker,[94] only entitled to do so if they possess sufficient resources not to become a burden on social assistance of the

state. Case C-20/12, *Giersch* and Case C-379/11, *Caves Krier Frères*.

86. See e.g. Case 207/78, *Even* (the right of war veterans to early retirement on full pension) and Case C-315/94, *de Vos* (pension contributions concerning military service).
87. Case 39/86, *Lair* and Case C-111/91 *Commission v. Luxembourg*.
88. Case 53/81, *Levin* and Case 139/85, *Kempf*.
89. Case C-138/02, *Collins*. Jobseekers have no right to social assistance in the host State. Art. 24(2) Dir. 2004/38. Job-seekers, however, may rely on Art. 45(2) TFEU in order to claim "a benefit of a financial nature intended to facilitate access to employment in the labour market of a Member State" when they have a "genuine link" with the employment market of the Member State concerned. Case C-138/02, *Collins*. Such allowances do not constitute social assistance for the purposes of Art. 24(2) of Dir. 2004/38. Joined Cases C-22/08 and C-23/08, *Vatsouras and Koupatantze*.
90. Case 316/85, *Lebon*.
91. Or, in relation to jobseekers, the extended period during which they may look for work.
92. Joined Cases C-22/08 and C-23/08, *Vatsouras and Koupatantze*.
93. Case 249/83, *Hoeckx* and Case C-326/90, *Commission v. Belgium*.
94. Or self-employed person, or family member of a worker or self-employed person.

host Member State.[95] If they do not satisfy this requirement, they have no right of residence on the basis of EU law and no claim to social assistance.[96] However, if they do possess the status of worker, Union citizens are entitled to right in the host State, even if their salary falls below minimum subsistence level[97] and even if they seek to supplement their income by "financial assistance drawn from the public funds of the State in which he resides".[98] In fact, as workers such Union citizens can invoke Article 7(2) of Regulation 492/2011 and claim social assistance under the same conditions as nationals of the host State.

Third, Article 7(2) has added value in comparison with Directive 2004/38 for frontier workers. Article 24(1) of Directive 2004/38 only applies to Union citizens who reside in the host Member State. Frontier workers, however, can invoke Article 7(2) to claim social advantages. Residence requirements, both for benefits granted to workers[99] and advantages awarded by virtue of residence,[100] constitute, absent justification, prohibited indirect discrimination on grounds of nationality.

Finally, Directive 2004/38 only applies to Union citizens who move to or reside in a Member State "other than that of which they are a national".[101] Hence, a Union citizen who lives in another Member State but works in his or her own Member State cannot benefit from Article 24(1) of Directive 2004/38. However, such a Union citizen is entitled to claim social advantages in the Member State of which he or she is a national under Article 7(2).[102]

6. Prohibition of direct discrimination, indirect discrimination, discrimination on grounds of migration and non-discriminatory obstacles to free movement

Article 45 TFEU prohibits first and foremost nationality discrimination. In work-related matters, the prohibition serves the interests of both migrant workers and national workers. It protects the former against potentially exploitative employers who might otherwise pay them less than, or offer them employment conditions inferior to those agreed upon with, national workers, whilst the prohibition frees the latter from the unfair competition of "cheap" workers from other Member States.[103]

The prohibition of nationality discrimination has been construed broadly. This holds true first as regards its addressees. These include all relevant actors, including legislatures and administrations, international and (sports) associations,[104] social partners,[105] employment offices[106] as well as individual employers.[107]

Further, the Court has extended the prohibition itself so as to cover not only direct but also indirect discrimination on grounds of nationality. The former concerns rules, measures or practices that differentiate between job-seekers, workers or persons on the sole ground of their nationality. Such differential treatment is "suspect" and in principle prohibited. The

---

95. Art. 7(1)(b) Dir. 2004/38.
96. Case C-333/13 *Dano*.
97. Case 53/81, *Levin*.
98. Case 139/85, *Kempf*.
99. Case C-57/96, *Meints*.
100. Case C-542/09, *Commission v. the Netherlands*.
101. Art. 3(1) Dir. 2004/38.
102. Case C-212/05, *Hartmann*.
103. S. Goedings, op. cit. *supra* note 5, at 122.
104. Case C-415/93, *Bosman*.
105. See Art. 7(4) Reg. 492/2011.
106. Art. 5 Reg. 492/2011.
107. Case C-281/98, *Angonese*.

classic rule is that nationality criteria can only be saved and lawfully applied when they fall within the scope of express Treaty derogations, more specifically the public service exception (Art. 45(4) TFEU) or, mainly in relation entry and residence rights, the public policy exception (Art. 45(3) TFEU). This orthodox understanding, however, does not present the full picture. First, nationality criteria may also be lawful when applied as regards rights (e.g. the right to vote and stand as a candidate in national elections) or benefits (e.g. benefits linked to the pursuit of military service) that fall outside the scope of the right to equal treatment or EU law.[108] Second, nationality criteria can possibly be saved when nationals and non-nationals do not find themselves in a comparable situation.[109] Third, the Court has accepted directly discriminatory rules by classifying them as obstacles to freedom of movement and justifying them under a "rule of reason-like approach".[110]

Indirect discrimination involves rules or measures that differentiate on the basis of criteria other than nationality but which in fact lead to the same result as nationality criteria do. More precisely, according to well-settled case law, national conditions, rules or practices must be regarded as indirectly discriminatory

> "where, although applicable irrespective of nationality, they affect essentially migrant workers [...] or the great majority of those affected are migrant workers, where they are indistinctly applicable but can more easily be satisfied by national workers than by migrant workers or where there is a risk that they may operate to the particular detriment of migrant workers".[111]

There is no need to prove that a national of another Member State is in practice actually affected. It suffices that the measure or rule is "intrinsically liable" to affect migrants more than non-mobile nationals.

From the case law one may deduce that the concept of indirect nationality discrimination may capture (durational)[112] residence requirements,[113] language requirements,[114] license or diploma requirements,[115] rules that for certain posts only allow for part-time contracts,[116] or rules that make a promotion,[117] increase in salary or entitlement to a bonus[118] conditional upon length of service but do not take consideration working period completed in other Member States. The possibilities for lawfully applying indirectly discriminatory measures are greater than in case of differential treatment directly based on nationality. According to well-established case law indirect discriminatory rules may be justified "by objective considerations independent of the

108. Case 207/78, *Even*, and Case C-315/94, *De Vos*.
109. See e.g. Opinion of 10 May 2016 of A.G. Bot in Case C-182/15, *Petruhhin*.
110. Case C-124/93, *Bosman* – national sports teams and Case C-182/15, *Petruhhin*, at 33. In addition, the Court has accepted nationality criteria by simply remaining silent or turning a blind to the presence of direct discrimination (Case C-336/96, *Gilly* – tax advantages), not applying Art. 18 TFEU (Case C-386/02, *Baldinger* – compensation for ex-prisoners of war – compare Opinion of 11 Dec. 2003 of A.G. Ruiz-Jarabo Colomer in that same case).
111. Case C-237/94, *O'Flynn*, at 18.
112. Case C-111/91, *Commission v. Luxembourg*.
113. See e.g. Case C-224/97, *Ciola* and Case C-350/96, *Clean Car*.
114. Case 379/87, *Groener* and Case C-202/11, *Las*.
115. Case 222/86, *Heylens* and Case C-340/89, *Vlassopoulou*.
116. Case 33/88, *Allué*.
117. Case C-15/96 *Schöning-Kougebetopolulou*.
118. Case C-224/01, *Köbler*.

nationality" and if they are necessary for, and proportionate to, the legitimate aim pursued by the national law.[119]

In addition, Article 45 TFEU may prohibit nationality-neutral measures that are "liable to restrict freedom of movement for workers".[120] A distinction can be made between national rules that can be said to discriminate on grounds of migration and national rules that are truly non-discriminatory. The former concern national rules that deny a given right or benefit to persons who have exercised free movement rights that is granted to those who do not move. The prohibition of such measures may imply a right to export benefits[121] or entitle nationals who return home to a given right.[122] The test for possible justification is essentially the same as the one applicable to measures that indirectly differentiate on grounds of nationality.

The prohibition of "truly" non-discriminatory obstacles, so rules that make no direct or indirect distinction between nationals and non-nationals or between mobile and immobile persons so far has proved not to have much practical significance. In fact, it is only in the famous *Bosman* ruling that the Court actually condemned such rules (*in casu* rules concerning the transfer system in professional football) on the ground that they directly affected access to the labour market in other Member States.[123]

7. Enforcement

In order to enhance the enforceability of the rights granted by Article 45 TFEU the EU legislature adopted in 2014 Directive 2014/54/EU.[124] The Directive aims to remove existing obstacles to the free movement of workers, such as the lack of awareness of EU rules among public and private employers and the difficulties faced by mobile citizens to get information and assistance in the host Member States. To overcome these barriers and prevent discrimination, the Directive requires Member States to ensure that: (i) one or more bodies at national level will provide support and legal assistance to EU migrant workers with the enforcement of their rights, (ii) effective legal protection of rights (including for example protection from victimization for EU migrant workers who seek to enforce their rights) is offered and (iii) easily accessible information in more than one EU language on the rights is enjoyed by EU migrant workers and jobseekers.[125]

8. Coordination of social security

8.1 Introduction

As stated in section 1 of this Chapter, Article 48 TFEU confers upon the EU legislature the power to adopt measures in the field of social security that are necessary to provide freedom of movement for workers. As far back as in 1958, thus a decade before free movement of workers

---

119. Case C-111/91, *Commission v. Luxembourg*, and Case C-237/94, *O'Flynn*.
120. Case C-40/05, *Lyyski*; Case C-379/09, *Casteels* and Case C-109/04, *Kranemann*. Any restriction however minor may be prohibited. Case C-212/06, *Government of the French Community and Walloon Government*.
121. Case C-406/04, *De Cuyper* and Case C-499/06, *Nerkowska*.
122. Case C-224/98, *D'Hoop*.
123. Case C-415/93 *Bosman*. For an unsuccessful application of reliance on the prohibition of non-discriminatory rules see Case C-190/98, *Graf*.
124. Directive 2014/54/EU of the European Parliament and of the Council of 16 Apr. 2014 on measures facilitating the exercise of rights conferred on workers in the context of freedom of movement for workers (O.J. 2014, L 128/8).
125. On this new Directive see further G. Brinkman, "Equal treatment on the ground of nationality for EU migrant workers", (2015) *European Journal of Migration and Law*, 239–257.

itself was realized,[126] the legislature already made use of this power by adopting Regulations 3 and 4, which set in place a regime for the coordination of the Member States' social security systems. These first regulations were replaced in the early 1970s by Regulations 1408/71[127] and 574/72, which were amended numerous times in order to give due regard to developments in the field of free movement of workers and persons as well as ever ongoing changes in the social security schemes of the Member States.[128] In 2010 the two regulations were replaced by Regulations 883/2004[129] and 987/2009,[130] which have modernized and simplified the coordination regime.[131] The former (the "basic regulation") contains beneficiaries' rights in the field of social security; the latter (the "implementing regulation") provides a detailed set of rules governing the administrative cooperation between the social security institutions of the Member States needed for implementing and effectuating the rights conferred by the "basic regulation".

Regulations 883/2004 and 987/2009 do not set up a common social security scheme nor do they harmonize the national systems.[132] The regulations leave the power of the Member States to organize and finance social security in the way they deem fit untouched. It is up to the Member States to determine whether or not benefit schemes are set in place, how these are financed, which persons are affiliated to the schemes, the conditions for entitlement to benefits and the level of the benefits and the contributions to be paid.[133] The Regulations merely seek to link the schemes to each other in such a way that the exercise of free movement rights does not lead to a loss of entitlement to social security rights or to duties to pay premiums in more than one Member State.

To be sure, the coordination regime does not guarantee its beneficiaries that a move to another Member State will be neutral in terms of social security.[134] Because the social security systems of the Member States differ, such a move may be more or less advantageous (e.g. higher benefits, lower premiums) or disadvantageous (lower benefits, higher premiums) for the person concerned.[135] What the coordination rules do (seek to) guarantee is that beneficiaries are (i) subject to the legislation of one Member State ("single State rule"),[136] (ii) not discriminated

---

126. This is explained by the fact that the Commission could take the European Convention on social security for migrant workers, which had been agreed upon in furtherance of Art. 69(4) ECSC Treaty in Dec. 1957, as the basis for its proposal. See X. Wattillon, "Le Règlement no. 3", (1958) *Revue belge de la Sécurité sociale*, 221–243.
127. Council Reg. (EEC) 1408/71 of 14 June 1971 on the application of social security schemes to employed persons, to self-employed persons and to members of their families moving within the Community (first published in O.J. 1971, L 149, at 2, and subsequently amended many times).
128. As to the challenges in forthcoming years see Y. Jorens et al., *Key Challenges for the Social Security Coordination Regulations in the Perspective of 2020* (trESS Think Tank Report, 2013), available at <www.tress-network.org/tress2012/EUROPEAN%20RESOURCES/EUROPEANREPORT/trESSIII_ThinkTank%20Report%202013.pdf>.
129. Reg. (EC) 883/2004 of the European Parliament and of the Council of 29 Apr. 2004 on the coordination of social security systems (O.J. 2004, L 166, at 1).
130. Reg. (EC) 987/2009 of the European parliament and of the Council of 16 Sept. 2009 laying down the procedure for implementing Reg. (EC), O.J. 2009, L 284.
131. For extensive discussions of the coordination regime, see F. Pennings, *European Social Security Law*, 5th ed. (Intersentia, 2010) and M. Fuchs and R. Cornelissen (Eds.), *EU Social Security Law – a Commentary on Regulations 883/2004 and 987/2009* (Beck, 2015).
132. Case C-331/06, *Chuck*.
133. Case C-388/09, *da Silva Martins*.
134. Case C-187/15, *Pöpperl*, at 24.
135. Case C-208/07, *von Chamier-Glisczinski* and Case C-345/09, *van Delft*.
136. Art. 11(1) Reg. 883/2004.

against on grounds of their nationality,[137] (iii) entitled to receive benefits even if they reside in another Member State ("portability")[138] and (iv) that the social security institutions in the State where they have moved to will take into consideration periods of insurance, work or residence completed in the Member State they moved from when establishing entitlement to or calculating a social security benefit ("aggregation").[139]

8.2 *Scope*

Regulation 883/2004 is not the sole source of EU law[140] from which individuals may derive social security rights. They may do so too from e.g. Regulation 492/2011 ("social advantages"),[141] Directive 2004/38 on the rights of residence,[142] the Treaty provisions on non-discrimination and freedom of movement and, where third country nationals are concerned, a series of migration instruments, association agreements and measures adopted within the framework of the latter agreements.[143] However, the coordination regime governed by Regulation 883/2004 is far more comprehensive and offers more social security protection than those others instruments. Hence, before discussing how the Regulation has worked out the above mentioned key principles, it is useful to first establish to whom and to what benefit schemes they apply.[144]

8.2.1 *Personal scope*

In the course of the years, the personal scope of the coordination regime has been attuned to the evolving scope of the right to freedom of movement. Thus, whereas Regulation 1408/71 first only applied to workers, and was subsequently extended to self-employed persons, civil servants and students, Regulation 883/2004 now applies to "all nationals of the Member States

---

137. Art. 4 Reg. 883/2004.
138. Art. 7 Reg. 883/2004.
139. Art. 6 Reg. 883/2004.
140. In addition, insured persons may possibly derive rights from bilateral or multilateral treaties on social security. Art. 8 provides that Reg. 883/2004 shall replace any social security convention applicable between Member States falling under its scope. However, certain provisions of social security conventions entered into by the Member States before the date of application of this Regulation continue to apply provided that they are more favourable to the beneficiaries or if they arise from specific historical circumstances and their effect is limited in time. For these provisions to remain applicable, they shall be included in Annex II. See e.g. Case C-227/89, *Rönfeldt* and Case C-475/93, *Thevenon*. Art. 8(2) states that two or more Member States may, as the need arises, conclude conventions with each other based on the principles of this Regulation and in keeping with the spirit thereof.
141. The relationship between Reg. 883/2004 and Reg. 492/2011 may be labelled as a *lex specialis-lex generalis* relationship. See Art. 36(2) Reg. 492/2011. Thus, a national rule that is compatible with the social security regulation cannot be successfully challenged under Reg. 492/2011. Compare Case C-57/96, *Meints*. Comparably, where a rule is at odds with Reg. 883/2004, there is in principle no need to establish whether it runs counter to Reg. 492/2011. See e.g. Case C-255/99, *Humer*.
142. See Art. 24(2) of this Directive.
143. These migration and association instruments are not discussed here. For an overview see K. Eisele, *The External Dimension of the EU's Migration Policy – Different Legal Positions of Third Country Nationals in the EU – A Comparative Perspective* (Wolf Legal Publishers, 2013), Part VI (with numerous literature references).
144. The territorial scope of Reg. 883/2004 covers the territory of the Member States (and the EEA States and Switzerland), including the continental shelf, Case C-347/10, *Salemink*. In addition, the coordination rules apply when work is performed outside that territory provided there is a sufficiently close link between EU territory and the employment relationship in question, Case C-106/11, *Bakker*; Case C-60/93, *Aldewereld* and Case 9/88, *Lopes Veiga*.

who are or have been subject to the legislation of one or more Member States"[145] and who find themselves in a cross-border situation.[146]

The fact that Regulation 883/2004 refers to "nationals of the Member States" does not imply that third country nationals[147] cannot benefit from the coordination regime. First, family members and survivors of Union citizens are, when they are defined or recognized as such by national legislation,[148] covered regardless of their nationality.[149] Second, the Agreement on the European Economic Area and the EC-Switzerland Agreement on the Free Movement of Persons have extended the scope Regulation 883/2004 to the nationals (and territories) of Iceland, Liechtenstein and Norway, and Switzerland respectively, when they move between their country and EU Member States.[150] Third, Regulation 1231/2010 has extended the coordination regime to third country nationals moving within the Union.[151]

8.2.2 *Substantive scope*

The coordination regime applies to the following branches of social security:[152] sickness benefits, maternity and equivalent paternity benefits, invalidity benefits, old-age benefits, survivor's benefits, benefits in respect of accidents at work and occupational diseases, death grants, unemployment benefits, pre-retirement benefits, family benefits[153] and "special non-contributory benefits".[154] Only statutory schemes are covered to the exclusion benefits awarded or schemes

145. Art. 2 Reg. 883/2004. The latter requirement is easily met. A national of a Member State can benefit from the coordination regime where s/he "is covered, even if only in respect of a single risk, compulsorily or on an optional basis, by a general or special social security scheme [...] irrespective of the existence of an employment relationship". Case 182/78, *Pierik II*; Joined Cases 82/86 and 103/86, *Laborero and Sabato* and Case C-85/96, *Martìnez Sala*.
146. Like the Treaty rules on freedom of movement and non-discrimination, Reg. 883/2004 does not apply in wholly internal situations. Case C-153/91, *Petit* and Case C-212/06, *Government of the French Community and Walloon Government v. Flemish Government*.
147. The Regulation also applies to stateless persons and refugees. Art. 2(1) Reg. 883/2004. See Case C-95/99, *Khalil*.
148. Art. 1(i) Reg. 883/2004.
149. Art. 2 Reg. 883/2004. See e.g. Joined Cases C-245/94 and C-312/94, *Hoever and Zachow*. Family members can benefit from the coordination regime with the exception of provisions specifically meant for (self-) employed persons, Case C-308/93, *Cabanis-Issarte*, such as unemployment benefits (Case C-189/00, *Ruhr*).
150. See Annex VI to the EEA Agreement (O.J. 1994, L 1, at 3) and Annex II to the EC-Switzerland Agreement (O.J. 2002, L 114, at 1). In Case C-431/11, *United Kingdom v. Council* and Case C-656/11, *United Kingdom v. Council*, the Court concluded that decision aimed at extending the coordination regime to the EEA and Switzerland could be lawfully based on Art. 48 TFEU.
151. Reg. (EU) 1231/2010 of the European Parliament and of the Council of 24 Nov. 2010 extending Reg. (EC) 883/2004 and Reg. (EC) 987/2009 to nationals of third countries who are not already covered by these Reg. solely on the ground of their nationality (O.J. 2010, L 344, at 1). To benefit from the Reg. third country nationals must be legally resident in a Member State and not find themselves in a wholly internal situation. Case C-247/09, *Xhymshiti* and Case C-45/12, *Hadj Ahmed*.
152. Art. 3 Reg. 883/2004. It is well established case law that a benefit may be regarded as a social security benefit falling within the ambit of Reg. 883/2004 when (i) it is granted, without any individual and discretionary assessment of personal needs, to beneficiaries on the basis of a legally defined position and (ii) that it relates to one of the risks expressly listed in Art. 3(1) of Reg. 883/2004. Case C-388/09, *da Silva Martins*, at 38. Such a determination must be based on the constituent elements of each particular benefit, in particular its purpose and the conditions on which it is granted. Case C-160/96, *Molenaar*, at 19 and Case C-361/13, *Commission v. Slovakia*, at 74–78.
153. Art. 3(1) Reg. 883/2004.
154. Art. 3(3) *juncto* Art. 70 Reg. 883/2004.

established by collective agreements, such as for example, supplementary pension schemes.[155] Social assistance[156] and benefit schemes for war victims are explicitly excluded from Regulation 883/2004;[157] other benefits, such as student financial aid or rental subsidies, are implicitly excluded as they are not among the above exhaustively listed[158] social security benefits.[159]

8.3 *Rules determining the applicable legislation*

The coordination regime aims to provide insured persons exercising their free movement rights "constant social security protection" first and foremost by determining the legislation applicable to insured persons. In essence, these rules seek to settle positive or a negative conflict of social security laws.[160] The former could arise, for example, in case a person works in a Member State that has chosen employment on the national territory as the criterion for compulsory affiliation to a given social security scheme, and lives in another Member State that for the same social security risk has opted for residence in national territory as the criterion for affiliation. On the basis of national legislation of the two States, the person concerned could thus be insured in, and thus may have to pay contributions, in both. In the reverse situation, in which a person works in a State that has chosen residence as the factor for affiliation and lives in a State that has set in place an employment based scheme, s/he is confronted with a negative conflict of laws: neither one of the two national legislations is applicable.

The rules determining the applicable legislation seek to ensure that beneficiaries are subject to the legislation of one Member State only, the so-called "single State rule". They prescribe[161] which Member State is the competent State that must apply its legislation. It is this Member State which can levy contributions, and it is most cases also this State which bears the costs of the benefits provided to beneficiaries. In situations of positive conflict of laws, the rules produce exclusive effect, which implies that the competent State must apply its own legislation whilst the other State involved is prohibited to do so. For the competent State, exclusive effect implies

---

155. Member States do have the option to bring within the scope of the coordination regime collective agreements which have been made obligatory or whose scope have been extended, by making a declaration to that effect. See Art. 3(l) Reg. 883/2004.
156. Art. 3(5) Reg. 883/2004.
157. See Case 79/76, *Fossi* and Case C-386/01, *Baldinger*.
158. Case 249/83, *Hoeckx*.
159. Art. 9 of Reg. requires from Member States to notify the Commission of which legislation is covered. Benefit systems that are notified are covered by the Reg. The reverse does not hold true (Case 35/77, *Beerens*: a benefit scheme that has not been notified may fall within the scope of the regulation when it satisfies the criteria for constituting a social security benefit. Where a Member State has refrained from declaring a national law under those regulations, the other Member States can, generally, infer from it that that law does not fall within the material scope of those regulations. Case C-12/14, *Commission v. Malta*, at 38. The formal classification of a given benefit or scheme under national law is irrelevant. Even a levy that is categorized by the Member State as a tax may be covered. Case C-34/98, *Commission v. France*.
160. The rules do not lay down the substantive conditions for entitlement to social security benefits. It is in principle for the legislation of each Member State to determine those conditions. Therefore, Reg. 883/2004 does not preclude for example national provisions that make entitlement to social benefits conditional upon the claimant having a right to reside lawfully in the Member State concerned. case C-308/14, *Commission v. United Kingdom*, at 63–69.
161. The rules are mandatory in nature and in particular do not allow individuals to choose the legislation of which Member State that will be applicable to them so as to for example escape from a duty to pay premiums. Case C-160/98, *Molenaar*. However, two or more Member States, the competent authorities of these Member States or the bodies designated by these authorities may by common agreement provide for exceptions to the rules determining the applicable legislation. See Art. 16(1) Reg. 883/2004, as interpreted in Case 101/83, *Brusse* and Case C-454/93, *Van Gestel*.

mandatory or imperative effect, whereas for the non-competent State it entails prohibitive effect. Thus, where the Regulation determines that the State of employment is the competent State, this Member State will have to apply its legislation to a person who works on its territory. If the person concerned lives in another Member State, the latter is prevented from applying its legislation even if it has chosen for a residence based scheme.[162] In situations of negative conflict of laws, the rules determining the applicable legislation produce binding effect. The competent State will have to apply its laws to a person even if s/he does not satisfy the criterion for affiliation laid down in its national legislation.[163]

The two main rules that determine the applicable legislation are the *lex loci laboris* (Art. 11(2)(a)) and the *lex loci domicilii* (Art. 11(2)(e). The former is the classic rule according to which workers and self-employed persons are subject to the legislation of the Member State where they perform their economic activities. The choice for this rule is motivated by the desire to ensure that employers pay the same premiums for all their employers, and thus do not have the option of employing foreign workers on cheaper conditions than national employees. The *lex loci laboris* rule seeks to avoid social dumping.[164] The *lex loci domicilii* applies to the economically inactive and entails that they are subject to the legislation of the State where they reside.[165]

The *lex loci laboris* does not always suffice for effectuating the single State rule for the simple reason that a person may perform activities in more than one Member States. Regulation 883/2004 therefore contains specific rules for persons who do so. Thus, a person who has one employer who employs him/her in more than one Member State is subject to the legislation of the State of residence, if he/she performs a substantial part of his/her activities there.[166] The State of residence is also the competent State if a person works in more than one Member State for more than one employer, even though there is no need that the activity can be labelled as "substantial".[167] Comparable rules apply to persons who are self-employed in more than one

162. For a long time the Court held on strictly to the exclusive effect of the rules determining applicable legislation by ruling that a Member State that is not assigned to be the competent one was prohibited to apply its legislation and to award benefits to persons falling under the legislation of another Member State. Case 302/84, *Ten Holder*. Recently, however, the Court seems to have mellowed its approach somewhat by ruling that Reg. 1408/71 does not prevent the Member State of residence from granting, pursuant to its legislation, benefits to a person falling under the legislation of another Member State. Case C-352/06, *Bosmann* and Joined Cases C-611/10 and C-612/10, *Hudziński and Wawrzyniak*. In essence, in these two cases the Court loosened the notion of prohibitive effect where it comes to the granting of benefits. This prohibitive effect still fully stands for duties to pay premiums. Case 102/76, *Perenboom*. See further N. Rennuy, "The emergence of a parallel system of social security coordination", 50 CML Rev. (2013), 1221–1266.
163. Case 276/81, *Kuijpers* and Case 2/89, *Kits van Heijningen*.
164. F. Pennings, op. cit. *supra* note 131, at 72.
165. Under the regime established by Art. 11 of Reg. 883/2004 this is a rest group, covering persons who do not pursue (self-) employed activities, are not civil servants (subject to the legislation of the administration in question), wholly unemployed frontier workers (who for purposes of unemployment benefit are referred to the State of residence) or persons called up for service in military forces (subject to legislation of State in question). The economically inactive are to be distinguished from the group of "post-actives", which covers who have worked before. The latter are when they receive cash benefits (with the exception of, *inter alia*, invalidity or old-age benefits) as a consequence of their previous activities, considered to be still pursuing those activities. Art. 11(2) Reg. 883/2004. This provision has simplified the legal status of the post-actives as compared with the complexities that arose under Reg.1408/71. See Case 302/84, *Ten Holder*; Case 245/88, *Daalmeijer*; Case C-275/96, *Kuusijjärvi* and Case C-227/03, *van Pommerden-Bourgondiën*.
166. Art. 13(1)a Reg. 883/2004 *juncto* Art. 14 Reg. 987/2009.
167. Art. 13(1)a Reg. 883/2004.

State,[168] whilst a person who is employed in one State and self-employed in another is subject to the legislation of the former.[169]

The *lex loci laboris* rule is not absolute. The most important[170] exception concerns posted workers.[171] The rule is based on the factual criterion where work is actually performed. As a result, in case an employer sends employees for short periods to various other Member State to perform activities on his or behalf, the competent State would change each time. This could lead not only to many administrative formalities but also, because the periods of activity may be too short, not to any rights to benefits for the posted workers. Regulation 883/2004 therefore makes it possible that the employee in question can remain subject to the legislation of the Member State where the employer normally carries out his activities.[172]

This "posting rule" is, however, limited in time. The rationale for this concerns the notion of social dumping. If employers could remain subject to the legislation of the State where they normally operate, they could easily relocate to and establish in State where the financial contributions to be paid to them are comparatively low and subsequently post their workers to the State from which they *de facto* originate. The posted workers would be the victim as the benefits they are entitled to in case a given social security risks occurs are likely to be less favourable than those in which they perform their work. Hence, the Regulation allows for a derivation of the *lex loci laboris* rule for a maximum period of 24 months.[173]

8.4 *Principles of coordination*

Regulation 883/2004's coordination regime is, in addition to the rules determining the applicable legislation, governed by a number of key principles, including the right to equal treatment regardless of nationality (Art. 4), equal treatment of benefits, income, facts or events (Art. 5), aggregation (Art. 6), and portability of benefits (Art. 7)[174] Phrased negatively, the right to equal treatment prohibits both direct[175] and indirect[176] nationality discrimination. Under the coordination regime[177] the notion of indirect discrimination plays a less prominent role than it does elsewhere in EU law. The legality of national rules or measures that are indirectly discriminatory is to be assessed under other provisions.

For example, residence criteria for entitlement to benefits are indirectly discriminatory, but these are in principle not be reviewed under Article 4 but under Article 7 of Regulation 883/2004 on the waiving of residence conditions. Article 7 stipulates, in brief, that benefits shall

---

168. Art. 13(2) Reg. 883/2004.
169. Art. 13(3) Reg. 883/2004. Under Reg. 1408/71 it was possible for such a person to be subject to the legislation of more than one Member State. Joined Cases C-393/99 and C-394/99, *Hervein and Lorthiios*. This exception to the single State rule and the notion of exclusive effect no longer exists under the new Regulation.
170. Another exception concerns wholly unemployed frontier workers who are subject to the legislation of the State of residence. Art. 11(3)c *juncto* Art. 65(5) Reg. 883/2004.
171. Art. 12 Reg. 883/2004.
172. These activities cannot be incidental but must be substantial. See Art. 14 Reg. 987/2009.
173. The posted worker cannot be sent to replace another posted worker. Art. 12(1) Reg. 883/2004.
174. Other principles, which will not be discussed here concern the non-overlap of benefits (Art. 10 Reg. 883/2004, which stipulates that "Unless otherwise specified, this Regulation shall neither confer nor maintain the right to several benefits of the same kind for one and the same period of compulsory insurance"), and the so-called "Petroni principle", Case 24/75, *Petroni* – "EU law must not deprive beneficiaries of rights acquired on the basis of national law alone".
175. Case C-346/05, *Chateignier*.
176. Case C-332/05, *Celozzi* and Case C-399/09, *Landtová*.
177. The prohibition has proved relevant for example in situations in which national authorities refuse to take into account pay earned (Case C-205/05, *Nemec*) or benefits received (C-507/06, *Klöppel*).

not be reduced, amended, suspended, withdrawn or confiscated because an insured person lives in another Member State. This export provision has priority over the non-discrimination provision[178] and this legally of the utmost relevance. Under Article 4 an indirectly discriminatory measure may possibly be justified when necessary for and proportional to the protection of a mandatory public interest. Article 7, however, does not allow for objective justifications. Regulation 883/2004 does leave room for application of residence criteria, but only when the provisions applicable to certain types of benefits (e.g. special non-contributory benefits)[179] specifically indicate so. Comparably, national rules that make entitlement to social security rights conditional upon completion of periods of insurance, employment or residence and do not take into consideration periods completed in other Member States can be regarded as indirectly discriminatory. However, their legality is to be assessed under the aggregation rule contained in Article 6 of Regulation 883/2004, or specific aggregation provisions applicable to specific benefits.[180]

8.5 *Coordination rules for specific types of social security benefits*

The above stated principles and rules apply to all benefits covered by Regulation 883/2004 and the chapters in which the coordination of these benefits is worked out in further detail. Below we will discuss the chapter on health care and insurance and unemployment benefits.

8.5.1 *Health care and health insurance*

The provisions of Regulation 883/2004 on health care[181] seek to ensure that persons who exercise their free movement rights are entitled to the medical treatment they need at the expense of the competent institutions they are affiliated to. In all cases covered by these provisions, medical care is offered in accordance with the legislation of the State of treatment; the costs are fully reimbursed by the competent institution.[182] Regulation 883/2004 governs a variety of situations.[183]

---

178. F. Pennings, op. cit. *supra* note 131, at 116.
179. Art. 70 Reg. 883/2004.
180. See e.g. Art. 61 Reg. 883/2004 on unemployment benefits. Similarly, it would seem that national rules that do not treat equally income, facts or events relevant for establishing a migrant's social security status are indirectly discriminatory, but they should or at least can now be reviewed under Art. 5 of Reg. 883/2004, which contains the principle of "equal treatment of income, facts or events".
181. Art. 17–35. In these provisions healthcare is referred to as "benefits in kind". Some of the provisions also apply to cash benefits, which in essence concern benefits that compensate for the loss of income in the event of sickness. See Case C-160/96, *Molenaar*. The borderline between cash benefits and benefits in kind is not always easy to draw, as the case law on long-term care benefits demonstrates. C-388/09, *da Silva Martins* and C-208/07, *Chamier-Glisczinski*. On the coordination of these benefits see further Y. Jorens et al., *Coordination of Long-term Care Benefits – Current Situation and Future Prospects* (trESS Think Tank Report, 2011), available at <www.tressnetwork.org/tress2012/EUROPEAN%20RESOURCES/EUROPEAN REPORT/trESSIII_ThinkTankReport-LTC_20111026FINAL_amendmentsEC-FINAL.pdf>.
182. Art. 35 Reg. 883/2004.
183. The Regulation contains separate provisions on the healthcare rights of pensioners. Arts.23–30 Reg.883/2004. The reason for this is not that the EU legislature has wished to grant more, less or other rights to pensioners than to other insured persons or to impose different conditions for the enjoyment of these rights. The rights awarded are in essence the same. The reason for the separate provisions concerns the assignment of the competent institution. In many Member States health insurance for pensioners is linked to not to residence but to entitlement or receipt of a pension. Therefore, the EU legislature has opted for the "*lex loci pensionado*" rather than the "*lex loci domicilii*". In brief, pensioners are insured for healthcare, and must pay contributions, in the State from which they receive a pension (or pensions) and it is this State that carries the burden of having to pay cross-border healthcare. See further A.P. van der Mei et al., "Pensioners and the financing of cross-border healthcare", (2011) *European Journal of Social Law*, 82–102, and S. Roberts

First, an insured person who resides in a Member State other than the competent one is entitled to health care in the State of residence, as though he or she were insured there.[184] Second, such an insured person is also entitled to obtain care in the competent State.[185] Frontier workers thus have a right to choose in which of the two States concerned they wish to obtain care.[186] Third, insured persons who have travelled to and are temporarily staying in another Member State are entitled to medical treatment which becomes "necessary on medical grounds during their stay, taking into account the nature of the benefits and the expected length of stay".[187] This right to so-called "unforeseen" or "unscheduled" treatment is to be distinguished from the right to "planned" or "scheduled" treatment, which applies to insured persons who are travelling to another Member State for the purpose of receiving medical treatment. Reimbursement of such planned treatment is conditional upon the grant of prior authorization by the competent institution. A right to get such prior authorization exists where the treatment "is among the benefits provided for by the legislation in the Member State where the person concerned resides" and where he or she "cannot be given such treatment within a time-limit which is medically justifiable", taking into account his or her state of health and the probable course of the illness.[188]

This latter phrase entails a codification of the "*Decker-Kohll*" case law of the Court of Justice. Prior to the rulings in these two cases, Regulation 1408/71 made the reimbursement of all planned treatment subject to prior authorization and only provided for a right to receive obtain authorization in exceptional cases.[189] Basically, the coordination regime left it to the Member States and their institutions to decide on the grant of prior authorization, which they as a rule only did so in exceptional cases. Authorization, and thus reimbursement of the costs of planned treatment, was a rarely granted privilege, not a right. In *Decker*[190] and *Kohll,*[191] however, the Court held that national rules making the reimbursement of the costs of healthcare outside the national territory conditional upon prior authorization are at odds with the Treaty rules on freedom of movement goods and services respectively. In essence, the Court transformed the aforementioned privilege into a legally enforceable right to be reimbursed for planned treatment that could only be denied or restricted when necessary for protecting the financial stability of health insurance schemes or the infrastructure of healthcare systems.

The controversial *Decker* and *Kohll* judgments triggered two reactions. First, in a series of cases the Court itself was asked to clarify the precise implications of the rulings. The Court, in brief, stuck to the view that prior authorization are at odds with the Treaty rules on free movement of services, but held that they can be justified and lawfully applied to types of medical care that are not included in national insurance packages, hospital care and "non-contracted" care.[192] Second, Member States insisted on a political response and this has ultimately led to the adop-

---

(Ed.), *Health Care for Pensioners* (trESS Think Tank Report, 2009), available at <www.tressnetwork.org/TRESSNEW/PUBLIC/EUROPEANREPORT/ThinkTank_Pensioners_2009.pdf>.

184. Art. 17 Reg. 883/2004, which confers the same right to family members.
185. Art. 18 Reg. 883/2004.
186. The same does not necessarily hold true for their family members. Member State may choose not to recognize the right of family members residing in another Member State to care in the latter State by indicating this in Annex III to Reg. 883/2004. Art. 18. Reg. 883/2004.
187. Art. 19 Reg. 883/2004.
188. Art. 20(2) Reg. 883/2004.
189. Art. 22(2) Reg. 1408/71.
190. Case C-120/95, *Decker.*
191. Case C-158/96, *Kohll.*
192. Case C-157/99, *Geraets-Smits and Peerbooms.* See further A.P. van der Mei, "Cross-Border access to health are within the European Union: Some reflections on *Geraets-Smits and Peerbooms* and *Vanbraekel*", 9 MJ (2002), at 189–213, at 199.

tion of Directive 2001/24/EU on the application of patients' rights in cross-border healthcare (Patients' Rights Directive – PRD),[193] which essentially has codified the most relevant aspects of the Court's case law.

The PRD and Regulation 883/2004 co-exist and now jointly govern the financial aspects[194] of cross-border care. The general rule established in *Decker* and *Kohll* is laid down in the PRD: the Member State of affiliation (competent State) shall reimburse an insured person the costs of health care he or she has received in another Member State, provided the insured person is entitled to this care in the State of affiliation.[195] Reimbursement may be limited up to the costs of the care in the State of affiliation.[196] In principle, this right to be reimbursed for cross-border care is not subject to prior authorization. Member States, however, are entitled to set in place a system of prior authorization for healthcare which is made subject planning requirements and involves "overnight hospital accommodation [...] for at least one night" or requires "use of highly specialized and cost-intensive medical infrastructure or medical equipment".[197] The PRD specifies, in a manner comparable to Regulation 883/2004, that authorization must be given when the care cannot be provided within a time limit which is medically justifiable.[198]

8.5.2 *Unemployment benefits*

The rules of Regulation 883/2004 on unemployment benefits[199] govern various situations, and in each of these they deviate, at least partly, from the general principles governing the coordination regime.[200]

The first situation concerns insured persons who reside in the competent State the moment they become unemployed. The right to unemployment benefit is governed by the legislation of this State. Regulation 883/2004, however, adds a specific aggregation rule: the competent

193. O.J. 2011, L 88, at 45. See further W. Palm and I. Glinos, "Enabling patient mobility in the EU: Between free Movement and coordination" in E. Mossialos et al. (Eds.), *Health Systems Governance in Europe – The Role of European Union Law and Policy* (CUP, 2010) and J. van den Gronden et al. (Eds.), *Health Care and EU Law* (Asser Press, 2011).
194. In addition, the PRD has introduced a series of "new" patients' rights (e.g. rights to information, good quality and safe care, to complain and be compensated for damage and data protection – see further L. Bongers and D. Townend, "The implementation of the Directive on the application of patients' rights in cross-border healthcare in the Netherlands", 21 *European Journal of Health Law* (2014), 65–78) and provided the framework for more intensive cross-border cooperation in healthcare (recognition of prescriptions, European reference networks, eHealth, health technology assessment – see further T. Hervey, "Cooperation between health care authorities in the proposed directive on patients' rights in cross-border healthcare" in J. van den Gronden et al. (Eds.), *Health Care and EU Law* (Asser Press, 2011), 162).
195. Art. 7(1) PRD.
196. Art. 7(4) PRD. See Case C-368/98, *Vanbraekel*.
197. See Art. 8(2) PRD, which also allows prior authorization for treatment presenting a particular risk for the patient or population and care provided by a provider that could give rise to serious and specific concerns relating to the quality and safety of care".
198. Art. 8(5) PRD.
199. Reg. 883/2004 does not define the term "unemployment benefit". From the case law it seems to follow, however, that it concerns benefit payable to persons who have reduced, ceased or suspended their remunerative activities, who are available to the labour market (Case C-66/92, *Acciardi* and which replace wages lost by unemployment, the objective of which is to provide an income for the costs of living of the employee (Case C-102/91, *Knoch*. The condition concerning availability for new work or the labour market is not always decisive. Case C-406/04, *De Cuyper*. Unemployment benefits may next to cash benefits also involve in kind benefits such as training or reintegration programmes. Case 375/85, *Campana*.
200. See further R. Cornelissen, "The new EU coordination system for workers who become unemployed", (2007) *European Journal of Social Security*, 187–220 and F. Pennings, "Coordination of unemployment benefits under Reg. 883/2004", (2009) *European Journal of Social Security*, 177–204.

institution must take into consideration periods of insurance, employment or self-employment fulfilled in other Member States. However, if, under the legislation it applies, the right to unemployment benefit is conditional upon completion of periods of insurance, the competent institution does not have to take into consideration periods (self-)employment fulfilled elsewhere if these would not have been considered to be insurance periods if they had been completed under its own legislation.[201]

The second situation involves unemployed persons who wish to look for work in another Member State. The basic premise is that such cross-border job-seekers have no right to claim unemployment benefits in the State where they search for work.[202] Rather, it is the competent State they have to turn to. Article 64 provides for a right to export unemployment benefits that, in comparison with the general export rule laid down in Article of Regulation 883/2004, is limited in three respects: (i) export is reserved for those who have become wholly unemployed, (ii) is limited to three months and (iii), in case, the job-seeker returns to the competent State after more than three months, s/he loses entitlement to unemployment benefit altogether. The rationale behind the second and third limitations lies in the duty to find new employment that all national laws impose on recipients of unemployment benefits. For this purpose, registration with and supervision by employment offices is crucial. As the employment offices in the State of the job-search have no (financial) incentive to strictly supervise whether the unemployed person in concerned actually seeks work, (competent) Member States wish to keep the duration of the right to export short.[203] In fact, for this reason, national legislation on unemployment benefits simply excludes a right to export benefits altogether. The right to export under consideration here is based exclusively on Regulation 883/2004. This also explains why the Court has accepted in *Testa*[204] that the right to unemployment benefit will be lost in case of a return to the competent State after three months. Article 64, as a whole, provides for a right that contributes to freedom of movement and in no way deprives job-seekers of a right they would otherwise not have.

The third group of situations concerns unemployed persons who, while last employed, resided in a Member State other than the competent State. The provision makes a distinction between those who are partially or intermittently unemployed, on the one hand, and wholly unemployed workers, on the other hand.

The former must make themselves available to the employment services in the competent State and shall receive benefits in accordance with that State's legislation (Art. 65(1)). As to the wholly unemployed, a distinction is made between frontier workers, *id est* workers who return home to the State of residence as a rule daily or at least once a week,[205] and wholly unemployed "non-frontier workers" who return less frequently. The latter are given a choice. Depending on in which of the two States involved they decide to live, they can claim unemployment benefit there.[206] Wholly unemployed frontier workers must make themselves available for new employment in the State of residence, and may, if they so wish, also do so in the State of former employment. As to entitlement to unemployment benefit, however, they have no choice: they are only entitled to claim benefit in the State of residence. This is deviation from the general *lex loci*

201. Art. 61(1) Reg. 883.2004. Case 126/77, *Frangiamore* and Case 388/87, *Warmerdam*.
202. See, implicitly, Art. 61(2) Reg. 883/2004.
203. R. Cornelissen, op. cit., *supra* note 200, at 218.
204. Joined Cases 41/79, 121/79 and 796/79, *Testa*.
205. Art. 1(f) Reg. 883/2004.
206. Case C-102/91, *Knoch*.

laboris,[207] which, according to the Court, is justified by the assumption that wholly unemployed frontier workers have the best chances of finding new work in the State where they live.[208]

Further reading

Essers, G., A.P. van der Mei and F. Van Overmeiren, *Vrij verkeer van personen in 60 arresten – De zegeningen van het Europees burgerschap* (Kluwer, 2012).

Fuchs, M. and R. Cornelissen, *EU Social Security law – A Commentary on EU Regulations 883/2004 and 987/2009* (Beck/Hart/Nomos, 2015).

Mei, A.P. van der, *Vrij Verkeer van Werknemers* (Sdu Uitgevers, 2003).

Minderhoud, P. and N. Trimikliniotis (Eds.), *Rethinking the Free Movement of Workers: The European Challenges Ahead* (Wolf Legal Publishers, 2009).

O'Brien, O., "Social blind spots and monocular policy making: The ECJ's migrant worker Model", 46 CML Rev. (2009), 1107.

O'Leary, S., "Free movement of persons and services" in P. Craig and G. de Búrca, *The Evolution of EU Law* (OUP, 2011), at 499, 546.

Pennings, F., *European Social Security Law*, 6th ed. (Intersentia, 2015).

---

207. On the moment the wholly unemployed frontier workers moves (residence) to the State of employment this exception ceases to exist. Case C-131/95, *Huijbrechts*. The exception is also subject to debate, however, and it has been proposed that the competent State should be exclusively responsible for unemployment benefits. C. Garcia De Cortazar and E. Rentola (Eds.), *Coordination of Unemployment Benefits* (Think Tank Report, 2012), available on <www.tressnetwork.org/tress2012/EUROPEAN%20RESOURCES/EUROPEANREPORT/trESS_ThinkTankReport2012.pdf>.

208. Case 39/76, *Mouthaan* and Case 227/81, *Aubin*. This assumption does not always hold true. In *Miethe*, a case decided under the former Reg. 1408/71, the Court held that in exceptional circumstances a wholly unemployed frontier worker who has maintained personal and business links in the State of employment may have a better chance of finding new employment there. The Court did not give such "atypical" frontier workers a right to choose in which of the two States involved to claim unemployment benefit, but it did rule that the provision applicable to wholly unemployed non-frontier worker could be applied to them, allowing for the grant of benefit by the State of employment. Case 1/85, *Miethe*, at 10–12. This "*Miethe*-case law" is no longer relevant under the new Reg. 883/2004. Wholly unemployed frontier workers may now also make themselves available for new employment in the competent State, but can only claim benefit in the State of residence. Case C-443/11, *Jeltes*.

CHAPTER 16
CITIZENSHIP OF THE UNION

*Annette Schrauwen**

1. The concept of "citizenship of the Union"

The concept of citizenship of the Union figures in Title II of the Treaty on European Union and in Part II of the Treaty on the Functioning of the European Union.[1] The Maastricht Treaty introduced EU citizenship as a legal concept into the EC Treaty in 1993, suggesting a transformation from an economic to a political organization that places the individual in the centre of Union law.[2] The political flag of citizenship[3] is more a question of additional citizenship: any person who holds the nationality of one of the Member States of the European Union is automatically also a citizen of the Union.[4] The Member States decide on questions of nationality (see section 2.1 below). Nationals of third countries, even if they are legally resident in a Member State, have no access to Union citizenship.[5] The additional character is emphasized in the Treaty text, with the words that citizenship of the Union shall not replace national citizenship.[6]

With the introduction of Union citizenship, the Member States were aiming primarily to bring the European Union closer to the citizens, and to make clear and more meaningful the rights citizens derive from the integration process (cf. Art. 1, para 2 TEU). The description "Union citizen" is intended to express the fact that the Union does not solely concern the Member

---

* Law Faculty, University of Amsterdam.

1. Art. 9 TEU (introduced by Lisbon), Art. 20 TFEU (ex 17 EC).
2. S. Kadelbach, "Union citizenship" in Von Bogdandy and Bast (Eds.), *Principles of European Constitutional Law*, revised 2nd ed. (Hart, 2010), 443–478.
3. As to how Union citizenship was introduced in the EC Treaty, see J. Cloos et al., *Le Traité de Maastricht: Genèse, analyse, commentaries* (Bruylant, 1993), 162–166. Cf. moreover contributions in D. O'Keeffe and P. Twomey, *Legal Issues of the Maastricht Treaty* (Wiley Chancery, 1994).
4. Art. 9 TEU, Art. 20 TFEU.
5. For a critical view, see P. van Dijk, "Free movement of persons: Towards European citizenship", (1992) SEW, 277–307; S. Besson and A. Utzinger, "Introduction: Future challenges of European citizenship – Facing a wide-open Pandora's box", (2007) ELJ, 573–590; D. Kochenov, "Ius Tractum of many faces: European citizenship and the difficult relationship between status and rights", (2009) CJEL, 169–237; D. Kochenov, "Rounding up the circle: The mutation of member states' nationalities under pressure from EU citizenship", 23 *EUI Robert Schuman Working Paper* (2010); A. Wiesbrock, "Granting citizenship-related rights to third-country nationals: An alternative to the full extension of European Union citizenship?", 14 EJML (2012), 63–94; A. Schrauwen, "Granting the right to vote for the European Parliament to resident third-country nationals: Civic citizenship revisited", (2013) ELJ, 201–218; S. Iglesias Sánchez, "Nationality: The missing link between citizenship of the European Union and European migration policy" in E. Guild, C.J. Gortázar Rotaeche and D. Kostakopoulou (Eds.), *The Reconceptualization of European Union Citizenship* (Brill Nijhoff, 2014), 65–87.
6. A. Schrauwen, "European Union citizenship in the Treaty of Lisbon: Any change at all?", (2008) MJ, 55–64.

States and their civil services, but also the citizens themselves, since they have rights directly conferred on them (Art. 20(2) TFEU). The introduction of European citizenship was greeted with some scepticism (see section 1.2.3 below), as being mainly a rhetorical exercise with little added value compared with the already existing *acquis communautaire*. Considering the controversial and at times spectacular evolution of the case law, Union citizenship did not remain an empty normative shell.[7]

1.1 *European citizenship before the Treaty of Maastricht*

The idea of a European citizenship has been part of the creation of the European Communities and has since lingered in the background before the concept was explicitly included in the Treaty texts in the Maastricht Treaty.[8] In the development of free movement rights, and especially the rights of service recipients, the personal scope of free movement was extended to the effect that the link with economic activity became more tenuous. In *Cowan*, for instance, a British tourist in Paris, was refused compensation for injury resulting from a violent assault, because France awarded such compensation only to French nationals or persons holding a residence permit.[9] As a tourist, he was a recipient of services The Court ruled that the prohibition of discrimination based on nationality of Article 7 EEC (now Art. 18 TFEU) applied, despite the fact that the French rule did not in any way hinder free movement.[10]

A much broader approach to European citizenship, encompassing the rights associated with citizenship in a liberal democratic state, can be found in documents that focus on developing the European Community beyond the economic field.[11] The political status of nationals of the Member States in the EEC became apparent with the first direct elections of the European Parliament in 1979, enhancing the democratic legitimacy of the Community, and making clear the intention to turn the Economic Community into a "citizens' Community".[12] In the same year, the Commission proposed a Directive on free movement of persons not engaged in economic activity, based on Article 235 EEC (now Art. 352 TFEU). It was seen as a first step towards the creation of European citizenship,[13] though in the end the proposal never got accepted. A few years later, in the run-up towards the Single European Act, other reports were added that again employed the rhetoric of a "Citizen's Europe" and argued for political integration and free travel between Member States.[14] In 1984, the European Parliament employed the term "citizenship of the Union" for the first time in its Draft Treaty on European Union. Article 3 of the draft defined

7. D. Thym, "Towards 'real' citizenship? The judicial construction of Union citizenship and its limits" in M. Adams et al., *Judging Europe's Judges. The Legitimacy of the Case Law of the European Court of Justice* (Hart, 2013), 155–174.
8. See A.C. Evans, "European citizenship", (1982) MLR, 497–515; A. Durand, "European citizenship", 4 EL Rev. (1979), 3; R. Plender "An incipient form of European citizenship" in F.G. Jacobs (Ed.) *European Law and the Individual* (North-Holland Publishing, 1976), 39–53.
9. Case C-186/87, *Cowan v. Le Trésor Public*.
10. See E. Spaventa, *Free Movement of Persons in the European Union. Barriers to Movement in their Constitutional Context* (Kluwer, 2007).
11. See for instance *Towards a Citizen's Europe*, Bull. E.C. Su 7/75 and *European Union, Report by Leo Tindemans,* (1976) *Ministry of Foreign Affairs*, 41.
12. W. Maas, *Creating European Citizens* (Rowan & Littlefield, 2007), 34.
13. See 13th General Report on the Activities of the European Economic Community, at 84 and Resolution of the European Parliament, O.J. 1980, C 117/48.
14. See notably the reports of the committees Adonnino and Dooge, Bull. E.C. 3/85.

it as being dependent upon citizenship of a Member State, and explicitly specified that citizenship of the Union may not be independently acquired or forfeited.[15]

The Single European Act inserted the aim of a European area without internal borders in Article 8A EEC (now Art. 26 TFEU), which formed one of the motives for the adoption of three Directives providing residence rights for economically inactive nationals of the Member States.[16] Though all this helped to remove the link between free movement and economic activity, it was only when the Spanish government proposed to introduce a formal European citizenship in the Treaty texts that voting rights and general free movement rights came to be understood as European citizenship rights.[17]

1.2 *Citizenship in the Treaty of Maastricht*

Article 8 EC (now as amended Art. 20 TFEU) reveals the Maastricht Treaty as the "constitutional moment" that created European citizens: "Citizenship of the Union is hereby established."[18] It thus created a new legal category that bundles pre-existing legal rights. It immediately raised questions to the added value of this new legal concept and the appropriateness of its introduction.[19]

1.2.1 *Why a notion of citizenship?*

With the development of free movement rights for economically inactive persons and the enactment of directives making it possible for nationals of Member States to participate in local and European elections when residing in a Member State other than that of their nationality,[20] the legal status of the European citizens in the European legal order went beyond that of a mere market participant. In general, literature discerns three elements that inspired the bundling of these rights under the status of citizenship of the Union in the Maastricht Treaty.[21] The first element, strengthening the position of citizens of the Union in their host country, is paramount in the Spanish proposals on citizenship of the Union. The second element, marking the transgression from an economic to a political order, was a key concern after the fall of the Berlin wall. The third element aims at identification with the Union and can be described as constitutional patriotism: fostering a feeling of belonging to one legal community. Their legal expression can be found in provisions on membership, rights and duties and participation.[22] The Maastricht Treaty formulated the Union's intentions as follows: "to strengthen the protection of the rights

15. *Draft Treaty Establishing the European Union*, O.J. 1984, C 77/33. The Draft Treaty is also known as the Spinelli Draft, after one of its authors. See also S. Kadelbach, op. cit. *supra* note 2.
16. Directive 90/364, 90/365 and 90/366 (replaced by 93/96) on the right of residence, the right of residence for retired persons, and the right of residence for students, O.J. 1990, L 180/26. These three directives have been repealed by Directive 2004/38, O.J. 2004, L 158/77.
17. See Document 12, Spanish Government, "Proposals towards a European citizenship, Sept. 1990" in R. Corbett (Ed.), *The Treaty of Maastricht: From Conception to Ratification: a Comprehensive Reference Guide* (Harlow, 1993), 156–158; L.J. van Middelaar, *The Passage to Europe. How a Continent became a Union* (YUP, 2013), 258; C. Closa, "The concept of citizenship in the Treaty on European Union", (1992) CML Rev., 1137–1169; S. O'Leary *The Evolving Concept of Community Citizenship. From the Free Movement of Persons to Union Citizenship* (Kluwer, 1996).
18. W. Maas, op. cit. *supra* note 12, at 45.
19. N. Reich, "Union citizenship – Metaphor or source of rights", (2001) ELJ, 4–23 at 5.
20. Directive 94/80/EC of 19 Dec. 1994, O.J. 1994, L 368/38 and Directive 93/109, O.J. 1993, L 329/34.
21. W. Maas, op. cit. *supra* note 12, 46–47; S. Kadelbach, op. cit. *supra* note 2, at 447; C. Barnard, *The Substantive Law of the EU. The Four Freedoms*, 4th ed. (OUP, 2013), 432; C. Closa op. cit. *supra* note 17.
22. According to the definition of citizenship by David Held, in "Between state and civil society: Citizenship" in G. Andrews (Ed.) *Citizenship* (Lawrence & Wishart, 1991), 20; cited by C. Barnard, op. cit. *supra* note 21.

and interests of the nationals of its Member States through the introduction of a citizenship of the Union".[23]

1.2.2 *Definition of citizenship of the Union*

Article 8 EC (Maastricht version) stipulated that every person holding the nationality of a Member State shall be a citizen of the Union, a phrase that nowadays can be found in Article 20 TFEU, and in slightly different wording in Article 9 TEU. The conferral of Union citizenship led to some confusion as it remained unclear what its scope was. It was one of the reasons why, as a consequence of the Danish initial rejection of the Treaty of Maastricht in a referendum, a sentence was added that citizenship of the Union does not replace national citizenship. The definition shows that the introduction of citizenship of the Union does not attribute rights to others than the nationals of the Member States.[24] Though several proposals have been made to broaden the scope of the definition, both in literature and during subsequent Treaty negotiations, the link with nationality remains.[25]

The definition in Article 20 TFEU is followed by a non-limitative enumeration of the rights citizens of the Union shall have. These are free movement rights, voting rights, the right to diplomatic protection by any Member State in the territory of a third country where the Member State of nationality has no representation and the right to petition the European Parliament, to apply to the European Ombudsman and to address institutions and advisory bodies of the Union. Moreover, the Council may adopt provisions to strengthen or add to the rights listed in Article 20 TFEU, based on the report on the application of the citizenship provisions that Article 25 TFEU requires the Commission to submit every three years.

1.2.3 *Reception of the concept*

Article 20 TFEU defines citizenship of the Union as a legal concept encompassing positive rights, and seems to add little new to the rights that already existed under Community law. Not surprisingly, many scholars saw it as a symbolic institution or worse, as a trivialization of the concept of citizenship "to the point of embarrassment".[26] Others pointed at the predominance of economic entitlements linked to citizenship and saw it as primarily designed to facilitate market integration.[27] It would have relevance only for those individuals who have the financial resources to move to another Member State and not benefit the non-migrant population. The initial scepticism faded with the judicial evolution of citizenship of the Union that shifted

---

23. Art. B, 3rd indent TEU (repealed).
24. See F. Goudappel, *The Effects of EU citizenship. Economic, Social and Political Rights in a Time of Constitutional Change* (TMC Asser Press, 2010), 5–6.
25. See for example A. Lansbergen and J. Shaw "National membership models in a multilevel Europe", 8 *International Journal of Constitutional Law* (2010); W. Maas, "Migrants, states, and EU Citizenship's unfulfilled promise", (2008) *Citizenship Studies*, 583–596 and the policy documents referred to at 590–591.
26. J.H.H. Weiler "To be a European citizen – Eros and civilization", (1997) *Journal of European Public Policy*, 495–519, at 499; see also C. Lyons, "Citizenship in the constitution of the European Union: Rhetoric or reality?" in R. Bellamy and A. Warleigh (Eds.) *Citizenship and Governance in the European Union* (Continuum, 2001), 93; U. J. d'Oliveira "Union citizenship: Pie in the sky?" in A. Rosas and E. Antola (Eds.), *A Citizen's Europe: In Search of a New Order* (Sage, 1995), 58; see also T. Kostakopoulou, "European Union citizenship: The journey goes on" in A. Ott and E. Vos (Eds.) *Fifty Years of European Integration: Foundations and Perspectives* (TMC Asser Press, 2009), 271–290, for a more detailed account of why scholars concluded that European citizenship was simply a symbolic and decorative institution.
27. M. Everson, "The legacy of the market citizen" in J. Shaw and G. More (Eds.) *New Legal Dynamics of European Union* (OUP, 1995), 73; T. Downes, "Market citizenship: Functionalism and fig-leaves" in R. Bellamy and A. Warleigh, op. cit. *supra* 26.

the economic paradigm of European integration away from market integration as the leading principle.[28]

The introduction of citizenship of the Union also inspired scholars to assess it in light of its future potential. On a more abstract level, the transformative potential of Union citizenship for the understanding of citizenship and non-state forms of governance was analysed.[29] Others looked at the membership element of citizenship and the (im-) possibility of forming a European demos and a European identity.[30] The disagreements and debates about EU citizenship have not gone silent while case law and legislative developments pushed forward the place of Union citizenship in the body of EU law.[31]

1.3.3 *Citizenship of the Union in the Lisbon Treaty*

The Treaties of Amsterdam and Nice did not add much to the provisions on citizenship of the Union. The "complementary" character explicitly included in the definition in Amsterdam was however re-defined in the Lisbon Treaty, as "additional", in order to express that EU citizenship can only add rights, and cannot detract from national citizenship.[32]

The Lisbon Treaty introduced Union citizenship in the Treaty on the European Union, under the Title "Provisions on democratic principles".[33] Here we find the provisions on the (political) relationship between the Union and the citizens (see section 9 below). They seem to be a far echo from the Laeken Declaration of 2000 that strongly called for a closer link between Union and citizens. Nevertheless indicative of a direct link between Union and citizens are textual references where the Union aims to offer internal and external security to *its* citizens[34] or to serve the interests of *its* citizens.[35]

The citizenship provisions in the TFEU brought few substantive changes to the pre-Lisbon provisions. A legal basis was added for the adoption of coordination and cooperation measures necessary to facilitate protection of Union citizens by diplomatic authorities of Member States

28. F. Wollenschläger, "A new fundamental freedom beyond market integration: Union citizenship and its dynamics for shifting the economic paradigm of European integration", (2011) ELJ, 1–34; but for an opposite view see N. Nic Shuibhne, "The resilience of EU market citizenship", 47 CML Rev. (2010), 1597.
29. A. Wiener, *Building Institutions. The Developing Practice of European Citizenship* (OUP, 1998); J. Shaw "The interpretation of European Union citizenship", 61 MLR (1998), 293–317; D. Kostakopoulou, "Co-creating European Union citizenship: Institutional *process* and crescive norms", (2013) CYELS, 255–281; see also the literature overview by D. Kostakopoulou, "Ideas, norms and European citizenship: Explaining institutional change", 68 MLR (2005), 233–267; J. Shaw, *The Transformation of Citizenship in the European Union* (CUP, 2007).
30. J.H.H. Weiler, "In defence of the status quo: Europe's constitutional Sonderweg" in J. Weiler and M. Wind (Eds.), *European Constitutionalism Beyond the State* (CUP, 2003), 7–24; J. Habermas "The crisis of the European Union in the light of a constitutionalization of International Law", (2012) EJIL, 335–348; R. Bellamy, "An ever closer union among the peoples of Europe: Republican intergovernmentalism and *demoi*cratic representation within the EU", (2013) *European Integration*, 499–516.
31. See the rich overview provided by D. Kochenov, "The essence of EU citizenship emerging from the last ten years of academic debate: Beyond the cherry blossoms and the moon?", (2013) ICQL, 97–136.
32. J. Shaw, "The Treaty of Lisbon and citizenship", *European Policy Brief Federal Trust*, available at <fedtrust.co.uk/content.php?content_id=127&cat_id=3> (last visited 18 Apr. 2014); A. Schrauwen, op. cit. *supra* note 6.
33. There had been no references to citizenship in the pre-Lisbon TEU.
34. Art. 3(2) and (5) TEU.
35. Art. 13 TEU. Shaw, op. cit. *supra* note 32, suggests these references reinforce a paternalistic notion of the Union as *protective* polity.

other than that of their nationality.[36] Furthermore, the exclusion of passports, identity cards, residence permits or any other such document in relation to the adoption of measures to facilitate the exercise of free movement rights under Article 21 (2) TFEU has been abolished, due to the introduction of a specific legal basis under Article 77 (3) TFEU. Measures with respect to social security and social protection in order to facilitate free movement, previously not covered under the citizenship provisions, may now be adopted according to a special legislative procedure.[37]

2. Acquisition and loss of Union citizenship

Access to Union citizenship is determined solely by reference to the nationality of the Member States. Member States decide on matters of nationality, and they may not "restrict the effects of the grant of nationality of another Member State [...]".[38] The absolute discretion of Member States has however consequences for other Member States, due to the fact that naturalized citizens as EU citizens enjoy free movement and residence rights.[39] However, the Court also made clear that the discretion to laying down conditions for the acquisition and loss of nationality was to be exercised "having due regard to Community law".

Though the Union has no competence to regulate issues of nationality, the Court in the *Rottmann* case has declared that loss or revocation of Member State nationality is a matter that is governed by requirements of EU law, because a possible loss of the status of Union citizen falls "by reason of its nature and its consequences within the ambit of Union law [...]" and therefore is "amenable to judicial review carried out in the light of European Union law".[40] States remain free to determine their own systems regarding acquisition and loss of nationality, but will have to observe limitations imposed by Union law such as proportionality, non-discrimination[41] and arguably fundamental rights.[42] This development could be seen as an affirmation of the autonomy of the content of Union citizenship, and as a legal manifestation of Union citizenship as the fundamental status of nationals of the Member States, as announced by the Court in *Grzelczyk*.[43]

Furthermore, though Union citizenship is additional to national citizenship, it may affect certain aspects of nationality law in other ways as well, notably restrictions on the use of surnames.[44] Moreover, it seemingly has also affected nationality laws in several Member States, who voluntarily established diverging and less strict naturalization requirements for EU citizens than those imposed on third-country nationals.[45] The one-way derivative nature of Union citizenship is under (slight) challenge.[46]

---

36. Art. 23 TFEU; Art. 35 TEU obliges Member States to contribute to the implementation of the right of Union citizens to protection in third countries.
37. Art. 21(3) TFEU.
38. Case C-369/90, *Mario Vicente Micheletti et al. v. Delegacion del Gobierno en Caniabria*, para 10. See also Case C-200/02, *Chen*.
39. S. Iglesiás Sanchez, op. cit. *supra* note 5 at 86; G.R. de Groot, "Latin-American European citizens: Some consequences of the autonomy of the Member States of the European Union in nationality matters", 9 MJ (2002), 115–120.
40. Case C-135/08, *Rottmann v. Freistadt Bayern*, paras. 42 and 48.
41. Case C-21/74, *Airola*.
42. S. Iglesías Sanchez, op. cit. *supra* note 5, at 86; N. Cambien, "The impact of Union citizenship on Member State immigration laws. Some potentially perverse side-effects resulting from recent ECJ case law", available at <ssrn.com/abstract=2189492> (last visited 29 Apr. 2014), at 30.
43. Case C-184/99, *Grzelczyk*, para 31.
44. Case C-148/02, *Garcia Avello*; Case C-353/06, *Grunkin and Paul*; Case C-208/09, *Sayn-Wittgenstein*.
45. D. Kochenov, op. cit. *supra* note 5, at 2.
46. See also D. Kochenov, op. cit. *supra* note 31.

3. Union citizenship as a legal status

Article 20(2) TFEU points at the legal consequences for those having Union citizenship: they shall enjoy the rights and be subject to the duties provided for in the Treaties. However, citizenship duties are nowhere to be found in the Treaties. Where some see the lack of duties as a sign of immaturity of EU citizenship, and others contest their need,[47] the evolution of EU citizenship shows unmistakably a rights-based approach. According to the Court of Justice, Union citizenship is destined to be the fundamental status of nationals of the Member States.[48] Moreover, national measures that would deprive citizens of the Union of the genuine enjoyment of the substance of the rights conferred by virtue of their status as EU citizens are precluded by that status.[49] And indeed, important rights result from this status.

The status has improved the position of economically inactive persons with regards to the right of residence and of non-discrimination, also because the Court has been creative in construing in favor of the Union citizen the condition of Article 18 TFEU according to which the prohibition of discrimination only bites in matters which come within the application of the Treaties. Furthermore, case law has constructed the right of free movement and residence granted to EU citizens under Article 21 TFEU as a directly enforceable Union law right.[50]

3.1 *Directive 2004/38: Personal scope and beneficiaries*

The Court's case law on free movement and residence rights attached to the status of Union citizen has been largely incorporated in Directive 2004/38. On 30 April 2006 the existing EU instruments dealing separately with workers, self-employed persons, as well as students and other inactive persons were codified and reviewed in a single legislative act, Directive 2004/38 on the right of citizens of the Union and their family members to move and reside freely within the territory of the Union.[51] It deals with three subjects related to the rights attached to the status of Union citizens: the conditions governing the exercise of free movement and residence rights, the right of permanent residence and the limits placed on these rights. Provisions on the personal scope of the Directive and on the beneficiaries precede these subjects. Finally, the Directive also includes procedural guarantees. The Court has repeatedly insisted that the provisions establishing the free movement of workers must be construed broadly[52] and has extended that principle to the provisions of the Directive.[53] It is in line with the aims of Directive 2004/38 to "simplify and strengthen the right of free movement and residence of all Union citizens".[54]

The Directive applies to Union citizens and their family members, irrespective of nationality. Article 2(2) of the Directive defines family members as the spouse or the registered partner, the direct descendants under the age of 21 or who are dependants and those of the spouse or partner, the dependent direct relatives in the ascending line and those of the spouse or partner. Furthermore, Article 3(2) of the Directive requires the host Member State to facilitate, in

---

47. D. Kochenov, "EU citizenship without duties", 20 ELJ (2014), 482–498.
48. Case C-184/99, *Grzelczyk*, N. Cambien, op. cit. *supra* note 42.
49. Case C-34/09, *Ruiz Zambrano*.
50. Case C-413/99, *Baumbast and R. v. Secretary of State for the Home Department*.
51. O.J. 2004, L 158/77; an instructive analysis of the process leading up to the Directive can be found in the institutional report by Michal Meduna included in the Union Citizenship report of the FIDE Congress 2014, which also contains national reports laying out application of the Directive in practice, U. Neergaard, C. Jacqueson and N. Holst-Christensen, *Union Citizenship: Development, Impact and Challenges. The XXVI FIDE Congress in Copenhagen, 2014. Congress Publications Vol. 2*, (DJØF Publishing, 2014).
52. Case C-139/75, *Kempf*; Case C-316/85, *Lebon*; Case C-1/05, *Jia*.
53. Case C-423/12, *Reyes*, para 23; Case C-127/08, *Metock*, para 84.
54. Recital 3 of the Preamble to Directive 2004/38.

accordance with its national legislation, entry and residence for any other family members who are dependants in the country from which they have come, or are members of the household of the Union citizen, or whose health condition strictly requires the personal care by the Union citizen and the partner (with no reference to gender) with whom the Union citizen has a durable relationship, duly attested. The Article gives expression to recital 6 of the Preamble that sets the objective to maintain the unity of the family in a broader sense.

Whether the concept of spouse also covers same sex marriages, made possible under the laws of some Member States, is unclear.[55] Inclusion of the registered partner as family member follows the Court's decision in *Reed*.[56] Recognition as family member is conditional on registration of the partnership on the basis of legislation of a Member State and treatment by the host state of registered partnerships as equivalent to marriage (and in accordance with the conditions laid down in the host state's legislation). Who is considered family member may thus differ from State to State. Divorce, annulment of marriage or termination of the registered partnership shall not affect the right of residence of the former spouse or partner (Art. 13). For non-EU former spouses or partners extra conditions as to duration of the marriage or relationship and time of residence in the host state are imposed (Art. 13(2)).

The concept of "dependant" qualifies which children above 21 and which relatives in the ascending line or which other family members may join the Union citizen under the terms of the Directive. The dependent status is the result of a factual situation characterized by the fact that material support for that family member is provided by the Union citizen who has exercised his right of free movement or by his spouse.[57] There is no need to show that the dependant has tried to obtain a job or subsistence support, all that matters is that the Union citizen regularly, for a significant period, pays a sum of money to the dependant, necessary in order for him to support himself in the State where the dependant resides. The dependency must exist at the time when he applies to join the Union citizen on whom he is dependent. Once he has joined the Union citizen, he will not lose residence status for being no longer dependent, as Article 23 of the Directive entitles family members who have a right of residence to take up employment or self-employment in the host State.[58]

Beneficiaries of the Directive are Union citizens[59] who move to or reside in a Member State other than that of their nationality[60] and the family members (as defined in Art. 2 point 2) who accompany or join them. The members of the extended family (as defined in Art. 3(2)) "are conferred a certain advantage, compared with applications for entry and residence of other nationals of third states".[61] Member States must ensure that their legislation contains criteria enabling applicants belonging to the extended family to obtain a decision that is founded on an extensive examination of their personal circumstances. Member States have a wide discretion as regards the selection of these criteria, provided they are consistent with the normal meaning of the term

55. The Court is asked to answer that question in Case C-673/16, *Coman*, pending.
56. Case C-59/85, *Reed*.
57. Case C-1/05, *Jia*; Case C-83/11, *Rahman*; Case C-423/12, *Reyes*, para 21.
58. Case C-423/12, *Reyes*, para 31–32.
59. In Case C-364/10, *Hungary v. Slovak Republic*, the Court stated that Heads of State have a status with a specific character capable of distinguishing the person who enjoys that status from all other Union citizens and therefore their access to the territory is not governed by the same conditions as those applicable to other citizens.
60. Directive 2004/38 has been incorporated in the European Economic Area Agreement, Annex VIII, point 3. Thus, nationals from Norway, Iceland and Liechtenstein are also beneficiaries of the Directive, even though they are not Union citizens.
61. Case C-83/11, *Rahman*, para 21.

"facilitate". Member States may include requirements to the nature and duration of dependence to satisfy themselves that dependence is not brought about with the sole objective to obtain entry and residence in the host State. Refusal of entry and residence must be motivated and applicants are entitled to judicial review.[62]

3.2 *Relationship between the Directive and the Treaty provisions*

Since the scope of application of the Directive is limited to situations where Union citizens are in a host State, the Treaty provisions on Union citizenship retain their relevance for Union citizens claiming rights in their State of nationality, irrespective of whether they never moved[63] or return to their home State.[64] Interpretation of Treaty provisions, as primary source of Union law, will prevail over and steer interpretation of the provisions of Directive 2004/38.[65] However, especially in cases of family rights of migrants, the Court has also referred to the Directive in order to give substance to Treaty provisions. Thus, Article 21(1) provides a derived right of residence for family members irrespective of nationality upon return to the State of nationality of the Union citizen, whereby no more strict conditions may be imposed than those imposed by the Directive.[66]

The Treaty provisions on free movement of workers, self-employed and freedom to provide services retain their relevance for the residence and equal treatment rights of Union citizens and their family members, as does secondary legislation based on those provisions.[67] Furthermore, in some instances provisions of the Directive and Treaty provisions may apply cumulatively.[68] Litigants therefore will likely continue to invoke Treaty provisions and other relevant secondary legislation next to provisions of the Directive.

4. Free movement rights

Of the rights laid down in Articles 20–25 TFEU, Article 21(1) TFEU appears as the first of rights ascribed to the status of citizens of the Union.[69] It gives Union citizens the right to move and reside freely within the territory of the Member States, subject to the limitations and conditions laid down in the Treaties and by the measures adopted to give them effect. As with the Treaty provisions on economic free movement, the presence of a cross-border element triggers the application of Union law. The Court confirmed the reading that citizenship of the Union was "not intended to extend the scope *ratione materiae* of the Treaty also to internal situations which have no link with Community Law".[70] As a consequence, in principle only citizens who have moved between Member States can invoke the special rights attached to their Union citizenship status. In *Walloon Government*, for instance, the Court distinguished two kinds of situations.[71] Where citizens have never exercised their freedom to move within the Union, Union law cannot apply. In situations where citizens have made use of their right to freedom of movement Union law

62. Ibid.
63. Case C-34/09, *Zambrano*.
64. Case C-456/12, *O. and B.*
65. Case C-75/11, *Commission v. Austria*.
66. Case C-456/12, *O. and B.*
67. Joined Case C-147/11 and C-148/11, *Czop and Punakova*.
68. Case C-73/08, *Bressol and others*.
69. A.G. Pergola describes it as a primary right, inseparable from citizenship of the Union in his Opinion in Case C-85/96, *Martínez Sala*, para 18.
70. Joined Cases C-64/96 and C-65/96, *Uecker and Jacquet*, para 23.
71. Case C-212/06, *Government of the French Community and Walloon Government v. Flemish Government*.

does apply. The result is in line with the principle of conferral, but it seems illogical and strange that fortuitous previous movement determines whether one has access to rights under EU law.[72]

The Court interprets Article 21 TFEU as a directly enforceable right.[73] Any conditions and limitations imposed on the exercise of the right to move and reside freely require a justification and must respect the principle of proportionality. Indeed, the Court interprets this right in quite a similar way to the approach followed for the economic fundamental freedoms under the Treaty (see Ch. 12–15 of this book on the economic freedoms), as implying a prohibition of unjustified restrictions of this right. This led to Union citizens challenging residence conditions for access to social benefits and rights – such as war pensions, unemployment benefits, invalidity benefits, student maintenance grants, tax benefits and surnames – from the Member State of their nationality.[74] The *sedes materiae* does not have to fall under Union law. Whenever social benefits are at stake, the concerned Member State may ensure that there is a connection between its society and the recipient of a benefit, as long as the conditions it imposes are proportionate. In *Tas-Hagen* the Court said that with regard to benefits not covered by Union law, Member States "enjoy a wide margin of appreciation in deciding which criteria are to be used when assessing the degree of connection to society, while at the same time complying with the limits imposed by [Union] law". The degree of connection to society as a legal standard is not without problems, and has been criticized for having a vague and flexible nature.[75]

4.1 *Rights of exit and entry*

Chapter II of Directive 2004/38 concerns rights of exit (Art. 4) and entry (Art. 5). Exit may be restricted on grounds of public policy, provided the measures restricting exit respect the general principles outlined in Article 27 of the Directive (see below section 6).[76] No visa or equivalent formality may be imposed on nationals of Member States leaving or entering another Member State; a valid identity card or passport is sufficient. Non-EU family members may be required to have an entry visa, but shall be exempted from the visa requirement once they have a residence card evidencing their right of residence as family member of an EU citizen.[77] In case family members do not have the necessary travel documents or necessary visa when they apply for a residence card as family member, they must get the opportunity to obtain those documents

72. A.G. Sharpston describes the result as "curiously random" in her Opinion in Case C-34/09, *Zambrano*, para 135. For a general critical analysis see A. Tryfonidou, *Reverse Discrimination in EC Law* (Kluwer, 2009).
73. Case C-413/99, *Baumbast and R.*
74. Case C-192/05, *Tas-Hagen*; Case C-499/06, *Nerkowska*; Case C-221/07, *Zablocka*; Case C-406/06, *De Cuyper*; Case C-503/09, *Stewart*; Joined Cases C-11/06 and C-12/06, *Morgan* and *Bucher*; Case C-135/99, *Elsen*; Case C-76/05, *Schwarz and Gootjes-Schwarz*; Case C-353/06, *Grunkin-Paul*; Case C-208/09, *Sayn-Wittgenstein*; Joined Cases C-523/11 and C-585/11, *Prinz* and *Seeberger.*
75. Case C-192/05, *Tas-Hagen*, para 36. The connection to the society of the Member State providing the benefit, whether this is the state of nationality or not, is also known as "the real link" case law. See further S. O'Leary "Solidarity and citizenship rights in the Charter of Fundamental Rights of the European Union" in G. de Búrca (Ed.), *EU Law and the Welfare State* (Hart, 2005); E. Spaventa and M. Dougan (Eds.), *Social Welfare and EU Law* (Hart, 2005); C. Nedwick, "The European Court of Justice, trans-national health care, and social citizenship: accidental death of a concept", 26 *Wisconsin International Law Journal* (2008), 844; A.P. van der Mei, *Free Movement of Persons within the European Community: Cross-border Access to Public Benefits* (Hart, 2003); A.P. van der Mei, "Union citizenship and the 'de-nationalisation' of the territorial welfare state", 7 *European Journal of Migration and Law* (2005), 203–211; G. Davies "The humiliation of the state as a constitutional tactic" in F. Ambtenbrink and P. van den Berg (Eds.), *The Constitutional Integrity of the European Union* (TMC Asser Press, 2010), 147–174; K. Lenaerts, "European Union citizenship, national welfare systems and social solidarity", 18 *Jurisprudencija* (2011), 397–422.
76. Case C-33/07, *Jipa*; Case C-430/10, *Gaydarov*; Case C-434/10, *Aladzhov*.
77. Case C-202/13, *McCarthy and Others.*

or to prove by other means their identity and status as family member of an EU citizen (Art. 5(4)).[78]

A condition of previous lawful residence in another Member State may not be imposed. In *Akrich*, a case preceding Directive 2004/38, the Court declared that the relevant provisions on free movement aimed to secure fee movement within the Union, and that non-EU family members could only derive free movement rights in case they already had a valid right to remain in a Member State.[79] The ruling implied that according to the division of competences between Member States and Union, the Union is competent to regulate movement of Union citizens and their family members within the Union only. In *Jia*, the Court attenuated the condition of prior lawful residence limiting the impossibility to derived rights of free movement to situations where previous residence was unlawful or seeking to evade national immigration rules illicitly.[80] In *Metock* the Court explicitly reconsidered its position, pointing at the aim of Directive 2004/38 to strengthen the free movement and residence rights of all Union citizens.[81] It declared the Union competent to regulate "the entry and residence of nationals of non-member countries who are family members of a Union citizen in the Member State in which that citizen has exercised his right of freedom of movement, including where the family members were not already lawfully resident in another Member State".[82] Moreover, the Court added that it makes no difference whether non-EU nationals enter the host State before or after the Union citizen or before or after becoming his family members.[83] After the *Metock* ruling, several Member States tried in vain to persuade the Commission to table a revision of the Directive in order to regain control over first access of non-EU family members to the territory of the Union. Moreover, the Court's reading of the aim of the Directive as "strengthening the rights of Union citizens" is seen as an illustration of the weak potential of the EU legislator to restrain a more expansive reading of Union citizenship.[84]

Article 21 TFEU not only encompasses the right to leave the home state[85] and to enter and reside in another Member State, but also the right to return to the home state. Whereas Directive 2004/38 elaborates the first and second group of rights, the right to return to the home state is covered by Article 21 TFEU. This implies that return to the home state cannot be restricted without justification. The grant of a derived right of residence in the home State to a third-country national who is a family member of a Union citizen and with whom that Union citizen has resided in a host State, can be based on Article 21(1) TFEU when a Union citizen, not economically active in the host State, returns to the Member State of nationality.[86] In such a situation the conditions of the residence of a Union citizen in a Member State other than that of which he is a national as elaborated in Directive 2004/38 (section 5.2 below) apply by analogy. However, a derived right of residence will only occur in case the residence in the host state has been "sufficiently genuine so as to enable the Union citizen to create or strengthen family life" in the host state.[87] Residence of three months or longer, and under the conditions of the Directive, is sufficient evidence of genuine residence in the host state. Whether shorter periods of

78. Case C-459/99, *MRAX*.
79. Case C-109/01, *Akrich*.
80. Case C-105, *Jia*, para 31.
81. Case C-127/08, *Metock*, paras. 58–59.
82. Ibid., para 65.
83. Ibid., para 93.
84. D. Thym, op. cit. *supra* note 7, esp. at 157–159.
85. Case C-249/11, *Byankov*.
86. Case C-456/12, *O.* and *B.*
87. Ibid., para 51.

residence might also qualify as "genuine" remains open. The next sections will discuss the conditions of those residence rights and how these can have a (sometimes problematic) impact on both the initial ambition to mark with Union citizenship the intention to move beyond market integration and the Member States' concern for their national welfare systems.

5. Residence rights

5.1 *Residence rights under the Treaty provisions*

As indicated above, citizenship of the Union was not intended to extend the scope *ratione materiae* of the Treaty to internal situations, which have no link with Union law. Nevertheless, the link with Union law can also be established in cases where the status of citizen of the Union itself is at stake. As we have seen, the loss of the status and thereby deprivation of the rights attaching to the status may fall within the ambit of EU law and it would be contrary to Article 20 TFEU not to observe the principle of proportionality when withdrawing nationality from a citizen of the Union.[88] This reasoning is taken a step further in situations where the status as such is not lost, but where measures have the effect of depriving citizens of the Union of "the genuine enjoyment of the substance of rights" attached to the status. In a controversial decision in *Ruiz Zambrano*, the Court interpreted Article 20 TFEU as precluding the refusal of a right of residence and a work permit to a third country national upon whom his minor children, who are Union citizens, are dependent, in so far as the refusal would deprive those children of the genuine enjoyment of the substance of the rights attaching to the status of European Union citizen.[89] The problem in the case at hand was that no free movement rights were used. To the surprise of many, the ECJ argued that denying a residence right to the third country national parents would "lead to a situation where those children, citizens of the Union, would have to leave the territory of the Union in order to accompany their parents." It extended the same reasoning to a refusal to grant a work permit to the third country national parent as this might lead to a lack of sufficient resources to provide for himself and his family, which in turn might lead to a decision to leave the Union territory. When the children have to leave the territory of the Union with their parents they "would, in fact, be unable to exercise the substance of the rights conferred on them by virtue of their status as citizens of the Union."[90] In subsequent case law the Court emphasized the exceptional nature of its ruling in the *Ruiz Zambrano* case, and that it would only apply in situations where the Union citizen will be *forced* to leave the Union territory.[91] In *O and S* the Court had to answer the question whether only biological parents could derive a residence rights from their Union citizen children under Article 20 TFEU.[92] The Court made clear that the principles stated in the *Ruiz Zambrano* judgment are not "confined to situations in which there is a blood relationship between the third country national for whom a right of residence is sought and the

---

88. Case C-135/08, *Rottmann*.
89. Case C-34/09, *Ruiz Zambrano*; I. Solanke "Using the citizen to bring the refugee in", 75 MLR (2010), 101–111; K. Hailbronner and D. Thym, "Comment on Case C-34/09 Ruiz Zambrano", 48 CML Rev. (2011), 1253; D. Kochenov and R. Plender "EU citizenship: From an incipient form to an incipient substance? The discovery of the Treaty text", 37 EL Rev. (2012), 369; H. van Eijken and S.A. de Vries, "A new route into the promised land? Being a European citizen after Ruiz Zambrano", 36 EL Rev. (2011), 704.
90. Case C-34/09, *Ruiz Zambrano*, para 44.
91. Case C-434/09, *McCarthy*; Case C-256/11, *Dereci*; Case C-40/11, *Iida*; Case C-87/12 *Kreshnik Ymeraga*. In C-86/12, *Alokpa*, the Court made clear that the responsibility for protecting the genuine enjoyment of the substance of the rights of Union citizens lies ultimately with the Member State of nationality.
92. Joined Cases C-356/11 and C-357/11, *O. and S.*, and *L.*

Union citizen who is a minor from whom that right of residence might be derived."[93] Instead, the legal, financial, or emotional dependency of the minor citizen on the third country national for whom a right of residence is sought has to be taken into consideration.

In its *Ruiz Zambrano* judgment and subsequent case law on residence rights derived from Article 20 TFEU, the ECJ did not refer to the EU Charter of Fundamental Rights nor to fundamental rights as general principles of Union law, even though national judges explicitly asked the Court how to interpret the citizenship provisions in conjunction with provisions of the EU Charter of Fundamental Rights.[94] Arguably, EU fundamental right protection does not apply in case a situation does not fall under the scope of EU law, and as a consequence EU fundamental right protection cannot be invoked as long as Union citizens are not forced to leave the territory of the Union as a consequence of not granting residence rights to their third country parent.[95] Thus, in *O.* and *S.*, the ECJ refers to Articles 7 and 24 of the EU Charter of Fundamental Rights that Member States must take into account when deciding on residence status of third country national family members on the basis of Directive 2003/86/EC on the right to family reunification,[96] whereas no such reference was made in the context of similar decisions based on Article 20 TFEU. The paradoxical result that EU fundamental rights apply to residence of family members of third country nationals but not to residence of family members of EU citizens in their State of nationality was said to sit ill with the idea that EU citizenship is destined to be the fundamental status of the nationals of the Member States.[97] However, six years after the *Zambrano* judgment, the Court recognized the relevance of Articles 7 and 24 of the EU Charter of Fundamental Rights in the context of residence rights for third country family members based on Article 20 TFEU. Interestingly, it did so in a case where the national judge did not refer to fundamental rights in the preliminary questions.[98]

5.2 *Residence rights under Directive 2004/38*

The Directive makes a distinction between residence up to three months and residence for more than three months and up to five years, imposing different conditions on these categories. It introduces a right of permanent residence for citizens and their family members who have resided legally for a continuous period of five years in a host Member States. In general the rights increase the longer one resides in a host Member State. Especially during the period from three months to five years, conditions differ according to whether citizens are economically active or not. As we will see, the formulation of these conditions in the Directive is sometimes vague and inconsistent.[99]

---

93. Ibid., para 55.
94. Case C-34/09, *Ruiz Zambrano*. See also Case C-87/12, *Kreshnik Ymeraga* and Case C-86/12, *Alokpa*.
95. See Case C-165/14, *Rendón Marín*, para 81; Case C-87/12, *Kreshnik Ymeraga*, paras. 42–43. By contrast, EU fundamental rights do apply when a third country parent with a derived right of residence is expelled, Case C- 304/14, *CS*, para 36; see also, Art. 51 EU Charter of Fundamental Rights on its scope of application.
96. O.J. 2004, L 158/77.
97. A.G. Sharpston in Case C-34/09, *Ruiz Zambrano*, at para 170; D. Kochenov, "Equality across the legal orders; Or voiding EU citizenship of content" in E. Guild, C.J. Gortàzar, and D. Kostakopoulou (Eds.), op. cit. *supra* note 5, 301–321.
98. Case C-133/15, *Chavez-Vilchez a.o.*, para 70.
99. See also the criticism of K. Hailbronner, "Union citizenship and access to social benefits", (2005) CML Rev., 1245–1267, esp. 1258–1264.

5.2.1 *Residence up to three months*

All Union citizens, whether economically active or not, and their family members enjoy a right of residence up to three months without any conditions or formalities other than the possession of a valid residence card or passport. If the person concerned cannot show a valid identity card or passport, but can provide unequivocal proof of his nationality by other means, a right of residence may not be refused on that basis.[100] The right to reside up to three months is not unlimited, as those enjoying it may not become, in the ambiguous terms of the Directive, an "unreasonable burden" on the social assistance system of the host Member State (Art. 14 (1)). They do however enjoy a right to equal treatment (Art. 24 (1)), but not a right to social assistance (Art. 24 (2)).[101]

5.2.2 *Residence longer than three months and up to five years*

Workers and self-employed have a right to reside longer than three months in the host state based on that status. Others must fulfil conditions of sufficient resources for themselves and their family not to become a burden on the social assistance system of the host state and must have comprehensive sickness insurance cover. Students have to fulfil special conditions of enrolment in an educational establishment and assuring relevant national authorities they have sufficient resources for themselves and their family members. Students can bring only their spouse/partner and children with them (Art. 7), whereas all other citizens may be accompanied or joined by dependent relatives in the ascending line as well.[102]

Administrative formalities are included in Articles 8 through 11. They concern registration with the relevant authorities, the issue of a registration certificate to Union citizens and their EU family members, and proof of sufficient resources. Any system for processing personal data relating to Union citizens in the host State to support national authorities responsible for applying the law with respect to residence may contain only data necessary for that application and may be kept only when a central register makes application of that law more effective. These data may not be stored and managed for statistical purposes, nor can they be used for the purpose of fighting crime unless similar data of nationals are kept.[103]

To determine sufficiency of the resources, Member States may not lay down a fixed amount, but they must take into account the personal situation of the person concerned. In any case, they may not determine that the amount is sufficient only if it is higher than the threshold below which their nationals become eligible for social assistance (Art. 8(4)). Non-EU family members must be issued with a residence card for family members in case the planned period for residence is for more than three months. Registration certificates and residence cards have a declaratory character. The declaratory character means that residence of a Union citizen or of a family member of a Union citizen may not be regarded as illegal within the meaning of European Union law solely on the ground that he does not hold a residence card, nor can it be regarded legal within the meaning of European Union law solely on the ground that such a card was issued to him.[104]

Article 14(2) provides that the right of residence is retained as long as the persons concerned meet the conditions set out in Article 7, e.g. being economically active or having sufficient

---

100. Case C-215/03, *Salah Oulane.*
101. See also Case C-299/14, *García-Nieto.*
102. See *supra*, section 3.2.1.
103. Case C-542/06, *Huber.*
104. Case C-325/09, *Dias*, para 49; Case C-456/12, *O. and B.*, para 60.

resources and a comprehensive sickness insurance.[105] Another person may provide the resources, as there is no condition that the person concerned must himself have such resources.[106] The conditions apply until the right of permanent residence is acquired, after a legal residence for a continuous period of five years. The conditions aim to prevent so-called social benefit tourism. Nevertheless, Article 24(2) limits the derogation from equal treatment in social benefits to the first three months of residence, or longer in case of jobseekers (see also part II, section 3). In the period between three months and five years, Union citizens or their family members may have recourse to the social assistance system of the host Member State, but they may not become an "unreasonable burden" for the host state. In this way, the Directive incorporates the case law developments with respect to equal treatment of Union citizens before 2004.[107] Article 14 of the Directive permits Member States to verify if the financial conditions are fulfilled in case of reasonable doubt, but these examinations may not be carried out systematically. Furthermore, expulsion measures may not be the automatic consequence of recourse to the social assistance system. Citizens and their family members may be a reasonable burden. It is a consequence of the principle that limitations and conditions to free movement rights must be construed narrowly and in compliance with the limits imposed by EU law and the principle of proportionality.[108] However, the Directive did not put a halt to discussions on what constitutes a reasonable burden and which benefits should be regarded as social assistance. It has been far from clear what criteria should be taken into consideration when assessing the proportionality of a refusal to grant social assistance. Furthermore, the case law is inconsistent in focusing on a broad interpretation of free movement rights in some cases and on the importance of the limitations and conditions in the interest of the Member States in others. It has led to incoherent and unpredictable outcomes. In particular it is not clear at what point economically inactive EU citizens who apply for social benefits can be said to no longer fulfil the conditions of having sufficient resources and therefore no longer enjoy a residence right based on Directive 2004/38.

In *Brey*, the Court defines social assistance as "covering all assistance introduced by the public authorities, whether at national, regional or local level, that can be claimed by an individual who does not have resources sufficient to meet his own basic needs and the needs of his family and who, by reason of that fact, may become a burden on the public finances of the host Member State during his period of residence which could have consequences for the overall level of assistance which may be granted by that State".[109] When the competent authorities of the host state examine an application of a Union citizen for a social benefit they must take into account *inter alia* the amount and the regularity of the income which he receives and the period during which the benefit applied for is likely to be granted in order to define whether the burden becomes "unreasonable". Furthermore, the proportion of the beneficiaries of the social benefit

---

105. In case the relationship with the Union citizen ends, or the Union citizen dies or departs, family members may keep their right of residence under the conditions of Arts. 12 or 13 of the Directive, see *infra*, section 8.
106. Case C-200/02, *Zhu and Chen*; Case C-408/03, *Commission v. Belgium*.
107. Case C-85/96, *Martínez Sala*; Case C-184/99, *Grzelczyk*; Case C-413/99, *Baumbast and R*; Case C-456/02, *Trojani*.
108. Case C-413/99, *Baumbast and R*; Case C-200/02; Case C-456/02, *Trojani*, para 34; Case C-200/02, *Zhu and Chen*, paras. 31 and 32.
109. Case C-140/12, *Brey*, para 61. In *Brey*, the Court also had to rule on the relationship between the entitlement to minimum social benefits under Reg. 883/2004 on the coordination of social security systems and the entitlement to social assistance under Directive 2004/38. The argument that its broad definition of "social assistance" in the specific context of Directive 2004/38 is not precluded by Reg. 883/2004 results in a limitation of the legal relevance of Reg. 883/2004 for economically inactive citizens. For a criticism of that argument see H. Verschueren, "Free movement or benefit tourism: The unreasonable burden of *Brey*", (2014) *European Journal of Migration and Law*, 147–179.

who are Union citizens may be relevant to define the extent of the burden.[110] On top of that, Recital 16 of Directive 2004/38 refers to duration of residence and personal circumstances that should be taken into account. Needless to say that the administrative costs of such an extensive assessment can be very high.[111] Once it is decided that the Union citizen becomes an unreasonable burden, the authorities may decide to withdraw or not renew his residence permit. However, as long as the Union citizen is lawfully residing in the host state, he may rely on EU law in order to receive social benefits, notwithstanding that this may subsequently compromise his right of residence.[112]

In *Dano*, the Court seems to shift its focus towards the interest of the Member States.[113] Where in earlier cases,[114] dating from before Directive 2004/38, the Court found that lawfully residing EU citizens could claim equal access to social benefits in a host State regardless of the basis of their lawful residence, in *Dano* the Court said that "so far as concerns access to social benefits [...], a Union citizen can claim equal treatment with nationals of the host Member State only if his residence in the host Member State complies with the conditions of Directive 2004/38".[115] The Court argued that "preventing Union citizens who are nationals of other Member States becoming an unreasonable burden on the social assistance system of the host Member State" is an objective of the Directive.[116] It contrasts with other Court's rulings, in which the Directive's aim to facilitate and strengthen free movement rights is paramount and where emphasis was put on restrictive interpretation of limitations and conditions to free movement. The circumstances in *Dano*, which concerned EU citizens living in an other Member State than that of their nationality who had never worked, never looked for a job and had no intention to do so, seemed to contribute to the Court's ruling. It is however questionable whether this ruling applies in all cases that concern economically inactive citizens with scarce resources.[117]

Whenever Union citizens are expelled on grounds that they do not (longer) fulfil the conditions for residence longer than three months and up to five years as outlined in Article 7 of the Directive, a ban on entry may not be imposed (Art. 15(3)).

5.2.3 *Right of permanent residence*

After a continuous period of five years legal residence, Union citizens and their (non-EU) family members who have legally resided with them for a continuous period of five years shall have a right of permanent residence in the host state (Art. 16).[118] When that right is acquired, with effect from the actual moment at which the five year period is completed,[119] the conditions of sufficient resources and sickness insurance no longer apply, and those enjoying the right of permanent residence enjoy equal treatment also in respect to social assistance. Furthermore, they are better protected against expulsion on grounds of public policy or public security (see below,

110. Case C-140/12, *Brey*, para 78.
111. H. Verschueren, op. cit. *supra* note 109, at 174.
112. Case C-184/99, *Grzelczyk*, para 42; Case C-456/02, *Trojani*, para 45; Opinion of A.G. Wahl in Case C-140/12, *Brey*, para 94.
113. Case C-333/13, *Dano*.
114. Case C-85/96, *Martinez Sala*; Case C-184/99 *Grzelczyk*; Case C-456/02, *Trojani*.
115. Case C-333/13, *Dano*, para 69.
116. Ibid., para 74.
117. For a detailed account of the ambivalence of the case law on access to social benefits and suggestions on how to bring coherence into that case law, see D. Thym, "The elusive limits of solidarity: Residence rights of and social benefits for economically inactive Union citizens", (2015) CML Rev., 17–50.
118. Case C-529/11, *Alarape*, para 34.
119. Case C-325/09, *Dias*, para 57.

section 6). As long as non-EU nationals keep their status as spouse of a Union citizen, they fulfil the condition of residing "with" the latter, even though the spouses decided to separate and commenced residing with other partners.[120]

In *Lassal*,[121] the Court referred to the integration-based reasoning behind the right of permanent residence. Its objective and purpose are to promote social cohesion and to strengthen the feeling of Union citizenship. Accordingly, loss of the right of permanent residence can only happen on account of absence of more than two consecutive years, justified because after that period the link with the host Member State is loosened. The integration-based reasoning explains why, for the purposes of the acquisition of the permanent right of residence, continuous periods of five years' legal residence completed before the date of transposition of Directive 2004/38, in accordance with the earlier EU law instruments, must be taken into account.[122] The earlier EU law instruments are those that Directive 2004/38 codified, revised and repealed.[123]

The text of the Directive refers to a five-year period of "legal residence" and seems to indicate that the integration objective that lies behind the right of permanent residence is based on territorial and time factors. However, the Court has argued that the integration objective is also based on qualitative elements.[124] Therefore, it said, only residence that complies with the conditions set out in Article 7 of the Directive (being economically active or having sufficient resources and a comprehensive sickness insurance) is considered to be legal residence within the meaning of Article 16 of the Directive.[125] Previous periods of residence by a national of an acceding State must, upon accession, be taken into account for the purpose of the acquisition of the right of permanent residence, provided those periods were completed in compliance with the conditions of Article 7 of the Directive.[126] Legal residence based on other instruments, for instance residence based on Article 12 of Regulation 1612/68 that entitles parents a derived right of residence based on the right of children to continue their education in the host Member State, does not lead to a right of permanent residence under Directive 2004/38.[127] Imposition of a prison sentence by a national court is considered to show the non-compliance with the values expressed by the society of a host Member State.[128] Therefore periods of imprisonment do not contribute to the degree of integration in the host State and interrupt the period of five years continuous residence upon which permanent residence is acquired.[129] The reading of "qualitative elements" into the integration-based reasoning behind Article 16 of the Directive is criticized for not being consistent with hermeneutic principles governing the interpretation of EU law, since it is a very restrictive interpretation that furthermore might open the door to executive discretion in the treatment of Union citizens.[130]

---

120. Case C-244/13, *Ogieriakhi*.
121. Case C-162/09, *Lassal*.
122. Ibid.
123. Case C-529/11, *Alarape*.
124. Case C-325/09, *Dias*, para 64.
125. Joined Cases C-424/10 and C-425/10, *Ziolkowski and Szeja*; Case C-529/11, *Alarape*, para 35.
126. Joined Cases C-424/10 and C-425/10, *Ziolkowski and Szeja*.
127. Case C-529/11, *Alarape*.
128. Case C-378/12, *Onuekwere*.
129. Thought the Court in *Onuekwere* referred to non-EU family members only, the Court seems to indicate that the same reasoning applies to EU citizens in Case C-400/12, *M.G.*, para 32.
130. E. Spaventa, "Earned citizenship – understanding Union citizenship through its scope" in D. Kochenov (Ed.), *EU Citizenship and Federalism: the Role of Rights* (CUP, 2017), at 178–203.

6. Limiting the right of residence and expulsion

The broad reading of entry and residence rights for EU citizens and their (non-EU national) family members leads to partial loss of Member State control over migration. However, Member States may deny entry to Union citizens or their family members on grounds of public policy, public security or public health (Arts. 27–29 of the Directive). Entry restrictions on grounds of public policy or public security must comply with the principle of proportionality and be based exclusively on the personal conduct of the individual concerned. That conduct must represent a genuine, present and sufficiently serious threat affecting one of the fundamental interests of society.[131] Within three months from the date of arrival of the person concerned on the territory of the host State, that State may request information from the home State or other Member States concerning previous police records of the person concerned. Such a request may not be a matter of routine and can only be made when it is considered "essential" (Art. 27(3)). Previous criminal convictions do not in themselves constitute grounds to restrict entry.[132] Entry restrictions based on public health may only be taken in case of diseases with epidemic potential as defined by the relevant instruments of the World Health Organization and other infectious diseases or contagious parasitic diseases, provided protection provisions apply to nationals as well. However, if diseases occur later than three months after arrival the individuals concerned may not be expelled. Article 35 of the Directive allows Member States to refuse entry in the case of abuse or fraud. Proof of abuse requires, first, a combination of objective circumstances in which, despite formal observance of the conditions laid down by the European rules, the purpose of those rules has not been achieved, and, secondly, a subjective element consisting in the intention to obtain and advantage from the European Union rules by artificially creating the conditions laid down for obtaining it.[133] Typical examples of abuse in obtaining entry rights are marriages of convenience. The Commission has provided guidance on how to identify abuse.[134] It signals that although the number of sham marriages is not very high, the implication of organized crime is a worrying factor and it suggests that Europol and Eurojust can offer assistance and support to national authorities.[135]

Article 27 of the Directive sets out the general principles applying to restrictive measures taken on grounds of public policy, public security and public health.[136] Member States remain competent to determine what conduct they consider contrary to public order and public security, and this may vary from one Member State to another and from one period to another.[137] Nevertheless the concept of public policy must be interpreted strictly.[138] Territorial restrictions on the right of residence may be imposed only when the same territorial restrictions apply to nationals (Art. 22).[139] Application of any restrictive measure taken on grounds of public order or public security must be in line with the principles set out in Article 27. These concern proportionality, the personal conduct that must be a genuine, present and sufficiently serious threat to a fundamental interest of society, the prohibitions to take general preventive measures and to take measures based on previous criminal convictions only. The grounds may not be invoked to

131. Case C-41/74, *Van Duyn*; Case C-30/77, *Bouchereau*; Case C-348/96, *Calfa*.
132. Art. 27(2) of Directive 2004/38; Case C-67/74, *Bonsignore*.
133. Case C-456/12, *O. and B.*, para 58.
134. COM(2009)313 and COM(2013)837.
135. COM(2013)837, at 8.
136. The same principles apply in case of restrictive measures taken against family members having a derived residence rights based on Art. 20 TFEU, Case C-165/14, *Rendón Marín* and Case C-304/14, *CS*.
137. Case C-30/77, *Bouchereau*, para 34.
138. Case C-41/74, *Van Duyn*; Case C-36/75, *Rutili*, para 27.
139. In contrast with Case C-100/01, *Oteiza Olazabal*.

serve economic ends. According to the Commission, in certain circumstances persistent petty criminality may represent a threat to public policy.[140] Expiry of the identity card or passport on the basis of which a registration certificate or residence card was issued shall not constitute a ground for expulsion (Art. 15 (2)). Article 27 also codifies the principle of international law that a State cannot refuse its own nationals the right of entry, and strengthens it by prohibiting such a refusal even if a passport is no longer valid or the nationality of the passport holder is in dispute (Art. 27(4)). Article 28 of the Directive lays down a framework for expulsion measures outlining the factors that Member States must take into account when they decide to expel EU citizens or their family members. EU citizens may be expelled only for conduct that the law of the host State condemns with repressive measures towards its own nationals, or with regard to which other genuine and effective measures intended to combat such conduct were taken.[141] Expulsion decisions must always consider individual circumstances.[142] Article 28 introduces distinct levels of protection according to the period of residence in the host State. After five years of residence, upon acquisition of the right of permanent residence, expulsion decisions against Union citizens or their family members may only be taken on "serious" grounds of public policy or public security (Art. 28 (2)). In case Union citizens have resided in the host State for a period of ten years, these grounds must be "imperative" and relate to public security only (Art. 28(3)). The latter provision applies only to Union citizens and not to their non-EU family members, unless they are minors. The status of Union citizens leads to more protection in this respect, in line with a "particularly restrictive interpretation of the derogations" from the freedom of movement.[143] However, the first rulings on Article 28 of the Directive have been criticized for making inexact the distinction between paragraphs 2 and 3 of Article 28 of the Directive, and for giving too much deference to the interpretative freedom of the Member States.[144]

The integration-based reasoning that underlies the acquisition of the right of permanent residence also applies to enhanced protection against expulsion, including the qualitative criteria the Court introduced next to the period of residence. Periods of imprisonment interrupt the continuity of residence leading to enhanced protection. However, the period before imprisonment in which the person concerned resided in the host State "may" be taken into consideration as part of an overall assessment required for determining whether the integrating links previously forged with the host state have been broken.[145] The Court has interpreted the concept of "imperative" grounds of public security as considerably stricter than that of "serious" grounds and limited to "exceptional circumstances".[146] The threat to public security must be of a particular high degree of seriousness. Public security covers both internal and external security. Public security may be affected by a "threat to the functioning of the institutions and essential public services and the survival of the population, as well as the risk of a serious disturbance to foreign relations or to peaceful coexistence of nations, or a risk to military interests".[147] The fight against crime in

140. COM(2009)313 def. "Communication from the Commission to the European Parliament and the Council on guidance for better transposition and application of Directive 2004/38/EC on the right of citizens of the Union and their family members to move and reside freely within the territory of the Member States", at 12; see also Case C-349/06, *Polat*.
141. Case C-115/81, *Adoui and Cournaille*, para 8.
142. Joined Cases C-482/01 and C-493/01, *Orfanopoulos and Oliveri*.
143. Ibid., para 65.
144. For a critical comment see D. Kostakopoulou and N. Ferreira, "Testing liberal norms: The public policy and public security derogations and the cracks in European Union citizenship", (2014) CJEL, 167–191.
145. Case C-400/12, *M.G.*, paras. 36–37.
146. Case C-145/09, *Tsakouridis*.
147. Ibid., para 44.

connection with dealing in narcotics as part of an organized group is covered by the concept of "imperative grounds of public security" as well as "serious grounds" of public policy or public security.[148] In *P.I.*, where sexual exploitation of children was at stake, the Court explicitly referred to Article 83(1) TFEU that provides a competence for the EU to harmonize in the areas of "particularly serious crimes" and lists sexual exploitation and illicit drug trafficking as particular serious crimes, even though Directive 2004/38 makes no reference to the type of crimes that can be qualified as a threat to public security. It refers only to the personal conduct of the individual concerned.[149] European Union law does not impose on Member States a uniform scale of values as regards the conduct that may be considered contrary to public security.[150] Nevertheless, the Court said that it is open to the Member States to regard criminal offences listed in the second paragraph of Article 83(2) TFEU imperative grounds of public security, as these "might pose a direct threat to the calm and physical security of the population", on condition that the manner in which these offenses were committed discloses particularly serious characteristics.[151]

The Directive provides in procedural guarantees in the context of expulsion decisions (Arts. 30–33). Persons concerned shall be notified in writing of any decision taken, whereby they must be able to comprehend its content and the implications for them. The procedural guarantees are read in the light of Article 47 of the Charter of Fundamental Rights of the EU (the right to an effective remedy and to a fair trial).[152] The notification must specify the court or administrative authority with which the person concerned may lodge an appeal, and the time limit for the appeal. Persons concerned shall have access to judicial and, where appropriate, administrative redress procedures in the host Member State.[153] The procedural guarantees equally apply when restrictions on free movement are based on other grounds (Art. 15), such as withdrawal of a residence permit in case a citizen residing in a host State between three months and five years no longer fulfils the conditions of Article 7. Where application is made for an interim order to suspend enforcement of an expulsion measure, actual removal from the territory may not take place, as a general rule, until such time as the decision on the interim order has been taken. Persons concerned may submit an application for lifting the exclusion order after a reasonable period, and in any event after three years from enforcement of the final exclusion order. Their application must be based on arguments to establish that there has been a material change in the circumstances that justified the exclusion order.

7. The right to equal treatment

7.1 The right to equal treatment under the Treaty provisions

Where residence periods determine access to rights, Union citizens can invoke the general prohibition on discrimination in Article 18 TFEU as soon as the discriminatory treatment of the Union's citizen is due to or related to the fact that he exercises or has exercised his right of free movement under Article 21 TFEU. In *Bressol*, students not residing in Belgium could

---

148. Ibid., para 56.
149. In Art. 27(2) of Directive 2004/38. For critical comment on the reference to Art. 83(2) TFEU see E. Spaventa, op. cit. *supra* note 130.
150. Case C-348/09, *P.I.*, para 21.
151. Ibid., para 28. For a critical comment see D. Kochenov and B. Pirker, "Deporting citizens within the European Union: A counterintuitive trend" in Case C-348/09 *PI v. Oberbürgermeisterin der Stadt Remscheid,* (2013) CJEL, 369.
152. Case C-300/11, *ZZ*.
153. The principle of procedural autonomy applies, under respect for the principles of equivalence and effectiveness, Case C-161/15, *Abdelhafid Bensada Benallal.*

invoke Articles 18 and 21 TFEU to challenge a Belgian rule that restricted access of non-resident students to (expensive) medical and paramedical courses.[154] In *D'Hoop*, a Belgian national was refused the so-called tideover allowance, an unemployment benefit granted under Belgian legislation to young people who have completed their studies and seeking their first employment.[155] The reason for that refusal was that Ms D'Hoop had obtained her secondary school diploma in France and not in Belgium. Consequently, it was because Ms D'Hoop had exercised her right of free movement under Article 21 TFEU that she could not receive the allowance. Because she had exercised her free movement right, her situation was considered to come within the scope of the Treaty – which allowed her to invoke the principle of non-discrimination under Article 18 TFEU. Again, as with claims that denial of benefits from the Member State of nationality might hinder free movement (see section 4.1 above), the question whether the *sedes materiae* itself, in the case of Ms D'Hoop an allowance such as the tideover allowance, falls within the scope of the Treaty, does not matter for reliance on Article 18 TFEU.[156]

It follows from the above that there are two ways for Union citizens to enforce specific rights through reliance on the Treaty provisions: first via the general prohibition on discrimination in Article 18 TFEU and second, as soon as there is a connecting factor with the right to move and reside freely, on the basis of Article 21 TFEU as a prohibition on unjustified restrictions of this right.[157]

7.2 *The Right to equal treatment under the Directive*

Article 24(1) of the Directive lays down a general right of equal treatment within the scope of the Treaty. According to the Court, inequality of treatment is contrary to the principles underpinning the status of citizen of the Union.[158] The principle of equal treatment requires that comparable situations must not be treated differently and that different situations must not be treated in the same way. Such treatment may be justified only if it is based on objective considerations independent of the nationality of the person concerned and is proportionate to the objective being legitimately pursued.[159] Union citizens and their family members residing on the basis of the Directive in the territory of the host State enjoy equal treatment with nationals of the host State, subject to such specific provisions as are expressly provided for in the Treaty and secondary law (Art. 24 of the Directive). Limits to equal treatment concern both the "scope of the Treaty" and express limitations in the Directive itself such as restrictions based on public policy, public security and public health, the requirement not to become an unreasonable burden on the social assistance system of the host State, or derogations for social assistance to jobseekers and student maintenance grants (Art. 24(2)) as well as express limitations in other secondary law instruments and express limitations in the Treaty such as access to employment in the

---

154. Case C-73/08, *Bressol a.o.*
155. Case C-224/98, *Marie-Nathalie D'Hoop v. Office national de l'emploi.*
156. See also Case C-274/96, *Bickel and Franz* (right to use one's own language in criminal proceedings); Case C-148/02, *Garcia Avello* (use of surname); Case C-103/08, *Gottwald* (free annual toll disc for disabled persons); Case C-164/07, *Wood* (compensation from a Guarantee fund for the victims of acts of terrorism and other crimes); Case C-524/06, *Huber* (registration of data).
157. See C. Timmermans, "*Martínez Sala* and *Baumbast* revisited" in M. Poiares Maduro and L. Azoulaï, *The Past and Future of EU Law. The Classics of EU Law Revisited on the 50th Anniversary of the Rome Treaty* (Hart, 2010), 345–355, at 352.
158. Case C-75/11, *Commission v. Austria (reduced transport fares for students)*, at 51.
159. Case C-274/96, *Bickel and Franz*, paras. 15 and 16; Case C-184/99, *Grzelczyk*, para 31; Case C-224/98, *D'Hoop*, paras. 29–30; Case C-148/02, *Garcia Avello*, para 31; Case C-164/07, *Wood*, para 13; Case C-524/06, *Huber*, para 75.

public sector (Art. 45(4) TFEU). The interpretation of Articles 18 TFEU and 21 TFEU where the question whether the *sedes materiae* itself falls within the scope of the Treaty does not matter for reliance on Article 18 TFEU (see section 4.1 above) seems to be applicable to Article 24 of Directive 2004/38 as well, since Article 24 of the Directive is "merely a specific expression" of the principle of equal treatment provided for in Article 18 TFEU.[160] Limits to equal treatment as provided by the Directive that are based on the argument that a situation does not fall under the scope of the Treaty seem rare,[161] as situations falling within the scope *ratione materiae* of Union law "include those involving the exercise of the fundamental freedoms guaranteed by the Treaty and those involving the exercise of the right to move and reside within the territory of the Member States.[162] Of course, Article 24 applies only in case Union citizens reside in the host State on the basis of the Directive, whereas in other cases Articles 18 and 21 TFEU provide the right to move and reside freely within the territory of a Member State without being subject to direct or indirect discrimination.[163] Article 24(1) thus specifies the legal effects of the general prohibition on discrimination under Article 18 TFEU in conjunction with the freedom of movement of EU citizens. Therefore, the prohibition on discrimination laid down in Article 18 TFEU and Article 24(1) of the Directive can be applied cumulatively.[164] However, family members who are not nationals of a Member State and have the (derived) right of residence or permanent residence seem to enjoy an independent right of equal treatment under Article 24(1) of the Directive, but not under Articles 18 and 21 TFEU.

Article 24(2) of the Directive excludes equal access to social assistance during the first three months of residence, or, in case of work-seekers, for a longer period (see section 5.2.2 above). It also limits access to maintenance aid for studies to economically inactive persons who have a right of permanent residence, normally acquired after five years residence. In this way, the Union legislator included the approach the Court took in its case law on the scope of application of the Treaty after the introduction of Union citizenship and whereby social security benefits,[165] social security allowances paid to jobseekers[166] and student maintenance grants paid to students[167] no longer fell outside the scope of application of Union law. Article 24(2) elaborates the way in which Member States may impose the condition on these allowances that there is a genuine link between the person claiming the allowance and the employment market or society of the host state, expressed by a period of residence in the host State. However, according to settled case law, the principle of proportionality demands that "the proof required to demonstrate the genuine link must be not too exclusive in nature or unduly favour one element which is not necessarily representative of the real and effective degree of connection between the claimant and the Member State, to the exclusion of all other representative elements".[168] An implicit test of

160. Case C-75/11, *Commission v. Austria (reduced transport fares for students)*, para 54.
161. One could think of the right to participate in national elections or certain rights linked to the performance of military service; see e.g. Case C-207/78, *Even* (the right of war veterans to early retirement on full pension) and Case C-315/94 *de Vos* (pension contributions concerning military service).
162. Case C-274/96, *Bickel and Franz* (right to use one's own language in criminal proceedings); Case C-148/02, *Garcia Avello* (use of surname); Case C-103/08, *Gottwald* (free annual toll disc for disabled persons); Case C-164/07, *Wood* (compensation from a Guarantee fund for the victims of acts of terrorism and other crimes); Case C-524/06, *Huber* (registration of data).
163. Case C-73/08, *Bressol and others*, paras. 30–39.
164. Ibid., para 39.
165. Case C-184/99, *Grzelczyk*.
166. Case C-138/02, *Collins*, para 63.
167. Case C-209/03 *Bidar*, paras. 38–42.
168. Case C-224/98, *D'Hoop*, para 39; Case C-503/09, *Stewart*, para 95; Case C-75/11, *Commission v. Austria*, para 62; Joined Cases C-523/11 and C-585/11, *Prinz* and *Seeberger*, para 37. See also *infra* section 5.2.2.

the legality of the five-year residence criterion to the exclusion of other elements representative of a genuine link for access to student maintenance grants was at issue in *Förster*.[169] The Court, as opposed to Advocate General Mazák, considered that a five-year residence requirement is proportionate to attain the objective of ensuring that students from other Member States are to a certain degree integrated into the society of the host State. It pointed out that in order to be proportionate, national authorities must apply a residence requirement on the basis of clear criteria known in advance.[170] The Court has adopted a similar approach with respect to the exclusion of jobseekers from access to social assistance, and added that the gradual system of Directive 2004/38 as regards the retention of the status of 'worker' sufficiently takes into account the individual situation of applicants.[171]

8. The position of family members under the Directive

Family members accompanying or joining a EU citizen have, based on the Directive, a right to equal treatment and a right to take up employment or self-employment in the host State that are both based on the Directive. As family members derive their residence rights from EU citizens, it might make their residence rights insecure in case the relationship ends or the Union citizen dies or leaves the host State, particularly in case of non-EU family members. The Directive offers some protection in Articles 12 and 13. Article 12 concerns rights after death or departure and makes a distinction between EU family members and those who are not nationals from a EU Member State. For EU family members, who obviously are Union citizens themselves, residence rights are not affected. They are however subjected to the same conditions of Article 7 as those of any other EU citizen. Non-EU family members do not lose the right of residence in case the Union citizen dies (departure is not mentioned), unless this happens before they have been residing in the host State as family members for at least one year (Art. 12(2)). These family members will retain the right of residence on a personal basis, subjected to the conditions of Article 7. Children who reside in the host State and are in school retain, together with the parent who has actual custody over them, the right of residence in case of death or departure of the Union citizen. This right is irrespective of nationality and financial resources. The right is retained until the completion of the studies.[172]

The different wording of paragraphs one and two of Article 12 implies that in case the Union citizen departs from the host State, the non-EU partner will lose the right of residence, unless there are school-going children (Art. 12(3)).[173] Furthermore, non-EU family members may not take into account their residence as a student for the purposes of acquisition of the right of permanent residence.[174]

Article 13 concerns cases of termination of the (marital) relationship and again makes a distinction between EU and non-EU nationals. The residence right of EU former partners is not affected and it is subjected to the conditions of Article 7 of the Directive. Non-EU former partners retain the right of residence only in case the marriage or registered partnership has lasted three years, including one year in the host State, or in case the non-EU partner has the custody over

169. Case C-158/07, *Förster*; F. Wollenschläger, "The Judiciary, the legislature and the evolution of Union citizenship" in P. Syrpis (Ed.), *The Judiciary, The Legislature and the EU Internal Market* (CUP, 2012), 302–330.
170. Ibid., para 56.
171. Case C-67/14, *Alimanovic*, para 60.
172. Children of workers and their primary caregivers obtain a similar right based on Art.10 of Reg. 492/2011, Case C-147/11, *Czop*.
173. Case C-115/15, *NA*.
174. Case C-529/11, *Alarape and Tijani*.

the children, or has the right of access to a minor child in the host State.[175] Furthermore, in cases of domestic violence the right of residence is retained after divorce, which prevents blackmail of non-EU family members with threats of divorce or termination of the relationship.

9. Political rights

Title II of the Treaty on European Union contains the provisions on democratic principles. It shows a commitment to participation of citizens in the democratic life of the Union. Article 9 TEU confirms that the Union must observe the principle of the equality of its citizens. Article 10 TEU makes clear that the Union has a dual legitimacy structure: citizens are directly represented at Union level in the European Parliament,[176] whereas those who represent the Member States in the European Council and the Council are accountable to their citizens, either directly or indirectly through the national Parliaments. Though representative democracy is the foundation of the functioning of the Union (Art. 10(1) TEU), provisions aiming at deliberative democracy are also present, such as Article 11 (1) TEU that obliges the institutions to give citizens and representative organizations the opportunity to exchange their views. Furthermore, the Lisbon Treaty introduced elements of participatory democracy with the provisions on the Citizens' initiative (Art. 11(4) TEU). The electoral rights and the right to participate in a Citizens' initiative are elaborated in the TFEU in part two on non-discrimination and citizenship of the Union.

9.1 Electoral rights

Article 20(2) under b) TFEU confers the right to vote and to stand as candidates in elections to the European Parliament and in municipal elections to Union citizens in the host Member State, under the same conditions as nationals of that State.[177] The enfranchisement of EU citizens in the host state is seen as part of the process of creating an ever-closer union among the peoples of Europe, as stated in the Preamble of the Treaty on European Union. Two Directives regulate the procedures,[178] allowing for exceptions to the principle of equal treatment between national and non-national voters where this is justified by problems specific to a Member State, notably where there are particularly high levels of non-national EU citizens. Luxembourg has availed itself of such derogation for European Parliament and municipal elections.[179] Belgium has the possibility to apply restrictions in municipal elections to a limited number of local governments, but has never invoked that derogation.[180]

Rules concerning voting rights in national elections are a national competence. However, the fact that several Member States disenfranchise their citizens if they move to another Member State has been criticized for being against the philosophy of EU citizenship.[181] The Commission

175. The right of residence will not be retained if the EU citizen, partner of the third country national, has left the host state before commencement of the divorce proceedings, Case C-218/14, *Kuldip Singh*.
176. The mirror provision is Art. 14(2) TEU: "The European Parliament shall be composed of representatives of the Union's citizens".
177. A comprehensive analysis is provided by J. Shaw, op. cit. *supra*, note 29; the voting rights are also included in the EUCFR under Arts. 39 and 40.
178. Directive 93/109/EC, O.J. 1993, L 329 (last amended by Directive 2013/1/EU, O.J. 2013, L 26; Directive 94/80/EC, O.J. 1994, L 368 (last amended by Directive 2013/19/EU, 2013, L 158).
179. COM(2013)126 final and COM(2012)99 final.
180. Art. 12(2) of Directive 94/80/EC; COM(2012)99 final.
181. D. Kochenov, "Free movement and participation in the parliamentary elections in the Member State of nationality: An ignored link?", (2009) MJ, 197–223.

therefore has urged these Member States to allow their citizens to exercise their free movement rights without being disenfranchised by national legislation.[182]

National law determines the beneficiaries of the right to vote in elections to the European Parliament. Member States must exercise that competence in compliance with EU law.[183] On 12 September 2006, the Court ruled in two cases on electoral procedures for the European Parliament. In *Spain v. United Kingdom (Gibraltar)*[184] the Court recognized that allowing certain commonwealth citizens, not being Union citizens, the right to vote was part of the constitutional tradition of the United Kingdom. It confirmed that Member States could, in compliance with Union law, extend the franchise for the European Parliament to non-EU citizens. Whether that judgment still stands in the light of Article 14(2) TEU, which provides that the European Parliament shall be comprised of representatives of the Union's citizens has not been clarified thus far. In *Eman and Sevinger*[185] the Court made clear that the extension of voting rights for the European Parliament to non-resident citizens (expatriate voting) was compatible with Union law, as long no arbitrary distinction was made.

Article 10(4) provides that political parties at European level contribute to forming European political awareness and to expressing the will of citizens of the Union. Though the electoral procedure for European Parliament elections is largely organized according to national procedures and comprising national party lists,[186] the decision of the political parties in the European Parliament to "nominate" candidates for the presidency of the European Commission in their 2014 election campaign could be seen as following the logic of Article 10(4) TEU.

9.2 *The citizens' initiative*

No less than one million citizens who are national of at least seven Member States may invite the Commission to submit a proposal for a legal act. The details of this so-called Citizens' initiative, introduced by Article 11(4) TEU, are elaborated in Regulation 2011/11, based on Article 24 TFEU.[187] In order to launch an initiative, an organizing committee must request its registration. The Commission will register the initiative provided it fulfils organizational conditions, is within the framework of the Commission's powers, is not "manifestly abusive, frivolous or vexatious", and is not manifestly contrary to the EU values as set out in Article 2 of the TEU.[188] Once registered, the organizers have one year to collect one million signatures, coming from at least one quarter of the Member States, with a set minimum of signatures per Member State. When an initiative has gathered the required number of signatures, the Commission must respond to it, however it is under no legal obligation to follow it up with a legislative proposal. The procedure as elaborated by Regulation 2011/211 has not been left without criticism.[189] The possibility

182. COM(2014)33 Communication from the Commission to the European Parliament, the Council, the European Economic and Social Committee and the Committee of the Regions, *Addressing the consequences of disenfranchisement of Union citizens exercising their right to free movement.*
183. Case C-650/13, *Delvigne.*
184. Case C-145/04, *Spain v. United Kingdom.*
185. Case C-300/04, *Eman and Sevinger.*
186. Act concerning the election of the representatives of the European Parliament by direct universal suffrage, annexed to Decision 76/787/ECSC, EEC, Euratom (amended by Council Decision 2002/772/EC, Euratom), O.J. 1976, L 278/1.
187. Reg. 2011/211/EU, O.J. 2011, L 65/1, Implementing Reg. 1179/2011/EU, O.J. 2011, L 301/3.
188. Art. 4(2) of Reg. 2011/211. The Commission must provide appropriate reasons when refusing to register a proposal, Case T-646/13, *Minority Safepack.*
189. M. Dougan, "What are we to make of the citizens' initiative?", 48 CML Rev. (2011), 1807–1848; L. Bouza Garcia and S. Del Rio Villar, "The ECI as a democratic innovation: Analyzing its ability to promote inclusion, empowerment and responsiveness", 13 *European Civil Society* (2012), 312–324.

to launch a citizens' initiative is only available since April 2012 and therefore it seems too soon to conclude whether it will enhance democratic participation and engagement with the Union.

10. The right to diplomatic protection and the right to address the institutions

Article 23 TFEU (and Art. 46 EUCFR) grants every citizen of the Union, in the territory of a third country in which the Member State of which he is a national has no representation, the right to protection by diplomatic or consular authorities of any Member State, on the same conditions as nationals of that State. The implementing measures for this right were adopted under the intergovernmental model (i.e. by the Member States) rather than by Community Institutions.[190] In order to secure the envisaged diplomatic protection, Member States must start international negotiations with the relevant third countries (Art. 23 TFEU). As yet there are little results in this field. The Lisbon Treaty added a new paragraph to Article 23 providing a legal basis for directives establishing the coordination and cooperation measures necessary to facilitate such protection. A first Directive to that effect has been adopted.[191] Furthermore, Article 35 TEU provides that diplomatic and consular missions of the Member States shall contribute to the implementation of the right to protection of Union citizens and of the measures adopted pursuant to Article 23 TFEU.

The right to petition the European Parliament, to apply to the European Ombudsman and to address any of the institutions and advisory bodies of the Union in one of the official languages and to receive a reply in that language are also conferred on non-citizens of the Union residing in one of the Member States and any legal person having its registered office in a Member State (Arts. 227 and 228 TFEU, Arts. 41(4), 43 and 44 EUCFR).[192] On the other hand, the right to petition the European Parliament and the right to apply to the Ombudsman are, by reference to Articles 227 and 228 TFEU, confined in their subject matter.

11. Citizenship reports and the possibility of extending citizenship rights

On the basis of the Report required to be presented every three years in accordance with Article 25 TFEU, "and without prejudice to the other provisions of the Treaty", the Council may adopt provisions to strengthen or add to the rights listed in Article 20(2) TFEU. The Council acts unanimously on the basis of a proposal of the Commission, after obtaining the consent of the European Parliament. The provisions shall only enter into force after their approval by the Member States in accordance with their respective constitutional requirements (Art. 25 TFEU). Article 25 shows that the concept of EU citizenship is open to further development.

Thus far, Article 25 TFEU has been brought up with respect to the extension of political rights. In the 2013 citizenship reports from the Commission,[193] Article 25 TFEU is mentioned in the context of examining ways to enable EU citizens to participate in national and regional

---

190. Decision 95/553, O.J. 1995, L 314/73.

191. Council Directive 2015/637 on the coordination and cooperation measures to facilitate consular protection for unrepresented citizens of the Union in third countries and repealing Decision 95/553/EC, O.J. 2015, L106/1.

192. The right to write the institutions in an official language and to receive an answer in the same language is conferred to "every person" under Art. 41(4) ECFR.

193. Report from the Commission to the European Parliament, the Council, the European Economic and Social Committee and the Committee of the Regions under Art. 25 TFEU *On Progress towards Effective EU Citizenship 2011–2013*, COM(2013)270 final; Report from the Commission to the European Parliament, the Council, the European Economic and Social Committee and the Committee of the Regions *EU Citizenship Report 2013. EU citizens: Your rights, your future*, COM(2013)269 final.

elections in their country of residence.[194] Also, a citizens' initiative, "Let me vote", with the same aim and proposing the use of Article 25 TFEU was launched in 2013, but did not succeed to collect the necessary one million signatures. Meanwhile, the Commission has presented enfranchisement in the host State as a longer-term vision and is recommending Member States not to disenfranchise their nationals who reside in other Member States.[195]

By its reference to "the rights listed in Article 20(2)", Article 25 TFEU appears to exclude the extension of Union citizenship to all natural persons residing in a Member State, in the way Articles 227 and 228 TFEU have done.[196]

12. Concluding remarks

The introduction of the concept of Citizenship of the Union proved to be the start of a very dynamic, and some would say unwarranted, development in case law.[197] Its success in realizing the intention to shift the paradigm away from economic integration might be disputed, as it emphasizes the material circumstances of free movement and predominantly brings rights to those who are economically active or have sufficient resources.[198] Nevertheless, Union citizenship certainly influenced the relationship between Member States and their own nationals in several ways. The promise of the Treaty text that EU citizenship will not replace national citizenship could not prevent that the demands of the useful effect of the citizenship provisions restrain the discretion of Member States in nationality issues as well as in deciding upon residence rights of non-EU family members of their own nationals or in granting economically inactive EU citizens limited access to national solidarity systems. In all those areas Member States show deep concern about the detrimental effects of these developments on domestic social and economic policy choices.[199] From a more legal perspective, the various legal standards developed in EU citizenship case law leaves one with a perception of confusion and unpredictability. Consider, for example, standards such as the "genuine link", the "deprivation of the substance of rights", "a genuine residence", and the ambiguous use of the proportionality principle that sometimes demands an assessment of individual circumstances, and in other instances allows general criteria regardless of personal circumstances because it makes the law predictable and manageable.

The codification of the case law in Directive 2004/38, and the addition of a status of permanent residence, has provided a major source of rights for EU citizens in Member States other than that of their nationality. However, it also explicitly conditions and restricts those rights. Through the demand that EU citizens may not become an "unreasonable burden" for the social assistance system of the host State, the legislator seemingly attempts to draw a red line as to how much solidarity Union citizenship encompasses. The red line is drawn more sharply in case of jobseekers' access to social benefits and students' access to maintenance grants, and has

---

194. See also M. Meduna, Institutional Report, as cited *supra* note 51, in particular 306–310.

195. COM(2014)33, cited *supra* note 182. See also Report from the Commission to the European Parliament, the Council, the European Economic and Social Committee and the Committee of the Regions under Art. 25 TFEU *On Progress towards Effective EU Citizenship 2013–2016*, COM(2017)32 final; European Commission, *EU Citizenship Report 2017. Strengthening Citizens' Rights in a Union of Democratic Change*, at 19.

196. Its predecessor, Art. 22 EC, referred to "the rights laid down in this part", and did not appear to exclude such an extension.

197. See M. Dougan, "The bubble that burst: Exploring the legitimacy of the case law on the free movement of Union citizens" in M. Adams a.o. (Eds.), *Judging Europe's Judges. The Legitimacy of the Case Law of the European Court of Justice* (Hart, 2013), 127–154.

198. See E. Spaventa, op. cit. *supra* note 130; M. Everson, "A citizenship in movement", (2014) GLJ, 965–984.

199. See also Editorial Comments "The free movement of persons in the European Union: Salvaging the dream while explaining the nightmare", (2014) CML Rev., 729–740.

been confirmed by the Court.[200] Moreover, the Court has made it clear that protection under the Directive is only for those who meet the economic and financial criteria of the Directive.[201]

Since its inception, Union citizenship certainly has developed in a spectacular way. Nevertheless, the fundamental status of citizenship still contains a worrying note of frailness, and its *telos* is far from certain.[202] Therefore it seems not audacious to expect that legislative and judicial developments in Union citizenship will continue to be ambivalent and contested.

Further reading

Dougan, M., N. Shuibhne and E. Spaventa, *Empowerment and Disempowerment of the European Citizen* (Hart, 2012).

Everson, M., "A Citizenship in Movement", (2014) GLJ, 965.

Guild, E., C. J. Gortázar Rotaeche and D. Kostakopoulou (Eds.), *The Reconceptualisation of European Union Citizenship* (Brill Nijhoff, 2014).

Kochenov, D. and R. Plender, "EU citizenship: From an incipient form to an incipient substance? The discovery of the treaty text", 37 EL Rev. (2012), 369.

Kochenov, D., "The essence of EU citizenship emerging from the last ten years of academic debate: Beyond the cherry blossoms and the moon?", (2013) ICQL, 97–136.

Kochenov, D. (Ed.), *EU Citizenship and Federalism: The Role of Rights* (CUP, 2017).

Kostakopoulou, D., "When EU citizens become foreigners", 20 ELJ (2014), 447–463.

Iglesias Sánchez, S., "Fundamental rights and citizenship of the Union at crossroads: A promising alliance or a dangerous liaison?", 20 ELJ (2014), 464–481.

Neergaard, U., C. Jacqueson and N. Holst-Christensen, *Union Citizenship: Development, Impact and Challenges. The XXVI FIDE Congress in Copenhagen, 2014* (DJØF Publishing, 2014).

Nic Shuibhne, N., "The resilience of EU market citizenship", 47 CML Rev. (2010), 1597.

Schrauwen, A., "Granting the right to vote for the European Parliament to resident third-country nationals: Civic citizenship revisited", (2013) ELJ, 201.

Tryfonidou, A., *Impact of Union Citizenship on EU's Market Freedoms* (Hart, 2016).

Wollenschläger, F., "A new fundamental freedom beyond market integration: Union citizenship and its dynamics for shifting the economic paradigm of European integration", (2011) ELJ, 1.

200. Case C-158/07, *Förster*; Case C-67/14, *Alimanovic*.

201. Case C-333/13, *Dano*; and by analogy, Case C-456/12, *O. and B.*

202. See N. Nic Shuibhne and J. Shaw, "General Report" in U. Neergaard, C. Jacqueson and N. Holst Christensen, op. cit. *supra* note 51, at 226 and D. Thym, op. cit. *supra* note 7.

CHAPTER 17
EUROPEAN MIGRATION AND ASYLUM LAW

*Jorrit J. Rijpma**

1. Introduction

This chapter examines European Migration and Asylum Law. More precisely it considers the EU's competence over borders, visa, migration and asylum. These powers form part of the so-called Area of Freedom, Security and Justice (AFSJ) and are found in Part Three, Title V, Chapter 2 of the Treaty on the Functioning of the European Union (TFEU). Although the way in which EU law treats nationals of non-Member States is not exclusively defined by this part of the Treaty, it is here that the general competence to regulate the entry, residence and rights of non-EU nationals is located.

Ever since the 1970s oil crisis Western European countries have adopted a restrictive labour migration policy, most legal immigration since then stemming from family reunification. An absolute increase in asylum seekers arriving in Western Europe since the late 1980s has induced these countries to discourage asylum requests, in particular by lowering their countries' relative attractiveness.[1] Globalization has not only increased the level of people crossing borders, it has also turned Europe from a sending region into a migration magnet.[2] While the economic crisis slowed down migration inflows, net migration remained positive overall.[3] The 2015 refugee crisis led to a significant increase in asylum applications in Europe and showed once more how politically sensitive questions of migration and asylum are. Much like the sovereign debt crisis, the refugee crisis shook the foundations of the European project, as borders were re-erected and common values were openly questioned.[4]

Migration and asylum touch upon Member States' core notion of sovereignty: the right to decide on the entry and residence of non-nationals. Yet, from the very beginning of European integration, EU law has imposed limits on this *ius excludendi* as regards the nationals of the Member States under the free movement of persons. The conclusion of Association Agreements under Article 217 TFEU has further limited Member States' power to regulate migration, to the extent that these agreements have extended the free movement of persons in the relation

---

* Associate Professor of EU law and Jean Monnet Professor, Europa Institute, Leiden Law School.

1. E.R. Thielemann, "Why asylum policy harmonization undermines refugee burden-sharing", 6 EJML (2004), 47–65, at 54.
2. M. de Haas and H. Czaika, "The globalization of migration: Has the world become more migratory?", 48 *International Migration Review* (2015), 283–323, at 294.
3. C. Tilly, "The impact of the economic crisis on international migration: A review", 25 *Work, Employ. Soc* (2011), 675–692, at 680.
4. J. Rijpma, "It's my party and I'll cry if I want to: 'Celebrating' thirty years of Schengen" in B. Steunenberg, W. Voermans & S. Van den Bogaert (Eds.), *Fit for the Future? Reflections from Leiden on the Functioning of the EU* (The Hague, 2016), 147–170. The present chapter takes into account developments until Sept. 2017.

with third countries. Although strictly speaking these agreements belong to the domain of external relations, they have had a profound impact on Member States' migration policies.[5]

It was not until the mid-1980s that the first steps towards a more Europeanized migration and asylum policy were made. Under the 1985 Schengen Agreement a number of Member States committed themselves to lifting checks at their internal borders.[6] This was subject to the adoption of common rules on visa, borders, migration and asylum and police cooperation in the 1990 Schengen Implementing Convention (CISA).[7] It was only with the Maastricht Treaty that migration and asylum were included as "areas of common interest" under the supranational third pillar of the newly established European Union.[8] The Amsterdam Treaty carried the powers in asylum and migration over to the supranational Community pillar and integrated the Schengen rules into the EU legal framework.[9]

Although the Lisbon Treaty completed the process of mainstreaming migration and asylum policies, bringing its institutional framework in line with other area of Union competence, European migration and asylum law remains fragmented.[10] There is no comprehensive migration or asylum code regulating the residence of TCNs. This explains that while goods, once customs-cleared and legally marketed in one of the Member States, must be considered in free circulation, a similar logic does not apply to TCNs.

2. The rationale behind a European migration and asylum policy

European migration and asylum law forms an integral part of the AFSJ, which comprises also cooperation in civil and criminal matters, police and judicial cooperation and the protection of fundamental rights. The official rationale considers EU competence in this field as the functional spill-over from the free movement of persons, more specifically the lifting of internal border controls under the Schengen agreements. This link is still visible in Article 3(2) TEU which states that "the Union shall offer its citizens an area of freedom, security and justice without internal frontiers in which the free movement of persons is ensured *in conjunction with appropriate measures* with respect to external border controls asylum, immigration and the prevention and combatting of crime".[11]

The internal market rationale does not however explain the inclusion of competences going beyond the power to regulate short-term visas, borders and the responsibility for asylum claims in the Maastricht Treaty. Moreover, the introduction of the AFSJ as a Treaty objective in the Treaty of Amsterdam, replacing the more neutral term of Justice and Home Affairs (JHA) cooperation, turned this policy field into a constitutional and political project.[12] The definition of the EU as an "area" also justifies a comparison with the introduction of EU citizenship aimed

5. The rights conferred on certain TCNs by virtue of EU free movement law or bilateral agreements are generally more beneficial and take precedence over more general measures of EU migration law.
6. Schengen Agreement of 14 June 1985, O.J. 2000, L 239/13.
7. Convention implementing the Schengen Agreement of 19 June 1990, O.J. 2000, L 239/19.
8. J. Rijpma, "The third pillar of the Maastricht Treaty: The coming out of Justice and Home Affairs" in M. de Visser and A.P. van der Mei (Eds.), *The Treaty on European Union 1993–2013: Reflections from Maastricht* (Intersentia, 2013), 269–288.
9. Council Decision 1999/435/EC concerning the definition of the Schengen acquis, O.J. 1999, L 176/1 and Council Decision 1999/436/EC determining the legal basis for each of the provisions or decisions which constitute the Schengen acquis, O.J. 1999, L 176/17.
10. J. Rijpma, "Institutions and agencies: Government and governance after Lisbon" in C.C. Acosta & D. Murphy (Eds.), *EU Security and Justice Law after Lisbon and Stockholm* (Hart, 2014), 54–76.
11. Emphasis added.
12. J. Monar, "The area of freedom, security and justice" in A. Bogdandy and J. Bast, *Principles of European Constitutional Law* (Hart, 2009), 551–585, at 552. For a critical note on the comparison with the internal market

to create a sense of belonging and to enhance the legitimacy of the EU.[13] By considering the different rationales behind the introduction of these competences, starting with its internal market origins, it will become clear that there are different, often conflicting interests underlying this policy area, which remain visible in the European migration and asylum *acquis*.

2.1 *Free movement and spill-over*

From the principled decision taken in 1985, it would take another decade before borderless travel would become reality. First, a series of so-called flanking measures, considered necessary to compensate for the absence of internal border checks, had to be adopted. These measures were laid down in the 1990 Schengen Implementing Convention (CISA). In terms of migration and asylum, it provided for common rules on visa, checks at the external borders and the responsibility of asylum claims. At the same time it provided for rules on police cooperation and created the Schengen Information System (SIS) which contained alerts on persons who should be refused entry to the Schengen area, otherwise wanted persons, stolen vehicles and identity documents, etc.

Meanwhile the 1986 Single European Act had defined the internal market as an area without internal frontiers.[14] From the outset, there was disagreement whether this implied also an obligation to lift checks at the internal borders. Not only did the UK fiercely oppose such interpretation, the fact that the free movement of persons was restricted to the nationals of the Member States lend support to the argument that this would require a minimum set of common rules on the external borders, as well as visa and asylum. The reasoning that borderless travel in the EU required the adoption of compensatory measures was later confirmed by the ECJ in *Wijsenbeek*.[15] The Court argued that in the absence on rules on the external borders, visa and asylum, the current Article 24(2) TFEU could not have direct effect. A similar, but *a contrario*, reasoning underlies the Court's approval of the exclusion of the UK from participating in certain compensatory measures, without lifting controls at its internal borders first.[16]

2.2 *Security*

From the outset, the notion that lifting checks at the internal borders would lead to a security deficit has been very much present. Flanking measures or compensatory measures would need to remedy this perceived security threat, preventing the free movement of those that should not benefit from borderless travel in Europe. However, as was pointed out by Costello: "any internal market rationale is agnostic as to the restrictiveness or otherwise of external barriers, but simply requires the application of common rules".[17] Yet, many of the common rules that have been adopted in the field of migration and asylum aim to limit the inflow of TCNs and to fight irregular migration, largely mirroring policy preferences at Member State level.

One explanation for the restrictiveness of the EU's policy in this area is that since the late 1980s migration and asylum have increasingly been looked at through a security lens. When

---

project: N. Walker, "In search of the area of freedom, security and justice: A constitutional odyssey" in N. Walker (Ed.), *Europe's Area of Freedom, Security and Justice* (OUP, 2004), 3–37, at 5.

13. P. Craig, *The Lisbon Treaty: Law Politics and Treaty Reform* (OUP, 2010), 331- 378, 375; S. Coutts, "Citizenship of the European Union" in C.C. Acosta and D. Murphy (Eds.), *EU Security and Justice Law after Lisbon and Stockholm* (Hart, 2014), 92–109, at 93.
14. Art 7a TEC, now Art. 24(2) TFEU.
15. Case C-378/97, *Wijsenbeek*, at para 40.
16. Case C-77/05, *UK v. Council* (Frontex), at para 63, Case C-137/05, *UK v. Council* (Passports), at para 50; C-482/08, *UK v. Council* (VIS), at para 47.
17. C. Costello, *The Human Rights of Migrants in European Law* (OUP, 2015), at 15.

host societies are ill-equipped to absorb newcomers, integration proves a slow process and populist parties exploit fear of the other, migration and asylum is often portrayed as a threat to public order, public health, employment of a country's own citizens and the host society's social cohesion. More recently these fears have found fertile ground in the threat of terrorism and the refugee crisis.

The security dimension of migration and asylum policies was reinforced at the European level for a number of reasons. The Schengen cooperation was largely shaped by security professionals rather than diplomats.[18] With no involvement of the European Parliament and the Court of Justice of the European Union (CJEU), Schengen formed a new policy venue shielded from national legal constraints and conflicting policy goals.[19] The fall of the Berlin wall redefined the concept of security, broadening its focus from military threats to new societal risks, and blurring internal and external security.[20] By juxtaposing migration and asylum to terrorism and organized crime, not only in discourse, but also institutionally, the regulation of migration and asylum became associated with policing and criminal justice.[21] With the introduction of the AFJS, security no longer exclusively served free movement, but became an objective on its own.

Mitsilegas in applying a broad definition of criminalization has argued that EU law has criminalized migration through the adoption of substantive criminal law, the application of criminal law enforcement instruments and the use of mechanisms of prevention and pre-emption.[22] Other scholars describe similar developments as proof of the "securitization" of this policy field or alternatively as a risk-based approach to migration and asylum.[23] Interestingly, in the refugee crisis, controlling migration and asylum was even brought back within the framework of external security, as evidenced for instance by the deployment of an Common Security and Defence Policy (CFSP) mission to tackle human smuggling.[24]

2.3 *Economics*

Whilst the lifting of internal border checks was considered to have clear economic benefits, migration itself has generally been considered a threat rather than an asset to Member States' economies. More recently, the restrictive nature of migration policies in Europe has been somewhat mitigated by an emerging consensus that migration may help to counter the negative effects of Europe's ageing population. An ageing population poses challenges to the sustainability of Member States' welfare systems which need to be supported by an increasingly small working-age population. Moreover, even in the aftermath of the economic crisis, despite overall

18. J. Huysmans, *The Politics of Insecurity: Fear, Migration and Asylum in the EU* (Routledge, 2006), 87 and D. Bigo, "Security and immigration: Toward a critique of the governmentality of unease", 27 *Alternatives*, Special Issue (2002), 63–92, at 77.
19. V. Guiraudon, "European integration and migration policy: Vertical policy-making as venue shopping", 38 JCMS (2000), 251–271, at 252.
20. H. Grabbe, "The sharp edges of Europe: Extending Schengen eastwards", 76 *International Affairs* (2000), 519–536, at 520.
21. J. Huysmans, op. cit. *supra* note 18, at 71 and D. Bigo, op. cit. *supra* note 18, at 65.
22. V. Mitsilegas, *The Criminalization of Migration in Europe: Challenges for Human Rights and the Rule of Law* (Springer, 2015).
23. N. Schmidthäussler and A. Niemann, "The logic of EU policy-making on (irregular) migration: Securitization or risk?", (2016) *Mainz Papers on International and European Politics*.
24. Council Decision (CFSP) 2015/778 on a European Union military operation in the Southern Central Mediterranean (EUNAVFOR MED), O.J. 2015, L 122/31.

unemployment at high levels, many Member States face labour shortages in specific sectors and are competing for highly skilled workers.[25]

Nonetheless, Member States have often questioned the appropriateness of EU intervention in this area. Article 79(5) TFEU explicitly reserves the power to determine the volumes of admission of TCNs for the purpose of labour. The principle of subsidiarity seems to argue against Union action, in light of the differences in Member States' economies and labour market needs.[26] The Commission itself argued that immigration does "not provide in itself a long-term solution to falling birth rates and an ageing population, but it is one of the available tools within a broader policy mix".[27] It has taken a sectoral over a horizontal approach, favouring "wanted" TCN migrants (skilled and educated).

The Commission's 2015 Agenda on Migration again placed the development of a policy for legal migration firmly within the economic needs of the Member States, but did emphasize that opportunities for legal migration may "foster circular growth and development" also in the countries of origin and importantly "reduce push factors towards irregular stay and entry".[28] In 2016 the Commission once more underlined the need for "*a more proactive labour migration policy*" and to "*improve the overall framework on legal and labour migration*".[29]

The economic rationale for labour migration has often been coupled to another rationale, namely the idea that the creation of opportunities for legal migration may constitute an alternative for irregular migration. This thinking is reflected in the change of name of the EU's overarching framework of the EU external migration and asylum policy from Global Approach to Migration (GAM) in 2005, to Global Approach to Migration and Mobility (GAMM) in 2011.[30] It also informs the conclusion of so-called Mobility Partnerships with third countries, a hybrid instrument under which Member State pledge to create opportunities for legal migration in combination with cooperation on irregular migration.[31] A similar approach is visible in the Valletta Action Plan, adopted by African and European leaders in 2015 and the Commission's Communication on a new Partnership Framework with third countries under the Agenda on Migration.[32]

2.4 *Solidarity, mutual recognition and trust*

Numerous European Council Conclusions have underscored the importance of solidarity between the Member States in the field of migration, asylum and borders. The Lisbon Treaty introduced an explicit reference in Article 67(2) TFEU and in Article 80 TFEU, which prescribes that policies in this area shall be "governed by the principle of solidarity and fair sharing of responsibility, including its financial implications". The notion of solidarity is closely linked to the notion of mutual recognition and trust. In the absence of full harmonization at EU level, Member States will need to recognize and trust the decisions of other Member States when delivering

25. B. Ryan, "The European Union and labour migration: Regulating admission or treatment" in A. Baldaccini et al. (Eds.), *Whose Freedom, Security and Justice?: EU Immigration and Asylum Law and Policy* (Hart, 2014), 489–515, at 490.
26. Study for the EP Committee on Employment and Social Affairs, "Labour Market Shortages in the European Union", PE 542.202(2015).
27. COM(2005)669 final, Policy Plan on Legal Migration, at 5.
28. COM(2015)240 final, A European Agenda on Migration, at 7 and 11.
29. COM(2016)197 final, at 14.
30. European Council (Council Document 15914/05); COM(2011)743 final.
31. COM(2007)248 final.
32. Valletta Summit Action Plan, 11–12 Nov. 2015, available at: <www.consilium.europa.eu/en/press/press-releases/2015/11/12-valletta-final-docs/>; COM(2016)385 final.

visa giving access to the Schengen area, when controlling their part of the external borders and when handling asylum claims in line with commonly agreed standards and procedures. In doing so, these Member States act in the interest of the EU as a whole and therefore may turn to the EU for support, especially when due to their geographical location, size or economic development they are carrying an unequal burden.

In practice, it is mostly financial and operational solidarity that have been reinforced. Currently, there are two main EU funding instruments in the AFSJ: the Asylum, Migration and Integration Fund and the Internal Security Fund, the latter comprising an instrument for funding of cooperation in the area of borders and visa.[33] In terms of operational and administrative cooperation, the European Border and Coast Guard Agency (Frontex) and the European Asylum Support Office (EASO) are semi-independent agencies, which coordinate and contribute to the financing of cooperation between national border guard authorities and asylum authorities respectively.[34]

In terms of physical solidarity, understood as effectively taking responsibility for asylum claims or the return of irregular migrants, little progress has been made. The clearest example is the effective sabotage of the emergency measures adopted during the refugee crisis, aimed at relocating asylum seekers across the Union in order to relieve some of the immediate pressure on Italy and Greece, by the opposing Member States.[35]

Many of the solidarity instruments simultaneously aim to enhance trust. For instance, the operational cooperation and the common training activities under the auspices of Frontex and EASO serve to foster a common culture and a more harmonized application of common rules. Yet, there have been many instances in which trust between the Member States has been put to the test. The regularization of irregular migrants in Italy (2002) and Spain (2005), led to fierce criticism from other Member States and resulted in the adoption of a Council Decision obliging Member States to inform each other of measures "likely to have a significant impact on several Member States or on the European Union as a whole".[36]

Also the failure of Member States to comply with EU law, in particular fundamental rights obligations, erodes trust, and puts pressure on the system of mutual recognition. This was shown in 2011 when judgments of the European Court of Human Rights and the European Court of Justice (ECJ) on the systemic failures in the Greek asylum system, lead to the suspension of transfers to Greece under the so-called Dublin Regulation, determining the Member States responsible for handling an asylum request.[37] In that same year, the Italian decision to grant temporary residence permits to mostly Tunisians in the wake of the Arab Spring, enabling them to travel onwards on Schengen territory, infuriated many Member States, France in particular. This eventually led to an overhaul of the rules on "Schengen Governance", first and foremost aimed at improving Member States' discipline in guarding the external borders.[38]

Finally, concerns as regards the rule of law and corruption in Bulgaria and Romania have effectively barred these Member States from lifting checks at their internal borders. Rather than further harmonization, these measures have sought to address Member States concerns

---

33. Reg. (EU) 516/2014, O.J. 2014, L 150/168; Reg. (EU) 515/2014, O.J. 2014, L 150/143.
34. Reg. (EU) 2016/1624, O.J. 2016, L 251/1 ("EBGC Reg."); Reg. (EU) 439/2010, O.J. 2010, L 132/11 ("EASO").
35. Joined Cases C-643/15 and Case C-647/15, *Slovak Republic and Hungary v. Council.*
36. Council Decision 2006/688/EC, O.J. 2006, L 283/2006.
37. ECtHR, *MSS v. Belgium and Greece*, Appl. No. 30696/09, judgment (Grand Chamber) of 21 Jan. 2011. See also ECtHR, *Tarakhel v. Switzerland*, Appl. No. 29217/12, Judgment (Grand Chamber) of 4 Nov. 2014 as regards the situation in Italy. Joined Cases C-411/10 and Cases C-493/10, *NS & ME.*
38. Council Reg. (EU) 1053/2013, O.J. 2013 L295/27 and Reg. (EU) 1051/2013, O.J. 2013, L295/1.

by triggering exceptional measures, such as the suspension of transfers of asylum seekers to the responsible Member States or the reinstatement of checks at internal borders.

2.5 *International human rights obligations and Union values*

European migration and asylum law is further motivated, shaped, but also constrained by the EU's fundamental rights, as part of the fundamental values upon which it is founded and which it is not merely to uphold, but also promote.[39] As such these provide for a countervailing force against restrictive tendencies in this field. The European Convention for the Protection of Human Rights and Fundamental Freedoms (ECHR) and the interpretation thereof by the Strasbourg Court remains of paramount importance for the development of European migration and asylum law. Article 67(1) TFEU explicitly states that in the AFSJ fundamental rights shall be respected. Article 78(1) TFEU provides that the EU's asylum policy must be in accordance with the Geneva Convention and other relevant treaties. The EU has repeatedly underlined that the goal of the EU's Common European Asylum System (CEAS) is to provide and area of protection and solidarity. The European Agenda on Migration explicitly refers to the EU's "duty to protect".[40]

One of the most important rights laid down in the Geneva Convention can be found in Article 33(1): the right not to be expelled or returned ("refouled") to a country where one's life or freedom is threatened. Although Article 18 of the Charter states that there is a right to asylum, the explanations to the Charter state merely refer back to the obligation to respect the Geneva Convention, implying that rather than a right to asylum there is a right to seek asylum.[41] Nonetheless, EU secondary law does provide for a right to international protection where the conditions laid down in those instruments are met. As such the EU's ambitions in the field of migration and asylum go beyond the mere respect of fundamental rights, and give expression to its aim to further these rights and interpret them broadly.

Another good example is the right to family life. This right must be respected in the application of the EU's rules on migration and asylum, but does not include a universally recognized right to family reunification.[42] Even so, the EU has adopted legislation, the Family Reunification Directive, that under conditions provides for such right.[43] Likewise, the adoption of the Long Term Residents Directive, aims to improve the status of legally resident TCNs, in line with the requirement of Article 79(1) TFEU that their treatment should be "fair" and earlier calls for "a set of uniform rights as near as possible to those enjoyed by EU citizens".[44]

Fundamental rights also play an important role in the interpretation of European legislation, as well as in assessing the legality of this legislation and its application by the Member States. The European Parliament unsuccessfully tried to challenge the provisions of the Family Reunification Directive allowing for integration requirements to be imposed on children older than twelve and restricting the right to family reunification with children above the age of fifteen. In this case the Court held that the Directive itself did not infringe the right to family life, the rights of the child or provisions of non-discrimination, but it did underscore that in the application of

39. Arts. 2 and 6 TEU, Art. 51(1) CFR.
40. COM(2015)240 final, at 12.
41. Explanations relating to the Charter of Fundamental Rights, O.J. 2007, L 303/17.
42. ECtHR, *Gül v. Switzerland*, Appl. No. 23218/94, judgment of 19 Feb. 1996, at para 46, and ECtHR, *Ahmut v. the Netherlands*, Appl. No. 21702/93, judgment of 28 Nov. 1996, at para 63; C-256/11, *Dereci*, at para 70.
43. Council Directive 2003/86/EC on the right to family reunification, O.J. 2003, L251/12.
44. Council Directive 2003/109/EC, O.J. 2004, L 16/44 ("Long Term Residents Directive"); Tampere European Council Conclusions, 15 and 16 Oct. 1999, at point 21.

these provisions the Member States would have to respect these rights.[45] Likewise, the Charter imposes limits on the way in which Member States may assess the credibility of an asylum seeker's sexual orientation.[46] Finally, the EU's fundamental rights *acquis* has imposed limits on the presumption of mutual trust in the context of the Dublin regime, ensuring that fundamental rights be respected at all times and ensuring that the transfer of an asylum seeker from one Member State to the other does not result in a violation of the prohibition of *refoulement*.[47]

3. Union competences in asylum and migration

The transfer of competences in the field of migration and asylum has been a gradual process bearing testimony to the sensitive nature of this policy field. Although most exceptions and transitional arrangements have with the entry into force of the Lisbon Treaty become a things of the past, a number of special features continue to the characterize AFSJ as a whole, albeit to a lesser degree in relation to the specific field of asylum and migration. Most important distinguishing feature is the variable geometry that applies in this area, which is a direct result of the unwillingness of some EU Member States to participate on rules on migration and asylum, as well as the association of a number of non-Member States with the Schengen *acquis*.

3.1 *Treaty framework*

Under Article 4(2)(j) TFEU, the AFSJ is an area of shared competence. With the entry into force of the Lisbon Treaty, the ordinary legislative procedure now applies to all competences in the field of migration and asylum, with a few exceptions in which special legislative procedures apply on non-legislative procedures.[48] Only few powers have been explicitly reserved for the Member States.[49] Importantly, in particular for the field of border management, the ultimate responsibility for internal security continues to lie with the Member States.[50]

In the legislative process, the Council working procedures continue to include an additional layer between working group level and COREPER, the so-called Strategic Committee on Immigration, Frontiers and Asylum (SCIFA), which was introduced in Amsterdam Treaty to allow the representatives of the national ministries of the interior to continue to exercise influence over this policy field alongside their counterparts in the foreign ministries.[51] The European Council continues to define the strategic guidelines for legislative and operational planning.[52] It has done so, since the entry into force of the Amsterdam Treaty in the form of five-year plans: the Tampere Agenda (1999), the Hague Programme (2004) and the Stockholm Programme (2009).[53] These programmes have largely shaped the development of the EU's migration and asylum *acquis*.

---

45. Case C-540/03, *Parliament v. Council*, at paras. 105–107.
46. Joined Cases C-148/13 to C-150/13, *A, B, C*. See also pending Case C-473/16, *F*, O.J. 2016, C 419/31.
47. Joined Cases C-411/10 and C-493/10, *NS & ME*; Case C-578/16, *CK*.
48. For instance: Art. 70 TFEU: adoption of evaluation mechanisms, Art. 74 TFEU: measures for ensuring administrative cooperation, Art. 78(3) TFEU: the adoption of emergency measures.
49. Art. 79(5) TFEU: determining the volumes of admission for the purpose of labour migration.
50. Art. 72 TFEU.
51. J. Monar, "Justice and Home Affairs" in G. Edwards and G. Wiessala (Eds.), *The European Union 1999/2000: JCMS Annual Review of Activities* (Blackwell, 2000), at 137.
52. Art. 68 TFEU.
53. European Council Conclusions, Tampere, 15–16 Oct. 1999; European Council, "The Stockholm Programme: An open and secure Europe serving and protecting citizens", Conclusions, 2009: O.J. 2009, C 115/1, 26; The Hague Programme, Annex to the European Council Conclusions, Brussels, 4–5 Nov. 2004.

The follow-up of the Stockholm Programme and the current framework for the overall development of the AFSJ, are the Strategic Guidelines adopted by the European Council in June 2014.[54] These are less ambitious and less elaborate than their predecessors for two apparent reasons. First, many of the measures proposed in the Stockholm Programme had only just been adopted or were still in the legislative process. The focus therefore shifted from legislation to implementation. Second, it formed an acknowledgement of "mainstreaming" of JHA policies after the entry into force of the Lisbon Treaty and the agenda setting role of the Commission.[55] Nonetheless, the European Council continues to play an important role, closely interacting with the Commission in response to crisis situations and even taking the lead during the 2015 refugee crisis.[56]

3.2 *Variable geometry*

The "communautarization" of the powers in asylum and migration allowed for the adoption of a protocol to the Amsterdam Treaty integrating the Schengen *acquis* into the EU's legal framework. In two decisions based on Article 2 of the Schengen Protocol, the Council identified the Schengen *acquis* and assigned a legal basis to the different parts thereof.[57] The integration of the Schengen *acquis* necessitated special arrangements. First, for the UK, which had chosen to remain outside the Schengen cooperation, and Ireland which did not wish to give up its Common Travel Area with the UK. Second, for Denmark which after the Maastricht Treaty had indicated it would only be willing to cooperate in justice and home affairs on an intergovernmental basis. Finally, for the non-Member States that had previously signed up to the Schengen agreements. This has resulted in a myriad of opt-outs and opt-ins and bilateral relations under public international law.

The United Kingdom and Ireland

The position of the UK and Ireland as regards the Schengen *acquis* is regulated in Protocol 19 ("Schengen Protocol"), while the position of the UK and Ireland in relation to the broader cooperation in the AFSJ has been regulated in protocol 21 ("AFSJ Protocol").[58] Under Article 4 of the Schengen Protocol, the UK and Ireland are allowed to opt-in to parts of the Schengen *acquis,* subject to a unanimous Council vote. Article 5 of the same protocol allows them also to opt-in to proposals and initiatives that build upon the Schengen measures. The Court interpreted this notion of "Schengen developing measures" broadly, covering any measure that, judged by its content and purpose, may render more effective parts of the Schengen *acquis.*[59] However, in order to participate in these Schengen developing measures, the UK and Ireland would first need to accept the underlying parts of the Schengen *acquis*. As the UK and Ireland did not lift checks

---

54. European Council, Conclusions of 26–27 June 2014 (European Council Document EUCO 79/14).
55. See for a different reading of the Guidelines: S. Guild & E. Carrera, "The European Council's guidelines for the area of freedom, security and justice 2020: Subverting the "Lisbonization" of Justice and Home Affairs?", (2014) CEPS.
56. See for instance the development of the GAM in response to the storming of the Spanish enclaves of Ceuta and Mellila in 2005 and its renewal as GAMM in reaction to the Arab Spring in 2011. See also D. Thym, "The 'refugee crisis' as a challenge of legal design and institutional legitimacy", 53 CML Rev. (2016), 1545–1574, at 1565.
57. Council Decision 1999/435/EC, O.J. 1999, L 176/1 and Council Decision 1999/436/EC, O.J. 1999, L 176/17.
58. E. Fahey, "Swimming in a sea of law: Reflections on water borders, Irish (-British)-Euro relations and opting-out and opting-in after the Treaty of Lisbon", 47 CML Rev. (2010), 673–707.
59. Case C-77/05, *UK v. Council* (Frontex), at para 85, Case C-137/05, *UK v. Council* (Passports), at para 65.

at their internal borders this effectively excluded them from a variety of measures developing the Schengen border *acquis*.[60]

When legislation to which the UK and Ireland has previously opted-in to is amended, the UK and Ireland may chose not to participate, unless the Council deems that this would make the application of that measure practically inoperable.[61] Importantly, the UK and Ireland have opted-in to most asylum measures, but only partially participate in the "second generation" instruments of the CEAS.[62] The prospect of Brexit will end the UK's limited participation under the terms of the Schengen and AFSJ protocols, but it is likely to raise new questions as the UK will seek continue its current participation. It is unlikely that Brexit will change Ireland's position in relation to the AFSJ.[63]

Denmark

On the basis of Article 1 of the Schengen Protocol the provisions of the Schengen *acquis* continue to bind Denmark. It has the right opt-in to measures developing the Schengen *acquis* within six months by implementing this measure in its national law. This then creates an obligation under public international law.

Denmark does not have the possibility to opt-in to measures that do not develop the Schengen *acquis*. In 2006 it therefore concluded an agreement under public international law with the EU participating in the Dublin rules.[64] An explicit exception to the Danish opt-out relates to the EU's common visa list or the uniform visa format in which Denmark does participate.[65]

Denmark may unilaterally end the Protocol or bring into effect the Annex to Protocol 22 ("Danish Protocol") which would allow it to opt-in to any measure adopted under the AFSJ in line with the rules applicable to the UK and Ireland.[66] On 3 December 2015 the Danish people rejected a proposal to use this possibility in a referendum.

Schengen associated countries

Since Norway and Iceland had already joined the Schengen cooperation prior to its incorporation into EU law, the conclusion of an international agreement between the EU and these countries was necessary.[67] In 2006, Switzerland joined the Schengen area by means of an agreement

60. The Court confirmed this interpretation in a case in which the UK fought its exclusion from the adoption of a measure that broadened the use of the Visa Information System (VIS) for criminal law enforcement, considering that the VIS itself had to be considered a Schengen developing measure: Case C-482/08, *UK v. Council* (VIS), at para 47. It was less strict in relation to a clause allowing for an agreement to be made with the UK and Ireland on its participation in the European Border Surveillance System (EUROSUR): Case C-44/14, *Spain v. Parliament and Council*, at para 53.
61. Art. 4a, Protocol 21.
62. Meaning that the UK remains bound to the original "first generation" instruments.
63. Even if Ireland does not intend to join Schengen, Brexit does raise fears of checks at the UK/Irish land border, although both countries have indicated the wish to keep an open border between them. See for the UK position: <www.gov.uk/government/uploads/system/uploads/attachment_data/file/638135/6.3703_DEXEU_Northern_Ireland_and_Ireland_INTERACTIVE.pdf>.
64. Agreement between the EC and Denmark, O.J. 2006, L 66/38.
65. Art. 6, Protocol 22.
66. Arts. 7 and 8, Protocol 22.
67. Schengen Association Agreement NO/IS, O.J. 1999, L 176/36.

with the EU.[68] Liechtenstein joined the Schengen area two years later on the basis of a Protocol to the Schengen agreement between the EU and Switzerland.[69]

The Schengen associated countries participate on the basis of a take it or leave approach. Although they can provide input on Schengen developing measures in the so-called mixed-Committee established by the agreements and intervene in cases before the CJEU, non-acceptance of subsequent legislation or the case law of the Court will almost inevitably result in the termination of the Schengen association.

In view of the clear link between the lifting of internal border checks and the Dublin mechanism, the Schengen associated countries have also associated themselves through international agreements with the Dublin regime on the allocation of responsibility for asylum claims.[70] This then required the conclusion of an agreement between the EU and the Schengen Associated countries, as well as the addition of a protocol making these rules applicable between the Schengen Associated Countries and Denmark, and the conclusion of an agreement between Schengen Associated Countries Norway and Iceland with Switzerland.[71]

Acceding Member States

New Member States do not have the option to opt-out from the Schengen cooperation.[72] Although they are required to participate fully in the AFSJ from day one, this does not mean that borders checks are immediately lifted upon accession. This requires a unanimous Council decision, based upon "careful examination of the legal and practical readiness of the new Member States" individually.[73] In the case of Bulgaria and Romania, despite having fulfilled all technical requirements, concerns over corruption and the rule of law in these Member States have effectively blocked such a decision. Croatia, being the most recent accession country, is still awaiting a Council Decision to be adopted. Cyprus is still not applying the Schengen *acquis* in full, and unlikely to do so in the near future, because of the fact that its government is not in effective control over part of its territory.

3.3 *The EU's policy agenda on migration and asylum*

In spring 2015, in the wake of another series of deadly shipwrecks off the coast Libya, the Commission published its European Agenda on Migration.[74] Although presented as a new and more European approach, it echoed earlier policy plans and repackaging existing initiatives. It called for progress in the four areas of EU competence in this field: irregular migration, asylum, borders legal migration (the agenda's four pillars). It also called for increased cooperation with third countries, which has been a key element of the EU's Global Approach since 2005. Whilst largely

68. The Schengen Association Agreement CH, O.J. 2008, L 53/52. Norway, Iceland and Switzerland are bound vis-à-vis each other in relation to the Schengen rules by separate agreements between themselves, as are Denmark and Switzerland.
69. Protocol between the EU, the EC, Switzerland and Liechtenstein, O.J. 2008, L 160/3.
70. See Art. 7 of the Schengen Association Agreement NO/IS. The Schengen Association Agreement CH/LI in Art. 15(4) states even more clearly that it shall only be applied if the Dublin rules are implemented.
71. Norway and Iceland associated themselves with the Dublin rules in 2001 (O.J. 2001, L 93/40), Switzerland did in 2008 (O.J. 2008, L 53/5). Norway, Iceland and Switzerland are bound vis-à-vis each other in relation to the Dublin rules by separate agreements between themselves. Their relation with Denmark is regulated in separate protocols.
72. Art. 7, Protocol 19.
73. Ch. 24 on Justice and Home Affairs, *acquis communautaire*: <europa.eu.int/comm/enlargement/negotiations_eu10_bg_ro/chapters/chap24/index.htm>.
74. COM(2015)240 final.

focusing on the short and medium term, for the longer term the plan indicated the need for a truly *common* European Asylum System, the shared management of the external borders and a new model of legal migration.

The European refugee crisis of 2015 lead to the *de facto* suspension of the Dublin-system and put a severe strain on the Schengen-system, as a number of Member States reintroduced checks at their internal borders in an attempt to gain control over refugee flows. This provided the momentum for more fundamental reforms, most notably in the field of borders and asylum. The Commission forcefully urged for a return to Schengen, safeguarding borderless travel within Europe, by strengthening the external borders.[75] A proposal for the creation of a European Border and Coast Guard Agency, reinforcing Frontex, introducing the notion of shared border management and tightening oversight over Member States' control of the external borders, swiftly made its way through the legislative process.[76] It was followed by much more contentious proposals for the reform of the CEAS, amending the Dublin-system, transforming EASO into a "European Asylum Agency", and providing for a further harmonization of the rules on qualification, procedure and reception.[77] Although these proposal entail significant amendments to the EU's asylum and immigration *acquis*, a comprehensive policy plan for the future shape of the CEAS remains lacking and developments continue largely event-driven. It is also far from certain these proposals will pass or, if so, will be successfully implemented. Once more the refusal of Hungary and Poland to abide by the EU's emergency relocation decisions of 2015 serves as an example.[78] Interestingly, the 2016 Communication that introduced the many proposals for the reform of the CEAS, also referred to the need for legal pathways for migration but stopped short of presenting any long term vision.[79]

Meanwhile, the closure of the "Balkan route" and a controversial agreement with Turkey, making this country responsible for the reception of Syrian refugees as a safe third country, is generally considered to have brought about a considerable reduction in the number of people reaching Europe from Turkey.[80] At the same time however, arrivals in Italy and Spain have been on the rise. Even if the implementation of the EU-Turkey statement remains problematic, it has been considered by European leaders as a source of inspiration for future relations with other third countries.[81] In its Communication on a new Partnership Framework with third countries the Commission focuses heavily on readmission and return.[82] It seeks to link cooperation in matters of migration and asylum with the Union's other external policies, notably trade and

75. COM(2016)120 final.
76. EBGC Reg., cited *supra* note 34.
77. COM(2016)270 final (Dublin Reg.), COM(2016)271 final (European Asylum Agency), COM(2016)466 final (Qualification), COM(2016)467 final (Procedures), COM(2016)468 final (Reception).
78. Joined Cases C-643/15 and C-647/15, *Slovak Republic and Hungary v. Council*.
79. COM(2016)197 final.
80. EU-Turkey Statement, European Council Press Release 144/16 (18 Mar. 2016). See however T. Spijkerboer, "Fact check: Did the EU-Turkey deal bring down the number of migrants and of border deaths?", *Border Criminologies Blog*, 28 Sept. 2016: <www.law.ox.ac.uk/research-subject-groups/centre-criminology/centreborder-criminologies/blog/2016/09/fact-check-did-eu>.
81. On the question of whether the agreement is to be considered an international agreement under public law: M. Den Heijer and T. Spijkerboer, "Is the EU-Turkey refugee and migration deal a treaty?", *EU Law Analysis*, 7 Apr. 2016, available at <eulawanalysis.blogspot.it/2016/04/is-eu-turkey-refugee-and-migration-deal.html>; The General Court held that the "deal" constitutes a measure adopted by the Member States and not the Union: Cases T-192/16, T-193/16 and T-257/16 T-192/16, *NF, NG and MN v. European Council* (appeals have been lodged before the European Court of Justice: Cases C-208/17 P, C-209/17 P and C-210/17 P).
82. COM(2016)385 final.

development, introducing an element of conditionality. Also in the reform of the CEAS, the emphasis on safe third countries is very much visible.[83]

4. EU migration and asylum law: Substantive rules

The substantive EU's migration and asylum *acquis* can be roughly divided along the legal bases contained in Part Three Title V, Chapter 2 TFEU: measures relating to borders and visa, regular and irregular migration and asylum. Most of the pre-Amsterdam Schengen *acquis*, which was given a legal basis by the Council upon its incorporation in the EU legal order, has now been recast as EU legislative acts.[84] Many of these measures have in fact been amended and supplemented by so-called "Schengen developing measures". In addition, the EU legislator has used its new competences under this title to adopt rules that do not necessarily develop the Schengen *acquis*, but supplement it by, for instance, providing harmonized rights for specific categories of TCN or bringing in line Member States' rules on asylum.

4.1 *Borders and Visa*

4.1.1 *Borders*

Despite the introduction of a "shared responsibility" for the management of the external borders in 2016, the prime responsibility for guarding their respective parts of the external borders continues to lie with the Member States.[85] They act in accordance with common rules in the interest of the whole Schengen area. A periodic Schengen Evaluation by the Commission and representatives of the Member States aims to assess whether Member States implement the Schengen *acquis*, including the rules on border control, correctly.[86] In 2004, the EU legislator established Frontex, an agency that should foster operational cooperation between national border guards at the external border, through common risk analyses, training and joint operational activity and exercises.[87] The agency does not have executive authority, although border guards from one Member States may in the context of joint operational activity exercise law enforcement powers in another Member State.[88] In addition, the European system for the surveillance of the external borders, links national border guards authorities in an information sharing environment, with Frontex as spider in the web.[89] In 2016, the EU legislator considerably strengthened the Agency's powers, officially renaming it the European Border and Coast Guard Agency and giving it a supervisory role in assessing possible vulnerabilities in Member States' border management.[90]

The main instrument regulating the control of the external borders is the Schengen Borders Code (SBC).[91] Border control consists of checks at designated border crossing points and surveillance in between these points.[92] Whilst rules on border surveillance remain limited, the Code exhaustively regulates entry and exit conditions. Upon entry and exit all persons are systematically checked for their identity, travel document and possible listing in relevant database, as well as whether they do not pose a genuine, present and sufficiently serious threat to the

83. See *infra*, section 4.3.6.
84. Council Decision 1999/436/EC, O.J. 1999, L 176/17.
85. Art. 5, EBCG Reg., cited *supra* note 34.
86. Council Reg. (EU) 1053/2013, O.J. 2013, L 295/27.
87. Council Reg. 2007/2004, O.J. 2004, L 349/1.
88. Art. 40, Reg. (EU) 2016/1624, O.J. 2016, L 251/1.
89. Reg. (EU) 1052/2013, O.J. 2013, L 295/11.
90. EBGC Reg., cited *supra* note 34. It will nonetheless continue to be referred to as Frontex.
91. Reg. (EU) 2016/399, O.J. 2016, L 77/1 ("SBC").
92. Art. 2(10), SBC.

internal security, public policy, international relations of the Member States or a threat to the public health.[93] The most important database in this regard is the SIS, which was initially set up under the CISA and has since been replaced by the SIS II.[94] It contains data on persons or objects, such as people against whom an arrest warrant or entry ban has been issued or stolen vehicles as recorded by the participant countries.[95]

TCNs are subject to a thorough check upon entry and exit.[96] Entry checks include, in addition to the minimum check, verification of whether the conditions of stay a fulfilled, which includes a verification of the visa. Exit checks may include also verification of the visa and/or possible overstay. A person that does not fulfil these conditions shall be refused entry and receive a substantiated decision stating the reason for denial of entry.[97] A Member State does not have the discretion to deny entry to a third-country national entry by applying a condition that is not laid down in the SBC.[98]

In order for the imposition of the Schengen rules not to disrupt local border communities, the EU legislator adopted the Local Border Traffic Regulation providing for a special permit for residents of border areas, allowing them to cross the external border in a particular border area more easily and to stay in that area for a period of three months.[99]

As a means of last resort, Member States are allowed to temporarily reinstate checks at their internal borders for reasons of public policy or national security, in which case the rules of the SBC apply *mutatis mutandis*.[100] The procedure for reinstatement of checks at the internal borders is regulated in Title III, Chapter 2 of the SBC and varies on whether this is done for foreseen or unforeseen threats, but may in any case not exceed a period of six months.[101] An additional procedure was introduced in 2011, allowing the Council to adopt a recommendation to one or more Member States to reintroduce border checks for a maximum period of two years in exceptional circumstances.[102] This would be the case where the overall functioning of the area without internal border control would be at risk as a result of persistent serious deficiencies in a Member States' border management system.[103] A finding of the existence of such deficiencies may follow from a Schengen Evaluation or the newly introduced Vulnerability Assessment.[104]

93. Art. 8(2), SBC. This systematic check against relevant data bases was introduced in response to the terrorist attacks carried out by "foreign fighters", EU nationals who had traveled to and returned from countries such as Syria: Reg. (EU) 2017/458, O.J. 2017, L 74/1. Note that TCN family members of EU citizens who have a derived right of free movement may only be refused entry on the basis of an entry in the SIS if they constitute a threat to public policy, public security or public health that would allow for their refusal of entry under Directive 2004/38: Case C-503/03, *Commission v. Spain*, at para 52.
94. Reg. (EC) 1987/2006, O.J. 2006, L 381/4 (border checks) and Council Decision 2007/533/JHA, O.J. 2007, L 205/63 (criminal matters).
95. Note the Commission has recently proposed three new regulations on the use of SIS II for return, border checks and in criminal matters respectively (COM(2016)881–883 final).
96. Art. 8(3), SBC.
97. Art. 14(1) and (2), SBC.
98. Case C-575/12, *Air Baltic*, at para 69.
99. Reg. (EC) 1931/2006, O.J. 2016, L 405/1. The Local Border Traffic regime is implemented through bi-lateral local border traffic agreements between a Member State and its neighbouring country on the basis of reciprocity: Art. 13.
100. Art. 32, SBC.
101. Art. 25(4) SBC.
102. Ibid.
103. Art. 29, SCB, introduced by Reg. (EU) 1051/2013, cited *supra* note 38.
104. Art. 13, Reg. (EU) 2016/1624, O.J. 2016, L 251/1.

A recent Commission proposal would further extend the period during which controls may be reinstated for reasons of public or internal security, to as long as three years in case of a persisting threat.[105]

The reinstatement of border checks should be distinguished from police controls in border areas. The SBC is without prejudice to Member States police powers with extend also to border areas.[106] These police controls may not however amount to *de facto* border controls and therefore need to be clearly circumscribed by law in terms of purpose, timing and location.[107]

4.1.2 *Visa*

Under Article 77(2) TFEU, the EU only has competence on short term visa, that is for stays of a maximum duration of 90 days within a 180 day period.[108] Long stay visas and visa with limited territorial validity remain national visas.[109] However, Member States may be bound by EU legislation to provide for a long term visa, for instance under the Blue Card Directive or Family Reunification Directive.[110] Long term visas may have a maximum duration of one year, after which they should be replaced with a residence permit.[111] Long term visa and residence permits are considered equivalent to a short-stay visa for the purpose of crossing the external borders.[112]

Regulation (EC) No 539/2001 determines the countries whose nationals must be in possession of a visa.[113] The decision to list a country is based on "a variety of criteria relating inter alia to illegal immigration, public policy and security, and to the European Union's external relations with third countries, consideration also being given to the implications of regional coherence and reciprocity".[114] The Regulation contains a so-called safeguard clause, which enables the Commission to adopt an implementing act suspending visa-free travel in an emergency situation characterized by a substantial and sudden increase in the number of irregular migrants, asylum applications with a low chance of success or rejected readmission applications from a particular third country. After this period it may propose a legislative amendment to end visa-free travel.[115]

A Schengen visa is issued on the basis of the provisions of the Community Visa Code.[116] An application must in principle be lodged with the consular authorities of the Member State of (main) or alternatively first destination.[117] A Member State may be represented by other Member States in countries where it does not have a consulate or visa.[118]

---

105. COM(2017)571 final.
106. Art. 23, SBC.
107. Joined Cases C-188/10 and C-189/10, *Melki & Abdeli*, at para 73, Case C-278/12 PPU, *Adil*, at para 87 and Case C-9/16, *Criminal Proceedings against A*, at para 57.
108. Art. 1(1), Reg. (EC) 810/2009, O.J. 2009, L 243/1 ("Visa Code"); all visa issued by the Member States follow the uniform format of Reg. (EC) 1683/95, O.J. 1995, L 164/1.
109. Art. 18(1) CISA.
110. See *infra*, section 4.4.
111. Art. 18(2) CISA.
112. Art. 6(1)(b), SBC.
113. Council Reg. (EC) 539/2001, O.J. 2001, L 81/1.
114. Recital 5, ibid.
115. Art. 1a, ibid. The article was introduced in 2014 after the visa liberalization for countries in the Western Balkans and strengthened in 2017 in the wake of the refugee crisis and further visa liberalization for amongst others Ukraine.
116. Visa Code, *supra* note 108. Proposals to simplify the rules and to introduce a touring visa are pending: COM(2014)163–164 final.
117. Art. 5, ibid.
118. Art. 8, ibid.

The conditions for granting a visa are similar to the entry conditions for TCNs, but much emphasis is placed on the evidence that an applicant has sufficient means of subsistence and will return home after his stay.[119] Article 32(1) lists the reasons for refusing a visa. A visa can only be refused on the ground given in the Visa Code.[120] However, Member States have a wide margin of discretion in ascertaining these conditions.[121] In particular, the concept of public policy does not require the person concerned to constitute a personal threat.[122] A refusal must however be based on "solid factual evidence", even if judicial review remains limited to the absence of a manifest error and respect for procedural guarantees.[123] A negative decision can take the form of a refusal, inadmissibility, refusal of extension, annulment or revocation.[124] An appeal in accordance national law is only foreseen in cases of refusal, annulment or revocation.[125]

In the *X&X*-Case, the Court held that Member States are not required to issue a short-term visa on humanitarian grounds to applicants that apply to seek international protection, as such application would need to be considered as an application for a long-term visa, the conditions for which had not been harmonized by the Member States.[126] As such it fell outside the scope of EU law and the Charter did not apply to the case at hand.[127]

Since 2008, the EU's visa policy is supported by the Visa Information System (VIS), which connects all consular authorities in third countries and which contains alphanumerical and biometric data of all TCN visa applicants.[128] The system should facilitate the work of border guards in checking the identity and validity of the visa of a TCN border crosser and prevent abuse and fraud. Law enforcement staff was granted access to the system from the start.[129]

4.1.3 *Entry-exit system and ETIAS*

Currently, a proposal to adopt a comprehensive entry-exit system is under consideration, mandating the registration of entry and exit of all TCNs with a view to identify more readily overstay, as a source of irregular migration, as well as irregularly present TCNs.[130] Again law enforcement staff would have access to this system. As such, the system would become a general surveillance tool, rather than an instrument for migration control. The proposal requires an amendment of the SBC and the system is envisaged to be interoperable with the VIS, in order to prevent duplication of data collection. In 2016, the Commission also revived a proposal for a European Travel Information and Authorization System (ETIAS), requiring all TCN that are not under a visa obligation to seek prior authorization before travelling to the EU.[131] Both the Entry-Exit System

119. Art. 21, ibid.
120. Case C-84/12, *Koushkaki*, at para 63.
121. Case C-84/12, *Koushkaki*, at para 60, C-544/15, *Fahimian*, at para 42.
122. Case C-544/15, *Fahimian*, at para 40.
123. Case C-544/15, *Fahimian*, at paras. 45 and 46.
124. Arts. 32, 33, 34, Visa Code.
125. Art. 32(3) and 34(7), Visa Code. See pending Case C-403/16, *El Hassani* regarding the question whether Art. 47 CFR (right to an effective remedy) requires an appeal possibility with a judicial rather than an administrative body.
126. Case C-638/16 PPU, *X&X*, at para 43.
127. Ibid., at paras. 44 and 45.
128. Reg. (EC) 767/2008, O.J. 2008, L 218/60.
129. Council Decision 2008/633/JHA, O.J. 2008, L 218/129.
130. COM(2016)194 final.
131. COM(2016)731 final.

and ETIAS raise important questions of compatibility with fundamental rights, in particular data protection rules.[132]

4.2 *Irregular migration*

In addition to its border and visa policy, the EU legislator has adopted a range of measures aimed at preventing and fighting irregular migration on the basis of Article 79(2) TFEU. These are on the one hand aimed at aimed at preventing people from reaching and entering EU and on the other hand at the return of irregular migrants.

4.2.1 *Preventing access to territory*

The main instrument to prevent irregular migration, putting the enforcement of the EU's visa policy in private hands, is the imposition of carrier sanctions and the obligation for airlines to transmit Advanced Passenger Information, which consists of the data contained in a person's passport.[133] Under Directive 2001/51, carriers (land, air and sea), are obliged to return any passenger that is refused entry into the Schengen area or, failing to do pay for the cost of stay and return of that person. Even if the directive states that this obligation is without prejudice to Member States' obligations vis-à-vis TCNs in need of international protection, the Directive in practice often forms an insurmountable barrier for refugees to access EU territory, also in the absence of an obligation on the Member States to provide for humanitarian visas.[134]

4.2.2 *Preventing human smuggling and trafficking*

Being a party to the Palermo Protocols against human smuggling and trafficking that supplement the UN Convention against Transnational Crime, the EU has criminalized both.[135] Directive 2002/90 obliges Member States to adopt "appropriate sanctions" for anyone who intentionally facilitates the irregular entry and stay within a Member State.[136] Member States *may* decide not to impose sanctions where the aim was to provide humanitarian assistance.[137] In case of human trafficking, Directive 2011/36, based on the EU's powers in criminal law, provides that Member States shall prescribe criminal sanctions, prescribing maximum penalties of a minimum of up to ten year imprisonment.[138] The directive also provides for support and assistance to the victims of trafficking and should be read in conjunction with Council Directive 2004/81/EC providing for a residence permit issued to third-country nationals who are victims of trafficking, who co-operate with the competent authorities.[139] Finally, the EU legislator has provided for sanctions against employers hiring irregular migrants, obliging the Member States to adopt "effective,

---

132. Studies for the EP Committee on Civil Liberties, Justice and Home Affairs, "Smart Borders Revisited: an assessment of the Commission's revised Smart Borders Proposal, PE 571 381 (2016) and "European Travel Information and Authorization System (ETIAS): Border management, fundamental rights and data protection", PE 583.148 (2017). See also Opinion 1/15, *Draft agreement between Canada and the European Union* (PNR).
133. Council Directive 2001/51/EC, O.J. 2001, L 187/45; Council Directive 2004/82/EC, O.J. 2004, L 261/24.
134. See above, section 4.1.2.
135. Smuggling Protocol, 2241 UNTS 507 (2000) and the Trafficking Protocol, 2237 UNTS 319 (2000).
136. Art. 1(1), Council Directive 2002/90/EC, O.J. 2002, L 328/17.
137. Art. 1(2), ibid.
138. Art. 4, Directive 2011/36/EU, O.J. 2011, L 101/1.
139. Art. 11, ibid. Council Directive 2004/81/EC, O.J. 2004, L 261/19.

proportionate and dissuasive sanctions", in particular financial sanctions.[140] Where the offence is committed intentionally by a natural person the directive prescribes criminal penalties.[141]

4.2.3 *Return*

If a TCN no longer fulfils the requirements for legal stay she is *normally* required to leave the Schengen area immediately.[142] Under international law, countries are obliged to readmit their own nationals but in practice this often proves problematic for instance due to a lack of proof of nationality or travel documents. So-called readmission agreements with third countries are meant to facilitate the return of their irregularly staying nationals. More importantly, EU readmission agreements extend their personal scope to non-nationals that have transited through the contracting party's territory. The Lisbon Treaty introduced an explicit external competence for the conclusion of readmission agreements in Article 79(3) TFEU. In practice, the conclusion of a readmission agreement is often a prerequisite for visa liberalization and accompanied with financial incentives for the third country in question.

The rules on return of TCNs, including their treatment in expulsion proceedings, detention, entry bans and procedural rights, have been regulated in the Return Directive of 2011.[143] It imposes on the Member States the obligation to issue a return decision, ordering an irregularly staying TCN to leave the territory of the Member States.[144] Such decision should allow for a period for voluntary return, unless the person involved constitutes a danger to public policy, public or national security, her application for legal stay was manifestly unfounded or fraudulent, or there is a risk of absconding.[145] The ECJ has held that, public policy under the Return Directive must be interpreted in line with the EU definition of public policy under EU free movement law, meaning that the person in question must constitute a present, genuine and sufficiently serious threat to a fundamental interest of society.[146]

In case no period for voluntary return is granted, or where the period for voluntary departure has passed, the Member State may proceed with the removal of the person in question ("forced return").[147] A return decision is accompanied by an entry ban if no period for voluntary return has been granted or the obligation to return has not been complied with.[148] In all other cases the imposition of an entry ban is optional, although in many Member States the imposition of an entry ban has become an automatism.[149] Because an entry ban is valid in the whole Schengen territory, it is generally accompanied by an entry in SIS II.[150] This is problematic as the conditions for entry in the SIS II are stricter than for which an entry ban can be imposed.[151] The

140. Art. 5(1), Directive 2009/52/EC, O.J. 2009, L 168/24.
141. Art. 10, ibid.
142. Art. 23(1), CISA.
143. Directive 2008/115/EC, O.J. 2008, L 348/98 ("Return Directive"). Note that Member States may draw inspiration from the Return Directive as regards the rules applicable to the expulsionof an EU citizen to the extent that is not precluded by any provision of EU law: Case C-184/16, *Petrea*, para 52.
144. Art. 6(1), ibid. A Return decision cannot be substituted by a fine: Case C-38/14, *Zaizoune*, at para 37.
145. Art. 7, ibid.
146. Case C-554/13, *Z.Zh. H & I.O.*, para 60.
147. Art. 8, Return Directive.
148. Art. 11, ibid.
149. Report for DG Home Affairs of the European Commission, "Evaluation on the application of the Return Directive (2008/115/EC)", 22 Oct. 2013, at 16, available at <ec.europa.eu/smart-regulation/evaluation/search/download.do?documentId=10737855>.
150. Arts. 21 and 24, Reg. (EC) 1987/2006, cited *supra* note 94.
151. Meijers Committee, "Note on the coordination of the relationship between the Entry Ban and the SIS-alert: an urgent need for legislative measures", CM1203 (8 Feb. 2012). Art. 11(2) Return Directive.

duration of an entry ban, which in principle may not exceed five years unless there is a serious threat to public policy, must be calculated from the date on which the TCN has actually left the territory of the Member States.[152]

The Return Directive also contains important procedural safeguards. As regards detention it has harmonized the Member States' rules on the maximum duration thereof.[153] Detention is only allowed in case of a risk of absconding or insufficient cooperation of the irregular migrant, and only if there are no other less coercive measures available.[154] The risk of absconding is to be assessed on a case-by-case basis on the basis of objective criteria defined by law.[155] Detention should take place in special detention centres and as a rule, irregular migrants detained under the Return Directive should be kept separate from ordinary criminals.[156] Detention is allowed for a six months, with a possible prolongation of twelve months in case of delays due to a lack of cooperation of the irregular migrant or the need to obtain necessary documents from third countries.[157] Detention is only possible as long as there is a reasonable prospect of removal.[158] If in the course of a return procedure an asylum request is made, the Return Directive ceases to apply, but Member States must ensure that the return procedure can be resumed in case the request is denied.[159] As such Member States are allowed to order the detention of an claimant for international protection against whom a return decision was issued prior to the request being made, where the person involved constitutes a risk to public policy and security or where the request was put forward solely to delay return proceedings.[160] The Directive requires that decisions under the Return Directive, including those on detention, are in writing, state reasons and provide information about available legal remedies.[161] An effective remedy must be made available before a judicial or administrative authority.[162]

The Return Directive does not harmonize all rules on the (irregular) stay of TCNs. Member States are therefore not banned from criminalizing re-entry in breach of an entry ban or criminalizing irregular stay as an infringement.[163] The application of national criminal law should not however stand in the way of effective return proceedings.[164] This means for instance that Member States cannot imprison an irregular migrant during return proceedings, as this would delay removal.[165] It does not prevent Member States from applying their criminal law rules to TCNs

---

152. Article 11(2), Return Directive. Case C-225/16, *Ouhrami*, para 52.
153. This resulted in the abolition of unlimited detention in nine Member States and an increase in the maximum period of detention in twelve Member States: Report for DG Home Affairs, *supra* note 149, at 48.
154. Art. 15(1), Return Directive.
155. Art. 3(7), Return Directive. See by analogy: Case C-528/15, *Al Chodor*, at para 34.
156. Art. 16(1), Return Directive. See on the absence of special detention centres: Joined Cases C-473/13 and C-514/13, *Bero & Bouzalmate* and the obligation to keep returnees apart from ordinary criminals: Case-474/13, *Pham*.
157. Art. 15(5) and 15(6), Return Directive.
158. Art. 15(4), Return Directive. Case C-357/09 PPU, *Kadzoev*, at paras. 62 and 67.
159. Case C-601/15, *J.N*, at para 75 and Case C-534/11, *Arslan*, at para 63. By analogy: Case C-329/11, *Achughbabian*, at para 30.
160. Case C-601/15, *J.N*, at para 67.
161. Arts. 12 and 15(2), Return Directive. This includes decisions on the further course of action once the maximum period of detention under Art. 15(6) of the Directive has expired: Case C-146/14 PPU, *Mahdi*, at para 52.
162. Art. 13(1), Return Directive.
163. Case C-290/14, *Celaj*, at para 20, Case C-329, *Achughbabian*, at para 28 and Case C-430/11, *Sagor*, at para 31.
164. Case C-290/14, *Celaj*, at para 21, Case C-430/11, *Sagor*, at para 32.
165. Case C-290/14, *Celaj*, at para 26, Case C-61/11 PPU, *El Dridi*, at para 59, Case C-329/11, *Achughbabian*, at paras. 37 to 39 and 45 and Case C-430/11, *Sagor*, at para 33.

to whom the return procedure was followed and terminated.[166] It also does not require Member States to provide for an autonomous title of stay upon expiry of the maximum detention period, if there is no reasonable prospect of return.[167]

The Commission's priorities for operational cooperation for the next years were set out in the 2015 Action Plan on Return and the 2017 Renewed Action Plan.[168] In 2015, the Commission also adopted the Return Handbook, a Commission recommendation containing common guidelines, best practices and recommendations for return procedures under the Return Directive.[169] The EU's tries to improve the effectiveness of its return policy by facilitating operational cooperation between Member States' authorities responsible for return. As early as 2001, a Directive was adopted on the mutual recognition of return decisions, followed by directives on assistance in removal by air and joint flights for removals.[170] In 2016, the Council adopted a regulation for a European travel document for the return of irregular TCNs, considering that the lack of travel documents is often an obstacle for return.[171]

In 2004, Frontex was given the power to provide assistance in the organization of joint return operations, since in most Member States this competence falls under the border guard authorities.[172] Although initially not a priority, it has steadily expanded its activities in this field as return became more and more central to the EU's policy on irregular migration. In 2011, it was given the power the power to organize and coordinate joint return operations upon initiative of Member States.[173] The new European Border and Coast Guard Agency will further strengthen the Agency's role with the establishment of a dedicated return office within the Agency, allowing it to propose return operations to the Member States.[174]

4.3 *Asylum policy*

Following the logic of flanking measures, the CISA contained rules on the allocation of responsibility for asylum claims amongst the Schengen countries. These rules were deemed necessary to prevent "asylum shopping" and a "race to the bottom" in an area without internal border checks and without harmonized standards for refugee protection. Recast as K.3 Convention after the Maastricht Treaty ("Dublin I"), and as Regulation following Amsterdam ("Dublin II"), the regulation is currently applied in its third version ("Dublin III").[175]

In 1999, the Tampere Agenda for the first time called for a broader set asylum rules and the establishment of the CEAS, which should ultimately lead to a "a uniform status of asylum [...] valid throughout the Union".[176] In the first phase of the CEAS, directives were adopted laying down minimum standards for the qualification, procedure and reception of asylum seekers and refugees. By 2013 these directives were revised and updated as part of the second phase of the

166. Case C-329/11, *Achughbabian*, at para 48. See *a contrario*: Case C-357/09 PPU, *Kadzoev*, at para 70.
167. Case C-146/14 PPU, *Mahdi*, at para 89. The Member State should however issue the TCN with a written confirmation of her situation.
168. COM(2015)453 final and COM(2017)200 final.
169. COM(2015)6250 final.
170. Council Directive 2001/40/EC, O.J. 2001, L 149/34; Council Directive 2003/110/EC, O.J. 2003, L 321/26; Council Decision 2004/573/EC, O.J. 2004, L 261/28.
171. Reg. (EU) 2016/1953, O.J. 2016, L 311/13.
172. Recital 11, Council Reg. (EC) 2007/2004, cited *supra* note 87.
173. Art. 9, Reg. (EU) 1168/2011, O.J. 2011, L 304/1;.
174. Art. 28 (1), EBCG Reg., cited *supra* note 34.
175. Reg. (EU) 604/2013, O.J. 2013, L 180/31 ("Dublin III").
176. European Council Conclusions, Tampere, 15–16 Oct. 1999, at point 15: <www.europarl.europa.eu/summits/tam_en.htm>. Now included in Art. 78(2)(a) TFEU.

CEAS, along with the Dublin Regulation.[177] However, the Dublin rules remained fundamentally unchanged, continuing to be a mechanism for the allocation of responsibility, rather than an instrument for sharing responsibility.

Despite the fact that the Lisbon Treaty increased powers for full harmonization in this area, the revision of the asylum directives did not result in the adoption of a truly uniform status. Whereas a negative decision is recognized as final, a positive decision remains valid only in the Member State that took the decision. These decisions can only be taken by national asylum authorities. In order to provide support to national authorities and to foster operational cooperation between them, EASO was established.[178]

4.3.1 *Dublin Regulation*

Article 3 of the Dublin Regulation determines that only one single Member State shall be responsible for processing a claim for international protection. Responsibility is allocated on the basis of a hierarchical set of criteria laid out in Chapter III.[179] First are the criteria that see to unaccompanied minors and applicants with close relatives in another Member State. Unaccompanied minors should as a rule not be transferred other than to a Member State where they have family members.[180] Application of the Dublin system should also not result in breaking up a family unit.[181] In principle a Member State is responsible if there are already family members present who either enjoy international protection or are in the process of having their claim assessed.[182] Under Article 16, Member States shall normally unite an applicant with a child, sibling or parent in case of dependency such as in case of pregnancy, illness, severe disability or old age.[183]

A second set of criteria makes the Member State responsible that facilitated legal entry for instance by issuing a residence permit or visa.[184] Finally, and in practice the most important criterion, is the one that makes the Member State through which the applicant has illegally entered the EU responsible.[185] It is this criterion that creates an inherent unfairness in the system, even if under the current regulation this responsibility ceases after twelve months.[186] The Eurodac system, supports the functioning of the Dublin rules, storing the fingerprints of asylum applicants

177. Directive 2013/32/EU, O.J. 2013, L 180/60 ("Procedures Directive"); Directive 2011/95/EU, O.J. 2011, L 337/9 ("Qualification Directive"); Directive 2013/33/EU, O.J. 2013, L 180/96 ("Reception Directive").
178. EASO Reg., cited *supra* note 34.
179. Art. 7(1), Dublin III Reg.
180. Art. 8, Ibid. See Case C-648/11, *MA*, at para 60.
181. Art. 11, ibid.
182. Arts. 9 and 10, ibid.
183. The Court interpreted the words "shall normally" under the Dublin II Reg. as constituting an obligation, unless there are exceptional circumstances. This also meant that a request from the responsible Member States could not be made a precondition. Case C-245/11, *K*, at paras. 46 and 51.
184. Arts. 12 and 14, Dublin III Reg. See P. Boeles et al., *European Migration Law* (Intersentia, 2014), at 259. During the 2015 refugees crises, a number of Member States, faced with an unusually large inflow of third country nationals, allowed for transit through their respective territories, enabling these people to request international protection in other Member States. The Court has held that in such situation the applicants should not be considered to have obtained a visa, but to have crossed irregularly the border of these Member States: Case C-646/16, *Jafari*, at paras. 58 and 102 and Case C-490/16, *AS*, at para 42.
185. Art. 13(1), ibid. Note that this article takes precedence over Art. 14 (Member State that delivered a visa).
186. Art. 13(2), ibid.

and people apprehended at the external borders.[187] As with the VIS, law enforcement staff has been given access to this database.[188]

Responsible Member States are required to accept requests for transfers ("take back") and to examine an application ("take charge"), where they are responsible on the basis of the allocation criteria.[189] There is however no obligation for a Member State to transfer. Article 17 provides for two discretionary clauses. First, the sovereignty clause allows a Member State take responsibility without any further conditions. Second, under the humanitarian clause, a Member State may ask another Member State to take responsibility upon the basis of further humanitarian reasons based in particular on family or cultural considerations. The Regulation does not impose an obligation to put forward such a request or to accept it.

Article 3(2) of the Dublin Regulation incorporates the rulings of the ECHR and the CJEU in *MSS v. Belgium and Greece* and *NS & ME* respectively.[190] It provides that where there are systemic flaws in the asylum procedure and in the reception conditions of the Member State normally responsible, resulting in a risk of inhuman or degrading treatment, the determining Member State should examine whether another Member State could be held liable on the basis of the allocation criteria, in the absence whereof it should ultimately take responsibility itself. More recent case law of the ECtHR, in particular *Tarakhel v. Italy*, raised doubts as to whether only a systemic flaw in a Member State's asylum system would be able to halt a transfer under the Dublin rules.[191] In *CK* the Court held that also in the absence of systemic flaws, a transfer that in an individual case would amount to a violation of Article 4 of the Charter would have to be suspended.[192]

The Dublin III Regulation introduced new procedural safeguards and reinforced existing ones. An applicant subject to a transfer decision now has the right to be informed, to be heard in a personal interview, and to an effective remedy before a court or tribunal.[193] As a result, and unlike under its predecessor, the allocation criteria do not merely regulate the relation between Member States, but allow asylum seekers to derive rights from them.[194] An incorrect application of the criteria can therefore be challenged before a court or tribunal.[195]

4.3.2 *Temporary Protection Directive and relocation decisions*

Following the Balkan wars of the 1990s, the Council adopted a Temporary Protection Directive, which allows for a temporary protection status in the Member States as soon as the Council triggers the mechanism contained in the Directive.[196] The temporary status is for a period of

187. Reg. (EU) 603/2013, O.J. 2013, L 180/1 ("Eurodac Reg."). See for the Commission's recast proposal: COM(2016)272 final.
188. Arts. 1(2) and 5–7, Eurodac Reg., ibid.
189. Art. 18, Dublin III Reg. Under Art. 21(1), a take charge request must be made as quickly as possible and in any event within three months, failing to do so means an applicant may rely, on the expiry of that period, even if the requested Member State is willing to take charge of the application: Case C-670/16, *Mengesteab*, at para 62.
190. ECtHR, *MSS v. Belgium and Greece*, Appl. No. 30696/09, judgment (Grand Chamber) of 21 Jan. 2011 and Joined Cases C-411/10 and C-493/10, *NS & ME*.
191. ECtHR, *Tarakhel v. Switzerland*, Appl. No. 29217/12, Judgment (Grand Chamber) of 4 Nov. 2014.
192. Case C-578/16 PPU, *CK*, at para 85; See also K. Lenaerts, "La vie après l'avis: Exploring the principle of mutual (yet not blind) trust", 54 CML Rev. (2017), 805–840, at 832.
193. Arts. 4, 5 and 27, Dublin III Reg.
194. Case C-394/12, *Abdullahi*, at para 60.
195. Case C-63/15, *Ghezelbash*, at para 61, Case C-155/15, *Karim*, at para 22. This was more recently confirmed in Case C-670/16, *Mengesteab*, at paras. 62 and Case C-490/16, *AS*, at para 35.
196. Art. 5(3), Council Directive (EC) 2001/55, O.J. 2001, L 212/12.

one year, with possible extensions up to three years.[197] At the end of the temporary protection, beneficiaries fall under the regular asylum rules.[198]

The Temporary Protection Directive has never been put to practice; not even at the height of the 2015 refugee crisis. It would have done little in distributing the responsibility for refugees more evenly, as it merely calls for "Community solidarity" and imposes information obligations.[199] It is here that the two Relocation Decisions, adopted by the Council using its emergency powers of Article 78(3) TFEU, differ.[200] These decisions provided for the relocation of a total number of 160,000 refugees, mainly from Italy and Greece, on the basis of a distribution key, based primarily on population size and GDP.[201] The decisions constitute a temporary and limited derogation of the Dublin Regulation. Only refugees with a *prima facie* successful claim are eligible for relocation, that is applicants from countries that have an average EU recognition rate of over 75%.[202] Four Central European Member States that fiercely opposed the compulsory redistribution mechanism, unsuccessfully challenged the decision before the ECJ. Even though relocation has taken place at a painfully slow pace, the Commission nonetheless proposed for a similar, but permanent emergency measure to be included in the recast of the Dublin Regulation.[203]

4.3.3 *Qualification Directive*

The Qualification Directive lays down the conditions for granting refugee protection or subsidiary status under EU law, as well as the rights connected to this status.[204] Refugee protection is essentially based on the same criteria as those of the 1951 Geneva Convention.[205] A refugee is someone who has a well-founded fear of persecution for reasons of race, religion, nationality, political opinion or membership of a particular social group.[206] Article 9(1) of the Qualification Directive defines an act of persecution as one that is "sufficiently serious by its nature or repetition as to constitute a severe violation of basic human rights" or by an accumulation of measures amounting to the same. The concept of basic human rights is illustrated by reference to the non-derogable rights in the ECHR.[207] The Court has clarified that Member States cannot expect asylum seekers to hide their sexual orientation or religion or even exercise restraint ("discretion") in order to evade persecution.[208]

Actors of prosecution do not necessarily have to be state actors, but may also be private actors if the state is incapable or unwilling to provide protection.[209] Likewise protection may be granted by non-state actors, such a multilateral forces, but this must be a genuine and

---

197. Art. 4(1) and 4(2), ibid.
198. Art. 20, ibid.
199. Art. 25, ibid.
200. Council Decision (EU) 2015/1523, O.J. 2015, L 239/146 and Council Decision (EU) 2015/1601, O.J. 2015, L 248/80.
201. In line with the Annex to the Commission Communication on the European Agenda on Migration, COM(2015)240 final.
202. Art. 3(2), Council Decision (EU) 2015/1523 and Art. 3(2) of Council Decision (EU) 2015/1601, cited *supra* note 200.
203. COM(2015)450 final.
204. Qualification Directive, cited *supra* note 177.
205. Art. 1A(2), Geneva Convention.
206. Art. 2(d), Qualification Directive.
207. In Joined Cases C-199/12, C-200/12, C-201/12, *X, Y, Z*, at para 57, the ECJ made clear the reference is merely to provide guidance.
208. Case C-71/11, *Y & Z* and Joined Cases C-199/12, C-200/12, C-201/12, *X, Y, Z*.
209. Art. 6(c), Qualification Directive.

non-temporary form of protection.[210] Member States may also apply the "internal flight alternative" holding that a person can find protection in a safe part of her country of origin.[211]

Subsidiary protection is a secondary protection status, granted where there are substantial grounds for believing that the person concerned faces a real risk – as opposed to a well-founded fear – of serious harm.[212] Serious harm consists of the death penalty or execution, torture, or other forms of inhumane and degrading treatment.[213] It also includes "a serious and individual threat to a civilian's life or person by reason of indiscriminate violence in situations of international or internal conflict".[214] The Court in *Elgafaji* explained how to interpret the apparent contradiction between the need for an *individual* threat resulting from *indiscriminate* violence.[215] It held that an individual threat could result from the degree of indiscriminate violence, if it was so serious that an individual on the sole account of his presence on the territory of his home country would face a real risk of being subject to serious harm.[216]

Like the Geneva Convention, the Qualification Directive contains cessation and exclusion clauses. Refugee status is refused or lost if there is no longer a need for protection (cessation) or where the person in question is excluded from protection *a priori*.[217] Article 12(2), based on Article 1F of the Refugee Convention, excludes claimants that have committed crimes against peace, war crimes and crimes against humanity, serious non-political crimes committed prior to or crimes contrary to the purposes and principles of the United Nations.[218] Particularly cruel terrorist acts, even if committed with a political objective, may nonetheless lead to exclusion for serious crimes.[219] Terrorist acts can also be considered as contrary to the UN's objectives, as may supporting activities such as recruitment of individuals for engaging in terrorist acts.[220]

Being exceptions, the cessation and exclusion clauses need to be interpreted narrowly.[221] However, the Qualification Directive does make the termination of a refugee status mandatory as soon as it transpires that a cessation or exclusion clause applies, leaving no room for humanitarian or proportionality considerations.[222] The Qualification Directive has in broad terms aligned the regime for cessation, exclusion and termination of subsidiary protection with that of the refugee status.[223]

Beneficiaries of international protection are entitled to a set of rights which "expand and complement" the rights granted under the Geneva Convention.[224] The recast of the Qualification Directive has largely aligned the rights of refugees and those receiving subsidiary protection.

---

210. Art. 7(2), ibid. See Joined Cases C-175/08, C-176/08, C-178/08, C-179/08, *Abdulla*, at para 73.
211. Art. 8, ibid.
212. Art. 2(f), ibid. The CJEU has noted that the Qualification Directive regulates "two distinct systems of protection": Joined Cases C-175/08, C-176/08, C-178/08, C-179/08, *Abdulla*, at para 77.
213. Art. 15, ibid.
214. Art. 15(c), ibid.
215. Case C-465/07, *Elgafaji*.
216. Ibid., at para 35.
217. Arts. 11 and 12, Qualification Directive. See on the application of the cessation clause: Joined Cases C-175/08, C-176/08, C-178/08, C-179/08, *Salahadin*, at paras. 73 and 100.
218. Art. 12(2), ibid.
219. Art. 12(2)(b), ibid.
220. Joined Cases C-57/09 and C-101/09, *B&D*, at para 84 and Case C-573/14, *Lounani*, at para 79. Exclusion does always remain conditional on an individual assessment of the specific facts (*B&D*, paras. 87 and 94; *Lounani*, at para 72).
221. Case C-31/09, *Bobol*, at para 51.
222. Art. 14(2) and 14(3)(a), Qualification Directive. Joined Cases C-57/09 and C-101/09, *B&D*, at para 109. P. Boeles et al., op. cit. *supra* note 184, at 335.
223. Arts. 16, 17 and 19, ibid.
224. P. Boeles et al., op. cit. *supra* note 184, at 336.

They must receive a residence permit and a travel document, and have the right to move freely within the Member State as any other legally TCN.[225] However, refugees are to receive a renewable right of residence of at least three years, as opposed to one year, renewable with at least two years, for beneficiaries of subsidiary protection.[226]

Refugees and beneficiaries of subsidiary protection shall have access to employment, education and health care under the same conditions as nationals.[227] Refugees shall have access to social welfare under the same conditions as nationals, whereas Member States may limit the granting of social welfare to core benefits for people with a subsidiary protection status.[228] All beneficiaries of international protection shall have access to housing on the same conditions as legally resident TCNs.[229] In its *Alo & Osso* judgment, the CJEU made it clear that Member States may impose certain residence requirements for the purpose of facilitating integration, to the extent that legally TCNs find themselves in a different position.[230] However, the recast Qualification Directive does no longer allow for a distinction to be made between refugees and beneficiaries of subsidiary protection.[231]

4.3.4 *Procedures Directive*

The recast Procedures Directive lays down common procedures for the handling of requests international protection, as well as for withdrawing protection status.[232] Although the Directive refers to common procedures, the current framework still allows for considerable leeway to accommodate differences in Member States' national legal systems.[233] The second-phase Procedures Directive has generally raised procedural safeguards, in particular strengthening information obligations of the Member State.[234] Contrary to its predecessor, it applies to all claims for international protection, including subsidiary protection.[235]

As a rule claims for refugee status must be examined before eligibility for subsidiary protection.[236] In principle, a procedure cannot take longer than six months, with a possible extension in where the facts are complicated, the Member States has to handle a large number of applicants or if the delay is attributable to the applicant.[237] The Directive allows for a prioritization of claims that are likely to be founded or where the applicant is vulnerable.[238] Accelerated procedures, subject to minimum procedural standards, are also allowed.[239]

Applications can be found inadmissible if under the Dublin Regulation another Member State is responsible, if a third country has previously provided protection (country of first

225. Arts. 24, 25 and 33, Qualification Directive.
226. Art. 24, ibid.
227. Arts. 26, 27 and 30, ibid.
228. Art. 29, ibid.
229. Art. 32, ibid.
230. Joined Cases C-443/14 and C-444/14, *Alo & Osso*, at para 64.
231. Ibid., at para 56.
232. Procedures Directive, cited *supra* note 177.
233. Art. 5, Procedures Directive e.g. allows Member States to introduce or maintain more favourable provisions.
234. Arts. 11 and 19, ibid.
235. Case C-277/11, *M*, at para 79 and Case C-604/12, *N*, at para 39. National procedures under the first Procedures Directive must in any case to ensure the effectiveness of subsidiary protection under the Qualification Directive: Case C-429/15, *Danqua*, at para 49.
236. Art. 10(2), Procedures Directive, confirming the subsidiary nature of subsidiary protection: Case C-604/12, *H.N*, para 30.
237. Art. 31(3), ibid. Art. 31(5), sets a maximum time limit of 21 months.
238. Art. 31(7), ibid.
239. Art. 31(8), ibid.

asylum) or if there is a third country with which the applicant has a connection and that could have provided protection in according with the standards of the Geneva Convention and fundamental rights standards (safe third country).[240] The notion of safe third country has played a central role in the EU-Turkey Statement and is increasingly presented as a way of limiting access to asylum in Europe whilst ensuring protection elsewhere.[241] Under the current Directive, Member States themselves designate safe third countries, but the 2016 Commission proposal for an Asylum Procedures Regulation provides for a harmonized list.[242] Whereas the notion of safe third country is relevant for the admissibility of an application, the notion of safe countries of origin creates a rebuttable presumption that the applicant does not qualify for asylum because the situation in his home country does not generally give grounds to believe there is a risk of persecution or ill-treatment.[243] The initial provision that allowed the Council to draw up such list was annulled by the Court as the Treaties, as it bypassed the Treaties rules on legislation and delegation.[244] In 2015, the Commission adopted a proposal to amended the Procedures Directive and adopt a harmonized list of safe countries of origin.[245]

Free legal aid is ensured at the stage of judicial review, but may be refused during the administrative phase.[246] There should be an effective remedy before a court or tribunal, against decisions taken on an application for international protection.[247] In *Samba Diouf* the Court held that this only applies to final decisions, and not a decision to use an accelerated procedure which could effectively be challenged at a later stage.[248] Article 47 of the Charter on the right to an effective remedy does not require two levels of judicial review.[249] Importantly, the recast Procedures Directive requires that appeals, at least in first instance, conduct a "full and *ex-tunc*" assessment" taking into account events and points of law that have arisen after the administrative decision on the application, allowing for new facts and points of law to be put forward.[250] Applicants are allowed to remain in the territory of the Member State pending the appeal.[251]

4.3.5 *Reception Directive*

Reception conditions for applicants for international protection are regulated in the Reception Directive.[252] Like the Procedures Directive, the second-generation Reception Directive has improved standards, importantly in extending its scope to applicants for subsidiary protection.

Applicants receive a document certifying their status as an applicant and confirming their right of residence.[253] They are allowed to move freely within the Member States or in any case within an assigned area, which allows them to access the rights under the Directive.[254] These

---

240. Art. 33, ibid. The notions of first country of asylum, European safe third country and safe third country have been defined in Arts. 35, 38 and 39 respectively.
241. Art. 39, ibid.
242. Art. 39(4), ibid. Art. 45, COM(2016)467 final.
243. Art. 36, Procedures Directive. See also Protocol (24) on asylum for nationals of Member States of the European Union.
244. Case C-133/06, *Parliament v. Council*.
245. COM(2015)452 final.
246. Art. 21(2), Procedures Directive.
247. Art. 46, ibid.
248. Case C-69/10, *Samba Diouf*, at para 70.
249. Ibid., at para 69.
250. Art. 46(3), ibid.
251. Art. 46(5), ibid.
252. Reception Directive, cited *supra* note 177.
253. Art. 6, ibid.
254. Art. 7, ibid.

rights include accommodation, access to employment, education for minors and health care.[255] Under the recast directive access to the education system shall be given no later than three months and access to the labour market no later than nine months.[256] Member States must also ensure access to necessary health care.[257] A Member State should seek to preserve applicants' family unit when present on its territory, but there is no right to family reunification.[258]

Member States may make material reception conditions dependent on the applicant's own means.[259] Material reception conditions may be offered in cash or in kind.[260] The level of assistance may be less favourable than what is provided to nationals of the Member States to ensure an adequate standard of living.[261] Material receptions conditions may be reduced or even withdrawn in specific circumstances, such as failing to meet reporting duties or serious breaches of the rules of the accommodation centres and seriously violent behaviour.[262]

Member States may decide on the residence of the applicant for reasons of public interest, public order or, when necessary, for the efficiency of the procedure.[263] Member States may make provision of the material reception conditions subject to residence in a specific place, such as a reception centre.[264] Detention for the mere fact that someone is an applicant for international protection is not allowed.[265] Unlike under the Return Directive there is no time limit for detention other than that detention should be for as short as possible.[266]

4.3.6 *A third phase for the Common European Asylum System*

Just years after the completion of the revision of the EU's asylum *acquis*, the 2015 refugee crisis created the impetus for a third round of reforms aimed at further harmonization. The aim is to minimize divergences in recognitions rates across the Member States, to provide for harmonized standards laid down by regulation instead of directive, and to remove incentives for asylum seekers to seek protection in Member States other than the one responsible for their request ("secondary movements").[267] However, instead of a fundamental reform of the Dublin Regulation, the Commission's proposal for a recast of the Dublin Regulation rather tightens existing rules, amongst others by curtailing Member States' discretion to take charge of an asylum claim irrespective of the allocation criteria.[268] The familiar Dublin rules would be complemented with a permanent emergency relocation mechanisms, much like the Council's emergency relocation decisions.[269] It would accommodate the cooperation with third country along the line of the EU-Turkey deal, by determining that before the allocation criteria will be applied, a Member States should assess whether an asylum seeker cannot be returned to a safe third country.[270]

255. Arts. 14, 15 and 17, ibid.
256. Arts. 14(2) and 15(1), ibid.
257. Art. 17, ibid.
258. Art. 12, ibid.
259. Art. 17(3), ibid.
260. Art. 17(5), ibid. Financial aid granted must be sufficient to ensure a dignified standard of living and adequate for the health of applicants and capable of ensuring their subsistence: Case C-79/13, *Saciri*, at para 40.
261. Ibid.
262. Art. 20, ibid.
263. Arts. 7(2), ibid.
264. Art. 7(3), ibid.
265. Art. 8(1), ibid.
266. Art. 9(1), ibid.
267. COM(2016)270 final, at 4.
268. Art. 19, ibid.
269. Art. 34, ibid.
270. Art. 3, ibid.

Mirroring the reform of Frontex, EASO would be reinforced and as the European Asylum Agency be given supervisory powers to detect and help remedy weaknesses in national asylum systems.[271] Although the proposal for a reform of the Dublin regulation is currently halted in the legislative process, progress is being made on the reform of the asylum directives.[272] Also here the trend emerging from these proposals is clear: more harmonization, stricter rules and accommodating cooperation with third countries.

4.4 *Legal migration*

As a general rule, admission for long term migration and access to the labour market remain firmly in the hands of the Member States. To the extent that the EU legislation has adopted harmonized rules, these can be roughly divided into two. A first category aims to facilitate the entry and residence of TCNs thought to be beneficial to the Member States. The main example is the directive covering highly-skilled workers, which with a nod to the United States' Green Card, is called the Blue Card Directive.[273] In addition, there are directives covering intra-corporate transferees, seasonal workers, as well as researchers, students, trainees and volunteers.[274] An exception to this "self-interest driven" legislation is the Family Reunification Directive that bears testimony to the importance given to family life in the EU legal order.[275] The Commission has proposed a recast of the Blue Card Directive.[276] It is also carrying out a "fitness check" of all legislation on legal migration.[277]

A second category aims to facilitate procedures for admission by the Member States and provides TCNs once admitted by a Member State with a harmonized set of rights. The Single Permit Directive prescribes a single permit (for entry, residence and work) for economic migrants and prescribes equal treatment with nationals in areas such as working conditions, workers' rights, education and tax benefits.[278] More generally, the Long Term Residents Directive provides legally resident TCNs, including the beneficiaries of international protection, with a more stable right of residence after five years.[279] Although this legislation aims to approximate the position of TCNs to that of EU citizens, their position remains remarkably less favourable and the rights provided for remain generally limited to the Member State of legal residence. These instruments are generally also without prejudice to more beneficial conditions under national law or EU law, such as Association Agreements concluded with specific third countries.

This section will first look at the Family Reunification Directive, followed by a discussion of Long Term Resident Directive, and conclude with a discussion of the Blue Card Directive, as an example of the sectoral "first admission directives". Despite the different personal scope of these measures, the CJEU's interpretation of one measure can often be applied by analogy to other measures in this area.[280]

---

271. COM(2016)271 final.
272. COM(2016)466 final (Qualification), COM(2016)467 final (Procedures), COM(2016)468 final (Reception).
273. Council Directive 2009/50/EC, O.J. 2009, L 155/17 ("Blue Card Directive").
274. Directive 2014/66/EU, O.J. L 157/1 (Intercorporate Transferees); Directive 2014/36/EU, O.J. 2014, L 94/375 (Seasonal Workers); Directive (EU) 2016/801, O.J. 2016, L 132/21 (Students and Researchers recast). Until 23 May 2018, Directive 2004/114, O.J. 2004, L 375/12 will apply.
275. Council Directive 2003/86/EC, O.J. 2003, L 251/12 ("Family Reunification Directive").
276. COM(2016)378 final.
277. See <ec.europa.eu/home-affairs/what-we-do/policies/legal-migration/fitness-check_en>.
278. Directive 2011/98/EU, O.J. 2011, L 343/1.
279. Council Directive 2003/109/EC, O.J. 2004, L 16/44 ("Long Term Residents Directive").
280. Art. 79(1) TFEU.

4.4.1 Family reunification

The Family Reunification Directive determines the conditions under which TCNs (the sponsor) have a right to family reunification.[281] Its objective is to promote family reunification.[282] Family reunification includes the right to bring over a TCN for the purpose of "family formation".[283] It only applies to TCNs who are in possession of a residence permit that is valid for at least one year or who have a reasonable prospects of obtaining the right of permanent residence.[284] Member States may require an additional maximum of two year legal residence of the sponsor.[285] They may also require that the sponsor and spouse to be of a minimum age, at maximum 21 years, in order to ensure better integration and prevent forced marriages.[286] In the words of the Court this age limit would ensure a person would be mature enough to object to a forced marriage, but also to integrate in a different country.[287] The directive does not apply to the nationals of the Member States and in fact many Member States have rules in place that are more beneficial to its own nationals.[288] It does apply with exceptions to recognized refugees, taking into account their special position, but does not apply to beneficiaries of subsidiary protection.[289]

The Directive provides a right to family reunification with a clearly defined core of family members: the spouse and the minor unmarried children of the sponsor and/or spouse.[290] Member States may extend this right to dependent parents of the sponsor or the spouse, adult children of the sponsor or spouse who are dependent for health reasons, as well as the duly attested long term partner of the sponsor.[291] Member States may retain national legislation requiring that a request for family reunification be made before the age of 15, but "shall authorize the entry and residence" on other grounds than family reunification.[292] They may verify whether a child is aged over 12 years which arrives independently from the rest of her family fulfils integration conditions set by existing legislation.[293] It was these provisions that the European Parliament unsuccessfully challenged before the ECJ for violating fundamental rights.[294]

Applications may be rejected on grounds of public policy, security and health, and residence permits for family members may be withdrawn or not renewed for the same reasons.[295] Member States may require evidence that the sponsor has suitable accommodation, health insurance, as well as stable and regular resources sufficient to prevent recourse to the social assistance system of the Member State.[296] Social assistance was defined by the Court as social assistance granted

281. Family Reunification Directive, cited *supra* note 275.
282. Case C-578/08, *Chakroun*, at para 43.
283. Ibid., para 61.
284. Art. 3(1), Family Reunification Directive.
285. Art. 8, ibid.
286. Art. 4(5), ibid.
287. Case C-338/13, *Noorzia*, at para 16. As regards EU citizens the ECJ has taken a somewhat different view, emphasizing the beneficial effects of family members' presence for integration in the host state: Case 59/85, *Reed*, at para 28 and recently Case C-127/08, *Metock*, at para 56.
288. C. Groenendijk et al., *The Family Reunification Directive in EU Member States; the First Year of Implementation* (Centre for Migration Law Nijmegen, 2007), at 12.
289. Art. 7(2), Family Reunification Directive.
290. Art. 4(1), ibid.
291. Art. 4(2), ibid.
292. Art. 4(6), ibid.
293. Art. 4(1), ibid.
294. Case C-540/03, *Parliament v. Council*, at paras. 105–107.
295. Art. 6, Family Reunification Directive.
296. Art. 7(1), ibid.

by public authorities, whether at national, local or regional level.[297] The Court made it clear that Member State are allowed to use a reference amount, but only as guidance as individual circumstances would need to be taken into account.[298] A sponsor's resources are to be evaluated in the light of their nature and regularity and may take into account the minimum national wages.[299] Member States may make a prospective assessment of the likelihood of the sponsor retaining stable and regular resources.[300]

Member States may impose integration measures on the family member.[301] These may be applied prior to granting family reunification, including in the country of origin, except where it concerns refugees.[302] The requirement may however not make the exercise of the right to family reunification excessively difficult. This could be the case where the costs constitute a serious obstacle or where no regard is had to special circumstances, such as age, literacy and health.[303] Importantly, the amount of the fees may not be such as to render family reunification impossible or excessively difficult.[304] A permit may be refused, withdrawn or not renewed in case the conditions for family reunification do no longer apply or in case of fraud.[305] The directive explicitly refers to a situation in which the family bond is broken, or in case of a marriage of convenience.[306]

4.4.2 *Long Term Residents Directive*

The Long Term Resident status opens up the possibility for TCNs who have resided "legally and continuously" for five years in a Member States to acquire the long-term resident status.[307] This includes beneficiaries of international protection.[308] The status grants more secure residence rights, as well as equal treatment with nationals in specific fields and residence rights in another Member State. TCNs who reside solely on temporary grounds are excluded, as well as persons whose residence permit is formally limited.[309] The five year period may include absences for up to six months, not exceeding ten months in a five year period.[310] The long term status is not automatically conferred, but must be applied for.[311] EU law does not allow for national rules that confer the status on family members of long term residents before these have themselves fulfilled the five year residence requirement.[312]

Applicants need to prove that they have for themselves and for their dependent family members stable and regular resources to prevent recourse to the social assistance system of the Member State.[313] These resources are to be evaluated in the light of their nature and regularity

297. Case C-578/08, *Chakroun*, at paras. 45–46.
298. Ibid., at para 48.
299. Art. 7(1)(c), ibid.
300. Case C-558/14, *Kachab*, at para 40. In that case the ECJ ruled that a Spanish rule taking a one year reference period, appeared reasonable and did not go beyond what was necessary.
301. Art. 7(2), Family Reunification Directive.
302. Art. 7(2), ibid. Case C-153/14, *K&A*, at para 49.
303. Ibid., at para 58.
304. Ibid., at paras. 64–65.
305. Art. 16(1), ibid.
306. Art. 16(2), ibid.
307. Art. 4(1), Long Term Residents Directive, *supra* note 279.
308. Directive 2011/51/EU, O.J. 2011, L132/1.
309. Art. 3(2), Long Term Residents Directive. See however: Case C-502/10, *Singh*, at para 50.
310. Art. 4(3), ibid.
311. Case C-40/11, *Iida*, at para 47.
312. Case C-469/13, *Tahir*, at para 43.
313. Art. 5(1)(a), Long Term Residents Directive.

and may take into account the minimum national wages and pensions.[314] They must also have health insurance.[315] Member States may further require that integration conditions are complied with.[316] Even where the status has already been awarded, Member States may still require that the holder to pass a civic integration examination, under pain of a fine.[317] As the Court held in relation to integration measures under the Family Reunification Directive, that requirement should not hinder the effectiveness of the directive, meaning that regard should be had to specific individual circumstances, as well as the overall costs, level of the fine and frequency with which a fine could be imposed.[318] Already at an earlier stage the Court had held that the Dutch fees for permits under the directive were "excessive and disproportionate" which were liable to deprive the directive of its effectiveness.[319]

Member States may refuse to grant long-term resident status on grounds of public policy or public security.[320] They must consider the seriousness of the danger the person concerned poses and take into due account the duration and ties with the Member State.[321] A TCN will lose her status in case of fraudulent acquisition, adoption of an expulsion measure or absence of the territory of the EU for twelve consecutive months.[322] Member States may also withdraw the status – without expelling the person in question – in case she constitutes a threat to public policy and security, not however reaching the threshold for expulsion under the Directive.[323] Expulsion is allowed only, echoing the Citizens' Directive, where she constitutes an actual and sufficiently serious threat to public policy or public security.[324]

Long term resident status grants equal treatment with nationals in a number of areas, including employment (although not as regards work that may involve the – even occasional – exercise of public authority), education, social security, social assistance and social protection as defined in national law, as well as tax benefits.[325] However, in most of these areas however Member States may impose residence requirements.[326] Importantly, they may limit equal treatment in respect of social assistance and social protection to core benefits.[327] In the *Kamberaj* case the ECJ held that core benefits must include in any case basic needs such as food, accommodation and health, in particular also in the light of the Charter's provisions on social housing and the integration objective of the Directive.[328]

Far from granting long term residents a right to free movement within the Union, the long term resident status allows for residence in a second Member State for both economic and non-economic purposes. Member States may limit the total number of long term residents for economic purposes on the basis of existing quota or apply a labour market test for reasons of labour

314. Ibid. By analogy with Case C-558/14, *Kachab*, one must assume a Member State is allowed to look at prospective resources.
315. Art. 15(1)(b), ibid.
316. Art. 15(2), ibid.
317. Case C-579, *P&S*, at paras. 43, 47–48.
318. Case C-153/14, *K&A*, at para 49; Case C-579, *P&S*, at para 49.
319. Case C-508/10, *Commission v. Netherlands*, at paras. 65 and 74.
320. Art. 6(1), Long Term Residents Directive.
321. Ibid.
322. Art. 9(1), ibid.
323. Art. 9(3), ibid.
324. Art. 12(1), ibid.
325. Art. 11(1), ibid.
326. Art. 11(2), ibid.
327. Art. 11(4), ibid.
328. In Case C-571/10, *Kamberaj*, at paras. 91–92.

market policy.[329] They may require that a long term resident have adequate resources and health insurance, as well as comply with integration requirements, unless these have already been complied with in the first Member State.[330] A Member State can refuse a long term resident and her family member not only on the basis of public policy and security, but also public health.[331] The "core" family members of the long term resident may join the long term resident if the family was already established in the first Member State.[332] Acquisition of a long term resident status in the second Member State is possible under the same conditions as in the first Member State.[333]

4.4.3 *Blue Card Directive*

After much political debate, the Blue Card Directive was adopted in 2009.[334] Despite providing for a preferential regime for highly qualified workers, the Directive has not been an overwhelming success. In many Member States competing national regimes actually offer more beneficial conditions for skilled labour migration.[335] In 2016 the Commission proposed a recast of the Directive, that should facilitate existing procedures and improve current benefits. It would extend the scope of the Blue Card to beneficiaries of international protection and limit the possibility for Member States to maintain parallel regimes.[336]

Highly qualified workers are defined as workers, in line with the definition under the EU rules on free movement, who have "the required adequate and specific competence, as proven by higher professional qualifications".[337] Member States shall issue a Blue Card to highly qualified workers, who present a contract or binding job offer with a minimum duration of one year, have sickness insurance and are not considered a risk to public policy, public security or health.[338] In addition minimum salary requirements apply (at least 1,5 times the average gross annual salary in the Member State) which may be derogated from for sectors in particular need of workers.[339] Member States shall grant Blue Card holders every facility to obtain a visa.[340]

Member States may refuse a Blue Card when the conditions for obtaining it are not fulfilled and in case of fraud.[341] In addition, Member States may carry out a labour market test before issuing or renewing a Blue Card during the first two years, in line with the principle of Community preference.[342] They may also refuse a card on the basis of their power to determine the volume of admission of highly qualified workers.[343] They may further deny an application in

329. Art. 14(3), 14(4) and 14(5), Long Term Residents Directive.
330. Art. 15(2) and (3), ibid. The same holds true for family members: Art. 16(4)(2), ibid.
331. Arts. 17 and 18, ibid.
332. Art. 16, Long Term Residents Directive.
333. Art. 23, ibid.
334. Blue Card Directive, *supra* note 273.
335. COM(2014)287 final, at 4.
336. COM(2016)348 final, at 14.
337. Art. 2(b), Blue Card Directive.
338. Art. 5, ibid. Under Directive 2004/114, O.J. 2004, L 375/12 (Students and Researchers), the ECJ has given a very broad reading to the public security exception. Although a decision would need to be based on sufficient grounds and a sufficiently solid factual basis, it does not require a sufficiently serious, individual and actual threat: Case C-544/15, *Fahimian*, at paras. 41–42 and 46. At the same time, once all conditions are met, Member States cannot refuse a residence permit for study purposes: Case C-491/13, *Ben Alaya*, at para 31.
339. Art. 5(3) and 5(5), Blue Card Directive.
340. Art. 7(1), ibid.
341. Art. 8(1), ibid.
342. Art. 8(2), ibid.
343. Arts. 8(3) and 6, ibid.

case of a possible brain drain in the country of origin ("unethical recruitment") or where the prospective employer has been sanctioned for undeclared work or illegal employment.[344] A Blue Card may be withdrawn in case of unemployment for more than three months, where the TCN has recourse to social assistance or where she becomes a danger to public policy, security or health.[345]

The validity of the card shall be between one and four years.[346] Like the Single Permit Directive, the Blue Card entitles the TCN to equal treatment in areas such as such as working conditions, workers' rights, education and tax benefits, albeit with more limited derogations.[347] After eighteen months in the Member State that issued the Blue Card, a card holder and her family member that were already present with her, may move to a second Member State for the purpose of highly qualified employment and apply for a Blue Card there.[348] The second Member State retains the right to refuse a card on the basis of its powers to decide on the volume of admission of highly skilled workers.[349]

The Blue Card Directive contains important derogations from the Family Reunification and Long Term Residents Directive favourable to the card holder. For family reunification for instance, the minimum period of residence and the requirement of a prospect of permanent residence do not apply.[350] For the necessary five years of residence required for acquisition of the long term resident-status, periods of residence in different Member States may be accumulated, requiring only two years of continuous residence in the Member State where the application is lodged.[351]

5. Concluding remarks

Providing an comprehensive, yet contained overview of this dynamic and rapidly developing field of EU policy is not an easy task, especially not at a time of heightened legislative activity. From its humble origins as flanking measures, facilitating borderless travel within Europe, it has become a rapidly growing policy area in its own right. On paper the EU's migration and asylum *acquis* appears a closed and almost watertight system. Secure borders filter out the dangerous TCN and welcome the *bona fide* migrant that comes to contribute to the Member States' societies. Those in protection are given sanctuary and those that (no longer) fulfil the conditions for legal stay are asked to leave or sent back to their home countries. But practice is unruly. Regulation can at most try to steer trends, but it dependent of a range of external factors that are largely out of control or outside the competence of the EU.

Although institutional framework of this area is now largely in line with more classic fields of EU competence, it has by no means become less contentious or political. The underlying, often conflicting, rationales of this policy area will continue to push the migration and asylum *acquis* forward, albeit not always in a single direction. If anything, the 2015 refugee crisis, the humanitarian crisis in the Mediterranean and the terrorist threat in Europe have raised the profile of this policy field and have laid bare the weaknesses of integration based upon limited harmonization and mutual recognition. They have made visible more structural problems with the rule of law and the respect for fundamental rights in various Member States. And finally, they have made

344. Art. 8(4) and 8(5), ibid.
345. Art. 9, ibid.
346. Art. 7(2), ibid.
347. Art. 14, ibid.
348. S. Peers, *EU Justice and Home Affairs* (OUP, 2016), at 381.
349. Arts. 18(1) and 19(1), Blue Card Directive.
350. Art. 15(2), ibid.
351. Art. 16(2), ibid.

painfully clear that solidarity is difficult to impose by means of Treaty provisions or secondary legislation. It is for these reasons that more harmonization and centralization may not in and of itself provide the desired outcomes.[352]

In an interconnected world, migration and asylum are a fact of life which must be expected to dominate the political agenda for years to come. The European Union, as a heaven of peace and prosperity in a structurally instable world, will continue to attract both those seeking international protection, as well as those looking for a better future. It will need to develop a strategy now to prepare for the reality of migration and asylum in the coming decades. Such strategy must not only responds to justified concerns of its citizens, but also do justice to its economic needs and uphold its fundamental values. It should prepare the Union and its Member States for increased inflows and "migratory pressure" at their external borders, not by fighting this phenomenon but by accommodating it to the best of its abilities.

Unfortunately, recent proposals seem to do little more than reaffirm existing restrictive trends, the shifting of borders inwards and outwards and a heavy reliance on surveillance and technology. Although the most recent initiatives by the European Commission, published late September 2017, constitute anything but fundamental overhaul of existing policies or a long-term vision for the future of EU migration and asylum policies, they do provide for the voluntary resettlement of refugees from areas of conflict and pilot projects on legal migration. The question that remains to be seen is to what extent they are only the proverbial drop in the ocean.

Further reading

Azoulai, L. and K. de Vries, *EU Migration Law: Legal Complexities and Political Rationales* (OUP, 2014).

Boeles, P., M. den Heijer, G. Lodder and K. Wouters, *European Migration Law* (Intersentia, 2014).

Cherubini, F., *Asylum Law in the European Union* (Routledge, 2015).

Costello, C., *The Human Rights of Migrants in European Law* (OUP, 2015).

Fletcher, M., C. Herlin-Karnell, E. Matera, *The European Union as an Area of Freedom, Security and Justice* (Routledge, 2017).

Hailbronner, K. and D. Thym, *EU Immigration and Asylum Law: A Commentary* (Nomos, 2016).

Mitsilegas, V., *The Criminalization of Migration in Europe: Challenges for Human Rights and the Rule of Law* (Springer, 2015).

Moreno-Law, V., *Accessing Asylum in Europe: Extraterritorial Border Controls and Refugee Rights Under EU Law* (OUP, 2017).

Peers, S., *EU Justice and Home Affairs Law: Volume I: EU Immigration and Asylum Law* (OUP, 2016).

Peers, S., V. Moreno-Lax, M. Garlick and E. Guild, *EU Immigration and Asylum Law* (Brill, 2015).

352. M. den Heijer et al., "Coercion, prohibition and great expectations. The continuing failure of the Common European Asylum System", 53 CML Rev. (2016), 607–642.

CHAPTER 18
JUDICIAL COOPERATION IN CIVIL MATTERS

*Xandra Kramer**

1. Introduction and institutional development

Judicial cooperation in civil matters in the European Union denotes cooperation between the Member States, their courts, and other judicial institutions in civil law cases having cross-border implications. This policy area includes instruments in the field of procedural law regarding, *inter alia,* the recognition and enforcement of judgments, the service of documents, and the taking of evidence, as well as the matter of the applicable law. These topics are regarded traditionally as private international law issues or, as far as they concern procedure, matters of international civil procedure. Prior to the EU involvement, on the international level a certain degree of harmonization on several of these issues had already been achieved by the conventions activities of the Hague Conference on Private International Law.[1] In the EU, the legislative competence in relation to judicial cooperation in civil matters was introduced in 1999 when the Treaty of Amsterdam entered into force. It is a part of the Area of Freedom, Security and Justice (AFSC) currently laid down in Section V of Part III of the TFEU.

In the pre-Amsterdam period, judicial cooperation in civil matters was limited, and was based on intergovernmental cooperation through conventions.[2] The only reference in the Rome Treaty concerned the recognition and enforcement of judgments. Article 220 thereof (later Art. 293 EC Treaty) provided the basis for Member States to enter into negotiations to simplify formalities governing the reciprocal recognition and enforcement of judgments and arbitral awards. On the basis of this provision, the 1968 Convention on jurisdiction and the enforcement of judgments in civil and commercial Matters (Brussels Convention) was established.[3]

---

* Professor Private Law at Erasmus University Rotterdam and Private International Law at Utrecht University. This chapter has been written as part of the project "Building EU Civil Justice: challenges of procedural innovations – bridging access to Justice" (www.euciviljustice.eu) financed by the European Research Council (ERC-Consolidator Grant no. 726032).

1. See <www.hcch.net> (last visited 1 June 2017). See on the relation between the EU and the Hague Conference *inter alia* M. Traest, *De Europese Gemeenschap en de Haagse Conferentie voor het Internationaal Privaatrecht* (Maklu, 2003); R. Wagner, "Die Haager Konferenz für Internationales Privatrecht zehn Jahre nach der Vergemeinschaftung der Gesetzgebungskompetenz in der justitiziellen Zusammenarbeit in Zivilsachen", (2009) *RabelsZ*, 216–240.
2. See for an extensive treatment T. Drappatz, *Die Überführung des internationalen Zivilverfahrensrechts in einen Gemeinschaftskompetenz nach Art. 65 EGV* (Mohr Siebeck, 2002), 5–25. In relation to European civil procedure: X.E. Kramer, *Eenvormige procedures voor de inning van vorderingen* (Kluwer, 2007), 18–19; E. Storskrubb, *Civil Procedure and EU Law. A Policy Area Uncovered* (OUP, 2008), 33–38.
3. Brussels Convention on Jurisdiction and the Enforcement of Judgments in Civil and Commercial Matters of 1968, O.J. 1972, L 299/32.

To further facilitate recognition and enforcement as well as the common market, a system of conflict of law rules on contracts was introduced by the 1980 Convention on the law applicable to contractual obligations (Rome Convention).[4] The 1992 Maastricht Treaty incorporated civil justice in the Third Pillar, thus creating the basis for more encompassing conventions.[5]

A breakthrough was the legislative competence resulting from the Treaty of Amsterdam, introducing Title IV (Arts. 61–69) on visas, asylum, immigration, and other policies related to the free movement of persons. Article 61 sub (c) in conjunction with Article 65 EC Treaty empowered the Community to establish measures in the field of judicial cooperation in civil matters having cross-border implications, needed for the proper functioning of the international market.[6] These include measures on the cross-border service of documents, the taking of evidence, recognition and enforcement, the conflict of laws, and international jurisdiction as well as measures eliminating obstacles to the good functioning of civil proceedings. The present provision, Article 81 TFEU, largely reiterates Article 65 EC Treaty, but adds a number of topics on which measures may be taken. It should be noted that due to the exceptions made for Denmark, the United Kingdom, and Ireland as regards the entire AFSJ, these Member States are not bound by instruments established on this basis.[7] To date, the United Kingdom and Ireland have opted in on most of the civil justice cooperation instruments. Denmark has a general opt-out, but participates in two key Regulations in this area as a result of parallel agreements.[8]

The new competence and strong policy initiatives have resulted in over twenty legislative instruments that together comprise the area of civil justice cooperation. At the same time, the extended competence affected the external competence. The *ERTA* ruling of 1971, introducing the implied powers doctrine, had already made clear that Member States cannot individually or collectively enter into obligations with third countries in areas that would affect Community rules.[9] Now that the EU has full competence in the area of judicial cooperation in civil matters, and the instruments cover a wide range of issues, the ERTA doctrine has become fully effective. In Opinion 1/03 of 2006, the ECJ concluded that the EU had the exclusive competence to conclude a new Lugano Convention on jurisdiction and recognition and enforcement[10] with

4. Convention 80/934/EEC on the Law Applicable to Contractual Obligations of 1980 (Rome Convention), O.J. 1980, L 266/1.
5. Art. K1 in conjunction with K3. Several conventions were proposed in this period, but were not adopted in view of the envisaged competence under the upcoming Treaty of Amsterdam.
6. See generally T. Drappatz, op. cit. *supra* note 2, 88–155; E. Storskrubb, "Civil justice – A newcomer and an unstoppable wave?" in P. Craig and G. de Búrca, *The Evolution of EU Law*, 2nd ed. (OUP, 2011), 303–307. From the perspective of private international law: P. Stone, *EU Private International Law*, 2nd ed. (Elgar, 2010), 4–6; M. Bogdan, *Concise Introduction to EU Private International Law*, 3rd ed. (Europa Law Publishing, 2016); A.P.M.J. Vonken (in collaboration with H.L.E. Verhagen, X.E. Kramer, S. van Dongen), *Mr. C. Assers Handleiding tot de beoefening van het Nederlands Burgerlijk recht* (Kluwer, 2013), 50–56. From the perspective of a European civil procedure: X.E. Kramer, op. cit. *supra* note 2, 19–25; E. Storskrubb, op. cit. *supra* note 2, 39–43; B. Hess, *Europäisches Zivilprozessrecht* (C.F. Müller, 2010), 25–45.
7. See Protocol 21 TEU and TFEU for the United Kingdom and Ireland and Protocol 22 for Denmark. It goes without saying that Brexit implies that United Kingdom is no longer bound by these instruments.
8. Agreement between the European Community and the Kingdom of Denmark on the service of judicial and extrajudicial documents in civil or commercial matters, O.J. 2005, L 300/55; Agreement between the European Community and the Kingdom of Denmark on jurisdiction and the recognition and enforcement of judgments in civil and commercial matters, O.J. 2005, L 299/62.
9. Case 22/70, *Commission v. Council*.
10. The Lugano Convention of 1988 is a parallel Convention to the Brussels Convention cited *supra* note 3, and the new Lugano Convention is intended to align it to the Brussels Reg. 44/2001. See also Council Decision of 15 Oct. 2007 on the signing, on behalf of the Community, of the Convention on jurisdiction and the recognition and enforcement of judgments in civil and commercial matters, O.J. 2007, L 339/1.

the EFTA States.[11] In 2007, the EU also became a member of the Hague Conference on Private International Law, alongside membership of the individual Member States, since the Member States can no longer freely engage with third countries in these matters.[12]

The present chapter will focus first on the policy initiatives and legislative developments in the area of judicial cooperation in civil matters (section 2). It will continue with a more in-depth analysis of Article 81 as the legislative basis for instruments (section 3). Next, the legislative framework will be discussed, focusing on the key areas and the instruments as well as the role of the ECJ in the development of this area (section 4). Lastly, the current debates and prospects for the further development will be addressed (section 5).

2. Policy background and pillars of judicial cooperation

The competence in the area of judicial cooperation in civil matters was backed up by strong policy impetus.[13] The 1998 Action Plan of the European Commission and the Council stated that the reinforcement of judicial cooperation in civil matters signifies a fundamental stage in the creation of a European judicial area.[14] The aim is to simplify and facilitate the legal environment of EU citizens, with legal certainty and equal access to justice as guiding principles.[15] This Action Plan laid the foundation and included a time plan for measures to be taken in this area, focusing on the main pillars of civil justice in the cross-border context: *i.e.* international jurisdiction, the applicable law and recognition and enforcement, and adding the availability of speedy and fair proceedings.[16]

The Tampere Presidency Conclusions of 1999 further boosted the development of EU civil justice.[17] These Conclusions underlined the need to improve access to justice, the mutual recognition of judgments, and generally a greater convergence in civil law. Specific aims were set as regards improving access to justice, including setting up an information system, measures on legal aid, and accelerated cross-border litigation procedures for small consumer claims, commercial uncontested claims, and family litigation.[18] The Council endorsed the principle of mutual recognition as the cornerstone of judicial cooperation and announced the further reduction of intermediate measures for the recognition and enforcement of judgments (abolition of *exequatur*).[19] The following Joint Programme of the Commission and the Council on the implementation of the Tampere principle of mutual recognition was adopted, and set concrete goals for the introduction of new instruments and the simplification of existing instruments.[20]

---

11. Opinion 1/03, *Lugano Convention*. See *inter alia* N. Lavranos, "Opinion 1/03, *Lugano Convention*", 43 CML Rev. (2007), 1067–1100; K. Boele-Woelki and R.H. van Ooik, "Exclusieve externe bevoegdheden van de EG inzake het Internationaal Privaatrecht", (2006) *Nederlands Tijdschrift voor Europees Recht*, 194–201.
12. Council Decision 2006/719/EC of 5 Oct. 2006 on the accession of the Community to the Hague Conference on Private International Law, O.J. 2006, L 297/1. See also Art. 3 Statute of the Hague Conference on Private International Law.
13. See for an overview E. Storskrubb, op. cit. *supra* note 2, 66–70; B. Hess, op. cit. *supra* note 6, 46–50.
14. Action plan of the Council and the Commission on how best to implement the provisions of the Treaty of Amsterdam on an area of freedom, security and justice, O.J. 1999, C-19/1, at 4, no. 16.
15. Ibid.
16. Action Plan cited *supra* note 14, nos. 39–40.
17. Tampere European Council, 15 and 16 Oct. 1999, Presidency Conclusions, see in particular nos. 28–39.
18. Tampere Presidency Conclusions, cited *supra* note 17, nos. 29–32.
19. See more in detail *inter alia* X.E. Kramer, "Cross-border enforcement in the EU: Mutual trust versus fair trial? Towards principles of European civil procedure", (2011) *International Journal of Procedural Law*, 202–230, in particular 207–215.
20. Programme of measures for implementation of the principle of mutual recognition of decisions in civil and commercial matters, O.J. 2001, C 12/1, at 8.

These policy documents were followed by a series of proposals introducing, *inter alia*, instruments on the service of documents, the taking of evidence, minimum standards for legal aid and jurisdiction and enforcement in certain family law matters.[21] To enhance access to justice and to implement the principle of mutual recognition, in its 2002 Green Paper the Commission presented its two-tiered approach to simplifying and speeding up cross-border litigation in uncontested and small claims.[22] The first tier was to abolish the *exequatur* for uncontested claims, and the second involved the creation of uniform procedures for the recovery of uncontested claims.[23]

The 2004 Hague Programme built upon the policy goals set out in the Tampere Programme.[24] Important themes in this Programme were to further enhance judicial cooperation by strengthening mutual trust and to complete the programme of mutual recognition. A new issue that was put forward was to ensure coherence of all private law instruments relating to judicial cooperation in civil matters, including for example the various directives on consumer contract law. The 2009 Stockholm Programme reiterated the importance of access to justice for European citizens along with the fundamental nature of the right to effective enforcement as well as the necessity of increasing coherence and of the evaluation of instruments.[25] In the Stockholm Action Plan, the Commission emphasized that the European judicial area is built on the cornerstone of mutual recognition and that the principle of mutual recognition "can only function effectively on the basis of mutual trust among judges, legal professionals, businesses and citizens".[26] Apart from proposing new legislation, this Action Plan includes a range of practical measures, including the introduction of e-justice and communication – such as the introduction of the e-Justice portal[27] – and the training of judges.

The recognition of the fundamental nature of effective access to justice is not new in the European procedural arena, since it already flows from Articles 6 and 13 of the European Convention on Human Rights (ECHR). These rights derived from the ECHR are an integral part of EU law. Moreover, Article 47 of the Charter of Fundamental Rights of the European Union (CFREU) lays down the right to an effective remedy and a fair trial, and forms the pillar upon which the judicial cooperation in the EU should be built.[28]

21. See further section 4.1 on the specific instruments.
22. Green Paper on a European order for payment procedure and on measures to simplify and speed up small claims litigation, 20 Dec. 2002, COM(2002)746 final.
23. Reg. (EC) 1896/2006 of the European Parliament and of the Council of 12 Dec. 2006 creating a European order for payment procedure, O.J. 2006 L 399/1 and Reg. (EC) 861/2007 of the European Parliament and of the Council of 11 July 2007 establishing a European Small Claims Procedure, O.J. 2007, L 199/1. See for a comprehensive study X.E. Kramer, op. cit. *supra* note 2; E.A. Ontanu, *Cross-Border Debt Recovery in the EU. A Comparative and Empirical Study on the Use of European Uniform Procedures*, PhD thesis Erasmus University Rotterdam (Intersentia, 2017). See also B. Hess, op. cit. *supra* note 6, 556–587; E. Storskrubb, op. cit. *supra* note 2, 203–232.
24. The Hague Programme: strengthening freedom, security and justice in the European Union, 13 Dec. 2004, O.J. 2005, C 53/1.
25. The Stockholm Programme – An open and secure Europe serving and protecting the citizen, O.J. 2010, C 115/1, at 5.
26. European Commission, Action Plan Implementing the Stockholm Programme, COM(2010)171 final, at 4.
27. See <e-justice.europa.eu/home.do> (last visited 1 June 2017).
28. See on Art. 47 in the ASFJ *inter alia* H. Raulus, "Fundamental rights in the area of freedom, security and justice" in S. Wolff, F.A.N.J. Goudappel and J.W. de Zwaan (Eds.), *Security and Justice after Lisbon and Stockholm* (Asser Press, 2011), 213–240, and in private law matters C. Mak, "Rights and remedies: Article 47 EUCFR and effective judicial protection in European private law matters" in H.-W. Micklitz (Ed.), *Constitutionalization of European private law* (OUP, 2014), 236–258.

As a result of the economic crisis, policy and legislative initiatives have also been presented in the economic context of the "Justice for Growth" Agenda.[29] In the area of civil procedure, the focus is on enabling a swift recovery of claims and on reducing costs. Examples of where this policy was expressed to underpin legislation are the amendment of the Regulation establishing a European Small Claims Procedure[30] and the adoption of the European Account Preservation Order.[31]

Lastly, in the EU Justice Agenda for 2020 the Commission presents as the main challenges the strengthening of mutual trust ("the bedrock upon which EU justice policy should be built"), the mobility of citizens (freedom of movement), and economic recovery and growth.[32] These should be tackled by a further consolidation, codification, and completion of EU legislation.[33] This present agenda will be discussed further in section 5.

It is along these cornerstones of mutual recognition and mutual trust, and with access to justice, predictability and legal certainty as guiding principles, that over twenty instruments have meanwhile been established that together comprise the area of civil justice cooperation.

3. Institutional framework: Scope and limits of Article 81 TFEU

Article 81 TFEU provides the Treaty basis for measures on judicial cooperation in civil matters. Article 67(4) TFEU states that the Union shall facilitate access to justice, in particular through the principle of mutual recognition of judicial and extrajudicial decisions in civil matters. In between the Amsterdam Treaty and the Lisbon Treaty, the Treaty of Nice brought about an institutional change by introducing the co-decision procedure. Since then, the tripartite decision-making has had an important influence on instruments in the civil justice area.

This subsection will discuss the scope and limits of Article 81 TFEU within the dynamics of the legislative process involving the various instruments based on this provision and its predecessor, Article 65 EC Treaty.

3.1 *Civil matters and judicial cooperation*

Article 81(1) TFEU provides that the Union shall develop judicial cooperation in civil matters having cross-border implications, based on the principle of mutual recognition of judgments and of decisions in extrajudicial cases. It adds that this may include the adoption of instruments for the approximation of the laws of the Member States. The competence extends to all civil and commercial matters, including family law, though the legislative process for family matters as laid down in Article 81(3) implies limits. Article 81(2) lists a series of issues on which measures may be taken, some of which are aimed at supporting the general goals of judicial cooperation in civil matters, in particular ensuring effective access to justice (sub e), the elimination of obstacles to the proper functioning of civil proceedings (sub f) and, on the practical level, judicial training (sub g). Others regard traditional private international law questions regarding the

29. See *inter alia* the Programme of the Irish Presidency of the Council of the European Union (1 Jan. – 30 June 2013) for stability, Jobs and Growth, at 21.
30. Reg. (EU) 2015/2421 amending Reg. (EC) 861/2007 establishing a European Small Claims Procedure and Reg. (EC) 1896/2006 creating a European order for payment procedure, O.J. 2015, L 341/1, and see the proposal COM(2013)794 final.
31. Reg. 6552014 establishing a European Account Preservation Order to facilitate cross-border debt recovery in civil and commercial matters, O.J. 2014, L 189/59.
32. Communication from the Commission to the European Parliament, the Council, the European Economic and Social Committee of the Regions, The EU Justice Agenda for 2020 – Strengthening Trust, Mobility and Growth within the Union, COM(2014)144 final, see point 3.
33. Communication EU Justice Agenda 2020 cited *supra* note 32, point 4.

applicable law, international jurisdiction, and recognition and enforcement (sub a and c), or specific issues of civil procedure, particularly the cross-border service of documents (sub b), the taking of evidence (sub d), and alternative dispute resolution (sub g).

3.2 *Cross-border dichotomy*

An important limitation to judicial cooperation in civil matters is that it should concern matters "having cross-border implications". The scope of this condition and its implications are politically controversial, and have been debated in the literature.[34]

The first confrontation with the prerequisite of the "cross-border implications" arose a few years after Article 65 EC Treaty was enacted. The Commission envisaged the Legal Aid Directive to cover both cross-border and domestic disputes.[35] However, this met with resistance from the Council, and this Directive was consequently restricted to cross-border disputes.[36] These are defined as disputes where the party applying for legal aid is domiciled or habitually resident in a Member State other than that where the court is sitting or where the decision is to be enforced. The argument was continued when the Commission proposed three other instruments that were not confined to cross-border cases. These were the two Regulations creating harmonized procedures – the European Order for Payment Procedure[37] and the European Small Claims Procedure[38] – and the Mediation Directive.[39] Discussions evolved around the wording of the Treaty text as well as the principle of subsidiarity and the requirements of the internal market.

Particularly in relation to the proposal for a European Order for Payment Procedure, the Commission reasoned extensively as to why this instrument should not be restrained to cross-border cases.[40] It stated that limiting the scope of this procedure would be inappropriate and counterproductive in view of the considerable differences between national procedures and the fundamental economic importance of an efficient procedure for the recovery of uncontested debts.[41] It would distort the internal market if economic operations were to have access to diverging mechanisms depending upon the cross-border or domestic nature of the case. The Commission argued further that the distinction between cross-border and domestic disputes was ambiguous, and that every case could potentially become cross-border if only for enforcement purposes. However, the vast majority of the Member States objected to the application

34. See *inter alia* P.A.M. Meijknecht, "Alleen voor grensoverschrijdende gevallen?" in R.J.C. Flach (Ed.), *Amice: Rutgers-bundel* (Kluwer, 2005), 223–231; X.E. Kramer, op. cit. *supra* note 2, 20–21; E. Storskrubb, op. cit. *supra* note 2, 41–43; B. Hess, op. cit. *supra* note 6, 34–36; G. Wagner, "Harmonisation of civil procedure: Policy perspectives" in X.E. Kramer and C.H. van Rhee (Eds.), *Civil Litigation in a Globalising World* (Asser Press, 2012), 97–99; P.P.M. van der Grinten, "Vraagpunten in het Europees procesrecht", (2007) *Tijdschrift voor Civiele Rechtspleging*, 68–69.
35. Proposal for a Council Dir. to improve access to justice in cross-border disputes by establishing minimum common rules relating to legal aid and other financial aspects of civil proceedings, COM(2002)13, and the adopted Dir. to improve access to justice in cross-border disputes by establishing minimum common rules relating to legal aid for such disputes 2002/8/EC, O.J. 2003, L 26/41.
36. See also E. Leroy, "L'aide juridique et judiciaire en droit européen" in G. Leval and M. Storme (Eds.), *Het Europees gerechtelijk recht en procesrecht* (Die Keure, 2003), 317.
37. Proposal for a Regulation of the European Parliament and of the Council creating a European Order for Payment Procedure, COM(2004)173 final/3.
38. Proposal for a Regulation of the European Parliament and of the Council establishing a European Small Claims Procedure, COM(2005)87 final.
39. Proposal for a Dir. of the European Parliament and of the Council on certain aspects of mediation in civil and commercial matters, 22 Oct. 2004, COM(2004)718 final.
40. Explanatory Memorandum to the Commission Proposal cited *supra* note 38, 7–8.
41. Explanatory Memorandum to the Commission Proposal cited *supra* note 38, at 7.

of these instruments to purely domestic cases, and so did the European Parliament.[42] All three instruments were therefor confined to cross-border cases. In the uniform European procedures, these are defined as cases in which at least one of the parties is domiciled or habitually resident in a Member State other than that of the court or tribunal seized.[43] The Mediation Directive generally regards disputes that involve parties domiciled or habitually resident in different Member States.[44]

The wording of Article 81 TFEU leaves little room to create instruments that apply to purely domestic cases. Past experiences have shown that with reference to the Treaty text and the principles of subsidiarity and proportionality, as laid down in Article 5(1) EU Treaty, most Member States are not in favour of a flexible interpretation. For several instruments, particularly the aforementioned, this implies that the scope of application and practical relevance is relatively limited. Additionally, it has been rightfully remarked that this limitation discriminates between domestic and cross-border disputes.[45] This complicates the creation of a coherent framework that would truly ensure equal and effective access to justice.

In recent years, the Commission has not openly challenged the "cross-border implications" prerequisite in Article 81 TFEU, though it did attempt to stretch the limits of the definition of a cross-border case. In particular in its proposal to amend the European Small Claims Regulation it proposed a negative definition of cross-border cases, meaning that this Regulation should apply unless a list of factors are all connected to only one Member State.[46] However this broad definition was not accepted in the legislative process and the amended Small Claims Regulation retains the previous limitation to cross-border cases.[47]

Additionally, several more recent instruments that generally fit under the heading of judicial cooperation in civil matters were not based on Article 81 TFEU but on the general basis of harmonization of laws of Article 114 TFEU. This provision usually provides the basis for directives on substantive private law matters, including consumer contract law. Examples are the Directive on Consumer Alternative Dispute Resolution (ADR),[48] the Regulation on Online Dispute Resolution (ODR),[49] and the Recommendation on collective redress.[50] Though these instruments are also interwoven with the consumer *acquis* and competition law, an additional reason to use Article 114 as the competence basis is that it does not limit legislation to cross-border cases.

---

42. See *inter alia* House of Lords (European Union Committee), European Small Claims Procedure, Report with Evidence, Minutes of Evidence, 15 Feb. 2006, at 2; European Parliament legislative resolution on the proposal for a regulation of the European Parliament and of the Council creating a European order for payment procedure, A6-0240/2005, 13 Dec. 2005; European Parliament legislative resolution on the proposal for a regulation of the European Parliament and of the Council establishing a European Small Claims Procedure, A6-0387/2006,14 Dec. 2006. See also P.P.M. van der Grinten, "Kroniek: Europese ontwikkelingen", (2005) *Tijdschrift voor Civiele Rechtspleging*, 83; P.A.M. Meijknecht, op. cit. *supra* note 34.
43. Art. 3 Reg. European Order for Payment and Reg. European Small Claims Procedure.
44. Art. 2 Dir. 2008/52/EC on certain aspects of mediation in civil and commercial matters, O.J. 2008, L 136/3.
45. M. Storme, "Closing comments: Harmonisation or globalisation of civil procedure" in X.E. Kramer and C.H. van Rhee (Eds.), *Civil Litigation in a Globalising World* (Asser Press, 2012), 382–383.
46. Art. 1(1) Commission proposal cited *supra* note 30, amending Art. 3 Reg. European Small Claims Procedure.
47. X.E. Kramer, "European procedures on debt collection: Nothing or noting? Experiences and future prospects", in B. Hess, M. Bergström and E. Storskrubb, *EU Civil Justice. Current Issues and Future Outlook* (Hart Publishing, 2016), 118–119.
48. Dir. 2013/11/EU on alternative dispute resolution for consumer disputes and amending Reg. (EC) 2006/2004 and Dir. 2009/22/EC (Dir. on consumer ADR), O.J 2013, L 165/63.
49. Reg. (EU) 524/2013 on online dispute resolution for consumer disputes and amending Reg. (EC) 2006/2004 and Dir. 2009/22/EC (Reg. on consumer ODR), O.J. 2013, L 165/1.
50. Commission Recommendation on common principles for injunctive and compensatory collective redress mechanisms in the Member States concerning violations of rights granted under Union Law, C(2013)3539/3.

3.3 *Decline of the internal market requirement*

The second condition relates to the functioning of the internal market (see Art. 81(2) TFEU). From the Tobacco Advertising ruling on the internal market requirement of measures based on Article 114 TFEU, it was clear that this requirement is not a mere formality.[51] In order to fulfil this requirement, the measure needs to genuinely have the objective to improve the functioning of the internal market, and should actually contribute to eliminating obstacles to the free movement.[52] In relation to the predecessor of Article 81 TFEU, Article 65 EC Treaty, it has rightfully been questioned whether this condition should be interpreted in the same way.[53] More importantly, there is a notable difference in the wording between Article 65 EC Treaty and the current Article 81(2) TFEU. While the EC Treaty enabled the taking of measures in this area "*insofar* as necessary for the functioning of the internal market", Article 81(2) states that measures shall be taken "*particularly* when necessary for the proper functioning of the internal market".

With relation to Article 65 EC Treaty, the internal market criterion was debated in the literature, but did in the end not create obstacles to the development of the civil justice area.[54] The preparatory documents for each instrument state why that instrument is necessary for the internal market, with additional reference to the principles of subsidiarity and proportionally. These reasons are also included in the Preambles of the various instruments, and range from ensuring equal access to justice, securing free movement and predictability of the outcome of litigations to putting a halt to distortion of competition. Discussions arose during the negotiations on the Rome II Regulation on the applicable law to torts under Article 65 EC Treaty.[55] It may well be argued that the internal market is not necessarily affected by differences in the law applicable to tortuous actions. Particularly in view of the universal territorial scope of the EU instruments on applicable law,[56] the connection with the EU may be very weak.[57] Several delegations as well as the Council's Legal Service were of the opinion that the scope of this Regulation should be limited to EU situations.[58] Nevertheless, the outcome of the negotiations was that the universal scope should be retained. It is submitted that this is a desirable outcome, since a distinction between EU and non-EU situations would undermine the uniform European system of conflict of laws.[59]

---

51. Case C-376/98, *Tobacco Advertising*. Dir. 98/43/EC on Tobacco sponsorship and advertising was annulled. See also Case C-380/03, *Germany v. European Parliament and Council*.
52. Case C-376/98, *Tobacco Advertising*, paras. 84 and 95.
53. See in relation to its predecessor, Art. 65 TFEU, B. Hess, "Die Integrationsfunktion des Europäischen Zivilprozessrechts", (2001) *Praxis des internationalen Privat- und Verfahrensrecht*, 389–396, at 393–394.
54. See *inter alia* T. Drappatz, op. cit. *supra* note 2, 93–100; M. Traest, op. cit. *supra* note 1, 87–88 with further references; A. Dickinson, "European private international law – Embracing new horizons or mourning the past?", (2005) *Journal of Private International Law*, 197–236, at 209; X.E. Kramer, op. cit. *supra* note 2, 21–23.
55. Reg. (EC) 864/2007 of the European Parliament and of the Council on the Law Applicable to Non-Contractual obligations (Rome II), O.J. 2007, L 199/40. Notably A. Dickinson, *The Rome II Regulation. The Law Applicable to Non-Contractual Obligations* (OUP, 2008), 69–85. See also *inter alia* M. Wilderspin, "The Rome II Regulation; Some policy observations", (2008) *Nederlands Internationaal Privaatrecht*, 408–413, at 410–412.
56. See Art. 3 Rome II which provides that the Regulation applies regardless of the law designated by this Regulation. This may also be the law of a third State. See also Art. 2 of Reg. (EC) 593/2008 of the European Parliament and of the Council on the Law Applicable to Contractual Obligations (Rome I), O.J. 2008, L 177/6.
57. A. Dickinson, op. cit. *supra* note 55, 72–73; X.E. Kramer, "The Rome II Regulation on the law applicable to non-contractual obligations: The European private international law tradition continued", (2008) *Nederlands Internationaal Privaatrecht*, 414–424, at 415.
58. Council Document 7015/04, 2 Mar. 2004 and 9009/04 ADD 15, 26 May 2004. See also M. Wilderspin, op. cit. *supra* note 55, at 411.
59. X.E. Kramer, op. cit. *supra* note 57, at 415.

To sum up, it is not to be expected that the reference to the internal market will form any impediment to the scope of instruments on the basis of Article 81 TFEU. It serves as an additional ground to take measures rather than a limitation.

3.4 *Special position of family law*

The activity of the EU in the area of family law has until recently been modest. However, as a result of the free movement of persons and Union citizenship, this is an area of growing importance.[60] It is a subject of different legislative instruments and initiatives. Article 81(2) TFEU subjects the adoption of measures in the area of judicial cooperation in civil matters to the ordinary co-decision procedure.[61] However, Article 81(3) makes an exception for family law matters. Pursuant to this provision, measures in the area of family law with cross-border implications are to be established by the Council subject to a special procedure.[62] It is to act unanimously after consulting the European Parliament. This unanimity is, however, not an absolute precondition for family law matters. On the basis of the "passerelle" clause included in the same provision, the Council, acting unanimously and after consultation with the Parliament, could decide to follow the ordinary legislative procedure with regard to a clearly determined aspect of family law. However, such a decision will not be adopted if it is opposed by national Parliaments within six months.

As is also evident from the troublesome legislative procedure of a regulation including conflict of law rules regarding divorce and legal separation, this special procedure makes the adoption of measures in the family law area more difficult.[63] The Rome III Regulation on the law applicable to divorce and legal separation was eventually adopted on the basis of enhanced cooperation pursuant to Articles 326–334 TFEU.[64] An obvious advantage of the procedure of enhanced cooperation is that it enables the establishment of desired instruments that will at least harmonize the rules for part of the EU. Evidently, this procedure also has its disadvantages, and it has rightfully been pointed out that this legislative technique results in a two-speed Europe.[65] In the case of Rome III, for instance, it accentuated the rift between the Member States. It is submitted that for the specific topic, the "agreement to disagree" is regrettable but does not impair the status quo. This is particularly true for the Rome III Regulation, where the possible negative effects of only partial harmonization are diminished by the jurisdiction and recognition rules included in the Brussels II-bis Regulation.[66] However, enhanced cooperation for measures of judicial cooperation in civil matters should only be applied as *ultimum remedium* where agreement on a highly necessary measure is not feasible.

---

60. X.E. Kramer, M. de Rooij, V. Lasic, E.N. Frohn, R.J. Blauwhoff, "A European framework for private international law: current gaps and future perspectives", (2012) *Study European Parliament*, 39–46.
61. In accordance with Arts. 289 and 294 TFEU. Currently, 17 Member States are bound by this Regulation.
62. A. Fiorini, "Which legal basis for family law? The way forward", (2012) *briefing note European Parliament*, in particular 12–14; N.A. Baarsma, *The Europeanisation of International Family Law* (Asser Press/Springer, 2011), 121–122.
63. See *inter alia* A. Fiorini, "Rome III – choice of law in divorce: Is the Europeanization of family law going too far?", (2008) *International Journal of Law*, Policy and the Family, 178–205; N.A. Baarsma, op. cit. *supra* note 62, 199–233.
64. Council Reg. (EU) 1259/2010 implementing enhanced cooperation in the area of the law applicable to divorce and legal separation, O.J. 2010, L 343/10.
65. K. Boele-Woelki, "To be, or not to be: Enhanced cooperation in international divorce law within the European Union", (2008–2009) *Victoria University Wellington Law Review*, 779–792, at 791. See generally M. Bordignon and S. Brusco: "On enhanced cooperation", (2006) *Journal of Public Economics*, 2063–2090.
66. X.E. Kramer, "Current gaps and future perspectives in European private international law: Towards a code on private international law?", (2012) *Briefing note European Parliament*, at 14.

4. Key areas of civil justice and the legislative framework

This section turns to the secondary law in the area of civil justice cooperation. It is not an easy task in the first place to establish which instruments may be gathered under the concept of judicial cooperation in civil matters. Strictly speaking, only the instruments based on Article 81 TFEU (ex Article 65 EC Treaty) can be regarded as instruments of civil justice cooperation. In a broader sense, other legislation that concerns private international law, civil procedure, or even substantive private law regarding the cross-border context may also be included in this area. The webpage dedicated to Judicial cooperation in civil matters[67] of the European Union website seems to take a broad approach by, for example, including the Directive on the compensation to crime victims.[68] This Directive is at the intersection of civil law and criminal law, and is based not on Article 81 TFEU but on Article 352 TFEU (formerly Art. 308 EC Treaty) on residual measures necessary to attain the objectives of the Treaty. This webpage also lists several conventions of the Hague Conference on Private International Law to which the Member States or the EU as an entity is a member. The Rome III Regulation on the law applicable to divorce and legal separation, which is at the heart of civil justice cooperation (see Art. 81(2) sub b TFEU), is not listed on this website. The reason is likely that this instrument is based on enhanced cooperation.[69] A European Commission webpage dedicated to Civil Justice in cross-border disputes offers yet other choices concerning instruments belonging to this area.[70]

This section focuses primarily on legislation established by virtue of Article 81 TFEU, but where necessary will also make reference to other EU instruments that belong to private international law or to international civil procedure. It will elaborate on the existing legislative framework and the legislative approach, and will briefly address the role of the ECJ.

4.1 *Key areas and the existing legislative framework*

A broad range of instruments has meanwhile been established on the basis of the competence in civil justice cooperation.[71] These instruments address all the different issues set out in Article 81(2) TFEU. The key areas may be grouped as follows: a) private international law measures, dedicated to the applicable law jurisdiction, and the recognition and enforcement; b) instruments on specific issues of civil procedure and uniform European procedures; and c) general measures to support the area of civil justice cooperation. These instruments rely on different main premises, but they all contribute to the objectives of creating and maintaining the genuine European judicial area in civil matters.

4.1.1 *Private international law instruments*

Traditionally, private international law is concerned with the applicable law, the regulation of international jurisdiction, and the recognition and enforcement of judgments and extrajudicial documents.[72] In this domain, nine regulations have thus far been established, while several pro-

---

67. See <europa.eu/legislation_summaries/justice_freedom_security/judicial_cooperation_in_civil_matters/index_en.htm> (last visited 1 June 2017). See also the webpage on Civil Justice <ec.europa.eu/justice/civil/index_en.htm> (last visited 1 June 2017).
68. Council Dir. 2004/80/EC of 29 Apr. 2004 relating to compensation to crime victims, O.J. 2004, L 261/15.
69. See section 3.4.
70. <ec.europa.eu/justice/civil/index_en.htm> (last visited 1 June 2015).
71. See also X.E. Kramer, "European private international law: The way forward", (2014) *Compilation of in depth analyses, workshop on upcoming issues of EU law*, at 77–105.
72. In the broader sense, the cross-border service of documents and the taking of evidence may also be included, but for the present purposes these are gathered under specific procedural law instruments (sub b).

posals are pending. Two instruments installed under Article 81 TFEU contain rules only on the applicable law; these are Regulation 593/2008 on the law applicable to contractual obligations (Rome I Reg.)[73] and Reg. 864/2007 on the law applicable to non-contractual obligations (Rome II Reg.).[74] These two instruments cover virtually the entire area of the law of obligations, with the exception of a few expressly excluded matters.[75] The third instrument that can be included in this category is Regulation 1259/2010 on the law applicable to divorce and legal separation (Rome III Reg.).[76] This is the family law instrument on which the required unanimity under Article 81(3) could not be reached, and is the first in this area that proceeded under enhanced cooperation (see section 3.4 above). The instruments on the applicable law create a uniform conflict of laws system, and they have the dual purpose of facilitating the mutual recognition of judgments and of supporting the proper functioning of the internal market by ensuring legal certainty and predictability of the outcome of litigation.[77]

Two key instruments in this area concern international jurisdiction and recognition and enforcement. The first one is Regulation 1215/2012 on jurisdiction and the recognition and enforcement of judgments in civil and commercial matters (Brussels I-bis).[78] The second instrument is Regulation 2201/2003 concerning jurisdiction and the recognition and enforcement of judgments in matrimonial matters and parental responsibility (Brussels II-bis Reg.).[79] The goal of these instruments is to facilitate the internal market by harmonizing the rules to distribute jurisdiction among the Member States' courts and to facilitate the free circulation of judgments. These implement the mutual recognition programme by simplifying the recognition and enforcement. In the Brussels I-bis Regulation the declaration of enforceability (*exequatur*) for the enforcement of a judgment or extrajudicial document in another Member State has been fully abolished.[80] In a number of specific instruments introducing uniform European procedures, the exequatur had already been abolished along with the grounds of refusal that have eventually

---

73. Reg. (EC) 593/2008 of the European Parliament and of the Council of 17 June 2008 on the law applicable to contractual obligations, Rome I cited *supra* note 56, O.J. 2008, L 177/6. This Regulation replaced the Rome Convention of 1980.
74. Reg. (EC) 864/2007 of the European Parliament and of the Council on the Law Applicable to Non-Contractual obligations (Rome II), O.J. 2007, L 199/40.
75. See Art. 1 Rome I and Rome II. Most of the excluded matters are willed exclusions in the sense that they are either subject to international conventions or to other specific regulations. Few result from a political compromise. This goes particularly for Art. 1(2)(g) Rome II, which excludes the violations of privacy and rights relating to personality, including defamation. An agreement on a choice of law rules for these matters could not be reached at the time.
76. Council Reg. (EU) 1259/2010 implementing enhanced cooperation in the area of the law applicable to divorce and legal separation ("Rome III"), O.J. 2010, L 343/10.
77. See Recitals 4 and 6 Rome I and Rome II, and Recital 9 of Rome III. The Preamble of the Rome III Reg. does not refer explicitly to the principle of mutual recognition or the free circulation of judgments.
78. Reg. 1215/2012 of the European Parliament and of the Council of 12 Dec. 2012 on jurisdiction and the recognition and enforcement of judgments in civil and commercial matters (recast), O.J. 2012, L 351/1.
79. Council Reg. (EC) 2201/2003 of 27 Nov. 2003 concerning jurisdiction and the recognition and enforcement of judgments in matrimonial matters and the matters of parental responsibility, repealing Reg. (EC) 1347/2000 ("Brussels II-bis"), O.J. 2003, L 338/1. It replaced Reg. 1347/2000 (Brussels I-bis) which had a narrower scope.
80. See *inter alia* L.J.E. Timmer, "Abolition of *exequatur* under the Brussels I Reg.: Ill conceived and premature?", (2013) *Journal of Private International Law*, 129–147; M.E. Hazelhorst & X.E. Kramer, "Afschaffing van het exequatur in Brussel I: daadwerkelijke verbetering of politiek gebaar?", (2013) *Tijdschrift voor Civiele Rechtspleging*, 37–46; X.E. Kramer, "Cross-border enforcement and the Brussels I-bis Regulation: Towards a new balance between mutual trust and national control over fundamental rights", (2013) *Netherlands International Law Review*, 343–373; M. E. Hazelhorst, *Free Movement of Civil Judgments in the European Union and the Right to a Fair Trial* (Asser Press, 2016).

been retained in the Brussels I-bis Regulation.[81] The Brussels II-bis Regulation has so far only abolished exequatur in relation to specific judgments, *i.e.* regarding rights of access to and return of the child.[82] However, this Regulation is also in the process of amendment.[83]

Three instruments cover all three aspects of private international law. The first instrument to encompass jurisdiction, the applicable law, and the recognition and enforcement of judgments is Regulation 2015/848 on Insolvency Proceedings and its predecessor.[84] The second one is Regulation 4/2009 on maintenance obligations (Maintenance Reg.).[85] Rules on jurisdiction and the recognition and enforcement for maintenance used to be included in the Brussels I Regulation. A separate regulation was necessary, however, in particular to include a general framework for the actual cooperation between the Member States to ensure the often problematic recovery of maintenance. For the purpose of enforcement, this Regulation also abolishes the exequatur proceedings. The third instrument is Regulation 650/2012 on matters of succession (Succession Reg.).[86] It has created an encompassing framework for jurisdiction, applicable law, recognition and enforcement of decisions, and the acceptance and enforcement of authentic instruments, and a European Certificate of Succession. In view of the wide diversity in succession law of the Member States, and the complexity of the matters concerned, the establishment of this instrument was a true accomplishment. Two earlier proposals for instruments encompassing all three private international law matters concern matrimonial property regimes[87] and the property consequences of registered partnerships.[88] However due to the complex and somewhat controversial nature, the legislative process has been put on hold.

The framework of private international law covers a broad range of issues, starting with non-family civil and commercial matters and, in more recent years, extending to particular matters of family law, family property, and succession. However, there are still gaps in the current framework. A 2012 study carried out at the request of the European Parliament identified systemic gaps in the following areas in non-family law: property law, trusts, agency, corporations, and to a certain extent arbitration.[89] In family law, EU rules are lacking in the area of registered partnerships and similar institutions, names of natural persons, adoption, parentage, protection of adults, status, and the capacity of natural persons in general. Conventions of the Hague Conference on Private International Law are in place on several of these topics;[90] however, these are not ratified by all Member States or do not cover all relevant aspects of private international law.

81. See section 4.1.2.
82. See Arts. 28 and 40–45 Brussels II-bis Reg.
83. Proposal for a Council Reg. on jurisdiction, the recognition and enforcement of decisions in matrimonial matters and the matters of parental responsibility, and on international child abduction (recast), COM(2016)411/2.
84. Reg. (EU) 2015/848 of the European Parliament and of the Council of 20 May 2015 on insolvency proceedings, O.J. 2015, L 141/19 as did its predecessor Reg. 1346/2000.
85. Council Reg. (EC) 4/2009 of 18 Dec. 2008 on jurisdiction, applicable law, recognition and enforcement of decisions and co-operation in matters relating to maintenance obligations, O.J. 2009, L 7/1.
86. Reg. (EU) 650/2012 of the European Parliament and of the Council of 4 July 2012 on jurisdiction, applicable law, recognition and enforcement of decisions, and acceptance and enforcement of authentic instruments in matters of succession and on the creation of a European Certificate of Succession, O.J. 2012, L 201/107.
87. Proposal for a Council Reg. on jurisdiction, applicable law and the recognition and enforcement of decisions in matters of matrimonial property regimes, COM(2011)126/2.
88. Proposal for a Council Reg. on jurisdiction, applicable law and the recognition and enforcement of decisions regarding the property consequences of registered partnerships, COM(2011)127/2.
89. X.E. Kramer op. cit. *supra* note 60.
90. See in particular Hague Convention of 14 Mar. 1978 on the Law Applicable to Agency, the Hague Convention of 29 May 1993 on Protection of Children and Co-operation in Respect of Intercountry Adoption and the Hague Convention of 13 Jan. 2000 on the International Protection of Adults.

4.1.2 *Instruments on specific procedural issues and European procedures*

Several instruments cover specific matters that are generally regarded as procedural law matters. They are intended to regulate cooperation in specific areas for the purpose of improving the functioning of the internal market and the efficiency of proceedings. An important regulation for judicial practice is Regulation 1393/2007 on the service of documents (Service Reg.).[91] The second regulation that facilitates cooperation in judicial practice is Regulation 1206/2001 on the taking of evidence.[92] Hague Conventions with a wide global reach already existed, both for the service of documents and the taking of evidence. However, these Regulations enable a more advanced cooperation between the Member States. Based upon a decentralized system of co-operation between service agencies and courts and the use of standard forms, these instruments have established a more efficient system regarding the service of documents and the taking of evidence.[93]

Apart from these two regulations implementing cooperation between authorities, three instruments have introduced uniform civil procedures for specific claims. Regulation 1896/2006 creating a European Order for Payment Procedure[94] and Regulation 861/2007 establishing a European Small Claims Procedure[95] were the first ones to introduce genuine European civil procedures. The European Order for Payment Procedure is a one-sided procedure for the collection of uncontested debts, while the Small Claims Procedure currently applies to claims up to € 5,000.[96] The aim of these European procedures is to simplify, speed up, and reduce the costs of procedures for the recovery of respectively uncontested and small claims.[97] The procedures contain rules to simplify the procedure and are conducted through standard forms in order to increase litigants' access to justice. In view of the "cross-border implications" requirement of Article 81 TFEU (see section 3.2), the scope of these procedures is limited to cross-border cases.[98] They are available to the claimant on an optional basis as an exponent of the subsidiarity and proportionality principle. In 2014, the third European procedure was adopted: namely, Regulation 655/2014 creating a European Account Preservation Order.[99] An attempt to create a European collective redress mechanism has not as yet succeeded, but the policy debate did result in a Recommendation on common principles for collective redress.[100]

A measure of its own kind is Directive 2008/52/EC on certain aspects of mediation (Mediation Directive).[101] It lays down minimum rules to support the use of mediation as an alternative to court litigation, especially as regards the suspension of limitation periods, confidentiality, and the recognition and enforcement of mediation settlements. Like the other instruments in

---

91. Reg. (EC) 1393/2007 of the European Parliament and of the Council of 13 Nov. 2007 on the service in the Member States of judicial and extrajudicial documents in civil or commercial matters (service of documents), and repealing Council Reg. (EC) 1348/2000, O.J. L 324/9.
92. Council Reg. (EC) 1206/2001 of 28 May 2001 on co-operation between the courts of the Member States in the taking of evidence in civil or commercial matters, O.J. L 174/1.
93. See Arts. 1–3 Service Reg. and 1–2 Evidence Reg.
94. Reg. (EC) 1896/2006 of the European Parliament and of the Council of 12 Dec. 2006 creating a European order for payment procedure, O.J. 2006, L 399/1.
95. Reg. (EC) 861/2007 of the European Parliament and of the Council of 11 July 2007 establishing a European Small Claims Procedure, O.J. 2007, L 199/1 as amended by Reg. (EU) 2015/2421, cited *supra* note 30.
96. Art. 2 European Small Claims Reg. as amended by Reg. (EU) 2015/2421.
97. Art. 1 European Order for Payment Reg. and European Small Claims Reg.
98. See Arts. 2 and 3 European Order for Payment Reg. and European Small Claims Reg.
99. Cited *supra* note 31. It has been applicable since 18 Jan. 2017.
100. Commission Recommendation on common principles for injunctive and compensatory collective redress mechanisms in the Member States concerning violations of rights granted under Union Law, C(2013)3539/3.
101. Dir. 2008/52/EC on certain aspects of mediation in civil and commercial matters, O.J. 2008, L 136/3.

this area, this Directive is confined to cross-border mediation.[102] As was mentioned in section 3.2, two subsequent instruments on alternative dispute resolution – the Directive on consumer ADR and the Regulation on ODR – have been adopted on the basis of Article 114 TFEU, and are not confined to cross-border cases.

4.1.3 *General measures to support the area of civil justice cooperation*

The primary instrument designed to promote access to justice is Directive 2002/8/EC on legal aid (Legal Aid Directive). This Directive establishes minimum rules for the provision of legal aid in all cross-border disputes.[103] An important institutional framework is the European Judicial Network in civil and commercial matters (EJN), which was set up in 2001.[104] The EJN organizes meetings of the national contact points, and liaises with magistrates and other authorities and professional associations designated by Member States to discuss and report on topics in the area of civil justice cooperation. Where required, it also prepares practice guidelines relating to the specific regulations, and the e-Justice portal has been set up to function as a "one stop to justice" portal.[105] Judicial training as referenced in Article 81(2) sub g is promoted by several Communications and has been put into practice.[106] This judicial training was a prominent feature in the Stockholm Programme and Action Plan to support the development of mutual trust.[107] The 2011 Commission Communication "Building trust in EU-wide justice" intends to have trained at least half of all legal professionals in the EU.[108] The Commission acts primarily as a collaborative party involved with training institutes and other networks, including the European Law Academy (ERA) and the European Judicial Training Network (EJTN).

4.2 *Legislative approach: In search of coherence*

As is clear from the overview in the previous section, the ambitious policy programmes have been translated into legislative initiatives resulting in a series of instruments covering all items listed in Article 81(2) TFEU. A clear priority in the activities cannot be distinguished, though enhancing access to justice and strengthening mutual trust are common threads in all initiatives. Only in one case, that of the Rome III Regulation, was a Commission proposal not adopted, and the initiative proceeded on the basis of enhanced cooperation. In other instances, the ambitions of the Commission were tempered by, *inter alia*, limiting the scope of particular procedural instruments to cross-border cases. In this respect, the initiatives may be called successful.

The legislative technique is not in all respects transparent. In by far the most cases, the regulation is the chosen instrument, even where some of these seem primarily to contain minimum rules. For some matters, the Commission opted for a directive, and several overarching measures to support the cooperation in civil matters result from Council decisions.[109] As was discussed earlier, not all instruments that may be regarded as dealing with judicial cooperation in civil matters have been established under Article 81 TFEU. Several sectorial instruments containing

---

102. See *supra*, section 3.2.
103. Council Dir. 2002/8/EC of 27 Jan. 2003 to improve access to justice in cross-border disputes by establishing minimum common rules relating to legal aid for such disputes, O.J. 2002, L 26/41.
104. Council Decision 2001/470/EC of 28 May 2001 establishing a European Judicial Network in civil and commercial matters, O.J. 2001, L 174/25, amended by Council Decision 568/09/EC, O.J. 2009, L 168/35.
105. See <e-justice.europa.eu/home.do> (last visited 1 June 2017).
106. See initially the Communication on judicial training in the European Union, COM(2006)356.
107. See *supra*, section 2.
108. Communication from the Commission, Building trust in EU-wide justice – a new dimension to European Judicial training, COM(2011)551 final.
109. See *supra*, section 4.1 for an overview of the relevant instruments.

important rules of civil procedure have been established under Article 114 TFEU. Reference was made to the consumer ADR and ODR instruments.[110] Another example is the Intellectual Property Enforcement Directive that includes important rules of harmonized civil procedure.[111] Unlike the instruments founded on Article 81 TFEU, these are not limited to cross-border cases. Additionally, the provisions on enhanced cooperation (Arts. 326–334 TFEU) were used to establish the Rome III Regulation, an instrument that undoubtedly belongs to the civil justice area. Reference may also be made to the rules of procedure for the Unified Patent Court based on enhanced cooperation in unitary patent protection.[112]

Taking into account the entire area of civil justice cooperation, including private international law and civil procedure, it is submitted that there is a lack of regulatory coherence.[113] The selected topics, the substantive and territorial scope of the various instruments, and the legislative methodology are to a certain extent *ad hoc*. The instruments regarding aspects of civil procedure also rely on different levels of harmonization, with several taking the form of traditional private international law rules that aim primarily to coordinate the different systems.[114] However, they also partially harmonize, or occasionally contain minimum rules of civil procedure.[115] Additionally, three instruments have introduced harmonized European civil procedures, though only for cross-border cases and on an optional basis.[116] This is of course part of a political reality, where limited competence and compromises come into play. However, it is clear that the area of civil justice is a work in progress and requires further consolidation.

4.3 *Contribution of ECJ case law*

Since the Lisbon Treaty entered into force, the ECJ has general competence to interpret the civil justice instruments pursuant to Article 267 TFEU. Prior to that, the competence in relation to civil justice cooperation instruments was limited to the highest courts.[117] Pursuant to a protocol, the ECJ already had jurisdiction in relation to the Brussels Convention and the Rome Convention. The rich body of case law on the Brussels Convention and its successor, the Brussels I Regulation and, more recently, on the series of civil justice regulations, is of great significance to the development of this area. The autonomous interpretation of concepts has given a true uniform reading of these instruments, while the teleological interpretation effectuates the policy objectives. On numerous occasions, the ECJ has underlined the objectives of legal certainty and

---

110. See *supra*, section 3.2.
111. Dir. 2004/48/EC of the European Parliament and of the Council of 29 Apr. 2004 on the enforcement of intellectual property rights O.J. 2004, L 157/32.
112. Reg. (EU) 1257/2012 of the European Parliament and the Council implementing enhanced cooperation in the area of the creation of unitary patent protection, O.J. 2012, L 361/1. The Council Agreement on a Unified Patent Court (O.J. 2013, C 175/1) includes important rules of civil procedure and embeds an exhaustive set of Rules of Procedure. See for the 16th Draft of 31 Jan. 2014, <unified-patent-court.org/images/documents/revised-draft-rules-of-procedure.pdf> (last visited 1 June 2017).
113. By way of an analogy with architecture, the present author has referred to these developments as procedural deconstructivism; see X.E. Kramer, *Procedure Matters: Construction and Deconstructivism in European Civil Procedure* (Eleven International Publishing, 2013), at 23.
114. E.g. the Brussels I and Brussels II-bis Reg.s, see *supra*, section 4.1.
115. E.g. the European Enforcement Order Reg., see *supra*, section 4.1.
116. The European Order for Payment Procedure, the European Small Claims Procedure and the European Account Preservation Order, see *supra*, section 4.1.
117. Art. 68 EC Treaty.

predictability, supported the aim of establishing efficient access to justice,[118] and given effect to the cornerstone of mutual trust.[119]

5. Current debates and prospects

Current policy and academic debates evolve around a couple of themes: in the first place, the principle of mutual recognition and mutual trust as a cornerstone of judicial cooperation. Mutual recognition is embedded in Article 81 TFEU and referenced to underpin all recent instruments. Mutual trust was first introduced as a seemingly inherent premise, and has been criticized in academic literature, while legislative negotiations also indicate that mutual trust is not always self-evident. In more recent years, the Commission has focused on the actual building of mutual trust by, *inter alia*, promoting judicial training and involving a wide audience in the policy debate.[120] A second recurring theme since the establishment of the Hague Programme is the need for coherence in the EU civil justice area, as its lack has been rightfully criticized.[121] In the area of private international law, the 2012 initiative by the European Parliament to examine the possibility of a European framework or even a Code of private international law is exemplary.[122] In 2013, a project was launched by the European Law Institute (ELI) and UNIDROIT to transform the ALI/UNIDROIT Principles of Transnational Civil Procedure into European rules of civil procedure that is expected to contribute to the coherence of European civil procedure.[123] A third string of activities, so far particularly pushed forward by the European Parliament, is the work on minimum standards of civil procedure in the EU with the aim of enhancing judicial cooperation

118. See, *inter alia*, Case C-215/11, *Szyrocka v. SiGer*, regarding the European Order for Payment Procedure. On a question as to whether national requirements to obtain an order for payment were relevant, the ECJ ruled that the requirements to obtain such an order are exhaustively regulated by Art. 7 of the Reg. It stated that the objective of this Regulation is to simplify and speed up the process, and reduce the costs of litigation, and that this objective would be undermined if Member States were to impose additional requirements (paras. 30 and 31).
119. See, *inter alia*, in the area of jurisdiction: Case C-281/02, *Owusu v. Jackson*, and Case C-185/07, *Westtankers*, in which the ECJ held the *forum non conveniens* contrary to the principle of mutual trust underlying the Brussels I Reg. and Case C-159/02, *Turner v. Grovit*, where it prohibited the anti-suit injunction for this reason. The much debated abolition of *exequatur* and the consequent prohibition of the Member State of enforcement to review a judgment on the ground of a possible public policy violation under the Brussels II-bis Reg. was upheld on the basis of the principle of mutual trust in Case C-491/10 PPU, *Aguirre Zarraga v. Pelz*.
120. See particularly, "Assises de la justice, Shaping Justice policies in Europe for the years to come", <ec.europa.eu/justice/events/assises-justice-2013/index_en.htm> (last visited 1 June 2017).
121. See *inter alia* M. Tulibacka, "Europeanization of civil procedures: In search of a coherent approach", 46 CML Rev. (2009), 1533–1535; S. Huber, "Koordinierung europäischer Zivilprozessrechtsinstrumente" in Geimer and Schütze (Eds.), *Recht ohne Grenzen. Festschrift für Athanassios Kaissis zum 65. Geburtstag* (Sellier, 2012), 413–429; X.E. Kramer, *Procedure Matters: Construction and Deconstructivism in European Civil Procedure* (Eleven International Publishing, 2013); J. von Hein & G. Rühl (Eds.), *Kohärenz im Internationalen Privat- und Verfahrensrecht der Europäischen Union* (Mohr Siebeck 2016).
122. X.E. Kramer, op. cit. *supra* note 60; J. von Hein & G. Rühl, "Towards a European code on private international law?", (2015) *Cross-border activities in the EU: Making life easier for citizens, Workshop for the JURI Committee*, at 8–53.
    See generally on the idea of such a codification M. Fallon, P. Lagarde and S. Poillot Peruzzetto (Eds.), *Quelle architecture pour un code européen de droit international privé?* (Peter Lang, 2011); E. Kieninger, "Das Europäische IPR vor der Kodifikation?" in H. Kronke & K. Thorn, *Grenzen überwinden – Prinzipien bewahren, Festschrift für Bernd von Hoffmann* (Gieseking, 2012), 184–197; M. Czepelak, "Would we like to have a European Code of Private International Law?", (2010) *European Review of Private Law*, 705–728.
123. See also X.E. Kramer, "The structure of civil proceedings and why it matters: Exploratory observations on future ELI-UNIDROIT European rules of civil procedure", (2014) *Uniform Law Review*, 1–22, at 22.

and mutual trust.[124] These soft law and legislative activities to create common standards should be strengthened by promoting best practices on civil justice cooperation.[125]

The EU Justice Agenda for 2020 mentions as the main challenges the strengthening of mutual trust, the mobility of citizens, and economic recovery and growth.[126] The Commission focuses on the further consolidation, codification, and completion of EU legislation.[127] It states that first and foremost the progress should be consolidated, with fundamental rights being upheld, and rights granted by EU legislation becoming a reality. If instruments are not implemented successfully by Member States, effective remedies should be available. To further mutual trust, the Commission provides financial support to training programmes. Information and communication technologies need to be further developed to make justice more effective. The Commission also addresses enhancing the operational cooperation by, *inter alia*, strengthening the role of the European Judicial Network. As to codification, the Commission briefly references the possibility of EU codification of the existing instruments, particularly regarding the conflict of laws. In relation to the completion of EU legislation, the Commission does not mention particular initiatives but addresses in general the need to adjust to the dynamics of the mobility of citizens and businesses.[128] It emphasizes that mutual trust requires justice systems to be independent, of a high standard, and efficient. Both parties' procedural rights should be protected, and the need to reinforce procedural rights should be examined, for example in relation to the service of documents and the taking of evidence, and in ensuring the best interests of the child in matters involving family law.

The 2020 Justice Agenda seems less ambitious than earlier programmes that fired new concepts and announced numerous concrete legislative initiatives. However, this is only partially true. After a flood of new instruments were established within a period of only fifteen years, the time has now come to implement, evaluate, reflect, and consolidate further. Still relatively little is known about the actual functioning and impact of particular instruments, and in any case there will be room for improvement if only by increasing coherence. The financial crisis and general scepticism also require a new approach to the question of legitimacy. In recent years, the economy has become more important as a driver of policy initiatives, and it will continue in this vein.[129] To some, the ideology of creating an area of freedom, security and justice has lost its magic and subsidiarity is high on the agenda of certain Member States. This makes it even more imperative to take seriously the seemingly less ambitious agenda of consolidation and building mutual trust.

---

124. See, *inter alia*, R. Mańko, "Europeanisation of civil procedure. Towards common minimum standards?", (2015) European Parliamentary Research Service; B. Hess, "Harmonized Rules and Minimum Standards in the European Law of Civil Procedure", (2016) In-depth analysis European Parliament; European Parliament, Report with recommendations to the Commission on common minimum standards of civil procedure in the EU (2015/2084(INL)), June 2017.
125. B. Hess and X.E. Kramer (Eds.), *From Common Rules to Best Practices in European Civil Procedure* (Nomos/Hart, 2017).
126. EU Justice Agenda 2020, cited *supra* note 32, point 3.
127. Cited *supra* note 32, point 4.
128. Cited *supra* note 32, point 4.3.
129. See also European Policy Center, Information Paper "The Stockholm programme: What's next?", Contribution to the informal meeting of Justice and Home Affairs Ministers (Vilnius, July 2013), at 4, where it is concluded that "the economic situation will have a crucial impact on the content of the guidelines".

Further reading

Bogdan, M., *Concise Introduction to EU Private International Law*, 3rd ed. (Europa Law Publishing, 2016).

van Calster, G., *European Private International Law* (Hart Publishing, 2016).

Fallon, M., P. Lagarde and S. Poillot Peruzzetto (Eds.), *Quelle architecture pour un code européen de droit international privé*? (Peter Lang, 2011).

Hazelhorst, M.E., *Free Movement of Civil Judgments in the European Union and the Right to a Fair Trial* (Asser Press, 2016).

Hess, B., *Europäisches Zivilprozessrecht* (C.F. Müller, 2010).

Hess, B., M. Bergström and E. Storskrubb, *EU Civil Justice. Current Issues and Future Outlook* (Hart Publishing, 2016).

Hess, B. and X.E. Kramer (Eds.), *From Common Rules to Best Practices in European Civil Procedure* (Nomos/Hart, 2017).

von Hein, J. and G. Rühl (Eds.), *Kohärenz im Internationalen Privat- und Verfahrensrecht der Europäischen Union* (Mohr Siebeck, 2016).

Kramer, X.E., *Eenvormige procedures voor de inning van vorderingen* (Kluwer, 2007).

Kramer, X.E., and C.H. van Rhee (Eds.), *Civil Litigation in a Globalising World* (Asser Press, 2012).

Kramer, X.E., M. de Rooij, V. Lasic, E.N. Frohn and R.J. Blauwhoff, "A European framework for private international law: Current gaps and future perspectives", (2012) *Study European Parliament.*

Kramer, X.E., *Procedure Matters: Construction and Deconstructivism in European Civil Procedure* (Eleven International Publishing, 2013).

Kramer, X.E., "European private international law: The way forward", (2014) *In-depth analysis European Parliament.*

Ontanu, E.A., *Cross-Border Debt Recovery in the EU. A Comparative and Empirical Study on the Use of European Uniform Procedures* (Intersentia, 2017)

Stone, P., *EU Private International Law*, 3rd edition (Edward Elgar Publishing, 2014).

Storskrubb, E., *Civil Procedure and EU Law. A Policy Area Uncovered* (OUP, 2008).

Storskrubb, E., "Civil justice – A newcomer and an unstoppable wave?" in P. Craig and G. de Búrca, *The Evolution of EU Law*, 2nd ed. (OUP, 2011), 299–321.

Tulibacka, M. "Europeanization of civil procedures: In search of a coherent approach", 46 CML Rev. (2009), 1533–1535.

CHAPTER 19
EU CRIMINAL LAW

*Jannemieke Ouwerkerk and Willem Geelhoed**

This Chapter presents the body of EU law affecting the national criminal justice systems of the Member States and their mutual cooperation. Section 1 describes EU criminal law competences, including their historical background. Section 2 presents the body of EU law in the field of substantive criminal law, followed by an account of EU procedural criminal law in section 3. Section 4 gives an overview of instruments for judicial cooperation in criminal matters based on the principle of mutual recognition. Section 5 provides a picture of EU agencies and bodies set up to perform specific tasks relating to cross-border cooperation in criminal matters.

1. The evolution of criminal law into an area of EU competence

The criminal justice systems of the EU Member States have long been influenced by European Union law. At first, this influence was mainly restricted to a negative effect: national rules on criminal offences and sanctions and on criminal procedure were disapplied in case of colliding EU rules, for instance regarding fundamental freedoms.[1]

Beyond this negative effect, the European Union has become more active in using criminal law measures to attain certain objectives. A few distinct underlying reasons can be identified. One common method of justifying the Union's involvement in the field of criminal law is to focus on the increasingly cross-border nature of crime in the Union, stimulated by the abolition of border controls within the Schengen Area.[2] Still, law enforcement activities are largely confined to national jurisdictions.

A more principled approach to criminal law matters, also justifying the introduction of EU measures, emerges from the Union's goal to offer its citizens an Area of Freedom, Security and Justice ("AFSJ").[3] This entails that the EU endeavours to promote the harmonization of criminal law provisions of the Member States as a means to protect citizens against crime and at the same time to provide them with adequate rights if they become involved with the criminal justice system of another Member State.[4] Essential in this respect is the definition of a catalogue

---

* J.W. Ouwerkerk: Law Faculty, University of Leiden; W. Geelhoed: Faculty of Law, University of Groningen.

1. Case C-8/74, *Procureur du Roi v. Benoît and Gustave Dassonville*; Case 55/94, *Reinhard Gebhard v. Consiglio dell'Ordine degli Avvocati e Procuratori di Milano*. See also A. Klip, *European Criminal Law. An Integrative Approach*, 3rd ed. (Intersentia, 2016), 85–94.
2. C. Harding and A.H.J. Swart, "Intergovernmental co-operation in the field of criminal law" in P. Fennell, C. Harding, N. Jörg and A.H.J. Swart (Eds.), *Criminal Justice in Europe. A Comparative Study* (Clarendon, 1995), 87–106.
3. Art. 3(2) TEU. See further Ch. 17, "European migration and asylum law", of this book.
4. Some argue that this line of reasoning potentially enables European law-making to touch national criminal justice systems in all possible ways, provided sufficient competences exist. See G. de Kerchove, "L'espace

of crimes that are serious enough to warrant the Union's attention,[5] and the definition of a catalogue of procedural rights.[6]

In the specific fields of EU fraud (i.e. fraud with EU subsidies and levies) and corruption in national and EU civil services, the rationale driving the development of European criminal law measures is to protect the financial interests of the European Union itself.

1.1 *Integration within the Schengen framework and the ne bis in idem principle*

The earliest forms of criminal law integration took place outside the Treaties, i.e. in the Schengen framework, which coupled the abolition of border controls with intensified police cooperation. An element of that framework that became very important for the development of European criminal law was the principle of *ne bis in idem*, protecting against multiple prosecutions for the same facts.[7] This principle was laid down in Article 54 CISA (Convention Implementing the Schengen Agreement), and became directly enforceable throughout the Schengen Area.[8] ECJ case law on the matter focused on two questions: firstly, when are facts considered to be finally judged, and, secondly, under what conditions can the facts be said to be the same?[9] A long line of case law shows that criminal proceedings are considered "final" if, according to the law of the Member State in which proceedings were followed, further prosecution is definitively barred, or where the accused has been finally acquitted (consequently, most cases settled out of court qualify as being finally judged). Moreover, the legal classification of the offence has turned out to be irrelevant for the purpose of assessing the sameness of facts, leaving the concrete circumstances of the case as the core of the second test.[10]

The EU Charter[11] also includes the *ne bis in idem* principle (Art. 50), giving it a slightly wider scope than the CISA does. Contrary to Article 54 CISA, the Charter does not require a sentence to be enforced before qualifying the initial judgment as a final decision. The "enforcement condition" of Article 54 CISA has, however, been held to constitute a justified restriction of Article 50 of the Charter.[12] The *ne bis in idem* principle is also enshrined in several instruments of judicial cooperation, as a ground for refusal. Depending on the circumstances, the ECJ requires the

---

judiciaire pénal européen après Amsterdam et le sommet de Tampere" in G. de Kerchove and A. Weyembergh (Eds.), *Vers un espace judiciaire pénal européen* (Editions de l'Université de Bruxelles, 2000), 3–17.

5. Art. 83(1) TFEU.
6. Art. 82(2) TFEU; see also the Council *Roadmap for strengthening procedural rights of suspected or accused persons in criminal proceedings*, O.J. 2009, C 295/1.
7. W.B. van Bockel, *The Ne Bis In Idem Principle in EU Law* (Kluwer Law International, 2010).
8. Most EU Member States have also ratified Protocol 7 to the ECHR, which includes the *ne bis in idem* principle (Art. 4). However, this provision only applies within the jurisdiction of a single Member State: it does not prevent a second prosecution in another State.
9. To some extent, this case law developed in dialogue with the ECtHR; see e.g. judgment of 10 Feb. 2009 in *Sergey Zolothukin v. Russia* (Application no. 14939/03).
10. Joined Cases C-187/01 and C-385/01, *Criminal proceedings against Hüseyin Gözütok and Klaus Brügge*; Case 469/03, *Criminal proceedings against Filomeno Mario Miraglia*; Case C-436/04, *Criminal proceedings against Leopold Henri Van Esbroeck*; Case C-467/04, *Criminal proceedings against Giuseppe Francesco Gasparini and Others*; Case C-150/05, *Jean Leon Van Straaten*; Case C-367/05, *Criminal proceedings against Norma Kraaijenbrink*; Case C-297/07, *Klaus Bourquain*; Case C-491/07, *Criminal proceedings against Vladimir Turanský*; Case C-489/10, *Criminal proceedings against Łukasz Marcin Bonda*; Case C-398/12, *Criminal proceedings against M.*; Case C-486/14, *Criminal proceedings against Piotr Kossowski.*
11. See further Ch. 4, "Fundamental rights", of this book on the Charter of Fundamental Rights. See also Case C-617/10, *Åklagaren v. Hans Åkerberg Fransson.*
12. Case C-129/14 PPU, *Criminal proceedings against Zoran Spasic.* See also Case C-288/05, *Criminal proceedings against Jürgen Kretzinger.*

executing state's criminal law authorities to request information about the earlier proceedings, and to accept the information given by the issuing state's judicial authorities.[13]

1.2 *From Maastricht to Amsterdam: Criminal law on an intergovernmental basis*

Criminal law matters first became a serious formal concern of the European Union with the Maastricht Treaty, which introduced the field of Justice and Home Affairs, the so-called Third Pillar.[14] The Maastricht Treaty included express competences for the Union to legislate on criminal law, subjected to some atypical institutional arrangements. Instead of regulations and directives, the main instruments for law-making were conventions, joint actions and common positions.[15] In the decision-making procedures, the European Parliament was virtually powerless and the Council could only decide in unanimity. The right of initiative lay exclusively with one or more of the Member States. Since the Commission could not use infringement proceedings to enforce implementation, its relevance was very limited, leaving the Council as prime actor in legislative proceedings.[16]

The Treaty of Amsterdam changed the institutional set-up in multiple ways. It introduced the AFSJ, an overarching policy area for police and criminal law cooperation, visa, asylum and border control issues,[17] and civil law cooperation.[18] In terms of legislative instruments, the Treaty of Amsterdam replaced conventions, joint actions and common positions by framework decisions and decisions.[19] The framework decision was a much-used legislative instrument. In comparison to Maastricht-era conventions, it did not need ratification by national parliaments, which could explain its popularity. It also lacked direct effect.[20]

The Treaty of Amsterdam contained an optional possibility for Member States to enable their courts to make preliminary references to the ECJ on questions of interpretation.[21] As quite a number of Member States used this possibility, the ECJ could play a role in developing EU criminal law. For example, in *Pupino* the ECJ ruled that national law had to be interpreted in conformity to framework decisions. In order to reach its decision, the Court extended Member States' loyal cooperation duties to also apply vis-a-vis the European Union.[22]

The Treaty of Nice slightly changed the institutional setup of the AFSJ, by introducing a legal basis for Eurojust.[23] This body for prosecutorial cooperation and coordination was set up provisionally in 2001. The Commission proposed to include a legal basis for the establishment of a European Public Prosecutor's Office, without success.[24]

1.3 *Criminal law competences under the Lisbon Treaty*

The Lisbon Treaty abolished the Pillar structure, in place since the Maastricht Treaty, thereby merging all policy areas of the European Union into a single institutional framework.[25]

---

13. Case C-261/09, *Gaetano Mantello*.
14. Art. K.1-K.9 TEU.
15. Art. K.3(2) TEU.
16. S. Miettinen, *Criminal Law and Policy in the European Union* (Routledge, 2013), 23–25.
17. See Ch. 17, "European migration and asylum law", of this book.
18. See Ch. 18, "Judicial cooperation in civil matters", of this book.
19. Art. 34(2) TEU (Amsterdam version).
20. Art. 34(2)(b) TEU (Amsterdam version).
21. Art. 35 TEU (Amsterdam version).
22. Case C-105/03, *Criminal proceedings against Maria Pupino*, para 42.
23. Art. 29(2), 31(1) and 31(2) TEU (Nice version).
24. COM(2000)608.
25. J. Salminen, "Depillarization and the shaping of AFSJ", (2011) MJ, 275–302.

Consequently, regular legislative instruments such as regulations and directives may be enacted, and regular procedures of interpretation and enforcement apply to all newly adopted instruments. On 1 December 2014, a transitional period expired during which the powers of the ECJ over "old" Third Pillar instruments were still restricted.[26] Nevertheless, the communitarization of the AFSJ, like other fields of EU action, is not complete, perhaps due to the sensitive nature of criminal law.[27] For instance, the Treaty explicitly respects the different legal systems and traditions of the Member States.[28] The institutional set-up reflects this: Member States share the power of initiative with the Commission,[29] subsidiarity objections for national parliaments require comparatively low thresholds,[30] and special emergency brake procedures are in place for Member States to safeguard fundamental aspects of their criminal justice systems.[31]

The Union's powers under the Treaty of Lisbon cover many elements of criminal law and criminal procedure. Its cornerstone is the principle of mutual recognition of judgments and judicial decisions.[32] Competences for regulating cooperation in criminal matters include: ensuring recognition of judgments and decisions, preventing and settling conflicts of jurisdiction, supporting the training of the judiciary and facilitating the cooperation between judicial authorities.[33] To exercise these competences, the Union may use any legislative instrument, while some specific procedural elements such as the emergency brake procedure do not apply.

Moreover, the Union is competent to create common norms regarding substantive criminal law (concerning the definitions of offences and sanction levels)[34] and regarding criminal procedure (including the mutual admissibility of evidence, defence rights, and rights of victims of crime).[35]

Further powers include the adoption of measures in the field of crime prevention[36] and the establishment of bodies and agencies active in criminal law cooperation, such as Eurojust[37] and the European Public Prosecutor's Office.[38] In matters of police cooperation, there is a Union competence on Europol[39] as well as a competence to legislate on the processing of criminal information and on common investigative techniques.[40] The Lisbon Treaty also envisages a supporting competence for the training and exchange of police staff, and cooperation on equipment and on research into crime detection.[41] Furthermore, the EU may legislate on operational cooperation between police authorities.[42]

---

26. Protocol no. 36 on transitional provisions, Art. 10(1).
27. V. Mitsilegas, "European criminal law and resistance to communautarisation after Lisbon", (2010) NJECL, 458–480; S. Peers, "Mission accomplished? EU Justice and Home Affairs Law after the Treaty of Lisbon", 48 CML Rev. (2011), 661–693.
28. Art. 67(1), 82(2) TFEU.
29. Art. 76 TFEU.
30. Art. 7(2), Protocol no. 2 on the application of the principles of subsidiarity and proportionality.
31. Art. 82(3), 83(3) TFEU.
32. Art. 82(1) TFEU.
33. Art. 82(1)(a)–(d) TFEU; see *infra* section 4 for an overview of measures adopted in these areas.
34. Art. 83 TFEU. Section 2 *infra* gives an overview of measures adopted under this provision.
35. Art. 82(2)(a)–(c) TFEU. As follows from Art. 82(2)(d) TFEU, any other aspect of criminal procedure can be added to these competences by a special procedure. See *infra* section 3 for an overview of measures adopted under Art. 82(2) TFEU.
36. Art. 84 TFEU.
37. Art. 85 TFEU; *see infra* section 5.2.
38. Art. 86 TFEU; see *infra* section 5.5.
39. Art. 88 TFEU; see *infra* section 5.1.
40. Art. 87(2)(a) and (c) TFEU.
41. Art. 87(2)(b) TFEU.
42. Art. 87(3) TFEU.

1.4 Jurisdiction of the ECJ over criminal law matters

Prior to the Lisbon Treaty, Member States could enable their courts to make preliminary references on the validity and interpretation of legislative acts adopted under the EU's Third Pillar.[43] Not all Member States did so, and even if they did, the highest courts were not obliged to refer a case to the ECJ. A transitional period left this untouched, but since December 2014, normal rules on preliminary references apply to old Third Pillar instruments.[44] The European Commission is also competent to start infringement proceedings against Member States for late or incorrectly transposing Third Pillar legislation. All directives adopted since 1 December 2009 are subject to normal ECJ oversight.

1.5 Opt-out arrangements for the UK, Ireland, and Denmark

The opt-out and opt-in arrangements in the AFSJ reveal its sensitive nature. In a protocol to the Lisbon Treaty, Ireland and the United Kingdom secured a renewal of their Amsterdam-era opt-in, which enabled them to take part in legislative instruments on a case-by case basis.[45] The United Kingdom could, uniquely, completely opt-out before 1 December 2014, and thereby cease to be bound to AFSJ legislation.[46] It exercised that option, and subsequently opted back in to a select number of measures.[47] Conversely, Denmark has a full opt-out of all legislative measures[48] but it normally accepts these on an intergovernmental basis.[49] The treaty enables Denmark to choose for an opt-in arrangement comparable to the one applicable to Ireland and the United Kingdom.[50]

2. Substantive criminal law of the EU

2.1 Influence of the EU on the general part of criminal law

The general part of criminal law consists of principles, rules and doctrines that apply to all crimes, or to broader categories of crime. This general part includes the principle of legality, *mens rea* and defences (the mental elements of an offence), *actus reus* and rules on commission, participation, and attempts (the physical elements of an offence, modes of liability). To date, EU legislation generally only refers to concepts in the general part, without defining them. Nevertheless, a nascent general part of EU criminal law can be construed from fundamental principles of EU law and ECJ case law. The following briefly mentions the most important concepts referred to in sources of EU law.

Article 49 of the EU Charter on Fundamental Rights (hereinafter: the Charter)[51] enshrines the *principle of legality* which recognizes the primacy of law in criminal justice.[52] The legality principle is commonly considered a key principle in communities governed by the rule of law. Fundamental values that can be deduced from the legality principle are: the *nullum crimen, nulla*

---

43. Art. 35 TEU (Nice version).
44. Protocol no. 36 on transitional provisions, Art. 10(3).
45. Protocol no. 21 on the position of the United Kingdom and Ireland in respect of the Area of Freedom, Security and Justice.
46. Protocol no. 36 on transitional provisions, Art. 10(4).
47. Notified in Council doc. no. 12750/13 and 15398/14, respectively.
48. Protocol no. 22 on the position of Denmark, Arts. 1–2.
49. On the basis of Protocol no. 22 on the position of Denmark, Art. 4.
50. Protocol no. 22 on the position of Denmark, Art. 8.
51. On the Charter, see Ch. 4, "Fundamental rights", of this book.
52. See also Joined Cases C-387/02, C-391/02 and C-403/02, *Criminal proceedings against Silvio Berlusconi, Sergio Adelchi, Marcello Dell'Utri and others*; Case C-42/17, Criminal Proceedings against M.A.S. and M.B..

poena sine lege principle (no crime and no punishment without law), the prohibition of retroactive application of criminal law, the *lex mitior* principle (application of the more lenient law) and the principle of legal certainty (accessibility and foreseeability).[53]

With regard to *actus reus* Article 49 of the Charter refers to both acts and omissions, which has led to the conclusion that both may be criminalized.[54] Moreover, many legislative instruments refer to modes of participation as well as inchoate offences (often attempt, sometimes preparatory offences). Definitions of these concepts have however not been provided in the Charter nor elsewhere in primary or secondary EU law.[55] Member States are free to interpret these concepts according to national law, subject to conformity with principles of EU law.

Regarding *mens rea*, most legislative instruments refer to intentionally committed conduct. Only a limited number of instruments have prescribed criminalization of negligent or reckless conduct.[56] Definitions of these concepts have, however, not been provided in any of these legislative instruments, nor elsewhere in EU law. The ECJ has interpreted these concepts in a few cases,[57] some of which were in the criminal law sphere; here the ECJ interpreted the concept of intent[58] and "an offence which was not intentionally committed" in the specific context of the instruments at stake.[59] A general ruling on the meaning of these concepts has however not been given so far. The same applies to defences that may negate elements of a criminal act such as intent. Although fragments of justifications and excuses can be deduced from ECJ case law, or have been laid down in legislative instruments,[60] they have neither been provided for systematically, nor interpreted autonomously at EU level.[61]

2.2 *Euro crimes*

In its 2011 Communication on EU Criminal Policy, the Commission used the term "Euro crimes" to refer to the offences covered by Article 83(1) TFEU.[62] This provision lays down a

---

53. Peristeridou qualifies the application and interpretation of the legality principle in EU criminal law as incoherent and incomplete. She therefore proposes to reshape the principle in this context so that the elements of foreseeability, transparency, and controllability are better secured, C. Peristeridou, *The Principle of Legality in European Criminal Law* (Intersentia, 2015).
54. A. Klip, op. cit. *supra* note 1, at 219.
55. Proposals for that aim have been put forward in: J. Keiler, *Actus Reus and Participation in European Criminal Law* (Intersentia, 2013).
56. See Directive 2008/99/EC, O.J. 2008, L 328/28 requiring the criminalization of "at least serious negligence" with regard to crimes committed in the sphere of environment protection; and Directive 2009/123/EC, O.J. 2009, L 280/52 which refers to criminalization of acts "if committed with intent, recklessly or with serious negligence".
57. See for cases outside the criminal law sphere: C-308/06, *The Queen on the application of International Association of Independent Tanker Owners (Intertanko) and Others v. Secretary of State for Transport*, paras. 76–77 (on negligence); Case C-40/04, *Criminal proceedings against Syuichi Yonemoto*, paras. 45–55 (on negligence); Case C-396/12, *A. M. van der Ham and A. H. van der Ham-Reijersen van Buuren v. College van Gedeputeerde Staten van Zuid-Holland*, para 37 (on intent).
58. See Case C-367/09, *Belgisch Interventie- en Restitutiebureau v. SGS Belgium NV and others*, para 57. See also on "knowingly and intentionally" as laid down in Framework Decision 2008/841/JHA, O.J. 2008, L 300/42: Case C-72/11, *Criminal proceedings against Mohsen Afrasiabi and others*, paras. 66–67.
59. Case C-157/80, *Criminal proceedings against Siegfried Ewald Rinkau*, para 11.
60. Klip mentions several examples: A. Klip, op. cit. *supra* note 1, 230–231.
61. For further reading on these issues, see: A. Klip, op. cit. *supra* note 1, 220–224; J.-M. ten Voorde, "The concept of intent in rulings of the Court of Justice of the European Union", (2015) EPL, 555–570; J. Blomsma, *Mens Rea and Defences in European Criminal Law* (Intersentia, 2012).
62. COM(2011)573, "Towards an EU Criminal Policy: Ensuring the effective implementation of EU policies through criminal law", at 5. The term Euro-crimes is not always reserved for the areas of crime covered by

competence to establish common minimum norms on offence definitions and sanctions in ten areas of crime: terrorism, trafficking in human beings, sexual exploitation of women and children, illicit drug trafficking, illicit arms trafficking, money laundering, corruption, counterfeiting of means of payment, computer crime, and organized crime.[63]

These areas of crime are considered to deserve an EU approach because of their "particularly serious nature" and their "cross-border dimension". According to Article 83(1) TFEU, the cross-border dimension of these crimes may follow from their nature or impact (e.g. cybercrime is borderless by nature) or from a "special need to combat them on a common basis" (e.g. in the eurozone Member States need to collectively fight euro-counterfeiting).[64]

All Euro-crimes, except illicit arms trafficking, were already the subject of pre-Lisbon legislation. Post-Lisbon directives mainly aim to update or extend the scope of already existing harmonization measures.

In the area of *terrorism*, Directive 2017/541/EU[65] replaces Framework Decisions 2002/475/JHA[66] and 2008/919/JHA.[67] Pursuant to the first of these former instruments, Member States were already obliged to qualify a number of criminal acts as terrorist offences if these acts were intentionally committed with one of a number of listed aims (Art. 1). Moreover, it defines "terrorist group" and calls for the criminalization of certain offences related to a terrorist group, such as directing such a group (Art. 2). It further contains provisions on offences linked to terrorism (Art. 3) and the level of penalties for terrorist offences (Arts. 5–6). The second instrument added to this the criminalization of public provocation to commit a terrorist offence, recruitment for terrorism, and training for terrorism. The newest directive partly implements new international standards and obligations. It additionally criminalizes travelling to third countries with terrorist intentions, being trained for terrorist purposes, and funding terrorism related offences.

Framework Decision 2002/629/JHA[68] and Directive 2011/36/EU[69] contain criminal law provisions with regard to *trafficking in human beings*. The provisions concern definitions of offences as well as minimum levels of maximum penalties. The purpose of "exploitation" constitutes an indispensable element of human trafficking offences. Whereas the 2002 Framework Decision was limited to exploitation in the sense of forced labour, slavery, forced prostitution or other forms of sexual exploitation (Art. 1), the 2011 Directive determines that exploitation also covers forced begging, exploitation of criminal activities, and the removal of organs (Art. 2).

Directive 2011/92/EU concerns *sexual abuse and sexual exploitation*,[70] replacing and extending offence definitions and sanction levels included in Framework Decision 2004/68/JHA.[71] The 2004 Framework Decision criminalized the sexual exploitation of children as well as the

---

Art. 83(1) TFEU. Klip, for instance, interprets Euro-crimes as covering all criminal offences regulated by EU Law, see A. Klip, op. cit. *supra* note 1, 231 et seq.

63. Additional areas of crime can be added to the list of Euro-crimes by a unanimous Council decision, with the Parliament's consent.
64. See also Mitsilegas who states that Art. 83(1) TFEU aims to address global security threats; he therefore characterizes criminalization under its heading as "securitized criminalization" (as the opposite of "functional criminalization"), V. Mitsilegas, "EU criminal law competence after Lisbon: From securitized to functional criminalization" in D.A. Arcarazo and C.C. Murphy (Eds.), *EU Security and Justice Law After Lisbon and Stockholm* (Hart Publishing, 2014).
65. O.J. 2017, L 88/6.
66. O.J. 2002, L 164/3.
67. O.J. 2008, L 330/21.
68. O.J. 2002, L 203/1.
69. O.J. 2011, L 101/1.
70. O.J. 2011, L 335/1.
71. O.J. 2004, L 13/44.

production, distribution, supplying, possession and acquisition of child pornography, and laid down minimum levels of maximum penalties (Arts. 2, 3, 5). The 2011 Directive broadens offence definitions (Arts. 3–5), but also criminalizes "grooming", i.e. the online solicitation of children for sexual purposes (Art. 6). Member States enjoy some discretion to apply these provisions to consensual sexual activities with a child that reached the age of sexual consent, or to activities between peers close in age and degree of psychological and physical development, provided that the sexual activities do not involve any abuse (Art. 8).[72]

Framework Decision 2004/757/JHA[73] contains drug offences, defining drugs as any of the substances covered by two UN Conventions[74] as well as the substances subject to controls under Joint Action 97/396.[75] It obliges Member States to criminalize a number of acts relating to drugs, such as production, manufacturing, offering (for sale), importation, exportation, etc. Moreover, it prescribes the minimum levels of maximum penalties which must be foreseen in national legislation. A new Directive[76] extends the existing scope of EU-level offences to new psychoactive substances (also known as "designer drugs") that pose severe health, social and safety risks, which are therefore submitted to permanent market restrictions under a Regulation.[77]

Pursuant to Articles 1–2 of the Second Protocol to the Convention on the Protection of the European Communities' Financial Interests (hereinafter called the PFI Convention),[78] Member States must criminalize *money laundering*, defined in the so-called first anti-money laundering Directive 91/308/EEC.[79] Framework Decision 2001/500/JHA additionally requires a maximum penalty of at least one year deprivation of liberty.[80] These rules will probably be replaced by criminal prohibitions on money laundering, proposed in a 2012 draft Directive on the fight against EU fraud by means of criminal law; this proposal aims to replace the PFI Convention.[81] Since this concerns combating illegal activities affecting the financial interests of the EU (taking Art. 325(4) TFEU as its legal basis), it can be qualified as an example of regulatory criminal law (dealt with in section 2.3.).

Corruption has been the subject of several instruments. The First Protocol to the aforementioned PFI Convention[82] criminalizes both passive corruption (accepting advantages) and active corruption (giving advantages) which damage the EU's financial interests. The PFI

72. See also recital 20 of the preamble to Directive 2011/92/EU, O.J. 2011, L 335/1: "This Directive does not govern Member States' policies with regard to consensual sexual activities in which children may be involved and which can be regarded as the normal discovery of sexuality in the course of human development, taking account of the different cultural and legal traditions and of new forms of establishing and maintaining relations among children and adolescents, including through information and communication technologies".
73. O.J. 2004, L 335/8.
74. The 1961 Single Convention on Narcotic Drugs and the 1971 Vienna Convention on Psychotropic Substances.
75. Joint Action 97/396 of 16 June 1997 envisages the creation of a mechanism for the rapid exchange of information on new synthetic drugs and their risk assessment, O.J. 1997, L 167/1.
76. O.J. 2017, L 305/12.
77. O.J. 2006, L 376/1, as amended by Regulation (EU) 2017/2101, O.J. 2017, L 305/1.
78. O.J. 1997, C 221/12.
79. O.J. 1991, L 166/77. Subsequent EU legislation to combat money laundering has been expanding the scope of money laundering activities that have to be prohibited, but so far it has been left within the discretion of Member States whether such prohibitions are of a criminal or administrative nature, see also the most recent anti-money laundering instrument, Directive 2015/849/EU, O.J. 2015, L 141/73. This may change in the near future, since a proposal for a directive on countering money laundering by means of criminal law has been submitted end of 2016, see COM(2016)826 final.
80. O.J. 2001, L 182/1, Art. 2.
81. See also Ch. 9, "Budget and finances", of this book.
82. O.J. 1996, C 313/1.

Directive somewhat broadens the scope of offences compared to the PFI Convention, e.g. where it suggests that corrupt conduct should no longer be required to be "in breach of official duties".[83] Again, this matter is more properly dealt with in section 2.3; the Directive is based on Article 83(2) TFEU.

Even broader definitions were included in the 1997 Convention on Corruption which criminalizes active and passive corruption as such, without requiring a negative effect on the EU's financial interests.[84] Moreover, Framework Decision 2003/568/JHA[85] criminalizes passive and active corruption in the private sector, thereby replacing Joint Action 98/742/JHA on that matter.[86] As Klip points out, there is also a criminal prohibition in Article 15 of the Convention on Mutual Assistance in Criminal Matters between the EU Member States.[87] This provision, which is phased out by Article 17 of Directive 2014/14/EU on the European Investigation Order,[88] requires criminal liability for offences against or by officials of a Member State during law enforcement operations on the territory of another Member State.[89]

Framework Decision 2000/383/JHA demands that Member States criminalize several activities relating to the *counterfeiting of currency*.[90] Directive 2014/62/EU adds more detailed provisions on the minimum levels of maximum penalties.[91] Additionally, Framework Decision 2001/413/JHA contains provisions on the criminalization and sanctioning of *fraud and counterfeiting of non-cash means of payment* (e.g. credit cards).[92]

As to *computer crime*, Directive 2013/40/EU[93] has replaced and expanded the scope of its predecessor Framework Decision 2005/222/JHA.[94] Under the heading "attacks against information systems", Member States must criminalize the illegal access to information systems, the illegal system or data interference, illegal interception, and the provision of tools (e.g. computer programmes) for the purpose of committing the aforementioned offences.

Framework Decision 2008/841/JHA relates to *organized crime*. It provides a definition of "criminal organization" and requires Member States to criminalize either participation in such a criminal organization (the civil law model), the conspiracy to commit crimes (the common law model), or both. It harmonizes minimum levels of maximum penalties for those offences as well (Articles 1–3).[95]

Directive 2014/42/EU requires Member States to enable the *freezing and confiscation of the proceeds from crime* in relation to so-called Euro-crimes (offences falling under the scope of Art. 83(1) TFEU).[96] While such an obligation already followed from Framework Decision 2005/212/JHA,[97] it was felt that the level of harmonization achieved under this instrument was disappointingly low and that the instrument was too limited in scope. Directive 2014/42/EU therefore replaced some of the 2005 provisions and included broader obligations for criminal

---

83. O.J. 2017, L 198/29, Art. 4.
84. O.J. 1997, C 195/1.
85. O.J. 2003, L 192/54.
86. O.J. 1998, L 358/2.
87. O.J. 2000, L 197/1.
88. O.J. 2014, L 130/1.
89. Cf. A. Klip, op. cit. *supra* note 1, 236–237.
90. O.J. 2000, L 140/1.
91. O.J. 2014, L 151/1.
92. O.J. 2001, L 149/1.
93. O.J. 2003, L 218/8.
94. O.J. 2005, L 69/67.
95. The Framework Decision replaces Joint Action 98/733/JHA, O.J. 1998, L 351/1.
96. O.J. 2014, L 127/39.
97. O.J. 2005, L 68/49.

asset recovery. The Directive adds provisions on extended confiscation (Art. 5),[98] third party confiscation (Art. 6), non-conviction based confiscation (Art. 4(2)), and freezing of property with a view to confiscation (Art. 7).

2.3 *Regulatory criminal law*

EU criminal law provisions may also be adopted to serve the effectiveness of EU law.[99] An express criminal law competence for that objective is laid down in Article 83(2) TFEU: in harmonized policy areas, minimum rules on offence definitions and on penalties may be established by means of directives, provided that such approximation "proves essential to ensure the effective implementation" of a Union policy (e.g. environmental policy).[100]

Several other Treaty provisions have been interpreted as providing a legal basis for regulatory criminal law, particularly Article 325(4) TFEU.[101] Aiming at countering fraud against the EU budget, this provision allows the adoption of "necessary measures" in order to afford "effective and equivalent protection in the Member States and in all the institutions, bodies, offices and agencies". Moreover, it has been stated that Articles 33, 79, 91, 103, 114, 192 TFEU and, finally, the catch-all provision of Article 352 TFEU also confer criminal law powers upon the EU.[102]

The overview below demonstrates that the EU's competences to legislate in the field of regulatory criminal law have been applied in a wide range of EU policy areas. As evident from pre-Lisbon initiatives in particular, the Commission has long favoured a broad interpretation of powers in this context.[103]

In order to contribute to the effective protection of the EU's *environmental policies*, Directive 2008/99/EC requires criminalization of various forms of "environmentally harmful activities".[104] Directive 2009/123/EC aims to reinforce *maritime safety*.[105] For the specific aim of preventing

98. Art. 3 of Framework Decision 2005/212/EU (*supra* note 85) required Member States to choose at least one of three types of extended confiscation. Extended confiscation powers allow confiscation of additional property – not related to a specific crime – which according to the court constitutes the proceeds of other crimes.
99. This is what Mitsilegas qualifies as "functional criminalization", see V. Mitsilegas, op. cit. *supra* note 64.
100. See Ch. 11, "Application and enforcement in the Member States", of this book. Art. 83(2) TFEU is considered a "quasi-codification" of the ECJ's case-law in the *Environment case* and the *Ship-source pollution case* (Case C-176/03, *Commission v. Council* and C-440/05, *Commission v. Council*), see e.g.: A. Weyembergh, "Approximation of substantive criminal law: The new institutional and decision-making framework and new types of interaction between EU actors" in F. Galli and A. Weyembergh (Eds.), *Approximation of Substantive Criminal Law in the EU. The Way Forward* (Editions de l'Université de Bruxelles, 2013), 16; V. Mitsilegas, op. cit. *supra* note 64, 117.
101. E.g. V. Mitsilegas, op. cit. *supra* note 64, 119; H. Satzger, *International and European Criminal Law* (C.H. Beck Verlag, 2012), 55–56, 81; and P. Asp, *The Substantive Criminal Law Competence of the EU* (Stockholm University, 2012), 142–154.
102. See (references in) J.W. Ouwerkerk, "Criminalization powers of the European Union and the risks of cherry-picking between various legal bases: The case for a single legal framework for EU-level criminalization", (2017) CJEL.
103. Under the pre-Lisbon pillar regime, the European Commission and the Council battled on whether criminal law provisions in the areas of environment protection had to be adopted under Community Law (former First Pillar) or Union Law (former Third Pillar). In the *Environment* and *Ship-source pollution* cases (Case C-176/03, *Commission v. Council* and C-440/05, *Commission v. Council*), the ECJ ruled in favour of a (then) Community criminal law competence if essential for the enforcement of EU policy objectives.
104. O.J. 2008, L 328/28. E.g. discharge of a quantity of materials or ionizing radiation into air, soil or water, or the production, processing, etc. of hazardous radioactive substances (Art. 3).
105. O.J. 2009, L 280/52.

ship-source pollution, it has amended Directive 2005/35/EC[106] and criminalizes, under well-defined circumstances, ship-source discharges of polluting substances into EU waters.

In order to preserve *market integrity*, Directive 2014/57/EU[107] obliges Member States to criminalize in their national laws the intentional commission of insider dealing, market manipulation, and the unlawful disclosure of inside information, laying down minimum levels of maximum penalties (Arts. 3–7). Prior to this Directive, Member States had to provide for administrative sanctions and measures for such infringements.[108] This obligation still exists, now under Regulation 596/2014/EU.[109] The Regulation and Directive are closely related, with a dual regime, so the Directive requires that the most serious violations are enforced by means of criminal law.[110]

In addition to the body of administrative law for the *protection of the financial interests of the EU*, criminal law provisions are provided for in the 1995 PFI Convention.[111] This Convention obliges Member States to impose criminal sanctions for serious cases of fraud affecting the EU's financial interests.[112] The PFI Convention applies to all EU Member States except Croatia and the UK.

In 2012, the Commission submitted a proposal for a Directive to replace the PFI Convention,[113] aiming to criminalize EU fraud, but also fraud-related acts negatively affecting the EU budget (e.g. money laundering and corruption).[114] Negotiations on the draft Directive culminated in the inclusion of VAT fraud.[115]

In the *fight against illegal immigration*, several instruments provide for criminal prohibitions. Framework Decision 2002/946/JHA[116] prescribes the criminalization of infringements defined in Articles 1 and 2 of Directive 2002/90/EC, concerning assistance to unauthorized entry, transit and residence. Moreover, Directive 2009/52/EC requires that Member States criminalize the employment of illegally staying third-country nationals (Art. 9).[117]

In order to *combat racism and xenophobia* across the EU, Framework Decision 2008/913/JHA[118] obliges Member States to criminalize public incitement to violence or hatred directed against a group of persons or a member of such a group. It also criminalizes publicly condoning, denying or grossly trivializing crimes of genocide, crimes against humanity and war crimes (Art. 1).

---

106. O.J. 2005, L 255/11.
107. O.J. 2014, L 173/179.
108. Cf. Directive 2003/6/EC, O.J. 2003, L 96/16.
109. Reg. 596/2014/EU, O.J. 2014, L 173/1 has repealed Directive 2003/6/EC, *supra* note 108.
110. For further reading on this, see M. Luchtman and J. Vervaele, "Enforcing the market abuse regime: Towards an integrated model of criminal and administrative law enforcement in the European Union?", (2014) NJECL, 192–220.
111. O.J. 1995, C 316/49.
112. See also Ch. 9, "Budget and finances", of this book.
113. COM(2012)363. The proposal is based on Art. 325(4) TFEU.
114. As already mentioned in section 2.2 *supra*, Protocol No. 1 to the PIF Convention obliges criminal sanctions for passive and active corruption which damages the EU's financial interests; Protocol No. 2 to the PIF Convention requires to impose criminal sanctions for money laundering activities which damages the EU financial interests, *supra* notes 82 and 78.
115. O.J. 2017, L 198/29. See on this, Ch. 9, "Budget and finances", of this book.
116. O.J. 2002, L 328/1.
117. O.J. 2009, L 168/24.
118. O.J. 2008, L 328/55. The Directive repeals Joint Action 96/443/JHA, O.J. 1996, L 185/5.

3. EU norms of criminal procedure

3.1 *Minimum standards of procedural rights for suspects and accused persons*

All EU Member States are a party to the ECHR, which provides an absolute minimum of rights and guarantees in criminal proceedings throughout the Union, in accordance with their interpretation by the ECtHR. These include: the absolute prohibition of torture and inhuman or degrading treatment or punishment (Art. 3); the right to liberty (Art. 5); the right to an effective legal remedy (Art. 13); and the right to a fair trial which includes the right to be presumed innocent until proved guilty, the right to legal assistance, and the right to interpretation for those who do not understand or speak the language of the criminal proceedings (Art. 6).

These procedural rights and guarantees are now also enshrined in the Charter, which is addressed to the EU's institutions, bodies, offices and agencies as well as to the Member States when they implement EU law (Art. 51(1) Charter). The meaning and scope of Charter rights corresponds to the equivalent provisions in the ECHR, but Art. 52(3) of the Charter enables a more extensive protection of those rights in the EU context.

Since 2009, the EU legislature is creating more detailed rules on some of the aforementioned procedural rights. This was considered necessary in order to strengthen mutual trust between Member States' criminal justice authorities, and to consequently facilitate the application of the principle mutual recognition in criminal matters. In a 2009 Resolution, the Council presented a Roadmap for the progressive creation of more detailed procedural rights.[119] Article 82(2)(b) TFEU provides a legal basis to adopt such minimum norms for the objective of smoothening judicial cooperation. Under this provision, the following initiatives have been taken.

Directive 2012/13/EU harmonizes the *right to information* for suspects and accused persons about their procedural rights and the accusations against them.[120] These persons must be informed of their right of access to a lawyer, the rules and conditions on free legal advice, the right to interpretation and translation, and the right to remain silent (Art. 3). Upon arrest, more extensive rights apply: Article 4 stipulates the prompt provision of a written Letter of Rights with information on the aforementioned procedural rights, supplemented with information on the right of access to the materials of the case, the right to have consular authorities and a third person informed, the right of access to urgent medical assistance, and, finally, on the maximum period of time a person may be deprived of his liberty before being brought before a judge. In surrender proceedings, the Letter of Rights must contain information on the rights of requested persons, in accordance with Framework Decision 2002/584/JHA,[121] and must be promptly provided upon arrest (Art. 5). The right to information also covers the right for suspects and accused persons to be informed of the nature of the suspicion or accusation (Art. 6), and the right to have access to case materials (Art. 7).

Directive 2016/343/EU[122] harmonizes some aspects of the *presumption of innocence* such as the right to remain silent and the right not to incriminate oneself (Art. 7). It also determines that the prosecution bears the burden of proof for establishing guilt (Art. 6). Moreover, Member States must avoid to publicly present suspected or accused persons as guilty, neither by public statements, nor by the use of measures of physical restraint (e.g. handcuffs, glass boxes, cages, iron legs),[123] unless strictly necessary (Arts. 4–5). These minimum standards do not seem to ex-

119. O.J. 2009, L 295/1.
120. O.J. 2012, L 142/1.
121. O.J. 2002, L 190/1.
122. O.J. 2016, L 65/1.
123. These examples are from recital 20 of the preamble to Directive 2016/343/EU.

ceed the level of protection required by ECtHR case-law on the presumption of innocence. This Directive also covers the *right to be present at trial* in criminal proceedings. Articles 8–9 contain circumstances that nevertheless justify trials in the absence of suspects or accused persons, as well as rules on the right to a new trial or another legal remedy enabling a "fresh determination of the merits of the case", in cases where persons were tried *in absentia*.

Pursuant to Article 2 of Directive 2010/64/EU,[124] suspected or accused persons who do not understand or speak the language of criminal proceedings are entitled to *oral interpretation*[125] including, where necessary in view of the fairness of the proceedings, during communicating with their legal counsel, or in relation to procedural applications (e.g. lodging an appeal).[126] The right to interpretation also applies in European arrest warrant proceedings.[127]

Article 3 of Directive 2010/64/EU further envisages the right to be provided with a *translation of essential documents*, defined as "all documents which are essential to ensure that [suspects and accused persons] are able to exercise their right of defence and to safeguard the fairness of the proceedings" (e.g. decisions on deprivation of liberty, charges or indictments, and judgments).[128] This also applies to European arrest warrants.

Upon deprivation of liberty, at whatever stage of criminal proceedings, suspects or accused persons have the right to have *at least one person informed* of their situation, pursuant to Article 5 of Directive 2013/48/EU.[129] They are free to decide who they wish to inform (their partner, another relative, their employer, etc.). Articles 6 and 7 provide non-nationals with *the right to communicate with third persons as well as with consular authorities*.

Directive 2013/48/EU further includes *the right of access to a lawyer*, in both criminal proceedings and surrender proceedings. In criminal proceedings, the right of access to a lawyer must be granted from the first stage of (police) questioning and in any case upon arrest (Art. 3). In surrender proceedings, this right applies upon being arrested for the execution of a European arrest warrant (Art. 10).

The right of access to a lawyer in criminal proceedings encompasses 1) the right to meet and communicate in private, also before being interrogated; 2) the right to have the lawyer present and participating when being interrogated; and 3) the right to have the lawyer attend certain investigative or evidence-gathering activities[130] insofar national law requires or permits suspects or accused persons to attend these activities (Art. 3). In surrender proceedings, the right of access to a lawyer entitles the requested person to meet and communicate with the lawyer, and have him present and participating during a hearing (Art. 10). Member States are obliged to safeguard confidentiality (Art. 4).

---

124. O.J. 2010, L 280/1.
125. The ECJ ruled that Directive 2010/64/EU does not apply to a national special procedure, as available in Hungary, for judicial recognition of a foreign conviction, see Case C-25/15, *István Balogh*.
126. That Art. 2 refers to oral interpretation of oral statements has explicitly been stated in Case C-216/14, *Criminal proceedings against Gavril Covaci*, para 30.
127. On the European arrest warrant, see *infra* section European arrest warrant.
128. The right to translation does not include the right to lodge an objection against a penalty order by the defendant in a language he understand, but which is not the language of the criminal proceedings concerned, Case C-216/14, *criminal proceedings against Gavril Covaci*, para 47. Moreover, the ruling in Case C-25/15, *István Balogh* applies accordingly.
129. O.J. 2013, L 294/1.
130. I.e. identity parades, confrontations, and reconstructions of the crime scene (Art. 3(3)(c) of Directive 2013/48/EU, cited *supra* note 129).

Directive 2016/1919/EU regulates *legal aid for suspects and accused persons*, both in criminal proceedings and in surrender proceedings.[131] The Directive leaves it to the Member States' discretion to use a means or a merits test, or both, to decide on eligibility for legal aid (Art. 4).

Directive 2016/800/EU envisages *specific procedural safeguards for children* in criminal proceedings and surrender proceedings.[132] These include the right to inform the holder of parental responsibility (Art. 5), the right to have this person present during court hearings (Art. 15), the right to an individual assessment in order to meet a child's specific needs for protection, education, training and social integration (Art. 7), the right to a medical examination (Art. 8), and several other specific rights. Logically, this also influences the scope of the right to information: under Article 4, children must also be informed of their specific rights.

3.2 *Minimum standards of procedural rights for victims of crime*

The current legal basis to adopt common minimum standards on the rights of crime victims is Article 82(2)(c) TFEU. That legal basis enables harmonization if necessary to facilitate mutual recognition of judicial decisions in criminal matters, and more generally, to advance police and judicial cooperation in cross-border criminal cases. Prior to the Lisbon Treaty, the EU legislature adopted Framework Decision 2001/220/JHA which obliges Member States to provide victims with a "real and appropriate role" in their criminal justice systems.[133] Some specific rights were articulated (e.g. rights to be heard, to supply evidence, to receive information). Following a 2011 Council Resolution containing a Roadmap for strengthening the rights of victims of crime,[134] Directive 2012/29/EU significantly expanded the rights of crime victims in criminal proceedings.[135]

Victims of crime have *the right to understand and to be understood* (Art. 3), requiring Member States to ensure accessible communication tailored to the specific needs of the individuals involved. Victims must be provided with *interpretation and translation services* if needed (Art. 7). They are also entitled to receive *information on their rights and on victim support* (Art. 4): Member States must guarantee actual and free *access to victim support services*, (Art. 8) which have to provide certain services in particular (Art. 9). The right to information also encompasses the *right to receive a written acknowledgement of a formal complaint* (Art. 5) and the *right to receive information about the criminal proceedings* (Art. 6). Victims have *the right to be heard* and to *supply evidence* (Art. 10). If an alleged offender is not prosecuted, victims are entitled to a *review* of such a decision (Art. 11).

There are *minimum requirements for safe and competent restorative justice services* (Art. 12). Restorative justice processes must be in the interest of the victim and must be based on their consent, while the offender must have acknowledged the basic facts of the case concerned.[136] Where victims are formally a party to the proceedings, they must have *access to legal aid* (Art. 13). Additionally, *expenses must be reimbursable* (Art. 14). Moreover, if recoverable property of victims was seized, this *property must in principle be returned* (Art. 15). Victims have a right to ob-

131. O.J. 2016, L 297/1.
132. O.J. 2016, L 132/1.
133. O.J. 2001, L 82/1, in particular Art. 2(1).
134. O.J. 2011, C 187/1.
135. O.J. 2012, L 315/57.
136. Based on earlier case-law in the context of the predecessor Framework Decision, it may fairly be concluded that it is left to the Member States' discretion to determine which types of offences are considered suitable for restorative justice processes/mediation, see Joined Cases C-483/09 and C-1/10, *Criminal proceedings against Magatte Gueye and Valentín Salmerón Sánchez*, paras. 71–76 and Case C-205/09, *Criminal proceedings against Emil Eerics, Mária Vassné Sápi*, para 40.

tain a *decision on compensation* by the offender (Art. 16). Member States must grant equal rights to victims resident in another Member State (Art. 17).[137] The Member State where the crime was committed is obliged to minimize any difficulties.

There is a general objective for the *protection of victims and their family members from secondary and repeat victimization, from intimidation and from retaliation* (Art. 18). To that end, Member States must take measures enabling victims and their family members to avoid contact with the offender within court premises. New court premises must have separate waiting areas for victims (Art. 19). Member States must provide special measures for victims with specific protection needs, such as children (Arts. 23 and 24).

4. Judicial cooperation on the basis of mutual recognition

4.1 *Mutual recognition as a cornerstone principle*

In 1999, the European Council proclaimed the principle of mutual recognition as the cornerstone of criminal law cooperation.[138] Applying this internal market principle to criminal law matters was expected to facilitate cross-border judicial cooperation significantly. Based on the presumption that Member States trust each other's criminal justice systems, the principle of mutual recognition basically envisages a "free movement of judicial decisions":[139] it obliges Member States to recognize and, if necessary, to enforce foreign judicial decisions, as if handed down in the domestic legal order.

A cooperation regime based on the principle of mutual recognition is characterized by a minimum of formalities and a limited number of exceptions compared to traditional cooperation instruments. In general, the reduction of formalities is expressed in the adoption of strict time limits for recognition, the creation of standard forms, accepting direct contact between judicial authorities therewith eliminating political or diplomatic authorities, and in abolishing the *exequatur* procedure. Decreasing exceptions has been effected through (partially) removing traditional sovereignty-related grounds for refusal, such as the political exception. Moreover, most of the mutual recognition instruments have abolished the double criminality requirement for a list of 32 offences.[140]

The overview below shows that the principle of mutual recognition applies to various types of judicial decisions in all stages of criminal proceedings, i.e. before, during and after conviction.[141]

---

137. As stated by Klip, Art. 17 provides "cross-border rights to victims", A. Klip, op. cit. *supra* note 1, at 328. See also Case C-186/87, *Ian William Cowan v. Le Trésor public* on the prohibition of discrimination in awarding compensation for persons who fall victim to crime while making use of their free movement rights.
138. Presidency Conclusions, Tampere European Council, 15–16 Oct. 1999, paras. 33–37.
139. As formulated in recital 5 of the preamble to Framework Decision 2002/584/JHA, O.J. 2002, L 190/1.
140. The exceptions are Framework Decisions 2008/909/JHA and 2008/947/JHA, see *infra* section 4.5.
141. For further reading on the development and meaning of mutual recognition in the context of criminal law, see W. van Ballegooij, *The Nature of Mutual Recognition in EU Law* (Intersentia, 2015); C. Janssens, *The Principle of Mutual Recognition in EU Law* (OUP, 2013); A. Suominen, *The Principle of Mutual Recognition in Cooperation in Criminal Matters* (Intersentia, 2011); J. Ouwerkerk, *Quid Pro Quo? A Comparative Law Perspective on the Mutual Recognition of Judicial Decisions in Criminal Matters* (Intersentia, 2011).

4.2 *European arrest warrant*

Framework Decision 2002/584/JHA[142] was the first legislative measure implementing the principle of mutual recognition in the field of criminal law.[143] In order to establish fast and simple surrender procedures, Member States are in principle obliged to recognize and execute *European arrest warrants,* i.e. to surrender requested persons to the issuing Member State. The system of surrender based on Framework Decision 2002/584/JHA replaces the traditional system of extradition.

Surrender may be sought for the purpose of criminal prosecution, or for the purpose of executing a custodial sanction (Arts. 1 and 2(1)). In a limited number of situations, surrender must or may be refused (Arts. 3–5). The final decision on surrender must be taken within 90 days upon arrest, or within 10 days if the requested person consents (Art. 17).[144]

4.3 *Cross-border gathering and use of evidence*

Directive 2014/41/EU[145] aims to establish a comprehensive system for obtaining evidence in cross-border cases, based on the principle of mutual recognition. It replaces the traditional multilateral legal framework on mutual assistance as well as Framework Decision 2003/577/JHA regarding the cross-border freezing of evidence[146] and Framework Decision 2008/978/JHA regarding the cross-border obtaining of already existing evidence.[147]

In comparison with the two framework decisions, Directive 2014/41/EU is much broader in scope: with the exception of setting up a joint investigation team and the gathering of evidence within such a team, it covers all types of investigative measures. It introduces the so-called *European Investigation Order,* which is a judicial decision issued by one Member State in order to have investigative measures carried out in another Member State, for the purpose of gathering evidence. There are some grounds for refusal (Art. 11). Refusal on other grounds is prohibited, although Article 10 entitles the executing authority to apply a less intrusive investigative measure, provided that identical results are achieved. Gathered evidence must be transferred to the issuing Member State without undue delay (Art. 13).

The Directive remains silent on the issue of the mutual admissibility of evidence. Article 82(2) TFEU provides a legal basis to establish common minimum norms, but so far no legislation has been adopted.

4.4 *Cross-border supervision of non-custodial pre-trial measures*

Framework Decision 2009/829/JHA[148] encourages the imposition of non-custodial measures pending trial. It is based on the assumption that foreign suspects (including Union citizens) are more likely to be taken into provisional detention than residents, for fear that the suspect

---

142. O.J. 2002, L 190/1. It has been amended by Art. 2 of Framework Decision 2002/299/JHA, O.J. 2009, L 81/24 which provides the criteria for refusing execution of European arrest warrants issued for the purpose of executing a sanction if the sentenced person did not appear at the trial resulting in that sanction.
143. It has engendered heated discussions, see e.g. E. Guild (Ed.), *Constitutional Challenges to the European Arrest Warrant* (Wolf Legal Publishers, 2006); S. Alegre and M. Leaf, "Mutual recognition in European judicial cooperation: A step too far too soon? Case study – the European arrest warrant", (2004) ELJ, 200–217.
144. Failure to comply with the time-limits prescribed does not relieve the executing Member State of its obligation to take a decision on the European arrest warrant, see Case C-237/15 PPU, *Minister for Justice and Equality v. Francis Lanigan*, paras. 34–42.
145. O.J. 2004, L 130/1.
146. O.J. 2003, L 196/45.
147. O.J. 2008, L 350/72.
148. O.J. 2009, L 294/20.

might abscond. In order to avoid differences in treatment, to stimulate alternatives to pre-trial detention (so-called "supervision measures"), and to ensure that non-resident suspects remain under supervision while awaiting trial, the Framework Decision enables the mutual recognition of *decisions on supervision measures*. These can include obligations not to enter certain areas, obligations to avoid contact with the alleged victim, and obligations to report to the police (Art. 8). The executing Member State monitors the suspect's compliance.

In 2011, Directive 2011/99/EU[149] introduced the mutual recognition of *criminal protection measures*: prohibitions imposed on a dangerous person in order to protect another person against criminal acts (Art. 2(2)). If the protected person decides to move abroad, a European protection order enables the Member State to which the protected person moves to continue protection and monitor the compliance of the person causing danger.[150]

4.5 *Transfer of execution of sanctions*

The principle of mutual recognition has also been applied to several types of sanctions. Framework Decision 2005/214/JHA concerns *financial penalties*, including court costs and compensation for victims (Art. 1(b)).[151] In order to facilitate the cross-border confiscation of the proceeds of crime (particularly organized crime and money laundering) Framework Decision 2006/783/JHA regulates the cross-border recognition and execution of *confiscation sanctions*.[152] A newly proposed Regulation for the mutual recognition of both freezing orders and confiscation orders is currently under negotiation;[153] it aims to strengthen the cross-border confiscation of the proceeds of crime and to bring the mutual recognition regime in line with the common standards regarding confiscation and freezing sanctions pursuant to Directive 2014/42/EU and Framework Decision 2005/212/JHA.[154]

Two other instruments relate to sanctions involving a restriction of individual freedom such as imprisonment: Framework Decision 2008/909/JHA[155] and Framework Decision 2008/947/JHA[156] aim to facilitate the enforcement of foreign sanctions in the sentenced persons' home state or state of residence, as this would serve their social rehabilitation.

Framework Decision 2008/909/JHA concerns *custodial sanctions*, i.e. sanctions involving deprivation of liberty. It replaces between Member States a number of Council of Europe conventions.

Framework Decision 2008/947/JHA relates to *alternative sanctions and probation measures*, e.g. carrying out community service, prohibitions on entering certain areas, reporting to the police, etc. (Art. 4). Such obligations are qualified as probation measures if they have been imposed in relation to a suspended sentence, conditional sentence, or conditional release (Art. 2). The mutual recognition of alternative sanctions and probation measures implies that the executing Member State monitors compliance.

Grounds for non-recognition have in principle exhaustively been provided for in both framework decisions. However, Member States may decide to add the absence of double

---

149. O.J. 2011, L 338/2.
150. See for critical reflection on the need of this instrument: S. van der Aa and J.W. Ouwerkerk, "The European Protection Order: No time to waste or a waste of time?", (2011) *European Journal of Crime, Criminal Law and Criminal Justice*, 267–287.
151. O.J. 2005, L 76/16.
152. O.J. 2006, L 328/59.
153. COM(2016)819.
154. Cited *supra* note 96 and 97.
155. O.J. 2008, L 327/27.
156. O.J. 2008, L 337/102.

criminality as an additional ground for refusal, even where the underlying offence is mentioned on the aforementioned list of 32 offences. Under both framework decisions, the executing Member State is not entitled to convert a foreign sanction into a sanction that fits within domestic standards; only if it is incompatible with the law of the executing Member State, either in terms of its duration, or its nature, the foreign sanction may be adapted before it is being enforced (Art. 8 of Framework Decision 2008/909/JHA; Art. 9 of Framework Decision 2008/947/JHA).

Framework Decision 2009/299/JHA specifically relates to the mutual recognition of *in absentia judgments*, i.e. judicial decisions rendered following a criminal trial at which the individual concerned did not appear in person.[157] This is an "umbrella instrument", amending the foregoing framework decisions simultaneously; it determines under what conditions *in absentia* judgments constitute a ground for non-recognition of financial penalties, confiscation sanctions, custodial sanctions, alternative sanctions, and probation measures.[158]

4.6 *Taking account of foreign convictions*

Framework Decision 2008/675/JHA[159] envisages that in the course of new criminal proceedings Member States take into account *previous convictions handed down in another Member State* to the extent national previous convictions are taken into account, and that the same consequences are attached to them as according to national law are attached to previous national convictions (e.g. if national law considers recidivism a ground for aggravated sentencing). The obligation to do so only exists if sufficient information on such previous convictions is available under the applicable instruments on the exchange of information from criminal records or on mutual legal assistance.

4.7 *The protection of fundamental rights in cross-border cooperation*

Almost all of the mutual recognition instruments lack an express ground to refuse recognition in case of an alleged (risk of) violation of fundamental rights.[160] Explicit human rights exceptions have largely been considered superfluous. The binding effect of the Charter and the role of the ECHR are enshrined in Article 6 TEU; moreover, all Member States are a party to human rights treaties, such as the ECHR.[161] Mere reference to those rights in the preambles has therefore been regarded as sufficient.[162] But the fact remains that in the cross-border context the exact scope of the Member States' responsibilities is still open to debate. The main question is whether and to what extent the executing Member State can be held liable for human rights violations in the issuing Member State.

The issue of human rights protection in cross-border cooperation in criminal affairs has been especially pronounced in the context of extradition and surrender. ECtHR case-law provides basic principles in this regard. The ECtHR is evidently not blind to the growing importance of international cooperation; thus, a basic level of mutual trust is considered reasonable and necessary.[163] However, in cases of flagrant denial of justice, the assumption of trust must be rebuttable,

---

157. O.J. 2009, L 81/24.
158. The criteria for non-recognition of foreign decisions in relations to decisions *in absentia* also apply to European arrest warrants issued for the purpose of execution of a sanction imposed in the issuing Member State, cited *supra* note 144.
159. O.J. 2008, L 220/32.
160. The only exception is Art. 11(1)(f) of Directive 2014/41/EU, O.J. 2014, L 130/1 on the European Investigation Order.
161. See Ch. 4, "Fundamental rights", of this book.
162. See e.g. recitals 12–13 in the preamble to Framework Decision 2002/584/JHA, O.J. 2002, L 190/2.
163. ECtHR, *Drozd and Janousek v. France and Spain*, Appl. No 12747/87, judgment of 26 June 1992, para 110.

and extradition or surrender refused.[164] In this context, the prohibition of torture and the right to a fair trial are the most likely rights to be at stake. It is settled ECtHR case-law that extradition or surrender must be refused where there are substantial grounds for believing that there is a real risk of inhuman or degrading treatment or punishment in the issuing state.[165] Moreover, Article 6 ECHR bars extradition or surrender if a suspect has suffered a flagrant denial of his right to a fair trial in the issuing state, or runs the risk of being denied one when he returns.[166] Issues may also arise under Articles 2 (right to life),[167] 5 (right to liberty),[168] and 8 (right to family and private life).[169] Outside the prohibition of torture, however, even higher standards apply for successful reliance on fundamental rights as a bar to extradition or surrender.[170] With regard to the right to a fair trial, the question is whether the issuing state provides an effective remedy; in the relationships with other state parties to the ECHR – including all EU Member States – such an effective remedy is generally considered to be available.[171]

It has been argued that the EU provides a "perfect platform" to develop a minimum level of protection of fundamental rights exceeding the minimum level required by the ECHR.[172] This may seem at odds with the aim of establishing simplified and efficient cooperation mechanisms based on the principles of mutual recognition and mutual trust.

The particularly sensitive relationship between mutual recognition and fundamental rights has been repeatedly recognized, predominantly in the context of surrender. The ECJ has affirmed that the execution of European arrest warrants may only be refused on the grounds listed in the underlying framework decision.[173] Adding other refusal grounds would "inevitably lead to the failure of the very system of surrender" and is therefore not easily accepted by the ECJ.[174] Following ECtHR case-law, claimed breaches of fundamental rights must in principle be brought before the courts of the issuing Member State. Recently, however, the ECJ has drawn a line in matters of inhumane prison conditions. In *Aranyosi and Căldăraru*, the question was whether the inadequate prison conditions in Hungary and Romania provide a ground to refuse the execution of the European arrest warrants, or to make this subject to the condition that the issuing Member States provide sufficient information to conclude that prison conditions are compatible with fundamental rights. The ECJ underlined the absolute character of Article 4

164. Idem; see also ECtHR, *Soering v. United Kingdom*, Appl. No. 14038/88, judgment of 7 July 1989, para 91.
165. ECtHR, *Soering v. United Kingdom*, Appl. No. 14038/88, judgment of 7 July 1989, para 91. That the *Soering* doctrine also applies in the context of surrender between EU Member States follows from ECtHR, *Robert Stapleton v. Ireland*, Appl. No. 56588/07, admissibility decision of 4 May 2010.
166. ECtHR, *Soering v. United Kingdom*, Appl. No. 14038/88, judgment of 7 July 1989, para 113. See also ECtHR, *Drozd and Janousek v. France and Spain*, Appl. No 12747/87, judgment of 26 June 1992, para 110; and ECtHR, *Mamatkulor and Askarov v. Turkey*, Appl. Nos. 46827/99 and 46951/99, judgment of 4 Feb. 2005.
167. Art. 2 ECHR only bars extradition where the extraditing state "knowingly puts the person concerned at such high risk of losing his life as for the outcome to be a near-certainty", see ECtHR, *Launder v. United Kingdom*, Appl. No. 27279/95, admissibility decision of 8 Dec. 1997.
168. ECtHR, *Drozd and Janousek v. France and Spain*, Appl. No 12747/87, judgment of 26 June 1992, para 110.
169. ECtHR, *Launder v. United Kingdom*, Appl. No. 27279/95, admissibility decision of 8 Dec. 1997; ECtHR, *King v. United Kingdom*, Appl. No. 9742/07, admissibility decision of 26 Jan. 2010, para 29.
170. This appears from the decisions referred to in footnotes 172–175.
171. See e.g. ECtHR *Einhorn v. France*, Appl. No. 71555/01, admissibility decision of 16 Oct. 2011; ECtHR, *Cenaj v. Greece and Albania*, Appl. No. 12049/06, admissibility decision of 4 Oct. 2007; ECtHR, *Robert Stapleton v. Ireland*, Appl. No. 56588/07, admissibility decision of 4 May 2010.
172. H. Battjes, E. Brouwer, P. de Morree and J. Ouwerkerk, *The Principle of Mutual Trust in European Asylum, Migration and Criminal Law. Reconciling Trust and Fundamental Rights* (Forum, 2011), at 51.
173. Case C-396/11, *Radu*, para 36; Case C-261/09, *Mantello*, paras. 36–37; C-388/08 PPU, *Leymann and Pustovarov*, para 51; Case C-237/15 PPU, *Minister for Justice and Equality v. Francis Lanigan*, para 40.
174. Case C-396/11, *Radu*, para 40.

of the Charter. It reaffirmed the executing state's responsibility to assess whether there are substantial grounds for believing that there is a real risk that the sought person will be subjected to inhumane or degrading treatment.[175] The executing Member State must ask the issuing Member State to provide the necessary information on the prison conditions.[176] If, in the light of this information or any other information, the executing Member State finds a real risk of inhuman or degrading treatment, it must suspend (not refuse) the execution of the European arrest warrant, until on the basis of additional information such a risk can be excluded. A refusal to execute the European arrest warrant is only allowed if that risk cannot be discounted within a reasonable period of time.[177]

The imperative character of the mutual recognition principle has been held to limit Member States' possibilities to surpass within their national legal orders the minimum level of protection required by the Charter and the ECHR. In cases of cross-border cooperation in criminal matters, higher national standards of procedural safeguards are only allowed insofar they do not compromise the principles of mutual recognition and mutual trust; in *Melloni* the ECJ held that surrender could not be made conditional on the right to have an *in absentia* conviction reviewed in the issuing Member State.[178]

5. European agencies and bodies for criminal justice cooperation

5.1 *Europol*

Europol (the European Police Office) is an EU agency, dedicated to criminal law enforcement. It is set up by Regulation 2016/794/EU, adopted on the basis of Article 88 TFEU.[179] Its main operational activities regard assisting national police authorities in collaborating in investigations in concrete cases and the more abstract collection of information and intelligence (Art. 4, Europol Regulation). Europol can also assist and participate in Joint Investigation Teams, and can request a certain Member State to start an investigation in a specific case (Arts. 5–6). Europol does not have executive powers which could enable it to actively use investigative measures. Its activities relating to collecting and processing information and intelligence may be carried out for crimes falling within the substantive competence of Europol (listed in an annex to the regulation), which covers various forms of serious, organized and transnational crime.[180]

The intelligence information collected by Europol is analysed within an Analysis Work File (AWF).[181] These AWFs cover all sorts of high-impact crime. The information can be shared with participating Member States, for instance through the liaison officers that every Member State has stationed at Europol's headquarters in The Hague (Art. 7).

Europol was originally set up on the basis of the Maastricht Treaty, which gave the Union the competence to act in matters of police cooperation. The Treaty's objective indicated that Europol was one of the means to combat terrorism, unlawful drug trafficking and other serious forms of international crime.[182] The body was first set up provisionally by Ministerial Agree-

175. Joined Cases C-404/14 and C-659/15 PPU, *Aranyosi and Căldăraru*, paras. 85–86, 89.
176. Ibid. paras. 94–95.
177. Ibid. paras. 98, 104.
178. Case C-399/11, *Melloni v. Ministerio Fiscal*, paras. 44–46, 22–64.
179. O.J. 2016, L 135/53 (hereinafter Europol Regulation).
180. Europol Regulation, Annex I.
181. For the legal framework, see Council Decision 2009/936/JHA of 30 Nov. 2009 adopting the implementing rules for Europol analysis work files, O.J. 2009, L 325/14.
182. Art. K.1(9) included a competence for "the organization of a Union-wide system for exchanging information within a European Police Office (Europol)".

ment, as the "Europol Drugs Unit".[183] This Unit was intended to assist national law enforcement agencies in their efforts to combat serious drug-related crime, and afterwards also for combating organized crime and money laundering.[184] Its tasks included information exchange between one or more participating Member States, as well as the preparation of general situation reports on the basis of non-personal information supplied by Member States and other sources.[185] Europol began its activities as a permanent body on 1 January 1999.[186] The convention[187] establishing it made it possible to set up a shared database containing intelligence information accessible to all Member States. Since 1 Jan. 2010, Europol is formally an agency of the European Union.[188]

5.2 *Eurojust*

Eurojust is the Union's agency for prosecutorial cooperation.[189] It comprises a College consisting of national members of the Member States, each of whom has assistants and is grouped in a national desk. Eurojust may assist national criminal law authorities in multiple ways and coordinate their work. It can act as a College, or through one or more of the national members.[190] Its competences include the possibility to ask a particular Member State to start an investigation or a prosecution, take special investigative measures or any other measure justified for investigations or prosecutions.[191] It is also equipped with an on-call coordination centre to assist in urgent matters. In multilateral contexts, Eurojust may ask a number of Member States to coordinate their investigative and prosecutorial efforts, and also to accept that one of them is better placed to start an investigation or a prosecution than the others.[192] It may request Member States to set up a Joint Investigation Team.[193]

Conversely, Eurojust can receive requests from Member States for purposes of coordination and cooperation in cases affecting multiple Member States, and it may assist Europol, and Member States on the basis of Europol's analyses.[194] It can request Member States to convey all information it needs in order to fulfil its task.[195] If some Member States cannot agree on the settlement of a conflict of jurisdiction, Eurojust may be asked to issue a non-binding decision on the settlement.[196] Moreover, where the execution of a European Arrest Warrant is problematic, Eurojust may be consulted in order to facilitate execution.[197]

Eurojust's substantive competence is contained in an annex to the decision and includes all forms of serious and cross-border crime.[198]

---

183. Signed in Copenhagen on 2 June 1993.
184. Enlarged to these fields by Joint Action 95/73/JHA, O.J. 1995, L 62/1.
185. Ministerial Agreement, at 2–3.
186. On the basis of the Convention establishing Europol, based on Art. K.3 TEU; O.J. 1995, C 316/1, entering into force on 1 Oct. 1998.
187. Complemented by three protocols, entering into force in 2007: O.J. 2002, C 358/2; O.J. 2002, C 312/2; O.J. 2004, C 2/3.
188. On that date the Europol Decision (O.J. 2009, L 121/37), entered into force, replacing the Eurojust Convention. The Decision has in 2016 been replaced by the Europol Regulation.
189. Set up by the "Eurojust Decision", O.J. 2002, L 63/1.
190. Eurojust Decision, Art. 5.
191. Eurojust Decision, Art. 6(1)(a)(i); Art. 7(1)(a)(i); Art. 6(1)(a)(vi); Art. 6(1)(a)(vii).
192. Eurojust Decision, Art. 6(1)(a)(iii); Art. 7(1)(a)(iii); Art. 6(1)(a)(ii); Art. 7(1)(a)(ii).
193. Eurojust Decision, Art. 6(1)(a)(iv); Art. 7(1)(a)(iv).
194. Eurojust Decision, Art. 6(1)(c); Art. 7(1)(c); Art. 7(1)(d); Art. 7(1)(f).
195. Eurojust Decision, Art. 6(1)(a)(v); Art. 7(1)(a)(v).
196. Eurojust Decision, Art. 7(2).
197. Eurojust Decision, Art. 7(3); Framework Decision 2002/584/JHA, Art. 16(2); Art. 17(7).
198. Eurojust Decision, Art. 4.

Eurojust was set up following the European Council in Tampere. In the context of discussions on the AFSJ, the establishment of a European cooperation unit for the purpose of assisting the prosecution services of the Member States was considered. A provisional unit "Pro-Eurojust" was set up, later made into the permanent body "Eurojust".[199] Eurojust has its own president, who is chosen by co-optation. There is an independent Joint Supervisory Body performing oversight tasks. At the moment of writing, negotiations are being held on a proposed regulation, replacing the current legal framework.[200]

5.3 *The European Judicial Network*

The European Judicial Network (EJN)[201] is a network of contact points, being officials in the criminal law authorities of the Member States.[202] Within the network, the national contact points facilitate the actual cooperation between the contact points and between the judicial authorities in the Member States by ensuring that the most appropriate authorities can establish direct contact with each other in order to effectively carrying out their tasks. Additionally, the national contact points provide other contact points and national authorities with legal and practical information relating to their national criminal justice system and to international criminal law cooperation mechanisms. The national contact points also have a task in promoting judicial training activities, if appropriate in cooperation with the European Judicial Training Network.[203] The European Judicial Network has its secretariat located at the offices of Eurojust in The Hague.

5.4 *OLAF*

OLAF is part of the European Commission, and carries out administrative investigations into cases of fraud and corruption affecting the EU's financial interests. Its activities can lead to follow-up investigations by national criminal law authorities. See further Chapter 9 of this manual.

5.5 *The future European Public Prosecutor's Office*

In 2013, the Commission presented a proposal for a Regulation establishing a European Public Prosecutor's Office ("EPPO") in order to fight fraud and corruption damaging the EU's financial interests. The Council adopted the Regulation in 2017.[204] The Regulation is based on Article 86 TFEU. Since it was impossible to reach unanimity in the Council, the Regulation has been adopted by enhanced cooperation.

Already in the 1990s, the fight against fraud and corruption led the Commission to invite academics to come forward with ideas for legislative measures or other solutions. This resulted in the Corpus Juris project, which included the idea of a European Prosecutor.[205] The Commission published a Green Paper[206] and a follow-up report,[207] after unsuccessfully trying to include

---

199. O.J. 2002, L 63/1.
200. See COM(2013)535. The framework is comprised of the Eurojust Decision, amended by Council Decision 2003/659/JHA, O.J. 2003, L 245/44 and Council Decision 2009/426/JHA, O.J. 2009, L 138/14.
201. Created in 1998 by Joint Action 98/428/JHA, O.J. 1998, L 191/4, which was replaced by Council Decision 2008/976/JHA, O.J. 2008, L 348/130.
202. Council Decision 2008/976/JHA, Art. 2.
203. Council Decision 2008/976/JHA, Art. 4.
204. O.J. 2017, L 283/1.
205. M. Delmas-Marty, *Corpus juris: portant dispositions pénales pour la protection des intérêts financiers de l'Union européenne* (Economica, 1997).
206. COM(2001)175.
207. COM(2003)128.

a legal basis for the European Prosecutor in the Nice Treaty.[208] Since the Lisbon Treaty, Article 86 TFEU provides a legal basis.[209]

The Office is intended to overcome problems in connecting OLAF's administrative investigations with national prosecutorial follow-ups.[210] The substantive competence of the EPPO will primarily be restricted to fighting offences damaging the Union's financial interests, but may be extended by the European Council to include other forms of serious crime with a cross-border dimension.[211] In the Regulation, the substantive competence is closely linked to the Directive on the fight against fraud to the Union's financial interests by means of criminal law, but also includes ancillary offences.[212]

The structure of the Office comprises a central office that takes policy decisions and in some cases case-specific decisions, and a level of Delegated European Public Prosecutors, leading the investigations and the prosecutions which take place in the national criminal courts. These delegated prosecutors are national prosecutors specifically given the additional task of performing the duties of a European prosecutor. In cases of conflict, they are to give priority to their European mandate.[213]

Procedural measures that are foreseen to be at the Office's disposal are only to a very limited extent laid down in the proposed regulation. For the majority of investigative measures, the Office should rely on national rules. This complicates judicial review of the lawfulness of investigations and, in connection, raises questions on the admissibility of evidence.[214] Other concerns surround the choice of forum to be made by the Office after completing a criminal investigation in a case for which multiple Member States may have jurisdiction. While some criteria may have been elaborated that apply to choice of forum decisions, a review of such a decision before the national court that has been chosen will probably not amount to an effective remedy. Alternatively, the ECJ could be entrusted with the review of decisions on forum choice decisions. This raises the question whether other issues should as well be subjected to judicial review before the ECJ.[215]

Further reading

Asp, P., *The Substantive Criminal Law Competence of the EU* (Jure, 2012).

Asp, P., *The Procedural Criminal Law Cooperation of the EU* (Jure, 2016).

Brière, C. and A. Weyembergh, *The Needed Balances in EU Criminal Law. Past, Present and Future* (Hart, 2017).

Hecker, B., *Europäisches Strafrecht* (Springer, 2015).

Janssens, C., *The Principle of Mutual Recognition in EU Law* (OUP, 2013).

Klip, A., *European Criminal Law. An Integrative Approach*, 3rd ed. (Intersentia, 2016).

Miettinen, S., *Criminal Law and Policy in the European Union* (Routledge, 2013).

Mitsilegas, V., M. Bergström and Theodore Konstadinides (Eds.), *Research Handbook on EU Criminal Law* (Edward Elgar Publishing, 2016).

Mitsilegas, V., *EU Criminal Law after Lisbon: Rights, Trust and the Transformation of Justice in Europe* (Hart, 2016).

---

208. COM(2000)608.
209. The Constitution for Europe also contained a legal basis: Art. III-274.
210. SWD(2013)274, at 15–17.
211. Art. 86(1) TFEU; Art. 86(4) TFEU.
212. O.J. 2017, L 198/29, O.J. 2017, L 283/1, Art. 22.
213. O.J. 2017, L 283/1, Art. 13(3).
214. See O.J. 2017, L 283/1, Arts. 30, 31, 37, 42.
215. See Council document 13732/15.

Ouwerkerk, J., *Quid Pro Quo? A Comparative Law Perspective on the Mutual Recognition of Judicial Decisions in Criminal Matters* (Intersentia, 2011).
Satzger, H., *International and European Criminal Law* (C.H. Beck/Hart/Nomos, 2012).
Sieber, U., H. Satzger and B. von Heintschel-Heinegg, *Europäisches Strafrecht* (Nomos, 2014).

CHAPTER 20
COMPETITION LAW AND POLICY

*Christof R.A. Swaak and Marc van der Woude**

1. General part: A system of undistorted competition[1]

1.1 The place of competition rules in the Treaty

The cornerstone of the European Union is its internal market. It is the basis of the Union's prosperity. In order to make this market work, the authors of the Treaty considered that prohibitions on public obstacles to trade, such as customs duties and quantitative restrictions, would not suffice. The laws of supply and demand needed to be protected from other types of intervention that could distort competition to ensure that the internal market would work as a market. This additional protection can be found in Title VII of Part III of the Treaty on the Functioning of the European Union ("TFEU"), and it deals with common rules on competition (Chapter 1), discriminatory indirect taxation (Chapter 2) and differences in regulatory standards that distort competitive conditions in the internal market (Chapter 3).

Chapter 1 distinguishes between two sorts of competition rules. Articles 101 to 106 TFEU are the first set of rules and primarily deal with the market conduct of firms, called "undertakings" in the Treaty's terminology. The second set of rules, which are discussed in Chapter 21 of this book, concerns State intervention in the form of aid to certain undertakings or productions. It is not always easy to draw a distinction between the two sets of rules, especially where States intervene in the economic process themselves, either through public undertakings and/or by granting undertakings exclusive or special rights. This grey area of direct intervention is covered by Article 106 TFEU, which is the subject of Chapter 22 of this volume.

The section of the chapter in the Treaty that deals with competition rules that apply to undertakings is relatively short. It contains, aside from Article 106 already referred to above, two substantive norms; Article 101 TFEU dealing with collusion between undertakings and Article 102 TFEU concerning the market conduct of dominant undertakings. The other three provisions are procedural in nature. Articles 104 and 105 TFEU are mainly of historical interest. They explain how Articles 101 and 102 TFEU were to be applied before the implementing legislation foreseen by Article 103 TFEU entered into force. The main regulation adopted on that legal basis

---

* Christof R.A. Swaak is a partner in the Practice Group Competition & Regulation at Stibbe, Amsterdam & Brussels. Marc van der Woude is a judge at the General Court of the European Union and a professor of Competition Law at the Erasmus School of Law of the Erasmus University in Rotterdam. The authors want to thank Maria Cabrera for her valuable contribution to this chapter.

1. For further reading, reference is made to G. Bellamy and G. Child, *European Law of Competition*, 7th ed. (OUP, 2013); D. Chalmers, D. Davies and G. Monti, *European Union Law*, 3rd ed. (CUP, 2014); P. Craig and G. de Búrca, *EU Law: Text, Cases and Materials*, 6th ed. (OUP, 2015); and A. Jones and B. Sufrin, *EU Competition Law: Text, Cases, and Materials*, 6th ed. (OUP, 2016).

is Regulation 1/2003,[2] which can be seen as the main portal for the application of Articles 101 and 102 TFEU by the European Commission, national competition authorities ("NCAs") and courts. This Regulation is of general application and covers all sectors of the economy. It should be noted, however, that according to Article 42 TFEU, special rules can apply for agriculture and fisheries.[3]

Unlike the former ECSC Treaty, the EU treaties do not contain rules on concentrations between undertakings. In the early days of the European Economic Community, concentrations were not perceived as incompatible with the common market. Larger firms were thought to be better equipped to meet the challenges of this integrated and expanded market.[4] This approach changed during the seventies and eighties. Finally, in 1989, the legislator adopted rules on the control of concentrations. These rules are now laid down in Regulation 139/2004,[5] which was adopted on the basis of Article 103 TFEU (former Art. 83 EC) and Article 352 TFEU (former Art. 308 EC), because Articles 101 and 102 TFEU are not sufficiently able to control all operations that may prove to be incompatible with the system of undistorted competition envisaged in the Treaty.

Finally, the system of EU competition law has served as a model for many national competition law regimes – in Europe and beyond. In fact, the system set up by Articles 101 and 102 TFEU and the Regulation on concentration control have been followed by nearly all Member States in an unprecedented wave of spontaneous harmonization.[6] In many Member States, legislators have expressed the view that the concepts upon which their national competition rules rely should be interpreted in the same manner as those used at the EU level. In such circumstances, the Court of Justice even agreed to interpret concepts of national law at the request of national courts under the preliminary reference procedure of Article 267 TFEU, if this was needed to ensure their uniform application.[7]

1.2 *The actors involved*

The present system of EU competition rules includes a wide variety of actors who interact with their counterparts at the national and international level in order to promote the proper functioning of markets within, but also beyond their jurisdiction.

The first group of actors can be found at the EU level. In this sphere, the European Commission ("the Commission") has the main role. Both in the provisional system of Article 105 TFEU and under Regulations 1/2003 and 139/2004, the Commission is entrusted with the practical application of competition rules. It prosecutes infringements and can impose injunctions and fines, albeit that its decisions can be challenged before EU courts pursuant to Article 263 TFEU.

2. Council Reg. (EC) 1/2003 of 16 Dec. 2002 on the implementation of the rules on competition laid down in Arts. 81 and 82 of the Treaty, O.J. 2003, L 1/1.
3. See Reg. (EU) 1379/2013 of the European Parliament and the Council of 11 Dec. 2013 on the common organization of the markets in fishery and aquaculture products, amending Council Reg.s (EC) 1184/2006 and (EC) 1224/2009 and repealing Council Reg. (EC) 104/2000, O.J. 2013, L 354/1.
4. Memorandum on the Problem of Concentration in the Common Market, Competition Series, Study No. 3, Brussels 1966.
5. Council Reg. (EC) 139/2004 of 20 Jan. 2004 on the control of concentrations between undertakings, O.J. 2004, L 24/1.
6. M. Danov, F. Becker, and P. Beaumont (Eds.), *Cross-Border EU Competition Law Actions* (Hart, 2013) and K. Cseres, *Questions of Legitimacy in the Europeanization of Competition Law Procedures of the EU Member States* (ACELG, 2013).
7. See Case C-8/08, *T-Mobile Netherlands BV, KPN Mobile NV, Orange Nederland NV and Vodafone Libertel NV v. Raad van bestuur van de Nederlandse Mededingingsautoriteit*, para 6.

The Commission is thus in charge of defining the competition policy of the Union.[8] In addition, the Commission has the power to propose new legislation to the Union legislator which, in the field of competition law, is usually the Council. Article 103 TFEU indeed limits the Parliament's right to be consulted. However, in other areas such as concentration control, the field of damages, or actions for competition law infringements, the Council and Parliament act as co-legislators.[9] Also, the Commission is politically accountable to the European Parliament, which it reports to on an annual basis.

The second group is composed of actors from the national sphere. These include national competition authorities and national courts that are competent to apply both national and European competition rules. In this respect, Article 1 of Regulation 1/2003 provides that Articles 101 and 102 TFEU are directly applicable in full. In quantitative terms, the enforcement activities of the NCAs have overtaken those of the Commission. The application of competition rules by national courts, which has been significant from the very beginning of the European integration process, is expected to increase even further after the implementation of Directive 2014/14/EU on private damages actions.[10] In this context, reference should also be made to the role of arbitration. Pursuant to the ruling of the ECJ in *Eco Swiss*, arbiters must, as a rule, take account of European competition rules.[11] By contrast, NCAs and national courts are not competent to assess concentrations which fall within the ambit of Regulation 139/2004. This Regulation provides, with certain exceptions, for one-stop shop approval of such concentrations by the Commission.

The third category of actors concerns the international arena. Reference should be made first to the EEA agreement, whose Articles 53 and 54 mirror Articles 101 and 102 TFEU, and which contains detailed rules governing cooperation between the EFTA-Surveillance Authority and the Commission. The decisions of that Authority are subject to appeal before the EFTA Court which, together with the ECJ, ensures uniform interpretation of the EEA Agreement and the Union Treaties (see Chapter 41). Second, all Member States of the EU adhere to the European Convention of Human Rights (see Chapter 1). Although the Union itself is not yet a member, the Convention's provisions are held in high regard as fundamental principles relevant to the application of national and EU competition rules. This holds true especially with regard to due process rules.[12] Third, the EU has concluded a series of bilateral cooperation agreements in the field of competition law. Some of these agreements – in particular those concluded with economically strategic countries such as Canada, Japan, South-Korea and the US – lay down detailed cooperation procedures which, *inter alia*, facilitate the exchange of information between enforcement authorities. Fourth, the Union participates in international cooperation agreements, sometimes formally in the context of the OECD Treaty and sometimes more informally in the context of the International Competition Network, which unites the world's competition authorities.[13]

---

8. Joined Cases 100-103/80, *SA Musique Diffusion française and Others v. Commission*, para 105.
9. Directive 2014/104/EU of 26 Nov. 2014 on certain rules governing actions for damages under national law for infringements of the competition law provisions of the Member States and of the European Union, O.J. 2014, L 349/1.
10. Directive 2014/104, ibid.
11. Case C-126/97, *Eco Swiss China Time Ltd v. Benetton International NV.*
12. E.g. ECtHR, *Société Colas Est and Others v. France*, Appl. 37971/97, judgment of 16 Apr. 2002 and ECtHR, *A. Menarini Diagnostics S.R.L. v. Italy*, Appl. 43509/08, judgment of 27 Sept. 2011.
13. For instance, the European Union and the US reached a Cooperation Agreement which provides for regular bilateral meetings to share information on enforcement activities and priorities. Available at <ec.europa.eu/competition/international/bilateral/usa.html>.

1.3 *The sources of law*

Although the Treaty chapter on competition rules for undertakings is relatively short, EU competition law has expanded recently to cover a fairly wide area. In the hierarchy of norms, reference has already been made to the two basic regulations – Regulation 1/2003 on the application of Articles 101 and 102 TFEU and Regulation 139/2004 on EU concentration control. Both Regulations authorize the Commission to adopt implementing regulations specifying certain procedural questions.[14] The Council has also enacted other basic regulations that empower the Commission to adopt its own regulations with respect to the application of the exception of Article 101(3) TFEU to certain categories of agreement.[15] These so-called block exemption Regulations mean that agreements falling within their scope are considered to be exempt from the prohibition laid down by Article 101(1) TFEU. Conversely, the fact that an agreement is not covered by such a block exemption does not mean that the prohibition necessarily applies.[16] The latest generation of block exemptions functions on the basis of market share thresholds; agreements below a certain market share are deemed to benefit from the exception, unless they contain hard-core restrictions such as price-fixing, export bans, or market and customer sharing.

Apart from the Council's basic regulations and the Commission's implementing regulations or block exemptions, EU competition law can be found in the so-called notices, communications or guidelines by which the Commission tries to clarify the state of the law and/or explain its policy. These explanatory documents are not legally binding on national and Union courts. They do however bind the Commission; by issuing such documents the Commission has given rise to legitimate expectations. In the field of Articles 101 and 102 TFEU, the Commission has published numerous notices on a wide range of issues, such as on the clarification of legal concepts (e.g. the Notice on agreements of minor importance),[17] the methodology of calculating fines (e.g. the fining guidelines),[18] the incentives it is prepared to offer to undertakings that are willing to denounce restrictive practices (the leniency Notice),[19] the priorities it will set in its enforcement policy (guidance on enforcement priorities in applying Article 102 TFEU to exclusionary conduct by dominant undertakings),[20] as well as sector specific questions, such as the application of competition rules in the postal sector.[21] The advantage of issuing such Notices, which often explain or codify the Commission's decisional practice and/or the case law of the Union courts, is that they give easy and didactic access to complex legal and factual questions.

14. E.g. Commission implementing Reg. (EU) 1269/2013 of 5 Dec. 2013 amending Reg. (EC) 802/2004, implementing Council Reg. (EC) 139/2004 on the control of concentrations between undertakings, O.J. 2013, L 336/1.
15. Council Reg. (EEC) 2821/71 of 20 Dec. 1971 on application of Art. 85(3) of the Treaty to categories of agreements, decisions and concerted practices, O.J. 1971, L 285/46 and Council Reg. (EEC) 19/65 of 2 Mar. 1965 on application of Art. 85(3) of the Treaty to certain categories of agreements and concerted practices, O.J. 1965, L 533/65.
16. Case C-41/96, *VAG-Händlerbeirat eV v. SYD-Consult*, para 16.
17. Commission Notice on agreements of minor importance which do not appreciably restrict competition under Art. 101(1) of the Treaty on the Functioning of the European Union (De *Minimis* Notice), O.J. 2014, C 291/1.
18. Guidelines on the method of setting fines imposed pursuant to Art. 23(2)(a) of Reg. 1/2003, O.J. 2006, C 210/02.
19. Commission Notice on Immunity from fines and reduction of fines in cartel cases, O.J. 2006, C 298/17 ("Leniency Notice").
20. Guidance on the Commission's enforcement priorities in applying Art. 82 of the EC Treaty to abusive exclusionary conduct by dominant undertakings, O.J. 2009, C 45/7.
21. Commission Notice on the application of the competition rules to the postal sector and on the assessment of certain State measures relating to postal services, O.J. 1998, C 39/2.

The same holds true for the notices published in the field of concentration control. For example, the two Notices on horizontal and non-horizontal concentrations give valuable insight into the Commission's past and future enforcement practices.[22] Last but not least, reference should be made to one specific notice – the Notice on the definition of the relevant market, which will be explained in further detail in section 1.5 below.[23] These Notices are important to all areas of EU competition law because they each concern the proper functioning of markets.

Similarly, the Commission's decisional practice and the case law of the Union courts are important sources of EU competition law. The same holds true – to a lesser extent – for the practice of NCAs, national courts, the EFTA surveillance authority and the EFTA court. Ultimately, however, the case law of the ECJ has the most clout. After all, it is the Court of Justice that has final say on the interpretation of EU (competition) law.

Finally, access to and hence the understanding of EU competition law has been greatly facilitated by the Commission's competition website. It provides easy access to all sources of EU and national competition law in a pragmatic and well-structured manner.[24]

1.4 *The objectives and effectiveness of the competition rules*

Before the Treaty of Lisbon came into force, the objectives of the competition rules could be found in Article 3(g) EC, which listed the various types of actions of the European Community. This provision referred to the fact that the internal market included a system of undistorted competition. Under the new Treaty structure there is no such list, although Title II of Part I TFEU lays down a few principles of general application. The objective of ensuring a system of undistorted competition in the internal market is not included in that title, but it is explicitly mentioned in Protocol 27 on the internal market and competition. The fact that the competition objective has been transferred – from the list of primary objectives to a protocol attached to the TFEU – does not affect its importance. Indeed, in case *C-496/09* dealing with recovery of State aid, the Court explicitly underlined the "vital nature" of the competition rules, which are "the expression of one of the essential tasks with which the European Union is entrusted".[25]

This means that the case law of the ECJ on the interaction between the objective of undistorted competition and the duty of Member States and the Union to cooperate within the meaning of Article 4(3) TEU, is still relevant. That case law confers a quasi-constitutional dimension on competition rules; it prohibits Member States from introducing or maintaining regulatory or legislative measures which may render the competition rules ineffective. This implies that Articles 101 TFEU or 102 TFEU, read in conjunction with Article 4(3) TEU, are infringed when a Member State requires or encourages conduct contrary to Article 101 TFEU or reinforces its effects, or when it divests its own rules of the character of legislation by delegating, to private economic operators, responsibility for taking decisions affecting the economic sphere, or requires or encourages the abuse of a dominant position.[26] Against this backdrop, it

---

22. Guidelines on the assessment of horizontal mergers under the Council Reg. on the control of concentrations between undertakings, O.J. 2004, C 31/5 ("Horizontal Merger Guidelines") and Guidelines on the assessment of non-horizontal mergers under the Council Reg. on the control of concentrations between undertakings, O.J. 2008, C 265/6 ("Non-horizontal Merger Guidelines").
23. Commission Notice on the definition of the relevant market for the purposes of Community competition law, O.J. 1997, C 372/5.
24. Available at <ec.europa.eu/competition/index_en.html>.
25. Case C-496/09, *Commission v. Italy*, para 60 and see also Case C-52/09, *Konkurrensverket v. TeliaSonera Sverige AB*, paras. 20 and 21.
26. Case C-327/12, *Ministero dello Sviluppo economico and Autorità per la vigilanza sui contratti pubblici di lavori, servizi e forniture v. SOA Nazionale Costruttori – Organismo di Attestazione SpA*, paras. 37 and 38.

should also be remembered that the Treaty's competition rules benefit from the principle of the primacy of European law and that in conflicts with national competition rules, European rules take precedence.[27]

The principle of effectiveness of the competition rules not only affects the way in which Member States apply national substantive law, but also impacts their procedural autonomy. The ECJ held, for example, that the effectiveness of the Commission's fining decisions and, hence, the coherent application of the competition rules would be significantly reduced if Member States were to allow companies to deduct the amount of those fines from their taxable profits.[28] Similarly, Member States may not enact procedural rules, such as limitation periods, which would make it practically impossible to exercise the right to seek compensation for the harm caused by a restrictive practice prohibited by Article 101(1) TFEU.[29]

As in other areas of European Union law, the Court follows a teleological interpretation method. The competition rules are interpreted in a manner that allows them to reach the objective of undistorted competition. This generally implies that the concepts underlying the competition rules are interpreted broadly. The evolution of the rules on concentration control offers a typical example of this approach. Even though the EEC Treaty itself did not contain provisions on concentration control, the Court considered that a system of undistorted competition implied that competition should not be eliminated and that Article 102 TFEU could apply to certain mergers.[30] Similarly, once the Commission had the power to control concentrations, the EU courts gave a broad interpretation of the dominance test allowing the Commission to examine concentrations that could lead to collective dominance.[31]

Despite their manifest importance, the objectives of the competition rules are not unambiguous. It is hard to define precisely what a system of undistorted competition might entail. Its interpretation evolves over time and is influenced by academic theories and socioeconomic developments. In the early years, the orientation of competition policy is said to have been influenced by German ordo-liberalism – which attaches normative importance to the value of competition as a process.[32] Gradually, this school of thought fell prey to the criticism of academics who insisted on the importance of consumer welfare as the main objective of EU competition policy.[33] It is submitted that the concept of "undistorted competition" is sufficiently broad as to include a plurality of objectives. These cannot be restricted to consumer welfare standards, as the Court recalled in *GlaxoSmithKline*: "Like other competition rules laid down in the Treaty, Article 81 EC aims to protect not only the interests of competitors or of consumers, but also the structure of the market and, in so doing, competition as such. Consequently, for a finding that an agreement has an anti-competitive object, it is not necessary that final consumers be deprived of the advantages of effective competition in terms of supply or price."[34] This does not mean that the Court rejects the idea that consumer welfare can play a role in defining the objectives of

27. Case C-14/68, *Walt Wilhelm and Others v. Bundeskartellamt*, para 6.
28. Case C-429/07, *Inspecteur van de Belastingdienst v. X BV*.
29. Joined Cases C-295-298/04, *Vincenzo Manfredi v. Lloyd Adriatico Assicurazioni SpA Antonio Cannito v. Fondiaria Sai SpA and Nicolò Tricarico and Pasqualina Murgolo v. Assitalia SpA*.
30. Case C-6/72, *Europemballage Corporation and Continental Can Company Inc. v. Commission*, para 25.
31. Case T-102/96, *Gencor Ltd v. Commission*.
32. S. Dullien and U. Guérot, *The Long Shadow of Ordoliberalism: Germany's Approach to the Euro Crisis* (Paper ECFR/49, European Council of Foreign Relations, 2012); and D. Gerber, *Constitutionalizing the Economy: German Neo-liberalism, Competition Law and the "New" Europe*, 42 AJCL (1994).
33. See in particular, D. Gerber, *Law and Competition in Twentieth Century Europe: Protecting Prometheus* (OUP, 1998). More recently, D. Zimmer (Ed.), *The Goals of Competition Law* (Edward Elgar, 2012).
34. Joined Cases C-501, 513, 515 & 519/06 P, *GlaxoSmithKline Services Unlimited v. Commission*, para 63.

competition rules. Market conduct that harms consumer welfare is indeed likely to give rise to competition concerns, as follows from the Court's ruling in *Post Danmark*.[35] However, conduct that does not harm consumers directly is not necessarily exempt from the scope of the competition rules, especially where that conduct seeks to partition the internal market.[36]

The open-ended nature of the objectives pursued by the competition rules entails the risk that they might conflict with other Treaty objectives, such as environmental or social policy considerations. The Court's case law on these conflicts is not entirely clear, and it takes various approaches in solving them.[37] In the early years it seemed to consider that other policy considerations could give rise to economic improvement within the meaning of the exception laid down in Article 101(3) TFEU.[38] Another method consists of discarding the application of competition rules altogether, for example by stating that the rules do not apply to collective labour agreements or by declaring that certain activities are not economic in nature.[39] Yet another approach is to declare the competition rules applicable, but to limit their scope thus allowing the other objective to prevail. In the *Wouters* case, for example, the Court considered that a rule of the bar that prevented lawyers from setting up joint practice with accountants did not go beyond what is necessary to ensure proper conduct of the legal profession.[40] Similarly, in *Meca-Medina*, the Court held that competition rules did not prevent anti-doping restrictions in sports competition.[41]

1.5 *Market definition*

EU competition rules do not apply in the abstract. They are about selling goods and services to consumers and, as mentioned above, protecting the competitive system against distortions. This competitive process naturally takes place in markets where supply meets demand. This in turn implies that, in a given case, the market in question – referred to as the relevant market – must be defined. Generally speaking, where the conduct of or between undertakings or concentrations does not significantly affect the laws of supply and demand, it is unlikely that competition concerns will arise. Market impact will depend to a large extent on the actual and potential constraints under which these undertakings operate. As will be discussed below,[42] competition rules rely in many respects on the use of market share as an indicator of market impact; for example, when defining the existence of agreements of minor importance, assessing the impact of agreements on inter-state trade, verifying the applicability of block exemption regulations, or determining the existence of dominant positions.

The correct definition of the relevant market is therefore of utmost importance when applying EU competition rules. In 1997 the Commission published a notice which explains its methodology.[43] This focuses on demand substitutability as the most immediate competitive constraint under which undertakings compete. If customer demand can easily switch to other goods, or suppliers from other areas, these should be included in the definition of the relevant

35. Case C-209/10, *Post Danmark A/S v. Konkurrencerådet*, para 42.
36. Joined Cases 56 & 58/64, *Établissements Consten S.à.R.L. and Grundig-Verkaufs-GmbH v. Commission.*
37. See C. Townley, *Art. 81 EC and Public Policy* (Hart, 2009).
38. Case 26/76, *Metro SB-Großmärkte GmbH & Co. KG v. Commission*, para 21.
39. E.g., Case C-413/13, *FNV Kunsten Informatie en Media v. Staat der Nederlanden* and Case C-205/03 P, *Federación Española de Empresas de Tecnología Sanitaria (FENIN) v. Commission.*
40. Case C-309/99, *J. C. J. Wouters, J. W. Savelbergh and Price Waterhouse Belastingadviseurs BV v. Algemene Raad van de Nederlandse Orde van Advocaten.*
41. Case C-519/04 P, *David Meca-Medina and Igor Majcen v. Commission.*
42. See *infra*, sections 2.7.2 and 3.3.
43. Commission Notice, cited *supra* note 23.

market. Other constraints such as supply-side substitutability and potential competition are considered to be less immediate and are, as a rule, not taken into consideration for the purposes of the market definition. They are usually taken into consideration at a later stage of the competitive analysis.

In order to define the goods that customers see as substitute goods offered by the undertakings being scrutinized, the Notice relies on the so called SSNIP ("Small but Significant and Non-Transitory Increase in Price") test. The idea is to measure how customers react to a hypothetical scenario – involving a small but lasting price increase of approximately 5% – designed to measure the cross-elasticity of demand. This exercise starts by analysing the type of products sold by the undertakings in the relevant market area. Additional products and areas may be included in the market definition depending on whether competition from these other products and areas sufficiently affects or restrains the pricing of the parties' products in the short-term. The exercise stops when customers cease to switch to the latest products or areas included in the test, because there is no substitutability between the products.

The 1997 Notice not only explains the methodology for defining the relevant market, but also gives practical information as to the type and intensity of evidence required. This evidence typically refers to market research and inquiries. The Notice also explains that market shares are usually calculated on the basis of total sales in terms of value and/or volume in the relevant market.[44]

Finally, although undertakings generally have a relatively good idea of the constraints under which they operate and, hence, of the markets in which they compete, the data referred to in the Notice is sometimes unavailable. In addition, it is not always obvious that such data can be adequately produced or used in national court proceedings. It is submitted that in such cases, parties can refer to (recent) decisions of the Commission and NCAs dealing with the same goods and services as those sold by the undertakings involved. The Commission's website, referred to in Section 1.3 above, gives relatively easy access to such precedents.

2. Anti-competitive collusion[45]

2.1 *The structure of Article 101 TFEU*

Article 101 TFEU consists of three paragraphs that provide for a prohibition, a sanction, and a possible exemption from the prohibition. Only the conduct (of undertakings) that meets the conditions of the prohibition described in Article 101(1) TFEU will be subject to the automatic sanction of Article 101(2) TFEU, or qualify for the exemption given in Article 101(3) TFEU.

The structure of Article 101 does not follow the example of its US counterpart. Section 1 of the Sherman Act does not have three separate paragraphs; it simply provides for a prohibition that needs to be applied – according to the US Supreme Court – taking into account a rule of reason doctrine by which the pro- and anti-competitive effects of any particular conduct are weighed when assessing the compatibility of such conduct.[46] This does not apply with respect to certain offenses *per se* which have been found to be "manifestly anti-competitive"[47] and are

44. Commission Notice, cited *supra* note 23, section IV Calculation of Market Share.
45. For further reading on Art. 101 TFEU, readers are referred to G. Amato, *Antitrust and the Bounds of Power* (Hart, 1997); O. Odudu, *The Boundaries of EC Competition Law: The Scope of Art. 81* (OUP, 2006); C. Townley, *Art. 81 EC and Public Policy* (Hart, 2009); J. Faull and A. Nikpay, *The EU Law of Competition*, 3rd ed. (OUP, 2014); R. Whish and D. Bailey, *Competition Law*, 8th ed. (OUP, 2015); and C. Harding and J. Joshua, *Regulating Cartels in Europe*, 2nd ed. (OUP, 2010).
46. *Standard Oil of New Jersey v. United States* (1911) 221 U.S. 1.
47. *Bus Elec Corp v. Sharp Elec Corp* (1988) 485 U.S. 717.

conclusively presumed – without elaborate inquiry into their likely competitive effects – to restrain trade unreasonably. The General Court has rejected a rule of reason doctrine under Article 101(1) TFEU and has pointed out that no rule exists according to which it is necessary, in the application of Article 101(1) TFEU, to weigh the pro- and anti-competitive effects of an agreement in order to determine whether it falls within the scope of the prohibition. The weighing of pro- and anti-competitive effects of a restriction of competition law should be considered in the context of Article 101(3) TFEU.[48] Article 101 TFEU is applied in its entirety by the European Commission, NCAs (such as the Dutch Competition Authority "ACM") and national courts.[49]

Article 101(1) TFEU determines that all agreements between undertakings, decisions by associations of undertakings and concerted practices which may affect trade between Member States and which have as their object or effect the prevention, restriction, or distortion of competition, are incompatible with the internal market. It then gives a few examples illustrating prohibited conduct such as price-fixing or other trading conditions, and the sharing of markets or sources of supply.

The text of Article 101(1) TFEU *explicitly* indicates that the prohibition: (i) is addressed to (associations of) undertakings; (ii) regards collusive conduct such as an agreement between undertakings, a decision by an association of undertakings or a concerted practice; (iii) which has as its object or effect the prevention, restriction or distortion of competition within the internal market; and (iv) may affect trade between Member States. For the prohibition to apply, an additional *implicit* condition has to be met, namely that it concerns an appreciable restriction of competition and an appreciable effect on trade between Member States. This implicit condition shows that the scope of the prohibition of Article 101(1) TFEU does not cover conduct which has an insignificant effect on competition.

An agreement that falls within the scope of the prohibition and does not meet the conditions of the exemption set out in Article 101(3) TFEU, is covered by the sanction in Article 101(2) TFEU and is therefore automatically null and void. If the provision in the agreement that violates Article 101(1) TFEU is severable, the rest of the agreement stands. If not, the whole agreement is to be considered null and void.[50] The practical result of such automatic nullity is decided by national courts under their national law within the relevant EU Member State.[51] The "absolute" nature of the sanction of Article 101(2) TFEU limits the national court's margin of discretion. For instance, the Dutch Supreme Court was very clear when it recognized the absolute character of the nullity sanction of Article 6(2) of the Dutch Competition Act (the Dutch equivalent of Article 101(2) TFEU) with the result that conversion of the contractual clause which violates competition law into a less restrictive clause in order to comply with such law, is not allowed.[52] It is submitted that Dutch courts will proceed in the same way as regards the nullity sanction of Article 101(2) TFEU.

---

48. See Case T-112/99, *Métropole télévision (M6), Suez-Lyonnaise des eaux, France Télécom and Télévision française 1 SA (TF1) v. Commission*, paras. 72–74 and Case T-65/98, *Van den Bergh Foods Ltd v. Commission*, para 106.
49. Pursuant to Art. 5 of Reg. 1/2003, cited *supra* note 2, the procedural powers of these authorities to apply Art. 101 TFEU are not the same. See Case C-375/09, *Prezes Urzędu Ochrony Konkurencji i Konsumentów v. Tele2 Polska sp. z o.o., devenue Netia SA*.
50. Case 56/65, *Société Technique Minière (LTM) v. Maschinenbau Ulm GmbH (MBU)*.
51. Case 319/82, *Société de Vente de Ciments et Bétons de l'Est SA v. Kerpen & Kerpen GmbH und Co. KG*.
52. HR 18 Dec. 2009 LJN BJ9439, NJ 2010, 140 (*Prisma Vastgoed/Slager*). The Dutch Supreme Court held: "3.7.2 Het onderdeel faalt omdat het hof terecht heeft geoordeeld dat toepassing van art. 3:42 BW onverenigbaar is met de op uitbanning van ongeoorloofde concurrentiebeperkende overeenkomsten gerichte, in art. 6 lid 2 Mw neergelegde absolute nietigheid".

In principle, all possible types of conduct that fall within the scope of Article 101(1) TFEU can qualify for the exemption of Article 101(3) TFEU. However, in order for an agreement that falls within the scope of the prohibition to be exempted, it must meet the two positive and two negative conditions of Article 101(3) TFEU. The agreement must: (i) contribute to improving the production or distribution of goods or to promote technical or economic progress; (ii) whilst allowing consumers a fair share of the resulting benefit; and (iii) refrain from imposing restrictions on the undertakings concerned which are not indispensable to the attainment of these objectives; and (iv) refrain from affording such undertakings the possibility of eliminating competition in a substantial part of the products in question.

In an effort to provide guidance on how to interpret and apply Article 101(3) TFEU in general and the aforementioned "positive" and "negative" conditions of Article 101(3) TFEU, the Commission has published a notice entitled "Guidelines on the application of Article 101(3) of the Treaty".[53] The undertakings claiming that an agreement meets the four conditions – and that consequently benefit from the exemption – bear the burden of proof.[54] These undertakings must be able to come up with arguments (and possibly factual evidence) to justify the conclusion that the agreement is sufficiently likely to give rise to pro-competitive effects. In practical terms, this means that undertakings entering into an agreement that potentially falls within the scope of Article 101(1) TFEU will have to carry out a thorough "self-assessment" of the agreement under Article 101(3) TFEU. The purpose of a "self-assessment" is to examine whether the claim that the agreement concerned meets the conditions of Article 101(3) TFEU can be substantiated and is therefore exempted. Such a "self-assessment" can be a complicated exercise, and may entail both a legal and economic analysis. As factual circumstances in a market tend to change, it may be necessary to periodically update the "self-assessment" to make sure that the agreement continues to fall under Article 101(3) TFEU.[55]

For the first positive condition ("efficiency gains") to be fulfilled, one should be able to show objective benefits emanating from the agreement. Efficiencies are not assessed from the subjective point of view of the parties. According to the Commission, the aim of the analysis is to ascertain whether any objective benefits are created by the agreement and what the economic importance is of such efficiencies. One needs to verify the nature of the claimed efficiencies, the link between them and the agreements, the likelihood and magnitude of each claimed efficiency, and how and when each might be achieved.[56]

The second positive condition ("fair share for consumers") implies that the fair share of benefits for the consumer must at least compensate for any actual or likely negative impact caused to consumers by the restriction of competition within the meaning of Article 101(1) TFEU. The net effect of the agreement concerned must at least be neutral for those consumers directly (or likely) affected by the agreement. There is a sliding scale, meaning that the greater the restriction, the greater the efficiencies and the pass-on to consumers must be.[57]

The first negative condition ("indispensability"), namely that the agreement must not impose any restrictions that are not indispensable to the attainment of the positive benefits,

---

53. Commission Guidelines on the application of Art. 81(3) of the Treaty, O.J. 2004, C 101/97 ("Art. 101(3) Guidelines"). It should be noted that the interpretation of Art. 101(3) TFEU proposed in the Guidelines is stricter than the one followed in the Commission's earlier decisional practice. In addition, this stricter interpretation has not yet been validated by the ECJ.
54. Art. 2 of Reg. 1/2003, cited *supra* note 2.
55. The assessment is sensitive to material changes in the facts. See Art. 101(3) Guidelines, cited *supra* note 53, para 44.
56. Art. 101(3) Guidelines, cited *supra* note 53, paras. 48–72.
57. Art. 101(3) Guidelines, cited *supra* note 53, paras. 83–104.

involves a two-fold test. First, it must be established whether the specific restrictive agreement is reasonably necessary in order to achieve the efficiencies. One must be able to show that the efficiencies are specific to the agreement in question; there are no other economically practicable and less restrictive means of achieving these benefits. Second, it must be determined whether the individual competitive restrictions that flow from the agreement are reasonably necessary for achieving the efficiencies. A restriction is considered to be indispensable if its absence would eliminate or significantly reduce any benefits that follow from the agreement, or would make it significantly less likely they will materialize.[58]

The second negative condition – namely that the agreement must not afford the undertakings any opportunity to eliminate competition with respect to a substantial portion of the products concerned ("no elimination of competition") – ensures that, ultimately, protection of the competitive process is given priority over any potentially pro-competitive efficiency gains that might result from restrictive agreements. A determination of whether competition is eliminated depends on the degree of competition that existed prior to the agreement, and on the reduction of competition that results from the agreement. According to the Commission, the second negative condition requires a realistic analysis of the various sources of competition on the market and the level of competitive constraint they impose on the contracting parties, and the impact of the agreement on this competitive restraint. Both actual and potential competition must be considered.[59]

As mentioned above, the Council of the European Union has granted the Commission the authority to put in place so-called block (or group) exemption regulations for certain categories of agreement.[60] Examples include the block exemptions for: (i) vertical agreements;[61] (ii) vertical agreements in the motor vehicle sector;[62] (iii) technology transfer agreements;[63] (iv) specialization agreements;[64] and (v) research and development agreements.[65] The provisions of block exemption regulations are binding and have direct effect in the EU Member States which makes it possible, for instance, to invoke them before national courts. Block exemptions create "safe havens" for agreements that fall within their scope and are presumed to meet the conditions of Article 101(3) TFEU and are therefore exempted from Article 101(1) TFEU. Most block exemptions provide for a list of "hard-core" restrictions that make it impossible for agreements including one or more of those restrictions to benefit from the block exemption concerned.

58. Art. 101(3) Guidelines, cited *supra* note 53, paras. 73–82.
59. Art. 101(3) Guidelines, cited *supra* note 53, paras. 105–116.
60. Art. 103(2)(b) TFEU. See e.g. Reg. 19/65, cited *supra* note 15, amended by Council Reg. (EU) 1215/1999 of 10 June 1999 amending Reg. 19/65/EEC on the application of Art. 85(3) of the Treaty to certain categories of agreements and concerted practices, O.J. 1999, L 148/1 and Reg. 2821/71, cited *supra* note 15.
61. Commission Reg. (EU) 330/2010 of 20 Apr. 2010 on the application of Art. 101(3) of the Treaty on the Functioning of the European Union to categories of vertical agreements and concerted practices, O.J. 2010, L 102/1, and Commission Guidelines on Vertical Restraints, O.J. 2010, C 130/1, ("Guidelines on Vertical Restraints").
62. Commission Reg. (EU) 461/2010 of 27 May 2010 on the application of Art. 101(3) of the Treaty on the Functioning of the European Union to categories of vertical agreements and concerted practices in the motor vehicle sector, O.J. 2010, L 129/52.
63. Commission Reg. (EC) 316/2014 of 21 Mar. 2014 on the application of Art. 101(3) of the Treaty on the Functioning of the European Union to categories of technology transfer agreements, O.J. 2014, L 93/17.
64. Commission Reg. (EU) 1218/2010 of 14 Dec. 2010 on the application of Art. 101(3) of the Treaty on the Functioning of the European Union to certain categories of specialisation agreements, O.J. 2010, L 335/43 ("the Specialisation Block Exemption Reg.").
65. Commission Reg. (EU) 1217/2010 of 14 Dec. 2010 on the application of Art. 101(3) of the Treaty on the Functioning of the European Union to certain categories of research and development agreements, O.J. 2010, L 335/36 ("the R&D Block Exemption Reg.").

Under certain circumstances, the European Commission and NCAs can intervene and decide to remove an agreement from the "safe haven".[66]

The fact that an agreement does not fulfil the conditions of a block exemption does not necessarily mean that it automatically falls within the scope of Article 101(1) TFEU. A separate and individual assessment will have to be made in order to determine whether this is the case. It could very well be the case that the individual agreement falls outside the scope of Article 101(1) TFEU or meets the cumulative conditions of Article 101(3) TFEU, and is therefore exempted.

2.2 *The concept of undertaking*

The prohibition of Article 101(1) TFEU is addressed to undertakings. But what does the concept of undertaking entail? The meaning of undertaking is independent of national law definitions that define what constitutes a company. The case law of the ECJ, has clarified that the concept of undertaking encompasses any entity engaged in economic activity regardless of the legal status of the entity and the way it is financed.[67] The nature of the activity is central to the concept of undertaking, and not the form or nature of the entity or entities engaged in the activity.[68] It is irrelevant whether the entity is a legal or a natural person, or whether or not it is profit-driven.[69] The concept of an undertaking entails designating an economic unit – even if, in legal terms, the economic unit consists of several natural or legal persons.[70]

Given that an entity can simultaneously be engaged in various activities of disparate nature, the entity could conceivably qualify as an undertaking for one activity, but not for another. The economic nature of the activity is crucial in this assessment. The ECJ held that an economic activity is any activity that consists of offering goods or services on a given market.[71] A public authority can also qualify as an undertaking if it is engaged in an economic activity offering goods or services.[72] To reiterate, the public or private legal status of an entity is irrelevant to the concept of undertaking.

Although the concept of undertaking is defined very broadly, it does have certain limits. A good example of this would be the entity that exercises *public powers* – or in other words, performs public tasks such as providing air navigation services[73] or carrying out anti-pollution surveillance.[74] This would encompass any activity that is a public task, meaning one that is in the public interest, fulfils an essential function of the State, and is connected by its nature, its aim, and the rules it must follow, with the exercise of powers that are typically entrusted to a public authority.[75]

---

66. Art. 29 of Reg. 1/2003, cited *supra* note 2.
67. See e.g. Case C-41/90, *Klaus Höfner and Fritz Elser v. Macrotron GmbH*, para 21.
68. See e.g. Case C-90/09 P, *General Quimica and Others v. Commission*, paras. 34–36.
69. See e.g. Case C-222/04, *Ministero dell'Economia e delle Finanze v. Cassa di Risparmio di Firenze SpA, Fondazione Cassa di Risparmio di San Miniato and Cassa di Risparmio di San Miniato SpA*, para 107 and Case C-205/03 P, *FENIN*, para 25.
70. See Case C-217/05, *Confederación Española de Empresarios de Estaciones de Servicio v. Compañía Española de Petróleos SA*, para 40.
71. Joined Cases C-180/98-184/98, *Pavel Pavlov and Others v. Stichting Pensioenfonds Medische Specialisten*, para 75.
72. Case C-41/90, *Höfner*.
73. Case C-364/92, *SAT Fluggesellschaft mbH v. Eurocontrol*, para 30.
74. Case C-343/95, *Diego Calì & Figli Srl v. Servizi ecologici porto di Genova SpA (SEPG)*, para 23.
75. Case C-343/95, *Diego Calì*, para 23.

Another example is provided by entities that exercise pension and insurance schemes that are based on *solidarity* and are supervised by the State.[76] An entity is not deemed to engage in economic activity if it operates a scheme that is based on solidarity; there is no real connection between the payments it receives, such as premiums, and the amounts going out.[77] The same is true for the procurement by public entities of goods and services for the purpose of providing health care on the basis of solidarity. In other words, providing health care cannot be considered an economic activity; therefore, the same would apply to the purchase of medicines and health services for use in the same context. According to the Court, the nature of the purchasing activity is determined by taking into account whether the subsequent use of the purchased goods amounts to an economic activity.[78] Entities operating social schemes need to be clearly distinguished from the majority of commercial pension and insurance schemes – which generally do not operate on the basis of solidarity. The latter qualify as entities engaged in economic activity and can therefore be considered "undertakings".

The prohibition given in Article 101(1) TFEU addresses collusion *between* undertakings. Therefore, the prohibition does not cover conduct within one and the same undertaking. This means that an undertaking is free to organize itself internally by allocating tasks and organizing its economic activity in the most efficient manner possible. For there to be one single undertaking, there must be a single economic entity; this is the case, for instance, within a corporate group if the ultimate parent company exercises decisive control, and its subsidiaries have no real freedom to determine their own conduct on the market.[79] In other words, a parent company and its subsidiaries form a single economic unit if the subsidiaries do not have any real autonomy with respect to their conduct on the market, but merely carry out instructions from the parent company.[80] The determination of whether this is the case depends on the factual situation – taking into consideration factors such as the corporate structure and where actual decision-making takes place within the group.

Furthermore, the prohibition does not apply to genuine agency relationships between genuine agents and their principals. An agency relationship can be of such a nature that the agent does not independently determine its own conduct in the market – it simply carries out instructions, and bears little or no financial or commercial risk for the activities it carries out as an agent of the principal.[81] In other words, under these circumstances, the principal and the genuine agent are seen as a single economic entity, namely as an undertaking.

The fact that a group of companies qualifies as a single economic unit may mean that the parent company can potentially be held jointly and severally liable for an infringement by one or more of its subsidiaries of Article 101(1) TFEU. This is the case if a subsidiary – even though it has a separate legal personality – does not independently determine how it will conduct itself on the market, and instead carries out, in all material respects, instructions given by its parent company. For quite some time, it was not clear whether a violation of competition rules by a subsidiary could be attributed to the parent company based solely on 100% shareholding, or whether it was also necessary to produce evidence that the parent company in fact exercised

76. See e.g. Case C-218/00, *Cisal di Battistello Venanzio & C. Sas v. Istituto nazionale per l'assicurazione contro gli infortuni sul lavoro (INAIL)* and Case C-350/07, *Kattner Stahlbau GmbH v. Maschinenbau – und Metal – Berufsgenossenschaft*, paras. 33–38.
77. Joined Cases C-159 & 160/91, *Christian Poucet v. Assurances Générales de France and Caisse Mutuelle Régionale du Languedoc-Roussillon.*
78. Case C-205/03 P, *FENIN*, para 26.
79. Case 15/74, *Centrafarm BV and Adriaan de Peijper v. Sterling Drug Inc*, para 41.
80. Case C-73/95 P, *Viho Europe BV v. Commission*, para 16.
81. See Guidelines on Vertical Restraints, cited *supra* note 61, paras. 12–21.

decisive influence over its subsidiary. There was also some uncertainty as to whether it was necessary to come up with additional factual evidence establishing that the parent company itself was in any way involved in the collusive behaviour.[82]

The ECJ provided clarity by holding that the fact that a parent company and its subsidiary constituted a single undertaking in the sense of Article 101 TFEU makes it possible to hold the parent company jointly and severally liable without having to establish the parent company's personal involvement in the infringement. According to the Court, it is sufficient to prove that the subsidiary is wholly owned by the parent company in order to *presume* that the parent exercises decisive influence over the commercial policy of the subsidiary. The parent company can be held jointly and severally liable unless the parent company, which has the burden of rebutting that presumption, adduces sufficient evidence to show that its wholly owned subsidiary acts independently on the market.[83] The presumption is also maintained if the parent company has an almost 100% shareholding in the subsidiary.[84] According to the European Commission, investment firms can also be held jointly and severally liable for the alleged involvement of a "portfolio company" in an infringement of Article 101(1) TFEU.[85]

It has proven very difficult, if not impossible, to rebut the presumption; the parent company has to show that the subsidiary that violated Article 101(1) TFEU was able to act with complete autonomy – not only at the operational level but also at the financial level.[86] The concept of undertaking has been stretched even further for the purpose of holding different companies jointly and severally liable for a violation of Article 101 TFEU, even when those companies do not belong to the same group. Generally speaking, joint and several liability issues arise when two or more companies are held jointly responsible for collusive conduct. In most cases, this happens to a parent company and its wholly owned subsidiary within one group of companies. "The presumption that the parent does in fact exercise decisive influence over the commercial conduct of its subsidiary is justified in so far as it covers typical situations as regards the relationship between a subsidiary and its single parent company, by providing that the ownership of all or virtually all the share capital by the single parent company means in principle that they pursue the same conduct on the market."[87] According to the ECJ, this can also transpire if two (or possibly more) independent companies cooperate in a joint venture that has been engaged in an infringement of Article 101(1) TFEU. More specifically, if two parent companies each have a 50% participation in a joint venture that has violated Article 101(1) TFEU, it is only for the purpose of establishing liability for participation in the infringement – and only in so far as it has been demonstrated on the basis of factual evidence – that both parent companies *did in fact* exercise decisive influence over the joint venture, that these three entities can be considered to form a single economic unit and therefore form a single undertaking for the purpose of Article 101 TFEU.[88] For two independent parent companies and their joint venture to be one undertaking, there must be direct evidence demonstrating the exercise of decisive influence by the parent

---

82. See in this context e.g. Case C-286/98 P, *Stora Kopparbergs Bergslags AB v. Commission* and Joined Cases T-109, 118, 122, 125, 126, 128, 129, 132 & 136/02, *Bollere SA and Others v. Commission*.
83. Case C-97/08 P, *Akzo Nobel NV and Others v. Commission*, paras. 60 and 61.
84. See, e.g., 98% in Case C-521/09 P, *Elf Aquitaine SA v. Commission*, para 63; 97% in Case T-299/08, *Elf Aquitaine SA v. Commission*, para 56 and 92–95% in Joined Cases T-379 & 381/10, *Keramag Keramische Werke AG and Others and Sanitec Europe Oy v. Commission*, para 315.
85. See e.g. Commission Decision of 2 Apr. 2014, *Power Cables*, O.J. 2014, C 319/10.
86. See Case C-508/11 P, *Eni SpA v. Commission*, para 68.
87. See Case T-541/08, *Sasol and Others v. Commission*, para 149.
88. Case C-172/12 P, *El du Pont de Nemours and Company v. Commission*, para 47. See also Case C-179/12 P, *The Dow Chemical Company v. Commission*, para 64.

companies. An abstract examination of decision-making procedures is not enough.[89] If only one of the parent companies is held liable for their joint venture's infringement, it must be shown that decisive influence on the joint venture's commercial conduct was exercised unilaterally by that parent company.[90]

The attribution of liability for acts of subsidiaries and joint ventures can have important consequences for parent companies – for instance, the imposition of much higher fines. The maximum fine that can be imposed is 10% of the worldwide turnover of an undertaking that violates Article 101(1) TFEU.[91] This maximum will be considerably higher if the turnover of the relevant undertaking is assessed based on the turnover of the parent company (and therefore most likely the entire corporate group) instead of only on the turnover of the subsidiary that was involved in the wrongful conduct.

The single economic entity concept can also result, ultimately, in attribution of the liability of a wholly owned subsidiary established in the EU to a parent company located outside the EU. In other words, a parent company residing outside the EU can be held jointly and severally liable for the conduct of its subsidiary in the EU.[92]

The further question arises of whether the attribution of liability under Article 101(1) TFEU should result in the parent company (also) being held liable for damages that are the result of wrongful conduct by a subsidiary. This is not necessarily the case. The liability of defendants in potential follow-on damage actions is determined according to the national law of each relevant EU Member State.[93] Most of these national laws are based on the principle that the legal entity involved in the violation is liable for the damages caused. It is therefore questionable whether a parent company can be held liable under national law for damages that are not the result of its own acts but caused by the conduct of a subsidiary.

Liability issues also arise in the context of corporate restructurings. As a general rule, a change in the legal form or name of an undertaking does not change liability. The succeeding entity remains liable for the wrongful act of its predecessor when, from an economic point of view, the two are identical.[94] For this to be the case, there should be, according to the Commission, a functional and economic continuity between the original infringer and the undertaking into which it was merged.[95] In principle, a parent company selling the business or subsidiary that was involved in an infringement, remains liable for as long as it exists.[96] The Commission may (but is not obliged to) impute liability for the conduct of a subsidiary to the former parent company for the period prior to the sale and impute liability to the new parent for the period thereafter.[97] The Commission can choose to hold liable either the subsidiary directly participat-

89. See Case T-541/08, *Sasol*, paras. 44–47 and 107.
90. See Case T-541/08, *Sasol*, para 54.
91. Art. 23(2) of Reg. 1/2003, cited *supra* note 2.
92. See e.g. Case 48/69, *Imperial Chemical Industries (ICI) Ltd. v. Commission.*
93. See Case C-352/13, *Cartel Damage Claims (CDC) Hydrogen Peroxide SA v. Akzo Nobel NV and Others*, paras. 21 and 22.
94. See e.g. Joined Cases C-125, 133, 135 & 137/07 P, *Erste Group Bank AG, Raiffeisen Zentralbank Österreich AG, Bank Austria Creditanstalt AG and Österreichische Volksbanken AG v. Commission*, para 79.
95. See e.g. Commission Decision of 21 Dec. 1989, *PVC I*, O.J. 1989 L 74/1, para 42 and Commission Decision of 27 July 1994, *PVC II*, O.J. 1994, L 239/94, paras. 14–34.
96. See e.g. Case C-279/98 P, *Cascades SA v. Commission*, para 78 and Case T-9/99, *HFB Holding für Fernwärmetechnik Beteiligungsgesellschaft mbH & Co. KG and Others v. Commission*, para 103.
97. See e.g. Joined Cases T-259-264 & 271/02, *Raiffeisen Zentralbank Österreich AG and Others v. Commission*, 331 and 332.

ing in the infringement or both the former and new parent company jointly and severally with the subsidiary concerned.[98]

Against the backdrop of the need for effective enforcement, and of avoiding the possibility of escaping liability for infringements of Article 101(1) TFEU, it may be necessary, by way of an exception, to attribute liability for an infringement to the new operator of the undertaking that participated in the infringement if the new operator can in fact be regarded as the successor of the original operator.[99] This is the case if the new operator continues to operate the undertaking that participated in the infringement.

2.3 *The concept of collusion*

The text of Article 101(1) TFEU refers to agreements between undertakings, decisions by associations of undertakings, and concerted practices. These are three different expressions of the concept of collusion and should not be seen as separate categories. Basically, an undertaking should decide independently and unilaterally on its commercial strategy without any knowledge of what its competitors will do on the market. Any form of collusion between undertakings that restricts competition is prohibited. The concept of collusion is broad and applies irrespective of form. There is no need for reciprocity.

An "agreement" is the first example of collusion mentioned in Article 101(1) TFEU that, according to the Court, centres around the existence of "[...] a concurrence of wills between at least two parties, the form in which it is manifested being unimportant so long as it constitutes the faithful expression of the parties' intention".[100] The form of the agreement is not relevant. It can be written or orally agreed upon,[101] it can be signed or just be a "gentlemen's agreement".[102] It can also be an "old" agreement with ongoing effects in the market.[103] Almost by definition, decisions by or other acts of associations of undertakings such as trade associations, can potentially be of a collusive nature. The mere setting up of a trade association,[104] and (even non-binding) recommendations can fall within the scope of Article 101(1) TFEU.[105]

Similarly, the meaning of "concerted practice" is very broad and takes no account of form; it also covers all other forms of collusion, particularly, according to the Court, "coordination between undertakings which, without having reached the stage where an agreement, properly so called, has been concluded, knowingly substitutes practical co-operation between them for the risks of competition".[106]

A concerted practice can even be established on the basis of one isolated exchange of information between competitors.[107]

---

98. See in this sense, Case T-541/08, *Sasol*, para 192.
99. Case T-161/05, *Hoechst GmbH v. Commission*, paras. 50–52. See also Case C-49/92 P, *Commission v. Anic Partecipazioni SpA*, para 145 and Joined Cases C-204, 205, 211, 213, 217 & 219/00 P, *Aalborg PortlandA/S, Irish Cement Ltd, Ciments français SA, Italcementi – Fabbriche Riunite Cemento SpA), Buzzi Unicem SpA and Cementir – Cementerie del Tirreno SpA v. Commission*, para 359.
100. Case T-41/96, *Bayer AG v. Commission*, para 69.
101. See e.g. Case 28/77, *Tepea BV v. Commission* and Case T-43/92, *Dunlop Slazenger International Ltd v. Commission*.
102. See e.g. Case T-141/89, *Tréfileurope Sales SARL v. Commission* and Case T-9/99, *HFB*, para 200.
103. Case 243/83, *SA Binon & Cie v. SA Agence et messageries de la presse*, para 17 and Case T-7/89, *SA Hercules Chemicals NV v. Commission*. See also Commission Decision of 17 Dec. 1990, *Soda-ash-Solvay*, O.J. 1990, L 152/1.
104. Commission Decision of 30 June 1970, *ASPA*, O.J. 1970, L 148/91.
105. See Joined Cases 209-215 & 218/78, *Heintz van Landewyck SARL and others v. Commission.*
106. Case 48/69, *ICI*, paras. 64 and 65.
107. Case C-8/08, *T-Mobile*, paras. 44–53.

The burden of proof to show that there is collusion between undertakings is borne by the authorities enforcing Article 101(1) TFEU. The burden of proof often proves difficult; illegal conduct generally takes place in secret, and is not often well documented. In practice, collusion takes place in various shapes and forms ranging from traditional "hard-core cartels" that engage in price-fixing and market allocation to more "atypical cartels" that conduct sophisticated exchanges of commercially sensitive information and signalling, for instance by means of press releases. When attempting to prove collusion, the authorities are not obliged to choose between the qualifications "agreement" and "concerted practice". Collusive conduct can fit both examples of collusion.[108] Furthermore, the Commission and European Courts have developed the concept of the single complex and continuous infringement ("SCCI"), which encompasses various expressions of collusive conduct forming part of an overall plan to distort competition. Undertakings participating in such an overall plan can be held liable for the whole of that conduct, even if their participation was limited to parts thereof.[109]

Unilateral conduct does not qualify as collusion – something more is required.[110] Collusion is "form free" and can be either explicit or tacit. Explicit collusion is relatively straightforward. It should however be distinguished from parallel market conduct. Such conduct may be an indication of explicit collusion, but can also be the result of specific features of the relevant market, especially if the market is oligopolistic in nature. Where there are few market players, they may be inclined to behave in the same way even in the absence of any type of prior contact. This situation is usually referred to as tacit collusion. However, it remains a challenge to distinguish tacit collusion – that violates Article 101(1) TFEU – from independent and unilateral conduct – that is the result of undertakings adapting to (developments in) the marketplace and is in compliance with competition rules. The ECJ has recognized that the parallel conduct of undertakings could provide circumstantial evidence of collusion but emphasized that such parallel conduct does not necessarily provide proof of violation of Article 101(1) TFEU if an alternative explanation can be provided for the conduct, such as market conditions.[111] If there is no such alternative explanation, parallel conduct can amount to illegal tacit collusion.[112] There are examples where the Commission concluded that, although certain conduct in a vertical distribution relationship gave the impression of being unilateral, in reality it could nonetheless be qualified as collusion between undertakings that fell within the scope of Article 101(1) TFEU.[113]

As a rule, if an undertaking is represented at a meeting where collusion in contravention of Article 101 TFEU takes place, it will be held liable for that conduct. It is only by explicitly and publicly distancing itself – *vis-à-vis* the other participant(s) – from the collusive conduct that

---

108. Case C-49/92 P, *Commission v. Anic Partecipazioni SpA*, paras. 132 and 133; Case C-238/05, *Asnef-Equifax, Servicios de Información sobre Solvencia y Crédito, SL v. Asociación de Usuarios de Servicios Bancarios (Ausbanc)*, para 32.

109. Joined Cases T-101 & 111/05, *BASF and UCB v. Commission* and Case C-287/11 P, *Commission v. Aalberts Industries NV and Others*. In order for the Commission to prove the continuous nature of an infringement, it must adduce factual evidence sufficiently proximate in time for it to be reasonably accepted that the infringement continued uninterruptedly between two specific dates. The period that can be considered as "sufficiently proximate" depends on the market context. See in this context Case T-655/11, *FSL Holdings, Firma Léon Van Parys and Pacific Fruit Company Italy SpA v. Commission*, para 476.

110. Case T-41/96, *Bayer*.

111. Joined Cases C-89, 104, 114, 116, 117 & 125-129/85, *Ahlström Osakeyhtiö and Others v. Commission* ("Wood Pulp II"), paras. 66–127.

112. Commission Decision of 16 July 2008, *CISAC*, O.J. 2008, C 323/12.

113. Joined Cases 25 & 26/84, *Ford v. Commission*.

an undertaking can escape liability from that point onwards.[114] In practice, a party's intention to publicly distance itself often takes the form of a declaration indicating that it does not wish to participate in, or no longer wishes to participate in, the collusive conduct. It is not always clear what type of action or statement is required to achieve that effect. The mere fact that an undertaking does not act in line with or does not actively participate in the collusive conduct, or has stopped doing so, is not enough. In one way or another, a clear and public message needs to be sent. A quiet withdrawal from collusive conduct will not suffice to end liability.[115]

Finally, collusive conduct by undertakings in consequence of government intervention is not necessarily covered by Article 101(1) TFEU. However, this is only the case if national law does not leave room for undertakings to act competitively on the market.[116] It is not enough that the State encourages – or even facilitates or approves of – collusive conduct. For instance, in situations where the State, for various reasons, does not want to legislate but instead chooses to encourage a particular sector to resolve a perceived problem by self-regulation, (associations of) undertakings must remain aware that Article 101(1) TFEU continues to apply. The fact that a representative of the State is present at meetings or actively participates in discussions leading up to the self-regulation is not a valid excuse for collusive conduct in the sense of Article 101 TFEU. EU Member States nonetheless need to be careful when they introduce legislative measures that leave no room for competition. The ECJ has held that Member States are not allowed to negatively influence the effectiveness ("*effet utile*") of competition rules by means of legislation.[117]

2.4 *The concept of effect on trade*

As mentioned in Section 1.1 above, EU competition rules were put in place to ensure that the internal market would work as one market. This internal market dimension is reflected in the condition that collusive conduct within the meaning of Article 101(1) TFEU "may affect trade between Member States". The inter-state trade condition thus limits the scope of the prohibition *vis-à-vis* application of national competition rules enacted by the Member States. This conflict rule is specified in Article 3 of Regulation 1/2003,[118] according to which national competition authorities and courts must apply Article 101 TFEU when they enforce their national competition rules in situations of collusive conduct that potentially affect trade between Member States. If there is a conflict between Art 101 and the relevant national law due to their simultaneous

114. Case T-9/99, *HFB*. See also Joined Cases C-204, 205, 211, 213, 217 & 219/00 P, *Aalborg PortlandA/S, Irish Cement Ltd, Ciments français SA, Italcementi – Fabbriche Riunite Cemento SpA, Buzzi Unicem SpA and Cementir – Cementerie del Tirreno SpA v. Commission.*
115. In Case C-373/14 P, *Toshiba Corporation v. Commission,* para 61, the ECJ considered that it is sufficient for the Commission to show that the undertaking concerned participated in meetings at which anticompetitive agreements were concluded, without manifestly opposing them, to prove to the requisite standard that the undertaking participated in a cartel. In Case C-74/14, *Eturas UAB and Others v. Lietuvos Respublikos konkurencijos taryba,* an online travel booking system had sent emails to other travel agents relating to the maximum amount of discounts that should be granted. The ECJ ruled that in cases where it is not possible to identify all addressees of a message sent by a cartel participant, it cannot be required that a company receiving it, distances itself in the eyes of all other addressees. A "clear and explicit objection" addressed to the system administrator (in this case Eturas) would be enough to rebut the presumption of awareness.
116. Joined Cases C-359 & 379/95 P, *Commission and France v. Ladbroke Racing LTD,* para 33; Case C-198/01, *Consorzia Industrie Fiammiferi (CIF) v. Autorità Garante della Concorrenza e del Mercato,* paras. 52–55; and Case T-228/97, *Irish Sugar plc v. Commission,* para 130.
117. Case C-35/96, *Commission v. Italy,* paras. 53 and 54 and Case C-267/86, *Van Eycke v. Society Anonymous ASPA,* para 16.
118. Reg. 1/2003, cited *supra* note 2.

application, the national authorities are required to respect the supremacy of EU competition law over their own national provisions.[119] In practice, however, the risk of conflict – and, hence, the relevance of the inter-state trade condition – has decreased. This is because Member States have aligned their competition laws with the EU model, particularly by introducing prohibitions in national competition laws that are similar or even identical (without the condition "affect trade") to Article 101 TFEU.[120] The Netherlands, for example, has even included definitions of key terms such as "agreement" and "undertaking" in the Dutch Competition Act that use the words "within the meaning of Article 101(1) TFEU".[121]

The ECJ allowed broad interpretation of the concept "may affect trade between Member States" when it held that this is fulfilled whenever it is possible "[…] to foresee with a sufficient degree of probability, on the basis of a set of objective factors of law or fact, that the agreement or concerted practice in question may have an influence, direct or indirect, actual or potential, on the pattern of trade in goods or services between Member States".[122] An influence that is purely hypothetical or speculative should not be taken into consideration. A similar approach can be found in other areas of EU law. For instance, in the context of free movement of goods and services (see Ch. 13 and 14), the Court defined "measures having an equivalent effect to quantitative restrictions on imports" as all "trading rules enacted by Member States which are capable of hindering, directly or indirectly, actually or potentially, intra-community trade are to be considered as measures having an effect equivalent to quantitative restrictions".[123]

The Commission has published a notice giving its interpretation of the relevant case law on effect on trade.[124] In that Notice, which attempts to infer several guiding principles from the Court's case law, the Commission points out that the concept of effect on trade is not limited to the exchange of goods and services, but in fact covers all cross-border economic activity, including the establishment by undertakings of agencies, branches or subsidiaries in other Member States. It also includes situations in which the competitive structure of the common market is affected.[125] It is enough that collusive conduct is *capable* of having an effect on trade.[126] An agreement can also fall within the scope of Article 101(1) TFEU if only one of its provisions is capable of having such effect on trade.[127] Also, the Notice refers to the case law pursuant to which trade can also be affected by collusion within (a part of) one Member State. Consequently, a purely national agreement can fall under the scope of Article 101(1) TFEU. The context of the collusive conduct is important for the assessment. On the one hand, even a relatively small-scale agreement (for instance, between a beer brewer and the owner of a local bar) may under certain circumstances, for example where it is part of a network or bundle of similar agreements, affect trade between Member States.[128] On the other hand, if there are in fact only limited possibilities for trade between Member States, the conclusion might be that the collusion does not affect

119. Case 14/68, *Walt Wilhelm*.
120. C. Kerse and N. Kahn, *EU Antitrust Procedure*, 6th ed. (Sweet & Maxwell, 2012).
121. Dutch Competition Act, Arts. 1(e) and 1(f).
122. Joined Cases 56 & 58/64, *Consten and Grundig*, at 341. See also Case 56/65, *LTM*, at 249.
123. Case 8/74, *Procureur du Roi v. Benoit and Gustave Dassonville*, para 5.
124. Commission Guidelines on the effect on trade concept contained in Arts. 81 and 82 of the Treaty, O.J. 2004, C 101/81 ("the Guidelines on inter-state trade").
125. Guidelines on inter-state trade, ibid., paras. 19–20 and 30.
126. Guidelines on inter-state trade, ibid., para 26.
127. Case 193/83, *Windsurfing International Inc. v. Commission*.
128. Case C-234/89, *Stergios Delimitis v. Henninger Bräu AG*, para 20 and 21. See also Case 23/67, *Brasserie De Haecht v. Consorts Wilkin-Janssen*, at 416.

trade between Member States.[129] An export ban imposed on undertakings outside the EU can have an appreciable effect on trade between Member States.[130]

For collusive conduct to fall under the scope of Article 101(1) TFEU, it needs to affect trade to an *appreciable* extent. In its Notice, the Commission notes that this "appreciability" condition should be assessed on a case-by-case basis by looking at the position and the importance of the colluding undertakings on the relevant market. The stronger the market position (for instance in terms of turnover or relative market share) the more likely it is that this condition will be fulfilled.[131] The Notice also provides specific guidance for small and medium-sized undertakings. It introduces to that effect a rebuttable presumption (based on whether the combined turnover of the undertakings involved is less or greater than 40 million Euro and whether the undertakings' aggregate market position is less or greater than 5%).[132]

2.5 *Within the internal market*

Article 101(1) TFEU covers the prevention, restriction, and distortion of competition within *the internal market* and is as such limited to the geographic territory of the European Union. In a globalizing worldwide economy, collusion can have a restrictive effect in many different jurisdictions both within and outside the EU. Competition authorities from various jurisdictions have investigated and fined the same collusive conduct in many cases where it resulted in restrictive effects being felt in several countries.

Similarly, collusive conduct that takes place outside the territory of the European Union can have restrictive effects within the internal market. One example would be an agreement concluded outside the EU between undertakings that are not established in the EU that aimed to fix prices and allocate customers for a product that is sold in a worldwide market that includes the EU. To address such a situation, the ECJ developed an "implementation doctrine" by holding that Article 101(1) TFEU is applicable when the collusive conduct (such as an agreement concluded outside the EU) is implemented in the internal market. According to the Court it "is immaterial [...] whether or not they had recourse to subsidiaries, agents, subagents, or branches within the Community in order to make their contacts with purchasers within the Community".[133] It however remains questionable whether an agreement concluded and implemented outside – but with effects on commerce in – the EU falls within the scope of Article 101(1) TFEU.

Nonetheless, the Commission seems to take the position that it can proceed on the basis of an "effects doctrine" for the application of Article 101 TFEU.[134] A good example of this is the *LCD* case, where the Commission first elaborates on the "implementation doctrine" and then turns its attention to the fact that the General Court held that application of the EU Merger Control Regulation is justified if the conduct at issue has immediate, foreseeable and substantial effect in the EU.[135]

---

129. Case C-215/96, *Carlo Bagnasco and Others v. Banca Popolare di Novara soc. coop. arl. (BNP)*, para 51.
130. Case C-306/96, *Javico International and Javico AG v. Yves Saint Laurent Parfums SA (YSLP)*.
131. Guidelines on inter-state trade, cited *supra* note 124, paras. 45–47.
132. Guidelines on inter-state trade, cited *supra* note 124, paras. 50–53.
133. Joined Cases 89/85 etc., *Wood Pulp II*, para 17. See in the context of merger control Case T-102/96, *Gencor*.
134. Guidelines on inter-state trade, cited *supra* note 124, para 100. See also Case T-102/96, *Gencor*, para 90, in which it was held that the application of the EU merger control regulation "is justified under public international law when it is foreseeable that a proposed concentration will have an immediate and substantial effect in the Community".
135. Commission Decision of 8 Dec. 2010, *LCD – Liquid Crystal Displays*, O.J. 2010, C 8761, paras. 230 and 231.

2.6 Restriction of competition

The concept of "restriction of competition" is, for various reasons, the most difficult to explain. First, it depends on another underlying concept: the notion of "competition that the conduct under scrutiny potentially restricts". Undertakings can compete with each other in many ways such as price, quality, and service. Moreover, competition can exist between producers, suppliers and distributors at both the inter-brand and intra-brand level. One should also bear in mind that competition can exist "between the parties" to the collusion as well as "between one of them and third parties".[136] Second, the concept of "competition worthy of protection" varies over time and is influenced by economic thinking. In its early days, the requirements of the internal market were the primary concern. In *Metro* for example, the ECJ held that the requirement that competition not be distorted implies the existence of workable competition within the market, defined as "the degree of competition necessary to ensure the observance of the basic requirements and the attainment of the objectives of the Treaty, in particular the creation of a single market achieving conditions similar to those of a domestic market".[137] While the objective of integration retains importance, the case law now also refers to consumer welfare as a prime objective – as has been observed in Section 1.4 above.[138] Third, whether or not competition is restricted is in many respects a fact-specific determination that depends on the economic and legal context in which the conduct under scrutiny is assessed.

The fourth complication results from the wording of Article 101(1) TFEU, which indicates that the prohibition concerns collusive conduct that has the object or effect of restricting competition. This means that infringements fall into two alternative categories.[139] The first is collusive conduct that has the object of restricting competition ("object infringement"). Certain types of collusive conduct reveal a sufficient degree of "harm to competition" which means there is no need to examine their effects. These are mostly "hard-core" infringements like price-fixing, the allocation of markets and customers, exchanges of commercially sensitive information, and fixing minimum resale prices. The second is collusive conduct that does not have restricting competition as its object, but nonetheless has that effect ("effect infringement"). This is the category of collusive conduct that falls short of causing a sufficient degree of "harm to competition" that would otherwise qualify it as an object infringement. For this type of collusion, one needs to consider the effects of the collusion. Before Article 101(1) TFEU is triggered, it is necessary to identify the factors that show that competition has in fact been prevented, restricted or distorted to an appreciable extent.

The case law on the definition of object infringements is unclear. Before the judgment of the ECJ in *Cartes Bancaires*, it was sufficient to establish that collusive conduct could potentially have a negative impact on competition. In *T-Mobile* the ECJ held that: "[...] a concerted practice pursues an anti-competitive object for the purpose [...] where, according to its content and objectives and having regard to its legal and economic context, it is capable in an individual case of resulting in the prevention, restriction or distortion of competition within the common market. It is not necessary for there to be actual prevention, restriction or distortion of competition or a direct link between the concerted practice and consumer prices. An exchange of information between competitors is tainted with an anti-competitive object if the exchange is capable of removing uncertainties concerning the intended conduct of the participating undertakings."[140]

---

136. Joined Cases 56 & 58/64, *Consten and Grundig*, at 339.
137. Case 26/76, *Metro*, para 20.
138. Joined Cases C-501, 513, 515 & 519/06 P, *GlaxoSmithKline*, and Case C-209/10, *Post Danmark*.
139. Case 56/65, *LTM*, at 249.
140. Case C-8/08, *T-Mobile*, para 43.

This is a very broad definition of the concept of object infringement, since any type of conduct is in some way capable of restricting competition. In *Cartes Bancaires*, the ECJ limited the scope by establishing that restrictions of competition by object should be interpreted restrictively, and by ruling that "the essential legal criterion for ascertaining whether coordination between undertakings involves [...] a restriction of competition 'by object' is the finding that such coordination reveals in itself a sufficient degree of harm to competition".[141] For an object infringement, it is necessary to demonstrate that the restriction of competition causes a sufficient degree of harm, and to determine the extent thereof, in order to be able to be characterized as a restriction "by object" within the meaning of Article 101(1) TFEU. Even when the ECJ refers to general experience showing that certain types of conduct lead to falls in production, price increases, and a poor allocation of resources, it still requires an assessment of the content of its provisions, its objectives, and the economic and legal context. When determining that context, it is also necessary to take into consideration the nature of the goods or services affected, as well as the real conditions of the functioning and structure of the market or markets in question.

If collusive conduct does not qualify as an object infringement, it may nonetheless still qualify as an effect infringement due to factors which indicate that competition has in fact been prevented, restricted or distorted to an appreciable extent.[142] For this purpose, it is necessary to perform a full and thorough analysis of the collusive conduct in its market context to determine whether the effect is a restriction of competition.[143] In the course of such an analysis, one has to look at the proper context and actual effects on the market. For instance, in *European Night Services and Others v. Commission,* the General Court noted that account should be taken of the actual conditions, in particular the economic context in which the undertakings operate, the products or services covered by the agreement and the actual structure of the market concerned. In addition, the General Court held that it is necessary to examine the conditions of existing and potential competition on the market in order to ascertain whether, in light of the structure of the market and the economic and legal context in which it functions, there are genuine opportunities for the undertaking to compete amongst themselves, or for a new competitor to penetrate the relevant market and compete with established undertakings.[144] During an assessment of the effects, it is also necessary to consider "counter-factual" scenarios, in other words what the market situation would be in the absence of conduct such as the agreement in question.[145]

In this context, reference should also be made to the concept of ancillary restraints. If such restrictions are necessary to achieve a legitimate commercial goal, they are not covered by Article 101(1) TFEU. This concept covers any alleged restriction of competition which is necessary and directly related to the implementation of a main, non-restrictive transaction, and proportionate to it. A good example of such an ancillary restraint would be a non-compete clause in a take-over agreement that is necessary to ensure the transfer of (the value of) the business from

---

141. Case C-67/13 P, *Groupement des carte bancaires (CB) v. Commission*, paras. 57 and 58. See also Case C-345/14, *SIA "Maxima Latvija" v. Konkurences padome*, para 20.
142. There is a fine line between restrictions of competition by object and by effect which has been highly debated in both the European court's case law and the academic sphere. The ECJ has given some guidance by establishing that "the distinction between "infringements by object" and "infringements by effect" arises from the fact that certain forms of collusion between undertakings can be regarded, by their very nature, as being injurious to the proper functioning of normal competition". See Case C-8/08, *T-Mobile*; Case C-67/13 P, *Cartes Bancaires*, para 50; and Case C-345/14, *Maxima Latvija*, para 18.
143. Case C-234/89, *Delimitis v. Henninger Bräu*. See also Case 23/67, *Brasserie De Haecht.*
144. Joined Cases T-374, 375, 384, & 388/94, *European Night Services Ltd (ENS) and Others v. Commission*, paras. 136 and 137.
145. Case 56/65, *LTM*, at 250. See also Case T-328/03, *O2 (Germany) GmbH & Co, OHG v. Commission*, paras. 71 and 72.

the seller to the purchaser.[146] Such an ancillary restraint should be objectively necessary for the implementation of the main transaction and proportionate to it. Therefore, in the case of a non-compete clause, it should not be formulated more broadly in terms of duration and scope than strictly necessary in order to make the transaction viable.[147] The Commission has indicated that, in principle, a non-compete period of up to two years is acceptable when a transfer only includes goodwill, but may be as long as three years if it involves the transfer of customer loyalty in the form of both goodwill and know-how.[148] In other contexts, certain ancillary restraints have been recognized as not falling within the scope of Article 101(1) TFEU, such as the functioning of franchise agreements[149] and cooperatives.[150]

Finally, for collusive conduct to fall under the scope of Article 101(1) TFEU it needs to result in an *appreciable* restriction of competition. This Treaty provision does not apply to collusive conduct which has an insignificant effect on the market.[151] In its *de minimis* Notice, the European Commission gives guidelines on what is and what is not likely to qualify as an appreciable restriction of competition under Article 101(1) TFEU.[152] According to the Notice, agreements between competitors with an aggregate market share that does not exceed 10% do not appreciably restrict competition. For agreements between non-competing undertakings, the Guidelines adhere to a market share threshold of 15% for each of the parties. If it is difficult to establish whether the parties to an agreement are competitors, the threshold of 10% applies. Relying on a broad interpretation of the ruling of the ECJ in *Expedia*, the Notice also explains that object restrictions do not benefit from its scope.[153]

2.7 *Horizontal agreements*

2.7.1 *Introduction*

There are many reasons for companies operating at the same level within an economy to work together. Such cooperation can be economically beneficial when it leads to a combination of complementary activities, skills, or assets. Horizontal cooperation can lead to economic efficiencies through the sharing of risks, cost savings, and the pooling of know-how. Such cooperation can take place between various companies, whether actual or potential competitors, or non-competitors.

However, horizontal cooperation can also seriously damage the competitive process. As a rule, price-fixing and the allocation of customers and territories between competitors both fall within the scope of Article 101(1) TFEU because they rarely lead to efficiencies. On the contrary, they generally lead to inefficient production, less innovation, higher prices, and limited consumer choice.[154] These types of cooperation lead to the formation of what is often referred to as hard-core cartels, seen by many as fraud and a form of "white collar crime".[155] It is for this reason that the "fight against cartels" has been a top priority for authorities around the world.

146. Case 42/84, *Remia BV and Others v. Commission.*
147. See in this context Commission Notice on restrictions directly related and necessary to concentrations, O.J. 2005, C 56/24 ("the Ancillary Restraints Notice"). See also Case 42/84, *Remia*, paras. 18–20 and Case T-112/99, *Métropole*, para 104.
148. Ancillary Restraints Notice, ibid., para 20.
149. Case 161/84, *Pronuptia de Paris GmbH v. Pronuptia de Paris Irmgard Schillgallis*, para 23.
150. Case C-250/92, *Gøttrup-Klim e.a. Grovvareforeninger v. Dansk Landbrugs Grovvareselskab AmbA*, para 45.
151. Case 5/69, *Franz Völk v. S.P.R.L. Ets J. Vervaecke*, at 302.
152. De *minimis* Notice, cited *supra* note 17.
153. Case C-226/11, *Expedia Inc v. Autorité de la concurrence and Others*, para 37.
154. L. Kaplow, *Competition Policy and Price Fixing* (Princeton University Press, 2013).
155. A. Papadopoulos, *The International Dimension of EU Competition Law and Policy* (CUP, 2010), at 89.

In the European Union, high fines are imposed for violation of the cartel prohibition. In jurisdictions – the United States and certain EU Member States such as the United Kingdom and Ireland – a violation of the cartel prohibition is a criminal offence and can lead to high fines for companies and prison sentences for individuals.

Between innocuous, efficiency-enhancing forms of cooperation on the one hand, and the ruthless form of hard-core cartels on the other, lies a wide spectrum of possibilities that, depending on the circumstances, could trigger Article 101(1) TFEU. In recognition of the need for safe havens, the Council of the European Union and the Commission have published block exemptions for certain categories of horizontal cooperation agreements such as research and development agreements, specialization agreements, special arrangements in the insurance sector,[156] agreements in the road and inland waterways sectors,[157] and consortia between liner shipping companies.[158] In its Horizontal Guidelines the Commission has, in addition, provided public guidance on how companies can cooperate whilst remaining in compliance with Article 101 TFEU.[159] These Guidelines deal with the most common forms of horizontal cooperation such as joint production, research and development ("R&D"), product standardization, certain types of exchange of information and joint purchasing. These types of cooperation can be advantageous for both the economy and the consumer. However, horizontal cooperation – especially between actual or potential competitors – can also lead to restrictions of competition within the meaning of Article 101(1) TFEU. Cooperation between competitors is by nature a sensitive matter as it may lead to less competition between cooperating competitors if, for instance, they disclose strategic information, achieve significant commonality of costs, contribute assets or obtain financial interests that reduce the incentive for independent decision-making. Horizontal cooperation can also have foreclosure effects, for example when it relies on exclusivity arrangements that limit the possibility of teaming up with other market players.[160] In order to assess horizontal cooperation under Article 101, all market characteristics such as market shares and entry barriers should be taken into account. Generally speaking, the more restrictive the cooperation, the less likely it will qualify for an exception within the meaning of Article 101(3) TFEU. However, there are examples of situations, for instance in the Dutch brick sector, in which the Commission allowed collusive conduct – under Article 101(3) – on the basis of a coordinated plan to reduce capacity in order to overcome the difficulties which had for several years affected that industry ("crisis cartel").[161] Finally, reference should be made to new forms of cooperation, which have drawn the attention of enforcers: such as "hub & spoke" situations, signalling, bench-marking, data gathering and facilitation.[162]

---

156. The R&D Block Exemption Reg., cited *supra* note 65; the Specialisation Block Exemption Reg., cited *supra* note 64; and Commission Reg. (EU) 267/2010 of 24 Mar. 2010 on the application of Art. 101(3) of the Treaty on the Functioning of the European Union to certain categories of agreements, decisions and concerted practices in the insurance sector, O.J. 2010, L 83/1.
157. Council Reg. (EC) 69/2009 of 26 Feb. 2009 applying rules of competition to transport by rail, road and inland waterway, O.J. 2009, L 61/1.
158. Commission Reg. (EC) 906/2009 of 28 Sep. 2009 on the application of Art. 81(3) of the Treaty to certain categories of agreements, decisions and concerted practices between liner shipping companies (consortia), O.J. 2009, L 256/31.
159. Commission Guidelines on the applicability of Art. 101 of the Treaty on the Functioning of the European Union to horizontal co-operation agreements, O.J. 2011, C 11/1 ("the Horizontal Guidelines").
160. Horizontal Guidelines, ibid., paras. 32–38.
161. See Commission Decision of 29 Apr. 1994, *Stichting Baksteen*, O.J. 1994, L 131/15.
162. See *infra*, section 2.8.

2.7.2 *Various common types of horizontal cooperation*

One frequently used type of horizontal cooperation concerns *information exchange*, which can take place in various shapes and forms; for instance within the context of trade associations, which tend to facilitate information exchange among members for various legitimate purposes such as technical meetings and lobby efforts. In theory, information exchange may lead to various efficiency gains for companies and consumers. For example, it could serve to solve information asymmetries on a market, improve internal efficiency in companies (i.e. bench-marking), reduce cost, or improve consumer choice.

Nonetheless, information exchange is likely to restrict competition if it creates transparency with regard to the future market strategy of competitors or if it is instrumental to collusive conduct such as price-fixing and the allocation of prices, customers, and territories. A disclosure of commercially sensitive information by one company, or an exchange amongst competitors, is likely to be problematic because it reduces the independence of competitors' conduct on the market and diminishes the incentive to compete.[163] This is particularly the case regarding information on future quantities, prices, and other commercial terms and conditions. The threshold for violation of Article 101(1) TFEU is low. In *Bananas*, for example, banana importers were fined because information was exchanged concerning general market conditions – market trends, weather conditions, imports of bananas, stocks, and other factors – which influenced supply and demand, as well as for the fact that they shared market forecasts with each other.[164] As mentioned previously in Section 2.6, the ECJ held in *T-Mobile* that communications – between competitors – *capable* of reducing uncertainty about the future market conduct of a competitor are restrictions by object within the meaning of Article 101(1).[165] There is a presumption that undertakings active in a certain market will take information exchanged with competitors into account and adapt their conduct accordingly. By contrast, the disclosure of information that is "genuinely public" does not normally constitute collusive conduct. The same applies to the exchange of aggregated data (not individualized at the company level) or historic data, which is unlikely to lead to a restriction of competition. However, the public disclosure of information can also be seen as signalling – an effort to reach a common understanding.[166]

Cooperation that takes place long before the final product reaches the consumer is generally perceived positively. This especially holds true for *joint research and development* for the purpose of improving existing technologies or developing entirely new products. The economic benefits of this type of cooperation are obvious because they include innovation, risk and cost reduction, and increased choice in products and services for consumers. In some circumstances, however, R&D cooperation may also tend to restrict competition if it slows down innovation, i.e. fewer – or worse – products are brought to market, there is reduced competition between the contracting companies outside the scope of their cooperation, or coordination is facilitated. The assessment of a particular R&D agreement under Article 101 TFEU has to take into account the characteristics of the market and the competitive position of the cooperating parties. In view of the substantial efficiencies involved, there is a block exemption regulation for R&D agreements between undertakings as long as their share in the relevant market does not exceed 25%.[167]

---

163. Horizontal Guidelines, cited *supra* note 159, paras. 61 and 62.
164. Commission Decision of 15 Oct. 2008, *Bananas*, Case COMP/39.188. See also Joined Cases C-293 & 294/13 P, *Fresh del Monte Produce Inc. v. Commission*; and Case C-286/13 P, *Dole Food and Dole Fresh Fruit Europe v. Commission.*
165. Case C-8/08, *T-Mobile*, para 43.
166. Horizontal Guidelines, cited *supra* note 159, para 63.
167. Art. 4 of the R&D Block Exemption Reg., cited *supra* note 65.

Agreements between parties with a higher market share will have to be individually assessed under Article 101(3) TFEU.

Joint production agreements are generally assessed more cautiously; this type of cooperation between competitors can cause efficiency by leading to cost reduction and better production technologies. Joint production can take place by pooling resources, setting up joint production structures, or entering into a more relaxed contractual arrangement such as subcontracting, where a contractor puts the sub-contractor in charge of the production of the goods. Horizontal subcontracting agreements are concluded between undertakings operating in the same product market and include unilateral and reciprocal specialization agreements and subcontracting agreements with a view to expanding production.[168] A production agreement may restrict competition when it results in coordination, creates a degree of alignment of competitively important parameters such as output levels, quality, and price, or leads to the foreclosure of third parties. Because of the increased risks involved in joint production agreements, the block exemption Regulation for specialization agreements (including joint production) is less generous than its counterpart for joint R&D agreements. Its "safe haven" is indeed limited to agreements between undertakings with a combined market share that does not exceed 20% of the relevant market.[169]

Horizontal cooperation by means of *joint purchasing arrangements* is aimed at creating buying power that leads to lower prices or better-quality products and services for consumers. However, joint purchasing that leads to a high degree of commonality of costs may lead to coordination and collusive conduct on the selling market. These arrangements may also lead to an exchange of commercially sensitive information (such as prices and volumes). Joint purchasing may become problematic if the cooperation leads to a significant degree of market power on the purchasing market by establishing considerable buying power. In most cases, such market power is unlikely where parties to a joint purchasing arrangement have a combined market share not exceeding 15% on the purchasing market(s) as well as a combined market share not exceeding 15% on the selling market(s).[170] In the event of higher market shares, the joint purchasing arrangement will have to be assessed individually under Article 101 TFEU.

Agreements on joint *commercialization* are generally more problematic, because they are likely to affect customers more directly. This includes cooperation between competitors in the selling, distribution, or promotion of their substitute products and can vary, for instance, from joint selling arrangements that lead to the joint determination of commercial aspects related to the sale of the product (such as price), to limited cooperation on one specific aspect such as distribution, after-sales, or advertising. Whether joint commercialization can lead to efficiency will depend on the nature of the activity and the parties to the cooperation. It is possible that the integration of economic activity such as joint distribution can lead to efficiencies for smaller producers because of economies of scale or scope. The main competitive concerns regard potential price-fixing, output limitation, the allocation of markets or customers, an increase in commonality of costs or an exchange of strategic information. However, commercialization agreements can only have restrictive effects on competition if the parties have some degree of market power. In most cases, such effects are likely to occur if the combined market share of the cooperating companies exceeds 15%.[171]

168. Horizontal Guidelines, cited *supra* note 159, paras. 150–154.
169. Art. 3 of the Specialisation Block Exemption Reg., cited *supra* note 64.
170. Horizontal Guidelines, cited *supra* note 159, para 208.
171. Horizontal Guidelines, cited *supra* note 159, para 240.

Another category of horizontal cooperation is *standardization* arrangements between competitors – with the primary objective of defining the technical or quality requirements with which current or future products, production processes, services or methods will comply. Once again, this type of cooperation takes many different shapes and forms, relating, for instance, to technical specifications, quality conditions, or standard terms and conditions. Standardization agreements and standard terms can be beneficial, for example when they facilitate technical interoperability and compatibility, reduce transaction costs for sellers and buyers and increase product quality. Standardization can also facilitate collusion, limit technical development and innovation by creating barriers of entry and by preventing certain companies from having access to the standards. It is generally recognized that there will not normally be any restriction of competition if participation in setting standards is unrestricted, and the procedure for adopting the standard in question is transparent – in other words, when there is no obligation to comply with the standard and access thereto is provided on fair, reasonable and non-discriminatory terms (FRAND terms).[172]

2.8 *Cartels*

The concept of *hard-core cartel* includes the more traditional forms of horizontal collusion between competitors in an effort to fix prices, allocate customers, divide territories, restrict output or organize a collective boycott. Hard-core cartels have been around for centuries and are not limited to one particular sector. There have been examples of hard-core cartels in many different sectors of the economy including banking, vitamins, cement, chemicals, televisions, tobacco, construction and auction houses. Most of these cartels were aimed at reducing competition, bringing stability to the market ("live and let live"), bringing price stability by avoiding a price war ("don't rock the boat") or keeping new competitors out of the market.

At a more abstract level, hard-core cartels involve coordination for the purpose of removing the risk of competition and related uncertainties of conduct by competitors. A good example of a traditional hard-core cartel is the organic peroxide cartel. For years, its participants went to Switzerland every few months for meetings organized by the consultant Fides/AC Treuhand for the legitimate purpose of receiving an aggregated factual overview of market developments ("white papers"). After the formal meeting, however, discussion continued: detailed overviews were given of prices and volumes for each product, customer and geographical region ("red papers"). As a result of these discussions there was a long period of collusion on price levels and market volume, and market share arrangements were made.[173]

The concept behind a hard-core cartel is relatively easy to understand. However, detecting cartels and finding evidence of their existence is not necessarily straightforward. According to established case law, it is up to the Commission to prove the existence of a cartel. The Commission must prove any infringement and adduce evidence capable of demonstrating – to the requisite legal standard – the existence of circumstances constituting an infringement. It is necessary for the Commission to produce precise and consistent evidence to support its firm conviction that an infringement has taken place.[174] Such evidence can come from various sources and may consist of a combination of communications such as email, (often hand-written) notes taken at meetings, agendas, internal memoranda, telephone data, documented communications in chat rooms, and declarations made by individuals. The existence of collusive conduct can be

172. Horizontal Guidelines, cited *supra* note 159, para 287.

173. Commission Decision of 10 Dec. 2003, *Organic Peroxides*, O.J. 2005, L 110/44. See also Commission Decision of 11 Nov. 2009, *Heat Stabilisers*, O.J. 2009, Case COMP/38.589.

174. See e.g. Case T-30/10, *Reagens SpA v. Commission*, paras. 117–128.

inferred from a number of coincidences and indicia which, taken together, may in the absence of another plausible explanation, constitute evidence of an infringement of Article 101(1) TFEU.[175] By providing evidence that supports another plausible explanation, an undertaking can call into question the Commission's finding that the facts cannot be explained other than by the existence of anti-competitive conduct within the meaning of Article 101(1) TFEU.

Obviously, the authorities can try to find evidence by wielding their investigatory powers such as conducting raids and issuing requests for information. However, amnesty or leniency programmes that provide an incentive for participants in cartels to come forward and self-report in exchange for lenient treatment have been by far the most successful means of detection. Applicants for lenient treatment need to admit to infringement of Article 101(1) TFEU and need to hand over all evidence of the violation. In practice, most investigations are triggered by an application for leniency.[176]

Hard-core cartels come in various shapes and forms and their character can change over time. Cartels can start covering one product and then expand to include several other products and services. Cartels can evolve from one isolated incident and then go on to include various related activities that ultimately display a well-organized and stable pattern of conduct. The number and role of participants can vary, and may change over time for as long as the cartel exists. This makes it a challenge for authorities to define and qualify the specific conduct that violates Article 101(1) TFEU. As mentioned above, the Commission can tie together the various elements of collusive conduct within the concept of a single complex and continuous infringement ("SCCI") of Article 101(1). This makes it possible for the Commission to put together or, in other words, "package" the different elements and characteristics of a cartel that form part of an overall plan to distort competition into a single infringement of Article 101(1) TFEU. For an SCCI there must be collusive conduct involving a single, overall plan which is in violation of Article 101(1). There has to be a common anti-competitive objective and a link of complementarity between the various elements of the conduct pursuing the anti-competitive effect. The participants in the cartel need to have actual or presumed knowledge that their acts will contribute to the single, overall plan, and they will have not taken any action to publicly distance themselves from it.[177] Public distancing effectively spells the end of the common understanding. An undertaking can only be held liable for participation in the SCCI if evidence arising from its conduct shows that it intended to contribute to the common objectives pursued by all participants, and that it was aware of the conduct planned or put into effect by other undertakings in pursuit of those same objectives – or that it could reasonably have foreseen this – and that it was prepared to take that risk.[178] It is up to the Commission to indicate and substantiate, based on the evidence, whether an undertaking violated Article 101(1) TFEU by either participating

---

175. See in this sense Joined Cases C-204, 205, 211, 213, 217 & 219/00 P, *Aalborg PortlandA/S, Irish Cement Ltd, Ciments français SA, Italcementi – Fabbriche Riunite Cemento SpA), Buzzi Unicem SpA and Cementir – Cementerie del Tirreno SpA v. Commission*, para 57 and Case T-30/10, para 119.
176. The Leniency Notice, cited *supra* note 19.
177. See in this sense Joined Cases T-101 & 111/05, *BASF*, paras. 159–161.
178. Case C-287/11 P, *Commission v. Aalberts Industries NV and Others*, para 63. In Case T-758/14, *Infineon Technologies AG v. Commission*, para 227, the General Court confirmed that participants of a cartel will be held liable only to the extent of their awareness of the infringement as a whole. In order to be qualified as a single and continuous infringement, the Commission has to show (i) that the participants shared a single and common anti-competitive objective and (ii) complementarity between the contacts as evidence that they were part of the same overall plan.

in the SCCI or only in certain specific elements thereof, and to attribute liability accordingly i.e. for the SCCI as a whole or the specific elements.[179]

Authorities have shifted their enforcement focus to include *atypical* cartels such as "hub & spoke" situations, facilitation, and signalling. Hub & spoke conduct can be described as an exchange of commercially sensitive information with a competitor that takes place via a third party such as a supplier or a customer. Instead of exchanging the information directly at the horizontal level, the exchange takes place via a third party at another level of (or outside) the distribution chain. A key element of a hub & spoke situation is that there is an intention or understanding, for instance between the supplier and the reseller, that the sensitive information concerned will be passed on by the supplier to the competing reseller (or possibly by the reseller to a competing supplier) with a view to coordinating the commercial conduct of the competing reseller.[180] A hub & spoke situation not only creates liability for the competing undertakings exchanging the information indirectly but also for the third "facilitating party". For instance, in *Organic Peroxides* and *Heat Stabilizers*, the Commission fined consultant AC-Treuhand for acting as the facilitator of the collusive conduct in the respective cartel.[181] Another atypical cartel situation can arise when competitors engage in signalling – exchanging information via public announcements. According to the Commission, there is no problem when an undertaking makes a unilateral announcement (on pricing or other commercial conditions) that is genuinely public, for instance by means of a press release or in a newspaper. However, the way competitors respond to each other's announcements can also amount to collusive conduct. It is possible for a competitor's response to a public announcement to be used as a strategy for reaching common understanding on the terms of coordination.[182] There are several examples of signalling cases that have become a subject of investigation.[183]

2.9 *Vertical agreements*

Manufactures can choose from among various methods of product distribution. They may decide to distribute their products or services in-house, meaning that although they bear the economic risk of distribution, they are generally shielded from application of Article 101 TFEU. This also holds true when a manufacturer appoints a commercial agent. By contrast, Article 101 TFEU will apply to vertical agreements concluded between independent undertakings, as the Court confirmed in *Consten & Grundig*.[184] Such agreements are entered into by undertakings operating at different levels of the production or distribution chain, and their main purpose is to facilitate the distribution of products and services from the manufacturing level to the end consumer. Vertical agreements can lead to economic efficiencies by facilitating better

---

179. See in this context Case T-68/09, *Soliver NV v. Commission*, paras. 62–67.
180. In the UK, an essential precondition for establishing a hub & spoke violation seems to be the understanding or intention of the parties involved. See e.g. CA/98/8/2003, *Agreements between Hasbro UK Ltd, Argos Ltd & Littlewoods Ltd fixing the price of Hasbro toys and games*, and related judgment in Case 2005/1071 and 1074, *Argos Ltd/Littlewoods v. Office of Fair Trading*.
181. See in this context Case T-99/04, *AC-Treuhand AG v. Commission*, Case T-27/10, *AC-Treuhand AG v. Commission*, and Case C-194/14 P, *AC-Treuhand v. Commission*. By contrast, see A.G. Wahl in Case C-194/14, *AC-Treuhand v. Commission* who opined that AC-Treuhand could not be held liable. See also Commission Press Release, "Commission fines broker ICAP Euro 14.9 million for participation in several cartels in Yen interest rate derivatives sector", IP/15/4104, (2015).
182. Horizontal Guidelines, cited *supra* note 159, para 63.
183. See e.g. Autoriteit Consument en Markt Press Release, "Commitments decision regarding mobile operators" Case 13.0612.53, (2014) and Commission Press Release "Antitrust: Commission confirms inspections in the sector of maritime transport services", (2012).
184. This was confirmed in Joined Cases 56 & 58/64, *Consten and Grundig*.

coordination, reducing transaction and distribution costs, and by optimizing sales and investment levels. However, they may also restrict intra-brand competition, for example when export bans or resale provisions prevent distributors from competing with each other. They can also restrict inter-brand competition, if an undertaking restricts the freedom of its distributors or suppliers to do business with its competitors.[185]

The Commission created a safe haven for categories of vertical agreements and published a block exemption for certain categories of vertical agreements. Block exemption Regulation 330/2010 and the related Guidelines on Vertical Restraints[186] provide guidance on how to assess vertical agreements under Article 101 TFEU. Over the years, the Commission shifted from taking a legalistic to a more economic approach in dealing with vertical agreements. This approach is based on the presumption that where the market share held by each of the contracting parties on the relevant market does not exceed 30% ("no market power"), vertical agreements generally lead to an improvement in production or distribution, unless they contain certain types of severe restrictions of competition. These "hard-core restrictions" include minimum and fixed resale prices (such as "resale price maintenance"), certain types of territorial protection (including "export bans"), restriction of active or passive sales to end-users by members at the retail level of a selective distribution system, restriction of cross-supplies between distributors within a selective distribution system, and restrictions that prevent buyers of components from selling them as spare parts to end-users or service providers such as repairers.[187] The presence of such stipulations implies that the agreement cannot benefit from the block exemption regulation. Furthermore, the block exemption does not apply to certain obligations, such as overly long non-compete obligations, without their presence implying the loss of the benefit of the exemption.[188]

A vertical agreement that is not covered by the block exemption will have to be assessed individually, first under Article 101(1) TFEU in order to establish whether it appreciably restricts competition and, if so, in order to assess whether it meets the conditions of Article 101(3). This implies an analysis of the features of the agreement, the parties and the market in which they operate. Such an assessment may have to be made on a periodic basis as it is sensitive to changes in the factual assumptions.[189]

Companies can make a choice, depending on the business model and characteristics of the product or service, between various types of distribution systems that bring their product or service to the consumer. They may also include various restrictions in their agreements. The focus of these restraints may be on pricing, customers, territories, products and possibly sales techniques. In the Guidelines on Vertical Restraints, the Commission elaborates on how the various distribution systems (and related vertical restraints) can be assessed under Article 101 TFEU, referring to distribution systems such as single branding, exclusive distribution, selective distribution and franchise.

The distribution arrangement in *single branding* means the buyer is obliged (or induced) to concentrate its orders for a particular product with one supplier. This can be organized by means of a non-compete arrangement that obliges or encourages the buyer to purchase nearly all of what it needs from one supplier. Another way to arrange single branding is by quantity-forcing

---

185. Case C-234/89, *Delimitis v. Henninger Bräu*, para 39.
186. Commission Reg. 330/2010, cited *supra* note 61, and Guidelines on Vertical Restraints, cited *supra* note 61.
187. Art. 4 of Commission Reg. 330/2010, cited *supra* note 61.
188. Art. 5(1) of Commission Reg. 330/2010, cited *supra* note 61.
189. Guidelines on Vertical Restraints, cited *supra* note 61, paras. 122–127.

on the basis of incentives or obligations that make the buyer concentrate its purchases, directing it to a large extent toward one supplier.[190]

In an *exclusive distribution* system, the supplier agrees to sell its products to a single distributor for resale in a particular territory; that distributor is usually restricted from making active sales to other (exclusively allocated) territories. Under an exclusive customer allocation arrangement, the supplier agrees to sell its products to a sole distributor for resale to a particular group of customers (with the distributor restricted from actively selling to other exclusively allocated groups of customers). These exclusivity arrangements allow the distributor to actively invest and focus on a particular territory or group of customers.[191]

A *selective distribution* system restricts the number of authorized distributors on the basis of qualitative (and possibly, quantitative) selection criteria (linked to the nature of the product), and obliges these selected distributors to only sell to appointed dealers and final customers (excluding non-authorized dealers). In practice, a selective distribution system is mostly used for exclusive, high-quality, branded final products such as cosmetics and high-end technology audio systems.[192] The choice for a selective distribution system is often made in an effort to ensure that the product is offered and sold to customers by well-trained employees with detailed knowledge of the product, in an exclusive environment that contributes to the "high-end" reputation of the "quality product". On the one hand, the block exemption exempts selective distribution agreements that meet the criteria – regardless of the nature of the product concerned and regardless of the nature of the selection criteria. On the other hand, there is some risk that the benefit of the block exemption can be withdrawn, for instance if the characteristics of the product do not require selective distribution or do not require the applied criteria.[193] Although under certain circumstances internet sales undermine the image and the quality-image of certain products, an absolute ban on internet sales restricts competition and constitutes an infringement of Article 101(1) TFEU.[194]

Franchising is often used for the creation of a uniform distribution network with a common identity and reputation. For this purpose, franchising combines the distribution of goods or services with the use of a particular business method (developed and maintained by the franchisor). Franchising agreements include intellectual property licences for trademarks or signs, and know-how for the use and distribution of goods or services in combination with commercial or technical assistance. Under the franchise agreement, the franchisee pays a franchise fee to the franchisor for the licence and assistance.[195]

For many years, there was a separate block exemption regulation for the distribution of automobiles. However, as of 1 June 2013 – and after a transitional period of three years – the purchase, sale and resale of new motor vehicles is covered by the vertical block exemption Regulation. Because of certain competition issues arising on the aftermarkets, such as access by independent

190. Guidelines on Vertical Restraints, cited *supra* note 61, paras. 129–150.
191. Guidelines on Vertical Restraints, cited *supra* note 61, paras. 151–173.
192. Case 26/76, *Metro* and Case C-230/16, *Coty Germany GmbH v. Parfümerie Akzente GmbH.*
193. Guidelines on Vertical Restraints, cited *supra* note 61, paras. 174–188.
194. Case C-439/09, *Pierre Fabre Dermo-Cosmétique SAS v. Président de l'Autorité de la concurrence and Ministre de l'Économie, de l'Industrie et de l'Emploi*, paras. 35–54. See also Case C-230/16, *Coty*. The Commission published its final report on e-commerce sector inquiry in May 2017 and in February 2017, it had opened three investigations into anti-competitive practices in e-commerce. See respectively Commission Press Releases, "Antitrust: Commission publishes final report on e-commerce sector inquiry", IP/17/1261 (2017) and "Antitrust: Commission opens three investigations into suspected anticompetitive practices in e-commerce", IP/17/201, (2017).
195. Guidelines on Vertical Restraints, cited *supra* note 61, paras. 189–191. See also Case 161/84, *Pronuptia*.

repairers to spare parts and other equipment, there is still a special block exemption regulation for vertical agreements that relate to spare parts and the provision of repair and maintenance services for motor vehicles. The Commission published supplementary guidelines in an effort to help companies make their own assessment of vertical agreements for the sale and repair of motor vehicles and for the distribution of spare parts.[196] In the Guidelines, the Commission gives its views on how to assess, under Article 101 TFEU, arrangements such as single branding and selective distribution in the motor vehicle sector.

2.10 *Licensing agreements*

Intellectual property rights ("IPRs") are the result of creative and innovative human activity and are of crucial importance to the consumer and the economy as a whole. In return for these efforts, the holder of an IPR – such as a copyright, trademark, patent, or breeders right – enjoys an exclusive right allowing him to prevent any other third party from infringing on this right. The holder of the right can decide to exploit the IPR himself, or can decide to involve third parties by granting licences under certain contractual conditions set out in licence agreements that may include provisions on the licence fee, restrictions on the relevant territory and the field of use, duration, and non-compete arrangements. The same can be done for know-how which is a collection of practical information resulting from experience and testing that is secret, substantial and identifiable.[197] Such licencing agreements between two or more undertakings can trigger Article 101(1) TFEU, especially when they grant the licensee absolute territorial protection or restrict his freedom to set prices.[198]

The Commission again sought to increase legal certainty when it adopted block exemption Regulation 316/2014 for technology transfer agreements and issued the Commission Guidelines on technology transfer agreements.[199] The block exemption only covers technology transfer agreements between two undertakings, namely the licensor permitting the licensee to exploit the licenced technology rights (possibly after further research and development by the licensee) for the purpose of producing goods or services. Technology transfer agreements between competitors can benefit from the block exemption where the combined share of the relevant markets accounted for by the parties does not exceed 20%. This threshold goes up to 30% for agreements concluded between non-competitors.[200] However, an agreement cannot benefit from the block exemption if it contains one or more hard-core restrictions such as pricing, output, markets or customer restrictions.[201] Certain restrictions that frustrate incentives to innovate cannot benefit from the block exemption, but they do not prevent the rest of an agreement from benefitting from the exemption. Examples are grant back obligations and non-challenge clauses.[202]

---

196. Commission Reg. 461/2010, cited *supra* note 62, and Commission Supplementary guidelines on vertical restraints in agreements for the sale and repair of motor vehicles and for the distribution of spare parts for motor vehicles, O.J. 2010, C 138/16.
197. See in this sense Art. 1(1)(i) of Commission Reg. 316/2014, cited *supra* note 63, See also in this context the Commission Guidelines on the application of Art. 101 of the Treaty on the Functioning of the European Union to technology transfer agreements, O.J. 2014, C 89/3, para 45.
198. See e.g. Joined Cases 56 & 58/64, *Consten and Grundig*; Case 258/78, *L.C. Nungesser KG and Kurt Eisele v. Commission*; Case 161/84, *Pronuptia*, and Case 27/87, *SPRL Louis Erauw-Jacquery v. La Hesbignonne SC*.
199. Commission Reg. 316/2014, note 63. See also in this context the Commission Guidelines, ibid., paras. 8 and 9.
200. Art. 3 of Commission Reg. 316/2014, cited *supra* note 63.
201. Art. 4 of Commission Reg. 316/2014, cited *supra* note 63.
202. Art. 5 of Commission Reg. 316/2014, cited *supra* note 63.

3. Abuses of dominant position[203]

3.1 The structure of Article 102 TFEU

For the prohibition of Article 102 TFEU to apply, several conditions must be fulfilled. First, unlike Article 101 TFEU, Article 102 does not apply to all undertakings. It requires the undertaking concerned to hold a dominant position. This implies that the market in which this dominance is allegedly present must be defined.[204]

Second, the dominant position must be held in the internal market or in a substantial part thereof. This raises the question of how to define "a large part of the internal market". Generally speaking, the territory of a Member State, including the smaller ones, is considered large enough.[205] This does not necessarily hold true for regions of Member States, even though some regions are themselves larger than the territory of certain Member States. For example, the ECJ held that Wallonia could be considered to represent a large part of the internal market, but this was not the case for the Alsace region.[206] Important infrastructure, such as large ports and airports, can also be qualified as comprising a large part of the internal market.[207]

Third, the undertaking or undertakings concerned must abuse their dominant position. Article 102 TFEU offers a non-exhaustive list of examples of abuse. Although the abusive conduct may consist of restrictive agreements, Article 102 TFEU primarily targets the conduct of the dominant undertaking(s). It can therefore be argued that by targeting unilateral conduct as well, Article 102 TFEU has a wider scope than Article 101 TFEU. It should also be noted that the text of Article 102 TFEU refers to an abuse by one or more undertakings. It follows from the case law that this collective aspect does not relate to the conduct, but to the dominant position which can be of an oligopolistic nature.[208]

Fourth, the contested abuse must affect trade between Member States. This condition is normally deemed to be met if the other conditions are already fulfilled. Indeed, the conduct of a dominant undertaking can be presumed to have an impact on the structure of competition, particularly where the conduct seeks to eliminate a competitor.[209] The ECJ has ruled, however, that the inter-state condition is not met if that trade only occurs as a result of the abusive conduct.[210]

The present section will focus on the two main conditions for application of Article 102 TFEU, i.e. those relating to dominance and the abuse thereof. It should be noted from the outset

---

203. For further reading on Art. 102 TFEU, readers are referred to P. Akman, *The Concept of Abuse in EU Competition Law* (Hart, 2012); S. Bishop, and M. Walker, *The Economics of EC Competition Law: Concepts, Application and Measurement*, 3rd ed. (Sweet & Maxwell, 2010); J. Faull and A. Nikpay, *The EU Law of Competition*, 3rd ed. (OUP, 2014); R. Nazzini, *The Foundations of European Union Competition Law: The Objective and Principles of Art. 102* (OUP, 2011); R. O'Donoghue, and A.J. Padilla, *The Law and Economics of Art. 102 TFEU*, 2nd ed. (Hart, 2013); P. Akman, *The European Commission's Guidance on Art. 102 TFEU: From Inferno to Paradiso*, 73 MLR (2010).

204. See *supra*, section 1.5.

205. Case 127/73, *Belgische Radio en Televisie and société belge des auteurs, compositeurs et éditeurs v. SV SABAM and NV Fonior*, para 5.

206. See respectively, Case 311/84, *Centre belge d'études de marché – Télémarketing (CBEM) SA v. Compagnie luxembourgeoise de télédiffusion SA* and Case 247/86, *Société alsacienne et lorraine de télécommunications et d'électronique (Alsatel) v. SA Novasam.*

207. See respectively, Case C-179/90, *Merci convenzionali porto di Genova SpA v. Siderurgica Gabrielli SpA* and Case C-163/99, *Portugal v. Commission.*

208. Case C-393/92, *Municipality of Almelo and Others v. NV Energiebedrijf Ijsselmij*, paras. 41 and 42.

209. Joined Cases 6 & 7/73, *Istituto Chemioterapico Italiano S.p.A. and Commercial Solvents Corporation v. Commission*, paras. 32 and 33. Conversely, abuses on purely local markets are unlikely to affect inter-state trade; see Guidelines on inter-state trade, cited *supra* note 124, paras. 97–99.

210. Case 22/78, *Hugin Kassaregister AB and Hugin Cash Registers Ltd v. Commission.*

that there is a close link between the two conditions. The analysis under Article 102 TFEU starts with the contested conduct of the undertaking concerned. It is for the goods and services concerned by this conduct that dominance must be established.

However, a dominant position does not necessarily have to be established on the same market as the market on which the contested conduct takes place. It can also be an adjacent market, especially in monopolization cases where dominance in one market is used as a leverage to distort competition in another. For example, in the *CBEM* case, the firm under scrutiny was dominant in the market for commercial television and was accused of monopolizing the adjacent market for telephony services related to television advertising.[211] Similarly, in the *Microsoft* case, the dominant firm was accused of abusing its dominance in the market for PC operating software in order to monopolize the adjacent market for group servers and Google was hit with a €2.42 billion fine for abusing its market dominance as search engine by giving a Google product an illegal advantage in the separate comparing shopping market.[212] It follows from *Tetra Pak II* that, even in the absence of monopolization attempts in adjacent markets, the abuse does not necessarily have to take place on the same market as the dominated market. The case concerned predatory pricing practices in the market for non-aseptic packaging materials where dominance was not established. The Court decided, however, that the disconnect between the abuse (in the non-aseptic products market) and dominance (on the market for aseptic packaging products) could only be justified in light of the special circumstances of the case.[213]

3.2 *The concept of dominance*

The ECJ has systematically referred to dominance as "a position of economic strength enjoyed by an undertaking which enables it to prevent effective competition being maintained on the relevant market by giving it the power to behave to an appreciable extent independently of its competitors, customers and ultimately of its consumers".[214] This concept of independence seems to refer to a degree of market power enabling the dominant undertaking to maintain prices above the competitive level or to reduce output without losing turnover.[215] However, this concept of independence is not incompatible with occasional fierce price competition or with occasionally incurring short term losses.[216] The idea is that the dominant firm has the ability to maintain its strong position over time.[217]

This temporal dimension is not always clear. In some cases, undertakings enjoy a dominant position due to exceptional circumstances such as strikes affecting competitors, transport problems, or public trade embargos. The Court of Justice did not rule out that taking advantage of such circumstances could constitute abuse.[218] Nor did it rule out that abuse can take place in the presence of potential competition, if the disciplinary influence is taking too long to exert its

211. Case 311/84, *CBEM v. CLT*.
212. Case T-201/04, *Microsoft Corp. v. Commission* and Commission decision of 27 Jun. 2017, *Google*, (AT.39740) pending appeal before the General Court.
213. Case C-333/94 P, *Tetra Pak International SA v. Commission*, ("Tetra Pak II"), para 27. In some respects, the relationship between dominance and abuse may lead to circular reasoning in the sense that a firm is held to be dominant precisely because it can engage in certain types of conduct.
214. Case C-27/76, *United Brands Company and United Brands Continentaal BV v. Commission*, para 65.
215. See also Commission Guidance Paper, cited *supra* note 20, paras. 10 and 11.
216. Case 322/81, *NV Nederlandsche Banden Industrie Michelin v. Commission*, ("Michelin I"), para 59.
217. Case 85/76, *Hoffmann-La Roche & Co. AG v. Commission*, para 44. See also Case T-321/05, *AstraZeneca AB and AstraZeneca plc v. Commission*, para 267.
218. Case 77/77, *Benzine en Petroleum Handelsmaatschappij BV and Others v. Commission*.

effect on the firm under scrutiny.[219] It should also be mentioned in this context that a finding of dominance in the concentration control proceedings does not provide conclusive evidence for the existence of a dominant position in an Article 102 TFEU case. This is because concentration control is prospective in nature, whilst Article 102 requires actual or past market conduct.[220]

The fact that an undertaking is found to be dominant is not an accusation – holding such a position is not prohibited. Many objective explanations can be given for a position of dominance – for instance, historical reasons and/or State intervention. This holds true particularly in sectors of the economy which were governed by State owned monopolies before they were opened to competition. Dominance can also result from the competitiveness of the firm in question. Companies such as Microsoft, Intel, and Google – that are or were considered "dominant" by the Commission – have rapidly expanded their market position by virtue of their innovative efforts. Although Article 102 TFEU does not prohibit their market dominance, it nevertheless considerably restricts their commercial freedom. The ECJ explains this additional burden on dominant firms by the special responsibility not "to impair genuine undistorted competition" in markets where competition is already weakened by the very presence of a dominant firm.[221]

Dominant positions can exist in many forms. First, it is possible to draw a distinction between horizontal and vertical forms of dominance. Horizontal dominance concerns the market power of the undertaking under scrutiny in comparison to its competitors on the same market. In these situations, it is very important to properly define the relevant market. The undertaking that is said to be dominant has an interest in arguing that the market should be defined broadly so as to minimize its position thereon, whereas the undertakings complaining about its conduct will claim that the market must be defined more narrowly so as to maximize that position.

Vertical dominance concerns the upstream and downstream relationship between the undertaking under scrutiny and its competitors. This implies that the undertaking under scrutiny commands access to an input or outlet against which its competitors need to compete. Input foreclosure cases sometimes lead to a very narrow definition of the upstream market. For example, a firm that produces a unique piece of equipment is likely to have a dominant position on the downstream market for spare parts for that equipment.[222] Such narrow market definitions can also result from regulatory intervention. For example, in *General Motors* the "regulated" market concerned the market for technical certificates which the owner of the car brand needed to deliver to be able to register the exported car in other Member States.[223] Intellectual property rights can also imply that the undertaking concerned commands access to an essential component of the downstream product. For example, in the *Magill* case, an independent producer of television programme guides needed access to the programming data of the three television companies then (i.e. the eighties) broadcasting in Ireland.[224] However, those "listings" were protected by copyright. Ten years later a comparable problem arose in *Microsoft*; the owner of the copyright on Windows operating software was accused of refusing access to elements of the

---

219. Case C-333/94 P, *Tetra Pak* II, para 29 and Case T-340/03, *France Télécom SA v. Commission*, para 111.

220. Case T-125/97, *The Coca-Cola Company and Coca-Cola Enterprises Inc. v. Commission*, para 81.

221. Case T-286/09, *Intel Corp. v. Commission*, paras. 90 and 91. See also Case 322/81, *Michelin I*, para 57.

222. Case 22/78, *Hugin*, and Case 53/87, *Consorzio italiano della componentistica di ricambio per autoveicoli and Maxicar v. Régie nationale des usines Renault*. See for a more nuanced approach, Pelikan/Kyocera, Commission 25th Annual Report on Competition Policy, 1995, para 87.

223. Case 26/75, *General Motors Continental NV v. Commission*. See also Case 226/84, *British Leyland Public Limited Company v. Commission*.

224. Joined Cases C-241 & 242/91 P, *Radio Telefis Eireann (RTE) and Independent Television Publications Ltd (ITP) v. Commission* ("Magill").

software ("interface information") which were required to connect group servers to individual PCs.[225]

Outlet foreclosure cases often concern so-called "essential facilities": infrastructure which is essential for access to the markets. These facilities are most often impossible to duplicate for technical, environmental or economic reasons. Typical examples are the electricity grid, gas transport pipelines and telecommunications networks which competitors need to access in order to be able to compete downstream on the markets for the supply of electricity, gas and electronic data. The fact that the pricing and access conditions of such networks are regulated by sector-specific rules does not preclude parallel application of Article 102 TFEU regarding the conduct of the owner of the infrastructure, unless that conduct was explicitly imposed by public regulation.[226] Other examples concern ports or airports; if the owner of such infrastructure also operates transport or ferry services, he may be tempted to offer his competitors disadvantageous access conditions.[227] However, the concept of "essential facility" can only be stretched so far. The Court made this clear in the *Bronner* case which concerned the refusal – by Mediaprint, the owner of a nationwide newspaper delivery scheme – to grant Mr Bronner access to its network. The ECJ noted that alternative forms of delivery, such as kiosks and shops, were available and that there were no technical, legal or economic obstacles preventing Mr Bronner from setting up his own delivery scheme. The Court added that "in order to demonstrate that the creation of such a system is not a realistic potential alternative and that access to the existing system is therefore indispensable, it is not enough to argue that it is not economically viable by reason of the small circulation of the daily newspaper or newspapers to be distributed".[228]

A second distinction concerns the difference between collective and sole dominance. Sole dominance refers to the dominant position of a single firm, whilst collective dominance refers to situations where two or more firms hold that position. The case law on collective dominance was initially prompted by arrangements made in a collusive context between the undertakings in question that were so strong as to give rise to a collective dominant position. Such links can exist for example in the context of a shipping line conference.[229] The case law extended the concept of collective dominance to tight oligopolies which are conducive to parallel behaviour – even in the absence of overt contacts. The General Court confirmed in *Gencor* that the concept of dominance includes this type of oligopoly, yet without limiting its application to concentration control.[230] It can therefore be argued that such oligopolistic situations also fall within the scope of Article 102 TFEU. A confirmation of this view can be found in the *Irish Sugar* case concerning the joint conduct of the leading Irish sugar producer and a smaller competitor in which the leading producer held a non-controlling stake.[231] The General Court considered that the economic independence of the two entities did not prevent them from holding the dominant position jointly, and that the mere independence of the economic entities in question was not sufficient

225. Case T-201/04, *Microsoft*.

226. Case C-280/08 P, *Deutsche Telekom AG v. Commission*, para 81. See also Case C-457/10 P, *AstraZeneca AB and AstraZeneca plc v. Commission*, para 132.

227. B&I/Sealink, Holyhead, 22nd Annual Report on Competition Policy, 1992, point 219. See also Commission Decision of 21 Dec. 1993, *Port of Rodby*, O.J. 1994, L 55/52.

228. Case C-7/97, *Oscar Bronner GmbH & Co. KG v. Mediaprint Zeitungs- und Zeitschriftenverlag GmbH & Co. KG, Mediaprint Zeitungsvertriebsgesellschaft mbH & Co. KG and Mediaprint Anzeigengesellschaft mbH & Co. KG*, para 45.

229. Joined Cases T-68, 77 & 78/89, *Società Italiana Vetro SpA, Fabbrica Pisana SpA and PPG Vernante Pennitalia SpA v. Commission* and Joined Cases C-395 & 396/96 P, *Compagnie Maritime Belge Transports SA and Others v. Commission*.

230. Case T-102/96, *Gencor*, paras. 273–277.

231. Case T-228/97, *Irish Sugar*.

to rule out the possibility of their holding a joint dominant position. The General Court also noted that the concept of joint dominance does not imply that the abuse itself must be collective as well: "Undertakings occupying a joint dominant position may engage in joint or individual abusive conduct. It is enough for that abusive conduct to relate to the exploitation of the joint dominant position which the undertakings hold in the market."[232]

3.3 *Proof of dominance*

The evidence required to establish the existence of a dominant position will depend to a large extent on the type of dominance at stake. Horizontal dominance can be hard to prove, especially when the parties disagree on the market definition and/or when the dominance is collective in nature. By contrast, vertical dominance is easier to prove. Once it is established that a certain input or access to certain infrastructure or outlets is required to compete on a market, the undertaking that owns that input or infrastructure is likely to hold a dominant position. Dominance is also relatively easy to prove when the undertaking concerned holds exclusive rights conferred by public authorities. However, intellectual property rights do not by themselves constitute evidence of a dominant position. That may be the case if no substitute for the goods or data protected by these rights is available, and the rights prevent third parties from copying the goods or data.[233]

In the absence of special circumstances, market shares are generally taken as the starting point of any analysis. This obviously requires that the relevant market first be defined. The 1997 Notice on the relevant market, covered in Section 1.5 above, lays down the methodology used by the Commission in competition cases – including those brought under Article 102 TFEU. Before adoption of the Notice, the EU Court's case law developed its own criteria, which are probably no longer relevant today. A good example of the prior approach can be found in the *United Brands* case, in which the ECJ had to decide whether bananas constituted a market of their own or whether they were part of the wider market for fruit in general. In its analysis, the Court focused on demand emanating from a very confined set of consumers – "the very young, the old and the sick", who presumably accept no substitute for bananas – without assessing whether that group was representative of total customer demand.[234] It is also unlikely that the approach taken by the Court in *Continental Can* as regards the inclusion of supply-side substitutability is likely to be followed in future cases. There, the ECJ considered that the Commission had failed to explain why the market for light metal containers for meat and fish was distinct from other metal packaging markets, since the suppliers in those other markets could, by simply adapting, pose a serious counterweight.[235] As mentioned above, the methodology proposed in the 1997 Notice focuses on demand and only includes supply-side substitutability if it has a disciplining effect as immediate as that resulting from consumer preference.[236] Recent cases decided under Article 102 TFEU are not likely to give useful extra guidance on defining the market. Those precedents are very fact specific and do not give insight into what the Commission's future decisional practice, and the Courts' future case law, will be.[237]

---

232. Case T-228/97, *Irish Sugar*, para 66.
233. See Joined Cases C-241 & 242/91 P, *Magill*, and Case C-418/01, *IMS Health GmbH & Co. OHG v. NDC Health GmbH & Co. KG*.
234. Case C-27/76, *United Brands*, para 31.
235. Case C-6/72, *Continental Can*, para 33.
236. Commission Notice, cited *supra* note 23.
237. For further reference see F. Gonzalez-Diaz, and R. Snelders (Ed.), *Abuse of Dominance under Art. 102 TFEU* (Claeys & Casteels, 2013). See also A. Jones and B. Sufrin, *EU Competition Law*, 5th ed. (OUP, 2014), at 61–87 and 198–334.

Assuming that the markets are defined both from a product point of view and from a geographical perspective, the question arises of how large a market share must be for it to be considered a valid indicator of a dominant position. The Courts have systematically considered that "very large market shares" held "over some time" "are in themselves, and save exceptional circumstances, evidence of the existence of a dominant position".[238] In *Akzo* the Court specified that 50% could be considered a "very large" market share.[239] The ECJ also attached considerable importance to the *relative* size of the market share: if the market shares of competing firms are very modest, a market share of less than 50% could also suffice to establish dominance.[240]

In its 2009 Guidance Paper, the Commission takes a different approach.[241] It does not state that very large market shares alone amount to conclusive evidence; rather, they merely give a useful preliminary indication. In addition, it approaches them in a negative way: i.e. low market shares are a good proxy for the absence of substantial market power, but high market shares cannot be said to be indicative of the presence of such. The Commission considers that, as a rule, dominance is not likely if the undertaking's market share is below 40%. It is submitted that the Commission is correct in taking a more cautious approach. Not even a market share of 100% is conclusive evidence of a dominant position if the undertaking concerned acts under competitive constraints which prevents it from increasing its prices without hurting demand for its products. These constraints can result from various factors: competing firms could enter the market or expand production in a manner that effectively deters the firm with the very large market share from increasing its own prices. Buying power can be another constraint: if the market share of the buyer on the demand side matches the market share of the supplier, and/or if that buyer is in a position to find alternative sources of supply, the supplier will be in no position to behave independently. Obviously, there will be no potential newcomers to the market in the presence of barriers to entry. Here again, the 2009 Guidance Paper offers a useful list of factors: legal barriers such as tariffs or quotas, economies of scale and scope, privileged access to essential inputs or natural resources, important technologies or an established distribution and sales network, network effects faced by customers in switching to a new supplier, the need to make significant investments and conclude long-term contracts that have appreciable foreclosing effects. The Guidance Paper also mentions that persistently high market shares may be indicative of the existence of barriers to entry and expansion.[242]

While this list refers to the Court's case law, it does not include all factors that EU courts have found to be relevant indicators of barriers to entry. For example, the 2009 Guidance Paper does not refer to high capital costs or the existence of spare capacity.[243] This is probably because economic thought has evolved as far as the phenomenon of capital as a barrier to entry is concerned. It is not so much the capital cost itself that is the problem, but rather the fact that a part of these costs is "sunk", i.e. cannot be recovered after market exit. This means that new entrants must ensure themselves of a sufficiently large customer base if they are to obtain a return on their investment.[244] In addition, the 2009 Guidance Paper fails to refer to other factors the Court

238. Case 85/76, *Hoffmann-La Roche*, para 41.
239. Case C-62/86, *Akzo Chemie BV v. Commission*, para 60.
240. See Case C-27/76, *United Brands*, where the dominance was established at 45% and Case T-219/99, *British Airways plc v. Commission*, para 183 where the market share of the accused undertaking hovered around 40%. See also Commission Decision of 24 Mar. 2004, *Microsoft*, Case COMP/C-3/37.792, para 435.
241. Commission Guidance Paper, cited *supra* note 20.
242. Commission Guidance Paper, cited *supra* note 20, para 17.
243. See respectively, Case C-27/76, *United Brands*, para 122 and Case 85/76, *Hoffmann-La Roche*, para 48.
244. See Case T-336/07, *Telefónica, SA and Telefónica de España, SA v. Commission*, para 121.

has identified as indicators of dominance, such as the vertical integration of the undertaking concerned, the strength of its distribution network and even its technological lead.[245]

To conclude, even though the concept of dominance is still largely determined by the Court's early case law, the same does not hold true for the evidence of dominance used therein. The factors the Court relied upon in past decades to define the relevant market and determine the position of the undertaking under scrutiny on that market do not correspond to present day economic thinking. Nor do they match the methodology proposed by the Commission in its 1997 Notice on the relevant market,[246] and to a lesser extent, in the 2009 Guidance Paper. It is submitted that this methodology, as well as the case law and decisional practice under Regulation 139/2004,[247] offers better insight into the type of evidence required to establish dominance than the Court's older case law.

3.4 *The concept of abuse*

Although the text of Article 102 TFEU suggests the existence of a causal relationship between the dominant position and the conduct which is held to be abusive, the abuse does not necessarily have to occur on the same market as the dominated market.[248] This relative disconnect between the concepts of abuse and dominance can be explained by the fact that the Court considers the concept of abuse objectively. It is the conduct itself that is assessed and not its cause. In *Hoffmann La Roche* the ECJ explained its position as follows: "The concept of abuse is an objective concept relating to the behaviour of an undertaking in a dominant position which is such as to influence the structure of a market where, as a result of the very presence of the undertaking in question, the degree of competition is weakened and which, through recourse to methods different from those which condition normal competition in products or services on the basis of the transactions of commercial operators, has the effect of hindering the maintenance of the degree of competition still existing in the market or the growth of that competition".[249]

The objective nature of the concept of abuse also implies that the conduct does not necessarily have to be intentional for it to trigger Article 102 TFEU. However, if it can be shown that the dominant firm behaved intentionally, that intent will be taken into consideration as a contributing factor.[250] In addition, if the objective of the contested conduct is to restrict competition and/or if that conduct restricts or merely tends to restrict competition, it is not necessary to show that these outcomes have actually ensued.[251] The General Court relied on its standard case law when it confirmed the Commission's decision in *Intel* "... for the purposes of applying Article 82 EC, showing an anti-competitive object and an anti-competitive effect may, in some cases, be one and the same thing. If it is shown that the object pursued by the conduct of an undertaking in a dominant position is to restrict competition, that conduct will also be liable to have such an effect".[252] It should be noted, however, that the judgment of the General Court in Intel was annulled by the Court on appeal. Although the Court's ruling focuses on a specific type of abuse, it conveys a message suggesting that effects have become more important. It held in grounds 138 and 139 that the *Hoffmann La Roche* case law mentioned above "must be further clarified in the

---

245. See respectively, Case C-27/76, *United Brands,* para 70. Also, Case 322/81, *Michelin I,* para 55 and 58.
246. Commission Notice, cited *supra* note 23.
247. Reg. 139/2004, cited *supra* note 5.
248. See *supra,* section 3.1.
249. Case 85/76, *Hoffmann-La Roche,* para 91.
250. Case C-549/10 P, *Tomra Systems ASA and Others v. Commission,* paras. 20 and 21. See also Case C-62/86, *Akzo.*
251. Case T-203/01, *Manufacture française des pneumatiques Michelin v. Commission,* ("Michelin II"), para 239.
252. Case T-286/09, *Intel,* para 203.

case where the undertaking concerned submits, during the administrative procedure, on the basis of supporting evidence, that its conduct was not capable of restricting competition and, in particular, of producing the alleged foreclosure effects", "the Commission is not only required to analyse, first, the extent of the undertaking's dominant position on the relevant market and, secondly, the share of the market covered by the challenged practice, as well as the conditions and arrangements for granting the rebates in question, their duration and their amount; it is also acquired to assess the possible existence of a strategy aiming to exclude competitors that are at least as efficient as the dominant undertaking from the market".[253]

Currently, the objective nature of the concept of abusive conduct does not give much insight into the type of conduct that could be prohibited by Article 102 TFEU. The definition taken from *Hoffmann La Roche* refers to methods different from those which apply to normal competition. Other cases refer to competition on the merits.[254] It is not clear, however, what "normal" or "merit based" competition means, especially in light of the consideration that the dominant undertaking bears a special responsibility. As discussed above, this responsibility implies that conduct which is considered normal and legal when it emanates from a non-dominant firm, ceases to be so if it emanates from a dominant undertaking. The criteria relating to normalcy or merits therefore do not relate to the conduct of the undertaking concerned, but to its dominant position. This begs the question of whether Article 102 TFEU penalizes dominant positions – a question which the Court answered in the negative.[255]

The lack of clarity and predictability attached to the concept of abuse in the Court's case law has provoked considerable criticism.[256] These doctrinal debates have also fuelled internal discussion within the Commission's services that ultimately led to the 2009 Guidance Paper, in which the Commission tried to create a yardstick for defining the concept of competition "on the merits". This yardstick is based on the notion that consumer welfare is the main objective competition rules must seek to protect.[257] These rules should not be invoked to protect competitors that are less efficient than the dominant undertaking. In addition, the form or external appearance of the conduct in question should not be relied upon to justify the presumption that harm to consumer welfare has occurred. Intervention should be restricted to cases where there is "cogent and convincing evidence" that such harm occurs or is likely to occur. In using this approach, interventions under Article 102 TFEU should be effects-based and not rely on the legal form of the conduct.

Until now, EU Courts have reacted ambiguously to the Commission's new approach. In some cases, they have applied the terms and tools proposed by the 2009 Guidance Paper. In *Post Danmark* for example, the ECJ explicitly mentioned that "competition on the merits may, by definition, lead to the departure from the market or the marginalisation of competitors that are less efficient and so less attractive to consumers [...]".[258] In other cases, the ECJ seem less inclined to follow the Commission's new approach.[259] The ECJ has provided more guidance in the area of rebates granted by dominant undertakings. In *Post Danmark II*, that Court held that practices must have an anti-competitive effect on the market to be considered abusive,

253. Case C-413/14, *Intel.*
254. Case C-457/10 P, *AstraZeneca*, para 134.
255. See *supra*, section 3.2.
256. See C. Ehlermann and M. Marquis (Eds.), *European Competition Law Annual 2007: A reformed approach to Art. 82 EC* (Hart, 2008). This book contains a series of articles criticizing the application of Art. 102 TFEU (then Art. 82 EC). See also R. O'Donoghue and J. Padilla, op. cit. *supra* note 203.
257. Commission Guidance Paper, cited *supra* note 20, para 19.
258. Case C-209/10, *Post Danmark*, para 22.
259. Case C-549/10 P, *Tomra*, paras. 73 and 79.

but that this effect only needs to be probable; therefore, there is no need to show that it is of a serious or appreciable nature.[260] However, the anticompetitive effect must not be of a "purely hypothetical nature".[261] The Court also considered that the "as-efficient competitor test", must be regarded as only one of several tools that can be used to assess whether there is abuse due to retroactive rebates. This approach seems to be confirmed by grounds 138 and 139 of the Court's judgment in Intel, quoted above. The as-efficient competitor test can be an important element contributing to the circumstances of the case which need to be taken into consideration by the Commission.[262]

The Court's judgment in *Intel* was preceded by both negative and positive commentary from the academic world on the General Court's judgment which held that an effects analysis was not required.[263] Although the Court's judgment shed some light on the effects issue, many other issues remain unresolved. For example, it is still unclear whether an as-efficient test is always required, and whether its outcome outweighs other elements of the overall assessment the Commission is supposed to make. It is submitted that the concept of abuse will never be crystal clear. Dealing with abuse of dominant positions involves complex economic phenomena which are perceived differently as a function of the interests defended by stakeholders, the prevailing societal concerns, and the leading schools of economic and philosophical thought. Any Article 102 TFEU case is "a child of its time" and should only be seen as such.[264] Fortunately, there is less of an intellectual divide as to how abuses should roughly be categorized. It is possible to distinguish between two broadly overlapping categories of abuse: exclusionary and exploitative. The first category, which is the subject matter of the 2009 Guidance Paper, concerns situations in which the dominant firm seeks to consolidate or extend its dominant position, whereas the second concerns situations in which competition has ceased to have any disciplinary effect thus leaving the undertaking concerned inclined to reap the benefits of its dominant position.

Finally, even if certain forms of conduct at first appear to be abusive in nature, the case law would seem to indicate that the dominant firm should be given a chance to justify its conduct on objective grounds. In *ABG* for example, BP was accused of abusing its dominant position by restricting sales to ABG to a much greater extent than it did to its other customers – without providing any objective reason for this behaviour. The ECJ did not agree: it noted the exceptional circumstances resulting from the oil embargo imposed on the Netherlands, and referred to the fact that ABG had only occasionally been a customer.[265] Ever since, although the matter of objective justification consistently comes up in the case law, dominant firms have met with little success when invoking objective grounds. In *Hilti*, the General Court made it clear that public safety considerations were a matter of concern for public authorities and could not justify the practices of the firm itself.[266] Even so, in *Post Danmark* the ECJ added a twist to its previous case law when it suggested the existence of an efficiency defence which could be seen as the corollary of the exception for dominant undertakings in Article 101(3) TFEU. After referring to its earlier case law, it went on to state that a dominant undertaking might be able to demon-

---

260. Case C-23/14, *Post Danmark v. A/S v. Konkurrencerådet*, paras. 70 and 74.
261. Case C-23/14, *Post Danmark II*, para 65.
262. C-413/14 P, *Intel*, paras. 142 and 143.
263. See e.g. the controversy between, on the one hand, W. Wils, "The judgment of the EU General Court in Intel and the so-called more economic approach to abuse of dominance", (2014) *World Competition*, at 405–434, and on the other hand, P. Rey, and J. Venit, "An effects-based approach to Art. 102: A response to Wouter Wils", (2015) *World Competition*, at 3–29.
264. G. Amato, *Antitrust and the Bounds of Power* (Hart, 1997).
265. Case 77/77, *BP*.
266. Case T-30/89, *Hilti AG v. Commission*, para 118.

strate "[...] that its conduct is objectively necessary or that the exclusionary effect produced may be counterbalanced, outweighed even, by advantages in terms of efficiency that also benefit consumers".[267] The 2009 Guidance Paper also refers to objective necessity on grounds beyond the dominant firm's control, and to efficiencies as a means of justifying *prima facie* abusive behaviour.[268] It is too early to draw conclusions on the practical relevance of the efficiency defence. In *Intel*, for example, the General Court noted that the dominant firm had not put forward any argument to that end.[269]

3.5 *Exclusionary practices*

Dominant firms can seek to reinforce their position in many ways. One of the main advantages of the 2009 Guidance Paper is that it offers an intellectual framework for the assessment of exclusionary practices, which it subdivides in two groups: anti-competitive foreclosure and price based conduct. With regard to the first group, which includes practices that prevent competitors from gaining access to certain inputs or to certain customers, the 2009 Guidance Paper enumerates a series of factors ("factors") that the Commission considers to be "generally relevant": the strength of the dominant position, the conditions on the relevant market (in particular the entry conditions), the position of competitors, customers and input suppliers, the duration and scope of the contested conduct, possible evidence that this conduct has produced actual effects on the market, as well as documentary evidence of an exclusionary strategy. With respect to the second group, the 2009 Guidance Paper states that the Commission will, as a rule, only intervene if the contested conduct affects competitors that are just as efficient as the dominant undertaking. It also offers cost-based criteria to carry out that test. The cost benchmarks are set by the average avoidable cost ("AAC") and the long-run average incremental cost ("LRAIC").[270] The 2009 Guidance Paper subsequently explains how these criteria can be used to assess specific forms of exclusionary conduct. Some of these will be discussed below.

In the first place, dominant firms can seek to foreclose their competitors by barring access to customers, for example by imposing exclusive purchasing obligations. In *Hoffmann La Roche* the ECJ held that such obligations fell afoul of Article 102 TFEU.[271] The Court condemned a similar practice in *United Brands*, where the dominant firm threatened to cut off one of its distributors if he continued to sell bananas obtained from competing suppliers.[272] Similarly, one of the abusive practices in the *Intel* case consisted of payments made to customers on the condition that they cease buying processors from Intel's competitors.[273] Imposing this type of *de facto* exclusivity also occurred in the *Irish freezer* case. Unilever, the dominant ice cream supplier in Ireland, offered to install freezers in its distributors' stores on the condition that the freezers be used exclusively for Unilever ice cream. Since the distributors did not at the time have sufficient space for freezers from competing suppliers, Unilever's freezer exclusivity requirement was tantamount to outlet exclusivity.[274] The 2009 Guidance Paper specifies, in light of the factors

---

267. Case C-209/10, *Post Danmark*, paras. 41 and 42.
268. Commission Guidance Paper, cited *supra* note 20, paras. 28–31.
269. Case T-286/09, *Intel*, para 94.
270. See footnote 2 under para 26 of the Commission Guidance Paper, cited *supra* note 20. It explains that AAC generally correspond to the average variable cost (AVC) and that average total cost (ATC) can be used as a proxy for LRAIC. Comparable proxies were used by the Court in *Akzo*, to determine when below-cost pricing is to be regarded as predatory in nature.
271. Case 85/76, *Hoffmann-La Roche*.
272. Case C-27/76, *United Brands*, paras. 163–196.
273. Case T-286/09, *Intel*.
274. Case T-65/98, *Van den Bergh Foods*.

mentioned above, that the relative strength of the dominant firm will determine whether anti-competitive foreclosure arises. This is particularly the case if the dominant undertaking is an "unavoidable trading partner" and/or where its brand is a "must stock item".[275]

In the second place, rebate schemes also offer an opportunity to foreclose competitors if the rebates are made conditional on an obligation for customers to acquire all or a significant portion of their requirements from the dominant supplier. Such rebates can indeed have a foreclosure effect if they apply to all purchases from the dominant firm. That they are retroactive implies that switching to a competing supplier becomes less attractive if the switch leads to the loss of rebates on all previous purchases from the dominant undertaking. The determination of whether or not foreclosure occurs depends on the modalities of the rebate scheme and, in particular, on how great a percentage of the total price is represented by the rebate. According to the 2009 Guidance Paper, the Commission will determine that such a scheme is capable of foreclosing equally efficient competitors if those competitors cannot make up the loss incurred in comparison with the customers willing to switch.[276]

However, up until now the Courts have refrained from applying the detailed analysis proposed by the 2009 Guidance Paper. Ever since *Hoffman La Roche*, EU courts have looked askance at rebate schemes which by virtue of their wording or "form" impose conditions demanding loyalty for all or a significant part of the customer's demand.[277] The General Court recalled this principle of case law in *Intel* by distinguishing three types of rebate scheme.[278] The first category concerns quantity rebate systems linked solely to the volume of purchases made from a dominant undertaking which are generally considered to not have a foreclosure effect on the market: "If increasing the quantity supplied results in lower costs for the supplier, the latter is entitled to pass on that reduction to the customer in the form of a more favourable tariff. Quantity rebates are therefore deemed to reflect gains in efficiency and economies of scale [...]".[279] The second category concerns loyalty or exclusivity rebates which are granted conditionally; the customer must obtain all or most of its requirements from the dominant undertaking. According to the General Court, such exclusivity rebates "are incompatible with the objective of undistorted competition within the common market, because they are not based — save in exceptional circumstances — on an economic transaction which justifies this burden or benefit but are designed to remove or restrict the purchaser's freedom to choose his sources of supply and to deny other producers access to the market", but they "are designed, through the grant of a financial advantage, to prevent customers from obtaining their supplies from competing producers".[280] The third category consists of rebate systems in which the financial incentive cannot be directly linked to a condition requiring that supplies be procured exclusively or quasi-exclusively from the dominant undertaking, even though the mechanism for granting the rebate is predicated on having a loyalty-building effect: "In examining whether the application of such a rebate constitutes an abuse of dominant position, it is necessary to consider all the circumstances, particularly the criteria and rules governing the grant of the rebate, and to investigate whether, in providing an advantage not based on any economic service justifying it, that rebate tends to remove or

---

275. Commission Guidance Paper, cited *supra* note 20, para 36. Please note that, until now, the Court considered Art. 102 TFEU to apply to exclusive purchasing obligations even in the absence of effects.
276. Commission Guidance Paper, cited *supra* note 20, paras. 37- 45.
277. See for a list of rebates covered by precedents, A. Jones and B. Sufrin, op. cit. *supra* note 237, at 455 and 456.
278. Case T-286/09, *Intel*.
279. Ibid., para 75.
280. Ibid., para 77.

restrict the buyer's freedom to choose his sources of supply, to bar competitors from access to the market, or to strengthen the dominant position by distorting competition."[281]

In its judgment on appeal, the Court neither rejected nor confirmed this categorization. It held that the Hoffmann La Roche case law needed to be "clarified" in situations where the undertaking concerned submits – and can substantiate – that its conduct was not capable of restricting competition or, in particular, of producing the alleged foreclosure effects.[282] It could therefore be argued that the loyalty rebates falling under the second category defined by the General Court could as such be considered abusive, unless the undertaking concerned presents alternative arguments supported by evidence. Since companies and their counsel are likely to raise such arguments whenever they are involved in an abuse of dominance case, it is reasonable to submit that a purely formal analysis will no longer suffice to characterize loyalty rebates as abusive conduct and, hence, that the second category of rebates defined by the General Court has become part of its third category, as suggested by Advocate general Wahl in his opinion in Intel.

In the third place, dominant firms can seek to foreclose their competitors by forcing tied sales on their customers. This can occur in many forms, and the *Hilti* case provides a good illustration of a dominant supplier's inventiveness. Hilti, a supplier of nail guns and cartridges used in the construction industry, made the sale of cartridges conditional upon the sale of a corresponding number of nails, either contractually or by reducing discounts. It also discouraged its distributors from selling competing Hilti-compatible nails by, for instance, refusing to sell them cartridges or by refusing to honour the guarantee on nail guns that had been used with nails from competing suppliers.[283] Similarly, in *Tetra Pak II*, the leading supplier of packaging machines offered to install and maintain packaging machines for its customers provided they bought the necessary cartons exclusively from Tetra Pak. The Courts rejected Tetra Pak's argument that it was not forcing the tied sale of different products, but rather selling one integrated packaging solution.[284] Another well-known example of a tied sale can be found in the *Microsoft* case; the dominant supplier of PC operating software (Windows) technically integrated the Windows Media Player ("WMP") into it, hence dampening the interest of computer manufacturers in installing competing media players on their devices. The Commission held that Windows and WMP were two separate products and that Microsoft was seeking to monopolize the market for media players by abusing its dominant position in the PC operating software market. The General Court upheld the Commission's finding that this form of technical bundling was abusive.[285]

The 2009 Guidance Paper explains various types of tied sale and bundling. Once again, the Commission displays a nuanced take on such practices. Despite the fact that Article 102(d) TFEU refers to tied sale as an example of abuse of a dominant position, the Commission will only intervene if the following two conditions are met: first, the products in question must be different in the sense that there is separate customer demand for each of them; and second, the anti-competitive foreclosure must occur either in the tied market, in a market in the process of becoming tied, or in both markets at the same time. Whether this is the case cannot be taken for granted but, rather, depends on the factors indicated above. The risk of anti-competitive foreclosure is considered to be the greatest if the technical bundling is costly to reverse, or makes resale of the individual components more difficult.

---

281. Ibid., para 78.
282. Case C-413/14 P, *Intel*, para 138.
283. Case C-53/92 P, *Hilti AG v. Commission*.
284. Case C-333/94 P, *Tetra Pak II*.
285. Case T-201/04, *Microsoft*.

In the fourth place, dominant firms can try to eliminate competition by selling below cost. Such predatory pricing is controversial since it also leads to lower prices, to the benefit of consumers. The competitive concern is, however, that after all competitors have been eliminated, the dominant firm will recover its losses by increasing prices. The undertaking will thus "recoup" its "sacrifice". The first time the Commission and Court dealt with predation in this sense was in the *Akzo* case, which concerned the market for a bleaching agent that could be used in both the flour-milling and chemical sectors. The dominant supplier of the bleaching agent, Akzo, concentrated its activities on the latter sector. When it noticed that ECS, a smaller UK competitor active in the flour sector, was starting to make incursions on the chemical sector, Akzo retaliated by making its own incursions on the bakery sector – mainly by offering to sell the bleaching agent to ECS's largest customers at a very low price point. The question was whether these prices were predatory in nature. The ECJ confirmed the Commission's decision that the conduct was abusive, but relied on the cost test developed by Areeda and Turner, two American academics.[286] On that basis, the Court held that any prices that did not cover Akzo's average variable costs ("AVC"), as a proxy of marginal costs, were presumed to be abusive because any sale implied a loss. By contrast, prices above AVC, but below average total costs ("ATC"), were considered illegal only "if they are determined as part of a plan of eliminating a competitor".[287] In that price range, predatory intent seems to be the decisive element. In two subsequent cases, the Court applied the same test it used in *Akzo*. It also made clear that this test did not require the Commission to show that the dominant firm would recover or "recoup" the losses incurred by selling below cost.[288]

The 2009 Guidance Paper provides further interpretation of the *Akzo* test. First, as mentioned above, the Commission now uses the concepts of AAC and LRAIC as alternatives to the notions of AVC and ATC. Second, it is not as categorical as the Court in *Akzo*; pricing below AAC is in itself abusive. Such pricing is considered to give a "clear indication of sacrifice" by the dominant firm. The Commission requires the existence of a likelihood that anti-competitive foreclosure will befall competitors that are as efficient as the dominant firm, and harm to the consumer. It also adds that is easier for dominant firms to engage in predatory conduct if they selectively target customers with low prices.

The case law confirms the latter finding. It is sometimes difficult to distinguish abusive predatory pricing practices from discriminatory pricing practices. In *Akzo* for example, the dominant firm targeted ECS's main customer in the flour sector. However, selective pricing may also be abusive in the absence of below-cost pricing. In *Compagnie Maritime Belge* for example, the Commission and Courts considered selective price undercutting by a liner conference (known as CEWAL) in order to eliminate outsider competition (from Grimaldi, not a member of the conference) to be abusive, without examining the question of whether the prices charged by the "fighting ships" (mobilized by CEWAL to target Grimaldi's customers) were loss-making. It should be noted, however, that the case had certain distinguishing features. The ECJ emphasized that the liner conference had a collective market share of 90% and that it collectively targeted one specific competitor.[289] In *Irish Sugar*, the General Court also upheld a Commission decision concerning a series of abusive practices including so-called "border rebates" that the dominant Irish supplier used to target customers close to the Northern Irish border; British

---

286. P. Areeda and D. Turner, "Predatory pricing and related practices under section 2 of the Sherman Act", 88 *Harvard Law Review* (1975).
287. Case C-62/86, *Akzo*, para 72.
288. Case C-333/94 P, *Tetra Pak II*, para 44 and Case C-202/07 P, *France Télécom SA v. Commission*, para 110.
289. Joined Cases C-395 & 396/96 P, *CMBT*, paras. 116–120.

suppliers had begun selling to customers in Ireland. The General Court rejected the arguments of the applicant claiming that the rebates did not lead to predatory pricing and that it was just reacting to competition. In doing so, the General Court referred to Article 102(c) TFEU and to the particular circumstances of the case: first, market partitioning contrary to the common market integration objective; second, Irish Sugar's very strong dominance with a market share of 88%; and third, the fact that Irish Sugar kept its prices at the pre-existing higher level for customers that could not benefit from imports.[290]

However, the *Post Danmark* case sheds a different light on the relationship between predatory and discriminatory pricing. In that case, one of its competitors complained that Post Danmark was selectively targeting three of its customers in the liberalized postal market. The Danish competition council found that Post Danmark was charging one of those customers prices below ATC but above AVC, although there was no evidence of exclusionary intent.[291] Nevertheless, it decided that Post Danmark's pricing for that customer was predatory in nature, particularly because the prices were selective and were not applied to Post Danmark's existing customers. In answering the questions referred by the Danish appeal court pursuant to Article 267 TFEU, the Court suggests that the selective nature of the prices is not sufficient to render those prices abusive: "[...] a pricing policy such as that in issue in the main proceedings cannot be considered to amount to an exclusionary abuse simply because the price charged to a single customer by a dominant undertaking is lower than the average total costs attributed to the activity concerned, but higher than the average incremental costs pertaining to the latter [...] Indeed, to the extent that a dominant undertaking sets its prices at a level covering the great bulk of the costs attributable to the supply of the goods or services in question, it will, as a general rule, be possible for a competitor as efficient as that undertaking to compete with those prices without suffering losses that are unsustainable in the long term."[292] This implies that pricing between AVC and ATC falls in a grey area; it is only abusive if it is has exclusionary effects for competitors that are just as efficient as the dominant undertaking. There is also the general suggestion that selective or discriminatory pricing is not a problem in the absence of such effects.

In the fifth place, pricing policies can become abusive in vertical relationships where competitors of the dominant undertaking need access to that firm's products or services in order to compete on downstream markets. This pricing question arose in the *British Sugar* case; competitors needed access to unprocessed industrial sugar from the dominant firm in order to compete on the downstream market for retail sugar. By selling the upstream product at a relatively high price and applying relatively low prices on the downstream market, British Sugar was in effect "squeezing" its competitors' margins.[293] Margin squeeze also occurs in situations where downstream suppliers need access to the infrastructure of the dominant firm – for instance, access to upstream telecommunications networks. Even in the absence of price discrimination, the owner of the infrastructure can influence a competitor's profit margin to a considerable extent since it is able to compensate the losses it makes on the downstream market with the relatively higher prices it charges for access to the upstream infrastructure. However, a margin squeeze alone does not suffice to demonstrate abuse. There must also be, at least potentially, an exclusionary effect on competitors that are just as efficient as the dominant firm.[294]

---

290. Case T-228/97, *Irish Sugar*, paras. 173–193.
291. The case refers to yet another cost concept: average incremental costs.
292. Case C-209/10, *Post Danmark*, paras. 37 and 38.
293. Commission Decision of 18 July 1988, *Napier Brown/British Sugar*, O.J. 1988, L 284/41.
294. Case C-280/08 P, *Deutsche Telekom*; Case C-52/09, *TeliaSonera*. The Commission Guidance Paper, cited *supra* note 20, does not deal with margin squeeze as a separate category of abuses, but sees it as a variation of

In the sixth place, dominant firms can exclude competitors by refusing them access to essential inputs. One of the very first cases dealing with Article 102 TFEU concerned refusal to sell an essential input. A dominant pharmaceutical company, Commercial Solvents, had ceased supplying aminobutanol – a substance required to make ethambutol – to Zoja, a smaller Italian company, after it decided to sell ethambutol itself.[295] A refusal to grant access to certain types of infrastructure can also be seen as a form of input foreclosure if the infrastructure is essential to making the product or reaching customers. As discussed in Section 3.2 above, not all networks can necessarily be considered essential facilities.[296] Although most likely to occur in the (former) utilities sector, essential facilities can also exist in other sectors, such as the financial sector. In the *Clearstream* case, the refusal to grant access concerned the sole central securities depository authorized under German law.[297] In its 2009 Guidance Paper, the Commission warns of the potential negative effects arising from interventions aimed at such refusals to sell. The imposition of supply obligations under Article 102 TFEU may indeed dampen the incentive to invest in the product or service concerned. The Commission will only intervene if three conditions are met: the refusal concerns an input that is objectively necessary to compete on a downstream market; is likely to eliminate effective competition on that market; and is likely to result in harm to the consumer.[298]

A specific form of input foreclosure concerns the refusal to licence intellectual property rights. The stream of case law dealing with such refusals started with cases involving car parts. Volvo and Renault refused to licence the design rights that would allow independent repairers to fabricate spare body parts for Volvo and Renault car models. The Court considered that a refusal under these circumstances could indeed be abusive if, for example "[…] the arbitrary refusal to supply spare parts to independent repairers, the fixing of prices for spare parts at an unfair level or a decision no longer to produce spare parts for a particular model even though many cars of that model are still in circulation […]".[299] A following series of cases dealt with the refusal to licence a specific type of copyright on listings or data. The previously mentioned Magill case concerned the refusal by Irish television broadcasters to grant Magill a copyright licence for television listings that would have allowed it to publish a comprehensive television guide – something that did not exist at the time in Ireland. The ECJ considered the refusal abusive because the listings were necessary to create a new product for which there was existing customer demand, and because there was no justification for refusal other than that television broadcasters wanted to reserve the secondary market for television guides for themselves.[300] The IMS case also deals with a derivative sort of copyright[301] – on the method IMS used to divide German territory into smaller geographical areas, which relies on postal codes, administrative regions, road infrastructure and the location of pharmacies and physicians. This data, combined with data obtained from pharmaceutical wholesalers, allowed IMS to compile and sell market studies on pharmaceutical sales. The pharmaceutical industry – which helped IMS to develop this database, known as a "brick structure" – used it as the standard for measuring the performance

---

refusal to supply. Indeed, by squeezing the margins of "just as efficient" competitors to unprofitable levels, this pricing practice can be seen as tantamount to a refusal to sell, see para 80.

295. Joined Cases 6 & 7/73, *Commercial Solvents*. See Case 311/84, *CBEM v. CLT*, for the refusal to sell essential services.

296. Case C-7/97, *Bronner*.

297. Case T-301/04, *Clearstream Banking AG and Clearstream International SA v. Commission*.

298. Commission Guidance Paper, cited *supra* note 20, paras. 75–88.

299. Case 238/87, *Volvo v. Veng*, para 9. See also Case 53/87, *CIRCA v. Renault*, para 16.

300. Joined Cases C-241 & 242/91 P, *Magill*.

301. Case C-418/01, *IMS*.

of its sales force. IMS refused to licence the data to NDC – a newcomer that wished to compete with IMS on the market for pharmaceutical sales studies. In answer to the question referred by the German court concerning the dispute between IMS and NDC, the ECJ applied the criteria it developed in Magill, albeit emphasizing two difficulties which the referring German court was requested to verify. First, could brick structures be seen as an upstream market separate from the downstream market for pharmaceutical studies? And second, could it be said that NDC intended to launch a new product, or did it simply intend to duplicate IMS' products?[302]

In *Microsoft*, the same criteria resurfaced, albeit that the nature of the copyright was entirely different from the rights invoked in *Magill* and *IMS*. The case concerned Microsoft's refusal to disclose interface information concerning its Windows operating system, which commanded a 90%-share of the market for PC operating software. The information was requested by producers of workgroup servers so they could ensure interoperability between their products and Windows-operated PC's. The Commission considered that access to the data was indeed necessary to be able to compete on an equal footing with Microsoft on the market for workgroup servers, and that elimination of competition on that market would be to the detriment of consumers and reduce Microsoft's incentive to innovate, hence reducing technical development. On appeal, the General Court found that the Commission had not made a manifest error of assessment in applying the *Magill* criteria to Microsoft's conduct. In line with the finding in *IMS*, it argued that the interface information could be seen as an upstream product. The General Court also agreed with the Commission that it was sufficient to demonstrate the existence of a risk that competition on the downstream market would be eliminated. As regards the question of whether Microsoft's refusal obstructed the introduction of a new product, the General Court referred to the importance, to consumers, of the quality of non-Microsoft group servers which they considered even better than Microsoft products. Microsoft's competitors would not be able to reproduce Microsoft products.[303]

A refusal to license IP rights need not be explicit; it also be implicit – for example where the holder of the IP right in question imposes licensing conditions that are unacceptable to the undertakings that need the licenses in order to gain access to the market. The question of which licensing conditions a patent holder can impose – and, hence, how the patent holder's right to royalties balances out against free competition – were the key issues in *Huawei*. That case concerned so-called standard essential patents ("SEP") which were essential for the implementation of telecommunications technology agreed upon by ETSI, an international standard setting organization. Operators participating in that standard, such as Huawei, had agreed to license the relevant patents subject to terms that were Fair Reasonable and Non-Discriminatory ("FRAND"). Upon noticing that ZTE was using its SEP before the conclusion of a license agreement, Huawei initiated patent infringement proceedings before a German court which then asked the ECJ, pursuant to Article 267 TFEU, if it would be considered abusive, under these conditions, to bring a patent infringement case. After it emphasized the special nature of a SEP, the ECJ replied that filing an infringement case without giving prior notice to or consulting with the alleged infringer is abusive. It also defined the basic principles by which parties can come to FRAND licensing terms.[304]

In the seventh place, dominant firms can also attempt to manipulate public procedures in order to exclude their competitors. In *Compagnie Maritime Belge*, for example, it was considered

302. Case C-418/01, *IMS*.
303. Case T-201/04, *Microsoft*.
304. Case 170/13, *Huawei*. See also Commission decisions of 29 Apr. 2014 in Motorola (AT.39985) and Samsung (AT.39939).

that the members of CEWAL had acted abusively by holding the Congolese authorities to a strict interpretation of an exclusivity agreement – thus preventing Grimaldi from obtaining Congolese business.[305] In *ITT*, the conduct at stake was vexatious litigation brought before Belgian courts against a newcomer on the market for telephone directories.[306] More importantly, the Courts upheld a Commission decision condemning a pharmaceutical company, AstraZeneca, for misleading the patent authorities, thereby artificially prolonging the duration of its patents, and for withdrawing market authorization for specific forms of packaging that generic entrants wanted to use.[307]

3.6 *Exploitative abuses*

The first example of abuse listed in Article 102 TFEU is the imposition of unfair prices or trading conditions. Fairness is a difficult criterion to apply because of its highly subjective and normative nature. The starting point is to find a benchmark to somehow measure "unfairness". It is submitted that this benchmark should not relate to monopolistic prices as such. To the extent that Article 102 TFEU does not condemn dominant positions, it should equally refrain from condemning the corresponding prices. The Court's case law seems to confirm this view. In its early case law, the Court refers to excessive prices as unfair. A price is deemed excessive if it bears no reasonable relation to the economic value of the service or good supplied.[308] But how does one measure economic value? In *United Brands* the ECJ developed a two-step test. The first step is to compare the price and the production costs. If the difference between the two is excessive, the second step assesses whether the price imposed is unfair, either inherently or when compared to competing products.[309] This comparison can be made in relation to competitors in the same market, different geographical markets, or to different situations over time.[310]

Since the 80s, there have been relatively few cases dealing with unfair or excessive pricing. This is probably due to a variety of reasons, such as the arrival of sector specific (price) regulation in the liberalized utilities sectors and the intrinsic difficulty of finding the right benchmark. One of the latest interventions can be seen in the *Scandlines* case in which the Commission was requested to assess the pricing conditions in effect at the port of Helsingborg. The case highlights the difficulties encountered in defining the right cost level. It also shows that demand-side considerations can also play a role, especially when customers are prepared to pay a premium for services offered by the dominant firm.[311] The problems in defining the right cost benchmark also led to the rejection of the complaint in the *IMAX* case.[312] No new excessive pricing cases have been taken up since.

A second category of exploitative abuse concerns conduct by a dominant firm that aims to prevent parallel trade in its products. Reference has already been made to the *General Motors* and *British Leyland* cases; those car producers were considered dominant because they were the only undertakings in a position to deliver the type of approval certificate needed for the registration of motor vehicles. By refusing to deliver the certificates (on reasonable terms) to

---

305. Joined Cases C-395 & 396/96 P, *CMBT*, paras. 77–88.
306. Case T-111/96, *ITT Promedia NV v. Commission.*
307. Case C-457/10 P, *AstraZeneca.*
308. Case 26/75, *General Motors,* and Case C-27/76, *United Brands.*
309. Case C-27/76, *United Brands,* paras. 251 and 252.
310. Joined Cases 110, 241 & 242/88, *François Lucazeau and Others v. Société des Auteurs, Compositeurs et Editeurs de Musique (SACEM) and Others,* para 25.
311. Commission Decision of 23 July 2004, *Scandlines Sverige AB v. Port of Helsingborg,* Case COMP/A.36.568/D3.
312. Commission Decision of 25 Mar. of 2004, *Euromax v. IMAX,* Case COMP/37.761.

traders operating outside the official dealer network, the firms were in a position to control parallel trade in their own products.[313] Another technique for preventing trade can be found in the *United Brands* case; the dominant firm forbade its distributors to resell bananas whilst they were still green.[314] The problem of parallel trade particularly arises in industrial sectors, such pharmaceuticals, where differences in public regulation lead to considerable price differences between Member States. Traders ship goods from low priced countries to high priced ones. In *Sot. Lelos* the ECJ considered that it was not necessarily abusive for a dominant firm to refuse to supply wholesalers involved in parallel exports: "... although a pharmaceuticals company in a dominant position, in a Member State where prices are relatively low, cannot be allowed to cease to honour the ordinary orders of an existing customer for the sole reason that that customer, in addition to supplying the market in that Member State, exports part of the quantities ordered to other Member States with higher prices, it is none the less permissible for that company to counter in a reasonable and proportionate way the threat to its own commercial interests potentially posed by the activities of an undertaking which wishes to be supplied in the first Member State with significant quantities of products that are essentially destined for parallel export."[315] In this case, the Court considered that, when striking a balance, account should be taken of the need to meet supply obligations on the domestic market, and the prior business relationship with the wholesalers in question.

In the third place, it follows from Article 102(c) TFEU that dominant firms bear a special responsibility to ensure undistorted competition on the downstream market where their customers compete with each other. In the context of exclusionary practices, as mentioned above, it is not entirely clear whether price discrimination between customers is prohibited as such, especially after the judgment of the Court in *Post Danmark*. Even so, EU courts have very infrequently chosen to apply Article 102(c) TFEU to cases involving price discrimination between customers. Some of these concern the combined application of Articles 106 and 102(c) TFEU to discriminatory tariff schemes for ports and airports.[316] By contrast, *British Airways* was a purely Article 102 TFEU case; the dominant carrier was accused, *inter alia*, of subjecting different travel agents to differing tariff conditions. The Court emphasized that this counted as discrimination that distorted competition between travel agents.[317]

Finally, the concept of abuse is a quite broad, encompassing many sorts of conduct. As a rule, it can be said that the conduct of a dominant firm can be taken into account if it directly affects the main objectives and principles of the Union Treaties, including market integration and the prohibition of discrimination on grounds of nationality. In *GVL* for example, the sole German copyright management agency refused to conclude management contracts with performing artists who were not German nationals or resident in Germany; nor would it do anything else to protect the rights of those artists in Germany. The ECJ upheld, with little debate, the Commission's decision holding that such discrimination constituted an abuse of GVL's dominant position.[318]

313. Case 26/75, *General Motors*, and Case 226/84, *British Leyland*.
314. Case C-27/76, *United Brands*.
315. Joined Cases C-468-478/06, *Sot. Lélos kai Sia EE and Others v. GlaxoSmithKline AEVE Farmakeftikon Proïonton*, para 71 in particular.
316. Case C-18/93, *Corsica Ferries Italia Srl v. Corpo dei Piloti del Porto di Genova* and Case C-163/99, *Portugal v. Commission*.
317. Case C-95/04 P, *British Airways plc v. Commission*, paras. 143 and 144.
318. Case 7/82, *Gesellschaft zur Verwertung von Leistungsschutzrechten mbH (GVL) v. Commission*.

4. Enforcement of antitrust rules[319]

4.1 The system set up by Regulation 1/2003

The system set up by Regulation 1/2003 and its predecessor Regulation 17/62,[320] is a curious one. It confers investigative and prosecutorial powers, as well as the authority to impose heavy fines, upon one and the same administrative body, i.e. the European Commission. Although the system has been heavily criticized,[321] and even though it has changed over the years, the Commission continues to combine the role of prosecutor (investigating and initiating administrative proceedings) and judge (imposing high fines) in the same case.

Under Regulation 17/62, the European Commission played a very prominent role in the application of Articles 101 and 102 TFEU. It became clear that this central role (and the procedures related to it) was not efficient and hampered the application of competition rules by the European Commission, the national courts and NCAs. For instance, under Regulation 17/62, the exception of Article 101(3) TFEU could only be obtained from and after prior notification to the Commission. As a result, the Commission was swamped with notifications and could no longer function properly. The system of Regulation 17/62 imposed considerable costs on undertakings and prevented the European Commission from concentrating its resources on curbing the most serious infringements.

Regulation 17/62 was ultimately replaced by Regulation 1/2003 and this changed the enforcement landscape. A directly applicable exception system was introduced and, as a result, national courts and NCAs now had the power to apply not only the prohibitions of Articles 101(1) and 102, but also the exception of Article 101(3) TFEU.[322] Regulation 1/2003 strengthened the position of national courts and NCAs in the enforcement of EU competition rules. In addition, Regulation 1/2003 introduced new forms of cooperation between the Commission and the NCAs. According to the Commission, the introduction of Regulation 1/2003 has considerably advanced enforcement of EU competition rules.[323] Mainly as a result of the prioritization of its activities, the Commission has become much less accessible for informal guidance and interactions with undertakings.[324]

---

319. For further reading on enforcement of antitrust rules, readers are referred to G. Bellamy and G. Child, op. cit. *supra* note 1; C. Kerse and N. Khan, *EU Antitrust Procedure*, 6th ed. (Sweet & Maxwell, 2012); I. Lianos and I. Kokkoris, *The Reform of Competition Law: New Challenges* (Kluwer, 2010); R. Wesseling and M. Van Der Woude, "The lawfulness and acceptability of enforcement of European Cartel Law", 35 *World Competition* (2012), 573, and W. Wils, "Antitrust compliance programmes and optimal antitrust enforcement", 1 *Journal of Antitrust Enforcement* (2013), 52.
320. Council Reg. (EEC) 17/62 of 21 Feb. 1962, First Reg. implementing Arts. 85 and 86 of the [EEC] Treaty, O.J. 1963 127/2268.
321. See e.g. I. Forrester, "Due Process in EC competition cases: A distinguished institution with flawed procedures", (2009) ELR, and D. Slater, S. Thomas and D. Waelbroek, "Competition law proceedings before the European Commission and the right to a fair trial: No need for reform?", (2008) *Global Competition Law Centre Working Paper.*
322. See in this context, Art. 1 of Reg. 1/2003, cited *supra* note 2.
323. Communication from the Commission the European Parliament and the Council, "Ten Years of Antitrust Enforcement under Reg. 1/2003: Achievements and Future Perspectives", COM(2014)453.
324. Commission Notice on informal guidance relating to novel questions concerning Arts. 81 and 82 of the EC Treaty that arise in individual cases (guidance letters), O.J. 2004, C 101/78.

4.2 *Enforcement by the Commission*

Regulation 1/2003 provides the Commission with powers enabling it to apply and enforce Articles 101 and 102 TFEU.[325] On the one hand, the Commission has far-reaching powers to investigate (and to impose fines on companies if they fail to comply with the Commission's requests). This includes conducting sector inquiries, sending out requests for information (by simple request or by formal decision), taking voluntary statements from individuals, and conducting inspections or so-called dawn raids.[326] In relation to the latter, the Commission has broad powers to search for, and seize, documents – especially in an IT environment. Commission officials can search servers, cloud services, mobile devices, hard disks including private devices and media that are used for professional reasons.[327]

The relevant legal framework and the case law impose certain limits on these far-reaching powers. One example is Article 20(4), which requires the Commission to state the subject matter and purpose of the inspection whenever it issues a decision ordering an investigation. This fundamental requirement was put in place to force the Commission to provide justification for any proposed entry onto the premises of the undertakings concerned, and also to enable those undertakings to assess the scope of their duty to cooperate whilst at the same time safeguarding their rights of defence.[328] Another important limitation is that, on the basis of the case law, the Commission is obliged to respect legal professional privilege and cannot have access to communications between the undertaking and outside counsel that is registered at the Bar of an EU Member State, or to documents drawn up exclusively for the purpose of seeking legal advice.[329]

The Commission must also respect the right to remain silent; undertakings cannot be forced to admit that they have committed an infringement, but they are obliged to answer factual questions and provide documents when requested.[330] However, there is no clarity on which questions can be classified as purely factual. To provide some guidance, Advocate General Wahl has stated that the salient point is whether an otherwise factual question could result in an answer being given which implies an admission of guilt.[331]

The Commission has the power to establish whether an infringement of Articles 101 and 102 TFEU has taken place, and it can also decide to put an end to it. It can also do this by means of taking interim measures, by accepting commitments, or through settlement proceedings.[332]

---

325. Art. 4 of Reg. 1/2003, cited *supra* note 2.
326. See in this context Arts. 17–21 of Reg. 1/2003. Sector inquiries generally have been followed by enforcement action by the Commission in the industry concerned. For instance, in May 2015 the Commission launched a sector inquiry into the e-commerce sector and in February 2017, it announced that it had started three separate investigations in this industry.
327. European Commission Explanatory note on Commission inspections pursuant to Art. 20(4) of Council Reg. 1/2003, 11 Sept. 2015.
328. See, in this sense, Case C-94/00, *Roquette Frères SA v. Commission*, para 47, Case C-37/13 P, *Nexans and Nexans France v. Commission*, para 34 and Case C-583/13 P, *Deutsche Bahn and others v. Commission*, para 56.
329. Case C-550/07 P, *Akzo Nobel Chemicals and Akcros Chemicals v. Commission*; Case 53/85, *AKZO Chemie v. Commission*; and Case C-155/79, *AM & S Europe Limited v. Commission*.
330. Preamble 23 of Reg. 1/2003, cited *supra* note 2.
331. A.G. Wahl in Case C-247/14 P, *HeidelbergCement AG v. Commission*, para 158. See also Case C-247/14 P, *HeidelbergCement AG v. Commission*.
332. Arts. 7–9 of Reg. 1/2003, cited *supra* note 2. See also Commission Reg. (EC) 773/2004 of 7 Apr. 2004 relating to the conduct of proceedings by the Commission pursuant to Arts. 81 and 82 of the EC Treaty, O.J. 2004, L 123/18; Commission Reg. (EC) 622/2008 of 30 June 2008 amending Reg. (EC) 773/2004, as regards the conduct of settlement procedures in cartel cases, O.J. 2008, L 171/3; and Commission Notice on the conduct of settlement procedures in view of the adoption of Decisions pursuant to Art. 7 and Art. 23 of Council Reg. (EC) 1/2003 in cartel cases, O.J. 2008, C 167/1.

At the end of an investigation, the Commission assesses whether to initiate formal proceedings *vis-à-vis* the relevant undertakings. If so, it prepares and sends out a statement of objections, and allows the undertakings concerned to respond within a certain timeframe. Subsequently, the undertakings will be given an opportunity to be heard on the matters to which the Commission has taken objection.[333] The Commission will then have to decide whether to proceed with the preparation, adoption and publication of a decision. Pursuant to Article 27(2) of Regulation 1/2003, the defence rights of the undertakings concerned have to be fully respected in the proceedings.[334] For instance, the Commission must provide access to its file on the undertakings (subject to the legitimate interest of undertakings in the protection of business secrets). An opportunity should be given to examine all evidence in the investigation that might be relevant to the defence. This relates to both inculpatory and exculpatory evidence, with the exception of business secrets of other undertakings, internal Commission documents, and other confidential information. During the proceedings, the hearing officer needs to ensure the effective exercise of the procedural rights of the undertakings concerned.[335]

Articles 23 and 24 of Regulation 1/2003 provide the Commission with the power to impose fines on undertakings. In particular, the Commission's use of the power to impose the fines set out in Article 23(2) of Regulation 1/2003 has had great impact on the effective enforcement of Articles 101 and 102 TFEU.[336] The Commission has wielded this power to create a deterrent effect by imposing record fines on undertakings that have violated Articles 101 and/or 102 TFEU.[337] These fines cannot exceed 10% of the undertaking's total turnover in the preceding business year. The statute of limitations for the Commission to impose penalties for infringements of Article 101 and/or 102 TFEU is five years.[338] Not wanting to run the risk of incurring high fines, an increasing number of companies have introduced internal measures to foster compliance with EU competition rules. These internal measures are usually taken in the context of a competition law compliance programme. This can consist of informing and training employees, implementing sanctions for violation of the rules, performing periodic audits ("trust but verify"), and introducing a hotline for employees who want to inform the employer of irregularities.[339]

Following the example of the US amnesty programme, the Commission has introduced the possibility for undertakings to apply for immunity or lenient treatment. Under the leniency programme, the first undertaking to disclose its participation in a hard-core cartel can be granted

---

333. Art. 27(1) of Reg. 1/2003, cited *supra* note 2. See also Commission Reg. 773/2004, cited *supra* note 332, and Commission Notice on best practices for the conduct of proceedings concerning Arts. 101 and 102 TFEU, O.J. 2011, C 308/6.

334. Case C-110/10 P, *Solvay v. Commission*, paras. 47 and 48 and Case T-485/11, *Akzo Nobel and Akcros Chemicals v. Commission*, paras. 67–72.

335. Decision of the President of the European Commission of 13 Oct. 2011 on the function and terms of reference of the hearing officer in certain competition procedures, O.J. 2011, L 275/29. See Case C-162/15 P, *Evonik Degussa GmbH v. Commission*, where the Court of Justice clarifies the Hearing Officer's competence to decide on confidentiality claims. The judgment also provides guidance on the type of information the Commission may disclose in a public version of an infringement decision.

336. Commission Guidelines, cited *supra* note 18, and Commission Information Note, *Inability to pay under paragraph 35 of the 2006 Fining Guidelines and payment conditions pre- and post-decision finding an infringement and imposing fines*, O.J. 2010, 737/2.

337. See cartel statistics, on DG Comp's website available at <ec.europa.eu/competition/cartels/statistics/statistics.pdf>

338. Art. 25(1)(b) of Reg. 1/2003, cited *supra* note 2.

339. See competition compliance guidance, on DG Comp's website available at <ec.europa.eu/competition/antitrust/compliance/index_en.html> and OECD Guidelines for Multinational Enterprises, available at <mneguidelines.oecd.org/text/>. See also, "Compliance is a Culture, Not Just a Policy", Brent Snyder, Department of Justice, Sept. 9, 2014, available at < www.justice.gov/atr/public/speeches/308494.pdf>.

immunity from fines if it submits information and evidence that enables the Commission to find an infringement of Article 101 or to carry out a targeted inspection. In order to qualify, an undertaking has to meet certain strict conditions including admitting its participation in a violation of Article 101(1) TFEU. Undertakings that are not the first to apply for immunity can qualify for fine reduction if they turn in evidence that represents significant added value. Depending upon the order in which applications for lenient treatment are received, the fine can be reduced anywhere from 30–50% for the first applicant, 20–30% for the second, and up to 20% for subsequent undertakings that provide evidence with significant added value. In relation to the probative value of a leniency application, the Court of Justice ruled that if the accuracy of a leniency application is contested by other undertakings similarly accused, the evidence cannot be regarded as constituting sufficient proof of an infringement unless it is supported by other evidence. The Court also clarified, that two leniency statements can constitute sufficient evidence if they corroborate each other.[340]

Over the years, the leniency option has increasingly proved to be a very successful enforcement tool. The vast majority of investigations conducted by the Commission are triggered by applications for leniency and not by *ex officio* investigations or complaints.[341] In view of this success, many other jurisdictions have introduced similar national leniency programmes. However, certain developments such as an increase in civil follow-on damage litigation have had an effect on the incentive to apply for lenient treatment. Depending on the circumstances, the upside of a possible fine reduction can be outweighed by the downside of applying for leniency.[342]

4.3 *Enforcement by NCAs and the ECN*

Under Regulation 1/2003, NCAs have an important role in the decentralized enforcement of Articles 101 and 102 TFEU. The Commission and NCAs are meant to work in close cooperation, forming a network of enforcers applying EU competition rules that is facilitated by arrangements for the exchange of information and consultation.[343] The Commission and NCAs also work together closely with regard to inspections.[344] This network, the European Competition

340. Case C-613/13 P, *Commission v. Keramag Keramische Werke GmbH and Others*, paras. 28 and 44..
341. Commission Notice on the handling of complaints by the Commission under Arts. 81 and 82 of the EC Treaty, O.J. 2004, C 101/65.
342. C. Swaak and R. Wesseling, "Reconsidering the leniency option: If not first in, good reasons to stay out", 36 ECLR (2015). In order to address this concern, the Commission introduced a series of amendments to primary antitrust legislation and "soft law" with the view of harmonizing Directive 2014/104/EU, cited *supra* note 9, with antitrust procedural rules. The main changes relate to "access to file" as they intend to safeguard leniency submissions by protecting them from disclosure. Moreover, new limitations have been introduced to the use of information obtained in the course of Commission proceedings; also, no corporate statement for leniency or settlement submission will be disclosed by the Commission (Commission Reg. (EU) 2015/1348 of 3 Aug. 2015 amending Reg. (EC) 773/2004 relating to the conduct of proceedings by the Commission pursuant to Arts. 81 and 82 of the EC Treaty, O.J. 2015, L 208/3). See also Commission Communication on amendments to the Commission Notice on Immunity from fines and reduction of fines in cartel cases, O.J. 2015, C 256/1.
343. See, in this sense, recital 15 in the preamble and in particular Arts. 11–14 of Reg. 1/2003, cited *supra* note 2. See also Commission Notice on cooperation within the Network of Competition Authorities, O.J. 2004, C 101/43. On 4 Nov. 2015, the Commission invited the general public and stakeholders to give feedback on potential EU legislative actions to further strengthen the enforcement and sanctioning tools of NCAs. Available at <ec.europa.eu/competition/consultations/2015_effective_enforcers/index_en.html>.
344. Arts. 20–22 of Reg. 1/2003, cited *supra* note 2. The Commission proposed a Directive to empower competition authorities of the Member States to be more effective enforcers and to ensure the proper functioning of the internal market, on 22 Mar. 2017. This Directive aims to provide NCAs with minimum means and instruments to detect competition law infringements and impose effective sanctions. The Proposal complements

Network ("ECN"), should ensure an efficient division of work and the effective and consistent application of EU competition rules. In practice, this can be a challenge; the Commission and NCAs have parallel competences that each allow application of Articles 101 and 102 TFEU. Consequently, the allocation of cases within the network is not always an easy task. Although Article 13 of Regulation 1/2003 provides some basic guidance on the suspension or termination of proceedings in the event more than one enforcer is dealing with the matter, the Commission and NCAs have broad discretion to coordinate and optimize their cooperation, thereby ensuring that the most appropriate authorities within the network deal with a particular matter.[345] Notwithstanding the parallel competences and the spirit of good cooperation, the Commission remains the first amongst equals. Article 11 of Regulation 1/2003 assigns the Commission a central role in directing the flow of information within the network. It also gives the Commission priority; NCAs are relieved of their competence to apply Articles 101 and 102 in the event the Commission initiates its own proceedings.

Cooperation between the Commission and NCAs within the network has led to various initiatives defining best practices (for instance in merger control). It has also yielded practical results such as the publication of the ECN Model Leniency Programme (as revised in November 2012) which confirms the commitment of ECN members to make best efforts to align their respective leniency programmes with the ECN Model Programme, and facilitates, for instance, summary leniency applications with NCAs in cases where the Commission is particularly well-situated to deal with the matter.[346] The ECN takes the initiative in addressing specific concerns, if need be.[347] However, instruments adopted in the context of the ECN, including the Model Leniency Programme, are not binding on NCAs, irrespective of the judicial or administrative nature of those authorities.[348] It should be added that over time, the International Competition Network ("ICN") has become more important, as a network for enforcers of competition law worldwide.[349]

4.4 *Enforcement by national courts*

As with any other directly applicable provision of EU law, Articles 101 and 102 TFEU can – and in certain circumstances must – be applied by national courts.[350] These articles can be directly relied upon in the context of cease and desist actions, damage claims, or in contractual disputes. In the latter scenario, the nullity sanction of Article 101(2) TFEU is often used as a defence to oppose the enforcement of a contract that runs afoul of Article 101(1) TFEU.[351] Where national rules favour restrictive conduct, Articles 101 and 102 TFEU can also be invoked in criminal pro-

---

the system of decentralised enforcement of Regulation 1/2003 and further harmonizes the procedural powers of the NCAs.

345. Case T-201/11, *Si.mobil telekomunikacijske storitve d.d. v. Commission*, paras. 36–41 and Case T-355/13, *easyJet Airline Co. Ltd v. Commission*, paras. 23–29.

346. Available at <ec.europa.eu/competition/ecn/model_leniency_en.pdf>.

347. See, in this context, the Resolution of the Meeting of Heads of the European Competition Authorities, "Protection of leniency material in the context of civil damages actions", (May 2012). Available at <ec.europa.eu/competition/ecn/leniency_material_protection_en.pdf>.

348. Case C-428/14, *DHL Express and Others v. Autorità Garante della Concorrenza e del Mercato and Others*, para 77. This judgment confirms that EU and Member States' leniency programmes are independent and therefore even if a leniency applicant obtains leniency or immunity in an EU cartel investigation this does not entail that the beneficiary will receive the same treatment in related national investigations.

349. Available at <www.internationalcompetitionnetwork.org/>.

350. Case C-126/97, *Eco Swiss*, para 40 and Joined Cases C-430 & 431/93, *Van Schijndel and Van Veen v. Stichting Pensioenfonds voor Fysiotherapeuten.*

351. See *supra*, section 2.1.

ceedings.[352] When national courts encounter difficulties in the interpretation of these treaty provisions, they can rely on the preliminary reference procedure laid down in Article 267 TFEU.[353] A substantial portion of the case law on EU competition law originates from this procedure.

Regulation 1/2003 actively encourages national courts to apply this law: first, Article 3 of the Regulation compels them to apply Articles 101 and 102 TFEU in cases where they apply national competition rules to conduct that has an effect on inter-state trade;[354] second, Article 15 of Regulation 1/2003 provides for practical cooperation between national courts, on the one hand, and the Commission and NCAs on the other. If requested to do so, the Commission can provide information or opinions that can be useful for the application of competition rules. Also, the Commission and NCAs can intervene in national court proceedings as *amicus curiae*. In a case dealing with the question of whether fines could be deducted from corporate tax, the Court extended this potential intervention to proceedings in which the effectiveness of the Commission's enforcement policy is at stake.[355]

However, Regulation 1/2003 also restricts the autonomy of national courts when they apply Articles 101 and 102 TFEU. Article 16 explicitly compels them to respect Commission decisions dealing with similar conduct. They must also refrain from taking decisions if the Commission can be expected to define its position in the same case. In addition, the autonomy of Member States to define the conditions under which Articles 101 and 102 TFEU can be applied is limited by the general principles of equivalence and effectiveness. For example, in *Courage*, the Court held that a contract party should also be able to rely on Article 101 TFEU to claim damages resulting from the performance of that contract; the full effectiveness of the prohibition laid down in Article 101(1) would be at risk if it were not open to individuals claiming damages for losses incurred due to a contract, or from conduct likely to restrict or distort competition.[356]

Over the last five years, litigation brought before national courts has increased significantly. Almost as a rule, cartel cases pursued by NCAs and the European Commission give rise to so called "follow-on" damages claims.[357] This has in its turn led to a series of preliminary reference proceedings – ranging from queries on private international law to requests for a definition of the damages that can be claimed or the evidence for which the applicant can request a court order.[358] The disclosure aspect is particularly delicate; the disclosure of documents submitted to

352. See e.g. Joined Cases 209-213/84, *Criminal proceedings against Lucas Asjes and Others, Andrew Gray and Others, Jacques Maillot and Others and Léo Ludwig and Others.*
353. In fact, the very first preliminary reference procedure related to a contractual dispute in which Art. 101(2) TFEU was invoked by the defendant. Case 13/61, *Kledingverkoopbedrijf de Geus en Uitdenbogerd v. Robert Bosch GmbH and Maatschappij tot voortzetting van de zaken der Firma Willem van Rijn*, at 50.
354. See *supra*, section 4.1.
355. Case C-429/07, *X BV.*
356. Case C-453/99, *Bernard Crehan v. Courage Ltd. and Others*, para 26. See also Joined Cases C-295-298/04, *Manfredi*, para 60. European Institutions can also be held liable under Art. 340 TFEU if they have engaged in unlawful conduct. See Case T-577/14, *Gascogne Sack Deutschland GmbH and Gascogne v. European Union*, where the General Court ordered the EU to compensate the undertaking for the damage suffered as a result of the Court's failure to adjudicate within a reasonable time.
357. E.g. Commission Decision of 09 Nov. 2010, *Air Freight*, O.J. 2010, C (2010) 7694. See for example the air freight civil litigation: In 2010, the Commission fined 11 air cargo carriers approximately €800 million for participating in an international cartel involving air cargo services. As a result, various claim vehicles initiated civil proceedings against the airlines and claimed a multiple of the fines already imposed by the Commission and other competition authorities. For instance, Deutsche Bahn Schenker brought legal actions in the US and in Germany, with claims of approximately $2.5 billion in damages from air cargo carriers.
358. Case C-352/13, *Cartel Damage Claims*; Case C-557/12, *Kone AG and Others v. ÖBB-Infrastruktur AG*; Case C-199/11, *Europese Gemeenschap v. OTIS NV and Others;* and Case C-681/11, *Bundeswettbewerbsbehörde, Bundeskartellanwalt v. Schenker and Others.*

the Commission or NCAs – especially those handed over in the context of a leniency application – may deter undertakings from filing leniency applications in future.[359] The issue of damage claims – and the need to strike a balance between ensuring effective public enforcement and the policy of encouraging private enforcement – led to the adoption of Directive 2014/104, which should have been implemented in national law by the end of 2016.[360]

Directive 2014/104 codifies the principle that any natural or legal person who has suffered harm caused by a competition law infringement is entitled to seek full compensation. It lays down specific rules regarding the disclosure of evidence, in particular documents held by competition authorities. For example, Article 6(6) explicitly rules out the disclosure of leniency statements. Another section of Directive 2014/14 deals with liability issues. It provides that the participants in a cartel are jointly and severally liable for harm caused by the infringement, implying that the victim has the right to require full compensation from any of the cartelists involved. However, the liability of the undertaking benefitting from immunity under a leniency programme is limited to the harm caused to its own customers. The last two sections of the Directive deal with the calculation of damages, and the issue of passing on overcharges.[361] One may expect that the new rules laid down in the Directive will inspire a new stream of case law on their interpretation and application.

4.5 *Judicial review*

As already mentioned, the system put in place by Regulation 1/2003, and its predecessor Regulation 17/62, confers investigative and prosecutorial powers, as well as the authority to impose heavy fines, upon the Commission. Despite criticism of this combination of apparently irreconcilable roles, most Member States have also adopted similar systems for the administrative enforcement of competition rules. It follows from *Menarini*, a landmark judgment of the European Court of Human Rights, that such systems do not necessarily run contrary to the due process rules laid down in Article 6 of the European Convention on Human Rights ("ECHR") if the decisions taken by the administrative authority can be challenged before a judicial body that exercises so-called "unlimited jurisdiction".[362] This implies that the judicial body has the power to review all aspects of the contested decision, and that it can annul or replace the fine. The legality of a system of administrative enforcement of competition rules thus depends on the intensity of judicial review.

Following the principles laid down in *Menarini*, the ECJ confirmed in the *KME* and *Chalkor* cases that judicial review by the General Court met the due process criteria laid down in Article 47 of the Charter of Fundamental Rights of the European Union, which mirrors – within the context of EU law – the conditions imposed by Article 6 ECHR.[363] It noted that the General Court controls the legality of the Commission's decisions pursuant to Article 267 TFEU and

359. Case C-360/09, *Pfleiderer AG v. Bundeskartellamt.*
360. Directive 2014/104, cited *supra* note 9.
361. See also Commission Communication on quantifying harm in actions for damages based on breaches of Art. 101 or 102 of the TFEU, O.J. 2013, C 167/19 and the Commission Study on the Passing-on of Overcharges, final report, 2016 Brussels. The Study provides national courts with guidelines on how to estimate the share of the overcharge which was passed on to the indirect purchaser. The Study includes a 39 step checklist with practical advice to national courts on issues such as the use of quantification methods and application of the disclosure provisions of the Directive.
362. ECtHR, *Menarini.*
363. Case C-386/10 P, *Chalkor AE Epexergasias Metallon v. Commission*; Case C-272/09 P, *KME Germany AG, KME France SAS and KME Italy SpA v. Commission*; and Case C-389/10 P, *KME Germany AG, KME France SAS and KME Italy SpA v. Commission.*

that this control is complemented by its unlimited jurisdiction within the meaning of Article 261 TFEU. However, it also pointed out that this control can only be exercised on the basis of arguments put forward by the applicant. Therefore, there is no *ex officio* re-examination of the case before the General Court. In addition, the power of this court to substitute its own view for the Commission's position is limited to the issue of the fine, and does not concern the finding of infringement itself.[364] The latter issue is assessed in the context of legality oversight, or "control". Although this type of control concerns the legality of the contested decision upon its date of adoption, it does not preclude applicants from raising arguments not raised during the administrative procedure before the Commission.[365]

5. Concentration control[366]

5.1 *Setting up the system*

As mentioned in Section 1.1 above, the competition rules of the TFEU primarily deal with the conduct of undertakings on the market. Unlike the former ECSC Treaty, this does not include rules dealing with concentrations of undertakings, i.e. with changes in the number of players on the market. Although the Commission acknowledged this issue in a 1966 study, it nevertheless sought to extend the use of Articles 101 and 102 TFEU to concentrations.[367] In *Continental Can,* the Commission and the Court considered that the acquisition of a competitor by an already dominant undertaking could be deemed to constitute abuse.[368] The ECJ also followed the Commission in *BAT and Reynolds v. Commission* concerning the application of Article 101 TFEU to situations in which an undertaking holds a minority stake in its competitor as a result of which competition between the two firms is weakened.[369]

It was only with the inauguration of the internal market project at the beginning of the eighties, which led to adoption of the Single Act, that the Member States thought it necessary to adopt a system of EU-wide concentration control. Regulation 4064/89 imposed a system of *ex ante* control by which undertakings must notify the Commission – as the central authority – of concentrations of a certain magnitude, i.e. those big enough to have a Community dimension.[370] The test the Commission was meant to apply referred to the terms of Article 102 TFEU: concentrations that created or strengthened dominant positions to the significant detriment of competition within the internal market were considered to be incompatible with the common market. Although there was some confusion in the early days about the exact scope of this test, its thrust was generally perceived to be the prevention of new (or the reinforcement of existing) dominant positions. In 2004, Regulation 4064/89 was replaced by Regulation 139/2004, which

364. Case C-295/12 P, *Telefónica SA and Telefónica de España SAU v. Commission.*
365. Case C-407/08 P, *Knauf Gips KG v. Commission,* para 90.
366. For further reading on concentration control, readers are referred to M. Broberg, *The European Commission's Jurisdiction to Scrutinise Mergers,* 4th ed. (Kluwer, 2013); C.J. Cook and C.S. Kerse, *EC Merger Control,* 5th ed. (Sweet & Maxwell, 2009); A. Jones and B. Sufrin, op. cit. *supra* note 237; I. Kokkoris, *Merger Control in Europe: The Gap in the ECMR and National Merger Legislations* (Routledge, 2012); U. Schwalbe and D. Zimmer, *Law and Economics in European Merger Control* (OUP, 2009) and B. Bishop and C. Caffara, *Merger control in new markets,* 31 ECLR (2001).
367. Commission Memorandum, cited *supra* note 4.
368. Case C-6/72, *Continental Can.*
369. Joined Cases 142 & 156/84, *British-American Tobacco Company Ltd and R. J. Reynolds Industries Inc. v. Commission,* para 30.
370. Council Reg. (EEC) 4064/89 of 21 Dec. 1989 on the control of concentrations between undertakings, O.J. 1989, L 395/1.

instituted a slightly different test.[371] Article 2(2) of that Regulation refers to concentrations which significantly impede effective competition in the common market or in a substantial part of it, in particular as a result of the creation or strengthening of a dominant position. The test now mainly focuses on impediments to effective competition – citing the creation or reinforcement of dominant positions as one of the principal causes of such impediments. The new test, which is reminiscent of the substantial lessening of competition test used in the US, makes it clear that the Commission can also prohibit concentrations that lead to oligopolies without coordinated effects.[372]

Another major change introduced by Regulation 139/2004 concerns the exceptions to the Commission's exclusive power to assess concentrations with a Community dimension. Member States can request referral of those concentrations to their NCAs in cases where the concentration affects competition on a market within a Member State that has all the hallmarks of a distinct market.[373] Member States can also refer a concentration that has no Community dimension to the Commission.[374] The new Regulation also allows parties to a concentration to present a referral request to the Commission if their concentration triggers concentration regimes in at least three Member States, or to request that the Commission refer a case with a Community dimension back to a Member State.[375]

The procedure that must be followed under Regulation 139/2004, and the notification forms – in particular Form CO – which must be submitted by the reporting undertaking(s), can be found in implementing Regulation 802/2004.[376] In addition, the Commission has published a wide range of notices in which it summarizes or codifies its existing decisional practice. These notices can be regrouped into three main categories. The first category is comprised of the consolidated jurisdiction notice which explains the concepts that trigger the Commission's competence to assess concentrations. The second set of notices regulates the Commission's proceedings. The third and last group deals with the substantive test to be applied by the Commission. Before briefly discussing the main features of these three sets of rules, a few preliminary questions need to be asked. The first is purely jurisdictional: does a particular transaction have to be reported to the Commission? The answer to this question does not depend on the potential market impact of the concentration – the Commission must even be notified of innocuous concentrations if they meet the relevant jurisdictional criteria. Conversely, concentrations that are potentially harmful yet have no Community dimension do not need to be reported to the Commission – although they may be subject to national concentration control. The second question asks which substantive test is to be applied by the Commission, and whether the undertakings can provide any remedies to allay the Commission's concerns. Finally, the last question concerns the procedure to be followed by the Commission when dealing with concentrations. Failure to comply with procedure can be a costly affair: failure to provide timely notification of a concentration can result in the imposition of fines of up to 10% of an undertaking's worldwide turnover. For instance, in May and July 2017, the Commission issued a statement of objections in

371. Reg. 139/2004, cited *supra* note 5.
372. OECD, *The standard for merger review, with a particular emphasis on country experience with the change of merger review standard from the dominance test to the SLC/SIEC test*, 2009.
373. Art. 9 of Reg. 139/2004, cited *supra* note 5. See also, Case T-119/02, *Royal Philips Electronics NV v. Commission*, paras. 321 and 322.
374. Art. 22 of Reg. 139/2004, cited *supra* note 5. See Case T-221/95, *Endemol Entertainment Holding BV v. Commission*, para 42 and Case T-22/97, *Kesko Oy v. Commission*, para 116.
375. See Arts. 4(4) and 4(5) of Reg. 139/2004, cited *supra* note 5.
376. Commission Reg. (EC) 802/2004 of 7 Apr. 2004 implementing Council Reg. (EC) 139/2004 on the control of concentrations between undertakings, O.J. 2004, L 133/1.

four cases, because the parties to a concentration had provided incorrect or misleading information during the investigation of their notified concentration.[377]

5.2 *Concentrations with a Community dimension*

Article 3(1) of Regulation 139/2004 defines a concentration as a change of control on a lasting basis resulting from either the merger of two or more previously independent undertakings or parts of undertakings, or the acquisition, by one or more persons already controlling at least one undertaking, or by one or more undertakings, whether by purchase of securities or assets, by contract or by any other means, of direct or indirect control of the whole or parts of one or more other undertakings. The decisive criterion relates to the change of control of undertakings that are already present on the market. It follows from Article 3(2) of the Regulation that the concept of control is relatively broad. It not only encompasses formal, legal voting rights, but can also include factual aspects ranging from a state of economic dependence to matters of inheritance.[378] Nor does the acquisition of control necessarily imply that the acquiring undertaking holds a share greater than 50% in another undertaking. The decisive percentage might be less than 50% if the remaining voting rights are dispersed among many other shareholders[379] or if the acquirer has obtained certain special rights in the undertaking that confer upon him, *de facto* or *de iure*, the right to determine the commercial strategy of the undertaking. Such special rights include, for example, the power to approve the business plan or the budget of the undertaking. The conferral of such veto rights implies that the company cannot be run without the consent of its owner.

The concept of control not only covers the acquisition of sole control – it also includes the acquisition of joint control; i.e. a situation where two or more undertakings jointly control another undertaking. In a joint control situation, the partners have no choice but to reach consensus on the commercial policy of the undertaking in question.[380] It should be noted that the Regulation only applies to joint control situations that have an impact on the structure of the market. The object of joint control therefore refers to the creation of joint ventures performing all the functions of an autonomous economic entity on a lasting basis.[381] Joint ventures that merely coordinate the conduct of their parent undertakings or that are dependent for their economic survival on input from or sales to their parents do not qualify as full function entities. Posing the requirement of structural market impact also implies that certain temporary acquisitions will not be deemed to give rise to a concentration.[382]

377. See e.g. for 'gun jumping' Case C-84/13 P, *Electrabel SA v. Commission*, and for provision of misleading or incorrect information, see Commission decision of 17 May 2017, *Facebook/WhatsApp*, (M.8228). For other cases relating to breaches of merger procedural rules, see European Commission Press Releases "Mergers: Commission alleges Altice breached EU rules by early implementation of PT Portugal acquisition", IP/17/1368, (2017) and "Mergers: Commission alleges Merck and Sigma-Aldrich, General Electric, and Canon breached EU merger procedural rules", IP/17/1924 (2017).
378. See Commission Consolidated Jurisdictional Notice under Council Reg. (EC) 139/2004 on the control of concentrations between undertakings, O.J. 2008, C 95/1, paras. 19–21.
379. By contrast, Reg. 139/2004, cited *supra* note 5, does not apply to minority shareholdings: e.g. Case T-411/07, *Aer Lingus Group plc v. Commission*. The Commission is consulting with stakeholders on the expediency of bringing such minority holdings within the ambit of the Reg.
380. Commission Consolidated Jurisdictional Notice, cited *supra* note 378, para 62.
381. Art. 3(4) of Reg. 139/2004, cited *supra* note 5.
382. Art. 3(5) of Reg. 139/2004, cited *supra* note 5. See Case T-279/04, *Éditions Odile Jacob SAS v. Commission*, paras. 119–144.

After having determined the existence of a concentration, which includes the ancillary restrictions to it,[383] the parties concerned must determine whether the concentration has a Community dimension. Article 1 of Regulation 139/2004 provides two definitions. First, where the undertakings party to the concentration have a combined worldwide turnover exceeding 5 billion euro and at least two of them achieve 250 million euro turnover in the Union, the concentration is deemed to have a Community dimension, unless each of the undertakings concerned achieves more than two-thirds of its aggregate Community-wide turnover within one and the same Member State. The second test, which may apply if the worldwide turnover of the parties to the undertakings exceeds 2.5 billion euro, is more complex. It requires that they have a combined turnover of more than 100 million euro in at least three Member States and that at least two of the undertakings achieve a turnover in those States higher than 25 million euro. Moreover, the Community-wide turnover of each of at least two of the undertakings must be more than 100 million euro, unless each of the undertakings concerned achieves more than two-thirds of its aggregate Community-wide turnover within one and the same Member State. Both sets of rules imply that the parties to a concentration must first define the undertakings concerned, then determine the turnover figures for each of them and, finally, define the geographical origin of that turnover.

Once the Commission's jurisdiction is established, on this basis or as a consequence of a referral (see above), Member States can no longer apply their own concentration control rules. It follows from Article 21(4), however, that they may take appropriate measures to protect legitimate interests other than those taken into consideration by this Regulation, such as public security, plurality of the media and prudential rules, subject to the Commission's prior approval of those interventions.[384]

5.3 *The notification system*

It follows from Article 4 of Regulation 139/2004 that the Commission must be notified of concentrations with a Community dimension before their implementation. Notification determines the starting date of the deadlines laid down in the Regulation. There are two basic deadlines, and extensions can be granted for both. The first deadline expires 25 working days following the filing. During that period the Commission must decide whether it has serious doubts about the compatibility of the concentration with the common market. If that is the case, it initiates proceedings for an in-depth investigation. This second phase, which leads to a final decision, can last up to 105 working days. Both first and second phase decisions can include the imposition of conditions. It should be noted, however, that the Commission can only adopt a negative decision after it has given the parties concerned the opportunity to be heard on the basis of a statement of objections.[385] Article 18 also grants third parties certain, more limited, rights to be involved.[386]

Although both Regulation 139/2004 and implementing Regulation 802/2004 lay down relatively detailed rules of procedure, such as the Commission's power to request information and to organize on the spot investigations, a significant portion of the procedure takes place before the official notification. The Commission will only accept notification if parties have presented

383. Ancillary Restraints Notice, cited *supra* note 147.

384. Case C-42/01, *Portugal v. Commission.*

385. Case C-413/06 P, *Bertelsmann AG and Sony Corporation of America v. Independent Music Publishers and Labels Association (Impala)*, paras. 61–76. The hearing officer is in charge of ensuring that the procedural safeguards duly apply (see above).

386. Case T-96/92, *Comité Central d'Entreprise de la Société Générale des Grandes Sources and Others v. Commission.*

a complete version of Form CO. In addition, failure to submit complete notification implies that the clock should not start running on the time limits referred to above. The question of whether notification is complete necessarily involves a margin of appreciation and hence a degree of subjectivity. The Commission has tried to objectivize these and other aspects of its procedure in a series of best practice guidelines which can be found on its website.

5.4 *The substantive test*

As mentioned above, concentration control is preventive in nature. It seeks to avoid the creation or reinforcement of dominant market positions. It is therefore not surprising that many of the concepts used in concentration control proceedings are identical or akin to those used for the purposes of Article 102 TFEU. It should be recalled however that these *ex ante* control proceedings are prospective in nature and relatively abstract to the extent they relate to any specific type of market conduct.[387] That being said, there must be a causal relationship between the concentration and the competition concern. The Commission is not empowered to regulate existing dominant positions.[388]

Concentration control proceedings usually start with an attempt to define the markets affected by the concentration. A precise definition is not required however, if, irrespective of the size of these markets, the concentration does not give rise to competition concerns.[389] As in the other areas of competition law, the Commission relies on the methodology laid down in the 1997 Notice on the definition of the relevant market.[390] After having defined the markets, the Commission usually identifies whether there are any particular markets amongst the markets concerned which require closer attention. In horizontal relationships, a market is deemed to be "affected" if the overlapping activities of the parties represents a combined market share of 20% or more. In vertical relationships, a market is deemed to be affected if one or more of the parties to the concentration has a market share exceeding 30% of a market which is upstream or downstream of a relevant market in which any other party to the concentration is engaged. For these markets, parties must supply a considerable amount of data in their notification form.

Market shares do play an important role in the assessment of horizontal concentrations. According to the horizontal merger guidelines,[391] market shares provide useful first indications of the market structure and the competitive importance of the merging parties and their competitors, especially where they exceed 50%. Market shares are also used to calculate concentration ratios, such as the Herfindahl-Hirschmann Index ("HHI") which reflects the sum of the squares of the individual market shares of all the firms in the market. While the absolute level of the HHI can give an initial indication of the competitive pressure in the market post-merger, the change in the HHI is a useful proxy for the change in concentration directly brought about by the merger.[392]

In relation to the competitive harm resulting from the reduction of competitive pressure, the guidelines refer in the first place to non-coordinated effects. These effects not only refer to price increases or output reductions by the new dominant entity, but also to the loss of competition which the parties to the concentration exerted on each other prior to the concentration.

---

387. Case T-125/97, *Coca-Cola*.
388. Joined Cases 19 & 20/74, *Kali und Salz AG and Kali-Chemie AG v. Commission*. See also Commission Decision of 14 Dec. 1993, *Kali+Salz*, O.J. 1994, L 186/38, para 71.
389. Case T-79/12, *Cisco Systems, Inc. and Messagenet SpA v. Commission*.
390. Commission Notice, cited *supra* note 23.
391. Horizontal Merger Guidelines, cited *supra* note 22.
392. Horizontal Merger Guidelines, cited *supra* note 22, para 16. See also Case T-282/06, *Sun Chemical Group BV and Others v. Commission*, paras. 133–141.

This latter situation may occur in oligopolistic situations in which these parties were each other's closest competitors.[393] The second type of competitive harm mentioned in the horizontal merger guidelines refers to coordinated effects, which occur when the concentration gives rise to or reinforces collective dominance. The guidelines codify and clarify the case law on oligopolistic dominance: "[...] three conditions are necessary for coordination to be sustainable. First, the coordinating firms must be able to monitor to a sufficient degree whether the terms of coordination are being adhered to. Second, discipline requires that there is some form of credible deterrent mechanism that can be activated if deviation is detected. Third, the reactions of outsiders, such as current and future competitors not participating in the coordination, as well as customers, should not be able to jeopardize the results expected from the coordination."[394]

The horizontal merger guidelines also list a series of factors which may compensate for the competitive concerns resulting from the concentration. These factors not only include typical market-related elements, such as countervailing buying power and entry conditions, but also refer to specific characteristics of the merging firms, such as the circumstance that the acquired entity is a "failing firm", or the efficiencies the concentration is likely to bring about. The efficiency defence is not an easy one to argue. It is subject to two cumulative conditions: the efficiencies must benefit consumers and be merger-specific.

With respect to mergers between non-competing firms, which include vertical and conglomerate mergers, the relevant guidelines state that they are, as a rule, less likely to give rise to competitive concerns than horizontal concentrations, and that they provide scope for efficiencies through the integration of complementary activities. However, they may lead to anti-competitive foreclosure if the market shares in the markets concerned exceed 30% and where these markets are relatively concentrated. Such foreclosure may relate either to customers or to inputs, which are important for competitors of the new entity and which enable it to raise their rival's costs. Whether such foreclosure will occur cannot be taken for granted and depends on the ability of the new entity to engage in effective foreclosure conduct, and its incentive to do so. And even if both conditions are fulfilled, the non-horizontal guidelines require the Commission to make an overall assessment which takes into account all relevant factors, such as entry which may counterbalance the effects of the foreclosure conduct as well as the efficiencies resulting from the merger. According to the guidelines, these foreclosure issues may ensue not only from vertical concentrations, but also from conglomerate ones.[395] It is submitted that applying this standard of review to conglomerate mergers is less likely to lead to prohibition decisions than in the past.[396]

As mentioned above, parties to a concentration can try to alleviate the Commission's possible concerns by submitting commitments, which the Commission can then impose as conditions or obligations attached to its approval decision. The so-called remedy notice contains a non-exhaustive list of such "commitments". These include structural commitments, such as divestitures, and conduct remedies relating to the future market conduct of the merged entity, such as the conclusion of long term (supply) contracts.[397]

393. Horizontal Merger Guidelines, cited *supra* note 22, paras. 24–38.

394. Horizontal Merger Guidelines, cited *supra* note 22, para 41 and in particular Case T-342/99, *Airtours plc v. Commission*, para 62 and Case C-413/06 P, *Bertelsmann*, para 123.

395. Non-horizontal Merger Guidelines, cited *supra* note 22.

396. See A. Jones and B. Sufrin, op. cit. *supra* note 237, at 1230.

397. Commission Notice on remedies acceptable under Reg. 139/2004 and under Commission Reg. 802/2004, O.J. 2008, C 267/1.

Further reading

Akman, P., *The Concept of Abuse in EU Competition Law* (Hart Publishing, 2012).
Akman, P., "The European Commission's guidance on Article 102 TFEU: From inferno to paradiso", 73 MLR (2010).
Bellamy, G. and G. Child, *European Law of Competition*, 7th ed. (OUP, 2013).
Bishop, S. and M. Walker, *The Economics of EC Competition Law: Concepts, Application and Measurement*, 3rd ed. (Sweet & Maxwell, 2010).
Brammer, S., *Co-operation between National Competition Agencies in the Enforcement of EC Competition Law* (Hart Publishing, 2009).
Broberg, M., *The European Commission's Jurisdiction to Scrutinise Mergers*, 4th ed. (Kluwer, 2013).
Chalmers, D., D. Davies and G. Monti, *European Union Law*, 3rd ed. (CUP, 2014).
Cook, C.J. and C.S. Kerse, *EC Merger Control*, 5th ed. (Sweet & Maxwell, 2009).
Craig, P. and G. de Búrca, *EU Law: Text, Cases and Materials*, 6th ed. (OUP, 2015).
Faull, J. and A. Nikpay, *The EU Law of Competition*, 3rd ed. (OUP, 2014).
Jones, A. and B. Sufrin, *EU Competition Law: Text, Cases, and Materials*, 6th ed. (OUP, 2016).
Kerse, C. and N. Khan, *EU Antitrust Procedure*, 6th ed. (Sweet & Maxwell, 2012).
Nazzini, R., *The Foundations of European Union Competition Law: The Objective and Principles of Article 102* (OUP, 2011).
O'Donoghue, R. and A.J. Padilla, *The Law and Economics of Article 102 TFEU*, 2nd ed. (Hart Publishing, 2013).
Ortiz Blanco, L., *EU Competition Procedure* 3rd ed. (OUP, 2013).
Townley, C., *Article 81 EC and Public Policy* (Hart Publishing, 2009).
Wesseling, R. and M. Van Der Woude, "The lawfulness and acceptability of enforcement of European Cartel Law", 35 *World Competition* (2012).
Whish, R. and D. Bailey, *Competition Law*, 8th ed. (OUP, 2015).
Wils, W., "Antitrust compliance programmes and optimal antitrust enforcement", 1 *Journal of Antitrust Enforcement* (2013).

CHAPTER 21
STATE AID LAW

*Tom Ottervanger and Maarten Aalbers**

1. Introduction

Articles 107 to 109 TFEU contain the substantive and procedural rules concerning distortions of competition as a result of state aid to undertakings. Article 107(1) TFEU stipulates that aid granted by a Member State or through state resources in any form whatsoever which distorts, or threatens to distort, competition by favouring certain undertakings or the production of certain goods is incompatible with the common market, insofar as such aid affects trade between Member States. The various substantive elements of the prohibition of state aid shall be discussed in section 3.

A robust regime of state aid control is considered essential to ensure economic and sustainable growth and the functioning of the internal market. Compared to other branches of EU substantive law, EU supervision of state aid is highly centralized and falls within the exclusive competences of the Commission. The Commission exercises broad discretion in reviewing and investigating all forms of state aid in almost every economic sector. There are several types of aid which are *de jure* exempted from the prohibition. These exemptions are enumerated in Article 107(2) TFEU. In addition, Article 107(3) TFEU provides for the possibility for exemption from the prohibition with the Commission's approval. The application of these exemptions falls within the discretionary powers of the Commission (section 4).

A supervisory mechanism is provided for in Article 108 TFEU. State aid control is founded on the principle of compulsory prior notification. Except in cases covered by a block exemption, any plans to grant aid must be notified to the Commission. Under the so-called "standstill obligation" of Article 108(3) TFEU the Member State must refrain from putting aid measures in effect until a Commission decision is rendered on its compatibility with the internal market (section 5).

The enforcement of Articles 107 and 108 TFEU is shaped by the extensive investigative powers the Commission enjoys based on the Procedural Regulation 2015/1589.[1] The Commission can open formal investigations into aid schemes. Member States, aid beneficiaries and competitors can be required to provide relevant information for purposes of this investigation. Along with the Commission, the national courts also play an additional role in the enforcement of Article 108 (3) TFEU (section 7), especially in ordering recovery of unlawful aid (section 6.2).

* T. Ottervanger: Europa Institute, Law Faculty, University of Leiden; M. Aalbers: Europa Institute, Law Faculty, University of Leiden.

1. Reg. (EU) 2015/1589 of 13 July 2015 laying down detailed rules for the application of Art. 108 TFEU, O.J. 2015, L 248, at 9–29.

The Council, on the proposal of the Commission, is authorized under Article 109 TFEU to proscribe implementing rules for the substantive or procedural aspects of the state aid provisions. The adoption by the Council of Regulation 733/2013, amending Council Regulation 994/98, authorizes the Commission to enact further rules on certain categories of horizontal state aid.[2]

In 2012 the Commission launched an ambitious state aid reform programme – the State Aid Modernization (SAM) – covering a large variety of substantive and procedural measures (regulations, guidelines and communications).[3] In 2015 these proposals were implemented (sections 2 and 8).

The Commission adopted Regulation 1407/2013 on *de minimis* aid[4] and a revised General Block Exemption Regulation 651/2014.[5] This regulation, considered a cornerstone of the modernization agenda, sets out conditions for categories of aid that can be exempted from prior notification and approval by the Commission. Next to this regulation the Commission adopted renewed regulations for aid to small and medium-sized agricultural enterprises (the Agricultural Block Exemption Regulation)[6] and *de-minimis* aid for agricultural enterprises.[7]

State aid law and policy is further shaped by numerous guidelines and communications and a growing body of case law by the Union courts.

Although Article 107 TFEU is not directly effective,[8] the standstill obligation laid down in Article 108(3) TFEU has direct effect.[9] State aid which may in itself be compatible under Article 107(2) and (3) TFEU, may nevertheless be unlawful when implemented prior to notification under Article 108(3) TFEU.

The case law also suggests that the provisions on free movement of goods and services are complemented by the provisions of Articles 107 and 108 TFEU, and that the free movement of goods and services would be seriously undermined if Member States were able to confer on their national trade and industry artificial advantages over their competitors in other Member States through the granting of state aid.[10] The state aid provisions thus play a direct role in maintaining a regime of undistorted competition in light of Protocol No. 27 annexed to the TFEU.[11]

Special state aid rules apply to the agricultural sector based on Article 42 TFEU[12] and to the transport sector, based on Article 96 TFEU.[13]

The supervision of national aid measures also involves the coordination of national economic policy, which is of increasing importance in the context of the Economic and Monetary Union. Effective control of state aid concentrates not only the intensity of the aid (scope and

2. O.J. 2013, L 204/11.
3. Communication on the EU State Aid Modernization (SAM), COM(2012)209.
4. Reg. 1407/2013, O.J. 2013, L 352/1.
5. Reg. 651/2014, L 187/1.
6. Reg. 702/2014, O.J. 2014, L193/1.
7. Reg. 1408/2013, O.J. 2013, L352/9.
8. Case C-78/76, *Steinike*; Case C-284/12, *Deutsche Lufthansa v. Flughafen Frankfurt-Hahn.*
9. Case C-78/76, *Steinike*; Case C-284/12, *Deutsche Lufthansa v. Flughafen Frankfurt-Hahn.*
10. Joined Cases C-197/11 & C-203/11, *Eric Libert v. Vlaams Gewest*; Case T-57/11, *Castelnou Energía v. Commission*; Joined Cases C-20/15 P & C-21/15 P; *Commission v. World Duty Free.*
11. L. Hancher, T. Ottervanger and P.J. Slot, *EU State Aids* (Sweet & Maxwell, 2016), at 383.
12. Reg. 26/62, O.J. 1962, B 30/1. See Case 177/78, *Pigs and Bacon v. Commission*; Case C-311/94, *IJssel-Vliet Combinatie BV v. Minister van Economische Zaken*; Case C-173/02, *Spain v. Commission.*
13. Reg. 1370/2007, O.J. 2007, 315/1 provides for a set of rules for the public passenger transport services by rail and by road (on compensation for public service obligations in transport); Guidelines concerning the application of Reg. (EC) 1370/2007 on public passenger transport services by rail and by road, O.J. 2014, C 92/1.

terms), but also on the total volume. Therefore state aid law may well take place as a part of budgetary control in the context of Articles 120 and 121 TFEU.

2. Developments in EU state aid law 2005–2017

The main developments in EU state aid law over the last decade have been the launch of the State Aid Action Plan (SAAP) in 2005; the application since 2008 of the State Aid Framework in the financial sector, introducing specific rules for rescue and restructuring of financial institutions; the contribution of state aid to the Europe 2020 strategy and the comprehensive State Aid Modernization Programme (SAM).

The SAAP reform has shifted the policy of the Commission towards a more refined economic approach in assessing state aid, while encouraging Member States and the Commission to operate within more effective procedures that will contribute to less and better targeted aid.[14] During the financial crisis of 2008–2013, the Commission approved a massive and unprecedented amount of aid to European financial institutions in the period after October 2008, resorting to Article 107(3)(b) and (c) TFEU.[15] This provision allows the Commission to declare aid to be compatible with the Treaty so as to remedy a serious disturbance in the economy of Member States.[16] To create guidance on its decision practice, the Commission adopted a new Banking Communication in 2013. The content of this communication was scrutinized and consequently declared in conformity with the Commission's powers under Article 107(3) sub (c) TFEU.[17]

As for the Europe 2020 strategy the Commission has laid down state aid instruments that can be used to enhance the so-called "flagship initiatives" (innovation, digital agenda, youth policy, sustainable growth, employment, green energy and competition). These goals were incorporated in the 2012 State Aid Modernization (SAM) strategy of the Commission (see also section 8). In 2013 and 2014 the Commission enacted new guidelines, communications and revised secondary legislation, aiming for more effective control. The modernized block exemptions have an increased substantive scope and provide Member States with enlarged exemption categories *inter alia* in the field of research & development, social policy objectives and culture.[18] In 2017 the Commission added new exemption categories concerning infrastructural aid for airports and harbours and types of aid for culture and sports.[19] This increase in scope is accompanied by an increased *ex post* control by the Commission and new procedural powers.[20]

14. L. Hancher, T. Ottervanger and P.J. Slot, op. cit. *supra* note 11, at 7–8.
15. See for instance Case C- 224/12 P, *Commission v. the Netherlands (ING)*; Case T-319/11, *ABN-AMRO v. Commission*.
16. The implementation of these decisions by the Member States resulted in several preliminary rulings by the ECJ. See for instance Case C-667/13, *Estado Português v. Banco Privado Português SA; Case* C-690/13, *Trapeza Eurobank v. ATE*; Case C-672/13, *OTP Bank*.
17. Communication on the application of the state aid rules to support measures in favour of banks in the context of the financial crisis (Banking Communication), O.J. 2013, C 216/01; Case C-526/14, *Kotnik v. Slovenia*.
18. See the General Block Exemption Reg./Commission Reg. (EU) 651/2014 of 17 June 2014 declaring certain categories of aid compatible with the internal market in application of Arts. 107 and 108 of the Treaty, O.J. 2014, L 187/1.
19. Commission Reg. (EU) 2017/1084 of 14 June 2017 amending Reg. (EU) 651/2014, C/2017/4213, at 1–18; See also press release Commission, Brussels 17 May 2017, available at <europa.eu/rapid/press-release_IP-17-1341_en.htm>.
20. See Council Reg. (EU) 734/2013, O.J. 2013, L 204/15.

3. Article 107(1) TFEU

3.1 Advantage

3.1.1 The concept of an advantage

Article 107(1) TFEU refers to advantages in any form whatsoever which distort competition. Economic or social policy objectives pursued by the state do not narrow the ambit of this provision.[21] Nor can it be accepted that Member States compensate real or supposed competitive disadvantages that "national champions" incur by the policies of neighbouring Member States.[22] The wording of Article 107(1) TFEU therefore stipulates that any advantage granted by the state falls within the scope of Article 107 TFEU.[23] Whether or not aid measures are intentionally designed to strengthen the market position of an undertaking is not important. Not the form but the potential effect of the aid is decisive for determining an advantage.[24] The concept of an advantage has been defined in the case law as any economic benefit granted by the state, which an undertaking would not have obtained under normal market conditions.[25] The sole fact that an undertaking financially benefits from an aid measure, has to be considered as the fulfilment of, at least, the advantage criterion.[26]

Advantages do include not only "positive" acts but can also consist of the mitigation of charges. Examples of the former case are subsidies, loans at lower than commercial rates of interest or guarantees.[27] In the latter case undertakings are relieved from certain economic duties, such as a taxes or debts.[28] An advantage may take the form of social security contributions;[29] export aid,[30] financial goodwill;[31] lower charges for goods or services delivered by the state or a public undertaking;[32] preferences for public undertakings;[33] rescue and restructuring aid;[34]

21. C-431/14 P, *Greece v. Commission*; Case C-63/14, *Commission v. France;* Joined Cases C-20/15 P & C-21/15 P, *Commission v. World Duty Free.*
22. Case C-431/14 P, *Greece v. Commission.*
23. Joined Cases C-399/10 P & C-401/10 P, *Bouyges*; Case C-279/08 P, *Commission v. the Netherlands,*
24. Case C- 730/79, *Philip Morris v. Commission*; Case T-298/97, *Alzetta v. Commission*; Case C-280/00, *Altmark*; Case C-351/98, *Spain v. Commission*; Case T 308/00 RENV, *Salzgitter v. Commission*; Cases T-385/12 and T-135/12, *France and Orange v. Commission*; Joined Cases C-20/15 P & C-21/15 P, *Commission v. World Duty Free;* Case C-150/16, *Fondul Proprietatea v. Complexul Energetic Oltenia*; Case C-124/10 P, *Commission v. EDF*, para 77; Case C-357/14 P, *Electrabel v. Commission.*
25. Joined Cases T- 319/12 & T-321/12, *Spain v. Commission*; Case T-52/12, *Greece v. Commission*; Cases C-533/12 P and C-536/12 P, *SNCM v. Commission*; Case C-522/13, *Navantia v. Concello de Ferrol*; Case C-211/15 P, *Orange v. Commission.*
26. Case T-150/12, *Greece v. Commission*; Case C-522/13, *Navantia v. Concello de Ferrol.*
27. Case T-387/11, *Nitrogénművek Veg v. Commisison*; Case C-559/12 P, *LaPoste*; Case C-242/13, *Commerz v. Havenbedrijf Rotterdam*; Case C-275/10, *Residex v. Rotterdam*; Case C-620/13 P, *British Telecommunications v. Commission*; Case C-559/12 P, *La Poste*; Case C-672/13, *OTP Bank.*
28. Case C-5/14, *Kernkrafwerke Lippe – Ems v. Hauptzollamt Osnabrück*; Case C-74/16, *Congregación de Escuelas Pías.*
29. Joined Cases 62/87 & 72/87, *Exécutif régional wallon and SA Glaverbel v. Commission*; Case C-369/07, *Commission v. Greece*; Case C-211/15 P, *Orange v. Commission.*
30. Commission communication on the application of Arts. 107 and 108 TFEU to short-term export-credit insurance O.J. 2012, C-392/1.
31. Case C-274/12 P, *Telefónica*; Joined Cases C-20/15 P & C-21/15 P, *Commission v. World Duty Free.*
32. Joined Cases 67, 68 & 70/85, *Van der Kooy*; Joined Cases T-295/12 & T-309/12, *ZT v. Commission.*
33. Case C-559/12 P, *France v. Commission (La Poste)*; C-284/12, *Deutsche Lufthansa v. Flughafen Frankfurt-Hahn.*
34. Joined Cases C-533/12 P & C-536/12 P, *Société nationale maritime Corse-Méditerranée (SNCM) and Corsica Ferries v. Commission*; Joined Cases C-399/10 P & C-401/10 P, *Bouygues Télécom v. Commisison*; Case

sales at lower prices or gifts of land;[35] and aid for privatization.[36] The concept of aid does not include advantages for a particular undertaking or branch of industry which result from legal or administrative measures but are not directly quantifiable in monetary terms (for example, certain employment conditions),[37] or whereby a transfer of income between undertakings takes place (for instance, by measures intended to promote the use of "green" electricity).[38]

To establish whether a measure constitutes an advantage the Court has developed two important tests in its case law. The first test is the market economy investor principle. Under this principle the Commission and the Court assesses whether the state acted as a normal undertaking would. The second test is the "Almark test". Under this test the Commission and the Court ascertains whether the state financially compensated an undertaking for discharging a service of general economic interest.

3.1.2 *The market economy investor test*

An important principle in assessing whether an aid measure qualifies as an advantage is the so-called market economy investor principle (MEIP).[39] The Court developed this principle as a test to determine whether public investments, for example capital injections, are made under normal market conditions.[40] If the investment took place under conditions under which a private investor would not have made capital available, then such action constitutes aid within the meaning of Article 107(1) TFEU. In the *EDF* case the Court made clear that the market economy investor test must be examined on an *ex-ante* basis, based on the information that is available at the time of the state investment.[41] Moreover, the General Court ruled in the *Leidschendam* case that the Commission must investigate all available economic and financial information in order to determine whether a Member State has acted as a market economy investor.[42] Accordingly the Commission must conduct an analysis of the relevant market as proof that a state did not act as a private operator lies with the Commission.[43]

This MEIP – test applies not just to investments or capital participations by governmental organizations but also to related practices, such as land sales,[44] public crediting[45] and public vending.[46] Applied to the financial markets a "*private creditor test*" examines for example whether debt renegotiations by public creditors involve state aid, comparing the behaviour of the public creditor to that of private creditors.[47]

T-487/11, *Banco Privado Portugues v. Commission.*

35. Case C-239/09, *Seydaland*; Case C – 39/14, *BVVG v. Jerichowerland.*
36. Case C-214/12 P, *Land Burgenland v. Commission.*
37. Joined Cases C-72/91 & C-73/91, *Sloman Neptun*; Joined Cases C-533/12 P & C-536/12 P, *SNCM v. Commission.*
38. Case C-329/15, *ENEA v. rezes Urzędu Regulacji Energetyki*; Case C-262/12, *Vent De Colère*; Case T-251/11, *Austria v. Commission.*
39. Case C-39/94, *SFEI and Others*, paras. 60–61.
40. Case C-142/87 *Tubemeuse*; Case C-305/89 *Italy v. Commission.*
41. Case C-124/10 P, *Commission v. EDF*, paras. 83–85 and 105.
42. Joined Cases T-186/13, T-190/13 & T-193/13, *Leidschendam – Voorburg v. Commission.*
43. Joined Cases T-186/13, T-190/13 & T-193/13, *Leidschendam – Voorburg v. Commission*; Case T-103/14, *Frucona Košice v. Commission.*
44. Case C-39/14, *BVVG v. Jerichowerland.*
45. Case C-525/04 P *Spain v. Commission*; Case C-73/11 P, *Frucona v. Commission.*
46. Joined Cases T-268/08 & T-281/08 *Land Burgenland and Austria v. Commission.*
47. Case C-300/16 P, *Commission v. Frucona Košice*; Case C-73/11 P, *Frucona Košice v. Commission*; Case C-150/16, *Fondul Proprietatea v. Complexul Energetic Oltenia.*

The MEIP – test applies to state intervention by means of ownership or control of certain assets or in decisions to purchase certain goods and services. Therefore it must be distinguished from public prerogative powers.[48] National authorities may not invoke public policy goals, such as full employment and access to social security, as a justification for financial risks which market operators normally would not take.[49] In such a case a national authority does not act as market economy investor.

3.1.3 *The Altmark test*

According to the landmark *Altmark* judgment, compensation for a public service obligation does *not* constitute state aid, *provided* that four cumulative criteria are met.[50] Control by the Commission and the Courts on the application of the Altmark criteria is limited to ascertaining whether there is a manifest error of assessment.[51]

Firstly, there must be a clear public service obligation. There must be an economic activity which can clearly distinguish itself from normal market activities, on account of a genuine general interest.[52] The General Court applied in several cases a market failure test to distinguish services of a general economic interest from normal market activities.[53] Secondly, prior to entrustment, objective and transparent criteria must be determined to calculate the total net costs that must cover the compensation. Thirdly, the compensation may not exceed the total net cost incurred by the SGEI provider, including a reasonable profit. The second and third conditions exclude the risk of retroactive compensation and demand that national authorities create a control mechanism that precludes overcompensation.[54] The fourth criterion provides that if the public service provider is not selected pursuant to a public tender, the compensation will need to be calculated based on the total net costs, which a well-run, average undertaking would make in carrying out the services. This condition, requiring a public tender or benchmarking, has led to a flow of highly technical case law on the interaction between EU state aid law and EU public procurement law.[55]

3.2 *State resources*

3.2.1 *Transfer of state resources*

Article 107(1) TFEU entails that an advantage must be provided by the state or through state resources. Pursuant to Article 107(1) TFEU, the concept of "state" includes not only central

48. L. Hancher, T. Ottervanger and P.J. Slot, op. cit. *supra* note 11, at 104.
49. Case C-533/12 P and C-536/12 P, *SNCM*; Cases T-385/12 and T-135/12, *France Télécom and Orange v. Commission.*
50. Case C-280/00, *Altmark Trans.*
51. Case T-388/03, *Deutsche Post and DHL International v. Commission*; Case C-446/14, *Germany v. Commission (Zweckverband Rhineland Palatinate).*
52. Case C-211/15 P, *Orange.*
53. Cases T-461/13 and T-462/13, *Spain and Comunidad Autónoma del País Vasco v. Commission;* Case T-289/03, *BUPA v. Commission;* Judgments in Cases T-79/10, *Colt Télécommunicatons France v. Commission*; T- 258/10 *Orange v. Commission* and T- 325/10, *Iliad and others v. Commission.*
54. Joined Cases T-309/04, T-317/04, T-329/04 & T-336/04, *TV2 Danmark v. Commisison*; Case T-137/10, *CBI v. Commission;* Case T-15/14, *Simet v. Commission.*
55. Joined Cases C-341/06 P & C-342/06 P, *Chronopost and La Poste v. UFEX;* Case T-289/03, *BUPA v. Commission;* Case T-354/05, *Télévision Française;* Case T-137/10, *CBI v. Commission;* Case T-454/13, *SNCM v. Commission.*

authorities, but also (independent) sub-entities such as regions,[56] municipalities,[57] public undertakings[58] or private bodies established or appointed by the state to administer certain resources.[59] Moreover, according to the wording of Article 107(1) TFEU, not only aid granted directly by the state itself but also aid financed out of the state budget is covered. Thus, aids granted by public or private bodies (whether or not specially established for this purpose),[60] financial bodies under the control of the state,[61] public holding companies,[62] and public companies,[63] are also covered by the provisions of Article 107(1) TFEU.

The same is true for aid measures which are not actually financed through state resources, but from the operating surplus of a public body under national law which acts under pressure from public authorities.[64] The Court confirmed that even if resources originate from private sources, they could still be deemed under public control.[65] However, in *Preussen Elektra* the Court held that an obligation imposed by a statutory measure on private electricity suppliers to purchase electricity produced from renewable energy sources at fixed minimum prices did not involve any state resources.[66]

An exception to the concept of state resources concerns the so-called self-financed aid in the form of taxes charged to undertakings on the basis of a legislative provision which are entirely re-distributed to the same sector.[67] The Court clarified the role of public authorities towards self-financed aid in the *Doux Elévages case*.[68] In this case the Court ruled that resources which are reserved by a private (trade) organization for a specific purpose in the interest of members of the organization, cannot be considered "state resources" as long as the Member State only plays an instrumental role by declaring a financial contribution to a trade organization compulsory.[69] However, if a fund would be under state control, and the obligation to pay into the fund as well as the right to receive payment from it are subject to state regulation, the measure would qualify as "state resources" according to the Court.[70] In *Vent de Colère* the Court made clear that advantages provided by private bodies financed from compulsory contributions must be

56. Cases T-214/95, *Vlaams Gewest (Flemish Region) v. Commission*; Joined Cases T-92/00 and T-103/00, *Territorio Histórico de Álava and others v. Commission.*
57. Joined Cases C-324/90 & C-342/90, *Germany and Pleuger Worthington v. Commission.*
58. Case C-242/13, *Commerz v. Havenbedrijf Rotterdam*; Case C-522/13, *Navantia v. Concello de Ferrol*; Commission Directive 2006/111/EC of 16 Nov. 2006 on the transparency of financial relations between Member States and public undertakings as well as on financial transparency within certain undertakings O.J. 2006, L 318.
59. Case C-76/76 *Steinike and Weinlig v. Germany*; Case C-345/02, *Pearle*; Case C-262/12, *Vent de Colère v. Ministre de l'Ecologie.*
60. Case 78/76, *Steinike und Weinlig v. Germany*; Case C-262/12, *Vent de Colère v. Ministre de l'Ecologie*; Case T-347/09, *Germany v. Commission.*
61. Case C-329/15, *ENEA v. rezes Urzędu Regulacji Energetyki.*
62. Case C-303/88, *Italy v. Commission*; Case C-305/89, *Italy v. Commission*; Case C-206/06, *Essent Netwerk Noord and Others.*
63. Joined Cases 67/85, 68/85 & 70/85, *Van der Kooy*; Case T-l06/95, *FFSA.*
64. Case C-37/14, *Commission v. France ("Plan de Campagne").*
65. Case C-258/08, *Ladbroke.*
66. Case C-379/98, *Preussen Elektra AG v. Schleswag AG.*
67. Case C-329/15, *ENEA v. rezes Urzędu Regulacji Energetyki*; Case C-379/98, *Preussen Elektra AG v. Schleswag AG.*
68. Case C-677/11, *Doux élevages v. Ministère de l'Agriculture.*
69. Case C-677/11, *Doux élevages v. Ministère de l'Agriculture.*
70. Case T-136/05, *Salvat père & fils v. Commission.*

considered as state resources, since the state appointed these entities to manage the provision of given advantages.[71]

3.2.2 *Imputability to the state*

Apart from involving state resources, a measure must be imputable to the state in order to fall under the scope of Article 107(1) TFEU. The concept of "aid imputable to the state" has been construed narrowly by the Court in comparison to the concept of "state resources".

In cases where public authorities designate a private or public entity to administer aid to undertakings, such a transfer of state resources is considered imputable to the state.[72] The imputability requirement is not easily met if the aid is granted through one or more intermediate public or private entities which are *not* directly designated by the state to provide such aid.

In general, the Court requires that the actual deployment of the state resources can be attributed to some form of government decision.[73] Whether the transfer of state resources through public or private entities is imputable to the state depends on public control.[74] Even if the state is in a position to exercise decisive influence over the operations of a public undertaking, actual exercise in a particular case cannot be automatically presumed.[75] On a case by case basis the Commission must assess whether measures taken by public undertakings are indeed imputable to the state.[76]

Relevant factors for imputability include: the degree of integration of the public undertaking;[77] the nature of the undertaking's activities;[78] the dependence of a body to make decisions based on the directives of public authorities;[79] and the extent to which the undertaking in question operates under normal conditions of competition with private market operators.[80] Moreover, even unauthorized guarantees, deliberately and secretly granted by officials of public undertakings, may result in aid that can be imputed to the state, unless the state can demonstrate that the aid would have been opposed by the responsible public authority, had it been aware of such conduct.[81]

3.3 *The selectivity criterion*

In order to fall within the scope of Article 107(1) TFEU a measure must confer a selective advantage favouring certain products or certain undertakings which may mean one or more undertakings, a particular group of undertakings or certain economic sector or region.[82] The selectivity test in Article 107(1) TFEU distinguishes aid measures from the general provisions on distortions of competition found in Articles 116 and 117 TFEU.[83]

---

71. Case C-262/12, *Vent de Colère v. Ministre de l'Ecologie.*
72. Case C-329/15,*ENEA v. rezes Urzędu Regulacji Energetyki*; Case T-251/11, *Austria v. Germany.*
73. Case C-482/99, *Stardust Marine*; Case T-251/11, *Austria v. Germany.*
74. Case C-482/99, *Stardust Marine*; Joined Cases T-267/08 & T-279/08, *Région Nord-Pas- de Calais v. Commission.*
75. Case C-242/13, *Commerz v. Havenbedrijf Rotterdam.*
76. Case C-206/06, *Essent Netwerk Noord*; Case C-242/13, *Commerz v. Havenbedrijf Rotterdam*; Case C-329/15,*ENEA v. rezes Urzędu Regulacji Energetyki.*
77. Case C-482/99, *Stardust Marine.*
78. Case T-387/11, *Nitrogenmuvek v. Commission*, para 63.
79. Case C-345/02, *Pearle.*
80. Case C-482/99, *Stardust Marine.*
81. Case C-242/13, *Commerz v. Havenbedrijf Rotterdam.*
82. Joined Cases C-110/09 P, & C-107/09 P, *Commission and Spain v. Gibraltar and the United Kingdom*; Case C-270/15 P, *Belgium v. Commission.*
83. Case T-349/03, *Corsica Ferries v. Commission*; Case C-148/04, *Unicrediio v. Agenzia delle Entrate.*

In essence the selectivity test resembles a non-discrimination analysis, under which the Commission and the Courts can assess whether undertakings, which operate under comparable legal and factual situations, are treated unequally by measures of state intervention.[84] An aid measure is therefore selective when it favours certain undertakings or the production of certain goods over other undertakings.[85] In cases of individual aid the Commission can, without further analysis, decide that there is *de facto* selectivity.[86] A clear example is a subsidy.[87] In case of a general measure, the Commission has to establish whether this measure confers "an advantage of general application" and if so, whether this advantage is also selective.[88] General horizontal measures of economic policy, such as a lowering of tax rates, which are *a priori* available to all the undertakings operating in a Member State's economy, fall in principle outside of the scope of Article 107(1) TFEU.[89] However, if these measures result in benefitting certain economic transactions or undertakings that represent a specific economic sector, for instance the export sector, they can still be selective.[90] The Court has drafted in its case law a three-tier test for determining whether general measures have a selective effect.[91] This test is called the material selectivity test. Although established by the Court in tax cases, this "material selectivity test" is applied by the Court beyond the domain of fiscal aids, for instance in the field of transport.[92] The first step for the Commission is to determine whether a state measure directly derives from a common legal framework that applies without distinction and is applicable to every market operator in the national territory.[93] In such a case Article 107(1) TFEU is not applicable. This common legal framework is the so-called "normal reference system". Particularly in matters concerning taxation the national fiscal system serves as the normal reference system.[94] The second step is to assess whether a derogation from this normal reference system leads to different treatment of undertakings, which, given the objective of the general measure, are in the same factual and legal situation.[95] In case there is an exception from the normal reference, this measure constitutes a *priori* selective advantage. This means that the measure is selective, unless objectively justified by the Member State.[96] Under these circumstances the Commission is required to assess, within the third and last tier, whether this exception was prescribed in the normal reference system and whether the exception has a legitimate objective and given this objective, whether undertakings in the same factual and legal situation are treated differently.[97]

84. See Case C-270/15 P, *Belgium v. Commission*; Case C-518/13, *Eventech*; Case C-15/14 P, *Commission v. MOL*; Case C-100/15 P, *NMTA v. Commission*; Joined Cases C-20/15 & C-21/15, *Commission v. World Duty Free*.
85. Case C-143/99 *Adria-Wien Pipeline*.
86. Joined Cases C-164/15 P & C-165/15 P, *Ryan Air and Aer Lingus v. Commission*.
87. Joined Cases C-164/15 P & C-165/15 P, *Ryan Air and Aer Lingus v. Commission*.
88. Case C-524/14 P, *Commission v. Hansestadt Lübeck*; Joined Cases C-164/15 P & C-165/15, P,*Ryan Air and Aer Lingus v. Commission*.
89. Case C-143/99, *Adria-Wien Pipeline*; Case C-279/08 P, *Commission v. Kingdom of the Netherlands*; Joined Cases C-20/15 &C-21/15, *Commission v. World Duty Free*.
90. Case C-143/99, *Adria-Wien Pipeline*, para 48; Joined Cases C-110/09 P & C-107/09 P, *Commission and Spain v. Gibraltar and the United Kingdom*.
91. Case C-143/99, *Adria-Wien Pipeline*; Case C-279/08 P, *the Netherlands v. Commission (NOx)*.
92. Case C-279/08 P, *NOx*; Case C-524/14 P, *Commission v. Hansestadt Lübeck*.
93. Joined Cases C-20/15 P & C-21/15 P, *Commission v. World Duty Free, Banco Santander and Santusa*.
94. Case T-308/00, *Salzgitter*.
95. Case C-270/15 P, 30 June 2016, *Belgium v. Commission*; Case C-518/13, *Eventech*; Case C-15/14 P, *Commission v. MOL*; Case C-100/15 P, *NMTA v. Commission*.
96. Case C-524/14 P, *Commission v. Hansestadt Lübeck*.
97. Joined Cases C-106/09P & C 107/09P, *Commission and Kingdom of Spain v. Gibraltar and United Kingdom*, paras. 146, 149–150; Joined Cases C-20/15 P & C-21/15 P, *Commission v. World Duty Free, Banco Santander and Santusa*.

The Court has held that measures have a selective nature where the structure of a measure, although formulated in a general and objective manner, effectively favours a particular undertaking or group of undertakings.[98] The Court ruled in the case of the *Gibraltar tax scheme*, that a "tax reduction, established for all the eligible undertakings in Gibraltar, *de facto* favoured offshore companies, since this group undertakings were taxed precisely on account of the specific features characteristic of that group".[99] The three-tier analysis can prove difficult to assess for the reviewing EU Courts. Especially in the *Banco Santander* and *Autogrill* judgments the General Court had a hard time in distinguishing between the first and second tier of the material selectivity test.[100] In these judgments the General Court had to review two decisions concerning a Spanish tax reduction of financial goodwill for foreign shareholding acquisitions.[101] The Commission decided that this tax reduction formed an exception to the general applicable corporate tax scheme in Spain and therefore constituted a selective advantage. Concerning the first tier of the material selectivity test the Commission decided that the reference framework, the general corporate tax scheme, was not selective. However in its assessment of the second tier, the Commission concluded that the tax reduction scheme constituted a derogation which discriminated between two categories of undertakings in comparable situations. Although the measure was applicable to every taxable undertaking in Spain, undertakings which acquire shareholdings abroad were treated differently compared to undertakings that did not acquire foreign shareholdings.[102] In its assessment of the measure the General Court came to a radically different outcome.[103] First of all the General Court considered that the measure did not favour a group of undertakings since the measure was *a priori* available to any undertaking.[104] Referring to the *Gibraltar* judgment, the General Court held that the Commission should have identified specific characteristics of the beneficiary undertakings distinguishing them from other undertakings, as the Court did with the offshore companies in Gibraltar. On appeal in the case *Commission v. World Duty Free and Banco Santander* the Court considered this interpretation to be in breach with the goals of Article 107(1) TFEU. The Court firstly distinguishes the first tier (establishing a normal reference system) from the second tier (establishing whether a derogation from the normal reference system is not discriminatory). The Court considered that, since the measure was only available to Spanish undertakings with financial assets abroad, the General Court misapplied this test. Therefore the Court held that the General Court had failed to examine the effects of the different treatment of undertakings by the tax reduction scheme. The Court further held that the concept of selectivity also includes economic transactions performed by undertakings. Most important the Court ruled that the General Court had misapplied the selectivity test by requiring the Commission to identify a specific group of undertakings of beneficiaries, rather than focusing on the different treatment of undertakings in comparable situations.[105]

---

98. Joined Cases C-106/09 P & C-107/09 P, *Commission and Spain v. Gibraltar and United Kingdom.*
99. Joined Cases C-106/09 P & C-107/09 P, *Commission and Spain v. Gibraltar and United Kingdom*, para 101.
100. P. Nicolaides, "New limits to the concept of selectivity: The birth of 'general exception' to the prohibition of state aid in EU competition law", (2015) JCEL & Pract., at 1–9.
101. See Cases T-219/10, *Autogrill España v. Commission* and T-399/11, *Banco Santander and Santusa v. Commission.*
102. See Opinion A.G. Wathelet, 28 June 2016 concerning Joined Cases C-20/15 P & C-21/15 P, *Commission v. World Duty Free, Banco Santander and Santusa*, para 49.
103. Cases T-219/10, *Autogrill España v. Commission* and T-399/11, *Banco Santander and Santusa v. Commission.*
104. See Joined Cases C-20/15 P & C-21/15 P, *Commission v. World Duty Free, Banco Santander and Santusa.*
105. Joined Cases C-20/15 P & C-21/15 P, *Commission v. World Duty Free, Banco Santander and Santusa*, para 104.

3.4 *Effect on interstate trade*

The prohibition of Article 107(1) TFEU only applies to measures which can affect trade between Member States. Due to the high level of economic integration within the EU, advantages for one or more undertakings may easily have an impact on intra-EU trade. In its assessment the Commission is not required to show an actual effect on interstate trade.[106] Establishing a *potential* effect on trade between Member States suffices. Moreover, whether the recipient of the aid is either directly involved in cross-border trade or not is of no consequence.[107] Only in cases of involvement of third countries is the Commission is obliged to explain why intra-EU trade is affected.[108]

However in situations where only Member States are involved, the Commission may simply accept that there is a potential effect on interstate trade when an advantage strengthens the position of an undertaking in a Member State.[109] Such an advantage can potentially hinder undertakings form other Member State in offering their services and goods in that Member State.[110]

Although the concept of an effect on interstate trade must be interpreted broadly, there are economic activities which are less likely to have such an effect since they have a predominantly local character. Whether an economic activity has a local scope can only be assessed by the Commission. In 2015 the Commission offered Member States some guidance on local public support measures that can be granted without prior Commission approval. The Commission adopted several decisions that clearly indicated that certain aid measures had a marginal effect on consumers and market operators in neighbouring Member States due to their local nature.[111] These aid measures comprised, amongst others, sport activities, local harbours and health activities with only marginally foreseeable effects on cross-border investments.[112]

3.5 *Distortion of competition*

An aid measure is considered to distort or threaten to distort competition when it is liable to improve the competitive position of an undertaking compared to other undertakings.[113] Where it is in competition with undertakings in other Member States there may be no need to define the relevant market or to investigate, in detail, the market position of the beneficiary and its competitors.[114] The mere fact that the aid allows the recipient undertaking to maintain a stronger competitive position than it would have had if the aid had not been provided is enough to

---

106. C-197/11, *Eric Libert.*
107. Case C-280/00, *Altmark Trans*, para 78; Case C-197/11, *Eric Libert.*
108. Case C-494/06P, *Commission v. Italy and WAM Spa.*
109. Case T-288/07, *Friulia Venezia Giulia*; Case C-222/04, *Cassa di Risparmio di Firenze*; Case C-150/16, *Fondul Proprietatea v. Complexul Energetic Oltenia.*
110. Case C-280/00, *Altmark Trans*, paras. 77 and 78.
111. Commission Decisions: *United Kingdom – Member-owned golf clubs* (SA.38208, O.J. JOCE C/277/2015); *United Kingdom – Glenmore Lodge* (SA. 37963, O.J. C/277/2015); *The Netherlands – Lauwersoog port* (SA.39403, O.J. C/259/2015); *Germany – Städtische Projektgesellschaft "Wirtschaftsbüro Gaarden – Kiel"* (SA.33149, O.J. C/188/2015); *Germany – Medical centre in Durmersheim* (SA.37904, O.J. C/188/2015); *Czech Republic – Hradec Králové public hospitals* (SA.37432, O.J. C/203/2015).
112. Commission Guidance on local public support measures that can be granted without prior Commission approval, 29 Apr. 2015, Press Release IP/15/4889.
113. Case C-197/11, *Eric Libert*; Case C-522/13, *Navantia v. Concello de Ferrol*; Case C-518/13, *Eventech v. Parking Adjudicator (Black Cabs)*; Joined Cases T-186/13, T-190/13 & T-193/13, *Leidschendam – Voorburg v. Commission.*
114. Case C-197/11, *Eric Libert*; Case C-522/13, *Navantia v. Concello de Ferrol.*

conclude that there is a possible distortion of competition.[115] Due to its very definition, an aid creates a competitive advantage, and therefore state aid law does not require a detailed analysis on the effects on competition as is the case with the Articles 101 and 102 TFEU.[116] It is not decisive for the outcome of a case whether a large or small amount of aid is at issue,[117] or whether a large or small undertaking is involved.[118] Therefore there are no requirements of "significance" or "appreciability" concerning possible distortion competition, although *de minimis* aid, on condition it fulfils all the conditions of the *de minimis* regulations does not distort competition (nor does it have an effect on interstate trade).[119] As a result the Commission only has to demonstrate that the aid *potentially* distorts competition.[120]

4. Exemptions

There are two groups of exceptions or exemptions which may apply to the prohibition contained in Article 107(1) TFEU: 1) measures for the purposes specified in Article 107(2) TFEU, which are *de jure* compatible;[121] and 2) measures which are declared by the Commission, on the basis of Article 107(3) TFEU, to be compatible in the framework of the supervision procedure. In this regard the Commission has broad discretionary powers.[122]

4.1 *Automatic exemptions: Article 107(2) TFEU*

Article 107(2) TFEU lists the following exempted categories. The first exemption concerns aid of a social character as specified in Article 107(2) (a) TFEU.[123] This provision can only be relied upon if aid is granted to individuals while not resulting in an indirect benefit to undertakings.[124] The second exemption concerns aid to make good damage caused by disasters or exceptional occurrences (Article 107(2) (b)) TFEU). Both derogations must be interpreted restrictively.[125] Article 107(2) (c) TFEU provides a mechanism to exempt aid granted in connection with the re-unification process of Germany which has lost its practical meaning.

4.2 *Exemptions granted by the Commission: Article 107(3) and Article 106(2) TFEU*

4.2.1 *General exemption regime under Article 107(3) TFEU*

Whereas Article 107(2) exempts specific forms of aid automatically, Article 107(3) TFEU applies to measures that can be approved by the Commission *or* can be approved collectively by the Council and, if so empowered, the Commission. The Commission enjoys a wide discretion

115. Case C-197/11, *Eric Libert*; Case C-518/13, *Eventech v. Parking Adjudicator (Black Cabs)*; Joined Cases T-186/13, T-190/13 & T-193/13, *Leidschendam – Voorburg v. Commission.*
116. Case 730/79, *Philip Morris Holland BV v. Commission*; Case C-142/87, *Belgium v. Commission*; Case C-74/16, *Congregación de Escuelas Pías.*
117. Case C-156/98, *Germanv. v. Commission* (tax concession); Case C-518/13, *Eventech v. Parking Adjudicator (Black Cabs).*
118. Case C-74/16, *Congregación de Escuelas Pías.*
119. Case T-527/13, *Italy v. Commission*; Case C-74/16, *Congregación de Escuelas Pías.*
120. Case C-197/11, *Eric Libert.*
121. See on the German clause – which is still in force – Joined Cases T-132 & 143/96, *Freistaal, Sachsen, Volkswagen v. Commission.*
122. Case 310/85, *Deufil*; Case T-182/10, *Aiscat v. Commission*; Case T-601/11, *Danske Automat Brancheforening v. Commission.*
123. See for example Case C-672/13, *OTP Bank.*
124. Joined Cases C-442/03P & C-471/03P, *P&O Ferries SV v. Commission.*
125. Case C-730/79, *Philip Morris v. Commission.*

in assessing the compatibility of aid under Article 107(3) TFEU.[126] To that end the Commission must conduct a *balancing test* between, on the one hand, economic and social interests against on the other hand, the effects on competition and trade between Member States.[127] Four major groups of aid measures can be distinguished: regional aid; sectoral aid; horizontal aid (such as for example environment and research and development aid); and "other" types of aid. The Commission has adopted policies for assessing specific types such as rescue and restructuring aid,[128] government guarantees,[129] and aid for the sale of land by public bodies.[130]

The Commission has published guidelines and communications to provide guidance and transparency on the preferred method to assess the compatibility of aid. The adoption of such instruments has enabled the Commission to develop detailed policies for assessing and coordinating the compatibility of (sub)categories of aid mentioned in Article 107(3) TFEU. In section 5 below the newly adopted guidelines will be discussed from the perspective of the State Aid Modernization Programme.

4.2.2 *Categories of exemptions under Article 107(3) TFEU*

Firstly, Article 107(3)(a) TFEU sets out cases relating to the underdeveloped areas of the Union where living standards are abnormally low or where there is serious underemployment. The Court has ruled that qualifications such as "serious" or "abnormal" are defined according to the Union, not national, averages, so as to limit the application of this exception by the wealthier Member States.[131]

Secondly, Article 107(3)(b) concerns aid to promote the execution of an important project of common European interest or to remedy a serious disturbance in the economy of a Member State. The Commission adopted a communication on eligible criteria for the assessment of state aid for important projects of common European interest.[132]

The third category can be found in Article 107(3)(c) TFEU which is the most frequently applied exception, covering both regional and sectoral aids.[133] This provision is interpreted broadly to permit certain differences with regard to the role of the national average.[134] The exception implies a balancing test to weigh the negative effect on the market against the positive contribution of the aid to the attainment of certain Union objectives in accordance with the principle of proportionality.[135]

The Commission's assessment of particular horizontal and sectoral categories of aid that fall within the scope of Article 107(3) (a) and (c) has been "codified" into various guidelines as

---

126. Case C-730/79, *Philip Morris v. Commission*; Case C-169/95, *Commission v. Spain.*
127. Joined Cases T-447/93 & T-449/93, *AITEC and others v. Commission*; Case T-457/09, *Westfälisch-Lippischer Sparkassen- und Giroverband v. Commission.*
128. Commission guidelines on state aid for rescuing and restructuring firms in difficulty, O.J. (2014), C 249/1.
129. Commission Notice on the application of Arts. 107 and 108 TFEU to state aid in the form of guarantees, O.J. 2000, C 71/14.
130. Commission Communication on state aid elements in sales of land and buildings by public authorities, O.J. 1997, C 209/3.
131. Case 248/84, *Germany v. Commission* (compatibility of a regional aid programme); Joined Cases C-278/92 to C-280/92, *Spain v. Commission* (capital contributions); Case C-169/95, *Pyrsa.*
132. Communication on the compatibility of State aid to promote the execution of important projects of common European interest, O.J. 2014, C 188/4.
133. Case C -284/84, *Germany v. Commission*; Case T-362/10, *Vtesse v. Commission.*
134. Joined Cases 296/82 & 318/82, *Leeuwarder Papierfabriek*; Case 259/85; Case C-113/00, *Spain v. Commission*; Guidelines on regional state aid for 2014–2020, O.J. 2013, C 209/1.
135. Case 730/79, *Philip Morris*; Communication on the compatibility of state aid to promote the execution of important projects of common European interest, O.J. 2014, C 188/4.

well as in the General Block Exemption Regulation (GBER). In the wake of the State Aid Modernization Programme, both the GBER and the applicable guidelines were revised to promote effectiveness in public spending through a better contribution of state aid to the objectives of common interests, increasing scrutiny on the incentive effect, on limiting the aid to the minimum, and on the potential negative effects of the aid on competition and trade. They deal with: aid for regional development;[136] aid for research and development;[137] aid for environmental protection and energy;[138] aid in the context of the EU Emissions Trading Scheme;[139] risk financing[140] and aid for rescuing and restructuring non-financial undertakings in difficulty.[141]

Several of these horizontal categories are also covered by the General Block Exemption Regulation. In addition, sector specific rules are applicable concerning the agricultural sector,[142] audiovisual production,[143] the deployment of broadband networks,[144] fisheries,[145] the financial sector[146] and the financing of airports.[147] Several sectorial types of aid have also been included in the Block Exemption Regulations.[148]

In the fourth place, Article 107(3) (d) TFEU allows cultural aid and aid for heritage conservation. With the adoption of the General Block Exemption Regulation specific forms of aid in this category, including aid for sport and multifunctional recreational infrastructures are exempted from notification.[149]The application of these exemptions in the regulation is conditional to specific thresholds and aid intensities, leaving a residual function for the application of Article 107(3) (d) TFEU.

Finally, Article 107(3)(e) TFEU empowers the Council to extend the grounds on which aid may be approved as compatible to other types of measures. This Article provides for the creation of "other discretionary exceptions" to the general prohibition of aids. Such categories of aids may be specified by a decision of the Council acting by a qualified majority on a proposal from the Commission. To that end the Council is solely permitted to create new categories of exceptions from the basic prohibitions of Article 107(1) TFEU; the application of the state aid rules to such categories is entrusted to the Commission.[150] Exempted categories that were

136. Guidelines on regional State aid for 2014–2020, O.J. 2013, C 209/1.
137. Framework for State aid for research and development and innovation, O.J. 2014, C 198/1.
138. Guidelines on State aid for environmental aid and energy, O.J. 2014, C 200/1.
139. Guidelines on certain State aid measures in the context of the greenhouse gas emission allowance trading scheme post 2012, O.J. 2012, C 154/4.
140. Guidelines on risk finance aid for 2014–2020, O.J. 2014, C 19/4-34.
141. Guidelines on State aid for rescuing and restructuring non-financial undertakings in difficulty, O.J. 2014, C 249/1.
142. Guidelines for State aid in the agricultural and forestry sectors and in rural areas 2014 to 2020, O.J. 2014, C 204/1.
143. Communication on State aid for audiovisual works, O.J. 2013, C 322/1.
144. Guidelines for the application of state aid rules for the deployment of broadband networks, O.J. 2013, C 25/1.
145. Guidelines for state aid in the fisheries sector O.J. 2015, C 217/01.
146. Banking Communication, O.J. 2013, C 216/01.
147. Guidelines on state aid to airports and airlines, O.J. 2014, C 99/3.
148. Reg. 702/2014/EU/, The Agricultural Block Exemption Reg., O.J. 2014, C L193/1-75; Reg. 1388/2014/EU, The Fisheries Block Exemption Reg., O.J. 2014, L 369/37e; Reg. 651/2014/ General Block Exemption Reg. O.J. 2014, L 187/1.
149. The General Block Exemption Reg. (GBER) exempts: aids for culture and heritage conservation (Art. 53 GBER); aid schemes for audiovisual works (Art. 54 GBER) and aids for sports and multifunctional recreational infrastructures (Art. 55 GBER).
150. Case C-272/12 P, *Commission v. Ireland*; Case T-176/11 R, *Castelnou Energia v. Commission* & Case C-99/14 P, *Carbunión v. Council*.

adopted by the Council which have remained in force are rare: in 2010 the Council adopted a decision on aid to facilitate the closure of the coalmine sector.[151]

4.2.3 *Exemption under Article 106(2) TFEU for services of general economic interest*

The concept of "services of general economic interest" (SGEI) is mentioned in Articles 14 and 106 (2) TFEU; however, this concept is not defined in the TFEU or in secondary legislation. Qualifying public service obligations and entrusting undertakings with a SGEI is left to the national authorities. As a result the concept of SGEI has developed into various areas of public services such as healthcare,[152] local transport services,[153] social services,[154] public broadcasting,[155] and public utilities such as postal services[156] and energy supply.[157] Member States have a wide discretion to define SGEI's, particularly in areas that fall almost exclusively within their competence, such as social policy and healthcare.[158]

Compensations for SGEI-providers that fail to satisfy the Altmark test constitute state aid but may be justified under Article 106(2) TFEU.[159] Article 106(2) TFEU is applicable to undertakings discharged with an SGEI, only insofar as they do not obstruct the legal or factual performance of the tasks assigned to those undertakings. State aid for an SGEI can only be exempted under this provision if the measure is suitable and necessary. In *Viasat* the Court was asked whether the Altmark test and the application of Article 106(2) TFEU constitute the same test.[160] In its judgment, the Court clearly separates the goals of the Altmark test and the proportionality test of Article 106(2) TFEU. The Court considers that both tests respond to fundamentally different questions. The Altmark test aims to assess whether a compensation for an SGEI constitutes an advantage, whilst the application of Article 106(2) TFEU exclusively allows the Commission to determine whether a state measure, constituting state aid, can be declared compatible with the internal market.

A different and more flexible approach was introduced by the Commission concerning small and local SGEI-compensations. The Commission adopted two exemptions from notification under Articles 106(2), 107(1) and 108(3) TFEU. The first exemption is the Commission regulation on *de-minimis aid* for an SGEI. The second exemption is the SGEI Exemption Decision. When only the first three Altmark conditions are met, no obligation to notify exists, provided that the measure falls within the substantive scope of the *de-minimis* regulation for SGEI's[161] or the SGEI Exemption Decision.[162]

The SGEI *de- minimis* rule excludes compensation not exceeding € 500,000 (during three years) from the application of Article 107(1) TFEU. The SGEI Exemption exempts compensation for SGEI's from notification, depending on the total amount of aid (up to € 15 million on an

---

151. Council Decision 2010/787/EU, O.J. 2010, L 336/24.
152. Case T-137/10, *CBI v. Commission.*
153. Case C-280/00, *Altmark*; Case C-303/13 P, *Commission v. Andersen.*
154. Case C-113/13, *ANPAS*; Case T-137/10, *CBI v. Commission.*
155. Case T-151/11, *Telefonica v. Commission*; Case T-533/10, *DTS v. Commission.*
156. Case C-559/12 P, *La Poste.*
157. Case T-57/11, *Castelnou Energía and Greenpeace – España v. Commisison.*
158. Case T- 289/03, *BUPA v. Commission.*
159. Case C-265/08, *Federutility v. Commission*; Case T-57/11, *Castelnou Energía v. Commission*; Case T-454/13, *SNCM v. Commission.*
160. Case C-660/15, *Viasat v. Commission.*
161. Commission Reg. (EU) 360/2012 on the application of Arts. 107 and 108. TFEU to *de minimis* aid granted to undertakings entrusted with an SGEI, O.J. 2012, L 114/8.
162. Commission Decision of 20 Dec. 2011 on the application of Art. 106(2) TFEU to State aid in the form of public service compensation granted to undertakings entrusted with an SGEI, O.J (2012), L 7/3.

annual basis).[163] Different thresholds apply for ports and airports, hospitals and social (including social housing and childcare). Compensation schemes for SGEI's that exceed the thresholds of the SGEI Exemption Decision must be notified. The Commission has adopted the SGEI Framework Decision to clarify the compatibility conditions for large compensations.[164] However, the Court did make it clear in *Viasat* that the conditions of this Framework Decision may not infringe the Courts case law on the application of Article 106(2) TFEU.[165]

4.2.4 *Special derogation*

There is a derogation provided for in Article 108(2) TFEU, which allows for the possibility for the Council to declare aid compatible with the internal market even if it does not satisfy the normal conditions of Article 107 TFEU or Regulation 2015/1589 based on Article 109 TFEU. Such a derogation may only be given in exceptional circumstances and the Court grants the Council wide discretion in this instance. The Council has used this competence in the agricultural sector in approving aid measures which deviate from the common market regulations, thus amending these regulations under Article 108(2) TFEU.[166]

5. Article 108 TFEU enforcement

5.1 *Introduction*

By virtue of Article 108 TFEU the Commission is responsible for enforcing Article 107 TFEU. The mechanism for applying the state aid rules has over the years been developed by Commission decisions and communications and the case law of the Union courts. Existing rules and procedures have to some extent been codified by Council Regulation 659/99, the "procedural regulation", and implementing Commission Regulation 794/2004. The procedural regulation has been amended in 2013 by Council Regulation 734/2013 which aims at strengthening the Commission's powers in light of the modernization programme (discussed in section 5 above).[167] In 2015 the Council codified the procedural regulation and the amended regulation by Council Regulation 2015/1589.[168]

The new procedural regulation 2015/1589 defines different concepts of aid, such as "existing aid", "new aid", "individual aid" and "unlawful aid". It further describes the different stages of the administrative procedure while the implementing regulation sets out detailed provisions for (compulsory) notification of aid measures by the member states. The procedural regulation further specifies the investigative powers of the Commission and the different types of decisions it can take, including the ordering of recovery of unlawful aid. Basically, the regulation provides for four different procedures: for duly notified aid, for unlawful aid, for so-called "misuse of aid", and for existing aid schemes.

In 2013 DG Competition has drafted a comprehensive working document ("State Aid Manual of Procedures") to give its staff practical guidance on how to conduct the procedures to apply Articles 107 and 108 TFEU. Although the Commission has published this document

---

163. Art. 2 (1) (d) and (e) Commission Decision of 20 Dec. 2011 on the application of Art. 106(2) TFEU to State aid in the form of public service compensation granted to certain undertakings entrusted with SGEI, O.J (2012), L 7/3.
164. Communication from the Commission, European Union framework for State aid in the form of public service compensation O.J. 2011, C8, at 15–22.
165. Case C-660/15, *Viasat v. Commission.*
166. See for instance Joined Cases C-111/10 C 117/10, C-118/10, C-121/10, *Commission v. Council.*
167. O.J 2013, L 204/15.
168. Commission Reg. (EU) 2015/1589, O.J. 2015, L 248/9.

in order to provide greater transparency of the way it handles state aid cases, the Commission emphasizes that it is not a formal Commission document but merely an internal tool.[169]

National courts have no jurisdiction to rule on the compatibility of aid with the internal market, which is the exclusive competence of the Commission.[170] However, as will be explained below, they do play a crucial role in the "private enforcement" of the state aid rules when it comes to preserving the rights of individuals in case of a breach by a member state of the prohibition of Article 108(3) TFEU. In addition, national courts have jurisdiction when it comes to the implementation of negative Commission decisions, especially concerning a recovery order, and with respect to the application of the provisions of block exemption regulations, such as the important General Block Exemption Regulation, that are directly applicable in litigation before national courts.[171]

5.2 *Ex-post supervision for existing aid*

The supervision framework makes a distinction between existing aid and new aid.[172] Existing aid is defined under Article 108(1) TFEU and Regulation 2015/15899 as aid which was in operation at the entry into force of the [then] EC Treaty in any given Member State (i.e. January 1958 for the original Member States and the date of accession for the other Member States[173]), as well as aid which is implemented in accordance with the Treaty provisions, having been notified to and approved by the Commission, or to which no objection has been raised.[174] Measures which originally did not qualify as state aid but became aid due to the evolution of the internal market, also constitute existing aid.[175] In contrast, if measures become aid due to liberalization by Union law, they shall not be considered existing aid after the date for liberalization. When a Member State alters an existing aid scheme, the latter is transformed into new aid and the normal procedure for new aid applies.[176]

Article 108(1) TFEU further provides that existing aid is (only) subject to *ex-post* supervision.[177] In other words, there will not be any recovery of aid granted in the past. Such an existing aid measure does not need to be notified and does not require Commission approval prior to implementation.[178] However, the Commission keeps existing aid *schemes* (as opposed to an existing *individual* aid measure) under constant review and may examine the measure under Article 108(1) to ensure compatibility with the internal market. When a measure is *prima facie* not compatible, the Commission will propose appropriate measures, which are not binding.[179] If the Member State does not accept the proposal, the Commission may initiate the formal investigation proceedings under Article 108(2) TFEU. If the Commission finds that the aid is incompatible, it shall require the Member State to alter it or completely abolish it.[180]

169. "State Aid Manual of Procedures", Commission document, 13 July 2013.
170. Case C-275/10, *Residex*; Case C-284/12, *Lufthansa v. Flughafen Frankfurt – Hahn.*
171. See Case C-493/14, *Dilly's Wellnesshotel.*
172. Case C-44/93, *Namur-Les Assurances du Crédit v. Belgium.*
173. Case T-468/08, *Tisza Eromu v. Commission.*
174. Case C-228/16 P, *DEI v. Commission.*
175. Art. 1(b) (v) of Reg. 2015/1589; Case C-89/08 P, *Commission v. Ireland;* Case C-357/14 P, *Electrabel v. Commission.*
176. For the meaning of alteration, see implementing Regulation 794/2004, Art. 4.
177. Arts. 13 (2) Reg., 2015/1589.
178. Case C-47/91, *Italy v. Commission;* Case C-387/92, *Banco de Credito.*
179. Case T-152/06, *NDSHT v. Commission;* Case T-203/10 RENV, *Woonpunt v. Commission.*
180. See for example Commission Decision SA 25338, 21 Jan. 2016, C (2016) 167 final, (corporate tax exemption for public undertakings in the Netherlands).

5.3 *Ex-ante supervision of new aid*

5.3.1 *Administrative procedure*

Article 108(3) TFEU, as further implemented by the procedural regulations, sets forth the notification requirements and the two-phase administrative procedure for new aid.[181] The notification system enables the Commission to examine the proposed aid measure's compatibility with Article 107 TFEU. The Commission must be informed in a timely and sufficiently detailed manner of any plan to grant new aid (unless the measure can benefit from the simplified procedure as described in the implementing Commission regulation).[182] Moreover, any plan to grant or alter existing aid[183] must also be notified.[184] New aid which has not been notified is considered to be unlawful.

In the course of the administrative procedure the Commission can request information from the Member State concerned. If the Member State fails to do so, the Commission is able to base its final decision on the information it has available. Pursuant to the 2013 amendments to the procedural regulation, as a result of the State Aid Modernization Programme, the powers of the Commission were considerably strengthened in this regard.[185] For example, during the second phase investigation it may request – informally or by decision – additional information from other Member States as well as from undertakings, including the beneficiary.[186] Moreover, undertakings must fully comply with information requests triggered by the Commission during the formal investigation. When supplying incorrect or misleading information the Commission may even impose fines.[187]

It is important to note that pursuant to Article 109 TFEU certain measures may be exempted from the obligation to notify. The most important exemptions are those contained in the General Block Exemption Regulation (GBER) and in the regulations concerning *de minimis* aid. The block exemption exempts categories that are considered unproblematic from the requirement of prior notification. Examples are investment aid for SME's, environmental aid and aid for renewable energy. At the same time the Commission has strengthened *ex-post* control of compliance with the conditions for exemption. Member States are required to comply with the procedural obligations of the GBER by submitting information on the implementation of exempted aid measures. If they fail to do so within the time limits of the GBER, Member States risk breaching the standstill clause of Article 108 (3) TFEU.[188] For clarification purposes the Commission created a handbook on the GBER and in addition the information interactive "State Aid Wiki".[189]

181. Arts. 2–11 Reg. 2015/1589.
182. Joined Cases T-126/96 & T-127/96, *BFM and ENIM*, from which it emerges that as long as the information provided is not complete, notification has not taken place.
183. Case C-272/12 P, *Commission v. Euralminia*; Case T-438/15, *Port de Namur*.
184. Case C-332/98, *CELF*.
185. See Ch. XIII and IX of Reg. 2015/1589.
186. Arts. 6 and 7 of Reg. 2015/1589.
187. Art. 8 Reg. 2015/1589.
188. Case C-493/14, *Dilly's Wellnesshotel*.
189. General Block Exemption Reg.; Frequent Asked Questions, available at <ec.europa.eu/competition/state_aid/legislation/practical_guide_gber_en.pdf>; Please see the website of the Commission: <ec.europa.eu/dpo-register/details.htm?id=41047>.

5.3.2 *Preliminary examination*

The Commission is empowered under Article 108(3) TFEU to submit its concerns on notified aid. Pursuant to the case law[190] as codified in the procedural regulation, this preliminary examination can lead to the conclusion that (1) either there is no aid, or (2) there is aid but it is compatible with the internal market, or (3) the compatibility raises doubts. In the latter case a formal investigation procedure under Article 108(2) TFEU must be opened. The Commission does not enjoy discretion in this matter.[191]

The preliminary examination procedure enables the Commission to ascertain whether the measure indeed constitutes state aid and, if so, whether the effect of the aid on competition and interstate trade is such as to prejudice the Union interest by assessing the aim of the measure and especially its economic consequences.[192]

A formal investigation procedure, if necessary, must be opened without delay, meaning within two months, as interpreted by the Court and corresponding with the appeal period laid down in Article 263 TFEU, starting from the receipt of a complete notification. The Commission is not obliged to hear complainants or other interested parties at this point, given the preliminary nature of the examination.[193] If the Commission does not express its views after two months the aid may be lawfully granted, on condition that the standstill clause was not breached.[194]

The Commission issues a decision in all three above-mentioned instances. When notified a decision is addressed to the Member State in question and constitutes a reviewable act vis-à-vis the Member State concerned and, in certain circumstances, vis-à-vis third parties.[195]

5.3.3 *Formal investigation procedure*

The formal investigation procedure aims to obtain legal certainty as to the compatibility of aid under Article 107 TFEU.[196] This is the exclusive competence of the Commission.[197] The procedure applies to both notified and non-notified aid.

These formal second phase proceedings differ from the preliminary first phase in that they are contentious in character.[198] The decision to open a formal investigation is a challengeable act in so far as it produces a legal effect. It must be immediate and sufficiently binding in relation to the Member State to which it is addressed and the beneficiary of the measure under examination. A state aid measure which can be considered as already implemented cannot entail any independent legal effects.[199]

---

190. Case C-198/91, *William Cook plc v. Commission*; Case C-225/91, *Matra*; Case T-49/93, *Société Internationale de Diffusion et d'Edition (SIDE) v. Commission*; Case T-11/95, *BP Chemicals.*
191. Case T-73/98, *Société Chimique Prayon v. Commission.*
192. Case C-518/13, *Black Cabs*; Case T-135/12, *Orange v. Commission*; Case C-211/15 P, *Orange v. Commission.*
193. Case T-109/01, *Fleuren Compost BV v. Commission*; Case C-362/09, *Athinaïki Techniki v. Commission.*
194. Otherwise, an official investigation procedure may be initiated by the Commission; see Case C-357/14 P, *Electrabel v. Commission*; Case T-176/01, *Ferriere Nord.*
195. See Case C-39/94, *SFEI*. In this case the Court held that a decision can also be understood as an implicit refusal to start the official investigation proceedings. See also Case C-228/16 P, *DEI v. Commission.*
196. Joined Cases C-164/15 P & C-165/15 P, *Ryan Air and Aer Lingus v. Commission*; Case T-79/14, *Secop v. Commission.*
197. Case C-39/94, *SFEI*; Case C-131/15 P, *Club Hotel Loutraki.*
198. Case C-367/95 P, *Sytraval*; Case C-78/03, *ARE v. Commission*; Case T-95/03, *AESCAM v. Commission.*
199. Case T-251/13, *Nijmegen v. Commission.*

The Commission may not rely on information against a Member State of which that Member State is not in possession and on which it has not had an opportunity to comment.[200] However, a Member State cannot criticize the Commission for failing to consider information that the Member State had not supplied to the Commission,[201] although the Commission cannot justify its decision by relying on this failure of the Member State if it had not actually ordered the production of this information.[202]

Article 108 TFEU requires respect for the rights of the defence; not only the Member State concerned but also other interested parties must be given the opportunity to be heard.[203] This primarily occurs through a Notice in the "C" series of the Official Journal. As a general rule, the Commission is obliged to complete the formal investigation procedure within eighteen months following a complete notification as set out under Regulation 2015/1589. Following that time period, the Commission must give a decision within two months at the request of the Member State.

The termination of the formal investigation procedure leads to a decision that (1) either there is no aid, or (2) that the aid is compatible (a positive decision), or (3) that the aid is compatible provided that certain conditions are met (a conditional decision), or (4) that the aid is incompatible (a negative decision).

6. Unlawful aid

6.1 *Definition*

The definition of unlawful aid is the key concept relevant for recovery. Pursuant to the Procedural Regulation, the Commission's power to order recovery is restricted to unlawful aid and cases of misuse of aid.

"Unlawful aid" is defined in Article 1(f) of the Procedural Regulation 2015/1589 as "new aid" put into effect in contravention of Article 108(3) TFEU. This definition covers, first, situations where aid is implemented without notification. According to case law a positive decision of the Commission does not have the effect of regularizing, retrospectively, implementing measures which were invalid because they had been taken in disregard of the prohibition laid down by Article 108(3) TFEU. However, the Commission itself may not order the repayment of unlawful aid which has been declared compatible in a positive decision. The Court ruled that as for recovery of unlawful aid which the Commission later declares to be compatible, the national courts are competent to order the payment of the interest advantage that the company has received in the period between the granting of the unlawful aid and the Commission's declaration of compatibility.[204]

Secondly, the term unlawful aid covers notified aid which is, notwithstanding the standstill obligation, implemented before the Commission has given its approval. Thirdly, aid can be considered to be unlawful when the aid is granted in breach of a negative Commission decision.[205]

200. Case C-418/15 P(I), *Cap Actions SNCM v. Commission.*
201. Case C-261/89, *Italy v. Commission*; Case C-364/90, *Italy v. Commission*; Case C-241/94, *France v. Commission*; Case C-382/99, *Kingdom of the Netherlands v. Commission.*
202. Case T-318/02, *Thüringen v. Commission.*
203. Also the initiation of the procedure is an act subject to appeal, see Case C-312/90, *Spain v. Commission.*
204. Case C-1/09, *CELF v. SIDE.*
205. Case C-37/14, *Commission v. France.*

6.2 *Recovery*

The Commission's power to recover aid where it takes a negative decision is laid down in the regulation: Article 16(1) provides that the Commission shall decide that the Member State concerned shall take all necessary measures to recover the aid. According to Article 16(2), the Commission shall also require interest to be paid from the date on which the unlawful aid was at the disposal of the beneficiary until the moment of recovery. According to Article 16(3), Member States shall effect recovery without delay and in accordance with the procedures under national law. Disputes arising in connection with the enforcement of recovery at the national level are a matter for the national courts alone.[206] Interest to be recovered on the sums unlawfully granted is aimed at eliminating any financial advantages incidental to such aid, that, in itself, would constitute aid.[207]

The policy of the Commission can be found in its Notice of 2007.[208] When ordering recovery, the Commission is not required to fix the exact amount to be recovered, as long as the recipient and the Member State are able, without too much difficulty, to calculate the amount to be repaid.[209] If unforeseen or unforeseeable difficulties should arise in recovering aid, the Court has consistently held that the Commission and Member States should "work together in good faith to overcome the difficulties in full compliance with the provisions of the Treaty, and in particular those on aid", in keeping with Article 4(3) TEU.[210] The only defence available to a Member State is that it is absolutely impossible for it to properly implement the decision.[211] The fact that a company is insolvent or bankrupt does not affect the obligation of repayment; removal of this obligation in the event of liquidation would render meaningless the state aid rules.[212]

If the Court finds that a Member State has failed to fulfil its obligation, the state shall, according to Article 260 TFEU, be required to take the necessary measures to comply with the judgment.[213] If the Commission then considers that the Member State concerned still has not taken the necessary measures to comply, it may (again) bring the case before the Court. If the Court finds that the Member State has not complied with its judgment it may ultimately impose a lump sum or penalty payment on it.[214]

Pursuant to Article 16(1) of the procedural regulation, legitimate expectations can only be invoked successfully if they are the result of conduct by the Commission, or other EU institutions, and if the aid is granted in compliance with the procedure laid down in Article 108.[215] A "diligent businessman" should normally be able to determine whether that procedure has been followed.[216] Legitimate expectations can only be invoked successfully if they are the result of conduct by the Commission, or other EU institutions, and if the aid is granted in compliance with the procedure laid down in Article 108 TFEU. It is important to note that even when the Member State or beneficiary concerned has not presented the Commission with any argument based on the existence of legitimate expectations, the Commission is, pursuant to Article 16(1),

206. Case C-574/14, *PGE v. URE*; Case C-33/14, *Mory v. Commission.*
207. Case C – 68/13, *Mediaset v. Commission.*
208. Notice "Towards an effective implementation of Commission decisions ordering member states to recover unlawful and incompatible State aid", O.J, 2007, C 272/4.
209. Case C-69/13, *Mediaset v. Ministero dello Sviluppo economico*; Case T-468/08, *Tisza Eromu v. Commission.*
210. Joined Cases C-485/03 to C-490/03, *Commission v. Spain*; also see Case C-672/13, *OTP Bank.*
211. Case T-220/13, *Scuola Elementare Maria Montessori v. Commission.*
212. Case C-63/14, *Commission v. France.*
213. Case C-591/14, *Commission v. Belgium (TSE).*
214. Case C-496/09, *Commission v. Italy*; Case C-184/11, *Commission v. Spain.*
215. Case C-272/12 P, *Commission v. Euralminia*; Cases T-179/09 and T-468/08, *Dunamenti Erömü v. Commission.*
216. Case T-421/07, *RENV, Deutsche Post v. Commission.*

required *ex officio* to take into consideration the exceptional circumstances that provide justification.[217] The fact that a company is insolvent or bankrupt does not affect the obligation of recovery.[218] The Court dismissed the defence of exceptional circumstances on many occasions, for instance when Member States invoked administrative policy or social reasons.[219]

6.3 *Procedure*

The procedural regulation provides for a separate procedure for unlawful aid. If the Commission is informed of any unlawful aid, it must investigate the matter without delay. The obligation to take a decision within two months is waived, given that the Member State has forfeited its right to speedy legal certainty by not complying with the standstill rule.[220]

During this investigation, the Commission may order suspension of the aid or issue interim orders for its recovery.[221] The Commission may apply directly to the Court if the Member State does not comply with the orders. The Commission is not bound to the term of eighteen months in assessing the compatibility of the unlawful aid in the formal investigation procedure.[222]

7. Judicial protection

7.1 *National courts*

Article 108(3) TFEU, providing the so-called standstill obligation, has direct effect. It may therefore be relied upon by individuals before the national courts. The role of the national courts in safeguarding plaintiffs' rights is fundamentally different from the Commission's role of assessing the compatibility of aids and in no way conflicts with that latter role.[223] As stated by the Court, their respective roles are complementary but separate.[224] The Commission has devoted a special notice to the role of national courts in state aid matters.[225]

With regard to deciding whether a state aid may be declared compatible under Article 107(2) and (3) TFEU, the national courts do not enjoy jurisdiction as this falls within the exclusive competence of the Commission.[226] However, they may have cause to interpret the concept of aid in order to determine, for example, whether an unnotified measure ought to have been subject to the administrative procedure.[227] The national courts also do not have jurisdiction to determine the validity of any Commission decision, particularly in relation to recovery of aid declared incompatible.[228]

Third parties, such as competitors, should be able to obtain an injunction from national courts preventing the actual granting of the aid.[229] In addition, as is pointed out by the

217. See case T-219/13, *Ferracci v. Commission.*
218. Case C-63/14, *Commission v. France.*
219. Case C-263/12, *Commission v. Greece*; Case C-63/14, *Commission v. France.*
220. Case C-39/94, *SFEI*. This can lead to problems for complainants, however, if the Commission fails to act, see Case T-17/96, *TF1.*
221. But not in the case of misuse of aid (Art. 20 Reg. 2015/1589), i.e. aid granted in contravention of the terms of a decision of approval.
222. Art. 9 (6) Reg. 2015/1589.
223. Case C-690/13, *Trapeza Eurobank v. ATE.*
224. Case C-284/12, *Deutsche Lufthansa v. Flughafen Frankfurt Hahn.*
225. Notice on the enforcement of State aid law by national courts, O.J 2009, C 85/1.
226. Case C-354/90, *FNCAEP*; Case C-44/93, *Namur*; Case T-49/93, *SIDE*; Case C-256/97, *DMT*.
227. Case C-690/13, *Trapeza Eurobank v. ATE.*
228. Case C-39/94, *SFEI*; Case C-24/95, *Alcan Deutschland.*
229. Case C-33/14, *Mory v. Commission.*

Commission in its Notice,[230] recovery is not the only means of guaranteeing the prohibition. The state may also, and independently of any obligation to recover the aid, be subject to claims for damages brought in the national courts on the basis of Union law by competitors who incur loss as a result of unlawfully implementing the aid. Other remedies include recovery of illegality interest, and interim measures against unlawful aid. In the *CELF* case the Court ruled that after a final positive Commission decision the national court is no longer under an EU law obligation to order full recovery.[231] However, in such circumstances the national court could order the aid recipient to pay the Member State interest in respect of the period of unlawfulness.

The new procedural regulation has introduced formal rules for cooperation between the Commission and the national courts. Article 29(2) of Regulation 2015/1589 now provides that the courts may ask the Commission for information or a non-binding opinion on the scope of Articles 107 and 108 TFEU and that, as in competition cases, the Commission may act as an *amicus curiae* by submitting written observations or making oral statements. In some instances a national court is encouraged by the Court to involve the Commission in a national procedure. When ordering provisional measures, pending a formal investigation by the Commission, national courts must either verify with the Commission, or put a preliminary question to the Court, in order to verify whether such measures do not obstruct the outcome of a formal investigation.[232] In practice, especially during proceedings for interim measures, a national court might opt to cooperate with the Commission.[233]

7.2 *The General Court and the Court of Justice*

The possibilities for appeal under Articles 263 and 265 TFEU are open to the Member States with respect to actions and inactions of the Commission relating to the supervisory mechanisms.[234] The validity of a decision addressed to a Member State cannot be contested later in an enforcement procedure under Article 108(2) TFEU, where the Member State had earlier failed to challenge the validity of that decision.[235] However, the Commission can bring an action to the Court right away under Article 108(2) TFEU against a Member State which fails to comply with a decision issued on the basis of this Article or Regulation 2015/1589.[236]

Interested parties other than Member States who are affected by the aid can only bring actions before the General Court if they are directly and individually concerned by the decision addressed to the Member State, as set forth in Article 263 TFEU.[237] In the case of the beneficiary of the aid these conditions are met. This is also true if a closed group of undertakings that benefit from a measure and that are individually identifiable is affected by a Commission decision.[238]

However, in the case of a competitor the question of direct and individual concern by a Commission decision is more complex. A distinction must be made between, on the one hand, the preliminary and, on the other hand, the formal investigation procedure. Where the

---

230. Commission notice on the enforcement of state aid law by national courts, O.J 2009, C 85/1.
231. Case C-1/09, *CELF v. SIDE.*
232. Case C-284/12, *Deutsche Lufthansa v. Flughafen Frankfurt-Hahn.*
233. Case C-574/14, *PGE v. URE.*
234. See Case 282/85, *DEFI.* Autonomous government bodies which grant aid have standing if they meet the requirements of direct and individual concern, see Joined Cases T-15/12 & T-16/12, *Provincie Groningen v. Commission.*
235. Case 52/84, *Commission v. Belgium*; Case C-188/92, *TWD Textilwerke Deggendorf.*
236. An individual cannot force the Commission to make use of this procedure, see Case T-277/94, *AITEC* and Case C-362/09, *Athinaïki Techniki v. Commission.*
237. Case C-33/14 P, *Mory v. Commission*; Case T-118/13, *Whirlpool v. Commission.*
238. See for example Case C-132/12P, *Woonpunt v. Commission.*

Commission, after a preliminary examination, finds that doubts are raised as to the compatibility with the internal market of a notified measure, it shall decide to initiate the formal investigation procedure.[239]

Competitors may become involved in state aid proceedings by lodging a complaint and/or by expressing their views in response to the publication by the Commission of its decision to initiate an investigation pursuant to Article 108(2) TFEU. Usually, competitors want to act against positive decisions, i.e. decisions declaring an aid measure compatible with the internal market after the Article 108(2) TFEU procedure has been brought to an end. They may also specifically wish to challenge the legality of the conditions of authorization imposed on a Member State. Competitors may not only want to bring proceedings against final decisions but may also want to act against decisions whereby the Commission has decided, for whatever reason, not to open the Article 108(2) TFEU procedure.

In a series of cases the Union Courts have upheld the rights of third-party complainants to challenge the Commission's decision not to open the adversarial Article 108(2) TFEU procedure with respect to individual aid measures.[240] Usually the complainant is informed by the Commission in a letter that the Commission has decided, by decision addressed to the Member State concerned, that the measure complained of does not constitute state aid, or is deemed to be compatible with the internal market.

The Union courts have held that the failure to open the procedure provided for in Article 108(2) TFEU deprives the parties concerned, within the meaning of that provision, of their rights. Therefore, they are also considered to be "individually concerned by the decision at the end of the preliminary phase not to open the contentious phase, to the extent that they seek to protect their procedural rights under the former provision". The Court has distinguished the following situations.

First, the persons entitled under the fourth paragraph of Article 263 TFEU to bring proceedings are those persons who seek to safeguard their procedural rights under Article 108(2) TFEU, i.e. the right to receive notice and participate in the procedure by submitting comments on the measure reviewed by the Commission; that procedure is obligatory if the Commission experiences serious difficulties in establishing whether or not there is state aid and whether or not it is compatible with the internal market. The Union Courts must therefore ascertain whether the assessments made by the Commission involved serious difficulties justifying the opening of the contentious procedure.

Secondly, however, if the applicant only calls into question the merits of the decision as such, the mere fact that the party may be "concerned" for the purposes of Article 108(2) TFEU cannot suffice to render the action admissible.[241] The complainant must then demonstrate a particular status, i.e. that its market position is substantially affected by the aid.[242]

The test for a complainant to challenge a first phase decision on its merits is in fact the same test as that which applies for the admissibility of actions against a second phase decision. The crucial issue for competitors who seek to show that they have standing to challenge a final decision taken after the procedure in Article 108(2) or to challenge the merits of a decision not to open the procedure in Article 108(2) TFEU is that their market position is substantially affected by the aid measure.[243] The Court confirmed in Case C-367/04 P that the simple fact of

239. See Art. 4 of Reg. 2015/1589.
240. Case C-362/09, *Athinaïki Techniki v. Commission*.
241. Case C-33/14, *Mory v. Commission*; Case T-251/13, *Nijmegen v. Commission*.
242. Case C-418/15 P(I), *Cap Actions SNCM v. Commission*.
243. Case T-193/06, *Télévision française v. Commission*.

being present in the same market as the beneficiary does not make a competitor individually concerned.[244]

8. State Aid Modernization Programme: New enforcement priorities

In 2013 the Commission adopted a Communication on State Aid Modernization (SAM), setting out three objectives to reform state aid law enforcement: 1) fostering growth in a strengthened, dynamic and competitive internal market; 2) prioritization enforcement on cases with the greatest impact on the internal market; and 3) streamlining rules and facilitating a faster decision making process.

In the broader context of the EU's 2020 agenda to foster growth and to cope with the increasing workload consisting of state aid notifications and *ex officio* investigations, the Commission has enacted a new legislation package that prioritizes large and potentially distortive aids concerning specific instruments and/or sectors. In 2016 the Commission concluded its *ex officio* investigations into the Spanish and Dutch professional football sectors.[245] The Commission decided that most of the restructuring aids to the Dutch football clubs were compatible with Article 107 paragraph 3(c) and Article 165 TFEU, whilst preferential taxes and guarantees for Primera Division clubs were declared incompatible.[246] Moreover a land transfer between the city of Madrid and Real Madrid was also declared to be incompatible.[247] Although these football cases raised a high profile in the news, the Commission especially prioritizes aid measures concerning regional investment aids, fiscal aids – the so-called "tax rulings"[248] and aids for rescue and restructuring of undertakings in financial difficulties.[249] In particular the recovery of preferential tax advantages to Apple, roughly estimated at €13 billion, requires the Commission's full attention.[250] Because of the persistence of the Irish Government not to comply with the *Apple* decision, the Commission referred Ireland to the ECJ for failure to recover aid.[251] Prioritization policies towards large and distortive aids are expected to develop further as of 2017. To that end the amended procedural regulation was designed to increase the Commission's

244. C-367/04 P, *Deutsche Post AG and DHL Express v. Commission.*
245. The Commission examined tax privileges in favour of Spanish football clubs FC Barcelona, Real Madrid, Athletic Bilbao and Atlético Osasuna; land transfers between Real Madrid and the City of Madrid and guarantees granted to Valencia, Elche and Hercules. See also press release European Commission, "Commission decides Spanish professional football clubs have to pay back incompatible aid", Brussels, 4 July 2016, IP/16/2401; Press release European Commission, "Commission clears support measures for certain football clubs in the Netherlands", Brussels, 4 July 2016, IP/16/2402.
246. See Commission Decisions SA.29769 (tax privileges for Real Madrid CF, FC Barcelona, Athletic Club Bilbao, Club Atlético Osasuna); SA.36387 (for Valencia, Hercules and Elche); SA.40168 (Willem II), SA.41612 (MVV), SA.41614 (Den Bosch), SA.41617 (NEC) and SA.41613 (PSV). In the case of the Dutch football clubs, the Commission even declared that a landscape transaction between the municipality of Eindhoven and PSV Eindhoven did not constitute state aid. The aid schemes for NEC Nijmegen, MVV Maastricht, Fc Den Bosch and Willem II Tilburg were declared compatible with the internal market.
247. See Commission Decision SA.33754 Aid to Real Madrid.
248. See for instance the Commission Decisions SA.38375 (Fiat) and SA.38374 (Starbucks), SA.37667 (Belgian "Excess profit" tax) in which the Commission on 21 Oct. 2015 and 23 Feb. 2016 decided that respectively Luxembourg, the Netherlands and Belgium granted selective tax advantages. The Commission decided that these measures constituted state aid. See also the speech by Eurocommissionair Margarethe Vestager, "Fighting for European values at a time of change", 14 June 2017, Europa Lecture Leiden University, available at <www.ec.europa.eu/competition>.
249. Speech by Gert-Jan Koopmans, 17 Nov. 2014, "2nd Dutch State Aid Network Convention".
250. See also Commission Decision SA. 38373 (Apple) of 30 Aug. 2016.
251. Press release European Commission, "Commission refers Ireland to Court for failure to recover illegal tax benefits from Apple worth up to €13 billion", 4 Oct. 2017, IP/17/3702.

investigative powers by introducing market information tools and sector inquiries in state aid.[252] Moreover, the Commission has streamlined the complaint-handling procedures.[253] Based on Article 8 of the new Procedural Regulation 2015/1589 the Commission may even impose fines on undertakings or any association of undertakings to enforce compliance with the requests for information. Member States will not be fined, since they are under a duty to cooperate sincerely with the Commission. The new investigative powers are comparable to those under the competition rules but do not introduce a decentralization of enforcement as under Regulation 1/2003. Concerning the cooperation with the Member States, the Commission expects that they will play a more distinct role in *ex ante* control, whereas the Commission will focus on *ex post* enforcement. As a result the Member States play their part in operationalizing the SAM objectives and are required to create effective control mechanisms for the application of block exemption regulations – the General Block Exemption Regulation[254] and the Agricultural Block Exemption Regulation.[255] The Commission retains however its exclusive power to declare aid compatible with the internal market but focuses on cases with the greatest impact.

Further reading

T. Ottervanger, L. Hancher and P.J. Slot (Eds.), *EU State Aids* (Sweet & Maxwell, 2016).
J. Piernas López, (Ed.), *The Concept of State Aid under EU Law* (OUP, 2016).
V. Verouden, P. Werner (Eds.), *EU State Aid Control. Law and Economics* (Kluwer, 2016).

252. Arts. 7 and 25 Reg. 2015/1599.
253. Arts. 12 (1) and 24 (2) Reg. 2015/1589.
254. Commission Reg. (EU) 651/2014, O.J. 2014, L 187.
255. Case C-493/14, *Dilly's Wellnesshotel*.

CHAPTER 22
PUBLIC PROCUREMENT

*Sarah Schoenmaekers**

1. Introduction

Public procurement is the process by which government departments or agencies purchase works, supplies or services from economic operators. A classic example is the purchase of new office chairs by a municipality for its personnel or the construction of a new road by the national government.

Public procurement affects a substantial share of world trade flows, amounting to € 1000 billion per year. In the EU, the public purchase of goods and services has been estimated to account for 16% of Union's GDP.[1] Since public authorities are in charge of the public purse, they should save public expenditure and seek to achieve best value for money when purchasing. To prevent corruption and favouritism, the procurement process is generally subject to specific rules and principles. These can be formulated at local, national or European level. In the European Union, public procurement rules seek to promote more competition by opening the procurement process to undertakings from other states. This should not only lead to lower prices and more choice, but also avoid discriminatory behaviour by procuring public authorities vis-à-vis non-national undertakings in contravention of the fundamental principles of the internal market.

2. History and international context of the EU public procurement regime

After the Second World War, Europe had to be rebuilt and its economic position in the world had to be strengthened again. A reduction of barriers to international trade was considered an appropriate way to reach this aim as it would increase competitiveness on the procurement markets. As these markets were characterized by high levels of corruption and protectionism, the creation of public procurement rules was even more desirable. Nevertheless, it took several decades before specific procurement legislation entered into force at international level.

The 1957 Treaty of Rome did not include specific provisions on public procurement due to a failure to reach agreement on a set of principles because of the complexity of the subject matter and the politically sensitive nature of such rules.[2] Nevertheless, the Treaty did contain a provision prohibiting discrimination on grounds of nationality, provisions on the free movement of

---

* Law Faculty, Maastricht University.

1. European Commission, "Public procurement in a nutshell", available at <ec.europa.eu/trade/policy/accessing-markets/public-procurement> (last visited 3 May 2016).
2. A. Reich, *International Public Procurement Law: The Evolution of International Regimes on Public Purchasing* (Kluwer, 1999), 71–72.

goods, services, workers and the freedom of establishment.[3] These offered a legal basis for future legislative action at EU level in the field of public procurement.

In the absence of specific rules, political capture and rent seeking behaviour caused Member States to discriminate against foreign undertakings on nationality grounds leading to a fragmentation of the common market. To cure such defects, the 1962 Council of Ministers adopted two General Programmes for the elimination of restrictions on interstate trade to provide guidance to Member States on the implementation of the rules on the right of establishment and the freedom to provide services. The Programmes envisaged a gradual removal of quotas established between Member States for public contracts and the coordination of national procedures for their award to persons or undertakings of other Member States.[4] Several Directives have been adopted ever since, the first Directive specifically concerning public procurement being Directive 70/32/EEC[5] on provision of *goods* to the State, local authorities and other official bodies. Together with Directives 71/304/EEC[6] and 71/305/EEC[7] concerning the procurement of *works* and Directive 77/62/EEC[8] on *public supply* contracts, Directive 70/32/EEC is said to form the first generation of the public procurement *acquis.*

In the 1960s and 1970s the international regulation of public procurement became an important item within the framework of the OEEC and the OECD. Even though the discussions did not result in a formal agreement, they were vital in paving the way for the successful negotiations in the Tokyo Round of GATT, leading to the conclusion of the Government Procurement Agreement (GPA) in 1979.[9] The GPA is a plurilateral agreement within the framework of GATT meaning that not all GATT members are also parties to the GPA. Its fundamental aim is to mutually open government procurement markets among its parties. Initially only procurement of goods by central government-controlled purchasing entities that were included in the Annex to the Agreement was covered, if a certain threshold was reached. Since the entire GPA negotiations were conducted by the Community rather than by each Member State individually, the international and European developments went hand in hand.[10] While the first public procurement Directives were not applicable to products originating in and supplied by third countries, the GPA provisions introduced more favourable conditions for tenders from outside the Community. The GPA was the vehicle for establishing an international framework of rights and obligations with respect to government procurement, to achieve liberalization and expansion of world trade.[11] Due to its reciprocity clause, signatories to the GPA who were no Community members had to open up their market to Community tenderers. Due to these developments,

3. See Arts. 7, 30, 48 and 52–66 of the Treaty of Rome respectively.
4. C. Bovis, *EU Public Procurement Law* (Elgar European Law, 2007), 17.
5. Commission Dir. 70/32/EEC of 17 Dec. 1969 on provision of goods to the State, to local authorities and other official bodies, O.J. 1970, L 13/1.
6. Council Dir. 71/304/EEC of 26 July 1971 concerning the abolition of restrictions on freedom to provide services in respect of public works contracts and on the award of public works contracts to contractors acting through agencies or branches, O.J. 1971, L 185/1.
7. Council Dir. 71/305/EEC of 26 July 1971 concerning the co-ordination of procedures for the award of public works contracts, O.J. 1971, L 185.
8. Council Dir. 77/62/EEC of 21 Dec. 1976 coordinating procedures for the award of public supply contracts, O.J. 1977, L 13. This Dir. was amended in 1980 by Council Dir. 80/767/EEC of 22 July 1980 adapting and supplementing in respect of certain contracting authorities Dir. 77/62/EEC coordinating procedures for the award of public supply contracts, O.J. 1980, L 215/1.
9. C. McCrudden, *Buying Social Justice* (OUP, 2007), 100.
10. Ibid., 106.
11. C. Bovis, op. cit. *supra* note 4, 34.

the supply Directive was amended in 1988 to include the GPA rules.[12] Accordingly, undertakings based in third countries with subsidiaries within the Community, had the same access to public supply contracts as Community undertakings and could enforce Community law.

Given the increasing significance of public procurement in the economic activity of Member States and the fact that the 1985 White Paper on the Internal Market proposed a deadline of 31 December 1992 to complete the internal market, it was felt that public procurement markets had to be opened up even further. To enhance transparency and non-discrimination the public supplies Directive and the public works Directives were modified[13] and a separate Directive[14] was adopted in the utilities sector.[15] These are called the second generation *acquis*.

The third generation of the public procurement *acquis* saw the light with the adoption of a Directive on the procurement of services in 1992[16] Services had gained a more prominent role in the economy and public authorities were awarding contracts in this field at an increasing pace. The large amount of legislation in the field of public procurement led to the adoption of a consolidated regime: for about a decade Directive 93/36/EEC[17] would be applicable to public supply contracts, Directive 93/37/EEC[18] to public work contracts and Directive 93/38/EEC[19] to utilities.

Meanwhile, at international level, the Uruguay Round led to the creation of the World Trade Organization in 1994, which aims at liberalizing international trade. Within the framework of the WTO, GATT remained the umbrella agreement for trade of goods. The Uruguay Round extended the GATT rules to trade in services and created GATS (General Agreement on Trade in Services). Public procurement is however still largely outside the scope of the general WTO rules, the main instrument on public procurement being the GPA. In 1994 a broader GPA was signed which reinforced the need to open up public procurement to international competition by ensuring effective market access to foreign bidders. This was strengthened by the most recent version that was concluded on 15 December 2011, with the final text of the revised GPA being signed on 30 March 2012 and entering into force on 6 April 2014 for the parties that have

---

12. Council Dir. 88/295/EEC of 22 Mar. 1988 amending Dir. 77/62/EEC relating to the coordination of procedures on the award of public supply contracts and repealing certain provisions of Dir. 80/767/EEC, O.J. 1988, L 127/1.
13. It concerns Council Dir. 88/295/EEC of 22 Mar. 1988 amending Dir. 77/62/EEC relating to the coordination of procedures on the award of public supply contracts and repealing certain provisions of Dir. 80/767/EEC, O.J. 1988, L 127/1 and Council Dir. 89/440/EEC of 18 July 1989 amending Dir. 71/305/EEC concerning coordination of procedures for the award of public works contracts, O.J. 1989, L. 210.
14. Council Dir. 90/531/EEC of 17 Sept. 1990 on the procurement procedures of entities operating in the water, energy, transport and telecommunications sectors, O.J. 1990, L 297/1.
15. Since the water, energy, transport and telecommunication sectors are characterized by their large scope and as they are important policy areas, they are subjected to a complex and separate regulatory regime in most Member States. See European Commission, "Statistical Performance Indicators for Keeping Watch over Public Procurement", 1992; C. Bovis, op. cit. *supra* note 4, 27.
16. Council Dir. 92/50/EEC of 18 June 1992 relating to the coordination of procedures for the award of public service contracts, O.J. 1992, L 209/1.
17. Council Dir. 93/36/EEC of 14 June 1993 coordinating procedures for the award of public supply contracts, O.J. 1993, L 199/1.
18. Council Dir. 93/37/EEC of 14 June 1993 concerning the coordination of procedures for the award of public works contracts, O.J. 1993, L 199/54.
19. Council Dir. 93/38/EEC of 14 June 1993 coordinating the procurement procedures of entities operating in the water, energy, transport and telecommunications sectors, O.J. 1993, L 199/84.

accepted the protocol of amendment. EU law has to comply with those international obligations as well.[20]

In 2000, the European Council held a special meeting in Lisbon to agree on a new strategic goal for the Union in order to strengthen employment, economic reform and social cohesion as part of a knowledge-based economy. In this light, the European Commission wanted to modernize the procurement directives. The entry into force of new public procurement rules, in particular to make them accessible to SMEs and to ensure that procurement could take place on-line was warranted. Directive 2004/18/EC[21] was created. It includes rules on public works, supply and service contracts in one legal document and thus entails an important simplification. Furthermore, Directive 2004/17/EC[22] on utilities was adopted. These Directives form the fourth generation of the procurement *acquis.* Even though they contain several simplifications and codify important case law of the Court of Justice, specifically with regard to sustainable procurement, a new procurement package was adopted by the European legislator in 2014.

3. Objectives of the EU public procurement regime

The EU's main priority in its public procurement regime is the removal of legal and administrative barriers to trade in government markets.[23]

Furthermore, the acquisition of better value for money and resulting economic growth is an important aim as well. More competition leads to more choice for the contracting authorities to decide which tender is the most advantageous and most suitable to reach their needs, lower prices and hence bring about more value for taxpayers' money.[24]

Next to purely economic goals, rules on public procurement aim to contribute to the avoidance of corruption, the creation of equal opportunities for economic operators, fair treatment and efficiency in evaluating tenders by focusing on transparency, equal treatment and non-discrimination.[25] Since modern procurement systems developed alongside the development of the welfare state, public procurement is increasingly focusing on social and environmental objectives. Since the late 1980s which were characterized by the end of the Cold War, the collapse of Communism, the expansion of market capitalism and the consequent growth of international trade and investment, governments realized that public procurement can contribute to Member States' social policy in relation to long-term unemployment, equal distribution of income, social exclusion and the protection of minorities. This phenomenon, which is called "social linkage"[26]

---

20. The revised GPA modernizes the text of the GPA. It is expected to bring extra procurement opportunities worth around € 80 billion in countries that are party to the agreement by adding numerous government entities and new services and other areas of public procurement activities to the GPA's scope of application.
21. Dir. 2004/18/EC of the European Parliament and of the Council of 31 Mar. 2004 on the coordination of procedures for the award of public works contracts, public supply contracts and public service contracts, O.J. 2004, L 134/114.
22. Dir. 2004/17/EC of the European Parliament and of the Council of 31 Mar. 2004 coordinating the procurement procedures of entities operating in the water, energy, transport and postal services sectors, O.J. 2004, L 134/1.
23. European Commission, "Statistical Performance for Keeping Watch over Public Procurement", 1992.
24. Case C-305/08, *CoNISMa*, para 37; Case C-147/06 and C-148/06, *SECAP*, para 29. It should be noted, however, that an increased number of participants brings about that contracting authorities will face more costs of tendering and costs relating to the evaluation of offers.
25. S. Arrowsmith, "Public procurement: Basic concepts and the coverage of procurement rules" in S. Arrowsmith (Ed.), *Public Procurement: An Introduction* (Asia Link – EuropeAid Co-operation Office, 2010), 4.
26. C. McCrudden, op. cit. *supra* note 9, 363.

gained popularity since the EC procurement reforms of the 1980s and 1990s.[27] Public procurement was generally considered to be a useful tool for helping to deliver these policies. This led to the development of the concept "sustainable public procurement" which entails that public authorities seek to achieve the appropriate balance between economic, social and environmental considerations. The increased importance of sustainability has been reflected clearly in the 2014 procurement Directives.

4. Principles and treaty provisions underlying the EU public procurement regime

The European public procurement regime is based on several fundamental principles which should be respected whenever there is a cross-border interest, even if the Directives are not applicable e.g. when a certain threshold is not met.[28] These can also be found in most national regulatory procurement systems. For reasons of legal certainty, the European legislator has codified these principles in the procurement Directives. As held by recital 1 of Directive 2014/24/EU of the European Parliament and of the Council on public procurement and repealing Directive 2004/18/EC (hereinafter: the General Directive),[29] "the award of public contracts by or on behalf of Member States' authorities has to comply with the principles of the Treaty on the Functioning of the European Union (TFEU), and in particular the free movement of goods, freedom of establishment and the freedom to provide services, as well as the principles deriving therefrom, such as equal treatment, non-discrimination, mutual recognition, proportionality and transparency". This list is non-exhaustive and in procurement literature other ground principles have been identified such as integrity, economy, openness, fairness, competition, accountability, objectivity, *de minimis* and the public interest function of Contracting authorities.[30] Non-discrimination, equal treatment, transparency and proportionality are generally identified as the four cornerstones of every procurement procedure. This is reflected in Article 18(1) alinea 1 of the General Directive which states that "Contracting authorities shall treat economic operators equally and without discrimination and shall act in a transparent and proportionate manner."[31]

4.1 *The principle of non-discrimination*

The prohibition of discrimination in public procurement focuses primarily on discrimination on the basis of nationality.

Every time a Contracting Authority purchases supplies, works or services, it has to ensure that it does not (in)directly discriminate between domestic and foreign products or service providers. This reflects the principle of national treatment as laid down in the GPA which entails that parties to the GPA must give the same treatment afforded to national providers and

27. The 1987 Single European Act held in Art. 130r(2) that environmental protection requirements shall be a component of the Community's other policies. This policy and the integration of environmental requirements into other policies has developed ever since. The increasing importance of social linkage went hand in hand with the growth of corporate social responsibility which gave buyers the power to force firms to comply with international and regional social and environmental norms.
28. This will be further discussed in paras. 4–6.
29. Dir. 2014/24/EU of the European Parliament and of the Council of 26 Feb. 2014 on public procurement and repealing Dir. 2004/18/EC, O.J. 2014, L 94/65–242.
30. C. Bovis, op. cit. *supra* note 4, 63–80; S. Arrowsmith, op. cit. *supra* note 25, 20; J. Lynch, *Public Procurement & Contract Administration: A Brief Introduction* (Lean Publication, 2013).
31. Art. IV(1) and (2) of the Revised GPA.

products to providers and products from other signatory states.[32] Even measures that are non-discriminatory in nature but hinder free movement are in principle forbidden

Examples of direct discriminatory behaviour in public procurement may relate to decisions to buy certain supplies only from the domestic market or to give preference to domestic service providers.[33] Applying certain qualifications conditions to foreign service providers only, also leads to discriminatory behaviour.[34] Indirect discrimination may occur if qualifications conditions are applied to domestic and foreign service providers alike, but in practice only national operators comply with these qualifications.[35] Free movement is hindered a well when contracting authorities ask for a disproportionate amount of experience or demand the use of a certain technology system to the exclusion of all other systems.[36]

The principle of non-discrimination cannot be interpreted restrictively. It implies an obligation of transparency to give tenderers insight in the decision-making process of contracting authorities and to enable contracting authorities to determine whether the non-discrimination principle has been complied with.[37] Contracting authorities have to ensure not to actually or potentially hinder free movement except if there is a valid justification and the proportionality principle is respected. Justifications that are often invoked are environmental concerns (e.g. the obligation to use renewable energy sources),[38] security issues (e.g. award of contracts only to firms in national public ownership based on the secrecy of data and the security of the state)[39] and regional development. Grounds of an economic nature can never justify a derogation form the Treaty.[40]

4.2 *The equal treatment principle*

The principle of equal treatment is much broader than the non-discrimination principle as it focuses on any type of discrimination or inequality. Comparable situations cannot be treated differently and different situations should be treated in the same way unless objectively justified.[41] This reflects the GPA's most favoured national (MFN) principle that guarantees treatment that is not less favourable than that afforded to other parties.

Even before its codification in the procurement Directives, the equal treatment principle was important in the field of public procurement. As held by the Court in *Storebaelt*,[42] the duty to observe the principle lies at the very heart of the Directive as the purpose of the Directive is to ensure the development of effective competition. Observance of the equal treatment principle requires that all the tenders comply with the tender conditions so as to ensure an objective comparison of the tenders submitted by the various tenderers. Furthermore, all tenderers must have equality of opportunity when formulating their tenders.[43] Accordingly, a person who has

32. Art. IV(1) and (2) of the Revised GPA.
33. Case C-21/88, *Du Pont de Nemours*; Case C-243/89, *Storebaelt*.
34. Case C-360/89, *Commission v. Italy*.
35. Case C-45/87, *Dundalk*. In this case only one national operator complied with the national qualifications; Case C-3/88, *Re Data Processing*; Case C-234/03, *Contse*; Case C-113/89, *Rush Portuguesa*.
36. Case C-359/93, *UNIX*; Case C-384/93 *Alpine Investments*; Case C-234/03, *Contse*.
37. Case 275/98, *Unitron*; Case C-324/98, *Telaustria*; Joined Cases C-285/99 and C-286/99, *Lombardini*.
38. Case C-379/98, *PreusenElektra*; Case C-513/99 *Concordia Bus Finland*.
39. Case C-3/88, *Re Data Processing*.
40. Case C-221/12, *INTEGAN*. In this case, economic grounds could not justify the direct grant of a contract or an exclusive right to engage in an activity of certain cross-border interest.
41. Case C-434/02, *Arnold André* and Case C-210/03, *Swedish Match*.
42. Case C-243/89, *Storebaelt*; Case C-513/99, *Concordia Bus Finland* and Case C-21/03, *Fabricom*.
43. Case C-87/94, *Commission v. Belgium*.

carried out certain preparatory work is not necessarily in the same situation as a person who has not.[44] Article 24 of the new General Directive indicates that Member States have to ensure that contracting authorities take appropriate measures to effectively prevent, identify and remedy conflicts of interest arising in the conduct of procurement procedures so as to avoid any distortion of competition and to ensure equal treatment of all economic operators. There is specifically a conflict of interest where staff members of the contracting authority who are involved in or may influence the outcome of the procurement procedure, have a financial, economic or other personal interest which might compromise their impartiality and independence.[45] It follows that direct grants or exclusive rights for certain operators are in principle forbidden. The equal treatment principle is also violated when a contracting authority alters the weighting of the award criteria following an initial review of the tenders submitted[46] or when it conducts negotiations with the selected consortium on the basis of a tender which did not comply with the tender conditions.[47]

4.3 *The principle of transparency*

The principle of non-discrimination implies an obligation of transparency imposed on the contracting authority. It ensures to the benefit of any potential tenderer, a degree of advertising sufficient to enable the market to be opened up to competition and the impartiality of procurement procedures to be reviewed.[48] Whether a certain level of advertisement can held to be sufficient is for the national court to decide.

If a public entity concludes an agreement without any recourse to competition, whereby it grants a licence or the exclusive right to engage in an economic activity of cross-border interest, any other economic operator in that Member State may before the courts of that State, allege an infringement of the transparency principle.[49] The same holds true if a contracting authority renews licences without inviting any competing bids.

4.4 *Treaty provisions*

The principles discussed above are interconnected and intertwined with the Treaty provisions on the internal market. Article 18 TFEU prohibits any discrimination based on nationality and Article 19 TFEU indicates that the Council may take appropriate action to combat discrimination based on sex, racial or ethnic origin, religion or belief, disability, age or sexual orientation.[50] Article 34 and 35 TFEU on the free movement of goods aim to combat discrimination on the basis of nationality and are a concretization of Article 18 TFEU. They are an important inspiration for the Directives on public procurement specifically with regard to the award of public supply contracts. Articles 50 and 59 provide the legal basis for the Directive in the field of the freedom of establishment and the freedom to provide services. These are relevant with regard to the award of public works and public service contracts. Behaviour of contracting authorities that violates one of the fundamental principles discussed above, generally also violates Article 18 TFEU and one of the free movement provisions.

---

44. Case C-21/03, *Fabricom*.
45. Art. 41 and 57(4) (f) of Dir. 2014/24/EU.
46. Case C-226/09, *European Commission v. Ireland;* Case C-331/04, *ATI EAC*.
47. Case C-243/89, *Storebaelt.;* Case C-336/12, *Manova* which is codified in Art. 56(3) of Dir. 2014/24/EU; Case C-387/14 *Esaprojekt*.
48. Case C-324/98, *Telaustria*; Case C-275/98, *Unitron*; Joined Cases C-285/99 and C-286/99, *Lombardini*.
49. Case C-221/12, *INTEGAN*; Case C-91/08, *Wall*.
50. Art. 20 and 21 jo. 51 of the Charter on Fundamental Rights of the European Union.

5. Public sector procurement: The new General Directive 2014/24/EU

5.1 *Introduction and rationale of the Directive*

Even though Directives 2004/17/EC and 2004/18/EU brought about considerable improvements and simplification, their application turned to be very complex, inflexible, filled with disproportionate obligations which were specifically felt by SMEs[51] and therefore not cost-efficient.[52] For this reason, a new procurement package – the fifth procurement *acquis* – was proposed by the European Commission in December 2011 and entered into force on 17 April 2014. It consists of Directive 2014/24/EU on public procurement, Directive 2014/25/EU[53] on procurement by entities operating in the water, energy, transport and postal services sectors and Directive 2014/23/EU[54] on the award of concession contracts. The 2014 procurement package aims for more transparency and efficiency, a smoother award of contracts, a better connection between price and quality, more competition and a growing economy.[55] Member States were required to implement most of the provisions by 18 April 2016. Changes at EU level are closely linked to changes at international level. In April 2014, the latest version of the GPA entered into force after two-third of the signatories signed it. 19 parties are currently part of the agreement, including the EU with respect to its 28 Member States. The 2014 GPA streamlined and modernized the text of the GPA. It is expected that businesses in signatory states will gain better market access since numerous government entities and new services and other areas of the public procurement activities have been added to its scope of application, leading to extra procurement opportunities worth around € 80 billion.

5.2 *Scope of application*

5.2.1 *Procurement of public contracts and design contests*

Directive 2014/24/EU has a broad scope of application. It establishes rules on the procedures for procurement with respect to public contracts and design contests, whose value is not less than the thresholds laid down in Article 4.[56] Public contracts are contracts for pecuniary interest concluded in writing between one or more economic operators and one or more contracting authorities and having as their object the execution of works, the supply of products or the provision of services.[57] The construction of social housing units[58] is a typical example of a works contract, the purchase of office supplies is a typical supply contract and hiring a company to

---

51. For example the submission of documents to demonstrate they hold certain capacities.
52. The costs involved rise to € 5.6 billion. See Commission Staff Working Paper, Executive Summary of the Impact Assessment, SEC(2011), 1586, final.
53. Dir. 2014/25/EU of the European Parliament and of the Council of 26 Feb. 2014 on procurement by entities operating in the water, energy, transport and postal services sectors and repealing Dir. 2004/17/EC, O.J. 2014, L 94/243–374.
54. Dir. 2014/23/EU of the European Parliament and of the Council of 26 Feb. 2014 on the award of concession contracts, O.J. 2014, L 94/1–64.
55. Communication of the Commission of 13 Apr. 2011, "The Single Market Act: Twelve levers to boost growth and confidence", IP/11/469.
56. Art. 1(1) Dir. 2014/24/EU.
57. Art. 2(6)–(9) provides a definition for public works contracts, public supplies contracts and public service contracts. Important to note is that "public works" means the outcome of building or civil engineering works taken as a whole which is sufficient in itself to fulfil an economic or technical function; Case C-451/08, *Helmut Müller*.
58. Case C-197/11, *Libertt*.

clean all offices is defined as a service contract.[59] Design contests are procedures enabling contracting authorities to acquire a plan or design selected by a jury after being put out to competition.[60] It is not of importance whether or not the works, supplies or services are intended for a public purpose.

Contracts which have as their subject two or more types of procurement (works, services or supplies), classify as mixed procurement contracts. The main subject of the contract in question will be relevant to determine the applicable provisions.[61] In the case of mixed contracts consisting partly of services and partly of supplies (e.g. the purchase of a new computer system (supplies) including the maintenance of that system (services) or partly of services and partly of social services, the main subject will be determined by looking at which part of the contract has the highest value.[62]

5.2.2 *Contracting authority*

Directive 2014/24/EU is applicable when contracting authorities conclude public contracts with economic operators. The concept "contracting authority" refers to the State,[63] regional or local authorities, bodies governed by public law (BGPL) or associations formed by one or more of such authorities or one or more of such bodies governed by public law.[64] As held by the Court in *Beentjes*, the term has to be interpreted in a *functional* manner. Accordingly, a local land consolidation committee with no legal personality having as a main task the financing and award of public works contracts, while depending on the relevant public authorities for the appointment of its members and its operations being subject to their supervision, falls within the notion of state, even though it is not part of the state administration in *formal* terms.[65]

BGPL are all entities that are not part of the "traditional state" apparatus of government departments and local authorities, but are closely dependent on the state so that there is a risk that they will be influenced to discriminate in their purchasing.[66] As indicated in Article 2(4) of the Directive, BGPL are bodies that have the following characteristics:

(a) they are established for the specific purpose of meeting needs in the general interest, not having an industrial or commercial character;
(b) they have legal personality; and
(c) they are financed, for the most part, by the State, regional or local authorities, or by other bodies governed by public law; or are subject to management supervision by those authorities or bodies; or have an administrative, managerial or supervisory board, more than half of whose members are appointed by the State, regional or local authorities, or by other bodies governed by public law.

Whether an entity is established to meet needs in the general interest (a) has been interpreted very broadly and in a functional manner by the Court. As held in *BFI*[67] such needs are those

59. Case C-386/11, *Piepenbrock.*
60. Art. 2(21) Dir. 2014/24/EU.
61. Art. 3(2) Dir. 2014/24/EU. This article is applicable in case of mixed contracts having as their subject-matter different types of procurement all of which are covered by this Dir. If this is not the case, Art. 3(3)–(5) is applicable.
62. The estimated value is the determining factor in case of mixed contracts consisting partly of services within the meaning of Chapter I of Title III and partly of other services.
63. Annex I to the Dir. contains a non-exhaustive list of central government authorities of the Member States.
64. Art. 2(1) Dir. 2014/24/EU.
65. Case C-31/87, *Gebroeders Beentjes;* Case C-353/96, *Teoranta.*
66. S. Arrowsmith, op. cit. *supra* note 25, 89; Case C-283/00, *SIEPSA.*
67. Case C-360/96, *BFI.*

which the State chooses to provide itself or over which it retains a decisive influence for reasons associated with the general interest. In this regard account must be taken of all the relevant legal and factual elements, such as the circumstances prevailing at the time when the body was established and the conditions under which it exercises its activity.[68] Specific attention has to be paid to the fact that the BGPL does not aim primarily at making a profit, the fact that it does not bear the risks associated with the activity, and any public financing of the activity. As held in *Agora*,[69] the fact that a body operates in a competitive environment tends to indicate that the entity cannot be qualified as a BGPL. Nevertheless, the fact that an entity that was established to meet needs in the general interest also carries out other profit-making activities, provided that it continues to attend to the needs which it is specifically required to meet, does not exclude it from the scope of the Directive.[70] The proportion of profit-making activities actually pursued by that entity as part of its activities as a whole is irrelevant for its classification as a BGPL.[71] Whether an entity has legal personality (b) depends on the national law of the Member States. It entails that the entity is capable of having legal rights and duties so that it can for example enter into contracts, sue and be sued. A close reading of (c) reveals that there must be a close dependency of BGPL on the state, in order to make the Directive applicable.[72]

With regard to the financial aspect, the Court held in *University of Cambridge*[73] that obtaining public funds from the state, such as grants for the support of research work or payments for the benefit of students who are not e able to meet tuition fees, may indicate that a body is a BGPL.[74] Not all payments made by a contracting authority have the effect of creating or reinforcing a specific relationship of subordination or dependency. Only payments made to finance or support the activities of the body concerned without any specific consideration therefor can be described as "public financing". Payments that constitute a consideration paid by a contracting authority for a contractual service provided by the university, such as the execution of research work, do not fall within the definition of public financing. The nature of the relationship is analogous to the dependency that exists in normal commercial relationships formed by reciprocal contracts freely negotiated between the contracting parties. For (c) to be applicable, the proportion of public finances received by an entity always needs to exceed 50 per cent.[75] The financing does not have to be direct. Indirect State financing exists when the State fixes the base and the amount of the contributions, or exercises such influence, by setting out precisely the services that the legal person must supply and controlling the determination of the amount of contributions so that the legal person only has narrow discretion in fixing the amount.[76] A State measure which confers on a body the right to raise contributions from its members but does not set the amount of those contributions or the extent of the services to be financed thereby does not create a link of close dependency on the public authorities.[77]

---

68. Case C-373/00, *Adolf Truly.*
69. Joined Cases C-223/99 and C-260/99, *Agorà.*
70. Even companies governed by private law established for the specific purpose of meeting needs in the general interest can be qualified as a contracting authority. See Case C-214/00, *Commission v. Spain*; Case C-18/01, *Korhone.*
71. Case C-393/06, *Aigner*; Case C-44/96, *Mannesmann*; Case C-373/00, *Adolf Truly*; Case C-18/01, *Korhonen.*
72. Case C-44/96, *Mannesmann.*
73. Case C-380/98, *University of Cambridge.*
74. Next to universities, statutory sickness insurance funds or public broadcasting bodies may be qualified as BGPL. Case C-300/07, *Oymanns*; Case C-337/06, *Bayerische Rundfunk.*
75. Case C-380/98, *University of Cambridge.*
76. Case C-300/07, *Oymanns*; Case C-337/06, *Bayerische Rundfunk.*
77. Case C-526/11, *Ärztekammer.*

With regard to the management aspect, the dependency test is fulfilled if the public authority can significantly influence the decisions of the entity in relation to public contracts.[78] The mere supervision of compliance with management rules may lead to significant influence being conferred on the public authorities if these rules are very detailed. This is certainly the case if this supervision is backed up by the important power to wind-up an entity or to suspend the managerial organs and appoint a provisional administrator.

The final alternative, disposing of a managerial board of which more than half of the members are appointed by a contracting authority, is straightforward. Just as with the financial requirement, it can be stated that "more than half" simply refers to more than 50 per cent.

5.2.3 *Thresholds*

In general, Directive 2014/24/EU is applicable to public contracts and design contests with a value net of value-added tax (VAT) estimated to be equal to or greater than the following thresholds:[79] EUR 5 548 000 for public works contracts; EUR 144 000 for public supply and service contracts awarded by central government authorities EUR 221 000 for public supply and service contracts awarded by sub-central contracting authorities; EUR 750 000 for public service contracts for social and other specific services listed in Annex XIV.

If the thresholds are not met, the Directive is not applicable and national procurement legislation will be relevant, if existing. It is presumed that contracts with a low value are not interesting for non-domestic operators. As there is always a possibility that foreign undertakings want to be involved in a tender process, specifically in border regions, the Treaty and general EU principles are applicable if a cross border interest can be demonstrated.

Compared to the 2004 Directive, the current General Directive contains an additional category for public service contracts for social and other specific services such as healthcare and education.[80] As these services are often provided within a national context and mostly do not have a cross border dimension, a high threshold of EUR 750 000 will exclude many of them from the procedural obligations from the Directive. Member States are required to put in place national rules for the award of such contracts and are free to determine the procedural rules applicable if these allow contracting authorities to take into account the specificities of the services in question and ensure that they comply with the principles of transparency and equal treatment. Certain[81] health, social and cultural services can be reserved for organizations that fulfil specific conditions to participate.

5.2.4 *Exceptions*

Directive 2014/24/EU contains several exceptions to its scope of application. Most notably, contracts in the utilities sector fall within the scope of Directive 2014/25/EU.[82] There are also some specific exclusions in the field of electronic communications, public contracts awarded and design contests organized pursuant to international rules and specific service contracts such

78. Case C-237/99, *OPAC*; Case C-373/00, *Adolf Truly*.
79. Art. 4 and 6(1) Dir. 2014/24/EU. Every two years from 30 June 2013, the Commission verifies whether the thresholds correspond to the thresholds established in the GPA and shall, where necessary, revise them. Commission Delegated Reg. 2017/2365 of 18 Dec. 2017 amending Dir. 2014/24/EU in respect of the application thresholds for the procedures for the award of contracts contains the current thresholds.
80. Dir. 2004/18/EC contained a difference between Annex IIA and Annex IIB services with regard to the scope of application of the Dir.
81. Art. 77 Dir. 2014/24/EU.
82. Art. 7 Dir. 2014/24/EU.

as contracts for certain legal services.[83] The latter are national in nature and cross border interest is deemed not to be expected. The Directive is not applicable to public service contracts awarded by a contracting authority to another one or to an association of contracting authorities on the basis of an exclusive right they enjoy which is compatible with the TFEU.[84] Furthermore, it is only applicable to a closed list of research and development services and to specific defence and security services.[85]

Public contracts between entities within the public sector do not fall within the scope of the Directive. As held by Article 12(1), a public contract awarded by a contracting authority to a legal person governed by private or public law falls outside the scope of the Directive where all of the following conditions are fulfilled:

(a) the contracting authority exercises over the legal person concerned a control which is similar to that which it exercises over its own departments;
(b) more than 80 % of the activities of the controlled legal person are carried out in the performance of tasks entrusted to it by the controlling contracting authority or by other legal persons controlled by that contracting authority; and
(c) there is no direct private capital participation in the controlled legal person with the exception of non-controlling and non-blocking forms of private capital participation required by national legislative provisions, in conformity with the Treaties, which do not exert a decisive influence on the controlled legal person.

Since the three conditions have to be applied cumulatively, it is not easy for contracts to be excluded from the scope of the Directive.

A contracting authority is deemed to exercise over a legal person a control similar (not comparable!) to that which it exercises over its own departments within the meaning of condition (a) where it exercises a decisive influence over both strategic objectives and significant management actions and decisions of that legal person.[86] Such control can also be exercised by another legal person, which is itself controlled in the same way by the contracting authority. Condition (a) is a literal codification of the Court's ruling in *Teckal*[87] in which it held that the procurement Directives are not applicable to in-house contracts. Public authorities are not obliged to purchase supplies, works or services from economic operators if they can arrange for those internally.[88] Condition (b) is equally inspired by the *Teckal* case as it was stated that the entity that was awarded the contract should carry out the essential part of its activities for the controlling entity. With regard to condition (c), the participation of a private company, even as a minority, in the capital of a company in which the contracting authority also participates renders the in-house exception inapplicable.[89] The Directive is thus applicable every time a contracting authority concludes a contract with a company that is legally distinct from it and in whose capital it has a holding together with one or more private undertakings.[90] It can thus equally apply to contacts concluded by two distinct public authorities.

---

83. Arts. 7–10 Dir. 2014/24/EU.
84. Art. 11 Dir. 2014/24/EU. Case C-220/06, *Asociaciòn Profesional de Empresas.*
85. Arts. 13–17 Dir. 2014/24/EU.
86. Case C-458/03, *Parking Brixen.*
87. Case C-107/98, *Teckal.*
88. Case C-18/01, *Korhonen.*
89. The fact that a contracting authority holds either by itself or with other contracting authorities 100% of share capital tends to indicate that it exercises sufficient control. Case C-295/05, *Asemfo*; Case C-410/04, *ANAV.*
90. Case C-26/03, *Stadt Halle*; Case C-231/03, *Coname.*

Article 12(4) contains specific grounds for the exclusion of a contract concluded exclusively between two or more contracting authorities (quasi in-house) from the scope of the Directive and Article 12(2) allows horizontal in-house contracts to escape from the application of the Directive. These will not be further discussed within the scope of this essay.

5.3 *Selection*

5.3.1 *Grounds for exclusion*

Before checking whether economic operators fulfil certain selection criteria, contracting authorities have to verify whether an exclusion ground is applicable. Article 57(1) of the Directive contains a list of situations which oblige contracting authorities to exclude untrustworthy operators from participation (mandatory exclusion grounds), Operators which have been convicted by a final judgment for reasons of participation in a criminal organization, corruption, fraud, terrorist offence, money laundering or child labour, have to be excluded.[91] An operator also has to be excluded where the contracting authority is aware that the economic operator is in breach of its obligations relating to the payment of taxes or social security contributions and where this has been established by a judicial or administrative decision having final and binding effect. Article 57(4) and 57(2) paragraph 2 refer to situations that allow the exclusion of economic operators (discretionary exclusion grounds).[92] These include the violation of environmental, social or labour law, grave professional misconduct or the conclusion of agreements with other economic operators aimed at distorting competition. The grounds mentioned in the Directive are exhaustive.[93] When implementing the Directive, Member States are free to turn the discretionary exclusion grounds into mandatory exclusion grounds.[94] They also have to determine the maximum period of exclusion. Where the period of exclusion has not been set by final judgment this cannot exceed five years in case of mandatory exclusion grounds and three years in case of discretionary exclusion grounds.[95] In all cases Member States have to respect the principles of proportionality and transparency. Despite the existence of a relevant ground for exclusion, operators have the possibility to demonstrate their reliability (self-cleaning).[96] If such evidence is considered as sufficient, the economic operator cannot be excluded from the procurement procedure.[97]

---

91. Art. 57(1) Dir. 2014/24/EU.
92. Member States may also require contracting authorities to exclude operators if any of these situations occurs. These grounds for exclusion are in any case optional for Member States; Joined Cases C-226/04 and C-228/04, *La Cascina*.
93. Joined Cases C-226/04 and C-228/04, *La Cascina*. In Case C-213/07, *Michaniki*, the Court held that whilst the exclusion grounds are exhaustive regarding grounds relating to professional qualities, they may also exclude for further reasons to ensure transparency and equal treatment in the procurement process. This case dates from 2008, so before the entry into force of the new Directive which already takes into account more grounds, such as the prevention of conflicts of interest; Joined Cases C-21/03 and C-41/03, *Fabricom*.
94. Art. 57(4) Dir. 2014/24/EU.
95. Art. 57(7) Dir. 2014/24/EU.
96. Case C-21/03, *Fabricom*, in which the Court held that an undertaking which has participated in the preparatory stages of a public contract and was for this reason precluded from submitting a tender,, should have the opportunity to prove that its previous involvement has not distorted competition. A tenderer cannot be eliminated automatically. Art. 41 Dir. 2014/24/EU and Joined Cases C-285/99 and C-286/99, *Lombardini*.
97. Art. 57(6) Dir. 2014/24/EU.

5.3.2 *Selection criteria*

As indicated in Article 58(1) of Directive 2014/24/EU, contracting authorities may impose selection criteria on candidates[98] or tenderers[99] as requirements for participation to ensure that they can perform the contract. These selection criteria may refer to:

(a) suitability to pursue the professional activity;
(b) economic and financial standing;
(c) technical and professional ability.

When contracting authorities impose such requirements, they have to ensure that those requirements are related and proportionate to the subject-matter of the contract. In line with the principle of transparency, the selection criteria have to be set in advance and made known to economic operators.

With regard to (a), contracting authorities may require economic operators to be enrolled in one of the professional or trade registers kept in their Member State of establishment. If membership of an organization or a particular authorization is mandatory in the country of origin, contracting authorities may require economic operators to prove that they hold such authorization or membership.[100]

With regard to (b), contracting authorities may require that economic operators have a certain minimum yearly turnover, including a certain minimum turnover in the area covered by the contract.[101] To ensure the participation of SME's, this minimum turnover can in principle not exceed two times the estimated contract value. Facilitating the participation of SMEs in public procurement is one of the core objectives of the Europe 2020 strategy. Accordingly, where a contract is divided into lots, which contracting authorities are "encouraged"[102] to do to enhance competition and to make the size of the individual contracts better correspond to the capacity of SMEs or to adapt the content of the individual contracts more closely to the specialized sectors of SMEs, the turnover requirement applies in relation to each individual lot.

With regard to (c), contracting authorities may impose requirements ensuring that economic operators possess the necessary human and technical resources and experience to perform the contract to an appropriate quality standard. Contracting authorities may require, in particular, suitable references from contracts performed in the past to prove that economic operators have a sufficient level of experience.[103] It is up to contracting authorities to determine whether firms fulfil these criteria. Article 60 and 62 of the Directive contains more specific rules on the means of proof and the reference to quality assurance and environmental management standards.

Directive 2014/24/EU has created an important new way for operators to prove that they fulfil the selection criteria and are not in one of the situations in which they can be or have to be excluded: the European Single Procurement Document (ESPD).[104] This is an updated self-declaration on the basis of an electronically available standard form that serves as preliminary

98. A candidate is an economic operator that has sought an invitation or has been invited to take part in a restricted procedure, in a competitive procedure with negotiation, in a negotiated procedure without prior publication, in a competitive dialogue or in an innovation partnership: Art. 2(1)(12) Dir. 2014/24/EU.
99. A tenderer is an economic operator that has submitted a tender: Art. 2(1)(11) Dir. 2014/24/EU.
100. Art. 58(2) Dir. 2014/24/EU.
101. Art. 58(3) Dir. 2014/24/EU. It is in principle up to national authorities to determine the relevant financial standards. See Joined Cases C-27/86-29/86, *CEI*.
102. As held by Art. 46(1) Dir. 2014/24/EU, contracting authorities have to provide reasons for their decision not to subdivide contracts into lots.
103. Case C-46/15, *Ambisig*.
104. Art. 59 Dir. 2014/24/EU.

evidence in replacement of certificates issued by public authorities or third parties confirming that the economic operator fulfils these conditions. This will be more efficient, less time consuming and less costly, which is of special importance to SMEs. Only the tenderer to whom the contract will be awarded has to submit up-to-date supporting documents[105] unless the contracting authority can obtain the information directly by accessing a national database. In e-Certis, Member States have to make available and keep up-to-date a complete list of databases containing relevant information on economic operators which can be consulted by contracting authorities from other Member States to facilitate cross border tendering.[106]

5.3.4 *Reduction of the number of candidates*

Next to the qualitative aspects of firms, there is also a quantitative element in the selection process. As held by Article 65(1), in certain procedures,[107] contracting authorities can limit the number of candidates meeting the selection criteria that they will invite to tender or to conduct a dialogue, provided the minimum number of qualified candidates is available. In the restricted procedure the minimum number of candidates shall be five. In the competitive procedure with negotiation, the competitive dialogue procedure and the innovation partnership the minimum number of candidates is three. In any event the number of candidates invited has to be sufficient to ensure genuine competition.[108]

5.4 *Award criteria*

As held by Article 67(1) contracting authorities are required to base the award of public contracts on the tender that is most economically advantageous from their point of view. This tender must be identified on the basis of the price or cost, using a cost-effectiveness approach, such as life-cycle costing[109] and may include the best price-quality ratio, which shall be assessed on the basis of criteria linked to the subject-matter of the public contract in question.[110] These criteria can relate to quality, aesthetic,functional, social, environmental and innovative characteristics, or after-sales service.[111] The list is not exhaustive which entails that award criteria should not be confused with selection criteria which do form a closed list.[112]

As quality and social aspects are continuously gaining importance, Member States can provide that contracting authorities may not use price or cost as the sole award criterion. This is important, since Directive 2004/18/EC did not foresee this possibility and the award on the basis of the economically most advantageous tender was seen as a separate award criteria next to the lowest price.[113]

Contracting authorities are free to determine which factors they want to apply in evaluating tenders and the Court has always applied a flexible and broad interpretation. Of course, award criteria cannot confer an unrestricted freedom of choice on the contracting authorities.[114] They allow contracting authorities to balance economic considerations with policy choices[115]

105. Art. 59(4) and (5) Dir. 2014/24/EU.
106. Arts. 59(6) and 61 Dir. 2014/24/EU.
107. These procedures will be discussed in para 5.5.
108. Art. 65(2) and 66 Dir. 2014/24/EU.
109. Art. 68 Dir. 2014/24/EU.
110. Case C-448/01, *Wienstrom*; Case C-87/94, *Commission v. Belgium.*
111. Art. 67(2) Dir. 2014/24/EU. This is a non-exhaustive list.
112. Case C-19/00, *SIAC*; Case C-71/92, *Commission v. Spain;* Case C-31/87, *Gebroeders Beentjes.*
113. Art. 56 Dir. 2004/18/EC.
114. Art. 67(3) and (4) Dir. 2014/24/EU.
115. C. Bovis, op. cit. *supra* note 4, 274.

and have to ensure the possibility of effective competition. They have to indicate the relative weighing of each criterion except where only price is considered. Where weighing is not possible for objective reasons, the criteria should be mentioned, in hierarchical order or descending sequence, in the invitation to tender or the contract documents.[116] The Directive contains specific rules on how to assess costs using a life-cycle costing approach.[117] Social criteria,[118] environmental conditions[119] and ecological criteria have been considered to be valid award criteria if they are of direct economic advantage to the contracting authority.

Where tenders appear to be abnormally low, contracting authorities are obliged to ask economic operators to explain the price or costs proposed.[120] There is no exact definition of what counts as "abnormally low". This has to be determined on a case by case basis by contracting authorities themselves. A tender can however only be rejected where the evidence supplied does not satisfactorily account for the low level of price or costs proposed.[121] Where a tender is abnormally low due to violation of labour, social or environmental law, it *has* to be rejected.[122] If it is abnormally low because the tenderer has obtained State Aid, it *may* be rejected on that ground alone only after consultation with the tenderer and the latter is unable to prove, that the aid in question was compatible with the internal market. In such case, the contracting authority has to inform the Commission.[123] Even in this situation there is no obligation to reject the tender.

5.5 *Procedures*

Title III of the Directive contains six procedures which may be used by contracting authorities when awarding contracts.

5.5.1 *Open procedure*

As held by Article 27 of Directive 2014/24/EU, in open procedures, any interested economic operator may submit a tender in response to a call for competition. When contracting authorities publish a contract notice, operators have 35 days to submit their tender.[124] An open procedure is a one staged procedure: after the reception of tenders, contracting authorities will apply the selection and award criteria and can conclude the contract.

5.5.2 *Restricted procedure*

In restricted procedures, any economic operator may submit a request to participate by providing the information for qualitative selection as requested by the contracting authority.[125] The minimum time limit for receipt of requests to participate (first stage of the procedure) is 30 days from the date on which the contract notice was sent. In the second stage, only those economic operators invited to do so by the contracting authority following its assessment of the information provided may submit a tender within 30 days from the date on which the invitation to

116. Case C-324/93, *R Evans;* Case C-448/01, *Wienstrom;* Case C-87/94, *Commission v. Belgium.*
117. Art. 68 Dir. 2014/24/EU.
118. Case C-31/87, *Gebroeders Beentjes.*
119. Case C-513/99, *Concordia Bus Finland.*
120. Joined Cases C-285/99 and C-286/99, *Lombardini.*
121. Case C- Case C-568/13, *Data Medical Service.*
122. Art. 69(3) Dir. 2014/24/EU.
123. Art. 69(4) Dir. 2014/24/EU.
124. In case a prior information was published, the minimum time limit may be shortened if certain conditions are fulfilled. The time limit may also be shortened in case of urgency and if tenders are submitted by electronic means. Art. 27(2)–(4) Dir. 2014/24/EU.
125. Art. 28 Dir. 2014/24/EU.

tender was sent.[126] Contracting authorities can limit the number of suitable candidates to be invited to participate in the procedure to five.

5.5.3 *Competitive procedure with negotiation*

In competitive procedures with negotiation, any economic operator may submit a request to participate by providing the requested information for qualitative selection.[127] The procedure can only be used in the specific cases mentioned in Article 26(4) of the Directive, for example if the complexity of the contract demands this. Contracting authorities have to provide a sufficiently precise description of their needs and the characteristics required of the supplies, works or services to be procured. The procedure can take place in successive stages: the minimum time limit for receipt of requests to participate is 30 days from the date on which the contract notice was sent and the minimum time limit for the receipt of initial tenders is 30 days from the date on which the invitation was sent. Only economic operators invited by the contracting authority following its assessment of the information provided may submit an initial tender. Next, the initial tender will be the basis for the subsequent negotiations. Contracting authorities will thus not only negotiate the initial tender but all subsequent tenders submitted by the tenderers to improve the content of the tenders. Only the final tender is not subject to negotiations. During the negotiations, contracting authorities are obliged to inform all tenderers of any changes to the technical specifications[128] or other procurement documents, other than those setting out the minimum requirements.[129] They have to provide sufficient time for tenderers to modify and re-submit amended tenders and are not allowed to reveal any confidential information communicated by a candidate or a tenderer without its agreement.

5.5.4 *Competitive dialogue*

In competitive dialogues, any economic operator may submit a request to participate in response to a contract notice within 30 days by providing the requested information for qualitative selection. In the contract notice, contracting authorities define their needs and set out the award criteria based on the best price-quality ratio. Only those economic operators invited by the contracting authority following the assessment of the information provided may participate in the dialogue which aims to identify and define the means best suited to satisfy the contracting authority's needs.[130] Competitive dialogues can take place in successive stages to reduce the number of solutions to be discussed during the dialogue stage by applying the award criteria. The dialogue continues until the contracting authority can identify the solutions which are capable of meeting its needs. Solutions proposed during the dialogue cannot be revealed to other participants unless this is agreed upon. After the dialogue is concluded, contracting authorities will ask each of the remaining participants to submit their final tender on the basis of the solution(s) presented during the dialogue.[131] The procedure can only be applied in limited circumstances, e.g. in case of particular complex contracts.[132]

---

126. If certain conditions are fulfilled, the time limits may be shortened. See Art. 28(3)–(6) Dir. 2014/24/EU.
127. Art. 29 Dir. 2014/24/EU.
128. Technical specifications lay down the characteristics of a work, service or supply. Art. 42 Dir. 2014/24/EU and Annex VII point 1.
129. The minimum requirements and award criteria are not subject to negotiations. Art. 29(3) Dir. 2014/24/EU.
130. Art. 30 Dir. 2014/24/EU.
131. A difference with the competitive procedure with negotiations is that in the latter, tenderers will first submit their initial tenders before negotiations have started.
132. Art. 26 (4) Dir. 2014/24/EU.

5.5.5 *Innovation partnership*

Directive 2014/24/EU has introduced a new procedure: the innovation partnership. Its use is characterized by the need for an innovative product, service or work that cannot be met by products, services or works already available on the market. The partnership aims at the development and the subsequent purchase of the supplies, services or works, provided that they correspond to the performance levels and maximum costs agreed between the contracting authorities and the participants.[133] The partnership is structured in successive phases. In the procurement documents, the contracting authority has to explain the nature and scope of the required solution and so that operators can decide whether to request to participate. This has to be done within 30 days from the date on which the contract notice is sent. In selecting candidates, contracting authorities will apply criteria concerning the candidates' capacity in the field of research and development and implementation of innovative solutions Only those operators invited after assessment may submit research and innovation projects.[134] Tenderers whose tenders have not been eliminated will be informed about any changes to the technical specifications or other procurement documents and will be granted sufficient time to modify and re-submit their amended tenders. Of course, confidential information cannot be disclosed without consent. To reduce the number of tenders to be negotiated by applying the award criteria, negotiations may take place in successive stages.[135] The innovation partnership sets intermediate targets to be attained by the partners and provides for payment in appropriate instalments. Based on those targets, the contracting authority may decide after each phase to terminate the innovation partnership or, in the case of an innovation partnership with several partners, to reduce the number of partners by terminating individual contracts, if those possibilities were indicated in the procurement documents.[136]

5.5.6 *Negotiated procedure without prior publication*

As the negotiated procedure without prior publication does not allow for true competition, it can be used only in very exceptional circumstances and when allowed for by national law. This can be the case when no (suitable) tenders or (suitable) requests to participate have been submitted in response to an open or restricted procedure or in cases of extreme urgency caused by an unforeseeable event.[137]

5.6 *Procurement tools*

Directive 2014/24/EU provides a few techniques and instruments for electronic and aggregated procurement to assist contracting authorities.

5.6.1 *Framework agreements*

A framework agreement is an agreement between one or more contracting authorities and one or more economic operators, to establish the terms governing contracts to be awarded during a given period, specifically regarding price and, where appropriate, the quantity envisaged.[138] It sets out the terms and conditions for subsequent call-offs that can be made throughout the term of the agreement but places no obligations on the authorities to buy. In principle, the agreement

133. Art. 31 (1) Dir. 2014/24/EU.
134. Art. 31 (6) Dir. 2014/24/EU.
135. Art. 31 (5) Dir. 2017/24/EU.
136. Art. 31 (2) Dir. 2014/24/EU.
137. Art. 32(2) Dir. 2014/24/EU.
138. Art. 33(1) Dir. 2014/24/EU.

cannot exceed four years and has to be published in the Official Journal if the threshold is exceeded and there is no specific exclusion. When assessing the total value of the framework, the estimate should include all the potential call-offs over the lifetime of the agreement that may be made by all contracting authorities that are permitted to use the framework, not just the intended call-offs by the contracting authority which is procuring the framework agreement.[139] A benefit is that there is no need to re-advertise and re-apply the selection and award criteria from the outset.[140]

Contracts based on a framework agreement can only be concluded between the contracting authorities clearly identified for this purpose in the call for competition or the invitation to confirm interest and those economic operators party to the framework agreement.[141] Accordingly, once the framework agreement is concluded, contracts based on it cannot be concluded with other parties. Where a framework agreement is concluded with a single economic operator, contracting authorities may consult this operator in writing, requesting it to supplement its tender as necessary. If the agreement is concluded with more than one economic operator, it has to be performed without reopening competition where it sets out all the terms and the objective conditions for determining which economic operator shall perform them. When not all the terms are laid down in the framework agreement, it can also be performed through (partial)[142] reopening of competition amongst the economic operators parties to it. Article 33 (5) of the Directive contains the procedure that has to be followed when awarding the contract.

5.6.2 *Dynamic purchasing systems*

Contracting authorities may use a dynamic purchasing system for commonly used purchases.[143] The system is completely electronic and relies on a list of registered suppliers that submit the terms on which they are willing to supply products or services.[144] As the rules of the restricted procedure are applicable,[145] any economic operator may request to participate in the system and all admitted participants will be invited to submit a tender for each specific procurement. Contrary to the situation under a framework agreement, contracting authorities have to publish a new tender for every order and initial tenders are not used to reduce the number of suppliers since new suppliers can be added to the list any time, regardless of the merits of the tender.[146]

5.6.3 *Electronic auctions*

Contracting authorities can in principle decide that the award of a public contract will be preceded by an electronic auction when the content of the procurement documents can be established with precision.[147] After the full initial evaluation of the tenders in accordance with the award criteria, all tenderers that have submitted admissible tenders will be invited simultaneously to participate in the electronic auction. The invitation is accompanied by the outcome of the full evaluation of the relevant tender and states the mathematical formula to be used in the electronic auction. After new prices, revised downwards, and/or new values concerning

139. Office of Government Commerce, *Framework Agreements OGC Guidance on Framework Agreements in the Procurement Regulations*, Sept. 2008, 5.
140. Office of Government Commerce, op. cit., *supra* note 139, 3.
141. Art. 33(2) Dir. 2014/24/EU.
142. Art. 33(4) Dir. 2014/24/EU.
143. Art. 34(1) Dir. 2014/24/EU.
144. S. Arrowsmith, op. cit. *supra* note 25, 257.
145. The time limits are not the same as those applied in the restricted procedure. Art. 34(2) Dir. 2014/24/EU.
146. S. Arrowsmith, op. cit. *supra* note 25, 257.
147. Art. 35(1) and (2) Dir. 2014/24/EU.

certain elements of the tender are presented, the auction allows for the automatic re-ranking of the tenders by using automatic evaluation methods. The mathematical formula on which these methods are based have to be communicated to the tenderers.[148] Throughout each phase of the auction, tenderers receive sufficient information to ascertain their relative ranking at any moment. The auction is a repetitive electronic process and will be closed at the time specified in advance or when no more valid new prices of values are submitted.[149] An advantage of electronic auctions is that suppliers can ascertain at any time their ranking and determine whether they have submitted the best offer.

5.6.4 *Electronic catalogues*

Where the use of electronic means of communication is required, contracting authorities may require tenders to be presented in the format of an electronic catalogue or to include an electronic catalogue.[150] Electronic catalogues can be qualified as permanent electronic auctions. Public authorities place their orders through them and are in charge of monitoring, approving, publishing and following the catalogues online. Companies display their offers via the platform, where maximum visibility is granted and receive their orders from the public sector electronically. This technique simplifies the processes followed by suppliers to create offers, while buyers can automate processes for reception, evaluation, purchasing and invoicing.[151]

5.6.5 *Centralized procurement and joint procurement*

Member States can provide that contracting authorities may acquire supplies and/or services from a central purchasing body offering the acquisition of supplies and/or services intended for contracting authorities. They may also provide that contracting authorities can acquire works, supplies and services by using contracts awarded by a central purchasing body.[152] These bodies will always use electronic means of communication.[153] This option brings about more homogeneity, relieves individual contracting authorities from conducting the procedures and saves time and costs. It is possible for two or more contracting authorities to agree to perform certain specific procurements jointly, even if they are located in different Member States.[154]

5.7 *Contract performance*

Contrary to Directive 2004/18/EC, Directive 2014/24/EU contains some specific clauses on contract performance. This is interesting, since the goal of the European Union has traditionally been to guarantee equal access to procurement procedures rather than a general harmonization.[155] Contracting authorities can lay down special conditions relating to the performance of a contract as long as these are linked to the subject-matter of the contract and indicated in the call for competition or in the procurement documents.[156] Such conditions may include economic, innovation-related, environmental, social or employment-related considerations. In this regard, there is a growing tendency to require companies entrusted with the execution of large public

148. Art. 35(6) Dir. 2014/24/EU.
149. Art. 35(8) Dir. 2014/24/EU.
150. Art. 36(1) Dir. 2014/24/EU.
151. European Communities, *Electronic catalogues in electronic public procurement*, 2007, 10.
152. Art. 37(1) Dir. 2014/24/EU.
153. Art. 37(3) Dir. 2014/24/EU.
154. Art. 38(1) and 39(1) Dir. 2014/24/EU.
155. F. Judo, "Uitkijken naar Sisyphus, Een eerste kennismaking met het voorstel van richtlijn betreffende het gunnen van overheidsopdrachten", (2012) *Tijdschrift voor Aannemingsrecht*, 49.
156. Art. 70 Dir. 2014/24/EU. Case C-552/13 *Grupo Hospitalario Quirón.*

works contracts to pursue corporate social responsibility (CSR).[157] The Directive contains rules on modification of contracts during their term which is only allowed for in limited circumstances.[158] It also contains provisions on subcontracting and the termination of contracts.[159]

6. Utilities procurement

The legislative package that was published on 28 March 2014 foresees in a new Directive on utilities procurement: Directive 2014/25/EU. This Directive replaces Directive 2004/17/EC and is applicable in the fields of gas and heat, electricity, water, transport services, ports and airports, postal services, extraction of oil and gas and exploration for, or extraction of, coal or other solid fuels.[160] The procurement principles that are applicable when Directive 2014/24/EU is used, are also applicable to these specific sectors.[161] The utilities directive contains comparable procedures and techniques. It will not be further discussed in this chapter.

7. Concessions

Service concessions were specifically excluded from the application of Directives 2004/18/EC and 2004/17/EC.[162] An important novelty that was brought about by the 2014 legislative package, was the introduction of Directive 2014/23/EU on the award of concession contracts. It is applicable to works and services concessions. These are contracts for pecuniary interest concluded in writing by means of which one or more contracting authorities or entities entrust the execution of works and the management of services to one or more economic operators. Under EU law, the service that is the subject of a service concession must be in the general interest, so that a public authority is institutionally responsible for providing it. The typical beneficiaries will be third-party members of the general public.[163] An example of a service concession is the exploitation for commercial purposes of an electronic telephone database.[164]

The consideration consists either solely in the right to exploit the works or in that right together with payment. The absence of (full), compensation to the concessionaire constitutes the essence of a concession. Since he only obtains income and generates profits if he can successfully exploit the services/works, a significant proportion of the risk is put on the concessionaire. Since concession contracts have a specific nature, they are generally used for complex, long-term and high value projects and to make public-private cooperation possible. Private capital and know-how is used to supplement the limited public capital. As this special nature calls for a more flexible regime, the concessions directive does not refer to standard procedures to award a contract but nevertheless offers some procedural guarantees.[165] Contracting authorities and contracting entities wishing to award a concession have to use a concession notice and the award of a contract has to be published.[166] Concessions have to be awarded on the basis of objective criteria which comply with the principles of equal treatment, non-discrimination and transparency. To identify an overall economic advantage for the contracting authority, tenders

157. C. McCrudden, op. cit. *supra* note 9, 404.
158. Art. 72 Dir. 2014/24/EU; Case C-454/06, *Pressetext;* Case C-549/14 *Finn Frogne.*
159. Art. 71 and 73 Dir. 2014/24/EU.
160. Arts. 8–14 Dir. 2014/25/EU.
161. Art. 36 Dir. 2014/25/EU.
162. Art. 17 Dir. 2004/18/EC and Art. 18 Dir. 2004/17/EC. Dir. 2004/18/EC did however include a chapter on works concessions. In case of cross border interest, the treaty principles will be applicable.
163. C. Bovis, op. cit. *supra* note 4, 336.
164. Case C-324/98, *Telaustria.*
165. Art. 37 Dir. 2014/23/EU.
166. Arts. 31 and 32 Dir. 2014/23/EU.

have to be assessed in conditions of effective competition/The award criteria have to be linked to the subject-matter of the concession, and cannot confer an unrestricted freedom of choice on the contracting authority/entity. They can include, *inter alia*, environmental, social or innovation-related criteria.[167]

8. Remedies

The European public procurement system has a specific set of remedies. Directives 89/665/EEC and 92/13/EEC relating to review procedures concerning the award of public contracts were both amended by Directive 2007/66/EC. As held by Article 2a of Directive 89/665/EEC, after the award decision is taken, the contract cannot be concluded before the expiry of at least 10 to 15 calendar days depending on the means of communication. This is the codification of the *Alcatel* judgment.[168] This gives bidders time to examine the decision and decide whether to initiate a review procedure. Member States are obliged to ensure that decisions taken by contracting authorities can be reviewed effectively and as rapidly as possible and that there is sufficient time for effective review to at least any person having or having had an interest in obtaining a particular contract and who has been or risks being harmed by an alleged infringement.[169] On the basis of the principle of procedural autonomy, Member States can organize such review procedures themselves. They can for example determine the time limit to enact a review procedure, provided that such period is at least 10 to 15 calendar days following the date on which the decision is sent and depending on the means of communication.[170] In case a review procedure is started, the procurement process will automatically be suspended until the review body has taken its decision. Review decisions include powers to take interim measures, to set aside unlawful decisions and to award damages.[171] Where damages are claimed on the grounds that a decision was taken unlawfully, Member States may provide that the contested decision must first be set aside by a review body.[172] It has been noted that while the requirement of proof of fault can be a substantial condition for a successful damages claim in some Member States, this does not satisfy the effective and rapid review mechanisms called for in Article 1 (1) of the Directive.[173]

If it considers that there was a serious infringement of procurement law during a contract award procedure, the European Commission can also start a special infringement procedure.[174]

After the contract is concluded it can be considered ineffective if certain conditions are fulfilled. This is for example the case when a contract has been awarded without prior publication. The consequences of an ineffective contract have to be provided for by national law.[175] Ineffectiveness can result in the retrospective in cancellation of contractual obligations or the reduction of contractual obligations. In the latter case Member State have to provide for alternative penalties such as the imposition of fines or the shortening of the duration of the contract.[176]

---

167. Art. 41 Dir. 2014/23/EU.
168. Art. 2a Dir. 89/665/EEC; Case C-81/98, *Alcatel.*
169. Art. 1(3) and 2a(1) Dir. 89/665/EEC.
170. Art. 2c Dir. 89/665/EEC; Case C-470/99, *Universale-Bau* and Case C-78/98, *Preston;* Case C-249/01, *Hackermüller.*
171. Art. 2 Dir. 89/665/EEC.
172. Art. 2(6) Dir. 665/89/EEC.
173. H. Schebesta, "Community law requirements for remedies in the field of public procurement: Damages", (2010) *European Procurement & Public Private Partnership Law Review,* 32; Case C-275/03, *Commission v. Portugal.*
174. Art. 3 Dir. 89/665/EEC.
175. Art. 2d (2) Dir. 89/665/EEC.
176. Art. 2e Dir. 89/665/EEC; C. Bovis, op. cit. *supra* note 4, 197.

It goes without saying that even though the European public procurement system knows a specific set of remedies, the general principles of effectiveness and equivalence have to be respected as well.

9. Future outlook and conclusion

The public procurement approaches as developed within the framework of the WTO and the European Union evolved in close relationship and cross-fertilized each other. They aim to remove legal and administrative barriers to trade in government markets by eliminating preferential and discriminatory purchase patterns. By increasing competitiveness contracting authorities will be better equipped to achieve value for money when purchasing goods, works or services. Even though the EU procurement market is open to foreign bidders, the markets of third countries remain to a large extent closed. For this reason, the Commission adopted on 21 March 2012 a proposal for a Regulation on the access of third-country goods and services to the Union, also called the proposal on an 'International Procurement Instrument'.[177] The proposal, which was amended in January 2016,[178] aims at encouraging partners to open participation for EU bidders in third countries' tenders by incorporating a price penalty to bidders, products or services of countries that apply barriers to EU participation in procurement if more than 50% of the total value of the tender originates in a third country.[179] Bidders can still be awarded the contract if their offer remains competitive in terms of price and quality despite the price penalty.

Economic goals are not the only ones that are pursued by procurement regimes. Since the late 1980s the European Union has developed its social dimension significantly and there has been an increasing emphasis on ethical and environmental concerns. Public procurement is seen as a useful tool to contribute to these policies. Increased attention to sustainability has been translated in the 2014 procurement package. It is expected that a(n electronic) procurement system that is business friendly and socially responsible will not only deliver cost efficiencies but also support innovation, investment and sustainable economic growth. Nevertheless, it remains up to the contracting authority to decide how much weight can be granted to those considerations.

The asylum crisis, which makes the European Union face numerous challenges due to a steeply increased influx of asylum seekers, has demonstrated the importance of public procurement. It has created an explosive need for infrastructure, supplies and services such as food, tents and medical services. The application of Directive 2014/24/EU allows contracting authorities to purchase these facilities in an economically responsible manner and react fast if required by applying an accelerated procedure or, if necessary, a negotiated procedure without publication.[180] It remains to be seen whether all needs can be satisfied in this way and whether the crisis will influence the application of the procurement system.

Further reading

Arrowsmith, S., *The Law of Public and Utilities Procurement* (Sweet & Maxwell, 2014).

Arrowsmith, S., "Public procurement: Basic concepts and the coverage of procurement rules" in S. Arrowsmith (Ed.), *Public Procurement: An Introduction* (Asia Link – EuropeAid Co-operation Office, 2010).

---

177. COM(2012)124 final.
178. COM(2016)34 final.
179. Art. 8 and 11 COM(2016)34 final.
180. Communication of 9 Sept. 2015 from the Commission to the European Parliament and the Council on Public Procurement rules in connection with the current asylum crisis, COM(2015)454 final.

Bovis, C., *EU Public Procurement Law* (Elgar European Law, 2007 and 2013).
Bovis, C., "Access to justice and remedies in public procurement", (2012) *European Procurement & Public Private Partnership Law Review*. 195–202.
Judo, F., "Uitkijken naar Sisyphus, Een eerste kennismaking met het voorstel van richtlijn betreffende het gunnen van overheidsopdrachten", (2012) *Tijdschrift voor Aannemingsrecht*, 34–53.
Lynch, J., *Public Procurement & Contract Administration: A Brief Introduction* (Lean Publishing, 2013).
McCrudden, C., *Buying Social Justice* (OUP, 2007).
Reich, A., *International Public Procurement Law: The Evolution of International Regimes on Public Purchasing* (Kluwer, 1999), 71–2.
Schebesta, H., "Community law requirements for remedies in the field of public procurement: Damages", (2010) *European Procurement & Public Private Partnership Law Review*, 23–37.

CHAPTER 23
TAXATION

*Dennis Weber**

1. Introduction

Within the EU, direct taxation (income tax, corporate tax, inheritance tax, etc.) is largely not regulated. EU law, however, is of great influence; the EU treaty freedoms, and the provisions concerning State Aid are increasingly having effect on domestic direct tax law. In the field of indirect taxation, there is unification (customs), harmonization (VAT) and coordination (energy taxation). The Customs Union is an exclusive Union Competence (Art. 3(1)(a) TFEU), the rest of direct and indirect taxation are shared competences with "preemption", which means that at the moment the Union exercises its competence, the Member States lose their competence in that field.

2. EU treaty freedoms in taxation cases

2.1 *Introduction*

The EU treaty freedoms have great influence on direct taxation (corporate taxation/income taxation). To date, in more than 335 judgments in 25 years, the Court has had to rule on the interpretation of the EU Treaty freedoms in direct tax cases.

In the absence of unifying or harmonizing measures adopted in the Union, the Member States remain competent to determine the criteria for taxation of income and wealth with a view to eliminating double taxation. In this context, the Member States are at liberty, to define, by treaty or unilaterally, the criteria for allocating their powers of taxation, according to the Court in cases such as *Gilly*, *Saint-Gobain* and *Van Hilten.*[1]

Although the Member States are thus at liberty to determine the criteria for taxation concerning the levy of direct taxation, the Member States may not restrict the free movement with their domestic measures.[2]

For the answer to the question which national tax provisions fall under the scope of application of the EU Treaty freedoms and which do not, a distinction must be drawn between disadvantages which arise in the exercising of the free movement and which can be traced back to:

a. the legislation of one Member State;

---

* Professor European Corporate tax law; Amsterdam Centre for Tax Law (ACTL) of the University of Amsterdam.

1. See Case C-307/97, *Saint-Gobain*, para 56, Case C-336/96, *Gilly*, paras. 24 and 30, and Case C-513/03, *Van Hilten*, para 47.
2. See, for example, Case C-307/97, *Saint-Gobain* and Case C-385/00, *De Groot*.

b. the existence within the EU of different kinds of tax systems (quasi-; restrictions/ disparity/dislocation).

The disadvantages under point a. are covered by the treaty freedoms and can be considered (discriminatory) restrictions of the free movement. Here below in section 2.2 a number of examples of suchlike restrictions will be provided. The disadvantages under point b. fall outside the scope of application of the treaty freedoms because they are inherent to the sovereign right to which the Member States are entitled to levy tax. The disadvantage, in other words, arises from a disparity (also called quasi-restriction or dislocation). In section 2.3. tax disparities will be discussed.

2.2 *Tax restrictions in the case law of the court*

2.2.1 *(Indirect) discrimination on grounds of nationality*

Any discrimination on grounds of nationality shall be prohibited (Art. 18 TFEU). In direct taxation cases, playing a role in this framework in particular is the fact that non-resident taxpayers are often treated differently and less favourably than resident taxpayers. This less favourable treatment on the basis of residence is considered by the Court as an indirect discrimination against nationality, because this distinction in particular has a detrimental effect for non-resident taxpayers who usually have the nationality of another Member State. In *Asscher,*[3] for example, a non-resident taxpayer was due 25% income tax, whereas a resident taxpayer was only due 6% income tax. The Court considered this an indirect discrimination against nationality. Although Article 18 TFEU prohibits *any* discrimination on grounds of nationality, in the case law of the Court we see especially that discrimination of nationals of other Member States is forbidden. The Court is milder when it concerns discrimination of own nationals (reverse discrimination). An example is *Van Hilten,*[4] which concerned an anti-abuse provision in Netherlands inheritance tax which laid down, in short, that the Netherlands could levy inheritance tax on the worldwide estate of an individual with Netherlands nationality when he dies within ten years after emigration from the Netherlands. Although with this provision the Netherlands clearly discriminated its own nationals (the estate of a German citizen whose death occurred within ten years after emigration from the Netherlands was not affected by the provision) the Court saw no discrimination.

2.2.2 *Allowances related to personal and family circumstances*

For benefits related to personal and family circumstances, the Court sets out a special approach in, *Schumacker.*[5] For benefits related to personal and family circumstances, we can think of tax free amounts, personal exemptions, (for example, exemptions which are dependent on the number of children or whether the person is married or not). These are allowances which enhance the taxpayer's ability to pay tax (see also *Schulz,*[6] para 39). In international tax law (OECD Model Tax Convention) such allowances are only taken into account by the Member State of the resident taxpayer. Personal and family allowances, therefore, are not taken into account for non-resident taxpayers. This creates a tension with the free movement of workers given that due to this, on the basis of residence, an indirect discrimination against nationality arises. In the *Schumacker* case, the Court ruled with regard to personal and family allowances that the

---

3. Case C-107/94, *Asscher.*
4. Case C-513/03, *Van Hilten.*
5. Case C-279/93, *Schumacker.*
6. Case C-240/10, *Schultz.*

situation of residents and non-resident taxpayers are not comparable. The Court considered (para 32): "Income received in the territory of a Member State by a non-resident is in most cases only a part of his total income, which is concentrated at his place of residence. Moreover, a non-resident's personal ability to pay tax, determined by reference to his aggregate income and his personal and family circumstances, is more easy to assess at the place where his personal and financial interests are centred. In general, that is the place where he has his usual abode. Accordingly, international tax law, and in particular the Model Double Taxation Treaty of the Organization for Economic Cooperation and Development (OECD), recognizes that in principle the overall taxation of taxpayers, taking account of their personal and family circumstances, is a matter for the State of residence".

Union law, therefore, respects the rule of international tax law that personal and family allowances should be taken into account only for resident taxpayers.

In the *Schumacker case,* however, the Court immediately made an exception to this: A Member State must also take into account personal and family allowances of a non-resident taxpayer, i. where the non-resident receives no significant income in the State of his residence and obtains the major part of his taxable income for an activity performed in the State of employment (major income test); and ii. where his personal and family allowances are not taken into account either in the State of residence or in the State of employment (no deduction test). In the *Schumacker* case, these conditions were satisfied: Schumacker resided in Belgium and worked in Germany. For Germany, he was a non-resident taxpayer and Germany did not in the first instance have to take into account the personal and family allowances. Schumacker, however, received 100% of his income in Germany (thus, satisfied the major income test) and in Belgium, account could not be taken of his personal and family allowances (after all, he had no income there).

The interpretation of the *Schumacker* exception is not always quite clear. For example, what is a major part of a person's taxable income? Is this 90%, is it 85%? It is made clear from *Gilly* that when a non-taxpayer derives 100% of his income in the State of employment, he has still not satisfied the *Schumacher* exception when his personal and family allowances are taken into account via deduction on the income of his partner (because the Member State of residence taxed the family income which allowed Gilly to shift her allowance to her partner[7]). In *Commission/Estonia,*[8] only 50% income was derived in the residence State (Finland) and 50% income in the work State (Estonia). It could be expected that in this case, Estonia would not have to take into account the personal and family allowances of a non-resident taxpayer given that only 50% of the income is derived in Estonia. The Court, nevertheless, ruled that because of "the modest amount of worldwide income", the income of the taxpayer was not taxable in Finland, such that "that State is not in a position to take into account the ability to pay tax and the personal and family circumstances of the person concerned". Because Finland as the resident State could thus not take into account the personal and family allowances, it was Estonia that had to take into account (despite the fact that only 50% of the income was derived in Estonia) the personal and family allowances. It would seem to follow from this that the major income test is no longer of such relevance, but that, according to the Court, it concerns if somewhere within the EU the personal and family allowances are taken into account. This is what some call the always-somewhere or one-market approach.[9]

The *Schumacker* case law can be criticized. The fact that no Member State at all takes account of the personal and family circumstances is namely not a discrimination which arises from the

7. Case C-336/96, *Gilly.*
8. Case C-39/10, *Commission v. Estonia.*
9. See P. Wattel and B. Terra, *European Tax Law* (Kluwer, 2008), 898.

legislation of one Member State, but is the cause of a disparity (the applicability of different tax systems). In addition, it would seem to be much more in accordance with national treatment to allocate the personal and family allowance to non-resident taxpayers pro-rata according to the national part of the world income. Under such a pro-rata system, when a non-resident earns, for example, 40% of his worldwide income in the work State, then he receives in the work State 40% of the personal and family allowances applicable there.[10]

2.2.3 *Horizontal discrimination*

One phenomenon which is called "horizontal discrimination" is that a national provision draws no distinction between a domestic situation and a foreign situation, but a distinction between two foreign situations. For example, Member State A taxes a source of income more heavily if that source belongs to a resident of Member State B, as compared to the case that the source belongs to a resident of Member State C.

When such a horizontal discrimination is the consequence of the application of a tax treaty then, according to the Court, there is no discrimination. This was at issue in Case C-376/03,[11] *D*. Mr D, resident in Germany, was not entitled to a tax allowance for the Netherlands wealth taxation, whereas a taxpayer, for that matter in the same situation, who was resident in Belgium, was entitled to a tax allowance on the basis of the tax treaty concluded between Belgium and the Netherlands. The Court rejected horizontal discrimination insofar as the disadvantage from a bilateral tax treaty arises on the basis of: i. the fact that the reciprocal rights and obligations in a tax treaty only apply to persons resident in one of the two Contracting Member States is an inherent consequence of bilateral double taxation conventions; and ii. when the rule cannot be regarded as a benefit separable from the remainder of the Convention, but is an integral part thereof and contributes to its overall balance.[12]

It appears from the *D* case that the Court is mild as concerns horizontal discrimination which finds its source in a tax treaty. When horizontal discrimination arises on the basis of national law, however, that discrimination is prohibited unless there is an objective difference. An example of this can be found in *Orange European Smallcap Fund*[13] and *Sopora.*[14] In this latter case, national legislation was at issue, by which the Netherlands provided that workers who resided in another Member State prior to taking up employment in the Netherlands are to be granted a tax advantage consisting of a flat-rate exemption of expenses in an amount up to 30% of the taxable income. This tax advantage was only granted on the condition that those workers resided at a distance of more than 150 km from the Netherlands border. This condition has as a consequence that most Belgian workers and some German, French, Luxembourgish and United Kingdom workers are excluded from the benefit of the flat-rate rule. Of importance was that in the judgment, the Court considered that the freedom of workers also prohibits discrimination *between* non-resident workers if such discrimination leads to nationals of certain Member States being unduly favoured in comparison with others. With this ruling, the Court has made clear that also horizontal discrimination on the basis of national law could be forbidden.

10. P. Wattel and B. Terra, op. cit. *supra* note 9, at 989.
11. Case C-376/03, *D.*
12. See for another example, Case C-374/04, *Test Claimants in Class IV of the ACT GLO.*
13. Case C-196/06, *Orange European Smallcap Fund.*
14. Case C-512/13, *Sopora.*

2.2.4 *Restriction of free movement*

In tax law, some violations of EU treaty freedoms can be traced back to (indirect) discrimination against nationality, but there are different national measures which do not discriminate against nationality as such, but which do render exercising the free movement less attractive. Such measures do not discriminate against *nationality*, but draw a distinction between a domestic and a foreign situation.

Good examples are exit taxes. Exit taxes are levied when a company or an individual relocates its place of residence to another State. Obviously, these levies do not apply to purely domestic situations. In cases such as *Lasteyrie*,[15] *N*[16] (for individuals) and *National Grid Indus*[17] (for companies) the Court considered such exit taxes (under certain conditions) a restriction of the free movement. In many cases, the Court has considered national provisions, which discriminate not so much against nationality but which do restrict the free movement because they draw a distinction between domestic and foreign situations, a restriction. We see this, for example, in cases concerning the prevention of economic double taxation. When a company has to pay company tax on profits made and that profit is distributed to the shareholder, so-called economic double taxation arises when this dividend is taxed again on the shareholder. Member States, therefore, often prevent double taxation by, for example, granting exemption to the shareholder from paying tax on the dividend, applying a low rate to the dividend, or by allowing set off of the double taxation already paid. In the past, this prevention of economic double taxation was only granted for domestic dividend and not for foreign dividends. In cases such as *Manninen*,[18] *Lenz*,[19] and *Haribo*,[20] the Court considered such distinction, under conditions, a restriction of the free movement.

The fact that a domestic loss is taken into account (for example, a loss on an immovable property situated in the Member State) and a foreign loss is not taken into account has also been the subject of many cases before the Court. The Court considers the not taking into account of foreign losses in such a case a restriction of the free movement. Examples of this are *Marks & Spencer* (loss of a foreign subsidiary),[21] *Lidl Belgium*[22] (loss of a foreign permanent establishment) and *K* (loss of foreign immovable property).[23] Note that the Court does accept a justification for the not taking into account of foreign loss, namely, the fact that this endangers the balanced allocation of the power to tax between the Member States (see further on this, section 2.5.).

Another question is if tax provisions which make no distinction between domestic and cross-border situations can constitute a restriction of the free movement. It is shown from *Viacom*[24] and *Mobistar*[25] that in tax cases, the Court is of the opinion that for a measure without distinction particularly a restriction is present if this makes in fact or in law the exercising of free movement more onerous.

---

15. Case C-9/02, *Lasteyrie.*
16. Case C-470/04, *N.*
17. Case C-371/10, *National Grid Indus.*
18. C-319/02, *Manninen.*
19. C-315/02, *Lenz.*
20. C-436/08, C-437/08, *Haribo.*
21. Case C-446/03, *Marks & Spencer.*
22. Case C-414/06, *Lidl Belgium.*
23. Case C-123/11, *K.*
24. Case C-134/03, *Viacom.*
25. C-544/03 and C-545/03, *Mobistar.*

Mobistar concerned a direct municipal tax which was levied on pylons, masts and antennas for GSM reception. In dealing with the question if this tax is in conflict with the freedom to provide services, the Court reiterates the case law in which it was ruled that measures without distinction which are applicable to domestic service providers and services to foreign providers can also constitute a restriction. In the judgment, the Court emphasizes that there can be a restriction if the national rule affects the provision of services between the Member States more adversely than the provision of services within a Member State. Furthermore, the Court emphasizes that "measures, the only effect of which is to create additional costs in respect of the service in question and which affect in the same way the provision of services between Member States and that within one Member State, do not fall within the scope of" the freedom to provide services.

Applied to the case in *Mobistar,* the Court ruled that the tax without distinction was applicable to domestic and foreign service providers and thus, the foreign operators in fact were even affected more adversely than the national operators. In addition, the Court considered the following:

> "it is necessary to point out that such taxes apply without distinction to all owners of mobile telephone installations within the commune in question, and that foreign operators are not, either in fact or in law, more adversely affected by those measures than national operators. Nor do the tax measures in question make cross-border service provision more difficult than national service provision. Admittedly, introducing a tax on pylons, masts and antennae can make tariffs for mobile telephone communications to Belgium from abroad and vice versa more expensive. However, national telephone service provision is, to the same extent, subject to the risk that the tax will have an impact on tariffs".

A measure without distinction which has exactly the same effect in domestic and in cross border situations (thus, which is neutral; such as in *Mobistar*) can, according to the Court, only constitute a restriction of free movement if the access to the market is endangered by the measure. An example is *Danske Bilimportører.*[26] The question in this case was if a Danish registration tax on new motor vehicles was in conflict with the provisions on the free movement. The Danish tax in the first tax bracket was 108% on the purchase price and 180% on the remainder. The Court first established that the tax was not in conflict with Article 110 TFEU (the prohibition on a higher tax on foreign products), given that Denmark did not have domestic production of cars and thus there could be no question of a discrimination within the meaning of Article 110 TFEU. But in the judgment the Court keeps open the possibility that despite the circumstance that a domestic tax is applicable without distinction and does not affect the free (cross border) movement more adversely than the domestic movement, there could be a restriction. This arises if "charges of such an amount" are levied that the free movement of goods within the common market could be endangered. In other words: if access to the market is obstructed. In *Danske Bilimportører,* this did not occur because according to the Court, it could in no way be derived from the figures on the number of new vehicles registered in Denmark and thus on the number of vehicles imported into the Member State, that the free movement of this type of goods between Denmark and the other Member States was endangered.

Examples of tax measures without distinction but which restrict the free movement, although scarce, are to be found in the case law of the Court.

26. Case C-383/01, *Danske Bilimportører.*

One example is *De Coster*,[27] another example is to be found in *Deutsche Shell*.[28] In this case, it had a registered office in Germany and a permanent establishment in Italy. A currency loss that was suffered on (a transfer) of capital (in Italian lira) from the Italian permanent establishment could not be deducted from the (worldwide) profit in Germany. A comparison with a purely German situation was not so obvious in this case, given that in the case of a permanent establishment in Germany, this cannot be financed so readily with Italian liras. If one should assume such a hypothetical situation, however, then the currency loss would be deductible in Germany. The problem that arises in this case is that the underlying issue only arises in fact in cross border situations. The Court ruled that there could be a restriction of the free movement "where, on account of a tax law, a company may be deterred from setting up subsidiary bodies such as permanent establishments in other Member States and from carrying on its activities through such bodies" (para 29) and went on to consider (para 30): "As the Advocate General observed in points 43 and 44 of her Opinion, the tax system concerned in the main proceedings increases the economic risks incurred by a company established in one Member State wishing to set up a body in another Member State where the currency used is different from that of the State of origin. In such a situation, not only does the principal establishment face the normal risks associated with setting up such a body, but it must also face an additional risk of a fiscal nature where it provides start-up capital for it".

Here, the Court would appear to take the middle ground as to whether there is a measure with distinction or without, and rules that in light of the fact that the disadvantage that arises from the German rule (non-deductible currency loss) only occurs in cross border situations, there is a restriction. In the approach of the Court, it would seem that the Court is of the opinion that a measure which is applicable without distinction but which hinders cross border situations particularly, is a prohibited restriction.

One of the most recent judgments is *Hervis*.[29] In this case, a Hungarian tax on the turnover of enterprises was applicable. The tax was applicable without distinction to both domestic enterprises and to foreign enterprises. The rate structure, however, was steeply progressive and the taxable basis for taxpayers who belonged to a company group was formed by the consolidated turnover of all the affiliated taxpayers of the group. This meant that the progressive rate was based on a notional turnover. For separate legal persons, such as independent franchisees, the progressive rate was only based on their own turnover. The Court considered (para 39): "In those circumstances, if it is established that, on the store retail market in the Member State concerned, the taxable persons belonging to a group of companies and covered by the highest band of the special tax are, in the majority of cases, "linked", within the meaning of the national legislation, to companies which have their registered offices in other Member States, the application of the steeply progressive scale of the special tax to a consolidated tax base consisting of turnover is liable to disadvantage, in particular, taxable persons "linked" to companies which have their registered office in another Member State". Here also, we see that a measure without distinction can in fact constitute a discrimination of foreign situations.

2.3 *Tax disparities in the case law of the Court*

Tax disparities (quasi-restrictions/dislocations) arise from national tax systems existing alongside each other and can have negative effects for the operation of the internal market (such as double taxation). Such negative effects have to be removed either by bilateral or multilateral

27. Case *C-17/00, De Coster.*
28. Case *C-293/06, Deutsche Shell.*
29. Case C-385/12, *Hervis.*

treaties or by Union law and cannot be regarded as a restriction of movement. That, in a nutshell, is what follows from the case law of the Court.

An example that disadvantages that arise from the legislation of two Member States do not constitute a restriction of the free movement is to be found in the problems concerning juridical double taxation. This was the question in *Kerckhaert-Morres.*[30] In this case, Kerckhaert-Morres, a married couple who resided in Belgium, received a dividend from France. In Belgium, dividends (both domestic and foreign) are taxed at a rate of 25%. Here thus, is a measure with no distinction. France levied 15% tax at source on the dividend. In this case, the question was if Belgium was obliged to credit this 15% tax. The Member States in this case argued, amongst others, that there was a disparity and that it was not Belgium but France which imposed the restriction. The European Commission, on the contrary, took the position that there was a restriction, the source of which was to be found in the applicability of the same rule to objectively different situations. According to the Commission, the domestic situation and the cross border situation are not comparable because French source tax is levied on the cross border dividend. It held the view that Belgium must take account of this inequality by crediting the French source tax. The Court, however, was of the opinion that there was no question of a prohibited restriction, but of an allowed disparity:

> "In circumstances such as those of the present case, the adverse consequences which might arise from the application of an income tax system such as the Belgian system at issue in the main proceedings result from the exercise in parallel by two Member States of their fiscal sovereignty".

In this case, we see an example of negative effects for the operation of the internal market which arises from national tax systems existing alongside each other. Such negative effects had to be removed either by bilateral or multilateral treaties or by Union law. If such a disadvantage should constitute a precluded restriction of the free movement, then the Court would have to take a political decision. The Court, namely, would have to identify which Member State may not levy tax. In that case, the Court would be taking the place of the legislature. In the literature, there is still an on-going discussion on the question of whether the negative consequences of quasi-restrictions (particularly double taxation and not being able to set off cross border loses) should be considered a prohibited restriction of the treaty freedoms. Vanistendael,[31] Kofler and Mason are of the opinion that double taxation must be considered a prohibited restriction.[32] Wattel is of the opinion that not being able to set off cross border losses is the consequence of a dislocation of the tax base and therefore, is allowed.[33]

In the literature, the disadvantages mentioned above are given different names such as: "disparity", "quasi-restriction", "distortion" or "dislocation". The term "disparity" is the most common but its meaning is not completely correct. The term "disparity", namely, is often used as a synonym for "different". Because of this, some assume that the disadvantage of the simultaneous application of the legislation of two Member States only occurs when the legislation of these two Member States is *different.*[34] That, in my view however, is incorrect: where the legislation of two Member States is completely identical, a disadvantage can also be present which arises from

30. Case C-513/04, *Kerckhaert-Morres.*
31. See: F. Vanistendael, "The ECJ at the crossroads: Balancing tax sovereignty against the imperatives of the single market", (2006) *European Taxation*, 418.
32. G.W. Kofler and R. Mason, "Double taxation: A European 'switch in time'?", 14 CJEL (2007).
33. P. Wattel and B. Terra, op. cit. *supra* note 9, at 94.
34. S. Douma, "The three D of direct tax jurisdiction: Disparity, discrimination and double taxation", (2006) *European Taxation*, 522.

the legislation of the Member States whereas that legislation *does not* contain a restriction. One example can be found in *Kerckhaert-Morres,*[35] discussed further above. In this case, there was an issue of juridical double taxation. The Court was of the opinion that there was no question of a restriction of the free movement given that the disadvantage is a "result from the exercise in parallel by two Member States of their fiscal sovereignty". If the legislation of these two Member States had been entirely the same, the disadvantage of the juridical double taxation would simply have remained, but there would still not have been a restriction, nor would there have been an allowed dislocation of the tax base; the double taxation is namely allowed because this results from the exercise in parallel of the fiscal sovereignty. In this framework, it is therefore probably better to call disadvantages which fall outside the scope of application of the treaty freedoms "quasi-restrictions". A.G. *Geelhoed* did so in his Opinion in *Test Claimants in Class IV of the ACT Group Litigation.*[36] With quasi-restrictions, he meant all disadvantages which arose from the different tax systems which existed alongside each other such as: i. double administrative red tape, ii. double taxation, iii. disparities (in the sense of differences), and iv. the necessity to divide the power to tax between these systems, with as consequence, dislocation of the tax base.

2.4 *Per country versus overall approach – always somewhere approach – neutralisation of restrictions*

As is observed above, there is a restriction if a disadvantage arises in the exercising of the free movement which can be traced back to the legislation of one Member State.

This implies that a restriction of the free movement is not dependent on the legislation of *another* Member State and thus, not on disparities between legislation of different Member States (also called the "per country approach"). Nevertheless, it can be derived from the case law of the Court that for the question whether there is or is not a restriction in a certain Member State, the Court, under certain circumstances, *does* take into account the tax treatment in another Member State. Thus, in some cases, the Court takes the tax treatment in two (and not only one) Member States into account to establish if there is a restriction. The Court then applies, as it were, an overall approach.

In cases such as Case *Schumacker,*[37] *Wallentin*[38] and *De Groot* (personal tax advantages),[39] and in *Marks & Spencer,*[40] *Deutsche Shell*[41] and Case *Lidl Belgium* (foreign losses of multinationals),[42] the Court takes account of the tax treatment in another Member State. The case law of the Court in these cases is, in short, that always somewhere in the EU (in the source State or the residence State) account is taken of the personal tax benefits (such as tax free amounts, etc.) and that somewhere in the EU, account should be taken of losses. Wattel calls this case law the "always somewhere approach".[43]

---

35. Case C-513/05, *Kerckhaert-Morres.*
36. Case C-374/04, *Test Claimants in Class IV of the ACT Group Litigation.*
37. Case C-279/93, *Schumacker.*
38. Case C-169/03, *Wallentin.*
39. Case C-385/00, *De Groot.*
40. Case C-446/03, *Marks & Spencer.*
41. Case C-293/06, *Deutsche Shell.*
42. Case C-414/06, *Lidl Belgium.*
43. P. Wattel and B. Terra, op. cit. *supra* note 9, 898.

In cases such as *Denkavit International*,[44] *Amurta*,[45] (cross border dividend) and *Miljoen*[46] the Court ruled that an obstacle raised by a Member State can be "neutralized" by obligations laid down in a bilateral tax treaty concluded with another Member State.

2.5 *Balanced allocation of the power to tax, prevention of tax avoidance, effectiveness of fiscal supervision: Justifications for restrictions*

The Court has accepted a number of imperative reasons in the public interest in order to justify restrictions of the free movement in tax cases. The most important are: i. the safeguarding of the "balanced allocation of the power to tax between the Member States"; ii. the prevention of tax avoidance; and iii. Effectiveness of fiscal supervision.

2.5.1 *Balanced allocation of the power to tax*

In, amongst others *Argenta*,[47] the Court made clear that the balanced allocation of the power to tax in particular provided for the "right of a Member State to exercise its powers of taxation in relation to activities carried out in its territory". In other words: income and capital which can be imputed to the territory of a certain Member State must be able to be taxed by the Member State. In cases such as *Marks & Spencer*, the Court ruled that not taking foreign losses into account constitutes a restriction of the free movement (see for this section 2.3.4.), in the same cases, however, the Court has also ruled that on the ground of the balanced allocation of the power to tax between the Member States the restriction is justified. The Court, therefore, obliges the Member States not to import foreign losses. To date, one exception has been made, namely, when the foreign subsidiary has exhausted all possibilities to set off losses (*Marks & Spencer* exception).[48] In such a situation, the Court finds it disproportionate not to take foreign losses into account. A.G. Kokott and A.G. Mengozzi have advised the Court to repeal the *Marks & Spencer* exception, particularly because it leads to import of foreign losses and the exception leads to legal uncertainty, but the Court has still refused to do so.[49] The *Marks & Spencer* exception is another example of what is called the always somewhere approach of the Court, which means that a taxpayer, in this case, can always take its losses into account somewhere within the EU (see also section 2.4).

2.5.2 *Prevention of tax avoidance*

The Court also provides the Member States with the possibility of fighting tax avoidance by means of anti-abuse provisions. In the direct taxation case law, the Court allows combating "wholly artificial arrangements". General anti-abuse provisions which are applicable to every situation (in other words, measures that do not take into account specific circumstances that indicate abuse) or are applicable "for whatever reason" (thus without taking into account the subjective intention to abuse) are, according to the Court, too general to prevent abuse. The denial of the deduction of interest paid on loans in a group because the main shareholder is

---

44. Case C-170/05, *Denkavit International.*
45. Case C-379/05, *Amurta.*
46. Case C-10/14, C-14/10 and C-17/14, *Miljoen*, para 53.
47. Case C-350/11, *Argenta.*
48. Case C-446/03, *Marks & Spencer.* para 55, and Case 123/11, *A OY*, para 49; see also: M. Lang, "Has the case law of the ECJ on final losses reached the end of the line?", (2014) *European Taxation*, 530.
49. See A.G. Kokott in her Opinion in Case C-123/11, *A Oy*, and in C-172/13, *Commission v. UK*, and A.G. Mengozzi in his Opinion in Case C-322/11, *K.*

established abroad (*Lankhorst-Hohorst*),[50] or an anti-abuse provision that is applicable to every cross-border lease of assets (*Jobra*)[51] are examples of anti-abuse measures that are too general to justify a restrictive treatment. In cases such as *Cadbury Schweppes* and *Test Claimant in the Thin Cap GLO*,[52] the Court accepts anti-abuse rules that provide for a legal presumption of abuse, but only when the taxpayer has the opportunity, without being subject to undue administrative constraints, to provide evidence of any commercial justification that there may be for that arrangement. It is thus permitted to impose a reasonable burden of proof on the taxpayer in the sense that he must prove that, in any situation, there is no question of a "wholly artificial arrangement". In *Cadbury Schweppes*, the question was whether setting up a financing company in Ireland was a "wholly artificial arrangement". According to the Court, this would not be the case if the incorporation of this company reflected economic reality. Whether there is an economic reality must be based on objective factors which are ascertainable by third parties and, of particular importance, whether the financing company physically exists in terms of premises, staff and equipment.[53]

2.5.3 *Effectiveness of fiscal supervision*

In cross border situations, Member States are confronted with administrative obstacles and in such circumstances, access to information relevant for tax assessments is also more difficult. For that reason, many tax treaties contain provisions on the exchange of information (compare, for example, Art. 26 OECD model treaty), and furthermore, the Directive regarding mutual assistance is applicable within the EU on the basis of which information can (sometimes obligatory) be exchanged. A Member State however will, preferably unilaterally, subject a taxpayer who carries out cross border activities, to strict supervision rules in order thus to overcome the information problems. The case law of the Court demonstrates that although the Court allows scope for such fiscal measures concerning the providing of information for the benefit of supervision, it will take a stance in the case of a difference between domestic and foreign situations.

The effectiveness of fiscal supervision in this framework is an overriding reason of public interest, which is accepted by the Court as justification for a restriction of the free movement (compare, amongst others, *Rewe-Zentral "Cassis de Dijon"*).[54] It follows from the case law that the Court applies this justification with great restraint. The *Baxter*[55] and *Fournier*[56] cases for instance, concerned tax measures which prevented a tax benefit in cross border situations. The Member State in that case invoked effective fiscal supervision as a justification of the restriction, but this was rejected by the Court given that the regulations concerned offered no possibility to demonstrate that, in a cross border situation, the conditions for obtaining the tax advantages had been satisfied. The regulation was considered disproportionate and therefore, could not be justified on the basis of the effectiveness of fiscal supervision.

It follows from the case law that the Member States may take measures by means of which income and expenditure can be ascertained clearly and precisely (see *Futura participations*).[57] The evidence required does not to take any particular form and the assessment must not be con-

50. Case C-324/00, *Lankhorst-Hohorst.*
51. Case C-330/07, *Jobra.*
52. C-196/04, *Cadbury Schweppes* and *Test Claimant in the Thin Cap GLO.*
53. D. Weber, "Abuse of law in European Tax Law: An overview and some recent trends in the direct and indirect tax case law of the ECJ", (2013) *European Taxation*, at 251 (part 1) and at 313 (part 2).
54. Case 120/78, *Rewe-Zentral "Cassis de Dijon"*.
55. Case C-254/97, *Baxter.*
56. Case C-39/04, *Fournier.*
57. Case 250/95, *Futura participations.*

ducted too formalistically and, furthermore, the evidence must not prove virtually impossible or excessively difficult to obtain (see: *Accor*[58]). In general, the Court is strict and requires that this supervision be conducted in domestic and cross border situations on the basis of the same conditions (see, for example, *Vestergaard*).[59] In joined cases *X and Passenheim-Van Schoot,*[60] the Court, nevertheless, allowed a longer period for additional assessment on foreign savings and the income therefrom when savings and income from these assets had been concealed from the tax authorities of a Member State and these authorities had no indication of their existence on the basis of which they could initiate investigation. In the case of concealment of income, where the tax authorities have no indication that it exists, longer periods for additional assessment are allowed; where the tax authorities do have a starting point, a longer period is not allowed (see *Halley*).[61]

The Court also allows the Member States more scope to justify rules by invoking the effectiveness of fiscal supervision if the free movement of capital between the Member States and third countries is applicable. The Directive regarding mutual assistance is not applicable to third countries, whereby the Member States could be confronted with problems in verifying any proof provided. The Member States may then set requirements (such as the existence of a tax treaty with the third country which contains an exchange of information provision), such that the Member State is given the opportunity to verify the proof put forward. An example is *Commission v. Italy.*[62]

3. State aid rules and harmful tax competition

EU Member States endeavour to attract economic activities and capital and thereby stimulate jobs by means of a competitive tax system. Competition between the Member States can be beneficial as the Member States are driven to deal efficiently with the tax collected), but it can also have harmful effects (rat race to the bottom), and that is why it is also called harmful tax competition.

3.1 *Harmful tax competition*

With the Code of Conduct for Business Taxation,[63] the Council is seeking to "curb harmful tax measures". This Code of Conduct is a political commitment (and thus not legally enforceable) and concerns those measures which affect, or may affect, in a significant way the location of business activity in the European Union. The Code contains a number of criteria to test a potentially harmful tax measure which are different from the criteria under the State aid provisions (such as no real economic activity, departure from internationally accepted tax rules, lack of transparency) and do not as such relate to the question of whether the measure is selective. Having said that, there is certainly an overlap, given that tax advantages which are afforded to offshore companies both under the State aid provisions and under the Code of Conduct can be

58. Case C-310/09, *Accor.*
59. Case C-55/98, *Vestergaard.*
60. C-155/08 and C-157/08, *X and Passenheim-Van Schoot.*
61. Case C-132/10, *Halley.*
62. Case C-540/07, *Commission v. Italy.*
63. Resolution of the Council and the representatives of the Governments of the Member States, meeting within the Council of 1 Dec. 1997 on the Code of Conduct for business taxation; O.J. 1998, C 2; W. Bratton and J. McCahery, "Tax coordination and tax competition in the European Union: Evaluating the code of conduct on business taxation", 38 CML Rev. (2001), 677.

suspect (see the *Gibraltar* case discussed above).[64] The Code has been applicable since 1998, and has been a powerful instrument of EU direct tax policy ever since. The Code of Conduct Group, consisting of high-level representatives from every Member State and a representative from the Commission, supervises whether certain national measures under the Code are harmful and have to be rolled back or may not be introduced. This Group reports to the Council. In the past years, the Code of Conduct Group has been focusing on the problems which, in taxation terms, are known as Base Erosion and Profit Shifting (BEPS), which has led, amongst others, to proposals to combat hybrid tax mismatches within the European Union and to a proposal on what favourable patent boxes must comply with within the EU.[65]

3.2 *State Aid*

In tax law, the importance of the State aid provisions (Art. 107 TFEU et seq.; see Ch. 21) has been growing rapidly these past years. One of the reasons is the combating of harmful tax competition within the EU (see 3.1.)Because of this, amongst others, the question has arisen whether and to what extent tax arrangements which Member States make with multinationals constitute forbidden State Aid. These are the questions surrounding cases such as *Starbucks, Amazon* and *Apple*.[66]

In the "Notice on the application of the State aid rules to measures relating to direct business taxation",[67] the European Commission addresses how it considers Article 107 TFEU should be interpreted in tax cases.

In tax cases particularly, the question is whether a measure is "selective". The determination of the reference framework has a particular importance in the case of tax measures, since the very existence of an advantage may be established only when compared with "normal" taxation, according to the Court in, amongst others, *Commission v. Portugal*.[68] In order to establish this, first, is it necessary to begin by identifying and examining the common or "normal" tax regime applicable in the Member State concerned? Second, it is that in relation to this common or "normal" tax regime it is necessary to assess and determine whether any advantage granted by the tax measure at issue may be selective by demonstrating that the measure derogates from that common regime inasmuch as it differentiates between economic operators who, in light of the objective assigned to the tax system of the Member State concerned, are in a comparable factual and legal situation.[69]

In the *Gibraltar* case,[70] the Court made an important exception to the rule that there must be a derogation on the common tax regime. In that case, Gibraltar wanted to introduce a new corporate tax regime, which consisted of a registration fee, a payroll tax and a business property occupation tax (BPOT). The tax could not be higher than 15% of the profits. This new system

64. P.J. Wattel, "Some fringe areas of EU State aid law in direct tax matters" in D. Weber (Ed.), "EU income tax law – Issues for the years ahead", 9 *EC and International Tax Law Series* (2013), 139.
65. Council of the European Union, 11 Dec. 2014, no. 16553/1/14, H&I 2015/45 (comments by J. van de Streek).
66. K. Desai, "A development in state aid practice – Tax rulings and settlements become a focus of attention", (2014) ECLR, 575. Alleged aid to Apple, Invitation to submit comments, O.J. 2014, C 369/22 and O.J. 2015, C 44/13. Luxembourg alleged aid to FFT, Commission Decision, O.J. 2014, C 369/05, Netherlands Alleged aid to Starbucks, Commission Decision, O.J. 2014, C 460/11.
67. Commission Notice of 11 Nov. 1998, press release IP/98/983. See also: "Report on the implementation of the Commission Notice on the application of the State Aid rules to measures relating to direct business taxation", COM(2004)434 final.
68. Case C-88/03, *Commission v. Portugal.*
69. See for instance: Joined Cases C-78/08 to C-80/08, *Paint Graphos and Others*, para 49.
70. Joined Cases C-106/09 and C-107/09 *P*.

favoured offshore companies particularly which, according to their nature, are not physically present in Gibraltar and thus, are not subject to the payroll tax and BPOT. The General Court found that there was no question of a selective measure because there was no derogation from the common tax system. In appeal, the Court of Justice dwelt more on the consequences of the legislation and not so much on the techniques used. The Court considered that it is apparent that "the regime at issue, by combining those bases, even though they are founded on criteria that are in themselves of a general nature, in practice discriminates between companies which are in a comparable situation with regard to the objective of the proposed tax reform, namely to introduce a general system of taxation for all companies established in Gibraltar. Combining those bases of assessment not only results in taxation according to the number of employees and the size of the business premises occupied, but also, due to the absence of other bases of assessment, excludes from the outset any taxation of offshore companies, since they have no employees and also do not occupy business property". Also of importance was, the fact that offshore companies were not taxed was not a random consequence of the regime but the "inevitable consequence" of that regime. The fact that offshore companies, which constitute a group of companies, avoid taxation precisely on account of the specific features characteristic of that group, was sufficient to conclude that there were selective advantages.

There are no selective advantages when the measure is justified by the nature or general scheme of the system. In *P Oy*,[71] the question was whether the granting of a certain tax advantage, whereby the tax authorities have discretional powers, can be justified by the nature or general scheme of the system. According to the Court there is here, in principle, no question of selectivity when the competent authorities have only a degree of latitude limited by objective criteria which are not unrelated to the tax system established by the legislation". However, when the tax authorities have "broad discretion" on the basis of criteria unrelated to the tax system, then selectivity is present.

4. Harmonization in taxation

4.1 *Decision-making in tax matters*

Article 113 TFEU lays down a legal basis for harmonization of the legislation concerning turnover taxes, excise duties and other forms of indirect taxation to "the extent that such harmonization is necessary to ensure the establishment and the functioning of the internal market and to avoid distortion of competition". The decision-making takes place on the basis of the consultation procedure which means that further to a proposal of the European Commission, the Council must first request advice from the European Parliament and the Economic and Social Committee before taking a decision on the proposal. A proposal must then be adopted by unanimous vote.

For direct taxation, no specific legal basis for harmonization is laid down in the Treaty on the Functioning of the European Union (TFEU). The directives adopted to date in the field of direct taxation find their basis in the general harmonization provisions, as laid down in Article 115 TFEU. On the basis of this article, under the consultation procedure, directives can be determined by unanimous vote for the approximation of laws, regulations or administrative provisions of the Member States as directly affect the establishment or functioning of the internal market.

71. Case C-6/12, *P Oy*.

Also, the Directive concerning administrative cooperation in the field of taxation[72] is based on Articles 113 and 115 TFEU, as are certain amendments to the Directive on Mutual Assistance for the recovery of tax claims[73] (both provisions provide for direct taxation and for indirect taxation).

Article 114, paragraph 1, TFEU, in derogation of Article 115 TFEU, lays down the "ordinary legislative procedure" (see for this procedure: Art. 294 TFEU) on the basis of which a directive can be adopted with a qualified majority. In Article 114, paragraph 2, TFEU, however, it is determined that Article 114, paragraph 1 shall not apply "to fiscal provisions". In *Commission v. Council,*[74] it is observed that "those words cover not only all fields of taxation, without drawing any distinction between the types of duties or taxes concerned, but also all aspects of taxation, whether material rules or procedural rules" (para 63) and that the words "fiscal provisions" contained in Article 95(2) EC (now: Art. 114, para 2, TFEU) must be interpreted as covering not only the provisions determining taxable persons, taxable transactions, the basis of imposition, and rates of and exemptions from direct and indirect taxes, but also those relating to arrangements for the collection of such taxes" (para 67).

On balance, therefore, decisions in the field of indirect taxation (Art. 113 TFEU) and decisions in the field of direct taxation (Art. 115 TFEU) are taken by means of the consultation procedure and by unanimous vote. On the basis of Article 115 TFEU, only *directives* can be adopted. Article 113 TFEU allows all kinds of measures for the indirect taxation mentioned in that provision, thus, both directives and regulations.

4.2 *Harmonization in direct taxation*

4.2.1 *Corporate taxation*

In the area of corporate taxation,[75] there are a number of tax directives which harmonize sub areas of corporate taxation within the EU. The most important is the so-called Parent-Subsidiary Directive.[76] The objective of this Directive is to exempt dividends and other profits distributions paid by subsidiary companies to their parent companies from withholding taxes and to eliminate double taxation of such income at the level of the parent company. By means of this common system, dividends can be distributed without withholding tax and without giving rise to double taxation within the European Union. This has created tax rules which are neutral from the point of view of competition and it allows enterprises to adapt to the requirements of the internal market, to increase their productivity and to improve their competitive strength at international level.

The Interest & Royalty Directive[77] provides for the elimination of withholding taxes on royalty and interest payments paid between associated companies. This to ensure that double

---

72. Directive 2011/16/EU of 15 Feb. 2011 on administrative cooperation in the field of taxation and repealing Directive 77/799/EEC.
73. Directive 76/308/EEC Mutual assistance: Council Directive 76/308/EEC of 15 Mar. 1976 on "Mutual assistance for the recovery of claims relating to certain levies, duties, taxes and other measures" [Integrated Text Including Last Amendment by Directive 2001/44/EC], O.J. 1976, L 73/18 and O.J. 2001, L 175/17.
74. C-338/01, *Commission v. Council.*
75. C.H.J.I Panayi, *European Union Corporate Tax Law* (CUP, 2013).
76. Council Directive of 30 Nov. 2011 on the common system of taxation applicable in the case of parent companies and subsidiaries of different Member States (2011/96/EU).
77. Council Directive of 3 June 2003 on a common system of taxation applicable to interest and royalty payments made between associated companies of different Member States (2003/49/EC).

taxation is eliminated for the purpose of preventing burdensome administrative formalities and cash flow problems which arise from withholding taxes for enterprises.

On the basis of the Business Restructuring Directive (also called the Merger Directive),[78] common rules are applicable to business restructuring which are neutral from the point of view of competition. The objective of the Directive is that taxation of the income, profits and capital gains from business reorganizations should be deferred and that at the same time, the taxing rights of the Member States are safeguarded. The Directive provides for deferral of taxation in the case of cross-border legal mergers, divisions, transfer of assets and exchange of shares. Because the directive provides only for deferral of taxation, the tax claim of the Member State after the restructuring is retained. When a Member State sees its tax claim disappear due to restructuring, the Directive provides that this Member State may still levy tax. The Directive also provides for deferral of taxation in the case of the transfer of the registered office of a Societas Europaea (SE) or European Cooperative Society (SCE).

Multinational enterprises charge to other group companies the prices they find reasonable in the group (because the price is not set by the market). This also means that multinationals can shift profits from one country to another, this by setting the prices such that the profits are made in a country with a low corporate tax rate. To prevent this, the prices which multinational enterprises charge in cross border situations to other group companies are often adjusted for tax law purposes. It is assumed in most of the Member States that a payment which is at arm's length (at arm's length principle) should be charged for goods, services and intangibles (copyrights, patents, brand names, etc.). This means that prices charged within a multinational group should be same as the prices charged to persons outside of the group (third parties) and consequently the multinational can no longer shift profits. Application of the at arm's length principle can lead to price adjustments being made by the tax authorities of a certain Member State (for fiscal reasons). Because all the Member States remain competent to determine their own criteria to levy corporation tax, they are not obliged to follow the price adjustment of another Member State. This could lead to double taxation. In 2017 the EU Council approved a Council Directive on Double Taxation Dispute Resolution Mechanisms in the European Union.[79] This Directive introduces improvements to the existing mechanisms intended to resolve disputes between Member States on the interpretation of bilateral tax treaties, including transfer pricing issues. The Directive makes dispute resolution mechanisms binding and mandatory. Additionally, the Directive introduces time limits and obliges Member States to resolve disputes related to double taxation. The Directive will result in more legal certainty in that it guarantees final and binding decisions for any dispute. The Directive enables any affected company to submit a complaint to the competent authorities of Member States. Such a complaint can lead to a mutual agreement procedure. If mutual agreement is not reached within two years, a mandatory arbitration procedure will be launched. In this procedure an officially appointed advisory commission will issue a binding opinion.

If you oversee the EU measures on corporate taxation the conclusion is that there is currently a lack of coordination in corporate taxation between the Member States. This creates obstacles for companies acting in the Single Market, as they are confronted with 28 different tax bases of corporate taxation, creating heavy compliance costs and administrative burdens which

78. Council Directive 90/434/EEC of 23 July 1990 on the common system of taxation applicable to mergers, divisions, partial divisions, transfer of assets and exchanges of shares concerning companies of different Member States and to the transfer of the registered office of an SE or SCE between Member States.
79. Proposal for a Council Directive on Tax dispute Resolution mechanisms in the European Union, 19 May 2017.

are detrimental to European competitiveness. It also allows companies to exploit mismatches. Intense competition for mobile tax bases has created new opportunities for aggressive tax planners, while other companies are still facing double taxation. For this reason, in June 2015, the European Commission published an action plan.[80] In this Action Plan, the Commission unfolds a new approach to corporate taxation in the EU, to meet the goal of fairer and more efficient taxation and to effectively tackle corporate tax avoidance. One the ambitious measures is to introduce one system of corporate taxation in the EU, the so-called Common Consolidated Corporate Tax Base (CCCTB). The first part of this Action plan was published in January 2016 when the Commission introduced an anti-Tax Avoidance Package.[81] Most important part of this package is a proposal for an Anti-Tax Avoidance Directive,[82] which was approved in June 2016.

4.3 *Indirect taxation*

4.3.1 *Union Customs Code*

Article 28 TFEU determines that the Union shall comprise a customs union.[83] This customs union covers all trade in goods and involves the prohibition between Member States of customs duties on imports and exports and of all charges having equivalent effect, and the adoption of a common customs tariff in their relations with third countries. To reach this goal, the Union Customs Code (UCC)[84] was adopted.[85] The UCC is laid down in a Regulation and thus is binding in its entirety and directly applicable in all Member States. There is, therefore, unification. The UCC serves as a framework Regulation on the rules and procedures for customs throughout the EU. Based on the concept of an internal market, that code contains the general rules and procedures which ensure the implementation of the tariff and other common policy measures introduced at Union level in connection with trade in goods between the Union and countries or territories outside the customs territory of the Union, taking into account the requirements of those common policies.[86]

The customs system within the EU is a so-called "closed system". A system of customs supervision is applicable at the moment that the goods are brought into the customs territory until these are released for free circulation. There is a diversity of rules for customs approved treatment such as release for free circulation, transit, customs warehousing, etc.

4.3.2 *Value Added Tax (VAT)*

Within the EU, a Value Added Tax (VAT[87]) is levied on transactions related to goods and services. The levy of VAT is laid down in a directive and is fully harmonized within the EU. The VAT system operates such, in short, that taxpayers (entrepreneurs) are VAT due to the Member States on the payments they receive for the supplies and services they have provided. On the

80. 17 June 2015, European Commission, Communication, "A fair and efficient corporate tax system in the European Union: Five key areas for action", SWD (2015) 121 final, COM(2015)302 final.
81. Commission Communication, "Anti-tax avoidance package: Next steps towards delivering effective taxation and greater transparency in the EU", COM(2016)23, 28 Jan. 2016.
82. Proposal for a Council Directive laying down rules against tax avoidance practices that directly affect the functioning of the internal market, COM(2016)26.
83. M. Fabro, *Customs Law of the European Union* (Kluwer, 2010).
84. Reg. (EU) No 952/2013 of 9 Oct. 2013 laying down the Union Customs Code.
85. The customs union used to be laid down in various regulations and directives. The rules have been recast a number of times to provide for a better overview, streamlining and modernization of the various rules and procedures.
86. T. Walsh, *European Union Customs Code* (Kluwer, 2015).
87. Council Directive 2006/112/EC of 28 Nov. 2006 on the common system of value added tax.

other hand, they have the right to deduct from the VAT they are due the VAT they have paid on the costs of supplies and services provided to them for their economic activities. This is called the right to the deduction of input tax. By the deduction of input tax, the entrepreneur in fact is not burdened with VAT.

To give a simple example: entrepreneur of "Fast-bike shop" sells bicycles. When he sells a bicycle for EUR 100 he has to charge 21% VAT (EUR 21). On the other hand, he pays VAT on the cost price of the bicycle which he buys direct from the bicycle manufacturer. As the cost price of the bicycle is EUR 75, he pays 21% VAT which is EUR 15.75; this is the "input tax" he can deduct form the VAT (EUR 21) he is due to the Member State. The VAT that Fast-bike shop is due to the Member State is EUR 5.25 euro (21 minus 15.75 input tax), thus, he only pays VAT on the *Value Added* (100 – 75 = 25).

The VAT is ultimately paid by the end consumer and in this manner, is strictly proportionate to the end price, which benefits the economic neutrality. Through this system, there is also no question of tax accumulation (double taxation). The levy of VAT takes place on the basis of the designated country principle, in other words, that the tax as a rule is for the benefit of the country where the supply of goods or services takes place. The aim is that the levy of VAT has no influence on fiscal neutrality, which means that levy of VAT may not have influence on competition relations between entrepreneurs and between suchlike products and services. Accordingly, similar entrepreneurs and products must be subject to the same tax burden. The Common EU system of VAT is full of exceptions and special rules and thereby, is perceived as complex.[88]

4.3.3 *Excises and energy taxation*

Excise duties in the EU are harmonized in several directives (based on Art. 113 TFEU). Excises are indirect taxes on the consumption or the use of certain products. In contrast to VAT, these are mainly specific taxes, not based on the (added) value of the product but expressed as a monetary amount per quantity of the product. The General Arrangements Directive[89] regulates the general provisions (chargeability, exemptions, etc.) for excise duty. In general, a distinction has to be made between commercial traffic (principle of taxation in the Member State of destination) and transport of goods by private people for their own use (the principle of taxation in the Member State of origin). There are also several directives in which excise duties for specific products are set out in further detail, such as the Alcohol and Alcohol Beverages Directives,[90] the Tobacco Directive[91] and the Energy Taxation Directive.[92]

4.4 *Administrative cooperation and recovery of tax claims*

The Directive on administrative cooperation provides for mandatory and voluntary exchange of information between the Member States (also information about tax rulings, which are

88. See for a comprehensive overview: B.J.M. Terra and J. Kajus, *A Guide to the European VAT Directives* (IBFD, 2016).
89. Directive 2008/118/EC of 16 Dec. 2008 concerning the general arrangements for excise duty and repealing Directive 92/12/EEC.
90. Council Directive 92/83/EEC of 19 Oct. 1992 on the harmonization of the structures of excise duties on alcohol and alcoholic beverages, O.J. 1992, L 316, and Council Directive 92/84/EEC of 19 Oct. 1992 on the approximation of the rates of excise duty on alcohol and alcoholic beverages, O.J. 1992, L 316, 29.
91. Council Directive 2011/64/EU of 21 June 2011 on the structure and rates of excise duty applied to manufactured tobacco (codification), O.J. 2011, L 176, 24.
92. Directive 2003/96/EC restructuring the Community framework for the taxation of energy products and electricity, O.J. 2003, L 283.

arrangements made between a taxpayer and a Member State regarding the taxpayer's tax position[93]). In 2011 2014 and 2015, the EU rules relating to administrative cooperation within the EU were tightened because in the current era of globalization, the Member States are increasingly invoking mutual assistance. The mobility of taxpayers, the number of cross border transactions, the internationalization of financial instruments, concerns about cross border tax fraud and tax avoidance are also contributing factors. For direct taxation, rules relating to mutual assistance are laid down in Directive 2011/16/EU.[94] Administrative cooperation in the fields of VAT and excise are regulated in separate regulations.[95] Within the EU, there is also a directive which regulates mutual assistance for the recovery of tax claims.[96]

5. Conclusion

In the EU, indirect taxation (Customs, VAT, Excises, energy taxation) has been unified, harmonized or coordinated for a long time. Direct taxation (income tax, corporate tax, inheritance tax, etc.) is still largely a national domain, but the Treaty freedoms and recently, State aid provisions, greatly influence the formation of national tax systems. The expectation is that the Member States will have to cooperate more closely in the fields of corporate taxation and international taxation, such in order to remove the disadvantages for the taxpayer of 28 tax systems and to remove abuse of tax mismatches. In 2015, the European Commission drew up an action plan and is to put forward concrete proposals in the coming years. The first part of this Action plan was published in January 2016 when the Commission introduced an anti-Tax Avoidance Package. Most important part of this package is a proposal for an Anti-Tax Avoidance Directive which was already approved by the EU Council in June 2016. In 2017 binding and mandatory procedures to solve double taxation disputes where approved. If more EU legislation in taxation matters will be approved in the near future will depend particularly on the political will of the Member States.

Further reading

Fabio, M., *Customs Law of the European Union* (KLI, 2010).
Helminen, M., *EU Tax Law* (IBFD, 2017).
Panayi, C.H.J.I., *European Union Corporate Tax Law* (CUP, 2013).
Terra, B.J.M. and P.J. Wattel, *European Tax Law* (Kluwer, 2018).
Terra, B.J.M. and J. Kajus, *A Guide to the European VAT Directives* (IBFD, 2016).

---

93. A "tax ruling", for instance, deals with the interpretation or application of a legal or administrative tax provision to a cross-border transaction.
94. Directive 2011/16/EU, O.J. 2011, L 64/1; see also: Council Directive 2014/107/EU of 9 December 2014 amending Directive 2011/16/EU as regards mandatory automatic exchange of information in the field of taxation, O.J. 2014, L 359/1.
95. Council Reg. 904/2010 of 7 Oct. 2010 on administrative cooperation and combating fraud in the field of value added tax (recast), O.J. 2011, L 268, at 1; Council Reg. 2073/2004 of 16 Nov. 2004 on administrative cooperation in the field of excise duties, O.J. 2004, L 359, at 1.
96. Council Directive 2010/24/EU of 16 Mar. 2010 concerning mutual assistance for the recovery of claims relating to taxes, duties and other measures, O.J. 2010, L 84/1.

CHAPTER 24
INTELLECTUAL PROPERTY

*Ana Ramalho**

1. Introduction

The umbrella term "intellectual property" refers to a range of rights – such as patents, trademarks, copyright or designs – that are granted to creations of the mind. These rights protect different subject-matters,[1] and have divergent requirements for, and scopes of, protection.[2] In procedural terms, the rights also differ – for example, while some have to be registered to come into existence (as is the case of trademarks or patents), others are granted independently of formalities (like copyright).

In practice, the same product can combine various types of protection. For instance, the technology of a smart phone might be protected by a patent, while its name is trademarked, its shape is design protected, and copyright will confer exclusive rights to the creator of the original ringtones of that same phone. Sometimes, the same feature can even attract different rights – e.g., shapes can be protected by design rights, but also by copyright and trademarks (provided of course that the respective requirements for protection are met).

Moreover, the different IP rights share common features. By its nature, the subject matter of the various IP rights – an intellectual creation – is intangible. Intellectual creations that attract IP rights are usually embodied in a physical object (such as, e.g., the smart phone that embodies the patented technology), but the physical object is distinct from the immaterial creation. IP is concerned with the latter. Should IP rights not exist, the result of the creator's intellectual effort – an invention, a book, a logo – could be freely appropriated by others due to its immateriality. This argument appeals directly to the importance of, and justification for, intellectual property: one the one hand, natural justice links the creator to her creation for ethical and moral reasons (i.e., having IP rights is just); on the other hand, granting certain rights to creators gives them

* Maastricht University, Department of International and European Law.

1. E.g., trademarks protect signs, like words or logos; patents are granted to inventions; copyright covers literary, artistic or scientific works; related rights (also called neighbouring rights) protect performances, phonograms and broadcasts; designs protect the outward appearance of products; geographical indications consist of signs used to convey the specific geographical origin of products; trade secrets protect confidential business information or know-how.
2. The requirements for protection concern the specific conditions for the grant of the right (for instance, a trademark must be distinctive and capable of being represented in the register in order to be registered; an invention is patentable provided that it is new, it has an inventive step and it has industrial application; literary, artistic or scientific works must be original to be afforded copyright protection). The scope of protection refers to the breadth of protection of the right, such as, e.g., its duration (compare, for example, the duration of patents – in general, 20 years – with that of copyright, which in the EU lasts for 70 years after the death of the author).

an incentive to create and innovate (i.e., having IP rights is efficient).[3] However, because IP rights could effectively exclude competitors and users from using the creation, they are limited in time[4] and are restricted by several exceptions (such as, e.g., the exception to copyright that allows users to make copies of a copyright-protected work for their private use).

Chiefly, IP rights are exclusive (they confer upon their owner certain exclusive rights that allow him to benefit from his creation, usually by commercially exploiting it and preventing others from doing so) and territorial (that is, they are granted for a certain territory). These particular characteristics can conflict with central EU objectives, such as establishing of the internal market (and securing that competition therein is not distorted). In fact, territorially defined exclusive rights are in theory not consistent with internal market goals and free movement principles It was exactly these challenges that prompted several EU institutions to take action in the IP field, either through negative or positive integration.

This chapter will examine the way in which EU law and institutions have addressed the conflict between the main IP rights and EU law rules and principles. Section 2 explores the provisions of the Treaties that are relevant to the field of IP. It is divided into negative integration (2.1.) and positive integration (2.2.). Section 3 analyses each IP right separately, focusing on relevant case law and examining how the conflict between Treaty provisions and national IP rights has been addressed by EU institutions. Section 4 draws some conclusions regarding IP in the EU context.

2. Intellectual property in the context of the EU Treaties

The territoriality of IP rights implies that each Member State defines its own legal regime for each of the IP rights, which are then valid along national borders. While several international treaties have set some common standards of protection that approximated the IP laws of many countries (including the Member States of the EU),[5] these international rules are most often minimum standards that allow parties to set higher levels of protection,[6] and they do not exhaustively regulate all aspects of a given IP right.[7]

The differences between the national IP regimes of EU Member States pose a challenge to certain key goals of the EU, such as the objective of establishing an internal market. Copyright, patents or trademarks comprise exclusive rights that are attached to or embedded in a good or a service. Since such rights are granted on a national basis, they can be at odds with free movement principles. The differences between national legal regimes may effectively impede cross-border trade, since the same work, product or trademark might be protected in one Member State but not in others, or it might be protected in different Member States to different degrees. Another

---

3. See, *inter alia*, L. Bently and B. Sherman, *Intellectual Property Law*, 3rd ed. (OUP, 2009), at 3–5; J. Hughes, "The philosophy of intellectual property", 77 *Georgetown Law Journal* (1988), 287–366; W. Dibble, "Justifying intellectual property", 1 *UCL Jurisprudence Review* (1994), 74–88.
4. Except for trademarks, which, albeit being valid for an initially limited period, can be indefinitely renewed.
5. See for example the Agreement on Trade-Related Aspects of IP, or TRIPs, of 1994 (covering all the main areas of IP).
6. See for instance the case of the Berne Convention, which sets in Art. 7(1) the general term of protection for copyright works at 50 years after the death of the author. This is a minimum standard, in that countries party to the Convention are allowed to establish longer periods for copyright duration. Following the breathing space left by the Convention, the EU has established a general term of protection of 70 years after the death of the author via the Term of Protection Dir. (Dir. 2006/116/EC of the European Parliament and of the Council of 12 Dec. 2006, O.J. 2006, L 372/12 (codified version), amended by Dir. 2011/77/EU of the European Parliament and of the Council of 27 Sept. 2011, O.J. 2011, L 265/1.).
7. An example is the enforcement of IP rights, the concrete rules of which are normally left to the national legislator.

consequence of exclusive rights granted on a territorial basis is the possibility they give the right holder to partition the market, e.g. by practicing price discrimination between Member States and subsequently preventing parallel imports (that is, preventing the resale of products across borders). Such division of markets also runs counter to the establishment of an EU internal market and the competition rules underlying it.

The next sections will provide an overview of Treaty provisions that are relevant to determine the relationship between IP and EU law. Section 2.1. describes the Treaty rules that can either conflict with or accommodate national IP rights. Section 2.2. examines the legal basis to regulate IP at the EU level.

2.1 *Negative integration: National IP rights and Treaty provisions*

Several Treaty provisions affect national IP rights. As mentioned, IP rights might constitute barriers to trade and be at odds with the establishment of the internal market. The Treaty outlaws restrictions to the free movement of goods and services – Article 34 TFEU prohibits quantitative restrictions on imports and all measures having equivalent effect; and Article 56 TFEU prohibits barriers to the freedom to provide cross-border services. However, the Treaty itself gives some legal coverage to national IP laws, even if they negatively impact the EU internal market.

First, Article 345 TFEU mandates that "the Treaties shall in no way prejudice the rules in Member States governing the system of property ownership". The Treaty does not clarify the scope of this rule, although the history of the provision can support an interpretation according to which "system of property ownership" refers primarily to the national rules regulating public or private allocation of property.[8]

Second, Article 36 TFEU permits certain derogations to the free movement of goods. Prohibitions of restrictions to the free movement of goods and services are thus not absolute. Restrictions on imports and exports can be admitted in certain circumstances, namely when they are in force for the protection of industrial and commercial property, provided that such restrictions are not a means of arbitrary discrimination nor a disguised restriction on trade between Member States. Similarly, in what concerns the free movement of services, the Treaty provides for exceptions to the prohibition of restrictions. The free movement of services can be restricted where an activity is connected with the exercise of an official authority (Art. 51 TFEU, applicable via Art. 62 TFEU), as well as in cases where public policy, public security or public health are at stake (Art. 52 (1) TFEU, applicable via 62 TFEU). There are no exceptions expressly granted with respect to industrial and commercial property. Still, the ECJ has considered that derogations from the free movement of services should also be accepted for reasons of "general interest,"[9] and it has expressly established that intellectual property could be a justification to restrict trade in services.[10]

---

8. See J. Schwarze, *EU-Kommentar* (Nomos, 2000), Art. 295, para 1. The origins of this provision date back to Art. 83 of the Treaty constituting the European Coal and Steel Community (ECSC Treaty), the aim of which was to leave to Member States the choice of whether undertakings subject to the ECSC Treaty should be publicly or privately owned. The ECJ has moreover ruled on the scope of Art. 345 along similar lines, stating that the provision covers questions of "establishing or maintaining a body of rules relating to the public ownership of private undertakings" (Joined Cases C-105/12 to C-107/12, *Nederland v. Essent*, paras. 29–31).
9. Case C-262/02, *Commission v. France*, at 23, and Case C-243/01, *Gambelli*, at 60.
10. See Case 62/79, *Coditel v. Ciné Vog (Coditel I)*, at 12–15. In this case, the matter was whether the ownership of copyright in a film could be used to prevent an unauthorized cable retransmission (in Belgium) of a broadcast which in turn had taken place with consent (in Germany). The Court established that, since public

In addition, the ownership of exclusive rights inherent to IP rights can give the right holder the ability to affect competition on the market with regard to the work or product that constitutes the subject matter of an IP right. Accordingly, the Treaty also puts forth competition rules that might clash with national IP rights. Article 101(1) TFEU prohibits agreements between undertakings which may affect cross border trade and whose object or effect is to prevent, restrict or distort competition within the internal market. Still, such practices may be accepted in certain conditions, namely if the agreement "contributes to improving the production or distribution of goods or to promoting technical or economic progress", subject to the condition that consumers get a fair share of that benefit, and provided that the restrictions are indispensable and do not eliminate competition in relation to a substantial part of the product concerned.[11] Article 101(1) may thus potentially affect licences for the exploitation of IP, if conditions therein are met; but those licences might still be admissible under the exception of paragraph 3 of the same provision. Further, the Commission adopted block exemptions, which apply Article 101(3) to certain types or categories of agreements. Most IP agreements are now covered by a number of block exemptions.[12]

Another competition-related provision that might affect national IP rights is Article 102 TFEU, which prohibits the abuse of a dominant position. By its very nature, IP rights imply some sort of exclusivity, which might put their owner in a dominant position on the market. The ownership and exercise of an (exclusive) IP right does not necessarily amount to an infringement of Article 102 TFEU.[13] If however that dominant position is abused, then Article 102 may come into play. This will typically happen when a company enjoying a dominant position on the market refuses to grant licences with regard to its IP rights,[14] although a few other situations involving conflicts between the exercise of IP rights and Article 102 TFEU have arisen.[15]

2.2 *Positive integration: The legal basis to regulate intellectual property in the EU*

The IP acquis is composed of a mix of Directives and Regulations, most of which have been enacted under previous versions of the Treaties. As a rule, Directives have been used to harmonize national IP laws, while Regulations have created unitary intellectual property titles, with a EU-wide validity.

The revision of the Treaty of Rome by the Single European Act (SEA), which was signed in 1986, was determinant to trigger the intervention of the EU (then EC) legislator in IP – the SEA prescribed as a goal of the EC the establishment of an internal market over a period expiring on

---

communications may be "infinitely repeated", the copyright holder has a "legitimate interest" in calculating the due fees on the basis of the actual or probable number of performances.

11. Cf. Art. 101 TFEU, para 3.
12. T. Cook, *EU Intellectual Property Law* (OUP, 2010), at 48. Block exemptions exist for several types of agreements, including vertical agreements, Research & Development agreements or technology transfer agreements – see in more detail R. Whish and D. Bailey, *Competition Law* (OUP, 2015) at 178 et seq.
13. As made clear early on by the ECJ – see Case 24/67, *Parke Davis v. Probel.*
14. See, e.g., Case 53/87, *CICRA v. Renault* (concerning the refusal to license the design for spare parts of cars); Joined Cases C-241 & C-242/91, *RTE and ITP v. Commission ("Magill")*(concerning refusals to grant licenses of copyright in television programme listings); Case C-418/01, *IMS Health* (involving a refusal to license a copyright-protected structure conveying a system for gathering sales data and other information).
15. It's the case of the practices of collecting societies in the field of copyright and related rights. Collecting societies are entities that represent categories of right holders, mainly for purposes of exploitation and management of their rights. Many of these societies enjoy a dominant position in the relevant market, and some of their practices might be at odds with Art. 102 TFEU – for a full account and relevant case law, see T. Cook, op. cit. *supra* note 12, at 63–66.

31 December 1992,[16] and, to accomplish this ambitious deadline, Article 100a of the EEC Treaty gave the EC the power to adopt harmonization measures by a qualified majority in the Council, a novelty in relation to the unanimity rule of the Treaty of Rome.

The possibility of harmonizing national IP laws was, and still is, connected to the making of an internal market. The ECJ has made clear that the provisions that recognize a place for national IP laws within the framework of the Treaties did not constitute any stronghold of Member States' powers. Regarding Article 345 TFEU (formerly Art. 295 EC Treaty), the Court stressed, in relation specifically to "industrial and commercial property", that the provision could not be interpreted as reserving to Member States the power to adopt measures that would adversely affect the free movement of goods.[17] In what concerns Article 36 TFEU (formerly Art. 30 EC Treaty), on the exceptions to the free movement of goods, the ECJ determined that the provision was not intended to grant Member States an exclusive competence in the matters contained therein.[18] The same argument should be applied to the exceptions to the free movement of services. This means that these provisions do not amount to a question of competence allocation between the EU and its Member States; instead, the free movement provisions and their exceptions mediate the relationship between EU law and national legislation on given areas, without prejudice to future intervention of the EU legislator in such areas.

The legal basis to regulate IP has thus to be found in other provisions. In the current version of the Treaties, Article 114(1) TFEU enables the European Parliament and the Council to jointly adopt harmonizing measures for the establishment and functioning of the internal market. This provision (and in previous versions of the Treaties its corresponding predecessors) has been the main legal basis relied upon to harmonize national IP laws. IP rights being territorial, cross-border trade of IP goods and services can be effectively impeded by national legislative differences. The IP laws of the Member States differed – and still do, in many aspects – from one another, in such fundamental features as the type and scope of the rights granted. The Directives currently in force were therefore justified due to the differences in national IP laws that were arguably hindering cross-border trade.

As a result, Article 114 TFEU will be a valid legal basis, first and foremost, where that cross-border relevance exists – i.e., where differences between national IP laws are an impediment to the internal market. The extensive body of ECJ case law on this provision should be taken into consideration when using the provision as a legal basis to harmonize IP laws.[19]

Second, Article 114 TFEU can also be used as a legal basis where national IP laws cause distortions to competition, since the ECJ has ruled that such situations also fall under the provision,[20] provided that the distortion is "appreciable".[21]

Next to Article 114 TFEU, some Directives – mostly in the field of copyright – have also used as legal bases for harmonization the facilitation of the taking-up and pursuit of activities of

---

16. Art. 8a of the EEC Treaty, as amended by the SEA.
17. Case C-30/90, *Commission v. UK*, at 18, and Case C-350/92, *Spain v. Council*, at 18.
18. Case 35/76, *Simmenthal*, at 14.
19. See, *inter alia*, Case C-376/98, *Germany v. Parliament and Council* (*Tobacco Advertising I*); Case C-380/03, *Germany v. Parliament and Council* (*Tobacco Advertising II*); Joined Cases C-465/00, C-138 & 139/01, *Österreichischer Rundfunk*; Case C-300/89, *Commission v. Council* (*Titanium Dioxide*); Case C-301/06, *Ireland v. Parliament and Council* (*Data Retention*); Case C-58/08, *Vodafone v. Secretary of State for Business, Enterprise and Regulatory Reform*; Joined Cases C-154 & 155/04, *Alliance for Natural Health and others v. Secretary of State for Health and others (Alliance for Natural Health)*; Case C-217/04, *UK v. Parliament and Council.*
20. See Case C-300/89, *Titanium Dioxide* at 15 and 23; Case C-376/98, *Tobacco Advertising I* at 95 and 106; Case C-301/06, *Data Retention* at 63. See also S. Weatherill, "Union legislation relating to the free movement of goods" in P. Oliver (Ed.), *Oliver on the Free Movement of Goods* (Hart, 2010) at 433 et seq.
21. Case C-376/98, *Tobacco Advertising I* at 106 and 109.

self-employed persons, in the context of the right of establishment (current Art. 53(1) TFEU) and the freedom to provide services (current Art. 62 TFEU). And in fact authors and artists, who are the centrepiece of copyright and related rights, are often self-employed persons and their activities frequently amount to the provision of services. However, these two bases have been used in an ancillary fashion. They have usually been invoked together with Article 114 TFEU.

In what concerns the creation of pan-European IP rights, the Treaty of Lisbon added a new provision – Article 118 TFEU – that empowers the Parliament and the Council to create IP rights (such as, e.g., a EU patent or a EU copyright) to provide for a uniform IP protection throughout the EU. The provision was drawn from the flexibility clause of the previous version of the Treaty (Art. 308 EC Treaty), which allowed the Council to unanimously pass Commission proposals (after consulting the Parliament), if necessary to attain one of the objectives of the Community in the course of the operation of the common market. It was under Article 308 EC Treaty that the Community trademark and the Community design – both unitary titles – were created. The flexibility clause continues to exist, though (Art. 352 TFEU) – it is just doubtful that any future unitary IP right can be created under it, as Article 118 is now the specific norm to do so.

The "unification" under Article 118 TFEU is different from the harmonization of pre-existing national laws enabled by Article 114 TFEU: the creation of a new, pan-European IP title adds a new form of right to the legal order (regardless of whether it replaces or not national IP entitlements), whereas harmonization of national IP laws is supposed to adjust existing national laws by approximating them. However, the use of Article 118 TFEU as a legal basis is also dependent on internal market considerations. The creation of a EU-wide IP title would have to be linked to the "context of the establishment and functioning of the internal market". The attachment of the competence of Article 118 TFEU to the building of an internal market was furthermore confirmed by the ECJ.[22] Most of the harmonized regimes of the several IP rights can serve as guidelines to future unified titles – presumably such regimes were aimed at improving the functioning of the internal market or the elimination of distortions to competition, and whether the concrete outcome met those expectations or not can serve as a valuable lesson in the context of unification.

The attachment of the competences of Articles 114 and 118 to the establishing and functioning of the internal market raises questions as to the normative content – or lack thereof – of the provisions.[23] Both can be termed as functional competences, as the Treaties grant the EU powers to achieve an objective (the establishment and functioning of the internal market), but leave the substantive choices to the legislator's discretion.[24] This can make the IP legislation greatly dependent on that discretion – for example, with regard to the specific regime of each IP right.

3. The development of an intellectual property acquis

As mentioned above, the main conflicts between EU rules and national IP rights arise in relation to free movement and competition provisions. Several EU institutions have taken action to address these conflicts. The ECJ has ruled on the interplay between the relevant provisions of the Treaties and national IP rights; the Commission, the Council and the European Parliament

22. Joined Cases C-274 & C-295/11, *Spain v. Council*, at 21.
23. A. Ramalho, *The Competence of the European Union in Copyright Lawmaking. A Normative Perspective of EU Powers for Copyright Harmonization* (Springer, 2016).
24. T. Quadra-Salcedo Janini, *El Sistema Europeo de Distribución de Competencias* (Thomson Civitas, 2006) at 68 et seq; S. Weatherill, "Competence creep and competence control", 23 *Yearbook of European Law* (2004), at 6–7.

have been involved in the creation of legislation in the field of IP, either with a view to harmonize national IP laws or to create new, pan-European IP rights; the Commission has issued several decisions on IP agreements and their effects on competition.

The following sections examine the judicial and legislative actions that aimed at conciliating IP rights with free movement principles and internal market goals, as these have been the primary focus of EU institutions when dealing with IP. The analysis concerns the IP fields where that activity has been most visible: trademarks (3.1.), patents (3.2.) and copyright (3.3).[25]

3.1 *Trademarks*

The first visible EU intervention in the field of trademarks came from the ECJ. The Commission had early on begun work on the harmonization or unification of industrial property law – which comprised trademarks and patents[26] – but it was not until December 1988 that a Directive on trademarks was passed.[27] Before that, the ECJ had had the opportunity to decide on the conflict between national trademark rights and the relevant provisions of the Treaties.

In one of the first IP-related cases, the Court confirmed that trademarks fell under the property clause (Art. 345 TFEU in the current version of the Treaties) in the *Consten and Grundig* case.[28] It involved the firms Grundig and Consten, which had an exclusive distribution agreement whereby Consten was appointed by Grundig as the exclusive distributor of its products in France. Grundig products were sold in France by Consten under the trademark "Gint". When a third company started to sell Grundig's products having imported these products from another Member State, Consten sued for unfair competition and trademark infringement. Despite the recognition that trademarks fell under the property clause of the Treaty, the Court considered that there was a difference between the existence and the exercise of such rights. In the Court's view, the Treaty's provision meant that the existence (i.e., the grant) of the trademark was a matter for national law, but the Community could control the exercise of the right where necessary to assure compliance with Treaty norms.[29] Based on this reasoning, the exclusive distribution agreement between the parties was annulled due to its incompatibility with market competition rules.

The Court did not provide a general definition of what existence and exercise of rights amounted to. But in subsequent cases it was faced with situations where the exercise of trademark

---

25. Other IP rights that have figured less prominently in the EU IP landscape – with little references to the Court of Justice, negligible legislative intervention from the EU and/or not many conflicts with EU law and principles to account for – are not going to be analysed here. These include designs, geographical indications or trade secrets. Likewise, the question of enforcement of IP rights (harmonized by Dir. 2004/48/EC of the European Parliament and of the Council of 29 Apr. 2004 on the enforcement of intellectual property rights, O.J. 2004, L 195/16) will not be examined. All these are covered in a previous version of the current chapter: A. Ramalho, "Intellectual Property", available at <papers.ssrn.com/sol3/papers.cfm?abstract_id=2723932>.
26. European Commission, Memorandum on the creation of an EEC trademark, SEC (76) 2462, Bulletin of the European Communities Supplement 8/76, 6 July 1976, p. 5. Note however that the Commission had already initiated work regarding a possible harmonization and unification of industrial property law (including trademarks) in 1959 – see, for a thorough description of this background, C. Gielen, "Harmonization of trade mark law in Europe: The first trade mark harmonization Dir. of the European Council", 14 *European Intellectual Property Review* (1992), 262–269.
27. First Council Dir. 89/104/EEC of 21 Dec. 1988 to approximate the laws of the Member States relating to trade marks, O.J. 1989, L 40/1, replaced on codification by Dir. 2008/95/EC of 22 Oct. 2008, O.J. 2008, L 299/25.
28. Joined Cases 56 & 58/64, *Consten and Grundig v. Commission.*
29. *Consten and Grundig* at 345. See also U. Loewenheim, "Intellectual property before the European Court of Justice", 26 *International Review of Intellectual Property and Competition Law* (1995), 829–850, at 830; and K. Shaw, "Likelihood of coexistence: A comparative analysis of the interplay between European trademark law and free competition", 18 *University of Baltimore Intellectual Property Law Journal* (2009), 51–77, at 62–63.

rights could be at odds with free movement principles and/or the Community system of competition, and it established certain principles that ought to govern that conflict. These cases concerned mainly what are now Articles 34 and 36 TFEU, and how the protection of trademarks can come under the exception of Article 36 TFEU for the "protection of industrial and commercial property". It was in this context that the Court ruled that, in order for the exercise of trademark rights to be a valid derogation from the principle of free movement of goods, such exercise has to amount to a safeguard of rights which constitute the "specific subject matter" of trademarks.[30] As clarified by the Court, the specific subject matter of trademarks consists of putting products protected by the trademark on the market for the first time, as well as protecting the reputation of the trademark, namely by preventing competitors from selling products illegally bearing the trademark.[31] Also part of the specific subject matter of trademarks is the right to prevent uses of the trademark which hinder the guarantee of origin that the trademark stands for.[32] This guarantee of origin of the trademarked product to the consumer was termed by the Court the "essential function of trademarks", therefore hinting that the rights comprised in the "specific subject matter" of a trademark are what enable such trademark to perform its "essential function".[33] In other words, if the exercise of national trademark rights is confined to the specific subject matter of trademarks (e.g., putting a product bearing the trademark on the market for the first time), then such exercise can legitimately constitute a barrier to cross-border trade, as it comes under the derogation of Article 36 TFEU. However, any trade-hindering act that does not fall under the notion of specific subject matter of trademarks – for example, preventing third parties from further reselling a product bearing the trademark, where the later was marketed with the trademark owner's consent – cannot be saved by Article 36 TFEU and will be prohibited under Article 34 TFEU.

Several rulings of the ECJ have expanded upon the notion of specific subject matter and have clarified how Article 36 TFEU is to be applied to IP rights in general and trademarks in particular. Most prominently, it is now settled case law that, once the trademark owner has put the product on the market anywhere in the European Economic Area (EEA), or has consented to a third party doing so, the rights conferred by the trademark – its specific subject matter – are deemed to be exhausted.[34] So, for example, if the right holder sells his trademarked product for EURO 100 in Member State A and for EURO 200 in Member State B, he cannot prevent a third party from buying his goods in Member State A and reselling them in Member State B for EURO 150. This is known as the principle of exhaustion. Its main rationale is that, absent such principle, the trademark owner would be able to partition national markets by preventing parallel imports of the goods that she (or someone with her expressed or implied consent)[35] placed on the market herself – a situation that would be clearly at odds with internal market goals.

30. Case 16/74, *Centrafarm*, para 7. The "specific subject matter" doctrine was confirmed in several later cases: see *inter alia* Case 102/77, *Hoffmann-La Roche*, para 6; Case 58/80, *Dansk Supermarked*, para 11; Case 1/81, *Pfizer*, para 6.
31. Case 16/74, *Centrafarm*, para 8; Case 102/77, *Hoffmann-La Roche*, para 7; Case 3/78, *American Home Products*, para 11.
32. Case 102/77, *Hoffmann-La Roche*, para 7; Case 3/78, *American Home Products*, para 12.
33. Case 102/77, *Hoffmann-La Roche*, para 7.
34. Case 16/74, *Centrafarm*, at 9–11; Case C-10/89, *HAG II*, at 12; Case 58/80, *Dansk Supermarked*, at 11.
35. Implied consent can however only be valid if "it can be inferred from facts and circumstances prior to, simultaneous with or subsequent to the placing of the goods on the market [...] which [...] unequivocally demonstrates that the proprietor has renounced his exclusive rights" – see case C-324/08, *Makro v. Diesel*, and case law cited therein.

The need to address the challenges posed by trademarks to the making of a common market led the Commission to produce a Memorandum on the creation of a pan-European trademark,[36] where the case for a unitary trademark – a Community trademark that would be valid in all the Member States – was presented. It was also stressed that the Community trademark, while being an autonomous system, would coexist with national trademarks.[37] This coexistence however meant that the conflicts between national trademarks and the free movement of goods would persist. Therefore, together with the creation of a Community trademark, the Commission suggested the harmonization of national trademark laws.[38] These solutions were again brought up and emphasized in the Commission's 1985 White Paper "Completing the Internal Market".[39]

As a result, the First Council Directive 89/104/EEC to approximate the trademark laws of the Member States ("Trademark Directive) was adopted on 21 December 1988;[40] and the Council Regulation (EC) No 40/94 on the Community trademark ("Trademark Regulation") was passed on 20 December 1993.[41] As their names suggest, the Directive harmonized national trademark laws, whereas the Regulation introduced a new pan-European right – the Community trademark – in the EU legal order. The Directive and the Regulation do not differ much on many of the substantive provisions. The points where they do differ concern mainly the procedural aspects: these are mostly absent from the Directive,[42] while the Regulation contains detailed procedural rules (e.g., relating to application and registration procedures). Chiefly, the Regulation provides for the Office for Harmonization in the Internal Market (OHIM, now European Union Intellectual Property Office, or EUIPO), the EU agency responsible for managing the Community trademarks and designs.

Regarding the substantive rules, both the Directive and the Regulation establish that, for a sign to be registered as a trademark, it must be capable of (1) being represented graphically[43] and (2) distinguishing the goods and services of a trader from those of another.[44] Both set out the grounds for refusal of registration or invalidity of trademarks (such as, e.g., the lack of distinctiveness of the trademark; the likelihood of confusion of the trademark with another trader's trademark; or the fact that the trademark takes unfair advantage of the distinctive character of a Community trademark that has a reputation, just to name a few).[45] Other corresponding provisions are the rights conferred by a trademark (which roughly amount to preventing the use of the same or similar trademark in relation to the same or similar goods or services so as to avoid confusion of consumers, unless the trademark has a reputation, in which case it is legitimate

---

36. European Commission, Memorandum on the creation of an EEC trademark, SEC (76) 2462, Bulletin of the European Communities Supplement 8/76, 6 July 1976.
37. Memorandum at 9.
38. Ibid. at 12.
39. White Paper from the Commission to the European Council "Completing the internal market", COM(85)310 final, para 146.
40. Trademark Directive: First Council Directive 89/104/EEC of 21 December 1988 to approximate the laws of the Member States relating to trade marks, O.J. 1989 L 40/1, replaced on codification by Directive 2008/95/EC of 22 October 2008, O.J. 2008, L 299/25.
41. O.J. 1994, L 11/1.
42. As revealed by Recitals 6, 8, 9 and 11 of the Dir.
43. This requirement has now been changed to "being capable of being represented in the Register of European Union trademarks" by Reg. (EU) 2015/2424 of the European Parliament and of the Council of 16 December 2015, O.J. 2015, L 341/21 ("Amending Reg.") and Dir. (EU) 2015/2436 of the European Parliament and of the Council of 16 December 2015, O.J. 2015, L 336/1 ("Amending Dir.").
44. Art. 2 of the Dir. and Art. 4 of the Reg.
45. Arts. 3 and 4 of the Dir., and Arts. 7, 8, 52 and 53 of the Reg.

for the owner to prevent use in relation to dissimilar goods or services as well);[46] the grounds for revocation of trademarks (e.g., due to its non-use);[47] or the limitation of the effects of the trademark (for example, the trademark owner cannot prohibit the use of a third party's own name in the course of trade).[48]

The principle of exhaustion has also been codified in both instruments,[49] and since then the ECJ has continued to sharpen it by reference to the relevant provisions. Thus, for instance, the Court has ruled out the possibility of the so-called "international exhaustion" (i.e., where the right holder has placed the goods on the market outside the EEA). In such cases, according to the Court, the right holder is able to prevent parallel imports, as her trademark rights have not been exhausted by the sale of the product outside the EEA.[50] The Court has also elaborated on the concept of "legitimate reasons" for the trademark owner to oppose further marketing of the goods (i.e., where exhaustion might not apply),[51] which include repackaging of the goods by the parallel importer that can mislead the consumer as to their origin,[52] or advertisement of the goods that seriously damages the reputation of the trademark.[53]

In 2011, the Commission revealed its intention to revise both the Directive and the Regulation, so as to modernize the trademark system at EU and Member State levels.[54] In 2013, the Commission presented its proposals to reform the Directive and the Regulation, which were finally adopted in December 2015.[55] Both proposals clarify existing provisions (namely in what concerns the scope and limitations of trademarks), streamline procedures (in the case of the Proposal for a Directive, procedural rules are introduced *ex novo*), and establish a framework for cooperation between the EUIPO and national offices.

3.2 *Patents and rights similar to patents*

Some principles and doctrines established by the ECJ in relation to trademarks have also been developed by the Court in the field of patents. The Court confirmed that, also when it comes to patents, the Treaty cannot affect the existence of national patent rights, but can nevertheless affect their exercise.[56] The Court stated as well that derogations to the free movement of goods should only be admitted where necessary to safeguard the "specific subject matter" of patents, which it deemed to be the exclusive right to produce and commercialize for the first time the patented product, as well as the right to oppose infringements.[57] Yet, the right owner cannot

46. Art. 5 of the Dir. and Art. 9 of the Reg.
47. Art. 12 of the Dir. and Art. 51 of the Reg.
48. Art. 6 of the Dir. and Art, 12 of the Reg.
49. Art. 7 of the Dir. and Art. 13 of the Reg.
50. Case C-355/96, *Hartlauer*, and Case C-173/98, *Dubois*.
51. Art. 7 para 2 of the Dir. and Art. 13 para 2 of the Reg.
52. Case 102/77, *Hoffmann-La Roche* paras. 7–9 and joined Cases C-427, 429 & 436/93, *Bristol-Myers Squibb and others v. Paranova*, para 47. The Court has however put forth an extensive list of requirements that, if met, render the repackaging legitimate and therefore conducive to an exhaustion of the owner's rights – see para 14 of *Hoffmann-La Roche* and para 79 of *Bristol-Myers Squibb and others v. Paranova*. For further development and clarification of the requirements, see case C-348/04, *Boehringer Ingelheim*.
53. Case C-337/95, *Parfums Christian Dior*, paras. 43–46.
54. Communication from the Commission to the Parliament, the Council the European Economic and Social Committee and the Committee of the Regions "A single market for intellectual property rights. Boosting creativity and innovation to provide economic growth, high quality jobs and first class products and services in Europe", COM(2011)287 final, at 9.
55. See *supra* note 43.
56. Case 15/74, *de Peijper*, para 7.
57. Case 15/74, *de Peijper*, paras. 8–9.

oppose further commercialization of the protected product, since, similarly to what happens with trademarks, rights are exhausted after the product is put on the market by her or with her consent, or by a person economically or legally dependent on her.[58]

However, as compared to trademarks, EU legislation on patents is sketchier. Five EU legislative measures are currently in force in the field of patents and rights similar to patents, all of them being quite sectorial: Directive 98/44/EC, on the legal protection of biotechnological inventions;[59] the Supplementary Protection Certificate Regulations for medicinal products[60] and plant protection products;[61] the Regulation on compulsory licensing of pharmaceutical patents;[62] and the Regulation on Community plant variety rights.[63]

As the name indicates, the Directive on the legal protection of biotechnological inventions aims at harmonizing patent protection for biological material.[64] The Supplementary Protection Certificate Regulations create a right akin to patents – the Supplementary Protection Certificate, or SPC – that confers the same rights as an original patent in relation to the relevant ingredient of the medicinal product or the plant protection product.[65] These certificates compensate patent owners for delays in marketing medicinal or plant protection products due to the (often lengthy) processes of getting regulatory approval for them, offering in practice an extension of protection of these products for up to 5 years (and thus being frequently referred to as "patent extensions").[66] The Regulation on compulsory licensing of patents harmonizes the conditions under which compulsory licenses are granted in relation to patents and SPCs concerning the manufacture and sale of pharmaceutical products, when the latter are to be exported to certain

58. Case 15/74, *de Peijper*, para 11; Case 187/80, *Merck*, paras. 9, 12; Case 19/84, *Hoechst*, para 22. Note however that, if the protected product is put on the market under a compulsory license, the right holder will not be considered to have consented on the commercialization, and there will be no exhaustion – see *Hoechst*, paras. 23–27.
59. Dir. 98/44/EC of the European Parliament and of the Council of 6 July 1998 on the legal protection of biotechnological inventions, O.J. 1998, L 213/13.
60. Reg. (EC) 469/2009 of the European Parliament and of the Council of 6 May 2009 concerning the supplementary protection certificate for medicinal products (Codified version), O.J. 2009, L 152/1.
61. Reg. (EC) 1610/96 of the European Parliament and of the Council of 23 July 1996 concerning the creation of a supplementary protection certificate for plant protection products, O.J. 1996, L 198/30.
62. Reg. (EC) 816/2006 of the European Parliament and of the Council of 17 May 2006 on compulsory licensing of patents relating to the manufacture of pharmaceutical products for export to countries with public health problems, O.J. 2006, L 157/1.
63. Council Reg. (EC) 2100/94 of 27 July 1994 on Community plant variety rights, O.J. 1994, L 227/1. Plant varieties and patent systems are mutually exclusive (see Art. 53 (b) of the European Patent Convention and Art. 92 para 1 of the Reg.) but their nature is somewhat similar – see T. Millett, "The Community system of plan variety rights", 24 EL Rev. (1999), 231–258, at 231.
64. Defined as "any material containing genetic information and capable of reproducing itself or being reproduced in a biological system" (Art. 2, para 1(a) of the Dir.). The Dir. however excludes from patentability: plant and animal varieties; essentially biological processes for the production of plants or animals; the human body and the simple discovery of one of its elements, including the sequence or partial sequence of a gene; and inventions contrary to *ordre public* or morality, such as processes for cloning human beings (Arts. 4, 5 and 6 of the Dir.). See, for an analysis of the Dir., G. Kamstra, *Patents on Biotechnological Inventions: The EC Directive* (Sweet & Maxwell, 2002).
65. See Art. 4 of both Regs.
66. Art. 13 of both Regs. In the case of the SPC for medicinal products, the SPC can last for an extra 6 months on top of those 5 years – see Art. 13(3) of Reg. (EC) 469/2009. For further comments and explanation of the main features of SPCs, see T. Cook, op. cit. *supra* note 12, at 542–561; L. Bently and B. Sherman, op. cit. *supra* note 3, at 602–606.

third countries in need of those products.[67] Finally, the Regulation on Community plant variety rights grants a pan-European right to new plant varieties (i.e., a unitary right valid throughout the EU, which, unlike the Community trademark, is not cumulative with national plant variety rights), and provides for the Community Plant Variety Office (CPVO), the EU agency responsible for managing the system of plant variety rights.[68]

Efforts to regulate the patent field more broadly have been quashed in one way or the other. The Commission set up a working group on patents early on, which resulted in the 1975 draft of the Community Patent Convention (CPC). The CPC provided for a Community patent of a unitary nature. However, the CPC didn't succeed for several reasons (including differences in the legal traditions of the Member States, high national thresholds for ratification and the absence of a clear mandate of the Community).[69]

Despite the absence of a more comprehensive legislative activity at the EU level, the European Patent Convention (EPC), to which all EU member states are parties (together with a few third countries) did in practice harmonize a number of substantive rules, namely those on patentability and scope of protection.[70] Moreover, the EPC created the European Patent Office (EPO), which is the granting authority of European patents. Nevertheless, these "European" patents are not pan-European as such – the EPO provides the contracting states with a single point of procedure for patent application, granting and post-grant oppositions; but after grant the patents are subject to national laws (so, for instance, infringement and invalidation actions must take place on a national basis). The applicant chooses the countries where she seeks protection when applying to the EPO, and those may or may not coincide with the EU territory in its entirety, depending on the applicant's choice. The current "European" patent thus amounts to a bundle of national patents, with a partly centralized procedural system. In other words, the EPC system dealt with territoriality issues only to a very limited extent.[71]

More recently, in 2012, all Member States except for Italy and Spain agreed on a "patent package", a legislative initiative comprising two Regulations and an international agreement. The "patent package" is geared towards the institution of a European patent with unitary effect, created by Regulation 1257/2012,[72] and a unified patent court, established by an international agreement.[73] The European patent with unitary effect is a patent granted by the EPO under the rules and procedures of the EPC, which benefits from unitary effect in the participating Member States by virtue of Regulation 1257/2012.[74] The unified patent court, as envisaged, will have exclusive jurisdiction both regarding the future unitary patent and the existing patents granted under the EPC.[75]

---

67. Art. 1 of the Reg. See, on the Reg., J. Cornides, "European Union adopts regulation on compulsory licensing of pharmaceutical products for export", 10 *Journal of World Intellectual Property* (2007), 70–77.
68. On Community Plant Variety Rights, see T. Millett, op. cit. *supra* note 63, at 231–258; B. Kiewiet, "The Community plant variety protection system", 1 *Irish Intellectual Property Law Quarterly* (2011), 168–171.
69. See J. Pila, "The European Patent: An old and vexing problem", 62 *International and Comparative Law Quarterly* (2013), 917- 940, and references cited therein; T. Cook, op. cit. *supra* note 12, at 533–534.
70. See Part II of the EPC.
71. Although, from an industry perspective, the advantages of the current "European patent" are not to be overlooked – e.g., the applicant can limit the geographical scope of the patent to countries where she has an actual commercial interest, which allows her to adopt more flexible patenting strategies (A. Kur and T. Dreier, *European Intellectual Property Law. Text, Cases and Materials* (Edward Elgar, 2013), at 88).
72. Reg. (EU) 1257/2012 of the European Parliament and of the Council of 17 Dec. 2012, implementing enhanced cooperation in the area of the creation of unitary patent protection, O.J. 2012, L 361/1.
73. Council of the European Union, Agreement on a Unified Patent Court, O.J. 2013, C 175/1.
74. Art. 2(b) and (c) of Reg. 1257/2012.
75. Agreement on a Unified Patent Court, Art. 1.

The patent package also includes Regulation 1260/2012,[76] dealing with the thorny issue of translation of patents.[77] The Regulation allows for the filing of applications for European patents with unitary effect in one of the official languages of the EPO (English, French and German), with no need for further translation into other EU official languages after a transitional period and save where a dispute arises.[78]

The benefits of the "patent package" to the establishment of an internal market are however undermined due to the opt-out of Italy and Spain.[79] The Regulations were passed under the enhanced cooperation procedure, a mechanism that allows Member States to cooperate in areas where the competence of the EU is not exclusive. However, acts adopted following the enhanced cooperation procedure are not binding on non-participating Member States (in this case, Spain and Italy),[80] which might run counter to internal market aims.[81] The international agreement creating a unified patent court will enter into force when it is ratified by at least 13 states, including France, Germany and the United Kingdom. The two Regulations will enter into force when the agreement does. At the time of writing, 12 countries had ratified the agreement (with Germany and the United Kingdom missing from the list).

3.3 *Copyright and related rights*

As in other fields of IP, the ECJ pioneered EU intervention in the area of copyright and related rights A few principles and doctrines were developed early on by the Court, much like what happened in relation to trademarks and patents. The existence versus exercise doctrine was transposed to the field of copyright and related rights in the *Deutsche Grammophon v. Metro* case.[82] Also in that decision, the Court ruled that the provisions referring to exceptions to the free movement of goods and to competition (Arts. 30, 81 and 82 EC Treaty, nowadays Arts. 36, 101 and 102 TFEU respectively) could be relevant to a right related to copyright.[83] The Court did not justify this stance, but a possible explanation might be that the right of a producer of phonograms (which was the right involved in the case) has some similarities to such rights as patents or trademarks, due to its economic nature – therefore being able to come under the definition of "industrial and commercial property".[84]

---

76. Council Reg. (EU) 1260/2012 of 17 Dec. 2012, implementing enhanced cooperation in the area of the creation of unitary patent protection with regard to the applicable translation arrangements, O.J. 2012, L 361/89.
77. Reportedly, disagreement regarding language regimes and translation has long been a considerable obstacle in the creation of a EU patent regime – see M. Lamping, "Enhanced cooperation – A proper approach to market integration in the field of unitary patent protection?", 42 *International Review of Intellectual Property and Competition Law* (2011), 879–925, at 900, and references cited therein. And, in fact, one of the arguments of Spain and Italy to oppose the patent package was exactly the language arrangements – see Joined Cases C-274 & C-295/11, *Spain and Italy v. Council.*
78. Arts. 3 paras. 1, 4 and 6 of the Reg.
79. Italy signed the Agreement on the Unified Patent Court, but did not take part in the rest of the patent package.
80. Art. 20 para 4 TEU.
81. As pointed out by R. Hilty et al., "The unitary patent package: Twelve reasons for concern", Max Planck Institute for Intellectual Property and Competition Law Research Paper No. 12–12, available at <papers.ssrn.com/sol3/papers.cfm?abstract_id=2169254> (last accessed 30 May 2017), at 1.
82. Case 78/70, *Deutsche Grammophon v. Metro*. See also Case 262/81, *Coditel v. Ciné Vog Films (Coditel II)*, where the ECJ considered that the distinction between existence and exercise of the right, developed in the framework of the free movement of goods, was applicable to the free movement of services as well (in this case, to the retransmission of a film's broadcast).
83. Case 78/70, *Deutsche Grammophon* at 11.
84. A. Françon, "Le droit d'auteur et le traité de Rome instituant la Communauté Economique Européenne", 100 *Revue internationale du droit d'auteur* (1979), 128–197, at 150–151.

The Court reasoned that restrictions to the free movement of goods based on the protection of industrial and commercial property were only justified when "safeguarding rights which constitute the specific subject matter of that property".[85] The meaning of "specific subject matter" was developed in subsequent cases and seems to be linked to the protection of certain core rights inherent to copyright and related rights. These core rights, according to the ECJ, are of two kinds: moral and economic.[86] While moral rights enable in particular authors and performers "to object to any distortion, mutilation or other modification of a work which would be prejudicial to their honour or reputation," economic rights grant them "the right to exploit commercially the marketing of the protected work" (which can be done *inter alia* by conferring licenses in return for payment of royalties).[87]

However, this is subject to the caveat of exhaustion: the right holder cannot prevent further distribution of the copyright goods when such goods were placed on the market by herself or by someone with her consent.[88] But here the Court has differentiated sale from other forms of commercial exploitation, namely rental. For purposes of the principle of exhaustion, the Court decided that the sale of a copyright product with the consent of the right holder did not have the effect of exhausting other forms of commercial exploitation such as rental[89] (and this lies at the heart of the justification for having a Directive on rental and lending rights, as seen below). National laws that granted rental rights aimed at providing right holders with an additional source of revenue that reflected the number of occasions of actual rental, allowing them to partake in the rental market.[90] If that right were to be exhausted by sale, it "would be rendered worthless," according to the Court.[91]

Following that argument, the outcome of cases in relation to services such as public communications of the copyright work was different. This was the question at stake in *Coditel I*.[92] The Court established that, since public communications may be "infinitely repeated", the problems that arise in that realm are different from the ones relating to works that are brought to the public in a material form (like books or records).[93] In such cases, the copyright holder has a "legitimate interest" in calculating the due fees on the basis of the actual or probable number of performances.

The legislative intervention in the field of copyright and related rights has been done through a series of Directives aiming at harmonizing specific aspects of national regimes. Each Directive reveals a particular vision and deals with specific aspects of copyright and/or related rights. As their names indicate – Computer Programs Directive,[94] Rental and Lending Rights Directive,[95]

---

85. See Case 78/70, *Deutsche Grammophon* at 11. See also along the same lines Case 58/80, *Dansk Supermarked*.
86. Joined Cases C-92 & 326/92, *Phil Collins*, at 20.
87. Joined Cases C-92 & 326/92, *Phil Collins* at 20, later confirmed by Joined Cases C-403 & 429/08, *Premier League & Karen Murphy*, at 107.
88. See, *inter alia*, Case 78/70, *Deutsche Grammophon* at 13; Joined Cases 55 & 57/80, *Musik-Vertrieb v. Gema*, at 10, 15, 27; *Dansk Supermarked*, at 11–12.
89. Case 158/86, *Warner* at 18–19.
90. Ibid., at 14–15.
91. Ibid., at 18.
92. See *supra* note 10.
93. See Case 62/79, *Coditel I* at 12.
94. Council Dir. 91/250/EEC of 14 May 1991 on the legal protection of computer programs, O.J. 1991, L 122/42, replaced on codification by Dir. 2009/24/EC of the European Parliament and of the Council of 23 Apr. 2009, O.J. 2009, L 111/16.
95. Rental and Lending Rights Directive: Council Directive 92/100/EEC of 19 November 1992 on rental right and lending right and on certain rights related to copyright in the field of intellectual property, O.J. 1992, L

Satellite and Cable Directive,[96] Term of Protection Directive,[97] Database Directive,[98] Information Society Directive,[99] Resale Right Directive,[100] Orphan Works Directive[101] and Collective Management Directive[102]–, the individual Directives cover specific features of copyright and related rights, such as protected subject matter (like computer programs or databases), exclusive rights (e.g., rental and lending), or duration (term of protection). In fact, the only Directive so far that has had a more horizontal approach is the Information Society Directive, as it concerns the main rights in copyright and exceptions thereof. But there is currently no truly horizontal instrument regulating copyright in a holistic fashion in the EU.

This piecemeal harmonization was chosen because it was felt that not all aspects of national laws would merit attention: on the one hand, Member States' legislation had already been approximated through international treaties; on the other hand, not all features of national copyright/related rights laws were considered to have cross-border relevance.[103] As a result, the EU legislative framework in copyright and related rights has left untouched certain parts of national regimes, such as moral rights of authors or copyright contracts. To add to the legislative patchwork, different Directives used different legislative techniques. In general, there is a tendency to use total harmonization in relation to the definition of protected subject matter and economic rights, while other aspects, such as exceptions to exclusive rights, are regulated using minimum or partial harmonization.[104] As a result, national laws on copyright and related rights are streamlined in some aspects but not in others – even in relation to subjects that have (supposedly) been harmonized by Directives.

It is also noteworthy that some of these legislative initiatives are to a certain extent a by-product of ECJ's decisions. It is the case of the Satellite and Cable Directive, which is an offspring of *Coditel I*.[105] There, the ECJ sided with the right holder of copyright in a film and ruled that it was

---

346/61, replaced on codification by Directive 2006/115/EC of the European Parliament and of the Council of 12 December 2006, O.J. 2006, L 376/28).

96. Council Dir. 93/83/EEC of 27 Sept. 1993 on the coordination of certain rules concerning copyright and rights related to copyright applicable to satellite broadcasting and cable retransmission, O.J. 1993, L 248/15.
97. See *supra* note 6.
98. Dir. 96/6/EC of the European Parliament and of the Council of 11 Mar. 1996 on the legal protection of databases, O.J. 1996, L 77/20.
99. Dir. 2001/29/EC of the European Parliament and of the Council of 22 May 2001 on the harmonization of certain aspects of copyright and related rights in the information society, O.J. 2001, L 167/10.
100. Dir. 2001/84/EC of the European Parliament and of the Council of 22 Sept. 2001 on the resale right for the benefit of the author of an original work of art, O.J. 2001, L 272/32.
101. Dir. 2012/28/EU of the European Parliament and of the Council of 25 Oct. 2012 on certain permitted uses of orphan works, O.J. 2012, L 299/5.
102. Dir. 2014/26/EU of the European Parliament and of the Council of 26 Feb. 2014 on collective management of copyright and related rights and multi-territorial licensing of rights in musical works for online use in the internal market, O.J. 2014, L 84/72.
103. European Commission, Green Paper on Copyright and the Challenge of Technology – Copyright issues requiring immediate action, COM(88)172, para 1.4.9.
104. This is however not always the case – see e.g. Art. 5 of the Term of Protection Dir. (2006), using a partial harmonization technique in relation to protected subject matter. The provision gives Member States the possibility of protecting critical and scientific publications of works that have come into the public domain – Member States have the option of implementing this protection or not.
105. See *supra* note 10. The Explanatory Memorandum to the Satellite and Cable Proposal (Proposal for a Council Dir. on the coordination of certain rules concerning copyright and neighbouring rights applicable to satellite broadcasting and cable retransmission, COM(91)276 final) states in para 61: "[G]iven the disparities that exist it is conceivable that the Court of Justice could follow its findings in *Coditel* [Case 62/79] and hold that there has not yet been established a single audiovisual area". The creation of an EU audiovisual area is one of the aims of the Dir. (see the Explanatory Memorandum, para 44 and 54).

possible for the right owner to forbid an unauthorized cable retransmission in another Member State. Likewise, the Rental and Lending Rights Directive was partially based on *Warner*.[106] In this case, the Court confirmed that a national copyright (in this particular context, Danish) could, in certain situations, restrict Community trade. The Term of Protection Directive was also a partial result of *EMI Electrola v. Patricia*,[107] where the Court ruled that the differences between national laws prevented the distribution of imported Danish records (where they were already in the public domain) in Germany (where copyright subsisted). In the decision, the ECJ suggested that this outcome – which of course was not the most desired for purposes of establishing an internal market – was due to the "lack of harmonization or approximation of legislation", which ascribed to Member States the determination of the conditions and rules for the protection of literary and artistic property.[108] The case was taken up by the Commission as one of the justifications to act, as shown in the Explanatory Memorandum to the Term of Protection Proposal.[109]

Some established principles in the field of copyright have been called into question, mainly due to the advent of the Internet. It is the case of the dividing line between goods and services, which has been challenged in recent years. Offering copyright goods online is characterized by an immateriality that is more compliant with the definition of a service than that of goods. Such offering can be "infinitely repeated", as it does not imply a physical copy. In that case, distributing copyright works online would not cause the right to be exhausted – with the result that a user who downloaded a copy of a protected copyright work would not be allowed to resell that digital copy. This was dealt with specifically by the Information Society Directive, where it is stated that exhaustion "does not arise in the case of services and on-line services in particular".[110] Nevertheless, due to the complex legislative map in copyright/related rights, the rule of no exhaustion in the online world is not transversal. In particular, it does not necessarily apply to computer programs made available online for users to download. As the ECJ made clear in *Usedsoft v. Oracle*,[111] the exhaustion of the distribution right of computer programs concerns both tangible and intangible copies of that program, and hence also copies of programs which, on the occasion of their first sale, have been downloaded from the Internet. The Court justified the compatibility of this decision with the Information Society Directive with the fact that the case came under the exhaustion rule of the Computer Programs Directive (and not the Information Society Directive). According to the Court, the Computer Programs Directive constitutes a *lex specialis* in relation to the provisions of the Information Society Directive.[112]

This and other cases on several provisions of the different Directives highlight the complex intricacies of the legislative patchwork in the field of copyright and related rights, and are a paramount justification for the public consultation on the review of the EU copyright rules,

106. See Explanatory Memorandum to the Proposal for a Council Dir. on rental right, lending right, and on certain rights related to copyright, COM(90)586 final, at 26–27, where the Commission refers expressly to this case.
107. Case 341/87, *EMI Electrola*.
108. *EMI Electrola* at 11.
109. See Explanatory Memorandum to the Proposal for a Council Dir. harmonizing the term of protection of copyright and certain related rights, COM(92)33 final, at 14–15.
110. Recital 29 of the Information Society Dir.
111. Case C-128/11, *Usedsoft v. Oracle*.
112. *Usedsoft* para 51.

launched by the Commission at the end of 2013.[113] The Commission has since proposed a Regulation on the cross border portability of online content services,[114] a Regulation on the exercise of copyright and related rights in the context of online transmissions of broadcasting organizations and retransmissions,[115] and a Directive on copyright in the Digital Single Market.[116] At the time of writing neither had yet been adopted.

4. Conclusion

The area of IP has over time gained prominence at the EU level. At the outset, awareness of the relevance of IP to the European project came mostly through the ECJ and its first decisions on the conflict between national IP rights and Treaty rules. The Commission started work in this field early on, but in previous versions of the Treaties the legislature's hands were tied for reasons of lack of, or burdensome, empowering norms. The legislative competence of the EU in internal market-related matters has however evolved, and the TFEU in particular marks a different stage of EU integration in what IP is concerned.

There is at the moment an array of secondary legislation in the IP field. Still, the IP legislative landscape has a couple of deficiencies. First, it lacks consistency, either from one IP area to another or even within the same IP subject. Different features of IP rights' regimes confer different spaces of regulatory freedom to Member States, which impair the harmonization project in a transversal manner. Moreover, piecemeal harmonization approaches, such as the one adopted in copyright, leave harmonization gaps within the same IP field. Consistency is also affected by the choice of the legislature to use different harmonization techniques in the same instrument. As a result, the topography of the EU IP field is less than homogeneous.

Second, and in connection therewith, the EU intervention in IP has hardly solved the problem of territoriality. Harmonization of national laws, which has been the preferred approach in most cases, does not change the fact that national IP rights are still defined along national borders. The approximation of national laws can to a certain extent address problems of cross-border trade; yet, due to the lack of consistency in most of the harmonization process, barriers to free movement of goods and services are likely to persist. The hindrance to the internal market caused by territoriality can be tackled by creating unitary IP titles, but that has only happened in a few cases (most notably, trademarks and designs).

However, a new wave of legislative intervention in the IP arena seems to be on its way, and it might just address the abovementioned shortcomings. On the one hand, new harmonizing measures can address problems of consistency, either through codification of existing Directives or through recasting.[117] On the other hand, Article 118 TFEU might change the stakes and cause more pan-European IP rights to be created, particularly in the fields of patents and copyright.

---

113. Public consultation on the review of EU copyright rules, available at <ec.europa.eu/internal_market/consultations/2013/copyright-rules/index_en.htm> (last accessed 13 Aug. 2015), at 2. See also Communication from the Commission to the European Parliament, the Council, the European Economic and Social Committee and the Committee of the Regions, A Single Market for Intellectual Property Rights. Boosting creativity and innovation to provide economic growth, high quality jobs and first class products and services in Europe, COM(2011)287 final, at 9–11, where the case for a copyright overhaul is made.
114. COM(2015)627 final, from 9.12.2015.
115. COM/2016/0594 final – 2016/0284 (COD), from 14.9.2016.
116. COM/2016/0593 final – 2016/0280 (COD), from 14.9.2016.
117. Codification replaces existing directives by one single act, but it does not alter their substance, nor does it comprise a change in policy. Recasting implies codification, but it also seeks to amend the directives in one single act – see Commission Communication on Updating and Simplifying the Community Acquis, COM(2003)71 final, at 12–13.

Further reading

Geiger, C., (Ed.), *Constructing European Intellectual Property. Achievements and New Perspectives* (Edward Elgar, 2013).

Kur, A., and Dreier, T., *European Intellectual Property Law. Text, Cases and Materials* (Edward Elgar, 2013).

Pila, J., and C. Wadlow, (Eds.), *The Unitary EU Patent System* (Hart/Bloomsbury, 2015).

Ramalho, A., *The Competence of the European Union in Copyright Lawmaking. A Normative Perspective of EU Powers for Copyright Harmonization* (Springer, 2016).

Seville, C., *EU Intellectual Property Law and Policy*, 2nd ed. (Edward Elgar, 2016).

CHAPTER 25
COMPANY LAW

*M.A. Verbrugh**

1. Introduction

Company laws of the Member States have to a great extent been shaped by EU legislation and have been influenced in important ways by the case law of the Court of Justice of the European Union (CJEU) on the right of establishment.

Apart from harmonization of company law in the EU through directives, the European legislator also adopted several regulations on supranational companies on the basis of Article 352 TFEU. Lastly, some influence on the company laws for listed companies in the Member States derives from recommendations from the Commission.[1]

In section 2, the freedom of establishment and case law on this provision will be discussed. Section 3 analyses the harmonization of company law through directives. Supranational companies will be dealt with in section 4. In section 5, the most important developments on the modernization of European company law are described.

2. Freedom of establishment and case law

2.1 *Introduction*

Articles 49 and 54 TFEU contain the right of establishment of companies or firms. The first provision grants legal persons the freedom of establishment, the second one sets the boundaries on companies or firms that can invoke this right (2.2). In a number of cases, the CJEU ruled on the compatibility of Member States' legislative choices to determine the applicable company law to legal persons. Therefore, before the case law will be dealt with (2.4), the two doctrines to determine the applicable company law will have to be clarified (2.3).

2.2 *Articles 49 and 54 TFEU*

Article 49 TFEU reads as follows:

> "[...] restrictions on the freedom of establishment of nationals of a Member State in the territory of another Member State shall be prohibited. Such prohibition shall also apply

* M.A. Verbrugh is Associate Professor in Company Law at the Erasmus School of Law at the Erasmus University Rotterdam, the Netherlands.

1. See Recommendation 2004/913/EC and Recommendation 2005/162/EC. Recommendations shall have no binding force. See Art. 288 TFEU. See for an alternative and supplement to the existing EU instruments for the convergence of company law, The European Model Company Act (EMCA; first edition 2017) and T. Baums and P. Krüger Andersen, "The European model Company Law Act Project", ECGI Law Working Paper No. 097/2008, Mar. 2008.

> to restrictions on the setting-up of agencies, branches or subsidiaries by nationals of any Member State established in the territory of any Member State.
>
> Freedom of establishment shall include the right to take up and pursue activities as self-employed persons and to set up and manage undertakings, in particular companies or firms within the meaning of the second paragraph of Article 54, under the conditions laid down for its own nationals by the law of the country where such establishment is effected, subject to the provisions of the Chapter relating to capital."

This provision shows that an important element in the prohibition on restrictions on the freedom of establishment entails a prohibition of discrimination: the provisions on freedom of establishment predominantly aim to ensure that foreign nationals and companies are treated in the host Member State in the same way as nationals of that State. Furthermore, the provisions prohibit the State of origin from hindering the establishment in another Member State of one of its nationals or of a company incorporated under its legislation.[2]

The CJEU grants a broad interpretation to the right of establishment: it covers all measures which permit or even merely impede access to another Member State, without formally distinguishing on the basis of the nationality of the legal persons concerned.[3]

In order to meet the criteria of an establishment, an economic activity should be involved by the undertaking with a presence in the Member State on a permanent basis.[4] In case the law of a Member State constitutes a restriction on the right of establishment, the CJEU assesses whether it pursues a legitimate objective compatible with the Treaty and is justified by Treaty derogations or by imperative reasons in the public interest.[5] In such a case, the CJEU further examines whether its application is applied in a non-discriminatory manner, is appropriate to ensure the attainment of the objective thus pursued and does not go beyond what is necessary to attain it.

According to Article 54(1) TFEU, companies or firms formed in accordance with the law of a Member State and having their registered office, central administration or principal place of business within the Union shall, for the purposes of the chapter on the right of establishment, be treated in the same way as natural persons who are nationals of Member States. Member States determine which companies or firms can be set up and under which conditions. The so called connecting or linking factors registered office, central administration *or* principal place of business have been put as alternatives and on the same footing in this provision, since the use of these factors differ in the Member States (see section 2.3 below).[6] "Companies or firms" means companies or firms constituted under civil or commercial law, including cooperative societies, and other legal persons governed by public or private law, save for those which are non-profit-making (Art. 54(2) TFEU).

---

2. See Case C-96/08, *CIBA*.
3. See also Case C-411/03, *Sevic*, para 18.
4. See Case C-221/89, *Factortame and Others*, para 20; Case C-246/89, *Commission v. United Kingdom*, para 21; Case C-196/04, *Cadbury Schweppes*, para 54 and Case C-378/10, *Vale*, para 34.
5. See also Art. 52 TFEU. As imperative reasons in the public interest the Court has accepted the protection of the interests of creditors, minority shareholders and employees, the preservation of the effectiveness of fiscal supervision and the fairness of commercial transactions. See amongst others Case C-208/00, *Überseering*, para 92; Case C-167/01, *Inspire Art*, para 132, and Case C-378/10, *Vale*, para 39. See also Case C-212/97, *Centros*, para 34.
6. See Case C-81/87, *Daily Mail*, paras. 19–21, Case C-208/00, *Überseering*, paras. 68–69 and Case C-210/06, *Cartesio*, paras. 105–109. See for these cases *infra*, section 2.4.

2.3 Incorporation doctrine and real seat doctrine

Only companies that are recognized by Member States can invoke the freedom of establishment. For both the recognition of the company by the Member State of origin as for the recognition by other Member States,[7] the incorporation doctrine and the real seat doctrine play an important role.

Companies are creatures of the law and only exist by virtue of national legislation which determines their incorporation and functioning. The legislation of the Member States varies widely in regard the factor providing a connection to the national territory required for the incorporation of a company.[8] In the EU, two doctrines are used as the connecting factor to determine the applicable company law: the incorporation doctrine and the real seat doctrine.[9] In the first doctrine, the company law rules of the Member State in which the company has lawfully been set up will be applicable.[10] In general, this Member State will require the registered office to be within its territory. In the real seat doctrine, the company law of the Member State where the real seat is situated will apply.[11] The exact meaning of "real seat" depends on the Member State applying the real seat doctrine, but in most cases it will refer to the place of the central administration and in some cases it will refer to the principal place of business. Real seat doctrine countries will require that the registered office is located in the same Member State or place as the real seat.

Although the real seat doctrine has traditionally been mostly applied in the EU, over the last years some Member States have changed to the incorporation doctrine due to the flexibility the incorporation doctrine provides to companies.[12] Furthermore, the use of the incorporation doctrine stimulates the setting up of companies from Member States applying this doctrine in other Member States and thereby competition between company laws in the EU.

Due to the application of the two doctrines in the EU problems can arise in practice when companies move their real seat to another Member State.[13] If the real seat is moved from a real seat doctrine country to an incorporation doctrine country, the home country will no longer apply its company law, but also the host country will not apply its own company law. In the opposite situation, where a company moves its real seat from an incorporation doctrine country to a real seat doctrine country and the doctrines are strictly applied, the first and the latter country will apply their own company law. In other words, after a company moves its real seat, a situation can occur where no company law is applicable, as well as a situation where two company laws are applicable. The CJEU dealt with these and similar situations in several cases in light of the freedom of establishment.

---

7. The *Convention on the Mutual Recognition of Companies and Legal Persons,* which was signed in 1968 by the original six Member States, never entered into force. See Bull. EC Supp. 2/89 and V. Edwards, *EC Company Law* (OUP, 1999), 384.
8. See Case C-81/87, *Daily Mail*, paras. 19–21.
9. Also known as statutory seat doctrine and siège réel doctrine. See also P. Paschalidis, "Freedom of establishment and private international law for corporations", (2012) *Oxford Private International Law Series,* Ch. 1–2 and S. Rammeloo, "Corporations in private international law. A European perspective", (2001) *Oxford Private International Law Series,* Ch. 2.
10. Amongst others The Netherlands, the United Kingdom and Ireland use the incorporation doctrine.
11. Amongst others France, Italy and Spain use the real seat doctrine.
12. Since Case C-208/00, *Überseering* (see *infra*, section 2.4) German stock companies are no longer required to have their real seat in Germany. After Case C-210/06, *Cartesio* (see *infra*, section 2.4) Hungary changed from the real seat doctrine to the incorporation doctrine. Belgium is planning to do the same.
13. See also E. Wymeersch, "The transfer of the company's seat in European company law", (2003) CML Rev., 661–695.

2.4 *Case law*

2.4.1 *Introduction*

In a number of cases, references for a preliminary ruling were sent to the CJEU, questioning whether a national law was in accordance with the right of establishment of Articles 49 and 54 TFEU. The case law of the CJEU has influenced the company laws of the Member States in important ways. It has amongst others increased cross-border mobility of companies in the EU and has stimulated Member States to deregulate company laws for private limited companies. The cases below will not be dealt with in chronological order in time but will be arranged according to their subject-matter.

2.4.2 *Cross border transfer of the real seat*

In *Daily Mail,* the company Daily Mail and General Trust PLC transferred its real seat from the UK to the Netherlands without prior consent of the H.M. Treasury. By establishing its residence abroad the company would no longer be liable to UK corporation tax but to Dutch corporation tax. The central question before the CJEU was whether (former) Articles 52 and 58 of the EEC Treaty (now Arts. 49 and 54 TFEU) preclude a Member State from prohibiting a company from transferring without prior consent the central management and control to another Member State.[14] The CJEU stated that the Treaty regards the differences in national legislation concerning the required connecting factor – i.e. the registered office, central administration and principal place of business – and the question whether the registered office or real head office may be transferred to another Member State as problems which must be dealt with by future legislation or conventions. The CJEU concluded that Articles 52 and 58 of the Treaty cannot be interpreted as conferring on companies incorporated under the law of a Member State a right to transfer their central management and control and their central administration to another Member State while retaining their status as companies incorporated under the legislation of the first Member State.[15]

Twenty years later this ruling was confirmed in *Cartesio.* The Hungarian company Cartesio filed an application with the commercial court for registration of the transfer of its (real) seat to Italy. That application was rejected on the ground that Hungarian law did not allow the company to transfer its seat abroad while continuing to be subject to Hungarian company law. The CJEU referred to its judgment in *Daily Mail* and decided that, as Community law now stands, (former) Articles 43 EC and 48 EC (now Arts. 49 and 54 TFEU) are to be interpreted as not precluding national legislation under which a company may not transfer its seat to another Member State whilst retaining its status as a company governed by the law of the Member State of incorporation.[16] In other words, the CJEU confirmed that the real seat doctrine was still valid for companies incorporated in the Member State applying this doctrine.

---

14. Although for UK company law the place of central management is not relevant and only for tax reasons consent was needed, the ruling of the ECJ is relevant for company laws of Member States using the real seat doctrine. See also C.W.A. Timmermans, "Impact of EU law on international company law", (2010) ERPL, 554.
15. Case C-81/87, *Daily Mail and General Trust PLC.* As follows from *supra,* section 2.3, this ruling is (for company law) only relevant for Member States using the real seat doctrine, since in the incorporation doctrine the place of central management and control is not relevant and can be placed outside the State of origin.
16. In answering the question whether (former) Art. 43 EC applies to a company, the ECJ speaks about "a preliminary matter which can only be resolved by the applicable national law". See Case C-210/06, *Cartesio,* para 109 and see critically M.A. Verbrugh, "*Cartesio*: baanbrekend of wegbereidend?", (2009) SEW, 419–428.

Überseering concerns a landmark case on the validity of the application of the real seat doctrine on companies incorporated in another Member State. After two German nationals acquired all the shares in the Dutch private limited company Überseering, the company sought compensation from a German company for breach of contract and brought an action before the German court. The German court found that Überseering had transferred its actual centre of administration (the real seat) from the Netherlands to Germany once its shares had been acquired by the German nationals but equally found that, as a company incorporated under Dutch law, Überseering did not have legal capacity in Germany and, consequently, could not bring legal proceedings there. In the preliminary ruling that followed, the CJEU decided that where a company is deemed to have moved its actual centre of administration to another Member State, Articles 49 and 54 TFEU preclude the latter Member State from denying the company legal capacity and, consequently, the capacity to bring legal proceedings before its national courts.[17]

With *Überseering* the real seat doctrine lost part of its meaning as described in section 2.3 above, since a Member State can no longer apply its own company law to companies from other Member States with their real seat in its territory.[18] Although the real seat doctrine is therefore still valid for "own companies", *Überseering* guaranteed the free movement of the real seat of companies from incorporation doctrine countries to real seat doctrine countries and thereby contributed to the mobility for these companies in the internal market.[19]

2.4.3 *Cross border merger and cross border conversion*

In *Sevic,* the application for registration of the merger of a German company and a Luxembourg company was rejected by the German court on the ground that the German Law on transforming companies provided that only legal entities established in national territory may merge and that, therefore, that law did not apply to cross border mergers. The CJEU ruled that Articles 49 and 54 TFEU preclude registration in the national commercial register of the merger from being refused in general in a Member State where one of the two companies is established in another Member State, whereas such registration is possible where the two companies participating in the merger are both established in the territory of the first Member State.[20]

Although *Sevic* lost much of its relevance after the adoption of the Tenth Directive on cross border merger in 2005, the judgment still has meaning. First, the Tenth Directive only applies to stock companies, whereas the definition of companies in Article 54 TFEU is much broader. Second, the case seems to be relevant for other ways of cross border transformation, such as cross border division and cross border conversion.[21]

The *Cartesio* case concerns the validity of the real seat doctrine (see section 2.4.2 above) but contains an important *obiter dictum* on cross border transfer of the registered office (cross border conversion). According to the CJEU in *Cartesio,* the situation where the company wants to move its real seat but does not want to change the applicable company law has to be distinguished from the situation where a company moves to another Member State with an attendant change as regards the national law applicable (a cross border conversion).[22] In that case, the

17. Case C-208/00, *Überseering.*
18. In practice this only relates to companies from incorporation doctrine countries since only these companies are allowed to have their real seat outside the State of origin.
19. Several years after Case C-208/00, *Überseering* the German legislator amended the German law and allowed German stock companies to bring their real seat outside Germany. See "Gesetz zur Modernisierung des GmbHRechts und zur Bekämpfung von Missbräuchen" (MoMiG).
20. Case C-411/03, *Sevic.*
21. See also Case C-411/03, *Sevic,* para 19.
22. See Case C-210/06, *Cartesio,* para 111.

Member State of incorporation cannot, by requiring the winding-up or liquidation, prevent that company from converting itself into a company governed by the law of the other Member State, to the extent that it is permitted under that law to do so. Such a barrier to the actual cross border conversion constitutes a restriction on the freedom of establishment which, unless it serves overriding requirements in the public interest, is prohibited under (former) Article 43 EC.[23]

Vale can in many respects be seen as a mirror image of *Cartesio*. The Italian company Vale moved its seat to Hungary and wanted to convert itself in a Hungarian company. The Hungarian court, however, rejected the registration of the cross border conversion. According to the court only Hungarian companies can be shown in the commercial register and, consequently, a company which is not Hungarian cannot be listed as a predecessor in law. In other words, only national conversions were permitted. Here a parallel can be seen with *Sevic*, where only national mergers were registered. Not surprisingly, the CJEU gave a similar judgment as it did in *Sevic*. The CJEU stated that Articles 49 and 54 TFEU must be interpreted as precluding national legislation which enables companies established under national law to convert, but does not allow, in a general manner, companies governed by the law of another Member State to convert to companies governed by national law by incorporating such a company.[24]

Assuming that all Member States will allow national conversions, *Cartesio* and *Vale* show that companies in the Member States can in principle be converted in a company type of another Member State. From *Cartesio*, it follows that Member States cannot preclude the company from leaving (outbound conversion) and from *Vale* is follows that the host Member State cannot preclude the company from coming in (inbound conversion).[25] The three cases show that the CJEU has played an important role in the possibilities for cross border mobility in the EU.

2.4.4 *Recognition of foreign companies using a branch*

In *Centros*, two Danish nationals set up a UK private limited company without conducting any business in the UK. By setting up a branch in Denmark the stricter rules in Denmark on, in particular, minimum capital, were circumvented. For this reason the Danish Department of Trade refused to register the branch in Denmark. According to the CJEU, it is contrary to (former) Articles 52 and 58 of the Treaty for a Member State to refuse to register a branch of a company formed in accordance with the law of another Member State in which it conducts no business where the branch is intended to enable the company to carry on its entire business in the State in which that branch is created, thus evading application of the rules governing the formation of companies which are more restrictive as regards the paying up of a minimum share capital. That interpretation does not, however, prevent the Member State from adopting any appropriate measure for preventing or penalizing fraud where it has been established that they are in fact attempting, by means of the formation of a company, to evade their obligations towards private or public creditors.[26]

Less than one year later than *Überseering* (see above) and in line with *Centros* the CJEU rendered another judgment that stimulated the use of companies from incorporation doctrine countries in *Inspire Art*. In this case the Netherlands imposed additional conditions on the

23. Case C-210/06, *Cartesio*. See critically on *Cartesio* P.M. Storm, "*Cartesio*: stapjes in de processie van Echternach", (2009) *Ondernemingsrecht*, 328–337.
24. Case C-378/10, *VALE Építési kft*.
25. Whether the real seat has to move with the cross border conversion depends on the host Member State: if it applies the real seat doctrine the real seat has to be moved. This follows from Case C-81/87, *Daily Mail* and Case C-210/06, *Cartesio*. If a company moves from a real seat doctrine country to an incorporation doctrine country, the real seat does not have to move. This follows from Case C-208/00, *Überseering*.
26. Case C-212/97, (*Centros*).

branch of the English limited company Inspire Art. The company fell under the definition of a "formally foreign company" of the Dutch Law on Formally Foreign Companies, since it carried on its activities entirely in the Netherlands and did not have any real connection with the UK. The law imposed the obligation to record, with its registration in the Dutch commercial register, its description as a "formally foreign company" and to use that description in its business dealings and imposed obligations concerning the minimum share capital and annual accounts. From *Inspire Art* it follows that it is contrary to (former) Articles 43 EC and 48 EC for national legislation to impose on a branch established in that State by a company formed in accordance with the law of another Member State certain conditions provided for in domestic company law in respect of company formation relating to minimum capital and directors' liability.[27] According to the CJEU, the reasons for which the company was formed in that other Member State, and the fact that it carries on its activities (almost) exclusively in the Member State of establishment, do not deprive it of the right to invoke the freedom of establishment, save where the existence of an abuse is established on a case-by-case basis.[28]

After *Centros* and even more after *Inspire Art* the number of UK companies being set up by non-UK nationals has increased significantly.[29] This triggered several Member States to deregulate the company law for private limited companies or to introduce alternative company types with less burdensome rules.[30]

2.4.5 *Conclusion*

The various cases above show that the CJEU has played an important role in the possibilities for cross border mobility in the EU. Based on the freedom of establishment companies can under certain circumstances participate in a cross border merger, a cross border division or a cross border conversion. Furthermore, nationals of a Member State can do business with any company type that fit their needs best from another Member State where the incorporation doctrine applies by using a branch in their own country. Additionally, companies from Member States using the incorporation doctrine are free to move their head office in the EU. On the other hand, the CJEU has upheld the real seat doctrine for companies being set up in Member States using the real seat doctrine.

3. Harmonization of company law

3.1 *Introduction*

Harmonization of company law in the Member States started in the sixties of the 20th century, with the First Directive being adopted in 1968. The mandate given to the European Parliament, the Council and the Commission to harmonize company law can be found in Article 50 (former Art. 44 EC) TFEU.

According to Article 50(1) TFEU, the main goal of the harmonization program in the field of company law is to attain freedom of establishment, in other words, to create the necessary

27. Furthermore, it is contrary to Art. 2 of the Eleventh Directive (89/666/EEC) to impose on this branch disclosure obligations not provided for by that directive.
28. Case C-167/01, *Inspire Art*.
29. See M. Becht, C. Mayer and H.F. Wagner, "Where do firms incorporate? Deregulation and the cost of entry", *ECGI Law Working Paper No.70/2006*, Aug. 2007, available at <www.ssrn.com>.
30. For example, the Netherlands in 2012 abolished many rules on capital protection for the "Besloten vennootschap", like on minimum share capital. Germany introduced the "Unternehmergesellschaft (haftungsbeschränkt) (UG)" in 2008 and Belgium introduced the "Starter-bvba" in 2010.

conditions for companies to be able fully to exercise the freedom of establishment granted by the Treaty.[31]

From the wording of the provision in Article 50(2)(g) TFEU, from policy documents and literature two other goals or sub-goals can be derived.[32] First, by harmonizing company law a "Delaware effect", whereby Member States would lower their standards for creditors and shareholders in order to attract companies from other Member States – a so called "race to the bottom"– would be prevented.[33] Second, harmonization would facilitate and encourage cross border businesses and reorganizations. Since the beginning of the 21st century, this last sub-goal seems to have become one of the main goals of the Commission.

3.2 *Company Law Directives*

Since the harmonization program started in 1962 until now, twelve directives in the field of company law have been adopted. Below, these directives and their amendments over the years will be described. Additionally, proposals for directives, either old and abandoned or new and under negotiation at this moment will be discussed.[34]

- The First Company Law Directive, Directive 68/151/EEC,[35] deals with the publication of documents and particulars concerning companies, the validity of obligations entered into by companies and the nullity of companies. The publication requirements provide (potential) creditors and others relevant information on the company and its financial situation, the provisions on representation restricts to a great extent the grounds on which obligations entered into are not valid and the rules on nullity limit the cases in which nullity can arise. The directive was amended by Directive 2003/58/EC in order to modernize the directive and to simplify the disclosure formalities and was codified by Directive 2009/101/EC.[36] The last directive has been amended by Directive 2012/17/EU to interconnect business registers within the EU in order to improve the availability of cross-border electronic access to business information.[37]
- The Second Company Law Directive, Directive 77/91/EEC,[38] relates to the formation of public limited companies and the maintenance and alteration in their capital. The directive harmonizes capital protection rules in the EU and deals with topics like minimum capital, distributions, acquisitions by a company of its own shares, consideration for shares, increase and reduction in capital and pre-emptive rights. Many Member States applied some or most of the provisions voluntarily to private limited companies. As described in section 2.4.4 above, some of these Member States have abolished part

31. See J. Wouters, "European company law: Quo vadis?", (2000) CML Rev., 289. To Timmermans it seems that the main reason why the harmonization of company law has never really been successful, is because there has never been consensus between Parliament, Council and Commission on the need and goals of the harmonization. See C.W.A. Timmermans, "Europees vennootschapsrecht", (2000) SEW, 249.
32. See: C.W.A. Timmermans, "Europees vennootschapsrecht", (2000) SEW, 249–250.
33. See critically L. Enriques, "EC company law and the fears for a European Delaware", (2004) EBLR, 1259–1274.
34. Below the order of the number of the directive will be followed, although the numbering of directives has been left aside some years ago.
35. O.J. 1968, L 65/8.
36. O.J. 2009, L 258/11. Although First Directive has been repealed, for practical reasons the enumeration above starts with "First Directive" and not with Directive 2009/101/EC. The same accounts for the other directives that have been codified.
37. O.J. 2012, L 156/1. At the moment the Business Registers Interconnection System (BRIS) is being set up.
38. O.J. 1977, L 26/1.

or many of these rules for private limited companies in the last years, which show a somewhat different and critical approach nowadays towards the rules on capital protection as provide by the Second Company Law Directive. Although Directive 2006/68/EC[39] resulted in less restrictions and more exemptions in the Second Company Law Directive, a fundamental amendment in the approach to capital protection by the European legislator is not expected in the short term. The Second Company Law Directive was codified by Directive 2012/30/EC.[40]

- The Third Company Law Directive, Directive 78/855/EEC,[41] covers mergers between public limited liability companies. The directive was amended by Directive 2007/63/EC,[42] easing the requirement of an independent expert's report, and by Directive 2009/109/EC,[43] easing reporting and documentation requirements, and was codified by Directive 2011/35/EU.[44]
- The Fourth Company Law Directive, Directive 78/660/EEC,[45] concerns the annual accounts of certain types of companies. The directive was amended several times and repealed in 2013 by Directive 2013/34/EU.[46] Directive 2013/34/EU was amended by Directive 2014/95/EU of 22 October 2014, as regards disclosure of non-financial and diversity information by certain large undertakings and groups.
- The Draft Fifth Company Law Directive concerns the structure of public limited companies and the powers and obligations of their organs. The first Proposal was submitted to the Council in 1972 and later several amendments to the Proposals were made, but in the end the Proposal has been withdrawn by the Commission. No new proposal on these topics from the Commission is to be expected. The main reason for the failure of the Fifth Directive is the fundamental difference in board structure for companies in Europe.[47]
- The Sixth Company Law Directive, Directive 82/891/EEC,[48] relates to the division of public limited companies. The directive was amended in the same way as the Third Directive by Directive 2007/63/EC and by Directive 2009/109/EC. There is no directive on cross border division. In its Action Plan of 2012 the Commission stated that it would consider an initiative to provide a framework for cross-border divisions in 2013 but no proposal has been published since then.[49]
- The Seventh Company Law Directive, Directive 83/349,[50] deals with consolidated accounts. The directive was amended several times and repealed in 2013 by Directive 2013/34/EU.[51] Directive 2013/34/EU was amended by Directive 2014/95/EU of 22

39. O.J. 2006, L 264/32.
40. O.J. 2012, L 315/74.
41. O.J. 1978, L 295/36.
42. O.J. 2007, L 300/47.
43. O.J. 2009, L 259/14.
44. O.J. 2011, L 110/1.
45. O.J. 1978, L 222/11.
46. O.J. 2013, L 182/19.
47. See K. Hopt and P. Davies, "Corporate boards in Europe – Accountability and convergence", (2013) AJCL, 301–376. See also *infra*, section 4.2.
48. O.J. 1982, L 378/47.
49. See further *infra*, section 5.
50. O.J. 1983, L 193/1.
51. O.J. 2013, L 182/19. See also Reg. (EC) 1606/2002 (IAS-Reg.) on the application of international accounting standards, O.J. 2002, L 243/1.

October 2014, as regards disclosure of non-financial and diversity information by certain large undertakings and groups.
- The Eight Company Law Directive, Directive 84/253,[52] concerns the approval of persons responsible for carrying out the statutory audits of accounting documents. The directive was repealed by Directive 2006/43.[53]
- The Draft Ninth Company Law Directive relates to corporate groups and has not even led to an official proposal from the Commission and since 1984 the draft is no longer under discussion.[54]
- The Tenth Company Law Directive, Directive 2005/56/EC,[55] concerns cross border merger of public and private limited liability companies. The directive was amended by Directive 2009/109/EC, easing reporting and documentation requirements.
- The Eleventh Company Law Directive, Directive 89/666,[56] deals with disclosure requirements in respect of branches opened by companies of another Member State. The directive has been amended by Directive 2012/17/EU to interconnect business registers within the EU in order to improve the availability of cross-border electronic access to business information.
- The Twelfth Company Law Directive, Directive 89/667/EEC,[57] relates to single member private limited companies. The directive was codified by Directive 2009/102/EC.[58] In April 2014 the Commission published a Proposal for a Directive on single-member private limited liability companies, as an alternative for the Proposal on the Statute for a European Private Company (see section 4 below).[59] This Proposal, once adopted, will repeal Directive 2009/102/EC.
- The Thirteenth Company Law Directive, Directive 2004/25,[60] relates to takeover bids for the securities of companies governed by the laws of Member States, where all or some of those securities are admitted to trading on a regulated market in one or more Member States. The objectives of the directive are, amongst others, facilitation of takeover bids and protection of the interests of (minority) shareholders. As a means of protecting the minority shareholders, a person who has acquired control of a listed company is required to make a bid to all the holders of those securities.
- Although the Commission held several consultations and promised in its Action Plan of 2003 (section 5) to come with a proposal in the near future, no directive exists (yet) on cross border transfer of the registered office (cross border conversion). Since there are two different company law systems involved in a cross border conversion, harmonization of the rules in the EU seems necessary.
- The Shareholder Rights Directive, Directive 2007/36/EC,[61] deals with the exercise of certain rights of shareholders in listed companies. The directive introduces, amongst

---

52. O.J. 1984, L 126/20.
53. O.J. 2006, L 157/87.
54. See V. Edwards, op. cit. *supra* note 7 391.
55. O.J. 2005, L 310/1.
56. O.J. 1989, L 395/36.
57. O.J. 1989, L 395/40.
58. O.J. 2009, L 258/20.
59. COM(2014)212 final. On 28 May 2015, the Council agreed on a compromise text for a draft directive. The agreement is based on a compromise text tabled by the presidency and will serve as the basis for forthcoming negotiations with the European Parliament.
60. O.J. 2004, L 142/12.
61. O.J. 2007, L 184/17.

others, minimum standards to ensure that shareholders of listed companies have timely access to the relevant information ahead of the general meeting, to put items on the agenda and are able to vote at a distance. In April 2014 the Commission published a Proposal for a Directive amending Directive 2007/36/EC as regards the encouragement of long-term shareholder engagement,[62] and in April 2017 the directive was adopted by the Council. This initiative can be seen as a reaction to the economic and financial crisis that started in 2008.
- Directive 2001/86/EC supplements the Regulation on the Statute for a European company with regard to the involvement of employees.[63]
- Directive 2003/72/EC supplements the Regulation on the Statute for a European Co-operative Society with regard to the involvement of employees.[64]
- In December 2015, the Commission adopted a proposal to codify and merge the First, Second, Third, Sixth, Tenth and Eleventh Directive.[65] The aim of this proposal, which does not involve any change to the substance of these directives, is to make EU company law more reader-friendly and to reduce the risk of future inconsistencies.

3.3 *Conclusion*

To what extent the harmonization programme has been successful is difficult to answer since the goals of the programme have never been completely clear and seem to have changed somewhat over time. As to the main goal of harmonization, to attain freedom of establishment, also the rulings of the CJEU played an important role. Many topics of company law have been harmonized for public companies and, to a lesser extent, for private companies. As a result, basic financial and non-financial information on companies and on branches is available and easily accessible, the rules on representation in the Member States are clear and stimulate business in the EU, and companies can easily restructure nationally and cross border. For cross border restructuring, however, more work has to be done by the European legislator.

Some important elements of national company law have been proven immune from European interference, like the structure of companies and the powers and obligations of their organs. This, however, does not make the harmonization programme unsuccessful, since no governance system has been proven to be superior.[66]

4. Supranational companies

4.1 *Introduction*

A substantial part of company law in the Member States has been harmonized through a number of directives. Although this helps companies to exercise freedom of establishment, differences between company laws and company types in the Member States remain. According to

62. COM(2014)213 final.
63. O.J. 2001, L 294/22. After putting the worker participation provisions in a separate directive, the Reg. on the Statute for a European company could finally be adopted. See for the European company (SE) section 4 below.
64. O.J. 2003, L 207/25. Directive 2003/72/EC follows the example of Directive 2001/86/EC. See for the European Cooperative Society (SCE) section 4 below.
65. Proposal for a Directive of the European Parliament and of the Council relating to certain aspects of company law (codification), COM(2015)616 final. See Directive 2017/1132 of 14 June 2017.
66. One of the explanations for the big differences that still exist in corporate governance systems is path dependence. See K. Heine, "European corporate laws, regulatory competition and path dependence", 13 *European Journal of Law and Economics* (2002), 47–71.

the Preamble of Regulation on the Statute for a European company (SE), restructuring and cooperation operations involving companies from different Member States give rise to legal and psychological difficulties and tax problems. In order to overcome these difficulties, EU regulations have been adopted for the creation of supranational companies.[67] The provisions of these regulations are directly applicable in the Member States and permit the creation of companies with a European dimension.

In section 4.2 below the existing supranational companies will be discusses, followed by proposals for new supranational companies in section 4.3.

4.2 *SE, SCE and EEIG*

Three regulations on supranational companies have been adopted so far: the Regulation on the European Economic Interest Grouping (EEIG) in 1985;[68] the Regulation on the Statute for a European company (*Societas Europaea* (SE)) in 2001;[69] and the Regulation on the Statute for a European Cooperative Society (*Societas Cooperativa Europaea* (SCE)) in 2003.[70] The SCE Regulation is in many ways similar to the SE Regulation. Since the SE plays the most important role in practice and has influenced the development of (proposals for) other supranational companies, most attention will be paid below to the SE.

The SE Regulation aims at creating a uniform legal framework within which companies from different Member States should be able to plan and carry out the reorganization of their business on a Community scale.[71] An SE has the form of a European public limited-liability company and has legal personality.[72] The subscribed capital shall not be less than EUR 120,000.[73]

An SE may be: a) created by the merger of two or more public companies; b) set up by two or more public or private companies as a holding SE; c) set up as a subsidiary SE by two or more "companies"; d) created by conversion of a public company into an SE. In all cases there should be companies from at least two Member States involved.[74] For an SE, the real seat doctrine applies: the registered office of an SE shall be located in the same Member State as its head office.[75] The registered office of an SE may be transferred to another Member State for which the Regulation provides extensive provisions.[76] Probably the most important advantage for the use of an SE is to show the truly European or international nature of the company, in other words, a more psychological motive. Furthermore, by establishing an SE, no choice has to be made for one of the participating national company types in a cross border merger, so the SE can play a neutral role. Lastly, the use of SEs in practice seems in some cases to be motivated to

67. The legal basis of these regulations is Art. 352 TFEU. For measures taken by the Council on the basis of Art. 352 TFEU unanimity is required.
68. Reg. 2137/85, O.J. 1985 L 1991/1.
69. Reg. 2157/2001, O.J. 2001 L 294/1.
70. Reg. 1435/2003, O.J. 2003 L 207/1. The SE and the SCE have a directive supplementing the Reg. on the involvement of employees. See *supra*, section 3.2.
71. See SE Reg., Preamble and Directive 2001/86/EC, Preamble (2). Since reference is made in a number of cases in the Reg. to national company law, the SE is, however, not a truly uniform legal person but influenced to a big degree by the Member State where the seat is located.
72. See Art. 1 SE Reg.
73. Art. 4 (2) SE Reg.
74. See Art. 2 SE Reg. An SE may itself set up one or more subsidiaries in the form of SEs. See Art. 3 SE Reg. The different ways of forming an SE are dealt with in different sections of Title II in the Reg.
75. See Art. 7 SE Reg. See for the enforcement of the real seat doctrine, Art. 64 SE Reg.
76. See Art. 8 SE Reg.

avoid national legislation.[77] In general, the creation of SEs so far is quite modest.[78] The relative increase in formation over the last years is promising however.[79]

In 2003, two years after the SE, the Regulation on the Statute for a European Cooperative Society (SCE) was adopted.[80] The most characteristic provision is to be found in Article 1(3) SCE Regulation: "an SCE shall have as its principal object the satisfaction of its members' needs and/or the development of their economic and social activities, in particular through the conclusion of agreements with them to supply goods or services or to execute work of the kind that the SCE carries out or commissions".[81] Rather uncommonly for most national cooperative societies, the SCE capital shall be divided into shares.[82] Unless otherwise provided by the statutes of the SCE, no member shall be liable for more than the amount he has subscribed.[83] An SCE may be formed by natural persons, companies and other legal bodies, provided that at least two of them are governed by different Member States.[84] The SCE must have its registered office in the same Member State as its head office[85] and may transfer its registered office to another Member State.[86]

The aim of the Regulation on the EEIG is to create a legal framework for natural persons, companies, firms and other legal bodies to be able to cooperate effectively across frontiers. The EEIG is used on a very limited scale in practice, which cannot surprise if one looks at various characteristic provisions of the Regulation. According to Article 3, the purpose of a grouping shall be to facilitate or develop the economic activities of its members and to improve or increase the results of those activities; its purpose is not to make profits for itself.[87] Furthermore, the members of a grouping shall have unlimited joint and several liability for its debts and other liabilities of whatever nature.[88]

4.3 *SPE, SUP and FE*

In addition to the abovementioned regulations being adopted, the EU proposed some legislative instruments that never resulted in supranational legislation. In 2008 a Proposal for a Regulation on the Statute for a European private company (*Societas Privata Europaea* (SPE)) was published.[89] According to the proposal, an SPE could be set up without a cross border element,

77. Apparently, the SE is also sometimes used in Germany in order to avoid the worker participation laws. In that case an SE is formed just before the threshold (amount of workers) for the application of these laws is reached.
78. See for an extensive study by Ernst & Young on the use of the SE, "Study on the operation and the impacts of the Statute for a European Company" (2009).
79. On 30 May 2017 in total 2803 SEs were set up. Available at <www.worker-participation.eu>.
80. The solution for the worker participation for the SE is also used for the SCE: a separate Directive was adopted. See for the SCE, W.J.M. van Veen (ed.), *De Europese coöperatieve vennootschap* (SCE) (Kluwer, 2006).
81. Furthermore, an SCE may also have as its object the satisfaction of its members' needs by promoting their participation in economic activities, in one or more SCEs and/or national cooperatives.
82. Art. 1(2) SCE Reg. The subscribed capital shall not be less than EUR 30,000 (Art. 3(2) SCE Reg.).
83. Where the members of the SCE have limited liability, the name of the SCE shall end in "limited". See Art. 1 SCE Reg.
84. See for the formation of an SCE Art. 2 SCE Reg.
85. See Art. 6 SCE Reg.
86. See Art. 7 SCE Reg.
87. Consequently, a grouping may not, amongst others exercise a power of management or supervision over its members' own activities or over the activities of another undertaking, hold shares of any kind in a member undertaking, or employ more than 500 persons.
88. Art. 24 EEIG Reg.
89. COM(2008)396/3. In 2009 the European Parliament proposed several amendments to the Statute and in 2011 a Presidency's compromise proposal was published. See for the SPE H. Hirte & C. Teichmann (Eds.),

with 1 Euro capital and Member States would not be allowed to apply the real seat doctrine. No political consensus could, however, be reached on a number of issues, which led to the withdrawal of the proposal by the Commission in 2014.[90]

In 2014, the Commission published an alternative for the SPE with a Proposal for a Directive on single-member private limited liability companies (*Societas Unius Personae* (SUP)).[91] The objective of the proposal is to make it easier to set-up companies in other Member States and to reduce operational costs, by a harmonized registration procedure, the possibility of online registration with a uniform template of articles of association and a legal capital of 1 Euro.[92]

Lastly, the proposal on a Statute for a European Foundation (*Fundatio Europaea* (FE)) of February 2012 can be mentioned.[93] According to the Commission, foundations cannot channel funds efficiently on a cross-border basis in the EU.[94] The Statute for a FE would create a new European legal form intended to facilitate foundations" establishment and operation in the single market. Since the Commission saw no prospects that an agreement could be reached, it withdrew the proposal at the end of 2014.[95]

5. Modernization of company law

From the First Directive in 1968 until 1989 nine company law directives were adopted but since then no further development seemed possible. Therefore the Commission in 2001 set up the High Level Group on Company Law Experts with the mandate to provide recommendations for a modern regulatory European company law framework. The High Level Group published an influential report in November 2002, dealing with a number of corporate governance and company law issues, amongst others general themes on harmonization, capital formation and maintenance, groups and pyramids and corporate restructuring and mobility.[96]

The Group recommended that particular attention should be given to eliminate obstacles for cross-border activities of business in Europe. Most of the recommendations of the High Level Group were adopted by the Commission in its Action Plan of May 2003.[97] Many actions from the Action Plan have been taken up successfully by the European legislator, like the adoption of the Tenth Directive. An important exception is a Directive on cross border transfer of the registered office (section 3.2).

The European Private Company – Societas Privata Europaea (SPE) (De Gruyter, 2013) and D.F.M.M. Zaman, C.A. Schwarz, M.L. Lennarts, H.J. de Kluiver and A.F.M. Dorresteijn (Eds.), *The European Private Company (SPE). A Critical Analysis of the EU Draft Statute* (Intersentia, 2009).

90. See O.J. 2014, C 153/6.
91. COM(2014)212 final.
92. See the Explanatory Memorandum, 3 (2014/0120 (COD)). At the Council (Competitiveness) on 28 May 2015 a general approach was agreed on the proposal. This compromise proposal of the Council has amended the original proposal on some elements. See for the proposal of May 2015, Council of the European Union 29 May 2015, 9050/15 DRS 41 CODEC 751.
93. COM(2012)35 final.
94. See the Explanatory Memorandum, (COM(2012)35 final). See for the feasibility study, "Max Planck Institute for Comparative and International Private Law and Universität Heidelberg, Centrum für soziale Investitionen und Innovationen, Feasibility Study on a European Foundation Statute, Final Report" (2008).
95. See Commission Work Programme 2015, "A new start, annex to the communication of the commission", COM(2014)910 final, Annex 2, under 61.
96. Report of the High Level Group of Company Law Experts on a Modern Regulatory Framework for Company Law in Europe (2002).
97. "Communication from the Commission to the Council and the European Parliament, Modernising Company Law and Enhancing Corporate Governance in the European Union – A Plan to Move Forward", 2003, COM(2003)284 final.

In 2007 the Commission published a report setting out its view on simplifying the rules governing company law.[98] In general, an important goal for the Commission from that period was to simplify existing company law and to reduce administrative burden.

On 5 April 2011 two important documents on European company law were published: a consultation document on corporate governance issues from the Commission[99] and a report of the Reflection Group "On the Future of EU Company Law".[100] The content of both documents are influenced by the economic and financial crisis that started in 2008. In 2012 the Commission launched a broad public consultation on European company law in general. The Commission took the results of the consultations of 2011 and 2012 together into account and published its "Action Plan: European company law and corporate governance" in December 2012.[101] The Action Plan outlines the initiatives which the Commission intends to take in order to modernize and enhance the current framework. In general, the Action Plan of 2012 can be characterized as quite modest and therefore no initiatives for major change have been initiated since then or can be expected in the near future. Until now, some of the initiatives have been taken up, like the proposal to amend the Shareholder Directive.

Further reading

Davies, P., K. Hopt, R. Nowak and G. van Solinge (Eds.), *Corporate Boards in Law and Practice* (OUP, 2013).

Dorresteijn, A., T. Monteiro, C. Teichmann and E. Werlauff, *European Corporate Law*, 2nd ed. (Kluwer Law International, 2009).

Dumoulin, S.H.M.A., *The European Company: Corporate Governance and Cross-Border Reorganisations from a Legal and Tax Perspective* (Boom Juridische uitgevers, 2005).

Ferrarini, G., K.J. Hopt, J.W. Winter and E. Wymeersch (Eds.), *Reforming Company and Takeover Law in Europe* (OUP, 2004).

van Gerven, D. and P. Storm (Eds.), *The European Company* (CUP, 2006 (Volume I) and 2008 (Volume II)).

Grundmann, S., *European Company Law*, 2nd ed. (Intersentia, 2012).

Hirte, H. and C. Teichman (Eds.), *The European Private Company – Societas Privata Europaea (SPE)* (De Gruyter, 2013).

Hopt, K.J., *The European Foundation: A New Legal Approach* (CUP, 2006).

Kraakman, R., J. Armour, P. Davies, L. Enriques, et al., *The Anatomy of Corporate Law, A Comparative and Functional Approach*, 3rd ed. (OUP, 2017).

Mellenbergh, R. and G. Raaijmakers (Eds.), *European Regulation of Company Law* (Ars Aequi, 2015).

Vossestein, G.-J., *Modernization of European Company Law and Corporate Governance. Some Considerations on Its Legal Limits* (Kluwer Law International, 2010).

98. See COM(2007)394 final.
99. "Green Paper. The EU corporate governance framework", COM(2011)164 final.
100. The report deals with cross border mobility, long term viability of shareholders and with groups of companies.
101. "Action Plan: European company law and corporate governance – a modern legal framework for more engaged shareholders and sustainable companies" of 12 Dec. 2012, COM(2012)740 final. See for a critical analysis.

CHAPTER 26
ECONOMIC AND MONETARY UNION[1]

*Fabian Amtenbrink**

1. A brief history of Economic and Monetary Union[2]

1.1 The original EEC Treaty

The coordination of economic and monetary policy was only summarily treated in the original EEC Treaty.[3] Among the policy provisions was Article 6 EEC, which laid down in general terms an obligation on the Member States to "coordinate their respective economic policies to the extent necessary to attain the objectives of the Treaty". As to the details, the first indent of Article 145 EEC endowed the Council with a responsibility to "ensure coordination of general economic policies of the Member States". As far as policy practice is concerned, Article 103 EEC, albeit primarily geared towards the coordination of short-term economic policy (conjunctural policy), was used as the legal basis for the secondary legislation, which in the 1970s was meant to lay the foundation for the first steps toward an economic and monetary union. Article 103(4) EEC acquired separate legal significance as the legal basis for Community action in case of problems encountered in supplying certain products, particularly during the first oil crisis in 1973, whereas Article 104 EEC was primarily declaratory in nature: it set out the general objectives of economic policy which the Member States had to follow as members of the EEC. Article 105 EEC primarily dealt with the procedural aspects of the coordination of economic and monetary policy.

Turning to monetary policy, Article 107 EEC dealt with the exchange rate policies of the Member States, which were nonetheless a matter of common concern. This implied that exchange rate policy was not to be used to create artificial competitive advantage in the common market. The importance of these provisions decreased steadily after the final implosion in 1973 of the Bretton Woods system of fixed exchange rates.[4] Articles 108 and 109 EEC provided assistance and safeguard procedures respectively, for Member States faced with serious balance

---

* Erasmus School of Law, Erasmus University Rotterdam.

1. This chapter reuses, builds on, and further develops the chapter on Economic and Monetary Union in the 4th edition of *The Law of the European Union and the European Communities* (2008).
2. See generally, D. Gros and N. Thygesen, *European Monetary Integration* (Longman, 1992), 3–56.
3. See the 2nd English edition of this work edited by L.W. Gormley, 598–600, 603–608 and 616–625, and literature cited there. It is remarkable that such a meagre and incomplete legal basis for economic and monetary policy integration should have led to so many thorough legal analyses. The incompleteness of the European integration process in an economic policy sense, resulting from the fact that the rules in the then EEC Treaty had serious *lacunae*, clearly formed a challenge in this respect.
4. For an account of the origins, workings and shortcomings of this system see M.D. Bordo, "The Bretton Woods International Monetary System: A historical overview" in M. D. Bordo and B. Eichengreen (Eds.),

of payment difficulties from which – possibly – adaptation of their exchange rates could result. Since the end of the 1960s, the practical importance of these provisions too gradually diminished.[5]

The 1986 Single European Act inserted Article 102a EEC into the Treaty, the most important legal significance of which was that its second paragraph stated expressly that insofar as further development in the field of economic and monetary policy (such as monetary cooperation between the Member States towards a monetary union) necessitated institutional change, amendment of the EEC Treaty would be required.

1.2 *Werner Report: The first plan to form a European Economic and Monetary Union*

As early as 1962, the Commission, in its memorandum on the working programme of the Community during the second stage of the transitional period, had argued that the customs union would need to evolve into an economic and monetary union, if achievements thus far attained were not to be jeopardized. By 1968 the Commission was openly propagating monetary unification, which in 1969 led to the so-called Barre Memorandum.[6] After the The Hague Summit in December 1969 which provided the first impulse in this direction, the Council on 6 March 1970 decided to set up a special working group, which – by reference to the various proposals – was assigned the task of identifying the fundamental options for a realization in stages of economic and monetary union. This so-called Werner Committee presented its final report on 8 October 1970,[7] highlighting the rationale for economic, monetary and social policy integration leading to an economic and monetary union; this has remained essentially unchanged since the 1970s: market integration presupposes a necessary complement in policy integration.

Based on a Commission proposal, on 22 March 1971 a corresponding resolution issued by the Governments of the Member States was adopted.[8] The economic and monetary union was to take shape as a system in which "the principal decisions of economic policy will be taken at Community level and therefore that the necessary powers will be transferred from the national plane to the Community plane".[9] As regards monetary union, the report argued that this "implies, internally, the total and irreversible convertibility of currencies, the elimination of margins of fluctuation in rates of exchange, the irrevocable fixing of parity ratios and the total liberation of movements of capital", whereby "considerations of a psychological and political order militate in favour of the adoption of a single currency which would guarantee the irreversibility of the undertaking".[10] Interestingly, the report pointed out that the implications of such a project resonated beyond the field of economic and monetary policy, an observation that is still valid

---

A Retrospective on the Bretton Woods System: Lessons for International Monetary Reform (University of Chicago Press, 1993), 3–108.

5. This does not diminish the great legal interest of these provisions, as they implied a considerable and far-reaching limitation of national powers concerning exchange rate policy and related policies. See in this context Joined Cases 6 & 11–69, *Commission v. France*.
6. Commission Memorandum to the Council on the co-ordination of economic policies and monetary cooperation within the Community, submitted 12 Feb. 1969.
7. Report to the Council and Commission on the Realization by Stages of Economic and Monetary Union in the Community (O.J. 1970, C 136/1) (Werner Report). In addition to its president, the then Prime Minister and Minister of Finance of Luxembourg, the committee included the presidents of the Monetary Committee, the Committee of Governors of the Central Banks, the Committee for Medium-Term Economic Policy, the Committee on Short-Term Economic Policy and the Budgetary Policy Committee, as well as a representative of the Commission.
8. O.J. 1971, C 28/1 (O.J. English Spec. Ed. 2nd Series, IX, at 40).
9. Werner Report, cited *supra* note 7, 26.
10. Ibid.

today: "These transfers of responsibility and the creation of the corresponding Community institutions represent a process of fundamental political significance which entails the progressive development of political cooperation. The economic and monetary union thus appears as a leaven for the development of political union which in the long run it will be unable to do without".[11] This call for the establishment of a political union can also be found in more recent, post-crisis documents, such as the June 2015 Five President's Report on "Completing Europe's Economic and Monetary Union", which *inter alia* refers to the political union that "provides the foundation for all of the above through genuine democratic accountability, legitimacy and institutional strengthening".[12]

Following the suggestions made in the Werner Report, the resolution envisaged the realization of economic and monetary union in subsequent stages, whereby it was expressly recognized that some of the necessary measures would require amendment of the EEC Treaty. For the initial three-year stage the resolution itself proposed a number of measures aimed in particular at strengthening the coordination of short-term economic policy measures, the promotion of the free movement of capital, and the coordination of the monetary and credit policies of the Member States. Moreover, the Council and, where necessary, the representatives of the Member States at the end of the resolution undertook to lay down before the end of the first stage, on a proposal from the Commission, the measures which after the transition to the second stage were to lead to the full realization of an economic and monetary union, even as far as this required amendments of the Treaty. Yet, these plans turned out to be short-lived.

In May 1971, the German Government was compelled by the growing flow of dollars to allow the exchange rate of the German mark to fluctuate freely instead of narrowing the reciprocal fluctuation margins, as had been agreed upon in March of that year. This was the forerunner of further unrest in the international monetary system, which in 1973 led to the final implosion of the Bretton Woods exchange rate system.[13] The first oil crisis at the end of 1973 was the beginning of the end of the nearly uninterrupted period of growth that the Community had enjoyed since 1958. As each national government attempted as best it could to limit the damage caused by the looming combination of inflation, stagnating economic growth and unemployment, the absence of exchange rate discipline was certainly not found to be a hindrance, as a lack of internal economic and monetary discipline could be as it were automatically corrected by an amendment of the now floating exchange rate parities. These disturbances at the global level go far in explaining why three years into the first stage of the envisaged EMU, the Council had made only minimal progress towards meeting the objectives it had introduced in its resolution of 22 March 1971. Taking into account the combination of a turbulent economic and political climate at the global level and a not very well-considered approach to deepening economic and monetary integration, the next steps taken by the Council in February and March 1974 were decidedly small-scale.[14]

---

11. Ibid.
12. Available at <ec.europa.eu/commission/publications/five-presidents-report-completing-europes-economic-and-monetary-union_en>.
13. For an economic analysis see M.D. Bordo, op. cit. *supra* note 4, 74 et seq.
14. Decision 74/120 on the attainment of a high degree of convergence of economic policies (O.J. 1974, L 63/16), amended by Decision 75/787 (O.J. 1975, L 330/52), supplemented by Decision 79/136 (O.J. 1979, L 305/8) and repealed by Decision 90/141 (O.J. 1990, L 78/23) on the attainment of progressive convergence of economic policies and performance in stage one of EMU; Directive 74/121 on stability, fall growth and employment in the Community (O.J. 1974, L 63/19), also repealed by Decision 90/141.

In the monetary field the Council adopted two decisions on 22 March 1971, one concerning strengthening cooperation between central banks[15] and one setting up a procedure for granting medium-term financial assistance.[16]

1.3 *The European Monetary System: An interlude*

After the monetary turmoil in the second half of 1971, agreement was reached by the Ministers of Finance and central bank governors of the "Group of Ten" on 18 December 1971 on new exchange rates with simultaneous widening of the fluctuation margins to 2.25% in both directions.[17] In fact, for a short while, progress towards monetary union seemed possible again and in March 1972 a new resolution on economic and monetary union was adopted by the Council.[18] This resolution strengthened the resolution adopted earlier that month on the coordination of the economic policies of Member States by providing for a top level coordination group in which the Commission was also represented. This group existed in relative obscurity for a number of years, being quickly eclipsed by the Economic Policy Committee established by Decision 74/122,[19] which is still in existence. Furthermore, a legislative initiative was taken to promote stability, growth, and full employment in the Community.[20]

With regard to exchange rates, agreement was again reached in the Basle Agreement of 10 April 1972 on a gradual reduction of the currency fluctuations between Member States, the final aim being the abolition of any fluctuation, although fluctuations *vis-à-vis* the external world only had to respect the wider fluctuation margins permitted by the International Monetary Fund (IMF), as part of the Bretton Woods exchange rate system.[21]

Based on a proposal by the Committee of Governors of the Central Banks (Committee of Governors),[22] a European Monetary Cooperation Fund (EMCF) was set up in early 1973 that was to form a prelude to a European central banking system.[23] The EMCF was set up in order to facilitate the operation of the exchange rate arrangements set out in the Basle Agreement and to contribute to the progressive establishment of an economic and monetary union as foreseen in the Werner Plan. In the end, the Werner Plan never got past the initial stage, as it had to be finally acknowledged that economic realities made any further development impossible.[24]

---

15. Decision 71/142 (O.J. 1971, L 73/14).
16. Decision 71/143 (O.J. 1971, L 73/15), revised on several occasions and finally replaced by Reg. 1969/88 (O.J. 1988, L 178/1) establishing a single medium term facility for financial assistance.
17. Communiqué from the "Group of Ten", Washington, 18 Dec. 1971. Also referred to as the Smithsonian Agreement. While referred to as the "Group of Ten" (G-10), this forum is made up of eleven countries, including Belgium, Canada, France, Germany, Italy, Japan, Sweden and the US. The Bank for International Settlements, the IMF, the OECD and the EU (European Commission) have observer status.
18. O.J. 1972, C 38/3 (O.J. English Spec. Ed., 2nd series IX, at 65).
19. Decision 74/122 (O.J. 1974, L 63/21). The Committee now closely works together with the Economic and Financial Committee, see section 5.3.3.
20. Leading to Council Directive 74/121/EEC on stability, growth and full employment in the Community (O.J. 1974, L 63/19).
21. This mechanism for the restriction of the cross-rates between the Member States' currencies within the exchange rate regime agreed upon in the Smithsonian Agreement, cited *supra* note 17, has also been referred to as "the Snake in the Tunnel". See e.g. B. Eichengreen, *International Monetary Arrangements for the 21st Century* (Brookings, 1994), 54.
22. Established by Decision 64/300/EEC (O.J. 1964, No. 77, at 1206/64), later amended by Decision 90/300 (O.J. 1990, L 78/25). This Committee ceased to exist at the start of the second stage of EMU on 1 Jan. 1994 (see Art. 117(1) EC in conjunction with 116(1) EC).
23. Reg. 907/73 of the Council establishing a European Monetary Cooperation Fund (O.J. 1973, L 89/2.).
24. See D. Gros and N. Thygesen, op. cit. *supra* note 2, 20, with reference to the Majolin Report of Mar. 1975.

However, new initiatives were taken in due course. In March 1979, the European Monetary System (EMS) with at its centre the European Exchange Rate Mechanism (ERM) was established.[25] Eventually, all Member States participated in a differentiated, partially more flexible and partially more rigid exchange rate and intervention system.[26] Based on a central rate, the exchange rates of the participating currencies of the Member States were kept within agreed-upon margins of fluctuation. As part of the ERM, participating national central banks were obliged to intervene on behalf of currencies that reached the "ceiling" or "floor" rate. In order to support the mechanism, the EMCF provided borrowing facilities. Despite certain legal and substantive weaknesses, the system worked relatively satisfactorily. With its grid of bilateral central rates and intervention obligations for central banks whenever actual exchange rates diverged – initially – more than 2.25% (for some participants 6%) from the central rate, the so-called European Currency Unit (ECU), the system contributed to a relatively large degree of exchange rate stability within the Community at the time, certainly when compared to the fluctuating exchange rates of the Bretton Woods system.[27] The intervention credits – in the form of very short-term facilities, short-term monetary support, and the medium-term financial assistance previously mentioned – all played a part. More importantly, the mechanism was proof of the willingness of the Member States to make active use of the intervention mechanism whenever a particular currency came under pressure. What is more, the fact that the central rate for each participating currency could only be changed (realigned) by unanimous decision is proof that the ERM Member States had already agreed to give up some degree of authority over monetary policy.[28]

A system of stable yet adjustable exchange rates as provided for in the EMS could not, however, avoid internal realignments of the central rates if inflationary movement in the participating Member States diverged. In this context, the convergence in real economic policy that could be observed in the Community from 1982 onwards contributed to the arguably rather positive results of the EMS.[29]

1.4 *From the Single European Act to the Treaty on European Union and the single European currency*

The Single European Act 1986 (SEA) recognized the goal of EMU in its preamble and explicitly acknowledged the existence of the EMS and the ECU. While this first major revision of the EEC Treaty did not result in any substantial broadening of Community competences, for the first time the aim of close cooperation between the Member States on matters relating to

---

25. See European Council Resolution on the establishment of the European Monetary System and related matters (*Bull.* EC 7/8-1978); European Council Resolution of 12/13 Mar. 1979 (*Bull.* EC 7-1979); Agreement between the central banks of the Member States of the EEC laying down the operational procedures for the European Monetary System; Council Reg. 3180/78, changing the value of the unit of account used by the European Monetary Cooperation Fund (O.J. 1978, L 379/1). Council Reg. 3181/78, relating to the European monetary system (O.J. 1978, L 379/2).
26. European Council Conclusions of 4 and 5 Dec. 1978 on the establishment of a European Monetary System. See also J.-V. Louis, "Het Europese monetaire stelsel", (1979) SEW, 441–458, and P. De Grauwe, "The EMS during 1979–1984", (1985) *International Economics Research Paper.*
27. The ECU was made up of a basket of the currencies of the Member States. Following the tumult in the ERM in the second half of 1993 the margins were widened to 15%, with the exception of the German Dmark and the Dutch Guilder. On the crisis of the ERM in 1992/93 see e.g. F. Ozkan and A. Sutherland, "A model of the ERM crisis", *CERP Discussion Paper No. 879* (1994).
28. F. Amtenbrink, *The Democratic Accountability of Central Banks. A Comparative Study of the European Central Bank* (OUP, 1999), 116.
29. See H. Hahn, "The European Central Bank: Key to European Monetary Union or target?", (1991) CML Rev., 783–820, 786. On the turbulences in the ERM in 1992 see section 4.2.

economic and monetary policy was acknowledged in primary Community law.[30] Moreover, with the entry into force of the SEA, after a long period during which little progress was made, the liberalization of capital movement within the Community was finally readdressed, albeit most notably "by the enactment of a programme of legislation" rather than a directly effective Treaty provision; the latter was only introduced by the Treaty on the European Union (Treaty of Maastricht).[31] The liberalization of capital movement had major consequences for national policy options in the monetary field, and also for the working of the EMS. It was thus no coincidence that during the decision-making on the liberalization of capital movement, the desirability of a fully-fledged EMU again became a live issue.[32] The basis of the negotiations on the EMU title of the Treaty of Maastricht was provided by the report on Economic and Monetary Union in the Community by the Delors Committee.[33] This committee, which had been set up in June 1988 by the Hannover European Council,[34] presented its report in April 1989, sketching the main aspects of EMU, which are still reflected in Title VIII of Part Three of the TFEU on economic and monetary policy.

The political negotiations on EMU[35] were accelerated by the collapse of the Eastern bloc, at which stage France agreed to German reunification allegedly in exchange for the latter's consent to the establishment of EMU.[36] Both the European Council of Madrid 1989 and the drafters of the Treaty of Maastricht adopted the proposal set out in the Delors Report for the introduction of a European economic and monetary union in three subsequent phases or stages. With the establishment of an EMU in steps it was recognized that additional measures would be required to improve the convergence of the economies of the Member States, as well as the working of the internal market, before a single currency area could be realized.

The first stage of EMU, which commenced on 1 July 1990, did not require the amendment of primary Community law, as it was geared towards the completion of the internal market and in particular the elimination of all existing measures restricting capital movements and payments. Moreover, greater economic and monetary policy coordination based on the legal framework existing at the time was envisaged. Finally, the necessary preparations had to be made for the introduction of the legal framework for EMU. This was achieved by means of the Intergovernmental Conference which led to the signing and subsequent ratification of the Treaty on European Union, which first and foremost introduced what is currently Title VIII of the Treaty on the Functioning of the European Union on economic and monetary policy, including the provisions on the legal and economic conditions for Member States to join the European single currency, the institutional framework necessary for the conduct of a single monetary policy, as well as a regulatory framework for the coordination of the economic policies of the Member States.[37] The Treaty of Maastricht gave legal effect to the approach chosen in the Delors Report

30. Art. 102a(1) EEC.
31. J. A. Usher, "The evolution of the free movement of capital", 31 *Fordham International Law Journal* (2007), 1533–1570, 1537. See further Ch. 14, "Free movement of services, establishment and capital", of this book.
32. See J. Cloos, G. Reinesch, D. Vignes, J. Weyland, *Le Traité de Maastricht* (Bruylant, 1993), 39–41.
33. Committee for the Study of Economic and Monetary Union, *Report on the Economic and Monetary Union in the European Communities* (EU Commission, 1989).
34. *Bull.* EC 6-1988, point 3.4.1.
35. As to important aspects of the negotiations see J. Cloos et al., op. cit. *supra* note 32, 96–101. R. Corbett, *Treaty of Maastricht – From Conception to Ratification: A Comprehensive Reference Guide* (Longman, 1993), provides also a thorough analysis of the genesis of the Treaty of Maastricht.
36. See J. Gillingham, *European Integration, 1950–2003 Superstate or New Market Economy* (CUP, 2004), 274–276; R. Vaubel, "The Euro and the German veto", 7 *Econ Journal Watch* (2010), 82–90, with further references.
37. Signed on 7 Feb. 1992 (O.J. 1992, C 191), the Treaty entered into force on 1 Nov. 1993. Much of the groundwork was laid in a report by the Committee of Governors of the Central Banks of the Member States on a

– a full EMU in stages – by effectively considering all Member States to be at stage two and thus in the antechamber to the third and final stage of EMU.

Stage two of EMU commenced on 1 January 1994, as originally foreseen by Article 116(1) EC.[38] Initially, the main purpose of this stage was twofold. First, the necessary institutional and legal framework for the establishment of a single currency area had to be actually set up, namely by creating a European monetary authority and adopting the necessary secondary Community law governing the technical aspects of the replacement of the national currencies of the participating Member States. At stage two, a system of coordination between the Member States' economies would apply, including seemingly strict budgetary rules, with the aim of ensuring that the Member States would fulfil the legal and economic criteria in time to qualify for the third and final stage of EMU within the rather strict timeframe foreseen by the drafters of the Treaty of Maastricht. In fact, while it de jure made participation in the third and final stage subject to the fulfilment of certain conditions and a qualified majority decision of the Council meeting in the composition of the Heads of State or Government, Article 121(4) EC Treaty at the same time stated that "If by the end of 1997 the date for the beginning of the third stage has not been set, the third stage shall start on 1 January 1999". At the start of the second stage, the European Monetary Institute (EMI) was established, taking over the functions of the Committee of Governors and the EMCF. It was to be directed and managed by a Council, consisting of a President and the Governors of the national central banks.[39] Its main task was to undertake the necessary preparatory work necessary for the establishment of the European System of Central Banks (ESCB) and the European Central Bank (ECB), as well as to coordinate the Member States' monetary policies during stage two.[40]

In the run-up to the decision on the first group of Member States to adopt the single European currency, Member States that hoped to join stage three of EMU from the start pointed to their improved budgetary positions (namely Italy, Spain and Portugal) and, in some instances, attempted to muster political support for a soft approach to the application of the convergence criteria by the Commission and Council. Both the legal and political margins of discretion for the Council were, however, relatively small.[41] The Council, based on reports by the Commission and the EMI,[42] forwarded its recommendations for each Member State to the Council in the composition of the Heads of State and Government.[43] The latter body confirmed the qualifica-

draft status and a draft Treaty on Economic and Monetary Union.

38. Ch. 4 of today's Title VIII TFEU on transitional provisions no longer states this deadline and does not explicitly refer to "stages".

39. Art. 117 EC. The EMI had legal personality. See Protocol on the Statute of the European Monetary Institute annexed to the Treaty of Maastricht (Statute EMI). The first president of the EMI was Alexandre Lamfalussy, followed by Willem Duisenberg.

40. F. Amtenbrink, op. cit. *supra* note 28, 118. Generally, on the tasks of the EMI: European Monetary Institute, *Role and Functions of the European Monetary Institute*, Feb. 1996; U. Häde, "Das Europäische Währungsinstitut und die Kommission", (1994) EuZW, 685–687.

41. Germany, in particular, insisted on strict application of Art. 121 EC, not surprising against the backdrop of the decision by the German Constitutional Court in the *Brunner* case (an English translation of the judgment has been published in (1994) CML Rev., 57–81, in particular its statements on price stability). Moreover, as has been observed above, Art. 88 of the German Basic Law makes the transfer of monetary policy authority to the ECB subject to the observance of price stability as the primary objective.

42. See European Monetary Institute, "Convergence Report (Report required by Art. 109j of the Treaty establishing the European Community" (European Commission, "Convergence Report", 1998).

43. Art. 121(1), (2) and (4) EC. See Council Recommendation 98/316/EC in accordance with Art. 109j(2) of the Treaty (O.J. 1998, L 139/21); Council Decision 98/317/EC in accordance with Art. 109j(4) of the Treaty (O.J. 1998, L 139/30).

tion for stage three of EMU for each Member State separately. This decision, which adopted the considerations made in the recommendations, stated that eleven of the then fifteen Member States had fulfilled "the necessary conditions for the adoption of a single currency",[44] despite the fact that Belgium and Italy continued to be burdened by government debt of more than twice the allowed 60% reference value and thus did not fulfil the criterion requiring a sustainable government financial position.[45] This required recourse to the possibility provided for in Article 104(2)(b) EC (now Article 126(2)(b) TFEU) of granting an exemption if the ratio of government debt to GDP is sufficiently diminishing and approaching the reference value at a satisfactory pace.[46]

The May 1998 decision by the Council in the composition of the Heads of State and Government on the first group of Member States to fulfil the convergence criteria and the subsequent decision on the irrevocable fixing of the exchange rates of the currencies of those countries as of 1 January 1999 marked the start of stage three of EMU. On 1 June 1998, the newly established ECB became operational, taking over all remaining tasks from the EMI.[47] Moreover, in accordance with Article 114(2) EC (now 134 TFEU) the Economic and Financial Committee was set up, which took over the tasks of the Monetary Committee which had been established at the start of stage two in order to promote the coordination of the (economic) policies of the Member States.[48]

The legal framework of the European single currency has been basically defined by three Regulations.[49] Regulation 1103/97 governed the transition from the ECU to the new single currency, the euro. Central to this secondary Community act has been the regulation of the legal continuity of contracts in which reference has been made to the ECU or a former national currency of a Member State participating in the euro area.[50] The actual introduction of the euro as the single currency and the replacement of the national currencies of the initial group of Member States participating in the euro area was governed by Regulation 974/98.[51] This regulation has been amended each time an additional Member State joins the euro area, and sets out the transitional regime which covers the period from the adoption of the euro as single currency (in the case of the initial group of countries joining the euro area: 1 January 1999) until the actual cash changeover from the national currency units to the euro.[52] The euro adoption date, the cash changeover date, and – where applicable – the phasing-out period for each participating Mem-

44. Art. 121(2) 2nd indent EC. In the preamble to this decision, the special position of Denmark and the UK was recalled. With regard to Greece and Sweden, the Council determined that those countries did not fulfil all convergence criteria.
45. Moreover, Italy had not participated in ERM for a full two years.
46. In its convergence report 1998, cited *supra* note 42, 16 and 22, the EMI urged these Member States to maintain their strict budgetary policies.
47. See former Art. 123 EC.
48. Art. 114(1) EC. With regard to the role of the Economic and Financial Committee in economic coordination see section 5.3.3.
49. Reg. 1103/97 on certain provisions relating to the introduction of the euro (O.J. 1997, L 162/1), as amended; Council Reg. 974/98 on the introduction of the euro (O.J. 1998, L 139/1), as amended; Council Reg. 2866/98 on the conversion rates between the euro and the currencies of the Member States adopting the euro (O.J. 1998, L 359/1), as amended.
50. This Reg. has been the subject of numerous publications: U. Wölker, "The continuity of contracts in the transition to the third stage of Economic and Monetary Union", (1996) CML Rev., 1107–1116; R. Dunnett, "Some legal principles applicable to the transition to the single currency", (1996) CML Rev., 1133–1167; W. Rank, *Geld, geldschuld en betaling* (Kluwer, 1996), 65–70.
51. See most recently Council Reg. 827/2014 amending Reg. 974/98 as regards the introduction of the euro in Lithuania (O.J. 2014, L 228/3).
52. Arts. 6–9 Reg. 974/98, as amended.

ber State are set out in an Annex. Banknotes and coins denominated in a national currency unit remain legal tender within the territory of the respective Member State until six months from the respective cash changeover date, whereby Member States can shorten this period.[53] Moreover, a Member States may for a period of up to six months from the respective cash changeover date lay down rules for the use of banknotes and coins denominated in its national currency unit and take any measures necessary to facilitate their withdrawal from circulation. Finally, Regulation 974/98 determines that with effect from the respective cash changeover date, the ECB and the central banks of the participating Member States have to put into circulation banknotes denominated in euro in the participating Member States.[54] The third regulation governing important aspects of the transition to the single currency is Council Regulation 2866/98 which actually determines the conversion rates between the euro and the currencies of the Member States adopting the euro.[55]

2. EMU as structured by the Treaty on European Union and the Treaty on the Functioning of the European Union

Economic policy as part of EMU as defined by the TFEU embraces a fully achieved internal market with free movement of products (goods and services) and factors of production (persons and capital), as well as free and undistorted competition.[56] Within this framework, the main features of the national economic policies are to be coordinated, and more or less stringent rules apply with respect to the budgetary policies of Member States. These rules are to a large extent laid down in secondary Union law, as well as – more recently – two intergovernmental treaties. Within the economic governance framework, Union and national policies may in principle be implemented, for example for the strengthening of the Union's economic structure and competitive position, and to promote well-balanced regional development. Only global economic policy coordination and the binding rules concerning the budgetary policy of the Member States are included in Title 1 of Chapter VIII TFEU on economic policy.[57] Yet, this certainly does not mean that the other objectives mentioned in Article 3(3) TEU are prevented from playing a role.[58] On the contrary, Articles 119 and 120 TFEU expressly refer to Article 3 TEU, and Article 120 TFEU states that Member States should conduct their economic policies "with a view to contributing" to these objectives.[59] Yet, as far as the EU is concerned, the TFEU also allows for the achievement of those other objectives by means other than those specified in the economic policy title.

53. Ibid., Art. 15.
54. Ibid., Arts. 10 and 11.
55. This Reg. is amended on the occasion of each new Member State joining the euro area. See most recently Council Reg. 851/2014 amending Reg. 2866/98 as regards the conversion rate to the euro for Lithuania (O.J. 2014, L 233/21).
56. It should be noted that Title VIII bears the title "economic and monetary policy", rather than referring to economic and monetary *union*.
57. Arts. 120–126 TFEU.
58. See P. VerLoren van Themaat, "Some preliminary observations on the intergovernmental conferences: The relations between the concepts of a common market, a monetary union, a political union and sovereignty", (1991) CML Rev., 302–308. He rightly observed for the old Art. 99(1) EC (now 121 TFEU) that given that an Economic and Monetary Union also encompasses the common (now internal) market, the substantive scope of EMU is much wider than the coordination of macroeconomic and fiscal policies alone. He argued that the concept of economic policies must be interpreted extensively, embracing both macro-economic and micro-economic or structural policies.
59. On Art. 3 TEU see section 5.1.

Monetary policy as defined by Title 2 of Chapter VIII of Part III of the TFEU stands for a single currency area (the euro area) within which monetary policy is centrally determined.[60] At the level of primary Union law, monetary policy for the euro area Member States is governed by Articles 127–133 TFEU as far as substantive provisions are concerned. Institutional provisions are furthermore provided for in Articles 13(1) TEU, Articles 282–284 TFEU, and the Statute of the European System of Central Banks and of the European Central Bank (Statute ESCB).[61] Liberalization of capital markets and movement of payments is provided for in Articles 63–66 TFEU.[62]

EMU as set out in primary Union law stands for a system that has been designed to combine the central monetary policy of an autonomous monetary authority at Union level with vertically cooperative coordination of the economic policies of the Member States. Before the reform of the economic policy coordination framework in response to the euro area sovereign debt crisis, it could already be observed that with respect to certain aspects of the budgetary policy of the Member States this coordination displayed traits of vertical subordination. This characteristic has become increasingly prominent as a result of the reform measures described in section 3 below. Nevertheless, formal reference to the economic policies of the Member States can still be found, namely in Articles 119 and 120 TFEU.

If the rules in the former Articles 102a–109 EEC were typical examples of a *traité-cadre* approach, which could be further filled in and worked out by the then Community institutions and the Member States, the present Treaty rules for EMU, in combination with the relevant Protocols, display all the facets of a *traité-loi*, which in places is worked out in considerable detail. However, this does not necessarily warrant the conclusion that the Union provisions on economic policy coordination have resulted in a stringent and enforceable system. Indeed, theoretical evidence and experience in practice in applying the Treaty system during the first 10 years of operation of the single currency suggest that at times the opposite has been the case. Even prior to the crisis this prompted attempts to strengthen the existing secondary Union law framework.[63]

Title VIII TFEU provides several legal bases for the adoption of detailed rules in the form of secondary Union law.[64] During the European financial and sovereign debt crisis, these legal bases gained considerable importance for the amendment and expansion of the system of economic policy coordination in EMU.

3. The *ad hoc* and structural European regulatory response to the European sovereign debt crisis

A brief history of EMU must include mention of the *ad hoc* and structural measures taken in response to the euro area debt crisis. This is even more so since several of these measures have proven to be rather controversial.[65]

60. Art. 127(1) TFEU. See further section 6.2.
61. Protocol (No. 4) annexed to the TEU and TFEU (O.J. 2012, C 326/1).
62. See Ch. 14, "Free movement of services, establishment and capital", of this book.
63. Namely through the amendment in 2005 of Council Reg. 1466/97 on the strengthening of the surveillance of budgetary positions and the surveillance and coordination of economic policies (O.J. 1997, L 209/1) by Council Reg. 1055/2005 (O.J. 2005, L 174/1), and Council Reg. 1467/97 on speeding up and clarifying the implementation of the excessive deficit procedure (O.J. 1997, L 209/6), by Council Reg. 1056/2005 (O.J. 2005, L 174/5).
64. *Inter alia* Arts. 121(6), 122(2), 125(2), 126(14), 127(6), 128(2), 129(4) 133 and 136 TFEU.
65. For a brief overview of the legal issues see e.g. J.-V. Louis, "Guest editorial: The no-bailout clause and rescue packages", (2010) CML Rev., 971–986. For a broader analysis see e.g. the contributions in M. Adams, F.

The initial response to the crisis came in the form of measures for dealing with the acute situation in Greece, and later in Ireland and Portugal. Since time was of the essence and the appropriate instruments were not thought to be readily available, financial assistance to Greece initially came in the form of bilateral loans from other Member States that were centrally pooled and coordinated and managed by the European Commission.[66] This was combined with a standby agreement with the International Monetary Fund (IMF).[67] Shortly thereafter, based on Article 122(2) TFEU, the European Financial Stabilization Mechanism (EFSM) was set up as a mechanism that would "allow the Union to respond in a coordinated, rapid and effective manner to acute difficulties in a particular Member State".[68] Such financial assistance could be granted to a Member State that was considered to be "seriously threatened with, a severe economic or financial disturbance caused by exceptional occurrences beyond its control" by qualified majority decision by the Council based on a Commission proposal.[69] As will be explained in greater detail in section 5.4., the choice of legal basis for the EFSM was not uncontroversial. Parallel to the ESFM, the European Financial Stabilization Facility (EFSF), a "special purpose vehicle", was set up as a public limited company (société anonyme) under Luxembourg law, based on an intergovernmental agreement between the euro area Member States.[70] Resources for the financial assistance of Member States were generated by issuing financial instruments (debt securities). As shareholders of the EFSF, euro area Member States have irrevocably and unconditionally guaranteed to contribute towards the payment of all amounts payable by the EFSF following the issuance of financial instruments.[71] Ireland, Portugal and Greece have all received financial assistance under the EFSF scheme in combination with EFSM assistance.

In October 2012 the European Stability Mechanism (ESM Treaty) was set up by means of an intergovernmental treaty as a permanent facility with the purpose of granting financial assistance to participating Member States that are "experiencing, or are threatened by, severe financing problems, if indispensable to safeguard the financial stability of the euro area as a whole and of its Member States".[72] Spain became the first euro area Member State to receive financial assistance from the ESM in late 2012 for the recapitalization of its financial institutions. Subsequently, Cyprus and Greece also became recipients of funding from the ESM.

Fabbrini and P. Larouche (Eds.), *The Constitutionalization of European Budgetary Constraints* (Hart Publishing, 2014); K. Tuori and K. Tuori, *The Eurozone Crisis* (CUP, 2014); A. Hinarejos, *The Euro Area Crisis in Constitutional Perspective* (OUP, 2015).

66. See the Intercreditor Agreement between Belgium, Germany, Ireland, Spain, France, Italy, Cyprus, Luxemburg, Malta, the Netherlands, Austria, Portugal, Slovenia, Slovakia, and Finland of 8 May 2010; see also the Loan Facility Agreement between these euro area countries (lenders) and the euro area country Greece (borrower). The initial amount was 80 billion euro. For a general assessment of the ad hoc and temporary financial assistance measures in the crisis see A. De Gregorio Merino, "Legal developments in the Economic and Monetary Union during the debt crisis: The mechanisms of financial assistance", (2012) CML Rev., 1613–1646.
67. 30 billion euro.
68. Reg. 407/2010 establishing a European financial stabilization mechanism (O.J. 2010, L118/1), preamble para 5.
69. Ibid., Art. 1.
70. EFSF Framework Agreement between Belgium, Germany, Ireland, Spain, France, Italy, Cyprus, Luxembourg, Malta, the Netherlands, Austria, Portugal, Slovenia, Slovakia, Finland, Greece and European Financial Stability Facility, 7 June 2010. Arts. of Incorporation of 15 Dec. 2010.
71. EFSF Framework Agreement, para 2(4)(a). The effective capacity of the EFSF was set at 440,000 million euro. The burden-sharing has been based on the ECB's capital key.
72. Treaty establishing the European Stability Mechanism (T/ESM 2012-LT/en 1), Art. 3. For further details on the working of the ESM and the controversy surrounding its compatibility with Union law see section 5.4.

In the domain of monetary policy, the ECB could be seen to be reacting to the changing macroeconomic environment in the euro area. Mirroring policy positions taken by the US Fed, the ECB cut key interest rates to historic lows from July 2008 onwards, which in the case of the deposit facility resulted starting in June 2014 in negative interest rates.[73] In addition, the ECB has implemented a number of so-called non-standard monetary policy measures entailing the purchase of public and private sector assets, which proved to be rather controversial.[74]

In addition to these *ad hoc* crisis measures, the European legislator as well as the Member States have taken a number of steps essentially geared towards improving economic governance in the Union "which should be built on stronger national ownership of commonly agreed rules and policies and on a more robust framework at the level of the Union for the surveillance of national economic policies", thereby learning from the "[E]xperience gained and mistakes made during the first decade of the economic and monetary union".[75] Measures taken at the Union level, the substance of which will be explained in more detail in subsequent sections, came mainly in the form of secondary Union law that was passed in two large legislative packages in 2011 and 2013 that are known as, respectively, Six Pack and Two Pack.[76] In fact, with the exception of the addition of a new paragraph 3 to Article 136 TFEU,[77] which now states that the euro area Member States may establish a stability mechanism, primary Union law has remained unaltered. This can largely be explained by the absence of political consensus among the Member States on whether and how to change primary Union law. Article 48 TEU sets high hurdles for any amendment of the Treaties. Instead, whenever the adoption of secondary Union law was not an option, recourse was sought to intergovernmental instruments. Cases in point are the aforementioned ESM Treaty and the Treaty on Stability, Coordination and Governance in Economic and Monetary Union (TSCG, Fiscal Compact).[78] The TSCG in essence aims at reinforcing the Treaty rules on budgetary discipline through intergovernmental commitments by the signatory Member States whereby, as has been observed elsewhere, the relationship between the TSCG and primary Union law is a delicate one, as also becomes clear from Article 2 TSCG.[79]

---

73. For a current overview of the key interest rates see <www.ecb.europa.eu/stats/monetary/rates/html/index.en.html>.
74. See further section 6.2.
75. Reg. 1173/2011 on the effective enforcement of budgetary surveillance in the euro area, (O.J. 2011, L 306/1), preamble no. 3.
76. Six Pack legislation: Reg. 1173/2011 on the effective enforcement of budgetary surveillance in the euro area (O.J. 2011, L 306/1); Reg. 1174/2011 on enforcement measures to correct excessive macroeconomic imbalances in the euro area (O.J. 2011, L 306/8); Reg. 1175/2011 amending Council Reg. 1466/97 on the strengthening of the surveillance of budgetary positions and the surveillance and coordination of economic policies (O.J. 2011, L 306/12); Reg. 1176/2011 on the prevention and correction of macroeconomic imbalances (O.J. 2011, L 306/25); Council Reg. 1177/2011 amending Council Reg. 1467/97 on speeding up and clarifying the implementation of the excessive deficit procedure (O.J. 2011, L 306/33); Council Directive 2011/85/EU on requirements for budgetary frameworks of the Member States (O.J. 2011, L 306/41). Two Pack legislation: Reg. 472/2013 on the strengthening of economic and budgetary surveillance of Member States in the euro area experiencing or threatened with serious difficulties with respect to their financial stability (O.J. 2013, L 140/1); Reg. 473/2013 on common provisions for monitoring and assessing draft budgetary plans and ensuring the correction of excessive deficit of the Member States in the euro area (O.J. 2013, L 140/11).
77. 2011/199/EU: European Council Decision amending Art. 136 of the Treaty on the Functioning of the European Union with regard to a stability mechanism for Member States whose currency is the euro (O.J. 2011, L 91/1). In this case the simplified Treaty amendment procedure provided for in Art. 48(6) TEU was utilized.
78. T/SCG/en 1. Signed on 2 Mar. 2012 by all Member States but the Czech Republic and the UK.
79. See F. Amtenbrink, "Legal developments", (2012) *JCMS Annual Review*, 132–146, 138; P. Craig, "The stability, coordination and governance treaty: Principle, politics and pragmatism", (2012) E.L. Rev., 231–248;

4. Legal status of non-euro area Member States and the legal and economic conditions for joining the single currency (convergence criteria)

Member States not yet participating in the euro area (non-euro area Member States) are subject to the legal regime applying in stage two of EMU until such time as they fulfil the legal and economic conditions set out in Article 140 TFEU and until a Council decision on their inclusion in the euro area has been taken.[80] Given that not all EU Member States have adopted the single currency (yet) and, moreover, given the prospect of further enlargement of the EU in future, the legal regime applicable to non-euro area Member States retains its practical relevance. It should also be noted that two Member States enjoy a special status under primary Union law that was negotiated at the time of the Treaty of Maastricht.

4.1 *Member States outside the euro area*

Any country acceding to the EU initially finds itself in the antechamber to the euro area until such time as it fulfils the convergence criteria explained below. Article 139(1) TFEU essentially defines such Member States as "Member States with a derogation". This status basically means that the legal regime introduced by Title VIII TFEU does not fully apply to those Member States.[81] In a nutshell, Article 140(2) TFEU excludes from the scope of application all those provisions that directly concern the euro area and euro area Member States both in the context of economic policy coordination and the single monetary policy. In particular, the punitive elements of the economic policy coordination framework that are geared towards the euro area Member States do not apply. Moreover, Member States with a derogation are not bound by the objectives and tasks of the ESCB and the acts of the ECB. Nor do they participate in the main decision-making bodies of the ECB, the Executive Board and the Governing Council. Member States with a derogation must however consider their exchange rate policy to be a matter of common interest.[82] This implies the existence of an exchange rate mechanism after the establishment of stage three of EMU and the euro area which has been provided by means of the ERM II. Based on a proposal of the EMI,[83] the main contours of the ERM II were determined in a Resolution by the Amsterdam European Council in December 1996. As such, ERM II effectively combines the characteristics of an intergovernmental agreement, Union law, and the agreement between central banks which governed the original EMS.[84] ERM II endeavours to ensure that non-euro area Member States orient their policies toward stability, and foster

---

V. Borger and A. Cuyvers, "Het Verdrag inzake Stabiliteit, Coördinatie en Bestuur in de Economische en Monetaire Unie: De juridische en constitutionele complicaties van de eurocrisis", (2012) SEW, 370–390.

80. On the question of participation of seceding State entities that were formerly part of an existing euro area Member State see P. Athanassiou and S. Laulhé Shaelou, "EU Accession from Within? – An Introduction", (2014) *Yearbook of European Law*, 1–50, 31 et seq.

81. See generally J. Cloos et al., op. cit. *supra* note 32, 224–226; R. Smits, "De monetaire unie van Maastricht", (1992) SEW, 715, 729–731; R. Smits, *The European Central Bank: Institutional Aspects* (Kluwer, 1997), 134–139; J-V Louis, M. Waelbroeck et al. (Eds.), *Union économique et monétaire. Cohésion économique et sociale. Poltitique industrielle et technologique européenne*, 2nd ed. (Université de Bruxelles, 1995) (Commentaire Mégret), 147–159.

82. Art. 142 TFEU.

83. European Monetary Institute, Monetary and Exchange Rate Policy Cooperation Between the Euro Area and the other EU-countries, Report of 7 Oct. 1996 to the Dublin European Council of 13 and 14 Dec. 1996 (*Europe*, Document no. 2015/2016, 9–12).

84. Resolution of the European Council on the establishment of an exchange-rate mechanism in the third stage of Economic and Monetary Union (O.J. 1997, C 236/5). This resolution replaces the Resolution of the European Council establishing the European Monetary System (EMS) (*Bull.* EC 6-1978, 1.5.2.). See also the Agreement between the European Central Bank and the national central banks of the Member States

convergence with the aim of eventually fulfilling the convergence criteria. While there is no legal obligation as such to join ERM II, participation in the exchange rate mechanism is a precondition for qualifying for participation in the euro area.[85]

Denmark and the United Kingdom occupy a special category of countries outside the euro area. At the time the Treaty of Maastricht was drafted, the governments of both countries expressed serious reservations about the creation of a single European currency and the loss of sovereignty over monetary policy that would have been the consequence thereof.[86] The option of making participation in the third and final stage of EMU subject to a separate decision in the Member States was rejected by a majority of Member States led by France, which wanted the whole process of the establishment of EMU to be regulated by what is now Union law. By ratifying the Treaty of Maastricht, the Member States thus had to politically and legally commit themselves to participation in the euro area. The risk of this all-or-nothing approach was that Member States which categorically, or as a result of domestic political pressure, rejected the idea of a single European currency would be forced to discard the Treaty of Maastricht as a whole, thereby blocking its adoption. To get around this problem, separate provisions for the United Kingdom and Denmark were agreed upon in two protocols.[87]

The Protocol on certain provisions relating to the United Kingdom recognizes that the latter is not obliged or committed to move to the third stage of EMU without a separate decision to do so by its government and parliament, and that it is under no obligation to join the euro area unless it has informed the Council that it intends to do so (opt in). The Protocol defines in detail the extent to which the provisions of EMU apply. What results from this is that in some regards the United Kingdom can be compared to a Member State with a derogation. This is in particular the case with regard to its participation in economic coordination. However, at the same time it is not fully subject to the legal requirements that Member States with a derogation have to fulfil. In the context of Article 126(1) TFEU the UK only needs to "endeavour to avoid an excessive government deficit". Moreover, Article 131 TFEU on the independence of national central banks does not apply.[88] The Protocol on certain provisions relating to Denmark allows that country to decide not to participate in the third stage of EMU (opt out). As Denmark notified the Council of such a decision, according to the Protocol Denmark must be treated like a Member State with a derogation.[89] Finally, Sweden can be considered a special case; despite the absence of any special agreement, that country is de facto a Member State that is not obliged to adopt the single currency. By remaining outside the single currency, the Swedish government gives effect to a referendum in 2003 in which the Swedish electorate voted against the adoption of the euro.[90]

---

outside the euro area laying down the operating procedures for an exchange rate mechanism in stage three of Economic and Monetary Union (O.J. 2006, C 73/21), as amended.

85. Art. 140(1) TFEU. At the time of writing of this chapter, Denmark is the only participating country.
86. See e.g. J.-V. Louis, op. cit. *supra* note 81, 148.
87. See Protocol (No. 15) on certain provisions relating to the United Kingdom of Great Britain and Northern Ireland (O.J. 2008, C 115/284); Protocol (No. 16) on certain provisions relating to Denmark (O.J. 2012, C 326/287).
88. Para 5 of the Protocol on certain provisions relating to the United Kingdom of Great Britain and Northern Ireland.
89. No. 2 of said Protocol. No. 4 implicitly provides for the possibility for Denmark to revise its decision by abrogating the exemption granted under the Protocol. In such a case the provisions of the Protocol would cease to apply (No. 5).
90. The turnout was 81.2%, whereby 56.2% voted against the adopting the euro. Generally, with regard to the legal position of Sweden: V. Miller, C. Taylor and E. Potton, "The Swedish referendum on the Euro", 3 *House of Common Library Research Paper* (2003).

The exclusion from the euro area of Member States with a derogation, the United Kingdom, Denmark, and Sweden results de facto in an EMU with varying degrees of integration. This poses a challenge to the governance of EMU, and not only in the context of the ESCB and the ECB as will be observed below, but also in the (ECOFIN-)Council. The above-mentioned Member States are excluded from certain decisions in the context of economic coordination and monetary union.[91] On the initiative of France, since 1997 the Ministers of Finance of the Member States participating in the euro area have convened regularly on issues relating to economic and monetary policy issues related to the euro area in the so-called Eurogroup.[92] While still considered to constitute an informal body in terms of the decision-making powers in the Union legal framework, its formal recognition through the Treaty of Lisbon in Article 137 TFEU and a Protocol attached to the Treaties highlights the growing importance of this informal gathering. This has only been strengthened as a result of the expansion of the euro area specific economic coordination framework and corresponding decision-making procedures by the Six Pack and Two Pack. In fact, in terms of its participants, the only real difference between a meeting of the Council in the composition of the Member States whose currency is the euro and the Eurogroup, aside from the labelling of the meeting, is the participation of the vice-president of the European Commission, the president of the ECB, and – as a matter of practice – the managing director of the ESM.[93]

It has been flagged as a point of concern that the euro area Member States are currently in a position to form a blocking majority on EU legislative proposals that would be applicable to all Member States: "If most or all Eurozone members were regularly to adopt the same position, whether as a result of prior concertation or from commonality of interests, the normal process of consensus-building within Council bodies would be liable to be subverted".[94] Moreover, it has been noted that this arrangement may effectively pave the way for the determination of economic policy outside the institutional framework of the Union – despite the fact that this has an impact on EMU which itself is an integral part of EU law.[95] Such criticism has only increased in the throes of the European financial and sovereign debt crisis, namely regarding the role of the Eurogroup in determining the macroeconomic conditionality attached to financial assistance to euro area Member States. In *Mallis* the General Court and on appeal the ECJ had an opportunity to reflect upon the legal nature and position of the Eurogroup in the Union legal order.[96] The ECJ sided with the General Court which characterized the Eurogroup as "a forum for discussion, at ministerial level, between representatives of the Member States whose currency is

---

91. With regard to economic policy see: Arts. 126(13) and 139(4) TFEU. With regard to monetary policy see: Arts. 139(2) and 283 TFEU.
92. Conclusions European Council of Amsterdam, 16 and 17 June 1997, pt. 1.5. (*Bull.* EU 6-1997, p. 10). Conclusions European Council of Luxemburg, 12 and 13 Dec. 1997, pt. 1.9 (43) (*Bull.* EU 12-1997, p. 13), and Resolution of the European Council of 13 Dec. 1997 on economic policy coordination in stage 3 of EMU and on Treaty Arts. 109 and 109b of the EC Treaty (O.J. 1998, C 35/1). Usually the meetings take place prior to the meetings of the ECOFIN Council.
93. See Arts. 1 and 2 of the Protocol on the Euro Group (O.J. 2004, C 310/341). The Eurogroup is supported by a Working Group consisting of representatives of the euro area member states of the Economic and Financial Committee, the Commission and the ECB. See <www.consilium.europa.eu/en/council-eu/eurogroup/eurogroup-working-group/>.
94. A. Dashwood, "Guest editorial: Living with the eurozone", (2016) CML Rev., 3–9, 7.
95. See A. Geelhoed in the 6th Dutch ed. of *Het recht van de Europese Unie en van de Europese Gemeenschappen* (Kluwer, 2003), 90–791 and 834–835.
96. Joined Cases C-105-109/15 *P, Mallis et al.*, on appeal from Case T-327/13, *Mallis and Malli*; Case T-328/13, *Tameio Pronoias Prosopikou Trapezis Kyprou*; Case T-329/13, *Chatzithoma*; Case T-330/13, *Chatziioannou*; Case T-331/13, *Nikolaou*. See further sections 5.4. and 6.1.3.

the euro, and not a decision-making body".[97] While Advocate General Wathelet recognizes the links between the Eurogroup and the Council due to their partially overlapping composition and the close proximity of their meetings, he stresses that the Eurogroup neither constitutes "a configuration of the Council" nor can it in his opinion be deemed an office, body or agency of the Union within the meaning of the first paragraph of Article 263 TFEU.[98] Finally, the General Court has also emphasized that despite its composition it "cannot be regarded as being under the control of the Commission or the ECB, or that it acts as an agent of those institutions".[99]

The stronger emphasis on differentiation between the euro area and non-euro area Member States through the Treaty of Lisbon also becomes apparent from the introduction of chapter 4 of Title VIII TFEU entitled "Provisions specific to Member States whose currency is the euro".[100] Article 136(1) TFEU, which allows for the adoption of measures specific to those Member States whose currency is the euro namely with the aim of strengthening the coordination and surveillance of their budgetary discipline has become the joint legal basis for most legal acts under the Six Pack and Two Pack reforming the economic policy coordination framework in EMU.[101] Moreover, use has been made of the possibility provided in Article 136(1) TFEU of establishing separate economic policy guidelines for the euro area.[102] Finally, the above-mentioned Article 136(3) TFEU allows for the establishment of a stability mechanism specifically for the euro area Member States.

4.2 *Legal and economic criteria for joining the single currency (convergence criteria)*

Article 140 TFEU identifies the applicable criteria and procedure for the adoption of decisions resulting in the accession of a Member State to the euro area. To be sure, countries do not have to fulfil the convergence criteria for joining stage three of EMU at the time of the accession to the EU. However, not in the least to rule out any opting out à la Denmark and the United Kingdom, the 1993 Copenhagen criteria unequivocally oblige states to commit to the aims of economic and monetary union and the eventual adoption of the single currency.[103] In the past, accession negotiations on the adoption and implementation of the *acquis communautaire* have included a separate chapter on economic and monetary union focusing, *inter alia*, on economic growth, the development of public finances, structural reforms, as well as the independent status of the national central bank.[104]

Article 140 TFEU entails a rather complex set of procedural and substantive legal and economic conditions for participation in the euro area. These conditions are generally referred to as convergence criteria and in sum impose far-reaching obligations on the national approach to economic and monetary policy.[105]

---

97. Case T-327/13, *Mallis*, para 41.
98. Opinion of Advocate General Wathelet delivered on 21 Apr. 2016, para 61 and 65.
99. Case T-327/13, para 44.
100. Arts. 136–138 TFEU.
101. Partly in conjunction with Art. 121(6) TFEU or Art. 126(14) TFEU.
102. Albeit that they have to be compatible with those adopted for the whole of the Union.
103. See e.g. Art. 4 of the Act concerning the conditions of accession of the Czech Republic, the Republic of Estonia, the Republic of Cyprus, the Republic of Latvia, the Republic of Lithuania, the Republic of Hungary, the Republic of Malta, the Republic of Poland, the Republic of Slovenia and the Slovak Republic and the adjustments to the Treaties on which the European Union is founded (O.J. 2003, L 236/33).
104. In the case of former Communist countries of Central and Eastern Europe, review included the progress made in the transition to a market economy.
105. Critically e.g. P. de Grauwe, "The Maastricht Treaty as an obstacle to monetary union", (1993) *International Economic Research Paper no. 94*.

As regards *legal conditions*, non-euro area Member States are required to observe the prohibition of overdraft facilities or other types of credit facilities with the ECB or with the central banks of the Member States (Art. 123 TFEU), as well as the prohibition of privileged access to financial institutions (Art. 124 TFEU). Pursuant to Article 139(2) TFEU both provisions also apply to non-euro area Member States. The same applies to Article 125 TFEU.[106] Article 131 TFEU requires Member States to ensure that their national legislation – including the statutes of national central banks – is compatible with the TFEU and the Statutes of the ESCB and the ECB.[107] While Member States with a derogation do not participate in the decision-making bodies of the ECB and are not subject to its single monetary policy, Article 139(2) TFEU does exclude Article 131 TFEU from the scope of application for these Member States. The actual extent of this obligation and its impact on the institutional arrangements laid down in the legal basis of a central bank can arguably only be found by using the ESCB and ECB as a yardstick. Certainly in the run up to the initial introduction of the single currency this requirement has triggered amendment of the legal basis of several national central banks, resulting in some instances in substantial alteration to their position *vis-à-vis* the government.[108]

With regard to *economic conditions*, Article 140(1) TFEU and the Protocol on the convergence criteria include the economic criteria Member States need to fulfil in order to demonstrate that they have achieved the degree of sustainable economic convergence envisaged by the TFEU. These include:

- The achievement of a *high degree of price stability* as reflected by a rate of inflation which is close to that of, at most, the three best performing Member States in terms of price stability. Article 1 of the Protocol on the convergence criteria explains that a Member State has to have sustainable price performance and an average rate of inflation, observed over a period of one year before the examination, that exceeds by no more than 1.5 percentage points that of, at most, the three best performing Member States in terms of price stability.[109] The term "best performing Member States" has to be read as Member States both inside and outside the euro area, whereby the reference value is calculated as the simple arithmetic average of the inflation rates of the three best performing Member States in terms of price stability plus 1.5 percentage points. Although it has received less attention in the literature than the condition relating to the government financial position, the importance of this condition should not be underestimated. Indeed, the degree to which a Member State achieves convergence in nominal price development is a good indicator of its ability to adjust its economy to the demands of EMU. The ability to achieve and maintain relative price stability is a good indication of whether a Member State will be able to muster the discipline required by a fully established EMU.[110]

106. For more details see section 5.2.
107. See Art. 130 TFEU and Art. 7 Statute ESCB and ECB. On the independence of the ESCB and the ECB see section 6.1.3.
108. With regard to the legal adjustments of the central banks of the Member States see F. Amtenbrink, op. cit. *supra* note 28.
109. Inflation is measured by the harmonized indices of consumer prices (HICPs) as defined in Reg. 2016/792 on harmonized indices of consumer prices and the house price index (O.J. 2016, L 135/11).
110. C. Maggiulli, "Convergence et union monétaire européenne", (1993) RMC, 620–627. Also T.H. Van Hoek and G. Zalm, "Nationaal begrotingsbeleid in Europees perspectief" in J. Alders et al. (Eds.), *Begrotingsbeleid en financiering Nederlandse staatsschuld, op weg naar de EMU* (NIBE, 1992), 34–51, and S. Brittan, "EMU in Perspective" in M. Andenas et al. (Eds.), *European Economic and Monetary Union: The Institutional Framework* (Kluwer Law International, 1997), 101–124, 109–112.

- The *sustainability of the government financial position*, as demonstrated by having achieved a government budgetary position without a deficit that is excessive as determined under Article 126(6) TFEU. According to Article 2 of the Protocol on the convergence criteria the Member State may not be the subject of an excessive deficit procedure. Accordingly, the reference values for the excessive deficit are 3% for the ratio of the planned or actual government deficit to gross domestic product at market prices and 60% for the ratio of government debt to gross domestic product at market prices, whereby it has to be noted that the substance of this criterion has aroused a fair amount of dispute among economists.[111] What is more, at the time of their formulation in the Treaty of Maastricht these government deficit criteria were rather ambitious. Most Member States nursed government deficits far in excess of the 3% threshold and government debt considerably above the 60% limit. By the end of 1997 most Member States had managed to comply with the government deficit criterion, but were still running excessive government debt. It was under these circumstances that the exception included in the former Article 104(1)(b) EC (now Article 126(1)(b) TFEU), allowing for a government debt above 60% if "[...] the ratio is sufficiently diminishing and approaching the reference value at a satisfactory pace" gained political and strategic importance.[112] In 1997 and 1998 the Council decided to abrogate decisions on the existence of excessive deficits for a number of Member States.[113]
- The observance of the *normal fluctuation margins* provided for by the exchange-rate mechanism of the EMS for at least two years without devaluing against the currency of any other Member State. This criterion now effectively refers to participation in the successor of the ERM, ERM II, and effectively supplements the first two convergence criteria. Article 3 of the Protocol on convergence criteria adds to this that the normal fluctuation margins must be observed "without severe tensions" and that the Member State must not have devalued its currency's bilateral central rate against any other Member State's currency "on its own initiative". What is arguably missing from this is the possibility that a devaluation of the currency of one or more Member States might result from a revaluation of the currencies of a number of other Member States.[114] At the time of the establishment of the legal framework for EMU, the inclusion of this criterion formed an insurmountable barrier for a vast majority of Member States. This was due to the turbulence in the ERM which reared its head in September 1992, leading to the departure of the United Kingdom and Italy from the system and considerable adjustment to the exchange rates of the Spanish Peseta and the Portuguese Escudo

111. W. Buiter, "De budgettaire voodoo van Maastricht", (1992) ESB, 268–272. See also T.H. Van Hoek and G. Zalm, op. cit. *supra* note 110; I. Harden and J. von Hagen, "National debt boards: An institutional route to fiscal discipline" in M. Andenas et al., op. cit. *supra* note 110, 270–286. A. Italianer, "Begrotingsbeleid in EMU: Safety first" in J. Alders et al., op. cit. *supra* note 110, 14–34, in particular 24–25; P. van den Bempt, "The impact of Economic and Monetary Union and Member States' fiscal policies" in K. Gretschmann (Ed.), *Economic and Monetary Union, Implications for National Policy Makers* (Nijhoff, 1993), 245–261.
112. Note for example the rather cautious way in which the EMI and the Commission handled this criterion: Commission's recommendation concerning the third stage of Economic and Monetary Union. Convergence Report 1998. Growth and employment in the stability-oriented framework of EMU, European Economy, No. 65, 1998.
113. See e.g. Council Decision 98/307/EC and 98/311/EC abrogating the decision on the existence of an excessive deficit in Belgium, as well as in Italy (O.J. 1998, L 139/9 and L 139/15). While the debt ratio was on a downward path, at the time both countries had a government debt of more than two times that of the reference value.
114. See J. Cloos et al., op. cit. *supra* note 32, 207.

within the system.[115] Given the deadlines foreseen in the former Article 121(4) EC this should not in itself have posed a serious problem for the Member States concerned. However, that changed following the turbulence of the summer of 1993 which resulted in a broadening of the fluctuation margins in ERM in most instances from 6 to 15%.[116] Given the vulnerability of a system of stable but adjustable exchange rates it was doubtful that it would be possible to return to the normal, i.e. previous, fluctuation margins in the ERM in time for a positive evaluation of the corresponding convergence criterion. To avoid a negative outcome, focus turned to the objective of this criterion, namely to ensure that Member States maintain discipline in conducting their monetary policy so as to prevent exchange rate fluctuations caused by a destabilizing monetary policy. This was effectively the approach favoured by the Member States in the period between 1993 and 1998. Despite the broad margins foreseen in ERM, in practice the exchange rates stuck relatively close to the normal central rate. Quite remarkably, in the last year before the changeover to the single currency, no significant speculations with ERM currencies took place on the financial markets. This suggests that the economic policies of the Member States enjoyed sufficient credibility in the marketplace. Consequently, in the run-up to the decision on the initial group of Member States to join the euro area, a rather flexible approach was also taken regarding fulfilment of this convergence criterion.[117]

- The *fourth* and final convergence criterion listed in Article 140(1) TFEU is the *durability of convergence* achieved by the Member State and of its participation in the exchange-rate mechanism of the European Monetary System as reflected in the long-term interest-rate levels. According to Article 4 of the Protocol on the convergence criteria, in assessing this criterion it is observed whether a Member State over a period of one year before the examination, has had an average nominal long-term interest rate that does not exceed by more than 2% that of the three best performing Member States in terms of price stability.[118] If the economies of the Member States are convergent in terms of the level of inflation and the government budgetary situation, the free movement of capital should also result in the convergence of the long-term interest rates. The interest rate is a reflection of the level of trust which the financial markets have in the soundness of the economic policy of the Member States.[119]

Finally, although not formally listed as one of the convergence criteria, the last sentence of Article 140(1) TFEU states that the Commission in its reports on the achievement of convergence of a Member State must also take account of the results of the *integration of markets*, the situation and development of the balances of payments on current account, and an examination of the development of unit labour costs and other price indices. This provision emphasizes the link between monetary and economic policy on the one hand, and market integration on the other.

---

115. See F. Ozkan and A. Sutherland, op. cit. *supra* note 27; H. Tietmayer, "Zur politischen Fundierung des monetären Integrationsprozesses in Europa" in O. Due et al. (Eds.), *Festschrift für Ulrich Everling* (Nomos, 1995), 1575–1585, 1580.
116. For the Dmark and the Dutch Guilder the margins remained at +/- 2.25%.
117. Of course, the convergence criterion was formally applied, thereby allowing Sweden, which had deliberately not participated in ERM I to stay outside the euro area. On the contrary, the fact that neither Finland nor Italy had stayed a full two years in ERM was not considered reason to reject them. See P. Beaumont and N. Walker, *Legal Framework of the Single European Currency* (Hart Publishing, 1999), 177.
118. Interest rates are measured on the basis of long-term government bonds or comparable securities, taking into account differences in national definitions.
119. T.H. Van Hoek and G. Zalm, op. cit. *supra* note 110, 37–38, and J.-V. Louis, op. cit. *supra* note 81, 140.

The actual procedure for the acceptance of a Member State into the euro area is laid down in Articles 140(2) and (3) TFEU and entails two separate basic decisions. First, on a proposal from the Commission, having consulted the European Parliament and after discussion in the European Council, the Council decides on the fulfilment of the criteria set out in Article 140(1) TFEU by a Member State with a derogation. The decision is to be taken by qualified majority of the euro area Member States within six months of the Commission's proposal. The qualified majority is determined in accordance with Article 238(3)(a) TFEU, whereby at least 72 % of the members of the Council representing the participating Member States, comprising at least 65 % of the population of these countries, must vote in favour.[120] Where the Council has decided on the acceptance of a new Member State into the euro area and thus formally speaking "to abrogate a derogation", a separate decision irrevocably fixing the rate at which the euro from that point on is substituted for the currency of the Member State concerned has to be taken in unanimity by the euro area Member States and the Member State in question. This decision is based on a proposal from the Commission, whereby the ECB is to be consulted.[121]

5. Economic policy inside and outside the euro area

The coordination of economic policy can be divided into a number of main segments relating to general objectives and principles applicable to EMU, the rules on government financing, and the actual system of economic policy coordination in EMU, as well as the legal framework for dealing with extraordinary economic situations in Member States inside and outside the euro area. What will become evident from the ensuing examination of these elements is that the provisions included in primary and secondary Union law, as well as in several intergovernmental treaties, even when considering the recent reforms, do not amount to an economic union in the sense of a unified single European economic policy pursued at the supranational level on behalf of the Member States. Having noted this, and as has already been hinted at in section 3, the European influence on national economic policy mainly of euro area Member States has certainly substantially increased in recent years, thereby widening the gap between the euro area and non-euro area Member States.

5.1 *Objectives and principles of economic policy coordination in the EU*

Article 119(1)–(2) TFEU sees to the adoption of economic policy at the Union level that is based on the close coordination of Member States' economic policies, on the internal market, and on the definition of common objectives. This entails the euro as the single currency, as well as the definition and conduct of a single monetary and exchange-rate policy with the primary objective of maintaining price stability and, without prejudice to this objective, to supporting the general economic policies of the Union. The latter requirements are reflected in Article 127(1) TFEU and Article 219(1) TFEU.[122]

Article 119 TFEU raises some important legal questions. The deliberate reference to the principle of an open market economy emphasizes that the necessary coordination of economic policies should be based on a well-functioning internal market. Therefore, coordination of economic polices not only involves macro-economic policy, but involves micro-economic policies directed at improving the functioning of the internal market and parts thereof as well. The

120. See most recently Council Decision 2014/509/EU on the adoption by Lithuania of the euro on 1 Jan. 2015 (O.J. 2014, L 228/29).
121. See most recently Council Reg. 851/2014 amending Reg. 2866/98 as regards the conversion rate to the euro for Lithuania (O.J. 2014, L 233/21).
122. See section 6.2.

qualification of the market economy as "open" implies a certain norm that instructs Member States and the Union, in the formation, attainment and implementation of their policies, to opt whenever possible for solutions that leave the operation of the market intact at the Union level.[123] Interpreted in such a manner, state intervention should thus be avoided as much as possible.[124] Past experience has demonstrated that disparities in the composition and use of economic steering instruments may cause major specific or generic distortions which could unnecessarily affect the functioning of the internal market. This point is of particular importance; in the course of the regulatory response to the European financial and sovereign debt crises, a certain trend towards further differentiation between euro area and non-euro area Member States both in relation to economic policy coordination and financial market supervision could be discerned.[125] What is more, this reference implicitly indicates that the coordination of economic policies is *not* limited to macro-economic policy in the narrowly applied sense of influencing macro-economic variables by, e.g. fiscal policy measures.[126] As the recent European sovereign debt crisis has highlighted, in the long run the institutional structure and operation of national economies is at least as important for the economic development of the euro area and the Union as a whole as the orchestration of national budgetary policies according to the different phases of the economic cycle.[127] Finally, it may be argued that the reference to an "open" market economy refers to the relationship with the global market and thus supports the principle set out in Article 206 TFEU of a liberal commercial policy.[128]

The phrase "favouring an efficient allocation of resources" which is found in Article 120 TFEU but not in Article 119(1) TFEU can, on the one hand, be interpreted to only set out an adjunct goal of free competition. Interpreted in such a manner, the phrase would be merely repetitious. On the other hand, the reference can also be read as an independent condition for the Member States and the Commission in the conduct of their economic policies: the authorities should use their – public – resources as efficiently as possible.[129] The real obligation to coordi-

123. J.-V. Louis, "Perspectives of the EMU after Maastricht" in J. Stuyck (Ed.), *Financial and Monetary Integration in the European Community: Legal, Institutional and Economic Aspects* (Kluwer, 1993), 1, 18, with reference to Arts. 4 and 98 EC (now Arts. 119 and 120 TFEU) has argued that the commitment to the principle of an open market economy with free competition appears to have been included for two reasons: first in order to prevent the adoption of quantitative measures of limitation of credit allowed by financial institutions, a favourite instrument of French monetary policy in the past, and, secondly, to protect against rescue operations by the ECB as lender of last resort. For a discussion of the lender of last resort function of the ECB and the national central banks in the euro area see A. Steinbach, "The lender of last resort in the Eurozone", (2016) CML Rev., 361–384.
124. H. Siekmann, "Art. 119" in H. Siekmann (Ed.), *EWU. Kommentar zur Europäischen Währungsunion* (Mohr Siebeck, 2013), 84.
125. With regard to financial market supervision and namely the geographic scope of application of the Single Supervisory Mechanism see Ch. 27, "Financial market regulation and supervision", of this book.
126. In the same sense: F. Van Estorff and B. Molitor in H. Von der Groeben, J. Thiesing, C.-D. Ehlermann (Eds.), *Kommentar zum EU-/EG-Vertrag*, 5th ed. (Nomos, 1999), 3/40.
127. Already illustrative in this regard Commission White Paper "Growth, Competitiveness and Employment" (COM(93)700(*Bull.* EU Supp. 6/93).
128. On the legal implications of this reference see also C. Ohler, "Art. 120" in H. Siekmann, op. cit. *supra* note 124, 98; D. Hattenberger, "Artikel 120 AEUV" in J. Schwarze (Ed.), *EU-Kommentar*, 3rd ed. (Nomos, 2012), 1495.
129. Although on grammatical grounds the first interpretation appears to be more obvious, there are also arguments in favour of the second view. Strictly speaking, an efficient allocation of resources is the consequence of an effective operation of the market. Understood in that way, the addition would be superfluous. It can have particular significance only if the desired efficient allocation is extended beyond the market sector. The history of the former Arts. 4 and 98 EC (now Arts. 119 and 120 TFEU) lend some support to this

nate economic policies according to a cyclical procedure can be read into the words: "Member States shall conduct their economic policies [...] in the context of broad guidelines referred to in Article 121(2)".[130]

Arguably, despite any explicit reference, in practice the Union concept of economic policy does not shy away from short-term macroeconomic policy. Thus, for example, in February 2001 the ECOFIN Council addressed a recommendation to Ireland in accordance with Article 121(4) TFEU to pursue a more restrictive budgetary policy in view of the inflationary tension on the Irish labour market, a clear example of Keynesian short-term macro-economic policy.[131] With the introduction of the macroeconomic imbalances procedure in the European Semester in reaction to the crisis it can be argued that, at least in the case of the euro area Member States, the monitoring of the short-term economic policies of Member States has been further institutionalized including the possibility of imposing penalties for non-compliance.[132]

Article 126(1) TFEU in conjunction with the Protocol on the excessive deficit procedure quantifies the guiding principle of sound public finances referred to in Article 119(3) TFEU by obliging Member States to avoid excessive government deficits. The term "excessive government deficit" is defined in Article 126(2) TFEU and Article 1 of the above-mentioned Protocol on excessive government deficit in terms of two values: the planned or actual government deficit and the government debt.[133] This exclusive focus of primary Union law on the government budgetary positions of the Member States highlights the preoccupation of the drafters of the Treaty of Maastricht, especially Germany, with ensuring the stability of the future single currency.[134] This focus has been further reinforced by the adoption of the TSCG, by which the signatory Member States have agreed to pursue balanced or surplus budgets.[135] According to Article 3(1)(a) TSCG the budgetary positions of the general government must be balanced or in surplus; this is deemed to be the case if the annual structural balance of the general government

interpretation, see J. Cloos et. al., op. cit. *supra* note 32, 234. On the meaning of this reference see also C. Ohler, op. cit. *supra* note 128, 98–99.

130. Brackets added. Interestingly, the wording of the former Art. 98 EC, first phrase, (now Art. 120 TFEU, first sentence) ignited intense debate in the Working Group on Economic Governance of the Convention on the Future of Europe in the context of the unsuccessful attempt to establish a Constitution for Europe. Some members of the Working Group considered that "in order to ensure economic growth, full employment and social cohesion, this should extend to bringing macro-economic policy within the shared competence of the Union and the Member States". However, in its final report to the Convention Plenary, the Working Group recommended that the current structure be kept, whereby the exclusive competence for monetary policy within the euro area lies with the Union, namely the European Central Bank, and economic policy with the Member States. In the final drafting stage, by the Intergovernmental Conference, of the envisaged Art. I-15, any reference to a competence for the Union to coordinate the economic policies of the Member States was meticulously avoided. See: P.J.G. Kapteyn, "EMU and Central Bank: Chances missed", (2005) EuConst, 123–130, 125; D. Servais and R. Ruggeri, "The EU Constitution: Its impact on Economic and Monetary Union and economic convergence", in European Central Bank, *Legal Aspects of the European System of Central Banks, Liber Amicorum Paolo Zamboni Caravelli* (European Central Bank, 2005), 43–71, 48–49.
131. Council Recommendation 2001/191/EC (O.J. 2001, L 69/22). The recommendation was later published, see Council Decision 2001/192/EC (O.J. 2001, L 69/24).
132. See further sections 5.3.2. and 5.3.3.
133. See already section 4.2.
134. The inclusion of an economic paradigm in legislation geared towards economic policy decision-making is not unproblematic, as politics or new scientific insights may change the approach to economic governance over time.
135. See also section 5.3.3.

is at its country-specific medium-term objective, as defined in Council Regulation 1466/97 (as amended), with a lower limit of structural deficit of 0,5 % of GDP at market prices.[136]

According to Article 120 TFEU Member States are supposed to conduct their economic policies with a view to contributing to the achievement of the objectives of the Union as defined in Article 3 TEU, whereby reference is once again made to the previously mentioned principles of an open market economy and free competition, as well as the principles set out in the above-mentioned Article 119 TFEU. As such, the exact scope of the second sentence of Article 120 TFEU is far from precise. This concerns in particular Article 119(3) TFEU, which incompletely summarizes the objectives of economic policy – including stable prices, sound public finances and monetary conditions and a sustainable balance of payments.[137] It is notable that no reference is made to "ensuring a high level of employment" in this account, despite the fact that a high level of employment is mentioned as one of the objectives of the Union in Article 3(3) TEU as part of the objective of establishing a highly competitive social market economy and, moreover, as one of the requirements the Union must take into account in defining and implementing its policies and activities. This objective is moreover included as a "horizontal clause" in Article 147(2) TFEU.[138] Its absence in Article 120 TFEU can be explained by the rather dogmatic debate on the aims of economic policy that accompanied the drafting of the EMU provisions as part of the Treaty of Maastricht. At the preparatory and negotiation stages, German views predominated in the discussion on the conditions which the economic policy of Member States should satisfy with a view to monetary union. In the German view the primary and central element of economic, financial and monetary policy was the maintenance of price stability. The realization of this objective is one of the preconditions for economic growth and, hence, for growth in employment. Those views tacitly implied the rejection of a counter-cyclical fiscal policy according to Keynesian prescriptions. While there was still not sufficient political will to include an explicit reference to a high level of employment as one of the objectives of economic policy coordination in EMU, in the face of a sharp rise in unemployment in the former Community, a title on employment policy was introduced into primary law thereafter by the Treaty of Amsterdam, which today can be found in Title IX TFEU.

Still, considering the deliberate reference in Article 120 TFEU to the objectives of the Union in Article 3 TEU, and moreover considering the scope of the newly established macroeconomic imbalances procedure explained later on in sections 5.3.2. and 5.3.3., it cannot be concluded from the absence of any deliberate mention of the employment objective in the former provision that employment falls outside the scope of economic policy coordination at the Union level. In fact, the Employment Title of the TFEU includes two systematic references, respectively in Article 146(1) and in Article 148(2) TFEU, to the broad guidelines for the economic policies of the Member States and of the Union (BEPG) mentioned in Article 121(2) TFEU, which were adopted upon the entry into force of the Treaty of Maastricht. The so-called employment guidelines are to be drafted in conformity with these guidelines. This furnishes further evidence as to why the absence of any mention of employment as one of the objectives of economic policy coordination in Articles 119–121 TFEU may be considered something of an anomaly. In the wake of the effects in the EU of the global economic slowdown in the early 2000s, namely growth and employment levels, and the relaunch of the Lisbon strategy, which aimed to "raise the Union's growth potential, while maintaining sound macroeconomic policies that underpin the success of reform efforts", systematic attention has been paid in the broad policy guidelines issued in

---

136. Art. 3(1)(b) TSCG, which effectively refers to Art. 5(1) Council Reg. 1466/97.
137. Similar objectives were already defined in Art. 104 of the original EEC Treaty.
138. Title IX TFEU.

accordance with Article 121(2) TFEU to the employment aspect and especially to measures that result in higher employment.[139] In fact, in 2005 the BEPGs and the employment guidelines were merged into "Integrated guidelines for jobs and growth".[140] The European Semester is geared towards further integration of the various instruments. Moreover, unemployment rates have been included as one of several indicators of macroeconomic imbalance as part of the macroeconomic imbalances procedure.

5.2 *The rules on deficit financing according to market principles*

In most Member States public authorities, bodies governed by public law, and public undertakings have since time immemorial enjoyed a privileged position in the financing of their deficits. The most important escape from the rigour of a highly disciplined budgetary policy is provided by so-called monetary deficit financing through credit facilities afforded by the national central bank. However, extensive monetary financing of government deficits poses grave risks to internal price stability, and thus to interest rate development on the money markets. For this reason, the drafters of Article 123 TFEU intended to prescribe a general prohibition of monetary deficit financing by the public sector in the broadest sense of the term,[141] and together with Article 126 TFEU and the Articles 124 and 125 TFEU discussed below to introduce a "Union legal framework for the fiscal and budgetary policies of the Member States".[142] The enclosed paradigm of government refinancing at market conditions has been contested given recent experience in the context of the European sovereign debt crisis.[143]

Besides the prohibition of extending overdraft or any other type of credit facility by the ECB or a central bank of any of the Member States in favour of national public authorities including mainly central or regional governments, or Union institutions, offices or agencies, Article 123(1) TFEU also prohibits the purchase on the primary market of public debt instruments by the ECB or national central banks. Consequently, what is in principle not barred by this provision is the purchase by central banks of public debt instruments on the secondary market and thus from sellers other than the issuer at the time of the introduction of the debt instrument to the public on the primary market. The prohibition of monetary financing moreover does not apply to publicly-owned credit institutions.[144]

In the course of the European financial and sovereign debt crisis the scope of Article 123(1) TFEU has become the subject of major academic debate and ultimately of judicial consideration by the ECJ, initially in the context of the establishment of the ESM Treaty and later as a consequence of the unconventional monetary policy measures by the ECB *inter alia* involving

139. See the Council's Recommendations as to the BEPG (O.J. 2005, L 205/28), for the 2005–2008 period.
140. European Commission, "Integrated Guidelines for Growth and Jobs (2005–2008)" (COM(2005)141 final), 6. Generally with regard to the EU employment policy K. van Duin, *Rethinking EU Employment Policy; A Legal and Economic Analysis*, PhD thesis (Erasmus University Rotterdam, 2013).
141. See Council Reg. 3603/93 (O.J. 1993, L 332/1) on definitions for the application of the prohibitions referred to in Arts. 104 and 104b(1) of the Treaty. Art. 8 of this regulation adopts the definition of public undertakings used in the old Directive 80/723 (O.J. 1980, L 195/35), which has since been repealed by Commission Directive 2006/111/EC on the transparency of financial relations between Member States and public undertakings as well as on financial transparency within certain undertakings (O.J. 2006, L 318/17). See generally J. Pipkorn, "Legal arrangements in the Treaty of Maastricht for the effectiveness of the Economic and Monetary Union", (1994) CML Rev., 263–291, 277.
142. Own translation. D. Hattenberger, op. cit. *supra* note 128, 1531.
143. F. Amtenbrink, R. Repasi, and J. de Haan, "Is there life in the old dog yet? Observations on the political economy and constitutional viability of common debt issuing in the Euro area", (2016) *Review of Law & Economics*, 605–633.
144. Art. 123(1) TFEU.

the purchase of public debt instruments of euro area Member States that are in economic difficulties. It has been argued that such purchases are at the very least a circumvention of what this provision aims to achieve: ensuring that Member States actually sustain the economic and budgetary consequences of their (unsound) budgetary policies, namely the higher risk premium the country may be faced with when borrowing.[145] In its ruling on the first ever preliminary reference by the German Federal Constitutional Court (*Bundesverfassungsgericht*) the ECJ observed in *Gauweiler* that Article 123(1) TFEU aims to encourage Member States "to follow a sound budgetary policy, not allowing monetary financing of public deficits or privileged access by public authorities to the financial markets to lead to excessively high levels of debt or excessive Member State deficits".[146] While the purchase of government bonds on the secondary market is thus not per se excluded by this provision, something the Court had already previously noted in the *Pringle* case, the ECJ in *Gauweiler* emphasized that "sufficient safeguards" must be put in place to ensure that such purchases do not "fall foul of the prohibition of monetary financing in Article 123(1) TFEU", namely by having "an effect equivalent to that of a direct purchase of government bonds from public authorities and bodies of the Member States".[147] In the view of the ECJ this would be the case "if the potential purchasers of government bonds on the primary market knew for certain that the ESCB was going to purchase those bonds within a certain period and under conditions allowing those market operators to act, de facto, as intermediaries for the ESCB for the direct purchase of those bonds from the public authorities and bodies of the Member State concerned".[148] According to the European judges this can be ensured by having measures in place that prevent markets from anticipating and thus already factoring in the price of such purchases on the primary market, *inter alia* by observing a minimum waiting period between the issue of a security on the primary market and its resale on the secondary market and, moreover, by refraining from any "prior announcement concerning either [the ECB's] decision to carry out such purchases or the volume of purchases envisaged".[149] Finally, in *Pringle* the ECJ had already observed that Article 123(1) TFEU does not extend to situations in which one Member State grants financial assistance to another Member State; the addressees of this provision are the ECB and the national central banks.[150]

Complementing the prohibition of monetary financing, Article 124 TFEU prohibits any measure not based on prudential considerations that establishes privileged access to financial institutions "by Union institutions or bodies, central governments, regional, local or other

---

145. On the aims of this provision: J.A. Kämmerer, "Art. 123 AEUV" in H. Siekmann, op. cit. *supra* note 124, 150, 152.
146. Case C-62/14, *Gauweiler*, para 100.
147. Ibid., para 102 and 104. As to the Court's assessment of the ECB's announcement of the Outright Monetary Transactions (OMT) programme, which formed the substance of this case, see section 6.2. See also Case C-370/12, *Pringle*, para 123.
148. Case C-62/14, *Gauweiler*, para 104.
149. Brackets added. Ibid., para 106. In the recently submitted second-ever preliminary reference by the German Federal Constitutional Court regarding the ECB's secondary market public sector purchase programme (ECB Decision 2015/774, O.J. 2015, L 121/20, as amended) and the eligibility of marketable debt instruments issued or fully guaranteed by Greece (ECB Decision 2016/104, O.J. 2016, L 169/14), the German judges once more refer to the scope of Art. 123(1) TFEU to question the legality of the ECB measures. For details on this – at the time of writing of this chapter – pending case see BVerfG, Beschluss des Zweiten Senats vom 18. Juli 2017 – 2 BvR 859/15 – Rn (1-137). The reference is pending before the ECJ as Case C-493/17, *Weiss et al.* See also the decision of the president of the ECJ of 18 Oct. 2017 rejecting the request by the German court for an application of the expedited preliminary reference procedure.
150. Case C-370/12, *Pringle*, para 125. C.A. Vassilopoulos and E. de Lhoneux, *The European Stability Mechanism before the Court of Justice of the European Union* (Springer, 2013).

public authorities, other bodies governed by public law or public undertakings".[151] Practices such as easing the borrowing requirements for public authorities, which was common in several Member States before 1994, is thus prohibited. Privileged treatment is only permissible if it results from normal business considerations based on the relatively high creditworthiness of the authority concerned as a debtor.[152]

To the extent that the rules for deficit financing on strictly market conditions contained in Articles 123 and 124 TFEU aim to confront national budgetary authorities with the financial consequences of a budgetary policy in deficit, this rests on the assumption that financial markets will indeed reflect their confidence in the authority concerned in the terms under which they are prepared to provide capital, namely in the risk premium (interest rates) that the country will be asked to pay when borrowing. The effectiveness of this as a corrective arguably depends on the existence of a credible mechanism ensuring that Member States cannot escape market logic. 125 TFEU was arguably put in place to provide such a mechanism by prohibiting both the Union and Member States from assuming liability for the commitments of central governments, regional, local or other public authorities, other bodies governed by public law, or public undertakings of any Member State. Excluded from the scope of Article 125 TFEU, however, are mutual financial guarantees for the joint execution of a specific project. Before the European sovereign debt crisis, the scope of Article 125 TFEU was not the subject of much debate. What was notable however was that this provision was soon labelled the no bail-out clause,[153] thereby suggesting – if one subscribes to a dictionary definition of the term – that Member States that are in financial difficulties cannot be saved or rescued by other Member States or by the Union, regardless of the actual circumstances or character of such assistance.[154] Article 125 TFEU became the subject of controversial debate, mainly among legal and economic academics and policy makers, initially when the Member States decided to grant bilateral loans to Greece in May 2010 and later when financial assistance was granted to several other countries under the EFSM/EFSF and ESM scheme. In fact the legality both under EU and national (constitutional) law of the sum of these measures was unsuccessfully challenged before several of the national highest (constitutional) courts *inter alia* with reference to violation of Article 125 TFEU, for example before the German Federal Constitutional Court (*Bundesverfassungsgericht*) regarding the constitutionality of the German (bilateral) financial aid to Greece and the German guarantee in the context of the EFSM[155] and the ratification of the ESM Treaty and the Fiscal Compact.[156] In *Pringle* the ECJ opted for a narrow interpretation of Article 125 TFEU, pointing out first of all with reference to Article 122(2) TFEU and the more restrictive wording of Article 123

151. See further Council Reg. 3604/93 specifying definitions for the prohibition of privileged access (O.J. 1993, L 332/4).
152. Art. 2 Council Reg. 3604/93 provides a definition of defines prudential considerations.
153. See already J. Pipkorn, op. cit. *supra* note 141, 275.
154. See e.g. M. Ruffert, "The European debt crisis and European Union law", (2011) CML Rev., 1777–1806; H. Kube and E. Reimer, "Grenzen des Europäischen Stabilisierungsmechanismus", (2010) *Neue Juristische Wochenschrift*, 1911–1916. Differently: M. Selmayr, "Die 'Euro-Rettung' und das Unionsprimärrecht: Von putativen, unnötigen und bisher versäumten Vertragsänderungen zur Stabilisierung der Wirtschafts- und Währungsunion", (2013) ZÖR, 259–318.
155. BVerfG 129, 124, Official English language version available at <www.bundesverfassungsgericht.de/SharedDocs/Entscheidungen/EN/2011/09/rs20110907_2bvr098710en.html;jsessionid=26991B1DF7A0770B53DE6F19DE070F74.2_cid392>.
156. BVerfG, Order of 12 Sept. 2012 – 2 BvR 1390/12. Official English language version available at <www.bundesverfassungsgericht.de/SharedDocs/Entscheidungen/EN/2012/09/rs20120912_2bvr139012en.html>. Generally, on the implications of the challenges of crisis measures before national courts F. Amtenbrink, "New economic governance in the European Union: Another constitutional battleground?" in K.

TFEU that this provision does not intend to "prohibit either the Union or the Member States from granting any form of financial assistance whatever to another Member State".[157] The ECJ considered that stability support and credit lines granted to Member States in financial difficulties in the context of the ESM do not violate Article 125 TFEU, as neither the Member States nor the Union or the ESM for that matter take on existing commitments or assume the debts of the recipient Member States.[158] Yet, from the considerations of the ECJ it can be deduced that to be in line with Article 125 TFEU the granting of financial assistance has to fulfil two conditions. First and most importantly, assistance must be subject to strict conditionality so as to prevent moral hazard and to incentivize Member States to conduct sound budgetary policy in line with primary Union law.[159] In this context the European judges have emphasized the objective pursued by Article 125 TFEU, namely to prohibit "the Union and the Member States from granting financial assistance as a result of which the incentive of the recipient Member State to conduct a sound budgetary policy is diminished".[160] What is more, the ECJ refers to situations where such financial assistance is "indispensable for the safeguarding of the financial stability of the euro area as a whole".[161] This is also reflected in Article 136(3) TFEU, which allows for the establishment of a stability mechanism that can be activated "if indispensable to safeguard the stability of the euro area as a whole", whereby the granting of such assistance must be subject to strict conditionality.[162] Whether the ECJ's considerations regarding Article 125 TFEU are to be interpreted as extending to any kind of financial assistance provided beyond the current ESM remains up for debate.[163]

While Article 125 TFEU is thus clearly interpreted as part of a set of Treaty rules designed to expose Member States to market forces so as to provide additional incentive to implement sound budgetary policies, the experiences of the first 10 years of existence of the single currency suggest that this mechanism has not necessarily worked as envisaged. Evidence of this can be found in the development of government bond yield spreads in the euro area. The considerable variation observed prior to the introduction of the single currency gave way to relatively high convergence thereafter that is not easily explained by economic fundamentals in some of the euro area Member States at the time. In this context, it has been observed that market behaviour did not suggest that in case a euro area Member State got into financial difficulties Article 125

Purnhagen and P. Roth (Eds.), *Varieties of European Economic Law and Regulation. Liber Amicorum for Hans Micklitz* (Springer, 2014), 207–234.

157. Case C-370/12, *Pringle*, para 130–132. For an analysis of the judgment see C. Koedooder, "The Pringle judgment: Economic and/or Monetary Union?", (2013) *Fordham International Law Journal*, 110–146; B. de Witte and T. Beukers, "The Court of Justice approves the creation of the European stability mechanism outside the EU legal order: Pringle", (2013) CML Rev., 805–848.
158. Ibid., para 139.
159. Ibid., para 142–143.
160. Ibid., para 135.
161. Case *Pringle*, para 136 and 142. The ECJ contrasts this with the situation wherein financial assistance is granted "as soon as a Member State whose currency is the euro is experiencing difficulties in obtaining financing on the market". Interestingly, to support this interpretation the ECJ refers to an ECB opinion: ECB Opinion on the draft European Council Decision amending Art. 136 of the Treaty on the Functioning of the European Union with regard to a stability mechanism for Member States whose currency is the euro.
162. European Council decision amending Art. 136 of the Treaty on the Functioning of the European Union with regard to a stability mechanism for Member States whose currency is the euro (2011/199/EU) (O.J. 2011, L 91/1).
163. This discussion is e.g. relevant in the context of proposals for the establishment in future of a system of common debt issuing in the euro area, such as through Eurobonds, Stability Bonds or a European Safe Asset. With regard to the latter see European Commission, "Reflection Paper on the Deepening of the Economic and Monetary Union" (COM(2017)291).

TFEU would actually be applied in a way that excluded any form of financial assistance, resulting in low risk aversion.[164] Consequently, the introduction of the euro lowered borrowing costs considerably for some euro area Member States, arguably providing the wrong kind of incentive.[165]

In principle, no further implementation measures are required for Articles 123 and 125 TFEU to take effect.[166] Still, Article 125(2) TFEU empowers the Council of the European Union to adopt secondary Union acts that "specify definitions" for the application of the prohibitions referred to in Articles 123–125 TFEU.[167]

5.3 *Economic policy coordination inside and outside the euro area*[168]

In the original legal framework introduced by the Treaty of Maastricht, coordination of the economic policies of the Member States of the EU was basically geared towards the prevention of, and thereafter dealing with, excessive government deficits as defined in Article 126(1) and (2) TFEU in conjunction with the Protocol on the excessive deficit procedure.[169] Correspondingly, the multilateral surveillance and excessive deficit procedures laid down in today's Articles 121 and 126 TFEU formed the two central segments of the coordination of economic policies laid down in primary Union law.

The Treaty legal framework has been further defined in several Protocols attached to the Treaties. From a practical point of view, the Protocol on the excessive deficit procedure, the Protocol on certain provisions relating to the United Kingdom of Great Britain and Northern Ireland, as well as the Protocol on certain provisions relating to Denmark could be considered the most important. These Protocols respectively define the reference values and terminology referred to in Article 126(1) and (2) TFEU, and determine how far the rules on economic policy coordination apply to the United Kingdom and Denmark.

As far as secondary Union law is concerned, next to the two – repeatedly revised – Council Regulations of the 1997 Stability and Growth Pact, today's legal framework is primarily defined by the above-mentioned Six Pack and Two Pack legislation that was adopted in the wake of the crisis.[170] Indeed, while Title VIII TFEU still sets out the basic framework as far as primary Union law is concerned, the structural regulatory response to the euro area debt crisis namely in the guise of secondary Union law measures and two related intergovernmental treaties has altered the legal landscape beyond what a study of the TEU and TFEU might lead one to expect. Relevant in this regard are the introduction of the obligation for signatory Member States of the Fiscal Compact to establish a balanced budget rule and automatic correction mechanism

---

164. See M. Buti and N. Carnot, "The EMU debt crisis: Early lessons and reforms", (2012) JCMS, 899–911, 903, who argue that it was to be expected that the Union would "renege" on a strict reading of Art. 125 TFEU if necessary.
165. On the initial convergence of long-term interest rates for sovereign debt bonds in the euro area and the subsequent dramatic increase in (certain) sovereign bond yields see K. Klose and B. Weigert, "Sovereign yield spreads during the Euro-crisis – Fundamental factors versus redenomination risk", 7 *German Council of Economic Experts Working Paper* (2012).
166. See already J. Pipkorn, op. cit. *supra* note 141, 275.
167. See Council Reg. 3604/93 (cited *supra* note 151), which was based on the old Art. 104a(2) EEC; Council Reg. 3603/93 (cited *supra* note 141).
168. This section is based, partially, on F. Amtenbrink and H.H.B. Vedder, *Recht van de Europese Unie*, 5th ed. (Boom, 2017), Ch. IX.
169. See *supra* section 3.1.
170. See *supra* note 76.

in national legislation,[171] and, importantly, the approach to economic policy coordination espoused by the European Semester.

5.3.1 *The European Semester*

Economic policy coordination in EMU currently takes place in the context of the so-called European Semester, which is geared towards an alignment of the various policy instruments through the introduction of "an overarching framework for integrated multilateral economic and budgetary surveillance".[172] This has resulted in a very complex annual surveillance cycle covering a period of six to eight months essentially aimed at ensuring that Member States act in conformity with the agreed-upon medium-term budgetary objectives and any necessary national reform programmes in line with the strategic objectives of the Union.[173] At the same time, the cycle is aimed at improving the monitoring of the implementation of the employment guidelines and the prevention and correction of macroeconomic imbalances in the Member States. In principle, four interconnected phases can be differentiated:[174]

- a preparatory phase (November-December) geared towards the gathering of relevant information by the European Commission on economic fundamentals of the Member States and the EU as a whole, that is published in the form of an Annual Growth Survey[175] and an Alert Mechanism Report,[176] as well as towards the issuing of general Commission recommendations specifically for the euro area;[177]
- a policy-guidance phase (January-April), in which the European Council, in conjunction with the Council and the European Parliament, formulates the Union strategic objectives, and in which the Commission undertakes any required in-depth reviews of the economic situation of euro area Member States as part of the macroeconomic imbalances procedure;[178]
- a country-specific policy-guidance phase (April-July), commencing with Member States identifying their specific objectives, priorities and plans in the context of the annual Stability and Convergence Programmes,[179] as well as the establishment of National Reform Programmes (describing planned structural reforms), followed by a

171. See *supra* section 3.
172. Council recommendation 2015/1184 on broad guidelines for the economic policies of the Member states and of the European Union (O.J. 2015, L 192/27), preamble no. 1.
173. While in publications reference is often made to a 6-month cycle, if the preparatory phase is included, the actual surveillance cycle covers 8–9 months (Nov. – June/July).
174. See the visual overview at <www.consilium.europa.eu/en/policies/european-semester/>.
175. See e.g. Communication from the Commission to the European Parliament, the Council, the European Central Bank, the European Economic and Social Committee, the Committee of the Regions and the European Investment Bank, Annual Growth Survey 2016. Strengthening the recovery and fostering convergence (COM(2016)690 final).
176. See Arts. 3 and 4 Reg. 1176/2011 (macroeconomic imbalances procedure).
177. See e.g. European Commission, Recommendation for a Council recommendation on the economic policy of the euro area (COM(2016)726 final).
178. See e.g. Communication from the Commission to the European Parliament, the Council, the European Central Bank and the Eurogroup, "2016 European semester: Assessment of progress on structural reforms, prevention and correction of macroeconomic imbalances, and results of in-depth reviews under Reg. (EU) No 1176/2011" (COM(2016)95 final/2).
179. In accordance with Arts. 3 and 7 Council Reg. 1466/97.

Council decision on country-specific recommendations that are based on a draft by the Commission and endorsed by the European Council;[180]
- an implementation phase (from August), during which the Member States draft their national budget for the next year and forward it to the European Commission for review.[181]

Rather than provide a detailed chronological account of the European Semester in the sections that follow, major features of the current system of economic policy coordination and the main differences with the original framework introduced by the Maastricht Treaty will be highlighted. Despite the many changes to the governance framework, the coordination system in essence continues to be made up of two main pillars: surveillance and enforcement.

5.3.2 *Multilateral surveillance of deficits, debts and macroeconomic (im)balances*

Currently, surveillance of the economic policies of the Member States extends to a relatively broad spectrum of macroeconomic developments that may exert a negative influence on the economic developments at the country level or "of the economic and monetary union, or of the Union as a whole".[182] What is particularly noteworthy about the introduction of the European Semester is the increased focus on the specific situation in the euro area and its Member States, as becomes *inter alia* clear from the introduction of euro area-specific recommendations.

Each year, euro area countries are required to submit their detailed draft budget for the coming year to both the European Commission and the Eurogroup. When drafting their budgets euro area Member States must take into account the general recommendations for the euro area, the Council's country-specific recommendations made in the context of the multilateral surveillance and macroeconomic imbalances procedures, and are also subject to the general obligation to reduce any public debt greater than 60% of GDP by on average 5% per year.[183] Budgetary plans are assessed by the European Commission which issues an opinion on their economic sustainability based on its own economic forecasts.[184] In exceptional cases the Commission may ask the Member State to submit a new draft budget at the latest within three weeks. This is the case if the Commission is of the opinion that the implementation of the draft budgetary plans submitted by the Member State could lead to "a particularly serious non-compliance with the budgetary policy obligations laid down".[185] Euro area Member States are also required to report their debt issuance plans to the European Commission and the Eurogroup "ex ante and in a timely manner".[186]

In the context of multilateral surveillance as laid down in Article 121 TFEU in conjunction with Council Regulation 1466/97 the European Commission and the Council monitor the implementation of economic policy by all Member States in accordance with agreed-upon plans, for instance involving fiscal targets, with a view to ensuring that no excessive government deficits emerge. This includes namely what Member States have laid down in their stability or

180. See e.g. Council recommendations on the 2016 National Reform Programme of the Netherlands and delivering a Council opinion on the 2016 Stability Programme of the Netherlands (COM(2016)339 final).
181. See namely Arts. 6–7 Reg. 473/2013 on common provisions for monitoring and assessing draft budgetary plans and ensuring the correction of excessive deficit of the Member States in the euro area (O.J. 2013, L 140/11).
182. Art. 2(1) Reg. 1176/2011.
183. Art. 4 TSCG. See also Art. 2(1a) Council Reg. 1467/97. With regard to the required information in the draft budgetary plans see Art. 6. See also Art. 5 Council Reg. 1466/97.
184. Ibid., Art. 7(1).
185. Ibid., Art. 7(2).
186. Ibid., Art. 8(1).

convergence programmes. In this context, it should be noted that the economic assumptions these programmes are based upon are scrutinized to determine whether an announced adjustment path towards a budgetary objective is appropriate and, moreover, to what extent the proposed measures are sufficient for the purpose of achieving the objectives within the economic cycle. The economic evaluations provided by the Member States are subjected to an independent assessment by Eurostat, the statistical office of the European Union.[187] To be sure, Eurostat must in principle be able to rely on the accuracy of the data provided by the Member States, which in the past has on occasion proven to be not entirely without problem.[188] However, as part of the Six Pack legislation, the possibility of issuing fines has been introduced for the manipulation of statistics by a Member State that "intentionally or by serious negligence misrepresents deficit and debt data" relevant for the application of the multilateral surveillance or excessive deficit procedure, whereby the ECJ has unlimited jurisdiction to review the decisions of the Council imposing fines.[189]

Another main innovation of the revised multilateral surveillance framework is the strengthening of the enforcement regime for euro area Member States. In fact, with the introduction of the Six Pack regulations it has become possible to impose penalties before the actual occurrence of an excessive deficit pursuant to Article 126(6) TFEU. In the context of the multilateral surveillance procedure the Commission can first address a warning to a Member State for which it has observed a significant deviation from the announced adjustment path towards the agreed-upon medium-term budgetary objectives with the aim of preventing the occurrence of an excessive deficit.[190] This has to be followed up by a Council recommendation calling upon the Member State concerned to take the necessary corrective policy measures. If no effective action is taken, the Commission can recommend that the Council adopt, by QMV, a decision verifying that indeed no effective action has been taken and to adopt revised recommendations. The inaction of the Council does not stall the procedure, as in the case of a subsequent second request by the Commission to the Council to adopt a decision, reversed qualified majority voting (RQMV) applies.[191] This means that the decision is deemed to be adopted by the Council unless the latter rejects the Commission's recommendation by qualified majority within 10 days of the Commission's adoption thereof.[192] In the case of euro area Member States the Commission is moreover obliged to recommend that the Council take a further decision within 20 days, requiring the euro area Member State concerned to lodge with the Commission an interest-bearing deposit amounting to 0,2 % of its GDP in the preceding year. RQMV also applies to this decision.[193] The interest-bearing deposit is only returned if the economic situation that gave rise to the decision has ceased to exist, whereas further deterioration of the situation may at some point result in a changeover to the excessive deficit procedure. The adoption of a decision on a deposit will also have consequences in the context of any subsequent excessive deficit procedure.[194]

With the introduction of the macroeconomic imbalances procedure as part of the Six Pack, the monitoring of all Member States now extends to a broader set of economic, financial and structural variables that can function as indicators of the existence of macroeconomic

---

187. Council Reg. 479/2009 provides for a uniform terminology to be applied also by the Member States in the context of the excessive deficit procedure.
188. See e.g. Report by Eurostat on the revision of the Greek government deficit and debt figures, 22 Nov. 2004.
189. Art. 8 Reg. 1173/11.
190. Art. 121(4) TFEU in conjunction with 6(2) Council Reg. 1466/97.
191. Art. 6(2) Council Reg. 1466/97.
192. Ibid.
193. Art. 5(1)–(2) Reg. 1173/11.
194. See section 5.3.3.

imbalances. Article 2(1) of Regulation 1176/11 defines such imbalances as "any trend giving rise to macroeconomic developments which are adversely affecting, or have the potential adversely to affect, the proper functioning of the economy of a Member State or of the economic and monetary union, or of the Union as a whole". The unwinding of such imbalances has been identified as having contributed to the European financial crisis and more broadly to the growing divergence between the economies of the Member States.[195] As part of the European Semester, the Commission prepares an annual Alter Mechanism Report for the purpose of the early identification and monitoring of imbalances in the Member States, which basically amounts to "a qualitative economic and financial assessment" which identifies Member States that "may be affected by, or may be at risk of being affected by, imbalances".[196] To this end, the Commission makes use of a so-called scoreboard consisting of macroeconomic and macro-financial indicators that are linked to internal and external imbalances. This includes for example the levels of public and private indebtedness, financial and asset market developments (including housing), the evolution of private sector credit flow, and the evolution of unemployment. Moreover, the evolution of current account and net investment positions of Member States, real effective exchange rates, export market shares, changes in price and cost developments, and non-price competitiveness are explicitly identified.[197] From Regulation 1176/11 it becomes clear that these indicators should not be applied mechanically by the Commission, as the development of the imbalances in the Union and in the euro area must be taken into account.[198] Considering the somewhat restricted scope of economic policy in EMU, the scope of indicators included in the analysis is remarkable; it signifies the recognition of the importance of labour markets and social aspects to EMU.[199]

The Annual Alert Report is evaluated by the Council as part of the multilateral surveillance procedure in the European Semester and, moreover, is discussed by the Eurogroup for the euro area Member States. This assessment can subsequently give rise to a so-called in-depth review, that is a detailed analysis of country-specific circumstances, with the aim of determining whether a Member State is indeed affected by imbalances, and if so, whether these imbalances are excessive.[200] The latter is the case if an imbalance is considered "severe" in the sense of Regulation 1176/11, which is to say that it jeopardizes or risks jeopardizing "the proper functioning of the economic and monetary union".

In the context of the multilateral surveillance procedure, the detection of a non-excessive imbalance can trigger Council recommendations, as the latter can (but is not obliged!) to take such a course of action based on a recommendation by the Commission. In any event, the Commission is obliged to inform not only the Council, but also the European Parliament, the Council and the Eurogroup.[201]

5.3.3 *Excessive deficit and excessive macroeconomic imbalances procedures*

While the reform of economic policy coordination in response to the European sovereign debt crisis has undoubtedly strengthened the preventive arm of the system, the effectiveness of the system arguably still to a large extent relies on the effectiveness of the measures set in place to

195. See e.g. European Commission, "The Macroeconomic imbalances procedure. Rationale, process, application: A compendium", 39 *Institutional Paper* (2016), 15–16.
196. Art. 3 Reg. 1176/11.
197. Ibid., Art. 4.
198. Art. 4(2) Reg. 1176/11.
199. European Commission, op. cit. *supra* note 195, 17.
200. Ibid., Art. 5.
201. Ibid., Art. 6.

address excessive government deficits or excessive macroeconomic imbalances, and thus, on the corrective arm of the system.

Concerning the budgetary situation of Member States, Article 126(1) TFEU obliges Member States to avoid government deficits that are "excessive".[202] The Commission monitors the development of the budgetary situation and of the stock of government debt in the Member States with a view to identifying gross errors. It examines in particular whether and to what extent Member States comply with budgetary discipline.[203] The Commission makes its assessment based on semi-annual reports which the Member States have to provide before 1 April and 1 October, and which must include, among other things, information concerning their planned and actual government deficits and the levels of government debt.[204]

Article 126(2) TFEU provides the Commission and subsequently also the Council with a certain degree of discretion in considering whether a government deficit above 3% of GDP exceeds the reference value if the deficit has declined substantially and continuously and reached a level that comes close to the reference value or if the excess over the reference value is only exceptional and temporary. Moreover, a government debt of above 60% may be deemed not to exceed the reference value if actual government debt has sufficiently diminished and is approaching the reference value at a satisfactory pace.[205] What can be concluded from this is that breaching the quantified government deficit limit does not *de jure* signify the existence of an excessive deficit, as the reference values for establishing an excessive deficit are not absolute.

The original Council Regulation 1467/97 aimed to clarify and tighten the conditions for the application of these exceptions. To this end, in deciding on its initial recommendation, the Commission was in the past only required to consider an economic downturn exceptional if there had been an annual fall of real GDP of at least 2%. The Council however was not bound by this rule as it could exercise discretion when deciding whether an annual fall of real GDP of less than 2% should be considered exceptional.[206] In making its overall assessment the Council had to take into account the observations made by the Member State concerned, thereby leaving some room for political bargaining. Arguably, the 2005 reform of Council Regulation 1467/97 resulted in a more flexible approach being taken to the evaluation of excessive deficits in the Member States. Commission and Council can consider an excess over the reference value resulting from a severe economic downturn to be exceptional if the excess over the reference value results from a negative growth rate or an accumulated loss of output during a protracted period of very low growth relative to potential growth.[207] The amendment of Council Regulation 1467/97 as part of the Six Pack moreover resulted in a new focus on government debt.[208] This is immediately apparent from the fact that secondary Union law now determines the circumstances that allow the ratio of government debt to GDP to be considered "sufficiently diminishing and approaching the reference value at a satisfactory pace" in accordance with Article 126(2) (b) TFEU. This is the case if the actual debt value in the previous three years has moved

---

202. With regard to the numeric values see section 4.2 above. Those parts of the excessive deficit procedure described in Art. 126(9) and (11) TFEU do not apply in the case of Member States with a derogation, nor in the UK and Denmark.
203. Art. 126(2) TFEU.
204. Art. 3 Council Reg. 479/2009.
205. Art. 126(2)(a) and (b) TFEU.
206. Art. 2(2) and (3) Council Reg. 1467/97 (before amendment).
207. Art. 2(2) Reg. Council 1467/97, as amended.
208. By means of Council Reg. 1177/2011 amending Council Reg. 1467/97 on speeding up and clarifying the excessive deficit procedure (O.J. 2011, L 306/33).

in the direction of the reference value of 60% at an average of rate of 5% as a benchmark.[209] While this provision on government debt is notably less flexible than the one on deficits, the overall flexibility in application of the exemption is arguably preserved by the fact that when evaluating the economic situation in a given Member State, the Commission must take into account numerous factors related to the development of the medium-term economic, budgetary and government debt position.[210] Against the background of the European financial and sovereign debt crisis it is interesting to note that the Commission must take into account "debt incurred in the form of bilateral and multilateral support between Member States in the context of safeguarding financial stability", as well as "debt related to financial stabilization operations during financial disturbances".[211] Overall it may be noted that while from an economic point of view it seems sensible to take diverging economic situations into account in determining whether a government deficit or debt must be considered excessive for the purpose of the excessive deficit procedure, the long list of factors to be considered risks blurring the overall assessment and offers multiple escape routes from stringent application of the economic coordination framework.[212]

Within two weeks of the adoption by the Commission of a report to the effect that a Member State has not fulfilled the requirements of Article 126(1) and (2) TFEU, the Economic and Financial Committee has to formulate an opinion on the report.[213] Taking that opinion into account, the Commission then has to address an opinion to the Council indicating the existence of or the risk entailed by an excessive deficit and moreover to forward a recommendation to the Council regarding the initiation of the excessive deficit procedure.[214] According to Article 3(3) Council Regulation 1467/97, the actual Council decision in accordance with Article 126(6) TFEU is taken as a rule within four months of the report of economic data by the Member State concerned.[215] This decision is taken by qualified majority vote, excluding the Member State concerned.[216] From the wording of Article 126(6) TFEU it can be concluded that it is up to the Council to decide, based on the Commission proposal, whether an excessive deficit exists and thus, whether to formally start the excessive deficit procedure. However, in the TSCG the signatory euro area Member States have committed themselves in principle to always support the proposals or recommendations of the Commission regarding the existence of an excessive deficit in a euro country, unless a qualified majority of euro area countries, excluding the euro area Member State concerned, opposes the proposal or recommendation. With the TSCG an attempt has thus been made to introduce RQMV to the main decisions of the excessive deficit procedure. Yet, considering the unambiguous wording of primary Union law on this point it is questionable whether any deviating decision-making procedure can be imposed by means of an

---

209. Art. 2(1a) Council Reg. 1467/97.
210. Art. 2(3) Council Reg. 1467/97, as amended.
211. Art. 2(3), last para, Council Reg. 1467/97, as amended.
212. M. Buti, S.C.W. Eijffinger and D. Franco, "The stability pact pains: A forward-looking assessment of the reform debate", (2005) *CEPR Discussion Paper no. 5216*, 22.
213. Art. 126(3) TFEU; Art. 3 Council Reg. 1467/97. With regard to the composition and tasks of the Economic and Financial Committee which was set up at the start of stage three of EMU: Art. 134 TFEU, Council Decision 98/743/EC on the detailed provisions concerning the composition of the Economic and Financial Committee (O.J. 1998, L 358/109) and Council Decision 1999/8/EC adopting the Statutes of the Economic and Financial Committee (O.J. 1999, L 5/71), as amended.
214. Arts. 126(3)–(6) TFEU and Art. 3 Council Reg. 1467/97.
215. Art. 3(3) of the original Council Reg. 1467/97 foresaw a period of 3 months. It is clear from the words "as a rule" that this barely amounts to a "hard" deadline.
216. Art. 126(13) TFEU. Before the amendment of Art. 126 TFEU by the Treaty of Lisbon, the Member State concerned was only excluded from the subsequent decisions taken in accordance with Arts. 126(7)–(11) TFEU.

intergovernmental treaty to the effect that an inaction by the Council amounts to a decision in support of the Commission recommendation. This is even more so the case since Article 2(2) TSCG states that its provisions only apply to the extent that they are compatible with the EU Treaties. In any event, primary Union law cannot effectively be altered or set aside by an intergovernmental treaty agreed upon by some but not all Member States and, moreover, outside the procedure of Article 48 TEU.

In an attempt to further reinforce the excessive deficit procedure for euro area Member States, the possibility has been introduced with the Six Pack legislation of applying penalties at the outset of the excessive deficit procedure in two situations, namely when a euro area Member State already had had to lodge an interest-bearing deposit in the context of the multilateral surveillance procedure, and in the case that the Commission establishes the existence of "particular[ly] serious non-compliance with the budgetary policy obligations" included in Council Regulation 1466/97.[217] To this end the Commission makes a recommendation to the Council within 20 days of the Council's decision on the existence of an excessive deficit for the lodging of a non-interest-bearing deposit that must in principle amount to 0,2 % of GDP of the country concerned in the preceding year. However, this amount can be reduced or even cancelled by the Council.[218] RQMV applies to any decision on the application of penalties.[219]

When a decision on an excessive deficit procedure has been taken, the Council is required to issue general recommendations in accordance with Article 126(7) TFEU with a view to bringing the excessive deficit to an end.[220] While according to this provision these recommendations are in principle not made public, it has nonetheless become established practice to publish them immediately.[221] The Member State is given a deadline of no more than six months in order to take effective action. In serious situations, this deadline may be as short as three months. Moreover, the Council recommendation must establish a deadline before which the excessive government deficit has to be corrected.[222] In principle, the excessive deficit or debt must be corrected in the year following its identification.[223] As to the contents of these recommendations, since the 2005 reform of Council Regulation 1467/97, Article 3(4) requires that the Member States concerned must be called upon to achieve a minimum annual improvement of at least 0.5% of GDP as a benchmark in the cyclically-adjusted balance.[224]

Once again, a special legal regime applies to euro area Member States by which they have to submit to the Commission and Council so-called economic partnership programmes that

217. Art. 5(1) Reg. 1174/11.
218. Ibid., Art. 5(4).
219. Ibid., Art. 5(2).
220. Despite what the wording of Arts. 126(6) and (7) TFEU and Art. 3(3) Council Reg. 1467/97 may suggest, the existence of an excessive deficit and the subsequent recommendations are not established in one and the same decision. The use of the word "shall adopt" (rather than "shall decide") suggests that the Council is obliged to adopt recommendations.
221. According to Art. 126(8) TFEU the publication is only foreseen after it has been established that the Member State has not taken any effective measures.
222. Art. 3(3) of the original Council Reg. 1467/97 foresaw a period of four months.
223. Art. 3(4) Council Reg. 1467/97, unless there are "special circumstances". An example of such an exemption can be found in the case of Hungary, where the Council allowed for an extended deadline due to its significant general government deficit upon EU accession and because of the ongoing structural shift to a modern service-oriented market economy accompanying the process of real convergence. See Council Recommendation to Hungary with a view to bringing an end to the situation of an excessive government deficit (11218/04) (ECOFIN 270/UEM 140).
224. For details see F. Amtenbrink and J. de Haan, "Reforming the stability and growth pact", (2006) EL Rev., 402–413, 409–410.

identify the policy measures and structural reforms they consider necessary "to ensure an effective and lasting correction of the excessive deficit"[225] while, moreover, remaining subject to reporting requirements in addition to those applicable to all Member States pursuant to Article 3(4a) Council Regulation 1467/97.[226]

The Member State's progress in correcting its excessive government deficit is monitored both by the Commission, which makes recommendations on the progress and possible further action to the Council, and the Council itself. Article 126(8) TFEU in conjunction with Article 126(13) TFEU implies that the Council must establish by formal vote that a Member State has not taken any effective corrective action in response to the general recommendations issued by the Council.[227] This has to take place immediately after the expiry of the deadline set by the Council and thus no later than six months after the recommendations in accordance with Article 126(7) TFEU have been issued. For Member States with a derogation, the Council decision under Article 126(8) TFEU effectively marks the end of the excessive deficit procedure, as the remaining escalation steps foreseen in primary and secondary Union law (described below) only apply to euro area Member States.[228]

For euro area Member States the Council must take a decision within two months of the decision under Article 126(8) EC giving the Member State concerned notice that it must within a specified time limit implement those deficit reduction measures that the Council considers necessary to remedy the situation. Once again the Member State is requested to meet specific annual budgetary targets, whereby the Council must identify concrete measures geared towards meeting them.[229] Euro area Member States moreover can be confronted with penalties in the form of a fine amounting to 0,2% of GDP of the Member State concerned.[230] This is subject to a separate Council decision on a Commission recommendation, whereby RQMV applies.[231] The application of such fines can be reduced or even cancelled by the Council on recommendation by the Commission on grounds of "exceptional economic circumstances or following a reasoned request by the Member State concerned".[232] This provides the Commission and Council with a considerable degree of discretion. On the one hand, it may be argued that this option reduces the stringency and hence deterrent effect of the excessive deficit procedure in the case of euro area Member States. On the other hand, it may be observed that it does not make much sense to reflexively impose fines when a Member State is simply unable to achieve the necessary corrections due to economic circumstances beyond its control.[233]

Article 126(11) TFEU also foresees in the possibility of applying sanctions if a Member State fails to comply with the successive recommendations issued pursuant to paragraphs 7 and 9 of Article 126 TFEU. Such a Council decision must as a rule be taken within sixteen months of the

---

225. Art. 9(1) Reg. 473/13. This is repeated in Art. 5 TSCG.
226. Art. 10 Reg. 473/13.
227. This is confirmed by the wording of Art. 5(1) Council Reg. 1467/97.
228. See Art. 139(2)(b) TFEU. For these Member States, at least in theory the incentive in correcting excessive deficits should be the fulfilment of the convergence criteria laid down in Art. 140(1), 2nd indent TFEU.
229. Art. 126(9) TFEU. Art. 5(1) Council Reg. 1467/97, as amended.
230. Whereby any non-interest-bearing deposit previously lodged is converted into a fine.
231. Art. 6(1)–(2) Reg. 1173/11.
232. Ibid., Art. 6(4).
233. For examples see Council implementing decision on imposing a fine on Portugal for failure to take effective action to address an excessive deficit (11554/16) (ECOFIN 744, UEM 284); Council implementing decision on imposing a fine on Spain for failure to take effective action to address an excessive deficit (11555/16) (ECOFIN 745, UEM 285).

initial report of economic data by the Member State concerned.[234] In principle, sanctions must be imposed in the form of fines allocated to the ESM.[235] In the case of a breach of the government deficit criterion, the initial deposit comprises a fixed component equal to 0.2% of GDP, and a variable component of 0.1% in the preceding year for each percentage point that the government deficit is above the reference value of 3% or, in the case of an excessive debt, or of the government balance as a percentage of GDP that should have been achieved in the same year according to the Council recommendation pursuant to Article 126(9) TFEU.[236] An upper limit for a single deposit is fixed at 0.5% of GDP.[237] These sanctions can be intensified if the Member State concerned fails to cooperate.[238] The option of issuing fines is also explicitly foreseen for excessive debt whereby the Six Pack legislation addresses a major deficiency of the previous legal framework, which did not specify the sanctions applicable in case of non-compliance with the criterion relating to government debt ratio, despite the fact that Article 126(11) TFEU in principle always applied in these situations as well.[239] If and as long as a Member States acts in accordance with Council recommendations pursuant to paragraph 7 or 9 of Article 126 TFEU, the excessive deficit procedure is held in abeyance.[240]

It becomes apparent from Article 126(13) TFEU that Council decisions in accordance with Articles 126(7)–(9), and (11) TFEU are to be taken on a Commission recommendation by the Council by qualified majority in accordance with Article 238(3)(a) TFEU and excluding the votes of the representative of the Member State concerned. Moreover, Member States with a derogation are excluded from voting in the context of Article 126(9) and (11) TFEU, as it has been observed above that they are not subject to this part of the excessive deficit procedure.[241] Thus, in a euro area of 19 Member States, excluding the Member State that is the subject of the procedure, 10 euro area countries (55% of the participating Member States), representing at least 65% of the combined population of those 18 countries have to vote in favour of the application of fines. A blocking majority requires at least the number of euro area Member States representing 35% of the combined total population of these countries, plus one additional euro area Member State. What becomes clear from this is that the decision to apply sanctions in case of non-compliance by a euro area Member State is a political process.

Turning to the macroeconomic imbalances procedure, if in the opinion of the Commission the in-depth review reveals imbalances that it considers excessive, i.e. severe,[242] it must inform the European Parliament, the Council and the Eurogroup, as well as the relevant European

234. Art. 7 Council Reg. 1467/96, which moreover foresees in an expedited procedure in case of a deliberately planned excessive deficit.
235. See Arts. 11, 12 and 16 Council Reg. 1467/97, as amended. Art. 16 refers to the EFSF, which has since been replaced by the ESM. At the time of the writing this section, this mechanism had not been applied on a single occasion.
236. Ibid., Art. 12(1).
237. Ibid., Art. 12(3).
238. Ibid., Art. 12(2).
239. Critical of this lacuna in the pre-crisis framework, F. Amtenbrink and J. de Haan, "Economic governance in the European Union – Fiscal policy discipline versus flexibility", (2003) CML Rev., 1075–1106, 1099–1100.
240. Art. 9 Council Reg. 1467/97.
241. See Arts. 139(2) TFEU. The same applies to the UK and Denmark. See Protocol on certain provisions relating to the United Kingdom of Great Britain and Northern Ireland and Protocol on certain provisions relating to Denmark. Nevertheless, in practice the United Kingdom in the past seems to have subjected itself also to Art. 126(9) TFEU. At the 2753rd ECOFIN Council meeting on 10 Oct. 2006 (13600/06 (Presse 278)), the application of Art. 104(9) EC (now 126(9) TFEU) was discussed, albeit in the end rejected.
242. See section 3.3.1.

Supervisory Authorities and the European Systemic Risk Board of this.[243] Moreover, the Commission can make a recommendation to the Council to adopt a recommendation establishing the existence of an excessive imbalance. The Council decides by qualified majority on the opening of an excessive macroeconomic imbalances procedure. This decision must also include "policy recommendations to be followed and a deadline within which the Member State concerned is to submit a corrective action plan".[244] This plan must identify the planned policy action and timing, whereby "account should be taken of the economic and social impact of the policy actions and shall be consistent with the broad economic policy guidelines and the employment guidelines".[245] The action plans are subject to review by the Commission and Council, as is their implementation thereafter.

Whereas non-euro area Member State in principle do not face any particular sanctions in case of non-compliance, a more stringent regime applies once again to euro area Member States based on Regulation 1176/11. In the first instance, when the Council concludes that the Member State concerned has not taken the corrective action it recommended, the Council must impose an interest-bearing deposit, acting on a recommendation from the Commission, amounting to 0,1 % of the GDP in the preceding year of the Member State concerned.[246] If the Council concludes on two successive occasions that a euro area Member State has not taken corrective action, or has not submitted a sufficient plan of action, the Council must decide to convert the interest-bearing deposit into an annual fine. Both the decision on the interest-bearing deposit and the fine are taken by RQMV.[247] Similar to what has already been observed about the excessive deficit procedure, the Commission can propose to reduce or even cancel the interest-bearing deposit or the annual fine "on grounds of exceptional economic circumstances or following a reasoned request by the Member State concerned".[248]

In conclusion, it can be observed that the Six Pack and Two Pack legislation and the TSCG are collectively a serious attempt to reinforce the excessive deficit procedure and to put the Commission more so than in the past in the driver's seat. Moreover, with the introduction of the macroeconomic imbalances procedure a broader spectrum of economic policy of the Member States has become subject to both the preventive and the persuasive aspects of the economic policy coordination framework in EMU. Yet, one aspect that had long been considered to be a main weakness of the coordination framework, namely the reliance on peer review in the context of the original excessive deficit procedure as introduced by the Maastricht Treaty and the Stability and Growth Pact, has not been entirely removed from the system. Indeed, Article 126 TFEU, which puts the Council at the helm of each main procedural step has not been amended. As far as the reference to RQMV in the TSCG is concerned, it has already been observed here that it is questionable whether this can effectively amend primary Union law.[249] What is more, while the votes of the Member State concerned are excluded from all Council decisions in the context of Article 126 TFEU, participation in the voting procedure by Member States that are themselves the subject of an excessive deficit or macroeconomic imbalances procedure can potentially reduce the efficiency of the system, both in deterring countries from conducting

243. Art. 7(1) Reg. 1176/11. On these bodies see Ch. 27, "Financial market regulation and supervision", of this book.
244. Ibid., Art. 7(2).
245. Ibid., Art. 7(3).
246. Ibid., Art. 3(1).
247. Ibid., Art. 3(2). Fines are allocated to the ESM.
248. Ibid., Art. 3(6).
249. A different conclusion may be drawn with regard to the additional procedural steps laid down in secondary Union law concerning the application of penalties.

unsound budgetary and more broadly macroeconomic policies and in strictly applying concrete sanctions.[250] The stringency of the procedures depends to a considerable extent on the political will of the Member States to apply the rules, which may depend on their particular economic and political situation.[251] In fact, the reformed system itself offers ample opportunity to take such extraneous considerations into account in the context of the decision to reduce or even cancel fines. The practical consequences of the system of peer review could be witnessed in 2003 in the context of the application of the excessive deficit procedure to Germany and France, which triggered a major inter-institutional conflict between the Commission and the Council.[252] The lack of any automatism in the procedure and the absence of an independent enforcer may increase the incentive for the Council to collude in subverting implementation of the rules.[253] Experience so far suggests that keeping the Council in charge of key decisions can aggravate enforcement problems and thus ultimately the sustained convergence of the economic performance of the Member States as well. This may not only be problematic for economic policy coordination in EMU, but also for monetary policy. Given the interconnectedness of economic and monetary policy, the weakness of the current system of economic coordination, together with the diverging economic situations in the Member States and the deficit situation in some Member States can result in spill over effects – not just on other Member States, but also on the single monetary policy in the euro area. Indeed, even before the outbreak of the European financial and sovereign debt crisis it had been observed that the ECB may feel compelled to tighten or loosen its monetary policy standards, thereby also affecting those Member States whose economic situation may require a different monetary policy stance.[254] Finally, it can be observed that while the option of abstaining from the application of penalties may make sense from an economic point of view, its existence arguably also suggests that the whole approach in EMU to achieving compliance through enforcement may be problematic in the first place.[255]

5.3.4 *Scope of judicial review in the multilateral surveillance, excessive deficit and macroeconomic imbalances procedure*

As far as Article 121 TFEU in conjunction with the secondary Union law instruments described in section 5.3.2. imposes legally binding obligations on Member States in the context of the

250. B. Irlenbusch et al., "Voting in EMU – An experimental study of institutional innovation and the role of communication in the stability and growth pact", (2003) JCMS, 645–664.
251. In this context R. Smits, "Some reflections on economic policy", (2007) *Legal Issues of European Integration*, 5–25, 14, who already observed that the old EC Treaty is "flawed in its basic structure of EMU" as it is based "on the misconception that enlightened self-interest will ensure coordination of economic policies".
252. Council Decision 2003/98/EC on the existence of an excessive deficit in Germany (O.J. 2003, L 34/16) and Council Decision 2003/487/EC on the existence of an excessive deficit in France (O.J. 2003, L 165/29). See also the subsequent Council recommendations (5506/03 (Presse 15)) and (9844/03 (Presse 149)). For more details see section 5.3.4. While the application of RQMV can in principle avoid the reoccurrence of such a situation, it must be recalled that its binding force in the excessive deficit procedure is not undisputed.
253. The original German proposal for a reinforcement of the excessive deficit procedure had called for an automatic application of the excessive deficit procedure. However, these ideas were resisted by a considerable number of Member States, not least because this would have essentially altered primary Community law, as Art. 104 EC (now 126 TFEU) did not foresee any such automatism. See F. Amtenbrink, J. de Haan and O. Sleijpen, "The stability pact: Placebo or panacea?", (1997) EBL Rev., 233–238, 234.
254. F. Amtenbrink and J. De Haan, op. cit. *supra* note 239, 1093, with further references. The unconventional monetary policy of the ECB may be considered a case in point, see section 6.2.
255. See in this regard F. Amtenbrink and R. Repasi, "Enforcement and compliance in economic policy coordination in EMU" in A. Jakab and D. Kochenov, *The Enforcement of EU Law and Values. Ensuring Member States' Compliance* (OUP, 2017), 145–181.

multilateral surveillance procedure, a failure to act may in principle become subject to an infringement procedure initiated by the Commission or even by another Member State pursuant to Article 258 or 259 TFEU.[256] In case of non-compliance by a Member State with a judgment by the ECJ declaring the Member State's omission in breach of Union law, sanctions could be applied to the Member State concerned as a result of the application of Article 260(2) TFEU. Yet, as has been observed elsewhere, such judicial review in the context of the multilateral surveillance procedure may be little more than a theoretical course of action and moreover cannot effectively prevent the emergence of an excessive government deficit or, for that matter, macroeconomic imbalances.[257] In contrast, Article 126(10) TFEU makes it clear that the Member States' obligation to avoid excessive government deficits, as well as to observe Council recommendations issued pursuant to Article 126(7) and, thereafter, Article 126(9) TFEU, are excluded from judicial review in the context of an infringement procedure.[258] Consequently, a Member State cannot be forced to comply with the excessive deficit rule laid down in Article 126(1) TFEU by means of sanctions based on Article 260(2) TFEU. In challenge of this view it has been argued that the 1997 Stability and Growth Pact has resulted in an objectification of the excessive deficit procedure in a normative sense, which makes Article 126(10) TFEU redundant.[259] Yet, even if this was the case and an action was deemed permissible despite the clear wording of Article 126 TFEU, its outcome would arguably remain uncertain. Unless a Member State has not acted at all, the assessment of whether a Member State has taken effective measures comes down to an economic evaluation by the Council, which involves a considerable degree of discretion.

As far as the additional legal regime introduced by the Six Pack and Two Pack for the euro area Member States, as well as by the TSCG for the signatory countries, is concerned it must be recalled that Article 126(10) TFEU states that this judicial action "may not be exercised within the framework of paragraphs 1 to 9 of this Article". This wording arguably supports the conclusion that any legal obligations arising in the context of and linked to the application of the procedures laid down in these paragraphs cannot be enforced by means of Articles 258–259 TFEU.[260] This would then arguably include the non-interest-bearing deposits and fines that Regulation 1173/11 links to the decisions pursuant to Article 126(7) and (8) TFEU.

Article 8(1) TSCG foresees in the jurisdiction of the ECJ, pursuant to Article 273 TFEU, in instances in which a contracting party does not comply with the obligation laid down in its Article 3(2) to introduce the balanced budget rule into national law, as well as the requirement to introduce an automatic correction mechanism into national law.[261] A case can be brought by any of the signatory Member States either on their own initiative or based on a Commission report concluding that a Member States has not complied with Article 3(2) TSCG. Non-compliance with a judgment by the ECJ can trigger financial sanctions.[262] This jurisdiction does not however extend to the actual observance of the budgetary rules laid down in the TSCG.

Legally binding measures by Union institutions in the context of the multilateral surveillance, excessive deficit and macroeconomic imbalance procedures can in principle be subject to judicial review in the context of an action for annulment in accordance with Article 263 TFEU. This thus excludes those measures in the context of Articles 121 and 126 TFEU and the related

---

256. Unlike Art. 126(10) TFEU, Art. 121 TFEU does not exclude the application of Arts. 258 and 259 TFEU.
257. F. Amtenbrink and J. de Haan, op. cit. *supra* note 239, 1083.
258. Excluded are Arts. 126(1)–(9) TFEU.
259. A. Geelhoed, op. cit. *supra* note 95, at 779, with reference to J.-V. Louis, op. cit. *supra* note 81, 22.
260. The Dutch language wording seems even clearer: "[...] in het kader van de toepassing van [...]".
261. Art. 3(1)(a)–(d) TSCG.
262. Art. 8(2) TSCG.

secondary Union law that come in the form of recommendations.[263] On the contrary, a decision by the Council in the context of Regulations 1173/11 and 1176/11 or Council Regulation 1467/97, to apply a (non) interest bearing deposit or a fine can in principle be challenged before the ECJ by the Member State concerned.

Finally, disputes concerning the application of a legal regime may also arise between Union institutions and bodies. In fact, the scope of the obligations of the Council in the context of the excessive deficit procedure, and thus, the legal stringency of an important part of economic coordination itself, formed the subject-matter of a dispute between the Commission and the Council that finally had to be resolved by the ECJ.[264] What triggered this open inter-institutional conflict, in the form of an annulment procedure was the failure of the Council in the case of Germany and France to adopt a decision pursuant to ex Article 104(8) EC (now 126(8) TFEU) and thereafter, ex Article 104(9) EC (now Art. 126(9) TFEU). Instead, by applying the voting rules which relate to the decisions envisaged by ex Article 104(9) EC (now 126(9) TFEU), the Council adopted conclusions with regard to each of the two Member States concerned which moreover deviated from the Commission recommendations. These conclusions stated that the Council had decided not to act on the basis of the Commission recommendation and, moreover, that the Council agreed "to hold the Excessive Deficit Procedure in abeyance for the time being".[265] From the Commission's perspective, the Council had effectively acted in contravention of the EC Treaty by deciding not to take the two relevant decisions and, moreover, by issuing conclusions. In its judgment the ECJ confirmed the binding character of the rules governing the excessive deficit procedure and the role assigned to the Commission therein by rejecting the Council's course of action with regard to the issuing of conclusions. The ECJ considered that the Council had effectively broken the rules governing the excessive deficit procedure by deciding to hold the procedure in abeyance and by making this subject to compliance by Germany and France with the Council recommendations included in these conclusions. Consequently, the ECJ annulled the conclusions. However, at the same time the European judges acknowledged that in circumstances where the Council does not succeed in adopting a decision because the required majority is lacking, the excessive deficit procedure is effectively held in abeyance. In this context, the ECJ did not follow the Commission's appraisal of the legal nature of such incapacity on the part of the Council. In the view of the ECJ, failure to reach a positive decision in the Council does not amount to a decision open to challenge under what is now Article 263 TFEU.

5.4 *Powers to deal with extraordinary economic circumstances inside and outside the euro area*

Article 122(1) TFEU allows the Council, acting by qualified majority on a proposal from the Commission, to decide on measures appropriate to an existing financial situation in a Member State, in particular if severe difficulties arise in the supply of certain products.[266] The lessons learned from the two oil crises of the 1970s, when a forerunner of this provision in the EEC

---

263. See Art. 288 TFEU.
264. Case C-27/04, *Commission v. Council*. Generally, on this decision: B. Dutzler and A. Hable, "The European Court of Justice and the stability and growth pact: Just the beginning?", (2005) EIoP; U. Häde, "Der EuGH und die Haushaltsdisziplin – Das Urteil vom 13.7.2004 zum Verfahren bei einem übermäßigen Defizit", (2004) EuR, 750–764; I. Maher, "Economic policy coordination and the European Court: Excessive deficits and ECOFIN discretion", (2005) EL Rev., 831–841; R. Smits, "Het Europese Hof beslecht geschil over communautair toezicht op begrotingsdiscipline", (2004) NTER, 221–227.
265. See 2546th Council meeting (14492/1/03 REV 1 (Presse 320)).
266. This provision, originally introduced by the Treaty of Maastricht, was amended by the Treaty of Nice, thereby lowering the voting requirement in the Council from unanimity to qualified majority.

Treaty was applied for the adoption of measures to ensure the oil supply in the Community, highlight the practical importance of having such a crisis mechanism.[267] Reflecting the particular purpose of the provision, an explicit reference to energy as one of the areas in which severe difficulties may arise was introduced into Article 122(1) TFEU by the Treaty of Lisbon. Moreover, a frank appeal was made to the "spirit of solidarity between Member States". The case law of the ECJ seems to indicate that the Council may choose the particular form of the measure it considers the most suitable.[268] As such, Article 122(1) TFEU may embrace any of the legally binding measures identified in Article 288 TFEU.[269]

Since both the subjection of government deficits and debts to Union norms and the prohibition of monetary financing can make it difficult for Member States to address the consequences of natural disasters or other exceptional occurrences beyond their control, which can trigger major economic shocks, Article 122(2) TFEU allows the Council, on a proposal from the Commission, to decide to grant financial assistance to any Member State under certain conditions. As pointed out in section 3, this legal basis was used at the height of the European financial and sovereign debt crisis to set up the EFSM, with Ireland being the first euro area Member State to receive financial assistance under this ad-hoc mechanism, followed shortly thereafter by Portugal.[270] The appropriateness of using Article 122(2) TFEU as a legal basis was contested both on grounds of the structural rather than ad hoc nature of the financial assistance mechanism, as well on grounds of the view that Member States that had become beneficiaries of the EFSM did not find themselves in the situation described by the provision.[271] In its decision on the legality under Union law of the Treaty establishing the ESM Treaty the ECJ did not zoom in on the scope of Article 122(2) TFEU as a legal basis, but instead focussed mainly on the question of whether that provision excluded the conclusion of an intergovernmental treaty by the euro area Member States. This was rejected by the ECJ, which argued that only financial assistance granted by the Union lies within the scope of Article 122(2) TFEU and, moreover, that "nothing in Article 122 TFEU indicates that the Union has exclusive competence to grant financial assistance to a Member State".[272]

In February 2012, after the European Council decision of March 2011 to amend Article 136 TFEU to include an explicit reference to the establishment by the euro area Member States of a stability mechanism,[273] it was agreed that the European Stability Mechanism would be established – by means of an intergovernmental treaty – with as its objective to "mobilise funding and provide stability support under strict conditionality, appropriate to the financial assistance instrument chosen, to the benefit of ESM Members which are experiencing, or are threatened by, severe financing problems, if indispensable to safeguard the financial stability of the euro

267. Art. 103(4) EEC.
268. Case 5/73, *Balkan*, para 18. In this case, the Court ruled on Art. 103(2) EEC which referred to "measures appropriate to the situation".
269. See also R. Smits, op. cit. *supra* note 81, 715.
270. 2011/77/EU: Council Implementing Decision on granting Union financial assistance to Ireland (O.J. 2011, L 30/34); 2011/344/EU: Council Implementing Decision on granting Union financial assistance to Portugal (O.J. 2011, L 159/88). Later on, as part of the second financial rescue programme, Greece also received assistance under the EFSM (Mar. 2012).
271. See F. Amtenbrink, "Legal developments", (2011) *JCMS Annual Review*, 165–186, 173–175, with further references; R. Palmstorfer, "To bail out or not to bail out? The current framework of financial assistance for the Euro area Member States measured against the requirements of EU primary law", (2012) EL Rev., 771–784.
272. Case C-370/12, *Pringle*, paras. 118 and 120. See also S. Adam and F.J. Mena Parras, "The European stability mechanism through the legal meanderings of the Union's constitutionalism: Comment on *Pringle*", (2013) EL Rev., 848–865.
273. See *supra* section 3.

area as a whole and of its Member States".[274] As foreseen by that legal instrument, the ESM has assumed the roles of the EFSM and EFSF. Yet, the latter will continue to exist as a legal entity until all outstanding loans have been repaid.[275] The ESM entered into force in September 2012 and has since been utilized for emergency loan packages for Spain and Cyprus, as well as for the third financial assistance programme for Greece.[276]

Seated in Luxemburg, the ESM has full legal personality.[277] It is governed by a Board of Governors which in practice consists of the Ministers of Finance of the euro area Member States, and a Board of Directors consisting of one representative from each euro area Member State – usually junior ministers or high ranking state officials with a background in economic and financial matters.[278] Major decisions on granting stability support by the ESM, including *inter alia* the economic policy conditionality attached to any assistance, changing the authorized capital stock and maximum lending volume of the ESM, and making capital calls, are the prerogative of the Board of Governors. The ESM Treaty foresees a capital stock of EUR 700,000 million, although initially only the EUR 80,000 million had to be paid up front by the Member States, with the remaining amount constituting so-called callable shares.[279] The ESM is entitled to finance its operations by "issuing financial instruments or by entering into financial or other agreements or arrangements with ESM Members, financial institutions or other third parties".[280] In this context it becomes clear from Article 8(5) ESM Treaty that this legal instrument carefully avoids creating a system of joint and several liability; the liability of each Member State is explicitly limited "in all circumstances" to its portion of the authorized capital stock at its issue price. What is more, no Member State is liable "by reason of its membership, for obligations of the ESM". As Advocate General Kokott explained in her reasoned opinion in *Pringle*, "nothing in the ESM Treaty can be construed to impose on any Member State an obligation of payment which exceeds its own share at any time in the authorised capital stock", meaning that "if a Member State has fully paid its own contribution, then no increased capital call can subsequently be made on it".[281] Furthermore, no decision to change the authorized capital stock or to adapt the maximum lending volume of the ESM can be made against the will of a euro area Member State; a unanimous decision by the Board of Governors is required.[282]

According to Articles 14–18 ESM Treaty, financial assistance can come in various forms including precautionary financial assistance, financial assistance for the re-capitalization of financial institutions, as well as by intervention on the primary or secondary market for the bonds of a euro area Member State. Whichever instrument is chosen, its application is restricted to addressing a situation in which a euro area Member State experiences, or is threatened by, severe financing problems, whereby financial assistance is "indispensable to safeguard the financial

---

274. Art. 3 ESM Treaty. On the significance of the departure from the Community method for "the normative grid of fiscal discipline" see K. A. Armstrong, "The new governance of EU fiscal discipline", (2013) EL Rev., 601–616, 616.
275. The ESM and the EFSF "share staff, facilities and operations". See <www.esm.europa.eu/about-us/history>.
276. As of 31 Dec. 2016. See European Commission, "The Financial Sector Adjustment Programme for Spain", (2012) *Occasional Papers 118*; European Commission, "The Financial Sector Adjustment Programme for Cyprus", (2013) *Occasional Papers 149*. See also the Financial Assistance Facility Agreement between the ESM, Greece, the Bank of Greece and the Hellenic Financial Stability Fund, executed in Athens and Luxembourg on 19 Aug. 2015.
277. Arts. 31–32 ESM Treaty.
278. Ibid., Arts. 5(1) and 6(1).
279. Ibid., Arts. 8 and 9.
280. Ibid., Art. 3(1). In practice this is done through the emission by the ESM of bills and bonds.
281. A.G. Kokott in Case C-370/12, *Pringle*, para 165.
282. Art. 5(6) ESM Treaty.

stability of the euro area as a whole and of its Member States".[283] Whether this is indeed the case is ultimately a decision to be taken by the Ministers of Finance of the euro area Member States, which in principle requires unanimity.[284] However, Article 4(4) ESM Treaty provides for an emergency voting procedure. If failure to speedily adopt a decision to grant or implement financial assistance "would threaten the economic and financial sustainability of the euro area", a qualified majority of 85% of the votes cast is sufficient for financial assistance to be granted. Considering that the voting rights of the Member States are linked to their capital subscriptions (number of shares allocated), this means that of all the euro area Member States only France, Germany and Italy can effectively exercise a veto, whereas other Member States can at least theoretically be outvoted. This has aroused controversy in some countries, taking centre stage in a number of cases before the highest national (constitutional) courts.[285] This procedure is not only remarkable for its potential consequences for democratic decision making in the smaller euro area Member States, but also when one considers that it is the European Commission and the ECB that trigger the procedure in the first place.[286]

The ESM Treaty follows the EFSM and EFSF in making financial assistance subject to several strict requirements.[287] First, financial assistance can only be granted to euro area Member States that have both ratified the TSCG and that comply with Article 3(2) TSCG.[288] Moreover, strict conditions "appropriate to the financial assistance instrument chosen" must be attached to any financial assistance. According to Article 12(1) ESM Treaty, this so-called conditionality can range from "a macro-economic adjustment programme to continuous respect of pre-established eligibility conditions". Details regarding the macroeconomic adjustment programme are laid down in Regulation 472/2013 and are closely related to the economic partnership programmes that Member States subject to an excessive deficit procedure must establish pursuant to Regulation 4734/2013.[289] Once the basic decision to grant stability support to a euro Member State has been taken by the Board of Governors, the European Commission "in liaison with the ECB and, wherever possible, together with the IMF", negotiates on behalf of the Board of Governors a memorandum of understanding (MoU) with the country in question that must "reflect the severity of the weaknesses to be addressed and the financial assistance instrument chosen". The MoU is signed by the Commission, but has to be approved by the Board of Governors and thus, the Ministers of Finance of the other euro area Member States. Concurrently, a financial assistance facility agreement has to be adopted by the Board of Governors that states the financial terms and conditions and the choice of instruments.[290] Moreover, it has become common practice for financial assistance to be paid out in instalments, depending on positive compliance reports based on monitoring by the European Commission and the ECB (and where applicable, the IMF).

The strict conditionality which has become common practice ever since the bilateral loans to Greece in 2010 has been the subject of much debate both with regard to the socio-economic consequences of the economic and financial reform measures required from the Member State concerned by the MoU, but also with regard to the applicable procedure for their adoption and monitoring. Namely the somewhat ambiguous roles foreseen for the ECB and the Eurogroup

283. Ibid., Art. 12(1).
284. Ibid., Art. 5(6).
285. For details see F. Amtenbrink, op. cit. *supra* note 156.
286. Art. 4(4) ESM Treaty.
287. F. Amtenbrink, op. cit. *supra* note 156.
288. Preamble no. 5 ESM Treaty.
289. Respectively Art. 7 Reg. 472/2013 and Art. 9 Reg. 473/2013.
290. Art. 13(2)–(4) ESM Treaty.

have been questioned.[291] In *Gauweiler*, concerning the compatibility with Union law of the announced unconventional monetary policy measures (OMT) of the ECB, Advocate General Cruz Villalón observed that "The ECB is [...] involved in the elaboration of the conditionality imposed on the State requesting assistance whilst, subsequently, it also takes part in the task of monitoring compliance with conditionality, which is crucial if the programme is actually to continue and eventually to come to an end".[292] Considering the independent position of the ECB within the European constitutional order and its somewhat narrow democratic accountability,[293] this extensive involvement is in itself already quite remarkable, even if legally speaking its role is restricted to acting as an expert advisor. What is more, it is questionable whether this involvement combined with the linking of (un)conventional monetary measures on behalf of euro area Member States subject to the compliance with the conditionality agreed under the ESM can still be reconciled with the monetary policy task assigned to the ECB by Article 127(1) TFEU.[294] Finally, it is not always entirely clear what the precise legal nature of the actions of the various actors is in the context of the adoption of financial assistance programmes, as is demonstrated in several cases brought before European courts; this can be problematic from the point of view of effective judicial protection.[295]

Along with Article 122 TFEU, Article 143 TFEU also provides a legal basis for mutual financial assistance. This provision can only be utilized in the case of a Member State with a derogation that is "in difficulties or is seriously threatened with difficulties as regards its balance of payments either as a result of an overall disequilibrium in its balance of payments, or as a result of the type of currency at its disposal, and where such difficulties are liable in particular to jeopardise the functioning of the internal market or the implementation of the common commercial policy".[296] To this end, the so-called medium-term financial assistance facility was set up by means of secondary Union law enabling loans to be granted to one or more non-euro area Member States which are experiencing, or are seriously threatened with, the above-mentioned difficulties.[297] Similar to what has been observed in the context of the ESM, the medium-term financial assistance (laid down in a loan agreement) comes with economic policy conditions agreed upon in an MoU "with a view to reestablishing or ensuring a sustainable balance of payments situation".[298] Financial assistance can be applied for by the Commission in agreement with a non-euro area Member State or by such a Member State on its own initiative, whereby

---

291. E.g. D. Schiek, "The EU Constitution of social governance in an economic crisis: In defence of a transnational dimension to social Europe", (2013) MJ, 185–208; C. Costamagna, "The impact of stronger economic policy coordination on the European social dimension: Issues of legitimacy" in M. Adams, F. Fabbrini, P. Larouche (Eds.), op. cit. *supra* note 65, 359–377; A. Poulou, "Financial assistance conditionality and human rights protection: What is the role of the EU Charter of Fundamental Rights?", (2017) CML Rev. 991–1025.
292. Brackets added. See the opinion by Advocate General Cruz Villalón in Case C-62/14, *Gauweiler*, para 144.
293. See section 6.1.3.
294. As is observed by Advocate General Cruz Villalón in Case C-62/14, *Gauweiler*, para 145.
295. Joined Cases C-8/15 P to C-10/15 P, *Ledra Advertisement et al.* on appeal from T-289/13, *Ledra Advertising*; T-291/13, *Eleftheriou and Papachristofi*; T-293/13, *Theophilou*. Joined Cases C-105-109/15 P, *Mallis et al.*, on appeal from T-327/13, *Mallis and Malli*; Case T-328/13, *Tameio Pronoias Prosopikou Trapezis Kyprou*; Case T-329/13, *Chatzithoma*; Case T-330/13, *Chatziioannou*; Case T-331/13, *Nikolaou*. A. Karatzia, "Cypriot depositors before the ECJ: Knocking on the wrong door?", (2015) *King's Law Journal*, 175–184. For a detailed assessment of all cases see R. Repasi, "Judicial protection against austerity measures in the euro area: Ledra and Mallis", (2017) CML Rev., 1123–1156. See further section 6.1.3.
296. Art. 143(1) TFEU.
297. Council Reg. 332/2002 establishing a facility providing medium-term financial assistance for Member States' balances of payments (O.J. 2002, L 53/1), as amended.
298. Art. 3(2) Reg. 332/2002.

the decision on granting financial assistance and the conditions attached thereto is taken by QMV in the Council on a proposal from the Commission and after consulting the Economic and Financial Committee.[299] The funds for the financial assistance are raised on the capital markets or with financial institutions by the Commission.[300] While Article 143 TFEU and the corresponding secondary Union law provide for financial assistance from the Union, in practice financial EU assistance can be accompanied by financial assistance from the IMF and the World Bank, as has for example been the case for Hungary.[301]

6. Monetary policy in the euro area[302]

Pursuant to Article 3(1)(c) TFEU the Union has exclusive competence over the monetary policy of the Member States whose currency is the euro. Thus, as soon as the rates at which the euro became the substitute for national currencies were irrevocably fixed, Member States participating in the monetary union gave up their autonomous competence relating to monetary policy.[303] The national monetary policy of the Member States participating in the euro area is replaced by a single monetary policy, with the primary objective of securing price stability.[304] In order to formulate and implement a specific monetary policy in the euro area, the ESCB and the ECB were established in accordance with ex Article 123(1) EC.[305]

Today, the primary Union law provisions governing the ESCB and the ECB can be found in Article 13 TEU, Articles 127–133, 282–284 TFEU and in the Protocol on the Statute of the

---

299. Ibid., Art. 8.
300. Ibid., Art. 1(2).
301. Council of the European Union, "The Council approves the grant of a loan to Hungary to support its medium term balance of payments", Brussels, 4 Nov. 2008, 15103/08 (Presse 313). Next to Hungary, since 2008, also Latvia and Romania have received financial assistance. Maximum volume of loans granted under this facility may not exceed EUR 50 billion in principal, see Art. 1(1).
302. This section on monetary policy reuses, updates and builds upon the corresponding section in the 4th ed. of *The Law of the European Union and the European Communities* (2008). Due to the limited space available, the external dimension of the euro cannot be dealt with. For an economic analysis see F. Di Mauro and R. Anderton, *The External Dimension of the Euro Area* (CUP, 2007). For a legal analysis see e.g. R. Smits, op. cit. *supra* note 81, 367–458; J.-V. Louis, op. cit. *supra* note 81, 82–84 and 159–166, J.-V. Louis, "Les relations internationales de l'Union économique et monétaire", (1999) *EUI Working Papers, LAW no. 99/10*; C. Zilioli and M. Selmayr, "The external relations of the Euro area: Legal aspects", (1999) CML Rev., 273–349; and *idem* "Recent developments in the law of the European Central Bank", (2006) *Yearbook of European Law*, 1–86, 77 et seq.; W. Weiss, "Kompetenzverteilung in der Währungspolitik und Aussenvertretung des Euro", (2002) EuR, 165–191. T. Padoa-Schioppa, "The external representation of the euro area", (1999) introductory statement at the Sub-Committee on Monetary Affairs of the European Parliament; W. Duisenberg, "The role of the ECB at the international level", speech delivered at the Annual Meeting of the Institute for International Finance, Inc. (IIF), Prague, 23 Sept. 2000; F. Amtenbrink, "EMU and the Overseas" in D. Kochenov (Ed.), *EU Law and the Overseas* (Kluwer, 2011), 271–290; European Central Bank, "The External Representation of the EU and EMU", Monthly Bulletin, May 2011, 87–97.
303. Generally, on the development of European monetary union see H. James, *Making the European Monetary Union* (HUP, 2014).
304. Consequently, the framework relating to the coordination of monetary policy applicable to Member States with a derogation, namely Art. 142 TFEU on exchange rate policy and any participation in ERM II, no longer applies.
305. The ESCB and the ECB became operational on 1 June 1998 after the appointment of the president, vice-president and the other members of the Executive Board. See Decision 98/345/EG (O.J. 1998, L 154/33). In the period between 1 June 1998 and 1 Jan. 1999 the national central banks remained in charge of the conduct of their independent monetary policies. Together with the ECB they made the necessary preparations for the changeover to the single currency. See ex Art. 123(1), last two sentences EC.

European System of Central Banks and the European Central Bank.[306] Together with the provisions in the TEU and TFEU, the Protocol enjoys the status of primary Union law.[307] Thus, as opposed to what can be observed about many national central bank systems outside the EU, the legal basis of the ESCB and the ECB has a quasi-constitutional status; any substantial amendments to the institutional structure of the ESCB and ECB or of its primary objective requires the application of the Treaty amendment procedure laid down in Article 48 TEU.[308] In order to provide for specific amendments to the legal basis without the need for recourse to Treaty revision, Article 129(3) TFEU allows a simplified revision procedure to be followed for the more technical aspects governed by the legal basis of the ECB.[309]

An overview of the legal framework of monetary union is provided below.[310] In this context it should be noted that the substantially increased role of the ECB in prudential supervision as a result of the emergence of the European Banking Union is discussed separately in Chapter 27 of this book.

6.1 *Legal nature, organizational structure and constitutional position of the ESCB and the ECB*

Situated at the centre of monetary union, the ESCB and particularly the ECB are effectively in charge of the formulation and implementation of monetary policy in the euro area.

6.1.1 *Legal nature*

The ESCB is a system currently composed of 29 central banks: the – at the time of writing of this chapter – 28 central banks of the current Member States (NCBs) of the EU and the ECB itself.[311] The legal personality of the national central banks derives from the respective national legal orders, whereas the ECB enjoys legal personality under Union law pursuant to Article 282(3) TFEU. The ESCB as such has no legal personality. The ECB has its seat in Frankfurt am Main, Germany. Details are laid down in a Headquarters Agreement between the German government and the ECB,[312] which – as far as its legal nature is concerned – is "part of the legal context created by the Protocol on privileges and immunities [of the European Union] and, more generally, part of European Union law, which constitutes the legal framework of reference for the purpose of interpreting its provisions".[313]

Article 13(1) TEU lists the ECB as one of the Union's institutions and thus, as part of the Union's institutional framework. As such, within the scope of its tasks, the ECB must "aim to

306. Protocol (No. 4) annexed to the TEU and TFEU (O.J. 2012, C 326/230).
307. Art. 51 TEU.
308. F. Amtenbrink, op. cit. *supra* note 28, 179.
309. Amendments of Art. 5.1, 5.2, 5.3, 17, 18, 19.1, 22, 23, 24, 26, 32.2, 32.3, 32.4, 32.6, 33.1(a) and 36 of the Statute of the ESCB can be initiated by means of the ordinary legislative procedure, either on recommendation from the ECB itself and after consulting the Commission or on a proposal from the Commission and after consulting the ECB.
310. For a detailed legal analysis of the institutions and the single monetary policy see e.g. R. Smits, op. cit. *supra* note 81; F. Amtenbrink, op. cit. *supra* note 28; C. Zilioli and M. Selmayr, *The Law of the European Central Bank* (OUP, 2001); S. Adalid, *La Banque centrale européenne et l'Eurosystème* (Bruylant, 2015). For an economic analysis see e.g. J. de Haan, S.C.W. Eijffinger and S. Waller, *The European Central Bank* (MIT Press, 2005); J. de Haan and J. Berger (Eds.), *The European Central Bank at Ten* (Springer, 2010). For a political science analysis see D. Howarth and P. Loedel, *The European Central Bank. The New European Leviathan?* (Palgrave, 2005).
311. Art. 282(1) TFEU.
312. SEC/GovC/4/98/7 (English language version).
313. Brackets added. As observed by A.G. Jääskinen in Case C-62/11, *Land Hessen v. Florence Feyerbacher*, para 47.

promote its values, advance its objectives, serve its interests, those of its citizens and those of the Member States, and ensure the consistency, effectiveness and continuity of its policies and actions". Until the amendment of primary Union law by the Treaty of Lisbon, the ECB, alongside the European Investment Bank, was listed separately from the institutions of the then Community.[314] This special treatment of the ECB by the former EC Treaty could first and foremost be interpreted as an expression of the independent position of the ECB in the Community institutional framework, which the drafters of the Treaty of Maastricht intended to emphasize. Moreover, unlike the previously existing Community institutions, the ECB was initially set up for the purpose of a single task within the then Community framework, that is the conduct of monetary policy for a single currency area.

Despite this distinct (independent) status and the separate legal personality of the constituting parts of the ESCB, it cannot be concluded that the ECB in the past or even presently enjoys a status separate from the Community/Union legal order,[315] as has been confirmed by the ECJ in *Commission v. ECB*.[316] In fact, it can be observed that the ESCB's main objective as defined in Article 127(1) TFEU is to pursue the main aims of the Union as identified in Article 3(3) TEU, that is "the sustainable development of Europe based on balanced economic growth and price stability". Moreover, the ECB is supposed to support the general economic policies in the Union with a view to contributing to the achievements of the objectives of the Union.[317] Placing the ESCB and ECB within the Union legal order is also supported by the genesis of its legal framework and the current structure of the TFEU provisions.[318] Yet, despite the fact the ECB forms part of the Union institutional legal order, its somewhat special status is still reflected in today's primary Union law by the fact that Article 13(3) TEU also identifies the ECB, together with the Court of Auditors, apart from the other Union Institutions.

As the ESCB comprises the ECB and the national central banks of all EU Member States, it could be argued that the ESCB constitutes a two-tier system. Yet, the power for conducting monetary policy is not equally or otherwise shared by the central and decentralized levels

314. See ex Arts. 7–8 EC. On the position prior to and after the introduction of the Treaty of Lisbon see also B. Krauskopf and C. Steven, "The institutional framework of the European system of Central Banks: Legal issues in the practice of the first ten years of its existence", (2009) CML Rev., 1143–1175.
315. Differently in the first instance C. Zilioli and M. Selmayr (1999), op. cit. *supra* note 303, and F. Amtenbrink and J. de Haan, "The European Central Bank: An independent specialized organization of Community law", (2000) CML Rev., 65–76 and 591–644, where the authors argued that the ECB has a "special status" outside the Community legal order. This view has been rightly rejected by R. Torrent, "Whom is the European Central Bank the Central Bank of?: Reaction to Zilioli and Selmayr", (1999) CML Rev., 1229–1241. See "The European Central Bank: An independent specialized organization of community law – A comment", (2002) CML Rev., 65–76; B. Dutzler, "Institutional framework of the EMU – Is the ECB a fourth pillar?" in F. Breuss, G. Fink and S. Griller (Eds.), *Institutional, Legal and Economic Aspects of EMU* (Springer, 2002), 3–35.
316. Case C-11/00, *Commission v. ECB*, which rejected the view that the ECB holds a special position outside the Community legal order. Informative is also the Opinion of A.G. Jacobs of 3 Oct. 2002.
317. On the objectives of the ECB see J.-V. Louis, op. cit. *supra* note 81, 55–57; R. Smits, op. cit. *supra* note 81; 93; F. Amtenbrink and J. de Haan, op. cit. *supra* note 315, 67–68.
318. On the genesis see J.-V. Louis, op. cit. *supra* note 81, 57. On the position of the ECB see also R. Smits, op. cit. *supra* note 81, 93; F. Amtenbrink and J. de Haan, op. cit. *supra* note 315, 73–75. See also D. Janzen, *Der neue Art. 88 Satz 2 des Grundgesetzes. Verfassungsrechtliche Anforderungen an die Übertragung der Währungshoheit auf die Europäische Zentralbank* (Duncker & Humblot, 1996), 100–101. Instructive in this context is also Case 85/86, *Commission v. Board of Governors of the European Investment Bank*, where the ECJ stated that the EIB's operational and institutional autonomy does not mean that it is totally separated from the Communities and exempted from every rule of Community law.

in the system.[319] In fact, the distribution of tasks follows a different logic, as the ECB constitutes the policy-making arm of the system, whereas the national central banks of the euro area Member States are mainly charged with the execution of the single European monetary policy decisions.[320] The ESCB thus includes features both of a centralized and a decentralized system, whereby the emphasis lies on the former. As to the motives for this hybrid setup it has been observed by de Lhoneux that "The ESCB was conceived to avoid the abrupt setting up of a new centralised European bureaucracy, to prevent the devastating social effects of an imposed merger of central banks, and to ensure the decentralization principle".[321]

To be sure, the functions of the NCBs are not limited to those assigned by primary Union law, as they are permitted to perform other functions outside the ESCB to the extent that these do not interfere with the objectives and tasks of the ESCB.[322] NCBs can thus fulfil tasks not related to the conduct of monetary policy, such as those related to the supervision of financial institutions. With the loss of the monetary policy function in stage three of EMU, the role of NCBs in this area has been consolidated in some instances,[323] whereby from November 2014 national central banks of euro area countries that fulfil the role of banking supervisor operate within the framework of the European Banking Union.

6.1.2 *Organizational structure*

The concentration of powers at the central level of the ESCB is rooted in its organizational structure, as it is governed by the decision-making bodies of the ECB. The NCBs are required to act in accordance with its guidelines and instructions.[324] The two main decision-making bodies of the ECB are the Executive Board and the Governing Council. Moreover, for as long as there are Member States with a derogation, the ECB features a General Council.[325]

The *Executive Board* is the managerial board of the ECB and comprises the President of the ECB, the vice-president and four additional members. They are appointed for a non-renewable period of eight years from among persons of recognized standing and professional experience in monetary and banking matters by qualified majority vote in the European Council, on a recommendation from the Council. The latter has to consult the European Parliament and the ECB's

319. Due to this, some authors in the past have characterized the ESCB as a "single-tier" system. See e.g. M. Potacs, "Nationale Zentralbanken in der Wirtschafts- und Währungsunion", (1993) EuR, 23–40, 32. With regard to the distribution of powers for the in the banking supervision tasks of the ECB see Ch. 27, "Financial market regulation and supervision", of this book.

320. See Arts. 12.1. and 14.3. ESCB Statute. With reference to Art. 12.1. ESCB Statute the role of the national central banks in the ESCB has been described as an expression of the subsidiarity principle laid down in Art. 5 EC. See e.g. Editorial Comment, "Executive Agencies within the EC: The European Central Bank – A model?", (1996) CML Rev., 623–631, 627; R. Smits (1992), op. cit. *supra* note 81, 717. Implicitly also J.-V. Louis, op. cit. *supra* note 81, 58. The execution of monetary policy by the NCBs in the ESCB can be viewed as a form of decentralized governance for which the ESCB as such remains responsible. Similar R. Smits (1997), op. cit. *supra* note 81, 112 with further references in footnotes 446 and 447. However, *sensu stricto* this cannot be considered as an example of the application of the subsidiarity principle, as today's Art. 5(3) TEU does not apply in areas where the Union has exclusive competences, such as for monetary policy in the euro area.

321. E. de Lhoneux, "The eurosystem", in European Central Bank, *Legal Aspects of the European System of Central Banks* (European Central Bank, 2005), 161–187, 163.

322. See Art. 14.4. ESCB Statute according to which such functions must be performed on the responsibility and liability of national central banks.

323. This development could for example be seen at *De Nederlandse Bank*, which in 2004 merged with the Dutch Pension and Insurance Supervisory Authority (PVK).

324. Ibid., Arts. 8 and 14.3. ESCB Statute.

325. Art. 141 TFEU and Arts. 10–14 and 44–46 ESCB Statute.

Governing Council.[326] In order to ensure continuity, the first-ever members of the Executive Board were appointed with staggered terms.[327] In addition to the rules of procedure of the ECB, the Executive Board has its own rules of procedure establishing a regime for the adoption of decisions by means of teleconferencing, as well as for the delegation of powers.[328] The main task of the Executive Board is to implement monetary policy based on the guidelines and decisions of the Governing Council of the ECB. It is the Executive Board which issues guidelines and instructions to the NCBs so that they can fulfil their executive tasks in the ESCB. Moreover, the Executive Board is responsible for the preparation of the meetings of the Governing Council of the ECB. As *primus inter pares,* the President of the ECB chairs both the Executive Board and the Governing Council of the ECB and represents the ECB externally, in particular in contacts with Union institutions, such as the Council and the European Parliament, but also the Eurogroup.[329] Decisions of the Executive Board are in principle taken by simple majority of votes cast, whereby each member has one vote. In the event of a tie, the President of the ECB casts a deciding vote.[330]

The *Governing Council* is the main policy-making body of the ECB. It consists of the members of the Executive Board and the governors of the NCBs of the euro area Member States. Given its mixed composition, the term of office and appointment procedures of the members of the Governing Council vary. The governors of the NCBs are appointed in accordance with the respective national provisions, as a result of which their terms of office can thus in principle vary, whereby Union law calls for a minimum term of five years.[331] The main task of the Governing Council is to take all necessary decisions to ensure the performance of the tasks entrusted to the ESCB under Union law. It takes the decisions concerning the definition (quantification) of the monetary policy objective and the actual implementation of monetary policy, namely relating to the determining of the key interest rates, open market and credit operations, as well as the supply of reserves in the ESCB. The Governing Council moreover also establishes the guidelines which are necessary for the implementation of its decisions. It can also delegate certain powers to the Executive Board.[332] According to Article 284(1) TFEU, the President of the Council and a member of the Commission are entitled to participate in meetings of the Governing Council. They do not, however, have a right to vote.[333]

---

326. Art. 11.2. ESCB Statute, which moreover states that only EU citizens can be members of the Executive Board. The European Parliament committee on Economic and Monetary Affairs invites candidates to appear for a statement and to answer questions. In case of a negative opinion, the president of the European Parliament asks for a nomination to be withdrawn, see Rule 122 of the Rules of Procedure of the European Parliament (8th parliamentary term), Jan. 2017.
327. As foreseen in Art. 50 ESCB Statute. Despite the fact that this provision foresaw the initial appointment of the President of the ECB for a full period of 8 years, the dispute around the person to first take this position resulted in France insisting on a political compromise allowing for replacement of the President – already – after 4 years. The decision on the appointment of the first president was controversial. See R. Smits, "Het begin van de muntunie: Besluitvorming en regelgeving", (1999) SEW, 2–12, 6.
328. Decision of the European Central Bank adopting the Rules of Procedure of the European Central Bank (ECB/2004/2) (O.J. 2004, L 80/33), as amended (current consolidated version available at <ecb.int>). Decision of the European Central Bank concerning the Rules of Procedure of the Executive Board of the European Central Bank (ECB/1999/7) (O.J. 1999, L 314/34).
329. Art. 13 ESCB Statute; Art. 1 Protocol (No. 14) on the Euro Group attached to the TEU and TFEU.
330. Ibid., Art. 11.5.; Art. 7 Rules of Procedure ECB.
331. Ibid., Art. 14.2., which also states the conditions under which a relieve from office is admissible.
332. Ibid., Art. 12.1. Guideline 2015/510 of the ECB on the implementation of the Eurosystem monetary policy framework (ECB/2014/60) (O.J. 2015, L 91/3), as amended.
333. The president of the Council may submit a motion for deliberation to the Governing Council, see Art. 284(1) TFEU.

Although the original provisions introduced by the Treaty on the European Union operated on the basis of a strict equality of all NCB governors, in the light of enlargement of the euro area and the feared loss of efficiency in the main decision-making organ of the ECB, the Treaty of Nice introduced new arrangements into the ESCB Statute, allowing the Council meeting in the composition of the Heads of State or Government to amend Article 10.2. ESCB Statute on the voting in the Governing Council by unanimous vote.[334] By Decision of 21 March 2003, based on a recommendation by the ECB,[335] the Council amended this provision introducing a rotation system. While the six members of the Executive Board retain their voting right when participating in Governing Council meetings, Article 10.2. ESCB Statute effectively limits the size of the Governing Council to 21 voting participants by applying a different voting regime from the time that the number of Member States – and thus NCBs – participating in the euro area exceeds 15. With the start of the rotation system initially being postponed until the number of NCB governors exceeded 18, it has been in operation since 1 January 2015, marking the date of the joining of Lithuania as the 19th member of the euro area.[336]

According to this voting arrangement, governors of the national central banks participating in the euro area only have a voting right on a rotation basis, whereby the frequencies depends – put in a nutshell – on an indicator of the relative size of the economies of the euro Member States.[337] Based on this indicator, NCB governors are allocated to different groups. The first group consists of the five NCB governors from the euro area Member States that occupy the highest positions in the country-ranking. They share four voting rights. The second group includes all other NCB governors. Between them, they share the remaining 11 voting rights. This allocation of votes, which is published in advance, determines how an NCB governor has the right to vote during a calendar year. Article 10.2. makes clear in this context that within each group these voting rights need to be distributed for an equal number of times.[338] Once the number of Member States participating in the euro area exceeds 22, three groups are foreseen: the first group will continue to consist of the five NCB governors from the participating Member States which occupy the highest positions in the country ranking on the basis of the economic indicators, sharing four voting rights between them. The second group will be made up of half of all national central bank governors, rounded up to the nearest whole number where necessary, selected from the subsequent positions of the country ranking. They will share eight voting rights. The remaining NCB governors make up a third group, and will have three voting rights.

---

334. See Art. 10.6. ESCB Statute, inserted by Art. 5 of the Treaty of Nice. This could take place either on a recommendation from the ECB and after consulting the European Parliament and the Commission, or on a recommendation from the Commission and after consulting the European Parliament and the ECB. It was up to the Council to recommend the amendments to the Member States for adoption in accordance with what is now Art. 48 TEU.
335. Council Decision 2003/223/EC (O.J. 2003, L 83/66), based on a Declaration on the new Art. 10.6. ESCB Statute annexed to the Treaty of Nice.
336. Art. 1 decision of the European Central Bank to postpone the start of the rotation system in the Governing Council of the European Central Bank (ECB/2008/29) (O.J. 2009, L 3/4).
337. The principal component of the indicator is the Member State's GDP. The second component is the total assets of the aggregated balance sheet of monetary financial institutions (TABS-MFI) within the territory of the Member State concerned. The relative weights of the two components are 5/6 for GDP and 1/6 for TABS-MFI. But see D. Gros, "Reforming the composition of the ECB Governing Council in view of enlargement: How not to do it!", Briefing paper for the Monetary Committee of the European Parliament, Feb. 2003, who criticizes this index, as it has arbitrary elements.
338. The ECB publishes the full schedule of the rotation of voting rights in the Governing Council for the current and subsequent year. See <ecb.int>.

Even when considering that all non-voting NCB governors can participate in the discussions, with the revision of the original system – for better or for worse – the large economies regain the upper hand at least as far as the formal voting power is concerned.[339] The amended voting procedure has also resulted in a (subtle) shift in the balance of power in the Governing Council. The power of the six permanently elected members of the Executive Board of the ECB, and thus of the central level, has increased relative to that of the NCB governors, the decentralized level, as the voting rights shared between the latter will not exceed 15 regardless of the number of Member States participating in the euro area.[340] To be sure, from a legal point of view, given the independent position of NCB governors, the required commitment to the objectives of the ESCB and the ECB, as well as the independence of the ESCB and the ECB as a whole, little stands in the way of introducing an institutional set-up as foreseen in the ESCB Statute whereby not all central bank governors participate in a vote, which should from the outset be in the common interest of the single monetary policy in the euro area.

The formal voting requirements in the Governing Council have not been altered and continue to be largely by simple majority vote of the members having a voting right, with the president having a deciding vote in case of a tie.[341] A quorum exists, if two-thirds of the members with a voting right participate in a decision. While meetings of the Governing Council are convened every two weeks, monetary policy decisions relating to the setting of key interest rates are currently taken only every six weeks, based on a predetermined and publicly available schedule. The other meetings are reserved for so-called non-monetary policy matters relating, *inter alia*, to the payment systems, financial stability and important legal affairs.

The *General Council* constitutes the third decision-making body of the ECB. The General Council has effectively taken over those functions of the former EMI that still had to be performed when the EMI was dissolved at the end of stage two of EMU.[342] In principle this is a temporary body geared towards integrating non- euro area NCB's into the ESCB.[343] It consists of the President and Vice-President of the ECB and *all* NCB governors, including those with a derogation, as well as the Danish central bank (*Danmarks Nationalbank*) and, for the time being, the Bank of England.[344] The specific tasks of the General Council are described in Article 47 ESCB Statute, the most important being its contribution to the preparation of Member States with a derogation for the third stage of EMU.[345] The General Council monitors the functioning of ERM II and serves as the forum for monetary and exchange rate policy coordination.

6.1.3 *ECB independence and accountability*

Whether and to what extent the position of the ECB highlighted hereafter can best be described as independent or autonomous may be a definitional matter rather than involving clear-cut legal

339. Critical in this regard: House of Lords Select Committee on the European Union, "Is the European Central Bank Working?", Session 2002–03, 42nd Report, part 3, which includes a detailed analysis of the adjusted voting system. It should be noted however that for certain decisions relating – *inter alia* – to the capital of the ECB and the transfer of foreign reserve assets from the NCBs to the ECB, the votes in the Governing Council are weighted according to the NCBs' shares in the subscribed capital of the ECB (Art. 10.3. ESCB Statute).
340. See Art. 10.2. ESCB Statute.
341. Ibid.
342. Art. 141 TFEU and Art. 44 ESCB Statute.
343. Similarly, J.-V. Louis, op. cit. *supra* note 81, 151.
344. Art. 45.2. ESCB Statute. The other members of the Executive Board and moreover the President of the Council and a member of the Commission are allowed to participate in the meetings, albeit without voting rights.
345. Ibid., Art. 47.3.

considerations. While Article 282(3) TFEU uses the term independence to describe the position of the ECB vis-à-vis other Union institutions and bodies, as well as the governments of the Member States, arguably the term autonomy may better describe the position of the ECB in the Union legal order, which allows this institution to fulfil its monetary policy related function to a large degree without influence from a European or national authority.[346] At the same time it can be noted that reference to the independence of the ECB both in the academic literature and by the ECJ cannot be understood to mean that the ECB is entirely free of control or outside influence.[347] In accordance with the mainly legal and economic literature several aspects of central bank independence can be distinguished relating to institutional, functional, organizational and financial aspects of the bank that cannot be described in more detail here.[348] What they all have in common is that they are geared towards insulating all aspects of the functioning of the ECB from political tampering.

Three main factors can be identified that have had a crucial impact on the position accorded the ECB in the Union legal order. Firstly, the establishment of an independent monetary authority was an important condition for Germany to accept the transfer of sovereignty over monetary policy in the first place. Against the background of the positive experience with the role of the Bundesbank in the stability of the German currency, an autonomous ECB was considered a crucial prerequisite for the establishment of an inflation-averse European central bank and a stable single currency.[349] At the time when the rules on EMU were drawn up, a majority of national central banks supported the establishment of an ECB, whose independent position would be secured in the legal basis of the bank.[350] The German position can also be explained by the extensive, albeit not always conclusive, theoretical and empirical evidence offered mainly by economists, which suggests that the conduct of an inflation-averse monetary policy requires the removal of that policy from the political arena.[351] Arguably, against the background of the budgetary rules geared towards fiscal discipline, the establishment of an independent ECB with an overriding single monetary policy objective also signifies the commitment of the drafters of the Treaty to monetary dominance in EMU.[352] Yet, despite its independence, the ECB does not

---

346. For this reason, A. Geelhoed, op. cit. *supra* note 95, argues in favour of using the term autonomy when referring to the position of the ECB.
347. In Case C-11/00, *Commission v. ECB*, the ECJ chooses the term "independence" to describe the position of the ECB.
348. See e.g. J.-V. Louis, *Vers un système européen de banques centrales: projet de dispositions organiques* (Université de Bruxelles, 1989), 25–28; S. Fischer, "Modern Central Banking" in F. Capie et al. (Eds.), *The Future of Central Banking* (CUP, 1994), 262–308; F. Amtenbrink, op. cit. *supra* note 28, 18 et seq.; S. Adalid, op. cit. *supra* note 310, 518 et seq.
349. See H. Tietmeyer, "The role of the independent Central Bank in Europe", (1990) *Contribution to the 1990 IMF Seminar on Central Banking.*
350. This preference can be clearly seen in draft ESCB Statute prepared by the Committee of Governors. R. Smits, op. cit. *supra* note 81, 159–160; but see also F. van Esch and E. de Jong, "Institutionalization without internalization. The cultural dimension of French-German conflicts on European Central Bank independence", (2012) *Int Econ Policy*, 631–648.
351. See e.g. S.C.W. Eijffinger and J. de Haan, "The political economy of Central-Bank independence", *Special Papers in Economics no. 19* (Princeton University, 1996), with further references; A. Alesina and G. Tabellini, "Bureaucrats or politicians?", (2004) *NBER Working Paper Series no. 10241*, with further references. Critical on the political economy rationale of central bank independence: W. Buiter, "How robust is the new conventional wisdom? The surprising fragility of the theoretical foundation of inflation targeting and Central Bank independence", (2006) *CEPR Discussion Paper No. 5772*; J. de Haan, D. Masciandaroc and M. Quintyn, "Does Central Bank independence still matter?", (2008) *European Journal of Political Economy*, 717–721.
352. On the relationship between fiscal and monetary dominance in EMU see D. Lombardi and M. Moschella, "The government bond buying programmes of the European Central Bank: An analysis of their policy

operate in an institutional and legal vacuum. First of all, a clear link exists between the monetary policy and the economic policy of the Union. What is more, the ECB is tied into the institutional structure of the Union, as it is at least to some degree accountable for the conduct of the tasks which have been assigned to it. From a legal perspective, this accountability includes the judicial review of ECB measures by the ECJ.[353] Essentially, the ECB fulfils both delegated legislative and executive functions within the Union framework, while at the same time being separated from these two branches of government, which are in any event not easily separable at the European level.

Still, arguably no aspect of the institutional structure of the ECB has been debated more controversially from the start of the ESCB than the issue of the democratic legitimacy and accountability of the ECB in the Union legal order.[354] In fact, if anything, the recent European financial and sovereign debt crisis, the monetary policy stands of the ECB in the crisis, its involvement in the financial assistance measures, but also its new task as the European banking supervisor, has reignited the debate.[355] The case for the democratic accountability of a central bank is based, on the one hand, on the legal nature of these bodies and their position within a democratic system, and on the other hand on the task with which they have been entrusted.[356] While the act of delegation of monetary policy by an act of parliament initially legitimizes the position of the central bank in a given constitutional system, this *ex ante* mechanism of accountability cannot suffice. Indeed, in order to ensure the democratic accountability, and with it the democratic legitimacy, of independent central banks certain conditions have to be met, such as access to information (transparency), the existence of a yardstick making it possible to judge whether the bank has properly discharged its duties and the existence of institutionalized contacts, which allow for the exchange of information. Moreover, effective accountability also requires the existence of legal instruments to hold the central bank to account. The distribution of these instruments between government and parliament provides for the democratic element in keeping the bank accountable. Examples of such instruments are the possibility to amend the

---

settings", (2015) *Journal of European Public Policy*, 1–20.

353. For that reason alone, the position of the ECB cannot be easily compared to that of the independent judiciary.

354. See e.g. R.M. Lastra, "The independence of the European system of central banks", (1992) Harv. Int'l L.J., 475–519; L.W. Gormley and J. de Haan, "The democratic deficit of the European Central Bank", (1996) EL Rev., 95–112; R. Smits, op. cit. *supra* note 81; F. Amtenbrink, op. cit. *supra* note 28; F. Amtenbrink, "The European Central Bank – democratically accountable or unrestrained?", (1999) NJB, 72–78; B. J. Laurens, M. Arnone and J.-F. Segalotto (Eds.), *Central Bank Independence, Accountability, and Transparency. A Global Perspective* (Palgrave, 2009). Generally, on the independence and accountability of EU agencies S. Peers and M. Costa, "Reassessing the accountability of European Union decentralized agencies: Mind the independence gap", (2016) EPL, 645–666.

355. See e.g. Transparency International EU, "Two sides of the same coin? Independence and accountability of the European Central Bank" (2017). See also F. Amtenbrink and M. Markakis "Towards a Meaningful Prudential Supervision Dialogue in the Euro Area?", ADEMU Working Paper Series, WP 2017/081, December 2017. Stressing the limitations is M. Goldoni, "On the limits of legal accountability of the European Central Bank", (2017) Geo. Mason L. Rev., 595–616. To be sure, the debate on central bank accountability predates the establishment of the ECB, see e.g. K. Bonin, *Zentralbanken zwischen funktioneller Unabhängigkeit und politischer Autonomie* (Nomos, 1979); R. Caesar, "Die Unabhängigkeit der Notenbank im demokratischen Staat", (1980) *Zeitschrift für Politik*, 347–377.

356. F. Amtenbrink and J. de Haan, op. cit. *supra* note 315, 65–66; T. Daintith, "Between domestic democracy and alien rule of law? Some thoughts on the "independence" of the Bank of England" in M. Andenas et al., op. cit. *supra* note 110, 355–372; F. Amtenbrink, "The three pillars of Central Bank governance – Towards a model Central Bank law or a Code of Good Governance?" in International Monetary Fund, *Current Developments in Monetary and Financial Law* (International Monetary Fund, 2005), 101–132.

legal basis of the central bank, the possibility of performance-based dismissals, the possibility of government or parliament to override central bank decisions.[357]

The choice which has been made by the drafters of the Treaty of Maastricht to define the independent position, the structure, competences and tasks of the ECB in primary Union law, has resulted in a supranational central bank system whose democratic link back to the European and national governments and parliaments is arguably relatively weak. By granting large parts of the ECB's legal framework a quasi-constitutional status, amendment of the legal basis of the bank via the Treaty amendment procedure is a rather unrealistic scenario and thus an ineffective instrument of democratic accountability in the hands of the Council and the European Parliament. While it will be observed hereafter that the ECB is to some extent subject to monitoring by the European Parliament, unlike national parliaments, the latter is not in the position to alter the legal basis of the ECB by itself. Moreover, given the extent to which the ECB and the NCBs are deliberately distanced from Union institutions and national governments, such as the Council and the Commission, neither national parliaments nor the European Parliament can hold these Union institutions effectively to account for a supervisory role which they effectively do not have *vis-à-vis* the ECB and NCBs. Finally, it can be observed that national parliaments and governments can hardly make their respective NCB governor personally responsible for a decision which has been collectively taken by the Executive Board of the ECB and the other NCB governors participating in the Governing Council and – considering the rotation system – possibly even without a voting right of the NCB governor concerned. What is more, the European Parliament's difficulties in holding the ECB to account for its conduct of monetary policy is not only of an institutional nature. The evaluation of the monetary policy in the national sphere takes place first and foremost in the light of economic policy pursued by national government. The consistency of monetary policy with economic policy constitutes an important yardstick. Yet, despite the strengthening of the economic policy coordination framework in EMU following the European financial and sovereign debt crisis, a clear-cut single European fiscal policy is still absent.[358] What is more, given the diminutive role of the European Parliament in European monetary policy, it has to review the ECB's performance based on a yardstick that has been established without the input of the European Parliament.

From the point of view of the ECB, the accountability requirements laid down in primary Union law focus on reporting requirements and on the exchange of information in the shape of dialogue with Union Institutions. The TFEU and the ESCB Statute introduce several reporting requirements, including the publication of weekly consolidated financial statements, quarterly reports on the activities of the ESCB and the drafting of an annual report on the activities of the ESCB and on the monetary policy of both the previous and current year addressed to the European Parliament, the Council and the Commission, and also to the European Council.[359] Following each meeting of the Governing Council at which monetary policy decisions have been taken, the president of the ECB holds a scheduled press conference. Both the President of the Council and a member of the Commission can also participate in meetings of the Governing Council, albeit without a voting right.[360] The President of the Council may submit a motion for deliberation to the Governing Council, but the Governing Council is neither obliged to take a decision on that motion for deliberation nor does the President of the Council or the member

357. For an extensive analysis of these and other elements in the context of the ESCB and the ECB see F. Amtenbrink, op. cit. *supra* note 28.
358. With regard to the development of a fiscal union see European Commission, cited *supra* note 164.
359. Art. 284(3) TFEU and Art. 15 ESCB Statute.
360. Art. 284(1) TFEU.

of the Commission for that matter have a right to override or postpone decisions taken by that decision-making body.[361]

The President of the ECB is invited to participate in Council meetings when the Council is discussing matters relating to the objectives and tasks of the ESCB.[362] In practice, the President of the ECB or his representative participate regularly in ECOFIN Council meetings and the ECB president also participates in the meetings of the Eurogroup. Considering that the drafters of the Treaty of Maastricht wanted to place the ECB at some distance from any political influence, these arrangements may seem somewhat surprising. However, adequate communication channels between the government, parliament and the central bank can help to avoid misunderstandings and false expectations in particular on the part of the government but also the public at large as to what monetary policy can and cannot do.[363] At the same time, such contacts ensure that the central bank does not operate in a political or social vacuum. Public support can be an important element in shielding a central bank from unwanted political influence.[364] Parliamentary support can be equally important, as can be the support of the public at large.

Against the background of the Treaty-based independence of the ECB, namely the instruments foreseen in primary Union law for holding the ECB accountable can only be considered somewhat underdeveloped in particular when compared to the legal arrangements of some other central bank systems.[365] Yet, this deficiency of the existing legal framework is partly – albeit certainly not fully – compensated by the actual practice that has developed over time. Two main features in this regard that cannot be easily deduced from primary Union law are the ECB's monetary policy dialogue with the European Parliament and the bank's publication of accounts of meetings of its Governing Council.

According to Article 284(3) TFEU the ECB President and the other members of the Executive Board may, at the request of the European Parliament or on their own initiative, be heard by the competent parliamentary committees. From the wording of this provision it cannot be concluded that the appearance before the European Parliament amounts to an obligation, and no further details are provided in primary Union law on the substance or procedure of such encounters.[366] Still, from the coming into operation of the ECB a practice has emerged whereby the president of the ECB appears before the European Parliament Committee on Economic and Monetary Affairs on a quarterly basis. This regular so-called monetary dialogue was established

---

361. A similar limited right of presence existed previously in the case of the Bundesbank, see F. Amtenbrink, op. cit. *supra* note 28, 222. While the existence of override mechanisms is generally considered problematic from the point of view of central bank independence, the example of the Reserve Bank of New Zealand Act 1989 (section 12) and the Bank of England Act 1998 (section 19 on "reserve powers") show that legal arrangements can be put in place to prevent the abuse of such a mechanism for short-term political ends. In line with the principle of ministerial responsibility, the previous Dutch Bank Act 1948 also provided for an override mechanism in favour of the Minister of Finance (Art. 26(1)). While this right has never been exercised it certainly functioned as an efficient deterrent.
362. Art. 284(2) TFEU.
363. F. Amtenbrink, op. cit. *supra* note 356, 113 et seq.
364. J.-V. Louis, op. cit. *supra* note 81, 75, in this context cites Goodhart: "An independent central bank will fail and be rejected, unless it can establish broadly-based public support".
365. F. Amtenbrink, op. cit. *supra* note 28, 359 et seq. with concrete proposals for improvements. For an early comparative indicator of central bank accountability see J. de Haan, F. Amtenbrink and S.C.W. Eijffinger, "Accountability of Central Banks: Aspects and quantifications", (1999) *Banca Nazionale del Lavoro Quarterly Review*, 167–193. For a different assessment see e.g. R. Smits, op. cit. *supra* note 81, 176–178; C. Zilioli and M. Selmayr, op. cit. *supra* note 310.
366. The European Parliament had suggested the introduction of a rule according to which the president of the ECB should be heard every 6 months or whenever the European Parliament considered it feasible. See Resolution of the European Parliament on EMU (O.J. 1990, C 284/62).

on the initiative of the European Parliament, which in its rules of procedure included a provision inviting the president of the ECB to attend the meetings of said committee "at least four times a year to make a statement and to answer questions.[367] A study of these hearings during the first decade highlights the vivid interest that MEPs take in the activities of the ESCB and ECB and in particular the latter's decisions on monetary policy.[368] In the European financial and sovereign debt crisis much attention has been given to the role of the ECB in addressing the crisis, including *inter alia* its unconventional monetary policy and its (future) role in European banking supervision.[369]

The regular appearances before the European Parliament combined with the reporting requirements form an important element in the actual accountability of the ECB. In more recent times central banks, including the ECB, have discovered transparency as an ally both in meeting demands of more openness and accountability, as well as in communicating monetary policy.[370] Indeed, transparency may not only refer to the degree to which a central bank provides information, but moreover to the public's understanding of the decisions taken by the monetary authorities and the reasoning behind them.[371] This includes in particular the quantification of the monetary policy objective and the strategy of the central bank in achieving the statutory objective. As such, communication is very much in a central bank's own interest, since it enhances the effectiveness and credibility of monetary policy, as the general public and even more so the financial markets (better) understand the banks' approach to monetary policy.[372]

Unlike some central banks outside the ESCB, until 2015 the ECB did not publish minutes of meetings of its Governing Council.[373] Article 10.4 ESCB Statute, which states that the "proceedings of the meetings shall be confidential" has for a long time been interpreted by the ECB to exclude the publication of any records of the meetings of the monetary policy decision making body at the ECB, and suggestions to publish such minutes have been considered controversial.[374] At the same time, in the European financial and sovereign debt crisis the secrecy surrounding these meetings combined with regular hints by NCB governors about disagreements in the Governing Council has given rise to undesirable speculation. Increasing transparency

---

367. See currently Rule 126 of the Rules of Procedure of the European Parliament (8th parliamentary term), Jan. 2017.
368. See generally with regard to these hearings F. Amtenbrink, "On the legitimacy and democratic accountability of the European Central Bank: Legal arrangements and practical experience" in A. Arnull and D. Wincott (Eds.), *Accountability and Legitimacy in the European Union* (OUP, 2002), 147–163, 157 et seq; F. Amtenbrink and K. van Duin, "The European Central Bank before the European Parliament: Theory and practice after ten years of monetary dialogue", (2009) EL Rev., 561–583; S.C.W. Eijffinger, "Monetary Dialogue 2009–2014: Looking backward, looking forward", (2015) *Credit and Capital Markets*, 1–10.
369. S. Collignon and S. Diessner, "The ECB's monetary dialogue with the European Parliament: Efficiency and accountability during the euro crisis?", (2016) JCMS, 1296–1312. The minutes of the hearings are available at <www.europarl.europa.eu/committees/nl/econ/monetary-dialogue.html>.
370. Generally, with regard to the transparency of the ECB see: European Journal of Political Economy, Vol. 23, Issue 1 (Mar. 2007), with numerous contributions on this topic.
371. R. Lastra, "How much accountability for central banks and supervisors?", (2001) *Central Banking*, 69–75; J. de Haan, F. Amtenbrink and S. Waller, "Transparency and credibility of the European Central Bank", (2004) JCMS, 775–794, with further references.
372. International Monetary Fund, "Supporting Document to the Code of Good Practices on Transparency in Monetary and Financial Policies", (2000) International Monetary Fund.
373. According to Art. 5.2. Rules of Procedure ECB minutes are internally drafted. Art. 23.1 allows the Governing Council to authorize the president of the ECB "to make the outcome of their deliberations public". Section 15(3) of the Bank of England Act 1998 provides an example of how the publication of such minutes can be achieved without compromising the objectives of the bank.
374. F. Amtenbrink, op. cit. *supra* note 368, 152.

and raising awareness of its monetary policy stands seems to also have been what the ECB had in mind when it decided in December 2014 to revise its position and announced it would start publishing regular accounts of Governing Council monetary policy discussions with the aim to "provide the rationale behind monetary policy decisions and enable members of the public to improve their understanding of the Governing Council's assessment of the economy and its policy responses in the light of evolving conditions".[375] Even when considering that the accounts do not specify which NCB governors or members of the ECB's Executive Board have taken what positions concerning a specific monetary policy decision, the publication of these accounts is an important improvement over the previous practice at the ECB, not least in providing valuable information for those in charge of holding the ECB to account.

The *ex post* democratic accountability in the form of the political control described above is complemented by *ex post* judicial control. Indeed, the independence of the ECB and its far-reaching competences and regulatory activities makes it indispensable that the ECB is subject to full judicial review. To this end Article 35.1 ESCB Statute states that the acts and omissions of the ECB are open to review or interpretation by the ECJ in the cases and under the conditions laid down in the TFEU. Paragraph 1 of Article 263 TFEU empowers the ECJ, *inter alia*, to review the legality of legally binding acts of the ECB.[376] The ECB itself can bring an action pursuant to paragraph 3 of Article 263 TFEU against legally binding acts adopted jointly by the European Parliament and the Council, acts of the Council, of the Commission and of the European Parliament for the purpose of protecting its prerogatives.[377] Moreover, according to Article 277 TFEU, in proceedings in which a regulation of the ECB is at issue, parties can plead the grounds specified in paragraph 2 of Article 263 TFEU (grounds of lack of competence, infringement of an essential procedural requirement, infringement of the TFEU or of any rule of law relating to its application, misuse of powers) in order to invoke the inapplicability of that regulation. The ECB can also become subject to an action for failure to act and can itself institute such an action.[378] Moreover, in the context of the preliminary reference procedure provided for by Article 267(b) TFEU, national courts and tribunals can direct questions to the ECJ concerning the validity or interpretation of ECB acts, if they consider that a decision on the question is necessary to enable them to give judgment. The first-ever preliminary reference to the ECJ by the German Federal Constitutional Court in case *Gauweiler* is a case in point.[379] Finally, according to paragraph 3 of Article 340 TFEU and Article 35.3 ESCB Statute, action by the ECB can become the subject of non-contractual liability for any damages caused by it or its staff. Whether and to what extent the NCBs are liable depends on their respective national laws; yet, as has been observed elsewhere, this non-contractual liability of NCBs should be limited to those activities which they undertake outside the ESCB and thus outside the control of the ECB.[380]

With regard to the conduct of monetary policy the ECJ made clear in *Gauweiler* that any measures must be proportionate to the objectives of that policy.[381] Moreover, the European court has emphasized in this decision that to the extent that the ESCB is required "to make

---

375. ECB, "ECB to publish accounts of monetary policy discussions from Jan.", Press release of 18 Dec. 2014. These accounts are available at <www.ecb.europa.eu/home/html/index.en.html >.
376. With regard to the consequences of a judgment see Arts. 264 and 266 TFEU.
377. According to Art. 35.5. ESCB Statute, decisions of the ECB to bring an action are taken by the Governing Council.
378. Art. 265 TFEU.
379. Case C-62/14, *Gauweiler*.
380. R. Smits, op. cit. *supra* note 81, 107–108.
381. Case C-62/14, *Gauweiler*, para 66–67. See also P. Craig and M. Markakis, "Gauweiler and the legality of outright monetary transactions", (2016) EL Rev., 4–24.

choices of a technical nature and to undertake forecasts and complex assessments, it must be allowed, in that context, a broad discretion", whereby an "adequate statement of the reasons of its decisions" must be provided.[382] Still, the institutional and substantive context of the ESCB is "juridified" to a larger extent than has been the case in the past in many instances for national central banks. As such, the extensive jurisdiction of the ECJ relating to the ECB is certainly more than merely symbolic, as it highlights the intention of the drafters of the Treaty of Maastricht to place the ECB as much as possible within the Union legal order.[383] The practical relevance of this has also become evident in the context of the ECB's involvement in the establishment of the MoU on specific economic policy conditionality in the context of the financial assistance granted by the ESM to Cyprus.[384]

Several cases were brought before the General Court by depositors that had suffered as a result of the restructuring of a number of large Cypriot banks aimed at the annulment of a Eurogroup statement, and the establishment of the non-contractual liability of the Union.[385] Limiting the observations on these cases presently to the ECB, in *Ledra Advertisement* the ECJ reiterated its view stated in *Pringle* that "first, the duties conferred on the Commission and ECB within the ESM Treaty do not entail the exercise of any power to make decisions of their own and, secondly, the activities pursued by those two institutions within the ESM Treaty commit the ESM alone".[386] While the ESM, being based on an intergovernmental Treaty, does not as such form part of the Union legal order, the ECJ has made clear that it "cannot prevent unlawful conduct [...] from being raised against the Commission and the ECB in an action for compensation under Article 268 TFEU and the second and third paragraphs of Article 340 TFEU".[387] The Court has emphasized that the fact that the intergovernmental ESM Treaty confers tasks on the ECB and the Commission for that matter does not mean that these institutions are no longer subject to obligations arising under primary Union law, including the observance of the Charter of Fundamental Rights of the European Union. For the Commission the ECJ in this context referred to Article 17(1) TEU and the obligation of the Commission to promote the general interest of the Union' and to ensure the application of Union law.[388] In observing Union law, the ECB is thus not only banned from certain activities even outside the Union legal framework, but any such activities may also give rise to a non-contractual liability, whereby the substantive conditions established by the ECJ have to be met.[389]

Finally, in internal disputes between the ECB and an NCB concerning the fulfilment by the latter of its obligations under the ESCB Statute, Article 35.6 ESCB Statute introduces a procedure which has similarities to the treaty infringement procedure in Article 258 TFEU. In such a case the ECB (rather than the Commission) has to deliver a reasoned opinion on the matter after giving the national central bank concerned the opportunity to submit its observations. If

---

382. Ibid., para 68–70. On the limitations of a judicial review of monetary policy see already T. Daintith, op. cit. *supra* note 356, 368–369; F. Amtenbrink, op. cit. *supra* note 28, 4–5, with references to attempts in the US to challenge decisions of the Fed.
383. See J.-V. Louis, op. cit. *supra* note 81, 75.
384. See *supra* section 5.4.
385. See the references cited *supra* note 295.
386. Joined Cases C-8-10/15 P, *Mallis*, para 53.
387. Ibid., para 54–55. Brackets added.
388. Ibid., para 56–59.
389. Ibid., para 64. Namely, the unlawfulness of the conduct alleged against the EU institution, the existence of a damage, as well as the existence of a causal link between the conduct of the institution and the damage complained of.

the national central bank concerned does not comply with the opinion within the period laid down by the ECB, the latter may than bring the matter before the ECJ.[390]

6.2 *Objectives and scope of monetary policy*

The primary objective of the ECB as set out in Articles 127(1) and 282(2) TFEU, as well as in Article 2 ESCB Statute, is to maintain price stability. As a secondary, subordinated, objective, the ECB must support the general economic policies of the Union with a view to contributing to the achievements of the Union's objectives as laid down in Article 3 TEU.[391] The inclusion of this overriding primary single monetary policy objective in primary Union law can be attributed above all to the influence of Germany, which was only willing to surrender the monetary policy authority of the Bundesbank if the new European monetary policy authority had a clear monetary policy objective.[392] With the reference to the economic policies of the Union not only the construction of an EMU that relies on the coordination of the economic policies of the participating Member States is acknowledged, but moreover also the close link between monetary and economic policy.[393] While an interventionist and protectionist general economic policy would almost inevitably result in a flanking protectionist external monetary policy, a monetary policy which relies on strong *dirigiste* instruments is in the long run not considered compatible with the principle of an open economy.[394]

Neither the TFEU nor the ESCB Statute quantify the primary monetary objective of "price stability". It is thus for the ECB itself to define what this actually amounts to in numerical terms. Put differently, the ECB enjoys both instrument-independence and goal-independence.[395] The ECB initially announced its quantitative definition of price stability as "[...] a year-on-year increase in the Harmonised Index of Consumer Prices (HICP) for the euro area of below 2%". Following concerns that, on the basis of this quantification the ECB may actually pursue a monetary policy which results in deflation, i.e. a decline in the level of prices, the ECB eventually adjusted this definition somewhat by emphasizing that it aims to maintain inflation rates below, *but close to*, 2% over the medium term.[396]

The unconventional monetary policy measures of the ECB during the European financial and sovereign debt crisis, foremost in the form of several outright asset purchase programmes from 2009 onwards, has triggered a fundamental debate on the scope and limits of monetary policy competence of the ECB.[397] Namely the economic effectiveness[398] and legal

390. The fact that the ECB brings the action against a NCB rather than a Member State underlines the independence of the NCB as part of the ESCB.
391. See *supra* section 5.1.
392. See in this context namely Art. 88 sentence 2 *Grundgesetz*, as amended by law of 21 Dec. 1992 (BGBl. I, p. 2086).
393. The same applies for the reference to the economic principles referred to in Art. 2 TFEU.
394. R. Smits, op. cit. *supra* note 81, 286, observes in this context that the requirement to observe the principle of open market economy has consequences for the policy instruments of the ECB, whereby the focus should rest on indirect instruments.
395. F. Amtenbrink, op. cit. *supra* note 28, 203 et seq.
396. See European Central Bank, *The Monetary Policy of the ECB* (European Central Bank, 2004), 50–51.
397. For an overview of the ECB's measures since 2012 see I. Alvarez et al., "The use of the Eurosystem's monetary policy instruments and operational framework since 2012", (2017) *ECB Occasional Paper Series No. 188*.
398. See e.g. L. Gambacorta, B. Hofmann and G. Peersman "The effectiveness of unconventional monetary policy at the zero lower bound: A cross-country analysis", (2012) *BIS Working Papers, No. 384*; G. Claeys and Z. Darvas, "The financial stability risk of ultra-loos monetary policy", (2015) *Bruegel Policy Contribution*; M. Demertzis and G.B. Wolff, "The effectiveness of the ECB's asset purchase programme", (2016) *Bruegel Policy Contribution*.

feasibility[399] of the programmes have been questioned. Whereas in the opinion of the ECB these measures have been necessary to ensure "the proper transmission of the ECB's interest rates to the euro area economy and the singleness of its monetary policy",[400] as well as to subsequently achieve the target inflation rate of below, but close to 2 percent,[401] critics have argued that the ECB has exceeded its monetary policy competence under primary Union law by effectively engaging in economic policy and, moreover, in acting in breach of the prohibition of monetary financing (Art. 123(1) TFEU) and the so-called no-bail-out clause (Art. 125 TFEU). While certainly not being limited thereto, the ECB's announcement of an Outright Monetary Transactions (OMT) programme in August 2012, followed in September of that year by the publication of "technical features of Outright Monetary Transactions"[402] took centre stage in this regard, as these announcements became the subject of constitutional challenges before the German Federal Constitutional Court, which – for the first time in its history – made a preliminary reference to the ECJ.[403]

In the course of the European financial and sovereign debt crisis monetary policy in the euro area has thus become subject to judicial consideration in two main areas relating to the scope of monetary and economic policy in the Union framework and its limitations in the light of the fiscal constraints foreseen in the TFEU. With regard to the former, already in *Pringle* the ECJ had to consider the scope of the exclusive monetary policy competence of the Union when deciding to what extent Member States were allowed to conclude the ESM Treaty.[404] The ECJ observed that rather than provide a clear definition, primary Union law refers to the objectives of monetary policy as stated in Articles 3(1)(c) and 127 TFEU.[405] In the view of the Court it is thus the objective(s) pursued with a measure and namely, whether and to what extent it aims at maintaining price stability, that determine(s) if the measure qualifies as monetary or economic policy. In this context, the European judges have emphasized that "an economic policy measure cannot be treated as equivalent to a monetary policy measure for the sole reason that it may have indirect effects on the stability of the euro" and thus, on price stability.[406] *A contrario sensu*, in *Gauweiler* the ECJ has observed that "a monetary policy measure cannot be treated as equiva-

---

399. From the numerous legal contributions see e.g. M. Seidel, "Der Ankauf nicht markt- und börsengängiger Staatsanleihen, namentlich Griechenlands, durch die Europäische Zentralbank und durch nationale Zentralbanken – rechtlich nur fragwürdig oder Rechtsverstoß?", (2010) EuZW, 521; C. Herrmann, "EZB-Programm für die Kapitalmärkte verstößt nicht gegen die Verträge – Erwiderung auf Martin Seidel, EuZW 2010, 521", (2010) EuZW, 645; M. Ruffert, "The European debt crisis and European Union law", (2011) CML Rev., 1777–1805; P. Athanassiou, "Of past measures and future plans for Europe's exit from the sovereign debt crisis: What is legally possible (and what is not)", (2011) EL Rev., 558–575; S. Grun and F. Grle, "The European Central Bank's public sector purchase programme (PSPP), the prohibition of monetary financing and sovereign debt restructuring scenarios", (2016) EL Rev., 781–803.

400. P. Cour-Thimann and B. Winkler, "The ECB's non-standard monetary policy measures. The role of institutional factors and financial structure", (2013) *Working Paper Series, No. 1528*, 5.

401. See ECB, "ECB announces expended asset purchase programme", Press release, 22 Jan. 2015.

402. Available at <www.ecb.europa.eu/press/pr/date/2012/html/pr120906_1.en.html>.

403. BVerfG, Order of the Second Senate of 14 Jan. 2014 – 2 BvR 2728/13 – paras. (1–24). For the background of this reference and the vast critique mainly in the German academic literature see the various contributions to the special issue "The OMT decision of the German Federal Constitutional Court", (2014) GLJ. Editorial Comment, "An unintended side-effect of Draghi's bazooka: An opportunity to establish a more balanced relationship between the ECJ and Member States' highest courts", (2014) CML Rev., 378–388; V. Borger, "Outright monetary transactions and the stability mandate of the ECB: *Gauweiler*", (2016) CML Rev., 139–196.

404. Case C-370/12, *Pringle*.

405. Ibid., para 53.

406. Ibid., para 56.

lent to an economic policy measure merely because it may have indirect effects on the stability of the euro area". Pointing out the obvious, namely that the ECB cannot exceed the powers conferred upon it by primary Union law, the Court states that "[T]he fact that a programme such as that announced in the press release might also be capable of contributing to the stability of the euro area, which is a matter of economic policy, does not turn the measure into an economic policy".[407] Approached in this way, the European judges sided with the ECB in considering that the aims of the announced outright monetary transaction could be considered as contributing to "an appropriate monetary policy transmission and the singleness of the monetary policy", mainly by being directed towards "rectifying the disruption to the monetary policy transmission mechanism caused by the specific situation of government bonds issued by certain Member States".[408] The ECJ did thus not follow the German Federal Constitutional Court's rather assertive reasoning that the announced technical features of the OMT, namely its selectivity and conditionality, would disqualify the programme as a measure that is covered by the scope of monetary policy as defined in primary Union law.[409] From a combined reading of *Pringle* and *Gauweiler* it can thus be concluded that whereas economic policy is geared towards the stability of the euro area as such, monetary policy in the euro area is geared towards the stability of the single currency, whereby indirect effects of a measure aimed at achieving the objectives of that policy on the other policy do not change its nature. If anything, it may be argued that with this approach the ECJ recognizes the interconnectedness of the two policy fields in reality and as perceived by the drafters of the provisions on EMU in primary Union law.[410] Be that as it may, as has been pointed out in section 5.2., the ECB's 2015 secondary markets public sector purchasing programme has triggered a new case before the German Federal Constitutional Court and the second-ever preliminary reference to the ECJ. The German judges once again raise the question of the compatibility of the ECB's monetary policy stands, on this occasion arguing that while the purchasing programme "officially pursues a monetary policy objective and that monetary policy instruments are used to achieve this objective", "the economic policy impacts stemming from the volume of the [purchases] and the resulting foreseeability of purchases of government bonds are integral features of the programme which are already inherent in its design". In this context the proportionality of the measure has been questioned, but it has also been argued that "the decisions on which the programme is based are lacking comprehensible reasons that would allow for an ongoing review, during the multi-year period envisaged for the implementation of these decisions, as to whether there remains a continued need for the programme".[411]

Turning to the compatibility of outright asset purchases with the prohibition of monetary financing (Art. 123(1) TFEU), in its preliminary ruling in *Gauweiler* the ECJ did not share the legal assessment of the referring German court that under the conditions announced by the ECB the purchase of government bonds on secondary markets had to be considered in contradiction to this prohibition. Pointing to the instruments at the disposal of the ECB,[412] the ECJ argued

407. Case C-62/14, *Gauweiler*, para 51–52.
408. Ibid., para 47–48, 55.
409. For these and other arguments submitted by the German court see BVerfG, Order of the Second Senate of 14 Jan. 2014 – 2 BvR 2728/13 – paras. (1–24).
410. On the point of interconnectedness see also P. Craig and M. Markakis, op. cit. *supra* note 381, 18–19. With regards to the ECJ's observations on scope and limits of discretion in monetary policy see *supra* section 6.1.3.
411. See German Federal Constitutional Court, "Proceedings on the European Central Bank's Expanded Asset Purchase Programme are Stayed: Referral to the Court of Justice of the European Union", Press release No. 70/2017 of 15 Aug. 2017 concerning Order of 18 July 2017 in Case 2 BvR 859/15, 2 BvR 980/16, 2 BvR 2006/15, 2 BvR 1651/15.
412. See further section 6.3.

that this provision "does not preclude, generally, the possibility of the ESCB purchasing from the creditors of such a State, bonds previously issued by that State", as long as this is not done in a way that effectively results in a circumvention of Article 123(1) TFEU, namely by having "an effect equivalent to that of a direct purchase of government bonds from the public authorities and bodies of the Member States".[413] In the view of the European judges this would in particular be the case if market participants are in a position to anticipate the timing and conditions of bond purchasing by the ECB, putting them de facto in the position of intermediaries for the ESCB.[414] A mere (indirect) influencing of the functioning of the primary and secondary sovereign debt markets is not considered sufficient reason to trigger the prohibition of monetary financing. Concerning the above-mentioned second preliminary reference by the German Federal Constitutional Court concerning the ECB's 2015 secondary markets public sector purchasing programme, the German judges once more raise the question whether the implementation of this programme by the ECB fulfils the conditions of Article 123(1) TFEU as interpreted by the ECJ.[415] All in all, it can be observed with Adamski that the preliminary reference by the German Federal Constitutional Court and the ruling by the ECJ highlights how "a common constitutional culture, at least in economic aspects, is still a very distant dream not only for the EU, but (more perplexingly) even for the closer circle of the euro area countries".[416]

Similar to what has been observed for the primary objective, the secondary monetary policy objective of the ECB stated in Article 127(1) TFEU, that is to support the general economic policies in the Union with a view to contribute to the achievements of the objectives of the Union, is not defined in any detail in the TFEU apart from the implicit reference to Article 3 TEU.[417] As has been observed, any obligation arising from this objective is subordinated to the objective of price stability. What is more, apart from arguably including an obligation to act, from the *Gauweiler* preliminary ruling it becomes clear that this also includes the obligation to refrain from any action that contravenes the effectiveness of the general economic policy in the Union, such as by removing incentives for Member States to pursue a sound budgetary policy in line with primary Union law.[418]

6.3 *Tasks of the ESCB and of the ECB*

Article 127 (2) TFEU in conjunction with Article 3.1. ESCB Statute lists the basic tasks that the ESCB has to carry out, including the implementation of monetary policy, the conduct of foreign-exchange operations and the holding and managing of foreign reserves, as well as the smooth operation and promotion of payment systems. Moreover, pursuant to Article 127(5) TFEU, the ESCB is given a role in "contributing to" the smooth conduct of the prudential supervision of credit institutions and the stability of the financial system. With the establishment of the Single Supervisory Mechanism based on Article 127(6) TFEU this task has been very substantially upgraded and as such is exclusively discussed in Chapter 27 of this book. Finally, the ECB fulfils advisory functions.

The monetary policy instruments available to the ECB are laid down in Article 127(2) TFEU and Articles 17–21 ESCB Statute. They cover open market operations, including main

413. Case C-62/14, *Gauweiler*, para 95–97.
414. Ibid., para 104.
415. C.A. Vassilopoulos and E. de Lhoneux, op. cit. *supra* note 150.
416. D. Adamski, "Economic constitution of the Euro area after the *Gauweiler* preliminary ruling", (2015) CML Rev., 1451–1490, 1453.
417. See *supra* section 6.1.
418. Case C-62/14, *Gauweiler*, para 109.

refinancing operations, longer-term refinancing operations, fine-tuning operations and structural operations, standing facilities, including a marginal lending facility and a deposit facility, as well as minimum reserve requirements applied to credit institutions in the euro area.[419] As far as the indirect instruments are concerned, i.e. open market operations and lending facilities, the ECB itself establishes the general guidelines which have to be observed by the ECB and the NCBs in carrying out such operations.[420] On the contrary, for direct instruments, which create direct obligations for third parties, such as minimum reserve requirements, the Council has adopted complementary legislation.[421] In *Gauweiler* the ECJ clarified that the buying and selling of government bonds, which constitute marketable instruments, is in principle covered by Article 18.1. ESCB Statute on open market and credit operations and thus, forms part of the instruments at the disposal of the ECB, albeit subject to the prohibition on monetary financing pursuant to Article 123(1) TFEU.[422]

Next to monetary policy operations, according to Article 127(2), second and third indent TFEU, the ECB conducts foreign-exchange operations that are consistent with the Council's prerogative laid down in Article 219 TFEU to conclude exchange rate agreements with third countries.[423] The reason for vesting this task with the ECB lies in the close link between external and internal monetary policy that may call for exchange rate interventions on behalf of the euro, for instance if the value of the currency of an important trading partner of the Union suddenly increases considerably, causing an increase in prices for imports, or if an overvalued euro put the euro area economies under pressure on global markets. Exchange rate operations by the ECB may be conducted through foreign reserve assets that are provided by the NCBs. According to Article 30 ESCB Statute, NCBs have to provide the ECB with foreign reserve assets up to an amount equivalent to 50,000 million euro. The individual contributions of the NCBs have been fixed in proportion to their share in the subscribed capital of the ECB.[424] Moreover, within the margins and under the conditions set by the Council, the ECB can demand additional foreign reserve assets.[425] Generally speaking, the foreign reserves consist of a number of major convertible currencies, namely US dollars, Japanese yen, Chinese renminbi, as well as gold, other foreign currency, reserve assets, and special drawing rights.[426]

419. For a more detailed account see European Central Bank, *The Implementation of the Monetary Policy in the Euro Area: General Documentation on the Eurosystem Monetary Policy Instruments and Procedures* (European Central Bank, 2006).
420. Guidelines of the European Central Bank on the implementation of the Eurosystem monetary policy framework (General Documentation Guideline) (ECB/2014/60), as amended. Guidelines of the European Central Bank on domestic asset and liability management operations by the national central banks (ECB/2014/9), as amended.
421. See e.g. Art. 19.2. ESCB Statute which refers to Art. 42 ESCB Statute for the applicable procedure. See Reg. 1745/2003 of the European Central Bank on the application of minimum reserves (ECB/2003/9), as amended.
422. Case C-62/14, *Gauweiler*, paras. 96–97.
423. Details to be found in Art. 23, 30 and 31 ESCB Statute.
424. With regard to the subscription of the ECB's capital in accordance with the procedure laid down in Art. 28.1. ESCB Statute. See Council Decision (2003/517/EC) of 15 July 2003 on the statistical data to be used for the adjustment of the key for subscription to the capital of the European Central Bank (O.J. 2003, L 181/43) and Decision of the ECB of 29 Aug. 2013 on the national central banks' percentage shares in the key for subscription to the ECB's capital (ECB/2013/28).
425. Art. 30.4. ESCB Statute.
426. For details see the ECB's template on international reserves and foreign currency liquidity available at <www.ecb.europa.eu/stats/balance_of_payments_and_external/international_reserves/templates/html/index.en.html>.

While the ECB in principle has the full right to hold and manage the foreign reserves that are transferred to it and to use them for the statutorily prescribed purposes, in practice the ECB involves the euro area NCBs in the operational management of the foreign reserve assets. NCBs can however decide to abstain from management or to pool such management with one or more other euro area NCBs.[427] Moreover, NCBs are permitted to hold and manage foreign-exchange assets (working balances) in accordance with Article 127(3) TFEU, albeit also subject to ECB Guidelines.[428] Finally, NCBs are at liberty to perform transactions in fulfilment of their obligations towards international organizations.[429]

Another task listed in Article 127(2) TFEU carried out by the ESCB is to promote the smooth operation of payment systems.[430] Interruptions in the payment systems are considered to result in frictions in trade and even serious disturbances in the financial markets with undesired effects on monetary policy.[431] The term payment system here is referred to as "the complete set of instruments, intermediaries, rules, procedures, processes and interbank funds transfer systems which facilitate the circulation of money in a country or currency area", including payment instruments (namely cash and non-cash payments), payment processing (namely clearing), and settlement.[432] From Article 22 ESCB Statute it becomes clear that the ECB and the NCBs have a facilitating role, whereby the ECB is given the competence to issue regulations to ensure efficient and sound clearing and payment systems within the Union and with third countries. The fact that the ECB has been given regulatory competence underlines the supervisory role entrusted to the ECB in this area, whereby this role also has to be seen in the broader context of EU financial services secondary law that deals with payments, clearing and settlement.[433]

The two main systems operating in the euro area are the Trans-European Automated Real-time Gross settlement Express Transfer system (TARGET), geared towards the processing of euro payments, and the corresponding central banking model (CCBM), geared towards "the cross-border transfer of collateral within the euro area in Eurosystem credit operations".[434] Initially TARGET stood for a decentralized structure linking together national real-time gross settlement (RTGS) systems and the ECB Payment Mechanism (EPM). Currently a revised version is in place (TARGET II), which is based on an integrated IT infrastructure and aims

427. See Arts. 9.2. and 12.1. ESCB Statute, according to which the ECB can manage certain of its activities through the NCBs. Art. 2 of the Guideline of the European Central Bank (ECB/2008/5) on the management of the foreign reserve assets of the European Central Bank by the national central banks and the legal documentation for operations involving such assets (recast) (ECB/2008/5), O.J. 2008, L 192/63, as amended.

428. Guideline of the European Central Bank for participating Member States' transactions with their foreign exchange working balances pursuant to Art. 31.3 of the Statute of the European System of Central Banks and of the ECB (ECB/2003/12) (O.J. 2003, L 283/81).

429. Art. 31.1. ESCB Statute.

430. Art. 127 (4) TFEU, Art. 3.1. ESCB Statute.

431. See H. Scheller, *The European Central Bank. History, Role and Function*, 2nd ed. (European Central Bank, 2006), 98 et seq.

432. European Central Bank, *The Payment System* (European Central Bank, 2010), 25.

433. E.g. Directive 2015/2366 on payment services in the internal market (O.J. 2015, L 337/35); Reg. 924/2009 on cross-border payments in the Community (O.J. 2009, L 266/11); Directive 2009/110/EC on the taking up, pursuit and prudential supervision of the business of electronic money institutions (O.J. 2009, L 267/7); Directive 98/26/EC on settlement finality in payment and securities settlement systems (O.J. 1998, L 166/45); Reg. 648/2012 on OTC derivatives, central counterparties and trade repositories (O.J. 2012, L 201/1); Reg. 909/2014 on improving securities settlement in the European Union and on central securities depositories (O.J. 2014, L 257/1).

434. European Central Bank, op. cit. *supra* note 432, 244.

at a greater harmonization of the component payments systems.[435] Together with several other payment systems not operated by the ECB, such as EURO1, that are categorized as systemically important payment systems (SIPS), TARGET II is subject to the oversight requirements for systemically important payment systems issued by the ECB itself.[436]

The final task mentioned in Article 127(2) TFEU and Article 4 ESCB Statute, is the fulfilment of its advisory role. Generally speaking, the ECB has to be consulted on any proposed Union act in its fields of competence, as well as by national authorities regarding any draft legislative provision in its fields of competence.[437] In several places spread throughout the TFEU it is determined that the ECB has to be consulted.[438] Consultation in those cases forms an integral part of the applicable Union decision-making procedure and the ECB's participation has to be considered an "essential procedural requirement".[439] The actual scope of this obligation must not be interpreted too narrowly, as it includes any measures in the field of competence of the ESCB and ECB, including among others those relating to exchange rate policy, payment systems, prudential supervision, and more generally the regulation of the EU capital market.[440] The ECB may also submit opinions to the appropriate Union institutions or bodies or to national authorities on matters in its fields of competence on its own initiative.

These formal advisory functions of the ECB have to be differentiated from the competence of the president of the ECB and the other members of the Executive Board and Governing Council of the ECB – quasi inherent to their function – to take a position on their own authority on the budgetary and economic policy of the Union. While the ECB does not hold any formal powers in this area, given the close relationship between economic policy, for which the Member States essentially remain responsible, and monetary policy, the conduct of which is entrusted to the ECB, the latter must have the right to express its views in this regard, be it in the European Parliament or in other public fora. As such the ECB keeps up the tradition that could be observed in some national central bank systems whereby central bank officials would at times be rather outspoken about the approach to economic policy chosen by government or parliament.[441]

Although listed separately, authorization for issuing banknotes within the euro area can be identified as another exclusive task of the ECB in the euro area. It is the ECB that decides on

---

435. Decision of the European Central Bank concerning the terms and conditions of TARGET2-ECB (ECB/2007/7), (O.J. 2007, L 237/71), as amended; Guidelines of the European Central Bank on a Trans-European Automated Real-time Gross Settlement Express Transfer system (TARGET2) (ECB/2012/27) (O.J. 2007, L 30/1), as amended. For more details see European Central Bank, "Blue Book. Payment and Securities Settlement Systems in the European Union", Volume I (Euro Area Countries) and Volume II (Non-Euro Area Countries) (European Central Bank, 2010), op. cit. *supra* note 434, 244 et seq. The Guideline and Decision are based on the abovementioned Art. 22 ESCB Statute.
436. Reg. 95/2014 on oversight requirements for systemically important payment systems (ECB/2014/28), O.J. 2014, L 217/16.
437. Art. 282 (5) TFEU; Council decision (98/415/EC) on the consultation of the European Central Bank by national authorities regarding draft legislative provisions (O.J. 1998, L 189/42); European Central Bank, *Guide to consultation of the European Central Bank by national authorities regarding draft legislative provisions* (European Central Bank, 2015); S.L. Lambrinoc, "The legal duty to consult the European Central Bank. National and EU consultations", (2009) *ECB Legal Working Paper Series, No. 9*.
438. See e.g. Art. 48(3) and (6) TEU; Arts. 66, 133, 134(3), 138(1), 140(3), 219, 289(4), 292, 294 TFEU.
439. Similar, R. Smits, op. cit. *supra* note 81, 212.
440. The close relationship between the proper functioning of the capital market and the efficiency of monetary policy supports the view that the consultation of the ECB in this field is mandatory.
441. Two examples of critical reflection are: J. Zijlstra, *Per Slot van Rekening* (Contact, 1992), 215–219 and 238–244; H. Tietmeyer, "Reflection on the German treaty negotiations of 1990" in S. Frowen and R. Pringle (Eds.), *Inside the Bundesbank* (Macmillan, 1998), 68–109.

the denominations and specifications of euro banknotes.[442] National central banks may issue such notes upon authorization by the ECB. Pursuant to Article 128(2) TFEU Member States in principle have the right to issue coins, albeit subject to approval by the ECB for the volume of the issue.[443] Moreover, the denominations and technical specifications of euro coins are governed by Council Regulation.[444]

6.4 *The ECB's legal instruments*

The instruments at the disposal of the ECB to fulfil its tasks are listed in Article 132(1) TFEU and Article 34.1. ESCB Statute and include regulations and decisions, as well as legally non-binding recommendations and opinions.[445] The ECB can make use of regulations only to the extent necessary to define and implement monetary policy, to calculate and determine minimum reserves requirements, for tasks related to managing sound clearing and payment systems, and in the context of any prudential supervisory tasks of credit institutions or other financial institutions that are vested in the ECB by Council Regulation.[446] The ECB can make use of decisions to the extent necessary for carrying out the tasks entrusted to the ESCB by the TFEU and the ESCB Statute. Finally, the ECB can make recommendations and deliver opinions. Unlike the former Article 110(2) EC, neither Article 132 TFEU nor Article 34.1. ESCB Statute define the various measures with regard to their legal effects. Yet it is presently argued that the legal effects of these instruments are similar to those described in Article 288 TFEU. While ECB regulations are generally applicable and binding in their entirety and directly applicable in all Member States, decisions are only binding in their entirety for those to whom they are addressed. Recommendations and opinions have no binding force. As for procedural requirements, Art. 132(2) TFEU and Art. 34.2. ESCB Statute leave it up to the discretion of the ECB to decide whether to publish its decisions, recommendations and opinions.

In addition to regulations and decisions which produce internal and external legal effect, the ECB has a number of instruments at its disposal, namely decisions, instructions, and guidelines, which are intended to address the various components of the ESCB itself.[447] While primarily producing legal effect within the system and namely *vis-à-vis* NCBs, which have to act in accordance with guidelines and instructions, they may under certain circumstances also bind the ESCB in relation to third parties.[448] Moreover, internal guidelines and instructions on the decentralized implementation of the monetary policy of the ECB can be of considerable importance to the different actors in the financial markets.

The ECB has decided to publish its acts and instruments in the Official Journal of the European Union.[449] Moreover, in principle, any EU citizen or natural or legal person residing in or

---

442. Decision of the European Central Bank on the denominations, specifications, reproduction, exchange and withdrawal of euro banknotes (ECB/2013/10) (O.J. 2013, L 118/37).
443. See e.g. Decision 2016/2164 of the European Central Bank on the approval of the volume of coin issuance in 2017 (ECB/2016/43) (O.J. 2016, L 133/73).
444. Council Reg. 729/2014 on denominations and technical specifications of euro coins intended for circulation (Recast) (O.J. 2014, L 194/1).
445. For a more detailed analysis see e.g. R. Smits, op. cit. *supra* note 81, 102–106, and C. Zilioli and M. Selmayr, op. cit. *supra* note 310, 91–131. The competences have to be differentiated from those special competences which Art. 41 ESCB Statute vests in the Union legislature for the subject matter identified in that provision.
446. Art. 132 TFEU.
447. Art. 12.1. and 14.3. ESCB Statute.
448. See C. Zilioli and M. Selmayr, op. cit. *supra* note 310, 108–111.
449. Decision of the ECB on the publication of certain legal acts and instruments of the European Central Bank (ECB/2000/12) (O.J. 2001, L 55/68).

having its registered office in a Member State has a right of access to ECB documents,[450] albeit subject to conditions and limitations.[451] Access can namely be refused if this would undermine the protection of public (or private) interests, *inter alia* as regards the confidentiality of the proceedings of the ECB's decision-making bodies or the financial, monetary, or economic policy of the Union or the Member States.[452] The ECB enjoys wide discretion in this regard.[453]

Further reading

Adalid, S., *La Banque centrale européenne et l'Eurosystème* (Bruylant, 2015).

Adams, M., F. Fabbrini and P. Larouche (Eds.), *The Constitutionalization of European Budgetary Constraints* (Hart Publishing, 2014).

Adamski, D., "Economic constitution of the Euro area after the *Gauweiler* preliminary ruling", (2015) CML Rev., 1451–1490.

Armstrong, K. A., "The new governance of EU fiscal discipline", (2013) EL Rev., 601–616.

Borger, V., "Outright monetary transactions and the stability mandate of the ECB: *Gauweiler*", (2016) CML Rev., 139–196.

Craig, P., "The stability, coordination and governance treaty: Principle, politics and pragmatism", (2012) EL Rev., 231–248.

Craig P. and M. Markakis, "Gauweiler and the legality of outright monetary transactions", (2016) EL Rev., 4–24.

Hinarejos, A., *The Euro Area Crisis in Constitutional Perspective* (OUP, 2015).

Howarth D. and P. Loedel, *The European Central Bank. The New European Leviathan?* (Palgrave Macmillan, 2005).

Müller-Graff, P.-C. (Ed.), *Europäisches Wirtschaftsordnungsrecht* (Nomos, 2015).

Poulou, A., "Financial assistance conditionality and human rights protection: What is the role of the EU Charter of Fundamental Rights?", (2017) CML Rev., 991–1025.

Repasi, R., "Judicial protection against austerity measures in the euro area: *Ledra* and *Mallis*", (2017) CML Rev., 1123–1156.

Siekmann, H. (Ed.), *EWU. Kommentar zur Europäischen Währungsunion* (Mohr Siebeck, 2013).

Smits, R., *The European Central Bank: Institutional Aspects* (Kluwer, 1997).

Tuori K. and K. Tuori, *The Eurozone Crisis* (CUP, 2014).

Zilioli C. and M. Selmayr, *The Law of the European Central Bank* (OUP, 2001).

---

450. As to the notion of "documents" see Case T-436/09, *Dufour*, para 54 et seq.

451. Decision of the ECB on public access to European Central Bank documents (ECB/2004/3) (O.J. 2004, L 80/42), as amended. Generally, on the ECB's access to document regime see D. Curtin, "Accountable independence of the European Central Bank: Seeing the logics", (2017) ELJ, 28–44.

452. Ibid., Art. 4.

453. See Case T-590/10, *Thesinger*, para 43 et seq. Upheld on appeal in Case C-28/13 P, *Thesinger*.

CHAPTER 27

FINANCIAL MARKET REGULATION AND SUPERVISION

*Matthias Haentjens, Jouke Tegelaar and Dorine Verheij**

1. Introduction

The basis of the EU legal framework regarding the financial markets is formed by the Treaty objective of constructing an internal market (Art. 3(3) TEU) and the fundamental freedoms, free movement of capital and services (Art. 26(2) TFEU).[1] This internal market objective and these freedoms have resulted in a legal framework that is thoroughly harmonized and sometimes even unified. But it has not been the consequence of a gradual process; perhaps no other area of law has witnessed such huge changes, as the area of financial markets.

This chapter deals with the European legal framework regarding financial markets.[2] It is a vast topic on which, moreover, numerous separate volumes have been written. In the context of this book, it seemed rational to concentrate on the institutional set-up in which European rules regarding the financial markets are created, applied and enforced, rather than on their substantive content. Also, we have chosen to focus on the application of European law at the European level, rather than at the national level. Consequently, we have divided this chapter into sections on regulation (section 3), supervision and enforcement (section 4), and legal protection (section 5). These sections are preceded by section 2, which provides an introduction to the institutional set-up of the European rules regarding the financial markets and explains it from a historic perspective.

2. Institutional structure and its development[3]

2.1 *Lamfalussy Report: 2001*

European financial market regulation is created in accordance with the so-called "Lamfalussy process", which resulted from the Lamfalussy Report.[4] This report was drafted by Baron

---

* Professor and PhD candidates, respectively, at the Hazelhoff Centre for Financial Law of Leiden University.

1. See, e.g., N. Moloney, *EU Securities and Financial Markets Regulation*, 3rd ed. (OUP, 2014), at 9; Ch. 12, "The functioning of the internal market" and Ch. 14, "Free movement of services, establishment and capital", of this book.

2. The pace and depth of the developments discussed in this chapter make it important to note that our research closed on 9 Apr. 2018. We have not been able to take into account any draft legislation published after that date. Moreover, given the large amount of (delegated) regulation in the field of law discussed in this chapter, relevant pieces have been taken into account, but in order to keep this chapter within manageable proportions not all drafts of regulations yet to be enacted could be included.

3. Part of this section has been based on M. Haentjens and P. de Gioia-Carabellese, *European Banking and Financial Law* (Routledge, 2015), 4–14.

4. Lamfalussy Report, Final Report of the Committee of the Wise Men in the Regulation of European Securities Markets, 15 Feb. 2001 <ec.europa.eu/internal_market/securities/docs/lamfalussy/wisemen/

Alexandre Lamfalussy and the group he chaired in 2000–2001. This group was appointed by the European Council and was entrusted with assessing the efficiency of the legislative progress in the financial sector. They concluded that the current legislative process was too slow and rigid to accomplish the European Commission's Financial Services Action Plan (FSAP)[5] in time. This plan aimed at stimulating European financial integration by means of, *inter alia*, harmonization of financial regulation. Consequently, the Lamfalussy Report details a set of recommended guidelines conducive to a more efficient lawmaking process in the Union. The EU legislature has embraced the recommended process, which is therefore now commonly referred to as the Lamfalussy process.

The Lamfalussy process discerns the following four levels of regulation:

- *Level 1:* The adoption of framework Directives or Regulations by the EU, in accordance with the co-decision procedure, currently: the ordinary legislative procedure.[6] This level expresses the more fundamental policy choices on the topic in question. The Level 1 instrument Markets in Financial Instruments Directive II ("MiFID II"),[7] for example, gives the following general rule: "An investment firm shall, when holding funds belonging to clients, make adequate arrangements to safeguard the rights of clients and, except in the case of credit institutions, prevent the use of client funds for its own account".[8]
- *Level 2:* The implementation of additional legislation at EU level, so-called Delegated and Implementing Directives/Regulations, the purpose of which is to fill in the details of the framework Directives and Regulations. Under Articles 290(1) and 291(2) TFEU, the European Commission can adopt "delegated acts" of general application to supplement or amend certain non-essential elements of legislative acts and "implementing acts" where uniform conditions for implementing legally binding Union acts are needed. Two types of delegated and implementing acts can be distinguished: delegated and implementing acts made by the European Commission, and delegated and implementing acts made by the European Commission in cooperation with the European Supervisory Authorities (ESAs).[9] With regard to the latter category, so-called regulatory technical standards and implementing technical standards (RTSs and ITSs, respectively) are proposed by one of the ESAs and submitted to the European Commission for endorsement.[10]

---

final-report-wise-men_en.pdf>.

5. Communication of the Commission, Financial Services: Implementing the Framework for Financial Markets: Action Plan, COM(1999)232 final.
6. Art. 289 TFEU.
7. Directive 2014/65/EU of the European Parliament and of the Council of 15 May 2014 on markets in financial instruments and amending Directive 2002/92/EC and Directive 2011/61/EU, O.J. 2014, L 173 ("MiFID II").
8. Art. 16(9) MiFID II.
9. See, with regard to delegated acts, E. Wymeersch, "The European Financial Supervisory Authorities or ESAs" in E. Wymeersch, K.J. Hopt and G. Ferrarini (Eds.), *Financial Regulation and Supervision. A Post-Crisis Analysis* (OUP, 2012), 250. Wymeersch calls them "Commission-only acts" and "ESA plus Commission acts".
10. See Arts. 10 and 15 ESA Reg. (Reg. (EU) 1093/2010 of the European Parliament and of the Council of 24 Nov. 2010 establishing a European Supervisory Authority (European Banking Authority), amending Decision 716/2009/EC and repealing Commission Decision 2009/78/EC, O.J. 2010, L 331; Reg. (EU) 1095/2010 of the European Parliament and of the Council of 24 Nov. 2010 establishing a European Supervisory Authority (European Securities and Markets Authority), amending Decision 716/2009/EC and repealing Commission Decision 2009/77/EC, O.J. 2010, L 331; and Reg. (EU) 1094/2010 of the European Parliament and of the Council of 24 Nov. 2010 establishing a European Supervisory Authority (European Insurance

Building on the above example of MiFID II and the general rule given therein, this rule has been further specified/substantiated in the accompanying Level 2 instrument, the MiFID II Delegated Directive 2017/593,[11] stating: "1. Member States shall require that investment firms comply with the following requirements: (a) they must keep records and accounts enabling them at any time and without delay to distinguish assets held for one client from assets held for any other client and from their own assets; [...]."

- *Level 3:* A focus on cooperation among national supervisors, so as to accomplish "[e]nhanced cooperation and networking among EU securities regulators to ensure consistent and equivalent transposition of Level 1 and 2 legislation".[12] This supervisory convergence is to be achieved by "soft law" instruments made by the ESAs, such as recommendations and guidelines,[13] Q&A's, interpretations, opinions, positions, supervisory briefings and reports.[14]

  Recommendations and guidelines address market participants and supervisors and are issued to ensure consistent and uniform implementation and cooperation between the Member States.[15] Formally, they are not legally binding, but if the addressed parties are not willing to comply, they have to explain their reasons ("comply or explain" mechanism).[16] Thus, they often function as hard law in practice. Again building on the above example of the MiFID, ESMA had published guidelines and recommendations on MiFID's suitability requirements under Article 19 of MiFID II's predecessor, MiFID, in 2012,[17] but many other examples could be referred to.

  Q&A's are specifically meant to ensure "consistent and effective application" of European financial market regulation.[18] They answer questions of the general public and the competent authorities on the practical application of European financial market regulation. Although Q&A's are not legally binding and the "comply or explain" mechanism does not apply, they can have significant relevance in practice. An example of a Q&A with great significance in practice is the Q&A on the Prospectus Directive.[19]
- *Level 4:* A more effective enforcement of the EU legislation by the Commission by checking Member States' compliance with Union law and by launching infringement procedures against a Member State which is suspected of a breach.

---

and Occupational Pensions Authority), amending Decision 716/2009/EC and repealing Commission Decision 2009/79/EC, O.J. 2010, L 331).

11. Art. 2 of Commission Delegated Directive (EU) 2017/593 of 7 April 2016 supplementing Dir. 2014/65/EU of the European Parliament and of the Council with regard to safeguarding of financial instruments and funds belonging to clients, product governance obligations and the rules applicable to the provision or reception of fees, commissions or any monetary or non-monetary benefits, C/2016/2031, O.J. 2017, L 87.
12. Lamfalussy Report, cited *supra* note 4, 19.
13. Art. 8(2)(c) and (d) ESA Reg.
14. E. Wymeersch, op. cit. *supra* note 9, 249.
15. <ec.europa.eu/finance/insurance/solvency/solvency2/index_en.htm>.
16. Art. 16(3) ESA Reg.
17. *Final report. Guidelines on certain aspects of the MiFID suitability requirements*, ESMA/2012/387. On 13 July 2017, ESMA published a consultation paper with a draft new version of these Guidelines, which are to be updated in conformity with MiFID II. A "Final report" was expected in Q1/Q2 2018.
18. See <www.eba.europa.eu/single-rule-book-qa>.
19. ESMA/2016/1674.

2.2 *De Larosière Report: 2009*

In October 2008, Jacques de Larosière de Champfeu was entrusted to draft a report with practical proposals in the area of financial regulation and supervision. The report was commissioned against the backdrop of the euro area crisis and the sovereign debt crisis in 2009.[20] The De Larosière Report essentially emphasized three steps to guard against a future collapse: (a) a new regulatory agenda; (b) stronger coordinated supervision; and (c) effective crisis management procedures.

The De Larosière Report emphasized that the regulatory framework in place prior to the crisis lacked "cohesiveness". As the EU Member States were afforded a significant degree of leeway over the extent to which they could implement and enforce the Directives, such "options [led] to a wide diversity of national transpositions related to local traditions, legislations and practices".[21] The reason for this lack of harmonization was the vagueness that characterized the first level of legislation where the national legislator had a multitude of options at his disposal. As a result, at Level 3 in the Lamfalussy structure, it was very difficult, if not impossible, to "impose a single solution", i.e. a sufficiently harmonized regime.[22]

First and most significantly, the report has resulted in the creation of a European System of Financial Supervision (ESFS). The ESFS consists of three European Supervisory Authorities: the European Banking Authority having its seat in London (but to be relocated to Paris) (EBA), the European Securities Markets Authority having its seat in Paris (ESMA) and the European Insurance and Occupational Pensions Authority seated in Frankfurt (EIOPA).[23] The relevant national supervisors participate in these authorities and, unlike their predecessors, the ESAs are empowered to issue binding Regulatory Technical Standards and Implementing Technical Standards in addition to non-binding guidelines and recommendations. Also, for specific instances, ESAs have been granted direct supervisory powers. ESMA, for instance, has been made exclusively responsible for the direct oversight of credit rating agencies and trade repositories.[24] As another example, on 27 March 2018, ESMA has partly prohibited the provision of contracts for differences and binary options to retail investors.[25] Also, a European Systemic Risk Board (ESRB) forms part of the ESFS, which is "responsible for the macro-prudential oversight of the financial system within the Union in order to contribute to the prevention or mitigation of systemic risks to financial stability in the Union that arise from developments within the financial system and taking into account macroeconomic developments, so as to avoid periods of widespread financial distress".[26]

Many areas of financial law underwent significant change so as to limit the level of discretion in the hands of each Member State. For instance, the deposit guarantee scheme which was previously based on a minimum harmonization Directive[27] and which thus left relative discretion

---

20. De Larosière Report, The High-Level Group on Financial Supervision in the EU, 25 Feb. 2009 <ec.europa.eu/info/system/files/de_larosiere_report_en.pdf>.
21. See De Larosière Report, cited *supra* note 20, 27.
22. Ibid.
23. See, respectively, Reg. (EU) 1093/2010, Reg. (EU) 1095/2010 and Reg. (EU) 1094/2010.
24. See also *infra*, section 4.2.1.
25. See <www.esma.europa.eu/press-news/esma-news/esma-agrees-prohibit-binary-options-and-restrict-cfds-protect-retail-investors> and *infra*, section 4.2.1.
26. Art. 3(1) Reg. (EU) 1092/2010 of the European Parliament and of the Council of 24 Nov. 2010 on European Union macro-prudential oversight of the financial system and establishing a European Systemic Risk Board, O.J. 2010, L 331.
27. Dir. 94/19/EC of the European Parliament and of the Council of 30 May 1994 on deposit-guarantee schemes, O.J. 1994, L 135.

to each Member State on the level of protection afforded to the depositor, has been replaced by a maximum harmonization Directive[28] where this discretion is significantly curtailed, if not entirely removed. In other cases, such as the Market Abuse Regulation replacing the Market Abuse Directive,[29] Directives have been or will be replaced by Regulations, so as to accomplish unification. Also, where no harmonization instrument was to be found,[30] a legislative framework is being, or has recently been, drafted and shall be announced to be published in the future. For an instrument that has recently been enacted for which there was no statutory predecessor, reference can, for instance, be made to the Regulation on Central Securities Depositories.[31]

2.3 *Banking Union, single supervision and crisis management: 2014–present*

2.3.1 *Banking Union*

As a consequence of the financial crisis, the European legislature considered that coordination between supervisors be vital but that there was no sufficient coordination yet. Especially in the context of a single currency, there was also a need for centralized decision-making.[32] In 2012 the European Commission concluded that the interdependency between the euro area Member States requires another approach to prudential banking supervision. Mere coordination between national supervisors through the ESAs would not suffice to effectively monitor and strengthen financial stability in the euro area.[33] In addition, merely harmonizing banking regulation would not reduce the presence of regulatory arbitrage and the risks associated with it. The European Banking Union has been designed as the solution to these issues.

More specifically, since so-called Super Tuesday 15 April 2014, a dramatic step was taken in the institutional landscape of the EU. On that date, measures were adopted that have created what is commonly referred to as the Banking Union. These measures specifically concern the euro area, but some apply to the Union as a whole. In general, the Banking Union, as initially envisaged by the European Commission, would consist of three pillars: (i) the Single Supervisory Mechanism (SSM); (ii) the Bank Recovery and Resolution framework and Single Resolution Mechanism (SRM); and (iii) the EU Deposit Guarantee Scheme (which is not in place yet).

2.3.2 *Single supervision*

Despite the tumultuous evolution of the financial sector over the past 30 years, prior to the recent financial crisis a truly European integration of supervisors had remained conspicuous by its absence. Therefore, until relatively recently, a paradox of sorts prevailed within the EU where, on the one hand, a fully integrated market of credit institutions reaped the benefits of a single market which afforded them the tools to expand and operate at a greater pace across the EU, while, on the other hand, the fragmented subsistence of a body of supervisors as numerous

---

28. Dir. 2009/14/EC of the European Parliament and of the Council of 11 Mar. 2009 amending Dir. 94/19/EC on deposit-guarantee schemes as regards the overage level and the payout delay, O.J. 2009, L 68.
29. Reg. (EU) 596/2014 of the European Parliament and of the Council of 16 Apr. 2014 on market abuse (market abuse regulation) and repealing Dir. 2003/6/EC of the European Parliament and of the Council and Commission Dir. 2003/124/EC, 2003/125/EC and 2004/72/EC, O.J. 2014, L 173.
30. For instance, a guarantee scheme in the insurance industry.
31. Reg. (EU) 909/2014 of the European Parliament and of the Council of 23 July 2014 on improving securities settlement in the European Union and on central securities depositories and amending Dir. 98/26/EC and 2014/65/EU and Reg. (EU) 236/2012, O.J. 2014, L 257.
32. Communication from the European Commission to the European Parliament and the Council, A roadmap towards a Banking Union, COM(2012)510 final, 3.
33. Communication from the European Commission to the European Parliament and the Council, A Roadmap towards a Banking Union, COM(2012)510 final, 3.

as the various countries constituting the EU was evident. This asymmetry, in hindsight may have been a contributory factor in the collapse of several major financial institutions in the late 2000s, too vast and pan-European to be supervised by the assemblage of authorities existing in each respective country. This flaw in the architecture of the EU banking system has recently been revisited by the creation of the SSM, the first pillar of the Banking Union.[34] The SSM has three main objectives: to ensure the safety and soundness of the European banking system, to increase financial integration and stability and to ensure consistent supervision.[35]

This first pillar is based on the Single Supervisory Mechanism Regulation (SSM Regulation),[36] transferring the prudential supervision of credit institutions within the euro area to the European Central Bank (ECB).[37] The ECB is responsible for the functioning of the SSM as a whole, although the direct supervision of credit institutions is divided between the ECB and the national competent authorities (NCAs) of participating Member States.[38] The ECB is the main supervisor of the so-called "significant credit institutions"[39] incorporated in the participating Member States, i.e. all EU Member States that use the euro as their currency and all other states that wish to accede to the SSM.[40] The NCAs are responsible for the direct supervision of the "less significant credit institutions".[41]

2.3.3 *Crisis management*

As the disorderly failure of the Fortis group has shown, cooperation between the relevant national authorities is critical when a cross-border operating bank fails.[42] Yet it is also fraught with conflicts, as the same authorities are expected to protect different (national) interests. The Banking Union's second pillar therefore brings about, for the Member States that use the euro as their currency and any other country that wishes to accede, the Single Resolution Mechanism (SRM).

The SRM is built on a Regulation and an intergovernmental agreement.[43] The Regulation has the same scope as the SSM Regulation, in that it also applies to credit institutions of the euro area, and it is characterized by the same distinction between "significant" and "less significant"

34. By virtue of Council Reg. (EU) 1024/2013 of 15 Oct. 2013 conferring specific tasks on the European Central Bank concerning policies relating to the prudential supervision of credit institutions, O.J. 2013, L 287.
35. European Central bank, Guide to Banking Supervision, available at <www.bankingsupervision.europa.eu/press/publications/html/index.en.html>, at 5; Art. 1 SSM Reg.
36. Council Reg. (EU) 1024/2013 of 15 Oct. 2013 conferring specific tasks on the European Central Bank concerning policies relating to the prudential supervision of credit institutions, O.J. 2013, L 287. The Regulation entered into force on 3 Nov. 2013.
37. On the ECB and its monetary function, see Ch. 26, "Economic and Monetary Union", of this book.
38. Depending on the way in which financial supervision is structured in a given Member State, the "competent authority", i.e. the authority responsible for prudential supervision of credit institutions in a Member State, can, for instance, be a central bank.
39. On the definition of "significant", see also more extensively *infra,* section 4.3.1.
40. E. Ligere, "Quo vadis, Europe?", (2015) JIBLR 30, 407–411.
41. See on the definition of "less significant", more extensively *infra,* section 4.3.1. European Central bank, Guide to Banking Supervision, available at <www.bankingsupervision.europa.eu/press/publications/html/index.en.html>, at 11.
42. See The Basel Committee on Banking Supervision, Report and Recommendations of the Cross-border Bank Resolution, June 2010, 10 et seq.
43. Reg. (EU) 806/2014 of the European Parliament and of the Council of 15 July 2014 establishing uniform rules and a uniform procedure for the resolution of credit institutions and certain investment firms in the framework of a Single Resolution Mechanism and a Single Resolution Fund and amending Reg. (EU) 1093/2010, O.J. 2014, L 225; Agreement on the transfer and mutualization of contributions to the Single Resolution Fund of 14 May 2014 (8457/14).

banks. Substantively it forms the SSM's corollary, for it was argued that credible single supervision of banks would require common crisis management of the same.[44] The intergovernmental agreement was a political emergency solution: certain Member States argued that there was no basis in the Treaties for an EU instrument to accomplish a Single Resolution Fund (SRF) as it is now established on the basis of the agreement. Consequently, the instrument of intergovernmental agreement was resorted to.[45]

As a result, credit institutions in Member States participating in the SSM and the SRM have become subject to unified and centralized supervision and resolution and enjoy a financial backstop arrangement at a European level in the form of the SRF, while credit institutions in Member States outside the SSM and the SRM are subject to national – albeit harmonized – arrangements for supervision and resolution under the Bank Recovery and Resolution Directive (BRRD).[46]

Within the SRM, the SRM Regulation[47] and the BRRD are applied by a new European resolution authority, viz. the Single Resolution Board (SRB). Thus, this SRB has become responsible for the resolution of cross-border and significant banks in the euro area. Together, the SRM and BRRD aim to prevent or minimize the negative effects of a disorderly liquidation of credit institutions. More generally, it was hoped that with the harmonized and modernized bank insolvency regime established by means of the BRRD and SRM, the financial support as was previously provided by Member State governments to failing banks could be avoided in the future. Thus, the so-called "doom-loop" or "vicious circle" between banks and sovereign debt was hoped to have been broken.[48]

2.4 *Future developments*

As the Banking Union's third pillar, the European Commission originally envisaged to create a common deposit guarantee scheme (DGS).[49] This common DGS would provide the euro area with a single backstop that would uniformly, and on the basis of the combined euro area Member States' finances, guarantee all depositors' claims on a bank to a certain amount in circumstances where his deposits are not available for retrieval. However, this common DGS proved to be politically too ambitious at the time so that the most recent legislative framework in this area

44. See, e.g., Y. Mersch, "Europe's ills cannot be healed only by monetary innovation", *Financial Times*, 25 Apr. 2013.
45. See, more extensively, e.g. G.S. Zavvos and S. Kaltsouni, "The single resolution mechanism in the European Banking Union: Legal foundation, governance structure and financing" in M. Haentjens and B. Wessels (Eds.), *Research Handbook on Crisis Management in the Banking Sector* (Edward Elgar, 2015), 141 et seq.
46. Dir. 2014/59/EU of the European Parliament and of the Council of 15 May 2014 establishing a framework for the recovery and resolution of credit institutions and investment firms and amending Council Dir. 82/891/EEC, and Dir. 2001/24/EC, 2002/47/EC, 2004/25/EC, 2005/56/EC, 2007/36/EC, 2011/35/EU, 2012/30/EU and 2013/36/EU, and Regs. (EU) 1093/2010 and (EU) 648/2012, of the European Parliament and of the Council, O.J. 2014, L 173.
47. The SRM Reg. applies as of 1 Jan. 2016. Some provisions, including certain provisions related to the powers of the Single Resolution Board to collect information and to cooperate with the national authorities, have applied since 1 Jan. 2015; Art. 88 SRM Reg.
48. See, e.g., M. Haentjens and P. de Gioia Carabellese, op. cit. *supra* note 3, 94; E. Wymeersch, "The Single Supervisory Mechanism or 'SSM', Part One of the Banking Union", (2014) *Financial Law Institute Working Paper Series*. For more information about the "vicious circle", see Memo European Commission, "Banking union: restoring financial stability in the Eurozone", 9 Mar. 2015.
49. Proposal for a Regulation of the European Parliament and of the Council amending Reg. 806/2014 in order to establish a European Deposit Insurance Scheme, COM(2015)586 final.

is the recast Deposit Guarantee Scheme Directive of 16 April 2014 (DGS Directive),[50] which now mainly further harmonizes the payout time and the way national Member States' DGSs are funded. Yet the original plan does not seem to have been definitively shelved and a renewed proposal for a common DGS has been published under the name of the European Deposit Insurance Scheme.[51]

Regarding current and future developments, mention must be made of the latest Commission Action Plan for the establishment of a "Capital Markets Union". More specifically, in September 2015, the Commission adopted an Action Plan "setting out a list of over 30 actions and related measures to establish the building blocks of an integrated capital market in the EU by 2019".[52] Where the Banking Union project focused on (strengthening) the EU's banking sector, the measures under this Action Plan mainly address the capital markets.

The institutional structure of European financial regulation and supervision has been one of increasing integration, and in that development, various milestones can be discerned. But these steps have – at least until now – never proven to be fully adequate to keep pace with the integration at a practical level. Where the Lamfalussy process, for instance, introduced the possibility to sidestep "cumbersome" parliamentary involvement, the set-up that followed from the De Larosière report resulted in the possibility to minimize "cumbersome" EU Commission involvement by means of RTSs and ITSs. In parallel, the European legislator introduced ever more statutory instruments in areas that were left unregulated before, while areas in which Directives of minimum harmonization existed, these were replaced by maximum harmonization Directives and Regulations replaced Directives. This has not been changed since the financial crisis.[53] As a great unknown, it remains to be seen what the consequences will be of the UK leaving the EU for the pace of the future integration of the EU's financial regulation

3. Regulation

3.1 Introduction

A discussion of the existing body of European financial market regulation can be organized in various ways. This section employs the European sectoral approach. This is the traditional way to organize financial markets regulation and supervision, and accords with the structure of the ESFS. The ESFS consists of EBA, ESMA and EIOPA, which all regulate different parts of the financial sector: banks (section 3.2.), securities and markets (section 3.3.) and insurers and pension funds (section 3.4.), respectively.

A discussion of European financial market regulation could, however, also have been structured in other ways. Moreover, the current financial markets, products and institutions cannot always be classified in a strict sectoral way.[54] Investment insurance products and bank insurer

---

50. Dir. 2014/49/EU of the European Parliament and of the Council of 16 Apr. 2014 on Deposit Guarantee Schemes (recast), O.J. 2014, L 173.
51. See the Proposal for a Reg. of the European Parliament and of the Council amending Reg. (EU) 806/2014 in order to establish a European Deposit Insurance Scheme, COM(2015)586 final – 2015/0270 (COD). This proposal is yet to be enacted; and on 11 Oct. 2017 the Commission published a Communication on completing the Banking Union in which it proposed options to facilitate progress on the dossier. See also <www.europarl.europa.eu/legislative-train/theme-deeper-and-fairer-economic-and-monetary-union/file-european-deposit-insurance-scheme-(edis)>.
52. See <ec.europa.eu/info/business-economy-euro/growth-and-investment/capital-markets-union/capital-markets-union-action-plan_en>.
53. Cf. N. Moloney, op. cit. *supra* note 1, 9.
54. See also V. Colaert, "European banking, securities, and insurance law: Cutting through sectoral lines?" (2015) CML Rev., 1579–1616.

groups, for example, could be classified as falling under the remit of both ESMA and EIOPA, and of both EBA and EIOPA, respectively. Therefore, in respect of financial regulation and supervision, not only a sectoral but also a functional approach can be used. In this functional approach, financial regulation is classified by determining whether the rules at stake establish prudential or conduct requirements.[55] Prudential rules include, *inter alia*, capital requirements for financial institutions in order to make the financial system resilient to shocks, and to enhance financial stability both on micro and macro, i.e. systemic, level.[56] Conduct rules regulate the "behaviour" of financial institutions. They aim to create orderly and transparent markets, to enhance integrity between market participants and to enhance consumer and investor protection.[57]

Since the body of European financial market regulation is enormous, this section 3 can only concentrate on the most important (framework) Regulations and Directives. Where relevant, a reference to Level 2 or Level 3 acts will be made.[58]

3.2 *Banks*

In the aftermath of the financial crisis the need for a deeper integration of the regulation and supervision of the banking system at the European level became clear. To that end, the European Commission took legislative initiatives "to create a safer and sounder financial sector".[59] More than ten years after the beginning of the financial crisis, these initiatives have resulted in a Single Rulebook for all Member States which forms the basis of the European Banking Union. In short, the Commission's initiatives focused on the prevention of bank crises, the improvement of depositors' protection, and the proper management of bank failures.[60] The legislative instruments relating to these three topics will be discussed hereafter in more detail.

First, the prudential requirements for the banking sector have been increased under the legal framework of the Capital Requirements Regulation (CRR)[61] and the ancillary Capital Requirements Directive IV (CRD IV),[62] together often referred to as "CRD IV".[63] The CRD

---

55. Another manner – and also a functional approach – to categorize financial regulation would be to distinguish between the two main categories of addressees of the instruments, i.e. whether public institutions or private parties should enforce the rules.
56. Notable examples of European directives and regulations that codify prudential rules, i.e. capital and liquidity requirements, are: CRR and CRD IV; Solvency II; and the IORP Directive.
57. Notable examples are: MiFID II, MiFIR, the Prospectus Directive, the Regulation on key information documents for packaged retail and insurance-based investment products (PRIIPs), EMIR, CSDR, the UCITS V Directive, the AIFMD and the CRA Regulation.
58. On Level 2 and 3, and on the Lamfalussy process, see *supra* section 2.1.
59. European Commission, "Updated version of first memo published on 15/04/2014 – Banking Union: restoring financial stability in the Eurozone", 24 Nov. 2015.
60. Cf. European Commission, "Updated version of first memo published on 15/04/2014 – Banking Union: restoring financial stability in the Eurozone", 24 Nov. 2015.
61. Reg. (EU) 575/2013 of the European Parliament and of the Council of 26 June 2013 on prudential requirements for credit institutions and investment firms and amending Reg. (EU) 648/2012, O.J. 2013, L 176.
62. Dir. 2013/36/EU of the European Parliament and of the Council of 26 June 2013 on access to the activity of credit institutions and the prudential supervision of credit institutions and investment firms, amending Dir. 2002/87/EC and repealing Dir. 2006/48/EC and 2006/49/EC, O.J. 2013, L 176.
63. The CRD IV framework calls for the adoption of delegated and implementing acts. Over the years, various Level 2 acts have been established. Also, EBA proposed many RTSs and ITSs – an overview of which can be found on <ec.europa.eu/internal_market/bank/docs/regcapital/acts/overview-crr-crdiv-rts_en.pdf> and <ec.europa.eu/internal_market/bank/docs/regcapital/acts/overview-crr-crdiv-its_en.pdf>. The delegated and implementing acts cover a wide range of topics, such as supervisory disclosures, passporting notifications, disclosure template of leverage ratios, and the authorization of credit institutions.

IV package forms "the legal framework governing the access to banking activities, the supervisory framework and the prudential rules" for credit institutions and investment firms.[64] Under Articles 8(1) and 9(1) CRD IV, banking is considered a reserved business on the ground that the typical banking activities such as money-lending and ancillary services are not available to anyone, "but rather exclusively to those who/which [...] are permitted to commence such a business by means of a license or authorization".[65] If such licence/authorization has been given in one Member State, the bank is allowed to conduct its business in all other Member States without further limitations ("passporting") as long as the relevant authorities in other Member States have been notified.[66]

Also, CRD IV implements capital and liquidity requirements that were established in Basel III.[67] Capital and liquidity requirements aim to avoid that, in times of financial instability, a bank ends up in a solvency or a liquidity crisis. Capital requirements specify the minimum amount of capital (for example, equity and subordinated loans) that banks have to hold against their risk-weighted assets.[68] The riskier the asset, the more capital the bank is required to hold against it.[69] If a bank suffers losses "on the asset side of its balance sheet", the capital can "absorb" them.[70] Examples of capital requirements are the standard total capital ratio of 8% of risk weighted assets, the capital conservation buffer and the capital surcharge for globally systemically important banks.[71] Liquidity requirements aim to protect a bank against sudden liquidity demands of depositors and other creditors of the bank. To that end, banks are, for instance, obliged to hold certain amounts of high-quality liquid assets which can be sold quickly if the bank suddenly needs cash to meet liquidity demands.[72]

Second, the legislative initiatives of the European Commission aimed to improve the protection of depositors. To that end, in 2014, Directive 94/19/EC on Deposit Guarantee Schemes was amended.[73] When a bank has failed, deposit guarantee schemes guarantee the (partial)

---

64. Recital 5 CRR. See also N. Moloney, op. cit. *supra* note 1, 381 et seq. On CRD IV, see extensively, R. Theissen, *EU Banking Supervision* (Eleven Publisher, 2013).
65. M. Haentjens and P. de Gioia Carabellese, op. cit. *supra* note 3, 11.
66. Cf. M. Haentjens and P. de Gioia Carabellese, op. cit. *supra* note 3, 8–10. The regime of passporting has already been introduced in the Second Banking Dir., Art. 18 of the Second Council Dir. 89/646/EEC of 15 Dec. 1989 on the coordination of laws, regulations and administrative provisions relating to the taking up and pursuit of the business of credit institutions and amending Dir. 77/780/EEC, O.J. 1989, L 386. See also on "passporting" more in general: N. Moloney, op. cit. *supra* note 1, 396 et seq.
67. See European Commission, "Updated version of first memo published on 15/04/2014 – Banking Union: Restoring financial stability in the Eurozone", 24 Nov. 2015. Basel III is one of the Basel Accords produced by the Basel Committee on Banking Supervision in Dec. 2010. The Basel Committee sets global standards for the prudential regulation of banks in the Basel Accords. The standards are not legally binding, but nevertheless have a large influence on many legal systems worldwide.
68. E.g., commercial loans provided by the bank. In Dec. 2017, the Basel Committee on Banking Supervision published standards on the calculation of risk-weighted assets, see in detail <www.bis.org/bcbs/publ/d424_hlsummary.pdf>.
69. M. Haentjens and P. de Gioia Carabellese, op. cit. *supra* note 3, 103.
70. Cf. recital 72 CRR. Cf. also J. Armour, D. Awrey, P. Davies et al., *Principles of Financial Regulation* (OUP, 2016), 296 and M. Haentjens and P. de Gioia Carabellese, op. cit. *supra* note 3, 103.
71. See further, M. Haentjens and P. de Gioia Carabellese, op. cit. *supra* note 3, 104 et seq., and J. Armour, D. Awrey, P. Davies et al., op. cit. *supra* note 70, 290 et seq.
72. Cf. J. Armour, D. Awrey, P. Davies et al., op. cit. *supra* note 70, 316–317 and 322–323. See further, M. Haentjens and P. de Gioia Carabellese, op. cit. *supra* note 3, 105 et seq.
73. Dir. 2014/49/EU.

compensation of depositors who lost their savings.[74] These schemes have two objectives: to protect depositors and to preserve financial market stability.[75] The underlying theory is that, as depositors are (at least partly) protected under the deposit guarantee schemes, they can be certain that their deposits are guaranteed (because they will be reimbursed) and would have less incentives to withdraw their deposits.[76] A key condition for deposit guarantee schemes to work, is that depositors have confidence in the financial safety net provided. Therefore, the amendments of 2014 have introduced rules that establish, *inter alia*, a higher minimum level of coverage for deposits and a faster payout.[77]

In addition to depositors, investors are protected under the Investor Compensation Scheme Directive (ICSD).[78] The ICSD offers protection to investors by requiring Member States to ensure an investor-compensation scheme is in place in case an investment firm is unable "to meet its obligations to its investor clients".[79] The ICSD does not offer protection against investment risks, but rather against situations in which the inability to return assets is caused by fraud at the investment firm or in which there are errors or problems in the investment firm's systems.[80] In 2010, the European Commission adopted a proposal to amend the ICSD establishing rules on, *inter alia*, a higher minimum level of coverage and a faster payout.[81] However, in March 2015, the European Commission withdrew the proposal as part of a more general operation to reduce the regulatory burden under its Work Programme 2015.[82]

The third purpose of the legislative initiatives developed by the European Commission, was to prevent and manage bank failures. Therefore, a single mechanism to deal with bank failures (a Single Resolution Mechanism (SRM)) within the Banking Union has been created.[83] In this regard, three pieces of legislation are vital: the Winding Up Directive,[84] the BRRD[85] and the SRM Regulation.[86]

---

74. See <ec.europa.eu/info/business-economy-euro/banking-and-finance/financial-supervision-and-risk-management/managing-risks-banks-and-financial-institutions/deposit-guarantee-schemes_en>.
75. Cf. recital 3 Directive on Deposit Guarantee Schemes.
76. Cf. M. Haentjens and P. de Gioia Carabellese, op. cit. *supra* note 3, 124 et seq. See also on this topic in general: R.A. Eisenbeis and G.G. Kaufman, "Deposit Insurance Issues in the Post 2008 Crisis World" in A.N. Berger, P. Molyneux and J.O.S. Wilson (Eds.), *The Oxford Handbook on Banking* (OUP, 2014).
77. Arts. 6, 8 and recital 7 Directive on Deposit Guarantee Schemes.
78. Dir. 97/9/EC of the European Parliament and of the Council of 3 Mar. 1997 on investor-compensation schemes, O.J. 1997, L 084.
79. Art. 2(2) and recital 4 and 5 Directive on investor-compensation schemes.
80. See, for the examples referred to, <europa.eu/rapid/press-release_MEMO-10-319_en.htm?locale=en> and N. Moloney, op. cit. *supra* note 1, 839.
81. See the amendments proposed to Art. 2, 4(3) and 9(2) in Proposal for a Directive of the European Parliament and of the Council amending Dir. 97/9/EC of the European Parliament and of the Council on investor-compensation schemes COM(2010)371, and, for a more detailed explanation, 8–9 and 11–12 of the Proposal.
82. See O.J. 2015, C 80/17, O.J. 2015, C 80/21 and Communication from the Commission to the European Parliament, the Council, the European Economic and Social Committee and the Committee of the Regions. Commission Work Programme 2015, COM(2014)910 final, 4.
83. See also *supra*, section 2.3.3, and *infra*, section 4.3.2, and extensively M. Haentjens and B. Wessels, op. cit. *supra* note 45.
84. Dir. 2001/24/EC of the European Parliament and of the Council of 4 Apr. 2001 on the reorganization and winding up of credit institutions, O.J. 2001, L 125.
85. Dir. 2014/59/EU.
86. Reg. (EU) 806/2014.

The Winding Up Directive has already been introduced in 2001.[87] It entails that, if a bank with branches in other Member States fails, reorganization measures and winding-up proceedings (bankruptcy proceedings) will be controlled by only one Member State, i.e. the home Member State.[88] The home Member State is the state where the bank has been authorized and has its registered office.[89] With regard to reorganization measures, under Article 3 of the Winding Up Directive, "the administrative or judicial authorities of the home Member State are empowered to decide on the implementation of reorganization measures with respect to a bank, including branches established in other Member States". In addition, under Articles 9 and 10 of the Winding Up Directive, the decision to open winding-up proceedings can solely be made by the administrative or judicial authorities of the home Member State that are responsible for winding up the bank and the winding-up proceedings will be governed by the laws, regulations and procedures applicable in the home Member State. Hence, bankruptcy proceedings will be governed by one single national bankruptcy regime.

More recently, in 2014, the BRRD and the SRM Regulation were adopted.[90] Whereas the Winding Up Directive concentrates on coordination and conflict of laws rules, the legal frameworks of the BRRD and the SRM Regulation provide harmonized rules on the prevention and management of bank failures and rules on the European institutional structure to apply the rules of the BRRD, respectively.[91] The BRRD has introduced rules to deal with banks in financial distress in order to "avoid destabilizing financial markets and minimize the costs for taxpayers".[92] It has established rules for banks in different stages of financial distress and involves "three pillars": (i) preparation (Title II of the BRRD); (ii) early intervention (Title III of the BRRD); and (iii) resolution (Title IV of the BRRD).[93] As part of the prevention of bank failures, banks and the resolution authorities are, for example, obliged to create "living wills" (recovery and resolution plans[94]) which provide an *ex ante* planning of how a bank in financial distress

---

87. See, extensively, G. Moss, I. Fletcher and S. Isaacs (Eds.), *The EU Regulation on Insolvency Proceedings*, 3rd ed. (OUP, 2016), 222 et seq.
88. Since the introduction of the BRRD, the Winding Up Directive also applies to investment firms, G. Moss, I. Fletcher and S. Isaacs (Eds.), op. cit. *supra* note 87, 223.
89. Art. 2 Winding Up Directive and Art. 6(2) of Dir. 2000/12/EC of the European Parliament and of the Council of 20 Mar. 2000 relating to the taking up and pursuit of the business of credit institutions, O.J. 2000, L 126.
90. See, extensively, G. Moss, I. Fletcher and S. Isaacs (Eds.), op. cit. *supra* note 87, 248 et seq. On 23 Nov. 2016, the European Commission issued a package of proposals to amend the CRR, the CRD, the BRRD and the SRM Reg. As regards the BRRD and SRM Reg., the package consisted of two draft Directives. Commission proposal 2016/0362 (COD), COM(2016)852 final, focuses on the "Minimum Requirement for own funds and Eligible Liabilities" (MREL) and aims to incorporate the global standard for "Total Loss Absorbing Capacity", which is similar, but not identical to MREL, into MREL as codified in the BRRD. Also, this draft Directive provides for a new moratorium tool to be employed in the pre-resolution phase, as an additional early intervention power. In Apr. 2018, this proposal was still being discussed within the Council. Moreover, the second Commission proposal 2016/0363 (COD), COM(2016)853 final was approved and resulted in Dir. (EU) 2017/2399 of the European Parliament and of the Council of 12 Dec. 2017 amending Dir. 2014/59/EU as regards the ranking of unsecured debt instruments in insolvency hierarchy, O.J. 2017, L 345. Under this Directive, Art. 108 BRRD on the ranking in insolvency hierarchy has been amended. Member States must now amend their national insolvency laws so that a category of ordinary unsecured claims have a higher priority ranking than that of unsecured claims resulting from debt instruments, provided they meet certain conditions.
91. G. Moss, I. Fletcher and S. Isaacs (Eds.), op. cit. *supra* note 87, 249.
92. Recital 5 BRRD.
93. G. Moss, I. Fletcher and S. Isaacs (Eds.), op. cit. *supra* note 87, 249.
94. Arts. 5 and 10 BRRD.

should be handled.[95] Furthermore, under Title III of the BRRD, supervisors can exercise early intervention powers as to be able to remedy the deterioration of a bank's financial and economic situation before that bank "reaches a point at which authorities have no other alternative than to resolve it".[96] Under Article 27(1)(a) and (d) of the BRRD, early intervention measures involve, for example, the power to require the bank to implement (parts of) the recovery plan and the power to replace members from the management body.[97] Finally, under Title IV of the BRRD, if the conditions for resolution under Article 32(1) of the BRRD and Article 18(1) of the SRM Regulation have been complied with,[98] the resolution authority can apply the resolution tools listed in Article 37(3) of the BRRD and Article 22(2) of the SRM Regulation.[99] The resolution tools are: the sale of business tool, the bridge institution tool, the asset separation tool and the bail-in tool.

Finally, the SRM Regulation not only harmonizes substantive rules on bank resolution, but also centralizes resolution decisions with the SRB. It has introduced the institutional framework of the SRM, the SRB and the SRF for the Banking Union.[100] The SRB is the central power of the SRM and bears responsibility for the effective and consistent functioning of the SRM.[101] It prepares resolution plans and may eventually employ the resolution tools listed in Article 37(3) of the BRRD and Article 22(2) of the SRM Regulation.[102] Furthermore, the SRM Regulation established the SRF, a fund financed by the banking sector to secure funding for the resolution of failing banks.[103]

3.3 *Securities and markets*

In a nutshell, financial instruments such as securities (shares and bonds) and derivatives are traded in the financial markets after being issued by issuers. This section explains the different legal instruments regulating the financial markets and the parties involved in transactions of financial instruments.

In general, investment firms and regulated markets are regulated by the Directive on Markets in Financial Instruments II (MiFID II)[104] and the Regulation on Markets in Financial Instruments (MiFIR).[105] They comprise a "regulatory framework for investment services in financial

95. Cf. J. Armour, D. Awrey, P. Davies et al., op. cit. *supra* note 70, 356. In Mar. 2016, a Level 2 Delegated Regulation has been adopted specifying, *inter alia,* the content of recovery plans, resolution plans and group resolution plans and the minimum criteria that the competent authority is to assess as regards recovery plans and group recovery plans (Commission Delegated Reg. (EU) 2016/1075, O.J. 2016, L 184).
96. Recital 40 BRRD. See also G. Moss, I. Fletcher and S. Isaacs (Eds.), op. cit. *supra* note 87, 252.
97. See also G. Moss, I. Fletcher and S. Isaacs (Eds.), op. cit. *supra* note 87, 252–253.
98. In short, the conditions for resolution are: (1) "the institution is failing or is likely to fail"; (2) "there is no reasonable prospect that any alternative private sector measures [...] would prevent the failure of the institution within a reasonable timeframe"; and (3) "a resolution action is necessary in the public interest". G. Moss, I. Fletcher and S. Isaacs (Eds.), op. cit. *supra* note 87, 253.
99. G. Moss, I. Fletcher and S. Isaacs (Eds.), op. cit. *supra* note 87, 253.
100. Art. 42 et seq. SRM Reg.
101. Cf. Art. 7(1) SRM Reg and recital 11 SRM Reg.
102. Arts. 8 and 22(1) SRM Reg.
103. Arts. 67, 70 and 71 SRM Reg.
104. Dir. 2014/65/EU of the European Parliament and of the Council of 15 May 2014 on markets in financial instruments and amending Dir. 2002/92/EC and Dir. 2011/61/EU, O.J. 2014, L 173. See also D. Busch, G. Ferrarini, *Regulation of the EU financial markets: MiFID II and MiFIR* (OUP, 2017) and D. Busch, *MiFID II/MIFIR: Nieuwe regels voor beleggingsondernemingen en financiële markten,* Preadvies van de Vereniging voor Financieel Recht (Kluwer, 2015).
105. Reg. (EU) 600/2014 of the European Parliament and of the Council of 15 May 2014 on markets in financial instruments and amending Reg. (EU) 648/2012, O.J. 2014, L 173.

instruments by banks and investment firms" and a regulatory framework for the operation of traditional stock exchanges (regulated markets) and alternative trading venues.[106] In 2004, MiFID I already introduced rules on investment services concerning financial instruments provided by banks and investment firms (e.g., investment advice) and rules on the operation of trading platforms.[107] In 2014, the rules of MiFID I were updated and further developed in MiFID II and MiFIR. The majority of these new rules became applicable as from January 2018.[108]

MiFID II contains harmonized rules on the authorization of investment firms and regulated markets[109] and on the operating conditions of investment firms.[110] As part of these operating conditions, conduct of business rules have been harmonized in order to provide a high level of investor protection.[111] Regarding the provision of investment services, MiFID II distinguishes three categories of clients, viz. retail clients, professional clients and eligible counterparties. With regard to each of its clients, an investment firm must "act honestly, fairly and professionally in accordance with the best interests of its clients".[112] Furthermore, investment firms have to comply with the "principles" set out in Articles 24 and 25 MiFID II. To that end, under Article 25(2), when providing investment advice or portfolio management, the investment firm must conduct a suitability test, i.e. an investment firm must obtain information "regarding the client's or potential client's knowledge and experience in the investment field relevant to the specific type of product or service, that person's financial situation including his ability to bear losses, and his investment objectives including his risk tolerance". Under Article 25(3), when providing "execution only" investment services, the investment firm shall conduct a less strict appropriateness test, i.e. an investment firm must ask the client "to provide information regarding that person's knowledge and experience in the investment field relevant to the specific type of product or service offered or demanded".[113]

In response to the financial crisis, MiFID II aims to strengthen the regulatory framework of markets in financial instruments and "to increase transparency, better protect investors, reinforce confidence, address unregulated areas, and ensure that supervisors are granted adequate powers to fulfil their tasks".[114] In order to achieve these objectives, MiFID II and MiFIR, *inter alia*, aim to ensure that trading in financial instruments "as far as possible" takes place at markets which are subject to regulation (whether stock exchanges or alternative trading systems).[115] Therefore, MiFID II and MiFIR have extended the scope of MiFID I by introducing a new type of trading venue: the organized trading facility (OTF).[116] Furthermore, MiFID II strengthens

---

106. Proposal for a Directive of the European Parliament and of the Council on markets in financial instruments repealing Directive 2004/39/EC of the European Parliament and of the Council (Recast), COM(2011)656 final, 1.
107. Cf. Proposal for a Dir. of the European Parliament and of the Council on markets in financial instruments repealing Dir. 2004/39/EC of the European Parliament and of the Council (Recast), COM(2011)656 final, 1.
108. Art. 93(1) MiFID II.
109. Art. 5 MiFID II and 44 MiFID II, respectively.
110. As from Art. 21 MiFID II.
111. As was already arranged for under MiFID I, cf. Recitals 1–2 MiFID I.
112. Art. 24(1) MiFID II.
113. An exception to carry out the appropriateness test can be made if the conditions under Art. 25(4) MiFID II are met.
114. Recital 4 MiFID II. See also D. Busch, op. cit. *supra* note 104.
115. Recital 6 MiFIR. See also recital 13 MiFID II and M. Haentjens and P. de Gioia Carabellese, op. cit. *supra* note 3, 206.
116. Recital 8 MiFIR.

investor protection by introducing more stringent rules on corporate governance,[117] more stringent organizational rules[118] and more stringent operating conditions for investment firms.[119] The MiFID II framework also codifies new rules on product governance, including the requirement for investment firms to identify the target market for each product and to ensure all relevant risks of the product are assessed and understood.[120]

The second category of legislative instruments that should be discussed in this section are concerned with the requirements for issuers who intend to offer financial instruments to investors on regulated markets: the Listing Directive, the Transparency Directive, the Prospectus Directive (as from 21 July 2019 onward, the Prospectus Regulation) and the Regulation on key information documents for packaged retail and insurance-based investment products (the PRIIPs Regulation).

Whenever an issuer wishes to have its securities traded on a regulated market (such as a stock exchange), the requirements as set by the Listing Directive[121] must be fulfilled.[122] The Listing Directive thus creates a level playing field with regard to the admission of securities to an official stock exchange and with regard to securities that have already been admitted to an official listing.[123]

In addition, the Transparency Directive and the Prospectus Directive are concerned with the provision of information to investors and the financial markets. Under the Transparency Directive,[124] issuers whose securities have been admitted to trading on an EU regulated market (the access to which is thus governed by the rules of the Listing Directive), are obliged to disclose information about their business.[125] The underlying rationale of the Transparency Directive is that if issuers are obliged to provide investors with "a regular flow of information" and thus provide investors with insight into their business, investor protection and market efficiency will be enhanced.[126] Under the Transparency Directive, issuers must, for instance, comply with periodic information requirements requiring the publication of annual financial reports[127] and half-yearly financial reports.[128]

---

117. Recital 5 MiFID II.
118. Art. 16 MiFID II.
119. Art. 21 et seq. MiFID II.
120. Arts. 16(3) and 24(2) MiFID II.
121. Dir. 2001/34/EC of the European Parliament and of the Council of 28 May 2001 on the admission of securities to official stock exchange listing and on information to be published on those securities, O.J. 2001, L 184.
122. Art. 5 Listing Directive.
123. Cf. M. Haentjens and P. de Gioia Carabellese, op. cit. *supra* note 3, 27.
124. Dir. 2004/109/EC of the European Parliament and the Council of 15 Dec. 2004 on the harmonization of transparency requirements in relation to information about issuers whose securities are admitted to trading on a regulated market and amending Dir. 2001/34/EC, O.J. 2004, L 390, in conjuction with Dir. 2013/50/EU of the European Parliament and of the Council of 22 Oct. 2013 amending Dir. 2004/109/EC of the European Parliament and of the Council on the harmonization of transparency requirements in relation to information about issuers whose securities are admitted to trading on a regulated market, Dir. 2003/71/EC of the European Parliament and of the Council on the prospectus to be published when securities are offered to the public or admitted to trading and Commission Dir. 2007/14/EC laying down detailed rules for the implementation of certain provisions of Dir. 2004/109/EC, O.J. 2013, L 294.
125. Cf. Recital 1 Transparency Directive.
126. Recitals 1–2 Transparency Directive.
127. Art. 4 Transparency Directive.
128. Art. 5 Transparency Directive.

Furthermore, issuers will often have to comply with the requirements of the Prospectus Directive.[129] A prospectus is a document required by law which contains information on (the securities offered by) the issuer that helps investors to decide whether or not to invest in the securities offered.[130] The Prospectus Directive *inter alia* sets rules on when the publication of a prospectus is required,[131] on the information that shall be included in a prospectus[132] and the approval of a prospectus and the corresponding "passporting" regime.[133] The rules of the Directive have been specified in various delegated and implementing acts[134] and, in addition, the Level 3 Q&A on the Prospectus Directive is of great practical significance.[135]

Yet, change is at hand, as, from 21 July 2019 onward, a new Prospectus Regulation will apply and will repeal the Prospectus Directive currently applicable.[136] The Prospectus Regulation aims to reduce the administrative burden placed on issuers by creating specific rules for specific types of issuers.[137] For instance, small and medium-sized entreprises (SMEs) are provided with the opportunity to draw up an EU Growth prospectus, which is a standard prospectus that SMEs can supposedly complete easily.[138] As another example, frequent issuers, who wish to issue securities several times a year, can draw up a universal registration document presenting relevant information on the issuer. When new securities are to be issued, the frequent issuer can then benefit from a faster approval track for the prospectus.[139]

Finally, issuers offering certain complex financial products to retail investors ("packaged retail and insurance-based investment products" or PRIIPs, such as structured deposits) are required to publish Key Information Documents (KIDs) under the PRIIPs Regulation.[140] The

129. Dir. 2003/71/EC of the European Parliament and of the Council of 4 Nov. 2003 on the prospectus to be published when securities are offered to the public or admitted to trading and amending Dir. 2001/34/EC, O.J. 2003 L 345 in conjuction with Dir. 2010/73/EU of the European Parliament and of the Council of 24 Nov. 2010 amending Dir. 2003/71/EC on the prospectus to be published when securities are offered to the public or admitted to trading and 2004/109/EC on the harmonization of transparency requirements in relation to information about issuers whose securities are admitted to trading on a regulated market, O.J. 2010, L 327. See extensively: M. Haentjens and P. de Gioia Carabellese, op. cit. *supra* note 3, 31 et seq., R. Veil, *European Capital Markets Law*, 2nd ed. (Hart Publishing, 2017), 281 et seq. and T.M.C. Arons, *Cross-border Enforcement of Listed Companies' Duties to Inform: A Comparative Research into Prospectus Liability Regimes and Private International Law Problems Arising in Collective Proceedings* (Diss. Rotterdam, Kluwer, 2012).
130. COM(2015)583 final, 1.
131. Arts. 3 and 4 Prospectus Directive.
132. Art. 5 et seq. Prospectus Directive.
133. Arts. 17 and 18 Prospectus Directive. See also M. Haentjens and P. de Gioia Carabellese, op. cit. *supra* note 3, 35–36.
134. For an oversight, see <ec.europa.eu/info/law/prospectus-directive-2003-71-ec/amending-and-supplementary-acts/implementing-and-delegated-acts_en>. See e.g. Commission Reg. (EC) 809/2004, O.J. 2004, L 149. Amended by Commission Delegated Reg. (EU) 2016/301, O.J. 2016, L 58; Commission Delegated Reg. (EU) 759/2013, O.J. 2013, L 213; Commission Delegated Reg. (EU) 862/2012, O.J. 2012, L 256; and Commission Delegated Reg. (EU) 486/2012, O.J. 2012, L 150.
135. ESMA-31-62-780.
136. Reg. (EU) 2017/1129 of the European Parliament and of the Council of 14 June 2017 on the prospectus to be published when securities are offered to the public or admitted to trading on a regulated market, and repealing Dir. 2003/71/EC, O.J. 2017, L 168. The new Prospectus Regulation has been developed in the context of the Capital Markets Union, COM(2015)583 final, 1 and Recital 1 Prospectus Regulation.
137. COM(2015)583 final, 1–2.
138. Art. 15 Reg. (EU) 2017/1129.
139. Art. 9 Reg. (EU) 2017/1129 and COM(2015)583 final, 15.
140. Art. 1–2 Reg. (EU) 1286/2014 on key information documents for packaged retail and insurance-based investment products (PRIIPs), O.J. 2014, L 352. See in detail V. Colaert, "The Regulation of PRIIPs: Great ambitions, insurmountable challenges?" (2016) *Journal of Financial Regulation*, 203–224.

PRIIPs Regulation's main objective is to enable retail investors to understand and compare PRIIPs through key information documents. To that end, its provisions lay down in detail what information shall be provided and in what format that information shall be presented.[141]

Furthermore, as a third category, European rules have been established on the integrity and transparency of the (secondary) markets[142] in order to protect investors and to improve market efficiency. In this regard, the Market Abuse Regulation, the Benchmark Regulation and the Directive on Short Selling should be mentioned.[143]

In July 2016, the EU regulatory framework on market abuse and market manipulation changed. The old Market Abuse Directive[144] and its Implementing Directive (level 2)[145] were replaced by the Market Abuse Regulation (MAR)[146] and the new Market Abuse Directive.[147] The rationale of the new regulatory framework however remained the same: the Market Abuse Regulation (MAR), together with the Market Abuse Directive (MAD), is to establish rules against insider dealing, unlawful disclosure of inside information, and market manipulation in order to ensure market integrity and investor protection and confidence.[148] The MAR and the MAD aim to address problems that were not, or insufficiently, addressed by the old regulatory framework, such as the emergence of new markets, platforms, and over-the-counter instruments, the gap of regulation for commodity markets and related derivative markets, and the tools to ensure effective enforcement by supervisors.[149]

The Regulation on benchmarks became applicable as from 1 January 2018 onward.[150] Benchmarks – LIBOR and EURIBOR are probably the most well-known examples – are indices "used as a reference price for a financial instrument or a financial contract".[151] The manipulations of LIBOR and EURIBOR revealed the vulnerability of benchmarks and caused the EU legislator to take action in this field.[152] The Benchmark Regulation's main objective is to ensure the

---

141. Art. 5 et seq. PRIIPs Regulation.
142. In the financial sector, the primary market and the secondary market have to be distinguished. When securities are issued and sold for the first time to investors, they are said to be traded in the primary market. The secondary market concerns the trade of securities which have already been issued and may be traded in a regulated market among investors.
143. In conjunction with the Transparency Directive mentioned *supra*.
144. Dir. 2003/6/EC of the European Parliament and of the Council of 28 Jan. 2003 on insider dealing and market manipulation (market abuse), O.J. 2003, L 96.
145. Commission Dir. 2003/124/EC of 22 Dec. 2003 implementing Dir. 2003/6/EC of the European Parliament and of the Council as regards the definition and public disclosure of inside information and the definition of market manipulation, O.J. 2003, L 339. See also N. Moloney, op. cit. *supra* note 1, 538 et seq.
146. Reg. (EU) 596/2014. See extensively N. Moloney, op. cit. *supra* note 1, 699 et seq., F.G.H. Kristen, H.J. de Kluiver, N. Lemmens, *Market abuse regulation: van Europese kaders naar uitleg en toepassing in Nederland: preadviezen voor de Vereniging voor Financieel Recht 2017* (Kluwer, 2017) and R. Veil, op. cit. *supra* note 129, p. 183 et seq.
147. Dir. 2014/57/EU of the European Parliament and of the Council of 16 Apr. 2014 on criminal sanctions for market abuse (Market Abuse Directive), O.J. 2014, L 173.
148. Art. 1 MAR. M. Haentjens and P. de Gioia Carabellese, op. cit. *supra* note 3, 43. See in more detail L. Gullifer and J. Payne, *Corporate Finance Law. Principles and Policy* (Hart Publishing, 2015), 578.
149. Proposal for a Regulation of the European Parliament and of the Council on insider dealing and market manipulation (market abuse), COM(2011)651 final – 2011/0295 (COD), 3. See also M. Haentjens and P. de Gioia Carabellese, op. cit. *supra* note 3, 43.
150. Reg. (EU) 2016/1011 of the European Parliament and of the Council of 8 June 2016 on indices used as benchmarks in financial instruments and financial contracts or to measure the performance of investment funds and amending Dir. 2008/48/EC and 2014/17/EU and Reg. (EU) 596/2014, O.J. 2016, L 171, in particular, Art. 59. See in detail R. Veil, op. cit. *supra* note 129, p. 692 et seq.
151. Impact Assessment, SWD(2013) 336 final, 1.
152. Cf. recital 1 Benchmark Regulation.

integrity of indices used as benchmarks, which should enhance the functioning of the internal market and the protection of consumers and investors.[153] To that end, the regulatory framework involves *inter alia* requirements with regard to the strengthening of the governance, and the avoidance of conflicts of interests for persons involved with the benchmark,[154] and rules on the methodology for determining a benchmark.[155]

Furthermore, the Regulation on Short Selling has restricted and set rules for the practice of short selling.[156] Short selling involves the sale of securities "which the seller does not own at the time of entering into the agreement to sell" – under Article 2(1)(b) of the Regulation on Short Selling. When the sale is concluded, the seller might have borrowed the securities from another investor (the actual owner). Alternatively, however, short selling can also be "uncovered" or "naked" without the seller having borrowed securities at the moment of entering into the agreement to sell.[157] Short sellers hope that the price of the securities decreases – as opposed to ordinary investors who hope the securities price increases – to make a profit out of the difference between the price for which they sold the borrowed securities initially and the price for which they have to buy the securities back in order to deliver them to the actual owner. In the aftermath of the financial crisis, short selling was thought to be able to aggravate the downward spiral in share prices "in a way which could ultimately threaten their viability and create systemic risks".[158] Therefore, the Regulation on Short Selling has established rules on the process of short selling in order to protect investors and to ensure the proper functioning of the financial markets.[159] As part of these rules, for example, naked short selling has been banned completely under Article 12 of the Regulation on Short Selling.[160]

In addition to the legislative instruments listed above, several European legislative instruments regulate the infrastructure of the "post-trading area", i.e. the clearing and settlement of transactions.[161] In this regard, the Settlement Finality Directive, the Regulation on OTC Derivatives, Central Counterparties and Trade Repositories (better known as the European Market Infrastructure Regulation or EMIR) and the Regulation on Central Securities Depositories will be discussed.

To begin with, the Settlement Finality Directive,[162] which was introduced in 1998, established European rules guaranteeing transfers and payments of financial products in order to minimize systemic risk.[163] To that end, the Directive entails that transfer orders and netting are

153. Cf. Art. 1 Benchmark Regulation.
154. Art. 4 Benchmark Regulation.
155. Art. 12–13 Benchmark Regulation.
156. Reg. (EU) 236/2012 of the European Parliament and of the Council of 14 Mar. 2012 on short selling and certain aspects of credit default swaps, O.J. 2012, L 86. See extensively N. Moloney, op. cit. *supra* note 1, 538 et seq.
157. Cf. N. Moloney, op. cit. *supra* note 1, 539. See also in detail J. Armour, D. Awrey, P. Davies et al., op. cit. *supra* note 70, 194 et seq.
158. Recital 1 Reg. on Short Selling.
159. Cf. recital 2 Reg. on Short Selling.
160. See also recital 18 Reg. on Short Selling and N. Moloney, op. cit. *supra* note 1, 555 et seq.
161. See, in detail on how clearing and settlement work precisely, M. Haentjens and P. de Gioia Carabellese, op. cit. *supra* note 3, 165–166 et seq.
162. Dir. 98/26/EC of the European Parliament and of the Council of 19 May 1998 on settlement finality in payment and securities settlement systems, O.J. 1998 L 166 in conjuction with Dir. 2009/44/EC of the European Parliament and of the Council of 6 May 2009 amending Dir. 98/26/EC on settlement finality in payment and securities settlement systems and Dir. 2002/47/EC on financial collateral arrangements as regards linked systems and credit claims, O.J. 2009, L 146.
163. Cf. recitals 2, 4 and 9 Settlement Finality Directive and M. Haentjens and P. de Gioia Carabellese, op. cit. *supra* note 3, 166–167.

legally enforceable even if participants of payment and securities settlement systems such as banks and central securities depositories[164] enter into insolvency proceedings.[165]

Furthermore, in 2012, the European Market Infrastructure Regulation (EMIR)[166] established rules on (reporting requirements for) derivative contracts and on central counterparties to be used in the clearing of derivatives transactions.[167] Very importantly, EMIR introduced mandatory centralized clearing for derivatives, meaning that the parties involved in a derivatives transaction must make use of a central counterparty to facilitate the clearing of the transaction.[168] This mechanism aims to reduce operational and systemic risk, as the central counterparty takes over the default risk of the original counterparties.[169] EMIR also establishes rules on the authorization and supervision of and organizational, business conduct and prudential requirements for central counterparties.[170] Due to the great importance of central counterparties in the post-trading area, the European Commission adopted a legislative proposal to arrange for the recovery and resolution of central counterparties in financial distress in November 2016.[171]

In addition, the Regulation on Central Securities Depositories (CSDR)[172] has introduced European rules on central securities depositories, i.e. central institutions where securities can be held and which operate securities settelement systems.[173] The CSDR aims to increase the safety, efficiency and smoothness of settlements by establishing an internal market for the operations of central securities depositories[174] and by introducing organizational, conduct of business and prudential requirements for central securities depositories.[175]

As final part of this section on securities and markets, European rules have been developed for collective investment schemes – for instance, regarding UCITSs (Undertakings for

---

164. Cf. Arts. 2(b) and (f) Settlement Finality Directive.
165. Art. 3 Settlement Finality Directive. See also M. Haentjens and P. de Gioia Carabellese, op. cit. *supra* note 3, 167.
166. Reg. (EU) 648/2012 of the European Parliament and of the Council of 4 July 2012 on OTC derivatives, central counterparties and trade repositories, O.J. 2012, L 201. Level 2 acts further detail the rules of EMIR. The European Commission has endorsed technical standards on, *inter alia*, the prudential requirements for central counterparties (Commission Delegated Reg. (EU) 152/2013, O.J. 2013, L 52), detailed rules on the clearing obligation (Commission Delegated Reg. (EU) 149/2013, O.J. 2013, L 52) and, more recently, rules on over the counter (OTC) interest rate derivative contracts that have to be cleared centrally (Commission Delegated Reg. (EU) 2015/2205, O.J. 2015, L 314 and Commission Delegated Reg. (EU) 2016/1178, O.J. 2016, L 195). It must be noted that, in May 2017, the European Commission adopted a proposal to simplify the current legal framework established by EMIR as part of the Regulatory Fitness and Performance (REFIT) programme. See Proposal for a Reg. of the European Parliament and of the Council amending Reg. (EU) 648/2012 as regards the clearing obligation, the suspension of the clearing obligation, the reporting requirements, the risk-mitigation techniques for OTC derivatives contracts not cleared by a central counterparty, the registration and supervision of trade repositories and the requirements for trade repositories, COM(2017)208, 3.
167. Art. 1 EMIR.
168. See M. Haentjens and P. de Gioia Carabellese, op. cit. *supra* note 3, 205.
169. See M. Haentjens and P. de Gioia Carabellese, op. cit. *supra* note 3, 206.
170. Art. 14 et seq., recital 49 and Art. 26 et seq. EMIR, respectively.
171. Proposal for a Reg. of the European Parliament and of the Council on a framework for the recovery and resolution of central counterparties and amending Regs. (EU) No 1095/2010, (EU) No 648/2012, and (EU) 2015/2365, COM(2016)856 final – 2016/0365 (COD).
172. Reg. (EU) 909/2014.
173. Cf. Recital 1 CSDR.
174. Art. 1 CSDR.
175. Recital 20 CSDR.

Collective Investment in Transferable Securities), AIFMs (Alternative Investment Fund Managers) and MMFs (money market funds) – and for market facilitators such as credit rating agencies.[176]

The UCITS V Directive[177] and the Directive on Alternative Investment Fund Managers (AIFMD)[178] are at the core of the European regulatory framework with respect to collective asset management.[179] As from 21 July 2018, this framework will be complemented by the new Regulation on money market funds.[180] Investment funds – UCITSs, AIFs (Alternative Investment Funds) and MMFs – raise assets from retail and/or professional investors (the clients of the investment fund) and, afterwards, invest these assets into the financial markets. Investment funds perform an important role in channeling assets to projects and parties in need of funding.

UCITSs have been regulated at the EU level already since 1985,[181] but in the aftermath of the financial crisis, the rules for UCITSs at the European level were changed, *inter alia*, because of the complexity of the financial products offered by UCITSs and because of the conflicts of interest that these funds and, more in particular, their managers have to deal with.[182] Conflicts of interest can arise in the course of investment decisions, for instance, if the manager can make "a financial gain, or avoid a financial loss" at the expense of a UCITS (and its clients) or if the manager "has an interest in the outcome of a service provided" to a UCITS (and its clients) which differs from the interest of the UCITS (and its clients).[183] In brief, the UCITS V Directive establishes, *inter alia*, rules on the authorization of UCITSs and passporting,[184] general conditions

---

176. Under the sectoral approach, it is difficult to put this kind of European regulation in one of the three categories (banking, markets or insurance/pension funds). But as these market participants are being supervised by ESMA, we will discuss their regulation in this section.
177. Dir. 2014/91/EU of the European Parliament and of the Council of 23 July 2014 amending Dir. 2009/65/EC on the coordination of laws, regulations and administrative provisions relating to undertakings for collective investment in transferable securities (UCITS) as regards depositary functions, remuneration policies and sanctions, O.J. 2014, L 257. See also M. Haentjens and P. de Gioia Carabellese, op. cit. *supra* note 3, 144 et seq. and N. Moloney, op. cit. *supra* note 1, 200 et seq.
178. Dir. 2011/61/EU of the European Parliament and of the Council of 8 June 2011 on Alternative Investment Fund Managers and amending Dir. 2003/41/EC and 2009/65/EC and Regs. (EC) 1060/2009 and (EU) 1095/2010, O.J. 2011, L 174. See also M. Haentjens and P. de Gioia Carabellese, op. cit. *supra* note 3, 148 et seq., N. Moloney, op. cit. *supra* note 1, 269 et seq., L. van Setten and D. Busch (Eds.), *Alternative Investment Funds in Europe* (OUP, 2014), E. Wymeersch (Ed.), *Alternative Investment Fund Regulation* (Kluwer, 2012) and D.A. Zetzsche (Ed.), *The Alternative Investment Fund Managers Directive* (Kluwer, 2012).
179. The frameworks are similar in many aspects, however, some important differences remain, see N. Moloney, op. cit. *supra* note 1, 283.
180. Reg. (EU) 2017/1131 of the European Parliament and of the Council of 14 June 2017 on money market funds, O.J. 2017, L 169.
181. Council Dir. 85/611/EEC of 20 December 1985 on the coordination of laws, regulations and administrative provisions relating to undertakings for collective investment in transferable securities (UCITS), O.J. 1985, L 375.
182. Cf. Proposal for a Directive of the European Parliament and of the Council amending Directive 2009/65/EC on the coordination of laws, regulations and administrative provisions relating to undertakings for collective investment in transferable securities (UCITS) as regards depositary functions, remuneration policies and sanctions, COM(2012)350 final, 2–3, which resulted in Directive 2014/91/EU of the European Parliament and of the Council of 23 July 2014 amending Dir. 2009/65/EC on the coordination of laws, regulations and administrative provisions relating to undertakings for collective investment in transferable securities (UCITS) as regards depositary functions, remuneration policies and sanctions, O.J. 2014, L 257.
183. See also the Financial Conduct Authority's Handbook of rules and guidance, Ch. 10 Conflicts of interest, available at <www.handbook.fca.org.uk/>.
184. Art. 5 UCITS V.

to take up business,[185] operating conditions (for instance rules on conflicts of interest),[186] remuneration principles applying to fund managers[187] and rules on depositaries of UCITSs.[188]

The AIFMD contains rules for the managers of collective investment funds that cannot be qualified as UCITSs, for instance, for hedge fund managers and private equity fund managers that were not subject to regulation before the introduction of the AIFMD in 2011.[189] Officially, the AIFMD does not entail maximum harmonization, but the AIFMD has established a high level of harmonization and its rules are extremely detailed.[190] The AIFMD has introduced requirements on the authorization of AIFMs and passporting,[191] operating conditions (for instance rules on best execution and conflicts of interest),[192] remuneration principles applying to fund managers,[193] organizational requirements[194] and rules regarding depositaries of AIFs.[195]

The Regulation on money market funds creates a legal framework for investment funds specialized in collecting and investing in short-term assets. According to the recitals of the Regulation, the key features of MMFs are that they "have the objective of offering returns in line with money market rates, or of preserving the value of the investment, and that seek to achieve those objectives by investing in short-term assets such as money market instruments or deposits, or entering into reverse repurchase agreements or certain derivative contracts with the sole purpose of hedging risks inherent to other investments of the fund".[196] MMFs shall not be understood as being different from UCITSs and AIFs. On the contrary, UCITSs and AIFs that comply with the key features of MMFs set out above, shall comply with the rules of the new Regulation in addition to the already existing regulatory framworks.[197] The Regulation on

185. Art. 6 et seq. UCITS V.
186. Art. 10 et seq. UCITS V.
187. Art. 14a UCITS V.
188. Art. 22 et seq. UCITS V. See in detail: Commission Delegated Reg. (EU) 2016/438, O.J. 2016, L 11. The regulatory framework of UCITSs has been extended by two Implementing Directives, two Implementing Regulations and one Delegated Regulation – still under Directive 2009/65/EC, which has now been amended by the UCITS V Directive. The Implementing acts cover requirements on key investor information (Commission Reg. (EU) 583/2010 of 1 July 2010, O.J. 2010, L 176), details on the notification procedure to competent authorities (Commission Reg. (EU) 584/2010, O.J. 2010, L 176), rules on the merger of UCITS (Commission Dir. 2010/44/EU, O.J. 2010, L 176) and detailed rules on organizational requirements, conflict of interests, conduct of business risk management and content of the agreement between a depositary and a management company (Commission Dir. 2010/43/EU, O.J. 2010, L 176).
189. European Commission, "Directive on Alternative Investment Fund Managers ('AIFMD'): Frequently Asked Questions", MEMO/10/527, 11 Nov. 2010. From 2013 to 2015, the regulatory framework was complemented with three regulations which particularly focused on rules regarding European venture capital funds (Reg. (EU) 345/2013 of the European Parliament and of the Council of 17 April 2013 on European venture capital funds, O.J. 2013, L 115), European social entrepreneurship funds (Reg. (EU) 346/2013 of the European Parliament and of the Council of 17 April 2013 on European social entrepreneurship funds, O.J. 2013, L 115) and European long-term investment funds (Reg. (EU) 2015/760 of the European Parliament and of the Council of 29 April 2015 on European long-term investment funds, O.J. 2015, L 123).
190. N. Moloney, op. cit. *supra* note 1, 284. The rules have been further detailed in various Level 2 acts. See, e.g., Commission Delegated Reg. (EU) 231/2013 of 19 Dec. 2012, O.J. 2013, L 83.
191. Arts. 6–8 AIFMD.
192. Arts. 12 and 14 AIFMD.
193. Art. 13 AIFMD.
194. Art. 18 et seq. AIFMD.
195. Art. 21 et seq. AIFMD.
196. Recital 13 Regulation on money market funds.
197. Cf. Recital 11–12 Regulation on money market funds.

money market funds provides for rules on, *inter alia*, the authorization of MMFs[198] and the investment policies adopted by MMFs.[199]

Also, European rules with regard to market facilitators such as credit rating agencies have been adopted. Credit rating agencies issue credit ratings on the creditworthiness of states, companies, financial institutions and financial instruments. They are market facilitators (also called gatekeepers or information intermediaries) in the sense that they provide market participants with information on issuers and their financial instruments, which enhances price forming mechanisms.[200] In response to the malpractices of credit rating agencies that were discovered in the aftermath of the financial crisis, the Regulation on Credit Rating Agencies (CRA Regulation)[201] provides a regulatory framework that aims "to enhance the integrity, transparency, responsibility, good governance and independence of credit rating activities".[202] To that end, rules have been established in order to manage and avoid conflicts of interest,[203] to increase the competition between credit rating agencies,[204] to reduce the over-reliance on credit ratings,[205] and to reduce (and eventually eliminate) the use of credit ratings for regulatory purposes.[206]

3.4 *Insurers and pension funds*

Insurers and pension funds collect assets (premiums and contributions) from their policy holders and members and pay out reimbursements and pensions to their beneficiaries. Insurers and pension funds can be considered financial intermediaries, as are banks. They owe obligations to many consumers, as they have promised to make payments to them upon the occurrence of certain future events.[207] At the same time, they are institutional investors that collectively invest and manage the assets provided to them by policy holders and members. Due to their key function in society and because their mismanagement could cause severe damage to many consumers, insurers and pensions funds have been made subject to European regulation.[208]

---

198. Art. 4 Regulation on money market funds.
199. E.g. Art. 8 et seq. and Art. 17 et seq. Regulation on money market funds.
200. Cf. J. Armour, D. Awrey, P. Davies et al., op. cit. *supra* note 70, 34.
201. Reg. (EC) 1060/2009 of the European Parliament and of the Council of 16 Sept. 2009 on credit rating agencies, O.J. 2009, L 302 (CRA Reg.). This Regulation has been amended twice by Reg. (EU) 513/2011 of the European Parliament and of the Council of 11 May 2011 amending Reg. (EC) 1060/2009 on credit rating agencies, O.J. 2011, L 145 (CRA II) and Reg. (EU) 462/2013 of the European Parliament and of the Council of 21 May 2013 amending Reg. (EC) 1060/2009 on credit rating agencies, O.J. 2013, L 146 (CRA III).
202. Art. 1 CRA Reg.
203. Art. 1 CRA Reg.
204. Recital 11 CRA III.
205. Recital 9 CRA III.
206. Recital 8 CRA III. With regard to the removal of references to credit ratings in legislation, ESMA has remarked in an evaluation in 2015 that "[t]he process to reduce reliance on ratings in a European context can [...] be said to be at an early stage", see ESMA/2015/1471, 36. The approach of CRA Reg. has been criticized for following a double strategy: on the one hand, the CRA Reg. includes provisions in order to improve the quality and reliability of credit ratings, while, on the other hand, the CRA Reg. attempts to reduce the overreliance on credit ratings by financial markets and legislators. See F. Amtenbrink and K. Heine, "Regulating credit rating agencies in the European Union. Lessons from behavioural science" (2013) *The Dovenschmidt Quarterly*, 10 et seq.
207. Cf. with respect to insurers J. Armour, D. Awrey, P. Davies et al., op. cit. *supra* note 70, 493–494. See, on whether systemic risk is involved with the insurer business, also ibid., 495 et seq. and F. Hufeld, R.S.J. Koijen and C. Thimann, *The Economics, Regulation, and Systemic Risk of Insurance Markets* (OUP, 2017).
208. Cf. Proposal for a Dir. of the European Parliament and of the Council on the taking-up and pursuit of the business of Insurance and Reinsurance Solvency II, p. 2 and Proposal for a Dir. of the European Parliament

The EU regulatory framework of insurers was established in the Solvency II Framework Directive.[209] The Directive entered into force in January 2016[210] and was amended by the Omnibus II Directive[211] in order to implement the powers of EIOPA.[212] The main purpose of Solvency II is to protect policy holders and beneficiaries and to protect financial stability.[213] To that end, Solvency II includes rules on the authorization of insurers and a corresponding "passporting" regime,[214] conditions governing the insurer business (for instance, on governance and public disclosure)[215] and prudential requirements for insurers.[216] The European Commission has adopted an extensive Delegated Regulation which forms "the core of the single prudential rulebook for insurance and reinsurance undertakings".[217]

The European regulatory framework of institutions for occupational retirement provisions (IORPs), i.e. pension funds, has been established in the IORP Directive of 2003.[218] A Commission proposal to amend the IORP Directive was adopted by the European Parliament and approved by the Council of the EU in December 2016,[219] and resulted in the IORP Directive (recast),[220] which must be implemented by the Member States before 13 January 2019.[221] The IORP Directive establishes rules regarding the taking-up and pursuit of activities carried out by pension funds,[222] thereby aiming to protect the interests of future pensioners and to enhance the efficient management of collective occupational pension schemes.[223] To that end, for instance, under Article 18 IORP Directive (Art. 19 IORP Directive (recast)), European pension funds must invest contributions as a prudent person would do so (the so called "prudent person" rule). With regard to the IORP Directive (recast), four main objectives have been formulated

---

and of the Council on the activities of institutions for occupational retirement provision COM(2000)507 final – COD 2000/0260.

209. Dir. 2009/138/EC of the European Parliament and of the Council of 25 Nov. 2009 on the taking-up and pursuit of the business of Insurance and Reinsurance (Solvency II), O.J. 2009, L 335.
210. Dir. 2013/58/EU of the European Parliament and of the Council of 11 Dec. 2013 amending Dir. 2009/138/EC (Solvency II) as regards the date for its transposition and the date of its application, and the date of repeal of certain Directives (Solvency I), O.J. 2013, L 341.
211. Dir. 2014/51/EU of the European Parliament and of the Council of 16 Apr. 2014 amending Dir. 2003/71/EC and 2009/138/EC and Regs. (EC) 1060/2009, (EU) 1094/2010 and (EU) 1095/2010 in respect of the powers of the European Supervisory Authority (European Insurance and Occupational Pensions Authority) and the European Supervisory Authority (European Securities and Markets Authority), O.J. 2014, L 153.
212. Cf. recital 7 Omnibus II Directive.
213. Recital 16 Solvency II Framework Directive.
214. Arts. 14 and 15 Solvency II Framework Directive.
215. Art. 40 et seq. Solvency II Framework Directive.
216. Art. 128 et seq. Solvency II Framework Directive.
217. European Commission – Fact Sheet. Solvency II Overview, MEMO 15-3120, 12 Jan. 2015, 2. Commission Delegated Reg. (EU) 2015/35, O.J. 2015, L 12 as amended by Commission Delegated Reg. (EU) 2016/467, O.J. 2016, L 6. In 2017, further amendments to the Delegated Regulation have been proposed (Commision Delegated Reg. (EU) 2017/1542 of 8 June 2017 amending Delegated Reg. (EU) 2015/35 concerning the calculation of regulatory capital requirements for certain categories of assets held by insurance and reinsurance undertakings (infrastructure corporates)).
218. Dir. 2003/41/EC of the European Parliament and of the Council of 3 June 2003 on the activities and supervision of institutions for occupational retirement provision, O.J. 2003, L 235.
219. Proposal for a Dir. of the European Parliament and of the Council on the activities and supervision of institutions for occupational retirement provision (recast), COM(2014)167.
220. Dir. (EU) 2016/2341 of the European Parliament and of the Council of 14 Dec. 2016 on the activities and supervision of institutions for occupational retirement provision (IORPs) (recast), O.J. 2016, L 354.
221. Art. 64 IORP Directive (recast).
222. Art. 1 IORP Directive.
223. Recital 7 IORP Directive.

in the Commission proposal: to remove the remaining prudential barriers for cross-border IORPs; to ensure good governance and risk management; to improve the provision of information to members and beneficiaries; and to provide supervisors with tools to supervise IORPs effectively.[224]

In addition to the regulatory framework for occupational pension funds, in June 2017, the European Commission launched a legislative proposal for a Regulation creating a new pan-European Personal Pension Product (PEPP).[225] As appears from the proposal, PEPPs are meant as an additional mode of pension saving for consumers introduced as part of the European Commission's Action Plan on the Capital Markets Union.[226]

4. Supervision and enforcement

4.1 Introduction

The regulatory dimension of the European financial markets has been sketched in brief in section 3. As shown, a high level of harmonization, and on some points even unification, has been achieved in EU financial regulation, both as regards prudential and conduct of business rules. However, to speak with the words of Moloney: "Regulation does not operate in a vacuum: it must be operationalized through supervision".[227] This quote underlines the traditional and fundamental distinction between regulation and supervision. Regulation refers to the applicable legal provisions which regulate financial activities, whereas supervision concerns enforcement of these legal provisions including monitoring, taking decisions and (criminal and administrative) sanctioning. Such strict distinction does not mirror practice as the border is regularly blurred, but will prove effective to understand the relation between sections 3 and 4.

To return to Moloney's quote: Regulation would remain a mere toothless tiger without effective supervision and enforcement, as the global financial crisis has painfully demonstrated. National procedural autonomy of the Member States lies at the heart of enforcing substantive Union law.[228] Therefore, Member States have been left a large degree of discretion as regards selecting enforcement instruments and supervisory approaches to apply EU legislation. The same applies to supervision and enforcement of financial regulation. As a result of national procedural autonomy in applying and enforcing EU financial regulation, a lack of consistent supervisory and sanctioning powers has continued (and still continues) to exist across the different Member States.[229] However, even if financial legislation is harmonized, financial supervisory practice remains characterized by wide discretionary powers of the supervisory authorities and national supervisory traditions of the Member States. Moreover, a great amount of financial regulation has been enacted in Directives which have to be implemented in the national laws of the Member States. The exercise of supervision, therefore, is not exhaustively determined by identical pan-European "hard rules", i.e. legislation. So even extensively harmonized financial regulation,

224. The Proposal for a Dir. of the European Parliament and of the Council on the activities and supervision of institutions for occupational retirement provision (recast), COM(2014)167, 3–4.
225. Proposal for a Reg. on a pan-European Personal Pension Product (PEPP), COM(2017)343 final.
226. COM(2017)343 final, 2–3.
227. N. Moloney, op. cit. *supra* note 1, 944.
228. However, once a particular procedural matter is regulated at Union level, the Member States lose their "procedural competence" with regard to this matter, see W. van Gerven, "Of rights, remedies and procedures", (2000) CML Rev., 502.
229. De Larosière Report, cited *supra* note 20, 28 and 41; Communication from the European Commission, Reinforcing sanctioning regimes in the financial services sector, COM(2010)716, 5–7.

such as current EU banking law, did not prevent fragmentation of supervisory practices across the EU.[230]

These inconsistencies in national supervisory regimes ultimately undermine financial stability in both Member States and the EU. Ineffective enforcement with regard to one or more individual financial institutions could lead to financial instability in one Member State and could ultimately spill over to financial stability in another. Moreover, such inconsistencies in supervisory regimes may also be a stimulus for "regulatory arbitrage", so that financial institutions elect the State with the most favourable and lax regime to do business in, ultimately undermining financial stability. The conclusion which should be drawn from the above, is that merely harmonizing financial regulation, without having regard to the financial supervisory practice, will not be sufficient to reduce the risk of regulatory arbitrage.[231]

To overcome these inconsistencies in supervisory regimes, the De Larosière Report recommended to complement the EU regulatory framework with a new supervisory architecture by means of a European System of Financial Supervision (ESFS).[232] All 28 Member States of the EU fall within the scope of the ESFS. As of 4 November 2014, the ECB, and as of 1 January 2016 the SRB, also form part of the financial supervisory architecture. The remit of both the ECB and the SRB covers the "participating Member States", which are currently only the 19 Member States within the euro area.[233] The ESAs, the ECB and the NCAs are primarily engaged in micro-prudential supervision: supervision that focuses on the stability of individual institutions. The ESRB in collaboration with the ECB has the responsibility for macro-prudential oversight, i.e. of the financial system's stability as a whole, with the aim of monitoring systemic risk. The SRB fulfils the role of centralized resolution authority with regard to euro area credit institutions.

This section will have its focus on the organization of supervision and enforcement of EU financial regulation by the ESAs, the ECB and the SRB. We understand "enforcement" here in a broad sense, so as to also include the SRB's application of EU law, mainly the SRM Regulation. The following subsections aim to provide an overview of the current supervisory structure and its key players, including the relevant national authorities.

The structure of this chapter could suggest that the ESAs are the main supervisory authorities within the European supervisory architecture. However, as will be elaborated on hereafter, the ESAs' primary task is of a regulatory, rather than of a supervisory nature. Within the SSM, it is the NCAs together with the ECB which should be regarded as the main supervisory authorities. In other sectors, for instance those concerning non-euro area banks or conduct of business supervision of (both euro area and non-euro area) banks, the national authorities have remained primarily responsible for financial supervision.

4.2 *European Supervisory Authorities*

As discussed above, in section 2.2, the three ESAs have been established as a result of the recommendations in the De Larosière Report. The ESAs are successors of the former "level 3 committees": the Committee of European Banking Supervision (CEBS), the Committee of European Insurance and Occupational Pensions Supervisors (CEIOPS), and the Committee of European Securities Regulators (CESR).[234] The De Larosière Report considered the structure and com-

---

230. E. Wymeersch, op. cit. *supra* note 48, 5.
231. Also E. Wymeersch, op. cit. *supra* note 48, 5.
232. See also *supra*, sections 2.2 and 3.1.
233. Therefore Bulgaria, Czech Republic, Croatia, Denmark, Hungary, Poland, Romania, Sweden and the United Kingdom fall outside the scope of the Banking Union.
234. Recital 10 ESA Reg.

petences of the Level 3 committees not sufficient to ensure financial stability in the EU and its Member States,[235] mainly because these networks of supervisors acted merely as advisory bodies to the European Commission and their actions did not have legally binding effects.[236] At first glance, the ESAs essentially followed in the footsteps of their predecessors with regard to the competences of the latter.[237] However, the ESAs have been fitted with additional legally binding powers, which clearly distinguishes them from the former Level 3 committees.[238]

The De Larosière Report emphasizes the fact that the formation of ESAs does not intend to transfer competences from the NCAs, including the day-to-day supervision, to the ESAs, while referring to the principles of subsidiarity and proportionality as enshrined in the Treaty on the Functioning of the European Union.[239] The relationship between the ESAs and the NCAs is sometimes referred to as a "hub-and-spoke" model; the ESAs as hubs in their regulatory capacity and the NCAs as spokes in their capacity as implementers.[240] However, this hub-and-spoke system does not prevent any hierarchy from existing in their relation.[241] The hierarchal structure, with the ESAs as higher-ranked, is reflected in their supervisory powers as will be described below.

Following the 2017 review of the ESAs,[242] the European Commission identified various problems and published on 20 September 2017 a proposal for a Regulation amending the ESAs' framework.[243] This proposes amendments to the ESA Regulations and to, *inter alia*, MiFIR and

---

235. De Larosière Report, cited *supra* note 20, 46–47.
236. De Larosière Report, cited *supra* note 20, 47.
237. Recital 10 ESA Reg.; Art. 8 ESA Reg.; De Larosière Report, cited *supra* note 20, 2; E. Ferran, "Understanding the New Institutional Architecture of EU Financial Market Supervision" in E. Wymeersch, K.J. Hopt and G. Ferrarini (Eds.), *Financial Regulation and Supervision. A Post-Crisis Analysis* (OUP, 2012), 137.
238. E. Ferran, op. cit. *supra* note 237, 138.
239. De Larosière Report, cited *supra* note 20, 47; Recital 9 ESA Reg. Ferran however argues that the step-by-step assumption of supervisory responsibilities by pan-European authorities is very likely to lead to the emergence of powerful European supervisory authorities and a "full federalization of supervisory responsibility", see E. Ferran, op. cit. *supra* note 237, 111–158. See also: E. Wymeersch, "The institutional reforms of the European financial supervisory system", (2010) *European Company and Financial Law*.
240. E. Wymeersch, op. cit. *supra* note 9, at 235 and 317; J. Black, "Restructuring global and EU financial regulation: Character, capacities and learning" in E. Wymeersch, K.J. Hopt and G. Ferrarini (Eds.), *Financial Regulation and Supervision. A Post-Crisis Analysis* (OUP, 2012), 32.
241. J. Black, op. cit. *supra* note 240, 32.
242. See European Commission, Staff Working Document, Impact Assessment accompanying a proposal for a Reg. of the European Parliament and of the Council amending Reg. (EU) 1093/2010 establishing a European Supervisory Authority (European Banking Authority), Reg. (EU) 1094/2010 establishing a European Supervisory Authority (European Insurance and Occupational Pensions Authority), Reg. (EU) 1095/2010 establishing a European Supervisory Authority (European Securities and Markets Authority), Reg. (EU) 345/2013 on European venture capital funds, Reg. (EU) 346/2013 on European social entrepreneurship funds, Reg. (EU) 600/2014 on markets in financial instruments, Reg. (EU) 2015/760 on European long-term investment funds, Reg. (EU) 2016/2011 on indices used as benchmarks in financial instruments and financial contracts or to measure the performance of investment funds, Reg. (EU) 2017/1129 on the prospectus to be published when securities are offered to the public or admitted to trading on a regulated market, SWD(2017)308 final (hereinafter: "ESAs Impact Assessment").
243. European Commission, Proposal for a Reg. of the European Parliament and of the Council amending Reg. (EU) 1093/2010 establishing a European Supervisory Authority (European Banking Authority), Reg. (EU) 1094/2010 establishing a European Supervisory Authority (European Insurance and Occupational Pensions Authority), Reg. (EU) 1095/2010 establishing a European Supervisory Authority (European Securities and Markets Authority), Reg. (EU) 345/2013 on European venture capital funds, Reg. (EU) 346/2013 on European social entrepreneurship funds, Reg. (EU) 600/2014 on markets in financial instruments, Reg. (EU) 2015/760 on European long-term investment funds, Reg. (EU) 2016/2011 on indices used as benchmarks in financial instruments and financial contracts or to measure the performance of investment

the Prospectus Regulation. The amendments concern: (i) the ESAs' powers in certain areas; (ii) the governance framework; and (iii) the funding framework. Where relevant for this section, reference will be made to specific proposed amendments.

4.2.1 *Supervisory powers*

As explained, as a matter of principle, the day-to-day supervision remains a competence of the NCAs. Moreover, the ESAs' primary task is of a regulatory nature aiming at supervisory convergence.[244] Under certain circumstances, however, they have also been entrusted with supervisory powers which may be legally binding towards either NCAs, or towards supervised institutions directly. First, the ESAs may have legally binding powers towards the NCAs in question in case of "breach of Union law",[245] in an emergency situation,[246] or if a disagreement continues to exist between NCAs in cross-border situations.[247] Second, the ESAs have the power to take legally binding decisions towards supervised institutions directly.[248] This competence is emergency-driven and only materializes in exceptional circumstances. Third, the ESAs have the power to temporarily prohibit or restrict certain financial activities that threaten the orderly functioning and integrity of financial markets or the stability of the financial system.[249] These legally binding supervisory powers will be discussed in more detail below. It will be shown that these competences predominantly have a "last resort" character, which is expressed in the conditions which have to be met in order to use them.[250]

The major supervisory decisions, including the above-mentioned categories, are taken by the main decision-making body of the ESAs, their respective Boards of Supervisors (BoSs).[251] These BoSs are composed of the representatives of the 28 respective NCAs as voting members.[252] The European Commission, the ECB, the ESRB and the two other ESAs each provide one representative, which together with the ESA non-voting Chairperson constitute the non-voting part of the BoSs.[253] Decisions are in general taken by simple majority.[254] With regard to most decisions[255] of EBA, a so-called "double majority" system of voting has been implemented as a consequence of the Banking Union.[256] This system aims at safeguarding non-euro area

funds, Reg. (EU) 2017/1129 on the prospectus to be published when securities are offered to the public or admitted to trading on a regulated market, COM(2017)536 final (hereinafter: Proposal to amend the ESAs' framework).

244. See more extensively on these regulatory powers, section 3.
245. Art. 17 ESA Reg.
246. Art. 18(3) ESA Reg.
247. Art. 8(1)(e) jo. Arts. 18(3) and 19(3) ESA Reg.; Art. 17(1)(2)(3) ESA Reg. Both illustrative for the "last resort" character of the legal binding powers of the ESAs.
248. Art. 8(1)(f) jo. Arts. 17(6), 18(4) and 19(4) ESA Reg.
249. Art. 9(5) ESA Reg.
250. E. Ferran, op. cit. *supra* note 237, 138.
251. Art. 43(1) ESA Reg.
252. Recital 52 ESA Reg.; Art. 40 ESA Reg.
253. Art. 40(1)(c)(d)(e) ESA Reg.
254. Art. 44(1) ESA Reg.
255. Decisions concerning breaches of Union law (Art. 17), settlement of disagreements (Art. 19) and actions in emergency situations (Art. 18) are taken by a simple majority including the double majority system. Decisions on technical standards (Arts. 10–16) and on measures and decisions concerning the prohibition and restriction of financial activities (Art. 9(5)) are taken by a qualified majority including the double majority system.
256. Art. 44(1) EBA Reg. as amended by Reg. (EU) 1022/2013 of the European Parliament and of the Council of 22 Oct. 2013 amending Reg. (EU) 1093/2010 establishing a European Supervisory Authority (European

Member States, particularly the United Kingdom, against a decision-making process which could be dominated by the 19 euro area Member States.

Part of the European Commission's proposal to enhance the governance structure of the ESAs is the establishment of Executive Boards within the ESAs. The Executive Board's main function will be preparing decisions to be taken by the BoS.[257] In addition, the Executive Boards are envisaged to have decision-making powers concerning certain non-regulatory tasks currently within the remit of the BoSs. Although the proposal still refers to the BoSs as the main body of the ESAs,[258] the Executive Boards will be granted decision-making powers in, among others, the areas of breach of Union law and settlement of disputes between NCAs.[259] As it is these areas where "incentive misalignments", between the EU and national interests, "are most problematic".[260] In other words: the composition of the BoSs, comprising representatives from the 28 NCAs as voting members, leads, in the view of the Commission, to a governance arrangement that is "dominated by national authorities and so does not foster effective and efficient decision making on matters where there is a strong EU interest."[261] The Executive Boards will therefore be composed of a Chairperson and a number of full-time members who are externally appointed.[262]

Breach of Union law (Art. 17 ESA Regulations)

If an NCA has incorrectly or insufficiently applied Union law, a "three-step mechanism"[263] applies aiming to resolve such breach: (i) the ESAs are empowered to investigate the alleged breach[264] and may address a recommendation to the NCA concerning measures to end this breach;[265] (ii) if the NCA does not comply with the recommendation, the European Commission is empowered to issue a formal opinion requiring the NCA to comply with Union law;[266] and (iii) in case of continual inaction, the ESAs may take an individual decision addressed towards a supervised institution, provided that such decision "is necessary to remedy in a timely manner such non-compliance in order to maintain or restore neutral conditions of competition in the market or ensure the orderly functioning and integrity of the financial system".[267] Such individual decision directed towards a supervised institution prevails over any previous decision adopted by the NCA on the same matter.[268] This action is sometimes referred to as the "knight's move", for it is as if the ESA jumps over, i.e. bypasses, the NCA. Such breach of "Union law" comprises Level 1 and Level 2 legislation, as well as the general principles of the TFEU,

---

Banking Authority) as regards the conferral of specific tasks on the European Central Bank pursuant to Council Reg. (EU) 1024/2013, O.J. 2013, L 287.

257. Proposal to amend the ESAs' framework, 22.
258. Proposal to amend the ESAs' framework, 23.
259. Proposal to amend the ESAs' framework, 20, 22–23.
260. Proposal to amend the ESAs' framework, 275.
261. ESAs Impact Assessment, 160.
262. Proposal to amend the ESAs' framework, 22–23.
263. Recital 28 ESA Reg. Although Ferran distinguishes four "stages" by dividing step i. in two stages, E. Ferran, op. cit. *supra* note 237, 145.
264. Art. 17(2)–(3) ESA Reg.
265. Art. 17(3)–(4) ESA Reg.
266. Art. 17(4)–(5) ESA Reg.
267. Art. 17(6) ESA Reg.
268. Art. 17(7) ESA Reg. Moloney points at the "invidious position" of a supervised entity if it is confronted with conflicting decisions of the ESA on the one hand and the NCA on the other, see N. Moloney, "The European Securities and Markets Authority and institutional design for the EU financial market – A tale of two competences: Part (2) rules in action", (2011) EBOR, 202.

but probably also soft law instruments issued by the respective NCA, such as guidelines and recommendations.[269] Including the latter in the definition of Union law will therefore result in ESAs enforcing NCAs to correctly apply their own NCA-issued rules. Hence, these supervisory powers may cover a wide range of breaches.

It follows from the regime described above that the competence to take an individual decision addressed to a supervised institution is only activated if the NCA does not comply with the European Commission's formal opinion and if the individual decision is necessary to remedy non-compliance in a timely manner in order to maintain or restore neutral conditions of competition or ensure the orderly functioning and integrity of the financial system. Ferran and Wymeersch both argue that step (iii) is most likely to be rarely used. Ferran highlights that this competence will only materialize in the unusual instance that the NCA does not comply with the European Commission's formal opinion.[270] She also emphasizes that the principle of "sincere cooperation" and the obligations of NCAs to share information and assist the ESAs in carrying out their tasks[271] will prevent escalating enforcement to the third step.[272] Wymeersch believes that enforcement actions on the basis of this provision will probably be uncommon due to the emergency-driven component.[273]

Another important limitation to the power to direct an individual decision towards a supervised institution, is the condition that ESAs in their capacity as "knights" may only apply directly applicable legislation. In other words: ESAs will remain powerless to apply EU legislation that must first be implemented in national law, such as Directives and Member States' options in Regulations. A more practical restraint to this competence is the absence of an enforcement power in cases where a supervised institution fails to comply with a decision addressed to it by an ESA.

In the Commission's proposal to amend the ESAs' framework, the Commission has proposed to broaden the ESAs' investigatory powers under Article 17 ESA Regulations to increase its effectiveness. The proposed amendment will empower the ESAs to request information not only from the NCA allegedly in breach of EU law, but also from other competent authorities, financial institutions and financial market participants.[274]

Action in emergency situations (Art. 18 ESA Regulations)

In an emergency situation, the ESA Regulations provide for a "two-step mechanism" to respond: (i) the ESAs have the power to take decisions addressed to an NCA;[275] and (ii) if the NCA does not comply with that decision, the ESA may take a decision directly addressed to a supervised institution.[276] For the "knight's move" competence of step (ii) to materialize, the NCA must be in breach of its legislative obligations and "urgent remedying is necessary to restore the orderly functioning and integrity of financial markets or the stability of the whole or part of the financial system in the Union".[277] Again, in this capacity ESAs are only empowered to apply directly applicable EU legislation.

---

269. E. Wymeersch, op. cit. *supra* note 9, 257.
270. E. Wymeersch, op. cit. *supra* note 9, 262.
271. Recital 46 ESA Reg.; Arts. 2(4), 17(2) etc. ESA Reg.
272. E. Ferran, op. cit. *supra* note 237, 146.
273. E. Wymeersch, op. cit. *supra* note 9, 262.
274. Proposal to amend the ESAs' framework, 20.
275. Art. 18(3) ESA Reg.
276. Art. 18(4) ESA Reg.
277. Art. 18(4) ESA Reg.

The power to address an "emergency decision" to an NCA materializes in two situations: after a formal declaration of emergency has been taken by the Council of the EU in consultation with the European Commission and the ESRB and, where appropriate, the ESAs;[278] and without such formal declaration, "in exceptional circumstances where coordinated action by national authorities is necessary to respond to adverse developments which may seriously jeopardize the orderly functioning and integrity of financial markets or the stability of the whole or part of the financial system in the Union".[279]

A decision triggered by a (formal or informal) emergency situation must encompass an obligation for the NCA "to take the necessary action in accordance with the legislation referred to in Article 1(2) to address any such developments by ensuring that financial market participants and competent authorities satisfy the requirements laid down in that legislation".[280] Article 1(2) refers to the relevant Level 1 legislation, "all directives, regulations, and decisions based on the mentioned Level 1 legislation" and "any further legally binding Union Act which confers tasks on the Authority": *inter alia*, Level 1 instruments, Level 2 instruments and RTSs/ITSs. The scope of this competence therefore is dependent on the obligations of the NCAs laid down in the relevant EU legislation.[281]

Settling disagreements between competent authorities (Art. 19 ESA Regulations)

A "two-step mechanism" has also been introduced to resolve issues as regards disagreements between NCAs in cross-border situations.[282] This mediatory function of the ESAs may result in (i) a decision addressed to the NCAs in question,[283] and (ii) a decision directly addressed to supervised institutions.[284]

The ESAs' competence to take a "mediatory" decision addressed to NCAs is activated, if the NCAs in question do not reach an agreement within the so-called conciliation period.[285] Legislation as mentioned in Article 1(2) needs to provide for this "mediation" competence and determines its conditions and scope.[286] The aim of such decision is to require the relevant NCAs to take or refrain from action in order to settle the matter "in order to ensure compliance with Union law".[287] If an NCA is in breach of such "mediatory" decision and as a result fails to ensure the compliance of a market participant with directly applicable legislation, the relevant ESA may, again, use its "knight's move" to directly address a decision to a supervised institution.[288]

In the Commission's proposal, amendments have been proposed to ensure that the ESAs may act and intervene decisively if a disagreement occurs. The amendments seek to clarify, *inter alia*, that settlements may also be triggered on initiative of the ESAs "where on the basis of objective criteria a disagreement can be determined" between NCAs.[289]

278. Art. 18(2) ESA Reg.
279. Art. 18(3) ESA Reg.
280. Art. 18(3) ESA Reg.
281. E. Wymeersch, op. cit. *supra* note 9, 245.
282. Art. 19 ESA Reg.
283. Art. 19(3) ESA Reg.
284. Art. 19(4) ESA Reg.
285. Art. 19(2)–(3) ESA Reg.
286. Art. 19(1) ESA Reg.; E. Wymeersch, op. cit. *supra* note 9, 266.
287. Art. 19(3) ESA Reg.
288. Art. 19(4) ESA Reg.
289. Proposal to amend the ESAs' framework, 20.

Financial activities (Art. 9 ESA Regulations)

A different type of supervisory powers is the power of the ESAs to act against dangerous financial activities that threaten the orderly functioning and integrity of financial markets or the stability of the financial system by either temporarily prohibiting or restricting them.[290] This tool may only be used by the ESAs in cases where legislation, as mentioned in Article 1(2) provides for it, or in the case of a formal emergency situation.[291] The power to prohibit or restrict certain financial activities may possibly qualify as an EU decision which is legally binding to the parties addressed, either NCAs or both NCAs and all supervised institutions involved.[292]

An example of the power to act against such dangerous financial activities has been provided for in Article 40 MiFIR, which confers on ESMA "temporary intervention powers", under certain conditions. On 27 March 2018, ESMA exercised this power by introducing measures concerning a temporary prohibition on the marketing, distribution or sale of binary options to retail investors and a temporary restriction on the marketing, distribution or sale of contracts for differences (CFDs) to retail investors.[293]

Exclusive supervisory powers: ESMA

ESMA has a special position among the other two ESAs, as it has been entrusted with direct and exclusive supervisory powers in relation to credit rating agencies (CRAs).[294] The contribution of CRAs to the global financial crisis has received extensive coverage in the political debate. Matters such as conflicts of interest embedded in the issuer-pays business model and the lack of market transparency led to the EU Regulation on credit rating agencies (CRA I) in 2009.[295] Whereas CRA I primarily allocated supervision of CRAs established in the Member States to the NCAs, the De Larosière Report advocated a centralized supervisory model.[296] This recommendation has been implemented in the Regulation amending CRA I (CRA II), which entrusts ESMA with the exclusive supervision of CRAs.[297] The supervisory competences include the registration of CRAs, ongoing monitoring of CRAs and sanctioning powers.[298] In the meanwhile, and as discussed above under section 3.2.2, CRA III has been adopted.[299]

The Commission's proposals to amend the ESAs' framework aim to expand ESMA's exclusive supervisory powers significantly. The proposals include designating ESMA as the competent authority for administrators of critical benchmarks, for benchmarks used in the EU but

290. Art. 9(5) ESA Reg.
291. Art. 9(5) ESA Reg.
292. E. Wymeersch, op. cit. *supra* note 9, 274.
293. ESMA, Additional information on the agreed product intervention measures relating to contracts for differences and binary options, 27 March 2018, ESMA35-43-1000, available at <www.esma.europa.eu/document/additional-information-agreed-product-intervention-measures-relating-contracts-differences>.
294. ESMA also has direct and exclusive supervisory powers in relation to trade repositories under EMIR, see Art. 55 et seq. EMIR.
295. Reg. (EC) 1060/2009 of the European Parliament and of the Council of 16 Sept. 2009 on credit rating agencies, O.J. 2009, L 302 (CRA I). See *supra*, section 3.2.2.
296. De Larosière Report, cited *supra* note 20, 19–20.
297. Reg. (EU) 513/2011 of the European Parliament and of the Council of 11 May 2011 amending Reg. (EC) 1060/2009 on credit rating agencies, O.J. 2011, L 145 (CRA II).
298. Arts. 5, 15–21, 24, 36a, b et seq. CRA II.
299. See also *supra*, section 3.3.2., Reg. (EU) 462/2013 of the European Parliament and of the Council of 21 May 2013 amending Reg. (EC) 1060/2009 on credit rating agencies, O.J. 2013, L 146 (CRA III).

administered outside the Union, for data reporting service providers, and with regard to certain categories of prospectuses.[300]

4.2.2 *Joint Committee of the ESAs*

The regulatory and supervisory functions of the ESAs have been divided by sector, symbolizing the classic organization of the financial industry: banks, markets and securities and insurers and pension funds.[301] However, this traditional division has been increasingly blurred since the end of the 20th century.[302] Notwithstanding this development, one fully integrated "super ESA"[303] nor setting up all ESAs in one Member State to further integration proved politically feasible. As a result, cross-sectoral issues are dealt with at the level of the individual ESAs. To (partly) fill in this supervisory gap of cross-sectoral issues a coordinating Joint Committee has been established, the successor of the former "Three Level 3 Committees" at the time of the Level 3 committees.[304] Recalling the blurring of sectors, it seems almost all issues in one sector will in one way or the other affect another.[305] A small amount of these cross-sectoral issues will however be dealt with at joint level.[306] Article 54(2) ESA Regulations illustrates the range of possible cross-sectoral issues which may be dealt with at the level of the Joint Committee, including: financial conglomerates, accounting and auditing and retail investment products. As the Joint Committee does not have the competence to take binding decisions, the Joint Committee will either result in reaching "joint positions" of the involved ESAs, or in measures which are "adopted in parallel" with regard to such issues.[307]

The Commission's proposal to amend the ESAs' framework includes amendments expanding the remit of the Joint Committee, so as to also include consumer and investor protection issues.[308]

4.3 Banking Union

4.3.1 *Single Supervisory Mechanism: ECB*

The SSM was established by the SSM Regulation, which centralizes prudential supervision of credit institutions in both the euro area Member States and other Member States that have elected to accede to the SSM (hereinafter together: "participating Member States") under the ECB.[309]

300. Proposal to amend the ESAs' framework, 28–30.
301. Even though the De Larosière Report emphasizes the future merits of a more functional approach to financial supervision, see De Larosière Report, cited *supra* note 20, 58.
302. See V. Colaert, op. cit. *supra* note 54, 1579–1616. See section 3.1.
303. E. Wymeersch, op. cit. *supra* note 9, 288.
304. Arts. 54–57 ESA Reg.
305. E. Wymeersch, op. cit. *supra* note 9, 289.
306. E. Wymeersch, op. cit. *supra* note 9, 289.
307. Art. 56 ESA Reg.
308. Proposal to amend the ESAs' framework, 24.
309. See, more extensively, E. Wymeersch, op. cit. *supra* note 48; E. Wymeersch, "The Single Supervisory Mechanism: Institutional aspects" in D. Busch and G. Ferrarini (Eds.), *European Banking Union* (OUP, 2015), 93–117; E. Ferran and V. Babis, "The European Single Supervisory Mechanism", (2013) *Journal of Corporate Law Studies*, 255–85; G. Ferrarini and L. Chiarella, "Common banking supervision in the Eurozone: Strengths and weaknesses", (2013) *ECGI Law Working Paper No 223*.

Scope: Prudential supervision of credit institutions

Article 4(1) of the SSM Regulation confers on the ECB the exclusive competence to carry out the tasks relating to credit institutions "for prudential supervisory purposes". Other financial institutions, shadow banking activities,[310] the prevention of money laundering and terrorist financing, consumer protection, the financial markets and conduct supervision with respect to credit institutions are not within the scope of the SSM and will therefore remain with the national authorities.[311] However, as the SSM Regulation does not contain a definition of what constitutes prudential supervision, the exact scope of the ECB's supervisory competences is not entirely clear. Will the ECB for instance be unable to enforce rules on money laundering, even though a violation of these rules often goes hand in hand with violation of prudential provisions on risk management?[312] These blurred lines are likely to cause tensions and uncertainties as to whether certain issues fall within the remit of the national authorities, or of the ECB.

As a truly revolutionary new feature of the SSM, the ECB applies "all relevant Union law", which explicitly includes national legislation that transposes either Directives or Member States' options in Regulations, to carry out its supervisory tasks.[313] Although "relevant Union law" has not been specified in the SSM Regulation, the ECB's supervisory task is to ensure that credit institutions comply with the Single Rulebook, i.e. CRD IV and CRR, which comprises most of the relevant banking regulation. The ECB is responsible for, *inter alia*, the authorization and withdrawal of authorizations of credit institutions, ensuring compliance with the rules imposing prudential requirements in several areas and to have robust governance arrangements in place, carrying out supervisory reviews and supervisory tasks in relation to so-called recovery plans, which set out the bank's arrangements and measures in case of financial difficulties, and certain early intervention measures.[314] The ECB may also instruct the NCAs to make use of their additional national powers in accordance with the conditions as set out in national law.[315] Such instructions must fill in the competence gap which may emerge if the SSM Regulation does not provide the ECB with the power to carry out one of its tasks.

Direct and indirect supervision

The SSM is composed of both the ECB and the NCAs and puts a strong emphasis on their cooperation.[316] The allocation of supervisory competences between the ECB and the NCAs is stipulated in the SSM Regulation and the SSM Framework Regulation.[317] Important to note

---

310. The Financial Stability Board ("FSB") defines shadow banking as follows: "credit intermediation involving entities and activities (fully or partially) outside the regular banking system", see FSB, Transforming Shadow Banking into Resilient Market-based Finance, An Overview of Progress, 12 Nov. 2015, 1, available at <www.fsb.org/wp-content/uploads/shadow_banking_overview_of_progress_2015.pdf>. Examples of shadow banking activities are: securitization transactions and collateralized finance transactions, such as repurchase agreements (repos) and securities lending.
311. Recital 28 SSM Reg.
312. Example derived from E. Wymeersch, op. cit. *supra* note 48, 13.
313. Art. 4(3) SSM Reg. See, more extensively, A. Witte, "The application of National Banking Supervision Law by the ECB: Three parallel modes of executing EU law?" (2014) MJ, 105 et seq. As opposed to the ESAs, whose power to take decisions towards supervised institutions only materializes if the relevant legislation is directly applicable, i.e. Regulations, see section 4.2.1.
314. Art. 4(1) SSM Reg.
315. Art. 9(1) SSM Reg.
316. Art. 6 SSM Reg.
317. Reg. (EU) 468/2014 of the European Central Bank of 16 Apr. 2014 establishing the framework for cooperation within the Single Supervisory Mechanism between the European Central Bank and national competent authorities and with national designated authorities, O.J. 2014, L 141.

is that, even though the SSM framework provides for an allocation of prudential supervisory responsibilities divided between the ECB and the NCAs, the General Court (GC) held on 16 May 2017 in *Landeskreditbank Baden-Württemberg – Förderbank v. ECB* that the ECB must be regarded as exclusively competent in respect of *all* euro area credit institutions.[318] In this view, the exclusive supervisory competences are conferred on the ECB and implemented in a decentralized manner by the "assisting" NCAs within the framework of the SSM.[319]

With regard to the prudential supervisory tasks of the ECB listed in Article 4(1) SSM Regulation, except for the competence to authorize and to withdraw authorizations of credit institutions and the competence to assess notifications of the acquisition and disposal of qualifying holdings in credit institutions, the responsibilities of the ECB and the NCAs are allocated on the basis of significance of supervised credit institutions: significant credit institutions (SIs) are "directly" supervised by the ECB, whereas less significant credit institutions (LSIs) are "indirectly" supervised by the ECB.[320] The significance of a credit institution is determined on a consolidated basis and is assessed based on the following criteria: (i) size; (ii) importance for the economy of the Union or any participating Member State; and (iii) significance of cross-border activities.[321] An NCA may also notify the ECB that it considers a certain credit institution of significant relevance with regard to the domestic economy. The ECB takes a decision confirming or rejecting such significance.[322] Even if none of these criteria have been met, the ECB may yet declare a credit institution significant "to ensure the consistent application of high-quality supervisory standards".[323] This assumption of power may be of great significance, because the ECB lacks disciplining competences in relation to the NCAs.

Common procedures

This differentiation of supervisory responsibilities on the basis of significance does not apply to the competence to authorize and to withdraw authorizations of credit institutions, and to the competence to assess notifications of the acquisition and disposal of qualifying holdings in credit institutions, known as the "common procedures".[324] Both are exclusive tasks of the ECB.[325] This exclusiveness does not exclude the NCAs from any involvement in these procedures; they have an important preparatory and assisting role. For instance, the NCAs assist the ECB in the authorization procedures by taking final decisions rejecting authorization and by drafting decisions granting authorization which are ultimately confirmed by the ECB.[326]

Day-to-day supervision

The principal method of supervision under the SSM is of an ongoing and preventive nature with the objective of preventing a bank failure by ensuring banks meet the regulatory requirements

318. *Landeskreditbank Baden-Württemberg – Förderbank v. ECB* (Case T-122/15). See, more extensively, R. Smits, "Competences and alignment in an emerging future. After L-Bank: how the Eurosystem and the Single Supervisory Mechanism may develop", (2017) *Ademu Working Paper Series*.
319. Case T-122/15, *Landeskreditbank Baden-Württemberg*, paras. 50–64.
320. Art. 6(4) SSM Reg.
321. Art. 6(4) SSM Reg.
322. Art. 6(4) SSM Reg.
323. Art. 6(5b) SSM Reg.; ECB, Guide to Banking Supervision, Sept. 2014, 9, available at <www.bankingsupervision.europa.eu/ecb/pub/pdf/ssmguidebankingsupervision201411.en.pdf>.
324. ECB, Guide to Banking Supervision, Sept. 2014, 26, available at <www.bankingsupervision.europa.eu/ecb/pub/pdf/ssmguidebankingsupervision201411.en.pdf>.
325. Art. 6(4) SSM Reg.
326. Art. 16 SSM Reg.

and that they are managed prudently. The ECB has general and broad investigatory powers to carry out its designated tasks as the direct supervisor of SIs, including information requests,[327] general investigations[328] and announced and unannounced on-site inspections.[329] To conduct these on-site inspections, the ECB appoints on-site inspection teams, which are separate from the Joint Supervisory Teams (JSTs).[330]

The day-to-day supervision of SIs is conducted by JSTs of the ECB, consisting of staff from both the NCAs and the ECB.[331] Each SI has its own JST, which is led by a coordinator at the ECB.[332] The coordinator is responsible for the implementation of the supervisory tasks and activities, as included in the so-called Supervisory Examination Programme for each individual institution. The supervisory tasks of the JSTs include, *inter alia*, performing the supervisory review and evaluation process (SREP), participating in the preparation and implementation of a supervisory examination programme and implementing any ECB decisions with respect to SIs.[333]

Administrative measures

In case irregularities are detected in the course of day-to-day supervision, the ECB has the power to impose specific supervisory measures for the purpose of its supervisory tasks.[334] This power materializes in the following circumstances: (i) the credit institution is not meeting the requirements of the relevant legislation or is likely to breach these requirements in the future; and (ii) based on determination in the framework of a supervisory review the arrangements, strategies, processes and mechanisms implemented by the credit institution and the own funds and liquidity held by it do not ensure a sound management and coverage of its risks.[335] Article 16(2) SSM Regulation lists possible measures, including the competence to require institutions to hold own funds in excess of the capital requirements laid down in the relevant legislation, to require the reduction of risk inherent in the activities, products and systems of institutions, and to remove members from the management body. The objective of these corrective measures is to require credit institutions to take the necessary measures at an early stage.

Administrative penalties

A sanctioning regime forms part of the ECB's enforcement mechanism as well. The SSM Regulation entrusts the ECB with the power to impose pecuniary penalties if an SI breaches a requirement of directly applicable Union law, provided that administrative pecuniary penalties are available to the NCAs under the relevant Union law.[336] In situations not covered by this sanctioning power, the ECB may require NCAs to initiate sanctioning proceedings provided

327. Art. 10 SSM Reg.
328. Art. 11 SSM Reg.
329. Art. 12 SSM Reg.
330. Art. 12(1) SSM Reg.; Art. 143(1) SSM Framework Reg.
331. Art. 3(1) SSM Framework Reg.; ECB, Guide to Banking Supervision, Sept. 2014, available at <www.bankingsupervision.europa.eu/ecb/pub/pdf/ssmguidebankingsupervision201411.en.pdf>, at 10 and 15.
332. ECB, Guide to Banking Supervision, Sept. 2014, available at <www.bankingsupervision.europa.eu/ecb/pub/pdf/ssmguidebankingsupervision201411.en.pdf>, at 16–17.
333. Art. 3(2) SSM Framework Reg.
334. Art. 16 SSM Reg.
335. Art. 16(1) SSM Reg. These measures may be complemented with the ECB's competence to take "early intervention measures" under the BRRD, see Art. 27 et seq. BRRD.
336. Art. 18(1) SSM Reg.

for in Union or national law.[337] The types of sanctions available to the ECB are: (a) a pecuniary penalty up to twice the amount of the profits gained or losses avoided; (b) up to 10% of the total annual turnover, as defined in the relevant Union law;[338] or (c) any other pecuniary penalty as provided for in the relevant Union law.[339]

4.3.2 *Single Resolution Mechanism: SRB*

The SSM constitutes the preventative phase of potential crisis management. However, these supervisory activities may not always prevent a bank from failing. Therefore, the SRM Regulation has been enacted, which became operational on 1 January 2016 and has resulted in the establishment of the SRB and the SRF. The ultimate decision-making with regard to the resolution of SIs and cross-border groups in the euro area has now been centralized with the SRB. The resolution tools provided for in the SRM Regulation, and which may be applied singularly or jointly, are: (a) the sale of business tool, (b) the bridge institution tool, (c) the asset separation tool (good bank-bad bank), and (d) the bail-in tool.[340] Tools (a), (b), and (c) result in a "gone concern scenario", in which the bank as an entity disappears. Tool (d) aims at preservation of the entity and therefore involves a "going concern scenario".[341]

The SRB is directly responsible for drawing up resolution plans and taking resolution decisions with regard to SIs and other cross-border groups in the euro area.[342] The resolution of LSIs and non-cross-border entities and groups falls within the resolution competence of the national resolution authorities (NRAs).[343] The BRRD complements the SRM Regulation, in that it covers the resolution of LSIs, credit institutions in non-participating Member States and in the States of the European Economic Area (EEA). The BRRD harmonizes resolution tools, but does not constitute a centralized resolution mechanism, therefore leaving discretion to the national authorities as regards resolution.

Resolution Decision: SRB, ECB, European Commission, Council and NRAs

A decision to put a failing credit institution "in resolution" and to apply one or more resolution tools may have dramatic consequences for the various relevant stakeholders, i.e. the respective credit institution, its shareholders, bondholders, depositors, other financial institutions and the financial system as a whole. The complex decision-making process of the resolution procedure within the SRM reflects this potential impact by numerous checks and balances, and is a result of political compromises.[344] Its complexity is primarily caused by the sheer number of participants in the decision structure, viz. the SRB, the ECB, the European Commission, the Council of the EU, and the NRAs. This system therefore entrusts the resolution decisions to the discretion of these authorities, "soft triggers" rather than to quantitative parameters, "hard triggers".[345]

337. Art. 18(5) SSM Reg.
338. If a subsidiary has committed the breach, the annual turnover will be calculated on the basis of the group's turnover which could lead to a large penalty, see Art. 18(2) SSM Reg.
339. Art. 18(1) SSM Reg.
340. Art. 22(2) SRM Reg.
341. G. Boccuzzi, *The European Banking Union. Supervision and Resolution* (Palgrave Macmillan, 2016), 78–79.
342. Art. 7(2) SRM Reg.
343. Art. 7(3) SRM Reg. The NRAs are, among others, responsible for adopting resolution plans and carrying out assessments of resolvability, adopting measures during early intervention, waiving the obligation to draft a resolution plan and setting the level of minimum requirements for own funds and eligible liabilities.
344. G.S. Zavvos and S. Kaltsouni, op. cit. *supra* note 45, 127, 136–137.
345. G. Boccuzzi, op. cit. *supra* note 341, 73.

More specifically, the SRB has the power to take a resolution decision, either on its own initiative after an assessment by its Executive Board,[346] provided that the conditions for resolution have been met, or after a communication from the ECB.[347] The cumulative conditions for resolution are: (a) the bank is failing or is likely to fail; (b) with regard to timing and other relevant criteria, there is no reasonable prospect that any alternative private sector or supervisory action would prevent the failure of the institution; and (c) a resolution is necessary in the public interest.[348]

Whether a credit institution is failing or is likely to fail, i.e. condition (a), must be determined by a detailed list of circumstances to be found in the SRM Regulation.[349] This assessment will be carried out by the ECB after consultation of the SRB.[350] The Executive Board of the SRB may also assess this condition, but only after informing the ECB of its intention to do so.[351] The ECB may supersede this intention by conducting the assessment itself within three calendar days after being notified of the intention.[352] If the ECB deems that the credit institution meets condition (a), it shall communicate this to the European Commission and the SRB.[353]

The assessment whether there is a reasonable private sector alternative or whether supervisory measures may prevent the credit institution from failing, i.e. condition (b), must be made by the SRB.[354] "Where applicable", it must be made by the NRAs in close cooperation with the ECB. The ECB may inform the SRB or the NRAs if it considers condition (b) to be met.

The SRB is exclusively responsible for the assessment whether the resolution action is in the public interest, i.e. condition (c). The SRB shall deem a resolution action necessary in the public interest if: (i) it is necessary for the achievement of one or more of the resolution objectives (Art. 14 SRM Regulation); (ii) it is proportionate to one or more of the resolution objectives; and (iii) the winding up of the entity under normal insolvency proceedings would not meet those resolution objectives.[355] It has been argued, however, that this condition (c) will virtually always be met, for normal insolvency proceedings have distinctively different objectives than the resolution objectives of the BRRD and SRM Regulation.[356]

Once the SRB has adopted a "resolution scheme", it must be transmitted to the European Commission immediately.[357] Within 24 hours after transmission, the European Commission must either endorse the resolution scheme or object to its "discretionary aspects", i.e. aspects which are characterized by a margin of political judgment, including the assessment whether the resolution is in the public interest.[358] If the European Commission endorses the resolution scheme, it will be deemed to be adopted. Within twelve hours from the transmission, the Eu-

346. Art. 53 et seq. SRM Reg.
347. Art. 18(1) SRM Reg.
348. Art. 18(1) SRM Reg.; G.S. Zavvos and S. Kaltsouni, op. cit. *supra* note 45, 129.
349. Art. 18(4) SRM Reg.
350. Art. 18(1) SRM Reg.; Zavvos and Kaltsouni argue that this central role for the ECB is consistent with the ECB's supervisory powers under the SSM; in this capacity the ECB will have access to the relevant tools, information and data, see G.S. Zavvos and S. Kaltsouni, op. cit. *supra* note 45, 130.
351. Art. 18(1) SRM Reg.
352. Art. 18(1) SRM Reg.
353. Art. 18(1) SRM Reg.
354. Art. 18(1) SRM Reg.
355. Art. 18(5) SRM Reg.; G.S. Zavvos and S. Kaltsouni, op. cit. *supra* note 45, 130.
356. See M. Haentjens, "National Insolvency Law in International Bank Insolvencies" in B. Santen and D.H. van Offeren (Eds.), *Perspectives on International Insolvency Law: A Tribute to Bob Wessels* (Kluwer, 2014), 78.
357. Art. 18(7) SRM Reg.
358. Art. 18(7) SRM Reg. Pursuant to the Meroni doctrine, the SRB in its capacity as EU agency, may not decide on such "discretionary aspects", see G.S. Zavvos and S. Kaltsouni, op. cit. *supra* note 45, 133.

ropean Commission may propose to the Council either to object to the resolution scheme on the ground that it does not fulfil condition (c), or to approve or object to a material modification of the amount of the Fund provided for in the resolution scheme.[359] If the Council deems the resolution not to be necessary in the public interest, the credit institution will be wound up in accordance with the applicable national (insolvency) law.[360] The European Commission may only object to the remaining discretionary aspects of the resolution scheme.[361] If either the European Commission has objected to its discretionary aspects or if the Council has approved the proposed modification of the scheme, the SRB must modify the resolution scheme in accordance with the reasons expressed within eight hours.[362]

If within 24 hours after transmission of the resolution scheme by the SRB there has been no objection by the Council or the European Commission, or if the scheme has been modified, the scheme may enter into force.[363] The adopted resolution scheme is addressed to the relevant NRA, which must then carry out the scheme taking all necessary measures to implement it in accordance with the implementation of the BRRD in national law.[364]

5. Legal protection

5.1 *Introduction*

This section maps out, in broad brushstrokes, the mechanisms for judicial redress regarding decisions of European financial authorities. So as to allow for legal protection, parties affected by decisions of European financial authorities may challenge these decisions, both in the form of judicial review of the decision and in the form of civil liability for damages. Under the so-called *locus standi* requirements of EU judicial review regimes, not only addressees may challenge a decision, but also parties who can demonstrate that the decision is of direct and individual concern to them.[365]

In this section, "judicial" is understood in the broadest sense, as we also include "administrative" appeal with the ECB's Administrative Board of Review. The scope of this administrative review pertains to the "procedural and substantive conformity" of the ECB's supervisory decisions with the SSM Regulation. In the following, judicial redress against decisions by the ESAs on the one hand, and by the ECB (in its role as prudential bank supervisor) and the SRB on the other are distinguished.[366] As the ECB's remit is identical to the SRB's, and the mechanisms of judicial redress against their decisions are similar, they are discussed together.

---

359. Art. 18(7) SRM Reg.
360. Art. 18(8) SRM Reg.
361. Art. 18(7) SRM Reg.
362. Art. 18(7) SRM Reg.
363. Art. 18(7) SRM Reg.
364. Art. 18(9) read with Art. 29 SRM Reg. For an example of such a resolution decision, see the SRB resolution decision of 7 June 2017 concerning Banco Popular Español S.A., available at <srb.europa.eu/sites/srbsite/files/resolution_decision.pdf>.
365. See e.g. Art. 263(4) TFEU, Art. 24(5) SSM Reg., Art. 60(1) ESA Reg., Art. 85(3) SRM Reg. In the *Plaumann* case, howevr, the ECJ held that the *locus standi* requirement should be applied in a very restrictive manner, leaving little room for parties to challenge a decision not addressed to them, the so-called *Plaumann* test; Case C-25/62, *Plaumann v. Commission*.
366. On the role of the SRB, see *supra*, section 4.3.2.

5.2 *ESAs*

As explained above in section 4.2.1., the three ESAs have been empowered to take decisions towards NCAs, and, in exceptional cases, towards supervised financial institutions. An appeal against these decisions is possible under certain circumstances. A joint Board of Appeal has been created to facilitate such an appeal under Articles 58 and 59 of the ESA Regulations. The CJEU has held that this Board of Appeal must be considered as an internal body of the relevant ESA.[367]

Pursuant to Article 60(1) of the ESA Regulations natural or legal persons, including competent authorities, may appeal against an ESA decision if they are the addressee, or if the decision is of direct and individual concern to them.

As stated in section 4.2.1., under Articles 17, 18 and 19 of the ESA Regulations,[368] an ESA can take legally binding decisions towards an NCA and, where this authority does not comply with this decision within the period of time specified therein, the ESA may adopt an individual decision addressed to a financial market participant[369] or financial institution.[370] Furthermore, appeal can be brought against other decisions of the ESAs taken within the scope of their powers,[371] such as decisions taken under Article 9(5) of the ESA Regulations, to temporarily prohibit or restrict certain financial activities.[372]

Under Article 60(3) of the ESA Regulations, an appeal lodged with the Board of Appeal does not have suspensive effect, but "the Board of Appeal may, if it considers that circumstances so require, suspend the application of the contested decision". Sections (4) and (5) of the same Article provide that the Board must first determine whether the appeal is admissible, and thereafter whether it is well-founded. The Board of Appeal may then confirm the decision taken by the relevant ESA, or remit the case back to the ESA.

Pursuant to Article 60(2) and (3) of the ESA Regulations, Member States and the Union institutions, as well as any natural or legal person, may institute proceedings before the General Court (GC) against decisions of the ESAs, also if an ESA has an obligation to act and fails to take a decision.[373] Pursuant to Article 61 of the ESA Regulations, if there is no right of appeal before the Board of Appeal, an action for annulment against an ESA decision may be brought directly before the GC in accordance with Article 263 TFEU.[374] But where an ESA decision is open to appeal before the Board of Appeal, it follows from Article 61(1) ESA Regulations that such an appeal is obligatory, i.e. such an appeal before the Board of Appeal is a mandatory requirement for any subsequent challenge with the GC. Thus, decisions taken by the Board of Appeal itself

---

367. GC 9 Sept. 2015, T-660/14, *SV Capital OÜ v. EBA*, no. 62. More extensively on judicial protection against ESA decisions, see P. Van Cleynenbreugel, *Market Supervision in the European Union: Integrated Administration Constitutional Context*, (Brill Nijhoff, 2015), 152–161.
368. Arts. 17(4)(6), 18(3)(4) and 19(3)(4) ESA Reg.
369. In accordance with the meaning of "financial market participant" under Art. 4(1) ESMA Reg.
370. In accordance with the meaning of "financial institutions" under Art. 4(1) EBA Reg. and EIOPA Reg.
371. Art. 1(2) ESA Reg.
372. E.J. van Praag, "Het grensoverschrijdend financieel toezicht loopt tegen grenzen aan", (2011) *Tijdschrijft voor Financieel Recht*, 266.
373. On 9 Sept. 2015, the first case against a Board of Appeal decision was rendered by the General Court (GC 9 Sept. 2015, T-660/14, *SV Capital OÜ v. EBA*). The appeal challenged the decision of the EBA not to initiate an investigation into the Finnish and Estonian supervisory authorities. The GC found that the challenge against the EBA decision was inadmissible, but the challenge against the Board of Appeal decision admissible. In that appeal, it found that the Board had no competence to decide as it did. On the more general issue of the admissibility requirements under Art. 263(4) TFEU, see Ch. 26, "Economic and Monetary Union", of this book.
374. Art. 256(1) TFEU jo. Art. 51 Statute CJEU.

may be challenged with the GC. In turn, decisions of the GC can be appealed before the Court of Justice.[375]

5.3 *ECB and SRB*

Regarding the ECB in its role as single prudential supervisory authority for credit institutions and the SRB, similar mechanisms for judicial redress have been introduced. The appropriate route to challenge *ex post*[376] a decision taken by the ECB or the SRB in the context of prudential supervision or resolution of a credit institution, respectively, depends on the category of credit institution in question. In the case of, in short, significantly important and cross-border operating banks,[377] the ECB and SRB are empowered to take decisions that directly address these institutions, while for other banks, the relevant national authority is initially responsible.[378]

If a national authority has taken the relevant decision, appeal must be lodged under national administrative law.[379] If a decision is taken by the ECB or SRB, appeal can be lodged with the internal ECB Administrative Board of Review or the SRB Appeal Panel, respectively. The cases in which appeal with this Board of Review and Appeal Boards are opened, are listed in Article 24(1) SSM Regulation and Article 85(3) SRM Regulation, respectively. Interestingly, under the SSM Regulation, preliminary appeal with the ECB Administrative Board of Review is not required to be allowed appeal with the GC, and the party in question is therefore free to decide whether to lodge (administrative) appeal with the ECB, or to forego that appeal and initiate proceedings with the GC directly. In contrast, an appeal with the SRB Appeal Panel must be lodged and decided first, so as to be admissible to appeal with the CJEU.[380]

The SRB Appeal Panel must be composed of five individuals of high repute from the Member States and with a proven record of relevant knowledge and professional experience, who are not working for authorities involved in the performance of resolution tasks.[381] The ECB Administrative Board is set up in a similar way.[382]

Pursuant to Article 24(7) SSM Regulation, the ECB Administrative Board of Review shall express an "opinion" no later than two months from the receipt of the appeal and remit the case for preparation of a new draft decision to the Supervisory Board of the ECB. The Supervisory Board shall then take into account the opinion of the Administrative Board of Review and shall promptly submit a new draft decision to the Governing Council of the ECB. The new draft decision shall abrogate the initial decision, replace it with a decision of identical content, or replace it with an amended decision. The new draft decision shall be deemed adopted unless the Governing Council objects within a maximum period of ten working days. Under Article 85(4) and (8) SRM Regulation, the SRB Appeal Panel shall decide upon the appeal within one month

375. Art. 256(1) TFEU jo. Art. 51 Statute CJEU.
376. Pursuant to Art. 86(1) BRRD, the decision to employ a "resolution tool" (as defined under the BRRD) may be challenged *ex ante* in court provided the relevant Member State has opted in to that possibility. Pursuant to Recital 92 BRRD, such a challenge should be adjudicated within 24 hours of the resolution authority decision. In as far as the SRM Reg. applies and the SRB takes the relevant decisions (i.e. in case of significantly important and cross-border banks), there is not such an option.
377. Art. 6(4) SSM Reg. sets out the criteria that determine whether a credit institution qualifies as "significant". Also, certain tasks, such as the authorization of credit institutions and the withdrawal of such authorization, are the ECB's responsibility, regardless of the relevant credit institution's qualification. The SRM follows the same division of powers: Art. 7(2) SRM Reg.
378. See also *supra*, sections 4.3.1 and 4.3.2.
379. See, e.g., Art. 85(2) BRRD.
380. Art. 86(1) SRM Reg.
381. See Art. 85 SRM Reg.
382. Art. 24(2) SSM Reg.

after the appeal has been lodged, while the Appeal Panel may confirm the decision taken by the SRB, or remit the case to the latter.

If the SRB has an obligation to act and fails to take a decision, proceedings for failure to act may be initiated before the CJEU.[383] Also in other cases, direct appeal at the CJEU may be admissible under Article 263 TFEU[384] in several instances, the ECB and the SRB instruct the national resolution authority to carry out certain measures regarding a specific credit institution. Pursuant to existing case law of the CJEU, it would probably depend on the margin of discretion the ECB's or SRB's instruction has left for the national authority where and under what law the credit institution in question should challenge the subsequent measures taken by the national authority. If the ECB's/SRB's instruction to the national authority does not leave much margin of discretion for the national authority, appeal must probably be lodged with the CJEU directly.[385] Hence, one could argue that such instruction, not leaving discretion to the national authorities, is of "direct and individual concern" to the institution which is addressed by the ultimate national decision. If, conversely, the ECB's/SRB's instruction to the national authority would leave the national authority a substantial margin of discretion, the national authority would probably be the appropriate forum to challenge it.[386] It has been argued that the complexity of this regime alone hampers effective legal protection.[387] Moreover, this situation could lead to parallel procedures at both national and Union level.

As a result of broad discretion conferred upon both the ECB and the SRB, and the complex assessments which characterize their decision making, the Court will, when reviewing a decision under Article 263 TFEU, apply a standard of review that takes into account that broad discretion. When reviewing the substance of such decision, the Court will thus only assess whether there is a manifest error, misuse of power, or clear excess in the bounds of discretion.[388] Review of compliance with procedural guarantees, such as the right to be heard, is therefore of fundamental importance for judicial protection against ECB and SRB decisions, as was also reiterated by the ECJ in *Gauweiler*.[389]

The SRB's contractual liability is governed by the law applicable to the contract in question, and its non-contractual liability is subject to the general principles common to the laws concerning the liability of public authorities of the Member States.[390] In the event of the latter, the SRB must, in accordance with such general principles, compensate any damage caused by

---

383. Art. 86(3) SRM Reg. A similar rule for the ECB may be assumed.
384. See, e.g., recital 120 SRM Reg. and S.M.C. Nuijten, "Legal protection against actions under the Single Resolution Mechanism – or the lack of it", (2015) *NautaDutilh paper*, available at <www.nautadutilh.com/>, 18–19 and 21.
385. See, e.g., G.J.S. ter Kuile, L. Wissink and W.H. Bovenschen, "Tailor-made accountability within the single supervisory mechanism" (2015) CML Rev., 184; S.M.C. Nuijten, "Rechtsbescherming bij toezicht onder het SSM", (2014) *Tijdschrift voor Financieel Recht*, 471; A. Witte, "The application of National Banking Supervision Law by the ECB: Three parallel modes of executing EU Law?", (2014) MJ, 102; T.M.C. Arons, "Judicial protection of supervised credit institutions in the European Banking Union" in D. Busch and G. Ferrarini (Eds.), *European Banking Union* (OUP, 2015), 459–460.
386. Parliamentary Proceedings, *Tweede Kamer*, 2014–2015, 34 208, no. 3, 31–33. See also, S.M.C. Nuijten, op. cit. *supra* note 385, 20 et seq. and T.M.C. Arons, op. cit. *supra* note 385, 433 et seq.
387. M. Haentjens, "'Judge-made law has played its part'; The changing role of the judiciary in bank insolvencies" in INSOL Europe Academic Forum Conference Proceedings, (2017) forthcoming.
388. P. Craig, *EU Administrative Law* (OUP, 2012), 408.
389. *Gauweiler and Others v. Deutscher Bundestag* (Case C-62/14).
390. Art. 87(1)(3) SRM Reg.

it or by its staff in the performance of their duties.[391] For the ECB, a similar obligation applies.[392] The ECB's non-contractual liability could either be the consequence of inadequate (prudential) supervision which has resulted in depositors seeking to cover their financial losses, or of a wrongful decision addressed towards a credit institution which as a result has incurred losses.[393]

The CJEU has exclusive jurisdiction over any dispute relating to contractual or non-contractual liability of the SRB.[394] The SSM Regulation does not provide for such exclusive jurisdiction. Therefore, in legal disputes regarding the liability of the ECB, save where jurisdiction has been conferred upon the ECJ,[395] the competent court must be determined by the conflict of laws rules of the (recast) Brussels I Regulation.[396] Disputes relating to the non-contractual liability of an NCA or NRA are within the jurisdiction of the relevant national court. Pursuant to the SRM Regulation, the SRB must compensate an NRA for the damages which it has been ordered to pay by a national court, or which it has agreed to pay pursuant to an amicable settlement agreement.[397] An exception applies when the NRA's act or omission constituted an infringement of the SRM, other EU law, a decision of the SRB, the Council, or the European Commission, and committed intentionally or with manifest and serious error of judgement.[398]

It follows from the above that both the SRB and the ECB can be held liable on the basis of the criteria for non-contractual liability of the EU laid down in Article 340(2) TFEU, which comprise the following:

- the rule of law infringed must be intended to confer rights on individuals;
- the breach must be sufficiently serious; and
- there must be a direct causal link between the breach of the ECB's or SRB's obligation and the loss or damage sustained by those affected (*condicio sine qua non*).

The requirement that the rule of law infringed must be intended to confer rights on individuals may cause difficulties for third parties, such as depositors of a failed bank, to claim damages from the ECB or the SRB. This is a result of the *Peter Paul* case of the ECJ in 2004, in which the ECJ held that the former Banking Directives and the DGS Directive did not intend to confer rights to depositors, so that the claimants did not meet the first requirement for non-contractual liability.[399] This case has since been used as a benchmark for liability of financial supervisory authorities for inadequate (prudential) supervision towards third parties. However, credit institutions to whom the ECB has addressed a wrongful decision directly, may hold the ECB liable.[400]

391. Art. 87(3) SRM Reg.
392. Recital 61 SSM Reg., which refers to Art. 340 TFEU.
393. T.M.C. Arons, op. cit. *supra* note 385, 469; E.J. van Praag, "Aansprakelijkheid van financiële toezichthouders naar Europees recht", (2014) SEW, 215.
394. T.M.C. Arons, op. cit. *supra* note 385, at 472; Art. 87(2) and (5) SRM Reg.
395. Art. 35(2) (Protocol No. 4) of the Statute of the European System of Central Banks and the European Central Bank.
396. T.M.C. Arons, op. cit. *supra* note 385, at 472; Council Reg. (EC) 44/2001 of 22 Dec. 2000 on jurisdiction and the recognition and enforcement of judgments in civil and commercial matters, O.J. 2001, L 12 (Brussels I Reg.). As from 10 Jan. 2015 Reg. (EU) 1215/2012 of the European Parliament and of the Council of 12 Dec. 2012 on jurisdiction and the recognition and enforcement of judgments in civil and commercial matters, O.J. 2012, L 351 (recast Brussels I Reg.) applies.
397. Art. 87(4) SRM Reg.
398. Art. 87(4) SRM Reg.
399. Case C-222/02, *Peter Paul and Others*.
400. T.M.C. Arons, op. cit. *supra* note 385, at 471.

Further reading

Armour, J., D. Awrey, P. Davies et al., *Principles of Financial Regulation* (OUP, 2016).
Bergström, C.F. and D. Ritleng (Eds.), *Rulemaking by the European Commission. The New System for Delegation of Powers* (OUP, 2016).
Binder, J.H., and D. Singh (Eds.), *Bank Resolution: The European Regime* (OUP, 2016).
Boccuzzi, G., *The European Banking Union. Supervision and Resolution* (Palgrave Macmillan, 2016).
Busch, D. and G. Ferrarini (Eds.), *European Banking Union* (OUP, 2015).
Colaert, V., "European banking, securities, and insurance law: Cutting through sectoral lines?", (2015) CML Rev., 1579–1616.
Gleeson, S. and R. Guynn, *Bank Resolution and Crisis Management* (OUP, 2016).
Haentjens, M. and P. de Gioia-Carabellese, *European Banking and Financial Law* (Routledge, 2015).
Haentjens, M. and B. Wessels (Eds.), *Research Handbook on Crisis Management in the Banking Sector* (Edward Elgar, 2015).
Moloney, N., *EU Securities and Financial Markets Regulation*, 3rd ed. (OUP, 2014).
Moss, G., I. Fletcher and S. Isaacs (Eds.), *The EU Regulation on Insolvency Proceedings*, 3rd ed. (OUP, 2016).
Moss, G., M. Haentjens and B. Wessels (Eds.), *EU banking and insurance insolvency* (OUP, 2017).
Theissen, R., *EU Banking Supervision* (Eleven Publishing, 2013).
Veil, R., *European Capital Markets Law*, 2nd ed. (Hart Publishing, 2017).
Wood, P.R., *Law and Practice of International Finance* (Sweet & Maxwell, 2008).
Wymeersch, E., K.J. Hopt and G. Ferrarini (Eds.), *Financial Regulation and Supervision. A Post-Crisis Analysis* (OUP, 2012).

CHAPTER 28
EU SOCIAL LAW AND POLICY

*Sacha Garben**

This chapter focuses on EU social law and policy, excluding the topic of non-discrimination.[1] After situating social policy in the Treaties (section 1) and a discussion of its distinguishing features (section 2), the main EU measures will be set out (section 3).

1. Social policy in the Treaties

The EU's social objectives feature prominently in the Treaties: in the TFEU's preamble as the resolve to ensure the "social progress of their States by common action to eliminate the barriers which divide Europe", in the TEU's preamble referring to "fundamental social rights as defined in the European Social Charter signed at Turin on 18 October 1961 and in the 1989 Community Charter of the Fundamental Social Rights of Workers" and the promotion of "social progress", and in the EU Charter that recognizes a wide range of social rights. Article 3 TEU conceptualizes the EU as "a social market economy", and provides that it "shall combat social exclusion and discrimination, and shall promote social justice and protection". These objectives are mainstreamed in accordance with Article 9 TFEU, providing that "in defining and implementing its policies and activities, the Union shall take into account requirements linked to the promotion of a high level of employment, the guarantee of adequate social protection, the fight against social exclusion [...]."

Article 4 TFEU lists "social policy, for the aspects defined in this Treaty" as a shared competence. These aspects are further defined in Title X. The central provision is Article 153 TFEU, which provides the legal basis for the Union "to support and complement the activities of the Member States" in several fields such as, improving working conditions, social security and social protection, workers' health and safety, information and consultation of workers, and the integration of persons excluded from the labour market. For all the fields listed in Article 153(1) TFEU, the EU "may adopt measures designed to encourage cooperation between Member States", excluding any harmonization. Rather than a shared competence, this bears all the features of a complementary EU competence.[2] Furthermore, the final paragraph of Article 153 TFEU declares that "the provisions of this Article shall not apply to pay, the right of association, the right to strike or the right to impose lock-outs", entailing a clear limit on the EU's power under this social competence. While in addition to these supporting powers the EU is also granted a law-making competence to adopt directives (except for the combating of social exclusion and

---

* Professor of EU law, College of Europe, Bruges. Nothing in the contribution represents the views of the European Commission, the views expressed are entirely personal.

1. See Ch. 29, "Equal treatment and non-discrimination", of this book.
2. See Ch. 3, "System of competences", of this book.

the modernization of social protection systems), this power is limited to establishing minimum requirements. EU action on this basis can thereby only partially pre-empt Member State action, since they retain the power to set stricter standards. Furthermore, in addition to Article 4 TFEU, Article 5 TFEU provides that "the Union may take initiatives to ensure coordination of Member States' social policies". This is further detailed in Article 156 TFEU, laying down the necessary infrastructure for a social Open Method of Coordination (OMC). Finally, the social chapter features a unique additional way for the EU to adopt legislation in this area, namely by the implementation of agreements concluded between the Social Partners, i.e. representatives of management and labour. All this makes that social policy is an area with a mixed competence-structure, located somewhere between shared and complementary, and with *sui generis* features.

Title X contains several other important provisions. This includes Article 157 on equal pay between men and women, which is often considered to be the origin of European social policy.[3] Article 151 TFEU provides important context to the powers conferred in Title X,[4] referring to the European Social Charter and the Community Charter of the Fundamental Social Rights of Workers, to the objective of improving European living and working conditions but also referencing "the need to maintain the competitiveness of the Union's economy". This concern about a potential tension between social protection and economic growth is echoed in Article 153 TFEU itself, providing that directives adopted on this basis shall avoid imposing administrative, financial and legal constraints which would hold back the creation and development of SME's. Articles 152, 154 and 155 TFEU provide the legal framework for European-level social dialogue, including the possibility for the Social Partners to conclude framework agreements. In the areas covered by Article 153 TFEU, such agreements "shall be implemented" "at the joint request of the signatory parties, by a Council decision".[5] Article 154 requires the Commission to consult the Social Partners before submitting any proposal in the social policy field (first phase consultation), and, if it then decides to put forward a proposal, to consult the Social Partners on its content (second phase consultation). The Social Partners may decide to take over and instead negotiate an agreement between themselves. The final provisions of Title X regulate the establishment of the Social Protection Committee (Art. 160 TFEU) and impose reporting duties on the European Commission (Arts. 159 and 161 TFEU).

Outside the Social Title, several other provisions are relevant. The social security and social protection of EU citizens in the context of their right to move and reside freely is dealt with under Article 21 TFEU, providing specific legislative powers to which the limitations of Article 153 TFEU (e.g. excluding the adoption of Regulations) do not apply. The social security of mobile EU workers is addressed in Article 48 TFEU.[6] Finally, Article 174 TFEU provides that in order to promote its overall harmonious development, the Union shall develop and pursue its actions leading to the strengthening of its economic, social and territorial cohesion. These objectives are mainly pursued through the European Structural and Investment Funds, which are the European Social Fund (ESF), the European Regional Development Fund, the Cohesion Fund, the European Agricultural Fund for Rural Development and the European Maritime and Fisheries Fund. These funds are governed by Common Provisions Regulation 1303/2013,[7] defining common principles, rules and standards for their implementation, and providing an overall

---

3. See Ch. 29, "Equal treatment and non-discrimination", of this book.
4. Case C-126/86, *Fernando Roberto Giménez Zaera v. Institut Nacional de la Seguridad Social and Tesorería General de la Seguridad Social*, para 14.
5. Art. 155(2) TFEU.
6. See Ch. 15, "Free movement of workers and coordination of social security", of this book.
7. O.J. 2013, L 347, at 320–469.

budget of € 454 billion for the period 2014–2020. 86 billion is allocated to the ESF, which has its own Treaty Title. Article 162 TFEU provides that in order to improve employment opportunities for workers in the internal market and to contribute thereby to raising the standard of living, the ESF is established aiming to render the employment of workers easier and to increase their geographical and occupational mobility within the Union, and to facilitate their adaptation to industrial changes and to changes in production systems, in particular through vocational training and retraining. Specific rules are found in Regulation 1304/2013.[8] In addition, a separate Fund for European Aid to the Most Deprived disposes of €3.8 billion for the 2014–2020 period to provide material assistance to the most deprived, in the form of food, clothing and other essential personal items.[9]

2. Rationale of EU action

EU action on social policy has always been, and remains, contested. This finds reflection in the very gradual development of EU law-making competence, which was originally limited to equal pay, and developed only slowly with the inclusion by the Single European Act of the health and safety of workers, via the Maastricht's Treaty's Social Protocol which excluded the UK, to the current Social Title as essentially founded by the Amsterdam Treaty. The EU social *acquis* therefore developed in a haphazard way, often under the guise of the internal market. While EU primary law now clearly bestows a social mission on the EU, the political salience of the issues means that it remains a difficult area for it to define its role in. Under application of the subsidiarity principle, it is not always clear to what extent the EU is better placed than the Member States to determine the appropriate level of social and labour protection. In some Member States, national governments are not even the primary actors in setting those standards, deferring instead to self-regulation by the social partners. As is commonly the case, the EU has found it easiest to legitimate its intervention in cases where there is a cross-border dimension in play, such as the social protection of mobile workers and their families, where there is a clear link to economic issues, such as in employment/labour law, or in relation to the non-discrimination principle.

Three different rationales can be distinguished to legitimize an active role for the EU. First, the social mandate defined in the Treaties enables and requires the EU to adopt policies ensuring social progress and improvement in living and working conditions. In the most general terms, it is a mission to foster the "European Social Model", understood as a commitment to social and employment rights, a universal and fair social protection system, inclusive labour markets, strong social-dialogue, high quality public services, and high levels of social inclusion and cohesion.[10] Second, EU social policy can be considered necessary to ensure an "equal level playing field" for economic actors in the internal market. Without certain minimum common labour rules, (companies in) countries with high levels of protection would potentially suffer a competitive disadvantage and these countries would thereby be incentivized to lower their standards. Such "social dumping" due to regulatory competition is considered undesirable, and therefore the EU should adopt minimum standards to prevent "a race to the bottom". Third, and more recently, the convergence of social and labour standards in the Member States is considered a pre-condition for economic stability in the Euro-zone and for the competitiveness of the European economy. Here, labour and social standards are seen in the context of economic

8. O.J. 2013, L 347, at 470–486.
9. Reg. 223/2014, O.J. 2014, L 72, at 1–41.
10. D. Vaughan-Whitehead (Ed.), *The European Social Model in Crisis, Is Europe Losing its Soul?* (Edward Elgar Publishing, 2015), at 1–10.

competitiveness and not necessarily as goals in themselves, and EU action based on this objective may therefore well focus on reducing these standards, rather than raising them.

These narratives are not always easy to reconcile. They lead to different conclusions as to the desirable nature and extent of EU action, and public intervention more generally. Issues of market regulation and wealth redistribution are of high political sensitivity on the national level, making it very difficult for the EU to define its role. In light of its imperfect democratic legitimacy, the EU often seeks to justify its action by reference to its output; as pursuing objectively "good", evidence-based policies that can, and perhaps should, be removed from the fickle nature of politics.[11] Much of EU (social) policy is therefore "masked" by economics, law and scientific evidence. Policies are presented not as a political choice, but as necessary to foster the competitiveness of the EU economy, to respect individual rights or to implement scientific findings. The so-called "flexicurity" approach to EU employment legislation is a good example: presenting a mix between security for workers and flexibility for employers not just as a political compromise but as the best outcome in objective terms. It can however be questioned whether any policy area is really suitable for such a "technocratic" approach, and in any event socio-economic questions are almost by definition of high political salience, which means that such depoliticization strategies can never be fully effective.[12] In the end, the political consequences of these policy choices will have to be owned, and the different narratives of EU action in this area will have to be mediated. It is only in awareness of these tensions that one can fully understand the nature and dynamics of this complex field, as well as the specific measures that it comprises.

3. The EU social *acquis* at a glance

3.1 Overview of main legislative and policy measures

3.1.1 Posting of workers

(i) Directive 96/71/EC

The Posting of Workers Directive 96/71/EC[13] regulates the situation where a worker, employed by an employer established in one Member State and under a contract which is most probably regulated by the law of that home State, is seconded for temporary work to another Member State. The central principle is that the host State is required to apply to that employment relationship certain basic standards of its own labour law system (e.g. minimum wage, working time, holidays, set out in Article 3 of the Directive) as laid down in national legislation or universally applicable collective agreement, even though these standards have not been agreed between the employee and the employer and even though the labour law system of the home State would not apply those standards. Therefore, the Directive constitutes, in essence, a labour law directive. However, it was based on Articles 57(2) and 66 EC (now Arts. 53 and 62 TFEU) on freedom of establishment and to provide services, and not the Treaty's social policy provisions and the (then applicable) Social Policy Agreement. This was because these internal market provisions

---

11. A. Moravcsik, "In defense of the 'Democratic deficit': Reassessing legitimacy in the European Union", 40 JCMS (2002), at 603–624.
12. A. Follesdal and S. Hix, "Why is there a democratic deficit in the EU: A reply to Moravcsik", 44 JCMS (2006), at 533–562.
13. O.J. 1997, L 18, at 1–6.

required only a qualified majority vote and the measures adopted would apply to the UK, which had opted-out of social policy at that time.[14]

(ii) Laval and Rüffert

In *Laval*,[15] the Court was called on to interpret the Directive in the context of industrial action by Swedish trade unions in the form of a blockade of work sites of a Latvian company, which due to its considerably lower labour costs won a construction contract to carry out temporary work in Sweden. The industrial action was aimed at forcing the company to sign a collective agreement in Sweden containing wage conditions and other terms of employment. Significantly, the Court interpreted the Directive in light of its legal basis. The Court held "[a]s regards the requirements as to pay which can be imposed on foreign service providers, it should be recalled that [...] Directive 96/71 relates only to minimum rates of pay. Therefore, [it] cannot be relied on to justify an obligation on such service providers to comply with rates of pay such as those which the trade unions seek in this case to impose in the framework of the Swedish system, which do not constitute minimum wages". As such, the Court interpreted Directive 96/71 as laying down mandatory rules for minimum protection which at the same time constituted maximum protection, since the host Member State was prohibited to make the provision of services in its territory conditional on the observance of additional employment conditions. The Court came to this conclusion as another interpretation "would amount to depriving the directive of its effectiveness". The internal market legal basis constituted an important reason to interpret the Directive as laying down a ceiling of labour rights, rather than the floor of rights that it was originally intended to be, and would have been if adopted on the Treaty's labour law provisions.

The *Laval* judgment caused significant controversy for its exceedingly wide definition of what constitutes a potential restriction of the free movement provisions to include industrial action by workers, and for its narrow scope for justification on social grounds. The Court took that latter approach further in *Rüffert*, however, holding that EU law precluded Member States from requiring in public procurement that foreign EU contractors pay their employees the remuneration prescribed by the collective agreement in force at the place where those services are performed.[16] The collective agreement in question had not been declared universally applicable, as is required under Article 3(8) of the Posting Directive for it to be able to set the "minimum rates of pay" that host states can impose on foreign companies. Especially striking was the Court's reasoning regarding the possible justification on grounds of worker protection: requiring a level of remuneration that exceeds the minimum rate of pay applicable pursuant to national legislation cannot be necessary for the protection of workers – otherwise the same rate of pay would be required nationally and/or for the whole sector, regardless of whether the worker is employed in the context of a private or a public contract.

(iii) Elektrobudowa and Regiopost

However, two recent judgments signal a change in the Court's restrictive approach. *Elektrobudowa* concerned Polish workers posted to Finland, who considered that they had not received

14. See J. Malmberg, "Posting post-Laval: Nordic responses" in M. Moreau (Ed.), *Before and After the Crisis, What Implications for the "European social Model"?* (Edward Elgar Publishing, 2011), at 28, and A.T. Davies, "Posted workers: Single market or protection of national labour law systems?", 34 CML Rev. (1997), at 571.
15. Case C-341/05, *Laval un Partneri Ltd v. Svenska Byggnadsarbetareförbundet, Svenska Byggnadsarbetareförbundets avdelning 1, Byggettan and Svenska Elektrikerförbundet.*
16. Case C-346/06, *Dirk Rüffert v. Land Niedersachsen.*

sufficient wages from their employer.[17] They assigned their claims to a Finnish trade union, who brought their claims to a national court. The ECJ confirmed the possibility of workers to assign their wage claims to trade unions if the law of the host Member State so provides, regardless of whether such a possibility is permitted under the legislation of the home State. Moreover, the Court gave a broad interpretation of what Member States could consider as part of the mandatory "minimum rates of pay". The Court held that the minimum wage could be calculated by categorizing workers into pay groups based on criteria such as qualifications, training, experience and type of work performed (as long as this was done in a transparent way), and – notably – that it could include a posting-specific flat-rate daily allowance.

This turn was followed through in *Regiopost*.[18] The Court held that the award of public contracts could be made subject by law to a public procurement-specific minimum wage. The Court accepted the requirement of a German region for tenderers to commit to paying (sub-)contractors the wage as stipulated in a regional law on public procurement. The Court considered that the provision was a "law" laying down a "minimum rate of pay" under Article 3(1) of the Directive, thereby distinguishing the situation from *Rüffert* where the minimum pay requirement was laid down in a collective agreement that had not been declared universally applicable as is required by Article 3(8) of the Posting Directive. The fact that the law in question only applied to public contracts did not make any difference, since the Directive made the criterion of "universal application" only applicable to collective agreements.

(iv) Revision of the posting of Workers Directive

The permissive signal to Member States and their courts is strong and *Elektrobudowa* and *Regiopost* may thereby already go a long way to address the political concerns about social dumping since *Laval* and *Rüffert*, although some stakeholders may insists on seeing the text of the Directive itself revised. Indeed, in response to the political fallout after *Laval* and *Rüffert*, the Commission has proposed a revision of the Posting of Workers Directive,[19] in addition to the already adopted Enforcement Directive allowing host States more effective methods of policing their legitimately imposed labour standards.[20] The aim is to strengthen host Member State's powers to impose labour conditions to companies posting workers to their territory. The proposal replaces the notion of "minimum rates of pay" of Article 3(1)(c) with "remuneration", and allows social standards to be imposed through other collective agreements than those declared universally applicable in the context of subcontracting. The proposal received the required number of negative opinions from national parliaments to trigger the yellow card procedure. The Commission nevertheless decided to go ahead with the proposal, and on 1 March 2018, the EU Institutions announced that a common understanding had been reached on the proposal, which "establishes the principle of equal pay for equal work on the same place, whilst providing more legal certainty for both workers and employers.[21]

---

17. Case C-396/13, *SähköalO.J.en ammattiliitto ry v. Elektrobudowa Spółka Akcyjna*.
18. Case C-115/14, *RegioPost GmbH & Co. KG v. Stadt Landau*.
19. Proposal for a Directive amending Directive 96/71/EC concerning the posting of workers in the framework of the provision of services, COM(2016)128 final.
20. Directive 2014/67/EU on the enforcement of Directive 96/71/EC concerning the posting of workers in the framework of the provision of services, O.J. 2014, L 159, at 11–31.
21. Joint statement on the revision of the Posting of Workers Directive, 01/03/2018, available at http://ec.europa.eu/social/main.jsp?langId=en&catId=89&newsId=9062&furtherNews=yes.

3.1.2 Working time

The EU measures on working time are of high importance for the EU's social *acquis*, both in symbolic and practical terms. Applicable to virtually all workers across Europe, determining their minimum rights to limited working time, adequate rest periods and paid holidays, these rules arguably affect many more Europeans in an important part of their daily lives than the bulk of EU law. Hotly contested by the UK ever since its original inception, the original 1993 Directive (93/104) was challenged for allegedly having been wrongly based on Article 118a EEC Treaty which allowed the adoption of measures for the protection of the health and safety of workers.[22] The UK argued that the Directive went beyond the protection of workers' health and safety, but the Court upheld the Directive for the most part, annulling only the provision that weekly rest had to be preferably taken on Sundays as unrelated to health protection.

Directive 2003/88/EC[23] replaces the original 1993 Directive. It provides a limit to average weekly working time of 48 hours. There can be an individual opt-out of this maximum through a written agreement between the worker and the employer, if the Member State has allowed the use of this derogation. This opt-out does not apply to the minimum rest provisions of the Directive, which prescribe a minimum daily rest period of 11 consecutive hours, a rest break during working hours if the worker is on duty for longer than 6 hours, and a minimum weekly rest period of 24 uninterrupted hours for each 7-day period. Several derogations exists to accommodate the need for flexibility, for instance to guarantee 24/7 service provision. For the purpose of the application of these provisions, the Court considers "working time" to include all on-call time where the worker is obliged to remain at the workplace, such as doctors on night duty in hospitals,23 as well as stand-by time where the worker is required not only to be contactable, but is objectively limited in his opportunities to devote himself to his personal and social interests, such as a fire-fighter who has to be able to reach his place of work within 8 minutes.[24]

In addition, the Directive lays down the right to minimum paid annual leave of 4 weeks. Also this right has been interpreted broadly.[25] In *Schultz-Hoff*,[26] the Court held that the right to paid annual leave remains unaffected by periods of sick leave, although in the case of long-term illness there can be a limit on the retention and accumulation of annual leave entitlements.[27] The Court considered in *Bollacke* that outstanding leave entitlements should not perish in the event of the worker's death, meaning that they should be inherited in the form of an allowance in lieu by the legal heirs.[28] In *Lock*, the Court held that in the case where a worker's salary is (partially) composed of performance-related pay such as sales commissions, the "normal remuneration" that has to be paid in relation to the worker's holidays should include the average amount of such commissions.[29] The practical significance of this ruling for the daily working lives of many citizens is not to be underestimated, with performance-related pay on the rise as a risk-shifting remuneration strategy of employers.

---

22. Case C-84/94, *United Kingdom of Great Britain and Northern Ireland v. Council of the European Union.*
23. O.J. 2003, L 299, at 9–19.
24. Case C-518/15, *Ville de Nivelles v. Rudy Matzak* ECLI:EU:C:2018:82, paras. 63–65.
25. See T. Nowak, "The working time Directive and the European Court of Justice", 15 MJ (2008), 447–471.
26. Joined Cases C-350/06 and C-520/06, *Gerhard Schultz-Hoff v. Deutsche Rentenversicherung Bund and Stringer and Others v. Her Majesty's Revenue and Customs.*
27. Case C-214/10, *KHS AG v. Winfried Schulte*. Such a limitation is not permissible in case the worker did not exercise his annual leave rights in respect of several consecutive reference periods because his employer refused to remunerate that leave: Case C-214/16, *Conley King v. The Sash Window Workshop Ltd, Richard Dollar*, ECLI:EU:C:2017:914.
28. Case C-118/13, *Gülay Bollacke v. K + K Klaas & Kock B.V. & Co. KG.*
29. Case C-539/12, *Z. J. R. Lock v. British Gas Trading Limited.*

In addition to the general Working Time Directive, specific measures apply by way of derogation to a number of transport sectors.[30] Furthermore, Directive 94/33/EC[31] on the protection of young people at work can be mentioned in this context, although it has a wider aim and context in that it also prohibits child labour. The Directive requires Member States to take the necessary measures to prohibit work by children, particularly that the minimum working age is not lower than the minimum age at which compulsory full-time schooling ends, or 15 years. Exceptions are allowed for occasional or short-term work, domestic service in a private household or work regarded as not being harmful, damaging or dangerous to young people in a family undertaking, for cultural, artistic, sporting or advertising activities, for children of at least 14 years of age working under a combined work/training scheme, and for children of at least 14 years of age performing light work. The Directive provides specific limits to maximum weekly working time, night work and minimum rest periods for children and adolescents. Interestingly, the Directive still contains the provision that the minimum rest period shall in principle include Sunday, which was annulled in the context of the general Working Time Directive, as it was never challenged.

3.1.3 Non-standard forms of employment

(i) Fixed-Term work

The Fixed-Term Work Directive 1999/70/EC[32] implements the Framework Agreement concluded by the Social Partners. Clause 4 lays down the principle of equal treatment, entailing that fixed-term workers should not be treated less favourably in their employment conditions than permanent workers, unless objectively justified. The Court has held that these employment conditions include pay and pensions, even though Article 153(5) TFEU excludes "pay" from the scope of application of this legal basis.[33] Clause 4 provides a directly effective right, in contrast to Clause 5[34] which obliges Member States to adopt measures to prevent abuse arising from successive fixed-term employment, and gives the choice between (i) requiring objective reasons for renewal, (ii), providing an overall limit of duration, and (iii) providing a maximum number of renewals of successive fixed-term employment. Member States have a wide margin of appreciation and may also provide other "equivalent" protection instead. Furthermore, while the remedies against abuse should be effective, Member States are not required to provide for the automatic conversion of fixed-term contracts into a permanent position after a certain time limit or as remedy for a breach of the limitations.[35]

The Court has not adopted a very protective approach in its interpretation of Clause 5. It has, for instance, held that successive fixed-term employment of 11 years could be justified in certain situations, and has accepted a wide range of objective justifications for otherwise unlimited fixed-term employment.[36] For the purpose of determining "successive" fixed-term employment,

---

30. Directive 2000/79/EC, Directive 2005/47/EC, Directive 2002/15/EC, Directive 1999/63/EC and Directive 2009/13/EC.
31. O.J. 1994, L 216, at 12–20.
32. O.J. 1999, L 175, at 43–48.
33. Case C-307/05, *Yolanda Del Cerro Alonso v. Osakidetza-Servicio Vasco de Salud*, Case C-268/06, *Impact v. Minister for Agriculture and Food and Others*. See on this issue C. Kilpatrick, "The ECJ and labour law: A 2008 retrospective", 38 *Industrial Law Journal* (2009), at 180–208.
34. Case C-307/05, *Yolanda Del Cerro Alonso v. Osakidetza-Servicio Vasco de Salud.*
35. Case C-212/04, *Konstantinos Adeneler and Others v. Ellinikos Organismos Galaktos (ELOG).*
36. Case C-586/10, *Bianca Kücük v. Land Nordrhein-Westfalen*, C-190/13, *Antonio Márquez Samohano v. Universitat Pompeu Fabra.*

the Court has accepted that an interruption of 60 days can be sufficient to break the link of continuous fixed-term employment, although this is likely to depend on the specific circumstances of employment in each case. The Court has come under some pressure in recent years, as the deterioration of working conditions following the economic crisis and a corresponding increase in fixed-term employment have led to amplified litigation on this subject. This has resulted in a stream of preliminary references, and has made fixed-term work one of the most active areas of EU social law. While the Court's approach remains rather deferential to the Member States, especially compared to its abovementioned judgments in working time, it has condemned the wide-scale (ab)use of fixed-term employment in the public sector in certain situations.[37]

(ii) Part-Time work

Directive 97/81/EC[38] implements the Framework Agreement on part-time work of the Social Partners. Similar to the Fixed-Term Work Directive, it provides that part-time workers are not to be treated less favourably in relation to employment conditions than full-time workers, although this is subject to the *pro rata temporis* principle. There is an overlap here with the principle of equal treatment between men and women, as the Court has since long held that because more women are engaged in part-time employment, it amounts to indirect gender discrimination to treat part-time work less favourably.[39] While the Directive therefore relates to the non-discrimination *acquis*, it is primarily a labour law directive on non-standard employment, bearing a high resemblance to the Fixed-Term Work Directive in form and content, although it is considerably less "suspicious" of part-time work than its counterpart is of fixed-term work. Indeed, the Directive does not contain a provision obliging Member States to prevent abuses arising from part-time employment, but instead a provision that employers should, as far as possible, facilitate voluntary part-time employment. The Directive offers a certain measure of protection as regards involuntary part-time employment, providing that "a worker's refusal to transfer from full-time to part-time work or vice-versa should not in itself constitute a valid reason for termination of employment" although this is "without prejudice to termination in accordance with national law, collective agreements and practice, for other reasons such as may arise from the operational requirements of the establishment concerned".

(iii) Temporary agency work

The Temporary Agency Work Directive 2008/104/EC[40] was adopted in 2008 after two decades of debate and failed negotiations.[41] It was adopted on the basis of (now) Article 153 TFEU for the protection of workers and in that vein Article 5 of the Directive provides the principle of equal treatment for temporary agency workers, entitling them to the same conditions of employment, including pay, as directly hired workers. Even if the strength of this provision is arguably weakened by the long list of ambiguously worded derogations in that same provision, it is an important right that can serve to improve the conditions of temporary agency workers as well as workers more generally, by discouraging the use of this precarious type of employment for "the wrong reasons", i.e. to undercut worker protection and labour standards.

---

37. Joined Cases C-22/13, C-61/13 to C-63/13 and C-418/13, *Raffaella Mascolo et al.*
38. O.J. 1998, L 14, at 9–14.
39. See Ch. 29, "Equal treatment and non-discrimination", of this book.
40. O.J. 2008, L 327, at 9–14.
41. N. Countouris and R. Horton, "The Temporary Agency Work Directive: Another broken promise?", 38 *Industrial Law Journal* (2009), at 329–338.

However, in line with the "flexicurity" approach, the Directive also contains a provision that is more difficult to consider as aimed at worker protection, namely Article 4 concerning a review of restrictions on temporary agency work, providing that "prohibitions or restrictions on the use of temporary agency work shall be justified only on grounds of general interest relating in particular to the protection of temporary agency workers, the requirements of health and safety at work or the need to ensure that the labour market functions properly and abuses are prevented" and that by 5 December 2011, Member States are to carry out a review to that purpose. The Court has held that Article 4 "is addressed only to the competent authorities of the Member States, imposing on them an obligation to review in order to ensure that any potential prohibitions or restrictions on the use of temporary agency work are justified, and, therefore, the provision does not impose an obligation on national courts not to apply any rule of national law containing prohibitions or restrictions on the use of temporary agency work which are not justified on grounds of general interest within the meaning of Article 4(1)".[42] The Court thereby denied direct effect to this provision, removing the poison from its bite. While the Commission can still institute infringement proceedings against Member States who have not properly carried out the review, it is an open question to what extent the Commission can also take up infringements for reasons beyond the procedural, for instance against a Member State when it adopts new restrictions that the Commission considers manifestly unjustified.

(iv) Other measures

Directive 91/383/EEC extends the protection afforded to workers under the EU occupational health and safety rules (see section 3.1.6. below) to fixed-term and temporary agency workers, of whom research indicates that they are more exposed to the risk of accidents at work and occupational diseases than other workers. Furthermore, the seasonal workers Directive 2014/36[43] deserves to be mentioned. While formally part of migration policy, it sets important labour standards for third country nationals engaging in seasonal work in the EU. The Directive seeks to respond to the needs of Member States for a source of labour for low skill, seasonal, and, typically, precarious, jobs that are difficult to fill with European workers, while simultaneously minimizing the possibility of economic and social exploitation of the third-country migrant workers.[44] Article 23 provides the principle of equal treatment, particularly as regards the freedom of association and the right to strike, concerning terms of employment, working conditions and in relation to "branches of social security". These important guarantees for this vulnerable group of workers were obtained throughout a contentious legislative process mainly by the Parliament's contribution, which significantly raised the level of protection compared to the original proposal.[45]

3.1.4 *Structural changes in the company*

(i) Insolvency

Directive 2008/94/EC[46] ensures payment of employees' outstanding claims in the event of employer insolvency, requiring Member States to set up an institution to guarantee these payments. The Directive, adopted on (now) Article 153 TFEU, replaces Directive 80/987/EEC. It was the

42. Case C-533/13, *Auto- ja Kuljetusalan Työntekijäliitto AKT ry v. Öljytuote ry and Shell Aviation Finland Oy*.
43. O.J. 1991, L 206, at 19–21. Deadline for transposition is 30 Sept. 2016.
44. J. Fudge and A.T. Herzfeld Olsson, "The EU Seasonal Workers Directive: When immigration controls meet labour rights", 16 *European Journal of Migration and Law* (2014), at 440.
45. Ibid., at 457–459.
46. O.J. 2008, L 283, at 36–42.

old Directive's lack of transposition in Italy that triggered the well-known *Francovich* case on state liability, where the Court held that the obligation to guarantee outstanding payments was sufficiently precise and unconditional regardless of the discretion of the Member State in giving effect to this obligation.[47] The minimum guarantee period covers the remuneration for the last three months (within a reference period of at least six months) or eight weeks (within a reference period of at least eighteen months). In addition, the Directive requires Member States to adopt the necessary measures to protect occupational supplementary pension entitlements. The Court ruled that Member States have considerable latitude in determining both the means and the level of protection of rights to old-age benefits under supplementary occupational pension schemes in the event of employer insolvency, precluding an obligation to guarantee in full.[48] However, a guarantee limited to less than half of the benefits to which an employee was entitled does not fall within the definition of the word "protect".[49]

(ii) Collective redundancies

The Collective Redundancies Directive 98/59/EC,[50] adopted on the basis of (now) Article 114 TFEU, replaces one of the oldest labour law directives (75/125) and regulates the situation of workers affected by decisions of employers to lay off a group of employees. According to the Court, by harmonizing the rules applicable to collective redundancies, the EU legislature intended both to ensure comparable protection for employees' rights in the different Member States and to harmonize the costs which such protective rules entail for EU undertakings.[51] In terms of the worker protection it affords, the Directive provides collective rather than individual rights, laying down rules for the information and consultation of workers' representatives before "collective redundancies" are made.

The Directive allows Member States to choose between two alternatives when declaring redundancies to be "collective": either (i) when in 30 days there are at least 10 redundancies in establishments[52] normally employing between 20 and 100 workers; at least 10% of the workers in establishments normally employing between 100 and 300 workers; at least 30 workers in establishments normally employing 300 workers or more, or (ii) when, over a period of 90 days, at least 20 workers are made redundant, whatever the number of workers normally employed. When an employer, unilaterally and to the detriment of the employee, makes significant changes to essential elements of his employment contract for reasons unrelated to the individual employee concerned, this constitutes a "redundancy".[53] In establishing whether "collective redundancies" have been effected, there is no need to take into account individual terminations of contracts concluded for limited periods or specific tasks, when they take place on the date of

47. Joined Cases C-6/90 and C-9/90, *Andrea Francovich and Danila Bonifaci and others v. Italian Republic.*
48. Case C-278/05, *Carol Marilyn Robins and Others v. Secretary of State for Work and Pensions.*
49. Ibid., and Case C-398/11, *Hogan et al.*
50. O.J. 1998, L 225, at 16–21.
51. Cases C-383/92, *Commission v. United Kingdom*; Case C-55/02, *Commission v. Portugal.*
52. Member States may limit the meaning of "establishment" to mean a single particular establishment of a large undertaking and not the whole undertaking at large, thereby limiting the Directive's scope of application. Case C-80/14, *Union of Shop, Distributive and Allied Workers (USDAW), B. Wilson v. WW Realisation 1 Ltd, in liquidation, Ethel Austin Ltd, Secretary of State for Business, Innovation and Skills.* Based on the internal market legal basis, the Directive can set ceilings of worker protection.
53. See Case C-422/14, *Cristian Pujante Rivera v. Gestora Clubs Dir, SL, Fondo de Garantía Salarial.*

expiry or completion.[54] Fixed-term workers however do count towards the minimum "normally employed" workers.[55]

Employers contemplating collective redundancies must hold consultations in good time with the workers' representatives, "with a view to reaching an agreement". These consultations must cover means of avoiding or reducing collective redundancies, and of mitigating the consequences, in particular by social measures redeploying or retraining affected workers. To ensure that the consultations are effective, even if there is no obligation to reach an agreement, employers must provide the workers' representatives with written information on *inter alia* the reasons for the redundancies, the number of workers affected, the period over which the projected redundancies are to be effected, the selection criteria proposed, and any extra redundancy payments. The employer is also required to notify the competent public authority in writing of any projected collective redundancies. In *AGET*, the Court recently condemned Greek rules concerning collective redundancies for being contrary to Article 49 TFEU. The rules specified that in the absence of an agreement with the workers' representatives on projected collective redundancies, an employer could effect such redundancies only if the competent national public authority did not object.[56]

(iii) Transfer of undertakings

Directive 2001/23/EC,[57] replacing another old directive (77/187/EEC), protects employees' rights when a workplace is transferred from one employer to another, stipulating that such a transfer does not in itself constitute valid grounds for dismissal. Nevertheless, dismissal may occur, for economic, technical or organizational reasons. In principle, the rights and obligations under the previous employment contract remain valid, and collective agreements continue to apply for at least a year. The Directive does not require the continued observation of rights to old-age, invalidity or survivors' benefits under non-statutory, supplementary pension schemes. Employees' representatives must be consulted in good time on any measures envisaged in relation to employees as a result of the transfer. Moreover, representatives and, in certain cases, employees themselves must be informed about the date, reasons and implications of the transfer as well as the measures envisaged in relation to the employees.

The Directive is applicable wherever there is a change in the natural or legal person responsible for carrying on the business who incurs the obligations of an employer towards employees of the undertaking.[58] The aim of the Directive is to ensure continuity of employment relationships within an economic entity, irrespective of any change of ownership. The decisive criterion is therefore the fact that the entity in question "retains its identity", as indicated by the fact that its operation is actually continued or resumed.[59] This can be assessed by considering all the facts characterizing the transaction, including: (i) the type of undertaking, (ii) whether its tangible assets are transferred, (iii) the value of its intangible assets, (iv) whether the majority of its employees are taken over by the new employer, (v) whether its customers are transferred, (vi) the degree of similarity between the activities carried on, and (vii) the period, if any, for

---

54. Case C-392/13, *Andrés Rabal Cañas v. Nexea Gestión Documental SA and Fondo de Garantía Salarial.*
55. Case C-422/14, *Cristian Pujante Rivera v. Gestora Clubs Dir, SL, Fondo de Garantía Salarial.*
56. Case C-201/15, *AGET Iraklis.* The judgment is also noteworthy for the ECJ remarkable approach to the Collective Redundancies Directive, which it considers may be deprived of its practical effect if no collective redundancies can take place.
57. O.J. 2001, L 82, at 16–20.
58. Cases C-171/94 and C-172/94, *Merckx and Neuhuys*; C-127/96, C-229/96 and C-74/97, *Hernández Vidal and Others* and Case C-458/12, *Amatori and Others.*
59. Cases 24/85, *Spijkers,* and C-232/04 and C-233/04, *Güney-Görres and Demir.*

which activities were suspended. However, all those circumstances are "merely single factors in the overall assessment which must be made and cannot therefore be considered in isolation".[60] The application of the Directive depends on a complex case-by-case analysis. The Court has confirmed that in these inherently uncertain circumstances, national courts of last instance are bound to make preliminary references and may incur the liability of the state if they fail to do so.[61]

3.1.5 *Information and consultation of workers*

Directive 2002/14/EC[62] establishes a general framework, setting out minimum principles, definitions and arrangements for information and consultation at enterprise level in the EU. Information and consultation are required on the recent and probable development of the activities and economic situation, the situation, structure and probable development of employment and any anticipatory measures envisaged, in particular where there is a threat to employment, and decisions likely to lead to substantial changes in work organization or in contractual relations. The Directive applies to undertakings employing at least 50 employees, or to establishments employing at least 20 employees, according to the choice made by the Member State.

Directive 2009/38/EC[63] on the establishment of a European Works Council applies to EU-scale undertakings or groups with at least 1000 employees and at least 150 employees in each of two Member States. It replaces the initial EU Directive (94/45/EC). European Works Councils are bodies representing the European employees of a company, informing and consulting these employees on the progress of the business and any significant decision at European level that could affect their working conditions. Works Councils are created at the request of 100 employees from two countries, or on the initiative of the employer. The composition and functioning of each European Works Council varies, as it is determined by a signed agreement between management and workers' representatives. The Directive however provides subsidiary requirements if such a signed agreement is lacking.

On a more individual basis, the worker is entitled to receive essential information relating to the employment relationship in writing. The Written Statement Directive (91/533/EEC)[64] prescribes that such information, including the description of the work, its duration, the amount of paid leave and the agreed working time, must be given when the employment starts or shortly after. After evaluation,[65] the has Commission concluded that many workers in the EU still do not receive a written confirmation of their working conditions, concerning mostly atypical workers such as casual workers and certain sectors, such as construction, agriculture, catering and domestic work. On the basis of a recent evaluation of the Directive, which has found "gaps in the personal scope of the Directive (e.g. domestic workers or some new forms of employment) and gaps in the 'information package' to be notified and issues of enforcement of the Directive", the Commission has proposed a revision of the Written Statement Directive. The newly proposed Directive on Transparent and Predictable Working Conditions 'updates' the existing information obligations and moreover creates new minimum standards to ensure that all workers, including those on atypical contracts, benefit from more predictability and clarity as regards their working conditions. In particular, the proposal aligns the notion of worker

60. Cases C-29/91, *Redmond Stichting*; Case C-13/95, *Süzen*, and Case C-340/01, *Abler and Others*.
61. Case C-160/14, *João Filipe Ferreira da Silva e Brito and Others v. Estado português*.
62. O.J. 2002, L 80, at 29–34.
63. O.J. 2009, L 122, at 28–44.
64. O.J. 1991, L 288, at 32–35.
65. REFIT Evaluation of the "Written Statement Directive" (Directive 91/533/EEC), C(2017)2611 final.

to the case-law of the CJEU, provides workers the right to information directly at the start of employment, the right to greater predictability of work for those working mostly with a variable schedule, the possibility to request transition to a more stable form of employment and receive a reply in writing, and the right to mandatory training without deduction from salary. The initiative is part of the European Pillar of Social Rights, discussed further below.[66]

The Commission has also initiated a first phase consultation on a possible consolidation of the existing EU legislation on worker information and consultation on collective redundancies, transfers of undertakings and on the general framework for information and consultation of workers.[67] This is in reaction to evaluation which found that there were gaps and inconsistencies as regards the definitions of the concepts of "information" and "consultation" under the different directives, and uncertainties as to the extent to which public administration falls within the scope of application of the Directives.[68] Directives 98/59/EC and 2001/23/EC (on collective redundancies and on the transfer of undertakings) do not provide for specific definitions of the concepts "information" and "consultation", while the general framework Directive 2002/14/EC does. However, these are different from the definitions in Directive 2009/38/EC on European Works Councils and the European Company Directive 2001/86/EC. The Commission considers that the addition of specific provisions defining the concepts "information" and "consultation" in the three Directives under consideration would enhance legal clarity and awareness.

3.1.6 OSH

The densest body of EU rules in the social policy area is probably that concerning occupational health and safety (OSH). Consisting of a single framework directive and numerous individual directives regulating specific risks or workplaces, it is a complex but important body of legislation for the protection of workers in Europe.[69] Similarly to what we have seen in other areas discussed above, the first directives on safety and health at work (e.g. Directive 77/576/EEC on safety signs in the workplace and Directive 78/610/EEC on occupational exposure limits to vinyl chloride monomers) were adopted on the basis of the general market harmonization provisions, due to a lack of an explicit legislative competence on OSH until the mid-1980s. The

66. See European Commission, Regulatory Fitness and Performance Programme REFIT and the 10 Priorities of the Commission, SWD/2016/0400 final, 20 and 346, European Commission, Recommendation on the European Pillar of Social Rights, C(2017) 2600 final, and Communication of 26 April 2017 establishing a European Pillar of Social Rights, COM(2017) 250 final, and European Commission, Proposal for a Directive of the European Parliament and of the Council on transparent and predictable working conditions in the European Union, COM(2017)797.
67. European Commission, *"First phase consultation of the Social Partners under Art. 154 TFEU on a consolidation of the EU Directives on information and consultation of workers"*, C(2015)2303 final.
68. SWD(2013)293 final.
69. Directives 89/391/EEC on health and safety at work; 89/654/EEC on minimum safety and health requirements for the workplace; 92/57/EEC on temporary or mobile construction sites; 92/91/EEC on the mineral-extracting industries through drilling; 92/104/EEC on workers in surface and underground mineral extracting industries; 93/103/EC on fishing vessels; 92/29/EEC on improved medical treatment on board vessels; 89/656/EEC on personal protective equipment; 90/269/EEC on the manual handling of loads; 90/270/EEC on work with display screen equipment; 92/58EEC on safety and/or health signs at work; 2009/104/EC on work equipment; 92/85/EEC on pregnant workers; 2013/35/EU on electromagnetic fields; 1999/92/EC on explosive atmospheres; 2002/44/EC on mechanical vibration; 2003/10/EC on noise; 2006/25/EC on artificial optical radiation; 2000/54/EC on biological agents at work; 2010/32/EU on sharp injuries in the hospital and healthcare sector; 98/24/EC on chemical agents; 2004/37/EC on carcinogens or mutagens; 2009/148/EC on asbestos.

insertion of a legal basis by the Single European Act in the form of Article 118a EEC Treaty (now Art. 153 TFEU) led to a flowering of the OSH *acquis*.

The most important legal act is the European Framework Directive (89/391/EEC), which establishes general principles for managing safety and health, such as responsibility of the employer, rights/duties of workers, using risk assessments to continuously improve company processes, and workplace health and safety representation. All subsequent Directives within the meaning of Article 16(1) of the Framework Directive follow these common principles. Directive 89/391/EEC applies to all sectors of activity, both public and private. Individual directives tailor the principles of the Framework Directive to specific tasks (e.g. manual handling of loads), specific hazards at work (e.g. exposure to dangerous substances or physical agents), specific workplaces and sectors (e.g. extractive industries), and specific groups of workers (e.g. pregnant women). The individual directives define how to assess these risks and, in some instances, set limit values for certain substances or agents. While the Framework Directive continues to apply to all areas covered by the individual directives, where individual directives contain more stringent and specific provisions, these special provisions prevail.

3.1.7 Social OMC

The OMC originated in the European Employment Strategy and was later expanded to other areas, including that of social and welfare policy.[70] Its key features of non-binding policy exchange towards commonly agreed indicators and benchmarks in an inter-governmental setting, are arguably very suitable for the kind of "soft" policy coordination that the Treaty mandates the EU to pursue in Articles 5(3), 153 and 156 TFEU especially where the EU lacks a direct law-making competence.[71] The OMC is, ostensibly, "owned" by the national actors, who are provided with a European-level infrastructure for their collaboration, with the Commission acting only in a facilitating monitoring capacity and without "hard" powers of enforcement. The overarching objectives are set by the European Council, and the OMC's flexibility allows it to be moulded by national policy-makers in a "bottom-up" fashion. With both sides of the political spectrum content to leave the controversial aspects of redistributive social and welfare policies largely outside the EU's power to set binding standards, the OMC is a way to for the EU to exert some control over these policies that are sensitive but also important for the inter-connected European economy and society.

A central player is the Social Protection Committee (SPC), an EU advisory policy committee for the Ministers in the Employment and Social Affairs Council (EPSCO) comprising 2 representatives of each Member State and the Commission.[72] Article 160 TFEU provides that the SPC shall promote cooperation on social protection policies between Member States and with the Commission, "to monitor the social situation and the development of social protection policies in the Member States and the Union" and to "promote exchanges of information, experience and good practice between Member States and with the Commission". The SPC is to establish appropriate contacts with management and labour in carrying out these activities.

---

70. See *inter alia*: K. Armstrong, *Governing Social Inclusion. Europeanization through Policy Coordination* (OUP, 2010); M. Dawson, *New Governance and the Transformation of European Law: Coordinating EU Social Law and Policy* (CUP, 2011).
71. The Commission has warned that the OMC should not be used where the Community Method is available. See European Commission, European Governance A White Paper, COM(2001)428.
72. J. Zeitlin and B. Vanhercke, "Economic governance in Europe 2020: Socializing the European semester against the odds?" in D. Natali and B. Vanhercke, *Social Policy in the European Union: State of Play 2015*, ETUI 16th Annual Report, at 65.

In addition to its key role in the Social OMC, the SPC is also an important actor in the context of the European Semester. The relation between these two separate governance processes is complex, due to a partial overlap in actors, subject matter and methodology. The European Semester, much larger in scope than the Social OMC, was introduced in 2010–2011 as a new institutional architecture for socio-economic policy coordination, especially in response to the Euro-crisis.[73] The Commission, Council and European Council set general priorities in the Annual Growth Survey, review national progress towards the achievement of these goals on the basis of Country Reports prepared by the Commission, and accordingly issue Country Specific Recommendations (CSRs) to Member States. As Zeitlin and Vanhercke note, the European Semester brings together within a single annual cycle a wide range of EU governance instruments with different legal bases and sanctioning authority, from the Stability and Growth Pact, the Macroeconomic Imbalances Procedure, and the Fiscal Treaty to the Europe 2020 Strategy and the Integrated Economic and Employment Policy guidelines. While some of the Semester's working methods resemble those of the OMC, it is more structured and more prescriptive, even if not legally binding. And while the Semester includes "a social dimension",[74] the overall rationale of the process is still economic, and national social and welfare policies are evaluated mainly through the prism of financial sustainability.

3.1.8 *The European Pillar of Social Rights*

On 26 April 2017, following a year-long preparatory phase,[75] the Commission officially launched a European Pillar of Social Rights,[76] with a Commission Recommendation adopted on the basis of Article 292 TFEU. On 17 November 2017, Commission, Parliament and Council signed an Inter-Institutional Proclamation on the Pillar. Both the Recommendation and the Inter-Institutional Proclamation are non-binding "soft law" instruments,[77] so the Pillar's legal value is limited to a source of interpretation of EU law, which the ECJ may or may not use, and which potentially circumscribes the actions of the signatories on the basis of the legal certainty principle.[78]

In a narrow sense, the Pillar is a set of 20 rights and principles, categorized in 3 chapters. Chapter I, entitled "Equal opportunities and access to the labour market" comprises the right to education, training and life-long learning, equal treatment between men and women, non-discrimination on grounds of gender, racial or ethnic origin, religion or belief, disability, age or sexual orientation, and "active support to employment". Chapter II, entitled "Fair working conditions", contains the rights to "secure and adaptable employment", fair wages, information about employment conditions and protection in case of dismissals, social dialogue and involvement of workers, work-life balance and healthy, safe and well-adapted work environment, and data protection. Chapter III, entitled "Social protection and inclusion" contains rights and

---

73. B. Vanhercke, J. Zeitin and A. Zwinkels, "Further socializing the European semester: Moving forward for the 'social triple A'?", European Social Observatory Report, 1 Dec. 2015.
74. J. Zeitlin and B. Vanhercke, "Socializing the European semester? Economic governance and social policy coordination in Europe 2020", (2014) *Swedish Institute for European Policy Studies.*
75. European Commission, Communication of 8 March 2016 launching a consultation on a European Pillar of Social Rights, COM(2016)127. For discussion see S. Garben, "The European Pillar of Social Rights: Effectively Addressing Displacement?" (2018) EuConst, forthcoming.
76. European Commission, Recommendation on the European Pillar of Social Rights, C(2017)2600 final, and Communication of 26 Apr. 2017 establishing a European Pillar of Social Rights, COM(2017)250 final.
77. Art. 288 TFEU states this explicitly for recommendations. Proclamations are not mentioned as a legal instrument in the Treaties, so their legal status is more obscure. See Z. Rasnača, "Bridging the gaps or falling short? The European Pillar of Social Rights and what it can bring to EU-level policymaking" (2017) ETUI Working Paper No. 5, p. 14.
78. See for a more elaborate analysis Z. Rasnača, op. cit. previous footnote.

principles on childcare and support for children, social protection, unemployment benefits, minimum income, old-age income and pensions, health care, inclusion of people with disabilities, long-term care, housing and assistance for the homeless, and access to essential services. In the accompanying staff working document,[79] each right or principle is explained by reference to its current status under the EU *acquis*.

For several rights and principles, concrete implementation measures at EU level are envisaged, and the proposals are conceptualized as part of the overall package. Some proposed measures are legislative, others are soft law, e.g. recommendations, communications, funding or foreseen as policy coordination in the EU's yearly cycle of economic governance (the European Semester). In a broader sense, the European Pillar of Social Rights can be understood as a larger package, or even an agenda or process, including those legislative and soft law proposals and initiatives as well as the 20 rights and principles. The main measures, to be adopted on the basis of the Treaty's Social Policy Title, are (i) an Initiative to support Work-Life Balance for parents and carers,[80] including a Proposal for a Directive on work-life balance for parents and carers,[81] (ii) an Access to social security initiative for a potential action addressing the challenges of access to social protection for people in all forms of employment and potentially also self-employment,[82] and (iii) a revision of the Written Statement Directive 91/533/EEC (in the form of a new Directive on Transparent and Predictable Working Conditions[83]) to introduce minimum standards applicable to every employment relationship and prohibiting abuse.

Various important legal instruments already exist containing by and large the same rights and principles as the European Pillar of Social Rights, most notably the EU Charter of Fundamental Rights, but also the European Social Charter of the Council of Europe and the many ILO Conventions. The Pillar's explanations indicate that it "draws on" these instruments and nothing in it may be interpreted as restricting or adversely affecting these principles and rights.[84] The Pillar "reaffirms the rights already present in the EU and in the international legal acquis and complements them to take account of new realities. As such, the Pillar does not affect principles and rights already contained in binding provisions of Union law: by putting together rights and principles which were set at different times, in different ways and in different forms, it seeks to render them more visible, more understandable and more explicit for citizens and for actors at all levels. [...] [T]he Pillar establishes a framework for guiding future action by the participating Member States".[85]

Thus, as the Commission indicates, the catalogue of 20 social rights and principles at the core of the Pillar initiative is not, "given the legal nature of the Pillar", directly enforceable, and "will require a translation into dedicated action and/or separate pieces of legislation, at the appropriate level".[86] As such, while the precedent of a "proclamation" was set by the EU Charter of Fundamental Rights,[87] the format of the overall Pillar initiative is perhaps more reminiscent

79. SWD(2017)201 final.
80. COM(2017)252 final.
81. COM(2017)253 final.
82. Commission Work Programme 2017 – Delivering a Europe that protects, empowers and defends, point 11.
83. Proposal for a Directive of the European Parliament and of the Council on transparent and predictable working conditions in the European Union, COM(2017)797.
84. Staff Working Document accompanying the Commission Communication establishing a European Pillar of Social Rights, p. 2 and 3.
85. See Commission Communication on the Pillar, COM(2016)127.
86. See Commission Staff Working Document, SWD(2017)201, p. 3.
87. The Commission draws this comparison itself, stating that "[a]s it was done for the Charter of Fundamental Rights, the proposal for an interinstitutional proclamation will be discussed with the European Parliament and the Council". See COM(2016)127.

of the Community Charter of the Fundamental Social Rights of Workers.[88] Most importantly, many rights listed in the Community Charter were implemented in secondary law through the Social Charter Action Programme,[89] such as on occupational health and safety, written statement, posted workers, working time, pregnant workers, and younger workers. In its broader sense, the Pillar resembles an Action Plan.

3.2 *Cross-cutting considerations*

3.2.1 *A uniform application of the labour law directives?*

In the context of Article 45 TFEU, the ECJ has since long held that the definition of "worker" is autonomous and defined at European level. This is however different in the context of the EU social *acquis*. In the TFEU's Social Policy Title, Article 151(2) obliges the EU "to take account of the diverse forms of national practices, in particular in the field of contractual relations". Perhaps in light thereof, several EU labour law directives refer to national law and practices, for instance to determine to which "employment relationships" they apply.[90] This deference to national regulators contrasts with the EU's habitual concern for effective and uniform application of EU law. For certain directives, the ECJ has decided to give an autonomous definition of their scope of application, such as for the Working Time Directive[91] and Directive 98/59 on collective redundancies,[92] but these measures do not refer to national law. By contrast, in the context of the Part-Time Work Directive which does refer to national law and practice, the Court confirmed in *Wippel* concerning a zero-hours contract that it was for the national level to determine whether the Directive applied, following national legal definitions and practices.[93]

The question to what extent Member States can limit the scope of application of the EU labour law directives by such references to their own national legislation is of mounting importance considering the increase (in the use) of non-standard forms of employment, such as "zero-hours contracts" in the UK and so-called "civil law contracts" in Poland.[94] It would seem harmful to the social objectives of the *acquis* if its scope of application could be unilaterally limited by Member States, excluding certain forms of work or workers regardless of the material conditions of their employment.[95] Indeed, even when a Directive refers to national definitions, the Member States' discretion is not "wholly unfettered", as the Court held in *Tümer*.[96] The Court ruled that an illegally resident third country nationals could not be excluded from the scope of

---

88. The 1989 Community Charter of the Fundamental Social Rights of Workers is a political declaration signed in 1989 by (then) all the EU MS except the UK, which signed in 1997. The Community Charter is declaratory, but it is a source of inspiration for the ECJ, especially when interpreting the rights in the EU Charter of Fundamental Rights that are based on rights first set out in the 1989 Charter.
89. COM(89)568.
90. E.g. the Fixed-Term Work Directive 1999/70/EC, the Part-Time Work Directive 97/81/EC, the Temporary Agency Work Directive 2008/104/EC, the Information and Consultation Directive 2002/14/EC, the Insolvency Directive 2008/94/EC and the Written Statement Directive 91/533/EEC.
91. Case C-428/09, *Union syndicale Solidaires Isère v. Premier ministre and Others*. The ECJ applies its case law concerning Article 45 TFEU.
92. Case C-55/02, *Commission of the European Communities v. Portuguese Republic*, and Case C-596/12, *European Commission v. Italian Republic*.
93. Case C-313/02, *Nicole Wippel v. Peek & Cloppenburg GmbH & Co. KG*, para 40.
94. See European Commission,"Employment and Social Developments in Europe 2015, Chapter 1.2. Labour Law", SWD(2016)7 final.
95. See Opinion of A.G. Saugmandsgaard of 06/07/2016, in Case C-216/15, *Betriebsrat der Ruhrlandklinik gGmbH v. Ruhrlandklinik gGmbH*.
96. Case C-311/13, O. *Tümer v. Raad van bestuur van het Uitvoeringsinstituut werknemersverzekeringen*.

the Insolvency Directive if a Member State had recognized such third-country nationals under its civil law as having the status of an "employee" with an entitlement to pay. Similarly, regarding the Part-Time Work Directive, the ECJ held that the Member States' freedom to define the concept of "worker" was "subject to the condition that that does not lead to the arbitrary exclusion of that category of persons from the protection offered by [the] Directive".[97] In *Ruhrlandklinik*,[98] the CJEU ruled on this issue regarding the Temporary Agency Work Directive. It held that the reference to national law "cannot be interpreted as a waiver on the part of the EU legislature of its power itself to determine the scope of that concept for the purposes of Directive 2008/104, and accordingly the scope ratione personae of that directive". The reference to national law only preserved Member States' power to determine who constitutes a "worker" for the purposes of national law.[99] The CJEU declared: "the essential feature of an employment relationship is that, for a certain period of time, a person performs services for and under the direction of another person, in return for which he receives remuneration, the legal characterization under national law and the form of that relationship, as well as the nature of the legal relationship between those two persons, not being decisive in that regard".[100]

Most recently, in *Ruhrlandklinik*, the ECJ ruled on this issue with regard to the Temporary Agency Work Directive, which similarly refers to "any person who, in the member state concerned, is protected as a worker under national employment law".[101] It held that such a reference "cannot be interpreted as a waiver on the part of the EU legislature of its power itself to determine the scope of that concept for the purposes of Directive 2008/104, and accordingly the scope ratione personae of that directive". The reference to national law meant only that the EU legislature intended to preserve the power of the MS to determine the persons falling within the scope of the concept of 'worker' for the purposes of national law and who must be protected under their domestic legislation. The ECJ declared that "the essential feature of an employment relationship is that, for a certain period of time, a person performs services for and under the direction of another person, in return for which he receives remuneration" and that "the legal characterisation under national law and the form of that relationship, as well as the nature of the legal relationship between those two persons [is not] decisive in that regard".

3.2.2 *The role of the EU Charter*

As we have seen, several of the social rights featured in the EU Charter are implemented by means of secondary law, often pre-dating the Charter itself. The relationship between the rights contained in the EU Charter and these measures is evolving. As was to be expected, the Charter is proving a source of inspiration in the interpretation of the rights and obligations laid down in secondary law, strengthening for instance the "fundamental social right" to paid annual leave.[102] Still, the Charter has not developed into the social safeguard or catalyst that some may have hoped it would be.

Firstly, an important question was whether the Charter would change anything regarding the (lack of) horizontal application of Directives, of high relevance in the area of labour law as it

97. Case C-393/10, *Dermod Patrick O'Brien v. Ministry of Justice*. The Court added: "An exclusion from that protection may be allowed only if the relationship between judges and the Ministry of Justice is, by its nature, substantially different from that between employers and their employees falling, according to national law, under the category of workers."
98. Case C-216/15, *Betriebsrat der Ruhrlandklinik gGmbH v. Ruhrlandklinik gGmbH*.
99. Case C-216/15, *Betriebsrat der Ruhrlandklinik gGmbH v. Ruhrlandklinik gGmbH*, para 31.
100. Case C-216/15, *Betriebsrat der Ruhrlandklinik gGmbH v. Ruhrlandklinik gGmbH*, para 27.
101. Case C-216/15, *Betriebsrat der Ruhrlandklinik gGmbH v. Ruhrlandklinik gGmbH*, ECLI:EU:C:2016:883.
102. See, *inter alia*, Joined Cases C-229/11 and C-230/11, *Heimann and Toltschin*.

often concerns claims against private employers. In *Dominguez,* the Court interpreted the right to paid annual leave under the Working Time Directive (contained in Article 31(2) of the Charter) to preclude national provisions or practices which make entitlement to paid annual leave conditional on a minimum period of ten days or one month's actual work during the reference period.[103] However, if national law did not provide this right, and could not be interpreted so as to provide this right, and if the employer was not to be considered an "emanation of the state", the individual worker was left only with the option to seek compensation through state liability under the *Francovich* doctrine. The Court thereby resisted the possibility to use the *Mangold* doctrine[104] in combination with the Charter to make the general right to paid annual leave a horizontally applicable EU right.[105] Contrary to the Advocate General,[106] the Court did not even mention the Charter in this respect. Furthermore, the Court has explicitly denied any direct effect to certain social rights in the Charter, such as Article 27 of the Charter on information and consultation.[107]

Secondly, the Court strictly adheres to the limitations on the applicability of the Charter in that it does not extend the existing competences of the EU, declining competence to rule on the compatibility of the controversial single-open ended contract with a year-long probation period in Spain[108] or on the issue of judicial fees and deposits required for lodging appeals in employment law cases.[109] Along those lines, the Court has refused to hear claims in relation to the changes to national labour and social systems under the financial assistance programmes.[110]

Thirdly, the Charter does not only contain social rights, but also economic ones, which might play out to the disadvantage of social secondary legislation. For instance, in *Alemo-Herron,*[111] the Court interpreted Directive 2001/23/EC on the transfer of undertakings in light of Article 16 of the Charter laying down the freedom to conduct a business, to preclude a Member State from providing, in the event of a transfer of an undertaking, that dynamic clauses referring to collective agreements negotiated and adopted after the date of transfer are enforceable against the transferee, where that transferee does not have the possibility of participating in the negotiation process of such collective agreements concluded after the date of the transfer. It remains to be seen whether the recently launched European Pillar of Social Rights, discussed in section 3.1.8. above, will serve to strengthen the social rights contained in the Charter. It may do so, as it aims to implement a number of these rights through the adoption of new legislation and soft law measures.

103. Case C-282/10, *Maribel Dominguez v. Centre informatique du Centre Ouest Atlantique and Préfet de la région Centre.*
104. Case C-144/04, *Werner Mangold v. Rüdiger Helm.*
105. D. Leczykiewicz, "Horizontal application of the Charter of Fundamental Rights", 38 EL Rev. (2013), at 480.
106. Opinion of A.G. Trstenjak, Case C-282/10, *Maribel Dominguez v. Centre informatique du Centre Ouest Atlantique and Préfet de la région Centre.*
107. Case C-176/12, *Association de médiation sociale v. Union locale des syndicats CGT and Others.*
108. For instance, in Case C-117/14, *Grima Janet Nisttahuz Poclava v. Jose María Ariza Toledano.*
109. Case C-265/13, *Emiliano Torralbo Marcos v. Korota SA, Fondo de Garantía Salarial.*
110. Case C-434/11, *Corpul Național al Polițiștilor v. Ministerul Administrației și Internelor (MAI) and Others;* Case C-134/12, *Ministerul Administrației și Internelor (MAI), Inspectoratul General al Poliției Române (IGPR) and Inspectoratul de Poliție al Județului Tulcea (IPJ) v. Corpul Național al Polițiștilor-Biroul Executiv. Central;* Case C-264/12, *Sindicato Nacional dos Profissionais de Seguros e Afins v. Fidelidade Mundial-Companhia de Seguros SA.*
111. Case C-426/11, *Mark Alemo-Herron and Others v. Parkwood Leisure Ltd.*

3.2.3 *A social deficit?*[112]

While, for the reasons indicated above, EU law and policy on social and employment matters often strikes an apolitical tone, scholars have suggested that there is in fact a highly political bias in the overall outcome of the European integration process, reflecting a "liberal" vision of the market and its place in society rather than a "social" one.[113] This is not because of any subjective preferences on the part of EU policy makers, but because of a structural asymmetry in the European integration process. The case law, constitutionalizing the free movement provisions[114] and defining "restrictions" of these freedoms widely, plays a crucial role in this dynamic. Striking down national social standards that do not pass the Court's strict proportionality test significantly limits Member States' social regulatory powers (negative integration). The EU in turn possesses only limited capacities to re-regulate by setting European social standards (positive integration), as its legal competence is limited and the high consensus threshold in this area of widely varying national preferences means that it is difficult to adopt legislation even where law-making competence exists. This imbalance results in a regulatory gap where significant non-economic interests risk to remain unprotected, potentially eroding social standards across Europe.

As an additional challenge, the EU's economic, monetary and employment policy has put pressure on national social and labour standards over the past decade. Firstly, the economic and sovereign debt crisis threatening the stability of the Euro-zone and the EU economy more generally has led to the adoption of harsh austerity measures in the affected countries. The Commission coordinates the financial support in the form of economic adjustment programmes, requiring reforms to address "economic imbalances", specified in the Memorandums of Understanding that the Commission signs with the countries in need. The detailed conditionalities specified therein have resulted in a significant and widely reported reduction of health, social protection and labour standards in these countries.[115] These events adversely affect the image and credibility of the EU, as for many they represent its ultimate failure to deliver on promises of an inclusive social market economy. Furthermore, in the European Semester there have been highly detailed CSRs concerning a range of labour market and social standards in a great number of Member States. While some of these recommendations encourage Member States to increase social inclusion and worker protection, many others entail the opposite. While steps have been taken to "socialize" the European Semester as a response "to rising social and political discontent with the consequences of post-crisis austerity policies",[116] the process still fundamentally challenges national social and labour standards on the basis of an approach that sees a liberal, market-oriented and business-friendly climate as the solution to most of Europe's problems.

4. Final considerations

While it could be argued that the social credentials of the EU leave somewhat to be desired, we have also seen that the EU still boasts an impressive social *acquis*, and recent developments in the case law of the Court in the areas of posting of workers and temporary agency work seem to

---

112. See generally S. Garben, "The constitutional (im)balance between 'the Market' and 'the Social' in the European Union", 13 EuConst (2017), 23–61.
113. F. Scharpf, "The European social model: Coping with the challenges of diversity", 40 JCMS (2002), at 645–670.
114. See Ch. 15, "Free movement of workers and coordination of social security", of this book.
115. The 2015 ILO Report on social protection provides a comprehensive, damning overview. ILO, World Social Protection Report, 2015, at xxv, 9, 24, 135, and 137.
116. J. Zeitlin and B. Vanhercke, op. cit. *supra* note 74.

indicate an increasing concern for the protection of Member States' social and labour standards. Equally, the Juncker Commission has launched certain interesting initiatives. Apart from the proposed revision of the Posting of Workers Directive, the Commission has launched a European Pillar of Social Rights.[117] As part of the Pillar initiative, the Commission proposed the abovementioned revision of the Written Statement Directive, in a way to include basic employment rights for precarious workers, which is a highly significant development. Furthermore, it has launched a first phase consultation to define new rules on access to social protection for people in self-employment and non-standard employment and a proposal for a Directive on Work-Life Balance for Parents and Carers. While the overall impact of the Pillar on the social dimension of European integration is not yet clear, it certainly marks a change in outlook compared to the past decade. It will be very interesting to see whether these developments will usher in a new period in the European integration process, (re-)establishing the social legitimacy of the EU, or not.

Further reading

Barnard, C., "EU employment law and the European social model: The past, the present and the future", 67 *Current Legal Problems* (2014), 199–237.

Bruun, N., K. Lörcher and I. Schömann, *The Lisbon Treaty and Social Europe* (Hart, 2012).

De Búrca, G., and B. de Witte (Eds.), *Social Rights in Europe* (OUP, 2005).

Cantillon, B., H. Verschueren and P. Ploscar (Eds.), *Social Inclusion and Social Protection in the EU: Interactions between Law and Policy* (Intersentia, 2012).

Copeland, P., "EU enlargement, the clash of capitalisms and the European social model", 10 *Comparative European Politics* (2012), 476–504.

Davies, G., "Democracy and legitimacy in the shadow of purposive competence", 21 ELJ (2015), 2–22.

Dawson, M., *New Governance and the Transformation of European Law: Coordinating EU Social Law and Policy* (CUP, 2011).

Dougan, M. and E. Spaventa, *Social Welfare and EU Law. Essays in European Law* (Hart, 2005).

Garben, S., "The constitutional (im)balance between 'the Market' and 'the Social' in the European Union", 13 *EuConst* (2017), 23–61.

Garben, S., 'The European Pillar of Social Rights: Effectively Addressing Displacement?' [2018] 14 *European Constitutional Law Review*, forthcoming.

Kilpatrick, C., "Are the bailouts immune to EU social challenge because they are not EU law?", 10 *European Constitutional Law Review* (2014), 393–421.

Kilpatrick, C., and B. de Witte (Eds.), "Social rights in times of crisis in the Eurozone: The role of fundamental rights' challenges", 5 *EUI Working Papers LAW* (2014).

Moreau, M.A. (Ed.), *Before and After the Economic Crisis, What Implications for the European Social Model"?* (Edward Elgar Publishing, 2011).

Scharpf, F., "The asymmetry of European integration, or why the EU cannot be a 'social market economy'", 8 *Socio-Economic Review* (2010), 211–250.

Vanhercke, B., J. Zeitin and A. *Zwinkels*, "Further socializing the European semester: Moving forward for the 'social triple A'?", *European Social Observatory Report*, 1 Dec. 2015.

117. COM/2017/0250 final.

CHAPTER 29
EQUAL TREATMENT AND NON-DISCRIMINATION

*Christa Tobler**

1. Introduction

Within the broad field of Union social law as discussed in the previous chapter, equal treatment and non-discrimination law is both the oldest and "arguably the area on which the social dimension of EU law and policy is most developed".[1] Originally, the only substantive provision in the Social Policy Chapter of the EEC Treaty concerned the right to equal pay for men and women workers, namely Article 119 (today, after amendment, Art. 157(1) and (2) TFEU). Subsequently, this provision was complemented by a number of sex equality directives in the field of employment. Since the Social Policy Chapter did not contain any specific legal basis provision enabling the adoption of such law, the first generation of secondary sex equality law developed in the "disguise" of economic law, based on general legal basis provisions. Today, Article 157(3) TFEU provides for a specific legal basis for sex equality legislation in the field of employment and occupation. Outside the ambit of the present Social Policy Title, and therefore not limited to social matters, Article 19 TFEU serves as a legal basis for the adoption of secondary law to combat discrimination on grounds of sex, racial or ethnic origin, religion or belief, disability, age and sexual orientation.

This development on the level of the Union's competences has resulted in an important body of law relating to the discrimination grounds listed in Article 19 TFEU, mostly in the form of secondary legislation. As the ECJ noted in *Coleman*,[2] Article 19 TFEU deals with Union competence only. Only for sex discrimination is there a substantive Treaty provision, namely Article 157 TFEU on equal pay. Present secondary sex equality law includes Directive 79/7 on statutory social security[3] (which is the only surviving Directive from the first generation of sex equality legislation), Directive 2004/113 on goods and services,[4] Directive 2006/54[5] on employment and

---

* Prof. Dr. Christa Tobler, LLM; Europa Institutes of the Universities of Leiden (the Netherlands) and Basel (Switzerland).

1. C. O'Cinneide, "Completing the picture: The complex relationship between EU anti-discrimination law and 'Social Europe'" in N. Countouris and M. Freedland (Eds.), *Resocialising Europe in a Time of Crisis* (CUP, 2013), 118–137, at 118.
2. Case C-303/06, *S. Coleman v. Attridge Law and Steve Law*.
3. O.J. 1979, L 6/24, Council Directive 79/7/EEC of 19 Dec. 1978 on the progressive implementation of the principle of equal treatment for men and women in matters of social security.
4. O.J. 2004, L 373/37, Council Directive 2004/113/EC of 13 Dec. 2004 implementing the principle of equal treatment between men and women in the access to and supply of goods and services.
5. O.J. 2006, L 204/23, Directive 2006/54/EC on the implementation of the principle of equal opportunities and equal treatment of men and women in matters of employment and occupation (recast).

occupation and Directive 2010/41 on self-employment.[6] Discrimination on grounds of racial or ethnic origin is prohibited in Directive 2000/43[7] and discrimination on grounds of religion or belief, disability, age and sexual orientation in Directive 2000/78.[8] A proposal intended to broaden the field of application of Union law with respect to the latter group of grounds has been pending for some time.[9] It seems conceivable that it might eventually be adopted in a modified version, in the shape of the European Union Accessibility Act[10] (though it should be noted that this proposal, whose legal basis is Art. 114 TFEU, reflects a positive integration approach through harmonization, rather than a negative integration approach through common prohibitions of discrimination).

This chapter focuses on the Union's law in relation to the Article 19 grounds as prime examples of prohibitions of discrimination that are relevant outside internal market and Union citizenship law. The reason for this choice is the fact that the law on the Article 19 grounds shares a common model that is more developed than that of other prohibitions of discrimination under Union law, even within the social field. For example, in other contexts there are no legal definitions of different forms of discrimination and fewer forms of discrimination have been legally recognized (e.g. Clause 4 in the Annex to Directive 97/81 on part-time work,[11] Clause 4 in the Annex to Directive 1999/70 on fixed-term work,[12] and Art. 5 of Directive 2008/104 on temporary work[13]).

The chapter aims to give an overview that will be useful in the practice of non-discrimination law. It begins with the larger context of international human rights law (below 2) and the layered system of Union law itself (below 3). It then turns to the legislation relating to the Article 19 grounds and discusses its field of application (below 4), the meaning of equal treatment and discrimination (below 5), duties and possibilities to treat differently (below 6 and 7) and enforcement (below 8). The conclusion provides some overall comments (below 9). As a final preliminary remark, it is important to note that the legislation discussed in this chapter provides for minimum protection only. Member States have the option of maintaining or introducing more favourable provisions. Further, they are bound by the principle of non-regression, meaning that implementation of the Directive must not lead to a reduction in the level of protection under national law (e.g. Art. 6 of Directive 2000/43).

---

6. O.J. 2010, L 180/1, Directive 2010/41/EU of the European Parliament and of the Council of 7 July 2010 on the application of the principle of equal treatment between men and women engaged in an activity in a self-employed capacity and repealing Council Directive 86/613/EEC.
7. O.J. 2000, L 180/22, Council Directive 2000/43/EC of 29 June 2000 implementing the principle of equal treatment between persons irrespective of racial or ethnic origin.
8. O.J. 2000, L 303/16, Council Directive 2000/78/EC of 27 November 2000 establishing a general framework for equal treatment in employment and occupation.
9. COM(2008)426, Proposal for a Council Directive on implementing the principle of equal treatment between persons irrespective of religion or belief, disability, age or sexual orientation.
10. COM(2015)615 final, Proposal for a Directive of the European Parliament and of the Council on the approximation of the laws, regulations and administrative provisions of the Member States as regards the accessibility requirements for products and services.
11. O.J. 1998, L 14/9, Directive 97/81/EC concerning the Framework Agreement on part-time work concluded by UNICE, CEEP and the ETUC.
12. O.J. 1999, L 175/43, Council Directive 1999/70/EC of 28 June 1999 concerning the framework agreement on fixed-term work concluded by ETUC, UNICE and CEEP.
13. O.J. 2008, L 327/9, Directive 2008/104/EC of the European Parliament and of the Council of 19 Nov. 2008 on temporary agency work.

2. The larger context of international law

At the background of Union non-discrimination law there are a number of international Conventions to which (some of) the Member States are parties, including most notably the UN's International Covenant on Civil and Political Rights (ICCPR), the International Covenant on Economic, Social and Cultural Rights (ICESC), the Convention on the Elimination of All Forms of Discrimination against Women (CEDAW), the Convention on the Rights of Persons with Disabilities (CRPD) and the various Conventions of the International Labour Organisation (ILO). The ECJ sometimes mentions these instruments as interpretative tools that support its own findings. Conversely, it rarely relies on them directly in order to arrive at a certain conclusion. This is, however, different in cases concerning disability. Since the Union itself is a party to the CRPD,[14] this Convention is an integral part of the Union legal order and takes primacy over secondary law which must be interpreted in a manner that is consistent with the Convention. The Court has relied on the Convention for example when defining "disability" (e.g. *Daouidi*)[15] and when explaining the purpose of positive action measures under Art. 7(2) of Directive 2000/78 (*Milkova*).[16]

On the regional level, Article 6(3) TEU states that the Union shall accede to the ECHR. Pending such accession, the Convention does not constitute a legal instrument, which has been formally incorporated into the Union legal order (Opinion 2/13).[17] Nevertheless, it takes a special place as part of the Union's general principles (Art. 6(2) TEU). The Court regularly refers to the ECHR, for example when defining the term "religion" (*Achbita*).[18]

Compared to the Union law discussed in this chapter, the scope of the international instruments is much broader, since they prohibit discrimination with respect to all aspects of life. The comparatively narrow scope of Union law as described in this chapter is partially due to the limited competences of the Union itself but partially also due to the fact that the Union has not used its competences to the full, and has used them unevenly for different discrimination grounds. With respect to the concept of "discrimination", the UN Conventions are broader, and the ECHR is narrower, than is Union law. In the case of the ECHR, the prohibition under Article 14 is more limited than that of the Union, notably because the former allows for broader justification possibilities in the case of direct discrimination. However, the fact that the ECHR provides for a minimum level of protection only means that there is room for the comparatively broader approach of the Union.[19] Conversely, Union law generally is less ambitious than are the UN Conventions, which are based on a very broad concept of "discrimination" and oblige the states to actively combat such discrimination.[20]

---

14. Approved on behalf of the European Community by O.J. 2010, L 23/35, Council Decision 2010/48/EU.
15. Case C-395/15, *Mohamed Daouidi v. Bootes Plus SL and Others.*
16. Case C-406/15, *Petya Milkova v. Izpalnitelen direktor na Agentsiata za privatizatsia i sledprivatizatsionen kontrol.*
17. Opinion 2/13, *Accession of the European Union to the European Convention for the Protection of Human Rights and Fundamental Freedoms.*
18. Case C-157/15, *Samira Achbita, Centrum voor gelijkheid van kansen en voor racismebestrijding v. G4S Secure Solutions NV.*
19. C. Tobler, "Equality and non-discrimination under the ECHR and EU law. A comparison focusing on discrimination against LGBTI Persons", 74 Zeitschrift für ausländisches öffentliches Recht und Völkerrecht (2014), 521–561; see also Advocate General Sharpston in Case C-188/15, *Asma Bougnaoui and Association de défense des droits de l'homme (ADDH) v. Micropole SA*, para 58 et seq., in the different context of a comparison of the freedom of religion under the Convention and the prohibition of discrimination on grounds of religion under Union law.
20. To take the example of the CEDAW, see generally M. Freeman, C.M. Chinkin and B. Rudolf (Eds.), *The UN Convention on the Elimination of All Forms of Discrimination Against Women: A Commentary* (OUP, 2012).

3. The layered system of Union non-discrimination law

Union non-discrimination law is a layered system, where specific provisions are expressions of general principles and fundamental rights.[21] Articles 20, 21 and 23 CFR, which deal with equality and non-discrimination, are expressions of general principles of equal treatment and non-discrimination that were recognized as part of EEC law long before the Charter was created. In this context, a distinction must be made between the general principle of equal treatment or non-discrimination in its broadest form, on the one hand, and various general principles linked to specific grounds, on the other hand. The former is independent of a specific ground and simply demands same or different treatment, depending on the comparability of the situations. The latter are characterized by a focus on a specific ground (e.g. sexual orientation, *Römer*).[22] They demand same treatment in that respect, which implies that factual differences in regard to that ground do not render situations non-comparable.

The general principles of equal treatment and non-discrimination fulfil the usual functions of the Union's general principles, i.e. they serve as an aim to interpretation, a constitutional framework and – occasionally – as a gap-filling tool.[23] For purposes of the practical application of the different levels of Union law, the starting point is the principle established in *Tedeschi*,[24] namely that insofar as there is specific secondary law on given matter, there is no room for the application of more general rules on the level of primary law. However, there are at least two special constellations.

First, the Court held in *Jenkins*[25] that the secondary law on equal pay for men and women workers then in force did not add to the scope of Article 119 of the EEC Treaty. This was important because the secondary law made reference not only to equal work but also to work of equal value, which was not mentioned in the Treaty at the time, and because in this manner the problem of the lack of horizontal direct effect of Directives could be avoided. Today, this means that Article 157(1) and (2) TFEU and the equal pay provision in Article 4 of Directive 2006/54 can be applied side by side.

Second, the Court found in *Mangold*[26] that the nature of Directive 2000/78 as a general framework Directive means that the prohibitions of discrimination with respect to the grounds covered do not flow from the Directive itself but rather from general principles, to which the Directive merely gives expression in the domain of employment and occupation. Accordingly, the law applicable in cases falling within the scope of the Directive is the relevant general principle, as now also enshrined in Article 21 CFR, and as given expression in the Directive. In *AMS*,[27] the Court stated that the general principle of non-discrimination on grounds of age is sufficient in itself to confer on individuals a right, which they may invoke. However, it is important to remember that a general principle can apply only where the matter at issue is within the scope of Union law. As the examples of *Kücükdeveci*[28] and *Kristensen*[29] show, this may be through

21. See C. Tobler, "The prohibition of discrimination in the Union's layered system of equality law: From early staff cases to the Mangold approach" in A. Rosas, E. Levits and Y. Bot (Eds.), *The Court of Justice and the Construction of Europe: Analyses and Perspectives on 60 years of Case-Law* (Asser Press/Springer, 2013), 443–467.
22. Case C-147/08, *Jürgen Römer v. Freie und Hansestadt Hamburg.*
23. See Ch. 6, "Sources of EU law", of this book.
24. Case 5/77, *Carlo Tedeschi v. Denkavit Commerciale s.r.l.*
25. Case 96/80, *J.P. Jenkins v. Kingsgate (Clothing Productions) Ltd.*
26. Case C-144/04, *Werner Mangold v. Rüdiger Helm.*
27. Case C-176/12, *Association de médiation sociale v. Union locale des syndicats CGT and Others.*
28. Case C-555/07, *Seda Kücükdeveci v. Swedex GmbH & Co. KG.*
29. Case C-476/11, *HK Danmark, acting on behalf of Glennie Kristensen v. Experian A/S.*

Directive 2000/78 itself, which appears to be rather circular. *Bartsch*[30] provides an example where the necessary link was missing.

More recently, *Schmitzer*[31] might indicate a change in direction. Here, the Court stated that it examines cases involving an individual and a public body solely in the light of Directive 2000/78, rather than also of the general principle. The fact that the Court in this context referred to case law involving collective agreements might be taken to imply that the same approach can also apply in cases between individuals. Important examples of more recent cases involving individuals which the Court examined in the light of the Directive are *Achbita*[32] and *Bougnaoui*.[33] More recent cases involving an individual and a public body are *de Lange*[34] and *Milkova*.[35] In the latter case, the Court, in spite of having found that there is no different treatment on grounds of disability under the Directive, proceeded to use the defence argument of the Bulgarian Government of positive action under Article 7(2) of the Directive to bring the case within the scope of Union law and, thereby, under the general principle of equal treatment (the Court applied a similar approach in the framework of the law of the internal market in *Hudzinksi*).[36]

4. Field of application

The field of application of Union non-discrimination law is the eye of the needle through which a case must pass before it can be assessed under this law. Article 157(1) TFEU and the Directives concern persons who find themselves in certain situations. Accordingly, the personal scope of Union non-discrimination law is closely linked with its material scope, as described below. As a general starting point, the Court has held that in view of the effectiveness of the prohibition of discrimination, the scope of the Union's non-discrimination law cannot be defined restrictively (e.g. *Runevič-Vardyn*).[37] However, an abuse of rights is not protected (*Kratzer*, with respect to a complainant who applied for a post solely for the purpose of acquiring the status of applicant in order to claim compensation for discrimination, without any real interest in the post).[38]

It should be noted that, different from internal market law, Union non-discrimination law relating to the Article 19 grounds field requires neither a cross-border element nor Union nationality of the person entitled to equal treatment. Rather, it is law that applies within the territory of the individual Member States and irrespective of the nationality of the persons concerned. Cases such as *Feryn*,[39] concerning discrimination against Moroccans, confirm that third-country nationals are included among those protected by the Directives.

---

30. Case C-427/06, *Birgit Bartsch v. Bosch und Siemens Hausgeräte (BSH) Altersfürsorge GmbH.*
31. Case C-530/13, *Leopold Schmitzer v. Bundesministerin für Inneres.*
32. Case C-157/15, *Samira Achbita, Centrum voor gelijkheid van kansen en voor racismebestrijding v. G4S Secure Solutions NV.*
33. Case C-188/15, *Asma Bougnaoui and Association de défense des droits de l'homme (ADDH) v. Micropole SA.*
34. Case C-548/15, *J.J. de Lange v. Staatssecretaris van Financiën.*
35. Case C-406/15, *Petya Milkova v. Izpalnitelen direktor na Agentsiata za privatizatsia i sledprivatizatsionen control.*
36. Joined Cases C-611/10 and C-612/10, *Waldemar Hudzinski v. Agentur für Arbeit Wesel – Familienkasse* (C-611/10) *and Jaroslaw Wawrzyniak v. Agentur für Arbeit Mönchengladbach – Familienkasse* (C-612/10).
37. Case C-391/09, *Malgožata Runevič-Vardyn and Łukasz Paweł Wardyn v. Vilniaus miesto savivaldybės administracija, Lietuvos Respublikos teisingumo ministerija, Valstybinė lietuvių kalbos komisija and Vilniaus miesto savivaldybės administracijos Teisės departamento Civilinės metrikacijos skyrius.*
38. Case C-423/15, *Nils-Johannes Kratzer v. R+V Allgemeine Versicherung AG.*
39. Case C-54/07, *Centrum voor gelijkheid van kansen en voor racismebestrijding v. Firma Feryn NV.*

4.1 *Personal scope*

Depending on their subject matter, the Directives give varying indications with respect to the persons covered, both those obliged and those protected. Two examples are "all persons who provide goods and services", in Article 3(1) of Directive 2004/113, and "all persons, as regards both the public and private sectors, including public bodies" in relation to the material issues listed thereafter, in Article 3(1) of Directives 2000/43 and 2000/78. With respect to the term "worker" (or "employment"), the Court often relies on the concept as developed in the context of the free movement for workers. The formal framework in which a person performs work is not relevant, as long as the characteristics of an employment relationship are present (e.g. *Danosa*).[40] However, there is no single definition of the term "worker" under Union law, whose meaning depends on the context (*Allonby*).[41]

Particularly important in practice, those obliged include the social partners. Whilst they enjoy the right of collective bargaining according to Article 28 CFR, this is strictly within the limits of Union law. Consequently, when the social partners adopt measures falling within the scope of a non-discrimination Directive, they must comply with that Directive (e.g. *Hennigs and Mai*).[42] As long as a collective agreement is not contrary to the relevant EU Directive, the Member State concerned is free to make it compulsory for persons who are not bound as parties to the agreement (*Rosenbladt*).[43]

4.2 *Material scope*

Different from the prohibition of discrimination on the basis of nationality, none of the Article 19 grounds relates to all matters falling under Union law. The oldest field of application is that of pay, followed by other employment conditions, including access to employment and dismissal. Today, this forms the nucleus common to all law prohibiting discrimination on the Article 19 grounds. In other respects, the scope of the law differs, which means that there is uneven protection. However, it needs to be remembered that the Member States are free to provide for a higher degree of protection by applying their national law to situations that are not covered by Union law.

4.2.1 *The oldest field: Pay*

Already Article 119 of the EEC Treaty stated the principle of equal pay for men and women. However, it was only after the ECJ decision *Defrenne II*[44] (declaring the provision to be directly effective both vertically and horizontally) and after the adoption of facilitating legislation that the principle became meaningful in practice. In spite of this, pay discrimination against women remains a persistent problem, which also has consequences in the field of pensions.[45]

According to Article 157(2) TFEU the term "pay" covers "the ordinary basic or minimum wage or salary and any other consideration, whether in cash or in kind, which the worker receives directly or indirectly, in respect of his employment, from his employer". In ECJ case law, this has led to a very broad concept covering any consideration, whether in cash or in kind, whether immediate or future, provided that the worker receives it, albeit indirectly, in respect

---

40. Case C-232/09, *Dita Danosa v. LKB Lizings SIA*.
41. Case C-256/01, *Debra Allonby v. Accrington & Rossendale College, Education Lecturing Services, trading as Protocol Professional and Secretary of State for Education and Employment*.
42. Joined Cases C-297/10 and C-298/10, *Sabine Hennigs v. Eisenbahn-Bundesamt, Land Berlin v. Alexander Mai*.
43. Case C-45/09, *Gisela Rosenbladt v. Oellerking Gebäudereinigungsges. mbH*.
44. Case 43/75, *Gabrielle Defrenne v. Société anonyme belge de navigation aérienne Sabena*.
45. See the Commission's Report on equality between women and men 2015, SWD(2016)54, at 18.

of the employment from the employer (e.g. *Gillespie*).[46] The Court held early on that benefits under occupational pension systems are covered (*Bilka*).[47] This was subsequently confirmed in *Barber*,[48] even though by that time there was a sex equality Directive on occupational pensions. The issue was decisive because the Directive allowed for different pension ages but Article 119 of the EEC Treaty did not. Today, the fixing of different ages with respect to occupational pensions is mentioned as an example of sex discrimination in Article 9(1)(f) of Directive 2006/54.

In Directive 2000/78, Recital 13 in the preamble explicitly includes in the scope of the Directive social security and social protection schemes that are income within the meaning of Article 157 TFEU. In *Maruko*,[49] the Court rejected the argument that a same-sex widower's pension cannot be covered in view of Recital 22 in the preamble to the Directive, according to which the Directive is without prejudice to national laws on marital status and the benefits dependent thereon. Rather, the Member State have to exercise their competence in this respect in a manner that is compatible with the Directive.

In contrast, the concept of pay excludes statutory social security benefits without any element of agreement within the undertaking or the occupational branch concerned (e.g. *Elbal Moreno*).[50] Neither are differences resulting from tax treatment covered, since they do not originate from the employer (though they may be related to other aspects relevant under the non-discrimination law, such as dismissal in *Vergani*[51] or vocational training in *de Lange*[52]). The European Parliament has called upon the Member States to remember their commitments regarding a review of the effect that their tax policies have on the gender pay gap.[53]

4.2.2 *Other issues related to employment and occupation*

Also covered for all discrimination grounds are certain employment-related issues other than pay, though to the exclusion of employment-related social security, which is covered only by some legislation. With respect to self-employment, Article 2 of Directive 2010/41 generally refers to persons pursuing "a gainful activity for their own account, under the conditions laid down by national law". The other Directives are more specific and list issues such as access to work, including promotion, employment conditions, including dismissal, vocational guidance and training as well as membership of and involvement in an organization of workers or employers (e.g. Art. 14 of Directive 2006/54).

In these contexts, other Union social law may also be relevant. For example, the working conditions covered by Directive 2006/54 include the conditions applicable to a worker who has taken parental leave and is returning to work (*Nadežda Riežniec*,[54] with respect to previous secondary law). Whilst other conditions for the implementation of such leave are outside the

46. Case C-342/93, *Joan Gillespie and others v. Northern Health and Social Services Boards, Department of Health and Social Services, Eastern Health and Social Services Board and Southern Health and Social Services Board.* Joined Cases C-216/12 and C-217/12, *Caisse nationale des prestations familiales v. Fjola Hliddal* and *Pierre-Louis Bornand.*
47. Case 170/84, *Bilka v. Karin Weber von Hartz.*
48. Case C-262/88, *Douglas Harvey Barber v. Guardian Royal Exchange Assurance Group.*
49. Case C-267/06, *Tadao Maruko v. Versorgungsanstalt der deutschen Bühnen.*
50. Case C-385/11, *Isabel Elbal Moreno v. Instituto Nacional de la Seguridad Social (INSS), Tesorería General de la Seguridad Social (TGSS).*
51. Case C-207/04, *Paolo Vergani v. Agenzia delle Entrate, Ufficio di Arona.*
52. Case C-548/15, *J.J. de Lange v. Staatssecretaris van Financiën.*
53. European Parliament Resolution of 24 May 2012 with recommendations to the Commission on application of the principle of equal pay for male and female workers for equal work or work of equal value.
54. Case C-7/12, *Nadežda Riežniece v. Zemkopības ministrija, Lauku atbalsta dienests.*

scope of that Directive, Member States are obliged under Directive 2010/18[55] to grant men and women workers parental leave of at least four months (although there is no obligation that it be paid leave).

Both Directives 2000/43 and 2000/78 specify in Article 3(2) that they are without prejudice to provisions and conditions relating to the entry into and residence of third-country nationals and stateless persons in the territory of Member States, and to any treatment which arises from the legal status of such persons. This must be understood as referring to matters of immigration law only.

Specifically with respect to Directive 2000/78, according to Article 3(4) Member States may provide that the Directive, in so far as it relates to discrimination on the grounds of disability and age, shall not apply to the armed forces. The same does not apply in other contexts, where employment in the army is covered, though depending on the circumstances justification based on occupational requirements may be possible.[56] In contrast, Union non-discrimination law does not cover compulsory army service, since this issue relates to the organization of the Member States' armed forces (*Dory*).[57]

4.2.3 *Employment-related social security*

Article 3(1)(e) of Directive 2000/43 includes social security in general in the scope of the Directive. In contrast, Article 3(3) of Directive 2000/78 provides that that Directive does not apply to payments of any kind made by state schemes or similar, including state social security or social protection schemes, and Recital 14 in the preamble states that the Directive does not affect the competence of the Member States to determine the pension age in that regard. However, the ECJ held in *Palacios de la Villa*[58] that this merely means that the Directive does not affect the competence of the Member States to determine the statutory pension age.

With respect to sex equality, Directive 2006/54 covers only occupational social security. Statutory social security falls under Directive 79/7, though the schemes covered are limited, as is illustrated by *Jackson and Cresswell*[59] (no coverage of the general risk of poverty). Further, Article 7 contains limitations, including notably the right of the Member States to exclude from the ambit of Directive 79/7 the determination of pensionable age for the purposes of granting old-age and retirement pensions and the possible consequences thereof for other benefits. However, this is confined to the determination of pensionable age as such, to the exclusion of other matters. For example, dismissal of a woman solely because she has attained the qualifying age for a state pension, which age is different under national law for men and women, constitutes sex discrimination under what is today Directive 2006/54 (*Marshall I*).[60]

4.2.4 *Other matters, in particular goods and services*

In addition to employment and social security, two Directives cover a number of further matters. Article 3(1)(e) to (h) of Directive 2000/43 lists social protection (including healthcare), social advantages, education and, finally, access to and supply of goods and services which are available to the public, including housing. Two examples in relation to services and ethnic origin

55. O.J. 2010, L 68/13, Council Directive 2010/18/EU of 8 Mar. 2010 implementing the revised Framework Agreement on parental leave concluded by BUSINESSEUROPE, UEAPME, CEEP and ETUC and repealing Directive 96/34/EC.
56. See *infra*, section 7.3.2.
57. Case C-186/01, *Alexander Dory v. Germany.*
58. Case C-411/05, *Félix Palacios de la Villa v. Cortefiel Servicios SA.*
59. Joined Cases 63 & 64/91, *Sonia Jackson and Patricia Cresswell v. Chief Adjudication Officer.*
60. Case 152/84, *M. H. Marshall v. Southampton and South-West Hampshire Area Health Authority (Teaching).*

are *Nikolova,*[61] concerning the measuring of the consumption of electricity, and *Jyske Finans,*[62] concerning a loan to purchase a car. Conversely, the Court held in *Runevič-Vardyn*[63] that national rules governing the manner in which surnames and forenames are to be entered on certificates of civil status does not fall within the scope of the term "services". The Court also noted that the preparatory work relating to the Directive indicates that the Council was unwilling to take into account an amendment proposed by the European Parliament whereby "the exercise by any public body, including police, immigration, criminal and civil justice authorities, of its functions" would have been included.

In the field of sex equality, Directive 2004/113 specifically covers the access to and supply of goods and services (though not education). Recital 11 in the preamble states that goods should be taken to be those within the (broad) meaning of the provisions of the TFEU relating to the free movement of goods,[64] and services should be taken to be those within the (broad) meaning of Article 57 TFEU[65] (though it should be remembered that this refers to the definition of the term itself, to the exclusion of the requirement of cross-border transactions that applies in the field of the internal market law). With respect to insurance, Article 5(2) of Directive 2004/113, allowing for different treatment based on actuarial factors in the field of insurance, was declared to be invalid by the ECJ in *Test-Achats.*[66] The question of actuarial factors also arose in the case of *X,*[67] in the context of Directive 79/7, which does not contain a derogation with respect to the use of such factors. The Court noted that differences in the average life expectancy of men and women cannot amount to an objective justification and that the calculation of a statutory social security benefit cannot be made on the basis of a generalization as regards the average life expectancy.

5. Equal treatment and non-discrimination

5.1 *Equality and discrimination under EU law: An Aristotelian understanding*

The interpretation of the concepts of equality and discrimination under Union law is based on the so-called Aristotelian model. According to settled ECJ case law, equality or equal treatment "requires that comparable situations must not be treated differently and that different situations must not be treated in the same way unless such treatment is objectively justified" (e.g. *Arcelor,*[68] *Chatzi*[69]). Consequently, discrimination "can arise only through the application of different rules to comparable situations or the application of the same rule to different situations" (e.g. *Commission v. Hungary*).[70]

61. Case C-83/14, *CHEZ Razpredelenie Bulgaria AD v. Komisia za zashtita ot diskriminatsia.*
62. Case C-668/15, *Jyske Finans A/S v. Ligebehandlingsnævnet, acting on behalf of Ismar Huskic.*
63. Case C-391/09, *Malgožata Runevič-Vardyn and Łukasz Paweł Wardyn v. Vilniaus miesto savivaldybės administracija, Lietuvos Respublikos teisingumo ministerija, Valstybinė lietuvių kalbos komisija and Vilniaus miesto savivaldybės administracijos Teisės departamento Civilinės metrikacijos skyrius.*
64. See Ch. 13, "Free movement of goods", of this book.
65. See Ch. 14, "Free movement of services, establishment and capital", of this book.
66. Case C-236/09, *Association Belge des Consommateurs Test-Achats ASBL and Others v. Conseil des ministres;* C(2011) 9497, Commission Communication of 22 Dec. 2011: Guidelines on the application of Council Directive 2004/113/EC to insurance, in the light of the judgment of the Court of Justice of the European Union in Case C-236/09, *Test-Achats.*
67. Case C-318/13, *X.*
68. Case C-127/07, *Société Arcelor Atlantique et Lorraine and Others v. Premier ministre, Ministre de l'Écologie et du Développement durable and Ministre de l'Économie, des Finances et de l'Industrie.*
69. Case C-149/10, *Zoi Chatzi v. Ipourgos Ikonomikon.*
70. Case C-253/09, *Commission v. Hungary.*

It has been observed that on this general level equality is "a loose principle that amounts to little more than a general standard of fairness and rationality".[71] The main problem lies in the fact that its constitutive elements, namely comparability and objective justification, remain undefined. The former in particular has proven to be elusive.

First, it may be difficult to find a suitable comparator. Under the single source principle, the comparator must be a person or group of persons who receives treatment by the same person as the alleged victim of discrimination (e.g. an employee of the same employer, though employment does not have to be simultaneous, e.g. *Lawrence*,[72] *Macarthys*[73]).

Second, deciding on comparability necessarily implies a value judgment. ECJ case law offers little practical guidance in that respect, other than stating that, first, what is required is not that the situations be identical, but only that they be comparable and, secondly, that the assessment of that comparability must be carried out not in a global and abstract manner, but in a specific and concrete manner in the light of the objective and of the aim of the national legislation creating the distinction at issue (e.g. *Milkova*).[74] To some extent, the law may provide clarification, by containing elements such as "equal work or work of equal value" in Article 157(1) TFEU, which means that the situations to be judged under this provision are comparable only if they concern either the same work or work of equal value. "Work of equal value" was explicitly added through the Amsterdam revision, though even before that it had been included through the Court's interpretation.[75] At the same time, explicit mention of elements of comparability does not exclude the relevance of further issues (e.g. the difference in the situations of female workers who had a baby and male workers who are recent fathers, with respect to a maternity benefit that is considered pay; *Abdoulaye*).[76] Further clarification may come from case law. For example, the Court has held that the concept of "work of equal value" relates to the nature of the work, rather than also to the level of its performance by individual workers (*Rummler*).[77]

In preliminary ruling cases, comparability is an issue of fact that is normally left to the national court. However, sometimes the ECJ itself indicates the decision to be taken in that regard (e.g. *Hay*,[78] concerning the comparability of married couples and registered partners of a French *Pacte civil de solidarité*, PACS).

5.2 *Discrimination grounds*

Article 21 CFR contains an open list of discrimination grounds, including even grounds that do not appear elsewhere in Union law, e.g. genetic features.[79] In contrast, other Union law relating to the Article 19 grounds is based on a closed system of grounds. For example, it does not

---

71. M. Bell, "The principle of equal treatment: Widening and deepening" in P. Craig and G. De Búrca (Eds.), *The Evolution of EU Law*, 2nd ed. (OUP, 2011), 611–639, at 626.
72. Case C-320/00, *A. G. Lawrence and Others v. Regent Office Care Ltd, Commercial Catering Group and Mitie Secure Services Ltd.*
73. Case 129/79, *Macarthys Ltd v. Wendy Smith.*
74. Case C-406/15, *Petya Milkova v. Izpalnitelen direktor na Agentsiata za privatizatsia i sledprivatizatsionen control.*
75. See *supra*, section 3.
76. Case C-218/98, *Oumar Dabo Abdoulaye and Others v. Régie nationale des usines Renault SA.*
77. Case 237/85, *Gisela Rummler v. Dato-Druck GmbH.*; COM(94)6, Memorandum on equal pay for work of equal value.
78. Case C-267/12, *Frédéric Hay v. Crédit agricole mutuel de Charente-Maritime et des Deux-Sèvres.*
79. See A. de Paor and D. Ferri, "Regulating genetic discrimination in the European Union", (2015) *European Journal of Law Reform*, 14–32.

mention intersexuality,[80] and Article 3(2) of Directive 2000/43 states that it does not cover differences of treatment based on nationality.

In a closed system, it is crucial how the discrimination grounds are interpreted. The Article 19 grounds are not as such defined in the relevant legislation. In practice, this does not normally raise particular problems. Rather, the meaning of these grounds appears to be taken as self-evident. In the cases before the ECJ, the debate rather focuses on the question of whether a given element is directly, i.e. inextricably, or only indirectly linked to a given ground.[81] Where the basic meaning of a discrimination ground is raised in a case, the Court usually applies a broad interpretation. Most notably, a broad approach is reflected in the case law where the concept of discrimination based on sex is interpreted as including not only disadvantageous treatment of men and women because of sex understood in the traditional, biological sense but also disadvantageous treatment of transgender persons who plan to undergo, or have already undergone, so-called gender reassignment procedures (*P. v. S.*,[82] *K.B.*,[83] and *Richards*[84]). Given the absence of explicit Union law on transgender discrimination, this allowed the Court to bring at least some such cases within the ambit of sex equality law. More fundamentally, it would be better to understand the concept of "sex" along the lines of the statement made by Advocate General Tesauro in the *P. v. S.* case, namely that biological sex should not be seen as a dichotomy but rather as a continuum, and further to include the concept of gender identity. In this manner, the entire body of Union sex equality law would apply to intersex and transgender people (and in the latter case notably independent of so-called gender reassignment procedures).

With respect to disability, the Court initially interpreted this concept in a narrow manner (*Chacón Navas*)[85] that was criticized as reflecting a medical, rather than a social model that would focus on what it means to have a disability in a particular society.[86] In *Ring*,[87] the ECJ referred to the broader definition under the UN Convention on the Rights of Persons with Disabilities. The definition under Directive 2000/78 is now that of a condition caused by an illness medically diagnosed as curable or incurable where that illness entails a limitation which results in particular from physical, mental or psychological impairments which in interaction with various barriers may hinder the full and effective participation of the person concerned in professional life on an equal basis with other workers, and the limitation is a long-term one. Depending on the circumstances, this may include obesity (*Kaltoft*).[88] At the same time, the requirement of effects on professional life means that not every limitation falls within the scope of the Directive (*Z.*,[89] concerning a female worker who had no uterus).

---

80. See M. Travis, "Accommodating intersexuality in European Union anti-discrimination law", 21 ELJ (2015), 180–199.
81. See *infra*, section 5.4.
82. Case C-13/94, *P. v. S. and Cornwall County Council.*
83. Case C-117/01, *K.B. v. National Health Service Pensions Agency, Secretary of State for Health.*
84. Case C-423/04, *Sarah Margaret Richards v. Secretary of State for Work and Pensions.*
85. Case C-13/05, *Sonia Chacón Navas Sonia Chacón Navas v. Eurest Colectividades SA.*
86. E.g. L. Waddington, *Implementing and Interpreting the Reasonable Accommodation Provision of the Framework Employment Directive: Learning from Experience and Achieving Best Practice* (European Commission, 2004), at 7.
87. Joined Cases C-335/11 and C-337/11, *HK Danmark, acting on behalf of Jette Ring, v. Dansk almennyttigt Boligselskab, and HK Danmark, acting on behalf of Lone Skouboe Werge, v. Dansk Arbejdsgiverforening, acting on behalf of Pro Display A/S, in liquidation.*
88. Case C-354/13, *Fag og Arbejde (FOA), acting on behalf of Karsten Kaltoft, v. Kommunernes Landsforening (KL), acting on behalf of the Municipality of Billund.*
89. Case C-363/12, *Z. v. A Government department and The Board of management of a community school.*

The same concern for a social approach applies, *mutatis mutandis,* in the context of other discrimination grounds, e.g. with respect to the difference between sex, understood as a biological term, and gender, understood as a social construct ("a constitutive element of social relationships" and "a primary way of signifying relationships of power").[90]

In most cases the person to whom the ground relates will be the victim of the alleged discrimination. However, discrimination can also be by association, as in *Coleman,*[91] where a mother complained of discrimination on grounds of disability resulting from the fact that she cared for her severely disabled son. Similarly, in *Nikolova*[92] the person who complained of discrimination on grounds of ethnic origin was not part of the relevant population. However, she had a shop in a city district that was mainly populated by Roma people. As such she suffered, together with that population, the less favourable treatment applied in that district.

5.3 *Multi-dimensional discrimination*

Non-discrimination cases may involve more than one discrimination ground, leading to multiple or multi-dimensional discrimination. In this context, two forms of such discrimination must be distinguished, namely, first, cumulative or aggregate discrimination, where two or more discrimination grounds are relevant side by side (e.g. sex and ethnic origin), and, second, intersectional discrimination, where it is the combination of two or more grounds that forms the basis for the disadvantageous treatment (e.g. only black women are treated differently, but neither black men nor women of another physical type).[93]

Since the time of the adoption of Directives on discrimination on grounds other than sex, multiple discrimination has become legally relevant also in the context of the European Union.[94] It is explicitly recognized in Recital 14 in the preamble to Directive 2000/43 and in Recital 3 in the preamble to Directive 2000/78, which state that "women are often the victims of multiple discrimination". The Court appears to interpret this as referring to cumulative discrimination, which may occur in the combination of different grounds of discrimination (i.e. beyond sex discrimination). So far, there is limited ECJ case law touching on the issue of cumulative discrimination (e.g. *Meister*[95] and *Odar*[96]). In practice, different fields of application for different types of discrimination and different justification grounds may present difficulties.

With respect to intersectional discrimination, *Parris*[97] is relevant. The case concerned a survivor's benefit which, under Irish law, was available for both married and registered couples, though only where the member of the scheme had married, respectively had the partnership registered, before the age of 60. Mr Parris was unable to meet this criterion because Irish law did

---

90. J.W. Scott, "Gender: A useful category of historical analysis", 91 *American Historical Review* (1986), 1053–1075, at 1067.
91. Case C-303/06, *S. Coleman v. Attridge Law and Steve Law.*
92. Case C-83/14, *CHEZ Razpredelenie Bulgaria AD v. Komisia za zashtita ot diskriminatsia.*
93. With respect to this example, see the foundational work by K. Crenshaw, "Mapping the margins: Intersectionality, identity politics, and violence against women of color", (1991) *Stanford Law Review,* 1240–1299.
94. See generally D. Schiek and V. Chege, *European Union Non-Discrimination Law. Comparative Perspectives on Multidimensional Equality Law* (Routledge-Cavendish, 2009) and with respect to intersectional discrimination D. Schiek and A. Lawson (Eds.), *European Union Non-Discrimination Law and Intersectionality. Investigating the Triangle of Racial, Gender and Disability Discrimination* (Ashgate, 2011), D. Schiek, "Intersectionality and the notion of disability in EU discrimination law", 53 CML Rev. (2016), 35–64, and S. Fredman, *Intersectional Discrimination in EU Gender Equality and Non-Discrimination Law* (Publications Office of the European Union, 2016).
95. Case C-415/10, *Galina Meister v. Speech Design Carrier Systems GmbH.*
96. Case C-152/11, *Johann Odar v. Baxter Deutschland GmbH.*
97. Case C-443/15, *David L. Parris v. Trinity College Dublin and Others.* See *infra,* section 5.4.1.

not allow him to have his same-sex partnership registered or to marry before he turned 60 years of age. In these circumstances, homosexual persons in a certain age cohort were unable to meet the requirement for an entitlement to the benefit in question. Asked by the national court about the relevance of the combined effect of sexual orientation and age in such a case, the Court held that under Directive 2000/78 there is no new category of discrimination resulting from the combination of more than one ground that may be found to exist where discrimination on the basis of those grounds taken in isolation has not been established (instead the Court found justifiable discrimination indirectly on grounds of age). Unfortunately, this means that an important part of the reality of discrimination in society remains outside the ambit of Union law.

5.4 *Forms of discrimination*

The most recent generation of the Union's secondary law on the Article 19 grounds mentions four basic forms of discrimination, namely direct discrimination, indirect discrimination, harassment and instruction to discriminate, with the first three of these being defined in the legislation. Outside the EU's internal employment law, harassment and instruction to discriminate appeared first in Directives 2000/43 and 2000/73. The distinction between direct and indirect discrimination is much older.[98] In academic writing, the failure to provide for reasonable accommodation for persons with disabilities has also been called a form of discrimination but it is not formally constructed as such under Directive 2000/78.[99]

The existence of four distinct forms of discrimination in the Union's secondary law relating to the Article 19 grounds means that this law differs from that on the internal market. There, only direct and indirect discrimination are relevant, though the prohibition of discrimination is supplemented by the prohibition of non-discriminatory restrictions, which is absent in the context of the Article 19 grounds.

5.4.1 *Direct discrimination*

Direct discrimination is defined in the non-discrimination Directives as the situation where one person is treated less favourably on a particular ground than another is, has been or would be treated in a comparable situation (e.g. Art. 2(2)(a) of Directive 2000/78). Such treatment is prohibited unless the law expressly provides for a possibility of justification.

According to ECJ case law, direct discrimination is either explicitly based on a prohibited ground or on a criterion that is inextricably linked to such a ground (e.g. *Tyrolean Airways*).[100] This is, for example, the case for pregnancy or maternity and sex, based on the argument that pregnant persons and recent mothers necessarily are women (*Dekker*).[101] Today, Article 2(2)(c) of Directive 2006/54 states that less favourable treatment of a woman related to pregnancy or maternity leave within the meaning of Directive 92/85[102] is discrimination directly based on

---

98. See generally C. Tobler, *Indirect Discrimination. A Case Study into the Development of the Legal Concept of Indirect Discrimination under EC Law* (Intersentia, 2005).
99. L. Waddington op. cit. *supra* note 86, at 7. See *infra*, section 6.
100. Case C-132/11, *Tyrolean Airways Tiroler Luftfahrt Gesellschaft mbH v. Betriebsrat Bord der Tyrolean Airways Tiroler Luftfahrt Gesellschaft mbH.*
101. Case C-177/88, *Elisabeth Johanna Pacifica Dekker v. VJV-Centrum.*
102. O.J. 1992, L 348/1, Council Directive 92/85/EEC of 19 Oct. 1992 on the introduction of measures to encourage improvements in the safety and health at work of pregnant workers and workers who have recently given birth or are breastfeeding (tenth individual Directive within the meaning of Art. 16 (1) of Directive 89/391/EEC).

sex under the former Directive. Conversely, the Court held in *Jyske Finans*[103] that the country of birth by itself is not inextricably linked to a given racial or ethnic origin.

Direct discrimination may also exist where another ground is used but where the group of persons excluded from an advantage consists in fact only of e.g. women (*Nikoloudi*),[104] or where only one particular group is unable to meet the condition whilst another group has a choice, e.g. homosexuals in the case of marriage under the law of certain Member States (*Maruko,*[105] *Römer,*[106] both with respect to survivor's pensions, and *Hay,*[107] with respect to marriage benefits). In *Hay,* the Court held that the fact that the disadvantaged group consisted of both heterosexual and homosexual couples did not change the direct nature of the discrimination against the latter since they, unlike heterosexual couples, could not, on the date of the facts in the main proceedings, legally enter into marriage. In the present writer's opinion, the same reasoning could also have been applied in the case of *Parris,*[108] in relation to a survivor's benefit that was available only where the employee had married, respectively had the partnership registered, before turning 60 years of age. Here, too, only homosexuals in the relevant age bracket had been unable to marry. However, the Court refused to find direct discrimination on grounds on sexual orientation based on the argument that the rule in question is neutral in that respect.

In *Feryn,*[109] the Court held that direct discrimination can take the form of a mere statement, i.e. a speech act, in this case with respect to ethnic origin. This was subsequently confirmed in the context of sexual orientation in *Asociaţia Accept.*[110]

A remarkable element with respect to direct discrimination was added through the *Nikolova*[111] decision, concerning the placement of meters to measure electricity consumption in a number of urban districts in Bulgaria which were known to be inhabited primarily by members of the Roma community, in a manner different from other districts. The Court held that, depending on the reasons for the differential treatment, such treatment could amount to either direct or indirect discrimination on grounds of ethnic origin. It constitutes direct discrimination within the meaning of that provision if that measure proves to have been introduced and/or maintained for reasons relating to the ethnic origin common to most of the inhabitants of the district concerned. Elements to be taken into account by the national court in this context include in particular stereotypes and prejudices on the side of the alleged perpetrator. At the same time, the reasons for disadvantageous treatment must not be equated with intention. Under Union law, a finding of discrimination does not depend on the intention to discriminate.

In practice, whether there is different treatment directly based of a given criterion depends on what precisely is the basis for the treatment. This is a question of fact which, in preliminary ruling cases, is for the national court to decide. For example, in *Bougnaoui* the ECJ merely stated that it is not clear from the order for reference whether the referring court's question is based on a finding of a difference of treatment based directly on religion or belief, or on a finding of

103. Case C-668/15, *Jyske Finans A/S v. Ligebehandlingsnævnet, acting on behalf of Ismar Huskic.*
104. Case C-196/02, *Vasiliki Nikoloudi v. Organismos Tilepikoinonion Ellados AE.*
105. Case C-267/06, *Tadao Maruko v. Versorgungsanstalt der deutschen Bühnen.*
106. Case C-147/08, *Jürgen Römer v. Freie und Hansestadt Hamburg.*
107. Case C-267/12, *Frédéric Hay v. Crédit agricole mutuel de Charente-Maritime et des Deux-Sèvres.*
108. Case C-443/15, *David L. Parris v. Trinity College Dublin and Others.*
109. Case C-54/07, *Centrum voor gelijkheid van kansen en voor racismebestrijding v. Firma Feryn NV.*
110. Case C-81/12, *Asociaţia Accept v. Consiliul Naţional pentru Combaterea Discriminării.*
111. Case C-83/14, *CHEZ Razpredelenie Bulgaria AD v. Komisia za zashtita ot diskriminatsia.* See C. McCrudden, "The new architecture of EU equality law after CHEZ: Did the Court of Justice reconceptualize direct and indirect discrimination?", 2016/1 European Equality Law Review (2016), 1–10.

a difference of treatment based indirectly on those criteria.[112] The case concerned the dismissal of a worker because she was wearing, as a female Muslim, a headscarf. It was disputed among the parties in the national proceedings whether the reason for the dismissal was specifically the wearing of an Islamic headscarf or rather a general ban on the wearing of religious signs.

5.4.2 *Indirect discrimination*

Indirect discrimination is a less obvious form of discrimination, brought about by the use of an apparently neutral criterion that, due to the circumstances in which it is used, in practice works (almost or largely) like the prohibited criterion. The classical example from the field of sex equality is the differentiation in pay between full-time workers and part-time workers for the same time unit. Since, due to the continuing influence of the traditional division of the roles within the family, it is often predominantly women who perform part-time work, such a differentiation works mainly to their detriment. The use of such criteria is prohibited (*prima facie* discrimination), unless there is objective justification (e.g. *Bilka*;[113] today, such discrimination is also covered by Clause 4 in the Annex to Directive 97/81, concerning part-time work).

Indirect discrimination is defined in the most recent generation of non-discrimination Directives as the situation where an apparently neutral provision, criterion or practice would put persons of a particular group at a particular disadvantage compared with persons of another group, unless that provision, criterion or practice is objectively justified by a legitimate aim, and the means of achieving that aim are appropriate and necessary (e.g. Article 2(b) of Directive 2004/113). Under this modern definition, proof of an actual disparate effect by statistics is no longer a precondition for a finding of *prima facie* indirect discrimination. Rather, the definition – in line with the definition that applies in the internal market law under the landmark decision of *O'Flynn*[114] – merely requires that an apparently neutral provision, criterion or practice "would" put persons of a particular group at a particular disadvantage (potential disparate impact). Statistics may still be used in this context (Recital 14 in Directive 2000/43 and Recital 15 in Directive 2000/78). However, proof by statistics under the old sex equality regime (i.e. before the adoption of the modern Directives) was shown to raise numerous difficult questions.[115] Unfortunately, recent case law sometimes appears to disregard the requirement of a merely potential, rather than actual, disparate effect (e.g. *Achbita*, para 34: "that the apparently neutral obligation it encompasses results, in fact, in persons adhering to a particular religion or belief being put at a particular disadvantage").[116]

It should be noted that in Article 2(2)(b) of Directive 2000/78, indirect discrimination is defined as disadvantageous treatment on grounds of "a particular religion or belief, a particular disability, a particular age, or a particular sexual orientation". This wording indicates that it would not be sufficient to argue that e.g. one religion is treated in a more favourable manner, leading to disadvantageous treatment of all the others. Rather, the unfavourable treatment must relate to a specific religion. The situation is the same with respect to racial or ethnic origin. Whilst Article 2(2)(b) of Directive 2000/43 refers to "persons of a racial or ethnic origin", the Court in *Jyske Finans*[117] interpreted this as relating to persons of a "given" or "particular" racial or ethnic origin.

112. Case C-188/15, *Asma Bougnaoui and Association de défense des droits de l'homme (ADDH) v. Micropole SA.*
113. Case 170/84, *Bilka v. Karin Weber von Hartz.*
114. Case C-237/94, *John O'Flynn v. Adjudication Officer.*
115. See e.g. C. Barnard and B. Hepple, "Indirect discrimination: Interpreting Seymour-Smith", (1999) CLJ, 399–412.
116. Case C-157/15, *Samira Achbita, Centrum voor gelijkheid van kansen en voor racismebestrijding v. G4S Secure Solutions NV.*
117. Case C-668/15, *Jyske Finans A/S v. Ligebehandlingsnævnet, acting on behalf of Ismar Huskic.*

As for sex equality, the Directives refer to "persons of the other sex" (e.g. Art. 2(b) of Directive 2004/13). Union law in this respect is based on the idea of only two possibilities of biological sexes, namely female and male. Even though ECJ case law on transgender persons adds a somewhat broader element,[118] seen from a modern scientific perspective the understanding of the concept of sex under Union law is simplistic.

Again, whether there is different treatment indirectly on the basis of a given criterion is a question of fact which depends on what precisely is the basis for the treatment and what, further, is the effect of that treatment. *Achbita,*[119] a case concerning the dismissal of a worker because she was wearing, as a female Muslim, a headscarf, provides an example. In this case, it was disputed whether the application of a general rule in force within the undertaking in question, prohibiting the wearing of any visible sign of political, philosophical or religious beliefs, indirectly amounted to different treatment based on a particular religion. The Court found that it is not inconceivable that the referring court might conclude that the rule at issue introduced a difference of treatment that is indirectly based on religion or belief, for the purposes of Article 2(2)(b) of Directive 2000/78, namely if it is established that the apparently neutral obligation it encompasses results, in fact, in persons adhering to a particular religion or belief being put at a particular disadvantage. Absent justification, such treatment amounts to indirect discrimination based on religion prohibited under the Directive.

5.4.3 *Harassment*

Harassment is defined as the situation where an unwanted conduct related to a discrimination ground takes place with the purpose or effect of violating the dignity of a person and of creating an intimidating, hostile, degrading, humiliating or offensive environment. In this context, the concept may be defined in accordance with the national laws and practice of the Member States (e.g. Art. 2(3) of Directive 2000/78).

In the field of sex equality, the legislation distinguishes between harassment and sexual harassment. For example, Article 2(1)(c) of Directive 2006/54 defines harassment as relating to the situation "where an unwanted conduct related to the sex of a person occurs with the purpose or effect of violating the dignity of a person, and of creating an intimidating, hostile, degrading, humiliating or offensive environment". The more specific notion of sexual harassment is defined in Article 2(1)(d) as relating to the situation "where any form of unwanted verbal, non-verbal or physical conduct of a sexual nature occurs, with the purpose or effect of violating the dignity of a person, in particular when creating an intimidating, hostile, degrading, humiliating or offensive environment".[120]

These definitions indicate that harassment is a type of discrimination that is not comparison-based.[121] Instead, the focus is put on a person's dignity, which is not an express element of the legal definitions of the other forms of discrimination under Union law. Further, the Court held in *Coleman*[122] that discrimination through harassment can be by association.

---

118. See *supra*, section 5.2.
119. Case C-157/15, *Samira Achbita, Centrum voor gelijkheid van kansen en voor racismebestrijding v. G4S Secure Solutions NV*.
120. See e.g. R. Holtmaat, "Sexual harassment and harassment on the ground of sex in EU law: A conceptual clarification", 2 *European Gender Equality Law Review* (2001), 4–13.
121. The foundational argument in this respect was made by C. MacKinnon, *Sexual Harassment of Working Women. A case of Sex Discrimination* (Yale University Press, 1979).
122. Case C-303/06, *S. Coleman v. Attridge Law and Steve Law*.

5.4.4 *Instruction to discriminate*

With respect to instruction to discriminate, the Directives simply state that this is a form of discrimination (e.g. Art. 2(2)(b) of Directive 2006/54). It concerns the situation where one person instrumentalizes another in order to cause discrimination.

6. Duty to treat differently

In certain, limited respects Union non-discrimination law specifically mandates differential treatment. In the framework of the present law, this concerns only the duty to provide reasonable accommodation for persons with a disability. Outside the formal framework of non-discrimination law, but linked to it in terms of substance, Directive 92/85 on the protection of the health and safety of pregnant workers and workers who have recently given birth also sets up a duty to treat differently. An obligation to provide for reasonable accommodation is also foreseen in the proposal for a Directive intended to extend the field of application of the prohibition of discrimination on grounds of religion or belief, disability, age or sexual orientation.

With respect to disability, Article 5 of Directive 2000/78 states that, in order to guarantee compliance with the principle of equal treatment, reasonable accommodation is to be provided in relation to persons with disabilities. Employers must take appropriate measures, where needed in a particular case, to enable a person with a disability to have access to, participate in, or advance in employment, or to undergo training, unless such measures would impose a disproportionate burden on the employer. This burden is not deemed to be disproportionate when it is sufficiently remedied by measures existing within the framework of the disability policy of the Member State concerned.

According to *Ring*,[123] the concept of reasonable accommodation refers to the elimination of the various barriers that hinder the full and effective participation of persons with disabilities in professional life on an equal basis with other workers. Recital 20 in the preamble to the Directive generally mentions a number of physical, organizational and educational measures that may be relevant in this context. Whether a measure is reasonable must be assessed in each individual case, taking into account in particular the costs entailed by such a measure, the scale and financial resources of the undertaking, and the possibility of obtaining public funding or any other assistance, as indicated in Recital 21.

According to Recital 17, the Directive does not require the recruitment, promotion or maintenance in employment of a person who is not competent, capable and available to perform the essential functions of the post concerned, though this is without prejudice to the obligation to provide reasonable accommodation for people with disabilities. Accordingly, dismissals due to the fact that the person concerned is not competent, capable and available to perform the essential functions of the post due to a disability, have to be judged in the light of the obligation to provide reasonable accommodation and can only be made after the employer has made reasonable accommodation for the specific needs of the employee in question (*Chacón Navas*).[124] It has been argued that this means that dismissal on the grounds of disability based on the employee being unable to perform non-essential functions, or on the basis of a comparison

123. Joined Cases C-335/11 and C-337/11, *HK Danmark, acting on behalf of Jette Ring, v. Dansk almennyttigt Boligselskab*, and *HK Danmark, acting on behalf of Lone Skouboe Werge, v. Dansk Arbejdsgiverforening, acting on behalf of Pro Display A/S, in liquidation.*

124. Case C-13/05, *Sonia Chacón Navas Sonia Chacón Navas v. Eurest Colectividades SA.*

between the employee and another employee who does not require reasonable accommodation, is prohibited.[125]

7. Grounds allowing for differential treatment (justification)

Many (though not all) Union non-discrimination provisions provide for derogations that can be relied on in order to justify differential treatment, without there being an obligation to do so. In addition to a legitimate aim, this requires that the measure taken in view of this aim be proportionate. With respect to the legitimate aim, Union law on the Article 19 grounds provides for a combination of a closed system of statutory grounds (where only the grounds specifically stated in the law can be relied on), a half-closed system (where unspecified grounds can be relied on as long as they relate to social policy objectives) and an open system (where in principle any legitimate ground can be relied on). In all of these cases, purely financial or budgetary considerations by themselves cannot serve as justification, though they can underpin a social policy (e.g. *Fuchs and Köhler*).[126] Further, in line with a general approach under EU law, derogations have to be interpreted strictly (e.g. *Prigge*).[127]

7.1 *Open system: Objective justification*

The broadest framework for justification is that where Union non-discrimination law provides for the possibility of unspecified objective justification. This concerns, first, direct sex discrimination in the context of goods and services. Article 4(5) of Directive 2004/113 provides that the Directive does not preclude differences in treatment, if the provision of the goods and services exclusively or primarily to members of one sex is justified by a legitimate aim and the means of achieving that aim are appropriate and necessary. The same approach of providing for objective justification for direct discrimination can be found in the Directives on part-time work (Directive 97/81) fixed-term work (Directive 1999/70) and temporary work (Directive 2008/104), which are not further discussed in this chapter. There is no ECJ case law on Article 4(5) of Directive 2004/113 yet.[128] Possible examples could be women-only times at sport facilities or women-only compartments in crowded trains.

An open possibility of objective justification also exists in the context of indirect discrimination, as part of the definition of the legal concept. This element was only gradually introduced into the definition, first as referring to objective differences (i.e. comparability) and only later as referring to justification within the proper meaning of the term (i.e. cross-cutting or countervailing reasons). Objective justification in the latter sense appeared first in sex equality law in *Jenkins*[129] (and only considerably later in economic law). In *Jenkins*, the Court referred to factors that are objectively justified and in no way related to discrimination based on sex. In this respect, mere generalizations are insufficient to show that the aim of the measure is unrelated to any discrimination on grounds of sex (*Nikoloudi*).[130]

With respect to the acceptable aim, in the context of Member State legislation, in particular in the field of social security, the rules must meet a necessary aim of the Member State's social

125. C. O'Cinneide, *The Evolution and Impact of the Case-law of the Court of Justice of the European Union on Directives 2000/43/EC and 2000/78/EC* (Office for Official Publications of the European Union, 2013), 42.
126. Joined Cases C-159/10 and C-160/10, *Gerhard Fuchs, Peter Köhler v. Land Hessen.*
127. Case C-447/09, *Reinhard Prigge and Others v. Deutsche Lufthansa AG.*
128. An infringement action by the Commission was withdrawn: Case C-328/09, *Commission v. Estonia.*
129. Case 96/80, *J.P. Jenkins v. Kingsgate (Clothing Productions) Ltd.*
130. Case C-196/02, *Vasiliki Nikoloudi v. Organismos Tilepikoinonion Ellados AE.*

policy (*Rinner-Kühn*).[131] In the context of private employment, the measure must correspond to a real need on the part of the undertaking (*Bilka*).[132] According to *Jenkins*, this may include economic considerations, an approach that must be criticised as undermining the effectiveness of the prohibition of indirect discrimination.

In preliminary ruling cases, the ECJ often leaves the assessment of the aim of the measure to the national court, including the judgment on its legitimacy. Where the Court gives specific indications, they are sometimes problematic, for example the Court's finding that the state of the employment market (i.e. scarcity of available workers) may constitute a legitimate ground for differential treatment (*Enderby*).[133] Similarly, the Court accepted the aim of fostering so-called minor employment in order to respond to a need for such employment (meaning for cheap employment of e.g. part-time cleaners, which is achieved, among others, by excluding them from social security if they work below a certain number of hours; *Nolte*[134]). Further, the Court held that the fact that the rates of pay are determined by collective bargaining or by negotiation at local level may be taken into account as a factor in the assessment of whether differences between the average pay of two groups of workers are due to objective factors unrelated to any discrimination (e.g. *Rosenbladt*).[135] More recently, the Court in *Achbita*[136] appears to give a particular weight to an employer's freedom to conduct a business under Article 16 CFR. According to the Court, an employer's wish to project an image of neutrality towards the customers is, in principle, a legitimate aim. This wish may find expression in a rule prohibiting the wearing of any religious, political or philosophical symbols at work, notably for workers who are required to come into contact with the customers. Such a rule in turn may subsequently justify the dismissal of a worker who does not respect the rule, provided that this measure is proportionate.

The Court appears to be stricter in *Nikolova*.[137] In this case, which concerned the measuring of the consumption of electricity, the Court accepted as legitimate the intention to ensure the security of the electricity transmission network and the due recording of electricity consumption. The Court added, however, that there is no objective justification if it is found that the measure prejudices excessively the legitimate interest of the consumers inhabiting the district concerned, mainly lived in by inhabitants of Roma origin, in having access to the supply of electricity in conditions which are not of an offensive or stigmatizing nature and which enable them to monitor their electricity consumption regularly.

7.2 *Half-closed system for age discrimination: Objective justification under Article 6(1) of Directive 2000/78*

In the case of age discrimination, justification for direct discrimination is based on a half-closed system. Article 6(1) of Directive 2000/78 refers to differences of treatment on grounds of age that, within the context of national law, are objectively and reasonably justified by a legitimate aim, including legitimate employment policy, labour market and vocational training objectives, and if the means of achieving that aim are appropriate and necessary. The Court has specified that the reference to employment policy, labour market and vocational training objectives means that legitimate aims under Article 6(1) are limited to social policy objectives. These must

---

131. Case 171/88, *Rinner-Kühn v. FWW Spezial Gebäudereinigung GmbH & Co. KG.*
132. Case 170/84, *Bilka v. Karin Weber von Hartz.*
133. Case C-127/92, *Dr. Pamela Mary Enderby v. Frenchay Health Authority and Secretary of State for Health.*
134. Case C-317/93, *Inge Nolte v. Landesversicherungsanstalt Hannover.*
135. Case C-45/09, *Gisela Rosenbladt v. Oellerking Gebäudereinigungsges. mbH.*
136. Case C-157/15, *Samira Achbita, Centrum voor gelijkheid van kansen en voor racismebestrijding v. G4S Secure Solutions NV.*
137. Case C-83/14, *CHEZ Razpredelenie Bulgaria AD v. Komisia za zashtita ot diskriminatsia.*

be in the public interest, which excludes purely employer-specific reasons such as costs or competitiveness. Apart from these limitations, Article 6(1) is not stricter than the objective justification test for indirect discrimination (*Age Concern England*).[138]

Article 6(1) of Directive 2000/78 gives examples of acceptable differences in treatment and of legitimate aims, e.g. the setting of special conditions on access to employment, occupation and vocational training, for young people, older workers and persons with caring responsibilities in order to promote their vocational integration or ensure their protection. There is extensive ECJ case law on the issue of legitimacy. For example, in the context of compulsory retirement, the Court found legitimate, among others, the regulation of the national labour market, in particular for the purposes of checking unemployment (*Palacios de la Villa*),[139] allocating posts for professors in the best possible way between the generations and promotion of an exchange of experiences and innovation and thereby the development of the quality of teaching and research at universities (*Georgiev*)[140] and counteracting the shortage of labour which would result from large numbers of forthcoming retirements and avoiding humiliation in individual terminations of employment (*Hörnfeldt*).[141]

Generally, the Court is generous with respect to the legitimacy of aims for the purposes of justification under Article 6(1) of Directive 2000/78, based on the consideration that, as Union law stands at present (i.e. given the limited Union competences in this field), the Member States and, where appropriate, the social partners at national level enjoy broad discretion in their choice to pursue a particular aim in the field of social and employment policy (e.g. *Toftgaard*).[142] Examples where the Court rejected a particular aim as not being legitimate are few, including notably *Prigge*,[143] concerning traffic safety since this aim is not of a social nature, and *Hennigs and Mai*,[144] concerning compensation for greater financial needs of older employees, since no direct correlation to age had been shown (i.e. life cycle arguments are not acceptable).

It is not necessary that the aim of a particular measure is specifically stated in the national law or in an agreement of the social partners. Rather, it is sufficient that the aim can be identified (*Palacios de la Villa*,[145] *Rosenbladt*[146]). Also, the aim can change over time and still be acceptable (*Fuchs and Köhler*).[147]

7.3 *Closed system of statutory grounds*

Outside the open and the half-closed system of justification grounds as just discussed, the Union non-discrimination law discussed in this chapter provides for a closed list of specific justification grounds that can be relied on depending on the Directive and/or the discrimination criterion. With the above-mentioned exceptions, only these specific grounds are available for direct discrimination (e.g. *Hay*).[148]

---

138. Case C-388/07, *The Queen, on the Application of The Incorporated Trustees of the National Council for Ageing (Age Concern England) v. Secretary of State for Business, Enterprise and Regulatory Reform.*
139. Case C-411/05, *Félix Palacios de la Villa v. Cortefiel Servicios SA.*
140. Joined Cases C-250/09 and C-268/09, *Vasil Ivanov Georgiev v. Tehnicheski universitet – Sofia, filial Plovdiv.*
141. Case C-141/11, *Torsten Hörnfeldt v. Posten Meddelande AB.*
142. Case C-546/11, *Dansk Jurist- og Økonomforbund, acting on behalf of Erik Toftgaard v. Indenrigs- og Sundhedsministeriet.*
143. Case C-447/09, *Reinhard Prigge and Others v. Deutsche Lufthansa AG.*
144. Joined Cases C-297/10 and C-298/10, *Sabine Hennigs v. Eisenbahn-Bundesamt, Land Berlin v. Alexander Mai.*
145. Case C-411/05, *Félix Palacios de la Villa v. Cortefiel Servicios SA.*
146. Case C-45/09, *Gisela Rosenbladt v. Oellerking Gebäudereinigungsges. mbH.*
147. Joined Cases C-159/10 and C-160/10, *Gerhard Fuchs, Peter Köhler v. Land Hessen.*
148. Case C-267/12, *Frédéric Hay v. Crédit agricole mutuel de Charente-Maritime et des Deux-Sèvres.*

7.3.1 *Genuine occupational requirements*

All non-discrimination Directives on the Article 19 grounds that cover employment contain a derogation concerning occupational requirements. For example, under Article 4 of Directive 2000/43 Member States may provide that a difference of treatment which is based on a characteristic related to racial or ethnic origin shall not constitute discrimination where, by reason of the nature of the particular occupational activities concerned or of the context in which they are carried out, the characteristic constitutes a genuine and determining occupational requirement, provided that the objective is legitimate and the requirement is proportionate.

The reference in the text of the law not only to the nature of the particular occupational activities concerned, but also more generally to the context in which they are carried out, led the Court to a broad application of the derogation where a very specific type of employment is at issue (*Sirdar,*[149] concerning access to employment in elite troops in the armed forces and the need for so-called interoperability, as opposed to *Kreil,*[150] concerning employment in the armed forces in general; both cases concerned legislation that preceded Directive 2006/54).

In the context of Directive 2000/78, the Court noted that it is not the ground on which the difference in treatment is based but a characteristic related to that ground which must constitute a genuine and determining occupational requirement, for example particular physical capabilities for fire fighters, pilots or police officers, as these may diminish with age. As a legitimate aim in whose context such characteristics can be relied on, the Court accepted the operational capacity and proper functioning of the professional fire service (*Wolf*),[151] air traffic safety (*Prigge*),[152] and the ability to perform the duties of the police (*Salaberria Sorondo*).[153] However, the Court emphasized the need to interpret Article 4(1) of Directive 2000/78 restrictively. In this context, it also pointed to Recital 23 in the preamble to the Directive, according to which it is only in "very limited" circumstances that a difference of treatment may be justified where a characteristic related, *inter alia,* to age constitutes a genuine and determining occupational requirement. This approach has since been confirmed in context of religion. In *Bougnaoui,*[154] the Court added that the concept of a "genuine and determining occupational requirement" refers to a requirement that is objectively dictated by the nature of the occupational activities concerned or of the context in which they are carried out. Conversely, it cannot cover subjective considerations, such as the willingness of the employer to take account of the particular wishes of the customer (in this case the wish of a customer not be served by an employee wearing, as a Muslim woman, a headscarf).

In Directive 2000/78, the general derogation for reasons of occupational requirements in Article 4(1) is followed by a further paragraph concerning employers with a religious ethos. According to Article 4(2), the Directive does not prejudice the right of churches and other public or private organizations, the ethos of which is based on religion or belief, acting in conformity with national constitutions and laws, to require individuals working for them to act in good faith and with loyalty to the organization's ethos. At the time of writing, a case concerning this provision is pending before the ECJ.[155]

---

149. Case C-273/97, *Angela Maria Sirdar v. The Army Board, Secretary of State for Defence.*
150. Case C-285/98, *Tanja Kreil v. Germany.*
151. Case C-229/08, *Colin Wolf v. Stadt Frankfurt am Main.*
152. Case C-447/09, *Reinhard Prigge and Others v. Deutsche Lufthansa AG.*
153. Case C-258/15, *Gorka Salaberria Sorondo v. Academia Vasca de Policía y Emergencias.*
154. Case C-188/15, *Asma Bougnaoui and Association de défense des droits de l'homme (ADDH) v. Micropole SA.*
155. Case C-68/17, *IR v. JQ.*

Directive 2000/78 also contains a special provision on the religion and the recruitment of teachers in Northern Ireland and in view of maintaining a balance of opportunity in employment for teachers in Northern Ireland while furthering the reconciliation of historical divisions between the major religious communities there, namely Article 15(2).

7.3.2 *Positive action*

Introduced through the Treaty revision of Amsterdam, Article 157(4) TFEU as well as all Directives with the exception of Directive 79/7 provide for the possibility of positive action. In the case of Directive 2000/78, Article 7 contains two parts, the first a general provision, and the second specifically about persons with a disability and Member State provisions to maintain or adopt provisions on the protection of health and safety at work and measures aimed at creating or maintaining provisions or facilities for safeguarding or promoting their integration into the working environment. In addition, Directive 2000/78 contains a special provision on Northern Ireland, which refers to tackling the under-representation of one of the major religious communities in the police service, namely Article 15(1). Further, the Commission's proposal for a Directive intended to improve the gender balance among non-executive directors of companies listed on stock exchanges[156] must also be seen in the context of positive action. Though formulated in a gender-neutral manner, it indirectly aims to improve the number of women on company boards.

For a long time, there was case law on positive action only in the context of sex equality. The Court has construed positive action as an exception, even though under previous secondary law it was mentioned as intending to ensure equal opportunities and under Article 157(4) TFEU as intending to ensure full equality in practice. Under the Court's case law positive action in the area of employment does not allow for automatic and unconditional preference for one sex even where women and men are equally qualified (*Kalanke*,[157] *Badeck*,[158] *Abrahamsson*[159]). However, more recently and outside the issue of access to employment, the emphasis is no longer on a narrow interpretation but rather on proportionality (*Lommers*).[160] In a case that arose under EEA law, the EFTA Court noted that the formulation of Article 157(4) TFEU calls for a more open interpretation (*Norwegian Quota*).[161] However, the ECJ so far shows no signs of such a change in interpretation (e.g. *Briheche*,[162] *Commission v. Greece*[163]). On a positive note, the Court

156. COM(2012)614, Proposal for a Directive of the European Parliament and of the Council on improving the gender balance among non-executive directors of companies listed on stock exchanges and related measures. See L. Senden and M. Visser, "Balancing a tightrope: The EU Directive on improving the gender balance among non-executive directors of boards of listed companies", (2013) *European Gender Equality Law Review*, 17–33. See also the European Commission's Report on "Women and men in leadership positions in the European Union – A review of the situation and recent progress" (Office for Official Publications of the European Union, 2013) and the Factsheet "Gender balance on corporate boards. – Europe is cracking the glass ceiling" of 2016, available at <ec.europa.eu/justice/gender-equality/files/gender_balance_decision_making/1607_factsheet_final_wob_data_en.pdf>.
157. Case C-450/93, *Eckhard Kalanke v. Freie und Hansestadt Bremen.*
158. Case C-158/97, *Georg Badeck and Others.*
159. Case C-407/98, *Katarina Abrahamsson and Leif Anderson v. Elisabet Fogelqvist.*
160. Case C-476/99, *H. Lommers v. Minister van Landbouw, Natuurbeheer en Visserij.*
161. Case E-1/02, *EFTA Surveillance Authority v. Norway*; annotation by C. Tobler, 41 CML Rev. (2004), 245–260.
162. Case C-319/03, *Serge Briheche v. Ministre de l'Intérieur, Ministre de l'Éducation nationale and Ministre de la Justice.*
163. Case C-559/07, *Commission v. Greece.*

held in *Roca Álvarez*[164] that granting a breastfeeding/bottle feeding leave to employed mothers, but to employed fathers only where the mother of the child is also employed (i.e. as a derived right), cannot be considered to be a measure eliminating or reducing existing inequalities in society within the meaning the Directive, nor as a measure seeking to achieve substantive as opposed to formal equality by reducing the real inequalities that can arise in society. Rather, it is liable to perpetuate a traditional distribution of the roles of men and women by keeping men in a role subsidiary to that of women in relation to the exercise of their parental duties.

In the context of disability and of Article 7(2) of Directive 2000/78, the Court held in *Milkova*[165] that the purpose of this provision is to authorize specific measures aimed at effectively eliminating or reducing actual instances of inequality affecting people with disabilities, which may exist in their social lives and, in particular, their professional lives. The case concerned the requirement of authorization in view of the dismissal of employees with a disability, in order to ensure that a specialized body assesses the impact of the dismissal on the health of the person concerned and decides whether or not to authorize that dismissal.

7.3.3 *Protection of women as regards pregnancy and maternity*

Article 28(1) of Directive 2006/54 states that the Directive is without prejudice to provisions concerning the protection of women, particularly as regards pregnancy and maternity. Similar provisions can be found in Article 4(2) of Directives 2004/113 and 79/7 (which, however, only mentions maternity). In its case law, the Court gives the same rationale for these provisions as with respect to maternity leave under Directive 92/85, namely recognizing the legitimacy, in terms of the principle of equal treatment of the sexes, of differential treatment of women under the derogation, namely the protection of a woman's biological condition during and after pregnancy and, further, the protection of the special relationship between a woman and her child over the period which follows pregnancy and childbirth (e.g. *Hofmann*,[166] though in this case, which concerned a young father willing to make it possible for his wife to return to paid work as quickly as possible by caring for the baby, unfortunately with the effect of reinforcing the traditional division of roles in the family).

The Court's case law on this derogation relates mostly to the legislation that preceded Directive 2006/54, for example in *Stoeckel*,[167] concerning a general ban of night-work for women, further in *Roca Álvarez*,[168] concerning "breastfeeding" leave for fathers, and in *Betriu Montull*,[169] concerning the transfer of part of the maternity leave to the father. Today, only matters not covered by specific law such as Directive 92/85 fall under Directive 2006/54. Examples concern maternity leave under national law that goes beyond the compulsory EU minimum of 14 weeks (*Boyle*),[170] further dismissal of a woman because of pregnancy or maternity, where the dismissal occurs outside the protection period set up by Directive 92/85 (*Paquay*),[171] and dismissal of a woman on sick leave in order to undergo in vitro fertilization treatment, at a stage where there was not yet a pregnancy within the meaning of Directive 92/85 (*Mayr*).[172]

---

164. Case C-104/09, *Pedro Manuel Roca Álvarez v. Sesa Start España ETT SA.*
165. Case C-406/15, *Petya Milkova v. Izpalnitelen direktor na Agentsiata za privatizatsia i sledprivatizatsionen kontrol.*
166. Case 184/83, *Ulrich Hofmann v. Barmer Ersatzkasse.*
167. Case C-345/89, *Alfred Stoeckel.*
168. Case C-104/09, *Pedro Manuel Roca Álvarez v. Sesa Start España ETT SA.*
169. Case C-5/12, *Marc Betriu Montull v. Instituto Nacional de la Seguridad Social (INSS).*
170. Case C-411/96, *Margaret Boyle and Others v. Equal Opportunities Commission.*
171. Case C-460/06, *Nadine Paquay v. Société d'architectes Hoet + Minne SPRL.*
172. Case C-506/06, *Sabine Mayr v. Bäckerei und Konditorei Gerhard Flöckner OHG.*

7.3.4 *Occupational social security under Article 6(2) of Directive 2000/78 and under Article 9(1)(g) of Directive 2006/54*

Both Directive 2000/78 and Directive 2006/54 contain specific derogations with respect to social security. According to Article 6(2) of Directive 2000/78, Member States may provide that the fixing for occupational social security schemes of ages for admission or entitlement to retirement or invalidity benefits, including the fixing under those schemes of different ages for employees or groups or categories of employees, and the use, in the context of such schemes, of age criteria in actuarial calculations, does not constitute discrimination on the grounds of age, provided this does not result in discrimination on the grounds of sex. Under Article 9(1)(h) of Directive 2006/54, the setting of different levels of benefit is acceptable in so far as may be necessary to take account of actuarial calculation factors which differ according to sex in the case of defined-contribution schemes. In the case of funded defined-benefit schemes, certain elements may be unequal where the inequality of the amounts results from the effects of the use of actuarial factors differing according to sex at the time when the scheme's funding is implemented.

So far, there is little ECJ case law on these provisions. In *Kristensen,*[173] the Court held that Article 6(2) applies only to occupational social security schemes that cover the risks of old age and invalidity, and only with respect to the fixing of ages for admission or entitlement to retirement or invalidity benefits, including the use of age criteria in actuarial calculations. In *Toftgaard,*[174] the provision was found not to be relevant, as the case did not concern an occupational social security scheme covering the risks of old age and invalidity. In *Parris,*[175] the Court held that an age requirement with respect to the entitlement to an occupational old age survivor's benefit is covered by Article 6(2) of Directive 2000/78 and capable of justifying differential treatment.

7.3.5 *Article 2(5) of Directive 2000/78*

Specifically for Directive 2000/78, Article 2(5) provides that this Directive is without prejudice to measures laid down by national law, which, in a democratic society, are necessary for public security, for the maintenance of public order and the prevention of criminal offences, for the protection of health and for the protection of the rights and freedoms of others.

This derogation has so far rarely appeared in ECJ case law. In *Prigge,*[176] an age discrimination case concerning compulsory retirement of pilots, the ECJ found that air traffic safety falls under the ground of public security. In *Petersen,*[177] another age discrimination case concerning the right of dentists to practice under the statutory health insurance system, the Court held that maintaining a high-quality medical service and prevention of the risk of serious harm to the financial balance of the social security system is a legitimate aim under the ground of public health. In this latter context, the Court made a link with previous case law from the field of the internal market where financial considerations were also accepted if they were linked to the non-financial aim of protecting public health (*Watts,*[178] *Hartlauer*[179]).

---

173. Case C-476/11, *HK Danmark, acting on behalf of Glennie Kristensen v. Experian A/S.*
174. Case C-546/11, *Dansk Jurist- og Økonomforbund, acting on behalf of Erik Toftgaard v. Indenrigs- og Sundhedsministeriet.*
175. Case C-443/15, *David L. Parris v. Trinity College Dublin and Others.*
176. Case C-447/09, *Reinhard Prigge and Others v. Deutsche Lufthansa AG.*
177. Case C-341/08, *Domnica Petersen v. Berufungsausschuss für Zahnärzte für den Bezirk Westfalen-Lippe.*
178. Case C-372/04, *The Queen, on the application of Yvonne Watts v. Bedford Primary Care Trust and Secretary of State for Health.*
179. Case C-169/07, *Hartlauer Handelsgesellschaft mbH v. Wiener Landesregierung and Oberösterreichische Landesregierung.*

7.4 An overarching issue: Proportionality

Proportionality being a general principle of Union law, all justification measures, whatever their legal basis, must be proportionate (e.g. *Johnston*).[180] This implies that the measure in question must be appropriate or suitable for achieving the aim, and necessary or requisite, i.e. that it is not possible to reach the aim with a less onerous measure. Further, in line with internal market law, a measure is appropriate for ensuring attainment of the objective pursued only if it genuinely reflects a concern to attain it in a consistent and systematic manner (e.g. *Petersen*).[181]

According to the Court, in the present state of Union law (i.e. again, given the limited competences of the Union in the field of social law) the Member States and, where appropriate, the social partners at national level enjoy broad discretion in their choice not only of their aims in the field of social and employment policy, but also in the definition of the measures capable of achieving it (e.g. *Toftgaard*).[182] For so far as the Court in its case law deals with proportionality, this generous approach is reflected in its decisions, though there appear to be differences between different categories of cases. This can be well illustrated with respect to justification for differential treatment on grounds of age.

In cases concerning compulsory retirement, the Court tends to accept as proportionate under the derogation provisions of Directive 2000/78 age limits that correspond to the national statutory retirement age or are higher than this age. According to the Court, it does not appear unreasonable in such cases for the Member State or the social partners to take the view that the measure is appropriate and necessary (e.g. *Palacios de la Villa*,[183] *Rosenbladt*,[184] *Fuchs and Köhler*,[185] all with regard to a retirement age of 65 years; *Hörnfeldt*,[186] with respect to a retirement age of 67; *Georgiev*,[187] with respect to a retirement age of 68, which was five years higher than the statutory retirement age; as opposed to *Prigge*,[188] with regard to a retirement age of 60 for airline pilots under a collective agreement, in a situation where national and international law fixed the retirement age at 65).

In contrast, in cases concerning issues other than compulsory retirement, the Court in general appears to be stricter on the issue of proportionality (e.g. *Hennigs and Mai*,[189] where it found that a salary system allegedly based on experience in fact provided for the stepping in the first salary group of an employee without experience based solely on age, and *Toftgaard*, where it found that the legitimate objectives could be attained by less restrictive, but equally appropriate, measures).

Overall, whilst proportionality is often the main battlefield in concrete cases, the outcome of a given case on this issue may be difficult to predict.

---

180. Case 222/84, *Marguerite Johnston v. Chief Constable of the RUC.*
181. Case C-341/08, *Domnica Petersen v. Berufungsausschuss für Zahnärzte für den Bezirk Westfalen-Lippe.*
182. Case C-546/11, *Dansk Jurist- og Økonomforbund, acting on behalf of Erik Toftgaard v. Indenrigs- og Sundhedsministeriet.*
183. Case C-411/05, *Félix Palacios de la Villa v. Cortefiel Servicios SA.*
184. Case C-45/09, *Gisela Rosenbladt v. Oellerking Gebäudereinigungsges. mbH.*
185. Joined Cases C-159/10 and C-160/10, *Gerhard Fuchs, Peter Köhler v. Land Hessen.*
186. Case C-141/11, *Torsten Hörnfeldt v. Posten Meddelande AB.*
187. Joined Cases C-250/09 and C-268/09, *Vasil Ivanov Georgiev v. Tehnicheski universitet – Sofia, filial Plovdiv.*
188. Case C-447/09, *Reinhard Prigge and Others v. Deutsche Lufthansa AG.*
189. Joined Cases C-297/10 and C-298/10, *Sabine Hennigs v. Eisenbahn-Bundesamt, Land Berlin v. Alexander Mai.*

8. Enforcement

8.1 Enforcement under specific secondary law

Most of the most recent generation of non-discrimination Directives contain a special chapter on remedies and enforcement and additional, relevant provisions in other parts of the Directives. To some extent, this is a codification of the Court's case law in the field of sex equality before the adoption of these Directives, in particular on the right to judicial access and on the burden of proof. At the same time, enforcement elements developed in the context of sex equality law have informed Union law more generally.[190] More recently, the model established by the non-discrimination Directives has been exported into the field of the free movement for workers, through Directive 2014/15.[191]

In the Directives dealing with the Article 19 grounds, judicial access now falls under a provision entitled "Defence of rights" (e.g. Art. 7 of Directive 2000/43). This obliges the Member States to ensure that judicial and/or administrative procedures, including where they deem it appropriate, conciliation procedures, for the enforcement of obligations under the Directive are available. The law does not specify the nature of the court to which the Member States must entrust the task of judicial procedure. So long as persons who consider themselves wronged by failure to apply the principle of equal treatment to them are able to pursue their claims effectively before a competent court, the requirements of the law are satisfied (*Schneider*).[192] The right to judicial access is without prejudice to time limits under national law for initiating proceedings (though such time limits must be reasonable; e.g. *Levez*).[193] As for the applicants, the Member States are obliged to ensure that associations, organizations or other legal entities which, under the national law, have a legitimate interest in ensuring that a Directive is complied with, may engage either on behalf or in support of the complainant in procedures provided for the enforcement of obligations under the Directive.

With respect to proof, according to the Court it is normally for the person alleging facts in support of a claim to adduce proof of such facts. In principle, this also applies in cases of alleged discrimination (e.g. *Brunnhofer*).[194] However, in most modern Directives there is now an express provision on the burden of proof which provides for a shifting of the burden of proof to the alleged perpetrator in the situation where the victim of the alleged discrimination has established facts from which it may be presumed that there has been direct or indirect discrimination (e.g. Art. 19 of Directive 2006/54). *Feryn*[195] is an example under Directive 2000/78, where the second part of the decision concerns the distribution of the burden of proof with respect to actual discrimination through a refusal to hire persons based on their ethnic origin (as opposed to the speech act, which is the subject of the first part of the decision).

190. See C. Tobler, "The impact of non-discrimination law in developing a general doctrine of enforcement under EU law" in E. Ellis and K. Benediktsdottír (Eds.), *Equality into Reality. Action for Diversity and Non-Discrimination in Iceland* (University of Iceland Press, 2011), 67–107.

191. O.J. 2014, L 128/8, Directive 2014/54/EU of the European Parliament and of the Council of 16 Apr. 2014 on measures facilitating the exercise of rights conferred on workers in the context of freedom of movement for workers. See E. Muir, "Procedural rules in the service of the "transformative function" of EU equality law: Bringing the prohibition of nationality discrimination along", *8 Review of European Administrative Law* (2015), 153–176.

192. Case C-380/01, *Gustav Schneider v. Bundesminister für Justiz.*

193. Case C-326/96, *B.S. Levez v. Jennings (Harlow Pools) Ltd.*

194. Case C-381/99, *Susanna Brunnhofer v. Bank der österreichischen Postsparkasse AG.*

195. Case C-54/07, *Centrum voor gelijkheid van kansen en voor racismebestrijding v. Firma Feryn NV.*

Where discrimination has been found, there must be penalties or sanctions that are effective, proportionate and dissuasive and which may comprise the payment of compensation to the victim (e.g. Art. 17 of Directive 2000/78). The nature of the sanctions is not specified on the level of Union law. However, the Court explained in *Marshall II*[196] that in the case of discriminatory dismissal a situation of equality cannot be restored without either reinstating the victim of discrimination or granting financial compensation for the loss and damage sustained. Where compensation is chosen, it must enable the loss and damage actually sustained as a result of the discriminatory dismissal to be made good in full. Accordingly, the fixing of an upper limit is not acceptable (this is now explicitly stated in Article 10 of Directive 2010/41). Conversely, Union law does not oblige the Member States to provide for punitive damages (*Arjona Camacho*).[197]

Since taking steps against discrimination may have negative effects on the complainant, most Directives contain provisions obliging the Member States to take the measures against victimization (i.e. measures necessary for the protection against adverse treatment by the alleged perpetrator as a reaction to a complaint because of discrimination; e.g. Art. 10 of Directive 2004/113).

Finally, so-called equality bodies established in the Member States may play a role in the enforcement of non-discrimination law. An obligation to set up or maintain national bodies for the promotion of equal treatment initially only existed with respect to discrimination on grounds of racial or ethnic origin (Art. 13 of Directive 2000/43). Subsequently, it was also introduced with respect to discrimination on grounds of sex (e.g. Art. 12 of Directive 2004/113). It is now also stated in the proposal for a new directive that would widen the scope of Directive 2000/78. In practice, national equality bodies often already now have a broader mandate. Member States enjoy a broad margin of discretion as regards the enforcement role of their equality bodies, either exercising quasi-judicial powers themselves and/or assisting or representing victims in challenges before courts. There is a European Network of Equality Bodies, Equinet.[198]

8.2 *General elements of enforcement of non-discrimination law*

With respect to issues that are not specifically regulated in secondary law, the Union's general enforcement principles apply, including notably the principles of equivalence and effectiveness[199] (e.g. *Bulicke*,[200] *Starjakob*[201]). Further, the Court held that where discrimination has been suffered, equal treatment in the concrete, individual case is to be achieved by placing the person discriminated against in the same situation as that of the comparators. In other words, the person discriminated against must be granted the same favourable treatment, resulting in so-called levelling up (e.g. *Jonkman*).[202] The same approach also applies in the Union's internal market law (e.g. *Pöpperl*).[203]

In relation to the general rule or measure that caused the discrimination, for as long as measures reinstating equal treatment have not been adopted, observance of the principle of equal treatment can be ensured only by granting persons within the disadvantaged category the same advantages as those enjoyed by persons within the favoured category (however, this applies

196. Case C-271/91, *M. Helen Marshall v. Southampton and South-West Hampshire Area Health Authority.*
197. Case C-407/14, *María Auxiliadora Arjona Camacho v. Securitas Seguridad España, SA.*
198. Information available at <www.equineteurope.org>.
199. See Ch. 11, "Application and enforcement of EU law in the Member States", of this book.
200. Case C-246/09, *Susanne Bulicke v. Deutsche Büro Service GmbH.*
201. Case C-417/13, *ÖBB Personenverkehr AG v. Gotthard Starjakob.*
202. Joined Cases C-231/06 to C-233/06, *Office national des pensions v. Emilienne Jonkman and Hélène Vercheval; Noëlle Permesaen v. Office national des pensions.*
203. Case C-187/15 *Joachim Pöpperl v. Land Nordrhein-Westfalen.*

only where there is a valid point of reference, i.e. an identifiable group of persons who enjoyed the more favourable treatment; *Specht*).[204] This also implies that in changing such a rule or measure, levelling down is possible, as long as it is general and does not cause new discrimination. This is, however, a common problem with an approach based on equal treatment. Indeed, any indication of a specific level of treatment would require harmonization.

Generally, whatever way out of the discrimination is chosen, the remedy must not in its turn lead to fresh discrimination (again *Jonkman*, which is a follow up of the *Defrenne* cases).

9. Conclusion

Compared to other Union law, but also to traditional public international law, Union equal treatment and non-discrimination law relating to the Article 19 grounds is highly developed, in particular with respect to the concept of discrimination and to enforcement. In spite of this, discrimination remains a persistent problem in the Union.[205] The importance of addressing it is recognized in a number of provisions of primary Union law, including in particular Articles 2 and 3(3) TEU as well as under Articles 8 and 10 TFEU. In this context, a special place is given to sex equality. Whilst to some extent this has historic reasons (i.e. it reflects the fact that the sex discrimination ground was covered from the inception of the EEC), it remains the case that stereotypes with regard to sex are at the basis of a number of other types of discrimination, which is why it is necessary to give special attention to this problem.

Within the comparatively sophisticated framework of Union law, the present chapter has told a tale of an uneven development. On the level of legislation, it was noted that the Union has not used its competences to combat discrimination to the full, and has used them unevenly for the discrimination grounds covered, which has resulted in a hierarchy of discrimination grounds. This situation appears to be due mainly to political pragmatism on the side of the Union institutions. The ECJ has recognized the institutions' wide margin of discretion in this regard, noting in *Test-Achats*[206] that, in the progressive achievement of equality mandated under Articles 3(3) TEU and 8 TFEU, it is the Union legislature which determines when it will take action, having regard to the development of economic and social conditions within the European Union. Further, where the Union legislator decides to act, it may be permissible to implement the principle of equality gradually, providing for transitional periods in the legislation. Insofar, it remains a matter for politics to decide on the "appropriate balance to be struck between consistency and coherence on the one hand, and targeted measures that reflect the diverse manifestations of discrimination on the other".[207]

An uneven development can also be discerned in the case law. On the one hand, this chapter has shown the important role of the ECJ case law in this field, ranging from the recognition of the direct effect of Article 119 of the EEC Treaty in the early times to the acknowledgment of the problem of stereotypes and the incorporation of this perspective into the existing legal framework more recently. Indeed, through its case law the ECJ has made a major contribution to the development of the concept of legal equality under Community and Union law and to

---

204. Joined Cases C-501/12 to C-506/12, C-540/12 and C-541/12, *Thomas Specht, Jens Schombera, Alexander Wieland, Uwe Schönefeld, Antje Wilke, Gerd Schini v. Land Berlin and Rena Schmeel, Ralf Schuster v. Bundesrepublik Deutschland.*

205. See *Discrimination in the EU 2015. Special Eurobarometer,* available at <ec.europa.eu/public_opinion/archives/ebs/ebs_393_en.pdf>, for further information, see e.g. <www.equineteurope.org/Discrimination-in-the-EU-in-2015>.

206. Case C-236/09, *Association Belge des Consommateurs Test-Achats ASBL and Others v. Conseil des ministres.*

207. M. Bell and Lisa Waddington, "Editorial: Equality and diversity: Challenges for EU anti-discrimination law", 13 MJ (2006), 277–278, at 278.

the effectiveness of that law. At the same time, there is a sizable number of problematic decisions which limits the power of Union non-discrimination law.

Overall, the Union's law relating to the Article 19 grounds aims to foster conditions of social inclusion (e.g. Recital 8 in the preamble to Directive 2000/43). In order to reach this aim, the law must recognize and combat the existence of unequal power relations in society as well as the existence of stereotypes. Stereotypes are often the root cause of discrimination and notably may lead to structural, systemic or institutional discrimination, i.e. discrimination arising from deeply rooted views, opinion and value judgments relied on in a given society or from societal, cultural, economic patterns and structures.[208] The present Union law is only to a certain extent able to address this problem. Structural discrimination is not explicitly mentioned in the non-discrimination law as discussed in this chapter, though it is linked to some of its concepts, in particular positive action (which is meant to be used to counteract instances of structural discrimination) and to indirect discrimination (a concept which was said to have been "invented in order to cater for the situation of institutional discrimination").[209] More recently, it has been suggested that a strategic use of the prohibition of harassment could help to combat structural discrimination.[210]

In contrast, structural discrimination is specifically addressed in international law in a manner that goes considerably further. Article 5(a) of the Convention on the Elimination of All Forms of Discrimination against Women (CEDAW) is an example. It obliges the Signatory States to engage in what is often referred to as social engineering, that is, to work towards modifying the social and cultural patterns of conduct of men and women, with a view to achieving the elimination of prejudices and customary and all other practices which are based on the idea of the inferiority or the superiority of either of the sexes or on stereotyped roles for men and women.[211] The UN Convention on the Rights of Persons with Disabilities (CRPD) contains a similar provision in Article 8.

There are no equivalent provisions in Union law. Given this and other limitations of Union law relating to the Article 19 grounds, it must be concluded that the power of this law to contribute to transformative equality, defined as seeking to accelerate equality for disadvantaged groups through changing existing social structures and the way how organizations and institutions function, remains limited. Much is, therefore, left to the Member States who may, and in the light of their obligations under international law, must go further than does Union law.

Further reading

Belavusau, Ulad/Kristin Henrard (Eds.), *EU Anti-Discrimination Law Beyond Gender* (Oxford, 2018).

Ellis, E. and P. Watson, *EU Anti-Discrimination Law*, 2nd ed. (OUP, 2012).

Fredman, S., *Discrimination Law*, 2nd ed. (OUP, 2011).

FRA/ECTHR, *Handbook on European Non-Discrimination Law* (Office for Official Publications of the European Union, 2011).

Schiek, D., L. Waddington and M. Bell (Eds.), *Cases, Materials and Text on National, Supranational and International Non-Discrimination Law* (Hart Publishing, 2007).

208. See notably C. McCrudden, "Institutional discrimination", 2 OJLS (1982), 303–367.
209. E. Ellis, "The definition of discrimination in European Community sex equality law", 19 EL Rev. (1994), 563–580, at 572.
210. M. Mercat-Bruns, "Racisme au travail: les nouveaux modes de détection et les outils de prevention", Droit Social (2017), 361–371.
211. See R. Holtmaat, "Art. 5" in M.A. Freeman, C. Chinkin and B. Rudolf op. cit. *supra* note 20, at 155.

The publications of the European Equality Law Network set up by the European Commission, available at <www.equalitylaw.eu/publications>.

CHAPTER 30
AGRICULTURE AND FISHERIES[1]

*Thomas van Rijn**

1. The nature of the agricultural problems

Public authorities have since time immemorial been concerned about agriculture. Already in the nineteenth century the specialty presently known as agricultural law was developed. It was principally concerned with the legal status of the farmer's land (title, mortgages and succession, etc.). At the beginning of the twentieth century, and particularly in the period between the two world wars, agricultural markets were subject to intensive government intervention. To an important extent, this market regulation was due to a number of specific characteristics of the agricultural sector compared with other sectors of the economy. Some of the structural causes of the permanent problems, which are relevant to an understanding of European agricultural policy, will be briefly mentioned here.[2]

Neither the demand for, nor the supply of, agricultural products is very susceptible to rises or falls in prices (this is known as low price elasticity of supply and demand). In the short term, the volume of production depends – particularly for plant products – mainly on climatological factors. In addition, there is a weak price elasticity (and for a number of products also a weak income elasticity) of demand, i.e. changes in price or income have little effect on demand. For generations already, the agricultural sector has been confronted with massive surpluses or sometimes massive shortages, resulting in unstable markets and price relationships. Many agricultural products are substitutable, both in terms of demand and supply, so that unstable situations for one product exercise a direct effect on the situation of other products. A surplus of milk, for example, may lead to the wholesale slaughter of milk cows, and an increase in the supply of beef can interfere with the market for pork.

In the long term these problems stem from the structure of supply and demand. On the demand side problems may arise through a low or stagnating population growth, so that the improvements in mechanization, intensive farming and productivity cannot be fully absorbed: structural surpluses then result. In many countries, principally the southern and eastern Member States, agricultural structures are relatively underdeveloped, primarily due to natural factors such as hill and mountain farming, climate, and inadequate infrastructure, and the level of organization of production and trade in agricultural products is relatively low. These structural weaknesses often go hand in hand with social inequalities and retarded economic development.

---

* Formerly: Legal Service, European Commission.

1. Parts of this chapter are based on René Barents' contribution to the previous edition of the book.
2. For more extensive discussion see M. Tracy, *Agriculture in Europe. Challenge and Response. 1880–1980*, 2nd ed. (Granada, 1982). More literature about the genesis of European agricultural policy is to be found in R. Barents, *The Agricultural Law of the EC* (Kluwer, 1994).

The new Member States in Central and Eastern Europe also have to face the problems linked to the transition from collective forms of organization to market economies. Another important element in the problem is the relative immobility of production. In some countries, agricultural land is scarce and more profitable production requires an active policy of land reallocation, infrastructural improvements and so on. It is still the case that most agricultural holdings are in the hands of marginal or almost marginal family enterprises, which, while economically of limited significance, have a social and electoral influence which should not be underestimated. Moreover, farmers are vitally important for management of the environment and natural surroundings.

This brief overview makes it clear that any form of intervention in the agricultural markets must deal not merely with short-term problems (market and price policies), it must also embrace the longer term (agricultural structures). Intervention in the context of market and price policies almost always aims to increase prices or producer incomes. Two types of short-term intervention should be distinguished: the first involves supplements to the income of the producers, in the form of subsidies – whether product-related or not. In this situation, there is free price formation for agricultural products, and farmers sell their products at market prices, but receive "deficiency payments" so as to assure them of a certain income. This was long the system followed in the United Kingdom, but even before its accession to the Communities the United Kingdom Government started to adapt this system to the Community system. The second type – which was the standard practice in most European countries apart from the United Kingdom and Ireland – involves a system of price interventions, whereby surplus production which would depress prices is taken out of the national market through government financed purchases. This of course requires effective prevention of the undermining of this equilibrium by much cheaper imports from third countries; variable import levies have thus been imposed to bring third-country imports up to the Community price level, and export subsidies have been paid to compensate farmers for the lower prices on the world market. In some cases this policy was accompanied by centralization of imports and exports of agricultural products. Price-stabilizing measures may also take the form of production quotas, which may be used in order to avoid disastrous price competition and the resulting demise of many marginal producers. The choice for one method or the other depends on a myriad of political, economic and financial considerations, and has been a subject of constant debate particularly in economic literature.[3] Agricultural structural policy has not only to offer a long-term perspective for short-term interventions and their effects on the structure of supply and demand, it must also contribute to a harmonious development of the agricultural sector in public policy as a whole. Such policy is often related to competition policy (for instance in relation to cooperatives), and production and marketing structures, and is closely linked to regional and environmental policy.

The fisheries sector demonstrates similar problems to those of agriculture described above: low price elasticity of supply and demand, substitutability of products; structural problems. However, the main problem is the decline of the fish stocks in the sea caused by overfishing of the stocks by the expanding fleet of ever more sophisticated vessels. Therefore, mere intervention in the functioning of the markets through price stabilization measures comparable to those in agriculture nor structural measures in the form of a modernization of the fleet were sufficient to reach the objective of a fair income for fishermen. Regulation of the "production" (catch) was indispensable to secure a viable fisheries sector in the long term.

---

3. Cf. M. Tracy, op. cit. *supra* note 2.

2. The place of the common agricultural and common fisheries policies in the TFEU

2.1 *Agriculture and fisheries*

Contrary to the EC-Treaty, Title III of the TFEU expresses clearly that it is not only dealing with agriculture, but also with fisheries. This is the confirmation of the commonly shared view which was based on the definition of agricultural products as referring to Annex-I products, thereby including fish, crustaceans and molluscs. Article 38(1) TFEU now states in its last sentence that the reference to "agriculture has to be understood as referring to fisheries as well, however 'taking into account of the special characteristics of the fisheries sector'". The TFEU differs also in another aspect from the EC-Treaty. Article 4(2) states clearly that the competence in the field of agriculture is shared between the Union and the Member States, even when agriculture is a common policy. However, the Member States may only exercise this competence to legislate as far as the Union has not exercised its competence (Art. 2(2) TFEU).[4] It is clear that the Union has regulated almost the entire policy area, which leaves the Member States only minor issues to legislate. The most important part of the fisheries sector, i.e. the measures relating to the conservation of marine biological resources, falls, according to Article 3(1) d), within the exclusive competence of the Union. The Member States have no competence to take measures in that area (Art. 2(1) TFEU).[5] For other matters falling within the fisheries policy the Union and the Member States share the competence to legislate.

2.2 *Internal market and common policy*

It follows from Article 26 TFEU that the agricultural and fisheries sectors form part of the internal market. This was by no means obvious, as is apparent from the fact that the second sentence of Article 38(1) explicitly states that the internal market extends to agriculture, fisheries and trade in agricultural products.[6] Given that for years all Member States had been regulating agricultural markets to a greater or lesser extent in the framework of various types of market regulation, the application of the free movement of goods provisions after the transitional period would have irrevocably led to the undermining of these national market organizations, which were primarily based on price interventions coupled with import and export regulation. The common market in the agricultural sector could therefore only be established by specific measures involving the communitarization of the national regulatory policies. What precisely these measures should be – which comprise "a" or "the" common policy – is not specified in the Treaty itself. These provisions only sketch a framework consisting of a number of objectives,[7] some global indication of instruments,[8] and a broad grant of powers.[9]

Article 38(2) and (4) TFEU do express the factually legally indissoluble link between the CAP and the internal market for agricultural products.[10] The one is unimaginable without the other, as is confirmed by Article 43(4)(b) TFEU, which provides that the Union policy in this

4. See already Case 237/82, *Jongeneel Kaas*, 141–143/81, *Holdijk* and C-158/89, *Dietz Matti.*
5. This is a codification of the case law of the Court of Justice, see Joined Cases 3, 4 & 6/76, *Kramer.*
6. Case 83/78, *Pigs Marketing Board v. Raymond Redmond* and Case 177/78, *Pigs and Bacon Commission v. McCorren and Company Ltd.*
7. Art. 39 TFEU.
8. Arts. 40–41 TFEU.
9. Art. 43 TFEU.
10. Case 250/84, *Eridania v. Cassa conguaglio zucchero,* Case C-27/90, *SITPA v. ONIFLHOR;* Joined Cases C-133,300 & 362/93, *Crispoltoni and others v. Fattoria Autonoma Tabacchi et al.*

sector has the objective of creating a situation which is comparable to that of a national market.[11] The CAP thus embodies the most far-reaching form of integration provided for in the Treaty, namely a total fusion of positive and negative integration.[12] It is particularly on that point that the CAP has great economic and also legal significance for the whole integration process. The CAP not only serves to establish the internal market, it is of essential importance for the whole of Union policy, in particular relating to the strengthening of economic and social cohesion, environmental policy, commercial policy, public health and consumer protection. The Court has recognized in very clear terms this connection between the CAP negative and positive integration aspects.[13]

The significance and connection of the internal market and the common policy has been clarified in the case law of the Court in two respects. First, since the end of the transitional period the Member States may not maintain in force any measures which conflict with the free movement of goods provisions.[14] This means in practical terms that national market organizations have become well-nigh impossible, a principle which applies also if the Union has not taken or been able to take common measures in a particular sector.[15] In relation to the Member States, the internal market takes precedence over national market organizations, although the exceptions of Article 36 TFEU remain applicable as long as the measures based thereupon have not been superseded by harmonization of laws.[16] In relation to the Union itself, however, the situation is different, and is actually to be regarded as the mirror image of the prohibition of unilateral intervention measures by the Member States. Although the Union is also bound by the free movement of goods provisions,[17] it is entitled, should the Union interest so require, to adopt measures on the basis of Article 43 TFEU, which in principle could involve a temporary division of the internal market. Apart from the monetary compensation measures, mentioned below, the case law has accepted the de facto division on national lines by production quotas

---

11. Case 31/74, *Galli* and Case 68/86, *United Kingdom v. Council.*
12. In relation to the common organizations of the markets, this principle means that after the end of the transitional period the free movement of goods provisions have become an integral part of these organizations, see Joined Cases 3, 4 & 6/76, *Kramer*, Case 83/78, *Pigs Marketing Board;* Case 251778, *Denkavit Futtermittel* and Case 29/82, *Van Luipen.* This integral part principle is confusingly sometimes referred to as the "open market" principle, see in particular Case 190/73, *Officier van Justitie v. Van Haaster,* and Case 111/76, *Officier van Justitie v. Van den Hazel;* Case. 94/79, *Vriend,* and Case C-44/94, *The Queen v. Minister of Agriculture, Fisheries and Food, ex parte Fishermen's Organisations et al.*
13. Joined Cases 80 & 81/77, *Commissionnaires réunis and Ramel v. Receveur des douanes;* Case 4/79, *Providence Agricole.*
14. Case 48/74, *Charmasson v. Ministre de l'économie and des finances;* Case 118/78, *Meijer v. Department of Trade et al.;* Case 232/78, *Commission v. France;* Joined Cases 194 & 241/85, *Commission v. Greece;* Case 119/86, *Spain v. Council et al.*
15. See Case 232/78, *Commission v. France.* In non-regulated sectors Art. 38 EC, which envisages the possibility of countervailing measures, retains some significance; this provision has only been applied in the alcoholic drinks sector, see Case 337/82, *St. Nikolaus Brennerei und Likörfabrik v. Hauptzollamt Krefeld;* Case 114/83, *Société d'initiatives and de cooperation agricoles v. Commission;* Case 181/85, *France v. Commission.*
16. E.g., see Case 251/78, *Denkavit Futtermittel;* Case 40/82, *Commission v. United Kingdom;* Case 261/85, *Commission v. United Kingdom;* Case 118/86, *Openbaar Ministerie v. Nertsvoederfabriek Nederland;* Case 29/87, *Dansk Denkavit v. Landbrugsministeriet;* Case C-5/94, *The Queen v. Ministry of Agriculture, Fisheries and Food, ex parte Hedley Lomas.*
17. Joined Cases 80 & 81/77, *Commissionnaires réunis and Ramel;* Case 179/78, *Procureur de la République v. Michelangelo Rivoira et al.;* Case 15/83, *Denkavit Nederland;* Case 199/84, *Procuratore della Republica v. Migliorini and Fischi.* See K.J.M. Mortelmans, "The relationship between the treaty rules and community measures for the establishment and functioning of the internal market: Towards a concordance rule," (2002) CML Rev., 1303–1346.

(e.g., sugar) or dual market organizations established per Member State.[18] An example of this latter approach can be seen in the old sheep meat market organization, which, as a result of political problems, was based on a system of premiums "per ewe" for the United Kingdom, and in the other Member States on a system of price intervention. This meant that mutton and lamb exported from the United Kingdom to the other Member States was subject to an export levy equal to the ewe premium received (the clawback system). In these and other cases the Court regarded such measures as permissible, as long as they were based on Community action which aimed to maintain the common market as much as possible, or to complete it at a later stage.[19]

In the fisheries sector the Court has, for administrative and conservation reasons, accepted the establishment of a system of national quotas in different sea areas, which have the effect that fishermen of different Member States do not have the same rights to fish in Union waters.[20]

3. Objectives

The connection between market integration and policy integration explained above is apparent from the objectives of the CAP and the CFP as set out in Article 39(1) TFEU and the general guidelines expressed in Article 39(2) TFEU. By their very nature these objectives, both as to the short term and the long term, and constituting an integral whole, can only be achieved in completely communitarized agricultural and fisheries markets. The Court has drawn the important conclusion from this that the concept of a CAP, which is not clearly defined anywhere in the Agriculture Title, has an objective and indivisible character. Thus all measures which relate to the realization of free movement of agricultural products contribute, by their nature, to these objectives, and as such constitute a matter falling within the competence of the Union under Articles 4(2)(d) and 43 TFEU. This is particularly true for the harmonization of national legislation relating to veterinary, health and phytosanitary matters, zoo technical and plant improvement questions, and the complex mass of legislation involving the production, composition, presentation of and trade in straight and compound animal feeding stuffs.[21]

As has been indicated above, these objectives cover all aspects of agricultural and fisheries policies. The objective specified in Article 39(1)(a) relates primarily to structural policy; the one in Article 39(1)(b) encompasses the income policy and those in Article 39(1)(c), (d) and (e) mainly concern market and price policy. The achievement of these objectives, which in some ways are even in conflict with one another, requires, according to long-established case law, that the Union legislature should possess a wide margin of discretion so that account may be taken of, as appropriate, the political, economic and budgetary situation, and priorities established.[22] This choice of priorities means that in order to ensure the maintenance of the internal market, it may even be split up, in principle on a temporary basis, by Union measures, if complete free movement is no longer possible for compelling reasons (e.g., crisis management in the framework of combating cattle diseases). Against this background, the Community was entitled to apply the monetary compensatory amounts which were necessary when the system of fixed

---

18. E.g., Case 138/79, *Roquette v. Council;* Case 139/79, *Maizena.*
19. Case 106/81, *Kind;* Case 61/86, *United Kingdom v. Commission;* Case 162/86, *Livestock Sales Transport v. Intervention Board for Agricultural Produce;* Joined Cases C-38/90 & C-151/90, *Lomas;* Case 212/94, *FMC.*
20. Case 46/86, *Romkes I.* Cf. Art. 5 (2) of Reg. 1380/2013.
21. Cf. Case 68/86, *United Kingdom v. Council;* Case 131/86, *United Kingdom v. Council;* Case C-131/87, *Commission v. Council;* Case C-11/88, *Commission v. Council;* Case C-180/96, *United Kingdom v. Commission.*
22. E.g., Case 5/67, *Beus v. Hauptzollamt München;* Joined Cases 63-69/72, *Wilhelm Werhahn Hansamühle et al. v. Council,* Joined Cases 197-200, 243, 245 & 247/80, *Ludwigshafener Walzmühle v. Council and Commission;* Case 59/83, *Biovilac v. EEC;* Case C-311/90, *Hierl v. Hauptzollamt Regensburg-,* Case C-353/92, *Greece v. Council;* Case C-280/93, *Germany v. Council.*

exchange rates became untenable at the beginning of the 1970s.[23] Another consequence of the competence to set priorities is that, within certain limits, Union legislation in the fields of agricultural and fisheries policy has to take account of certain "horizontal" interests, such as the protection of animal welfare, public health, environment and other aspects.[24]

The precise relationship between short-term and long-term policies is not clearly expressed in the objectives. On the one hand it can be deduced from the introductory word "thus" in Article 39(l)(b) TFEU that increasing the individual "earnings of persons engaged in agriculture or fishery should principally be achieved by structural measures".[25] On the other hand, the improvement of individual earnings can also be seen in a normative context, in the sense that there is an obligation to realize such an increase, which implies a more or less permanent income policy. The relationship between the two components is a matter for the Council's discretionary power.[26] This background explains why the Court has never accepted that Article 39 TFEU could be a source of individual rights relating to income (with, as a consequence, a certain intervention policy) or economic freedom (with, as a consequence, the absence or limitation of such an intervention policy).[27] Thus Article 39 TFEU forms an obligation for the Union and the Member States to take various steps, but it does not confer direct rights on operators in the agricultural sector.[28] In any event, both limbs of Article 39 TFEU make it plain that the CAP and the CFP, in legal terms as in other terms, cannot only consist of a market and price policy. The factual accuracy of this legal statement has been confirmed in more than 50 years of the existence of the CAP.

The general nature of the objectives has led the Council to indicate previously in different market organizations more specific goals to be achieved by the market organizations.[29] The most pronounced specification of the objectives to be pursued in a particular sector can be seen in the fisheries sector, where the basic regulation defines a number of specific objectives for the common fisheries policy in which the relationship with the objectives laid down in Article 39 TFEU is not always easy to determine.[30]

4. Scope

As has been noted above, the TFEU Treaty is silent as to what is meant by "a" or "the" Common Agricultural Policy (CAP). Article 38(2) and (3) TFEU do give a description of what are

23. E.g., Case 5/73, *Balkan Import Export v. Hauptzollamt Berlin Packhof*; Joined Cases 80 & 81/77, *Commissionnaires réunis and Ramel v. Receveur des douanes.*
24. Joined Cases 141-143/81, *Holdijk*; Case C-146/91, *KYDEP v. Council and Commission;* Case C-336/00, *Huber;* Case C-189/01, *Jippes.* See also Arts. 9, 11, 12 and 13 TFEU. For the limits see Case T-576/08, *Germany v. Commission.*
25. Joined Cases 36 & 71/80, *Irish Creamery Milk Suppliers Association et al. v. Government of Ireland et al.;* Case 297/82, *De Samvirkende Danske Landboforeninger v. Ministry of Fiscal Affairs.*
26. E.g., Case 114/76, *Bela-Mühle Josef Bergmann v. Grows-Farm.* The Court annulled the contested Regulation finding that there was a discriminatory distribution of the burden of costs between the various agricultural sectors, and that the obligation involved was not necessary to attain the objective in view. Temporary precedence can therefore be given to the attainment of one particular objective over another, see e.g. Case C-280/93, *Germany v. Council.*
27. E.g., Case 139/79, *Maizena v. Council;* Case 106/81, *Kind v. EEC;* Case 281/84, *Zuckerfabrik Bedburg v. Council and Commission;* Case C-280/93, *Germany v. Council.*
28. Case 114/76, *Bela-Mühle;* Case 138/78, *Stölting v. Hauptzollamt Frankfurt-Jonas;* Case 237/82, *Jongeneel Kaas.*
29. Cf. Commissions decisions (*European sugar industry*), O.J. 1973, L 140/17 and O.J. 1988, L 262/27 (*Bloemenveilingen Aalsmeer*).
30. See Art. 2 of Reg. 1380/2013.

agricultural products, referring to the list of products contained in Annex I to the TFEU Treaty.[31] The text of both these parts of Article 38 TFEU together with the case law, makes it clear that whether or not a product is on that list is decisive.[32] This limitative list did not, though, prevent products being brought within the scope of application of the Title on Agriculture which are not specified therein, but which are economically or functionally of essential importance to the products which are mentioned therein.[33] A practical consequence of this demarcation of the Title on Agriculture by means of a list of agricultural products is that the TFEU does not make clear what should be understood by the concepts of agricultural holding or producers of agricultural products; this can lead to problems in relation to measures which are not linked to products but to groups of people.[34]

According to the text of Article 38 TFEU and the list of fish, crustaceans and molluscs in Annex I, the provisions of the Title on Agriculture apply to saltwater and freshwater fisheries.

The territorial scope of the common fisheries policy extends to the territorial sea, the economic exclusive zone[35] and for fishing activities of EU-vessels and nationals to third country waters and to the High Sea.

5. Instruments and their development

The basic instruments to achieve the objectives of the common agricultural policy and common fisheries policy are laid down in the TFEU. They have been developed in regulations and directives adopted by the legislator on the basis of the general mandate laid down in Article 43 TFEU.

The main instrument mentioned in the Treaty is the *common organization of agricultural markets* (Art. 40 TFEU), for which three forms, in ascending order of integration, are provided: common rules on competition, coordination of national market organizations and a European market organization. In practice the latter form has taken precedence. A market organization has been defined by the Court as "a totality of legal devices placing the regulation of the market in the products in question under the control of the public authority, with a view to ensuring, by means of an increase in productivity and of optimum utilization of the factors of production, in particular of manpower, a fair standard of living for producers, the stabilization of markets, the assurance of supplies and reasonable prices to the consumers".[36] An important aspect of the common market organization is the obligation to exclude discrimination between producers or consumers (Art. 40(2), second subparagraph).[37] This provision extends the general ban on discrimination on grounds of nationality to discrimination between producers or between consumers, even within Member States. The principle of proportionality between the measures taken and the objectives to be achieved is also laid down in this provision.

31. Case 61/80, *Coöperatieve Stremsel- en Kleurselfabriek v. Commission;* Case 123/83, *BNIC v. Clair,* Case T-61/89, *Dansk Pelsdyravleiforening v. Commission.*
32. Case 61/80, *Coöperatieve Stremsel- en Kleurselfabriek;* Case 77/83, *CILFIT;* Case C-295/88, *Corman v. Belgian State and Grand Duchy of Luxembourg.*
33. Cf. the full list of agricultural products covered by the CMO in Annex I to Reg. 1308/2013, O.J. 2013, L 347/671.
34. As to this problem, see Case 85/77, *Société Azienda Avicola Sant'Anna v. Istituto Nazionale della Previdenza Sociale (INPS) and Servizio Contributi Agricoli Unificati (SCAU);* Case 139/77, *Denkavit v. Finanzamt Warendorf;* Case 312/85, *Villa Banfi v. Regione Toscana,* Case C-162/91, *Tenuta in Bosco v. Ministero delle finanze dello Stato;* Case C-403/98, *Monte Arcosu.*
35. In 1977, the EC – following the example of many third countries – extended its fishing waters to 200 sea miles from the coast, see the so-called The Hague Council Resolution of 29 Oct. 1976, O.J. 1981, C 105/1 (but the important annexes were not published).
36. Case 48/74, *Charmasson.*
37. Case 5/73, *Balkan Import Export;* Case C-306/93, *SMW Winzersekt.*

A second basic instrument is the *structural policy*, not expressly mentioned in the Treaty, but to be deducted from the objectives (especially Art. 39(1)(a) TFEU) and from the obligation to take account of the "structural and natural disparities between the various agricultural regions" when establishing the common agricultural policy (Art. 39(2)(a) TFEU).

A third instrument provided for by the TFEU is the coordination of efforts in the sphere of vocational training, research, dissemination of agricultural knowledge and the promotion of the consumption of certain agricultural products (Art. 41 TFEU).[38]

Finally, two general Treaty instruments have played an important role in establishing the common agricultural policy: the *harmonization of laws* (Art. 43 TFEU) and the *application of the competition rules* (Art. 42 TFEU).

In the more than 50 years of CAP, the above-mentioned instruments of agricultural law have seen an important development, which went as far as introducing a new instrument: the direct income support. We will give a brief sketch of the instruments and their development in the following paragraphs.

5.1 *Common market organization*

The common market organization as a basic instrument of the CAP has been elaborated via a complex and intricate set of Council regulations covering different agricultural products.[39] A detailed description of those regulations would exceed the scope of this book, but it is worthwhile to consider the developments they have undergone.

At the initial stages, the central objective of agricultural policy was to raise productivity. The growth in agricultural production was needed to keep pace with population growth in order to maintain food security. Farmers' incomes were expected to rise as a natural result. To raise productivity a number of market regulation mechanisms were created in the common market organizations: guaranteed common prices; public purchase of agricultural products and public and private storage (intervention), whenever prices were too low; measures to restrict imports and promote exports.[40] Those mechanisms – classical instruments of the former national market organizations – were already mentioned in Article 40(2) EEC.

This policy was so successful that the objective of stabilization of the markets was threatened. Towards the end of the 1970s production exceeded demand, especially for certain basic commodities such as wheat, milk or meat, triggering intervention purchases at guaranteed prices, which in turn led to stocks of surplus commodities known as grain mountains and milk lakes. At this point the need was felt to develop, in the main market organizations, mechanisms to stabilize the markets. In 1984 a system of production quotas for milk and milk products was introduced.[41] Incidentally this mechanism was not new in European agricultural law: the market organization for sugar had known production quotas ever since it had been established.[42] In the market organizations for cereals and beef meat, stabilizing mechanisms were introduced aimed at curbing production once a certain production level was exceeded.[43]

---

38. This instrument is mainly pursued through other instruments of agricultural and fisheries policies as well as through other Union policies (e.g. research).
39. A list can be found in recital 2 of Reg. 1234/2007.
40. See for example Reg. 120/76/EEC, O.J. 1967, 117/2269, English special edition: Series V Chapter 1952–1972 at 21.
41. See Art. 5c of Reg. (EEC) 804/68 as inserted by Reg. (EEC) 856/84, O.J. 1984, L 90/10.
42. See Reg. 1009/76/EEC, O.J. 1967, 308/1, English special edition: Series V Chapter 1967 at 304.
43. These consisted of maximum guaranteed quantities, which, once exceeded, caused intervention prices and/or production subsidies to be reduced, and in some instances increased with a co-responsibility levy. See for example Art. 4a of Reg. (EC) 2727/75 as amended by Reg. (EEC) 1579/86, O.J. 1986, L 139, at 29.

In 1992, the instruments of agricultural policy underwent a third phase of development: an important change from market policy to income policy took place with the introduction of direct premiums for producers, in particular in the market organizations for cereals and certain meat products. These premiums, based on historical production, were granted to wheat producers for setting aside land and to beef producers for keeping (a limited number of) animals. The premiums were intended to compensate for the fact that guaranteed prices were simultaneously being lowered.[44] Direct premiums therefore contained a strong element of income support.

The final phase (for the time being?) has been the introduction of the single payment scheme (SPS) in 2003 (later called Direct Payments Scheme),[45] a further move from market policy to income policy. This entitlement was introduced for the benefit of all farmers, irrespective of the nature or size of their production, provided they held the required acreage of arable land and kept it in good agricultural condition. With the introduction of the SPS, nearly all intervention prices were lowered and made subject to purchase ceilings. A difference with previous reforms is that the SPS has not been introduced as part of the market organizations, but in a separate regulation thereby stressing that it is a different instrument of agricultural policy than the common market organizations.

The reduced importance of the market organizations as an instrument of agricultural policy led in 2007 to their fusion into one common organization of the markets (the so-called single CMO-Regulation), reproducing faithfully the different still existing provisions of those market organizations.[46] In 2009[47] and 2013[48] the regulation was simplified, harmonizing some provisions and improving their presentation, but essentially leaving the instruments of the different market organizations intact.

It can be concluded that as the main instrument of the CAP to attain the objective of ensuring a reasonable standard of living for those working in the agricultural sector, the common organization of the markets has been superseded by other instruments and mainly by the direct income support. This can be seen as a revolution in EU agricultural law and policy.

In fisheries a classical organization of the markets (guaranteed common prices; private storage and regulation of import and export) existed until 2013, when it was brought in line with the CMO in agriculture.[49]

5.2 *Structural measures*

Structural policy aims at improving the structure of European agriculture and fisheries in order to make agricultural and fishery products more competitive on the market. The instrument of structural policy has essentially remained unchanged over the years. It consists of subsidies granted to producers in support of structural measures, which they undertake. Structure has to be considered in a wide sense: it is not only about increasing the size of holdings or the innovation of production methods, but social support and environmental measures are important elements of structural policy. An example is income support to facilitate the closure of holdings or the start-up of new ones. Over the years, measures to protect and improve the environment have played an increasingly important role.

44. Cf. Reg. (EEC) 1765/92, O.J. 1992, L 181, at 12 and Reg. (EEC) 1766/92, O.J. 1992, L 181, at 21. See D. Bianchi, *La politique agricole commune (PAC). Toute la PAC, rien d'autre que la PAC!* (Bruylant, 2006), at 30 et seq.
45. Reg. (EC) 1782/2003, O.J. 2003, L 270, at 1 and Reg. (EU) 1307/2013, O.J. 2013, L 347/608.
46. Reg. 1234/2007. See R. Mögele and F. Erlbacher, *The Single Common Market Organisation* (C.H. Beck, 2011).
47. Reg. 72/2009.
48. Reg. 1308/2013.
49. Reg. (EU) 1379/2013.

Structural policy in agriculture began to acquire real importance after 1988, in the framework of the limitation of the expenditure for market measures and the increase in the expenditure in the context of the Structural Funds in order to improve economic and social cohesion.

From the very beginning, structural measures have taken mainly the form of indirect Union support. This means that the decision to create certain support schemes is taken at Union level, while the Member States decide if and how to apply them to their own producers. The Member States have to bear a proportion of the support they grant, as the Union does not cover the full 100%.

The legal form of these instruments has changed over time. Initially there was a clear preference for directives, but since the integration of Union policy on agricultural structures into the overall Community structural policy, regulations have taken over.

The structural measures in the fisheries sector – always in the form of indirect Union support – have, since the beginning in 1983,[50] rested on two pillars: on the one hand measures for the modernization, renewal and development of the fleet and the port infrastructure as well as for the development of aquaculture. On the other hand measures were taken to keep the fishing capacity in line with the available fish stocks. With the declining fish stocks the latter pillar became more and more important so that the modernization and renewal of the fleet became increasingly conditional upon the strict respect of measures restricting the fishing capacity.

5.3 *Approximation of laws*

As mentioned earlier, the rules of the common market apply to agriculture and fishery (Art. 38 TFEU). This implies the free movement of agricultural products (Art. 34 TFEU). However, Member States are entitled to introduce restrictions in order to protect the health and life of humans, animals and plants (Art. 36 TFEU). Member States have indeed used this prerogative in the past to combat animal and plant disease or take measures in respect of plant protection products. The measures taken have varied from Member State to Member State, and restricted the intracommunity trade as certain products marketed in one Member State did not meet the marketing requirements of another.

The TFEU provides for a general tool to approximate laws, which is intended to eliminate such restrictions (Art. 114). Since the ECJ has ruled that agricultural legislation can be approximated on the basis of Article 43 TFEU,[51] approximation has become another instrument of agricultural law. Before the Maastricht Treaty (1991), the latter legal basis had the advantage of enabling the Council to take decisions on the basis of a qualified majority, while under Article 100 EEC providing for approximation of laws in general, decisions had to be taken unanimously. Since that Treaty, Article 43 TFEU differs from Article 114 TFEU in that it does not enable the Member States to maintain or introduce stricter provisions than those contained in harmonized legislation.

At first, approximation was an uphill struggle, mainly because of the unanimity requirement. However, the Europe 1992[52] programme and the introduction of qualified majority voting speeded up the process considerably. Around 1992 many directives were introduced that harmonized national legislation on animal and plant disease,[53] animal welfare[54] and plant protection

50. Reg. 2908/83, O.J. 1983, L 290/1. At the moment Reg. (EU) 508/2014.
51. Case 68/86, *United Kingdom v. Council.*
52. European Commission: White Paper on completing the internal market, COM(85)310 final.
53. See for instance the Veterinary Directives 91/492 to 91/498, O.J 1991, L 268, and Directive 92/33/EEC, O.J. 1992, L 157/1.
54. Directives 91/628–91/360, O.J. 1991, L 340.

products,[55] giving a boost to the free movement of agricultural products. The Member States could still restrict this free movement, but only within the limits set by various Community directives.

Over the following years the Community gradually limited the freedom these directives left to the Member States, in particular as a result of the BSE crisis, the ultimate result of which was a common policy implemented by the Member States.[56] This development was fostered by the fact that by the 1997 Amsterdam Treaty a provision was included in the Treaty (now Art. 168(4)(b) TFEU) under which the Council and the Parliament were given powers to adopt veterinary and phytosanitary measures directly aimed at protecting public health. This has resulted, among other things, in four regulations designed to promote food safety.[57]

The same development as with the structural measures has taken place with regard to the shift in legal instruments from directives to regulations, the latter being directly applicable and therefore, not necessitating implementation by the Member States, which simplified their application.

5.4 *Competition rules*

Article 42 TFEU states that the competition rules are applicable only to the extent determined by the legislator. With regard to state aid, in different legislative acts Articles 107–109 TFEU are declared applicable.[58] The Commission's guidelines on how it would assess state aid in the light of these articles direct the national structural aid along the lines of the Union's structural policy.[59] Commission Regulation No. 702/2014 declares certain categories of state aid compatible with the state aid rules.[60] However, national aid granted in accordance with the Regulations on rural development support and on structural measures in the fisheries sector is expressly declared not to constitute state aid under Articles 107 to 109 TFEU.[61]

With regard to cartels, the common market organizations declare Articles 101 to 106 TFEU in principle applicable, but special rules have been provided for in respect of certain agreements and decisions of producer organizations, whereby certain objectives of agricultural or fishery policy are pursued.[62]

6. Pillars of the actual agricultural law

European agricultural law currently rests on five pillars: direct income support; regulation of the markets; rural development support; promotion of product quality and measures combating animal and plant diseases and promoting animal welfare.

---

55. Directive 91/414/EEC of 15 July 1991, O.J. 1991, L 230/1.
56. See for example Reg. (EC) 999/2001, O.J. 2001, L 147/1.
57. Regs. (EC) 852/2004 to 854/2004, O.J. 2004, L 139; Reg. (EC) 882/2004, O.J. 2004, L 165/1.
58. Art. 211 (1) of Reg. 1308/2013; Art. 8 of Reg. 508/2014. However, Articles 107–109 TFEU do not apply to certain national payments which under Reg. 1308/2013 are (partially) financed by the Union (Art. 211 (2)(a) of Reg. 1308/2013).
59. 59 Community guidelines for State aid in the agriculture and forestry sector 2014 to 2020, O.J. 2014, C 204/1.
60. O.J. 2014, L 193/1.
61. Art. 81(2) Reg. 1305/2013 and Art. 8 (2) Reg. 508/2014, O.J. 2014, L 149/1.
62. Arts. 206–210 of Reg. (EU) 1308/2013, O.J. 2013, L 347/760; Arts. 40 and 41 of Reg. 1379/2013. See also Guidelines on the application of the specific rules set out in Arts. 169, 170 and 171 of the CMO Reg. for the olive oil, beef and veal and arable crops sectors, O.J. 2015, C 431/1.

6.1 *Direct income support*

Direct income support is nowadays the most important instrument of agricultural policy. It pursues the objective laid down in Article 39(1)(b) TFEU, i.e. ensure a fair standard of living, in particular by increasing the individual earning of farmers. As mentioned above, direct income support has been developed over the years as a compensation for the decrease in market support.

The basic payment scheme is the most important support measure. Under this scheme, support from the Union budget is granted to active farmers in order to keep their income at an acceptable level. To that end each active farmer has been allocated payment entitlements corresponding to the number of eligible hectares which are at his disposal, irrespective of the products or quantities he produces.[63] This makes the scheme "WTO proof", which was a condition to prepare the agricultural policy for the likely outcome of the Doha-Round negotiations under the auspices of the World Trade Organization. The rules of the WTO would no longer allow States to have product-linked support measures in agriculture above a certain threshold. The unit value of the payment entitlement is calculated by dividing a fixed percentage for each Member State of the national envelop for direct payments laid down in the Regulation by the total number of payment entitlements in the Member State.[64] Member States may apply this system on a regional basis. This means that, apart for the exceptions provided for, every farmer will have in principle the same support per hectare on a national or regional basis. This is different than under the single payment system, the previous direct support scheme, under which the value of the payment entitlements could vary between farmers according to their historic support level or to differences between regions.[65] A transitional system running until 2019 is instituted for the Member States which in 2014 have applied the single payment system.[66] Another transitional system running until 2021 governs the Member States[67] which applied, in 2014, the single area payment scheme according to which the value of the farmer's payment entitlement was fixed by dividing the total amount of direct payments by the total acreage of agricultural land in the Member State, eventually adapted through a certain percentage.[68]

In addition to the basic payments, the Member States have the option to grant other direct aid: redistributive payments, payment for agricultural practices beneficial for the climate and the environment, payment for areas with natural constraints and payment for young farmers.[69] Finally, support linked to production may be granted to certain important agricultural sectors or products, which undergo certain difficulties.[70]

To qualify for all types of direct income support, farmers must render public services, respect certain rules regarding the environment, animal and public health and animal welfare (a requirement known as "cross-compliance") and must observe best agricultural practices.[71] Failure to meet these requirements results, in principle, in a reduction or exclusion of the support.[72]

---

63. See Art. 24(2) of Reg. 1307/2013, O.J. 2013, L 347/608.
64. Art. 25 of Reg. 1307/2013.
65. See Arts. 43, 58, 59 and 63–65 of Reg. 1782/2003 and Arts. 33, 46 and 47 of Reg. 73/2009, O.J. 2009, L 30/16.
66. Art. 26 of Reg. 1307/2013.
67. Those which acceded to the Union in 2004, 2007 and 2013.
68. Art. 122 of Reg. 73/2009.
69. Arts. 41, 43 et seq., 48 and 50 of Reg. 1307/2013.
70. Arts. 52 and 56 of Reg. 1307/2013.
71. Arts. 93 and 94 of Reg. 1306/2013, O.J. 2013, L 347/592.
72. Arts. 97 and 99 of Reg. 1306/2013.

6.2 Regulation of the market

The regulation of the agricultural markets is the main objective of the common organization of the markets. After the liberalization of the agricultural policy at the beginning of this century, market regulation was reduced to some basic instruments, necessary to permit the markets to operate smoothly, which are laid down in the CMO-Regulation:[73] rules on market intervention (public intervention, private storage, aid schemes for certain sectors, planting rights for vines), marketing rules (marketing standards, designation of origin and labelling of wine, contracts for sugar and milk, sugar quotas (until 2017), rules for producers' and interbranch organizations), rules on trade with third countries (import and export licences, import duties, tariff quota, export refunds) and competition rules specific to agriculture.

The rules on market intervention have the function of a safety net: in the case of an extreme fall of market prices products can be taken off the market through intervention buying by the public sector or private storage.

Rationalizing the agricultural production is the aim of the marketing rules. Their importance increases in a more and more liberalized market.

Export refunds have been a long-standing classical instrument of market regulation: surplus products were disposed of on the world market with a subsidy to compensate for the difference in price between the prices in the Union and the world market. The instrument can now be operated only in the case of market disturbance or specific problems in a sector.

6.3 Rural development support

Rural development policy is the second pillar of the agricultural policy next to the common organization of the markets and direct payment system, which form the first pillar. It encompasses the agricultural structural policy and emphasizes, through its name, the broad framework for such policy.

Rural development financial support is granted to projects which can be brought under one of the six priority areas indicated in Regulation No. 1305/2013.[74] [75] The choice of the projects is with the Member States. Each Member State draws up, at the beginning of the seven year programming period (2014–2020), a programme of the categories of measures which it wants to promote. The programme has to be approved by the Commission. Union support is granted via the Member State to projects which are featured in the programme, are approved by the Member State and have received also Member State financial support.

6.4 Promotion of product quality

Product quality has become increasingly important since agricultural policy has become more liberalized and the farmers are submitted to market forces. On the European market, farmers can get added value for their products and therefore a better income by producing quality products rather than bulk products. The promotion of product quality is a "common action to develop the consumption of agricultural products in the sense of Art. 41 under (b) TFEU". Since recent years it is an important element of the CAP.

---

73. Reg. 1308/2013. See for an analysis of the 2009 CMO, op. cit. *supra* note 46.
74. O.J. 2013, L 347/487.
75. These priority areas are: fostering knowledge transfer and innovation, enhancing farm viability and competitiveness, promoting food chain organization, restoring, preserving and enhancing ecosystems, promoting resource efficiency and supporting the shift towards a low carbon and climate resilient economy and promoting resource efficiency, and supporting the shift towards a low carbon and climate resilient economy (Art. 5 of Reg. 1305/2013).

The main instrument of the policy is the system of protected designations of origin, protected geographical indications and traditional specialities,[76] which has been created to encourage producers in a particular area or of a traditional speciality to define the distinctive character of their products and to protect their designation of origin, their geographical indication or traditional speciality. These products constitute an important asset that expresses the distinctive character of European agriculture. Inclusion in the Union registers of protected designations of origin and protected geographical indications or traditional specialities restricts their use to well-defined groups of producers in a way similar to the protection of intellectual property. In this way, the system gives consumers the assurance of the qualitative characteristics of the products.

Rules on organic farming constitute another instrument of promoting the quality of agricultural products.[77] These rules restrict the use of the label "organic" to products made by using specific methods, subject to a set of prescribed control procedures. The purpose is to encourage organic production by giving a quality label to the product, and to ensure consumers that these labelled products are really organic.

Finally, marketing standards have been defined under the common market organization, giving an indication of the quality of the products in question.[78]

6.5 *Measures combating animal and plant diseases and promoting animal welfare*

As mentioned earlier, the Union has issued regulations and directives laying down the measures Member States are to take to combat and prevent animal and plant diseases as well as Union measures to promote animal welfare. Their primary aim is to ensure that any restrictions on the free movement of agricultural products are kept to a minimum. An evenly important agricultural policy objective is the safeguarding of agricultural production and consumer confidence in the safety of products. The BSE crisis in the 1990s was exemplary in this regard. The disease not only caused extensive hindrances of intra-community trade, but through the massive destruction of cattle and the loss of confidence of consumers also a large drop in the production of beef products, thereby causing an important income reduction for certain farmers.

For this reason on the basis of rather summarily described emergency powers, the Union, in particular the Commission, has taken the lead in organizing the fight against animal and plant diseases leaving the Member States more and more in the role of implementing Union measures.

Rules on animal welfare reflect the integration of the considerations referred to in Article 13 TFEU in agricultural policy. The aim from the viewpoint of agricultural policy lies in the promotion of positive consumer perception towards meat products and of the quality of the products when animals are feeling better.

At this point the measures protecting feed and food safety, already referred to above,[79] can be mentioned. They are situated at the border between agricultural, health and consumer policy, combining elements of all those policies.

7. Pillars of the actual fisheries law

Since the origin of the fisheries policy of the EU in the 1970s, the pillars of fisheries law have been: conservation of fish stocks, fleet restructuring, market regulation and international

76. Regs. (EU) 110/2008, O.J. 2008, L 39/16 and 1151/2012, O.J. 2012, L 343/1.
77. Reg. (EC) 834/2007, O.J. 2007, L 189/1 and implementing Reg. (EC) 889/2008, O.J. 2008, L 250/1.
78. See Reg. 543/2011, O.J. 2011, L 157/1.
79. See section 5.3.

relations. After the last 10-yearly reform of the policy those matters still determine the law of fisheries in the EU.

7.1 Conservation

Conservation of fish stocks is an essential pillar of every fisheries policy. Fish stocks are precious resources which have to be kept in a good state in order to be able to reap the benefits from them. This has been especially noticed since the last decade of the last century, when scientific studies revealed that many fish stocks were in danger of collapse. This situation still exists.[80]

The classical instrument to preserve fish stocks is to limit the catches. Every year the Council fixes, in a regulation under Article 43 (3) TFEU, the total amount of fish that may be taken from a fish stock, a fish stock being a certain fish species within a predetermined geographical area (e.g. herring in area ICES IV = the North Sea). That amount is called the total allowable catch (TAC). The TAC is distributed among the Member States according to a percentage key. On this basis the Member States obtain a quota of the fish – expressed in tons or species – which their vessels may catch from a certain fish stock during that year. The percentage key is determined on the basis of the catches of the relevant fish stock by the vessels of a Member State in a given historical period. For most fish stocks that period goes back to the years 1975–1977.[81] This is called the principle of relative stability.[82] The percentage key is stable, but the quantity of fish that may be fished every year fluctuates according to the TAC figure.

A complement to the TAC and quota system is the limitation of fishing effort.[83] The observance of the quota is difficult, in particular in sea areas where more than one species can be fished by the same vessels. Restricting the time a vessel may fish in such an area is then a complementary instrument to limit catches.

The continuous depletion of fish stocks demonstrated that the yearly fixing of the TAC, quota and fishing effort were not the most effective instruments for the conservation and management of fisheries. For that reason a system of multiannual management plans for the most perished fish stocks has been introduced.[84] These plans establish objective criteria for the fixing of the TAC and total fishing effort for one or more fish stocks with the objective of re-establishing the state of the fish stock. The criteria are linked to the evolution of the mortality rate of the stock so that the variation in the mortality rate is reflected in the level of the TAC and fishing effort.

The 2013 reform of the fisheries policy has brought a new instrument for the conservation of fish stocks: the landing obligation.[85] It appeared that much fish was discarded immediately after the catch because it was undesired "by-catch", outwith the quota, commercially not interesting and/or not corresponding to the minimum size. An obligation to land all caught fish should encourage fishermen to improve the selectivity of their fishing techniques.

So-called technical measures constitute a last instrument to preserve fish stocks.[86] These measures are aimed to protect juvenile fish and concern the technics of fishing (mainly fishing gear), but include also temporary or permanent bans of fishing in certain areas. The aim of

---

80. European Commission Green Paper "Reform of the Common Fisheries Policy", Doc. COM(2009)163 final.
81. See Reg. 172/83, O.J. 1983, L 24/30 fixing for the first time the percentage key.
82. See C-61/96, *Spain v. Council*.
83. Reg. 1954/2003, O.J. 2003, L 289/1.
84. Art. 9 ff of Reg. 1380/2013, O.J. 2013, L 354/33.
85. Art. 15 of Reg. 1380/2013, O.J. 2013, L 354/35.
86. Reg. 850/98, O.J. 1998, L 125/1.

these measures is to limit the catch of fish which is too young to be able to reproduce, causing a decrease of the stock.

7.2 *Fleet restructuring*

Structural policy in fisheries concentrates mainly on the fishing fleet. A balance has to be found between the necessary modernization of the vessels and the restriction of the fishing capacity of the fleet. The profitability of the sector needs modern, more efficient vessels, while those modern vessels have a larger fishing capacity and therefore could form a danger for the conservation of the fish stocks. The instruments for this policy reflect this balance: aid for modernization of vessels on the one hand and a strict regime of limiting the access of new vessels to the fleet.[87]

Other structural measures are directed to the sustainable development of the fisheries and aquaculture sectors.[88]

7.3 *International relations*

European Union fisheries policy finds its origin in the unilateral declaration by third countries that the exploitation of fisheries and other resources within the 200-mile zone from their coast would be reserved for nationals of the coastal state. Breaking with the existing principle of the *mare librum,* access to the 200-mile zone was forbidden for vessels from other countries. This practice has been codified in 1982 in the Convention on the Law of the Sea.[89]

For the European Community the declaration of the 200-mile zone in the Atlantic Ocean and the North Sea by neighbouring countries meant the loss of rich fishing grounds. Therefore, in an action coordinated by the European Community, the Member States on their part declared a 200-mile zone in the Atlantic Ocean and the North Sea and prohibited the access of vessels of third countries to their zones.[90] Traditional fishing patterns were preserved through the conclusion of agreements between the European Community and the neighbouring third countries, in particular Norway, granting each other's vessels access to their respective waters on the basis of a quota (reciprocal access agreements) and organizing the common management of certain common fish stocks.[91]

Community vessels are active in all the oceans and therefore agreements also needed to be concluded with different states around the world, in order for Union vessels to be able to continue or to expand their fishing activities. Those agreements targeting mainly the catch of wide-ranging fish species like tuna, fix the tonnage of Union vessels allowed to fish in the exclusive zone of the third countries for a number of years, the technical conditions for the access and the financial compensation. The compensation is partly paid by the vessel owners through the price for fishing licences and partly by the Union budget. The latter part of the financial compensation must, for an agreed amount, be spent on structural measures in the fishing sector in the third country involved (partnership agreements).[92]

Fisheries agreements are concluded by the European Union as a consequence of the declaration by the Court of Justice in the *Kramer* judgment that the exploitation of the living resources of the sea is an exclusive Union competence.[93] That judgment has been codified in Article 3(1)

87. See Reg. 508/2014, O.J. 2014, L 149/1 and Art. 22 et seq. of Reg. 1380/2013, O.J. 2013, L 354/39.
88. See Art. 24 et seq. of Reg. 508/2014, O.J. 2014, L 149/1.
89. O.J. 1998, L 179/1.
90. Cited *supra* note 35.
91. Agreement with Norway, O.J. 1980, L 226/47.
92. Art. 32 of Reg. 1380/2013, O.J. 2013, L 354/22.
93. Joined Cases 3, 4 and 6/76, *Kramer and others.*

(d) TFEU. The exclusive competence makes the EU also a contracting party to regional fisheries organizations.[94] Those organizations regulate the fisheries in different parts of the oceans. Member States may only be members of such organizations when the scope of the organization is wider than the conservation of fisheries resources.[95]

On account of its exclusive competence in matters of conservation of marine resources, the European Union is a contracting party to certain agreements on fisheries matters concluded on a global scale. The most important of those agreements is the Convention on the Law of the Sea[96] and the implementing agreement relating to the conservation and management of straddling stocks and highly migratory fish stocks.[97] Both agreements are mixed agreements, the first one also covering matters other than fisheries, such as the environment and deep sea mining, the latter for the control issues incorporated in the agreement.[98]

7.4 *Market regulation*

The common organization of the markets in fish and fishery products[99] relies heavily on the role of producer organizations. Their main instruments for the regulation of the markets are the establishment of catch plans and the purchase of fish for destruction or for the production of fishmeal when the market price goes below a certain yearly fixed level for each fish species. Imports are regulated in the CMO through a reference price.

8. Decision making

Since the Lisbon Treaty is the legislative procedure also applicable to agriculture and fisheries (Art. 43(2)). Until that Treaty the Council decided solely, with Parliament acting in an advisory role.[100] However, Article 43(3) TFEU provides for decisions by the Council without involvement of the European Parliament.

The legislative procedure is prescribed for "the establishment of the common organisation of the markets and the other provisions necessary for the attainment of the objectives of the common agricultural (and fisheries) policy". Therefore, the general policy lines have to be laid down by acts of the Council and European Parliament together. Under Article 43(3) the Council is authorized, without involvement of the European Parliament, to establish the measures on fixing prices, levies, aid and quantitative limitations as well as on the fixing and allocation of fishing opportunities. The distinction between these measures and those which are the subject of the legislative acts is not completely clear. The Court has declared that measures entailing a political choice are to be adopted under the legislative procedure, while the measures referred to in Article 43(3) TFEU are mainly of a technical nature and intended to implement the policy

94. For an overview see R. Churchill and D. Owen, *The EC Common Fisheries Policy* (OUP, 2010), at 359 et seq. and T. van Rijn, "Anhang Art. 38–44 AEUV" in von der H. Groeben, J. Schwarze and A. Hatje (Eds.), *Europäisches Unionsrecht*,, 7th ed. (Nomos, 2015).
95. See the GFCM, the fisheries organization of the Mediterranean Sea (industry policy objectives), O.J. 1998, L 190/34 and CCAMLR, fisheries organization of the Antarctic (environmental objectives) O.J. 1981, L 252/26.
96. O.J. 1998, L 179/1.
97. O.J. 1998, L 189/14.
98. However, those aspects are purely accessory to the substance of the Agreement. Moreover, rules regulating the way Member States have to organize the control on fishing activities are extensively laid down in Reg. (EC) 1224/2009.
99. Reg. 1379/2013, O.J. 2013, L 354/1.
100. See Art. 37(2) EC.

measures adopted under Article 43(2).[101] There is no hierarchical relationship between acts adopted under Article 43(2) and measures adopted under Article 43(3); therefore, the Council may adopt measures under the last provision even if the legislator has not established a legal framework for the subject in question.[102]

The legislative acts have attributed powers to the Commission to complement provisions of those acts through delegated acts and to lay down common provisions for the application of the acts through implementing acts. Council acts under Article 43(3) also attribute powers to the Commission to implement those acts.[103]

9. Implementation, application, control

Under Article 291 TFEU the Member States have to take the measures necessary for the implementation and application of Union acts. Although in the agricultural and fisheries fields the Union legislative, delegated and implementing acts are very detailed, implementing rules by the Member States are necessary to regulate the application of the Union acts. Member States have to set up the administrative structure capable of granting direct payments and other aids to agricultural producers, of organizing the purchase of intervention and public and private storage of agricultural products, of granting subsidies to producer organizations, for rural development projects and structural reform of the fishing fleet, of managing the fishing quota system and finally of controlling the observance by beneficiaries and other producers of the obligations laid down in Union legislation.

The control function is very important because of the amount of Union money involved. Therefore, the way the control has to be exercised is specified in Union regulations in great detail.[104] Those regulations also contain provisions on the administrative sanctions Member States have to apply in cases of non-compliance. In the agricultural area the sanctions are of a pecuniary nature and distinguish according to the gravity of the infringement.[105] In the fisheries area the Union has established a list of serious infringements and has specified the non-pecuniary sanctions the Member States have to apply as a minimum.[106]

10. Financing

Expenditure for direct payments and the regulation of the agricultural and fishery markets is financed from the European Agricultural Guarantee Fund (EAGF), which forms part of the EU budget. The dimension of the EAGF – and therefore the maximal admissible expenditure – is fixed for each year in the multi-annual financial framework 2014–2020.[107] The amounts are lower than in the past seven years, but still form about 40% of the EU budget.

Rules regarding the financial management of the EAGF are laid down in the basic regulation on the financing of the CAP.[108] Expenditure is carried out by *paying agencies* designated by the Member States; these are charged with the approval of payment requests for the numerous subsidies, the bookkeeping and the organization of administrative and physical checks. Finan-

101. Joined Cases C-103/12 & C-165/12, *European Parliament and Commission v. Council*; C-124/13 & C-125/13, *European Parliament and Commission v. Council.*
102. See Case C-113/14, *Germany v. European Parliament and Council.*
103. E.g. Art. 2(3) of Council Reg. 1370/2013, O.J. 2013, L 346/12.
104. See for instance Arts. 67–74 and 96–102 of Reg. (EU) 1306/2013 and Reg. (EC) 1224/2009.
105. Art. 97 of Reg. (EU) 1306/2013, O.J. 2013, L 347/549.
106. Arts. 3, 42 and 45 of Reg. 1005/2008, O.J. 2008, L 286/1.
107. Reg. 1311/2013, O.J. 2013, L 347/884.
108. See Reg. (EU) 1306/2013, O.J. 2013, L 347/549.

cing takes place by means of advances made available to the Member States by the Commission. At the end of each financial year, the Member States forward to the Commission their annual statement of expenditure together with an attestation regarding the completeness, accuracy and veracity of the accounts transmitted. On the basis of this statement, the Commission operates two audit procedures: it controls the financial reports (clearance of accounts) and it verifies whether the material conditions for granting the expenses and their control have been respected (conformity clearance). Each year the latter procedure leads to reductions in the financial allocations for many Member States. This procedure is an effective way to promote observance of Union law by the Member States, much more so than the infringement procedure laid down in Article 258 TFEU. The financial regulation provides for a dispute settlement procedure in case the Member States do not agree with the envisaged reductions. The final decision of the Commission may be appealed to the Court of Justice, which has led to a large amount of case law over the years, in which the Court has defined further the consequences of the strict liability of the Member States for payments made in breach of Union legislation.[109] The clearance of accounts procedure concerns exclusively the Member States and the Commission; individuals have no possibility to challenge, before the Community courts, decisions relating to this procedure, even if they are indirectly affected by such decisions.[110]

The expenditure on rural development is channelled through the European Agricultural Fund for Rural Development (EAFRD). The Fund is part of the Union budget and its finances are fixed – on the basis of the Union's multi-annual financial framework 2014–2020 – in Regulation No. 1305/2013, which also determines the repartition of the amounts between the Member States.[111] The European Maritime and Fisheries Fund regulates the expenditure for structural measures in the fisheries and aquaculture field.[112] Both Funds are governed by the common rules laid down for the European Structural and Investment funds.[113]

11. Outlook

As the objectives of the CAP are chiselled into stone in the TFEU, the policy instruments will not vary much in the future: on the one hand instruments of income policy, mainly direct income support and market support, and on the other hand structural policy measures, including quality policy. However, because of budgetary constraints and the wishes of Member States to set their own priorities within their respective budgets, there will be a tendency to decentralize more elements to the Member States. This will raise the question of up to which point will decentralization be possible without creating unequal treatment between producers and a distortion of the internal market. Indeed, the objective of maintaining the internal market is a fundamental Treaty objective and has to be respected in all instances. That objective will necessitate laying down the main features of agricultural income and structural policies in Union acts. A Union policy of combating diseases and promoting animal welfare will also remain necessary for the good functioning of the internal market. Finally, environmental policy considerations will occupy an increasingly important place in the future CAP.

---

109. See e.g. Case C-247/98, *Greece v. Commission* and Case C-373/99, *Greece v. Commission.*
110. Joined Cases 89 & 91/86, *Étoile commerciale and CNTA v. Commission;* Case T-244/00, *Coillte Teoranta v. Commission.*
111. Art. 58 and Annex I of Reg. 1305/2013.
112. Reg. 508/2014, O.J. 2014, L 149/1.
113. Reg. 1303/2013, O.J. 2013, L 347/320.

The main objective of the common fisheries policy, the conservation of the fish stocks, will probably not change over the coming years, as the depletion of many stocks is still a real danger. This makes the actual instruments a necessity for the future.

Further reading

Andreoso-O'Callaghan, B., *The Economics of European Agriculture* (Springer, 2003).

Bianchi, D., *La politique agricole commune (PAC)* (Bruylant, 2012).

Churchill, R. and D. Owen, *The EC Common Fisheries Policy* (OUP, 2010).

Danielson, J.H., *EU Agricultural Law* (Kluwer, 2013).

Hill, B., *Understanding the Common Agricultural Policy* (Routledge, 2012).

McMahon, J.A. and M.N. Cardwell, *Research Handbook on EU Agricultural Law* (Edward Elgar Publishing, 2015).

Mögele, R. and F. Erlbacher (Eds.), *Single Common Market Organisation – Article by Article Commentary of the Legal Framework for Agricultural Markets in the European Union* (C.H. Beck/Hart Publishing/Nomos, 2011).

Norer, R. (Ed.), *Handbuch des Agrarrechts*, 2nd ed. (Springer, 2012).

van Rijn, T., "Article 38–44 AEUV" in von der H. Groeben, J. Schwarze and A. Hatje (Eds.), *Europäisches Unionsrecht*, 7th ed. (Nomos, 2015).

Wakefield, J., *Reforming the Common Fisheries Policy* (Edward Elgar Publishing, 2016).

CHAPTER 31
TRANSPORT POLICY

*Pablo Mendes de Leon**

1. Particularities of transport services

The transport chains and modes keep the EU internal market together, and form the basis for external links. The transport sector comprises five modes, to wit road, rail, inland waterways, maritime and air transport. The operation of transport services is a complex, multifaceted economic and cross border activity.

The transport sector significantly depends on infrastructure and the associated differences of cost allocation. This allocation does not take place in the same way in each Member State, despite being linked with the common transport policy, particularly in respect of road transport, which is by far the most used mode of transport,[1] and rail transport. Moreover, it does not take place in the same way within the various Member States. Hence, the existence of strongly divergent national intervention systems has affected the establishment of a common transport policy. Thus, national railways are still subsidized in virtually all of the Member States.[2] The waterway transport sector is far less significant; the problems in this sector are primarily caused by the relatively small size of the sector. Finally, the international character of sea and air transport requires special attention.

2. The development of a common transport policy

The framers of the EEC Treaty felt it necessary to establish a common policy for the transport sector.[3] The special status of transport in the Treaty was due to the fact that the transport sector was highly regulated in the original Member States. The TFEU also deals with transport in a separate Title.

The transport policy proceeds from a regulated market economy orientation in which price and capacity rules from the national regulatory system have largely disappeared. It does not only focus on liberalizing market access but also on other objectives including the protection of safety, security, the environment and passengers, and the conduct of social and external policies. In

---

* Law Faculty, University of Leiden. The author is grateful to Miss Merinda Stewart and Mr Benjamyn Scott, both holding an Advanced LLM degree in Air and Space Law at the University of Leiden, for their accurate and comprehensive contribution to the completion of this Chapter.

1. See EU Commission, *Road Freight Transport Vademecum* (2010), confirming that road transport is the most used means of transport but also reveals a stronger recover of the other (less used) inland means of transport.
2. See M. Scharf in L. Hancher, T.R. Ottervanger, and P.J. Slot, *E.U. State Aids*, 4th ed. (Sweet & Maxwell, 2012), Ch. 17–35, 524.
3. See Art. 3(1)(e) EC.

addition, the role of the EU in the world has changed dramatically since the original six Member States set out to develop a common transport policy, and the EU's transport policy increasingly reflects this trend.[4]

3. The relationship between the general principles of the TFEU and the special provisions of the transport title

The Transport Title contains no provisions regulating this relationship. Article 58(1) TFEU provides that the free movement of services in the field of transport is governed by the provisions in the title relating to Transport. In a transport policy case,[5] the Court ruled that pursuant to Article 91(1)(a) and (b) TFEU, the Council is obliged to bring about the free movement of services in the transport sector. Otherwise, the general treaty rules are applicable to transport, as confirmed in various judgments.[6]

The Court of Justice decided in *Corsica Ferries I* that on the basis of Article 100(2) TFEU, the freedom to provide services in the areas covered by that provision needed to be implemented by the Council.[7] For these sectors, the use of Article 18 TFEU as a legal basis for the application of the freedom to provide services is excluded.[8] The Court's ruling in the same transport policy case also made it clear that Articles 56 and 57 TFEU are not directly applicable in the transport sector: specific measures were needed.

The non-discrimination principle laid down in Article 18 TFEU cannot provide a legal basis for the realization of the freedom to provide services in this area. While it is true that as a general rule of the Treaty,[9] Article 18 applies to transport,[10] questions relating to the freedom to provide services in the transport sector fall under Articles 90, 91 and 100(2) TFEU by virtue of Article 58(1) TFEU – as the Court has confirmed in *Corsica Ferries II*.[11]

4. Principal provisions of the title on transport

4.1 *Establishment of a common transport policy*

Article 90 TFEU confirms the rule laid down in Article 58(1) that the freedom to provide services in the field of transport is to be achieved in the context of the common transport policy. It also places that policy in the perspective of the general objectives of the TFEU.

The Commission has produced various papers and communications elaborating the common transport policy.[12] The concept was extensively discussed in the transport policy case,[13] in which the common transport policy was described as "a coherent set of rules".[14] The importance of a correct definition of the concept was somewhat diminished by the Court's conclusion that it was for the Council to determine the objectives and means of that policy. As a result of that

4. See *infra* section 5.4 on external relations.
5. Case 13/83, *Parliament v. Council* at para 64.
6. Case 167/73, *Commission v. France*; Case 156/77, *Commission v. Belgium*; Joined Cases 209-213/84, *Ministère public v. Asjes*; Case 66/86, *Ahmed Saeed Flugreisen v. Zentrale zur Bekämpfung unlauteren Wettbewerbs.*
7. Case C-49/89, *Corsica Ferries France v. Direction générale des douanes.*
8. Case C-18/93, *Corsica Ferries Italia.*
9. Case 167/73, *Commission v. France.*
10. See Opinion of A.G. van Gerven, in Case C-18/93, *Corsica Ferries v. Corpo dei piloti del porto di Genova.*
11. Case C-18/93, *Corsica Ferries v. Corpo dei piloti del porto di Genova.*
12. Of which the most important one is the White Paper, "Roadmap to the single European Transport Area", COM(2011)0144 final, 28 Mar. 2011.
13. Case 13/83, *Parliament v. Council.*
14. At para 46.

judgment, the Council proceeded to draw up programmes for the achievement of a common policy in the various branches of transport.[15]

4.2 *Articulation of the characteristics of transport*

Article 91(1)(a) and (b) prescribe that in any event common rules must be established for international transport to or from the territory of a Member State or passing across the territory of one or more Member States, and that those rules must be established for the conditions under which non-resident carriers may operate transport services within – another – Member State (*cabotage*). According to the Court, liberalization measures may be based on Article 91(1)(d) TFEU while "taking into account the distinctive features of transport" in the first sentence of Article 91(1) TFEU.[16] Hence, the Council has a wide margin of discretion on this point.[17] The Council may decide what degree of market intervention is necessary.

4.3 *Equal treatment of transporters*

Article 92 TFEU obliges the Member States not to introduce provisions which make the conditions of transport for undertakings from other Member States less favourable.[18] In Case C-195/90, *Commission v. Germany*, the Court gave a broad interpretation of this obligation designed to place carriers on an equal footing with national undertakings. The same provision is directly effective[19] and ceases to have effect when the measures specified in Article 91(1) TFEU are adopted.

4.4 *Measures on State aid*

Article 93 TFEU provides that aid measures which meet the needs of coordination of transport, or which represent reimbursement "for the discharge of certain obligations inherent in the concept of a public service" are compatible with the Treaty; these principles are further elaborated in Regulation 1370/2007,[20] pursuant to which national authorities may allow for the provision of services of general interest which are more numerous, safer, of a higher quality or provided at lower cost than those that market forces alone would have permitted. Operators of such public service obligations may be compensated for their service provision under the conditions laid down in this regulation. The regulation applies to operators of national and international rail and other track-based modes of transport, and of road transport; EU States may apply it to providers of inland waterways and national sea waters.[21]

Article 93 supplements the exceptions to the prohibition on State aid listed in Article 107(2) and (3) TFEU, and may also be seen as an exception to Article 106(2) TFEU.[22] Articles 107 and 108 TFEU are otherwise applicable to the transport sector.[23] Moreover, the provisions in the

15. The most recent one being: EU Commission, "Roadmap to a single European Air Transport Area", COM(2011)0144.
16. In the *transport policy* case, see Case 13/83, *Parliament v. Council.*
17. The Court confirmed this in Case C-17/90, *Pinaud Wieger.*
18. See Case C-320/03 R, *Commission v. Austria*, the Court ruled that the Austrian ban was contrary to Arts. 34 and 35 TFEU.
19. As appears from Joined Cases C-184 & 221/91, *Oorburg and Van Messem v. Wasser- und Schiffahrtsdirektion Nordwest.*
20. Reg. 1370/2007 on public passenger transport services by rail and by road and repealing Council Reg. (EEC) 1191/69 and 1107/70. See *infra* sections 5.1 and 5.3.
21. Without prejudice to Reg. 3577/92/EEC on maritime transport.
22. See Case C-387/92, *Banco Exterior de España v. Ayuntamiento de Valencia.*
23. See Case 156/77, *Commission v. Belgium.*

fields of public service and competition, discussed in subsections 5.1 and 5.2 below, are important for the interpretation of this provision.

4.5 *Establishment of charges, rates and conditions*

Article 94 TFEU provides that measures taken within the framework of the Treaty in respect of transport rates and conditions must take account of the economic circumstances of carriers. This is a distinct obligation which the Council has to take into account in the adoption of measures under Article 91 TFEU.[24] Article 95 TFEU requires the abolition of discriminatory carriage rates and conditions for the carriage of identical goods over the same transport links based on the country of origin or destination; it is a *lex specialis* in relation to Article 18 TFEU and is implemented in Regulations 11/60 and 3626/84.

Article 96 TFEU contains a prohibition on Member States allowing or imposing, in respect of transport operations carried out within the Union, rates and conditions involving any element of support or protection in the interest of one or more particular undertakings or industries. To the extent that such support or protection constitutes aid in the sense of Article 107 TFEU – which, in view of the wide definition of State aid which the Court applies, is very likely – Articles 107 and 108 TFEU will apply in addition to Article 93, as will the case law and legislation on services of general economic interest as to which see section 5.1, below.

4.6 *Specific procedures for sea and air transport*

Article 101(2) comprises the legal basis for adopting provisions for sea and air transport. In addition, it prescribes the ordinary legislative procedure for the adoption of new legislation by the European Parliament and Council.

5. Particular subjects pertaining to transport

5.1 *Public services and services of general economic interest*

The notion of public services, or services of general economic interest, has become a key concept in Union law and politics and is particularly important in all sectors that have been the target of liberalization, that is, transport, energy, telecommunications, postal services and broadcasting. The Treaty of Amsterdam of 1997 added Article 16, according to which

> "the Community and the Member States, each within their respective powers and within the scope of application of this Treaty, shall take care that such services operate on the basis of principles and conditions which enable them to fulfil their missions."

Article 36 of the EU Charter of Fundamental Rights recognizes services of general economic interest. The European Council of 20–21 June 2007 adopted a Protocol on *Services of General Interest* which is now part of the Lisbon Treaty.[25] Public service obligations are closely related to services of general economic interest. This tool enables governments of EU States to secure the maintenance of services that are deemed essential for the harmonious development of their territory.[26] For inland transport, the Council made provision for the removal of differences between the Member States' legislation concerning the treatment of public service obligations in the transport sector.[27] In that sector such differences are capable of significantly distorting

24. See also, the judgment in Case C-17/90, *Pinaud Wieger.*
25. See Protocol 9 on *Services of General Interest.*
26. See Art. 16 of EU Reg. 1008/2008.
27. Reg. 1191/69.

competition. In order to attain the desired aim, common principles for the removal or treatment of public service obligations have been established.[28]

The proper function of public services and the extent to which such services are exempt from the competition and the State aid rules are largely dealt with by reference to Article 106(2) TFEU.[29] An additional element was introduced by the Court's judgment in the *Altmark* case[30] which provides important guidelines for the compatibility of financial compensation for such services with the State aid rules.

In 2005, the EU adopted a Community Framework for State aid given in the form of public service compensation, the validity of which has been prolonged by a Communication from the Commission in 2011.[31] The Framework addresses situations that do not fall within the scope of application of the above-mentioned decision and specific projects that Member States have decided to notify.[32] The Commission enacted a directive repealing the Financial Transparency Directive,[33] and published further relevant documents in November 2007.[34] It can be gleaned from State aid decisions based on Article 106(3) TFEU that the Commission considers that in those instances where the *Altmark* conditions are not fulfilled, an exemption from the effects of Article 107(2) TFEU is justified, provided that the compensation is commensurate with the extra cost of providing the public service. Regulation 1370/2007 provides for the follow-up of the *Altmark* case law in the inland transport sector.

5.2 *Competition*

Until 1 May 2004, the transport sector was subject to special competition rules, diverging from those which were applicable to other sectors. Since this date, the general rules of Regulation 1/2003 as amended also apply to the transport sector.

Inland transport is now subject to the latter Regulation pursuant to the provisions of Regulation 169/2009.[35] Article 2 of this Regulation provides for an exemption for technical agreements; Article 3 provides for an exemption for groups of small and medium-sized undertakings from Article 101(1) TFEU; Article 4 provides for a conditional exemption of agreements from Article 101(1). Specified activities pertaining to the joint operation of international shipping services are exempted under Article 101(3).[36]

5.3 *State aid*

Articles 107 and 108 TFEU apply to the transport sector, albeit supplemented by Article 93 TFEU.[37] Those special provisions are made in, for instance, Regulation 1370/2007 laying down the conditions under which competent authorities may compensate for the costs incurred when

---

28. As for the rail sector, common rules and methods for the financial compensations arising from the normalization of railway accounts were laid down in Reg. 1192/69 as amended.
29. Art. 106(2) TFEU deals with undertakings entrusted with the operation of services in the general interest.
30. Case C-280/00, *Altmark Trans and Regierungspräsidium Magdeburg*.
31. Community Framework for State aid in the form of public service compensation, the validity of which prolonged by the Communication from the Commission, C 337/2.
32. Para 21 of the preamble of the decision.
33. Dir. 80/723/EEC amended by Dir. 2005/81/EC, repealed by Commission Dir. 2006/111/EC.
34. Services of general interest, including social services of general interest as to which see "A new European commitment", COM(2007)725 final; accompanying document SEC(2007)1516.
35. Reg. 169/2009; see also, Reg. (EC) 1/2003 and Reg. (EEC) 1017/68.
36. By virtue of Commission Reg. 906/2009/EC.
37. According to the Commission Guidelines on regional State aid for the period 2014–2020, which entered into force on 1 July 2014, special rules apply to the transport sector.

imposing or contracting public services obligations. Article 3 of that regulation indicates when aid measures are permissible.

5.4 *External Relations*

Two fundamental decisions of the ECJ, namely, the judgment in the *ERTA* case[38] and *Opinion 1/76 on* the *European Laying-up Agreement for Inland Waterway Vessels*[39] – concern international transport. These decisions of the Court indicate that the Union has competence to conclude international agreements in order to implement existing Union transport policy, and to put new policy into effect. In *Opinion 1/94 on the WTO*, the Court ruled that international agreements in transport matters are not covered by Article 207 TFEU.[40] The ECJ also found that when internal competence are effectively exercised at the same time as external competence, then the latter will be exclusive.[41]

6. Measures applying to the transport modes

6.1 *Road transport*

6.1.1 *Economic regulation*

A common transport policy has been more or less established for professional freight transport by road.[42] Given that road freight transport forms a very large part of the professional freight transport sector, the economic importance of this system is great. Regulation 1072/2009 (as amended) establishes a system of Community licences, based on qualitative criteria. Directive 2006/1 sets rules for the use of vehicles hired without drivers for the carriage of goods by road.[43]

General measures have the effect of bringing the competitive conditions between the Member States closer together. The first of these regards the introduction of a Union driving licence.[44] The Union has also taken action on the harmonization of the technical control of motor vehicles and their trailers, being that the original directive introduced the obligation of mutual recognition of roadworthiness tests according to Union rules.[45] As a result of these measures, lorries are assured of free movement. The formalities for the cross-frontier transport of goods have been adapted to the development of the internal market within the Union.[46] A particular milestone in the economic achievement of the common transport policy was the adoption of Directive 85/3 on weights, dimensions and certain other technical characteristics, later replaced by Directive 96/53 and then amended by Directive (EU) 2015/719.[47] The long-running debate on this subject matter demonstrates the competing interests of transporters who are anxious to transport goods as efficiently and cheaply as possible, freight vehicle manufacturers who are seeking to gain market dominance through their own standards and safety considerations, and, last but not least, those seeking to minimize the environmental impact.

---

38. Case 22/70, *Commission v. Council (ERTA)*.
39. Opinion 1/76, *European Laying-up Agreement*. These principles have been reiterated in the ECJ's judgments in Case C-266/03, *Commission v. Luxembourg* and Case C-433/03, *Commission v. Germany*.
40. Opinion 1/94, *WTO*, para 48.
41. Opinion 1/94, *WTO*, para 89.
42. Transport on road has been liberalized ever since 1962; see Reg. 1072/2009.
43. Dir. 2006/1.
44. See, now, Dir. 91/439 amended by Dir. 96/47 and Dir. 97/26 and Dir. 2006/126.
45. Dir. 77/143, now replaced by Dir. 2009/40 on roadworthiness tests for motor vehicles and their trailers.
46. Dir. 91/432 amending Dir. 83/643.
47. Dir. 2015/719; Member States had until 7 May 2017 to bring the provisions of the Directive into force.

The regime for the carriage of passengers by road is based on controlling access to the occupation of a passenger transport operator pursuant to requirements of good repute, appropriate financial standing and professional competence.[48] Once a road haulage operator has a Union authorization, he or she may freely undertake international transport throughout the Union in accordance with Regulation 1072/2009. International coach and bus transport is governed by Regulation 1073/2009.

The holder of a Union authorization may carry out the operation of domestic services in another State throughout the Union. Member States remain competent to introduce tolls or other road user charges, although they may not discriminate on the ground of carrier nationality or consignment origin or destination, nor may they give rise to any undue hindrance.[49] This directive also contains certain rules to ensure uniform application.

For international transport there are no common rules for rates and contractual conditions: Regulation 4058/89 prescribes that the rates for international carriage are to be freely fixed between the parties to the haulage contract,[50] and the Member States have to establish a system whereby the rates charged are communicated to the national authorities, pending the introduction of a definitive system of market observation.[51] By virtue of agreements with Switzerland this country has become part of the EU road transport market.[52]

6.1.2 *Safety and security*

Directive 2008/68 lays down rules for the transport of dangerous goods by road, by rail or by inland waterways within or between Member States. For road traffic those rules have been drawn up by the Economic Commission for Europe of the UN (UN-ECE).[53]

6.1.3 *Protection of the environment*

The directives on the protection of ambient air quality play a vital role in the road transport sector.[54] In a remarkable judgment, the ECJ ruled that Austria was entitled to implement more stringent environmental standards ahead of the deadline set by Directive 96/62.[55] Over the past decades, road transport has grown much faster than the other inland transport modes. Since road transport causes more pollution than the other modes of transport, shifting the balance between the modes of transport is therefore at the heart of the sustainable development strategy. Regulation 1692/2006, establishing the *Marco Polo II* programme, implements this strategy.

48. Reg. 1071/2009.
49. See Art. 7 of Dir. 1999/62.
50. Reg. 4058/89, Art. 2.
51. Ibid., Art. 3.
52. Agreement between the European Community and the Swiss Confederation on the Carriage of Goods and Passengers by Rail and Road.
53. See also, Dir. 95/50 and Dir. 98/91.
54. Dir. 2008/50; see also, Case C-34/11 *European Commission v. the Portuguese Republic.*
55. Dir. 96/62 on ambient air quality assessment and management repealed by Dir. 2008/50; in Case C-320/03, *Commission v. Austria* the ECJ ruled against the Austrian ban on driving because it failed the proportionality test.

6.1.4 *Social policies*

As there are many small firms in this sector measures were adopted with a view to protecting them against cut-throat competition. The Commission has established sectoral committees promoting the dialogue between social partners.[56]

It was in this field that the celebrated litigation in Case 22/70 *Commission v. Council* took place, relating to the ERTA Agreement which governs international road transport involving through third countries.[57]

Regulation 561/2006 contains the provisions relating to manning, driving times, breaks and rest periods. Other aspects of working time in relation to road transport are regulated in Directive 2002/15.

6.1.5 *External relations*

Transport to third countries remains dependent on the agreements which have been concluded with those countries. For instance, the *Agreement on the International Carriage of Passengers by Road by Means of Occasional Coach and Bus Services* was concluded for transport to, via, or from third countries.

6.2 *Rail transport*

6.2.1 *Economic regulation, including social policies and consumer protection*

The main objective of the policy in this sector has been the promotion of the healthy financial position of the railways to guarantee reasonable conditions of competition vis-à-vis transport by road and inland waterways. The fact that railways have been and for the most part still are public undertakings has been an important factor in this policy. The Member States take on an important part of the infrastructure costs, which makes the competitiveness of this transport mode with other modes very difficult. Various measures of Union secondary law are therefore directed towards achieving transparency in regard to the financial relations between the railways and the Member States.

Directive 2012/34 requires a clear separation to be made between the management and accounts concerning the various functions of the railways: on the one hand the provision of transport services, and on the other hand the management of railway infrastructure.[58] Article 10 ensures equitable and non-discriminatory access to infrastructure for all railway undertakings. Directive 2012/34 contains conditions and procedures for granting a Union railway licence.[59] Rules for the allocation of railway infrastructure capacity and the levying of charges for the use of railway infrastructure are laid down in Chapter 4 of Directive 2012/34. It also regulates the basic activity principles of the Member States' regulatory bodies, entrusted with the tasks of promoting safety standards and competitiveness, and of reviewing and monitoring matters relating to the infrastructure managers.[60] Common rules for the normalization of the accounts of railway undertakings have long been in force.[61]

---

56. Commission Decision 98/500/EC on "the establishment of Sectoral Dialogue Committees promoting the Dialogue between the social partners at European level".
57. The "European Agreement concerning the Work of Crews of Vehicles engaged in International Road Transport" (Geneva, 1 Jul. 1970 to 31 Mar. 1971, TS 103(1978); Cmnd 7401), ERTA.
58. Dir. 2012/34/EU.
59. Chapter 3 of the Directive 2012/34/EU.
60. In Arts. 6–7 and Arts. 55–57 of Dir. 2012/34/EU.
61. Reg. 1192/69. See also, Commission proposal for repealing this regulation (COM(2013)26 final – 2013/0013 COD).

Regulation 1/2003 also applies to the rail sector.[62] Freight carried by rail[63] and international passenger services[64] have been fully liberalized. However, domestic transport by rail is still closed to competition. In practice, Member States have not yet implemented the provisions coming from EU law. The rail sector is excluded from the obligation to award Public Service Obligations (PSO),[65] which are available in inland, maritime and air transport.

Directive 2007/59 contains rules for the certification of train drivers.

Regulation 1371/2007 lays down rules on rail passengers' rights and obligations.

6.2.2 *Safety and security*

The considerable increase in the transportation of dangerous goods by rail led to the adoption of Directive 2008/68 which regulates the transport of dangerous goods, including loading and unloading, by road, rail or inland waterways within or between Member States. Rules for ensuring the safe transport of dangerous goods by rail have been drawn up by the *Intergovernmental Organization for International Carriage by Rail* (OTIF). As in other transport modes, National Safety Authorities must supervise safety of the railway system and check the certification of the railway undertakings, which is based on mutual recognition. Here again, supervision is hampered by budgetary and human resources constraints.

6.2.3 *External relations*

In the field of external relations, the Intergovernmental Organization for International Carriage by Rail (OTIF) was set up on 1 May 1985.[66] The EU is a member of OTIF.[67]

6.3 *Inland waterway transport*

6.3.1 *Economic regulation, including social policies and consumer protection*

Rules on access to the market in the international transport of goods and passengers by inland waterways are laid down in Regulation 1356/96.[68] This regulation implements the principle of freedom to provide services in this sector, allowing for full liberalization of the market. However, inland waterway transport in the Union occupies a special position insofar as one of the most important inland waterway routes in the Union, the Rhine and its tributaries, is governed by the *Mannheim Convention*, which makes it subject to participation from third countries, in particular Switzerland. This Convention guarantees free navigation of the Rhine not simply for the riparian States, but also for other countries; as a result of the opening of the Rhine-Main-Danube canal, giving East European inland waterway fleets access to the Rhine waterway network, the traditional free navigation was confined to vessels having a real connection with one of the contracting parties to the Convention. Community carriers enjoy cabotage rights.[69]

---

62. Recital 36 of Reg. 1/2003; Joined Cases T-374, 375, 384 & 388/94, *European Night Services et al. v. Commission*; Case T-14/93, *Union internationale des chemins de fer v. Commission* and Case C-264/95 P, *Commission v. Union internationale des chemins de fer*, Case T-229/94, *Deutsche Bahn AG v. Commission* and Case C-436/97 P, *Deutsche Bahn v. Commission*; Joined Cases T-79 & 80/95 *SNCF and British Railways v. Commission*.
63. See Dir. 2004/51/EC amending Dir. 91/440/EEC. See also, Reg. 913/2010.
64. See Dir. 91/440/EEC amended by, among others, Dir. 2007/58/EC.
65. See Reg. 1370/2007.
66. As a consequence of the convention of 9 May 1980 (COTIF).
67. Dec. 2013/103/EU.
68. Reg. 1356/96.
69. Reg. 3921/91. In Cases C-266/03, *Commission v. Luxembourg* and C-433/03, *Commission v. Germany*, the ECJ ruled that this regulation does not govern transport by carriers in non-Member States.

There are also rules relating to access to the occupation of carrier of goods by waterways in national and international transport, and on mutual recognition of diplomas, certificates and other titles relating to this occupation.[70] Article 3 of the relevant directive sets professional competence as the condition for access to the occupation. Article 7 of the Directive states that diplomas and certificates issued in accordance with the directives are to be mutually recognized. Directive 96/50 sets the conditions for granting national boat masters' certificates for the carriage of goods and passengers by inland waterway in the Union. Directive 2009/100 regulates reciprocal recognition of navigability licences,[71] whereas Directive 2016/1629 lays down technical requirements for inland waterways vessels.[72] To cope with structural overcapacity of the inland waterway transport rules for the restructuring have been laid down in Regulation 1101/89 as variously amended.[73]

Passengers are protected pursuant to the provisions of Regulation 1177/2010.[74]

6.3.2 *Safety and security*

Rules for ensuring the safe transport of dangerous goods by rail have been drawn up by the UN Economic Commission for Europe (UN-ECE).

6.3.3 *Protection of the environment*

Under the above Mannheim Convention, internalization of external, that is, environmental costs, is forbidden. Hence, consent from Switzerland is required to mitigate the damaging effects of inland waterway navigation through the imposition of higher charges. The same goes for navigation on the Danube which is also governed by an international convention to which non-EU States, including Moldova, Russia, Ukraine and Serbia are parties.

6.3.4 *External relations*

The Central Commission for Navigation on the Rhine, in which the Union also has observer status, is an important forum.[75] This Commission is responsible for implementing and promoting free navigation on the Rhine, as laid down in the Convention of Mannheim.

6.4 *Maritime transport*

6.4.1 *Economic regulation, including consumer protection*

The internal market of the EU for maritime transport is now characterized by free access to the market and the protection of this free market. Regulation 4057/86 is the only regulation specifically applicable to liner services.[76] Cabotage has also been liberalized, but Member States retain the option to impose public service obligations.[77] Under the "Blue Belt" and "Blue Lanes" policies intra-EU maritime transport must be performed as smoothly as possible, that is, by reducing administrative burdens, in order to facilitate swift transit.[78]

---

70. Dir. 87/540.
71. As amended by Dir. (EU) 2016/1629.
72. Dir. 2016/1629 amending Dir. 2009/100/EC and repealing Dir. 2006/87/EC.
73. Reg. 1101/89.
74. Reg. 1177/2010.
75. France, Germany, Belgium, the Netherlands and Switzerland are members. The special problems concerning Switzerland were dealt with in Opinion 1/76, *European Laying-up Agreement*.
76. Tramp shipping services do not come under Reg. 954/79 and Reg. 4057/86.
77. See Case C-205/99, *Analir.*
78. See Commission Implementing Reg. 2016/481.

As to the protection of the free market by the application of the EU competition law regime, it appeared to be impossible for the Member States to fulfil their obligations under the Convention on a Code of Conduct for Liner Conferences whereas the Council concluded that shipping conferences no longer fulfil the conditions for the exemptions from the competition regime.[79] Hence, the EU decided that the mechanisms of Regulation 1/2003 should also be applied to the maritime sector and abolished the exemption for cabotage and tramp vessels,[80] whereas the Council empowered the Commission to grant a block exemption for liner consortia.[81] This exemption is the only remaining special feature of the application of the competition rules in the maritime sector.

Since 1985, the now Articles 107 and 108 TFEU have been applied on myriad occasions in the shipping sector.[82] Community guidelines on State aid to maritime transport were adopted in 1997 and revised in 2004. These guidelines lay down a more flexible approach than in other sectoral regimes. Due to this, the great difference in competitiveness between ships registered in the Union and those outside – which frequently sail under a low-cost flag – operating aid is permitted by way of exception; this must be exceptional, temporary and degressive. Regulation 4057/86 on unfair pricing practices in the maritime sector amounts to the establishment of anti-dumping rules in liner transport.

While ports have been called "natural monopolies", competition as between them can be fierce. Hence the Commission calls for transparency by maintaining separate accounts for activities which receive public funding and those which do not.[83]

An important body of case law has built up on the compatibility of exclusive rights in ports with provisions of the Treaty.[84] The exclusive rights of certain dock-workers in the Port of Genoa were found to be in breach of Article 106(1) TFEU.[85] In various judgments, lines have been drawn, with gradually increasing clarity, between activities which can be categorized as a typical exercise of State authority which therefore fall outside the scope of the prohibitions of the competition rules,[86] entrepreneurial activities in the form of exclusive rights which can be justified under Article 106(2) TFEU,[87] and entrepreneurial activities which do not deserve any kind of special treatment.[88]

Port services are recognized as *Services of General Economic Interest.*[89] A Commission decision exempts compensation for smaller ports from the prohibition of Article 106 TFEU.[90]

National legislation concerning these activities is also assessed on the basis of principles developed in case law on Articles 3(1)(g) and 101 and 102 TFEU, that is, preventing distortions of competition.[91] The Commission has also applied the State aid rules in relation to seaports.[92] Sometimes, ports still apply rules which involve differences in treatment that are incompatible

79. See Art. 101(3) TFEU.
80. Art. 2 of Reg. 1419/2006, abolishes Art. 32 of Reg. 1/2003 excluding these services from Reg. 1/2003.
81. Reg. 246/2009.
82. M. Scharf op. cit. *supra* note 2.
83. See Dir. 2006/111/EC.
84. See, P.W. de Langen and A.A. Pallis, "Entry barriers in seaports", 34 *Maritime Policy and Management* (2007), 427–440.
85. Case C-179/90, *Merci Convenzionali Porto di Genova v. Siderurgica Gabrielli.*
86. Case C-343/95, *Cali & Figli v. Servizi Ecologici Porto di Genova*; see *also* Case C-22/98, *Becu et al.*
87. Case C-266/96, *Corsica Ferries France,* mooring services and the prices charged for such services.
88. Case C-35/96, *Commission v. Italy,* on the activity of customs agents.
89. See section 5.1.
90. Dec. 2012/21/EU; see *also,* the judgment in Case C-280/00, *Altmark,* cited *supra* note 32.
91. This is especially so when exclusive or special rights are involved.
92. See the Decision on tugboats in the port of Rotterdam.

with the general Treaty rules; for instance, a surcharge on normal duties applying to goods coming from other Member States is obviously not permitted under Article 110 TFEU.[93]

The Commission must urge the Member States to comply with the general Treaty rules in the implementation of maritime policy. This mainly involves the infringement of the principle of freedom of establishment in national legislation on registration of vessels.[94]

Since 31 December 2012, passengers by sea are also covered by Regulation 392/2009, which addresses the liability of carriers in case of loss or damage resulting from an accident.[95]

6.4.2 *Safety and security*

There has been a sharp increase in measures on safety and environmental issues which, since the Second World War, were regulated by the IMO whereas the Member States' traditional shipping policies strongly supported this worldwide regulatory system. A shift away from this worldwide approach began to take place as a result of the public opinion, which was no longer satisfied with the EU's hesitancy in the areas of safety and environmental pollution. The frequent and well-publicized large-scale shipping disasters – disasters in both human and environmental terms – have played a very important role.

EU policy in this area is characterized by deference to the basic principles drawn up by the International Maritime Organization (IMO) which is a part of the UN, although there is a certain tension between the two organizations.[96] The cautious start to this policy consisted of two directives, concerning the pilotage of vessels by deep-sea pilots in the North Sea and the English Channel, and minimum requirements for certain tankers entering or leaving Community ports, respectively.[97]

Meanwhile, the linchpin of Union policy is laid down in Directive 2009/16.[98] This directive obliges Member States to inspect vessels calling at their ports in order to enforce compliance with the safety, environmental and social, that is, living and working, conditions, contained in various IMO conventions and implicitly also the relevant EU directives mentioned below. The principle of port state control is an important deviation from the usual principle of international public law under which treaties are only binding on the parties to them. The "no more favourable treatment" principle, which is set out in various IMO and International Labour Organization (ILO) conventions concerning maritime transport, means that ships registered in a State which is not a party to the convention may also be inspected in order to ensure compliance with the rules laid down in the conventions. For maritime transport, where large numbers of vessels are registered in States with low-cost flags, the principle is of great importance for these States who are usually not a party to the conventions mentioned here. Article 16 of the directive provides that authorities of the Member States shall ban sub-standard ships. The Commission must publish a list of such ships.

---

93. Joined Cases C-114 & 115/95, *Texaco*; Joined Cases C-430 & 431/99, *Sea-Land Service and Nedlloyd Lijnen*; Case C-435/00, *Geha Naftiliaki et al.*
94. Case C-334/94, *Commission v. France*; see also, Cases C-62/96, *Commission v. Greece* and Case C-151/96, *Commission v. Ireland*; C-290/94, *Commission v. Greece*; C-90/94, *Haahr Petroleum v. Abenra Havn et al.*; C-114 & 115/95, *Texaco v. Middelfart Havn and Olieselskabet Danmark v. Trafikministeriet*, and C-242/95, *GT-Link v. De Danske Statsbaner*.
95. Reg. 392/2009 on the liability of carriers of passengers by sea in the event of accidents.
96. See, F. Hoffmeister and P.J. Kuijper, "The status of the EU at the UN: Institutional ambiguities and political realities" in J. Wouters, F. Hoffmeister and T. Ruys (Eds.), *EU-UN: An Ever Growing Partnership* (T.M.C. Asser Press, 2006).
97. Dir. 79/115 and Dir. 79/116 amended by Dir. 2002/59.
98. Amended by Dir. 2013/38 which repealed Dir. 95/21.

The Union safety policy may look impressive if measured in terms of legislation, but it has two fundamental flaws: one is that enforcement will always lag behind legislation, and this is particularly true in the field of international shipping where it is difficult for one jurisdiction to impose its enforcement policy; and the second, and probably more important flaw, is the fact that it has so far been impossible to *pierce the corporate veil* when it comes to punishing the real culprits. As a result, *mala fide* ship-owners can hide behind corporate structures set up in countries hosting flags of convenience. The United Nations Conference on Trade and Development (UNCTAD) convention on registration of ships, which was designed to tackle this problem, has remained a dead letter. The Union has attempted to remedy this by its port state control policy and in particular the Directive 95/21 repealed by Directive 2009/16 which has been discussed above in this section.

The fight against terrorism in the Union increasingly leaves its mark in the maritime sector with the adoption of rules intended to enhance ship and port facility security.[99] Directive 2005/65 introduces Union measures to enhance port security in the face of threats of security incidents.[100] In addition, the Union has concluded an important agreement with the USA on container security.[101]

Security is not only increasingly relevant in the air transport sector but also in the maritime sector. Under Article 222 TFEU, the EU and its Member States must act jointly in a spirit of solidarity if a Member State is the subject of a terrorist attack.

6.4.3 *Protection of the environment*

In the field of safety and the protection of the marine environment, the IMO is the competent body. Port charging of ships has been used as a tool to reduce the damaging effects of emissions.[102] Operators of ships must demonstrate that they produce reduced quantities of ship-generated waste.

6.4.4 *Infrastructure*

Ports are usually natural monopolies which qualification holds both for sea transport (seaports) and air transport (airports). This monopoly position is strengthened by the fact that it is increasingly difficult to construct new ports, for reasons of environmental protection and spatial planning. Strictly speaking, ports fall outside the scope of application of the transport Title of the Treaty. Nevertheless, port activities are intimately connected with transport. As a result of the completion of the internal market and the considerable growth in transport, there is an increasingly urgent need to address the position of ports within the Union.

Hence, in 1997 the Commission issued a Green Paper on Sea Ports and Maritime Infrastructure.[103] The key elements in the Green Paper concern the role of ports in the trans-European Transport Network as to which see section 7, below, EU enlargement and connections to neighbouring third countries, the role of ports as transfer points in the intermodal transport chain, the development of short sea shipping, maritime safety, and protection of the environment. In addition, attention is paid to financing and charging for the use of ports and maritime

---

99. Reg. 725/2004.
100. Dir. 2005/65/EC.
101. "Agreement between the EC and the United States of America on intensifying and broadening the agreement on customs cooperation and mutual assistance in customs matters to include cooperation on container security and related matters".
102. See Dir. 2000/59.
103. COM(97)678 final of 10 Dec. 1997.

infrastructure. This last subject crops up regularly in the context of application of the State aid rules. In the second decade of the 21st century the approach to this issue has started to change. In 2011, market access to port services was included in the agenda of another White Paper[104] for the purpose of subsequently resolving and adapting new legislation. In 2016, the Commission published a document on the implementation of the 2011 White Paper (2011) which outlined that although there has been little progress on the goals set in 2011, the situation has evolved since the publishing of the White Paper.[105]

6.4.5 *Social policies*

The harmonization of social policies plays an important role in the maritime sector because of the growing shortage of seafarers in combination with the rapid growth of the maritime industry and the existence of "flags of convenience" providing for low labour and safety standards. The EU works together with the IMO and ILO to address these problems.

The Maritime Labour Convention (ILO) has formed the basis for EU legislation on the minimum requirements for seafarers working on board a ship.[106] Questions remain on the harmonized enforcement of this convention as the participation from the Flag State, the Port State and the State providing the labour forces is required. An EU register and EU flag for shipping would help to achieve a level playing field in this sector.[107] A European flag would not be a substitute for national flags but stand for mutual recognition and harmonization of standards. Here too, national policy objectives prohibit rapid progress.

6.4.6 *External relations*

The EU has observer status in the IMO. Given the worldwide nature of the IMO, EU legislation in this area may take rules laid down by this body as basis for more far-reaching rules; nevertheless, with the continuing growth of EU policy, there is increasing tension as also noted in section 6.1, above.

The Organization for Economic Cooperation and Development (OECD) plays an important role in the preparation of the decision-making by the Western countries (the so-called B Group) in the UNCTAD framework and in the adoption of its own policies, as demonstrated by the Code of Liberalization of Current Invisible Operations. The Union also has observer status in the OECD, but the Commission plays an active role in the OECD's work. The maritime transport division of the UNCTAD has drafted a number of conventions, the most important of which is that laying down a code of conduct for Liner Conferences.[108]

Regulation 4055/86 on the freedom to provide services aims to apply this principle to maritime transport between them and third countries. The regulation provides for the gradual abolition of unilateral national restrictions. The regulation also governs the conditions under which Member States may conclude cargo-sharing arrangements with third countries.[109] Article 3 of the regulation provides that the Member States must abolish rules on cargo-sharing arrangements contained in existing bilateral agreements. The Commission has brought infringement

104. 2011 White Paper, "Roadmap to a single European Transport Area", COM(2011)0144 final.
105. SWD(2016)226 final.
106. See Dir. 2009/13.
107. See, Dir. 2009/21/EC.
108. UNCTAD Convention on a *Code of Conduct for Liner Conferences* (1974).
109. In Case 355/87, *Commission v. Council*, the Commission challenged Council Decision 87/475 which authorized Italy to conclude a bilateral marine transport agreement with Algeria.

proceedings a number of times in order to make Member States comply with this obligation.[110] Also, a number of proceedings have been brought in which differences in harbour dues and charges for vessel traffic services were challenged.[111]

Regulation 4058/86 on free access to cargoes is intended to coordinate the individual reactions of the various Member States to restrictions imposed on their vessels in maritime transport to third countries where such restrictions result from government measures. In 2002, the EC and its Member States, and China, made an agreement designed to strengthen and consolidate their relations, to promote multimodal transport involving a sea leg in order to increase efficiencies in the transport chain, and to recognize the importance of further developing a flexible and market-oriented approach and the benefits to economic operators of both parties of controlling and operating their own international cargo transport services in the context of an efficient international maritime transport system. The agreement entered into force on 1 March 2008.[112]

6.5 Air transport

6.5.1 Economic regulation, including social policies

The EU internal air transport market is now governed by EU Regulation 1008/2008 on *common rules for the operation of air services in the EU*. In order to complete the creation of a "level playing field". This Regulation lays down rules on substantial ownership and effective control on the licensing of air carriers which must be in the hands of EU States or their nationals.[113] Public service obligations (PSO) can be applied on intra-EU routes.[114]

Subject to reciprocity, non-EU air carriers also enjoy freedom of pricing.[115] Importantly, the final price (fare) must include all charges, including airport charges, surcharges, fees and taxes. This is a matter of consumer protection.[116]

Articles 101 and 102 TFEU, as well as Article 107 TFEU governing State aid have been applied to air transport.[117] The definition of "undertaking" has relevance for the air transport sector as airlines, at least EU airlines, are "undertakings" pursuant to Article 2 of EU Regulation 1008/2008, and so are airports following the decision of the ECJ in, among others, the case of *Aéroports de Paris*,[118] but Air Traffic Control (ATC) agencies are not.

Since the entry into force of EU Regulation 1/2003, the air transport sector is fully subject to the EU rules on competition.

The alleged anticompetitive behaviour, where concerted practices or abuse of dominant position (Art. 102 TFEU), must be assessed in a *relevant services market*. The determining factor consists of *interchangeability*: air services which are interchangeable fall within one services market. Hence, in the market for the operation of air services, the question is whether direct air services can be substituted with indirect air services, and air transport with surface transport. Whether one of those alternatives forms an alternative for the direct air route depends on a

110. Joined Cases C-176 & 177/97, *Commission v. Belgium and Luxembourg*; Joined Cases C-62 & 84/98, *Commission v. Portugal* (agreement with Angola and former Yugoslavia); Case C-295/00, *Commission v. Italy*.
111. Joined Cases C-430 & 431/99, *Sea-Land Service and Nedlloyd Lijnen*; Case C-435/00, *Geha Naftiliaki et al.*
112. Agreement on maritime transport between the European Community and its Member States, of the one part, and the government of the People's Republic of China, of the other part.
113. See Art. 4 of Reg. 1008/2008.
114. See Arts. 16–18 of Reg. 1008/2008.
115. See Art. 22(1) of Reg. 1008/2008.
116. See Art. 23 of Reg. 1008/2008.
117. See J. Milligan, *European Union Competition Law in the Airline Industry* (Kluwer Law International, 2017).
118. See ECJ, Case C-82/01 P, *Aéroports de Paris v. Commission of the European Communities*.

multiplicity of factors, such as the overall travel time, frequency of services and the price of different alternatives.[119]

There is little case law on Article 102 TFEU.[120]

EU Council Regulation 487/2009 on *the application of Article 101(3) of the TFEU to certain categories of agreements and concerted practices in the air transport sector* is the only air transport specific regulation still in place. It empowers the EU Commission to exempt specified practices from the scope of Article 101 TFEU on the prohibition of concerted practices. So far, the Commission has not adopted any specific exemption and there are no indications that it intends to do so.

The EU Commission has built a wealth of experience regarding *airline alliances*. It distinguishes between product or services and geographical markets and between business/time sensitive and leisure/price sensitive passengers in relation to the dominance on those markets. If needed, airlines participating in the alliance are requested to remedy their potentially anti-competitive behaviour by surrendering slots at hub airports, freezing capacity and/or fares and granting interline opportunities to new entrants. Generally speaking, the EU Commission supports consolidation, with due regard for global developments in this field. The anti-competitive effects of such alliance agreements must now be self-assessed by airlines. Following the entry into force of EU Regulation 1/2003, the EU Commission has made its decisions in relation to the above three alliance agreements, namely, the oneworld case (2010),[121] the Star alliance case (2013)[122] and the Skyteam alliance case (2015)[123] by making the commitments proposed by the alliance members legally binding.

Merger control is a special issue in international air transport as it bears a close relationship with the relevance of nationality requirements under which international air transport operates for the purpose of designation under bilateral air services agreements. Since the adoption of Merger Regulation 139/2004, the EU Commission has reviewed some 30 airline mergers. Significant cross border merger activity started to take place in the 21st century with the merger between Air France and KLM.[124] In the *Etihad/Alitalia* merger of 2014 the Commission concluded that the marketing carrier does not exert more than a residual constraint on the operating carrier.[125] Thus, the EU Commission imposes restrictions on the merger in order to remedy the potential anti-competitive effects of the venture. The approach is similar to that adopted in alliances cases.

The Commission's *Aviation Strategy for Europe* (2015) addresses these challenges by, among others, highlighting the objective of accessing growth markets by improving market access, services and investment opportunities with third countries.

The economic crises in the last decade of the 20th century, and at the end of the first decade of the 21st century, forced many airlines to restructure their operations. The acute fall-off in demand exposed many failings in the industry: overcapacity, low productivity, high costs and undercapitalization. Successful restructuring required public money, particularly on the part of those airlines that were wholly or partially owned by their governments. Hence, next to mergers and takeovers, undertakings, including airlines and airports, tried to compensate for losses by

---

119. See Commission Notice on the *definition of the relevant market*, para 13.
120. But see a case on the refusal to interline in the Commission's Decision 92/213, *British Midland/Aer Lingus* (1992).
121. See COMP/39569, EU Commission Decision of 14 July 2010.
122. See, EU Commission, Press Release of 23 May 2013.
123. See EU Commission, Press Release of 15 May 2015, Antitrust.
124. Case No COMP/M.3280, *Air France/KLM*, dated 11 February 2005.
125. See EU Commission Decision of 14 Nov. 2014.

taking recourse to *State aid*. The EU Commission has monitored State aid granted to airlines since 1989. Aid was in most cases given to the national "flag" carrier for rescuing it from bankruptcy. The Commission has authorized aid to airlines as "exceptional measures" designed to assist the restructuring of the airlines concerned, with a view to completing the liberalization of the internal market.

In 2014, the Commission published its *Guidelines on State aid to airports and airlines*, which also focus on financing of airports and start up aid to airlines departing from regional airports which are mostly public owned and managed under local or regional administration and have a public interest in attracting traffic, and therefore subsidize those airports they serve, under the mentioned State aid Guidelines, a "General Economic Interest".[126]

Directive 2000/79 sets out rules for an agreement on the organization of working time of *mobile workers* in civil aviation. The EU attempts to improve the regulations on flight and duty time limitations, taking into account the latest scientific and technical evidence.

6.5.2 *Safety and security*

In 2002, the European Aviation Safety Agency (EASA) was mandated to deal with certification, operation and maintenance of aircraft, the licensing of aviation personnel and the adoption of standards relating to air navigation infrastructure, that is, aerodromes and air traffic services, and environmental protection.[127]

Following the events in the USA in September 2001, the Council established the principal regulation governing aviation security in the EU, that is, Regulation 2320/2002[128] establishing common rules in the field of civil aviation security, as amended and replaced by EC Regulation 300/2008 as further amended and constantly updated.

6.5.3 *Protection of the environment*

Regulation 598/2014[129] seeks to ensure that similar solutions are applied to similar problems at EU airports for *noise* abatement, and that sustainable development of airport capacity is facilitated on the basis of a *balanced approach* developed by ICAO by considering the available measures to address the noise problem at an airport, including reduction of noise at source, land-use planning and management, operational procedures and other noise management methods such as economic incentives and operational restrictions.

The EU Commission has chosen a market based trade mechanism in order to combat global warning as a consequence of *aircraft emissions*. The "permit to emit" greenhouse gasses has been made subject to an Emission Trade System (ETS). In 2008, the EU adopted Directive 2008/101 pursuant to which all flights arriving at or departing from an airport located in an EU State are included within the scope of the Directive.[130] Most important aviation States and trading partners of the EU and its Member States have criticized this Directive which they consider as unilateral actions infringing international law.[131] Confronted with the risk of a trade war on a global scale, and retaliation measures, the EU Council and Parliament Decision decided on 26

---

126. See Case C-280/00, *Altmark* cited in section 5.1.
127. See Reg. 216/2008 amended by EC Reg. 1108/2009 and Commission Reg. 690/2009 and 6/2013.
128. See also Commission Reg. 133/2010 amending EU Reg. 820/2008.
129. Reg. 598/2014 of 16 Apr. 2014.
130. See P. Mendes de Leon, "Nouvelles frontières: Trading international law and European law in the context of the establishment of an emission trade system" in M. Bulterman, L. Hancher, A. McDonnell and H. Sevenster, *Views of European Law from the Mountain* (Kluwer Law International, 2009).
131. See P. Mendes de Leon, "Enforcement of the EU ETS: The EU's convulsive efforts to export its environmental values", 37 *Air and Space Law* (2012), 287–306; B.F. Havel & J.Q. Mulligan, "The triumph of politics:

April 2013 to *stop the clock*, that is, to temporarily exempt international flights from some of the EU ETS obligations.[132] Meanwhile ICAO has prepared a global agreement, named CORSIA.[133] The EU institutions consider continuing the "stop the clock" regime which effectively means that the EU ETS will apply to the operation of intra-European flights by all carriers, thus assuring a level playing field among them. For intra-EEA flights whether operated by EU air carriers or other air carriers, it is proposed that the EU ETS regime will stay in place.

6.5.4 *Infrastructure*

Member States are also entitled to distribute air traffic between various airports which are part of one airport system.[134] The way in which Italian authorities exercised this power led to considerable conflict at the time the new Malpensa airport near Milan came into use.[135] In 2009, the EU adopted Directive 2009/12 on *airport charges* which applies to airports in the EU with annual traffic of over 5 million passenger movements per year. It prohibits discrimination among airport users, although they may be modulated on the basis of relevant, objective and transparent criteria for reasons of public and general interests, including protection of the environment. Airport charges must be set in a transparent fashion, following consultations between the airport operator and users, resulting in an agreement between the two parties, whilst Member States must establish procedures for resolving disagreements between these parties.[136]

Another piece of legislation pertaining to infrastructure comprises Council Directive 96/67/EC of 15 October 1996 *on access to the ground handling market at EU airports* which provides that at the larger airports in the EU ground handling of aircraft should be provided by more than one supplier so as to remove the previous monopoly position held by the airport authority or the resident, principal carrier. Self-handling by airlines must be allowed under specified conditions. Subject to review by the EU Commission, exemptions based on safety or capacity arguments may be made.

The EU Commission is undertaking further measures to improve aviation infrastructure as to which see the Airport Package of 2011. The package is intended to improve not only the slot allocation process but also the provision of ground handling services in which sector monopolization at certain airports should be avoided.

Air Traffic Management (ATM) in Europe is a fast-developing field of air transport which is supported by the regulatory framework governing the Single European Sky (SES). The SES regime forms the starting point for the EU's involvement with ATM.[137] Under the European Common Aviation Area (ECAA) agreement, the SES includes western Balkan States and Norway, Switzerland and Iceland. The SES regime is now covered by Regulation 1070/2009 – *Improving the Performance of European Aviation System*, amending and supplementing the four basic regulations of 2004. Regulation 1070/2009 is designed to improve the performance and

---

Reflections on judgment of the Court of Justice of the European Union validating the inclusion of non-EU airlines in the emissions trading scheme", 37 *Air and Space Law* (2012), 3–33.

132. See EU Dec. 377/2013, and EU Reg. 2014/2014 amending Dir. 2003/87.
133. On 6 October 2016, the 39th session of the ICAO Assembly adopted Resolution 39-3 on a Global Market-Based Measure scheme. The Resolution establishes a global Carbon Offsetting and Reduction Scheme for International Aviation (CORSIA), under which aircraft operators will be required to purchase offsets for the increase in total CO_2 emissions from international civil aviation above 2020 levels.
134. Art. 19 of Reg. 1008/2008.
135. See Case C-361/98, *Italy v. Commission.*
136. See Dir. 2009/12 on airport charges.
137. See Reg. 549/2004, 550/2004, 551/2004 and 552/2004 which were revised and extended in 2009 with Reg. 1070/2009 aimed at increasing the overall performance of the air traffic management system in Europe.

sustainability of the European aviation system in the key areas of safety, environment, capacity and cost-efficiency.[138] It was also necessary to adapt the Single European Sky legislation to technical progress and to create a single safety framework in the EU. This second legislative package also includes Regulation 1108/2009, extending EASA remit to airports and ATM. This second legislative package became known under the heading Single European Sky II.

Inevitably, the development of the SES regulations has not been without its difficulties and serious concerns have been raised with regard to certain aspects of the proposals. It is challenging to reconcile the position of Member States possessing sovereignty over their airspace under the Chicago Convention of 1944, which is considered as the constitution of international civil aviation, with the need for willingness to transfer decision-making powers over that same airspace to the EU institutions and to move beyond the traditional national approach to air traffic management. Other concerns are expressed by air traffic services unions in some EU States at the prospect of service providers from other States gaining the right to provide air traffic services in their country's airspace.

6.5.6 *Consumer protection*

As part of a policy to increase protection to passengers, Regulation 261/2004 on compensation for denied boarding, cancellation and delays of flights was adopted.[139] This regulation increases the airlines' responsibilities considerably, which led the International Air Transport Association (IATA) and the European Association of Low Cost Airlines to challenge the legality of the regulation on a number of grounds.[140] According to the associations, the regulation was incompatible with Articles 19 and 22(1) of the Montreal Convention. The ECJ did not find a conflict between the rules of the regulation and those of the Montreal Convention.

Meanwhile the scope of this regulation has been expanded by subsequent decisions of the European Court for the benefit of consumer protection and equal treatment;[141] these decisions have been frequently criticized.[142] In order to ensure clarity, common understanding and proper enforcement of these decisions, the European Commission has published interpretation guidelines on Regulation 261/2004.[143]

6.5.7 *External relations*

Air transport between the Union and third countries is subject to bilateral air services agreements between Member States and third countries – which is the usual mode in air transport. However, the rules governing the internal aviation market and the general Treaty rules also have

---

138. See D. Calleja and P.M.J. Mendes de Leon (Eds.), *Achieving the Single European Sky: Goals and Challenges* (Kluwer Law International, 2011), at 17–32.

139. Reg. 261/2004 of the European Parliament and of the Council establishing common rules on compensation and assistance to passengers in the event of denied boarding and of cancellation or long delay of flights, and repealing Reg. (EEC) 295/91.

140. See Case C-344/04, *IATA and ELFAA*; the Court rejected all the arguments of the parties, and upheld the Regulation. See case note by K. Bradley, (2006) CML Rev., 1101–1124 and J. Balfour, (2007) CML Rev., 555–560.

141. See notably: Joined Cases C-402/07 and C-432/07 *Sturgeon v. Condor* and *Böck and Lepuschitz v. Air France*; Cases C-581/10 and C-629/10, *TUI Travel plc, British Airways plc, easyJet Airline Co. Ltd, International Air Transport Association, The Queen v. Civil Aviation Authority.*

142. See, for instance, J. Balfour, "Airline liability for delays – the European Court of Justice re-writes EC Reg. 261/2004", 35 *Air & Space Law* (2010), 71–76; J. Wegter, "The ECJ Decision of 10 January 2006 on the Validity of Reg. 261/2004: Ignoring the Exclusivity of the Montreal Convention", 31 *Air & Space Law* (2006), 133–148.

143. See Interpretative Guidelines on Reg. (EC) 261/2004, C(2016)3502 final.

consequences for relations with third countries as explained in the "*Open Skies*" judgments of the Court of Justice.[144] The Commission argued that in the *Open Skies* Agreements with the US the Member States had infringed their obligations under Union law. The Commission based its case primarily on the existence of an exclusive external competence of the Union in the sense of *Opinion 1/76*.[145] The Court rejected this argument but accepted certain other claims made by the EU Commission. Principally, the Court accepted the Commission's argument that the clause on the ownership and control of airlines in the bilateral agreements was contrary to the freedom of establishment laid down in Article 49 TFEU. However, the Court disagreed with the Commission, and sided with Member States on the matter of the core provisions of said agreements on market access which are subject to traffic rights remaining the prerogative of Member States.

Since the *Open Skies* decisions of the Court in 2002, the Commission's external policies are based on three pillars which focus on (I) the alignment of nationality clauses in bilateral air services agreements with the Freedom of Establishment, (II) the conclusion of all-encompassing agreements with third States of which the EU-US agreement of 2007 as amended in 2010 is the principal one, and (III) the neighbourhood policy designed to create an European Common Aviation Area, encompassing the – then – 27 EU States plus the States in the South Eastern part of Europe. Agreements with Mediterranean States, including Morocco, Israel and Jordan, are drawn up on a similar model.[146]

7. Combined Transport and Trans-European Networks

The Commission's Green Paper on Sea Ports and Maritime Infrastructure addresses the role of ports in the trans-European Transport Network (TEN), EU enlargement and connections to neighbouring third countries, the function of ports as transfer points in the intermodal transport chain, and protection of the environment.[147] In 2004, the Union adopted a directive on minimum safety requirements for tunnels in the Trans-European Road Network.[148] While the European rail network sponsored under the TEN-T policy has been enlarged significantly on certain connections, and the enlargement of the EU in 2004 has been greatly supported by the TEN-T project, progress has been hampered by budgetary constraints.[149]

Directive 92/106 provides for liberalization of combined transport. The EU Commission also fosters intermodal interurban travel by improving technologies and integrating the various surface modes of transport as this policy may reduce the use of energy recourses. Those technologies must reduce inefficiencies due to differences with respect to technical specifications and lack of interoperability. The two Directives aim to stimulate the interoperability of trans-European high-speed railway systems.[150]

144. Case C-466/98, *Commission v. United Kingdom*; Case C-467/98, *Commission v. Denmark*; Case C-468/98, *Commission v. Sweden*; Case C-469/98, *Commission v. Finland*; Case C-471/98, *Commission v. Belgium*; Case C-472/98, *Commission v. Luxembourg*; Case C-475/98, *Commission v. Austria*; Case C-476/98, *Commission v. Germany*.
145. See section 5.4.
146. Communication *The EU's External Aviation Policy – Addressing Future Challenges*, COM(2012)556 final.
147. COM(97)678 final of 10 Dec. 1997.
148. Dir. 2004/54.
149. See EU Commission Working Document, "Roadmap to a Single European Transport Area – Towards a competitive and resource efficient transport system", SEC(2011)391 final, at 9.
150. Dir. 96/48 and Dir. 2001/16 amended by Dir. 2004/50 and Dir. 2007/32.

Further reading

Bianco, L.O. and B. Van Houtte (Eds.), *EU Regulation and Competition Law in the Transport Sector* (OUP, 2017).

Bulterman, L., L. Hancher, A. McDonnell and H. Sevenster (Eds.), *Views of European Law from the Mountain* (Kluwer Law International, 2009).

Calme, S., "Relationship between the European Union Railway Transport Law and the Railway Protocol", available at <www.law.ox.ac.uk/sites/files/oxlaw/sandie_calme_-_relationship_between_eu_railway_transport_law_and_the_rail_protocol_0.pdf>, last accessed on 8 May 2017.

Correia, V., *L'Union européenne et le droit international de l'aviation civile* (Bruylant, 2014).

Hobe, S., N. von Ruckteschell and D. Hefferman (Eds.), *Cologne Compendium on Air Law in Europe* (Heymanns, 2013).

Hooydonk, E. van, *The Impact of EU Environmental Law on Waterways and Ports: Including a Proposal for the Creation of Portus 2010* (Maklu, 2006).

Jesse, H. and M.J. Werner, *EU Maritime Transport Law* (C.H. Beck/Hart/Nomos, 2016).

Langen, P.W. de and A.A. Pallis, "Entry barriers in seaports", 34 *Maritime Policy and Management* (2007), 427–440.

Milligan, J., *European Union Competition Law in the Airline Industry* (Kluwer Law International, 2017).

CHAPTER 32
EUROPEAN ENERGY LAW – FROM MARKET TO UNION?

*Leigh Hancher**

1. Introduction

In July 2014 the incoming President of the Commission announced that he intended to reform Europe's energy policy into a new European Energy Union– by pooling resources, connecting networks and uniting Europe's power when negotiating with non EU countries.[1] A reader unfamiliar with the history of European energy law and policy might be excused for having assumed that given that two of the founding European treaties dealt specifically with energy issues that such an "Energy Union" is already in place. This is however not the case. In recent decades, and aligned to the wider Single Market initiative launched in 1986,[2] the focus of European energy law and policy has been on creating a single internal energy market for electricity, gas, and in so far as barriers to trade remain, for coal and oil. A fully liberalized, common energy market would deliver lower prices and enhance Europe's competiveness on global markets. The new emphasis on a "European Energy Union" might indicate that more interventionist action is now needed. An internal energy market, although a cornerstone of European policy cannot necessarily deliver on the other two of Europe's ambitious energy policy goals – that is to achieve de-carbonization by 2050[3] and to enhance security of supply for the Member States – given that over 50% of gas, oil and other fuels originate from third countries.[4]

The development of EU energy and related climate change policies over the last two decades has generated a complex and not necessarily coherent body of harmonizing legislation. Article 194 TFEU provides the Union with an express but shared competence to adopt legislation in the field of energy. Nevertheless much of the legislation adopted to meet the so-called "20–20–20 targets" announced in 2007[5] has been based on the Treaty's environmental policy provisions.

---

* Professor of European Law, University of Tilburg, Professor of European Energy Law, EUI, Florence.

1. Available at <ec.europa.eu/priorities/docs/pg_en.pdf#page=6> (last visited 12 Feb. 2017).
2. For a discussion see Ch. 12, "The functioning of the internal market", of this book.
3. These goals are expressed in the EU Commission's Communication "Energy Roadmap 2050". The EU is committed to reducing greenhouse gas emissions to 80–95% below 1990 levels by 2050. 15 Dec. 2011, COM(2011)885.
4. The EU is highly dependent on energy from abroad, importing 53% of all the energy it consumes at a cost of more than one billion euros per day. This 42% of its solid fuels such as coal and 95% of its uranium. See further the Commission's Communication on the European Energy Security Strategy, 28 May 2014, COM(2014)330.
5. European Council 8/9 Mar. 2007 (7724/1/07 REV.1, 2 May 2007). These targets include a unilateral cut to greenhouse gas emissions by 20 per cent by 2020 compared to 1990 levels, to raise the share of renewable energy to 20 per cent by 2020 and to improve energy efficiency to save 20 per cent of EU energy consumption compared to forecasts compared to forecasts for 2020.

A truly integrated and competitive internal energy market not only needs a common legislative framework (often referred to as the "software" of European energy policy) but also significant physical interconnections (the "hardware") between Member States. The Commission estimates that some € 200 billion in investment is required up to 2020 in this respect. As such the Treaty provisions on trans-European energy networks are also an important component of the governance framework for the delivery of a European energy policy. Given that the TFEU now confers exclusive competence on the Union in respect of Foreign Direct Investment [FDI], the potential impact of Article 207 TFEU on external energy policy cannot be overlooked.

This chapter focuses on the growing body of secondary legislation adopted on the basis of these various Treaty provisions. Section 2 examines the constitutional framework for EU energy policy. Section 3 then turns to a more detailed explanation of the novel legal features of recent internal energy market legislation. Section 4 deals with the external dimension of EU energy policy while section 5 explores some of the tensions between various national measures to promote EU energy and climate goals and the Treaty rules.

As will become apparent, the numerous legislative measures adopted to pursue energy policy goals are based on a number of different Treaty provisions, even after the entry into force of the Lisbon Treaty. Energy Union policy is now intricately linked with climate change policy and while the former has traditionally focused on liberalizing energy supply the latter is increasingly focused on the demand side of the equation: to secure the most efficient use of energy by its users, thus reducing its adverse environmental impact. But national prerogatives may still legitimately predominate on both the supply and the demand side of the energy policy equation. Despite adoption of numerous harmonization packages over the past two decades, and perhaps in continuing deference to national sensitivities, the European courts have proven reluctant to undermine this state of affairs.

2. The constitutional framework

Historical reasons partially explain why the original EEC Treaty did not identify energy as one of its main policy areas. When the Treaty of Rome was concluded in 1957 energy was at the centre of the attention of the Member States, and coal was the most important source of primary energy. The six founding Member States had pooled their interests in that area in the context of the now defunct European Coal and Steel Community (ECSC).[6] In addition, the European Atomic Energy Community Treaty (EAEC) – the Euratom Treaty – concluded in 1957, ensured cooperation in the field of the nuclear energy as the other primary energy source which could give the Community its energy independence. In 1957 natural gas was not an important source of primary energy, and mineral oil was dealt with by the rules on the free movement of goods. The state of technical development of electricity grids hardly allowed large scale trans-frontier electricity trading. So, in 1951 the ECSC Treaty and in 1957 the Euratom Treaty offered a sufficient legal basis for a common energy policy of the day, with EEC Treaty articles on free movement, competition and state aids available for "plugging the gaps".[7] In addition the European institutions adopted a number of measures as a response to oil shortages and to secure adequate oil stocks.[8]

---

6. On the expiry of the ECSC in 2001, coal is now subject to the TFEU, albeit with some transitional measures in relation to state aid.
7. For a detailed overview see T. Daintith and L. Hancher, *Energy Strategy in Europe: The Legal Framework* (De Gruyter, 1986).
8. Council Directive 68/414/EEC of 20 Dec. 1968 imposing an obligation on Member States of the EEC to maintain minimum stocks of crude oil and/or petroleum products, O.J. 1986, 308/14; Council Directive

The Treaty on the European Union of 1992 did not further address or identify energy as a policy issue,[9] merely listing it as a "common policy" (Art. 3(u) EC). The list of objectives laid down in Article 2 EC did not refer to energy at all.[10] The absence of a specific competence was not an obstacle to the adoption of an important body of law as the legal foundation for European energy policy. The European institutions adopted successive packages of common rules for the internal gas and electricity market, based on Article 110 TFEU and in so far as promoting renewable energy and energy efficiency is concerned, on the basis of Article 191 TFEU. Security of supply legislation has been adopted in the past on the basis of Article 122 TFEU[11] and in adopting various measures aimed at increasing fuel price transparency,[12] general powers given in provisions such as Article 213 EEC were relied upon.

2.1 *The Treaty of Lisbon*

Energy now receives an explicit recognition in Article 4 of Part I of the Treaty as one of the Union's shared competences. A separate energy title XXI is now included consisting of a single Article – Article 194 – specifying how competence is to be shared.[13] Thus, Article 194 sets out the four main aims of Union policy on energy: to ensure the functioning of the energy market, to ensure security of supply of the Union; to promote energy efficiency and saving and the development of new and renewable forms of energy, and finally to promote the interconnection of energy networks. These aims are to be executed in a "spirit of solidarity" between the Member States.

Importantly, Article 194(2) stipulates that Union legislation shall not affect a Member State's choice between different energy sources and the general structure of its supply, without prejudice to Article 192(2) (dealing with environmental policy).[14] The Member States therefore appear to retain extensive competence to determine their "energy mix". Legislation furthering the objectives of Article 194(1) TFEU can be adopted by the ordinary legislative procedure but any matter falling within the scope of Article 194(3) is subject to unanimity.[15] This leaves a question mark as to the scope of Article 194(2). Would a measure potentially affecting a Member State's rights to determine its energy mix be subject to the rule on unanimity, giving every Member State a veto right or is the provision to read as a form of "opt-out" for a Member State to avoid the national application of an EU legislative measure adopted in accordance with the ordinary

---

73/238/EEC of 24 July 1973 on measures to mitigate the effects of difficulties in the supply of crude oil and petroleum products, O.J. 1973, L 228/1.

9. In a Declaration on Art. 231 EC attached to the Final Act on the occasion of signature of the SEA in 1986 the then Intergovernmental Conference confirmed that the Community's activities in the sphere of the environment may not interfere with national policies regarding the exploitation of energy resources, a declaration which the national governments regarded as confirming their sovereignty over mineral resources.
10. A new provision on trans-European networks was however included – Art. 154 EC.
11. Directive 2004/67/EC of 26 Apr. 2004 concerning measures to safeguard security of natural gas supply, O.J. 2004, L 127/47.
12. Directive 90/377/EEC of 29 June 1990 concerning a Community procedure to improve the transparency of gas and electricity prices charged to industrial end-users, O.J. 1990, L 185/1.
13. In the so-called Reform Treaty, the predecessor to the Lisbon Treaty, the Title was XX and the Art. number was 176 A (see <www.consilium.europa.eu/uedocs/cmsUpload/cg00014.en07.pdf> last visited 12 Feb. 2017).
14. Art. 192(2) TFEU derogates from the ordinary co-decision procedure (laid down in Art. 192(1) TFEU) for EU legislation in the environmental sphere, requiring the Council to act unanimously after consulting (*inter alia*) the European Parliament where they seek to adopt measures significantly affecting a Member State's choice between different energy sources and the general structure of its energy supply.
15. See Ch. 5, "The political institutions", of this book.

procedure? The wording of Article 194(2) TFEU has led some commentators to speak of a "*domaines sancturisés*" and "zones de competence national exclusive".[16] Yet a wide interpretation curtailing or even excluding the EU's competence on energy could be in conflict with the aims of the EU policy on energy to which the EU is committed in Article 194(1) TFEU.

This is not merely an academic question but one which has taken on increasing importance as the EU presses forward with plans for a low carbon energy economy by 2050. Can legislation require a Member State to relinquish its domestic coal supplies for renewable energy? Can it mandate the substitution of one fuel such as gas for another, such as nuclear?[17] Given that, as explained below, Article 194 TFEU has not been the only legal basis used for the adoption of energy and climate change legislation, this is a complex issue.

The text of Article 194(2) TFEU is not dissimilar to that found for the legal basis of the EU's policy on environment in Article 192(2)(c) TFEU, which also makes reference to "a Member State's choice between different energy sources and the general structure of its energy supply". Yet, in contrast to acts based on Article 194 TFEU, the EU's environmental measures may affect "significantly" these national domains.[18] Hence, both limitations serve to protect national sovereignty with regard to the Member States' choice of energy supply and the general or global structure of its energy supply, but Article 194(2) is even more rigorous: it appears to forbid any EU measure affecting, whether significantly or not, this national reservation, and this prohibition cannot be overcome by unanimity in the Council.

In *Case T-370/11*,[19] Poland challenged a Commission decision adopted under Directive 2003/87 as an infringement of Article 194(2) TFEU, on the basis that the decision affects a Member State's right to determine the conditions for exploiting its energy resources, its choice between different energy sources and the general structure of its energy supply. Poland alleged that the Commission had focused on natural gas to the detriment of other fuels such as coal, and as a consequence increases the natural gas needs of the State concerned, disrupt its energy balance and force it to redefine its overall energy policy. The contested decision implemented a Directive which took as its legal basis what is now Article 191 TFEU and not Article 194(2) TFEU (the choice of legal basis being not disputed by Poland). The Court rejected Poland's complaint alleging infringement of Article 194(2) TFEU. Poland maintained that Article 194(2) TFEU remained relevant, and measures adopted in the context of other policies cannot affect the rights conferred by Article 194(2) TFEU. The General Court held that there was no reason to suppose that Article 194(2) applied in the area of the environment.[20]

The final text of the new energy title was intended as a carefully crafted compromise between national sovereignty over natural resources and the energy mix and energy taxation issues and a shared Union competence for the rest. Article 194 confirms the Union's competence to adopt preventative measures to avoid security threats and may well provide a basis for political backing for more far-reaching measures to establish a true European Energy Union in the future.[21]

16. See C. Blumann, "Les compétences de l'Únion européenne dans le domaine de l'énergie", (2009) *R.A.E.-L.A.E.*, at 737–745.
17. A. Johnston and E. van der Marel, "Ad Lucem? Interpreting the new EU energy provision, and in particular the meaning of Art. 194(2) TFEU", 22 *European Energy and Environmental Law Review*, at 181.
18. See TFEU, Art. 192(2)(c).
19. Case T-370/11, *Republic of Poland v. European Commission*. See also Case C-226/16, *Eni SpA v. Premier ministre, Ministre de l'environnement*, paras. 21-22.
20. Ibid., para 17.
21. Art. 122 TFEU states that "without prejudice to any other procedures provided for in the Treaties, the Council, on a proposal from the Commission, may decide, in a spirit of solidarity between Member States,

2.2 Nuclear energy: The Euratom Treaty

Under the Euratom Treaty, the EU has an extensive legal competence to protect the general public throughout Europe from ionizing radiation, even if the choice of energy mix is a national competence.[22] Fourteen Member States have nuclear power plants. On the basis of the Euratom Treaty, the EU can ensure the safe and sustainable use of nuclear energy across Europe and pursue high standards of safety, security and non-proliferation through the adoption of nuclear safeguards measures to ensure that nuclear materials are used only for the purposes declared by the users.

Although the Euratom Treaty is a "lex specialis" it does not entirely derogate from the TFEU. The Euratom Treaty adopts no particular policy towards nuclear power, but rather lays down certain conditions for its use.[23] Its overall objectives are listed in Article 1 and the tasks to be performed in accordance with its Article 2 include, *inter alia*, the promotion of research, the establishment of uniform safety standards to protect workers and the general public, to facilitate investment and to ensure the non-diversion of nuclear materials and the peaceful uses of nuclear energy. Ten separate chapters, set out in Title II of the Treaty, are devoted to each task. In an important ruling in Case C-29/99, *Commission v. Council*, the ECJ confirmed that the EAEC's competences covered technological as well as radiological safety, allowing the EAEC to go on to conclude further measures on nuclear safety.[24] Recent legislation has focused on this latter objective.

2.2.1 Nuclear safety

The Fukushima Daiichi accident in 2011 led to an overhaul of a number of existing health and safety measures, including Council Directive 2013/59/EURATOM[25] laying down basic safety standards for protection against the dangers arising from exposure to ionizing radiation updated earlier legislation, and Council Directive 2013/51/EURATOM[26] laying down requirements for the protection of the health of the general public with regard to radioactive substances in water intended for human consumption.

The Nuclear Safety Directive 2009[27] introducing a common safety framework and making international nuclear safety principles legally binding in all Member States, also required amendment.[28] The new Directive, strengthens the power and independence of national regulatory authorities, introduces a high-level EU-wide safety objective to prevent accidents and avoid radioactive releases, sets up a European system of peer reviews on specific safety issues every six

upon the measures appropriate to the economic situation, in particular if severe difficulties arise in the supply of certain products, notably in the area of energy".

22. As recognized by the Court in Case C-29/99, *Commission v. Council*, para 82–89.
23. In so far as measures are aimed at the energy sector in general, including nuclear generation, and fulfil the objectives set out in Art. 194(1) TFEU, then the relevant legislation must be adopted on that legal basis and not on the basis of any specific provision in the Euratom Treaty – see Case C-490/10, *Parliament v. Commission*, para 82.
24. Case C-29/99, *Commission v. Council*, paras. 82–89.
25. This Directive repeals Directives 89/618/Euratom, 90/641/Euratom, 96/29/Euratom, 97/43/Euratom and 2003/122/Euratom.
26. Council Directive 2013/51/Euratom, O.J. 2013, L 296/12.
27. Council Directive 2009/71/Euratom, O.J. 2009, L 172/18.
28. The amendment is based on the lessons learned from the Fukushima nuclear accident, EU nuclear stress tests, and the safety requirements of the Western European Nuclear Regulators Association (WENRA) and the International Atomic Energy Association (IAEA).

years, increases transparency on nuclear safety matters by informing and involving the public and promotes an effective nuclear safety culture.[29]

It may be argued that nuclear energy is likely to remain a special case in that the TFEU rules on state aid (Arts. 107–108 TFEU) at least cannot be straightforwardly and directly applied to evaluate aid to this sector.[30] The application of the competition rules and the rules regarding merger clearance have not proved problematic: the Commission has consistently applied Articles 101 and 102 TFEU as well as its powers under EU Regulation 139/04 to the nuclear sector.[31]

2.2.2 *The Supply Agency*

The Euratom Treaty establishes a common policy on supplies, founded on equal access to sources of supply (Art. 52(1) Euratom). The Euratom Supply Agency (ESA) is charged with ensuring a regular and equitable supply of ores and nuclear fuels for all users in the EAEC, pursuing the longer term aim of security of supply through reducing dependence upon any one source and diversifying sources of supply. The Treaty grants the ESA wide powers to achieve these goals but in practice these have been used sparingly.[32]

2.3 *Energy, SGEI and the Lisbon Treaty*

Member States have been equally reluctant to let go of national powers to guarantee that their domestic consumers could receive electricity and gas on fair and reasonable terms if the national markets do not deliver leading to the inclusion of Article 16 TFEU as well as a separate Protocol (no. 26) on Services of General Interest (SGI).[33]

The Protocol does not deal with the financing of such services, so that the Treaty rules on state aids (now Articles 107–109 TFEU) continue to apply as before. But is clear that despite the adoption of successive packages of secondary legislation on the internal energy market, Member States can still legitimately impose a range of public service obligations (PSO) on energy companies as confirmed in the *Federutility* case.[34] Indeed the Commission has relied on Article 106(2) TFEU to endorse government measures on the operation of an LNG plant in order to guarantee diversity of supply.[35] The General Court confirmed that the Commission was entitled to rely upon Article 106(2) to approve state aid to the Spanish coal sector as a form of back-up supply to support the increased use of renewable energy.[36]

---

29. Council Directive 2014/87/Euratom of 8 July 2014 amending Directive 2009/71/Euratom establishing a Community framework for the nuclear safety of nuclear installations, O.J. 2014, L 219/42.
30. See L. Hancher and F.M. Salerno, "EU energy policy" in A Biondi et al. (Eds.) *The Future of the EU after Lisbon* (OUP, 2012), Ch. 18. See also Commission Decision SA.34947(2013/C) (ex 2103/N) – United Kingdom – Support to the Hinkley Point C Nuclear Power Station. This decision is now under appeal in Case T-356/15, *Austria v. Commission*, action brought on 6 July 2015. This is the first time a Member State has challenged a Commission decision approving aid granted by another Member State.
31. See for example, Case COMP/M.4839, *AREVA NP MHI/ATMEA*, O.J. 2007, C 61/01.
32. As endorsed by the ECJ in Joined Cases C-123 and 124/04, *Industrias Nucleares do Brasil and Siemens*.
33. This Protocol recognizes that such services are shared values of the Union and the essential role and wide discretion of national, regional and local authorities in providing, organizing and commissioning these services is underlined, including the high level of quality, safety and affordability and the promotion of universal access and user rights.
34. Case C-265/08, *Federutility and Others v. Autorità per l'energia elettrica e il gas*, paras. 29 and 30. See however the subsequent Case C-36/14, *Commission v. Poland* of 10 Sept. 2015 in which the Court held that the application of price controls to wholesale markets could not be justified as necessary and proportionate.
35. Case SA.36740, *Lithuania LNG*.
36. Case T-57/11, *Castelnou Energía v. Commission*.

2.4 *The inter-relationship between Article 194 and climate change policy*

Article 11 TFEU provides: "Environmental protection requirements must be integrated into the definition and implementation of the Community policies and activities, in particular with a view to promoting sustainable development This "mainstreaming" principle is not new,[37] and it is of particular importance in the energy sector given the adverse impact of most types of fossil fuel on the environment. To date a series of important measures, which are briefly described below, have been adopted on the basis of Article 192 TFEU.

2.4.1 *Article 192 TFEU: Renewables, emissions and efficiency*

This Article (and its predecessors) provided the legal basis for harmonizing legislation directly impacting the energy market, including the Renewables (or "RES") Directive 2009/28[38] as well as on the promotion of energy efficiency,[39] in furtherance of the "20–20–20" goals.

In addition the EU's flagship initiative – the Emission Trading Scheme (ETS)[40] – is based on Article 191 TFEU. EU Directive 2004/8 – also adopted on the basis of Article 192(1) TFEU promotes co-generation and district heating as environmentally friendly and efficient forms of electricity generation.[41] Furthermore, the Directive 2009/31 on Geological Storage of Carbon Dioxide – which in promoting carbon capture and storage (CCS) – may have substantial impact on generation based on indigenous fossil fuels – takes the environmental title as its legal basis.[42] These measures promote the supply of sustainable energy. The Commission adopted an ambitious Energy Efficiency Plan in 2011, focusing on six areas of competence: the public sector, the building industry; European industry in general, financial support measures; the role of consumers and the transport sector.[43] Its overall aim is to ensure 20% energy saving by 2020. A new Directive intended to implement these targets into binding measures was proposed by the Commission in June 2011. In its final version Directive 2012/27 abandoned the proposed binding targets due to lack of political support, although the Directive imposes a number of binding measures.[44]

---

37. See for an early application in relation to the promotion of renewable energy, A.G. Jacob's Opinion in Case C-379/98, *Preussen Elektra*.
38. Directive 2009/28/EC of the European Parliament and of the Council of 23 Apr. 2009 on the promotion of the use of energy from renewable sources O.J. 2009, L 140/52.
39. One of the first directives being Directive 2002/91/EC of the European Parliament and of the Council of 16 Dec. 2002 on the energy performance of buildings O.J. 2002, L 1/65. Directive 2006/32/EC of the European Parliament and of the Council of 5 Apr. 2006 on energy end-use efficiency and energy services and repealing Council Directive 93/76/EEC, O.J. 2006, L 114/64.
40. Directive 2003/87 as amended by Directive 2009/27, O.J. 2009, L 140/63. For an evaluation see, C. Poncelet, "The ETS: Analysis of some contentious points", 20 *European Energy and Environmental Law Review* (2011), at 245–254. See also Case C-5/16, *Poland v. European Parliament and Council of the EU*, pending.
41. Directive 2004/8/EC of the European Parliament and of the Council of 11 Feb. 2004 on the promotion of cogeneration based on a useful heat demand in the internal energy market and amending Directive 92/42/EEC, O.J. 2004, L 52/50.
42. Directive 2009/31/EC of the European Parliament and of the Council of 23 Apr. 2009 on the geological storage of carbon dioxide O.J. 2009, L 140/114.
43. Energy Efficiency Plan, COM/2011/109, 8 Mar. 2011.
44. A review of each Member State's progress towards the European 20% objective will take place in 2014. Directive 2012/27/EU entered into force on 4 Dec. 2012. Member States have to transpose the Directive into national law by 5 June 2014 at the latest.

2.5 *Energy networks*

Although Article 194(1) makes reference to the promotion of energy network interconnection, the EU has used a separate legal basis – Article 170 TFEU[45] – to adopt Regulation 347/2013 in April 2013[46] as part of the so called Energy Infrastructure package.[47] Indeed the Treaty provisions on trans-European networks, should be regarded as a supplement to the achievement of the internal market for transport, telecommunications and energy.

As required by the Regulation, the European Commission adopted on 14 October 2013[48] a list of some 250 key energy infrastructure projects.[49] These "projects of common interest" (PCI) will benefit from accelerated licensing procedures and improved regulatory conditions and may have access to financial support from the Connecting Europe Facility (CEF), under which a €5.85 billion budget has been allocated to trans-European energy infrastructure for the period 2014–20.[50] Selection is carried out in a two-stage process. The project promoter will submit its proposal to the relevant regional group. The final decision on the Union-wide list of projects of common interest is taken by the Commission.

Member States must designate a single competent authority responsible – "a one stop shop" – for the completion of the entire permit granting process, which should not exceed 3 years.[51] Where a PCI encounters significant implementation difficulties the Commission can designate a European coordinator. The coordinator has no powers however to require the realization of the projects in question. The Regulation confers important tasks on national transmission system operators (TSOs), national energy regulators as well as the European energy agency – ACER. In accordance with Article 3(6) of Regulation 347/2013 PCIs included on the Union list shall become an integral part of the relevant national 10-year network development plans[52] and other national infrastructure plans concerned, as appropriate. Those projects must be part of the EU-wide 10 year network development plan. In turn the EU-wide 10 year plan must include a

45. The Title XV on trans-European networks was added to the EC Treaty by the Treaty of Maastricht; See further Ch. 33, "Cohesion policy and geographic differentiation", of this book.
46. Reg. (EU) 347/2013 of the European Parliament and of the Council of 17 Apr. 2013 on guidelines for trans-European energy infrastructure and repealing Decision 1364/2006/EC and amending Reg. (EC) 713/2009, (EC) 714/2009 and (EC) 715/2009 Text with EEA relevance, O.J. 2013, L 115/39.
47. This Regulation is anchored in the Europe 2020 Strategy for smart, sustainable and inclusive growth, which put energy infrastructures at the forefront as part of the flagship initiative "Resource efficient Europe". It forms an integrated package with the "Connecting Europe Facility" (CEF). See also the Commission Communication, Long term infrastructure vision for Europe and beyond, COM/2013/0711 final 14 Oct. 2013.
48. Commission Delegated Reg. (EU) 1391/2013 of 14 Oct. 2013 amending Reg. (EU) 347/2013 of the European Parliament and of the Council on guidelines for trans-European energy infrastructure as regards the Union list of projects of common interest, O.J. 2013, L 349/28 establishes the list of the projects now designated as PCIs.
49. Subsequent lists will be drawn up every two years. Six months after the adoption of the first list, the Commission must establish a publicly accessible infrastructure transparency platform containing information on projects of common interest. No later than 2017, the Commission will publish a report on the implementation of these projects.
50. Reg. 1316/2013 of the European Parliament and of the Council of 11 Dec. 2013 establishing the Connecting Europe Facility, amending Reg. (EU) 913/2010 and repealing Regulations (EC) 680/2007 and (EC) 67/2010, O.J. 2013, L 348/12.
51. Member States may elect between integrated, co-ordinated and collaborative schemes in order to organize the permit granting process. The duration and implementation is further regulated by Art. 10.
52. As required under Art. 22 of the Parliament and Council Directive (EC) 2009/72 concerning common rules for the internal market in electricity and repealing Directive (EC) 2003/54, O.J. 2009, L 211/55 and the Parliament and Council Directive (EC) 2009/73 concerning common rules for the internal market in natural gas and repealing Directive (EC) 2003/55, O.J. 2009, L 211/94.

harmonized methodology for an energy system wide analysis of the costs and benefits of a PCI. In an integrated market the costs of a PCI should be borne by all the users of the infrastructure and not just by a single TSO's national customers, especially as the benefits of an interconnector may occur in one Member State in the form of lower energy prices, while another Member State bears the largest proportion of the costs. Regulation 347/2013 aims to introduce clear and transparent rules for cost allocation across borders.[53]

2.6 *Article 194 TFEU: What difference does it make?*

Subsequent to its entry into force, Article 194 is now used as the primary legal basis for measures relating to the functioning of the internal energy market, such as the Regulation on Market Integrity and Transparency (REMIT) 2011 and on security of supply including the Regulation on Security of Supply for Gas 2010, both discussed below in Part 2.

In *Case C-490/10*,[54] the Parliament successfully challenged the failure of the Commission and the Council to choose Article 194 TFEU as the proper legal basis for Council Regulation 617/2010 on the notification of investment projects in energy infrastructure. The Court held that "[...] that provision constitutes the legal basis for European Union acts which are "necessary" to achieve the objectives assigned to that policy by Article 194(1) TFEU". The latest package of legislative measures, "The Clean Energy Package", adopted by the Commission in December 2016 all take Article 194 TFEU as their legal basis,[55] as does the newly adopted Regulation 2017/1938 on security of gas supply.[56]

Although Commission has acknowledged that Article 194(2) allows the Member States to determine their own "energy mix", and choose, for example, to opt for nuclear energy if they so wish, public intervention to support particular sources of energy nevertheless remains subject to the Treaty rules on free movement, competition and state aid.[57] This follows from the text of Article 194(2), which does not provide for a derogation from any other Treaty rules.

3. The third energy package legislation – building the internal market

3.1 *The third energy package*

The so-called third package of internal energy market measures,[58] adopted in 2009 was based on Article 114 TFEU. The scope of this legislation confirms that the European institutions already

---

53. Art. 11 of the Regulation requires that by 16 Nov. 2013, the ENTSOs shall publish and submit to Member States, the Commission and ACER their respective methodologies, for a harmonized energy system-wide cost-benefit analysis at Union level for projects of common interest. Those methodologies, which must be reviewed by ACER and by the Commission, shall be applied for the preparation of each subsequent 10-year network development plan developed by the ENTSOs. Methodologies shall be drawn up in line with the principles laid down in Annex V and be consistent with the rules and indicators set out in Annex IV.
54. *C-490/10 European Parliament v. Council of the European Union.*
55. The Clean Energy Package "Clean Energy for All Europeans", comprises some 1000 pages of text and puts forward ten legislative measures: see <eur-lex.europa.eu/resource.html?uri=cellar:fa6ea15b-b7b0-11e6-9e3c-01aa75ed71a1.0001.02/DOC_1&format=PDF>.
56. O.J. 2017, L 280/1.
57. EC Communication, *Delivering the internal electricity market and making the most of public intervention*, C[2013]7243 final, 5 Nov. 2013; EC Staff Working Document, *Generation Adequacy in the internal electricity market – guidance on public interventions*, SWD[2013]438 final, 5 Nov. 2013.
58. See (i) Parliament and Council Directive (EC) 2009/72 concerning common rules for the internal market in electricity and repealing Directive (EC) 2003/54, O.J. 2009, L 211/55; (ii) Parliament and Council Directive (EC) 2009/73 concerning common rules for the internal market in natural gas and repealing Directive (EC) 2003/55, O.J. 2009, L 211/94; (iii) Parliament and Council Reg. (EC)713/2009 establishing an

enjoyed extensive competence in the matter of energy policy before the adoption of Article 194 TFEU, to influence the organization of national energy markets is potentially considerable. The Third Energy Package has built on the two previous packages of harmonizing measures.[59] The first internal electricity and gas directives adopted in 1996 and 1998 respectively essentially required a minimal level of harmonization and a gradual opening up of national markets.[60] National import and export monopolies had to be removed[61] and third party access rights to transmission networks for competing suppliers had to be introduced. Third party access – "TPA" – is the cornerstone of the liberalization of Europe's electricity and gas markets. The Court of Justice has held that "for competition to function, non-discriminatory, transparent and fairly priced network access is of paramount importance in bringing about the internal electricity market".[62] The Court has refused to "grandfather" contractual rights of access granted on the basis of commitments entered into before liberalization of the electricity market.[63] Subsequent directives were adopted in 2003 requiring Member States to open their markets in full so that all domestic customers could purchase electricity or gas from the supplier of their choice by 1 July 2007. Network access rights were strengthened and energy utilities were required to separate their transmission functions into distinct legal entities.[64] National regulatory institutions were required to supervise access rights and network tariffs.[65]

An exhaustive analysis of the two directives and three regulations that constitute the Third Package is beyond the scope of this chapter but a short account of several aspects of the Package illustrates the dilution of national sovereignty on energy market organizational issues. Three themes are addressed: a) the new unbundling regime, b) the role and duties of national regulators and c) the creation of the new Agency for the Cooperation of Energy regulators ("ACER").

3.1.1 *The unbundling regime*

A controversial element of the Third package is Article 9 of Directive 72/009 and Directive 73/009. This article introduces "ownership" unbundling for Transmission System Operators (TSOs). The Commission concluded in various reports, including the Sector Enquiry Report of 2007, that mere legal unbundling of national energy companies was insufficient to guarantee the objectives of the internal energy market exercise.[66] During negotiations on the draft

---

Agency for the Cooperation of Energy Regulators, O.J. 2009, L 211/1; (iv) Parliament and Council Reg. (EC) 714/2009 on conditions for access to the network for cross border exchanges in electricity and repealing Reg. (EC) 1228/2003, O.J. 2009, L 211/15; (v) Parliament and Council Reg. (EC) 715/2009 on conditions for access to the natural gas transmission networks and repealing Reg. (EC) 1775/2005, O.J. 2009, L 211/36.

59. The "First" package comprised a Directive 96/92 on internal electricity market and a Directive 98/30 on the internal gas market. In 2003 a subsequent Directive 2003/54 (electricity) and Directive 2003/55 (gas) were adopted together with Reg. 1228/2003 (cross border electricity) and later Reg. 715/2005 (gas).
60. Initially this right was restricted to large industrial consumers and distribution companies.
61. In 1994 the ECJ had ruled that the Commission was not entitled to rely on Arts. 37 and 106(1) TFEU to require Member States to remove exclusive import and export rights conferred on their national electricity and gas companies. See Case C-157/94, *Commission v. Netherlands*.
62. Case C-439/06, *Citiworks AG v. Flughafen Leipzig/Halle GmbH*.
63. Case C-17/03, *VEMW*. See also Case C-264/09 *Commission v. Slovakia*.
64. Case C-274/08, *Commission v. Sweden*.
65. See Case C-239/07, *Julius Satauskas* on the importance of published network tariffs.
66. See the DG Comp report on the energy sector inquiry (SEC(2006)1724, 10 Jan. 2007) which found, among other things, that there was poor integration between European energy markets and barriers to entry for new entrants. The Commission considered that this was partly caused by vertical foreclosure and concluded that further unbundling would help address these problems by improving the independence of the networks.

directives Member States gained some flexibility in choosing between the various unbundling models – full ownership unbundling (FOU),[67] the Independent System operator (ISO),[68] and the Independent Transmission Operator (ITO),[69] and finally the so-called ITO+,[70] so that a number of Member States were prepared to withdraw their objections to the Community's exercise of its powers to interfere with matters of national property law and the protection conferred by Article 345 TFEU.

In order to ensure full compliance with the unbundling rules, TSOs must now also be certified by the national regulatory authority (NRA) The decision is forwarded to the European Commission to deliver an opinion on compliance with the directives' requirements.[71] An NRA will be required to take the "utmost account" of this opinion. The unbundling rules are also extended to third country companies, via the certification procedures. Where certification is requested by a TSO which is controlled by a person or persons from a third country,[72] the NRA shall refuse certification if has not been demonstrated that the entity concerned complies with the requirements of Article 9 and that the granting of certification will not put at risk the security of energy supply of the Member State and the Union.[73] The rationale for this clause is to ensure that European transmission systems are not controlled by vertically integrated third country suppliers.[74]

3.1.2 *National regulatory authorities*

Given the detail and complexity of EU internal market energy legislation, its effective enforcement and application is dependent on effective, sector- specific regulation at national level. Member States must designate a single national regulatory authority at national level. The Directives impose a large list of duties and obligations on the NRAs and require that they are entrusted with sufficient resources and powers to carry out these duties. In particular, Article 37(4)(d) of Directive 72/09 (electricity) and Article 41(3)(d) of Directive 73/09 (gas) require the NRAs to impose effective, proportionate and dissuasive penalties on undertakings not complying with their obligations under the Third Package. The directly applicable Regulations 714/2009 (electricity) and 715/2009 (gas) require NRAs to incorporate various common principles in their

---

67. FOU requires that ownership and operation of the transmission system is carried out by a company that is independent from supply or generation.
68. Technically a derogation from FOU, ISO option allows the ownership of the assets to remain with a vertically integrated undertaking (VIU) but requires that an independent system operator is full responsible for operation.
69. The ITO allows both ownership and operation to remain within a legally unbundled subsidiary of a VIU subject to strict regulation and oversight by the NRA.
70. Art. 9(9) allows the status quo to be maintained, insofar as the transmission system belonged to a VIU on 3 Sept. 2009 and there are arrangements in place which guarantee more effective independence.
71. The Commission may, if it considers it appropriate, request that the Agency for the Cooperation of Energy Regulators (ACER) provide an opinion. If so, the two-month period shall be extended for a further two months.
72. For an application of the concept of control in this respect, see further the Commission's opinion on the certification of Gaz-Sytem as the operator of the Polish section of the Yamal-Europe pipeline, C(2014)6463, 9 Sept. 2014.
73. Security of supply concerns in relation to the certification of the Greek TSO, DEFSA, which had been acquired by the Azeri state oil company SOCAR prompted the Commission to request the Greek regulatory authorities to take a number of far reaching measures into account in its certification decision, including the suspension of SOCAR's voting rights in DEFSA – see Opinion C (2014) 5483 of 28 July as corrected by C(2014)7734 of 17 Oct. 2014.
74. Directive 2003/55/EC of the European Parliament and of the Council of 26 June 2003 concerning common rules for the internal market in natural gas and repealing Directive 98/30/EC, O.J. 2003, L 176/57, Recital 22.

tariff methodologies and network access rules. For example with respect to electricity network tariffs, these must not be distance-related, and gas network tariffs must be set separately for each point of entry or exit of its gas transmission network.

A major innovation of the Third Energy Package is that national regulators must not only be independent from the industry, which they regulate, they must also enjoy a certain amount of independence from their national governments. Thus, according to Article 35(4)–(5) of Directive 72/09 (electricity) NRAs shall "[...] not seek or take direct instructions from any government or other public or private entity when carrying out the regulatory tasks. [...] The regulatory authority can take autonomous decisions, independently from any political body [...]".[75] This means that national governments' scope to determine or otherwise influence transmission tariffs is now heavily circumscribed: NRAs cannot be subject to specific veto rights although Member States may issue general policy guidelines to these bodies.[76]

In order to gauge the extent to which these provisions limit Member States' ability to influence key aspects of national energy markets policy, suffice it to compare with analogous provisions on NRAs in the field of telecoms.[77] Moreover, only NRAs (and not government officials) may participate in the new Agency for the Cooperation of Energy Regulators ("ACER"). Finally the NRAs are required to closely consult and co-operate with each other and with ACER on a variety of cross-border issues.

3.2 *The New Agency – the ACER*

The Agency for the Co-operation of Energy Regulators – ACER- is essentially an advisory body to provide both the Commission and the NRAs with opinions on various issues including the monitoring of TSOs and their cooperation at the regional or at Union level through the European Networks of TSOs – the ENTSOs.

The creation of a new Agency by Regulation 713/2009 was facilitated by a high level of political support but the powers eventually conferred on the ACER are minimal due to the Commission's insistence on a narrow interpretation of the so-called "Meroni doctrine", which sets limit on the Commission's ability to delegate powers to agencies.[78] ACER may provide an opinion or recommendation "on any issue relating to the purpose for which it has been established" either at the request of the European Parliament, the Council or the Commission, or on its own initiative. It must also perform a general reporting and monitoring role with regard to the internal markets in electricity and gas, providing a public annual report, including identifying any barriers to the completion of the internal market and possible proposals for tackling these difficulties. ACER may only take legally binding decisions, subject to Commission veto, on cross border infrastructures when the NRAs concerned have failed to reach agreement or where these NRAs jointly request ACER to take a decision. However, ACER has acquired important powers and duties in relation to the implementation of REMIT as well as the development of network planning.

---

75. Art. 39 of Directive 2009/73/EC of the European Parliament and of the Council of 13 July 2009 concerning common rules for the internal market in natural gas and repealing Directive 2003/55/EC, O.J. 2009, L 211/94 has identical provisions.
76. Case C-474/08, *Commission v. Belgium.*
77. See further L. Hancher and P. Larouche, "The coming of age of EU network regulation" in P. Craig and G. de Búrca (Eds.) *The Evolution of EU Law*, 2nd ed. (OUP, 2011), at 743–781.
78. See Ch. 8, "The EU administration", of this book.

3.3 ACER, network codes and comitology

Another distinctive characteristic of the Third Energy Package is the extensive delegation of regulatory powers by the Council to the Commission by way of comitology procedures, and in particular the so-called regulatory procedure to adopt guidelines and network codes, and to amend the various annexes to the Directives and the Regulations. Network codes can be adopted to harmonize a range of essentially technical issues relating to the operation of gas and electricity transmission networks. The network codes are highly technical instruments, requiring extensive involvement from the TSOs who have the necessary expertise but who are also entrusted with the obligation to act in the general interest of system users and to facilitate market integration.[79] A novel feature of the Third package is the creation of European Networks of Transmission System Operators for Electricity (ENTSO-E) and gas (ENTSO-G). These private law organizations are entrusted with the obligation to develop both network codes and plans for the development of a fully interconnected European market for electricity and gas. ACER has an important role to play in the process of the adoption of network codes. Despite their technical nature these complex network codes have a far-reaching impact on the operation of the internal gas and electricity markets and are considered to be an essential component of the so-called Electricity and Gas Target Models.[80] The process of establishing network codes is defined in Article 6 and 8 of the Regulation (EC) 714/2009 (Electricity) and of the Regulation (EC) 715/2009 (Gas) Regulation. The areas in which network codes can be developed are set out in Article 8(6) of the Electricity Regulation and the Gas Regulation. The adoption of controversial codes – for example on gas tariff principles – has proven to be particularly arduous. Furthermore the adoption of the first network code for gas also revealed that not only technical standards and regulatory procedures but also private contracts would be impacted.

3.4 REMIT

Regulation 1227/2010 on Energy Market Integrity and Transparency (REMIT)[81] introduces a tailor-made regime for the oversight of trading of wholesale energy products on power exchanges and in the over-the-counter (OTC) markets and takes its inspiration from similar measures adopted to deal with such behaviour in financial markets. The definition of wholesale energy product under REMIT covers contracts for the supply of electricity and natural gas where delivery occurs in the Union as well as contracts relating to the transportation of electricity or natural gas in the Union. In both cases, REMIT covers contracts for physical delivery or for financial settlement.

REMIT therefore establishes a uniform EU-wide framework to deal with market abuse, in the form of market manipulation, attempted market manipulation and insider trading, in wholesale energy markets. Importantly it establishes a complex framework for the monitoring of wholesale energy markets to detect and deter market manipulation and insider trading. Finally it provides for the sanctioning of breaches of market abuse rules at national level. ACER is now responsible for collecting and analysing wholesale markets data and other relevant data to

---

79. Art. 12 of Parliament and Council Directive (EC) 2009/72 concerning common rules for the internal market in electricity and repealing Directive (EC) 2003/54, O.J. 2009, L 211/55 and Art. 13 of Parliament and Council Directive (EC) 2009/73 concerning common rules for the internal market in natural gas and repealing Directive (EC) 2003/55, O.J. 2009, L 211/94.
80. The Gas Target Model and the Electricity Target Model have been developed by the national energy regulators as part of their informal co-operation through the Council of European Energy Regulators (CEER).
81. Reg. (EU) 1227/2011 of the European Parliament and of The Council of 25 Oct. 2011 on wholesale energy market integrity and transparency, O.J. 2011, L 326/1.

identify possible instances of market abuse.[82] It will notify the concerned NRAs when there are grounds to believe that abusive behaviour has actually occurred. NRAs then carry out investigations and impose appropriate penalties.

3.5 *The gas security of supply regulation*

The Third Energy Package introduces provisions to improve the coordination of national measures to deal with security of supply problems, but did not allow for a specific policy for security of gas supply to be defined at Union level, Regulation 994/2010[83] places a shared responsibility to ensure security of gas supply on national gas undertakings, the Commission and competent national authorities. Article 6 of the Gas Directive 2009/73 obliges Member States to co-operate on their national emergency plans but the Regulation goes further. It introduces various measures to enable and even require permanent bi-directional flows on all cross-border interconnections to enable reverse flows between Member States.[84]

3.6 *Conclusion*

The adoption of the Third Energy Package, in addition to the Infrastructure Regulation 347/2013, REMIT, and the Security of Supply of Gas Regulation 994/2010 confirm the considerable progress made before and after Lisbon towards creating the legal basis for an internal energy market, serviced by interconnected networks. European legislation has become complex and technical, and heavily reliant on specialized regulatory bodies, working in co-ordination with ACER, to ensure its implementation and enforcement. Nevertheless the role of the Commission should not be underestimated, not only in relation to the adoption of further delegated legislation, but also to ensure that the Member States transpose European legislation into national law.

4. External energy policy

4.1 *Introduction*

Energy security was once one of the major components of early European energy policy in the wake of the oil crises of the 1970s, and resulted in the early adoption of internal co-ordination measures, for example, on oil stocks. From the mid- 1980s, European policy tended to focus on the creation of a genuine internal energy market even if the external dimension did not disappear entirely from the political agenda. In 1997 for example, the Council adopted a Regulation containing a programme to promote international cooperation in the energy sector.[85]

The Commission's Communication on security of energy supply and international cooperation, adopted in 2011 set out the first comprehensive strategy for the EU's external relations in energy. Improved coordination among EU Member States in identifying and implementing clear priorities in external energy policy was declared to be central. This strategy is based on four main objectives:

---

82. On 17 Dec. 2014 the Commission adopted an implementing regulation further specifying the extensive data reporting framework for the operation of REMIT.
83. Council Reg. (EU, Euratom) 617/2010 of 24 June 2010 concerning the notification to the Commission of investment projects in energy infrastructure within the European Union and repealing Reg. (EC) 736/96, O.J. 2010, L 180/7. The 2010 Regulation has in turn been repealed by EU Reg. 2017/1938 of 25 October 2017, O.J. 2017, L 280/1. See also Case C-226/16, *Eni SpA*.
84. See further L. Hancher and F. Salerno, op. cit. *supra* note 30, at 384–387 for a detailed account.
85. Council Reg. (EC) 701/97 of 14 Apr. 1997 amending a programme to promote international cooperation in the energy sector – Synergy programme, O.J. 1997, L 104/1.

- Building up the external dimension of the EU's internal energy market;
- Strengthening partnerships for secure, safe, sustainable and competitive energy;
- Improving access to sustainable energy for developing countries;
- Better promoting EU policies beyond its borders.[86]

Nevertheless it is difficult to conclude that on energy related matters, Europe speaks with a common voice.[87]

4.2 *Shared competence*

The conclusion of external agreements in the sphere of "*energy*" is a shared competence, as confirmed by Article 4(2)(i) TFEU. In the field of energy, (I) international agreements are usually "*mixed*" agreements entered into by both the EU and the Member States; and (ii) insofar as the Member States remain competent to enter into or maintain external bilateral agreements, they must not endanger the realization of the objectives of EU law and policy.

The internal competence for the EU translates into an external competence by virtue of Article 216(1) TFEU.[88] This may happen because the internal competence expressly allows for external action, as is the case with Article 191(4) TFEU on external environmental action. There is no equivalent in Article 194 TFEU to Article 191(4) TFEU for external energy action, but the objective in Article 194(1)(b) TFEU concerning "*security of energy supply*" equally implies external action given the EU's dependence on third countries for energy even if this is not an exclusive competence. Article 194 TFEU is the legal basis for the Decision No 994/2012/EU of 25 October 2012 establishing an information exchange mechanism with regard to intergovernmental agreements between Member States and third countries in the field of energy.[89]

Member States are required to submit all existing intergovernmental agreements, including all annexes and amendments to these agreements to the Commission. The recitals indicate that, in the event of incompatibility, Member States should take all necessary steps to find a suitable solution to eliminate the incompatibility, and that the Commission has the right to launch infringement proceedings in accordance with Article 258 TFEU to enforce this obligation. With respect to new intergovernmental agreements the Member state concerned *may* inform the Commission of the objectives of, and the provisions to be addressed in, the negotiations. A Member State *may* also request the assistance of the EC in those negotiations.[90]

4.2.1 *Strategic Partnerships*

As for the second objective, in the specific energy field a large number of bilateral initiatives including Strategic Partnerships with major supplier states have been brokered, including a Partnership and Cooperation Agreement with Russia, Free Trade Agreements and various

86. In Sept. 2013, the Commission adopted a report on the implementation of the Sept. 2011 Communication -Report from the Commission on the Implementation of the Communication on Security of Energy Supply and International Cooperation and of the Energy Council Conclusions of Nov. 2011, COM(2013)638.
87. See further: Notre Europe, "Towards a European Energy Community: A policy proposal", Study 76, 2009.
88. Art. 216(1) TFEU provides: "The Union may conclude an agreement with one or more third countries or international organisations where the Treaties so provide or where the conclusion of an agreement is necessary in order to achieve, within the framework of the Union's policies, one of the objectives referred to in the Treaties, or is provided for in a legally binding Union act or is likely to affect common rules or alter their scope".
89. Decision 994/2012/EU of the European Parliament and of the Council of 25 Oct. 2012 establishing an information exchange mechanism with regard to intergovernmental agreements between Member States and third countries in the field of energy, O.J. 2012, L 299/13, as amended by Decision 2017/684, O.J. 2017, L 99/1.
90. Decision 994/2012/EU, Art. 5.

Partnership and Cooperation Agreements concluded in the context of European Neighbourhood Policy (ENP). A number of countries have concluded an ENP Action Plan (AP), which include action on energy (e.g. Egypt) whereas other major supplier states to the EU have not (e.g. Russia). These APs are political commitments and are primarily couched in diplomatic terms. In essence a unilateral approach on the part of Member States to secure their energy supply remains the rule.

4.2.2 *The Energy Community Treaty*

EU trade agreements may eventually replace mixed trade agreements, but energy agreements often cover more than one policy dimension and the dividing line between trade related and other policy measures such as security of energy transit or market governance has always been rather vague. The Energy Community Treaty, for example, between the European Community and Albania, Bosnia, Croatia, the former YRM, Montenegro, Serbia and UNMIK of 2006 was entered into on the basis of Articles 133 and 175 EC.[91] This Treaty represents a concrete attempt to extend the European energy "acquis" for oil, gas and electricity to non-EU countries. The Treaty parties are obliged to adopt the internal energy market legislation under the supervision of the institutions established by the Treaty for that purpose.[92]

4.3 *Foreign direct investment*

The extension of the Common Commercial Policy ("CCP") to include Foreign Direct Investment ("FDI") in Article 207(1) TFEU could have important repercussions for the energy sector. The scope of the CCP competence is clarified in Article 207(1) TFEU to cover foreign direct investment (FDI) and the achievement of uniformity in measures of liberalization. The clarification of the scope of the CCP and the fact that all aspects of the CCP now fall under the exclusive competence of the EU are expected to contribute to a streamlining of the conduct as well as the coherence of EU trade policy and this may also be of relevance to external energy policy. The extension of the scope of exclusive competence could significantly reduce, but not necessarily eliminate the need of further mixed (multi-lateral) agreements on investment protection in the energy sector (a prominent example being the Energy Charter Treaty).[93] It is evident that despite the reference to the requirement to act in a "spirit of solidarity" in Article 194(1) TFEU, Member States have not been prepared to surrender sovereignty on external energy policy to the European level. The export of the European energy "acquis" to certain neighbouring countries is an important innovation.

5. The future of EU energy law and policy

EU energy policy goals are ambitious but not entirely consistent. This can weaken the political prospects for a true "European Energy Union" and creates legal uncertainty as to the enforceability of numerous national measures. European energy legislation – even where it is updated

---

91. Council Decision 2006/500/EC of 29 May 2006 on the conclusion by the European Community of the Energy Community Treaty, O.J. 2006, L 198/15.
92. For an overview of the Energy Community Treaty and its objectives, see the annual reports published by the Energy Community Secretariat, available at <www.energy-community.org/portal/page/portal/ENC_HOME/DOCUMENTS> (last visited 12 Feb. 2017).
93. All Member States and the European Communities are Parties to the Energy Charter Treaty – see 98/181/EC, ECSC, Euratom: Council and Commission Decision of 23 Sept. 1997 on the conclusion, by the European Communities, of the Energy Charter Treaty and the Energy Charter Protocol on energy efficiency and related environmental aspects O.J. 1998, L 69/1.

and amended by successive packages – does not always impose full harmonization. A Union policy which seeks to replace conventional fuels with renewable energy sources by requiring Member States to meet binding targets does not fit easily with the parallel aim of securing the completion of the internal energy market, which does not prioritize any particular type of fuel. Moreover energy remains a sensitive national policy issue and governments will be more likely to pursue their own, invariably protectionist prerogatives, where possible. National resources are likely to be preferred over uncertain supplies of imported energy in the event of an energy crisis. Even if Article 194(1) TFEU requires Member States to "act in a spirit of solidarity", the necessary instruments to co-ordinate such action are not in place.

The realization of the ambitious "20–20–20" targets have required large amounts of financial support which must comply with the Treaty state aid rules.[94] This raises the question of whether Member States can be obliged to accept and/or subsidize renewable energy production outside their own territory in order to meet EU targets. The Renewable Energy Sources (RES) Directive 2009/28 does not appear to compel them to do so,[95] but any restrictions on the importation of renewable energy must still be assessed under the Treaty rules on free movement.

The *Ålands Vindkraft*[96] case and that of *Essent (Belgium)*[97] both concerned national restrictions on imports of renewable energy which arose from the application of territorial restrictions in the operation of green certificate schemes. Only domestic green energy could qualify for such a certificate. Advocate General Bot in his opinion in *Ålands Vindkraft* had urged the ECJ to rule on the validity of the Directive 2009/78, finding that the relevant sub-article of the Directive and the national measure at issue were caught by Article 34 TFEU. In his view, it would appear "somewhat paradoxical to assert that the importation of green energy from other Member States might undermine environmental protection" and could somehow be justified on the basis of the "rule of reason" or Article 36.

The Court confirmed that the national measures were indeed restrictions to the free movement of goods, but as the national schemes designed to achieve binding targets could be justified on the basis of Article 36 TFEU, if the relevant tests of necessity and proportionality were met. In this respect it held that: "The finding made by the Court in paragraph 79 of the judgment in PreussenElektra — to the effect that the nature of electricity is such that, once it has been allowed into the transmission or distribution system, it is difficult to determine its origin and in particular the source of energy from which it was produced — remains valid".[98]

6. Conclusion

This chapter has examined the evolution of EU energy policy and its elevation to a Treaty Title. It has indicated that the numerous legislative measures adopted to pursue energy policy

---

94. The Third Energy Package does not exclude a certain preference for domestic energy production – indeed Art. 11 of Directive 2009/73 allows Member States to give priority to the dispatch of a limited percentage of domestically produced fuels.
95. Directive 2009/28/EC, Art. 3(3) provides: "Without prejudice to Arts. 87 and 88 of the Treaty [now Arts. 107 and 108 TFEU], Member States shall have the right to decide, in accordance with Arts. 5 to 11 of this Directive, to which extent they support energy from renewable sources which is produced in a different Member State". This Article should be read in the light of recital 25 of the preamble to the RES Directive which recognizes that "it is essential that Member States are able to determine if and to what extent their national support schemes apply to energy from renewable sources produced in other Member States and to agree on this by applying the cooperation mechanisms provided for in this Directive".
96. Case C-573/12, *Ålands Vindkraft AB v. Energimyndigheten*, para 104.
97. Case C-204/12, Essent (Belgium).
98. Case C-573/12, *Ålands Vindkraft AB v. Energimyndigheten*, paras. 87 and 119.

goals are based on a number of different Treaty provisions, even after the entry into force of the Lisbon Treaty. This is perhaps inevitable given the multi-faceted dimensions of energy policy – which involves much more than the creation of an internal energy market. Energy policy is now intricately linked with climate change policy and while the former has traditionally focused on liberalizing energy supply the latter is increasingly focused on the demand side of the equation: to secure the most efficient use of energy, thus reducing its adverse environmental impact. National prerogatives still predominate on both the supply and the demand side of the energy policy equation, and despite adoption of numerous harmonization packages over the past two decades, the European courts have proven reluctant to undermine this state of affairs.

Further reading

De Búrca (Eds.), *The Evolution of EU Law*, 2nd ed. (OUP, 2011), 743–781.

Hancher L. and P. Larouche, "The coming of age of EU network regulation" in P. Craig and G. Talus, K. *Introduction to EU Energy Law* (OUP, 2016).

Hancher, L. and F.M. Salerno, "EU energy policy" in A Biondi et al. (Eds.) *The Future of the EU after Lisbon* (OUP, 2012).

Hones, C. (Ed.), *EU Energy Law Vol. 1, The Internal Energy Market,* 3rd ed. (Claeys and Castells, 2010).

Johnson, A. and G. Block, *EU Energy Law* (OUP, 2014).

Leal-Arcase, R., et al., *Energy Security Trade and the European Union* (Edward Elgar, 2016).

Leal-Arcase, R., et al., *Research Handbook on EU Energy Law and Policy* (Edward Elgar, 2017).

CHAPTER 33
THE REGIONAL DIMENSION OF EU LAW: COHESION POLICY AND GEOGRAPHICAL DIFFERENTIATION

*Thomas Vandamme**

1. Introduction: "A Europe of the Regions"?

When it comes to the regional dimension of the European Union, the EU is traditionally criticized for reflecting primarily the model of a classic international organization with little visibility of the regions and other subnational actors. In this respect, the term "regional blindness" was first introduced as early as 1966 by Ipsen and has since been often repeated in many a study on the role of regional actors in the EU.[1] Amongst the grounds for such criticism one often finds the untapped potential of strong regional involvement for enhancing the legitimacy of the EU and its policies.[2] The most notable exceptions to this regional blindness are probably the Outermost Regions (OMRs) and the Overseas Countries and Territories (OCTs). Their special characteristics have been acknowledged from the early days of European integration in the sense that they call for geographical differentiation of European law.

Nevertheless, over time changes have been made to the EU institutional architecture that improved the position of the regions and other sub-national entities such as provinces and communes. One such institutional achievement is the establishment of the Committee of the Regions, added to the EU institutional architecture by the Treaty of Maastricht, the powers and budget of which have subsequently increased. Moreover, in the "post-Lisbon era" the subsidiarity principle (Art. 5(3) TEU) as well as respect for constitutional identity (Art. 4(2) TEU) both include a direct reference to the regional divisions of the Member States.[3] The Lisbon Treaty also granted the Committee of the Regions for the first time direct access to the ECJ for challenging EU acts amounting to a form of "collective legal redress" for sub-state agents.[4]

---

* Amsterdam Centre for European Law and Governance, Law Faculty, University of Amsterdam.

1. See H.-P. Ipsen, "Als Bundessstaat in der Gemeinschaft" in E. von Caemmerer et al. (Eds.), *Probleme des Europäischen Rechts: Festschrift für Walter Hallstein* (Klostermann, 1966), at 248–265. See also S. Weatherill, "The challenge of the regional dimension in the European Union" in S. Weatherill and U. Bernitz (Eds.), *The Role of the Regions and Sub-National Actors in Europe* (Hart, 2005), at 1.
2. See P. Popelier and W. Vandenbruwaene, "The subsidiarity mechanism as a tool for inter-level dialogue in Belgium: On regional blindness and co-operative flaws", 7 EuConst (2011), at 204.
3. See C. Panara, "The Contribution of local self-government to constitutionalism in the Member States in the EU multilayered system of governance" in C. Panara and M. Varney (Eds.), *Local Government in Europe, the "Fourth Level" in the EU Multi-layered System of Governance* (Routledge, 2013), at 236.
4. See also A. Cygan, "The regions within multi-level governance: Enhanced opportunities for improved accountability", 21 MJ (2014), at 265. It should also be noted that the new right for the Committee to challenge EU acts only serves to challenge the application of the (newly formulated) subsidiarity norm.

Many substantive issues of EU law such as agricultural policy, fisheries, infrastructure, public services, environment, education, culture and state aid may have strong repercussions on regions depending on the legislative and executive powers allotted to them domestically. To influence these policies they enjoy to a variable degree direct access to the European institutions (by lobbying, or through the Committee of the Regions) but in addition to those methods their position also still depends heavily upon the means they derive from national (constitutional) constellations. In that sense, the extent to which the Member State central government can be a gateway for channelling regional interests differs considerably.[5]

These different routes to influencing EU law-making do not mutually exclude each other. In fact, the acknowledgment of the importance of the regional actors in the EU, next to the Member states and the EU Institutions themselves has given rise to the concept of Multi-level Governance (MLG) in political science. A concept nowadays used to cover a whole array of different stakeholders (including civil society) in the co-establishment and implementation of European policy but that originated in studies of the sub-national actors.[6]

Despite improvements to their position in the EU institutional architecture, regions are far from satisfied. Also today, the EU can still be said to build upon the Member States as the focal point for input in European decision taking.[7] The external responsibility for the implementation of EU law (although often an internal responsibility of local or regional authorities) lies entirely with the Member States.[8] Regional *in*visibility is also clear in terms of legal protection. Regions, being non-privileged applicants, enjoy only limited *locus standi* before the ECJ when they wish to challenge EU acts under Article 263 TFEU. This is also true for the OCTs and OMRs despite their special status in EU law.[9] Case law demonstrates the tough implications this may have, especially in the context of cohesion policy.[10]

Although many fields of EU law are highly relevant to the regional and local entities in Europe, hereafter the main focus will be on the one EU policy area that primarily targets the regions: EU cohesion policy and its financial instruments (section 2 and 3). Section 4 focuses on the geographical differentiation of EU law, in particular in relation to the OMRs and OCTs. Their specific characteristics are acknowledged by the Treaties and justify a separate treatment.

---

5. See for example Art. 117 of the Italian Constitution. See also M. Suszycka-Jasch and H.-C. Jasch, "The participation of the German *Länder* in formulating German EU policy", (2009) *German Law Journal*, at 1215. For a regional constitution this matter, see Art. 186 of the 2006 Catalan Constitution.
6. Gary Marks first started studying cohesion policy through the lens of "MLG" in the late 1980s following the major reforms of cohesion policy in 1988, see M. Stein and L. Turkewitsch, *The Concept of Multi-level Governance in Studies of Federalism*, Paper presented at the 2008 International Political Science Association (IPSA), Concordia University, Montreal, at 7. On "MLG" and cohesion policy, see also European Commission, "European Governance, A White Paper", of 25 July 2001, COM(2001)428, at 4 and S. Piattoni, *The Theory of Multilevel Governance* (OUP, 2010), at 83–173.
7. See also Case C-95/97, *Région Wallonne v. Commission*, para 6: "It is not possible for the European Communities to comprise of a greater number of Member States than the number of states between which they were established".
8. See for a classic example Case C-111/00, *Commission v. Austria*, para 12 where some of the Austrian *Länder* had not yet implemented Directive 97/65EC into regional legislation and Case C-383/00, *Commission v. Germany*. In the latter case, the federal German Government had to take full responsibility, despite its misgivings that the Commission infringes the principle of sincere cooperation (Art. 4(3) TEU) by disregarding Germany's complex federal makeup.
9. See for example T-32/98 and 41/98, *Government of the Netherlands Antilles v. Commission*, para 45.
10. See D. Caruso, "Direct concern in regional policy: The European Court of Justice and the Southern question", 17 ELJ (2011), at 804. See also Case C-15/06 P, *Regione Siciliana v. Commission*.

2. Economic, social and territorial cohesion

After the Treaty of Lisbon, regional policy has been restyled as "Economic, Social and Territorial Cohesion" in Article 3(3) TEU and Title XVIII of Part Three of the TFEU.[11] Although the Treaties lack an official definition of "Economic, Social and Territorial Cohesion",[12] it follows descriptively from Article 174 TFEU that it entails "policy aimed at reducing disparities between the levels of development of the various regions and the backwardness of the least favoured regions". It should be stressed that Article 174 TFEU maintains that cohesion policy is to diminish the disparities in *levels of development* rather than merely reducing disparities. This indicates that merely a redistributive policy is not the primary target of cohesion policy. Furthermore, the inclusion of the word "territorial" in Title XVIII by the Lisbon Treaty further cemented what political scientists call the place-based narrative of cohesion policy. It implies that the local dimension should be strongly integrated into the operationalization of all European Structural and Investment Funds.[13] This becomes apparent from the focus not only on "least favoured regions", but also on "rural areas", "areas affected by industrial transition" and regions "with severe and permanent natural or demographic handicaps such as the northernmost regions with very low population density and island, cross-border and mountain regions". Hereafter, the term "cohesion policy" will be used as a *pars pro toto* for the collective policies on economic, social and territorial cohesion.

To cushion the frictions of market integration, cohesion policy has been devised, not merely for infusion of capital and income into the weaker regions (social cohesion) which at best should be a temporal solution but primarily, and increasingly, to create better infrastructures that help exploit resources in weaker regions that might otherwise remain untapped (economic cohesion).[14] These funds described below in subsections 3.1 and 3.2 allow the EU to stimulate financially the weaker regions' and Member States' infrastructures physically, technologically and educationally. Cohesion policy thus aims at various, often interconnected, goals such as restructuring regional economies that lag behind; support regions that undergo a transition in economic activities like urban areas with declining industries; help rural areas that suffer deprivation or areas where income from fisheries is dropping dramatically.

Giving concrete shape to these aims may give rise to daunting political and practical entanglements. Of the various recognized risks associated with cohesion policy, the most salient are the following:

(1) The increase in funding of cohesion policy should not result in overstretching the Member State's absorption capacity, possibly resulting in useless projects and mismanagement of funds (the "Cathedrals in the desert" phenomenon).

---

11. Arts. 174 to 178 TFEU.
12. In literature, the terms "regional policy" may be used synonymously with "cohesion policy" and "structural policy". See for example D. Caruso, op. cit. *supra* note 10, at 806.
13. The pre-Lisbon Art. 158 EC only referred to economic and social cohesion. See for the "place based" discourse C. Mendez, "The post-2013 reform of EU cohesion policy and the place-based narrative", 20 *Journal of European Public Policy* (2013), at 639.
14. See for an interesting (and different) take Strumia who placed cohesion policy under the lens of the "right not to move" in the internal market, see F. Strumia, "Remedying the inequalities of economic citizenship in Europe: Cohesion policy and the negative right to move", 17 ELJ (2011), at 725. Some even venture to call cohesion policy the "bribe to stay at home" by curbing immigration of the lower skilled European citizens who might otherwise burden social security systems of the receiving states, see R. Fenge and V. Meier, "Regional policy as a means to curb immigration" in G. Gelauff, I. Grilo and A. Lejour (Eds.), *Subsidiarity and Economic Reform in Europe* (Springer, 2008), at 317.

(2) Member States may become "addicted" to cohesion funding, rendering their budgets extra vulnerable.
(3) Cohesion policy is prone to political horse-trading when its transfers become bargaining chips, extending to policy fields outside the cohesion policy area.
(4) It may lead to reluctance amongst the "poor" Member States to admit "new poor" states to the EU as that may dissipate the total amount of available funding.

A further difficult issue in cohesion policy is the tension between its redistributive nature, favouring the weaker regions and its goal to use the funds as efficient as possible. Efficiency may demand the concentration of resources where they most likely yield maximum benefit. That may induce policy makers to spend funds in areas where certain sectors are already strongly developed (e.g. for research and innovation). At present, this dilemma seems mitigated by allowing all types of regions (rich and poor) to benefit from the funds, be it with different "investment priorities" depending on the state of development of the region(s) concerned.[15] The lion's share of the funds is however tagged for the poorest regions.

Although the different EU funds may be the most visible feature of cohesion policy, it encompasses a lot more. The policy's key Treaty provision, Article 175 TFEU, is coordinative in the sense that the Member States too must take the regional policy concerns into account when they coordinate their economic policies, thus bridging economic policy coordination (ex. Art. 120 TFEU) with cohesion policy. Article 174 TFEU also addresses the EU Institutions by means of an integration clause obliging them to take cohesion objectives into account when devising other policies, for instance macro-economic and internal market policies. One area of EU law where the regional agenda is particularly prominent in both EU and Member State policies is state aid with its specific exception for regional aid (Art. 107(3) (a) TFEU).

Cohesion policy in its turn needs to take into account non-discrimination and gender equality as well as sustainable development and environmental protection. These objectives are even more closely integrated under the current framework for cohesion policy due to its firm positioning under the overall umbrella of the "Europe 2020" strategy for smart, sustainable and inclusive growth (see *infra,* subsection 3.1).[16]

3. Funding economic, social and territorial cohesion

The instruments to fund EU cohesion policy are laid out in Article 175 TFEU as the *structural funds, other financial instruments and the EIB*. The structural funds are thereby defined as the *European agricultural guidance and guarantee fund, guidance section,* the *European Social Fund* and *the European Regional Development Fund*. These funds have operated on the basis of four consecutive framework programs that stretch several years each. Every new framework program was encompassed with a reform of the entire system. In 1988 the framework program established better coordination of the EU and Member States' expenses; the 1993 program introduced the Cohesion Fund for Member States with a Gross National Income (GNI) of less than 90 % of the EU average and the 1999 program prepared cohesion policy for the Eastern enlargement.

The big innovation of the current framework for 2014–2020 is its target to firmly embed cohesion policy within the "Europe 2020 agenda". Cohesion policy is now to be regarded a means to achieve the overarching goal of "Smart, Sustainable and Inclusive Growth",[17] the motto of "Europe 2020". Thus, the new framework for cohesion policy goes well beyond purely economic

15. See Art. 96(1) Reg. 1303/2013.
16. See Art. 7, 8 and 9, Reg. 1303/2013.
17. See Council Recommendations on broad guidelines for employment policies of 13 July 2010, O.J. 2010, L 191/28 and Council Decision 2010/707, O.J. 2010, L 308/46.

issues and includes topics like research, the low carbon economy, efficient public administration, social inclusion, climate change adaptation and better ICT.[18] Regulation 1303/2013 provides the common provisions on all relevant EU Funds (hereafter "Common Provisions Regulation").[19] In line with the broader "2020 approach, it has a wider scope than its predecessor. It not only establishes the framework for cohesion policy *strictu sensu* (the European Regional Development Fund or "ERDF", the European Social Fund, or "ESF" and the Cohesion Fund, or "CF") but also for the European Agricultural Fund for Rural Development ("EAFRD") and the European Maritime and Fisheries Fund ("EMFF"). By coordinating all EU funds more closely, it is hoped they can be mobilized better to address the financial and economic crisis ravaging the EU economy since 2008. Evidently, the interweaving of Cohesion policy with the wider "Europe 2020" Agenda provided compelling reasons to retain the enormous cohesion policy budget.[20] This new framework also led to a new nomenclature: all funds combined are designated as the "European Structural and Investment Funds" or "ESI-Funds".[21] The traditional term "Structural Funds" remains reserved for the ERDF and the ESF whereas these two together with the CF are simply referred to as "the Funds".[22]

The Common Provisions Regulation thus operates as a "multi-tiered constitution" of the different funding sources. Its Part II contains general provisions applicable to all "ESI Funds". Part III provides for additional rules common to "the Funds" whereas Part IV gives general provisions for the "Funds" and the European Maritime and Fisheries Fund. The European Agricultural Fund for Rural development, an integral part of the Common Agricultural Policy (CAP), is only covered by the general provisions in Part II. For each fund a specific regulation provides additional rules for that fund only ("fund specific regulations").[23] Article 175, third paragraph, TFEU provides for a legal basis for additional actions if these "prove necessary outside the Funds". This power was in fact used to establish EU donations to an organization focused on bringing peace and prosperity in Northern Ireland.[24]

Cohesion policy is impressive in terms of its resources. Transfers through the funds have increased steadily since the first package of measures adopted under the Delors Commission in 1988 curtailing the *juste retour* principle (the principle that there should be some correlation between the amount of money that a Member State injects into the Union and what it receives through the ESI funds or as other Union expenditures). For 2014–2020 a total of 351 billion is

---

18. See Art. 9 Common Provisions Reg., translating "smart, sustainable and inclusive growth including economic social and territorial cohesion" into 11 "thematic objectives".
19. Reg. 1303/2013 of the European Parliament and the Council of 17 Dec. 2013 laying down common provisions on the European Regional Development Fund, the European Social Fund the Cohesion Fund and the European Agricultural Fund for Rural Development and the European Maritime and Fisheries Fund and laying down general provisions on the European Regional Development Fund, the European Social Fund and the European Maritime and Fisheries Fund, O.J. 2013, L 347/32.
20. See C. Mendez, op. cit. *supra* note 13, at 555.
21. From a legal-technical standpoint the new nomenclature is remarkable as it gives the impression of secondary EU law overhauling primary law. The Common Provisions Reg. tags the ERDF and ESF as the "Structural Funds", but Art. 175 TFEU still includes the European Agricultural Guidance and Guarantee Fund, Guidance Section (now the EAFRD), as the third "structural fund". Art. 177 TFEU allows for the Structural Funds to be "grouped" but it does not seem to authorize splitting away the European Agricultural Guidance and Guarantee Fund, Guidance Section (or its renaming to "EAFRD" for that matter).
22. See Art 1, para 2 of the Common Provisions Reg. Nevertheless the preamble uses the term "cohesion policy" for all policies supported by the ERDF, ESF and CF.
23. They are based on Arts. 178 TFEU (ERDF), 43 TFEU (EAFRD and EMFF), 164 TFEU (ESF) and Art. 177, second sentence, TFEU (CF), respectively.
24. Although the ECJ later held that Art. 352 TFEU had to be used as additional legal basis, see Case 166/07, *European Parliament v. Council*, para 59.

coined for the allocations under Cohesion Policy proper and another 100 billion for the rural development and fisheries funds, totalling over 453 billion for all ESI Funds. As can be expected in such a sensitive, and valuable, policy field, it involves fierce competition amongst the stakeholders. Thus, the influence of the Commission, vis-à-vis that of the Member States, has shifted back and forth over the consecutive programming periods for cohesion policy, in particular as regards the eligibility rules for regions.[25]

3.1 *Structural Funds and Cohesion Fund: General and operational principles*

Part III of the Common Provisions Regulation is dedicated to the cohesion policy proper. Apart from pursuing their original purpose of economic, social and territorial cohesion, the three "Funds"[26] are also to contribute to the "Europe 2020" strategy for smart sustainable and inclusive growth.[27] They do this by aiming for two official "goals":

(1) the *Investment for Growth and Jobs* goal; and
(2) the *European Territorial Cooperation* goal.

The "investment for growth and jobs" goal is supported by all three funds. In fact, they may do so simultaneously.[28] The "European territorial cooperation goal" is solely supported by the ERDF.[29]

In terms of operationalization, the CF functions on a Member State basis whereas the Structural Funds (ERDF and ESF) operate on a regional basis following the so-called NUTS classification system (*Nomenclature des unités territoriales statistiques*).[30] The NUTS units are always identical to, or composed of, existing national administrative entities. "NUTS 1" regions are the largest units, "NUTS 2" regions represent the intermediate level and "NUTS 3" regions the smallest territorial units. Under the *Investment for Growth and Jobs* goal[31] the Structural Funds operate on the "NUTS 2" level. For this goal (that covers the largest amount of resources), regions must be classified according to their Gross Domestic Product: (1) *more developed* (GDP more than 90% of the EU average, (2) *transition* (GDP between 75 and 90% of the EU average) and (3) *less developed* (GDP lower than 75% of the EU average).[32] Immediately after the adoption of the Common Provisions Regulation, the Commission adopted a comprehensive decision listing these three categories of regions for the 2014–2020 term.[33]

Another general feature of cohesion policy is its increased linkage with *"Sound Economic Governance"*. This is now part and parcel of the required "Partnership Agreements" in which Member States set out how they will implement and operationalize ESI Funds. Member States must implement ESI Funds in full consistency with the "European Semester",[34] the annual

25. In the 2006–2013 period Member States regained full control over the designation of regions for the "regional competitiveness objective" (now a part of the "investment for growth and jobs goal"). See however for several arguments countering the "renationalization thesis" J. Bachtler and C. Mendez, "Who governs EU cohesion policy? Deconstructing the reforms of the Structural Funds", 45 JCMS (2007), at 535.
26. See Art. 1, second para, Common Provisions Reg.
27. See Art. 89(1), second para, Common Provisions Reg.
28. See Art. 98(1) Common Provisions Reg.
29. See Reg. 1299/2013, O.J. 2013, L 347/259.
30. Reg. 1059/2003 of the European Parliament and Council on a common classification of territorial units for statistics, O.J. 2003, L 154/1 as amended by Reg. 105/2007.
31. See Art. 90(1) Common Provisions Reg.
32. See Art. 90(2) Common Provisions Reg.
33. See Commission Implementing Decision 2014/99/EU, O.J. 2014, L 50/22. A possible Brexit would however change the EU-average GDP and result in a reclassification of some of the regions.
34. See point 2.3 of the Common Strategic Framework (Annex I to Reg. 1303/2013).

review of Member State's macroeconomic policies that incorporates all the new governance measures that were adopted to counter the economic and financial crisis. Specifically, the Commission may request an alteration of the Partnership Agreement and the ensuing operational programmes (see *infra* section 3.1.3) in order to align the use of the ESI funds with the plethora of different (preventive or corrective) measures for "sound economic governance".[35] These include the Council Recommendations under Article 121(2) TFEU (setting out economic policy guidelines), under Article 148(4) TFEU (on national employment policies), conditions under Regulation 332/2002[36] (for non-Euro Member States with medium term financial assistance), conditions under Regulation 407/2010 (for Member States supported by the financial stability mechanism),[37] macroeconomic adjustment programmes for Euro-Member States that are under enhanced budgetary surveillance following Regulation 472/2013[38] or as required by a Council recommendation under the Macro Economic Imbalances Procedure of Regulation 1176/2011.[39]

The "Lisbonization" of Cohesion policy is not beyond criticism. It may potentially require national policy revisions that sit uneasily with the multiannual programming basis on which cohesion policy is to operate. Moreover, it provides the "power of the purse" to achieve policy ends (fiscal discipline and economic reform) for which the EU only has coordinative powers and that are as such unrelated to the territorial, place based, narrative that should be underpinning cohesion policy in the first place.[40] This increased alignment of cohesion policy with the "Europe 2020" goals as well as its recruitment as a means to impose European fiscal discipline regimens as part of the new economic governance policies (the "European Semester") are particularly important for the Cohesion Fund as it is the one fund that operates on a Member State rather than regional basis. Thus, the Council for the first time suspended payments in 2012 to Hungary when it failed to meet requirements of fiscal discipline. Yet, sanctions like these to enforce macroeconomic governance rules are criticized for exacerbating Member States' already precarious fiscal positions.[41] The current framework of the Common Provisions Regulation tries to mitigate these negative consequences. Today, such suspension must take into account the economic and social circumstances of the Member State concerned as well as the economic impact it already suffers from the application of the excessive deficit procedure (EDP) or the excessive imbalances procedure (EIP).[42] Furthermore, programmes and priorities of "critical importance" remain unaffected by the suspension, e.g. the Youth Employment Initiative (see *infra* subsection 3.2.2.).

35. See Art. 23 to 25 Common Provisions Reg.
36. Reg. 332/2002 of the Council of 18 Feb. 2002 establishing a facility providing medium-term financial assistance for Member States' balances of payments, O.J. 2002, L 53/1.
37. Reg. 407/2010 of the Council of 11 May 2010 establishing a European Financial Stabilization Mechanism, O.J. 2010, L 118/1.
38. Reg. 472/2013 of the European Parliament and the Council of 23 May 2013 on the strengthening of economic and budgetary surveillance of Member States in the euro area experiencing or threatened with serious difficulties with respect to their financial stability, O.J. 2013, L 140/1.
39. Reg. 1176/2011 of the European Parliament and the Council of 16 Nov. 2011 on the prevention and correction of macro-economic imbalances, O.J. 2011, L 306/25. See in particular Art. 7(2) and 8(2).
40. See C. Mendez, op. cit. *supra* note 13, at 651.
41. See D. Adamski, "Europe's misguided constitution of economic prosperity", (2013) CML Rev, at 47.
42. See point 24 of the preamble and Annex III of the Common Provisions Reg.

3.1.1 *The additionality principle*

A vital prerequisite for the effectiveness of the Funds is that they are additional to national investments and do not simply replace them.[43]

In the past, the operationalization of the additionality principle had proved to be tricky. The structural expenditure by Member States must be assessed by reference to the period prior to the start of the new programming term, but what to do if the Member State later reduces dramatically the national expenditure? To avoid that risk, strong verification requirements are put in place: an *ex ante* verification when the Partnership Agreement has been submitted, a midterm verification of national structural expenditure in 2018 and an *ex post* assessment in 2022.[44] In case later verifications prove that Member State expenditure was not in pace with the prognoses at the start of the programming period, the Commission may impose "a financial correction".[45]

In the UK, a (hard) Brexit scenario may lead to an abrupt end of the EU flow of funds to projects already approved. Reassurances were made by the UK Government that projects started before autumn 2016 will be fully financed by UK funds for the remainder of the duration.[46]

3.1.2 *The complementarity principle*

Where the additionality principle prevents EU funding from replacing national investment efforts, the complementarity principle makes sure that such Member State effort is substantial enough to keep the Member States selective and critical when it comes to proposing projects. As the principle is applicable to all ESI funds it is stated in the general principles section of the Common Provisions Regulation: "ESI Funds shall provide support […] which *complements* national, regional or local intervention".[47] It is believed that "co-ownership" (in financial terms) will increase overall effectiveness of the project and prevent possibly useless projects; the "cathedrals in the desert phenomenon").

The downside to this is that sometimes the Member State or regional authorities lack the means to "considerably" co-finance projects. Thus, to avoid the situation that certain Member States' budgets would be overburdened, provision is made to increase the co-financing rate for the ESI funds on a sliding scale where the co-financing rate can go up to a maximum of 85% of the total expenditure.[48]

3.1.3 *The programming principle*

Ever since the 1988 reforms, it is a basic requirement for structural funds' spending to be embedded in multiannual "operational programmes" rather than on an individual project basis. Although the operationalization of the programming principle has changed over the consecutive cohesion policy frameworks (with arguably varying degrees of influence of the Commission over Member State priorities) it has remained a structural feature designed to strengthen the coherence of separate individual projects. The multiannual operational programs need the approval of the Commission[49] who keeps oversight over implementation and monitoring of the

43. See Art. 95(2) Common Provisions Reg.
44. See Art. 15, 95(5) and para 87 of the preamble Common Provisions Reg.
45. See Art. 95(6) Common Provisions Reg.
46. Available at <www.gov.uk/government/publications/autumn-statement-2016-documents/autumn-statement-2016>.
47. See Art. 4(1) Common Provisions Reg.
48. See Arts. 120 and 121 Common Provisions Reg.
49. See Art. 29(4) Common Provisions Reg. In fact the Commission has on several occasions rejected proposed programmes, see C. Mendez, op. cit. *supra* note 13, at 552.

programmes, rendering Member States more accountable.[50] The programmes must cover the entire "programming period", currently the 2014–2020 term.

Article 4 of the Common Provisions Regulation requires the programmes to "deliver the Lisbon Strategy for smart, sustainable and inclusive growth as well as the fund specific missions, including economic, social and territorial cohesion taking into account (…) country specific recommendations under Article 121(2) TFEU and 148(4) TFEU and, where appropriate, the national reform programmes". Although there is much to be said for coherence, the downside could be that the combination of "Europe 2020", "sound economic governance" as well as cohesion policy proper have become somewhat conflated. Cohesion policy appears a bit lost in the amalgam of objectives.[51] Furthermore, unlike the previous cohesion policy framework, the Common Provisions Regulation allows for operational programmes to be supported by different funds for the purposes of "Investment for growth and Jobs" thus necessitating the observation of different "fund specific rules" simultaneously.[52]

To facilitate this daunting task of integrating the various goals of both achieving "Smart Sustainable and Inclusive Growth" ("Europe 2020") as well as the Cohesion policy proper, a Common Strategic Framework (CSF) is established.[53] This guiding document provides the basis for the adoption of the operational programmes. It requires the operational programmes to run along a multi-tiered system, whereby each programme adopts "priority axes", each of which concerns one fund, one type of region ("less developed", "transition" or "more developed") and one (of eleven) "thematic objectives" as set out in art 9 of the Common Provisions Regulation that translate into one or more "investment priorities" as established by the fund specific regulations (see *infra*).[54]

3.1.4 *The principle of partnership*

The principle of partnership, applicable to all ESI Funds, elevates Multi-level Governance to a legal standard underpinning Cohesion policy. The previously mentioned Common Strategic Framework requires all operational programmes to be preceded by a "Partnership Agreement" setting out the Member State's strategy, priorities and arrangements for using the EFI Funds.[55] These agreements must ensure the alignment between the "Europe 2020" goals and the "Fund specific missions". The Partnership Agreement must specify the different partners (regions, urban and other authorities, economic and social partners and relevant bodies representing civil society) involved in the preparation, implementation and monitoring of the operational programmes.[56] Further rules on identification of relevant "partners", their involvement, their conflict management etc. are laid down in a Commission delegated regulation establishing a "code of conduct".[57]

---

50. See for example Joined Cases C-383/06 and C-385/06, *Vereniging Nationaal Overlegorgaan Sociale Werkvoorziening a.o. v. Minister van Sociale Zaken en Werkgelegenheid.*
51. See for a similar critique M. Baun and D. Marek, *Cohesion Policy in the European Union* (Palgrave, 2014), at 2.
52. See Art. 98 Common Provisions Reg.
53. See Art. 10 and Annex I Common Provisions Reg.
54. See Art. 96(1) Common Provisions Reg.
55. Art. 2(20) Common Provisions Reg.
56. See Art. 5 Common Provisions Reg.
57. See Commission Delegated Reg. 240/2014 on the European Code of Conduct on Partnership in the Framework of the European Structural and Investment Funds, O.J. 2014, L 74/1 and point 5.1 of Annex I to the Common Provisions Reg.

3.2 *The Structural Funds and Cohesion Fund*

3.2.1 *The European Regional and Development Fund*

Despite a hesitant start in 1975, the ERDF is today the largest of the ESI Funds. According to Article 176 TFEU it is intended to "redress the main regional imbalances in the Union" by helping regions whose development is lagging behind or who are faced with declining industries that need conversion. Today, its contribution to "Smart, Sustainable and Inclusive Growth" as set out by the Common Provisions Regulation is achieved by helping small and medium sized enterprises (SMEs), invest in physical infrastructures, ICT, education, research and innovation, etc. It is the only fund that supports the "European Territorial Cooperation" goal by supporting regions with shared land- or maritime borders to establish cooperation concerning facilities, human resources and infrastructural projects.[58]

For the "Investment in Growth and Jobs" goal, the ERDF's financial infusions serve all three categories of regions ("more developed", "transition" and "less developed"). Yet, the type of activities that can be subsidized are different (the ERDF Regulation tags this "thematic concentration") and there is a more restrained choice of investment priorities depending on the level of development of the region concerned.[59] The operational programmes for the wealthier regions need to concentrate their efforts on research and development, ICT, competitiveness of SMEs and especially the shift to a low carbon economy.[60] The *transition regions* and less *developed regions* are allowed more variety in the choice and importance of individual investment priorities.[61] For the regions with natural or demographic handicaps, northernmost regions (in Finland and Sweden) and the Outermost Regions (see *infra*), the possibilities in terms of activities to be supported are wider still.[62]

3.2.2 *The European Social Fund*

The ESF is the oldest of the ESI Funds, established in 1957 with a separate Title in the Treaty (Title X; Arts. 162–164 TFEU).[63] According to the Treaty, its mission is to increase the mobility of workers (both geographically and occupationally) and to facilitate their "adaptation to industrial changes and changes in production systems". Although primarily an instrument of European social policy, its activities are firmly integrated in the cohesion policy since the 1988 cohesion policy reforms.

The system for designing operational programs funded by the ESF, resembles that for the ERDF. The funded activities must befit the following "thematic objectives" as identified by the Common Provisions Regulation: "sustainable and quality employment and labour mobility", "social inclusion combatting poverty and any discrimination", "education, training and lifelong learning" and "institutional capacity building and efficient public administration".[64] As with the

58. See Reg. 1299/2013 on specific provisions for support from the European Regional Development Fund to the European Territorial Cooperation Goal, O.J. 2013, L 347/259.
59. See Reg. 1301/2013 of the European Parliament and the Council of 17 Dec. 2013 on the European Regional Development Fund and on specific provisions concerning the Investment for Growth and Jobs Goal and repealing Reg. 1880/2006, O.J. 2013, L 347/289.
60. See Art. 5 of Reg. 1301/2013.
61. These "investment priorities" are established by Art. 9, first paras. (1)–(4) Common Provisions Reg.
62. See Arts. 10 to 12 of Reg. 1301/2013.
63. Reg. 1304/2013 of 17 Dec. 2013 on the European Social Fund, O.J. 2013, L 347/470.
64. See Art. 9(1) Common Provisions Reg. (objectives 8 to 11 respectively) and Art. 3(1) of Reg. 1304/2013.

ERDF, these thematic objectives are translated into more concrete "investment priorities" in Article 3 of the ESF Regulation.[65]

The designs of the operational programmes are further curtailed by the general requisite that they must reserve at least 20% of the ESF allocations (on Member State basis) to "social inclusion, combatting poverty and discrimination".[66] Furthermore (and again like the ERDF Regulation), the ESF Regulation requires a higher level of concentration for "more developed" regions, as they must spend 80% of all allocated ESF funds on a maximum of five "investment priorities". A wider spread of funds is allowed in "transition regions" and "less developed regions".[67]

In response to the financial crisis and its soaring youth unemployment rates in certain Member States, the ESF Regulation made specific arrangements for extra funding under the "Youth Employment Initiative". Extra resources are set aside to help persons under the age of 25 who are unemployed or not in education or training and reside in regions with a youth unemployment rate of over 25%.[68]

3.2.3 *The Cohesion Fund*

The Cohesion Fund ("CF") differs from the structural funds proper as it was only established in the wake of the Maastricht Treaty as part of the roadmap towards the establishment of the EMU. This is still reflected in the Treaty architecture that mentions the ERDF, EAFRD and ESF as "Structural Funds" but not the more recently established CF. It is therefore not a structural fund *strictu senso*. Initially destined to help only those Member States that expected great difficulties in preparing themselves for accession to the EMU (at the time Spain, Greece, Portugal and Ireland) the CF seemed to have a limited lifespan. Yet, over time it acquired permanent status and received a proper legal basis in art 177, second paragraph, TFEU.

Thus, unlike the structural funds (ERDF and ESF) that operate on the basis of identified eligible regions, the resources of the CF are earmarked for Member States. Under the current rules, the eligible Member States are those with a gross national income ("GNI") of less than 90% of the EU average.[69] For the 2014–2020 period, 15 Member States are eligible for CF support.[70] As the UK is not amongst the current eligible Member States, "Brexit" would have little impact in this regard.[71]

The CF funds two goals only: (1) improvement of the environment and (2) transport infrastructure.[72] If EU environmental policy (adopted pursuant to Art. 191 TFEU) proves too costly for a specific Member State, it may provide for CF support.[73] CF sponsored environmental projects should primarily benefit the shift to a low carbon economy, promote climate change adaptation and resource efficiency.[74] Furthermore, Title XVI (Arts. 170–172 TFEU) on Trans-

65. Mismanagement of ESF resources leads to a duty to recover sums, see Joined Cases C-383/06 and C-385/06, *Vereniging Nationaal Overlegorgaan Sociale Werkvoorziening v. Minister van Sociale Zaken en Werkgelegenheid*, para 40.
66. See Art. 4(2) Reg. 1304/2013. This corresponds to "thematic objective" 9 Common Provision Reg.
67. See Art. 4(3) Reg. 1304/2013.
68. See Arts. 16–18 of Reg. 1304/2013.
69. See Art. 90(3) Common Provisions Reg. The "90% rule" has been given the status of primary law in Protocol 28 on Economic, Social and Territorial Cohesion annexed to the Treaty of Lisbon.
70. See Commission Decision 2014/99 of 18 Feb. 2014, O.J. 2014, L 50/22 see also Art. 90(5) Reg. 1303/2013.
71. For the EU-27, a Brexit would mean a decrease of the GNI average, yet this would seem insufficient to change the number of current eligible states.
72. See Reg. 1300/2013 of 17 Dec. 2013, O.J. 2013, L 347/281.
73. See Art. 192(5), second indent, TFEU.
74. Se Art. 4 Reg. 1300/2013. These goals are subdivided in to various "investment priorities" corresponding to the "thematic objectives" in Art. (1), (5) and (6) Common Provisions Reg.

European Networks links the CF with the attainment of the goals of EU transport infrastructure policy where "projects of common interest" need Union financing.[75] It particularly should concern low carbon transportation (sustainable transport), remove bottlenecks and increase interoperability of transport systems.[76] For the 2014–2020 period, the CF is financially linked to the policy on Trans-European Networks by means of the newly established "Connecting Europe Facility". Although this Facility is established to serve all types of Trans-European Networks (energy and telecommunications infrastructures) in *all* Member States, a budget of 11.3 billion (transferred from the CF) is ring-fenced for Member States eligible for CF support.[77]

3.3 *Other financial instruments*

3.3.1 *The European Agricultural Fund for Rural Development*

With the reform of the Common Agricultural Policy (CAP) the former *European Agricultural Guidance and Guarantee Fund, Guarantee section* and the *European Agricultural Guidance and Guarantee Fund, Guidance section* (both established in 1962) are replaced by the European Agricultural Guarantee Fund (EAGF) and the European Agricultural Fund for Regional Development (EAFRD) respectively.[78] Whereas the first fund concentrates on direct payments to farmers and measures to regulate agricultural markets (e.g. export refunds), the EAFRD concentrates on improving the rural economies (competitiveness; ecology; social environment).[79]

As it is primarily one of the two pillars of the CAP, the EAFRD is less integrated in cohesion policy. It should be remembered that the CAP is a policy area that fundamentally differs from cohesion policy as it is by "occupation of the field" a largely Europeanized policy area whereas cohesion policy depends largely on Member State decisions in the field of regional economic planning. Consequently the funding from the EAFRD is much less of a complimentary nature as that emanating from the Structural Funds or the Cohesion Fund. It is for that reason only partially covered by the Common Provisions Regulation.[80]

3.3.2 *The European Maritime and Fisheries Fund*

The EMFF is set up to deliver the goals of the Common Fisheries Policy (CFP) as well as the "Europe 2020" Strategy for smart inclusive and sustainable growth.[81] In particular, it aims for environmentally sustainable, resource efficient, innovative, competitive and knowledge based fisheries and aquaculture in the EU's maritime economy. Its link with cohesion policy is mainly through its ambition to increase economic growth, social inclusion, job creation and support employability and labour mobility in coastal and inland communities.[82] The EMFF is covered by Parts II and IV of the Common Provisions Regulation.

---

75. See Art. 171(1), third indent, TFEU. Transport infrastructure projects of "common interest" are further specified in Reg. 1315/2013 on Union Guidelines for the development of the trans-European transport network, O.J. 2013, L 348/1.
76. These investment priorities correspond to the Thematic Objective in Art. 9(7) of the Reg. 1303/3013.
77. See Arts. 5(1)(a) and 11 of Reg. 1316/2013 establishing the "Connecting Europe Facility", O.J. 2013, L 348/1129.
78. See Arts. 40(3) and 43(2) TFEU and Reg. 1305/2013 of the European Parliament and the Council on support for rural development by the European Agricultural Fund for Rural Development (EAFRD), O.J. 2013, L 347/487.
79. See Reg. 1290/2005 of 21 June 2005 on the financing of the Common Agricultural Policy, O.J. 2005, L 209/1, Arts. 3 (EAGF expenditure) and 4 (EAFRD expenditure).
80. Only Part II Common Provisions regulation.
81. See Reg. 508/2014, O.J. 2014, L 149/1, Arts. 5 and 6.
82. See Art. 6(4) Reg. 508/2014.

The specific nature of the fisheries sector accounts for certain divergences from the general operationalization of the ESI Funds.[83] Instead of multiple operational programmes, Member States draw up a single operational programme.[84] Furthermore, a distinction is made between measures under shared management, following the "Multi-Level Governance" model (the general rule for all ESI Funds) and the measures under direct management by the Union. The latter relate to the Integrated Maritime Policy (IMP), mostly covering measures that stimulate co-operation (both cross border and cross-sectoral), dialogue and network building for maritime affairs.[85]

3.4 *The European Investment Bank*

Article 175 TFEU names the European Investment bank (EIB) as one of the instruments of the EU to establish its cohesion policy. Established as early as 1957, the EIB is a typical product of its time. There was then a widespread belief that public investment banks were the proper vehicle to stimulate (regional) economic growth and development.[86] Its shareholders are the Member States and it operates on a non-profit basis.[87]

The EIB can be classified as a "policy driven public bank" providing loans and loan-guarantees for projects in "all sectors of the economy", ranging from investments in education or infrastructure to environmental projects. Its close connection with cohesion policy and trans-European networks[88] is apparent from its mission: the "balanced and steady development of the internal market" (Art. 309 TFEU). It does so by facilitating projects for (a) developing less developed regions; (b) modernizing or converting undertakings or developing fresh activities called for by the establishment and functioning of the internal market; or (c) projects of common interest to several Member States. These projects are subject to the proviso that they cannot be financed by the Member States themselves due to their size or nature.[89] EIB activities must be carried out in conjunction with assistance from the ESI Funds. In 1994 a new instrument was added to the European Investment Bank Group: the European Investment Facility ("EIF") which specifically targets the small and medium sized enterprises (SME) through loan guarantees and participation in venture capital.

The EIB's operating principles are not unlike those underlying cohesion policy as they too include additionality and complementarity. Its funding may be called for "to the extent that other funds are not available on reasonable terms" and it finances always partly the project concerned (Art. 309 TFEU speaks of "facilitating financing").[90] A second parallel is that also the EIB may be instrumental in sanctioning "sound economic governance" on Member States (i.e. "reconsidering its lending policy") that fail to put in practice "recommendations" in the course of the excessive deficit procedure.[91]

The main difference with the ESI Funds is of course that loans of the EIB must (eventually) be paid back. The EIB finances its activities through the capital furnished by the Member

83. See for a description of the predecessor of the EMFF, the European Fisheries Fund (EFF), T. Markus, *European Fisheries Law* (Europa Law Publishing, 2009), at 203–223.
84. Art. 17 Reg. 508/2014.
85. See Art 24 et seq. (shared management) and Art. 81 et seq. (direct management) Reg. 508/2014.
86. See W. Rostow, *The Stages of Economic Growth: A non-Communist Manifesto* (CUP, 1960).
87. See Art. 308 and 309 TFEU and Protocol No. 5.
88. See Art. 171 TFEU and its reference to "loan guarantees" for projects of "common interest".
89. Art. 309, sub (b) and (c) TFEU state as much. For projects covered by Art. 309 sub a TFEU the same condition applies following Art. 18 Statute EIB.
90. See Art. 16(1) Statute EIB.
91. Art. 126 (11), second indent, TFEU.

States[92] and, to a larger extent, by having recourse to the capital markets. The EIB enjoys the "triple A" rating, hence it can easily attract external resources and subsequently borrow these funds to its lenders under moderate interest rates. In fact, in terms of lending capacity the EIB is presently the world's largest multilateral lending institution surpassing other institutions like the World Bank.[93] In the UK there is considerable concern that post "Brexit", this source of financing will disappear completely as there is no obvious alternative for the EIB in terms of expertise and lending capacity.[94]

Another difference is that, unlike the ESI Funds that operate on a programmatic basis, the EIB co-finances *individual* projects. The projects may be public or private as long as they are ultimately backed by the Member State concerned, by other adequate guarantees or by the sheer strength of the debtor.[95] On average, the leverage of the EIB is that for every euro it lends, 3.6 euros are covered by another source.[96]

To operate independently (and in that sense operate as a "normal" bank), the EIB enjoys legal personality and indeed an amount of independence instrumental to its banking activities.[97] Yet, although an independent financial institution, the EIB must also carry out its public task assigned to it by the Treaties. At this point there is some ambiguity in the setup of the EIB.[98] Also the requirement that funding through the EIB must operate in a coordinated fashion with the ESI Funds can be at odds with the EIB's functional independence.

A specific institutional feature of the EIB that is worth mentioning is the possible legal recourse from its actions. For a EU body whose actions have potentially such a wide impact, it is striking that the *lex specialis* in Article 271 TFEU (diverging from Art. 263 TFEU) is rather restrictive, especially towards private parties. It reserves *locus standi* for the Commission, the Member States and the Board of Governors or the Board of Directors of the EIB.[99]

4. Geographical differentiation: "Overseas Europe"

4.1 *Introduction*

EU law does not apply *ratione loci* to the entire aggregate of the territories of the EU Member States. In those Member States still exercising sovereignty over remnants of their former colonial empires (Denmark, The Netherlands, The United Kingdom and France) EU law may not apply to the fullest extent, if at all. Although the topic may be considered somewhat of a "niche" of EU law, the overall importance of "overseas Europe" (the outermost regions and overseas countries and territories) should not be underestimated. Over six million people, the vast majority of which EU citizens, live in these parts, covering a landmass of more than four million square kilometres, giving control over a joint exclusive economic zone of more than 21 million square kilometres.

92. Art. 4 Statute EIB.
93. For instance in 2013 it provided loans up to 71.7 billion EUR, see <www.EIB.org>.
94. Between 2011 and 2015, EUR 29 billion was borrowed to UK actors by the EIB/EIF.
95. See Art. 16(3) Statute EIB.
96. Although in this respect differences between the different Member State are great, see N. Robinson, "The European Investment Bank: The EU's neglected institution", 47 JCMS (2009), at 651–662.
97. See Case 85/86, *Commission v. Board of Governors*, paras. 28–29 and Case C-449/99 P, *EIB v. Hautem*.
98. On the EIB's governance, see N. Hachez and J. Wouters, "A responsible lender? The European Investment Bank's environmental, social and human rights accountability", 49 CML Rev. (2012), at 47–96.
99. See for example T-460/93, *Etienne Tête et al v. EIB*.

With the Treaty of Lisbon the general provisions on "overseas Europe" can be found in three interlinked provisions that cover different legal regimes as far as the geographical scope of the TEU and the TFEU is concerned.[100] Basically there are four categories of Union territories:

(1) the metropolitan areas of the 28 Member States (Art. 52 TEU);
(2) the outermost regions (hereafter "OMRs"; Art. 349 TFEU);
(3) the overseas countries and territories (hereafter "OCTs"; Art. 355(2) TFEU); and
(4) a miscellaneous category of *sui generis* territories (Art. 355 (3)(4) and (5) TFEU.[101]

As a "rule of thumb" EU law applies to a varying degree to the different territories. Article 52 TEU specifies that the TEU and TFEU apply in full to the territories of the metropolitan areas of the 28 Member States except for the odd exception.[102] Article 355(1) TFEU brings the OMRs (see section 4.3) under the scope of the Treaties subject to special provisions laid down in accordance with Article 349 TFEU ("Yes, except"). The OCTs as listed in Annex II to the Treaties (see section 4.4) are by principle excluded from the application of EU law unless specific arrangements provide otherwise ("No, unless"). These arrangements are established by consecutive association arrangements that each span a timeframe of 10 years.

Yet, even within these different categories there are considerable differences regarding important issues such as the Schengen acquis, VAT, the economic freedoms, the customs union or the Eurozone. For example, the Portuguese Azores are part of the Union's VAT area whereas the Spanish Canary Islands (also an OMT) are not. In the French OCT of Saint Pierre and Miquelon the euro is the official tender whereas in the Dutch Antilles, also an OCT, other currencies are used. Portuguese Madeira, an OMR, is part of the Schengen zone whereas the French Département of Martinique, an OMR too, is not. It may also be mentioned that the personal status of the inhabitants of these territories may differ considerably, depending on the peculiarities of nationality legislation. Some inhabitants of OCTs may thus be citizens of a Member State and thus officially EU citizens (as is the case with the "nationals" of the Dutch Antilles) whereas residents of other OCTs may be deprived of such status, like the "nationals" of the British Cayman Islands or even the Danish citizens resident on the Faroe Islands.[103] Since this latter aspect concerns the personal application of EU law rather than its geographical application, it will not be further discussed in this section.

Amongst the miscellaneous category of *sui generis* territories one finds the "European territories for whose external relations a Member State is responsible" (Art. 355(3) TFEU). Contrary to what is sometimes assumed, this provision does not cover the European microstates

100. Before "Lisbon" the EU Treaty contained no provision on its territorial scope whereas only the TEC (TFEU) contained a clause on territorial scope with specifications for the OMR and OCT. This gave rise to the assumption that the former "Second and Third Pillars" of the EU were applicable to the entire territories of the Member States with associated territories overseas, see M. Fletcher, "EU crime and policing and the OCTs" in D. Kochenev (Ed.), *EU Law of the Overseas, Outermost Regions, Associated Overseas Countries and Territories, Territories Sui Generis* (Kluwer, 2011), at 291 and 293–294.
101. On the territorial scope of application of the Treaties more generally, see J. Ziller, "Outermost regions, overseas countries and territories and others after the entry into force of the Lisbon Treaty" in D. Kochenev, op. cit. *supra* note 100, at 79.
102. Particularly when it comes to VAT (not applicable to mount Athos in Greece or to the German island of Heligoland) and the customs Union (not applicable to the German town of Büsingen and Heligoland and the Italian towns of Livigno and Campione d'Italia). The Spanish exclaves of Ceuta and Melilla, although officially covered by EU law in full, are excluded from the customs union, the Common Agricultural Policy and the Common Fisheries Policy (see Art. 25 of the 1985 Act of Accession of Portugal and Spain and Protocol 2 annexed to that Treaty) and from the Union's VAT area (Art. 6 (2)(c) and (d) of Directive 2006/112.
103. Whereas the Danish citizens living in Greenland, an OCT since 1985, do enjoy the status of EU citizens.

(Monaco, San Marino or the Vatican) as these countries manage their own external relations nor does it cover the Principality of Andorra.[104] The only territory today covered by this provision is Gibraltar.[105] Gibraltar is therefore covered by the Treaties subject to derogations.[106] For the Finnish Åland archipelago (normally covered by the same provision as Gibraltar as Finland manages its external relations) special provision is made in Article 355(4) TFEU with a similar legal effect: the islands are covered by the Treaties subject to certain conditions most notably an exemption from EU VAT legislation.[107] Due to their military (non-economic) nature, the UK Sovereign Base Areas on Cyprus, Dhekelia and Akrotiri, are in principle excluded from the EU Treaties.[108] The British Crown Dependencies of Jersey, Guernsey and the Isle of Man are legally bound to observe EU law on the free movement of goods (including agricultural produce) and are within the customs union.[109] Finally, the Danish Faroe Islands, anxious to protect their fishing grounds, are excluded from the scope of the Treaties unreservedly.[110]

4.2 *The passerelle clause to change a territory's status*

The Treaty of Lisbon introduced an interesting innovation in the form of a simplified Treaty amendment procedure allowing the OCTs to change to OMRs and *vice versa*. By unanimous European Council Decision the list of OMRs in Article 349 and of OCTs in Annex II to the TFEU can now be changed under Article 355(6) TFEU for Danish, French or Netherlands territories. Interestingly this rule is not applicable to UK territories since none of the UK territories was interested in a possible change of status during the negotiations on the Lisbon Treaty. Unlike the simplified revision procedure in Article 48(6) TEU this amendment requires no national round of ratifications. In fact this new "passerelle" has already been put to use in both directions. The French island of Saint Barthélemy, originally an OMR,[111] became an OCT in 2012.[112] By contrast, the French island of Mayotte became a new *Département d'outre-mer* and again EU law followed suit, "promoting" Mayotte from OCT to OMR as of 1 January 2014.[113]

The examples of Saint Barthélemy and Mayotte illustrate that constitutional change on the national plane is not automatically translated to the EU level. The Member State concerned may not (right away) submit a proposal for status change to the European Council. Today, Saint Martin, no longer a *Département d'outre-mer* under French law, is still qualified under EU law as

---

104. See F. Murray, *The European Union and Member State Territories: A New Legal Framework under the EU Treaties* (Asser Press, 2012), at 38.
105. Although even that argumentation is not watertight; see F. Murray, op. cit. *supra* note 104, at 47.
106. To the extent that it is *not* excluded, see *Matthews v. United Kingdom*, ECHR No. 24833/94 (on the question whether the Gibraltese should be enfranchised for EP elections under the First Protocol to the ECHR).
107. See for other exemptions Protocol 2 on the Åland Islands, O.J. 1994, C 241/352.
108. See Art. 355 (5)(b) TFEU. However, the Protocol on the Sovereign Bases annexed to the 2003 Treaty of accession of *inter alia* Cyprus may provide otherwise, see also S.L. Shaelou, "The principle of territorial exclusion in the EU, sovereign base areas in Cyprus, a special case of sui generis territories" in D. Kochenev, op. cit. *supra* note 100, at 153.
109. See Art. 355 (5)(c) TFEU which refers to Protocol No. 3 to the 1972 Act of Accession of the UK to the EEC. See also Case C-293/02, *Jersey Potatoes v. States of Jersey and Jersey Potato Marketing Board*.
110. See Art. 355 (5)(a) TFEU and the Protocol on the Faroe Islands, O.J. 1972, L 73/163.
111. More precisely, it was part of the *Département d'outre-mer* of Guadeloupe (an OMR). As a new *Collectivité d'outre-mer* Saint Barthélemy regained the power to adopt customs policies while retaining the Euro as currency.
112. See European Council Decision 2010/718/EU of 29 Oct. 2010, O.J. 2010, L 325/4. This proves wrong the assumption that OMRs could not benefit from the passerelle.
113. See European Council Decision 2012/419/EU, O.J. 2012, L 204/131.

OMR in Article 349 TFEU.[114] The Dutch Antillean islands of Bonaire, Sint Eustatius and Saba, although since 2010 more closely tied to metropolitan Netherlands as "special municipalities" are still OCTs like the other Dutch Caribbean islands of Aruba, Sint Maarten and Curaçao.

4.3 *The Outermost Regions*

The OMRs are covered by the more detailed provision of Article 349 TFEU that mentions them by name: the French *Départements d'outre-mer* of Guadeloupe, French Guyana, Martinique, Mayotte, Réunion and Saint Martin,[115] the Portuguese Archipelagos of Madeira and the Azores and the Spanish Canary Islands. The provision lists the specific physical, economic and social challenges that the outermost regions face: "their remoteness, insularity, small size, difficult topography and climate and economic dependence on a few products".[116] The provision mirrors the general consideration in Article 174 TFEU about the "least favoured regions" in the EU proper (that also mentions the natural or demographic handicaps, insularity or mountainous terrain). However, the situation of the OMRs is considered to be more precarious and permanent compared to that of "least favoured regions" in general. With the EU enlargements after 2004, bringing to the EU regions that are worse off than some of the OMRs, the latter's special position has been contested at times.[117]

As a general rule, EU law applies to the OMRs in the absence of specific rules adopted under Article 349 TFEU.[118] Although the Treaties in principle apply to OMRs, the Council on a proposal of the Commission and after consultation of the European Parliament may adopt specific measures as to the application of the Treaties and EU common policies, "taking into account the special characteristics and constraints" of the OMRs.[119] These specific measures require the less democratic consultation procedure.[120] When the Council had adopted a whole array of amendments to existing secondary legislation due to the status change of Mayotte into an OMR (see subsection 4.2), the European Parliament challenged the use of Article 349 TFEU as the legal basis. The Court did not follow suit however, reaffirming that Article 349 TFEU is the appropriate legal basis to determine the geographical scope of the Treaties (including the *acquis*) in relation to the OMRs. Furthermore, these measures may take different forms (permanent derogations or temporary postponements of EU law) as long as these are justified by the "structural, economic and social situation of the OMR".[121] Although Article 349 TFEU mentions certain policy areas specifically (state aid, customs, fiscal policy, access to the structural funds etc.), the

---

114. In fact before "Lisbon" there was some debate on the this issue as the former text of Art. 299 (2) TEC did not mention the French *départements d'outre-mer* by name, hence giving rise to the theory that by internal constitutional reshuffle, France could *ipso facto* change the status of its territories under EU law.
115. Saint Martin is no longer part of the *Département* of Guadeloupe but a separate *Collectivité d'outre-mer* since 2007. Now that the OMRs are mentioned by name, an internal chance of legal status cannot be said to result automatically in a change of status under EU law.
116. This list is of course not exhaustive as one can for instance also mention their proximity to less developed third countries with limited trade possibilities.
117. See the Opinion of A.G. Wahl in Joined Cases C-132/14 to 136/14, *European Parliament and Commission v. Council* ("Mayotte"), para 48.
118. See Case 1489/77 *Hansen & O.C. Balle GmbH v. Hauptzollamt Flensburg*, paras. 11 and 12.
119. This duty upon the Council to heed the OMRs' interests does not guarantee their *locus standi* before the ECJ, see Case C-444/08 P, *Autonomous Region of the Azores v. Council.*
120. There is no consensus on the meaning (or added value even) of the second sentence of Art. 349 TFEU. See para 52 of the Opinion A.G. Wahl in Joined Cases C-132/14 to 136/14, *European Parliament and Commission v. Council.*
121. See Joined Cases C-132/14 to 136/14, *European Parliament and Commission v. Council.*

possible exemptions for the OMRs are not restricted to these fields[122] and might even extend to CFSP and the AFSJ.[123] The main restriction on this legislative power is that the Council should refrain from "undermining the integrity of the coherence of the Union legal order, including the internal market and common policies". An important example thereof is making sure the help extended to OMRs does not result in deflections of trade.[124]

Since the OMRs are part of the customs union, free flow of goods to and from these areas must be upheld. Moreover, financial dues imposed upon "imports" into the OMRs from the metropolitan part of the same Member State ("internal customs duties") are prohibited, a rule later extended to the internal market more generally.[125] However, Article 349 TFEU also allows the Council to adopt specific measures that may restrict free movement of goods.[126]

One policy field that deserves specific mention is state aid as the Treaty of Lisbon also recognized its importance for OMRs. Thus, OMRs are now listed as regions whose economic aid may be exempted from the ban on state aid. They form a separate category in Article 107(3) TFEU, next to areas "where the standard of living is abnormally low" or where there is "serious underemployment". Many OMRs lobbied for this adaptation of 107 TFEU, as they feared that the accession of new Member States with weaker economies and the consequent lowering of the average threshold might jeopardize their qualification as regions eligible for state aid.[127]

4.4 *The Overseas Countries and Territories*

The OCTs, listed in Annex II to the Treaties, consist of a long list of British, French, Dutch, and Danish possessions that span the globe. For the United Kingdom these are the Cayman Islands, Anguilla, the Turks and Caicos Islands, Montserrat, the British Virgin Islands, (all in the Caribbean area), South Georgia and the South Sandwich Islands, Saint Helena, the Falklands and Bermuda[128] (all in the Atlantic), Pitcairn (in the Pacific) and the British Indian Ocean Territories.[129] No less impressive are the listed French possessions: the *Collectivités d'outre-mer* of New Caledonia, French Polynesia, Wallis and Futuna, the Southern and Antarctic Territories (TAAF),[130] Saint Pierre et Miquelon, and Saint Barthélemy.[131] The list also contains the Dutch Caribbean islands of Curaçao, Aruba and Sint Maarten (with the status of "countries") as well as Bonaire, Saint Eustatius and Saba (with the status of "special municipalities") and the Danish territory of Greenland.

---

122. See Case 58/86, *Avirons*. Examples of areas not mentioned in 349 TFEU are the freedom of establishment and the freedom to provide services.
123. Since the Lisbon Treaty, Art. 349 TFEU refers to "conditions of application of the "Treaties"", thus including CFSP as regulated by the TEU.
124. See for instance Council Reg. 645/2008, O.J. 2008, L 180/1 on tariff quotas on imports of fishery products into the Canary Islands, specifically para 8 of the preamble.
125. See Joined Cases C-363/93 and 407 to 411/93, *Lancry*, para 31 and, for the internal market more generally, Joined Cases C-485 and 486/93, *Kos*.
126. See on the power of the Council to do so under Art. 349 TFEU Case C-212/96, *Chevassus-Marche*. See on the *octroi de mer* (or dock dues), imposed in the French DOMs Council Decision 2004/162 of 10 Feb. 2004, O.J. 2004, L 52/64.
127. See J. Ziller, op. cit. *supra* note 101, at 81.
128. Bermuda is today effectively an OCT as it has signed up to OCT Decision 2013/755/EU. The preceding Decision 2001/822 did not apply to Bermuda.
129. The rule in Art. 355 (2) second sentence TFEU that the British OCTs not mentioned in Annex II shall be subject to the Treaties was designed to cover Hong Kong and Rhodesia and is therefore today obsolete.
130. The *Terres Australes et Antarctiques Françaises*, is a *Collectivité d'outre-mer* subdivided in five districts.
131. The French island of Clipperton is not listed in Annex II and therefore not subject to the EU-OCT Association.

Unlike the OMRs, the OCTs are excluded from EU law unless specific arrangements provide otherwise. The main basis for such arrangement is the EU-OCT Association in Part Four TFEU (Arts. 198 to 204). Article 198 TFEU provides for the OCTs to be associated with the Union, the purpose of which is to "promote the economic and social development of the OCTs and to establish close economic relations between them and the Union as a whole".[132] Geographically, the EU-OCT association covers all the inhabited OCTs listed in Annex II, except for Greenland.[133] Instead, a separate decision governs EU-Greenlandic relations since 2014.[134] As of 2014 also Bermuda joined the EU-OCT association.

The EU-OCT association is periodically renewed (usually every ten years) by a new OCT Decision based on Article 203 TFEU. The current EU-OCT association regime is established by Decision 2013/755 (hereafter: "the OCT Decision").[135] It is based on three pillars: (1) enhancing the OCTs' competitiveness; (2) strengthening their resilience and reducing their vulnerability (this includes the sustainable development goals as well as education improvement goals); and (3) promoting cooperation, including cooperation with neighbouring regions.[136] In terms of domestic legal effect, the ECJ has clarified that clear and unconditional provisions of the OCT Decision may be relied upon in court.[137]

The relationship between the EU and the OCTs was very much modelled on that of the ACP countries (African, Caribbean and Pacific countries), a model that does not befit the situations of OCTs.[138] Thus, the current OCT Decision reduces the traditional parallelism between the EU-ACP and the EU-OCT relations, allowing for more preferential treatment of OCT originating products. Nevertheless the financial assistance to the OCTs is still funded by the European Development Fund, the instrument that also provides development aid to the ACP countries. The European Development Fund is financed directly by the Member States and requires a separate international agreement to be renewed with certain intervals. It is managed outside the general framework for the EU budget.[139]

In terms of operationalization, the new OCT Decision seeks more alignment with the functioning of the ESI Funds. Key is the "Partnership Principle" whereby the main responsibility for the programming and implementing the funds furnished by the European Development Fund rests with the OCTs themselves, thus moving away from the previous mechanisms that were more akin to traditional development cooperation.[140]

---

132. See Case C-390/95P, *Antillean Rice Mills v. Commission*, para 36 and Case C-17/98, *Emesa Sugar v. Aruba*, para 28.
133. The general provisions for OCTs in Arts. 198 to 203 TFEU apply to Greenland, yet subject to the special provisions in the Protocol for Greenland, see Art. 204 TFEU.
134. See Council Decision 2014/137/EU, O.J. 2014, L 76/1. Fisheries is regulated in a separate protocol granting access to Greenlandic fishing grounds in exchange for financial compensation to the Greenlandic Fisheries sector.
135. Council Decision 2013/755/EU of 25 Nov. 2013 on the association of the overseas countries and territories with the European Union, O.J. 2013, L 344/1. It replaces Decision 2001/822, O.J. 2001, L 314/1. The very first Association regime for the OCTs was established by international agreement at the Paris Conference of 20 Feb. 1957 after which the consecutive OCT regimes were laid down in unanimous acts of the Council. Since the 1991 OCT Decision, these decisions have a lifespan of 10 years.
136. See Art. 3(2) Decision 2013/755.
137. See Joined Cases C-100 and C-101/89, *Kaefer and Procacci*, para 23.
138. See the Commission's Green Paper, COM(2008)383(final) of 25 June 2008.
139. The current Agreement on the 11th European Development Fund entered into force on 1 Mar. 2015 after ratification by all EU Member States, O.J. 2013, L 210/1.
140. See para 5 and 34 of the Preamble and Art. 1(1) to the OCT Decision 2013/755.

Although the OCTs are excluded from substantive areas of EU law,[141] their relationship with the EU in terms of free movement resembles somewhat that of a "one way street". According to Article 199 TFEU the Member States "shall apply to their trade with the countries and territories the same treatment as they accord to each other pursuant to the Treaties", a duty the OCTs need not reciprocate. This special position of the OCTs is particularly visible when it comes to the free movement of goods. Although not part of the customs union, products originating in the OCTs are exempt from any customs duties and charges having equivalent effect[142] when entering the EU's metropolitan area. Yet, the OCTs may still impose duties on EU products provided they "meet the needs for their development and industrialization" *or* "produce revenue for their budget".[143] When levying such duties, the OCTs must treat all EU Member States equally.[144] If the OCT's import duties on products from third countries are such that EU Member States suffer deflections of trade, the affected Member State(s) may ask the Commission to propose measures to remedy the situation.[145]

Equally, the freedom to provide services and free establishment are not applicable *as such* in the OCTs unless provision is made to such effect in the OCT Decision. In fact, for establishment Article 199(5) TFEU expects the Association to deal with establishment "in accordance with" the regular internal market legal basis applying a "non-discriminatory basis". Despite this call for alignment, the OCT Decision treats services and establishment in an asymmetrical way, stimulating the OCTs' development while simultaneously taking into account their vulnerabilities. The EU should, as a minimum, offer OCTs the "most favourable treatment" it accords to natural and legal persons in any third country. By contrast, the most favoured nation clause for the OCTs has a more restricted formulation: they should extend to the EU at least the same treatment granted to (legal) persons in "any major trading economy with whom an economic integration agreement was concluded after 1 January 2014". Moreover, they are allowed to adopt regulations to aid local natural persons and local activities, subject to Commission notification.[146]

Free movement of capital between the OCTs and the EU seems to be only partially liberalized under the OCT Association. Even though there is full free movement of payments, free movement of capital is restricted to "direct investments in companies", excluding measures such as portfolio investments or investments in real estate.[147] Yet, considering that Article 63 TFEU has a global reach, also liberalizing free movement of capital with third countries, the more restricted rule under the EU-OCT Association appears odd.[148] Indeed, the ECJ has brought the

---

141. See the 2009 Communication Elements for a new Partnership between the EU and the OCTs, COM(2009)623 final, see in particular at 4 and 7.
142. As first established in Joined Cases C-363 and 407–411, *Lancry*. See Art. 40(2) and 70 and 71 OCT Decision. See today Art. 43 and 44 Decision 2013/755. Although Art. 200 TFEU only mentions customs duties, "charges having equivalent effect" are also covered by the provision, see Case C-260/90, *Leplat*.
143. See Art. 200(3) TFEU and Art. 45(1) OCT Decision which does not repeat the point on the OCT's budget.
144. Thus not giving any favorable treatment to the state with which it has special relations, see Art. 200(3) TFEU. This most favoured nation treatment is extended to that given by the OCT to any "major trading economy", see Art. 45 (2) and (4) OCT Decision.
145. See Art. 201 TFEU.
146. See respectively Art. 51(1) and (3) OCT Decision. Art. 52 requires further Council measures on the liberalization of medical professions. The non-discrimination clause in the preceding version of this provision (Art. 45(2)(b) of the 2006 OCT Decision) has not been repeated in the current OCT Decision.
147. See Art. 59 OCT Association Decision. See for the nomenclature on what constitutes "direct investment" Directive 88/361, O.J. 1988, L 178/5.
148. As also stated by W. Geurtsen, "The free movement of capital with the OCTs" in D. Kochenev, op. cit. *supra* note 100, at 255 and 264.

capital movements between a Member State and an OCT (with which it has no special ties)[149] in the ambit of Article 63 TFEU stating that OCTs are to profit from the rules on free movement of capital as if they were "third countries".[150] As some OCTs are considered "tax havens", it is important to note that the OCT Decision allows Member States to maintain certain rules combatting tax evasion.[151]

Since Lisbon, the legal basis for the OCT Decision (Art. 203 TFEU) may also regulate the free movement of workers between the EU and the OCTs and between the OCTs *inter se*. Before 2009 this required an international agreement.[152] The current OCT Decision does not do so however, restricting itself to goods, services, establishment and capital.

The EU-OCT Association seems to be limited to economic integration. For instance, it does not indicate that OCTs are subject to the Area of Freedom, Security and Justice. Quite the contrary, it states in Article 40 that efforts "may" be made towards capacity building in the OCTs on fighting serious forms of crime (such as human trafficking, organized crime, anti-terrorism measures etc.) and to develop means of police and judicial cooperation in these fields. As regards money laundering and terrorism financing the OCT Decision is more adamant: OCTs "shall" cooperate with the EU in these areas. The same is true more generally for international standards on regulation and supervision of financial services (on tax cooperation, transparency, anti-terrorism and money laundering) where the EU and the OCTs "shall" promote regulatory convergence.[153]

Yet, it would go too far to regard Part Four TFEU (and the concomitant OCT Decision) as a "comprehensive *lex specialis*". Since the ruling of the ECJ in *Eman and Sevinger* it is clear that Part Two TFEU (non-discrimination and EU citizenship) applies to the OCTs.[154] In the previous *Kaefer* and *Procacci* case the ECJ had already done so for Parts Six TFEU (Institutions) and Seven TFEU (General and Final Provisions).[155] Thus, it became clear that courts in the OCTs may refer preliminary questions to the ECJ under Article 267 TFEU as they qualify as "courts or tribunals of a Member State".[156]

Some authors even argue that the EU-OCT arrangements must be perceived as an exception to the main rule that EU law *does* apply in full to the OCTs. Not just the general principles of EU law, rules on EU citizenship and non-discrimination[157] but even substantive areas like the area of freedom security and justice would therefore apply.[158] Indeed, it may be wondered if the acknowledgement of the EU citizenship status of the OCT nationals may not be an increasingly solid ground to start extending the 'AFSJ' geographic scope towards the OCTs. The same is true

149. It concerned French taxation on investment in real estate owned by a company on the British Virgin Islands, which is a British OCT.
150. See Case C-384/09, *Prunus and Polonium*, para 20.
151. See Art. 66 OCT Decision. See Joined Cases C-24/12 and C-27/12, *X BV and TBG Ltd* on a Dutch measure restricting capital movement to the Dutch Antilles. It was upheld be resorting to Art. 66 OCT Decision.
152. See Art. 202 TFEU.
153. See Art. 71 OCT Decision.
154. See J. Ziller, op. cit. *supra* note 101, at 76.
155. See Joined Cases C-100/89 and C-101/89, *Kaefer and Procacci*.
156. See Joined Cases C-100/89 and C-101/89, *Kaefer and Procacci* on a preliminary reference of the administrative court in Papeete (French Polynesia), para 8. It must be noted that the ECJ seemed to attach great importance to the possibility of an appeal before a court in Metropolitan France, which, as M.P. Broberg states, cannot be the exclusive reason to regard the courts in the OCTs as courts "of a Member State", see M.P. Broberg and N. Fenger, *Preliminary References to the European Court of Justice* (OUP, 2010).
157. See Case C-300/04, *Eman and Sevinger*.
158. See M. Fletcher, op. cit. *supra* note 100, at 299 and M.P. Broberg, "Access to the European Court of Justice by courts in overseas countries and territories" in D. Kochenev, op. cit. *supra* note 100, at 144.

for the geographic scope of application of the Charter of Fundamental Rights. Even if it follows from Article 355(2) TFEU that the Charter is geographically not applicable to the OCTs, it might be increasingly difficult to reconcile that with the EU citizenship status as enjoyed by many OCT nationals.

Further reading

Baun, M. and D. Marek, *Cohesion Policy in the European Union* (Palgrave, 2014).

Caruso, D., "Direct concern in regional policy: The European Court of Justice and the Southern question", 17 ELJ (2011).

Hachez, N. and J. Wouters, "A responsible lender? The European Investment Bank's environmental, social and human rights accountability", 49 CML Rev. (2012), at 47–96.

Kochenev, D. (Ed.), *EU law of the Oversees, Outermost Regions, Associated Countries and Territories, Territories Sui Generis* (Kluwer, 2011).

König, P., "Reform of the EU cohesion policy", 20 *European Review* (2012), at 252.

Mendez, C., "The post-2013 reform of EU cohesion policy and the place-based narrative", 20 *Journal of European Public Policy* (2013), at 639.

Murray, F., *The European Union and Member State Territories, A New Legal Framework under the EU Treaties* (Asser Press, 2012).

Piattoni, S., *The Theory of Multilevel Governance* (OUP, 2010).

Strumia, F., "Remedying the inequalities of economic citizenship in Europe: Cohesion policy and the negative right to move", 17 ELJ (2011), at 725.

CHAPTER 34
EU HEALTH LAW AND POLICY

*Anne Pieter van der Mei and Ellen Vos**

1. Introduction

Article 168 TFEU instructs the European Union (hereafter EU) to pursue a public health policy and confers upon its institutions specific, mostly supplementary, powers for this purpose. EU action will be aimed at improving public health, preventing physical and mental illnesses and diseases and obviate sources of danger to physical and mental health. In furtherance of this task the Union has adopted numerous programmes and measures that are mainly aimed at inciting Member States to act and to cooperate on topics concerning health protection and promotion, prevention of diseases and encouragement of healthy lifestyles.

The EU's engagement in health however, entails more than the activities triggered by Article 168 TFEU. Most importantly, the EU is obliged to ensure a high level of human health protection in the definition and implementation of all its policies and activities.[1] Thus, health protection is an inherent part of the internal market as well as the EU's policies in the fields of agriculture, environmental protection, transport, labour law, intellectual property law[2] and external relations.[3] Moreover, the TFEU guarantees health providers and patients freedom of movement, it entitles pharmaceutical companies to sell their products all over the EU and the Treaty's rules on competition policy and fiscal governance have a profound impact on the functioning and financing of national health care sectors.

Hence, EU health law and policy cut across almost all, if indeed not all, areas of EU activity. They constitute a patchwork of numerous substantive health topics, which are regulated by a voluminous body of rules, decisions and policy instruments set in place by a myriad of actors ranging from EU institutions to agencies to private sector organizations.

This Chapter provides a bird's-eye view on these highly fragmented areas of EU health law and policy. After a historical overview of the EU's involvement in health matters, it presents some key topics of EU health law and policy under the headings of "health and the internal market" (section 3) and health policy *stricto sensu* (section 4).

---

* Law Faculty, Maastricht University.

1. See Art. 9 TFEU.
2. See e.g. Case C-34/10, *Oliver Brüstle v. Greenpeace e.V.*, and Case C-364/13, *International Stem Cell Corporation v. Comptroller General of Patents, Designs and Trade Marks* (on the patentability of "human embryo's" for purposes of Directive 98/44/EC of the European Parliament and of the Council of 6 July 1998 on the legal protection of biotechnological inventions – O.J. 1998, L 213, at 13).
3. See further T. Hervey and J. McHale, *European Health Law – Themes and Implications* (CUP, 2015), 433–532.

2. EU health law and policy: A brief history

The thinking on an EU health policy can be traced back to 1952. In December of that year the French Government convened a conference in Paris, which was attended by representatives of various States, including the six ECSC members.[4] Topic on the agenda: a proposal to create a "European Health Community". After a passionate opening statement in which Foreign Affairs Minister Robert Schuman called for "*un front commun de l'Europe contre la maladie*",[5] Paul Ribeyre, French Minister for Public Health and the Population and the "Monnet-like mastermind" of the proposal, presented the main features of the envisaged organization. The Health Community would be given two tasks.[6] The first concerned the creation of a common health market, which would encompass "medicinal products, medical and surgical equipment, pharmaceutical production plants and climatic and thermal resources", and enable "all doctors to practise indiscriminately in each participating country". The proposal assigned a key role to a "High Authority", which would have to take the binding decisions necessary for enforcing the common market rules and be assisted by a Consultative Committee composed of persons having "specialist knowledge of health-related sciences or industries".

The second task of this Health Community would consist of measures aimed at promoting cooperation among participating States on topics like coordination of medical research, hospital planning and combatting epidemics. Schuman and Ribeyre envisaged the creation of a Council of Ministers, which would be entrusted with the task of bringing the action of the High Authority "into line with the health policy of the various governments".

The Health Community, or the so-called "white pool",[7] however, never saw the light of day, *inter alia* because it was vigorously opposed by chemical, pharmaceutical and medical equipment industries.[8] The Schuman-Ribeyre proposal was shelved and never reconsidered again. When one takes the proposal of the shelves again, blows off the dust and re-reads it, at least two elements become visible that have been characteristic for the role the European institutions have actually played in health matters ever since the late 1950s.

First, the proposal reflected the notion that market integration does not only constitute, a potential threat to health values and health care systems. Freedom of movement and competition also offer opportunities for increasing efficiency, stimulating innovation and growth in health sectors. Second, the proposal embodied the idea that health aims and the pooling of "white sources" may have to be pursued by different means or along diverging paths. Thus, as regards the creation of a common health market, supranational decision-making was chosen for. At the same time, however, as to health policy *stricto sensu*, which may entail the making of delicate social, ethical or political choices, mere cooperation was chosen for, leaving national competences untouched.

---

4. See further A.P. van der Mei and E. Vos, "The state of the European Health Union – The Maastricht contribution to EU health policy" in M. de Visser & A.P. van der Mei (Eds.), *The Treaty on European Union 1993–2013: Reflections from Maastricht* (Intersentia, 2013), 623–642.
5. *Exposé de Robert Schuman à la conférence préparatoire à la Communauté européenne de la santé* (Paris, 12 Dec. 1952), available at <www.cvce.eu/collections/unit-content/-/unit/02bb76df-d066-4c08-a58a-d4686a-3e68ff/f49cf794-1504-41c6-8486-2402bc929f52/Resources#1fba65da-1ae8-45a4-beb5e299ed4b4c6c_fr&overlay>.
6. Ibid.
7. In addition to the ECSC ("black pool") and the European Health Community ("white pool"), plans were circulating for an agricultural community ("green pool"), a transport community, and a European Defence Community. See G. Parsons, *A Certain Idea of Europe* (Cornell University Press, 2003), 83–86.
8. G. Parsons, op. cit. *supra* note 7, 86–87.

Clearly, the 1957 Rome Treaty set economic goals, not health goals and did not provide for specific health powers. Yet, three aspects made the EEC's involvement in health matters inevitable. First, the common market rules were defined generally in the sense that they applied to all goods, services, persons and companies to the exclusion of, in principle, none. In other words, while not specifically designed for it, the EEC Treaty did apply to the health sector and thus essentially called for what Ribeyre had in mind: the realization of a common health market.[9] Second, the free movement rules expressly left room for the justification of national rules hampering freedom of movement on health protection grounds[10] and conferred upon the EEC legislature the power to approximate national health protection laws to actually realize free movement.[11] Third, health issues were bound to arise in a number of policy areas included in the EEC Treaty, like agriculture[12] and social policy.[13]

During the first three decades the EEC institutions did indeed get involved in health matters. For example, a coordination regime for health insurance aimed at facilitating free movement of workers was set in place,[14] the freedom of health professionals was realized upon the establishment of a complex system for the mutual recognition of health diploma's[15] and qualifications and, in response to the "Thalidomide crisis", the foundations were laid for a Community system for the marketing authorization of medicines.[16] All in all, however, progress remained modest and this was largely due to the fact that former Article 100 EEC (now Art. 115 TFEU) prescribed unanimity for decision-making in the Council, which indeed proved to be a formidable obstacle for the adoption of positive integration measures.

It was only in the mid- and late-1980s that the European institutions' involvement in health issues intensified. The turning point was the Single European Act (SEA) of 1986, which made two significant changes.

First, the SEA empowered the Council to adopt harmonization measures needed for the establishment and functioning of the internal market by qualified majority vote[17] and ordered the Commission, in its proposals for harmonization measures, to strive for a high level of protection of health and safety.[18] Virtually all measures proposed in the Commission's 1985 White Paper,[19] many of which contained measures involving health protection, could now be, and indeed were, quickly adopted. Health protection acquired a prominent place on the European agenda. The Community developed itself into a "leader" with regard to ensuring product safety, and medicines and foodstuffs especially.[20]

---

9. Art. 117 EEC et seq.
10. E.g., Art. 36 EEC.
11. Art. 100 EEC.
12. Art. 39 EEC.
13. Art. 117 EEC.
14. Reg. 3 of the Council of 25 Sept. 1958 concerning social security for migrant Workers, O.J. 1958, 30/561 as later replaced by Reg. (EEC) 1408/71 of the Council of 14 June 1971 on the application of social security schemes to employed persons and their families moving within the Community, O.J. English Special Edition (II), at 416.
15. See W. Berg, *Gesundheitsschutz als Aufgabe der EU – Entwicklung, Kompetenzen, Perspektiven* (Nomos, 1997), and H. Schneider, *Die Anerkennung von Diplomen in der Europäischen Gemeinschaft* (Maklu, 1995), 99–160.
16. See W. Berg, op. cit. *supra* note 15.
17. Art. 100a(1) EEC.
18. Art. 100a(3) EEC.
19. Commission's White Paper on the Completion of the Internal Market of June 1985, COM(85)310 final.
20. G. Permanand, and E. Vos, "EU regulatory agencies and health protection" in E. Mossialos et al. (Eds.), *Health Systems Governance in Europe – The Role of European Union Law and Policy* (CUP, 2010), at 134–185 and 156.

Second, the SEA introduced provisions offering the EU institutions new competences in policy areas in which health protection plays a key role, such as environmental policy[21] and health and safety of workers in the workplace.[22]

In the following years, it was foremost the internal market agenda that continued to drive the Community's involvement in health matters. With the new decision-making procedure, EU health policy rapidly matured in the late 1980s. The EU did not, and could not, pursue a health policy *stricto sensu* as it had no formal competences to for example, coordinate medical research, hospital planning and combat epidemics, as Schuman and Ribeyre had envisaged. In practice, however, the Member States and the Community had already taken a few initiatives solely motivated by health promotion motives, most notably[23] including the Europe against Cancer[24] and Europe against Aids programmes.[25] Subsequently, the Maastricht Treaty offered a legal basis and powers for health initiatives. It tasked the Community to "contribute towards a high level of human health protection by encouraging cooperation between Member States, and, if necessary, lending support to their action" on issues concerning the improvement of public health, prevention of illness and diseases, and combatting epidemics and encourage cooperation among the Member States.[26] To achieve these objectives, the Treaty entrusted the Commission with the task of proposing measures of cooperation and it empowered the Council and the Parliament to adopt "incentive measures", excluding "any harmonization of the laws and regulations of the Member States".[27]

Since the entry into force of the Maastricht Treaty the European institutions continued to use their internal market and sectoral powers. This led, among others, to a strengthening of the regime for the production and marketing of healthy and safe medicinal products and an extensive body of legislation ensuring workers a healthy and safe working place. It took some time, however, before the EU institutions commenced developing a health policy *stricto sensu*. They only did so in response to two unforeseen events.

The first concerned the French blood transmission scandals and the BSE crisis. The Amsterdam Treaty responded to these crises by ordering the institutions not just to *contribute* to but rather to *ensure* health protection and to work also on health promotion.[28] In addition, "Amsterdam"[29] conferred upon the European Parliament and the Council the power to adopt measures setting high standards of quality and safety of organs and substances of human origin,

---

21. Art. 130s EEC.
22. Art. 118a EEC.
23. Another example is Resolution of the Council and of the representatives of the Governments of the Member States, meeting within the Council of 29 May 1986 on alcohol abuse, O.J. 1986, C 184/3. In addition, one month before the Maastricht Summit, Resolution of the Council and of the representatives of the Governments of the Member States, meeting within the Council of 11 Nov. 1991 concerning fundamental health-policy choices was adopted, O.J. 1991, C 304/5.
24. Resolution of Council and the Representatives of the Governments of the Member States on a programme of action of the European Communities against cancer, O.J. 1986, C 184/9. Notably, this programme was initiated by Italian Prime Minister Craxi and French President Mitterand, after the latter had been diagnosed with cancer.
25. Decision 91/317/EEC of the Council and the Ministers of Health of the Member States, meeting within the Council adopting a plan of action in the framework of the 1991 to 1993 "Europe against AIDS" programme, O.J. 1991, L 175/26.
26. Art. 129(1) EC.
27. Art. 129(4) EC.
28. Art. 152 EC, ex Art. 129 EC.
29. A.P. van der Mei and L. Waddington, "Public health and the Treaty of Amsterdam", (1998) *European Journal of Health Law*, 129–154.

blood and blood derivatives[30] as well as measures in the veterinary and phytosanitary field aiming at protection of public health.[31]

The second "event" involved the 1998 ruling in *Kohll*[32] in which the Court of Justice read in the Treaty provisions on free movement of services a right to freedom of movement for patients. These rulings caused a stir in governmental and health care circles.[33] The subsequent political debates, which took more than a decade, culminated in 2011 in the adoption of the Patients' Rights Directive (PRD).[34] Notably, next to rules on the (reimbursement of the costs of) cross-border healthcare, the PRD includes some health measures *stricto sensu* including a set of "new" patient rights, rules aimed at promoting health cooperation and provisions on health technology assessment.

The Lisbon Treaty did not bring about fundamental changes. Two points are worth mentioning though. The first concerns the nature of competences in health related fields. Thus, the EU's competences in the area of "common safety concerns in public health matters" are classified as shared competences, whereas the "protection and improvement of human health" is regarded as an area in which the EU merely has the power to support, coordinate or supplement action by the Member States. Second, the EU Charter on Fundamental Rights, which has becoming legally binding, contains rights to human dignity, life and access to preventive care[35] which may have potential significance for health law and policy.

All in all, EU health policy and law have not been shaped in a pro-active "Ribeyrean-like" manner on the basis of a pre-conceptualized vision on how best to protect, promote or improve the health of Europe's citizens. Rather, in the EU, health law and policy have largely developed in re-active manner and in response to sometimes foreseen, sometimes unforeseen health issues and incidents that have arisen in the course of the European market integration process as well as developments in other EU policy areas. It is only since the late 1990s, early 2000s that the European institutions commenced developing a policy that, on the one hand, encompasses health policy measures *stricto sensu* and, on the other hand, seeks to streamline all EU health activities and to develop a more coherent approach to the Union's contribution to health.

3. Health and the internal market

EU health law and policy are to a large extent products of the market integration process. From a health or health care perspective, this process may be viewed from two angles.

First, market integration offers opportunities to further health objectives. For example, by eliminating obstacles to trade in medicines the EU expands the selling market for pharmaceuticals, and thus enables the pharmaceutical companies to increase their profits, which they, in turn, can invest in the development of new, better or cheaper medicines. Comparably, freedom of movement does not only offer doctors, nurses and other health professionals to find better (paid) jobs, but also enables hospitals and other employers in the health sector to hire the best doctors and nurses or to solve problems of shortages in their national health labour market so as

30. Art. 152(4a) EC.
31. Art. 152 (4b) EC.
32. Case C-158/96 *Raymond Kohll v. Union des caisses de maladie*. See also Case C-120/95, *Nicolas Decker v. Caisse de maladie des employés privés*.
33. Ibid.
34. Directive 2011/24/EU of the European Parliament and of the Council of 9 Mar. 2011 on the application of patients' rights in cross-border healthcare O.J. 2011, L 88/45.
35. See Arts. 1, 2 and 33 of the Charter respectively. See further J. McHale, "Fundamental rights and health care" in E. Mossialos et al., op. cit. *supra* note 20, 282–314, and T. Hervey and G. McHale, op. cit. *supra* note 3, Ch. 7.

to maintain or improve the quality of the health services they deliver. Essentially, the EU shares the "Ribeyrean" view that by pooling "white resources" through the creation of an "internal health market" health goals can be achieved.

Second, EU internal market law rests on the premise that the "health and life of humans rank foremost among the assets and interests protected by the Treaty".[36] Health values carry more weight than free trade values. Free movement for medicines, foodstuffs or toys cannot be pursued at the expense of the health of patients, consumers or children. The internal market must be a "healthy one". Member States can lawfully oppose free trade or cross-border movement in the name of health for as long, and in as far, as the European legislature has not yet taken over responsibility for health protection. The main tool the EU legislature has at its disposal to set such European health standards concerns the harmonization power granted by Article 114 TFEU.

Surely, this is an economic power for adopting measures that "have as their object the establishment and functioning of the internal market". Yet, because diverging health protection rules may affect the functioning of the market, the harmonization power granted by Article 114 TFEU can be used as an instrument for health policy.[37] In practice the EU indeed has made extensive use of internal market legislation to pursue health objectives.[38]

To illustrate the significance of internal market law for the EU's health law and policy, the remainder of this section discusses internal market law[39] in as far as relevant for pharmaceuticals, foodstuffs, tobacco products, health care providers and patients.

3.1 *Pharmaceuticals*

As noted above, from the 1960s the EC/EU has been working on, and progressively developed, a comprehensive body of legislation on the production, marketing and monitoring of pharmaceuticals. The need to regulate such products became apparent in the 1950s after the *Thalidomide* tragedy, in which a sedative used by pregnant women led to fetal loss and major birth defects.[40] This "sharpest possible wake-up call regarding the need to regulate medicines",[41] led national authorities to set strict regulatory measures and regimes at national level, with regard to market access and post-market control. In order to protect health and to ensure free movement of

36. Joined Cases C-570/07 and C-571/07, *José Manuel Blanco Pérez and María del Pilar Chao Gómez v. Consejería de Salud y Servicios Sanitarios and Principado de Asturias*, at 44.
37. This is clearly confirmed by Art. 114(3) TFEU, which instructs the Commission to take a high level of protection in its proposals concerning health, safety, environmental and consumer protection.
38. As such, this has never aroused much controversy. B. de Witte, "A competence to protect: The pursuit of non-market aims through internal market legislation" in P. Syrpis (Ed.), *The Judiciary, the Legislature and the EU Internal Market* (CUP, 2012), at 25–45. Two other things have been controversial though. The first concerns the precise reach of the internal market harmonization power. See the discussion by S. Garben in this volume of Case C-376/98, *Federal Republic of Germany v. European Parliament and Council of the European Union*. The second controversial issue involves the level of health protection, and the so-called "opt-out" clauses contained in Art. 100a(4) EEC (now Art. 114(4) and (5) TFEU), which allow Member States to maintain or adopt national measures that set higher health protection standards upon authorization by the Commission. See, I. Maletic, *The Law and Policy of Harmonisation in Europe's Internal Market* (Edward Elgar, 2013).
39. This section focuses on free movement law. For an overview and analysis of the application of the EU competition rules to the healthcare sector, see L. Hancher and W. Sauter, *EU Competition and Internal Market Law in the Healthcare Sector* (OUP, 2012).
40. S. Krapohl, "Thalidomide, BSE and the single market: An historical-institutionalist approach to regulatory regimes in the European Union", (2007) *European Journal of Political Research*, 25–46.
41. G. Permanand and E. Vos, "EU regulatory agencies and health protection" in E. Mossialos et al., op. cit. *supra* note 20, at 157.

medicines on the European market, the Community legislature adopted in 1965 a first directive defining medicinal products and stipulating rules regarding their development and production, along with initial guidelines for post-market controls. Importantly, the directive established safety, efficacy and therapeutic benefit as grounds for marketing approval.[42] This directive was the beginning of a long and thorny process towards the creation of an internal market for pharmaceuticals. To speed up marketing applications for new medicines and to alleviate the burden of applications being made separately to each national authority, the Community/EU created various procedures to remove the trade barriers that existed due to the strict national regulatory schemes.[43] However, faced with the distrust of Member States in each other's authorization schemes, the EU decided in 1993 to set up a centralized authorization procedure for the marketing of medicinal products together with a new agency, the *European Agency for the Evaluation of Medicinal Products* (EMEA), currently called the European Medicines Agency (EMA).[44] Together with the decentralized procedure that was set up to reinforce mutual recognition of national marketing authorizations, the centralized procedure up until to date constitutes the centre of the body of EU legislation on pharmaceuticals.[45] The centralized procedure is compulsory for a biotechnological and high tech medicines and may be used for a number of other medicines.[46] Directive 2001/83 stipulates that no medicinal product may be placed on the market without a prior marketing authorization. The authorization decisions are taken either by a national competent authority or by the Commission upon advice from the EMA. Marketing authorizations are assessed on criteria of quality, safety and efficacy of the medicinal products concerned. Importantly, the EU regime leaves untouched the powers of the Member States to set prices of medicines or to include medicines in the scope of national health systems or social security schemes.[47] Today, the EU has set a wide range of legislative and non-legislative meas-

---

42. Council Directive 65/65/EEC of 26 Jan. 1965 on the approximation of provisions laid down by law, regulation or administrative action relating to proprietary medicinal products (O.J. 1965, L 22), at 369.
43. Namely, a mutual recognition procedure Council Directive 75/319/EEC of 20 May 1975 on the approximation of provisions laid down by law, regulation or administrative action relating to medicinal products (O.J. 1975, L 147), at 13, the multi-state procedure Council Directive 83/570/EEC of 26 Oct. 1983 amending 65/65/EEC (O.J. 1983, L 332), at 1 and the concertation procedure: Council Directive 87/22/EEC of 22 Dec. 1986 on the approximation of national measures relating to the placing on the market of high-technology medicinal products, particularly those derived from biotechnology (O.J. 1987, L 15), at 38.
44. Council Reg. (EEC) 2309/93 of 22 July 1993 laying down Community procedures for the authorization and supervision of medicinal products for human and veterinary use and establishing a European Agency for the Evaluation of Medicinal Products O.J. 1993, L 214/1. This Regulation has been replaced by Reg. (EC) 726/2004 Of The European Parliament And Of The Council of 31 Mar. 2004 laying down Community procedures for the authorization and supervision of medicinal products for human and veterinary use and establishing a European Medicines Agency (O.J. 2004, L 136/1).
45. Today, the main pieces of legislation of pharmaceuticals are constituted by Directive 2001/83/EC Of The European Parliament And Of The Council Of 6 Nov. 2001 On The Community Code Relating To Medicinal Products For Human Use, (O.J. 2001, L 311/67), amended by various directives and Directive 2001/82/EC Of The European Parliament And Of The Council Of 6 Nov. 2001 On The Community Code Relating To Medicinal Products For Veterinary Use, (O.J. 2011, L 311/1) and Reg. (EC) 726/2004, cited *supra* note 44.
46. In relation to medicines for human use, these are for example: human medicines for the treatment of human immunodeficiency virus (HIV) or acquired immune deficiency syndrome (AIDS), cancer, diabetes, neurodegenerative diseases, auto-immune and other immune dysfunctions, and viral diseases; veterinary medicines for use as growth or yield enhancers; medicines derived from biotechnology processes, such as genetic engineering; advanced-therapy medicines, such as gene-therapy, somatic cell-therapy or tissue-engineered medicines and so called "orphan drugs" (medicines used for rare human diseases).
47. See Art. 1, Reg. (EC) 726/2004 of the European Parliament and of the Council of 31 Mar. 2004 laying down Community procedures for the authorization and supervision of medicinal products for human and veterinary use and establishing a European Medicines Agency (O.J. 2004, L 136/01).

ures on pharmaceuticals in relation to health protection,[48] ranging from pharmacoviligence,[49] transparency of pricing of pharmaceuticals,[50] advanced therapy medicines[51] and orphan drugs.[52]

3.2 *Foodstuffs*

Since the 1960s the Community/Union has been working on an internal market for foodstuffs. As early as 1962, the Community legislature adopted the first directive on colouring matters of foodstuffs laying down lists of colouring matters which could be used to treat foodstuffs, together with their conditions of use.[53] The Directive put the protection of health protection first, although it did recognize that the protection of the consumer against falsification and the needs of the economy were also be taken into consideration. From then onwards, the EU actively pursued a full harmonization programme on foodstuffs with the aim to adopt harmonization measures laying down compositional rules for individual foods. It sought to replace all national legislation in the food area with detailed EU legislation, for example precise requirements on the composition of chocolate. It was this kind of legislation that made commentators fear of having only "Euro-food".[54] The slow and cumbersome decision-making process of this "traditional approach" together with the recognition of the mutual recognition principle by the Court in *Cassis de Dijon*,[55] pushed the institutions to adopt in 1985 a New Approach to harmonization and technical standards.[56] This approach abandoned the detailed regulation of compositional rules and concentrated on a horizontal approach regulating the substances processed into food

---

48. See for an overview of the legislation concerning pharmaceutical products for human use: Compendium of EU pharmaceutical law, EudraBook V1 – May 2015, available at <ec.europa.eu/health/documents/eudralex/cd/index_en.htm>. Mention may further be made of the REACH programme, which aims to improve the protection of human health and the environment through the better and earlier identification of the intrinsic properties of chemical substances. Reg. (EC) 1907/2006 of the European Parliament and of the Council of 18 Dec. 2006 concerning the Registration, Evaluation, Authorization and Restriction of Chemicals (REACH), establishing a European Chemicals Agency, amending Directive 1999/45/EC and repealing Council Reg. (EEC) 793/93 and Commission Reg. (EC) 1488/94 as well as Council Directive 76/769/EEC and Commission Directives 91/155/EEC, 93/67/EEC, 93/105/EC and 2000/21/EC, O.J. 2006, L 396/1.
49. Directive 2010/84/EU of the European Parliament and of the Council of 15 Dec. 2010 amending, as Regards Pharmacovigilance, Directive 2001/83/EC on the Community Code Relating to Medicinal Products for Human Use (O.J. 2010, L 348/74).
50. Council Directive 89/105/EEC of 21 Dec. 1988 Relating to the Transparency of Measures Regulating the Prices of Medicinal Products for Human Use and their Inclusion in the Scope of National Health Insurance Systems (O.J. 1989, L 40/8).
51. Reg. 1394/2007/EC of the European Parliament and of the Council of 13 Nov. 2007 on advanced therapy medicinal products and amending Directive 2001/83/EC and Reg. (EC) 726/2004 (O.J. 2007, L 324/121).
52. Reg. 141/2000/EC of the European Parliament and of the Council of 16 Dec. 1999 on Orphan Medicinal Products (O.J. 2000, L 18/1).
53. Council Directive 62/2645/EEC of 23 Oct. 1962 on the approximation of the rules of the Member States concerning the colouring matters authorized for use in foodstuffs intended for human consumption, O.J. 1962, L 115.
54. D. Welch, "From "Euro beer" to "Newcastle brown": A Review of European Community Action to dismantle divergent 'food' laws", (1983) JCMS, 22.
55. Case 120/78, *Rewe-Zentral AG v. Bundesmonopolverwaltung für Branntwein*.
56. Council Resolution on a New Approach to technical harmonization and standards, O.J. 1985, C 136/2 and Commission Communication on technical harmonization and standards, a new approach COM(85)19 final.

to ensure their safety.[57] This New Approach subsequently formed the main device for the EU of food issues from the mid-1980s till the mid-1990s, enabling the EU institutions to concentrate on the adoption of only a "few" horizontal directives.

However mid-1990, the BSE crisis demonstrated the deficiencies of this approach to foodstuffs.[58] An Inquiry Committee of the European Parliament thus revealed that the EU suffered from poor internal management and obscure decision-making procedures. Moreover it concluded that the EU had used politically coloured scientific opinions and had failed to take protection of public health seriously, having attached greater importance to national agricultural and industrial interests.[59] Unsurprisingly, these shortcomings triggered an unprecedented crisis of confidence and credibility in EU law and policy relating to food. The formal condemnation of the EU's approach to food safety by the European Parliament's Inquiry Committee forced the EU to drastically reform both its foundations and its institutional arrangements on food safety.[60]

In the aftermath of the BSE crisis, the EU adopted in 2002 Regulation 178/2002 ("the General Food Law"),[61] which provided for a new, more coherent body of food safety governance arrangements and established a new European agency, the European Food Safety Authority (hereinafter EFSA).[62] The primary goal of the General Food Law is establish a high level of protection of both health and consumers' interests, relegating the effective functioning of the internal market to second place.[63] Next to protect consumers' health, the General Food law aims to protect consumers against fraudulent practices, adulteration of food, and other misleading practices. It also requires that fair trade, animal health and welfare, plant health, and the environment to be taken into account, where appropriate.[64] The general food law introduces important concepts as risk analysis and the precautionary principle and lays down the foundation of a genuine EU policy on foods, the bottom line being that "food shall not be placed on the market if it is unsafe".[65] Being based on agricultural, commercial, internal market and public health policies, the General Food Law forms the underpinning of a comprehensive set of EU measures on health in relation to foods, varying from chemical and biological safety of foods,[66]

---

57. See European Commission, "Communication from the Commission on the Free Movement of Foodstuffs within the Community", O.J. 1989, C 271/3.
58. See E. Vos, "EU Food safety regulation in the aftermath of the BSE crisis", (2000) *Journal Of Consumer Policy*, at 227–255.
59. O.J. 1996, C 261/132. See also European Parliament Resolution on the Commission's information policy on BSE since 1988 and the measures it has taken to ensure compliance with the export ban and to eradicate the disease, O.J. 1996, C 261/75.
60. See, *inter alia*, C. Joerges, "The law's problems with the governance of the European market" in C. Joerges and R. Dehousse (Eds.), *Good Governance in Europe's Integrated Market* (OUP, 2002), 3–31.
61. Reg. (EC) 178/2002 laying down the general principles and requirements of food law, establishing the European Food Safety Authority and laying down procedures in matters of food safety O.J. 2002, L 31/1.
62. See e.g. A. Alemanno & S. Gabbi (Eds.), *Foundations of EU Food Law and Policy* (Ashgate, 2014); C. MacMaoláin, *Food Law: European, Domestic and International Frameworks* (Hart, 2015); C. Ansell and D. Vogel (Eds.), *What's the Beef? The Contested Governance of European Food Safety* (MIT, 2006); E. Vos & F. Wendler (Eds.), *Food Safety Regulation In Europe: A Comparative Institutional Analysis* (Intersentia, 2006).
63. Art. 1, Reg. 178/2002, cited *supra* note 61.
64. Art. 8, Reg. 178/2002, cited *supra* note 61.
65. Art. 14, Reg. 178/2002, cited *supra* note 61.
66. For example, Reg. (EC) 1935/2004 Of The European Parliament And Of The Council of 27 Oct. 2004 on materials and articles intended to come into contact with food and repealing Directives 80/590/EEC and 89/109/EEC (O.J. 2004, L 338, at 4).

genetically modified foods and feeds,[67] novel foods[68] to food improvement agents, such as flavourings[69] and additives.[70]

3.3 *Tobacco*

From the early years of the integration process, the Community/Union has developed policies concerning tobacco. Notably, its first initiatives did not target tobacco as a product that may cause sickness and death, but rather involved the award of subsidies to farmers producing raw tobacco under the Common Agricultural Policy (CAP). In fact, it is only since 2010 that the EU has "de-coupled" CAP financial aid from tobacco production.[71]

Especially since the late 1980s, early 1990s, however, the EU institutions have adopted a long series of measures that pro-actively seek to discourage the use of tobacco products. EU legislation[72] includes labelling directives requiring health warnings on tobacco products, advertising directives banning tobacco advertising on TV, radio and internet and in the press, tax directives setting minimum levels of excise duties on tobacco products, directives prohibiting smoking in the workplace, resolutions inviting Member States to adopt measures to protect people from exposure to smoke in public places and public transport, and regulations prescribing maximum levels of tar and nicotine in cigarettes.[73]

The latest piece of legislation is the Tobacco Products Directive (TPD).[74] The TPD illustrates two features of EU decision-making on tobacco products. First, being based on *inter alia* Article 114 TFEU,[75] the TPD is a typical example of health policy being pursued by use of the EU's economic competences.[76] The Directive aims to approximate national laws concerning tobacco-related topics "in order to facilitate the smooth functioning of the internal market for tobacco and related products, taking as a base a high level of protection of human health". Second, the process that led to the adoption once more showed the political sensitivity of tobacco regulation with the tobacco industry using all its powers to avoid or to delay adoption of the

67. Reg. (EC) 1829/2003 of the European Parliament and of the Council of 22 Sept. 2003 on genetically modified food and feed (O.J. 2003, L 268/1).
68. Reg. (EU) 2015/2283 of the European Parliament and of the Council of 25 Nov. 2015 on novel foods, amending Reg. (EU) 1169/2011 of the European Parliament and of the Council and repealing Reg. (EC) 258/97 of the European Parliament and of the Council and Commission Reg. (EC) 1852/2001 (O.J. 2015, L 327/1).
69. Reg. (EC) 1334/2008 of the European Parliament and of the Council of 16 Dec. 2008 on flavourings and certain food ingredients with flavouring properties for use in and on foods and amending Council Reg. (EEC) 1601/91, Reg.s (EC) 2232/96 and (EC) 110/2008 and Directive 2000/13/EC (O.J. 2008, L 354/34-50).
70. Reg. (EC) 1333/2008 of the European Parliament and of the Council of 16 Dec. 2008 on food additives (O.J. 2008, L 354/16–33).
71. Available at <ec.europa.eu/agriculture/tobacco/index_en.htm>.
72. For an overview see <ec.europa.eu/health/tobacco/key_documents/index_en.htm#anchor1>.
73. For an overview and discussion see T. Hervey and G. McHale, op. cit. *supra* note 3, 390–403 and A. Gilmore and M. McKee, "Tobacco policy in the European Union" in E.A. Feldman and R. Bayer (Eds.), *Unfiltered: Conflicts over Tobacco Policy and Public Health* (Harvard University Press, 2004).
74. Directive 2014/40/EU of the European Parliament and of the Council of 3 Apr. 2014 on the approximation of the laws, regulations and administrative provisions of the Member States concerning the manufacture, presentation and sale of tobacco and related products and repealing Directive 2001/37/EC, O.J. 2014, L 127/1.
75. In addition, the TPD is based on Art. 53(1) (establishment) and Art. 62 (services) TFEU.
76. In Case C-547/14, *Philip Morris Brands SARL, Philip Morris Limited, British American Tobacco UK Limited v. Secretary of State for Health*, at the time of writing still pending, the Court of Justice has asked a series of question concerning this directive including its validity.

Directive. The process even led to the resignation[77] of Commissioner Dalli, who was accused of holding informal meetings with tobacco industry lobbyists.

In terms of substance, the TPD replaces[78] earlier legislation and lays down more stringent norms.[79] The TPD sets maximum levels of tar or nicotine for cigarettes and bans tobacco products with certain additives, such those with a given flavour and/or ease inhalation (e.g. menthol). In addition, the TPD has made more strict rules concerning marketing, labelling and packaging of tobacco products. Thus, packages of cigarettes and other tobacco products must include text-warnings like "Smoking kills – quit now" and "Tobacco smoke contains over 70 substances known to cause cancer" as well as photographs showing what smoking can actually do to health.

3.4 *Healthcare providers*

From the 1970s, the European institutions have sought to facilitate health professionals' mobility[80] mainly by adopting rules aimed at mutual recognition of diploma's and professional qualifications.[81] The relevant rules are now laid down in Directive 2005/36 on the recognition of professional qualifications,[82] as recently amended by Directive 2013/55.[83] Two approaches have been followed. The first may be labelled as the "sectoral approach", which implies that separate directives were adopted for specific groups of health professionals, such as doctors, nurses, midwives, dentists and pharmacists. For each of these two directives were adopted.[84] The first contained minimum requirements for access to the profession in question, and Member States were expected, if need be, to adjust their medical training programmes to these requirements. The second directive listed by official professional title the diploma's that satisfy these requirements, and the basic starting point was that diploma's obtained in one Member State should be automatically recognized by or in other Member States. For other professions, such as psychologists and physiotherapists, the "general system" applicable to other professions has been followed. In essence, this system requires from competent authorities to assess the diplomas and qualifications of individuals on a case-by-case basis and to establish whether or to what extent these satisfy national minimum requirements as to the required training. There is no obligation to recognize foreign qualifications automatically; rather, if the national requirements are not wholly met, an aptitude test or an adaptation period may be prescribed.

As regards health professionals, the system for the recognition of diplomas and qualifications does not function perfectly.[85] Several problems exist. A first flaw of the system is that it

---

77. T-562/12, *John Dalli v. European Commission.*
78. More specifically, this happened on 20 May 2016, *id est* the date at which the implementation period expired.
79. Stricter tobacco regulation may raise questions concerning fundamental rights. See D. Uwer, "The new EU Tobacco Products Directive and European Fundamental Rights", 40 *European Law Review* (2014), 35–51.
80. See further M. Peeters et al., "EU law and health professionals" in E. Mossialos et al., op. cit. *supra* note 20; M. Wismar et al. (Eds.), *Health Professional Mobility and Health Systems: Evidence from 17 European Countries* (European Observatory on Health Systems and Policies, 2011), and J. Buchan et al. (Eds.), *Health Professional Mobility in a Changing Europe – New Dynamics, Mobile Individuals and Diverse Responses* (European Observatory on Health Systems and Policies, 2014).
81. Another issue that has attracted a lot of debate concerns the application of Directive 2003/88/EC of the European Parliament and of the Council of 4 Nov. 2003 concerning certain aspects of the organization of working time (O.J. 2003, L 299, at 9) to the organization of the working time of health professionals. See e.g. Case C-87/14, *Commission v. Ireland* and Case C-151/02, *Landeshauptstadt Kiel v. Norbert Jaeger.*
82. O.J. 2005, L 255.
83. O.J. 2013, L 354.
84. See H. Schneider, op. cit. *supra* note 15, 99–160.
85. T. Hervey and G. McHale, op. cit. *supra* note 3, 142–153.

rests on mutual recognition of diplomas acquired by health professionals at the end of their initial education. It does not include rules and policies on the continuous professional training, which differ significantly from Member State to Member State. Second, there is not yet sufficient protection against "rogue" professionals who have been faced with disciplinary or criminal sanctions and subsequently wish to continue to practise in other Member States. A final problem, which does not concretely concern the skills and minimum training of individual doctors, relates to asymmetries in the mobility of health professionals. Especially since the 2004 enlargement, it has become clear that the higher salaries and better career opportunities in some of the "old" Member States have had a magnetic effect on health professionals from the "new" Member States, confronting the latter with an outflow of qualified health personnel.

3.5 *Patients*

For a long period of time, till 1998, patients could not benefit from the free movement rules. In the late 1950s, the European legislature had already set in place a regime coordinating national social security regimes, including health (insurance) systems, with a view to facilitating the exercise of free movement rights. That regime, however, merely intended to ensure that citizens who, during a temporary or longer stay in another Member States would become in need of medical care, could obtain the treatment needed. The coordination regime did not allow citizens to move to other States for the sole purpose of receiving, at the expense of the sickness fund or other health institutions they were affiliated to, medical treatment. Such a right was deliberately denied. Reimbursement of the costs of what nowadays is often referred to as "planned" or "scheduled" treatment was subject to prior authorization by sickness funds and a right to obtain such permission only existed in exceptional cases or circumstances. Authorization was a rarely given privilege. Free movement of patients did not exist.[86]

In 1998, however, in *Kohll* the Court of Justice established that the fact that health care and insurance systems are solidarity-based schemes does not imply that they fall outside the scope of the free movement rules. In the words of Advocate General Tesauro, such systems do not constitute "islands beyond the reach" of internal market law.[87] The Court effectively created freedom of movement for patients by holding that national rules which make reimbursement of the cost of cross-border care subject to the grant of prior authorization, hamper the free movement of (medical) services. Absent justification, prior authorization rules were said to be incompatible with Article 49 EC (now Art. 56 TFEU).[88] In essence, the Court transformed the aforementioned privilege into a legally enforceable right to be reimbursed for planned treatment.

Formally, a right to freedom of movement for patients can now be said to exist, but this is not to say that the Court has had no eye on health values. In *Kohll* the Court already recognized, in quite general terms, that national rules restricting freedom of movement in services can be justified when necessary for protecting the financial stability of health insurance schemes or the infrastructure of healthcare systems. In subsequent cases, notably including *Gereats-Smits and Peerbooms,* the Court showed due respect for Member States' concerns as regards their ability to keep up adequate health care systems by holding that prior authorization rules can be lawfully

86. A.P. van der Mei, *Free Movement of Persons within the European Community – Cross-Border Access to Public Benefits* (Hart, 2003), Ch. 4, and W. Palm and I. Glinos, "Enabling patient mobility in the EU: Between free movement and coordination" in E. Mossialos et al., op. cit. *supra* note 20, 509–560.
87. Opinion Advocate General Tesauro in Case C-120/95, *Decker*, para 17.
88. Case C-158/96, *Kohll*.

applied to types of medical care that are not included in national insurance packages and hospital care.[89]

Today, the "*Kohll*-case law" is largely codified in Directive 2001/24/EU on the application of patients' rights in cross-border healthcare (Patients' Rights Directive – PRD).[90] The PRD and Regulation 883/2004 co-exist and jointly govern the financial aspects of cross-border care. The general rule established in *Kohll* is laid down in the PRD: the Member State of affiliation (competent State) shall reimburse an insured person the costs of health care he or she has received in another Member State, provided the insured person is entitled to have this care in the State of affiliation.[91] Reimbursement may be limited up to the costs of the care in the State of affiliation.[92] In principle, this right to be reimbursed for cross-border care is not subject to prior authorization. Member States, however, are entitled to set in place a system of prior authorization for healthcare which is made subject planning requirements and involves "overnight hospital accommodation [...] for at least one night" or requires "use of highly specialized and cost-intensive medical infrastructure or medical equipment".[93] The PRD specifies, in a manner comparable to Regulation 883/2004, that authorization must be given when the care cannot be provided within a time limit which is medically justifiable.[94] When authorization is granted, the insured person is entitled, in accordance with Regulation 883/2004, to have the costs fully reimbursed by the organ he or she is affiliated to.

Notably, the PRD does not only include rules on the financing of cross-border care, but also contains provisions aimed at health cooperation[95] (e.g. European reference networks between health care providers and centres of expertise in the Member States, ICT and eHealth[96] and health technology assessment) and new rights for patients' rights,[97] including those that do not cross borders (e.g. rights concerning quality of care, patient safety, and confidentiality of personal data). Strikingly, the process that has led to the adoption of the PRD in 2011 was triggered by a critique on the application of the internal market rules to solidarity-based healthcare and health insurance schemes, but it has ultimately resulted in a comprehensive package of measures that seem above all concerned with health aims *stricto sensu*. The inter-linkage between the two pillars of EU health law and policy is well illustrated by the legal basis of the PRD: Article 114 TFEU plus Article 168 TFEU.

89. Case C-157/99, *Gereats-Smits and Peerbooms*. See further A.P. van der Mei, op. cit. *supra* note 86, and W. Palm and I. Glinos, op. cit. *supra* note 86.
90. O.J. 2011, L 88, at 45. See further W. Palm and I. Glinos, op. cit. *supra* note 86.
91. Art. 7(1) PRD.
92. Art. 7(4) PRD. See Case C-368/98, *Vanbraekel*.
93. See Art. 8(2) PRD, which also allows "prior authorization for treatment presenting a particular risk for the patient or population and care provided by a provider that could give rise to serious and specific concerns relating to the quality and safety of care".
94. Art. 8(5) PRD.
95. T. Hervey, "Cooperation between health care authorities in the proposed Directive on Patients' Rights in cross-Border healthcare" in J. van den Gronden et al. (Eds.), *Health Care and EU Law* (Asser Press, 2011), 162.
96. On this topic see further S. Callens, "The legal framework on E-health" in E. Mossialos et al., op. cit. *supra* note 20, at 509–560.
97. W. Sauter, "Harmonization in healthcare: The EU Patients' Rights Directive", (2011) *TILEC Discussion Paper 2011-0030*, available at <papers.ssrn.com/sol3/papers.cfm?abstract_id=1859251>, and L. Bongers and D. Townend, "The implementation of the Directive on the application of patients' rights in cross-border healthcare in the Netherlands", 21 *European Journal of Health Law* (2014), 65–78.

4. Health policy *stricto sensu*

As noted above, the European Health Community, as proposed by Schuman and Ribeyre more than six decades ago, would, in addition to common health market, encompass cooperation among Member States on issues like coordination of medical research, hospital planning and combatting epidemics. What the French Ministers had in mind was "joint planning and studies" and exchanges between health practitioners and professionals and coordination of research that would enable national governments to base their national policies on solid scientific foundations.[98]

While it took a long time, in Maastricht the EU Member States did take up the task of stimulating health cooperation and to develop a European health policy *stricto sensu* by inserting in the Treaty a public health provision, which is now contained in Article 168 TFEU.

Apart from the general mainstreaming duty to ensure a "high level" of human health protection in all its policies and activities, the EU's activities conducted in furtherance of the health mandate mainly focus on health promotion. As indicated above, this requires EU activities to be "directed towards improving public health, preventing physical and mental illness and diseases, and obviating sources of danger to physical and mental health".[99] Such activities shall cover "the fight against the major health scourges, by promoting research into their causes, their transmission and their prevention, as well as health information and education, and monitoring, early warning of and combating serious cross-border threats to health".[100] In principle, it is the Member States that have to act. They shall coordinate "among themselves" their policies and programmes, and they are only required to do so "in liaison" with the Commission".[101] The EU's action merely complements national policies. The Union "shall encourage" cooperation between the Member States and the Commission may take "any useful initiative" to promote such cooperation or coordination. It is thus plain that the prime responsibility for health policy in the strict sense lies with the Member States, not with the Union.

For certain topics the European Parliament and the Council may co-adopt "incentive measures" designed to protect and improve human health, excluding however any harmonization of the laws and regulations of the Member States. Such measures may be adopted in particular to combat the major cross-border health scourges, measures concerning monitoring, early warning of and combatting serious cross-border threats to health, and measures which have as their direct objective the protection of public health regarding tobacco and the abuse of alcohol.[102]

A typical example[103] of an EU policy that is being pursued by means of the soft law powers provided by Article 168 TFEU concerns alcohol consumption.[104] The EU's strategy regarding alcohol and health concentrates in terms of substance on topics like raising awareness on the

---

98. In addition, the Community would have to work on a programme for the building of "medical establishments", which could provide financial assistance to national governments and would intervene in existing hospital establishments so that they would be as effectively as possible. Statement by Paul Ribeyre on the creation of a European Health Community (Sept. 1952), available at <www.cvce.eu/viewer/-/content/abdcf030-7e1b-4947-ab88-e6d93400370f/5350cea3-b096-47f5-9d4b-062dd139d934/en>.
99. Art. 168(1), second sentence TFEU. For an overview of EU activities see e.g. the website of the European Centre for Disease Prevention and Control: <ecdc.europa.eu/en/activities/diseaseprogrammes/Pages/Activities_DiseaseProgrammes.aspx>.
100. Art. 168(1) TFEU, third sentence.
101. Art. 168(2) TFEU, third sentence.
102. Art. 168(5) TFEU.
103. Another example concerns the fight against obesity. See A. Garde, *EU Law and Obesity Prevention* (Kluwer, 2010).
104. See further T. Hervey and G. McHale, op. cit. *supra* note 3, 418–423.

impact of alcohol consumption on health, reducing such consumption in the workplace, decreasing the number of drink-driving accidents and discouraging the youth to drink.[105] These goals are pursued through recommendations, data gathering and the bringing together of stakeholders (industry, health professionals, consumers, NGOs) in a "European Alcohol and Health Forum" to discuss issues such as the afore-mentioned. The EU could adopt binding anti-alcohol measures under Article 114 TFEU, as it has done as regards tobacco, but the "political will" to do so seems, to the disappointment of many critics, absent.[106]

For a few topics the EU legislature is empowered to adopt "hard" legal measures. These include measures to set high quality and safety standards of organs and substances of human origin, blood and blood derivatives, and medicinal products and devices as well as measures concerning veterinary and phytosanitary issues directly aimed at protecting public health.[107] Notably, the HIV/AIDS blood contamination episodes in France triggered the adoption of measures, including the Blood Safety Directive,[108] the Human Tissue Directive[109] and more recently the Transplantation of Human Organs Directive.[110]

More generally, the EU has sought to implement its health mandate by adopting Health programmes[111] that aim to contribute to a series of generally defined health objectives like "fostering good health in an ageing Europe", "protecting citizens from health threats" and "supporting dynamic health systems and new technologies",[112] and they are to be pursued by concrete measures and projects for which EU funding is made available.

5. EU health law and policy: Future

From its inception, it already soon became clear that the EEC would need to become involved in regulation of the health aspects of the internal market. The spill-over effects from the free movement of goods and persons made the EU to actively legislate in various policy areas, such as pharmaceuticals, health care providers and patients, so as to achieve an internal market. Nowadays, the mainstreaming obligation of health protection pushes the EU to ensure human health

---

105. Communication from the Commission to the Council, the European Parliament, the European Economic and Social Committee and the Committee of the Regions An EU strategy to support Member States in reducing alcohol related harm COM(2006)625.
106. See e.g. J. Gornall, "Europe under influence", (2014) *British Medical Journal,* 498.
107. Art. 168(4).
108. Directive 2002/98/EC of the European Parliament and the Council of 27 Jan. 2003 setting standards of quality and safety for the collection, testing, processing, storage and distribution of human blood and blood components, O.J. 1998, L 33/30. On this Directive, and the question of whether it precludes a national rule temporarily deferring from blood donation men who have had sexual relations with other men, See Case C-528/13, *Geoffrey Léger v. Ministre des Affaires sociales, de la Santé et des Droits des femmes and Etablissement français du sang.*
109. Directive 2004/23/EC of the European Parliament and of the Council of 31 Mar. 2004 on setting standards of quality and safety for the donation, procurement, testing, processing, preservation, storage and distribution of human tissues and cells, O.J. 2004, L 102/48.
110. Directive 2010/53/EU of the European Parliament and of the Council of 7 July 2010 on standards of quality and safety of human organs intended for transplantation O.J. 2010, L 207/14.
111. Decision 1786/2002/EC of the European Parliament and of the Council of 23 Oct. 2002 adopting a programme of Community action in the field of public health (2003–2008) – Commission Statements, O.J. 2002, L 271/1; Decision 1350/2007/EC of the European Parliament and of the Council of 23 Sept. 2007 establishing a second programme of Community action in the field of health (2008–13), O.J. 2007, L 301/3 and Reg. (EU) 282/2014 of the European Parliament and of the Council of 11 Mar. 2014 on the establishment of a third Programme for the Union's action in the field of health (2014–2020) and repealing Decision 1350/2007/EC, O.J. 2014, L 86/1.
112. White Paper – "Together for Health: A Strategic Approach for the EU 2008–2013", COM(2007)630 final.

protection in the definition and implementation of all Union policies and activities. Market integration has thus provided for ample opportunities to pursue health objectives. This has led to the evolvement of both a healthy internal market and an internal health market, thus blurring traditional, separate notions of internal market policy and health policy.

The introduction of a formal competence on health policy by the Maastricht Treaty has required the EU to further evolve a health policy *stricto sensu.* Although this competence is a supplementary one, the EU has wholeheartedly embraced this area and has unfolded many activities, mainly to support or to instigate coordination of Member State action. The increasing globalization of markets together with global health incidents, however, make clear that in various instances action would be needed beyond national borders. The EU is significantly constrained in its responses to global health threats given its limited competences. The same may be true in relation to the increasing preoccupation with health diseases due to changing life style patterns, that may need a more common approach trangressing national health policies. Such demands may ultimately prove necessary the EU to develop an appropriate all-encompassing EU health law and policy. In view of the political sensitivities, this outlook seems unlikely to occur in the near future. Until that time, EU health law and policy will in all likelihood evolve slowly in a patchy manner in response to crises and incidents. Thus, the EU is working on, but has not yet set in place a genuine "*front commun de l'Europe contre la maladie*", as the French Ministers Schuman and Ribeyre had called for more than six decades ago.[113]

Further reading

Berg, W., *Gesundheitsschutz als Aufgabe der EU – Entwicklung, Kompetenzen, Perspektiven* (Nomos, 1997).

De Rujiter, A., *A Silent Revolution: The Expansion of EU Power in the field of Human Health – A Rights-Based Analysis of EU Health Law and Policy* (University of Amsterdam, 2015).

Greer, S., et al., *Everything You Always Wanted to Know about European Union Health Policies but Were Afraid to Ask* (European Observatory on Health Systems and Policies, 2014).

Hervey, T. and J. McHale, *EU Health law – Themes and Implications* (CUP, 2015).

Mossialos, E., et al. (Eds.), *Health Systems Governance in Europe – The Role of European Union Law and Policy* (CUP, 2010).

Van de Gronden, J., et al. (Eds.), *Health Care and EU Law* (Asser Press, 2010).

113. *Exposé de Robert Schuman à la conférence préparatoire à la Communauté européenne de la santé*, cited *supra* note 5.

CHAPTER 35
CONSUMER PROTECTION IN THE EU

*K.J. Cseres**

1. Introduction

The most important characteristic of the EU consumer protection is that it has developed as part of the internal market process. Its direct link to market integration has determined its role in EU law: it is a legal instrument to build, support, and expand the internal market.[1] Accordingly, the consumer is not conceived as a passive actor in need of social protection but as an active market actor who contributes to the well-functioning of markets. This instrumentalist character is reflected in the fact that consumer law did not develop as an autonomous area of EU law but on the legal basis of the internal market Article 114 TFEU. Accordingly, the harmonization of consumer rules was not an end in itself, and consumers were merely regarded as the passive beneficiaries of free trade and market integration.

EU consumer law as it stands today has developed through three major phases from 1970 to present. In the first phase of 1970s – early 1980s, consumer protection has developed through soft law documents without a legislative basis. The legislative basis was laid down in the late 1980s and in this second phase EU consumer protection was established as an autonomous area of EU law. The third phase from 2000 on can be characterized by the re-orientation of the internal market itself, where liberalization and marketization of public services resulted in a new body of consumer law in specific sectors such as energy, telecommunications or financial services. The most recent years are characterized by the challenges of economic crisis, climate change and most notably digitalization. These challenges have not only increased the market orientation of EU consumer law, but it also increased the role of fundamental rights. The new legislative technique of full-harmonization was implemented along with a new regulatory approach endorsing consumer empowerment. At the same time, social policy considerations gained relevance, for example for vulnerable consumers. Moreover, EU courts have actively shaped procedural guarantees and fundamental rights protection. This chapter is structured along the three phases of EU consumer law and is completed with two more sections on the regulatory model of EU consumer law and the enforcement of consumer law.

---

* Associate Professor, Amsterdam Centre for European Law and Governance, University of Amsterdam.

1. C.U. Schmid, "The instrumentalist conception of the acquis communautaire in consumer law and its implications on a European contract law code", (2005) *European Review of Contract Law*, DOI <doi.org/10.1515/ercl.2005.1.2.211>; H.-W. Micklitz, "Do consumers and businesses need a new architecture of consumer law? A thought-provoking Impulse", 32 *Yearbook of European Law* (2013), 266.

2. The development of consumer law in the EU

2.1 *First phase: No legal basis – consumer law as soft law*

The Treaty of Rome did not provide a legal basis for consumer protection. In fact, the word "consumer" was only used in two provisions: as one of the several beneficiaries of a common agricultural policy Articles 39 and 40 EEC (now Arts. 39 and 40 TFEU) and in competition law, Article 85 EEC (now Art. 101 TFEU).

Although consumer interests were increasingly recognized in the 1970s, it was unclear whether the Commission had competence to take specific measures of consumer protection. The EU legislator remained inactive until 1975, when a Preliminary Programme for consumer protection and information policy was adopted. It recognized the need for specific consumer policy in the European Community.[2] It stated five basic consumer rights, that emerged from President Kennedy's message to the US congress in 1962.[3] After this programme the Commission became active in laying down the first pillars of EU consumer law and policy.[4] In 1981 a Second Action Plan was adopted[5] repeating the five fundamental consumer rights and emphasizing the relevance of effective enforcement. By the 1980s the Commission became the driving force behind both EU and national consumer laws. In the absence of an explicit legal basis for consumer law, Article 100 EEC (subsequently Art. 94 EC, now Art. 115 TFEU) was used. However, Article 100 and later 100a EEC (now Art. 114 TFEU) aimed at the adoption of measures which had as their object the functioning of the internal market. This legal basis could only be used by relying on the argument that the diverging national consumer laws resulted in market distortion, which had to be remedied by harmonization.[6] Article 100 EEC (now Art. 114 TFEU) required a direct link with the internal market and thus consumer law measures were bound to the realization of the internal market project.

The process of market integration had undeniable benefits for consumers; abolishing national rules and creating a larger market was to benefit consumers by widening consumer choice and increasing quality of consumer products and services. Still, consumer protection and rules of free movements and free competition proved to be conflicting objectives. National provisions that protected consumers but restricted the free movement rules and formed obstacles to cross-border trade were condemned by the ECJ. The Court established a distinctive place for consumer protection in the Community legal order by balancing national consumer protection

---

2. Council Resolution of 14 Apr. 1975 on a preliminary programme of the European Economic Community for a consumer protection and information policy, O.J. 1975, C 92/1.
3. The right to health and safety protection, the right to protection of economic interests, the right of redress, the right to information and education and the right of representation (the right to be heard).
4. For example, in many of the Member States product liability had been on the agenda since the 1960s. With the acceptance of the EC's first consumer programme it was believed that the product liability issue would be solved at the Community level. Within a couple of years the Commission indeed took over the political initiative and made an attempt to combine the different national regulations. H.-W. Micklitz, "The necessity of a new concept for the further development of the consumer law in the EU", 4 GLJ (2003), 1043–1064, at 1048.
5. Council Resolution of 19 May 1981 on a second programme of the European Economic Community for a consumer protection and information policy, O.J. 1981, C 133/1.
6. H.-W. Micklitz and S. Weatherill, "Consumer policy in the European Community: Before and after Maastricht", 16 *Journal of Consumer Policy* (1993), 185–321, at 291.

measures and the free movement rules.[7] These judgments constituted new individual rights for consumers and further developed the EU concept of consumer protection.[8]

This has often been illustrated by *Cassis de Dijon,*[9] where the ECJ acknowledged consumer protection as a *rule of reason* exception to the free movement rules. In this and similar cases the ECJ found national consumer protection rules overprotective and (mis)using consumer protection as a justification for distorting competition and holding back relevant information for consumers. Where national rules barred the cross-border flow of products and where adequate information provision would have been sufficient to protect consumers, the Court has not hesitated to rule against the national consumer measure. At the same time, this line of case law has also raised serious concerns of race to the bottom, i.e. higher national standards of consumer protection had to give way to lower consumer standards.[10]

However, the contours of EU consumer law were not only shaped in an indirect way through negative integration. Positive harmonization measures were also adopted even though in a modest way due to the limited constitutional structure of the Treaty and the fact that consumer policy was a shared competence between the Member States and the EU. Accordingly, consumer protection developed through soft law and later as secondary law in the form of Directives. The directives that were adopted in this period were Directive 84/450 on misleading advertising,[11] Directive 85/374 on product liability, Directive 85/577 on doorstep selling and Directive 87/102 on consumer credit.[12] These directives focused on improved transparency in transactions, hence facilitating consumer choice.[13]

2.2 *Second phase: Establishing a legal basis*

Consumer protection became an autonomous policy aim in 1987 with the adoption of the Single European Act. However, the Single Act still did not provide a specific legal basis for consumer law. Its goal was the progressive establishment of the internal market The Single Act inserted Article 95 EC (now Art. 114 TFEU) and expanded Community policies to health, safety, environmental protection and consumer protection. It did require the Commission to take a high level of protection in the fields of health, safety, the environment and consumer protection as a basis for its proposals concerning single market legislation. Consumer protection was from that moment on adopted on the basis of Article 95 EC (now Art. 114 TFEU), which required qualified majority voting instead of unanimity in the European Council.

While consumer protection remained in the shadow of the internal market process, the rhetoric changed and it was acknowledged that consumers had a decisive role to play in the completion of the internal market, which would not operate properly without their active participation. By the end of the 1980s the importance of consumer protection in the Community

7. N. Reich, *Wirtschaftsrecht, Verbraucherinteressen und EU-Integration, Europäisches Verbraucherrecht* (Nomos, 2003), at 1.4.
8. O. Gerstenberg and G. De Búrca, "The denationalization of constitutional law", 47 Harv.Int.'l L.J. (2006), at 223.
9. Case C-120/78, *Rewe Zentral AG v. Bundesmonopolverwaltung für Branntwein.*
10. I. Benöhr, "Consumer law and the market" in I. Benöhr, *EU Consumer Law and Human Rights* (OUP, 2013), at 21.
11. Council Directive 84/450/EEC of 10 Sept. 1984 relating to the approximation of the laws, regulations and administrative provisions of the Member States concerning misleading advertising, O.J. 1984, L 250/17.
12. J. Stuyck adds the Directive 79/112 on the labelling of foodstuffs (O.J. 1979, L 33/1). J. Stuyck, "European consumer law after the treaty of Amsterdam: Consumer policy in or beyond the internal market?", 37 CML Rev. (2000), 367–400, at 377.
13. H.-W. Micklitz and S. Weatherill, op. cit. *supra* note 6, at 294.

grew significantly and a basic set of rules was created in order to improve consumers' confidence in cross-border shopping.[14] A new concept of consumer protection emerged: consumers needed a minimum set of Community measures in order to enter transactions cross-border. Consumer information and consumer choice became the cornerstones of a well-functioning internal market. with the recognition that consumers "may make or break" the internal market.[15]

The new concept was reflected in *GB-INNO*, where the Court banned a Luxembourg law, which was protecting consumers against confusion by prohibiting special offers of reduced prices. The Court clearly stated that the provision of information to consumers is a fundamental requirement and national legislation that denies consumers' access to information may not be justified.[16]

In a line of similar cases,[17] where free movement rules had to be balanced with national measures that arguably protected consumers, the ECJ began to establish individual consumer rights, most notably the right to information. In these cases the ECJ has also gradually defined the normative concept of the consumer as a reasonably circumspect and well-informed person. This concept became a building block of the EU's regulatory approach to consumer law, which will be discussed in section 3.2.

The Maastricht Treaty extended the Community competence beyond market integration and thus included explicit provisions on consumer protection in Article 3(t) EC and contained a special Title IX on consumer protection. Article 129a EC[18] became the most important provision in the Treaty with regard to consumer protection. Article 129(1)(b) recognized, for the first time, the Community's power to act in order to protect consumers, independent of the internal market. While Article 129 1 (a) EC still referred to Article 95EC (now Art. 114 TFEU), Article 129 (1) (b) EC contained an independent legal basis. Consumer protection became an internal market policy as well as a supporting policy for the Member States' corresponding actions. In this way the Maastricht Treaty re-emphasized the "assistance character" of consumer policy, which meant that it contributed to and pursued the tasks of other policy areas.[19]

However, the Community's competence under Article 129 (1) (b) EC proved to be limited. Article 129 (1) (b) EC did not confer a general competence but rather paved the way for a minimum harmonization approach.[20] As a legal basis it was hardly used in the development of consumer law. Only one directive, Directive 98/6/EC on the indication of prices of products offered to consumers[21] was adopted on the basis of Article 129 EC. Other directives were

14. The White Paper for completing the internal market opened the door for the Commission to realize different projects of consumer protection with the help of the qualified majority voting procedure. "Completing the internal market: White paper from the Commission to the European Council", COM(85)310.
15. S. Weatherill, "The Commission's options for developing EC consumer protection and contract law: Assessing the constitutional basis", 13 EBLR (2002), 497–515, at 510.
16. Case C-362/88, *GB-INNO-BM v. Confédération du commerce luxembourgeois*, para 19.
17. Case C-126/91, *Schutzverband gegen Unwesen in der Wirtschaft v. Y.Rocher GmbH*; Case C-315/92, *Verband Sozialer Wettbewerb e.V. v. Clinique Laboratories SNC*.
18. Art. 129 a, provided that the Community shall contribute to the attainment of a high level of consumer protection through:
    "(a) measures adopted pursuant to Art. 100a in the context of the completion of the internal market;
    (b) specific action which supports and supplements the policy pursued by the Member States to protect health, safety and economic interests of consumers and to provide adequate information to consumers".
19. N. Reich, op. cit. *supra* note 7, at 1.8.
20. I. Benöhr, op. cit. *supra* note 10, 24.
21. Directive 98/6/EC of the European Parliament and of the Council of 16 Feb. 1998 on consumer protection in the indication of the prices of products offered to consumers, O.J. 1998, L 80/21.

still adopted on the basis of Article 95 EC, although the Commission's proposal was initially based on Article 129 EC.[22] This implied that the Community continued to address consumer protection rules through its internal market competence. While the Maastricht Treaty has made consumer law a key policy area of Community law, the new Treaty title did not contain any directly effective, substantive provision. In fact, the status of consumer protection law remained unchanged even after the Lisbon Treaty.

Still, the EU started to set a strongly pro-consumer agenda. In the 1990s many directives were adopted, such as Directive 90/314/EEC on package travel,[23] Directive 92/59 on general product safety,[24] Directive 93/13/EEC on unfair contract terms,[25] Directive 94/19 on deposit-guarantee schemes,[26] Directive 94/47/EC on timesharing, Directive 97/7 on distant contracts, Directive 98/6 on consumer protection with regard to the indication of prices of products,[27] Directive 98/27/EC on injunctions, Directive 99/44/EC on the sale of consumer goods and associated guarantees, 2002/65/EC on distance marketing of financial services.[28]

Another relevant legal issue of the Maastricht Treaty was the institutionalization of the principle of subsidiarity. Article 3(b)(2) EC formally introduced the subsidiarity principle and aimed to clarify the division of competences between the Community and its Member States. The Commission's proposals had to be justified by complementing, rather than replacing the efforts of Member States to defend, for example, consumers' rights.

An important modification to the consumer Treaty rules was introduced by the Amsterdam Treaty. The protection of health, safety, economic interests and information became part of Community policy in Article 153EC (ex. Art. 129). Additionally, information has now been drafted as a consumer right not as a consumer interest.[29] The objectives of consumer protection have been enlarged in the Amsterdam Treaty, adding education and the self-organization of consumers.

Finally, Article 153(2) EC was completely new and implemented a horizontal clause: the Community shall take the requirements of consumer protection into account when it defines or

22. The directives on timesharing (Directive 94/47/EC of the European Parliament and the Council of 26 Oct. 1994 on the protection of purchasers in respect of certain aspects of contracts relating to the purchase of the right to use immovable properties on a timeshare basis, O.J. 1994, L 280/83), distance selling (Directive 97/7/EC of the European Parliament and of the Council of 20 May 1997 on the protection of consumers in respect of distance contracts, O.J. 1997, L 144/19), guarantees (Directive 1999/44/EC of the European Parliament and of the Council of 25 May 1999 on certain aspects of the sale of consumer goods and associated guarantees, O.J. 1999, L 171/12), court actions (Directive 98/27/EC of the European Parliament and of the Council of 19 May 1998 on injunctions for the protection of consumers' interests, O.J. 1998, L 166/51) were adopted on the basis of Art. 95.
23. Council Directive 90/314/EEC of 13 June 1990 on package travel, package holidays and package tours, O.J. 1990, L 158/59.
24. Council Directive 92/59/EEC of 29 June 1992 on general product safety, O.J. 1992, L 228/24.
25. Council Directive 93/13/EEC of 5 Apr. 1993 on unfair terms in consumer contracts, O.J. 1993, L 95/29.
26. Directive 94/19/EC of the European Parliament and of the Council of 30 May 1994 on deposit-guarantee schemes, O.J. 1994, L 135/5.
27. Directive 98/6/EC of the European Parliament and of the Council of 16 Feb. 1998 on consumer protection in the indication of the prices of products offered to consumers, O.J. 1998, L 80/21.
28. Directive 2002/65/EC of the European Parliament and of the Council of 23 Sept. 2002 concerning the distance marketing of consumer financial services and amending Council Directive 90/619/EEC and Directives 97/7/EC and 98/27/EC, O.J. 2002, L 271/16.
29. Although health, safety and economic interests of consumers are still regarded as interests, they play a relevant role in relation to other Treaty provisions. Health and safety provide grounds to justify restrictions of free movement rules. Economic interests of consumers were regarded by the ECJ to justify non-discriminatory obstacles to the free movement of goods and services. J. Stuyck, op. cit. *supra* note 12, at 384.

implements other Community policies and activities. The relevance of this provision remained limited.[30] It has received more practical application after the Lisbon Treaty.

The growing competence of the EU in consumer matters has raised concerns of the Member States with regard to the attribution of powers and the principle of proportionality under Article 5 EC (now Art. 1 TEU). These concerns were reflected in the CJEU's "Tobacco Advertising" Directive judgment.[31] Germany sought an annulment of this Directive arguing that it was adopted on an incorrect legal basis: the Directive aimed at the protection of public health and not at harmonization of national laws as required under Article 95 EC (now Art. 114 TFEU). The ECJ annulled the Directive[32] as having been invalidly adopted under Article 95 EC (now Art. 114 TFEU) and reasoned that measures referred to under Article 114 TFEU "must genuinely have that object, actually contributing to the elimination of obstacles to the free movement of goods or to the freedom to provide services, or to the removal of distortions of competition". The ECJ added that "recourse to Article 95 EC as a legal basis is possible if the aim is to prevent the emergence of future obstacles to trade resulting from multifarious development of national laws, the emergence of such obstacles must be likely and the measure in question must be designed to prevent them".[33]

The judgment has narrowly defined the competencies of the Union institutions *vis-à-vis* the Member States.[34] The Commission had to define precisely which consumer problems arose by providing clear evidence of their nature and magnitude and identifying the incentives of affected entities and their consequent behaviour.[35]

In sum, in this second phase consumer protection developed into a true Community policy and consumers were granted EU rights to enable them to actively participate in the internal market.

2.3 *Third phase: Re-orientation of the internal market*

While the internal market programme has always focused on removing trade barriers, the vision of the internal market that emerged in the last two decades seemed to be more impact driven, guided by consumers' and citizens' needs. This re-orientation not only focuses on satisfaction of economic well-being of consumers but more increasingly on fundamental rights protection and also citizenship norms such as solidarity, inclusion and sustainability.[36]

This reorientation was reflected in the Lisbon Treaty and the Charter of Fundamental Rights. The Lisbon Treaty made the system of EU competences more transparent. Consumer protection is now explicitly mentioned as a shared competence of the EU and its Member States in Article 4(2)(f) TFEU. The Lisbon Treaty made the Charter a binding instrument.[37] Consumer

---

30. J. Stuyck, op. cit. *supra* note 12, at 386.
31. Case C-376/98, *Germany v. Parliament and Council.*
32. Directive 98/43 on tobacco advertising, O.J. 1998, L 213/9.
33. Case C-376/98, *Germany v. Parliament and Council,* para 84 cited in Case C-491/01 *British American Tobacco,* paras. 60–61.
34. See more recently Case C-58/08, *Vodafone and Others v. Secretary of State for Business, Enterprise and Regulatory Reform.*
35. Case C-376/98, *Germany v. Parliament and Council,* para 84.
36. K.J. Cseres and A. Schrauwen, "Empowering consumer-citizens: Changing rights or merely discourse?" in D. Schiek, *The EU Social and Economic Model After the Global Crisis: Interdisciplinary Perspectives* (Ashgate, 2013).
37. According to Art. 52 of the Charter, both the EU institutions and the Member States are bound by it, though the latter only "when implementing Union law". *Test-Achats* illustrates the importance of the Charter of Fundamental Rights in this context. See also I. Benöhr, op. cit. *supra* note 10, Ch. 2, 5, 6, 7 and 8.

protection has been implemented as a fundamental right in the Charter of Fundamental Rights, however, Article 38 is more an EU policy guideline[38] than a subjective right. Still, it indicates that consumer protection has become an autonomous social objective of the EU and in combination with other Charter provisions like Article 47 on procedural rights, Article 36 on services of general economic interest, Article 3 on physical integrity, Article 12 on freedom of assembly or Article 8 on data protection it can develop into a broader EU model of consumer protection. It has been argued that the Charter could further develop this broader framework through its influence on EU and national law, contractual relationships between consumers and businesses and possible exceptions to the free movement rules.[39]

However, the Lisbon Treaty brought neither any changes in relation to the extent of the competence of the EU nor regarding the legislative procedure that is applicable in Article 169 TFEU. The legislative procedure that applied under Articles 114 and 169 TFEU is the co-decision procedure, post-Lisbon called the ordinary legislative procedure.[40]

The Lisbon Treaty also left the substantive Treaty provisions unchanged. Article 12 TFEU functions as a horizontal clause, which is echoed, in Article 38 of the Charter of Fundamental Rights. In fact, Article 12 TFEU forms a constitutional basis to weigh the interests of consumers in the assessment of other EU policies, for example in possible infringements to competition law.[41]

Besides these constitutional changes, a new set of consumer rules emerged in the public utilities sectors, which were liberalized from the end of 1990s.

In these sectors the EU adopted a market-oriented approach and the main regulatory instruments were implemented by aiming at activating competition and customer choice. The (de)regulatory approach focused on supply side market failures and on the creation of a competitive market structure by introducing specific regulatory frameworks.

Even though consumer benefit has always been the main objective of market opening, concrete consumer interests have not been directly addressed[42] and enforceable consumer rights were only introduced in the later stage of the liberalization process.

Sector specific consumer rules were enacted only from the 2000s on, when regulated markets were moving from a single focus on market access and market opening to a more complex policy setting – which Hancher and Larouche termed "managed competition".[43] This explains on the one hand, the late development of sector-specific consumer rules and consumer protection issues as elements of the EU liberalization,[44] and on the other, the fact that the main consumer interests in the liberalized markets were first laid down by focusing on customer choice and from the second generation of Directives on, centring around the switching of providers.[45]

---

38. Art. 38 of the Charter says: "Union policies shall ensure a high level of consumer protection".
39. I. Benöhr, op. cit. *supra* note 10, at 57, 66.
40. Under this procedure, the European Parliament and the Council of Ministers act as co-legislators. Adoption by the Council requires a qualified majority. The Lisbon Treaty introduces from Nov. 2014 a new formula on weighing the votes.
41. Case T-224/10, *Association belge des consommateurs test-achats ASBL v. Commission*, para 43.
42. K. Cseres, "What has competition done for consumers in liberalised markets?", 4 *Competition Law Review* (2008), at 77–121.
43. P. Larouche and L. Hancher, "The coming of age of EU regulation of network industries and services of general economic interest" in P. Craig and G. de Búrca (Eds.), *The Evolution of EU Law*, 2nd ed, (OUP, 2010).
44. L.A. Reisch and H.W. Micklitz, "Consumers and deregulation of the electricity market in Germany", 29 *Journal of Consumer Policy* (2006), at 399–415.
45. Initially issues connected to consumer protection remained at national level of legislation as the energy systems were still state owned and public service obligations were also determined by Member States. A.

The emerging sectoral consumer rules consist of regulatory law to complete the internal market and strengthen competition building a new "horizontal" regime of consumer contract law.[46]

A clear EU policy concerning sector specific consumer law has been absent until 2002, when a first set of consumer rights were included in several secondary legislation.[47]

2.3.1 *Full harmonization: A new regulatory approach*

A new regulatory approach has been put forward by the Commission in the 2002–2006 Consumer Policy Strategy:[48] full harmonization. This was further pursued in other legislations such as the Directive 2002/65 on distance marketing of consumer financial services,[49] the Directive 2005/29 on unfair commercial practices,[50] the revised Directive 2008/48 on consumer credit[51] and the Directive 2011/83 on consumer rights.[52]

Full harmonization has raised many concerns. It did strengthen the internal market orientation of EU consumer protection. Under Article 169(4) TFEU only measures that are adopted in order to complete the internal market may be based on full harmonization. Hence, the legal basis for consumer measures adopted on the basis of full harmonization had to be Article 114 TFEU.[53]

Second, the typical approach in EU consumer law used to be minimum harmonization. Full harmonization has been developed in the field of technical standards, where directives contain mandatory requirements. In consumer law full harmonization restricts the possible beneficial effects of regulatory diversity and regulatory competition among Member States. It does simplify the regulatory scene across the various national regimes.

Third, full harmonization has been heavily criticized for decreasing the protection of consumers. Producing common standards that attract widespread support from business and consumers in all the Member States may prove to be unfeasible and lead to solutions that are the result of political compromises instead of careful legal and economic considerations. Such an

---

Johnston, "Seeking the EU 'consumer' in services of general economic interest" in D. Leczykiewicz and S.Weatherill (Eds.), *The Images of the Consumer in EU Law* (Hart Publishing, 2015), at 112, 114.

46. N. Reich, "Harmonisation of European contract law: With special emphasis on consumer law", 1 *China-EU Law Journal* (2011), 55–94, at 71.
47. See the second and then the Third package of Directives in the Energy and telecommunications markets. Directive 2002/22 on universal services, O.J. 2002, L 108/51.
48. COM(2002)208 final at 9.
49. Directive 2002/65/EC of the European Parliament and of the Council of 23 Sept. 2002 concerning the distance marketing of consumer financial services and amending Council Directive 90/619/EEC and Directives 97/7/EC and 98/27/EC, O.J. 2002, L 271/16.
50. Directive 2005/29/EC of the European Parliament and of the Council of 11 May 2005 concerning unfair business-to-consumer commercial practices in the internal market and amending Council Directive 84/450/EEC, Directives 97/7/EC, 98/27/EC and 2002/65/EC of the European Parliament and of the Council and Reg. (EC) 2006/2004 of the European Parliament and of the Council ("Unfair Commercial Practices Directive"), O.J. 2005, L 149/22.
51. Directive 2008/48/EC of the European Parliament and of the Council of 23 Apr. 2008 on credit agreements for consumers and repealing Council Directive 87/102/EEC, O.J. 2008, L 133/66.
52. Directive 2011/83/EU of the European Parliament and of the Council of 25 Oct. 2011 on consumer rights, amending Council Directive 93/13/EEC and Directive 1999/44/EC of the European Parliament and of the Council and repealing Council Directive 85/577/EEC and Directive 97/7/EC of the European Parliament and of the Council, O.J. 2011, L 304/64. See also M. Loos, "Full harmonisation as a regulatory concept and its consequences for the national legal orders: The example of the Consumer Rights Directive", (2010) *Centre for the Study of European Contract Law Working Paper Series No. 3*.
53. M. Loos, op. cit. *supra* note 52 and M.P. Rott, "Minimum harmonization for the completion of the internal market? The example of consumer sales law", 40 CML Rev. (2003), 1107–1135, at 1130.

approach might sacrifice the higher levels of consumer protection in certain Member States to meet lower levels of protection. Full harmonization leaves little or no room for the Member States' particularities in the cultural, political, linguistic or legal determinants of consumer interests and behaviour.[54]

The Product Liability Directive[55] well illustrates the implications of full-harmonization for national consumer rules and ultimately what it means for the effective protection of consumers. In its case law the ECJ has consistently argued that the Product Liability Directive seeks to achieve, in the matters regulated by it, full harmonization.[56] Accordingly, the Member States cannot apply a general system of product liability that would go beyond the level of protection established in the Directive. In *Medicina Asturiana*[57] the ECJ answered the question whether Article 13 of the Product Liability Directive must be "interpreted as precluding the restriction or limitation, as a result of transposition of the Directive, of rights granted to consumers under the legislation of the Member State". The ECJ stated that this provision could not be interpreted as giving Member States the possibility of maintaining a general system of product liability different from that provided for in the Directive.

Similarly, concerning the full harmonization character of the Directive on unfair commercial practices the ECJ has condemned several national provisions that maintained or introduced a *per se* prohibition of a commercial practice that was not on the Directive's blacklist even though they provided a higher level of consumer protection.[58] Critics emphasized that the EU's full harmonization approach lowers the overall level of consumer protection in the Member States.

Whether full harmonization "upgrades" or "levels down" consumer protection standards[59] also depends on the scope of application of EU legislation. The drafting process of Directive on Consumer Rights 2011/83 well illustrates how the full harmonization approach can undermine the initial aim of bringing coherence in the EU consumer *acquis*. This Directive has been initially proposed as the review and restructuring of eight Directives. Fearing that the new Directive would lower the level of protection guaranteed in certain countries in the areas of the Directives that were adopted as minimum harmonization measures, the political compromise reduced the original eight Directives to two; on doorstep selling and distance selling. The Directives on unfair contract terms and sales and guarantees were removed from the reform that should have been established by the Consumer Rights' Directive.[60]

Another illustration is the Directive 2008/48 on consumer credit, the scope of which was limited to pre-contractual and contractual information by creditors and intermediaries,

---

54. K.J. Cseres and H.A. Luth,"The DCFR and consumer protection: An economic assessment" in F. Chirico and P. Larouche (Eds.), *Economic Analysis of the DCFR, The Work of the Economic Impact Group within CoPECL* (De Gruyter, 2010), at 235–276. V. Mak, "Review of the consumer acquis: Towards maximum harmonization?", 17 E.R.P.L. (2009), 55–73; J.M. Smits, "Full harmonization of consumer law? A critique of the draft directive on consumer rights", 18 E.R.P.L. (2009), 5–14.
55. Case C-183/00, *Maria Victoria González Sánchez v. Medicina Asturiana*; Cases C-52/00, *Commission v. France* and C-154/00, *Commission v. Greece*. See for more details I. Benöhr, op. cit. *supra* note 10, at 34–38. M. Tulibacka, *Product Liability Law in Transition: A Central European Perspective* (Ashgate, 2009), at 123.
56. Cases C-52/00, *Commission v. France* and C-154/00, *Commission v. Greece.*
57. Case C-183/00, *Medicina Asturiana*; Cases C-52/00, *Commission v. France* and C-154/00, *Commission v. Greece*. See for more details I. Benöhr, op. cit. *supra* note 10, at 34–38.
58. Case C-322/01, *Deutscher Apothekerverband*; Case C-205/07, *Gysbrechts*; Case C-522/08, *Telecomunikacja Polska*. Case C-304/08, *Plus Warenhandelsgesellschaft*; Case C-540/08, *Mediaprint*; Case C-206/11, *Köck*.
59. N. Reich, op. cit. *supra* note 46, at 58.
60. S. Weatherill, "The Consumer Rights Directive: How and why a quest for 'coherence' has (largely) failed", 49 CML Rev. (2012), 1287–1288. K. Tonner and K. Fangerow, "Directive 2011/83/EU on consumer rights: A new approach to European consumer law?", (2012) EUVR, 67–81.

withdrawal rights, linked transactions and left many core issues of consumer credit to be regulated by the Member States.[61] Similarly, Directive 2005/29 on Unfair Commercial Practices left the issues of enforcement to the Member States.[62] Accordingly, even though these are measures of full harmonization their scope is limited and the Member States retain the competence to adopt measures "around" the Directives that protect their own consumers at higher level than the Directive.[63] Still, the ECJ has in judgments such as *Mediaprint*, *Plus Warenhandelsgesellschaft* and *VTB: VAB*[64] went further and it not only struck down general prohibitions that went beyond the blacklist of the Directive, but by doing so it has focused on the outcome of the Directive and not on its legal basis.[65]

The next two sections it will, first, analyse the EU's regulatory model of consumer protection and then examine the EU measures on the enforcement of EU consumer law.

3. EU regulatory model of consumer protection

The model of EU consumer protection can be best captured along two lines. On the one hand, by examining the balance European consumer law establishes between default and mandatory rules. On the other hand, by examining the intervention it imposes on the laws of the Member States. EU consumer law has been characterized as instrumental,[66] as its primary goal is to facilitate the internal market. Hence, its normative concept is closer to market mechanisms than social policy concepts. The consumer has primarily been seen as an active market participant: the "marketized consumer".[67] However, positive and negative measures of harmonization take significantly different stances on the image of the consumer and the level of intervention required at EU level.[68] Positive measures of harmonization follow a more consumer protective approach and consider consumers as weak parties, while negative harmonization measures are based on a benchmark of the assertive and active consumer.

This regulatory fuzziness remains one of the reasons that the EU law of consumer protection exists as a fragmented patchwork of various consumer related issues. While, a considerable number of EU directives exist on matters of consumer protection, they merely address particular aspects of consumer law. Consequently, the EU has so far not introduced a coherent and compound consumer protection legislation.

As an illustration of the above, the following sections will examine the information based regulatory model of EU consumer law and then analyse the normative concept of the consumer in EU law.

---

61. Ibid., at 59.
62. V. Mak, op. cit. *supra* note 54.
63. K. Tonner and K. Fangerow op. cit. *supra* note 60, at 75.
64. Joint Cases C-261/07, *VTB:VAB NV v. Total Belgium NV* and C-299/07, *Galatea BVBA v. Sanoma Magazines Belgium NV*. Case C-304/08, *Plus Warenhandelsgesellschaft*; Case C-540/08, *Mediaprint*.
65. See also V. Mak, "Full harmonization in European private law: A two-track concept", 20 E.R.P.L. (2012), 213–235.
66. H.-W. Micklitz, "The consumer: Marketized, fragmentized, constitutionalized" in D. Leczykiewicz and S. Weatherill, *The Images of the Consumer in EU Law* (Hart Publishing, 2015), 21–41, at 23.
67. H.-W. Micklitz op. cit. *supra* note 66.
68. H. Unberath and A. Johnston, "The double-headed approach of the ECJ concerning consumer protection", 44 CML Rev. (2007); V. Mak, "The consumer in European regulatory private law" in D. Leczykiewicz, S. Weatherill (Eds.), *The Images of the Consumer in EU Law*, 1st ed. (Hart Publishing, 2015), 381–401, at 382.

3.1 *Regulatory approach: Information paradigm*

EU consumer protection is characterized by a normative concept of the well informed and confident consumer and by the adoption of information provisions instead of corrective legal measures. The ECJ developed a neo-liberal concept of the consumer by emphasizing consumers' own responsibility in markets and the beneficial working of market forces. This model is based on the idea that consumers are able to make informed choices rather than government regulation defining that choice. Mandatory information disclosure creates a more informed bargaining environment, improves transparency and it is a less interventionist instrument than a simple ban. It does not restrict consumer choice and reflects the least political resistance.

Information disclosure has been characterized as a *conditio sine qua non* of well- functioning EU markets[69] and as a core element of EU consumer protection. Information disclosure as a preferred regulatory technique was already apparent in *Cassis de Dijon* where the Court argued that information improves transparency of the market and it is less culturally sensitive than substantive rules.[70]

Accordingly, information disclosure and the right of withdrawal have always been fundamental elements of EU Directives such as Directive 85/577 on doorstep selling, Directive 90/314 on package travel, Directive 87/102 on consumer credit, Directive 97/7 on distance contracts or Directive 97/5 on cross-border credit transfers. Directive 94/47 on timeshare and Directive 84/450 on misleading and comparative advertising also focuses on information disclosure. Directives that address the content of particular contracts and aspects of performance also pursue transparency, such as the Directive 93/13 on Unfair Contract Terms with regard to monitoring the fairness of contract terms, which were not individually negotiated and the Directive 99/44 on Consumer Sales, which focuses on the obligations of a seller to supply goods which meet certain expectations as to quality and fitness, and provides remedies for circumstances where these expectations have not been met.[71]

Over the years information provisions have become more detailed reaching its top in Articles 5 and 6 of the Directive 2011/83/EU on Consumer rights, that respectively lay down 8 different categories of information which need to be provided to a consumer before a contract which is not an off-premises or distance contract is concluded and 20 categories of information for off-premises and distance contracts. There are also specific information duties in Article 4 of Directive 2002/65/EC on the Distance Marketing of Financial Services and in Articles 3–5 of Directive 2008/122/EC Timeshare and In Article 4 and Annex II of Directive 2008/48/EC Consumer Credit. Besides defining the various categories of information that the consumer must be provided, the Directives also contain rules on the form and method of how information provision for example that information is given in "plain and intelligible language".[72]

Recital 20 of Directive 93/13 on unfair contract terms basically states that before a consumer concludes a contract, he should be able to familiarize himself with all the terms of that contract. As the ECJ held in *RWE Vetrieb* "[i]nformation, before concluding a contract, on the terms of the contract and the consequences of concluding it is of fundamental importance for a

69. This principle was recognized by the ECJ in *GB-INNO*.
70. S. Weatherill, op. cit. *supra* note 15, at 454.
71. C. Twigg-Flesner, "The importance of law and harmonisation for the EU's confident consumer" in D. Leczykiewicz and S. Weatherill (Eds.), *The Images of the Consumer in EU Law* (Hart Publishing, 2015).
72. Ibid.

consumer. It is on the basis of that information in particular that he decides whether he wishes to be bound by the terms previously drawn up by the seller or supplier".[73]

The ECJ has turned transparency requirements into a positive information obligation as only transparent information allows the consumer to make use of his/her rights. Moreover, in *Kásler* the ECJ has amplified the requirement of Article 5, stating that the requirement that a term is in plain and intelligible language had to be understood in broad sense and not merely limited to the question whether term is "formally and grammatically intelligible", and that a consumer must be able to evaluate on the basis of clear, intelligible criteria, the economic consequences resulting from the term.[74] Recent preliminary rulings on Directive 93/13 such as *Mohamed Aziz*[75] show that informing consumers about unfair contract terms has become a fundamental question of consumers' effective judicial protection.

Similarly, informing the consumer about his withdrawal right has also become a fundamental requirement. In *Pia Messner* the ECJ confirmed that consumers are in principle able to withdraw from distance contracts without paying compensation for use to the seller. The ECJ stated that a different judgment would harm the effectiveness of the consumers' very right to withdraw by imposing a financial burden on consumers.[76] In *Walter Endress* the ECJ held that a national provision, under which a right of withdrawal lapses one year after payment of the first premium, where the consumer has not been informed about the right of cancellation, was contrary to EU law.[77]

In *Schulte*[78] and *Heininger*[79] the ECJ went even so far that it extended the right of withdrawal concerning the Directive on doorstep selling to enable consumers not only to get out of contractual obligations years after the conclusion of the contract, but also to get out of so-called linked contracts.

Finally, in *Martín Martín* the ECJ stated that the national court may also *ex officio* raise the infringement of Article 4 of Directive 85/577/EC and declare the contract void if the consumer was not informed of his right of withdrawal in a doorstep selling contract.[80] These cases show that ECJ has made information provisions and transparency requirements fundamental elements of consumer protection.

3.2 *The normative concept of the consumer in EU law*

The normative concept of the consumer developed in the ECJ's free movement case law. According to this jurisprudence EU law relies on the benchmark of an "average consumer", who is a

73. Case C-92/11, *RWE Vetrieb AG v. Verbraucherzentrale NRW*, para 44. The ECJ went on explaining "that it is of fundamental importance for that purpose, first, whether the contract sets out in transparent fashion the reason for and method of the variation of the charges for the service to be provided, so that the consumer can foresee, on the basis of clear, intelligible criteria, the alterations that may be made to those charges and, secondly, whether consumers have the right to terminate the contract if the charges are in fact altered". Case C-92/11, *RWE Vetrieb AG v. Verbraucherzentrale NRW*, para 49 and Case C-472/10, *Nemzeti v. Invitel*, paras. 24, 26, 28.
74. Case C-26/13, *Árpád Kásler, Hajnalka Káslerné Rábai v. OTP Jelzálogbank Zrt*, paras. 71 and 73.
75. Case C-415/11, *Mohamed Aziz v. Caixa d´Estalvis de Catalunya, Tarragona i Manresa (Catalunyacaixa)*; Case C-226/12, *Constructora Principado SA v. José Ignacio Menéndez Álvarez*.
76. Case C-489/07, *Pia Messner v. Firma Stefan Krüger*, para 6.
77. Case C-209/12, *Walter Endress v. Allianz Lebensversicherungs AG*.
78. Case C-350/03, *Elisabeth Schulte and Wolfgang Schulte v. Deutsche Bausparkasse Badenia AG*.
79. Case 481/99, *Georg Heininger and Helga Heininger v. Bayerische Hypo- und Vereinsbank AG*.
80. Case C-227/08, *Eva Martín Martín v. EDP Editores SL*.

well informed, reasonable and circumspect market actor. In cases, such as *Pall Corp*,[81] *Clinique*,[82] *Mars*[83] and *Procureur de la Republique v. X.*,[84] the ECJ has condemned national rules for alleged consumer protection as being over-regulatory and relied on the "reasonably circumspect consumer" who is able to process information and make informed choices.[85] In *Gut Springheide* the Court explained that "[…] in order to determine whether a particular description, trade mark, promotional description or statement is misleading, it is necessary to take into account the presumed expectations of an average consumer, who is reasonably well informed and reasonably observant and circumspect."[86]

3.2.1 *The average consumer*

The average consumer in EU law and the case law of the Courts is that of the active consumer who is confident to conduct transactions cross-border. This is reflected in the legislation, which heavily relies on mandatory information disclosure as a regulatory technique. Properly disclosed information enables an active consumer to engage in effective transactions.

The concept of the average consumer defines the extent to which national consumer protection laws can restrict the EU free movement rules and it draws the borderline between the rights and duties of parties in B2C transactions.[87] The average consumer is granted mandatory rights[88] in order to realize market integration. Consumers are addressed as regulatory subjects who are empowered to contribute both to EU market integration and to European society.

The active consumer first appeared in the Commission's 1994 report on the Single market, which emphasized that consumers have a crucial role to pursue the single market objectives "The single market was not created for the benefit of business alone, and it will not function properly without the active and genuine participation of consumers."[89]

Consumers were addressed as market actors who actively search markets, monitor firms and switch providers. In fact, regulators used consumers' purchasing power and regulatory function as the source of justifying and legitimizing market processes.[90] Accordingly, in liberalized markets the main consumer interests were legislated first as customer choice and later as switching of providers.[91] In the regulatory framework of these sectors economic, social and

81. Case C-238/89, *Pall Corp. v. P. J. Dahlhausen & Co.*
82. Case C- 315/92, *Verband Sozialer Wettbewerb e.V. v. Clinique Laboratories SNC.*
83. Case C-470/93, *Verein gegen Unwesen in Handel und Gewerbe Köln e.V. v. Mars GmbH.*
84. Case C-373/90, *Procureur de la Republique v. X.*
85. Case C-126/91, *Schutzverband gegen Unwesen in der Wirtschaft v. Yves Rocher GmbH*, para 17.
86. Case C-210/96, *Gut Springenheide GmbH and Rudolf Tusky v. Oberkreisdirektor des Kreises Steinfurt – Amt für Lebensmittelüberwachung*, paras. 31, 32; See also Case C-540/08, *Mediaprint Zeitungs- und Zeitschriftenverlag GmbH & Co. KG*, para 103.
87. V. Mak, op. cit. *supra* note 68.
88. H.-W. Micklitz, "An expanded and systemized Community consumer law as alternative or complement?", 13 EBLR (2002), 583–598, at 588.
89. Commission, "The single market in 1994", COM(1995)238 final, para 319: "The citizen as consumer has a right to the benefits generated by increased competition and a wider choice of goods and services, while enjoying adequate protection of his safety and his other essential interests. In addition, the buying choices of well-informed consumers can speed up the positive economic effects of an integrated market."
90. T. Williams, "Empowerment of whom and for what? Financial literacy education and the new regulation of consumer financial services", 29 *Law & Policy* (2007), at 226–256.
91. A. Johnston, "Seeking the EU "consumer" in services of general economic interest" in D. Leczykiewicz and S. Weatherill (Eds.), *The Images of the Consumer in EU Law*, 1st ed. (Hart Publishing, 2015), at 112, 114.

political rights became increasingly blended in the internal market approach based on access to markets and universal services.[92]

Throughout the years the concept of the average consumer has been challenged from different perspectives. First, the impact of the economic and financial crises in 2008 on consumer confidence and purchasing power was considerable. Second, widespread liberalization of certain sectors has significantly increased the amount and complexity of information consumers have to process when entering transactions in the global marketplace. Third, as a reaction to these economic and social changes a new stream of economic theory has developed: behavioural economics, which challenges the rationality of consumers.[93] And last, in the age of technological innovations consumer law and notion of consumer faces fundamental challenges as a result of increased digitalization.[94] The need to adapt EU law to these changes in undeniable in light of the growing number of disadvantaged consumers, changing needs and interest of consumers extending to issues such as ethical and social objectives, insights on the irrational or bounded rationality of consumers in processing information.

Moreover, the EU concept of the rational, empowered consumer can conflict with the more protective standard of the Member States.[95] This has been acknowledged in *Buet*, the first case in 1989, where the Court has considered different categories of consumers and made reference to vulnerable consumers.[96]

3.2.2 *The vulnerable consumer*

The notion of the disadvantaged or vulnerable consumer is now part of EU law. However, the exact definition of who a vulnerable consumer is and what kind of intervention his position requires is far from clear.

The vulnerable consumer was first mentioned in *Buet*, where the Court made reference to people who are behind with their education as the potential purchasers of educational material, that makes them particularity vulnerable *vis-à-vis* the salesmen who can easily persuade them to buy the educational material which will improve their employments prospects.[97]

Still, the case law of the ECJ on the interpretation of the consumer notion continued to rely on the active consumer rather than the weak consumer.[98] This line of interpretation took a more consumer protective direction concerning the interpretation of Directive 93/13 on unfair contract terms. Already in *Océano Grupo*,[99] the Court of Justice stressed that the system introduced by the Directive is based on the idea that the consumer is in a weak position *vis-à-vis* the seller or supplier, as regards both his bargaining power and his level of knowledge. Consequently, the consumer may agree to terms drawn up in advance by the seller or supplier without being able

92. The provision of SGEI underlined the relationship on the one hand, between individual, the market and the EU and on the other hand, between citizenship access rights and consumer protection J. Davies, *The European Consumer Citizen in Law and Policy* (Palgrave, 2011), at 128.
93. Commission, "A European consumer agenda – Boosting confidence and growth" (Communication), COM(2012)225 final, "Consumer policy as an essential contribution to Europe 2020".
94. See the COM(2015)634 final. Proposal for a Directive of the European Parliament and of the Council on certain aspects concerning contracts for the supply of digital content.
95. H.-W. Micklitz argues that EU consumer law is market bound, in national law it is social policy bound. Ibid., at 589; H.-W. Micklitz, op. cit. *supra* note 88; V. Mak, op. cit. *supra* note 68.
96. Case C-382/87, *Buet*, see para 13 of the judgment.
97. Case C-382/87, *Buet*, see para 13 of the judgment.
98. Case 481/99, *Georg Heininger and Helga Heininger v. Bayerische Hypo- und Vereinsbank AG.*
99. Joined Cases C-240/98 and C-244/98, *Océano Grupo*.

to influence the content of those terms.[100] It is because of the consumer's weaker position that Article 6(1) of the Directive provides that unfair terms are not binding on the consumer. This is a mandatory rule which aims to re-establish equality between the contracting parties.[101]

Similarly the ECJ's case law on consumer sales protects the weak consumers as recently illustrated in *Soledad Duarte Hueros v. Autociba.*[102] The ECJ has so far mainly interpreted the concept of weak consumer, and as a general principle the definition of vulnerability is a Member State competence.

The "particularly vulnerable consumer" is referred to in Article 5(3) of the Unfair Commercial Practices Directive 2005/29: vulnerable consumers are those more exposed to a commercial practice or a product because of their: (a) mental or physical infirmity, (b) age or (c) credulity. While Recital 34 of the Preamble of the Consumer Rights Directive 2011/83 also refers to vulnerable consumers, the notion has not been implemented in the text of the Directive. Furthermore, Recital 8 of the Preamble of the General Product Safety Directive 2001/95 mentions vulnerable consumers.[103]

The notion of the vulnerable consumer has, however, been the most notably recognized in the Directives of specific sector regulation. The Universal Service Directive grants special rights to vulnerable consumers.[104] Both the Second and the Third Energy and Gas Package, has introduced particular protection for vulnerable consumers. Article 3(7) of Directive 2009/72[105] refers to the necessary safeguards to protect vulnerable consumers with regard to transparency regarding contractual terms and conditions, general information and dispute settlement mechanisms and switching. Member States should also define the concept of vulnerability by referring to, for example, energy poverty and, *inter alia*, to the prohibition of disconnection of electricity to such customers in critical times.

The gap between the "vulnerable" consumer standard in EU legislation and the "weaker" consumer standard of the ECJ's jurisprudence show that the concept of vulnerability needs to be made concrete by national legislation and case law.

4. Enforcement of consumer law

Consumers' access to justice and consumer redress has been part of the Union's policies since 1975 but it has only been reinforced in soft law documents. A specific legal basis for consumer

---

100. Joined Cases C-240/98 and C-244/98, *Océano Grupo* para 25; see also Case C-168/05, *Mostaza Claro*; Case C-40/08, *Asturcom Telecommunications,* para 29; Case C-243/08, *Pannon GSM,* para 25; Case C-137/08 (Grand Chamber), *VB Pénzügyi Lizing v. Ferenc Schneider,* para 46.
101. Case C-137/08 (Grand Chamber), *VB Pénzügyi Lizing v. Ferenc Schneider,* paras. 46–48.
102. Case C-32/12, *Soledad Duarte Hueros v. Autociba.*
103. L. Waddington, "Reflections on the protection of "vulnerable" consumers under EU Law", (2013) *Maastricht Working Papers No. 2.*
104. See both Art. 2 of Directive 2002/22/EC of the European Parliament and of the Council of 7 Mar. 2002 on universal service and users' rights relating to electronic communications networks and services (Universal Service Directive) and Arts. 7 and 23a of Directive 2009/136/EC of the European Parliament and of the Council of 25 Nov. 2009 amending Directive 2002/22/EC on universal service and users' rights relating to electronic communications networks and services, Directive 2002/58/EC concerning the processing of personal data and the protection of privacy in the electronic communications sector and Reg. (EC) 2006/2004 on cooperation between national authorities responsible for the enforcement of consumer protection laws.
105. Directive 2009/72/EC of the European Parliament and of the Council of 13 July 2009 concerning common rules for the internal market in electricity and repealing Directive 2003/54/EC (Text with EEA relevance), O.J. 2009, L 211/55.

redress is absent in the EU Treaties.[106] Although EU consumer protection was established as an independent legal area as outlined in section 2, the European Commission did not have a supervisory competence in consumer law. Even after the Lisbon Treaty, which transferred competences to the EU and thus made consumer protection a shared competence, the Member States retain almost exclusive competence in the way they enforce EU consumer rules. This is in line with the principle of national procedural autonomy.[107] Accordingly, the enforcement of EU consumer law is fragmented: there are harmonized substantive EU rules and decentralized national procedures, remedies and institutions of enforcement. This fragmentation is also challenged by a multi-level system of vertical (European and national law) and horizontal (general and sector-specific rules). EU directives generally did not foresee remedies and sanctions for infringements of consumer rights and there was no or little guidance from the EU on how to enforce EU consumer law. However, law enforcement is increasingly creeping into the EU agenda,[108] especially since the adoption of the Directive on unfair commercial practices. Moreover, the ECJ has taken an active role to lay down procedural safeguards to ensure effective judicial protection of consumers.

Since the entry into force of the Amsterdam Treaty in 1999 judicial cooperation in civil law matters became a new area of EU policy. After the Lisbon Treaty Article 81(2) TFEU also broadened the EU's competence in civil law matters and further measures can be based on the combination of Article 81 and 169 TFEU.[109] Since 2007 the enforcement of consumer law has become one of the key priorities of the Commission.[110] Access to justice was behind the adoption of Directive 98/27 EC on injunctions and later Regulation 2006/2004 on consumer protection cooperation. However, the main question was damages claims should be also available. In 2009 the Consumer Enforcement Package raised, two core issues of consumer law enforcement: effective means of collective redress and the deterrent effect of remedies and sanctions.

Accordingly, the Commission has worked on two enforcement issues: voluntary dispute resolutions schemes and collective actions. The Commission has adopted two Recommendations on minimum quality criteria for the establishment and operation of ADR schemes.[111] Later the Directive on ADR[112] and a Regulation on ODR was adopted,[113] that are to help European consumers to resolve their disputes out-of-court, covering online and offline, domestic and cross-border disputes. The ODR Regulation makes online out-of-court dispute resolution possible by the establishing the EU-wide online platform, which facilitates consumers to solve their

106. See Art. 169 TEU.
107. Case 33/76, *Rewe-Zentralfinanz eG and Rewe-Zentral AG v. Landwirtschaftskammer für das Saarland (Rewe I)*, para 5, Case C-261/95, *Palmisani*, para 27, Case C-453/99, *Courage and Crehan*, para 29.
108. A. de Moor-van Vugt, "Handhaving en toezicht in een Europese context" in Pront-van Bommel (Ed.), *De Consument en de Andere Kant van de Elektriciteitsmarkt: Inleidingen op het Openingscongres van het Centrum voor Energievraagstukken Universiteit van Amsterdam op 27 januari 2010* (Universiteit van Amsterdam, Centrum voor Energievraagstukken, 2011), at 62–95.
109. I. Benöhr, op. cit. *supra* note 10, at 191.
110. Communication of 13 March 2007 from the Commission to the Council, the European Parliament and the European Economic and Social Committee, "EU Consumer Policy Strategy 2007–2013", COM(2007)99 final.
111. Commission Recommendation 98/257/EC of 30 Mar. 1998 on the principles applicable to the bodies responsible for out-of-court settlement of consumer disputes O.J. 1998, L 115/31; Commission Recommendation 2001/310/EC of 4 Apr. 2001 on the principles for out-of-court bodies involved in the consensual resolution of consumer disputes, O.J. 2001, L 109/56.
112. Directive 2013/11 on alternative dispute resolution in consumer disputes, O.J. 2013, L 165/1.
113. Reg. 524/2013 on online dispute resolution in consumer disputes, O.J. 2013, L 165/1.

disputes online that arise from online sales or service contracts by directing the dispute to the appropriate national ADR entity.

With regard to damages claims, consumers' access to justice through compensatory claims is based on the right to an effective remedy before a national court or a tribunal in case of violation of rights and freedoms guaranteed by EU law. This is a fundamental right enshrined in Article 47 of the Charter of Fundamental Rights of the EU.[114]

In EU competition law the Green Paper in 2005[115] and in a White Paper in 2008[116] addressed collective actions as one of the key issues in private enforcement of competition law, but Directive 2014/104/EU on damages actions do not contain provisions on collective actions. Instead the EU has taken a more horizontal approach culminating in 2013 in a Communication[117] and a Recommendation on collective consumer redress.[118] This Recommendation merely consists of non-binding soft law without any obligation for the Member States to implement them in their legal system.

In the liberalized sectors, such as financial services, transport, telecommunications and energy Member States were required to establish independent regulatory authorities to monitor markets and compliance with consumer laws. The EU has encouraged certain minimum standards for consumer law enforcement. While the E-commerce Directive,[119] the Postal Services Directive[120] and the Markets in Financial Instruments Directive[121] encouraged Member States to establish ADR schemes, other Directives such as the Directives in telecom[122] and the energy

---

114. K.J. Cseres, "Harmonizing private enforcement of competition law in Central and Eastern Europe: The effectiveness of legal transplants through consumer collective actions", (2015) *Yearbook of Antitrust and Regulatory Studies*, 31–66. K.J. Cseres, "Collective consumer actions: A competition law perspective" in W. H. Van Boom and M. Loos (Eds.), *Collective Consumer Interests and How They are Served Best in Europe; Legal Aspects and Policy Issues on the Border between Private Law and Public Policy* (Europa Law Publishing, 2007), at 125–176.
115. Green Paper Damages actions for breach of the EC anti-trust rules, COM(2005)672 final.
116. White Paper on Damages Actions for Breach of the EC antitrust rules, COM(2008)165; Commission Staff Working paper accompanying the White Paper on damages, COM(2008)165 final, SEC(2008)404.
117. In 2011 the European Commission has published a public consultation working document entitled "Towards a Coherent European Approach to Collective Redress" SEC(2011)173, indicating change from a sectoral to a horizontal approach towards collective redress. This was followed in 2013 by the Communication "Towards a European Horizontal Framework for Collective Redress", COM(2013)401 final.
118. In the debate on the private enforcement of EU competition law the most important issue was whether group actions should be based on an opt-out or an opt-in principle. The Commission Recommendation on common principles for injunctive and compensatory collective redress mechanisms now follows the opt-in approach. Commission Recommendation of 11 June 2013 on common principles for injunctive and compensatory collective redress mechanisms in the Member States concerning violations of rights granted under Union Law, O.J. 2013, L 201/60.
119. Directive 2000/31/EC of the European Parliament and of the Council of 8 June 2000 on certain legal aspects of information society services, in particular electronic commerce, in the Internal Market, O.J. 2000, L 178/1.
120. Directive 2008/6/EC of the European Parliament and of the Council of 20 Feb. 2008 amending Directive 97/67/EC with regard to the full accomplishment of the internal market of Community postal services, O.J. 2008, L 52/3.
121. Directive 2004/39/EC of the European Parliament and of the Council of 21 Apr. 2004 on markets in financial instruments amending Council Directives 85/611/EEC and 93/6/EEC and Directive 2000/12/EC of the European Parliament and of the Council and repealing Council Directive 93/22/EEC, O.J. 2004, L 145/1.
122. Directive 2009/136/EC of the European Parliament and of the Council of 25 Nov. 2009, amending Directive 2002/22/EC on universal service and users' rights relating to electronic communications networks and services, Directive 2002/58/EC concerning the processing of personal data and the protection of privacy in the

sector,[123] the Consumer Credit Directive[124] and the Payment Services Directive[125] require that adequate and effective ADR schemes are put in place.

The enforcement of consumer rights has only been limited by the principles of effectiveness and equivalence. However, the ECJ's recent case law have considerably intruded this procedural autonomy. This case law, is based on the premise that national procedural rules cannot restrict consumers' possibility to make use of their substantive rights as enshrined in the EU Directives. The ECJ has incorporated a process of "proceduralization"[126] by claiming that national procedural issues should not restrict the substantive high level of consumer protection.[127] While most of these cases deal with the scope of consumer rights under national and EU law, the ECJ has, indirectly, addressed the question of which national procedural rules and remedies should be provided for the enforcement of those consumer rights under EU law.[128] In *Scarpelli*[129] concerning Directive 87/102 on consumer credit and *Caja de Ahorros y Monte de Piedad de Madrid*[130] concerning Directive 93/13 on unfair contract terms the ECJ confirmed that Member States may derogate from a minimum harmonization directive by introducing or retaining remedies which go beyond the harmonized standard of the directive and thus by providing a higher level of consumer protection.

In cases concerning consumers' rights of withdrawal such as *Messner*[131] and *Heine*[132] the ECJ has also defined the minimum scope of rights and remedies deriving from EU Directives and limited Member States' competence to determine the specific conditions when consumers exercise their rights of withdrawal.[133] However, with regard to the Product Liability Directive the ECJ has consistently stated that national rights and remedies which go beyond the maximum harmonization standards of the Directive must be reduced to the exact level provided for by this Directive.[134]

Concerning "proceduralization" the most remarkable line of cases, however, is related to the judicial review of unfair contract terms and the *ex officio* assessment of unfair contract terms. In a line of cases starting with *Océano*[135] the ECJ has established that the national must examine of its own motion whether a certain contract term is considered to be unfair under Article 3 of

---

electronic communications sector and Reg. (EC) 2006/2004 on cooperation between national authorities responsible for the enforcement of consumer protection laws O.J. 2009, L 337/37.

123. Directive 2009/72/EC of the European Parliament and of the Council of 13 July 2009 concerning common rules for the internal market in electricity, O.J. 2009, L 211/94.
124. Directive 2008/48/EC of the European Parliament and of the Council of 23 Apr. 2008 on credit agreements for consumers and repealing Council Directive 87/102/EEC, O.J. 2008, L 133/66.
125. Directive 2007/64/EC of the European Parliament and of the Council of 13 Nov. 2007 on payment services in the internal market amending Directives 97/7/EC, 2002/65/EC, 2005/60/EC and 2006/48/EC, O.J. 2007, L 319/1.
126. F.D. Negra, "The uncertain development of the case law on consumer protection in mortgage enforcement proceedings: *Sánchez Morcillo* and *Kušionová*", 52 CML Rev. (2015), 1009–1032, at 1010.
127. V. Mak, op. cit. *supra* note 68, at 392.
128. V. Trstenjak and E. Beysen, "European consumer protection law: *Curia semper dabit remedium?*", 48 CML Rev. (2011), 95–124.
129. Case C-509/07, *Scarpelli*.
130. Case C-484/08, *Caja de Ahorros y Monte de Piedad de Madrid*.
131. Case C-489/07, *Pia Messner v. Firma Stefan Krüger*.
132. Case C-511/08, *Handelsgesellschaft Heinrich Heine*.
133. V. Trstenjak and E. Beysen, op. cit. *supra* note 128, 115–117.
134. Case C-183/00, *Gonzalez Sanchez*, para 25; Case C-154/00, *Commission v. Greece*, paras. 12 and 20; Case C-52/00, *Commission v. France*, paras. 16 and 24; Case C-402/03, *Skov and Bilka*, paras. 22–23; Case C-285/08, *Moteurs Leroy Somer*, paras. 20–21.
135. Joined Cases C-240/98 to 244/98, *Océano Grupo Editorial SA v. Roció Murciano Quintero*.

Directive 93/13.[136] The ECJ stated that if consumers were obliged to raise the unfair nature of such terms themselves, there is a "real risk" that they will not do so either because of ignorance of their rights or because the fees for obtaining expert assistance are too high in comparison to the amount at stake in the litigation.[137] The ECJ stated in *Pannon GSM*[138] that national court's role is not limited to a mere power to rule on the possible unfairness of a contractual term, but also consists of the obligation to examine that issue of its own motion, where it has available to it the legal and factual elements necessary for that task, including when it is assessing whether it has territorial jurisdiction.[139]

The proceduralization of unfair terms has been opened by the ECJ in *Mohamed Aziz*,[140] where the national court was allowed to suspend mortgage enforcement proceedings in order to establish the unfairness of a term upon which enforcement was initiated. Such an interim relief was considered to ensure the judicial review of unfair terms. This "proceduralization" of the Directive has been continued in *Sánchez Morcillo*[141] and *Kušionová*[142] by assessing whether national procedural law governing mortgage enforcement proceedings ensures the effective judicial review of unfair terms in consumer contracts. These two cases also make a significant new contribution concerning the effects and function of the horizontal application of fundamental rights.

Likewise, the *ex officio* assessment of contract terms and the protection of consumers in a weaker procedural position, which restricts their use of substantive rights, has been extended to Directives 85/577 on distance contracts,[143] Directive 87/102 on consumer credit[144] and Directive 44/99 on consumer sales.[145] However, under these Directives the national courts are not obliged to raise the unfairness of contract terms and thus whether national rules restrict the effectiveness of substantive consumer rights based on EU law.

Further reading

Benöhr, I., *EU Consumer Law and Human Rights* (OUP, 2013).

Chirico, F. and P. Larouche (Eds.), *Economic Analysis of the DCFR, The work of the Economic Impact Group within CoPECL* (Sellier European Publishing, 2010).

Cseres, K.J. and A. Schrauwen, "Empowering consumer-citizens: Changing rights or merely discourse?" in D. Schiek, *The EU Social and Economic Model After the Global Crisis: Interdisciplinary Perspectives* (Ashgate, 2013).

136. Case C-168/05, *Elisa María Mostaza Claro v. Centro Móvil Milenium SL*, para 27; Case C-40/08, *Asturcom Telecomunicaciones SL v. Cristina Rodríguez Nogueira*. In this case the ECJ added that "Article 6 of the Directive must be regarded as a provision of equal standing to national rules which rank, within the domestic legal system, as rules of public policy", para 52.
137. Joined Cases C-240/98 to 244/98, *Océano Grupo*, para 26. Also Case C-473/00, *Cofidis SA v. Jean-Louis Fredout*.
138. Case C-243/08, *Pannon GSM Zrt v. Erzsébet Sustikné Győrfi*, para 32.
139. See also CJEU, Case C-137/08, *Pénzügyi Lízing*.
140. Case C-415/11, *Mohamed Aziz v. Caixa d´Estalvis de Catalunya, Tarragona i Manresa (Catalunyacaixa)*; Case C-226/12, *Constructora Principado SA v. José Ignacio Menéndez Álvarez*.
141. Case C-169/14, *Juan Carlos Sánchez Morcillo and María del Carmen Abril García v. Banco Bilbao Vizcaya Argentaria SA*.
142. Case C-34/13, *Monika Kušionová v. SMART Capital, a.s.*
143. Case C-227/08, *Eva Martín Martín v. EDP Editores SL*.
144. Case C-429/05, *Max Rampion and Marie-Jeanne Godard, née Rampion v. Franfinance SA and K par K SAS*.
145. Case C-32/12, *Soledad Duarte Hueros v. Autociba SA, Automóviles Citroën España SA*, and most recently C-497/13, *Froukje Faber*.

Leczykiewicz, D. and S. Weatherill (Eds.), *The Images of the Consumer in EU Law*, 1st ed. (Hart Publishing, 2015).
Mak, V., "Full harmonization in European private law: A two-track concept", 20 *European Review of Private Law* (2012).
Micklitz, H.-W., "Do consumers and business need a new architecture for consumer law? A thought provoking impulse", 32 *Yearbook of European Law* (2013), at 266–367.
Micklitz, H.-W., N. Reich, P. Rott and K. Tonner, *European Consumer Law*, 2nd ed. (Intersentia, 2014).
Negra, F.D., "The uncertain development of the case law on consumer protection in mortgage enforcement proceedings: *Sánchez Morcillo* and *Kušionová*", 52 CML Rev. (2015), 1009–1032.
Tonner, K. and K. Fangerow, "Directive 2011/83/EU on consumer rights: A new approach to European consumer law?", 2 *Journal of European Consumer and Market Law* (2012), 67–80.
Trstenjak, V. and E. Beysen, "European consumer protection law: *Curia semper dabit remedium?*", 48 CML Rev. (2011).
Weatherill, S.R., *EU Consumer Law and Policy*, 2nd ed. (Elgar European Law, 2013).

CHAPTER 36
ENVIRONMENTAL POLICY

*Suzanne Kingston**

1. History and development

There was no express mention of environmental policy in the original EEC Treaty, in part due to the essentially economic aims of that Treaty, and in part because, when the Treaty was drawn up in the late 1950s, the field of "environmental" law, in the sense of a discrete body of rules governing the way that we interrelate with our natural surroundings, barely existed in the signatory Member States (though national laws had long existed governing certain aspects of the current field, in the form of rules on private property and public health).[1] At international level, a collection of rules was just beginning to emerge in discrete environment-related areas, a process which had begun with the bilateral fisheries treaties of the mid-nineteenth century and in which the 1949 United Nations Conference on the Conservation and Utilization of Resources (UNCCUR) was a landmark event. These developments undoubtedly contributed to the subsequent emergence of Community environmental law.

Though environmental discourse became increasingly prevalent in the late 1950s and in the 1960s at international level,[2] there was little appetite for Community activity in the environmental field, as the institutions and Member States alike were immersed in the task of defining the Community legal and political order in this period. Nonetheless, a small amount of Community legislation was adopted in these years on what would now be considered to be environmental matters. In this period, and up to the entry into force of the Single European Act in 1987, two legal bases were used for such legislation, each requiring unanimity of voting in the Council. The first was Article 100 (now, in amended form, Art. 115 TFEU). The second was Article 235 (now, in amended form, Art. 352 TFEU). The Community's first legislative attempt to address environment-related issues was the 1967 adoption of a Directive on the classification, packaging and labelling of dangerous substances:[3] as it was based on Article 100, however, it was expressed to be aimed at removing the hindrances to trade caused by differing national legislation on the matter, rather than at environmental protection *per se*.[4] This early legislation, therefore, was premised on economic, rather than environmental, reasoning – any achievement of environmental improvement by Community legislation was, in principle, a side effect.

---

* School of Law, University College Dublin.

1. See for example in the UK, at 101–107 of the Public Health Act 1936, which were replaced by the Clean Air Act 1956.
2. See P. Sands and J. Peel, *Principles of International Environmental Law*, 3rd ed. (CUP, 2012), Ch. 2.
3. Directive 67/548 O.J. 1967, L 196/1 (subsequently amended).
4. However, protection of public health was mentioned as an aim in the preamble.

The first real sign of a distinct Community environmental policy came in the run-up to the landmark 1972 United Nations Conference on the Human Environment in Stockholm, convened in 1968 by the United Nations General Assembly.[5] In this way, the birth of Community environmental law occurred simultaneously with the beginning of a new period in international environmental law: as concern mounted for the "continuing and accelerating impairment of the quality of the human environment",[6] the impetus for international and regional environmental action grew. Thus, while Article 2 of the Treaty of Rome, which set out the EEC's aims, had listed among these aims "a harmonious development of economic activities, a continuous and balanced expansion, an increase in stability, and accelerated raising of the standard of living", the 1972 Paris Summit of the European Council made clear that to focus solely on economic growth was wrong-headed, declaring that "economic expansion is not an end in itself. Rather, its aim is to reduce disparities in living conditions and to improve the quality and standard of living". The Declaration continued, "as befits the genius of Europe, particular attention will be given to intangible values and to protecting the environment so that progress may really be put to the service of mankind".[7]

The Commission had already, however, got the ball rolling: the Paris Declaration followed the Commission's 1970 announcement that it would draw up a Community action programme on the environment, and the 1971 Commission Communication on Community environmental policy, in which it proposed using Article 235 (now, in amended form, Art. 352 TFEU) as a legal basis for potential Community environmental measures.[8] In 1973, the first Action Programme for the Environment was adopted, in the form of a political declaration by the Council and the representatives of Member States' governments meeting in the Council, sparked by France's concern that the Treaty provisions were, in their then form, not an appropriate basis for a European environmental policy.[9] In setting out the Community's environmental programme for the next four years, the First Action programme specified that the Community's Article 2 task of promoting throughout the Community a harmonious development of economic activities and a continuous and balanced expansion "cannot now be imagined in the absence of an effective campaign to combat pollution and nuisances or of an improvement in the quality of life and the protection of the environment".[10]

By thus reading in environmental protection as a necessary component of the aim of achieving economic growth, despite the fact that it was not expressly mentioned as an Article 2 aim of the Community, the programme opened the way for the adoption of Community environmental legislation.

Following the first Action programme, three further Action programmes were adopted between 1972 and 1987.[11] More than 150 pieces of Community environmental legislation were passed between 1972 and 1987, covering such diverse areas as environmental impact

5. UNGA Res. 2398 (XXIII)(1968).
6. Resolution adopted in July 1968 and a precursor to the convening of the Stockholm Conference: ECOSOC Res. 1346 (XLV)(1968).
7. Paris Declaration of the European Council, cited in the preamble to the First Action Programme on the Environment, O.J. 1973, C 112/1.
8. Commission Communication on a Community Policy for the Environment SEC(71)2616 (July 22, 1971).
9. See S. Kingston, V. Heyvaert and A. Čavoški, *European Environmental Law* (CUP, 2017), Ch. 1.
10. Preamble to the First Action Programme on the Environment, O.J. 1973, C 112/1.
11. Second Programme (1977–1981) O.J. 1977, C 399/1, Third Programme (1982–1986) O.J. 1983, C 46/1, Fourth Programme (1987–1992) O.J. 1987, C 328/1.

assessments, waste control, the protection of flora and fauna, and water and air quality.[12] In addition, the Community signed its first international environmental treaties in this period.[13] Such legislation was, by necessity, based on either Article 100 (where it could be argued that the legislation aimed to help achieve the common market)[14] or Article 235 (where no common market rationale could reasonably be found, but there were non-economic reasons for action at Community level);[15] indeed, most legislation was based on both articles.[16] In 1985, the ECJ in the landmark *ADBHU* case confirmed the validity of using Article 235 EC as a legal basis for environmental legislation on the basis that environmental protection was "one of the Community's essential objectives" justifying certain limits on the principle of freedom of trade.[17]

The rather uncertain status of Community environmental policy was formalized by Article 25 of the Single European Act (SEA) 1986, which inserted a new Title VII on the Environment into the Treaty,[18] making environmental protection an express objective of the Community. While it was clear that this remained an ancillary flanking policy to the primary Community aim of achieving the internal market, the Title nonetheless contained a specific legal basis for environmental legislation (Art. 130s), making it unnecessary to find an economic justification for the legislation or to use the "catch-all" Article 235 provision. Voting remained, however, subject to unanimity under Article 130s, though Member States could maintain or introduce more stringent protective measures than those passed on the basis of Article 130s, if compatible with the Treaty and notified to the Commission (Art. 130t, one of the so-called "environmental guarantee" or safeguard provisions).

Crucially, however, the SEA introduced a new Article 100a allowing internal market legislation (with some exceptions) to be passed by qualified majority. Environmental measures based on internal market objectives were therefore subject to qualified majority voting in the Council and thus be adopted with more ease. Moreover, environmental measures passed under this provision had to take "as a base a high level of environmental protection"[19] and Member States had the possibility of notifying the Commission if they deemed it necessary to "apply" national provisions in order to protect the environment despite the adoption of Community harmonizing legislation (another environmental guarantee provision).[20] The insertion of Article 100a led to a myriad of legal basis disputes before the ECJ on the question whether a given piece of environmental legislation ought to have been passed on the basis

---

12. See, for example, Directive 85/337 on environmental impact assessments O.J. 1985, L 175/40, Directive 75/442 on waste O.J. 1975, L 194/23, Directive 79/409 on the conservation of wild birds O.J. 1979, L 103/1, Directive 75/440 on surface water O.J. 1975, L 194/26, Directive 84/360 on the combating of air pollution from industrial plants O.J. 1984, L 188/20.
13. See, for example, the Paris Convention for the Prevention of Marine Pollution from Land-Based Sources, Decision 75/437 O.J. 1975, L 194/5.
14. For example, Directive 80/778 on drinking water O.J. 1980, L 229/11, Directive 73/404 on detergents O.J. 1973, L 347/51. The practice of basing such legislation on Art. 100 was in principle confirmed as compatible with the Treaty by the ECJ in Case 92/79, *Commission v. Italy*.
15. See, for example, Directive 79/409 on the conservation of wild birds O.J. 1979, L 103/1.
16. See, for example, Directive 85/337 on environmental impact assessments O.J. 1985, L 175/40, Directive 84/360 on combating air pollution from industrial plants O.J. 1984, L 188/20, and Directive 78/319 on toxic and dangerous waste O.J. 1978, L 84/43.
17. Case 240/83, *ADBHU*, para 13.
18. Arts. 130r-t – in amended form, present Arts. 191–193 TFEU.
19. Arts. 100a(3).
20. See Art. 100a(4).

of Article 130t (unanimous voting, consultation of the Parliament) or Article 100a (qualified majority voting, cooperation procedure with the Parliament).[21]

The SEA expressly set out the objectives of the newly formalized Community environment policy in Article 130r(1)), namely, preserving, protecting and improving the quality of the environment, contributing towards protecting human health, and ensuring a prudent and rational utilization of natural resources. Importantly, it also set out a number of what it termed "principles", which were to form a foundation of the Community's environmental policy (Art. 130r(2)), namely: the preventive principle, the source principle, and the polluter pays principle, each discussed below. The SEA also included a type of integration principle, requiring that environmental considerations be "a component of the Community's other policies", which was the first formalization of the obligation of environmental policy integration, discussed further below, at Treaty level. Although not forming part of Article 130r(2), another *de facto* "principle" of environmental law formalized by the SEA was that of subsidiarity (Art. 130r(4)).[22] The SEA also made express provision for the Community to participate in international environmental agreements (Art. 130r(4)).

These developments had a momentous effect on the development and formalization of the Community's environmental policy. The changes led, amongst other things, to a steady increase in the amount and scope of Community environmental legislation, and to the creation of a separate Directorate-General for the Environment (DG XI) in the Commission.[23] This was followed by the creation of the European Environment Agency (EEA), which is tasked with gathering data on the state of the EU's environment.[24]

The entry into force of the Maastricht Treaty brought with it a subtle upgrade in the perceived importance of the Community's environmental policy compared to other policies. The most significant (at least politically) was the first insertion into Article 2 EC, i.e., the fundamental objectives of the Community, of an express reference to environmental protection, including as one of the objectives of the Community "the promotion, throughout the Community, of a harmonious and balanced development of economic activities, sustainable and non-inflationary growth respecting the environment". Maastricht also introduced substantial, more practical, changes for the Community's environmental policy – most notably, the introduction of qualified majority voting for the environment legal basis (Art. 130s EC, subject to certain express exceptions);[25] the formalization of the status of the environmental action programme; and the addition of the precautionary principle to the principles of the Community's environmental policy. The principle of subsidiarity, which had been inserted by the SEA into the title

---

21. See, for instance, Case C-300/89, *Commission v. Council (Titanium Dioxide)*, discussed in Ch. 7, "Lawmaking", of this book.
22. Art. 130r(4) provided that, "The Community shall take action relating to the environment to the extent to which the objectives [of Community environmental policy, set out above] can be attained better at Community level than at the level of the individual Member States". The notion of subsidiarity had been present from the beginning in the Community's environment policy, featuring prominently in the Community's First Environment Programme. See Ch. 3, "System of competences", of this book for subsidiarity in general.
23. Significant legislation passed included legislation creating the European Environment Agency and legislation introducing an eco-label for environmentally-friendly products (Reg. 1210/90 O.J. 1990, L 120/1, Reg. 880/92, O.J. 1992, L 99/1).
24. Council Reg. (EEC) 1210/90 of 7 May 1990 on the establishment of the European Environment Agency and the European Environment Information and Observation Network O.J. 1990, L 120/1. In contrast to typical national environmental agencies, Member States have never been willing to give the EEA inspection or enforcement powers.
25. Namely, fiscal measures and measures concerning town and country planning, land use other than waste management, and management of water resources remained subject to unanimity of voting.

on the environment, was elevated to Part One of the Treaty, on the fundamental "*Principles*" of the Community (Art. 3b). In addition, Community financial support for environmental projects was bolstered by the insertion of Article 130d(2) (present Art. 177(2) TFEU)), providing for a Cohesion Fund to be set up in the field of the environment.

The Treaty of Amsterdam marked a further promotion and concretization of the Community's environmental aims. Specifically, it introduced the promotion of a "high level of protection and improvement of the quality of the environment" as an Article 2 EC objective of the Community, and modified the wording of Article 2 EC to refer to the aim of promoting a "harmonious, balanced and sustainable development of economic activities" (in place of the SEA's reference to "balanced development" and "sustainable growth"). The Treaty on European Union was amended to include among its objectives the promotion of "economic and social progress and [of achieving] balanced and sustainable development".[26] Further, the integration principle followed subsidiarity in being upgraded from its position in the Environment Title (former Art. 130r EC) to be included in Part One of the Treaty on the "Principles" of the Community (what was then Art. 6 EC).

No significant change was made to the environmental provisions by the Treaty of Nice. The Lisbon Treaty, however, made some changes deserving mention. Environmental values do not feature in the Article 2 TEU list of values upon which the Union is "founded". However, Article 3(3) TEU repeats the Treaty of Amsterdam's formulation of the balance between the EU's environmental, social and economic aims,[27] and it is for the first time specified that one of the goals of the Union's external relations policy is the "sustainable development of the Earth" (Art. 3(5) TEU). This is confirmed, and more detail added, by Article 21(2) TEU.[28] In the TFEU, Article 191(1) added the aim of combatting climate change to the EU's environmental policy aims, and added a *passerelle* clause in the environmental legal basis provision, discussed further below. Further, the newly inserted Title on Energy Policy includes "the development of new and renewable forms of energy" within the aims of the EU's policy in this field (Art. 194(1) TFEU). Finally, Article 37 of the Charter of Fundamental Rights of the EU effectively repeats the integration requirement of Article 11 TFEU (previously Art. 6 EC), discussed below.

2. Aims

The overarching aim of the Union's environmental policy is set out in Article 3(3) TEU, as further specified in Article 191(2) TFEU: "a high level of protection taking into account the

---

26. Art. 2, TEU, from the Maastricht version of promotion of "economic and social progress which is balanced and sustainable". Further important environmental changes brought about by Amsterdam were: (1) the "environmental guarantee" provisions of what is now Art. 114 TFEU were expanded to specify that Member States could, despite the passing of Community harmonization measures, maintain in force existing environmental measures or introduce new environmental measures, as long as the conditions set out therein were satisfied; and (2) the switch in decision-making procedures for (as it then was) Art. 130s EC (present Art. 192 TFEU) from the co-operation procedure to the co-decision procedure.
27. The relevant extract provides that that the Union "shall work for the sustainable development of Europe based on balanced economic growth and price stability, a highly competitive social market economy, aiming at full employment and social progress, and a high level of protection and improvement of the quality of the environment".
28. Art. 21(2) TEU includes within the aims of the EU's external action fostering the "sustainable economic, social and environmental development of developing countries" (though this is explicitly "*with the primary aim of eradicating poverty*") and helping to develop "international measures to preserve and improve the quality of the environment and the sustainable management of global natural resources, in order to ensure sustainable development".

diversity of situations in the various regions of the Union".[29] This aim effectively subsumes the four further aims set out in Article 191(1) TFEU, namely:

(1) Preserving, protecting and improving the quality of the environment;
(2) Protecting human health;
(3) Prudent and rational utilization of natural resources; and
(4) Promoting measures at international level to deal with regional or worldwide environmental problems, and in particular combating climate change.

As already mentioned, the fourth aim in this list was added by the Treaty of Lisbon. While not expressly an aim of the EU's environmental policy pursuant to Article 191 TFEU, the aim of sustainable development, as an aim of the EU (Art. 3(3) TEU), is also highly relevant here. The aim of sustainable development has been defined, at EU and international levels, as meeting the needs of the present generation without compromising those of future generations.[30] The Community (in conjunction with the Member States) issued a first Community sustainable development programme in 1993,[31] in the wake of the 1992 UN Conference on Environment and Development in Rio. Following the inclusion of sustainable development in the EU's aims with the Treaty of Amsterdam, the Gothenburg strategy adopted by the European Council in 2001 adopted a Sustainable Development Strategy (SDS) in 2001, declaring that it was adding a third, environmental, limb to the EU's Lisbon Strategy for socio-economic progress.[32] The EU SDS was reviewed in 2005, renewed in 2006, and reviewed again in 2009.[33] Despite all this policy activity, the precise benefits of the sustainable development aim from the environmental protection perspective remain largely unclear. The main practical import of sustainable development in the EU is a procedural one, namely, an ex-ante impact assessment must be undertaken by the Commission when proposing initiatives expected to have significant direct economic, social or environmental impacts.[34] The substantive aspect of the environmental pillar of sustainable development is given greater specification in the Article 11 TFEU integration requirement, discussed below.

3. Competence and external action

Article 4(2)(e) TFEU confirms that environmental policy constitutes a shared competence between the Union and its Member States. As a result, the Article 5(3) TEU subsidiarity principle applies throughout EU environmental policy. An exception lies in the field of conservation of marine biological resources under the common fisheries policy, where Article 3(1)(d) TFEU grants the Union exclusive competence. Further, as the ECJ has confirmed, international trade agreements making trade liberalization subject to compliance with the parties' international

---

29. See similarly, Art. 114(3) TFEU. The aim of achieving a high level of protection does not require an EU measure to aim for the highest level of protection that is technically possible: see Case C-341/95, *Bettati v. Safety Hi-Tech SRL*, para 47.
30. Conclusions of the Gothenburg European Council, 15 and 16 June 2001, SN200/1/01; G.H. Brundtland et al., *Our Common Future* (OUP, 1987).
31. See the Resolution of the Council and the Representatives of the Governments of the Member States O.J. 1993, C 138/1.
32. Conclusions of the Gothenburg European Council, 15 and 16 June 2001, SN 200/1/01.
33. COM(2005)37; Council Doc. 10117/06 of 9 June 2006; COM(2009)400; and Presidency Report on the 2009 Review of the EU Sustainable Development Strategy, Council of the EU, 1 Dec. 2009, 16818/09. No review of the Strategy has taken place since 2009.
34. See the Commission's Impact Assessment Guidelines, SEC(2009)92; Commission Communication on Impact Assessment, COM(2002)276.

environmental protection obligations fall within the Union's common commercial policy, and thereby constitute an exclusive competence of the Union.[35]

Article 191(4) TFEU provides that, within their respective spheres of competence in environmental matters, the Union and the Member States shall cooperate with third countries and with the competent international organizations. It also empowers the Union to enter into agreements with third parties in the course of such cooperation. Such power, however, is expressly without prejudice to Member States' competence to negotiate in international bodies and to conclude international agreements, thus emphasizing the shared nature of the EU's external, as distinct from internal action, in this field. In furtherance of this, the Union has entered into a wide range of international environmental agreements, alongside its Member States.[36]

In *PFOS*, however, the ECJ interpreted the Article 4(3) TEU duty of sincere cooperation to mean that, despite the shared nature of competence in the field, Member States were effectively obliged not to act in an international context once the EU had internally started the process for the formation of a concerted strategy on a topic (in that case, the EU had agreed not to make a proposal to add a specific pollutant to the Stockholm Convention on Persistent Organic Pollutants).[37] As a practical matter, this places obvious limitations on Member States' power of action in the environmental field (and other areas of shared competence: see Chapters 39 and 41.

4. Principles

Article 191(2) TFEU provides for four principles on which the Union's environmental policy "shall be based": the precautionary principle, the principle that preventive action should be taken (the "preventive principle"), the principle that environmental damage should as a priority be rectified at source (the "rectification at source principle"; and the principle that the polluter should pay (the "polluter pays principle"). To these must be added the Article 11 TFEU requirement to integrate environmental protection requirements into the definition and implementation of all Union policies and activities (the "integration principle"). Each of these is considered below.

While no longer a principle specific to Union environmental policy, the principle of subsidiarity, now contained in Article 5(3) TEU, should also be given special mention. This principle is discussed in detail in Chapter 3. Its application gives rise to particular controversy in the environmental context, in part because it can often be very difficult to assess whether environmental protection aims can be "better achieved" at Union level – coming, for instance, from the vantage point of a Member State with a tradition of a higher level of environmental protection than the EU average.[38] This underlines the importance of the particular environmental guarantee mechanisms built in to the Treaty for EU environmental policy, discussed below.

As mentioned above, in the case of the four principles set out in Article 191(2) TFEU, the Treaty states that the Union's "policy on the environment" "shall be based" on these principles. This mandatory directive to EU policy-makers leaves, however, a further question about the legal status of the principles of the Union's environmental policy. As discussed further

---

35. See *Opinion 2/15* (Singapore Free Trade Agreement), para 166.

36. See generally, E. Morgera (Ed.), *The External Environmental Policy of the European Union – EU and International Law Perspectives* (OUP, 2012).

37. Case C-246/07, *Commission v. Sweden* (PFOS). See M. Cremona, "Case C-246/07 *Commission v. Sweden*", 48 CML Rev. (2011), 1639.

38. Such as Denmark, Sweden, Austria or Germany. See, for instance, *The European Environment – State and Outlook Report 2015* (European Environment Agency, 2015) and the environmental section of European Commission, 34th Annual Report on Monitoring the Application of EU Law (General Secretariat, 2017).

below, the status of the principles as interpretative aids is clear: the ECJ has frequently made use of the principles to interpret provisions of EU law.[39] Due in particular to the Article 11 TFEU integration principle, this includes measures going outside the realms of EU environmental law in the sense of measures based on Article 192 TFEU.[40] In terms of their potential use as a self-standing ground of review of legality of EU law and/or of Member State action falling with the scope of EU law, it would seem from the ECJ's case-law to date that this will only be possible in case of a manifest failure to respect the principle at issue.[41] This is consistent with the notion that policy-makers enjoy a wide discretion in deciding how best to implement the principles at issue in practice. Again, such a legality review would not be restricted to review of EU measures passed on the basis of Article 192 TFEU.

In addition to the above-mentioned principles of Union environmental policy, Article 191(3) TFEU provides that, in preparing its policy on the environment, the Union "shall take account" of available scientific and technical data, environmental conditions in the various regions of the Union, the potential benefits and costs of action or lack of action, the economic and social development of the Union as a whole and the balanced development of its regions.

4.1 *The precautionary principle*

The precautionary principle was inserted into what is now Article 191 TFEU by the Treaty of Maastricht. Although this is not defined anywhere in the Treaty, the ECJ has held that that, as a matter of EU law, the precautionary principle requires that, "where there is uncertainty as to the existence or extent of risks to the health of consumers, the institutions may take protective measures without having to wait until the reality and the seriousness of those risks become fully apparent".[42] It is well-established that, although the principle appears in Title XX TFEU, on environmental policy, it is also a vital principle in the fields of public health and the common agricultural policy.[43] Indeed, the General Court has held that the principle constitutes a general principle of EU law.[44] Within the environmental context, the principle has been particularly important in interpreting the environmental guarantee clauses, discussed below, permitting Member States under certain conditions to prefer a higher level of environmental protection. It has also been crucial in the field of habitat protection, discussed below.

According to the ECJ, the precautionary principle requires a two-stage analysis.[45] First, the potentially negative consequences for the environment or health (as the case may be) must be identified. Secondly, it requires a "comprehensive assessment of the risk" to the environment or health, "based on the most reliable scientific data available and the most recent

39. See, for instance, Case C-2/90, *Commission v. Belgium* ("Walloon Waste"); Case C-379/98, *PreussenElektra*; Case C-127/02, *Landelijke Vereniging tot Behoud van de Waddenzee*; Case C-573/12, *Ålands Vindkraft v. Energimyndigheten*.
40. See Case C-77/09, *Gowan*, at para 71.
41. See, for instance, Case C-341/95, *Bettati v. Safety Hi-Tech SRL*; Case C-77/09, *Gowan*, Opinion of A.G. Geelhoed in Case C-161/04, *Austria v. Parliament and Council*, paras. 59–60.
42. Case C-77/09, *Gowan*, para 73; Case C-241/01, *National Farmers' Union*, para 63; Case C-180/96, *United Kingdom v. Commission*, para 99; Case C-236/01, *Monsanto Agricoltura Italia*, para 111. Compare the definition of the principle at international level in e.g., the Rio Declaration on Environment and Development of 1992, Principle 15.
43. See, for instance, Case C-241/01, *National Farmers' Union*, para 64, and Case C-282/15.
44. Joined Cases T-74/00, T-76/00, *Artegodan v. Commission*.
45. Case C-77/09, *Gowan*, paras. 75–78; Case C-333/08, *Commission v. France*, paras. 92–93. Compare the Commission's definition of the principle in its Communication on the Precautionary Principle (COM(2000)1final).

results of international research".[46] If, following this analysis, it proves "impossible to determine with certainty the existence or extent of the alleged risk because of the insufficiency, inconclusiveness or imprecision of the results of studies conducted", but there remains a "likelihood of real harm" to the environment or public health if the risk materializes, the precautionary principle will apply to justify objective and non-discriminatory measures that would otherwise be prima facie precluded due to their restrictive nature.[47] Further, the ECJ will only annul a decision to apply the precautionary principle in this manner in case of manifest error.[48] By contrast, the precautionary principle will not justify action taken where the evidence shows that the risks to the environment or human health are merely hypothetical.[49]

4.2 *The preventive principle*

The principle that "preventive action should be taken" has been present in what is now Article 191 TFEU since the environmental title was first inserted into the Treaty with the Single European Act. The idea behind the preventive principle is the simple adage that prevention is better than cure, i.e., it is simpler, and probably cheaper and more effective, to avoid pollution in the first place than to try and clean it up afterwards. This philosophy can be seen underlying a great many of the EU's environmental laws and policies, particularly those involving pollution control such as the Industrial Emissions Directive, the Environmental Liability Directive and the Waste Directive.[50] Despite the principle's long pedigree, it has received less attention in the case-law and literature than the precautionary principle, due in large part to its essential ambiguity: it offers no solution, for instance, to the question of what should be done once pollution has occurred.[51]

4.3 *The rectification at source principle*

The principle that environmental damage should "as a priority be rectified at source" has, like the preventive principle, been in the Treaty since the Single European Act, but has never been the subject of much jurisprudence or debate. Again, this is in large part because it is rather ambiguous by nature. One can extract from this principle, for instance, that a polluter should bear responsibility for cleaning up its own pollution (viz. the Environmental Liability Directive), and a polluting region should bear responsibility for cleaning up pollution coming from within its jurisdiction. The latter point is present in what remains the leading ECJ judgment on the topic, *Walloon Waste*. In this judgment, the ECJ held that, while a regional ban on imports of hazardous waste amounted to a restriction on free movement of goods that was *prima facie* contrary to what is now Article 34 TFEU, interpreting this Article in light of the rectification at source principle, the ban should not be considered to be discriminatory, and could be justified on environmental protection grounds.[52] In contrast, in *Sydhavnens*, the rectification at source

---

46. Ibid.
47. Ibid.
48. *Gowan*, para 79; Case C-341/95, *Bettati v. Safety Hi-Tech SRL*, para 35.
49. See, for instance, Case T-229/04, *Sweden v. Commission*, para 161.
50. Directive 2010/75 on industrial emissions O.J. 2010, L 334/17; Directive 2004/35 on environmental liability regarding the prevention and remedying of environmental damage O.J. 2004, L 143/56, and Directive 2008/89 on waste O.J. 2008, L 312/3. See e.g., Opinion of A.G. Kokott, Case 378/08, *Raffinerie Mediterranee*, paras. 54–76.
51. V.N. de Sadeleer, *Environmental Principles: From Political Slogans to Legal Rules* (OUP, 2002), at 61.
52. Case C-2/90, *Commission v. Belgium* ("Walloon Waste"), paras. 34–35.

principle did not justify a restriction on export of non-hazardous waste, where such waste was destined for recovery.[53]

4.4 *The polluter pays principle*

Prior to its insertion into the Treaty with the Single European Act, the polluter pays principle was already well-established as a principle of international environmental law and indeed as a first principle of environmental economics, insofar as it requires those who cause environmental damage to pay for it.[54] It had also been embraced by the Commission as early as its first Environmental Action Programme of 1973.[55] This led to a Commission Communication on the matter subsequently endorsed by the Council in a 1975 Recommendation. The Communication defined the polluter pays principle as meaning that,

> "natural or legal persons governed by public or private law who are responsible for pollution must pay the costs of such measures as are necessary to eliminate that pollution or to reduce it so as to comply with the [relevant standards]."[56]

In practice, EU environmental law as it stands implements the polluter pays principle only imperfectly, and there are many exceptions where society at large ends up bearing the cost of pollution caused by a sub-section of the population. A good example is the EU's State aid policy, where a polluter pays approach is evident in some of the Commission and ECJ case-law (especially on the definition of aid),[57] but is notably absent in other areas.[58] Thus, under the EU's Guidelines on State aid for environmental protection and energy, it is still permissible for the State to subsidize a company's own waste management, and even for the State to grant subsidies to environmentally damaging activities, as long as the conditions set out in Article 107 TFEU are otherwise met.[59] More broadly, however, the effect of a polluter pays approach can be seen clearly in the EU's embrace of market-based instruments (such as emissions trading) in environmental policy, which instruments aim to factor in the cost of environmental damage within the market's price mechanism. One important example of such an instrument, emissions trading, is discussed below.

Of further relevance here is Article 192(4) TFEU, which provides that, "without prejudice to certain measures adopted by the Union", the Member States shall finance and implement the EU's environmental policy. An important caveat to this principle is added by Article 192(5) TFEU, enabling derogation from Member States' Article 192(4) TFEU obligations, and/or financial support from the EU's Cohesion Fund, if national authorities are faced with costs "deemed disproportionate". While this provision is expressed to be "without prejudice to" the

53. Case C-209/98, *Sydhavnens*. See also, Case C-292/12, *Ragn-Sells*.
54. See the 1972 OECD Council Recommendation on Guiding Principles Concerning the International Economic Aspects of Environmental Policies, and the 1974 OECD Council Recommendation on the Implementation of the Polluter Pays Principle. See, subsequently, Principle 16 of the 1992 Rio Declaration on Environment and Development.
55. O.J. 1973, C 112/1.
56. Annex to Council Recommendation 75/436/Euratom, ECSC, EEC regarding cost allocation and action by public authorities on environmental matters O.J. 1975, L 194/1, point 2.
57. See S. Kingston, *Greening EU Competition Law and Policy* (OUP, 2012), Ch. 12.
58. See further, the observations of A.G. Jacobs in Case C-126/01, *GEMO*. Another example is seen in Art. 9 of the Water Framework Directive which outlines full-cost pricing for water in accordance with the polluter pays principle: Directive 2000/60/EC of the European Parliament and of the Council establishing a framework for the Community action in the field of water policy, O.J. 2000, L 327/1.
59. Commission Communication, Guidelines on State aid for environmental protection and energy 2014–2020, O.J. 2014, C 200/1, para 6 and 158–159.

polluter pays principle, it effectively implies that, as a matter of EU constitutional law, Member States will not be responsible for the costs of cleaning up pollution in their own jurisdiction where such costs are "deemed" disproportionate.

4.5 *The integration principle*

As already noted, the Article 11 TFEU integration principle states that "environmental protection requirements must be integrated into the definition and implementation of the Union policies and activities, in particular with a view to promoting sustainable development". A weaker version of this provision, requiring only that environmental considerations be a "component" of other Community policies, was inserted by the Single European Act into the environmental title of the Treaty. The Treaty of Amsterdam, however, elevated the principle to Part One of the Treaty.

Aside from its position in the Treaty, the language of Article 11 TFEU makes clear that it is of a different nature to the Article 191(2) TFEU principles. Rather than simply stating that EU "policy" must be "based on" the principle, it goes much further, mandating that environmental protection requirements be integrated into the "definition *and implementation*" of the EU's "policies *and activities*" (emphasis added). It is evident, therefore, that this is not just a high-level directive to policy-makers, but is a mandatory requirement for all decisions taken by EU bodies. The distinctive strength of the provision is further highlighted by comparison with the "integration" clauses inserted by the Treaty of Lisbon for other policy areas such as consumer protection, discrimination and social protection, which are phrased in far weaker terms.[60]

Despite the strength of the legal provision, the practical implementation of the integration principle has been rather disappointing to date. In 1998, the European Council launched the Cardiff process, by which different formations of the Council of Ministers were requested to develop strategies to achieve environmental integration, starting with energy, transport and agriculture.[61] This led, at the Council of Ministers level, to the development of bilateral integration strategies and programmes for a wide number of Council formations, including the internal market (which encompasses competition policy),[62] industry,[63] development,[64] fisheries,[65] general affairs and external relations[66] and economic and financial affairs[67] formations, in addition to the energy,[68] transport[69] and agriculture[70] formations. More recently, the "Greening the European Semester" initiative aims at integrating environmental concerns into the Union's macroeconomic policies. At the Commission level, a variety of bilateral sectoral environmental integration strategies have been developed in a wide range of policy areas, mirroring the Council's sectoral strategies.[71] In 2004, the Commission undertook to

---

60. Arts. 8–10 and 12–13 TFEU, discussed in Ch. 28, 29 and 35 of this book. See *contra*, however, J. Jans, "Stop the integration principle?", 33 *Fordham Int'l L.J.* (2011), 1533.
61. The Cardiff Summit followed a Commission Communication, "Partnership for Integration" (COM(98)333).
62. See the Council's report to the Helsinki European Council, Nov. 1999, doc. 13622/99.
63. Ibid.
64. Ibid.
65. See the Council Conclusions on integration of environment and sustainable development into the Common Fisheries Policy, Apr. 26, 2001, doc. 7885/01.
66. See the COREPER Report 7791/01 of 4 Apr. 2001, adopted at the General Affairs Council of 10 Apr. 2001.
67. See the Council's Report to the Nice European Council of Nov. 27, 2000 doc. 13054/1/00.
68. See the Council's adoption of an energy integration strategy, Nov. 1999, doc. 9994/99.
69. See, for example, Council Resolution, "Follow-up to the Cardiff/Helsinki Summit on the integration of environment and sustainable development into the transport policy", doc. 7329/01.
70. See the Council's adoption of an agriculture integration strategy, Nov. 15, 1999, doc. 13078/99.
71. Commission Communication, "Partnership for Integration" COM(98)333 final.

carry out an annual stocktaking of the progress of the Cardiff process, but this was never followed up.[72] The main cross-cutting practical effort to implement Article 11 TFEU, however, is again the procedural requirement that the Commission must undertake an impact assessment when proposing all major policy measures, discussed above.

At the ECJ level, the integration principle has been relied upon in cases on the relationship between EU internal market law and environmental protection, such as *PreussenElektra*, where the ECJ relied on the principle to support its conclusion that German rules favouring locally-generated renewable electricity did not breach what is now Article 34 TFEU.[73] This approach has been further vindicated in the decision of *Ålands Vindkraft*, where the ECJ ruled that a national renewable energy support scheme was compatible with Article 34 TFEU even where the green energy certificates at issue were only awarded for the production of renewable energy within the territory of that Member State, and not for renewable energy produced in other EU Member States.[74] Similarly, as concerns the Union's external trade policy, the integration principle has been relied on by the ECJ in concluding that sustainable development forms an "integral part" of the Union's common commercial policy.[75]

An integration approach is also evident in fields such as public procurement and State aid.[76] In addition, the ECJ has relied on the integration principle in a number of legal basis judgments, and has used it as an aid to the interpretation of secondary legislation,[77] including when deciding how to apply the Article 191(2) TFEU principles of EU environmental policy.[78] To date, however, the ECJ has stopped short of pronouncing the integration principle to form a self-standing ground of annulment of EU legislation, though some of its Advocates General would have gone this far.[79]

5. Legal bases and environmental guarantee provisions

5.1 *General legal bases*

As noted above, in the past, environmental measures frequently gave rise to legal basis disputes before the ECJ, particularly when what is now Article 114 TFEU (entailing qualified majority voting in the Council) was used instead of what is now Article 192(1) TFEU (which originally required unanimity).[80] With the move to qualified majority voting in Article 192(1) TFEU accomplished by the Treaty of Maastricht, however, legal basis disputes are less frequent in this

72. See "Integration of Environmental Considerations into other Policy Areas – A Stocktaking of the Cardiff Process" COM(2004)394 final, and S. Kingston, op. cit. *supra* note 57, Ch. 3.
73. Case C-379/98, *PreussenElektra*. An integration approach is also evident in, for instance, Case C-28/09, *Commission v. Austria (Inn Valley)*.
74. Case C-573/12, *Ålands Vindkraft v. Energimyndigheten*. See also, Case C-204/12, *Essent Belgium* (where the ECJ declined to follow the opinion of A.G. Bot opining that the finding in *PreussenElektra* was no longer good law), Case C-549/15, *E.ON Biofor Sverige*, and S. Kingston, "The uneasy relationship between the EU's economic and environmental policies: The role of the Court of Justice" in B. Sjåfjell and A. Wiesbrock (Eds.), *Sustainable Public Procurement in EU Law: New Perspectives on the State as Stakeholder* (OUP, 2015).
75. *Opinion 2/15* (Singapore Free Trade Agreement), para 147.
76. See, e.g., Case C-513/99, *Concordia Bus*.
77. See, for example, the Opinion of A.G. Kokott, Case C-304/01, *Spain v. Commission* (interpretation of fisheries legislation).
78. See, e.g. T-76/00, *Artegodan v. Commission*.
79. See, e.g., A.G. Cosmas in Case C-321/95P, *Greenpeace*, stating that the integration principle should be capable of direct effect; A.G. Geelhoed in Case C-161/04, *Austria v. Parliament and Council*, stating that review should be on the basis of manifest error.
80. See, for instance, Case C-300/89, *Commission v. Council (Titanium Dioxide)*.

field, although disputes between the use of Article 192(1) and Article 352 TFEU still occur.[81] Post-Lisbon, Article 192(1) TFEU remains the key legal basis for environmental provisions, and provides for the ordinary legislative procedure after consultation with ECOSOC and the Committee of the Regions.

By way of derogation, however, Article 192(2) TFEU provides that a special legislative procedure requiring unanimity of voting in the Council, and consultation of the European Parliament, ECOSOC and the Committee of the Regions, applies in the case of (a) provisions "primarily of a fiscal nature"; (b) measures affecting town and country planning, the quantitative management of water resources or affecting, directly or indirectly, the availability of those resources, and land use, with the exception of waste management; and (c) measures significantly affecting a Member State's choice between different energy sources and the general structure of its energy supply. This provision applies "without prejudice to Article 114", i.e., in the case of legislation that falls within these categories, but also falls within the scope of Article 114 TFEU, precedence should be given to the latter legal basis.

The Lisbon Treaty added a *passerelle* clause to Article 192(2) TFEU, whereby the areas listed may be made subject to qualified majority voting following a unanimous decision of the Council and after consultation of the European Parliament, ECOSOC and the Committee of the Regions, without the necessity for Treaty amendment.

Article 192(3) TFEU contains a legal basis provision for the adoption of the EU's multiannual Environmental Action Programmes, discussed above, to which the ordinary legislative procedure applies.

5.2 *Environmental guarantee provisions and minimum harmonization*

Where environmental legislation is passed on the basis of Article 192 TFEU or Article 114 TFEU, the Treaty expressly allows Member States, subject to compliance with certain conditions, to prefer a higher level of environmental protection via national measures. As noted above, these provisions are consistent with the EU's stated aim of promoting a "high level of protection taking into account the diversity of situations in the various regions of the Union" (Art. 191(2) TFEU).

First, Article 191(2) TFEU provides that harmonization measures "answering environmental protection requirements" shall include, "where appropriate", a safeguard clause allowing Member States to take provisional measures, for non-economic environmental reasons, subject to a procedure of inspection by the Union.

Secondly, Article 193 TFEU provides that the protective measures adopted pursuant to Article 192 shall not prevent any Member State from "maintaining or introducing more stringent protective measures", as long as they are compatible with the Treaties and notified to the Commission. The ECJ has held that the principle of proportionality does not apply to measures falling within this provision.[82]

Thirdly, Article 114(4) TFEU provides that if, after the adoption of a harmonization measure by the European Parliament and the Council, by the Council or by the Commission, a Member State deems it necessary to maintain national provisions on *inter alia* grounds "relating to the protection of the environment or the working environment", it shall notify the Commission of these provisions as well as the grounds for maintaining them.

Fourthly, without prejudice to Article 114(4) TFEU, Article 114(5) TFEU provides that if, after such a harmonization measure, a Member State deems it necessary to introduce national

81. See, for instance, Opinion 2/00, *Cartagena Protocol.*
82. Case C-6/03, *Deponiezweckverband Eiterköpfe.*

provisions based on new scientific evidence relating to *inter alia* the protection of the environment "on grounds of a problem specific to that Member State arising after the adoption of the harmonization measure", it shall notify the Commission of the envisaged provisions as well as the grounds for introducing them.

It is clear from the above that the conditions for introducing new national measures (Art. 114(4) TFEU) are stricter than those for maintaining existing measures (Art. 114(5) TFEU). For instance, the ECJ has affirmed that a ban on the use of genetically modified organisms in Upper Austria did not fall under Article 114(5) TFEU, because it did not raise any issues specific to that Member State.[83] The *Dutch Diesel Engine* cases also make clear that the problem giving rise to the proposed more stringent national measure need not have occurred exclusively in that Member State to qualify for the derogation.[84]

5.3 *Governance and enforcement*

A major theme within EU environmental law and policy in recent years has been the need to improve governance and enforcement. This has focused on efforts to improve the rather poor record of under-enforcement of EU environmental law,[85] and efforts to improve environmental governance by bringing the EU's laws, and those of its Member States, into line with the 1998 Aarhus Convention.[86] In 2012, the Commission issued a Communication[87] in which it specified the principal ways in which it intended to deal with the under-enforcement issue. This included improving knowledge of what is going on "on the ground", by putting more effective information systems in place at EU and national levels, and improving national inspections aimed at enforcing EU environmental law.[88] In February 2017, the Union adopted the so-called "Environmental Implementation Review" ("EIR") package, which is a new tool aimed at improving implementation of Union environmental law. EIR involves a two-yearly cycle of analysis, peer-to-peer dialogue and expert group meetings, with publication of country reports by Member States.[89] It is too early to tell whether EIR will, in practice, result in any significant improvements in the implementation of Union environmental law.

A further issue targeted by the Commission is the mechanism used by Member States for handling complaints made at national level. At EU level, large changes have occurred in recent years in complaint handling via the institution of the EU Pilot scheme, which has been in operation since 2008 (and is not confined to environmental law).[90] Essentially, the idea of the Pilot scheme is, once a complaint at EU level has been registered, it is transferred to the relevant Member State for their input – whether in the form of clarification, information or potential solutions to the problem. The Member State may communicate directly with the complainant to this end. In the absence of (what the Commission deems to be) a satisfactory solution, the Commission retains the power to commence infringement proceedings in the

83. Joined Cases C-439/05 P and C-454/05 P, *Land Oberösterreich and Austria v. Commission*.
84. Case T-182/06, *Netherlands v. Commission* and on appeal, Case C-405/07 P *Netherlands v. Commission*.
85. See the EU's Seventh Environmental Action Programme (O.J. 1973, C 112/1.), where improving enforcement is identified as a priority action from 2013–2020.
86. UNECE Convention on Access to Information, Public Participation in Decision-making and Access to Justice in Environmental Matters.
87. COM(2012)95. See also, the 2008 Communication on improving implementation of EU environmental law, COM(2008)773.
88. See Recommendation 2001/331/EC providing for minimum criteria for environmental inspections in Member States O.J. 2001, L 118/41.
89. See Commission Communication, "The EU Environmental Implementation Review" COM(2017)63.
90. See Commission Communication "A Europe of Results: Applying Community Law" COM(2007)502.

normal fashion. The 2012 Communication re-affirms the Commission's belief in "delegating" complaint-handling responsibilities to national authorities in this manner, especially in those fields of environmental enforcement which are not of strategic importance to the Commission.[91] While efforts to improve enforcement are in principle to be welcomed, the increased delegation of enforcement to Member States carried with it evident risks, and it is critical that the Commission supervises Member States carefully in this context.[92]

Alongside these efforts to improve environmental enforcement, the EU has been striving to improve environmental governance in recent years. In part, this has been driven by the 1998 Aarhus Convention of the UN Economic Commission for Europe, which lays down obligations for its signatories to ensure access to information, public participation and access to justice in environmental matters. Since May 2005, the Community (and subsequently the Union) has been a party to the Convention, alongside its Member States,[93] and has implemented it on two levels. First, in terms of measures directed at Member States, it has passed two Directives implementing the Convention's access to information and public participation principles,[94] although the latter applies only in narrowly designated fields of EU environmental law, namely, environmental impact assessment (EIA) and integrated pollution prevention and control (IPPC, now covered by the Industrial Emissions Directive), discussed below. Due to opposition from certain Member States, no Directive on the third pillar of the Convention, access to justice, has been passed. Secondly, in terms of measures directed at EU institutions and bodies, the EU passed a Regulation in 2006 aimed at implementing all of the three pillars of the Convention.[95]

Despite the lack of specific EU legislation on access to justice in Member States, a variety of recent ECJ judgments have gone some way to implement this aspect of the Convention in EU law. One of the most important of these was the 2011 *LZ I* judgment,[96] where the ECJ declined to find Article 9(3) of the Aarhus Convention to be directly effective, but held that, despite the fact that the Habitats Directive does not include any access to justice provisions, it was incumbent on Member States to ensure that the rights provided therein are "effectively protected in each case".[97] In practical terms, this meant that the national court had a duty to interpret national law "in a way which, to the fullest extent possible, is consistent with the objectives laid down in Article 9(3) of the Aarhus Convention" and the objective of effective judicial protection of the relevant EU law rights "so as to enable" an environmental

91. 2012 Communication, at 8; 2008 Commission Communication on implementing environmental law COM(2008)773.
92. See further, S. Kingston, V. Heyvaert and A. Čavoški, op. cit. *supra* note 9, Ch. 6.
93. Council Decision O.J. 2005, L 124/1. See generally, S. Kingston, V. Heyvaert and A. Čavoški, op. cit. *supra* note 9, Ch. 5 and 7.
94. Directive 2003/4/EC of the European Parliament and of the Council of 28 Jan. 2003 on public access to environmental information O.J. 2003, L 41/26; Directive 2003/35/EC of the European Parliament and of the Council of 26 May 2003 providing for public participation in respect of the drawing up of certain plans and programmes relating to the environment O.J. 2003, L 156/17. On Directive 2003/4, see Case C-204/09, *Flachglas Torgau*, Case C-279/12, *Fish Legal* and Case C-442/14, *Bayer CropScience*.
95. Reg. 1367/2006 of the European Parliament and of the Council on the application of the provisions of the Aarhus Convention O.J. 2006, L. 264/13. See Joined Cases C-401/12 P, C-402/12 P and C-403/12 P, *Council and Ors v. Vereniging* Milieudefensie *Stichting Stopluchtverontreiniging Utrecht*; Joined Cases C-404/12 P and C-405/12 P, *Council and Commission v. Stichting Natuur en Milieu and Pesticide Action Network Europe v. Commission*; and Case C-60/15, *Saint-Gobain Glass Deutschland*.
96. Case C-240/09, *Lesoochranárske zoskupenie*.
97. Ibid., para 47.

association such as that at issue to challenge the disputed measure.[98] This strong version of the duty of consistent interpretation effectively obliges national courts, therefore, to achieve via interpretative means the aims of this aspect of the Aarhus Convention in the absence of applicable EU legislation on access to justice, unless this would require a *contra legem* interpretation of national law. In *LZ II*, the ECJ applied the right to an effective remedy contained in Article 47 of the Charter of Fundamental Rights in conjunction with the Aarhus Convention, to hold that Union law precluded the Slovak procedural rules which made it impossible for the applicant environmental NGO to participate in the administrative permit procedure at issue in that case.[99]

The *LZ* judgments are complemented by a number of other judgments giving a robust interpretation of those few individual EU measures – namely, the IPPC Directive and EIA Directive – which do include express access to justice provisions. This has included conditions of access to justice relating to standing,[100] costs of legal proceedings,[101] level of competent tribunal,[102] availability of compensatory damages,[103] and the scope of application of these access to justice provisions.[104] Particularly notable in this regard is the ECJ's judgment in *Edwards*, concerning the meaning of the obligation to ensure that judicial proceedings should not be "prohibitively expensive" under the IPPC and EIA Directives.[105]

Separately, the Aarhus Convention Compliance Committee has found that the EU's own restrictive conditions of *locus standi* under Article 263 TFEU actions, discussed at Chapter 10, are contrary to that Convention's access to justice rules.[106] Nor, in the Committee's view, does Regulation 1367/2006 compensate for these shortcomings, as that Regulation has been interpreted by the CJEU as restricting internal review of administrative acts to those of individual scope, in apparent contradistinction to Article 9(3) of the Aarhus Convention.[107] In so finding, the Committee directly criticized the jurisprudence of the ECJ on the matter. In turn, the September 2017 Meeting of the Parties to the Aarhus Convention (a majority of which are Union Member States) declined to "endorse" the findings of the Committee, in favour of merely "noting" them.[108] This remarkable situation has cast a significant shadow over the Union's relationship with the Aarhus Convention.

---

98. Ibid., paras. 50–51.
99. Case C-243/15, *Lesoochranárske zoskupenie*.
100. Namely, Case C-115/09, *Bund für Umwelt und Naturschutz Deutschland, Landesverband Nordrhein-Westfalen (Trianel)* (German law restricting standing in EIA and IPPC matters to those environmental associations who can demonstrate impairment of rights is contrary to EIA/IPPC access to justice provisions).
101. Case C-260/11, *Edwards*.
102. Case C-416/10, *Križan* (access to justice provisions of IPPC directive allow Member State discretion as to level of tribunal competent to regularize breach of access to information provisions, as long as principles of effectiveness and equivalence of remedies are respected).
103. Case C-420/11, *Leth* (failure to carry out EIA does not in principle in itself confer right to compensation on individual for pecuniary damage caused by decrease in value of property due to negative environmental effects).
104. Joined Cases C-128/09 to C-131/09, C-134/09 and C-135/09, *Boxus* and Case C-182/10, *Solvay* (fact that approval for a prect that would otherwise be subject to EIA was given by legislative measure cannot exclude EIA access to justice provisions).
105. Case C-260/11, *Edwards*.
106. See Case ACCC/C/2008/32, Findings and recommendations adopted on 14 Apr. 2011 (Part I) and on 17 Mar. 2017 (Part II).
107. See *Council and Ors v. Vereniging Milieudefensie Stichting Stopluchtverontreiniging Utrecht;* and C-405/12 P, *Council and Commission v. Stichting Natuur en Milieu and Pesticide Action Network Europe v. Commission.*
108. The Commission's proposal to reject the findings of the Committee (COM(2017)366) was not accepted by the Council, which preferred to propose the deletion of the references to the ECJ in the Committee's

6. Overview of selected sectoral environmental policies

6.1 Climate and energy

In February 2010, the importance of climate policy to the EU was marked at an institutional level by the creation of a specific directorate-general of the European Commission devoted to climate issues (abbreviated as DG CLIMA). The creation of DG CLIMA followed the publication of the EU's flagship climate and energy package in 2009, aimed at reaching the so-called 20–20–20 targets by 2020 (i.e., achieving a 20% reduction in the EU's greenhouse gas (GHG) emissions compared to 1990 levels, achieving a 20% share of the EU's energy consumption for renewables and achieving a 20% improvement in the EU's energy efficiency).[109] The EU's flagship regulatory instrument for combating climate change has been the 2003 Emissions Trading Scheme (ETS) Directive, which created the world's first international emissions trading scheme covering, at least in its initial incarnation, carbon dioxide emissions from around 11,000 large industrial installations, amounting to around 40% of the EU's total greenhouse gas (GHG) emissions.[110] The aim of the EU ETS is essentially to put a price on GHG emissions, thus constituting a "market-based instrument" implementing the polluter pays principle, and incentivizing operators to reduce such emissions in a cost-effective way. Following considerable teething problems with the 2003 Directive – which meant, amongst other things, that the EU carbon price remained persistently low – it was revised in 2009.[111] The ETS has continued to suffer from problems, in part because the global recession has led to oversupply of allowances.

The ECJ has issued a number of judgments on the ETS, the most high-profile of which was the *ATAA* judgment,[112] where a challenge by the Air Transport Association of America and a number of US airlines to the inclusion of third country airlines within the scope of the ETS failed. In a lengthy and complex judgment, the Grand Chamber of the ECJ held that the application of the EU ETS to third country airlines was compatible with international law and, in particular, with the principle of territoriality, given that the scheme only applies to commercial aircraft that arrive at or depart from a Member State airport.[113]

Beyond the EU ETS, the EU's policy on renewable energy, energy efficiency and energy taxation, which also form part of its climate and energy package, are discussed at Chapter 32. Despite the challenges, there is evidence that the Union is succeeding in the aim of decoupling economic growth from increased carbon emissions. In 2016, Union greenhouse gas emissions were 23% below 1990 levels, in the context of a 53% increase in the size of the economy during this period.[114] Under the Paris Agreement of the United Nations Framework Convention on Climate Change, the Union has committed to achieve a 40% reduction in emissions, compared to 1990 levels, by 2030.[115]

6.2 Industrial pollution control

The principal legislation governing emissions from industrial installations is now the Industrial Emissions Directive, known in its former incarnation as the Integrated Pollution Prevention

---

findings, on grounds of separation of powers: Council Decision 2017/1346, O.J. 2017, L 186/15.

109. See Presidency Conclusions of the Council of the EU, 13 Feb. 2009, 17271/1/08.
110. Directive 2003/87/EC, O.J. 2003, L 275/23.
111. Directive 2009/29/EC, O.J. 2009, L 140/63.
112. Case C-366/10, *ATAA*.
113. Ibid., para 127.
114. Commissions Report to the Parliament and Council "Two years after Paris – Progress towards meeting the EU's climate commitments" (2017), available at <ec.europa.eu/clima>.
115. See also, the EU's Strategy on Adaptation to Climate Change COM(2013)216.

and Control (IPPC) Directive.[116] A key aim was to move away from sectoral, medium-specific emissions control (i.e., air emissions, water emissions, and so on) to regulating all of the emissions from large industrial installations in an integrated way. Individual licence conditions are decided on the basis of the Best Available Technique (BAT) standard, which varies depending on the industry at issue. The process of identifying the BAT for a specific industry is a reflexive one arrived at by a process of information exchange between regulators, regulates and environmental NGOs.[117]

6.3 *Control of chemical substances*

This field is now largely covered by the behemoth of the Regulation on the Registration, Evaluation Authorization and Restriction of Chemicals (REACH), which came into force on 1 June 2007.[118] REACH established a registration obligation for chemical substances in order to document the safe use of such substances and to provide information on their hazards, enabling manufacturers to outline risk management measures. This is part of a four-step process – registration, evaluation, authorization and restriction of chemicals.

The Regulation places the onus on the manufacturers and importers of chemicals to research and gather information on the substance and to register this with European Chemicals Agency, which was established in 2007 by Title X of the Regulation. Registration is required for substances placed on the market or produced in the EU in quantities of more than one tonne a year.[119] Information on chemicals is to be generated wherever possible by means other than animal testing.[120] Substances are then evaluated by the Agency, in conjunction with the Member States via, in particular, the Agency's Member State Committee. Substances of "very high concern" are subject to authorization pursuant to Title VII of the Regulation, and Article 55 thereof encourages manufacturers and importers to seek viable alternatives to such substances. Further, under the restriction procedure, substances on the Annex XVII by Commission Decision where it is found to pose an unacceptable risk to human health or the environment. Where this occurs, the substance shall not be placed on the market, manufactured or used unless it complies with the restriction.[121] REACH is considered to be one of the flagship examples of the EU's precautionary approach to environmental and health hazards.

6.4 *Environmental impact assessment and Strategic environmental impact assessment*

The procedural requirement to carry out an environmental impact assessment applies, by virtue of the Environmental Impact Assessment (EIA) Directive, to projects likely to have significant effects on the environment.[122] The impact assessment must be carried out prior to grant of development consent.[123] For certain projects, listed in Annex I, an impact assessment is mandatory; for others, listed in Annex II, the Member State determines whether an assessment is necessary on a case-by-case basis.[124] As noted above, the EU amended the EIA Directive in 2003 to implement the Aarhus Convention requirements of public participation and access

116. Directive 2010/75/EU O.J. 2010, L 334/17; Directive 2008/1/EC, O.J. 2008, L 24/8 (as codified).
117. Industrial Emissions Directive, O.J. 2010, L 334/17, Art. 13(1).
118. Reg. (EC) 1907/2006 L 396/1.
119. Ibid., Arts. 5 and 6.
120. Ibid., Art. 13.
121. Ibid., Art. 67.
122. The original EIA Directive dates from 1985, but is now codified in Directive 2011/92/EU O.J. 2012, L 26/1, as amended.
123. EIA Directive, Art. 2(1).
124. Ibid., Art. 4(2).

to justice, meaning that stricter EU law requirements apply in this regard here than in other areas of EU environmental law. The Strategic Environmental Assessment (SEA) Directive requires an environmental impact assessment to be carried out at the higher level of policy formation, namely in the case of plans and programmes prepared by public authorities and likely to have significant environmental effects.[125] However, it remains the case that each of these Directives impose largely procedural obligations, and do not require decision-makers to take whatever decision is best for the environment.

6.5 *Biodiversity and nature conservation*

The EU's flagship nature conservation laws remain the 1979 Birds Directive and the 1992 Habitats Directive,[126] which each follow a broadly similar regulatory technique. In the case of the Birds Directive, Member States are obliged *inter alia* to take special conservation measures for a number of bird species listed in Annex I of the Directive. This includes designating suitable territories for these species as Special Protection Areas (SPAs).[127] In the case of the Habitats Directive, Member States are obliged to designate Special Areas of Conservation (SACs) to protect the habitats and species listed in Annex I and Annex II respectively, with some of these singled out as priority habitats/species for protection.[128] Together, the designated SPAs and SACs form a network of nature conservation zones spanning the EU known as the Natura 2000 network, which accounts for 18% of the Union's terrestrial land and almost 6% of its marine territory.

Article 6 of the Habitats Directive specifies a range of heightened conservation obligations incumbent on Member States within SACs and (following amendment of the Birds Directive) SPAs. These include broadly-worded obligations, such as establishing the "necessary conservation measures", and taking "appropriate steps to avoid" deterioration of habitats and species. However, more precise obligations are contained in Article 6(3), which provides that the competent national authorities may only authorize a plan or project not directly connected with or necessary to the management of the site but likely to have a significant effect thereon after having ascertained, by means of an appropriate assessment of the implications of that plan or project for the site, that it will not adversely affect the integrity of the site. In *Waddenzee*, the ECJ interpreted Article 6(3) in light of the precautionary principle, discussed above, to hold that an appropriate assessment of the implications of a plan or project for a site's conservation objectives must be carried out if it "cannot be excluded, on the basis of objective information, that it will have a significant effect on that site, either individually or in combination with other plans or projects".[129] Following such assessment, the activity could be authorized only if the national authorities "have made certain that it will not adversely affect the integrity of the site", meaning that "no reasonable scientific doubt remains as to the absence of such effects".[130] Where a Member State can show that their plan or project is necessary for imperative requirements of

---

125. Directive 2001/42/EC, O.J. 2001, L 197/30.
126. Council Directive 79/409/EEC of 2 Apr. 1979 on the conservation of wild birds O.J. 1979, L 103/1; Council Directive 92/43/EEC of 21 May 1992 on the conservation of natural habitats and of wild fauna and flora O.J. 1992, L 206/7.
127. Wild Birds Directive, Art. 4.
128. Habitats Directive, Art. 3.
129. Case C-127/02, *Landelijke Vereniging tot Behoud van de Waddenze*, para 45.
130. Ibid., para 61. In *Sweetman v. An Bord Pleanála*, the ECJ interpreted the requirement not to adversely affect the "integrity of the site" as requiring the "the lasting preservation of the constitutive characteristics of the site concerned that are connected to the presence of [the] natural habitat type" being protected: Case C-258/11.

public interest, however, Article 6(4) permits them to go ahead as long as they take "compensatory measures" to ensure that the overall coherence of Natura 2000 is protected.[131]

In December 2016, following a so-called "fitness check" of the Habitats and Birds Directives pursuant to the Commission's broader Regulatory Fitness and Performance (REFIT) Programme, the Commission concluded that the Directives remain "fit for purpose", despite significant under-implementation problems.[132]

Further reading

Brundtland, G.H. et al., *Our Common Future* (OUP, 1987).

Clément, M., *Droit européen de l'environnement*, 3rd ed. (Éditions Larcier, 2017).

De Sadeleer, N., *Environnement et marché intérieur*, 3rd ed. (Commentaire J. Mégret, 2010)

Hedemann-Robinson, M., *Enforcement of European Union Environmental Law* 2nd ed. (Routledge, 2015).

Jones, G. (Ed.) *The Habitats Directive: A Developer's Obstacle Course?* (Hart, 2012).

Jordan, A. and C. Adelle, *Environmental policy in the European Union: actors, institutions and processes*, 3rd ed. (Routledge, 2013).

Kingston S. (Ed.), *European Perspectives on Environmental Law and Policy* (Routledge, 2013).

Kingston, S., V. Heyvaert and A. Čavoški, *European Environmental Law* (CUP, 2017).

Morgera E. (Ed.), *The External Environmental Policy of the European Union – EU and International Law Perspectives* (CUP, 2012).

Sands P. and J. Peel, *Principles of International Environmental Law*, 3rd ed. (CUP, 2012).

Verschuuren, J., "Innovatie en milieuregelgeving", 42 *Milieu & recht* (2015), 596.

131. In the case of priority species, the permissible justifications are more narrowly defined: see Art. 6(4) and see, interpreting that provision, Case C-399/14, *Grüne Liga Sachsen*.

132. Commission Staff Working Document SWD(2016)472.

CHAPTER 37
RESEARCH AND TECHNOLOGY

*Morag Goodwin**

1. Introduction

The Lisbon Agenda, agreed at the 2000 European Council meeting in Lisbon, set the new strategic goal of improving the competitiveness of the European economy to become the most competitive and dynamic knowledge economy in the world. This required, *inter alia*, a shift to a "dynamic, knowledge-based economy", a focus on the "knowledge triangle" of education, research and innovation, and the establishment of a European area for research and innovation, thereby placing policy in the areas of research and technology at the heart of the EU's strategic goals.[1] This position was maintained in the follow-up Europe 2020 strategy, launched in 2010.[2] The Lisbon Agenda has seen a shift from a position in which the Commission was restricted by the need to demonstrate that European co-ordination "added value" at each stage of policy-making to one in which the Union gained shared competences with the Member States in the area of Research and Development in the Lisbon Treaty.

The connection between the Union's commitment to industrial competitiveness and technological progress entails that research and technology have played a central role in realizing the Union's most fundamental objectives from the beginning, although a dedicated title did not appear in the treaties until the Single European Act. However, recognition of the need to better co-ordinate research and technology policies at the European level and efforts to facilitate it begin at the end of the 1950s with the EURATOM Treaty. The need to better co-ordinate research and technology policies so as to improve European competitiveness against its main international rivals of the U.S. and Japan is a recurrent theme of European research policy debates, re-stated with each new initiative calling for further co-operation and co-ordination. Yet despite the creation of the European Research Area in 2000, its re-launch under the Ljubljana Process in 2008 and its centrality to the 2020 Strategy, Member States continue to resist attempts by the Commission to integrate research and technology policy, preferring to limit such efforts to the Framework Programmes and to maintain decentralized, national efforts. The compatibility of Commission efforts with national rules and procedures remains a constant problem. The failure of the Member States to co-ordinate their activities in this area has thus ensured that EU efforts

---

* Law Faculty, University of Tilburg.

1. Lisbon European Council, Presidency Conclusions, 23–24 Mar. 2000. See also the 2004 W. Kok report reviewing the Lisbon Strategy, which suggested the need for urgent action and the making of research and development a top priority at all levels: "Facing the challenge – The Lisbon strategy for growth and employment", report from the High Level Group chaired by W. Kok (European Communities, 2004), 6.
2. Commission Communication, Europe 2020: "A strategy for smart, sustainable and inclusive growth", COM(2010)2020 final.

remain largely restricted to exhortatory documents and initiatives and to funding programmes, through which efforts are made to co-ordinate activities and secure better co-operation.

The European Union has a range of competences in the area of research and technology, primarily in order to facilitate co-operation and fund initiatives according to the priorities laid down by the Council and Parliament. The purpose of the Union's competences in this area is largely related to the furtherance of the Union's economic objectives, notably competitiveness at the international level.[3] The 2020 Strategy, however, has broadened the aims of research and technology policy to include social cohesion and jobs; and the Lisbon Treaty has removed the explicit connection between research and competitiveness, highlighting instead the need to promote all research activities required by commitments in the treaty, for example in health.

In addition to Union activities in research, innovation and technology, there are important inter-governmental initiatives at a broader European level that are worth mentioning: COST (European Co-operation in Science and Technology) and EUREKA. These networks are dedicated to international co-operation in long-term application-orientated research bridging private and public partnerships. The membership of both networks is broader than the EU Member States, with COST boasting 35 members and EUREKA slightly more, with 41 members drawn from the wider geographical Europe.[4]

2. Legal framework[5]

Article 4 of the Treaty on the Functioning of the European Union places research and technology, including policy in relation to outer space, within the ambit of shared competences. Specifically, it provides that "the Union shall have competence to carry out activities, in particular to define and implement programmes; however, the exercise of that competence shall not result in Member States being prevented from exercising theirs".[6] This wording makes it clear that, contrary to the "pre-emptive clause" in Article 2 TFEU,[7] the Union's competences in the area of research and development do not pre-empt Member State competence but are complementary to the activities of the Member States. In addition to shared competences, the Union enjoys a role in co-ordinating and supporting research in specific areas in a number of separate fields that span exclusive, shared and co-ordinating competences; for example, public health, crime prevention and agricultural policy.[8]

Title XIX TFEU is dedicated to Research and Technological Development and Space and determines the scope and possibilities for all Union activities within this field.[9] It is clear from Article 179 TFEU that one of the key purposes of Union action in this field is to enhance industrial competitiveness and that it is to achieve this by strengthening the European scientific and technological base and by establishing a European Research Area that enables the free circulation of researchers. To this end, the Union is obligated to "encourage undertakings, including small and medium-sized undertakings, research centres and universities in their research and technological development activities of high quality" throughout the Union. This, however, is not sufficient to achieve the research goals laid down in the Treaty; instead, competitiveness requires co-operation and thus Article 179 TFEU instructs the Union to provide support to

3. As part of the Europe 2020 strategy, Member States committed to increasing investment in R&D to 3% of GDP, in line with spending in the US and Japan.
4. See <www.cost.eu> and <www.eurekanetwork.org> (last accessed 8 Jan. 2015).
5. For more on the general competences of the Union, see Ch. 3, "System of competences", of this book.
6. Art. 4(3) TFEU.
7. As provided in Art. 2(2) TFEU.
8. Arts. 168, 87(2)(b), 41 TFEU respectively.
9. Art. 179(3) TFEU.

research actors in cooperating with one another across the internal market. This support is to include the implementation of research, technological development and demonstration programmes, the promotion of cooperation with third countries and international organizations, the dissemination and optimization of research results and the stimulation of the training and mobility of researchers.[10] In addition, emphasis in achieving greater competitiveness is laid upon the opening-up of national public contracts i.e. procurement,[11] the definition of common standards and the removal of legal and fiscal obstacles to cooperation in this area, such as divergent national patent protection rules.[12]

Title XIX no longer makes explicit the link between research and technology and the formation of the internal market and competition policy: under the Lisbon Treaty, Article 179 TFEU balances the reference to enhancing competitiveness with the need to promote "all the research activities deemed necessary by virtue of other Chapters of the Treaties." Instead this link is found in Title XVII of the TFEU on Industry, Research and Technology, which obligates the Union and the Member States to ensure the necessary conditions for industrial competitiveness. It is this title that provides the legal basis for some elements of the research and innovation framework, such as the European Institute of Innovation and Training (EIT) (see section 4.3 below). There remains, though, a strong link between the goals laid down for the European Research Area and the application of competition policy under Article 101 and 102 TFEU.[13] Similarly, there is a clear connection with rules on state aid, with reforms to the state aid regime resulting in the creation of a block exemption for activities for which the market failed to provide the necessary incentives, including research and development, innovation, and support to small- and medium-sized enterprises.[14]

The particular nature of shared competences, made clear by Article 4 TFEU, does not prevent the Union from taking the lead in large-scale, expensive projects. Article 187 empowers the Union to establish joint undertakings "or any other structure necessary for the efficient execution of Union research, technological development and demonstration programmes". For example, Joint Technology Initiatives (JTIs) – public-private partnerships, involving industry, the research community and public authorities – were established in 2007 on the basis of Article 187 to support large-scale multi-national research activities in areas considered key to European industrial competitiveness and issues of high societal relevance; Nanoelectronics Technologies

---

10. Art. 180 TFEU.
11. For more on the rules of public procurement, see Ch. 22, "Public procurement", of this book.
12. See, e.g., Case C-10/10, *Commission v. Austria,* para 37 (a free movement of capital case), in which the ECJ found that despite its earlier finding in Case C-39/04, *Laboratoires Fournier,* para 23, that research and development could constitute an over-ridding public interest for restricting free movement, Austria's actions in limiting tax deductibility to national research activities directly contradicted the objectives laid down in Art. 179, which explicitly encourages co-operation in research precisely by removing legal and fiscal obstacles.
13. S. Bishop and M. Walker, *The Economics of EC Competition Law: Concepts, Application and Measurement,* 3rd ed. (Sweet & Maxwell, 2010).
14. State Aid Action Plan, "Less and better targeted state aid: A roadmap for state aid reform 2005–2009", COM(2005)107 final. Commission Reg. (EC) 800/2008 of 6 Aug. 2008 declaring certain categories of aid compatible with the common market in application of Arts. 87 and 88 of the Treaty (General Block Exemption Reg.), O.J. 2008, L 214/3. This regulation was amended by Commission Reg. (EU) 651/2014 of 17 June 2014 declaring certain categories of aid compatible with the internal market in application of Arts. 107 and 108 of the Treaty, O.J. 2014, L 187/1. See, also, recent unsuccessful actions for annulment before the General Court concerning alleged state aid to research institutions: Case T-198/09, *UOP Ltd. v. European Commission,* 7 Mar. 2013; Case T-488/11, *Scheepsbouwkundig Advies- en Rekencentrum (Sarc) BV v. European Commission,* 12 June 2014. My thanks to Andrea Gideon for drawing my attention to these cases.

2020 (ENIAC) is a good example of a Joint Undertaking established under this part of the 7th Framework Programme.[15]

A large proportion of the provisions under Title XIX, Articles 182–186, provide for and lay down the extent of co-operation within the Union's frameworks programmes. The level of detail accorded the Framework Programmes in the treaty indicates the importance of these instruments as the main means of realizing the Union's research and development goals. Article 190 TFEU requires the Commission to report annually to the Council and the Parliament on the Union's research and technology activities of the preceding year and the plans for the up-coming year.

A number of EU instruments detail rights for researchers at the European level, with the most important being Article 13 of the Charter of Fundamental Rights.[16] This provision commits the Union institutions and Member States to respecting academic freedom. This freedom is re-stated in the Charter for European Researchers,[17] which provides, in addition, a set of general principles and requirements specifying the roles, responsibilities and entitlements of researchers as well as of employers and of funders. This latter Charter, unlike the Charter of Fundamental Rights, is a voluntary code and thus has no binding force even upon those institutions or bodies that have endorsed it.

3. Decision-making procedure

Under the Lisbon Treaty, decision-making in the area of research and technology now takes the form of a combination of the ordinary legislative procedure, the special legislative procedure and the Open Method of Co-ordination (OMC). Article 182(5) TFEU provides that measures necessary for the establishment of the European Research Area (ERA) will be adopted by means of the ordinary legislative procedure. Likewise, Article 189(2) TFEU lays down that actions in the area of space research and policy-making, including any harmonization of Member State laws and regulations, are subject to the ordinary legislative procedure. The adoption of the multi-annual funding programmes under Article 182 TFEU is, under the terms of Article 182(4) TFEU, subject to a special legislative procedure; this takes the form of a unanimous decision by the Council following consultation with the Parliament and the Economic and Social Committee. The details of the framework programmes, such as the rules for participation in and dissemination of research, the creation of supplementary programmes and joint programming, are, however, subject to the ordinary legislative procedure, following consultation with the Economic and Social Committee.[18] The establishment of Joint Undertakings (such as Joint Technology Initiatives (JTIs) – see section 4.4 below) under the terms of Article 187 TFEU is also, as provided in Article 188 TFEU, subject to a special legislative procedure, again following consultation not only with the Parliament but also with the Economic and Social Committee. The changes under Lisbon, noted above, have thus given the European Parliament a greater say in policy-making in this area, although the shift to co-decision procedure began with the Treaties of Maastricht and Amsterdam.

---

15. Established by Council Reg. 72/2008 (O.J. 2008, L 30.21. For this JU project website, available at <www.eniac.eu/web/index.php>.
16. Charter of the Fundamental Rights of the European Union (2012/C 326/02), O.J. 2010, C 326/391. Formally, of course, the Charter does not create any new rights (see the preamble) and it only applies where Member States act within the scope of EU law.
17. Available at <ec.europa.eu/euraxess/index.cfm/rights/europeanCharter>.
18. Art. 188 TFEU (ex Art. 172 TEC), referring to Arts. 183, 184 and 185 TFEU respectively.

In keeping with the retention by Member States of competence in the area of research and technology policy at the national level (where most policy-making in this area remains) and the preference of Member States for maintaining the independence of national research policies, the decision was taken by the Competitiveness Council in 2002 to apply the Open Method of Co-ordination to the area of Research and Development and to make it the main means of realizing the ERA (after the Framework Programmes).[19] This decision has been seen by at least one commentator as undermining the ERA and a rejection of the Commission's attempts to introduce legislative measures in the area of research and development.[20] The EU's Scientific and Technical Research Committee (CREST) was entrusted as the interface between Member States in applying OMC; an example of early OMC in this area is the CREST Collaboration Decision Guide, which is designed to help potential R&D collaborators decide on the best way to manage their collaboration.[21] CREST was renamed the European Research Area Committee (ERAC) in a 2010 Resolution of the Competitiveness Council, which laid down a new mandate for the body that better accommodates the shared competences in this area.[22]

4. European Research Area

The European Research Area (ERA) was introduced by the European Commission in 2000 and adopted by the European Council in the same year.[23] It has been described as a "sweeping reform" to European R&D policy-making – one that, it is claimed, took the research community in Europe by surprise.[24] The ERA forms an integral part of the Lisbon Strategy. Although the ERA was absent from the 2005–2008 Lisbon Integrated Guidelines (which spoke instead of a European Knowledge Area), in the 2008–2010 Community Lisbon Programme (CLP) the ERA merits a specific objective: objective 6 provides that "the Community will make the "fifth freedom", the free movement of knowledge, a reality and create a genuine European Research Area".[25] As Prange-Gstöhl notes, this is the first time that the so-called "fifth freedom" is presented as a clear objective in an official EU document and the realization of the ERA is presented as a necessary part of integration and the internal market.[26]

The aim of the ERA, as expressed in the original Commission proposal, is to give research a more central role in the European economy and in society by strengthening co-operation and

19. Council Conclusions of 26 Nov. 2002 on progress made in the development of the European Research Area and on providing it with new momentum, 5742/03, 28 Jan. 2003.
20. H. Prange-Gstöhl (Ed.), *International Science and Technology Cooperation in a Globalized World* (European Commisson, 2010), 5.
21. Report of the CREST OMC Expert Group on Intellectual Property (2nd Cycle), Cross-Border Collaboration between Publicly Funded Research Organisations and Industry and Technology Transfer Training, 1st Sept. 2006; available at <ec.europa.eu/invest-in-research/pdf/download_en/crestreport.pdf>.
22. Resolution on the developments in the governance of the European Research Area, 3016th Competitiveness Council meeting, Brussels, 26 May 2010; available at <ec.europa.eu/research/era/docs/en/council-resolution-on-era-governance_26-05-10.pdf >.
23. European Commission, "Towards a European research area"; European Council, Council Resolution of 15 June 2000 on establishing a European area of research and innovation (2000/C 205/01).
24. S. Kuhlmann and J. Edler, "Changing governance in European research and technology policy. Possible trajectories and the European research area" in J. Edler, S. Kuhlmann and M. Behrens (Eds.), *Changing Governance of Research and Technology Policy* (Edward Elgar, 2003), 3.
25. European Commission, "Proposal for a Community Lisbon programme 2008–2010", COM(2007)804 final (European Communities, 2007), 14. See also, European Commissioner for Science and Research J. Potočnik, "The EU's fifth freedom: Creating free movement of knowledge", speech delivered at Würzburg (Germany) on 26 Apr. 2007.
26. H. Prange-Gstöhl, op. cit. *supra* note 20, 6.

optimizing the allocation of resources. The ERA is structured around three "ideals": the creation of an "internal market" in research, which consists in a genuine area of free movement of knowledge, researchers and technology; a restructuring of the European research space, by improving the coordination of national research activities and policies; and the development of a European research policy that goes beyond the simple funding of research activities but extends to the development of shared values. An example of the latter is the emphasis on encouraging the participation of women in science and the concern with gender equality and gender mainstreaming across European and national research activities.[27] The ERA was expected to lead to a common European model for research by overcoming the "fragmentations" of the European research space into national/European, public/private and university/enterprise divisions; initiatives here include the European Charter for Researchers and the Code of Conduct for the Recruitment for Researchers, both of which are voluntary but which are implemented through the ERA's funding instruments.[28]

The concept of the ERA got off to a slow start but was given new life with the Commission's 2007 Green Paper "The European Research Area: New Perspectives", proposals given concrete form in the 2008 "Ljubljana Process". At the June 2008 Council meeting, Member States recommitted themselves to developing a "common vision and effective governance of the European Research Area".[29] This commitment took the form of inviting the Commission, through the Competitiveness Council, to propose new instruments capable of realizing the coherence in synergy between research policies recognized as vital to improving European competitiveness.[30]

Despite the importance attached to enhancing co-ordination between research policies in order to achieve the large-scale necessary to challenge the competitive dominance of Japan and the US, the Member States retain their central role. As the original Commission ERA proposal noted, national research activities constitute the great majority of spending on research and technology and much of the ERA has thus been directed towards national research policies, with the emphasis being on co-operation rather than co-ordination. In its 2014 Conclusions on the ERA, the Council emphasizes the central role of the Member States, noting that while "EU funding programmes foster transnational cooperation of research among the Member States, it is primarily for the Member States to define shared strategies and unlock national resources to achieve higher impact of research in a context of limited public research funding available".[31] The Council thus calls upon the Commission together with the Member States to establish an ERA-roadmap by mid-2015 with the main purpose of agreeing a set of tools and best practices "to support the Member States in developing and implementing their national policies in ways which correspond with their respective specificities and priorities". It is thus Member State priorities that are to continue to lead the further development of the ERA.

---

27. Available at <ec.europa.eu/research/era/gender-equality-and-gender-mainstreaming_en.htm>; however, the commitment by the Commission to produce a proposal for a Recommendation to Member States with common guidelines on institutional change to promote gender equality in universities and research institutions is apparently yet to materialize (as of Nov. 2014). Gender mainstreaming does, though, form a key part of Horizon 2020.
28. The Charter and Code of Conduct are available at <ec.europa.eu/euraxess/index.cfm/rights/europeanCharter> (last accessed 29 Nov. 2014).
29. Council Conclusions, doc. 10231/08, 3 June 2008, at 3.
30. Examples include the Communication on a European Partnership for Researchers, adopted on 23 May 2008 (COM2008317 final); "Towards Joint Programming of Research", adopted on 15 July 2008 (COM2008468 final) and "A communication on a strategic framework for international science and technology co-operation", adopted on 24 Sept. 2008, COM2008588 final.
31. Council Conclusions of 21 Feb. 2014, 3.

An important part of the ERA is the commitment to open access, with the goal of creating a digital ERA in which information moves freely throughout the ERA digital space.[32] Breaking onto the agenda in 2006, open access enjoys a prominent place in Horizon 2020.

The ERA also has an external dimension. Where early efforts in developing an international science and technology (S&T) policy were based on *ad hoc* initiatives through the Framework Programmes, and most of the early efforts on the part of the Commission to internationalize the ERA were thwarted by the Members States,[33] the re-vamping of the ERA in the Ljubljana Process saw Member States more willing to take a strategic approach to international S&T co-operation.[34] Using the OMC, Member States and associated countries set up a CREST working group in 2007 to identify areas and countries were joint action would generate the most added value. The external dimension of the ERA mirrors the internal structure, fostering co-operation between research institutions, public and private, inside and outside the Union and facilitating access to knowledge, resources and infrastructures.

Given the continuing centrality of Member States' individual research priorities, and thus their unwillingness to commit to collective goals and standards, the role of the Union in attempting to realize the ERA is confined to providing funding to stimulate the co-operation that it cannot mandate. The Framework Programmes, notably FP6 and FP7, constituted the main financial instrument of the ERA's realization; this has now been replaced by Horizon 2020. What follows in this section is an overview of the main funding instruments, and the bodies created to manage them, that form the backbone of the Union's efforts to create the ERA.

4.1 *The Framework Programmes and Horizon 2020*

The multi-annual Framework Programmes (FP) constitute the main instrument of a common European research policy. Started in 1983 on the basis of Article 166(1) TEC with a budget of €3.75 billion, the aim was to integrate the already existing Community technology programmes. Following reforms in the Maastricht Treaty, FPs were able to pursue research activities at the EU level beyond those necessary only to meet research-related goals explicitly provided for in the treaty. The seventh FP (2007–2013) brought major changes, notably a significant budget increase from €16.2 billion under FP6 to €50 billion under FP7. In addition, new instruments were introduced to better co-ordinate research programmes and policies. ERA-NETs-PLUS were introduced to complement the ERA-NETs, established under FP6 to coordinate the national and regional programmes of the Member States; these new instruments provide Community funds to finance joint calls with national and regional programmes and attempt to integrate national research programmes into new joint programmes under Article 169.

Horizon 2020 is the successor funding framework to the Framework Programmes.[35] It is to run from 2014–2020 and has a budget of €80 billion of public funding.[36] The Horizon 2020 framework is complemented by separate work programmes for the European Research Council,

---

32. See Commission Recommendation of 17 July 2012 on access to and preservation of scientific information (2012/417/EU); O.J. 2012, L 194/39; also Commission Communication, "Towards better access to scientific information: Boosting the benefits of public investments in research", 17 July 2012, COM(2012)401 final.
33. H. Prange-Gstöhl, op. cit. *supra* note 20, 11–12. H. Prange-Gstöhl notes "[i]t is not presumptuous to claim that an international EU research policy or strategy hardly existed".
34. The Commission's proposals for a strategic European framework for international S&T co-operation were finally endorsed by the Member States at the Competitiveness Council in Dec. 2008; Council Conclusions concerning a European partnership for international scientific and technological co-operation, 2891st Competitiveness Council meeting, Brussels, 2 Dec. 2008.
35. Horizon 2020 – The Framework Programme for Research and Innovation, COM(2011)808 final.
36. It is expected that private funding shall be additional.

Euratom, the Joint Research Centre and the Strategic Innovation Agenda for the European Institute of Innovation and Technology (EIT). Horizon 2020 is dedicated primarily to the realization of the "Innovation Union", one of the flagship initiatives of the Europe 2020 Strategy. It is divided into multi-annual work programmes. In Horizon 2020 the emphasis is upon eight "key drivers" identified by the Commission as essential in helping Europe exit the current economic crisis and build smart, sustainable and inclusive growth. These drivers are:

- focusing on parts of the societal challenges with high potential for sustainable competiveness, innovation and growth;
- using dedicated measures to leverage and boost engagement of industry, including SMEs;
- providing access to finance, which is an essential condition for successful innovation;
- developing the new knowledge and contributing to skills, which underpin excellent research and innovation, and promoting EU excellence;
- boosting the industrial deployment of enabling technologies;
- addressing the research and innovation divide;
- supporting strong partnership with Member States; and
- ensuring a strategic approach to international cooperation, strengthen the EU"s scientific excellence and its economic competitiveness, to jointly tackle global societal challenges and contribute to the EU's external policies.

These drivers form the basis of Horizon 2020 and are the focus of its first Work Programme.

In drawing up the first Work Programme for 2014–2015, the Commission has taken a new approach to programme design. The aim of this approach is to increase impact through integration, coherence and evidence-based implementation. This approach is to be underpinned by strategic programming, which includes fewer funding opportunities ("calls"), fewer topics and fewer types of action than under FP7; for example, the introduction of ERA-NETs-PLUS under FP7 to complement the already existing ERA-NETs has been slimmed down under Horizon 2020 into a single instrument with one substantial funding call.[37] Horizon 2020 approach is also said to adopt a challenge-based approach to call design. The purpose of the challenge-based approach is intended to stimulate more multi-disciplinary and more multi-sectoral proposals. The integrated approach is seen by the Commission to be essential in areas of cross-cutting activities and finds representation in the "focus areas" that translate into specific calls within the part of the Programme dedicated to societal challenges. The aim for the focus areas is that they enable scale and critical mass. In addition, cross-cutting challenges, such as gender or international strategy, have been mainstreamed across the different sections of the Work Programme. Smart integration with other initiatives, such as the Joint Programming Initiatives (JPI), is also an important goal of Horizon 2020.

Horizon 2020 has a three pillar structure: the first pillar "Excellent Science" has a budget of 24 billion euro and is dedicated to funding basic scientific research, notably Future and Emerging Technologies (FETs), large European research infrastructures as well as researcher mobility through the Marie Skłodowska-Curie Action programmes. In addition, the European Research

37. This simplified approach addresses one of the main criticisms of the Framework Programmes: that they were too complex for researchers to navigate. See, for one version of this criticism, Green Paper, *From Challenges to Opportunities: Towards a Common Strategic Framework for EU Research and Innovation funding* (Austrian Research Promotion Agency, 2011). Similar arguments have been made for a number of years by Science Europe – a body representing 51 European research funding organizations; see interview with Science Europe President, Prof. P. Boyle, 13 Mar. 2013; <horizon2020projects.com/pr-interviews/interview-supporting-science> (last accessed 17 Feb. 2015).

Council (ERC) operates under this first pillar to deliver €13 billion to individual researchers and teams of researchers based on scientific excellence. The second pillar, run by DG Enterprise, is entitled "Leadership in Enabling and Industrial Technologies (LEIT)" and is directed particularly towards funding for SMEs. The six sub-themes of the second pillar – ICT; Nanotechnologies; Advanced materials; Advanced manufacturing and processing; Biotechnology; and Space – all have a corresponding European Technology Platform (ETP) and a number have a corresponding Joint Technology Initiative (JTI) (see section 4.4. below). The third Horizon 2020 pillar addresses "Societal Challenges" and is split into seven sub-themes: Health; Food, water, forestry, bio-economy; Energy; Transport; Environment including climate change adaptation and raw materials; European society; and Security.

The Framework Programmes faced a number of criticisms; the most common concerned the complexity of the instruments (as noted above) and their impenetrability to non-insiders. A more fundamental criticism is that the Framework Programmes themselves simply have not achieved their goal of enhancing European competitiveness; quite simply, it has been claimed, no supranational European integration has taken place within research policy.[38] A more cutting critique has suggested that the Framework Programmes themselves are largely to blame for this failure, undercutting the formation of a European Research Area by creating clientele networks designed primarily to meet FP call criteria and by distracting the energies of the Commission in these excessively large and complex programmes.[39] It is for this reason that the Commission has proclaimed Horizon 2020 as a "break from the past";[40] it is of course too soon to say whether this self-declared optimism is justified.

The response to the first sets of calls under Horizon 2020, however, has been, in the widely reported words of Robert-Jan Smits, director-general of DG Research and Innovation, "overwhelming".[41] In the first round that closed in June 2014, 16,000 applications for funding were received, meaning that the programme was over-subscribed by a factor of nine. Yet the Commission's success in attracting applicants has reportedly dropped the success rate of those same applicants from 22% under FP7 to just 11% under the new programme.[42] The second wave in September 2014 appears to have been as successful, with, for example, the Executive Agency for SMEs (EASME) recording an additional 1,900 applications.[43] Much of this new enthusiasm for the EU funding programme is likely to be a result of severe cut-backs in public funding for research right across Europe but particularly in countries such as Greece, Italy and Spain. Yet the figures also suggest that the number of industry participants in consortium proposals has risen significantly, as has the number of proposals submitted by SMEs – both of which were goals of the new programme. The number of submissions from women is also up slightly, from 20% under FP7 to 23% in the first round of Horizon 2020.

---

38. This critique in particular has been made by T. Banchoff, "Institutions, inertia and European Union research policy", 40 JCMS (2002), 1.
39. Ibid.
40. Horizon 2020, "The framework programme for research and innovation", COM(2011)808 final, at 2.
41. Smits was speaking at the 2014 Euroscience Open Forum in Copenhagen, 24 June 2014. His comments were reported; see, for example, <www.linkedin.com/groups/Record-numbers-apply-Horizon-2020-4660030.S.5895184765836869635> (last accessed 18 Feb. 2015).
42. Thus while the programme can be said to be successful in attracting applicants, perhaps because of the heralded simplifications, a great deal of potential research time has been invested in preparing proposals that have little chance of success.
43. Available at <ec.europa.eu/easme/en/news/sme-instrument-more-1900-new-applications-received> (last accessed 18 Feb. 2015).

4.2 *Competitiveness and Innovation Programme*

A number of existing programmes were realigned under the Lisbon Strategy to operate in conjunction with the Seventh Framework Programme. The Competitiveness and Innovation Programme (CIP) was one of these and was presented as one of the Union's main tool for supporting progress towards achieving the goals of the Lisbon Strategy.[44] The CIP ran from 2007 to 2013 with a budget of €3621 million. The CIP was targeted at small and medium-sized enterprises (SMEs) and was designed to support innovation activities (including eco-innovation), provide better access to finance and deliver business support services in the regions. One of its main activities was to encourage a better take-up and use of information and communication technologies (ICT) among SMEs. It was divided into three operational programmes: the Entrepreneurship and Innovation Programme (EIP); the Information Communication Technologies Policy Support Programme (ICT-PSP); and the Intelligent Energy Europe Programme (IEE).

The CIP was replaced under Horizon 2020 with COSME. Created under Articles 173 and 195 TFEU, COSME is the EU programme for the Competitiveness of Enterprises and Small and Medium-sized Enterprises (SMEs).[45] As with Horizon 2020, it runs from 2014 to 2020 and it has a planned budget of €2.3 billion. According to its founding instrument, COSME is to "address market failures which affect the competitiveness of the Union economy on a global scale".

4.3 *European Institute of Innovation and Training*

The European Institute of Innovation and Training (EIT) is an independent body of the EU, founded in 2008 and operational since 2010 with the goal of spurring innovation in Europe.[46] The EIT forms part of Horizon 2020 and is intended to play a key part in realizing the Innovation Union by taking a leading role in fostering the integration of the "knowledge triangle": higher education, research and innovation. As would be expected for an entity that has its legal basis in Article 173(3) TFEU, the EIT's priority lies in transferring research and innovation to the business context and to commercial applications, as well as with the creation of and support for SMEs.

Its main tool in bolstering innovation is the creation of Knowledge and Innovation Communities (KICs). According to the amended foundational regulation, KICs are "autonomous partnership[s] of higher education institutions, research organisations, companies and other stakeholders in the innovation process in the form of a strategic network".[47] There are currently (as of the end of 2014) seven operational KICs; typical of the type of instrument is Climate-KIC, one of the first KICs to be launched, which has a partnership comprised of 47 per cent business, 32 per cent academia, and 21 per cent public bodies.[48] Climate-KIC funds innovative projects, supports the creation of new start-ups and sponsors education and training at all levels of higher education, as well as providing network connections between the various parts.

---

44. Decision 1639/2006/EC of the European Parliament and of the Council of 24 Oct. 2006 establishing a Competitiveness and Innovation Framework Programme (2007 to 2013), O.J. 2006, L 310/15.
45. Reg. (EU) No 1287/2013 of the European Parliament and of the Council of 11 Dec. 2013 establishing a Programme for the Competitiveness of Enterprises and small and medium-sized enterprises (COSME) (2014–2020) and repealing Decision 1639/2006/EC; O.J. 2013, L 347/33.
46. Reg. (EC) 294/2008 of the European Parliament and the Council of 11 Mar. 2008 establishing the European Institute of Innovation and Technology; O.J. 2008, L 97/1, as amended by Reg. (EU) 1292/2013 of the European Parliament and of the Council of 11 Dec. 2013 amending Reg. (EC) 294/2008 establishing the European Institute of Innovation and Technology; O.J. 2013, L 347/174.
47. Reg. (EU) 1292/2013, Art. 1(b).
48. <www.climate-kic.org> (last accessed 3 Jan. 2015).

4.4 *Joint Programming, JTIs and ETPs*

In recent years, the Commission has introduced new instruments outside the Framework Programme structure designed to stimulate research co-ordination between the Member States and at the same time to bring Europe's public research facilities – primarily universities – into long-term strategic partnerships with European industry and other private actors.

Based on the Joint Undertaking provision in Article 187 TFEU, Joint Technology Initiatives are long-term public-private partnerships designed to support large-scale multinational research activities in areas of major interest to European industrial competitiveness and issues of high societal relevance where national research policies lack the necessary scale. Under FP7, six areas were identified under "Co-operation" as particularly relevant for a JTI: fuel cells and hydrogen; aeronautics; innovative medicines; embedded computing systems; nano-electronics; GMES (global monitoring for environment and security).[49] This has led to the creation of five JTIs: the Innovative Medicines Initiative (IMI); Aeronautics and Air Transport (Clean Sky); Fuel Cells and Hydrogen (FCH); Embedded Computing Systems (ARTEMIS); Nanoelectronics Technologies 2020 (ENIAC).

With their focus on the needs of industry, JTIs are an instrument for realizing the ambitions of the European Technology Platforms (ETPs).[50] ETPs are industry-led stakeholder groups that develop both short- and long-term research and innovation agendas on a sectoral basis.[51] Not all ETPs qualify for a JTI, however. As the Commission itself notes, only a small number of ETPs are expected to achieve the necessary "scale and scope" to justify the mobilization of the high level of public and private investments that JTIs represent to implement important elements of their Strategic Research Agendas.[52] Each JTI is subject to a founding Council Regulation creating the necessary Joint Undertaking. These JTI JUs are independent legal entities, with a dedicated staff, budget and framework that governs the co-operation between the involved public and private entities. Each JTI JU is made up of the EU (represented by the European Commission), Member or Associated States to the Seventh Framework Programme and R&D actors (Corporate companies, SME's, research organizations and universities) that perform research activities in Europe. Funding of each JTI is provided by the EU as well the participating Member and Associated States; in-kind contributions, such as equipment, personnel and know-how are provided by industry and are expected to cover at least 50% of the total cost of the research projects.

---

49. Decision 1982/2006/EC of the European Parliament and of the Council of 18 Dec. 2006 concerning the Seventh Framework Programme of the European Community for research, technological development and demonstration activities (2007–2013), O.J. 2006, L 412. The last of these, GMES, has however not been the subject of a JTI but is contained in a separate agreement with the European Space Agency. NB.: GMES has been re-named the Copernicus programme.
50. European Technology Platforms (ETPs) were first formulated in 2003 and are bottom-up industry initiatives with the Commission playing only a facilitating role; European Commission, "Technology Platforms. From Definition to Implementation of a Common Research Agenda", 21 Sept. 2004, available at <ftp://ftp.cordis.europa.eu/pub/etp/docs/report-defweb_en.pdf>; European Commission, "Report on European Technology Platforms and Joint Technology Initiatives: Fostering Public-Private R&D Partnerships to Boost Europe's Industrial Competitiveness", Commission Staff Working Document, 10 June 2005, SEC(2005) 800.
51. As of the end of 2014, there were thirty-seven ETPs organized across six sectors – Bio-based economy; Energy; Environment; ICT; Production and Processes; and Transport – with three cross-sectoral initiatives: Nanofutures; Industrial Safety and PROSUMER.net, available at <cordis.europa.eu/technology-platforms/individual_en.html>.
52. European Commission, Roadmap for Joint Technology Initiatives, 9 Nov. 2006; available at <ec.europa.eu/research/jti/pdf/roadmap_jtis_en.pdf#view=fit&pagemode=none>.

Launched by the Commission at the end of 2008, Joint Programming is designed to make the most of limited public R&D funds by facilitating co-operation between the national research strategies of Member States.[53] Unlike JTIs and ETPs, Joint Programming is solely concerned with co-operation between public bodies in the Member States. The initiative is an explicit recognition that the OMC method of decision-making in this area has not led to concrete national research policy coordination initiatives between Member States or to common agenda setting in areas of strategic importance.[54] Joint Programming is based on Article 185 TFEU and is a voluntary process whereby Member States form partnerships to draw up and implement Strategic Research Agendas (SRA) that address major societal challenges. Suitable areas for JPIs are identified by the High Level Group on Joint Programming, made up of members nominated by the Member States and by the Commission; the process of developing a SRA is facilitated by the Commission and its implementation may receive Commission financial support. Some ten JPIs have been launched on topics ranging from healthy diets to cultural heritage and productive oceans.[55]

4.5 *European Research Council*

The European Research Council (ERC) and the Basic Research Fund that it manages forms a key part of the European Research Area. Created in 2007 as an Executive Agency, the ERC was established in order to realize the "Ideas" action of FP7;[56] it has been integrated into Horizon 2020 by means of a successor ERC that has replaced the agency created in 2007.[57] The Executive Agency, charged with implementation of the ERC's strategy, is now complemented by a governing Scientific Council, comprised of researchers of global standing.

The ERC is intended to address the bias in research and technology policies of the Member States towards applied research and technological and industrial development. The ERC is thus to focus on basic research across all fields, including the social sciences and humanities. Unlike any other European funding instrument, the grants offered by the ERC to European researchers at all stages of their careers have no pre-determined priorities or criteria other than research excellence and that projects be ground-breaking in their field.

5. European Space Policy

Article 189 TFEU lays down Union competence in drawing up a European space policy. For the purposes of creating and implementing such a policy, the Union is empowered to promote joint initiatives, support research and technological developments and to co-ordinate the exploration and exploitation of space. The Lisbon Treaty reforms, notably Article 4(3) TFEU, has given the Union a stronger role in the area of space policy, with its own competence to carry out activities and to define a European space strategy; Article 189 TFEU indeed requires the Union to create

53. Communication from the Commission to the European Parliament, the Council, the European Economic and Social Committee and the Committee of the Regions, "Towards joint programming in research: Working together to tackle common challenges more effectively", COM(2008)468 final.
54. Ibid., 6.
55. Available at <ec.europa.eu/research/era/joint-programming-initiatives_en.html>.
56. Commission Decision of 2 Feb. 2007 establishing the European Research Council (Text with EEA relevance) (2007/134/EC), O.J 2007, L 57/14; implementing Council Decision of 19 Dec. 2006 concerning the specific programme: "Ideas" implementing the Seventh Framework Programme of the European Community for research, technological development and demonstration activities (2007 to 2013), O.J. 2006, L 400/243, at 243.
57. Commission Decision of 12 Dec. 2013 establishing the European Research Council (2013/C 373/09; 2013/C 373/23).

a European space policy. The creation and implementation of policy in this area, including the creation of a European space programme, is determined via the ordinary legislative process, and allows for the harmonization of the laws of Member States so as to achieve policy objectives set at the European level. The shared competences in this area mean that the substance of the European Space Policy is jointly determined by the Union, the Member States and the European Space Agency (ESA).

Policy in this area is conducted in co-operation with the ESA – an independent intergovernmental body based in Darmstadt, with its own membership and competences. This co-operation is regulated by a Framework Agreement, adopted in 2004, under which the Commission and ESA agreed to co-ordinate their actions through a Joint Secretariat. The Agreement also created a ministerial-level Space Council, which is a meeting of the EU and ESA Councils, prepared by Member States representatives in the High-level Space Policy Group (HSPG).[58]

Space is understood as directly benefiting European citizens at three levels: social, economic and strategic. In particular, the space sector is understood as crucial to improving competitiveness and innovation within Europe; the link to industry is underlined by the decision to place space policy within the "Industrial Policy" section of Europe 2020, rather than the "Innovative Union",[59] with space understood as bringing benefits across all sectors of the economy, including transport, telecommunications, the environment and security. The importance of space at the strategic, economic and social levels and the recognition of this by all political actors at the European level is laid down in the European Space Policy. This Policy was launched in 2007, a co-creation of the Commission and the ESA and approved by the Space Council.[60]

The European Space Policy centres around two flagship initiatives: Galileo, which concerns the creation of a civilian satellite navigation system, and Copernicus (previously known as GMES), a programme that is designed to guarantee continuous access to information about the environment and on security issues by providing permanent space-based observation and in-situ infrastructures.[61] The main thrust of the policy is to retain independent access to space and space exploration, and to create independence from the US GPS system by establishing a European network of satellites. Support for ISS (the International Space Station) is also a key part of the Policy.

Space research is funded under the second pillar of Horizon 2020 – Leadership in Enabling and Industrial Technologies – and is thus strongly connected with Europe's industrial policy.[62] Space policy and research within the Commission is located in DG Enterprise and Industry. Space was one of the ten prioritized themes under FP7 and €1.4 billion was allocated for space-related projects, of which 85% was spent on Copernicus and the remaining 15% was used to support space science and exploration, space transportation and space technology.

---

58. Decision of the Council of the European Union on the signing of the Framework Agreement between the European Community and the European Space Agency, Brussels 7 Oct. 2003, 12858/03.
59. Communication from the Commission to the Council, the European Parliament, the European Economic and Social Committee and the Committee of the Regions, "Towards a Space Strategy for the European Union that Benefits its Citizens", COM(2011)152 final.
60. Resolution of the European Council, 25 May 2007, 10037/07, based on a resolution drafted at the Fourth Space Council.
61. Commission, "Towards a Space Strategy for the European Union that Benefits its Citizens", cited *supra* note 50.
62. See, for example, Communication from the Commission to the European Parliament, the Council, the European Economic and Social Committee and the Committee of the Regions, "EU Space Industrial Policy: Releasing the Potential for Economic Growth in the Space Sector", COM(2013)108 final.

On 18 December 2007, a network of European regions using space technologies known as NEREUS, was established. The network aims to provide a forum for dialogue between the regions and stakeholders in European space policy (the EU, the ESA, the Member States, and the space industry), as well as to provide representation of the regions in decision-making in the field of space policy at the European level.

Further reading

Banchoff, T., "Institutions, inertia and European Union research policy", 40 JCMS (2002), 1.

Edler, J., S. Kuhlmann and M. Behrens (Eds.), *Changing Governance of Research and Technology Policy* (Edward Elgar, 2003).

Guzzetti, L., *A Brief History of European Union Research Policy* (European Commission, October 1995).

Pavitt, K., "The inevitable limits of EU R&D funding", 27 *Research Policy* (1998), 559–568.

Prange-Gstöhl, H. (Ed.), *International Science and Technology Cooperation in a Globalized World. The External Dimension of the European Research Area* (Edward Elgar, 2010).

Van Vught, F., "The EU Innovation Agenda: Challenges for European higher education and research", (2009) *Higher Education and Policy.*

CHAPTER 38
SUPPORTING POLICIES

*Sacha Garben**

1. Introduction

This introductory section will explain what is covered by "supporting policies", how they relate to other areas and indicate their common characteristics.

1.1 *Complementary competences*

Article 6 TFEU provides that the EU "shall have competence to carry out actions to support, coordinate or supplement the actions of the Member States. The areas of such action shall, at European level, be (a) protection and improvement of human health; (b) industry; (c) culture; (d) tourism; (e) education, vocational training, youth and sport; (f) civil protection; (g) administrative cooperation". This category of competence is often referred to as "complementary", and for the purposes of this Chapter the policies that ensue from these competences shall be called "supporting policies".

In accordance with Article 2(5) TFEU, supporting policies are not to "supersede" the competence of the Member States in the area concerned. Moreover, the measures that can be adopted on the Treaty provisions relating to these areas cannot harmonize Member States' laws or regulations. Underlining the importance attached to it, this limitation is reiterated in each of the specific Treaty provisions relating to these policy areas.[1] These national autonomy clauses and harmonization prohibitions are a fundamental characteristic of complementary competence and betray its complex, two-sided nature: it is often as much directed at *authorizing* EU action as at *containing* it.

1.2 *The place of supporting policies in the Treaties*

As first sight, Article 6 TFEU seems to provide a finite list of complementary competences. This impression is reinforced by Article 4 TFEU, which establishes shared competence as a residual category, comprising all competences conferred by the Treaty that "do not relate to the areas referred to in Articles 3 and 6" TFEU. The truth is more complex. There are several other TFEU provisions, relating to policy areas not listed in Article 6 TFEU and instead classified as a shared competence, that confer only a limited, supporting competence on the EU.

For instance, Article 79 TFEU provides that the EU "may establish measures to provide incentives and support for the action of Member States with a view to promoting the integration

* Legal Studies Department, College of Europe. Nothing in the contribution represents the views of the European Commission, the views expressed are entirely personal.

1. Arts. 168(5), 173(3), 167(5), 195(2), 165(4), 196(2) and 197(2) TFEU.

of third-country nationals residing legally in their territories, excluding any harmonization of the laws and regulations of the Member States". Similar powers are provided in Article 84 TFEU in the field of crime prevention. Furthermore, as an ambiguous addition to the hard competence provided in its first paragraph, Article 19(2) TFEU stipulates that the EU "may adopt the basic principles of Union incentive measures, excluding any harmonization of the laws and regulations of the Member States", supporting Member State action to combat discrimination based on sex, racial or ethnic origin, religion or belief, disability, age or sexual orientation.

While strictly speaking inconsistent with the clear-cut categorization introduced in Articles 2–6 TFEU, the preceding examples are still relatively unproblematic. In essence, it concerns specific, limited parts of broader policy areas, where these limited parts exhibit traits of a complementary competence while the policy area as a whole can be classified as a shared competence.[2] The situation becomes more complex in other areas.

Firstly, Article 4 TFEU features two policy areas that as a whole do not fit the profile of either complementary or shared competence. Article 4(3) TFEU stipulates that in the areas of research, technological development and space, the Union shall have competence to carry out activities, but adds that the exercise of that competence shall not result in Member States being prevented from exercising theirs. Article 4(4) TFEU provides the same for development cooperation and humanitarian aid. These competences are further elaborated in several provisions under Titles III and XIX TFEU. The focus of EU action in these fields is on coordination and cooperation, but in contrast with complementary competences *stricto sensu*, the EU also possesses a hard legislative competence. At the same time, any EU action on these provisions, legislative or not, is not to pre-empt Member States from exercising their own competence. This contrasts with one of shared competence's defining features, that Member States shall exercise their competence only to the extent that the Union has not (i.e. "pre-emption").[3] The fact that continued Member State regulation is allowed regardless of the adoption of EU measures can perhaps be explained by the specific nature of these policy fields, where concurring action by several actors is unlikely to cause any regulatory conflict and instead contributes to the objectives of that policy. It does however show that the Lisbon Treaty's competence classification does not exactly fit the variety of competences featured in the EU legal order.

A different example illustrating that finding can be found in Article 153 TFEU on social policy, stating that "the Union shall support and complement the activities of the Member States" in a number of fields such as, *inter alia*, improving working conditions, social security and social protection, workers' health and safety, information and consultation of workers, and the integration of persons excluded from the labour market. For all the fields listed in Article 153(1) TFEU, the EU "may adopt measures designed to encourage cooperation between Member States through initiatives aimed at improving knowledge, developing exchanges of information and best practices, promoting innovative approaches and evaluating experiences, excluding any harmonization of the laws and regulations of the Member States". This bears all the features of a complementary competence. Furthermore, the final paragraph of Article 153 TFEU declares that "the provisions of this Article shall not apply to pay, the right of association, the right to strike or the right to impose lock-outs". While this does not constitute a prohibition of harmonization in

2. Arts. 79 and 84 TFEU are both part of the area of freedom, security and justice (Title V), which Art. 4(2)(j) TFEU classifies as shared.
3. Art. 2(2) TFEU states: "When the Treaties confer on the Union a competence shared with the Member States in a specific area, the Union and the Member States may legislate and adopt legally binding acts in that area. The Member States shall exercise their competence to the extent that the Union has not exercised its competence. The Member States shall again exercise their competence to the extent that the Union has decided to cease exercising its competence".

a traditional sense, it does mean that Article 153 TFEU cannot be used as a basis for EU action on these issues. However, in addition to these supporting powers, in all the listed fields except the combating of social exclusion and the modernization of social protection systems, the EU is also granted a hard competence to adopt directives. Still, these are limited to establishing minimum requirements. EU action on this basis can thereby only partially pre-empt Member State action, since they retain the power to set stricter standards. Furthermore, and rather confusingly, while Article 4 TFEU on shared competence features "social policy, for the aspects defined in this Treaty", Article 5 TFEU provides that "the Union may take initiatives to ensure coordination of Member States' social policies". All this makes that social policy is an area with a mixed competence-structure, located somewhere between shared and complementary.[4]

Article 5 TFEU, placed in the middle of, yet separate from, the three categories of Article 3, 4 and 6 TFEU, features two more competences that do not fit the mould. Article 5(2) TFEU provides that the EU shall contribute to a high level of employment by encouraging cooperation between Member States and supporting and complementing their action. This competence is further elaborated in Articles 145–149 TFEU, which provide that the EU may adopt incentive measures and initiatives aimed at developing exchanges of information and best practices, excluding harmonization and stipulating that the competences of the Member States shall be respected. While this therefore exhibits the characteristics of a complementary competence, it is not listed in Article 6 TFEU. Secondly, Article 5(1) TFEU provides that the "Member States shall coordinate their economic policies within the Union. To this end, the Council shall adopt measures, in particular broad guidelines for these policies. Specific provisions shall apply to those Member States whose currency is the euro." Strictly speaking, this is therefore not an EU competence at all, but instead allows the Member States and the Council to use the Union framework for the purposes of economic policy coordination. Still, the fact that it is not listed as a "mere" complementary competence was a conscious political decision, considering the importance of the coordination done by the EU institutions in this area.[5] It seems fair to say that with the adoption of measures like the Sixpack and Twopack,[6] EU-level action is this area indeed goes beyond a mere supporting policy. However, as we shall come to see in this Chapter, similar things could also be said about several other areas that are nevertheless listed in Article 6 TFEU.

1.3 *Between authorization and restraint*

The foregoing shows that the variety of different competences featured in the EU legal order makes it difficult to establish a watertight categorization. Nevertheless, this was one of the Lisbon Treaty's most important reforms, resulting from the decade-long "Debate on the Future of Europe",[7] supposed to make the competence division between the EU and the Member States more transparent, coherent and more effective at containing EU integration, particularly in sensitive policy fields. This latter objective is very pronounced in the case of complementary competence, constituting its defining characteristic.[8]

---

4. Art. 169 TFEU on consumer protection constitutes a similar example.
5. J. Piris, *The Lisbon Treaty: A Legal and Political Analysis* (CUP, 2011), 77.
6. See on this issue Ch. 26, "Economic and Monetary Union", of this book.
7. See: Laeken Declaration on the Future of the European Union, annex I to the Conclusions of the Laeken European Council, 14–15 Dec. 2001, SN 300/1/01 REV 1.
8. In the words of Schütze, the "essence of complementary competences is limited legislative powers". R. Schütze, "Co-operative federalism constitutionalized: The emergence of complementary competences in the EC legal order", 31 EL Rev. (2006), 167.

This approach is however not new, but instead carries on the tradition established by the introduction of the first complementary competences in the Maastricht Treaty (even if they were not yet named as such). Maastricht created new competences in culture, education, health and industrial policy, but each came with the specific proviso that legal measures adopted on these provisions could not harmonize national laws.[9] This reflected a more cautious approach than before, showing that Member States were at least as much concerned with setting down boundaries, establishing what the EU cannot do, as with creating scope for future EU initiatives.[10] The Lisbon Treaty has reaffirmed and extended this technique, applying it also to the four new complementary competences that it has created in sport, tourism, civil protection and administrative cooperation.

One might wonder why these complementary competences were created at all, if the Member States were so eager to retain their competence and restrain EU action. Apart from constituting a reluctant recognition that the EU may play a useful role in these areas, it also seems that they had little choice, since a *de facto* EU policy had already developed in these areas. A substantial body of higher education law and policy had emerged well before the Maastricht Treaty. Also in the areas of public health and culture there were numerous legal measures adopted in the absence of a specific legal basis. The new competences thus codified existent practice, legitimizing the policy that had come into existence, while at the same time trying to establish that that was as far as it should go. As shall be explored in the rest of this Chapter, this has put the complementary competences in the difficult position of simultaneously serving two masters: of authorization and restraint.

2. European integration in supporting policy areas

This section will reflect on the degree and kind of European integration in the supporting policy areas of Article 6 TFEU, discussing both negative integration, i.e. the disapplication of national rules that conflict with an EU rule, and positive integration, i.e. the creation of common standards or rules through the adoption of EU measures.

2.1 *Limited competence but extensive integration?*

Considering that the essential feature of supporting policy areas is the EU's limited competence, it might be surprising that there exists a substantial body of case law, legislation and other legal measures in most of these areas, both pre-dating and post-dating the introduction of the explicit legal bases. This has several explanations.

Firstly, in the application of *other* Treaty provisions, the limits stipulated in the complementary competences do not apply. This means that other Treaty provisions, such as the prohibitions on obstacles to free movement, can lead to the disapplication of national rules on education, sport, health, culture, civil protection, tourism and industry. Furthermore, it means that legal acts, including harmonization measures, regulating (aspects of) a supporting policy area, can be adopted on other provisions regardless of the harmonization prohibitions.[11]

Secondly, while the harmonization prohibitions limit direct legislation (as opposed to indirect legislation on other provisions), this does not mean that no legal acts can be adopted on the

---

9. Arts. 149(4), 150(4), 151(4), 152(4)(c) EC Treaty.
10. See, for culture: N. Nic Shuibhne, *Minority Language Policy: Culture, Citizenship and Fundamental Rights* (Kluwer Law International, 2002), 119.
11. Except for the flexibility clause of Art. 352 TFEU: "Measures based on this Article shall not entail harmonisation of Member States' laws or regulations in cases where the Treaties exclude such harmonisation."

basis of the complementary competences. Conversely, as we shall come to see, many supporting actions have been adopted by means of legal instruments such as Decisions and Regulations.

Thirdly, also "soft" measures, setting up informal coordination and cooperation, can be far-reaching; limiting and circumscribing national law and policy to a significant degree in practice. Especially European economic governance, in the form of Euro crisis financial assistance measures as well as the yearly policy coordination in the European Semester, is having far-reaching consequences for a number of the supporting policy areas such as health and education.

Finally, European integration in these areas can take place outside the EU institutional framework. The limited nature of EU competence in these fields might constitute a push-factor for such intergovernmental action, which can be broad and fundamental in scope, and can have a significant impact on both national and EU action.

2.2 *Negative integration*

In 1968, the Court of Justice was faced with the question whether an Italian tax on the export to other Member States of articles having an artistic, historic, archaeological or ethnographic value was caught by the prohibition on export restrictions in the EEC Treaty.[12] Italy argued that such articles could not be assimilated to "consumer goods or articles of general use" and were therefore not subject to the Treaty provisions which applied only to "ordinary merchandise". The Court firmly rejected the idea that there was a general cultural exemption.[13] In subsequent years, the Court has continuously confirmed that practices, goods and services are not excluded from the Treaty simply because they fall in areas where the competence of the EU is limited, or even non-existent. The Court has held that teachers qualify as "workers" in the sense of Article 45 TFEU,[14] and that privately funded education constitutes a "service" in the meaning of Article 56 TFEU.[15] Similarly, it qualifies medical care as a "service"[16] and has held that the activities of tourist guides cannot exempted from the Treaty.[17] This shows that in all the supporting policy areas listed in Article 6 TFEU, the application of other Treaty provisions can lead to the disapplication of national rules, thereby arguably "superseding" national competence in those areas.

Perhaps one of the best-known examples, in EU law and beyond, is the *Bosman* case.[18] At issue were certain transfer rules in professional football that restricted the free movement of workers in the EU. Several governments argued that Article 45 TFEU was not applicable to sporting activities as in most cases sport was not an economic activity, and since sport and culture fell within Member State autonomy and should therefore be shielded from EU interference. The Court replied that, considering the EU's objectives at that time when there was not yet an EU complementary competence in this field, "sport is subject to [EU] law only in so far as it constitutes an economic activity". As regards the difficulty of severing the economic from the sporting aspects, the Court held that EU law does not "preclude rules or practices justified

---

12. Case 7/68, *Commission v. Italy.*
13. R. Craufurd-Smith, "Community intervention in the cultural field" in R. Craufurd-Smith (Ed.), *Culture and European Union Law* (OUP, 2004), 28.
14. Case 66/85, *Deborah Lawrie-Blum v. Land Baden-Württemberg.*
15. Case C-76/05, *Herbert Schwarz and Marga Gootjes-Schwarz v. Finanzamt Bergisch Gladbach.*
16. Case C-158/96, *Raymond Kohll v. Union des caisses de maladie.*
17. Cases C-154/89, *Commission of the European Communities v. French Republic*, Case C-180/89, *Commission of the European Communities v. Italian Republic* and Case C-198/89, *Commission of the European Communities v. Hellenic Republic.*
18. Case C-415/93, *Union royale belge des sociétés de football association ASBL* v. *Jean-Marc Bosman, Royal club liégeois SA v. Jean-Marc Bosman and others and Union des associations européennes de football (UEFA) v. Jean-Marc Bosman.*

on non-economic grounds which relate to the particular nature and context of certain matches". However, this could not "be relied upon to exclude the whole of a sporting activity from the scope of the Treaty". Also the argument based on the limitation of EU competence was firmly rejected, since the question was not about "the conditions under which [EU] powers of limited extent, such as those based on Article [167 TFEU], may be exercised but on the scope of the freedom of movement of workers guaranteed by Article [45 TFEU], which is a fundamental freedom". Because of the judgment, the entire football transfer system had to be changed.[19]

As *Bosman* clearly shows, the Court is highly reluctant to carve policy areas out of the scope of the Treaty, even if they fall within Member State competence.[20] The Court explicitly separates the question of positive and negative integration, making clear that the fundamental freedoms fully apply even if they cut through areas where the EU possesses no, or only limited, legislative powers. The Court does recognize that certain non-economic objectives might have to be considered, but refers to the possibility of objective justification to accommodate these concerns. In that justification assessment, the Court does not explicitly consider whether an area falls within the scope of EU competence or not. While it could be argued that the Court is slightly more deferential in the application of the proportionality test in these areas,[21] being less hostile towards justifications of an economic nature[22] or towards directly discriminatory measures[23] than it is in other areas, the rigour with which the Court applies the Treaty provisions and the proportionality assessment in these policy areas remains striking.

This approach has had far-reaching consequences in public health.[24] By qualifying restrictions on (reimbursement of) care obtained abroad as restrictions of the services provision, the case law has meant that individuals may access other treatments than those allocated in the national package and they can escape waiting lists, having profound consequences for national health systems by challenging domestic practices governing the allocation of these public

19. See S. Van den Bogaert, *Practical Regulation of the Mobility of Sportsmen in the EU Post Bosman* (Kluwer Law International, 2005).
20. See also L. Azoulai, "The 'retained powers' formula in the case law of the European Court of Justice: EU Law as total law?", 2 *European Journal of Legal Studies* (2011), 192.
21. See L. Boucon, "EU Law and Retained Powers of Member States" in L. Azoulai, *The Question of Competence in the European Union* (OUP, 2014).
22. The Court has recognised the risk of "seriously undermining the financial balance of the social security system" in health care cases and the objective of avoiding "an unreasonable burden which could have consequences for the overall level of assistance" in student maintenance. See Case C-157/99, *B.S.M. Geraets-Smits v. Stichting Ziekenfonds VGZ and H.T.M. Peerbooms v. Stichting CZ Groep Zorgverzekeringen*, Case C-209/03, *The Queen, on the application of Dany Bidar v. London Borough of Ealing and Secretary of State for Education and Skills*.
23. In sport cases, the Court has allowed directly discriminatory measures to be considered under the objective justifications scheme, even if these have not always passed the proportionality test. See e.g. Case C-415/93, *Bosman*, Case C-176/96, *Jyri Lehtonen and Castors Canada Dry Namur-Braine ASBL v. Fédération royale belge des sociétés de basket-ball ASBL (FRBSB)*, Case C-438/00, *Deutscher Handballbund eV v. Maros Kolpak*, Case C-325/08, *Olympique Lyonnais SASP v. Olivier Bernard and Newcastle UFC*. K. Pijetlovic "Another classic of EU sports jurisprudence: Legal implications of *Olympique Lyonnais SASP v. Olivier Bernard ad Newcastle UFC* (C-325/08)", 35 EL Rev. (2010), 857. In cultural cases, the Court has generally been less lenient, but see on fixed book prices: Case C-531/07, *Fachverband der Buch- und Medienwirtschaft v. LIBRO Handelsgesellschaft mbH.*
24. See: G. Davies, "Welfare as a service", 29 LIEI (2002), 27; P. van Nuffel, "Patients free movement rights and cross-border access to health-care", 12 MJ (2005), 253; C. Newdick, "Citizenship, free movement and health care: Cementing individual rights by corroding social solidarity", 43 CML Rev. (2006), 1645.

services.[25] National autonomy to decide on important political questions, weighing the cost and benefit of health care to the public and the individual, is thereby limited by EU law. Furthermore, even though certain restrictions can be justified to protect the stability of the health care system, the Court imposes high standards of rationality through a strict proportionality assessment, which most of the national arrangements have failed.

The same holds true for the area of education. Although the Court has held that unlike medical treatment, publicly funded education does not constitute a "service",[26] the case law has arguably had an even greater impact on national education systems than it has had on health systems. Firstly, privately funded education does constitute a service.[27] Secondly, the Court's judgments on diploma recognition for professional and academic purposes require transparent and reasonable procedures operating from the assumption that equivalent diplomas should be recognized as such.[28] Most importantly, the Court has developed a progressive line of case law on mobile students' right to equal treatment, which has meant in particular that Member States cannot impose restrictions or higher fees on mobile EU students.[29] This is controversial because neither the economically inactive students nor their parents will have paid taxes in the host state, and there is no guarantee that they will settle there after their studies.[30] As such, EU law requires Member States which choose to devote significant public resources to maintaining a high quality further education system for the benefit of their own populations to subsidize, through the principle of equal access, in addition potentially large numbers of foreign students.[31] As an important illustration, in the situation of Austria and Belgium, which were flooded by German and French medical students that were escaping their country's *numerus clausus* system, this led to a situation where it became impossible to maintain their deeply valued tuition fee-free and open-access higher education systems.[32]

2.3 *Positive integration*

Let us recall Article 2(5) TFEU: "In certain areas and under the conditions laid down in the Treaties, the Union shall have competence to carry out actions to support, coordinate or supplement the actions of the Member States, without thereby superseding their competence in these areas. Legally binding acts of the Union adopted on the basis of the provisions of the Treaties relating to these areas shall not entail harmonization of Member States' laws or regulations". What does this mean for positive integration in the supporting policy areas?

As explained in section 2.1, the fact that in the application of *other* Treaty provisions the limits stipulated in the complementary competences do not apply means that legal acts, including

25. D. Martinsen, "Inter-institutional dynamics in the cross-border provision of healthcare services", (2009) ARENA Working Paper 5/2009, 6.
26. Case C-263/86, *Belgian State v. René Humbel and Marie-Thérèse Edel.*
27. Case C-76/05, *Herbert Schwarz and Marga Gootjes-Schwarz v. Finanzamt Bergisch Gladbach.*
28. Case C-313/01, *Christine Morgenbesser v. Consiglio dell'Ordine degli avvocati di Genova* and Case C-19/92, *Dieter Kraus v. Land Baden-Württemberg.*
29. Case C-293/83, *Françoise Gravier v. City of Liège.* See: G. Davies, "Higher education, equal access, and residence conditions: Does EU law allow member states to charge higher fees to students not previously resident?", 12 MJ (2005), 227, M. Dougan, "Fees, grants, loans and dole cheques: Who covers the costs of migrant education within the EU?", 42 CML Rev. (2005), 943, A.P. van der Mei, "EU law and education: Promotion of student mobility versus protection of the education systems" in M. Dougan and E. Spaventa (Eds.), *Social Welfare and EU Law* (Hart, 2005).
30. A.P. van der Mei, op. cit. *supra* note 37.
31. M. Dougan, op. cit. *supra* note 37.
32. See S. Garben, "Case C-73/08, *Nicolas Bressol and Others, Céline Chaverot and Others v. Gouvernement de la Communauté française*", 47 CML Rev. (2010), 1493.

harmonization measures regulating a supporting policy area, can be adopted on such other provisions, like the internal market. Indeed, in the following sections, where positive integration in every supporting area will be discussed in turn, we shall see that the most significant integration has taken place through "the back door" on the basis of other Treaty provisions, and that this is still happening regardless of the introduction of specific complementary competences and their harmonization prohibitions. Strictly speaking this is not contradicted by Article 2(5) TFEU, when it says that Union acts "*adopted on the basis of the provisions of the Treaties relating to these areas* shall not entail harmonization".[33]

To the extent that EU action is undertaken on the provisions relating to the supporting policy areas themselves, Article 2(5) TFEU provides that such action should be directed at "supporting, coordinating or supplementing the actions of the Member States" without "superseding their competence". The concrete legal significance of these statements is unclear, but these stipulations express the idea that EU action is not to replace or pre-empt national (scope for) action. For instance, while the EU may adopt a measure facilitating academic diploma recognition like a common diploma template, this should not prevent Member States from using other templates (in addition). Or while the EU may set up a scheme for coordination of civil protection interventions in case of natural disasters, this does not prevent Member States from intervening in other ways than through the common mechanism. Or while the EU may run an anti-smoking campaign, this does not prevent Member States from running their own national campaign in parallel. This freedom on the part of the Member States is not unlimited, however, since they are under a general duty of sincere cooperation which means that they cannot undertake action that would undermine the EU action in question, regardless of its complementary nature.[34]

The fact that Member States remain free to act in parallel of course does not mean that such EU measures are not binding on the Member States. On the contrary, many of these measures constitute traditional "hard law", adopted by means of Regulations or Decisions. As we shall see below, the above examples of a common diploma template and a civil protection mechanism have been adopted by means of Decisions, as has the funding necessary for EU anti-smoking campaigns. This means that Member States are fully bound to adopt the necessary measures for the implementation of these initiatives in their own legal/institutional order, and that infringement proceedings can be brought against them if they fail to do so. Nevertheless, supporting action often also entails the adoption of non-binding "soft law" measures, such as Recommendations. Such measures can however still be far-reaching, circumscribing national law and policy to a significant degree in practice. For example, the introduction of smoke-free public environments across Europe has been based on a "mere" Council Recommendation.[35]

One important form of "soft" supporting action is the so-called Open Method of Coordination (OMC), which constitutes an intergovernmental framework for cooperation between the Member States within which national policies are directed towards certain common objectives on a voluntary basis.[36] The OMC was developed in the context of employment policy, and is

---

33. Emphasis added.
34. Art. 4(3) TEU. On the principle of sincere cooperation, see Ch. 11, "Application and enforcement of EU law in the Member States", of this book.
35. Council Recommendation of 30 Nov. 2009 on Smoke-free Environments. A Commission report found that all EU countries have now adopted anti-exposure measures. As a result, the actual exposure rates have dropped significantly, e.g. for citizens visiting bars from 46% to 28%. See European Commission, Report on the implementation of the Council Recommendation of 30 Nov. 2009 on Smoke-free Environments, SWD (2013) 56 final/2.
36. On the OMC, see Ch. 28, "Social policy", of this book.

now used for social policy – which includes a limited health care policy element-,[37] culture, education, vocational training and youth.[38] The OMC is not mentioned expressly in the Treaties, but only in an indirect way, where it refers to "the organization of exchange of best practice" in the provisions relating to employment, social policy, health, research and technological development, and industry. Curiously, the Treaty does not contain such a reference in the provisions on culture, education,[39] vocational training and youth, while this area features a well-established OMC. A particularly powerful form of policy coordination has emerged since the onset of the financial and economic crisis: economic governance in the so-called European Semester. The Commission, the Council, and the European Council set general priorities in the Annual Growth Survey, review national progress towards the achievement of these goals on the basis of Country Reports prepared by the Commission, and accordingly issue Country Specific Recommendations (CSRs) to MS. As Zeitlin and Vanhercke note, the European Semester brings together within a single annual cycle a wide range of EU governance instruments with different legal bases and sanctioning authority, from the Stability and Growth Pact, the Macroeconomic Imbalances Procedure, and the Fiscal Treaty to the Europe 2020 Strategy and the Integrated Economic and Employment Policy guidelines.[40] As the CSRs are non-binding, they leave the ultimate decision to the Member States, although the political pressure they exert on national standards should not be underestimated, especially since in some cases non-compliance may lead to financial sanctions. The CSR's concern a wide range of national policies, including where the EU has only complementary, or no, direct competence, such as health, education, wages and social protection.

Finally, it should be noted that the provisions on education, culture and public health make reference to the term "incentive measures", without this terms being explained in more detail. In the case of education and culture it appears that EU action on this provision is limited to such "incentive measures". The other supporting policy provisions instead allow the adoption of: "specific measures in support of action taken in the Member States",[41] "specific measures to complement actions within the Member States",[42] "the measures necessary to help achieve the objectives",[43] and "the necessary measures to this end".[44] Still, it does not appear that the term "incentive measures" has a specific, more restrictive meaning in practice than the other formulations,[45] but this inconsistent use of terminology in the Treaty provisions is to be deplored.

---

37. One of the identified targets is providing accessible, high-quality and sustainable health care and long-term care. Commission Communication of 22 Dec. 2005 "A new framework for the open coordination of social protection and inclusion policies", COM(2005)706.
38. Youth policy does not entail the setting of targets, and it is up to the Member States to decide on objectives without the need for any European-level coordination of national action plans.
39. Art. 165 TFEU does mention "developing exchanges of information and experience on issues common to the education systems of the Member States".
40. Jonathan Zeitlin and Bart Vanhercke, "Socializing the European Semester? Economic Governance and Social Policy Coordination in Europe 2020" [2014] Swedish Institute for European Policy Studies 7.
41. Art. 173(3) TFEU on industry.
42. Art. 195(2) TFEU on tourism.
43. Art. 196(2) TFEU on civil protection.
44. Art. 197 TFEU on administrative cooperation.
45. In Case C-42/97, *Parliament v. Council*, the Parliament argued that Council Decision 96/664/EC on the adoption of a multiannual programme to promote linguistic diversity in the information society had to be annulled as it was wrongly based on the industry provision and should instead have been based on culture, as the fact that it "promoted" linguistic diversity made it an incentive measure in the sense of (now) Art. 167(5) TFEU. The Court simply held that "the wording of the title of a measure cannot by itself determine

3. The protection and improvement of human health[46]

In light of the degree and extent of EU action in this field, of all the supporting policy areas public health is the one that is the most difficult to distinguish from a shared competence.

3.1 *The place of health in the Treaties*

The Maastricht Treaty added a Title on public health containing a single article (now Art. 168 TFEU). The content of the provision has changed overtime, with the Amsterdam Treaty adding legislative powers partly as a reaction to a number of high-profile events, such as the BSE crisis and AIDS contamination scandals.[47] In a resolution annexed to the 2000 Nice European Council Conclusions, attention was paid to the precautionary principle, which now plays an important role in EU health policy. The EU Charter of Fundamental Rights that was also adopted in 2000, but only became legally binding upon the entry into force of the Lisbon Treaty in 2009, provides in Article 35 that everyone has the right of access to preventive health care and the right to benefit from medical treatment under the conditions established by national laws and practices. It also states that a high level of human health protection shall be ensured in the definition and implementation of all the Union's policies and activities. This mainstreaming obligation is echoed in Article 9 TFEU.

Furthermore, the TFEU now classifies a part of public health policy, namely that of "common safety concerns in public health matters", as a shared competence under Article 4(2)(k) TFEU. Indeed, this makes public health an area with an explicit mixed competence-structure. Article 168(4) declares that the EU may adopt (a) minimum harmonization measures setting high standards of quality and safety of organs and substances of human origin, blood and blood derivatives;[48] (b) full harmonization measures in the veterinary and phytosanitary fields which have as their direct objective the protection of public health;[49] and (c) full harmonization measures setting high standards of quality and safety for medicinal products and medical devices.[50] By contrast, such harmonization is not permitted for the "incentive measures designed to protect and improve human health and in particular to combat the major cross-border health scourges, measures concerning monitoring, early warning of and combating serious cross-border threats to health, and measures which have as their direct objective the protection of public health regarding tobacco and the abuse of alcohol" that Article 168(5) TFEU authorizes the EU to adopt.

---

its legal basis and, in this case, that the words 'to promote [...] linguistic diversity appearing in the title of the contested decision cannot be isolated from the measure as a whole and interpreted independently", upholding the Decision.

46. See on EU health law and policy in more detail also Ch. 34 of this book.
47. See Case C-180/96, *United Kingdom v. Commission*. E. Vos, "EU food safety regulation in the aftermath of the BSE crisis", 23 *Journal of Consumer Policy* (2000), 227.
48. E.g. Directive 2002/98/EC on human blood and of blood components and Directive 2004/23/EC on human tissues and cells intended for human applications. While these measures may only constitute minimum harmonization, such standards will have to comply with the internal market, and the adoption of a common standard, even if minimum, may influence the Court in its proportionality assessment of a more restrictive measure, as illustrated in Case C-421/09, *Humanplasma* (ECR I-12869).
49. E.g. Reg. 726/2004 laying down Community procedures for the authorization and supervision of medicinal products for human and veterinary use and establishing a European Medicines Agency and Reg. 470/2009 laying down Community procedures for the establishment of residue limits of pharmacologically active substances in foodstuffs of animal origin.
50. Rules relating to the safety and performance of medical devices were harmonized in the EU in the 1990s on the internal market legal base, by Directive 90/385/EEC, Directive 93/42/EEC and Directive 98/79/EC. Revisions were adopted by Reg. 2017/745 on medical devices and Reg. 2017/746 on in vitro diagnostic medical devices, on a joint legal basis of Articles 114 and 168 TFEU.

While this already shows that the EU has a relatively extensive mandate for action, perhaps the most important power in this field derives from another provision: Article 114 TFEU on the internal market.[51] Article 114(3) TFEU explicitly provides that within their respective powers, the Commission, the Parliament and the Council, in adopting harmonization measures on this provision concerning health, will take as a base a high level of protection. In addition, the more specific internal market legal bases can also be used to adopt measures that have a bearing on health. As a result, there are numerous directives and regulations concerning health aspects of free movement of goods,[52] persons[53] and free movement in the health sector.[54] This possibility to harmonize national rules on health in the context of the internal market is a pertinent one, especially since the Member States may derogate from the free movement provisions on grounds of public health. Unless the EU adopts a commonly applicable standard in such instances, obstacles to the fundamental freedoms will remain. Furthermore, the deregulation resulting from the exclusion of a national rule may have to be compensated by re-regulation on the European level, to avoid a regulatory gap.[55] However, at the same time, this harmonization possibility is difficult to reconcile with the harmonization prohibition of Article 168 TFEU, and has given rise to disputes in several high-profile Court cases, discussed below.

Finally, it deserves mentioning that Article 153 TFEU on social policy features an important health aspect, as one of the objectives for which the EU can adopt minimum harmonization measures on the basis of that provision is the protection of workers' health and safety.[56] Similarly, Article 169 TFEU on consumer protection authorizes the EU to adopt minimum harmonization for the protection of consumers' health and safety.

3.2 *Specific areas of EU health law and policy*

As a more systematic and detailed discussion of the various, fragmented areas of EU health law and policy is offered in Chapter 34 of this book, the following section merely aims to provide some key insights demonstrating how an area considered primarily as only a supporting competence nevertheless features a high degree of EU integration.

---

51. See G. Davies, "The community's internal market-based competence to regulate healthcare: Scope, strategies and consequences", 4 MJ (2007), 215.
52. E.g. Directive 2001/95/EC on general product safety, Reg. 1169/2011 concerning consumer information on foodstuffs, Reg. 1830/2003 concerning the traceability and labelling of genetically modified organisms and the traceability of food and feed products produced from genetically modified organisms, Council Directive 90/496/EEC on nutrition labelling rules of foodstuffs, Reg. 178/2002 laying down the general principles and requirements of food law, establishing the European Food Safety Authority and laying down procedures in matters of food safety.
53. E.g., the annex to Directive 64/221 contained a list of diseases, which could form an obstacle to free movement for the person in question. The Directive was repealed by Directive 2004/38/EC on the right of EU citizens and their family to move and reside freely. In accordance with Art. 29, the only diseases justifying measures restricting freedom of movement shall be the diseases with epidemic potential as defined by the World Health Organization and other infectious diseases or contagious parasitic diseases if they are the subject of protection provisions applying to nationals of the host Member State.
54. On (now) Art. 53 TFEU on the free movement of professionals, two directives (93/61 and 85/584) were issued on medical doctors and on pharmacies respectively. See also the Directive on Patient Mobility.
55. M. Poires Maduro, "Reforming the market or the state, Art. 30 and the European constitution, economic freedom and political rights", 3 ELJ (1997), 55.
56. In particular Council Directive 89/391/EEC of 12 June 1989 on the introduction of measures to encourage improvements in the safety and health of workers at work.

3.2.1 *Free movement of patients*

Essentially a codification of ECJ case law on patient mobility in the context of services,[57] the 2011 Patient's Rights Directive,[58] based on Article 114 and 168 TFEU, shows how negative integration may lead to positive integration.[59] In line with the case law, the Directive provides that the Member State of affiliation shall ensure reimbursement of cross-border care, on the condition that the insured person has the right to the type of care received. While regarding certain treatments, the State of affiliation can implement a system of prior authorization to avoid the risk of undermining the planning and financing of their health system, it may refuse this authorization only in very specific cases and not when this healthcare cannot be provided on its territory within a medically justifiable period.

Commentators have mentioned that the reference to "patient's rights" in the title of the Directive is misleading, since it only recognizes some values and principles but no patients' rights in the sense they commonly have, and some therefore see it as a "trick to mask the real intentions of the Directive, namely organizing the harmonization of healthcare services which failed on the occasion of the General Services Directive".[60] In any event, patient mobility in the EU shows that building a European health policy is a matter of trade-offs: between the constraints of the economic freedoms and the historical competence of the Member States, between the social values of the EU and the weakness of its powers to express these values, between national and European solidarity, and the Directive had tried to pay due consideration to these conflicting demands.[61] While it constitutes an important EU level regulation of the health care sector, it is true that it "fails to transcend the logic inherent in the legal system of mobility to help create a genuine policy of care in Europe", for which it would be necessary to "go beyond the legal mechanism of the internal market".[62] As such, it serves well to show what is and what is not possible under the current mix of complementary and shared, direct and indirect competence in the area of public health.

3.2.2 *Tobacco regulation*

One of the most important bodies of EU health policy is that in the field of tobacco.[63] Article 168(5) TFEU authorizes the EU to adopt incentive measures for the protection of public health regarding tobacco, but the most important regulation has instead been based on the internal market. This has caused controversy, that the Court has had to resolve.

In 1998, Parliament and Council adopted the Tobacco Advertisement Directive 98/43/EC,[64] prohibiting all advertising of tobacco products. As a minimum harmonization measure, it did not preclude Member States from laying down stricter requirements. Germany challenged the Directive arguing that the internal market provisions did not constitute the appropriate legal

57. See further Ch. 14, "Free movement of services, establishment and capital", of this book.
58. O.J. 2011, L 88/45.
59. See further Ch. 12, "The functioning of the internal market", of this book.
60. N. De Grove-Valdeyron, "La directive sur les droits des patients en matière de soins de santé transfrontaliers. Véritable statut juridique européen du patient ou simple clarification d'un régime de mobilité?", (2011) RTDE, 305 ; H. Nys, "The transposition of the Directive on patients' rights in cross-care healthcare in national law by the member states: Still a lot of effort to be made and questions to be answered", 21 EJHL (2015), 1.
61. S. de la Rosa, "The Directive on cross-border healthcare or the art of codifying complex case law", 49 CML Rev. (2012), 45.
62. Ibid.
63. See further Ch. 34, "EU health law and policy", of this book.
64. O.J. 1992, L 213/9.

basis. The Court agreed, at least to a certain extent, and annulled the Directive.[65] In coming to that conclusion, the Court considered that particularly the prohibition of advertising on posters, parasols, ashtrays and the prohibition of advertising spots in cinemas in no way helped to facilitate trade in these products. Hence, the prohibitions were not justified by the need to eliminate obstacles to the free movement of advertising media or advertising services. Nevertheless, as an important *obiter dictum*, the Court held that "provided that the conditions for recourse to [Article 114 TFEU] as a legal basis are fulfilled, the Community legislature cannot be prevented from relying on that legal basis on the ground that public health protection is a decisive factor in the choices to be made".

Following this much-discussed ruling,[66] Directive 2003/33/EC[67] was enacted, concerning specific advertising measures instead of a general ban. Germany again brought an application for annulment, arguing that this new, more limited directive still concerned EU health policy, and could therefore not be based on Article 114 TFEU. This time, Germany was unsuccessful.[68] The Court confirmed its approach as indicated in the *obiter dictum* in the first Tobacco Advertisement judgment, meaning that as long as the measure in question contributes to the functioning of the internal market, it can be based on the internal market provisions, regardless of its (fundamental) impact on health policy. Also subsequent cases brought against another important piece of EU tobacco legislation, the Tobacco Products Directive 2001/37 on manufacture, presentation and sale of tobacco products, were unsuccessful.[69] This has re-solidified the EU's basis for legislative action in this area, and for (indirect) positive integration of supporting policy areas in general.

In March 2014, a revision of the Tobacco Products Directive was adopted, "in order to reflect scientific, market and international developments".[70] Because of the fact that the old Directive constituted full harmonization on certain points, Member States had been prevented from adapting their labelling rules and strengthening protection. Central features of this new measure are the prohibition of characterizing flavours (e.g. menthol) and the mandatory large picture and text warnings. Together with the prohibition of "lipstick-style" packs and statements such as "free of additives", the Directive aims to put an end to products which entice children and teenagers into starting to smoke.

3.2.3 *Protection of workers' health and safety: The Working Time Directive*

Germany's main argument against the Tobacco Advertisement Directive was that it pretended to be an internal market regulation, while actually it constituted health policy. The UK made the opposite argument in another case, against the Working Time Directive.[71] The UK argued that this legislative measure, laying down minimum requirements regarding maximum working

---

65. Case C-376/98, *Germany v. European Parliament and Council of the European Union*, para 88.
66. See also Ch. 34, "EU health law and policy", of this book.
67. O.J. 2003, L 152/16.
68. Case C-380/03, *Germany v. European Parliament and Council of the European Union.*
69. Case C-491/01, *The Queen v. Secretary of State for Health, ex parte British American Tobacco (Investments) Ltd and Imperial Tobacco Ltd*, Case C-210/03, *The Queen, on the application of: Swedish Match AB and Swedish Match UK Ltd v. Secretary of State for Health*, Case C-434/02, *Arnold André GmbH & Co. KG v. Landrat des Kreises Herford.*
70. Directive 2014/40/EU, O.J. 2014, L 127/1–38, para 1 of the preamble.
71. Council Directive 93/104/EC replaced by Directive 2003/88/EC concerning certain aspects of the organization of working time, O.J. 2003, L 299/9–19.

hours, minimum rest periods and paid annual leave, pretended to be health policy but instead constituted social policy.[72]

The Directive was adopted on Article 118a EEC (now Art. 153 TFEU) concerning the protection of workers' health and safety, following qualified majority voting. The UK resisted the adoption of the Directive from the outset and argued that Article 235 EEC (now Article 352 TFEU) should have been used, requiring unanimity.[73] The UK argued that the Council had misused its power by using Article 118a EEC in order to avoid the unanimity requirements, claiming that working time, paid annual leave and rest periods were only remotely related to health and safety. The Court disagreed on all points except one, holding that the provision which stated that weekly rest periods should in principle include Sunday was unconnected to health and safety issues, and therefore this provision was annulled.

Although applicable to the entire economy, the Directive has arguably had the largest impact in the health care sector. After some transitional arrangements, the Directive now fully applies to all hospital doctors, including those in training. Long working hours have been a characteristic feature of this profession in many Member States. Moreover, a number of judgments on the issue of on-call time, which is a working arrangement often used in the health care sector where the worker is at the workplace ready to respond to a call but not necessarily working actively the whole time, have had a profound impact.[74] The fact that following the judgments, all time spent at the workplace, whether active or inactive, has to be fully considered as working time for applying the limits to working hours and the minimum rest periods of the Directive, has necessitated some structural reorganization of 24-hour care provision.

3.2.4 *Fiscal sustainability of national health care systems*

Article 168(7) TFEU provides that "Union action shall respect the responsibilities of the Member States for the definition of their health policy and for the organization and delivery of health services and medical care" and, further, that these national responsibilities "shall include the management of health services and medical care and the allocation of the resources assigned to them". While the measures and policies discussed in the preceding section could already be argued to challenge these statements of national autonomy, this could be said to apply with even more force to the EU's economic governance in recent years.[75] Firstly, the support provided to Member States in financial difficulties has taken the form of economic adjustment programmes, requiring reforms to address economic imbalances, specified in Memoranda of Understanding.[76] The detailed conditionalities specified therein have significantly affected national competences in the area of health, with rather controversial results. The European Centre for Disease Control has warned that serious health hazards have emerged because of the fiscal consolidation measures introduced since 2008, "more specifically, in Greece, Spain and Portugal citizens' access to public health care services has been seriously constrained, to the extent that there are

---

72. Case C-84/94, *United Kingdom of Great Britain and Northern Ireland v. Council of the European Union.*
73. T. Nowak, "The working time Directive and the European Court of Justice", 15 MJ (2008), 447.
74. Case C-303/98, *Sindicato de Médicos de Asistencia Pública (Simap) v. Conselleria de Sanidad y Consumo de la Generalidad Valenciana* and Case C-151/02, *Landeshauptstadt Kiel v. Norbert Jaeger.*
75. See for this argument also S. Greer, "The three faces of European Union health policy: Policy, markets and austerity" 33 *Policy and Society* (2014), 13.
76. The European Stability Mechanism (ESM) and the European Financial Stability Facility (EFSF) are intergovernmental support mechanisms created by the euro Member States in response to the financial crisis. EFSF is a temporary rescue mechanism. In October 2010, it was decided to create a permanent rescue mechanism, the ESM, on the basis of an international Treaty. See Ch. 26, "Economic and Monetary Union", of this book.

reported increases in mortality and morbidity".[77] In January 2013, doctors from Portugal, Spain, Ireland and Greece sent an open letter in which they deplored the effects that financial and economic decisions were having on the health of the populations of their countries, calling for immediate action to reverse the situation.[78] Secondly, health systems are increasingly featured in the Country Specific Recommendations (CSRs) issued in the context of the European Semester, usually "framed in the discourse of sustainability of public finances".[79]

4. Education, vocational training, youth and sport

These four fields lumped together in Article 6 TFEU constitute different but related areas, featuring various degrees and kinds of integration. They were introduced at different stages in the integration process: vocational training being the only supporting policy present from the beginning, education and youth being introduced by the Maastricht Treaty, and sport constituting the most recent addition by the Lisbon Treaty. The competences are further elaborated in the two articles of Title XII: Article 165 TFEU on education, sport and youth, and Article 166 TFEU on vocational training. Policy wise, they are now merged in the new ERASMUS+ Programme.[80]

4.1 Education and vocational training

The 1957 Rome Treaty did not confer any specific powers for the development of a common educational policy, but this did not deter the Court to expand its influence and to help establish a "Community law of education",[81] stating that "although educational and training policy is not as such included in the spheres which the Treaty has entrusted to the Community Institutions, it does not follow that the exercise of powers transferred to the Community is in some way limited if it is of such a nature as to affect the measures taken in the execution of a policy such as that of education and training".[82] Moreover, there was not a complete lack of explicit competence in educational matters. Article 57 EEC (now Art. 53 TFEU) granted legislative powers for the mutual recognition of diplomas. Furthermore, the EEC Treaty also provided for competence in vocational training. It is in fact on this provision that the EU's initial education law was developed.

4.1.1 ERASMUS

In its consequential *Gravier* judgment, where the Court held that Member states cannot charge higher enrolment fees to non-national EU students, the Court interpreted vocational training to include an element of "general education".[83] Shortly afterwards, the Commission presented the ERASMUS programme for student exchange solely under Art. 128 EC.[84] The Council however modified the legal basis, adding Art. 235 EC (now Art. 352 TFEU), considering that the planned

---

77. As reported by the International Labour Organization, World Social Protection Report, 2015, p. 135.
78. See <www.epha.org/spip.php?article5563>.
79. N. Azzopardi-Muscat and H. Brand, "EU Country Specific Recommendations for health systems in the European Semester process: Trends, discourse and predictors" 119 *Health Policy* (2015), 375.
80. Reg. 1288/2013 establishing "'Erasmus+': The Union programme for education, training, youth and sport", O.J. 2013, L 347/50-73.
81. B. de Witte (Ed.), *European Community Law of Education* (Nomos, 1989).
82. Case 9/74, *Donato Casagrande v. Landeshauptstadt München.*
83. Case 293/83, *Gravier*. Further developed in Case 24/86, *Blaizot v. University of Liege*, clarifying that this could also include university education whenever it prepares students for an occupation.
84. L. Pépin, "The history of EU cooperation in the field of education and training: How lifelong learning became a strategic objective", 42 *European Journal of Education* (2007), 124.

measures exceeded the scope of vocational training.[85] The Commission disagreed and brought an action for annulment regarding the inclusion of Article 235.[86] The Court found for the Council and upheld the Decision as based on both provisions,[87] but only because elements of the ERASMUS programme dealt with scientific research, which could not be considered part of vocational training. The Court sided with the Commission on the other crucial points, holding that the fact that the ERASMUS programme applied to all university studies did not mean that the measure exceeded the scope of vocational training. Even if this specific legal basis discussion has been long superseded since the introduction of a specific legal basis for education (the most recent incarnation of the programme, ERASMUS, is based on both Arts. 165 and 166 TFEU), it remains interesting as it shows the dynamics behind the evolution of these areas.

ERASMUS establishes a European University Network, encouraging universities by means of financial incentives to set up student and teacher exchange agreements. It gives out grants to the participating students; covering the cost of linguistic preparation for the studies abroad, travel expenditure and compensation for the higher cost of living in the host state. ERASMUS is very much a success story, both in terms of numbers, outcomes and public perception.[88] It has served not only to create a favourable public image of the role of the EU in educational matters, but arguably also of the EU generally.

4.1.2 *Professional diploma recognition*

The Rome Treaty featured another competence related to education: Article 53 TFEU on professional recognition of diplomas. Professional recognition deals with the rules of Member States that make access to or pursuit of a regulated profession in their territory contingent on possession of professional qualifications.[89] Article 53 TFEU provides an explicit legal basis for legislative action, approaching the issue from an internal market logic. Considering that currently around 800 professions are regulated by one or more Member States, the establishment of a common employment market would be fundamentally impaired if Member States could "carve out" these professions by applying their different statutory regimes. This has allowed for far-reaching measures. The numerous directives on co-ordination of training and recognition of qualifications obviously have a direct impact on content of courses.[90] For instance, Directive 78/687 caused the entire dentistry curriculum of Italian universities to be recreated.[91]

Over the years, the EU has pursued various regulatory strategies. The approach that was adopted in the '70 aimed at tackling recognition problems profession-by-profession and which entailed minimum harmonization of the education required for the respective profession was eventually abandoned as it proved too arduous. The strategy changed to a mutual recognition approach, resulting in the adoption of "umbrella" Directive 2005/36/EC.[92] This complex

---

85. Council Decision 87/327/EEC adopting the European Community Action Scheme for the Mobility of University Students, O.J. 1987, L 166/20.
86. K. Lenaerts, "Erasmus: Legal basis and implementation" in B. de Witte (Ed.), *European Community Law of Education* (Nomos, 1989), 116; J. Shaw, "Education and the law in the European Community", 21 *Journal of Law & Education* (1992), 420.
87. Case 242/87, *Commission v. Council (Erasmus)*.
88. See European Commission, *Erasmus: Success stories. Europe Creates Opportunities* (Office for Official Publications of the European Communities, 2007).
89. H. Schneider, *Die Anerkennung von Diplomen in der Europäischen Gemeinschaft* (Intersentia, 1995).
90. J. Lonbay, "Education and the law: The Community context", 14 EL Rev. (1989), 368.
91. C. Zilioli, "The recognition of diplomas and its impact on educational policies" in B. De Witte (Ed.), *European Community Law of Education* (Nomos, 1989), 51.
92. O.J. 2005, L 255/22-142. See also the discussion on the Internal Market Information System further below.

measure consolidated almost all the previous legislation, except for the specific directives on the provision of services and establishment of lawyers.[93] This directive does not substantially impact the higher education systems of the Member States in a direct way. As it does not propose the harmonization of new professions, but simply applies a mutual recognition approach to the non-coordinated professions, it is less intrusive and less contested. Still, the mechanism of mutual recognition might have an important effect on the national higher education systems, as it could put pressure on the national higher education systems that are less competitive, attractive or "efficient".

4.1.3 *Academic diploma recognition*

In contrast to professional recognition, academic recognition is concerned with the academic status of obtained degrees. Academic recognition is often regarded to lie outside the scope of formal EU powers. Although it could be argued that this distinction is unfounded,[94] no EU legislation concerning the academic recognition of diplomas has been adopted. That is not to say that no European integration has taken place in this area. Firstly, to refuse recognition of academic diplomas or titles can constitute a restriction of the fundamental freedoms.[95] Secondly, the EU has adopted a number of supporting measures to facilitate academic recognition, such as the European Credit Transfer System for higher education (ECT)[96] and for vocational training (ECVET),[97] Europass,[98] the European Qualifications Framework[99] and the Diploma Supplement.[100] Thirdly, significant European integration has taken place in this area in an intergovernmental way, most notably in the context of the Council of Europe, which has adopted the Lisbon Recognition Convention,[101] and the independent Bologna Process.[102]

The Bologna Process, a non-binding intergovernmental project including all EU Member States, aims to create a European Higher Education Area, with at its core common Bachelor-Master-Doctorate system. The Sorbonne and Bologna Declarations, which constitute the basis of the process, are "political artefacts"[103] that may be regarded as "public international soft law".[104] It could be said that the Bologna Process constitutes both a result and an illustration of the strong

---

93. Directives 77/249/EEC and 98/5/EC.
94. S. Garben, "On recognition of qualifications for academic and professional purposes", 16 *Tilburg Law Review* (2011), 127.
95. Case C-19/92, *Dieter Kraus v. Land Baden-Württemberg*, Case C-153/02, *Valentina Neri v. European School of Economics*. The non-recognition on equal terms of secondary school qualifications was considered a restriction of Arts. 18 and 21 TFEU on equal treatment of EU citizens, in Cases C-65/03, *Commission v. Belgium* and C-147/03, *Commission of the European Communities v. Republic of Austria*, and Case C-73/08, *Nicolas Bressol and Others, Céline Chaverot and Others v. Gouvernement de la Communauté française*.
96. ECTS was developed by the Commission in the context of ERASMUS to enable students to take the credits obtained during their period of study abroad and use them within their home curriculum.
97. Recommendation on the establishment of a European Credit system for Vocational Education and Training (ECVET), O.J. 2009, L 155.
98. Decision 2241/2004/EC.
99. *Recommendation of the European Parliament and of the Council of 23 Apr. 2008 on the establishment of the European Qualifications Framework for lifelong learning*, O.J. 2008, C 111/1-7. The EQF constitutes a European reference framework, consisting of 8 levels, based on "learning outcomes".
100. The Diploma Supplement is a European administrative annex to diplomas, which has been elaborated jointly by a working group of the European Commission, Council of Europe and UNESCO.
101. Convention on the Recognition of Qualifications concerning Higher Education in the European Region.
102. S. Garben, op. cit. *supra* note 105.
103. A. Amaral and A. Magalhaes, "Epidemiology and the Bologna saga", 48 *Higher Education* (2004), 84.
104. E. Hackl, "Towards a European area of higher education: Change and convergence in European higher education", EUI Working Paper, 9 RSC (2001), 28.

counter-forces in this area. On the one hand, it *de*-nationalizes higher education policy, as it lifts the organization of higher education systems to a European level. At the same time, from an EU perspective, Bologna constitutes a *re*-nationalization. The Process withdraws the important areas of teacher and student mobility and diploma recognition from the supranational spheres of EU influence, moving them to the intergovernmental realm where state autonomy still reigns. But although the Process takes place outside the EU framework, there is considerable material and institutional interaction. The Commission is heavily involved in by means of funding and steering, and characterizes its contribution to the Process as part of the Europe 2020 Strategy.[105] The follow-up relies heavily on the EU presidency and the European Credit Transfer System has been transposed into the Bologna Process' Bachelor-Master system. Furthermore, since 2015, the EU offers a Student Loan Guarantee Facility, which provides partial guarantees to financial intermediaries in respect of loans granted to students undertaking a second-cycle degree, such as a Master's degree, which is neither their country of residence nor the country in which they obtained their qualification granting access to the Master's programme.[106] This EU measure is of course an important support for the system and the goals of the Bologna Process. All of this makes the exact status of the Bologna Process obscure.[107]

Where the Court's aforementioned case law in *Gravier* and ERASMUS blurred the legal distinction between (university) education and vocational training, the Bologna Process has been responsible for merging them in practice. While there is a specific Copenhagen Process for vocational training, the Bologna Process has altered the meaning of vocational training in many Member States by requalifying higher vocational institutions as "universities" which can offer either special Bachelor degrees or regular Bachelor and even Master degrees.

4.1.4 *Student residence*

Further EU measures concerning mobile students include the Student Residence Directives. Directive 93/96 granted students the right of residence in the Member State of study, but under the conditions of sufficient health insurance and sufficient resources to avoid becoming a burden on the host State's social assistance schemes. This Directive was repealed by Directive 2004/38/EC on the right of citizens to move and reside freely within EU territory. The Directive constitutes a consolidation and clarification of all the legislation on the right of entry and residence for Union citizens. It indicates specifically that host Member States are not required, prior to the acquisition of the permanent right of residence, to grant maintenance aid for studies, including for vocational training, in the form of grants or loans. Remarkably, this provision led the Court to hold in *Bidar*[108] that maintenance grants were included in the scope of EU law for the purposes of the non-discrimination principle. The Court has however allowed a relatively wide derogation, meaning that Member States may require at least 5 years of prior residence.[109]

Directive 2004/114/EC concerns students from third countries. The rationale behind the Directive is, according to its preamble, to "promote Europe as a whole as a world centre of excellence for studies and vocational training" by promoting the mobility of third-country nationals

105. European Commission, *Realising the European Higher Education Area*, Contribution of the European Commission to the Berlin Conference of European Higher Education Ministers on 18/19 Sept. 2003.
106. Reg. 1288/2013 establishing "'Erasmus+': The Union programme for education, training, youth and sport", O.J. 2013, L 347/50–73.
107. S. Garben, "The Bologna process: From a European law perspective", 16 ELJ (2010), 186.
108. Case C-209/03, *The Queen, on the application of Dany Bidar v. London Borough of Ealing and Secretary of State for Education and Skills.*
109. Case C-158/07, *Jaqueline Förster v. IB-Groep.*

to the EU for the purpose of studies,[110] or, in the words of a commentator "to facilitate the admission and residence of groups of third-country nationals whose presence is welcome for economic reasons".[111] The Directive distinguishes four categories of third-country nationals, to wit students, pupils, unpaid trainees and volunteers. The conditions for entry of students and pupils are that they have a valid travel document and, if minors, come with parental authorization, that they have sickness insurance and sufficient resources to cover their stay and that they have been accepted by a higher educational establishment or school.

4.1.5 *Education of migrant children*

Finally, one of the most obvious categories of individuals that have been granted educational rights by means of EU legislation is that of migrant workers and their children. The worker itself is the least disputed beneficiary of equal treatment in relation to education, for he is the embodiment of the free movement of persons in the internal market. Realizing that the achievement of this objective would be undermined if the worker were to be separated from his family, Community law also provided for accommodation of the family members of the worker in the host state, which was a breakthrough development at the time. One of the most important pieces of legislation in this context was Regulation 1612/68, replaced by Regulation 492/2011.[112] In accordance with Article 10, the children of a national of a Member State who is or has been employed in the territory of another Member State shall be admitted to that State's general educational, apprenticeship and vocational training courses under the same conditions as the nationals of that State, if such children are residing in its territory. In addition, the children of migrant workers have been the subject of a legal measure constituting a piece of veritable education policy, namely the Directive on language teaching for the children of migrant workers.[113] This Directive of 25 July 1977 contains an obligation to take positive action, namely to promote teaching of the mother tongue and culture of their country of origin.

4.1.6 *Cost-effectiveness of education systems*

In recent years, education has become included in the European Semester, where it is being considered as a factor of economic stability and growth. Apart from enhancing inclusion policies, overall, the Country Specific Recommendations (CSRs) are predominantly concerned with the "cost-effectiveness" and "employability" of Member States' education systems. For instance, Denmark has been told that "[c]ontinued efforts are [...] needed to improve the quality and cost-effectiveness of its education and training systems",[114] Estonia to "[l]ink training and education more effectively to the needs of the labour market"[115] and Malta that it should "focus education outcomes more on labour market needs".[116] The CSRs can be remarkably de-

110. Preamble of *Council Directive 2004/114/EC of 13 Dec. 2004 on the conditions of admission of third-country nationals for the purposes of studies, pupil exchange, unremunerated training or voluntary service*, O.J. 2004, L 375/12-18.
111. G. Fitchew, "European policy and legislation on immigration", (2009) Migration Watch UK Briefing Paper 4.12.
112. O.J. 2011, L 141/1–12.
113. Directive 77/486 (O.J. 1977, L 199/32).
114. Council Recommendation of 9 July 2013 on the National Reform Programme 2013 of Denmark and delivering a Council opinion on the Convergence Programme of Denmark, 2013-2016, O.J. 2013, C 217/18, point 12.
115. Council Recommendation of 10 July 2012 on the National Reform Programme 2012 of Estonia and delivering a Council Opinion on the Stability Programme of Estonia, 2012-15, O.J. 2012, C 219/25–27, point 14.
116. Council Recommendation of 12 July 2011 on the National Reform Programme 2011 of Malta and delivering a Council opinion on the updated Stability Programme of Malta 2011-2014, O.J. 2011, C 215/10–12, point 3.

tailed and specific on the required reforms concerning various aspects of national education systems, which could be said to sit uncomfortably with the national autonomy clause in Article 165(1) TFEU that EU action should fully respect the responsibility of the Member States for the content of teaching and the organization of education systems. For example, the Commission's proposed CSR in 2017 for Croatia states: "Since 2015, as part of the implementation of the education, science and technology strategy, a reform of the school curricula was launched to improve on content and teaching of transferable skills. After ambivalent stakeholder reactions, the curricular reform was revised, and implementation has been significantly delayed. The process now needs to continue in line with the original objectives".[117] Furthermore, the CSRs reflect a clear policy to increase the involvement of the private sector in higher education and to make the funding of higher education "competitive". In this vein, Bulgaria has received the recommendation that "frameworks fostering collaboration between universities and the private sector have to be further developed, and funding should be allocated in a competitive, merit-based and transparent way", and to "pursue the reform of higher education, in particular through better aligning outcomes to labour market needs and strengthening cooperation between education, research and business",[118] Estonia to "enhance cooperation between businesses and academia",[119] and Italy to address the "underperformance of the tertiary education system" *inter alia* by creating "a stronger link between universities' performance and the allocation of public funding".[120]

4.2 *Youth*

According to Article 165(2) TFEU, Union action on youth shall be directed at encouraging the development of youth exchanges and of exchanges of socio-educational instructors, and encouraging the participation of young people in democratic life in Europe. In addition, Article 47 TFEU provides that Member States shall, within the framework of a joint programme, encourage the exchange of young workers. In the context of humanitarian aid, Article 214(5) TFEU states that to establish a framework for joint contributions from young Europeans to the humanitarian aid operations of the Union, a European Voluntary Humanitarian Aid Corps shall be set up.[121] Finally, the Charter of Fundamental rights features the rights of the child (Art. 24) and the prohibition of child labour and protection of young people at work (Art. 32). This latter right is given more concrete expression in Directive 94/33/EC on the protection of young people at work, adopted on Article 153 TFEU on social policy.[122] The Directive obliges Member States to prohibit work by children, and to ensure that work by adolescents is strictly regulated. Working with several harmful substances is prohibited.

---

117. Recommendation for a Council Recommendation on the 2017 National Reform Programme of Croatia and delivering a Council opinion on the 2017 Convergence Programme of Croatia, COM(2017)510 final.
118. Council Recommendation of 10 July 2012 on the National Reform Programme 2012 of Bulgaria and delivering a Council opinion on the Convergence Programme of Bulgaria, 2012-15, O.J. 2012, C 219/9–12, point 16 and Council Recommendation of 9 July 2013 on the National Reform Programme 2013 of Bulgaria and delivering a Council opinion on the Convergence Programme of Bulgaria, 2012-2016, O.J. 2013, C 217/10–13, point 4.
119. Council Recommendation of 10 July 2012 on the National Reform Programme 2012 of Estonia and delivering a Council Opinion on the Stability Programme of Estonia, 2012-15, O.J. 2012, C 219/25–27, point 14.
120. Council Recommendation of 10 July 2012 on the National Reform Programme 2012 of Italy and delivering a Council opinion on the Stability Programme of Italy, 2012-2015, O.J. 2012 C 219/46–49, point 16.
121. Reg. (EU) No. 375/2014 establishing the European Voluntary Humanitarian Aid Corps ("EU Aid Volunteers initiative"), O.J. 2014, L 122/1–17.
122. O.J. 1994, L 216/12–20.

In response to the high levels of youth unemployment as a consequence of the economic and financial crisis, this area has become a more defined political priority in recent years. As part of the "Youth Employment Package", in April 2013 the Council adopted the Recommendation on establishing a Youth Guarantee,[123] calling on Member States to ensure that all young people under 25 receive a good quality offer of employment, continued education, an apprenticeship or a traineeship within four months of leaving formal education or becoming unemployed. While not legally binding, the EU is seeking to enforce the implementation of the Youth Guarantee via other means. Firstly, the Youth Guarantee is supported by EU Structural Funds and the €6.4 billion Youth Employment Initiative agreed by the Council in 2013. Furthermore, the Country Specific Recommendations for 2014,[124] proposed by the Commission and endorsed by the European Council as part of the European Semester, urged 18 Member States to take urgent steps to combat youth unemployment by improving transitions from school to work, proposing specific recommendations on implementation of the Youth Guarantee to 8 countries.[125] In March 2013, as a supporting measure in the context of the Youth Guarantee, the Council adopted a Recommendation on a Quality Framework for Traineeships,[126] providing a common set of guidelines, inviting Member States to ensure that traineeships are based on a written agreement, better learning content and respect for the rights and working conditions of trainees, reasonable duration of traineeships and their proper recognition, and increased cross-border mobility of trainees.

Other notable measures include the Daphne Programme to prevent and combat violence against children, young people and women, Council Decision of 29 May 2000 to combat child pornography on the Internet,[127] and Directive 2011/93/EU of the European Parliament and of the Council of 13 December 2011 on combating the sexual abuse and sexual exploitation of children and child pornography,[128] based on Article 82(2) and Article 83(1) TFEU, which establishes minimum rules concerning the definition of criminal offences and sanctions in the area of sexual abuse and sexual exploitation of children, child pornography and solicitation of children for sexual purposes.

4.3 *Sport*

Despite the initial absence of any reference to sport in the Treaties, a significant body of European sport's law and policy has steadily been built over the years. First and foremost, the Commission and the Court apply the free movement and competition law rules to sporting rules.[129] The impact of such indirect, negative integration can hardly be overstated.[130] While the Court has generally excluded discriminatory nationality rules in the context of national teams from the scope of the Treaty,[131] it has firmly applied the free movement provisions to such measures

---

123. O.J. 2013, C 120/1–6.
124. See Commission Communication, *2014 European Semester: Country-specific recommendations*, COM(2014)400 final.
125. Spain, Italy, Slovakia, Croatia, Portugal, Poland, Bulgaria and Ireland.
126. O.J. 2014, C 88/1–4.
127. O.J. 2000, L 138/1–4.
128. O.J. 2011, L 335, replacing Council Framework Decision 2004/68/JHA.
129. See e.g. Case C-176/96, *Jyri Lehtonen and Castors Canada Dry Namur-Braine ASBL v. Fédération royale belge des sociétés de basket-ball ASBL*, Case C-438/00, *Deutscher Handballbund eV v. Maros Kolpak*, Case C-265/03, *Igor Simutenkov v. Ministerio de Educación y Cultura and Real Federación Española de Fútbol* In Case C-519/04 P, *David Meca-Medina*, Case C-325/08, *Olympique Lyonnais SASP v. Olivier Bernard.*
130. S. Van den Bogaert and A. Vermeersch, "Sport and the EC Treaty: A tale of uneasy bedfellows", 32 EL Rev. (2006), 821.
131. Case 36/74, *Walrave and Koch.*

at club level. And while it has been willing to accept the specificity of sport to a certain extent in some cases, the Court has not granted an outright exemption to sport, regardless of the consistent efforts of especially sporting bodies and their representatives to prevent the application of EU rules to sporting activities. In addition, as regards the passive enjoyment of sport there is a clear impact of the rules on media and supporter mobility.

Regarding positive integration, the importance of sport for the development of European integration has been acknowledged and the EU has developed a "moderate direct sports policy", emphasizing sport's cultural, educational and social functions, primarily through the "creative use"[132] of the EU's competences in other supporting policy areas such as culture, education and health, and the internal market.[133] As regards sport's societal role, there are a number of actions focusing on sport's capacity to improve social inclusion, particularly in relation to people with a disability, and those from minority groups.[134] Furthermore, in the context of the increasing societal problem of obesity, a large part of EU activities in the field of sport now focus on implementing the Council's Recommendation on promoting health-enhancing physical activity across sectors,[135] including a monitoring framework that takes into account the 2008 EU Physical Activity Guidelines.[136] The EU also plays a role in combatting match fixing,[137] through the coordination of EU legislation in related areas as well as cooperation with international bodies such as the International Olympic Committee and the Council of Europe. In 2012, the Commission published a study mapping national criminal law provisions applicable to match fixing,[138] and it is planning a Recommendation on best practices in the prevention and combating of betting-related match fixing.[139]

Article 165 TFEU now provides that the Union "shall contribute to the promotion of European sporting issues, while taking account of the specific nature of sport, its structures based on voluntary activity and its social and educational function". As such, EU action shall be directed at "developing the European dimension in sport, by promoting fairness and openness in sporting competitions and cooperation between bodies responsible for sports, and by protecting the physical and moral integrity of sportsmen and sportswomen, especially the youngest sportsmen and sportswomen". The insertion of this sports article by the Lisbon Treaty was considered desirable from the viewpoint of legal certainty and the legitimacy of already existing and future EU action in this area, and to a certain extent to provide a firmer legal and financial basis for certain actions. However, as is the case for the other supporting policies, it seems that the introduction

132. S. Van den Bogaert and A. Vermeersch, op. cit. *supra* note 129, at 822.
133. E.g., specific rules applicable to equestrian sports have been adopted on the agriculture/market provisions. Directive 90/428/EEC governs trade in equidae intended for competitions and establishes the conditions for their participation in competitions. Decision 93/195/EEC lays down the animal health conditions for the re-entry of registered horses for racing, competition and cultural events after temporary export to non-EU countries, and Decision 92/260/EEC, mainly used in the arrival from and return to their home countries outside the EU of sport horses.
134. Council conclusions on the role of sport as a source of and a driver for active social inclusion, O.J. 2010, C 326/5–8.
135. 2013/C 354/01.
136. EU Physical Activity Guidelines, 2008, available at <ec.europa.eu/sport/library/policy_documents/eu-physical-activity-guidelines-2008_en.pdf>.
137. See e.g. Council conclusions on combating match-fixing, O.J. 2011, C 378/1–2 and European Parliament resolution on the European dimension in sport, O.J. 2013, C 239E/46–60.
138. Available at <ec.europa.eu/sport/library/studies/study-sports-fraud-final-version_en.pdf>.
139. Available at <ec.europa.eu/sport/policy/organisation_of_sport/match_fixing_en.htm>.

of an explicit legal basis has not made a big difference in the scope and direction of EU sports law and policy, is not expected to do so in the near future.[140]

5. Culture

The initial Treaty only contained two scant references to culture, in Article 36 EEC which permitted Member States to restrict imports and exports in order to protect national treasures, and in Article 131 EEC which enabled the Member States to extend the benefits to associated countries in order to further the "economic, social and cultural development [...] which they desire".[141] For many years, national cultural bodies or those pleading of their behalf claimed that their cultural policy was not, and should not be, affected by European law. However, as has proven to be the case for so many other supporting policy areas, the case law of the Court and indirect legislation having a bearing on culture[142] had already removed any doubt on this point before the Maastricht Treaty's insertion of an explicit competence in the form of (now) Article 167 TFEU. The new provision thus did little more than legitimizing existing practice and attempting to draw sharper boundaries for future initiatives.

Article 167(1) TFEU provides that the EU "shall contribute to the flowering of the cultures of the Member States, while respecting their national and regional diversity and at the same time bringing the common cultural heritage to the fore". As such, EU action shall be aimed at encouraging cooperation between Member States and, if necessary, supporting and supplementing their action, for the improvement of the knowledge and dissemination of the culture and history of the European peoples, the conservation and safeguarding of cultural heritage of European significance, non-commercial cultural exchanges, and artistic and literary creation.

EU law does not attempt to define "culture", and as such it depends on one's own definition to what extent EU rules and policies affect it. In its widest understanding, there is hardly anything that escapes culture, as any act of regulation could somehow be argued to be a part, reflection of consequence of a region's/country's culture and identity.[143] Under a more focused but still broad interpretation of the term, EU rules and case law on e.g. the mutual recognition of foodstuffs and beverages and their denomination of origin,[144] media,[145] tourism[146] and

---

140. See to this effect also S. Weatherill, "EU sports law: The effect of the Lisbon Treaty" in A. Biondi, P. Eeckhout and S. Ripley (Eds.), *EU Law After Lisbon* (OUP, 2012).
141. R. Craufurd-Smith, "The evolution of cultural policy in the European Union" in P. Craig and G. de Búrca, *The Evolution of EU Law* (OUP, 2011), 869.
142. Such as the Television Without Frontiers Directive 89/552/EEC, Directive 2001/84 on the resale right for the benefit of the author of an original work of art, Directive 2006/116 on the term of protection of copyright and certain related rights, and the Audiovisual Media Services Directive 2010/13/EU.
143. As such, only in exceptional cases will this constitute a reason to derogate from the Treaty provisions. See on Sunday trading rules, predating *Keck*: Case C-145/88, *Torfaen Borough Council v. B & Q plc*. On a prohibition of games involving simulated killings: Case C-36/02, *Omega Spielhallen- und Automatenaufstellungs-GmbH v. Oberbürgermeisterin der Bundesstadt Bonn*. On abortion, see: Case C-159/90, *The Society for the Protection of Unborn Children Ireland Ltd v. Stephen Grogan and others*.
144. Case 170/78, *Commission of the European Communities v. United Kingdom of Great Britain and Northern Ireland*, Case 178/84 *Commission of the European Communities v. Federal Republic of Germany*, Case 237/82, *Jongeneel Kaas BV and others v. State of the Netherlands and Stichting Centraal Orgaan Zuivelcontrole*. Council Reg. (EC) No. 510/2006 on the protection of geographical indications and designations of origin for agricultural products and foodstuffs and Council Reg. (EC) No. 509/2006 on agricultural products and foodstuffs as traditional specialities guaranteed.
145. See e.g. Case C-288/89, *Stichting Collectieve Antennevoorziening Gouda and others v. Commissariaat voor de Media*, and the directives cited *supra* note 151.
146. See section 2.2.5.

on languages[147] should be included. Under the narrowest definition, one would only look at the EU's impact on the arts (fine arts, music, dance, theatre, literature)[148] and cultural[149]/archaeological[150] heritage.

No matter what definition one adopts, however, the underlying tension becomes clear: while perhaps there is nothing more distinctively and characteristically European than its deeply rich and diverse cultures, from the viewpoint of European integration, national cultures are perhaps the biggest and least surmountable obstacle. Culture is what both binds and divides Europeans. To a certain extent, the EU's strategy in dealing with this tension has been to focus on culture's economic manifestations, where it could make a stronger case for its involvement. This however has fed into a second underlying tension in this area: between culture's economic and explicitly *non*-economic aims and character. While the EU has been criticized for adopting a liberal approach, prioritizing trade over less easily quantifiable cultural interest, it has been pointed out that the EU "has not been completely blind to the fact that competitive pressures and the operation of consumer choice can diminish as well as enhance cultural diversity".[151]

---

147. It has been said that there is undoubtedly EU language law, but that one may doubt whether there is a coherent positive language policy. See B. de Witte, "Language law of the European Union" in R. Craufurd-Smith, *Culture and European Union Law* (OUP, 2004), 205. Relevant cases include: Case C-379/87, *Anita Groener v. Minister for Education and the City of Dublin Vocational Educational Committee*, Case C-366/98, *Criminal proceedings against Yannick Geffroy and Casino France SNC*, Case C-424/97, *Salomone Haim v. Kassenzahnärztliche Vereinigung Nordrhein*, Case C-281/98, *Roman Angonese v. Cassa di Risparmio di Bolzano SpA*, Case C-222/07, *Unión de Televisiones Comerciales Asociadas (UTECA) v. Administración General del Estado*. Relevant EU measures include: EEC Council: Reg. No. 1 determining the languages to be used by the European Economic Community (O.J. 1958, L 17/385–386), Commission Communication, A New Framework Strategy for Multilingualism, COM/2005/596 final. Art. 22 of the EU Charter states that the Union shall respect cultural, religious and linguistic diversity. See also Case C-361/01 P, *Christina Kik v. OHIM*, concerning the rules in force governing languages at the Office for Harmonisation in the Internal Market.
148. See e.g. Directive 2014/60/EU on the return of cultural objects unlawfully removed from the territory of a Member State and amending Reg. (EU) No. 1024/2012 (O.J. 2014, L 159/1–10), Council Reg. (EC) No. 116/2009 on the export of cultural goods (O.J. 2009, L 39/1–7), Council Resolution implementing the work plan on European cooperation in the field of culture: European added value and mobility of persons and circulation of works in the cultural sector (O.J. 2003, C 13/5–7), Council Resolution on the promotion of the free movement of persons working in the cultural sector, European Parliament resolution on the importance and dynamics of the theatre and the performing arts in an enlarged Europe (O.J. 2003, C 300E/156–162), Council Resolution on exchange of information and experience concerning conditions for professional artists in the context of EU enlargement (O.J. 2001, C 213/9–10). See also Case C-17/92, *Federación de Distribuidores Cinematográficos v. Estado Español and Unión de Productores de Cine y Televisión*, Joined Cases 60 and 61/84, *Cinéthèque SA and others v. Fédération nationale des cinémas français*.
149. See e.g. the Capitals of Culture initiative. Decision No. 1622/2006/EC establishing a Community action for the European Capital of Culture event for the years 2007 to 2019.
150. Although primarily the responsibility of the Council of Europe (see European Convention on the Protection of the Archaeological Heritage), heritage is also a priority for the EU. Action takes place through the OMC, funding and mainstreaming. Cultural heritage benefits from EU investments in 2014–2020 through the European Structural and Investment Funds (€ 351 billion for regional policy), Horizon 2020 (€ 80 billion for research) and Creative Europe (€ 1.5 billion for cultural and creative industries). Regarding mainstreaming, the EU's Environmental Impact Assessment Directive 2014/52 requires consideration of a project's impact on cultural heritage, and General Block Exemption Reg. 651/2014 allows state aid. See Council conclusions on cultural heritage as a strategic resource for a sustainable Europe adopted 21 May 2014 and Commission Communication "Towards an integrated approach to cultural heritage for Europe" COM(2014)477 final.
151. R. Craufurd-Smith, op. cit. *supra* note 146.

The EU's main incentive measure in this policy area today is "Creative Europe", with a budget of € 1.46 billion, providing support to the audio-visual and culture sector aiming to protect and promote European culture heritage, while additionally supporting the cultural and creative industries, seeing them as a driver for growth and job creation.[152] These funds are also used to support the Open Method of Coordination in culture, launched in 2008 on the basis of a proposal made by the Commission in the European Agenda for Culture.[153] The Member States agree on the themes on which the OMC should focus every four years, in the framework of the Work Plan for Culture.[154] Under the OMC, national authorities appoint representatives and individuals to be part of specialized working groups. There have been more than ten culture OMC groups, working on *inter alia* the mobility of culture professionals,[155] artists' residencies and the promotion of Creative Partnerships. Complementing the OMC dialogue between decision-makers, the Commission organizes a bi-annual Culture Forum, bringing together stakeholders and decision-makers.

In addition, the Commission represents the interests of the EU in international initiatives, such as those headed by the United Nations Educational, Scientific and Cultural Organization (UNESCO). Indeed, more than perhaps in other supporting policy areas, EU action in culture takes place in the context of action by other international players, in particular the Council of Europe and UNESCO, which could be said to have a more direct mandate for developing cultural policies and instruments. Of the various external binding instruments in the field, the UNESCO Convention on the Protection and Promotion of the Diversity of Cultural Expressions should be mentioned, to which the EU became a signatory in 2006,[156] as well as the Council of Europe Cultural Convention, to which all EU Member States are signatories.

6. Industry

Article 173 TFEU provides that "the Union and the Member States shall ensure that the conditions necessary for the competitiveness of the Union's industry exist", for which purpose their action shall be aimed at speeding up the adjustment of industry to structural changes, encouraging an environment favourable to initiative and to the development of undertakings throughout the Union, particularly small and medium-sized undertakings, encouraging an environment favourable to cooperation between undertakings, and fostering better exploitation of the industrial potential of policies of innovation, research and technological development. The second paragraph indicates that the Member States shall consult each other in liaison with the Commission and, where necessary, shall coordinate their action. The Commission may take any useful initiative to promote such coordination, in particular initiatives aiming at the establishment of

---

152. Reg. (EU) No. 1295/2013 establishing the Creative Europe Programme (2014 to 2020) and repealing Decisions No. 1718/2006/EC, No. 1855/2006/EC and No. 1041/2009/EC.
153. Commission Communication on a European agenda for culture in a globalizing world, SEC(2007)570.
154. The 2015–18 Work Plan for Culture, adopted by EU Culture Ministers in December 2014, sets out four main priorities for European cooperation in cultural policy-making: 1) Accessible and inclusive culture, 2) Cultural heritage, 3) Cultural and creative sectors: creative economy and innovation, 4) Promotion of cultural diversity, culture in EU external relations, and mobility.
155. Report and recommendations to the Cultural Affairs Committee on improving the conditions to support the mobility of artists and culture professionals, available at <ec.europa.eu/culture/policy/cultural-creative-industries/documents/artist-mobility_en.pdf>, and Report on building a strong framework for artists' mobility: 5 key principles, 2012, available at <ec.europa.eu/culture/library/reports/artist-mobility-report_en.pdf>.
156. Council Decision 2006/515/EC on the conclusion of the Convention on the Protection and Promotion of the Diversity of Cultural Expressions, O.J. 2006, L 201/15–30.

guidelines and indicators, the organization of exchange of best practice, and the preparation of the necessary elements for periodic monitoring and evaluation.

Considering its economic nature, one may wonder why industry is only a complementary competence. The text of Article 173 TFEU clearly bears the traces of a compromise between the age-old difference of views about the need for an industrial policy and the form it should take. The conflict was principally between the more *dirigiste* approach based on southern European thinking, and the liberal non-interventionist approach. The original draft was much more *dirigiste* in nature, but resistance from the northern, more market-oriented Member States led to the present text. All the actions that can be undertaken on Article 173 TFEU take place in accordance with a system of open and competitive markets. This point is emphasized by the last paragraph of the provision, which provides that this title "shall not provide a basis for the introduction by the Union of any measure which could lead to a distortion of competition". This confirms the free-market philosophy of the more liberally-minded Member States.

In July 2005, a Commission communication for the first time set out an integrated approach to industrial policy based on a concrete work programme of cross-sectoral and sectoral initiatives.[157] The 2007 "mid-term review of industrial policy" concluded that the actions described in the 2005 communication had benefited Europe's industries, with regard to both large companies and SMEs, and emphasized that the integrated approach had proved successful and had the support of Parliament and the Member States.[158] In the context of Europe 2020, the flagship initiative "An industrial policy for the globalization era" focuses on 10 actions to promote European industrial competitiveness, thus placing more emphasis on factors such as SME growth and the supply and management of raw materials.[159] In January 2014 the Commission launched the communication "For a European Industrial Renaissance"[160] focusing on reversing industrial decline and reaching the target of 20% of GDP for manufacturing activities by 2020. The Commission states that to attract new investments and create a better business environment, the EU needs more coherent politics in the field of the internal market, including European infrastructure such as energy, transport and information networks, as well as for goods and services. The importance of improved cooperation in the areas of good quality public administration, trade, research and raw materials is also mentioned.

7. Tourism

Introduced by the Lisbon Treaty, Article 195 TFEU provides that the Union shall complement the action of the Member States in tourism, particularly by promoting the competitiveness of Union undertakings. To that end, Union action shall be aimed at: "(a) encouraging the creation of a favourable environment for the development of undertakings in this sector; (b) promoting cooperation between the Member States, particularly by the exchange of good practice". The Parliament and the Council, under the ordinary legislative procedure, shall establish specific measures to complement actions within the Member States, excluding harmonization.

As in the case of the other supporting policy areas, there was already some EU integration in this field before the introduction of this specific legal basis. Many tourists have been able to

157. "Implementing the Community Lisbon Programme: A policy framework to strengthen EU manufacturing — towards a more integrated approach for industrial policy" (COM(2005)474).
158. COM(2007)374.
159. COM(2010)614. See also Commission Communication "Industrial Policy: Reinforcing competitiveness" (COM(2011)642), Commission Communication "A Stronger European Industry for Growth and Economic Recovery", COM(2012)582) and European Parliament resolution on an Industrial Policy for the Globalized Era (O.J. 2012, C 199E/131).
160. COM(2014)14.

make use of the freedom to receive services as well as the free movement of persons,[161] which for example means that Member States may not charge higher museum fees to EU citizens than to nationals.[162] Furthermore, in the tourist guide cases the Court held the activities of tourist guides fall within the freedom to provide services under Article 56 TFEU, meaning that licensing and other restrictions will be closely scrutinized and are likely to be prohibited by EU law.[163] Other relevant measures are the consumer protection directives on package tours[164] and on timesharing,[165] and a 2011 Regulation on statistical information on tourism.[166]

In 2010 the Commission adopted a Communication laying down a comprehensive strategy to boost the competitiveness of the sector, to promote sustainability, and to maximize the potential of EU financial policies.[167] The area is receiving increasing policy attention in recent years, which is not surprising considering its high economic significance, not least in the EU Member States that have been particularly hit in the economic crisis. In 2014, the Commission adopted a Green Paper on the safety of tourism accommodation,[168] a proposal for a Council Recommendation on European Tourism Quality Principles,[169] and a Communication on a European Strategy for more Growth and Jobs in Coastal and Maritime Tourism.[170]

8. Civil protection

Civil protection assistance consists of governmental aid delivered in the immediate aftermath of a disaster. It can take the form of in-kind assistance, deployment of specially-equipped teams, or assessment and coordination by experts sent to the field. Ever since the terrorist attacks of 11 September 2001, the subject of civil protection is receiving more attention in the EU, with numerous legal instruments and initiatives being adopted, providing a more structured European framework. This is an area where EU action is firmly supported by citizens, who see a clear added value in coordinated responses to disasters.[171] Also the Member States have shown a sustained willingness to enhance the EU's crisis management capacities. After a large-scale crisis or disaster, they routinely call for additional EU capacities to coordinate, link, or integrate their response capacities, and few European Council meetings conclude without some call for more crisis cooperation.[172]

161. Case 186/87, *Cowan v. Trésor Publique.*
162. Case C-45/93, *Commission v. Kingdom of Spain*, C-388/01, *Commission v. Italian Republic.*
163. Case C-154/89, *Commission v. French Republic*, Case C-180/89, *Commission v. Italian Republic*, Case C-198/89, *Commission v. Hellenic Republic*, Case C-375/92, *Commission v. Kingdom of Spain.*
164. Council Directive 90/314/EEC on package travel, package holidays and package tours, O.J. 1990, L 158/59–64, adopted on the basis of (now) Art. 114 TFEU.
165. Directive 2008/122/EC on the protection of consumers in respect of certain aspects of timeshare, long-term holiday product, resale and exchange contracts.
166. Reg. (EU) No. 692/2011 concerning European statistics on tourism, O.J. 2011, L 192/17–32.
167. Commission Communication, "Europe, the world's No. 1 tourist destination – a new political framework for tourism in Europe", COM(2010)352 final.
168. European Commission, Green Paper on Safety of Tourism Accommodation Services, COM/2014/464 final.
169. COM(2014)85 final – 2014/43 (NLE).
170. COM(2014)86 final.
171. 82% of EU citizens agree that a coordinated EU action in dealing with disasters is more effective than actions by individual countries, 2012 Eurobarometer.
172. A. Boin, M. Ekengren and M. Rhinard, *The European Union as Crisis Manager: Patterns and Prospects* (CUP, 2013).

Council Decision 2001/792 established an EU Mechanism to facilitate cooperation in civil protection interventions.[173] The Mechanism was set up to enable coordinated assistance from the participating states to victims of natural and man-made disasters in Europe and elsewhere, and it currently includes all 28 EU Member States as well as Iceland, Norway, and Macedonia. The EU Civil Protection legislation was revised in 2013 by Decision 1313/2013/EU of the European Parliament and of the Council on a Union Civil Protection Mechanism,[174] placing greater emphasis on disaster prevention, risk management, and disaster preparedness, including the organization of trainings, simulation exercises and the exchange of experts, but also developing new elements, such as a voluntary pool of pre-committed response capacities by the Member States. The "operational hub" of the EU Civil Protection Mechanism is the Emergency Response Coordination Centre (ERCC)[175] which monitors emergencies around the world on a 24/7 basis, and coordinates the response of the participating countries in case of a crisis. The ERCC teams are ready to intervene at short notice both within and outside the EU. They undertake specialized tasks such as search and rescue, aerial forest fire fighting, advanced medical posts and more. Since its launch in 2001, the EU Civil Protection Mechanism has monitored over 300 disasters and has received more than 180 requests for assistance.[176] The Mechanism also intends to help in marine pollution emergencies, where it works closely with the European Maritime Safety Agency.

In November 2017, the Commission put forward a proposal for a targeted revision of Decision 1313/2013. [add footnote: "European Commission, Proposal for a Decision amending Decision No. 1313/2013/EU on a Union Civil Protection Mechanism, COM(2017)0772 final." The explanatory memorandum indicates that the revision would be mainly aimed at reinforcing the Union and Member States' collective ability to respond to disasters, and addressing recurrent and emerging capacity gaps, especially with the creation of a dedicated reserve of response capacities at Union level, with decisions on deployment taken by the Commission, which retains command and control (to be known as rescEU). rescEU will be equipped with selected emergency capacities to respond to wildfires, floods, earthquakes and health emergencies as appropriate. Following discussion with Member States, a field hospital that can rapidly be deployed inside or outside the Union as part of the European Medical Corps should also be foreseen for cases of epidemics.

The increasing EU-level activities in this area were given a more solid basis by the Lisbon Treaty in Article 196 TFEU, which provides that the Union shall encourage cooperation between Member States to improve the effectiveness of systems for preventing and protecting against natural or man-made disasters. Union action shall aim to: "(a) support and complement Member States' action at national, regional and local level in risk prevention, in preparing their civil-protection personnel and in responding to natural or man-made disasters within the Union; (b) promote swift, effective operational cooperation within the Union between national civil-protection services; (c) promote consistency in international civil-protection work". The Parliament and the Council, under the ordinary legislative procedure, shall establish the measures necessary to help achieve these objectives, excluding harmonization.

173. O.J. 2001, L 297/7–11, adopted on (now) 352 TFEU.
174. O.J. 2013, L 347.924–947, adopted on Art. 196 TFEU.
175. Replacing and upgrading the functions of the previous Monitoring and Information Centre. See <ercportal.jrc.ec.europa.eu/>.
176. It has intervened e.g. in Hurricane Katrina in the USA (2005), the earthquake in Haiti (2010), the triple-disaster in Japan (2011), and typhoon Haiyan that hit the Philippines (2013).

9. Administrative cooperation

The effectiveness of the many rights and obligations under EU law rests on a legal framework consisting of direct application of Treaty rules, harmonized European rules, national rules, and mutual recognition, and the task of implementing and ensuring compliance with these rules lies, in practice, with a large number of public authorities in the Member States.[177] In order to carry out this task, Member States' authorities need to cooperate closely, meaning that administrative cooperation is not only desirable but is required by the very nature of the EU. In the context of the free movement of goods, many circulation regimes are accompanied by their own specific mechanism of administrative cooperation.[178] In the context of services, three important recent directives emphasized implementation through cooperation between Member States, to wit the revised Professional Qualifications Directive,[179] the Services Directive and the Patient's Rights Directive.[180] All three rely on the Internal Market Information system, developed to improve communication between Member State administrations.[181]

Introduced by the Lisbon Treaty, Article 197 TFEU provides that the "effective implementation of Union law by the Member States, which is essential for the proper functioning of the Union, shall be regarded as a matter of common interest". On this basis, the Union "may support the efforts of Member States to improve their administrative capacity to implement Union law. Such action may include facilitating the exchange of information and of civil servants as well as supporting training schemes.[182] No Member State shall be obliged to avail itself of such support. The European Parliament and the Council, acting by means of regulations in accordance with the ordinary legislative procedure, shall establish the necessary measures to this end, excluding any harmonization of the laws and regulations of the Member States". The third paragraph provides that this Article shall be without prejudice to the obligations of the Member States to implement Union law or to the prerogatives and duties of the Commission. It shall also be without prejudice to other provisions of the Treaties providing for administrative cooperation among the Member States and between them and the Union.[183]

While it cannot be considered irrelevant that the Lisbon Treaty created a specific provision in this area, Article 197 TFEU does not seem to have added or changed much, instead reiterating

177. F. Lafarge, "Administrative cooperation between member states and implementation of EU law", 16 EPL (2010), 598.

178. E.g. veterinary checks, waste, explosives, and dangerous/hazardous goods. Council Reg. (EC) 515/97 creates one of the currently most elaborated cooperation mechanisms, which are used by other regulations related to circulation of special goods, such as the export of cultural goods (Council Reg. 3911/92), dual use items (Council Reg. 1334/2000) and drug precursors (Council Reg. 111/2005).

179. Directive 2013/55/EU on the recognition of professional qualifications and Reg. (EU) No. 1024/2012 on administrative cooperation through the Internal Market Information System, O.J. 2013, L 354/132–170.

180. See section 3.2.1 *supra*.

181. F. Lafarge, op. cit. *supra* note 183. See Reg. 1024/2012 on administrative cooperation through the Internal Market Information System and repealing Commission Decision 2008/49/EC (O.J. 2012, L 316/1–11).

182. E.g., the Seconded National Experts and Experts in Training, who work for a national, regional or local public administration and are temporarily assigned to the Commission. See: Commission Decision of 12.11.2008 laying down rules on the secondment to the Commission of national experts and national experts in professional training C(2008) 6866 final. For a study on the impact of such exchanges: J. Trondal, "Is the European Commission a 'hothouse' for supranationalism? Exploring actor-level supranationalism", 45 JCMS (2007), 1111.

183. Art. 74 TFEU in the area of freedom, security and justice provides: "The Council shall adopt measures to ensure administrative cooperation between the relevant departments of the Member States in the areas covered by this Title, as well as between those departments and the Commission. It shall act on a Commission proposal, subject to Art. 76, and after consulting the European Parliament."

the status quo. It has been regretted that the Lisbon Treaty has not properly extended the EU legal basis for action in the area of European administrative law, particularly in order to allow the Union to codify the basic principles of European administration, pointing out that this would be desirable and much less intrusive than the extremely detailed provisions for the implementation of rules regarding specific matters which can currently be found as an annex to the various substantial rules of secondary EU law.[184]

10. Concluding Remarks

Of course, the various supporting policy areas all have a different scope and character. The degree and forms of integration differ, with public health on one side of the spectrum being very close to a shared competence, and on the other side of the spectrum areas like industry, where EU-level action is more limited. Some of the supporting policies were explicitly present from the beginning (vocational training), while others have only recently been added by the Lisbon Treaty (sport, tourism, civil protection and administrative cooperation). In some areas, EU-level action remains highly contested (education, sport), while in other areas it is generally welcomed (civil protection). While some areas seem inherently destined to be at odds with European integration (culture), for others it appears that the path towards becoming a shared EU competence is not necessarily blocked (health).

Keeping in mind these differences, in discussing these various supporting policy areas, one is nevertheless struck by several important commonalities. In practically all these fields, the most important European influence has taken place on other Treaty provisions, either via negative or positive integration. In that context, especially the internal market provisions have been the main "backdoor". The insertion of specific legal bases for action in these areas has therefore generally been regarded as a necessary legitimization of pre-existing practice rather than a gateway for further integration. Most, if not all, of these complementary competences have been as much directed at containing the development of supporting policies as at authorizing it. But it seems that the complementary competences have not fully succeeded in legitimizing, authorizing or containing European integration in these areas. Indirect legislation through other Treaty provisions continues, meaning that such action has neither been legitimized by the complementary competences, nor effectively contained. While the competences sometimes do provide for a firmer basis for the development of European-level initiatives and incentive measures, the introduction of harmonization prohibitions excludes the development of comprehensive and holistic European-level policies that take due account of the non-economic objectives and characteristics of the policy areas concerned.

The foregoing discussion shows that regardless of assurances to the contrary, areas that fall primarily in Member States' competence can still be deeply affected by European integration. Negative integration through case law limits the capacity of national communities to organize these sensitive areas in the way they see fit, which is difficult to reconcile with the stipulation that EU action shall not "supersede" national competence in these areas. Harmonization prohibitions prevent these communities from re-arranging or addressing the ensuing problems holistically on the European level, leading to a regulatory gap. This also has the effect of pushing harmonization through the back door, not prevented by the harmonization prohibitions, which does not sit easily with national autonomy clauses, harmonization prohibitions and the conferral principle. Although legally permissible, this kind of EU action clearly poses problems of transparency and accountability. Furthermore, because it often entails the use of the internal

184. J. Schwarze, "European administrative law in the light of the treaty of Lisbon", 18 EPL (2012), 285.

market or economic policy provisions, there is a danger of economic bias in the adoption of these measures, risking overlooking or undervaluing the socio-cultural values at stake. In addition, harmonization prohibitions push harmonization out of the EU legal framework into an intergovernmental one, either inside or outside the EU institutional framework. Both alternatives pose legitimacy problems of their own. The lack of a true harmonization possibility on the basis of the complementary competences has therefore been deplored,[185] and it has been suggested that the right way forward in these areas is to abolish the harmonization prohibitions, allowing for the adoption of legislative measures where necessary.[186] Instead of expecting (complementary) competences to contain EU integration and to protect Member State autonomy, which they have consistently failed to do, it would arguably make more sense to invest efforts in the democratization of the EU legislative process instead.[187] Such an approach would shift the focus from limiting the *existence* of competence to limiting its *exercise*, which would arguably better reflect and suit the dynamics of the EU legal order.[188]

Further reading

Boucon, L., "EU law and retained powers of Member States" in L. Azoulai (Ed.), *The Question of Competence in the European Union*, (OUP, 2014).

Van den Bogaert, S. and A. Vermeersch, "Sport and the EC Treaty: A tale of uneasy bedfellows", 31 EL Rev. (2006), 821–840.

Craufurd-Smith, R., *Culture and European Union Law*, (OUP, 2004).

Davies, G., "The Community's internal market-based competence to regulate healthcare: Scope, strategies and consequences", 14 MJ (2007), 215–238.

Garben, S., "Case C-73lo8, *N. Bressol and Others, C. Chaverot and Others v. Gouvernement de la Communauté française*", 47 CML Rev. (2010), 1493–1510.

Garben, S., *EU Higher Education Law. The Bologna Process and Harmonization by Stealth* (Kluwer Law International, 2011).

Garben, S., "The case to correct some of Maastricht's mistakes: A critical assessment of Article 165 TFEU on education and suggestions for reform" in M. de Visser and A.P. van der Mei (Eds.), *Treaty on European Union 1993–2013: Reflections from Maastricht* (Intersentia, 2013).

Romainville, C., (Ed.), *European Law and Cultural Policies, Droit européen et politiques culturelles* (Peter Lang, 2015).

Schütze, R., "Co-operative federalism constitutionalized: The emergence of complementary competences in the EC legal order", 31 EL Rev. (2006), 167–184.

Vadi, V. and B. de Witte (Eds.), *Culture and International Economic Law* (Routledge, 2015).

Weatherill, S., "EU sports law: The effect of the Lisbon Treaty" in A. Biondi, P. Eeckhout and S. Ripley (Eds.), *EU Law After Lisbon* (OUP, 2012).

De Witte, B., "A competence to protect: The pursuit of non-market aims through internal market legislation" in P. Syrpis (Ed.), *The Judiciary, The Legislator and The Internal Market* (CUP, 2012), 25–46.

---

185. R. Craufurd-Smith, op. cit. *supra* note 146; S. Van den Bogaert and A. Vermeersch, "Sport and the EC Treaty: A tale of uneasy bedfellows", 32 EL Rev. (2006), 838, J. Schwarze, "European administrative law in the light of the Treaty of Lisbon" 18 EPL (2012), 285.
186. S. Garben, "Confronting the competence conundrum: Democratizing the European Union through an expansion of its legislative powers", (2015) 35(1) *OJLS* 55.
187. Ibid.
188. K. Nicolaidis and R. Howse (Eds.), *The Federal Vision: Legitimacy and Levels of Governance in the United States and the European Union* (OUP, 2001), 451.

CHAPTER 39

AN INTRODUCTION TO UNION EXTERNAL ACTION, ITS SCOPE, ITS INSTITUTIONS AND ITS INSTRUMENTS

*Pieter Jan Kuijper**

1. The background to the Treaty provisions

One of the avowed goals of the Treaty of Lisbon was to create a more unified and forceful external presence of the EU by creating a single legal personality for the EU and a strong external figurehead, the High Representative, who is at the same time Vice-President of the Commission (HR/VP).

In spite of the demise of the different "pillars" created in Maastricht, the Lisbon Treaty still divides the external affairs of the EU over two different treaties, characterized by different decision-making procedures: the TEU and the TFEU. The corresponding branches of external relations, the Common Foreign and Security Policy (CFSP) and TFEU external action (TFEU EA) are nevertheless supposed to give rise to a single "external action", co-ordinated by a single "office" or person, the HR, and carried out by a single service, the European External Action Service (EEAS), often complemented by the Commission, and sometimes by the Member States collectively. Each of the two branches of external action responds to its own logic.

The TFEU EA responds to a logic which is inherent in the fact that the EU originally was a customs union and later became an internal market. The need for an external barrier is inherent in a customs union, since a common external tariff is a requirement in order to be able to profit from the customs union exception of the GATT.[1] This translated into exclusive Union competence for the common commercial policy (CCP), originally extrapolated by the Court from the customs union in goods[2] and firmly inscribed in Article 3(1)(e) TEU among the exclusive competences. The Treaty of Lisbon (Art. 207 TFEU) also included in the CCP, next to trade in goods, all the external aspects of the internal market in the field of services, investment and intellectual property, to which was also added foreign direct investment.

A similar logic demands that internal legislation that has been enacted in areas of shared competence can be protected or, if necessary, modified externally only by the Union in international negotiations. Internal legislation, therefore, creates the same phenomenon of an external barrier, since individually, or even collectively, Member States cannot dispose of Union legislation in force in international relations; only the Union institutions can.[3] Hence the Un-

---

* Law Faculty, University of Amsterdam.

1. See Art. XXIV: 5(a) GATT. This common external tariff shall not on the whole be higher than the general incidence of the separate external tariffs of the Members.
2. Opinion 1/75, *OECD Local Cost Standard,* 1975 ECR 1355, at 1364.
3. Case 22/70, *Commission v. Council (ERTA)*, paras. 17–18, and many later cases, consolidated in Opinion 1/03, *New Lugano Convention*, paras. 114–133.

ion institutions have an exclusive power to deal with this part of external action more or less according to the normal (formerly) Community ways of deciding matters.[4] It has been the ECJ in particular that has been active in defending the inherent logic in Union external relations as described above, now firmly embedded in Article 3(2) TFEU. In the long run third States are forced to recognize this shift in power from the Member States to the Union and to deal with the Union rather than the Member States, since otherwise they will find no negotiation partner on crucial international questions.

However, the "political foreign policy" of the CFSP responds to no such inherent logic, directly linked to its subject matter. It is supremely political in nature. The Member States want it because they hope thus to wield more political clout on the world scene. It is accepted by third States only insofar as it is convenient for them to speak to 1 figure instead of to 28 states, or even a few big Member States, and insofar as they are prepared to recognize the Union as an entity on the same level as States in specific circumstances. This is well illustrated by the case of the Caribbean States, united in Cariforum, that have been happy to conclude a European Partnership Agreement (EPA) with the EU at an early stage, but were among the States most opposed to granting the EU enhanced observer status in the UN General Assembly.[5]

Member States as constitutional legislators have left this branch of foreign policy firmly in the intergovernmental domain. They do not accept the "Community method" there,[6] largely excluding the Commission, the Parliament and the Court from this domain. The European Council and the Council of Ministers are the sole deciders in the field of the CFSP, operating largely on the basis of unanimity. The HR, as we will see later on, is at the same time the President of the Foreign Affairs Council and largely its creature.

In order to make the separation between the two domains of foreign policy complete Article 40 TEU states that the implementation of the CFSP shall not affect "the application of the procedures and the extent of the powers of the institutions" under the TFEU and *vice versa*. This two-way protection of the Community method against CFSP intergovernmentalism and of the latter against the "Community method" is new.[7] Old Article 47 TEU (Nice) only protected the "Community method" against the intergovernmental approach. In the light of this change, the sole test case that the Commission brought (and won) under this old article is of limited validity for future cases. Only insofar as the Court seemed to rely on its classic approach on the centre of gravity of a Community/Union act for determining its legal basis, not just between two articles of the same Treaty, but also between two articles in different Treaties, it gives an important hint as to what might be its approach to such cases in future.[8]

Other elements, similar to those that have determined the evolution of foreign policy and diplomacy in the Member States, have inevitably influenced the development of EU external relations. First of all, the increased tasks of modern government have led to a broadening of the field of foreign policy of the Member States. This has given rise to the distinction between high foreign policy (classic diplomacy and power politics) and low foreign policy (the technical and trade realms of foreign policy, including private and criminal law cooperation, which in many

---

4. That is to say largely in conformity with the ordinary legislative procedure and subject to full judicial control by the EUCJ.
5. EPA between the Cariforum States, of the one part, and the European Community and its Member States, of the other part, O.J. 2002, L 289/3 and Caricom document on EU request for enhanced observer status UN doc. A/65/834.
6. See, *inter alia*, Art. 31(1), first sentence, TEU, requiring unanimity and excluding the legislative character of CFSP acts decided by the Council.
7. Cf. Art. 40 TEU (Lisbon) with Art. 47 TEU (Nice).
8. See Case C-91/05, *Commission v. Council (ECOWAS)*, para 78.

Member States are not handled by the Ministry of Foreign Affairs). Another oft-made distinction is that between hard power (military might and prowess) and soft power (socio-economic and cultural projection). The creation of the EEC and its expansion into the present-day Union is an expression of these trends and distinctions.[9]

States have long striven to unite all the old and new elements and the hard and soft power aspects of foreign policy, if not into one broad Ministry of Foreign Affairs, then at least to have all these elements firmly directed and co-ordinated by the Ministry of Foreign Affairs, both at home and in the embassies abroad. The new integrated "external action" of the EU, bolstered by the principle of coherence, as laid down in Article 21 of the Lisbon Treaty, can be seen as another attempt, this time at European level, to reach this old ideal and thus to achieve a greater and better recognized presence on the international scene for the EU.

Secondly, this expansion of the field of foreign relations has been followed by an increased democratization of foreign policy. The diversification of constituencies involved in different elements of foreign policy and the confrontation of nearly all citizens with the internal regulatory consequences of expanded international trade and technology are at the root of this development. National Parliaments that had always been relatively restrained in "meddling" in foreign policy and that in some Member States did not even have the right of approval of all treaties,[10] became more vocal and acquired new rights of treaty approval. This trend in the Member States has been followed by similar developments in the Union, beginning with the Treaty of Maastricht. More and more powers have been given to the European Parliament in an attempt to enhance the democratic legitimacy of the Union, including of its external action. The Treaty of Lisbon granted the Parliament the right of approval for nearly all agreements concluded by the Union, including those relating to the common commercial policy.[11] Moreover, its new provisions on delegated power and uniform implementation (former comitology),[12] have had a "civilizing" influence on the great diversity and the considerable divergence from the norm, which hitherto prevailed in external relations implementing legislation.[13]

The period of implementation following the entry into force of the Lisbon Treaty has shown that Member States in the Council are not ready to draw the full consequences of their own decision to create a stronger and more unified EU presence on the international scene.[14] Many Member States have concluded that a loyal implementation of Lisbon would lead to a too visible loss of sovereignty on the international scene. Hence there is a continuing search for a workable balance between a genuine EU foreign policy across the whole breadth of high and low foreign policy and continued state sovereignty. This search for internal balance inevitably comes up

9. These notions have been developed to a large extent by J.S. Nye, see R.O. Keohane & J.S. Nye, *Power and Interdependence: World Politics in Transition* (Little-Brown, 1977) and J.S. Nye, "Soft Power", *Foreign Policy* (Autumn 1990), 153–177 and numerous other articles by Nye on the subject.
10. An example used to be the UK until the Constitutional Reform and Governance Act of 2010. Before then the Crown had the power to conclude treaties, and Parliament only became involved when treaties needed to be implemented in national law.
11. Art. 207(3) and (4) and 218(6)(a) TFEU. Before the Treaty of Lisbon the European Parliament formally did not even have the right to be consulted on trade agreements.
12. Art. 290 and 291 TFEU.
13. See Ch. 41, "Union external relations under the TFEU", section 2.3.3 of this book, on commercial defence.
14. For a mild rebuke by the ECJ of this unwillingness of the Member States to do what they promised on trade policy, see Case C-414/11, *Dai Ichi Sankyo*, Case C-137/12, *Commission v. Council (Conditional Access Services)*. See L. Ankersmit, "The scope of the common commercial policy after Lisbon: The *Daiichi Sankyo* and *Conditional Access Services* Grand Chamber judgments", 41 *Legal Issues of Economic Integration* (2014), 193–209. The most recent attempt of the Court to maintain internal balance in trade policy is Opinion 2/15 *FTA Singapore*.

against the realities of the world of international power politics, where the participants are sovereign states that do not envisage quietly making place for a newly minted "supranational entity". All the less so because classic international law continues to reflect this world of sovereign states and is adapting only very slowly to organizations to which important powers of Member States have been transferred. Classic international law, and in particular diplomatic law, gives them ample ammunition for opposing the fuller participation of the EU in international relations.[15]

2. Union external powers: Their structure and foundations in the EU treaties

After the Amsterdam Treaty, the European Union, though still not explicitly equipped with personality under international law, had been bestowed with treaty-making power. Hence the European Union and the European Community each concluded their own international agreements and developed separate international personalities. The Treaty of Lisbon has put an end to this. According to Article 1 TEU, the EU is based on two treaties, the TEU and the TFEU, that have equal value. The EU replaces and succeeds the European Community and it is the EU that has legal personality (Art. 47 TEU). The EU has implemented these basic provisions in the wider world by addressing diplomatic notes to all countries with which it maintains diplomatic relations and to all international organizations and treaty regimes to which it is affiliated in one way or another. After some further discussion and negotiation with some third States and international organizations, this succession of the European Union to the European Community has been generally accepted.[16]

The foundations of the EU's external action are laid down by Articles 2, 3(5) and 21 TEU, of which the last one is directly linked to Part V of the TFEU on the Union's external action. The values on which the Union is founded are mentioned in Article 2 TEU and include respect for human dignity, freedom, democracy, the rule of law and human rights. Article 3(5) TEU then states that these values shall be upheld and promoted in the framework of the EU's external action. In addition the Union shall contribute to peace, security, sustainable development and free and fair trade and, of particular importance from a legal point of view, "to the strict observance and development of international law, including respect for the principles of the United Nations Charter". These last words are repeated in slightly different form in Article 21 TEU.

Article 21 is of particular importance, as it ventures to set out the principles of an integrated external action that includes elements from both treaties on which the EU is built. From the TEU and its CFSP, there are references to the safeguarding the Union's values, references to peace and security based on the UN Charter, the OSCE and the Helsinki Final Act and its Charter of Paris,[17] references to the consolidation of and support for democracy, the rule of law, human rights and "the principles of international law".[18] From the TFEU and the external powers mentioned in that treaty there are references to fostering the balanced development of developing countries, with an emphasis on eradicating poverty, the integration of all countries

15. See for example R.A. Wessel and B. van Vooren, "The EEAS's diplomatic dreams and the reality of European and international law", (2013) *Journal of European Public Policy*, 1350–1367.
16. See also Ch. 41, "Union external relations under the TFEU", section 5, of this book on the special case of the UN and restrictive measures.
17. The Final Act of the Conference on Security and Cooperation in Europe (signed 1 Aug. 1975), available at <www.osce.org/mc/39501?download=true> (Helsinki Act, last visited 28 Aug. 2016); Charter of Paris for a New Europe (signed 21 Nov. 1990), available at <www.osce.org/mc/39516?download=true> (last visited 28 Aug. 2016).
18. See subparas. (a), (b) and (c) of Art. 21 TEU. The wording on international law is annoying in its imprecision. Whereas Art. 3(5) demands its strict observance, Art. 21 merely evokes the consolidation and support for its "principles".

into the world economy, in particular through free trade, the preservation of the environment and the sustainable management of global resources, and assistance to populations, countries and regions confronted by natural or man-made disasters.[19] Finally there is a reference to an objective that could fall both under the TEU and the TFEU, namely the promotion of an international system based on stronger multilateral cooperation and good global governance.[20]

Only the European Council may set out the strategic interests and objectives of the Union over the whole spectrum of external action, including both CFSP and TFEU powers. Such strategy decisions may deal with a specific country or region or a particular theme.[21] Before Lisbon such strategy decisions were already possible under the CFSP alone, but in reality were used very sparingly.[22] All indications are that at the integrated external action level under the Lisbon Treaty, they will not be used any more frequently. One reason for that may be the complicated decision-making procedure laid down in Article 22 TEU, which grapples, not very successfully, with the complications of requiring unanimity at the European Council level and the different decision-making procedures in the field of the CFSP and the TFEU at the level of making a proposal and implementing it. Below the level of strategic decision-making, the specific powers in the field of external action are set out in each of the two treaties, preceded by identical provisions recalling that the Union's external action shall be guided by the principles, pursue the objectives and be conducted in accordance with the general provisions of Article 2, 3(5) and 21 TEU.[23]

The powers granted by the TEU for the conduct of the CFSP and CSDP are defined in simple fashion as covering "all areas of foreign policy and all questions relating to the Union's security" (Art. 24(1) TEU). This is so broad and vague a mandate that one can hardly square it with the principle of conferral laid down in Article 5 TEU. Obviously the rule of unanimous decision-making is considered sufficient as a check on any abuse, since the Court has extremely limited jurisdiction in the field of CFSP.[24]

In the TFEU the specific external powers can be found in Part V of that Treaty, which includes the Common Commercial Policy (CCP), the Development Policy and the Cooperation with Developed Countries, as well as Humanitarian Aid and Economic Sanctions.[25] However, external powers that are linked to internal powers, such as the freedom of capital movements inside the Union and with third countries, asylum and immigration, monetary policy, education, trans-European networks, research and development and environmental policy are to be found in the different provisions dealing with these internal matters in the TFEU.[26] These are the external powers that are explicitly mentioned in the TFEU, but there are many aspects of

19. See subparas. (d), (e), (f) and (g) of Art. 21 TEU.
20. See subpara (h) of Art. 21 TEU.
21. See Art. 22 TEU.
22. From the period before Lisbon there are only three such Common Strategies of the European Council, relating to Russia, Ukraine and the Mediterranean Region.
23. See Art. 23 TEU and 205 TFEU.
24. Art. 24(1) TEU *in fine*.
25. See Arts. 206–207 TFEU (Common Commercial Policy), Arts. 208–211 TFEU (development cooperation), Arts. 212–213 TFEU (economic, financial and technical cooperation with third countries, Art. 214 (humanitarian aid), Art. 215 (restrictive measures).
26. Art. 64(2) TFEU (restrictions of free movement of capital, access for foreign banks etc), Art. 66 (safeguard measures on the freedom of movement of capital with third countries) Arts. 78 and 79 (asylum and immigration), Art. 138 TFEU (monetary policy), Art. 165 (3) TFEU (education), Art. 166(3) TFEU (vocational training), Art. 167(3) TFEU (culture), Art. 168 (3) TFEU (public health), Art. 171 (3) TFEU (trans-European networks), Art. 180(b) TFEU (research and development), Art. 191(1) and (4) TFEU (environmental policy). It is interesting to note that Arts. 64(2), 66. 78 and 79 concern all primarily autonomous measures and other Arts. explicitly mention treaty-making power broadly defined.

the internal market, especially insofar as they have led to harmonization, such as the maritime and aviation policy, competition policy, including state aids, the various policies in the field of freedom, security and justice outside asylum and immigration, which all have an external aspect without it being explicitly mentioned in the treaty.[27]

3. The instruments of external action

These substantive powers in the field of external action are carried out by three instrumental powers: the autonomous decision-making power with intended or unintended external effect, the treaty-making power and the power of external representation. These instrumental powers transcend the boundary between the two treaties and can be resorted to under both. We will here just draw the outlines of these instrumental powers and give greater substance to them, when discussing external action under each of the two treaties.

Autonomous action in the field of external relations of the Union are such actions that are unilateral foreign policy measures, such as recognition of states, the imposition of embargoes, or are legislative acts on which further external economic actions can be based, such as the basic anti-dumping regulation and the secondary anti-dumping decisions actually imposing duties on certain imported products. These examples have intentional external effects. It also happens that internal legislation or decisions have external effect that is largely incidental and mostly unintended, such as legislation on climate change and decisions in the field of competition law relating to foreign companies operating in the EU. It is obvious that such autonomous action can fall under the CFSP or under the TFEU; the problems flowing from that will be discussed in greater depth in the two following chapters.

The treaty-making power is laid down in Article 37 TEU for the CFSP and in Article 216 TFEU for the other aspects of external action. The latter article declares that the EU may conclude an agreement with one or more third countries, when the Treaties (plural) so provide. In spite of the additional ways in which treaty-making power may come about according to Article 216,[28] this restriction to the treaty-making powers explicitly mentioned in both Treaties is incomprehensible in the light of the treaty-making practice that the Union has followed hitherto, and continues to follow, on the basis of the case law of the Court, in particular the classic ERTA case.[29]

That case stands for the proposition that, since the EEC (now the Union) was equipped with international personality according to the Treaty (presently Article 47 TEU) and, since this was a general provision, this meant "that in its external relations the Community (now the Union) enjoys the capacity to establish contractual links with third countries over the whole field of [its] objectives [...]". There is reason to assume that ERTA in this respect is still good law, since Art 47 is identical to and has a comparable place in the system of the Treaties as the

27. Art. 100 TFEU (maritime and aviation policies), Art. 101 et seq. TFEU (cartels and abuse of dominant position), Art. 107 TFEU (State aids), Arts. 81 and 82 TFEU (respectively civil law and criminal law cooperation) and this list is not exhaustive. For the subsumption of the cooperation in these areas (and those mentioned in fn. 26) with third States under EU development policy and Art. 208 TFEU, see Case C-377/12, *Commission v. Council* (Framework Agreement with the Philippines on partnership and cooperation).
28. Art. 216 TFEU in addition mentions "or where the agreement of an agreement is necessary in order to achieve, within the framework of the Union's policies, one of the objectives referred to in the Treaties, or is provided for in a legally binding Union act or is likely to affect common rules or alter their scope". These phrases, however, all come from parts of Court judgments, which are concerned with exclusive treaty-making power, whereas Art. 216 lays down the procedures for the general (both exclusive and shared) treaty-making power.
29. Case 22/70, *Commission v. Council (ERTA)*.

old article on personality of the EEC. Seen in that light the following statement from the Court retains its full authority: "The Court has concluded *inter alia* that whenever Community law has created for the institutions of the Community powers within its internal system for the purpose of attaining a specific objective, the Community has authority to enter into the international commitments necessary for the attainment of that objective even in the absence of an express provision in that connexion".[30] Therefore the seemingly exhaustive reference to treaty-making powers to "when the Treaties so provide" in Article 216 in the end remains an illustrative list.[31]

Moreover, while Article 37 TEU merely lays down the treaty-making power as such in the field of CFSP only, Article 218 TFEU harks back to the ambition to create an integrated external action for the EU voiced in Article 21 TEU. It provides for detailed prescriptions on how to negotiate and conclude international agreements with third States and other international organizations on behalf of the Union and covering all aspects of external action, including the CFSP. The allocation of the power to negotiate and to propose signature and/or conclusion of an international agreement to either the Commission or the High Representative (HR) is dependent on whether the purpose of the agreement exclusively or predominantly relates to the CFSP.[32]

Where the third instrumental power of the Union's external action is concerned, namely the power of external representation, the Lisbon Treaty mentions three representatives, operating at different levels. First there is the President of the European Council who, at his level and in that capacity, shall ensure the external representation of the Union in the field of CFSP.[33] Secondly there is the HR who, presumably at her somewhat lower level, shall carry out the CFSP and to that end shall represent the EU externally, assisted by the EEAS. Moreover, the HR has the duty to maintain consistency in the external action of the EU, presumably primarily the consistency between CFSP and TFEU external action, between the high and low politics of external action.[34] To this effect she disposes of a coordinating power, which enables her to harmonize the CFSP with other areas of external action, supported also by such provisions as Article 205 TFEU, which declare that other external relations of the EU shall be conducted in accordance with the general provisions of external action, as laid down in Articles 2, 3(5) and 21 TEU.[35] Finally the Commission shall be responsible for the external representation of the Union, but the CFSP is explicitly excepted from this Commission power.[36]

In brief, the President of the European Council is responsible for international representation at the level of Head of States and Government, such as meetings with, for example, the President of the United States, whereas the HR is doing the same at the level of Ministers of Foreign Affairs, such as the Secretary of State of the US. However this is restricted for both to "high" foreign and defence policy. The Commission is responsible for external representation as far as "low" foreign policy is concerned, but does so at all levels. As a consequence, at meetings of the G-20, where both "high" and "low" foreign policy is discussed, for instance pure foreign

30. Opinion 1/76, *Laying-up Fund for the Rhine*, para 3.
31. There are indications in Opinion 2/15, *FTA Singapore*, para 243, that the Court may be of another view.
32. Art. 218 (3) et seq. TFEU. See Case C-263/14, *European Parliament v. Council (Tanzania Agreement)*, paras. 44–49.
33. Art. 15(6) TFEU. There is a remarkable parallel with the special external relations powers of the President of France laid down in Art. 52 of the French Constitution.
34. Art. 18 and 27 TEU. See also on this topic C. Hillion, "Fighting terrorism through the common foreign and security policy" in I. Govaere and S. Poli (Eds.), *EU Governance of Global Emergencies* (Brill, 2014), 75.
35. See also Arts. 207(1), 208(1), 212(1) and 214(2) TFEU.
36. Art. 17(1) TEU.

policy and e.g. climate change, the Union is represented by the two Presidents, of the European Council and of the Commission.[37]

4. External relations powers in the system of exclusive, shared and supplementary powers of the TFEU

Now that it is clear that autonomous and contractual external powers exist over the whole breadth of both the TEU and TFEU, the next step is to analyse where these powers fall in the categories of exclusive, shared and complementary powers of the Union, as laid down in Articles 3 through 6 TFEU.

An allocation of the Union's powers over these three categories does not apply to the powers under the TEU and thus is not applicable to the CFSP, including the Common Security and Defence Policy (CSDP). The CFSP is subject to "specific rules and procedures", meaning not the rules and procedures in force elsewhere in the Union under the TFEU. Moreover the acts adopted in the framework of CFSP cannot be of a legislative character and the Court of Justice cannot review them, except in specific cases.[38] In addition, as was already stated earlier, the CFSP powers are very broad and vague and thus largely unsuitable to judicial review in the light of the principle of conferral anyway. CFSP acts are of a decisional nature only and they are either used or not depending on whether the necessary unanimity can be marshalled.[39] In such a situation the differentiation between exclusive, shared or complementary powers does not make much sense. Although the principle of sincere cooperation covers both the CFSP and the TFEU external action, it is the Court's strong interpretation of this principle that has given it a hard edge in the field of external relations under the TFEU – which is inevitably lacking in the CFSP.[40]

In the realm of external action covered by the TFEU, the Court developed over many years an important body of case law on the question in which cases an expressly conferred or derived external competence would have an exclusive character.

First, in certain exceptional cases a derived external competence may be *ipso facto* exclusive, where it is necessary for the attainment of an objective of the Treaty that the external competence is exercised by the Community alone, to the exclusion of the Member States.[41] This was the case, for instance, when the overcapacity of shipping on the Rhine needed to be eliminated: an agreement with Switzerland was indispensable. The Court made it clear that cases where an exclusive power can be implicitly derived in such a direct manner will remain extremely limited, i.e. to those cases when there is an almost physical necessity,[42] and later took an even more restrictive view, requiring that the internal competence and the "necessary" external competence be exercised simultaneously.[43]

Secondly, Treaty provisions may confer an exclusive character on internal competence with effect from a particular time, and thereby also involve the exclusivity of the external powers

37. See also section 6.2 *infra*.
38. Art. 24(1) TEU.
39. For the possibility of "constructive abstention" see Art. 31(1) 2nd al. TEU and *infra* at section 5.
40. See *infra* section 7.
41. Opinion 1/76, *Laying-up fund for the Rhine*.
42. Opinion 1/94, *WTO – GATS and TRIPs*.
43. Opinion 1/03, *New Lugano Convention*. In this way, this approach to the exclusivity of external powers becomes indistinguishable from the *ERTA* approach discussed *infra*, since an exercise of internal powers is now necessary for the exercise of the corresponding external powers, the latter no longer being completely independent from the former.

derived from these.[44] In practice, this category is very similar to the first: the Act of Accession (1972), concerning the UK, Ireland and Denmark, provided for an exclusive competence of the Community in the area of fish conservation measures at the latest from the sixth year after accession. It was clear to the Court that this also necessitated EU agreements with third countries in this field.

The third possibility, as the Court ruled in *ERTA*, is that the *exercise* of internal competence may lead to the exclusivity of the derived external competence linked to it. This is the case, if and in so far as the internal measures taken as a result of the exercise of the internal competence could be affected or their scope be altered by a Member State concluding an agreement with a third country concerning the same subject matter, either on its own or together with other Member States.[45] In such a case, this would endanger the attainment of the objectives of the Community rules, and prevent the Community as such from protecting the Community interest.[46] After first having made an attempt to systematize its case law since *ERTA* in a set of judgments handed down in November 2002,[47] the Court produced a new restatement of its *ERTA* case law in its *Lugano Convention* Opinion of 2006.[48] This restatement runs broadly as follows.

The crucial question is: in what circumstances can Union rules be affected or their scope altered by international obligations undertaken by Member States? According to the Court's case law, this is the case where the international obligations fall within the scope of Union rules (regardless of whether these are rules resulting from a common policy mentioned in the Treaty, such as agriculture or transport, or other common rules)[49] or within an area which is already covered to a large extent by Union rules, especially in the case of progressive harmonization on the road to the internal market.[50] In such cases, the Member States can no longer enter into international commitments outside the framework of the Union, not even in the absence of conflict or identity between these commitments and the internal Union rules.[51] Such parallel international action by the Member States could interfere with the unhindered exercise of the internal Union competence.

In its *Lugano Convention* Opinion, the Court consolidates three situations that it also previously considered decisive for exclusive external competence (clauses granting negotiating powers with third states to the Union, usually represented by the Commission; clauses concerning the treatment of third state nationals; and situations of complete harmonization of a sector)[52] into one. It refers back to *ERTA* itself, where it said that the conclusion of an agreement by the Member States that is incompatible with the unity of the common market and the uniformity of Union law is not allowed.[53] On the other hand, harmonization at the level of

44. Joined Cases 3, 4 & 6/76, *Kramer*.
45. Case 22/70, *Commission v. Council (ERTA)*.
46. Case C-471/98, *Commission v. Belgium (Open skies)*.
47. Case C-471/98, *Commission v. Belgium (Open skies)*. The other seven open skies judgments handed down on the same day were, with some differences, essentially along the same line.
48. Opinion 1/03, *New Lugano Convention*. As appears from Opinion 2/15, *FTA Singapore*, paras. 181 and 201, Opinion 1/03 remains of considerable importance.
49. See Case 22/70, *Commission v. Council (ERTA)* and Opinion 2/91, *ILO Convention*.
50. Opinion 1/03, *New Lugano Convention*, recalling Opinion 2/91, *ILO Convention*. The criterion "largely covered by Union rules" has been broadly interpreted by the Court in Opinion 2/15 *FTA Singapore*, para 168 et seq.
51. Opinion 2/91, *ILO Convention* and Opinion 1/03, *New Lugano Convention*.
52. Opinion 1/94, *WTO – GATS and TRIPS*. The latter two are now characterized as situations where the nature of the existing Community rules is such that any agreement in that area would necessarily affect the relevant Community rules within the meaning of the *ERTA* judgment.
53. Opinion 1/03, *New Lugano Convention*, referring to para 31 of Case 22/70, *Commission v. Council (ERTA)*.

minimum standards (minimum harmonization) leads to the conclusion that the Member States wished to reserve the competence to negotiate with third countries, at least partially: they may legitimately apply stricter rules in conformity with Union law, and may undertake international commitments in relation to those stricter rules without altering the scope of the Union rules.[54] Such minimum harmonization is foreseen in the field of social policy (Art. 153(2)(b) TFEU), consumer protection (Art. 169(4) TFEU), and environmental protection (Art. 193 TFEU), but in practice also occurs in the harmonization of technical standards (Art. 114 TFEU).[55] In all these areas it will generally not be easy to arrive at an exclusive external competence of the Union; at best, the Council could agree voluntarily to apply the potential competence of the Community in such fields – which Member States in the Council will normally not allow. This situation seems anomalous in domains where Union legislation is often very intense (e.g. in the area of the environment), but where the Union is doomed to remain an international nonentity as a consequence of this approach.

Finally, the Court made it clear that no exclusive external Union competence is established as a consequence of distortions in the internal market (in particular, in relation to the freedom to provide services and freedom of establishment), which result from commitments undertaken by Member States with third countries.[56] On the other hand, it is not self-evident that where Member States are given the task of implementing provisions of an international agreement, such an agreement also comes within the competence of the Member States as such, so that it would have to be concluded as a mixed agreement. Where an agreement comes within the exclusive external competence of the Union, the fact that the Member States must take implementing measures or amend their national legislation does not alter this fact; it is the Union that remains competent to negotiate at international level.[57]

It is this extensive and nuanced body of case law of the Court relating to the implied exclusive external relations powers of the Union that Article 3(2) TFEU tries to capture in a single phrase, with the predictable result that the text of the Treaty is found wanting.[58] The text of Article 3(2), however, is clear enough that one can recognize many elements from the *ERTA* case and its progeny.[59] That is equally true of the elements of external policy that are declared to be exclusive Union powers in Article 3(1) TFEU, such as the common commercial policy and the conservation of marine biological resources under the common fisheries policy.[60] It was clearly not the intention of the treaty drafters to deviate from the Court's case law. At best, the Court, on the basis of the new text of Article 207 on the common commercial policy, has become more generous in drawing the contours of this policy in relation to other treaty provisions[61] and in accepting that internal legislation in neighbouring areas of trade policy, such as air and maritime transport, covers essentially all of these domains mentioned in the trade agreement and thus leads to an exclusive external power in that domain.[62]

---

54. Opinion 2/91, *ILO Convention*, accepted by Opinion 1/03, *New Lugano Convention*.
55. Here the situation has been changed after the entry into force of Lisbon, see the relation between Art. 207 TFEU on trade policy and Art. 114 TFEU in Case C-414/11, *Dai-ichi Sankyo*, paras. 56–60.
56. Cf. Case C-471/98, *Commission v. Belgium (Open Skies)*, para 70.
57. Opinion 2/91, *ILO Convention*.
58. For criticism of the drafting, see M. Cremona, "Defining competence in EU external relations: Lessons from the treaty reform process" in A. Dashwood and M. Maresceau (Eds.), *Law and Practice of EU External Relations. Salient Features of a Changing Landscape* (CUP, 2008), 34.
59. See Case 22/70, *Commission v. Council (ERTA)*, para 18 and Opinion 1/76, *Laying-up Fund*, para 3.
60. See Opinion 1/75 *Local Cost Standard* and Cases 3, 4 and 6/76, *Kramer*.
61. Opinion 2/15, *FTA Singapore*, e.g. para 131 et seq. on competition and 139 et seq. on sustainable development.
62. Opinion 2/15, ibid., para 175 et seq. for maritime transport, para 195 et seq. for rail transport and para 204 et seq. for road transport.

Where the CCP and Article 3(1) TFEU is concerned, the ECJ has made it clear that it is drawing consequences from the new language on TRIPs and services in Article 207 TFEU, but for the rest will not deviate from its well-established precedents.[63] Neither is there any indication that this would be any different where the conservation of marine biological resources under the EU fisheries policy is concerned.[64]

Therefore, the Court equally found no reason in the language of the newly minted Article 3(2) TFEU to deviate from the line of its established case law on the division of powers in external relations in the areas of shared powers. To the contrary, since that article was inspired by its case law, the EUCJ decided that it had to be interpreted in light of its jurisprudence.[65]

The common monetary policy of the euro-zone as an exclusive power of the Union is not derived from any existing case law of the Court. As in monetary policy the internal and external aspects are inextricably linked, there can be little doubt that the external monetary policy of the euro-zone is also an exclusive external power, to be carried out by Union institutions. The practical arrangements laid down in the TFEU for the exercise of this power, however, do not do justice to its exclusive nature, as we will see below.[66]

Article 4 TFEU gives a list of the powers that are shared between the Union and the Member States. In these areas in principle the powers are shared as well in external relations, except insofar as internal legislation in the field of shared powers would be affected or altered by an international agreement.[67] In that case shared powers will become exclusive powers for the purpose of external action in conformity with Article 3(2) TFEU, unless the shared powers in question provide for minimum norms and the proposed international agreement does so as well – which will prevent the Union's legislation from being affected or altered by the international agreement.[68] Article 4 also mentions two areas, one internal, namely research, technical development and space, and the other external, economic development and humanitarian assistance, where "internal" or rather autonomous legislation and the development of programmes or a common policy does not have a pre-emptive effect on the powers of the Member States in these areas of external action. External power in these areas of common policy is of a parallel nature so that external action of the Member States and of the Union can proceed in parallel fashion, without hurting each other and while striving for the same goal. When a Member State disburses a certain amount of money and sends technical experts, while the Union does the same for the same broad development programme, there is not normally an affectation (in a legal sense) of the Union action.[69] This is likely to be radically different, if a Member State concludes an agreement on, for instance, safety requirements for toys with the US, which touches upon Union legislation in this field and thus alters the latter's nature or scope. That would place the

63. See Case C-414/11, *Dai-ichi Sankyo* on TRIPs and Case C-137/12, *Commission v. Council (Conditional Access Services)* on an agreement on broadcasting services.
64. Joined Cases 103 and 165/12, *European Parliament & Commission v. Council*. These cases where about a choice of legal basis; at no time was the classic position on fisheries conservation put in question.
65. Case C-114/12, *Commission v. Council (Negotiation of a CoE Convention)*, paras. 65–67. See also Opinion 1/13 *Hague Convention on Child Abduction*.
66. See Art. 219 TFEU.
67. See Case 22/70, *ERTA*, para 17, and Ch. 26, "Economic and Monetary Union", of this book.
68. See Opinion 2/91, *ILO Convention*.
69. Case C-268/94, *Portugal v. Council (Agreement with India)*. The only limit a Member State would be held to in such a situation is that flowing from its obligation of sincere cooperation of Art. 4(3) TEU. This case was confirmed also on other points after the Lisbon Treaty in Case C-377/12, *Commission v. Council (Framework Agreement with the Philippines)*, see Ch. 41, "Union external relations under the TFEU", section 3.1.1 of this book.

Member State concerned immediately in breach of an exclusive external power of the Union, as was just mentioned above.

Beyond the dichotomy between exclusive EU powers and powers shared with the Member States, there is the coordinating power in the field of economic policy (Art. 5 TFEU) and the so-called supplementary powers of Article 6 TFEU. Insofar as these limited Union powers generate common rules, admittedly of quite a limited nature, it remains possible that such rules may be affected by Member State action or agreements on the international plane and that thus the derived exclusive external relations power of Article 3(2) TFEU is triggered and the international freedom of action of the Member States is circumscribed in that way. This is a rather theoretical possibility.

Having thus analysed how the external relations powers fit – and do no fit as far as the CFSP is concerned – into the system of exclusive, shared and supplementary powers introduced by the Treaty of Lisbon, it is now time to look into the question of how external relations powers are handled by the Union's Institutions and how they are integrated into the standard pattern of (partially new) decision-making procedures ushered in by the Lisbon Treaty.

5. The Union's institutions and decision-making in the field of external action

Different institutions and offices dominate the decision-making process in the CFSP on the one side and in the domain of external relations under the TFEU on the other. CFSP decisions are taken, at the initiative of the HR/VP or one of the Member States, by the European Council or the Council of Ministers on the basis of unanimity (with a number of exceptions). This is true both for autonomous acts, such as the general guidelines, the actions and the positions of the Union,[70] and for international agreements concluded by the Union.[71] These CFSP acts are decreed to be of a non-legislative nature. Accordingly the Parliament plays no role in the adoption of any CFSP acts, but has a number of possibilities to be kept abreast of the CFSP and to make recommendations. As we saw earlier the Court is also excluded from the area of CFSP and CSDP, but is charged with the surveillance of the border between the CFSP and the TFEU external relations and in one instance can annul CFSP acts that affect individuals subjected to restrictive measures.[72] By contrast the TFEU external relations function entirely according to the "Community method". Regulations, directives[73] and decisions are adopted on a proposal of the Commission by the ordinary legislative procedure, in which the Council, deciding by qualified majority and the European Parliament collaborate. The resulting Union acts are subject to the normal rules of judicial review. The procedure for adopting treaties also requires collaboration between Council and Parliament, but Parliament can only give an up or down vote to the treaty in question (Art. 218(6)(a) TFEU).

Before we look in greater detail at the decision-making procedures, it is important to point out that in the field of external action non-legal documents and soft law instruments play a considerable role in decision-making. Most Council meetings end with a *communiqué* about what the Council has done, whether or not it has adopted any formal acts of a legal nature. In the case of the press releases issued after a Foreign Affairs Council, these are often of greater importance than simply a brief record of what was discussed and a list of formal acts adopted. They contain relatively few items relating to formal Council acts, but many so-called "conclusions" and occasionally they contain or are accompanied by "declarations", either of the Council itself or of

70. See Art. 25 jo. 30 and 31 TEU.
71. See Art. 25 jo. 30, 37 TEU and Art. 218 TFEU.
72. Art. 275 TFEU jo. Art. 40 TEU.
73. There are few directives with immediate external effects, primarily in the field of migration and asylum.

the HR/VP. The conclusions normally give the views of the Council on a specific foreign policy problem as it is developing at the moment of the Council meeting and contain indications as to how the EU will approach the problem in question. They may also contain directives for action by the HR or by the competent special representative of the EU for the region or for the specific foreign policy problem in question.[74] Declarations are obviously of a more solemn nature than conclusions, but both have become, without doubt, instruments of a non-binding nature to steer the EU CFSP from month to month, between two meetings of the Foreign Affairs Council.[75]

Sometimes so-called strategies are adopted during a Council meeting and then attached to the press release of that meeting. Such strategies are elaborate documents that contain a long-term policy approach to a specific region or foreign policy problem. They have normally been developed by the HR, often together with the Commission if the matter sits astride the CFSP and the TFEU.[76] Such strategy documents are *not* the strategic decisions to be taken under Article 22 TEU by the European Council, as they have not been taken at that level. In their spirit they are like the definitions of an EU approach to a foreign policy problem to be adopted by the Council under Article 29 TEU, but they are not given any legal form.[77]

All formally non-binding instruments, such as those discussed above, have to be adopted by consensus, that is to say that none of the Member States in the Council explicitly states not to be able to support the consensus. Though officially consensus is not the same as unanimity,[78] in reality in the Council of Ministers of the EU both methods of decision-making are near-identical. The President of the Council, the HR, in practice will never proceed to a vote in order to have a unanimous decision; she will simply say that she is informed that there is general agreement on a proposed act or informal document and only exceptionally she will ask whether anyone is opposed to a CFSP decision. The same method is used to verify whether consensus exists. It is, of course, also possible for one or more Member States to declare during the debate in Council that they will break the unanimity or the consensus.

The above also applies to formally binding CFSP/CSDP decisions. However, there are important possibilities to mitigate the consequences of unanimity included in the TEU. First of all, there is the possibility of constructive abstention, which has been included in the Treaty since Amsterdam.[79] In such cases a Member State may declare that it abstains from voting without wanting to block the consensus. The result will be that the decision is adopted without creating any obligation on the abstaining State Member, but that the decision commits the Union and binds the non-abstaining Member States. Moreover, the abstaining Member State shall not

---

74. For example the Press Release of the Foreign Affairs Council of 17 Mar. 2014 contains "conclusions" *inter alia* on Ukraine, on the Sahel, on South Sudan and on the Central African Republic, Council doc. 7764/14, PRESSE 153, PR CO 17.
75. For example the Declaration of 27 May 2013 on the prospective prolongation of restrictive measures against Syria, Press Release of the Foreign Affairs Council of 27–28 May 2013, doc. 9977/13.
76. Two examples of such strategies are the EU Strategy on the Gulf of Guinea (adopted 17 Mar. 2014) and the Strategy for Security and Development in the Sahel (adopted 2011).
77. This may have to do with the fact that they often cover the two areas of external action and it would be problematic to base them on both CFSP and TFEU legal bases because the separation between these two domains maintained by Art. 40 TEU.
78. Footnote 1 to Art. IX:1 WTO Agreement contains a definition of consensus, which is considered of general validity in the law of international organizations and reads as follows: "The body concerned shall be deemed to have decided by consensus on a matter submitted for its consideration, if no Member, present at the meeting when the decision is taken, formally objects to the proposed decision".
79. It is likely that the introduction of the constructive abstention mechanism was inspired by Art. 6(2) of the OECD Convention.

take any action that would undermine or impede the Union's action. However, if the number of abstaining Member States goes beyond one third of the total number of Member States and one third of the population of the Union, the proposal is not adopted.[80] This flexibility is of great importance for the effectiveness of the Union, especially in the case of CFSP actions on the ground, for instance in Kosovo.[81]

In addition the TEU makes it possible to adopt CFSP decisions on the basis of qualified majority in specific cases, in particular when the decisions taken are based on an earlier basic decision either by the European Council or by the Council of Ministers itself, and when they concern the appointment of EU Special Representatives.[82] The reasons for this are obvious: the nomination of a special representative, often in a crisis situation, should not be unduly delayed by opposition of a few Member States. In the other cases, the decision of principle has been taken and its implementation should not again be subject to obstruction.

In the domain of TFEU external relations, acts take the form of regulations, directives or decisions insofar as they are autonomous in nature. All such acts, taken pursuant to the main external powers of the Union as laid down in Part V of the TFEU, such as the common commercial policy, development cooperation, cooperation with developed countries and humanitarian aid, follow the ordinary legislative procedure[83] and are subject to the normal, full judicial review under Union law. Examples of such acts are the basic regulations concerning safeguards and anti-dumping and countervailing duties in the field of trade and so-called financial instruments in the field of development, cooperation and humanitarian aid.[84]

Provisions mentioning the fostering of cooperation of the Union (and occasionally the Member States) with third States and international organizations in Part III of the TFEU in such areas as education, vocational training, culture, public health, Trans-European Networks (TENs), research, technological development and space, and the environment[85] seem in all their brevity and generality to leave room for autonomous measures and international agreements, although agreements are explicitly mentioned only in connection with the last two.[86] In all these areas the ordinary legislative procedure applies in case autonomous external measures would be necessary.

There is no doubt that the Union is competent to conclude agreements all across the spectrum of its powers both in the TEU and TFEU. Together with the imposition of restrictive

80. Art. 31(1) 2nd para.
81. Council Joint Action 2008/124/CFSP on the European Union Rule of Law Mission in Kosovo, EULex Kosovo, was adopted on 4 Feb. 2008 with constructive abstention by Spain, Greece and Cyprus, which also invoked the condition that participation in the mission was voluntary. See P.J. Kuijper, "And in the meantime [...] Kosovo (Editorial Comments)", 46 CML Rev (2009), at 377.
82. Art. 31(2) TEU. Another example of resort to qualified majority voting is the amendment of lists of individuals or entities subjected to restrictive measures by the Council. Indeed, once these lists have been established by unanimity, demanding unanimity for their amendment would seem useless. This is well illustrated in: Council Implementing Decision 2011/736/CFSP, which specifically refers to Art. 31(2) TFEU in its preamble. Compare R. Wessel and R. Böttner, "Art. 31 – Procedures for the adoption of CFSP measures" in H.-J. Blanke and S. Mangiameli (Eds.), *The Treaty on European Union (TEU). A Commentary* (Springer, 2013), 1051.
83. See Ch. 7, "Lawmaking", section 4 of this book.
84. See Ch. 41, "Union external relations under the TFEU", sections 2.3.2, 2.3.3, and 3.1.2 of this book.
85. To be found in Arts. 165(3), 166(3), 167(3), 168(3), 171(3), 186, 189(3) and 191(4) TFEU respectively.
86. See Arts. 186 and 191(4). It is difficult, however, to believe that fostering cooperation with third countries and international organizations, such as the Council of Europe and the European Space Agency could be done without international agreements. It is unlikely that the drafters of the Treaty had this in mind when they chose slightly different wording in these provisions. See also the view on the generality of the treaty-making power all across the board of the TFEU above at section 3.

measures on trade, finance and the admission of persons (Art. 215 TFEU), the procedure to negotiate and conclude treaties on the part of the Union, as laid down in Article 218 TFEU, is the only provision that seems to take the integrated nature of the Union's external action seriously. Both articles recognize that autonomous acts like decisions imposing sanctions on third States or individuals and companies with third States and contractual instruments like international agreements can and often must contain elements from the high and the low forms of foreign policy at the same time. And, as a natural consequence of the single international personality of the Union, it is no longer conceivable to split up such measures. Yet at the same time some accommodation has to be found for the separation between the two foundational Treaties (Art. 40 TEU) and justice has to be done to the phrase that "[t]he common foreign and security policy is subject to specific rules and procedures" (Article 24 TEU).

In the case of so-called restrictive measures this dilemma is solved by having two separate decisions, one under the TEU, taking the "political" decision to impose restrictive measures on third States, companies or individuals. Subsequently the Council has the obligation under Article 215 to adopt the "necessary measures" after a joint proposal by the HR and the Commission. This shall be done by qualified majority and will thus take care of the partial or complete interruption of economic or financial relations with a third country. In this way the two-way non-affectation clause of Article 40 TEU is supposed to be respected. In reality, however, the economic implementation under the TFEU of the political decision imposing restrictive measures taken under the TEU is clearly subservient to the latter. That is where the center of gravity of the restrictive measures that the two combined acts initiate, lies.[87]

Article 218 TFEU on the procedures for the negotiation, signature and conclusion of international agreements of the Union is written so as to find a solution by way of the center of gravity of the agreement in question. The proposal for the initiation for negotiations should come from the Commission or the High Representative, depending on whether or not the envisaged agreement relates exclusively or principally to the CFSP. Presumably based on the same criterion the Council appoints the negotiator, either the Commission or the HR (and perhaps in some instances both) and authorizes either of them to open the negotiations. Subsequently it is the negotiator which proposes to the Council such steps as the signature, the provisional application and the conclusion of the agreement. The Council takes all these steps deciding by qualified majority, except when the agreement covers a field for which unanimity is required for the adoption of a Union act. This is obviously the case for CFSP and CSDP acts. In addition Article 218(8) mentions a number of other cases in which the Council shall act unanimously.[88] The Parliament must give its consent to most international agreements now (Art. 218(6)(a)), but not to agreements of which the center of gravity lies in the CFSP area.

It is clear, therefore, that the center of gravity will decide whether an act concluding an EU international agreement will in its entirety be based on a CFSP or a TFEU provision.[89] This has been confirmed by the Court's approach to the agreements concerning the transfer of alleged pirates apprehended in the framework of the CSDP Atalanta operation against piracy off the

87. For more details on restrictive measures, see Ch. 41, "Union external relations under the TFEU", section 5 of this book. On the center of the gravity test used by the Court as the way to decide the correct legal basis of an act relying on objective criteria, see Ch. 7, "Lawmaking", of this book.
88. Association agreements, Cooperation Agreements with candidate Member countries and the agreement on the EU's accession to ECHR.
89. This can be seen as a codification of the approach of the Court in Case C-91/05, *Commission v. Council (ECOWAS)*, where the Court already had recourse to this approach in a trans-treaty fashion.

coast of Somalia[90] to nearby countries, such as Mauritius and Tanzania. Such transfer of alleged pirates to be prosecuted and judged had obviously strong links with cooperation in the criminal justice sector. As these agreements were totally dependent on the existence of the Atalanta mission both as to their contents and their aim, however, the Court decided that the CSDP aspects were preponderant for the conclusion of the transfer agreements as well.[91] However, now that the protection of the TEU against the TFEU rules and procedures is equally strong to the protection of the latter against the former (which used to have priority),[92] it remains unclear for the moment what the Council or the Court will decide in a situation in which the TFEU and CFSP/CSDP aspects of an EU act are deemed of equal weight.

As all legal acts, whether autonomous or contractual, those in the field of external action are prepared in the Council with the help of the system of working parties and committees. Between the working parties and the Council stands the Coreper (Coreper II), but in the field of external action also the Political and Security Committee (PSC) that is supposed to deal exclusively with CFSP matters.[93] Like Coreper it consists of persons with (in this case: junior) ambassadorial rank, but formally all CFSP questions, after having passed the PSC, have to transit through Coreper before they can go up to the Council for final (but in many cases purely formal) decision. Among the some 33 working parties that operate in the field of foreign affairs, there are some 10 that operate in the domain of trade and development and are chaired by the rotating 6 months presidency, as was the case before Lisbon. There are some 7 or 8 groups which work on matters of a military nature, such as disarmament etc. that functionally belong to the CFSP/CSDP. They are presided by representatives of the HR (from the EEAS). The largest group of working parties are regional in nature or concern international organizations of a broad remit, like the UN and the Council of Europe. They too are chaired by officers of the EEAS and thus demonstrate the integrative and coordinating role that the HR is supposed to play.

As in other domains of European law, this set-up is supposed to arrive at decisions at the lowest possible level and after that has happened, the rest of the trajectory of a Union act, also in case of external action, becomes a written procedure and thereby a mere formality. It is only by breaking a consensus or a putative qualified majority that a Member State can still provoke a discussion in the Council.

The European Parliament is now bestowed with the power of consent over most international agreements of the Union. Such consent shall be given by the majority of the votes cast (Art. 231 TFEU). The different cases in which such consent is required according to Article 218(6)(a) speak largely for themselves.[94] Sub-paragraph iii) is meant to refer to cooperation agreements that are different from association agreements only in name, but in reality are of the same importance. And "important budgetary consequences" in subparagraph iv) have to

90. For more details on Operation Atalanta, see the Ch. 40, "Common foreign and security policy and common security and defence policy", section 3.5 of this book.
91. Case C-263/14, *European Parliament v. Council (Operation Atalanta)*, paras. 43–54. See also Case C-658/11, *European Parliament v. Council (Mauritius Agreement)*, which is less explicit on the question of the CSDP nature of the agreement. Further on this case and its consequence for the right of information of the EP, see fn. 98 *infra* and accompanying text.
92. Cf. old Art. 47 TEU and new Art. 40 TEU (Lisbon).
93. The meetings of the PSC are prepared by Relex Counselors. On the various high level preparatory Council groups, see Ch. 5, "The Political Institutions", section 3 of this book.
94. These categories are: (i) association agreements; (ii) agreement on Union accession to the European Convention for the Protection of Human Rights and Fundamental Freedoms; (iii) agreements establishing a specific institutional framework by organizing cooperation procedures; (iv) agreements with important budgetary implications for the Union; (v) agreements covering fields to which either the ordinary legislative procedure applies, or the special legislative procedure where consent by the European Parliament is required.

be established with respect to the size of the budget as a whole and not just a chapter of it.[95] Consent of Parliament is expressed by a normal parliamentary majority and is obtained after the normal parliamentary procedure. This means that the proposed agreement is subject to a report from a rapporteur from the competent parliamentary committee (which also collects the opinions of other relevant committees). This report proposes the line the EP should take with respect to its consent.[96] There are well-known examples in recent years of critical reports that have led to the rejection by the European Parliament of important draft agreements, such as the SWIFT agreement with the USA, concerning access of US authorities to the payments data in the so-called SWIFT inter-bank system, and ACTA, the multilateral agreement on trade in counterfeit goods.[97] Both were rejected for reasons related to fundamental rights.

It has already been mentioned that the EP has in principle no right of being involved in the adoption of treaties and other legal acts in the field of CFSP. However, the Court recently confirmed that the Parliament's right to be informed of the different stages that a treaty goes through from recommendation for starting negotiations to conclusion extends also to treaties falling wholly under the CFSP. This is based on the fundamental democratic principle that the people should participate in the exercise of power through the intermediary of a representative assembly, which in the case of the CFSP/CSDP serves primarily to verify of the choice of legal basis for acts in this field is justified.[98]

The Court has constantly played an important role in defining the external powers of the Union and, therefore, in the vertical division of powers between the Union and the Member States. The Court has also been watching over "the institutional balance between the Institutions" in the field of external action. First of all, in deciding about the direct effect of certain agreements, notably the WTO Agreements, the Court is very conscious of the fact that in granting direct effect to treaty provisions it could be seen to be usurping the Commission's position as negotiator or the Council's and Parliament's position as legislators.[99] It also has defended the balance between the Institutions, where it concerns the negotiation of agreements, in respect of the Commission's duty to make recommendations to open negotiations,[100] as well as in respect of the Council's right to subject the Commission as negotiator to directives, while protecting the Commission's margin of discretion in carrying out such directives,[101] in respect of the Commission's task to represent the EU in litigation in international and foreign courts[102] and finally in defending the Council's powers in the conclusion of international agreements.[103]

95. In Case C-189/97, *Parliament v. Council (Important budgetary consequences)*, the Court ruled that a sum representing 1% of the whole of the payment appropriations allocated for external operations of the Community does not have important implications for the Community budget. The Court rejected a comparison with the overall Community budget as a basis for "important implications". The consequence is that this limit will not easily lead to a requirement of consent, as the threshold will be high.
96. On parliamentary procedure see Ch. 5, "The political institutions", section 5 of this book.
97. Reports Hennis-Plasschaert on SWIFT (A7-0013/2010) and Rapport Martin on ACTA (A7-0204/2012).
98. Case C-658/11, *European Parliament v. Council (Mauritius Agreement)*. This was confirmed in Case C-263/14, *European Parliament v. Council (Operation Atalanta)*, para 68 et seq., in particular 70–71.
99. Case C-307/02, *Van Parijs*, para 48. See P.J. Kuijper, "It shall contribute to [...] the strict observance and development of international law [...]", The role of the Court of Justice" in A. Rosas, E. Levits, Y. Bot (Eds.), *The Court of Justice and the Construction of Europe: Analyses and Perspectives on Sixty Years of Case-Law* (Asser/Springer, 2013), 589–612, at 604.
100. Case 22/70, *ERTA*, paras. 86–90, can be interpreted this way, when the Court scolds the Commission for not coming forward with a recommendation to the Council.
101. Case C-425/13, *Commission v. Council (Negotiation Directives)*, paras. 85 and 89–92.
102. Case C-73/14, *Council v. Commission (ITLOS)*. The Court developed its earlier judgment in C-131/03 P, *Reynolds Tobacco et al. v. Commission*, para 94.
103. Cases C-327/91, *France v. Commission (Competition Cooperation Agreement)* and Case C-322/02, *France v.*

After this overview of a number of general aspects of the (ideally) integrated external action of the Union, it is important to dwell on two consequences of the vertical and horizontal division of powers in the field of external action, namely the conclusion of mixed agreements and the mixed representation in international organizations and treaty bodies. Moreover, it is in fashioning its practice of mixed agreements that the Union came up against the realities of international politics and the seeming immutability of a system that is still based primarily on the fully sovereign State as the "natural" building block of international society. In short, the foreign relations law of the EU is not determined simply by EU law and its interpretation by the ECJ, but also by international law and politics.

6. Mixed agreements and mixed membership of international organizations

6.1 Mixed agreements

Mixed Agreements were foreseen in Article 102 of the Euratom Agreement, but were not mentioned in the EEC Treaty and never introduced later on, not even in the failed Constitution for Europe. They crept in by analogy and by practice, simply because during negotiations it became clear that the agreement envisaged between the parties, one of which was the EU, was not fully covered by the powers conferred on the EU. From very early on, it was also the political wish of the Member States that played a role, in particular in the conclusion of association agreements.[104]

Various typologies of mixed agreements have been devised.[105] Let it suffice here to say that there is only one case in which mixity is inevitable for legal reasons and that is when both exclusive powers of the Union on the one hand and exclusive powers of the Member States on the other are required in order to conclude the agreement in question. In all other cases Member States act as if there is a choice, even if there are no exclusive powers on their part in play at all. Even in cases where exclusive EU powers and shared EU powers combined are perfectly capable of supporting a sole Union agreement, they will reserve the shared powers to themselves and demand mixity. It is interesting to note that older case law of the Court, notably Opinion 1/76, says that Member States are only to be let into the agreement, if their presence in it is absolutely required, but in practice this seems to have become a dead letter.[106] Similarly the motive behind the possibility created by the Lisbon Treaty to conclude agreements covering CFSP and TFEU external relations powers at the same time, namely to reduce the number of mixed agreements,[107] was ignored by opting for the old-fashioned mixed agreement instead.[108] An internal reason is that, since it is difficult to demonstrate beyond doubt that there is exclusive power under the

---

Commission (Transatlantic Regulatory Cooperation). Post-Lisbon: Case C-660/13, *Council v. Commission (Signature of an Addendum to an MOU with Switzerland)*, paras. 42–46.

104. Among the early association agreements with Greece, Turkey, Cyprus and Malta, the first two were mixed and the latter two sole Community agreements. The importance of the treaty partners was the decisive element.
105. See A. Rosas, "Mixed Union – Mixed agreements" in M. Koskenniemi (Ed.), *International Law Aspects of the European Union* (Nijhoff, 1998), 125.
106. See Opinion 1/76, *Laying-up Fund for the Rhine*, paras. 6 and 7. Opinion 2/15, *Singapore FTA*, paras. 238–244, however, seem to exclude that Member States in the Council could decide to use a shared competence, in this case non-direct investment, as another legal basis next to an exclusive legal basis, like the CCP, to conclude an agreement on trade and investment broadly interpreted with a third country. The doctrine has always been overwhelmingly of another opinion.
107. In the past many agreements had been made mixed by including so-called political consultation provisions in the agreement at the behest of Member States in the Council.
108. See, for example, the EU-Korea FTA (14 May 2011) O.J. 2011, L 127/6, which was signed "between the European Union and its Member States, of the one part, and the Republic of Korea, of the other part".

implied power rule of Article 3(2) TFEU without going to the Court, the Commission and the Council prefer to tolerate ambiguity.[109] An external reason is that the Member States want to remain as much visible on the international scene as they can and that mixed agreements are a good way of doing this and having the best of both worlds from their perspective.

Third States parties to multilateral treaties and international organizations have regularly accepted the mixed nature of EU participation. They had, under international law, no obligation to accept the EU as a party, next to its Member States. In most instances the other parties to the agreement or members of an organization had to decide to modify the agreement concerned in order to provide for the acceptance/admission of so-called Regional (Economic) Integration Organizations (R[E]IOs) as parties to the Treaty or as Members to the organization.[110] Although this is a general category, in reality so far the EU is the only organization that is generally accepted as belonging in this category. If third States accepted to negotiate a mixed agreement with the EU and its Member States or to facilitate the accession of the EU, next to the Member States, it was because they accepted that there had been a genuine transfer of competences. Moreover, it was in their self-interest to accept the EU, since it was likely to lighten their negotiation burden if in nearly all areas covered by the agreement they would have only one interlocutor instead of many.[111] Nevertheless mixed agreements remain a bit of a nuisance with many complications for the EU and its treaty partners. Only some of the problems can be mentioned here.[112]

First and foremost is the division of competences between EU and Member States. Is the EU obliged to give full disclosure on this score to its treaty partners? Is that even possible given the changing scope of exclusive external powers following new internal legislation (Art. 3(2) TFEU and *ERTA* case law)? The EU has had to make declarations of competence primarily in cases where it wanted to become a party, with its Member States, to multilateral agreements. But bringing such declarations constantly up to date is illusory given the internal and external burden of negotiation that would necessarily be involved.

The declaration of competence may have all kinds of consequences for the actual life of the international agreement in question or of the international organization concerned. Who may speak on certain subjects in the treaty bodies or the organs of the international organization, the EU or its Member States? Who may vote on certain subjects? How many votes should there be for the Union, one or 28, or even 29?[113] In order to find answers to such questions internal codes of conduct between the Council, the Commission, and the Member States (and possibly

109. It is questionable whether such mixity based on tolerated ambiguity agreed between Council and Commission is in conformity with the balance between the institutions, as these two institutions in this way have implicitly bargained away the power of the European Parliament to express its consent with the Union part of the agreement, as the national Parliaments normally approve the entirety of the agreement (not just the "national part" of it) and thus diminish the powers of the EP.

110. The term REIO occurs for the first time in the revised Art. II(3) –(9) of the FAO Constitution.

111. This is very much the case in the WTO, where Member States hardly ever speak in meetings and where the other Members have repeatedly said that they do not want to deal any longer with 28 or 29 entities, when engaging in trade negotiations.

112. There is extensive literature on mixed agreements and the problems they entail, e.g. C. Hillion and P. Koutrakos (Eds.), *Mixed Agreements Revisited. The EU and its Member States in the World* (Hart, 2010).

113. The usual solution has become that the number of votes of the Union and its Member States will be that of the number of the Member States. However, refinements are possible: in some instances third States have forced the Union to accept that it will only have the number of votes of the Member States that are present in a meeting, even if a vote of the Union engages all Member States.

in future also the EP) are necessary to provide answers in the context of a specific agreement.[114] Such internal agreements are enforceable before the Court, even if they have no legal form and have not been published in the OJ, as long as they were intended to be binding.[115] Equally what one might call external rules of conduct are necessary and are often included in the agreement relating to the accession of the EU to an international organization and may contain stifling conditions for the EU and its Member States for the right to speak and to enjoy certain procedural rights during a debate, for the right to vote etc.[116]

Should the declaration of competence also have consequences for the division of responsibility between Union and Member States, or is that something that should be decided purely on the basis of the rules of attribution of unlawful acts as laid down in the rules of responsibility of States and of International Organizations?[117]

Directly linked to this last question is the question whether mixed agreements create obligations not only between the Union and the Member States on the one hand and third States on the other, but also between the Member States *inter se*. In bilateral mixed agreements this is normally clear from the title of the agreement which speaks of the Union and its Member States on the one side, mentioning the Member States by name as one group, and the third State on the other side. In multilateral treaties with many third States it is difficult to achieve this effect, because the EU Member States traditionally are mentioned alphabetically and interspersed among the third States, creating the impression that this is a normal multilateral agreement. The EU has occasionally used so-called disconnection clauses or declarations to clarify that the EU and its Member States are one group and that the Member States among themselves will apply the EU implementing legislation of the multilateral agreement in question, but not the agreement itself.[118]

Finally there is the problem of the conclusion of mixed agreements, which has both internal and external aspects. First of all both for reasons of EU law and international law, the EU and the Member States must all conclude or ratify the mixed agreement.[119] This will normally take three years at least (which is one reason to want to avoid mixed agreements) and provisional application may not always be an option. The Lisbon Treaty provides for provisional application procedures, but several Member States' constitutions or organic laws do not provide for

114. See for example the Code of Conduct agreed between the Council, the Member States and the Commission for the participation of the Community and its Member States in meetings regarding the implementation of the Convention on the Protection and Promotion of the Diversity of Cultural Expressions, Council Doc 5914/07, 1 Feb. 2007, reproduced in P.J. Kuijper, J. Wouters et al., *The Law of EU External Relations, Cases, Materials, and Commentary on the EU as an International Actor*, 2nd ed. (OUP, 2015), at 154.
115. Case C-25/94, *Commission v. Council (FAO)*, paras. 40–51.
116. Especially in the early cases of accession to treaty bodies (Annex IX of UNCLOS) and to an international organization as the FAO, such rules were extremely restrictive.
117. For a more elaborate discussion of this question, see P.J. Kuijper, "Responsibility for mixed agreements" in C. Hillion and P. Koutrakos (Eds.), *Mixed Agreements Revisited. The EU and its Member States in the World* (Hart, 2010), 208.
118. See the Unilateral Declaration on Behalf of the Community in Connection with Deposition of the Instrument of Accession, Annex II to the Decision on the Conclusion of the Convention on the Protection and Promotion of the Diversity of Cultural Expressions (UNESCO), Decision 2006/515/EC, O.J. 2006, L 201/15. Such declarations should probably be made in all such cases.
119. Note that in some instances, mixed agreements with a limited geographic scope, only certain Member States may accompany the Union as party to the mixed agreement. Examples of such treaties are the 1992 Convention on the Protection of the Marine Environment of the Baltic Sea Area, O.J. 1994, L 73, to which both the EU and several Union Member States bordering the Baltic Sea such as Germany, Finland, Sweden, Estonia, and Denmark are parties. The same applies to the Convention for the protection of the Mediterranean Sea against pollution, O.J. 1977, L 240.

this possibility.[120] Provisional application of only those parts of the agreement which fall undisputedly under Union exclusive competence may not always be politically feasible. This is a technique that has been applied with developing countries without much hesitation, but with developed countries or other countries, like the BRICs, it may severely affect the overall balance of the agreement to the detriment of the Union.[121]

Another major question is whether the EU should always be the last to ratify, after all Member States have done so. Normally the Commission and Council try to keep to this scenario, but there have been instances where the Union has used the qualified majority for a ratification decision and actually executed it before all the Member States had deposited their instrument of ratification.[122] It will be interesting to see whether the ECJ agrees with the Commission that the duty of cooperation of the Member States goes as far as that.

In order to avoid all these problems with delays caused by ratifications by the Member States, the Council has been rather creative by reverting to an old legal technique from the EEC's early days, namely by putting the ratification by the Member States in a decision of the representatives of the Member States meeting within the Council.[123] Contrary to the practice of those days the Council integrated the decision of the representatives of the Member States with the EU decision concluding the agreement into one hybrid act. However, the unanimity required for the decision of the Member States was incompatible with the qualified majority for the Union decision in Article 218(8) TFEU. For these reasons the hybrid decision was quashed by the Court of Justice.[124]

Furthermore, it is important to realize that the accession of the Union to a mixed multilateral agreement is dependent not only on the ratifications of the Member States, but also on reaching the number of ratifications of the EU's treaty partners required under the agreement itself for the amendment enabling the accession of the Union to enter into force. A good example of the difficulties that may ensue is the Convention on International Trade in Endangered Species (CITES). Its treaty body already in 1983 adopted an amendment to the convention, allowing the accession of regional economic integration organizations. This amendment entered into force in early 2014, when finally the required 54 ratifications had accumulated.[125] If it takes 30 years to collect the ratifications in a non-controversial case like CITES, one can imagine that the task before the EU of joining a large number of important existing international conventions will be daunting.

---

120. See Art. 218(5) TFEU. Among the Member States where provisional application is not foreseen or only foreseen for certain treaties are: Portugal, France, Austria, Italy, Finland, and others.
121. A far-reaching example of a regime close to provisional application, is the grant of rights akin to Membership offered to the EU, pending its accession to the World Customs Organization, see Council Decision 2007/668/EC, O.J. 2007, L 274/11-12.
122. For instance, UNCLOS was ratified by the Union before Germany and Denmark did so. Presently the Commission has engaged an infringement procedure against Germany for not having proceeded to the ratification of the mixed Open Skies Agreement with the US after more than seven years. See for the announcement of initiation of the infringement procedure the press release by the European Commission of 28 Oct. 2010, IP/10/245/.
123. See, for example, the Partnership and Cooperation Agreement between the European Communities and their Member States, of the one part, and the Republic of Armenia, of the other part, which was entered by both the ECSC Member States separately and the Council of the EEC, O.J. 1999, L 239/38.
124. Case C-28/12, *Commission v. Council (Hybrid Agreement)*, paras. 48–53.
125. The number of 54 ratifications fortunately was based on two thirds of the total number of 80 ratifications of the CITES Convention on the date of the adoption of the amendment in April 1983. The text of the Gaborone Amendment is available at <www.cites.org/eng/disc/gaborone.php> (last visited 28 Aug. 2016).

6.2 *Mixed membership in international organizations*

Founding treaties of international organizations are also international agreements, hence they can be concluded as mixed agreements, too. However, international organizations are also organizations, with, just as the EU itself, certain constitutional traits and a status of membership for which new Members must fulfil certain conditions. If the EU wants or even needs to become a Member, there is not just the possibility for accession for international organizations, which needs to be created, but also the conditions for membership which need to be fulfilled, which in the case of international organizations are more stringent than for States.[126] In some cases membership for international organizations remains excluded and a status as observer is all that remains. On the side of the Union, Article 220 TFEU simply states that the Union shall establish all appropriate forms of cooperation with the organs of the UN and its specialized agencies, as well as with the Council of Europe, the OSCE and the OECD. The same also applies to other international organizations. The HR and the Commission are supposed to implement such appropriate forms of cooperation – which is normally done through the conclusion of agreements between the EU and the organizations in question. Moreover, Union delegations to such international organizations, under the authority of the HR, are supposed to represent the Union in the organs of the organizations (Art. 221 TFEU).

It is important here to discuss the problems of mixed membership (or even mixed observership) in international organizations; other legal aspects of the EU's relationship with international organizations will be discussed in the following chapters. As has already been mentioned, the most difficult cases are the early cases, in which the Union desired to adhere to an international organization next to its Member States which already were Members of that organization, essentially the accession to the FAO and to its daughter organization with the WHO, the Codex Alimentarius Commission.[127] These are the accessions in which great emphasis was placed on international organizations as second rank creatures of international law, which would have to prove that they had received transferred powers from their Member States and in respect of which these Member States had to confirm that they had indeed transferred the mentioned powers which fell into the purview of the FAO, to the EU. Extensive declarations of competence were required and should be kept up to date. These declarations of competence would determine who was entitled to speak and vote on certain issues. The rights to speak and vote could not be exercised at the same time by the EU and its Member States. The declaration of competence would also have consequences for the responsibility of the EU and its Member States respectively for breach of their obligations under the FAO Agreement. The rights of the EU as a Member were considerably curtailed in respect of its membership in the committees of the FAO.[128]

The position of the EU in other organizations, where it was an original Member of the organization, or where it had enjoyed a particular status from the beginning, is considerably better. Examples are the WTO and the OECD. As far as the WTO is concerned, the EU participated from the beginning in the Uruguay Round, which spawned this organization. Also in the WTO's predecessor organization, the GATT, the EEC had been present as a *de facto* Member from the

---

126. See the special conditions with relation to competence declarations etc. laid down in Art. II (revised) of the FAO Constitution and Annex IX of the UNCLOS.

127. Similarly difficult and complicated was the adhesion to UNCLOS, which was basically the adhesion to a treaty, but with some organization-like traits, such as treaty organs. See Annex IX to UNCLOS.

128. Cf. Art. II(3)–(9) FAO Constitution and FAO Rules of Procedure. The Commission, the Council and the Parliament are seeking agreement on a new declaration of competence and a new internal arrangement on the Union's participation in the FAO, see doc. COM(2013) 333 final. There is no agreement yet on this document. For the internal arrangement on the EU's participation in the Codex Alimentarius Commission, see Annex III to Council Decision 2003/822/EC, O.J. 2003, L 309/14-21.

moment the Common External Tariff had been formed and had to pass the test of the Union being a customs union under Article XXIV:5 and 6 GATT, of which the external tariff was on the whole not higher than the average incidence of the tariffs of the Member States previously. The familiarity of the States represented in the GATT with the representatives of the Commission in their midst made it much easier for the EC at the time and the EU after Lisbon to be accepted as a Member that acted and spoke "on behalf of" all WTO Members who were Member States of the EU. Hardly any restrictive rules applied to the capacity of the EU to act in the WTO, to speak and participate fully in the debate. The only anomaly that remained, was that the Member States continued to pay their dues to the WTO, while the EU only paid an additional fee as payment for the additional administrative costs that its membership caused the organization to incur.[129]

The OECD is an example of an organization that was used to the presence of the EU, in the person of the representative from the Commission, in its midst from the moment of its creation as successor to the OEEC. The observership of the Commission actually is in between a normal status of observer and the rights of a Member State; on the other hand, it is always rather difficult to maintain a clear EC/Union standpoint in the discussions in the OECD Council. Given the high number of EU Member States among the membership of the OECD from the beginning, having a fully-fixed EU position was seen by the other OECD Member States a sure conversation stopper and hence inimical to having a serious debate. Since the OECD is more important as an organization for the quality of the studies of its Secretariat and takes relatively few decisions that are binding on the Members, this is not seen as a big problem.[130]

In the field of monetary matters – formally one of the exclusive powers of the Union – one would expect that such exclusivity would also have consequences for the external powers of the Union and would lead in the long run to a Union membership of the IMF, replacing the Member States. Nothing could be farther from the truth. Article 219 derogates extensively from Article 218, where the normal treaty-making procedure is concerned, when an exchange rate system for the Euro in relations to other currencies would have to be negotiated, or when agreements concerning monetary or foreign exchange rate regimes need to be negotiated more generally with third States. Especially the usual role of the Commission as negotiator in TFEU matters is severely curtailed and the Member States retain the power to negotiate in international bodies (read: the IMF) and to conclude international agreements, as long as these remain without prejudice to monetary union and Union agreements. Accordingly the Member States using the euro are still Members of the IMF, where many of them have an Executive Director, though the ECB is represented in such IMF bodies as the monetary committee etc.[131]

In the field of private international law, the Union had acquired considerable powers after the Amsterdam Treaty that in principle are shared under the Treaty, but had become exclusive in those areas that were covered by important internal legislation.[132] In view of these developments

129. This separate payment of their contribution assessed on the basis of the volume of their external trade by the Member States was advantageous for the WTO itself and the other Members, since the intra-Community trade was included in the basis of the assessment. This would not have been the case, if only the trade between the Union and third States had been taken as basis for the assessment of a Union contribution, replacing the MS contributions.
130. For more information on the relation between the EU and the OECD, see the website of the European External Action Service, "The OECD & the EU. Institutional Framework", available at <www.eeas.europa.eu/delegations/oecd_unesco/oecd_eu/political_relations/institutional_framework/index_en.htm> (last visited 28 Aug. 2016).
131. See R. Smits, "International representation of Europe in the area of Economic and Monetary Union: Legal issues and practice in the first ten years of the Euro", 56 *Euredia* (2009), 297.
132. Declaration 36 to the Lisbon Treaty, contained in the Final Act, states that Member States retain the right to negotiate and conclude agreements in the field of private international law, but only "insofar as such

the EC (at the time) decided to apply for membership in The Hague Conference on private international law (HCCH), an organization whose main vocation is to maintain a network of international conventions on private international law. The EU became a party to the HCCH fairly quickly, given that only a limited number of ratifications of the necessary amendments to the HCCH Convention were necessary.[133]

It is important to note that all accessions to a mixed membership international organization are different and the number of cases of mixed membership is limited. Thus no clear model that is easily applicable to other cases has been set.[134]

As a final element that determines the scope of the competences of the EU, especially in relation to its Member States, we need to pay attention here to the principle of community loyalty or sincere cooperation, as it is called in the Treaty of Lisbon. Like the implied powers doctrine this is largely judge-made law and it has found application primarily in connection with mixed agreements. Obviously, in areas where the division of competences is not always fully clear, the notion of sincere cooperation will be more easily invoked than in areas where exclusive powers are or should be applied and where thus breach of such exclusive powers would be the claim.

7. Loyalty and sincere cooperation in external relations

The general duty of sincere cooperation of Article 4(3) TFEU has developed strongly in the field of external relations and, as was noted above, notably where mixed agreements are at issue.[135] Moreover, in external relations there is a special duty of cooperation between the Member States, if they, in conformity with Article 351 TFEU, must adapt, or rid themselves of, treaty obligations towards third States, which antedate the Treaty of Rome or their accession to the EU and are incompatible with the Treaty.

It is important to note that already the classical *ERTA* case referred to Community loyalty, as it was then called, and not so much in order to condemn Member States for lack of such loyalty, but to excuse them for having first breached the exclusive power of the EC based on implied powers reasoning and then for having acted together outside the framework of the Council in order to take a minimum position on the common ratification of the European Road Transport Agreement. At least by taking this common approach they showed some Community loyalty, whilst the Commission had shown its lack of such loyalty by failing to put a recommendation before the Council for conclusion of ERTA by the EEC.[136] Apart from sparing the Council and the Member States a formal defeat, after having confronted them with its new theory of implied

---

agreements comply with Union law". Since Union law includes Art. 3(2) TFEU and the ERTA and Lugano Convention case law that goes with that Article, this declaration doe not change anything to the normal division of treaty-making capacity between the Union and the Member States.

133. Council Decision of 5 Oct. 2006 on the Accession of the Community to the Hague Conference on Private International Law, O.J. 2006, L 297. In spite of this accession the Member States remain parties to many HCCH Conventions concluded before the accession, which do not have a provision allowing EU to accede. The ensuing complications are the subject of Opinion 1/13, *Convention on Child Abduction.*

134. If one counts the OECD and the WCO as a kind of half membership and one discounts treaty bodies in UNCLOS, in multilateral environmental agreements (MEA's) and commodity agreements (some of which are no longer mixed), because they are not considered real international organizations, there remain barely four serious cases of mixed membership: FAO, Codex Alimentarius, the HCCH and WTO (of which the last one after Lisbon and Opinion 2/15, *FTA Singapore*, strictly speaking, should no longer be mixed).

135. On the duty of sincere cooperation in EU external relations: E. Neframi, "The duty of loyalty: Rethinking its scope through its application in the field of EU external relations", 47 CML Rev. 2010, 323–359.

136. Case 22/70, *(ERTA)*, paras. 88 and 90. See also P.J Kuijper, "Re-reading external relations cases in the field of transport: The function of community loyalty" in M. Bulterman et al. (Eds.), *Views of European Law from the Mountain. Liber Amicorum for Piet-Jan Slot* (Kluwer, 2009), 291–300.

exclusive competence for the Union (now enshrined in Article 3(2) TFEU), the Court thus managed to inspire proper respect for the correct procedures underpinning the cooperation between the institutions and the Member States in the field of external relations by mobilizing the doctrine of loyalty to that effect. This was to remain an important element in the Court's case law in external relations.

The Council thus was censured by the Court, for instance, for not having respected the internal arrangements that it had informally agreed with the Commission on the rules for speaking and casting votes in FAO organs. This case also shows that the duty of loyalty has roots in the good faith rule of international law, as the Council was not allowed to go against its own promise.[137] A somewhat comparable case also concerned a more or less informal agreement in the Council concerning the placing of a dangerous organic pollutant (PFOS) on the "prohibited list" of Persistent Organic Pollutants Convention (Convention of Rotterdam), to which the EU was a party. The Council agreed that the Union would take an initiative to do so, but only during the following year's Conference of the Parties (CoP). In spite of this agreement Sweden went ahead and proposed the measure that year, invoking the freedom to do so under the flexibility clause of Article 194(2), 2nd al. TFEU. The ECJ ruled, however, that Sweden did not have this right, once there had been an agreement (even if only informal in nature) in the Council that decided otherwise. Sweden's unilateral action made it impossible for the Union to act as it had been agreed.[138] That loyalty to the Union counts even in organizations of which the Union is not even a Member, but where it is merely an observer, is borne out by the so-called *IMO case*. In this case Greece presented a proposal of its own to the Maritime Safety Committee, after the Commission had refused Greece permission to do so. Although the flat refusal of the Commission could perhaps be criticized, the unilateral action of Greece was clearly contrary to its duty of cooperation, especially since the power in the domain of maritime safety was an exclusive one based on the *ERTA* doctrine.[139]

It is obvious that the case law of the ECJ on Union loyalty and sincere cooperation has a seriously constraining effect on the freedom of action of the Member States, even in those cases where the Union is not a Member of the organizations in question.

8. The place of international law in the law of the EU[140]

8.1 International law as law of the Union

Apart from the provision stating that international agreements concluded by the Union are binding on the Union's institutions and on the Member States (now Art. 216(2) TFEU), the Treaty of Rome was absolutely mum about how such international agreements would relate to the Treaty itself or to the regulations, directives and other acts adopted pursuant to the Treaty. This omission was never rectified in later versions of the Treaties, including the TEU and TFEU.

137. Case C-25/94, *Commission v. Council (FAO)*, para 50.
138. Case C-246/07, *Commission v. Sweden (PFOS)*. This case has been fairly severely criticized from the side of the Member States, but also in the literature. See M. Cremona, "Case C-246/07, *Commission v. Sweden* (PFOS), judgment of the Court of Justice (Grand Chamber) of 20 Apr. 2010", 48 CML Rev. (2011), 1639; C. Hillion, "Mixity and coherence in EU external relations: The significance of the duty of cooperation" in C. Hillion and P. Koutrakos (Eds.), *Mixed Agreements Revisited – The EU and its Member States in the World* (Hart, 2010). More recently: E. Neframi, "Principe de coopération loyale et principe d'attribution dans le cadre de la mise en œuvre du droit de l'union", (2016) *Cahiers de droit européen*, 221–251.
139. Case C- 45/07, *Commission v. Greece (IMO)*, paras. 21–23 and 30–33.
140. See for a more ample treatment specifically of the role of the ECJ in dealing with international law, P.J. Kuijper, op. cit. *supra* note 99, at 589–612. This section is based in large part on that chapter.

Thus the ECJ inevitably became the arbiter of this question. Already in the early 'seventies the Court, in the framework of a preliminary question procedure, was confronted by the question of whether it could interpret an international agreement. The Court replied in the affirmative. It took the view that the agreement had been approved by an act of the Council and thus had become an integral part of Community law.[141] Therefore is was not some act of legislative transformation that made the agreement part of Community law, but the act of conclusion of the Council – which nowadays requires prior approval of the European Parliament in most cases (Art. 218(6)(a) TFEU). In principle, therefore, the Community was, and the Union still is, a monist system, or at least a system of automatic incorporation of international into Union law.[142] Whether this monism stretches much beyond the mere reception of international agreements in the Union legal order is a question that will be confronted later.

In preliminary question and infringement procedures the Court accepted that all kinds of treaties in the different and expanding domains of competence of the Union,[143] whether mixed agreements or not,[144] were *ipso facto* part of the law of the Union and hence could be interpreted by the ECJ. This also applies to decisions of a binding character taken by a body established by an agreement concluded by the Union. By thus assuming jurisdiction over the interpretation and the question of the validity of these agreements and the decisions taken by their organs, the ECJ aims to guarantee the uniform interpretation and application of this part of Union law throughout the Union and in relation to the treaty partners of the Union.[145]

Institutions operating in the field of external relations, such as the Council and the Commission, have never had the slightest inclination to deny that customary international law was binding on first the Community and later the Union. This was only natural, as all the Member States were bound by it.[146] The Court was also of this view and simply accepted customary international law as part of Union law on the same basis as it had accepted international agreements as such.[147]

It is implicit in Article 218(11) TFEU that international agreements concluded by the Union should respect the Union Treaties. Therefore, as in most States, international agreements do

---

141. Case 181/73, *Haegeman v. Belgium*, paras. 3–5.
142. For a detailed study of these terms, see M. Mendez, *The Legal Effects of EU Agreements, Maximalist Treaty Enforcement and Judicial Avoidance Techniques* (OUP, 2013).
143. For specific sectors see Case 87/75, *Bresciani*, (multilateral association agreement); Case C-104/81, *Kupferberg*, (free trade agreement); Case C-459/03, *Commission v. Ireland*, (Law of the Sea, UNCLOS Convention); Case C-344/04, *IATA and ELFAA*, (air transport, Montreal Convention); Case C-182/10, *Solvay and Others*, (environment, Aarhus Convention).
144. Only, when it is crystal clear that a particular part of a mixed agreement is clearly Member State competence or non-utilized shared competence, will the Court leave the answer to a preliminary question about the interpretation or the validity of an international agreement to the national courts, see Case C-431/05, *Merck v. Merck Genericos*, paras. 46–48.
145. Case C-192/89, *Sevince v. Staatssecretaris van Justitie*, paras. 8–11.
146. The institutions could have a different view of what *was* customary international from the position of (some of) the Member States. In the 'sixties and 'seventies, for instance, the Commission in its role of competition authority and inspired by the terminology of the present Art. 101(1) was inclined to defend the "effects" approach to jurisdiction, while some Member States, notably France, the Netherlands and later the UK, strenuously argued otherwise and adhered to the territorial principle. See the Dyestuffs cases (*inter alia* Case 48/69, *ICI v. Commission*) and the Woodpulp cases (Joined Cases 89,104,114,116,117 and 125–129/85, *Ahlstrom et al. v. Commission*).
147. The classic case is Case C-286/90, *Anklagemyndigheden v. Poulsen and Diva Navigation*, paras. 9–11. The Court relied heavily on a number of ICJ judgments on the law of the sea for its view that specific provisions from the 1958 Geneva Convention on the Law of the Sea and of the draft UNCLOS represented customary international law.

not trump the constitution. The ECJ has strongly upheld this principle, with a specific concern for the integrity of its own composition and its own role as upholder of the law of the Union in the application and interpretation of the Treaties, in particular during the preliminary question procedure.[148]

Where the relation between international law and Union law is concerned, Article 216(2) TFEU declares that Union concluded agreements are binding on the Union's institutions and on the Member States. The Union courts have concluded from this that they should give precedence to agreements concluded by the Union over secondary Union law and, mostly through answers to preliminary questions from national courts, also over national law.[149] Moreover, this provision of Article 216(2), according to the ECJ, that Member States have a duty to respect such agreements as an obligation on their part to the Union, which will be held responsible by its treaty partners for such breaches on the part of the Member States.[150] Hence the Commission can bring infringement proceedings under Article 258 ff TFEU against Member States breaching agreements concluded by the Union. The Commission has used its power to bring such infringement proceedings sparingly, not only to induce Member States to respect their obligations under Union agreements, but also to act in conformity with Union law when allegedly applying an agreement concluded by the Union.[151]

It is implicit in the preceding discussion that the normal remedies available to the Court both under the direct actions and under the preliminary question procedures can in principle be used in bringing a case based on an agreement that is considered part of Union law but of higher rank than normal secondary Union law. This way is also open to individuals and companies under the general rules of Article 263 and 267 TFEU. The so-called privileged parties before the Court (i.e. institutions and Member States) have a special procedure available to them to have the Court test the constitutionality of an international agreement that is about to be concluded in the light of the TFEU (Art. 218(11) TFEU). That procedure has been specifically devised to avoid causing embarrassment to the political institutions of the Union involved in negotiating and in managing treaties once they have been concluded. It spares these institutions having to face up to claims linked to the Union's responsibility because of a Union agreement being found incompatible with the TFEU during the life of the agreement by deciding that question before the agreement is concluded by the Council on a proposal of the Commission and after consent of Parliament. Because the Court has accepted that the question of competence of the Union to conclude the agreement may be one of the constitutional issues to be considered in the framework of this procedure, it has become the favorite procedure for deciding on the division of competence between the Union and the Member States in the field of EU external relations. By now hardly a year goes by without at least one such request for an Opinion being filed with the ECJ by one of the Institutions (mostly the Commission) or by one or more Member States.

---

148. Opinion 1/91 *EEA Agreement*, Opinion 1/2009 *European Patent Court*, and Opinion 2/13 *Accession to the ECHR*. It must be noted that recently the ECJ has gone quite far in erecting the preliminary question procedure into a barrier for the jurisdiction of courts and arbitral tribunals instituted by international agreements, see Case C-284/16, *Slovak Republic v. Achmea*, paras. 52-56. That can be explained probably by the fact that the Bilateral Investment Agreement (BIT) in question had become an agreement between Member States after Slovakia's accession to the EU. It remains to be seen how this doctrine will be applied to EU or mixed agreements with third States, which on purpose set aside the doctrine of the exhaustion of local remedies in whole or in part, as most BITs do, see para 57 of Case C-284/16.
149. See M. Mendez, op. cit. *supra* note 142, Ch. II.
150. See Case 104/81, *Kupferberg*, paras. 11–13.
151. Case C-51/94, *Commission v. Germany (Dairy Agreement)* and Case C-459/03, *Commission v. Ireland (MOX-plant)*.

Before turning to the question of how the ECJ deals with such cases involving arguments of international law as may be brought before it and on the basis of which principles it does so, it is important to recall that a lot of work aimed at respecting the Union's obligations under international law is going on within the Union's political institutions. All the Commission's own decisions directly based on the Treaty, in particular in the field of competition law and State aids, are vetted by its Legal Service for conformity with Union law itself, but also with international law. The same is true for the Commission's regulations or decisions under delegated and implementing powers, primarily in the field of trade law, where conformity with WTO law is of particular importance, given the effective dispute settlement system of the WTO. In the case of legislative proposals with international repercussions, matters of international law, questions of conformity with international agreements or with customary international law may be successively vetted by the Legal Services of the Commission, of the Council of Ministers and of the Parliament. Their legal memoranda may be subject of discussion in the deliberations of all three institutions and ideally this should ensure that outright breaches of rules of international law will be few and far between.

8.2 *Harmonious interpretation and direct effect*

Harmonious interpretation, that is to say interpretation of the national laws or regulations in the light of international legal rules, is often the favoured treatment that national courts give to international agreements or international customary law. That stands to reason, since in that way the courts avoid placing the State in a position of international responsibility for breach of a treaty or a customary norm of international law, while at the same time leaving the national law or regulation intact. In doing so, moreover, the courts respect the separation of powers, as it spares the executive the annoyance of having to deal with a complaint of treaty infringement and the parliament the effort of modifying a national law. The courts of the Union are no exception to this general rule. For the purposes of harmonious interpretation the ECJ uses the elements of treaty interpretation derived from the Vienna Convention: text, context, object and purpose and, if this does not yield a reasonable result, the *travaux préparatoires*.[152]

On the basis of harmonious interpretation the ECJ has accepted, for instance, that Union law on the coordination of social security applies on the continental shelf of the Member States to the advantage of off-shore workers, as the continental shelf automatically accrues to the Member States according to the law of the sea. This approach to the problem was based initially on international customary law, inspired by the language of the Geneva Convention on the Law of the Sea and the Judgment of the ICJ in the *North Sea Continental Shelf cases*,[153] and later, once UNCLOS had entered into force for the (then) EC, on the text of Article 76 of UNCLOS.[154]

Similarly, the ECJ has accepted the so-called *clausula rebus sic stantibus* as a rule of customary international law that the EC could invoke to justify the suspension, and later the termination, of its trade and cooperation agreement with the former Yugoslavia immediately after the outbreak of the civil war and without following the rules on suspension and termination laid down in the agreement in question.[155] In the case of the application of rules of customary international law and given the complexity of those rules and the imprecision of the concepts used, the Court jus-

152. See Vienna Convention on the Law of Treaties, Arts. 31 and 32.
153. See Case C-37/00, *Weber v. Universal Ogden Services*, paras. 33–36. For the *North Sea Continental Shelf cases* see ICJ Reports 1969, at 3.
154. Case C-347/10, *Salemink v. Raad van Bestuur van het UWV*, paras. 31–36. The Court also refers again to the *North Sea Continental Shelf cases*.
155. Case C-162/96, *Racke v. Hauptzollamt Mainz*, paras. 45–46.

tified limiting its judicial review to the question whether, by adopting the suspending regulation, the Council made manifest errors of assessment concerning the conditions for applying those rules.[156] The Court reconfirmed this limited approach to judicial review, based on the habitual vagueness of customary international law, in 2011, but with the necessary nuance. There can be customary rules or principles of international law that are crystal-clear, such as the sovereignty of States over their airspace, and that need to be applied by the Court without reserve.[157]

This kind of reduced judicial review is not applied by the Court in the case of international agreements concluded by the Union and to the question whether individuals can invoke provisions of such agreements so that conflicting provisions of Union law or national law should not be applied by the Court (commonly called the question of direct effect). The ECJ has limited direct effect of international agreements in a different way, by developing a two-stage approach. The first stage requires an analysis of the international agreement as a whole in order to determine whether text, context and object and purpose of the agreement in question allow it to be accorded direct effect at all. Once that hurdle has been overcome, the second stage kicks in, requiring analysis of specific provisions on the basis of criteria that are well-known from many national jurisdictions: does the provision in question contain a clear and precise obligation which is not subject, in its implementation or effects, to the adoption of any subsequent measure?[158]

The GATT was the first agreement that was subjected to this first stage analysis and failed to pass it, as the Court considered that mutual bargaining was so pervasive in the application of the GATT that none of its provisions could be considered clear and unconditional, even if, like Article XI on the prohibition of quantitative restrictions, they were unconditional on their face.[159] The ECJ continued with this approach after the GATT became the WTO, an instrument that was much more like a classic treaty than the GATT had ever been, but now based its analysis of lack of direct effect more on the balance between the institutions and hence showed deference to the Commission as the negotiator and the Council as the legislator (now the Parliament ought to be included in that deference). There was also a hefty dose of reciprocity, as the courts of other major trading powers, such as the US, Japan and China, did not accord direct effect to the WTO provisions at all.[160]

Initially this GATT/WTO case law simply co-existed with cases in which the ECJ granted direct effect to provisions of international agreements or to decisions of treaty bodies, provided that they were written in unconditional language and were clearly intended to benefit individuals or economic operators. Such provisions occurred fairly frequently in free trade and association agreements or decisions of their treaty bodies.[161] The present two-stage approach was only fully developed by the ECJ in the early 2000s, when it felt that the WTO was not the sole case of an agreement that was inherently incapable of having direct effect, but that there was a larger cat-

156. Ibid., paras. 51–52.
157. Case C-366/10, *Air Transport Association of America et al. v. Secretary of State for Energy and Climate Change*, paras. 107–111. The contested extraterritorial effect of the EU's Energy Trading System (ETS) for aviation survived the reduced standard for judicial review.
158. An example is Case C-262/96, *Sema Sürül*, para 60.
159. See Joined Cases 21-24/72, *International Fruit*, paras. 20–27. Another motive for the Court may have been fear of contamination; important provisions of GATT (Arts. III:2, XI:1, XVII:1, XX and XXI) served as inspiration (even textually) for crucial articles of the EEC Treaty (now resp. Arts. 110, 34, 106, 36 and 346 TFEU).
160. Case C-377/02, *Van Parijs v. BIRB*, para 54.
161. Of particular importance are non-discrimination provisions benefiting workers from Turkey, e.g. Case C-192/89, *Sevince*; Case C-237/91, *Kus* and from the Maghreb countries, e.g., Case C-18/90, *Kziber*; Case C-58/93, *Yousfi*. Later similar declarations of direct effect emerged from the pre-accession agreements with the East-European countries: Case C-238/00, *Deutscher Handballbund eV. v. Marcos Kolpak*.

egory of such agreements, if one analysed their structure, object and purpose carefully. On this basis, the Court decided that the UN Convention on the Law of the Seas (UNCLOS) should be deemed to fall in this category.[162]

This case law on GATT/WTO and recently on other law-making conventions can be characterized as a judicial avoidance technique allowing the ECJ to shy away from the ultimate consequences of its self-created monism.[163] On the other hand, the ECJ case law continues to take monism seriously insofar as it rigorously applies harmonious interpretation to conventions to which it *ipso facto* denies direct effect, such as WTO and UNCLOS. In some preliminary question cases on TRIPs, for example, the instructions to the national judges went so far that the difference with direct effect seemed to disappear.[164] Similarly, the ECJ, while rejecting the direct effect of Article 9(3) of the Aarhus Convention on access to the courts in environmental cases because of lack of sufficient clarity, has mobilized Article 47 of the Charter on the right to an effective remedy and a fair hearing in conjunction with national procedural law to arrive an interpretation of Article 9(3) that seeks to be in harmony with the objective of that provision.[165]

8.3 *Agreements of the Member States*

What happens to the international agreements of the Member States, which touch upon the areas covered by the Union Treaties, once they have become Members of the Union? The situation is simple, when the agreements are between the Member States. The Union Treaty is later in time and, according to the rules of the law of treaties, prevails over earlier treaties covering the same subject matter. This was probably considered so obvious that it was not even mentioned in the Treaty of Rome. That Treaty, however, did include a provision on the international agreements of the Member States with third States (now Art. 351 TFEU).[166] This provision initially restates the well-known rule that third parties will neither derive benefits from nor assume obligations under the TFEU (para 1). It then continues to struggle mightily with the question what to do if the agreements with third States included obligations on the Member States, which are incompatible with the TFEU (para 2). In the final analysis it appears that also on this point the TFEU is not a "normal" treaty for the founding States: the incompatibilities must be eliminated in favour of the Union. If necessary, the Member States shall assist each other and shall develop a common attitude. And if reinterpretation or renegotiation with the third State in question turns out not to be possible, the "elimination of incompatibilities" may lead to termination of the agreement with the third States. Whether the third State is objectively in a difficult situation or is merely making difficulties, the obligation to eliminate incompatible provisions remains,[167] and so does the requirement to ultimately terminate the agreement in question, if the third State remains uncooperative.[168]

The Court has always interpreted Article 351 rather literally. Hence it can only be applied to situations, where there are incompatible provisions in an agreement with a third State concluded before accession of the Member State concerned. It has never considered the situation

162. Case C-308/06, *Intertanko et al. v. Secretary of State for Transport*, paras. 54–64.
163. See M. Mendez, op. cit. *supra* note 142, passim.
164. Case C-89/99, *Schieving-Nijstad v. Groeneveld.*
165. Cases C-240/09, *Lesoochranarske zoskupenie VLK I* and C-243/15, *Lesoochranarske zoskupenie VLK II.*
166. For a full treatment of the problems inherent in Art. 351 there is the excellent monograph by J. Klabbers, *Treaty Conflict and the European Union* (CUP, 2009). For a good overview on the basis of documents, see P.J. Kuijper, J. Wouters et al., *The Law of EU External Relations,* Cases, *Materials, and Commentary on the EU as an International Actor,* 2nd ed. (OUP, 2015), Ch. 13.
167. Case C-170/98, *Commission v. Belgium (Discriminatory cargo-sharing clause)*, paras. 41–43.
168. Case C-205/06, *Commission v. Austria (Investment Agreements)*, para 25 et seq.

in which new internal legislation of the Union creates new exclusive external powers of the EU under Article 3(2) TFEU and the *ERTA* doctrine. Nevertheless such instances are now legion and create difficult situations for the Union and the Member States, when the latter are all or in large majority parties to international conventions in these fields. This is the case for instance with the UN and many of its specialized agencies, and with many agreements in the field of maritime transport matters and aviation. Such agreements often date from before the creation of the EU and contain as yet no clauses to make accession possible for entities such as the EU. This is sometimes called the problem of "treaty arrears" of the Union. It cannot be solved by succession of the Union to the rights and obligations of the Member States, since the Court has always rejected this after having accepted it in the single case of GATT.[169] Such situations can be summed up as follows: important multilateral conventions, often of a legislative character, to which the Union as yet cannot become a party, while it does have often extensive legislation in the field covered and the Member States are all parties. What is the ECJ to do, when in such a situation there are allegations that the EU legislation is not in conformity with such multilateral convention?

The answer from the Court in such situations has been pretty broad-minded, if one considers that the Union is not and cannot (at least within the near future) become a party. However, given that the Union legislation in question often strives to implement the convention in question at the Union level, the ECJ decided that the customary principle of good faith in international law, which is reflected in Article 4(3) TEU, compelled it to interpret the provisions of Union law falling in the domain of such an international convention, while taking account of the latter.[170] This is not the same as a fully-fledged harmonious interpretation and there is certainly no room for any direct effect, but the chances that Union law will be interpreted in a way which is directly opposed to the thrust of the provisions of the relevant law-making convention is hereby strongly curtailed. However, the full meaning of the words "taking account of" in this context will be revealed only in later case law.

9. Conclusion. Great expectations inspired and frustrated by the two Treaties

The Lisbon Treaties inspired great expectations for what was called the external action of the European Union: a well-construed and well-co-ordinated foreign policy of the Union that was to include both low (TFEU) and high (TEU – CFSP) foreign policy and would be executed by a single diplomatic service, the EEAS, composed of professionals from the Council Secretariat, the Commission and Member States, manning true EU delegations (not mere Commission missions). Driven by a treaty-supported wish for consistency and coherence, the EEAS would project a stronger and more unified voice on the international scene.

However, these high expectations could not but be frustrated by the self-imposed division between high and low foreign policy as between the two Treaties: the TEU and the TFEU, each with their own rules and style of decision-making – that had to be kept strictly separate for fear of infection of the supra-national style of decision-making of the TFEU by the intergovernmental style of taking decisions of the TEU and vice-versa. All the while under the surface the trends of specialization and especially of democratization continued, being fed not merely by treaty language but by the evolution of foreign policy everywhere in the world.

---

169. Case C-308/06, *Intertanko et al. v. Secretary of State for Transport,* para 48 is a clear example of such rejection.
170. Ibid., para 52. This concerned the status of the International Convention for the Prevention of Pollution from Ships (MarPol Convention), to which all Member States were parties, but not the EU.

Mixed agreements are a continuing reality, contrary to expectations. The difficulties that flow from this so-called "mixity" both at the internal and the external level continue to be a severe handicap for the external representation and the single voice for the Union.

On the other hand Union loyalty and sincere cooperation between Union Institutions themselves are fast gaining in importance. The Court has strengthened these principles in the field of external relations of the Union and has fashioned them into a weapon for coherence.

As far as the place of international law in foreign relations is concerned, it is important to realize that the EU is not merely subjected to rules of international law and a passive consumer of these rules. The Union participates actively in the process of forming international law, simply by applying international law in its own way, by participating in its codification in the UN and through pleading international law not only before its own Court, but also before the WTO dispute settlement bodies, the ITLOS and by intervening before investment tribunals. As to the place of international law in the legal order of the Union, one can characterize it as mitigated monism – a mitigation that the ECJ has brought about by limiting the direct effect of international agreements. It has to be said that the ECJ is not exactly the only Supreme Court in the world that feels the need to do so.[171]

Further reading

De Baere, G., *Constitutional Principles of EU External Relations* (OUP, 2008).

Cannizzaro, E., P. Palchetti and R.A. Wessel (Eds.), *International Law as Law of the European Union* (Brill/Nijhoff, 2012).

Cardwell, P.J., (Ed.), *EU External Relations Law in the Post-Lisbon Era* (T.M.C. Asser Press & Springer, 2012).

Cremona, M. and A. Thies, *The European Court of Justice and External Relations Law* (Hart, 2015).

Czuczai, J. and F. Naert (Eds.), *The EU as Global Actor: Bridging Legal Theory and Practice*, (Brill/Nijhoff, 2017).

Eeckhout, P., *EU External Relations Law*, 2nd ed. (OUP, 2011).

Eeckhout, P. and M. Lopez-Escudero (Eds.), *The European Union's External Action in Times of Crisis* (Hart, 2016).

Evans, M. and P. Koutrakos, *The International Responsibility of the European Union, European and International Perspectives* (Hart, 2013).

Koutrakos, P., *EU International Relations Law* (Hart, 2006).

Kuijper, P.J., J. Wouters, F. Hoffmeister, G. De Baere, and T. Ramopoulos, *The Law of EU External Relations, Cases, Materials, and Commentary on the EU as an International Actor*, 2nd ed. (OUP, 2015).

Lock, T. *The European Court of Justice and International Courts* (OUP, 2015).

Wessel, R.A. and S. Blockmans (Eds.), *Between Autonomy and Independence: The EU Legal Order under the Influence of International Organisations* (T.M.C. Asser Press & Springer, 2012).

171. For the US, see D.L. Sloss, *The Death of Treaty Supremacy. An Invisible Constitutional Change* (OUP, 2016).

CHAPTER 40
THE COMMON FOREIGN AND SECURITY POLICY AND THE COMMON SECURITY AND DEFENCE POLICY

*Pieter Jan Kuijper**

1. Background and introduction

The beginnings of the CFSP in the form of the European Political Cooperation (EPC) and its formalization into the second pillar of the three-pillar structure created at the Maastricht IGC and its substantial amendment in the Treaty of Amsterdam have already been sketched in the preceding chapter. The most important improvements for the CFSP at Amsterdam were the introduction of an embryonic CSDP by inclusion of the so-called Petersberg tasks[1] into the Treaty and the bestowal of executive tasks, including a right of proposal, on the Council Secretariat under its Secretary-General, who was also to be High Representative for the CFSP. The appointment of the experienced former Spanish Minister of Foreign Affairs and former Secretary-General of NATO, Javier Solana, to this new position contributed to the dynamic development of the CFSP in the years that followed and in particular to the integration of the political and military aspects of security and foreign policy. It was during the stewardship of Solana that the important document on the European Security Strategy (ESS) was adopted by the European Council in December 2003.[2] It was an exercise that was undertaken in the period when the EU had been plunged into political disarray by the second Iraq war. Its function was to restore a minimum of unity, mainly around common objectives. This is again the case with the European Council's new CFSP Global Strategy, which was agreed in the summer of 2016. The title "Shared Vision, Common Action: A Stronger Europe" again expresses a wish rather than a reality. Compared to the first Security Strategy the emphasis is much more on hard power: the CSDP and the realization of agreed objectives in defence spending. Massive migration flows and the renewed Russian military pressure on the EU are also new challenges that come on top of the threats to the security of the EU that were mentioned in earlier Security Strategies, such as terrorism, organized crime and non-proliferation.[3]

* Law Faculty, University of Amsterdam.

1. The Petersberg tasks (so named for having been agreed at Petersberg, near Bonn in Germany) were included in a ministerial declaration of the Western European Union (WEU) and mentioned the tasks for which the WEU Member States were willing to deploy military units, namely (1) humanitarian and rescue tasks, (2) conflict prevention and peace-keeping tasks, and (3) tasks of combat forces in crisis management, including peace-making. They were included in Art. 17 TEU of the Treaty of Amsterdam.
2. "A secure Europe in a better world", European Security Strategy, Brussels 12 Dec. 2003. This document was updated in 2008.
3. "Shared vision, common action: A stronger Europe. A global strategy for the European Union's foreign and security policy", available at <europa.eu/global strategy/en>.

As the Treaty of Nice barely touched the CFSP, it was up to the Constitutional Treaty and the subsequent Treaty of Lisbon to modernize the CFSP and CSDP. Only thus could one arrive at a more integrated approach between the high foreign and security policy of the Union and the low external relations of the Community, so as to form a coherent and consistent external action of the European Union. As explained in the preceding chapter, in an attempt to bring about such an integrated external action and reduce the institutional rivalry between Commission and Council Secretariat, the High Representative (HR) was given a status between the two institutions, but linked to both: appointed by the Council and vice-president (VP) of the Commission. Hence the abbreviation HR/VP. The European External Action Service (EEAS) was similarly not linked to either of the two institutions and the HR/VP and the EEAS were put in an office building, that was neither a Commission nor a Council building.[4] In addition the CFSP provisions of the TEU were modified and the CSDP provisions expanded with three other military tasks beyond those agreed at Petersberg.[5] Furthermore the CFSP provisions have become more elaborate, as some of them now codify pre-existing secondary law in the field of CFSP, such as the provision on the European Defence Agency (EDA), another example of the surfeit of constitutional rules in EU external action.

This chapter first of all will go into greater detail about the institutions, bodies or services that are specific to the CFSP and CSDP and the role they play within this realm. In addition, the most important agencies and connected services will be discussed. Although there are no longer specific names for specific types of CFSP acts, as in the past, this chapter distinguishes between decisions of different types and analyses the most important examples. Important operational decisions, whether of a primarily civilian nature or of a military character will need some closer scrutiny, as they have often created important (legal) problems, such as the "frozen conflict" in Kosovo, and the fair adjudication of alleged pirates. At the same time it is vital to study non-binding documents. One way they have been used is to build a near complete legal policy in certain areas of international law that fall within the ambit of the CFSP/CSDP, such as international humanitarian law.

2. Bodies, Institutions and Agencies

The CFSP and CSDP are "conducted" by the HR/VP "as mandated by the Council", but developed by the proposals of the HR/VP herself. In addition the HR/VP serves as president of the Foreign Affairs Council, "without prejudice to the normal tasks of the General Secretariat of the Council" and she is Vice-President of the Commission and as such she fulfils within the Commission the responsibilities incumbent on it in external relations and coordinates other aspects of the EU's external action "without prejudice to the normal tasks of the services of the Commission".[6] It is the EEAS that supports the HR/VP in all these tasks and that also assists the President of the European Council, the President of the Commission and the Commission (i.e. the other Commissioners and their DGs) in the exercise of their respective functions in the area

4. However, the present HR/VP, Mrs. Mogherini, has been giving full weight to her VP-side, by establishing her office on the upper floor of the Berlaymont, next to other Commissioners. She is said to be putting also a lot of effort in her task of coordinating external action inside the Commission, in the so-called External Relations group of Commissioners, and with the CFSP/CSDP. See S. Blockmans and S. Russack, *The Commissioner's Group on External Action – Key political facilitator* (CEPS, 2015).
5. These three new tasks are included in Art. 43(1) TEU, next to the original Petersberg tasks mentioned in *supra* note 1, and are: (4) joint disarmament operations, (5) military advice and assistance tasks, and (6) post-conflict stabilization tasks.
6. See Art. 2 of Council Decision establishing the organization and functioning of the European External Action Service (2010/427/EU), O.J. 2010, L 201/30, Art. 2(1) (hereinafter the "EEAS Decision").

of external relations.[7] The EEAS is described in its foundational instrument as "a functionally autonomous body" of the EU, separate from the General Secretariat of the Council and from the Commission. It is said to have the legal capacity necessary to perform its tasks and attain its objectives.[8] There thus can be little doubt that under the new formulation of the action for annulment (Art. 263 TFEU), the EEAS has the capacity to sue and be sued, as long as that takes place within the performance of its tasks and the attainment of its objectives.

All the tasks of conception and execution of the CFSP and CSDP, which in the years between the Amsterdam and Lisbon treaties were exercised by the General Secretariat of the Council were transferred to the EEAS. However, the EEAS has no decision-making powers of its own or any powers transferred from the major EU institutions. Van Vooren has accordingly characterized the EEAS "as functionally akin to a Commission Directorate-General, without the legal advantage of being part of an institution with decision-making powers proper, accountable to Parliament, while being placed under the HR's authority with a broad mandate of support within the chalk lines set by the Council and the European Council".[9]

The relation of the HR/VP and the EEAS with the Commission is of a most complicated nature. Such typically external Commission DGs or services, as Development and Cooperation,[10] Humanitarian Aid and Civil Protection, Neighbourhood Policy and Enlargement, and Trade, are not integrated into the EEAS. Their policies were always within the Community ambit and now in TFEU. They thus remain within the Commission, but it is self-evident that the coordination powers of the HR/VP are of great importance with respect to these departments. In addition there is a service of the Commission, the Service for Foreign Policy Instruments (FPI), which is so closely bound up with the work of the EEAS and its delegations that it is located in the same building and operates *de facto* as a direction of the EEAS under the direct authority of the HR/VP, presumably in her quality of member of the Commission. The FPI is said to be primarily an operational service. It is responsible for a number of financial instruments that are closely linked to similar instruments in the field of development, namely the so-called Stability and Partnership Instruments.[11] It also organizes election observation missions.[12] It is in charge of the execution of the CFSP sanctions policy, which in the end rests on implementation under the TFEU[13] and also carries out the Kimberley Process certification scheme that distinguishes "clean" rough diamonds from so-called "blood or conflict diamonds".[14] It also takes on the op-

7. Ibid., Art. 2(2).
8. Ibid., Art. 1(2). This capacity should not be confused with legal personality, which the EEAS clearly has not.
9. B. van Vooren, "A legal-institutional perspective on the European External Action Service", 48 CML Rev. (2011), 475–502, at 500–501. The ECJ was equally of the opinion that the EEAS had to work within the chalk lines set by the Council, when it made the Council responsible, rather than the EEAS, for fully keeping the European Parliament informed of the progress of negotiations in the field of the CFSP under Art. 218(10) TFEU, see Case C-263/14, *European Parliament v. Council (Agreement with Tanzania)*, paras. 73–74.
10. The EEAS shares the work on the planning cycles of development aid with DG DEVCO. This is in many ways a natural consequence of the decentralization of the execution of development aid to the delegations of the EU, which are now part of the EEAS instead of the Commission.
11. See Reg. (EU) 230/2014 Establishing an Instrument contributing to Stability and Peace, O.J. 2014, L 77/1 and Reg. (EU) 234/2014 Establishing an Instrument for Cooperation with Third Countries, O.J. 2014, L 77/77, which replaced Reg. (EC) 1934/2006 Establishing an Instrument for Cooperation with Industrialized and other High Income Countries and Territories, O.J. 2006, L 405/41. See Ch. 41, "Union external relations under the TFEU", section 3.1.2 of this book.
12. Based on Reg. (EU) 235/2014, Establishing a Financing Instrument for Democracy and Human Rights Worldwide (EIDHR), O.J. 2014, L 77/85.
13. See Ch. 41, "Union external relations under the TFEU", section 5.1 of this book.
14. See Reg. (EC) No 2368/2002 Implementing the Kimberley Process Certification Scheme for the International Trade in Rough Diamonds, O.J. 2002, L 358/28.

erational side of the CFSP insofar as that is paid for by the Commission's budget. Finally it manages the export restrictions on goods that could be used for capital punishment and torture.[15]

Apart from the FPI and the separate Security Policy and Military structures of the CSDP, the EEAS is organized broadly as any Ministry of Foreign Affairs, with a central Political Affairs Department, five Regional DGs, a Global and Multilateral DG and a Budget and Administrative DG.[16] This Foreign Policy core of the EEAS conceives and proposes the CFSP as such, although it does not have a monopoly of proposal, as the Commission traditionally has had under the TFEU; Member States also often take initiatives. It carries out the bulk of the CFSP orientations and decisions with the help of the (at present) 139 offices and delegations of the EU.[17] Also in these respects the EEAS resembles a Ministry of Foreign Affairs, only there is the constant need for coordination with the Commission services during the conception of external policies of the TFEU or CFSP policies close to them and with the Commission and the Member States during implementation and execution on the ground through the EU delegations.

The delegations are opened or closed by the HR/VP in agreement with the Council and the Commission.[18] They do have the usual privileges and immunities that embassies have pursuant to bilateral agreements between the EU and the host State.[19] The General Court does not regard the EU delegations as having an independent legal personality or as a body, agency or office of the Union within the meaning of Article 263(5) and hence actions brought against a delegation are inadmissible.[20]

Just like the central administration of the EAAS, the delegations are all originally of a tripartite composition: people who have come from the General Secretariat of the Council, especially the directorates-general involved in the CFSP and CSDP; people from the Commission, especially the old DG Relex; and staff originating from the diplomatic service of the Member States.[21] The EEAS may not be an EU institution according to the Treaties, but it is an institution for the purpose of the EU Staff Regulations, which apply to all EEAS staff members, and as a

---

15. See Reg. 1236/2005 Concerning Trade in Certain Goods Which Could be Used for Capital Punishment, Torture or Other Cruel, Inhuman or Degrading Treatment or Punishment, O.J. 2005, L 200/1.
16. The regional divisions are: Asia and the Pacific; Africa; North Africa and the Middle East, Europe and Central Asia, and the Americas. The Global and Multilateral Division is in charge of the policy within international organizations, in particular the UN system, on global issues, such as counter-terrorism, development, as well as on human rights and democracy. See also Art. 4 of the EEAS Decision, which lays down the organization of the central administration of the EEAS in great detail – a consequence of the fact that what normally is decided internally by the Commission and the Council Secretary-General, here had to be laid down in a Council Decision.
17. Some of these delegations cover more than one country so that altogether nearly 170 countries have diplomatic relations with the EU. The 4 EU offices are in Hong-Kong, Taiwan, Kosovo and the West Bank/Gaza.
18. Art. 5(1) of the EEAS Decision, cited *supra* note 6.
19. The Union included the desire to obtain the usual privileges and immunities that States grant each other for its delegations in the notes that it sent to the Host States, in which it announced the replacement of the Commission delegations by EU delegations. See also Art. 5(6) of the EEAS Decision.
20. See Case T-395/11, *Elti v. Delegation of the European Union to Montenegro*, paras. 33–46. Only insofar as persons within the delegation have delegated authority to execute the part of the Commission budget that is specifically reserved for the EEAS or for local projects, for instance in the framework of Commission tendering procedures, the Commission must be considered responsible for the execution of such tendering procedures and any proceedings should hence be instituted against the Commission, ibid., paras. 66–71.
21. See recital 11 EEAS Decision, cited *supra* note 6. Later, after full capacity is reached, the composition will be at least 30% personnel seconded from the diplomatic services of the Member States and the rest permanent officials of the Union, see Art. 6(9) of the EEAS Decision.

consequence also the Protocol on Privileges and Immunities.[22] EEAS personnel shall conduct themselves solely with the interest of the Union in mind, they are independent and shall not seek or receive any instructions from anybody except the HR/VP, which guarantees that the EEAS remains entirely separate from both the Commission and the Council.[23] In the same way the Financial Regulation applies to the EEAS and will be amended accordingly to have a separate section for the EEAS.[24] There seems to be an informal understanding with the Commission and Parliament that they will exercise their budgetary responsibilities and powers in relation to the EEAS in a restrained manner so as to guarantee a steady functioning of the EEAS.

The delegations, which are part of the EEAS and under the authority of the HR, also carry out TFEU foreign relations, notably in trade, development policy, accession, and the external aspects of TFEU policies, such as transport, agriculture, environment, competition etc. Commission civil servants, who are part of the delegation, often carry out these aspects of external action. It is obviously of great importance that the head of delegation and his counterparts at EEAS headquarters in Brussels are continuously abreast of what is going on in a delegation. Hence any instructions from the Commission should reach them at the same time as they reach the Commission civil servants in the delegation; detailed rules were agreed to this effect.[25]

According to the EEAS decision, the organization and functioning of the EEAS had to be reviewed by mid-2013.[26] Much preparation was invested in this review: external reports were commissioned[27] and the EEAS advanced a number of proposals for reforming itself.[28] The EP Committee on Foreign Affairs prepared a report, resulting in Recommendations to the HR/VP, the Council and the Commission.[29] The Council in the end could broadly agree to the short term proposals of the HR/VP, which were largely of an internal organizational nature, but merely took note of the medium term recommendations, which required changes in EU law and attempted to clarify the relation between EU delegations and Member State embassies in the field of mixed external competence.[30] Lady Ashton, with the agreement of the Council, decided that a complete overhaul of the EEAS after barely two years would not be in the interest of the organization. Thus, only the piece-meal reforms were carried out. In parallel with the discussions in the Institutions on the EEAS review, the Court of Auditors also undertook an audit of the establishment of the EEAS, which was critical, but also realistic about the neigh impossible constraints under which the EEAS had to be set up and hit the ground running within

22. Recitals 8, 16 and 17 and Art. 6 of the EEAS Decision. The Conditions of Employment of Other Servants of the EEC apply to temporary agents. The HR fulfils the role of appointing authority.
23. Art. 6(4) of the EEAS Decision.
24. Art. 8 of the EEAS Decision.
25. See recital 13 and Art. 3(3) of the EEAS Decision; on this episode, see T. Blom and S. Vanhoonacker, "The European External Action Service (EEAS), the new kid on the block", Paper prepared for the ECPR Conference, Glasgow, 3–6 Sept. 2014, at 10 et seq.
26. Recital 19 and Art. 13(3) of the EEAS Decision.
27. For example: S. Blockmans et al., *EEAS 2.0, Draft Recommendations for the 2013 EEAS Review*, CEPS, Brussels.
28. *EEAS Review*, July 2013, see <collections.internetmemory.org/haeu/20160313172652/http://eeas.europa.eu/library/publications/2013/3/2013_eeas_review_en.pdf>.
29. See Recommendation [...] on the 2013 review of the organization and functioning of the EEAS, Committee on Foreign Affairs, Co-rapporteurs E. Brok and R. Gualtieri, text adopted on 13 June 2013, doc. P7_TA(2013) 0278.
30. Council Conclusions on the EEAS Review, General Affairs Council of 17 Dec. 2013, <www.consilium.europa.eu/uedocs/cms_data/docs/pressdata/EN/genaff/140141.pdf>.

the two years before the review.[31] Mrs. Mogherini, the new HR/VP, was under pressure from the Parliament in her confirmation hearings to finalize the implementation of the short-term reforms review by the end of 2015, but again the result has been discrete steps and no further grand scale reform.[32]

A special trait of the CFSP and the EEAS is the presence of so-called European Special Representatives (EUSRs) for specific problems (Human Rights) or regions (e.g. Afghanistan, Kosovo, Bosnia and Herzegovina, South Caucasus etc.), next to the normal regional or country desks in the EEAS and often also covering problems that are subject to a EU civil or military mission. The EUSRs are appointed by Council Decision (in the past by a Joint Action)[33] and are what in classic diplomacy are called "roving ambassadors". The present HR/VP has brought them within the organization chart of the EEAS, directly reporting to her. There is no doubt that the individual EUSRs will continue appearing before the Foreign Affairs Council to report on their work, but a strong link with EEAS and the missions that EEAS directs is thus established and this may improve coordination.[34]

The EEAS is surrounded by agencies, especially in the field of the CSDP: the EU Institute for Security Studies (EUISS),[35] a research institute in the field of defence and security, and the EU Satellite Centre (SatCen),[36] both created in July of 2001; the European Security and Defence College (ESDC), which in reality is a network among institutes, colleges, (military) academies, universities and institutions in the EU, which together will provide training on European Security and Defence Policy.[37] The former HR/SG and the Secretariat of the Council had certain functions that they needed to exercise according to these various Joint Actions and these were to be taken over by the HR/VP and the EEAS.[38]

The most important of these agencies, however, is the European Defence Agency (EDA), originally created in 2004 by secondary legislation only, but after Lisbon given treaty rank (Arts. 42(3) and 45 TEU). Accordingly the EDA was given a new basis in secondary law in July of 2011.[39] The EDA is intended to assist the Council and the Member States in improving the defence capabilities of the EU by research and development of armaments and their acquisition, in particular in relation to crisis management. The Agency will also identify and implement any measure that might be needed to strengthen the industrial and technological base of the

---

31. European Court of Auditors, *The establishment of the European External Action Service*, Special report 11/2014.
32. S. Blockmans et al., "Mogherini's first 100 days: Not the quiet diplomat", (2015) *CEPS Commentary*.
33. E.g. Council Decision 2012/440/CFSP Appointing the European Union Special Representative for Human Rights, O.J. 2012, L 200/21-23. Note that this formal decision appointed Mr. Stavros Lambrinidis, whose mandate, laid down in Art. 3 of the Decision, referred to the EU Strategic Framework and EU Action Plan on Human Rights and Democracy, which was adopted by the Council without any formal act the same day as the nomination of the EUSR and published in a press release. His mandate was prolonged from 1 July 2014 until 30 June 2019. See <eeas.europa.eu/headquarters/special representatives>.
34. This is in conformity with point 4 of the Council conclusions mentioned in note 30 above. Similarly point 6 of those conclusions have been embraced by F. Mogherini and J.-C. Juncker in making her coordinating tasks as VP of the Commission more central to her variegated functions.
35. Council Joint Action 2001/554/CFSP on the Establishment of a European Union Institute for Security Studies, O.J. 2001, L 200/1.
36. Council Joint Action 2001/555/CFSP on the Establishment of a European Union Satellite Center, O.J. 2001, L 200/5.
37. The ESDC had first been created in 2005, but after two years already needed an overhaul, see Council Joint Action 2008/550/CFSP Establishing a European Security and Defence College, O.J. 2008, L 176/20.
38. See recital 7 of the EEAS Decision, cited *supra* note 6.
39. Council Decision 2011/411/CFSP Defining the Statute, Seat and Operational Rules of the European Defence Agency and Repealing Joint Action 2004/551/CFSP, O.J. 2011, L 183/16.

defence industry in the Union. Obviously the Agency's mission in these sensitive areas will be without prejudice to the competences of the Member States in defence matters.[40] The EDA is open to all EU Member States, but not necessarily all participate in it[41] and even the participating Member States need not take part in all so-called *ad hoc* projects; they may opt out of such projects, even if the presumption is that all participating Member States will be in the project. On the other hand participating Member States may opt into an *ad hoc* project that is started by a limited number of participating Member States.[42] The EDA, according to its founding decision, is placed under particularly close political control of the Council, in its composition of Ministers of Defence, while the HR/VP is supposed to provide the "essential link" between the EDA and the Council. The Council should issue guidelines to the Agency. In issuing these guidelines all the preparatory organs of the Council's machinery should be fully involved: in this case, the Coreper, the PSC and the EUMC.[43] The Council also keeps a firm grip on the power of the EDA, which has been granted legal personality, to conclude so-called "administrative arrangements" with third countries, organizations and entities.[44]

It would carry matters too far to discuss the EDA here in further detail[45] but it is important to refer briefly to a potential point of friction between EDA's approach to defence procurement with the TFEU exception for the production and trade in arms and other military materiel and the rather restrictive interpretation that the Court and the Commission have given of this provision (Art. 346 TFEU). EDA developed a Code of Conduct on Defence Procurement for the participating Member States in EDA, which was approved on 21 November 2005. It is a purely voluntary code; no legal commitment is involved or implied. Those of the participating Member States, which subscribed to it, would extend fair and equal treatment to other subscribing Member States and would exercise mutual transparency and accountability through EDA on such matters as selection criteria for companies, specifications of products and award criteria.[46] The EDA Code covers only procurement that is exempted from the normal procurement directives and relates to products with military purposes under Article 346(1)(b) TFEU.[47]

The problem with this Treaty provision is that it is, at least in part, self-judging; accordingly the Commission and the ECJ have taken care to limit any abuse that could be made of it. The special directive on defence-related procurement contains a narrow definition of military equipment, namely equipment specifically designed or adapted for military purposes and intended

---

40. Arts. 1 and 2 of Council Decision 2011/411/CFSP, ibid.
41. By now all Member States participate except Denmark. Switzerland, Norway and Serbia have concluded special arrangements with EDA. See *infra* note 45.
42. Arts. 19 and 20 of Council Decision 2011/411/CFSP, ibid.
43. It is remarkable that this is laid down in detail in recitals 9–14 of Decision 2011/411/CFSP. There must have been a worry that the political and security side of the Council would otherwise escape the general political control of the Coreper.
44. See Art. 24 of Decision 2011/411/CFSP.
45. See N. Karampekios and I. Oikonomou (Eds.), *The European Defence Agency. Arming Europe* (Routledge, 2015).
46. For the Code of Conduct, see <www.eda.europa.eu/docs/documents/CoC.pdf> (last visited 16 June 2015). Because it was desirable that suppliers to the big defence contractors should also benefit from the code, a Code of Best Practice in the Supply Chain was issued in June 2006 to complement the Code of Conduct. See <www.eda.europa.eu/docs/documents/CoBPSC_final> (last visited 16 June 2015). These two Codes can be seen as follow-ups to an earlier Commission initiative for a European Defence Equipment Market (EDEM), COM(2003)113, 11 Mar. 2003, and a Commission Green Paper on Defence Procurement, COM(2004)608, 23 Sept. 2004, which tended to show that the existing legislative framework for defence procurement was not functioning well.
47. See Art. 10 of Dir. (EC) 2004/18 on the coordination of procedures for the award of public works contracts, public supply contracts and public service contracts, O.J. 2004, L 134/114 (Procurement Directive).

for use as arms, munitions or military material.[48] The Court has broadly followed the same line.[49] Only such material, therefore, can be covered by the EDA Code of Conduct on Defence Procurement.

3. CFSP and CSDP policies and actions

3.1 *Introductory remarks*

As mentioned in Chapter 39 CFSP and CSDP actions can be of many kinds. There can be declarations and policy statements from the HR/VP. There can be Council Declarations of various kinds: some are of great policy importance, such as the EU Maritime Security Strategy adopted in June 2014;[50] others carry less weight. As shown in the chapter above, at all monthly Foreign Affairs Council meetings Council conclusions are drawn up on virtually all agenda points and they have become an instrument for carrying on European Foreign Policy from month to month. As we will see in the following, such Council declarations and conclusions often work in tandem with formal legal acts, which however are in the minority during Foreign Affairs Council meetings. In this sense the Foreign Affairs and Defence Councils are unique in the EU, compared to the other Council configurations.

The formal acts of the Council fall into two legal categories: contractual acts, i.e. international agreements for the external aspects of the CFSP and CSDP and autonomous acts, i.e. decisions. We will not dwell further here on the international agreements. Normally the political CFSP aspects of an agreement will be integrated in a broader EU agreement, often mixed; this has already been discussed in the preceding chapter. The different types of CSDP agreements will come to the fore by themselves in the discussion of civilian and military CSDP missions below.

The Decisions that the Council may take in the framework of the CFSP are divided into decisions which lay down an approach of the Union in respect of a matter of a geographical or a thematic nature (Art. 29 TEU, the former "common position") and decisions undertaking operational action (Art. 28 TEU, the former "joint action"). In the framework of the CSDP there is a distinction between decisions setting up civilian missions and decisions setting up military missions (Art. 42(3) TEU). In the following sections (3.2 through 3.5) we will discuss an example of each of the four types of decisions and this will hopefully provide a deeper insight into the functioning of the CFSP and CSDP. However, before doing so a few remarks on the relation between CFSP/CSDP are in order.

Within the CSDP a progressive development towards a common defence policy should be put in motion. So far no formal decisions have been taken on this score. It should be noted that the future common defence policy should not affect the specific character of the security and defence policy of certain Member States (i.e. the so-called neutral Member States) or the obligations certain Members have taken upon themselves in the framework of NATO (Article 42(2) TEU).[51] Moreover, the CSDP should not diminish the right – and the terms of Article 42

---

48. See recital 10 and Art. 1(6) of Directive (EC) 2009/81 on the Coordination of Procedures for the Award of Certain Works Contracts, Supply Contracts and Service Contracts by Contracting Authorities or Entities in the Fields of Defence and Security, O.J. 2009, L 216/76.
49. See e.g. Case C-615/10, *Insinööritoimisto InsTiimi Oy*, para 46, where the Court defined purely military material "by virtue of its intrinsic characteristics [...] as having been specially designed and developed, also as a result of substantial modifications, for such [military] purposes".
50. See Council doc. 11205/14, "European Union Maritime Security Strategy", of 24 June 2014.
51. See on the relationship between the EU and NATO in security matters e.g. H. Ojanen, "The EU and NATO: Two competing models for a common defence policy", 44 JCMS (2006), 57–76 and L. Simon, *Geopolitical Change, Grand Strategy and European Security: The EU-NATO Conundrum* (Palgrave Macmillan, 2013).

TEU even make it an obligation – to exercise their power of individual or collective self-defence in accordance with Article 51 of the UN Charter (Art. 42(7) TEU). Thus Article 42 attempts to reconcile the views of NATO Member States, of neutral Member States, and of Member States that, in their defence policy, rely primarily on the UN Charter. Although paragraph 7 creates the impression that providing assistance in a situation of self-defence of a Member State is a duty, nevertheless the choice of means is in the hands of the Member State providing assistance, as it is in Article 51 Charter (and also Art. 5 NATO). Thus the obligations under both articles can in reality be severely reduced.

Article 42(7) has been invoked only once, when President Hollande relied on it after the terrorist attacks of 13 November 2015 in Paris. The reaction of the Council of Ministers (Defence) of 17 November 2015 was unanimous and positive. The HR/VP pointed out on that occasion, however, that the treaty provision, on its face, does not lead to a CSDP decision; but its invocation triggers bilateral aid and assistance.[52]

The mutual assistance clause of Article 42(7) TEU is the activation of intergovernmental discussions between the "victim state" and other Member States. This is fundamentally different from the solidarity clause of Article 222 TFEU, which can be invoked in case of a terrorist attack, a natural and a man-made disaster. Here the reaction of the Union is in the foreground, especially in case of terrorism, but individual Member States may also provide assistance in the three mentioned cases (Art. 222 (1) and (2)). Pursuant to paragraph 2 of Article 222, the application of this provision is laid down in a Council Decision proposed by the Commission and the HR/VP – which illuminates the hybrid character of the solidarity clause. Indeed, the relevant Council decision states explicitly that the EU should use all available means, including those of the CSDP, in combating a terrorist attack, or a natural or man-made disaster.[53] As in the application of Article 42(7) TEU, the Member States have complete freedom to decide by which means they intend to fulfil their obligation of assistance to the "victim State".[54] It would seem that Member States especially in the case of terrorist attacks, have a choice between Article 42(7) TEU and Article 222 TFEU. This choice is determined largely by a preference for an intergovernmental, bilateral approach or for following a Union method and adopting Union acts.[55]

Finally, before discussing the different types of decisions under CFSP and CSDP, it is important to dwell for a moment on the relative failure of the attempt to set-up an embryonic EU standing army that would permanently stand in wait for any oncoming major external military crisis: the European Battle Groups (EUBGs). After a preparation in the EUMS of two years the EUMC approved a Single Battlegroup Concept Document (SBCD) on 5 October 2006.[56]

With respect to the "neutral" status of some countries, see e.g. J. Beyer and S. Hofmann, "Varieties of neutrality: Norm revision and decline", 46 *Cooperation and Conflict* (2011), 285–311. On the CSDP in general see also C. Bickerton, B. Irondelle and A. Menon, "Security co-operation beyond the Nation-State: The EU's common security and defence policy", 49 JCMS (2011), at 1–21 and P. Koutrakos, *The EU Common Security and Defence Policy* (OUP, 2013).

52. Outcome of the Meeting of the Council of Ministers of Foreign Affairs and Defence, 16 and 17 Nov. 2015, Doc. 14120/15 Presse 69, at 6.
53. Council Decision 2014/415/EU on the arrangements for the implementation by the Union of the solidarity clause, O.J. 2014, L 192/53.
54. Declaration (no. 37) on Art. 222 of the TFEU.
55. More generally on Art. 42 TEU and Art. 222 TFEU, see S. Blockmans. "L'Union fait la force: Making the most of the solidarity clause (Art. 222 TFEU)" in I. Govaere and S. Poli (Eds.), *EU Management of Global Emergencies; Legal Framework for Combating Threats and Crises* (Brill, 2014), at 111–135 and P. Hilpold, "Filling a buzzword with life. The implementation of the solidarity clause in Art. 222 TFEU", 42 *Legal Issues of Economic Integration*, (2015), 209–239.
56. Council Document 13618/06.

There is thus no formal legal act establishing the Battle Groups. Battle Groups are an amalgam of military units and support units consisting of around 1500 troops, which are fully self-supporting, are mobile over land or sea or in the air and can be deployed within a matter of days. Battle group "packages" may be offered by single Member States or by a coalition of Member States and will be on call during a period of half a year. Although they are not based on a formal Council act, they are supposed to remain within the confines of Article 42 and 43 TEU. They are not supposed to do territorial defence, as that is in the hands of NATO, and they are characterized as rapid reaction forces. Although they are supposed to serve the common defence, their financing falls on the participating states, according to normal financing rules for military operations.[57] The EUBGs have never been called upon; the Member States in the Council have always preferred to go for *ad hoc* missions, even in such extreme emergency situations as arose in Chad and the Central African Republic in recent years.

3.2 *CFSP: The common policy with respect to the International Criminal Court (ICC)*

The common policy on the ICC started out in mid-2001 as a fairly general common endeavor to stimulate other States to ratify the Rome Statute of the ICC. It developed further in sharp opposition to the frontal attack of the US Bush administration on the ICC, largely succeeded in blunting the impact of this attack, and it then returned to calmer waters.

During the Rome Conference for the drafting of the ICC Statute, the EU did not manage to maintain a single front, especially the Security Council permanent members, France and the UK, were in a special position.[58] By the early summer of 2001, the Rome Statute of the ICC had been signed by 139 States and ratified or acceded to by 32. The number of required ratifications for the entry into force of the Statute and the start of the activities of the ICC was 60. It was at this juncture that the Council decided to adopt a common position under Article 15 (now 29) TEU in order to ensure that the number of 60 would be reached quickly and that the first steps towards an effective functioning of the new court would follow suit. This was a typical decision that would "define the approach of the Union to a particular matter of a geographical or thematic nature," as Article 29 TEU now puts it; all Member States were bound to ensure that their national policies conform to it. This common position was to be reviewed every six months.[59]

A year later the number of ratifications (69) had crossed the threshold of 60 and the entry into force was about to take place on 1 July 2002. In the meantime 9/11 had happened and a steady campaign in conservative circles within the Republican caucus in the US Senate against the ICC was bearing fruit. President Bush had withdrawn in May 2002 the signature that President Clinton had affixed on the Rome Statute on 31 December 2000. Moreover, the Senate was studying a bill called the American Service members Protection Act (ASPA). This bill foresaw a number of sanctions, such as loss of US military aid, against countries that had ratified the Rome Statute and observed their duty to the transfer of information to the ICC. In the meantime the European Parliament had also become vocal on the matter and in February 2002 called for an

---

57. Costs of EUGBs do not fall under Council Decision (CFSP) 2015/528 establishing a mechanism to administer the financing of the common costs of the European Union operations having military or defence implications (Athena), O.J. 2015, L 84/39-63.
58. See M. Groenleer and L. van Schaik, "United we stand? The European Union's external actorness in the cases of the International Criminal Court and the Kyoto Protocol", 45 JCMS (2007), 969–998, at 976–983, which gives an interesting political science perspective on the same episode discussed here. M. Groenleer and D. Rijks, "The European Union and the International Criminal Court: The politics of international criminal justice" in K.E. Joergensen (Ed.), *The European Union and International Organizations* (Routledge, 2009).
59. Council Common Position 2001/443/CFSP on the International Criminal Court, O.J. 2011, L 76/56.

action plan to follow up on Common Position 2001/443/CFSP. In April of the same year the Foreign Affairs Council took note of this resolution and the Action Plan, which did not have any official status, was finalized on 15 May 2002.[60] Further to these developments the Council of Ministers adopted conclusions on 17 June 2002, in which it expressed its concern about ASPA and the withdrawal of the US signature and urged the US administration "to give full weight" to these EU concerns. These conclusions were followed three days later by an amendment of the Common Position of a year earlier.[61] This amendment sought to support the early establishment and effective functioning of the Court and to advance universal support for the Court and the widest possible participation in the Statute.

The US resistance to the ICC took even stronger forms during the summer of 2002 and developed into a campaign of concluding bilateral agreements between the US and States parties to the Rome Statute on the non-delivery of US nationals to the ICC and of putting great pressure on the UN to exempt US citizens participating in UN operations from possible delivery to the ICC for war crimes.[62] In response the EU defined its opposition in much stronger terms through Council conclusions adopted on 30 September. These conclusions were accompanied by policy guidelines that not only could be used to set policy, but also applied, when – in spite of EU opposition – individual countries (notably the candidate countries of Central Europe) – might feel compelled to give in to US pressure for a non-delivery agreement. The guidelines clearly stated that the draft agreements that the US at the time sought to conclude with States parties to the Rome Statute were contrary to the obligations flowing from that Statute. They pointed out that impunity could never be the result of any agreement to be concluded and only citizens of non-parties could be subject to a non-delivery obligation.

It goes beyond the scope of this chapter to go further into detail on these conclusions.[63] They did, however, become the focal point of the EU's policy in this field, which remained strongly opposed to the line followed by the Bush administration, while it tried to keep the door open for a US return to the ICC machinery. The EU accepted that the US initially might assist as observer to the Meeting of the Parties; that it might cooperate in the work of the ICC, especially through providing information to its prosecutors, and later hopefully as party to the Statute again. These conclusions and guidelines were also referred to in the new Common Position of

---

60. The Action Plan was only adopted on 4 Feb. 2004, see recital 16 of Council Decision 2011/168/CFSP of 21 Mar. 2011 on the International Criminal Court and repealing Common Position 2003/444/CFSP, O.J. 2011, L 76/56. See the draft version of the Action Plan in Council doc. 5742/04, "Draft Action Plan to follow-up on the Common Position on the International Criminal Court" (28 Jan. 2004). In 2011, the original Action Plan was adapted following Council Decision 2011/168/CFSP. See Council doc. 12080/11 "Action Plan to follow-up on the Decision on the International Criminal Court" (12 July 2011). For a general overview of (the history of) EU – ICC relations see "The European Union and the International Criminal Court" (Brussels, 2010).
61. Council Conclusions on the International Criminal Court and the Draft US American Service members Protection Act of 17 June 2002, Council doc. 9717/02 (Presse 178), at 23; and Council Common Position 2002/474/CFSP of 20 June 2002 amending Common Position 2001/443/CFSP on the International Criminal Court, O.J. 2002, L 164/1, see in particular Art. 1.
62. The US threatened to veto all resolutions on UN peace-keeping operations, if it did not obtain ICC-immunity for all US citizens participating in such operations and actually did veto the prolongation of the operation in Bosnia and Herzegovina on July 2, 2002, see statement by Human Rights Watch "US betrays Bosnian people" of 2 July 2002. This blackmail found a "solution" in SC/Res. 1442 (2002), which gave immunity to US citizens for one year, which period was renewable.
63. See Council Conclusions of 30 Sept. 2002, Council doc. 12134/02 (Presse 279), <www.consilium.europa.eu/uedocs/cms_data/docs/pressdata/en/gena/72321.pdf>.For an overview of these events see e.g. D. Thomas, "Rejecting the US challenge to the International Criminal Court: Normative entrapment and compromise in EU policy-making", 46 *International Politics* (2009), 376–394.

the Council of June 2003,[64] which was adopted with a view to replacing the earlier common positions. However, the conclusions and guidelines of 30 September 2002 were not included as such in the new Common Position, but they were mentioned as the basis for advice to parties that had come under US pressure.[65] The common position concentrated rather on the long-standing objective of the widest possible ratification and acceptance of the Rome Statute and its related instruments, and in particular on the political and technical support in connection with ratification and implementation of the Statute by specific States and groups of States.[66] It also signalled a number of actions to be encouraged by the EU and the Member States in order to support the independence of the Court. If third States were to transfer their financial contributions early and in full to the ICC, if they were to ratify quickly the agreement on the privileges and immunities of the ICC, and if they were to school judges, prosecutors and officials in work related to the Court, that would signify an enormous boost to the ICC's independent existence.[67]

True to its support for the ICC, the EU was relatively quick to conclude an agreement with the Court on cooperation and assistance. This was a CFSP agreement based on Article 24 (now 37) TEU. This agreement, which exists in parallel to such agreements concluded by the Member States, is concerned with the exchange of information and documents which may help the Court and its Prosecutor in their tasks.[68]

During the second term of President Bush the fraught relationship between the EU and the US over the ICC began to normalize somewhat. This development continued under President Obama. Given the views of the majority of the US Senate, accepting the Rome Statute was not on the cards for the US, but cooperation became possible. On the European side the Common Position of 2003 went through a renewal and became a "normal" decision in conformity with Article 29 of the Lisbon text of the TEU.[69] The important new developments, such as the definition of aggression and the Review Conference were referred to in the recitals, while the end of impunity for the crimes included in the Rome Statute, the preservation of the independence of the ICC and the integrity of the Rome Statute were also mentioned as key elements. The core of the operative paragraphs, however, remained largely the same. This Council Decision of March 2011 is still in force today and on the whole one can say that the EU's policy on the ICC has been a qualified success, insofar as it has contributed to some inflection of the US hard line policy already during the second term of President G.W. Bush. It remains to be seen how the EU's policy on the ICC will be able to stop the growing tendency among African countries to leave the ICC.

If one analyses this evolution of the successive Common Positions and the Decision of 2011, it is striking that, though this is called initially a common position, which it substantively remains after the entry into force of the Lisbon Treaty, it is a common position not only of the Union, but also of the Member States. The different provisions are nearly all directed at the Union and the Member States, whereas, according to Article 29 TEU, a common position of the Union has to be followed by the Member States. This way of formulating such decisions confirms once more that the CFSP is a parallel policy between Union and Member States, without any pre-emption. As results from one particular provision that recurs in nearly all these

64. Council Common Position 2003/444/CFSP of 16 June 2003 on the International Criminal Court, O.J. 2003, L 150/67.
65. See Art. 5 of Common Position 2003/444/CFSP, cited *supra* note 60.
66. See Art. 2 of Common Position 2003/444/CFSP, ibid.
67. See Art. 3 of Common Position 2003/444/CFSP, ibid.
68. Council Dec. 2006/313/CFSP concerning the conclusion of the Agreement between the International Criminal Court and the European Union on cooperation and assistance, O.J. 2006, L 115/49.
69. Council Dec. 2011/168/CFSP of 21 Mar. 2011 on the International Criminal Court and repealing Common Position 2003/444/CFSP, O.J. 2011, L 76/56.

decisions, the Council, where appropriate, is supposed to operate as the coordinator of the policies of the Union and of the Member States with respect to the creation and functioning of the ICC, except in the last one where, next to the Council, the High Representative is mentioned in this coordinating role.[70]

Another common feature of the older decisions is the provision in which the Council notes that the Commission will also try to contribute to the objectives of the common position, where appropriate, by pertinent Community action.[71] The decision of 2011 marks the complete banishment of the Commission from the domain of the CFSP and CSDP after Lisbon by omitting this clause and instead including an article that charges the Union with ensuring the consistency and coherence across the board of its external and internal action.[72]

Finally the above rendering of this episode demonstrates once again how in the CFSP formal decisions and informal texts, such as Council conclusions, and the *sui generis* Action Plan serve together to create a Union policy, in this case in relation to the ICC and in opposition to US policy. One may even say that, on the whole, the Council Conclusions of 30 September 2002 were more important than any of the formal decisions.

3.3 *CSDP military common policy: The EU's non-proliferation policies*[73]

Non-proliferation is a word that originally was applied primarily in connection with nuclear weapons and it was in this sense that it was used when the Member States first created a Working Party on non-proliferation in 1981 in the framework of the European Political Cooperation (EPC).[74] When the European Council made its first declaration on the subject at the Dublin Summit of 1990 this was still the case.[75] By December 2003, some nine months after the invasion of Iraq by US and coalition troops, the European Council found another subject, next to its general European Security Strategy, on which it could show unity, and that was what by now was called the Strategy against the proliferation of Weapons of Mass Destruction (WMD). That is to say that chemical, biological, radiation and nuclear weapons and their precursors had all been thrown in the same basket, together with their delivery vehicles, ballistic missiles and their technology. This is motivated primarily by the indiscriminate and largely uncontrollable nature of these weapons, which inherently do not distinguish between combatants and non-combatants, one of the core principles of the law of war.[76] Whether all the different WMDs really belong

70. Compare Art. 4 of the 2001 Common Position mentioned in *supra* note 9 and Art. 6 of the 2011 Decision mentioned in *supra* note 67. Given the system of the Lisbon TEU, according to which the HR takes over the executive function in CFSP and CSDP from the Council Secretariat, one suspects that the Council should no longer have been mentioned in the 2011 decision at all.
71. Cf. Art. 5 of the 2001 Common Position and Art. 6 of the 2003 Common Position.
72. Art. 8 of the Decision of 2011, mentioned in *supra* note 69.
73. This section voluntarily does not include the EU's participation, through the HR/VP, in the negotiations on the so-called Nuclear Deal with Iran.
74. The existence of this and other working groups was formalized in Art. 30(10)(f) of the Single European Act of 1986.
75. Declaration on Nuclear Non-Proliferation, Annex VI to the Conclusions of the Presidency, Dublin, June 25–26 1990.
76. For this principle in international armed conflicts see Arts. 48, 51, 52 and 57 of the Additional Protocol to the Geneva Conventions of 12 Aug. 1949, and Relating to the Protection of Victims of International Armed Conflicts (Protocol I), 8 June 1977; for non-international armed conflicts, see Arts. 13–16 of the Additional Protocol to the Geneva Conventions of 12 Aug. 1949 and Relating to the Protection of Victims of Non-International Armed Conflicts (Protocol II), 8 June 1977.

together in the same basket is doubtful; this is illustrated by the fact that they are regulated by different international conventions and organizations.[77]

By necessity – given the different international regimes for non-proliferation -, but also by temperament – after all the CFSP is strongly embedded in international cooperation by the Treaties – this strategy was first of all to be carried out by "efficient multilateralism".[78] This implied coherent and consistent action by the EU and its Member Organizations in the different organizations, such as the UN, OPCW and the IAEA. This was secured, even before the official enunciation of the Strategy, by the adoption of a Common Position in November 2003 with a rather grandiose title,[79] but with the very practical aim of achieving universal ratification of the NPT, of the IAEA additional protocols relating to the safeguards regime, of the Chemical Weapons Convention (CWC), and of the Biological and Toxin Weapons Convention (BTWC), to encourage adherence to the Hague Code of Conduct against ballistic missile proliferation (HCoC),[80] and to promote early entry into force of the Comprehensive Nuclear Test Ban Treaty (CBTB).[81] Moreover, in doing all this, the EU and its Member States must especially pay attention to detection of breaches and strengthening enforcement of these instruments. Second, and equally important, all Member States had to become parties to the relevant conventions. Thus France, to give an important example, had to decide to give up its resistance to acceding to the NPT, which it did in 2006.[82]

The EU also sought to employ another of its existing strong points, the so-called Neighbourhood Policy, as well as its broader treaty-making programme and its Financing Instruments as a second way of reinforcing non-proliferation everywhere. This was called "the promotion of a regionally and internationally stable environment". One of the important elements of this approach was the inclusion of an anti-WMD provision in most regional and wider agreements that the EU was seeking to conclude, but this was a wish that was to encounter many obstacles. One can perhaps say that the adoption by the UN Security Council in April 2004 of S/Res 1540 on the risks of use of and trafficking in WMD by non-State organizations or private persons was an early harvest of the world-wide efforts of the EU Strategy.

Finally, the third way in which the strategy had to be carried out was by working closely with key partners, "such as the USA, Russia, the UK or NATO" as countries or organizations playing a major role in non-proliferation.

---

77. These are: the Chemical Weapons Convention 1993 (CWC) administered and supervised by the Organisation for the Prohibition of Chemical Weapons (OPCW), the Biological and Toxin Weapons Convention 1972 (BTWC), administered by the UN Office for Disarmament Affairs (UNODA) and the Non-Proliferation Treaty 1968 (NPT), administered also by UNODA and safeguarded through inspections by the International Atomic Energy Organization (IAEA).
78. EU Strategy Against Proliferation of Weapons of Mass Destruction, Annex to Council doc. 15708/03 of 12 Dec. 2003.
79. Council Common Position 2003/805/CFSP on the universalization and reinforcement of multilateral agreements in the field of non-proliferation of Weapons of Mass Destruction and means of delivery, O.J. 2003, L 302/34.
80. The HCoC is a fairly generally worded instrument discouraging the spread of ballistic missiles and their technology. It is not a full treaty; one "subscribes" to it, one does not "ratify" it. It has 137 subscribers at the moment. It is not to be confused with the Missile Technology Control Regime, the legal status of which is equally vague, but which in practice operates a stringent collective export controls regime that is also implemented by the EU.
81. This last point was the reconfirmation of an earlier Common Position 1999/533/CFSP on the same matter, O.J. 1999, L 204/1.
82. This enabled the EU *inter alia* to develop a common approach to NPT problems that was upheld during the NPT Review Conference of spring 2015.

Although this was a "strategy" adopted by the European Council, this was not a decision identifying the strategic interests of the EU, as foreseen in Article 26(1) TEU. It was a policy document without a legal basis or any particular status.[83] As was shown in discussing the policy with respect to the ICC, this does not need to be a weakness, but we will have to outline the inter-action of informal, but high-level documents without legal status with legal instruments of a more working level character such as TEU decisions and TFEU regulations or directives. This interaction was generally felicitous where the ICC was concerned; but how did the EU fare on non-proliferation?

After five years the review of the Strategy and the resulting document, issued by the Council of Ministers and again of an informal, non-binding nature, was called "New Lines for Action by the EU in combating the proliferation of weapons of mass destruction and their delivery systems".[84] From the document it is clear that the original strategy was perhaps too much directed to the external world and a turn to internal consciousness-raising and internal measures were announced, in conformity with the bleak view that the Council took of the risk of WMD falling into the hands of terrorists and shady dealers. The goals set in this "New Lines" document, which in reality was more of an action plan with a semi-annual reporting requirement,[85] were supposed to be reached by the end of 2010. The one page document that reviewed this objective by December 2010 made clear that the goals of the "New Lines" document were not reached and that even some of the earlier objectives of 2003 had remained unimplemented.[86] The Council noted "the ongoing efforts towards implementing this action plan, but realized that some aspects of the action plan need further efforts". Competent EU institutions and Member States were encouraged by the Council to continue their efforts towards complete implementation of the action plan in each policy sector by the end of 2012.[87] Actually it was only in October 2013 that the Council looked at the matter of non-proliferation of WMD again and concluded right away that much remained to be done to achieve a fully efficient, collective approach to fighting proliferation of WMD by the EU. And a number of old and new measures were mentioned in this new document that was, once again, of a non-binding character.[88]

The text of these later documents indicates that there was no full implementation of the EU's anti-proliferation policy for WMD, insofar as it was laid down in informal, non-binding, documents. From the beginning, there were also accompanying measures of a formal nature both under the TEU and the TFEU, but these were only broadly alluded to in the strategy documents.

In the TEU field, apart from the Common Position of November 2003,[89] these were primarily financial support actions taken by individual Council decisions, for instance in support of certain research projects relating to the Hague Code of Conduct against Ballistic Missile

83. This was seen by at least one scholar as a disadvantage, see P. van Ham, "The European Union's WMD strategy and the CFSP: A critical analysis", EU Non-Proliferation Consortium, Non-Proliferation Papers no. 2, at 5–6. On the other hand it is interesting to note that later TEU decisions based on either Art. 26(2) or 28 TEU even in their titles referred to the EU Strategy against the proliferation of weapons of mass destruction, as if it was a European Council strategy within the meaning of Art. 26(1) TEU. See the TEU decisions mentioned in note 90 below and accompanying text.
84. Council doc. 17172/08, 17 Dec. 2008.
85. For a recent example of such progress report, see Six-monthly Progress Report on the Implementation of the EU Strategy against the Proliferation of Weapons of Mass Destruction (2013/II), O.J. 2014, C 54/1.
86. Council doc. 17078/10, of 16 Dec. 2010.
87. Ibid.
88. Council doc, 15104/13 of 21 Oct. 2013.
89. See note 79 and accompanying text.

Proliferation.[90] Another example is the still ongoing project giving support to the World Health Organization in carrying out certain pilot projects in specific countries or regions in respect of the countering and management of so-called "biorisk" in laboratories.[91] One source mentions more than 20 different such financial subsidy decisions during the period up to 2011.[92] In addition there was also the occasional Council Decision on a common position to be followed in specific instances at meetings in the relevant organizations or conferences of the parties.[93]

Where accompanying TFEU measures are concerned, they were of two kinds: financial and legislative. The financial support relied on mobilization of sums from the large Financing Instruments of the EU, in particular the Stability Instrument and the Partnership Instrument.[94] Among the legislative efforts a prominent example was the new regime for dual use goods that was adopted on the legal basis for the common commercial policy and that included many precursor products for WMD and rocket technology and other delivery systems and thus plays an important role in maintaining the EU's and Member States' non-proliferation efforts.[95]

In conclusion, it appears that the anti-proliferation policy of the EU in respect of WMD is built on a similar mix of informal, non-binding texts and TEU and TFEU secondary legislation to the ICC policy. The link between the two kinds of instruments is almost equally close, with especially frequent references in the secondary legislation to the initial Strategy of 2003 and the "New Lines" document of 2008. The sheer weight of the informal texts that succeed each other in a straight line, always referring back to a preceding informal text and never to secondary legislation, shows that the non-legal texts dominate in this case.

However, these successive informal documents also show that there is a persistent underperformance in achieving the objectives of the Strategy against WMD proliferation.[96] For lawyers it is then tempting to conclude that somehow the "mix" in this case was not right and that it should be "tweaked" so as to be "right" in future cases. That would be wrong, simply because the two problems are so different and the non-proliferation of WMD demands an expertise over a broad front of very different problems that the combination of EAAS, at this stage of its development, and Commission simply could not fully cover at a sufficient level to the satisfaction of the Member States.[97] In addition there is the obvious problem of the two nuclear weapons States, which are also permanent members of the Security Council and somehow sit on two sides of

---

90. Council Decision 2008/974/CFSP in support of the Hague Code of Conduct against Ballistic Missile Proliferation in the framework of the implementation of the EU Strategy against Proliferation of Weapons of Mass Destruction, O.J. 2008, L 345/91; and Council Decision 2012/423/CFSP in support of ballistic missile non-proliferation in the framework of the implementation of the EU Strategy against Proliferation of Weapons of Mass Destruction and of Council Common Position 2003/805/CFSP, O.J. 2012, L 196/74.
91. Council Decision 2013/668/CFSP in support of World Health Organization activities in the area of biosafety and biosecurity in the framework of the EU Strategy against Proliferation of Weapons of Mass Destruction, O.J. 2013, L 310/13.
92. See P. van Ham, op. cit. *supra* note 83, at 8.
93. As an example: Council Decision 2010/212/CFSP relating to the position of the European Union for the 2010 Review Conference of the Parties to the Treaty on the Non-Proliferation of Nuclear Weapons, O.J. 2010, L 90/8. This decision based on Art. 29 TEU mentions no less than seven priorities and 56 essential issues for the EU to take care of.
94. For these instruments and their discussion see Ch. 41, "Union external relations under the TFEU", section 3.1.2 of this book.
95. For a discussion of the "Dual use Regulation", i.e. Council Reg. (EC) 428/2009, O.J. 2009, L 131/1. See Ch. 41, "Union external relations under the TFEU", section 2.3.1 of this book.
96. A judgment that is shared by P. van Ham, op. cit. *supra* note 83.
97. The Commission had pre-existing and recognized expertise in nuclear safeguards and inspections (from Euratom) and trade and export controls, but that did not include the core of nuclear disarmament. The EEAS and its predecessors in the Council Secretariat had not really had the time and the manpower (with

the table. Especially these two, but probably also many of the others, simply preferred at decisive moments to keep their margin of manoeuvre.

3.4 *CFSP/CSDP Civilian Action: EU-Lex Kosovo*[98]

If one wants to give an example of an important civilian CFSP/CSDP action, the EU-Lex Kosovo mission in the field of justice and police assistance must have pride of place; it was the biggest civilian operation ever mounted by the EU. The way this mission came about and how it functioned in practice is illustrative of some of the strong and weak points of the EU external action in the relations with different actors in Europe (the Balkan States, in particular Serbia, and Russia) and the world (the UN) in the face of considerable internal EU dissension on the crucial question of Kosovar independence.

EU-Lex Kosovo had to operate in a situation largely determined by Security Council Resolution 1244 of 10 June 1999 (S/Res/1244). That resolution foresaw, *inter alia*, a "substantial measure of self-government" for Kosovo as a kind of interim goal of the UN operation (UNMIK), taking full account of the "principles of sovereignty and territorial integrity of the Federal Republic of Yugoslavia" (Serbia and Montenegro).[99] The interim administration and peacekeeping was to be assured by UNMIK in cooperation with relevant international organizations: essentially KFOR as off-shoot of NATO for the internal security and border patrols,[100] and the European Union (primarily the Commission) for the social and economic administration of Kosovo, the so-called pillar IV, of UNMIK.[101]

It was Martti Ahtisaari, the former President of Finland, who was charged with finding a way of reconciling a "substantial measure of self-government" with the territorial integrity and sovereignty of Serbia. He discovered that this was not possible and concluded that a controlled transition to independence limited by extensive minority rights and protection for Kosovar Serbs was the only option. This so-called Ahtisaari plan "was not endorsed by the Security Council". The "troika" consisting of the EU, Russia and the US was then charged with writing a report, which concluded that "neither party was willing to cede its position on the fundamental question of sovereignty". This was in late 2007.

The Ahtisaari report also contained a recommendation to the effect that the administration of the socio-economic sector should be passed to the government of the newly-independent Kosovo and that the EU should take over the training and oversight of the Justice and Police sector through an EU-led rule of law mission. In addition, the UN Secretariat signalled that it could

---

the exception of some respected individuals) to build up (or even buy up) expertise in nuclear, biological and chemical warfare, as well as in missile technology with sufficient depth of understanding.

98. The following account is based primarily on E. Milano, "Il trasferimento di Funzioni di UNMIK a EULEX in Kosovo", (2008) *Rivista di Diritto Internazionale*, 967–990; P. Koutrakos, *The EU Common Security and Defence Policy* (OUP, 2013), at 168–177; and Editorial, "And in the meantime? Kosovo?", 46 CML Rev. (2009), 377–382. Also M. Karnitschnig, "The United Nations and the European Union in Kosovo – The challenges of joint nation-building" in J. Wouters, F. Hoffmeister and T. Ruys (Eds.), *The United Nations and the European Union: An Ever Stronger Partnership* (T.M.C. Asser Press, 2006), at 323–351, at 327.
99. See S/Res/1244, 10th recital and Annex I, indent 6.
100. The basis for these tasks was to be found in paras. 6–9 of S/Res/1244.
101. The support for UNMIK Pillar IV started out as a succession of short term CFSP Joint Actions in 1999 and was then changed to a Community Reg. (Council Reg. (EC) 1080/2000, O.J. 2000, L 122/27) based on Art. 308 EC Treaty (later amended by Council Reg. (EC) 2098/2003, O.J. 2003, L 316/1). On the basis of these Regulations, the Commission was authorized, on behalf of the Community, to conclude financing agreements with UNMIK and the Office of the UN High Representative. The Commission also seconded many of its civil servants and civil servants of the Member States to UNMIK.

not envisage maintaining a substantial long-term peace-keeping operation in Kosovo, next to all the other operations going on.

So how to carry out some version of Ahtisaari's "controlled transition to independence" without antagonizing Serbia and Russia completely, and requiring the EU and the US to obtain a new Security Council mandate for a Kosovo operation that would not be hit by a Russian veto? The solution lay in taking a number of steps that exploited the flexibility in Security Council Resolution 1244, while leaving Russia the satisfaction that the whole operation remained *de iure* a UN operation under the authority of the Security Council and hence subject to a Russian veto for any change in the existing text of the Resolution. The flexibility of S/Res. 1244 could be found in provisions leaving considerable freedom to UN Member States and relevant international organizations to establish a security presence in Kosovo and to the Secretary-General to establish an international civil presence there, with the assistance of relevant international organizations, in order to establish an interim administration.[102] It was in particular this relative autonomy of the Secretary-General in establishing an interim administration with the help of other international organizations that proved important. To understand this it is necessary to return to the events of late 2007 and the first half of 2008 in relation to Kosovo.

In its meeting of 14 December 2007, the European Council declared that the EU was ready to play a role in the solution of the Kosovo problem and to contribute an ESDP mission and a contribution to an international civilian office.[103] Presidential elections were held in Serbia on 3 February 2008 and won by President Tadic, who was regarded as broadly pro-European. In the light of this "positive" result for the EU, the Foreign Affairs Council decided the next day on two Joint Actions, one establishing the EU-Lex Kosovo Mission[104] and the other appointing a EU Special Representative (EUSR) for Kosovo.[105] Two weeks later on 18th February, Kosovo declared independence. The declaration contained a (5th) paragraph which welcomed important aspects of the Ahtisaari plan, including "a European Union led rule of law mission". This assured that EU-Lex was welcome and would be able to operate on Kosovar territory. So the operation could go ahead, in spite of the lack of a new Security Council Resolution.

During the rest of 2008 consultations among the troika and with the UN continued. Secretary-General Ban Ki-Moon prepared two successive reports on the restructuring of UNMIK. The first one, published in early June, showed in passing that the Secretary-General had been notified by the European Commission that it was no longer prepared to pay for Pillar IV of UNMIK.[106] The second one, published in November 2008, was along largely the same lines, with cosmetic differences to make it more palatable to all sides. The S-G was using his powers of organization of the UNMIK operation by reducing UNMIK proper to a minimum, under the cover of which NATO's KFOR would remain responsible for "hard security", in particular border patrol. The Kosovar government would exercise economic and social administration (ex-Pillar IV) and EU-Lex would take on the police and the public ministry, as well as the

102. See respectively paras. 7 and 9 (military presence) and 10 (civil presence) of S/Res/1244.
103. Presidency Conclusions of the European Council of 14 Dec. 2007, point 70.
104. Council Joint Action 2008/124/CFSP on the European Rule of Law Mission in Kosovo, EULEX KOSOVO, O.J. 2008, L 42/92.
105. The Dutchman Peter Feith was so appointed, Council Joint Action 2008/123/CFSP appointing the European Special Representative in Kosovo, O.J. 2008, L 42/88. His mandate was later extended by several later decisions. Samuel Žbogar served as Special Representative during 2012 -2016. The Council appointed Natalya Apostolova to serve in this capacity as from 1 Sept. 2016; she also is head of the EU Office in Kosovo.
106. See UN doc. S/2008/354, point 9.

judicial sector. Both documents contained so-called six points plans, which were rejected by the Kosovar government.[107]

In spite of this resistance from the Kosovar side, the latter S-G report became the object of a discussion in the Security Council in late November 2008, which ended with a mere Chairman's statement, because there was still no agreement on the need for a new resolution on the Kosovo operation. This statement was a marvel of creative ambiguity and read in part as follows: "The Security Council welcomes the cooperation between the UN and other international actors, within the framework of S/Res/1244, and also welcomes the continuing efforts of the European Union to advance the European perspective on the whole of the Western Balkans, thereby making a decisive contribution to regional stability and prosperity".[108]

On this basis, which allows one side to claim that the EU-Lex operation can continue operating in Kosovo only on the basis of S/Res/1244[109] and the other side to argue that is has been invited in by paragraph 5 of the Kosovar Declaration of Independence, EU-Lex Kosovo has continued its work in that territory until today. The original decision of 2008 has gone through more than 10 rounds of amendments and extensions of the mission and supplementary budgetary allocations. The last renewal of the mission for a period of two years was decided in June 2016.[110] Over that period the Council Joint Action, though advertised as an ESDP mission in Article 6, was originally based principally on the CFSP provision for operational action (Art. 14 TEU old, now Art. 28 TEU), but was later modified by decisions based on the same article, but also on Articles 42(4) and 43(2) TEU and thus more clearly brought within the new CDSP provisions, thereby reinforcing the tendency that any action under the TEU that is operational in nature is in principle a CSDP operation.[111]

It is also clear that the operation is learning from its experience. One example is the attention that is paid to the chain of command and the interaction between its different components: thus the articles on the Civilian Operation Commander (in Brussels) (Art.6), the Head of Mission (Art. 8), the political control and strategic direction (Art. 12) and security (Art 14) were all revised in order to reinforce the position of the Head of Mission, but also to reinforce control from Brussels both at the administrative level (Civilian Operations Commander) and at the political level (PSC and HR/VP).

Another learning process is hiding behind the new Article 15a and the change in paragraphs 4–6 of Article 16, introduced in June 2014, which states *inter alia* that EULex Kosovo has all kinds of legal capacities (contractual, administrative, buy and sell assets, hold bank accounts etc.), in particular "to discharge its liabilities and to be a party to legal proceedings, as required

---

107. These points were: (1) Kosovo police in Serb-majority areas; (2) Courts in Serb-majority areas; (3) Customs, allowing Kosovo to function as a single customs area; (4) Transportation and infrastructure and the cooperation in that respect; (5) KFOR's continued surveillance of Kosovo's boundaries; (6) Protection of Serbian (religious) patrimony.
108. UN doc. S/prst/2008/44.
109. Note that one of the amending decisions of the Council includes a footnote to the word "Kosovo" in the title of the original Joint Action as follows: "This designation is without prejudice to positions on status, and is in line with UNSCR 1244 (1999) and the ICJ Opinion on the Kosovo declaration of independence". Council Dec. 2014/349/CFSP, O.J. 2014, L 174/42, note 1.
110. Council Dec. 2016/947/CFSP amending Joint Action 2008/124/CFSP on the European Union Rule of Law Mission in Kosovo, O.J. 2016, L 157/26.
111. This is perhaps not entirely fortuitous, as it would be easy to regard EULex Kosovo as an external aspect of the police and judicial cooperation of Title V of the TFEU instead of as a typical CSDP operation. Hence, also the stress placed in the last recital of Joint Action 2008/124/CFSP and all renewal decisions on the risky environment and the chance of deterioration of the situation, which could impede the achievement of the objectives of the UE's external action.

in order to implement its mandate" and grants greater autonomy from the Commission in the execution of EULex's budget.[112] This seems to be a legislative reaction of the Council to a judgment of the General Court of a year earlier in a case in which a private party attacked the decision of the Head of Mission on bids for tender of helicopter services to EULex Kosovo, as well as an action for damages. The General Court declared both actions inadmissible, because EULex Kosovo does not have legal capacity to be a defendant. In the Court's view, the Head of Mission, in his capacity as budget holder, was discharging delegated responsibilities for the implementation of the relevant part of the Commission budget and thus the Commission as institution should have been the defending party.[113]

Another jurisprudential development that is important for the EULex operation and for military and civil CFSP/CSDP operations generally, was caused by a transfer of a seconded member of personnel in the EU Police Mission (EUPM) in Bosnia-Herzegovina. When it concerns the treatment of an individual EU member of personnel (from Commission, EEAS or Council Secretariat), the application of the Statute of EU personnel and the access to the ECJ under that Statute prevails over the lack of competence of the Court in CFSP matters.[114] The Court then regards the principle of equal treatment of persons in the same situation as decisive for the treatment of Member State seconded personnel in the service of a EU mission set up under the CFSP, including their right of access to the ECJ.[115] The decisions of the Head of Mission are and remain acts of staff management, even if they take place in the context of a CFSP mission. Hence the General Court, and on appeal the Court of Justice have jurisdiction to review such acts for their legality under actions for annulment and for non-contractual liability, also if seconded personnel is involved.[116]

Finally, EULex Kosovo has also been able to adapt to new needs in the field of prosecution of serious crime, crimes of war and organized crime, when a report for Assembly of the Council of Europe by the Swiss special rapporteur Dick Marty[117] caused a great stir about alleged atrocities and "harvesting" of human organs from prisoners of the Kosovo internal wars held in the north of Albania, in which prominent members of the Kosovo Liberation Army (KLA) allegedly had been directly involved. This led to the creation of the so-called Special Investigative Task Force (SITF) that was admitted into the "big tent" of EULex Kosovo by the inclusion of new Article 3a in Decision 2008/124/CFSP, while at the same time guaranteeing the independence of the prosecutors and (later to be nominated) judges of the Task Force. The future judicial

112. Art. 15a of Council Joint Action 2008/124/CFSP as introduced by Council Dec. 2014/349/CFSP, O.J. 2014, L 174/42. Linked to this new provision were also new paras. 4 et seq. of Art. 16, which *inter alia* included a passage making EULex Kosovo responsible for any claims and obligations arising from the implementation of its mandate.
113. Case T-213/12, *Elitaliana SpA v. EULex Kosovo*, paras. 30–35. Cf. Case T-395/11, discussed *supra* note 20 and accompanying text, which applies the same approach to Union delegations.
114. This is laid down, by the way, in the relevant CFSP decisions and entails a right of access to the Court, flowing from the Staff Regulations. See Case C-455/14 P, *H. v. Council, Commission and EUPM in Bosnia/Herzegovina*, paras. 54 et seq.
115. *H. v. Council, Commission and EUPM in Bosnia/Herzegovina*, para 57.
116. Ibid. *H. v. Council, Commission and EUPM in Bosnia/Herzegovina*, para 58. The judgment is also a welcome reinforcement of the authority of the Head of Mission, who was being undercut in this case by an intervention of the Italian authorities, to whom the seconded member of personnel had also addressed her complaints. For the rather fascinating factual and procedural background of the case, see paras. 13–19 of the case.
117. Report for the Committee on Legal Affairs and Human Rights of the Parliamentary Assembly of the Council of Europe titled "Inhuman treatment of people and illicit trafficking in human organs in Kosovo", Doc 12462, 7/1/2011.

proceedings against some of the alleged perpetrators of these crimes will be relocated to EU Member States, given the security risks inherent in holding their trials in Kosovo itself.

In conclusion, EULex Kosovo started out as a civilian CFSP/ESDP mission and became a civilian CSDP mission. It is quite likely that other civilian police missions and similar operational ventures will continue to be set up as civilian CSDP missions, because many of such missions are undertaken in insecure countries or areas. It is also clear that EULex Kosovo was undertaken at the limit of what could legally and practically be done without modifying the existing mandate for the Kosovo operation, as laid down in S/Res. 1244 (1999). The EU, because of the predisposition in favour of international legality for its external action ingrained in the TEU and because the UN involvement in Kosovo was a fact, had no other option than to respect at least the letter of the existing Security Council resolution, when it became clear that a new resolution was not in the cards.[118] The evolution of the mission through its amendments has also confirmed its increasing military character, as far as the organization of the lines of command is concerned and the stringent supervision from Brussels administrative and political organs, such as the civil operations commander and the PSC. Giving EULex a capacity to shoulder its responsibility and to sue and be sued is good for its accountability vis-à-vis its contractual partners and at the same time makes missions like EULex more autonomous in their relations to the Commission and more truly TEU CSDP bodies.

3.5 *Military CSDP mission: Atalanta*

Looking at a large military, principally naval, operation like Atalanta will give us the opportunity to see the military side of the CFSP/CDSP in full action, the military organs, the military planning and command structure, the recourse to the special mechanism to administer the financing of military missions, the special agreements with outside contributors, the Status of Forces Agreements with host States, the problems related by bringing to justice those on both sides that have breached rules of international law, such as those prohibiting piracy and international humanitarian law.

Somalia has been the object of attention from many sides: the UN, the African Union, other international organizations in their specialized fields, and finally also the EU and individual countries. The EU alone ended up with three missions in Somalia, while also giving support to the African force in Somalia, AMISOM. These missions are EU NAVCO/Atalanta, the anti-piracy mission (2009), EUTM Somalia, a military training mission (2010), and finally EUCAP Nestor, a naval capacity building mission (2012).[119]

By mid-2008 many sea-faring States had become seriously worried about the scale and frequency of pirate attacks around the Horn of Africa originating principally in Somalia. The matter was being discussed simultaneously in the UN Security Council and in the EU Foreign Affairs Council. The Security Council decided on a short term authorization to countries cooperating with the Transitional Federal Government (TFG) of Somalia in its fight against piracy and armed robbery at sea to act against piracy and use all necessary means to do so, in the same

118. The interpretation now given to that resolution allowed at least some implementation of the main points of the Ahtisaari report, but in the end may not prevent turning Kosovo into another "frozen conflict" on the border between Russia and the rest of the world, in the mould of Transnistria, Abkhazia, Nagorno-Karabakh, and perhaps Eastern Ukraine. With the difference that in this case the "advantage on the ground" is not in favour of Russia, as in the relations with Moldova and Georgia.

119. There was also the appointment of an EUSR for the Horn of Africa, Council Dec. 2011/819/CFSP, O.J. 2011, L 327/62. The Atalanta mission is analysed within the broader context of all the other EU activities in Somalia by H.-G. Ehrhart and K. Petretto, "The EU, the Somalia challenge, and counter-piracy: Towards a comprehensive approach?", 17 EFA Rev. (2012), 261–284.

way as they already had this right on the high seas, also within the territorial waters of Somalia.[120] In response to this authorization the EU took two quick successive steps. First the creation, in September 2008, of a military coordination action in support of the Security Council Resolution, basically aimed at better coordination of anti-piracy action undertaken by navy ships of Member States, which were already operating in the area.[121] Secondly, the absorption of this action, after a few months, within a much broader military operation for the deterrence, prevention and repression of piracy off the coast of Somalia was adopted in early November; this was operation Atalanta.[122] It operates in tandem with a similar mission undertaken by NATO: Ocean Shield.[123] These missions were well received by the Security Council[124] and, given the simplicity and clarity of the authorization given and the broad support from all permanent members, unlike the case of EULex Kosovo, there was no problem to make the mission conform to the resolutions adopted.[125]

Since Atalanta and its short-lived predecessor were defined in their titles as military missions, it is important to point out where such missions differ from other CFSP decisions. First of all, there is the absence of Denmark. Pursuant to Article 6 of the Protocol on the position of Denmark, it cannot participate in the military side of the EU and hence it does not participate in the implementation and financing of the Joint Action.[126] As in the case of EULex Kosovo, the military character of the mission was reinforced by the post-Lisbon amendments to the Atalanta decision which were clearly based on the CSDP articles, in particular Article 43(3) TEU.[127]

In the case of military missions, it is obvious that planning and launch, which are different from the adoption or entry into force of the operation, are of a special character, even if EULex Kosovo had a special provision on launch as well.[128] The planning begins long before the adoption of the Joint Action and the launch falls some time after it, in the case of Atalanta about one month later. From the launch decision it appears that not only the completion of an Operations

120. On the high seas international law already permitted such action under Art. 100 et seq. UNCLOS, which is considered declaratory of international customary law. See S/Res/1816 (2008), para 7 (2 June 2008).
121. Council Joint Action 2008/749/CFSP on the European Union military coordination action in support of UN Security Council Resolution 1816/2008, O.J. 2008, L 252/39.
122. Council Joint Action 2008/851/CFSP on a EU military operation to contribute to the deterrence, prevention and repression of acts of piracy and armed robbery off the Somali coast, O.J. 2008, L 301/33. In the meantime, the Joint Action has been amended several times, most recently in Nov. 2014 by Council Dec. 2014/827/CFSP, O.J. 2014, L 335/19.
123. See NATO website: <www.mc.nato.int/missions/operation-ocean-shield.aspx>. This mission was initially concentrating on escorting ships bringing in foodstuffs intended for the Somali population from the WFP. Atalanta also engaged in this task.
124. See S/Res/1846(2008), paras. 6 and 7.
125. See also Art. 5 of Joint Action 2008/851/CFSP, cited *supra* note 110, on the planning and launch of the Operation, which refers explicitly to point 7 of S/Res/1816.
126. Last recitals of Joint Action 2008/749/CFSP, cited *supra* note 121, and of Joint Action 2008/851/CFSP cited *supra* note 122. This does not apply to civilian CSDP missions; such recitals are not found in the Kosovo Decision and have not been introduced as a consequence of post-Lisbon amendments of that decision based on Arts. 42 and 43 TEU. The third legal basis, Art. 28 TEU, is "civilian" and remained decisive of the civilian nature of the decision.
127. Council Dec. 2009/907/CFSP amending Joint Action 2008/851/CFSP on a European Union military operation to contribute to the deterrence, prevention and repression of acts of piracy and armed robbery off the Somali coast, O.J. 2009, L 322/27, was adopted 8 days after the entry into force of the Lisbon Treaty and was based on that Art. next to Art. 28 TEU.
128. See Art. 5 of Council Joint Action 2008/124/CFSP, cited *supra* note 104.

Plan (OPLAN), as in the Kosovo operation, but also the typically military need for the adoption of the rules of engagement is indispensable for actually proceeding to launch.[129]

The command structure is also different from that of a civilian action, insofar as the EU Military Committee (EUMC) also gets its place. As in civilian CSDP missions, the HR/VP and the Council have the highest responsibility, but the PSC actually exercises political control and strategic direction over Atalanta. To this end the PSC gets a certain number of powers under Article 38 TEU delegated to it, such as amending the planning documents, the chain of command and the rules of engagement.[130] The PSC must report regularly to the Council and receives reports from the Chair of EUMC on the military aspects of the operation.[131]

The EU Operation Commander, who is the equivalent of the Civilian Operation Commander, is not part of EEAS and located in Brussels, but in a military headquarters somewhere in Europe, in the case of Atalanta a naval base in the UK. (This demonstrates in passing that the EU military organization is far less integrated and "supranational" than NATO, with its Supreme Allied Commander Europe, SACEUR, and a complete Headquarters in Mons, Belgium.) He reports to the EUMC, through its Chair. He remains fully responsible for the military operation; EUMC will merely "monitor" its proper execution.[132] Finally, there is the EU Force Commander, who is the commander in the field and who is in regular contact on the daily operations with the EU Operation Commander. Both these commanders may be invited to appear in the EUMC or the PSC.[133]

An important aspect of the civilian as well as the military crisis management operations is the possibility to accept the participation of third States, in the operations themselves, or only in the funding of the operations. In military operations third States contribute from time to time special troop contingents. In Atalanta for instance, Montenegro contributed a vessel and its crew. The PSC had anticipated this by taking a decision setting up a Committee of Contributors (CoC), which would consist of the Member States, representatives of all outside contributors, the EU Operation Commander, the DG of the European Military Staff or their representatives, and of the Commission and would be chaired by the HR/VP or her representative.[134] When the offer of Montenegro, after an invitation by the EU, was extended, it was officially accepted by the PSC, and Montenegro made a member of the CoC for Atalanta. The most important legal aspect, however, is the agreement between the EU and Montenegro on participation of the latter in operation Atalanta.[135] This agreement – and others like it with other contributors of contingents, such as Croatia, Korea and New-Zealand – includes provisions on the obligation

129. The planning is referred to in the 5th recital of Joint Action 2008/851/CFSP and mentions the adoption of a crisis management concept by the Council on 5 Aug. 2008, Council doc. 12335/08. For the launch, see Council Dec. 2008/918/CFSP on the launch of a European military operation to contribute to the deterrence, prevention and repression of acts of piracy and armed robbery off the Somali coast (Atalanta) of 8 Dec. 2008, O.J. 2008, L 330/19, Arts. 1 and 2.

130. See for example PSC Decision Atalanta/2/2010 on the appointment of an EU Force Commander for [...] Atalanta (2010/185/CFSP), O.J. 2010, L 83/22.

131. Art. 6 Council Joint Action 2008/851/CFSP, cited *supra* note 122.

132. Art. 7 Council Joint Action 2008/851/CFSP.

133. Art. 8 and Arts. 6(3) and 7(3) of Council Joint Action 2008/851/CFSP.

134. PSC Decision Atalanta/3/2009 on the setting up of the Committee of Contributors for the EU military operation to contribute to the deterrence, prevention, and repression of acts of piracy and armed robbery off the Somali coast (Atalanta) (2009/369/CFSP), O.J. 2009, L 112/9. It is remarkable that the Commission should be a Member of this Committee in the field of CSDP, but it probably is for its budgetary duties.

135. Council Dec. 2010/199/CFSP of 22 March 2010 on the signing and conclusion of the Agreement between the European Union and Montenegro on the participation of Montenegro in the European Union military operation to contribute to the deterrence, prevention and repression of acts of piracy and armed robbery

of the contributing State to follow the Joint Action, the OPLAN and their implementing measures, on the status of the forces of the contributing State (to be governed by the EU SOFA with Somalia), on the conditions of transfer of persons arrested and detained with a view to their prosecution (as pirates), on the chain of command, on some further financial aspects etc. This list of issues usually covered by Contribution Agreements brings to the fore two issues that also deserve further mention here, namely Status of Forces Agreements (SOFAs) and the particular problem bedevilling the Atalanta operation, i.e. what to do with apprehended pirates, these so-called *hostes generis humani*.

In the case of military, but also of civilian crisis operations, the status of forces or of the mission (Status of Mission Agreements, SOMAs) is of utmost importance. Without them there would be no mission. In the sea-borne mission that is Atalanta, the problem is that, although Somalia is the object of the Mission, it cannot be the only host State, given the large sea area that the operation must cover. In the end SOFAs were negotiated also with Djibouti and the Seychelles. The content of all three agreements was broadly similar and the privileges and immunities granted to the "European Union-led Naval Force (EUNAVFOR)", as the agreement calls Atalanta, are close to full diplomatic privileges and immunities, as will be briefly shown below. The national contingents belonging to EUNAVFOR are defined as including also the contingents of the third contributing States so as to ensure that these are also covered by the agreements[136] without the contributing States needing to conclude separate SOFAs with the three States.

The agreements begin by setting out the basic obligations of EUNAVFOR and its personnel. The personnel must respect the laws and regulations of the host State and shall not do anything incompatible with the objective of the operation. They must carry identity. The vessels and aircraft must be marked by distinctive EUNAVFOR identification. Such identification also must be affixed to the uniforms of personnel.[137] Personnel can rely on their national driving licences, ship master's certificates and pilot licenses and will not be subject to the host state's requirements for entry and stay.[138] On the part of the host State, EUNAVFOR itself, its vessels and aircraft, archives etc. will be inviolable, immune from search, requisition, attachment or execution and from any form of legal process. EUNAVFOR personnel will not be subject to arrest or detention by the host State and will enjoy immunity from the criminal, civil and administrative jurisdiction of the host State; they are not obliged to act as a witness; they cannot be subjected to measures of execution and shall be free from any taxation and imposition of customs duties. They remain subject to the jurisdiction of their sending States and in particular subject to the criminal (court martial) jurisdiction of the sending State.[139]

In the case of civilian CSDP missions, SOMAs are concluded broadly along the same lines. This did not apply in the case of EULex Kosovo, since concluding an agreement with Kosovo on this matter would have implied some recognition of Kosovo as an international person and this was impossible given the so-called status neutrality of the mission. However, as if by magic,

---

off the Somali coast (Operation Atalanta), O.J. 2010, L 88/1. The legal bases for this agreement were Art. 37 TEU (treaty-making power) and Arts. 218(5) and (6) TFEU (treaty-making procedure).

136. Agreement between the EU and the Somali Republic on the status of forces of the European Union-led naval force in the Somali Republic in the framework of the EU military operation Atalanta, O.J. 2009, L 10/29, Art. 1(3) (a) and (f).
137. Art. 3 of the EU-Somalia Agreement, ibid.
138. Art. 4 of the EU-Somalia Agreement, ibid.
139. Arts. 5, 6 and 7 of the EU-Somalia Agreement, ibid. In addition the sending State or the relevant EU institution may lift the immunity of its own personnel, but in practice the preference is normally given to repatriate the member of personnel concerned and to exercise criminal jurisdiction at home.

the Kosovo Parliament adopted "Law nr3/L033 on the status immunities and privileges of diplomatic and consular missions and personnel in the Republic of Kosovo" less than two weeks after the Joint Action was adopted; it contained a provision that applied the regime set out in the law to EULex Kosovo and its personnel.[140]

Finally, the issue of pirates arrested and to be tried has been important from the beginning. The Security Council was concerned by it, especially once it was discovered that many States had not managed to take up the crime of piracy in their criminal codes, contrary to their obligation (Art. 100 UNCLOS) to cooperate in the suppression of piracy on the high seas outside the jurisdiction of any State.[141] Article 12 of the Atalanta Decision considered the different modalities of transfer of alleged pirates from Somalia and other countries in the region to EU Member States or to other third States participating in Atalanta.[142] However, to cut a long story short, these modalities were largely unrealistic for practical and legal reasons. Warships are not equipped to hold prisoners for a long time, while continuing operations. Moreover carrying prisoners home at the end of the tour of duty of a ship exposed the trial of such prisoners to the risk of an excessively long pre-trial detention without any processing of their case. Hence the only reasonable solution was to deliver the alleged pirates to countries in the region where piracy was a crime subject to universal jurisdiction and which were known for a decent criminal law system.[143]

An example of such an agreement is the Agreement between the EU and Mauritius on the conditions of transfer of suspected pirates. The core article is the one on treatment, prosecution and trial of transferred persons, which contains a complete catalogue of the rights of the accused in line with the relevant provisions of the ECHR, as further developed in the case law of the ECtHR.[144] There is some case law in various pirate cases, but it would go too far to discuss that here in detail. There is little doubt, however, that the EU has been awake to the risks inherent in the treatment of the apprehended pirates and has made *bona fide* efforts to combat these risks.[145]

In conclusion the Atalanta mission has developed into a remarkable military mission under an unproblematic authorization (compared to EULex Kosovo). It has worked in close association with other EU programmes related to Somalia, both CFSP (Nestor) and TFEU development programmes. At the time of writing a consensus is forming that the emphasis should be falling on these other programmes, which concentrate on combating the underlying causes of piracy and that Atalanta can be built down and even terminated – which can be seen as an indication of its success. Although there has been some understandable criticism of the way in which pirates have been brought to judgment in Western Europe and in the region, it remains a

---

140. See <www.mfa-ks.netrepository/docs/2008_03-L033_en1.pdf>.
141. Hence many Security Council Resolutions after S/Res/1816 called upon all States to criminalize piracy. For example, S/Res/1918 (2010), para 2.
142. Art. 12(1) and (2) of the Atalanta Council Joint Action 2008/851/CFSP, cited *supra* note 122.
143. Art. 12(3) of the Atalanta Joint Action provides that alleged pirates could only be delivered for trial by third States if the conditions for the transfer were agreed with the third State in a manner consistent with international law, notably the international law of human rights. On this the extensive jurisdiction claimed by the ECtHR over actions of party states' armies abroad played a role. See e.g. ECtHR, *Turkey v. Cyprus*, Appl. 25781/94, Judgment of 10 May 2001, para 80.
144. Art. 4 of the Agreement between the EU and the Republic of Mauritius on the conditions of transfer of suspected pirates and associated seized property from the European Union-led naval force to the Republic of Mauritius and on the condition of the suspected pirates thereafter, annexed to Council Dec. 2011/640/CFSP on the signing and conclusion of the said agreement, O.J. 2011, L 254/1. This agreement was subject of Case C- 658/11 *Parliament v. Council*, concerning the Parliament's right to be informed of the agreement, even if it was an agreement entirely in the CFSP domain – which it was according to the Court.
145. See e.g. Judgment of 19 Oct. 2012, *Landgericht Hamburg*; Judgment of 16 June 2010, *Rechtbank Rotterdam*.

positive point that the proper treatment of those suspected of piracy has been a matter of attention throughout the mission.

4. Conclusion

The discussion above of the bodies, institutions and agencies and of the different types of measures that have been taken under the CFSP and CSDP shows that these two areas of EU policy are still in full development. This certainly has a lot to do with the continuing hesitation between two visions of the CFSP. Is it supposed to be an improved version of the old EPC, i.e. essentially a better and closer coordination between national foreign policies? Or is it aiming at a truly integrated European Foreign Policy? We saw this being expressed in the formulation of certain Common Positions relating to the ICC, which were not only drafted as decisions of the Union, but also as co-ordination of the positions of the Member States. It is also expressed in the way the EEAS is organized, with one third of the personnel obligatorily flowing in and out on loan from national diplomatic services. One may wonder whether this aspect of the EEAS's organization, laudable as it may be from certain viewpoints, will not turn out to be a birth defect. This constant in- and outflow of personnel, combined with the regular rotation that is normal for any Foreign Ministry and diplomatic service, must make it very difficult to impart some stability and *esprit de corps* to the EEAS and to make it into a relatively smoothly operating service. In addition, the EEAS has a need, again like any diplomatic service, to recruit and nurture a stable group of specialists of non-Western cultures, religions and languages and of arcane subjects like arms control and cyber war. Under circumstances where upheaval of personnel is the near-normal condition, finding, recruiting and retaining such specialists may be quite difficult.

As far as the conduct of the CFSP is concerned, it appears that it has evolved in a direction slightly different from the TEU, in particular where the leading role of the European Council is concerned. This may be temporary, due to the Eurocrisis and its aftermath, but since the entry into force of Lisbon the European Council has taken up its role in setting the strategy of the CFSP and CSDP only after a serious delay. Thus it has been left largely to the Council for Foreign Affairs, which has produced strategies in the form of declarations on the basis of an outdated legal basis. In addition the rather doubtful pattern of behaviour has developed that in real crisis situations, notably the aggressive actions and annexations (whether through agents or for itself) by Russia against Georgia and Ukraine, the heavy lifting is done by one (Sarkozy in the case of Georgia) or two (Merkel and Hollande) big Member States. These may be cases of "when the going gets tough, the tough get going", but very "common" or "European" as a foreign or defence policy it is not. The European Council is not even used as a serious back-stop in these cases.

It has been shown, moreover, that in the case of largely "political" policies, i.e. policies which require nearly exclusively diplomatic action, sometimes accompanied by financial or development support, such as the policy in respect of the ICC and the non-proliferation of weapons of mass destruction, the contribution of non-legal, informal texts adopted in the Foreign Affairs Council to the policy is more or equally important to the formal decisions passed by the Council. As soon as the operational content of the foreign policy action increases, however, the formal, legal texts increase in number and importance. This is only natural; the operational aspects, especially if they are military in nature need to be laid down in detail and are in need of all kinds of legal support texts, such as SOFAs and SOMAs, contribution agreements with third States etc. which are of a recurring nature, though slightly different in content from one operation to another.

It is also evident that the integrating stimulus that should come from the coordinating powers of the HR is of great importance in creating interventions which consist not only of recourse to military means, but which are supported by other TFEU actions and project or program money from TFEU financing instruments, as was the case in Somalia.

Further reading

Gatti, M., *European External Action Service. Promoting Coherence through Autonomy and Coordination* (Brill/Nijhoff, 2016).

Gosalbo Bono, R., "Reflections on the CFSP legal order", 43 CML Rev. (2006), 337.

Govaere, I. and S. Poli (Eds.), *EU Management of Global Emergencies. Legal Framework for Combating Threats and Crises* (Brill/Nijhoff, 2014).

Koutrakos, P. *The EU Common and Security Policy* (OUP, 2013).

Merket, H., *The EU and the Security Development Nexus. Bridging the Legal Divide* (Brill/Nijhoff, 2016).

Naert, F., *International Law Aspects of the EU's Security and Defence Policy, with a Particular Focus on the Law of Armed Conflict and Human Rights* (Intersentia, 2010).

Van Vooren, B., S. Blockmans, and J. Wouters (Eds.),*The EU's Role in Global Governance. The Legal Dimension, Part II The EU and Global Security Governance* (OUP 2013).

CHAPTER 41
UNION EXTERNAL ACTION UNDER THE TFEU

*Pieter Jan Kuijper**

1. Introduction

The external action of the EU (Part V of the TFEU) includes first of all the common commercial policy (CCP), which still remains very much the core of the Union's external policy. Furthermore Part V TFEU contains the so-called cooperation policies, i.e. development cooperation, economic, financial and technical cooperation with developed countries, and humanitarian aid. In addition Part V contains provisions on restrictive measures, international agreements and the external representation of the Union, all matters that have been discussed in Chapter 39 and are included in their specific context in the chapter on CFSP and this chapter. The TFEU solidarity clause (Art. 222) is discussed entirely in the chapter on CFSP (Ch. 40, section 3.1).

In the fields of trade and development the EU is without doubt among the major players in the world. It is actually the largest importer and exporter of goods and services (2013), in spite of the strong rise by China, especially in the goods sector.[1] It was also the largest provider of Official Development Aid (ODA) in 2016 and of development aid overall.[2]

It is important to recall that the CCP and the EU development and cooperation policies remain the core of EU external action for the simple reason that these two form the carrot and stick with which the Union can easily mete out approval and disapproval on the international scene. This is so, not only because of the EU's size, even after a Brexit, but also because the CCP is an exclusive EU power directly linked to the internal core of the EU, the internal market. This power can be used quite effectively, as the normal legislative procedure applies to the prime legislative texts, and the new Lisbon rules on delegation of legislative power and on implementing powers make the Commission into a stronger executive that is also well controlled. In the field of development assistance the EU and its Member States have considerable financial resources for development. Moreover the EU disposes of the legal instruments to disburse these resources in furtherance of the EU development policy goals. These goals are based on a solid long term consensus between the EU and the Member States, built on the UN Millennium goals and expressed in the so-called "European Consensus on Development" agreed between the major EU

---

* Law Faculty, University of Amsterdam.

1. Eurostat, *The EU in the World. 2016 Edition* (Eurostat Statistical Books, Publications Office of the European Union, 2016), Ch. 7 on International Trade.
2. European Commission Publication of figures on 2016 Official Development Assistance (ODA), fact sheet. Available at <europa.eu/rapid/press-release_MEMO-17-949_en.pdf>. ODA is a measurement of development aid unpolluted by military aid etc. agreed by the OECD Development Aid Committee (DAC). In 2016 total EU ODA (EU Institutions, including the EIB and the then 28 Member States) amounted to 75.5 billion and over 50 % of total world ODA.

institutions (Commission, Council and Parliament) and the Member States.[3] The renewal of the Millennium goals under the title "Transforming our world: the 2030 Agenda for Sustainable Development" has recently resulted in a new European Consensus.[4]

2. The common commercial policy

2.1 *The commercial policy competence of the Community*

2.1.1 *The concept of commercial policy and its scope. Article 207 TFEU*[5]

First of all it is important to note that the common commercial policy (CCP) from the beginning has had a liberalization bias, in the sense of wanting to contribute to a progressive reduction of restrictions on international trade and (now also) foreign direct investment, insofar as this is in the common interest.[6] As we saw earlier, the CCP is now clearly embedded in the principles and objectives of the Unions' external action.[7] And it remains based on uniform principles – which implies that differentiation within the CCP can only be limited.

Article 207(1) TFEU does not contain a definition of commercial policy but provides a non-exhaustive[8] list of subject matters: changes in tariff rates, the conclusion of tariff and trade agreements, foreign direct investment, the achievement of uniformity in measures of liberalization, export policy and measures to protect trade such as those to be taken in case of dumping or subsidies. The tariff and trade agreements can relate to trade in goods and services and the commercial aspects of intellectual property, i.e. all the subjects covered by the WTO Agreements. This outlines the core of the CCP, but does not fix its outer boundaries. First the core will be discussed below, followed by a few remarks about the outer boundaries.

This core of the CCP has been expanded, compared to the text of Article 133 (EC) of the Nice Treaty. Next to the commercial aspects of intellectual property also trade in services and foreign direct investment has become fully part of the commercial policy. In the light of Article 3(1)(c) TFEU this means that all these subjects have become part of the exclusive competence of the Union. In the past this was not the case. Opinion 1/94 handed down by the Court on the occasion of the conclusion of the WTO Agreements by the Union declared that only trade in goods (including agricultural goods) and in direct cross-border services fell within the scope of the CCP. Hence the logic of the *ERTA* doctrine on implied exclusive external powers of the Union, presently codified in Article 3(2) TFEU applied to most trade in services and commercial aspects of intellectual property. Since internal legislation covered only limited areas of trade in services and trade-related intellectual property rights, commercial policy as it existed in the real world, in particular in the WTO, did not correspond (any longer) to the notion of commercial policy in the EC Treaty. The Treaty of Lisbon aims to remedy this situation.

---

3. For the text of the European Consensus O.J. 2006, C 46/01. Updated by the Agenda for Change, doc. COM(2011)637 final.
4. See UNGA Res. 70/1 of 21/10/2015. For the new EU Development Consensus, see: Joint statement of the European Parliament, Council, European Commission, The New European Consensus on Development "Our World, Our Dignity, Our Future", O.J. 2017, C 210/1.
5. For a treatment at greater length of the themes discussed here see P. Didier et al., *Politique commerciale commune, Commentaire J. Mégret,* 3rd ed. (Éditions de l'Université de Bruxelles, 2014), 1–68.
6. Art. 206 TFEU. Note that this article, which goes back to Art. 111 of the Treaty of Rome has not been fully adapted to the new realities by referring to the customs union instead of the internal market.
7. Art. 207(1), second sentence, TFEU.
8. Cf. Opinion 1/78, *International Agreement on Natural Rubber*.

In two recent cases, one on intellectual property rights[9] and one on the regulation of television services,[10] the Court has removed any doubt on this score, against the wish of a large number of intervening Member States.

In the first case, *Dai-ichi Sankyo,* the Court was particularly clear, declaring that with the new Article 207 there had been "a significant development of primary law" and implied that the old case law relating to its predecessor provisions, such as Opinion 1/94, could no longer be relied upon to decide questions relating to the scope of the CCP.[11] The Court, falls back on existing criteria for deciding the question whether an EU act falls within the CCP, namely that such an act must have not only have the intention to promote, facilitate or govern trade, but also direct and immediate effects on trade. Only rules on intellectual property with a specific link to international trade will fall under the notion of 'commercial aspects of intellectual property' in Article 207(1). This is true for all rules of the TRIPs Agreement. The context of those rules is the liberalization of international trade, not the harmonization of the laws of the EU Member States.[12]

Along the same lines the Court analysed the second case, concerning the Council of Europe Convention on the legal protection of services based on, or consisting of, conditional access.[13] It was even more obvious than the first case a question of a choice between a legal basis in the CCP or one in the internal market provisions (Art. 114 TFEU). Since the regime of the Convention was broadly in line with the relevant EU Directive (98/84), it would ensure a comparable minimum level of protection all across Europe. Such an outward projection of the Union regime, according to the Court, had a clear link with international trade in those services and hence fell under the common commercial policy.[14]

Both cases thus grapple with the problem that internal and external aspects of the same subject matter have different legal bases, a different vertical division of competences and different decision-making procedures depending on whether the internal or external aspects are the subject of the Union act. However, the Court had already accepted this situation from the beginning of the WTO with respect to the internal and external aspects of agricultural policy.[15] The problem of different decision-making procedures is now solved in Article 207(4), where a parallelism of procedures in the Council is prescribed for trade measures, if corresponding internal measures require unanimity. The problem no longer exists for the role of Parliament now that autonomous legislation in trade policy is adopted by the ordinary legislative procedure and trade agreements require the consent of Parliament.

These cases were confirmed in the Court's long awaited Opinion 2/15 on the Free-Trade Agreement (FTA) with Singapore, together with the Court's view on foreign direct investment.[16] The Court confirmed that foreign direct investment falls under the common commercial policy. The Union has exclusive competence to conclude an agreement,[17] with the exception of non-direct foreign investment, so called "portfolio investment", where the Union shares the

9. Case C-414/11, *Daiichi Sankyo Co et al v. DEMO.*
10. Case C-137/12, *Commission & Parliament v. Council.*
11. Case C-414/11, *Daiichi Sankyo Co et al v. DEMO,* paras. 46–48. This contrasted with the Court's view in Opinion 1/94 *WTO* to the effect that the TRIPs Agreement was a world-wide minimum harmonization of intellectual property.
12. Ibid., paras. 51–52 and 58–60.
13. Case C-137/12, *Commission and Parliament v. Council,* paras. 58–63.
14. Ibid., paras. 64–66.
15. Opinion 1/94, *WTO,* para 29.
16. Opinion 2/15, *Singapore FTA,* paras. 35–36. On the content of the FTA see *infra* section 2.3.5.
17. Opinion 2/15, paras. 81–83.

competence with the Member States.[18] Furthermore, rules on dispute settlement, in the form of institutional provisions linked to the substantive rules on foreign direct investment, are 'ancillary' to these rules and thus fall under the exclusive competence of the Union.[19] However, not where it concerns Investor-State dispute settlement, which enables investors (companies and individuals) to keep cases outside national courts, which would otherwise have had jurisdiction over such cases.[20] Lastly, the Court showed great flexibility in the interpretation of Article 3(2) TFEU, in particular with respect to the criterion that internal rules should broadly cover a certain sector. Unlike in previous cases, it came to the conclusion that existing internal rules on different types of transport (maritime, rail, road etc.) were of this nature, thus leading to the conclusion that the FTA's provisions in these domains were covered by exclusive external competence.[21]

Development policy and environmental policy are integral aspects of a modern concept of commercial policy. Thus the Court has ruled that the Community system of generalized tariff preferences for developing countries (the GSP)[22] and restrictions in trade flows in connection with environmental disasters (e.g. Chernobyl) are part of the common commercial policy, and it is sufficient for these measures to be based on Article 133 EC, without the need to use other provisions of the EC Treaty as joint legal bases.[23] In Opinion 1/78 which concerned the Community's competence relating to an international rubber agreement, the Court saw no reason to exclude the agreement from the domain of the common commercial policy because of its possible repercussions on certain sectors of economic policy, such as the supply of certain raw materials to the Union or because the building up of stocks of a product might have a general political importance.[24]

Ever since the Treaty included provisions on external competence in the area of environmental policy (Arts. 191 et seq. TFEU), and on development cooperation (Arts. 208–211 TFEU), the choice of correct legal basis is determined by the question which aspect can be said, on objective grounds, to be dominant in a legal act of the Union. Recent case law of the Court reveals that only a careful analysis of the text, context, subject matter and objectives of the agreement can determine the ultimate choice of legal basis. This can lead to divergent results. For instance, the Court ruled that the Cartagena Protocol on Biosafety had to be concluded on the basis of 175 EC,[25] but the so-called Energy-Star agreement[26] on energy-efficient labelling programmes for office equipment had to be concluded on the basis of Article 133 EC. In the long run the Court has rather tended towards a double legal basis, since the cases in which trade and environmental matters are of equal weight and highly intertwined within one and the same agreement seem more prevalent among the newer agreements on the borderline between the two policy areas.[27]

As far as other provisions of Article 207 TFEU are concerned, a number of important (mostly new) points need to be signalled. Paragraph 2 makes it clear that the ordinary legislative procedure applies to Union legislation, which will define the framework for *implementing*

18. Ibid., paras. 227, 238.
19. Ibid., para 276.
20. Ibid., para 292.
21. Ibid., para 168 et seq.
22. See *infra* section 2.2.
23. Case 45/86, *Commission v. Council* (GSP) and Case C-62/88, *Greece v. Commission (Chernobyl)*.
24. Opinion 1/78, *International Agreement on Natural Rubber*.
25. Opinion 2/00, *Cartagena protocol*.
26. Case C-281/01, *Commission v. Council* (Energy Star).
27. Case C-94/03, *Commission v. Council* (PICs).

the CCP. It is important to note the term *implementing* here, as this is a reference to Article 291 TFEU on implementing powers. Therefore the actual commercial policy measures, such as the imposition of anti-dumping and countervailing duties and safeguard measures are implementing acts that in principle should be taken by the Commission.[28]

Paragraph 3 lays down the points on which the conclusion of trade agreements differs from the general treaty-making procedure of Article 218 TFEU. What used to be called the *113 or 133 Committee*, the *Trade Advisory Committee* as it is now called, is maintained. As its name implies it gives advice and takes no decisions. It follows generally the development of the Union's trade policy as carried out by the Commission. To this end it meets in different compositions (from Directors-General for Trade of the Member States, to middle level national officials, to simple trade attachés) in many different places in the world, in Brussels, in Geneva at the WTO, in all places in the world where the Union has delegations. This constant activity shows how, even if trade policy is an exclusive power where normally only the Commission is the external actor for the Union, the Member States, through this Committee, are constantly involved in the forming of and checking on the implementation of this policy, even if no formal negotiations are going on.

Paragraph 3 also contains the strange provision that the Council and the Commission shall be responsible for ensuring that the trade agreements negotiated are compatible with existing EU policies and rules. It is obviously the dream of every EU trade negotiator to come to an agreement that requires no changes in EU law. It is also obviously a pipe dream. This provision, therefore, is better read by the negotiators (the Commission) as a warning to be extremely cautious in negotiating those parts of a trade agreement that may affect internal rules and to verify carefully with the Council, and also the Parliament, which must now approve every trade agreement, whether the necessary changes would be acceptable.[29] The provision is all the stranger if one considers that paragraph 4 of Article 207 TFEU contains many safeguards that nothing untoward will happen by requiring unanimity of the Council in cases in which the internal rules require unanimity and in other sensitive areas, in particular in the cultural, audiovisual, social, educational and health services. Moreover, paragraph 5 scrupulously follows the long-standing case law of the Court in respect of international transport services, excluding these services from trade policy because they have their own place in the Treaty.[30] As we saw, recently this formal approach has been much relaxed by the Court with the help of a generous application of Article 3(2) TFEU.

Finally paragraph 6 of Article 207 TFEU protects the Member States from any reflexive effect of the exclusive nature of the CCP, which might render corresponding internal competences exclusive as well,[31] while it also excludes internal harmonization as a consequence of the CCP, where the Treaty excludes such harmonization, i.e. principally in the field of supporting policies mentioned in Article 6 TFEU.[32]

---

28. See *infra* section 2.3.2, at 2 et seq.
29. Cf. in relation to investment law, J. Kleinheisterkamp, "European policy space in international investment law", 27 *ICSID Review* (2012), 416–431, at 425–427.
30. Actually this approach by the Court formally has been maintained ever since Case 22/70, *ERTA*. See also Opinion 1/94, *WTO,* para 53 and Opinion 1/08 *Consolidated GATS Schedule*, paras. 152–173, and most recently Opinion 2/15, *Singapore FTA,* para 54.
31. This is controversial, see W. Weiss, "Common commercial policy in the European constitutional area: EU external trade competence and the Lisbon decision of the German Federal Constitutional Court" in M. Bungenberg and C. Herrmann (Eds.), *European Yearbook of International Economic Law, Special Issue Common Commercial Policy after Lisbon* (Springer, 2013), 29–47, at 35–39.
32. See on these policies and their *de facto* harmonization, Ch. 38, "Supporting policies", of this book.

Returning to the perspective sketched at the beginning of Chapter 39, Article 207 TFEU is indeed representative of the democratization of the Union and in particular in the external relations field. There is also a confirmation of the tendency to have a stronger and more cohesive external action, witness the elimination of the gaps in the exclusive CCP powers, not only in trade in services and trade related intellectual property, but also in the field of foreign direct investment. On the other hand some of the new elements in Article 207 also show a tendency to enhance Member State control over the CCP, in particular by guaranteeing continued mixity in certain respects (exclusion of transport policy[33] and, portfolio investment) and by introducing important safeguards, such as those in paragraphs 4 and 6.

Over the last years, the Juncker Commission sought to modernize trade policy under the slogan "Trade for All", a report released in October 2015.[34] After demonstrating that trade has indeed on the whole been positive for the EU, the report seeks to tackle the new realities in international trade (the growing importance of services and of so-called value chains in international trade) by conducting a new and more transparent trade policy, a value-oriented trade and investment policy and a program of negotiations that can serve to stimulating the international trading system of the WTO and to concluding bilateral or plurilateral trade agreements.

2.1.2 *The exclusivity of Community competence in the field of commercial policy*

Classic case law showed that in the field of commercial policy the Community has exclusive competence in relation to conventional as well as autonomous measures.[35] In Opinion 1/75[36] the Court based this exclusivity on the ground that the common commercial policy was conceived "in the context of the operation of the Common Market, for the defence of the common interests of the Community, within which the particular interests of the Member States must endeavour to adapt to each other". The outward unity of the Union would be threatened if a parallel competence were to be accepted.[37] That is, unless it can be guaranteed that the parallel competences of the Member States are only exercised in accordance with Community law.[38]

Even though the exclusivity of the CCP has now been codified in Article 3(1)(e) TFEU, it is still important to keep in mind the Court's rationale for making it so. In Opinion 1/75, the Court found that no obstacle to the exclusivity of the Union's common commercial policy competence arises from the fact that the obligations and financial burdens inherent in the execution of trade agreements are borne directly by the Member States; such obligations and burdens do not necessarily have to be transferred to the EU Institutions,[39] nor does the implementation of the obligations have to be completely the task of these Institutions.[40] The EU does have the power, however, to enter into financial obligations charged to the Union budget arising from an instrument of the common commercial policy.[41]

33. This exclusion is now mitigated by the broad interpretation of "implied" external competence in the transport field under Art. 3(2) TFEU in Opinion 2/15, *EU –Singapore FTA*, para 54 ff.
34. "Trade for all: Towards a more responsible trade and investment policy", Oct. 2015, available at <trade.ec.europa.eu/doclib/html/153846.htm> (last visited 30 Nov. 2016).
35. Case 41/76, *Suzanne Criel, née Donckerwolcke and Henri Schou v. Procureur de la République au tribunal de grande instance de Lille and Director General of Customs*.
36. Opinion 1/75, *Local cost Standard*, part B.2.
37. Opinion 1/75, *Local cost Standard*, part B.2.
38. More on parallel powers that are presumed to be mutually supportive in section 3.2 *infra* on EU development policy.
39. Opinion 1/75, *Local cost Standard*.
40. Opinion 2/91, *ILO Convention*.
41. Opinion 1/78, *International Agreement on Natural Rubber*. Even if such outlays are not incidental or subsidiary obligations but are an essential part of the system set up, as, for example, in the case of a buffer

In fact, Opinion 1/78[42] reveals that in certain circumstances the question whether the financial burdens arising from an agreement fall on the Member States is nevertheless relevant for the exclusivity or otherwise of the competence.[43] In the case of the financing of buffer stocks in the framework of the international rubber agreement, at issue in Opinion 1/78, the Court held that if the agreement was to be financed from the budgets of the Member States, it was not possible to establish an exclusive competence of the Community to conclude the agreement. Later, in Opinion 1/94, *WTO*, the Court rejected an abusive use of its Opinion 1/78; given that in the case of the WTO, where there is merely an operating budget of the organization, and no quasi-independent funds or buffer stocks, there is not a sufficient financial interest to justify the conclusion of the agreement jointly by the Member States.[44] There is, therefore, no longer any justification under EU law that, in particular in the WTO, the Member States remain Members, next to the Union. Since they will still remain Members of the WTO as a matter of international law, it is unlikely that there will be any change very quickly. Nevertheless the theoretical prospect alone has filled the constitutional court of at least one Member State with great concern.[45]

A wholly different threat to the exclusive character of the CCP as such may come from the side of the national constitutional courts of the Member States and from national parliaments or referendums. In particular the German Constitutional Court (GCC) in its Lisbon judgment stressed that, if the participation of Germany in the WTO were to become merely ceremonial, the loss of statehood would become too great and would be contrary to the German Constitution.[46] One wonders to what extent in the eyes of the GCC the Union can carry through a true implementation of the exclusive nature of the CCP, even without thinking of having the Member States removed from the WTO organs. In the long run a major clash between GCC and ECJ on the common commercial policy cannot be excluded. Furthermore, the Walloon Parliament's refusal to accept the ratification of the Comprehensive Economic and Trade Agreement with Canada (CETA) and the Dutch referendum on the agreement with Ukraine show that national reservations against Union agreements with third States might threaten a successful implementation of that policy.

As always with Union law, it is important to recall that, even in the case of exclusive Union powers, such as the CCP, the actual application of Union law is primarily in the hands of the authorities of the Member States. In the case of the CCP, these are primarily customs, border police, export control authorities and the competent courts of the Member States.

---

stock mechanism which has to be financed as part of the regulatory system of an international commodity agreement.

42. Ibid., para 60.
43. Compare with the findings in Opinion 1/75, *Local cost Standard*, just discussed.
44. Opinion 1/94, *WTO*, paras. 19–21. This may be the position under Union law, but at the international level, i.e. in the WTO itself, third states preferred a situation where the Member States would continue to pay into the WTO budget rather than the Community. Since contributions are trade-weighted in the WTO, the sum of the individual contributions of the Member States is higher than the contribution of the Community would be, as it would be based on its trade with third States only, and not include the trade between Member States. This is an interesting example of a more wide-spread phenomenon, namely that so-called "international realities" may stand in the way of the normal respect for Union law as interpreted by the Court.
45. See the Lisbon Judgment of the German Constitutional Court, 2BvE 2/08, BVerfGE 123, 267, available at <www.bverfg.de/entscheidungen/es20090630_2bve000208.html> (last visited 30 Nov. 2016), discussed immediately *infra*.
46. Ibid., paras. 371–376. See also W. Weiss, op. cit. *supra* note 31.

2.2 *Principles and development of the common commercial policy*

In the arrangements for commercial policy relations by means of autonomous measures, for instance changes in external tariffs or measures concerning imports (autonomous commercial policy), or the conclusion of agreements with third countries (conventional commercial policy), the Union is bound by the applicable international rules, in particular initially the GATT and later the WTO Agreements.

At the heart of the GATT 1947, and thus also of the WTO Agreement, lie the core standards of the most-favoured nation principle (Art. I), the national treatment principle (Art. III) and the prohibition of quantitative restrictions (Art. XI). The first obliges the contracting parties to grant the advantages, of whatever kind, which they grant to any other country relating to the import or export of goods, and now also of services, to all other members of the WTO. Thus, tariff concessions or agreed treatment of providers of services do not merely benefit the contracting party to which they are accorded, but all Members of the WTO. The national treatment principle requires each WTO member to grant national treatment to its partners in respect of internal taxation and legislation. In this manner, trade advantages which have been accorded cannot be in fact rendered nugatory through discriminatory national taxation or legislation. Under the national treatment clause in Article XVII GATS, this principle is conditional as far as services are concerned, i.e. national treatment is only accorded to undertakings in those sectors which a country has inscribed in its Schedule of commitments. The third principle, the prohibition of quantitative restrictions, speaks for itself.[47]

An extremely important exception as far as the Union is concerned is the exception relating to the formation of customs unions and free trade areas which satisfy certain conditions.[48] On the occasion of the establishment, and later of the enlargement, of the Community, the Member States relied on the provision concerning customs unions as against their other GATT partners. Thus they are not obliged to grant the advantages which they accord each other in the Union framework to all their GATT and now WTO partners. The exception for customs unions and free trade areas remains important for the Union, as it has concluded many such agreements with its neighbouring states and with developing countries.[49]

Another important exception to the core principles of the GATT is the Union's Generalized System of Preferences (GSP). This concept, developed and accepted in the United Nations Conference on Trade and Development (UNCTAD), seeks to abolish tariffs for imports from developing countries in order to raise the export revenue of these countries, to promote their industrialization and to accelerate their economic growth. The GATT authorized such preferences – which are clearly in conflict with the most favoured nation principle – originally by means of a so-called "waiver" under Article XXV: 5 GATT, and later by adopting a more general exception for differentiated and more favourable treatment of developing countries.[50] These tariff prefer-

47. Art. XI GATT actually served as model for Art. 34 TFEU and its predecessors. Generally on the influence of the WTO on EU primary and secondary law, see P.J. Kuijper and F. Hoffmeister, "WTO influence on EU law: Too close for comfort?" in R. Wessel and S. Blockmans (Eds.), *Between Autonomy and Dependence. The EU Legal Order under the Influence of International Organisations* (Asser, 2013), at 131–158.
48. Art. XXIV(4)–(8) GATT and Articles V and Va GATS.
49. The EEA Agreement (creating the European Economic Area with Norway, Iceland and Liechtenstein) establishes a free trade area in goods and a common market in other sectors of the economy. The agreement with Switzerland concerning trade in goods is a free trade agreement. The Agreements concluded with countries of the former Yugoslavia also aim to create a free trade area between the Union and each individual country; only the Association agreement with Turkey provides for a customs union with the EU, which was realized in 1995.
50. The so-called Enabling Clause, see BISD 26S, at 203.

ences were to be introduced autonomously by all industrialized countries, on a non-reciprocal basis and on the basis of non-discrimination. In 1971 the Community was one of the first developed economies to make use of the possibility to introduce such a GSP.

Presently, preferences are granted to more than 140 developing countries, including so-called economies in transition, certain Eastern European countries and countries of the former Soviet Union. Of all these countries, 50 so-called "least-developed countries" according to the criteria of the UN profit from the total freedom of customs duties for "everything but arms". This initiative by Commissioner Lamy was first enacted in 2001 and is now an integral part of the latest GSP Regulation.[51] The Union, like the United States, has always sought to discriminate between different groups of countries profiting from the GSP, but it has normally followed the road of positive discrimination. The principle of such positive discrimination has been upheld by a WTO Panel and the Appellate Body in a case brought by India against the old GSP regime of the Community that expired in 2004.[52]

Next to "everything but arms" for the least-developed countries, there is now a special incentive arrangement (GSP+), which provides for additional preferences for countries that have ratified a number of core human rights and labour conventions, as well as a number of international conventions in the field of environmental protection and good governance (mainly relating to combating illicit drugs and corruption).[53] The special incentive arrangement may be withdrawn when its conditions are no longer fulfilled.[54] In addition the Commission may also apply a special safeguard procedure when imports of products under the GSP regime cause serious difficulties to Community producers of like products.[55]

Finally, the dispute settlement system of the WTO should be mentioned as an important external element influencing the EC's commercial policy.[56] The reports and decisions of the panels and the Appellate Body of the WTO are binding, and can be enforced insofar as the country which has "won" the case may request an authorization to apply trade sanctions from the WTO Dispute Settlement Body.[57] The Union is represented before the panels and the Appellate Body by the Commission. If the Union wants to start a case against a third country or appeal a report from a panel, the Commission discusses the matter with the Trade Advisory Committee of the Council before going ahead.[58]

---

51. Reg. (EU) 978/2012, O.J. 2012, L 303/1, Art. 1(2)(c) and Arts. 17–18.
52. See Cases WT/DS 242 and 246, *EC – Generalized System of Preferences.* For more detail see J. Harrison, "Incentives for development: The EC's generalized system of preferences, India's WTO challenge and reform", 42 CML Rev. (2005), 1663 et seq.
53. This "special incentive arrangement" is laid down in Art. 1(2)(b) and Arts. 9–16 Regulation 978/2012, O.J. 2012, L 303/1. The relevant conventions are listed in Annex 9.
54. For the full Commission procedure for such temporary withdrawal see Arts. Arts 19 and 21 of Reg. (EU) 978/2012.
55. See Art. 22 et seq. of Reg. (EU) 978/2012.
56. For a comparative approach see P.J. Kuijper, "The Court of Justice and the Appellate Body: Between constitutionalism and dispute settlement" in S. Gaines, B. Olsen and K. Sørensen (Eds.), *Liberalising Trade in the EU and the WTO: Comparative Perspectives* (CUP, 2012), at 99–138.
57. See Arts. 21 and 22 WTO Dispute Settlement Understanding.
58. In case the Union is defendant, there is little time, as the deadlines of the WTO procedures, especially before the Appellate Body, are exceedingly short and the Commission has to prepare its defence as soon as it is notified of the case against it. In specific cases the Commission works closely together with Member States that are particularly affected, in order to clarify the facts of the case. An example is the so-called *Airbus* case, Case WT/DS 316, *EC – Measures Affecting Trade in Large Civil Aircraft,* where the Member States of the Airbus consortium, France, Germany, Spain and the UK were indispensable to mounting a complete defence.

The WTO dispute settlement system has contributed to reappraisal of the non-reciprocal character of the preferential system of cooperation with the ACP countries and the countries in the Mediterranean area. In a series of panel proceedings, concerning the EC banana policy[59] in favour of certain ACP countries, first the non-reciprocal character of these preferences was characterized as discriminatory vis-à-vis the developing countries that are not part of these systems of cooperation; such discrimination could not be considered permissible under certain GATT provisions. In addition, the specific authorization by the WTO of the retention of the non-reciprocal character of the cooperation with ACP countries turned out eventually to be insufficient. Although undoubtedly there were also political reasons for a re-examination of the non-reciprocal nature of ACP and Mediterranean cooperation, these panel proceedings certainly also had a contributory effect.[60] The banana case itself was finally settled after repeated interventions by special mediators and protracted negotiations.[61]

Also internal trade rules may fall foul of the WTO's rules, especially those on TBT and SPS. The *Hormones* case is an example. In this case the EU had placed a ban on the importation of beef from the US and Canada that had been treated with certain growth-inducing hormones. The panel and the Appellate Body found that a proper risk assessment as required by Articles 5.1 and 5.2 of the SPS Agreement was lacking, when the Union imposed its ban. Moreover, the EU had relied too lightly on the precautionary principle according to the Appellate Body.[62] The EU was thus obliged to remove the ban, but was not willing to do this. Instead it commissioned new scientific studies and took a new decision banning imports of hormone-treated beef from the US and Canada – which was not acceptable to the panel that had to check on the implementation by the EU of the earlier panel and Appellate Body reports. That led to a situation in which the EU maintained its ban and at the same time had to accept trade sanctions from the US and Canada authorized by the responsible WTO bodies. A satisfactory solution was found by agreements concluded between the EU and first the US (2009) and later Canada (2011), although that did not lead to a removal of the ban – which was politically unthinkable in the EU.[63]

Where a Commission regulation is sufficient to modify a Council Regulation, the Union is usually capable of implementing the necessary modification of its legislation within the period set by the DSU of normally 15 months from the adoption of the panel report.[64] In other cases where a basic Regulation adopted by the ordinary legislative procedure by Council and Parliament needs to be amended on the basis of a proposal of the Commission it will be extremely difficult to respect this deadline. In order to simplify a speedy implementation of panel or Appellate Body rulings a special procedure has been devised in the field of anti-dumping and countervailing duties, which will be discussed further below. Recently a similarly speedy procedure for the implementation of rights obtained through panel and Appellate Body reports in other areas has been introduced (see sect 2.3.4 below).

59. See Case WT/DS 27, *EC – Regime for the Importation, Sale and Distribution of Bananas.*
60. On the EU-ACP Cotonou Convention and the so-called Economic Partnership Agreements (EPAs), see *infra* section 4.2.5.
61. WTO Doc. WT/L/784. The compromise formula consisted of a banana tariff of Euro 148 per tonne to be reduced to Euro 114 over 8 years, while the ACP countries would be compensated for their loss of preferences by extra financial assistance, see Reg. (EU) 1341/2011 amending Reg. (EC) 1905/2006 establishing a financing instrument for development cooperation, O.J. 2011, L 347/34.
62. Case WT/DS 26 and WT/DS 48, *EC – Measures concerning meat and meat products (Hormones).*
63. See press releases IP/09/707 (US) and of 17 Mar. 2011 (Canada).
64. Art. 21(3)(c) DSU.

2.3 Commercial policy arrangements

2.3.1 Autonomous commercial policy: Regulation of imports and exports

The EU's regime for imports and exports of goods has been much simplified over the last twenty years because of the following developments inside and outside the Union. (1) At the beginning of 1993 the single market was "completed" and this made it impossible over time that Member States could maintain individual quantitative restrictions in respect of third countries and the concomitant barriers inside the single market. Article 134 EC (previously Art. 115 EEC) that allowed this disappeared from the Treaty entirely after Lisbon. (2) At the same time the Communist system of planned economies and planned international trade between the countries of the so-called Comecon started to disintegrate. (3) Shortly afterwards the Uruguay round was completed, which made many quantitative restrictions, especially so-called "voluntary" export restraints on textile trade, agreed between many developing countries on the one side and the US or the EC on the other, disappear over a period of ten years, as agreed in the Agreement on Textiles and Clothing (ATC) of the WTO. (4) The formerly Communist States, notably the big trading powers China (2002) and Russia (2012) became WTO Members and thus had to be treated, in principle, as all other WTO Members.

Long before the simplification of external policy in relation to quantitative restrictions that resulted from the above developments took place, the Common Customs Tariff was established, much earlier than envisaged in the EEC Treaty, on 1 July 1968. Furthermore, harmonized or common rules have been adopted in the field of customs legislation, and were codified in the Community Customs Code, in parallel with the completion of the Community's internal market.[65]

The import and export regime of the EU was codified in 2009 and as a consequence of these developments is now quite simple to understand for WTO Members, as it conforms to the prohibition of quantitative restrictions of Article XI GATT. The import regime, which is combined with the rules for safeguards is completely liberalized,[66] except for certain quantitative restrictions on textile products that have remained since they were not covered by the ATC and for the special regime set up for countries that are in the process of accession to the WTO or are still in a transitional period after accession.[67] Insofar as there are still restrictions on textile trade these have been consolidated into one Regulation that basically maintains a general system of surveillance over a limited number of sensitive textile products from all origins and contains a system of textile quota based on an agreement with Serbia.[68]

---

65. Since then the Customs Code has been modernized in 2008 and recast in 2013, Reg. (EU) 952/2013, O.J. 2013 L 269/1. The Customs Code entered into force only on May 1, 2016, after all delegated acts and implementing acts, replacing earlier comitology decisions, had been taken pursuant to the new powers of Arts. 290 and 291 TFEU. See Ch. 12, "The functioning of the internal market", of this book.
66. Council Reg. (EU) 2015/478 on common rules for imports (codified version), O.J. 2015, L 83/16, Art. 1.
67. Council Reg. (EC) 625/2009 on common rules for imports from certain third countries (codified version), O.J. 2009, L 185/1. This regulation differs only little from Reg. (EC) 260/2009. The countries covered are all ex-USSR states in the process of accession to the WTO and North Korea.
68. Council Reg. (EEC) 3030/93 for import of certain textile products from third countries. A consolidated version is available at <trade.ec.europa.eu/doclib/docs/2006/august/tradoc_129742.pdf> (last visited 30 Nov. 2016).

The Community's export regime has been based already since 1969 on the principle that exports to third countries are unrestricted.[69 70]

However, the common rules on imports and exports contain a number of exceptions. Some of them run parallel not only to Article XX and XXI GATT but also to Articles 30 and 347 TFEU, in that they may be unilaterally invoked by the Member States. They are clauses which permit each of the Member States to apply quantitative restrictions or supervisory measures justified on the grounds of public policy, public morality, public security; the health and life of humans, animals and plants; the protection of national treasures possessing artistic, historic or archaeological value; or the protection of industrial and commercial property.[71] In addition the export regime includes the exception on the ground of a "critical shortage" of certain essential products in the Union: in such cases quantitative restrictions may be introduced.[72] At the moment no use is made of this provision, which is an exception that has to be invoked at the Community level. Furthermore, Member States may also impose restrictions on imports or exports in connection with special formalities which are introduced, in conformity with the TFEU, on the ground of international agreements.[73] This latter category embraces in particular matters such as trade restrictions applying to certain endangered species and hazardous waste.

The general regulations on the import and export regimes play only a supplementary role as far as imports and exports of agricultural products are concerned. These are governed in first instance by the relevant provisions of the rules for the common organization of agricultural markets.[74] The rules for processed agricultural products also establish a special regime for those products. For both types of product this system has been based on a so-called Union preference for products in the common market, the subsidized export of Union surpluses, and specific protective measures against imports from third countries, as long as certain conditions are fulfilled.[75]

As to the manner in which the Member States promote exports to third countries relatively little has been done in the way of introducing uniform principles in the sense of Article 207 TFEU. Pure *export promotion*, in the sense of propaganda for national products is probably still permissible for the Member States. But once propaganda for a Member State's own products develops into the provision of substantive advantages, the realm of distortion of competition between Union undertakings is reached and the national aid measures for exports to third countries[76] should be harmonized. In addition, it cannot be excluded that the competitive relationships within the Union are distorted by national aids to exports, and thus Article 107 TFEU on

69. Council Reg. (EU) 2015/479 on common rules for exports (codification), O.J. 2015, L 83/34, Art. 1. As to the export of dual-use goods, see *infra* note 83, et seq.
70. The exception, allowing Member States to maintain unilateral export restrictions for a small number of products, including petroleum, lapsed in 1991, Reg. (EEC) 3918/91, O.J. 1991, L 372/31. The Member States retain only the limited possibility to take measures restricting exports in the framework of the "sharing system" of the International Energy Agency, see Art. 8 of Reg. (EC) 2015/479.
71. See Art. 24(2) Reg. (EC) 260/2009 and Art. 10 Reg. (EC) 1061/2009.
72. Art. 5 Reg. (EU) 2015/479.
73. Art. 24(1) Reg. (EU) 2015/478.
74. See e.g. Art. 25 Reg. (EC) 260/2009 and Art. 10 Reg. (EU) 2015/479. As of 1 Jan. 2008, Reg. (EC) 1234/2007 replaced previous individual common organizations of the market by one horizontal regulation, O.J. 2007, L 299/1; see in particular Part III, Trade with Third Countries.
75. See Ch. 30, "Agriculture and fisheries", of this book.
76. See former Art. 132 EC. The tying of bilateral (development) aid to purchases in the donor country can come within this, but a Commission initiative to come to an "unbundling" of development aid at Community level was not dealt with by the Council, cf. Doc. SEC(91)2273. The Parliament subsequently adopted a Resolution calling for the complete untying of all official aid, see A5/2003/190, Bulletin/2003/9, 1.6.64.

state aids may be brought into play.[77] Proposals from the Commission on harmonization of the causes of this problem have not met with success.

However, in respect of export credits, in 1978 the Council adopted on behalf of the Community the OECD consensus on an Arrangement on Guidelines for Officially Supported Export Credits. This was done on the basis of the Community's exclusive competence recognized by the Court's Opinion 1/75.[78] The EU recently has developed the unusual legislative technique of annexing the Guidelines to a Regulation, which states that the Arrangement applies in the Union and delegates the power of adopting the OECD's recurring modifications to the Guidelines under certain conditions to the Commission. This makes the Guidelines and their regular adaptations, which formally are not binding, obligatory for the Union.[79] This is not as odd as it might seem, as specific parts of the Guidelines have already been rendered binding for the Union by the Subsidies Agreement of the WTO.[80]

Financial instruments relating to the development of trade with particular countries or territories remain in the hands of the Member States. This can only tally with the Community's exclusive competence in the field of export policy as long as the rules governing the use of such instruments provide for "a strict uniformity of credit conditions granted to undertakings in the Community whatever their nationality" as required by the Court in Opinion 1/75.[81] A first step in this direction has been taken by the adoption of a directive on the harmonization of the most important provisions concerning export credit insurance for transactions with medium and long-term cover.[82]

Finally there are export restraints that Member States used to maintain for strategic reasons purely at the national level. Some of these were indeed purely national, but many were based or became to be based on international agreements, such as the Chemical Weapons Convention and the Biological and Toxin Weapons Convention, or on informal arrangements, such as the Missile Technology Control Regime (MCTR) and the Nuclear Suppliers Group (NSG). The purely military goods fall under the general exception for such goods of Article 346 TFEU, but the so-called precursors and dual use goods, i.e. goods that are used in the production of military goods and goods that have both civil and military uses do not. When the ECJ decided that export of such goods fell within the exclusive power of the Union's CCP in the *Werner and Leifer* cases,[83] this led to the adoption of a EU export regulation for dual use goods. The present version of this regulation[84] covers the export, transfer, brokering, technical assistance and transit of dual use items. The dual use items listed in Annex I are subject to an export authorization that will be issued by the authorities of the relevant Member State. In specific instances Member States may refuse export authorizations for all or specific destinations even for non-listed dual use goods.[85] For a limited number of these goods a "Community General Export Authoriza-

77. Case C-142/87, *Belgium v. Commission.*
78. Opinion 1/75, *Local cost Standard.*
79. For this post-Lisbon method see Reg. (EU) 1233/2011, O.J. 2011, L 326/45, et seq. It is interesting to note that delegated legislative power is used to reach the same effect as the procedure of Art. 218(7) TFEU.
80. See item (k) of the illustrative list of export subsidies in Annex I of the SCM Agreement. Art. 3(2) of that agreement prohibits such export subsidies.
81. See Opinion 1/75, *Local cost Standard.*
82. Dir. (EC) 98/29, O.J. 1998, L 148/22.
83. See Cases C-70/94, *Werner v. Germany* and C-83/94, *Criminal Proceedings against Peter Leifer, Reinhold Otto Krauskopf and Otto Holzer.*
84. Reg. (EC) 428/2009 setting up a Community regime for the control of exports, transfer, brokering and transit of dual use items, O.J. 2009, L 134/1.
85. Art. 3(2) and 4 of Reg. (EC) 428/2009. This is limited to the components of nuclear, chemical and biological and toxin weapons and their delivery vehicles. Se also Art. 8 which also opens this possibility for reasons

tion" is available for a small group of trusted third countries.[86] The Commission is authorized to modify the list of dual use items under delegated powers pursuant to Article 290 TFEU.[87]

In early 2016 the Commission published a Communication on the review of the EU's export control policy, which sought to reconcile the emergence of new security risks and threats and rapid technological and scientific developments on the one hand and the increasing importance of global supply chains in the production of sophisticated equipment on the other hand.[88] This has resulted in a Commission proposal for an important overhaul of the 2009 regime for export control.[89]

Another example of a general restraint on export, which Member States used to employ individually and which has gradually been "communitarized" after the achievement of the internal market, is the control of export of cultural goods. The system is the same as for strategic goods, with annexes containing lists of the controlled goods and a procedure for granting individual licenses by the authorities of the Member States.[90] A similar regime has also been introduced for goods to be used in the execution of capital punishment and torture.[91] This is clearly linked to the prohibition of capital punishment and of torture in Articles 2(2) and 4 of the EU Charter of Fundamental Rights. The export interdiction of chemical substances that can be used in administering capital punishment under this Regulation has been quite effective in limiting the number of executions in the United States for example.

2.3.2 *Autonomous commercial policy: Safeguard measures*

The basic Regulation on the common rules for imports[92] provides for the possibility of keeping a weather eye on the import of industrial products – which has been liberalized within the Union framework. First, there are provisions on a EU information and consultation procedure, which forms the first step towards the adoption of surveillance or safeguard measures. In the context of this procedure the Member States may provide information to the Commission and request that such measures be adopted. Such a request is discussed in the Committee on Safeguards, which is a Committee within the meaning of Regulation 182/2011, and oversees the Commission's implementing powers.[93]

If the discussion in the committee gives cause, and if the Commission is of opinion that there is sufficient evidence, a Community investigation procedure may be initiated. The Commission is charged with undertaking this investigation, and is bound to follow the rules laid down in the basic regulation on the common rules for imports.

---

of public security and human rights considerations.

86. Annex II of Reg. 428/2009. This group of countries consists of Australia, Canada, Japan, New Zealand, Norway, Switzerland and the United States.
87. Art. 15 and 23a of Reg. 428/2009.
88. In spite of the problems signalled by the Commission in its Communication, there has been no case law on Reg. 428/2009.
89. For the Communication, see doc. COM(2016)244 final and for the proposal doc. COM(2016)616 final.
90. Reg. (EC) 116/2009 on the export of cultural goods (Codified version), O.J. 2009, L 39/1.
91. Reg. (EC) 1236/2005 concerning trade in certain goods which could be used for capital punishment, torture or other cruel and inhuman or degrading treatmemt, O.J. 2005, L 200/1. For a broader treatment of these special export regimes, see P. Didier et al., *Politique commerciale commune, Commentaire J. Mégret*, 3rd ed. (Éditions de l'Université de Bruxelles, 2014), 244–254.
92. Reg. (EU) 2015/478, cited *supra* note 66.
93. Reg. (EU) 182/2011 of the EP and the Council laying down the rules and general principles concerning mechanisms for control by Member States of the Commission's exercise of implementing powers, O.J. 2011, L 55/13. More generally on the subject of implementing powers, see Ch. 7, "Lawmaking", of this book.

Surveillance measures may take one of two forms: Union retrospective surveillance or Union prior surveillance. The latter measures are clearly more restrictive, requiring the presentation of an import document in order to place the goods in free circulation within a Member State, even though the document is to be endorsed free of charge and within five days of request by the importer. In certain cases the Commission may decide to impose regional surveillance measures, which are limited to one or two regions (often Member States) of the Union.

Safeguard measures may be adopted by the Commission for protection of the interests of the Union if a product is imported into the Union in such increased quantities and/or[94] under such conditions that Union producers of like or directly competing products are seriously injured or if such serious injury threatens to occur. Such measures are adopted by the Commission after having followed the examination procedure in the Safeguards Committee. The measures may be of a Union or regional nature and may also have a preventative character.[95]

After the strict interpretation given by the WTO Appellate Body of the requirements for imposing safeguards[96] in the late 1990s, safeguards are no longer used very frequently anywhere. This is also true for the EU; in the early 2000s there are still three cases, covering certain steel products, mandarins and farmed salmon. Since the codified version of the Regulation on the common rules for imports entered into force in January 2010 no safeguards have been imposed at all. Surveillance often has a chilling effect on imports already and anti- dumping duties are considered more effective.[97]

Of somewhat more practical importance is the regulation on common rules for imports from state trading countries.[98] Here the conditions for instituting surveillance measures and for the application of safeguard measures are less stringently formulated, as most of the countries to which that regulation applies are not yet members of the WTO and, if they are, a transitional special safeguard clause may apply for a period agreed in their WTO accession agreements.[99] Union surveillance may be instituted simply whenever the interests of the Union so require, no threat of injury required.[100] In case safeguard measures are taken, their adoption may be justified either by reference to the conditions *or* to the increased quantities in which the relevant product is imported. Regional surveillance or safeguard measures are possible under this regulation as well.[101]

94. Art. 16(1) Reg. (EU) 2015/478, is to a large extent taken from Art. XIX GATT; this makes both conditions mandatory; see also Art. 16(2) of the regulation. Case law of the WTO has put renewed emphasis on the unforeseen circumstances in which the increase in imports takes place under Art. XIX GATT, see Case WT/DS 98, *Korea-Dairy*. An amendment of the regulation still seems necessary.
95. Arts. 16, 17 and 18 of Reg. (EU) 2015/478.
96. For a critical account of this jurisprudence, see J. Greenwald, "WTO dispute settlement: An exercise in trade law legislation?", 6 *Journal of International Economic Law* (2003), 113. See also Case WT/DS 98, *Korea-Dairy* for an example of such strict interpretation.
97. See the story of the farmed salmon case. Commission Reg. (EC) 206/2005 imposing definitive safeguard measures against imports of farmed salmon, O.J. 2005, L 33/8-29, revoked less than two months later by Commission Reg. (EC) 627/2005, O.J. 2005, L 104/4 and "succeeded" by Council Reg. (EC) 85 imposing a definitive anti-dumping duty and collecting definitively the provisional duty imposed on imports of farmed salmon originating in Norway, O.J. 2006, L 15/1-23. The EU lost the subsequent WTO case started by Norway, see WT/DS 337.
98. Council Reg. (EU) 2015/755 on common rules for imports from certain third countries, O.J. 2015, L 123/33.
99. As a consequence there was a special regulation on a transitional product-specific safeguard mechanism for China, Reg. (EC) 427/2003, O.J. 2003, L 65/1 which was used only once and has expired in 2004.
100. Art. 7 Reg. (EU) 2015/755, O.J. 2009, L 185/1, as modified by Reg. (EU) 37/2014, O.J. 2014, L 18/1, Art. 1.
101. See Arts. 4 and 13 Reg. (EC) 2015/755, as modified.

In the framework of the common rules for imports of textile products, in spite of the integration of textile products into the WTO, surveillance is pretty well permanent. Textiles and clothing remain a sensitive sector of the EU economy. The Member States have to provide the Commission with monthly reports of the quantities and origin of imports of textiles covered by the regulation, and with annual information about the export of textile products.[102] In this manner the Commission can evaluate at any given moment whether a Union investigation procedure should be initiated; a Member State may also request that this occur. Such a procedure runs in a broadly similar manner to that provided for in the general rules on imports.[103]

Again, measures against textile imports from non-market economy countries may be adopted under less stringent conditions than those applicable to imports from market economy countries. The Commission has received delegated legislative powers pursuant to Article 290 TFEU and in taking the various steps in starting investigations, taking surveillance measures and imposing safeguards it follows the rules of the relevant Regulation 182/2011.[104]

Imposition and management of import restrictions on textiles is now regulated at Union level. At the request of the Member States the authorizations are granted centrally by the Commission on a first-come, first-served basis. An advanced data processing system has been set up in the Union for this purpose. If the authorizations are not used within a brief period of validity, they must be returned to the Member State concerned, which returns them to the pool of available central authorizations. Thus, after the Court on grounds of principle had found against the division of quotas among Member States,[105] even in one of the most sensitive sectors of the economy, for which the Court had originally been prepared to countenance an exception, it has proved possible to introduce a real Union system of quota management for textiles.

More generally, the management of quantitative quotas is governed by Regulation 717/2008.[106] In addition to the first-come, first-served technique, two other methods of quota management are prescribed in this Regulation, depending on the circumstances. (1) The method of allocation of quotas according to traditional trade flows. This method has been codified in the WTO Agreement on Safeguards and is used for safeguards against WTO Members.[107] (2) Distribution in relation to the quantities requested. This method is primarily applied in cases in which the quota will probably be quickly exhausted.

---

102. Art. 6 Reg. (EU) 2015/936 on common rules for imports of textile products from certain third countries not covered by bilateral agreements, protocols or other arrangements or by other specific Union import rules, O.J. 2015, L 160/1-54.
103. Compare Arts. 6–10 Reg. (EU) 2015/936 with Arts. 5–10 Reg. (EC) 260/2009.
104. See Reg. (EU) 2015/9 *supra* note 103. The import regime for textiles has thus become a nice case study in delegated legislation and the advisory and examination procedures for implementing legislation at the same time.
105. See Case 51/87, *Commission v. Council.*
106. Reg. (EC) 717/2008 establishing a Community procedure for administering quantitative quota, O.J. 2008, L 198/1, codifying Reg. 520/94, O.J. 1994, L 66/1. Quantitative quota stand in contrast to tariff quota, which are quota within which lower or no tariffs apply than above the quota level. The latter are considered tariffs in the WTO/GATT, the former are in principle quantitative restrictions contrary to Art. XI GATT, but justified in exceptional circumstances.
107. Cf. Arts. 6–11 Reg. (EC) 717/2008 with Art. 5 of the Agreement on Safeguards of the WTO. In addition, the regulation takes account of individual traditional importers and not just traditional trade flows in general.

2.3.3 Anti-dumping duties and countervailing duties

Anti-dumping

Dumping and the use of subsidies are regarded as unfair trading practices because a company or a country does not, unlike in the case of safeguards, simply use its comparative advantage to export large quantities of products at low prices, but in fact artificially changes its comparative costs. In the case of subsidization this occurs through state subsidies; in the case of dumping this occurs because a company is prepared to export a product for a long period at a lower price than the sales price applicable on its domestic market, and sometimes even at a lower price than the cost price.[108] It will be evident that this is only possible if the products cannot flow back onto the company's domestic market, and that dumping presupposes a certain division of markets, which in international trade is frequently present in the form of tariffs.[109]

The present EU Regulations on anti-dumping[110] and on protection against subsidized imports[111] together with the regulations on the common rules for import and export were subject to a major modification in early 2014, when they were adapted to the post-Lisbon system of implementing powers. This was an important modification, as it meant that in principle anti-dumping and countervailing duties are imposed henceforth by the Commission in a domain that heretofore was considered too political to be left fully to it alone, even if its work was instrumental in doing the anti-dumping and countervail investigations and producing the regulations that contained the results from these investigations. It is remarkable how closely the text of the two regulations hews to the wording of the WTO Agreements on anti-dumping and on subsidies. This is openly acknowledged in the preamble of both regulations,[112] in response to provisions in the two WTO Agreements which insist that Members shall make their legislation conform fully to the text of the agreements.[113]

Under Article 1(1) of Regulation 2016/1036, anti-dumping duties "may be applied to any dumped product whose release for free circulation in the Community causes injury". The concepts of dumping and injury are thus the crucial concepts in the regulation. Under Article 1(2) of the Regulation a product is considered to have been dumped "if its export price to the Community is less than a comparable price for the like product, in the ordinary course of trade, as established for the exporting country". This is the so-called "normal value" of the product, and is "based on the prices paid or payable, in the ordinary course of trade, by independent customers in the exporting country", according to Article 2(1). The export price is the "price actually paid or payable for the product when sold for export from the exporting country to the

---

108. For a limited period of time, sales at prices below the cost of production or below marginal cost may be a legitimate market strategy, see A. Deardorff, "Economic perspectives on antidumping law" in J. Jackson and E. Vermulst (Eds.), *Antidumping Law and Practice, A Comparative Study* (Ann Arbor, 1990), at 23–39.
109. Within a common market like the EU anti-dumping measures are justified only during a transitional period, when market separation is still possible, cf. the old Art. 91 EC which was repealed by the Treaty of Amsterdam.
110. Council Reg. (EU) 2016/1036 on protection against dumped imports from countries not members of the European Community, O.J. 2016, L 176/21-54, codified version (basic anti-dumping regulation).
111. Council Reg. (EU) 2016/1037 on protection of subsidized imports from countries not members of the European Community, O.J. 2009, L 188/93-126, codified version (basic countervailing duty regulation).
112. See 3rd preambular para of Reg. (EU) 2016/1036 and 3rd preambular para of Reg. (EU) 2016/1037, O.J. 2009, L 188/93 which state that it is desirable that the text of the regulations should stay as close as possible to those of the WTO Agreements.
113. Art. 18.4 of the Anti-Dumping Agreement and Art. 32.5 of the Agreement on Subsidies and Countervailing Duties.

Community".[114] The difference between the normal value and the export price is what is called the dumping margin.[115] The anti-dumping duty may not be higher than the dumping margin. In the EU – unlike the United States – the practice has developed of imposing anti-dumping duties that are lower than the dumping margin, but adequate to remove the injury to Union industry.[116] This brings us back to the other crucial concept in the Regulation: injury, which – according to Article 3 of the Regulation – means, material injury to the Union industry, or the threat of such injury, or even the material retardation of the establishment of such an industry. This involves both the volume and price of the dumped imports on the Union market, on the one hand, and the consequent impact on the relevant branch of the Union industry, on the other. In addition to the presence of dumping and injury, it is also required to establish that the imposition of anti-dumping duties is in the EU interest. The most recent version of the Regulation includes, in Article 21, extensive provisions on this score.

Anti-dumping law as set out above might appear fairly simple, but it is in reality extremely complex, as the establishment of the normal value and the export price is usually far from straightforward, particularly in the case of trade within or between different entities of large multinationals. On their domestic markets they may distribute their products through subsidiaries rather than to independent buyers directly, and on their export markets this also often occurs. In non-market economy countries neither domestic prices nor costs are of much use. In these circumstances recourse is had to a constructed normal value, which is calculated on the basis of production costs plus a reasonable amount for selling, general and administrative costs and for profits, or on the basis of export prices to an appropriate third country,[117] or else to a constructed export price calculated on the basis of the price at which the imported products are first resold to an independent buyer.[118] Furthermore, in order to achieve a valid comparison at the same level of trade between the normal value and the export price, adjustments are often necessary on account of discounts and rebates, indirect taxes, transport costs, and differences in physical characteristics of the products concerned between products sold on the domestic market and products sold to the Community market.[119]

It is obvious that the question of non-market economy status, either as a country or as a sector in the economy of a country or as individual enterprise due to the governmental or quasi governmental status of a company is already now and will continue to be one of the hottest issues in the anti-dumping practice of the Commission and in the case law of the Court of Justice.[120] With a view to China's losing its non-market economy status at the end of 2016, according

114. Art. 2(8) Reg. (EU) 2016/1036.
115. Art. 2(12) Reg. (EU) 2016/1036. The Commission's practice of calculating the dumping margin without taking account of the so-called positive dumping margin (the so-called zeroing technique) has been condemned by a WTO panel and the Appellate Body, see WT/DS 141, *EC-Bed Linen*.
116. Art. 9(4) Reg. (EU) 2016/1036. The Commission has proposed to make this rule optional. See I. Van Bael and J.-F. Bellis, *EU Anti-Dumping and Other Trade Defence Instruments* (Wolters/Kluwer, 2011).
117. Art. 2(3) Reg. (EU) 2016/1036. Since such constructed normal value may make it easier to find dumping; countries considered non-market economies strive to be omitted from the list attached to the Reg., see e.g. Reg. (EC) 2117/2005 through which Ukraine was so omitted, O.J. 2005, L 340/17. According to its accession agreement to the WTO China will have to be omitted from the list by 31 Dec. 2016.
118. Art. 2(9) Reg. (EU) 2016/1036.
119. Art. 2(10) Reg. (EU) 2016/1036.
120. The Commission often relies on presumptions in these matters, which the Court seems less and less willing to accept. See R. Denton, "The non-market economy rules of the European Community's anti-dumping and countervailing duties legislation", 36 ICLQ (1987), 198–239; E. Vermulst, "The 10 major problems with the anti-dumping instrument in the European Community", 39 JWT (2005), 105–113, at 110. See also, for example, Case T-498/04, *Zhejiang Xinan Chemical Industrial Group Co. Ltd v. Council*, appealed as C-337/09,

to its accession agreement to the WTO, the Commission has made a proposal for an amendment to the basic anti-dumping regulation that would enable the Commission to decide during an investigation that certain sectors of a country's economy are distorted due to government interference or massive presence of state-owned and state-run enterprises. On that basis normal value would be based on undistorted prices or benchmarks, found on the international market or in an appropriate representative country with a similar level of development as the exporting country[121] This proposal builds on earlier Commission proposals of April 2013 on the modernization of the trade defence instruments which included proposals for increased transparency of the procedure, the elimination of the "lesser duty rule" and a number of smaller improvements in the procedure.[122] These two sets of proposals have led to an agreement in principle on the alternative for across-the-board non-market-economy treatment per country,[123] while the older proposals of 2013 are still being discussed between the institutions.

Subsidies and countervailing measures

The current version of the Agreement on Subsidies and Countervailing Measures, concluded in the framework of the WTO, contrary to the preceding version dating back to the Tokyo Round (1979) provides for a definition of a subsidy. Thus Articles 2 and 3 of the basic Subsidy Regulation largely reflect the definition of a subsidy in the new Agreement, and the conditions under which a subsidy is or is not countervailable. A subsidy is deemed to exist whenever there is "financial contribution by a government in the country of origin or export,"[124] and a benefit is thereby conferred on the subsidized enterprise or body. Subsidies only lead to the imposition of countervailing duties if they are specific, i.e. where access to a subsidy is explicitly limited to certain enterprises and there is no general availability of subsidies according to objective and neutral criteria.[125] Article 3(4) of the Regulation provides that certain types of subsidies, such as those contingent upon export performance or on the use of domestic rather than imported goods, are deemed to be specific. On the other hand, certain specific subsidies are exempt from the possible application of countervailing duties: subsidies for research and technological development up to certain levels, subsidies for regional development subject to stringent conditions, and certain environmental subsidies. Similar exceptions in the WTO Agreement on Subsidies and Countervailing Measures, however, were limited in time and it proved impossible to reach agreement on their prolongation. This has led to a WTO vulnerability of such EU subsidies, including state aids given for projects with a Community interest, which can be approved

---

Council v. Zhejiang Xinan Chemical Industrial Group Co. Ltd on the question of government authority over companies; Case T-512/09, *Rusal Armenal v. Council,* appealed as Case C-21/14 P, *Commission v. Rusal Armenal* on the question whether the special rules for non-market economies, sectors or companies can give rise to the application of the *Nakajima* doctrine, see *infra* note 135 and accompanying text.

121. See the Communication from the Commission "Towards a robust trade policy for the EU in the interest of jobs and growth", doc. COM(2016)690 final and Proposal for a Regulation amending Reg. (EU) 2016/1036 on Protection from Dumped Imports etc., doc. COM(2016)721 final of 18 Oct. and 9 Nov. 2016 respectively.
122. See Communication from the Commission on "Adapting Trade Defence Instruments to the current needs of the European Economy", COM(2013)191(final) and a Proposal for a Regulation amending Reg. (EU) 1225/2009, COM(20013)192(final).
123. EUObserver 18/11/2017, retrieved at <euobserver.com/economic/139866>.
124. This means not just obvious financial benefits, either by means of direct transfers of revenue or non-collection of taxes or levies, but also the provision of goods or services other than general infrastructure, or financial contributions through intermediaries or funding mechanisms, see Reg. (EC) 2026/97, O.J. 1997, L 288, Art. 2(1)(a)(i)–(iv).
125. Art. 4(1) Reg. (EU) 2016/1037.

according to the Union's state aid rules.[126] Regulation 597/2009 also contains, in Article 4, detailed criteria as to the calculation of the amount of the countervailable subsidy, derived from the relevant WTO Agreement.

The determination of injury, the definition of the concept of the Union industry affected and the procedures leading to the imposition of anti-dumping and countervailing duties are dealt with more or less identically in the two regulations.[127]

In order to establish the existence of material damage, factors have to be taken into account such as whether there has been a significant increase in the import of dumped or subsidized products, significant price undercutting by these imports as compared with the price of a like product of the Union industry, and their influence on the development of production, capacity utilization, inventories, sales, market share, productivity, return on investments, and profitability of the relevant branch of Union industry. Of course, a causal link must be demonstrated between the dumping or subsidies and the damage. Damage caused by other factors – such as the amount or prices of imports which are not being dumped or subsidized, or decrease in demand – which either separately or in combination also have negative effects on the industry, may not be attributed to the dumped or subsidized imports.

The term "Community/Union industry" refers to the Union producers of the like products as a whole, or a number of them whose collective output of the products constitutes a major proportion of the total Union production.

Anti-dumping or anti-subsidy proceedings

Anti-dumping or anti-subsidy proceedings may be opened *inter alia* on the basis of a complaint filed with the Commission by an undertaking or an association of undertakings.[128] In this case the so-called sector or representative requirement applies:[129] the natural or legal person or association not having legal personality must be acting on behalf of a Community industry in the sense of the regulation, as set out above. The Commission is the institution carrying out the anti-dumping or anti-subsidy investigation. Next to the complainants and the third country exporter, there are other interests that are potentially affected by the outcome of the investigation: the downstream industry and retailers in the EU, the EU consumers, often represented by consumer organizations (such as BEUC). All these have a role to play in the procedure, can make representations to, and may be heard by, the Commission. On the basis of their participation in the procedure, the Court has recognized the standing of these entities as parties or interveners in cases relating to the outcome of the investigation.[130]

Towards the end of the procedure the Commission is required to consider whether the imposition of anti-dumping duties is in the interest of the Union. This requires a weighing up of the interest of the complaining Union producers and the general interest of the economy of

126. See Art. 107(3)(b) TFEU. A well-known example of state aids approved on the basis of the "Community interest exception" are the Airbus producing countries' financing schemes, which caused considerable problems in the WTO Airbus case, see DS/316, *European Communities and Certain Member States – Measures affecting Trade in Large Civil Aircraft.*
127. Compare Arts. 3–21 of Reg. (EU) 2016/1036 with Arts. 8–30 of Reg. (EU) 2016/1037.
128. For the details of the investigation procedure the reader is referred to T. Giannakopoulos, *Safeguarding Companies' Rights in Competition and Anti-dumping/Anti-subsidies Proceedings* (Kluwer, 2011), at 331 et seq.
129. For long-standing criticism on the requirement of branch or representativeness in relation to the right of appeal and right to damages, see M. Bronckers, B. Ter Kuile and J. Steenbergen, "Ondernemingen en handelspolitieke instrumenten", (1985) SEW, 599–672, at 641 et seq.
130. For a summary of this case law see Case C-239/99, *Nachi Europe*. However in specific circumstances even independent importers can be individually concerned, see C-358/89, *Extramet.*

the Union, which includes the repercussions of the anti-dumping duties on the downstream sectors of the Union industry and of consumers. Obviously more general considerations of a commercial policy character and/or related to foreign policy considerations may play a role as well in establishing what is the Union interest in any particular case. Any decision taken by the Commission at the end of the procedure, therefore, has a strong discretionary character.[131]

Anti-dumping and anti-subsidy investigations may also end with a decision of the Commission that there are no protective measures necessary. The third possible outcome in anti-dumping cases is that the company investigated for dumping offers an "undertaking", essentially promising the Commission to end its dumping practices by increasing its prices to above normal value, which is accepted by the Commission.

Originally most decisions in the field of anti-dumping and anti-subsidy law were taken by the Council on proposal of the Commission. Now the Commission exercises implementing powers in both domains, supervised by a Committee of the Member States pursuant to Article 191(3) TFEU. The examination procedure is followed by this Committee, when the Commission is about to take decisions of a final nature: the imposition of anti-dumping duties, the termination of procedures with or without undertakings by the companies, prolongation of anti-dumping duties that have expired; reinvestigations and the extension of anti-dumping duties to other companies in the case of intervention. In the case of the imposition of definitive duties, the examination procedure has a special twist: recourse may be had to the special Appeals Committee procedure, if a proposed definitive imposition of anti-dumping duties leads to no opinion or a negative opinion in the Anti-Dumping Committee.[132] The advisory procedure is followed in all decisions with a more procedural character.

Complainants sometimes allege that Union anti-dumping measures are incompatible with the WTO Anti-Dumping Agreement. The question then arises whether that Agreement is directly effective; it is a question which has long been the subject of debate, but which has been answered negatively by the Court ever since 1996 in relation to all of the WTO Agreement and its annexes, including the Anti-Dumping Agreement.[133] Once, in *Nakajima,* however, the Court was willing to examine the anti-dumping regulation in the light of the then GATT Anti-Dumping Code, in the context of a plea of illegality under Article 277 TFEU, in view of the fact that the basic anti-dumping regulation stated explicitly that it was supposed to implement the WTO Anti-Dumping Agreement.[134] Recently the Court has given a restrictive interpretation to the notion of implementation of the WTO Anti-Dumping Agreement in another anti-dumping case.[135]

2.3.4 *The exercise of the EU's rights and implementation of its duties under International Trade Agreements*

With the increasing number of trade and cooperation agreements that the EU has negotiated over the last ten years next to the WTO, and that have been equipped with elaborate dispute settlement and enforcement procedures inspired by the WTO, the question arises how the EU should organize itself in such fashion that it can claim these rights, and once it has claimed and obtained them, how to enforce them effectively. One of the legal instruments to do this has a

---

131. Case C 191/82, *EEC Seed Crushers' and Oil Processors' Federation (Fediol) v. Commission.*
132. See Arts. 5(5) and 6 of Reg. 182/2011, O.J. 2012, L 55/13.
133. Case C-149/96, *Portuguese Republic v. Council.*
134. See Case C-69/89, *Nakajima All Precision Co. Ltd v. Council* and Case C-76/00, *Petrotub and Republica v. Council.*
135. Case C-21/14 P, *Council v. Rusal Armenal,* paras. 45–55. See also *supra* note 120.

long history and sets out how not just Member States, but also EU enterprises and branches of industry may complain about the abridgment of their rights under the WTO and other trade agreements: the so-called Trade Barriers Regulation (TBR).[136] The second instrument has been only recently adopted by the Council and the EP and concentrates on the later phase of applying and enforcing the rights, once they have been recognized by panels or the Appellate Body (AB) of the WTO or comparable dispute settlement organs of other trade agreements: the Application and Enforcement Regulation (AER).[137]

The TBR was originally intended as a reply to section 301 of the US Trade Act and like that provision also had the function to stimulate complaints from industry and lock the trade authorities into an elaborate procedure which almost "had" to be followed by action in the WTO; it gives rights to complaining enterprises and branches of industry, which can be enforced before the Union courts. The AER is a technical instrument that is primarily about delegation of implementing powers to the Commission so that rights the Union has obtained can be quickly and efficiently realized. This is a common trait with another more technical instrument that will also be briefly sketched below and that allows simplified and speedy procedures to repeal or amend Union disputed measures in the field of anti-dumping and countervail in cases where the EU has been condemned by a WTO Panel or AB report.[138]

Trade Barrier Regulation

The TBR is intended to permit the exercise of the above-mentioned rights of the EU, with two aims in mind a) to remove obstacles to trade that have an effect on the EU market, with a view to removing the material injury resulting therefrom; b) removing obstacles to trade that have an effect on the market of a third country, with a view to cancelling the adverse trade effects on EU exports resulting therefrom.[139]

"Obstacles to trade" means any trade practice adopted or maintained by a third country in respect of which international trade rules – that is to say the WTO Agreement or bilateral or multilateral treaties of the EU – establish a right of action, i.e. a right to contest the breach of the rules directly, or a right to seek to eliminate the consequences of the measure.[140] The consequences of such obstacles to trade may be felt directly on the internal market[141] or indirectly through the effects of such measures felt by EU undertakings on the market in third countries.[142] The TBR enables the EU primarily to combat illicit obstacles to Union exports in so far as these are to be imputed to third states. The dispute settlement procedures of the appropriate trade

136. Reg. (EC) 3286/94, O.J. 1994, L 349/71. See R. MacLean and B. Volpi, *EU Trade Barrier Regulation, Tackling Unfair Foreign Trade Practices* (Palladian, 2000) and G. Zonnekeyn and J. Van Eeckhaute, "De handelsbarrièreverordening en de vernieuwde markttoegangsstrategie van de EC", (1998) SEW, 80–91.
137. Reg. (EU) 654/2014 concerning the exercise of the Union's rights for the application and enforcement of international trade rules etc. O.J. 2014, L 189/50. This Regulation is coordinated with the TBR through a slight modification of Art. 13(3) of the latter by Art. 11 of the former.
138. Reg. (EC) 1515/2001 on the measures that may be taken by the Community following a report adopted by the WTO Dispute Settlement Body concerning anti-dumping and anti-subsidy matters (as amended), O.J. 2001, L 201/10.
139. Art. 1 Reg. (EC) 3286/94, O.J. 1994, L 349. The concept "adverse trade effects" comes from the WTO agreement on subsidies and countervailing measures, see Art. 5.
140. The last-mentioned is connected with the so-called "non-violation" complaints in the framework of the GATT, see Art. XXIII(1)(b).
141. Injury, Art. 2(3) Reg. (EC) 3286/94.
142. Adverse trade effects, Art. 2(4) Reg. (EC) 3286/94.

agreements, particularly those of the WTO and of the newer bilateral free trade and cooperation agreements, must be respected.[143]

The Commission conducts the so-called "Community examination procedure", assisted by the Trade Barriers Committee, a committee of the Member States controlling the Commission's implementing powers. If the examination procedure leads to the conclusion that dispute settlement mechanisms need to be activated, the Commission may directly initiate these procedures.[144] In case retaliatory commercial policy measures (i.e. suspension or revocation of trade concessions, the raising or introduction of customs duties or levies, or the imposition of quantitative restrictions) are required, the Commission should follow the normal procedure of Article 207 EC and make the relevant proposal.[145]

From the one case in which a decision under the TBR was attacked before the CFI (now the GC) – it concerned a Commission decision terminating a case without further action – one may conclude, on the one hand, that the Commission has a considerable discretion in fashioning its decisions under the TBR Regulation but, on the other hand, that the General Court is willing to go into painstaking detail in order to establish that this discretion has been properly used on the basis of all the facts and in respect of all the procedures.[146]

In 19 years (1995–2014) some 26 cases were examined under the TBR, of which 11 led to published decisions. The instrument seems to be used mainly for its intended aim, i.e. removing obstacles to trade or unfair commercial practices in third countries. Virtually all the procedures led to an improvement in the situation of Community exporters. The most spectacular cases were undoubtedly those which led to a GATT or WTO panel, with varying success.[147] Over the last years, however, the importance of the TBR as an instrument to which exporters have regular recourse has been declining slowly but surely.[148]

Application and Enforcement Regulation

The AER was enacted in the summer of 2014 and serves primarily to simplify the application and enforcement of the EU's right to suspend concessions or other obligations vis-a-vis another party to a WTO dispute settlement procedure, pursuant to an authorization of the WTO's Dispute Settlement Body. The same applies to retaliation, as it is commonly called, authorized in the framework of dispute settlement procedures under other trade agreements. A secondary aspect of the AER is the simplification of so-called rebalancing of concessions and other obligations in the framework of safeguard measures taken by third countries, if these countries fail to carry out this obligation themselves under the WTO Agreement on Safeguards or under the

143. Art. 12(2) Reg. (EC) 3286/94. In the more recent free trade and cooperation agreements, such as the agreement with Korea, elaborate dispute settlement procedures based on the WTO model have been included. Cf. the EU-Korea Free Trade Agreement, O.J. 2011, L 127/6, and more specifically its fourteenth chapter (Dispute Settlement).
144. Art. 13(1) Reg. (EC) 3286/94.
145. Art. 13(2) and 11(2)(c) of Reg. (EC) 3286/94.
146. See Case T-317/02, *Fédération des Industrie Condimentaires de France v. Commission.* A claim for damages from the same trade association was also rejected: Case T-90/03.
147. See GATT Panel US-Section 337 of the Trade Act, BISD 36S, at 345 and WTO Panels, DS 136, US-Anti-Dumping Act of 1916 (both won by the EC); DS 160, US-Section 110 of the Copyright Act (mixed result, but broadly favourable to the EC); DS 155, Argentina-Bovine Hides (mixed result), DS 193, Chile-Swordfish (panel proceeding discontinued after reaching agreement with Chile), DS 273 Korea-Commercial Vessels (negative result); DS 332, Brazil-Retreaded Tyres (mixed result, mostly favourable to the EC).
148. This has to do with the greater attention given to bilateral agreements and to informal mechanisms for market opening. See European Commission, "Global Europe: A Stronger Partnership to Deliver Market Access for European Exporters", COM(2006)567 and *idem*, COM(2007)183 final.

safeguard provisions of other trade agreements. The same applies, when the EU has a rebalancing right, in case a third state wants to modify existing concessions under the GATT and fails to fulfil its obligation to agree on compensation for the Union.[149] In all these cases retaliation and rebalancing decisions are to be taken by Commission implementing acts following the examination procedure or the urgency procedure, when circumstances justify it.[150]

This delegation of implementing power is strictly circumscribed both as to the measures that may be taken and the conditions under which they may be taken.[151] Obviously the Union's legislative power, i.e. the Council and Parliament, as well as the Member States, were somewhat concerned about the importance of this delegation to the Commission. This appears from a Statement by the Commission that is attached to the text of the Regulation in the Official Journal and in which the Commission makes a number of important promises on how it will apply this delegation in order to make it palatable to the other institutions and the Member States.[152]

Trade Implementation Regulation

This regulation enables the Commission, in case a Union measure in the field of anti-dumping or countervail is condemned in a WTO Panel or AB report, to repeal or amend the disputed measure or to adopt any other implementing measure that it deems appropriate in the circumstances with a view to bringing the Union into conformity with the recommendations and rulings contained in the report.[153] This Regulation was the direct consequence of the EC losing the WTO *Bed-Linen case* against India, in which the Panel and the AB rejected the so-called zeroing method of calculating anti-dumping duties. Since then (2001) the Commission has used these powers under the old comitology procedure in all the different hypotheses foreseen in the Regulation, both in anti-dumping and in countervailing duty cases.[154] This has hardly caused any problem and it is likely that this will also be true of the application of the AER, although the latter is primarily an instrument oriented towards obtaining rights, whereas the instrument discussed here is directed to fulfilling obligations effectively.

2.3.5 *EU policy on foreign direct investment: Two preconditions*

Two questions had to be answered before the EU could conclude any agreement on the conditions of access to and protection of FDI, whether as a mixed agreement or not (see section 2.1.2 above), including provisions for dispute settlement on the treatment of FDI. The first question was: what would be the relationship between new EU-wide agreements and existing Bilateral Investment Treaties (BITS) of the Member States? And the second question was: who would bear the responsibility for breaches of EU investment agreements: the EU itself or its Member States, or perhaps both?

Transitional Regulation on BITs

The first question is answered in Regulation 1219(2012) on the transitional arrangement for the Member States BITs during the period when the EU will begin to conclude investment

149. Art. 3 Reg. (EU) 654/2014. This relates to the procedure of re-balancing foreseen in Arts. XXVIII GATT.
150. Art. 5 and 8 Reg. (EU) 654/2014.
151. The details can be found in Arts. 4, 5 and 10 of Reg. (EU) 654/2014.
152. Extensive consultations with all relevant interests are promised; timely information of Member States will be provided; Parliament and Council will also receive the draft decisions that are sent to the Committee assisting the Commission in the exercise of its implementing power; structured dialogue with the EP on dispute settlement and enforcement issues will take place, see *supra* note 149.
153. Art. 1 Reg. (EC) 1515/2001, O.J. 2001, L 201/10.
154. For some more detail see P.J. Kuijper and F. Hoffmeister, op. cit. *supra* note 47, at 145–148.

agreements or investment chapters in broad trade and cooperation agreements.[155] The existence of this regulation and the one on the division of responsibility, to be discussed below, is testimony to the changed balance between the institutions in the field of trade. If the Parliament would not have been implicated in the adoption of these instruments it is far from certain that these regulations would have been adopted at all and certainly not within the time in which they were adopted now, such was initially the resistance of the Member States in the Council and especially of the heavy users of BITs.[156]

The transitional regulation establishes a notification requirement for the Member States for all the BITs they want to have continued validity. Once notified, any BIT will remain in force until it has been replaced by an EU BIT with the same country. The Commission may scrutinize all BITs notified and check whether they are contrary to other obligations of the Member States under EU law and also make an assessment whether a BIT would constitute a serious obstacle to the negotiation of conclusion of a Union BIT in the future. In that case the Member State shall cooperate with the Commission in order to find a solution to its objections.

The transitional regulation provides for the possibility that Member States, though under stringent conditions, negotiate about new BITs and in the end sign and conclude them.[157] These conditions are (1) that the agreement would not be contrary to EU law, except the exclusive powers of Article 207 TFEU, (2) the agreement would not clash with a Commission recommendation to negotiate a Union BIT with the country concerned, (3) the agreement would be consistent with the EU's principles and objectives for external action (in practice Art. 21 TEU); (4) the agreement would not constitute a serious obstacle to the negotiation and conclusion of Union BITs in general.[158] It is the Commission that will apply these criteria under implementing powers, following the advisory procedure.[159]

This aspect of the transitional regulation can be characterized as a law circumscribing and modifying the Commission's exercise of the infringement procedure. Criterion (1) whitewashes a clear infringement of the EU's exclusive competence in the field of the CCP, but not in other areas of EU law. Criteria (2) and (4) are derived from cases, where the Court has in the past ruled that Member States' duty of sincere cooperation in the field of external relations was infringed.[160] Criterion (3) is remarkable in that it permits the Commission – which for the rest has a very limited role in the CFSP – to take a decision with legal effects for a Member State on the basis of an alleged breach of Article 21 TEU. The procedure as a whole changes the balance between the institutions in normal infringement procedures by enabling the Commission, after a committee procedure, to take an immediate decision that will decide the infringement, which may then be attacked before the Court by the Member State(s) concerned. This raises a number of questions. The first one is whether the interest of organizing an appropriate transition allows the legislator to set aside the application of an exclusive power of the EU. The second is whether the Court will have jurisdiction insofar as the Commission has based its decision on criterion (3) relating to the principles of EU external action. The third one is whether the advisory

155. Reg. (EU) 1219/2012 establishing transitional arrangements for bilateral investment agreements between Member States and third countries, O.J. 2012, L 351/40.
156. The most important users of BITs are Germany (about 130 BITs), France and the UK (each about 110), the Netherlands (about 90) and Belgium. All Member States together have concluded some 1400 BITs.
157. See Arts. 8, 9, 11 and 12 of Reg. (EU) 1219/2012 for the procedures to be followed and the conditions to be respected by the MS. Member States have used this possibility with some regularity.
158. See Art. 9(1)(a)–(d) of Reg. (EU) 1219/2012.
159. See Arts. 9(3) and 12(4) together with Art. 16 of Reg. (EU) 1219/2012.
160. See e.g. Case C-266/03, *Commission v. Luxembourg (Transport Inland Waterways)*, paras. 57–67.

procedure is justified in an implementation committee, when the criteria for the implementing decision of the Commission give so much latitude as the four criteria mentioned above.[161]

Responsibility Regulation

The second question was answered, when the Council and the Parliament adopted Regulation No. 912/2014 during the summer of 2014. This regulation lays down a framework for managing financial responsibility as between the Union and its Member States in case of adverse judgments brought by foreign investors against the EU and/or its Member States.[162] This is of great importance, since investment disputes, contrary to WTO disputes which usually require specific performance, nearly always end in the award of money damages. Like the transition regulation, the responsibility regulation does not imply that the institutions and the Member States agree on the question of the division of competences in the field of FDI and ISDS. Both regulations contain an explicit mention in their Article 1 stating that the regulations are "without prejudice to the division of competences established by the TFEU". It remains to be seen whether the Court's Opinion 2/15 will need to have repercussions on these regulations[163]

The responsibility regulation contains a fairly simple rule on the apportionment of the financial responsibility, extensive rules on the conduct during dispute settlement proceedings, some detailed rules on settling disputes out of court or during the proceedings, and finally rules on the payment of the arbitral awards. The rules on the apportionment of financial responsibility are based on the criterion of who afforded the unlawful treatment, the Union or one or more of the Member States. In case EU law required the treatment afforded by a Member State, the EU and not the latter will bear responsibility. On the other hand a Member State will bear financial responsibility, if it has accepted such responsibility in cases where the Union acts as respondent or in cases where it wishes to negotiate a settlement of a claim relating to treatment by that Member State.[164]

The rules on who will play the role of respondent in an ISDS dispute are more complicated than those on the apportionment of the financial responsibility; there is no full parallelism between the two. The matter is simple if the litigious treatment has been afforded by the institutions, bodies, offices or agencies of the Union: the Union will act as the respondent, represented by the Commission, which will immediately notify the Council and the EP when it receives a request for consultations or a notice of initiation of arbitration proceedings from a claimant. In a case concerning treatment entirely or partially afforded by a Member State, the Commission and the Member State concerned will cooperate as required by the principle of sincere cooperation during the preliminary steps, including consultations, that will precede actual litigation. At that stage the Member State concerned will be the respondent, unless it notifies the

161. The answer to the first question is probably positive as long as the exclusion of an infringement of Art. 207 is truly linked to a well-ordered transition to the full effect of Art. 207 TFEU within a reasonable period of time. The second question may be answered positively as Art. 275 TFEU seems to refer to the CFSP in a narrow sense, as laid down in Ch. 2 of Title V of the TEU. As to the third question, the Statement of the two co-legislators and the Commission attached to Reg. (EU) 1219/2012 provides an answer of sorts to this question: this light procedure was justified because the Regulation allowed the Member States to ignore an exclusive power of the Union.

162. It is inherent in the Investor-State Dispute Settlement (ISDS) that the investor is always the complainant and the State or, in this case, the EU is always the defendant.

163. As is explained elsewhere, Opinion 2/15, *Singapore FTA,* decided that the competence of the Union over FDI is exclusive, but that portfolio investment is not part of FDI and that dispute settlement in this field is in principle ancillary to this exclusive competence, except to the extent that it led to the exclusion of the jurisdiction of Member States courts in investment cases, see section 2.1.1 above and references there.

164. See Art. 3 of Reg. (EU) 912/2014.

Commission that it does not want to act as such. The same applies if the Commission takes an implementing act in consultation with the Committee for Investment Agreements to the effect that the Union should be the respondent, since (1) the Union would bear at least part of the financial responsibility, or (2) the dispute also concerns treatment afforded by the institutions etc. of the Union (the advisory procedure would apply in these two cases), or (3) there is a parallel WTO panel seized of a related claim against the EU concerning the same specific legal issue, requiring a consistent defence in both cases (the examination procedure would apply in this case). Finally there are elaborate rules for cooperation between the Member States and the Commission during the conduct of an arbitration wherein either a Member State or the Union is respondent. The same applies to the negotiated settlement of a dispute by the Commission or a Member State. The financial settlement of the awarded damages largely follows the rules of the Financial Regulation.

Now that these two regulations have entered into force, the EU can go ahead and conclude international investment agreements, including ISDS. Two of such agreements have already been negotiated and their text has been finalized: the Free-Trade Agreement (FTA) with Singapore[165] and the Comprehensive Economic and Trade Agreement with Canada (CETA)[166] contain elaborate chapters on investment access, investment protection and ISDS, which is kept separate from the dispute settlement clauses relating to the trade chapters of the agreements. In the meantime, however, criticism of BITs and ISDS, which had been brewing in international legal circles for some time reached the political class and general public in Europe, when negotiations were started with the US on the Transatlantic Trade and Investment Pact (TTIP). This criticism related to substantive norms of investment protection, such as fair and equitable treatment (FET) and indirect expropriation and their creative interpretation by arbitral tribunals, as well as to the expansive view such tribunals habitually took of their competence, especially by a 'creative use' of the most-favoured nation principle to vest jurisdiction. Conflicts of interest were said to be rife. Moreover the methods of selection of the arbitral tribunals were also increasingly subject to criticism.[167]

The investment chapters and the ISDS provisions of the EU-Singapore FTA and of CETA are striking in that they seek to remedy such objections. They contain more precise definitions of FET by limiting it to specific instances of wrongful action by the authorities, such as denial of justice, fundamental breach of due process, manifestly arbitrary treatment, harassment, coercion, abuse of power and other bad faith conduct and a breach of a strictly circumscribed notion of legitimate expectations.[168] Both agreements contain a clear definition of what constitutes indirect expropriation.[169] This is to ensure that arbitral tribunals will remain within

165. EU-Singapore Free Trade Agreement. Authentic text available at <trade.ec.europa.eu/doclib/press/index.cfm?id=961> (last visited Aug. 2017).
166. For the near-final version of CETA: <ec.europa.eu/trade/policy/in-focus/ceta/ceta-chapter-by-chapter/>; for the interpretative instrument of CETA: Council doc. 13541/16.
167. There is wide-spread criticism of the over-representation of a certain type of male commercial lawyer with little knowledge of international law from North-America and Europe and an almost total absence of women, see e.g. C. Georgetti, "Is the truth in the eyes of the beholder? The perils and benefits of empirical research in international investment arbitration", 12 *Santa Clara Journal of International Law* (2013), 263.
168. See Art. 9.4 EU – Singapore FTA and Art. 8.10 CETA.
169. See Annex 9-A to the Investment Protection Section of the EU-Singapore FTA and Annex 8.12 and Annex 8-A to CETA, where indirect expropriation is defined as a measure or a series of measures that has an effect equivalent to direct expropriation, substantially depriving the owner of the attributes of property in its investment, such as the right to use, enjoy and dispose of the investment without a formal transfer of title or outright seizure. Moreover legitimate public policy measures taken to protect health, safety or the environment do not constitute indirect expropriation.

certain bounds, when using these notions. The Singapore agreement also ventures to change the selection of members of the arbitral tribunals by having recourse to lists of qualified people who are more diverse in gender and ethnic background and by formulating clearer rules on incompatibilities and conflicts.[170] Both agreements also make the proceedings of the (arbitral) tribunals largely transparent.[171] The CETA and also the proposed chapter on investment dispute settlement in the Commission's TTIP proposal create a Permanent Investment Tribunal and an Appellate Tribunal, thus completely judicializing the dispute settlement procedure and excluding the well-known problems of the present selection of arbitrators in respect of conflict of interest and issue conflict.[172] In order to discourage "frivolous" claims that are brought merely to exercise political pressure, the two agreements furthermore contain trip-wire provisions against "claims manifestly without legal merits" and against "claims unfounded as a matter of law".[173] Both agreements await final conclusion, after the rendering of Opinion 2/15 on the Singapore FTA in December 2017 and a pending request for an Opinion by the Belgian government on CETA respectively.

2.4 *Conclusion*

On the whole this section on the CCP confirms trends that were already signalled in Chapter 39 The CCP's legal instruments show that this policy is, at least in law, seriously constrained by the framework for international trade created and enforced in the WTO. Article 206 TFEU contains a clear allusion to the WTO principles, whereas Article 205 TFEU refers back to the international and Union principles of Article 21 TEU. In particular in safeguards, anti-dumping and countervail the conformity to the WTO instruments in these domains is a clear legal requirement. The EU is also equipped with legal instruments that enable it easily to assert its rights and fulfil its duties under international trade law, as laid down under the WTO, but also under many new bilateral trade agreements or other contractual instruments, such as association agreements of which comprehensive trade chapters form often the core. The instrument to fulfil the EU's duties in the field of trade would gain in credibility by having a broader scope than just the anti-dumping and anti-subsidies agreements of the WTO. In the field of international trade the Commission fulfils the role of executive in most of the classic autonomous instruments where the implementing powers are delegated in line with Article 291 TFEU.

Returning to the core question of the scope of the CCP, there is clarity in the WTO-covered part of the CCP: in some sensitive areas unanimity may still be necessary in the Council, but after recent post-Lisbon judgments of the ECJ there is no doubt: within the WTO the CCP is fully an exclusive power. After Opinion 2/15 it is clear that foreign direct investment in the literal sense is included in the CCP, but not portfolio investment. Investor-State Dispute Settlement (ISDS) is excluded because it diminishes the jurisdiction of national courts by excluding the exhaustion of local remedies and thus escapes the jurisdiction of the ECJ under the preliminary questions procedure.[174]

Foreign direct investment is also a field that has still to go through a long process of adaptation of the existing pattern of international agreements and international arbitration, in which

170. Art. 8.30 Ethics of CETA and Annex 9B to the ISDS section of the EU-Singapore FTA on the Code of Conduct for Arbitrators and Mediators.
171. Annex 9C to the ISDS section of the EU-Singapore FTA paras. 78-110, 225-256 and 285-293. On the preliminary question procedure as a bar to international dispute settlement, see Ch. 39, note 148.
172. Art. 8.27–8.29 of CETA.
173. See, for instance, Arts. 9.23 and 9.24 of the Investment chapter of the EU-Singapore FTA.
174. Opinion 2/15, *EU-Singapore FTA*. The Court never mentions the second point explicitly.

there is basically no place for international organizations, let alone for a *sui generis* international operator with real power in the field, such as the EU. Given the generally felt need to modernize investment (protection) agreements, there is a good chance that this will help the full introduction of the EU into a new international environment for investment protection and investment arbitration, characterized by a better balance between investors' rights and States' policy autonomy than is presently perceived to be the case.

3. Development and other cooperation policies

3.1 Development cooperation and other cooperation policies

3.1.1 Objectives and scope of development cooperation and other cooperation policies. A brief overview

Development cooperation, now laid down in Articles 208–211 TFEU, was introduced into the EC Treaty at Maastricht. For many years the EEC had based its cooperation with the African, Caribbean and Pacific (ACP) States on the association article (now Art. 217 TFEU) and on autonomous instruments under the CCP, such as the Generalized System of Preferences (GSP) and the commodity stabilization programme.[175] Economic, financial and technical cooperation with other third states was added officially in the Treaty of Nice (Art. 181a TEC, now Art. 212 TFEU). Finally Lisbon added a specific power for Humanitarian aid (Art. 214 TFEU).

Development cooperation should have as its main objective the reduction and in the end the eradication of poverty, according to Article 209 TFEU. Just as trade policy, the EU's development cooperation must be conducted within the framework of the principles and objectives of the EU's external action. EU development cooperation should work in tandem with the Member States' development policies, but will also comply with the commitments and the objectives which the EU and its Member States have consented to in the UN and in other international organizations dealing with development policy.[176] This is expressed in the "European Consensus on Development" of 2016, in a response to the new UN development strategy.

Like trade policy, development cooperation can be carried out by both autonomous and contractual measures. In addition the European Investment bank (EIB) can contribute to the implementation of both kinds of measures.[177] The autonomous measures take the form of so-called financing instruments, while the contractual instruments are agreements concluded under the general provision on treaties (Art. 218 TFEU), but also under the association provision (Art. 217 TFEU).

Development cooperation was originally largely a contractual policy based on the above-mentioned association provision. Moreover, insofar as it required money from the Community budget and in part also from the Member States, it was also based on contractual provisions and autonomous acts based on the flexibility clause (Art. 352 TFEU). The successive association agreements with the ACP States, the Conventions of Yaoundé, Lomé and Cotonou based on Article 217 TFEU, were accompanied by Financial Protocols which laid down the overall

---

175. The first GSP dates back to 1971 when it was created following UNCTAD recommendations and was seen by the ECJ to be properly part of the CCP in Case 45/86, *Commission v. Council (GSP),* para 21. For the Commodity stabilization programme recall Opinion 1/78, *International Agreement on Natural Rubber,* at 2884, in which the ECJ gave a broad interpretation to the CCP in order to accommodate this programme and its fund.

176. All this is explicitly laid down in Art. 208 TFEU. Further detail on the cooperation between EU and the Member States in respect of development policy is laid down in Art. 210 TFEU.

177. See Art. 209 TFEU. The terms for such contributions are fixed in Arts. 16–18 of the Statute of the EIB.

size of the Community's financial assistance to the ACP states and how much of that would be provided by the European Development Fund (EDF). The EDF, consisting of Union and Member State contributions and of EIB contributions, was and is based on an internal agreement between the Union and the Member States.[178] Nowadays the allocation of its funds is largely subject to Union implementing procedures following the model of Article 291 TFEU, but also based on an internal agreement. It has now reached its 11th edition, covering the period 2014–2020 and totalling some 30.5 billion euros.[179] This model is maintained for the development relation with the ACP States, but nowadays complemented by the so-called Economic Partnership Agreements (EPAs) with different groups of ACP countries, which concentrate on improving trade relations.[180] As we will see later, the development relation with the ACP countries has remained primarily contractual to this day, whilst the development relationship with other developing countries is rather a mix of contractual and autonomous elements, of on the one hand international agreements defining the relationship and on the other autonomous financial instruments providing the financial means and laying down the conditions on which they will be provided.

As to the scope of the development policy, it was very broadly defined in former Article 130y, later Article 177, TEC before Lisbon, combining sustainable economic and social development of the developing countries, smooth and gradual integration of their economies into the world economy and action against poverty. Article 209 TFEU at first sight seems to have been formulated more narrowly than Article 177 TEC, concentrating as it does on poverty eradication as the primary goal of European development policy. However, by referring back implicitly to Articles 3(5) and 21 TEU, Article 209 TFEU actually includes the same elements that were present in Article 177 TEC, namely sustainable social, economic and environmental development and the gradual integration of developing countries in the world economy, as well as the protection of human rights.[181] This was reason for the Court in *Portugal v. Council* to give a broad interpretation to development cooperation.[182] In this case he agreement contained a number of clauses that referred in very general terms to cooperation between the EC and India on such specific matters as energy, intellectual property, tourism, culture drug abuse control and human rights. In Portugal's view these needed each their own specific legal basis or, for human rights, a reference to the flexibility clause of Article 235 TEC.[183]

It is not surprising that the ECJ upheld and expanded the precedent of *Portugal v. Council* in a case litigated after the entry into force of the Lisbon treaty by accepting that provisions on readmission of third country nationals, on transport and on the environment were not so extensive as to constitute distinctive objectives of the Agreement and thus could be covered

178. All attempts at "communitarising" and thereby "budgetising" the EDF have failed, see Case C-316/91, *Parliament v. Council*, at paras. 21–27. See also on EDF Ch. 9, "Budget and Finances", of this book.
179. For the legal basis of the 11th EDF see Dec. (EU) 1/2014 of the ACP-EU Council of Ministers (revised Cotonou Agreement), O.J. 2014, L 196/40. See also Internal Agreement between the Representatives of the Governments of the Member States of the European Union, O.J. 2013, L 210/1 and Council Reg. (EU) 567/2014, O.J. 2014, L 157/52 for the financial regulation of the transition period between the 10th and the 11th EDF.
180. The only fully operational EPA is the one with Caricom, see O.J. 2008, L 289/I/3, signed on 15 Oct. 2008; entry into force still pending. Provisional application since 29 Dec. 2008. The EPA with Eastern and Southern Africa (ESA) has been provisionally applied since 14 May 2012; the one with Central Africa since 4 Aug. 2014. None of them have fully entered into force. For up-to-date information see <trade.ec.europa.eu/doclib/docs/2009/september/tradoc_144912.pdf> (last visited 30 Nov. 2017).
181. See Art. 21(2)(d) and (e) TEU and Art. 3(5) TEU.
182. Case C-268/94, *Portugal v. Council (Agreement with India)*.
183. Case C-268/94, *Portugal v. Council (Agreement with India)*, paras. 18, 23 and 24.

by the trade and development provisions of the TFEU.[184] As in the field of trade,[185] the Court emphasizes the continuity between the Treaty of Lisbon and preceding Treaties and sees no reason – to the obvious disappointment of many intervening Member States – to change the line of its case law.

The growing awareness that there can be no sustainable development and eradication of poverty as long as there is not a minimum of peace and security in and around a developing country and a basic level of the rule of law thus remains out of reach, forged a link between development and security policy (both internal and external), which was made explicit in the European Development Consensus.[186] The delimitation between the two pairs was at the basis of two ECJ judgments which once again used the Court's methods of interpretation when deciding on the proper legal basis of a Union act, as the instrument where the boundary between development on the one hand and international peace and security[187] or national security policy,[188] on the other hand, had to be drawn. In the latter case, it was relatively easy for the Court to annul a Commission decision financing a project for enhancing Philippines' border security, since the financing instrument serving as basis for the decision had not been brought up to date yet with the Development Consensus.[189] The former case was more difficult as both the introductory articles of the Cotonou agreement, the Development Consensus and other documents seemed to confirm that the EU could have recourse both to the CFSP and to the development provisions of the TFEU in carrying out the project in support of the elimination of small arms and light weapons in West-Africa through ECOWAS. As explained earlier, it was only the formulation of Article 40 (formerly Art. 47) TEU, which in such cases prescribed a preference for the Community legal basis, that made the Court decide for the development chapter as legal basis for this measure.[190]

During the 1990s it became clear very quickly, especially as a consequence of the disintegration of the Soviet Union and the rise of some developing nations to higher income levels that there was a need for economic, financial and technical assistance very much akin to development aid. Hence the European Bank for Reconstruction and Development (EBRD), a European institution comparable to the World Bank, but directed mainly at Eastern Europe, was founded.[191] Financial aid to higher income countries was initially given on the basis of the flexibility provision of the Treaty (now Art. 352 TFEU). An additional, special legal basis was introduced into the Nice Treaty. As to the relationship between development cooperation under Artcle 209 TFEU and the economic, financial and technical cooperation with developed countries under Article 212 TFEU, the difference is clear enough on the face of both articles. In reality, however, the secondary legislation based on Article 209(1) TFEU (or old Art. 179(1) EC) is used exclusively for any aid to developing countries that is considered ODA according to the

---

184. Case C-377/12, *Commission v. Council (Framework Agreement with the Philippines)*, paras. 48–59.
185. See the discussion of the Court's view of Art. 3(2) TFEU in Ch. 39, "An introduction to Union external action", section 4, of this book.
186. See European Development Consensus, cited *supra* note 3.
187. Case C-91/05, *Commission v. Council (ECOWAS)*.
188. Case 403/05, *Parliament v. Commission (Philippines border security)*.
189. In other words Reg.(EEC) 443/92 on Community Cooperation with the Asian and Latin American developing countries had not yet been succeeded by Reg. (EC) 1943/2006 which will be discussed below. Moreover Reg. (EEC) 443/92 did not contain a reference to the fight against terrorism and when the Commission proposed that it be inserted as one of the objectives, it failed.
190. Case C-91/05, para 77.
191. The EBRD was founded in 1991, see Agreement Establishing the European Bank for Reconstruction and Development (adopted 29 May 1990, entered into force 28 Mar. 1991).

criteria of the DAC (OECD), while the legislation based on Article 212(2) TFEU (or old Art. 181(a) EC) is used for aid to developed countries and non-ODA aid to developing countries.[192]

There are two policies that can illustrate the difference between Articles 209 and 212 TFEU: the Neighbourhood and Pre-accession policies. The latter is restricted to European countries that are officially candidate for accession and is based on Article 212 TFEU alone, while the former is aimed at countries from the "neighbourhood" which includes countries of the former Soviet Union and countries of the Mediterranean basin and the Middle East and is based on both articles.

Humanitarian aid will undoubtedly become more and more important in the future, given that climate change will entail a greater frequency of natural disasters and man-made disasters connected to it. The EU has over the years devoted increasing resources to it and the Treaty of Lisbon has created a separate legal basis for it in Article 214 TFEU.

3.1.2 Autonomous measures: Financing instruments

Next to the EDF adopted in the framework of the Cotonou Agreement, which contains a contractually agreed sum for development finance to the ACP countries, there are presently four *autonomous* financing instruments in the framework of the EU's development and cooperation policy: two general financing instruments – one for development cooperation[193] and one for cooperation with industrialized and high-income countries, now called the Partnership instrument[194] – and two specific ones – one for the promotion of democracy and human rights worldwide (EIDHR)[195] and the other for enhancing stability and peace.[196] Two comparable financing instruments enacted at the same time support the Accession (IPA) and Neighbourhood Policies.[197] The regulations concerned will be briefly set out here in general terms. They are linked to the long term seven year budget cycle of the EU and each has received a certain indicative sum for these seven years laid down in the relevant regulation.[198] Given this linkage they will be renewed or replaced by the end of 2020. They are held together by a common instrument laying down uniform rules and procedures for the implementation of all six financing instruments.[199] Separate from the six instruments there is a special financing instrument for humanitarian aid that is not linked in the same way to the budget cycle.[200]

192. See Reg. (EU) 233/2014, establishing a financing instrument for development cooperation O.J. 2014, L 77/44, and Reg. (EU) 234/2014 establishing a Partnership instrument for cooperation with third countries, O.J. 2014, L 77/77.
193. Reg. (EU) 233/2014, O.J. 2014, L 77/44.
194. Reg. (EU) 234/2014, O.J. 2014, L 77/77.
195. Reg. (EU) 235/2014, O.J. 2014, L 77/85, establishing a European Instrument for promoting Democracy and Human Rights (EIDHR).
196. Reg. (EU) 230/2014, O.J. 2014, L 77/1, the so-called Stability Instrument.
197. Reg. (EU) 231/2014 establishing an Instrument for Pre-accession Assistance (IPA II), O.J. 2014, L 77/11 and Reg. (EU) 232/2014 establishing a European Neighbourhood Instrument, O.J. 2014, L 77/27.
198. See for example Art. 20(1) of Reg. (EU) 233/2014, and Art. 8 of Reg. (EU) 234/2014.
199. Reg. (EU) 236/2014 laying down common rules and procedures for the implementation of the Union's instruments financing external action, O.J. 2014, L 77/95.
200. Reg. (EC) 1257/1996 concerning humanitarian aid, O.J. 1996, L 163/1. Another financing instrument that is often mentioned in the six financing instruments mentioned in the text, but stands slightly apart from them is the Instrument for Nuclear Safety Cooperation Reg. (Euratom) 300/2007, O.J. 2007, L 81/1, which replaces a number of post-Chernobyl instruments and continues to be aimed largely at assistance to the decommissioning of nuclear reactors of the Chernobyl type, which are considered inherently unsafe and outdated.

The six financing instruments and the common instrument are all based on Articles 209(1) and 212(2) TFEU together, except for the pre-accession instrument that is based on Article 212(2) TFEU alone, as the countries covered cannot be seen as developing countries. In the case of the Partnership instrument Article 207(2) TFEU is added to the two other legal bases, as such agreements are often WTO+ agreements or even FTAs. The six instruments are supposed to play a particular role in the coordination of the Union's external action through the High Representative and the EEAS.[201]

The Regulation on development cooperation is the most detailed of these financing instruments and the others are inspired by its provisions to a larger or smaller degree. The four development oriented instruments refer to the Millennium Development Goals of the UN General Assembly on the one hand and on the European Consensus on Development on the other.[202] For obvious reasons this is not the case for the pre-accession and neighbourhood instruments, which aim to reduce the distance both in economic and governance terms between the EU and the third countries eligible for support from these instruments[203] and therefore refer rather to Council declarations and other documents on the enlargement strategy, the Eastern Partnership and the Union for the Mediterranean.[204]

Mention is often made in the preambles of the development instruments of the WTO's aim of mainstreaming trade in development strategies. In addition recitals also mention the idea that a political environment respectful of democratic principles, human rights and fundamental freedoms is particularly conducive to stable, long-term development. This is, of course, the idea underlying the instrument for democracy and human rights and is mentioned as one of the fundamental elements of EU external action overall (see Arts. 21 TEU and 208 TFEU). Untying aid, following the best practices supported by the OECD DAC, is also advanced as an important element in the development instruments.[205] Where implementation is concerned, the financial support should be managed in conformity with the Financial Regulation.[206] Beyond loans or grants, aid can also consist of the procurement of goods and services or of contracts with individuals (for services, studies etc.). For recipients of aid are not limited to States, their subdivisions and institutions, but can also include private and moral persons, including companies and NGOs.[207] This is true in particular for the instrument for democracy and human rights that explicitly aims, if necessary, to provide assistance independently of the consent of the governments and authorities of the third countries concerned.[208]

The planning cycle is important, since it is the instrument by which the Commission spends development and cooperation money in a planned and controlled way, year after year, on goals that have been agreed with the recipients and that will contribute to the overall development

---

201. See Art. 9 of Council Dec. (EU) 2010/427 establishing the EEAS, O.J. 2010, L 201/30. This provision is explicitly referred to in all six instruments, see e.g. Art. 12 of Reg (EU) 230/2014, the Stability Instrument.
202. See in particular in the Development Cooperation Instrument, recitals 2 and 3 and recital 7 of Reg. (EU) 235/2014.
203. Both the Neighbourhood and the Pre-accession Instrument have an annex that lists the countries and territories (Kosovo!) that may benefit from support under those instruments. The four development instruments have no such lists attached to them.
204. See recitals 3 and 4 of Reg. (EU) 231/2014 and recitals 3–5 of Reg. (EU) 232/2014.
205. See Art. 2(3) Reg. (EU) 233/2014 and recitals 2 and 4 of Reg. (EU) 234/2014.
206. See the reference to Reg. (EU, Euratom) 966/2012, O.J. 2012, L 298/1, in recital 2 and Art. 1(3) of Reg. (EU) 236/2014.
207. Hence the need for the detailed rules on eligibility in the common instrument (Reg. (EU) 236/2014) mentioned above.
208. Recital 1 of Reg. (EU) 235/2014.

objectives of the country or countries concerned and will actually result in disbursement of the sums allocated to certain programmes and projects within the seven year budget cycle.[209]

The six instruments discussed here are all drafted in broad terms, where their strategies, themes, geographic concentration and overall objectives are concerned. In order to give greater precision, nearly all of them have an annex attached to them that sets some clearer priorities.[210] These priorities can be changed during the life of the instruments.

It is on these two points, the carrying out of the planning cycle from broad strategies, through programmes to projects and their funding on down and the re-ordering of priorities of the instruments, that these financial instruments show an interesting mix of delegating legislative powers and of granting implementing powers to the Commission. The amendment of the annexes that contain priorities is seen as a delegation of legislative power and is granted to the Commission under conditions that broadly follow the Common Understanding on Delegated Acts, leaving a waiting period of two months to both the Council and the Parliament to oppose a proposed Commission decision.[211] On the other hand the different steps in the programming cycles laid down in these instruments are viewed as implementing powers to be carried out by the Commission in consultation with a Committee (there is one for each instrument), normally through the examination procedure.[212]

The development cooperation instrument disposes of 19.6 billion euros over 7 years and divided this up over geographic and thematic programmes. The geographic programme covers Latin America, the different regions of Asia, the Middle East and Africa (primarily for trans-regional, continental and global problems, the African ACP countries being essentially covered by the Cotonou Agreement and the EDF). The thematic programme relates *inter alia* to health, education, environment and sustainable management of natural resources, food security, asylum and migration.[213]

The Partnership Instrument is the smallest of these instruments; it falls just short of 1 billion euros over seven years and provides non-ODA to higher income developing and developed countries, much of it to trade-related purposes and the improvement of economic relations; in many ways it is the external dimension of the "Europe 2020" programme.

The instrument for Democracy and Human Rights (EIDHR) is the next bigger instrument, endowed with 1.3 billion euros. The scope of the instrument is so broad (Art. 2) that special delegated power is granted to the Commission to change the scope after the mid-term review.

---

209. However, for many years in the 1990s and the early 2000s the Commission's development cooperation policy was marred by an ever increasing backlog in disbursements, sometimes resulting in an outright failure of spending a large part of the budget available for development cooperation. A conscious effort was made to remedy this, *inter alia* by making Europe Aid into a separate DG, next to DG DEV.
210. The one exception is Reg. (EU) 230/2014, the Instrument for Stability and Peace, since it is applied to specific post-conflict situations. This means that priorities are established by deciding to apply it to one such situation.
211. Common Understanding on Delegated Acts, later modified by the Annex to the Interinstitutional Agreement on Better Regulation, see Ch. 7, "Law-making" and Ch. 8, "The EU Administration", of this book.
212. Art. 5 of Reg. (EU) 182/11, O.J. 2011, L 55/13.
213. An important objective of the previous development cooperation instrument was providing adjustment assistance to the ACP countries that could no longer profit from the privileged access that their sugar and banana producers enjoyed to the EU market under the Cotonou agreement as a consequence of procedures under the WTO dispute settlement system, but this has disappeared. See Arts. 17 and 17a of Reg. (EC) 1905/2006. The relevant procedures under the WTO Dispute Settlement System are WT/DS/27 *EC-Bananas*; WT/DS/165 US – *Measures on certain products from the EU*; WT/DS/265, 266, 283, *EU Subsidies on Sugar*.

Given that EIDHR is used primarily for such purposes as election supervision,[214] it is clear that the association of the EEAS to the programmes and actions financed by EIDHR is particularly close. This is even more the case for the instrument for stability and peace, which finances programmes and projects relating to post-conflict situations, rehabilitation and peace-building after civil wars and the disintegration of society. All these instruments, except the IPA, refer back to to the provision in the decision establishing the EEAS that submits these instruments, in spite of the delegated and implementing powers, to the overall coordination power of the EEAS. The IPA is not subject to this power, as (pre)-accession is formally not part of the external action of the EU.

The Union is also a large-scale provider of food aid, in part on the basis of the World Food Programme and obligations undertaken towards UNRWA. The general rules governing such food aid are now included in the general financing instrument for development cooperation. Much of this aid is given in the form of emergency aid. For these purposes the Commission has established the ECHO, which is a semi-independent service and is in a position to make money and goods available at short notice to assist in coping with the consequences of disasters.[215]

3.1.3 *Contractual measures: International Agreements*

It is useful to recall all the above-mentioned autonomous financing instruments[216] have as contractual counterparts international agreements of a certain type concluded individually with countries that fall into groups defined according to their relation with the Union: the acceding countries, the neighbourhood countries, which fall into two sub-groups, the European ones and the Mediterranean and Middle-Eastern ones etc. It is in discussing the system of these groups of treaties below in section 4, that the agreements that are part of the European development cooperation will be further analysed.

3.2 *Conclusion*

The broad interpretation of development and other cooperation policies that the Court had developed before Lisbon has survived after. As long as development objectives are being pursued by cooperation in such fields as environmental, social and asylum and migration policies, it remains development cooperation. This gives the EU a welcome margin of manoeuvre. The cooperation and institutional provisions of agreements have formed the framework for many and variegated forms of cooperation with many different countries. However, the actual amount of aid, with the exception of the EDF which was and is linked to the association agreement with the ACP countries, has always remained autonomous and thus in the nature of a quasi-sovereign munificence. Both agreements and autonomous instruments frequently refer to and remain firmly anchored in international guidelines, such as the UN Millennium goals and its successor and thus give an aspect of continuity and international legitimacy to EU development cooperation.

The governance of the development and other cooperation policies shows an interesting mix of delegated powers and implementing powers in the same instruments and again, as in

---

214. See the Joint Declaration of the European Parliament, the Council of the European Union and the European Commission on Election Observation Missions, attached to Reg. (EU) 235/2014, which states that up to 25% of the budget over the seven year period will be devoted to election observation, depending on annual election priorities.

215. The ECHO is primarily applying Reg. (EC) 1257/96 concerning humanitarian aid, O.J. 1996, L 163/1.

216. Except the EDF that forms a contractual whole with the ACP Cotonou Agreement.

trade policy, formalizes and reinforces the position of the Commission as that of the executive in this policy field.

4. The System of European Union Agreements

4.1 The system viewed geographically

The system of agreements that the EU has concluded over the years is built up in concentric circles. The innermost circle consists of the European Economic Area (EEA) Agreement. This establishes a free trade area for goods and a common market in the area of the other freedoms: workers, establishment, and the provision of services. This most far-reaching form of cooperation with the economies of a number of the Union's immediate neighbours, together with a special institutional apparatus, now encompasses Norway, Iceland and Liechtenstein. Switzerland remained outside, following the negative decision given at a referendum, and – after Austria, Finland and Sweden acceded to the EU – a set of separate agreements was concluded with Switzerland. Sometimes these countries are contractually linked to specific aspects of the *acquis communautaire*, such as the Schengen system and the 'European Skies' project. If one wants to characterize the present remaining Member States of the EEA and Switzerland, one would say that they are countries that do not (yet) or no longer want to accede to the European Union.[217] Seen from that perspective, this would be the ideal solution for the UK after Brexit, although for political reasons this seems unlikely.

The second circle of countries is formed by those that are officially recognized as being candidates for accession or of having the calling of becoming a Member. These are the countries of the Western Balkans and Turkey. Croatia has recently become a Member and accession negotiations have begun with Turkey, Iceland, Montenegro, and Serbia. Albania has been officially accepted as a candidate country. Macedonia and Bosnia/Herzegovina are merely in dialogue with the Commission about membership. Kosovo is still in part under UN and EU tutelage. All these countries and Kosovo may profit from financing under the Instrument for Pre-accession Assistance (IPA) and they are subject to the finely balanced accession policy of the EU.[218] This accession policy is based on a number of criteria which were developed by the European Councils of Copenhagen (1993), Madrid (1995) and Helsinki (1999). According to the Copenhagen criteria, a candidate Member State must first have stable institutions guaranteeing democracy, the rule of law, human rights and respect for minorities; in addition, the country must have a functioning market economy, and the capacity to cope with competition from the common market; finally, the country must be able to undertake the obligations of membership, including adherence to the various political, economic and monetary aims of the EU. In Madrid, a "good governance" criterion was added: incorporation of the EU *acquis* is as such not enough; it must be possible for the *acquis* to be implemented and applied by competent administrative and judicial structures. Last, but not least, in Helsinki, the emphasis was again put on the importance of the political criteria for accession: the candidate countries should share the common values and objectives laid down in the Treaties. The Luxembourg European Council (1997) also made a link between accession and the reform of the Institutions of the Union.

---

217. Iceland has applied for membership in 2009, but it does not seem fully committed to this application any longer.

218. For IPA see *supra* note 197. A good summary of the official EU accession policy is to be found in "European Union Enlargement: A Historic Opportunity", published by the European Commission in 2001. Available at <ec.europa.eu/neighbourhoodenlargement/sites/near/files/archives/pdf/press_corner/publications/corpus_en.pdf>.

The third circle is formed by the countries of the former Soviet Union (except the central-Asian ones) and the countries falling under the Mediterranean Policy of the EU. They are the object of the European Neighbourhood Policy and have a common financial instrument to serve them: the European Neighbourhood Policy Instrument (ENPI).[219] This policy is under considerable pressure because of the events in Georgia and the Ukraine, in particular the annexation of the Crimea by Russia, as well as the reversals suffered by the Arab spring and the chaos and civil war prevailing in Libya, Syria and Iraq.[220]

Somewhat outside this third circle stand Russia and the countries of the Cotonou Partnership and Association Agreement, the latter being the original example of a development association. The renegotiation of the 1994 PCA (that entered into force in 1997) with Russia has been on the rocks for quite some time now. Initially there was a link with Russia's slow-moving accession to the WTO, but after that hurdle was overcome in 2012, the annexation of the Crimea and the outbreak of the Russo-Ukrainian war and the ensuing sanctions against Russia put an end to any serious chance for a further development of EU-Russian relations.

The ACP-EC partnership agreement of Cotonou is a multilateral association agreement with more than 70 countries from Africa, the Caribbean and the Pacific (hence ACP countries). It had its roots in the association with overseas countries and territories of the Member States with colonies at the time of the Treaty of Rome (now Art. 198 ff. TFEU), but has gone through constant changes and renewal since then.

Finally, the outermost circle of the EU's agreements, geographically, politically and legally, consists of the diverse forms of trade and cooperation agreements with countries of the Americas, the Arabian Peninsula, Asia and the Far East and South Africa. These agreements are usually based on Articles 207 and/or 352 TFEU, and, to the extent they concern development, also on Article 212 TFEU.

4.2 *Agreements based on Article 217 TFEU*

4.2.1 *Article 217 TFEU*

The characteristics of an association agreement under Article 217 EC lie in the reciprocal rights and obligations – even if that is true of all agreements – and in joint action and special procedures. Given the pluriformity of agreements concluded on the basis of Article 217 TFEU, it is difficult to point out specific characteristics which these agreements have in common as against other forms of cooperation agreements, and indeed the distinction between association agreements and those other forms has always been a problem for the Union Institutions. On the basis of EU practice and of the case law, the following appears to apply: association agreements are concluded with countries with which the EU has or wishes to establish particularly close links. These links may have historic roots, as in the case of the ACP, the Maghreb and the Mashreq countries; they may be geographical or political in nature, as in the case of the EEA countries. Association agreements may involve the whole gamut of Community competence, and thus often embrace broad fields.[221] Nevertheless, they are in practice mostly concluded as mixed agreements; only those with Cyprus and Malta in their time were concluded solely by the Community. Also, as the Court has put it, association agreements presuppose a certain participation in the EU system; certain fundamental rules of EU law, even if sometimes only in the form

219. For ENPI, see ibid.
220. This has led to a fracturing of the Neighbourhood Policy, which is influenced not only by the unpropitious political situation in the Middle East and Eastern Europe and the South Caucasus, but also by the more basic question which of the countries concerned have already acceded to the WTO.
221. Case 181/73, *Haegeman v. Belgium* and Case 12/86, *Demirel v. Stadt Schwäbisch Gmünd.*

of free trade, are extended to the association partner. That does not mean, though, that such rules have to be interpreted in the framework of the association in the same manner as in the framework of the Community itself.[222] Finally, association agreements are characterized by their strong institutional structure: they are often equipped with several bodies, including a Parliamentary Assembly, an Association Council at ministerial level and an Association Committee at the level of ambassadors or senior civil servants. The Association Council is often endowed with decision-making powers, and its decisions are binding on the participants in the association. The decisions of the Association Council form an integral part of Community law, without having to be transposed; they can thus be interpreted by the Court of Justice.[223]

Since the entry into force of the SEA the assent of the European Parliament has been required for the conclusion of association agreements. This requirement is currently to be found in Article 218(8) TFEU and is also applied to cooperation agreements with countries that are candidates for accession.

4.2.2 *The EEA Agreement*

Initially the Community had simple free trade agreements with its non-communist neighbours in Europe, which were members of the EFTA. The EEA Agreement, however, was designed to create "a homogeneous European Economic Area",[224] and to this end created an association which provides for the same freedoms as are found in the EU Treaty, although the free movement of goods remains limited to a free trade area as opposed to a customs union. There is as yet no complete free trade in agricultural products. A system is established whereby undistorted competition and equal compliance with the rules on competition is ensured. There is also provision for close cooperation in fields such as research and technological development, environment, education and social policy.

In order to achieve all this, the EEA Agreement contains a great many provisions which are identical, or virtually so, to the fundamental provisions on the freedoms in the EU Treaty, as well as to its competition provisions for undertakings and state enterprises, and the provisions on state aids. The EEA partners also take on board almost the whole *acquis communautaire*. For this purpose a number of Protocols and Annexes to the Agreement contain long lists with references to EU secondary legislation in all sorts of areas, which has force in the EEA partner states, sometimes with accompanying notes on the conditions under which this will occur, or with textual adaptations.

From the institutional viewpoint, the EEA is extremely well-equipped. There is an EEA Council, consisting of the members of the Council of the European Union, members of the Commission of the European communities, and one member of the government of each of the EFTA States which are parties to the EEA Agreement. The EEA Council meets twice a year, and is responsible for giving the general political impetus in the implementation of the EEA Agreement and for laying down general guidelines for the Joint Committee. This Joint Committee consists of representatives of the contracting parties, with the Commission representing the Community; it meets in principle at least once a month. Its main task is to keep track of legislative and jurisprudential developments within the Union, and continually adapt EEA law

---

222. Case 270/80, *Polydor and RSO Records Inc. v. Harlequin Records Shops Ltd and Simons Records Ltd*; Case 104/81, *Hauptzollamt Mainz v. Kupferberg*; Case C-207/91, *Eurim-Pharm GmbH v. Bundesgesundheitsamt*.
223. Case 181/73, *Haegeman* and Case C-192/89, *S.Z. Sevince v. Staatssecretaris van Justitie*. See also Ch. 39, "An introduction to Union external action", notes 141 and 161 and accompanying text, of this book.
224. Art. 1(1) EEA, see O.J. 1994, L 1. See also S. Norberg et al., *The European Economic Area, EEA Law, A Commentary of the EEA Agreement* (Fritzes, 1993).

to secondary EU law. The relevant Protocols and Annexes to the EEA Agreement are revised accordingly. There is also a Joint Parliamentary Committee, which consists of members of the European Parliament on the one hand and MPs of the EFTA States which are parties to the EEA on the other.

The EEA Agreement also creates bodies which are competent only in relation to the EFTA States which are parties to the EEA Agreement. Thus the EFTA Surveillance Authority has a role which is somewhat similar to that of the Commission in the Community, namely supervision of the implementation and fulfilment of EEA law by the EFTA States which are parties to the EEA Agreement, and, in particular, supervision of the implementation of competition law. The EFTA Court deals with appeals against the surveillance procedure regarding the EFTA States concerned, appeals concerning decisions in the competition field taken by the EFTA Surveillance Authority, and the settlement of disputes between two or more of the EFTA States concerned. Most importantly it also decides cases in the framework of a preliminary reference procedure in collaboration with the national courts of the Member States.[225]

Given that the intention is to maintain a homogeneous interpretation of Community law and EEA law which is identical to it, a special procedure for this purpose has been established. Accordingly, one of the tasks of the Joint Committee is to keep the development of the case law of the Court of Justice and of the EFTA Court under constant review, and to do what may be necessary in order to preserve the homogeneous interpretation of the Agreement.[226]

A special agreement was concluded with Iceland and Norway in the area of asylum and immigration policy – which was brought within the Union system by the Treaty of Amsterdam – as a kind of equivalent of the EEA Agreement.[227]

As mentioned earlier, Switzerland remained outside the EEA, but in the course of 1999, a set of seven core agreements were concluded with this country – alongside the old free trade agreement – on free movement of persons, air transport, overland transport (of goods and persons), trade in agricultural products, technical barriers to trade (mutual recognition of conformity to standards), public procurement, research and technological cooperation. Taken together, the substantive content of these agreements does not differ much from the EEA Agreement. The agreements entered into force on 1 June 2002.[228] The agreement on the free movement of persons and Switzerland's participation in the Schengen system is under pressure after the Swiss referendum on the limitation of immigration of February 2014. Some kind of renegotiation is necessary, but has as yet not been completed. The repercussions on the other agreements with Switzerland are uncertain, since in principle they are considered an unseverable whole.[229]

---

225. For the functioning of the EFTA Court, see C. Baudenbacher, *The EFTA Court in Action. Five Lectures* (German Law Publishers, 2010).

226. In practice, the EFTA Court has so far revealed itself to be very inclined to follow the case law of the Court of Justice: it created quasi-primacy and quasi-direct effect and developed an EEA version of state liability for breach of EEA law, see E. Mendez-Pinedo, *EC and EEA Law, A Comparative Study of the Effectiveness of European Law* (Europa Law Publishing, 2009).

227. This agreement was concluded on the basis of Art. 6 Schengen Protocol, see Dec. (EC) 1999/439, O.J. 1999, L 176/5.

228. The seven agreements are published and commented in D. Felder and C. Kaddous (Eds.), *Accords bilatéraux Suisse – UE (Commentaires)* (Helbing & Lichtenhahn/Bruylant, 2001). For information on the entry into force and the official publication of the agreements, see O.J. 2002, L 114. S. Breitenmoser, "Sectoral Agreements between the EC and Switzerland: Contents and context", 40 CML Rev. (2003), 1137–1186.

229. See Art. 25 of the Agreement on the Free Movement of Persons, which has a counterpart in the other seven bilateral agreements of 2002, O.J. 2002, L 114/6-72.

4.2.3 *The Association Agreements with the Eastern European and Southern Caucasus countries*

Very shortly after the first signs of reform appeared in Central and Eastern Europe, the Community concluded trade and cooperation agreements, the so-called Europe agreements, with countries such as Hungary, Poland, Czechoslovakia, Bulgaria and Romania.[230] These agreements have now served their purpose as instruments preparatory to accession. By contrast the present agreements with Eastern-European countries, Ukraine, Belarus (with which the Partnership Agreement has never been finalized for political reasons), Moldova, and similar agreements with the South Caucasus countries, Armenia, Azerbaijan, and Georgia have as their main aim to link these countries strongly to the European Union in the framework of the European Neighbourhood Policy and to grant them considerable financial assistance with the help of the corresponding financial instrument,[231] without giving them an immediate perspective of accession. However, political reality has forced the EU to take a two-pronged approach to these countries concluding or offering to some of them a new generation of associations, including a DCFTA, a Deep and Comprehensive Free Trade Area linked to an Association Agreement, and leaving others with the old cooperation agreements or proposing merely an update of these.

Taking the new Association Agreement, including the DCFTA, with Georgia[232] as an example, the following picture of these agreements can be sketched. The agreement contains an opening clause that states that democratic principles, respect for human rights and market economy principles underpin the relationship. Breach of these principles can lead to the unilateral suspension or termination of the agreement. The human rights and democratic principles are based on the UN Charter, the Helsinki Final Act and the Charter of Paris for a new Europe.[233] The Association contains a substantive part on political cooperation and cooperation in the field of the CFSP, immediately followed by a title concerning cooperation in the field of the Area for Freedom Security and Justice. There can be little doubt that the part on trade, which contains the DCFTA covering goods, services and intellectual property, is the most important part of the agreement covering well over half of its provisions and numerous annexes. It contains a binding dispute settlement chapter, with a procedure which has been inspired by the WTO dispute settlement system. Directly linked to trade are provisions on cooperation in the field of economic policy, in particular public finances and financial control, taxation and statistics

For the rest, these new Association Agreements provide for cooperation in a large number of sectors, from "hard" transport and industrial cooperation to "soft" tourism and cultural cooperation. Such provisions are well-known from many cooperation agreements. Naturally there is also a financial title, which not only lists the many funding mechanisms and instances (EIB, BERD) from which the associated country can draw, but also many rules to protect both parties from fraud and misappropriation.

The Association has an elaborate institutional structure, with an Association Council at Ministerial level at the top, which has the power to take decisions that bind the two parties. This power can be delegated to the Association Committee at ambassadorial level. Both the Association Council and Committee can create subsidiary committees. In addition the Association has

---

230. The first example was the agreement with Hungary (21 Nov. 1988), O.J. 1988, L 327/1. These agreements were still based on the old Arts. 113 and 235 EC. Similar agreements were concluded with the Baltic States in 1992, see O.J. 1992, L 403.
231. Reg. (EC) 232/2014 establishing a European Neighbourhood Policy Instrument, cited *supra* note 197.
232. See the texts of the DCFTA with Georgia and Moldova, cited *infra* note 234. For the old agreement with Ukraine see O.J. 1998, L 49/1; the new agreement has not yet been published in the O.J.
233. See Art. 2. As to the Charter of Paris, see Bull. EC 11-1990, at 130–148, point 2.2.1; 30 ILM 190 (1991).

advisory organs of a parliamentary nature and representative of civil society; the latter is a new feature among association agreements.

These new Associations are concluded by "double mixity", that is to say that they are mixed as between Union and Member States and as between TEU and TFEU. As far as the latter aspect is concerned, they are based on the general treaty-making power under the TEU (Art. 31) and on the association power (Art. 217 TFEU).[234] Since both articles require unanimity in the Council, this poses no problem. However, the association power requires consent of the European Parliament, which formally has no such power over the CFSP aspects of the agreement. It is clear that the mixity of CFSP and TFEU powers will still pose some problems in the future.[235]

4.2.4 *Association with a view to accession*

It was observed above that the Europe Agreements were a type of pre-accession association; the earliest examples of such associations, however, were with Greece, in 1961 (until Greece acceded to the Communities in 1981) and Turkey, in 1963. The association with Turkey has a simple structure in that the agreement limits itself to setting out the objectives in the field of the four freedoms which then have to be achieved through decisions of the Association Council. Moreover, it contains asymmetrical obligations concerning tariff concessions. The original Agreement with Turkey proved however too simple, and a Protocol was concluded in 1970 which brought a transitional phase into being, designed to lead to a customs union over 20 years. The objectives of the Agreement remained unaltered: a customs union, with free movement of workers, services and capital, as well as freedom of establishment, modelled on the EC Treaty. The association was "frozen" for political reasons for a long time in the 1980s. Moreover, the limited degree of liberalization for Turkish workers lawfully employed in a Member State caused such problems,[236] that full free movement of workers does not seem to be a realistic proposition for the foreseeable future. In acknowledgment of this situation the ECJ has recently refrained from granting further rights to Turkish workers migrating within the Union.[237]

In the meantime, at the end of the 1980s, Turkey applied to accede.[238] Only at the end of 1995 was the Association Council able to take a decision on the implementation of the final phase of the customs union.[239] The most difficult problem was the necessity of establishing a common commercial policy, which is a *sine qua non* for a customs union. It is astonishing that

---

234. See Council Dec. (EU) 2014/494 on the signing, on behalf of the European Union, and provisional application of the Association Agreement between the European Union and the European Atomic Energy Community and their Member States, of the one part, and Georgia, of the other part, O.J. 2014, L 261/1.

235. See the problems caused by the Walloon Parliament regarding the ratification of the CETA. For a more general view of the problems involved: Guillaume van der Loo and Ramses A. Wessel, "The non-ratification of mixed agreements: Legal consequences and solutions", 54 CML Rev. (2017), 735–770.

236. A number of judgments of the ECJ in which the Decisions of the Association Council concerning the right of access to other employment within the Community were granted direct effect led to an unprecedented strong political reaction from the German authorities. See Case C-192/89, *Sevince*, and Case C-237/91, *Kazim Kus v. Landeshauptstadt Wiesbaden,* and many other such cases, see e.g. D. Martin and E. Guild, *Free Movement of Persons in the European Union* (Butterworths, 1996), Ch. 13; A. Schrauwen and T. Vandamme, "Towards a citizenship of association? On the future of non-discrimination, preferential treatment and the standstill clauses in the EU-Turkey association regime" in E. Guild, C. Gortázar and D. Kostakopoulou (Eds.), *The Reconceptualization of EU Citizenship* (Brill Nijhoff, 2014); O. Yalincak, "Freedom of movement rights of Turkish nationals in the European Union", 19 CJEL (2013), 391–422.

237. See Case C-221/11, *Demirkan.*

238. Bull. EC 4-1987, points 1.3.1 and 1.3.2. The Commission originally gave its opinion that while accession was in principle possible, it would only be feasible after a number of years. Bull. EC 12/89, at 88.

239. Decision 1/95 of the Association Council EC-Turkey, O.J. 1995, L 5/1.

a country with such increasing economic significance as Turkey should adopt the greatest part of the Community's common commercial policy, without being able to exert much influence on it; only the Joint Committee of the customs union and the Association Council offer limited possibilities for this.[240] This can only be explained in the light of a soon-to-follow accession. Since this is now unlikely because of the political developments in Turkey, the customs union may start to unravel.[241]

Nevertheless, the European Council in Helsinki (1999) decided that Turkey could, in principle, accede. The Council has followed an interesting legal course on this issue, whereby first a Regulation based on Article 308 EC (now 352 TFEU) was adopted in February 2001, which laid down that as part of the pre-accession strategy in relation to Turkey, an accession partnership with that country would be realized. That partnership could be adopted by the Council by qualified majority, and would lay down the objectives, principles and priorities and interim objectives for the accession partnership. After discussions with Turkey, the framework for the possible coming accession was laid down in a unilateral legal act of the Council. Many of the same elements found in the old Europe Agreements and the new DCFTA's are met within that framework, including the basic principles of democracy, rule of law, human rights and protection of minorities.[242]

A new version of the pre-accession association was invented when the Community decided to conclude a series of so-called Stabilization and Association Agreements (SAAs) with the countries of the Western Balkans which were considered candidates for accession in the short run (Croatia and possibly Macedonia) or in the longer run (Serbia, Montenegro, Bosnia and Herzegovina and Albania). These SAAs are clearly more ambitious than the old PCAs with the East-European and South Caucasian countries, but seem to fall slightly short of the new DCFTAs signed with some of those countries. For the moment, the SAAs do not go further than to aim for a free trade area in full conformity with the relevant articles of the GATT and the GATS in 6 to 10 years. They are founded on a strongly worded opening article stating that democracy and human rights in line with the Universal Declaration of Human Rights, the Helsinki Final Act and the Paris Charter, as well as the principles of the market economy in line with the OSCE Bonn principles,[243] underlie the association. Another important provision is the one on cooperation with the other countries of the Western Balkans, with which SAA agreements have been concluded. The high ambitions of the agreements are also expressed in provisions on the movement of workers, establishment and trans-border services. In addition, there are elaborate chapters on approximation of laws and law enforcement, as well as on Justice and Home Affairs. In the SAAs, the Association Councils have the power to take decisions that are binding on both parties.[244] The SAAs are mixed agreements based on Article 217 TFEU.

---

240. See Arts. 54–60 of Decision 1/95.
241. See "From the Board", "Happy Golden Anniversary, EU-Turkey Customs Union!", 40 LIEI (2013), 291–296.
242. See Reg. (EC) 390/2001, O.J. 2001, L 58/1 and the Council Dec. (EC) 2001/235, O.J. 2001, L 85/13-23, based on it. These accession partnerships have become a general feature of relations between the EU and countries that are officially candidates for accession.
243. Document of the Bonn Conference on Economic Cooperation in Europe convened in accordance with the relevant provisions of the concluding document of the Vienna Meeting of the Conference on Security and Co-operation in Europe (19 Mar. – 11 Apr. 1990), available at <www.osce.org/eea/14081> (last visited 30 Nov. 2016). This document treated the necessary economic reforms in Eastern Europe at the time in relation to the political reforms.
244. Examples are the SAA with FYROM, O.J. 2004, L 84/13, and with Croatia, O.J. 2005, L 26/1, which has in the meantime acceded.

4.2.5 Development association

The classic examples of development association are the successive Yaoundé and Lomé Conventions and the Cotonou Partnership Agreement. After the independence of the French-African states it was felt necessary to continue the association provided for in Article 182 EC in some other way. This took the form of a combination of a free trade area and the grant of financial and technical assistance, initially contained in the Yaoundé Conventions (1964 and 1971). After four Lomé Conventions (1975–2000)[245] the Cotonou Agreement was signed on 2 June 2000, between the Community, its Member States, and more than seventy developing countries in Africa, the Caribbean and the Pacific (the ACP countries). The Agreement entered into force on 1 March 2003.[246] The Cotonou Agreement has clearly gained a political dimension as a result of the insertion of a number of articles concerning political dialogue, prevention and resolution of armed conflicts, and peace-building initiatives between the parties. Moreover, the provision included in Lomé IV on respect for human rights, democratic principles and the rule of law has been retained. This has been classified as an "essential element" of the agreement, so that a breach in this area could be a reason for unilateral suspension of the agreement, or even its termination.[247] It also contains a very elaborate system for sanctioning countries that do not conform to the democracy, human rights and rule of law provision which is laid down in Article 96. This provision has been activated for many African countries, when *coups d'état* occurred or civil war broke out.[248]

The cooperation provisions of the Association cover a multitude of areas which are important for development, such as agriculture, fisheries, industrial development, mining, energy, the environment and so on. In the sphere of financial development the European Development Fund has been created in order to support development activities under soft conditions. The amount of this development aid is laid down by a Protocol for five years, and thus grants the ACP countries a degree of the certainty which they need.

Two cases on bananas and ACP (cane) sugar,[249] which caused controversy within and outside the Community,[250] made clear that the asymmetrical nature of the trade provisions of the Association, which meant that the Union opened up its market without demanding concessions from the ACP countries, would no longer be tolerated by its partners in the WTO, not even through a special waiver. This led to a radical change of EU policy from which resulted the offer of Economic Partnership Agreements (EPAs) to regional groups or existing free-trade

245. After the first Lomé Convention the integration of most British ex-colonies in Africa and the Caribbean into the system was completed.

246. Text available at <ec.europa.eu/development/body/cotonou/index_en.htm> (last visited 30 Nov. 2016). For the conclusion and entry into force, see Council Dec. (EC) 2003/159, O.J. 2003, L 65/27, read with Art. 93(3) Cotonou. See K. Arts, "ACP-EU relations in a new era: The Cotonou Agreement", 40 CML Rev. (2003), 95–116.

247. See Art. 60 Vienna Convention on the Law of Treaties 1969. See further on this, B. Brandtner and A. Rosas, "Human rights and the external relations of the European Community: An analysis of doctrine and practice", (1998) EJIL, 437.

248. See on the application of Art. 96, L. Laakso, T. Kivimäki and M. Seppänen, "Evaluation of coordination and coherence in the application of Art. 96 of the Cotonou Partnership Agreement", *Studies in European Development Cooperation Evaluation No. 6* (European Union, 2007). A large number of African states have at one time or another been hit by the application of Art. 96, for instance Niger, Ivory Coast, Togo, Comores, Chad, Zimbabwe etc.

249. See Reg. (EEC) 404/93, O.J. 1993, L 47/1, and Case C0280/93 R, *Germany v. Council.*

250. See the series of decisions of the WTO Panels and the Appellate Body in the so-called Bananas Case (WT/DS 29) and the Sugar case (WT/DS 265, 266 and 283).

zones of its partners. These EPAs should contain advanced FTAs that would fully satisfy the WTO's requirements of eliminating all tariffs on substantially all the trade between the partners.

The most important institutions of the partnership are the Council of Ministers, the Committee of Ambassadors and the Joint Parliamentary Assembly. Meetings of the Heads of States and Governments of the Parties are also possible. The members of the Council of the European Union and the members of the Commission on the one hand, and a member of the government of each of the ACP states on the other, comprise the Council of Ministers. The Joint Parliamentary Assembly is composed of representatives of the European Parliament on the one hand, and members of parliament (or in their absence other representatives) designated by the ACP states on the other.

In order to have a clear view of the relation between the Cotonou Agreement and its EPAs it is also necessary to look at the provisions of the EPAs themselves. New Articles 36 and 37 of Cotonou provide for the negotiation of WTO-compatible FTAs, whilst Article 37a leaves the ACP countries free to be parties to other trading arrangements. The institutions of both agreements will work together with a view to ensuring coordination, coherence and complementarity (new Art. 14(2) Cotonou). The EPAs contain a provision stating that they shall prevail over the trade provisions of the Cotonou Agreement, except for the development cooperation articles.[251] The EPAs themselves are WTO-compatible free trade zones, where the EU liberalizes its market access immediately (normally the EU goods market is already open to the ACP countries) and the ACP countries have a transition period of 15 to 20 years to do the same.[252]

The trade provisions on goods and related matters of the agreement are largely modelled on the relevant WTO provisions with some small elaborations. The provisions on trade in services, e-commerce and investment create possibilities to go beyond the WTO and strive earnestly to enable further services commitments between the parties in order to satisfy the FTA requirements of Article Va of GATS. Insofar as investment is also covered in this chapter it is restricted to establishment in the field of services through commercial presence. There is an important chapter on binding dispute settlement, broadly based on the WTO procedure, but without an appellate instance. There are also rules on avoiding clashes between simultaneous dispute settlement regarding the same issue in the EPA dispute settlement mechanism and that of the WTO.[253]

The EPAs have their own institutional structure, which is broadly identical to that of the Cotonou Agreement.[254]

Associations similar to the Cotonou Agreement, with a clear development character, have existed for a long time with the Maghreb and Mashreq countries. The last "generation" of these – which were drawn up in the framework of the Mediterranean policy and now function within the European Neighbourhood Policy – are called Euro-Mediterranean agreements. The agreement with Tunisia may serve as example.[255] First of all, the agreement contains numerous references to the WTO, the GATT (in particular the provisions on free trade areas) and the GATS. As far as trade in goods is concerned, a free trade area must come into existence within

251. Arts. 2(2) and 241 of the EPA with Cariforum, OJ 2008, L 289/I/3.
252. Art. 21 of the Interim Agreement for an Agreement with the Central African Party, with a 10 to 15 year transition period for the central African side, OJ 2009, L57/1.
253. Ch. 3 on Settlement of Disputes and Art. 86 on the relationship to WTO obligations, in the EPA with the Central African Party, ibid.
254. Part V of the EPA with Cariforum, *loc. cit.* fn. 251.
255. O.J. 1998, L 97/1. As was noted above, Tunisia has been offered a DCFTA. Other Mediterranean countries that are Members of WTO and with a stable internal situation, such as Morocco and possibly Jordan, may be offered the same.

a period of 12 years – although Tunisia is granted abundant possibilities for temporarily raising customs duties or re-imposing them in favour of "infant industries" or restructuring with large scale social consequences. It should also be noted that the free trade in agricultural products is still very limited. In the area of establishment and services, the liberalization is intended to come about through recommendations of the Association Council. In addition, the agreement contains extensive provisions in the area of economic, social and cultural cooperation. The Court has recognized the direct effect of these provisions.[256]

Similar association agreements exist with the Mashrek countries: Egypt Syria, Lebanon, Jordan, as well as with Israel. These agreements have all been renegotiated between 1997 and 2004 and only the agreement with Syria has never been finalized due to political considerations and the subsequent civil war.[257] In the framework of the Euro-Mediterranean policy, the Community also concluded a so-called Euro-Mediterranean interim association agreement with the PLO for the benefit of the Palestinian Authority, at the time Palestinian autonomy began to be realized in 1997. This agreement is not based on the Treaty's association provision (Art. 310 EC, now 217 TFEU), but on the commercial policy and international cooperation provisions (now Arts. 207 and 212(1) TFEU).[258] The relation of the EU with Israel and the Palestinian Authority has been marked over the last few years by the Court's judgment in the *Brita* case.[259] From that case it results that the customs authorities of the Member States may not grant the preferential treatment under the EU-Israel agreement to goods that in reality come from the West Bank, whilst they are not obliged to follow the determination of origin from the Israeli authorities to the contrary as authoritative, if there are indications that they are not credible. This has given rise to movements different indications of origin to be affixed on products from Israel and the occupied territories.

4.3 *Other cooperation agreements*

4.3.1 *Partnership agreements with Russia and Central Asia*

The meeting of the European Council on Corfu in June 1994 saw the signature of the Partnership and Cooperation Agreement with Russia.[260] This mixed agreement was later embedded in the Common Strategy which the European Council adopted in the course of 1999.[261]

One of its first articles (Art. 2) states explicitly that respect for democratic principles and human rights underpins the internal and external policies of the Parties and constitutes an essential element of the partnership and of the agreement. In this context, reference is made to the Helsinki Final Act and the Charter of Paris for a new Europe.[262] The agreement is economically

256. See Case C-18/90, *Office national de l'emploi v. Kziber* and Case C-58/93, *Zoubir Yousfi v. Belgian State*. Just like Case C-192/89, *Sevince* and Case C-237/91, *Kazim Kus v. Landeshauptstadt Wiesbaden*, these decisions led to rather negative reactions, this time from the French authorities.
257. The agreement with Jordan is a good example, see O.J. 2002, L 129/1. The agreement with Israel is slightly different, O.J. 2000, L 147/1 and has been complemented with an important agreement on cooperation in science and technology.
258. See O.J. 1997, L 187/1, amended by exchange of letters, O.J. 2005, L 2/6.
259. Case C-186/08, *Brita v. Hauptzollamt Hamburg-Hafen*, paras. 47–53 and 70–73.
260. See O.J. 1997, L 327/1.
261. See Ch. 39, "An introduction to Union external action", notes 21 and 22 and accompanying text, of this book.
262. Such clauses were not included at the time in the contemporaneous Europe agreements, but were included in agreements with Latin-American countries. This "essential elements" formula is a reference to Art. 62(1)(a) VCLT on fundamental change of circumstances, and therefore puts either party ina position to abrogate the agreement in case such essential elements are no longer respected by the other party. The EU has so far has not invoked this clause.

and politically outdated because of Russia's membership in the WTO since 2012 and because of Russia's annexation of Crimea and policy of destabilization and conquest by proxy in the east of Ukraine.[263]

The institutional structure of the agreement resembles that of association agreements, with a Cooperation Council at ministerial level, and a Cooperation Committee at the level of senior civil servants, and a Parliamentary Cooperation Committee. Although the Cooperation Council may make recommendations, it has no power, unlike most association councils, to adopt binding decisions.

Similar partnership agreements have been concluded with a number of Central Asian ex USSR countries: Kazakhstan, Kyrgyzstan, Tajikistan, Turkmenistan and Uzbekistan, and they entered into force on 1 July 1999.[264] Kazakhstan and Belarus have joined the new Russian – founded FTA (the Eurasian Customs Union). As soon as it became clear that Kazakhstan was om its way to join the WTO in the course of 2015, the negotiation of an Enhanced Partnership and Cooperation Agreement with Kazakhstan was announced in January of that year.

4.3.2 *Diverse trade and cooperation agreements*

Since the mid-1970s, the Community, and later the Union, has hardly signed any classic trade agreements with non-European States which do not fall under development association. One of the earliest examples was the Cooperation Agreement with Canada (1976), but that has remained an exception. The so-called Transatlantic Declarations were drawn up with the United States and Canada, and a Transatlantic Dialogue was kept going, accompanied by an early warning system for trade conflicts. Comparable declarations were agreed with Japan, Australia and New Zealand.[265] This policy has been drastically changed over the last few years; the EU has come to the conviction that, given the slow progress of negotiations in the WTO it would make sense to conclude far-reaching trade agreements with major industrialized countries.

The first of these agreements was the free-trade agreement with Korea concluded in 2010.[266] It is a free-trade agreement that is in principle WTO-compliant, which means that in particular in services (including important provisions on transport services) the reciprocal commitments are considerable. The agreement also contains an important chapter on intellectual property that clearly goes further than the WTO TRIPs agreement. Of considerable interest is the chapter on trade and sustainable development, which includes both environmental and social aspects of sustainability, but which is outfitted with a soft dispute settlement mechanism through a panel of experts. This stands in sharp contrast to the chapter on dispute settlement on trade, which is modelled on the WTO-procedure and gives rise to binding panel decisions that are enforceable. The Korea FTA has become a mixed agreement mainly because of the Cultural

263. No official statements have been made on the relation between the Partnership Agreement and the sanctions against Russia.
264. For an example of one of these agreements, see O.J. 1999, L 196/1 (Kazakhstan). Of these countries Kazachstan, Kyrgyzstan and Tajikistan are already WTO Members, Uzbekistan is still negotiating its accession and Turkmenistan has not applied for membership yet.
265. 24th General report 1990, para 693 (US) and para 712 (Canada); 25th General report 1991, para 859 (Japan). Unfortunately, these declarations – which are full of consultation clauses and intentions as to cooperation, and which were stepped up even further in the mid 1990s – have not led in practice to a less confrontational type of trade policy, particularly between the US and the EU. The joint declarations with Australia and New Zealand date from 1997 and 1999 respectively.
266. See O.J. 2010, L 127/1. See also M. Elsig and C. Dupont, "European Union meets South Korea: Bureaucratic interests, exporter discrimination and the negotiations of trade agreements", 50 JCMS (2012), 492–507.

Protocol and is based, next to Article 207 TFEU, on the transport (Arts. 91 and 100 TFEU) and cultural (167 TFEU) provisions of the Treaty.[267]

The Comprehensive Economic and Trade Agreement (CETA) with Canada dwarfs the FTA with Korea in its scope and detail.[268] For instance, instead of a short chapter on trade and sustainable development that encompasses both labour and the environment, CETA has individual chapters of some length devoted to trade and sustainable development, trade and the environment and trade and labour. Moreover, CETA contains a separate chapter on investment and on investor-state dispute settlement (ISDS); this ISDS procedure is entirely separate from the binding dispute settlement procedure in the field of trade, which like the FTA with Korea is modelled on the WTO procedure. This is the simple consequence of the fact that in ISDS natural and legal persons can claim against a State, whereas the WTO procedure is entirely state-to-state. Both procedures, however, broadly share the same exception that resembles GATT Article XX and the same security exception modeled after GATT Article XXI. The Commission has *in extremis* renegotiated the investment dispute settlement system with the new Canadian government in order to make it conform to the model of an investment court system, with an Appeals Tribunal, which it had offered to the US in the TTIP negotiations.[269] CETA recently has been provisionally applied by the Council after consent from the EP. Only then the long process of approval by the Member States under their national procedures will follow. The tribulations with this process because of resistance by the Walloon Parliament in Belgium are well-known.[270]

The Trans-Atlantic Trade and Investment Pact (TTIP) that is under negotiation with the USA promises to be even more elaborate and wide-ranging than CETA and is extremely contentious both in US and European public opinion.[271] Furthermore, the new Trump administration has serious problems with this agreement.

Where Latin-America is concerned, in 1998–1999 the EU had renewed its series of so-called framework agreements with the states parties of three regional economic organizations, the Andean Community the Central America Common Market (CACM) and MERCOSUR. All these agreements had a commercial and development character. The EU has now again embarked on a round of renewal of the treaty relations with these countries. For the moment, the EU has succeeded in concluding a new trade agreement with Colombia and Peru in 2012, to which Ecuador has acceded at the end of 2014.[272] The old agreement with Chile of 2005 estab-

267. It is not to be excluded that a Cultural Protocol will become, like the political consultation clauses of old, the standard instrument to make a mixed agreement out of an agreement that is fundamentally a trade and transport agreement in which the transport provisions relate essentially to those aspects of transport covered by Union legislation.

268. For the text of CETA, see <trade.ec.europa.eu/doclib/docs/2014/september/tradoc_152806.pdf> (last visited 30 Nov. 2016). For a first legal assessment of CETA see L. Biuković, "Transparency norms, the world trade system and free trade agreements: The case of a CETA", 39 LIEI (2012), 93–107.

269. On CETA and ISDS, see *supra* section 2.3.5.

270. See P.J. Kuijper, "Post-CETA: How we got there and how to go on", (2017) RTDEur, 181–187.

271. For an overview of the contested points see e.g. C. Tietje and F. Baetens, *The Impact of Investor-State-Dispute Settlement (ISDS) in the Transatlantic Trade and Investment Partnership*, Study prepared for the Minister for Foreign Trade and Development Cooperation and the Ministry of Foreign Affairs, The Netherlands (2014) available at <www.rijksoverheid.nl/documenten/rapporten/2014/06/24/the-impact-of-investor-state-dispute-settlement-isds-in-the-ttip> (last visited 30 Nov. 2016).

272. See Council Dec. (EU) 2012/735 on the on the signing, on behalf of the Union, and provisional application of the Trade Agreement between the European Union and its Member States, of the one part, and Colombia and Peru, of the other part, O.J. 2012, L 354. Information on the accession of Ecuador can be found on the website of DG Trade, available at <trade.ec.europa.eu/doclib/press/index.cfm?id=1129&title=EU-and-Ecuador-conclude-negotiations-for-trade-and-development-agreement> (last visited 30 Nov. 2016).

lished an association of a political and economic nature between the Community and its Member States on the one hand and Chile on the other. Its trade part establishes a free trade area.[273] As we have seen this is a model that is now followed in many instances. An extremely ambitious agreement was signed with Mexico in 1997 on economic partnership, political coordination and cooperation, but entered into force only on 1 October 2000.[274] It aged well, probably because the Joint Committee established by the agreement was able to take binding decisions on progressive liberalization of trade, resulting in a free-trade area. Both countries recently decided to set up a committee to consider a further development of their relationship.[275] As far as Mercosur is concerned, the EU has a number of outdated old trade and cooperation agreements with the individual Member States (Argentina, Brazil, Uruguay and Paraguay) and the agreement with Mercosur itself also dates back to 1995. Since 2010 the two parties have decided to bring about a so-called Bi-regional Association Agreement, but even after a re-affirmation of this objective in early 2013 not much progress has been realized. By contrast the old agreement with the countries of the CACM has been expanded in 2011 to include all states of Central-America (Costa Rica, El Salvador, Guatemala, Honduras, Nicaragua and Panama) and to establish an FTA, within an Association Agreement that also includes cooperation provisions and political dialogue. The FTA is asymmetrical, i.e. immediate access of Central-American goods to the EU market and introduction of near-full liberalization on the part of the Central-American countries over a period of 10 or 17 years.[276] The cooperation provisions of the agreement are new, but along the lines of, the Korea FTA described above. There are also resemblances with the agreement with the Andean countries, which is broadly contemporaneous.

As far as relations with Asian countries are concerned, the EU has had a cooperation agreement with the five original ASEAN countries jointly (Indonesia, Malaysia, the Philippines, Singapore and Thailand) since 1980. In 2007 the EU announced that it would like to negotiate a region-to-region FTA with the newly expanded ASEAN (then including also Brunei, Burma, Cambodia, Laos and Vietnam) as it later succeeded concluding with the Central American countries. When not much progress was made during two years, the EU changed tack and announced it wanted to conclude comprehensive FTA's with the individual Members of ASEAN, starting with Singapore. That FTA was completed in two years (2012).[277] According to the Commission it is a pure trade agreement that should solely be based on Article 207 TFEU; Member States maintain that it should be mixed. The Court has delivered Opinion 2/15 on the matter and decided that it is a mixed agreement.[278] This will have great influence on a similar agreement with Vietnam,[279] and other future FTA's.

The Union has also completed a revision of the cooperation agreements with the South Asian states: India,[280] Pakistan, Nepal and Sri Lanka. These agreements are all based on Articles

273. See for signature and provisional application, as well as the text of the Decision: Dec. (EC) 2002/979, O.J. 2002, L 352.
274. See O.J. 2000, L 276/45.
275. See DG Trade website under Mexico, available at <ec.europa.eu/trade/policy/countries-and-regions/countries/mexico/> (last visited 30 Nov. 2016).
276. See Agreement establishing an Association between the European Union and its Member States, on the one hand, and Central America on the other, O.J. 2012, L 346.
277. The provisional text of the Agreement is available at <trade.ec.europa.eu/doclib/press/index.cfm?id=961> (last visited 30 Nov. 2016).
278. See *supra* note 174 and accompanying text.
279. The provisional text of that agreement is available at <ec.europa.eu/trade/policy/countries-and-regions/countries/vietnam> (last visited 30 Nov. 2016). The Commission proposal for conclusion, signature and provisional application will probably after the ECJ's Opinion 2/15 will have been issued.
280. See Case C-268/94, *Portuguese Republic v. Council (Agreement with India)*.

133 and 181 TEC (Arts. 207 and 211 TFEU) and also contain a clause on democracy and human rights. The Joint Committee of these cooperation agreements does not have decision-making power. Negotiations with India on an FTA have begun, but not progressed. There is an old trade agreement with China (1985), but relations are primarily governed by the WTO agreements, While the EU presently seeks to conclude a comprehensive investment agreement with China, trade and economic relations with Taiwan are regulated on the basis of autonomous measures – even though they are often preceded by unofficial negotiations. In this manner the EU takes account of China's sensitivities, but at the same time it can seek a *modus vivendi* with Taiwan, which is of great importance in all trade.

Relations between the Union and the countries of the Arab world beyond the Maghreb and Mashrek have not yet been highly developed in contractual terms. A Euro-Arab dialogue has existed since 1976 in the context first of European political cooperation, now of CFSP, with the objective, among other things, of contributing to the Middle Eastern peace process. The old cooperation agreement with North Yemen, dating from 1984, was extended with effect from 1995 to embrace the new Republic of Yemen, resulting from unification of the two Yemens.[281] Finally, in 1989 the Community concluded a cooperation agreement with the states of the Gulf Cooperation Council (Saudi Arabia, Kuwait, Bahrain, Qatar, United Arab Emirates, Oman), which may ultimately to lead to the creation of a free trade area.[282] However, these negotiations have been suspended by the GCC in 2008.

4.4 *Conclusion*

Two trends emerge from the overview. One is the increased bilateralization of trade, which is of course a global trend and a consequence of the incapacity of the WTO to agree on anything of note in the framework of the (*de facto* defunct) Doha Development Agenda. This is exemplified by the increasing number of highly substantive trade chapters found in previously rather general Association or Cooperation agreements and by the conclusion of EPA's within the framework of the Cotonou Agreement. The other, more recent one, is to include trade provisions equivalent to a DCFTA in association agreements which have CFSP provisions in them. As was noted above, such agreements are so structured as to minimize the conflict between the procedures under the TFEU and the TEU and have become very popular because of this.

5. Restrictive measures

5.1 *Introduction and overview of restrictive measures (sanctions)*

The first time the awareness dawned that UN economic sanctions ought to be implemented by the EU under the CCP, since otherwise such sanctions might be less effective than required because of different interpretations of the decision of the Security Council by the Member States, arose in the case of the UN sanctions against Rhodesia (1966, 1970).[283] The first time the EU actually took sanctions under the CCP – more specifically autonomous European sanctions- was against Argentina during the Falklands/Malvinas war, out of solidarity with its Member, the UK. Before the regulation imposing the sanctions under the present Article 207 TFEU was

281. See the exchange of letters in O.J. 1993, C 310/19.

282. O.J. 1989, L 54/1, see esp. Art. 11 of the Agreement. Given the continuous civil strife in this country, this agreement probably leads a paper existence.

283. See P.J. Kuijper, "Sanctions against Rhodesia: The EEC and the implementation of general international legal rules", 12 CML Rev. (1975), 231.

taken, however, there was discussion among the Member States under (now) Article 247 TFEU and a political decision that economic sanctions under the CCP were necessary was taken.[284]

Since then there has always been a unanimous political decision by the Member States preceding the adoption of sanctions under Community/Union law. Initially as described above, later such decisions were initiated under Political Cooperation, followed by measures under the CCP, and finally under the CFSP provisions, succeeded by actions under specific sanctions provisions included in the TEC and later the TFEU. Both UN ordered or authorized sanctions and autonomous EU sanctions are taken this way. The provisions on restrictive measures have followed the evolution of the practice of sanctions in the UN and the CFSP. This evolution can be sketched as follows.

First of all there has been an enormous growth of sanctions and restrictive measures. There are now well over 30 sanctions regimes that are maintained by the EU.[285] This is a consequence of the increased willingness of the UN Security Council to use this weapon because there has been less recourse to the veto in the Council since the 1990s. Autonomous restrictive measures also grew, since the Union had included more and more provisions in its development and cooperation agreements that authorized the (partial) suspension of provisions of these agreements, if either of the parties did not hew to the "essential elements" at the basis of these agreements, such as the human rights and democracy clauses.[286]

Secondly, there has been an increasing variety in the kinds of sanctions and how they are targeted. Initially sanctions were largely concentrated in the field covered by the CCP and directed at countries or territories. Especially the negative experience with such sanctions in Saddam's Iraq in the 1990s and in some African countries under predatory dictators and warlords, who were in a position to have the burden of economic sanctions shouldered largely by the common citizens, and in particular the sick and women and children, while they themselves still had access to untold wealth and ostentation, made the UN and the EU look for alternatives. These were found in so-called targeted sanctions directed at the leaders and the elites of these countries and their wealth. A technique that was soon, when the so-called war on terror broke out after the attack on the Twin Towers, also used against named suspected terrorist leaders and their families. This made instrument of sanctions shift from trade to financial measures, such as asset freezes and banking restrictions, and travel bans.

Thirdly, precisely because of this shift to individualized sanctions, especially in combating terrorism, greater attention was paid to the legality of such sanctions. Since so-called asset freezes against named individuals lasted longer and longer, it became more and more difficult to maintain that such measures were only preventive and temporary in nature and that hence not much attention needed to be paid to fundamental rights, such as the right of the targeted person to be informed of the charge against him or her and the reasons and facts on which these restrictive measures were based.[287] This has led to the well-known Kadi cases that will be discussed below and ultimately led to the quashing of the asset freeze against Mr. Kadi.[288] Since 2005 the ECJ, especially the General Court, has been subject to an ever higher wave of cases concerning these targeted sanctions and, in line with the Kadi cases, many of these cases have been decided

284. This was controversial at the time, see J. Verhoeven, "Communautés Européennes et Sanctions Internationales", 18 *Revue belge de droit international* (1984), 79–94.
285. See the list of sanctions regimes in force as available at <europeansanctions.com> (last visited August 2017), where 34 sanctions regimes are mentioned.
286. See section 3.1.1 on the ACP Convention.
287. Joined Cases C-584/10 P, C-593/10 P and C-595/10 P, *Kadi II* (ECJ 2013), para 156.
288. Joined Cases C-402/05 P and C-415/05 P, *Kadi I*, para 372. In the end Mr. Kadi was taken off the list by the UN Security Council even before the Court's judgment in *Kadi II*.

in favour of the complainant because of a lack of reasoning or a lack of evidence that the Court could have access to.[289]

It is interesting to note that given the difficulties surrounding targeted sanctions against individuals, recently they have been employed with greater moderation, insofar as the EU acted autonomously. They continue to be used also in the most recent sanctions against Iran until recently (non-proliferation) and against Russia (over its policy of aggression in relation to the Ukraine), but the emphasis is now shifted to the industries that one wants to hit and that are of special importance to these countries and their governing classes. These are general banking, investment and financial restrictions and restrictions on special technologies, such as those relating to nuclear installations (Korea) and exploration and exploitation of fossil fuels (both countries). These do not raise the same questions of fundamental rights as targeted sanctions, while they are still likely to hit primarily the governing elites without unduly hurting the general population.[290]

5.2 *Legal basis and adoption of sanctions regimes*

As already mentioned above, restrictive measures, whether binding UN sanctions[291] or autonomous measures, are taken in the same two step procedure: first a CFSP decision on the basis of Article 29 TEU, followed by a Council Regulation, adopted on the joint proposal of the Commission and the HR, under Article 215 TFEU. It is obvious that Article 215 TFEU deviates from the normal legislative procedure.[292] The fact that normally speed and surprise are of the essence in the adoption of sanctions and the origin of sanctions in a CFSP decision justify the absence of the EP in this procedure and justify the presence of the HR as co-proposer of the measures. The EP has argued that Article 75 TFEU on financial sanctions should give it a grip on all financial sanctions, including the implementation by the EU of the UN sanctions against Al-Qaeda. However, the Court has rejected this, contrasting the broad scope of Article 215 TFEU to the rather narrow ambit of Article 75, which is directly linked to Article 67 setting out the fundamental aspects of the area of freedom, security and justice.[293] In the domain of restrictive measures the EP is therefore limited to the right of being informed and the exercise of its general political oversight over TFEU matters.[294]

The Council has to a very large extent streamlined and standardized the procedures for the adoption of autonomous restrictive measures and the implementation of UN decided sanctions. Documents containing guidelines and best practices have been produced by the Council

---

289. The law of restrictive measures has thus become a sub-specialization of European law, with specialized lawyers, its own blog, available at <europeansanctions.com> (last visited Aug 2017). It represents a considerable litigation burden to the Council and the Commission.
290. See Reg. (EU) 833/2014, O.J. 2014, L 229/1 (sanctions against Russia).
291. The sanctions taken by the Security Council are binding within the meaning of Art. 25 Charter on the Members of the UN, but they are not binding on the EU as such, since the EU is not and cannot become a Member of the UN. The Court of Justice explicitly rejected the General Court's attempt to construct such binding character in *Kadi I*; see para 327 of that judgment. This does not alter the fact that Art. 29 TEU and Art. 215 TFEU combined make it possible for the EU to carry out such sanctions.
292. A good recent overview article is C. Eckes, "EU restrictive measures against natural and legal persons: From counterterrorist to third country sanctions", 51 CML Rev. (2014), 869.
293. Case C-130/10, *European Parliament v. Council*, paras. 55–66 (on the interpretation of Art. 215 TFEU) and 81–82 (on the role of the EP).
294. For an example of the exercise of such general oversight, see EP recommendation to the Council P7_TA(2012)0018, "European Parliament recommendation to the Council of 2 Feb. 2012 on a consistent policy towards regimes against which the EU applies restrictive measures, when their leaders exercise their personal and commercial interests within EU borders".

Secretariat and are regularly updated.[295] Whereas in the preparation of implementation of UN sanctions the measures have already been defined and circumscribed in the Security Council Resolution, this work has to be done in the instances of the Council, notably the Political and Security Committee and its working groups. In this preparation the EAAS plays an important role, which is logical given that the first decision on restrictive measures is taken in the framework of CFSP and that the subsequent EU regulation is based on a joint proposal from the Commission and the HR. Moreover, the preparatory steps to both legal acts require either close contact with the EU's UN delegation or with the EU and Member State delegations in the probable target State(s) and these EU delegations are directed by the EEAS. The Guidelines attach importance to guaranteeing that the countermeasures are in conformity with international law, in particular fundamental rights as laid down in the Charter on Human Rights and in the ECHR. Moreover, they have to be in line with the WTO Agreements, in particular the so-called security exception of Article XXI GATT and Article XIVbis GATS,[296] and with the customary rules of international law on jurisdiction as interpreted in the EU's own instruments directed at blocking the effects of the extra-territorial application of legislation adopted by a third country (so-called "Blocking Regulation").[297]

The Guidelines show that the Council has developed a very elaborate model for restrictive measures decisions under CFSP and for the corresponding Regulation based on Article 215, whether or not it concerns targeted measures. It is not useful to summarize it here in its entirety. Some aspects will be highlighted. The kind of measures that are taken can be: arms embargoes; restrictions on equipment used for internal repression and other specific import or export restrictions; restrictions on admission (visa refusal or travel ban); and financial restrictions. The CFSP decision and the way it is drafted is of particular importance for those measures that do not fall under EU competence, such as arms embargoes, the non-visa aspects of travel bans and some financial restrictions, since they must be implemented by the Member States on the basis of that Decision. All other measures are taken by Regulation and are immediately applicable in the Member States. They merely need to be complemented by sufficiently strong criminal sanctions from the Member States.

The sanctions measures are normally accompanied by humanitarian and other exemptions, by clauses on the absence of liability for having observed sanctions and on the protection of persons and enterprises having done so against any claim. The CFSP decision and the Regulation based on Article 215, may be linked to two or more annexes, one listing the targeted persons and/or companies, another the targeted categories of goods and/or services. Sanctions are often changed, both by UN decision and autonomous action by changing the persons, goods or services listed in these Annexes. In the case of autonomous sanctions the Council normally reserves these modifications of the annexes to itself, where it concerns the lists of persons and of goods.[298] In the case of the implementation of targeted UN sanctions, the Commission is

295. See Council of the European Union, Doc. 11205/12, "Guidelines on implementation and evaluation of restrictive measures (sanctions) in the framework of the EU CFSP" and Doc. 15530/16 "Best Practices for the effective implementation and evaluation of restrictive measures".
296. These two articles state in essence that WTO Members may take any restrictive measure on trade in arms and military equipment or imposed in pursuance of obligations under the UN Charter.
297. Reg. (EC) 2271/96 and Joint Action 996/668/CFSP, O.J. 1996, L 309/1 and 309/7.
298. For example, Art. 14(1) of Reg. (EU) 269/2014 concerning restrictive measures in respect of actions undermining or threatening the territorial integrity, sovereignty and independence of Ukraine, O.J. 2014, L 78/6.

empowered by the Council, to make changes in the list of names pursuant to any modifications decided by the Security Council or its Sanctions Committee.[299]

5.3 *Judicial review of restrictive measures: The Kadi cases and beyond*

The second alinea of Article 275 TFEU, introduced at Lisbon, allows the Court to review the legality of decisions imposing restrictive measures on natural or legal persons adopted by the Council on the basis of the CFSP provisions of the TEU, if they fulfil the requirements of Article 263(4) TFEU. Obviously that is also true for any such restrictions based on Article 215. There might be a slight question whether the right for the Court to review CFSP decisions is restricted to those CFSP decisions which are implemented by a Regulation explicitly based on Article 215(2), the provision which refers unambiguously to the power to target individuals, legal persons and non-State entities, whereas Article 215(1) is drafted so generally that could encompass this power as well. Since most such Regulations are based on Article 215 as a whole, the question is largely theoretical.[300]

Especially if natural or legal persons are listed by name in one of the Annexes of the Council CFSP decision and the Article 215 TFEU Regulation, there can be no doubt that they have access to the Court in order to request annulment of the act in question, except if it concerns one of the matters of which we have already seen above that they fall within the sphere of Member State competence, such as the arms trade or non-visa aspects of a travel ban.[301] Over the years a considerable body of case law has been produced by the General Court and the Court of Justice, largely constructed around the two seminal Kadi cases. An attempt will be made to set down the present state of this case law in brief.

In *Kadi I*, concerning the implementation of Security Council (UNSC) sanctions that demanded the freezing of Mr. Kadi's assets, the General Court accepted that measures taken for the implementation of Security Council resolutions under Chapter VII of the Charter would be exempt from judicial review in case of alleged breaches of fundamental rights. The General Court struggled mightily with the relationship between the Security Council resolution placing Mr. Kadi on the so-called sanctions list and the Community acts implementing this resolution, because it believed that they were *de facto* indistinguishable and that quashing the EC implementation measure implied that the Security Council resolution was also undermined.[302] The General Court felt that even by implication it should not review a Security Council resolution, except possibly on the basis of *ius cogens* to which in its view the Security Council was bound just as much as any subject of international law.[303]

---

299. For example Art. 7(1) of Reg. (EU) 881/2002 imposing certain specific restrictive measures directed against certain persons and entities associated with Usama bin Laden, the Al Qaida network, the Taliban etc., O.J. 2002, L 139/9.
300. See on this issue in greater detail also C. Eckes, "EU restrictive measures against natural and legal persons: From counter-terrorist to third country sanctions", 51 CML Rev. (2014), 869 et seq., at 882–883. See also recently Case C-72/15, *Rosneft v. HM Treasury*, paras. 58–81 on admissibility and the relation between Art. 24 TEU and Art. 275 TFEU.
301. Case C-348/12 P, *Council v. Manufacturing Support & Procurement Kala Naft*.
302. See T-315/01, *Kadi v. Council of the European Commission and Commission of the European Communities*, para 215. It should be noted in passing that the CFI gave an extra-ordinarily broad interpretation to the notion of *ius cogens*, including in it by implication the right to property and the fundamental rights of procedure of Mr. Kadi, only to come to the conclusion that even in this (overly) broad conception of *ius cogens* these rights had not been violated.
303. Ibid. paras. 226-231. However, even *ius cogens* was of no avail, according to the General Court.

The conception of the Union as, on the one hand, autonomous to a certain degree, but on the other hand, as subservient to the UN Security Council, became an issue in the appeals procedure before the European Court of Justice launched by Mr. Kadi. Stimulated by the radical position of A.G. Maduro, the ECJ took the view that the relative autonomy of the European Community/Union in respect of the UN ought to have consequences for its acceptance of implementing measures of Security Council resolutions, which breached the fundamental rights of Mr. Kadi, where it concerned his right to a proper procedure and his right to property.[304] Here the Court relied on the formal distinction that the General Court had so struggled with, namely the distinction between the UNSC resolution and the Community implementation measures. The Court emphasized that it confined its judgment strictly to the legality of the Community implementation measures and that this was no reflection on the Security Council resolution, even if the contents of the latter were in reality largely identical to those of the former.

The Security Council, perhaps reluctantly, realized that something had to be done about the method of putting natural and legal persons on the list, but more importantly about how to get them off the list. This led to the creation of the function of the Ombudsperson occupied by Mrs. Kimberley Prost, a Canadian judge, who had also served as *ad litem* judge in the ICTY. She served as a kind of representative of the interests of persons who claimed to be on the list without any justification, and a go-between in their relations with the Security Council and its Sanctions Committee. She and her successors managed to change the rules on delisting, which had initially been stacked against people who were listed, and in a later phase managed to have many people delisted.[305]

When the Kadi case returned to the European Courts, after the Commission had ventured to implement the first Kadi judgment and the Council decided to keep Mr. Kadi on the list, the General Court did not hesitate to draw the conclusion that Kadi's rights of defence had been infringed once again. This was based on the fact that Mr. Kadi was put through a new procedure both at the UN and at the EU level before the Office of the UN Ombudsperson became operational. Therefore his procedure followed the Focal Points mechanism in the UN, which had already been implicitly rejected by the Court of Justice in *Kadi I* 2008 as inadequate. Moreover, he had only been advised of a summary of the reasons why he was placed on the list. The General Court took the view that Mr. Kadi's renewed procedure was marked by an absence of effective judicial review that could remedy or sanction the lack of a guarantee of the rights of defence at the level of the administrative procedure. In the end the General Court thus came easily to the conclusion that Mr. Kadi had once more been the victim of a breach of his rights of defence and of judicial protection and that also his right to property had been infringed in breach of the principle of proportionality.[306]

When the Court of Justice was faced with the appeal in *Kadi II*, it was confronted by an attempt of A.G. Bot to devise a reduced level of judicial scrutiny in cases such as the one of Mr. Kadi in which there was a Security Council resolution that fixed the names of those who were subject to the sanction of an asset freeze. This constituted another attempt, as advanced by the General Court in *Kadi I*, to reconcile the autonomy of the EU legal system with the

---

304. See C-415/05 P, *Kadi I*, paras. 334, 361, 368–370.

305. This was a big improvement over the so-called Focal Point procedure that existed previously as the way to have people delisted. For Mrs. Prost and her important work as Ombudsperson, see L. Boisson de Chazournes and P.J. Kuijper, "Mr. Kadi and Mrs. Prost. Is the Ombudsperson going to find herself between a rock and a hard place?" in E. Rieter and H. De Waele (Eds.) *Evolving Principles of International Law. Studies in Honour of Karel C. Wellens* (Nijhoff, 2012). The website of the Ombudsperson is available at <www.un.org/en/sc/ombudsperson> (last visited 30 Sept. 2017).

306. Case T-85/09, *Kadi II*, paras. 179, 181, 193 and 194.

binding authority of Security Council decisions, which set aside all other international agreements between Member States pursuant to Article 103 Charter. The Court once again rejected this approach and insisted on the full autonomy of the EU legal system. The Ombudsman procedure was considered inadequate, falling short of a proper judicial protection of the rights of the individual. And although the Court of Justice did not follow the General Court in accepting Kadi's plea that his rights of defence had been breached, it did rule that there was insufficient information and proof to substantiate the allegations. This lack of information resulted largely from the unwillingness of the security services of many States, including of Member States, to have information that is primarily gathered by them discussed in open Court.

This last mentioned aspect has been subject to informal discussions between the Court and other Institutions as well as the Member States and has resulted in a new Article 105 of the Rules of Procedure of the General Court, which enables the Court to see such confidential or secret information and to decide to follow one of two courses. Either the Court decides that the information is relevant to the case and not confidential and should be shown to the person or company concerned. If the party concerned does not consent to this, the Court will not take such document into consideration. Or the Court decides that the information is relevant to the case and confidential, in which case it will not communicate that information to the person or company concerned and will deliberate how the requirements of effective judicial protection, in particular the adversarial principle, should be weighed up against the interest of safeguarding the security of the Union and the Member States, or of the conduct of their international relations. This deliberation should result in a reasoned decision of the Court specifying the procedures to be adopted in the circumstances and notably that the Member State party to the procedure produce a non-confidential summary that could be communicated to the person or company concerned.[307]

If this provision is adopted, ideally a fairer review by the EU Courts of targeted sanctions may be possible without the frequent dismissals for lack of sufficiently credible information, as the Courts of the Union have developed a well-defined approach to sanctions, both autonomous and UN induced, The Courts accept that, when it concerns the first time application of sanctions, there is no need to warn the targeted persons beforehand and to give information over the reasons for the imposition of sanctions. However, when they are maintained or re-imposed, the need for giving warning and communicating reasons reasserts itself.[308] As far as the targeted persons and companies are concerned the Courts have become more stringent over time whether family ties or links to the government of a repressive regime created a presumption of suspicion of terrorist activities or of active support of such regime.[309] The Courts, as in other cases that require complicated assessments of economic facts, are prepared to grant considerable discretion to the Council and will not substitute their own appreciation of the facts for that of the Council.[310] However, as we saw above, the main reason why a considerable number of sanctions regulations have been quashed is simply the seeming absence of, or unwillingness of the Member State authorities to produce, the elements of fact that have been

307. The new Art. 105 of the General Court's rules of procedure was adopted by the Council in Feb. 2015.The Court of Justice's Rules of Procedure were amended in 2016 by insertion of Art. 190a which laid down rules for the treatment of information or material produced before the General Court in accordance with Art. 105. Both Courts adopted quasi-identical Decisions concerning the security rules applicable to the handling of such information or material, see Decisions (EU) 2016/2386 and 2016/2387, O.J. 2016, L 355/5 et seq.
308. For example Joined Cases C-584/10 P, C-593/10 P and C-595/10 P, *Kadi II*, para 113, citing precedents.
309. For example Case C-376/10 P, Pye PhyoTay Za *v.* Council, paras. 68–72.
310. See Joined Cases T-208/11 and T-508/11, *LTTE v. Council*, para 220.

taken into account in imposing sanctions on a natural or legal person.[311] The only way out of that dilemma is the new procedure of Article 105 of the Rules of Procedure of the General Court. However it remains uncertain whether the secret services of Member States and third States will have sufficient trust in this procedure to accept recourse to it by their authorities. Moreover, one may wonder whether the application of Article 105 can be made to satisfy fully the requirements of fundamental rights.[312]

5.4 *Restrictive measures: Some conclusions*

Restrictive measures in the field of trade, investment and financial relations have become the most readily available measure to express the Union's displeasure with the policies and actions of third countries, once diplomatic and political sanctions, such as the recall of ambassadors, non-recognition and public rejection of statements or actions of the other side have been exhausted. It is used as a reaction to non-observance of core treaty provisions (the Cotonou Agreement and many others), to deadly force used by terrorist groups and to wholesale, but unacknowledged, invasion of another State's territory. Since the Union does not dispose of the means and the power to brandish forcible action other than in a reactive and defensive way, such restrictive measures have to be very carefully calibrated in order to be able to threaten effectively that stronger actions of an economic nature could still be taken. In short, the restrictive measures of the EU run the risk of becoming a blunt instrument very quickly, unless very finely tuned.

In addition the EU meets certain fundamental obstacles related to the rule of law in following UN so-called targeted sanctions and using such sanctions itself. Since such sanctions are an appropriate reaction to the indiscriminate nature of economic sanctions against a country as a whole – which in the past have led to unexpected solidarity within a target country or led to extreme misery of important segments of the population, whereas the elite was capable of minimizing the effects on them – it is highly desirable that everything is done to make targeted sanctions workable. At the moment of writing it is far from certain that such a solution can be made to work. One is, therefore, already discerning the beginning of a new form of targeted sanctions, not against individual natural and corporate persons, but against precise economic sectors, such as the oil and gas industry and the financial sector in the case of the sanctions against Russia over its actions in the Russo-Ukrainian war.

6. Overall conclusion

This chapter on TFEU external relations confirms the tendencies that were foreshadowed in the introductory chapter on external action. Trade which was the most "abnormal" sector in external relations, since there were no powers whatsoever for the EP and there were numerous special implementing procedures which deviated from even the old comitology procedures, has been strongly normalized, not just by granting more legislative powers, and granting the right of approval of trade agreements to the EP, but also by extensive use of the implementing powers within the framework of Article 291 TFEU in in the existing EU autonomous trade policy

311. Such unlawfulness is not necessarily followed by an award of damages for non-contractual liability, as an institution's infringement of EU secondary law or even of fundamental rights "may constitute an irregularity that an [...] authority exercising ordinary care and diligence could have committed in similar circumstances", Case T-341/07, *Sison v. Council (damages)*, para 73.

312. For a critical appraisal of the revised Art. 105 of the General Court's Rules of Procedure, see e.g. A. Cuyvers, "Give me one good reason: The unified standard of review for sanctions after *Kadi II*", 51 CML Rev. (2014) 1759–1788, at 1778–1779.

legislation on safeguards, anti-dumping and countervail. The same applies to the development and cooperation policy of the Union: there implementing powers under Article 291 are also extensively used, and even delegated legislative powers are granted to the Commission in situations which resemble the procedure foreseen in Article 218(7) for cases of minor amendment to international agreements and their annexes. In respect of countermeasures the EP has not acquired more powers and the Commission is only granted implementing powers insofar there is no margin of manoeuvre left to the EU at all in implementing UN sanctions, e.g. when the Security Council adds names to the list of natural and moral persons that are to be subjected to sanctions.

As far as the scope of the external action of the Union is concerned, there is little doubt that the Treaty of Lisbon aimed at establishing broader and better integrated and coordinated powers in the field of external relations. There is little doubt that the Member States, once Lisbon entered into force, looked to minimize these improvements of external action, but that it has been the Court that, in the field of development and other cooperation, has continued its existing case law on the scope of the relevant treaty articles, as it did also in the field of restrictive measures: Kadi II is not fundamentally different from Kadi I. It has also been the ECJ that has kept the Member States true to their original intentions with respect to the broadening of the EU's powers in the field of trade policy. In this respect a fairly literal interpretation of the new text of Article 207 TFEU was sufficient.

On the other hand the Member States so far have been successfully engaged in attempts to maintain the prevalent pattern of mixed competences in the conclusion of international agreements also after Lisbon, even if one of the ostensible objectives of the new text of Article 207 and of the possibility to combine elements from the CFSP and the 'classic' external relations powers in one international agreement was to reduce the need for recourse to mixed competences. The Court has censored some aspects of this tendency towards the "new mixity", but it would seem that the Member States have found a new way to "classic mixity" by construing many recent agreements as association agreements under the TFEU. However, although association agreements require unanimity according to Article 352 TFEU, just as the CFSP parts of such agreements, they do not require "mixity". On that point an intervention by the Court may be needed to confirm this. For "deep and comprehensive trade agreements" like CETA and TTIP, the 'association route' is obviously closed and hence the importance of the Court's Opinion 2/15.

Further reading

Balleix, C., *L'aide européenne au développement* (La Documentation Française, 2010).

Bungenberg, M. and C. Herrmann (Eds.), *Common Commercial Policy after Lisbon, European Yearbook of International Economic Law, Special Issue* (Springer, 2013).

Bungenberg, M., A. Reinisch and C. Tietje (Eds.), *EU and Investment Agreements, Open Questions and Remaining Challenges* (Nomos, 2013).

De Búrca, G. and J. Scott (Eds.), *The EU and the WTO. Legal and Constitutional Issues* (Hart, 2001).

Didier, P. et al., *Politique commerciale commune, Commentaire J. Mégret* (Editions de L'Université de Bruxelles, 2014).

Dimopoulos, A., *EU Foreign Investment Law* (OUP, 2011).

Gaines, S. et al., *Liberalising Trade in the EU and the WTO, Comparative Perspectives* (CUP, 2012).

Hermann, C., B. Simma and R. Streinz (Eds.), *Trade Policy between Law, Diplomacy and Scholarship, Liber amicorum in memoriam Horst G. Krenzler* (Springer, 2015).

Merket, H., *The EU and the Security-Development Nexus. Bridging the Legal Divide* (Brill-Nijhoff, 2016).

Strik, P., *Shaping the Single European Market in the Field of Foreign Direct Investment,* (Hart, 2014).

Thies, A., *International Trade Disputes and EU Liability* (CUP, 2014).
Van der Loo, G., *The EU-Ukraine Association Agreement and Deep and Comprehensive Free Trade Area, A New Legal Instrument for EU Integration without Membership* (Brill-Nijhoff, 2015).

TABLE OF SELECTED CASES (NUMERICAL ORDER)

Judgments of the Court of Justice

Case 9/56, *Meroni v. ECSC High Authority* ECLI:EU:C:1958:7, **90, 292, 372**

Case 25/62, *Plaumann v. Commission* ECLI:EU:C:1963:17, **371, 375, 988**

Case 26/62, *Van Gend en Loos v. Administratie der Belastingen* ECLI:EU:C:1963:1, **46, 418, 427, 429, 459, 493**

Case 6/64, *Costa v. E.N.E.L.* ECLI:EU:C:1964:66, **46, 389, 392, 393, 396, 413, 418, 422**

Joined Cases 56 and 58/64, *Consten and Grundig v. Commission* ECLI:EU:C:1966:41, **721, 733, 735, 743, 746, 855**

Case 56/65, *Société Technique Minière v. Maschinenbau Ulm* ECLI:EU:C:1966:38, **723, 733, 735, 736**

Case 5/67, *Beus v. Hauptzollamt München* ECLI:EU:C:1968:13, **204, 1051**

Case 24/67, *Parke, Davis & Co. v. Probel and others* ECLI:EU:C:1968:11, **852**

Case 7/68, *Commission v. Italy* ECLI:EU:C:1968:51, **486, 528, 1203**

Case 14/68, *Walt Wilhelm and others v. Bundeskartellamt* ECLI:EU:C:1969:4, **80, 443, 477, 733**

Case 24/68, *Commission v. Italy* ECLI:EU:C:1969:29, **493–495**

Joined Cases 2 and 3/69, *Sociaal Fonds voor de Diamantarbeiders v. Brachfeld and others* ECLI:EU:C:1969:30, **487, 493, 494**

Case 15/69, *Württembergische Milchverwertung Südmilch v. Ugliola* ECLI:EU:C:1969:46, **592**

Case 29/69, *Stauder v. Stadt Ulm* ECLI:EU:C:1969:57, **99, 190, 196**

Case 11/70, *Internationale Handelsgesellschaft v. Einfuhr- und Vorratsstelle für Getreide und Futtermittel* ECLI:EU:C:1970:114, **99, 123, 391, 423**

Case 22/70, *Commission v. Council (ERTA)* ECLI:EU:C:1971:32 **71, 77, 359, 371, 674, 1072, 1074, 1231, 1236, 1239–1241, 1247, 1254, 1295**

Case 25/70, *Einfuhr- und Vorratsstelle für Getreide und Futtermittel v. Köster* ECLI:EU:C:1970:115, **271, 274**

Case 39/70, *Norddeutsches Vieh- und Fleischkontor v. Hauptzollamt Hamburg St.Annen* ECLI:EU:C:1971:16, **299**

Case 78/70, *Deutsche Grammophon v. Metro* ECLI:EU:C:1971:59, **438, 861, 862**

Case 48/71, *Commission v. Italy* ECLI:EU:C:1972:65, **58, 366**

Joined Cases 51/71 to 54/71, *International Fruit Company and others v. Produktschap voor groenten en fruit* ECLI:EU:C:1971:128, **299, 443**

Case 94/71, *Schlüter & Maack v. Haupzollamt Hamburg* Jonas ECLI:EU:C:1972:45, **299**

Case 6/72, *Europemballage Corporation and Continental Can Company v. Commission* ECLI:EU:C:1973:22, **205, 359**

Joined Cases 21 to 24/72, *International Fruit Company and others v. Produktschap voor Groenten en Fruit* ECLI:EU:C:1972:115, **372, 391, 392, 1259**

Case 44/72, *Marsman v. Rosskamp* ECLI:EU:C:1972:120, **592**

Case 77/72, *Capolongo v. Azienda Agricola Maya* ECLI:EU:C:1973:65, **431, 493, 505**
Case 2/73, *Geddo v. Ente Nazionale Risi* ECLI:EU:C:1973:89, **505**
Case 4/73, *Nold KG v. Commission* ECLI:EU:C:1974:51, **505**
Case 152/73, *Sotgiu v. Deutsche Bundespost* ECLI:EU:C:1974:13, **592, 593**
Case 167/73, *Commission v. France* ECLI:EU:C:1974:35, **364, 592, 1068**
Case 2/74, *Reyners v. Belgian State* ECLI:EU:C:1974:68, **474, 478, 480, 489, 548, 557**
Case 8/74, *Dassonville* ECLI:EU:C:1974:82, **157, 301, 478, 479, 491, 507, 510, 532, 551, 733**
Case 9/74, *Casagrande v. Landeshauptstadt München* ECLI:EU:C:1974:74, **1214**
Case 15/74, *Centrafarm and others v. Sterling Drug* ECLI:EU:C:1974:114, **727, 858, 859**
Case 16/74, *Centrafarm and others v. Winthorp* ECLI:EU:C:1974:115, **856**
Case 33/74, *Van Binsbergen* v. *Bedrijfsvereniging voor de Metaalnijverheid* ECLI:EU:C:1974:131, **489, 545, 547, 548, 550, 551, 560**
Case 36/74, *Walrave and Koch v. Association Union Cycliste Internationale and others* ECLI:EU:C:1974:140, **438, 474, 492, 548, 593, 1219**
Case 48/74, *Charmasson v. Ministre de l'économie et des finances* ECLI:EU:C:1974:137, **1050, 1053**
Case 23/75, *Rey Soda v. Cassa Conguaglio Zucchero* ECLI:EU:C:1975:142, **271, 273, 274, 399**
Case 24/75, *Petroni v. ONTPS* ECLI:EU:C:1975:129, **605**
Case 43/75, *Defrenne II v. SABENA* ECLI:EU:C:1976:56, **75, 225, 400, 438, 1022**
Case 26/76, *Metro v. Commission* ECLI:EU:C:1977:167, **721, 735, 745**
Case 27/76, *United Brands v. Commission* ECLI:EU:C:1976:51, **748, 751–753, 756, 763, 764**
Case 33/76, *Rewe v. Landwirtschaftskammer für das Saarland* ECLI:EU:C:1976:188, **446, 464, 1160**
Case 35/76, *Simmenthal Spa v. Ministero delle finanze* ECLI:EU:C:1976:180, **418, 853**
Case 39/76, *Bedrijfsvereniging voor de Metaalnijverheid v. Mouthaan* ECLI:EU:C:1976:181, **610**
Case 45/76, *Comet BV v. Produktschap voor Siergewassen* ECLI:EU:C:1976:191, **446, 464**
Case 71/76, *Thieffry* v. *Conseil de l'ordre des avocats de la Cour de Paris* ECLI:EU:C:1977:65, **548, 553**
Case 79/76, *Fossi* ECLI:EU:C:1977:59, **63**
Case 102/76, *Perenboom* ECLI:EU:C:1977:71, **604**
Case 5/77, *Tedeschi v. Denkavit* ECLI:EU:C:1977:144, **274, 478, 525, 540, 1020**
Case 35/77, *Beerens* ECLI:EU:C:1977:194, **603**
Case 38/77, *Enka v. Inspecteur der Invoerrechten en Accijnzen Arnhem* ECLI:EU:C:1977:190, **208, 434**
Joined Cases 80/77 and 81/77, *Commissionaires réunis* ECLI:EU:C:1978:87, **491**
Case 102/77, *Hoffmann-La Roche v. Centrafarm* ECLI:EU:C:1978:108, **856, 858**
Case 106/77, *Amministrazione delle finanze dello Stato v. Simmenthal* ECLI:EU:C:1978:49, **394, 418, 419, 422, 443**
Case 126/77, *Frangiamore* ECLI:EU:C:1978:64, **609**
Case 148/77, *Hansen v. Hauptzollamt Flensburg* ECLI:EU:C:1978:173, **499**
Case 156/77, *Commission v. Belgium* ECLI:EU:C:1978:180, **1068, 1069**
Case 3/78, *Centrafarm* ECLI:EU:C:1978:174, **856**
Case 83/78, *Redmond* ECLI:EU:C:1978:214, **489, 1049, 1050**
Case 115/78, *Knoors* v. *Staatssecretaris van Economische Zaken* ECLI:EU:C:1979:31, **482, 546**
Case 120/78, *Rewe v. Bundesmonopolverwaltung für Branntwein* ECLI:EU:C:1979:42, **301, 476, 479, 509–511, 529, 532, 535, 551, 839, 1136**
Case 132/78, *Denkavit Loire* ECLI:EU:C:1979:139, **504**
Case 148/78, *Ratti* ECLI:EU:C:1979:110, **434, 525**
Case 182/78, *Pierik* ECLI:EU:C:1979:142, **602**
Case 207/78, *Ministère public v. Even* ECLI:EU:C:1979:144, **595, 596, 598**
Case 232/78, *Commission v. France* ECLI:EU:C:1979:215, **366, 1050**

Case 251/78, *Denkavit Futtermittel* ECLI:EU:C:1979:252, **510, 328, 1050**
Case 15/79, *Groenveld* ECLI:EU:C:1979:253, **491, 522**
Joined Cases 41/79, 121/79 and 796/79, *Testa* ECLI:EU:C:1980:163, **609**
Case 44/79, *Hauer v. Land Rheinland-Pfalz* ECLI:EU:C:1979:290, **99**
Case 62/79, *Coditel v. Ciné Vog Films* ECLI:EU:C:1980:84, **560, 851, 862, 863**
Case 138/79, *Roquette v. Council* ECLI:EU:C:1980:249, **90, 170, 249, 250, 372, 1051**
Joined Cases 55/80 and 57/80, *Musik-Vertrieb Membran v. GEMA* ECLI:EU:C:1981:10, **862**
Case 58/80, *Dansk Supermarked* ECLI:EU:C:1981:17, **490, 529, 856, 862**
Joined Cases 36 and 71/80, *Irish Creamery Milk Supplies Association* ECLI:EU:C:1981:62, **1052**
Case 98/80, *Romano* ECLI:EU:C:1981:104, **293**
Case 113/80, *Commission v. Ireland* ECLI:EU:C:1981:139, **511, 526, 527, 531**
Case 187/80, *Merck v. Stephar and Exler* ECLI:EU:C:1981:180, **859**
Case 244/80, *Foglia v. Novello II* ECLI:EU:C:1981:302, **394, 395**
Case 1/81, *Pfizer v. Eurim-Pharm* ECLI:EU:C:1981:291, **856**
Case 53/81, *Levin v. Staatssecretaris van Justitie* ECLI:EU:C:1982:105, **541, 591, 595–597**
Case 60/81, *IBM v. Commission* ECLI:EU:C:1981:264, **306**
Case 65/81, *Reina v. Landeskreditbank Baden-Württemberg* ECLI:EU:C:1982:6, **595**
Case C-104/81, *Hauptzollamt Mainz v. Kupferberg & Cie.* ECLI:EU:C:1982:362, **1256**
Joined Cases 115 and 116/81, *Adoui and Cornuaille v. Belgian State* ECLI:EU:C:1982:183, **593**
Joined Cases 141 to 143/81, *Holdijk* ECLI:EU:C:1982:122, **527, 1049, 1052**
Joined Cases 205/81 to 215/82, *Deutsche Milchkontor* ECLI:EU:C:1983:233, **299**
Case C-262/81, *Coditel v. Ciné Vog Films* ECLI:EU:C:1982:334, **861**
Case 227/81, *Aubin* ECLI:EU:C:1982:209, **610**
Case 230/81, *Luxembourg v. Parliament* ECLI:EU:C:1983:32, **78, 84**
Case 276/81, *Kuijpers* ECLI:EU:C:1982:317, **604**
Case 283/81, *CILFIT v. Ministero della Sanità* ECLI:EU:C:1982:335, **396–398, 466**
Case 322/81, *Michelin v. Commission* ECLI:EU:C:1983:313, **748, 749, 753**
Case 132/82, *Commission v. Belgium* ECLI:EU:C:1983:135, **495**
Case 174/82, *Sandoz* ECLI:EU:C:1983:213, **511, 527**
Case 286/82, *Luisi and Carbone v. Ministero dello Tesoro* ECLI:EU:C:1984:35, **548, 574**
Case 13/83, *Parliament v. Council (Common transport policy)* ECLI:EU:C:1985:220, **157, 243, 1068, 1069**
Case 14/83, *Von Colson and Kamann v. Land Nordrhein-Westfalen* ECLI:EU:C:1984:153, **435, 453**
Case 101/83, *Brusse* ECLI:EU:C:1984:187, **603**
Case 107/83, *Ordre des avocats au barreau de Paris v. Klopp* ECLI:EU:C:1984:270, **541**
Case 249/83, *Hoeckx v. Openbaar Centrum voor Maatschappelijk Welzijn Kalmthout* ECLI:EU:C:1985:139, **595, 596, 603**
Case 261/83, *Castelli v. ONTPS* ECLI:EU:C:1984:280, **595**
Case 294/83, *Les Verts v. Parliament* ECLI:EU:C:1986:166, **371, 374, 376, 380, 442**
Case 19/84, *Pharmon v. Hoechst* ECLI:EU:C:1985:304, **859**
Joined Cases 60/84 and 61/84, *Cinéthèque v. Fédération nationale des cinémas français* ECLI:EU:C:1985:329, **508, 513, 530, 737, 745, 746, 1222**
Case 94/84, *ONEM v. Deak* ECLI:EU:C:1985:264, **595**
Case 112/84, *Humblot v. Directeur des services fiscaux* ECLI:EU:C:1985:185, **500**
Case 137/84, *Ministère public v. Mutsch* ECLI:EU:C:1985:335, **595**
Joined Cases 142 and 156/84, *BAT and Reynolds v. Commission* ECLI:EU:C:1987:490, **204, 772**
Case 152/84, *Marshall v. Southampton and South West Hampshire Area Health Authority (Marshall I)* ECLI:EU:C:1986:84, **433–436, 438, 548, 1024**

Case 157/84, *Frascogna v. Caisse des dépôts et consignations* ECLI:EU:C:1985:243, **595**
Joined Cases 209 to 213/84, *Ministère public v. Asjes* ECLI:EU:C:1986:188, **770, 1068**
Case 222/84, *Johnston v. Chief Constable of the Royal Ulster Constabulary* ECLI:EU:C:1986:206, **110, 433, 435, 447, 448, 1041**
Case 302/84, *Ten Holder v. Nieuwe Algemene Bedrijfsvereniging* ECLI:EU:C:1986:242, **604**
Case 307/84, *Commission v. France* ECLI:EU:C:1986:222, **594**
Case 1/85, *Miethe v. Bundesanstalt für Arbeit* ECLI:EU:C:1986:243, **610**
Case 59/85, *Netherlands v. Reed* ECLI:EU:C:1986:157, **595, 667**
Case 66/85, *Lawrie-Blum v. Land Baden-Württemberg* ECLI:EU:C:1986:284, **592, 594, 1203**
Joined Cases 67/85 R, 68/85 R and 70/85 R, *Van der Kooy v. Commission* ECLI:EU:C:1985:173, **785**
Joined Cases C-89/85, 104/85, 114/85, 116/85, 117/85, 125 to 129/85, *Ahlström Osakeyhtiö and Others v.Commission* ECLI:EU:C:1988:447, **731**
Case 121/85, *Conegate v. HM Customs & Excise* ECLI:EU:C:1986:114, **526, 532, 563**
Case 139/85, *Kempf v. Staatssecretaris van Justitie* ECLI:EU:C:1986:223, **591, 596, 597**
Case 184/85, *Commission v. Italy* ECLI:EU:C:1987:207, **498, 501**
Case 193/85, *Co-Frutta v. Amministrazione delle finanze dello Stato* ECLI:EU:C:1987:210, **487, 497, 504**
Case 225/85, *Commission v. Italy* ECLI:EU:C:1987:284, **592**
Case 314/85, *Foto-Frost v. Hauptzollamt Lübeck-Ost* ECLI:EU:C:1987:452, **88, 355, 392, 458**
Case 316/85, *CPAS de Courcelles v. Lebon* ECLI:EU:C:1987:302, **596, 617**
Case 375/85, *Campana v. Bundesanstalt für Arbeit* ECLI:EU:C:1987:253, **608**
Case 14/86, *Pretore di Salò v. X* ECLI:EU:C:1987:275, **435, 437**
Joined Cases 27/86, 28/86 and 29/86, *CEI v. Association intercommunale pour les autoroutes des Ardennes* ECLI:EU:C:1987:355, **818**
Case 39/86, *Lair v. Universität Hannover* ECLI:EU:C:1988:322, **595, 596**
Case 45/86, *Commission v. Council* ECLI:EU:C:1987:163, **1294, 1319**
Case 46/86, *Romkes v. Officier van Justitie* ECLI:EU:C:1987:287, **506, 1051**
Case 66/86, *Ahmed Saeed Flugreisen and others v. Zentrale zur Bekämpfung unlauteren Wettbewerbs* ECLI:EU:C:1989:140, **1068**
Case 68/86, *United Kingdom v. Council* ECLI:EU:C:1988:85, **75, 1050, 1051, 1056**
Case 80/86, *Kolpinghuis Nijmegen* ECLI:EU:C:1987:431, **433, 435, 437**
Joined Cases 82 and 103/86, *Laborero and Sabato* ECLI:EU:C:1987:356, **602**
Case 85/86, *Commission v. EIB* ECLI:EU:C:1988:110, **930, 1120**
Case 222/86, *Unectef v. Heylens* ECLI:EU:C:1987:442, **110, 445, 598**
Case 3/87, *The Queen v. Ministry of Agriculture, Fisheries and Food, ex parte Agegate* ECLI:EU:C:1989:650, **593**
Case 18/87, *Commission v. Germany* ECLI:EU:C:1988:453, **494**
Case 31/87, *Beentjes v. Netherlands State* ECLI:EU:C:1988:422, **813**
Case 45/87, *Commission v. Ireland* ECLI:EU:C:1988:435, **511**
Joined Cases 46/87 and 227/88, *Hoechst v. Commission* ECLI:EU:C:1989:337, **101**
Case C-81/87, *Treasury and Commissioners of Inland Revenue, ex parte Daily Mail and General Trust PLC* ECLI:EU:C:1988:456, **868–870, 872**
Case 142/87, *Belgium v. Commission* ECLI:EU:C:1990:125, **790, 1303**
Case 196/87, *Steymann v. Staatssecretaris van Justitie* ECLI:EU:C:1988:475, **542, 593**
Case 242/87, *Commission v. Council* ECLI:EU:C:1989:217, **337, 1214**
Case 341/87, *EMI Electrola v. Patricia Im- und Export and others* ECLI:EU:C:1989:30, **864**
Case 344/87, *Bettray v. Staatssecretaris van Justitie* ECLI:EU:C:1989:226, **593**
Case 355/87, *Commission v. Council* ECLI:EU:C:1989:220, **246, 1080**

Case 379/87, *Groener v. Minister for Education and City of Dublin Vocational Education Committee* ECLI:EU:C:1989:599, **476, 592, 598, 1222**
Case C-382/87, *Buet and others v. Ministère public* ECLI:EU:C:1989:198, **1158**
Case 388/87, *Bestuur van de Nieuwe Algemene Bedrijfsvereniging v. Warmerdam-Steggerda* ECLI:EU:C:1989:196, **609**
Case 2/88 IMM, *Zwartweld and others* ECLI:EU:C:1990:440, **85, 153, 187, 415**
Case 3/88, *Commission v. Italy* ECLI:EU:C:1989:606, **557**
Case 5/88, *Wachauf v. Bundesamt für Ernährung und Forstwirtschaft* ECLI:EU:C:1989:321, **108**
Case 9/88, *Lopes da Veiga v. Staatssecretaris van Justitie* ECLI:EU:C:1989:346, **601**
Case 16/88, *Commission v. Council* ECLI:EU:C:1989:397, **271, 337**
Case 21/88, *Du Pont de Nemours Italiana v. USL di Carrara* ECLI:EU:C:1990:121, **490, 511, 810**
Case 33/88, *Allué and others v. Università degli studi di Venezia* ECLI:EU:C:1989:222, **592, 598**
Case 68/88, *Commission v. Greece* ECLI:EU:C:1989:339, **342, 453**
Case 103/88, *Fratelli Costanzo v. Comune di Milano* ECLI:EU:C:1989:256, **300, 301, 419, 428, 433, 439**
Joined Cases 143/88 & C-92/89, *Zuckerfabrik Süderdithmarschen AG et al. v. Hauptzollamt Itzehoe et al.* ECLI:EU:C:1991:65, **400**
Case 245/88, *Daalmeijer v. Sociale Verzekeringsbank* ECLI:EU:C:1991:66, **604**
Case C-322/88, *Grimaldi v. Fonds des maladies professionnelles* EU:C:1989:646, **218, 391**
Case 362/88, *GB-INNO-BM v. Confédération du commerce luxembourgeois* ECLI:EU:C:1990:102, **511, 1148**
Case C-2/89, *Bestuur van de Sociale Verzekeringsbank v. Kits van Heijningen* ECLI:EU:C:1990:183, **604**
Case C-10/89, *CNL-SUCAL v. HAG* ECLI:EU:C:1990:359, **856**
Case C-49/89, *Corsica Ferries France v. Direction générale des douanes* ECLI:EU:C:1989:649, **471, 1068**
Joined Cases C-100/89 and C-101/89, *Kaefer and Procacci v. French State* ECLI:EU:C:1990:456, **431, 1127**
Case C-106/89, *Marleasing v. Comercial Internacional de Alimentación* ECLI:EU:C:1990:395, **435, 436, 441**
Case C-113/89, *Rush Portuguesa v. Office national d'immigration* ECLI:EU:C:1990:142, **546, 555, 560, 810**
Case C-188/89, *Foster and others v. British Gas* ECLI:EU:C:1990:313, **433, 439**
Case C-192/89, *Sevince v. Staatssecretaris van Justitie* ECLI:EU:C:1990:322, **1256, 1259, 1328, 1331, 1335**
Case C-221/89, *The Queen v. Secretary of State for Transport, ex parte Factortame* ECLI:EU:C:1991:320, **541, 868**
Case C-227/89, *Rönfeldt v. Bundesversicherungsanstalt für Angestellte* ECLI:EU:C:1991:52, **601**
Case C-238/89, *Pall v. Dahlhausen* ECLI:EU:C:1990:473, **529, 531, 1157**
Case C-243/89, *Commission v. Denmark* ECLI:EU:C:1993:257, **366**
Case C-260/89, *ERT v. DEP* ECLI:EU:C:1991:254, **108, 365, 430, 441, 550, 557, 567**
Case C-292/89, *The Queen v. Immigration Appeal Tribunal, ex parte Antonissen* ECLI:EU:C:1991:80, **219, 592**
Case C-300/89, *Commission v. Council* ECLI:EU:C:1991:244, **90, 237, 853, 1168, 1176**
Case C-309/89, *Codorníu v. Council* ECLI:EU:C:1994:197, **372, 375, 376**
Case C-340/89, *Vlassopoulou v. Ministerium für Justiz, Bundes- u. Europaangelegenheiten Baden-Württemberg* ECLI:EU:C:1991:193, **476, 554, 598**
Case C-348/89, *Mecanarte-Metalurgica da Lagoa v. Alfandega do Porto* ECLI:EU:C:1991:278, **421**
Case C-360/89, *Commission v. Italy* ECLI:EU:C:1992:235, **810**
Case C-2/90, *Commission v. Belgium* ECLI:EU:C:1992:310, **473, 486, 531, 1172, 1173**
Joined Cases C-6/90 and C-9/90, *Francovich and Bonifaci v. Italy* ECLI:EU:C:1991:428, **459, 1005**
Case C-17/90, *Pinaud Wieger v. Bundesanstalt für den Güterfernverkehr* ECLI:EU:C:1991:416, **1069, 1070**
Case C-18/90, *Office national de l'emploi v. Kziber* ECLI:EU:C:1991:36, **391, 1259, 1335**

Case C-30/90, *Commission v. United Kingdom* ECLI:EU:C:1992:74, **853**
Joined Cases C-38/90 and C-151/90, *Lomas and others* ECLI:EU:C:1992:116, **1051**
Case C-41/90, *Höfner and Elser v. Macrotron* ECLI:EU:C:1991:161, **481, 726**
Case C-76/90, *Säger v. Dennemeyer* ECLI:EU:C:1991:331, **551, 558–560, 562, 563**
Case C-179/90, *Merci Convenzionali Porto di Genova v. Siderurgica Gabrielli* ECLI:EU:C:1991:464, **747, 1077**
Case C-208/90, *Emmott v. Minister for Social Welfare and Attorney General* ECLI:EU:C:1991:333, **448**
Case C-213/90, *ASTI v. Chambre des employés privés* ECLI:EU:C:1991:291, **593**
Case C-240/90, *Germany v. Commission* ECLI:EU:C:1992:408, **454, 455**
Case C-260/90, *Leplat v. Territoire de la Polynésie française* ECLI:EU:C:1992:66, **395, 1126**
Joined Cases C-320–322/90, *Telemarsicabruzzo* ECLI:EU:C:1993:26, **393**
Case C-326/90, *Commission v. Belgium* ECLI:EU:C:1992:419, **596**
Case C-332/90, *Stehen v. Deutsche Bundespost* ECLI:EU:C:1992:40, **593**
Case C-97/91, *Oleificio Borelli v. Commission* ECLI:EU:C:1992:491, **307, 308, 443**
Case C-102/91, *Knoch v. Bundesanstalt für Arbeit* ECLI:EU:C:1992:303, **608, 609**
Case C-111/91, *Commission v. Luxembourg* ECLI:EU:C:1993:92, **596, 598, 599**
Case C-126/91, *Schutzverband gegen Unwesen i.d. Wirtschaft v. Rocher* ECLI:EU:C:1993:191, **511, 1148, 1157**
Case C-153/91, *Petit v. Office national des pensions* ECLI:EU:C:1992:354, **602**
Joined Cases C-181/91 and C-248/91, *Parliament v. Council and Commission (Emergency aid)* ECLI:EU:C:1993:271, **222, 321**
Joined Cases C-184/91 and C-221/91, *Oorburg and Van Messem v. Wasser- und Schiffahrtsdirektion Nordwest* ECLI:EU:C:1993:121, **1069**
Case C-237/91, *Kus v. Landeshauptstadt Wiesbaden* ECLI:EU:C:1992:527, **391, 1259, 1331, 1335**
Joined Cases C-241/91 and C-242/91, *RTE and ITP v. Commission* ECLI:EU:C:1995:98, **222**
Joined Cases C-267/91 and C-268/91, *Keck and Mithouard* ECLI:EU:C:1993:905, **473, 508, 511, 514–518**
Case C-271/91, *Marshall v. Southampton and South West Hampshire Area Health Authority* ECLI:EU:C:1993:335, **453, 1043**
Case C-310/91, *Schmid v. Belgian State* ECLI:EU:C:1993:221, **593**
Case C-19/92, *Kraus v. Land Baden-Württemberg* ECLI:EU:C:1993:125, **476, 551, 552, 560, 1205, 1215**
Case C-66/92, *Acciardi v. Commissie beroepszaken administratieve geschillen in de provincie Noord-Holland* ECLI:EU:C:1993:341, **608**
Case C-71/92, *Commission v. Spain* ECLI:EU:C:1993:890, **819**
Case C-91/92, *Faccini Dori v. Recreb* ECLI:EU:C:1994:292, **439, 461**
Joined Cases C-92/92 and C-326/92, *Collins and Patricia Im- und Export v. Imtrat and EMI Electrola* ECLI:EU:C:1993:847, **560, 862**
Case C-137/92 P, *Commission v. BASF and others* ECLI:EU:C:1994:247, **145**
Case C-275/92, *H.M. Customs and Excise v. Schindler* ECLI:EU:C:1994:119, **486, 541, 543, 545, 559–561, 565, 566**
Case C- 315/92, *Verband Sozialer Wettbewerb v. Clinique Laboratories and Estée Lauder* ECLI:EU:C:1994:34, **511, 516, 1148, 1157**
Case C-350/92, *Spain v. Council* ECLI:EU:C:1995:237, **853**
Case C-379/92, *Peralta* ECLI:EU:C:1994:296, **477, 508, 514**
Case C-388/92, *Parliament v. Council* ECLI:EU:C:1994:213, **249**
Case C-18/93, *Corsica Ferries v. Corpo dei piloti del porto di Genova* ECLI:EU:C:1994:195, **471, 530, 560, 764, 1068**
Joined Cases C-46/93 and C-48/93, *Brasserie du pêcheur v. Bundesrepublik Deutschland and The Queen v. Secretary of State for Transport, ex parte Factortame and others* ECLI:EU:C:1996:79, **358, 465**

Case C-60/93, *Aldewereld v. Staatssecretaris van Financiën* ECLI:EU:C:1994:271, **601**
Case C-65/93, *Parliament v. Council* ECLI:EU:C:1995:91, **241, 250**
Case C-279/93, *Schumacker* ECLI:EU:C:1995:31, **581, 830, 837**
Case C-308/93, *Bestuur van de Sociale Verzekeringsbank v. Cabanis-Issarte* ECLI:EU:C:1996:169, **602**
Case C-312/93, *Peterbroeck, Van Campenhout & Cie v. Belgian State* ECLI:EU:C:1995:437, **447, 448**
Case C-324/93, *The Queen v. Secretary of State for the Home Department, ex parte Evans Medical and Macfarlan Smith* ECLI:EU:C:1995:84, **486, 490, 507, 820**
Joined Cases C-358/93 and C-416/93, *Bordessa and others* ECLI:EU:C:1995:54, **486, 571, 578, 583, 585**
Case C-359/93, *Commission v. Netherlands* ECLI:EU:C:1995:14, **810**
Case C-384/93, *Alpine Investments v. Minister van Financiën* ECLI:EU:C:1995:126, **471, 477, 547, 551, 559, 810**
Joined Cases C-363, C-407/93, C-408/93, C-409/93, C-410/93 and C-411/93, *Lancry and others v. Direction générale des douanes and others* ECLI:EU:C:1994:315, **481, 1124**
Case C-415/93, *Union royale belge des sociétés de football association and others v. Bosman and others* ECLI:EU:C:1995:463, **394, 438, 474, 492, 593, 597, 599, 1203, 1204**
Joined Cases C-427/93, C-429/93 and C-436/93, *Bristol-Myers Squibb and others v. Paranova* ECLI:EU:C:1996:282, **478, 858**
Joined Cases C-430/93 and C-431/93, *Van Schijndel v. Stichting Pensioenfonds voor Fysiotherapeuten* ECLI:EU:C:1995:441, **435, 447–449, 769**
Case C-454/93, *Rijksdienst voor Arbeidsvoorziening v. Van Gestel* ECLI:EU:C:1995:205, **603**
Case C-470/93, *Verein gegen Unwesen in Handel und Gewerbe Köln v. Mars* ECLI:EU:C:1995:224, **511, 516, 1157**
Case C-473/93, *Commission v. Luxembourg* ECLI:EU:C:1996:263, **222, 363, 594**
Case C-475/93, *Thévenon and Stadt Speyer-Sozialamt v. Landesversicherungsanstalt Rheinland-Pfalz* ECLI:EU:C:1995:371, **222, 601**
Case C-25/94, *Commission v. Council (Fishery agreement)* ECLI:EU:C:1996:114, **139, 1250, 1255**
Case C-39/94, *SFEI and others* ECLI:EU:C:1996:285, **783, 797, 800**
Case C-55/94, *Gebhard v. Consiglio dell'Ordine degli Avvocati e Procuratori di Milano* ECLI:EU:C:1995:411, **472, 541, 544, 551, 691**
Case C-58/94, *Netherlands v. Council* ECLI:EU:C:1996:171, **77**
Case C-84/94, *United Kingdom v. Council* ECLI:EU:C:1996:431, **204, 1001, 1212**
Case C-87/94, *Commission v. Belgium* ECLI:EU:C:1996:161, **810, 819, 820**
Case C-107/94, *Asscher v. Staatssecretaris van Financiën* ECLI:EU:C:1996:251, **552, 593, 830**
Case C-157/94, *Commission v. Netherlands* ECLI:EU:C:1997:499, **527, 1098**
Joined Cases C-163/94, C-165/94 and C-250/94, *Sanz de Lera and others* ECLI:EU:C:1995:451, **572, 578, 584**
Joined Cases C-178/94, C-179/94, C-188/94 and C-190/94, *Dillenkofer and others v. Bundesrepublik Deutschland* ECLI:EU:C:1996:375, **460, 461**
Case C-194/94, *CIA Security International v. Signalson and Securitel* ECLI:EU:C:1996:172, **440**
Case C-237/94, *O'Flynn v. Adjudication Officer* ECLI:EU:C:1996:206, **595, 598, 599, 1031**
Joined Cases C-245/94 and C-312/94, *Hoever and Zachow v. Land Nordrhein-Westfalen* ECLI:EU:C:1996:379, **602**
Case C-268/94, *Portugal v. Council* ECLI:EU:C:1996:461, **1241, 1320, 1338**
Case C-290/94, *Commission v. Greece* ECLI:EU:C:1996:265, **594, 1078**
Case C-315/94, *de Vos v. Stadt Bielefeld* ECLI:EU:C:1996:104, **596, 598, 632**
Case C-333/94 P, *Tetra Pak v. Commission* ECLI:EU:C:1996:436, **748, 749, 758, 759**
Case C-334/94, *Commission v. France* ECLI:EU:C:1996:90, **1078**
Case C-18/95, *Terhoeve* ECLI:EU:C:1999:22, **593**

Case C-32/95 P, *Commission v. Lisrestal and others* ECLI:EU:C:1996:402, **307**
Case C-72/95, *Kraaijeveld and others* ECLI:EU:C:1996:404, **431, 434, 435, 442, 449**
Joined Cases C-114/95 and 115/95, *Texaco v. Middelfart Havn and others and Olieselskabet Danmark v. Trafikministeriet and others* ECLI:EU:C:1997:371, **1078**
Case C-120/95, *Decker v. Caisse de maladie des employés privés* ECLI:EU:C:1998:167, **528, 530, 531, 607, 1134, 1140**
Case C-131/95, *Huijbrechts v. Commissie voor de behandeling van administratieve geschillen ingevolge artikel 41 der Algemene Bijstandswet in de provincie Noord-Brabant* ECLI:EU:C:1997:147, **610**
Case C-189/95, *Franzén* ECLI:EU:C:1997:504, **511, 534–536**
Case C-265/95, *Commission v. France* ECLI:EU:C:1997:595, **365, 474, 486, 490, 527**
Case C-321/95 P, *Greenpeace and others v. Commission* ECLI:EU:C:1998:153, **374, 1176**
Case C-337/95, *Parfums Christian Dior v. Evora* ECLI:EU:C:1997:517, **511, 858**
Case C-341/95, *Bettati v. Safety Hi-Tech* ECLI:EU:C:1998:353, **530, 1170, 1172, 1173**
Case C-343/95, *Cali & Figli v. Servizi Ecologici Porto di Genova* ECLI:EU:C:1997:160, **726, 1077**
Case C-368/95, *Vereinigte Familiapress Zeitungsverlags- und vertriebs GmbH v. Bauer Verlag* ECLI:EU:C:1997:325, **108, 511, 516, 517, 529, 530, 567**
Case C-390/95 P, *Antillean Rice Mills and others* ECLI:EU:C:1999:66, **1125**
Case C-408/95, *Eurotunnel and others v. SeaFrance* ECLI:EU:C:1997:532, **246, 249**
Case C-15/96, *Schöning-Kougebetopolulou v. Freie und Hansestadt Hamburg* ECLI:EU:C:1998:3, **598**
Case C-35/96, *Commission v. Italy* ECLI:EU:C:1998:303, **732, 1077**
Case C-44/96, *Mannesmann Anlagenbau Austria and others v. Strohal Rotationsdruck* ECLI:EU:C:1998:4, **814**
Joined Cases C-51/96 and C-191/97, *Deliège* ECLI:EU:C:2000:199, **438, 474, 542, 548, 552**
Case C-57/96, *Meints v. Minister van Landbouw, Natuurbeheer en Visserij* ECLI:EU:C:1997:564, **592, 597, 601**
Joined Cases C-61/96, C-132/97, C-45/98, C-27/99, C-81/00 and C-22/01, *Spain v. Council* ECLI:EU:C:2002:230, **1061**
Case C-85/96, *Martínez Sala v. Freistaat Bayern* ECLI:EU:C:1998:217, **590, 595, 602, 619, 625, 626**
Case C-90/96, *Petrie and others v. Università degli studi di Verona and Bettoni* ECLI:EU:C:1997:553, **592**
Case C-129/96, *Inter-Environnement Wallonie v. Région wallonne* ECLI:EU:C:1997:628, **209, 436**
Case C-149/96, *Portugal v. Council* ECLI:EU:C:1999:574, **85, 1311**
Case C-158/96, *Kohll v. Union des caisses de maladie* ECLI:EU:C:1998:171, **530, 531, 548, 557–560, 607, 1133, 1140, 1203**
Case C-160/96, *Molenaar v. Allgemeine Ortskrankenkasse Baden-Württemberg* ECLI:EU:C:1998:84, **602, 606**
Case C-180/96, *United Kingdom v. Commission* ECLI:EU:C:1998:192, **371, 1051, 1172, 1208**
Case C-210/96, *Gut Springenheide and Tusky v. Oberkreisdirektor des Kreises Steinfurt* ECLI:EU:C:1998:369, **529, 1157**
Case C-266/96, *Corsica Ferries France v. Gruppo Antichi Ormeggiatori del porto di Genova and others* ECLI:EU:C:1998:306, **514, 557, 558, 1077**
Case C-275/96, *Kuusijärvi v. Riksförsäkringsverket* ECLI:EU:C:1998:279, **604**
Case C-336/96, *Gilly v. Directeur des services fiscaux du Bas-Rhin* ECLI:EU:C:1998:221, **598, 829, 831**
Case C-350/96, *Clean Car Autoservice v. Landeshauptmann von Wien* ECLI:EU:C:1998:205, **598**
Case C-353/96, *Commission v. Ireland* ECLI:EU:C:1998:611, **813**
Case C-355/96, *Silhouette International Schmied v. Hartlauer Handelsgesellschaft* ECLI:EU:C:1998:374, **435, 858**
Case C-360/96, *Gemeente Arnhem and Gemeente Rheden v. BFI Holding* ECLI:EU:C:1998:525, **813**
Case C-7/97, *Bronner* ECLI:EU:C:1998:569, **750, 761**

Case C-35/97, *Commission v. France* ECLI:EU:C:1998:431, **592**
Case C-95/97, *Région wallonne v. Commission* ECLI:EU:C:1997:184, **1108**
Case C-126/97, *Eco Swiss v. Benetton* ECLI:EU:C:1999:269, **396, 717, 769**
Joined Cases C-176/97 and 177/97, *Commission v. Belgium and Luxembourg* ECLI:EU:C:1998:285, **1081**
Case C-212/97, *Centros* ECLI:EU:C:1999:126, **483, 868, 872**
Case C-224/97, *Ciola* ECLI:EU:C:1999:212, **419, 561, 598**
Case C-307/97, *Saint-Gobain* ECLI:EU:C:1999:438, **829**
Case C-378/97, *Wijsenbeek* ECLI:EU:C:1999:439, **480, 512, 641**
Case C-439/97, *Sandoz* ECLI:EU:C:1999:499, **572, 579, 580, 582**
Case C-17/98, *Emesa Sugar* ECLI:EU:C:2000:70, **1125**
Case C-22/98, *Becu and others* ECLI:EU:C:1999:419, **1077**
Case C-34/98, *Commission v. France* ECLI:EU:C:2000:84, **603**
Case C-35/98, *Verkooijen* ECLI:EU:C:2000:294, **574, 579, 581**
Case C-78/98, *Preston and others* ECLI:EU:C:2000:247, **574, 579, 581**
Case C-81/98, *Alcatel Austria and others* ECLI:EU:C:1999:534, **454, 826**
Case C-107/98, *Teckal* ECLI:EU:C:1999:562, **816**
Case C-173/98, *Sebago and Maison Dubois* ECLI:EU:C:1999:347, **858**
Case C-190/98, *Graf* ECLI:EU:C:2000:49, **553, 599**
Case C-209/98, *Sydhavnens Sten & Grus* ECLI:EU:C:2000:279, **522, 1174**
Case C-224/98, *D'Hoop* ECLI:EU:C:2002:432, **593, 599, 631, 632**
Joined Cases C-240/98 to 244/98, *Océano Grupo Editorial and Salvat Editores* ECLI:EU:C:2000:346, **1158, 1159, 1162, 1163**
Case C-251/98, *Baars* ECLI:EU:C:2000:205, **576**
Case C-254/98, TK-*Heimdienst* ECLI:EU:C:2000:12, **511, 516, 518**
Case C-275/98, *Unitron Scandinavia and 3-S* ECLI:EU:C:1999:567, **811**
Case C-281/98, *Angonese* ECLI:EU:C:2000:296, **395, 438, 474, 549, 597, 1222**
Case C-303/98, *Simap* ECLI:EU:C:2000:528, **1212**
Case C-324/98, *Telaustria and Telefonadress* ECLI:EU:C:2000:669, **556, 810, 811, 825**
Case C-332/98, *France v. Commission* ECLI:EU:C:2000:338, **796**
Case C-352/98 P, *Bergaderm et al. v. Commission* ECLI:EU:C:2000:361, **386, 461**
Case C-361/98, *Italy v. Commission* ECLI:EU:C:2001:29, **1084**
Case C-368/98, *Vanbraekel and others* ECLI:EU:C:2001:400, **559, 608, 1141**
Case C-376/98, *Germany v. Parliament and Council (Tobacco Advertising)* ECLI:EU:C:2000:544, **74, 76, 79, 372, 477, 479, 680, 853, 1134, 1150, 1211**
Case C-379/98, *PreussenElektra* ECLI:EU:C:2001:160, **473, 486, 528, 785, 810, 1095, 1172, 1176**
Case C-380/98, *University of Cambridge* ECLI:EU:C:2000:529, **814**
Case C-411/98, *Ferlini* ECLI:EU:C:2000:530, **438, 593**
Case C-466/98, *Commission v. United Kingdom* ECLI:EU:C:2002:624, **1086**
Case C-467/98, *Commission v. Denmark* ECLI:EU:C:2002:625, **1086**
Case C-468/98, *Commission v. Sweden* ECLI:EU:C:2002:626, **1086**
Case C-469/98, *Commission v. Finland* ECLI:EU:C:2002:627, **1086**
Case C-471/98, *Commission v. Belgium* ECLI:EU:C:2002:628, **1086**
Case C-472/98, *Commission v. Luxembourg* ECLI:EU:C:2002:629, **1086**
Case C-475/98, *Commission v. Austria* ECLI:EU:C:2002:630, **1086**
Case C-476/98, *Commission v. Germany* ECLI:EU:C:2002:631, **1086**
Case C-29/99, *Commission v. Council* ECLI:EU:C:2002:734, **1093**
Case C-54/99, *Église de scientology* ECLI:EU:C:2000:124, **578, 583, 585**

Joined Cases C-95/99 to C-98/99 and C-180/99, *Khalil and others* ECLI:EU:C:2001:532, **602**
Case C-143/99, *Adria-Wien Pipeline and Wietersdorfer & Peggauer Zementwerke* ECLI:EU:C:2001:598, **787**
Case C-157/99, *Smits and Peerbooms* ECLI:EU:C:2001:404, **473, 475, 542, 557–560, 607, 1141, 1204**
Case C-184/99, *Grzelczyk* ECLI:EU:C:2001:458, **474, 616, 617, 625, 626, 631, 632**
Case C-255/99, *Humer* ECLI:EU:C:2002:73, **601**
Joined Cases C- 223/99 and C-260/99, *Agorà and Excelsior* ECLI:EU:C:2001:259, **814**
Case C-237/99, *Commission v. France* ECLI:EU:C:2001:70, **815**
Joined Cases C-285/99 and C-286/99, *Impresa Lombardini* ECLI:EU:C:2001:640, **810, 811, 817, 820**
Case C-393/99 and C-394/99, *Hervein and others* ECLI:EU:C:2002:182, **604**
Case C-413/99, *Baumbast and R* ECLI:EU:C:2002:493, **474, 617, 620, 625**
Joined Cases C-430/99 and 431/99, *Sea-Land Service and Nedlloyd Lijnen* ECLI:EU:C:2002:364, **394, 395, 557, 1078, 1081**
Case C-449/99 P, *EIB v. Hautem* ECLI:EU:C:2001:502, **98, 1120**
Case C-453/99, *Courage v. Crehan* ECLI:EU:C:2001:465, **457, 770, 1160**
Case C-470/99, *Universale-Bau and others* ECLI:EU:C:2002:746, **826**
Case C-476/99, *Lommers* ECLI:EU:C:2002:183, **1038**
Case C-481/99, *Heininger* ECLI:EU:C:2001:684, **1156, 1158**
Case C-50/00 P, *Unión de Pequeños Agricultores (UPA) v. Council* ECLI:EU:C:2002:462, **377, 389, 390, 443–445, 510**
Cases C-52/00, *Commission v. France* ECLI:EU:C:2002:252, **1153, 1162**
Case C-60/00, *Carpenter* ECLI:EU:C:2002:434, **108, 470, 567**
Case C-99/00, *Kenny Roland Lyckeskog* ECLI:EU:C:2002:329, **396, 1120**
Case C-112/00, *Schmidberger* ECLI:EU:C:2003:333, **108, 394, 470, 487, 490, 491, 514, 527, 530, 533, 534**
Case C-154/00, *Commission v. Greece* ECLI:EU:C:2002:254, **1153, 1162**
Case C-183/00, *Medicina Asturiana* ECLI:EU:C:2002:255, **1153, 1162**
Case C-189/00, *Ruhr* ECLI:EU:C:2001:583, **602**
Case C-208/00, *Überseering* ECLI:EU:C:2002:632, **483, 868, 869, 871, 872**
Case C-214/00, *Commission v. Spain* ECLI:EU:C:2003:276, **814**
Case C-280/00, *Altmark Trans and Regierungspräsidium Magdeburg* ECLI:EU:C:2003:415, **782, 784, 789, 793, 1071, 1077, 1083**
Case C-283/00, *Commission v. Spain* ECLI:EU:C:2003:544, **813**
Case C-373/00, *Adolf Truly* ECLI:EU:C:2003:110, **814, 815**
Case C-378/00, *Commission v. Parliament and Council* ECLI:EU:C:2003:42, **275**
Case C-435/00, *Geha Naftiliaki and others* ECLI:EU:C:2002:661, **1078, 1081**
Case C-453/00, *Kühne & Heitz* ECLI:EU:C:2004:17, **399, 449, 451**
Joined Cases C-465/00, C-138/01 and C-139/01, *Österreichischer Rundfunk and others* ECLI:EU:C:2003:294, **853**
Case C-472/00 P, *Commission v. Fresh Marine* ECLI:EU:C:2003:399, **386**
Case C-18/01, *Korhonen and others* ECLI:EU:C:2003:300, **814, 816**
Case C-100/01, *Oteiza Olazabal* ECLI:EU:C:2002:712, **588, 628**
Case C-126/01, *GEMO SA* ECLI:EU:C:2003:622, **1174**
Case C-167/01, *Inspire Art* ECLI:EU:C:2003:512, **868, 873**
Joined Cases C-187/01 and C-385/01, *Gözütok and Brügge* ECLI:EU:C:2003:87, **692**
Case C-215/01, *Schnitzer* ECLI:EU:C:2003:662, **545**
Case C-224/01, *Köbler* ECLI:EU:C:2003:513, **365, 397, 444, 451, 460, 462, 465, 598**
Case C-236/01, *Monsanto Agricoltura Italy and others* ECLI:EU:C:2003:431, **1172**
Case C-241/01, *National Farmers' Union* ECLI:EU:C:2002:604, **392, 1172**

Case C-243/01, *Gambelli and others* ECLI:EU:C:2003:597, **560, 562, 566, 851**

Case C-249/01, *Hackermüller* ECLI:EU:C:2003:359, **826**

Case C-304/01, *Spain v. Commission* ECLI:EU:C:2004:495, **1176**

Joined Cases C-397/01 to C-403/01, *Pfeiffer and others* ECLI:EU:C:2004:584, **436, 437, 439, 442**

Case C-413/01, *Ninni-Orasche* ECLI:EU:C:2003:600, **595**

Case C-418/01, *IMS Health* ECLI:EU:C:2004:257, **751, 761, 762, 852**

Case C-448/01, *EVN and Wienstrom* ECLI:EU:C:2003:651, **819, 820**

Case C-36/02, *Omega Spielhallen* ECLI:EU:C:2004:614, **475, 534. 545, 557–559, 1221**

Case C-47/02, *Anker and others* ECLI:EU:C:2003:516, **594**

Case C-127/02, *Waddenvereniging and Vogelsbeschermingvereniging* ECLI:EU:C:2004:482, **434, 1172, 1183**

Case C-138/02, *Collins* ECLI:EU:C:2004:172, **596, 632**

Case C-151/02, *Jaeger* ECLI:EU:C:2003:437, **1139, 1212**

Case C-153/02, *Neri* ECLI:EU:C:2003:614, **1215**

Case C-159/02, *Turner* ECLI:EU:C:2004:228, **688**

Joined Cases C-189/02 P, C-202/02 P, C-205/02 P to C-208/02 P and C-213/02 P, *Dansk Rørindustri and others v. Commission* ECLI:EU:C:2005:408, **220**

Case C-222/02, *Paul and Others* ECLI:EU:C:2004:606, **461, 992**

Case C-262/02, *Commission v. France* ECLI:EU:C:2004:431, **557, 562, 563, 566, 851**

Case C-281/02, *Owusu* ECLI:EU:C:2005:120, **688**

Case C-293/02, *Jersey Produce Marketing Organisation* ECLI:EU:C:2005:664, **81, 1122**

Case C-315/02, *Lenz* ECLI:EU:C:2004:446, **581, 833**

Case C-319/02, *Manninen* ECLI:EU:C:2004:484, **833**

Case C-377/02, *Van Parys* ECLI:EU:C:2005:121, **1259**

Case C-386/02, *Baldinger* ECLI:EU:C:2004:535, **598**

Joined Cases C-387/02, C-391/02 and C-403/02, *Berlusconi and others* ECLI:EU:C:2005:270, **101, 435, 453, 695**

Case C-434/02, *Arnold André* ECLI:EU:C:2004:800, **74, 479, 810, 1211**

Case C-456/02, *Trojani* ECLI:EU:C:2004:488, **593, 625, 626**

Case C-6/03, *Deponiezweckverband Eiterköpfe* ECLI:EU:C:2005:222, **1177**

Joined Cases C-21/03 and C-34/03, *Fabricom* ECLI:EU:C:2005:127, **810, 811, 817**

Case C-26/03, *Stadt Halle and RPL Lochau* ECLI:EU:C:2005:5, **816**

Case C-17/03, *VEMW and others* ECLI:EU:C:2005:362, **1098**

Case C-72/03, *Carbonati Apuani* ECLI:EU:C:2004:506, **481, 488, 493**

Case C-105/03, *Pupino* ECLI:EU:C:2005:386, **217, 436, 437, 693**

Case C-176/03, *Commission v. Council (environmental crimes)* ECLI:EU:C:2005:542, **456, 700**

Case C-209/03, *Bidar* ECLI:EU:C:2005:169, **632, 1204, 1216**

Case C-210/03, *Swedish Match* ECLI:EU:C:2004:802, **74, 79, 479, 491, 810, 1211**

Case C-227/03, *van Pommerden-Bourgondiën* ECLI:EU:C:2005:431, **604**

Case C-231/03, *Coname* ECLI:EU:C:2005:487, **556, 816**

Case C-234/03, *Contse and others* ECLI:EU:C:2005:644, **810**

Case C-275/03, *Commission v. Portugal* ECLI:EU:C:2004:632, **826**

Case C-350/03, *Schulte* ECLI:EU:C:2005:637, **1156**

Case C-376/03, *D* ECLI:EU:C:2005:424, **832**

Case C-380/03, *Germany v. Parliament and Council* (*Tobacco Advertising II*) ECLI:EU:C:2006:772, **79, 680, 853, 1211**

Case C-411/03, *SEVIC Systems* ECLI:EU:C:2005:762, **868, 871**

Case C-446/03, *Marks & Spencer* ECLI:EU:C:2005:763, **833, 837, 838**

Case C-458/03, *Parking Brixen* ECLI:EU:C:2005:605, **556, 816**

Case C-459/03, *Commission v. Ireland* ECLI:EU:C:2006:345, **1256, 1257**

Case C-470/03, *A.G.M.-COS.MET* ECLI:EU:C:2007:213, **458, 461, 464**

Case C-513/03, *van Hilten-van der Heijden* ECLI:EU:C:2006:131, **575, 580, 829, 830**

Case C-540/03, *Parliament v. Council (Family Reunification Directive)* ECLI:EU:C:2006:429, **104, 108, 646, 667**

Case C-27/04, *Commission v. Council (Stability and Growth Pact)* ECLI:EU:C:2004:436, **75, 155, 371, 923**

Case C-109/04, *Kranemann* ECLI:EU:C:2005:187, **528, 584, 593, 599**

Joined Cases C-123/04 and 124/04, *Industrias Nucleares do Brasil and Siemens* ECLI:EU:C:2006:542, **1094**

Case C-144/04, *Mangold* ECLI:EU:C:2005:709, **426, 438, 441, 1014, 1020**

Joined Cases C-154/04 and C-155/04, *Alliance for Natural Health and others* ECLI:EU:C:2005:449, **79, 479, 491, 853**

Case C-161/04, *Austria v. Parliament and Council* ECLI:EU:C:2006:512, **1172, 1176**

Case C-196/04, *Cadbury Schweppes and Cadbury Schweppes Overseas* ECLI:EU:C:2006:544, **575, 839, 868**

Case C-217/04, *United Kingdom v. Parliament and Council* ECLI:EU:C:2006:279, **291–294, 853**

Joined Cases C-226/04 and C-228/04, *La Cascina and others* ECLI:EU:C:2006:94, **817**

Case C-234/04, *Kapferer* ECLI:EU:C:2006:178, **451**

Case C-265/04, *Bouanich* ECLI:EU:C:2006:51, **574**

Joined Cases C-295/04 to C-298/04, *Manfredi* ECLI:EU:C:2006:461, **457, 720, 770**

Case C-300/04, *Eman and Sevinger* ECLI:EU:C:2006:545, **635, 1127**

Case C-331/04, *ATI EAC and others* ECLI:EU:C:2005:718, **811**

Case C-344/04, *IATA and ELFAA* ECLI:EU:C:2006:10, **154, 170, 1085, 1256**

Case C-348/04, *Boehringer Ingelheim and others* ECLI:EU:C:2007:249, **858**

Case C-367/04 P, *Deutsche Post and DHL Express v. Commission* ECLI:EU:C:2006:126, **803**

Case C-372/04, *Watts* ECLI:EU:C:2006:325, **542, 548, 558, 559, 1040**

Case C-406/04, *De Cuyper* ECLI:EU:C:2006:491, **599, 608**

Case C-410/04, *ANAV* ECLI:EU:C:2006:237, **816**

Case C-432/04, *Commission v. Cresson* ECLI:EU:C:2006:455, **145**

Case C-436/04, *Van Esbroeck* ECLI:EU:C:2006:165, **692**

Case C-446/04, *Test Claimants in the FII Group Litigation* ECLI:EU:C:2006:774, **463, 573, 575, 576, 579**

Case C-452/04, *Fidium Finanz* ECLI:EU:C:2006:631, **476, 477, 539, 545, 575, 576**

Case C-513/04, *Kerckhaert and Morres* ECLI:EU:C:2006:713, **579, 836**

Case C-10/05, *Mattern and Cikotic* ECLI:EU:C:2006:220, **593**

Case C-40/05, *Lyyski* ECLI:EU:C:2007:10, **599**

Case C-77/05, *United Kingdom v. Council* ECLI:EU:C:2007:803, **641, 647**

Case C-91/05, *Commission v. Council (ECOWAS)* ECLI:EU:C:2008:288, **179, 1232, 1245, 1321**

Case C-110/05, *Commission v. Italy* ECLI:EU:C:2009:66, **472, 508, 511, 519–521, 533, 534**

Case C-112/05, *Commission v. Germany* ECLI:EU:C:2007:623, **572, 576, 578**

Case C-119/05, *Lucchini* ECLI:EU:C:2007:434, **88, 443, 451**

Case C-142/05, *Mickelsson and Roos* ECLI:EU:C:2009:336, **472, 509, 511, 514, 519–521, 530**

Case C-168/05, *Mostaza Claro* ECLI:EU:C:2006:675, **449, 1159, 1163**

Case C-170/05, *Denkavit Internationaal and Denkavit France* ECLI:EU:C:2006:783, **838**

Case C-205/05, *Nemec* ECLI:EU:C:2006:705, **605**

Case C-208/05, *ITC* ECLI:EU:C:2007:16, **301, 436, 592**

Case C-212/05, *Hartmann* ECLI:EU:C:2007:437, **550, 593, 597**
Case C-213/05, *Geven* ECLI:EU:C:2007:438, **595**
Case C-282/05 P, *Holcim v. Commission* ECLI:EU:C:2007:226, **187, 386**
Case C-295/05, *Asociación Nacional de Empresas Forestales* ECLI:EU:C:2007:227, **816**
Case C-307/05, *Del Cerro Alonso* ECLI:EU:C:2007:509, **1002**
Case C-332/05, *Celozzi* ECLI:EU:C:2007:35, **605**
Case C-341/05, *Laval un Partneri* ECLI:EU:C:2007:809, **92, 438, 474, 475, 492, 534, 546, 549, 557, 561, 563, 999**
Case C-346/05, *Chateignier* ECLI:EU:C:2006:711, **605**
Case C-379/05, *Amurta* ECLI:EU:C:2007:655, **579, 838**
Case C-392/05, *Alevizos* ECLI:EU:C:2007:251, **588**
Joined Cases C-402/05 P and C-415/05 P, *Kadi and Al Barakaat International Foundation v. Council and Commission* ECLI:EU:C:2008:461, **107, 1340**
Case C-403/05, *Parliament v. Commission (Philippines)* ECLI:EU:C:2007:624, **1321**
Case C-432/05, *Unibet* ECLI:EU:C:2007:163, **383, 390, 414, 444, 445, 448**
Case C-438/05, *The International Transport Workers' Federation and The Finnish Seamen's Union (Viking)* ECLI:EU:C:2007:772, **92, 438, 475, 492, 534, 546, 549**
Joined Cases C-439/05 P and C-454/05 P, *Land Oberösterreich v. Commission* ECLI:EU:C:2007:510, **1178**
Case C-440/05, *Commission v. Council (ship-source pollution)* ECLI:EU:C:2007:62577, **456, 700**
Case C-1/06, *Bonn Fleisch* ECLI:EU:C:2007:396, **300**
Case C-15/06 P, *Regione Siciliana v. Commission* ECLI:EU:C:2007:183, **1108**
Case C-133/06, *Parliament v. Council (Safe countries of origin)* ECLI:EU:C:2008:257, **236, 241, 664**
Joined Cases C-147/06 and C-148/06, *SECAP and others* ECLI:EU:C:2008:277, **808**
Case C-210/06, *Cartesio* ECLI:EU:C:2008:723, **389, 420, 868–872**
Case C-212/06, *Gouvernement de la Communauté française and Gouvernement wallon* ECLI:EU:C:2008:178, **481, 483, 599, 602, 619**
Case C-220/06, *Asociaciòn Profesional de Empresas de Reparto y Manipulado de Correspondencia* ECLI:EU:C:2007:815, **816**
Case C-301/06, *Ireland v. Parliament and Council* ECLI:EU:C:2009:68, **853**
Case C-308/06, *Intertanko and others* ECLI:EU:C:2008:312, **120, 696, 1260, 1261**
Case C-331/06, *Chuck* ECLI:EU:C:2008:188, **600**
Case C-337/06, *Bayerische Rundfunk and others* ECLI:EU:C:2007:786, **814**
Case C-346/06, *Rüffert* ECLI:EU:C:2008:189, **555, 999**
Joined Cases C-350/06 and C-520/06, *Schultz-Hoff and others* ECLI:EU:C:2009:18, **1001**
Case C-352/06, *Bosmann* ECLI:EU:C:2008:290, **604**
Joined Cases C-383/06 to C-385/06, *Vereniging Nationaal Overlegorgaan Sociale Werkvoorziening and others* ECLI:EU:C:2008:165, **1115, 1117**
Case C-393/06, *Ing. Aigner* ECLI:EU:C:2008:213, **814**
Case C-414/06, *Lidl Belgium* ECLI:EU:C:2008:278, **833, 837**
Case C-439/06, citiworks ECLI:EU:C:2008:298, **1098**
Case C-454/06, *pressetext Nachrichtenagentur* ECLI:EU:C:2008:351, **825**
Case C-499/06, *Nerkowska* ECLI:EU:C:2008:300, **599, 620**
Case C-507/06, *Klöppel* ECLI:EU:C:2008:110, **605**
Case C-155/07, *Parliament v. Council (EIB guarantee)* ECLI:EU:C:2008:605, **237**
Case C-166/07, *Parliament v. Council* ECLI:EU:C:2009:499, **237, 1111**
Case C-205/07, *Ghysbrechts and Santurel Inter* ECLI:EU:C:2008:730, **522, 523, 531, 1153**
Case C-208/07, *von Chamier-Glisczinski* ECLI:EU:C:2009:455, **600, 606**

Case C-213/07, *Michaniki* ECLI:EU:C:2008:731, **817**
Case C-239/07, *Sabatauskas and others* ECLI:EU:C:2008:551, **1098**
Case C-246/07, *Commission v. Sweden* ECLI:EU:C:2010:203, **1171, 1255**
Case C-300/07, *Hans & Christophorus Oymanns* ECLI:EU:C:2009:358, **814**
Case C-343/07, *Bavaria and Bavaria Italia* ECLI:EU:C:2009:415, **308**
Case C-370/07, *Commission v. Council (CITES)* ECLI:EU:C:2009:590, **75, 236, 237**
Joined Cases C-402/07 and C-432/07, *Sturgeon and others* ECLI:EU:C:2009:716, **1085**
Case 405/07 P, *Netherlands v. Commission* ECLI:EU:C:2008:613, **372, 1178**
Case C-465/07, *Elgafaji* ECLI:EU:C:2009:94, **662**
Case C-489/07, *Messner* ECLI:EU:C:2009:502, **1156, 1162**
Joined Cases C-514/07, C-528/07 and C-532/07 P, *Kingdom of Sweden v. API, European Commission* ECLI:EU:C:2010:541, **369, 409**
Case C-567/07, *Woningstichting Sint Servatius* ECLI:EU:C:2009:593, **578, 584**
Joined Cases C-570/07 and C-571/07, *Blanco Pérez and Chao Gómez* ECLI:EU:C:2010:300, **559, 563, 1134**
Case C-2/08, *Fallimento Olimpiclub* ECLI:EU:C:2009:506, **450–452**
Case C-8/08, *T-Mobile Netherlands and others* ECLI:EU:C:2009:343, **716**, 730, 735, **736**, 739
Joined Cases C-22/08 and C-23/08, *Vatsouras and Koupatantze* ECLI:EU:C:2009:344, **596, 1153**
Case C-40/08, *Asturcom Telecomunicaciones* ECLI:EU:C:2009:615, **449, 452, 1159, 1163**
Case C-58/08, *Vodafone and others* ECLI:EU:C:2010:321, **79, 84, 479, 853, 1150**
Case C-73/08, *Bressol and others* ECLI:EU:C:2010:181, **74, 550, 619, 631, 632, 1205, 1215**
Case C-91/08, *Wall* ECLI:EU:C:2010:182, **811**
Case C-127/08, *Metock and others* ECLI:EU:C:2008:449, **483, 617, 621, 667**
Case C-135/08, *Rottmann* ECLI:EU:C:2010:104, **226, 616, 622**
Case C-137/08, *VB Pénzügyi Lizing* ECLI:EU:C:2010:659, **1159, 1163**
Case C-227/08, *Martín Martín* ECLI:EU:C:2009:792, **1156, 1163**
Case C-265/08, *Federutility and Others* ECLI:EU:C:2010:205, **793, 1094**
Case C-274/08, *Commission v. Sweden* ECLI:EU:C:2009:673, **1098**
Case C-305/08, *CoNISMa* ECLI:EU:C:2009:807, **808**
Case C-314/08, *Filipiak* ECLI:EU:C:2009:719, **420**
Case C-324/08, *Makro Zelfbedieningsgroothandel and others* ECLI:EU:C:2009:633, **856**
Case C-333/08, *Commission v. France* ECLI:EU:C:2010:44, **510, 1172**
Case C-378/08, *ERG and others* ECLI:EU:C:2010:126, **1173**
Joined Cases C-403/08 and 429/08, *Football Association Premier League* ECLI:EU:C:2011:631, **545, 547, 560, 862**
Case C-451/08, *Helmut Müller* ECLI:EU:C:2010:168, **812**
Case C-474/08, *Commission v. Belgium* ECLI:EU:C:2009:681, **1100**
Case C-482/08, *United Kingdom v. Council* ECLI:EU:C:2010:631, **56, 641, 648**
Case C-515/08, *dos Santos Palhota and others* ECLI:EU:C:2010:589, **555, 565**
Case C-540/08, *Mediaprint Zeitungs- und Zeitschriftenverlag* ECLI:EU:C:2010:660, **1153, 1154**
Case C-543/08, *Commission v. Portugal* ECLI:EU:C:2010:669, **572, 576, 578**
Case C-578/08, *Chakroun* ECLI:EU:C:2010:117, **667, 668**
Case C-14/09, *Genc* ECLI:EU:C:2010:57, **595**
Case C-34/09, *Ruiz Zambrano* ECLI:EU:C:2011:124, **470, 482, 617, 619, 620, 622, 623**
Case C-45/09, *Rosenbladt* ECLI:EU:C:2010:601, **1022, 1035, 1036, 1041**
Joined Cases C-57/09 and C-101/09, *B and D* ECLI:EU:C:2010:661, **662**
Case C-77/09, *Gowan Comércio Internacional e Serviços* ECLI:EU:C:2010:803, **1172**

Joined Cases C-92/09 and C-93/09, *Volker und Markus Schecke and Eifert* ECLI:EU:C:2010:662, **124**
Joined Cases C-106/09 P and C-107/09 P, *Commission and Spain v. Government of Gibraltar and United Kingdom* ECLI:EU:C:2011:732, **786–788, 841**
Case C-108/09, *Ker-Optika* ECLI:EU:C:2010:725, **511, 516, 518, 529, 545**
Case C-115/09, *Bund für Umwelt und Naturschutz Deutschland, Landesverband Nordrhein-Westfalen* ECLI:EU:C:2011:289, **1180**
Joined Cases C-128/09 to C-131/09, C-134/09 and C-135/09, *Boxus and others* ECLI:EU:C:2011:667, **1180**
Case C-145/09, *Tsakouridis* ECLI:EU:C:2010:708, **108, 629**
Case C-204/09, *Flachglas Torgau* ECLI:EU:C:2012:71, **1179**
Case C-226/09, *Commission v. Ireland* ECLI:EU:C:2010:697, **811**
Case C-240/09, *Lesoochranárske zoskupenie* ECLI:EU:C:2011:125, **1179, 1260**
Case C-247/09, *Xhymshiti* ECLI:EU:C:2010:698, **602**
Case C-261/09, *Mantello* ECLI:EU:C:2010:683, **693, 709**
Case C-264/09, *Commission v. Slovakia* ECLI:EU:C:2011:580, **1098**
Case C-345/09, *van Delft and others* ECLI:EU:C:2010:610, **600**
Case C-379/09, *Casteels* ECLI:EU:C:2011:131, **599**
Case C-399/09, *Landtová* ECLI:EU:C:2011:415, **89, 427, 605**
Case C-447/09, *Prigge and others* ECLI:EU:C:2011:573, **1034, 1036, 1037, 1040, 1041**
Case C-539/09, *Commission v. Germany* ECLI:EU:C:2011:733, **327, 339, 345**
Case C-542/09, *Commission v. Netherlands* ECLI:EU:C:2012:346, **597**
Case C-34/10, *Brüstle* ECLI:EU:C:2011:669, **1129**
Case C-130/10, *Parliament v. Council* ECLI:EU:C:2012:472, **78, 237, 1341**
Case C-163/10, *Patriciello* ECLI:EU:C:2011:543, **161**
Joined C-188/10 and 189/10, *Melki and Abdeli* ECLI:EU:C:2010:363, **389, 421, 653**
Case C-282/10, *Dominguez* ECLI:EU:C:2012:33, **437, 458, 459, 1014**
Case C-347/10, *Salemink* ECLI:EU:C:2012:17, **610, 1258**
Case C-355/10, *Parliament v. Council (Schengen Borders Code)* ECLI:EU:C:2012:516, **238, 280, 372**
Case C-378/10, *VALE Építési* ECLI:EU:C:2012:440, **868, 872**
Case C-388/09, *da Silva Martins* ECLI:EU:C:2011:439, **600, 602, 606**
Case C-69/10, *Samba Diouf* ECLI:EU:C:2011:524, **664**
Case C-124/10 P, *Commission v. EDF* ECLI:EU:C:2012:318, **782, 783**
Case C-182/10, *Solvay and others* ECLI:EU:C:2012:82, **1180, 1256**
Case C-209/10, *Post Danmark* ECLI:EU:C:2012:172, **721, 735, 754, 756, 760**
Case C-214/10, *KHS* ECLI:EU:C:2011:761, **1001**
Case C 275/10, *Residex Capital IV* ECLI:EU:C:2011:814, **782, 795**
Case C-366/10, *Air Transport Association of America and others* ECLI:EU:C:2011:864, **106, 1181, 1259**
Case C-371/10, *National Grid Indus* ECLI:EU:C:2011:785, **833**
Joined Cases C-411/10 and C-493/10, *N.S. and others* ECLI:EU:C:2011:865, **96, 122, 644, 646, 660**
Case C-456/10, *ANETT* ECLI:EU:C:2012:241, **521, 528, 534–536**
Case C-472/10, *Invitel* ECLI:EU:C:2012:242, **1156**
Case C-489/10, *Bonda* ECLI:EU:C:2012:319, **346, 455, 692**
Case C-490/10, *Parliament v. Council* ECLI:EU:C:2012:525, **237, 1097**
Case C-491/10 PPU, *Aguirre Zarraga* ECLI:EU:C:2010:828, **688**
Case C-571/10, *Kamberaj* ECLI:EU:C:2012:233, **112, 669**
Joined Cases C-581/10 and C-629/10; *Nelson and others* ECLI:EU:C:2012:657, **1085**
Case C-586/10, *Kücük* ECLI:EU:C:2012:39, **1002**

Joined Cases C-608/10, C-10/11 and C-23/11, *Südzucker and Others* ECLI:EU:C:2012:444, 300
Joined Cases C-611/10 and C-612/10, *Hudziński and Wawrzyniak* ECLI:EU:C:2012:339, **604, 1021**
Case C-617/10, *Åklagaren Fransson* ECLI:EU:C:2013:105, **112, 122, 124, 346, 415, 430, 692**
Case C-61/11 PPU, *El Dridi* ECLI:EU:C:2011:268, **414, 657**
Case C-92/11, *RWE Vetrieb* ECLI:EU:C:2013:180, **1156**
Case C-106/11, *Bakker* ECLI:EU:C:2012:328, **601**
Case C-128/11, *Usedsoft* ECLI:EU:C:2012:407, **864**
Case C-171/11, *Fra.bo* ECLI:EU:C:2012:453, **440, 489, 492, 548**
Joined Cases C-197/11 and C-203/11, *Libert and others* ECLI:EU:C:2013:288, 780
Case C-202/11, *Las* ECLI:EU:C:2013:239, **592, 598**
Case C-221/11, *Demirkan* ECLI:EU:C:2013:583, **1331**
Case C-258/11, *Sweetman and others* ECLI:EU:C:2013:220, **1183**
Case C-260/11, *Edwards and Pallikaropoulos* ECLI:EU:C:2013:221, **1180**
Joined Cases C-274/11 and C-295/11, *Spain and Italy v. Council* ECLI:EU:C:2013:240, **55, 233, 854, 861**
Case C-329/11, *Achughbabian* ECLI:EU:C:2011:807, **456, 657, 658**
Case C-379/11, *Caves Krier Frères* ECLI:EU:C:2012:798, **592, 596**
Case C-386/11, *Piepenbrock* ECLI:EU:C:2013:385, **813**
Case C-398/11, *Hogan and others* ECLI:EU:C:2013:272, **1005**
Case C-399/11, *Melloni* ECLI:EU:C:2013:107, **100, 123, 421, 423, 710**
Case C-414/11, *Daiichi Sankyo and Sanofi-Aventis Deutschland* ECLI:EU:C:2013:520, **1233, 1240, 1241, 1293**
Case C-415/11, *Aziz* ECLI:EU:C:2013:164, **452, 1156, 1163**
Case C-420/11, *Leth* ECLI:EU:C:2013:166, **1180**
Case C-426/11, *Alemo-Herron and others* ECLI:EU:C:2013:521, **1014**
Case C-431/11, *United Kingdom v. Council* ECLI:EU:C:2013:589, **602**
Case C-443/11, *Jeltes and others* ECLI:EU:C:2013:224, **610**
Case C-526/11, *IVD* ECLI:EU:C:2013:543, **814**
Case C-583/11 P, *Inuit Tapiriit Kanatami and Others v. Parliament and Council* ECLI:EU:C:2013:625, **202, 372, 375, 378, 380, 381, 383, 389, 390, 444**
Case C-656/11, *United Kingdom v. Council* ECLI:EU:C:2014:97, **237 602**
Case C-658/11, *Parliament v. Council* ECLI:EU:C:2014:2025, **179, 237, 1246, 1247, 1287**
Case C-20/12, *Giersch and others* ECLI:EU:C:2013:411, **596**
Joined Cases C-24/12 and C-27/12, *X and TBG* ECLI:EU:C:2014:1385, **1127**
Case C-32/12, *Duarte Hueros* ECLI:EU:C:2013:637, **1159, 1163**
Case C-45/12, *Hadj Ahmed* ECLI:EU:C:2013:390, **602**
Case C-84/12, *Koushkaki* ECLI:EU:C:2013:862, **654**
Joined Cases C-105/12 to C-107/12, *Essent and others* ECLI:EU:C:2013:677, **574, 576, 584, 851**
Case C-114/12, *Commission v. Council* ECLI:EU:C:2014:2151, **80, 1241**
Case C-131/12, *Google Spain and Google* ECLI:EU:C:2014:317, **96**
Case C-137/12, *Commission & Parliament v. Council (European Convention on Conditional Access Services* ECLI:EU:C:2013:675, **237, 1233, 1241, 1293**
Case C-176/12, *Association de médiation sociale* ECLI:EU:C:2014:2, **437, 441, 442, 459, 463, 1014, 1020**
Joined Cases C-199/12 to C-201/12, *X and others* ECLI:EU:C:2013:720, **661**
Case C-204/12, *Essent Belgium* ECLI:EU:C:2014:2192, **1105, 1176**
Case C-209/12, *Endress* ECLI:EU:C:2013:864, **1156**
Case C-221/12, *Belgacom* ECLI:EU:C:2013:736, **556, 558**
Case C-226/12, *Constructora Principado* ECLI:EU:C:2014:10, **1156, 1163**

Case C-270/12, *United Kingdom v. Parliament and Council* ECLI:EU:C:2014:18, 199, 292, 372
Case C-279/12, *Fish Legal and Shirley* ECLI:EU:C:2013:853, 433, 1179
Case C-284/12, *Deutsche Lufthansa* ECLI:EU:C:2013:755, 780, 782, 795, 800, 801
Case C-292/12, *Ragn-Sells* ECLI:EU:C:2013:820, 1174
Joined Cases C-293/12 and C-594/12, *Digital Rights Ireland and Seitlinger* ECLI:EU:C:2014:238, 84, 96, 119, 381, 399
Case C-336/12, *Manova* ECLI:EU:C:2013:647, 811
Case C-370/12, *Pringle* ECLI:EU:C:2012:756, 36, 63, 74, 231, 392, 907, 909, 924, 925, 943
Case C-377/12, *Commission v. Council (PCA Philippines)* ECLI:EU:C:2014:1903, 237, 1236, 1241, 1321
Case C-390/12, *Pfleger and others* ECLI:EU:C:2014:281, 108, 471, 565
Joined Cases C-401/12 P, C-402/12 P and C-403/12 P, *Council and others v. Vereniging Milieudefensie and Stichting Stop Luchtverontreiniging Utrecht* ECLI:EU:C:2015:4, 1179
Joined Cases C-404/12 P and C-405/12 P, *Stichting Natuur en Milieu and Pesticide Action Network Europe* ECLI:EU:C:2015:5, 1179, 1180
Case C-427/12, *Commission v. Parliament and Council (Biocides)* ECLI:EU:C:2014:170, 280, 281
Case C-456/12, *O.* ECLI:EU:C:2014:135, 483, 619, 621, 624, 628, 638
Case C-573/12, *Ålands Vindkraft* ECLI:EU:C:2014:2037, 475, 478, 491, 511, 525, 529, 531, 1105, 1172, 1176
Case C-507/12, *Saint Prix* ECLI:EU:C:2014:2007, 595
Case C-575/12, *Air Baltic Corporation* ECLI:EU:C:2014:2155, 652
Case C-26/13, *Kásler and Káslerné Rábai* ECLI:EU:C:2014:282, 1156
Case C-34/13, *Kušionová* ECLI:EU:C:2014:2189, 1163
Case C-65/13, *Parliament v. Commission (EURES)* ECLI:EU:C:2014:2289, 297
Case C-67/13 P, *CB v. Commission* ECLI:EU:C:2014:2204, 736
Case C-69/13, *Mediaset* ECLI:EU:C:2014:71, 799
Case C-112/13, *A* ECLI:EU:C:2014:2195, 421
Case C-146/13, *Spain v. Parliament and Council* ECLI:EU:C:2015:298, 228, 281, 414
Joined Cases C-148/13 to C-150/13, *A* ECLI:EU:C:2014:2406, 120, 646
Case C-190/13, *Márquez Samohano* ECLI:EU:C:2014:146, 1002
Case C-270/13, *Haralambidis* ECLI:EU:C:2014:2185, 594
Case C-333/13, *Dano* ECLI:EU:C:2014:2358, 597, 626, 638
Case C-364/13, *International Stem Cell* ECLI:EU:C:2014:2451, 1129
Case C-396/13, *SähköalO.J.en ammattiliitto* ECLI:EU:C:2015:86, 445, 1000
Case C-409/13, *Council v. Commission (Macro-financial assistance)* ECLI:EU:C:2015:217, 154, 157, 181, 182, 241, 243, 246
Case C-425/13, *Commission v. Council* ECLI:EU:C:2015:483, 1247
Case C-456/13 P, *T & L Sugars and Sidul Açúcares v. Commission* ECLI:EU:C:2015:284, 379
Case C-497/13, *Faber* ECLI:EU:C:2015:357, 1163
Case C-508/13, *Estonia v. Parliament and Council* ECLI:EU:C:2015:403, 82, 84
Case C-512/13, *Sopora* ECLI:EU:C:2015:108, 832
Case C-528/13, *Léger* ECLI:EU:C:2015:288, 1143
Case C-530/13, *Schmitzer* ECLI:EU:C:2014:2359, 1021
Case C-533/13, *AKT* ECLI:EU:C:2015:173, 441, 1004
Case C-552/13, *Grupo Hospitalario Quirón* ECLI:EU:C:2015:713, 824
Case C-554/13, *Zh. and O.* ECLI:EU:C:2015:377, 656
Case C-568/13, *Data Medical Service* ECLI:EU:C:2014:2466, 820
Case C-5/14, *Kernkraftwerke Lippe-Ems* ECLI:EU:C:2015:354, 421, 782
Case C-10/14, C-14/14 and C-17/14, *Miljoen* ECLI:EU:C:2015:608, 838

Case C-12/14, *Commission v. Malta* ECLI:EU:C:2016:135, **603**
Case C-33/14 P, *Mory and others v. Commission* ECLI:EU:C:2015:609, **799–802**
Case C-36/14, *Commission v. Poland* ECLI:EU:C:2015:570, **1094**
Case C-48/14, *Parliament v. Council* ECLI:EU:C:2015:91, **241**
Case C-61/14, *Orizzonte Salute* ECLI:EU:C:2015:655, **450**
Case C-62/14, *Gauweiler and others* ECLI:EU:C:2015:400, **36, 73, 394, 426, 427, 907, 927, 940, 944–946, 991**
Case C-67/14, *Alimanovic* ECLI:EU:C:2015:597, **592, 633, 638**
Case C-73/14, *Council v. Commission (ITLOS)* ECLI:EU:C:2015:663, **241, 1247**
Case C-87/14, *Commission v. Ireland* ECLI:EU:C:2015:449, **1139**
Case C-88/14, *Commission v. Parliament and Council (visa requirement)* ECLI:EU:C:2015:499, **280**
Case C-105/14, *Taricco and Others* ECLI:EU:C:2015:555, **100, 122, 345, 424, 435, 455, 457**
Case C-115/14, *RegioPost* ECLI:EU:C:2015:760, **1000**
Case C-129/14 PPU, *Spasic* ECLI:EU:C:2014:586, **353, 692**
Joined Cases C-132/14 to 136/14, *Parliament v. Council (Mayotte)* ECLI:EU:C:2015:813, **1123**
Case C-146/14 PPU, *Mahdi* ECLI:EU:C:2014:1320, **657, 659**
Case C-160/14, *Ferreira da Silva e Brito and others* ECLI:EU:C:2015:565, **397, 465, 466, 1007**
Case C-169/14, *Sánchez Morcillo and Abril García* ECLI:EU:C:2014:2099, **907, 1163**
Case C-179/14, *Commission v. Hungary* ECLI:EU:C:2016:108, **567, 569, 570**
Case C-216/14, *Covaci* ECLI:EU:C:2015:686, **703**
Case C-286/14, *Parliament v. Commission (delegated regulation)* ECLI:EU:C:2016:183, **280**
Case C-293/14, *Hiebler* ECLI:EU:C:2015:843, **558, 563, 567–569**
Case C-298/14, *Brouillard* ECLI:EU:C:2015:652, **594**
Case C-299/14, *García-Nieto and others* ECLI:EU:C:2016:114, **592, 624**
Case C-308/14, *Commission v. United Kingdom* ECLI:EU:C:2016:436, **603**
Case C-333/14, *The Scotch Whiskey Association* ECLI:EU:C:2015:845, **348, 510, 529, 534**
Joined Cases C-340/14 and C-341/14, *Trijber* ECLI:EU:C:2015:641, **481, 547, 567, 568**
Case C-362/14, *Schrems* ECLI:EU:C:2015:650, **100, 211, 445**
Case C-387/14, *Esaprojekt* ECLI:EU:C:2017:338, **811**
Case C-399/14, *Grüne Liga Sachsen and others* ECLI:EU:C:2016:10, **1184**
Case C-441/14, *DI* ECLI:EU:C:2016:278, **89, 439, 459**
Case C-442/14, *Bayer CropScience and Stichting De Bijenstichting* ECLI:EU:C:2016:890, **1179**
Joined Cases C-443/14 and C-444/14, *Alo & Osso* ECLI:EU:C:2016:127, **663**
Case C-547/14, *Philip Morris Brands and others* ECLI:EU:C:2016:325, **83, 1138**
Case C-549/14, *Finn Frogne* ECLI:EU:C:2016:634, **825**
Joined Cases C-8/15 P to C-10/15 P, *Ledra Advertising v. Commission and ECB* ECLI:EU:C:2016:701, **106, 231, 386, 444, 463, 927**
Case C-15/15, *New Valmar* ECLI:EU:C:2016:464, **523, 531**
Joined Cases C-20/15 P and C-21/15 P, *Commission v. World Duty Free Group* ECLI:EU:C:2016:981, **780, 782, 787, 788**
Case C-46/15, *Ambisig* ECLI:EU:C:2016:530, **818**
Case C-60/15 P, *Saint-Gobain Glass Deutschland v. Commission* ECLI:EU:C:2017:540, **1179**
Case C-63/15, *Ghezelbash* ECLI:EU:C:2016:409, **96, 445, 660**
Joined Cases C-105/15 P to C-109/15 P, *Mallis and Malli v. Commission and ECB* ECLI:EU:C:2016:702, **386**
Case C-133/15, *Chavez-Vilchez and others* ECLI:EU:C:2017:354, **623**
Joined Cases C-145/15 and C-146/15, *Ruijssenaars and Jansen* ECLI:EU:C:2016:187, **454, 467**

Case C-148/15, *Deutsche Parkinson Vereinigung* ECLI:EU:C:2016:776, **510, 522, 532**
Case C-157/15, *G4S Secure Solutions* ECLI:EU:C:2017:203, **96, 1019, 1021, 1031, 1032, 1035**
Case C-182/15, *Petruhhin* ECLI:EU:C:2016:630, **598**
Case C-187/15, *Pöpperl* ECLI:EU:C:2016:550, **600, 1043**
Case C-188/15, *Bougnaoui and ADDH* ECLI:EU:C:2017:204, **96, 1019, 1021, 1031, 1037**
Case C-201/15, *AGET Iraklis* ECLI:EU:C:2016:972, **109, 541, 576, 1006, 1223, 1250**
Case C-213/15 P, *Commission v. Breyer* ECLI:EU:C:2017:563, **410**
Case C-243/15, *Lesoochranárske zoskupenie VLK* ECLI:EU:C:2016:838, **445, 1180, 1260**
Case C-268/15, *Ullens de Schooten* ECLI:EU:C:2016:874, **465**
Cases C-404/15 and C-659/15 PPU, *Aranyosi and Căldăraru* ECLI:EU:C:2016:198, **96**
Case C-406/15, *Milkova* ECLI:EU:C:2017:198, **1019, 1021, 1026, 1039**
Case C-424/15, *Ormaetxea Garai and Lorenzo Almendros* ECLI :EU:C:2016:780, **210**
Case C-443/15, *Parris* ECLI:EU:C:2016:897, **1028, 1030, 1040**
Case C-544/15, *Fahimian* ECLI:EU:C:2017:255, **654, 670**
Case C-549/15, *E.ON Biofor Sverige* ECLI:EU:C:2017:490, **1176**
Case C-601/15 PPU, *N.* ECLI:EU:C:2016:84, **113, 127, 657**
Case C-643/15, *Slovakia v. Council* ECLI:EU:C:2017:631, **38, 230, 239, 243, 244, 246, 249, 644, 650**
Case C-682/15, *Berlioz Investment Fund* ECLI:EU:C:2017:373, **430, 444, 445**
Case C-578/16 PPU, *C.K. and others* ECLI:EU:C:2017:127, **122, 646, 660**
Case C-638/16 PPU, *X and X* ECLI:EU:C:2017:173, **654**
Case C-42/17, *M.A.S. and M.B.* ECLI:EU:C:2017:936, **89, 90, 419, 424, 425, 427, 429, 455, 695**
Case C-493/17, *Weiss and others (pending)*, **907**

Opinions of the Court of Justice

Opinion 1/75, *OECD Understanding on a Local Cost Standard* ECLI:EU:C:1975:145, **1231, 1240, 1296, 1297, 1303**
Opinion 1/76, *Agreement on the establishment of a European Laying-up Fund for Inland Waterway Vessels* ECLI:EU:C:1977:63, **1072, 1076, 1237, 1238, 1240, 1248**
Opinion 1/78, *International Agreement on Natural Rubber* ECLI:EU:C:1979:224, **1292, 1294, 1296, 1319**
Opinion 1/91, *First Opinion on the EEA Agreement* ECLI:EU:C:1991:490, **16, 46, 1257**
Opinion 1/94, *Agreements annexed to the WTO Agreement* ECLI:EU:C:1994:384, **184, 1072, 1238, 1239, 1293, 1297**
Opinion 2/94, *Accession of the Community to the ECHR (ECHR I)* ECLI:EU:C:1996:140, **102, 103**
Opinion 2/00, *Cartagena Protocol on Biosafety* ECLI:EU:C:2001:664, **236, 237, 1178, 1294**
Opinion 1/03, *New Lugano Convention* ECLI:EU:C:2006:81, **81, 675, 1231, 1238, 1239, 1240**
Opinion 1/08, *Agreements modifying the Schedules of Specific Commitments under the GATS* ECLI:EU:C:2009:739, **236, 1295**
Opinion 1/09, *Agreement creating a Unified Patent Litigation System* ECLI:EU:C:2011:123, **228, 414, 442, 444, 458, 465**
Opinion 2/13, *Accession to the European Convention on Human Rights (ECHR II)* ECLI:EU:C:2014:2454, **95, 115, 123, 234, 421, 469, 1019, 1257**
Opinion 2/15, *EU-Singapore Free Trade Agreement* ECLI:EU:C:2017:376, **1171, 1176, 1317**

Judgments of the Court of First Instance

Case T-450/93, *Lisrestal and others v. Commission* ECLI:EU:T:1994:290, **307, 1038**
Case T-346/94, *France-Aviation v. Commission* ECLI:EU:T:1995:187, **307**
Case T-42/96, *Eyckeler & Malt v. Commission* ECLI:EU:T:1998:40, **307**
Case T-50/96, *Primex Produkte Import-Export and others v. Commission* ECLI:EU:T:1998:223, **307**

Case T-102/96, *Gencor v. Commission* ECLI:EU:T:1999:65, **720, 734, 750**
Case T-188/97, *Rothmans v. Commission* ECLI:EU:T:1999:156, **276**
Case T-290/97, *Mehibas Dordtselaan v. Commission* ECLI:EU:T:2000:8, **307**
Joined Cases T-74/00, T-76/00, T-83/00, T-84/00, T-85/00, T-132/00, T-137/00 and T-141/00, *Artegodan v. Commission* ECLI:EU:T:2002:283, **288, 1172, 1177**
Case T-193/04, *Tillack v. Commission* ECLI:EU:T:2006:292, **353, 355, 415**
Case T-201/04, *Microsoft v. Commission* ECLI:EU:T:2007:289, **748, 750, 758, 762**
Case T-229/04 *Sweden v. Commission* ECLI:EU:T:2007:217, **1173**
Case T-48/05, *Franchet and Byk v. Commission* ECLI:EU:T:2008:257, **352–354**
Case T-182/06, *Netherlands v. Commission* ECLI:EU:T:2007:191, **1178**
Case T-187/06, *Schräder v. CPVO* ECLI:EU:T:2008:511, **293**
Case T-411/07, *Aer Lingus Group v. Commission* ECLI:EU:T:2010:281, **774**
Case T-286/09, *Intel Corp. v. Commission* ECLI:EU:T:2014:547, **749, 753, 756, 757**
Case T-590/10, *Thesing and Bloomberg Finance v. ECB* ECLI:EU:T:2012:635, **950**
Case T-57/11, *Castelnou Energía v. Commission* ECLI:EU:T:2014:1021, **780, 793, 1094**
Case T-370/11, *Poland v. Commission* ECLI:EU:T:2013:113, **1092**
Case T-512/12, *Front Polisario v. Council* ECLI:EU:T:2015:953, **107**
Case T-562/12, *Dalli v. Commission* ECLI:EU:T:2015:270, **147, 1139**
Case T-102/13, *Heli-Flight v. AESA* ECLI:EU:T:2014:1064, **286**
Case T-289/13, *Ledra Advertising v. Commission and ECB* ECLI:EU:T:2014:981, **927**
Case T-291/13, *Eleftheriou and Papachristofi v. Commission and ECB* ECLI:EU:T:2014:978, **459, 927**
Case T-293/13, *Theophilou v. Commission and ECB* ECLI:EU:T:2014:979, **927**
Case T-327/13, *Mallis and Malli v. Commission and ECB* ECLI:EU:T:2014:909, **897, 927**
Case T-328/13, *Tameio Pronoias Prosopikou Trapezis Kyprou v. Commission and ECB* ECLI:EU:T:2014:906, **897, 927**
Case T-329/13, *Chatzithoma v. Commission and ECB* ECLI:EU:T:2014:908, **897, 927**
Case T-330/13, *Chatziioannou v. Commission and ECB* ECLI:EU:T:2014:904, **897, 927**
Case T-331/13, *Nikolaou v. Commission and ECB* ECLI:EU:T:2014:905, **897, 927**
Case T-660/14, *SV Capital v. ABE* ECLI:EU:T:2015:608, **989**
Case T-356/15, *Austria v. Commission* (pending), **1094**

Cases from other jurisdictions

European Court of Human Rights

M.S.S. v. Belgium and Greece, Appl. No 30696/09, 21 Jan 2011, **118**

Germany

Judgment of the Second Senate of 12 September 2012 - 2 BvR 1390/12, **908**
Order of the Second Senate of 14 January 2014 - 2 BvR 2728/13, **944**
Order of the Second Senate of 18 July 2017 - 2 BvR 859/15, 2 BvR 980/16, 2 BvR 2006/15, 2 BvR 1651/15, **944**

United Kingdom

R (Miller) v. Secretary of State for exiting the European Union UKSC 5, **422**

SUBJECT INDEX

A

Aarhus Convention (on access to information, public participation and access to justice in-environmental matters), 1179
Abuse of rights, 358–359, 388, 1021
Accession, 15–18
  Act of, 17
  agreement, 115, 116, 1309
  to the ECHR, 76, 115–116
  of the EU to multilateral agreements, 1250–1252
  to the EU, 64–66
  European Parliament, 28, 31
  negotiations, 16, 18, 1326
  partnership, 1332
  policy, 1326
  size of the Commission, 143
  Treaty of, 17
  and Treaty change, 59
  WTO, 1305
Access to courts, 309, 381. *See also* Access to justice
Access to information, 299, 318, 340, 699, 839, 936, 1148, 1179, 1197
Access to justice, 357, 361, 373–377, 388 442–443, 675–677, 679–680, 685–686, 688, 1042, 1159–1161, 1179–1180. *See also* Judicial protection
Accidents at work, 602, 1004
Acquis communautaire, 17, 25, 28, 129, 591, 612, 898, 1326, 1328
Action
  for annulment, 87, 142, 193, 194, 252, 355, 358, 369–383, 385, 392, 400, 922, 989, 1214, 1265, 1282
  for damages, 90, 193, 354, 361, 385–388, 405, 451, 457, 466, 1282
  for failure to act, 157, 383–385, 940
  for infringement. *See* infringement action
Acts. *See* also Secondary law
  Approval by Member States, 259–260
  decision-making procedures, 256–259
  of the EU institutions, 119, 236, 287, 373, 400
  of the European Council, 214–216
  ordinary legislative procedure
    Conciliation Committee, 254
    European Parliament and Council, 251–253
Additionality principle, 1114, 1119
Administration of the EU. *See* Chapter 36 *passim*
  Agencies (*see* Agencies)
  Commission, 302–304
    Directorates-General (DGs), 302
  Comitology (*see* Comitology)
  constitutional framework, 271–272
  Council, 304–305
  direct administrative effect, 300–301
  Economic and Financial Committee, 305
  Eurogroup Working Group, 305
  European administrative space, 267, 298
  executive federalism model, 268–270
  informal networks, 297–298
  institutional and procedural autonomy of Member States, 299–300
  legal issues
    composite administration and integrated administration, 305–306
    composite procedures, procedural rights and judicial review, 306–308
    fragmentation and codification, 309–310
    transparency, accountability and efficiency, 308–309
  national administrative acts, 301
  networks, 295–298
Administrative cooperation, 306, 415, 569, 600, 644, 843, 846–847, 1199, 1202, 1227–1228
Administrative integration, 295, 299
Administrative law, 453, 701, 990, 1228
Administrative tax cooperation, 847
Advance Passenger Information (API), 369, 409
Advantage
  artificial competitive, 883
  domestic products, 502, 535
  economic, 24, 346, 825

industry artificial, 780
private enforcement, 458
social, 589, 590, 592, 594–597, 1024
in state aid, 782–784
Altmark test, 784
market economy investor test, 783–784
tax, 579, 580, 803, 832, 839, 840, 842
Africa, the Caribbean and the Pacific countries (ACP), 1125, 1300, 1333–1334
Age
discrimination on grounds of, 89, 437, 1018, 1024, 1031, 1035–1036, 1040
Framework Directive 2000/78, 1041
non-discrimination, 441, 1020
pension, 1024
relevance for family reunification, 667
retirement, 1040, 1041
Agencies, 85, 189, 199, 207, 267, 283–295, 302, 309, 691, 710–713
accountability, 294
international dimension, 294–295
legal bases, 291–292
legal limits to agencies' powers, 292–294
organization, 285–287
powers, 287–291
rationales and types, 283–285
Agency for the Cooperation of Energy Regulators (ACER), 286, 287, 290, 1096, 1098, 1100–1102
Agenda on Migration, 643, 645, 649–651
Agreement(s)
accession, 17, 59–66, 113–116, 1305, 1309
draft accession, 114
between EU Member States *inter se*, 56–57, 221–234
in the context of competition
horizontal, 737–743
vertical, 743–746
inter-institutional, 241
international agreements
association (*see* Cooperation Policy)
conclusion of, 48, 52, 58, 71, 81, 92, 107, 113, 157, 171, 227, 249, 256, 321, 435, 1072, 1171, 1234, 1237, 1245, 1247, 1252, 1253, 1256, 1259, 1347
of the Member States with third states, 1260–1261
mixed agreements
accession, 1249, 1250, 1252, 1254
conclusion, 227, 391, 1063, 1103, 1240, 1248, 1250, 1252, 1256, 1314, 1327
declaration of competences, 1249, 1250, 1252
obligations under, 1252
negotiation, 26, 180, 227, 247, 1171, 1234, 1237, 1245, 1247, 1253, 1259
inter se agreements (*see* agreements between EU Member States *inter se*)
licensing, 746
Agriculture
approximation of laws, 1056–1057
common organization, agricultural markets, 1054–1055
competition rules, 1057
decision making, 1063–1064
development, product quality, 1059–1060
direct income support, 1058
financing, 1064–1065
implementation, application and control, 1064
income, 1065
internal market, 1065
markets, 273, 1047–1049, 1053, 1059, 1118, 1302
measures, 1060
objectives, 1051–1052
policies, 1049
prices, 1047
problems, 1047–1048
products, 315, 328, 486, 490, 1047–1049, 1051, 1053–1054, 1056–1057, 1059–1060, 1064, 1302, 1328, 1329, 1335
regulation, market, 1059
rural development, 1059
scope, 1052–1053
structural measures, 1047, 1048, 1055–1056
Alcohol,
EU policy, 1142–1143, 1208
national measures, 477, 498, 502, 505, 509–510, 517, 534–535, 552, 562, 846
Alert mechanism (economic coordination), 911
Alternative dispute resolution, 678, 679, 686, 687, 1160–1162
Alternative Investment Fund (Manager) Directive, 970, 971
Animal welfare, 1052, 1056–1058, 1060, 1065
Annual Growth Survey, 911, 1010, 1207
Annual work programme, 156, 244, 286, 1192
Anti-competitive collusion
Art. 101 TFEU, 722–726
cartels, 741–743
collusion, concept, 730–732
effect on trade, 732–734
horizontal agreements, 737–741

internal market, 734
licensing agreements, 746
restriction, 735–737
undertaking, concept, 726–730
vertical agreements, 743–746
Anti-dumping policy
definition of dumping, 1307
export price, 1301–1304
non-market economy status, 1308
normal value, 1307–1308, 1311
procedure (internal), 1309
proceedings against third country producers, 1310
undertaking, 1302–1304, 1310–1311
Appeal Committee (comitology), 278–279
Application and Enforcement Regulation (AER), (trade policy), 1312–1314
Approximation of laws, 415, 842, 1056–1057, 1332. *See* also Harmonization
Aquaculture, 1056, 1062, 1065, 1118
Architecture (of the Treaties), 45–51
Area of Freedom, Security and Justice (AFSJ), 103, 133, 141, 382, 469, 574, 639–640, 673, 689, 691, 1127, 1341
Asylum. *See* Migration and Asylum Law
Attribution of competences. *See* Principle of conferral
Autonomy of EU law, 126–127, 228, 418

B

Balance of payments, 11, 474, 571, 905, 927
Banking Union, 955–958, 959–963, 982–988
crisis management, 956
Deposit Guarantee Scheme, 957
institutional structure and development, 955
Single Resolution Board (SRB), 986
Single Resolution Mechanism, 986–988
Single Supervisory Mechanism (SSM)
administrative measures, 985
administrative penalties, 985–986
day-to-day supervision, 984–985
direct and indirect supervision, 983–984
prudential supervision of credit institutions, 983
Bank Recovery and Resolution Directive, 957
Barre Memorandum, 884
Barriers to trade, 493, 808, 827, 851, 1089, 1329
Basel Committee on Banking Supervision, 960
Benefit tourism, 590, 591, 596, 625
Better Regulation, 149, 245, 249
Beyen Plan, 8–9
Bilateral loans, in finacnial crisis 893, 908, 926
Biodiversity, 1183–1184
Biological and Toxin Weapons Convention (BTWC), 1276
Biotech Directive 98/44 (on the legal protection of biotechnological inventions), 859
Blood and blood derivatives, 1133, 1143, 1208
Blue Card Directive, 653, 666, 670–671
Body of European Regulators for Electronic Communications (BEREC), 286
Bovine spongiform encephalopathy crisis (BSE crisis), 1057, 1060, 1132, 1137, 1208
Bretton Woods, 323, 883, 885–887
Brexit, 36–38, 58–59, 66, 116, 184, 226, 648, 1114, 1117, 1120, 1291, 1326
Brussels Convention, 221, 673, 687
Brussels Regulation, 681–684, 687, 992
Budget
budgetary principles, 321–325
Council Decision 70/243, 314
Delors I Package of 1988, 315–317
discharge procedure, 341
ECSC Treaty, 313, 314
European Court of Auditors, 338–341
financial interests, EU, 342–347
implementation, 336
legal framework, 319–320
multi-annual financial framework, 313
objectives, 911, 913
policy, 891, 892, 903, 904, 906–909, 912, 917, 945
principle of
annuality, 322
equilibrium, 323
sound financial management, 324–325
specification, 324
transparency, 325
unit of account, 323
universality, 324
procedure, 331–335
sound financial management, 324–325
unity and budgetary accuracy, 321–322
value-added tax (VAT), 314
Budgetary. *See* Budget
Bundesverfassungsgericht (BVerfG). *See* Germany
Burden of proof, 448, 534, 702, 724, 731, 839, 1042

C

Capital
direct investments, 574, 576, 578, 1126
financial loan, 579
free movement
capital *vs.* establishment, 576–577
capital *vs.* services, 575–576

direct effect, 572
historical overview, 571–572
justifications, 581–586
material scope, 574–575
restrictions, 577–580
territorial scope, 572–574
third countries (*see* territorial scope)
investments in real estate, 574, 578, 1126
markets, 321, 570, 573, 892, 928, 958, 974, 1120
mortgages, 579
portfolio investment, 576, 1126
Capital Requirements Directive (CRD IV), 959–960, 983
Cartel, 212, 731, 737–738, 741–743, 767, 770, 771, 1057
Central counterparty, 969
Central Securities Depositories (Regulation on), 955, 968, 969
Charter of Fundamental Rights of the EU
applied by ECJ, 358
effect of, 105, 195, 429, 1304
limitations, 110
origins, 103–104
rights and principles, 111–112
scope of application
EU institutions & bodies, 104–107
Member States, 107–110
source of EU law, 195–196
Chemical Weapons Convention (CWC), 1276
Churchill, 2, 7
Citizenship of the Union. *See* Chapt. 16 *passim*
concept, 611–616
electoral rights, 634–635
free movement, 619–622
introduction by Maastricht Treaty, 25–26
national citizenship, 611, 614–616, 637
non-discrimination, 616, 617, 631, 634, 645
political rights, 634–636
protection by diplomatic/consular authorities, 636
Citizens' Initiative, 244, 262, 635–636
Citizens' Rights Directive 2004/38, 480, 587, 617, 620–621, 623–627, 630, 632–634, 637–638
family members, 633–634
free movement rights, 620–622
personal scope and beneficiaries, 617–619
relationship with Treaty, 619
residence rights, 623–627
restrictive measures, 628–630
right to equal treatment, 631–633
Civic integration, 669
Civil justice, 674–675, 677, 680, 682–689, 1025
Civil matters, 673–689
Civil protection, 1199, 1202, 1206, 1225–1226, 1228, 1265
Civil remedies, 457–458
Civil service, EU, 151–153, 692
Classification of Territorial Units for Statistics (NUTS classification), 1112
Climate and energy, 1181
Climate change, 294, 1089, 1090, 1092, 1095, 1106, 1111, 1117, 1145, 1169, 1170, 1181, 1193, 1236, 1238, 1322
Coal, 1, 3–7, 45, 48, 51, 77, 143, 163, 268, 292, 313, 825, 1089, 1090, 1092, 1094
Co-decision procedure. *See* Ordinary legislative procedure
Cohesion policy
Cohesion Fund (CF), 1110–1118
European Agricultural Fund for Rural Development (EAFRD), 1118
economic, social and territorial, 1109–1110
European Investment Bank (EIB), 1119–1120
European Maritime and Fisheries Fund (EMFF), 1118–1119
EU regions, 1107–1108
Europe 2020 agenda, 1110–1111
and geographical differentiation (*see* Geographical differentiation)
juste retour principle, 1111
reform, 1110
regulation, 1111
Collective action, 448, 549, 561, 1160, 1161
Collusion. *See* Anti-competitive collusion
Combined Transport Directive 92/106, 1086
Comitology, 273–282,
Appeal Committee, 278–279
comitology committees, 85, 273–282
delegated acts, 282
distinction between delegated and implementing acts, 275–276, 279
functions and functioning, 276–277
organic traits, 276
origins, rationale and tensions, 273–275
procedures, 277–278
scope of, 279–281
transparency, 279
Comitology Regulation (2011), 277
Commission. *See* European Commission
Committee of Governors of teh Central Banks, 886, 888
Committee of the Regions (CoR), 129, 184–186, 218, 249, 250, 373, 1107, 1108, 1177

Common Agricultural Policy (CAP), 10, 14, 17, 328, 839, 1049–1055, 1059, 1064, 1065, 1111, 1118, 1138, 1146, 1172
Common Commercial Policy
 and ACP countries, 1300
 autonomous measures,
  anti-dumping (*see* anti-dumping policy)
  import and export regime, 1301–1304
  safeguard measures, 1304–1306
  for state-trading measures, 1305
  subsidies and countervailing measures
  definition, 1309
  determination of injury, 1310
  procedures (internal), 1310
  proceedings against 3rd country producers, 1310
  surveillance measures, 1305–1306
 and development policy, 1235, 1291, 1294
 and environmental policy, 1171, 1176, 1235, 1294
 and the European Parliament, 30, 1233
 exclusive character of, 1297
 and foreign direct investment, 1104, 1231, 1292, 1293
 and GATT/WTO, 1298, 1300
 principles and development
 and trade in goods, 485–486, 1231, 1292
 and trade in services, 30, 1292, 1296
 and trade related international property rights, 1292, 1296
 and transport policy, 71, 1296
Common European Asylum System (CEAS), 645, 648, 650, 651, 658, 659, 665–666
Common Foreign and Security Policy (CFSP)
 agencies, 1268
 decisions, 1270
 EU-Lex Kosovo operation
  Ahtisaari report, 1279
  becoming a CSDP civilian action, 1279–1283
  EUSR for Kosovo, 1280
  KFOR, relation with, 1279, 1280
  legal capacity, 1281, 1282
  Security Council Resolution 1244, 1279–1280
  UNMIK, relation with, 1279–1280
 High Representative/Vice President (HR/VP), 1231, 1263–1265, 1275
 institutions, 1265, 1266
 legislation, absence of, 1341, 1342
 policy on International Criminal Court (ICC)
  common position 2001/443/CFSP, 1273, 1274
  court on cooperation and assistance, 1274
  decision of 2011, 1274, 1275
  Rome Statute, 1272, 1274
  transfer of information, 1272
  US resistance to, 1273
 role of the Council of Ministers
  conclusions, 1242, 1270, 1273, 1288
  declarations, 1270, 1288
  strategies, 1263, 1288
 role of the European Council
  strategy decisions, 1263, 1288
Common market
 in the agricultural sector, 1049
 concept of, 485
 functioning of, 535, 571
 historical bases, 10–12
 and internal market, 469, 473, 480
 integration objective, 760
 transitional period, 473, 489
Common market organizations, 1054–1055, 1057
Common Security and Defence Policy (CSDP)
 Atalanta military mission (EUNAVFOR)
  Committee of Contributors, 1285
  criminal prosecution of pirates, 1286–1287
  and EUCAP Nestor, 1283
  and EUMC, 1285
  and EUTM Somalia, 1283
  and Ocean Shield/NATO., 1284
  SOFA/SOMA, 1286, 1288
 EU-Lex Kosovo, civilian action, 1279–1283
 European Battle groups, 1271
 and NATO, 1263, 1270–1272, 1276, 1279–1280, 1284–1285
 non-proliferation policies, 1275–1279
  cooperation with other international organizations, 1276
  use of financing instruments, 1278
  WMD, 1275–1278
 and solidarity clauses
  Art. 42(7) TEU, 1271
  Art. 222 TFEU, 1271
Common Transport Policy, 11, 384, 1067–1069, 1072
Common Travel Area, 223, 647
Common Understanding on Delegated Acts, 282
Commonwealth, 5, 13, 14, 635

Community design, 854
Community method, 25, 28–29, 34, 47, 56, 134, 182, 233, 242, 1232, 1242
Community Patent Convention (CPC), 860
Community plant variety rights, 859, 860
Community trademark, 854, 857, 860
Community Visa Code, 653
Company. *See* also Establishment, freedom of
structural changes
collective redundancies, 1005–1006
employer insolvency, 1004–1005
transfer of undertakings, 1006–1007
Company law
company law directives
cross border merger and conversion, 871–872
cross border transfer of the real seat, 870–871
recognition of foreign companies, 872–873
harmonization of, 873–877
modernization, 880–881
supranational company forms, 878–880
European Economic Interest Grouping (EEIG), 878
Societas Europaea (SE), Societas Cooperativa Europaea (SCE), 878–879
Compensation. *See also* Damages
for investors, 961
in state aid, 793, 794
Competence. *See also* Conferral (principle of)
complementary competences, 1199–1203, 1205–1026, 1224, 1228–1229
concurrent competences, 80–81
control by national bodies
constitutional courts, 88–90
national parliaments, 86–88 (*see also* Subsidiarity, role of national parliaments)
exclusive competences, 79–80, 92, 228, 232, 239, 400, 478, 674, 1292–1294, 1296
implicit, implied 71
shared competence, 74–75, 79–81, 84
pre-emption under shared competence, 80–82, 222
in specific policy areas
asylum and migration, 646–647
consumer protection, 1147, 1150
in criminal law matters, 693–694
in EMU, 904, 995
in energy law, 1091, 1103
in external action, 1231, 1238–1242, 1249, 1292, 1294, 1296
ERTA doctrine, 1239–1240, 1255, 1261
external environmental action, 1170–1171
internal market, 469
in health policy, 1133
taxation, 829
system of competences (*see* Chapter 3 *passim*)
historical development, 70–73
judicial control 78–79
principle of conferral, 73–79
principle of proportionality, 84
principle of sincere cooperation, 84–85
principle of subsidiarity, 82–83
Competition law and policy *See* Chapter 20 *passim*.
abuse of a dominant position
Art. 102 TFEU, 747–748
concept, 753–756
dominance, concept, 748–751
exclusionary practices, 756–763
exploitative abuses, 763–764
proof of dominance, 751–753
actors, 716–717
collusion (*see* Anti-competitive collusion)
concentration control
community dimension, 774–775
notification system, 775–776
setting up, system, 772–774
substantive test, 776–777
enforcement of antitrust rules
Commission, 766–768
judicial review, 771–772
national courts, 769–771
NCAs and the ECN, 768–769
Regulation 1/2003, 765
hard-core restriction (*see* Hard-core restriction)
leniency
at EU courts, 768
ECN Model Programme, 769
market definition, 721–722
objectives and effectiveness of rules, 719–721
place in Treaty system, 715
sources of law, 718–719
Complementarity principle, 1114
Complementary competence, 1199–1203, 1205–1026, 1224, 1228–1229
Composite administration, 85, 268, 305–310
Comprehensive Nuclear Test Ban Treaty (CBTB), 1276

Concerted practice, 723, 730, 731, 733, 735, 1081, 1082
Conciliation Committee, 166, 170, 172, 176, 180, 254, 319, 334, 335
Concurrent competences, 80–81. *See also* Competence
Conditionality, 64, 106, 232, 651, 897, 909, 924–927, 941, 944
Conferral (principle of), 71, 73–79, 88, 90, 91, 198, 199, 231, 235, 236, 371, 372, 620, 1228, 1235, 1238
Confiscation Directive 2014/42, 699
Conflict of rights, 112, 122
Conflict rules, 732
Congress of Europe, 2
Consent procedure, 171, 251, 255–256, 258
Conservation of marine biological resources, 1049, 1170, 1240, 1241
Consistent interpretation, 435–437, 459, 1180. *See also* Direct effect; Directives
  of directives, 435–437, 459
  limits of, 436–437
  principle, 436–437, 459
Constitutional change, 45, 59–66, 75, 1122, 1151
Constitutional courts
  authority of, 420
  dialogue, 85, 413, 426
  domestic, 119
  German Federal, 26, 72, 73, 99, 110, 160, 396, 907, 908, 943–945
  Italian, 99
  national, 73, 88–90, 121, 411, 420–427, 926, 1297
  Poland, 417
  Spanish, 125
Constitutional identity, 88, 89, 419, 424, 425, 1107
Constitutional law, 45, 56, 59, 88, 90, 121, 160, 204, 209, 223, 365, 417–427, 908, 1175
Constitutional Treaty. *See* Treaty establishing a Constitution for Europe
Consultative Assembly, 3
Consumer protection
  average consumer, 1157–1158
  consumer confidence, 1158
  development of consumer law, EU
    Art. 100 EEC, 1146
    free movement rules, 1147
    full harmonization, 1152–1154
    legal basis, 1147–1150
    market integration, 1146
    market liberalization, 1151
    national, 1146
    preliminary programme, 1146
    re-orientation, internal market, 1150–1151
  enforcement, 1159–1163
  internal market, 1145
  regulatory approach, 1155–1156
  vulnerable consumer, 1158–1159
Convergence
  in Economic and Monetary Union, 887–890, 895–902, 909, 911, 913, 921
  in the internal market, 475–476, 540
Cooperation policy
  with Asian countries, 1338
  association agreements
    Eastern Europe and Southern Caucasus, 1330
    EEA Agreement, 1328–1329
    Stability and Association Agreement (SAA), 1332
    with Turkey, 1331
  with Canada
    Comprehensive Trade and Economic Agreement (CETA), 1337
    Cooperation Agreement, 1336
  Deep and Comprehensive Free Trade Agreement (DCFTA), 1330
  development association
    Cotonou Partnership Agreement (*see* Cotonou Partnership Agreement)
    Euro-Mediterranean Agreement, 1334
  financial and technical assistance, 1333
  financing instruments, 1322, 1323, 1325
  partnership agreements
    Central Asian countries, 1336
    Russia, 1336
  Trans-Atlantic Trade and Investment Pact (TTIP), US, 1337
Coordination of social security, 255, 587–610, 1258
  rules determining the applicable legislation, 603–605
Copenhagen criteria, 64, 101, 898, 1326
Copyright and related rights, 854, 861–865
Copyright Directive 2001/29 (on the harmonization of certain aspects of copyright and related rights in the information society), 863
Copyright goods online, 864
Coreper, 135, 138–140, 142, 253, 646, 1246, 1269
Correction mechanism (own resources), 328–329, 356
Cotonou Partnership Agreement
  EPA, 1333
  institutions, 1334
  Inter-parliamentary Assembly, 167, 1334

Council (Council of Ministers). *See* Council of the European Union
Council of Europe, 3, 7, 45, 98–99, 113, 121, 135, 707, 1011, 1215, 1220, 1223, 1246, 1252, 1282, 1292
Council of the European Union
  agenda setting, 133
  auxiliary bodies, 138–140
  composition, 136
  establishment, 135–136
  internal organization, 135–40
  legislation, 133
  Luxembourg accord, 21
  non-legislation, 134
  presidency (rotating), 177, 178, 189, 253
  QMV (*see* Voting)
  voting, 136–138
Court of Justice of the European Union (ECJ or CJEU). *See* Chapter 10 *passim*
  action for annulment (annulment action), 369–383
    direct and individual concern, 374–377
    grounds for annulment, 371–373
    non-privileged applicants, 374
    reviewable acts, 370–371
    standing requirements, 374–379
    time limits, 370
  action for damages, 386–388 (*see also* Action for damages)
  action for failure to act, 383–385
  EU Charter of Fundamental Rights, 358
  European Central Bank, 373
  illegality (*see* plea of illegality)
  infringement proceedings, 361–369
    administrative stage, 362–364
    judicial stage, 364–367
    procedures, 368–369
    financial sanctions, 367
  inter-institutional accountability, 401–402
  inter-state legal transactions, 358
  judicial procedure, 98, 299, 300, 309, 389, 1042
  judicial protection, 361–388
  judicial selection committee, 402–403
  linguistic regime, 189–190
  national identity clause, 425
  openness in judging, 407–411
    access to documents, 407–408
    case publicity, 408–409
    Charter of Fundamental Rights, 410
    European Court of Human Rights, 409
    oral hearing, 409
  plea of illegality, 385–386
  preliminary reference procedure, 388–401 (*see* also Preliminary reference procedure)
  primacy, development of principle of, 420–22
  relations with *Bundesverfassungsgericht*, 425–426
  reform of EU courts, 403–407
  regulatory acts, 378
  role in boundary between CFSP and TFEU, 1238, 1321, 1343
Courts
  Civil Service Court, 188, 357
  Court of Auditors, 104, 129, 172, 187–188, 250, 313, 315, 317–318, 324, 338–341, 373, 383, 930, 1267
  Court of First Instance, 23, 30, 104, 126, 163, 403
  Court of Justice (*see* Court of Justice of the European Union)
  General Court (formerly: Court of First Instance), 23, 30, 104, 163, 403
  national, 78, 89, 95, 100, 116, 119, 121, 124, 126, 157, 187, 207, 211, 293, 307, 357–358, 364, 373, 382, 388–401, 418–422, 427, 429–435, 438, 442–452, 461, 465, 471, 492, 535, 557, 717, 725, 769–771, 799–801, 1161, 1294, 1329
Credit facilities, 899, 906
Credit rating agencies, 957, 972, 981
Criminal law
  in AFSJ, 691
  competences, since Lisbon Treaty, 693–694
  cooperation (*see* Judicial cooperation)
  ECJ jurisdiction, 695
  fraud, 692
  measures, 691
  minimum standards of procedural rights
    suspects and accused persons, 702–704
    victims of crime, 704–705
  opt-out and opt-in arrangements, 695
  Schengen framework and *ne bis in idem* principle, 692–693
  substantive 217, 642, 691, 694–701
    Euro crimes, 696–700
    influence on national, 695–696
    regulatory, 700–701
Cross-border
  conversion of companies, 871–872

element in internal market (*see* Free movement of goods, Free movement of services)
merger of companies, 871–872
movement of goods, 487–489
trade, 523, 789, 850, 852, 853, 856, 1146
transfer
of the real seat, 870–871
of the registered office, 871, 876, 880
Culture, 19, 73, 102, 530, 781, 945, 1108, 1202, 1203, 1207, 1217, 1221–1223, 1228, 1244, 1320
Currency. *See* Single currency
Customs duties, 187, 314–315, 326, 487, 492–494, 496–497, 715, 845, 1124, 1126, 1286, 1299, 1313, 1335
Customs Union, 5, 10, 17, 156, 302, 485–488, 829, 845, 884, 1121, 1122, 1124, 1126, 1231, 1253, 1298, 1328, 1331–1332, 1336
Cyprus, 17–18, 160, 305, 649, 893, 925, 941, 1122, 1327

D

Damages
claims against the EU,
actions for, 193, 354, 361, 385–388, 459, 1282 (*see also* Court of Justice of the EU, The action for damages)
non-contractual liability, 386–388
claims against Member States (*see* State liability)
for competition infringements, 211, 769–771
compensatory, 1180
private enforcement, 457, 458, 463
risk of reputational, 168
Decentralized agencies, 284–286. *See also* Agencies
Decision-making procedures. *See* Chapter 7 *passim*
composite procedures, 306
consent procedure, 255–256
consultation, 248–251
Court of Justice, 241
initiative, 242–248
Commission, 243
Community method, 242
Council and Commission, 246
European Central Bank (ECB), 247
European Supervisory Authorities (ESAs), 245
monopoly of legislative initiative, 242
non-legislative acts, 242
inter-institutional agreements, 241
mutual sincere cooperation, 241
non-legislative procedure, 240
ordinary legislative procedure, 240, 251–255
special legislative procedure, 240, 257–258
unanimity requirement 258–259
Decisions. *See* Legal instruments
Decisions addressed to Member States, effect, 213, 432
Deep and Comprehensive Free-Trade Agreements (DCFTA), 1330
Defence rights (Rights of the defence), 363, 196, 447, 694, 767, 799
Deficit
accountability, 294
budget, 323
and debt data, 913
excessive (government), 155–158, 303, 896, 900–904, 913–926, 1113, 1119
financing, 906–910
De Gaulle. *See* France
De Larosière Report, 954–955, 958, 975, 976, 981
Delegated acts, 105, 156, 202, 215, 236, 239, 240, 245, 256, 271, 275, 279–282, 952, 1064, 1324. *See also* Implementing acts
Delimitation of competences, 34, 74, 81
Delors report, 571, 888
De minimis, 508, 521, 525, 552, 737, 780, 790, 793, 796, 809
Democracy, 17, 28, 31, 34, 64, 91, 95–96, 106, 120, 164, 167, 214, 260–261, 263–265, 409, 416–417, 634, 1234, 1322–1324, 1326, 1332–1333, 1339–1340
Democratic legitimacy, 24, 27, 32, 159, 260–265, 380, 612, 936, 1233
democratic deficit, 179, 261
European integration, 260
normative commitment through legitimacy, 260
pluralism, 262–264
problems of translation, 261
scale, 261–262
sense of political community, 264
transnational issues, 265
Denmark, 3, 13–15, 22, 26, 28, 53, 56, 225, 328, 648, 649, 674, 695, 834, 872, 890, 896–898, 910, 1120, 1217, 1239, 1284
Deposit Guarantee Scheme (DGS), 954, 955, 957, 958, 960, 961, 1149
Derivatives, 616, 761, 963, 967–969, 971, 1133, 1143, 1208
Derogation,
free movement of goods, 525–531
free movement of services, 580–584
non-participation in euro, 895–897

Designations of origin, 415, 511, 1060
Development cooperation, 1319–1325, 1333–1335
Differentiation, 45, 51–59, 270–273, 500, 502, 581, 898, 903, 984, 1031, 1107–1128
Diplomatic protection, 614, 636
Direct applicability, 89, 206, 207, 300, 428, 432, 434
Direct effect
Charter of Fundamental Rights, 429–430
conditions, 430–431
decisions, 432
direct applicability, 432
of directives, 432–435
freedoms
free movement of goods
expiry of transitional period, 489
horizontal direct effect, 491–492
measures, 489–491
horizontal, 437–442, 474
indirect, 435–437
international agreements, 435, 1259 (*see also* External relations)
inverse vertical, 433, 435
regulations, 432–435
state, concept of, 428
Treaty provisions, 428–429
triangular relations, 439
vertical, 425, 433–435, 474
Directives, 208–211, 432–435
binding force, 208
effect in national legal order, 432–435, 435–439
horizontal direct effect, 439 (*see also* Direct effect)
implementation (transposition)
transposition into national law, 208–209, 478
failure to implement, 462
legal instrument, 199–211
procedure for adoption (*see* Legislative procedure)
regional or local authorities, 210
result to be achieved, 206, 208
sanctions, 432–435
triangular relations (*see* Direct effect)
vertical direct effect (*see* Direct effect)
Direct payments, 118, 1055, 1058, 1059, 1064
Disability, 111, 441, 659, 811, 1010, 1017–1019, 1021, 1024, 1027, 1028, 1031, 1033, 1038, 1039, 1220
Discharge (of the budget),
powers of parliament, 172–173
procedure, 341
Disclosure obligations, 873
Discretion,
of EU institutions
choice of delegated or implementing power, 280–282,
choice of technique to achieve harmonization, 291–292
Commission's discretion in infringement proceedings, 362–364
Commission's discretion in competition enforcement, 769
Commission's discretion in state aid 792–794
of Member States
in implementation of EU law, 108, 430–432
in proportionality test, 563–566
in protection of fundamental rights, 124
Discrimination
aggregate, 1028
cumulative, 1028
direct discrimination, 499, 506, 577, 597, 1029–1031
direct effect, 437
discrimination by association, 1028, 1032
on grounds of migration, 597–598
on grounds of nationality, 98, 438, 500, 548, 550, 551, 597, 764, 805, 830
harassment, 1029, 1032–1033
horizontal, 832
indirect, 499–501, 524, 597, 598, 605, 632, 833, 1029, 1031–1032
instruction to discriminate, 1029, 1033
intersectional, 1028
multidimensional/multiple, 1028–1029
reverse discrimination, 480, 482–483, 488, 830
Division of competences (distribution of competences), 31, 75, 91. *See also* Competence
Dooge report, 22
Dublin Regulation, 118, 122, 207, 644, 659–660, 663, 665, 666
Duty of sincere cooperation, 176, 183, 207, 1171, 1206, 1254, 1315
Duty to state reasons, 159, 204, 205

E

Early warning system/mechanism, 73, 1336
E-commerce Directive, 1161
Economic and Financial Affairs Council (ECOFIN), 136, 897, 904, 938

Economic and Financial Committee, 305, 890, 916, 928
Economic and Monetary Union (EMU)
 ad hoc crisis, 892–894
 economic policy, euro area
  European Semester, 911–912
  excessive deficit (*see* Deficit, excessive (government))
  excessive deficit and excessive macroeconomic imbalances procedures, 914–921
  macroeconomic imbalances, 912–914
  multilateral surveillance of deficits, 912–914
  objectives and principles, 902–906
  powers to deal with extraordinary economic circumstances, 923–928
  rules on deficit financing, 906–910
 European Currency Unit (ECU), 887
 European Monetary System (EMS), 886–887
 European single currency (*see* Single currency)
 in-depth review of Member State in case of fundamental imbalances, 911, 914, 919
 legal status, non-euro area
  legal and economic criteria, single currency, 898–902
  Member States, 895–898
 monetary policy in the euro area
  ECB independence and accountability, 934–942
  ECB's legal instruments, 949–950
  ESCB and ECB, 945–949
  legal nature, 929–931
  objectives and scope, 942–945
  organizational structure, 931–934
  secondary markets, 906, 907, 925, 944, 945, 967
 original EEC Treaty, 883–884
 political negotiations, 888
 structural measures, euro area debt crisis, 892–894
 Werner report, 884–886
Economic and Social Committee (ECOSOC or ESC), 121, 129, 184–186, 188, 1177
Economic Partnership Agreement (EPA), 1333
Economic Partnership Programme, 917, 926
Economic Policy Committee, 886
Economic, social and territorial cohesion, 332, 996, 1109–1120. *See also* Cohesion policy
Education, 1213–1218
 competence, 82
 cost-effectiveness, 1217
 as economic service, 542
 ERASMUS Programme, 1213–1214
 establishment, 624
 freedom of movement, 554
 funding programmes, 207
 of migrant children, 1217
 minors and health care, 665
 national system, 542, 1205, 1218
 public service exception, 594
 quality, 561
 and tax benefits, 666, 671
 and vocational training (*see* Vocational training)
EEC Treaty
 history, 8, 10, 12, 13, 22, 33, 46, 51, 52
Effectiveness, principle of, 446–450. *See* Principle of effectiveness
Effective judicial protection, principle of 444–446. *See* Principle of effective judicial protection
Electoral rights. *See* Citizenship
Electricity, 1089–1091, 1094, 1095, 1098–1101
Emergency brake, 255, 263, 694
Employment
 access to, 663, 665, 1038
 conditions, 249, 530, 549, 555, 559, 587, 592, 594, 597, 783, 999, 1022
 contract of, 592, 594, 595, 824
 cross-border, 89
 and dismissal, 1022
 and economic policy, 215
 EU civil service, 151
 EURES, 296
 full, 589, 784, 886
 guidelines, 905, 906, 911, 920
 high level of, 905, 995, 1201
 illegal, 671, 701
 law, 137, 211, 1029
 market, 560, 632, 1035
 minimum period of, 596
 minor, 1035
 mobility of workers, 297, 1116
 non-standard forms of (*see* Non-standard forms of employment)
 and occupation, 1017, 1020, 1023–1024, 1036
 policy, 29, 82, 134, 186, 219, 905, 1010, 1015, 1035, 1036, 1041, 1113, 1206, 1207
 programmes, 593
 re-employment, 593

relationship, 438, 592, 593, 1012, 1013, 1022
rights, 997, 1016
scheme, 603
self-employment, 609, 618, 1016, 1018
social security, 1015, 1024
State of, 604, 831
terminations of, 1036
Youth Employment Package, 1219
Empty chair policy, 19
Energy policy. *See also* Chapter 32 *passim*
constitutional framework
Art. 194 TFEU, 1097
changes brought by Lisbon Treaty, 1091–1092, 1094
EAEC (Euratom), 1090
energy networks, 1096–1097
Euratom Treaty, 1090, 1093
governance, 1090
renewables, emissions and efficiency, Art. 192 TFEU, 1095
Services of General Interest (SGI), 1094
Energy Union 149, 1089
and environmental policy, 1095
external aspects (*see* External energy policy)
internal energy market, 1089–1090
nuclear energy (*see* Nuclear energy)
policy, 9, 1089–1092, 1098, 1102–1106, 1169
taxation, 829, 846, 847, 1092, 1181
Energy networks, 1090, 1091, 1096–1097
Enforcement
of antitrust rules, competition law, 765–769 (*see* Competition law and policy)
Application and Enforcement Regulation, 1312–1314
in a composite legal order, 413
of consumer law, 1159–1163
and effective application by Member States, 416, 443–444
of equal treatment and non-discrimination, 1042–1044
of EU fundamental rights, 119–120
of financial market rules, 974–988
of free movement of workers, 499
of environmental law, 1178–1180
private, 120, 457, 458, 771, 795, 1161
of State aid rules, 794, 803 (*see* State aid)
Enhanced cooperation, 30, 53–57, 137, 233, 256, 681–683, 686, 687, 712, 861
Enlargement, 12–18, 28, 29, 31, 33, 53, 64, 96, 134, 146, 150, 224, 318, 368, 403, 591, 895, 933, 1079, 1086, 1110, 1123, 1140, 1265, 1298, 1323. *See also* Accession
Entry-Exit System for Third Country Nationals, 654–655
Environmental policy. *See* Chapter 36 *passim*
aims (Art. 191(1) and Art. 191(2) TFEU), 1169–1170
biodiversity and nature conservation, 1183–1184
chemical substances control, 1182
climate and energy, 1181
competence and external action, 1170–1171
environmental protection, 1165–1168, 1170–1177
general legal bases, 1176–1177
governance and enforcement, 1178–1180
guarantee provisions and minimum harmonization, 1177–1178
history, 1165–1168
impact assessment, EIA and strategic, 1182–1183
industrial pollution control, 1181–1182
principles, 1171
integration, 1175–1176
polluter pays, 1174–1175
precautionary, 1172–1173
preventive, 1173
rectification at source principle, 1173–1174
values, 1169
Equal treatment
duty, 1033–1034
international law, 1019, 1044
justifications
public order, 1040
genuine occupational requirements, 1037–1038
objective justification, 1034–1035
occupational social security, Art. 6(2) of Directive 2000/78, 1040
positive action, 1038–1039
protection of women (pregnancy and maternity), 1039
layered system of Union non-discrimination law, 1024–1025
material scope
employment and occupation, 1023–1024
employment-related social security, 1024
goods and services, 1024–1025
pay, 1022–1023
and non-discrimination
discrimination grounds, 1026–1028

EU law, 1025–1026
forms of discrimination (*see* Discrimination)
multi-dimensional discrimination, 1028–1029
personal scope, 1022
proportionality, 1041
Equivalence, principle of, 446–450. *See* Principle of equivalence
Establishment, freedom of
and capital, 540
companies, 540
concept of, 541
cross-border element, 546–547
horizontal direct effect, 548–549
justifications (*see* also Justifications)
compliance with fundamental rights, 566–567
exceptions, 558–561
multiple legitimate aims, 561–562
proportionality assessment, 562–566
rule of reason, 561
treaty-based derogations, 557–558
and nationality, 546
restrictions
discriminatory, 549–550
limits to the concept of, 552–553
posting of workers, 555
recognition of diplomas and professional qualifications, 553–555
Säger approach, 551–552
transparency, 556
right of establishment, Arts. 49–55 TFEU, 540
and services, 544–545
EU Administration. *See* Administration of the EU
Euratom Treaty. *See* European Atomic Energy Community
Euro area
cooperation, 59
countries, 58, 945
crisis, 954
European Central Bank (ECB), 956
economic policy (*see* Economic and Monetary Union (EMU))
economy, 943
financial stability, 229, 230, 944
macroeconomic environment, 894
powers in special circumstances 924–928
sovereign debt crisis, 892
specific legislation, economic governance, 55
Euro crimes, 696–700
Eurodac, 659
Eurogroup, 218, 305, 897, 898, 912, 914, 919, 926, 932, 938, 941
Eurojust, 290, 628, 693, 694, 711–712
Europe 2020, 781, 818, 1010–1113, 1115, 1118, 1185, 1192, 1197, 1207, 1216, 1224, 1324
flagship initiatives, 781
Europe against Aids, 1132
Europe against Cancer, 1132
European Agency for the Evaluation of Medicinal Products (EMEA), 1135
European Agricultural Fund for Rural Development (EAFRD), 996, 1065, 1111, 1117, 1118
European Anti-Fraud Office (OLAF)
competences, 349–351
conduct of investigations, 351–353
creation and legal framework, 347–348
judicial control, 354–355
procedural guarantees, 353–354
structure and organization, 348–349
supervision, 354
European army, 7, 8. *See also* European Defence Community
European arrest warrant, 123, 125, 217, 424, 703, 706, 709–711
European Asylum Support Office (EASO), 290, 644, 650, 659, 666
European Atomic Energy Community (EAEC, Euratom), 10–12, 45, 46, 48, 186, 227, 1090, 1093–1094
European Banking Authority (EBA), 954, 958, 959, 977
European Border and Coast Guard Agency (Frontex), 105, 644, 650, 651, 658
European Central Bank (ECB), 36, 104, 106, 129, 186, 189, 200, 240, 247, 259, 304, 370, 373, 886, 889, 892, 929, 935, 956
Governing Council, 932
legal personality, 929
European civil procedure, 685, 687, 688
European Coal and Steel Community (ECSC), 5–12, 14, 45, 46, 48, 99, 143, 163, 167, 268, 314, 323, 1090, 1130
High Authority, 143, 292
European Commission
and administration/non-legislative acts
delegated powers, 157
implementing powers, 156
censure, 143–144, 149
characteristics, 146–149
collegiality, 145–146

composition, appointment and censure, 143–144
independence, 144–145
and Member States, 143–149, 152, 155–158
President of the Commission, 147–148
reduction of numbers of Commissioners, 143
right of proposal (right of initiative), 155, 156
right of withdrawal, 154, 182
services of the Commission
EU civil service, 151–153
organization, 149–151
tasks and functions
administration, 156–157
legislative process, 154–156
supervision, 157–159
European Community, 45–50,
European Competition Network, 295
European Conservatives and Reformists (ECR), 164
European Constitution. *See* Treaty establishing a Constitution for Europe
European Convention for the Protection of Human Rights and Fundamental Freedoms (ECHR)
accession of EU
background, 113–114
Draft Accession Agreement, 114
Opinion 2/13, 115–116
European Court of Human Rights (ECtHR), 112–119, 121, 122, 126, 410, 702, 703, 708, 709
European Social Charter (ESC), 98, 106
interrelationship EU, ECHR and national protection, 121–127
Member States acting within scope of EU law, 117–118
source of EU fundamental rights, 112–113
European Council
auxiliary bodies, 132–133
composition, 131
establishment, 130
internal organization, 130
political powers and functions, 133–135
powers
absence of legislative functions, 134–135
agenda setting, 133
President of, 131
qualified majority, 137–138
relation to Council of Ministers, 175, 177, 178, 1175, 1232, 1242, 1244
voting, 132, 136–137
European Court of Auditors. *See* Courts
European Court of Justice. *See* Court of Justice of the European Union
European Currency Unit (ECU), 323, 887, 890
European Defence Agency (EDA)
and Council, 1269
and EEAS, 1264, 1268
procurement
and Art. 346 TFEU, 1269
Code of Conduct, 1269, 1270
European Defence Community (EDC), 7–10, 12, 99
European Development Funds, 321, 1125, 1320, 1333
European Economic Area (EEA), 16, 17, 37, 46, 476, 477, 591, 602, 717, 856, 858, 986, 1038, 1084, 1168, 1326–1331
European Economic Community (EEC), 10–14, 22, 23, 26, 45, 46
European Economic Interest Grouping (EEIG), 878–879
European Environment Agency, 288, 1168
European Exchange Rate Mechanism (ERM), 887, 895, 896, 900, 901, 934
European Exchange Rate System, 886, 1253
European External Action Service (EEAS)
composition, 1261, 1266
functioning, 1246, 1264, 1265, 1267, 1268
internal organization
dependent agencies, 348
EU delegations, 1261, 1266, 1267, 1342
EU special representatives, 1268
service for foreign policy instruments, 1265
relation with Commission, 179, 1231, 1237, 1264–1267, 1282
relation with Council, 179, 1261, 1264–1268
review of, 1267
European Financial Stabilization Facility (EFSF), 327, 893, 908, 925, 926
European Financial Stabilization Mechanism (EFSM), 893, 908, 924–926
European Freedom and Direct Democracy Party (EFDD), 164
European Free Trade Association (EFTA), 13, 15, 16, 675, 717, 719, 1038, 1328, 1329
European Health Community, 1130, 1142
European Information Observation Network, 295
European Instrument for Democracy and Human Rights (EIDHR), 1322, 1324, 1325

European Insurance and Occupational Pensions Authority (EIOPA), 954, 958, 959, 973
European integration, 1–5, 7–9, 45, 47, 50–54, 57, 59, 66,
European Investment Bank (EIB), 186, 188, 247, 322, 336, 340, 344, 930, 1110, 1119–1120, 1319, 1320, 1330
European Judicial Network (EJN), 712
European Maritime and Fisheries Fund (EMFF), 996, 1065, 1111, 1118–1119
European Market Infrastructure (Regulation) (EMIR), 968, 969
European Medicines Agency (EMA), 289, 1135
European Monetary Cooperation Fund (EMCF), 886, 887, 889
European Monetary Institute (EMI), 864, 889, 890, 895, 934
European Monitoring Centre for Drugs and Drug Addiction, 288
European network of employment services (EURES), 296
European Ombudsman, 26, 107, 152, 284, 310, 369, 614, 636
European Parliament
composition and election, 159–165
elections, 161–163
General Secretariat
Secretary-General, 167–168
information, right to be informed, 1247
internal organization
Bureau (of the Parliament), 166, 167
delegations, 167
General Secretariat of the Parliament, 167–168
plenary meeting, 168–169
President, 165–168
Special Committees, 166
Standing Committees, 166
Members (MEPs)
immunity (Parliamentary), 161
incompatibilities, 160
number, 160
Statute, 159–161
national parliaments (relation with)
Conference of Parliamentary Committees for Union Affairs (COSAC), 173–174
Protocol (No. 1), 173,
plenary meeting, 168–169
political and judicial functions, 160
political groups and parties, 163–165
powers and functions
budgetary power, 171–172
consultation procedure, 169–170
co-operation procedure, 170
general power of deliberation, 171
national parliaments, 173–174
ordinary legislative procedure/co-decision, 170
petitions, 169
supervision and control, 172–173
Protocol on the Privileges and Immunities of the European Communities, 161
representatives of the Union's citizens, 159–160
European Patent Convention (EPC), 860
European Patent Office (EPO), 860, 861
European Political Community (EPC), 7–10, 99
European Political Cooperation (EPC), 18–23, 47, 1263, 1275, 1339
and European Council, 18–21
The Single European Act (1986), 21–23
European Public Prosecutor's Office (EPPO), 256, 319, 342, 356, 693, 694, 712–713
European Regional Development Fund (ERDF), 996, 1110–1112, 1116, 1117
European Research Area (ERA). *See also* Research and Technology
allocation of resources, 1189–1190
competitiveness and innovation programme, 1193
concept of, 1190
co-ordination, 1190
digital space, 1191
European Institute of Innovation and Training (EIT), 1194
European Research Council (ERC), 1196
European space policy (*see* Policy)
framework programmes and Horizon 2020, 1191–1193
international science and technology (S&T) policy, 1191
joint programming, JTIs and ETPs, 1195–1196
Lisbon Strategy, 1189
European Securities and Markets Authority (ESMA), 290–294, 953, 954, 958, 959, 981–982
European Semester, 302, 904, 906, 911–912, 914, 1010, 1011, 1015, 1112, 1113, 1175, 1203, 1207, 1213, 1217, 1219
European Social Fund (ESF), 268, 996, 997, 1110–1112, 1116–1117
European Space Agency (ESA), 1197

European Space Policy. *See* Research and Technology
European Stability Mechanism (ESM), 36, 57, 58, 63, 106, 158, 229–232, 322, 327, 893, 894, 897, 906, 908, 909, 919, 924–927, 941, 943
European Structural and Investment Funds (ESI funds), 996, 1065, 1109, 1111–1116, 1119, 1120, 1125
European Supervisory Authorities (ESAs), 245, 952–955, 975–982, 988–990
European Surveillance System (EUROSUR), 648
European Systemic Risk Board (ESRB), 920, 954, 975, 977, 980
European System of Central Banks (ESCB), 889, 892, 895, 897, 899, 907, 928–932, 934, 936–942, 945–949
European System of Financial Supervision (ESFS), 954, 958, 975
European Territorial Cooperation-goal, 1112, 1116
European Travel Information and Authorization System (ETIAS), 654–655
European Union Charter of Fundamental Rights. *See* Charter of Fundamental Rights of the EU
European Union Intellectual Property Office (EUIPO). *See* Intellectual property
European Union Oversees Countries and Territories Association (EU-OCT Association), 1125–1127
Europol, 188, 189, 222, 232, 290, 296, 628, 694, 710–711
Eurostat, 913
Eurozone. *See* Economic and Monetary Union
Excessive deficit procedure (EDP), 158, 572, 900, 904, 910, 913, 916–923, 926, 1113, 1119
Excessive macroeconomic imbalances procedure, 914–921
Exchange rate(s)
  interventions, 946
  mechanism (ERM), 887, 895, 896, 900
  operations, 886, 946
  regimes, 1253
Excises, 842, 846, 847, 1138
Exclusive competence. *See* Competences
Exclusive economic zone, 1120
Executive agencies, 284, 285, 293, 336, 1193, 1196. *See also* Agencies
Executive federalism, 268–272, 305
Exhaustion of IP rights
  caveat of, 862
  principle of, 856, 858, 862
  rule, 864
Exit taxation, 833
Ex officio application, 435, 448, 449, 452, 465, 768, 772, 800, 803, 1156, 1162, 1163. *See* also National Courts
Explanatory memorandum, 169, 245, 310, 864, 1226
Export
  intra-EU
    abuse of law, 483
    agricultural products, 1048, 1302
    authorization, 1303
    data, 211, 749
    free movement, 471, 486, 491, 505, 506, 525, 535, 585, 599, 609, 851, 1042, 1049
    import *vs.* export restrictions, 522–523
    market shares, 914
    prohibitions and restrictions, 187, 526, 1206
    regulation, 606, 609, 698, 718, 744, 764, 845, 859, 914, 1049, 1054, 1055, 1059,
  to third countries, 1301–1304, 1306, 1307, 1309, 1310, 1312, 1342
Expulsion, 625, 626, 628–630, 656, 669
External action
  agreements, Member States, 1260–1261
  association agreements based on Art. 217 TFEU, 1327–1335
  autonomous, 1322–1325
  commercial policy (*see* Common Commercial Policy)
    anti-dumping duties and countervailing duties, 1307–1311
    autonomous commercial policy, 1301–1306
  contractual, 1325
  cooperation agreements, 1335–1339
  development and other cooperation policies, 1319–1326
  expectations, 1261
  foreign direct investment, 1314–1318
  foundations of, 1234
  harmonious interpretation and direct effect, 1258–1260
  instruments of, 1236–1237
  international law as law of the Union, 1255–1258
  loyalty and cooperation, 1254–1255
  mixed agreements, 1248–1251, 1262
  mixed membership in international organizations, 1252–1254
  powers

exclusive, shared/complementary, 1238–1242
Treaty structure and foundations, 1234–1236
sanctions and restrictive measures, 1339–1346
Union institutions and decision-making, 1242–1248
External competence, 34, 70, 80, 81, 656, 674, 1072, 1086, 1103, 1238–1240, 1267, 1294
External energy policy
competence, 1103
Energy Community Treaty, 1104
foreign direct investment, 1104
oil crises, 1102
security, energy supply, 1102
strategic partnerships, 1103–1104
strategies, 1102–1103
External relations
and exclusive powers, 1238–1242
and parallel powers, 1241
and shared powers, 1238–1242
and supplementary powers, 1238–1242

F
Family benefits, 602
Family members
Blue Card Directive, 671
Citizens' Rights Directive, 633–634
Dublin Regulation, 659
education, 1217
expulsion measures, 629
free movement and residence rights, 617–619
identity and status, 621
long term residents, 668, 670
position of, 633–634
public security, 629
reunification, 667, 668
right to equal treatment, 631, 632
social advantages, 589
social assistance system, 625
and survivors of Union citizens, 602
third country nationals, 620, 621, 623, 624, 626, 628, 629
victimization, 705
Family reunification, 667–668
Family Reunification Directive, 645, 653, 666–669
Federalism
competences, EU administration, 270–271
constitutional framework, EU administration, 271–272
cooperative, 73, 82
executive federalism model, 268–270, 305
political safeguards, 83
Financial assistance
to ACP states, 1320
ESM Treaty, 925, 926, 941
EU political groups and parties, 163
euro area Member State, 232
host State, 597
measures, 936, 1203
mechanism, 924
medium-term, 886, 887, 927, 928, 1113
OCTs, 1125
programmes, 1014
Financial crisis 2007. *See* Sovereign debt crisis
Financial markets
behaviour, 1101
Commission's services, 149
ECB, 949
ERM currencies, 901
integrity of, 290
legislation, 35
monetary policy, 939, 947
private creditor test, 783
public authorities, 907
regulation (*see* Financial markets regulation)
supervision (*see* Supervision of financial markets)
territorial scope, 572
Financial markets regulation
banking regulations, 959–963
ESFS, 958
EU legal framework, 951
institutional structure and development
Banking Union, 955
crisis management, 956–957
De Larosière Report (2009), 954–955
Deposit Guarantee Scheme (DGS), 957–958
Lamfalussy Report (2001), 951–953
single supervision, 955–956
insurers and pension funds, 972–974
legal protection
ECB and SRB, 990–992
ESAs, 989–990
securities and markets, 963–972
supervision and enforcement
Banking Union, 982–988
ESAs, 975–982
Member States, 974, 975
powers, 977

Fiscal Compact, 36, 57, 58, 231, 894, 908, 910. *See also* Treaty on Stability, Coordination and Governance in Economic and Monetary Union
Fiscal Supervision, 529, 558, 838–840
Fisheries
- conservation, fish stocks, 1061–1062
- decision making, 1063–1064
- financing, 1064–1065
- fleet restructuring, 1062
- international relations, 1062–1063
- market regulation, 1063
- policies
  - implementation, application and control, 1064
  - objectives, 1066
  - origin of, 1060–1061

Fishing capacity, 1056, 1062
Fishing effort, 1061
Five President's Report, 885
Fluctuation margins, 885, 886, 900, 901
Foodstuffs, 527, 1131, 1134, 1136–1138, 1221
Foreign Direct Investment
- EU Policy, 1314–1318
- Investor-States Dispute Settlement, 1316, 1318
- Responsibility Regulation, 1316–1318
- Transitional Regulation, 1314–1316

Foreign policy
- democratization of, 1233
- "high" foreign policy, 1232, 1233, 1237, 1261
- "low" foreign policy, 1232, 1233, 1237, 1261

Formal investigation. *See* State aid
Fouchet Commission, 19
Framework decision on European Arrest Warrant. *See* European Arrest Warrant
Framework decisions, 50, 201
France, 13, 14, 19–21, 422
Fraud, 314, 318, 320, 327, 331, 342, 343, 345, 346, 348, 350, 351
Free movement of capital. *See* Capital, free movement
Free movement of goods. *See* Chapter 13 *passim*
- burden of proof, 534
- concept of customs union, 485–486
- concept of "goods", 486–487
- cross-border movement, 487–489
- direct effect (*see* Direct effect)
- financial restrictions
  - internal taxation (*see* Internal taxation)
  - tariff barriers (*see* Tariff barriers)
- intra-Community trade, 485
- justifications, 525–533 (*see* also Justifications)
  - mandatory requirements, 529–530
  - necessity test, 584
  - proportionality test, 531–533
  - rule of reason, 530
  - suitability test, 584
  - Treaty derogations (Art. 36 TFEU), 526–529
- non-tariff barriers (*see* Non-tariff barriers)
  - non-tariff and tariff restrictions, 523–524
- obstacle to freedom of movement, 530
- relationship with Art. 110 TFEU, 503–505
- restrictions, 524–525
- state-owned/state-backed commercial monopolies, 534–536
- third countries, 487

Free movement of services. *See also* Services Directive
- concept of, 540
- cross-border element, 546–547
- economic activity, 541–544
- and freedom of establishment (*see* Establishment, freedom of)
- and goods, 545
- internal market, 539
- market integration, 539
- public services, 539–540
- recipients, 547–548

Free movement of workers. *See* Chapter 15 *passim*
- Art. 45 TFEU, 587–588
- development, labour markets, 589
- enforcement, 499
- exception, public service, 593–594
- historical development, 588–591
- justifications (*see* also Justifications)
- Member States, 588–589
- prohibitions
  - direct discrimination, 597–598
  - indirect discrimination, 598
  - migration, 598–599
  - non-discriminatory obstacles, 599
- right to work, 592–593
- social advantages, 595–597
- social security (*see* Coordination of social security)
- status of worker, 594–595

Frontex. *See* European Border and Coast Guard Agency
Frontier worker, 597, 607, 609

Fundamental rights. *See* Chapter 4 *passim*. *See* also *Human rights*
coexistence of national constitutional rights, 125–127
coexisting human rights, EU perspectives, 121–125
enforcement of (*see* Enforcement)
as general principles, 100–102, 118–119
genesis of, 98–102
human rights law, 97–98
market rights (free movement of goods), 533–534
protection and promotion of, 95
sources of
Charter of Fundamental Rights (*see* Charter of Fundamental Rights)
European Convention for the Protection of Human Rights and Fundamental Freedoms (ECHR)
general principles of EU law, 118–119
Treaty basis, 95–96
Fundamental Rights Agency, 95, 96, 110, 221, 288

G

Gas
and electricity market, 1091, 1094, 1098
essential services, 750
and exploration, 825
greenhouse gas (GHG) emissions, 1083, 1181
industry, 1346
markets, 584
natural, 527, 1090, 1092
network tariffs, 1100
Regulation on Security of Supply for Gas 2010, 1097
security of supply regulation, 1102
transport pipelines, 750
Generalized System of Preferences (GSP)
commodity stabilization programme, 1319
"everything but arms," 1299
regulation, 1299
and trade policy, 1294, 1298, 1299
General Principles of EU law
applied by Court of Justice of the EU, 372
direct effect, 429
horizontal direct effect, 437
ECHR, 101
source of EU law, 196–198
source of fundamental rights, 100, 102–103, 118–119, 419
unwritten source, 91
Union non-discrimination law, 1020
General principles of law
applied by Court of Justice of the EU, 358
General Secretariat of the Council, 132, 1264–1266
Geneva Convention (Refugees), 120, 645, 661, 662, 664
Genuine link, 632, 633, 637
Genuine occupational requirements, 1037–1038
Geographical differentiation
EU Member states, 1120
OCTs, 1124–1128
OMRs, 1123–1124
passerelle clause to change a territory's status, 1122–1123
Germany
Bundesverfassungsgericht, 33, 88, 99, 100, 124, 423–426, 907, 908 (*see also* Constitutional courts, German Federal)
Franco-German relations, 3–4
Schuman Plan, 7, 51
Global Approach to Migration and Mobility (GAMM), 643
Golden shares, 572, 578, 584, 585
Goods, definition, 486
Governing Council of the ECB
and Executive Board, 895, 931, 932
meetings, 933, 937–939
monetary policy, 940
participation, 937
policy-making, 932
power, 934
role in SRM, 990
voting, 933, 934
Government
debt, 890, 900, 904, 915, 916, 919
deficit, 896, 904, 906, 910, 912, 915–919, 922, 924
Greenland, 1124, 1125
Group of Ten, 886

H

Hague Programme (2004), 646, 676, 688. *See also* Tampere Agenda *and* Stockholm Programme.
Harassment, 1029, 1032–1033, 1045, 1317
Hard-core restriction, 718, 725, 744, 746
Harmful tax competition, 840–841
Harmonization. *See also* Approximation of laws
absence of, 515, 525–526, 556
agriculture, 1050, 1051, 1054,
civil procedure, 467, 679, 687
common transport policy, 10
company law, 873–877
degree of, 673

directives, 158, 207–208
exclusion, 415, 1224, 1226, 1227
financial regulation, 952, 1072
full (total), 643, 659, 863, 1105, 1131, 1136, 1145, 1152–1154, 1208, 1211, 1214
healthcare services, 1210
internal market, 1239
lack of, 581, 864, 954
laws and regulations, Member State, 1188, 1197, 1200, 1205
maximum, 955, 958, 971, 1162
measures, 23, 185, 291, 292, 456, 480, 697, 1202, 1209
minimum, 57, 81, 82, 209, 954, 958, 1098, 1148, 1177–1178, 1208–1210, 1240
negative, 1154
partial, 582, 681
positive, 1147
prohibition of, 74, 1199, 1202, 1206, 1209, 1228, 1229
rules, 650, 1145
social policies, 1080
substantive, 211
taxation, 258, 842–847
and uniform legislation, 477–479

Health
common health market, 1130–1131, 1142
health care, 542, 543, 564, 606–608, 663, 665, 727, 1011, 1129–1134, 1140, 1205, 1207, 1208, 1210, 1212
health care providers, 1134, 1139–1141, 1143
health cooperation, 1133, 1141, 1142
insurance, 606–608
patients, 11140–1141
policy, 1142–1144

Hierarchy
of law, 75, 98, 195
of sources, 193–194, 198

High Authority. *See* European Coal and Steel Community (ECSC)

High Representative (of the Union for Foreign Affairs and Security Policy (HR/VP/HR)), 143, 174, 1231, 1243, 1264–1271, 1281, 1285

HIV/AIDS, 1143

Horizon 2020. *See* Research and Technology

Horizontal agreements, 737–741. *See also* Anti-competitive collusion

Human rights. *See* Chapter 4 *passim. See also* Fundamental rights
CDDH (Council of Europe Steering Committee for Human Rights), 113
cross-border cooperation in criminal affairs, 708
ECtHR, 96, 99, 112–119, 121, 122, 126, 410, 702, 703, 708, 709
as foundation of EU, 95, 97
in external relations, respect 1234
association agreements, 1333, 1335
instrument for Democracy and Human Rights (EIDHR), 1322, 1324, 1325
international human rights, 645–646
and labour conventions, 1299
policies, 96
protection of, 3, 95, 98, 101, 113, 469, 645, 1138, 1320
relationship with fundamental freedoms, 470
Universal Declaration of Human Rights, 97, 1332

Human Tissue Directive 2004/23, 1143

I

Immigration rules, 621

Impact assessment
Commission proposal, 156
environmental (EIA), 1179, 1182–1183
ex ante, 1170
external, 407
fundamental rights, 105
human rights, 107, 110
inception impact assessment, 245
TFEU integration principle, 1176

Implementation
of directives, 206, 209–211, 366, 446, 461, 1018
of the EU budget, 335–338, 341
general duty of Member States, 414, 431, 434, 435, 443, 452, 457, 460
implementing powers of the Union, 202, 270–280, 285, 292
Commission, 275–281
exceptional power of Council, 142

Implementing act(s), 111, 156, 157, 201, 202, 217, 232, 236, 240, 245, 259, 272, 275–281, 303, 310, 373, 382, 383, 385, 390, 414, 431, 653, 952, 966, 1064, 1295, 1317. *See also* Delegated acts

Implementing technical standard (ITS), 952, 954

Implied powers, 71, 77–79, 674, 1249, 1254

Import *vs.* export restrictions, 522–523

Imputability, 786

Incorporation doctrine, 869, 871–873

Independent Data Supervisor, 129

Indirect effect, 435–437, 440, 943, 944

Industrial and commercial property. *See* Intellectual property
Industrial emissions, 1173, 1179, 1181
Industrial policy, 1197, 1202, 1224
Industrial pollution control, 1181–1182
Information and Consultation, 111, 768, 995, 1005, 1007–1008, 1014, 1200, 1304
Information paradigm, 1155–1157
Information Society Directive, 863, 864
Infrastructure
    airports, 1079, 1084–1085
    energy networks 1096–1097
    ports, 747, 750, 1079, 1086
    Trans-European transport Network, 1086
Infringement action, 120, 454, 1160 *See also* Court of Justice of the EU
Institutional and procedural autonomy of Member States, 299–300
Institutional balance, 30, 90, 197, 215, 240, 241, 246, 355, 381, 1247
Institutions
    Common rules of the EU Institutions, 186–190
        linguistic regime, working languages, 189–190
        privileges and immunities, 186–188
        seat of the institutions, 188–189
    decision making powers, 251–259
    political (*see* Political institutions)
Institutions for occupational retirement provisions Directive (IORP II), 973
Integration
    civic, 669
    market, 23, 539, 614, 615, 760, 764, 884, 901, 1101, 1109, 1130, 1133, 1144–1146, 1148, 1157
    negative integration, 92, 471, 473, 477, 485, 571, 850–852, 1015, 1018, 1050, 1147, 1202–1205, 1210, 1219, 1228
    positive integration, 477–479
    mutual recognition principle, 479–480
    process, 13, 15, 23, 45, 50, 51, 54, 59, 302, 411, 611, 717, 1015, 1016, 1050, 1138, 1213
    supporting policy areas, EU, 1205–1207, 1211
Integration principle, 1168, 1169, 1171, 1172, 1175–1176
Intellectual property. *See* Chapter 24 *passim*. *See also* Copyright; Patents; TRIPS
    copyright and related rights, 861–865
    disputes, 260, 855
    enforcement, 211, 416, 457, 560, 687, 862, 1060
    licences, 745
    negative integration, 851–852
    patents, 858–861
    positive integration, legislation, 852–854, 865
    rights (IPRs), 560, 746, 749, 751, 761, 849–850, 1293
    scope, 849
    trademarks, 849, 850, 855–858
        European Union Intellectual Property Office, or EUIPO, 857
        Office for Harmonization in the Internal Market (Trade Marks and Designs) OHIM, 289, 857
    trade-related, 1292, 1296
Interest and Royalty Directive, 843
Interest-bearing deposit, 913, 917, 920
Intergovernmental
    Committee, 10, 13
    cooperation, 3, 10, 47
    decision-making model, 29
    framework, 19, 25, 47
    method, 25, 36
Intergovernmental conference (IGC), 12, 18, 24, 25, 27, 29, 31, 47, 52, 54, 61, 229, 318, 417, 888
Interim measures, relief, 446, 448, 457, 1163
    uniform conditions national courts and ECJ, 400–401,
    remedies, 457, 766, 801
Interinstitutional agreements (IIAs), 214–215, 316, 317, 333, 348–350
Inter-institutional relations, political
    budgetary process, 175–176
    Commission's services, 149
    legislative process, 176–182
Internal market
    abuse of law, 483
    competition aspects, 481–482, 734
    convergence of the freedoms and exceptions, 473–476
    EEA rules, 476–477
    fundamental freedoms, 469–471
    harmonization and uniform legislation, 477–479
    mutual recognition principle, 479–480
    purely internal situation 480–482 (*see also* Internal situation)
    re-importation, 482
    REMIT, 1101–1102
    reverse discrimination, 482–483
    types of barriers to free movement, 471
Internal situation, 464, 480–482, 488, 546, 547, 619, 622
Internal taxation
    Art. 110(1) TFEU
        discrimination, 499–500

justification, 500–501
similar products, 497–499
Art. 110(2) TFEU, 501–502
domestic and imported products, 496
indirect fiscal protectionism, 501
measures of, 486, 493, 504, 524
national treatment principle, 1298
remedies, 503
International jurisdiction, 674, 675, 678, 682, 683
International law
direct effect, 1258–1260
harmonious interpretation, 1258–1260
jurisdiction of ECJ, 391
as law of the EU, monism, 1255–1258, 1262
place in EU law, 1255–1261
private, 682–684
International Monetary Fund (IMF), 230, 886, 893, 926, 928, 1253
International organizations
mixed membership of
FAO, 1252
HCCH, 1254
OECD, 1252, 1253
WTO, 1252, 1253
Union membership of, 1252–1254
International private law. *See* private international law
Inter se agreements. *See* Agreements between EU Member States *inter se*
Intra-EU trade, 491, 533, 789
Invalidity benefits, 602, 620, 1040
Investment for growth and jobs
goal, 1112
purposes of, 1115
Investment fund, 573, 970, 971, 996, 1065, 1109, 1111
Investment priorities (cohesion policy), 1110, 1115–1117
Investor Compensation Scheme Directive (ICSD), 961
Ioannina Declaration, compromise, 17, 138. *See also* Council of the EU
Irregular migration
access EU territory, 655
human smuggling and trafficking, 655–656
return, 656–658
Islamic headscarf, 1031
Italy
Corte Costituzionale, 99, 421, 423
financial position, 890
patent package, 860, 861

J

Jobseekers, 592, 599, 625, 631–633, 637–638
Joint Committee ESAs, 982
Joint venture, 728, 729, 774
Judicial cooperation 28, 34, 37, 55,
in civil matters (*see* Chapter 18 *passim*)
area of, 675
Art. 81 TFEU, 677–678, 688
case law developments, 687–688
cross-border dichotomy, 678–679
family law, 681
general measures, 686
institutional development, 673–675
instruments, specific procedural issues and European procedures, 685–686
internal market, 680–681
jurisction, 683, 684, 687
2020 Justice Agenda, 689
legislative approach, 686–687
mutual trust, 688–689
policy, 676–677
private international law instruments, 682–684
criminal matters
European Arrest Warrant (*see* European Arrest Warrant)
EJN, 712
EPPO, 712–713
Eurojust, 711–712
Europol, 710–711
mutual recognition (*see* Mutual recognition in criminal matters)
OLAF, 712
in migration and asylum law, 640
mutual trust (*see* Mutual trust)
and OCTs, 1127
preliminary reference procedure, 388 (*see* Preliminary reference procedure)
Judicial dialogue, 381, 467
Judicial error, 465–466
Judicial protection, 361–388, 444–446 (*see also* Access to justice)
complete system of remedies, 377, 390, 442
right to an effective remedy (Charter Article 47), 446, 450
Judicial review, 73, 83, 105, 112, 116, 221, 280, 293, 294, 307, 370, 378, 380, 390, 424, 444, 664, 771, 1238, 1242, 1259, 1343, 1344
Jurisdiction. *See* Brussels Convention; Brussels Regulation; Judicial cooperation.
Justice and Home Affairs (JHA)
configuration of Council, 136
history, 25, 46, 47, 182, 640

judicial cooperation (*see* Judicial cooperation)
replaced by AFSJ, 640
Justifications (in framework of free movement of goods, free movement of services and freedom of establishment)
absence of EU harmonization legislation, 525–526
direct discriminatory national measures, 530–531
fundamental freedoms and fundamental human rights, 533–534
mandatory requirements, general interest, 529–530
test of necessity, 532–533
test of suitability, 532
legal certainty, 585–586
mandatory requirements in the general interest, 506, 525, 529–530
necessity, 532–533
overriding requirements in the general interest, 556, 558
proportionality test
consistency, 475
suitability, 532
Treaty derogations, 438, 526–529, 580–583, 868

K

Korean conflict, 7

L

Labour law, 37, 568, 817, 997–999, 1003, 1005, 1012–1014, 1129
Lamfalussy process, 951, 952, 958
Lamfalussy report, 951–953
Legal basis
constitutional significance, 75, 236
Council Regulation, 1097
case law rules for determining the legal basis, 237
economic governance reforms, 55
EU institutions, 74
European administrative law, 1228
existence and nature of competence to act, 236–237
financial regulation, 320
incorrect,
ground for annulment, 371–372
minimum harmonization, 209
principle of conferral, 236
special legislative procedure/non-legislative procedure, 240
type of instrument, 237
Legal certainty
and competence, 81
conflict of laws system, 683
in Court of Justice reasoning, 358, 359, 373
EU legal order, 375, 392
formal investigation procedure, 797
interest of producers, 11
as justification, 586
and legitimacy, 1220
principle 81, 91 (*see also* legal certainty, Principle of)
res judicata, 451
Legal instruments, 198–221
Art. 288, incomplete list, 199–200
budget instruments, 335
decisions, 211–214, 1203
directives, 208–211
ECB, 949–950
EU legal instruments
EU legal acts, 198, 203–205
European Parliament and Council, 198
European Council, 215–216
European pillar of social rights, 1011
(former) second and third pillars, 216–218
Interinstitutional agreements (IIAs), 214–215
non-binding instruments, 218–221
reform under Lisbon Treaty, 200–203
regulations, 206–207, 1203
secondary law, procedures 235, 239–260
Legal migration, 666–671
Blue Card Directive, 670–671
family reunification, 667–668
Long Term Residents Directive, 668–670
Legal protection, 196, 426, 437, 442, 443, 599, 859, 951, 988–992, 1108, 1293. *See also* Judicial protection
Legislative acts, 237–239
of the Council, 141
legally binding Union acts, 280
legislative deliberations of the Council, 141
adopted by legislative procedure, 142
regulatory acts, 142
Legislative procedure, process, 172, 175, 239–260, 952 (*see also* Political institutions)
first reading, 252
second reading, 181, 253
third reading, 246
Legislative proposal, 35, 105, 150, 156, 166, 181, 185, 250, 263, 265, 310, 325, 407, 415, 635, 897, 969, 974, 1258

Lex loci domicilii, 604
Lex loci laboris, 604, 605
Liability of Member States. *See* State liability
Liquidity requirements, 960
Lisbon Agenda. *See* Research and Technology
Listing Directive, 965
Locus Standi, 239, 376, 988, 1108, 1120, 1180
Long Term Residents Directive, 645, 666, 668–671
Loyal Cooperation. *See* Sincere cooperation, principle of

M

Macroeconomic imbalances
procedure, 604, 905, 906, 911–923, 1010, 1207
Margin of discretion, 124, 291, 294, 387, 431, 462, 478, 532, 533, 564, 566, 654, 723, 991, 1043, 1044, 1051, 1069, 1247
Market citizenship, 590
Market economy investor, 783–784
Market integration. *See* Free movement; Internal market;
Market organizations
common, 1053–1055, 1057, 1060
national, 1049, 1050, 1053, 1054
Market regulation
agriculture, 1063
financial (*see* Financial markets regulation)
social policy, 998
Markets in Financial Instruments Directive (MiFID I, MIFID II), 952, 963
Markets in Financial Instruments Regulation, 963, 976
Marshall Plan, Aid, 2
Maternity benefits, 1026
Measures having equivalent effect(to quantitative restrictions) (MEEQR)
case law definition, 506
dual regulatory burden, 512, 551
non-tariff barriers, 506–523
product requirements, 476
rules of use, 507
Medium-term financial assistance facility, 927
Member States
agreements between (*see* Agreements between EU Member States *inter se*)
composite EU legal order, 413–415
effective application and enforcement, 416
EU and national law, 419–421
implement, duty to (*see* Implementation)
liability of (*see* State liability)
role of founding values, 416–417
unconditional primacy and the duty of national courts, 418–419
Memorandum of Understanding (MoU), 215, 221, 232, 926, 927, 941
Mergers. *see* Competition law and policy, concentration control, 772–777
Messina Resolution, 10
Migration and Asylum Law. *See* Chapter 17 *passim*
AFSJ, 639
asylum policy, 658–665
bodies
EASO (*see* European Asylum Support Office)
European Border and Coast Guard Agency (Frontex) (*see* European Border and Coast Guard Agency)
competences, 646–649
economics, 642–643
free movement and spill-over, 641
international human rights and union values, 645–646
legal (*see* Legal migration)
rationale, 640
right to return to home state, 621
restrictive labour migration policy, 639
security, 641–642
solidarity, mutual recognition and trust, 643–645
substantive rules
borders, 651–653
CEAS, 658
Dublin Regulation, 659–660
entry-exit system and ETIAS, 654–655
irregular migration (*see* Irregular migration)
visas (*see* Visas)
Monetary deficit financing, 906
Monnet, Jean, 12
Moral hazard, 909
Morocco, 15, 107, 1086
Multi-Annual Financial Framework (MFF), 331–333
Multiannual programming, 154, 244, 1113
Multi-level governance (MLG), 1108, 1115, 1119
Mutual recognition
criminal matters
cross-border gathering and use of evidence, 706
cross-border supervision, non-custodial pre-trial measures, 706–707
European arrest warrant, 706

foreign convictions, 708
principle of, 705
protection of fundamental rights, cross-border, 708–710
transfer, execution of sanctions, 707–708
internal market
diplomas, 553–555
national product rules, 509–512
goods produced or previously imported in another Member State, 510
migration, asylum and borders, 643–645
Mutual trust, 115, 417, 646, 676–677, 688–689

N
Nassau Agreements, 13–14
National Central Banks (NCB)
Eurosystem, 304
national legislation, 899
public debt instruments, 906
Union institutions and national governments, 937
National Competent Authority (NCA) (in SSM)
breach of Union law, 977, 978
emergency decision, 980
Executive Boards, 978
"hub-and-spoke" model, 976
organization of supervision, 975
supervision of credit institutions, 956
National Competition Authority (NCA)
application of EU competition rules, 716–717, 765
and ECN, 768–769
Regulation 139/2004, 717, 773
National courts
access, 800–801
application EU law, 418–419, 424, 426, 428, 429, 442
cooperation with Court of Justice of the EU (*see* Preliminary reference procedure)
effective judicial protection, 444–446
ex officio application EU law, 448, 452
interim relief, 400, 401, 446, 448, 1163 (*see also* Interim relief)
remedies, 390, 392, 442, 444, 445
res judicata, 450–452
Nationality
direct and indirect discrimination, 524, 569
loss of nationality of a Member State, 616
non-discrimination on grounds of, 89, 198, 224, 438, 447, 548, 550, 556, 597
National Parliaments
relationship with European Parliament, 173–174
role in legislative procedure, 250–251 (*see also* Subsidiarity)
role in system of competences, 83, 85, 86–87
early warning system, 73
post-Lisbon system, 70
yellow card, 226
role in Treaty revision, 60, 62
National procedural autonomy, 300, 443, 446–450, 453, 467, 974, 1160. *See also* Principle of equivalence; Principle of effectiveness
National reform programme, 911, 1115
Nature conservation, 1183–1184
Ne bis in idem principle, 343, 346, 455, 692–693
Networks in EU administration, 295–298
No bail-out clause, 892, 908, 924, 943
Non-binding acts and instruments, 77, 78, 199, 218–221, 1243
Non-interest-bearing deposit, 917, 922, 923
Non-legislative act, 156, 157, 203, 237–239, 242, 245, 248, 257, 271, 275, 310, 380
Non-regulatory competences, 82
Non-standard forms of employment, 1002–1004
fixed-term work, 1002–1003
part-time work, 1003
temporary agency work, 1003–1004
Non-tariff barriers
boundaries, 523–524
import *vs.* export restrictions, 522–523
MEEQR in *Cassis de Dijon*
Keck & Mithouard, 514–522
mutual recognition of national product rules, 509–510
post-cassis case law of the court, 510–514
MEEQR in *Dassonville,* 507–508
quantitative restrictions, 505–506
North Atlantic Treaty Organization (NATO), 7, 9, 19, 1263, 1271, 1272, 1276, 1279, 1280, 1284, 1285
Norway, 3, 13–17, 591, 602, 648, 649, 1062, 1084, 1226, 1326, 1329
Nuclear energy, 37, 1090, 1093, 1094, 1097
Euratom Treaty (*see* European Atomic Energy Community)
safety, 1093–1094
supply agency, 1094
Nuclear Safety Directive 2014/87/euratom, 1093–1094

O
Obesity, 1027, 1220

Objective justification, 1034–1036
Objectives
agricultural and fisheries, 1051–1052
competition rules, 719–721
development cooperation and other cooperation policies, 1319–1322
economic policy coordination in the EU, 902–906
EU public procurement regime, 808–809
monetary policy, 942–945
in relation to competence, 77
Union objectives, 50, 133–134
Occupational diseases, 602, 1004
Occupational health and safety, 1004, 1008, 1012
Office for Harmonisation in the Internal Market (Trade Marks and Designs) OHIM. *See* Intellectual property, trademarks.
Oil crisis, 639, 883, 885
OLAF. *See* European Anti-Fraud Office (OLAF)
Old-age benefits, 602, 1005
Omnibus II Directive (financial regulation) 2014/51, 973
Open market economy, 902, 903, 905
Open Method of Coordination (OMC), 219, 295, 996, 1206
Opt-in, 647, 648, 695
Opt-out, 28, 53, 56–57, 213, 647–649, 674, 695, 861, 1001, 1091
Orange card, 86, 87, 174, 250–251
Ordinary legislative procedure, 34, 62, 86, 141, 170–172, 176, 179, 186–187, 198, 200, 202, 218, 229, 238–240, 246, 251–258, 263, 276, 358, 646, 681, 843, 952, 1070, 1091, 1151, 1177, 1188, 1224, 1226, 1232, 1242, 1244, 1293, 1294, 1300. *See also* European Parliament
Organization for Economic Cooperation and Development (OECD)
OECD Model treaty, 839. *See also* Taxation
Organization for European Economic Cooperation (OEEC), 4, 5, 10, 12–13, 806, 1253
Outermost Regions (OMRs), 304, 1107, 1108, 1116, 1121–1125
Outright Monetary Transactions (OMT), 73, 426, 927, 943, 944, 1121
Overfishing, 1048
Overseas Countries and territories (OCTs)
Decision 2013/755, 1125
ESI Funds, 1125
international agreement, 1127
and OMRs, 1107–1108
simplified Treaty amendment procedure 1122
Own resources
collection, 329–331
Council Decision 70/243, 314, 325–328
European Parliament, 326
GNI-based own resource, 327
juste retour principle, 328–329
multi-annual financial framework (MFF), 62, 325, 338
traditional own resources, 326
VAT own resource, 326–327

P
Palermo Protocols, 655
Parallel competences, 81–82, 769, 1296
Parent subsidiary directive, 843
Partnership agreements, 1062, 1112–1115, 1232, 1320, 1327, 1330, 1333–1336
Part-time work, 595, 1003, 1012, 1013, 1018, 1031, 1034
Passenger compensation, 1085
Passenger Name Records (PNR), 655. *See also* Advanced Passenger Information
Passerelle
change of status for OCTs and OMRs 1122–1123
environmental policy, 1177
simplified Treaty amendment procedure, 62
Patents, 849–855, 858–861
European Patent Convention, 860
Fair Reasonable and Non-Discriminatory (FRAND), 762
intellectual property rights, 849
licensing, 762
Patent Court Opinion (1/09), 85, 414, 442
Regulation 816/2006 on compulsory licensing of patents relating to the manufacture of pharmaceutical products for export to countries with public health problems, 859
Supplementary protection certificate for medicinal products, 859
Supplementary protection certificate for plant protection products, 859
uniform patent protection, 228, 687
Paternity benefits, 602
Patients' Rights Directive, 608, 1133, 1141
Pension Funds, 958, 972–974, 982
Permanent residence, 3, 617, 623, 625–627, 629, 632, 633, 637, 667, 671
Pharmaceuticals, 283, 761–764, 859, 1129, 1130, 1133–1136, 1143
Pillar structure, 46–51, 693, 1192, 1263
Pleven Plan, 7

Poland
Polish Constitutional Tribunal, 420
Police and Judicial Cooperation in Criminal Matters (PJCCM), 28, 34, 386
Political and Security Committee (PSC), 139, 1246, 1269, 1281, 1283, 1285, 1342
Political dialogue, 85, 87, 1333, 1338
Political institutions
administration/governance, 142
advisory bodies
common provisions, 184–185
Committee of the Regions, 186
Economic and Social Committee, 185–186
agenda setting, 141
appointment, representation and responsibility, 174–175
Commission, 181–182
European Council, 129, 176–178
European Parliament, 179–181
inter-institutional relations (*see* Inter-institutional relations, political)
legislation, 141–142
linguistic régime, 189–190
powers and functions, 133, 141–142, 169–173
privileges and immunities, 186–188
seat of the institutions, 188–189
Political rights, 111, 634–636, 1157–1158
Polluter pays principle, 458, 1168, 1171, 1174–1175, 1181
Positive action, 365, 383, 1019, 1021, 1038–1039, 1045, 1217
Posted workers, 416, 555, 568, 605, 1012
Precautionary principle, 1137, 1168, 1171–1173, 1183, 1208, 1300
Pre-emption, 81, 222, 223, 642, 1200, 1274
Pregnancy and maternity. *See* Protection of women as regards pregnancy and maternity
Preliminary examination (in state aid procedure), 797
Preliminary reference procedure, 126, 269, 306, 308, 370, 380–382, 388–401, 404, 427, 429, 716, 770, 940, 1329
complete system of remedies (*see* Judicial protection)
Court of Justice and national courts, 392–395
effects of, 398–400
interim measures, 400–401
national courts and tribunals, 395–398
obligation to refer, 395
Preliminary rulings. *See* Preliminary reference procedure
Pre-retirement benefits, 602
Prevention of tax avoidance, 838–840
Preventive principle (environmental policy), 1168, 1171, 1173
Price stability, 741, 899, 901, 902, 905, 906, 928, 930, 942, 943, 945
Primacy/priority of Union law, 32, 44, 88, 100, 123, 124, 413, 417–427, 720
Primary law. *See* Direct effect; Hierarchy; Treaty Amendment
Primary market (EMU), 906, 907
Principle
of conferral, 71, 73–79, 88, 90, 91, 197–199, 231, 235, 236, 371, 372, 620, 1235, 1238
of effective judicial protection, 196–197, 375, 377, 444–446, 450
of effectiveness, 90, 300, 324–325, 443, 447, 451, 452, 455, 720
of equivalence, 300, 447, 449, 451
of legal certainty, 81, 91
of legality, 89, 90, 424, 455, 695
of primacy, 32, 81, 91, 100, 123, 223, 417, 418, 451 (*see also* Primacy/priority of Union law)
of proportionality, 84, 110, 197, 198, 250, 388, 475, 505, 513, 525, 527, 531–533, 562, 565, 584, 585, 620, 622, 625, 628, 632, 791, 1053, 1150, 1177, 1344
of relative stability, 1061
of sincere cooperation (*see* Sincere cooperation, principle of)
of solidarity (*see* Solidarity)
of subsidiarity, 26, 35, 71, 82–84, 86, 87, 90, 104, 109, 198, 202, 204, 214, 239, 250, 251, 372, 415, 643, 678, 1149, 1168, 1171 (*see also* Subsidiarity, principle of)
Private International Law, 28, 479, 568, 673, 675, 677, 682–684, 687, 688, 770, 1253, 1254. *See also* Judicial cooperation, civil matters
Private law, 28, 71, 188, 336, 479, 492, 676, 679, 682, 868, 1101, 1174
Procedural autonomy, principle of. *See* National procedural autonomy
Procedures Directive (asylum), 663–664
Procurement
award criteria, 819–820
concessions, 825–826
contracting authority, 813–815
contract performance, 824–825
contracts and design contests, 812–813
exceptions, 815–817

GPA and third country, 806, 807
history and international context, 805–808
objectives, 808–809
principles
equal treatment, 810–811
non-discrimination, 809–810
transparency, 811
Treaty provisions, 811
procedures
competitive dialogues, 821
competitive procedures with negotiation, 821
innovation partnership, 822
negotiated procedure without prior publication, 822
open, 820
restricted, 820–821
remedies, 826–827
selection, 817–819
thresholds, 815
tools
centralized procurement and joint procurement, 824
dynamic purchasing systems, 823
electronic auctions, 823–824
electronic catalogues, 824
framework agreement, 822–823
utilities, 825
Programming principle, 1114–1115
Proposal, withdrawal of. *See* European Commission, right of withdrawal
Prospectus Directive, 953, 965, 966
Protection and improvement of human health
fiscal sustainability, national health care systems, 1212–1213
free movement of patients, 1210
place of health policy in treaties, 1208–1209
tobacco regulation, 1210–1211
Working Time Directive, 1211–1212
Protection of human rights. *See* Human rights; Fundamental rights
Protection of the financial interests of the EU
PFI Convention, 343–345
Protection of women as regards pregnancy and maternity, 1029, 1039
Protocol on the application of the principles of subsidiarity and proportionality, 245
Protocol on the Internal Market and Competition, 469
Protocol No. 9 on the Ioannina compromise, 138
Protocol on the excessive deficit procedure, 904, 910
Protocol on Services of General Interest, 1070
Protocols
primary law source, 195, 197
Prudential supervision of credit institutions, 258, 945, 956, 982, 983
Publication of EU acts, 203–205
Public health. *See* Protection and improvement of human health
Public participation, 1179, 1182–1183
Public policy
agricultural structural policy, 1048
arbitration award, 449
national security, 652
and public security, 583, 585, 628
Public procurement. *See* Procurement
Public security, 476, 527, 557, 570, 582, 583, 585, 626, 628–631, 669, 670, 775, 851, 1040, 1302
Public Service Obligations (PSO), 784, 793, 1069–1071, 1075, 1076, 1081, 1094
Purely internal situation. *See* Internal situation

Q

Qualification Directive (asylum), 661–663
Qualified majority voting (QMV). *See* Voting
Quantitative import and export restrictions, 505, 525
Quotas
agricultural sector, 1048, 1050, 1051, 1054, 1059
commercial policy, 1306
competition rules, 752, 806
free movement of goods, 505, 535

R

Race and ethnic origin, 811, 1010, 1017, 1018, 1030, 1031, 1037, 1043, 1200
Race to the bottom, 658, 840, 874, 997, 1147
Regulation on the Registration, Evaluation Authorization and Restriction of Chemicals (REACH), 1182
Real seat doctrine, 869–871, 873, 878, 882
Reception Directive (asylum), 664–665
Recognition and enforcement of judgments (civil law), 673–675, 678, 682–685
Recognition of diplomas and professional qualifications, 553–555, 1139
Recognition of foreign companies, 872–873
Recovery of tax claims, 843, 846–847
Rectification at source principle, 1171, 1173–1174
Referendum(s), 15–18, 22, 26, 33, 35, 36, 49, 58, 66, 146, 226, 227, 543, 583, 614, 648, 896, 1297, 1326, 1329
Refugee crisis, 38, 417, 639, 642, 644, 647, 650, 661, 665, 671

Registered office, 569, 636, 835, 844, 868–871, 876, 878–880, 950, 962
Regulation on Market Integrity and Transparency (REMIT), 1097, 1100–1102
Regulations
 binding nature, 432
 direct applicability, 432
 effect (*see* Direct effect, regulations)
 implementation, 207, 1314
 judicial review, 371
 legal instrument, 206–207
 place in system of secondary law, 199–205
 procedure for adoption (*see* Legislative procedure)
Regulatory criminal law, 698, 700–701
Regulatory Scrutiny Board, 245
Regulatory technical standard (RTS), 952, 954, 958, 980
Relance européenne, 8–10, 12
Relevant market,
  competition rules, 719, 721, 722, 731, 744, 746–748, 751, 753, 776, 789
Religion/belief, 441, 811, 1010, 1017, 1018, 1030–1033, 1037, 1200
Relocation Decision (asylum), 650, 660–661, 665
Remedies. *See* National courts
REMIT. *See* Regulation on Market Integrity and Transparency (REMIT)
Remuneration
 definition of a service 495, 541–545, 574,
 free movement of workers 587, 592, 593, 999–1001, 1005, 1013
 of MEPs 160,
Res judicata, 394, 450–452
Research and Technology. *See* Chapter 37 *passim*.
 competences, 1186
 decision-making procedure, 1188–1189
 EURATOM Treaty, 1185
 external aspects
  framework programmes, Horizon 2020
  funding, 1191
  joint undertakings, 1187, 1188, 1195
  Lisbon Agenda, 1185
  shared competence, 1185–1187, 1189, 1197
 industrial competitiveness, 1185
 legal framework, 1186–1188
 2020 Strategy, 1186
  activities, Union policy, 1186
  decision-making, 1188–1189
  European Research Area (ERA), 1189–1196
  European Space Policy, 1196–1198
Residence
 requirements, 577, 578, 597, 598, 633, 663, 668
 rights, 483, 597, 598, 613, 616, 617, 621–627
Resolution decision (banking), 963, 986–988
Responsibility of Member States. *See* State liability
Restrictions in the internal market
 prohibitions under the four freedoms, 473–474
 non-tariff barriers, 505–506
 tariff barriers, 492–496
Return Directive, 656–658, 665
Reviewable act. *See* Court of Justice of the European Union, annulment action
Revision (of the Treaties). *See* Treaty amendment.
Revision (simplified procedure). *See* Treaty amendment, simplified procedure
Right of initiative, 26, 28, 154, 162, 242–244, 246, 247, 333, 334, 589, 693
Rule of law. *See also* General principles of EU law
 accession, 64
 challenge to fundamental values in Poland and Hungary, 38
 Charter of Fundamental Rights, 149
 Commission, 148
 European Council of Copenhagen (1993), 17
 enforcement in Member States, 416, 417
 fundamental rights, 106, 120
Rule of reason. *See* Free movement of goods, justifications
Rules on criminal procedure, 691
Rural development, 996, 1057, 1059, 1064, 1065, 1112, 1118

S

Safeguard clauses (intra-EU), 11, 65, 146, 156, 474, 653, 1035, 1177
Safeguard measures (trade policy), 1304–1306
Same-sex partnerships, 1029
Sanctions
 administrative, 452–454
 in national legal system, 413
 penal, 456–457
 restrictive measures, 1339–1346
  CFSP and UN, 1340
  EU legal bases, 1341–1343
  judicial review, 1343–1346
  targeted sanctions, 1340, 1341

Schengen
  Schengen Agreement, 56, 640, 647, 649, 692
  Schengen Associated Countries, 648–649
  Schengen Borders Code, 651
  Schengen Implementing Convention (CISA), 640, 641, 652, 658
  Schengen Information System (SIS), 641, 652
Schuman plan, declaration. 1, 4–7, 51
Scope of EU law, 96, 107, 109, 110, 115, 117, 120, 121, 124, 197, 430, 441, 465, 470, 623, 654, 1172, 1216
Secondary law. *See* Direct effect; Hierarchy; Legal instruments
Securities (UCITS V Directive), 970
Securities and markets, 963–972
Security of supply, 559, 1089, 1091, 1094, 1097, 1102
Selectivity, 786–788, 842, 944
Selling arrangements, 507, 515–521, 524, 740
Services
  beneficiaries, 545–549
  concept, 541–545
  freedom to provide, free movement of (*see* Free movement of services)
  of general economic interest, 558, 568, 570
  service recipients, 548–549
  Services Directive 2006/123, 567–570
    administrative simplification and cooperation, 568–569
    authorizations, prohibited and suspect restrictions, 569
    internal market, 567
    restrictions, 570
    scope, 568
Settlement
  New Settlement for the United Kingdom, 226, 251
  Settlement Finality Directive, 968
  transactions, 968
Sex
  discrimination, 811, 1017, 1023, 1024, 1027, 1028, 1034, 1043, 1044, 1200
  equality, 1023–1025, 1031, 1032, 1034, 1042, 1044
  Sexual orientation, 441, 646, 661, 811, 1010, 1017, 1018, 1020, 1029–1031, 1200
Shared competences. *See* Competence
Short Selling Directive, 967
Sickness benefits, 602
Simplified revision procedure. *See* Treaty amendment, simplified procedure
Sincere cooperation, principle of
  in external relations, 1254–1255
  negative obligations, 85
  positive obligations, 85
Single currency, 884, 886–892, 895–902, 904, 909, 927, 928, 930, 935, 944, 946, 947, 955. *See also* Economic and Monetary Union
Single European Act (SEA), 21–23, 130, 274, 888–891
Single Resolution Board (SRB), 957, 986–988
Single Resolution Mechanism (Regulation), 229
Single Rulebook, 959, 983
Single Supervisory Mechanism (Regulation), 982–986
Six Pack, 55, 158, 894, 897, 898, 910, 913, 915, 917, 919, 920, 922
Smuggling, human, 642, 655–656
Social
  advantages, 595–597
  assistance, 592, 595–597, 603, 624
  benefits, 591, 592, 595
  deficit, 1015
  EU Charter of Fundamental Rights, 1013–1014
  labour law directives, 1012–1013
  market economy, 905, 995, 1015
  non-standard forms, employment (*see* Non-standard forms of employment)
  OMC, 219, 295, 996, 1009–1010, 1206, 1223
  OSH, 1008–1009
  partner, 597, 996, 997, 1002, 1003, 1022, 1036, 1041
  policies, 1074, 1075, 1080, 1081, 1201
  rationale of EU action, 997–998
  rights
    Pillar of Social Rights, 1010–1012, 1014, 1016
  structural changes, company (*see* Company)
  treaties, 995–997
  working time, 1001–1102
Social security. *See also* Coordination of social security
  coordination 599–610
    competent state, 603–605, 607–609, 1141
    health care, 606–608
    principles, 605–606
    scope, 601–603
    unemployment benefits, 608–610
  equal treatment in employment, 1023–1025
  internal market justifications, 473, 530, 543
  migration, 669
  unanimous voting, 30, 258
Societas Cooperativa Europaea (SCE), 878–879

Societas Europaea (SE), 844, 878–879
Soft law. *See* Non-binding instruments
Solidarity
  asylum claims, 644
  community, 661
  financial and operational, 644
  health care, 727, 1140, 1141
  pension and insurance schemes, 727, 1141
  principle of, 106, 643
  spirit of, 1104, 1105
Solvency II Framework Directive, 973
Sovereign debt crisis, 35, 223, 229–230, 444, 639, 892–895, 897, 903, 906, 908, 914, 916, 921, 924, 936, 937, 939, 942, 943, 954, 1015
Soviet Union, 16, 1299, 1321, 1322, 1327
Spaak report, 10–12, 588
Special legislative procedure, 141, 170, 172, 175, 176, 202, 238–240, 248, 256–258, 326, 331, 333, 646, 1177, 1188, 1412, 381616
Special non-contributory cash benefits, 602, 606
Spinelli Report, 22
Sport, 593, 789, 792, 1034, 1202, 1213, 1219–1221
Stability and Growth Pact (SGP), 35, 304, 910, 920, 922, 1010, 1207
State aid
  compatible aid, 792–794, 798
  developments in EU, 781
  elements of
    advantage, 782–784
    distortion of competition, 789–790
    effect on interstate trade, 789
    selectivity criterion, 786–788
    state resources, 784–786
  enforcement, Art. 108 TFEU
    ex-ante supervision, 796–798
    ex-post supervision, 795
  exempted aid, 779, 796
  exemptions
    Art. 106(2) TFEU, 793–794
    Art. 107(2) TFEU, 790
    Art. 107(3) TFEU, 790–793
    Art. 108(2) TFEU, 794
  existing aid, 794, 795
  formal investigation
    Commission, 780, 795, 796, 801
    procedure, 797–798, 800–802
  incompatible aid, 795, 798
  judicial protection, 800–803
  modernization programme, 803–804
  new aid, 794–798
  recovery, 779, 794, 795, 799–800
  in transport, 780, 787, 793
  unlawful aid, 798–799
State-backed commercial monopolies, 534–536
State liability. *See also* Damages
  conditions, 197, 460, 461–464
  Francovich, 414, 459–465
  judicial errors, 465–466
  national courts, 465
  parallel with non-contractual liability of EU, 387
  principle, 459, 460, 466
State resources. *See* State aid, elements of
Stockholm Programme, 646, 647, 676, 686. *See also* Tampere Agenda *and* Hague Programme
2020 Strategy. *See* Research and Technology
Structural funds
  additionality principle, 1114
  cohesion fund, 1117–1118
  complementarity principle, 1114
  economic and social cohesion, 1056
  ERDF, 1111, 1112, 1116
  ESF, 1111, 1112, 1116–1117 (*see* European Social Fund (ESF))
  EU cohesion policy, 1110
  "Europe 2020" strategy, 1112
  investment, growth and jobs, 1112
  lisbonization, 1113
  macroeconomic policies, 1113
  NUTS classification system, 1112
  principle of partnership, 1115
  programming principle, 1114–1115
Students, 212, 542, 553, 601, 613, 617, 624, 631–633, 666, 814, 1205, 1213, 1214, 1216, 1217
Study grants, 595
Subsidiarity, principle of
  decisions taken close to the citizen, 90
  EU institutions and bodies, 104
  at ECJ, 372
  history, 26, 71–72, 84, 214
  judicial cooperation on civil matters, 679, 680, 685
  lawful exercise of competences, 82–83
  role of national parliaments, 85–87, 173–174, 202
    Protocol (No 1) on the role of National Parliaments in the European Union, 173
    Protocol (No. 2) on the Application of the Principles of Subsidiarity and Proportionality, 83, 202
  procedures for implementing, 202, 204, 239, 245, 250
  UK draft settlement, 226

Substantive criminal law. *See* Criminal law, substantive
Suez crisis, 12
Sufficient resources (for free movement), 596, 622, 624, 625, 627, 637, 1099, 1216
Supervision of financial markets, 245, 582, 583, 931, 1127
  Banking Union (*see* Banking Union)
  European Supervisory Authorities (ESAs)
    De Larosière Report, 975–977
    Joint Committee, 982
    powers, 977–982
Supporting policies. *See also* Chapter 38 *passim*
  common characteristics, 1199–1207
  competence, 1199, 1201
  negative integration, 1203–1205
  positive integration, 1205–1207
  place in Treaty system, 1199
  specific areas
    administrative cooperation, 1227–1228
    civil protection, 1225–1226
    culture, 1221–1223 (*see also* Culture)
    education and vocational training (*see* Education; Vocational training)
    human health (*see* Protection and improvement of human health)
    industry, 1223–1224 (*see also* Industrial policy)
    sport, 1219–1221 (*see also* Sport)
    tourism, 1224–1225 (*see also* Tourism)
    youth, 1218–1219
Supranational companies. *See* Company law, supranational company forms, 867, 877–880
Supremacy. *See* Primacy/priority of Union law
Survivors' benefits, 1006
Sustainable development, 930, 1062, 1073, 1083, 1095, 1110, 1125, 1169, 1170, 1175, 1176, 1234, 1292, 1321, 1336, 1337
Switzerland, 13, 15, 16, 122, 477, 591, 602, 648, 649, 741, 1073, 1075, 1076, 1084, 1238, 1326, 1329
System of competences. *See* Competences

T

Tampere Agenda, 646, 658 (*see also* Hague Programme *and* Stockholm Programme).
Tariff barriers, 471, 481, 492–496
  boundaries, 523–524
  charges
    equivalent effect, 493–494
    permissible, 494–496
    recovery of unlawful changes, 496
  customs duties, 493
  inspections, 494
Taxation
  corporate tax, 580, 770, 788, 829, 841, 843–845, 847
  disparities, 835–837
  effectiveness of fiscal supervision, 839–840
  EU Treaty Freedoms, 829
  harmful tax competition, 840–841
  harmonization
    decision-making, 842–843
    direct taxation, 843–845
    indirect taxation, 845–847
  income tax, 829, 830, 836, 847
  power to tax, allocation of, 833, 838
  prevention of tax avoidance, 838–839
  state aid, 841–842
  tax allowance, 830, 832
  tax restrictions
    allowances, 830–832
    discrimination on grounds of nationality, 830
    free movement, 833–835
    horizontal discrimination, 832
Temporary Protection Directive, 660–661
Territorial scope
  application of EU law, 65, 76, 1120–1128
  extraterritorial effect, 107
    effects approach to jurisdiction, 734, 1256
  geographical scope of treaties, 1121–1122, 1123–1128 (*see also* OCTs and OMRs)
  territoriality of intellectual property rights, 850
Thalidomide crisis, 1131
Third pillar instruments, 56, 201, 217, 694, 695
Tindemans report, 21
Tobacco Products Directive, 1138, 1139, 1211
Tourism, 548, 559, 574, 590, 591, 596, 625, 1202, 1221, 1224–1225, 1228, 1320, 1330
Trade agreements
  bilateral/plurilateral, 1296
  Energy Community Treaty, 1104
  Free Trade Agreements (FTAs), 1293, 1317 (*see also* Common Commercial Policy; Agreements, international agreements)
Trade Barrier Regulation, 1312–1313
Trade Implementation Regulation, 1314
Trademarks. *See* Intellectual Property, trademarks
Trade-related Intellectual Property Rights (TRIPS), 1241, 1260, 1292–1293, 1336
Trafficking, human, 103, 655, 697, 1127

Trans-European Networks, 186, 1086, 1096, 1117–1119, 1235, 1244
Transparency
administrative action, 308
comitology committees, 279
concessions, 825
decision-making process, 263
financial, 1071
judicial, 408
market, 981
MiFID II, 964
nuclear safety, 1094
obligation, 556, 810
pricing of pharmaceuticals, 1136
principle of, 325, 556, 811, 815, 818
2014 procurement package, 812
procurement procedure, 809
Transparency Directive, 965, 1071
Transplantation of Human Organs, 1143
Transport. *See also* Chapter 31 *passim*
air transport, 1081–1085
common transport policy, 1067, 1068
competition rules and transport, 1071, 1082
consumer protection in transport, 1074–1078, 1085
environmental protection, 1073, 1076, 1079, 1083–1084
external relations and transport, 1072, 1074–1076, 1080–1081, 1085–1086
inland waterway, 1075–1076
maritime transport, 1076–1081
public service obligations, 1070
rail transport, 1067, 1069, 1073–1076
road transport, 1072–1074
safety and security, 1073, 1075, 1076, 1078–1079, 1083
state aid, 1071–1072
Trans-European networks, 1086
Treaty amendment, 45, 195, 196, 260, 403
content of amendments, 60
passerelle clauses (*see Passerelle*)
procedure 27, 59–64,
role of European Council, 134
simplified procedure, 62–63, 216, 260, 894, 929, 1122
structure and objectives of the ESCB and ECB, 929
Treaty establishing a Constitution for Europe, 31–38, 44–45, 49, 104, 238, 280
Treaty of Amsterdam
history, 27–30, 48, 54, 56, 173, 182, 215,
Treaty of Lisbon
history, 32–35, 44–46, 48, 50
Treaty of Maastricht
history, 23–28, 45–51
Treaty of Nice
history, 18, 29–31, 35, 54
Treaty of Paris. *See* European Coal and Steel Community
Treaty of Rome. *See* EEC Treaty
Treaty on European Union. *See* Treaty of Maastricht.
Treaty on Stability, Coordination and Governance in Economic and Monetary Union (TSCG) (Fiscal compact), 894, 904, 916
Treaty on the Functioning of the European Union (TFEU)
history, 34, 43, 45, 49, 50
Treaty provisions, effect of, 428–429, 491, 492
Trilogue, 166, 253, 254, 256, 381
Turkey,
accession to the European Union, 64
association agreement, 1331
Two Pack, 55, 158, 894, 897, 898, 910, 920, 922

U

Ultra vires review by German Federal Constitutional Court, 72, 73, 88, 89, 425, 426
Undertakings for Collective Investment in Transferable Securities (UCITSs), 969–971
Unemployment benefits, 602, 606, 608–610, 620, 631, 1011
Unfair contract terms, 1149, 1153, 1155, 1156, 1158, 1162
Uniform European procedures (in asylum), 679, 682, 683
Union citizenship. *See* Citizenship of the Union
Union loyalty. *See* Sincere cooperation, principle of
United Kingdom, 5, 12–20, 25, 30, 51, 56, 59, 66, 225, 226, 328, 647, 695, 896, 910, 1124
United Nations (UN)
Conference on Environment and Development in Rio, 1170
Convention on the Rights of Persons with Disabilities, 106, 1027, 1045
Convention on the Law of the Seas (UNCLOS), 1252, 1258, 1260, 1284, 1287
development strategy, 1319
Economic Commission for Europe, 1073, 1076
EU membership of UN bodies, 1279 (*see also* International organizations, EU membership of)

Member States, 1280
peace and security, 1234
sanctions, 1347
Security Council, 1276, 1283, 1340, 1344
UNMIK, 1279–1283
United States (US), 2, 3, 12–14, 19, 717, 738, 1079, 1086, 1146, 1272–1275, 1279, 1280, 1300, 1308, 1336, 1337

V
Valletta Action Plan, 643
Value-added tax (VAT)
common EU system, 846
fraud prosecution, 89, 327
harmonization, 314
own resource, 326–328
Variable geometry, 45, 51–59, 646–649
Vertical agreement (collusive practice), 725, 743–746
Victimization, 599, 705, 1043
Victims' rights, 704–705
Visas, 653–654
common visa list, 648
Community Visa Code, 653
Schengen visa, 653
verification, 652
Visa Information System (VIS), 654, 660
Vocational training
access for migrant workers, 589
diploma recognition, 1215–1216
education for children of migrant workers, 1217
student residence, 1216–1217
Voting
qualified majority voting (QMV), 6, 17, 21, 32, 35, 54, 55, 62, 137, 138, 233, 240, 258, 338, 913, 916, 928, 931, 999, 1056, 1131, 1147, 1167, 1168, 1176, 1177, 1212
reversed qualified majority voting (RQMV), 913, 916–918, 920
rights, 120, 162, 285, 613, 614, 634, 635, 774, 926, 933, 934, 937
unanimity, 26, 60, 62, 63, 182, 254, 256–258, 260, 326, 416, 1232, 1242
Vulnerability assessment (managing external borders), 652

W
Water Framework Directive, 297
Weapons of Mass Destruction (WMD), 1275
Werner Report, 884–886
Westendorp Report, 27
Western European Union (WEU), 9, 10, 20
Winding up Directive, 961, 962
Withdrawal (from the Union), 37, 66
Withdrawal (of legislative proposal). *See* European Commission, right of withdrawal
Worker
Community Charter of the Fundamental Social Rights, 121, 1012
employment opportunities, 997
free movement (*see* Free movement of workers)
health and safety, 997, 1033, 1132
information and consultation, 1007–1008
posted workers, 555, 564, 998–1000, 1016
Posted Workers Directive 96/71/EC, 998–1000
protection (*see* Worker protection)
retention of the status, 633
temporary agency, 1003, 1004
Worker protection, 999, 1003–1005, 1008, 1015, 1209, 1211–1212
Working time, 254, 998, 1001–1003, 1007, 1012, 1014, 1074, 1083, 1211–1212
Working Time Directive, 1211–1212
Work-seekers. *See* Jobseekers
World Trade Organization (WTO), 326, 807, 1058

Y
Yellow card, 86, 174, 226, 250, 1000 (*see also* Subsidiarity, role of national parliaments)
Youth Employment Package, 1220